SMITH & ROBERSON'S

Business Law

EIGHTEENTH EDITION

RICHARD A. MANN

Professor of Business Law
The University of North Carolina at Chapel Hill
Member of the North Carolina Bar

BARRY S. ROBERTS

Professor of Business Law
The University of North Carolina at Chapel Hill
Member of the North Carolina and Pennsylvania Bars

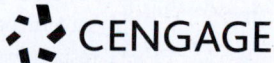

Australia · Brazil · Japan · Korea · Mexico · Singapore · Spain · United Kingdom · United States

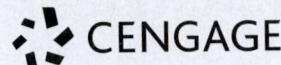

Smith & Roberson's Business Law
Eighteenth Edition
Richard A. Mann and Barry S. Roberts

SVP, Higher Education Product Management: Erin Joyner

VP, Product Management, Learning Experiences: Thais Alencar

Product Director: Joseph Sabatino

Product Manager: Abbie Schultheis

Product Assistant: Nick Perez

Learning Designer: Mara Vuillaume

Senior Content Manager: Cheri Plasse

Digital Delivery Quality Partner: Mark Hopkinson

VP, Product Marketing: Jason Sakos

Director, Product Marketing: Danae April

Product Marketing Manager: Anthony Winslow

IP Analyst: Ashley Maynard

Production Service: Straive

Designer: Sara Greenwood

Interior image Source: Ida Jarosova/iStock/Getty Images Plus/Getty Images

Africa Studio/ShutterStock.com

For product information and technology assistance, contact us at Cengage Customer & Sales Support, 1-800-354-9706 or support.cengage.com.

For permission to use material from this text or product, submit all requests online at www.copyright.com.

Library of Congress Control Number: 2021921566

ISBN: 978-0-357-36400-0

Cengage
200 Pier 4 Boulevard
Boston, MA, 02210
USA

Cengage is a leading provider of customized learning solutions with employees residing in nearly 40 different countries and sales in more than 125 countries around the world. Find your local representative at **www.cengage.com**.

To learn more about Cengage platforms and services, register or access your online learning solution, or purchase materials for your course, visit **www.cengage.com**.

Notice to the Reader

Publisher does not warrant or guarantee any of the products described herein or perform any independent analysis in connection with any of the product information contained herein. Publisher does not assume, and expressly disclaims, any obligation to obtain and include information other than that provided to it by the manufacturer. The reader is expressly warned to consider and adopt all safety precautions that might be indicated by the activities described herein and to avoid all potential hazards. By following the instructions contained herein, the reader willingly assumes all risks in connection with such instructions. The publisher makes no representations or warranties of any kind, including but not limited to, the warranties of fitness for particular purpose or merchantability, nor are any such representations implied with respect to the material set forth herein, and the publisher takes no responsibility with respect to such material. The publisher shall not be liable for any special, consequential, or exemplary damages resulting, in whole or part, from the readers' use of, or reliance upon, this material.

Printed in the United States of America
Print Number: 01   Print Year: 2021

About the Authors

Richard A. Mann received a B.S. in mathematics from the University of North Carolina at Chapel Hill and a J.D. from Yale Law School. He is professor emeritus of business law at the Kenan-Flagler Business School, University of North Carolina at Chapel Hill, and is past president of the Southeastern Regional Business Law Association. He is a member of Who's Who in America, Who's Who in American Law, and the North Carolina Bar.

Professor Mann has written extensively on a number of legal topics, including bankruptcy, sales, secured transactions, real property, insurance law, and business associations. He has received the *American Business Law Journal*'s award both for the best article and for the best comment and has served as a reviewer and staff editor for the publication. Professor Mann is a coauthor of *Business Law and the Regulation of Business* (Thirteenth Edition), *Essentials of Business Law and the Legal Environment* (Thirteenth Edition), and *Contemporary Business Law.*

Barry S. Roberts received a B.S. in business administration from Pennsylvania State University, a J.D. from the University of Pennsylvania, and an LL.M. from Harvard Law School. He served as a judicial clerk for the Pennsylvania Supreme Court prior to practicing law in Pittsburgh. Barry Roberts is professor emeritus of business law at the Kenan-Flagler Business School, University of North Carolina at Chapel Hill, and is a member of Who's Who in American Law and the North Carolina and Pennsylvania Bars.

Professor Roberts has written numerous articles on such topics as antitrust, products liability, constitutional law, banking law, employment law, and business associations. He has been a reviewer and staff editor for the *American Business Law Journal*. He is coauthor of *Business Law and the Regulation of Business* (Thirteenth Edition), *Essentials of Business Law and the Legal Environment* (Thirteenth Edition), and *Contemporary Business Law.*

Contents in Brief

Preface		*xiv*
Table of Cases		*xix*
Table of Illustrations		*xxii*

PART 1

The Legal Environment of Business — 1

1	Introduction to Law	2
2	Business Ethics and the Social Responsibility of Business	14
3	Civil Dispute Resolution	42
4	Constitutional Law	67
5	Administrative Law	90
6	Criminal Law	107
7	Intentional Torts	125
8	Negligence and Strict Liability	147

PART 2

Contracts — 171

9	Introduction to Contracts	172
10	Mutual Assent	190
11	Conduct Invalidating Assent	213
12	Consideration	234
13	Illegal Bargains	254
14	Contractual Capacity	275
15	Contracts in Writing	290
16	Third Parties to Contracts	315
17	Performance, Breach, and Discharge	334
18	Contract Remedies	352

PART 3

Agency — 371

19	Relationship of Principal and Agent	372
20	Relationship with Third Parties	395

PART 4

Sales — 421

21	Introduction to Sales and Leases	422
22	Performance	444
23	Transfer of Title and Risk of Loss	465
24	Products Liability: Warranties and Strict Liability in Tort	484
25	Sales Remedies	511

PART 5

Negotiable Instruments — 535

26	Form and Content	536
27	Transfer and Holder in Due Course	552
28	Liability of Parties	583
29	Bank Deposits, Collections, and Funds Transfer	602

PART 6

Unincorporated Business Associations — 623

30	Formation and Internal Relations of General Partnerships	624
31	Operation and Dissolution of General Partnerships	648
32	Limited Partnerships and Limited Liability Companies	675

PART 7

Corporations — 705

33	Nature, Formation, and Powers	706
34	Financial Structure	730
35	Management Structure	753
36	Fundamental Changes	785

PART 8

Debtor and Creditor Relations 805

37 Secured Transactions and Suretyship 806
38 Bankruptcy 839

PART 9

Regulation of Business 871

39 Protection of Intellectual Property 872
40 Antitrust 895
41 Consumer Protection 919
42 Employment Law 947
43 Securities Regulation 983
44 Accountants' Legal Liability 1021
45 Environmental Law 1035
46 International Business Law 1055

PART 10

Property 1073

47 Introduction to Property,
   Property Insurance, Bailments, and
   Documents of Title 1074
48 Interests in Real Property 1101
49 Transfer and Control of Real Property 1121
50 Trusts and Decedents' Estates 1139

Appendices A-1

A The Constitution of the
   United States of America A-2
B Dictionary of Legal Terms B-1

Index I-1

Contents

Preface   *xiv*
Table of Cases   *xix*
Table of Illustrations   *xxii*

PART 1

The Legal Environment of Business   1

1 Introduction to Law   2
Nature of Law   2
Classification of Law   4
Sources of Law   5
Legal Analysis   9
Chapter Summary   *11*
Cases   *12*

2 Business Ethics and the Social Responsibility of Business   14
Law Versus Ethics   15
Ethical Theories   15
Ethical Standards in Business   18
Ethical Responsibilities of Business   19
Corporate Governance   20
Chapter Summary   *23*
Cases   *24*
Questions   *24*
Business Ethics Cases   *26*

3 Civil Dispute Resolution   42
The Court System   42
The Federal Courts   42
State Courts   44
Jurisdiction   45
Subject Matter Jurisdiction   45
Jurisdiction Over the Parties   47
Civil Dispute Resolution   49

Civil Procedure   50
Alternative Dispute Resolution   53
Chapter Summary   *57*
Cases   *59*
Questions   *64*
Case Problems   *65*
Taking Sides   *66*

4 Constitutional Law   67
Basic Principles of Constitutional Law   68
Powers of Government   69
Limitations on Government   72
Chapter Summary   *77*
Cases   *78*
Questions   *86*
Case Problems   *86*
Taking Sides   *89*

5 Administrative Law   90
Operation of Administrative Agencies   91
Limits on Administrative Agencies   94
Chapter Summary   *96*
Cases   *97*
Case Problems   *103*
Taking Sides   *106*

6 Criminal Law   107
Nature of Crimes   107
White-Collar Crime   110
Crimes Against Business   111
Defenses to Crimes   114
Criminal Procedure   115
Chapter Summary   *117*
Cases   *118*

Questions 122

Case Problems 123

Taking Sides 124

7 Intentional Torts **125**

Intent 126

Harm to the Person 127

Harm to the Right of Dignity 129

Harm to Property 131

Harm to Economic Interests 132

Defenses to Intentional Torts 134

Chapter Summary 135

Cases 136

Questions 142

Case Problems 143

Taking Sides 146

8 Negligence and Strict Liability **147**

Negligence **148**

Breach of Duty of Care 148

Factual Cause 153

Scope of Liability (Proximate Cause) 153

Harm 154

Defenses to Negligence 155

Strict Liability **157**

Activities Giving Rise to Strict Liability 157

Defenses to Strict Liability 158

Chapter Summary 159

Cases 160

Questions 167

Case Problems 168

Taking Sides 170

PART 2

Contracts 171

9 Introduction to Contracts **172**

Development of the Law of Contracts 172

Definition of a Contract 174

Requirements of a Contract 174

Classification of Contracts 175

Promissory Estoppel 178

Quasi Contracts or Restitution 178

Chapter Summary 179

Cases 180

Questions 186

Case Problems 186

Taking Sides 189

10 Mutual Assent **190**

Offer 190

Essentials of an Offer 191

Duration of Offers 193

Acceptance of Offer **196**

Communication of Acceptance 197

Variant Acceptances 198

Chapter Summary 200

Cases 201

Questions 208

Case Problems 210

Taking Sides 212

11 Conduct Invalidating Assent **213**

Duress 213

Undue Influence 214

Fraud 214

Nonfraudulent Misrepresentation 217

Mistake 218

Chapter Summary 220

Cases 221

Questions 228

Case Problems 229

Taking Sides 233

12 Consideration **234**

Legal Sufficiency 234

Bargained-For Exchange 239

Contracts without Consideration 240

Chapter Summary 243

Cases 244

Questions 249

Case Problems 251

Taking Sides 253

13 Illegal Bargains **254**

Violations of Statutes 254

Violations of Public Policy 256

Effect of Illegality 258

Chapter Summary 259

Cases 260

Questions 270

Case Problems 271

Taking Sides 274

14 Contractual Capacity   **275**

Minors   275

Incompetent Persons   278

Intoxicated Persons   278

Chapter Summary   279

Cases   280

Questions   286

Case Problems   287

Taking Sides   289

15 Contracts in Writing   **290**

Statute of Frauds   **290**

Contracts within the Statute of Frauds   291

Compliance with the Statute of Frauds   296

Effect of Noncompliance   297

Parol Evidence Rule   **298**

The Rule   298

Situations to Which the Rule Does Not Apply   298

Supplemental Evidence   299

Interpretation of Contracts   **299**

Chapter Summary   301

Cases   303

Questions   310

Case Problems   311

Taking Sides   314

16 Third Parties to Contracts   **315**

Assignment of Rights   315

Delegation of Duties   319

Third-Party Beneficiary Contracts   320

Chapter Summary   322

Cases   324

Questions   329

Case Problems   330

Taking Sides   333

17 Performance, Breach, and Discharge   **334**

Conditions   334

Discharge by Performance   336

Discharge by Breach   336

Discharge by Agreement of the Parties   338

Discharge by Operation of Law   339

Chapter Summary   341

Cases   343

Questions   347

Case Problems   349

Taking Sides   351

18 Contract Remedies   **352**

Interests Protected by Contract Remedies   352

Monetary Damages   352

Remedies in Equity   356

Restitution   357

Limitations on Remedies   358

Remedies for Misrepresentation   359

Chapter Summary   361

Cases   362

Questions   367

Case Problems   369

Taking Sides   370

PART 3

Agency   **371**

19 Relationship of Principal and Agent   **372**

Nature of Agency   372

Creation of Agency   374

Duties of Agent to Principal   375

Duties of Principal to Agent   378

Termination of Agency   380

Chapter Summary   382

Cases   384

Questions   391

Case Problems   392

Taking Sides   394

20 Relationship with Third Parties   **395**

Relationship of Principal and Third Persons   **395**

Contract Liability of Principal   395

Tort Liability of Principal   401

Criminal Liability of Principal   404

Relationship of Agent and Third Persons   **405**

Contract Liability of Agent   405

Tort of Liability of Agent   407

Rights of Agent Against Third Person   407

Chapter Summary   407

Cases   409

Questions   416

Case Problems   417

Taking Sides   419

PART 4

Sales   421

21 Introduction to Sales and Leases   422

Nature of Sales and Leases   422
Definitions   423
Fundamental Principles of Article 2 and Article 2A   424
Formation of Sales and Lease Contracts   427
Manifestation of Mutual Assent   427
Consideration   429
Form of the Contract   431
Chapter Summary   433
Cases   434
Questions   440
Case Problems   441
Taking Sides   443

22 Performance   444

Performance by the Seller   444
Performance by the Buyer   449
Obligations of Both Parties   451
Chapter Summary   454
Cases   455
Questions   460
Case Problems   461
Taking Sides   464

23 Transfer of Title and Risk of Loss   465

Transfer of Title   465
Risk of Loss   469
Sales of Goods in Bulk   472
Chapter Summary   474
Cases   475
Questions   481
Case Problems   482
Taking Sides   483

24 Products Liability: Warranties and Strict Liability in Tort   484

Warranties   484
Types of Warranties   485
Obstacles to Warranty Actions   487
Strict Product Liability in Tort   490
Requirements of Strict Liability   491
Obstacles to Recovery Under Second Restatement   493
Restatement (Third) of Torts: Products Liability   494
Chapter Summary   496

Cases   498
Questions   506
Case Problems   507
Taking Sides   510

25 Sales Remedies   511

Remedies of the Seller   512
Remedies of the Buyer   516
Contractual Provisions Affecting Remedies   520
Chapter Summary   522
Cases   524
Questions   530
Case Problems   531
Taking Sides   534

PART 5

Negotiable Instruments   535

26 Form and Content   536

Negotiability   536
Types of Negotiable Instruments   538
Formal Requirements of Negotiable Instruments   540
Chapter Summary   545
Cases   546
Questions   549
Case Problems   550
Taking Sides   551

27 Transfer and Holder in Due Course   552

Transfer   552
Negotiation   552
Indorsements   555
Holder in Due Course   559
Requirements of a Holder in Due Course   559
Holder in Due Course Status   563
The Preferred Position of a Holder in Due Course   563
Limitations Upon Holder in Due Course Rights   566
Chapter Summary   569
Cases   571
Questions   578
Case Problems   580
Taking Sides   582

28 Liability of Parties   583

Contractual Liability   583
Signature   583
Liability of Primary Parties   585

Liability of Secondary Parties 585

Termination of Liability 588

Liability Based on Warranty **589**

Warranties on Transfer 589

Warranties on Presentment 590

Chapter Summary *593*

Cases *594*

Questions *599*

Case Problems *600*

Taking Sides *601*

29 Bank Deposits, Collections, and Funds Transfer **602**

Bank Deposits and Collections **602**

Collection of Items 602

Relationship between Payor Bank and its Customer 606

Electronic Fund Transfer **608**

Types of Electronic Funds Transfer 609

Consumer Funds Transfer 609

Wholesale Funds Transfer 611

Chapter Summary *614*

Cases *615*

Questions *619*

Case Problems *621*

Taking Sides *622*

PART 6

Unincorporated Business Associations **623**

30 Formation and Internal Relations of General Partnerships **624**

Choosing a Business Association **624**

Factors Affecting the Choice 625

Forms of Business Associations 626

Formation of General Partnerships **628**

Nature of Partnership 628

Formation of a Partnership 629

Relationships Among Partners **632**

Duties Among Partners 632

Rights Among Partners 634

Chapter Summary *638*

Cases *640*

Questions *645*

Case Problems *646*

Taking Sides *647*

31 Operation and Dissolution of General Partnerships **648**

Relationship of Partnership and Partners with Third Parties **648**

Contracts of Partnership 648

Torts and Crimes of Partnership 651

Notice to a Partner 652

Liability of Incoming Partner 652

Dissociation and Dissolution of General Partnerships under the RUPA **652**

Dissociation 652

Dissolution 653

Dissociation without Dissolution 655

Dissolution of General Partnerships under the UPA **656**

Dissolution 656

Winding Up 658

Continuation after Dissolution 658

Chapter Summary *659*

Cases *661*

Questions *670*

Case Problems *673*

Taking Sides *674*

32 Limited Partnerships and Limited Liability Companies **675**

Limited Partnerships 675

Limited Liability Companies 681

Other Types of Unincorporated Business Associations 686

Chapter Summary *687*

Cases *691*

Questions *700*

Case Problems *701*

Taking Sides *702*

PART 7

Corporations **705**

33 Nature, Formation, and Powers **706**

Nature of Corporations **707**

Corporate Attributes 707

Classification of Corporations 708

Formation of a Corporation **710**

Organizing the Corporation 710

Formalities of Incorporation 712
Recognition or Disregard of Corporateness **714**
Defective Incorporation 714
Piercing the Corporate Veil 715
Corporate Powers **716**
Sources of Corporate Powers 716
Ultra Vires Acts 717
Liability for Torts and Crimes 717
Chapter Summary 718
Cases 720
Questions 725
Case Problems 726
Taking Sides 729

34 Financial Structure **730**
Debt Securities **731**
Authority to Issue Debt Securities 731
Types of Debt Securities 731
Equity Securities **732**
Issuance of Shares 732
Classes of Shares 735
Dividends and Other Distributions **736**
Types of Dividends and Other Distributions 737
Legal Restrictions on Dividends and
Other Distributions 738
Declaration and Payment of Distributions 741
Liability for Improper Dividends and Distributions 741
Chapter Summary 742
Cases 743
Questions 749
Case Problems 750
Taking Sides 752

35 Management Structure **753**
Corporate Governance **753**
Role of Shareholders **756**
Voting Rights of Shareholders 756
Enforcement Rights of Shareholders 760
Role of Directors and Officers **761**
Function of the Board of Directors 762
Election and Tenure of Directors 763
Exercise of Directors' Functions 764
Officers 765
Duties of Directors and Officers 766
Chapter Summary 770

Cases 771
Questions 781
Case Problems 782
Taking Sides 784

36 Fundamental Changes **785**
Amendments to the Articles of Incorporation 785
Combinations 786
Dissolution 791
Chapter Summary 793
Cases 794
Questions 800
Case Problems 801
Taking Sides 803

PART 8
Debtor and Creditor Relations **805**
37 Secured Transactions and Suretyship **806**
Secured Transactions in Personal Property **806**
Essentials of Secured Transactions 807
Classification of Collateral 807
Attachment 809
Perfection 811
Priorities Among Competing Interests 814
Default 818
Suretyship **820**
Nature and Formation 820
Duties of Surety 822
Rights of Surety 823
Defenses of Surety and Principal Debtor 823
Chapter Summary 826
Cases 829
Questions 834
Case Problems 836
Taking Sides 838

38 Bankruptcy **839**
Federal Bankruptcy Law **839**
Case Administration—Chapter 3 840
Creditors, the Debtor, and the Estate—Chapter 5 842
Liquidation—Chapter 7 847
Reorganization—Chapter 11 851
Adjustment of Debts of Individuals—Chapter 13 854
Creditors' Rights and Debtor's Relief
Outside of Bankruptcy **856**

Creditors' Rights   856
Debtor's Relief   857
Chapter Summary   858
Cases   860
Questions   866
Case Problems   867
Taking Sides   869

PART 9

Regulation of Business   871

39 Protection of Intellectual Property   872

Trade Secrets   872
Trade Symbols   874
Trade Names   877
Copyrights   878
Patents   880
Chapter Summary   883
Cases   884
Questions   891
Case Problems   892
Taking Sides   894

40 Antitrust   895

Sherman Act   895
Clayton Act   901
Robinson-Patman Act   903
Federal Trade Commission Act   904
Chapter Summary   906
Cases   907
Questions   915
Case Problems   916
Taking Sides   918

41 Consumer Protection   919

State and Federal Consumer
Protection Agencies   919
Consumer Purchases   924
Consumer Credit Transactions   927
Creditors' Remedies   932
Chapter Summary   933
Cases   935
Questions   942
Case Problems   943
Taking Sides   946

42 Employment Law   947

Labor Law   947
Employment Discrimination Law   949
Employee Protection   955
Chapter Summary   959
Cases   960
Questions   977
Case Problems   978
Taking Sides   982

43 Securities Regulation   983

Securities Act of 1933   **985**
Definition of a Security   985
Registration of Securities   986
Exempt Securities   988
Exempt Transactions for Issuers   988
Exempt Transactions for Nonissuers   993
Liability   995
Securities Exchange Act of 1934   **996**
Disclosure   997
Liability   1002
Chapter Summary   1008
Cases   1010
Questions   1018
Case Problems   1019
Taking Sides   1020

44 Accountants' Legal Liability   1021

Common Law   1021
Federal Securities Law   1024
Chapter Summary   1027
Cases   1028
Questions   1032
Case Problems   1033
Taking Sides   1034

45 Environmental Law   1035

**Common Law Actions for
Environmental Damage**   **1035**
Nuisance   1035
Trespass to Land   1036
Strict Liability for Abnormally
Dangerous Activities   1036
Problems Common to Private Causes of Action   1036
Federal Regulation of the Environment   **1036**
The National Environmental Policy Act   1037

The Clean Air Act   1038
The Clean Water Act   1040
Hazardous Substances   1042
International Protection of the Ozone Layer   1046
Chapter Summary   *1047*
Cases   *1048*
Questions   *1052*
Case Problems   *1052*
Taking Sides   *1054*

46 International Business Law   **1055**
The International Environment   1055
Jurisdiction Over Actions of Foreign Governments   1057
Transacting Business Abroad   1059
Forms of Multinational Enterprises   1064
Chapter Summary   *1065*
Cases   *1067*
Questions   *1070*
Case Problems   *1071*
Taking Sides   *1072*

PART 10

Property   **1073**

**47 Introduction to Property,
   Property Insurance, Bailments,
   and Documents of Title**   **1074**
Introduction to Property and Personal Property   **1074**
Kinds of Property   1075
Transfer of Title to Personal Property   1076
Property Insurance   **1078**
Fire and Property Insurance   1078
Nature of Insurance Contracts   1079
Bailments and Documents of Title   **1081**
Bailments   1081
Documents of Title   1085
Chapter Summary   *1087*
Cases   *1090*
Questions   *1095*
Case Problems   *1098*
Taking Sides   *1100*

48 Interests in Real Property   **1101**
Freehold Estates   1101
Leasehold Estates   1103

Concurrent Ownership   1107
Nonpossessory Interests   1109
Chapter Summary   *1112*
Cases   *1113*
Questions   *1118*
Case Problems   *1119*
Taking Sides   *1120*

49 Transfer and Control of Real Property   **1121**
Transfer of Real Property   **1121**
Contract of Sale   1121
Deeds   1122
Secured Transactions   1124
Adverse Possession   1126
Public and Private Controls   **1126**
Zoning   1126
Eminent Domain   1127
Private Restrictions Upon Land Use   1128
Chapter Summary   *1129*
Cases   *1131*
Questions   *1135*
Case Problems   *1136*
Taking Sides   *1138*

50 Trusts and Decedents' Estates   **1139**
Trusts   **1139**
Types of Trusts   1139
Creation of Express Trusts   1141
Termination of a Trust   1142
Decedents' Estates   **1143**
Wills   1143
Intestate Succession   1147
Administration of Estates   1147
Chapter Summary   *1148*
Cases   *1150*
Questions   *1155*
Case Problems   *1157*
Taking Sides   *1158*

Appendices   **A-1**
Appendix A: The Constitution of the
United States of America   A-2
Appendix B: Dictionary of Legal Terms   B-1

Index   **I-1**

Preface

The format of the *Eighteenth Edition* continues the tradition of accuracy, comprehensiveness, and authoritativeness established by prior editions. This text covers the fundamentally important statutory, administrative, and case law that affects business in a succinct and nontechnical but authoritative manner and provides depth sufficient to ensure easy comprehension by students. Chapters contain learning objectives, narrative text, illustrations, cases consisting of selected court decisions, chapter summaries, and end-of-chapter questions and case problems.

Topical Coverage

This text is designed for use in business law and legal environment of business courses generally offered in universities, colleges, schools of business and commerce, community colleges, and junior colleges. By reason of the text's broad and deep coverage, instructors may readily adapt this text to specially designed courses in business law or the legal environment of business by assigning and emphasizing different combinations of chapters.

Emphasis has been placed upon the regulatory environment of business law: the first eight chapters introduce the legal environment of business, and *Part 9* (*Chapters 39 through 46*) addresses government regulation of business.

Uniform Certified Public Accountant Examination Preparation

As updated effective July 1, 2021, the Uniform CPA Examination is composed of four sections: Auditing and Attestation (AUD), Business Environment and Concepts (BEC), Financial Accounting and Reporting (FAR), and Regulation (REG). This textbook covers material included in Area II (Business Law) of the Regulation section of the CPA Exam.

In general, the Area II of the REG section blueprint covers topics of business law, including the following:

- Knowledge and understanding of the legal implications of business transactions, particularly as they relate to accounting, auditing and financial reporting
- Areas of agency, contracts, debtor–creditor relationships, government regulation of business, and business structure
  - The Uniform Commercial Code under the topics of contracts and debtor–creditor relationships
  - Nontax-related business structure content
- Federal and widely adopted uniform state laws and references as identified in [the following] References
  - Revised Model Business Corporation Act
  - Revised Uniform Limited Partnership Act
  - Revised Uniform Partnership Act
  - Uniform Commercial Code
  - Current textbooks covering business law…

More specifically, the Area II of the REG section blueprint includes the following topics, which are covered in this textbook:

II Business Law

A. Agency
1. Authority of agents and principals
2. Duties and liabilities of agents and principals

B. Contracts
1. Formation
2. Performance
3. Discharge, breach, and remedies

C. Debtor–Creditor Relationships
1. Rights, duties, and liabilities of debtors, creditors, and guarantors
2. Bankruptcy and insolvency
3. Secured transactions

D. Federal Laws and Regulations

E. Business Structure
1. Selection and formation of business entity and related operation and termination
2. Rights, duties, legal obligations, and authority of owners and management

For more information, visit www.aicpa.org/becomeacpa/cpaexam.html.

Up-to-Date

The *Eighteenth Edition* has been extensively updated and includes the following:

- The constitutional law chapter (*Chapter 4*) discusses recent U.S. Supreme Court decisions holding that (1) the anticommandeering doctrine invalidated a Federal statute that prohibited States from authorizing sports gambling schemes, (2) Internet retailers can be required to collect sales taxes in States where they have no physical presence, and (3) public employees who choose not to join unions may not be required to help pay for collective bargaining.

- The criminal law chapter (*Chapter 6*) discusses the recent U.S. Supreme Court decisions holding that (1) in both Federal and State courts the Sixth Amendment right to a jury trial requires a unanimous verdict to convict a defendant of a serious offense and (2) the government must obtain a search warrant to access wireless carriers' historical cell site records revealing the location of a user's cell phone whenever it made or received calls.

- The limited partnership and LLC chapter (*Chapter 32*) covers the 2001 ReRULPA and low-profit limited liability companies.

- The corporations chapters (*Chapters 33–36*) cover the 2016 Revised Model Business Corporation Act.

- The bankruptcy chapter (*Chapter 38*) discusses the Small Business Reorganization Act of 2019 and the U.S. Supreme Court decision holding that in Chapter 11 cases, including structured dismissal cases, a bankruptcy court cannot confirm a plan that contains distributions that violate the priority rules over the objection of an impaired creditor class.

- The intellectual property chapter (*Chapter 39*) includes the Copyright Alternative in Small-Claims Enforcement Act of 2019, the Music Modernization Act, and the Marrakesh Treaty of 2013 and discusses the U.S. Supreme Court cases involving the patent exhaustion

doctrine, *inter partes* review, and the Lanham Act's (1) disparagement clause and (2) immoral, deceptive, or scandalous clause.

- The consumer protection chapter (*Chapter 41*) covers the Consumer Review Fairness Act of 2016; the Economic Growth, Regulatory Relief Act; the Consumer Protection Act of 2018; and the U.S. Supreme Court case addressing whether the Dodd-Frank Act violates the separation of powers by prohibiting the President from removing the Director of the Consumer Financial Protection Bureau except for "inefficiency, neglect of duty, or malfeasance in office."

- The employment law chapter (*Chapter 42*) discusses the U.S. Supreme Court decisions holding (1) that nonunionized private-sector employers may enforce employment agreements that require employees to settle employment disputes through individual arbitration rather than in class or collective actions and (2) that public employees who choose not to join unions may not be required to help pay for collective bargaining.

- The securities regulation chapter (*Chapter 43*) (1) covers the U.S. Securities and Exchange Commission's amendments to Regulation A, to Rule 147, to Rule 504, and to rules regarding solicitations of interest prior to a registered public offering and smaller reporting companies, and (2) discusses the U.S. Supreme Court decision holding that under the Securities Litigation Uniform Standards Act of 1998, State courts have jurisdiction over class actions alleging violations of only the 1933 Act and defendants are not permitted to remove such actions from State court to Federal court.

- The environmental law chapter (*Chapter 45*) covers (1) the Chemical Safety for the 21st Century Act, (2) the EPA's Affordable Clean Energy (ACE) Rule, Safer Affordable Fuel-Efficient (SAFE) Vehicles Rule, and Navigable Waters Protection Rule, and (3) the U.S. Supreme Court decision holding that the Clean Water Act requires a permit when there is a direct discharge from a point source into navigable waters or when there is the functional equivalent of a direct discharge.

- The international business law chapter (Chapter 46) covers the United States–Mexico–Canada Agreement (USMCA), the Better Utilization of Investments Leading to Development (BUILD) Act, the U.S. International Development Finance Corporation (DFC), the Export Controls Act of 2018, and the International Antitrust Enforcement Assistance Act of 1994.

- The transfer and control of real property chapter (*Chapter 49*) covers the Economic Growth, Regulatory Relief Act; the Consumer Protection Act of 2018; and the Model Residential Mortgage Satisfaction Act.

- The trusts and decedents' estates chapter (*Chapter 50*) covers the Uniform Trust Code and discusses the U.S. Supreme Court decision holding that the retroactive application of Minnesota's revocation-upon-divorce statute, which automatically nullifies the designation of an ex-spouse as the beneficiary of a life insurance policy or other will substitute, does not violate the Contracts Clause of the U.S. Constitution.

Readability of Narrative Text

To make the text as readable as possible, all unnecessary "legal-ese" has been omitted, and necessary legal terms have been printed in boldface and clearly defined, explained, and illustrated. Each chapter is carefully organized with sufficient levels of subordination to enhance the accessibility of the material. The text is enriched by numerous illustrative hypothetical and case examples, which help students relate the material to real-life experiences. The end-of-chapter cases are cross-referenced in the text, as are related topics covered in other chapters.

Chapter Learning Objectives

Each chapter begins with a list of learning objectives for students.

Applying the Law

The Applying the Law feature provides a systematic legal analysis of a realistic situation that focuses on a specific concept presented in the chapter. It consists of (1) the facts of a hypothetical case, (2) an identification of the broad legal issue presented by those facts, (3) a statement of the applicable rule—or applicable legal principles, including definitions, which aid in resolving the legal issue, (4) the application of the rule to the facts, and (5) a legal conclusion or decision in the case. The Applying the Law feature appears in fourteen chapters. We wish to acknowledge and thank Professor Ann Olazábal, University of Miami, for her contribution in preparing this feature.

Practical Advice

Each chapter has a number of statements that illustrate how legal concepts covered in the chapter can be applied to common business situations.

Case Treatment

Relevant, carefully selected, and interesting cases illustrate how key principles of business law are applied. All the cases have been edited carefully to preserve the actual language of the court and to show the essential facts of the case, the issue or issues involved, the decision of the court, and the reason for its decision. We have retained the landmark cases from the prior edition. In addition, we have a number of recent cases, including the following U.S. Supreme Court cases: *Murphy v. National Collegiate Athletic Assn.; South Dakota v. Wayfair, Inc.; Janus v. State, County, and Municipal Employees; Carpenter v. United States; Cyan, Inc. v. Beaver County Employees Retirement Fund; Jam v. International Finance Corp.; and Sveen v. Melin.*

Illustrations

We have used more than 210 visually engaging, classroom-tested figures, diagrams, charts, tables, and chapter summaries. The figures and diagrams help students conceptualize the many abstract concepts in the law; the charts and tables not only summarize prior discussions but also help to illustrate relationships among legal rules. Moreover, each chapter has a summary in the form of an annotated outline of the entire chapter, including key terms.

End-of-Chapter Questions and Case Problems

Classroom-proven questions and case problems appear at the end of chapters to test students' understanding of major concepts. Almost all of the chapters include one or more new questions and/or case problems. We have used the questions (based on hypothetical situations) and the case problems (taken from reported court decisions) in our own classrooms and consider them excellent stimulants to classroom discussion. Students, in turn, have found the questions and case problems helpful in enabling them to apply the basic rules of law to factual situations.

Taking Sides

Each chapter—except *Chapters 1 and 2*—has an end-of-chapter feature that requires students to apply critical-thinking skills to a case-based fact situation. Students are asked to identify the relevant legal rules and develop arguments for both parties to the dispute. In addition, students are asked to explain how they think a court would resolve the dispute.

Appendices

The appendices include the Constitution of the United States and a comprehensive Dictionary of Legal Terms.

Pedagogical Benefits

Classroom use and study of this book should provide students with the following benefits and skills:

1. Perception and appreciation of the scope, extent, and importance of the law.
2. Basic knowledge of the fundamental concepts, principles, and rules of law that apply to business transactions.
3. Knowledge of the function and operation of courts and government administrative agencies.
4. Ability to recognize the potential legal problems which may arise in a doubtful or complicated situation and the necessity of consulting a lawyer and obtaining competent professional legal advice.
5. Development of analytical skills and reasoning power.

Additional Course Tools

CENGAGE INFUSE

Cengage Infuse for Business Law is the first-of-its-kind digital learning solution that uses your learning management system (LMS) functionality so you can enjoy simple course set-up and intuitive management tools. Offering just the right amount of auto-graded content, you'll be ready to go online at the drop of a hat.

SERIOUSLY SIMPLE COURSE SETUP

Get up and running quickly and easily. Search content organized by chapter and infuse publisher-provided readings and assessments straight into your course in just a few clicks.

LEVERAGES THE FUNCTIONALITY OF YOUR LMS

No need to learn a new technology; utilize the familiar functionality your LMS provides, enabling you to use content as-is from day one.

JUST THE RIGHT AMOUNT OF AUTO-GRADED CONTENT

Let us take care of the basics so you can focus on teaching. Infuse textbook chapter readings, comprehension checks, or end-of-chapter quizzes personalized to this text.

SUPPORT AT EVERY STEP

Access award-winning support 24/7, or take advantage of on-demand resources, including user guides and more.

INSTRUCTOR RESOURCES

Additional instructor resources for this product are available online. Instructor assets include an Instructor's Manual, Educator's Guide, PowerPoint® slides, and a test bank powered by Cognero®. Sign up or sign in at www.cengage.com to search for and access this product and its online resources.

Acknowledgments

We are grateful to those who provided us with comments for previous editions of the book: Miriam R. Albert, Fordham University; Mark Altieri, Cleveland State University; Wm. Dennis Ames, Indiana University of Pennsylvania; Albert Anderson, Mount Aloysius College; Albert Andrews, Jr., University of Minnesota; Michael Balsamo, SUNY–Old Westbury; Denise A. Bartles, Missouri Western State College; Lois Yoder Beier, Kent State University; Monika Lovewell Bellows, SUNY–Canton; Robert Bing, William Paterson College; Joell Bjorke, Winona State University; William N. Bockanic, John Carroll University; Andrea Boggio, Bryant University; Donald Boren, Bowling Green State University; Joyce Boland-DeVito, Esq., St. John's University; Joe Boucher, University of Wisconsin–Madison; L. Brooks, Nichols College; Nicolaus Bruns, Jr., Lake Forest Graduate School of Management; Mark A. Buchanan, Boise State University; Deborah Lynn Bundy, Marquette University; Michael Burg, University of St. Thomas; Debra Burke, Western Carolina University; Thomas J. Canavan, Long Island University–C. W. Post Campus; Regina W. Cannon, University of Georgia; Donald Cantwell, University of Texas–Arlington; John P. Carnasiotis, University of Missouri; Albert L. Carter, Jr., University of the District of Columbia; Thomas D. Cavenagh, North Central College; Jennifer Chapman, Georgia Gwinnett College; Jeff Charles, Bowling Green State University; John Cirace, CUNY–Lehman College; Richard R. Clark, University of the District of Columbia; Arlen Coyle, University of Mississippi; Mitchell F. Crusto, Washington University–St. Louis; Richard Dalebout, Brigham Young University; Arthur S. Davis, Long Island University; John Davis, Ashland Community & Technical College; Kenneth R. Davis, Fordham School of Business; William Day, Cleveland State University; Alex DeVience, Jr., DePaul University; Craig Disbrow, Plymouth State College, New Hampshire; Robert H. Doud, Adelphi University; William G. Elliott, Saginaw Valley State University; Edward Eramus, State University of New York–Brockport; Kurt Erickson, South West Michigan College; Jay Ersling, University of St. Thomas, Minnesota; Robert Evans, Rockford College; Alfred E. Fabian, Ivy Tech Community College; J. Royce Fichtner, Drake University; Thomas Fitzpatrick, Assumption College; Joe W. Fowler, Oklahoma State University–Stillwater; Karla H. Fox, University of Connecticut; Stanley Fuchs, Fordham University;

Samuel B. Garber, DePaul University; Nathan T. Garrett, Esq., North Carolina Central University; Michael J. Garrison, North Dakota State University; Daniel Gillespie, DePaul University; Dr. Roy Girasa, Pace University; Marvin Gordon, Loyola Chicago University; Sue Gragiano, Bowling Green State University; James Granito, Youngstown State University; John Gray, Faulkner University; Sally Terry Green, Texas Southern University; Dale A. Grossman, Cornell University; Donald Haley, Cleveland State University; Marc Hall, Auburn University Montgomery; Brian Hanlon, North Central College; Dr. Ivan Harber, Indian River State College; James V. Harrison, St. Peter's State College; Lori K. Harris-Ransom, Caldwell College; Edward J. Hartman, St. Ambrose University; Frances J. Hill, University of Wisconsin–Whitewater; Telford F. Hollman, University of Northern Iowa–Cedar Falls; Georgia L. Holmes, Mankato State University; James Holzinger, Muhlenberg College; Norman Hope, Tabor College; Sarah H. Hudwig, Mary Baldwin College; Velma Jesser, Lane Community College; Theresa Johnson, Cleveland State University; Marilee Jones-Confield, California State University–Long Beach; Al Joyner, Eastern Illinois University; Mary C. Keifer, Ohio University; Randall Kilbourne, Northwestern State University; Barbara Kirkpatrick, Virginia Intermont College; Edward M. Kissling, Ocean County College, New Jersey; Robert Klepa, UCLA Extension; Louise Knight, Bucknell University; William J. Koval, Jr., Notre Dame College; Duane R. Lambert, California State University–Hayward; Joseph F. Lenius, Northeastern Illinois University; Andrew Liput, Felician College; Avi Liveson, Hunter College; Romain Lorentz, University of St. Thomas; Sarah H. Ludwig, Mary Baldwin College; Richard Luke, Ricks College; Tanya M. Marcum, Bradley University; Pat Maroney, Florida State University; Sharon Martin, Empire State College–Brooklyn Unit; Bruce Marx, SUNY–Old Westbury; Michael A. Mass, American University; Cheryl Massingale, University of Tennessee–Knoxville; Greg K. McCann, Stetson University; Bruce McClain, Cleveland State University; Ann L. McClure, Fort Hays State University; James McGee, College of Westchester; Charles R. McGuire, Illinois State University; Herbert McLaughlin, Bryant College; James Molloy, University of Wisconsin–Whitewater; Sebrena R. Moten, Troy University; Donald Nelson, University of Denver; Carol L. Nielsen, Bemidji State University; Christopher J. Nyhus, University of Mary; L. K. O'Drudy, Jr., University of Virginia; Ann Morales Olazabal, University of Miami; David Oliveiri, University of Rochester; Richard Paxton, San Diego Community College; Gail P. Petravick, Bradley University; Jim Pingel, Everest University–Brandon; Jonathan Politi, Columbus College of Art & Design; James L. Porter, University of New Mexico; Lisa Rackley, Rich Mountain Community College; Elinor Rahm, Central Missouri State University; Samuel H. Ramsay, Jr., Bryant College; Decateur Reed, Boise State University; Richard E. Regan, St. John Fisher College; Roger Reinsch, Emporia State University; L. Reppert, Marymount University; Caroline Rider, Marist College; Roland W. Riggs, Marietta College; George Roe, University of Illinois–Chicago; Stanford Rosenberg, La Roche College; Alan Ross, University of California–Berkeley; Mark Rossi, Briar Cliff University; Tim Rueth, Marquette University; Stuart Schafer, University of Mississippi; Eric D Schwartz, LaRoche College; Donald H. Shoop, North Dakota State University; Carol Wahle Smith, Central Florida Community College; Peter Smithfield, Argyle Academy; Michael J. Sovansky, Saginaw Valley State University; Janis Stamm, Edinboro University of Pennsylvania; Beverly E. Stanis, Oakton Community College; James Staruck, DePaul University; Al Stauber, Florida State University; David Steele, University of Wisconsin–Eau Claire; Lowell E. Stockstill, Wittenberg University; Peter Strohm, Georgian Court College; Al Talarczyk, Edgewood College; James D. Taylor, Claremont McKenna College; Kevin M. Teeven, Bradley University; Robert J. Tepper, University of New Mexico; Dale B. Thompson, University of St. Thomas; Leonard Tripodi, St. Joseph's College; Alix Valenti, University of Houston–Clear Lake; Karen Vitori, Schoolcraft College; Nancy A. Wainwright, Eastern Washington University; Charles H. Walker, University of Mississippi; Michael G. Walsh, Villanova University; Daniel Warner, Western Washington University; Peter M. Wasemiller, Fresno Pacific College; David Webster, University of South Florida–Tampa; Scott A. White, University of Wisconsin; E. Marshall Wick, Gallaudet University; John G. Williams, Northwestern State University; Amy Wilson, Zane State College; Wells J. Wright, University of Minnesota; Rizvana Zameeruddin, University of Wisconsin–Parkside; and James B. Zimarowski, University of Notre Dame.

For their support, we extend our thanks to Karlene Fogelin Knebel, Joanne Erwick Roberts, and Susan Sklar. And we are grateful to Abbie Schultheis and Cheri Plasse of Cengage Learning for their invaluable assistance and cooperation in connection with the preparation of this text.

This text is dedicated to our children—Lilli-Marie Knebel Mann-Jackson, Justin Erwick Roberts, and Matthew Charles Roberts—and to our grandchildren.

Richard A. Mann
Barry S. Roberts

Table of Cases

Cases in italic are the principal cases included at the end of the chapters. Reference numbers indicate the pages on which the cases appear.

A.E. Robinson Oil Co., Inc. v. County Forest Products, Inc. 415

Alcoa Concrete & Masonry v. Stalker Bros. 260

Aldana v. Colonial Palms Plaza, Inc. 324

Alexander v. Fedex Ground Package System, Inc. 384

Alpert v. 28 Williams St. Corp. 794

Alzado v. Blinder, Robinson & Co., Inc. 691

American Manufacturing Mutual Insurance Company v. Tison Hog Market, Inc. 833

American Needle, Inc. v. National Football League 907

Anderson v. Mcoskar Enterprises, Inc. 266

Any Kind Checks Cashed, Inc. v. Talcott 575

Arrowhead School District No. 75, Park County, Montana, v. Klyap 364

Association For Molecular Pathology v. Myriad Genetics, Inc. 889

Bagley v. Mt. Bachelor, Inc. 267

Beam v. Stewart 779

Belden Inc. v. American Electronic Components, Inc. 498

Berardi v. Meadowbrook Mall Company 221

Berg v. Traylor 280

Bibi v. Elfrink 262

Bigelow-Sanford, Inc. v. Gunny Corp. 525

Border State Bank of Greenbush v. Bagley Livestock Exchange, Inc. 829

Borton v. Forest Hills Country Club 1117

Bouton v. Byers 183

Brehm v. Eisner 776

Brentwood Academy v. Tennessee Secondary School Athletic Association 80

Brown v. Board of Education of Topeka 84

Brown v. Entertainment Merchants Association 83

Burlington N. & S. F. R. Co. v. White 963

Burningham v. Westgate Resorts, Ltd. 227

Cappo v. Suda 1133

Carter v. Tokai Financial Services, Inc. 434

Catamount Slate Products, Inc. v. Sheldon 201

Chapa v. Traciers & Associates 832

Coastal Leasing Corporation v. T-Bar S Corporation 528

Coleman, Inc. v. Nufarm Americas, Inc. 436

Commerce & Industry Insurance Company v. Bayer Corporation 438

Conklin Farm v. Leibowitz 663

Connes v. Molalla Transport System, Inc. 413

Conway v. Cutler Group, Inc. 1131

Cooke v. Fresh Express Foods Corporation, Inc. 798

Cooperatieve Centrale Raiffeisen-Boerenleenbank B.a. v. Bailey 548

Coopers & Lybrand v. Fox 721

Cox Enterprises, Inc. v. Pension Benefit Guaranty Corporation 745

Dahan v. Weiss 307

Davis v. Watson Brothers Plumbing, Inc. 596

Deiter v. Coons 475

Denney v. Reppert 245

Department of Revenue of Kentucky v. Davis 81

Detroit Lions, Inc. v. Argovitz 388

Dilorenzo v. Valve And Primer Corporation 248

Directv, Inc. v. Imburgia 62

Dixon, Laukitis And Downing v. Busey Bank 615

Dodge v. Ford Motor Co. 747

Donahue v. Rodd Electrotype Co., Inc. 774

Donald R. Hessler v. Crystal Lake Chrysler-Plymouth, Inc. 459

Drake Mfg. Co., Inc. v. Polyflow, Inc. 720

Eastman Kodak Co. v. Image Technical Services, Inc. 911

Ed Nowogroski Insurance, Inc. v. Rucker 884

Enea v. The Superior Court of Monterey County 644

Environmental Protection Agency v. Eme Homer City Generation, L. P. 1048

Ernst & Ernst v. Hochfelder 1030

Estate of Countryman v. Farmers Coop. Ass'n 697

Faragher v. City of Boca Raton 969

Fcc v. Fox Television Stations, Inc. 101

Federal Ins. Co. v. Winters 326

Ferrell v. Mikula 137

First Bank v. Brumitt 327

First State Bank of Sinai v. Hyland 285

Fox v. Mountain West Electric, Inc. 180

Frank B. Hall & Co., Inc. v. Buck 139

Freeman v. Quicken Loans, Inc. 938

Furlong v. Alpha Chi Omega Sorority 456

Gaddy v. Douglass 389

Georg v. Metro Fixtures Contractors, Inc. 573

Greene v. Boddie-Noell Enterprises, Inc. 504

Griffin v. Jones 695

Hadfield v. Gilchrist 1093

Hamilton v. Lanning 864

Harris v. Looney 722

Harris v. Viegelahn 863

Heinrich v. Titus-Will Sales, Inc. 478

Heritage Bank v. Bruha 546

Herron v. Barnard 1090

Hochster v. De La Tour 344

Home Rentals Corp. v. Curtis 1113

Hospital Corporation of America v. Ftc 913

Household Credit Services, Inc. v. Pfennig 937

Husky International Electronics, Inc., v. Ritz 860

In Re Apa Assessment Fee Litigation 185

In Re L.b. Trucking, Inc. 499

In Re Magness 324

In Re The Score Board, Inc. 281

Inter-Tel Technologies, Inc. v. Linn Station
    Properties, Llc 723

In The Matter of 1545 Ocean Ave., Llc 698

In The Matter of The Estate of Rowe 1151

Jasper v. H. Nizam, Inc. 974

Jenkins v. Eckerd Corporation 308

Jerman v. Carlisle, Mcnellie, Rini,
    Kramer & Ulrich Lpa 940

Kalas v. Cook 306

Keeney v. Keeney 1150

Kelo v. City of New London 1132

Kelso v. Bayer Corporation 503

Kimbrell's of Sanford, Inc. v. Kps, Inc. 831

King v. Verifone Holdings, Inc 771

Kirtsaeng v. John Wiley & Sons, Inc. 887

Klein v. Pyrodyne Corporation 166

Leegin Creative Leather Products, Inc. v. Psks, Inc. 909

Lefkowitz v. Great Minneapolis Surplus Store, Inc. 203

Leibling, P.c. v. Mellon Psfs (Nj) National Association 616

Louisiana v. Hamed 121

Love v. Hardee's Food Systems, Inc. 162

Mackay v. Four Rivers Packing Co. 305

Madison Square Garden Corp., Ill. v. Carnera 366

Mark Line Industries, Inc. v. Murillo
    Modular Group, Ltd. 594

Maroun v. Wyreless Systems, Inc. 225

Martin v. Melland's Inc. 480

Matrixx Initiatives, Inc. v. Siracusano 1013

Mayo Foundation For Medical Education And Research v.
    United States 97

Mcdowell Welding & Pipefitting, Inc. v. United States Gyp-
    sum Co 345

Merritt v. Craig 362

Metropolitan Life Insurance Company v.
    Rjr Nabisco, Inc. 743

Midwest Hatchery v. Doorenbos Poultry 526

Miller v. Mcdonald's Corporation 386

Mims v. Arrow Financial Services, LLC 59

Mirvish v. Mott 1092

Montana Food, LLC v. Todosijevic 693

Moore v. Kitsmiller 164

Morrison v. National Australia Bank Ltd. 1068

Mountain Peaks Financial Services, Inc. v.
    Roth-Steffen 325

Murphy v. Bdo Seidman, LLP 1028

Nationsbank of Virginia, N.a. v. Barnes 547

Neugebauer v. Neugeb Auer 223

New England Rock Services, Inc. v. Empire Paving, Inc. 246

Nichols v. Healthsouth Corporation 773

Norcia v. Samsung Telecommunications America,
    LLC 206

Northern Corp. v. Chugach Electrical Association 346

Obb Personenverkehr Ag v. Sachs 1067

Omnicare, Inc. v. Laborers District Council Construction
    Industry Pension Fund 1011

O'neil v. Crane Co. 502

Palsgraf v. Long Island Railroad Co. 163

Palumbo v. Nikirk 167

Parker v. Twentieth Century-Fox Corp. 61

Parlato v. Equitable Life Assurance Society of The United
    States 411

Payroll Advance, Inc. v. Yates 264

Peace River Seed Co-Op. v. Proseeds Mktg. 524

Perez v. Mortgage Bankers Ass'n. 99

Philip Morris Usa v. Williams 136

Pittsley v. Houser 435

Prestenbach v. Collins 365

Prine v. Blanton 1153

Radlax Gateway Hotel, Llc v. Amalgamated Bank 861

Reed v. King 226

Re Keytronics 640

Ricci v. Destefano 967

Rnr Investments Limited Partnership v. Peoples First Community Bank 661

Robertson v. Jacobs Cattle Co. 665

Robinson v. Durham 477

Rosewood Care Center, Inc. v. Caterpillar, Inc. 303

Ryan v. Friesenhahn 12

Sackett v. Environmental Protection Agency 100

Salman v. United States 1015

Schoenberger v. Chicago Transit Authority 409

Schreiber v. Burlington Northern, Inc. 1016

Sec v. Edwards 1010

Shawnee Telecom Resources, Inc. v. Brown 796

Shaw v. United States 118

Sherrod v. Kidd 204

Silvestri v. Optus Software, Inc. 343

Soldano v. O'daniels 160

South Florida Water Management District v. Miccosukee Tribe of Indians 1050

Standards Ftc v. Wyndham Worldwide Corp. 935

State of Qatar v. First American Bank of Virginia 572

State of South Dakota v. Morse 119

Steinberg v. Chicago Medical School 182

The Hyatt Corporation v. Palm Beach National Bank 571

Thomas v. Lloyd 642

Thor Properties v. Willspring Holdings Llc 205

Travelers Indemnity Co. v. Stedman 597

Triffin v. Cigna Insurance 577

Tucker v. Hayford 1114

Union Planters Bank, National Association v. Rogers 617

Vance v. Ball State University 964

Vanegas v. American Energy Services 244

Waddell v. L.v.r.v. Inc. 457

Wal-Mart Stores, Inc. v. Samara Brothers, Inc. 886

Warnick v. Warnick 667

Whatley v. Estate of Mcdougal 1154

White v. Samsung Electronics America, Inc. 140

Williamson v. Mazda Motor of America, Inc. 78

Wilson v. Scampoli 455

Womco, Inc. v. Navistar International Corporation 501

Wood v. Pavlin 1116

World-Wide Volkswagen Corp. v. Woodson 60

Wyler v. Feuer 692

Young v. United Parcel Service, Inc. 971

Zarda v. Altitude Express, Inc. 960

Zelnick v. Adams 283

Table of Illustrations

1-1	Law and Morals	4
1-2	Classification of Law	4
1-3	Comparison of Civil and Criminal Law	5
1-4	Hierarchy of Law	6
2-1	Kohlberg's Stages of Moral Development	18
2-2	The Stakeholder Model	22
2-3	Pharmakon Employment	27
2-4	Pharmakon Affirmative Action Program	27
2-5	Mykon R&D Expenditures	29
2-6	Global Summary of the AIDS Epidemic	31
2-7	Regional Statistics for HIV and AIDS End of 2018	31
2-8	Stock Price of Vulcan, Inc. (note irregular intervals on time axis)	40
2-9	Average Daily Volume of Vulcan, Inc., Stock for Week (in 1,000s)	40
2-10	Purchases of Vulcan Stock by Selected Executives	41
3-1	Federal Judicial System	43
3-2	Circuit Courts of the United States	44
3-3	State Court System	45
3-4	Federal and State Jurisdiction	47
3-5	Subject Matter Jurisdiction	47
3-6	*Stare Decisis* in the Dual Court System	48
3-7	Jurisdiction	49
3-8	Stages in Civil Procedure	54
3-9	Comparison of Court Adjudication, Arbitration, and Mediation/Conciliation	55
4-1	Separation of Powers: Checks and Balances	69
4-2	Powers of Government	72
4-3	Limitations on Government	73
5-1	Administrative Rulemaking	93
5-2	Limits on Administrative Agencies	94
6-1	Degrees of Mental Fault	108
6-2	Constitutional Protection for the Criminal Defendant	115
7-1	Intent	127
7-2	Privacy	130
7-3	Intentional Torts	134
8-1	Negligence and Negligence *Per Se*	150
8-2	Defenses to a Negligence Action	156
9-1	Law Governing Contracts	174
9-2	Contractual and Noncontractual Promises	175
9-3	Validity of Agreements	176
9-4	Contracts, Promissory Estoppel, and Quasi Contracts (Restitution)	178
10-1	Duration of Revocable Offers	197
10-2	Mutual Assent	199
10-3	Offer and Acceptance	199
11-1	Misrepresentation	218
12-1	Consideration in Unilateral and Bilateral Contracts	236
12-2	Modification of a Preexisting Contract	238
12-3	Consideration	242
14-1	Incapacity: Minors, Nonadjudicated Incompetents, and Intoxicated Persons	279
15-1	The Statute of Frauds	295
15-2	Parol Evidence Rule	300
17-1	Discharge of Contracts	341
18-1	Contract Remedies	358
19-1	Duties of Principal and Agent	379
20-1	Contract Liability of Disclosed Principal	397
20-2	Contract Liability of Unidentified Principal	398
20-3	Contract Liability of Undisclosed Principal	399
20-4	Tort Liability	402
21-1	Law of Sales and Leases	423
21-2	Selected Rules Applicable to Merchants	426
21-3	Battle of the Forms	430
21-4	Contract Law Compared with UCC Law of Sales and Leases	432
22-1	Tender of Performance by the Seller	447
22-2	Performance by the Buyer	452

23-1	Passage of Title in Absence of Agreement by Parties	467
23-2	Void Title	468
23-3	Voidable Title	468
23-4	Entrusting of Goods to a Merchant	469
23-5	Passage of Risk of Loss in Absence of Breach	473
24-1	Warranties	489
24-2	Product Liability	495
25-1	Remedies of the Seller	516
25-2	Remedies of the Buyer	521
26-1	Use of Negotiable Instruments	537
26-2	Order to Pay: Draft or Check	538
26-3	Draft	538
26-4	Check	539
26-5	Promise to Pay: Promissory Note or Certificate of Deposit	539
26-6	Note	540
26-7	Certificate of Deposit	540
27-1	Bearer Paper	553
27-2	Negotiation of Bearer and Order Paper	553
27-3	Stolen Order Paper	554
27-4	Indorsements	557
27-5	Placement of Indorsement	558
27-6	Rights of Transferees	560
27-7	Effects of Alterations	566
27-8	Alteration	567
27-9	Availability of Defenses Against Holders and Holders in Due Course	568
27-10	Rights of Holder in Due Course Under the Federal Trade Commission Rule	568
28-1	Contractual Liability	588
28-2	Liability on Transfer	591
28-3	Liability Based on Warranty	592
29-1	Bank Collections	604
29-2	Parties to a Funds Transfer	613
29-3	Credit Transaction	613
30-1	General Partnership, Limited Partnership, Limited Liability Company, and Corporation	625
30-2	Tests for Existence of a Partnership	630
30-3	Partnership Property Compared with Partner's Interest	636
31-1	Contract Liability	649
31-2	Tort Liability	651
31-3	Dissociation and Dissolution Under RUPA	657
32-1	Comparison of General and Limited Partners	680
32-2	Comparison of Member-Managed and Manager-Managed LLCs	683
32-3	Liability Limitations in LLPs	687
33-1	Promoter's Preincorporation Contracts Made in the Corporation's Name	711
33-2	Comparison of Articles of Incorporation and Bylaws	713
34-1	Issuance of Shares	734
34-2	Debt and Equity Securities	737
34-3	Key Concepts in Legal Restrictions upon Distributions	739
34-4	Liability for Improper Distributions	741
35-1	Management Structure of Corporations: The Statutory Model	755
35-2	Management Structure of Typical Closely Held Corporation	755
35-3	Management Structure of Typical Publicly Held Corporation	755
35-4	Concentrations of Voting Power	759
35-5	Shareholder Suits	761
36-1	Fundamental Changes under the RMBCA	792
37-1	Fundamental Rights of Secured Party and Debtor	807
37-2	Requisites for Enforceability of Security Interests	812
37-3	Methods of Perfecting Security Interests	815
37-4	Priorities	819
37-5	Suretyship Relationship	821
37-6	Assumption of Mortgage	822
37-7	Defenses of Surety and Principal Debtor	825
38-1	Collection and Distribution of the Debtor's Estate	849
38-2	Comparison of Bankruptcy Proceedings	856
39-1	Intellectual Property	883
40-1	Sherman Act Violations Yielding a Corporate Fine of $300 Million or More	896
40-2	Restraints of Trade under the Sherman Act	900
40-3	Meeting Competition Defense	905
41-1	Magnuson-Moss Warranty Act	926
41-2	Consumer Rescission Rights	926
42-1	Unfair Labor Practices	949
42-2	Charges Filed with the EEOC from 2012 to 2019	951
42-3	Federal Employment Discrimination Laws	954
43-1	Registration and Exemptions under the 1933 Act	989
43-2	Exempt Transactions for Issuers Under the 1933 Act	994
43-3	Registration and Liability Provisions of the 1933 Act	997
43-4	Applicability of the 1934 Act	998
43-5	Disclosure Under the 1934 Act	999
43-6	Parties Forbidden to Trade on Inside Information	1004
43-7	Civil Liability Under the 1933 and 1934 Acts	1007

44-1 Accountants' Liability to Third Parties
for Negligent Misrepresentation 1023

44-2 Accountants' Liability under
Federal Securities Law 1026

45-1 Major Federal Environmental Statutes 1045

47-1 Kinds of Property 1076

47-2 Duties in a Bailment 1083

48-1 Freehold Estates 1104

48-2 Assignment Compared with Sublease 1105

48-3 Rights of Concurrent Owners 1108

49-1 Fundamental Rights of Mortgagor
and Mortgagee 1125

49-2 Eminent Domain 1128

50-1 Trusts 1140

50-2 Allocation of Principal and Income 1143

50-3 *Per Stirpes* and *Per Capita* 1148

The Legal Environment of Business

CH 1 INTRODUCTION TO LAW

CH 2 BUSINESS ETHICS AND THE SOCIAL RESPONSIBILITY OF BUSINESS

CH 3 CIVIL DISPUTE RESOLUTION

CH 4 CONSTITUTIONAL LAW

CH 5 ADMINISTRATIVE LAW

CH 6 CRIMINAL LAW

CH 7 INTENTIONAL TORTS

CH 8 NEGLIGENCE AND STRICT LIABILITY

CHAPTER 1

Introduction to Law

CHAPTER OUTCOMES

After reading and studying this chapter, you should be able to:

- Describe the basic functions of law.

- Distinguish between (1) law and justice and (2) law and morals.

- Distinguish between (1) substantive and procedural law, (2) public and private law, and (3) civil and criminal law.

- Describe the sources of law.

- Explain the principle of *stare decisis*.

L aw concerns the relations of individuals with one another as such relations affect the social and economic order. It is both the product of civilization and the means by which civilization is maintained. As such, law reflects the social, economic, political, religious, and moral philosophy of society. The laws of the United States influence the lives of every U.S. citizen. At the same time, the laws of each State influence the lives of its citizens and the lives of many noncitizens as well. The rights and duties of all individuals, as well as the safety and security of all people and their property, depend upon the law.

The law is pervasive. It interacts with and influences the political, economic, and social systems of every civilized society. It permits, forbids, or regulates practically every human activity and affects all persons either directly or indirectly. Law is, in part, prohibitory: certain acts must not be committed. For example, one must not steal; one must not murder. Law is also partly mandatory: certain acts must be done or be done in a prescribed way. Taxes must be paid; corporations must make and file certain reports with State or Federal authorities; traffic must keep to the right. Finally, law is permissive: individuals may choose to perform or not to perform certain acts. Thus, one may or may not enter into a contract; one may or may not dispose of one's estate by will.

Because the areas of law are so highly interrelated, an individual who intends to study the several branches of law known collectively as business law should first consider the nature, classification, and sources of law as a whole. This enables the student not only to understand any given branch of law better but also to understand its relation to other areas of law.

1-1 Nature of Law

The law has evolved slowly, and it will continue to change. It is not a pure science based upon unchanging and universal truths. Rather, it results from a continuous effort to balance, through a workable set of rules, the individual and group rights of a society.

1-1a DEFINITION OF LAW

A fundamental but difficult question regarding law is this: what is it? Numerous philosophers and jurists (legal scholars) have attempted to define it. American jurists and Supreme Court Justices Oliver Wendell Holmes and Benjamin Cardozo defined law as predictions of the way that a court will decide specific legal questions. William Blackstone, an English jurist, on the other hand, defined law as "a rule of civil conduct prescribed by the supreme power in a state, commanding what is right, and prohibiting what is wrong." Similarly, Austin, a nineteenth-century English jurist, defined law as a general command that a state or sovereign makes to those who are subject to its authority by laying down a course of action enforced by judicial or administrative tribunals.

Because of its great complexity, many legal scholars have attempted to explain the law by outlining its essential characteristics. Roscoe Pound, a distinguished American jurist and former dean of the Harvard Law School, described law as having multiple meanings:

> First, we may mean the legal order, that is, the regime of ordering human activities and relations through systematic application of the force of politically organized society, or through social pressure in such a society backed by such force. We use the term "law" in this sense when we speak of "respect for law" or for the "end of law."
>
> Second, we may mean the aggregate of laws or legal precepts; the body of authoritative grounds of judicial and administrative action established in such a society. We may mean the body of received and established materials on which judicial and administrative determinations proceed. We use the term in this sense when we speak of "systems of law" or of "justice according to law."
>
> Third, we may mean what Mr. Justice Cardozo has happily styled "the judicial process." We may mean the process of determining controversies, whether as it actually takes place, or as the public, the jurists, and the practitioners in the courts hold it ought to take place.

1-1b FUNCTIONS OF LAW

At a general level, the primary function of law is to maintain stability in the social, political, and economic system while simultaneously permitting change. The law accomplishes this basic function by performing a number of specific functions, among them dispute resolution, protection of property, and preservation of the state.

Disputes, which inevitably arise in a society as complex and interdependent as ours, may involve criminal matters, such as theft, or noncriminal matters, such as an automobile accident. Because disputes threaten the stability of society, the law has established an elaborate and evolving set of rules to resolve them. In addition, the legal system has instituted societal remedies, usually administered by the courts, in place of private remedies such as revenge.

The recognition of private ownership of property is fundamental to our economic system, based as it is upon the exchange of goods and services among privately held units of consumption. Therefore, a second crucial function of law is to protect the owner's use of property and to facilitate voluntary agreements (called contracts) regarding exchanges of property and services. Accordingly, a significant portion of law, as well as this text, involves property and its disposition, including the law of property, contracts, sales, commercial paper, and business associations.

A third essential function of the law is preservation of the state. In our system, law ensures that changes in leadership and the political structure are brought about by political actions such as elections, legislation, and referenda, rather than by revolution, sedition, and rebellion.

1-1c LEGAL SANCTIONS

A primary function of the legal system is to make sure that legal rules are enforced. **Sanctions** are the means by which the law enforces the decisions of the courts. Without sanctions, laws would be ineffectual and unenforceable.

An example of a sanction in a civil (noncriminal) case is the seizure and sale of the property of a debtor who fails to pay a court-ordered obligation, called a judgment. Moreover, under certain circumstances, a court may enforce its order by finding an offender in contempt and sentencing him to jail until he obeys the court's order. In criminal cases, the principal sanctions are the imposition of a fine, imprisonment, and capital punishment.

1-1d LAW AND MORALS

Although moral and ethical concepts greatly influence the law, morals and law are not the same. They may be considered as two intersecting circles, as shown in *Figure 1-1*. The area common to both circles includes the vast body of ideas that are both moral and legal. For instance, "Thou shall not kill" and "Thou shall not steal" are both moral precepts and legal constraints.

On the other hand, the part of the legal circle that does not intersect the morality circle includes many rules of law that are completely unrelated to morals, such as the rules stating that you must drive on the right side of the road and that you must register before you can vote. Likewise, the portion of the morality circle which does not intersect the legal circle includes moral precepts not enforced by law, such as the moral principle that you should not silently stand by and watch a blind man walk off a cliff or that you should provide food to a starving child.

♦ SEE FIGURE 1-1: *Law and Morals*

1-1e LAW AND JUSTICE

Law and justice represent separate and distinct concepts. Without law, however, there can be no justice. Although justice has at least as many definitions as law does, justice may be defined as fair, equitable, and impartial treatment of the competing interests and desires of individuals and groups with due regard for the common good.

FIGURE 1-1 Law and Morals

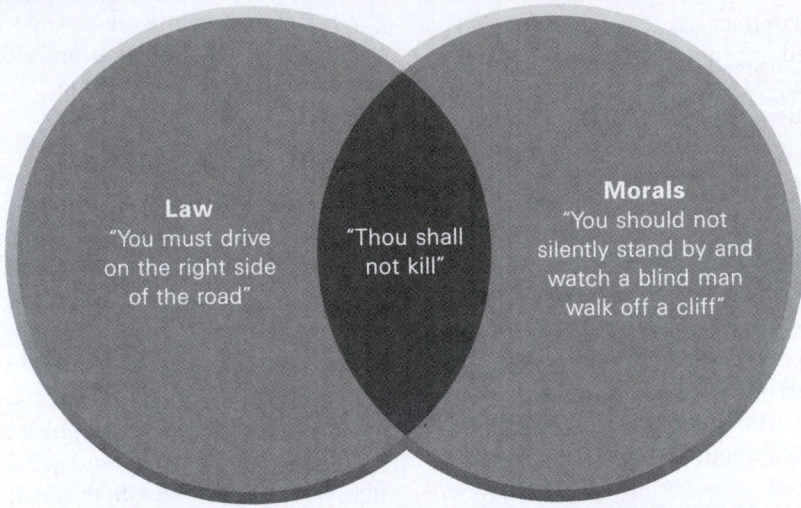

On the other hand, law is no guarantee of justice. Some of history's most monstrous acts have been committed pursuant to "law." Examples include the actions of Nazi Germany during the 1930s and 1940s and the actions of the South African government under apartheid from 1948 until 1994. Totalitarian societies often have shaped formal legal systems around the atrocities they have sanctioned.

1-2 Classification of Law

Because the subject is vast, classifying the law into categories is helpful. Though a number of classifications are possible, the most useful categories are (1) substantive and procedural, (2) public and private, and (3) civil and criminal.

Basic to understanding these classifications are the terms *right* and *duty*. A **right** is the capacity of a person, with the aid of the law, to require another person or persons to perform, or to refrain from performing, a certain act. Thus, if Alice sells and delivers goods to Bob for the agreed price of $500 payable at a certain date, Alice has the capability, with the aid of the courts, of enforcing the payment by Bob of the $500. A **duty** is the obligation the law imposes upon a person to perform, or to refrain from performing, a certain act. Duty and right are correlatives: no right can rest upon one person without a corresponding duty resting upon some other person or, in some cases, upon all other persons.

◆ SEE FIGURE 1-2: *Classification of Law*

FIGURE 1-2 Classification of Law

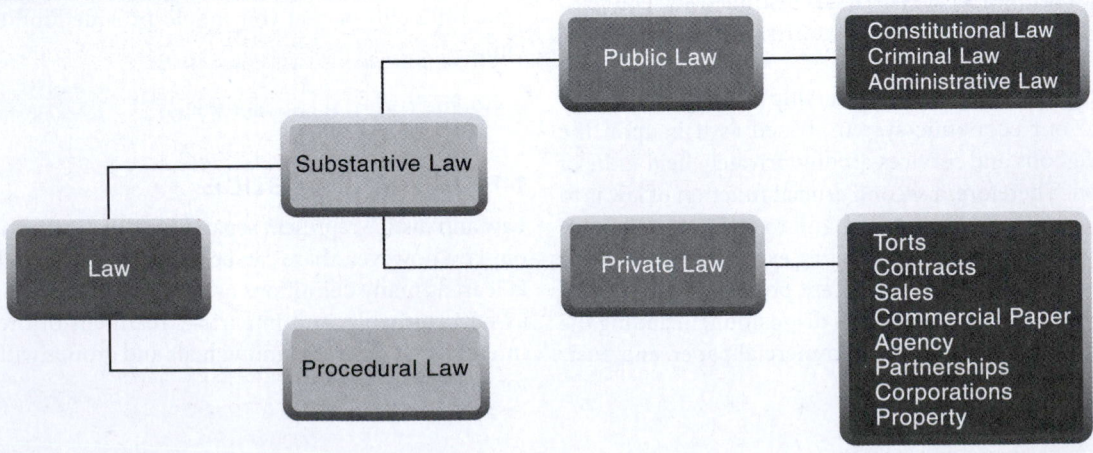

1-2a SUBSTANTIVE AND PROCEDURAL LAW

Substantive law creates, defines, and regulates legal rights and duties. Thus, the rules of contract law that determine when a binding contract is formed are rules of substantive law. This book is principally concerned with substantive law. On the other hand, **procedural law** establishes the rules for enforcing those rights that exist by reason of substantive law. Thus, procedural law defines the method by which one may obtain a remedy in court.

1-2b PUBLIC AND PRIVATE LAW

Public law is the branch of substantive law that deals with the government's rights and powers in its political or sovereign capacity and in its relation to individuals or groups. Public law consists of constitutional, administrative, and criminal law. **Private law** is that part of substantive law governing individuals and legal entities (such as corporations) in their relations with one another. Business law is primarily private law.

1-2c CIVIL AND CRIMINAL LAW

The **civil law** defines duties the violation of which constitutes a wrong against the party injured by the violation. In contrast, the **criminal law** establishes duties the violation of which is a wrong against the whole community. Civil law is a part of private law, whereas criminal law is a part of public law. (The term *civil law* should be distinguished from the concept of a civil law *system*, which is discussed later in this chapter.) In a civil action the injured party **sues** to recover **compensation** for the damage and injury he has sustained as a result of the defendant's wrongful conduct. The party bringing a civil action (the **plaintiff**) has the burden of proof, which he must sustain by a **preponderance** (greater weight) of the evidence. Whereas the purpose of criminal law is to punish the wrongdoer, the purpose of civil law is to compensate the injured party. The principal forms of

relief the civil law provides are a judgment for money damages and a decree ordering the defendant to perform a specified act or to desist from specified conduct.

A crime is any act or omission that public law prohibits in the interest of protecting the public and that the government makes punishable in a judicial proceeding brought (**prosecuted**) by it. The government must prove criminal guilt **beyond a reasonable doubt**, which is a significantly higher burden of proof than that required in a civil action. The government prohibits and punishes crimes upon the ground of public policy, which may include the safeguarding of the government itself, human life, or private property. Additional purposes of criminal law include deterrence and rehabilitation.

♦ SEE FIGURE 1-3: *Comparison of Civil and Criminal Law*

1-3 Sources of Law

The sources of law in the U.S. legal system are the Federal and State constitutions, Federal treaties, interstate compacts, Federal and State statutes and executive orders, the ordinances of countless local municipal governments, the rules and regulations of Federal and State administrative agencies, and an ever-increasing volume of reported Federal and State court decisions.

The *supreme law* of the land is the U.S. Constitution. The Constitution provides that Federal statutes and treaties shall be the supreme law of the land. Federal legislation and treaties are, therefore, paramount to State constitutions and statutes. Federal legislation is of great significance as a source of law. Other Federal actions having the force of law are executive orders of the President and rules and regulations of Federal administrative officials, agencies, and commissions. The Federal courts also contribute considerably to the body of law in the United States.

FIGURE 1-3 Comparison of Civil and Criminal Law

	Civil Law	Criminal Law
Commencement of Action	Aggrieved individual (plaintiff) sues	State or Federal government prosecutes
Purpose	Compensation Deterrence	Punishment Deterrence Rehabilitation Preservation of peace
Burden of Proof	Preponderance of the evidence	Beyond a reasonable doubt
Principal Sanctions	Monetary damages Equitable remedies	Capital punishment Imprisonment Fines

FIGURE 1-4   Hierarchy of Law

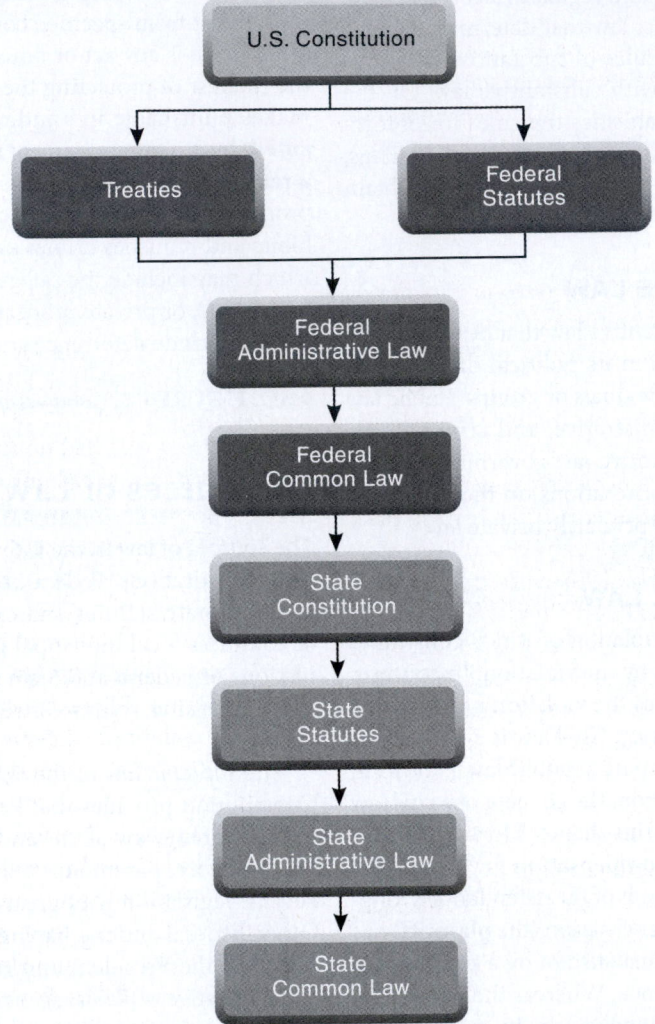

The same pattern exists in every State. The paramount law of each State is contained in its written constitution. (Although a State constitution cannot deprive citizens of Federal constitutional rights, it can guarantee rights beyond those provided in the U.S. Constitution.) State constitutions tend to be more specific than the U.S. Constitution and, generally, have been amended more frequently. Subordinate to the State constitution are the statutes that the State's legislature enacts and the case law that its judiciary develops. Likewise, State administrative agencies issue rules and regulations having the force of law, as do executive orders promulgated by the governors of most States. In addition, cities, towns, and villages have limited legislative powers within their respective municipal areas to pass ordinances and resolutions.

♦ **SEE FIGURE 1-4:** *Hierarchy of Law*

1-3a CONSTITUTIONAL LAW

A **constitution**—the fundamental law of a particular level of government—establishes the governmental structure and allocates power among the levels of government, thereby defining political relationships. One of the fundamental principles on which our government is founded is that of separation of powers. As detailed in the U.S. Constitution, this means that the government consists of three distinct and independent branches: the Federal judiciary, the Congress, and the executive branch.

A constitution also restricts the powers of government and specifies the rights and liberties of the people. For example, the Constitution of the United States not only specifically states what rights and authority are vested in the national government but also specifically enumerates certain rights and liberties of the people. Moreover, the Ninth Amendment to the U.S. Constitution makes it clear that this enumeration of rights does not in any way deny or limit other rights that the people retain.

All other law in the United States is subordinate to the Federal Constitution. No law, Federal or State, is valid if it violates the Federal Constitution. Under the principle of **judicial review**, the Supreme Court of the United States determines the constitutionality of *all* laws.

1-3b JUDICIAL LAW

The U.S. legal system is a **common law system**, first developed in England. It relies heavily on the judiciary as a source of law and on the adversary system for the adjudication of disputes. In an **adversary system**, the parties, not the court, must initiate and conduct litigation. This approach is based upon the belief that the truth is more likely to emerge from the investigation and presentation of evidence by two opposing parties, both motivated by self-interest, than from judicial investigation motivated only by official duty. In addition to the United States (except Louisiana) and England, the common law system is used in other countries previously colonized by England—including Canada (except Quebec), Australia, India (except Gao), Pakistan, Hong Kong, and New Zealand.

In distinct contrast to the common law system are civil law systems, which are based on Roman law. **Civil law systems** depend on comprehensive legislative enactments (called codes) and an inquisitorial method of adjudication. In the **inquisitorial system**, the judiciary initiates litigation, investigates pertinent facts, and conducts the presentation of evidence. The civil law system prevails in most of Europe, Scotland, the State of Louisiana, the province of Quebec, Latin America, and parts of Africa and Asia.

COMMON LAW The courts in common law systems have developed a body of law, known as "case law," "judge-made law," or "common law," that serves as precedent for determining later controversies. In this sense, common law is distinguished from other sources of law such as legislation and administrative rulings.

To evolve steadily and predictably, the common law has developed by application of *stare decisis* (to stand by the decisions). Under the principle of **stare decisis**, courts, in deciding cases, adhere to and rely on rules of law that they or superior courts announced and applied in prior decisions involving similar cases. Judicial decisions thus have two uses: (1) to determine with finality the case currently being decided and (2) to indicate how the courts will decide similar cases in the future. *Stare decisis* does not, however, preclude courts from correcting erroneous decisions or from choosing among conflicting precedents. Thus, the doctrine allows sufficient flexibility for the common law to change.

The strength of the common law is its ability to adapt to change without losing its sense of direction. As Justice Cardozo

said, "The inn that shelters for the night is not the journey's end. The law, like the traveler, must be ready for the morrow. It must have a principle of growth."

EQUITY As the common law developed in England, it became overly rigid and beset with technicalities. Consequently, in many cases, the courts provided no remedies because the judges insisted that a claim must fall within one of the recognized forms of action. Moreover, courts of common law could provide only limited remedies; the principal type of relief obtainable was a monetary judgment. Consequently, individuals who could not obtain adequate relief from monetary awards began to petition the king directly for justice. He, in turn, came to delegate these petitions to his chancellor.

Gradually, there evolved a supplementary system of judicial relief for those who had no adequate remedy at common law. This new system, called **equity**, was administered by a court of chancery presided over by a chancellor. The chancellor, deciding cases on "equity and good conscience," afforded relief in many instances in which common law judges had refused to act or in which the remedy at law was inadequate. Thus, two systems of law administered by different tribunals developed side by side: the common law courts and the courts of equity.

An important difference between law and equity was that the chancellor could issue a **decree**, or order, compelling a defendant to do or refrain from doing a specific act. A defendant who did not comply with the order could be held in contempt of court and punished by fine or imprisonment. This power of compulsion available in a court of equity opened the door to many needed remedies not available in a court of common law.

Equity jurisdiction, in some cases, recognized rights that were enforceable at common law but for which equity provided more effective remedies. For example, in a court of equity, for breach of a land contract, the buyer could obtain a decree of **specific performance** commanding the defendant seller to perform his part of the contract by transferring title to the land. Another powerful and effective remedy available only in the courts of equity was the **injunction**, a court order requiring a party to do or refrain from doing a specified act. Still another remedy not available elsewhere was reformation, in which case, upon the ground of mutual mistake, contracting parties could bring an action to reform or change the language of a written agreement to conform to their actual intentions. Finally, an action for **rescission** of a contract allowed a party to invalidate a contract under certain circumstances.

Although courts of equity provided remedies not available in courts of law, they granted such remedies only at their discretion, not as a matter of right. The courts exercised this discretion according to the general legal principles, or **maxims**, that they formulated over the years. A few of these familiar maxims of equity are the following: Equity will not suffer a wrong to be without a remedy. Equity regards the substance rather than the form. Equity abhors a forfeiture. Equity delights to do justice and not by halves. He who comes into equity must come with clean hands. He who seeks equity must do equity.

In nearly every jurisdiction in the United States, courts of common law and courts of equity have united to form a single court that administers both systems of law. Vestiges of the old division remain, however. For example, the right to a trial by jury applies only to actions at law but not, under Federal law and in almost every State, to suits filed in equity.

RESTATEMENTS OF LAW The common law of the United States results from the independent decisions of the State and Federal courts. The rapid increase in the number of decisions by these courts led to the establishment of the American Law Institute (ALI) in 1923. The ALI was composed of a distinguished group of lawyers, judges, and law professors who set out to prepare

> an orderly restatement of the general common law of the United States, including in that term not only the law developed solely by judicial decision, but also the law that has grown from the application by the courts of statutes that were generally enacted and were in force for many years. Wolk, "Restatements of the Law: Origin, Preparation, Availability," 21 *Ohio B.A. Rept.* 663 (1940).

As set out in its charter, the ALI's mission is "to promote the clarification and simplification of the law and its better adaptation to social needs, to secure the better administration of justice, and to encourage and carry on scholarly and scientific legal work." The ALI is limited to 3,000 elected members in addition to *ex officio* members and life members, for a total membership of nearly 4,600. Regarded as the authoritative statement of the common law of the United States, the Restatements cover many important areas of the common law, including torts, contracts, agency, property, and trusts. Although not law in themselves, they are highly persuasive and frequently have been used by courts in support of their opinions. Because they state much of the common law concisely and clearly, relevant portions of the Restatements are frequently relied upon in this book.

1-3c LEGISLATIVE LAW

Since the end of the nineteenth century, legislation has become the primary source of new law and ordered social change in the United States. The annual volume of legislative law is enormous. Justice Felix Frankfurter's remarks to the New York City Bar in 1947 are even more appropriate in the twenty-first century:

> Inevitably the work of the Supreme Court reflects the great shift in the center of gravity of law-making. Broadly speaking, the number of cases disposed of by opinions has not changed from term to term. But even as late as

1875 more than 40 percent of the controversies before the Court were common-law litigation, fifty years later only 5 percent, while today cases not resting on statutes are reduced almost to zero. It is therefore accurate to say that courts have ceased to be the primary makers of law in the sense in which they "legislated" the common law. It is certainly true of the Supreme Court that almost every case has a statute at its heart or close to it.

This modern emphasis upon legislative or statutory law has occurred because common law, which develops evolutionarily and haphazardly, is not well suited for making drastic or comprehensive changes. Moreover, courts tend to be hesitant about overruling prior decisions, whereas legislatures frequently repeal prior enactments. In addition, legislatures are independent and able to choose the issues they wish to address, while courts may deal only with issues that arise in actual cases. As a result, legislatures are better equipped to make the dramatic, sweeping, and relatively rapid changes in the law that enable it to respond to numerous and vast technological, social, and economic innovations.

While some business law topics, such as contracts, agency, property, and trusts, still are governed principally by the common law, most areas of commercial law have become largely statutory, including partnerships, corporations, sales, commercial paper, secured transactions, insurance, securities regulation, antitrust, and bankruptcy. Because most States enacted statutes dealing with these branches of commercial law, a great diversity developed among the States and hampered the conduct of commerce on a national scale. The increased need for greater uniformity led to the development of a number of proposed uniform laws that would reduce the conflicts among State laws.

The most successful example is the **Uniform Commercial Code (UCC)**, which was prepared under the joint sponsorship and direction of the ALI and the Uniform Law Commission (ULC), which is also known as the National Conference of Commissioners on Uniform State Laws (NCCUSL). All fifty States (although Louisiana has adopted only Articles 1, 3, 4, 4A, 5, 7, 8, and 9), the District of Columbia, and the Virgin Islands have adopted the UCC. The underlying purposes and policies of the Code are as follows:

1. simplify, clarify, and modernize the law governing commercial transactions;
2. permit the continued expansion of commercial practices through custom, usage, and agreement of the parties; and
3. make uniform the law among the various jurisdictions.

Established in 1892, the ULC is composed of more than three hundred lawyers, judges, and law professors appointed by each State. It has drafted more than three hundred uniform laws for the States to consider and enact. Its most widely adopted uniform acts include the Uniform Partnership Act, the Uniform Limited Partnership Act, the Uniform Electronic Transactions Act, the Uniform Trade Secrets Act, and the Uniform Probate Code. The text of many of the uniform acts is available on the ULC's website.

The ULC also promulgates a "model" act when an act's principal purposes can be substantially achieved even if the act is not adopted in its entirety by every State. The ALI has developed a number of model statutory formulations, including the Model Code of Evidence, the Model Penal Code, a Model Land Development Code, and a proposed Federal Securities Code. In addition, the American Bar Association has promulgated the Model Business Corporation Act.

TREATIES A **treaty** is an agreement between or among independent nations. Article II of the U.S. Constitution authorizes the President to enter into treaties with the advice and consent of the Senate, "providing two thirds of the Senators present concur."

Only the Federal government, not the States, may enter into treaties. A treaty signed by the President and approved by the Senate has the legal force of a Federal statute. Accordingly, a Federal treaty may supersede a prior Federal statute, while a Federal statute may supersede a prior treaty. Like statutes, treaties are subordinate to the Federal Constitution and subject to judicial review.

EXECUTIVE ORDERS In addition to his executive functions, the President of the United States also has authority to issue laws, which are called executive orders. Typically, Federal legislation specifically delegates this authority. An executive order may amend, revoke, or supersede a prior executive order. An example of an executive order is the one issued by President Johnson in 1965 prohibiting discrimination by Federal contractors on the basis of race, color, sex, religion, or national origin in employment on any work the contractor performed during the period of the Federal contract.

The governors of most States enjoy comparable authority to issue executive orders. Depending on the State, the authority for governors to issue executive orders comes from State constitutions, statutes, or case law.

1-3d ADMINISTRATIVE LAW

Administrative law is the branch of public law that is created by administrative agencies in the form of rules, regulations, orders, and decisions to carry out the regulatory powers and duties of those agencies. Administrative functions and activities concern matters of national safety, welfare, and convenience, including the establishment and maintenance of military forces, police, citizenship and naturalization, taxation, coinage of money, elections, environmental protection, and the regulation of transportation, interstate highways, waterways, television, radio, trade and commerce, and, in general, public health, safety, and welfare.

To accommodate the increasing complexity of the social, economic, and industrial life of the nation, the scope of administrative law has expanded enormously. Justice Jackson stated, "the rise of administrative bodies has been the most significant legal trend of the last century, and perhaps more values today are affected by their decisions than by those of all the courts, review of administrative decisions apart." *Federal Trade Commission v. Ruberoid Co.*, 343 U.S. 470 (1952). This is evidenced by the great increase in the number and activities of Federal government boards, commissions, and other agencies. Certainly, agencies create more legal rules and adjudicate more controversies than all the legislatures and courts combined.

1-4 Legal Analysis

Decisions in State trial courts generally are not reported or published. The precedent a trial court sets is not sufficiently weighty to warrant permanent reporting. Except in New York and a few other States where selected trial court opinions are published, decisions in trial courts are simply filed in the office of the clerk of the court, where they are available for public inspection. Decisions of State courts of appeals are published in consecutively numbered volumes called "reports." Court decisions are found in the official State reports of most States. In addition, West Publishing Company publishes State reports in a regional reporter, called the National Reporter System, composed of the following: Atlantic (A., A.2d, or A.3d), South Eastern (S.E. or S.E.2d), South Western (S.W., S.W.2d, or S.W.3d), New York Supplement (N.Y.S. or N.Y.S.2d), North Western (N.W. or N.W.2d), North Eastern (N.E. or N.E.2d), Southern (So., So.2d, or So.3d), Pacific (P., P.2d, or P.3d), and California Reporter (Cal.Rptr., Cal.Rptr.2d, or Cal.Rptr.3d). At least twenty States no longer publish official reports and have designated a commercial reporter as the authoritative source of State case law. After they are published, these opinions, or "cases," are referred to ("cited") by giving (1) the name of the case; (2) the volume, name, and page of the official State report, if any, in which it is published; (3) the volume, name, and page of the particular set and series of the National Reporter System; and (4) the volume, name, and page of any other selected case series. For instance, *Lefkowitz v. Great Minneapolis Surplus Store, Inc.*, 251 Minn. 188, 86 N.W.2d 689 (1957) indicates that the opinion in this case may be found in Volume 251 of the official Minnesota Reports at page 188; and in Volume 86 of the North Western Reporter, Second Series, at page 689.

The decisions of courts in the Federal system are found in a number of reports. U.S. District Court opinions appear in the Federal Supplement (F.Supp. or F.Supp.2d). Decisions of the U.S. Court of Appeals are found in the Federal Reporter (Fed., F.2d, or F.3d), and the U.S. Supreme Court's opinions are published in the U.S. Supreme Court Reports (U.S.), Supreme Court Reporter (S.Ct.), and Lawyers Edition (L.Ed.). While all U.S. Supreme Court decisions are reported, not every case decided by the U.S. District Courts and the U.S. Courts of Appeals is reported. Each circuit has established rules determining which decisions are published.

In reading the title of a case, such as *"Jones v. Brown,"* the "v." or "vs." means "versus" or "against." In the trial court, Jones is the plaintiff, the person who filed the suit, and Brown is the defendant, the person against whom the suit was brought. When a case is appealed, some, but not all, courts of appeals place the name of the party who appeals, or the appellant, first, so that *"Jones v. Brown"* in the trial court becomes, if Brown loses and becomes the appellant, *"Brown v. Jones"* in the appellate court. But because some appellate courts retain the trial court order of names, determining from the title itself who was the plaintiff and who was the defendant is not always possible. The student must read the facts of each case carefully and clearly identify each party in her mind to understand the discussion by the appellate court. In a criminal case, the caption in the trial court will first designate the prosecuting government unit and then will indicate the defendant, as in *"State v. Jones"* or *"Commonwealth v. Brown."*

The study of reported cases requires the student to understand and apply legal analysis. Normally, the reported opinion in a case sets forth (1) the essential facts, the nature of the action, the parties, what happened to bring about the controversy, what happened in the lower court, and what pleadings are material to the issues; (2) the issues of law or fact; (3) the legal principles involved; (4) the application of these principles; and (5) the decision.

A serviceable method by which students may analyze and brief cases after reading and comprehending the opinion is to write a brief containing the following:

1. the facts of the case,
2. the issue or question involved,
3. the decision of the court, and
4. the reasons for the decision.

By way of example, the edited case of *Ryan v. Friesenhahn* (see *Case 1-1*) is presented after the chapter summary and then briefed using the suggested format.

♦ See Case 1-1

You can and should use this same legal analysis when learning the substantive concepts presented in this text and applying them to the end-of-chapter questions and case problems. By way of example, in a number of chapters throughout the text, we have included a boxed feature called **Applying the Law**, which provides a systematic legal analysis of a single concept learned in the chapter. This feature begins with the **facts** of a hypothetical case, followed by an identification of the broad legal issue presented by those facts. We then state the **rule of law**—or applicable legal principles, including definitions, which aid in resolving the legal issue—and **apply** it to the facts. Finally, we state a legal **conclusion**, or decision in the case. An example of this type of legal analysis follows.

APPLYING THE LAW   Introduction to Law

FACTS Jackson bought a new car and planned to sell his old one for about $2,500. But before he did so, he happened to receive a call from his cousin, Trina, who had just graduated from college. Among other things, Trina told Jackson she needed a car but did not have much money. Feeling generous, Jackson told Trina he would give her his old car. But the next day a coworker offered Jackson $3,500 for his old car, and Jackson sold it to the coworker.

ISSUE Did Jackson have the right to sell his car to the coworker, or legally had he already made a gift of it to Trina?

RULE OF LAW A gift is the transfer of ownership of property from one person to another without anything in return.

The person making the gift is called the donor, and the person receiving it is known as the donee. A valid gift requires (1) the donor's present intent to transfer the property and (2) delivery of the property.

APPLICATION In this case, Jackson is the would-be donor and Trina the would-be donee. To find that Jackson had already made a gift of the car to Trina, both Jackson's intent to give it to her and delivery of the car to Trina would need to be demonstrated. It is evident from their telephone conversation that Jackson did intend at that point to give the car to Trina. It is equally apparent from his conduct that he later changed his mind, because he sold it to someone else the next day. Consequently, he did not deliver the car to Trina.

CONCLUSION Because the donor did not deliver the property to the donee, legally no gift was made. Jackson was free to sell the car.

NATURE OF LAW

Definition of Law "a rule of civil conduct prescribed by the supreme power in a state, commanding what is right, and prohibiting what is wrong" (William Blackstone)

Functions of Law to maintain stability in the social, political, and economic system through dispute resolution, protection of property, and the preservation of the state, while simultaneously permitting ordered change

Legal Sanctions are means by which the law enforces the decisions of the courts

Law and Morals are different but overlapping; law provides sanctions, while morals do not

Law and Justice are separate and distinct concepts; justice is the fair, equitable, and impartial treatment of competing interests with due regard for the common good

CLASSIFICATION OF LAW

Substantive and Procedural Law
- *Substantive Law* law creating rights and duties
- *Procedural Law* rules for enforcing substantive law

Public and Private Law
- *Public Law* law dealing with the relationship between government and individuals
- *Private Law* law governing the relationships among individuals and legal entities

Civil and Criminal Law
- *Civil Law* law dealing with rights and duties the violation of which constitutes a wrong against an individual or other legal entity
- *Criminal Law* law establishing duties which, if violated, constitute a wrong against the entire community

SOURCES OF LAW

Constitutional Law fundamental law of a government establishing its powers and limitations

Judicial Law
- *Common Law* body of law developed by the courts that serves as precedent for determination of later controversies
- *Equity* body of law based upon principles distinct from common law and providing remedies not available at law

Legislative Law statutes adopted by legislative bodies
- *Treaties* agreements between or among independent nations
- *Executive Orders* laws issued by the President or by the governor of a State

Administrative Law body of law created by administrative agencies to carry out their regulatory powers and duties

CASES

RYAN v. FRIESENHAHN
Court of Appeals of Texas, 1995
911 S.W.2d 113

Rickhoff, J.

This is an appeal from a take-nothing summary judgment granted the defendants in a social host liability case. Appellants' seventeen-year-old daughter was killed in a single-car accident after leaving appellees' party in an intoxicated condition. While we hold that the appellants were denied an opportunity to amend their pleadings, we also find that their pleadings stated a cause of action for negligence and negligence per se. We reverse and remand.

Todd Friesenhahn, son of Nancy and Frederick Friesenhahn, held an "open invitation" party at his parents' home that encouraged guests to "bring your own bottle." Sabrina Ryan attended the party, became intoxicated, and was involved in a fatal accident after she left the event. According to the Ryans' petition, Nancy and Frederick Friesenhahn were aware of this activity and of Sabrina's condition.

Sandra and Stephen Ryan, acting in their individual and representative capacities, sued the Friesenhahns for wrongful death, negligence, and gross negligence. * * *

* * *

a. The Petition The Ryans pled, in their third amended petition, that Todd Friesenhahn planned a "beer bust" that was advertised by posting general invitations in the community for a party to be held on the "Friesenhahn Property." The invitation was open and general and invited persons to "B.Y.O.B." (bring your own bottle). According to the petition, the Friesenhahns had actual or constructive notice of the party and the conduct of the minors in "possessing, exchanging, and consuming alcoholic beverages."

The Ryans alleged that the Friesenhahns were negligent in (1) allowing the party to be held on the Friesenhahn property; (2) directly or indirectly inviting Sabrina to the party; (3) allowing the party to continue on their property "after they knew that minors were in fact possessing, exchanging, and consuming alcohol"; (4) failing "to provide for the proper conduct at the party"; (5) allowing Sabrina to become intoxicated and failing to "secure proper attention and treatment"; (6) and allowing Sabrina to leave the Friesenhahn property while driving a motor vehicle in an intoxicated state. * * *

b. Negligence Per Se Accepting the petition's allegations as true, the Friesenhahns were aware that minors possessed and consumed alcohol on their property and specifically allowed Sabrina to become intoxicated. The Texas Alcoholic Beverage Code provides that one commits an offense if, with criminal negligence, he "makes available an alcoholic beverage to a minor." [Citation.] The exception for serving alcohol to a minor applies only to the minor's adult parent. [Citation.]

An unexcused violation of a statute constitutes negligence per se if the injured party is a member of the class protected by the statute. [Citation.] The Alcoholic Beverage Code was designed to protect the general public and minors in particular and must be liberally construed. [Citation.] We conclude that Sabrina is a member of the class protected by the Code.

In viewing the Ryans' allegations in the light most favorable to them, we find that they stated a cause of action against the Friesenhahns for the violation of the Alcoholic Beverage Code.

c. Common Law Negligence The elements of negligence include (1) a legal duty owed by one person to another; (2) breach of that duty; and (3) damages proximately caused by the breach. [Citation.] To determine whether a common law duty exists, we must consider several factors, including risk, foreseeability, and likelihood of injury weighed against the social utility of the defendant's conduct, the magnitude of the burden of guarding against the injury and consequences of placing that burden on the defendant. [Citation.] We may also consider whether one party has superior knowledge of the risk, and whether one party has the right to control the actor whose conduct precipitated the harm. [Citation.]

As the Supreme Court in [citation] explained, there are two practical reasons for not imposing a third-party duty on social hosts who provide alcohol to adult guests: first, the host cannot reasonably know the extent of his guests' alcohol consumption level; second, the host cannot reasonably be expected to control his guests' conduct. [Citation.] The Tyler court in [citation] relied on these principles in holding that a minor "had no common law duty to avoid making alcohol available to an intoxicated guest [another minor] who he knew would be driving." [Citation.]

We disagree with the Tyler court because the rationale expressed [by the Supreme Court] in [citation] does not apply to the relationship between minors, or adults and minors. The adult social host need not estimate the extent of a minor's alcohol consumption because serving minors any amount of alcohol is a criminal offense. [Citation.] Furthermore, the social host may control the minor, with whom there is a special relationship, analogous to that of parent-child. [Citation.]

* * *

As this case demonstrates, serving minors alcohol creates a risk of injury or death. Under the pled facts, a jury could find that the Friesenhahns, as the adult social hosts, allowed open invitations to a beer bust at their house and they could foresee, or reasonably should have foreseen, that the only means of arriving at their property would be by privately operated vehicles; once there, the most likely means of departure would be by the same means. That adults have superior knowledge of the risk of drinking should be apparent from the legislature's decision to allow persons to become adults on their eighteenth birthday for all purposes but the consumption of alcohol. [Citations.]

While one adult has no general duty to control the behavior of another adult, one would hope that adults would exercise special diligence in supervising minors—even during a simple swimming pool party involving potentially dangerous but legal activities. We may have no special duty to watch one adult to be sure he can swim, but it would be ill-advised to turn loose young children without insuring they can swim. When the "party" is for the purpose of engaging in dangerous and illicit activity, the consumption of alcohol by minors, adults certainly have a greater duty of care. [Citation.]

* * * Accordingly, we find that the Ryans' petition stated a common-law cause of action.

* * *

We reverse and remand the trial court's summary judgment.

Brief of Ryan v. Friesenhahn
I. Facts
Todd Friesenhahn, son of Nancy and Frederick Friesenhahn, held an open invitation party at his parents' home that encouraged guests to bring their own bottle. Sabrina Ryan attended the party, became intoxicated, and was involved in a fatal accident after she left the party. Sandra and Stephen Ryan, Sabrina's parents, sued the Friesenhahns for negligence, alleging that the Friesenhahns were aware of underage drinking at the party and

of Sabrina's condition when she left the party. The trial court granted summary judgment for the Friesenhahns.

II. Issue
Is a social host who serves alcoholic beverages to a minor liable in negligence for harm suffered by the minor as a result of the minor's intoxication?

III. Decision
In favor of the Ryans. Summary judgment reversed and case remanded to the trial court.

IV. Reasons
Accepting the Ryans' allegations as true, the Friesenhahns were aware that minors possessed and consumed alcohol on their property and specifically allowed Sabrina to become intoxicated. The Texas Alcoholic Beverage Code provides that a person commits an offense if, with criminal negligence, he "makes available an alcoholic beverage to a minor." A violation of a statute constitutes negligence per se if the injured party is a member of the class protected by the statute. Since the Alcoholic Beverage Code was designed to protect the general public and minors in particular, Sabrina is a member of the class protected by the Code. Therefore, we find that the Ryans stated a cause of action against the Friesenhahns for the violation of the Alcoholic Beverage Code.

In considering common-law negligence as a basis for social host liability, the Texas Supreme Court has held that there are two practical reasons for not imposing a third-party duty on social hosts who provide alcohol to adult guests: first, the host cannot reasonably know the extent of his guests' alcohol consumption level; second, the host cannot reasonably be expected to control his guests' conduct. However, this rationale does not apply where the guest is a minor. The adult social host need not estimate the extent of a minor's alcohol consumption because serving minors any amount of alcohol is a criminal offense. Furthermore, the social host may control the minor, with whom there is a special relationship, analogous to that of parent-child.

CHAPTER 2

Business Ethics and the Social Responsibility of Business

CHAPTER OUTCOMES

After reading and studying this chapter, you should be able to:

- Describe the differences between law and ethics.

- List and contrast the various ethical theories.

- Explain cost-benefit analysis and its appropriate use.

- Explain Kohlberg's stages of moral development.

- Explain the ethical responsibilities of business.

Business ethics is a subset of ethics: no special set of ethical principles applies only to the world of business. Immoral acts are immoral, whether or not a businessperson has committed them. In the past few years, countless business wrongs—such as insider trading, fraudulent earnings statements and other accounting misconduct, price-fixing, concealment of dangerous defects in products, reckless lending and improper foreclosures in the housing market, and bribery—have been reported almost daily. Companies including Enron, WorldCom, Adelphia, Parmalat, Arthur Andersen, and Global Crossing have violated the law, and some of these firms no longer exist as a result of these ethical lapses. In 2004, Martha Stewart was convicted of obstructing justice and lying to investigators about a stock sale. More recently, Bernie Madoff perpetrated the largest Ponzi scheme in history with an estimated loss of $20 billion in principal and approximately $65 billion in paper losses. In May 2011, Galleon Group (a hedge fund) billionaire, Raj Rajaratnam, was found guilty of fourteen counts of conspiracy and securities fraud. In 2013, large international banks faced a widening scandal—and substantial fines—over attempts to rig benchmark interest rates, including the London Interbank Offered Rate (LIBOR).

Unethical business practices date from the very beginning of business and continue today. As one court stated in connection with a securities fraud,

Since the time to which the memory of man runneth not to the contrary, the human animal has been full of cunning and guile. Many of the schemes and artifices

have been so sophisticated as almost to defy belief. But the ordinary run of those willing and able to take unfair advantage of others are mere apprentices in the art when compared with the manipulations thought up by those connected in one way or another with transactions in securities.

Ethics can be broadly defined as the study of what is right or good for human beings. It pursues the questions of what people ought to do, what goals they should pursue. In *Business Ethics*, 5th ed., Richard T. DeGeorge provides the following explanation of ethics:

In its most general sense *ethics is a systematic attempt to make sense of our individual and social moral experience, in such a way as to determine the rules that ought to govern human conduct, the values worth pursuing, and the character traits deserving development in life. The attempt is systematic and therefore goes beyond what reflective persons tend to do in daily life in making sense of their moral experience, organizing it, and attempting to make it coherent and unified.... Ethics concerns itself with human conduct, taken here to mean human activity that is done knowingly and, to a large extent, willingly. It does not concern itself with automatic responses, or with, for example, actions done in one's sleep or under hypnosis.*

Business ethics, as a branch of applied ethics, is the study and determination of what is right and good in business settings. Business ethics seeks to understand the moral issues that arise from business practices, institutions, and decision making and their relationship to generalized human values. Unlike the law, analyses of ethics have no central authority, such as courts or legislatures, upon which to rely; nor do they have clear-cut, universal standards. Despite these inherent limitations, making meaningful ethical judgments is still possible. To improve ethical decision making, it is important to understand how others have approached the task.

Some examples of the many ethics questions confronting business may clarify the definition of business ethics. In the employment relationship, countless ethical issues arise regarding the safety and compensation of workers, their civil rights (such as equal treatment, privacy, and freedom from sexual harassment), and the legitimacy of whistle-blowing. In the relationship between business and its customers, ethical issues permeate marketing techniques, product safety, and consumer protection. The relationship between business and its owners bristles with ethical questions involving corporate governance, shareholder voting, and management's duties to the shareholders. The relationship among competing businesses involves numerous ethical matters, including efforts to promote fair competition over the temptation of collusive conduct. The interaction between business and society at large has additional ethical dimensions: pollution of the physical environment, commitment to the community's economic and social infrastructure, and the depletion of natural resources. At the international level, these issues not only recur but also couple themselves to additional ones, such as bribery of foreign officials, exploitation of developing countries, and conflicts among differing cultures and value systems.

In resolving the ethical issues raised by business conduct, it is helpful to use a seeing-knowing-doing model. First, the decision maker should *see* (identify) the ethical issues involved in the proposed conduct, including the ethical implications of the various available options. Second, the decision maker should *know* (resolve) what to do by choosing the best option. Finally, the decision maker should *do* (implement) the chosen option by developing strategies for implementation.

This chapter first surveys the most prominent ethical theories, then examines ethical standards in business, and concludes by exploring the ethical responsibilities of business.

2-1 Law Versus Ethics

As discussed in *Chapter 1*, the law is strongly affected by moral concepts, but law and morality are not the same. Although it is tempting to say "if it's legal, it's moral," such a proposition is inaccurate and generally too simplistic. For example, it would seem gravely immoral to stand by silently while a blind man walks off a cliff if one could prevent the fall by shouting a warning, even though one is under no legal obligation to do so. Similarly, moral questions arise concerning "legal" business practices, such as failing to fulfill a promise that is not legally binding; exporting products banned in the United States to developing countries, where they are not prohibited; manufacturing and selling tobacco or alcohol products; or slaughtering baby seals for fur coats. The mere fact that these practices may be legal does not prevent them from being challenged on moral grounds.

Just as it is possible for legal acts to be immoral, it is equally possible for illegal acts to seem morally preferable to following the law. It is, for example, the moral conviction of the great majority of people that those who sheltered Jews in violation of Nazi edicts during World War II and those who committed acts of civil disobedience in the 1950s and 1960s to challenge racist segregation laws in the United States were acting properly and that the laws themselves were immoral.

2-2 Ethical Theories

Philosophers have sought for centuries to develop dependable universal methods for making ethical judgments. In earlier times, some thinkers analogized the discovery of ethical principles with the derivation of mathematical proofs. They asserted that people could discover fundamental ethical rules by applying careful reasoning *a priori*. (*A priori* reasoning is based on theory rather than experimentation and deductively draws conclusions from cause to effect and from generalizations to particular instances.) In more recent times, many philosophers have concluded that although careful reasoning and deep thought assist substantially in moral reasoning, experience reveals that the complexities of the world defeat most attempts to fashion precise, *a priori* guidelines. Nevertheless, reviewing the most significant ethical theories can aid analysis of business ethics issues.

2-2a ETHICAL FUNDAMENTALISM

Under **ethical fundamentalism**, or absolutism, individuals look to a central authority or set of rules to guide them in ethical decision making. Some look to the Bible; others look to the Koran, or the writings of Karl Marx, or to any number of living or deceased prophets. The essential characteristic of this approach is a reliance upon a central repository of wisdom. In some cases, such reliance is total. In others, it occurs to a lesser degree: followers of a religion or a spiritual leader may believe that all members of the group have an obligation to assess moral dilemmas independently, according to each person's understanding of the dictates of certain fundamental principles.

2-2b ETHICAL RELATIVISM

Ethical relativism is a doctrine asserting that individuals must judge actions by what they feel is right or wrong for themselves. It holds that both parties to a disagreement regarding a moral question are correct, because morality is relative. While ethical relativism promotes open-mindedness and tolerance, it has limitations. If each person's actions are always correct for that person, then his behavior is, by definition, moral, and no one can truly criticize it. If a child abuser truly felt it right to molest children, a relativist would accept the proposition that the child abuser was acting properly. As almost no one would accept the proposition that child abuse could ever be ethical, few can truly claim to be relativists. Once a person concludes that criticizing or punishing behavior is, in some cases, appropriate, he abandons ethical relativism and faces the task of developing a broader ethical methodology.

Although bearing a surface resemblance to ethical relativism, situational ethics actually differs substantially. **Situational ethics** holds that developing precise guidelines for navigating ethical dilemmas is difficult because real-life decision making is so complex. To judge the morality of someone's behavior, the person judging must actually put herself in the other person's shoes to understand what motivated the other to choose a particular course of action. In this respect, situational ethics shares with ethical relativism the notion that we must judge actions from the perspective of the person who actually made the judgment. From that point on, however, the two approaches differ dramatically. Ethical relativism passes no judgment on what a person did other than to determine that he truly believed the decision was right for him. Much more judgmental, situational ethics insists that once a decision has been viewed from the actor's perspective, a judgment can be made as to whether or not her action was ethical. Situational ethics does not cede the ultimate judgment of propriety to the actor; rather, it insists that another evaluate the actor's decision or act from the perspective of a person in the actor's shoes.

2-2c UTILITARIANISM

Utilitarianism is a doctrine that assesses good and evil in terms of the consequences of actions. Those actions that produce the greatest net pleasure compared with the net pain are better in a moral sense than those that produce less net pleasure. As Jeremy Bentham, one of the most influential proponents of utilitarianism, proclaimed, a good or moral act is one that results in "the greatest happiness for the greatest number."

The two major forms of utilitarianism are act utilitarianism and rule utilitarianism. **Act utilitarianism** assesses each separate act according to whether it maximizes pleasure over pain. For example, if telling a lie in a particular situation produces more overall pleasure than pain, then an act utilitarian would support lying as the moral thing to do. Rule utilitarians, disturbed by the unpredictability of act utilitarianism and by its

potential for abuse, follow a different approach by holding that general rules must be established and followed even though, in some instances, following rules may produce less overall pleasure than not following them. In applying utilitarian principles to developing rules, **rule utilitarianism** thus supports rules that on balance produce the greatest satisfaction. Determining whether telling a lie in a given instance would produce greater pleasure than telling the truth is less important to the rule utilitarian than deciding whether a general practice of lying would maximize society's pleasure. If lying would not maximize pleasure generally, then one should follow a rule of not lying, even though telling a lie occasionally would produce greater pleasure than would telling the truth.

Utilitarian notions underlie cost-benefit analysis, an analytical tool used by many business and government managers today. **Cost-benefit analysis** first quantifies in monetary terms and then compares the direct and indirect costs and benefits of program alternatives for meeting a specified objective. Cost-benefit analysis seeks the greatest economic efficiency, given the underlying notion that acts achieving the greatest output at the least cost promote the greatest marginal happiness over less efficient acts, other things being equal.

The primary purpose of cost-benefit analysis is to choose from alternative courses of action the program that maximizes society's wealth. For example, based on cost-benefit analysis, an auto designer might choose to devote more effort to perfecting a highly expensive air bag that would save hundreds of lives and prevent thousands of disabling injuries than to developing an improved car hood latching mechanism that would produce a less favorable cost-benefit ratio.

The chief criticism of utilitarianism is that in some important instances, it ignores justice. A number of situations would maximize the pleasure of the majority at great social cost to a minority. Under a strict utilitarian approach, for example, it would be ethical to compel a few citizens to undergo painful, even fatal medical tests to develop cures for the rest of the world. For most people, however, such action would be unacceptable. Another major criticism of utilitarianism is that measuring pleasure and pain in the fashion its supporters advocate is extremely difficult, if not impossible.

2-2d DEONTOLOGY

Deontological theories (from the Greek word *deon*, meaning "duty" or "obligation") address the practical problems of utilitarianism by holding that certain underlying principles are right or wrong regardless of calculations regarding pleasure or pain. Deontologists believe that actions cannot be measured simply by their results but must be judged by means and motives as well.

Our criminal laws apply deontological reasoning. Knowing that John shot and killed Marvin is not enough to tell us how to judge John's act. We must know whether John shot Marvin in anger, in self-defense, or by mistake. Although under any of these motives Marvin is dead, we judge John quite differently depending on the mental process that we believe led him to commit the act. Similarly, deontologists judge the morality of acts not so much by their consequences, but by the motives that lead to them. To act morally, a person not only must achieve just results but also must employ the proper means.

The eighteenth-century philosopher Immanuel Kant proffered the best-known deontological theory. Kant asserted what he called the categorical imperative, which has been summarized as follows:

1. Act only according to that maxim by which you can, at the same time, will that it should become a universal law.

2. Act as never to treat another human being merely as a means to an end.

Thus, for an action to be moral, it (1) must possess the potential to be made a consistently applied universal law and (2) must respect the autonomy and rationality of all human beings and avoid treating them as an expedient. That is, one should avoid doing anything that he or she would not have everyone do in a similar situation. For example, you should not lie to colleagues unless you support the right of all colleagues to lie to one another. Similarly, you should not cheat others unless you advocate everyone's right to cheat. We apply Kantian reasoning when we challenge someone's behavior by asking, what if everybody acted that way?

Under Kant's approach, it would be improper to assert a principle to which one claimed personal exception, such as insisting that it was acceptable for you to cheat but not for anyone else to do so. Because everyone would then insist on similar rules by which to except themselves, this principle could not be universalized.

Kant's philosophy also rejects notions of the end justifying the means. To Kant, every person is an end in himself or herself and deserves respect simply because of his or her humanity. Thus, any sacrifice of a person for the greater good of society would be unacceptable to Kant.

In many respects, Kant's categorical imperative is a variation of the Golden Rule. Like the Golden Rule, the categorical imperative reflects the idea that people are, to a certain extent, self-centered. As one writer on business ethics notes, this is what makes the Golden Rule so effective:

It is precisely this self-centeredness of the Golden Rule that makes it so valuable, and so widely acknowledged, as a guide. To inquire of yourself, "How would I feel in the other fellow's place?" is an elegantly simple and reliable method of focusing in on the "right" thing to do. The Golden Rule works not in spite of selfishness, but because of it. Tuleja, *Beyond the Bottom Line.*

As does every theory, Kantian ethics has its critics. Just as deontologists criticize utilitarians for excessive pragmatism and flexible moral guidelines, utilitarians and others criticize deontologists for rigidity and excessive formalism. For example, if one inflexibly adopts as a rule to tell the truth, one ignores situations in which lying might well be justified. A person hiding a terrified wife from her angry, abusive husband would seem to be acting morally by falsely denying that the wife is at the person's house. Yet, a deontologist, feeling bound to tell the truth, might ignore the consequences of truthfulness, tell the husband where his wife is, and create the possibility of a terrible tragedy. Less dramatically, one wonders whether the world would effect a higher ethical code by regarding as immoral "white lies" concerning friends' appearance, clothing, or choice of spouse.

2-2e SOCIAL ETHICS THEORIES

Social ethics theories assert that special obligations arise from the social nature of human beings. Such theories focus not only on each person's obligations to other members of society but also on the individual's rights and obligations within society. For example, **social egalitarians** believe that society should provide all persons with equal amounts of goods and services regardless of the contribution each makes to increase society's wealth.

Two other ethics theories have received widespread attention in recent years. One is the theory of **distributive justice** proposed by Harvard philosopher John Rawls, which seeks to analyze the type of society that people in a "natural state" would establish if they could not determine in advance whether they would be talented, rich, healthy, or ambitious, relative to other members of society. According to Rawls, the society contemplated through this "veil of ignorance" should be given precedence in terms of development because it considers the needs and rights of all its members. Rawls did not argue, however, that such a society would be strictly egalitarian. That would unfairly penalize those who turned out to be the most talented and ambitious. Instead, Rawls suggested that such a society would stress equality of opportunity, not of results. On the other hand, Rawls stressed that society would pay heed to the least advantaged to ensure that they did not suffer unduly and that they enjoyed society's benefits. To Rawls, society must be premised on justice. Everyone is entitled to her fair share in society, a fairness all must work to guarantee.

In contrast to Rawls, another Harvard philosopher, Robert Nozick, stressed liberty, not justice, as the most important obligation that society owes its members. **Libertarians** stress market outcomes as the basis for distributing society's rewards. Only to the extent that one meets the demands of the market does one deserve society's benefits. Libertarians oppose interference by society in their lives as long as they do not violate the rules of the marketplace, that is, as long as they do not cheat others and as long as they honestly disclose the nature of their transactions with others. The fact that some end up with fortunes while others accumulate little simply proves that some can play in the market effectively while others cannot. To libertarians, this is not unjust.

What is unjust to them is any attempt by society to take wealth earned by citizens and then distribute it to those who did not earn it. These theories and others (e.g., Marxism) judge society in moral terms by its organization and by its method of distributing goods and services. They demonstrate the difficulty of ethical decision making in the context of a social organization: behavior that is consistently ethical from individual to individual may not necessarily produce a just society.

2-2f OTHER THEORIES

The preceding theories do not exhaust the possible approaches to evaluating ethical behavior but represent the most commonly cited theories advanced over the years. Several other theories also deserve mention. **Intuitionism** holds that a rational person possesses inherent powers to assess the correctness of actions. Though an individual may refine and strengthen these powers, they are just as basic to humanity as our instincts for survival and self-defense. Just as some people are better artists or musicians, some people have more insight into ethical behavior than others. Consistent with intuitionism is the **good persons** philosophy, which declares that individuals who wish to act morally should seek out and emulate those who always seem to know the right choice in any given situation and who always seem to do the right thing. One variation of these ethical approaches is the "**Television Test**," which directs us to imagine that every ethical decision we make is being broadcast on nationwide television. Adherents of this approach believe an appropriate decision is one we would be comfortable broadcasting on television for all to witness.

2-3 Ethical Standards in Business

This section explores the application of the theories of ethical behavior to the world of business.

2-3a CHOOSING AN ETHICAL SYSTEM

In their efforts to resolve the moral dilemmas facing humanity, philosophers and other thinkers have struggled for years to refine the various systems discussed previously. No one ethical system is completely precise, however, and each tends occasionally to produce unacceptable prescriptions for action. But to say that a system has limits is not to say it is useless. On the contrary, many such systems provide insight into ethical decision making and help us formulate issues and resolve moral dilemmas. Furthermore, concluding that moral standards are difficult to articulate and that the boundaries are imprecise is not the same as concluding that moral standards are unnecessary or nonexistent.

Research by noted psychologist Lawrence Kohlberg provides insight into ethical decision making and lends credibility to the notion that moral growth, like physical growth, is part of the human condition. Kohlberg observed that people progress through stages of moral development according to two major variables: age and education. During the first level—the **preconventional level**—a child's conduct is a reaction to the fear of punishment and, later, to the pleasure of reward. Although people who operate at this level may behave in a moral manner, they do so without understanding why their behavior is moral. The rules are imposed upon them. During adolescence—Kohlberg's **conventional level**—people conform their behavior to meet the expectations of groups, such as family, peers, and eventually society. The motivation for conformity is loyalty, affection, and trust. Most adults operate at this level. According to Kohlberg, some people reach the third level— the **postconventional level**—at which they accept and conform to moral principles because they understand *why* the principles are right and binding. At this level, moral principles are voluntarily internalized, not externally imposed. Moreover, individuals at this stage develop their own universal ethical principles and even question the laws and values that society and others have adopted.

Kohlberg believed that these stages are sequential and that not all people reach the third or even the second stage. He therefore argued that exploring ways of enabling people to develop to the advanced stage of postconventional thought was essential to the study of ethics. Other psychologists assert that individuals do not pass from stage to stage but rather function in all three stages simultaneously.

♦ SEE FIGURE 2-1: *Kohlberg's Stages of Moral Development*

Whatever the source of our ethical approach, we cannot avoid facing moral dilemmas that challenge us to recognize and to do the right thing. Moreover, for those who plan business careers, such dilemmas will necessarily have implications for many others: employees, shareholders, suppliers, customers, and society at large.

FIGURE 2-1 Kohlberg's Stages of Moral Development		
Levels	**Perspective**	**Justification**
Preconventional (Childhood)	Self	Punishment/reward
Conventional (Adolescent)	Group	Group norms
Postconventional (Adult)	Universal	Moral principles

2-3b CORPORATIONS AS MORAL AGENTS

Because corporations are not persons but rather artificial entities created by the State, it is not obvious whether they can or should be held morally accountable. As Lord Chancellor Thurlow lamented two hundred years ago, "A company has no body to kick and no soul to damn, and by God, it ought to have both." Clearly, individuals within corporations can be held morally responsible, but the corporate entity presents unique problems.

Commentators are divided on the issue. Some, like philosopher Manuel Velasquez, insist that only people can engage in behavior that can be judged in moral terms. Opponents of this view, like philosophers Kenneth Goodpaster and John Matthews, Jr., concede that corporations are not persons in any literal sense, but insist that the attributes of responsibility inherent in corporations are sufficient in number to permit judging corporate behavior from a moral perspective.

2-4 Ethical Responsibilities of Business

Many people assert that the only responsibility of business is to maximize profit and that this obligation overrides any other ethical or social responsibility. Although our economic system of modified capitalism is based on the pursuit of selfinterest, it contains components to check this motivation of greed. Our system always has recognized the need for some form of regulation, whether by the "invisible hand" of competition, the self-regulation of business, or government regulation.

2-4a REGULATION OF BUSINESS

As explained and justified by Adam Smith in *The Wealth of Nations* (1776), the capitalistic system is composed of six "institutions": economic motivation, private productive property, free enterprise, free markets, competition, and limited government. Economic motivation assumes that a person who receives an economic return for his effort will work harder; therefore, the economic system should provide greater economic rewards for those who work harder. Private productive property, the means by which economic motivation is exercised, permits individuals to innovate and produce while securing to them the fruits of their efforts. Jack Behrman, a professor of business ethics, has described how the four other institutions combine with these two to bring about industrialized capitalism:

Free enterprise permits the combination of properties so people can do things together that they can't do alone. Free enterprise means a capitalistic combination of factors of production under decisions of free individuals. Free enterprise is the group expression of the use of private property, and it permits greater efficiency in an industrial setting through variation in the levels and kinds of production.

… The free market operates to equate supply and demand—supply reflecting the ability and willingness to offer certain goods or services and demand reflecting the consumer's ability and willingness to pay. Price is adjusted to include the maximum number of *both* bids and offers. The market, therefore, is *the* decision-making mechanism outside the firm. It is the *means* by which basic decisions are made about the use of resources, and all factors are supposed to respond to it, however they wish.

… Just in case it doesn't work out that way, there is one more institution—the *Government—which* is supposed to set rules and provide protection for the society and its members. That's all, said Smith, that it should do: it should set the rules, enforce them, and stand aside. J. Behrman, *Discourses on Ethics and Business*, pp. 25-29.

As long as all these constituent institutions continue to exist and operate in a balanced manner, the factors of production—land, capital, and labor—combine to produce an efficient allocation of resources for individual consumers and for the economy as a whole. To achieve this outcome, however, Smith's model requires the satisfaction of several conditions: "standardized products, numerous firms in markets, each firm with a small share and unable by its actions alone to exert significant influence over price, no barriers to entry, and output carried to the point where each seller's marginal cost equals the going market price." E. Singer, *Antitrust Economics and Legal Analysis*, p. 2.

History has demonstrated that the actual operation of the economy has satisfied almost none of these assumptions. More specifically, the actual competitive process falls considerably short of the classic economic model of perfect competition:

Competitive industries are never perfectly competitive in this sense. Many of the resources they employ cannot be shifted to other employments without substantial cost and delay. The allocation of those resources, as between industries or as to relative proportions within a single industry, is unlikely to have been made in a way that affords the best possible expenditure of economic effort. Information is incomplete, motivation confused, and decision therefore ill informed and often unwise. Variations in efficiency are not directly reflected in variations of profit. Success is derived in large part from competitive selling efforts, which in the aggregate may be wasteful, and from differentiation of products, which may be undertaken partly by methods designed to impair the opportunity of the buyer to compare quality and price. C. Edwards, *Maintaining Competition.*

In addition to capitalism's failure to allocate resources efficiently, it cannot be relied on to achieve all of the social and public policy objectives a pluralistic democracy requires. For example, the free enterprise model simply does not comprehend or address equitable distribution of wealth, national defense, conservation of natural resources, full employment, stability in economic cycles, protection against economic dislocations, health and safety, social security, and other important social and economic goals. Because the "invisible hand" and self-regulation by business have failed not only to preserve the competitive process in our economic system but also to achieve social goals extrinsic to the efficient allocation of resources, governmental intervention in business has become increasingly common. Such intervention attempts to (1) regulate both "legal" monopolies, such as those conferred by law through copyrights, patents, and trade symbols, and "natural" monopolies, such as utilities, transportation, and communications; (2) preserve competition by correcting imperfections in the market system; (3) protect specific groups, especially labor and agriculture, from failures of the marketplace; and (4) promote other social goals. Successful government regulation involves a delicate balance between regulations that attempt to preserve competition and those that attempt to advance other social objectives. The latter should not undermine the basic competitive processes that provide an efficient allocation of economic resources.

2-5 Corporate Governance

In addition to the broad demands of maintaining a competitive and fair marketplace, another factor demanding the ethical and social responsibility of business is the sheer size and power of individual corporations. The five thousand largest U.S. firms currently produce more than half of the nation's gross national product. Statutorily, their economic power should be delegated by the shareholders to the board of directors, who in turn appoint the officers of the corporation.

> In reality, this legal image is virtually a myth. In nearly every large American business corporation, there exists a management autocracy. One man—variously titled the President, or the Chairman of the Board, or the Chief Executive Officer—or a small coterie of men rule the corporation. Far from being chosen by the directors to run the corporation, this chief executive or executive clique chooses the board of directors and, with the acquiescence of the board, controls the corporation. R. Nader, M. Green, and J. Seligman, *Taming the Giant Corporation.*

In a classic study published in 1932, Adolf Berle and Gardiner Means concluded that significant amounts of economic power had been concentrated in a relatively few large corporations, that the ownership of these corporations had become widely dispersed, and that the shareholders had become far removed from active participation in management. Since their original study, these trends have steadily continued. The large publicly held corporations—numbering five hundred to one thousand—own the great bulk of the industrial wealth of the United States. Moreover, these corporations are controlled by a small group of corporate officers.

Historically, the boards of many publicly held corporations consisted mainly or entirely of inside directors (corporate officers who also serve on the board of directors). During the past two decades, however, as a result of regulations by the U.S. Securities and Exchange Commission and the stock exchanges, the number and influence of outside directors has increased substantially. Now the boards of the great majority of publicly held corporations consist primarily of outside directors, and these corporations have audit committees consisting entirely of outside directors.

Nevertheless, a number of instances of corporate misconduct have been revealed in the first years of this century. In response to these business scandals—involving companies such as Enron, WorldCom, Global Crossing, Adelphia, and Arthur Andersen—in 2002, Congress passed the Sarbanes-Oxley Act. This legislation seeks to prevent these types of scandals by increasing corporate responsibility through the imposition of additional corporate governance requirements on publicly held corporations. (This statute is discussed further in *Chapters 6, 35, 43,* and *44.*)

Moreover, in July 2010, the Dodd-Frank Wall Street Reform and Consumer Protection Act (Dodd-Frank Act) was enacted, representing the most significant change to U.S. financial regulation since the New Deal. Its purposes include improving accountability and transparency in the financial system, protecting consumers from abusive financial services practices, and improving corporate governance in publicly held companies. (The Dodd-Frank Act is discussed further in *Chapters 3, 29, 34, 35, 36, 41, 43,* and *49.*)

These developments raise social, policy, and ethical issues about the governance of large, publicly owned corporations. Many observers insist that companies playing such an important role in economic life should have a responsibility to undertake projects that benefit society in ways that go beyond mere financial efficiency in producing goods and services. In some instances, the idea of corporate obligation comes from industrialists themselves. Andrew Carnegie, for example, advocated philanthropy throughout his life and contributed much of his fortune to educational and social causes.

2-5a ARGUMENTS AGAINST SOCIAL RESPONSIBILITY

Among the arguments opposing business involvement in socially responsible activities are profitability, unfairness, accountability, and expertise.

PROFITABILITY As economist Milton Friedman and others have argued, businesses are artificial entities established to permit people to engage in profit-making, not social, activities. Without profits, they assert, there is little reason for a corporation to exist and no real way to measure the effectiveness of corporate activities. Businesses are not organized to engage in social activities; they are structured to produce goods and services for which they receive money. Their social obligation is to return as much of this money to their direct stakeholders as possible. In a free market with significant competition, the selfish pursuits of corporations will lead to maximizing output, minimizing costs, and establishing fair prices. All other concerns distract companies and interfere with achieving these goals.

UNFAIRNESS Whenever companies stray from their designated role of profit-maker, they take unfair advantage of company employees and shareholders. For example, a company may support the arts or education or spend excess funds on health and safety; however, these funds rightfully belong to the shareholders or employees. The company's decision to disburse these funds to others who may well be less deserving than the shareholders and employees is unfair. Furthermore, consumers can express their desires through the marketplace, and shareholders and employees can decide independently whether they wish to make charitable contributions. In most cases, senior management consults the board of directors about supporting social concerns but does not seek the approval of the company's major stakeholders. Thus, these shareholders are effectively disenfranchised from actions that reduce their benefits from the corporation.

ACCOUNTABILITY Corporations, as previously noted, are private institutions that are subject to a lower standard of accountability than are public bodies. Accordingly, a company may decide to support a wide range of social causes and yet submit to little public scrutiny. But a substantial potential for abuse exists in such cases. For one thing, a company could provide funding for causes its employees or shareholders do not support. It also could provide money "with strings attached," thereby controlling the recipients' agendas for less than socially beneficial purposes. For example, a drug company that contributes to a consumer group might implicitly or explicitly condition its assistance on the group's agreement never to criticize the company or the drug industry.

This lack of accountability warrants particular concern because of the enormous power corporations wield in modern society. Many large companies—like Walmart, Berkshire Hathaway, Facebook, ExxonMobil, and Apple—generate and spend more money in a year than all but a handful of the world's countries. If these companies suddenly began to pursue their own social agendas vigorously, their influence might well rival, and perhaps undermine, that of their own governments. In a country like the United States, founded on the principles of limited government and the balance of powers, too much corporate involvement in social affairs might well present substantial problems. Without clear guidelines and accountability, the corporate pursuit of socially responsible behavior might well distort the entire process of governance.

There is a clear alternative to corporations engaging in socially responsible action. If society wishes to increase the resources devoted to needy causes, it has the power to do so. Let corporations seek profits without the burden of a social agenda, let the consumers vote in the marketplace for the products and services they desire, and let the government tax a portion of corporate profits for socially beneficial causes.

EXPERTISE Even though a corporation has an expertise in producing and selling its product, it may not possess a talent for recognizing or managing socially useful activities. Corporations become successful in the market because they can identify and meet customers' needs. Nothing suggests that this talent spills over into nonbusiness arenas. In fact, critics of corporate engagement in social activities worry that corporations will prove unable to distinguish the true needs of society from their own narrow self-interest.

2-5b ARGUMENTS IN FAVOR OF SOCIAL RESPONSIBILITY

First, it should be recognized that even business critics acknowledge that the prime responsibility of business is to make a reasonable return on its investment by producing a quality product at a reasonable price. They do not suggest that business entities be charitable institutions. They do assert, however, that business has certain obligations beyond making a profit or not harming society. Critics contend that business must help to resolve societal problems, and they offer a number of arguments in support of their position.

THE SOCIAL CONTRACT Society creates corporations and accords them a special social status, including the grant of limited liability, which insulates the owners from liability for debts the organization incurs. Supporters of social roles for corporations assert that limited liability and other rights granted to companies carry a responsibility: corporations, just like other members of society, must contribute to its betterment. Therefore, companies owe a moral debt to society to contribute to its overall well-being. Society needs a host of improvements, such as pollution control, safe products, a free marketplace, quality education, cures for illness, and freedom from crime. Corporations can help in each of these areas. Granted, deciding which social needs deserve corporate attention is difficult; however, this challenge does not lessen a company's obligation to choose a cause. Corporate America cannot ignore the multitude of pressing needs that still remain, despite the efforts of government and private charities.

A derivative of the social contract theory is the **stakeholder model** for the societal role of the business corporation. Under the stakeholder model, a corporation has fiduciary responsibilities to all of its stakeholders, not just its stockholders. Historically, the stockholder model for the role of business has been the norm. Under this theory, a corporation is viewed as private property owned by and for the benefit of its owners—the stockholders of the corporation. (For a full discussion of this legal model, see *Chapter 35*.) The stakeholder model, on the other hand, holds that a corporation is responsible to society at large, and more directly, to all those constituencies on which it depends for its survival. Thus, it is argued that a corporation should be managed for the benefit of all of its stakeholders—stockholders, employees, customers, suppliers, and managers, as well as the local communities in which it operates. Compare *Figure 2-2* with *Figure 35-1*.

♦ **SEE FIGURE 2-2:** *The Stakeholder Model*

LESS GOVERNMENT REGULATION According to another argument in favor of corporate social responsibility, the more responsibly companies act, the less regulation the government must provide. This idea, if accurate, would likely appeal to those corporations that typically view regulation with distaste, perceiving it as a crude and expensive way of achieving social goals. To them, regulation often imposes inappropriate, overly broad rules that hamper productivity and require extensive recordkeeping procedures to document compliance. If companies can use more flexible, voluntary methods of meeting a social norm such as pollution control, then government will be less tempted to legislate norms.

The argument can be taken further. Not only does anticipatory corporate action lessen the likelihood of government regulation, but social involvement by companies creates a climate of trust and respect that reduces the overall inclination of government to interfere in company business. For example, a government agency is much more likely to show some leniency toward a socially responsible company than toward one that ignores social plights.

LONG-RUN PROFITS Perhaps the most persuasive argument in favor of corporate involvement in social causes is that such involvement actually makes good business sense. Consumers often support good corporate images and avoid bad ones. For example, consumers generally prefer to patronize stores with "easy return" policies. Even though the law does not require such policies, companies institute them because they create goodwill—an intangible though indispensable asset for ensuring repeat customers. In the long run, enhanced goodwill often leads to stronger profits. Moreover, corporate actions to improve the well-being of their communities make these communities more attractive to citizens and more profitable for business.

FIGURE 2-2   The Stakeholder Model

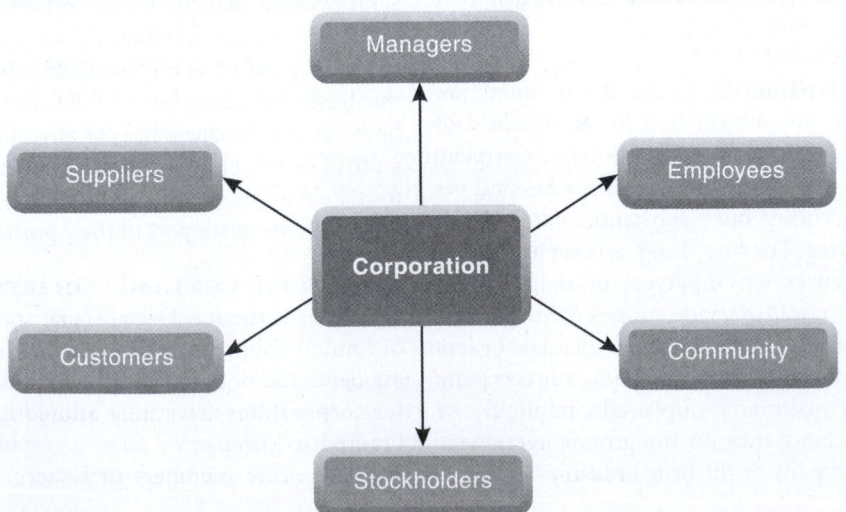

C H A P T E R   S U M M A R Y

DEFINITIONS	**Ethics** study of what is right or good for human beings
	Business Ethics study of what is right and good in a business setting

ETHICAL THEORIES	**Ethical Fundamentalism** individuals look to a central authority or set of rules to guide them in ethical decision making

Ethical Relativism actions must be judged by what individuals subjectively feel is right or wrong for themselves

Situational Ethics one must judge a person's actions by first putting oneself in the actor's situation

Utilitarianism moral actions are those that produce the greatest net pleasure compared with net pain
- *Act Utilitarianism* assesses each separate act according to whether it maximizes pleasure over pain
- *Rule Utilitarianism* supports rules that on balance produce the greatest pleasure for society
- *Cost-Benefit Analysis* quantifies the benefits and costs of alternatives

Deontology actions must be judged by their motives and means as well as their results

Social Ethics Theories focus is on a person's obligations to other members in society and on the individual's rights and obligations within society
- *Social Egalitarians* believe that society should provide all its members with equal amounts of goods and services regardless of their relative contributions
- *Distributive Justice* stresses equality of opportunity rather than results
- *Libertarians* stress market outcomes as the basis for distributing society's rewards

Other Theories
- *Intuitionism* a rational person possesses inherent power to assess the correctness of actions
- *Good Person* individuals should seek out and emulate good role models

ETHICAL STANDARDS IN BUSINESS	**Choosing an Ethical System** Kohlberg's stages of moral development is a widely accepted model (see *Figure 2-1*)

Corporations as Moral Agents because a corporation is a statutorily created entity, it is not clear whether it should be held morally responsible

ETHICAL RESPONSIBILITIES OF BUSINESS	**Regulation of Business** governmental regulation has been necessary because all the conditions for perfect competition have not been satisfied and free competition cannot by itself achieve other societal objectives

Corporate Governance vast amounts of wealth and power have become concentrated in a small number of corporations, which in turn are controlled by a small group of corporate officers

Arguments against Social Responsibility
- *Profitability* because corporations are artificial entities established for profitmaking activities, their only social obligation should be to return as much money as possible to shareholders
- *Unfairness* whenever corporations engage in social activities such as supporting the arts or education, they divert funds rightfully belonging to shareholders and/ or employees to unrelated third parties
- *Accountability* a corporation is subject to less public accountability than public bodies are

- *Expertise* although a corporation may have a high level of expertise in selling its goods and services, there is absolutely no guarantee that any promotion of social activities will be carried on with the same degree of competence

Arguments in Favor of Social Responsibility

- *The Social Contract* because society allows for the creation of corporations and gives them special rights, including a grant of limited liability, corporations owe a responsibility to society
- *Less Government Regulation* by taking a more proactive role in addressing society's problems, corporations create a climate of trust and respect that has the effect of reducing government regulation
- *Long-Run Profits* corporate involvement in social causes creates goodwill, which simply makes good business sense

C A S E S

Throughout this book, the authors have included court cases dealing with ethical or social issues. Every chapter has at least one case relating to ethical or social issues; in a number of chapters, all of the cases address these issues.

Q U E S T I O N S

1. You have an employee who has a chemical imbalance in the brain that causes him to be severely emotionally unstable. The medication that is available to treat this schizophrenic condition is extremely powerful and decreases the taker's life span by one to two years for every year that the user takes it. You know that his doctors and family believe that it is in his best interest to take the medication. What course of action should you follow?

2. You have a very shy employee who is from another country. After a time, you notice that the quality of her performance is deteriorating. You find an appropriate time to speak with her and determine that she is extremely distraught. She informs you that her family has arranged a marriage for her and that she refuses to obey their contract. She further informs you that she is contemplating suicide. Two weeks later, with her poor performance continuing, you determine that she is on the verge of a nervous breakdown; once again she informs you that she is going to commit suicide. What should you do? Consider further that you can petition a court to have her involuntarily committed to a mental hospital. You know, however, that her family would consider such a commitment an extreme insult and that they might seek retribution. Does this prospect alter your decision? Explain.

3. You receive a telephone call from a company you never do business with requesting a reference on one of your employees, Mary Sunshine. You believe that Mary is generally incompetent and would be delighted to see her take another job. You give her a glowing reference. Is this right? Explain.

4. You have just received a report suggesting that a chemical your company uses in its manufacturing process is very dangerous. You have not read the report, but you are generally aware of its contents. You believe that the chemical can be replaced fairly easily but that if word gets out, panic may set in among employees and community members. A reporter asks if you have seen the report, and you say no. Is your behavior right or wrong? Explain.

5. You and Joe Jones, your neighbor and friend, bought lottery tickets at the corner drugstore. While watching the lottery drawing on television with you that night, Joe leaps from the couch, waves his lottery ticket, and shouts, "I've got the winning number!" Suddenly, he clutches his chest, keels over, and dies on the spot. You are the only living person who knows that Joe, not you, bought the winning ticket. If you substitute his ticket for yours, no one will know of the switch, and you will be $10 million richer. Joe's only living relative is a rich aunt whom he despised. Will you switch his ticket for yours? Explain.

6. Omega, Inc., a publicly held corporation, has assets of $100 million and annual earnings in the range of $13 to $15 million. Omega owns three aluminum plants, which are profitable, and one plastics plant, which is losing $4 million a year. The plastics plant shows no sign of ever becoming profitable because of its very high operating costs, and there is no evidence that the plant and the underlying real estate will increase in value. Omega

decides to sell the plastics plant. The only bidder for the plant is Gold, who intends to use the plant for a new purpose, to introduce automation, and to replace all current employees. Would it be ethical for Omega to turn down Gold's bid and keep the plastics plant operating indefinitely for the purpose of preserving the employees' jobs? Explain.

7. You are the sales manager of a two-year-old electronics firm. At times, the firm has seemed to be on the brink of failure but recently has begun to be profitable. In large part, the profitability is due to the aggressive and talented sales force you recruited. Two months ago, you hired Alice North, an honor graduate from State University who decided that she was tired of the research department and wanted to try sales.

    Almost immediately after you send Alice out for training with Brad West, your best salesperson, he begins reporting to you an unexpected turn of events. According to Brad, "Alice is terrific: she's confident, smooth, and persistent. Unfortunately, a lot of our buyers are good old boys who just aren't comfortable around young, bright women. Just last week, Hiram Jones, one of our biggest customers, told me that he simply won't continue to do business with 'young chicks' who think they invented the world. It's not that Alice is a know-it-all. She's not. It's just that these guys like to booze it up a bit, tell some off-color jokes, and then get down to business. Alice doesn't drink, and although she never objects to the jokes, it's clear she thinks they're offensive." Brad believes that several potential deals have fallen through "because the mood just wasn't right with Alice there." Brad adds, "I don't like a lot of these guys' styles myself, but I go along to make the sales. I just don't think Alice is going to make it."

    When you call Alice in to discuss the situation, she concedes the accuracy of Brad's report but indicates that she's not to blame and insists that she be kept on the job. You feel committed to equal opportunity but do not want to jeopardize your company's ability to survive. What should you do?

8. Major Company subcontracted the development of part of a large technology system to Start-up Company, a small corporation specializing in custom computer systems. The contract, which was a major breakthrough for Start-up Company and crucial to its future, provided for an initial development fee and subsequent progress payments, as well as a final date for completion.

    Start-up Company provided Major Company with periodic reports indicating that everything was on schedule. After several months, however, the status reports stopped coming, and the company missed delivery of the schematics, the second major milestone. As an in-house technical consultant for Major Company, you visit Startup Company and find not only that they are far behind schedule but also that they lied about their previous progress. Moreover, you determine that this slippage has put the schedule for the entire project in jeopardy. The cause of Start-up's slippage was the removal of personnel from your project to work on short-term contracts to obtain money to meet the weekly payroll.

    Your company decides that you should stay at Startup Company to monitor its work and to assist in the design of the project. After six weeks and some progress, Start-up is still way behind its delivery dates. Nonetheless, you are now familiar enough with the project to complete it in-house with Major's personnel.

    Start-up is still experiencing severe cash flow problems and repeatedly requests payment from Major. But your CEO, furious with Start-up's lies and deceptions, wishes to "bury" Start-up and finish the project using Major Company's internal resources. She knows that withholding payment to Start-up will put them out of business. What do you do? Explain.

9. A customer requests certain sophisticated tests on equipment he purchased from your factory. Such tests are very expensive and must be performed by a third party. The equipment was tested as requested and met all of the industry standards but showed anomalies that could not be explained. Though the problem appears to be minor, you decide to inspect the unit to try to understand the test data—a very expensive and timeconsuming process. You inform the customer of this decision. A problem is found, but it is minor and highly unlikely ever to cause the unit to fail. In addition to the time and expense required to rebuild the equipment, notifying the customer that you are planning to rebuild the unit would also put your overall manufacturing procedures in question.

    Should you fix the problem, ship the equipment as is, or inform the customer? Explain.

10. You are a project manager for a company making a major proposal to a Middle Eastern country. Your major competition is from Japan.

    a. Your local agent, who is closely tied to a very influential sheikh, would receive a 5 percent commission if the proposal were accepted. Near the date for the decision, the agent asks you for $150,000 to grease the skids so that your proposal is accepted. What do you do?

b. What do you do if, after you say no, the agent goes to your vice president, who provides the money?

c. Your overseas operation learns that most other foreign companies in this Middle Eastern location bolster their business by exchanging currency on the gray market. You discover that your division is twice as profitable as budgeted due to the amount of domestic currency you have received on the gray market. What do you do?

11. Explain what relevance ethics has to business.

12. How should the financial interests of stockholders be balanced with the varied interests of stakeholders? If you were writing a code of conduct for your company, how would you address this issue?

13. A company adopts a policy that (a) prohibits romantic relationships between employees of different ranks and (b) permits romantic relationships between employees of the same rank only if both employees waive in writing their rights to sue the company should the relationship end. Violation of this rule is grounds for dismissal. Is this rule ethical? If not, how should it be revised? Explain.

14. A company prohibits any employee from making disparaging comments about the company through any social media—including online blogs, email, tweets, and other electronic media. Violation of this rule is grounds for dismissal. Explain whether this rule is ethical. If not, how should it be revised? Explain.

BUSINESS ETHICS CASES

The business ethics cases that follow are based on the kinds of situations that companies regularly face in conducting business. You should first read each case carefully and completely before attempting to analyze it. Second, you should identify the most important ethical issues arising from the situation. Often it is helpful to prioritize these issues. Third, you should identify the viable options for addressing these issues and the ethical implications of the identified options.

This might include examining the options from the perspectives of the various ethical theories as well as the affected stakeholders. Fourth, you should reach a definite resolution of the ethical issues by choosing what you think is the best option. You should have a well-articulated rationale for your resolution. Finally, you should develop a strategy for implementing your resolution.

PHARMAKON DRUG COMPANY

BACKGROUND
William Wilson, senior vice president of research, development, and medical (RD&M) at Pharmakon Drug Company, received both his Ph.D. in biochemistry and his M.D. from the University of Oklahoma. Upon completion of his residency, Dr. Wilson joined the faculty at Harvard Medical School. He left Harvard after five years to join the research group at Merck & Co. Three years later, he went to GlaxoSmithKline as director of RD&M, and after eight years, Dr. Wilson joined Pharmakon in his current position.

William Wilson has always been highly respected as a scientist, a manager, and an individual. He has also been an outstanding leader in the scientific community, particularly in the effort to attract more minorities into the field.

Pharmakon concentrates its research efforts in the areas of antivirals (with a focus on HIV), the cardiovascular system, the respiratory system, muscle relaxants, the gastrointestinal system, the central nervous system, and consumer health care (i.e., nonprescription and over-the-counter [OTC] medicines). Dr. Wilson is on the board of directors of Pharmakon and the company's executive committee. He reports directly to the chairman of the board and CEO, Mr. Jarred Swenstrum.

DECLINING GROWTH
During the previous eight years, Pharmakon experienced tremendous growth: 253 percent overall, with yearly growth ranging from 12 percent to 25 percent. During this period, Pharmakon's RD&M budget grew from $79 million to $403 million, and the number of employees rose from 1,192 to 3,273 (see *Figure 2-3*). During the previous two years, however, growth in revenue and earnings slowed considerably. Moreover, in the current year, Pharmakon's revenues of $3.55 billion and earnings before taxes of $1.12 billion were up only 2 percent from the previous year. Furthermore, both revenues and earnings are projected to be flat or declining for the next five years.

♦ SEE FIGURE 2-3: *Pharmakon Employment*

The cessation of this period's tremendous growth and the likelihood of future decline have been brought about principally by two causes. First, a number of Pharmakon's most important patents have expired. Competition from generics has begun and could continue to erode its products' market shares. Second, as new types of health-care delivery organizations evolve, pharmaceutical companies' revenues and earnings will in all likelihood be adversely affected.

FIGURE 2-3 Pharmakon Employment

Attribute/Years Ago	1	2	3	4	5	6	7	8
Total Employment	3,273	3,079	2,765	2,372	1,927	1,618	1,306	1,192
Minority Employment	272 (8.35%)	238 (7.7%)	196 (7.15%)	143 (6.0%)	109 (5.7%)	75 (4.6%)	53 (4.1%)	32 (2.7%)
Revenue ($ million)	3,481	3,087	2,702	2,184	1,750	1,479	1,214	986
Profit ($ million)	1,106	1,021	996	869	724	634	520	340
RD&M Budget ($ million)	403	381	357	274	195	126	96	79

PROBLEM AND PROPOSED SOLUTIONS

In response, the board of directors has decided that the company must emphasize two conflicting goals: increase the number of new drugs brought to market and cut back on the workforce in anticipation of rising labor and marketing costs and declining revenues. Accordingly, Dr. Wilson has been instructed to cut costs significantly and to reduce his workforce by 15 percent over the next six months.

Dr. Wilson called a meeting with his management team to discuss the workforce reduction. One of his managers, Leashia Harmon, argued that the layoffs should be made "so that recent gains in minority hiring are not wiped out." The percentage of minority employees had increased from 2.7 percent eight years ago to 8.3 percent in the previous year (see *Figure 2-3*). The minority population in communities in which Pharmakon has major facilities has remained over the years at approximately 23 percent. About 20 percent of the RD&M workforce have a Ph.D. in a physical science or in pharmacology, and another 3 percent have an M.D.

Dr. Harmon, a Ph.D. in pharmacology and head of clinical studies, is the only minority on Dr. Wilson's seven-member management team. Dr. Harmon argued that RD&M has worked long and hard to increase minority employment and has been a leader in promoting Pharmakon's affirmative action plan (see *Figure 2-4*). Therefore, she asserted, all layoffs should reflect this commitment, even if it means disproportionate layoffs of nonminorities.

Dr. Anson Peake, another member of Dr. Wilson's management team and director of new products, argued that

FIGURE 2-4 Pharmakon Affirmative Action Program

Pharmakon Drug Company
Equal Employment Opportunity Affirmative Action Program

POLICY

It is the policy of Pharmakon Drug Co. to provide equal employment opportunities without regard to race, color, religion, sex, national origin, sexual orientation, disability, and veteran status. The Company will also take affirmative action to employ and advance individual applicants from all segments of our society. This policy relates to all phases of employment, including, but not limited to, recruiting, hiring, placement, promotion, demotion, layoff, recall, termination, compensation, and training. In communities where Pharmakon has facilities, it is our policy to be a leader in providing equal employment for all of its citizens.

RESPONSIBILITY FOR IMPLEMENTATION

The head of each division is ultimately responsible for initiating, administering, and controlling activities within all areas of responsibility necessary to ensure full implementation of this policy.

The managers of each location or area are responsible for the implementation of this policy.

All other members of management are responsible for conducting day-to-day activities in a manner to ensure compliance with this policy.

Pharmakon's RD&M division has never discharged a worker except for cause and should adhere as closely as possible to that policy by terminating individuals based solely on relative merit. Dr. Rachel Waugh, director of product development, pointed out that the enormous growth in employment over the past eight years—almost a trebling of the workforce—had made the company's employee performance evaluation system less than reliable. Consequently, she contended that because laying off 15 percent of her group would be extremely difficult and subjective, she preferred to follow a system of seniority.

Dr. Wilson immediately recognized that any system of reducing the workforce would be difficult to implement. Moreover, he was concerned about being fair to employees and maintaining the best qualified group to carry out the area's mission. He was very troubled by a merit or seniority system if it could not maintain the minority gains. In fact, he had even thought about the possibility of using this difficult situation to increase the percentage of minorities to bring it more in line with the minority percentage of the communities in which Pharmakon had major facilities.

MYKON PHARMACEUTICALS, INC.

MYKON'S DILEMMA

Jack Spratt, the newly appointed CEO of Mykon Pharmaceuticals, Inc., sat at his desk and scratched his head for the thousandth time that night. His friends never tired of telling him that unless he stopped this habit, he would remove what little hair he had left. Nevertheless, he had good reason to be perplexed—the decisions he made would determine the future of the company and, literally, the life or death of thousands of people.

As a young, ambitious scientist, Spratt had gained international fame and considerable fortune while rising quickly through the ranks of the scientists at Mykon. After receiving a degree from the Executive MBA program at the Kenan Flagler Business School, University of North Carolina at Chapel Hill, he assumed, in rapid succession, a number of administrative positions at the company, culminating in his appointment as CEO. But no one had told him that finding cures for previously incurable diseases would be fraught with moral dilemmas. Although it was 3:00 A.M., Spratt remained at his desk, unable to stop thinking about his difficult choices. His preoccupation was made worse by the knowledge that pressure from governments and consumers would only increase each day he failed to reach a decision. This pressure had mounted relentlessly since the fateful day he announced that Mykon had discovered the cure for AIDS. But the cure brought with it a curse: there was not enough to go around.

COMPANY BACKGROUND

Mykon, a major international research-based pharmaceutical group, engages in the research, development, manufacture, and marketing of human health-care products for sale in both the prescription and OTC markets. The company's principal prescription medicines include a range of products in the following areas: antiviral, neuromuscular blocking, the cardiovascular system, anti-inflammatory, immunosuppressive, systemic antibacterial, and the central nervous system. Mykon also manufactures other products such as muscle relaxants, antidepressants, anticonvulsants, and respiratory stimulants. In addition, the company markets drugs for the treatment of congestive heart failure and the prevention of organ rejection following transplant.

Mykon's OTC business consists primarily of cough and cold preparations and several topical antibiotics. The company seeks to expand its OTC business in various ways, including the reclassification of some of its prescription drugs to OTC status. Mykon's OTC sales represented 14 percent of the company's sales during last year.

Mykon has a long tradition of excellence in research and development (R&D). The company's expenditures on R&D for the last three financial years constituted 15 percent of its sales.

Mykon focuses its R&D on the following selected therapeutic areas, listed in descending order of expenditure amount: antivirals and other antibiotics, cardiovascular, central nervous system, anticancer, anti-inflammatory, respiratory, and neuromuscular.

Mykon sells its products internationally in more than 120 countries and has a significant presence in two of the largest pharmaceutical markets—the United States and Europe— and a growing presence in Japan. It generated approximately 43 percent and 35 percent of the company's sales from the previous year in the United States and Europe, respectively. The company sells essentially the same range of products throughout the world.

PRODUCTION

Mykon carries out most of its production in Rotterdam in the Netherlands and in Research Triangle Park, North Carolina, in the United States. The latter is the company's world headquarters. The company's manufacturing processes typically consist of three stages: the manufacture of active chemicals, the incorporation of these chemicals into products designed for use by the consumer, and packaging. The firm has an ongoing program of capital expenditure to provide up-to-date production facilities and relies on advanced technology, automation, and computerization of its manufacturing capability to help maintain its competitive position.

Production facilities are also located in ten other countries to meet the needs of local markets and to overcome legal restrictions on the importation of finished products. These facilities engage principally in product formulation and packaging, although plants in certain countries manufacture active chemicals. Last year, Mykon had more than seventeen thousand employees, 27 percent of whom were in the United States. Approximately 21 percent of Mykon's employees were engaged in R&D, largely in the Netherlands and the United States. Although unions represent a number of the firm's employees, the firm has not experienced any significant labor disputes in recent years, and it considers its employee relations to be good.

RESEARCH AND DEVELOPMENT

In the pharmaceutical industry, R&D is both expensive and prolonged, entailing considerable uncertainty. The process of producing a commercial drug typically takes between eight and twelve years as it proceeds from discovery through development to regulatory approval and finally to the product launch. No assurance exists that new compounds will survive the development process or obtain the requisite regulatory approvals. In addition, research conducted by other pharmaceutical companies may lead at any time to the introduction of competing or improved treatments.

Last year, Mykon incurred approximately 95 percent of its R&D expenditures in the Netherlands and the United States. *Figure 2-5* sets out the firm's annual expenditure on R&D in dollars and as a percentage of sales for each of the last three financial years.

JACK SPRATT

Every society, every institution, every company, and most important, every individual should follow those precepts that society holds most dear. The pursuit of profits must be consistent with and subordinate to these ideals, the most important of which is the Golden Rule. To work for the betterment of humanity is the reason I became a scientist in

the first place. As a child, Banting and Best were my heroes. I could think of no vocation that held greater promise to help mankind. Now that I am CEO I intend to have these beliefs included in our company's mission statement.

These sentiments, expressed by Jack Spratt in a newsmagazine interview, capture the intensity and drive that animate the man. None who knew him was surprised when he set out years ago—fueled by his prodigious energy, guided by his brilliant mind, and financed by Mykon—for the inner reaches of the Amazon Basin to find naturally occurring medicines. Spratt considered it to be his manifest destiny to discover the cure for some dread disease.

His search was not totally blind. Some years earlier, Frans Berger, a well-known but eccentric scientist, had written extensively about the variety of plant life and fungi that flourished in the jungles of the Bobonaza River region deep in the Amazon watershed. Although he spent twenty years there and discovered nothing of medical significance, the vast number and intriguing uniqueness of his specimens convinced Spratt that it was just a matter of time before a major breakthrough would occur.

Spratt also had some scientific evidence. While working in Mykon's laboratory to finance his graduate education in biology and genetics, Spratt and his supervisors had noticed that several fungi not only could restore damaged skin but also, when combined with synthetic polymers, had significant effects on internal cells. Several more years of scientific expeditions and investigations proved promising enough for Mykon to send Spratt and a twenty-person exploration team to the Amazon

FIGURE 2-5 Mykon R&D Expenditures

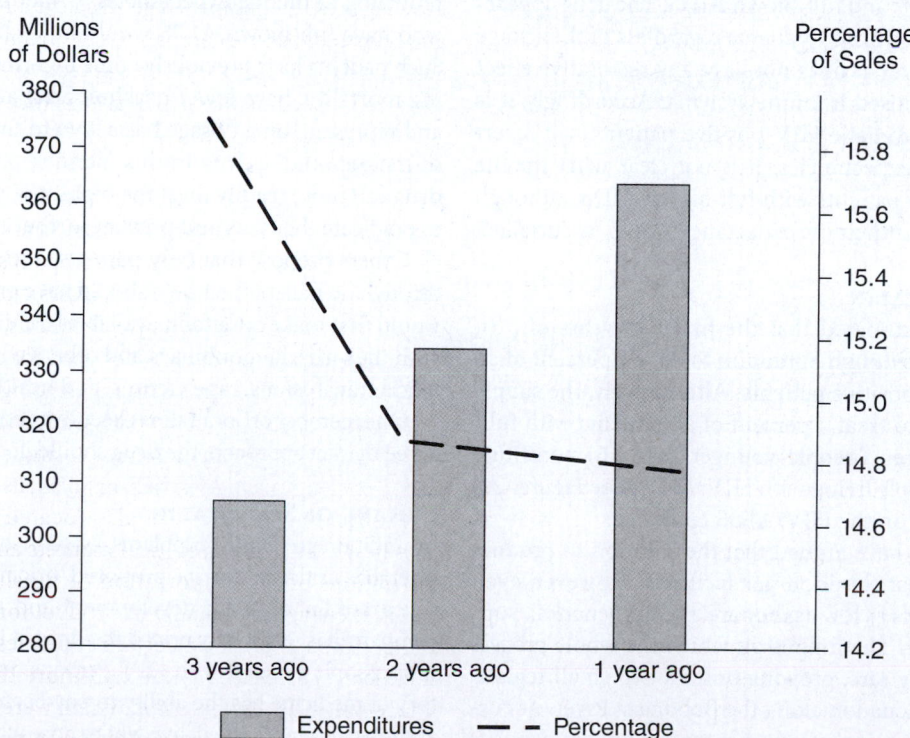

Basin for two years. Two years became five, and the enormous quantity of specimens sent back eventually took over an entire wing of the company's sizable laboratories in Research Triangle Park, North Carolina.

Upon Spratt's return, he headed up a group of Mykon scientists who examined the Amazonian fungi for pharmacological activity. After several years of promising beginnings and disappointing endings, they discovered that one fungus destroyed the recently identified virus HIV. Years later, the company managed to produce enough of the drug (code named Sprattalin) derived from the fungus to inform the Food and Drug Administration (FDA) that it was testing what appeared to be a cure for HIV. It was the happiest moment of Jack Spratt's life. The years of determined effort, not to mention the $800 million Mykon had invested, would now be more than fully rewarded.

Spratt's joy was short-lived, though. Public awareness of the drug quickly spread, and groups pressured the FDA to shorten or eliminate its normal approval process, which ordinarily takes more than seven years. People dying from the virus's effects demanded immediate access to the drug.

THE DRUG

Mirroring the insidiousness of HIV itself, the structure of Sprattalin is extraordinarily complex. Consequently, it takes four to seven months to produce a small quantity, only 25 percent of which is usable. It is expensive; each unit of Sprattalin costs Mykon $20,000 to produce. The projected dosage ranges from ten units for asymptomatic HIV-positive patients who have normal white blood cell counts to fifty units for patients with low white blood cell counts and full-blown AIDS. The drug appears to eliminate the virus from all patients regardless of their stage of the disease. However, it does not have any restorative effect on patients' compromised immune systems. Accordingly, it is expected that asymptomatic HIV-positive patients will revert to their normal life expectancies. It is not clear what the life expectancy will be of patients with full-blown AIDS, although it is almost certain that their life expectancy would be curtailed.

SUPPLY OF SPRATTALIN

The company has estimated that the first two years of production would yield enough Sprattalin to cure 6 percent of all asymptomatic HIV-positive patients. Alternatively, the supply would be sufficient to treat 4 percent of all patients with full-blown AIDS. Children (people younger than 15) constitute 4.5 percent of all people living with HIV/AIDS. See *Figures 2-6* and *2-7* for statistics on the HIV/AIDS epidemic.

Interested parties have argued that the solution to production problems is clear: build larger facilities. However, even with production levels as low as they are, the bottleneck in supply occurs elsewhere. The fungus on which the whole process depends is incredibly rare, growing only in two small regions near Jatun Molino, Ecuador, along the Bobonaza River. At current harvesting rates, scientists predict that all known deposits will be depleted in three years, and many of them insist that production should be scaled back to allow the fungus to regenerate.

Presently there are no known methods of cultivating the fungus in the laboratory. Apparently, the delicate ecology that allows it to exist in only one region of the earth is somehow distressed enough by either transport or lab conditions to render it unable to grow and produce the drug's precursor. Scientists are feverishly trying to discover those factors that will support successful culture. However, with limited quantities of the starting material and most of that pressured into production, the company has enjoyed no success in this endeavor. Because of Sprattalin's complexity, attempts to synthesize the drug have failed completely, mainly because it is not known how the drug works; thus, Sprattalin's effectiveness remains shrouded in mystery.

ALLOCATION OF SPRATTALIN

In response to the insufficient supply, a number of powerful consumer groups have made public their suggestions regarding the allocation of Sprattalin. One proposition advanced would use medical records to establish a waiting list of possible recipients based on the length of time they have been in treatment for the virus. The argument is that those people who have waited the longest and are most in danger of dying should be the first to find relief.

Other groups propose an opposite approach, arguing that because supply is so drastically short, Mykon should make Sprattalin available only to asymptomatic HIV patients. They require the least concentrations of the drug to become well, thus extending the drug's supply. They also have the greatest likelihood of returning to full life expectancies. Under this proposal, people who have full-blown AIDS would be ineligible for treatment. Such patients have previously come to terms with their impending mortality; have fewer psychological adjustments to make; and represent, on a dosage basis, two to five healthier patients. In meting out the drug in this manner, proponents argue, the drug can more readily meet the highest public health objectives to eradicate the virus and prevent further transmission.

Others propose that only patients who contracted the virus through no fault of their own should have priority. This approach would first make Sprattalin available to children who were born with the virus, hemophiliacs and others who got the virus from blood transfusions, rape victims, and health-care workers.

One member of Sprattalin's executive committee has suggested a free market approach: the drug should go to the highest bidder.

PRICING OF SPRATTALIN

In addition to supply problems, Mykon has come under considerable criticism for its proposed pricing structure. Because of extraordinarily high development and production costs, the company has tentatively priced the drug at levels unattainable for most people afflicted with HIV. Perhaps never before in the history of medicine has the ability to pay been so starkly presented, as those who can pay will live while those who cannot pay will die.

FIGURE 2-6 Global Summary of the AIDS Epidemic

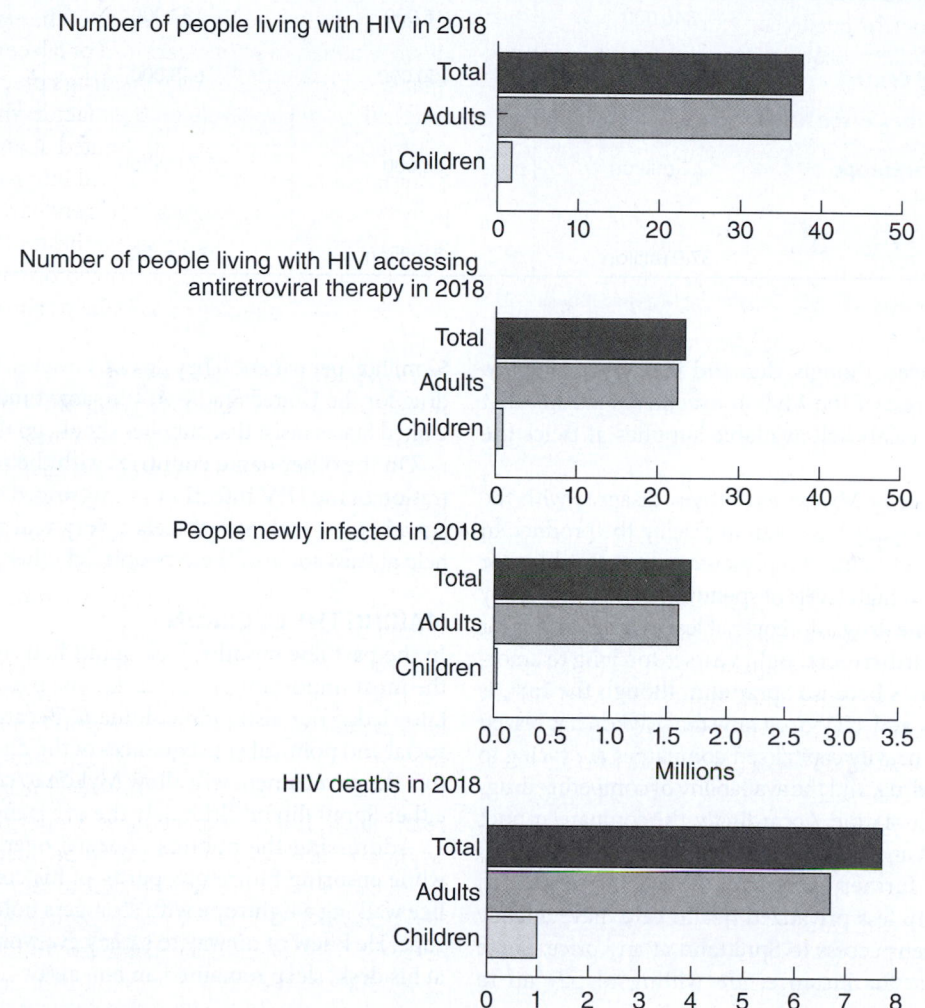

FIGURE 2-7 Regional Statistics for HIV and AIDS End of 2018

Region	People Living with HIV/AIDS	People Newly Infected	People with HIV Accessing Treatment	AIDS-Related Deaths
Eastern and Southern Africa	20.6 million	800,000	13.8 million	310,000
North Africa and Middle East	240,000	20,000	78,800	8,400
Western and Central Africa	5.0 million	280,000	2.6 million	160,000
Asia and Pacific	5.9 million	310,000	3.2 million	200,000
Latin America	1.9 million	100,000	1.2 million	35,000

(Continued)

FIGURE 2-7 Continued

Region	People Living with HIV/AIDS	People Newly Infected	People with HIV Accessing Treatment	AIDS-Related Deaths
Caribbean	340,000	16,000	187,000	6,700
Eastern Europe and Central Asia	1.7 million	150,000	648,000	38,000
Western and Central Europe and North America	2.2 million	68,000	1.7 million	13,000
Global Total	37.9 million	1.7 million	23.3 million	770,000

Source: World Health Organization, HIV/AIDS Department (accessed February 2020).

Even at these prices, though, demand far exceeds supply. Jack Spratt and the rest of the Mykon executives predict that the company could easily sell available supplies at twice the proposed price.

A growing number of Mykon executives disagree with the passive stance the company has taken in pricing the product. In their view, a 20 percent markup represents a meager return for the prolonged risk and high levels of spending that the company incurred to develop the drug. Moreover, it leaves little surplus for future investment. Furthermore, eight years is too long to amortize the R&D expenses because Sprattalin, though the first, is unlikely to be the last anti-HIV drug now that Mykon has blazed a path. Other, more heavily capitalized companies are racing to reverse engineer the drug, and the availability of competing drugs remains only a matter of time. Accordingly, the company cannot realistically count on an eight-year window of opportunity.

Foreign markets further exacerbate the pricing perplexity. Other countries, with less privatized health care, have already promised their citizens access to Sprattalin at any price. Some industrial countries, for instance, are willing to pay up to $2 million per patient. They do not, however, wish to subsidize the drug for the United States. At the same time, some voices in the United States insist that supplies should go first to U.S. citizens.

On the other hand, countries with the most severe concentration of the HIV infection cannot afford to pay even Mykon's actual costs. Jack Spratt feels a very real moral obligation to help at least some of these people, whether they can pay or not.

MAKING THE DECISION

In the past few months, Jack Spratt had seen many aspects of the most important project in his life become not only public knowledge but also public domain. Because of the enormous social and political consequences of the discovery, it is unlikely that the government will allow Mykon to control the destiny of either Sprattalin or ultimately the company.

Addressing the public's concern over access to the drug while ensuring future prosperity of his company had become like walking a tightrope with strangers holding each end of the rope. He knew of no way to satisfy everyone. As Jack Spratt sat at his desk, sleep remained an eon away.

OLIVER WINERY, INC.

BACKGROUND

Paul Oliver, Sr., immigrated to the United States from Greece. After working for several wineries, he started Oliver Winery, Inc., which eventually found a market niche in non-varietal jug wines. Through mass-marketing techniques, the company established a substantial presence in this segment of the market. Ten years ago, Paul, Jr., joined the firm after receiving a degree in enology (the study of wine making). He convinced his father of the desirability of entering a different segment of the wine market: premium varietals. To do this, the company needed a large infusion of capital to purchase appropriate vineyards. Reluctantly, Paul, Sr., agreed to take the company public. The initial public offering succeeded, and 40 percent of the company's stock went into outsiders' hands. Also, for the first time, outsiders served on the board of directors. Although Paul, Jr., wanted to use a new name for the premium varietal to appeal to a more upscale market, his father insisted on using the name Oliver.

BOARD MEETING

The board of directors met, along with Janet Stabler, the director of marketing of Oliver Winery, Inc. The following directors were in attendance:

Paul Oliver, Sr., chairman of the board and founder of the company

Paul Oliver, Jr., CEO, has an advanced degree in enology

Cyrus Abbott, CFO, has an MBA

Arlene Dale, comptroller, has a CPA with a master's degree in accounting

Raj Ray, COO, has a master's degree in industrial engineering

LaTasha Lane, vice president legal, has a J.D. degree

Elisabeth Constable, union representative to the board, has a GED degree

Rev. John W. Calvin, outside director, has a Doctor of Divinity degree

Carlos Menendez, outside director, has an MFA degree

Oliver, Sr.: The next item on the agenda is a proposal to develop a new line of wines. Janet Stabler will briefly present the proposal.

Stabler: Thank you. The proposal is to enter the fortified wine market. It's the only type of wine in which unit sales are increasing. We'll make the wines cheaply and package them in pint bottles with screw-on caps. Our chief competitors are Canandaigua with Richard's Wild Irish Rose, Gallo with Thunderbird and Night Train Express, and Mogen David with MD 20/20. We'll market the wine with little or no media advertising by strategically sampling the product to targeted consumers. That's it in a nutshell.

Oliver, Sr.: Any questions before we vote?

Menendez: Who'll buy this wine?

Calvin: From what I know about the consumers of your competitors, it appears to me that it's bought by homeless winos.

Stabler: Not entirely. For example, pensioners on a fixed income would find the price of the wine appealing. Thunderbird has been recently introduced into England and has become very popular with the yuppie crowd.

Calvin: Then why put it in pint bottles?

Stabler: For the convenience of consumers.

Menendez: Why would pensioners want a small bottle?

Calvin: Homeless people want it in pints so they can fit it in their hip pockets. They obviously don't have a wine cellar to lay away their favorite bottles of Mad Dog.

Stabler: The pint size also keeps the price as low as possible.

Calvin: Translation: The homeless don't have to panhandle as long before they can make a purchase. Also, why would you increase the alcoholic content to 18 percent and make it so sweet if it weren't for the wino market?

Stabler: Many people like sweet dessert wines, and 18 percent is not that much more than other types of wines that have 12 percent alcohol.

Menendez: Is it legal?

Lane: Sure. We sell to the retailers. It may be against the law to sell to intoxicated persons, but that's the retailers' business. We cannot control what they do.

Calvin: Isn't this product intended for a perpetually intoxicated audience that many people consider to be ill? Wouldn't we be taking advantage of their illness by selling highly sugared alcohol that suppresses their appetite? I've spoken to drinkers who claim to live on a gallon of this type of product a day.

Oliver, Jr.: What will this do to our image? We're still trying to get our premium wines accepted.

Stabler: Of course, we won't use the Oliver name on these wines. We will use another name.

Menendez: Is it okay to do that?

Stabler: Why not? Canandaigua, Gallo, and Mogen David all do the same thing. None of them put their corporate name on this low-end product.

Abbott: We're getting away from the crux of the matter. Profit margins would be at least 10 percent higher on this line than our others. Moreover, unit sales might increase over time. Our other lines are stagnant or decreasing. The public shareholders are grousing.

Dale: Not to mention that our stock options have become almost worthless. I'm only a few years from retirement. We need to increase the profitability of the company.

Ray: Operationally, this proposal is a great fit. We can use the grapes we reject from the premium line. It will also insulate us from bad grape years because any grape will do for this wine. We can fill a lot of our unused capacity.

Constable: And hire back some of the workers who were laid off!

Stabler: It's a marketing dream. Just give out some samples to "bell cows."

Menendez: What are bell cows?

Stabler: Opinion leaders who will induce other consumers to switch to our brand.

Calvin: You mean wino gurus?

Oliver, Sr.: Look, if we don't do it, others will. In fact, they already have.

Abbott: And they'll get richer, and we'll get poorer.

Lane: Gallo pulled out of several of these skid-row markets, as did Canandaigua. Little good it did. The alcoholics just switched to malt liquor, vodka, or anything they could get their hands on.

Dale: I think our concern is misplaced. These people are the dregs of society. They contribute nothing.

Calvin: They're human beings who need help. We're profiting off their misfortune and misery.

Oliver, Sr.: We can take that up when we decide on what charities to support. Anyone opposed to the proposal?

Calvin: Is this a done deal? I believe we should contribute half of our profits from this product to support homeless shelters and other programs that benefit indigent and homeless people. If not, I must resign from this board.

SOURCES

Carrie Dolan, "Gallo Conducts Test to Placate Critics of Its Cheap Wine," *Wall Street Journal*, June 16, 1989, p. B3.

Frank J. Prial, "Experiments by a Wine Maker Fails to Thwart Street Drunks," *New York Times*, February 11, 1990, p. A29.

Alix M. Freedman, "Winos and Thunderbird Are a Subject Gallo Doesn't Like to Discuss," *Wall Street Journal*, February 25, 1988, p. 1.

JLM, INC.

BACKGROUND

Sitting in her office, Ellen Fulbright, director of human resources (HR) for JLM, Inc., thought over the decisions confronting her. To help her decide, she mentally reviewed how they had arisen.

After receiving her MBA and J.D. degrees from a highly regarded university, she joined a prestigious New York law firm, where she specialized in employment law. After seven years at the law firm, she was hired by one of the firm's clients as general counsel. When that company was acquired by JLM, she joined its legal staff and within a few years was promoted to her current position.

Fulbright's rapid advancement resulted from her having made a positive impression on Rasheed Raven, JLM's CEO. Raven is a hard-driving, bottom-line-oriented pragmatist in his early forties. Raven, a graduate of Howard University, had begun his business career on Wall Street, which he astounded with his aggressive but successful takeover strategies. After acquiring fifteen unrelated manufacturing companies, he decided to try his hand at the turnaround business. He organized JLM as an umbrella for his acquired companies. Soon he earned the reputation as the best in the business by transforming JLM into the leader in the industry.

JLM is a highly successful turnaround company. Typically, JLM purchases companies that are in serious financial trouble and manages them until they become successful companies. At that time, JLM either retains them in its own portfolio of companies or sells them off to other enterprises.

REFERENCE LETTER POLICY

About a year after Fulbright had become HR director, Raven called her into his office and showed her a newspaper article. It reported, in somewhat sensational fashion, that several defamation suits had resulted in multimillion-dollar judgments against companies that had written negative letters of references about former employees. Raven told her that he was concerned about this and that he wanted her to develop an HR policy covering letters of reference.

In researching the issue, she discovered several articles in which the authors decried the recent spate of companies that had decided to stop writing letters of reference. According to their data, they believed that these companies had overreacted to the actual risk posed by defamation suits. Based on these articles and her own inclination toward full disclosure, she proposed that the company continue to permit letters of reference but that all letters with negative comments must be reviewed by her.

Raven did not receive her proposal favorably and sought a second opinion from her old law firm. His analysis of the firm's advice was, "We get nothing but brownie points for writing reference letters, but we face the possibility of incurring the cost of a legal defense or, worse yet, a court judgment. This is a no-brainer. We have no upside and all downside." Raven ordered that, henceforth, company employees would no longer write letters of reference but would simply verify dates of employment.

Although Fulbright was personally and professionally miffed by his decision, she drew up the policy statement as directed. Fulbright believed that because JLM frequently took over companies that needed immediate downsizing, this policy would be unfair and extremely detrimental to longtime employees of newly purchased companies.

TAKEOVER OF DIVERSIFIED MANUFACTURING, INC.

After a number of years of steady growth, Diversified Manufacturing began experiencing huge financial losses, and its immediate survival was in serious doubt. After careful consideration, Raven decided that Diversified was an ideal takeover target in that its core businesses were extremely strong and presented great long-term economic viability.

Upon acquiring Diversified, JLM quickly decided that it had to rid Diversified of some of its poorly performing companies and that it had to reduce the size of Diversified's home office staff by 25 percent. Raven relentlessly orchestrated the reduction in force, but at Fulbright's urging, he provided the discharged executives with above-average severance packages, including excellent outplacement services.

THE PROBLEM

The reduction in force was disruptive and demoralizing in all the usual ways. But for Fulbright, there was a further complication: the no-reference-letter policy. She was extremely troubled by its application to three discharged Diversified employees and to one discharged JLM employee.

THE SALACIOUS SALES MANAGER

Soon after taking over Diversified, Fulbright became all too aware of the story of Ken Byrd, then Diversified's national sales manager. Ken is an affable man of fifty who had been an unusually effective sales manager. Throughout his career, his sales figures were always doubled those of his peers. He achieved rapid advancement despite a fatal flaw: he is an inveterate and indiscreet womanizer. He could not control his hands, which slapped backs so well, nor his tongue, which persuaded so eloquently. He had two approaches to women. With a woman of equal or superior rank in the company, he would politely but inexorably attempt to sweep her off her feet. With these women, he would be extremely charming and attentive, taking great care to avoid being offensive or harassing. In contrast, with a woman of subordinate rank, he would physically harass her. Less openly but much too often, he would come up behind a woman, reach around her, and grab her. He invariably found this amusing—his victims, however, did not.

Fulbright could not believe that such a manager had stayed employed at Diversified so long, let alone been repeatedly promoted to positions of greater responsibility and power. As Fulbright investigated the situation, she discovered that numerous sexual harassment complaints had been filed with Diversified concerning Byrd's behavior. To protect Byrd, Diversified dealt with these complaints by providing money and undeserved promotions to the complainants to smooth over their anger. Thus, Diversified successfully kept the complaints in-house and away from the courts and the Equal Employment Opportunity Commission.

After JLM's takeover of Diversified, Fulbright quickly discharged Byrd. Her satisfaction in getting rid of him was short-lived, however. His golden tongue and stellar sales record had landed him several job offers. Her dilemma was that she was uncomfortable about unleashing this deviant on an unsuspecting new employer. But JLM's policy forbade her from writing any letters or answering questions from prospective employers.

THE FRUITLESS JUICE

Melissa Cuthbertson had been a vice president in procurement for Diversified's Birch-Wood division, with direct responsibility over the ordering of supplies and raw materials. Birch-Wood manufactured a full line of baby food products, including fruit drinks that were labeled "100% fruit juice." To cut costs, Stanley Aker, the division's president, had arranged for an unscrupulous supplier to provide high-fructose corn syrup labeled as juice concentrate. Because standard testing in the industry was unable to detect the substitution, the company did not get caught. Emboldened, Aker gradually increased the proportion of corn syrup until there were only trace amounts of fruit juice left in the "juice." A company employee discovered the practice and after the takeover brought the matter to Fulbright's attention through JLM's internal whistle-blowing channel, which Fulbright had established. She referred the matter to Raven, who called in Aker and Cuthbertson and confronted them with the accusation. They admitted it all, explaining that nutritionally the corn syrup was equivalent to the fruit juice. But at 60 percent of the cost of fruit juice, the corn syrup made a big difference to

the bottom line. Raven told them that such conduct was not permitted and that they must properly dispose of the adulterated juice.

That night Aker and Cuthbertson had the juice moved from Birch-Wood's New York warehouse and shipped to its Puerto Rico warehouse. Over the course of the next few days, the "juice" was sold in Latin America as "apple juice." Aker reported to Raven that the juice had been properly disposed of and that Birch-Wood had sustained only a small loss during that quarter. When Raven discovered the truth, he immediately discharged Aker and Cuthbertson, telling them that if he "had anything to do with it, neither of them would ever work again." Fulbright was to meet soon with Raven to discuss what should be done about Aker and Cuthbertson.

THE COMPASSIONATE CFO

Jackson Cobb, JLM's former chief financial officer, is a brilliant analyst. Through hard work, he had earned an excellent education that honed his innate mathematical gifts. His natural curiosity led him to read widely, and this enabled him to bring disparate facts and concepts to bear on his often-novel analyses of financial matters. But he had no interest in implementing his insights, for his only enjoyment was the process of discovering connections. Fortune—or fate—had brought him together with Raven, who is twenty years younger than Cobb. Theirs was definitely a case of opposites attracting. Raven cared little about ideas; he cared primarily about money. Cobb cared little about money; he cared primarily about ideas. Raven took Cobb's insights and translated them into action with spectacular success. Their relationship brought new meaning to the concept of synergy. When Raven formed JLM, he brought Cobb on as chief financial officer and installed him in an adjoining office.

Their relationship continued to flourish, as did JLM's bottom line, until Cobb's wife became terminally ill. During the eighteen months she languished, Cobb spent as much time as he could taking care of her. After forty years of marriage, he was unwilling to leave her welfare to the "kindness of strangers." At his own expense, he installed a state-of-the-art communication center in his home. By virtue of the internet, he had available to him the same data and information as he had at his office. Moreover, he could be reached at all times. But he was not in the office next to Raven; he was not present at Raven's daily breakfast meetings; he was not on the corporate jet en route to business meetings. After their many years of working together, Raven was enraged at the loss of immediate access to Cobb. He felt that Cobb had betrayed him and demanded that Cobb resume his old working hours. Cobb refused, and Raven fired him. Because of his age, Cobb was experiencing difficulty in finding new employment, and Fulbright wanted to write a letter on his behalf.

SWORD TECHNOLOGY, INC.

BACKGROUND

Sitting in his office, Stephen Hag, CEO of Sword Technology, Inc., contemplated the problems that had been perplexing him for some time. They had begun when he took his company international, and they kept coming. But today he was no more successful in devising a solution than he had been previously. Slowly, his thoughts drifted to those early days, years ago, when he and his sister Marian started the company.

The company's first product was an investment newsletter stressing technical analysis in securities investing. A few years later, he developed what became a "killer app": a computer program that defines an entirely new market and through customer loyalty substantially dominates that market. His software program enabled investors to track their investments in stocks, bonds, and futures. By combining powerful analytical tools with an accessible graphical interface, it appealed to both professional and amateur investors. Moreover, it required users to download information from the company's database. With one of the most extensive databases and the cheapest downloading rates in the industry, the company soon controlled the U.S. market. Sword then went public through a highly successful IPO (an initial public offering of the company's common stock). Currently, its stock is traded on the NASDAQ Stock Market. The company is required to file periodic reports with the Securities and Exchange Commission.

The company used cash from sales of software, online charges, and the IPO to try to enter the hardware side of the computer industry. It began manufacturing modems and other computer peripherals. A nagging problem, however, plagued the company's manufacturing efforts. Although Sword's modem could convert data more quickly and efficiently than most of its competitors, because of high labor costs, it was unable to market its modem successfully. To reduce manufacturing costs, especially labor costs, the company decided to move its manufacturing facilities overseas. And that's when the trouble began.

Stephen's thoughts returned to the present. He reopened the folder labeled "Confidential: International Issues" and began perusing its contents.

TRANSFER PRICING

The first item he saw was an opinion letter from the company's tax attorney. It dealt with Excalibur Technology, the first overseas company Sword established. Excalibur, a wholly owned subsidiary of Sword, is incorporated in Tolemac, an emerging country with a rapidly growing economy. To encourage foreign investment, Tolemac taxes corporate profits at a significantly lower rate than the United States and other industrial nations. Excalibur manufactures modems for Sword pursuant to a licensing agreement under which Excalibur pays Sword a royalty equal to a specified percentage of the modems' gross sales. Excalibur sells all of its output at a fair market price to Sword, which then markets the modems in the United States. Stephen had been closely involved in structuring this arrangement and had insisted on keeping the royalty rate low to minimize taxable income for Sword. Stephen reread the opinion letter:

> Section 482 of the Internal Revenue Code authorizes the Internal Revenue Service to allocate gross income, deductions, credits, and other common allowances among two or more organizations, trades, or businesses under common ownership or control whenever it determines that this action is necessary "in order to prevent evasion of taxes or clearly to reflect the income of any such organizations, trades, or businesses." IRS Regulation 1.482-2(e) governing the sale or trade of intangibles between related persons mandates an appropriate allocation to reflect the price that an unrelated party under the same circumstances would have paid, which normally includes profit to the seller. The Regulations provide four methods for determining an arm's-length price. In our opinion, under the only method applicable to the circumstances of Sword Technology, Inc., and Excalibur Technology, the royalty rate should be at least three times the current one. If the IRS were to reach the same conclusion, then the company would be liable for the taxes it underpaid because of the understatement of income. Moreover, the company would be liable for a penalty of either 20 percent or 40 percent of the tax deficiency, unless the company can show that it had reasonable cause and acted in good faith.

Stephen had spoken to the tax attorney at length and learned that the probability of an audit was about 10 percent and that many multinational companies play similar "games" with their transfer pricing. The attorney also told him that he believed that if the company were audited, there was at least a 90 percent probability that the IRS would agree with his conclusion and at least a 70 percent probability that it would impose a penalty. Because the dollar amount of the contingent tax liability was not an insignificant amount, Stephen had been concerned about it for the six weeks since he had received the letter.

CUSTOMS AND CUSTOMS

Soon after Excalibur had manufactured the first shipment of modems, a new problem arose: getting them out of Tolemac. They took far too long to clear customs, thus undermining

Excalibur's carefully planned just-in-time manufacturing schedules. Stephen hired a local export broker, who distributed cash gifts to customs officials. Miraculously, the clearance time shortened and manufacturing schedules were maintained. The export broker billed the company for his services and the amount of the cash gifts. Although the broker assured Stephen that such gifts were entirely customary, Stephen was not entirely comfortable with the practice.

THE THORN IN HIS SIDE

Tolemac was not Stephen's only problem. Six months after commencing operations in Tolemac, Sword began serious negotiations to enter the Liarg market. Liarg is a developing country with a large population and a larger national debt. Previously, Sword had encountered great difficulties in exporting products to Liarg. Stephen's sister, Marian, COO of Sword, took on the challenge of establishing a Liarg presence.

They decided that setting up a manufacturing facility in Liarg would achieve two objectives: having greater access to the Liarg marketplace and lower manufacturing costs for modems. At first, the Liarg government insisted that Sword enter into a joint venture, with the government having a 51 percent interest. Sword was unwilling to invest in such an arrangement, countering with a proposal for a wholly owned subsidiary. Marian conducted extensive negotiations with the government, assisted by a Liarg consulting firm that specialized in lobbying governmental officials. As part of these negotiations, Sword made contributions to the reelection campaigns of key Liarg legislators who were opposed to wholly owned subsidiaries of foreign corporations. After the legislators' reelection, the negotiations quickly reached a successful conclusion. On closing the contract, Sword flew several Liarg officials and their wives to Lake Tahoe for a lavish three-day celebration. All of these expenses were reported in the company's financial statements as payments for legal and consulting services.

Marian then hired an international engineering firm to help design the manufacturing plant. Two weeks later, they submitted plans for the plant and its operations that fully complied with Liarg regulations regarding worker health and safety as well as environmental protection. But as Marian had explained to Stephen, the plant's design fell far short of complying with U.S. requirements. Marian noted that under the proposed design, the workers would face exposure to moderately high levels of toxic chemicals and hazardous materials. The design also would degrade the water supply of nearby towns. However, the design would generate significant savings in capital and operational costs as compared with the design used in Sword's U.S. facility. Marian assured Stephen that all quality control systems were in place so that the modems produced in this plant would be indistinguishable from their U.S. counterparts. Stephen and Marian have had long discussions about what to do about the plant.

Stephen then took from the folder an article that had appeared in a number of U.S. newspapers.

Children and Chips

A twelve-year-old Liarg child recently spoke at an international conference in New York denouncing the exploitation of children in the Liarg computer chip industry. The child informed the outraged audience that he had worked in such a plant from age four to age ten. He asserted that he was just one of many children who were so employed. He described the deplorable working conditions: poor ventilation, long hours, inadequate food, and substandard housing. The pay was low. But because their families could not afford to keep them at home, the children were hired out to the factory owners, who especially wanted young children because their small fingers made them adept at many assembly processes.

Stephen had read the article countless times, thinking about his own children. He knew that if they set up a plant in Liarg, they would have to buy chip components from Liarg suppliers. He also knew that there would be no way for Sword to ensure that the chips had not been made with child labor.

Another labor issue troubled Stephen. Marian told him that she had met considerable resistance from the Liarg executives they had hired when she suggested that women should be hired at the supervisory level. They maintained that it was not done and would make it impossible to hire and control a satisfactory workforce at the plant. Moreover, they insisted on hiring their relatives as supervisors. When Marian protested this nepotism, they assured her that it was customary and asserted that the executives could not trust anyone not related to them.

TO OUTSOURCE OR NOT TO OUTSOURCE

Once again Stephen glanced over the cost data. Sword's labor costs for supporting its database services and hardware were eviscerating the company's profits. After racking his brain endlessly, he had concluded that wherever it made financial and strategic sense, Sword should utilize business process outsourcing (BPO), that is, long-term contracting out of non-core business processes to an outside provider in order to lower costs and thereby increase shareholder value.

Stephen had examined a number of potential countries on the basis of many factors, including time zone, communications infrastructure, technical training, English language skills of the workforce, and—most critically—costs. Liarg had emerged as the optimal choice. He anticipated reducing labor and associated overhead costs by 45 to 50 percent.

He planned to start by offshoring half of the call center operations, soon to be followed by a third of the low-end software development such as maintenance and coding. Assuming all went as he envisioned, he expected to move offshore both back-office operations and higher-level software development. As his imagination soared, he saw the potential to amplify the company's operations with round-the-clock development.

Stephen realized that embarking on this course would result in reducing the staffing at the company's U.S. call centers. He expected he could achieve some reductions through attrition and reassignment, but considerable layoffs would be necessary. He hoped that outsourcing the low-end software development would enable the company to redeploy its software developers to higher-level and more profitable assignments. Moreover, the recent rollback in the number of visas had resulted in difficulty in hiring sufficient numbers of software developers with the necessary skills. If Sword were to offshore back-office operations, Stephen expected an impact on current employees comparable to offshoring the call centers.

On top of all these concerns had come a letter from the company's outside legal counsel regarding payments made to foreign officials.

Memorandum of Law

The Foreign Corrupt Practices Act makes it unlawful for any person, and certain foreign issuers of securities, or any of its officers, directors, employees, or agents or its stockholders acting on its behalf to offer or give anything of value directly or indirectly to any foreign official, political party, or political official for the purpose of

1. influencing any act or decision of that person or party in his or its official capacity,
2. inducing an act or omission in violation of his or its lawful duty, or
3. inducing such person or party to use its influence to affect a decision of a foreign government in order to assist the domestic concern in obtaining or retaining business.

An offer or a promise to make a prohibited payment is a violation even if the offer is not accepted or the promise is not performed. The 1988 amendments explicitly excluded facilitating or expediting payments made to expedite or secure the performance of routine governmental actions by a foreign official, political party, or party official. Routine governmental action does not include any decision by a foreign official regarding the award of new business or the continuation of old business. The amendments also added an affirmative defense for payments that are lawful under the written laws or regulations of the foreign official's country. Violations are punishable by fines of up to $2 million for companies; individuals may be fined a maximum of $100,000 or imprisoned up to five years or both. Moreover, under the Alternative Fines Act, the actual fine may be up to twice the benefit that the person sought to obtain by making the corrupt payment. Fines imposed upon individuals may not be paid directly or indirectly by the domestic company or other business entity on whose behalf the individuals acted. In addition, civil penalties of up to $21,663 per violation, as adjusted for inflation in January 2021, may be imposed.

The statute also imposes internal control requirements on all reporting companies. Such companies must

1. make and keep books, records, and accounts that in reasonable detail accurately and fairly reflect the transactions and dispositions of the assets of the company; and
2. devise and maintain a system of internal controls that ensure that transactions are executed as authorized and recorded in conformity with generally accepted accounting principles, thereby establishing accountability with regard to assets and ensuring that access to those assets is permitted only with management's authorization.

Any person who knowingly circumvents or knowingly fails to implement a system of internal accounting controls or knowingly falsifies any book, record, or account is subject to criminal liability.

VULCAN, INC.

THE COMPANY
Vulcan, Inc., is a multinational *Fortune* 200 company engaging principally in the exploration for and extraction of minerals. It is listed on the New York Stock Exchange and has more than 615 million shares outstanding.

THE MEETING (MARCH 7)
On March 5, Stewart Myer, the company's CEO, personally telephoned Martha Bordeaux, the vice president for finance; Lamont Johnson, the chief geologist; and Natasha Bylinski, the vice president for acquisitions, to arrange a March 7 meeting at the Atlanta

airport. He emphasized to each of them the need for the utmost secrecy, directing them to arrange their travel to Atlanta as a connection to other and different destinations. When they all arrived at the meeting room, Myer reemphasized the need for complete secrecy. He then asked Johnson to present his report.

THE REPORT
Johnson read his report:

Over the past few years, we have conducted extensive aerial geophysical surveys of the areas west of the Great

Plains. These revealed numerous anomalies or extreme variations in the conductivity of rocks. One appeared particularly encouraging, so late last year we began a ground geophysical survey of the southwest portion of the Z segment in Montana. This survey confirmed the presence of anomalies. Accordingly, on January 14, we drilled some core samples and sent them to our lab. The results were so extraordinarily promising that on February 10, we obtained more core samples and had them chemically assayed. On February 25, we received the assay, which revealed an average mineral content of 1.17 percent copper and 8.6 percent zinc over 600 feet of the sample's 650-foot length.

Johnson then commented, "In my forty years in the business I have never seen such remarkable test results. On a scale of one to ten, this is an eleven."

THE REACTION
Bordeaux exclaimed, "Our stock price will go through the roof!" Bylinski retorted, "So will land prices!"

THE STRATEGY
Myer interrupted, "Look, we're not here to celebrate. There are many better places to do that. We can't keep a lid on this very long, so we have to strike soon. We need to line up the right agents to acquire the land. We must fragment the acquisitions to keep the sellers in the dark. Most critical is maintaining absolute secrecy. No one else in the company must know this. I will decide who needs to know, and I will tell them. It is your duty to the company to keep quiet. Now, let's discuss the acquisition plan."

When asked how he had managed to obtain core samples without tipping off the owners of the land, Johnson explained, "We pretended to be a motion picture company looking for locations to remake the movie *High Noon*. We drilled the samples in isolated areas and quickly filled the holes. To further cover our tracks, we drilled some barren core samples from land we owned and hid the cores on our land."

THE PLAN
Bylinski outlined the plan to acquire the land. "We only own about 20 percent of the land we want, and we have options on another 15 percent. However, we currently own none of the principal portion. So, we have a lot of work to do. We will employ several agents to negotiate the purchases. We will instruct them not to disclose that they are acting for us. In fact, we will order them not to disclose they are acting for anyone. We need to acquire approximately twenty square miles of additional land."

Bordeaux asked, "What if the locals start getting curious?" Myer replied, "I'll deal with that later if it arises."

STOCK OPTIONS
On March 15, Vulcan issued stock options at $23.50 per share to thirty of its executives, including Myer, Bordeaux, Johnson, and Bylinski. At this time, neither the stock option committee nor the board of directors had been informed of the strike or the pending land acquisition program.

THE RUMORS
While the land acquisition plan was nearing completion, rumors about a major strike by Vulcan began circulating throughout the business community. On the morning of March 20, Bordeaux read an account in a national newspaper reporting that ore samples had been sent out of Montana and inferring from that fact that Vulcan had made a rich strike. Bordeaux called Myer and told him about the article.

THE PRESS RELEASE
Myer prepared the following press release, which appeared in morning newspapers of general circulation on March 21:

During the past few days, the press has reported drilling activities by Vulcan and rumors of a substantial copper discovery. These reports are greatly exaggerated. Vulcan has engaged in normal geophysical explorations throughout the West. We routinely send core samples to verify our visual examinations. Most of the areas drilled have been barren or marginal. When we have additional information, we will issue a statement to shareholders and the public.

LAND ACQUIRED
On April 6, Vulcan completed its land acquisition program. It had employed seven different agents. In total, it had acquired thirty-seven parcels from twenty-two different sellers at prices ranging from $300 to $600 per acre. The land cost a total of approximately $6 million.

OFFICIAL ANNOUNCEMENT
At 10:00 A.M. on April 11, Myer released on behalf of Vulcan an official announcement of a strike in Montana containing at least 30 million tons of high-grade copper and zinc ore. The release appeared on the wire services at 10:30 A.M. The price of Vulcan stock shot up eleven points to $38 by the close of business that day and continued to rise, reaching a price of $56 on May 16. (*Figures 2-8* and *2-9* show the price and volume of Vulcan stock.)

LOOSE LIPS
Prior to the April 11 official announcement, a number of people purchased Vulcan stock with knowledge of the mineral

FIGURE 2-8 Stock Price of Vulcan, Inc. (note irregular intervals on time axis)

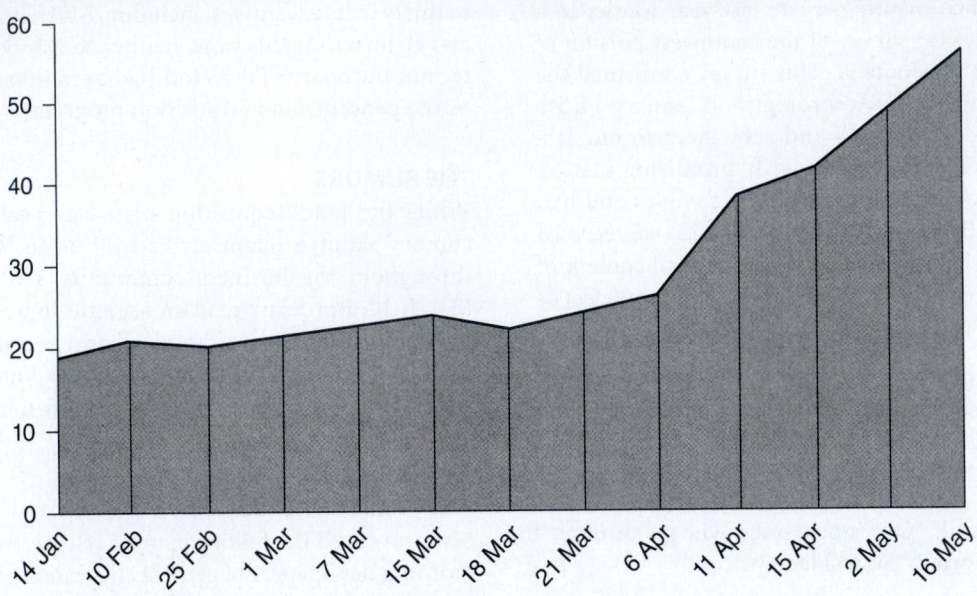

FIGURE 2-9 Average Daily Volume of Vulcan, Inc., Stock for Week (in 1,000s)

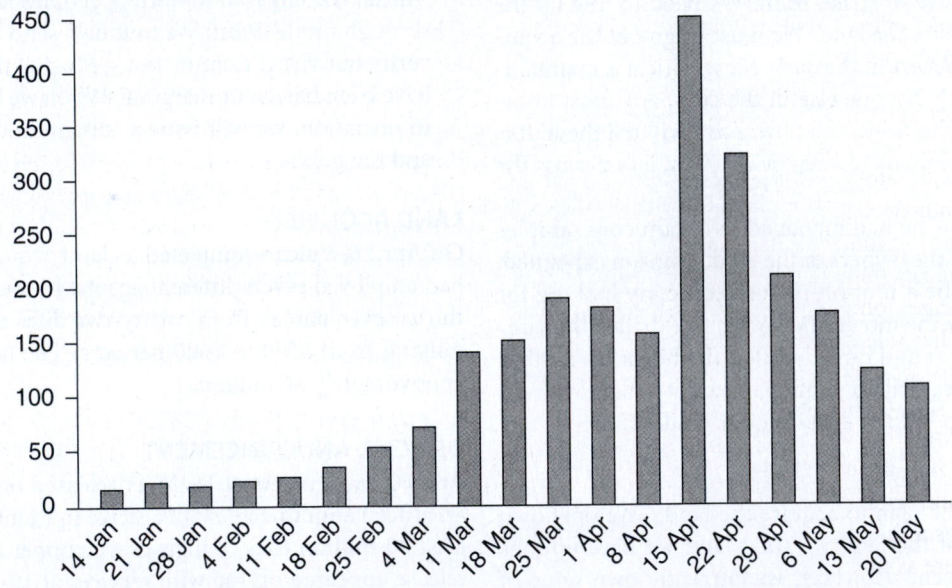

discovery. Some people also purchased land adjacent to Vulcan's holdings in Montana. These purchasers included the following:

THE VULCAN EXECUTIVES
Myer, Bordeaux, Johnson, and Bylinski each purchased shares or calls on several occasions during this time period. See *Figure 2-10* for a listing of their purchases.

THE EAGER EAVESDROPPER
After leaving the March 7 meeting, Bordeaux and Bylinski went to the airport lounge to wait for their flights. They excitedly—and loudly discussed what they had learned at the meeting. Several people overheard their remarks, and one of them, Rae Bodie, immediately called her broker and bought one thousand five hundred shares of Vulcan stock. Ms. Bodie also

FIGURE 2-10	Purchases of Vulcan Stock by Selected Executives				
Purchaser	**Date**	**Shares**	**Price**	**Calls**	**Price**
Myer	Jan. 20	10,000	18.00		
	Feb. 25	10,000	20.00		
	March 2	15,000	21.25		
	March 7			5,000	22.25
	March 15			5,000	23.75
Bordeaux	March 7	10,000	22.00		
	March 15			7,500	23.75
	March 18	5,000	24.00		
Johnson	Jan. 20	5,000	18.00		
	Feb. 25	8,000	20.00		
	March 1	12,000	21.00		
	March 7	6,000	22.00		
	March 15	4,000	23.50		
Bylinski	March 7	5,000	22.00		
	March 15	3,000	23.50		
	March 18			4,000	24.25

purchased a large tract of land next to Vulcan's site in Montana for approximately $600 per acre.

THE CRESTFALLEN SECURITY GUARD

On March 9, Johnson went into the home office very early to finish up the exploratory work on the new find. At the elevator, he encountered Celia Tidey, one of the company's security guards. Johnson knew her fairly well, since they both had worked for Vulcan for more than fifteen years. Noting her despondent visage, Johnson asked her what was wrong. She related to him her tale of woe: her husband had become disabled and lost his job while her son needed an expensive medical procedure that their health insurance did not cover. Johnson felt great empathy for her plight. He told her that big doings were afoot at Vulcan and that if she bought Vulcan stock soon, she would make a lot of money in a month or so. She took her savings and bought two hundred shares of Vulcan stock, which were as many shares as she could buy.

THE AVARICIOUS AGENT

William Baggio, one of the agents hired to acquire the land, inferred that whatever was up had to be good for Vulcan. Accordingly, on March 21, he purchased two thousand five hundred shares of Vulcan and five thousand acres of land adjacent to the Vulcan property.

THE TRUSTED TIPPEE

On March 8, Myer called Theodore Griffey, his oldest and dearest friend. After getting Griffey to swear absolute confidentiality, Myer told him all the details of the strike. After hanging up the telephone, Griffey immediately purchased fifteen thousand shares of Vulcan stock. Griffey then told his father and sister about the land; each of them bought fifteen thousand shares.

THE SCAMPERING STOCKBROKER

Morris Lynch, Myer's stockbroker, was intrigued by Myer's purchases of an unusually large volume of Vulcan shares. During the last two weeks of March, he put a number of his other clients into Vulcan, telling them, "I've looked at this stock, and it's good for you." About a dozen of his clients purchased a total of eight thousand shares.

THE LAND GRAB

After the official announcement on April 11, several of Vulcan's competitors began exploring the area and purchased large tracks of land, bidding up the price of land to $2,250 per acre. Both Bodie and Baggio sold their newly acquired land to Vulcan competitors at this higher price.

CHAPTER 3

Civil Dispute Resolution

CHAPTER OUTCOMES

After reading and studying this chapter, you should be able to:

- Describe the courts in the Federal court system and in a typical State court system.

- Distinguish among exclusive Federal jurisdiction, concurrent Federal jurisdiction, and exclusive State jurisdiction.

- Distinguish among (1) subject matter jurisdiction and jurisdiction over the parties and (2) the three types of jurisdiction over the parties.

- Explain the various stages of a civil proceeding.

- Compare litigation, arbitration, conciliation, and mediation.

As discussed in *Chapter 1*, substantive law establishes the rights and duties of individuals and other legal entities while procedural law determines the means by which these rights are asserted. Procedural law attempts to accomplish two competing objectives: (1) to be fair and impartial and (2) to operate efficiently. The judicial process in the United States represents a balance between these two objectives as well as a commitment to the adversary system.

The first part of this chapter describes the structure and function of the Federal and State court systems. The second part of this chapter deals with jurisdiction; the third part discusses civil dispute resolution, including the procedure in civil lawsuits.

THE COURT SYSTEM

Courts are impartial tribunals (seats of judgment) established by government bodies to settle disputes. A court may render a binding decision only when it has jurisdiction over the dispute and the parties to that dispute; that is, when it has a right to hear and make a judgment in a case. The United States has a dual court system: The Federal government has its own independent system, as does each of the fifty States plus the District of Columbia.

3-1 The Federal Courts

Article III of the U.S. Constitution states that the judicial power of the United States shall be vested in one Supreme Court and such lower courts as Congress may establish. Congress has established a lower Federal court system consisting of a number of special courts, district courts, and courts of appeals. The Federal court system is staffed by judges who receive lifetime appointments from the President, subject to confirmation by the Senate.

♦ **SEE FIGURE 3-1:** *Federal Judicial System*

3-1a DISTRICT COURTS

The district courts are the general trial courts in the Federal system. Most cases begin in a district court, and it is here that issues of fact are decided. The district court is generally presided over by *one* judge, although in certain cases, three judges preside. In a few cases, an appeal from a judgment or decree of a district court is taken directly to the Supreme Court. In most cases, however, appeals go to the Circuit Court of Appeals of the appropriate circuit, the decision of which, in most cases, is final.

Congress has established ninety-four judicial districts, each of which is located entirely in a particular State. All States have at least one district; about half of the States contain more than one. For instance, California and New York each have four districts, Illinois has three, and Wisconsin has two, while about half of the States each make up a single district.

3-1b COURTS OF APPEALS

Congress has established twelve judicial circuits (eleven numbered circuits plus the D.C. Circuit), each having a court known as the Court of Appeals, which primarily hears appeals

FIGURE 3-1 Federal Judicial System

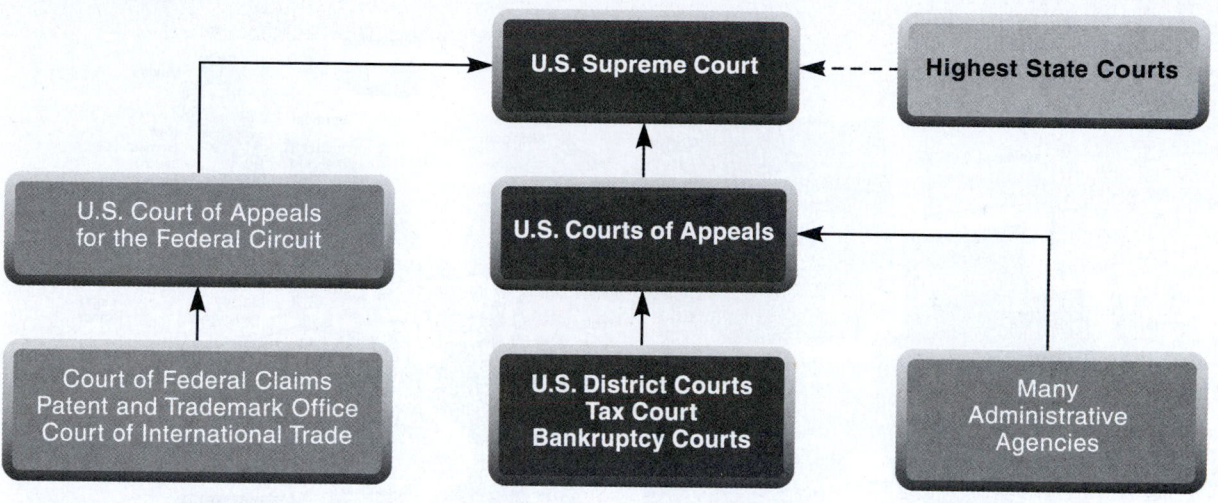

from the district courts located within its circuit. In addition, these courts review decisions of many administrative agencies, the Tax Court, and the Bankruptcy Court. Congress has also established the U.S. Court of Appeals for the Federal Circuit, which is discussed in the section on "Special Courts." The U.S. Courts of Appeals generally hear cases in panels of *three* judges, although in some instances, all of the judges of the circuit will sit *en banc* to decide a case.

The function of appellate courts is to examine the record of a case on appeal and to determine whether the trial court committed prejudicial error. If so, the appellate court will **reverse** or **modify** the judgment and if necessary **remand** it (send it back) to the lower court for further proceeding. If no prejudicial error exists, the appellate court will **affirm** the decision of the lower court.

♦ SEE FIGURE 3-2: *Circuit Courts of the United States*

3-1c THE SUPREME COURT

The nation's highest tribunal is the U.S. Supreme Court, which consists of nine justices (a Chief Justice and eight Associate Justices) who sit as a group in Washington, D.C. A quorum consists of any six justices. In certain types of cases, the U.S. Supreme Court has original jurisdiction (the right to hear a case first). The Court's principal function, nonetheless, is to review decisions of the Federal Courts of Appeals and, in some instances, decisions involving Federal law made by the highest State courts. Cases reach the Supreme Court under its appellate jurisdiction by one of two routes. Very few come by way

of **appeal by right**—cases the Court must hear should a party request the review. In 1988, Congress enacted legislation that almost completely eliminated the right to appeal to the U.S. Supreme Court.

The second way in which the Supreme Court may review a decision of a lower court is by the discretionary **writ of certiorari**, which requires a lower court to produce the records of a case it has tried. Now almost all cases reaching the Supreme Court come to it by means of writs of *certiorari*. The Court uses the writ as a device to choose the cases it wants to review. The Court grants writs for cases involving a Federal question of substantial importance or a conflict in the decisions of the U.S. Circuit Courts of Appeals. Only a small percentage of the petitions to the Supreme Court for review by *certiorari* are granted, however. The vote of four justices is required to grant a writ.

3-1d SPECIAL COURTS

The special courts in the Federal judicial system include the U.S. Court of Federal Claims, the U.S. Tax Court, the U.S. Bankruptcy Courts, the U.S. Court of International Trade, and the U.S. Court of Appeals for the Federal Circuit. These courts have jurisdiction over particular subject matter. The U.S. Court of Federal Claims has national jurisdiction to hear claims against the United States. The U.S. Tax Court has national jurisdiction over certain cases involving Federal taxes. The U.S. Bankruptcy Courts have jurisdiction to hear and decide certain matters under the Federal Bankruptcy Act, subject to review by the U.S. District Court. The U.S. Court of International Trade has nationwide jurisdiction over cases involving international trade

FIGURE 3-2 **Circuit Courts of the United States**

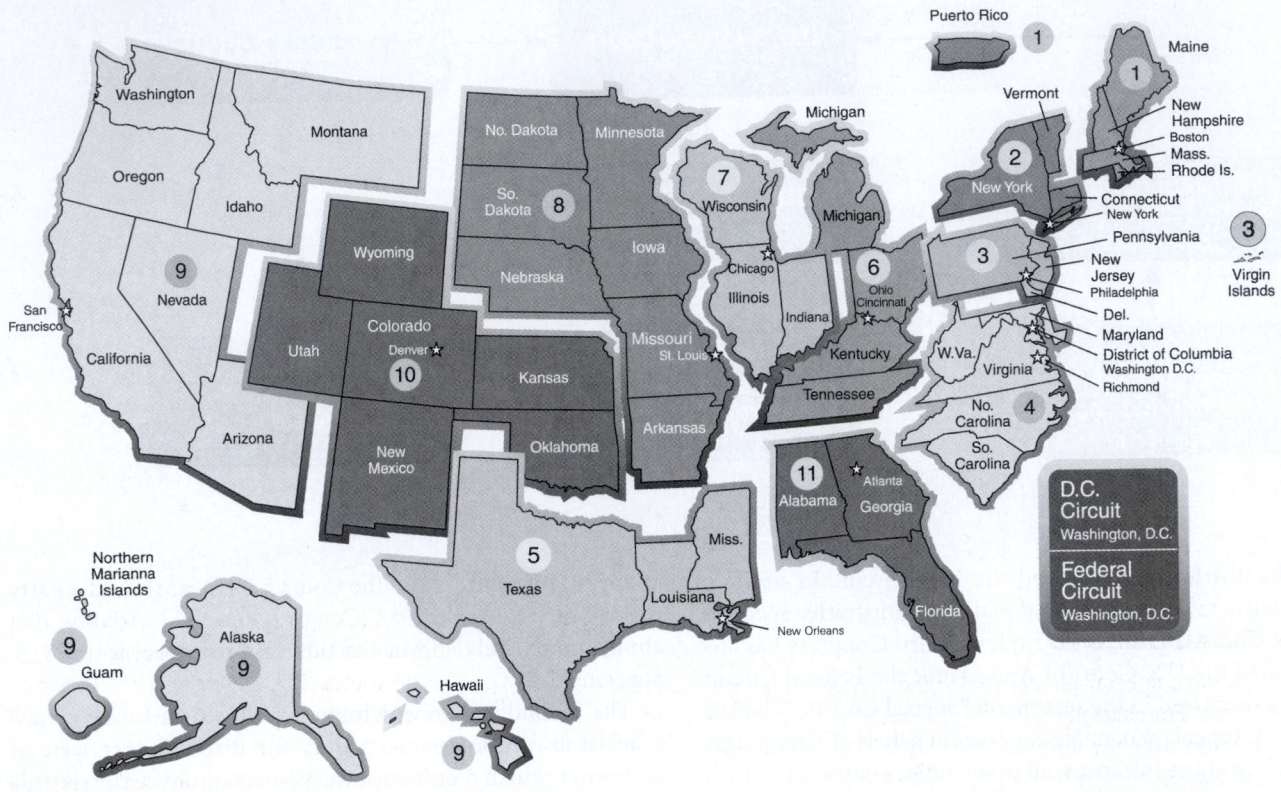

Source: Administrative Office of The United States Courts,
http://www.uscourts.gov/sites/default/files/u.s._federal_courts_circuit_map_1.pdf

and customs issues. The U.S. Court of Appeals for the Federal Circuit has nationwide jurisdiction and reviews decisions of the Court of Federal Claims, the Patent and Trademark Office, the U.S. Court of International Trade, the Merit Systems Protection Board, and the U.S. Court of Veterans Appeals, as well as patent cases decided by the U.S. District Court.

3-2 State Courts

Each of the fifty States and the District of Columbia has its own court system. In most States, the voters elect judges for a stated term.

◆ SEE FIGURE 3-3: *State Court System*

3-2a INFERIOR TRIAL COURTS

At the bottom of the State court system are the **inferior trial courts**, which decide the least serious criminal and civil matters. Usually, inferior trial courts do not keep a complete written

record of trial proceedings. Such courts, which are referred to as municipal courts, justice of the peace courts, or traffic courts, hear minor criminal cases such as traffic offenses. They also conduct preliminary hearings in more serious criminal cases.

Small claims courts are inferior trial courts that hear civil cases involving a limited amount of money. Usually there is no jury, the procedure is informal, and neither side employs an attorney. An appeal from small claims court is taken to the trial court of general jurisdiction, where a new trial (called a trial *de novo*), in which the small claims court's decision is given no weight, is begun.

3-2b TRIAL COURTS

Each State has trial courts of general jurisdiction, which may be called county, district, superior, circuit, or common pleas courts. (In New York, the trial court is called the Supreme Court.) These courts do not have a dollar limitation on their jurisdiction in civil cases and hear all criminal cases other than minor offenses. Unlike the inferior trial courts, these trial courts of general jurisdiction maintain formal records of their proceedings as procedural safeguards.

FIGURE 3-3 State Court System

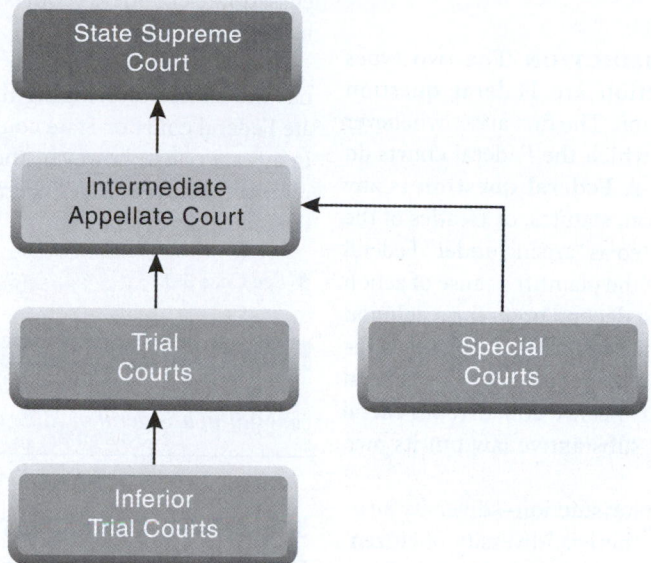

3-2c SPECIAL COURTS

Many States have special courts that have jurisdiction over particular areas. For example, many States have probate courts with jurisdiction over the administration of wills and estates. Many States also have family courts, which have jurisdiction over divorce and child custody cases. Appeals from these special courts go to the general State appellate courts.

3-2d APPELLATE COURTS

At the summit of the State court system is the State's court of last resort, a reviewing court generally called the Supreme Court of the State. Except for those cases in which review by the U.S. Supreme Court is available, the decision of the highest State tribunal is final. Most States also have created intermediate appellate courts to handle the large volume of cases seeking review. Review by such a court is usually by right. Further review is in most cases at the highest court's discretion.

JURISDICTION

Jurisdiction means the power or authority of a court to hear and decide a given case. To resolve a lawsuit, a court must have two kinds of jurisdiction. The first is subject matter jurisdiction. Where a court lacks jurisdiction over the subject matter of a case, no action it takes in the case will have legal effect.

The second kind of jurisdiction is over the parties to a lawsuit. This jurisdiction is required for the court to render an enforceable judgment that affects the rights and duties of the parties to the lawsuit. A court usually may obtain jurisdiction over the defendant if (1) the defendant lives or is present in the court's territory or (2) the transaction giving rise to the case has a substantial connection to the court's territory. The court obtains jurisdiction over the plaintiff when he voluntarily submits to the court's power by filing a complaint with the court.

3-3 Subject Matter Jurisdiction

Subject matter jurisdiction refers to the authority of a particular court to adjudicate a controversy of a particular kind. Federal courts have *limited* subject matter jurisdiction, as set forth in the U.S. Constitution, Article III, Section 2. State courts have jurisdiction over *all* matters that the Constitution or Congress has not given exclusively to the Federal courts or expressly denied the State courts.

3-3a FEDERAL JURISDICTION

The Federal courts have, to the exclusion of the State courts, subject matter jurisdiction over some areas. Such jurisdiction is called **exclusive Federal jurisdiction**. Federal jurisdiction is exclusive only if Congress so provides, either explicitly or implicitly. If Congress does not so provide and the area is one over which Federal courts have subject matter jurisdiction, they share this jurisdiction with the State courts. Such jurisdiction is known as **concurrent Federal jurisdiction**.

EXCLUSIVE FEDERAL JURISDICTION The Federal courts have exclusive jurisdiction over Federal criminal prosecutions; admiralty, bankruptcy, antitrust, patent, trademark, and copyright cases; suits against the United States; and cases arising under certain Federal statutes that expressly provide for exclusive Federal jurisdiction.

CONCURRENT FEDERAL JURISDICTION The two types of concurrent Federal jurisdiction are Federal question jurisdiction and diversity jurisdiction. The first arises whenever there is a Federal question over which the Federal courts do not have exclusive jurisdiction. A **Federal question** is any case arising under the Constitution, statutes, or treaties of the United States. For a case to be treated as "arising under" Federal law, either Federal law must create the plaintiff's cause of action or the plaintiff's right to relief must depend upon the resolution of a substantial question of Federal law in dispute between the parties. There is no minimum dollar requirement in Federal question cases. When a State court hears a concurrent Federal question case, it applies Federal substantive law but its own procedural rules.

The second type of concurrent jurisdiction—diversity jurisdiction—arises in cases in which there is "diversity of citizenship" *and* the amount in controversy exceeds $75,000. Then private litigants may bring an action in a Federal district court or a State court. **Diversity of citizenship** exists (1) when the plaintiffs are all citizens of a State or States different from the State or States of which the defendants are citizens, (2) when a foreign country brings an action against citizens of the United States, or (3) when the controversy is between citizens of a State and citizens of a foreign country. The citizenship of an individual litigant is the State in which the litigant resides or is domiciled, whereas that of a corporate litigant is both the State of incorporation and the State in which its principal place of business is located. On the other hand, a non-corporate entity, such as a limited partnership, takes the citizenship of each of its members.

For example, if the amount in controversy exceeds $75,000, then diversity of citizenship jurisdiction would be satisfied if Ada, a citizen of California, sues Bob, a citizen of Idaho. If, however, Carol, a citizen of Virginia, and Dianne, a citizen of North Carolina, sue Evan, a citizen of Georgia, and Farley, a citizen of North Carolina, diversity of citizenship would not exist because both Dianne, a plaintiff, and Farley, a defendant, are citizens of North Carolina.

The $75,000 jurisdictional requirement is satisfied if the plaintiff makes a good faith claim to the amount in the complaint, unless it is clear to a legal certainty that the claim does not exceed the required amount.

When a Federal district court hears a case solely under diversity of citizenship jurisdiction, no Federal question is involved, and, accordingly, the Federal court must apply substantive State law. The conflict of laws rules of the State in which the district court is located determine which State's substantive law the court will use. (Conflict of laws is discussed later.) Federal courts apply Federal procedural rules in diversity cases.

In any case involving concurrent jurisdiction, the plaintiff has the choice of bringing the action in either an appropriate Federal court or State court. If the plaintiff brings the case in a State court, however, the defendant usually may have it removed (shifted) to a Federal court for the district in which the State court is located.

◆ *See Case 3-1*

Practical Advice

If you have the option, consider whether you want to bring your lawsuit in a Federal or State court.

3-3b STATE JURISDICTION

EXCLUSIVE STATE JURISDICTION The State courts have exclusive jurisdiction over *all other matters* not granted to the Federal courts in the Constitution or by Congress. Accordingly, exclusive State jurisdiction would include cases involving diversity of citizenship in which the amount in controversy is $75,000 or less. In addition, the State courts have exclusive jurisdiction over all cases to which Federal judicial power does not reach. These matters include, but are by no means limited to, property, torts, contracts, agency, commercial transactions, and most crimes.

◆ **SEE FIGURE 3-4:** *Federal and State Jurisdiction*

◆ **SEE FIGURE 3-5:** *Subject Matter Jurisdiction*

CHOICE OF LAW IN STATE COURTS A court in one State may be a proper forum for a case even though some or all of the relevant events occurred in another State. For example, a California plaintiff may sue a Washington defendant in Washington over a car accident that occurred in Oregon. Because of Oregon's connections to the accident, Washington may choose, under its conflict of laws rules, to apply the substantive law of Oregon. Conflict of laws rules vary from State to State.

Practical Advice

Consider including in your contracts a choice-of-law provision specifying which jurisdiction's law will apply.

FIGURE 3-4 Federal and State Jurisdiction

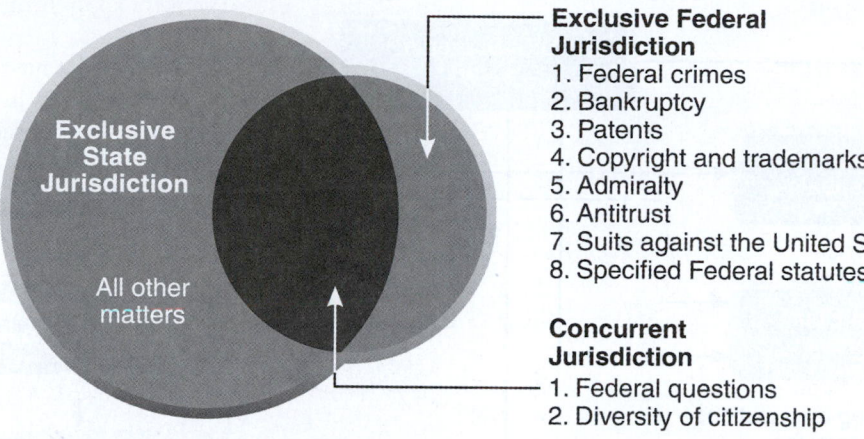

Exclusive Federal Jurisdiction
1. Federal crimes
2. Bankruptcy
3. Patents
4. Copyright and trademarks
5. Admiralty
6. Antitrust
7. Suits against the United States
8. Specified Federal statutes

Concurrent Jurisdiction
1. Federal questions
2. Diversity of citizenship

3-3c STARE DECISIS IN THE DUAL COURT SYSTEM

The doctrine of *stare decisis* presents certain problems when there are two parallel court systems. Consequently, in the United States, *stare decisis* functions approximately as follows:

1. The U.S. Supreme Court has never held itself to be bound rigidly by its own decisions, and lower Federal courts and State courts have followed that course with respect to their own decisions.

2. A decision of the U.S. Supreme Court on a Federal question is binding on all other courts, Federal or State.

3. On a Federal question, although a decision of a Federal court other than the Supreme Court may be persuasive in a State court, the decision is not binding.

4. A decision of a State court may be persuasive in the Federal courts, but it is not binding except in cases in which Federal jurisdiction is based on diversity of citizenship. In such a case, the Federal courts must apply State law as determined by the highest State court.

5. Decisions of the Federal courts (other than the U.S. Supreme Court) are not binding upon other Federal courts of equal or inferior rank, unless the latter owe obedience to the deciding court. For example, a decision of the Fifth Circuit Court of Appeals binds district courts in the Fifth Circuit but binds no other Federal court.

6. A decision of a State court is binding upon all courts inferior to it in its jurisdiction. Thus, the decision of the highest court in a State binds all other courts in that State.

7. A decision of a State court is not binding on courts in other States except in cases in which the latter courts are required, under their conflict of laws rules, to apply the law of the former State as determined by the highest court in that State. For example, if a North Carolina court is required to apply Virginia law, it must follow decisions of the Supreme Court of Virginia.

◆ SEE FIGURE 3-6: Stare Decisis *in the Dual Court System*

3-4 Jurisdiction Over the Parties

In addition to subject matter jurisdiction, a court also must have jurisdiction over the parties, which is the power to bind the parties involved in the dispute. The court obtains jurisdiction over

FIGURE 3-5 Subject Matter Jurisdiction

Types of Jurisdiction	Court	Substantive Law Applied	Procedural Law Applied
Exclusive Federal	Federal	Federal	Federal
Concurrent: **Federal Question**	Federal State	Federal Federal	Federal State
Concurrent: **Diversity**	Federal State	State State	Federal State
Exclusive State	State	State	State

FIGURE 3-6 *Stare Decisis* **in the Dual Court System**

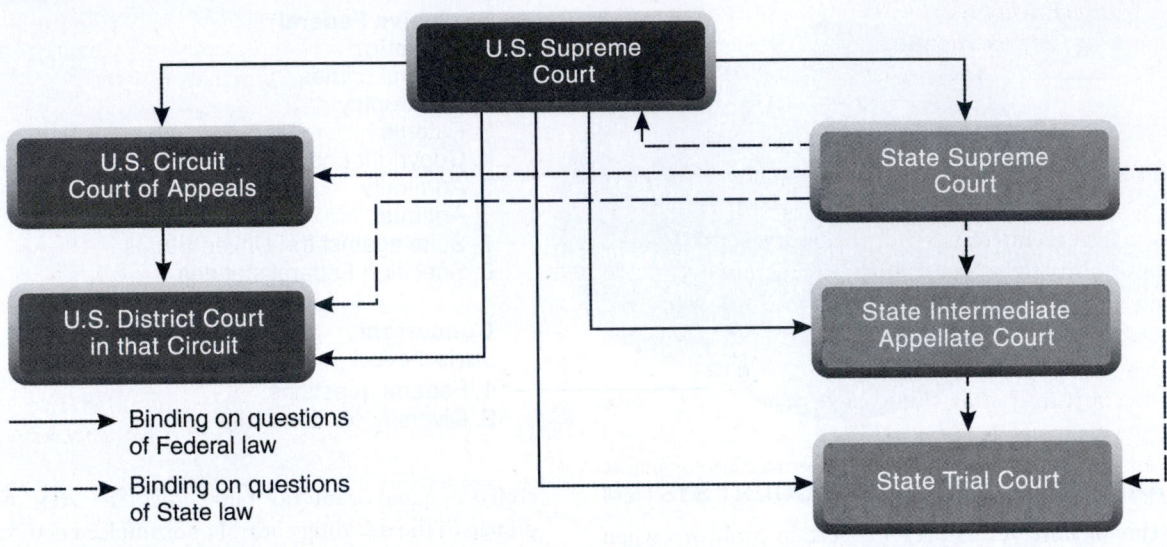

the *plaintiff* when she voluntarily submits to the court's power by filing a complaint with the court. A court may obtain jurisdiction over the *defendant* in three possible ways: (1) *in personam* jurisdiction, (2) *in rem* jurisdiction, or (3) attachment jurisdiction. In addition, the exercise of jurisdiction over a defendant must satisfy the constitutionally imposed requirements of due process: reasonable notification and a reasonable opportunity to be heard. Moreover, the court's exercise of jurisdiction over a defendant is valid under the Due Process Clause of the U.S. Constitution only if the defendant has minimum contacts with the State sufficient to prevent the court's assertion of jurisdiction from offending "traditional notions of fair play and substantial justice." For a court constitutionally to assert jurisdiction over a defendant, the defendant must have engaged in either purposeful acts in the State or acts outside the State that are of such a nature that the defendant could reasonably foresee being sued in that State. This overriding limitation on jurisdictional power is imposed upon the Federal and State courts through the U.S. Constitution, as discussed more fully in *Chapter 4*.

What notice is due depends on several factors, but generally must be "notice reasonably calculated, under the circumstances, to apprise interested parties of the pendency of the action and afford them the opportunity to present their objections."

◆ *See Case 3-2*

3-4a *IN PERSONAM* JURISDICTION

In personam jurisdiction, or personal jurisdiction, is jurisdiction of a court over the parties to a lawsuit, in contrast to jurisdiction over their property. A court obtains *in personam*

jurisdiction over a defendant either (1) by serving process on the party within the State in which the court is located or (2) by reasonable notification to a party outside the State in those instances where a "long-arm statute" applies. To *serve process* means to deliver a summons, which is an order to respond to a complaint lodged against a party. (The terms *summons* and *complaint* are explained more fully later in this chapter.)

Personal jurisdiction may be obtained by personally serving a person within a State if that person is domiciled in that State. The U.S. Supreme Court has held that a State may exercise personal jurisdiction over a nonresident defendant who is temporarily present if the defendant is personally served in that State. Personal jurisdiction also may arise from a party's consent. For example, parties to a contract may agree that any dispute concerning that contract will be subject to the jurisdiction of a specific court.

Most States have adopted **long-arm statutes** to expand their jurisdictional reach beyond those persons who may be personally served within the State. These statutes allow courts to obtain jurisdiction over nonresident defendants whose contacts with the State in which the court is located are such that the exercise of jurisdiction does not offend traditional notions of fair play and substantial justice. The typical long-arm statute permits a court to exercise jurisdiction over a defendant, even though process is served beyond its borders, if the defendant (1) has committed a tort (civil wrong) within the State, (2) owns property within the State and that property is the subject matter of the lawsuit, (3) has entered into a contract within the State, or (4) has transacted business within the State and that business is the subject matter of the lawsuit.

3-4b *IN REM* JURISDICTION

Courts in a State have the jurisdiction to adjudicate claims to property situated within the State if the plaintiff gives those persons who have an interest in the property reasonable notice and an opportunity to be heard. Such jurisdiction over property is called **in rem jurisdiction**, from the Latin word *res*, which means "thing." For example, if Carpenter and Miller are involved in a lawsuit over property located in Kansas, then an appropriate court in Kansas would have *in rem* jurisdiction to adjudicate claims with respect to this property so long as both parties are given notice of the lawsuit and a reasonable opportunity to contest the claim.

3-4c ATTACHMENT JURISDICTION

Attachment jurisdiction, or **quasi *in rem* jurisdiction**, is jurisdiction over property rather than over a person. Attachment jurisdiction is invoked by seizing the defendant's property located within the State to obtain payment of a claim against the defendant that is *unrelated* to the property seized. For example, Allen, a resident of Ohio, has obtained a valid judgment in the amount of $20,000 against Bradley, a citizen of Kentucky. Allen can attach Bradley's automobile, which is located in Ohio, to satisfy his court judgment against Bradley.

♦ **SEE FIGURE 3-7:** *Jurisdiction*

3-4d VENUE

Venue, which often is confused with jurisdiction, concerns the geographic area in which a lawsuit *should* be brought. The purpose of venue is to regulate the distribution of cases within a specific court system and to identify a convenient forum. In the Federal court system, venue determines the district or districts in a given State in which a suit may be brought. State rules of venue typically require that a suit be initiated in a county where one of the defendants resides. In matters involving real estate, most venue rules require that a suit be initiated in the county where the property is situated. A defendant, however, may object to the venue for various reasons.

CIVIL DISPUTE RESOLUTION

As mentioned in *Chapter 1*, one of the primary functions of law is to provide for the peaceful resolution of disputes. Accordingly, our legal system has established an elaborate set of government mechanisms to settle disputes. The most prominent of these is judicial dispute resolution, called *litigation*. The rules of civil procedure, discussed in the first part of this section, govern judicial resolution of civil disputes. Judicial resolution of criminal cases is governed by the rules of criminal procedure, which are covered in *Chapter 6*. Dispute resolution by administrative agencies, which is also common, is discussed in *Chapter 5*.

As an alternative to government dispute resolution, several nongovernment methods of dispute resolution, such as arbitration, have developed. These are discussed in the second part of this section.

FIGURE 3-7 Jurisdiction

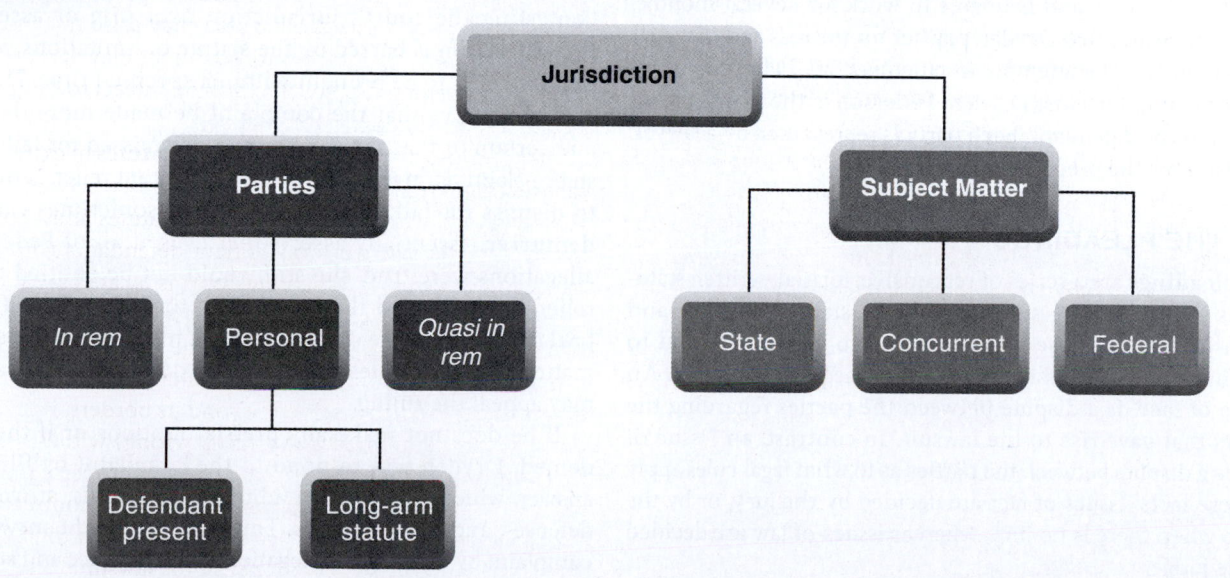

3-5 Civil Procedure

Civil disputes that enter the judicial system are subject to the rules of civil procedure. These rules are designed to resolve the dispute justly, promptly, and inexpensively. In addition, the Federal court system and most State court systems provide for **class action** lawsuits in which one or more plaintiffs may file suit on behalf of similarly situated individuals who are referred to as "the class." When a class action is permitted, the group files the lawsuit with a representative plaintiff, called the "named plaintiff" or "lead plaintiff." If the court certifies an action as meeting the criteria for a class action lawsuit and the plaintiffs prevail or reach a settlement, members of the class may obtain relief without bringing their own lawsuits. Conversely, if the defendant prevails in a certified class action lawsuit, members of the class may be bound by the decision and thus precluded from bringing their own lawsuits with respect to the claims in the class action lawsuit.

To acquaint the student with civil procedure, it will be helpful to carry a hypothetical action through the trial court to the highest court of review in the State. Although there are technical differences in trial and appellate procedure among State and Federal courts, the following example will provide a general understanding of the trial and appeal of cases. Assume that Pam Pederson, a pedestrian, while crossing a street in Chicago, is struck by an automobile driven by David Dryden. Pederson suffers serious personal injuries, incurs heavy medical and hospital expenses, and is unable to work for several months. Pederson desires that Dryden pay her for the loss and damages she sustained. After attempts at settlement fail, Pederson brings an action at law against Dryden. Pederson is the plaintiff, and Dryden is the defendant. Each party is represented by a lawyer. Let us follow the progress of the case.

3-5a THE PLEADINGS

The **pleadings** are a series of responsive, formal, written statements in which each side to a lawsuit states its claims and defenses. The purpose of pleadings is to give notice and to establish the issues of fact and law that the parties dispute. An "issue of fact" is a dispute between the parties regarding the events that gave rise to the lawsuit. In contrast, an "issue of law" is a dispute between the parties as to what legal rules apply to these facts. Issues of fact are decided by the jury, or by the judge when there is no jury, whereas issues of law are decided by the judge.

COMPLAINT AND SUMMONS A lawsuit commences when Pederson, the plaintiff, files with the clerk of the trial court a **complaint** against Dryden which contains (1) a statement of the claim and supporting facts showing that she is entitled to relief and (2) a demand for that relief. Pederson's complaint alleges that while exercising due and reasonable care for her own safety, she was struck by Dryden's automobile, which was negligently being driven by Dryden, causing her personal injuries and damages of $50,000, for which Pederson requests judgment.

Once the plaintiff has filed a complaint, the clerk issues a **summons** to be served upon the defendant to notify him that a suit has been brought against him. If the defendant has contacts with the State sufficient to show that the State's assertion of jurisdiction over him is constitutional, proper service of the summons establishes the court's jurisdiction over the person of the defendant. The sheriff of the county or a deputy sheriff serves a summons and a copy of the complaint upon Dryden, the defendant, commanding him to file his appearance and answer with the clerk of the court within a specific time, usually thirty days from the date the summons was served. A number of States permit the server to leave a copy of the summons at the defendant's home with a person of "suitable age and discretion." Most long-arm statutes allow service of the summons to be sent to out-of-state defendants by registered mail. If the defendant is a corporation, the statutes typically authorize actual service to the company's general or managing agent. When direct methods of notifying the defendant are unavailable, service by publication may be allowed.

RESPONSES TO COMPLAINT At this point, Dryden has several options. If he fails to respond at all, a **default judgment** will be entered against him for the relief the court determines in a hearing. He may make **pretrial motions** contesting the court's jurisdiction over him or asserting that the action is barred by the statute of limitations, which requires suits to be brought within a specified time. Dryden also may move that the complaint be made more definite and certain or that the complaint be dismissed for failure to state a claim upon which the court may grant relief. A motion to dismiss for failure to state a claim, sometimes called a **demurrer**, essentially asserts that even if all of Pederson's allegations were true, she still would not be entitled to the relief she seeks and that, therefore, there is no need for a trial of the facts. The court rules on a motion to dismiss as a matter of law. If it rules in favor of the defendant, the plaintiff may appeal the ruling.

If he does not make any pretrial motions or if they are denied, Dryden will respond to the complaint by filing an answer, which may contain admissions, denials, affirmative defenses, and counterclaims. Thus, Dryden might answer the complaint by denying its allegations of negligence and stating, on the other hand, that he, Dryden, was driving his car at a low speed and with reasonable care (a **denial**) when his car struck Pederson (an **admission**), who had dashed across the street in front of Dryden's car without looking in any direction to see whether cars or other vehicles were approaching; that, accordingly, Pederson's injuries were caused by her own negligence (an **affirmative defense**); and that, therefore, she should not be permitted to recover any damages. Dryden might further state that Pederson caused damages to his car and request a judgment for $2,000 (a **counterclaim**). These pleadings create an issue of fact regarding whether Pederson or Dryden, or both, failed to exercise due and reasonable care under the circumstances and were thus negligent and liable for their carelessness.

If the defendant counterclaims, the plaintiff must respond by a **reply**, which may also contain admissions, denials, and affirmative defenses.

3-5b PRETRIAL PROCEDURE

JUDGMENT ON PLEADINGS After the pleadings, either party may move for **judgment on the pleadings**, which requests the judge to rule as a matter of law whether the facts as alleged in the pleadings, which for the purpose of the motion are taken to be as the nonmoving party alleges them, form a sufficient basis to warrant granting the requested relief.

DISCOVERY In preparation for trial and even before completion of the pleadings stage, each party has the right to obtain relevant evidence, or information that may lead to evidence, from the other party. This procedure is known as **discovery**. It includes (1) pretrial **depositions** consisting of sworn testimony, taken out of court, of the opposing party or other witnesses; (2) sworn answers by the opposing party to **written interrogatories**; (3) **production** of documents and physical objects in the possession of the opposing party or, by a court-ordered subpoena, in the possession of nonparties; (4) a relevant court-ordered physical and/or mental **examination**, by a physician, of the opposing party; and (5) admissions of facts obtained by a **request for admissions** submitted to the opposing party. By properly using discovery, each party may become fully informed of relevant evidence and avoid surprise at trial. Another purpose of this procedure is to encourage and facilitate settlements by providing both parties with as much relevant information as possible.

PRETRIAL CONFERENCE Also furthering these objectives is the **pretrial conference** between the judge and the attorneys representing the parties. The basic purposes of the pretrial conference are (1) to simplify the issues in dispute by amending the pleadings, admitting or stipulating facts, and identifying witnesses and documents to be presented at trial and (2) to encourage settlement of the dispute without trial. (More

than 90 percent of all cases are settled before going to trial.) If no settlement occurs, the judge will enter a pretrial order containing all of the amendments, stipulations, admissions, and other matters agreed to during the pretrial conference. The order supersedes the pleadings and controls the remainder of the trial.

SUMMARY JUDGMENT The evidence disclosed by discovery may be so clear that a trial to determine the facts becomes unnecessary. Thus, after discovery, either party may move for a summary judgment, which requests the judge to rule that because there are no issues of fact to be determined by trial, the party thus moving should prevail as a matter of law. A **summary judgment** is a final binding determination on the merits made by the judge before a trial.

◆ *See Case 3-3*

3-5c TRIAL

In all Federal civil cases at common law involving more than $20, the U.S. Constitution guarantees the right to a jury trial. In addition, nearly every State constitution provides a similar right. In addition, Federal and State statutes may authorize jury trials in cases not within the constitutional guarantees. Under Federal law and in almost all States, jury trials are *not* available in equity cases. Even in cases in which a jury trial is available, the parties may waive (choose not to have) a trial by jury. When a trial is conducted without a jury, the judge serves as the fact finder and will make separate findings of fact and conclusions of law. When a trial is conducted with a jury, the judge determines issues of law and the jury determines questions of fact.

JURY SELECTION Assuming a timely demand for a jury has been made, the trial begins with the selection of a jury. The jury selection process involves a *voir dire*, an examination by the parties' attorneys (or in some courts, by the judge) of the potential jurors. Each party may make an unlimited number of **challenges for cause**, which prevent a prospective juror from serving if the juror is biased or cannot be fair and impartial. In addition, each party has a limited number of **peremptory challenges**, which allow the party to disqualify a prospective juror without showing cause. The Supreme Court has held that the U.S. Constitution prohibits discrimination in jury selection on the basis of race or gender.

CONDUCT OF TRIAL After the jury has been selected, both attorneys make an **opening statement** concerning the facts that they expect to prove in the trial. The plaintiff and her witnesses then testify upon **direct examination** by the plaintiff's attorney. Each is then subject to **cross-examination** by the defendant's attorney. Thus, in our hypothetical case, the plaintiff and her witnesses testify that the traffic light at the street intersection where Pederson was struck was green for traffic in the direction in which Pederson was crossing but changed to yellow when she was about one-third of the way across the street.

During the trial, the judge rules on the admission and exclusion of evidence on the basis of its relevance and reliability. If the judge does not allow certain evidence to be introduced or certain testimony to be given, the attorney must make an offer of proof to preserve the question of admissibility for review on appeal. An **offer of proof** consists of oral statements of counsel or witnesses showing for the record the evidence that the judge has ruled inadmissible; it is not regarded as evidence and is not heard by the jury.

After cross-examination, followed by redirect examination of each of her witnesses, Pederson rests her case. At this point, Dryden may move for a directed verdict in his favor. A **directed verdict** is a final binding determination on the merits made by the judge after a trial but before the jury renders a verdict. If the judge concludes that the evidence introduced by the plaintiff, which is assumed for the purposes of the motion to be true, would not be sufficient for the jury to find in favor of the plaintiff, then the judge will grant the directed verdict in favor of the defendant. In some States, the judge will deny the motion for a directed verdict if there is *any* evidence on which the jury might possibly render a verdict for the plaintiff. If a directed verdict is reversed on appeal, a new trial is necessary.

If the judge denies the motion for a directed verdict, the defendant then has the opportunity to present evidence. The defendant and his witnesses testify that Dryden was driving his car at a low speed when it struck Pederson and that Dryden at the time had the green light at the intersection.

After the defendant has presented his evidence, the plaintiff and the defendant may be permitted to introduce rebuttal evidence. Once both parties have rested (concluded), either party may move for a directed verdict. By this motion, the party contends that the evidence is so clear that reasonable persons could not differ as to the outcome of the case. If the judge grants the motion for a directed verdict, he takes the case away from the jury and enters a judgment for the party making the motion.

If the judge denies the motion, the plaintiff's attorney makes a **closing argument** to the jury, reviewing the evidence and urging a verdict in favor of Pederson. Dryden's attorney then makes a closing argument, summarizing the evidence and urging a verdict in favor of Dryden. Pederson's attorney is permitted to make a short argument in rebuttal.

JURY INSTRUCTIONS The attorneys previously have tendered possible written jury instructions on the applicable law to the trial judge, who gives to the jury those instructions he approves and denies those he considers incorrect. The judge also may give the jury instructions of his own. **Jury instructions** (called "charges" in some States) advise the jury of the particular rules of law that apply to the facts the jury determines from the evidence.

VERDICT The jury then retires to the jury room to deliberate and to reach a **general verdict** in favor of one party or the other. If it finds the issues in favor of the defendant, its verdict is that the defendant is not liable. If, however, it finds the issues for the plaintiff and against the defendant, its verdict will hold the defendant liable and will specify the amount of the plaintiff's damages. In this case, the jury found that Pederson's damages were $35,000. Upon returning to the jury box, the foreman either announces the verdict or hands it in written form to the clerk to give to the judge, who reads the general verdict in open court. In some jurisdictions, the jury must reach a **special verdict** by making specific written findings on each factual issue. The judge then applies the law to these findings and renders a judgment. In the United States, the prevailing litigant is ordinarily *not* entitled to collect attorney's fees from the losing party, unless otherwise provided by statute or an enforceable contract allocating attorney's fees.

MOTIONS CHALLENGING THE VERDICT The unsuccessful party then may file a written motion for a new trial or for judgment notwithstanding the verdict. The judge may grant a **motion for a new trial** if (1) the judge committed prejudicial error during the trial, (2) the verdict is against the weight of the evidence, (3) the damages are excessive, or (4) the trial was not fair. The judge has the discretion to grant a motion for a new trial (on grounds 1, 3, or 4) even if substantial evidence supports the verdict. On the other hand, he must deny a motion for judgment notwithstanding the verdict (also called a judgment n.o.v.) if any substantial evidence supports the verdict. This motion is similar to a motion for a directed verdict, only it is made *after* the jury's verdict. To grant the **motion for judgment notwithstanding the verdict**, the judge must decide that the evidence is so clear that reasonable people could not differ as to the outcome of the case. If a judgment n.o.v. is reversed on appeal, a new trial is *not* necessary, and the jury's verdict is entered. If the judge denies the motions for a new trial and for a judgment n.o.v., he enters **judgment on the verdict** for $35,000 in favor of Pederson.

3-5d APPEAL

The purpose of an **appeal** is to determine whether the trial court committed prejudicial error. Most jurisdictions permit an appeal only from a final judgment. As a general rule, an appellate court reviews only errors of law. Errors of law include the judge's decisions to admit or exclude evidence; the judge's instructions to the jury; and the judge's actions in denying or granting a motion for a demurrer, a summary judgment, a directed verdict, or a judgment n.o.v. Appellate courts review errors of law *de novo*. An appellate court will reverse errors of fact only if they are so clearly erroneous that the court considers them to constitute an error of law.

Assume that Dryden directs his attorney to appeal. The attorney files a notice of appeal with the clerk of the trial court within the prescribed time. Later, Dryden, as appellant, files in the reviewing court the record on appeal, which contains the pleadings, transcript of the testimony, rulings by the judge on motions made by the parties, arguments of counsel, jury instructions, verdict, posttrial motions, and judgment from which the appeal is taken. In States having an intermediate court of appeals, such court usually will be the reviewing court. In States having no intermediate courts of appeal, a party may appeal directly from the trial court to the State supreme court.

Dryden, as appellant, is required to prepare a condensation of the record, known as an abstract, or pertinent excerpts from the record, which he files with the reviewing court together with a brief and argument. His **brief** contains a statement of the facts, the issues, the rulings by the trial court that Dryden contends are erroneous and prejudicial, grounds for reversal of the judgment, a statement of the applicable law, and arguments on his behalf. Pederson, the appellee, files an answering brief and argument. Dryden may, but is not required to, file a reply brief. The case is now ready for consideration by the reviewing court.

The appellate court does not hear any evidence; rather, it decides the case upon the record, abstracts, and briefs. After **oral argument** by the attorneys, if the court elects to hear one, the court takes the case under advisement and makes a decision based upon majority rule, after which the court prepares a written opinion containing the reasons for its decision, the applicable rules of law, and its judgment. The judgment may **affirm** the judgment of the trial court, or if the appellate court finds that reversible error was committed, the judgment may be **reversed**, or the case may be **reversed and remanded** for a new trial. In some instances, the appellate court will affirm the lower court's decision in part and reverse it in part. The losing party may file a petition for rehearing, which is usually denied.

If the reviewing court is an intermediate appellate court, the party losing in that court may decide to seek a reversal of its judgment by filing within a prescribed time a notice of appeal, if the appeal is by right, or a petition for leave to appeal to the State supreme court, if the appeal is by discretion. This petition corresponds to a petition for a writ of *certiorari* in the U.S. Supreme Court. The party winning in the appellate court may file an answer to the petition for leave to appeal. If the petition is granted or if the appeal is by right, the record is certified to the State supreme court, where each party files a new brief and argument. Oral argument may be held, and the case is taken under advisement. If the State supreme court concludes that the judgment of the appellate court is correct, it affirms. If the State supreme court decides otherwise, it reverses the judgment of the appellate court and enters a reversal or an order of remand. The unsuccessful party may again file a petition for

a rehearing, which is likely to be denied. Barring the remote possibility of an application for still further review by the U.S. Supreme Court, the case either has reached its termination or, upon remand, is about to start its second journey through the courts, beginning, as it did originally, in the trial court.

3-5e ENFORCEMENT

If Dryden does not appeal or if the reviewing court affirms the judgment if he does appeal and Dryden does not pay the judgment, the task of enforcement remains. Pederson must request the clerk to issue a **writ of execution**, demanding payment of the judgment, which is served by the sheriff upon the defendant. If the writ is returned "unsatisfied," Pederson may post bond or other security and order a levy on and sale of specific nonexempt property belonging to Dryden, which is then seized by the sheriff, advertised for sale, and sold at public sale under the writ of execution. If the proceeds of the sale do not produce sufficient funds to pay the judgment, plaintiff Pederson's attorney may institute a supplementary proceeding in an attempt to locate money or other property belonging to Dryden. In an attempt to collect the judgment, Pederson's attorney also may proceed by **garnishment** against Dryden's employer to collect from Dryden's wages or against a bank in which Dryden has an account.

If Pederson cannot satisfy the judgment with Dryden's property located within Illinois (the State where the judgment was obtained), Pederson will have to bring an action on the original judgment in other States where Dryden owns property. Because the U.S. Constitution requires each State to accord judgments of other States **full faith and credit**, Pederson will be able to obtain a local judgment that may be enforced by the methods described previously.

◆ SEE FIGURE 3-8: *Stages in Civil Procedure*

3-6 Alternative Dispute Resolution

Litigation is complex, time-consuming, and expensive. Furthermore, court adjudications involve long delays, lack special expertise in substantive areas, and provide only a limited range of remedies. In addition, the litigation process offers little opportunity for compromise and often causes or exacerbates animosity between the disputants. Consequently, in an attempt to overcome some of the disadvantages of litigation, several nonjudicial methods of dealing with disputes have developed. The most important of these alternatives to litigation is arbitration. Others include conciliation, mediation, "mini-trials," and summary jury trials.

The various techniques differ in a number of ways, including (1) whether the process is voluntary, (2) whether the process is binding, (3) whether the disputants represent themselves or

FIGURE 3-8 **Stages in Civil Procedure**

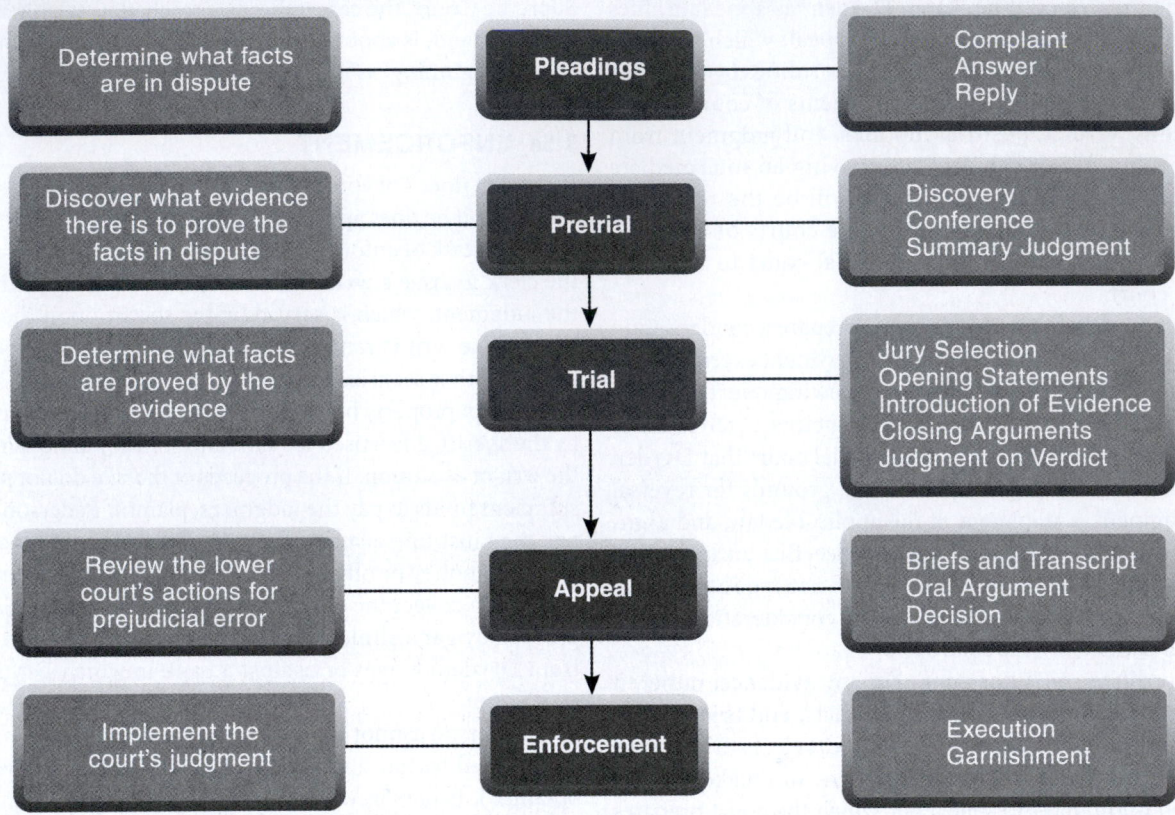

Determine what facts are in dispute	**Pleadings**	Complaint Answer Reply
Discover what evidence there is to prove the facts in dispute	**Pretrial**	Discovery Conference Summary Judgment
Determine what facts are proved by the evidence	**Trial**	Jury Selection Opening Statements Introduction of Evidence Closing Arguments Judgment on Verdict
Review the lower court's actions for prejudicial error	**Appeal**	Briefs and Transcript Oral Argument Decision
Implement the court's judgment	**Enforcement**	Execution Garnishment

are represented by attorneys, (4) whether the decision is made by the disputants or by a third party, (5) whether the procedure used is formal or informal, and (6) whether the basis for the decision is law or some other criterion.

Which method of civil dispute resolution—litigation or one of the nongovernmental methods—is better for a particular dispute depends on several factors, including the financial circumstances of the disputants, the nature of their relationship (commercial or personal, ongoing or limited), and the urgency of their need for a quick resolution. Alternative dispute resolution methods are especially suitable in cases in which privacy, speed, preservation of continuing relations, and control over the process—including the flexibility to compromise—are important to the parties. Nevertheless, the disadvantages of using alternative dispute mechanisms may make court adjudication more appropriate. For example, except for arbitration, only courts can compel participation and provide a binding resolution. In addition, only courts can establish precedents and create public duties. Furthermore, the courts provide greater due process protections and uniformity of outcome. Finally, the courts are independent of the disputants and are publicly funded.

◆ **SEE FIGURE 3-9:** *Comparison of Court Adjudication, Arbitration, and Mediation/Conciliation*

Practical Advice

Consider including in your contracts a provision specifying what means of dispute resolution will apply to the contract.

3-6a ARBITRATION

In **arbitration**, the parties select a neutral third person or persons (the arbitrators) who render(s) a binding decision after hearing arguments and reviewing evidence. Because the presentation of the case is less formal and the rules of evidence are more relaxed, arbitration usually takes less time and costs less than litigation. Moreover, in many arbitration cases, the parties can select an arbitrator with special expertise concerning the subject of the dispute. Thus, the quality of the arbitrator's decision may be higher than that available through the court system. In addition, arbitration normally is conducted in private, which enables the parties to avoid unwanted publicity. Arbitration is commonly used in commercial and labor management disputes.

FIGURE 3-9 Comparison of Court Adjudication, Arbitration, and Mediation/Conciliation

	Court Adjudication	Arbitration	Mediation/Conciliation
Binding	Yes	Yes	No
Public Proceedings	Yes	No	No
Special Expertise	No	Yes	Yes
Publicly Funded	Yes	No	No
Precedents Established	Yes	No	No
Time Consuming	Yes	No	No
Long Delays	Yes	No	No
Expensive	Yes	No	No

TYPES OF ARBITRATION Arbitration is of two basic types—consensual, which is by far the most common, and compulsory. **Consensual arbitration** occurs whenever the parties to a dispute agree to submit the controversy to arbitration. They may do this in advance by agreeing in their contract that disputes arising out of the contract will be resolved by arbitration. Or after a dispute arises, they may agree to submit the dispute to arbitration. In either instance, such agreements are enforceable under the Federal Arbitration Act (FAA) and State statutes.

Arbitration agreements give each party two distinct contractual rights. First, either party can file claims against the other in arbitration and obtain a binding decision from the arbitrator. Second, if one party sues the other party in court, the defendant can invoke the arbitration clause to require that the dispute be resolved in arbitration.

Forty-nine States adopted the Uniform Arbitration Act of 1956 (UAA). (In 2000, the Uniform Law Commission, also known as the National Conference of Commissioners on Uniform State Laws, promulgated the Revised UAA to provide State legislatures with a more up-to-date statute to resolve disputes through arbitration. At least twenty States have adopted the Revised UAA.

In a significant development, the U.S. Supreme Court held that the FAA preempted State law that would have prohibited the enforcement of a consumer arbitration clause requiring consumer complaints to be arbitrated individually instead of on a class-action basis. *AT&T Mobility LLC v. Concepcion*, 563 U.S. 333 (2011). In the Dodd-Frank Wall Street Reform and Consumer Protection Act of 2010, Congress required the Consumer Financial Protection Bureau (CFPB) to study the use of arbitration clauses in consumer financial markets and gave the CFPB the power to issue regulations that are in the public interest, for the protection of consumers, and consistent

with the study's findings. The CFPB's study—released in March 2015—showed that arbitration clauses restrict consumers' access to relief for disputes with financial service providers by allowing companies to prohibit class action lawsuits. In July 2017, the CFPB issued rules that ban consumer financial companies from using arbitration clauses to block consumers from suing in groups to obtain relief. On November 1, 2017, pursuant to the Congressional Review Act discussed in *Chapter 5*, Congress disapproved this rule stating that it "shall have no force or effect." Nevertheless, Congress had already prohibited agreements that require arbitration or any other nonjudicial procedure in the largest market that the CFPB oversees—the residential mortgage market.

In **compulsory arbitration**, which is relatively infrequent, a Federal or State statute requires arbitration for specific types of disputes, such as those involving public employees like police officers, teachers, and firefighters.

PROCEDURE Usually the parties' agreement to arbitrate specifies how the arbitrator or arbitrators will be chosen. If it does not, the FAA and State statutes provide methods for selecting arbitrators. Although the requirements for arbitration hearings vary from State to State, they generally consist of opening statements, case presentation, and closing statements. Case presentations may include witnesses, documentation, and site inspections. The parties may cross-examine witnesses, and the parties may be represented by attorneys.

The decision of the arbitrator, called an **award**, is binding on the parties. Nevertheless, it is subject to very limited judicial review. Under the FAA and the Revised UAA, grounds for review include (1) the award was procured by corruption, fraud, or other undue means; (2) the arbitrators were partial or corrupt; (3) the arbitrators were guilty of misconduct prejudicing the rights of a party to the arbitration proceeding; and (4) the arbitrators exceeded their powers. Historically, the courts were unfriendly to arbitration; now, however, they favor the procedure.

INTERNATIONAL ARBITRATION Arbitration is a commonly used means for resolving international disputes. The United Nations Commission on International Trade Law (UNCITRAL) and the International Chamber of Commerce have promulgated arbitration rules that have won broad international adherence. The FAA has provisions implementing the United Nations Convention on the Recognition and Enforcement of Foreign Arbitral Awards. A number of States have enacted laws specifically governing international arbitration; some of the statutes have been based on the Model Law on International Arbitration drafted by UNCITRAL.

COURT-ANNEXED ARBITRATION A growing number of Federal and State courts have adopted court-annexed arbitration in civil cases in which the parties seek limited amounts of damages. The arbitrators are usually attorneys. Appeal from this type of *nonbinding* arbitration is by trial *de novo*.

Many States have enacted statutes requiring the arbitration of medical malpractice disputes. Some States provide for mandatory nonbinding arbitration before bringing a case to court. Other States provide for voluntary but binding arbitration agreements, which patients sign before receiving medical treatment.

◆ *See Case 3-4*

3-6b CONCILIATION

Conciliation is a nonbinding, informal process in which the disputing parties select a neutral third party (the conciliator) who attempts to help them reach a mutually acceptable agreement. The duties of the conciliator include improving communications, explaining issues, scheduling meetings, discussing differences of opinion, and serving as an intermediary between the parties when they are unwilling to meet.

3-6c MEDIATION

Mediation is a process in which a neutral third party (the mediator) selected by the disputants helps them to reach a voluntary agreement resolving their disagreement. In addition to employing conciliation techniques to improve communications, the mediator, unlike the conciliator, proposes possible solutions for the parties to consider. Like the conciliator, the mediator lacks the power to render a binding decision. Because it is a voluntary process and has lower costs than a formal legal proceeding or arbitration, mediation has become one of the most widespread forms of dispute resolution in the United States. Mediation commonly is used by the judicial system in such tribunals as small claims courts, housing courts, family courts, and neighborhood justice centers. In 2001, the Uniform Law Commission promulgated the Uniform Mediation Act, which was amended in 2003. The Act establishes a privilege of confidentiality for mediators and participants. At least eleven States have adopted it.

Sometimes the techniques of arbitration and mediation are combined in a procedure called "med-arb." In **med-arb**, the neutral third party serves first as a mediator and if all issues are not resolved through such mediation, then serves as an arbitrator authorized to render a binding decision on the remaining issues.

3-6d MINI-TRIAL

A mini-trial is a structured settlement process that combines elements of negotiation, mediation, and trials. Mini-trials are most commonly used when both disputants are corporations. In a mini-trial, attorneys for the two corporations conduct limited discovery and then present evidence to a panel consisting of managers from each company, as well as a neutral third party, who may be a retired judge or another attorney. After the lawyers complete their presentations, the managers try to negotiate a settlement without the attorneys. The managers may consult the third party on how a court might resolve the issues in dispute.

3-6e SUMMARY JURY TRIAL

A summary jury trial is a mock trial in which the parties present their case to an advisory jury. Though not binding, the jury's verdict does influence the negotiations in which the parties must participate following the mock trial. If the parties do not reach a settlement, they may have a full trial *de novo*.

3-6f NEGOTIATION

Negotiation is a consensual bargaining process in which the parties attempt to reach an agreement resolving their dispute. Negotiation differs from other methods of alternative dispute resolution in that no third parties are involved.

C H A P T E R S U M M A R Y

THE COURT SYSTEM

FEDERAL COURTS	**District Courts** trial courts of general jurisdiction that can hear and decide most legal controversies in the Federal system
	Courts of Appeals hear appeals from the district courts and review orders of certain administrative agencies
	The Supreme Court the nation's highest court, whose principal function is to review decisions of the Federal Courts of Appeals and the highest State courts
	Special Courts have jurisdiction over cases in a particular area of Federal law and include the U.S. Court of Federal Claims, the U.S. Tax Court, the U.S. Bankruptcy Courts, the U.S. Court of International Trade, and the U.S. Court of Appeals for the Federal Circuit

STATE COURTS	**Inferior Trial Courts** hear minor criminal cases, such as traffic offenses, and civil cases involving small amounts of money; conduct preliminary hearings in more serious criminal cases
	Trial Courts have general jurisdiction over civil and criminal cases
	Special Courts trial courts, such as probate courts and family courts, having jurisdiction over a particular area of State law
	Appellate Courts include one or two levels; the highest court's decisions are final except in those cases reviewed by the U.S. Supreme Court

JURISDICTION

SUBJECT MATTER JURISDICTION	**Definition** authority of a court to decide a particular kind of case
	Federal Jurisdiction
	• *Exclusive Federal Jurisdiction* Federal courts have sole jurisdiction over Federal crimes, bankruptcy, antitrust, patent, trademark, copyright, and other specified cases
	• *Concurrent Federal* Jurisdiction authority of more than one court to hear the same case; State and Federal courts have concurrent jurisdiction over (1) Federal question cases (cases arising under the Constitution, statutes, or treaties of the United States) that do not involve exclusive Federal jurisdiction and (2) diversity of citizenship cases involving more than $75,000
	State Jurisdiction State courts have exclusive jurisdiction over all matters to which the Federal judicial power does not reach

JURISDICTION OVER THE PARTIES	**Definition** the power of a court to bind the parties to a suit
	In Personam **Jurisdiction** jurisdiction based upon claims against a person, in contrast to jurisdiction over the person's property
	In Rem **Jurisdiction** jurisdiction based on claims against property
	Attachment Jurisdiction jurisdiction over a defendant's property to obtain payment of a claim not related to the property
	Venue geographic area in which a lawsuit should be brought

CIVIL DISPUTE RESOLUTION

CIVIL PROCEDURE	**Pleadings** a series of statements that give notice and establish the issues of fact and law presented and disputed

- *Complaint* initial pleading by the plaintiff stating his case
- *Summons* notice given to inform a person of a lawsuit against her
- *Answer* defendant's pleading in response to the plaintiff's complaint
- *Reply* plaintiff's pleading in response to the defendant's answer

Pretrial Procedure process requiring the parties to disclose what evidence is available to prove the disputed facts; designed to encourage settlement of cases or to make the trial more efficient

- *Judgment on Pleadings* a final ruling in favor of one party by the judge based on the pleadings
- *Discovery* right of each party to obtain evidence from the other party
- *Pretrial Conference* a conference between the judge and the attorneys to simplify the issues in dispute and to attempt to settle the dispute without trial
- *Summary Judgment* final ruling by the judge in favor of one party based on the evidence disclosed by discovery

Trial determines the facts and the outcome of the case

- *Jury Selection* each party has an unlimited number of challenges for cause and a limited number of peremptory challenges
- *Conduct of Trial* consists of opening statements by attorneys, direct and cross-examination of witnesses, and closing arguments
- *Directed Verdict* final ruling by the judge in favor of one party based on the evidence introduced at trial
- *Jury Instructions* judge gives the jury the particular rules of law that apply to the case
- *Verdict* the jury's decision based on those facts the jury determines the evidence proves
- *Motions Challenging the Verdict* include motions for a new trial and a motion for judgment notwithstanding the verdict

Appeal determines whether the trial court committed prejudicial error

Enforcement a plaintiff with an unpaid judgment may resort to (1) a writ of execution to have the sheriff seize property of the defendant and (2) garnishment to collect money owed to the defendant by a third party

ALTERNATIVE DISPUTE RESOLUTION	**Arbitration** a nonjudicial proceeding in which a neutral party selected by the disputants renders a binding decision (award)

Conciliation a nonbinding process in which a third party acts as an intermediary between the disputing parties

Mediation a nonbinding process in which a third party acts as an intermediary between the disputing parties and proposes solutions for them to consider

Mini-Trial a nonbinding process in which attorneys for the disputing parties (typically corporations) present evidence to managers of the disputing parties and a neutral third party, after which the managers attempt to negotiate a settlement in consultation with the third party

Summary Jury Trial mock trial followed by negotiations

Negotiation consensual bargaining process in which the parties attempt to reach an agreement resolving their dispute without the involvement of third parties

CASES

Concurrent Federal Jurisdiction
MIMS v. ARROW FINANCIAL SERVICES, LLC
Supreme Court of the United States, 2012
565 U.S. 368, 132 S.Ct. 740, 181 L.Ed.2d 881

Ginsburg, J.

This case concerns enforcement * * * of the Telephone Consumer Protection Act of 1991 (TCPA or Act), [citation]. Voluminous consumer complaints about abuses of telephone technology—for example, computerized calls dispatched to private homes—prompted Congress to pass the TCPA. Congress determined that federal legislation was needed because telemarketers, by operating interstate, were escaping state-law prohibitions on intrusive nuisance calls. The Act bans certain practices invasive of privacy and directs the Federal Communications Commission (FCC or Commission) to prescribe implementing regulations. It authorizes States to bring civil actions to enjoin prohibited practices and to recover damages on their residents' behalf. The Commission must be notified of such suits and may intervene in them. Jurisdiction over state-initiated TCPA suits, Congress provided, lies exclusively in the U.S. district courts. Congress also provided for civil actions by private parties seeking redress for violations of the TCPA or of the Commission's implementing regulations.

Petitioner Marcus D. Mims, complaining of multiple violations of the Act by respondent Arrow Financial Services, LLC (Arrow), a debt-collection agency, commenced an action for damages against Arrow in the U.S. District Court for the Southern District of Florida. Mims invoked the court's "federal question" jurisdiction, *i.e.*, its authority to adjudicate claims "arising under the … laws … of the United States," [citation]. The District Court, affirmed by the U.S. Court of Appeals for the Eleventh Circuit, dismissed Mims's complaint for want of subject-matter jurisdiction. Both courts relied on Congress' specification, in the TCPA, that a private person may seek redress for violations of the Act (or of the Commission's regulations thereunder) "in an appropriate court of [a] State," "if [such an action is] otherwise permitted by the laws or rules of court of [that] State." [Citation.]

* * *

We granted certiorari, [citation], to resolve a split among the Circuits as to whether Congress granted state courts exclusive jurisdiction over private actions brought under the TCPA. [Citations.] We now hold that Congress did not deprive federal courts of federal-question jurisdiction over private TCPA suits.

Federal courts, though "courts of limited jurisdiction," [citation], in the main "have no more right to decline the exercise of jurisdiction which is given, then to usurp that which is not given." [Citation.] Congress granted federal courts general federal-question jurisdiction in 1875. [Citation.] * * * "The district courts shall have original jurisdiction of all civil actions arising under the Constitution, laws, or treaties of the United States." 28 U.S.C. § 1331. * * *

Because federal law creates the right of action and provides the rules of decision, Mims's TCPA claim, in 28 U.S.C. § 1331's words, plainly "aris[es] under" the "laws… of the United States." * * *

Arrow agrees that this action arises under federal law, [citation], but urges that Congress vested exclusive adjudicatory authority over private TCPA actions in state courts. In cases "arising under" federal law, we note, there is a "deeply rooted presumption in favor of concurrent state court jurisdiction," rebuttable if "Congress affirmatively ousts the state courts of jurisdiction over a particular federal claim." [Citation.] * * *

* * *

Arrow's arguments do not persuade us that Congress has eliminated § 1331 jurisdiction over private actions under the TCPA.

* * *

Nothing in the permissive language of § 227(b)(3) makes state-court jurisdiction exclusive, or otherwise purports to oust federal courts of their 28 U.S.C. § 1331 jurisdiction over federal claims. * * *

Title 47 U.S.C. § 227(b)(3) does not state that a private plaintiff may bring an action under the TCPA "only" in state court, or "exclusively" in state court. * * *

* * *

Nothing in the text, structure, purpose, or legislative history of the TCPA calls for displacement of the federal-question jurisdiction U.S. district courts ordinarily have under 28 U.S.C. § 1331. In the absence of direction from Congress stronger than any Arrow has advanced, we apply the familiar default rule: Federal courts have § 1331 jurisdiction over claims that arise under federal law. Because federal law gives rise to the claim for relief Mims has stated and specifies the substantive rules of decision, the Eleventh Circuit erred in dismissing Mims's case for lack of subject-matter jurisdiction.

* * *

For the reasons stated, the judgment of the United States Court of Appeals for the Eleventh Circuit is reversed, and the case is remanded for further proceedings consistent with this opinion.

Jurisdiction
WORLD-WIDE VOLKSWAGEN CORP. v. WOODSON
Supreme Court of the United States, 1980
444 U.S. 286, 100 S.Ct 559, 62 L.Ed.2d 490

White, J.

The issue before us is whether, consistently with the Due Process Clause of the Fourteenth Amendment, an Oklahoma court may exercise *in personam* jurisdiction over a nonresident automobile retailer and its wholesale distributor in a products-liability action, when the defendants' only connection with Oklahoma is the fact that an automobile sold in New York to New York residents became involved in an accident in Oklahoma.

Respondents Harry and Kay Robinson purchased a new Audi automobile from petitioner Seaway Volkswagen, Inc. (Seaway), in Massena, N.Y., in 1976. The following year the Robinson family, who resided in New York, left that State for a new home in Arizona. As they passed through the State of Oklahoma, another car struck their Audi in the rear, causing a fire which severely burned Kay Robinson and her two children.

The Robinsons subsequently brought a products-liability action in the District Court for Creek County, Okla., claiming that their injuries resulted from defective design and placement of the Audi's gas tank and fuel system. They joined as defendants the automobile's manufacturer, Audi NSU Auto Union Aktiengesellschaft (Audi); its importer, Volkswagen of America, Inc. (Volkswagen); its regional distributor, petitioner World-Wide Volkswagen Corp. (World-Wide); and its retail dealer, petitioner Seaway. Seaway and World-Wide entered special appearances, claiming that Oklahoma's exercise of jurisdiction over them would offend the limitations on the State's jurisdiction imposed by the Due Process Clause of the Fourteenth Amendment.

The facts presented to the District Court showed that World-Wide is incorporated and has its business office in New York. It distributes vehicles, parts, and accessories, under contract with Volkswagen, to retail dealers in New York, New Jersey, and Connecticut. Seaway, one of these retail dealers, is incorporated and has its place of business in New York. Insofar as the record reveals, Seaway and WorldWide are fully independent corporations whose relations with each other and with Volkswagen and Audi are contractual only. Respondents adduced no evidence that either World-Wide or Seaway does any business in Oklahoma, ships or sells any products to or in that State, has an agent to receive process there, or purchases advertisements in any media calculated to reach Oklahoma. In fact, as respondents' counsel conceded at oral argument, [citation], there was no showing that any automobile sold by World-Wide or Seaway has ever entered Oklahoma with the single exception of the vehicle involved in the present case.

* * *

The Supreme Court of Oklahoma [held] that personal jurisdiction over petitioners was authorized by Oklahoma's "long-arm" statute, [citation]. * * *

* * *

The Due Process Clause of the Fourteenth Amendment limits the power of a state court to render a valid personal judgment against a nonresident defendant. [Citation.] A judgment rendered in violation of due process is void in the rendering State and is not entitled to full faith and credit elsewhere. [Citation.] Due process requires that the defendant be given adequate notice of the suit, [citation], and be subject to the personal jurisdiction of the court, [citation]. In the present case, it is not contended that notice was inadequate; the only question is whether these particular petitioners were subject to the jurisdiction of the Oklahoma courts.

As has long been settled, and as we reaffirm today, a state court may exercise personal jurisdiction over a nonresident defendant only so long as there exist "minimum contacts" between the defendant and the forum State. [Citation.] The concept of minimum contacts, in turn, can be seen to perform two related, but distinguishable, functions. It protects the defendant against the burdens of litigating in a distant or inconvenient forum. And it acts to ensure that the States, through their courts, do not reach out beyond the limits imposed on them by their status as coequal sovereigns in a federal system.

The protection against inconvenient litigation is typically described in terms of "reasonableness" or "fairness." We have said that the defendant's contacts with the forum State must be such that maintenance of the suit "does not offend 'traditional notions of fair play and substantial justice.'" [Citation.] The relationship between the defendant and the forum must be such that it is "reasonable * * * to require the corporation to defend the particular suit which is brought there." [Citation.] Implicit in this emphasis on reasonableness is the understanding that the burden on the defendant, while always a primary concern, will in an appropriate case be considered in light of other relevant factors, including the forum State's interest in adjudicating the dispute, [citation]; the plaintiff's interest in obtaining convenient and effective relief, [citation], at least when that interest is not adequately protected by the plaintiff's power to choose the forum, [citation]; the interstate judicial system's interest in obtaining the most efficient resolution of controversies; and the shared interest of the several States in furthering fundamental substantive social policies, [citation].

* * *

Thus, the Due Process Clause "does not contemplate that a state may make binding a judgment in personam against an individual or corporate defendant with which the state has no contacts, ties, or relations." [Citation.] * * *

* * *

Applying these principles to the case at hand, we find in the record before us a total absence of those affiliating circumstances that are a necessary predicate to any exercise of state-court jurisdiction. Petitioners carry on no activity whatsoever in Oklahoma. They close no sales and perform no services there. They avail themselves of none of the privileges and benefits of Oklahoma law. They solicit no business there either through salespersons or through advertising reasonably calculated to reach the State. Nor does the record show that they regularly sell cars at wholesale or retail to Oklahoma customers or residents or that they indirectly, through others, serve or seek to serve the Oklahoma market. In short, respondents seek to base jurisdiction on one, isolated occurrence and whatever inferences can be drawn there from: the fortuitous circumstance that a single Audi automobile, sold in New York to New York residents, happened to suffer an accident while passing through Oklahoma.

* * *

Because we find that petitioners have no "contacts, ties, or relations" with the State of Oklahoma, [citation], the judgment of the Supreme Court of Oklahoma is Reversed.

CASE 3-3

Pretrial Procedure: Summary Judgment
PARKER v. TWENTIETH CENTURY-FOX CORP.
Supreme Court of California, 1970
3 Cal.3d 176, 89 Cal.Rptr. 737,474 P.2d 689

Burke, J.

Defendant Twentieth Century-Fox Film Corporation appeals from a summary judgment granting to plaintiff [Shirley MacLaine Parker] the recovery of agreed compensation under a written contract for her services as an actress in a motion picture. As will appear, we have concluded that the trial court correctly ruled in plaintiff's favor and that the judgment should be affirmed.

Plaintiff is well known as an actress, and in the contract between plaintiff and defendant is sometimes referred to as the "Artist." Under the contract, dated August 6, 1965, plaintiff was to play the female lead in defendant's contemplated production of a motion picture entitled "Bloomer Girl." The contract provided that defendant would pay plaintiff a minimum "guaranteed compensation" of $53,571.42 per week for 14 weeks commencing May 23, 1966, for a total of $750,000. Prior to May 1966 defendant decided not to produce the picture and by a letter dated April 4, 1966, it notified plaintiff of that decision and that it would not "comply with our obligations to you under" the written contract.

By the same letter and with the professed purpose "to avoid any damage to you," defendant instead offered to employ plaintiff as the leading actress in another film tentatively entitled "Big Country, Big Man" (hereinafter, "Big Country"). The compensation offered was identical, as were 31 of the 34 numbered provisions or articles of the original contract. Unlike "Bloomer Girl," however, which was to have been a musical production, "Big Country" was a dramatic "western type" movie. "Bloomer Girl" was to have been filmed in California; "Big Country" was to be produced in Australia. Also, certain terms in the proffered contract varied from those of the original. Plaintiff was given one week within which to accept; she did not and the offer lapsed. Plaintiff then commenced this action seeking recovery of the agreed guaranteed compensation.

The complaint sets forth two causes of action. The first is for money due under the contract; the second, based upon the same allegations as the first, is for damages resulting from defendant's breach of contract. Defendant in its answer admits the existence and validity of the contract, that plaintiff complied with all the conditions, covenants and promises and stood ready to complete the performance, and that defendant breached and "anticipatorily repudiated" the contract. It denies, however, that any money is due to plaintiff either under the contract or as a result of its breach, and pleads as an affirmative defense to both causes of action plaintiff's allegedly deliberate failure to mitigate damages, asserting that she unreasonably refused to accept its offer of the leading role in "Big Country."

Plaintiff moved for summary judgment under Code of Civil Procedure section 437c, the motion was granted, and summary judgment for $750,000 plus interest was entered in plaintiff's favor. This appeal by defendant followed.

The familiar rules are that the matter to be determined by the trial court on a motion for summary judgment is whether facts have been presented which give rise to a triable factual issue. The court may not pass upon the issue itself. Summary judgment is proper only if the affidavits or declarations in support of the moving party would be sufficient to sustain a judgment in his favor and his opponent does not by affidavit show facts sufficient to present a triable issue of fact. The affidavits of the moving party are strictly construed, and doubts as to the propriety of summary judgment should be resolved against granting the motion. Such summary procedure is drastic and should be used with caution so that it does not become a substitute for the open trial method of determining facts. The moving party cannot depend upon allegations in his own pleadings to cure deficient affidavits, nor can his adversary rely upon his own pleadings in lieu or in support of affidavits in opposition to a motion; however, a party can rely on his adversary's pleadings to establish facts not contained in his own affidavits. [Citations.] Also, the court may consider facts stipulated to by the parties and facts which are properly the subject of judicial notice. [Citations.]

* * *

Applying the foregoing rules to the record in the present case, with all intendments in favor of the party opposing the summary judgment motion—here, defendant—it is clear that the trial court correctly ruled that plaintiff's failure to accept defendant's tendered substitute employment could not be applied in mitigation of damages because the offer of the "Big Country" lead was of employment both different and inferior, and that no factual dispute was presented on that issue. The mere circumstance that "Bloomer Girl" was to be a musical review calling upon plaintiff's talents as a dancer as well as an actress, and was to be produced in the City of Los Angeles, whereas "Big Country" was a straight dramatic role in a "Western type" story taking place in an opal mine in Australia, demonstrates the difference in kind between the two employments; the female lead as a dramatic actress in a western style motion picture can by no stretch of imagination be considered the equivalent of or substantially similar to the lead in a song-and-dance production.

Additionally, the substitute "Big Country" offer proposed to eliminate or impair the director and screenplay approvals accorded to plaintiff under the original "Bloomer Girl" contract * * * and thus constituted an offer of inferior employment. No expertise or judicial notice is required in order to hold that the deprivation or infringement of an employee's rights held under an original employment contract converts the available "other employment" relied upon by the employer to mitigate damages, into inferior employment which the employee need not seek or accept. [Citation.]

* * *

The judgment is affirmed.

CASE 3-4

Arbitration
DIRECTV, INC. v. IMBURGIA
Supreme Court of the United States, 2015
577 U.S. ____, 136 S.Ct. 463, 193 L.Ed. 365

Breyer, J.

DIRECTV, Inc., the petitioner [defendant], entered into a service agreement with its customers, including respondents [plaintiffs] Amy Imburgia and Kathy Greiner. Section 9 of that contract provides that "any Claim either of us asserts will be resolved only by binding arbitration." [Citation.] It then sets forth a waiver of class arbitration, stating that "[n]either you nor we shall be entitled to join or consolidate claims in arbitration." [Citation.] It adds that if the "law of your state" makes the waiver of class arbitration unenforceable, then the entire arbitration provision "is unenforceable." [Citation.] Section 10 of the contract states that §9, the arbitration provision, "shall be governed by the Federal Arbitration Act." [Citation.]

In 2008, the two respondents brought this lawsuit against DIRECTV in a California state court. They seek damages for early termination fees that they believe violate California law. * * * DIRECTV, pointing to the arbitration provision, asked the court to send the matter to arbitration. The state trial court denied that request, and DIRECTV appealed.

The California Court of Appeal thought that the critical legal question concerned the meaning of the contractual phrase "law of your state," in this case the law of California. * * *

At one point, the law of California would have made the contract's class-arbitration waiver unenforceable. In 2005, the California Supreme Court held in *Discover Bank v. Superior Court*, [citation], that a "waiver" of class arbitration in a "consumer contract of adhesion" that "predictably involve[s] small amounts of damages" and meets certain other criteria not contested here is "unconscionable under California law and should not be enforced." [Citations.] But in 2011, this Court held that California's *Discover Bank* rule "'stands as an obstacle to the accomplishment and execution of the full purposes and objectives of Congress'" embodied in the Federal Arbitration Act. *AT&T Mobility LLC* v. *Concepcion*, [citations]. The Federal Arbitration Act therefore pre-empts and invalidates that rule. [Citations.]

The California Court of Appeal subsequently held in this case that, despite this Court's holding in *Concepcion*, "the law of California would find the class action waiver unenforceable." [Citation.] The court noted that *Discover Bank* had held agreements to dispense with class-arbitration procedures unenforceable under circumstances such as these. [Citation.] It conceded that this Court in *Concepcion* had held that the Federal Arbitration Act invalidated California's rule. [Citation.] But it then concluded that this latter circumstance did not change the result—that the "class action waiver is unenforceable under California law." [Citation.]

* * *

The court reasoned that just as the parties were free in their contract to refer to the laws of different States or different nations, so too were they free to refer to California law as it would have been without this Court's holding invalidating the *Discover Bank* rule. The court thought that the parties in their contract had done just that. And it set forth two reasons for believing so.

First, §10 of the contract, stating that the Federal Arbitration Act governs §9 (the arbitration provision), is a *general* provision. But the provision voiding arbitration if the "law of your state" would find the class-arbitration waiver unenforceable is a *specific* provision. The court believed that the specific provision "'is paramount to'" and must govern the general. [Citation.]

Second, the court said that "'a court should construe ambiguous language against the interest of the party that drafted it.'" [Citation.] DIRECTV had drafted the language; to void the arbitration provision was against its interest. Hence the arbitration provision was void. The Court of Appeal consequently affirmed the trial court's denial of DIRECTV's motion to enforce the arbitration provision.

The California Supreme Court denied discretionary review. [Citation.] DIRECTV then filed a petition for a writ of certiorari, noting that the Ninth Circuit had reached the opposite conclusion on precisely the same interpretive question decided by the California Court of Appeal. [Citation.] We granted the petition.

No one denies that lower courts must follow this Court's holding in *Concepcion*. The fact that *Concepcion* was a closely divided case, resulting in a decision from which four Justices dissented, has no bearing on that undisputed obligation. Lower court judges are certainly free to note their disagreement with a decision of this Court. But the "Supremacy Clause forbids state courts to dissociate themselves from federal law because of disagreement with its content or a refusal to recognize the superior authority of its source." [Citation.] The Federal Arbitration Act is a law of the United States, and *Concepcion* is an authoritative interpretation of that Act. Consequently, the judges of every State must follow it. [Citation.]

While all accept this elementary point of law, that point does not resolve the issue in this case. As the Court of Appeal noted, the Federal Arbitration Act allows parties to an arbitration contract considerable latitude to choose what law governs some or all of its provisions, including the law governing enforceability of a class-arbitration waiver. [Citation.] In principle, they might choose to have portions of their contract governed by the law of Tibet, the law of prerevolutionary Russia, or (as is relevant here) the law of California including the *Discover Bank* rule and irrespective of that rule's invalidation in *Concepcion*. The Court of Appeal decided that, as a matter of contract law, the parties did mean the phrase "law of your state" to refer to this last possibility. Since the interpretation of a contract is ordinarily a matter of state law to which we defer, [citation], we must decide not whether its decision is a correct statement of California law but whether (assuming it is) that state law is consistent with the Federal Arbitration Act.

Although we may doubt that the Court of Appeal has correctly interpreted California law, we recognize that California courts are the ultimate authority on that law. While recognizing this, we must decide whether the decision of the California court places arbitration contracts "on equal footing with all other contracts." [Citation.] And in doing so, we must examine whether the Court of Appeal's decision in fact rests upon "grounds as exist at law or in equity for the revocation of any contract." [Federal Arbitration Act, §2.] That is to say, we look not to grounds that the California court might have offered but rather to those it did in fact offer. * * *

We recognize * * * that when DIRECTV drafted the contract, the parties likely believed that the words "law of your state" included California law that then made class-arbitration waivers unenforceable. But that does not answer the legal question before us. That is because this Court subsequently held in *Concepcion* that the *Discover Bank* rule was invalid. Thus the underlying question of contract law at the time the Court of Appeal made its decision was whether the "law of your state" included *invalid* California law. * * * After examining the grounds upon which the Court of Appeal rested its decision, we conclude that California courts would not interpret contracts other than arbitration contracts the same way. Rather, several considerations lead us to conclude that the court's interpretation of this arbitration contract is unique, restricted to that field.

* * *

* * * California's interpretation of the phrase "law of your state" does not place arbitration contracts "on equal footing with all other contracts," [Citation.] For that reason, it does not give "due regard ... to the federal policy favoring arbitration." [Citation.] Thus, the Court of Appeal's interpretation is pre-empted by the Federal Arbitration Act. [Citation.] Hence, the California Court of Appeal must "enforc[e]" the arbitration agreement. [Citation.]

The judgment of the California Court of Appeal is reversed, and the case is remanded for further proceedings not inconsistent with this opinion.

QUESTIONS

1. On June 15, a newspaper columnist predicted that the coast of State X would be flooded on the following September 1. Relying on this pronouncement, Gullible quit his job and sold his property at a loss so as not to be financially ruined. When the flooding did not occur, Gullible sued the columnist in a State X court for damages. The court dismissed the case for failure to state a cause of action under applicable State law. On appeal, the State X Supreme Court upheld the lower court. Three months after this ruling, the State Y Supreme Court heard an appeal in which a lower court had ruled that a reader could sue a columnist for falsely predicting flooding.

   a. Must the State Y Supreme Court follow the ruling of the State X Supreme Court as a matter of *stare decisis*?

   b. Should the State Y lower court have followed the ruling of the State X Supreme Court until the State Y Supreme Court issued a ruling on the issue?

   c. Once the State X Supreme Court issued its ruling, could the U.S. Supreme Court overrule the State X Supreme Court?

   d. If the State Y Supreme Court and the State X Supreme Court rule in exactly opposite ways, must the U.S. Supreme Court resolve the conflict between the two courts?

2. State Senator Bowdler convinced the legislature of State Z to pass a law requiring all professors to submit their class notes and transparencies to a board of censors to be sure that no "lewd" materials were presented to students at State universities. Professor Rabelais would like to challenge this law as violating his First Amendment rights under the U.S. Constitution.

   a. May Professor Rabelais challenge this law in the State Z courts?

   b. May Professor Rabelais challenge this law in a Federal district court?

3. While driving his car in Virginia, Carpe Diem, a resident of North Carolina, struck Butt, a resident of Alaska. As a result of the accident, Butt suffered more than $80,000 in medical expenses. Butt would like to know, if he personally serves the proper papers to Diem, whether he can obtain jurisdiction against Diem for damages in the following courts:

   a. Alaska State trial court

   b. U.S. Court of Appeals for the Ninth Circuit (includes Alaska)

   c. Virginia State trial court

   d. Virginia Federal district court

   e. U.S. Court of Appeals for the Fourth Circuit (includes Virginia and North Carolina)

   f. Virginia equity court

   g. North Carolina State trial court

4. Sam Simpleton, a resident of Kansas, and Nellie Naive, a resident of Missouri, each bought $85,000 in stock at local offices in their home States from Evil Stockbrokers, Inc. ("Evil"), a business incorporated in Delaware, with its principal place of business in Kansas. Both Simpleton and Naive believe that they were cheated by Evil Stockbrokers and would like to sue Evil for fraud. Assuming that no Federal question is at issue, assess the accuracy of the following statements:

   a. Simpleton can sue Evil in a Kansas State trial court.

   b. Simpleton can sue Evil in a Federal district court in Kansas.

   c. Naive can sue Evil in a Missouri State trial court.

   d. Naive can sue Evil in a Federal district court in Missouri.

5. The Supreme Court of State A ruled that under the law of State A, pit bull owners must either keep their dogs fenced or pay damages to anyone bitten by the dogs. Assess the accuracy of the following statements:

   a. It is likely that the U.S. Supreme Court would issue a writ of *certiorari* in the "pit bull" case.

   b. If a case similar to the "pit bull" case were to come before the Supreme Court of State B in the future, the doctrine of *stare decisis* would leave the court no choice but to rule the same way as the "pit bull" case.

6. The Supreme Court of State G decided that the U.S. Constitution requires professors to warn students of their right to remain silent before questioning the students about cheating. This ruling directly conflicts with a decision of the U.S. Court of Appeals for the circuit that includes State G.

   a. Must the U.S. Circuit Court of Appeals withdraw its ruling?

   b. Must the Supreme Court of State G withdraw its ruling?

7. Thomas Clements brought an action to recover damages for breach of warranty against defendant Signa Corporation. (A warranty is an obligation that the seller of goods assumes with respect to the quality of the goods sold.) Clements had purchased a motorboat from Barney's Sporting Goods, an Illinois corporation. The boat was manufactured by Signa Corporation, an Indiana corporation with its principal place of business in Decatur, Indiana. Signa has no office in Illinois and no agent authorized to do business on its behalf within Illinois. Clements saw Signa's boats on display at the Chicago Boat Show. In addition, literature on Signa's boats was distributed at the Chicago Boat Show. Several boating magazines, delivered to Clements in Illinois, contained advertisements for Signa's boats. Clements also had seen Signa's boats on display at Barney's Sporting Goods Store in Palatine, Illinois, where he eventually purchased the boat. A written warranty issued by Signa was delivered to Clements in Illinois. Although Signa was served with a summons, it failed to enter an appearance in this case. The court entered a default order and, subsequently, a judgment of $6,220 against Signa. Signa appealed. Decision?

8. Mariana Deutsch worked as a knitwear mender and attended a school for beauticians. The sink in her apartment collapsed on her foot, fracturing her big toe and making it painful for her to stand. She claims that as a consequence of the injury she was compelled to abandon her plans to become a beautician because that job requires long periods of standing. She also asserts that she was unable to work at her current job for a month. She filed a tort claim against her landlord, Hewes Street Realty, for negligence in failing to maintain the sink properly. She brought the suit in Federal district court, claiming damages of $25,000. Her medical expenses and actual loss of salary were less than $1,500; the rest of her alleged damages were for loss of future earnings as a beautician. Hewes Street moved to dismiss the suit on the basis that Deutsch's claim fell short of the jurisdictional requirement, which then was $10,000, and that the Federal court therefore lacked subject matter jurisdiction over her claim. Decision?

9. Vette sued Aetna under a fire insurance policy. Aetna moved for summary judgment on the basis that the pleadings and discovered evidence showed a lack of an insurable interest in Vette. (An "insurable interest" exists where the insured derives a monetary benefit or advantage from the preservation or continued existence of the property or would sustain an economic loss from its destruction.) Aetna provided ample evidence to infer that Vette had no insurable interest in the contents of the burned building. Vette also provided sufficient evidence to put in dispute this factual issue. The trial court granted the motion for summary judgment. Vette appealed. Decision?

10. Mark Womer and Brian Perry were members of the U.S. Navy and were stationed in Newport, Rhode Island. On April 10, Womer allowed Perry to borrow his automobile so that Perry could visit his family in New Hampshire. Later that day, while operating Womer's vehicle, Perry was involved in an accident in Manchester, New Hampshire. As a result of the accident, Tzannetos Tavoularis was injured. Tavoularis brought action against Womer in a New Hampshire superior court, contending that Womer was negligent in lending the automobile to Perry when he knew or should have known that Perry did not have a valid driver's license. Womer sought to dismiss the action on the ground that the New Hampshire courts lacked jurisdiction over him, citing the following facts: (a) he lived and worked in Georgia, (b) he had no relatives in New Hampshire, (c) he neither owned property nor possessed investments in New Hampshire, and (d) he had never conducted business in New Hampshire. Did the New Hampshire courts have jurisdiction?

11. Kenneth Thomas brought suit against his former employer, Kidder, Peabody & Company, and two of its employees, Barclay Perry and James Johnston, in a dispute over commissions on sales of securities. When he applied to work at Kidder, Peabody & Company, Thomas had filled out a form, which contained an arbitration agreement clause. Thomas had also registered with the New York Stock Exchange (NYSE). Rule 347 of the NYSE provides that any controversy between a registered representative and a member company shall be settled by arbitration. Kidder, Peabody & Company is a member of the NYSE. Thomas refused to arbitrate, relying on Section 229 of the California Labor Code, which provides that actions for the collection of wages may be maintained "without regard to the existence of any private agreement to arbitrate." Perry and Johnston filed a petition in a California State court to compel arbitration under Section 2 of the Federal Arbitration Act. Should the petition of Perry and Johnston be granted?

12. Steven Gwin bought a lifetime termite protection plan for his home from the local office of Allied-Bruce, a franchisee of Terminix International Company. The plan provided that Allied-Bruce would "protect" Gwin's house against termite infestation, reinspect periodically, provide additional treatment if necessary, and repair damage caused by new termite infestations. Terminix International guaranteed the fulfillment of these contractual provisions. The plan also provided that all disputes arising out of the contract would be settled exclusively by arbitration. Four years later Gwin had Allied-Bruce reinspect the house in anticipation of selling it. Allied-Bruce gave the house a "clean bill of health." Gwin then sold the house and transferred the Termite Protection Plan to Dobson. Shortly thereafter, Dobson found the

house to be infested with termites. Allied-Bruce attempted to treat and repair the house, using materials from out of state, but these efforts failed to satisfy Dobson. Dobson then sued Gwin, Allied-Bruce, and Terminix International in an Alabama state court. Allied-Bruce and Terminix International asked for a stay of these proceedings until arbitration could be carried out as stipulated in the contract. The trial court refused to grant the stay. The Alabama Supreme Court upheld that ruling, citing a state statute that makes predispute arbitration agreements unenforceable. The court found that the Federal Arbitration Act, which preempts conflicting state law, did not apply to this contract because its connection to interstate commerce was too slight. Was the Alabama Supreme Court correct? Explain.

13. Eddie Lee Howard and Shane D. Schneider worked for Nitro-Lift Technologies LLC. As a condition of employment, they entered into confidentiality and noncompetition agreements that contained a clause requiring any dispute between Nitro-Lift and its employees to be settled in arbitration. After working for Nitro-Lift on wells in Oklahoma, Texas, and Arkansas, the plaintiffs quit and began working for one of Nitro-Lift's competitors. Claiming that the plaintiffs had breached their noncompetition agreements, Nitro-Lift served them with a demand for arbitration. The plaintiffs then filed suit in the District Court of Johnston County, Oklahoma, asking the court to declare the noncompetition agreements null and void and to enjoin their enforcement. The court dismissed the complaint, finding that the contracts contained valid arbitration clauses under which an arbitrator, and not the court, must settle the parties' disagreement. On appeal, the Oklahoma Supreme Court reversed, holding that despite the "[U.S.] Supreme Court

cases on which the employers rely," the "existence of an arbitration agreement in an employment contract does not prohibit judicial review of the underlying agreement." Finding that the arbitration clauses were no obstacle to its review, the Oklahoma Supreme Court held that the noncompetition agreements were "void and unenforceable as against Oklahoma's public policy," expressed in an Oklahoma statute. Did the Oklahoma Supreme Court err in preventing the arbitration of the noncompetition agreement?

14. Llexcyiss Omega and D. Dale York, both residents of Indiana, jointly listed a Porsche automobile for sale on eBay, a popular auction website. The listing stated that the vehicle was located in Indiana and that the winning bidder would be responsible for arranging and paying for delivery of the vehicle. The Attaways, residents of Idaho, entered a bid of $5,000 plus delivery costs. After being notified that they had won the auction, the Attaways submitted payment to Omega and York through PayPal, which charged the amount to the Attaways' Master-Card account. The Attaways arranged for CarHop USA, a Washington-based auto transporter, to pick up the Porsche in Indiana and deliver it to their Idaho residence. After taking delivery of the Porsche, the Attaways filed a claim with PayPal, asking for a refund of its payment to Omega and York because the Porsche was "significantly not-as-described" in its eBay listing. PayPal informed the Attaways via email that their claim was denied. The Attaways convinced MasterCard to rescind the payment that had been made to Omega and York. Omega and York filed suit against the Attaways in small claims court in Indiana, demanding $5,900 in damages. Explain whether the Indiana courts have jurisdiction over the Attaways.

TAKING SIDES

John Connelly suffered personal injuries when a tire manufactured by Uniroyal failed while his 1969 Opel Kadett was being operated on a highway in Colorado. Connelly's father had purchased the automobile from a Buick dealer in Evanston, Illinois. The tire bore the name "Uniroyal" and the legend "made in Belgium" and was manufactured by Uniroyal, sold in Belgium to General Motors, and subsequently installed on the Opel when it was assembled at a General Motors plant in Belgium. The automobile was shipped to the United States for distribution by General Motors. It appears that between 1968 and 1971, more than four thousand Opels imported into the United States from Antwerp, Belgium, were delivered to dealers in Illinois each year; that in each of those years, between 600 and 1,320 of the Opels delivered to Illinois dealers were equipped with tires manufactured by Uniroyal; and that the estimated number of Uniroyal tires mounted on Opels delivered in Illinois within each of those

years ranged from 3,235 to 6,630. Connelly brought suit in Illinois against Uniroyal to recover damages for personal injuries. Uniroyal asserted that it was not subject to the jurisdiction of the Illinois courts because it is not registered to do business and has never had an agent, an employee, a representative, or a salesperson in Illinois; that it has never possessed or controlled any land or maintained any office or telephone listing in Illinois; that it has never sold or shipped any products into Illinois, either directly or indirectly; and that it has never advertised in Illinois.

a. What arguments could Connelly make in support of its claim that Illinois courts have jurisdiction over Uniroyal?

b. What arguments could Uniroyal make in support of its claim that Illinois courts do not have jurisdiction over it?

c. Who should prevail? Explain.

CHAPTER 4

Constitutional Law

CHAPTER OUTCOMES

After reading and studying this chapter, you should be able to:

- Explain the basic principles of constitutional law.

- Describe the sources and extent of the power of the Federal and State governments to regulate business and commerce.

- Distinguish the three levels of scrutiny used by the courts to determine the constitutionality of government action.

- Explain the effect of the First Amendment on (1) corporate political speech, (2) commercial speech, and (3) defamation.

- Explain the difference between substantive and procedural due process.

As mentioned in *Chapter 1*, public law is that branch of substantive law that deals with the rights and powers of government in its political or governing capacity and in its relation to individuals or groups. Public law consists of constitutional law, administrative law, and criminal law. The first is discussed in this chapter; *Chapter 5* addresses administrative law, and *Chapter 6* covers criminal law.

As the fundamental and organic law of particular jurisdictions, constitutions serve a number of critical functions. They are the supreme law of their respective jurisdictions. In addition, they establish the structure of and allocate power among the various levels of government. They also impose restrictions upon the powers of government and enumerate the rights and liberties of the people.

The Constitution of the United States (reprinted in *Appendix A*) was adopted on September 17, 1787, by representatives of the thirteen newly created States. Its purpose is stated in the preamble:

> We the People of the United States, in Order to form a more perfect Union, establish Justice, insure domestic Tranquility, provide for the common defence, promote the general Welfare, and secure the Blessings of Liberty to ourselves and our Posterity, do ordain and establish this Constitution for the United States of America.

Although the framers of the U.S. Constitution enumerated precisely what rights and authority were vested in the new national government, they considered it unnecessary to list those liberties the people were to reserve for themselves. As Alexander Hamilton, a coauthor of *The Federalist*, explained, "Here in strictness the people surrender nothing; and as they retain everything, they have no need of particular reservations." Nonetheless, during the State conventions to ratify the Constitution, people expressed fear that the Federal government might abuse its powers. To calm these concerns, the first Congress approved ten amendments to the U.S. Constitution, now known as the Bill of Rights, which were adopted on December 15, 1791.

The Bill of Rights restricts the powers and authority of the Federal government and establishes many of the civil and political rights enjoyed in the United States, including the right to due process of law and freedoms of speech, press, religion, assembly, and petition. Although the Bill of Rights does not apply directly to the States, the Supreme Court has held that the Fourteenth Amendment incorporates most of the principal guarantees of the Bill of Rights, thus making them applicable to the States.

This chapter discusses constitutional law as it applies to business and commerce. It begins by surveying some of the basic principles of constitutional law. Then it examines the allocation of power between the Federal and State governments with respect to the regulation of business. Finally, it discusses the constitutional restrictions on the power of government to regulate business.

4-1 Basic Principles of Constitutional Law

The delegates to the constitutional convention desired a stronger national government but feared the accumulation of government power in the hands of one person or group. These two concerns underlie several principles basic to the U.S. Constitution: Federalism, Federal supremacy, judicial review, and separation of powers. An additional basic principle of constitutional law is State action.

4-1a FEDERALISM

Federalism is the division of governing power between the Federal government and the States. The U.S. Constitution enumerates the powers of the Federal government and specifically reserves to the States or the people the powers it does not expressly delegate to the Federal government. Accordingly, the Federal government is a government of enumerated, or limited, powers, and a specified power must authorize each of its acts. The doctrine of enumerated powers does not, however, significantly limit the Federal government because a number of the enumerated powers, in particular the power to regulate interstate and foreign commerce, have been broadly interpreted.

Furthermore, the Constitution grants Congress not only specified powers but also the power "[t]o make all Laws which shall be necessary and proper for carrying into Execution the foregoing Powers, and all other Powers vested by this Constitution in the Government of the United States, or in any Department or Officer thereof." In the Supreme Court's view, the Necessary and Proper Clause enables Congress to legislate in areas not mentioned in the list of enumerated powers as long as such legislation reasonably relates to some enumerated power. As Chief Justice John Marshall noted in the landmark case of *McCulloch v. Maryland*, 17 U.S. (4 Wheat.) 316 (1819), "[l]et the end be legitimate, let it be within the scope of the constitution, and all means which are appropriate, which are plainly adapted to that end, which are not prohibited, but consist with the letter and spirit of the constitution, are constitutional."

4-1b FEDERAL SUPREMACY AND PREEMPTION

Although under the U.S. Federalist system the States retain significant powers, the **Supremacy Clause** of the U.S. Constitution provides that within its own sphere, Federal law is supreme and State law must, in case of conflict, yield. Accordingly, any State constitutional provision or law that conflicts with the U.S. Constitution or valid Federal laws or treaties is unconstitutional and may not be given effect. In *McCulloch v. Maryland*, Chief Justice Marshall stated, "This great principle is, that the Constitution and the laws made in pursuance thereof are supreme; that they control the Constitution and laws of the respective states, and cannot be controlled by them."

♦ *See Case 3-4*

Under the Supremacy Clause, whenever Congress enacts legislation within its constitutional powers, the Federal action **preempts** (overrides) any conflicting State legislation. Even a State regulation that is not obviously in conflict must give way if Congress clearly has intended that its enactment should preempt the field. In such an instance, nonconflicting State legislation would be prohibited. This intent may be stated expressly in the legislation or inferred from the pervasiveness of the Federal regulation, the need for uniformity, or the danger of conflict between concurrent Federal and State regulation.

When Congress has *not* intended to displace all State legislation, nonconflicting State legislation is permitted. State legislation is conflicting if (1) compliance with both State and Federal law is impossible or (2) the State law "stands as an obstacle to the accomplishment and execution of the full purposes and objectives of Congress."

When Congress has not acted, the fact that it has the power to act does not prevent the States from acting. Until Congress exercises its power to preempt, State regulation is permitted.

♦ *See Case 4-1*

4-1c JUDICIAL REVIEW

Judicial review describes the process by which the courts examine government actions to determine whether they conform to the U.S. Constitution. If government action violates the U.S. Constitution, under judicial review, the courts will invalidate that action. Judicial review extends to legislation, acts of the executive branch, and the decisions of inferior courts. Such review scrutinizes actions of both the Federal and State governments and applies to both the same standards of constitutionality. The U.S. Supreme Court is the final authority as to the constitutionality of any Federal and State law. The U.S. Constitution does not expressly provide for judicial review, but in 1803, Chief Justice John Marshall, speaking for the Court, declared the existence of such authority in the landmark case of *Marbury v. Madison*, 5 U.S. (1 Cranch) 137 (1803).

4-1d SEPARATION OF POWERS

Another fundamental principle on which the U.S. government is founded is that of separation of powers. The U.S. Constitution vests power in three distinct and independent branches of government: the executive, legislative, and judicial branches. The doctrine of separation of powers prevents excessive power from concentrating in any group or branch of government. Basically, the legislative branch is granted the power to make the law, the executive branch to enforce the law, and the judicial branch to interpret the law. The separation of powers is not complete, however, and in some instances, two or more branches share power. For example, the executive branch has veto power over legislation enacted by Congress, the legislative branch must approve many executive appointments, and the judicial branch may declare both legislation and executive actions unconstitutional. Nevertheless, shared powers usually operate as checks and balances on the power of the branches sharing them.

♦ **SEE FIGURE 4-1:** *Separation of Powers: Checks and Balances*

4-1e STATE ACTION

Most of the protections provided by the U.S. Constitution and its amendments apply only to Federal or State government action, collectively referred to as state action. Only the Thirteenth Amendment, which abolishes slavery or involuntary servitude, applies to the actions of private individuals. By statute, however, the government may extend to private activity some or all of the protections that guard against state action. **State action** includes any actions of the Federal and State governments, as well as their subdivisions, such as city or county governments and agencies. For example, when a legislature, an executive officer, or a court takes some official action against an individual, state action has occurred.

In addition, action taken by private citizens may constitute state action if the State exercised coercive power over the challenged private action, encouraged the action significantly, or was substantially entangled with the action. For example, the Supreme Court found state action when the Supreme Court of Missouri ordered a lower court to enforce an agreement among white property owners that prohibited the transfer of their property to nonwhites. *Shelley v. Kraemer,* 334 U.S. 1 (1948). Moreover, if "private" individuals or entities engage in public functions, their actions may be considered state action subject to constitutional limitations. For example, in *Marsh v. Alabama,* 326 U.S. 501 (1946), the Supreme Court held that a company

town was subject to the First Amendment because the State had allowed the company to exercise all of the public functions and activities usually conducted by a town government. Since that case, the Supreme Court has been less willing to find state action based upon the performance of public functions by private entities; the Court now limits such findings to functions "traditionally exclusively reserved to the State." For instance, in *Jackson v. Metropolitan Edison Co.,* 419 U.S. 345 (1974), the Court held that a privately owned electric utility was *not* subject to the Due Process Clause, even though the State had granted the utility a monopoly, because operating a utility is *not* state action. In reaching this conclusion, the Court held that the fact that the State could have operated its own utilities did not make the activity of providing electric services state action.

♦ *See Case 4-2*

4-2 Powers of Government

As previously stated, the U.S. Constitution created a Federal government of enumerated powers. Moreover, as the Tenth Amendment declares, "[t]he powers not delegated to the United States by the Constitution, nor prohibited by it to the States, are reserved to the States respectively, or to the people." For example, not included in the powers given to Congress is the power to issue direct orders to the governments of the states, i.e., the power to control State lawmaking. This *anticommandeering doctrine* was applied by the U.S. Supreme Court to invalidate a Federal statute that prohibited States from authorizing sports gambling schemes. *Murphy v. National Collegiate Athletic Assn.,* 584 U. S. ____ (2018). Consequently, legislation Congress enacts must be based on a specified power granted to the Federal government by the Constitution or be reasonably necessary to carry out an enumerated power.

FIGURE 4-1 Separation of Powers: Checks and Balances

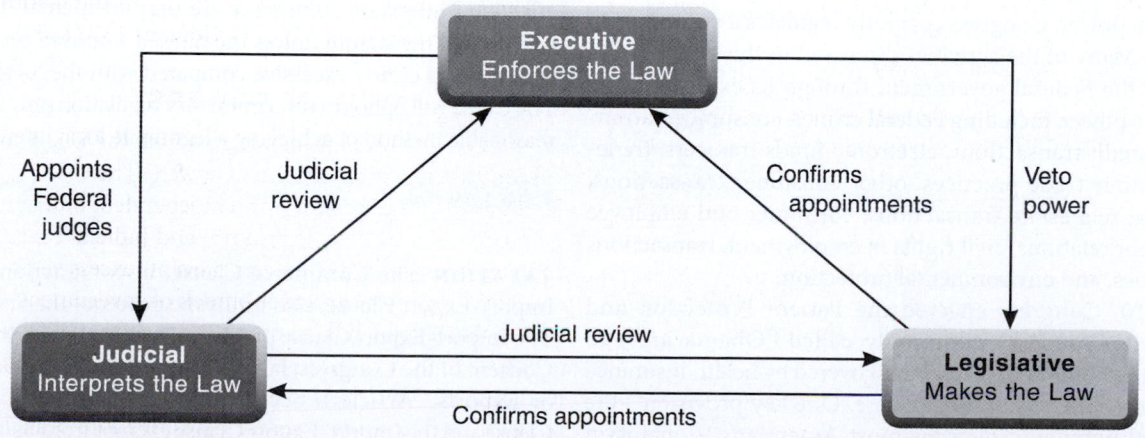

Some government powers may be exercised only by the Federal government. These exclusive Federal powers include the power to establish laws regarding bankruptcy, to establish post offices, to grant patents and copyrights, to coin currency, to wage war, and to enter into treaties. Other government powers are concurrent and may be exercised by both the Federal government and the States. Concurrent powers include taxation, spending, and the exercise of police power (regulation of public health, safety, and welfare).

This part of the chapter examines the sources and extent of the powers of the Federal government—as well as the residual power of the States—to regulate business and commerce.

4-2a   FEDERAL COMMERCE POWER

The U.S. Constitution provides that "[t]he Congress shall have Power … To regulate Commerce with foreign Nations, and among the several States." Article I, Section 8. This Commerce Clause has two important effects: (1) it provides the Federal government with a broad source of power for regulating the economy, and (2) it restricts State regulations that obstruct or unduly burden interstate commerce. As the U.S. Supreme Court has stated, "The Clause is both a prolific sourc[e] of national power and an equally prolific source of conflict with legislation of the state[s]." This section discusses the first of these effects; the next section discusses the second effect.

The U.S. Supreme Court interprets the Commerce Clause as granting virtually complete power to Congress to regulate the economy and business. More specifically, under the Commerce Clause, Congress has the power to regulate (1) the channels of interstate commerce, (2) the instrumentalities of interstate commerce, and (3) those activities having a substantial relation to interstate commerce. A court may invalidate legislation enacted under the Commerce Clause only if it is clear either that (1) there is no rational basis for a congressional finding that the regulated activity affects interstate commerce or (2) there is no reasonable connection between the selected regulatory means and the asserted ends.

Because of the broad and permissive interpretation of the commerce power, Congress currently regulates a vast range of activities. Many of the activities discussed in this text are regulated by the Federal government through its exercise of the commerce power, including Federal crimes, consumer warranties and credit transactions, electronic funds transfers, trademarks, unfair trade practices, other consumer transactions, residential real estate transactions, consumer and employee safety, labor relations, civil rights in employment, transactions in securities, and environmental protection.

In 2010, Congress enacted the Patient Protection and Affordable Care Act (commonly called "Obamacare") to increase the number of Americans covered by health insurance and decrease the cost of health care. One key provision—the *individual mandate*—requires most Americans to maintain "minimum essential" health insurance coverage or make a "shared responsibility payment" to the Federal government. The constitutionality of the individual mandate was challenged as beyond the commerce and taxing powers of Congress. In deciding the Commerce Clause question, the U.S. Supreme Court explained that the Commerce Clause presupposes the existence of commercial activity to be regulated:

> The individual mandate, however, does not regulate existing commercial activity. It instead compels individuals to *become* active in commerce by purchasing a product, on the ground that their failure to do so affects interstate commerce. Construing the Commerce Clause to permit Congress to regulate individuals precisely *because* they are doing nothing would open a new and potentially vast domain to congressional authority.

Accordingly, in a 5–4 vote, the Court held that the individual mandate was *not* a valid exercise of the commerce power. *National Federation of Independent Business v. Sebelius*, 567 U.S. 1 (2012). The Court's decision regarding the taxing power of Congress is covered later in this chapter.

4-2b   STATE REGULATION OF COMMERCE

The Commerce Clause, as previously discussed, specifically grants to Congress the power to regulate commerce among the States. In addition to acting as a broad source of Federal power, the clause also implicitly restricts the States' power to regulate activities if the result obstructs or unduly burdens interstate commerce.

REGULATIONS   The U.S. Supreme Court ultimately decides the extent to which State regulation may affect interstate commerce. In doing so, the Court weighs and balances several factors: (1) the necessity and importance of the State regulation, (2) the burden it imposes upon interstate commerce, and (3) the extent to which it discriminates against interstate commerce in favor of local concerns. The application of these factors involves case-by-case analysis. In general, in cases in which a State statute regulates evenhandedly to accomplish a legitimate State interest and its effects on interstate commerce are only incidental, the Court will uphold the statute unless the burden imposed on interstate commerce is clearly excessive compared with the local benefits. The Court will uphold a discriminatory regulation only if no other reasonable method of achieving a legitimate local interest exists.

♦ *See Case 4-3*

TAXATION   The Commerce Clause, in conjunction with the Import-Export Clause, also limits the power of the States to tax. The Import-Export Clause provides: "No State shall, without the Consent of the Congress, lay any Imposts or Duties on Imports or Exports." Article I, Section 10. Together, the Commerce Clause and the Import-Export Clause exempt from State taxation goods that have entered the stream of commerce, whether they are interstate or foreign, imports or exports. The purpose of this immunity is to protect goods in commerce from both discriminatory and cumulative State taxes. Once the goods enter the stream of interstate or foreign commerce, the power of the State to tax ceases and does not resume until the goods are delivered to the purchaser or the owner terminates the movement of the goods through commerce.

In applying the Commerce Clause to the validity of State taxes, the U.S. Supreme Court has held that a State may tax exclusively interstate commerce so long as it (1) applies to an activity with a substantial nexus with the taxing State, (2) is fairly apportioned, (3) does not discriminate against interstate commerce, and (4) is fairly related to the services the State provides. In a 5-4 decision addressing a Commerce Clause challenge, the U.S. Supreme Court upheld a South Dakota statute that required certain out-of-state sellers to collect and remit sales tax on goods sold to South Dakota consumers. This decision overruled earlier cases in which the Court had held that an out-of-state seller's liability to collect and remit the tax to the consumer's State depended on whether the seller had a physical presence in that State but that mere shipment of goods into the consumer's State did not constitute a physical presence in the consumer's State. *South Dakota v. Wayfair, Inc.*, 585 U. S. ____ (2018).

The Due Process Clause of the Fourteenth Amendment also restricts the power of States to tax. Under the Due Process Clause, for a State tax to be constitutional, sufficient nexus must exist between the State and the person, thing, or activity to be taxed.

4-2c FEDERAL FISCAL POWERS

The Federal government exerts a dominating influence over the national economy through its control of financial matters. Much of this impact, as previously discussed, results from the exercise of its regulatory powers under the Commerce Clause. In addition, the government derives substantial influence from powers that are independent of the Commerce Clause. These include (1) the power to tax, (2) the power to spend, (3) the power to borrow and coin money, and (4) the power of eminent domain.

TAXATION The Federal government's power to tax, although extremely broad, is subject to three major limitations: (1) direct taxes other than income taxes must be apportioned among the States, (2) all custom duties and excise taxes must be uniform throughout the United States, and (3) no duties may be levied upon exports from any State.

Besides raising revenues, taxes also have regulatory and socioeconomic effects. For example, import taxes and custom duties can protect domestic industry from foreign competition. Graduated or progressive tax rates and exemptions may further social policies seeking to redistribute wealth. Tax credits encourage investment in favored enterprises, to the disadvantage of unfavored ones. The Court will uphold a tax that does

more than just raise revenue "so long as the motive of Congress and the effect of its legislative action are to secure revenue for the benefit of the general government." *J.W. Hampton Co.* v. *United States*, 276 U.S. 394 (1928).

The Patient Protection and Affordable Care Act's individual mandate provision requires most Americans to maintain "minimum essential" health insurance coverage or make a "shared responsibility payment" to the Federal government. The constitutionality of the individual mandate was challenged as beyond the commerce and taxing powers of Congress. In deciding the taxing power question, in a 5–4 vote, the U.S. Supreme Court held that requiring certain individuals to "pay a financial penalty for not obtaining health insurance may reasonably be characterized as a tax. Because the Constitution permits such a tax, it is not our role to forbid it, or to pass upon its wisdom or fairness." *National Federation of Independent Business v. Sebelius*, 567 U.S. 1 (2012). In 2017, Congress repealed the individual mandate provision, effective in 2019.

SPENDING POWER The Constitution authorizes the Federal government to pay debts and to spend for the common defense and general welfare of the United States. Article I, Section 8. The spending power of Congress, which is extremely broad, will be upheld so long as it does not violate a specific constitutional limitation upon Federal power.

Furthermore, through its spending power, Congress may accomplish indirectly what it may not do directly. For example, in *South Dakota v. Dole*, 483 U.S. 203 (1987), the Supreme Court held that Congress could condition a State's receipt of Federal highway funds on that State's mandating twenty-one as the minimum drinking age, even though the Twenty-First Amendment grants the States significant powers with respect to alcohol consumption within their respective borders. As the Court noted, "Constitutional limitations on Congress when exercising its spending power are less exacting than those on its authority to regulate directly."

BORROWING AND COINING MONEY The U.S. Constitution also grants Congress the power to borrow money on the credit of the United States and to coin money. Article I, Section 8. These two powers have enabled the Federal government to establish a national banking system, the Federal Reserve System, and specialized Federal lending programs such as the Federal Land Bank. Through these and other institutions and agencies, the Federal government wields extensive control over national fiscal and monetary policies and exerts considerable influence over interest rates, the money supply, and foreign exchange rates.

EMINENT DOMAIN The government's power to take private property for public use, known as the power of **eminent domain**, is recognized as one of the inherent powers of government in the U.S. Constitution and in the constitutions of the States. Nonetheless, the power is carefully limited. The

Fifth Amendment to the Constitution contains a Takings Clause that specifies that "nor shall private property be taken for public use, without just compensation." Although this amendment applies only to the Federal government, the Supreme Court has held that the Takings Clause is incorporated through the Fourteenth Amendment and is therefore applicable to the States. Moreover, similar or identical provisions are found in State constitutions.

As the language of the Takings Clause indicates, the taking must be for a public use. Public use has been held to be synonymous with public purpose. Thus, private entities such as railroads and housing authorities may use the government's power of eminent domain so long as the entity's use of the property benefits the public. When the government or a private entity properly takes property under the power of eminent domain, the owners of the property must receive just compensation, which has been interpreted as the fair market value of the property.

The U.S. Supreme Court has held that the Takings Clause requires just compensation only if a government taking actually occurs, not if government regulation only reduces the value of the property. If, however, a regulation deprives the owner of all economic use of the property, then a taking has occurred. Eminent domain is discussed further in *Chapter 49.*

◆ *See Case 49-2*

◆ **SEE FIGURE 4-2:** *Powers of Government*

4-3 Limitations on Government

The Constitution of the United States grants certain enumerated powers to the Federal government while reserving other powers, without enumeration, to the States. The Constitution and its amendments, however, impose limits on the powers of both the Federal government and the States. This part of the chapter discusses those limitations most applicable to business: (1) the Contract Clause, (2) the First Amendment, (3) due process, and (4) equal protection. The first of these—the Contract Clause—applies only to the actions of State governments, whereas the other three apply to both the Federal government and the States.

None of these restrictions operates as an absolute limitation, but instead triggers scrutiny by the courts to determine whether the government power exercised encroaches impermissibly upon the interest the Constitution protects. The U.S. Supreme Court has used different levels of scrutiny, depending on the interest affected and the nature of the government action. Although the Court has differentiated levels of scrutiny most thoroughly in the area of equal protection, such differentiation also occurs in other areas, including substantive due process and protection of free speech.

The least rigorous level of scrutiny is the **rational relationship test**, which requires that government action conceivably bear some rational relationship to a legitimate government interest that the government action proposes to

---

FIGURE 4-2   **Powers of Government**

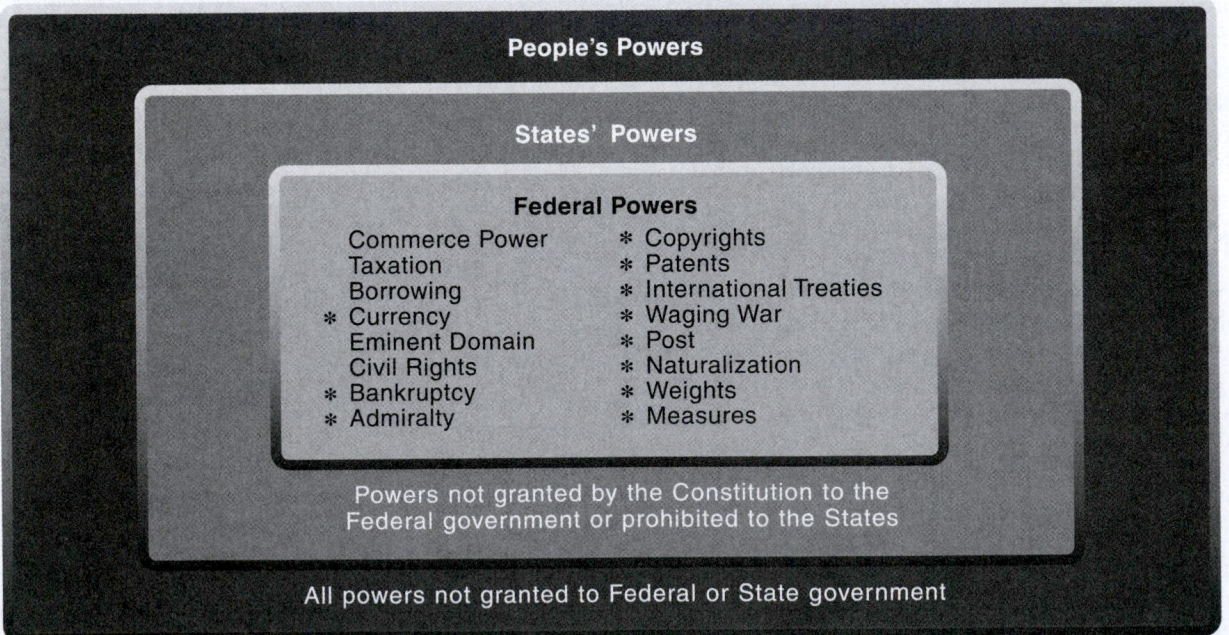

People's Powers

States' Powers

Federal Powers

Commerce Power	* Copyrights
Taxation	* Patents
Borrowing	* International Treaties
* Currency	* Waging War
Eminent Domain	* Post
Civil Rights	* Naturalization
* Bankruptcy	* Weights
* Admiralty	* Measures

Powers not granted by the Constitution to the Federal government or prohibited to the States

All powers not granted to Federal or State government

*Exclusive power

FIGURE 4-3	Limitations on Government		
Test/Interest	**Equal Protection**	**Substantive Due Process**	**Free Speech**
Strict Scrutiny	Fundamental rights Suspect classifications	Fundamental rights	Protected noncommercial speech
Intermediate	Gender Legitimacy		Commercial speech
Rational Relationship	Economic regulation	Economic regulation	Nonprotected speech

further. The most exacting level of scrutiny is the **strict scrutiny test**, which requires that the government action be necessary to promote a compelling government interest. Finally, under the **intermediate test**, the government action must have a substantial relationship to an important government objective. These standards will be explained more fully later.

◆ **SEE FIGURE 4-3:** *Limitations on Government*

4-3a CONTRACT CLAUSE

Article I, Section 10, of the Constitution provides: "No State shall … pass any … Law impairing the Obligation of Contracts." The U.S. Supreme Court has used this clause to restrict States from retroactively modifying public charters and private contracts. For example, the Contract Clause protects against impairing the charter of a corporation formed under a State incorporation statute. Although the Contract Clause does not apply to the Federal government, due process limits the Federal government's power to impair contracts.

Moreover, the U.S. Supreme Court has held that the Contract Clause does not preclude the States from exercising eminent domain or their police powers. As the Supreme Court stated, "No legislature can bargain away the public health or the public morals." *Stone v. Mississippi*, 101 U.S. (11 Otto) 814 (1879).

Practical Advice
The Federal Constitution protects you from a State law that impairs a preexisting contract.

4-3b FIRST AMENDMENT

The First Amendment states: "Congress shall make no law respecting an establishment of religion, or prohibiting the free exercise thereof; or abridging the freedom of speech, or of the press; or the right of the people peaceably to assemble, and to petition the Government for a redress of grievances."

The First Amendment's protection of free speech is not absolute. Some forms of speech, such as obscenity, receive no protection. Most forms of speech, however, are protected by the

strict or exacting scrutiny standard, which requires the existence of a compelling and legitimate State interest to justify a restriction of speech. In furthering such an interest, the State must use means that least restrict free speech.

◆ *See Case 4-4*

This section examines the application of the First Amendment's guarantee of free speech to (1) corporate political speech, (2) commercial speech, and (3) defamation.

CORPORATE POLITICAL SPEECH Freedom of speech is indispensable to the discovery and spread of political truth; indeed, "the best test of truth is the power of the thought to get itself accepted in the competition of the market." *Abrams v. United States*, 250 U.S. 616 (1919) (Holmes's dissent). To promote this competition of ideas, the First Amendment's guarantee of free speech applies not only to individuals but also to corporations. Accordingly, corporations may not be prohibited from speaking out on political issues. For example, in *First National Bank v. Bellotti*, 435 U.S. 765 (1978), the U.S. Supreme Court held unconstitutional a Massachusetts criminal statute that prohibited banks and business corporations from making contributions and expenditures with regard to most referenda issues. The Court in *Bellotti* held that if speech is otherwise protected, the fact that the speaker is a corporation does not alter the speech's protected status.

The Supreme Court retreated somewhat from its holding in *Bellotti* when it upheld a State statute prohibiting corporations, except media corporations, from using general treasury funds to make independent expenditures in elections for public office but permitting such expenditures from segregated funds used solely for political purposes. The Court held that the statute did not violate the First Amendment because the burden on corporations' exercise of political expression was justified by a compelling State interest in preventing corruption in the political arena: "the corrosive and distorting effects of immense aggregations of wealth that are accumulated with the help of the corporate form and that have little or no correlation to the public's support for the corporations' political ideas." The Court held that the statute was sufficiently narrowly tailored because it "is precisely targeted to eliminate the distortion caused by corporate spending while also allowing corporations to express their political views" by making expenditures through segregated funds. *Austin v. Michigan Chamber of Commerce*, 494 U.S. 652 (1990).

In a landmark 5–4 decision, *Citizens United v. Federal Election Commission*, 558 U.S. 310 (2010), the U.S. Supreme Court explicitly overruled the *Austin* case. *Citizens United* involved a First Amendment challenge to a Federal law that prohibited corporations and unions from using their general funds to make independent expenditures for speech defined as an "electioneering communication" or for speech expressly advocating the election or defeat of a candidate. (An electioneering communication is "any broadcast, cable, or satellite communication" that "refers to a clearly identified candidate for Federal office" and is made within thirty days of a primary election.) The Supreme Court invalidated these provisions as conflicting with the First Amendment, holding: "We return to the principle established in... *Bellotti* that the Government may not suppress political speech on the basis of the speaker's corporate identity. No sufficient government interest justifies limits on the political speech of nonprofit or for-profit corporations."

The ruling in *Citizens United*, however, did not apply to the two types of Federal statutory limits on direct contributions by individuals to Federal candidates and political parties. The first limit, called base limits, restricts how much money an individual may contribute to a particular candidate or committee. The second limit, called aggregate limits, restricts how much money an individual donor may contribute in total to all candidates or committees during a political cycle. In 2014, the U.S. Supreme Court considered a challenge to the aggregate limits in the case of *McCutcheon v. Federal Election Commission*, 572 U.S. 185. In a 5–4 decision, the Supreme Court invalidated the aggregate limits under the First Amendment. This decision did *not* involve any challenge to the base limits, which have been upheld previously as serving the permissible objective of combatting corruption. In addition, this decision concerned only contributions from *individuals*; Federal law continues to ban direct contributions by corporations and unions. Nevertheless, the *Citizens United* decision holds that political spending is a form of protected speech under the First Amendment and that the government may not prevent corporations or unions from spending money to advocate the election or defeat of a candidate.

COMMERCIAL SPEECH Commercial speech is expression related to the economic interests of the speaker and her audience, such as advertisements for a product or service. Since the mid-1970s, U.S. Supreme Court decisions have eliminated the doctrine that commercial speech is wholly outside the protection of the First Amendment. Instead, the Court has established the principle that speech proposing a commercial transaction is entitled to protection, which, though extensive, is less considerable than that accorded to political speech. Protection is accorded to commercial speech because of the interest such communication holds for the advertiser, consumer, and general public. Advertising and similar messages convey important information for the proper and efficient distribution of resources in a free market system. At the same time, commercial speech is less valuable and less vulnerable than other varieties of speech and therefore does not merit complete First Amendment protection.

In commercial speech cases, a four-part analysis has developed. First, the court must determine whether the expression is protected by the First Amendment. For commercial speech to come within that provision, such speech, at the least, must concern lawful activity and not be misleading. Second, the court must determine whether the asserted government interest is substantial. If both inquiries yield positive answers, then, third, the court must determine whether the regulation directly advances the government interest asserted and, fourth, whether or not the regulation is more extensive than is necessary to serve that interest. The Supreme Court recently held that government restrictions of commercial speech need not be absolutely the least severe so long as they are "narrowly tailored" to achieve the government objective.

In 2018, the U.S. Supreme Court applied the commercial speech standard to an Illinois law that requires public employees who choose not to join a union to "pay their proportionate share of the costs of the collective bargaining process, contract administration and pursuing matters affecting wages, hours and other conditions of employment." In a 5—4 decision, the Court ruled that this statute violates the free speech rights of nonmembers by compelling them to subsidize private speech on matters of substantial public concern. *Janus v. State, County, and Municipal Employees*, 585 U.S. ____.

Because the constitutional protection extended to commercial speech is based on the informational function of advertising, governments may regulate or suppress commercial messages that do not accurately inform the public about lawful activity. "The government may ban forms of communication more likely to deceive the public than to inform it, or commercial speech related to illegal activity." *Central Hudson Gas and Electric Corp. v. Public Service Commission*, 447 U.S. 557 (1980). Therefore, government regulation of false and misleading advertising is permissible under the First Amendment.

DEFAMATION Defamation is a civil wrong or tort that consists of disgracing or diminishing a person's reputation through the communication of a false statement. An example would be the publication of a false statement that a person had committed a crime or had a loathsome disease. For further discussion of defamation, see *Chapter 7*.

Because defamation involves a communication, it receives the protection extended to speech by the First Amendment. Moreover, in the case of *New York Times Co. v. Sullivan*, 376

U.S. 254 (1964), the U.S. Supreme Court held that a public official who was defamed in regard to his conduct, fitness, or role as public official could not recover in a defamation action unless the statement was made with *actual malice*, which requires clear and convincing proof that the defendant had knowledge of the falsity of the communication or acted in reckless disregard of its truth or falsity. This restriction upon the right to recover for defamation is based on "a profound national commitment to the principle that debate on public issues should be uninhibited, robust and wide-open, and that it may well include vehement, caustic and sometimes unpleasantly sharp attacks on government and public officials." The communication may deal with the official's qualifications for and his performance in office, which would likely include most aspects of character and public conduct.

In addition, the U.S. Supreme Court has extended the same rule to public figures and candidates for public office. The Supreme Court, however, has not precisely defined the term *public figure*. In a defamation suit brought by a private person (one who is neither a public official nor a public figure), the plaintiff must prove that the defendant published the defamatory and false comment with either malice *or* negligence.

4-3c DUE PROCESS

The Fifth and Fourteenth Amendments prohibit the Federal and State governments, respectively, from depriving any person of life, liberty, or property without due process of law. Due process has two different aspects: *substantive* due process and *procedural* due process. As discussed in *Chapter 1*, substantive law creates, defines, or regulates legal rights, whereas procedural law establishes the rules for enforcing those rights. Accordingly, **substantive due process** concerns the compatibility of a law or government action with fundamental constitutional rights such as free speech. In contrast, **procedural due process** involves the review of the decision-making process that enforces substantive laws and results in depriving a person of life, liberty, or property.

SUBSTANTIVE DUE PROCESS Substantive due process, which involves a court's determination of whether a particular government action is compatible with individual liberties, addresses the constitutionality of the substance of a legal rule, not the fairness of the process by which the rule is applied. Legislation affecting economic and social interests satisfies substantive due process so long as the legislation relates rationally to legitimate government objectives.

Nonetheless, courts will strictly scrutinize legislation that affects the fundamental rights of individuals under the Constitution to determine whether such legislation is necessary to promote a compelling or overriding government interest. Included among the fundamental rights that trigger the strict scrutiny standard of substantive due process are (1) the First Amendment rights of freedom of speech, religion, press, peaceful assembly, and petition; (2) the right to engage in interstate travel; (3) the right to vote; (4) the right to privacy; and (5) the right to marry. For example, the U.S. Supreme Court overturned the Federal Defense of Marriage Act (DOMA), which defines marriage as the union of a man and a woman for purposes of Federal benefits. DOMA thus denies Federal benefits to persons in same-sex marriages made lawful by some of the States. The Court held DOMA unconstitutional as a deprivation of the liberty of the person protected by the Fifth Amendment of the U.S. Constitution. *United States v. Windsor,* 570 U.S. 12 (2013).

Moreover, in a 5–4 decision, the U.S. Supreme Court held that the Due Process Clause of the Fourteenth Amendment requires a State to license a marriage between two people of the same sex and to recognize a marriage between two people of the same sex when their marriage was lawfully licensed and performed in another State. *Obergefell v. Hodges,* 576 U.S. ___ (2015).

◆ *See Case 7-1*

PROCEDURAL DUE PROCESS Procedural due process pertains to the government decision-making process that results in depriving a person of life, liberty, or property. As the Supreme Court has interpreted procedural due process, the government is required to provide an individual with a fair procedure if, but only if, the person faces deprivation of life, liberty, or property. When government action adversely affects an individual but does not deny life, liberty, or property, the government is not required to give the person any hearing at all.

Liberty, for the purposes of procedural due process, generally includes the ability of individuals to engage in freedom of action and choice regarding their personal lives. Any significant physical restraint constitutes a deprivation of liberty, which requires procedural safeguards. The most important and common examples of proceedings involving deprivation of liberty are criminal proceedings, discussed more fully in *Chapter 6*. In addition, civil proceedings that result in depriving a person of freedom of action are subject to the requirements of procedural due process. Liberty also includes an individual's right to engage in the fundamental rights described previously.

Property, for the purposes of procedural due process, includes not only all forms of real and personal property but also certain entitlements conferred by the government, such as social security payments and food stamps. In *Logan v. Zimmerman Brush Co.,* 455 U.S. 422 (1982), the Supreme Court stated, "The hallmark of property... is an individual entitlement grounded in state law, which cannot be removed except 'for cause.'" Under this interpretation of property, the Court has, for example, found protected property interests in high school education, when attendance is required; welfare benefits, when the individual has previously been found to meet the statutory requirements; social security payments; and a driver's license. On the other hand, if a public employee's job is terminable at any time, he has no property interest in his employment; accordingly, he may lose his job without any procedural due process protections.

When applicable, procedural due process requires that the procedure be fundamentally fair and impartial in resolving the factual and legal basis for the government actions that result in the deprivation of life, liberty, or property. The Supreme Court generally considers three factors in determining which procedures are required: the importance of the individual interest involved; the adequacy of the existing procedural protections and the probable value, if any, of additional safeguards; and the government interest in fiscal and administrative efficiency.

◆ *See Cases 3-2 and 7-1*

4-3d EQUAL PROTECTION

The Fourteenth Amendment states that "nor shall any State … deny to any person within its jurisdiction the equal protection of the laws." Although this amendment applies only to the actions of State governments, the Supreme Court has interpreted the Due Process Clause of the Fifth Amendment to subject Federal actions to the same standards of review. The most important constitutional concept protecting individual rights, the guarantee of equal protection requires that government action provide similar treatment for similarly situated persons.

For example, in a 5–4 decision, the U.S. Supreme Court held that the Equal Protection Clause of the Fourteenth Amendment requires a State to license a marriage between two people of the same sex and to recognize a marriage between two people of the same sex when their marriage was lawfully licensed and performed in another State. *Obergefell v. Hodges,* 576 U.S. ___ (2015).

When government action involves the classification of people, the equal protection guarantee comes into play. In determining whether government action satisfies the equal protection guarantee, the Supreme Court uses one of three standards of review, depending on the nature of the right involved: (1) the rational relationship test, (2) the strict scrutiny test, or (3) the intermediate test.

RATIONAL RELATIONSHIP TEST The rational relationship test, which applies to cases not subject to either the strict scrutiny test or the intermediate test, requires that the classification conceivably bear some rational relationship to a legitimate government interest that the classification proposes to further. Under this standard of review, government action is permitted to attack part of the evil to which the action is addressed. Moreover, there is a strong presumption that the

action is constitutional. Therefore, the courts will overturn the government action only if clear and convincing evidence shows that there is no reasonable basis justifying the action.

For example, the U.S. Supreme Court overturned the Federal Defense of Marriage Act (DOMA) also for violating the constitutional guarantee of equal protection. By defining marriage as the union of a man and a woman, DOMA denies Federal benefits to persons in same-sex marriages made lawful by some of the States. The Court held that DOMA denies equal protection of the laws, stating:

> The class to which DOMA directs its restrictions and restraints are those persons who are joined in same-sex marriages made lawful by the State. DOMA singles out a class of persons deemed by a State entitled to recognition and protection to enhance their own liberty. It imposes a disability on the class by refusing to acknowledge a status the State finds to be dignified and proper. DOMA instructs all federal officials, and indeed all persons with whom same-sex couples interact, including their own children, that their marriage is less worthy than the marriages of others. The federal statute is invalid, for no legitimate purpose overcomes the purpose and effect to disparage and to injure those whom the State, by its marriage laws, sought to protect in personhood and dignity. By seeking to displace this protection and treating those persons as living in marriages less respected than others, the federal statute is in violation of the Fifth Amendment. *United States v. Windsor,* 570 U.S. 12 (2013).

STRICT SCRUTINY TEST The strict scrutiny test is far more exacting than the rational relationship test. Under this test, the courts do not defer to the government; rather, they independently determine whether a classification of persons is constitutionally permissible. This determination requires that the classification be necessary to promote a compelling or overriding government interest.

The strict scrutiny test is applied when government action affects fundamental rights or involves suspect classifications. Fundamental rights include most of the provisions of the Bill of Rights and some other rights, such as interstate travel, voting, and access to criminal justice. Suspect classifications include those made on the basis of race or national origin. A classic and important example of strict scrutiny applied to classifications based upon race is the 1954 school desegregation case, *Brown v. Board of Education of Topeka,* 347 U.S. 483, in which the Supreme Court ruled that segregated public school systems violated the equal protection guarantee. Subsequently, the Court has invalidated segregation in public beaches, buses, parks, public golf courses, and courtroom seating.

A more recent U.S. Supreme Court case again addressed the application of strict scrutiny to public schools. School districts in Seattle, Washington, and metropolitan Louisville,

Kentucky, had voluntarily adopted student assignment plans that relied on race to determine which schools certain children may attend. In a 5–4 decision, the Court held that public school systems may not seek to achieve or maintain integration through measures that take explicit account of a student's race. The Court reaffirmed that when the government distributes burdens or benefits on the basis of individual racial classifications, that action is reviewed under strict scrutiny requiring the most exact connection between justification and classification. Therefore, the school districts must demonstrate that the use of individual racial classifications in their school assignment plans is narrowly tailored to achieve a compelling government interest. In reversing the lower courts' decisions upholding the schools' plans, the Court held: "The [school] districts have also failed to show that they considered methods other than explicit racial classifications to achieve their stated goals. Narrow tailoring requires 'serious, good faith consideration of workable race-neutral alternatives.'" *Parents Involved in Community Schools v. Seattle School District No. 1,* 551 U.S. 701 (2007).

Moreover, in reviewing the use of race by the University of Texas at Austin as one of various factors in its undergraduate admissions process, the U.S. Supreme Court held that strict scrutiny must be applied to any admissions program using racial categories or classifications. In this case, the Court reaffirmed that "all racial classifications imposed by government 'must be analyzed by a reviewing court under strict scrutiny.'" *Fisher v. University of Texas at Austin,* 570 U.S. 297 (2013).

In the case of *Schuette v. BAMN,* 572 U.S. 291 (2014), the U.S. Supreme Court in a 6–2 ruling upheld a Michigan constitutional amendment, approved and enacted by its voters, that bans affirmative action in admissions to the State's public universities. In holding that the amendment was *not* invalid under the Equal Protection Clause of the Fourteenth Amendment, the Supreme Court stated:

> In *Fisher* [*v. University of Texas at Austin*], the Court did not disturb the principle that the consideration of race in admissions is permissible, provided that certain conditions are met. In this case, as in *Fisher*, that principle is not challenged. The question here concerns not the permissibility of race-conscious admissions policies under the Constitution but whether, and in what manner, voters in the States may choose to prohibit the consideration of racial preferences in governmental decisions, in particular with respect to school admissions…. This case is not about how the debate about racial preferences should be resolved. It is about who may resolve it. There is no authority in the Constitution of the United States or in this Court's precedents for the Judiciary to set aside Michigan laws that commit this policy determination to the voters.

♦ *See Case 4-5*

INTERMEDIATE TEST An intermediate test applies to government action based on gender and legitimacy. Under this test, the classification must have a substantial relationship to an important government objective. The intermediate standard eliminates the strong presumption of constitutionality to which the rational relationship test adheres.

For example, in *Orr v. Orr,* 440 U.S. 268 (1979), the Court invalidated an Alabama law that allowed courts to grant alimony awards only from husbands to wives and not from wives to husbands. Similarly, in *Reed v. Reed,* 404 U.S. 71 (1971), where an Idaho statute gave preference to males over females in qualifying for selection as administrators of estates, the Court invalidated the statute because the preference did not bear a fair and substantial relationship to any legitimate legislative objective. More recently, the Court invalidated a State university's (Virginia Military Institute) admission policy excluding all women. *U.S. v. Virginia,* 518 U.S. 515 (1996). On the other hand, not all legislation based upon gender is invalid. For example, the Court has upheld a California statutory rape law that imposed penalties only upon males, as well as the Federal military selective service act, which exempted women from registering for the draft.

C H A P T E R   S U M M A R Y

BASIC PRINCIPLES

Federalism the division of governing power between the Federal government and the States

Federal Supremacy Federal law takes precedence over conflicting State law

Federal Preemption right of the Federal government to regulate matters within its power to the exclusion of regulation by the States

Judicial Review examination of government actions to determine whether they conform to the U.S. Constitution

Separation of Powers allocation of powers among executive, legislative, and judicial branches of government

State Action actions of governments to which constitutional provisions apply

POWERS OF GOVERNMENT	**Federal Commerce Power** exclusive power of the Federal government to regulate commerce with other nations and among the States
	State Regulation of Commerce the Commerce Clause of the Constitution restricts the States' power to regulate activities if the result obstructs interstate commerce
	Federal Fiscal Powers

- *Taxation and Spending* the Constitution grants Congress broad powers to tax and spend; such powers are important to Federal regulation of the economy
- *Borrowing and Coining Money* enables the Federal government to establish a national banking system and to control national fiscal and monetary policy
- *Eminent Domain* the government's power to take private property for public use with the payment of just compensation

LIMITATIONS ON GOVERNMENT	**Contract Clause** restricts States from retroactively modifying contracts
	Freedom of Speech First Amendment protects most speech by using a strict scrutiny standard

- *Corporate Political Speech* First Amendment protects a corporation's right to speak out on political issues
- *Commercial Speech* expression related to the economic interests of the speaker and its audience; such expression receives a lesser degree of protection
- *Defamation* a tort consisting of a false communication that injures a person's reputation; such a communication receives limited constitutional protection

Due Process Fifth and Fourteenth Amendments prohibit the Federal and State governments from depriving any person of life, liberty, or property without due process of law

- *Substantive Due Process* determination of whether a particular government action is compatible with individual liberties
- *Procedural Due Process* requires the government decision-making process to be fair and impartial if it deprives a person of life, liberty, or property

Equal Protection requires that similarly situated persons be treated similarly by government actions

- *Rational Relationship Test* standard of equal protection review applicable to cases not subject to either the strict scrutiny test or the intermediate test, such as economic regulation
- *Strict Scrutiny Test* exacting standard of equal protection review applicable to regulation affecting a fundamental right or involving a suspect classification
- *Intermediate Test* standard of equal protection review applicable to regulation based on gender and legitimacy

C A S E S

CASE 4-1

Federal Preemption
WILLIAMSON v. MAZDA MOTOR OF AMERICA, INC.
Supreme Court of the United States, 2011
562 U.S. 323, 131 S.Ct. 1131, 179 L.Ed.2d 75

Breyer, J.
Federal Motor Vehicle Safety Standard 208 (1989 version) requires, among other things, that auto manufacturers install seatbelts on the rear seats of passenger vehicles. They must install lap-and-shoulder belts on seats next to a vehicle's doors or frames. But they have a choice about what to install on rear inner seats (say, middle seats or those next to a mini-van's aisle). There they can install either (1) simple lap belts or (2) lap-and-shoulder belts. [Citation.]

* * *

In 2002, the Williamson family, riding in their 1993 Mazda minivan, was struck head on by another vehicle. Thanh Williamson was sitting in a rear aisle seat, wearing a lap belt; she died in the accident. Delbert and Alexa Williamson were wearing lap-and-shoulder belts; they survived. They, along with Thanh's estate, subsequently brought this California tort suit against Mazda. They claimed that Mazda should have installed lap-and-shoulder belts on rear aisle seats, and that Thanh died because Mazda equipped her seat with a lap belt instead.

The California trial court dismissed this tort claim on the basis of the pleadings. And the California Court of Appeal affirmed. The appeals court noted that in *Geier v. American Honda Motor Co.*, [citation], this Court considered whether a different portion of (an older version of) Federal Motor Vehicle Safety Standard 208 (FMVSS 208)—a portion that required installation of passive restraint devices—pre-empted a state tort suit that sought to hold an auto manufacturer liable for failure to install a particular kind of passive restraint, namely, airbags. * * *

* * *

* * * [W]e granted certiorari * * *.

* * *

Under ordinary conflict pre-emption principles a state law that "stands as an obstacle to the accomplishment and execution of the full purposes and objectives" of a federal law is preempted. [Citations.] In *Geier* we found that the state law stood as an "'obstacle' to the accomplishment" of a significant federal regulatory objective, namely, the maintenance of manufacturer choice. [Citation.] We must decide whether the same is true here.

* * *

Like the regulation in *Geier,* the regulation here leaves the manufacturer with a choice. And, like the tort suit in *Geier,* the tort suit here would restrict that choice. But unlike *Geier,* we do not believe here that choice is a significant regulatory objective.

* * * In 1984, DOT [Department of Transportation] rejected a regulation that would have required the use of lap-and-shoulder belts in rear seats [Citation.] Nonetheless, by 1989 when DOT promulgated the present regulation, it had "concluded that several factors had changed." [Citation.]

DOT then required manufacturers to install a particular kind of belt, namely, lap-and-shoulder belts, for rear outer seats. In respect to rear inner seats, it retained manufacturer choice as to which kind of belt to install. * * * DOT here was not concerned about consumer acceptance; it was convinced that lap-and-shoulder belts would increase safety; it did not fear additional safety risks arising from use of those belts; it had no interest in assuring a mix of devices; and, though it was concerned about additional costs, that concern was diminishing.

* * *

The more important reason why DOT did not require lap-and-shoulder belts for rear inner seats was that it thought that this requirement would not be cost-effective. * * * But that fact—the fact that DOT made a negative judgment about cost effectiveness—cannot by itself show that DOT sought to forbid common-law tort suits in which a judge or jury might reach a different conclusion.

For one thing, DOT did not believe that costs would remain frozen. Rather it pointed out that costs were falling as manufacturers were "voluntarily equipping more and more of their vehicles with rear seatlap/shoulderbelts." [Citation.] For another thing, many, perhaps most, federal safety regulations embody some kind of cost-effectiveness judgment. While an agency could base a decision to preempt on its cost-effectiveness judgment, we are satisfied that the rulemaking record at issue here discloses no such pre-emptive intent. And to infer from the mere existence of such a cost-effectiveness judgment that the federal agency intends to bar States from imposing stricter standards would treat all such federal standards as if they were maximum standards, eliminating the possibility that the federal agency seeks only to set forth a minimum standard potentially supplemented through state tort law. We cannot reconcile this consequence with a statutory saving clause that foresees the likelihood of a continued meaningful role for state tort law. [Citation.]

Finally, the Solicitor General tells us that DOT's regulation does not pre-empt this tort suit. As in *Geier,* "the agency's own views should make a difference." [Citation.]

* * *

Neither has DOT expressed inconsistent views on this subject. In *Geier,* the Solicitor General pointed out that "state tort law does not conflict with a federal 'minimum standard' merely because state law imposes a more stringent requirement." [Citation.] And the Solicitor General explained that a standard giving manufacturers "multiple options for the design of" a device would not pre-empt a suit claiming that a manufacturer should have chosen one particular option, where "the Secretary did not determine that the availability of options was necessary to promote safety." [Citation.] This last statement describes the present case.

In *Geier,* then, the regulation's history, the agency's contemporaneous explanation, and its consistently held interpretive views indicated that the regulation sought to maintain manufacturer choice in order to further significant regulatory objectives. Here, these same considerations indicate the contrary. We consequently conclude that, even though the state tort suit may restrict the manufacturer's choice, it does not "stan[d] as an obstacle to the accomplishment … of the full purposes and objectives" of federal law. [Citation.] Thus, the regulation does not preempt this tort action.

The judgment of the California Court of Appeal is reversed.

CASE 4-2

State Action

BRENTWOOD ACADEMY v. TENNESSEE SECONDARY SCHOOL ATHLETIC ASSOCIATION

Supreme Court of the United States, 2001
531 U.S. 288, 121 S.Ct. 924, 148 L.Ed.2d 807

Souter, J.

The issue is whether a statewide association incorporated to regulate interscholastic athletic competition among public and private secondary schools may be regarded as engaging in state action when it enforces a rule against a member school. The association in question here includes most public schools located within the State, acts through their representatives, draws its officers from them, is largely funded by their dues and income received in their stead, and has historically been seen to regulate in lieu of the State Board of Education's exercise of its own authority. We hold that the association's regulatory activity may and should be treated as state action owing to the pervasive entwinement of state school officials in the structure of the association, there being no offsetting reason to see the association's acts in any other way.

Respondent Tennessee Secondary School Athletic Association (Association) is a not-for-profit membership corporation organized to regulate interscholastic sport among the public and private high schools in Tennessee that belong to it. No school is forced to join, but without any other authority actually regulating interscholastic athletics, it enjoys the memberships of almost all the State's public high schools (some 290 of them or 84% of the Association's voting membership), far outnumbering the 55 private schools that belong. A member school's team may play or scrimmage only against the team of another member, absent a dispensation.

The Association's rulemaking arm is its legislative council, while its board of control tends to administration. The voting membership of each of these nine-person committees is limited under the Association's bylaws to high school principals, assistant principals, and superintendents elected by the member schools, and the public school administrators who so serve typically attend meetings during regular school hours. Although the Association's staff members are not paid by the State, they are eligible to join the State's public retirement system for its employees. Member schools pay dues to the Association, though the bulk of its revenue is gate receipts at member teams' football and basketball tournaments, many of them held in public arenas rented by the Association.

The constitution, bylaws, and rules of the Association set standards of school membership and the eligibility of students to play in interscholastic games. Each school, for example, is regulated in awarding financial aid, most coaches must have a Tennessee state teaching license, and players must meet minimum academic standards and hew to limits on student employment. Under the bylaws, "in all matters pertaining to the athletic relations of his school," [citation], the principal is responsible to the Association, which has the power "to suspend, to fine, or otherwise penalize any member school for the violation of any of the rules of the Association or for other just cause," [citation].

* * *

The action before us responds to a 1997 regulatory enforcement proceeding brought against petitioner, Brentwood Academy, a private parochial high school member of the Association. The Association's board of control found that Brentwood violated a rule prohibiting "undue influence" in recruiting athletes, when it wrote to incoming students and their parents about spring football practice. The Association accordingly placed Brentwood's athletic program on probation for four years, declared its football and boys' basketball teams ineligible to compete in playoffs for two years, and imposed a $3,000 fine. When these penalties were imposed, all the voting members of the board of control and legislative council were public school administrators.

Brentwood sued the Association and its executive director in federal court * * * claiming that enforcement of the Rule was state action and a violation of the First and Fourteenth Amendments. The District Court entered summary judgment for Brentwood and enjoined the Association from enforcing the Rule. [Citation.] * * *

The United States Court of Appeals for the Sixth Circuit reversed. [Citation.] It recognized that there is no single test to identify state actions and state actors but applied three criteria * * *, and found no state action under any of them. It said the District Court was mistaken in seeing a symbiotic relationship between the State and the Association, it emphasized that the Association was neither engaging in a traditional and exclusive public function nor responding to state compulsion. * * *

We granted certiorari, 528 U.S. 1153 (2000), to resolve the conflict and now reverse.

* * * Thus, we say that state action may be found if, though only if, there is such a "close nexus between the State and the challenged action" that seemingly private behavior "may be fairly treated as that of the State itself." [Citation.]

* * *

Our cases have identified a host of facts that can bear on the fairness of such an attribution. We have, for example, held that a challenged activity may be state action when it results from the State's exercise of "coercive power," [citation], when the State provides "significant encouragement, either overt or covert," [citation], or when a private actor operates as a "willful participant in joint activity with the State or its agents," [citation]. We have treated a nominally private entity as a state actor when it is controlled by an "agency of the State," [citation], when it has been delegated a public function by the State, [citations], when it is "entwined with governmental policies" or when government is "entwined in [its] management or control," [citation].

* * *

* * * [T]he "necessarily fact-bound inquiry," [citation], leads to the conclusion of state action here. The nominally private character of the Association is overborne by the pervasive entwinement of public institutions and public officials in its composition and workings, and there is no substantial reason to claim unfairness in applying constitutional standards to it.

The Association is not an organization of natural persons acting on their own, but of schools, and of public schools to the extent of 84% of the total. Under the Association's bylaws, each member school is represented by its principal or a faculty member, who has a vote in selecting members of the governing legislative council and board of control from eligible principals, assistant principals and superintendents.

Although the findings and prior opinions in this case include no express conclusion of law that public school officials act within the scope of their duties when they represent their institutions, no other view would be rational, * * *. Interscholastic athletics obviously play an integral part in the public education of Tennessee, where nearly every public high school spends money on competitions among schools. Since a pickup system of interscholastic games would not do, these public teams need some mechanism to produce rules and regulate competition. The mechanism is an organization overwhelmingly composed of public school officials who select representatives (all of them public officials at the time in question here), who in turn adopt and enforce the rules that make the system work. Thus, by giving these jobs to the Association, the 290 public schools of Tennessee belonging to it can sensibly be seen as exercising their own authority to meet their own responsibilities.

* * *

In sum, to the extent of 84% of its membership, the Association is an organization of public schools represented by their officials acting in their official capacity to provide an integral element of secondary public schooling. There would be no recognizable Association, legal or tangible, without the public school officials, who do not merely control but overwhelmingly perform all but the purely ministerial acts by which the Association exists and functions in practical terms.

* * *

To complement the entwinement of public school officials with the Association from the bottom up, the State of Tennessee has provided for entwinement from top down. State Board members are assigned ex officio to serve as members of the board of control and legislative council, and the Association's ministerial employees are treated as state employees to the extent of being eligible for membership in the state retirement system.

* * *

The entwinement down from the State Board is therefore unmistakable, just as the entwinement up from the member public schools is overwhelming. Entwinement will support a conclusion that an ostensibly private organization ought to be charged with a public character and judged by constitutional standards; entwinement to the degree shown here requires it.

* * *

The judgment of the Court of Appeals for the Sixth Circuit is reversed, and the case is remanded for further proceedings consistent with this opinion.

CASE 4-3

State Regulation of Commerce
DEPARTMENT OF REVENUE OF KENTUCKY v. DAVIS
Supreme Court of the United States, 2008
553 U.S. 328, 128 S.Ct. 1801, 170 L.Ed.2d 685

Souter, J.

Like most other States, the Commonwealth of Kentucky taxes its residents' income. [Citation.] The tax is assessed on "net income," which excludes "interest on any State or local bond" ("municipal bond," for short), [citation]. Kentucky piggybacks on this exclusion, but only up to a point: it adds "interest income derived from obligations of sister states and political subdivisions thereof" back into the taxable net. [Citation.] Interest on bonds issued by Kentucky and its political subdivisions is thus entirely exempt, whereas interest on municipal bonds of other States and their subdivisions is taxable. (Interest on bonds issued by private entities is taxed by Kentucky regardless of the private issuer's home.)

The ostensible reason for this regime is the attractiveness of tax-exempt bonds at "lower rates of interest … than that paid on taxable. bonds of comparable risk." [Citation.] Under the Internal Revenue Code, for example, [citation], "if the market rate of interest is 10 percent on a comparable corporate bond, a municipality could pay only 6.5 percent on its debt and a purchaser in a 35 percent marginal tax bracket would be indifferent between the municipal and the corporate bond, since the after-tax interest rate on the corporate bond is 6.5 percent." [Citation.] The differential tax scheme in Kentucky works the same way; the Commonwealth's tax benefit to residents who buy its bonds makes lower interest rates acceptable, while limiting the exception to Kentucky bonds raises in-state demand for them without also subsidizing other issuers.

The significance of the scheme is immense. Between 1996 and 2002, Kentucky and its subdivisions issued $7.7 billion in long-term bonds to pay for spending on transportation, public safety, education, utilities, and environmental protection, among other things. [Citation.] Across the Nation during the same period, States issued over $750 billion in long-term bonds, with nearly a third of the money going to education, followed by transportation (13%) and utilities (11%). [Citation.] Municipal bonds currently finance roughly two-thirds of capital expenditures by state and local governments. [Citation.]

* * *

The Commerce Clause empowers Congress "[t]o regulate Commerce … among the several States," Art. I, § 8, cl. 3, and although its terms do not expressly restrain "the several States" in any way, we have sensed a negative implication in the provision since the early days, [citation]. The modern law of what has come to be called the dormant Commerce Clause is driven by concern about "economic protectionism—that is, regulatory measures designed to benefit in-state economic interests by burdening out-of-state competitors." [Citation.] The point is to "effectuat[e] the Framers' purpose to 'prevent a State from retreating into [the] economic isolation,'" [citation], "that had plagued relations among the Colonies and later among the States under the Articles of Confederation," [citation].

* * *

Under the resulting protocol for dormant Commerce Clause analysis, we ask whether a challenged law discriminates against interstate commerce. [Citation.] A discriminatory law is "virtually *per se* invalid," [citation], and will survive only if it "advances a legitimate local purpose that cannot be adequately served by reasonable nondiscriminatory alternatives," [citation]. Absent discrimination for the forbidden purpose, however, the law "will be upheld unless the burden imposed on [interstate] commerce is clearly excessive in relation to the putative local benefits." *Pike v. Bruce Church, Inc.*, [citation]. State laws frequently survive this *Pike* scrutiny, [citation], though not always, as in *Pike* itself, [citation].

Some cases run a different course, however, and an exception covers States that go beyond regulation and themselves "participat[e] in the market" so as to "exercis[e] the right to favor [their] own citizens over others." [Citation.] This "market participant" exception reflects a "basic distinction … between States as market participants and States as market regulators," [citation], "[t]here [being] no indication of a constitutional plan to limit the ability of the States themselves to operate freely in the free market," [citations].

Our most recent look at the reach of the dormant Commerce Clause came just last Term, in a case decided independently of the market participation precedents. *United Haulers* upheld a "flow control" ordinance requiring trash haulers to deliver solid waste to a processing plant owned and operated by a public authority in New York State. We found "[c]ompelling reasons" for "treating [the ordinance] differently from laws favoring particular private businesses over their competitors." [Citation.] State and local governments that provide public goods and services on their own, unlike private businesses, are "vested with the responsibility of protecting the health, safety, and welfare of [their] citizens," [citation], and laws favoring such States and their subdivisions may "be directed toward any number of legitimate goals unrelated to protectionism," [citation]. That was true in *United Haulers*, where the ordinance addressed waste disposal, "both typically and traditionally a local government function." [Citation.] And if more had been needed to show that New York's object was consequently different from forbidden protectionism, we pointed out that "the most palpable harm imposed by the ordinances—more expensive trash removal—[was] likely to fall upon the very people who voted for the laws," rather than out-of-state interests. [Citation.] Being concerned that a "contrary approach … would lead to unprecedented and unbounded interference by the courts with state and local government," [citation], we held that the ordinance did "not discriminate against interstate commerce for purposes of the dormant Commerce Clause," [citation].

It follows *a fortiori* from *United Haulers* that Kentucky must prevail. In *United Haulers*, we explained that a government function is not susceptible to standard dormant Commerce Clause scrutiny owing to its likely motivation by legitimate objectives distinct from the simple economic protectionism the Clause abhors, [citations]. This logic applies with even greater force to laws favoring a State's municipal bonds, given that the issuance of debt securities to pay for public projects is a quintessentially public function, with the venerable history we have already sketched, [citation]. By issuing bonds, state and local governments "sprea[d] the costs of public projects over time," [citation], much as one might buy a house with a loan subject to monthly payments. Bonds place the cost of a project on the citizens who benefit from it over the years, * * * and they allow for public work beyond what current revenues could support. [Citation.] Bond proceeds are thus the way to shoulder the cardinal civic responsibilities listed in *United Haulers*: protecting the health, safety, and welfare of citizens. It should go without saying that the apprehension in *United Haulers* about "unprecedented … interference" with a traditional government function is just as warranted here, where the Davises would have us invalidate a century-old taxing practice, [citation], presently employed by 41 States, [citation], and affirmatively supported by all of them, [citation].

* * * [T]he Kentucky tax scheme parallels the ordinance upheld in *United Haulers:* it "benefit[s] a clearly public [issuer, that is, Kentucky], while treating all private [issuers] exactly the same." [Citation.]

* * * Kentucky's tax exemption favors a traditional government function without any differential treatment favoring local entities over substantially similar out-of-state interests. This type of law does "not 'discriminate against interstate commerce' for purposes of the dormant Commerce Clause." [Citation.]

* * *

A look at the specific markets in which the exemption's effects are felt both confirms the conclusion that no traditionally forbidden discrimination is underway and points to the distinctive character of the tax policy. The market as most broadly conceived is one of issuers and holders of all fixed-income securities, whatever their source or ultimate destination. In this interstate market, Kentucky treats income from municipal bonds of other States just like income from bonds privately issued in Kentucky or elsewhere; no preference is given to any local issuer, and none to any local holder, beyond what is entailed in the preference Kentucky grants itself when it engages in activities serving public objectives. * * * These facts suggest that no State perceives any local advantage or disadvantage beyond the permissible ones open to a government and to those who deal with it when that government itself enters the market. [Citation.]

* * *

In sum, the differential tax scheme is critical to the operation of an identifiable segment of the municipal financial market as it currently functions, and this fact alone demonstrates that the unanimous desire of the States to preserve the tax feature is a far cry from the private protectionism that has driven the development of the dormant Commerce Clause. * * *

The judgment of the Court of Appeals of Kentucky is reversed, and the case is remanded for further proceedings not inconsistent with this opinion.

CASE 4-4

First Amendment
BROWN v. ENTERTAINMENT MERCHANTS ASSOCIATION

Supreme Court of the United States, 2011
564 U.S. 786, 131 S.Ct. 2729, 180 L.Ed.2d 708

Scalia, J.

California Assembly Bill 1179 (2005), [citation], (Act), prohibits the sale or rental of "violent video games" to minors, and requires their packaging to be labeled "18." The Act covers games "in which the range of options available to a player includes killing, maiming, dismembering, or sexually assaulting an image of a human being, if those acts are depicted" in a manner that "[a] reasonable person, considering the game as a whole, would find appeals to a deviant or morbid interest of minors," that is "patently offensive to prevailing standards in the community as to what is suitable for minors," and that "causes the game, as a whole, to lack serious literary, artistic, political, or scientific value for minors." [Citation.] Violation of the Act is punishable by a civil fine of up to $1,000. [Citation.]

Respondents, representing the video-game and software industries, brought a preenforcement challenge to the Act in the United States District Court for the Northern District of California. That court concluded that the Act violated the First Amendment and permanently enjoined its enforcement. [Citation.] The Court of Appeals affirmed, [citation], and we granted certiorari, [citation].

California correctly acknowledges that video games qualify for First Amendment protection. The Free Speech Clause exists principally to protect discourse on public matters, but we have long recognized that it is difficult to distinguish politics from entertainment, and dangerous to try. * * * Like the protected books, plays, and movies that preceded them, video games communicate ideas—and even social messages—through many familiar literary devices (such as characters, dialogue, plot, and music) and through features distinctive to the medium (such as the player's interaction with the virtual world). That suffices to confer First Amendment protection. * * * And whatever the challenges of applying the Constitution to ever-advancing technology, "the basic principles of freedom of speech and the press, like the First Amendment's command, do not vary" when a new and different medium for communication appears. [Citation.]

The most basic of those principles is this: "[A]s a general matter, … government has no power to restrict expression because of its message, its ideas, its subject matter, or its content." [Citation.] There are of course exceptions. "'From 1791 to the present,' … the First Amendment has 'permitted restrictions upon the content of speech in a few limited areas,' and has never 'include[d] a freedom to disregard these traditional limitations.'" [Citations.] These limited areas—such as obscenity, [citation], incitement, [citation], and fighting words, [citation]—represent "well-defined and narrowly limited classes of speech, the prevention and punishment of which have never been thought to raise any Constitutional problem," [citation].

Last Term, in [citation], we held that new categories of unprotected speech may not be added to the list by a legislature that concludes certain speech is too harmful to be tolerated. * * *

* * *

The California Act * * * does not adjust the boundaries of an existing category of unprotected speech to ensure that a definition designed for adults is not uncritically applied to children. * * * Instead, it wishes to create a wholly new category of content-based regulation that is permissible only for speech directed at children.

That is unprecedented and mistaken. "[M]inors are entitled to a significant measure of First Amendment protection, and only in relatively narrow and well-defined circumstances may government bar public dissemination of protected materials to them." [Citation.] No doubt a State possesses legitimate power to protect children from harm, [citation], but that does not include a free-floating power to restrict the ideas to which children may be exposed. "Speech that is neither obscene as to youths nor subject to some other legitimate proscription cannot be suppressed solely to protect the young from ideas or images that a legislative body thinks unsuitable for them." [Citation.]

California claims that video games present special problems because they are "interactive," in that the player participates in the violent action on screen and determines its outcome. The latter feature is nothing new * * * As for the argument that video games enable participation in the violent action, that seems to us more a matter of degree than of kind. * * *

Because the Act imposes a restriction on the content of protected speech, it is invalid unless California can demonstrate that it passes strict scrutiny—that is, unless it is justified by a compelling government interest and is narrowly drawn to serve that interest. [Citation.] The State must specifically identify an "actual problem" in need of solving, [citation], and the curtailment of free speech must be actually necessary to the solution, [citation]. That is a demanding standard. "It is rare that a regulation restricting speech because of its content will ever be permissible." [Citation.]

California cannot meet that standard. At the outset, it acknowledges that it cannot show a direct causal link between violent video games and harm to minors. * * *

* * *

California's effort to regulate violent video games is the latest episode in a long series of failed attempts to censor violent entertainment for minors. While we have pointed out above that some of the evidence brought forward to support the harmfulness of video games is unpersuasive, we do not mean to demean or disparage the concerns that underlie the attempt to regulate them—concerns that may and doubtless do prompt a good deal of parental oversight. We have no business passing judgment on the view of the California Legislature that violent video games (or, for that matter, any other forms of speech) corrupt the young or harm their moral development. Our task is only to say whether or not such works constitute a "well-defined and narrowly limited clas[s] of speech, the prevention and punishment of which have never been thought to raise any Constitutional problem," [citation] (the answer plainly is no); and if not, whether the regulation of such works is justified by that high degree of necessity we have described as a compelling state interest (it is not). Even where the protection of children is the object, the constitutional limits on governmental action apply.

California's legislation straddles the fence between (1) addressing a serious social problem and (2) helping concerned parents control their children. Both ends are legitimate, but when they affect First Amendment rights they must be pursued by means that are neither seriously underinclusive nor seriously overinclusive. [Citation.] As a means of protecting children from portrayals of violence, the legislation is seriously underinclusive, not only because it excludes portrayals other than video games, but also because it permits a parental or avuncular veto. And as a means of assisting concerned parents it is seriously overinclusive because it abridges the First Amendment rights of young people whose parents (and aunts and uncles) think violent video games are a harmless pastime. And the overbreadth in achieving one goal is not cured by the underbreadth in achieving the other. Legislation such as this, which is neither fish nor fowl, cannot survive strict scrutiny.

We affirm the judgment below.

	Equal Protection
CASE **4-5**	**BROWN v. BOARD OF EDUCATION OF TOPEKA** Supreme Court of the United States, 1954 347 U.S. 483, 74 S.Ct. 686, 98 L.Ed. 873

Warren, C. J.

These cases come to us from the States of Kansas, South Carolina, Virginia, and Delaware. They are premised on different facts and different local conditions, but a common legal question justifies their consideration together in this consolidated opinion.

In each of the cases, minors of the Negro race, through their legal representatives, seek the aid of the courts in obtaining admission to the public schools of their community on a nonsegregated basis. In each instance, they have been denied admission to schools attended by white children under laws requiring or permitting segregation according to race. This segregation was alleged to deprive the plaintiffs of the equal protection of the laws under the Fourteenth Amendment. In each of the cases other than the Delaware case, a three-judge federal district court denied relief to the plaintiffs on the so-called "separate but equal" doctrine announced by this Court in *Plessy v. Ferguson,* [citation]. Under that doctrine, equality of treatment is accorded when the races are provided substantially equal facilities, even though these facilities be separate. In the Delaware case, the Supreme Court of Delaware adhered to that doctrine, but ordered that the plaintiffs be admitted to the white schools because of their superiority to the Negro schools.

The plaintiffs contend that segregated public schools are not "equal" and cannot be made "equal" and that hence they are deprived of the equal protection of the laws. Because of the obvious importance of the question presented, the Court took jurisdiction. * * *

Reargument was largely devoted to the circumstances surrounding the adoption of the Fourteenth Amendment in 1868. It covered exhaustively consideration of the Amendment in Congress, ratification by the states, then existing practices in racial segregation, and the views of proponents and opponents of the Amendment. This discussion and our own investigation convince us that, although these sources cast some light, it is not enough to resolve the problem with which we are faced. At best, they are inconclusive. The most avid proponents of the post-War Amendments undoubtedly intended them to remove all legal distinctions among "all persons born or naturalized in the United States." Their opponents, just as certainly, were antagonistic to both the letter and the spirit of the Amendments and wished them to have the most limited effect. What others in Congress and the state legislatures had in mind cannot be determined with any degree of certainty.

An additional reason for the inconclusive nature of the Amendment's history, with respect to segregated schools, is the status of public education at that time. In the South, the movement toward free common schools, supported by general taxation, had not yet taken hold. Education of white children was largely in the hands of private groups. Education of Negroes was almost nonexistent, and practically all of the race were illiterate. In fact, any education of Negroes was forbidden by law in some states. Today, in contrast, many Negroes have achieved outstanding success in the arts and sciences as well as in the business and professional world. It is true that public school education at the time of the Amendment had advanced further in the North, but the effect of the Amendment on Northern States was generally ignored in the congressional debates. Even in the North, the conditions of public education did not approximate those existing today. The curriculum was usually rudimentary; ungraded schools were common in rural areas; the school term was but three months a year in many states;

and compulsory school attendance was virtually unknown. As a consequence, it is not surprising that there should be so little in the history of the Fourteenth Amendment relating to its intended effect on public education.

In the first cases in this Court construing the Fourteenth Amendment, decided shortly after its adoption, the Court interpreted it as proscribing all state-imposed discriminations against the Negro race. The doctrine of "separate but equal" did not make its appearance in this Court until 1896 in the case of *Plessy v. Ferguson,* involving not education but transportation. American courts have since labored with the doctrine for over half a century. In this Court, there have been six cases involving the "separate but equal" doctrine in the field of public education. * * * In none of these cases was it necessary to reexamine the doctrine to grant relief to the Negro plaintiff. And in *Sweatt v. Painter,* [citation], the Court expressly reserved decision on the question whether *Plessy v. Ferguson* should be held inapplicable to public education.

In the instant cases, that question is directly presented. Here, unlike *Sweatt v. Painter,* there are findings below that the Negro and white schools involved have been equalized, or are being equalized, with respect to buildings, curricula, qualifications and salaries of teachers, and other "tangible" factors. Our decision, therefore, cannot turn on merely a comparison of these tangible factors in the Negro and white schools involved in each of the cases. We must look instead to the effect of segregation itself on public education.

* * *

Today, education is perhaps the most important function of state and local governments. Compulsory school attendance laws and the great expenditures for education both demonstrate our recognition of the importance of education to our democratic society. It is required in the performance of our most basic public responsibilities, even service in the armed forces. It is the very foundation of good citizenship. Today it is a principal instrument in awakening the child to cultural values, in preparing him for later professional training, and in helping him to adjust normally to his environment. In these days, it is doubtful that any child may reasonably be expected to succeed in life if he is denied the opportunity of an education. Such an opportunity, where the state has undertaken to provide it, is a right which must be made available to all on equal terms.

We come then to the question presented: Does segregation of children in public schools solely on the basis of race, even though the physical facilities and other "tangible" factors may be equal, deprive the children of the minority group of equal educational opportunities? We believe that it does.

In *Sweatt v. Painter,* [citation], in finding that a segregated law school for Negroes could not provide them equal educational opportunities, this Court relied in large part on "those qualities which are incapable of objective measurement but which make for greatness in a law school." In *McLaurin v.*

Oklahoma State Regents, [citation], the Court in requiring that a Negro admitted to a white graduate school be treated like all other students, again resorted to intangible considerations: "* * * his ability to study, to engage in discussions and exchange views with other students, and, in general, to learn his profession." Such considerations apply with added force to children in grade and high schools. To separate them from others of similar age and qualifications solely because of their race generates a feeling of inferiority as to their status in the community that may affect their hearts and minds in a way unlikely ever to be undone. The effect of this separation on their educational opportunities was well stated by a finding in the Kansas case by a court which nevertheless felt compelled to rule against the Negro plaintiffs:

> Segregation of white and colored children in public schools has a detrimental effect upon the colored children. The impact is greater when it has the sanction of the law, for the policy of separating the races is usually interpreted as denoting the inferiority of the Negro group. A sense of inferiority affects the motivation of a child to learn. Segregation with the sanction of law, therefore, has a tendency to (retard) the educational and mental development of Negro children and to deprive them of some of the benefits they would receive in a racial(ly)-integrated school system.

Whatever may have been the extent of psychological knowledge at the time of *Plessy v. Ferguson,* this finding is amply supported by modern authority. Any language in *Plessy v. Ferguson* contrary to this finding is rejected.

We conclude that in the field of public education the doctrine of "separate but equal" has no place. Separate educational facilities are inherently unequal. Therefore, we hold that the plaintiffs and others similarly situated for whom the actions have been brought are, by reason of the segregation complained of, deprived of the equal protection of the laws guaranteed by the Fourteenth Amendment. This disposition makes unnecessary any discussion whether such segregation also violates the Due Process Clause of the Fourteenth Amendment.

QUESTIONS

1. In May, Patricia Allen left her automobile on the shoulder of a road in the city of Erehwon after the car stopped running. A member of the Erehwon city police department came upon the car later that day and placed on it a sticker that stated that unless the car was moved, it would be towed. After a week, the car had not been removed, and the police department authorized Baldwin Auto Wrecking Co. to tow it away and store it on its property. Allen was told by a friend that her car was at Baldwin's. Allen asked Baldwin to allow her to take possession of her car, but Baldwin refused to relinquish the car until the $70 towing fee was paid. Allen could not afford to pay the fee, and the car remained at Baldwin's for six weeks. At that time, Baldwin requested that the police department issue a permit to dispose of the automobile. After the police department tried unsuccessfully to telephone Allen, the department issued the permit. In late July, Baldwin destroyed the automobile. Allen brings an action against the city and Baldwin for damages for loss of the vehicle, arguing that she was denied due process. Decision?

CASE PROBLEMS

2. In 1967, large oil reserves were discovered in the Prudhoe Bay area of Alaska. As a result, State revenues increased from $124 million in 1969 to $3.7 billion in 1981. In 1980, the State legislature enacted a dividend program that would distribute annually a portion of these earnings to the State's adult residents. Under the plan, each citizen eighteen years of age or older receives one unit for each year of residency subsequent to 1959, the year Alaska became a State. Crawford, a resident since 1978, brings suit challenging the dividend distribution plan as violative of the equal protection guarantee. Did the dividend program violate the Equal Protection Clause of the Fourteenth Amendment? Explain.

3. Maryland enacted a statute prohibiting any producer or refiner of petroleum products from operating retail service stations within the State. The statute also required that any producer or refiner discontinue operating its company-owned retail service stations. Approximately 3,800 retail service stations in Maryland sell more than twenty different brands of gasoline. All of this gasoline is brought in from other States, as no petroleum products are produced or refined in Maryland. Only 5 percent of the total number of retailers are operated by a producer or refiner. Maryland enacted the statute because a survey conducted by the State comptroller indicated that gasoline stations operated by producers or refiners had

received preferential treatment during periods of gasoline shortage. Seven major producers and refiners bring an action challenging the statute on the ground that it discriminated against interstate commerce in violation of the Commerce Clause of the U.S. Constitution. Are they correct? Explain.

4. The Federal Aviation Act of 1958 provides that "the United States of America is declared to possess and exercise complete and exclusive national sovereignty in the airspace of the United States." The city of Orion adopted an ordinance that makes it unlawful for jet aircraft to take off from its airport between 11:00 P.M. of one day and 7:00 A.M. of the next day. Jordan Airlines, Inc., is adversely affected by this ordinance and brings suit challenging it under the Supremacy Clause of the U.S. Constitution as conflicting with the Federal Aviation Act or preempted by it. Is the ordinance valid? Explain.

5. The Public Service Commission of State X issued a regulation completely banning all advertising that "promotes the use of electricity" by any electric utility company in State X. The commission issued the regulation to conserve energy. Central Electric Corporation of State X challenges the order in the State courts, arguing that the commission has restrained commercial speech in violation of the First Amendment. Was the corporation's freedom of speech unconstitutionally infringed? Explain.

6. E-Z-Rest Motel is a motel with 216 rooms located in the center of a large city in State Y. It is readily accessible from two interstate highways and three major State highways. The motel solicits patronage from outside State Y through various national advertising media, including magazines of national circulation. It accepts convention trade from outside State Y, and approximately 75 percent of its registered guests are from out of State Y. An action under the Federal Civil Rights Act has been brought against E-Z-Rest Motel alleging that the motel discriminates on the basis of race and color. The motel contends that the statute cannot be applied to it because it is not engaged in interstate commerce. Can the Federal government regulate this activity under the Interstate Commerce Clause? Why?

7. State Z enacted a Private Pension Benefits Protection Act requiring private employers with one hundred or more employees to pay a pension funding charge upon terminating a pension plan or closing an office in State Z. Acme Steel Company closed its offices in State Z, whereupon the State assessed the company $185,000 under the vesting provisions of the act. Acme challenged the constitutionality of the Act under the Contract Clause (Article I, Section 10) of the U.S. Constitution. Was the Act constitutional? Explain.

8. A State statute empowered public school principals to suspend students for up to ten days without any notice or hearing. A student who was suspended for ten days challenges the constitutionality of his suspension on the ground that he was denied due process. Was due process denied? Explain.

9. Iowa enacted a statute prohibiting the use of sixty-five-foot double-trailer-truck combinations. All the other midwestern and western States permit such trucks to be used on their roads. Despite these restrictions, Iowa's statute permits cities abutting the State line to enact local ordinances adopting the length limitations of the adjoining State. In cases in which a city has exercised this option, otherwise oversized trucks are permitted within the city limits and in nearby commercial zones. Consolidated Freightways is adversely affected by this statute and brings suit against Iowa, alleging that the statute violates the Commerce Clause. The District Court found that the evidence established that sixty-five-foot doubles were as safe as the shorter truck units. Does the statute violate the Commerce Clause? Explain.

10. Metropolitan Edison Company is a privately owned and operated Pennsylvania corporation subject to extensive regulation by the Pennsylvania Public Utility Commission. Under a provision of its general tariff filed with the commission, Edison had the right to discontinue electric service to any customer on reasonable notice of nonpayment of bills. Catherine Jackson had been receiving electricity from Metropolitan Edison when her account was terminated because of her delinquency in payments. Edison later opened a new account for her residence in the name of James Dodson, another occupant of Jackson's residence. In August of the following year, Dodson moved away, and no further payments were made to the account. Finally, in October, Edison disconnected Jackson's service without any prior notice. Jackson brought suit claiming that her electric service could not be terminated without notice and a hearing. She further argued that such action, allowed by a provision of Edison's tariff filed with the commission, constituted "state action" depriving her of property in violation of the Fourteenth Amendment's guarantee of due process of law. Should Edison's actions be considered state action? Explain.

11. Miss Horowitz was admitted as an advanced medical student at the University of Missouri-Kansas City. During the spring of her first year, several faculty members expressed dissatisfaction with Miss Horowitz's clinical performance, noting that it was below that of her peers, that she was erratic in attendance at her clinical sessions, and that she lacked a critical concern for personal hygiene. Upon the recommendation of the school's

Council on Evaluation, she was advanced to her second and final year on a probationary basis. After subsequent unfavorable reviews during her second year and a negative evaluation of her performance by seven practicing physicians, the council recommended that Miss Horowitz be dismissed from the school for her failure to meet academic standards. The decision was approved by the dean and later affirmed by the provost after an appeal by Miss Horowitz. She brought suit against the school's Board of Curators, claiming that her dismissal violated her right to procedural due process under the Fourteenth Amendment and deprived her of "liberty" by substantially impairing her opportunities to continue her medical education or to return to employment in a medically related field. Is her claim correct? Explain.

12. The McClungs owned Ollie's Barbecue, a restaurant located a few blocks from the interstate highway in Birmingham, Alabama, with dining accommodations for whites only and a takeout service for blacks. In the year preceding the passage of the Civil Rights Act of 1964, the restaurant had purchased a substantial portion of the food it served from outside the state. The restaurant had refused to serve blacks since its original opening in 1927 and asserted that if it were required to serve blacks it would lose much of its business. The McClungs sought a declaratory judgment to render unconstitutional the application of the Civil Rights Act to their restaurant because their admitted racial discrimination did not restrict or significantly impede interstate commerce. Decision?

13. Drug compounding is a process by which a pharmacist or doctor combines, mixes, or alters ingredients to create a medication tailored to the needs of an individual patient. Compounding is typically used to prepare medications that are not commercially available, such as medication for a patient who is allergic to an ingredient in a mass-produced product. The Federal Food, Drug, and Cosmetic Act of 1938 (FDCA) regulates drug manufacturing, marketing, and distribution, providing that no person may sell any new drug unless approved by the Food and Drug Administration (FDA). The Food and Drug Administration Modernization Act of 1997 (FDAMA), which amends the FDCA, exempts compounded drugs from the FDCA's requirements provided the drugs satisfy a number of restrictions, including that the prescription must be "unsolicited," and the provider compounding the drug may "not advertise or promote the compounding of any particular drug, class of drug, or type of drug." The provider, however, may "advertise and promote the compounding service."

A group of licensed pharmacies that specialize in drug compounding challenged the FDAMA's requirement that they refrain from advertising and promoting their products if they wish to continue compounding on the basis that it violates the Free Speech Clause of the First Amendment. What test should the court apply in determining the validity of the FDAMA?

14. A Massachusetts statute established differential methods by which wineries may distribute wines in Massachusetts. The statute allows only "small" wineries, defined as those producing 30,000 gallons or less of grape wine a year, to obtain a "small winery shipping license." This license allows them to sell their wines in Massachusetts in three ways: through shipments made directly to consumers, through wholesaler distribution, and through retail distribution. All of Massachusetts's wineries are "small" wineries. Some out-of-state wineries also meet this definition. Wines from "small" Massachusetts wineries compete with wines from "large" wineries, which Massachusetts has defined as those producing more than 30,000 gallons of grape wine annually. These "large" wineries must choose between relying upon wholesalers to distribute their wines in-state or applying for a "large winery shipping license" to sell directly to Massachusetts consumers. They cannot, by law, use both methods to sell their wines in Massachusetts, and they cannot sell wines directly to retailers under either option. Plaintiffs, a group of California winemakers and Massachusetts residents, assert that the statute was designed with the purpose, and has the effect, of advantaging Massachusetts wineries to the detriment of those wineries that produce 98 percent of the country's wine, in violation of the Commerce Clause. Decision? Explain.

15. American Express Travel Related Services ("Amex") sells Amex Travelers Cheques ("TCs"), which are preprinted checks for specified amounts with a unique serial number and no expiration date. Amex is able to sell TCs for their face value because Amex's contract with TC owners gives Amex the right to retain, use, and invest funds from the sale of TCs until the date the TCs are cashed.

All States have unclaimed property laws requiring abandoned property to be turned over to the State while the original property owner still maintains the right to the property. The purpose of unclaimed property laws is to provide for the safekeeping of abandoned property and then to allow the rightful owner to claim the abandoned property. As these laws are applied to TCs, Amex sends the funds held as TCs to the State as unclaimed property with the serial number, amount, and date of sale since the name of the TC owner is not known. When one of these TCs is cashed, Amex seeks to reclaim those funds from that State. In New Jersey, the Treasurer returns the funds with interest. Until recently, all States had a fifteen-year abandonment period for travelers checks. In 2010, New Jersey passed Chapter 25, shortening the abandonment period for travelers checks to three years. Amex challenges the constitutionality of the amendment. Explain whether the amendment violates any of the following provisions of the U.S. Constitution: (a) Due Process Clause, (b) Contract Clause, (c) Takings Clause, or (d) Commerce Clause.

TAKING SIDES

Alabama was one of only sixteen States that permitted commercial hazardous waste landfills. From 1985 through 1989, the tonnage of hazardous waste received per year more than doubled. Of this, up to 90 percent of the hazardous waste was shipped in from other States. In response, Alabama imposed a fee of $97.60 per ton for hazardous waste generated outside Alabama compared with a fee of $25.60 per ton for hazardous wastes generated within Alabama.

Chemical Waste Management, Inc., which operates a commercial hazardous waste land disposal facility in Emelle, Alabama, filed suit asserting that the Alabama law violated the Commerce Clause of the U.S. Constitution.

a. What arguments could Chemical Waste Management, Inc., make in support of its claim that the statute is unconstitutional?

b. What arguments could Alabama make to defend the constitutionality of the statute?

c. Who should prevail? Explain.

CHAPTER 5

Administrative Law

CHAPTER OUTCOMES

After reading and studying this chapter, you should be able to:

- Explain the three basic functions of administrative agencies.

- Distinguish among the three types of rules promulgated by administrative agencies.

- Explain the difference between formal and informal methods of adjudication.

- Identify (1) the questions of law determined by a court in conducting a review of a rule or an order of an administrative agency and (2) the three standards of judicial review of factual determinations made by administrative agencies.

- Describe the limitations imposed on administrative agencies by the legislative branch, the executive branch, and laws that require disclosure of information.

Administrative law is the branch of public law that is created by administrative agencies in the form of rules, regulations, orders, and decisions to carry out the regulatory powers and duties of those agencies. Administrative agencies are government entities—other than courts and legislatures—having authority to affect the rights of private parties through their operations. Such agencies, often referred to as commissions, boards, departments, administrations, government corporations, bureaus, or offices, regulate a vast array of important matters involving national safety, welfare, and convenience. For instance, Federal administrative agencies are charged with responsibility for national security, citizenship and naturalization, law enforcement, taxation, currency, elections, environmental protection, consumer protection, regulation of transportation, telecommunications, labor relations, trade, commerce, and securities markets, as well as with providing health and social services.

Because of the increasing complexity of the social, economic, and industrial life of the nation, the scope of administrative law has expanded enormously. Justice Jackson stated that "the rise of administrative bodies has been the most significant legal trend of the last century, and perhaps more values today are affected by their decisions than by those of all the courts, review of administrative decisions apart." *Federal Trade Commission v. Ruberoid Co.*, 343 U.S. 470 (1952). This observation is even truer today, as evidenced by the dramatic increase in the number and activities of Federal government boards, commissions, and other agencies. Certainly, agencies create more legal rules and adjudicate more controversies than all of the nation's legislatures and courts combined.

State agencies also play a significant role in the functioning of our society. Among the more important State boards and commissions are those that supervise and regulate banking, insurance, communications, transportation, public utilities, pollution control, and workers' compensation.

Countless administrative agencies establish much of the Federal, State, and local law in this country. These agencies, which many label the "fourth branch of government," possess tremendous power and have long been criticized as being "in reality miniature independent governments. . . [which are] a haphazard deposit of irresponsible agencies." 1937 Presidential Task Force Report.

Despite the criticism against them, these agencies clearly play a significant and necessary role in our society. Administrative agencies relieve legislatures of the impossible burden of fashioning legislation that deals with every detail of a specific problem. As a result, Congress can enact legislation, such as the Federal Trade Commission Act, which prohibits unfair and deceptive trade practices, without having to define such practices specifically or to anticipate all the particular problems that may arise. Instead, Congress may enact an **enabling statute** that creates an agency—in this example, the Federal Trade Commission (FTC)—to which it can delegate the power to issue rules, regulations, and guidelines to carry out the statutory mandate. In addition, the establishment of separate, specialized bodies enables administrative agencies to be staffed by individuals with expertise in the field being regulated. Administrative agencies thus can develop the knowledge and devote the time necessary to provide continuous and flexible solutions to evolving regulatory problems.

This chapter focuses on Federal administrative agencies, which can be classified as either independent or executive. Executive agencies are those housed within the executive branch of government, whereas independent agencies are not. Many Federal agencies are discussed in other parts of this text. More specifically, the FTC and the Justice Department are discussed in *Chapter 40*; the FTC, the Consumer Financial Protection Bureau (CFPB), and the Consumer Product Safety Commission (CPSC) in *Chapter 41*; the Department of Labor, the National Labor Relations Board (NLRB), and the Equal Employment Opportunity Commission in *Chapter 42*; the Securities and Exchange Commission (SEC) in *Chapters 43 and 44*; and the Environmental Protection Agency (EPA) in *Chapter 45*.

5-1 Operation of Administrative Agencies

Most administrative agencies perform three basic functions: (1) rulemaking, (2) enforcement, and (3) adjudication. The term *administrative process* refers to the activities in which administrative agencies engage while carrying out their rulemaking, enforcement, and adjudicative functions. Administrative agencies exercise powers that the Constitution has allocated to the three separate branches of government. More specifically, agencies exercise legislative power when they make rules, executive power when they enforce their enabling statutes and their rules, and judicial power when they adjudicate disputes. This concentration of power has raised questions regarding the propriety of having the same bodies that establish the rules also act as prosecutors and judges in determining whether those rules have been violated. To address this issue and bring about certain additional procedural reforms, Congress enacted the Administrative Procedure Act (APA) in 1946.

5-1a RULEMAKING

Rulemaking is the process by which an administrative agency enacts or promulgates rules of law. Under the APA, a rule is "the whole or a part of an agency statement of general or particular applicability and future effect designed to implement, interpret, or process law or policy." Section 551(4). Once promulgated, rules are applicable to all parties. Moreover, the rulemaking process notifies all parties that the agency is considering the impending rule and provides concerned individuals with an opportunity to be heard. Administrative agencies promulgate

three types of rules: legislative rules, interpretative rules, and procedural rules.

LEGISLATIVE RULES Legislative rules, often called *regulations*, are in effect "administrative statutes." **Legislative rules** are those issued by an agency that is able, under a legislative delegation of power, to make rules having the force and effect of law. For example, the FTC has rulemaking power with which to elaborate upon its enabling statute's prohibition of unfair or deceptive acts or practices. Legislative rules, which are immediately binding, generally receive greater deference from reviewing courts than do interpretative rules.

Legislative rules have the force of law if they are constitutional, within the power granted to the agency by the legislature, and issued according to proper procedure. To be constitutional, regulations must not violate any provisions of the U.S. Constitution, such as due process or equal protection. In addition, they may not involve an unconstitutional delegation of legislative power from the legislature to the agency. To be constitutionally permissible, the enabling statute granting power to an agency must establish reasonable standards to guide the agency in implementing the statute. Statutes have met this requirement through such language as "to prohibit unfair methods of competition," "fair and equitable," "public interest, convenience, and necessity," and other equally broad expressions. In any event, an agency may not exceed the actual authority granted by its enabling statute.

In 2015, the U.S. Supreme Court addressed the validity of an IRS rule that made the Patient Protection and Affordable Care Act's (more commonly called the Affordable Care Act or Obamacare) tax credits available in those States that have a Federal health insurance exchange. In a 6–3 decision, the Court upheld the IRS rule but based its decision on the Court's own interpretation of the Act without deferring to the agency's interpretation. The Court stated, "Congress passed the Affordable Care Act to improve health insurance markets, not to destroy them." *King v. Burwell*, 576 U.S. 988 (2015).

When analyzing an agency's interpretation of a statute, we often apply the two-step framework ***. Under that framework, we ask whether the statute is ambiguous and, if so, whether the agency's interpretation is reasonable. *** This approach "is premised on the theory that a statute's ambiguity constitutes an implicit delegation from Congress to the agency to fill in the statutory gaps." *** "In extraordinary cases, however, there may be reason to hesitate before concluding that Congress has intended such an implicit delegation." ***

This is one of those cases. The tax credits are among the Act's key reforms, involving billions of dollars in spending each year and affecting the price of health insurance for millions of people. Whether those credits are available on Federal Exchanges is thus a question of deep "economic and political significance" that is central to this statutory scheme; had Congress wished to assign that question to an agency, it surely would have done so expressly. *** It is especially unlikely that Congress would have delegated this decision to the *IRS*, which has no expertise in crafting health insurance policy of this sort. *** This is not a case for the IRS.

It is instead our task to determine the correct reading of [the Act].

Legislative rules must be promulgated in accordance with the procedural requirements of the APA, although the enabling statute may impose more stringent requirements. Most legislative rules are issued in accordance with the **informal rulemaking** procedures of the APA, which require that the agency provide the following:

1. prior notice of a proposed rule, usually by publication in the *Federal Register;*

2. an opportunity for interested parties to participate in the rulemaking; and

3. publication of a final draft containing a concise general statement of the rule's basis and purpose at least thirty days before its effective date. Section 553.

In some instances, the enabling statute requires that an agency make certain rules only after providing the opportunity for a hearing. This formal rulemaking procedure, which is far more complex than the informal procedures, is governed by the same APA provisions that govern adjudication, discussed later. In **formal rulemaking**, when an agency makes rules, it must consider the record of the trial-type agency hearing and include a statement of "findings and conclusions, and the reasons or basis therefor, on all the material issues of fact, law, or discretion presented on the record." Section 557(c).

Some enabling statutes direct that the agency, in making rules, follow certain procedures that are more formal than those the agency uses in informal rulemaking but do not compel the full hearing that formal rulemaking requires. This intermediate procedure, known as **hybrid rulemaking**, results from combining the informal procedures of the APA with additional procedures specified by the enabling statute. For example, an agency may be required to conduct a legislative-type hearing (formal) that permits no cross-examination (informal).

In 1990, Congress enacted the Negotiated Rulemaking Act to encourage the involvement of affected parties in the initial stages of the policy-making process prior to the publication of notice of a proposed rule. The Act authorizes agencies to use negotiated rulemaking but does not require it. If an agency decides to use negotiated rulemaking, the affected parties and the agency develop an agreement and offer it to the agency. If accepted, the agreement becomes a basis for the proposed regulation, which is then published for comment.

♦ *See Case 5-1*

Practical Advice

Participate as early as possible in the rulemaking process of administrative agencies that affect your business.

INTERPRETATIVE RULES Interpretative rules are "issued by an agency to advise the public of the agency's construction of the statutes and rules which it administers." Attorney General's Manual on the Administrative Procedure Act. Interpretative rules, which are exempt from the APA's procedural requirements of notice and comment, are not automatically binding on private parties the agency regulates or on the courts, although they are given substantial weight. As the Supreme Court has stated,

> The weight of such [an interpretative rule] in a particular case will depend upon the thoroughness evident in its consideration, the validity of its reasoning, its consistency with earlier and later pronouncements, and all those factors which give it power to persuade. *Skidmore v. Swift & Co.*, 323 U.S. 134 (1944).

♦ *See Case 5-2*

PROCEDURAL RULES Procedural rules are also exempt from the notice and comment requirements of the APA and are not law. These rules establish rules of conduct for practice before the agency, identify an agency's organization, and describe its method of operation. For example, the SEC's Rules of Practice deal with such matters as who may appear before the commission; business hours and notice of proceedings and hearings; settlements, agreements, and conferences; the presentation of evidence and taking of depositions and interrogatories; and the review of hearings.

♦ **SEE FIGURE 5-1:** *Administrative Rulemaking*

5-1b ENFORCEMENT

Agencies also investigate to determine whether certain conduct has violated the statute or the agency's legislative rules. In carrying out this executive function, the agencies traditionally have been accorded great discretion to compel the disclosure of information, subject to constitutional limitations. These limitations require that (1) the investigation be authorized by law

FIGURE 5-1 Administrative Rulemaking

Rule	Procedure	Effect
Legislative	Subject to APA	Binding
Interpretative	Exempt from APA	Persuasive
Procedural	Exempt from APA	Persuasive

and undertaken for a legitimate purpose, (2) the information sought be relevant, (3) the demand for information be sufficiently specific and not unreasonably burdensome, and (4) the information sought not be privileged.

For example, the following explains some of the SEC's investigative and enforcement functions:

> All SEC investigations are conducted privately. Facts are developed to the fullest extent possible through informal inquiry, interviewing witnesses, examining brokerage records, reviewing trading data, and other methods. With a formal order of investigation, the Division's staff may compel witnesses by subpoena to testify and produce books, records, and other relevant documents. Following an investigation, SEC staff present their findings to the Commission for its review. The Commission can authorize the staff to file a case in federal court or bring an administrative action. In many cases, the Commission and the party charged decide to settle a matter without trial. SEC, http://www.sec.gov.

5-1c ADJUDICATION

After concluding an investigation, the agency may use informal or formal methods to resolve the matter. Because the caseload of administrative agencies is vast, indeed far greater than that of the judicial system, agencies adjudicate most matters informally. Informal procedures include advising, negotiating, and settling. In 1990, Congress enacted the Administrative Dispute Resolution Act to authorize and encourage Federal agencies to use mediation, conciliation, arbitration, and other techniques for the prompt and informal resolution of disputes. The Act does not, however, require agencies to use alternative dispute resolution, and the affected parties must consent to its use.

Practical Advice

When available, consider using alternative methods of dispute resolution with administrative agencies.

The formal procedure by which an agency resolves a matter (called **adjudication**) involves finding facts, applying legal rules to the facts, and formulating orders. An **order** "means the whole or a part of a final disposition, whether affirmative,

negative, injunctive or declaratory in form, of an agency." APA Section 551(6). In essence an administrative trial, adjudication is used when required by the enabling statute.

The procedures the administrative agencies employ to adjudicate cases are nearly as varied as the agencies themselves. Nevertheless, the APA does establish certain mandatory standards for those Federal agencies the Act covers. For example, under the Act, an agency must give notice of a hearing. The APA also requires that the agency give all interested parties the opportunity to submit and consider "facts, arguments, offers of settlement, or proposals of adjustment." Section 554(c). In many cases this involves testimony and cross-examination of witnesses. If no settlement is reached, a hearing must be held.

The hearing is presided over by an administrative law judge (ALJ) and is prosecuted by the agency. The agency appoints ALJs through a professional merit selection system and may remove them only for good cause. There are more than twice as many ALJs as there are Federal judges. Hearings never use juries; thus, the agency serves as both the prosecutor and decisionmaker. To reduce the potential for a conflict of interest, the APA provides for a separation of functions between those agency members engaged in investigation and prosecution from those involved in decision making. Section 544(d). Either party may introduce oral and documentary evidence, and the agency must base all sanctions, rules, and orders upon "consideration of the whole record or those parts cited by a party and supported by and in accordance with the reliable, probative, and substantial evidence." Section 556(d). All decisions must include a statement of findings of fact and conclusions of law and the reasons or bases for them, as well as a statement of the appropriate rule, order, sanction, or relief.

If authorized to do so by law and within its delegated jurisdiction, an agency may impose in its orders sanctions such as penalties; fines; the seizure of property; the assessment of damages, restitution, compensation, or fees; and the requirement, revocation, or suspension of a license. Sections 551(10) and 558(b). In most instances, orders are final unless appealed, and failure to comply with an order subjects the party to a statutory penalty. If the order is appealed, the governing body of the agency may decide the case *de novo*. Section 557(b). Thus, the agency may hear additional evidence and arguments in deciding whether to revise the findings and conclusions made in the initial decision.

Although administrative adjudications mirror to a large extent the procedures of judicial trials, the two differ substantially:

Agency hearings, especially those dealing with rulemaking, often tend to produce evidence of general conditions as distinguished from facts relating solely to the respondent. Administrative agencies in rulemaking and occasionally in formal adversarial adjudications more consciously formulate policy than do courts. Consequently, administrative adjudications may require that the administrative law judge consider more consciously the impact of his decision upon the public interest as well as upon the particular respondent. . . . An administrative hearing is tried to an administrative law judge and never to a jury. Since many of the rules governing the admission of proof in judicial trials are designed to protect the jury from unreliable and possibly confusing evidence, it has long been asserted that such rules need not be applied at all or with the same vigor in proceedings solely before an administrative law judge. . . . Consequently, the technical common law rules governing the admissibility of evidence have generally been abandoned by administrative agencies. *McCormick on Evidence*, 4th ed., Section 350, p. 605.

5-2 Limits on Administrative Agencies

An important and fundamental part of administrative law is the limits judicial review imposes upon the activities of administrative agencies. On matters of policy, however, courts are not supposed to substitute their judgment for that of an agency. Additional limitations arise from the legislature and the executive branch, which, unlike the judiciary, may address the wisdom and correctness of an agency's decision or action. Moreover, legally required disclosure of agency actions provides further protection for the public.

♦ **SEE FIGURE 5-2:** *Limits on Administrative Agencies*

5-2a JUDICIAL REVIEW

As discussed in *Chapter 4*, judicial review describes the process by which the courts examine government action. Judicial review, which is available unless a statute precludes such review or the agency action is committed to agency discretion by law, acts as a control or check on a particular rule or order of an administrative agency. Section 701.

GENERAL REQUIREMENTS Parties seeking to challenge agency action must have standing and must have exhausted their administrative remedies. Standing requires that the

FIGURE 5-2 Limits on Administrative Agencies

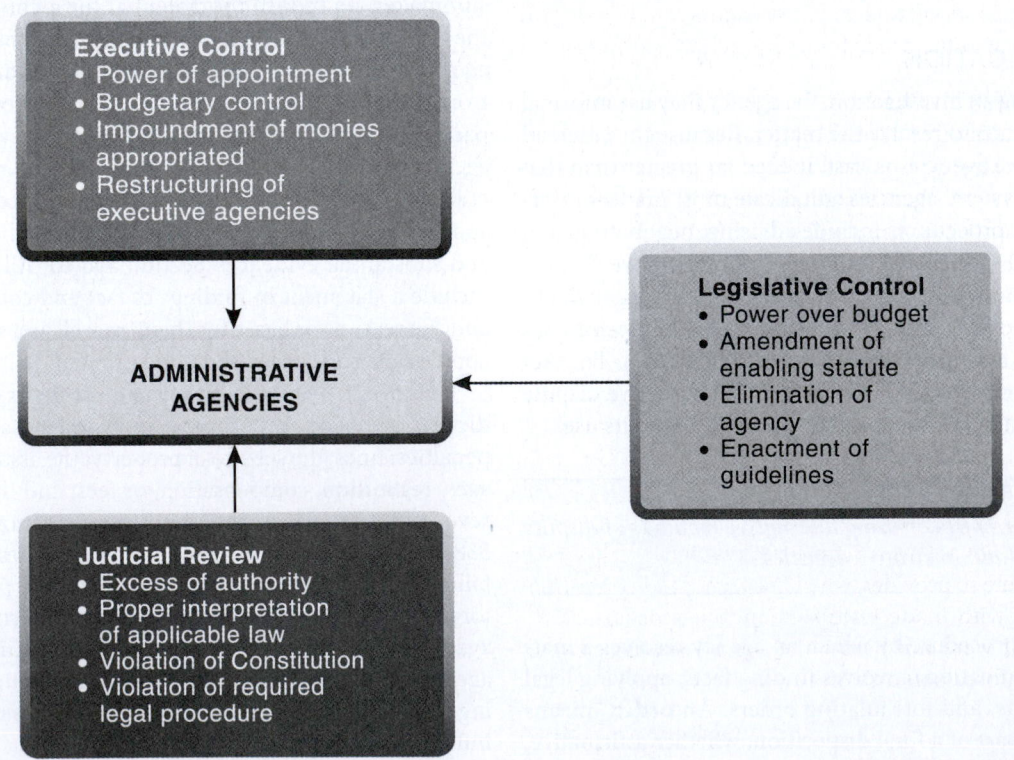

agency action injure the party in fact and that the party assert an interest that is in the "zone of interests to be protected or regulated by the statute in question." Judicial review is ordinarily available only for *final* agency action. Section 704. Accordingly, if a party seeks review while an agency proceeding is in progress, a court will usually dismiss the action because the party has failed to exhaust his administrative remedies.

◆ *See Case 5-3*

Practical Advice

Be sure to exhaust all of your administrative remedies before seeking judicial review of action taken by an administrative agency.

In exercising judicial review, the court may decide either to compel agency action unlawfully withheld or to set aside impermissible agency action. In making its determination, the court must review the whole record and may set aside agency action only if the error is prejudicial.

QUESTIONS OF LAW When conducting a review, a court decides all relevant questions of law, interprets constitutional and statutory provisions, and determines the meaning or applicability of the terms of an agency action. This review of questions of law includes determining whether the agency has (1) exceeded its authority, (2) properly interpreted the applicable law, (3) violated any constitutional provision, or (4) acted contrary to the procedural requirements of the law.

QUESTIONS OF FACT When reviewing factual determinations, the courts use one of three different standards. In cases in which informal rulemaking or informal adjudication has occurred, the standard generally is the **arbitrary and capricious** test, which requires only that the agency had a rational basis for reaching its decision. Where an agency has held a formal hearing, the **substantial evidence** test usually applies. It also applies to informal or hybrid rulemaking, if the enabling statute so requires. The substantial evidence test requires that the agency support its conclusions with "such relevant evidence as a reasonable mind might accept as adequate to support a conclusion." *Consolidated Edison Co. v. NLRB*, 305 U.S. 197 (1938). Finally, in rare instances, the reviewing court may apply the **unwarranted by the facts** standard, which permits the court to try the facts *de novo*. This strict review is available only when the enabling statute so provides, when the agency has conducted an adjudication with inadequate fact-finding procedures, or when issues that were not before the agency are raised in a proceeding to enforce non-adjudicative agency action.

◆ *See Case 5-4*

5-2b LEGISLATIVE CONTROL

The legislature may exercise control over administrative agencies in various ways. Through its budgetary power, it may greatly restrict or expand an agency's operations. Congress may amend an enabling statute to increase, modify, or decrease an agency's authority. Even more drastically, it may completely eliminate an agency. Or Congress may establish general guidelines to govern agency action, as it did by enacting the APA. Moreover, it may reverse or change an agency rule or decision through specific legislation. In addition, each house of Congress has oversight committees that review the operations of administrative agencies. Finally, the Senate has the power of confirmation over some high-level appointments to administrative agencies.

In 1996, Congress enacted the Congressional Review Act (CRA), which subjects most rules to an extensive form of legislative control. With limited exceptions, the CRA requires agencies to submit newly adopted rules to each house of Congress before they can take effect. If the rule is a major rule, it does not become final until Congress has had an opportunity to disapprove it. A **major rule** is any rule that the Office of Management and Budget (OMB) finds has resulted in or is likely to result in (1) an annual effect on the economy of at least $100 million; (2) a major increase in costs or prices; or (3) a significant adverse effect on competition, employment, investment, productivity, innovation, or international competitiveness of U.S. enterprises. If the rule is not a major rule, it takes effect as it otherwise would have after its submission to Congress and it is subject to possible disapproval by Congress. A rule covered by the CRA will not take effect if Congress adopts a joint resolution of disapproval within sixty legislative days. The President may veto the joint resolution, but Congress may then vote to override the veto. A rule that has been disapproved under the CRA is treated as though it had never taken effect, and no substantially similar rule may be issued without subsequent approval by Congress. Prior to 2017, the CRA had been used only once. In 2017, President Trump signed fifteen congressional resolutions disapproving rules issued at the end of the Obama administration.

5-2c EXECUTIVE BRANCH CONTROL

By virtue of their power to appoint and remove their chief administrators, U.S. Presidents have significant control over administrative agencies housed within the executive branch. With respect to independent agencies, however, Presidents have less control because commissioners serve for a fixed term that is staggered with a President's term of office. Nevertheless, the power of Presidents to appoint agency chairs and to fill vacancies confers considerable control, as does their power to remove commissioners for statutorily defined cause. The Presidents' central role in the budgeting process of agencies also enables them to exert great control over agency policy and operations. Even more extreme is a President's power to impound monies appropriated to an agency by Congress. In addition, a President may radically alter, combine, or even abolish agencies of the executive branch unless either house of Congress disapproves such an action within a prescribed time.

5-2d DISCLOSURE OF INFORMATION

Requiring administrative agencies to disclose information about their actions makes them more accountable to the public. Accordingly, Congress has enacted disclosure statutes to enhance public and political oversight of agency activities. These statutes include the Freedom of Information Act (FOIA), the Privacy Act, and the Government in the Sunshine Act.

FREEDOM OF INFORMATION ACT First enacted in 1966, FOIA gives the public access to most records in the files of Federal administrative agencies. Once a person has requested files, an agency must indicate within ten working days whether it intends to comply with the request and must within a reasonable time respond to the request. The agency may charge a fee for providing the records.

FOIA permits agencies to deny access to nine categories of records: (1) records specifically authorized in the interest of national defense or foreign policy to be kept secret, (2) records that relate solely to the internal personnel rules and practices of an agency, (3) records specifically exempted by statute from disclosure, (4) trade secrets and commercial or financial information that is privileged or confidential, (5) inter- or intra-agency memorandums, (6) personnel and medical files the disclosure of which would constitute a clearly unwarranted invasion of personal privacy, (7) investigatory records compiled for law enforcement purposes, (8) records that relate to the regulation or supervision of financial institutions, and (9) certain geological and geophysical information and data.

The Electronic Freedom of Information Act Amendments of 1996 require agencies to provide public access to information in an electronic format. Agencies must, within one year after their creation, make records available by computer telecommunications or other electronic means.

Practical Advice

Be aware that the Freedom of Information Act may give the public access to information you provide to administrative agencies.

PRIVACY ACT The Privacy Act of 1974 protects certain government records pertaining to individuals that a Federal agency maintains and retrieves by an individual's name or other personal identifier, including social security number. In general, the Privacy Act prohibits unauthorized disclosures of those records covered by the Act. It also gives individuals the right to review and copy records about themselves, to find out whether these records have been disclosed, and to request corrections or amendments of these records, unless the records are legally exempt. It also requires agencies to maintain in their records only that information about an individual that is relevant and necessary to accomplish an agency function and to collect information to the greatest extent practicable directly from the individual.

GOVERNMENT IN THE SUNSHINE ACT The Government in the Sunshine Act requires meetings of many Federal agencies to be open to the public. This Act applies to multimember bodies whose members the President appoints with the advice and consent of the Senate, such as the SEC, the FTC, the Federal Communications Commission, the CPSC, and the Commodity Futures Trading Commission. The Act does not cover executive agencies such as the EPA, the Food and Drug Administration, and the National Highway Traffic Safety Administration.

Agencies generally may close meetings on the same grounds that they may refuse disclosure of records under FOIA. In addition, agencies such as the SEC and the Federal Reserve Board may close meetings to protect information if disclosure would lead to financial speculation or endanger the stability of financial institutions. The Sunshine Act also permits agencies to close meetings that concern agency participation in pending or anticipated litigation.

CHAPTER SUMMARY

OPERATION OF ADMINISTRATIVE AGENCIES

Rulemaking process by which an administrative agency promulgates rules of law
- *Legislative Rules* substantive rules issued by an administrative agency under the authority delegated to it by the legislature
- *Interpretative Rules* statements issued by an administrative agency indicating how it construes the statutes and rules that it administers
- *Procedural Rules* rules issued by an administrative agency establishing its organization, method of operation, and rules of conduct for practice before the agency

Enforcement process by which agencies determine whether their rules have been violated

Adjudication formal methods by which an agency resolves disputes

LIMITS ON ADMINISTRATIVE AGENCIES

Judicial Review acts as a control or check by a court on a particular rule or order of an administrative agency

Legislative Control includes control over the agency's budget and enabling statute

Executive Branch Control includes the President's power to appoint members of the agency

Disclosure of Information congressionally required public disclosure enhances oversight of agency activities

C A S E S

CASE 5-1

Legislative Rules

MAYO FOUNDATION FOR MEDICAL EDUCATION AND RESEARCH v. UNITED STATES

Supreme Court of the United States, 2011
562 U.S. 44, 131 S.Ct. 704, 178 L.Ed.2d 588

Roberts, C. J.

I

Most doctors who graduate from medical school in the United States pursue additional education in a specialty to become board certified to practice in that field. Petitioners Mayo Foundation for Medical Education and Research, Mayo Clinic, and the Regents of the University of Minnesota (collectively Mayo) offer medical residency programs that provide such instruction. Mayo's residency programs, which usually last three to five years, train doctors primarily through hands-on experience. Residents often spend between 50 and 80 hours a week caring for patients, typically examining and diagnosing them, prescribing medication, recommending plans of care, and performing certain procedures. Residents are generally supervised in this work by more senior residents and by faculty members known as attending physicians. In 2005, Mayo paid its residents annual "stipends" ranging between $41,000 and $56,000 and provided them with health insurance, malpractice insurance, and paid vacation time.

Mayo residents also take part in "a formal and structured educational program." [Citation.] Residents are assigned textbooks and journal articles to read and are expected to attend weekly lectures and other conferences. Residents also take written exams and are evaluated by the attending faculty physicians. But the parties do not dispute that the bulk of residents' time is spent caring for patients.

Through the Social Security Act and related legislation, Congress has created a comprehensive national insurance system that provides benefits for retired workers, disabled workers, unemployed workers, and their families. [Citation.] Congress funds Social Security by taxing both employers and employees under FICA on the wages employees earn. [Citations.] Congress has defined "wages" broadly, to encompass "all remuneration for employment." § 3121(a). The term "employment" has a similarly broad reach, extending to "any service, of whatever nature, performed . . . by an employee for the person employing him." § 3121(b).

Congress has, however, exempted certain categories of service and individuals from FICA's [and Social Security Act] demands. As relevant here, Congress has excluded from taxation "service performed in the employ of . . . a school, college, or university . . . if such service is performed by a student who is enrolled and regularly attending classes at such school, college, or university." § 3121(b)(10). * * *

* * *

On December 21, 2004, the Department adopted an amended rule prescribing that an employee's service is "incident" to his studies only when "[t]he educational aspect of the relationship between the employer and the employee, as compared to the service aspect of the relationship, [is] predominant." [Citation.] The rule categorically provides that "[t]he services of a full-time employee"—as defined by the employer's policies, but in any event including any employee normally scheduled to work 40 hours or more per week—"are not incident to and for the purpose of pursuing a course of study." [Citation,] (the full-time employee rule). The amended provision clarifies that the Department's analysis "is not affected by the fact that the services performed . . . may have an educational, instructional, or training aspect." [Citation.] The rule also includes as an example the case of "Employee E," who is employed by "University V" as a medical resident. [Citation.] Because Employee E's "normal work schedule calls for [him] to perform services 40 or more hours per week," the rule provides that his service is "not incident to and for the purpose of pursuing a course of study," and he accordingly is not an exempt "student" under § 3121(b)(10). [Citation.]

After the Department promulgated the full-time employee rule, Mayo filed suit seeking a refund of the money it had withheld and paid on its residents' stipends during the second quarter of 2005. [Citation.] Mayo asserted that its residents were exempt under § 3121(b)(10) and that the Treasury Department's fulltime employee rule was invalid.

[The District Court granted Mayo's motion for summary judgment. The Government appealed, and the Court of Appeals reversed.]

We granted Mayo's petition for certiorari. [Citation.]

II

We begin our analysis with the first step of the two-part framework announced in *Chevron [USA Inc. v. Natural Resources Defense Council, Inc.]*, [citation], and ask whether Congress has "directly addressed the precise question at issue." We agree with the Court of Appeals that Congress has not done so. The statute does not define the term "student," and does not otherwise attend to the precise question whether medical residents are subject to FICA. [Citation.]

* * *

In the typical case, such an ambiguity would lead us inexorably to *Chevron* step two, under which we may not disturb an agency rule unless it is "'arbitrary or capricious in substance, or manifestly contrary to the statute.'" [Citation.] In this case, however, the parties disagree over the proper framework for evaluating an ambiguous provision of the Internal Revenue Code.

* * *

The principles underlying our decision in *Chevron* apply with full force in the tax context. *Chevron* recognized that "[t]he power of an administrative agency to administer a congressionally created . . . program necessarily requires the formulation of policy and the making of rules to fill any gap left, implicitly or explicitly, by Congress." [Citation.] * * * Filling gaps in the Internal Revenue Code plainly requires the Treasury Department to make interpretive choices for statutory implementation at least as complex as the ones other agencies must make in administering their statutes. [Citation.] We see no reason why our review of tax regulations should not be guided by agency expertise pursuant to *Chevron* to the same extent as our review of other regulations.

* * * We have held that *Chevron* deference is appropriate "when it appears that Congress delegated authority to the agency generally to make rules carrying the force of law, and that the agency interpretation claiming deference was promulgated in the exercise of that authority." * * *

* * * The Department issued the full-time employee rule pursuant to the explicit authorization to "prescribe all needful rules and regulations for the enforcement" of the Internal Revenue Code. [Citation.] * * *

* * *

The full-time employee rule easily satisfies the second step of *Chevron*, which asks whether the Department's rule is a "reasonable interpretation" of the enacted text. [Citation.] To begin, Mayo accepts that "the 'educational aspect of the relationship between the employer and the employee, as compared to the service aspect of the relationship, [must] be predominant'" in order for an individual to qualify for the exemption. [Citation.] Mayo objects, however, to the Department's conclusion that residents who work more than 40 hours per week categorically cannot satisfy that requirement. Because residents' employment is itself educational, Mayo argues, the hours a resident spends working make him "more of a student, not less of one." [Citation.] Mayo contends that the Treasury Department should be required to engage in a case-by-case inquiry into *what* [each] employee does [in his service] and *why*" he does it. [Citation.] Mayo also objects that the Department has drawn an arbitrary distinction between "hands-on training" and "classroom instruction." [Citation.]

We disagree. Regulation, like legislation, often requires drawing lines. Mayo does not dispute that the Treasury Department reasonably sought a way to distinguish between workers who study and students who work, [citation]. * * * The Department reasonably concluded that its full-time employee rule would "improve administrability," [citation], and it thereby "has avoided the wasteful litigation and continuing uncertainty that would inevitably accompany any purely case- by-case approach" like the one Mayo advocates, [citation].

* * *

We do not doubt that Mayo's residents are engaged in a valuable educational pursuit or that they are students of their craft. The question whether they are "students" for purposes of § 3121, however, is a different matter. Because it is one to which Congress has not directly spoken, and because the Treasury Department's rule is a reasonable construction of what Congress has said, the judgment of the Court of Appeals must be affirmed.

CASE
5-2

Interpretative Rules
PEREZ v. MORTGAGE BANKERS ASS'N.
Supreme Court of the United States, 2015
575 U.S. 92, 135 S.Ct. 1199, 191 L.Ed.2d 186

Sotomayor, J.

These cases began as a dispute over efforts by the Department of Labor to determine whether mortgage-loan officers are covered by the Fair Labor Standards Act of 1938 (FLSA), [citation]. [This statute is discussed in *Chapter 42*.] The FLSA "establishe[s] a minimum wage and overtime compensation for each hour worked in excess of 40 hours in each workweek" for many employees. [Citation.] Certain classes of employees, however, are exempt from these provisions. Among these exempt individuals are those "employed in a bona fide executive, administrative, or professional capacity . . . or in the capacity of outside salesman . . . ." [Citation.] The exemption for such employees is known as the "administrative" exemption.

The FLSA grants the Secretary of Labor authority to "defin[e]" and "delimi[t]" the categories of exempt administrative employees. [Citation.] The Secretary's current regulations regarding the administrative exemption were promulgated in 2004. As relevant here, the 2004 regulations differed from the previous regulations [issued in 1999 and 2001] in that they contained a new section providing several examples of exempt administrative employees. [Citation.] One of the examples is "[e]mployees in the financial services industry," who, depending on the nature of their day-to-day work, "generally meet the duties requirements for the administrative exception." [Citation.] The financial services example ends with a caveat, noting that "an employee whose primary duty is selling financial products does not qualify for the administrative exemption." [Citation.]

[In 2006, the Department issued an opinion letter finding that mortgage-loan officers fell within the administrative exemption. In 2010, however, the Wage and Hour Division again altered its interpretation of the FLSA's administrative exemption as it applied to mortgage-loan officers, concluding that mortgage-loan officers "have a primary duty of making sales for their employers, and, therefore, do not qualify" for the administrative exemption. The Department accordingly withdrew its 2006 opinion letter. Like the 1999, 2001, and 2006 opinion letters, the 2010 Administrator's Interpretation was issued without notice or an opportunity for comment.

MBA filed a complaint in federal District Court challenging the 2010 Administrator's Interpretation. MBA contended that the 2010 Administrator's Interpretation was procedurally invalid in light of the D.C. Circuit's decision in *Paralyzed Veterans*, which holds that an agency must use notice-and-comment procedures when an agency wishes to issue a new interpretation of a regulation that deviates significantly from a previously adopted interpretation. The District Court granted summary judgment to the Department. On appeal, the D.C. Circuit applied *Paralyzed Veterans* and reversed. The Department appealed to the U.S. Supreme Court.]

When a federal administrative agency first issues a rule interpreting one of its regulations, it is generally not required to follow the notice-and-comment rulemaking procedures of the Administrative Procedure Act (APA or Act). [Citation.] The United States Court of Appeals for the District of Columbia Circuit has nevertheless held, in a line of cases beginning with *Paralyzed Veterans of Am. v. D.C. Arena L. P.*, [citation], that an agency must use the APA's notice-and-comment procedures when it wishes to issue a new interpretation of a regulation that deviates significantly from one the agency has previously adopted. The question in these cases is whether the rule announced in *Paralyzed Veterans* is consistent with the APA. We hold that it is not.

The APA establishes the procedures federal administrative agencies use for "rule making," defined as the process of "formulating, amending, or repealing a rule." [Citation.] "Rule," in turn, is defined broadly to include "statement[s] of general or particular applicability and future effect" that are designed to "implement, interpret, or prescribe law or policy." [Citation.]

Section 4 of the APA, [citation], prescribes a three-step procedure for so-called "notice-and-comment rule-making." First, the agency must issue a "[g]eneral notice of proposed rule making," ordinarily by publication in the Federal Register. [Citation.] Second, if "notice [is] required," the agency must "give interested persons an opportunity to participate in the rule making through submission of written data, views, or arguments." [Citation.] An agency must consider and respond to significant comments received during the period for public comment. [Citation.] Third, when the agency promulgates the final rule, it must include in the rule's text "a concise general statement of [its] basis and purpose." [Citation.] Rules issued through the notice-and-comment process are often referred to as "legislative rules" because they have the "force and effect of law." [Citation.]

Not all "rules" must be issued through the notice-and-comment process. Section 4(b)(A) of the APA provides that, unless another statute states otherwise, the notice-and-comment requirement "does not apply" to "interpretative rules, general statements of policy, or rules of agency organization, procedure, or practice." [Citation.] The term "interpretative rule," or "interpretive rule," is not further defined by the APA, * * * it suffices to say that the critical feature of interpretive rules is that they are "issued by an agency to advise the public of the agency's construction of the statutes and rules which it administers." [Citation.] The absence of a notice-and-comment obligation makes the process of issuing interpretive rules comparatively easier for agencies than issuing legislative rules. But that convenience comes at a price: Interpretive rules "do not have the force and effect of law and are not accorded that weight in the adjudicatory process." [Citation.]

* * *

* * * This exemption of interpretive rules from the notice-and-comment process is categorical, and it is fatal to the rule announced in *Paralyzed Veterans*.

Rather than examining the exemption for interpretive rules contained in §4(b)(A) of the APA, the D.C. Circuit in *Paralyzed Veterans* focused its attention on §1 of the Act. That section defines "rule making" to include not only the initial issuance of new rules, but also "repeal[s]" or "amend[ments]" of existing rules. [Citation.] Because notice-and-comment requirements may apply even to these later agency actions, the court reasoned, "allow[ing] an agency to make a fundamental change in its interpretation of a substantive regulation without notice and comment" would undermine the APA's procedural framework. [Citation.]

* * * Because an agency is not required to use notice-and-comment procedures to issue an initial interpretive rule, it is also not required to use those procedures when it amends or repeals that interpretive rule.

The straightforward reading of the APA we now adopt harmonizes with longstanding principles of our administrative law jurisprudence. Time and again, we have reiterated that the APA "sets forth the full extent of judicial authority to review executive agency action for procedural correctness." *Fox Television Stations, Inc.,* [citation]. Beyond the APA's minimum requirements, courts lack authority "to impose upon [an] agency its own notion of which procedures are 'best' or most likely to further some vague, undefined public good." [Citation.] To do otherwise would violate "the very basic tenet of administrative law that agencies should be free to fashion their own rules of procedure." [Citation.]

These foundational principles apply with equal force to the APA's procedures for rulemaking. We explained in [citation] that §4 of the Act "established the maximum procedural requirements which Congress was willing to have the courts impose upon agencies in conducting rulemaking procedures." [Citation.] "Agencies are free to grant additional procedural rights in the exercise of their discretion, but reviewing courts are generally not free to impose them if the agencies have not chosen to grant them." [Citation.]

The *Paralyzed Veterans* doctrine creates just such a judge-made procedural right: the right to notice and an opportunity to comment when an agency changes its interpretation of one of the regulations it enforces. That requirement may be wise policy. Or it may not. Regardless, imposing such an obligation is the responsibility of Congress or the administrative agencies, not the courts. We trust that Congress weighed the costs and benefits of placing more rigorous procedural restrictions on the issuance of interpretive rules. [Citation.] In the end, Congress decided to adopt standards that permit agencies to promulgate freely such rules—whether or not they are consistent with earlier interpretations. That the D.C. Circuit would have struck the balance differently does not permit that court or this one to overturn Congress' contrary judgment. [Citation.]

* * *

For the foregoing reasons, the judgment of the United States Court of Appeals for the District of Columbia Circuit is reversed.

CASE 5-3	Judicial Review: Standing **SACKETT v. ENVIRONMENTAL PROTECTION AGENCY** Supreme Court of the United States, 2012 566 U.S. 120, 132 S.Ct. 1367, 182 L.Ed.2d 367	

Scalia, J.

[The Clean Water Act (Act) prohibits "the discharge of any pollutant by any person," without a permit, into the "navigable waters," which the Act defines as "the waters of the United States." If the Environmental Protection Agency (EPA) determines that any person is in violation of this restriction, the Act directs the agency either to issue a compliance order or to initiate a civil enforcement action. When the EPA prevails in a civil action, the Act provides for a civil penalty not to exceed $37,500 per day for each violation. According to the government, when the EPA prevails against any person who has been issued a compliance order but has failed to comply, that amount is increased to $75,000.

The Sacketts own a two-thirds-acre residential lot in Bonner County, Idaho. Their property lies just north of Priest Lake, but it is separated from the lake by several lots containing permanent structures. In preparation for constructing a house, the Sacketts filled in part of their lot with dirt and rock. Some months later, they received from the EPA a compliance order, which stated that their residential lot contained navigable waters and that their construction project violated the Act by placing fill material on the property. On that basis the order directs them immediately to restore the property pursuant to an EPA work plan and to provide the EPA with access to the site and all records and documents related to the conditions at the site.

The Sacketts, who do not believe that their property is subject to the Act, asked the EPA for a hearing, but that request was denied. They then brought an action in the U.S. District Court for the District of Idaho, seeking declaratory and injunctive relief. Their complaint contended that the EPA's issuance of the compliance order was "arbitrary [and] capricious" under the Administrative Procedure Act (APA) and that it deprived them of "life, liberty, or property, without due process of law," in violation of the Fifth Amendment. The District Court dismissed the claims for want of subject-matter jurisdiction. The U.S. Court of Appeals for the Ninth Circuit affirmed, concluding that the Act "preclude[s] pre-enforcement judicial review of compliance orders" and that such preclusion does not violate the Fifth Amendment's due process guarantee. The U.S. Supreme Court granted *certiorari.*]

The Sacketts brought suit under Chapter 7 of the APA, which provides for judicial review of "final agency action for which there is no other adequate remedy in a court." [Citation.] We consider first whether the compliance order is final agency action. There is no doubt it is agency action, which the APA defines as including even a "failure to act." [Citation.] But is it *final?* It has all of the hallmarks of APA finality that our opinions establish. Through the order, the EPA "'determined'" "'rights or obligations.'" [Citation.] * * * Also, "'legal consequences . . . flow'" from issuance of the order. [Citation.] * * *

The issuance of the compliance order also marks the "'consummation'" of the agency's decisionmaking process. [Citation.] As the Sacketts learned when they unsuccessfully sought a hearing, the "Findings and Conclusions" that the compliance order contained were not subject to further agency review. * * *

The APA's judicial review provision also requires that the person seeking APA review of final agency action have "no other adequate remedy in a court," [Citation.] In Clean Water Act enforcement cases, judicial review ordinarily comes by way of a civil action brought by the EPA under [citation]. But the Sacketts cannot initiate that process, and each day they wait for the agency to drop the hammer, they accrue * * * an additional $75,000 in potential liability. The other possible route to judicial review-applying to the Corps of Engineers for a permit and then filing suit under the APA if a permit is denied—will not serve either. * * *

Nothing in the Clean Water Act *expressly* precludes judicial review under the APA or otherwise. But in determining "[w]hether and to what extent a particular statute precludes judicial review," we do not look "only [to] its express language." [Citation.] The APA, we have said, creates a "presumption favoring judicial review of administrative action," but as with most presumptions, this one "may be overcome by inferences of intent drawn from the statutory scheme as a whole." The Government offers several reasons why the statutory scheme of the Clean Water Act precludes review. [The Supreme Court found that these arguments did not support an inference that the Clean Water Act's statutory scheme precluded APA review.]

* * *

We conclude that the compliance order in this case is final agency action for which there is no adequate remedy other than APA review, and that the Clean Water Act does not preclude that review. We therefore reverse the judgment of the Court of Appeals and remand the case for further proceedings consistent with this opinion.

CASE 5-4

Judicial Review: Questions of Fact
FCC v. FOX TELEVISION STATIONS, INC.
Supreme Court of the United States, 2009
556 U.S. 502, 129 S.Ct. 1800, 173 L.Ed.2d 738

Scalia, J.

Federal law prohibits the broadcasting of "any . . . indecent . . . language," [citation], which includes expletives referring to sexual or excretory activity or organs, see [citation]. This case concerns the adequacy of the Federal Communications Commission's explanation of its decision that this sometimes forbids the broadcasting of indecent expletives even when the offensive words are not repeated.

* * *

* * * Congress has given the Commission various means of enforcing the indecency ban, including civil fines, see § 503(b)(1), and license revocations or the denial of license renewals, [citation].

The Commission first invoked the statutory ban on indecent broadcasts in 1975, declaring a daytime broadcast of George Carlin's "Filthy Words" monologue actionably indecent. [Citation.] At that time, the Commission announced the definition of indecent speech that it uses to this day, prohibiting "language that describes, in terms patently offensive as measured by contemporary community standards for the broadcast medium, sexual or excretory activities or organs, at times of the day when there is a reasonable risk that children may be in the audience." [Citation.]

* * *

In the ensuing years, the Commission took a cautious, but gradually expanding, approach to enforcing the statutory prohibition against indecent broadcasts. * * *

Although the Commission had expanded its enforcement beyond the "repetitive use of specific words or phrases," it preserved a distinction between literal and nonliteral (or "expletive") uses of evocative language. [Citation.] The Commission explained that each literal "description or depiction of sexual or excretory functions must be examined in context to determine whether it is patently offensive," but that "deliberate and repetitive use . . . is a requisite to a finding of indecency" when a complaint focuses solely on the use of nonliteral expletives. [Citation.]

In 2004, the Commission took one step further by declaring for the first time that a nonliteral (expletive) use of the F- and S-Words could be actionably indecent, even when the word is used only once. The first order to this effect dealt with an NBC broadcast of the Golden Globe Awards, in the performer Bono commented, "'This is really, really, f* * *ing brilliant.'" * * *

* * *

This case concerns utterances in two live broadcasts aired by Fox Television Stations, Inc., and its affiliates prior to the Commission's Golden Globes Order. The first occurred during the 2002 Billboard Music Awards, when the singer Cher exclaimed, "I've also had critics for the last 40 years saying that I was on my way out every year. Right. So f* * * 'em." [Citation.] The second involved a segment of the 2003 Billboard Music Awards, during the presentation of an award by Nicole Richie and Paris Hilton, principals in a Fox television series called "The Simple Life." Ms. Hilton began their interchange by reminding Ms. Richie to "watch the bad language," but Ms. Richie proceeded to ask the audience, "Why do they even call it 'The Simple Life?' Have you ever tried to get cow s* * * out of a Prada purse? It's not so f* * *ing simple." [Citation.] Following each of these broadcasts, the Commission received numerous complaints from parents whose children were exposed to the language.

On March 15, 2006, the Commission released Notices of Apparent Liability for a number of broadcasts that the Commission deemed actionably indecent, including the two described above. [Citation.] * * *

The order first explained that both broadcasts fell comfortably within the subject-matter scope of the Commission's indecency test because the 2003 broadcast involved a literal description of excrement and both broadcasts invoked the "F-Word," which inherently has a sexual connotation.

[Citation.] The order next determined that the broadcasts were patently offensive under community standards for the medium. * * *

* * *

The order explained that the Commission's prior "strict dichotomy between 'expletives' and 'descriptions or depictions of sexual or excretory functions' is artificial and does not make sense in light of the fact that an 'expletive's' power to offend derives from its sexual or excretory meaning." * * * Although the Commission determined that Fox encouraged the offensive language by using suggestive scripting in the 2003 broadcast, and unreasonably failed to take adequate precautions in both broadcasts, [citation], the order * * * declined to impose any forfeiture or other sanction for either of the broadcasts, [citation].

* * * The [Second Circuit] Court of Appeals reversed the agency's orders, finding the Commission's reasoning inadequate under the Administrative Procedure Act. [Citation.] The majority was "skeptical that the Commission [could] provide a reasoned explanation for its 'fleeting expletive' regime that would pass constitutional muster," but it declined to reach the constitutional question. [Citation.] We granted certiorari, [citation].

The Administrative Procedure Act, [citation], which sets forth the full extent of judicial authority to review executive agency action for procedural correctness, [citation], permits (insofar as relevant here) the setting aside of agency action that is "arbitrary" or "capricious," [citation]. Under what we have called this "narrow" standard of review, we insist that an agency "examine the relevant data and articulate a satisfactory explanation for its action." *Motor Vehicle Mfrs. Assn. of United States, Inc. v. State Farm Mut. Automobile Ins. Co.,* [citation]. We have made clear, however, that "a court is not to substitute its judgment for that of the agency," [citation], and should "uphold a decision of less than ideal clarity if the agency's path may reasonably be discerned," [citation].

In overturning the Commission's judgment, the Court of Appeals here relied in part on Circuit precedent requiring a more substantial explanation for agency action that changes prior policy. * * *

We find no basis in the Administrative Procedure Act or in our opinions for a requirement that all agency change be subjected to more searching review. * * * The statute makes no distinction, however, between initial agency action and subsequent agency action undoing or revising that action.

To be sure, the requirement that an agency provide reasoned explanation for its action would ordinarily demand that it display awareness that it *is* changing position. An agency may not, for example, depart from a prior policy *sub silentio* or simply disregard rules that are still on the books. [Citation.] And of course the agency must show that there are good reasons for the new policy. But it need not demonstrate to a court's satisfaction that the reasons for the new policy are better than the reasons for the old one; it suffices that the new policy is permissible under the statute, that there are good reasons for it, and that the agency *believes* it to be better, which the conscious change of course adequately indicates. This means that the agency need not always provide a more detailed justification than what would suffice for a new policy created on a blank slate. * * * In such cases it is not that further justification is demanded by the mere fact of policy change; but that a reasoned explanation is needed for disregarding facts and circumstances that underlay or were engendered by the prior policy.

Judged under the above described standards, the Commission's new enforcement policy and its order finding the broadcasts actionably indecent were neither arbitrary nor capricious. First, the Commission forthrightly acknowledged that its recent actions have broken new ground, taking account of inconsistent "prior Commission and staff action" and explicitly disavowing them as "no longer good law." [Citation.] * * * There is no doubt that the Commission knew it was making a change. That is why it declined to assess penalties * * *.

Moreover, the agency's reasons for expanding the scope of its enforcement activity were entirely rational. * * * Even isolated utterances can be made in "pander[ing,] . . . vulgar and shocking" manners, [citation], and can constitute harmful "'first blow[s]'" to children, [citation]. It is surely rational (if not inescapable) to believe that a safe harbor for single words would "likely lead to more widespread use of the offensive language." [Citation.]

* * *

The judgment of the United States Court of Appeals for the Second Circuit is reversed, and the case is remanded for further proceedings consistent with this opinion.

[In deciding this case on remand, the Second Circuit Court of Appeals found the Federal Communications Commission's (FCC) policy unconstitutionally vague and invalidated it in its entirety. The U.S. Supreme Court vacated the Second Circuit's decision but ruled against the FCC's imposing sanctions against Fox. The Supreme Court explained that under the Due Process Clause laws must give fair notice of conduct that is forbidden or required and laws that are impermissibly vague must be invalidated. The Court held that because the FCC failed to give Fox fair notice prior to the broadcasts in question that fleeting expletives could be found actionably indecent, the FCC's standards as applied to these broadcasts were vague, and therefore the FCC's orders must be set aside. The Supreme Court noted that its decision (1) does not address the First Amendment implications of the FCC's indecency policy; (2) leaves the FCC free to modify its current indecency policy in light of its determination of the public interest and applicable legal requirements; and (3) leaves the courts free to review the current policy or any modified policy in light of its content and application. *FCC v. Fox Television Stations, Inc.*, 567 U.S. 239 (2012).]

C A S E   P R O B L E M S

1. In 1942, Congress passed the Emergency Price Control Act in the interest of national defense and security. The stated purpose of the Act was "to stabilize prices and to prevent speculative, unwarranted and abnormal increases in prices and rents." The Act established the Office of Price Administration, which was authorized to establish maximum prices and rents that were to be "generally fair and equitable and [were to] effectuate the purposes of this Act." Convicted for selling beef at prices in excess of those set by the agency, Stark appeals on the ground that the Act unconstitutionally delegated to the agency the legislative power of Congress to control prices. Is Stark correct in this contention? Explain.

2. The Secretary of Commerce (Secretary) published notice in the *Federal Register* inviting comments regarding flammability standards for mattresses. Statistical data were compiled, consultant studies were conducted, and seventy-five groups submitted comments. The Secretary then determined that all mattresses, including crib mattresses, must pass a cigarette test, consisting of bringing a mattress in contact with a burning cigarette. The department's staff supported this position by stating: "Exemption of youth and crib mattresses is not recommended. While members of these age groups do not smoke, their parents frequently do, and the accidental dropping of a lighted cigarette on these mattresses while attending to a child is a distinct possibility." Bunny Bear, Inc., now challenges the cigarette flammability test, asserting that the standard was not shown to be applicable to crib mattresses, because "infants and young children obviously do not smoke." Bunny Bear argues that the Secretary has not satisfied the burden of proof justifying the inclusion of crib mattresses within this general safety standard. Is Bunny Bear correct? Explain.

3. Reagan National Airport in Washington, D.C., ("National") is one of the busiest and most crowded airports in the nation. Accordingly, the Federal Aviation Administration (FAA) has restricted the number of commercial landing and takeoff slots at National to forty per hour. Allocation of the slots among the air carriers

serving National had been by voluntary agreement through an airline scheduling committee (ASC). When a new carrier requested twenty slots during peak hours, National's ASC was unable to agree on a slot allocation schedule. The FAA engaged in informal rulemaking and invited public comment as a means to solve the slot allocation dilemma. The FAA then issued Special Federal Aviation Regulation 43 (SFAR 43) based on public comments and a proposal made at the last National ASC meeting, thereby decreasing the number of slots held by current carriers and shifting some slots to less desirable times. SFAR 43 also granted eighteen slots to the new carrier. More specifically, SFAR 43 requires five carriers to give up one or more slots in specific hours during the day, requires twelve carriers to shift one slot to the latest hour of operations, and then reserves and allocates the yielded slots among the new entrants and several other carriers. An adversely affected carrier seeks judicial review of SFAR 43, claiming that it is arbitrary, capricious, and not a product of reasoned decision making, and that it capriciously favors the Washington-New York market as well as the new carrier. What standard would apply to the agency's actions? Should the rule be upheld? Explain.

4. Bachowski was defeated in a United Steelworkers of America union election. After exhausting his union remedies, Bachowski filed a complaint with Secretary of Labor Dunlop. Bachowski invoked the Labor–Management Reporting and Disclosure Act, which required Dunlop to investigate the complaint and determine whether to bring a court action to set aside the election. Dunlop decided such action was unwarranted. Bachowski then filed an action in a Federal district court to order Dunlop to file suit to set aside the election. What standard of review would apply and what would Bachowski have to prove to prevail under that standard?

5. The Federal Crop Insurance Corporation (FCIC) was created as a wholly government-owned corporation to insure wheat producers against unavoidable crop failure. As required by law, the FCIC published in the *Federal Register* conditions for crop insurance. Specifically, the FCIC published that spring wheat reseeded on winter wheat acreage was ineligible for coverage. When farmer Merrill applied for insurance on his wheat crop, he informed the local FCIC agent that 400 of his 460 acres of spring wheat were reseeded on the winter wheat acreage. The agent advised Merrill that his entire crop was insurable. When drought destroyed Merrill's wheat, Merrill tried to collect the insurance, but the FCIC refused to pay, asserting that Merrill was bound by the

notice provided by publication of the regulation in the *Federal Register*. Is the FCIC correct? Explain.

6. The Department of Energy (DOE) issued a subpoena requesting information regarding purchases, sales, exchanges, and other transactions in crude oil from Phoenix Petroleum Company (Phoenix). The aim of the DOE audit was to uncover violations of the Emergency Petroleum Allocation Act (EPAA), which provided for summary, or expedited, enforcement of DOE decisions. However, after the subpoena was issued but before Phoenix had responded, the EPAA expired. The EPAA provided that:

> The authority to promulgate and amend any regulation, or to issue any order under this Chapter shall expire at midnight September 30, 1981, but such expiration shall not affect any action or pending proceedings, administrative, civil or criminal action or proceeding, whether or not pending, based upon any act committed or liability incurred prior to such expiration date.

Using the summary enforcement provisions of the now-defunct EPAA, the DOE sues to enforce the subpoena. Phoenix argues that because the EPAA has expired, the DOE lacks the authority either to issue the subpoena or to use the summary enforcement provisions. Is Phoenix correct? Why or why not?

7. Under the Communications Act, the Federal Communications Commission may not impose common carrier obligations on cable operators. A common carrier is one that "makes a public offering to provide [communication facilities] whereby all members of the public who choose to employ such facilities may communicate or transmit." In May 1976, the Commission issued rules requiring cable television systems of a designated size (a) to develop a minimum twenty-channel capacity by 1986, (b) to make available on a first-come, nondiscriminatory basis certain channels for access by third parties, and (c) to furnish equipment and facilities for such access. The purpose of these rules was to ensure public access to cable systems. Midwest Video Corporation claimed that the access rules exceeded the Commission's jurisdiction granted it by the Communications Act of 1934, because the rules infringe upon the cable systems' journalistic freedom by in effect treating the cable operators as "common carriers." The Commission contended that its expansive mandate under the Communications Act to supervise and regulate broadcasting encompassed the access rules. Did the Commission exceed its authority under the Act? Why or why not?

8. Congress enacted the National Traffic and Motor Vehicle Safety Act of 1966 (the Act) for the purpose of reducing

the number of traffic accidents that result in death or personal injury. The Act directs the Secretary of Transportation to issue motor vehicle safety standards in order to improve the design and safety features of cars. The Secretary has delegated authority to promulgate safety standards to the National Highway Traffic Safety Administration (NHTSA) under the informal rulemaking procedure of the APA. The Act also authorizes judicial review under the provisions of the Administrative Procedure Act (APA) of all orders establishing, amending, or revoking a Federal motor vehicle safety standard issued by the NHTSA.

Pursuant to the Act, the NHTSA issued Motor Vehicle Safety Standard 208, which required all cars made after September 1982 to be equipped with passive restraints (either automatic seat belts or airbags). The cost of implementing the standard was estimated to be around $1 billion. However, early in 1981, due to changes in economic circumstances and particularly due to complaints from the automotive industry, the NHTSA rescinded Standard 208. The NHTSA had originally assumed that car manufacturers would install airbags in 60 percent of new cars and passive seat belts in 40 percent. However, by 1981, it appeared that manufacturers were planning to install seat belts in 99 percent of all new cars. Moreover, the majority of passive seatbelts could be easily and permanently detached by consumers. Therefore, the NHTSA felt that Standard 208 would not result in any significant safety benefits.

State Farm Mutual Automobile Insurance Company (State Farm) and the National Association of Independent Insurers (NAII) filed petitions in Federal court for review of the NHTSA's rescission of Standard 208. What standard of review would apply to the rescission? Should it be set aside? Explain.

9. David Diersen filed a complaint against the Chicago Car Exchange (CCE), an automobile dealership, alleging that the CCE fraudulently furnished him an inaccurate odometer reading when it sold him a 1968 Dodge Charger, in violation of the Vehicle Information and Cost Savings Act (the Odometer Act or the Act). The Odometer Act requires all persons transferring a motor vehicle to give an accurate, written odometer reading to the purchaser or recipient of the transferred vehicle. Under the Act, those who disclose an inaccurate odometer reading with the intent to defraud are subject to a private cause of action by the purchaser and may be held liable for treble damages or $1,500, whichever is greater. The CCE had purchased the vehicle from Joseph Slaski, who certified to the CCE that the mileage was approximately 22,600. The CCE did not suspect that the

odometer reading was inaccurate. After purchasing the vehicle, Diersen conducted an extensive investigation and discovered that the vehicle's title documents previously listed its mileage as 75,000. Before Diersen filed this lawsuit, the CCE offered to have Diersen return the car for a complete refund. Diersen refused this offer and decided instead to sue the CCE under the Act. The district court granted the defendant's motion for summary judgment, relying upon a regulation promulgated by the National Highway Traffic Safety Administration (NHTSA) which purports to exempt vehicles that are at least ten years old (such as the one Diersen purchased from the CCE) from the Act's odometer disclosure requirements. Diersen then filed a motion for reconsideration of the court's summary judgment order, arguing that the older-car exemption created by the NHTSA lacked any basis in the Act and was therefore invalid. Should Dierson's motion for reconsideration be granted? Explain.

10. The Public Company Accounting Oversight Board (PCAOB) was created as part of a series of accounting reforms in the Sarbanes-Oxley Act of 2002. The PCAOB is a governmentally created entity with expansive powers to regulate the entire accounting industry. Every accounting firm that audits public companies under the securities laws must register with the PCAOB, pay it an annual fee, and comply with its rules and oversight. The PCAOB may inspect registered firms, initiate formal investigations, and issue severe sanctions in its disciplinary proceedings. Although the Securities and Exchange Commission (SEC) appoints PCAOB members and has oversight of the PCAOB, it cannot remove PCAOB members at will, but only "for good cause shown," and "in accordance with" specified procedures. The SEC Commissioners, in turn, cannot themselves be removed by the President except for "inefficiency, neglect of duty, or malfeasance in office." Parties with standing have challenged in a U.S. District Court the constitutionality of the Sarbanes-Oxley Act's creation of the PCAOB because it conferred executive power on PCAOB members without subjecting them to presidential control. What should the court decide? Explain.

11. Present and former law review editors who were researching disciplinary systems and procedures at the military service academies for an article requested, but were denied, access to case summaries of honor and ethics hearings maintained in the U.S. Air Force Academy's Honor and Ethics Code reading files. Personal references and other identifying information are deleted from these summaries. It was the Academy's practice to

post copies of such summaries on forty squadron bulletin boards throughout the Academy and to distribute copies to Academy faculty and administration officials. The editors brought an action under the Freedom of Information Act (FOIA) against the Department of the Air Force to compel disclosure of the case summaries. Which exemptions to FOIA are most applicable? Explain whether any of these exemptions would enable the Academy to withhold the requested case summaries.

T A K I N G   S I D E S

Section 7(a)(2) of the Endangered Species Act of 1973 (ESA) provides (in relevant part) that:

> Each Federal agency shall, in consultation with and with the assistance of the Secretary (of the Interior), insure that any action authorized, funded, or carried out by such agency . . . is not likely to jeopardize the continued existence of any endangered species or threatened species or result in the destruction or adverse modification of habitat of such species which is determined by the Secretary, after consultation as appropriate with affected States, to be critical.

In 1978, the Fish and Wildlife Service and the National Marine Fisheries Service, on behalf of the Secretary of the Interior and the Secretary of Commerce respectively, promulgated a joint regulation stating that the obligations imposed by Section 7(a)(2) extend to actions taken in foreign nations. In 1983, the Interior Department proposed a revised joint regulation that would require consultation only for actions taken in the United States or on the high seas. Shortly thereafter, Defenders of Wildlife and other organizations filed an action against the Secretary of the Interior, seeking a declaratory judgment that the new regulation is in error as to the geographic scope of Section 7(a)(2) and an injunction requiring the Secretary to promulgate a new regulation restoring the initial interpretation. The Secretary asserted that the plaintiffs did not have standing to bring this action.

a. What arguments would support the plaintiff's standing to bring this action?

b. What arguments would support the Secretary's claim that the plaintiffs did not have standing to bring this action?

c. Which side's arguments are most convincing? Explain.

CHAPTER 6

Criminal Law

After reading and studying this chapter, you should be able to:

- Describe criminal intent and the various degrees of mental fault.

- Identify the significant features of white-collar crimes, corporate crimes, and the Racketeer Influenced and Corrupt Organizations Act (RICO).

- Define the crimes against business.

- Describe the defenses of person or property, duress, mistake of fact, and entrapment.

- Explain the constitutional amendments affecting criminal procedure.

As discussed in *Chapter 1*, the civil law defines duties the violation of which constitutes a wrong against the injured party. The criminal law, on the other hand, establishes duties the violation of which is a societal wrong against the whole community. Civil law is a part of private law, whereas criminal law is a part of public law. In a civil action, the injured party sues to recover compensation for the damage and injury that he has sustained as a result of the defendant's wrongful conduct. The party bringing a civil action (the plaintiff) has the burden of proof, which he must sustain by a preponderance (greater weight) of the evidence. The purpose of the civil law is to compensate the injured party.

Criminal law, by comparison, is designed to prevent harm to society by defining criminal conduct and establishing punishment for such conduct. In a criminal case, the defendant is prosecuted by the government, which must prove the defendant's guilt beyond a reasonable doubt, a burden of proof significantly higher than that required in a civil action. Moreover, under our legal system, guilt is never presumed. Indeed, the law presumes the innocence of the accused, and the defendant's failure to testify in her own defense does not affect this presumption. The government still has the burden of affirmatively proving the guilt of the accused beyond a reasonable doubt.

Of course, the same conduct may, and often does, constitute both a crime and a tort, which is a civil wrong. (Torts are discussed in *Chapters 7* and *8*.) But an act may be criminal without being tortious; by the same token, an act may be a tort but not a crime.

Because of the increasing use of criminal sanctions to enforce government regulation of business, criminal law is an essential part of business law. Moreover, businesses sustain considerable loss as victims of criminal actions. Accordingly, this chapter covers the general principles of criminal law and criminal procedure as well as specific crimes relevant to business.

6-1 Nature of Crimes

A **crime** is any act or omission forbidden by public law in the interest of protecting society and made punishable by the government in a judicial proceeding brought by it. Punishment for criminal conduct includes fines, imprisonment, probation, and death. In addition, some States and the Federal government have enacted victim indemnification statutes that establish funds, financed by criminal fines, to provide indemnification in limited amounts to victims of criminal activity. Crimes are prohibited and punished on grounds of public policy, which may include the protection and safeguarding of government (as in treason), human life (as in murder), or private property (as in larceny). Additional purposes of the criminal law include deterrence, rehabilitation, and retribution.

Historically, criminal law was primarily common law. In the twenty-first century, however, criminal law is almost exclusively statutory. All States have enacted comprehensive criminal law statutes (or codes) covering most, if not all, common law crimes. Since its promulgation in 1962, the American Law Institute's Model Penal Code has played an important part in the widespread revision and codification of the substantive criminal law of the United States. (In 2017, the ALI approved revisions to the sentencing provisions of the 1962 Model Penal Code.) Moreover, these statutes have made the number of crimes defined in criminal law far greater than the number of crimes defined under common law. Some codes expressly limit crimes to those included in the codes, thus abolishing common law crimes. Nonetheless, some States do not statutorily define all of their crimes; their courts, therefore, must rely on the common law definitions. Because there are no Federal common law crimes, all Federal crimes are statutory.

Within recent times, the scope of criminal law has increased greatly. The scope of traditional criminal conduct has been expanded by numerous regulations and laws that contain criminal penalties pertaining to nearly every phase of modern living. Typical examples in the field of business law are those laws concerning the licensing and conduct of a business, antitrust laws, and the laws governing the sales of securities.

6-1a ESSENTIAL ELEMENTS

In general, a crime consists of two elements: (1) the wrongful or overt act (*actus reus*) and (2) the criminal intent (*mens rea*). For example, to support a larceny conviction it is not enough to show that the defendant stole another's goods; it also must be established that he intended to steal the goods. Conversely, criminal intent without an overt act is not a crime. For instance, Ann decides to rob the neighborhood grocery store and then really "live it up." Without more, Ann has committed no crime.

Actus reus refers to all the nonmental elements of a crime, including the physical act that must be performed, the consequences of that act, and the circumstances under which it must be performed. The *actus reus* required for specific crimes will be discussed later in this chapter.

Mens rea, or mental fault, refers to the mental element of a crime. Most common law and some statutory crimes require subjective fault, other crimes require objective fault, while some statutory crimes require no fault at all. The Model Penal Code and most modern criminal statutes recognize three possible types of **subjective fault**: purposeful, knowing, and reckless. A person acts *purposely* or *intentionally* if his conscious object is to engage in the prohibited conduct or to cause the prohibited result. Thus, if Arthur, with the desire to kill Donna, shoots his rifle at Donna, who is seemingly out of

gunshot range, and in fact does kill her, Arthur had the purpose or intent to kill Donna. If Benjamin, desiring to poison Paula, places a toxic chemical in the water cooler in Paula's office and unwittingly poisons Gail and Victor, Benjamin will be found to have purposefully killed Gail and Victor because Benjamin's intent to kill Paula is transferred to Gail and Victor, regardless of Benjamin's feelings toward Gail and Victor.

A person acts *knowingly* if he is aware that his conduct is of a prohibited type or that a prohibited consequence is practically certain to result. A person acts *recklessly* if he consciously disregards a substantial and unjustifiable risk (1) that his conduct is prohibited or (2) that it will cause a prohibited result.

Objective fault involves a gross deviation from the standard of care that a reasonable person would observe under the circumstances. Criminal statutes refer to objective fault by such terms as *carelessness* or *negligence*. Such conduct occurs when a person *should* be aware of a substantial and unjustifiable risk that his conduct is prohibited or will cause a prohibited result. Examples of crimes requiring objective fault are involuntary manslaughter (negligently causing the death of another; carelessly driving an automobile; and in some States, issuing a bad check.

Many regulatory statutes have totally dispensed with the mental element of a crime by imposing criminal liability without fault. Without regard to the care that a person exercises, criminal liability without fault makes it a crime for a person to commit a specified act or to bring about a certain result. Statutory crimes imposing **liability without fault** include the sale of adulterated food and the sale of alcoholic beverages to a minor. Most of these crimes involve regulatory statutes dealing with health and safety and impose only fines for violations.

◆ **SEE FIGURE 6-1:** *Degrees of Mental Fault*

6-1b CLASSIFICATION

Historically, crimes were classified *mala in se* (wrongs in themselves or morally wrong, such as murder) or *mala prohibita* (not morally wrong but declared wrongful by law, such as the prohibition against making a U-turn). From the standpoint of the seriousness of the offense, a crime is also classified as a

FIGURE 6-1 Degrees of Mental Fault

Type	Fault Required	Examples
Subjective Fault	Purposeful Knowing Reckless	Larceny Embezzlement
Objective Fault	Negligent Careless	Careless driving Issuing bad checks (some States)
Liability Without Fault	None	Sale of alcohol to minor Sale of adulterated food

felony (a serious crime punishable by death or imprisonment in the penitentiary) or as a **misdemeanor** (a less serious crime punishable by a fine or imprisonment in a local jail).

6-1c VICARIOUS LIABILITY

Vicarious liability is liability imposed upon one person for the acts of another. Employers are vicariously liable for any authorized criminal act of their employees if the employer directed, participated in, or approved of the act. For example, if an employer directs an employee to fix prices with the employer's competitors and the employee does so, both the employer and employee have criminally violated the Sherman Antitrust Act. On the other hand, employers are ordinarily not liable for the unauthorized criminal acts of their employees. As previously discussed, most crimes require mental fault; this element is absent, so far as criminal responsibility of the employer is concerned, in cases in which the employee's criminal act was not authorized.

Employers, however, may be subject to a criminal penalty for the unauthorized act of a manager acting in the scope of employment. Moreover, employers may be criminally liable under liability without fault statutes for certain unauthorized acts of their employees, whether or not those employees are managerial. For example, many States have statutes that punish "every person who by himself or his employee or agent sells anything at short weight" or "whoever sells liquor to a minor and any sale by an employee shall be deemed the act of the employer as well."

Practical Advice
Because employers may be criminally liable for the acts of their employees, you should exercise due diligence in adequately checking the backgrounds of prospective employees.

6-1d LIABILITY OF THE CORPORATION

Historically, corporations were not held criminally liable because under the traditional view, a corporation could not possess the requisite criminal intent and, therefore, was incapable of committing a crime. The dramatic growth in size and importance of corporations changed this view. Under the modern approach, a corporation may be liable for violation of statutes imposing liability without fault. In addition, a corporation may be liable in cases in which the offense is perpetrated by a high corporate officer or the board of directors. The Model Penal Code provides that a corporation may be convicted of a criminal offense for the conduct of its employees if

1. the legislative purpose of the statute defining the offense is to impose liability on corporations and the conduct is within the scope of the [employee's] office or employment;

2. the offense consists of an omission to discharge a specific, affirmative duty imposed upon corporations by law; or

3. the offense was authorized, requested, commanded, performed, or recklessly tolerated by the board of directors or by a high managerial agent of the corporation.

Punishment of a corporation for crimes is necessarily by fine, not imprisonment. Nonetheless, individuals bearing responsibility for the criminal act face fines, imprisonment, or both. The Model Penal Code provides that the corporate agent having primary responsibility for the discharge of the duty imposed by law on the corporation is as accountable for a reckless omission to perform the required act as though the law imposed the duty directly upon him.

On November 1, 1991 (updated in 2004 and 2010), the Federal Organizational Corporate Sentencing Guidelines took effect. The overall purpose of the guidelines is to impose sanctions that will provide just punishment and adequate deterrence. The guidelines provide a base fine for each criminal offense, but that fine can be increased or reduced. Factors that can increase a corporate fine include the corporation's involvement in or tolerance of criminal activity, its prior history, and whether it has obstructed justice. On the other hand, corporations can reduce their punishment by implementing an effective compliance and ethics program reasonably designed to prevent potential legal violations by the corporation and its employees.

An effective compliance and ethics program should include the following:

1. standards and procedures to prevent and detect criminal conduct;
2. responsibility at all levels and adequate resources, and authority for the program;
3. personnel screening related to program goals;
4. training at all levels;
5. auditing, monitoring, and evaluating program effectiveness;
6. nonretaliatory internal reporting systems;
7. incentives and discipline to promote compliance; and
8. reasonable steps to respond to and prevent further similar offenses upon detection of a violation.

The 2010 amendments to the guidelines expanded the availability of reduced sentencing for corporations meeting additional requirements. Under the previous guidelines, convicted corporations could receive a reduced fine for having an effective compliance and ethics program *only if* no high-level personnel were involved in, or were willfully ignorant of, the crime. Under the 2010 amendments, a corporation can be eligible for a reduced fine based on an effective compliance and ethics program *despite* the involvement or willful ignorance of high-level personnel if the convicted corporation satisfies four additional criteria:

1. a direct and prompt communication channel exists between compliance personnel and the organization's

governing authority (e.g., the board of directors or the audit committee of the board);

2. the compliance program discovered the criminal offense before discovery outside the company was reasonably likely;

3. the corporation promptly reported the offense to appropriate government authorities; and

4. no individual with operational responsibility for the compliance program participated in, condoned, or was willfully ignorant of the offense.

Practical Advice
Companies should ensure that they have a satisfactory corporate compliance program.

6-2 White-Collar Crime

White-collar crime has been defined in various ways. The Justice Department defines it as nonviolent crime involving deceit, corruption, or breach of trust. It also has been defined to include crimes committed by individuals, such as embezzlement and forgery, as well as crimes committed on behalf of a corporation, such as commercial bribery, product safety and health crimes, false advertising, and antitrust violations. The FBI includes in its definition of white-collar crime: public corruption, money laundering, corporate fraud, securities and commodities fraud, mortgage fraud, financial institution fraud, bank fraud and embezzlement, fraud against the government, election law violations, mass marketing fraud, identity theft, and health-care fraud. A less precise definition is crime "committed by a person of respectability and high social status in the course of his occupation," while a narrower definition identifies white-collar crime as fraud or deceit practiced through misrepresentation to gain an unfair advantage.

Regardless of its definition, such crime costs society billions of dollars; according to the Federal Bureau of Investigation, white-collar crime is estimated to cost the United States between $300 and $660 billion per year. Historically, prosecution of white-collar crime was de-emphasized because such crime was not considered violent. Now, however, many contend that white-collar crime often inflicts violence but does so impersonally. For example, unsafe products cause injury and death to consumers while unsafe working conditions cause injury and death to employees. Indeed, many contend that white-collar criminals should receive stiff prison sentences due to the magnitude of their crimes.

Fraud and economic crime are increasing in both the United States and the rest of the world. In a 2018 survey of 325 U.S. companies, 53 percent reported that during the previous twenty-four months they had suffered from fraud or economic crime—defined as the theft of assets, business misconduct, cybercrime, or consumer fraud—up from 38 percent in 2016. During the same period, the global percentage rose to 49 percent from

36 percent. In the United States, 43 percent of fraud and economic crime was committed by people within the company, up from 29 percent in 2016. Globally, the figure rose to 52 percent in 2018 from 46 percent in 2016. Moreover, 31 percent of U.S. respondents to the survey said their organization was asked to pay a bribe, compared with 7 percent in the 2016 survey.

In response to the business scandals involving companies such as Enron, WorldCom, Global Crossing, Adelphia, and Arthur Andersen, in 2002, Congress passed the Sarbanes-Oxley Act. This Act, according to former President George W. Bush, constitutes "the most far-reaching reforms of American business practices since the time of Franklin Delano Roosevelt [President from 1932 until 1945]." The legislation seeks to prevent such scandals by increasing corporate responsibility, adding new financial disclosure requirements, creating new criminal offenses and increasing the penalties of existing Federal crimes, and creating a powerful new five-person Accounting Oversight Board with authority to review and discipline auditors.

The Sarbanes-Oxley Act establishes new criminal penalties, including the following: (1) imposing fines and/or imprisonment of up to twenty-five years for defrauding any person or obtaining any money or property fraudulently in connection with any security of a public company and (2) imposing fines and/or imprisonment of up to twenty years for knowingly altering, destroying, mutilating, or falsifying any document with the intent of impeding a Federal investigation. In addition, the Act substantially increases the penalties for existing crimes, including the following: (1) mail and wire fraud (five-year maximum increased to twenty-five-year maximum) and (2) violation of the Securities and Exchange Act (ten-year maximum increased to twenty-year maximum). The Act is discussed further in *Chapters 35, 43*, and *44*.

In December 2008, Bernard L. Madoff admitted to perpetrating a massive Ponzi scheme with estimated losses of $20 billion in principal and approximately $65 billion dollars in paper losses from almost five thousand clients. As a result, in 2010, the Securities and Exchange Commission began reforming and improving the way it operates to reduce the chances that such frauds will occur or be undetected in the future.

♦ *See Case 6-1*

6-2a COMPUTER CRIME

One special type of white-collar crime called **computer crime**, or **cybercrime**, is best categorized based on whether the computer was the instrument or the target of the crime. Examples of cybercrimes using computers as the **instrument** of the crime include the distribution of child pornography; money laundering; illegal gambling; copyright infringement; illegal communication of trade secrets; identity theft; and fraud involving credit cards, e-commerce, or securities. Cybercrime with a computer as a **target** of the crime attacks a computer's confidentiality, integrity, or availability; examples of computer intrusion include theft or destruction of proprietary information, vandalism, denial of service, website defacing and interference, and implantation of malicious code. Detecting crimes involving computers is extremely difficult. In addition, many businesses, loath to imply that their security is lax, often do not report computer crimes. Nonetheless, losses due to computer crimes are estimated to be in the tens of billions of dollars. Moreover, given society's ever-increasing dependence upon computers, this type of crime will in all likelihood continue to increase.

Computer crimes already have become commonplace. Examples abound. Software piracy (the unauthorized copying of copyrighted software) is now so widespread that an estimated two out of every three copies of software are illegally obtained. A computer consultant hired by Security Pacific Bank wrongfully transferred $10 million from the bank to his own Swiss bank account. Six employees stole TRW's credit-rating data and offered to repair poor credit ratings for a fee. Disgruntled or discharged employees have used computer programs to destroy company software.

As a consequence, enterprises are spending large sums of money to increase computer security. In addition, every State has enacted computer crime laws. Originally passed in 1984, the Federal Computer Fraud and Abuse Act protects a broad range of computers that facilitate interstate and international commerce and communications. The Act was amended in 1986, 1994, 1996, 2001, 2002, and 2008. The Act makes it a crime with respect to any computer that is used in interstate commerce or communications (1) to access or damage it without authorization, (2) to access it with the intent to commit fraud, (3) to traffic in passwords for it, or (4) to threaten to cause damage to it with the intent to extort money or anything of value. Furthermore, depending on the details of the crime, cybercriminals also may be prosecuted under other Federal laws, such as copyright, mail fraud, or wire fraud laws. **Spam**—unsolicited commercial electronic mail—is currently estimated to account for well over half of all electronic mail. Congress has concluded that spam has become the most prevalent method used for distributing pornography; perpetrating fraudulent schemes; and introducing viruses, worms, and Trojan horses into personal and business computer systems. In response, Congress enacted the Controlling the Assault of Non-Solicited Pornography and Marketing Act of 2003, also known as the CAN-SPAM Act of 2003, which went into effect on January 1, 2004. In enacting the statute, Congress determined that senders of spam should not mislead recipients as to the source or content of such mail and that recipients of spam have a right to decline to receive additional spam from the same source.

Practical Advice
Adequately protect the safety and security of all company electronic data and records.

6-2b RACKETEER INFLUENCED AND CORRUPT ORGANIZATIONS ACT

The Racketeer Influenced and Corrupt Organizations Act (RICO) was enacted in 1970 with the stated purpose of terminating the infiltration of organized crime into legitimate business. The Act imposes severe civil and criminal penalties on enterprises that engage in a pattern of racketeering, defined as the commission of two or more predicate acts within a period of ten years. A "predicate act" is any of several criminal offenses listed in RICO. Included are nine major categories of State crimes and more than thirty Federal crimes, such as murder, kidnapping, arson, extortion, drug dealing, securities fraud, mail fraud, and bribery. The most controversial issue concerning RICO is its application to businesses that are not engaged in organized crime but that do meet the "pattern of racketeering" test under the Act. Criminal conviction under the law may result in (1) fines of up to $250,000 ($500,000 for an organization) or twice the amount of gross profits or other proceeds from the offense and/or (2) a prison term of up to twenty years or for life if the violation is based on a racketeering activity for which the maximum penalty includes life imprisonment. In addition, businesses will forfeit any property obtained due to a RICO violation, and individuals harmed by RICO violations may invoke the statute's civil remedies, which include treble damages and attorneys' fees.

Other areas of Federal law that impose both civil and criminal penalties include bankruptcy (*Chapter 38*), intellectual property (*Chapter 39*), antitrust (*Chapter 40*), securities regulation (*Chapter 43*), and environmental regulation (*Chapter 45*).

6-3 Crimes Against Business

Criminal offenses against property greatly affect businesses, amounting to losses in the hundreds of billions of dollars each year. This section covers the following crimes against property: (1) larceny, (2) embezzlement, (3) false pretenses, (4) robbery, (5) burglary, (6) extortion and bribery, (7) forgery, and (8) bad checks.

6-3a LARCENY

The crime of larceny is the (1) trespassory (2) taking and (3) carrying away of (4) personal property (5) of another (6) with the intent to deprive the victim permanently of the goods. All six elements must be present for the crime to exist. Thus, if Barbara pays Larry $5,000 for an automobile that Larry agrees to deliver the following week and Larry does not do so, Larry is *not* guilty of larceny because he has not trespassed on Barbara's property. Larry has not taken anything from Barbara; he has simply refused to turn the automobile over to her. Larceny applies only when a person takes personal property from another without the other's consent. Here, Barbara voluntarily paid the money to Larry, who has not committed larceny but who may have obtained the $5,000 by false pretenses (which is discussed later). Likewise, if Carol takes Dan's 1968 automobile without Dan's permission, intending to use it for a joyride and then return it to Dan, Carol has not committed larceny because she did not intend to deprive Dan permanently of the automobile. (Nevertheless, Carol has committed the crime of unauthorized use of an automobile.) On the other hand, if Carol left Dan's 1968 car in a junkyard after the joyride, she most likely would be held to have committed a larceny because of the high risk that her action would permanently deprive Dan of the car.

6-3b EMBEZZLEMENT

Embezzlement is the fraudulent conversion of another's property by one who was in lawful possession of it. A **conversion** is any act that seriously interferes with the owner's rights in the property, such as exhausting the resources of the property, selling it, giving it away, or refusing to return it to its rightful owner. This statutory crime was first enacted in response to a 1799 English case in which a bank employee was found not guilty of larceny for taking money given to him for deposit in the bank because the money had been handed to him voluntarily. Thus, embezzlement is a crime intended to prevent individuals who are lawfully in possession of another's property from taking such property for their own use.

The key distinction between larceny and embezzlement, therefore, is whether the thief is in lawful possession of the property. While both crimes involve the misuse of another's property, in larceny, the thief unlawfully possesses the property, whereas in embezzlement, the thief possesses it lawfully. A second distinction between larceny and embezzlement is that, unlike larceny, embezzlement does not require the intent to deprive the owner permanently of his property. Nonetheless, to constitute embezzlement, an act must interfere significantly with the owner's rights to the property.

6-3c FALSE PRETENSES

Obtaining property by **false pretenses**, like embezzlement, is a crime addressed by statutes enacted to close a loophole in the requirements for larceny. False pretenses is the crime of obtaining title to property of another by making materially false representations of an existing fact, with knowledge of their falsity and with the intent to defraud. Larceny does not cover this situation because here the victim voluntarily transfers the property to the thief. For example, a con artist who

goes door to door and collects money by saying he is selling stereo equipment, when he is not, is committing the crime of false pretenses. The test of deception is *subjective*: if the victim is actually deceived, the test is satisfied even though a reasonable person would not have been deceived by the defendant's lies. Therefore, the victim's gullibility or lack of due care is no defense.

Many courts hold that a false statement of intention, such as a promise, does not constitute false pretenses. In addition, a false expression of opinion regarding value is usually not considered a misrepresentation of fact and thus will not suffice for false pretenses.

Other specialized crimes that are similar to false pretenses include mail, wire, and bank fraud as well as securities fraud. **Mail fraud**, unlike the crime of false pretenses, does not require the victim to be actually defrauded; it simply requires the defendant to use the mails (or private carrier) to carry out a scheme that attempts to defraud others. Due to its breadth and ease of use, mail fraud has been a charge brought extensively by Federal prosecutors. The **wire fraud** statute prohibits the transmittal by wire, radio, or television in interstate or foreign commerce of any information with the intent to defraud. The Federal statute prohibiting **bank fraud** makes it a crime knowingly to execute or attempt to execute a scheme to defraud a financial institution or to obtain by false pretenses funds under the control or custody of a financial institution. Securities fraud is discussed in *Chapter 43*.

◆ *See Case 6-2*

6-3d ROBBERY

Under the common law as well as most statutes, robbery is a larceny with the additional elements that (1) the property is taken directly from the victim or in the immediate presence of the victim and (2) the act is accomplished through either force or the threat of force, which need not be against the person from whom the property is taken. For example, a robber threatens Sam, saying that unless Sam opens his employer's safe, the robber will shoot Maria. Moreover, the victim's presence may be actual or constructive. *Constructive presence* means that the defendant's actual or threatened force prevents the victim from being present. For example, if the robber knocks the victim unconscious or ties her up, the victim is considered constructively present.

Many laws distinguish between simple robbery and aggravated robbery. Robbery can be aggravated by any of several factors, including (1) the use of a deadly weapon, (2) the robber's intent to kill or to kill if faced with resistance, (3) serious bodily injury to the victim, *or* (4) commission of the crime by two or more persons.

6-3e BURGLARY

At common law, **burglary** was defined as breaking and entering the dwelling of another at night with the intent to commit a felony. Many modern statutes differ from the common law definition by requiring merely that there be (1) an entry (2) into a building (3) with the intent to commit a felony in the building.

Thus, these statutory definitions omit three elements of the common law crime: the building need not be a dwelling house, the entry need not be at night, and the entry need not be a technical breaking. Nonetheless, so greatly do the modern statutes vary (except for the idea that each contains some, but not all, of the common law elements) that generalization is nearly impossible.

APPLYING THE LAW — Criminal Law

FACTS Bivens worked as an accounts payable clerk for C&N Construction. Every Wednesday morning, the site foreman would call Bivens and give her the names of the employees working on the job and the number of hours they had worked. Bivens would then convey this information to a paycheck processing company, which would return unsigned payroll checks to C&N. After a designated officer of the company signed them, Bivens would forward the checks to the job site for distribution by the foreman. After working for the company for nearly eight years, Bivens began sending false information to the payroll service about employees and hours worked. The resulting checks were typically payable to employees who had worked for C&N in the recent past but who were not active on the current job. Bivens would intercept these "fake" checks after they were signed, forge the payees' names, and either cash them or deposit them into her bank account. Over a period of seventeen months, Bivens diverted tens of thousands of dollars to herself by forging more than one hundred fake paychecks. She spent all but a few hundred dollars of the money on meals and entertainment, jewelry, clothing, and shoes. C&N's vice president ultimately discovered Bivens's practice, fired her, and notified the authorities of her conduct.

ISSUE Has Bivens committed the crime of embezzlement?

RULE OF LAW A crime consists of two elements: (1) *actus reus*, or a wrongful act, and (2) *mens rea*, or criminal intent. The crime of embezzlement occurs when a person who is in lawful possession of another's property intentionally misuses the property or seriously interferes with the owner's rights in it. Possible defenses to a crime include defense of person or property, duress, and mistake of fact.

APPLICATION The *actus reus* in this case is exercising wrongful dominion and control over the property of another while in legal possession of it. Bivens was lawfully in possession of C&N's property in the form of the payroll checks. While her job description certainly did not authorize her to keep any of the checks or payroll funds for herself, Bivens's position at C&N did require her to record and transmit payroll information as well as to handle the checks themselves. While in legal possession of C&N paychecks, Bivens misused or seriously interfered with C&N payroll funds. Without permission or right, she cashed some of the checks and diverted to herself money that belonged to C&N. She has committed the necessary wrongful act.

The next question is whether she had the requisite state of mind. Bivens's paycheck scheme also reflects mens *rea*, or subjective fault. Her conduct with regard to the checks was clearly purposeful or intentional. While it might be possible to make an error in transmitting employee names or hours worked occasionally, Bivens could not have negligently transmitted incorrect information about former employees in more than one hundred instances. Moreover, the fact she separated the fake checks from the genuine paychecks, surreptitiously took them from work, falsely endorsed them with the names of the former employee payees, and then cashed them and spent the money indicates she intended to steal the funds. This series of events benefiting Bivens could not possibly have happened unintentionally or through carelessness alone. Therefore the necessary *mens rea* is present.

Moreover, none of the defenses to a crime is applicable here. Bivens was not acting to protect herself, another person, or her property. Nor was she under duress; she was not threatened with immediate, serious bodily harm when she engaged in the paycheck scam. Finally, there is nothing to indicate that Bivens was mistaken about C&N's ownership of the payroll funds, that she was mistaken about the names or hours worked by employees any given week, or that she could have mistakenly thought she was expected to or permitted to falsify payroll records so as to cause paychecks to be issued to former employees, paychecks which she would then take and cash for herself. Thus, Bivens has no valid legal defense.

CONCLUSION Bivens's conduct with regard to these checks constitutes embezzlement.

6-3f EXTORTION AND BRIBERY

Although frequently confused, extortion and bribery are two distinct crimes. **Extortion**, or blackmail, as it is sometimes called, is generally held to be the making of threats for the purpose of obtaining money or property. For example, Lindsey tells Jason that unless he pays her $10,000, she will tell Jason's customers that he was once arrested for disturbing the peace. Lindsey has committed the crime of extortion. In a few jurisdictions, however, the crime of extortion occurs only if the defendant actually causes the victim to give up money or property.

Bribery, on the other hand, is the act of offering money or property to a public official to influence the official's decision. The crime of bribery is committed when the illegal offer is made, whether accepted or not. Thus, if Andrea offered Edward, the mayor of New Town, a 20 percent interest in Andrea's planned real estate development if Edward would use his influence to have the development proposal approved, Andrea would be guilty of criminal bribery. In contrast, if Edward had threatened Andrea that unless he received a 20 percent interest in Andrea's development, he would use his influence to prevent the approval of the development, Edward would be guilty of criminal extortion. Bribery of foreign officials is covered by the Foreign Corrupt Practices Act, discussed in *Chapters 43 and 46*.

Some jurisdictions have gone beyond traditional bribery law by adopting statutes that make commercial bribery illegal. **Commercial bribery** is the use of bribery to acquire new business, obtain secret information or processes, or receive kickbacks.

6-3g FORGERY

Forgery is the intentional falsification or false making of a document with the intent to defraud. Accordingly, if William prepares a false certificate of title to a stolen automobile, he is guilty of forgery. Likewise, if an individual alters some receipts to increase her income tax deductions, she has committed the crime of forgery. The most common type of forgery is the signing of another's name to a financial document.

6-3h BAD CHECKS

A statutory crime that has some relation to both forgery and false pretenses is the passing of **bad checks**; that is, writing a check on an account containing funds insufficient to cover the check. All jurisdictions have now enacted laws making it a crime to issue bad checks; however, these statutes vary greatly from jurisdiction to jurisdiction. Most jurisdictions simply require that the check be issued; they do not require that the issuer receive anything in return for the check. Also, although most jurisdictions require that the defendant issue a check with knowledge that she does not have enough money to cover the check, the Model Penal Code and a number of States provide that knowledge is presumed if the issuer had no account at the bank or if the check was not paid for lack of funds and the issuer failed to pay the check within ten days.

◆ *See Case 6-3*

6-4 Defenses to Crimes

Even though a defendant is found to have committed a criminal act, he will not be convicted if he has a valid defense. The defenses most relevant to white-collar crimes and crimes against business include defense of property, duress, mistake of fact, and entrapment. In some instances, a defense proves the absence of a required element of the crime; other defenses provide a justification or excuse that bars criminal liability.

6-4a DEFENSE OF PERSON OR PROPERTY

Individuals may use reasonable force to protect their property. This defense enables a person to commit, without any criminal liability, what the law would otherwise consider the crime of assault, battery, manslaughter, or murder. Under the majority rule, deadly force is *never* reasonable to safeguard property, because life is deemed more important than the protection of property. For this reason, individuals cannot use a deadly mechanical device, such as a spring gun, to protect their property. If, however, the defender's use of reasonable force in protecting his property is met with an attack upon his person, then he may use deadly force if the attack threatens him with death or serious bodily harm.

6-4b DURESS

A person who is threatened with immediate, serious bodily harm to himself or another unless he engages in criminal activity has the valid defense of duress (sometimes referred to as compulsion or coercion) to criminal conduct other than murder. For example, Ann threatens to kill Ben if he does not assist her in committing larceny. Ben complies. Because of duress, he would not be guilty of the larceny.

6-4c MISTAKE OF FACT

If a person reasonably believes the facts surrounding his conduct to be such that his conduct would not constitute a crime, then the law will treat the facts as he reasonably believes them to be. Accordingly, an honest and reasonable **mistake of fact** will justify the defendant's conduct. For example, if Ann gets into a car that she reasonably believes to be hers—the car is the same color, model, and year as hers; is parked in the same parking lot, and is started by her key—she will be relieved of criminal responsibility for taking Ben's automobile.

6-4d ENTRAPMENT

The defense of **entrapment** arises when a law enforcement official induces a person to commit a crime when that person would not have done so without the persuasion of the police official. The rationale behind the rule, which applies only to government officials and agents, not to private individuals, is to prevent law enforcement officials from provoking crime and from engaging in reprehensible conduct.

6-5 Criminal Procedure

Each one of the States and the Federal government has procedures for initiating and coordinating criminal prosecutions. In addition, the first ten amendments to the U.S. Constitution, called the Bill of Rights, guarantee many defenses and rights of an accused. The Fourth Amendment prohibits unreasonable searches and seizures to obtain incriminating evidence. The Fifth Amendment requires indictment for capital crimes by a grand jury, prevents double jeopardy and self-incrimination, and prohibits deprivation of life or liberty without due process of law. The Sixth Amendment requires that an accused receive a speedy and public trial by an impartial jury and that he be informed of the nature of the accusation, be confronted with the witnesses who testify against him, be given the power to obtain witnesses in his favor, and have the right to competent counsel for his defense. The Eighth Amendment prohibits excessive bail, excessive fines, and cruel or unusual punishment.

Most State constitutions have similar provisions to protect the rights of accused persons. In addition, the Fourteenth Amendment prohibits State governments from depriving any person of life, liberty, or property without due process of law. Moreover, the U.S. Supreme Court has held that almost all of the Constitutional protections just discussed apply to the States through the operation of the Fourteenth Amendment.

Although the details of criminal process differ in various jurisdictions, the process retains several common objectives. In every jurisdiction, the primary purpose of the process is to enforce the criminal law, but this purpose must be accomplished within the limitations imposed by other goals. These goals include advancing an adversary system of adjudication, requiring the government to bear the burden of proof, minimizing erroneous convictions, minimizing the burdens of defense, respecting individual dignity, maintaining the appearance of fairness, and achieving equality in the administration of the process.

We will first discuss the steps in a criminal prosecution; we will then focus on the major Constitutional protections for the accused in our system of criminal justice.

◆ SEE FIGURE 6-2: *Constitutional Protection for the Criminal Defendant*

6-5a STEPS IN CRIMINAL PROSECUTION

Although the particulars of criminal procedure vary from State to State, the following provides a basic overview. After arrest, the accused is booked and appears (first appearance) before a magistrate, commissioner, or justice of the peace, where formal notice of the charges is given, the accused is advised of his rights, and bail is set. Next, a **preliminary hearing** is held to determine whether there is probable cause to believe the defendant is the one who committed the crime. The defendant is entitled to be represented by counsel.

If the magistrate concludes that probable cause exists, she will bind the case over to the next stage, which is either an indictment or information, depending upon the jurisdiction. The Federal system and some States require indictments for all felony prosecutions unless waived by the defendant, while

FIGURE 6-2	Constitutional Protection for the Criminal Defendant
Amendment	**Protection Conferred**
Fourth	Freedom from unreasonable search and seizure
Fifth	Due process Right to indictment by grand jury for capital crimes* Freedom from double jeopardy Freedom from self-incrimination
Sixth	Right to speedy, public trial by jury Right to be informed of accusations Right to present witnesses Right to competent counsel
Eighth	Freedom from excessive bail Freedom from cruel and unusual punishment Freedom from excessive fines

*This right has *not* been applied to the States through the Fourteenth Amendment.

the other States permit but do not mandate **indictments**. A grand jury, which is not bound by the magistrate's decision at the preliminary hearing, issues an indictment, or true bill, if it finds sufficient evidence to justify a trial on the charge brought. Unlike the preliminary hearing, the grand jury does not hear evidence from the defendant, nor does the defendant appear before the grand jury. A grand jury traditionally consisted of not less than sixteen and not more than twenty-three people. Today, many States use a smaller grand jury, not infrequently composed of twelve members. An **information**, by comparison, is a formal accusation of a crime brought by a prosecuting officer, not a grand jury. Such a procedure is used in misdemeanor cases and in some felony cases in those States that do not require indictments. The indictment or information at times precedes the actual arrest.

At the **arraignment**, the defendant is brought before the trial court, where he is informed of the charge against him and where he enters his plea. The arraignment must be held promptly after the indictment or information has been filed. If his plea is "not guilty," the defendant must stand trial. He is entitled to a jury trial for all felonies and for misdemeanors punishable by more than six months of imprisonment. Most States also permit a defendant to request a jury trial for lesser misdemeanors. If the defendant chooses, however, he may have his guilt or innocence determined by the court sitting without a jury, which is called a "bench trial."

In the great majority of criminal cases, defendants enter into a plea bargain with the government instead of going to trial. In a 2012 case, the U.S. Supreme Court stated, "Ninety-seven percent of federal convictions and ninety-four percent of state convictions are the result of guilty pleas."

A criminal trial is somewhat similar to a civil trial, but with some significant differences: (1) the defendant is presumed innocent, (2) the burden of proof on the prosecution is to prove criminal guilt beyond a reasonable doubt, and (3) the defendant is not required to testify. The trial begins with the selection of the jury and the opening statements by the prosecutor and the attorney for the defense. The prosecution presents evidence first; then the defendant presents his. At the conclusion of the testimony, closing statements are made, and the jury, instructed as to the applicable law, retires to arrive at a verdict. If the verdict is "not guilty," the case is over. The State has no right to appeal from an acquittal, and the accused, having been placed in "jeopardy," cannot be tried a second time for the same offense. If the verdict is "guilty," the judge will enter a judgment of conviction and set the case for sentencing. The defendant may make a motion for a new trial, asserting that prejudicial error occurred at his original trial, necessitating a retrial of the case. He also may appeal to a reviewing court, alleging error by the trial court and asking for either his discharge or a remand of the case for a new trial.

6-5b FOURTH AMENDMENT

The Fourth Amendment, which protects all individuals against unreasonable searches and seizures, is designed to safeguard the privacy and security of individuals against arbitrary invasions by government officials. Although the Fourth Amendment by its terms applies only to acts of the Federal government, the Fourteenth Amendment makes it applicable to State government action as well.

When evidence has been obtained in violation of the Fourth Amendment, the general rule prohibits the introduction of the illegally seized evidence at trial. The purpose of this **exclusionary rule** is to discourage illegal police conduct and to protect individual liberty, not to hinder the search for the truth. In *Weeks v. United States*, 232 U.S. 383 (1914), the U.S. Supreme Court ruled,

> If letters and private documents can thus be seized and held and used in evidence against a citizen accused of an offense, the protection of the Fourth Amendment declaring his right to be secure against such searches and seizures is of no value, and, so far as those thus placed and concerned, might as well be stricken from the Constitution. The efforts of the courts and their officials to bring the guilty to punishment, praiseworthy as they are, are not to be aided by the sacrifice of those great principles established by years of endeavor and suffering which have resulted in their embodiment in the fundamental law of the land.

Nonetheless, in recent years, the U.S. Supreme Court has limited the exclusionary rule.

To obtain a warrant to search a particular person, place, or thing, a law enforcement official must demonstrate to a magistrate that he has probable cause to believe that the search will reveal evidence of criminal activity. **Probable cause** means "[t]he task of the issuing magistrate is simply to make a practical, commonsense decision whether, given all the circumstances set forth … before him, … , there is a fair probability that contraband or evidence of a crime will be found in a particular place." *Illinois v. Gates*, 462 U.S. 213 (1983).

Even though the Fourth Amendment generally requires a valid search warrant be obtained before a search and seizure, in some instances, a search warrant is not necessary. For example, it has been held that a warrant is not necessary when (1) there is hot pursuit of a fugitive, (2) the subject voluntarily consents to the search, (3) an emergency requires such action, (4) there has been a lawful arrest, (5) evidence of a crime is in plain view of the law enforcement officer, or (6) delay would significantly obstruct the investigation.

In a 5–4 decision, the U.S. Supreme Court held that the government must obtain a search warrant to access historical wireless carrier cell-site records revealing the location of a user's cell phone whenever it made or received calls. *Carpenter v. United States*, 585 U. S. _____ (2018).

6-5c FIFTH AMENDMENT

The Fifth Amendment protects persons against self-incrimination, double jeopardy, and being charged with a capital or infamous crime except by grand jury indictment.

The prohibitions against self-incrimination and double jeopardy also apply to the States through the Due Process Clause of the Fourteenth Amendment; the Grand Jury Clause, however, does not.

The privilege against self-incrimination extends only to testimonial evidence, not to physical evidence. The Fifth Amendment "privilege protects an accused only from being compelled to testify against himself, or otherwise provide the State with evidence of a testimonial or communicative nature." *Schmerber v. California*, 384 U.S. 757 (1966). Therefore, a person can be forced to stand in a lineup for identification purposes, provide a handwriting sample, or take a blood test. Most significantly, the Fifth Amendment does not protect the records of a business entity such as a corporation or partnership; it applies only to papers of individuals. Moreover, the Fifth Amendment does not prohibit examination of an individual's business records as long as the individual is not compelled to testify against himself.

The Fifth Amendment and the Fourteenth Amendment also guarantee due process of law, which is basically the requirement of a fair trial. Every person is entitled to have the charges or complaints against him made publicly and in writing, whether in civil or criminal proceedings, and to receive the opportunity to defend himself against those charges. In criminal prosecutions, due process includes the right to counsel; to confront and cross-examine adverse witnesses; to testify on one's own behalf, if desired; to produce witnesses and offer other evidence; and to be free from any and all prejudicial conduct and statements.

6-5d SIXTH AMENDMENT

The Sixth Amendment specifies that the Federal government shall provide the accused with a speedy and public trial by an impartial jury, inform her of the nature and cause of the accusation, confront her with the witnesses against her, have compulsory process for obtaining witnesses in her favor, and allow her to obtain the assistance of counsel for her defense. The Fourteenth Amendment extends these guarantees to the States.

The Supreme Court has explained the purpose of guaranteeing the right to a trial by jury as follows:

[T]he purpose of trial by jury is to prevent oppression by the Government by providing a safeguard against the corrupt or overzealous prosecutor and against the compliant, biased, or eccentric judge . . . [T]he essential factors of a jury trial obviously lie in the interposition between the accused and his accuser of the common sense judgment of a group of laymen. *Apodaca v. Oregon*, 406 U.S. 404 (1972).

Nevertheless, a defendant may forgo her right to a jury trial.

Historically, juries consisted of twelve jurors, but the Federal courts and the courts of certain States have since reduced the number to six. Noting no observable difference between the results reached by a jury of twelve and those reached by a jury of six, nor any evidence to suggest that a jury of twelve is more advantageous to a defendant, the Supreme Court has held that the use of a six-member jury in a criminal case does not violate a defendant's right to a jury trial under the Sixth Amendment. The jury need only be large enough "to promote group deliberation, free from outside attempts at intimidation, and to provide a fair possibility for obtaining a representative cross section of the community." Moreover, State court jury verdicts need not be unanimous, provided the vote is sufficient to ensure adequate deliberations. Thus, the Supreme Court has upheld jury votes of 11–1, 10–2, and 9–3, but has rejected as insufficient a 5–1 vote.

CHAPTER SUMMARY

NATURE OF CRIMES **Definition** any act or omission forbidden by public law
Essential Elements
- **Actus Reus** wrongful or overt act
- **Mens Rea** criminal intent or mental fault
Classification
- *Felony* a serious crime
- *Misdemeanor* a less serious crime
Vicarious Liability liability imposed for acts of employees if the employer directed, participated in, or approved of the acts
Liability of a Corporation under certain circumstances, a corporation may be convicted of crimes and punished by fines

WHITE-COLLAR CRIME	**Definition** nonviolent crime involving deceit, corruption, or breach of trust **Computer Crime** use of a computer to commit a crime **Racketeer Influenced and Corrupt Organizations Act (RICO)** Federal law intended to stop organized crime from infiltrating legitimate businesses
CRIMES AGAINST BUSINESS	**Larceny** trespassory taking and carrying away of personal property of another with the intent to deprive the victim permanently of the property **Embezzlement** taking of another's property by a person who was in lawful possession of the property **False Pretenses** obtaining title to property of another by means of representation one knows to be materially false; made with intent to defraud **Robbery** committing larceny with the use or threat of force **Burglary** under most modern statutes, an entry into a building with the intent to commit a felony **Extortion** making threats to obtain money or property **Bribery** offering money or property to a public official to influence the official's decision **Forgery** intentional falsification of a document to defraud **Bad Checks** knowingly issuing a check without funds sufficient to cover the check
DEFENSES TO CRIMES	**Defense of Person or Property** individuals may use reasonable force to protect themselves, other individuals, and their property **Duress** coercion by threat of serious bodily harm; a defense to criminal conduct other than murder **Mistake of Fact** honest and reasonable belief that conduct is not criminal **Entrapment** inducement by a law enforcement official to commit a crime
CRIMINAL PROCEDURE	**Steps in Criminal Prosecution** generally include arrest, booking, formal notice of charges, preliminary hearing to determine probable cause, indictment or information, arraignment, and trial **Fourth Amendment** protects individuals against unreasonable searches and seizures **Fifth Amendment** protects persons against self-incrimination, double jeopardy, and being charged with a capital crime except by grand jury indictment **Sixth Amendment** provides the accused with the right to a speedy and public trial, the opportunity to confront witnesses, a process for obtaining witnesses, and the right to counsel **Eighth Amendment** protects against excessive bail, excessive fines, and cruel or unusual punishment

C A S E S

CASE
6-1

White-Collar Crime
SHAW v. UNITED STATES
Supreme Court of the United States, 2016
580 U. S. ___, 137 S. Ct. 462, 196 L. Ed. 2d 373

Breyer, J.

A federal statute makes it a crime "knowingly [to] execute[e] a scheme … to defraud a financial institution,"[citation], for example, a federally insured bank, [citation]. [Lawrence Shaw,

defendant/petitioner, obtained the identifying numbers of a Bank of America account belonging to a bank customer, Stanley Hsu. Shaw used those numbers and other related information in a scheme to transfer funds from Hsu's account to other accounts at other institutions, from which Shaw then was able to obtain Hsu's funds.] The petitioner *** was convicted of violating this provision. He argues here that the provision does not apply to him because he intended to cheat only a bank depositor, not a bank. *** [The Ninth Circuit affirmed. Shaw filed a petition for writ of certiorari which was granted.]

The relevant criminal statute makes it a crime:

> "knowingly [to] execut[e] a scheme…
> "(1) to defraud a financial institution; or
> "(2) to obtain any of the moneys, funds, credits, assets, securities, or other property owned by, or under the custody or control of, a financial institution, by means of false or fraudulent pretenses, representations, or promises." [Citation.]

* * *

Shaw makes several related arguments in favor of his basic claim, namely, that the statute does not cover schemes to deprive a bank of customer deposits. First, he says that subsection (1) requires "an intent to wrong a victim bank [a 'financial institution'] *in its property rights*…." [Citation.] He adds that the property he took, money in Hsu's bank account, belonged to Hsu, the bank's customer, and that Hsu is not a "financial institution." [*Citation.*] Hence Shaw's was a scheme "designed" to obtain only "a bank *customer's* property," not "a bank's *own* property." [*Citation.*]

The basic flaw in this argument lies in the fact that the bank, too, had property rights in Hsu's bank account. When a customer deposits funds, the bank ordinarily becomes the owner of the funds and consequently has the right to use the funds as a source of loans that help the bank earn profits (though the customer retains the right, for example, to withdraw funds). [Citations.] *** Thus, Shaw's scheme to cheat Hsu was also a scheme to deprive the bank of certain bank property rights.

Hence, for purposes of the bank fraud statute, a scheme fraudulently to obtain funds from a bank depositor's account normally is also a scheme fraudulently to obtain property from

a "financial institution," at least where, as here, the defendant knew that the bank held the deposits, the funds obtained came from the deposit account, and the defendant misled the bank in order to obtain those funds.

*** Shaw [also] says he did not intend to cause the bank financial harm. Indeed, the parties appear to agree that, due to standard banking practices in place at the time of the fraud, no bank involved in the scheme ultimately suffered any monetary loss. [Citation.] But the statute, while insisting upon "a scheme to defraud," demands neither a showing of ultimate financial loss nor a showing of intent to cause financial loss.

* * *

Shaw further argues that the instructions the District Court gave the jury were erroneous. He points out that the District Court told the jury that the

> "phrase 'scheme to defraud' means any deliberate plan of action or course of conduct by which someone intends to deceive, cheat, *or* deprive a financial institution of something of value." [Citation.]

This instruction, Shaw says, could be understood as permitting the jury to find him guilty if it found no more than that his scheme was one to deceive the bank but not to *"deprive"* the bank of anything of value. The parties agree, as do we, that the scheme must be one to deceive the bank *and* deprive it of something of value.

For reasons previously pointed out, we have held that a plan to deprive a bank of money in a customer's deposit account is a plan to deprive the bank of "something of value" within the meaning of the bank fraud statute. The parties dispute whether the jury instruction is nonetheless ambiguous or otherwise improper. We leave to the Ninth Circuit to determine whether that question was fairly presented to that court and, if so, whether the instruction is lawful, and, if not, whether any error was harmless in this case.

For these reasons, the judgment of the Ninth Circuit is vacated, and the case is remanded for further proceedings consistent with this opinion.

CASE 6-2

False Pretenses
STATE OF SOUTH DAKOTA v. MORSE
Supreme Court of South Dakota, 2008
753 N.W.2d 915, 2008 SD 66

Konenkamp, J.
[Janice Heffron orally contracted with her neighbor, Wyatt Morse, to convert her second-floor bedroom into a bathroom in five weeks for $5,000. According to Janice, Morse repeatedly stated that he could do it "easy, quick, cheap." Janice told her mother, Maxine Heffron, who would finance the project, about Morse's offer. Maxine and Janice then went to Morse's

home, where he showed them the bathroom he had restored. Janice and Maxine were impressed. Morse also told them that he had plumbing experience, that his work would be above and beyond code, and that the local inspector did not inspect his work because he was so good. Maxine wanted to pay using personal checks to assure a paper trail, but Morse convinced her to pay him with cash. According to Janice, he wanted to be paid in cash to avoid the Internal Revenue Service. They agreed that Morse would convert the room into a bathroom, install an antique claw-foot tub (one that he would provide personally), put wainscoting on the walls, install an old tin ceiling like the one in his bathroom, and install crown molding.

Morse began work in January 2006. His efforts continued until the second week of March. He installed plumbing fixtures and he removed the old water heater and installed a new one. He ran a freeze-proof spigot outside the house. He put in a bathroom vent with an antique vent cover. He custom built a bathroom cabinet at no extra cost to the Heffrons. He mounted wainscoting and crafted a surrounding shelf with rope lighting. He put in a faux tin ceiling, with crown molding and trim. He installed water pipes and a new drain stack. The project took longer and cost more than originally agreed. Morse ran into difficulties when he attempted to install a tank-less water heater. He was never able to install the tankless heater and ended up installing a traditional tanked water heater. Morse also experienced problems with some of the pipes he installed. Janice told him that they were leaking. He repaired them and blamed the leaks on bad batches of solder.

Maxine paid Morse somewhere between $6,000 and $6,500 cash. In March 2006, Morse fell and aggravated his already bad back. Before Janice and Maxine hired him, Morse had told them that he had a back condition. After his fall in March, he came to the job site less and less. Then, after the second week in March he stopped coming entirely. The Heffrons tried contacting him through phone calls, personal visits, and certified mail. He never responded. After Morse abandoned the project, Janice contacted a licensed plumber, who examined Morse's work and gave Janice an estimate on the cost of completing the project. The plumber pointed out several deficiencies in Morse's work. In particular, Morse incorrectly installed the water heater, the pipes for the sink, lavatory, and bathtub. He used S-traps, illegal in South Dakota, and improperly vented the floor drains. Because he installed the water heater incorrectly, carbon monoxide was leaking into Janice's home. In sum, Morse's work on the bathroom, in the opinion of the licensed plumber, had no value to the home.

On October 12, 2006, Morse was indicted for grand theft by deception in violation of South Dakota law. A jury returned a guilty verdict. Morse was sentenced to five years in prison. He appealed asserting that the evidence was insufficient to sustain the verdict.]

Morse argues that the State failed to prove he had the requisite intent to defraud the Heffrons. He does not dispute that the work he did on Janice's home was faulty and resulted in the Heffrons having to pay considerably more in repairs. Nonetheless, he claims that his faulty work created a classic breach of contract claim, because when he entered into the agreement to remodel the bathroom, he believed he was capable of doing quality work and fully intended on completing the project. The State, on the other hand, argues that Morse "created and

reinforced the false impression in the minds of Jan and Maxine Heffron that he was licensed to, and capable of, installing a second floor bathroom." More particularly, the State contends that Morse "deceived" the Heffrons on his ability to do the work, "misled" them with his statements that his work would be above code, and "took actions to further reinforce the false impression that he was able to properly install the bathroom."

Theft by deception is a specific intent crime. [Citation.] Intent to defraud "'means to act willfully and with the specific intent to deceive or cheat, ordinarily for the purpose of either causing some financial loss to another or bringing about some financial gain to one's self.'" [Citation.] Therefore, Morse must have had the "purpose to deceive." [Citation.] "'It is only where [actors do] not believe what [they] purposely caused [their victims] to believe, and where this can be proved beyond a reasonable doubt, that [these actors] can be convicted of theft.'" [Citation.]

* * *

There are a number of cases involving construction contracts where courts have found the evidence sufficient to prove deceptive theft, or related criminal conduct. In those cases, however, there was either circumstantial or direct evidence to establish the requisite intent. For example, in [citation], an appeals court held that the jury could infer intent when *at the time* Cash obtained the money he had no intention to complete the work because he took the money and *never* performed. In *State v. Rivers*, the Iowa Supreme Court upheld the defendant's conviction for theft by deception because he had a pattern of deceptive conduct. [Citation.] Rivers was a self-employed contractor, who obtained multiple remodeling jobs, took money as a down payment, persuaded his customers to give him more money, and then never completed the work. * * *

Here, Morse was convicted of theft by deception, defined in SDCL 22-30A-3. It states in part:

> [a]ny person who obtains property of another by deception is guilty of theft. A person deceives if, with *intent to defraud*, that person:
>
> (1) Creates or reinforces a false impression, including false impressions as to law, value, intention, or other state of mind. However, as to a person's intention to perform a promise, deception may not be inferred from the fact alone that that person did not subsequently perform the promise; ...
>
> (3) Fails to correct a false impression which the deceiver previously created or reinforced, or which the deceiver knows to be influencing another to whom the deceiver stands in a fiduciary or confidential relationship; .
>
> The term, deceive, does not, however, include falsity as to matters having no pecuniary significance or puffing by statements unlikely to deceive reasonable persons.

* * *

Based on our review of the record, in a light most favorable to the verdict, Morse: (1) failed to complete the project in five weeks for $5,000 as promised; (2) performed work that was not "above and beyond code" as promised; (3) lied about obtaining a building permit; (4) lied about the reasons he could not get the tankless water heater installed and why the pipes were leaking; (5) returned the water heater and did not give the $186 refund to Maxine; (6) never provided Janice or Maxine receipts for materials purchased; (7) quit working on the project prematurely and without explanation; and (8) never responded to the Heffrons' attempts to contact him.

These facts do not prove the elements of theft by deception. There is no evidence that Morse had a purpose to deceive or intended to defraud the Heffrons when he agreed to remodel Janice's bathroom. Although his work was not above and beyond code, the State never argued that Morse *knew* he would do faulty work. Janice and Maxine both testified that Morse took them up to his house and showed him the remodeling that he did to his own bathroom. They both said they were impressed. It cannot be inferred that Morse intended to defraud the Heffrons because his work product was not up to code.

Moreover, the State never argued or presented evidence that Morse took Maxine's money with the intention of never performing under their agreement. * * * The parties made their agreement in December 2005, and no one disputes that Morse worked regularly on the project from January 2006 until the second week of March. While Morse failed to complete the project in five weeks for $5,000 as promised, the State never claimed that he *knew* it would take longer and charge more, and tricked the Heffrons into believing him. Neither Janice nor Maxine claimed that Morse deceived them into paying him more money when the project took longer than anticipated. * * *

To sustain a conviction, each element of an offense must be supported by evidence. [Citation.] Theft by deception is a specific intent crime, and therefore, the State was required to prove beyond a reasonable doubt that Morse had the specific intent to defraud the Heffrons when he agreed to remodel the bathroom. Here the evidence offered by the State "is so insubstantial and insufficient, and of such slight probative value, that it is not proper to make a finding beyond a reasonable doubt that [Morse] committed all of the acts constituting the elements of the offense[.]"

Reserved

CASE 6-3

Bad Checks
LOUISIANA v. HAMED
Court of Appeal of Louisiana, Fourth Circuit, 2014
147 So.3d 1191

Belsome, J.
The defendant, Zuhair Hamed, was charged by bill of information with one count of issuing a worthless check in the amount of five hundred dollars or more. The bill was later amended to indicate that the worthless check was in the amount of fifteen hundred dollars or more.

* * *

On September 18, 2007, Little Castro, L.L.C. (doing business as Discount City) entered into a credit sales agreement with fuel supplier, Ballard Petroleum, Inc. Ballard Petroleum agreed to provide fuel and Discount City would pay the obligation within ten days from the date of the invoice or next load. Ameer Hamed, the defendant's son, personally guaranteed payment on behalf of his establishment, Discount City. The defendant was listed as a contact on the credit application filed by his son.

During October of 2007, Ballard Petroleum made six fuel deliveries in a twelve-day period. However, the checks for those deliveries totaling approximately $126,000 were returned for nonsufficient funds (NSF). On November 1, 2007, the defendant rode with Mr. Jim Ballard, the owner of Ballard Petroleum,

to the bank, where he issued him a cashier's check in the amount of $126,061.30 to cover the returned checks. On the next day, another NSF check in the amount of $20,597.08 was returned to Ballard Petroleum. The check, dated October 26, 2007, was for a fuel delivery on October 16, 2007. The defendant was not a member of Silwady's Group L.L.C., the listed account holder on the check. Also, he was not a member of Little Castro, L.L.C. (Discount City). Thus, he was acting as an agent for these businesses.

In an effort to resolve the matter, Mr. Ballard made several attempts to contact the defendant, but he was unable to reach him. On November 6, 2007, pursuant to instruction from the Worthless Check Division of the District Attorney's office, Ballard Petroleum sent a certified letter notifying Discount City of the dishonored check. In response to the letter, the defendant acknowledged the debt and advised Mr. Ballard that he would reimburse him. By April of 2009, after the District Attorney's office became involved, the defendant paid $7,000.00 towards the balance. There were no additional payments made, and charges were eventually filed against the defendant in October of 2011.

[The defendant pled not guilty at arraignment. After a motions hearing, the trial court found no probable cause to substantiate the charges. The defendant subsequently waived his right to a jury trial and elected to proceed with a bench trial. At the conclusion of trial, the trial court found the defendant guilty as charged. The trial court denied all post-verdict motions, and the defendant was sentenced to four years in the Department of Corrections, suspended, with four years of active probation, as well as a $1,000.00 fine, court costs, and restitution costs. After a hearing, the magistrate court ordered the defendant to pay $13,626.08 in restitution. The defendant appealed.]

The defendant first argues that the evidence was insufficient for a rational trier of fact to find that the elements of the crime of issuing worthless checks were proven beyond a reasonable doubt.

The court in [citation] recognized the elements required to convict a defendant for issuing a worthless check as follows:

> Under [Louisiana Statute], to obtain a conviction for issuing of a worthless check the state is required to prove beyond a reasonable doubt that: (1) defendant issued, in exchange for anything of value, whether the exchange is contemporaneous or not; (2) a check, draft or order for the payment of money upon any bank or other depository; (3) knowing at the time of the issuing that the account on which drawn has insufficient funds with the financial institution on which the check is drawn to have the instrument paid in full on presentation; and (4) the instrument was issued with intent to defraud.

The proper inquiry under [the Louisiana statute] is whether a defendant knew that he had not sufficient credit with the bank, not whether his actual monetary balance was sufficient to cover a check, draft or order for payment issued by him. [Citation.]

In this case, the knowledge element is lacking. The State points to two facts to support its argument that the knowledge element was met: 1) the multitude of NSF checks written to the victim before and after the date of the check at issue; and 2) the defendant's acknowledgment that he owed the debt and would reimburse Ballard Petroleum.

First, there is no evidence in the record that the defendant knew there were insufficient funds in the bank on August 26, 2007. While Mr. Ballard testified that he went to the bank with the defendant, who issued him a cashier's check for the returned checks on November 1, 2007; this took place after the checks had already been written. Thus, it does not serve to establish that the defendant had knowledge of the insufficient funds at the time the checks were written. Likewise, the defendant's acknowledgement of the debt after he received the certified letter does not prove the defendant's knowledge at the time the check was issued.

* * * this was not the defendant's personal (or business) account. Significantly, the account holder, here, was Silwady's Group, a limited liability company that was not owned by the defendant [but did involve the defendant's son]. Thus, it is reasonable to conclude that the defendant was merely an agent, who was directed to write checks without knowledge of the status of the account. The fact that he continually attempted to reimburse Ballard Petroleum supports this conclusion. Under these circumstances, presenting account records alone is insufficient to prove the defendant's knowledge.

The record fails to provide sufficient evidence for a rational trier of fact to conclude that defendant had the knowledge that Silwady Group did not have sufficient funds with the bank for payment of the check when he signed it. [Citation.] Accordingly, we find that the evidence was legally insufficient to convict the defendant of issuing worthless checks. In light of this conclusion, we pretermit any discussion of the defendant's remaining assignments of error.

For these reasons, we reverse the defendant's conviction and sentence.

QUESTIONS

1. Sam said to Carol, "Kim is going to sell me a good used car next Monday; then I'll deliver it to you in exchange for your microcomputer, but I'd like to have the computer now." Relying on this statement, Carol delivered the computer to Sam. Sam knew Kim had no car, and would have none in the future, and he had no such arrangement with her. The appointed time of exchange passed and Sam failed to deliver the car to Carol. Has a crime been committed? Discuss.

2. Sara, a lawyer, drew a deed for Robert by which Robert was to convey land to Rick. The deed was correct in every detail. Robert examined and verbally approved it but did not sign it. Sara erased Rick's name and substituted her own. Robert signed the deed with all required legal formalities without noticing the change. Was Sara guilty of forgery? Discuss.

3. Ann took Bonnie's watch before Bonnie was aware of the theft. Bonnie discovered her loss immediately and pursued Ann. Ann pointed a loaded pistol at Bonnie, who, in fear of being shot, allowed Ann to escape. Was Ann guilty of robbery? Of any other crime?

4. Jones and Wilson were on trial, separately, for larceny of a $10,000 bearer bond (payable to the holder of the bond, not a named individual) issued by Brown, Inc. The Commonwealth's evidence showed that the owner of the bond had dropped it accidentally in the street enclosed in an envelope bearing his name and address; that Jones found the envelope with the bond in it; that Jones could neither read nor write; that Jones presented the envelope and bond to Wilson, an educated man, and asked Wilson what he should do with it; that Wilson told Jones that the finder of lost property becomes the owner of it; that Wilson told Jones that the bond was worth $1,000 but that the money could only be collected at the issuer's home office; that Jones then handed the bond to Wilson, who redeemed it at the corporation's home office and received $10,000; and that Wilson gave Jones $1,000 of the proceeds. What rulings?

5. Truck drivers for a hauling company, while loading a desk, found a $100 bill that had fallen out of the desk. They agreed to get it exchanged for small bills and divide the proceeds. En route to a bank, one of them changed his mind and refused to proceed with the scheme, whereupon the other pulled a knife and demanded the bill. A police officer intervened. It turned out that the bill was counterfeit money. What crimes have been committed?

6. Peter, an undercover police agent, was trying to locate a laboratory where it was believed that methamphetamine, or "speed"—a controlled substance—was being manufactured illegally. Peter went to Mary's home and said that he represented a large organization that was interested in obtaining methamphetamine. Peter offered to supply a necessary ingredient for the manufacture of the drug, which was very difficult to obtain, in return for one-half of the drug produced. Mary agreed and processed the chemical given to her by Peter in Peter's presence. Later, Peter returned with a search warrant and arrested Mary. Charged with various narcotics law violations, Mary asserted the defense of entrapment. Should Mary prevail? Why or why not?

7. The police obtained a search warrant based on an affidavit that contained the following allegations: (a) Donald was seen crossing a State line on four occasions during a five-day period and going to a particular apartment, (b) telephone records disclosed that the apartment had two telephones, (c) Donald had a reputation as a bookmaker and as an associate of gamblers, and (d) the Federal Bureau of Investigation was informed by a "confidential reliable informant" that Donald was conducting gambling operations. When a search was made based on the warrant, evidence was obtained that resulted in Donald's conviction of violating certain gambling laws. Donald challenged the constitutionality of the search warrant. Were Donald's constitutional rights violated? Explain your answer.

8. A national bank was robbed by a man with a small strip of tape on each side of his face. An indictment was returned against David. David was then arrested, and counsel was appointed to represent him. Two weeks later, without notice to David's lawyer, an FBI agent arranged to have the two bank employees observe a lineup, including David and five or six other prisoners. Each person in the lineup wore strips of tape, as had the robber, and each was directed to repeat the words "Put the money in the bag," as had the robber. Both of the bank employees identified David as the robber. At David's trial, he was again identified by the two, in the courtroom, and the prior lineup identification was elicited on cross-examination by David's counsel. David's counsel moved the court to grant a judgment of acquittal or alternatively to strike the courtroom identifications on the grounds that the lineup had violated David's Fifth Amendment privilege against self-incrimination and his Sixth Amendment right to counsel. Decision?

C A S E   P R O B L E M S

9. Waronek owned and operated a trucking rig, transporting goods for L.T.L. Perishables, Inc., of St. Paul, Minnesota. He accepted an offer to haul a trailer load of beef from Illini Beef Packers, Inc., in Joslin, Illinois, to Midtown Packing Company in New York City. After his truck was loaded with ninety-five forequarters and ninety-five hindquarters of beef in Joslin, Waronek drove north to his home in Watertown, Wisconsin, rather than east to New York. While in Watertown, he asked employees of the Royal Meat Company to butcher and prepare four hindquarters of beef—two for himself and two for his friends. He also offered to sell ten hindquarters to one employee of the company at an alarmingly reduced rate. The suspicious employee contacted the authorities, who told him to proceed with the deal. When Waronek arrived in New York with his load short nineteen hindquarters, Waronek telephoned L.T.L. Perishables in St. Paul. He notified them "that he was short nineteen hindquarters, that he knew where the beef went, and that he would make good on it out of future settlements."

L.T.L. told him to contact the New York police, but he failed to do so. Shortly thereafter, he was arrested by the Federal Bureau of Investigation and indicted for the embezzlement of goods moving in interstate commerce. Explain whether Waronek was guilty of the crime of embezzlement.

10. Four separate cases involving similar fact situations were consolidated as they presented the same constitutional question. In each case, police officers, detectives, or prosecuting attorneys took a defendant into custody and interrogated him in a police station to obtain a confession. In none of these cases did the officials fully and effectively advise the defendant of his rights at the outset of the interrogation. Police interrogations produced oral admissions of guilt from each defendant, as well as signed statements from three of them, which were used to convict them at their trials. The defendants appeal, arguing that the officials should have warned them of their constitutional rights and the consequences of waiving them before the questionings began. It was contended that to permit any statements obtained without such a warning violated their Fifth Amendment privilege against self-incrimination. Were the defendants' constitutional rights violated? Discuss.

11. Officer Cyril Rombach of the Burbank Police Department, an experienced and well-trained narcotics officer, applied for a warrant to search several residences and automobiles for cocaine, methaqualone, and other narcotics. Rombach supported his application with information given to another police officer by a confidential informant of unproven reliability. He also based the warrant application on his own observations made during an extensive investigation: known drug offenders visiting the residences and leaving with small packages, as well as a suspicious trip to Miami by two of the suspects. A State superior court judge issued a search warrant to Rombach based on this information. Rombach's searches netted large quantities of drugs and other evidence, which produced indictments of several suspects on charges of conspiracy to possess and distribute cocaine. The defendants moved to exclude the evidence on the grounds that the search warrant was defective in that Rombach had failed to establish the informant's credibility and that the information provided by the informant about the suspect's criminal activity was fatally stale. Explain whether the evidence should be excluded.

12. Raymond Johnson snatched a purse that had been left in an unattended car at a gas station. The purse contained both money and a firearm. Johnson was convicted for the crimes of grand theft of property (cash and payroll check) and grand theft of a firearm. Johnson appealed, arguing that this conviction is a double jeopardy violation in that it constitutes multiple convictions for a single act. Should he be convicted of two separate crimes for stealing the purse? Why or why not?

13. On February 10, Kelm secured a loan for $6,000 from Ms. Joan Williams. Kelm told Williams that the loan was to finance a real estate transaction. Five days later, Ms. Williams received a check drawn by Kelm in the amount of $6,000 from Kelm's attorney. Although the check was dated February 15, Kelm claims that she delivered the check to her attorney on February 10. The following week, Ms. Williams learned the check was uncollectible. Subsequently, Williams received assurances from Kelm but was unsuccessful in her efforts to obtain money from the drawee's bank. When Williams deposited the check, it was returned with a notation that it should not be presented again and that no account was on file. Bank records show that the account was closed on March 8 and that it had negative balances since February 10. Did Kelm illegally issue a bad check? Explain.

TAKING SIDES

Olivo was in the hardware area of a department store. A security guard saw him look around, take a set of wrenches, and conceal it in his clothing. Olivo looked around once more and proceeded toward an exit, passing several cash registers. The guard stopped him short of the exit.

a. What argument would support the prosecutor in finding Olivo guilty of larceny?

b. What argument would you make as Olivio's defense counsel for finding him not guilty of larceny?

c. Which side's argument do you find most convincing? Explain.

Intentional Torts

CHAPTER OUTCOMES

After reading and studying this chapter, you should be able to:

- Describe the torts that protect against intentional harm to personal rights.

- Explain the application of the various privileges to defamation suits and how they are affected by whether the plaintiff is (1) a public figure, (2) a public official, or (3) a private person.

- Distinguish the four torts comprising invasion of privacy.

- Describe the torts that protect against harm to property.

- Distinguish among interference with contractual relations, disparagement, and fraudulent misrepresentation.

A ll forms of civil liability are either (1) voluntarily assumed, as by contract, or (2) involuntarily assumed, as imposed by law. Tort liability is of the second type. Tort law gives persons redress from civil wrongs or injuries to their person, property, and economic interests. Examples include assault and battery, automobile accidents, professional malpractice, and products liability. The law of torts has three principal objectives: (1) to compensate persons who sustain harm or loss resulting from another's conduct, (2) to place the cost of that compensation only on those parties who should bear it, and (3) to prevent future harms and losses. The law of torts therefore reallocates losses caused by human misconduct. In general, a tort is committed when:

1. a duty owed by one person to another
2. is breached and
3. proximately causes
4. injury or damage to the owner of a legally protected interest.

Each person is legally responsible for the damages his tortious conduct proximately causes. Moreover, as discussed in *Chapter 20*, businesses that conduct their business activities through employees are also liable for the torts their employees commit in the course of employment. The tort liability of employers makes the study of tort law essential to business managers.

Injuries may be inflicted intentionally, negligently, or without fault (strict liability). This chapter discusses intentional torts; the following chapter covers negligence and strict liability.

The same conduct may, and often does, constitute both a crime and a tort. An example would be an assault and battery committed by Johnson against West. For the commission of this crime, the State may take appropriate action against Johnson. In addition, however, Johnson has violated West's right to be secure in his person and so has committed a tort against West, who may, regardless of the criminal action by the State against Johnson, bring a civil action against Johnson for damages. On the other hand, an act may be criminal without being tortious, and by the same token, an act may be a tort but not a crime.

In a tort action, the injured party *sues* to recover *compensation* for the injury sustained as a result of the defendant's wrongful conduct. The primary purpose of tort law, unlike criminal law, is to compensate the injured party, not to punish the wrongdoer. In certain cases, however, courts may award **punitive** or exemplary damages, which are damages over and above the amount necessary to compensate the plaintiff. In cases in which the defendant's tortious conduct has been intentional—or, in some States, reckless—and outrageous, exhibiting "malice" or a fraudulent or evil motive, most courts permit a jury to award punitive damages. The allowance of punitive damages is designed to deter the defendant and others from similar conduct by punishing and making an example of the defendant.

◆ *See Case 7-1*

125

Tort law is primarily common law. The Restatement of Torts provides an orderly presentation of this law. From 1934 to 1939, the American Law Institute (ALI) adopted and promulgated the first Restatement. Since then, the Restatement has served as a vital force in shaping the law of torts. Between 1965 and 1978, the institute adopted and promulgated a second edition of the Restatement of Torts, which revises and supersedes the first Restatement. This text refers to the second Restatement simply as the Restatement.

In 1996, the ALI approved the development of a new Restatement, called Restatement Third, Torts: Liability for Physical and Emotional Harm, which addresses the general or basic elements of the tort action for liability for accidental personal injury, property damage, and emotional harm but does not cover liability for economic loss. This work replaces comparable provisions in the Restatement Second, Torts. The final work is published in two volumes. Volume 1 was released in 2010 and primarily covers liability for negligence causing physical harm, duty, strict liability, factual cause, and scope of liability (traditionally called proximate cause). Volume 2 covers affirmative duties, emotional harm, land possessors' liability, and liability of actors who retain independent contractors. Volume 2 was approved in 2011 and published in 2012. Because this new Restatement primarily applies to nonintentional torts, it is covered extensively in the next chapter, and it is cited as the "Third Restatement." A few of its provisions, however, do apply to intentional torts and are included in this chapter.

The Institute has begun work on the Restatement Third, Torts: Intentional Torts to Persons, which is the latest installment of the ALI's ongoing revision of the Restatement Second of Torts. This new project will complete the major avenues of recovery for physical and emotional harm to persons with a focus on assault, battery, and false imprisonment, as well as consent, self-defense, and other privileges. Portions of all three chapters have been drafted, and some sections of chapters 1 and 2 have been approved.

In 2018, the ALI approved the final portions of the Restatement Third, Torts: Liability for Economic Harm which updates coverage on torts that involve economic loss or pecuniary harm *not* resulting from physical harm or physical contact to a person or property. The project updates coverage of economic torts in Restatement Second, Torts and addresses some topics not covered in prior Restatements. This project covers fraud, breach of fiduciary duty, interference with contract, unjustifiable litigation, injurious falsehood, and interference with the right to possession of personal property. It also addresses *unintentional* infliction of economic loss, including professional negligence,

negligent misrepresentation, negligent performance of services, and public nuisance.

In 2019, the ALI approved three more projects as part of its ongoing revision of the Restatement Second of Torts. (1) The Restatement Third, Torts: Defamation and Privacy addresses torts dealing with personal and business reputation and dignity, including defamation, business disparagement, and rights of privacy. (2) The Restatement Third, Torts: Remedies covers tort damages and other remedies including the types of recoverable damages and the measurement of damages. (3) The Restatement Third, Torts: Concluding Provisions deals with topics not covered otherwise in the Restatement Third of Torts that either require updating or were not previously included.

State legislatures and, to a lesser extent, courts have actively assessed the need for tort reform. In general, tort reform has focused on limiting liability by restricting damages or narrowing claims. The majority of States have enacted at least one piece of legislation that falls into the broad category of tort reform, but these States have enacted different changes or different combinations of changes affecting specific aspects of tort law. Approaches to tort reform that have been taken at the State level include the following:

1. Laws that address specific types of claims (e.g., limits on medical malpractice awards or on the liability of providers of alcohol).

2. Laws abolishing joint and several liability or limiting the application of this rule. Where joint and several liability is abolished, each one of the several defendants is liable only for his share of the plaintiff's damages.

3. Laws adding defenses to certain types of tort actions.

4. Laws capping noneconomic damages—so-called pain and suffering awards.

5. Laws to abolish or limit punitive damages or to raise the standard of proof beyond the preponderance of the evidence.

6. Laws aimed at attorneys' fees; for example, laws that directly regulate contingent fees.

7-1 Intent

Intent, as used in tort law, does not require a hostile or evil motive; rather, the term denotes either that the actor desires to cause the consequences of his act or that he believes that those consequences are substantially certain to result from it. Restatement, Section 8A. The Third Restatement provides that "[a] person acts with the intent to produce a consequence if: (a) the person acts with the purpose of producing that consequence; or (b) the person acts knowing that the consequence is substantially certain to result." Section 1.

The following examples illustrate the definition of intent: (1) If A fires a gun in the middle of the Mojave Desert, he intends to fire the gun, but when the bullet hits B, who is in the desert without A's knowledge, A does not intend that result. (2) A throws a bomb into B's office to kill B. A knows that C is in B's office and that the bomb is substantially certain to injure C, although A has no desire to harm C. A, nonetheless, is liable to C for any injury caused C. A's intent to injure B is *transferred* to C.

Infants (persons who have not reached the age of majority, which is eighteen years in almost all States) are held liable for their intentional torts. The infant's age and knowledge, however, are critical in determining whether the infant had sufficient intelligence to form the requisite intent. Incompetents, like infants, are generally held liable for their intentional torts.

A number of established and specifically named torts protect an individual from various intentional interferences with his person, dignity, property, and economic interests. Because the law of torts is dynamic, new forms of relief continue to develop. To guide the courts in determining when they should impose liability for intentionally inflicted harm that does not fall within the requirements of an established tort, Section 870 of the Restatement provides a general catch-all intentional tort: "One who intentionally causes injury to another is subject to liability to the other for that injury, if his conduct is generally culpable and not justifiable under the circumstances. This liability may be imposed although the actor's conduct does not come within a traditional category of tort liability."

This section also provides a unifying principle both for long-established torts and for those that have developed more recently. The Third Restatement has a similar provision. Section 5.

♦ **SEE FIGURE 7-1:** *Intent*

7-2 Harm to the Person

The law provides protection against intentional harm to the person. The primary interests protected by these torts are freedom from bodily contact (by the tort of battery), freedom from apprehension (assault), freedom from confinement (false imprisonment), and freedom from mental distress (infliction of emotional distress). Generally, intentional torts to the person entitle the injured party to recover damages for bodily harm, emotional distress, loss or impairment of earning capacity, and reasonable medical expenses as well as for harm the tortious conduct caused to property or business.

7-2a BATTERY

Battery is an intentional infliction of harmful or offensive bodily contact. It may consist of contact causing serious injury, such as a gunshot wound or a blow to the head with a club. Or it may involve contact causing little or no physical injury, such as knocking a hat off of a person's head or flicking a glove in another's face. Bodily contact is offensive if it would offend a reasonable person's sense of dignity, even if the defendant intended the conduct only as a joke or a compliment. Restatement, Section 19. For instance, kissing another without permission would constitute a battery. Bodily contact may be accomplished by the use of objects, such as Arthur's throwing a rock at Bea with the intention of hitting her. If the rock hits Bea or any other person, Arthur has committed a battery. Nonetheless, in a densely populated society, one cannot expect

---

FIGURE 7-1 Intent

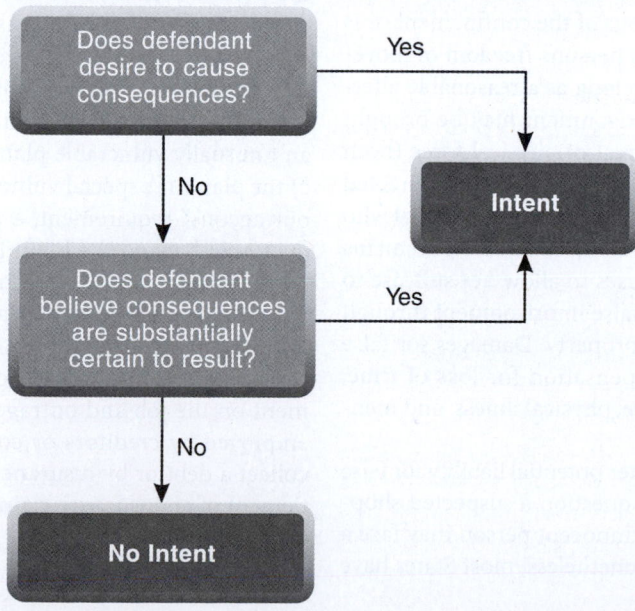

complete freedom from personal contact with others. Accordingly, neither casually bumping into another in a congested area nor gently tapping that other on the shoulder to get her attention would constitute a battery.

7-2b ASSAULT

Assault is intentional conduct by one person directed at another that places the other in apprehension of imminent (immediate) bodily harm or offensive contact. It is usually committed immediately preceding a battery, but if the intended battery fails, the assault remains. Assault is principally a mental rather than a physical intrusion. Accordingly, damages for assault may include compensation for fright and humiliation. The person in danger of immediate bodily harm must have *knowledge* of the danger and be apprehensive of its imminent threat to his safety. For example, if Joan aims a loaded gun at Kelly's back but Pat subdues her before Kelly becomes aware of the danger, Joan has not committed an assault upon Kelly.

Historically, it has been said that words alone do not constitute an assault. Nonetheless, spoken words must be taken in context, and if as taken cause apprehension, these spoken words will constitute an assault. On the other hand, words sometimes will negate an apparent threat so that there is no assault. This does not mean that a defendant can avoid liability for an assault by making his threat conditional. The threat "If you do not give me your book, I will break your arm" constitutes an assault.

7-2c FALSE IMPRISONMENT

The tort of **false imprisonment**, or false arrest, is the intentional confining of a person against her will within fixed boundaries if the person is conscious of the confinement or is harmed by it. Merely obstructing a person's freedom of movement is not false imprisonment so long as a reasonable alternative exit is available. False imprisonment may be brought about by physical force, by the threat of physical force (both express and implied), by physical barriers, or by force directed against the plaintiff's property. For instance, an individual who remains in a store after his wallet is confiscated or who remains on a train after the conductor refuses to allow her suitcase to be removed are both examples of false imprisonment through the use of force against personal property. Damages for false imprisonment may include compensation for loss of time, physical discomfort, inconvenience, physical illness, and mental suffering.

Merchants occasionally encounter potential liability for false imprisonment when they seek to question a suspected shoplifter. A merchant who detains an innocent person may face a lawsuit for false imprisonment. Nonetheless, most States have statutes protecting the merchant, provided she detains the suspect upon probable cause, in a reasonable manner, and for not more than a reasonable time.

♦ *See Case 7-2*

Practical Advice

When detaining a suspected shoplifter, be careful to conform to the limitations of your State's statutory privilege.

7-2d INFLICTION OF EMOTIONAL DISTRESS

Under the Second and Third Restatements, a person is liable for **infliction of emotional distress** when that person by extreme and outrageous conduct intentionally or recklessly causes severe emotional distress to another. The person is liable for that emotional distress and, if the emotional distress causes bodily harm, also for the resulting bodily harm. **Recklessness** is conduct that evidences a conscious disregard of or an indifference to the consequences of the act committed. With respect to infliction of emotional distress, the Third Restatement explains that an

actor acts recklessly when the actor knows of the risk of severe emotional disturbance (or knows facts that make the risk obvious) and fails to take a precaution that would eliminate or reduce the risk even though the burden is slight relative to the magnitude of the risk, thereby demonstrating the actor's indifference.

Damages may be recovered for severe emotional distress even in the absence of any physical injury. Liability for infliction of emotional distress, however, arises only when the person seeking recovery has suffered severe emotional disturbance and when a reasonable person in the same circumstances would suffer severe disturbance. Thus, the Third Restatement imposes an objective—not a subjective—test. Accordingly, there is no liability for mental harm suffered by an unusually vulnerable plaintiff, unless the defendant knew of the plaintiff's special vulnerability. Under the "extreme and outrageous" requirement, a person is liable only if the conduct goes beyond the bounds of human decency and would be regarded as intolerable in a civilized community. Ordinary insults and indignities are not enough for liability to be imposed, even if the person desires to cause emotional disturbance. Examples of this tort would include sexual harassment on the job and outrageous, prolonged bullying tactics employed by creditors or collection agencies attempting to collect a debt or by insurance adjusters trying to force a settlement of an insurance claim.

♦ *See Case 7-2*

7-3 Harm to the Right of Dignity

The law also protects a person against intentional harm to his right of dignity. This protection includes a person's reputation, privacy, and right to freedom from unjustifiable litigation.

7-3a DEFAMATION

The tort of defamation is a false communication that injures a person's reputation by disgracing him and diminishing the respect in which he is held. An example would be the publication of a false statement that a person had committed a crime or had a loathsome disease. In *Beckman v. Dunn*, 276 Pa.Super. 527, 419 A.2d 583 (1980), the court stated, "A communication is defamatory if it tends to harm the reputation of another so as to lower him in the estimation of the community or deter third persons from associating or dealing with him, and necessarily involves the idea of disgrace."

ELEMENTS OF DEFAMATION The elements of a defamation action are (1) a false and defamatory statement concerning another; (2) an unprivileged publication (communication) to a third party; (3) depending on the status of the defendant, negligence or recklessness on her part in knowing or failing to ascertain the falsity of the statement; and (4) in some cases, proof of special harm caused by the publication. Restatement, Section 558. The burden of proof is on the plaintiff to prove the falsity of the defamatory statement.

If a defamatory communication is handwritten, typewritten, printed, pictorial, or in another medium with like communicative power, such as a television or radio broadcast, it is designated **libel**. If it is spoken or oral, it is designated **slander**. Restatement, Sections 568 and 568A. In either case, it must be communicated to a person or persons other than the one who is defamed, a process referred to as *publication*. If Maurice hands or mails to Pierre a defamatory letter he has written about Pierre's character, this is not a publication, as it is intended only for Pierre. The publication must have been intentional or the result of the defendant's negligence.

Any living person, as well as corporations, partnerships, and unincorporated associations, may be defamed. Restatement, Sections 561 and 562. Unless a statute provides otherwise, no action may be brought for defamation of a deceased person. Restatement, Section 560.

A significant trend affecting business has been the bringing of defamation suits against former employers by discharged employees.

◆ *See Case 7-3*

Practical Advice

Consider whether you should provide employment references for current and former employees, and if you decide to do so, take care in what you say.

DEFENSES TO DEFAMATION The defense of **privilege** is immunity from tort liability granted when the defendant's conduct furthers a societal interest of greater importance than the injury inflicted upon the plaintiff. Three types of privileges apply to defamation: absolute, conditional, and constitutional.

Absolute privilege protects the defendant regardless of his motive or intent. This type of privilege, which has been confined to those few situations in which public policy clearly favors complete freedom of speech, includes (1) statements made by participants in a judicial proceeding regarding that proceeding, (2) statements made by members of Congress on the floor of Congress and by members of State and local legislative bodies, (3) statements made by certain executive branch officers in the discharge of their government duties, and (4) statements regarding a third party made between spouses when they are alone.

Qualified or **conditional privilege** depends upon proper use of the privilege. A person has conditional privilege to publish defamatory matter to protect his own legitimate interests or, in some cases, the interests of another. Conditional privilege also extends to many communications in which the publisher and the recipient have a common interest, such as in letters of reference. A publisher who acts in an excessive manner, without probable cause, or for an improper purpose forfeits conditional privilege.

The First Amendment to the U.S. Constitution guarantees freedom of speech and freedom of the press. The U.S. Supreme Court has applied these rights to the law of defamation by extending a form of constitutional privilege to defamatory and false statements regarding public officials, candidates for public office, or public figures so long as the statements are made without actual malice. Restatement, Section 580A. For these purposes, *actual malice* is not ill will but clear and convincing proof that the publisher had knowledge of the falsity of the communication or acted in reckless disregard of its truth or falsity. Thus, under **constitutional privilege**, a public official, candidate for public office, or public figure must prove that the defendant published the defamatory and false comment with knowledge or in reckless disregard of the comment's falsity and its defamatory character. However, in a defamation suit brought by a private person (one who is not a public official, a candidate for public office, or a public figure), the plaintiff must prove that the defendant published the defamatory and false comment with either actual malice *or* negligence.

Congress enacted Section 230 of the **Communications Decency Act of 1996 (CDA)**, granting immunity to Internet service providers (ISPs) from liability for defamation when publishing information originating from a third party. A court has interpreted this provision of the CDA as immunizing an ISP that refused to remove or retract an allegedly defamatory posting made on its bulletin board. The immunity granted by the CDA to ISPs has spawned a number of lawsuits urging ISPs to reveal the identities of subscribers who have posted allegedly defamatory statements. To date, ISPs have complied, generating additional litigation by angry ISP patrons attempting to keep their identities protected by asserting that their right to free speech is being compromised.

Because Section 230 of the CDA grants immunity only to ISPs, there is the possibility that employers will be held liable for some online defamatory statements made by an employee. Section 577(2) of the Restatement of Torts provides that a person who intentionally and unreasonably fails to remove defamatory matter that she knows is exhibited on property in her possession or under her control is liable for its continued publication. Therefore, employers in control of e-forums, such as electronic bulletin boards and chat rooms, should act quickly to remove any defamatory statement brought to their attention.

7-3b INVASION OF PRIVACY

The invasion of a person's right to privacy consists of four distinct torts: (1) appropriation of a person's name or likeness, (2) unreasonable intrusion upon the seclusion of another, (3) unreasonable public disclosure of private facts, or (4) unreasonable publicity that places another in a false light in the public eye. Restatement, Section 652A.

It is entirely possible and not uncommon for a person to invade another's right of privacy in a manner entailing two or more of these related torts. For example, Cindy forces her way into Ozzie's hospital room, takes a photograph of Ozzie, and publishes it to promote Cindy's cure for Ozzie's illness along with false statements about Ozzie that a reasonable person would consider highly objectionable. Ozzie would be entitled to recover on any or all of the four torts comprising invasion of privacy.

♦ SEE FIGURE 7-2: *Privacy*

APPROPRIATION The tort of appropriation is the unauthorized use of the plaintiff's name or likeness for the defendant's benefit, as, for example, in promoting or advertising a product or service. Restatement, Section 652C. The tort of appropriation, also known as the **right of publicity**, seeks to protect the individual's right to the exclusive use of his identity. In the earlier example, Cindy's use of Ozzie's photograph to promote Cindy's business constitutes the tort of appropriation.

♦ *See Case 7-4*

Practical Advice
When using another person's identity for your own purposes, be sure to obtain that person's written consent.

INTRUSION The tort of intrusion is the unreasonable and highly offensive interference with the solitude or seclusion of another. Restatement, Section 652B. Such unreasonable interference would include improper entry into another's dwelling, unauthorized eavesdropping upon another's private conversations, and unauthorized examination of another's private papers and records. The intrusion must be highly offensive or objectionable to a reasonable person and must involve matters that are private. Thus, there is no liability if the defendant examines public records or observes the plaintiff in a public place. This form of invasion of privacy is committed once the intrusion occurs, as publicity is not required.

PUBLIC DISCLOSURE OF PRIVATE FACTS Under the tort of public disclosure of private facts, the courts impose liability for publicity given to private information about another if the matter made public would be highly offensive and objectionable to a reasonable person. Like intrusion, this tort applies only to private, not public, information regarding an individual; unlike intrusion, it requires publicity. Under the Restatement, the publicity required differs in degree from the "publication" required under the law of defamation. This tort requires that private facts be communicated to the public at large or that they become public knowledge, whereas publication of a defamatory statement need only be made to a single third party. Section 652D, Comment a. Some courts, however, have allowed recovery where the disclosure was made to only one person. Thus, under the Restatement approach, Kathy, a creditor of Gary, will not invade Gary's privacy by writing a letter to Gary's

FIGURE 7-2   Privacy

	Appropriation	Intrusion	Public Disclosure	False Light
Publicity	Yes	No	Yes	Yes
Private Facts	No	Yes	Yes	No
Offensiveness	No	Yes	Yes	Yes
Falsity	No	No	No	Yes

employer to inform the employer of Gary's failure to pay a debt, but Kathy would be liable if she posted in the window of her store a statement that Gary will not pay the debt he owes to her. Also, unlike defamation, this tort applies to truthful private information if the matter published would be offensive and objectionable to a reasonable person of ordinary sensibilities.

FALSE LIGHT The tort of false light imposes liability for publicity that places another in a false light that is highly offensive if the defendant *knew* or acted in *reckless disregard* of the fact that the matter publicized was false. Restatement, Section 652E. For example, Linda includes Keith's name and photograph in a public "rogues' gallery" of convicted criminals. Because Keith has never been convicted of any crime, Linda is liable to him for placing him in a false light. Other examples include publicly and falsely attributing to a person an opinion, a statement, or a written work, as well as the unauthorized use of a person's name on a petition or on a complaint in a lawsuit.

Like defamation, the matter must be untrue; unlike defamation, it must be "publicized," not merely "published." Restatement, Section 652D, Comment a. Although the matter must be objectionable to a reasonable person, it need not be defamatory. In many instances, the same facts will give rise to actions both for defamation and for false light.

DEFENSES The defenses of absolute, conditional, and constitutional privilege apply to publication of any matter that is an invasion of privacy to the same extent that such defenses apply to defamation.

7-3c MISUSE OF LEGAL PROCEDURE

Three torts comprise the misuse of legal procedure: malicious prosecution, wrongful civil proceedings, and abuse of process. Each protects an individual from being subjected to unjustifiable litigation. Malicious prosecution and wrongful civil proceedings impose liability for damages caused by improperly brought proceedings, including harm to reputation, credit, or standing; emotional distress; and the expenses incurred in defending against the wrongfully brought lawsuit. Abuse of process is a tort consisting of the use of a legal proceeding (criminal or civil) to accomplish a purpose for which the proceeding is not designed. Abuse of process applies even when there is probable cause or when the plaintiff or prosecution succeeds in the litigation.

7-4 Harm to Property

The law also provides protection against invasions of a person's interests in property. Intentional harm to property includes the torts of (1) trespass to real property, (2) nuisance, (3) trespass to personal property, and (4) conversion.

7-4a REAL PROPERTY

Real property is land and anything attached to it, such as buildings, trees, and minerals. The law protects the possessor's rights to the exclusive use and quiet enjoyment of the land. Accordingly, damages for harm to land include compensation for the resulting diminution in the value of the land, the loss of use of the land, and the discomfort caused to the possessor of the land. Restatement, Section 929.

TRESPASS TO REAL PROPERTY Section 158 of the Restatement provides:

One is subject to liability to another for trespass, irrespective of whether he thereby causes harm to any legally protected interest of the other, if he intentionally

(a) enters land in the possession of the other, or causes a thing or a third person to do so, or

(b) remains on the land, or

(c) fails to remove from the land a thing which he is under a duty to remove.

It is no defense that the intruder acted under the mistaken belief of law or fact that he was not trespassing. If the intruder intended to be upon the particular property, his reasonable belief that he owned the land or had permission to enter upon the land is irrelevant. Restatement, Section 164. An intruder is not liable if his own actions do not cause his presence on the land of another. For example, if Carol throws Ralph onto Tim's land, Ralph is not liable to Tim for trespass, although Carol is.

A trespass may be committed on, beneath, or above the surface of the land, although the law regards the upper air, above a prescribed minimum altitude for flight, as a public highway. Therefore, no aerial trespass occurs unless the aircraft enters into the lower reaches of the airspace and substantially interferes with the landowner's use and enjoyment. Restatement, Section 159.

NUISANCE A nuisance is a nontrespassory invasion of another's interest in the private use and enjoyment of land. Restatement, Section 821D. In contrast to trespass, nuisance does not require interference with another's right to exclusive possession of land, but rather imposes liability for significant and unreasonable harm to another's use or enjoyment of land. Examples of nuisances include the emission of unpleasant odors, smoke, dust, or gas, as well as the pollution of a stream, a pond, or an underground water supply. In one case, a computer's serious disturbance of a television retailer's signal reception was considered a nuisance.

> **Practical Advice**
>
> *In using, manufacturing, and disposing of dangerous, noxious, or toxic materials, take care not to create a nuisance.*

7-4b PERSONAL PROPERTY

Personal property, or chattel, is any type of property other than an interest in land. The law protects a number of interests in the possession of personal property, including an interest in the property's physical condition and usability, an interest in the retention of possession, and an interest in its availability for future use.

TRESPASS TO PERSONAL PROPERTY The tort of trespass to personal property consists of the intentional dispossession or unauthorized use of the personal property of another. Though the interference with the right to exclusive use and possession may be direct or indirect, liability is limited to instances in which the trespasser (1) dispossesses the other of the property; (2) substantially impairs the condition, quality, or value of the property; (3) deprives the possessor of the use of the property for a substantial time; or (4) causes harm to the possessor or to some person or thing in which the possessor has a legally protected interest. Restatement, Section 218. For example, Albert parks his car in front of his house. Ronald pushes Albert's car around the corner. Albert subsequently looks for his car but cannot find it for several hours. Ronald is liable to Albert for trespass.

CONVERSION The tort of conversion is an intentional exercise of dominion or control over another's personal property that so seriously interferes with the other's right of control as to justly require the payment of full value for the property. Restatement, Section 222A. Thus, all conversions are trespasses, but not all trespasses are conversions.

Conversion may consist of the intentional destruction of personal property or the use of property in an unauthorized manner. For example, Ken entrusts an automobile to Barbara, a dealer, for sale. After she drives the car eight thousand miles on her own business, Barbara is liable to Ken for conversion. On the other hand, in the example in which Ronald pushed Albert's car around the corner, Ronald would not be liable to Albert for conversion. Moreover, a person who buys stolen property is liable to the rightful owner for conversion even if the buyer acquires the property in good faith and without knowledge that it was stolen. Restatement, Section 229.

7-5 Harm to Economic Interests

Economic interests account for a fourth set of interests the law protects against intentional interference. Economic or pecuniary interests include a person's existing and prospective contractual relations, a person's business reputation, a person's name and likeness (previously discussed under the section titled "Appropriation"), and a person's freedom from deception. Business torts—those torts that protect a person's economic interests—are discussed in this section under the

following headings: (1) interference with contractual relations, (2) disparagement, and (3) fraudulent misrepresentation.

7-5a INTERFERENCE WITH CONTRACTUAL RELATIONS

To conduct business, it is necessary to establish trade relations with employees, suppliers, and customers. Though these relations may or may not be contractual, those that are, or are capable of being established by contract, receive legal protection against interference. Section 766 of the Restatement provides:

> One who intentionally and improperly interferes with the performance of a contract (except a contract to marry) between another and a third person by inducing or otherwise causing the third person not to perform the contract, is subject to liability to the other for the pecuniary loss resulting to the other from the failure of the third person to perform the contract.

The law imposes similar liability for intentional and improper interference with another's prospective contractual relation, such as a lease renewal or financing for construction. Restatement, Section 766B.

In either case, the rule requires that a person act with the purpose or motive of interfering with another's contract or with the knowledge that such interference is substantially certain to occur as a natural consequence of her actions. The interference may occur by threats or by prevention through the use of physical force. Frequently, interference is accomplished through inducement, such as the offer of a better contract. For instance, Edgar may offer Doris, an employee of Frank, a salary of $5,000 more per year than the contractual arrangement between Doris and Frank. If Edgar is aware that a contract exists between Doris and Frank and of the fact that his offer to Doris will interfere with that contract, then Edgar is liable to Frank for intentional interference with contractual relations.

To be distinguished is the situation in which the contract may be terminated at will or in which the contractual relation is only prospective. In these cases, competition is a proper basis for interference; for if one party is pursuing a contractual relation, others also are free to pursue a similar arrangement. For example, Amos and Brenda are competing distributors of transistors. Amos induces Carter, a prospective customer of Brenda, to buy transistors from Amos instead of Brenda. Amos has no liability to Brenda because his interference with Brenda's prospective contract with Carter is justified on the basis of competition, so long as Amos does not use predatory means such as physical violence, fraud, civil suits, or criminal prosecution to persuade Carter to deal with him.

Damages for interference with contractual relations include the pecuniary loss of the benefits of the contract, consequential losses caused by the interference, and emotional distress or actual harm to reputation. Restatement, Section 774A. In one case, Pennzoil had orally entered into a contract to merge with Getty Oil. Before the merger was consummated, however, Texaco induced Getty to merge with Texaco instead. Pennzoil sued Texaco for tortious interference with the merger contract and was awarded $7.53 billion in compensatory damages and $3 billion in punitive damages. *Texaco, Inc. v. Pennzoil, Co.*, 729 S.W.2d 768 (1987).

Practical Advice

Recognize that inducing another person's employees to breach a valid agreement not to compete or not to disclose confidential information may be improper interference with contractual relations.

7-5b DISPARAGEMENT

The tort of **disparagement** or injurious falsehood imposes liability upon a person who publishes a false statement that results in harm to another's interests which have pecuniary value, if the publisher knows that the statement is false or acts in reckless disregard of its truth or falsity. This tort most commonly involves false statements that the publisher intends to cast doubt upon the title or quality of another's property or products. Thus, Adam, while contemplating the purchase of merchandise that belongs to Barry, reads a newspaper advertisement in which Carol falsely asserts she owns the merchandise. Carol has disparaged Barry's property in the goods. Similarly, Marlene, knowing her statement to be false, tells Lionel that Matthew, an importer of wood, does not deal in mahogany. As a result, Lionel, who had intended to buy mahogany from Matthew, buys it elsewhere. Marlene is liable to Matthew for disparagement.

Absolute, conditional, and constitutional privileges apply to the same extent to the tort of disparagement as they do to defamation. In addition, a competitor has conditional privilege to compare her products favorably with those of a rival, even though she does not believe that her products are superior. No privilege applies, however, if the comparison contains false assertions of specific unfavorable facts about the competitor's property. For example, a manufacturer who advertises that his goods are the best in the market, even though he knows that a competitor's product is better, is not liable for disparagement. If he goes further, however, by falsely stating that his product is better because his competitor uses shoddy materials, then his disparagement would no longer be privileged, and he would be liable to his competitor for disparagement.

The pecuniary loss an injured person may recover is that which directly and immediately results from impairment of the marketability of the property disparaged. The injured party also may recover damages for expenses necessary to counteract the false publication, including litigation expenses, the cost of

notifying customers, and the cost of publishing denials. Thus, Ursula publishes in a magazine an untrue statement that cranberries grown during the current season in a particular area are unwholesome. Shortly thereafter, the business of Victor, a jobber who has contracted to buy the entire output of cranberries grown in this area, falls off by 50 percent. If no other facts account for this decrease in his business, Victor is entitled to recover the amount of his loss from Ursula, plus the expenses necessary to counteract the misinformation published.

Practical Advice

When commenting on the products or services offered by a competitor, take care not to make any false statements.

7-5c FRAUDULENT MISREPRESENTATION

With respect to intentional, or fraudulent, misrepresentation, Section 525 of the Restatement provides:

> One who fraudulently makes a misrepresentation of fact, opinion, intention, or law for the purpose of inducing another to act or to refrain from action in reliance upon it, is subject to liability to the other in deceit for pecuniary loss caused to him by his justifiable reliance upon the misrepresentation.

The Third Restatement of Torts: Liability for Economic Harm continues this general rule of liability for fraud. Section 9. A misrepresentation is *fraudulent* if the maker of it (1) knows or believes that the matter is not as he represents it to be, (2) knows that he does not have the confidence in the accuracy of his representation that he states or implies, or (3) knows that he does not have the basis for the representation that he states or implies. Third Restatement of Torts: Liability for Economic Harm, Section 10.

For example, Smith represents to Jones that a tract of land in Texas is located in an area where oil drilling had recently commenced. Smith makes this statement knowing it to be false. In reliance upon the statement, Jones purchases the land from Smith, who is liable to Jones for fraudulent misrepresentation. Although fraudulent misrepresentation is a tort action, it is closely connected with contractual negotiations; the effects of such misrepresentation on assent to a contract are discussed in *Chapter 11*.

◆ **SEE FIGURE 7-3:** *Intentional Torts*

Practical Advice

When describing your products or services, take care not to make any false statements.

7-6 Defenses to Intentional Torts

Even though the defendant has intentionally invaded the interests of the plaintiff, the defendant will not be liable if such conduct was privileged. A defendant's conduct is privileged if it furthers an interest of such social importance that the law confers immunity from tort liability for the damage the conduct causes to others. Examples of privilege include self-defense, defense of property, and defense of others. In addition, the plaintiff's consent to the defendant's conduct is a defense to intentional torts.

7-6a CONSENT

If one consents to conduct resulting in damage or harm to his own person, dignity, property, or economic interests, no liability will generally attach to the intentional infliction of injury. **Consent**, which signifies that one is willing for an act to occur, negates the wrongfulness of the act. A person may manifest consent expressly or impliedly, by words or by conduct.

Consent must be given by an individual with capacity to do so. Consent given by a minor, a mental incompetent, or an intoxicated individual is invalid if he is not capable of appreciating the nature, extent, or probable consequences of the conduct to which he has consented. Consent is not effective if

given under duress, by which one constrains another's will by compelling that other to give consent unwillingly.

7-6b PRIVILEGE

A person who would otherwise be liable for a tort is *not* liable if he acts pursuant to and within the limits of a privilege. Restatement, Section 890. Conditional privileges, as discussed in the section on defamation, depend upon proper use of the privilege. Absolute privilege, on the other hand, protects the defendant regardless of his purpose. Examples of absolute privilege include untrue, defamatory statements made by participants during the course of judicial proceedings, by legislators, by certain governmental executives, and between spouses. Absolute immunity also protects a public prosecutor from civil liability for malicious prosecution.

One conditional privilege—self-defense—entitles an individual to injure another's person without the other's consent. The law created the privilege of **self-defense** to enable an individual to protect himself against tortious interference. By virtue of this privilege, an individual may inflict or impose what would otherwise constitute battery, assault, or false imprisonment.

Section 63 of the Restatement provides: "An actor is privileged to use reasonable force, not intended or likely to cause death or serious bodily harm, to defend himself against

FIGURE 7-3   Intentional Torts

Interest Protected	Tort
Person	
Freedom from contact	Battery
Freedom from apprehension	Assault
Freedom of movement	False imprisonment
Freedom from distress	Infliction of emotional distress
Dignity	
Reputation	Defamation
Privacy	Appropriation
	Intrusion
	Public disclosure of private facts
	False light
Freedom from wrongful legal actions	Misuse of legal procedure
Property	
Real	Trespass to real property
	Nuisance
Personal	Trespass to personal property
	Conversion
Economic	
Contracts	Interference with contractual rights
Goodwill	Disparagement
Freedom from deception	Fraudulent misrepresentation

unprivileged harmful or offensive contact or other bodily harm which he reasonably believes that another is about to inflict intentionally upon him."

The privilege of self-defense exists whether or not the danger actually exists, provided that the defendant reasonably believed self-defense was necessary. The reasonableness of the defendant's actions is based upon what a person of average courage would have thought under the circumstances. A possessor of property is also permitted to use reasonable force, not intended or likely to cause death or serious bodily harm, to protect his real and personal property.

CHAPTER SUMMARY

HARM TO THE PERSON	**Battery** intentional infliction of harmful or offensive bodily contact
	Assault intentional infliction of apprehension of immediate bodily harm or offensive contact
	False Imprisonment intentional confining of a person against her will
	Infliction of Emotional Distress extreme and outrageous conduct intentionally or recklessly causing severe emotional distress
HARM TO THE RIGHT OF DIGNITY	**Defamation** false communication that injures a person's reputation
	• *Libel* written or electronically transmitted defamation
	• *Slander* spoken defamation
	• *Defenses* truth, absolute privilege, conditional privilege, and constitutional privilege are defenses to a defamation action
	Invasion of Privacy
	• *Appropriation* unauthorized use of a person's identity
	• *Intrusion* unreasonable and highly offensive interference with the seclusion of another
	• *Public Disclosure of Private Facts* highly offensive publicity of private information
	• *False Light* highly offensive and false publicity about another
	Misuse of Legal Procedure torts that protect an individual from unjustifiable litigation
HARM TO PROPERTY	**Real Property** land and anything attached to it
	• *Trespass to Real Property* wrongfully entering on land of another
	• *Nuisance* a nontrespassory interference with another's use and enjoyment of land
	Personal Property any property other than land
	• *Trespass to Personal Property* an intentional taking or use of another's personal property
	• *Conversion* intentional exercise of control over another's personal property
HARM TO ECONOMIC INTERESTS	**Interference with Contractual Relations** intentionally causing one of the parties to a contract not to perform
	Disparagement publication of false statements about another's property or products
	Fraudulent Misrepresentation a false statement, made with knowledge of its falsity, intended to induce another to act
DEFENSES TO INTENTIONAL TORTS	**Consent** a person may not recover for injury to which he willingly and knowingly consents
	Self-Defense a person may take appropriate action to prevent harm to himself where time does not allow resort to the law

C A S E S

CASE

7-1

Punitive Damages
PHILIP MORRIS USA v. WILLIAMS
Supreme Court of the United States, 2007
549 U.S. 346, 127 S.Ct. 1057, 166 L.Ed.2d 940

Breyer, J.

This lawsuit arises out of the death of Jesse Williams, a heavy cigarette smoker. Respondent [plaintiff at trial], Williams' widow, represents his estate in this state lawsuit for negligence and deceit against Philip Morris, the manufacturer of Marlboro, the brand that Williams favored. A jury found that Williams' death was caused by smoking; that Williams smoked in significant part because he thought it was safe to do so; and that Philip Morris knowingly and falsely led him to believe that this was so. The jury ultimately found that Philip Morris was negligent (as was Williams) and that Philip Morris had engaged in deceit. In respect to deceit, the claim at issue here, it awarded compensatory damages of about $821,000 (about $21,000 economic and $800,000 noneconomic) along with $79.5 million in punitive damages.

The trial judge subsequently found the $79.5 million punitive damages award "excessive," [citation], and reduced it to $32 million. Both sides appealed. The Oregon Court of Appeals rejected Philip Morris' arguments and restored the $79.5 million jury award. Subsequently, [the State Supreme Court rejected Philip Morris' arguments that the trial court should have instructed the jury that it could not punish Philip Morris for injury to persons not before the court, and that the roughly 100-to-1 ratio the $79.5 million award bore to the compensatory damages amount indicated a "grossly excessive" punitive award].

* * *

Philip Morris then sought certiorari. It asked us to consider, among other things, (1) its claim that Oregon had unconstitutionally permitted it to be punished for harming nonparty victims; and (2) whether Oregon had in effect disregarded "the constitutional requirement that punitive damages be reasonably related to the plaintiff's harm." [Citation.] We granted certiorari limited to these two questions.

* * *

This Court has long made clear that "punitive damages may properly be imposed to further a State's legitimate interests in punishing unlawful conduct and deterring its repetition." [Citations.] At the same time, we have emphasized the need to avoid an arbitrary determination of an award's amount. Unless a State insists upon proper standards that will cabin the jury's discretionary authority, its punitive damages system may deprive a defendant of "fair notice … of the severity of the penalty that

a State may impose," [citation]; it may threaten "arbitrary punishments," i.e., punishments that reflect not an "application of law" but "a decision maker's caprice," [citation]; and, where the amounts are sufficiently large, it may impose one State's (or one jury's) "policy choice," say as to the conditions under which (or even whether) certain products can be sold, upon "neighboring States" with different public policies, [citation].

For these and similar reasons, this Court has found that the Constitution imposes certain limits, in respect both to procedures for awarding punitive damages and to amounts forbidden as "grossly excessive." [Citation] (requiring judicial review of the size of punitive awards); [citation] (review must be de novo); [citation] (excessiveness decision depends upon the reprehensibility of the defendant's conduct, whether the award bears a reasonable relationship to the actual and potential harm caused by the defendant to the plaintiff, and the difference between the award and sanctions "authorized or imposed in comparable cases"); [citation] (excessiveness more likely where ratio exceeds single digits). Because we shall not decide whether the award here at issue is "grossly excessive," we need now only consider the Constitution's procedural limitations.

In our view, the Constitution's Due Process Clause forbids a State to use a punitive damages award to punish a defendant for injury that it inflicts upon nonparties or those whom they directly represent, i.e., injury that it inflicts upon those who are, essentially, strangers to the litigation. * * *

* * *

* * * [W]e can find no authority supporting the use of punitive damages awards for the purpose of punishing a defendant for harming others. We have said that it may be appropriate to consider the reasonableness of a punitive damages award in light of the *potential* harm the defendant's conduct could have caused. But we have made clear that the potential harm at issue was harm potentially caused *the plaintiff*. [Citation.] ("We have been reluctant to identify concrete constitutional limits on the ratio between harm, or potential harm, *to the plaintiff* and the punitive damages award"). * * *

* * * Evidence of actual harm to nonparties can help to show that the conduct that harmed the plaintiff also posed a substantial risk of harm to the general public, and so was particularly reprehensible—although counsel may argue in a particular case that conduct resulting in no harm to others nonetheless posed a grave risk to the public, or the converse. Yet for the reasons given above, a jury may not go further than this and use a punitive damages verdict to punish a defendant directly on account of harms it is alleged to have visited on nonparties.

* * * We therefore conclude that the Due Process Clause requires States to provide assurance that juries are not asking the wrong question, *i.e.*, seeking, not simply to determine reprehensibility, but also to punish for harm caused strangers.

* * *

The instruction that Philip Morris said the trial court should have given distinguishes between using harm to others as part of the "reasonable relationship" equation (which it would allow) and using it directly as a basis for punishment. The instruction asked the trial court to tell the jury that "you *may* consider the extent of harm suffered by others *in determining what [the] reasonable relationship is*" between Philip Morris' punishable misconduct and harm caused to Jesse Williams, "*[but] you are not to punish the defendant for the impact of its alleged misconduct on other persons, who may*

bring lawsuits of their own in which other juries can resolve their claims . . ." [Citation.] And as the Oregon Supreme Court explicitly recognized, Philip Morris argued that the Constitution "prohibits the state, acting through a civil jury, from using punitive damages to punish a defendant for harm to nonparties." [Citation.]

* * *

As the preceding discussion makes clear, we believe that the Oregon Supreme Court applied the wrong constitutional standard when considering Philip Morris' appeal. We remand this case so that the Oregon Supreme Court can apply the standard we have set forth. Because the application of this standard may lead to the need for a new trial, or a change in the level of the punitive damages award, we shall not consider whether the award is constitutionally "grossly excessive." We vacate the Oregon Supreme Court's judgment and remand the case for further proceedings not inconsistent with this opinion.

CASE
7-2

False Imprisonment/Infliction of Emotional Distress
FERRELL v. MIKULA
Court of Appeals of Georgia, 2008
295 Ga.App. 326, 672 S.E.2d; reconsideration denied, 2008; *certiorari* denied 2009

Barnes, C. J.

Racquel Ferrell and the parents of Kristie Ferrell sued Ruby Tuesday, Inc. and its manager Christian Mikula for false imprisonment, intentional infliction of emotional distress, * * *. After extensive discovery, the defendants moved for summary judgment on all counts. In a one-page order stating only that no genuine issues as to any material fact existed, the trial court granted the motion, and the Ferrells' appeal. For the reasons that follow, we affirm the trial court's grant of summary judgment to the defendants on the Ferrells' claim for intentional infliction of emotional distress * * * but reverse the grant on the false imprisonment claim.

* * *

* * * [T]he evidence shows that on Friday night, August 6, 2006, 18-year-old Racquel Ferrell and 13-year-old Kristie Ferrell went to Ruby Tuesday. After they ate and paid their bill, the girls left the restaurant, got into their car, and drove out of the parking lot. As they began to enter the highway, Racquel noticed a black truck following her very closely with its headlights on high. She could not see well out of her rearview mirror with the bright lights behind her, so she changed lanes, but the truck changed lanes with her and stayed close behind. She switched lanes again, and the truck did too. A marked police car by the side of the road pulled onto the highway between the girls' car and the following truck and pulled the car over. After

asking Racquel if she had any drugs or weapons, the officer pulled her out of the car, placed her in handcuffs, and put her in the back seat of his patrol car. Another officer removed Kristie from the car, placed her in handcuffs, and put her in the back of another patrol car.

All of the police officers gathered to talk to the driver of the truck that had been following the Ferrells, who turned out to be a uniformed off-duty police officer working as a security guard for Ruby Tuesday. The officer who arrested Racquel returned to the patrol car where she was being held and told her if she had not paid her Ruby Tuesday bill she was going to jail. She protested, and the officer conferred again with the other officers, then returned to the car and said, "It was a mistake." He explained that the manager at the restaurant had sent the off-duty officer after them because he said the girls had not paid their bill, but they did not fit the description of the two people who had walked out without paying. The officers removed the handcuffs from Racquel and Kristie and returned them to their car. After asking for Racquel's driver's license and obtaining information about both girls, the officer told them they were free to go.

Mikula had been an assistant manager for about a month, and was the only manager at Ruby Tuesday that night. One of the servers, Robert, reported that his customers at Table 24 had a complaint, so Mikula talked to the couple and told them he would "take care of" the food item in question. The customers were a man and a woman in their late 20s to early 30s. Mikula left the table to discuss the matter with Robert, after which server Aaron told Mikula that the patrons at Table 24 had left without paying. Mikula looked at the table, confirmed they had not left any money for the bill, and went out the main entrance. He saw a car pulling out of the parking lot, and said to the off-duty officer, "Hey, I think they just left without paying." The officer said, "Who, them?" Mikula said, "I think so," and the officer got up and went to his vehicle.

* * *

Mikula knew the officer was going to follow the people in the car and would stop them, but did not ask the officer if he had seen who got into the car. He did not give the officer a description of the people at Table 24, and did not know the race, age, gender, or number of people in the car being followed. He did not know if there were people in any of the other cars in the parking lot. He did not ask any other people in the restaurant if they had seen the people at Table 24 leave the building, which had two exits. He did not know how long the people had been gone before Aaron told him they left, or whether another customer had picked up money from Table 24. He could have tried to obtain more information to determine whether the people in the car he pointed out were the people who had been sitting at Table 24, but did not do so.

* * *

In this case, the Ferrells were detained without a warrant, and thus have a claim for false imprisonment * * *. [Citation.] "False imprisonment is the unlawful detention of the person of another, for any length of time, whereby such person is deprived of his personal liberty." [Citation.] "The only essential elements of the action being the detention and its unlawfulness, malice and the want of probable cause need not be shown." [Citations.]

The evidence in this case clearly establishes that the Ferrells were detained. "* * * under modern tort law an individual may be imprisoned when his movements are restrained in the open street, or in a traveling automobile." [Citation.] Ruby Tuesday does not argue otherwise, but instead argues that the evidence established sufficient probable cause and the plaintiffs failed to establish that Mikula acted with malice. But malice is not an element of false imprisonment, * * *. Further, * * * the mere existence of probable cause standing alone has no real defensive bearing on the issue of liability [for false imprisonment]. [Citation.]

* * *

Arresting or procuring the arrest of a person without a warrant constitutes a tort, "unless he can justify under some of the exceptions in which arrest and imprisonment without a warrant are permitted by law, [citations]." Generally, one "who causes or directs the arrest of another by an officer without a warrant may be held liable for false imprisonment, in the absence of justification, and the burden of proving that such imprisonment lies within an exception rests upon the person ... causing the imprisonment." [Citations.] * * *

Accordingly, as the Ferrells have established an unlawful detention, the next issue to consider is whether Mikula "caused" the arrest. Whether a party is potentially liable for false imprisonment by "directly or indirectly urg[ing] a law enforcement official to begin criminal proceedings" or is not liable because he "merely relates facts to an official who then makes an independent decision to arrest" is a factual question for the jury. [Citation.] The party need not expressly request an arrest, but may be liable if his conduct and acts "procured and directed the arrest." [Citation.]

* * *

Here, Mikula told the officer that the car leaving the parking lot contained people who left without paying for their food, although he did not know or try to ascertain who was in the car. He also knew the officer was going to detain the people in the car and could have tried to stop him, but made no attempt to do so. Accordingly, the trial court erred in granting summary judgment to the defendants on the plaintiffs' false imprisonment claim.

* * *

The Ferrells also contend that the trial court erred in granting summary judgment to the defendants on their claim for intentional infliction of emotional distress. The elements of a cause of action for intentional infliction of emotional distress are: (1) intentional or reckless conduct; (2) that is extreme and outrageous; (3) a causal connection between the wrongful conduct and the emotional distress; and (4) severe emotional distress. [Citation.] Further,

[l]iability for this tort has been found only where the conduct has been so outrageous in character, and so extreme in degree, as to go beyond all possible bounds of decency, and to be regarded as atrocious, and utterly intolerable in a civilized community. Generally, the case is one in which the recitation of the facts to an average member of the community would arouse his resentment against the actor, and lead him to exclaim, "Outrageous!"

[Citation.]

In this case, the action upon which the Ferrells base their emotional distress claim is being stopped by the police, placed in handcuffs, and held in a patrol car for a short period of time before being released. While this incident was unfortunate, the question raised by the evidence was whether the restaurant manager's actions were negligent, not whether he acted maliciously or his conduct was extreme, atrocious, or utterly intolerable. Accordingly, the trial court did not err in granting the defendants' motion for summary judgment on the Ferrells' claim for intentional infliction of emotional distress.

* * *

Judgment affirmed in part and reversed in part.

CASE
7-3

Defamation
FRANK B. HALL & CO., INC. v. BUCK
Court of Appeals of Texas, Fourteenth District, 1984
678 S.W.2d 612; *certiorari* denied, 472 U.S. 1009, 105 S.Ct. 2704, 86 L.Ed.2d 720 (1985)

Junell, J.

[On June 1, 1976, Larry W. Buck, an established salesman in the insurance business, began working for Frank B. Hall & Co. In the course of the ensuing months, Buck brought several major accounts to Hall and produced substantial commission income for the firm. In October 1976, Mendel Kaliff, then president of Frank B. Hall & Co. of Texas, informed Buck that his salary and benefits were being reduced because of his failure to generate sufficient income for the firm. On March 31, 1977, Kaliff and Lester Eckert, Hall's office manager, fired Buck. Buck was unable to procure subsequent employment with another insurance firm. He hired an investigator, Lloyd Barber, to discover the true reasons for his dismissal and for his inability to find other employment.

Barber contacted Kaliff, Eckert, and Virginia Hilley, a Hall employee, and told them he was an investigator and was seeking information about Buck's employment with the firm. Barber conducted tape-recorded interviews with the three in September and October of 1977. Kaliff accused Buck of being disruptive, untrustworthy, paranoid, hostile, untruthful, and of padding his expense account. Eckert referred to Buck as "a zero" and a "classical sociopath" who was ruthless, irrational, and disliked by other employees. Hilley stated that Buck could have been charged with theft for certain materials he brought with him from his former employer to Hall. Buck sued Hall for damages for defamation and was awarded over $1.9 million by a jury—$605,000 for actual damages and $1,300,000 for punitive damages. Hall then brought this appeal.]

Any act wherein the defamatory matter is intentionally or negligently communicated to a third person is a publication. In the case of slander, the act is usually the speaking of the words. Restatement (Second) Torts § 577 comment a (1977). There is ample support in the record to show that these individuals intentionally communicated disparaging remarks to a third person. The jury was instructed that "Publication means to communicate defamatory words to some third person in such a way that he understands the words to be defamatory. A statement is not published if it was authorized, invited or procured by Buck and if Buck knew in advance the contents of the invited communication." In response to special issues, the jury found that the slanderous statements were made and published to Barber.

Hall argues that Buck could and should have expected Hall's employees to give their opinion of Buck when requested to do so. Hall is correct in stating that a plaintiff may not recover for a publication to which he has consented, or which he has authorized, procured or invited, [citation]; and it may be true that Buck could assume that Hall's employees would give their opinion when asked they do so. However, there is nothing in the record to indicate that Buck knew Hall's employees would defame him when Barber made the inquiries. The accusations made by Kaliff, Eckert and Hilley were not mere expressions of opinion but were false and derogatory statements of fact.

* * *

A defamer cannot escape liability by showing that, although he desired to defame the plaintiff, he did not desire to defame him to the person to whom he in fact intentionally published the defamatory communication. The publication is complete although the publisher is mistaken as to the identity of the person to whom the publication is made. Restatement (Second) of Torts § 577 comment e (1977). Likewise, communication to an agent of the person defamed is a publication, unless the communication is invited by the person defamed or his agent. Restatement § 577 comment e. We have already determined that the evidence is sufficient to show that Buck did not know what Kaliff, Eckert or Hilley would say and that he did not procure the defamatory statements to create a lawsuit. Thus, the fact that Barber may have been acting at Buck's request is not fatal to Buck's cause of action. There is absolutely no proof that Barber induced Kaliff, Eckert or Hilley to make any of the defamatory comments.

* * *

When an ambiguity exists, a fact issue is presented. The court, by submission of proper fact issues, should let the jury render its verdict on whether the statements were fairly susceptible to the construction placed thereon by the plaintiff. [Citation.] Here, the jury found (1) Eckert made a statement calculated to convey that Buck had been terminated because of serious misconduct; (2) the statement was slanderous or libelous; (3) the statement was made with malice; (4) the statement was published; and (5) damage directly resulted from the statement. The jury also found the statements were not substantially true. The jury thus determined that these statements, which were capable of a defamatory meaning, were understood as such by Burton.

* * *

We hold that the evidence supports the award of actual damages and the amount awarded is not manifestly unjust. Furthermore, in responding to the issue on exemplary damages, the jury was instructed that exemplary damages must be based on a finding that Hall "acted with ill will, bad intent, malice or gross disregard to the rights of Buck." Although there is no fixed ratio between exemplary and actual damages, exemplary damages must be reasonably apportioned to the actual damages sustained. [Citation.] Because of the actual damages [$605,000] and the abundant evidence of malice, we hold that the award of punitive damages [$1,300,000] was not unreasonable.

The judgment of the trial court is affirmed.

CASE

7-4

Appropriation
WHITE v. SAMSUNG ELECTRONICS AMERICA, INC.
United States Court of Appeals, Ninth Circuit, 1992
971 F.2d 1395; *certiorari* denied, 508 U.S. 951, 113 S.Ct. 2443, 124 L.Ed.2d 660 (1993)

Goodwin, J.

This case involves a promotional "fame and fortune" dispute. In running a particular advertisement without Vanna White's permission, defendants Samsung Electronics America, Inc. (Samsung) and David Deutsch Associates, Inc. (Deutsch) attempted to capitalize on White's fame to enhance their fortune. White sued, alleging infringement of various intellectual property rights, but the district court granted summary judgment in favor of the defendants. We affirm in part, reverse in part, and remand.

Plaintiff Vanna White is the hostess of "Wheel of Fortune," one of the most popular game shows in television history. An estimated forty million people watch the program daily. Capitalizing on the fame which her participation in the show has bestowed on her, White markets her identity to various advertisers.

The dispute in this case arose out of a series of advertisements prepared for Samsung by Deutsch. The series ran in at least half a dozen publications with widespread, and in some cases national, circulation. Each of the advertisements in the series followed the same theme. Each depicted a current item from popular culture and a Samsung electronic product. Each was set in the twenty-first century and conveyed the message that the Samsung product would still be in use by that time. By hypothesizing outrageous future outcomes for the cultural items, the ads created humorous effects. For example, one lampooned current popular notions of an unhealthy diet by depicting a raw steak with the caption: "Revealed to be health food, 2010 A.D." Another depicted irreverent "news"-show host Morton Downey Jr. in front of an American flag with the caption: "Presidential candidate. 2008 A.D."

The advertisement which prompted the current dispute was for Samsung videocassette recorders (VCRs). The ad depicted a robot, dressed in a wig, gown, and jewelry which Deutsch consciously selected to resemble White's hair and dress. The robot was posed next to a game board which is instantly recognizable as the Wheel of Fortune game show set, in a stance for which White is famous. The caption of the ad read: "Longest running game show. 2012 A.D." Defendants referred to the ad as the "Vanna White" ad. Unlike the other celebrities used in the campaign, White neither consented to the ads nor was she paid.

Following the circulation of the robot ad, White sued Samsung and Deutsch in federal district court under: * * * the California common law right of publicity; * * *. The district court granted summary judgment against White on each of her claims. White now appeals.

* * *

White * * * argues that the district court erred in granting summary judgment to defendants on White's common law right of publicity claim. In *Eastwood v. Superior Court*, [citation], the California court of appeal stated that the common law right of publicity cause of action "may be pleaded by alleging (1) the defendant's use of the plaintiff's identity; (2) the appropriation of plaintiff's name or likeness to defendant's advantage, commercially or otherwise; (3) lack of consent, and (4) resulting injury." [Citation.] The district court dismissed White's claim for failure to satisfy *Eastwood's* second prong, reasoning that defendants had not appropriated White's "name or likeness" with their robot ad. We agree that the robot ad did not make use of White's name or likeness. However, the common law right of publicity is not so confined.

The *Eastwood* court did not hold that the right of publicity cause of action could be pleaded only by alleging an appropriation of name or likeness. *Eastwood* involved an unauthorized use of photographs of Clint Eastwood and of his name. Accordingly, the *Eastwood* court had no occasion to consider the extent beyond the use of name or likeness to which the right of publicity reaches. That court held only that the right of publicity cause of action "may be" pleaded by alleging, *inter alia*, appropriation of name or likeness, not that the action may be pleaded only in those terms.

The "name or likeness" formulation referred to in *Eastwood* originated not as an element of the right of publicity cause of action, but as a description of the types of cases in which the cause of action had been recognized. The source of this formulation is Prosser, *Privacy*, 48 Cal.L.Rev. 383, 401-07 (1960), one of the earliest and most enduring articulations of the common law right of publicity cause of action. In looking at the case law to that point, Prosser recognized that right of publicity cases involved one of two basic factual scenarios: name appropriation, and picture or other likeness appropriation. [Citation.]

Even though Prosser focused on appropriations of name or likeness in discussing the right of publicity, he noted that "[i]t is not impossible that there might be appropriation of the plaintiff's identity, as by impersonation, without use of either his name or his likeness, and that this would be an invasion of his right of privacy." [Citation.] At the time Prosser wrote, he noted however, that "[n]o such case appears to have arisen." [Citation.]

Since Prosser's early formulation, the case law has borne out his insight that the right of publicity is not limited to the appropriation of name or likeness. In *Motschenbacher v. R.J. Reynolds Tobacco Co.*, [citation], the defendant had used a photograph of the plaintiff's race car in a television commercial. Although the plaintiff appeared driving the car in the photograph, his features were not visible. Even though the defendant had not appropriated the plaintiff's name or likeness, this court held that plaintiff's California right of publicity claim should reach the jury.

In *Midler*, this court held that, even though the defendants had not used Midler's name or likeness, Midler had stated a claim for violation of her California common law right of publicity because "the defendants * * * for their own profit in selling their product did appropriate part of her identity" by using a Midler sound-alike. [Citation.]

In *Carson v. Here's Johnny Portable Toilets, Inc.*, [citation], the defendant had marketed portable toilets under the brand name "Here's Johnny"—Johnny Carson's signature "Tonight Show" introduction—without Carson's permission. The district court had dismissed Carson's Michigan common law right of publicity claim because the defendants had not used Carson's "name or likeness." [Citation.] In reversing the district court, the sixth circuit found "the district court's conception of the right of publicity * * * too narrow" and held that the right was implicated because the defendant had appropriated Carson's identity by using, *inter alia*, the phrase "Here's Johnny." [Citation.]

These cases teach not only that the common law right of publicity reaches means of appropriation other than name or likeness, but that the specific means of appropriation are relevant only for determining whether the defendant has in fact appropriated the plaintiff's identity. The right of publicity does not require that appropriations of identity be accomplished through particular means to be actionable. It is noteworthy that the *Midler* and *Carson* defendants not only avoided using the plaintiff's name or likeness, but they also avoided appropriating the celebrity's voice, signature, and photograph. The photograph in *Motschenbacher* did include the plaintiff, but because the

plaintiff was not visible the driver could have been an actor or dummy and the analysis in the case would have been the same.

Although the defendants in these cases avoided the most obvious means of appropriating the plaintiffs' identities, each of their actions directly implicated the commercial interests which the right of publicity is designed to protect. As the *Carson* court explained,

> [t]he right of publicity has developed to protect the commercial interest of celebrities in their identities. The theory of the right is that a celebrity's identity can be valuable in the promotion of products, and the celebrity has an interest that may be protected from the unauthorized commercial exploitation of that identity. * * * If the celebrity's identity is commercially exploited, there has been an invasion of his right whether or not his "name or likeness" is used.

[Citation.] It is not important how the defendant has appropriated the plaintiff's identity, but whether the defendant has done so. *Motschenbacher*, *Midler*, and *Carson* teach the impossibility of treating the right of publicity as guarding only against a laundry list of specific means of appropriating identity. A rule which says that the right of publicity can be infringed only through the use of nine different methods of appropriating identity merely challenges the clever advertising strategist to come up with the tenth.

Indeed, if we treated the means of appropriation as dispositive in our analysis of the right of publicity, we would not only weaken the right but effectively eviscerate it. The right would fail to protect those plaintiffs most in need of its protection. Advertisers use celebrities to promote their products. The more popular the celebrity, the greater the number of people who recognize her, and the greater the visibility for the product. The identities of the most popular celebrities are not only the most attractive for advertisers, but also the easiest to evoke without resorting to obvious means such as name, likeness, or voice.

Consider a hypothetical advertisement which depicts a mechanical robot with male features, an African-American complexion, and a bald head. The robot is wearing black hightop Air Jordan basketball sneakers, and a red basketball uniform with black trim, baggy shorts, and the number 23 (though not revealing "Bulls" or "Jordan" lettering). The ad depicts the robot dunking a basketball one-handed, stiffarmed, legs extended like open scissors, and tongue hanging out. Now envision that this ad is run on television during professional basketball games. Considered individually, the robot's physical attributes, its dress, and its stance tell us little. Taken together, they lead to the only conclusion that any sports viewer who has registered a discernible pulse in the past five years would reach: the ad is about Michael Jordan.

Viewed separately, the individual aspects of the advertisement in the present case say little. Viewed together, they leave little doubt about the celebrity the ad is meant to depict. The female-shaped robot is wearing a long gown, blond wig, and large jewelry. Vanna White dresses exactly like this at times, but so do many other women. The robot is in the process of turning a block letter on a game-board.

Vanna White dresses like this while turning letters on a game-board but perhaps similarly attired Scrabble-playing women do this as well. The robot is standing on what looks to be the Wheel of Fortune game show set. Vanna White dresses like this, turns letters, and does this on the Wheel of Fortune game show. She is the only one. Indeed, defendants themselves referred to their ad as the "Vanna White" ad. We are not surprised.

Television and other media create marketable celebrity identity value. Considerable energy and ingenuity are expended by those who have achieved celebrity value to exploit it for profit. The law protects the celebrity's sole right to exploit this value whether the celebrity has achieved her fame out of rare ability, dumb luck, or a combination thereof. We decline Samsung and Deutsch's invitation to permit the evisceration of the common law right of publicity through means as facile as those in this case. Because White has alleged facts showing that Samsung and Deutsch had appropriated her identity, the district court erred by rejecting, on summary judgment, White's common law right of publicity claim.

QUESTIONS

1. The Penguin intentionally hits Batman with his umbrella. Batman, stunned by the blow, falls backwards, knocking Robin down. Robin's leg is broken in the fall, and he cries out, "Holy broken bat bones! My leg is broken." Who, if anyone, is liable to Robin? Why?

2. CEO was convinced by his employee, M. Ploy, that a coworker, A. Cused, had been stealing money from the company. At lunch that day in the company cafeteria, CEO discharges Cused from her employment, accuses her of stealing from the company, searches through her purse over her objections, and finally forcibly escorts her to his office to await the arrival of the police, which he has his secretary summon. Cused is indicted for embezzlement but subsequently is acquitted upon establishing her innocence. What rights, if any, does Cused have against CEO?

3. Ralph kisses Edith while she is asleep but does not waken or harm her. Edith sues Ralph for battery. Has a battery been committed? Explain.

4. Claude, a creditor seeking to collect a debt, calls on Dianne and demands payment in a rude and insolent manner. When Dianne says that she cannot pay, Claude calls Dianne a deadbeat and says that he will never trust her again. Is Claude liable to Dianne? If so, for what tort? Explain.

5. Lana, a ten-year-old child, is run over by a car negligently driven by Mitchel. Lana, at the time of the accident, was acting reasonably and without negligence. Clark, a newspaper reporter, photographs Lana while she is lying in the street in great pain. Two years later, Perry, the publisher of a newspaper, prints Clark's picture of Lana in his newspaper as a lead to an article concerning the negligence of children. The caption under the picture reads: "They ask to be killed." Lana, who has recovered

from the accident, brings suit against Clark and Perry. What result? Explain.

6. In 1963 the *Saturday Evening Post* featured an article entitled "The Story of a College Football Fix," characterized in the subtitle as "A Shocking Report of How Wally Butts and Bear Bryant Rigged a Game Last Fall." Butts was athletic director of the University of Georgia, and Bryant was head coach of the University of Alabama. The article was based on a claim by one George Burnett that he had accidentally overheard a long-distance telephone conversation between Butts and Bryant in the course of which Butts divulged information on plays Georgia would use in the upcoming game against Alabama. The writer assigned to the story by the *Post* was not a football expert, did not interview either Butts or Bryant, and did not personally see the notes Burnett had made of the telephone conversation. Butts admitted that he had a long-distance telephone conversation with Bryant but denied that any advance information on prospective football plays was given. Has Butts been defamed by the *Post*? Why or why not?

7. Joan, a patient confined in a hospital, has a rare disease that is of great interest to the public. Carol, a television reporter, requests Joan to consent to an interview. Joan refuses, but Carol, nonetheless, enters Joan's room over her objection and photographs her. Joan brings a suit against Carol. Is Carol liable? If so, for what tort? Explain.

8. Owner has a place on his land where he piles trash. The pile has been there for three months. John, a neighbor of Owner and without Owner's consent or knowledge, throws trash onto the trash pile. Owner learns that John has done this and sues him. What tort, if any, has John committed? Explain.

9. Chris leaves her car parked in front of a store. There are no signs that say Chris cannot park there. The store owner, however, needs the car moved to enable a delivery truck to unload. He releases the brake and pushes Chris's car three or four feet, doing no harm to the car. Chris returns and sees that her car has been moved and is very angry. She threatens to sue the store owner for trespass to her personal property. Can she recover? Explain.

10. Carr borrowed John's brand-new car for the purpose of going to the store. He told John he would be right back. Carr then decided, however, to go to the beach while he had the car. Can John recover from Carr the value of the automobile? If so, for what tort? Explain.

CASE PROBLEMS

11. Marcia Samms claimed that David Eccles had repeatedly and persistently called her at various hours, including late at night, from May to December, soliciting her to have illicit sexual relations with him. She also claimed that on one occasion, Eccles came over to her residence to again solicit sex and indecently exposed himself to her. Mrs. Samms had never encouraged Eccles but had continuously repulsed his "insulting, indecent, and obscene" proposals. She brought suit against Eccles, claiming she suffered great anxiety and fear for her personal safety and severe emotional distress, demanding actual and punitive damages. Can she recover? If so, for what tort? Explain.

12. National Bond and Investment Company sent two of its employees to repossess Whithorn's car after he failed to complete the payments. The two repossessors located Whithorn while he was driving his car. They followed him and hailed him down to make the repossession. Whithorn refused to abandon his car and demanded evidence of their authority. The two repossessors became impatient and called a wrecker. They ordered the driver of the wrecker to hook Whithorn's car and move it down the street while Whithorn was still inside the vehicle. Whithorn started the car and tried to escape, but the wrecker lifted the car off the road and progressed seventy-five to one hundred feet until Whithorn managed to stall the wrecker. Has National Bond committed the tort of false imprisonment? Explain.

13. In March, William Proxmire, a U.S. senator from Wisconsin, initiated the "Golden Fleece of the Month Award" to publicize what he believed to be wasteful government spending. The second of these awards was given to the Federal agencies that had for seven years funded Dr. Hutchinson's research on stress levels in animals. The award was made in a speech Proxmire gave in the Senate; the text was also incorporated into an advance press release that was sent to 275 members of the national news media. Proxmire also referred to the research in two subsequent newsletters sent to one hundred thousand constituents and during a television interview. Hutchinson then brought this action alleging defamation resulting in personal and economic injury. Assuming that Hutchinson proved that the statements were false and defamatory, would he prevail? Explain.

14. Capune was attempting a trip from New York to Florida on an eighteen-foot-long paddleboard. The trip was being covered by various media to gain publicity for Capune and certain products he endorsed. By water, Capune approached a pier owned by Robbins, who had posted signs prohibiting surfing and swimming around the pier. Capune was unaware of these notices and attempted to continue his journey by passing under the pier. Robbins ran up yelling and threw two bottles at Capune. Capune was frightened and tried to maneuver his paddleboard to go around the pier. Robbins then threw a third bottle that hit Capune in the head. Capune had to be helped out of the water and taken to the hospital. He suffered a physical wound that required twenty-four sutures and, as a result, had to discontinue his trip. Capune brought suit in tort against Robbins. Is Robbins liable? If so, for which tort or torts? Explain.

15. Ralph Nader, who has been a critic of General Motors Corp. for several years, claims that when General Motors learned that Nader was about to publish a book entitled *Unsafe at Any Speed*, criticizing one of its automobiles, it decided to conduct a campaign of intimidation against him. Specifically, Nader claims that GMC (a) conducted a series of interviews with Nader's acquaintances, questioning them about his political, social, racial, and religious views; (b) kept him under surveillance in public places for an unreasonable length of time, including close observation of him in a bank; (c) caused him to be accosted by women for the purpose of entrapping him into illicit relationships; (d) made threatening, harassing, and obnoxious telephone calls to him; (e) tapped his telephone and eavesdropped by means of mechanical and electronic equipment on his private conversations with others; and (f) conducted a "continuing" and harassing

investigation of him. Nader brought suit against GMC for invasion of privacy. Which, if any, of the alleged actions would constitute invasion of privacy?

16. Bill Kinsey was charged with murdering his wife while working for the Peace Corps in Tanzania. After waiting six months in jail, he was acquitted at a trial that attracted wide publicity. Five years later, while a graduate student at Stanford University, Kinsey had a brief affair with Mary Macur. He abruptly ended the affair by telling Macur he would no longer be seeing her because another woman, Sally Allen, was coming from England to live with him. A few months later, Kinsey and Allen moved to Africa and were subsequently married. Soon after Bill ended their affair, Macur began a letterwriting campaign designed to expose Bill and his mistreatment of her. Macur sent several letters to both Bill and Sally Kinsey, their parents, their neighbors, their parents' neighbors, members of Bill's dissertation committee, other faculty, and the president of Stanford University. The letters contained statements accusing Bill of murdering his first wife, spending six months in jail for the crime, being a rapist, and exhibiting other questionable behavior. The Kinseys brought an action for invasion of privacy, seeking damages and a permanent injunction. Will the Kinseys prevail? If so, for what tort? Explain.

17. The Brineys (defendants) owned a large farm on which was located an abandoned farmhouse. For a ten-year period the house had been the subject of several trespassings and housebreakings. In an attempt to stop the intrusions, Briney boarded up the windows and doors and posted "no trespassing" signs. After one break-in, however, Briney set a spring gun in a bedroom. It was placed over the bedroom window so that the gun could not be seen from outside, and no warning of its presence was posted. The gun was set to hit an intruder in the legs. Briney loaded the gun with a live shell, but he claimed that he did not intend to injure anyone.

   Katko (plaintiff) and a friend, McDonough, had broken into the abandoned farmhouse on an earlier occasion to steal old bottles and fruit jars for their antique collection. They returned for a second time after the spring gun had been set, and Katko was seriously wounded in the leg when the gun discharged as he entered the bedroom. He then brought action for damages. Decision?

18. Plaintiff, John W. Carson, was the host and star of *The Tonight Show*, a well-known television program broadcast by the National Broadcasting Company. Carson also appeared as an entertainer in nightclubs and theaters around the country. From the time he began hosting *The Tonight Show*, he had been introduced on the show each night with the phrase "Here's Johnny." The phrase "Here's Johnny" is still generally associated with Carson by a substantial segment of the television viewing public. To earn additional income, Carson began authorizing use of this phrase by outside business ventures.

   Defendant, Here's Johnny Portable Toilets, Inc., is a Michigan corporation engaged in the business of renting and selling "Here's Johnny" portable toilets. Defendant's founder was aware at the time he formed the corporation that "Here's Johnny" was the introductory slogan for Carson on *The Tonight Show*. He indicated that he coupled the phrase with a second one, "The World's Foremost Commodian," to make "a good play on a phrase." Carson brought suit for invasion of privacy. Should Carson recover? If so, for which tort? Explain.

19. Susan Jungclaus Peterson was a twenty-one-year-old student at Moorhead State University who had lived most of her life on her family farm in Minnesota. Though Susan was a dean's list student during her first year, her academic performance declined after she became deeply involved in an international religious cult organization known locally as The Way of Minnesota, Inc. The cult demanded an enormous psychological and monetary commitment from Susan. Near the end of her junior year, her parents became alarmed by the changes in Susan's physical and mental well-being and concluded that she had been "reduced to a condition of psychological bondage by The Way." They sought help from Kathy Mills, a self-styled "deprogrammer" of minds brainwashed by cults.

   On May 24, Norman Jungclaus, Susan's father, picked up Susan at Moorhead State. Instead of returning home, they went to the residence of Veronica Morgel, where Kathy Mills attempted to deprogram Susan. For the first few days of her stay, Susan was unwilling to discuss her involvement. She lay curled in a fetal position in her bedroom, plugging her ears and hysterically screaming and crying while her father pleaded with her to listen. By the third day, however, Susan's demeanor changed completely. She became friendly and vivacious and communicated with her father. Susan also went roller-skating and played softball at a nearby park over the following weekend. She spent the next week in Columbus, Ohio, with a former cult member who had shared her experiences of the previous week. While in Columbus, she spoke daily by telephone with her fiance, a member of The Way, who begged her to return to the cult. Susan expressed the desire to get her fiance out of the organization, but a meeting between them could not be arranged outside the presence of other members of The Way. Her parents attempted to persuade Susan to sign an agreement releasing them from liability for their actions, but Susan refused. After nearly sixteen days of "deprogramming," Susan left the Morgel residence and returned to her fiancee and The Way. Upon the direction of The Way ministry, she brought this action against her parents for false imprisonment. Will Susan prevail? Explain.

20. Debra Agis was a waitress in a restaurant owned by the Howard Johnson Company. On May 23, Roger Dionne, manager of the restaurant, called a meeting of all waitresses at which he informed them that "there was some stealing going on." Dionne also stated that the identity of the party or parties responsible was not known and that he would begin firing all waitresses in alphabetical order until the guilty party or parties were detected. He then fired Debra Agis, who allegedly "became greatly upset, began to cry, sustained emotional distress, mental anguish, and loss of wages and earnings." Mrs. Agis brought a complaint against the Howard Johnson Company and Roger Dionne, alleging that the defendants acted recklessly and outrageously, intending to cause emotional distress and anguish. The defendants argued that damages for emotional distress are not recoverable unless physical injury occurs as a result of the distress. Will Agis be successful on her complaint? Why or why not?

21. On July 31, Amanda Vaughn and Jason Vaughn accompanied their mother, Emma Simpson Vaughn, to a Walmart store. Amanda's friend, Kimberly Dickerson, was also with them. Once they entered the store, Mrs. Vaughn and Jason went into separate areas of the store. The two girls remained together in the front of the store and selected a stamp album to purchase. Kimberly took the album to the checkout register, and while she was at the register, she also selected a pack of gum. Once Kimberly paid for her two items, they were placed in a bag and she was given her change. Kimberly testified that she did not immediately put the change in her wallet while she was at the register. Instead, Kimberly walked back into the merchandise area where Amanda had remained. Kimberly was in the merchandise area, away from the registers, when she placed her change in her purse. Kimberly proceeded to place her hand in the Walmart bag to retrieve the gum she had just purchased.

At this time, Ms. Clara Lynn Neal, a customer service manager, observed Kimberly's hand coming out of her Walmart bag. According to Ms. Neal, because the two girls were in a somewhat-secluded area of the store, Ms. Neal walked past the two girls twice to observe them before she walked over to them.

Ms. Neal testified that she asked Kimberly if she could see her bag and her receipt and that Kimberly voluntarily gave her the bag. Plaintiffs alleged that Ms. Neal "detained the girls, snatched Kimberly's bag from her, searched the bag, discovered a receipt, tied the bag, and then personally escorted the girls to an area near the front door away from the registers." However, Kimberly's testimony stated that "[Ms. Neal] said she was going to have to check my bag because she doesn't know if I'm stealing something. So I didn't say anything. I didn't really give it to her because I was shocked. So she took it, and she was like searching through it."

Once Ms. Neal checked the purchases with the receipt, the girls were told to go to the front of the store and wait for their party. The girls were never told that they could not leave the store, and the girls were not detained by anyone else. According to all parties, from the time Ms. Neal walked up to the girls, verified the purchases, and returned the bag to Kimberly, the entire incident only lasted about one minute. While the girls were waiting at the front of the store, Jason was asked by his mother to inform the girls that she was ready to go. Jason approached the girls, and they responded that they could not leave. When Jason reported to his mother that the girls stated they could not leave the area, Mrs. Vaughn then went to the front of the store to investigate. Before Mrs. Vaughn took the children home, she explained to a store manager what had occurred. Do the girls have a cause of action against Walmart? Why or why not?

22. Pro Golf Manufacturing, Inc., manufactures and repairs golf equipment as well as gives golf lessons. On September 27, the *Tribune Review* newspaper published an article stating that several historic buildings, including the building housing Pro Golf's business, were set for demolition. On February 18 of the following year, the *Tribune Review* published another newspaper article, stating that the building containing Pro Golf's business had been demolished. However, the building containing Pro Golf's business neither had been scheduled for demolition nor had been demolished. Pro Golf seeks to recover for the financial loss that these false publications caused. Explain which tort offers the best likelihood of recovery and what Pro Golf would have to prove to recover.

Edith Mitchell, accompanied by her thirteen-year-old daughter, went through the checkout at Walmart and purchased several items. As they exited, the Mitchells passed through an electronic antitheft device, which sounded an alarm. Robert Canady, employed by Walmart as a "people greeter" and security guard, forcibly stopped Edith Mitchell at the exit, grabbed her bag, and told her to step back inside. The security guard never touched Edith or her daughter and never threatened to touch either of them. Nevertheless, Edith Mitchell described the security guard's actions in her affidavit as "gruff, loud, rude behavior." The security guard removed every item Mitchell had just purchased and ran it through the security gate. One of the items still had a security code unit on it, which an employee admitted could have

been overlooked by the cashier. When the security guard finished examining the contents of Mitchell's bag, he put it on the checkout counter. This examination of her bag took ten or fifteen minutes. Once her bag had been checked, no employee of Walmart ever told Mitchell she could not leave. Mitchell was never threatened with arrest. Mitchell brought a tort action against Walmart.

a. Explain on which torts Mitchell should base her claim against Walmart.

b. What arguments would support Walmart's denial of liability for these torts?

c. Which party should prevail? Explain.

Negligence and Strict Liability

Whereas intentional torts deal with conduct that has a substantial certainty of causing harm, negligence involves conduct that creates an unreasonable risk of harm. The basis of liability for negligence is the failure to exercise reasonable care, under given circumstances, for the safety of another person or his property, which failure causes injury to such person or damage to his property, or both. Thus, if the driver of an automobile intentionally runs down a person, she has committed the intentional tort of battery. If, on the other hand, the driver hits and injures a person while driving without reasonable regard for the safety of others, she is negligent.

Strict liability is not based upon the negligence or intent of the defendant but rather upon the nature of the activity in which he is engaging. Under this doctrine, defendants who engage in certain activities, such as keeping animals or carrying on abnormally dangerous conditions, are held liable for the injuries they cause, even if they have exercised the utmost care. The law imposes this liability to effect a just reallocation of loss, given that the defendant engaged in the activity for his own benefit and is in a better position to manage, by insurance or otherwise, the risk inherent in the activity.

As mentioned in *Chapter 7*, the American Law Institute (ALI) has published the Restatement Third, Torts: Liability for Physical and Emotional Harm (the "Third Restatement"). This new Restatement addresses the general or basic elements of the tort action for liability for accidental personal injury, property damage, and emotional harm, but does not cover liability for economic loss. "Physical harm" is defined as bodily harm (physical injury, illness, disease, and death) or property damage (physical impairment of real property or tangible personal property). The Third Restatement replaces comparable provisions in the Restatement Second, Torts.

In 2018, the ALI approved the final portions of the Restatement Third, Torts: Liability for Economic Harm, which updates coverage on torts that involve economic loss or pecuniary harm *not* resulting from physical harm or physical contact to a person or property. The project updates coverage of economic torts in Restatement Second, Torts and addresses some topics not covered in prior Restatements. This project covers fraud, breach of fiduciary duty, interference with contract, unjustifiable litigation, injurious falsehood, and interference with the right to possession of personal property. It also addresses *unintentional* infliction of economic loss—including professional negligence, negligent misrepresentation, negligent performance of services, and public nuisance.

In 2019, the ALI approved three more projects as part of its ongoing revision of the Restatement Second of Torts. (1) The Restatement Third, Torts: Defamation and Privacy addresses torts dealing with personal and business reputation and dignity—including defamation, business disparagement, and rights of privacy. (2) The Restatement Third, Torts: Remedies covers tort damages and other remedies including the identification of the types of recoverable damages and the measurement of damages. (3) The Restatement Third, Torts: Concluding Provisions deals with topics not covered otherwise in the Restatement Third of Torts that either require updating or were not previously included.

NEGLIGENCE

A person acts negligently if the person does not exercise reasonable care under all the circumstances. Third Restatement, Section 3. Moreover, the general rule is that a person is under a duty to all others at all times to exercise reasonable care for the safety of the others' person and property. Third Restatement, Section 7. On the other hand, a person is *not* under a general duty to avoid the *unintentional* infliction of economic loss. Restatement Third, Torts: Liability for Economic Harm, Section 1. A duty of care with respect to economic loss is recognized, however, in limited specific circumstances, the most important of which is an action to recover for economic loss caused by professional negligence (malpractice). Restatement Third, Torts: Liability for Economic Harm, Sections 1 and 4.

An action for negligence consists of five elements, each of which the plaintiff must prove:

1. **Duty of care:** that a legal duty required the defendant to conform to the standard of conduct established for the protection of others;

2. **Breach of duty:** that the defendant failed to exercise reasonable care;

3. **Factual cause:** that the defendant's failure to exercise reasonable care in fact caused the harm the plaintiff sustained;

4. **Harm:** that the harm sustained is of a type protected against negligent conduct; and

5. **Scope of liability:** that the harm sustained is within the "scope of liability," which historically has been referred to as "proximate cause." Third Restatement, Section 6, comments.

The first two elements are discussed in the next section "Breach of Duty of Care"; the last three elements are covered in subsequent sections.

8-1 Breach of Duty of Care

Negligence consists of conduct that creates an unreasonable risk of harm. In determining whether a given risk of harm was unreasonable, the law considers the following factors: (1) the foreseeable probability that the person's conduct will result in harm, (2) the foreseeable gravity or severity of any harm that may follow, and (3) the burden of taking precautions to eliminate or reduce the risk of harm. Third Restatement, Section 3. Thus, the standard of conduct, which is the basis for the law of negligence, is usually determined by a cost-benefit or risk-benefit analysis.

8-1a REASONABLE PERSON STANDARD

The duty of care imposed by law is measured by the degree of carefulness that a reasonable person would exercise in a given situation. The reasonable person is a fictitious individual who is always careful and prudent and never negligent. What the judge or jury determines a reasonable person would have done in light of the facts disclosed by the evidence in a particular case sets the standard of conduct for that case. The reasonable person standard is thus external and *objective*, as described by Justice Holmes:

If, for instance, a man is born hasty and awkward, is always hurting himself or his neighbors, no doubt his congenital defects will be allowed for in the courts of Heaven, but his slips are no less troublesome to his neighbors than if they sprang from guilty neglect. His neighbors accordingly require him, at his peril, to come up to their standard, and the courts which they establish decline to take his personal equation into account. Holmes, *The Common Law.*

CHILDREN A child is a person below the age of majority, which in almost all States has been lowered from twenty-one to eighteen. The standard of conduct to which a child must conform to avoid being negligent is that of a reasonably careful person of the same age, intelligence, and experience under all the circumstances. Third Restatement, Section 10. For example, Alice, a five-year-old girl, was walking with her father on the crowded sidewalk along Main Street when he told her that he was going to take her to Disney World for her birthday next week. Upon hearing the news, Alice became so excited that she began to jump up and down and run around. During this fit of exuberance, Alice accidentally ran into and knocked down an elderly woman who was passing by. Alice's liability, if any, would be determined by whether a reasonable five-year-old person of like age, intelligence, and experience under like circumstances would have the capacity and judgment to understand the increased risk her enthusiastic display of joy caused to others.

The law applies an individualized test because children do not possess the judgment, intelligence, knowledge, and experience of adults. Moreover, children as a general rule do not engage in activities entailing high risk to others, and their conduct normally does not involve a potential for harm as great as that of adult conduct. A child who engages in a dangerous activity that is characteristically undertaken by adults, however, such as flying an airplane or driving a boat or car, is held in almost all States to the standard of care applicable to adults. Finally, some States modify this individualized test by holding that under a minimum age, most commonly the age of seven, a child is incapable of committing a negligent act. The Third

Restatement further provides that a child less than five years of age is incapable of negligence. Section 10.

PHYSICAL DISABILITY If a person is ill or otherwise physically disabled, the standard of conduct to which he must conform to avoid being negligent is that of a reasonably careful person with the same disability. Third Restatement, Section 11(a). Thus, a blind man must act as a reasonable man who is blind, and a woman with multiple sclerosis must act as a reasonable woman with multiple sclerosis. However, the conduct of a person during a period of sudden incapacitation or loss of consciousness resulting from physical illness is negligent only if the sudden incapacitation or loss of consciousness was reasonably foreseeable to the actor. Examples of sudden incapacitation include heart attack, stroke, epileptic seizure, and diabetes. Third Restatement, Section 11(b).

MENTAL DISABILITY A person's mental or emotional disability is not considered in determining whether conduct is negligent unless the person is a child. Third Restatement, Section 11(c). The defendant is held to the standard of conduct of a reasonable person who is not mentally or emotionally disabled, even though the defendant is, in fact, incapable of conforming to the standard. Thus, an adult with the mental acumen of a six-year-old will be held liable for his negligent conduct if he fails to act as carefully as a reasonable adult of normal intelligence. In this case, the law may demand more of the individual than his mental limitations permit him to accomplish. When a person's intoxication is voluntary, it is not considered as an excuse for conduct that is otherwise lacking in reasonable care. Third Restatement, Section 12, Comment c.

SUPERIOR SKILL OR KNOWLEDGE If a person has skills or knowledge beyond those possessed by most others, these skills or knowledge are circumstances to be taken into account in determining whether the person has acted with reasonable care. Third Restatement, Section 12. Thus, persons who are qualified and who practice a profession or trade that calls for special skill and expertise are required to exercise that care and skill that members in good standing of their profession or trade normally possess. This standard applies to such professionals as physicians, surgeons, dentists, attorneys, pharmacists, architects, accountants, and engineers and to those who perform skilled trades, such as airline pilots, electricians, carpenters, and plumbers. A member of a profession or skilled trade who possesses greater skill than that common to the profession or trade is required to exercise that skill.

STANDARD FOR EMERGENCIES An emergency is a sudden and unexpected event that calls for immediate action and permits no time for deliberation. In determining whether a defendant's conduct is reasonable, the law takes into consideration the fact that he was at the time confronted with a sudden and unexpected emergency. Third Restatement, Section 9. The standard is still that of a reasonable person under the circumstances—the emergency is simply part of the circumstances. If, however, the defendant's own negligent or tortious conduct created the emergency, he is liable for the consequences of this conduct even if he acted reasonably in the resulting emergency situation. Moreover, failure to anticipate an emergency may itself constitute negligence.

VIOLATION OF STATUTE The reasonable person standard of conduct may be established by legislation or administrative regulation. Third Restatement, Section 14. Some statutes expressly impose civil liability upon violators. Absent such a provision, courts may adopt the requirements of the statute as the standard of conduct if the statute is designed to protect against the type of accident the defendant's conduct causes and the accident victim is within the class of persons the statute is designed to protect.

If the statute is found to be applicable, the majority of the courts hold that an unexcused violation is **negligence *per se***; that is, the violation conclusively constitutes negligent conduct. In a minority of States, the violation is considered merely to be evidence of negligence. In either event, the plaintiff must also prove legal causation and injury.

For example, a statute enacted to protect employees from injuries requires that all factory elevators be equipped with specified safety devices. Arthur, an employee in Freya's factory, and Carlos, a business visitor to the factory, are injured when the elevator fails because the safety devices have not been installed. The court may adopt the statute as a standard of conduct as to Arthur and hold Freya negligent *per se* to Arthur, but not as to Carlos, because Arthur, not Carlos, is within the class of persons the statute is intended to protect. Carlos would have to establish that a reasonable person in the position of Freya under the circumstances would have installed the safety device.

On the other hand, compliance with a legislative enactment or administrative regulation does not prevent a finding of negligence if a reasonable person would have taken additional precautions. Third Restatement, Section 16. For instance, driving at the speed limit may not constitute due care when traffic or road conditions require a lower speed. Legislative or administrative rules normally establish *minimum* standards.

◆ SEE FIGURE 8-1: *Negligence and Negligence* Per Se

◆ *See Case 1-1*

FIGURE 8-1   Negligence and Negligence *Per Se*

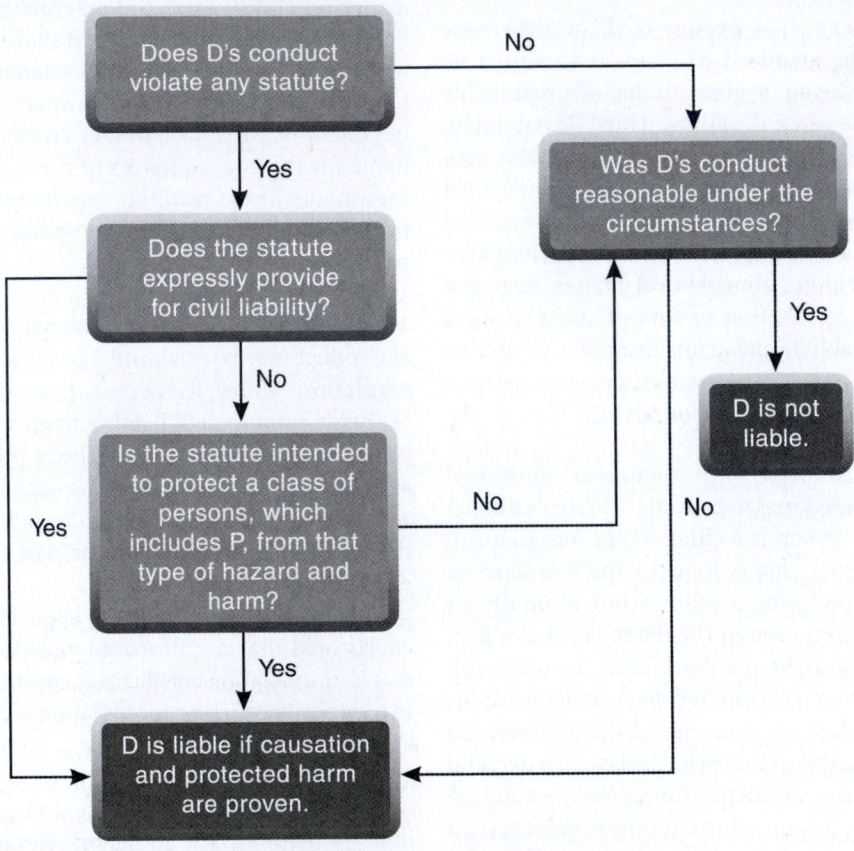

8-1b DUTY TO ACT

As stated previously, the general rule is that a person is under a duty to all others at all times to exercise reasonable care for the safety of the others' person and property. On the other hand, subject to several exceptions, a person (A) does not have a duty of care when the other's (B's) person or property is at risk for reasons other than the conduct of A. Third Restatement, Section 37. This rule applies even though the person may be in a position to help another in peril. As William Prosser, an authority on tort law, has stated, "The law has persistently refused to recognize the moral obligation of common decency and common humanity, to come to the aid of another human being who is in danger, even though the outcome is to cost him his life." For example, Toni, an adult standing at the edge of a steep cliff, observes a baby carriage with a crying infant in it slowly rolling toward the edge and certain doom. Toni could easily prevent the baby's fall at no risk to her own safety. Nonetheless, Toni does nothing, and the baby falls to his death. Toni is under no legal duty to act and, therefore, incurs no liability for failing to do so.

Nonetheless, special relations between the parties may impose an affirmative duty of reasonable care upon the defendant to aid or protect the other with respect to risks that arise within the scope of the relationship. Thus, if in the previous example, Toni were the baby's mother or babysitter, Toni would be under a duty to act and therefore would be liable for not taking action. The special relations giving rise to an affirmative duty to aid or protect another include (1) a common carrier to its passengers, (2) an innkeeper to its guest, (3) an employer to its employees, (4) a school to its students, (5) a landlord to its tenants with respect to common areas under the landlord's control, (6) a business open to the public to its customers, and (7) a custodian to those in its custody including parents to their children. Third Restatement, Section 40. The Third Restatement leaves it to the courts whether to recognize additional relationships as sufficient to impose an affirmative duty. Furthermore, State and Federal statutes and administrative regulations as well as local ordinances may impose an affirmative duty to act for the protection of another.

In addition, when a person's prior conduct, even though not tortious, creates a continuing risk of physical harm, the person has a duty to exercise reasonable care to prevent or minimize the harm. Third Restatement, Section 39. For example, Dale innocently drives her car into Bob, rendering him unconscious. Dale leaves Bob lying in the middle of the road, where he is run over by a second car driven by Chen. Dale is liable to Bob for the additional injuries inflicted by Chen.

Moreover, a person who voluntarily begins a rescue by taking charge of another who is imperiled and unable to protect himself incurs a duty to exercise reasonable care under the circumstances. Furthermore, a person who discontinues aid or protection is under a duty of reasonable care not to leave the other in a worse position. Third Restatement, Section 44. For example, Ann finds Ben drunk and stumbling along a dark sidewalk. Ann leads Ben halfway up a steep and unguarded stairway, where she abandons him. Ben attempts to climb the stairs but trips and falls, suffering serious injury. Ann is liable to Ben for having left him in a worse position. Most States have enacted Good Samaritan statutes to encourage voluntary emergency care. These statutes vary considerably, but they typically limit or disallow liability for some rescuers under specified circumstances.

There are special relationships in which one person has some degree of control over another person, including (1) a parent with dependent children and (2) an employer with employees when the employment facilitates the employee's causing harm to third parties. The parent and the employer each owe a duty of reasonable care under the circumstances to third persons with regard to foreseeable risks that arise within the scope of the relationship. Third Restatement, Section 41. Depending on the circumstances, reasonable care may require controlling the activities of the other person or merely providing a warning. Generally, the duty of parents is limited to dependent children; thus, when children reach majority or are no longer dependent, parents no longer have control and the duty of reasonable care ceases.

The duty of employers includes the duty to exercise reasonable care in the hiring, training, supervision, and retention of employees. This duty of employers is independent of the vicarious liability of an employer for an employee's tortious conduct during the course of employment and extends to conduct by the employee that occurs both inside and outside the scope of employment so long as the employment facilitates the employee causing harm to third parties. The Third Restatement provides the following example of an employer's duty:

Don is employed by Welch Repair Service, which knows that Don had several episodes of assault in his previous employment. Don goes to Traci's residence, where he had previously been dispatched by Welch, and misrepresents to Traci that he is there on Welch business to check repairs that had previously been made in Traci's home. After Traci admits Don, he assaults Traci. Welch is subject to a duty under this subsection with regard to Don's assault on Traci.

◆ *See Case 8-1*

8-1c DUTIES OF POSSESSORS OF LAND

The right of possessors of land to use that land for their own benefit and enjoyment is limited by their duty to do so in a reasonable manner; that is, by the use of their land, they cannot cause unreasonable risks of harm to others. Liability for breach of this obligation may arise from conduct in any of the three areas of torts discussed in this and the preceding chapter: intentional harm, negligence, or strict liability. Most of these cases fall within the classification of negligence.

In conducting activities on her land, the possessor of land is required to exercise reasonable care to protect others who are not on her property. For example, a property owner who constructs a factory on her premises must take reasonable care that it is not unreasonably dangerous to people off the site. Moreover, a business or other possessor of land that holds its premises open to the public owes those who are lawfully on the premises a duty of reasonable care with regard to risks that arise within the scope of the relationship.

In most States and under the Second Restatement, the duty of a possessor of land to persons who come upon the land depends on whether those persons are trespassers, licensees, or invitees. In about fifteen States, however, licensees and invitees are owed the same duty. In addition, at least nine States have abandoned these distinctions and simply apply ordinary negligence principles of foreseeable risk and reasonable care to all entrants on the land including trespassers. The Third Restatement has adopted this last—the unitary—approach.

SECOND RESTATEMENT In accordance with the historical—and still majority—approach to the duties of possessors of land, the Second Restatement provides for varying duties depending on the status of the entrant on the land.

A **trespasser** is a person who enters or remains on the land of another without the possessor's consent or a legal privilege to do so. The possessor of the land is not liable to adult trespassers for her failure to maintain the land in a reasonably safe condition. Nonetheless, trespassers are not criminals, and the possessor is not free to inflict intentional injury on them. Moreover, most courts hold that upon discovering the presence of trespassers on her land, the lawful possessor is required to exercise reasonable care for their safety in carrying on her activities and to warn the trespassers of potentially highly dangerous conditions that the trespassers are not likely to discover.

A **licensee** is a person who is privileged to enter or remain upon land only by virtue of the lawful possessor's consent. Restatement, Section 330. Licensees include members of the possessor's household, social guests, and salespersons calling at private homes. A licensee will become a trespasser, however, if he enters a portion of the land to which he is not invited or remains upon the land after his invitation has expired. The possessor owes a higher duty of care to licensees than to trespassers. The possessor must warn a licensee of dangerous activities and conditions (1) of which the possessor has knowledge or has reason to know and (2) which the licensee does not and is not likely to discover. A licensee who is not warned may recover if the activity or dangerous condition resulted from the possessor's failure to exercise reasonable care to protect him from the danger. Restatement, Section 342. To illustrate: Jose invites a friend, Julia, to his place in the country at 8:00 P.M. on a winter evening. Jose knows that a bridge in his driveway is in a dangerous condition that is not noticeable in the dark. Jose does not inform Julia of this fact. The bridge gives way under Julia's car, causing serious harm to Julia. Jose is liable to Julia.

An **invitee** is a person invited upon land as a member of the public or for a business purpose. An invitee is either a public invitee or a business visitor. Restatement, Section 332. A **public invitee** is a person invited to enter or remain on land as a member of the public for a purpose for which the land is held open to the public. Such invitees include those who use public parks, beaches, or swimming pools, as well as those who use government facilities, such as a post office or an office of the Recorder of Deeds, where business with the public is transacted openly. A **business visitor** is a person invited to enter or remain on the premises for a purpose directly or indirectly concerning business dealings with the possessor of the land, such as one who enters a store or a tradesperson who enters a residence to make repairs. With respect to the condition of the premises, the possessor of land is under a duty to exercise reasonable care to protect invitees against dangerous conditions they are unlikely to discover. This liability extends not only to those conditions of which the possessor knows but also to those she would discover by the exercise of reasonable care. Restatement, Section 343. For example, at the front of Tilson's supermarket is a large glass front door that is well lit and plainly visible. Johnson, a customer, nonetheless mistakes the glass for an open doorway and walks into it, injuring himself. Tilson is not liable to Johnson. If, on the other hand, the glass was difficult to see and a person might foreseeably mistake the glass for an open doorway, then Tilson would be liable to Johnson if Johnson crashed into the glass while exercising reasonable care.

THIRD RESTATEMENT The status-based duty rules just discussed have been rejected by the Third Restatement, which adopts a unitary duty of reasonable care to people entering the land. Section 51.

> [Except for "flagrant trespassers,"] a land possessor owes a duty of reasonable care to entrants on the land with regard to:
> (1) conduct by the land possessor that creates risks to entrants on the land;
> (2) artificial conditions on the land that pose risks to entrants on the land;
> (3) natural conditions on the land that pose risks to entrants on the land;...

This rule is similar to the duty land possessors owed to invitees under the Second Restatement except that it extends the duty to all who enter the land, including trespassers, with the exception of "flagrant trespassers." This rule requires a land possessor to use reasonable care to investigate and discover dangerous conditions and to use reasonable care to eliminate or improve those dangerous conditions that are known or should have been discovered by the exercise of reasonable care. However, some risks cannot reasonably be discovered, and the land possessor is not subject to liability for those risks. In addition, a land possessor is not liable to an ordinary trespasser whose unforeseeable presence results in an unforeseeable risk.

A different rule applies to "flagrant trespassers." The Third Restatement requires that a land possessor only (1) refrain from intentional, willful, or wanton conduct that harms a flagrant trespasser and (2) exercise reasonable care on behalf of flagrant trespassers who are imperiled and helpless. Third Restatement, Section 52. The Third Restatement does not define "flagrant trespassers" but instead leaves it to each State to determine at what point an ordinary trespasser becomes a "flagrant trespasser." Comment a to Section 52 of the Third Restatement explains:

> The idea behind distinguishing particularly egregious trespassers for different treatment is that their presence on another's land is so antithetical to the rights of the land possessor to exclusive use and possession of the land that the land possessor should not be subject to liability for failing to exercise the ordinary duty of reasonable care otherwise owed to them as entrants on the land. It stems from the idea that when a trespass is sufficiently offensive to the property rights of the land possessor it is unfair to subject the possessor to liability for mere negligence.

The Third Restatement provides an illustration of a flagrant trespasser: "Herman engaged in a late-night burglary of the Jacob liquor store after it had closed. While leaving the store after taking cash from the store's register, Herman slipped on a slick spot on the floor, fell, and broke his arm. Herman is a flagrant trespasser."

Practical Advice

Take care to inspect your premises regularly to detect any dangerous conditions and either remedy the danger or post prominent warnings of any dangerous conditions you discover.

♦ *See Case 8-2*

8-1d RES IPSA LOQUITUR

A rule of circumstantial evidence has developed that permits the jury to infer both negligent conduct and causation from the mere occurrence of certain types of events. This rule, called **res ipsa loquitur,** meaning "the thing speaks for itself," applies "when the accident causing the Plaintiffs physical harm is a type of accident that ordinarily happens as a result of the negligence of a class of actors of which the defendant is the relevant member." Third Restatement, Section 17.

For example, Abrams rents a room in Brown's motel. During the night, a large piece of plaster falls from the ceiling and injures Abrams. In the absence of other evidence, the jury may infer that the harm resulted from Brown's negligence in permitting the plaster to become defective. Brown is permitted, however, to introduce evidence to contradict the inference of negligence.

8-2 Factual Cause

Liability for the negligent conduct of a defendant requires that the conduct in fact caused harm to the plaintiff. The Third Restatement states: "Tortious conduct must be a factual cause of physical harm for liability to be imposed." Section 26. A widely applied test for causation in fact is the **but-for test**: a person's conduct is a cause of an event if the event would not have occurred *but for* the person's negligent conduct. That is, conduct is a factual cause of harm when the harm would not have occurred absent the conduct. Third Restatement, Section 26. For instance, Arnold fails to erect a barrier around an excavation. Doyle is driving a truck when its accelerator becomes stuck, and he and the truck plummet into the excavation. Arnold's negligence is not a cause in fact of Doyle's death if the runaway truck would have crashed through the barrier that Arnold could have erected. Similarly, the failure to install a proper fire escape on a hotel is not the cause in fact of the death of a person who is suffocated by smoke while sleeping in bed during a hotel fire.

If the tortious conduct of Adam is insufficient by itself to cause Paula's harm, but when Adam's conduct is combined with the tortious conduct of Barry, the combined conduct is sufficient to cause Paula's harm, then Adam and Barry are each considered a factual cause of Paula's harm. Third Restatement, Section 26, Comment c.

The but-for test, however, is not satisfied when there are two or more causes, each of which is sufficient to bring about the harm in question and each of which is active at the time the harm occurs. For example, Wilson and Hart negligently set fires that combine to destroy Kennedy's property. Either fire would have destroyed the property. Under the but-for test, either Wilson or Hart or both could argue that the fire caused by the other would have destroyed the property and that he, therefore, is not liable. The Third Restatement addresses this problem of multiple *sufficient* causes by providing, "If multiple acts exist, each of which alone would have been a factual cause under [the but-for test] of the physical harm at the same time, each act is regarded as a factual cause of the harm." Section 27. Under this rule, the conduct of both Wilson and Hart would be found to be a factual cause of the destruction of Kennedy's property.

8-3 Scope of Liability (Proximate Cause)

As a matter of social policy, legal responsibility has not followed all the consequences of a negligent act. Tort law does not impose liability on a defendant for all harm factually caused by the defendant's negligent conduct. Liability has been limited— to a greater extent than with intentional torts—to those harms that result from the risks that made the defendant's conduct tortious. Third Restatement, Section 29. This "risk standard" limitation on liability also applies to strict liability cases. Third Restatement, Section 29, Comment l. The Third Restatement provides the following example:

> Richard, a hunter, finishes his day in the field and stops at a friend's house while walking home. His friend's nine-year-old daughter, Kim, greets Richard, who hands his loaded shotgun to her as he enters the house. Kim drops the shotgun, which lands on her toe, breaking it. Although Richard was negligent for giving Kim his shotgun, the risk that made Richard negligent was that Kim might shoot someone with the gun, not that she would drop it and hurt herself (the gun was neither especially heavy nor unwieldy). Kim's broken toe is outside the scope of Richard's liability, even though Richard's tortious conduct was a factual cause of Kim's harm.

8-3a FORESEEABILITY

Determining the liability of a negligent defendant for unforeseeable consequences has proved to be troublesome and controversial. The Second Restatement and many courts have adopted the following position:

1. If the actor's conduct is a substantial factor in bringing about harm to another, the fact that the actor neither foresaw nor should have foreseen the extent of the harm or the manner in which it occurred does *not* prevent him from being liable.

2. The actor's conduct may be held not to be a legal cause of harm to another where, after the event and looking back from the harm to the actor's negligent conduct, it appears to the court highly extraordinary that it should have brought about the harm. Restatement, Section 435.

Comment j to Section 29 of the Third Restatement explains that

> the foreseeability test for proximate cause is essentially consistent with the standard set forth in this Section. Properly understood, both the risk standard and a foreseeability test exclude liability for harms that were sufficiently unforeseeable at the time of the actor's tortious conduct that they were not among the risks—potential harms—that made the actor negligent. Negligence limits the requirement of reasonable care to those risks that are foreseeable.

For example, Albert, while negligently driving an automobile, collides with a car carrying dynamite. Albert is unaware of the contents of the other car and has no reason to know about them. The collision causes the dynamite to explode, shattering glass in a building a block away. The shattered glass injures Betsy, who is inside the building. The explosion also injures Calvin, who is walking on the sidewalk near the collision. Albert would be liable to Calvin because Albert should have realized that his negligent driving might result in a collision that would endanger pedestrians nearby. Betsy's harm, however, was beyond the risks posed by Albert's negligent driving and he, accordingly, is not liable to Betsy.

◆ *See Case 8-3*

8-3b SUPERSEDING CAUSE

An intervening cause is an event or act that occurs after the defendant's negligent conduct and, together with the defendant's negligence, causes the plaintiff's harm. If the intervening cause is deemed a superseding cause, then it relieves the defendant of liability for harm to the plaintiff caused in fact by both the defendant's negligence and the intervening event or act. For example, Carol negligently leaves in a public sidewalk a substantial excavation without a fence or warning lights, into which Gary falls at night. Darkness is an intervening, but not a superseding, cause of harm to Gary because it is a normal consequence of the situation caused by Carol's

negligence. Therefore, Carol is liable to Gary. In contrast, if Carol negligently leaves an excavation in a public sidewalk into which Barbara intentionally shoves Gary, under the Second Restatement as a matter of law, Carol is not liable to Gary because Barbara's conduct is a superseding cause that relieves Carol of liability. The Third Restatement rejects this exception to liability, stating,

> Whether Gary's harm is within the scope of Carol's liability for her negligence is an issue for the factfinder. The factfinder will have to determine whether the appropriate characterization of the harm to Gary is falling into an unguarded excavation site or being deliberately pushed into an unguarded excavation site and, if the latter, whether it is among the risks that made Carol negligent. Section 34, Comment e.

An intervening cause that is a foreseeable or normal consequence of the defendant's negligence is not a superseding cause. Thus, a person who negligently places another person or his property in imminent danger is liable for the injury sustained by a third-party rescuer who attempts to aid the imperiled person or his property. Third Restatement, Section 32. The same is true of attempts by the endangered person to escape the peril, as, for example, when a person swerves off the road to avoid a head-on collision with an automobile driven negligently on the wrong side of the road. It is commonly held that a negligent defendant is liable for the results of necessary medical treatment of the injured party, even if the treatment itself is negligent. Third Restatement, Section 35.

8-4 Harm

The plaintiff must prove that the defendant's negligent conduct proximately caused harm to a legally protected interest. Certain interests receive little or no protection against such conduct, while others receive full protection. The courts determine the extent of protection for a particular interest as a matter of law on the basis of social policy and expediency. For example, negligent conduct that is the proximate cause of harmful contact with the person of another is actionable. Thus, if Bob, while driving his car, negligently runs into Julie, a pedestrian who is carefully crossing the street, Bob is liable for physical injuries Julie sustains as a result of the collision. On the other hand, if Bob's careless driving causes the car's side-view mirror to brush Julie's coat but results in no physical injuries to her or damage to the coat, thus causing only offensive contact with Julie's person, Bob is not liable because Julie did not sustain harm to a legally protected interest.

The courts traditionally have been reluctant to allow recovery for negligently inflicted emotional distress. Nevertheless, this view has changed gradually during this century, and the majority of courts now hold a person liable for negligently causing emotional distress if bodily harm—such as a heart attack—results from the distress. Restatement, Section 436. In the majority of States, a defendant is not liable for negligent conduct resulting solely in emotional disturbance. Restatement, Section 436A. Some courts, however, have recently allowed recovery of damages for negligently inflicted emotional distress even in the absence of resultant physical harm when a person's negligent conduct places another in immediate danger of bodily harm. The Third Restatement follows the minority approach: a person whose negligent conduct places another in immediate danger of bodily harm is subject to liability to the other for serious emotional disturbance caused by reaction to the danger even though the negligent conduct did not cause any impact or bodily harm to the other. Third Restatement, Section 46. Furthermore, in a majority of States and under the Third Restatement, liability for negligently inflicted emotional distress arises in the following situation: Aldana negligently causes serious bodily injury to Bernard. If Charlize is a close family member of Bernard and witnesses the injury to Bernard, then Aldana is liable to Charlize for serious emotional disturbance she suffers from witnessing the event. Third Restatement, Section 47.

8-5 Defenses to Negligence

A plaintiff who has established by the preponderance of the evidence all the required elements of a negligence action may, nevertheless, be denied recovery if the defendant proves a valid defense. As a general rule, any defense to an intentional tort is also available in an action in negligence. In addition, contributory negligence, comparative negligence, and assumption of risk are three defenses available in negligence cases that are not defenses to intentional torts.

8-5a CONTRIBUTORY NEGLIGENCE

The Restatement, Section 463, defines contributory negligence as "conduct on the part of the plaintiff which falls below the standard to which he should conform for his own protection, and which is a legally contributing cause cooperating with the negligence of the defendant in bringing about the plaintiff's harm." The Third Restatement's definition of negligence as the failure of a person to exercise reasonable care under all the circumstances applies to the contributory negligence of the plaintiff. Section 3, Comment b. In those few States that have not adopted comparative negligence (Alabama, Maryland, North Carolina, and Virginia, as well as Washington, D.C.), the contributory negligence of the plaintiff, whether slight or extensive, prevents him from recovering *any* damages from the defendant.

In these jurisdictions, despite the contributory negligence of the plaintiff, if the defendant had a **last clear chance** to avoid injury to the plaintiff but did not avail himself of such chance, the plaintiff's contributory negligence does not bar his recovery of damages. Restatement, Section 479.

8-5b COMPARATIVE NEGLIGENCE

The harshness of the contributory negligence doctrine has caused all but a few States to reject its all-or-nothing rule and to substitute the doctrine of comparative negligence, which is also called comparative fault or comparative responsibility. (In States adopting comparative negligence, the doctrine of last clear chance has also been abandoned.) Approximately a dozen States have judicially or legislatively adopted "pure" comparative negligence systems. (The Third Restatement of Torts: Apportionment of Liability advocates this form of comparative negligence.) Under **pure comparative negligence**, the law apportions damages between the parties in proportion to the degree of fault or negligence found against them. For instance, Matthew negligently drives his automobile into Nancy, who is crossing against the light. Nancy sustains damages in the amount of $10,000 and sues Matthew. If the trier of fact determines that Matthew's negligence contributed 70 percent to Nancy's injury and that Nancy's contributory negligence contributed 30 percent to her injury, then Nancy would recover $7,000.

Most States have adopted the doctrine of "modified" comparative negligence. Under modified comparative negligence, the plaintiff recovers as in pure comparative negligence unless her contributory negligence was "as great as" or "greater than" that of the defendant, in which case the plaintiff recovers nothing. Thus, in the previous example, if the trier of fact determined that Matthew's negligence contributed 40 percent to Nancy's injury and Nancy's contributory negligence contributed 60 percent, then Nancy would recover nothing from Matthew.

8-5c ASSUMPTION OF RISK

A plaintiff who has *voluntarily* and *knowingly* assumed the risk of harm arising from the negligent or reckless conduct of the defendant cannot recover from such harm. Restatement, Section 496A. In **express** assumption of the risk, the plaintiff expressly agrees to assume the risk of harm from the defendant's conduct. Usually, but not always, such an agreement is by contract. Courts usually construe these exculpatory contracts strictly and will hold that the plaintiff has assumed the risk only if the terms of the agreement are clear and unequivocal. Moreover, some contracts for assumption of risk are considered unenforceable as a matter of public policy. See *Chapter 13*.

In **implied** assumption of the risk, the plaintiff voluntarily proceeds to encounter a known danger. Thus, a spectator entering a baseball park may be regarded as consenting that

FIGURE 8-2   Defenses to a Negligence Action

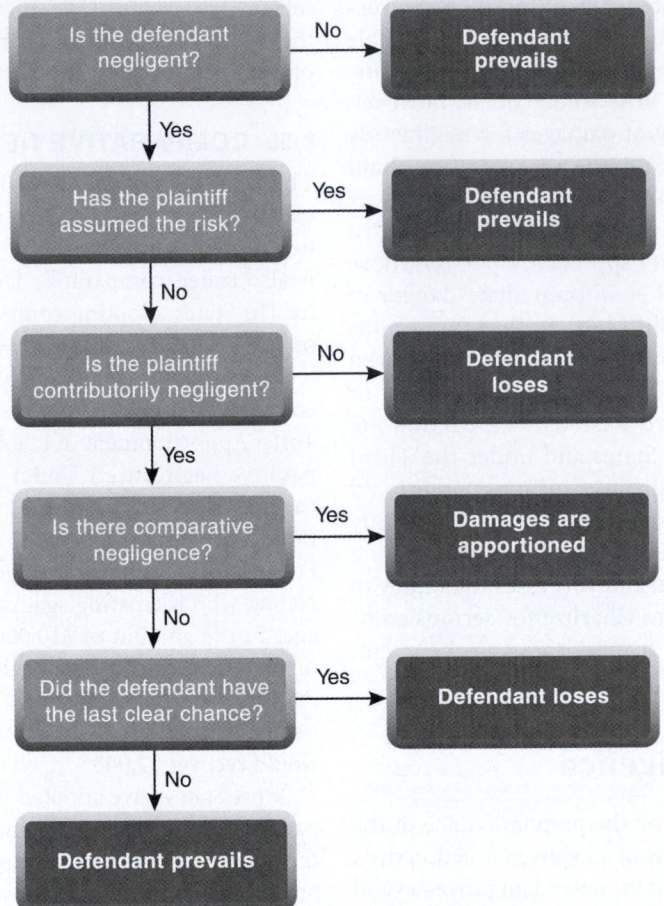

the players may proceed with the game without taking precautions to protect him from being hit by the ball. Most States have abolished or modified the defense of implied assumption of risk. Some have abandoned it entirely, while others have merged implied assumption of risk into their comparative negligence systems.

Reflecting this general trend, the Third Restatement of Torts: Apportionment of Liability has abandoned the doctrine of implied voluntary assumption of risk: it is no longer a defense that the plaintiff was aware of a risk and voluntarily confronted it. But if a plaintiff's conduct in the face of a known risk is unreasonable, it might constitute contributory negligence, thereby reducing the plaintiff's recovery under comparative negligence. This new Restatement limits the defense of assumption of risk to express assumption of risk, which consists of a contract between the plaintiff and another person to absolve the other person from liability for future harm.

Section 2. Contractual assumption of risk may occur by written agreement, express oral agreement, or conduct that creates an implied-in-fact contract, as determined by the applicable rules of contract law. Some contractual assumptions of risk, however, are not enforceable under other areas of substantive law or as against public policy.

♦ **SEE FIGURE 8-2:** *Defenses to a Negligence Action*

♦ *See Case 8-4*

Practical Advice

Consider having customers and clients sign waivers of liability and assumption of risk forms, but realize that many courts limit their effectiveness.

STRICT LIABILITY

In some instances, people may be held liable for injuries they have caused even though they have not acted intentionally or negligently. Such liability is called strict liability, absolute liability, or liability without fault. The law has determined that because certain types of otherwise socially desirable activities pose sufficiently high risks of harm regardless of how carefully they are conducted, those who perform these activities should bear the cost of any harm they cause. The doctrine of strict liability is not predicated upon any particular fault of the defendant, but rather upon the nature of the activity in which he is engaging.

8-6 Activities Giving Rise to Strict Liability

The following activities giving rise to strict liability are discussed in this section: (1) activities that are, in themselves, abnormally dangerous and (2) the keeping of animals. In addition, strict liability is imposed upon other activities. Nearly all States have imposed a limited form of strict product liability upon manufacturers and merchants who sell goods in a *defective condition* unreasonably dangerous to the user or consumer. This topic is covered in *Chapter 24.* All States have enacted workers' compensation statutes that make employers liable to employees for injuries arising out of the course of employment. Because the law imposes this liability without regard to the employer's negligence, it is a form of strict liability. Workers' compensation is discussed in *Chapter 42.* Moreover, the liability imposed upon an employer for torts that employees commit in the scope of their employment is a type of strict liability, as discussed in *Chapter 20.* Additional instances of strict liability include innocent misrepresentation (*Chapter 11*), some violations of the securities laws (*Chapter 43*), and carriers and innkeepers (*Chapter 47*).

8-6a ABNORMALLY DANGEROUS ACTIVITIES

A person who carries on an abnormally dangerous activity is subject to strict liability for physical harm resulting from the activity. Third Restatement, Section 20(a). "An activity is abnormally dangerous if: (1) the activity creates a foreseeable and highly significant risk of physical harm even when reasonable care is exercised by all actors; and (2) the activity is not one of common usage." Third Restatement, Section 20(b). The court determines whether an activity is abnormally dangerous by applying these factors. Activities to which the rule has been applied include collecting water or sewage in such quantity and location as to make it dangerous, storing explosives or flammable liquids in large quantities, blasting or pile driving, crop dusting, drilling for or refining oil in populated areas, and emitting noxious gases or fumes into a settled community. On the other hand, courts have refused to apply the rule where the activity is a "natural" use of the land, such as drilling for oil in the oil fields of Texas, collecting water in a stock watering tank, or transmitting gas through a gas pipe or electricity through electric wiring.

♦ *See Case 8-5*

Practical Advice

Determine whether any of your activities involve abnormally dangerous activities for which strict liability is imposed and be sure to obtain adequate insurance.

8-6b KEEPING OF ANIMALS

Strict liability for harm caused by animals existed at common law and continues today with some modification. As a general rule, those who possess animals for their own purposes do so at their peril and must protect against the harm those animals may cause to people and property.

TRESPASSING ANIMALS Owners and possessors of animals, except for dogs and cats, are subject to strict liability for physical harm their animals cause by trespassing on the property of another. Third Restatement, Section 21. There are two exceptions to this rule: (1) keepers of animals are not strictly liable if those animals incidentally stray upon land immediately adjacent to a highway on which they are being lawfully driven, although the owner may be liable for negligence if he fails to properly control them, and (2) keepers of farm animals, typically cattle, in some western States are not strictly liable for harm caused by trespassing animals that they allow to graze freely.

NONTRESPASSING ANIMALS Owners and possessors of wild animals are subject to strict liability for physical harm caused by such animals, whether they are trespassing or not. Third Restatement, Section 22(b). Accordingly, the owner or possessor is liable even if she has exercised reasonable care in attempting to restrain the wild animal. **Wild animals** are defined as those that, in the particular region in which they are kept, are known to be likely to inflict serious damage and cannot be considered safe, no matter how domesticated they become. The Third Restatement has a similar definition: "A wild animal is an animal that belongs to a category of animals that have not been generally domesticated and that are likely, unless restrained, to cause personal injury." Section 22(b). The court determines whether a category of animals is wild. Animals that have been determined to be wild include bears, lions, elephants, monkeys, tigers, wolves, zebras, deer, and raccoons. On the other hand, iguanas, pigeons, and manatees are not considered wild animals because they do not pose a risk of causing substantial personal injury. Third Restatement, Section 22, Comment b.

DOMESTIC ANIMALS are those that are traditionally devoted to the service of humankind and that as a class are considered safe. Examples of domestic animals are dogs, cats, horses, cattle, and sheep. Owners and possessors of domestic animals are subject to strict liability if they knew, or had reason to know, that the animal had dangerous tendencies abnormal for the animal's category. Restatement, Section 509; Third Restatement, Section 23. The animal's dangerous propensity must be the cause of the harm. For example, merely because he knows that a dog has a propensity to fight with other dogs, a keeper is not liable when the dog bites a human. On the other hand, a person whose 150-pound sheepdog has a propensity to jump enthusiastically on visitors would be liable for any damage caused by the dog's playfulness. About half of the States statutorily impose strict liability in dog cases even where the owner or possessor does not know, and did not have reason to know, of the dog's dangerous tendencies.

◆ *See Case 8-6*

8-7 Defenses to Strict Liability

This section discusses the availability in a strict liability action for abnormally dangerous activities and keeping of animals of the following defenses: (1) contributory negligence, (2) comparative negligence, and (3) assumption of risk.

8-7a CONTRIBUTORY NEGLIGENCE

Because the strict liability of one who carries on an abnormally dangerous activity or keeps animals is not based on his negligence, the ordinary contributory negligence of the plaintiff is not a defense to such liability. In imposing strict liability, the law places on the defendant the full responsibility for preventing harm. For example, Adrian negligently fails to observe a sign on a highway warning of a blasting operation conducted by Benjamin. As a result, Adrian is injured by these operations; nonetheless, he may recover from Benjamin.

8-7b COMPARATIVE NEGLIGENCE

Despite the rationale that disallows contributory negligence as a defense to strict liability, some States apply the doctrine of comparative negligence to some types of strict liability. The Third Restatement provides that if the plaintiff has been contributorily negligent in failing to take reasonable precautions, the plaintiff's recovery in a strict-liability claim for physical harm caused by abnormally dangerous activities or keeping of animals is reduced in accordance with the share of comparative responsibility assigned to the plaintiff. Section 25.

8-7c ASSUMPTION OF RISK

Under the Second Restatement of Torts, voluntary assumption of risk is a defense to an action based upon strict liability. If the owner of an automobile knowingly and voluntarily parks the vehicle in a blasting zone, he may not recover for harm to his automobile. The assumption of risk, however, must be voluntary. For example, the possessor of land located near a blasting operation is not required to move away; she may, in fact, recover for harm she suffers because of the operation.

The more recent Third Restatement of Torts: Apportionment of Liability has abandoned the doctrine of implied voluntary assumption of risk in tort actions generally: it is no longer a defense that the plaintiff was aware of a risk and voluntarily confronted it. This new Restatement limits the defense of assumption of risk to express assumption of risk, which consists of a contract between the plaintiff and another person to absolve the other person from liability for future harm. Section 2.

The Third Restatement: Liability for Physical and Emotional Harm recognizes a limitation on strict liability for abnormally dangerous activities and keeping of animals when the victim suffers harm as a result of exposure to the animal or activity resulting from the victim's securing some benefit from that exposure. Section 24(a). The Third Restatement gives the following example: "if the plaintiff is a veterinarian or a groomer who accepts an animal such as a dog from the defendant, the plaintiff is deriving financial benefits from the acceptance of the animal, and is beyond the scope of strict liability, even if the dog can be deemed abnormally dangerous."

C H A P T E R   S U M M A R Y

NEGLIGENCE

BREACH OF DUTY OF CARE	**Definition of Negligence** conduct that falls below the standard established by law for the protection of others against unreasonable risk of harm

Duty of Care a person is under a duty to all others at all times to exercise reasonable care for the safety of the others' person and property; however, except in special circumstances, no one is under a general duty to (1) avoid the unintentional infliction of economic loss or (2) aid another in peril

Reasonable Person Standard degree of care that a reasonable person would exercise under all the circumstances
- *Children* must conform to conduct of a reasonable person of the same age, intelligence, and experience under all the circumstances
- *Physical Disability* a disabled person's conduct must conform to that of a reasonable person under the same disability
- *Mental Disability* a mentally disabled person is held to the reasonable person standard
- *Superior Skill or Knowledge* if a person has skills or knowledge beyond those possessed by most others, these skills or knowledge are circumstances to be taken into account in determining whether the person has acted with reasonable care
- *Standard for Emergencies* the reasonable person standard applies, but an unexpected emergency is considered part of the circumstances
- *Violation of Statute* if the statute applies, the violation is negligence *per se* in most States

Duties of Possessors of Land
- *Second Restatement* a land possessor owes the following duties: (1) not to injure *trespassers* intentionally, (2) to warn *licensees* of known dangerous conditions licensees are unlikely to discover for themselves, and (3) to exercise reasonable care to protect *invitees* against dangerous conditions land possessor should know of but invitees are unlikely to discover
- *Third Restatement* adopts a unitary duty of reasonable care to all entrants on the land except for flagrant trespassers: a land possessor must use reasonable care to investigate and discover dangerous conditions and must use reasonable care to eliminate or improve those dangerous conditions that are known or should have been discovered by the exercise of reasonable care

Res Ipsa Loquitur permits the jury to infer both negligent conduct and causation

FACTUAL CAUSE AND SCOPE OF LIABILITY	**Factual Cause** the defendant's conduct is a factual cause of the harm when the harm would not have occurred absent the conduct

Scope of Liability (Proximate Cause) liability is limited to those harms that result from the risks that made the defendant's conduct tortious
- *Foreseeability* excludes liability for harms that were sufficiently unforeseeable at the time of the defendant's tortious conduct that they were not among the risks that made the defendant negligent
- *Superseding Cause* an intervening act that relieves the defendant of liability

HARM	**Harm to Legally Protected Interest** courts determine which interests are protected from negligent interference **Burden of Proof** plaintiff must prove that defendant's negligent conduct caused harm to a legally protected interest
DEFENSES TO NEGLIGENCE	**Contributory Negligence** failure of a plaintiff to exercise reasonable care for his own protection, which in a few States prevents the plaintiff from recovering anything **Comparative Negligence** damages are divided between the parties in proportion to their degree of negligence; applies in almost all States **Assumption of Risk** plaintiff's express consent to encounter a known danger; some States still apply implied assumption of the risk

STRICT LIABILITY

ACTIVITIES GIVING RISE TO STRICT LIABILITY	**Definition of Strict Liability** liability for nonintentional and nonnegligent conduct **Abnormally Dangerous Activity** strict liability is imposed for any activity that (1) creates a foreseeable and highly significant risk of harm and (2) is not one of common usage **Keeping of Animals** strict liability is imposed for wild animals and usually for trespassing domestic animals
DEFENSES TO STRICT LIABILITY	**Contributory Negligence** is not a defense to strict liability **Comparative Negligence** some States apply this doctrine to some strict liability cases **Assumption of Risk** express assumption of risk is a defense to an action based upon strict liability; some States apply implied assumption of risk to strict liability cases

C A S E S

<table>
<tr><td>CASE
8-1</td><td>Duty to Act
SOLDANO v. O'DANIELS
California Court of Appeal, Fifth District, 1983
141 Cal.App.3d 443, 190 Cal.Rptr. 310</td><td></td></tr>
</table>

Andreen, J.

Does a business establishment incur liability for wrongful death if it denies use of its telephone to a good samaritan who explains an emergency situation occurring without and wishes to call the police?

This appeal follows a judgment of dismissal of the second cause of action of a complaint for wrongful death upon a motion for summary judgment. The motion was supported only by a declaration of defense counsel. Both briefs on appeal adopt the defense averments:

This action arises out of a shooting death occurring on August 9, 1977. Plaintiff's father [Darrell Soldano] was shot and killed by one Rudolph Villanueva on that date at defendant's Happy Jack's Saloon. This defendant owns and operates the Circle Inn which is an eating establishment located across the street from Happy Jack's. Plaintiff's second cause of action against this defendant is one for negligence.

Plaintiff alleges that on the date of the shooting, a patron of Happy Jack's Saloon came into the Circle Inn and informed a Circle Inn employee that a man had been threatened at Happy Jack's. He requested the employee either call the police or allow him to use the Circle Inn phone to call the police. That employee allegedly refused to call the police and allegedly refused to allow the patron to use the phone to make his own call. Plaintiff alleges that the actions of the Circle Inn employee were a breach of the legal duty that the Circle Inn owed to the decedent.

We were advised at oral argument that the employee was the defendant's bartender. The state of the record is unsatisfactory in that it does not disclose the physical location of the telephone—whether on the bar, in a private office behind a closed door or elsewhere. The only factual matter before the trial court was a verified statement of the defense attorney which set forth those facts quoted above. Following normal rules applicable to motions for summary judgment, we strictly construe the defense affidavit. [Citation.] Accordingly, we assume the telephone was not in a private office but in a position where it could be used by a patron without inconvenience to the defendant or his guests. We also assume the call was a local one and would not result in expense to defendant.

There is a distinction, well rooted in the common law, between action and nonaction. [Citation.] It has found its way into the prestigious Restatement Second of Torts (hereafter cited as "Restatement"), which provides in section 314: "The fact that the actor realizes or should realize that action on his part is necessary for another's aid or protection does not of itself impose upon him a duty to take such action." * * *

* * *

As noted in [citation], the courts have increased the instances in which affirmative duties are imposed not by direct rejection of the common law rule, but by expanding the list of special relationships which will justify departure from that rule. * * *

* * *

Section 314A of the Restatement lists other special relationships which create a duty to render aid, such as that of a common carrier to its passengers, an innkeeper to his guest, possessors of land who hold it open to the public, or one who has a custodial relationship to another. A duty may be created by an undertaking to give assistance. [Citation.]

Here there was no special relationship between the defendant and the deceased. It would be stretching the concept beyond recognition to assert there was a relationship between the defendant and the patron from Happy Jack's Saloon who wished to summon aid. But this does not end the matter.

It is time to re-examine the common law rule of nonliability for nonfeasance in the special circumstances of the instant case.

* * *

We turn now to the concept of duty in a tort case. The [California] Supreme Court has identified certain factors to be considered in determining whether a duty is owed to third persons. These factors include:

the foreseeability of harm to the plaintiff, the degree of certainty that the plaintiff suffered injury, the closeness of the connection between the defendant's conduct and the injury suffered, the moral blame attached to the defendant's conduct, the policy of preventing future harm, the extent of the burden to the defendant and consequences to the community of imposing a duty to exercise care with

resulting liability for breach, and the availability, cost, and prevalence of insurance for the risk involved. [Citation.]

We examine those factors in reference to this case. (1) The harm to the decedent was abundantly foreseeable; it was imminent. The employee was expressly told that a man had been threatened. The employee was a bartender. As such he knew it is foreseeable that some people who drink alcohol in the milieu of a bar setting are prone to violence. (2) The certainty of decedent's injury is undisputed. (3) There is arguably a close connection between the employee's conduct and the injury: the patron wanted to use the phone to summon the police to intervene. The employee's refusal to allow the use of the phone prevented this anticipated intervention. If permitted to go to trial, the plaintiff may be able to show that the probable response time of the police would have been shorter than the time between the prohibited telephone call and the fatal shot. (4) The employee's conduct displayed a disregard for human life that can be characterized as morally wrong: he was callously indifferent to the possibility that Darrell Soldano would die as the result of his refusal to allow a person to use the telephone. Under the circumstances before us the bartender's burden was minimal and exposed him to no risk: all he had to do was allow the use of the telephone. It would have cost him or his employer nothing. It could have saved a life. (5) Finding a duty in these circumstances would promote a policy of preventing future harm. A citizen would not be required to summon the police but would be required, in circumstances such as those before us, not to impede another who has chosen to summon aid. (6) We have no information on the question of the availability, cost, and prevalence of insurance for the risk, but note that the liability which is sought to be imposed here is that of employee negligence, which is covered by many insurance policies. (7) The extent of the burden on the defendant was minimal, as noted.

* * *

We acknowledge that defendant contracted for the use of his telephone, and its use is a species of property. But if it exists in a public place as defined above, there is no privacy or ownership interest in it such that the owner should be permitted to interfere with a good faith attempt to use it by a third person to come to the aid of another.

* * *

We conclude that the bartender owed a duty to the plaintiff's decedent to permit the patron from Happy Jack's to place a call to the police or to place the call himself.

It bears emphasizing that the duty in this case does not require that one must go to the aid of another. That is not the issue here. The employee was not the good samaritan intent on aiding another. The patron was.

* * *

We conclude there are sufficient justiciable issues to permit the case to go to trial and therefore reverse.

CASE 8-2

Duty to Invitees
LOVE v. HARDEE'S FOOD SYSTEMS, INC.
Court of Appeals of Missouri, Eastern District, Division Two, 2000
16 S.W.3d 739

Crane, J.

At about 3:15 P.M. on November 15, 1995, plaintiff, Jason Love, and his mother, Billye Ann Love, went to the Hardee's Restaurant in Arnold, Missouri, which is owned by defendant, Hardee's Food Systems, Inc. There were no other customers in the restaurant between 3:00 P.M. and 4:00 P.M., but two or three workmen were in the back doing construction. The workmen reported that they did not use the restroom and did not see anyone use the restroom. After eating his lunch, plaintiff, who was wearing rubber-soled boat shoes, went to use the restroom. He opened the restroom door, took one step in, and, upon taking his second step, slipped on water on the restroom floor. Plaintiff fell backwards, hit his head, and felt a shooting pain down his right leg. He found himself lying in an area of dirty water, which soaked his clothes. There were no barricades, warning cones, or anything else that would either restrict access to the bathroom or warn of the danger.

Plaintiff crawled up to the sink to pull himself up and made his way back to the table and told his mother that his back and leg were "hurting pretty bad." His mother reported the fall to another employee.

Plaintiff's mother went back to the men's restroom and looked at the water on the floor. She observed that the water was dirty. The restaurant supervisor came out and interviewed plaintiff and viewed the water in the restroom. * * * The supervisor then filled out an accident report form, which reported that the accident occurred at 3:50 P.M. The supervisor testified that the water appeared to have come from someone shaking his hands after washing them. The supervisor told plaintiff he could not recall the last time the restroom had been checked. Plaintiff was taken to a hospital emergency room. As a result of his injuries, plaintiff underwent two back surgeries, missed substantial time from work, and suffered from continuing pain and limitations on his physical activities.

Defendant had a policy requiring that the restroom was to be checked and cleaned every hour by a maintenance man. The maintenance man was scheduled to work until 3:00 P.M., but normally left at 1:00 P.M. The supervisor could not recall whether the maintenance man left at 1:00 P.M. or 3:00 P.M. on November 15. The time clock activity report would show when the maintenance man clocked out, but defendant was unable to produce the time clock report for November 15.

It was also a store policy that whenever employees cleaned the tables, they would check the restroom. The restrooms were used by customers and employees. If an employee had to use the restroom, then that employee was also supposed to check the restroom. The restaurant supervisor did not ask if any employees had been in the restroom, or if they had checked it in the hour prior to the accident, and did not know if the restroom was actually inspected or cleaned at 3:00 P.M.

The restaurant had shift inspection checklists on which the manager would report on the cleanliness of the restrooms and whether the floors were clean and dry. However, the checklists for November 15 were thrown away. * * *

Plaintiff subsequently filed the underlying lawsuit against defendant to recover damages for negligence. The jury returned a verdict in plaintiff's favor in the amount of $125,000. * * *

* * * [Defendant] argues that plaintiff failed to make a submissible case of negligence because plaintiff failed to prove that defendant had actual or constructive notice of the water on the restroom floor in that there was no evidence showing the source of the water or the length of time the water had been on the floor.

* * *

In order to have made a submissible case, plaintiff had to show that defendant knew or, by using ordinary care, could have known of the dangerous condition and failed to use ordinary care to remove it, barricade it, or warn of it, and plaintiff sustained damage as a direct result of such failure. [Citation.]

"In order to establish constructive notice, the condition must have existed for a sufficient length of time or the facts must be such that the defendant should have reasonably known of its presence." [Citation.] [Prior] cases * * * placed great emphasis on the length of time the dangerous condition had been present and held that times of 20 or 30 minutes, absent proof of other circumstances, were insufficient to establish constructive notice as a matter of law. [Citations.]

* * *

Defendant's liability is predicated on the foreseeability of the risk and the reasonableness of the care taken, which is a question of fact to be determined by the totality of the circumstances, including the nature of the restaurant's business and the method of its operation. [Citations.]

In this case the accident took place in the restaurant's restroom which is provided for the use of employees and customers. The cause of the accident was water, which is provided in the restroom. The restaurant owner could reasonably foresee that anyone using the restroom, customers or employees, would use the tap water provided in the restroom and could spill, drop, or splash water on the floor. Accordingly, the restaurant owner was under a duty to use due care to guard against danger from water on the floor.

There was substantial evidence to support submissibility. First, there was evidence from which the jury could infer that the water came from the use of the restroom. It was on the floor of the restroom and the supervisor testified it appeared that someone had shaken water from his hands on the floor.

Next, there was evidence from which the jury could infer that, if the water was caused by a non-employee, the water was on the floor for at least 50 minutes, or longer, because there was evidence that no other customers were in the store to use the restroom after 3:00 P.M. and the workmen on the site advised that they had not used the restroom.

In addition, plaintiff adduced evidence from which the jury could have found that defendants' employees had the opportunity to observe the hazard. The restroom was to be used by the employees and was supposed to be checked by them when they used it; employees cleaning tables were supposed to check the restroom when they cleaned the tables; and a maintenance man was supposed to check and clean the restroom every hour.

There was evidence from which the jury could have inferred that the maintenance man charged with cleaning the restroom every hour did not clean the restroom at 3:00 P.M. as scheduled on the day of the accident. There was testimony that the maintenance man usually left at 1:00 P.M. * * * This could have created a span of 2 hours and 50 minutes during which there was no employee working at the restaurant whose primary responsibility was to clean the restroom. [Citation.]

There was also evidence from which the jury could have inferred that the restroom was not inspected by any employee who had the responsibility to inspect it during that same time period. The supervisor testified that he could not recall the last time the restroom had been checked and did not ask any employees if they had been in the restroom or had checked it in the hour before the accident. * * *

* * *

The judgment of the trial court is affirmed.

CASE 8-3

Scope of Liability (Proximate Cause)
PALSGRAF v. LONG ISLAND RAILROAD CO.
Court of Appeals of New York, 1928
248 N.Y. 339, 162 N.E. 99

Cardozo, C. J.

Plaintiff was standing on a platform of defendant's railroad after buying a ticket to go to Rockaway Beach. A train stopped at the station, bound for another place. Two men ran forward to catch it. One of the men reached the platform of the car without mishap, though the train was already moving. The other man, carrying a package, jumped aboard the car, but seemed unsteady as if about to fall. A guard on the car, who had held the door open, reached forward to help him in, and another guard on the platform pushed him from behind. In this act, the package was dislodged, and fell upon the rails. It was a package of small size, about fifteen inches long, and was covered by a newspaper. In fact it contained fireworks, but there was nothing in its appearance to give notice of its contents. The fireworks when they fell exploded. The shock of the explosion threw down some scales at the other end of the platform many feet away. The scales struck the plaintiff, causing injuries for which she sues.

The conduct of the defendant's guard, if a wrong in its relation to the holder of the package, was not a wrong in its relation to the plaintiff, standing far away. Relatively to her it was not negligence at all. Nothing in the situation gave notice that the falling package had in it the potency of peril to persons thus removed. Negligence is not actionable unless it involves the invasion of a legally protected interest, the violation of a right. "Proof of negligence in the air, so to speak,

will not do." [Citations.] "Negligence is the absence of care, according to the circumstances." [Citations.]

* * *

If no hazard was apparent to the eye of ordinary vigilance, an act innocent and harmless, at least to outward seeming, with reference to her, did not take to itself the quality of a tort because it happened to be a wrong, though apparently not one involving the risk of bodily insecurity, with reference to someone else. "In every instance, before negligence can be predicated of a given act, back of the act must be sought and found a duty to the individual complaining, the observance of which would have averted or avoided the injury." [Citations.]

* * *

A different conclusion will involve us, and swiftly too, in a maze of contradictions. A guard stumbles over a package which has been left upon a platform. It seems to be a bundle of newspapers. It turns out to be a can of dynamite. To the eye of ordinary vigilance, the bundle is abandoned waste, which may be kicked or trod on with impunity. Is a passenger at the other end of the platform protected by the law against the unsuspected hazard concealed beneath the waste? If not, is the result to be any different, so far as the distant passenger is concerned, when the guard stumbles over a valise which a truckman or a porter has left upon the walk? The passenger far away, if the victim of a wrong at all, has a cause of action, not derivative, but original and primary. His claim to be protected against invasion of his bodily security is neither greater nor less because the act resulting in the invasion is a wrong to another far removed. In this case, the rights that are said to have been violated, the interests said to have been invaded, are not even of the same order. The man was not injured in his person nor even put in danger. The purpose of the act, as well as its effect, was to make his person safe. If there was a wrong to him at all, which may very well be doubted, it was a wrong to a property interest only, the safety of his package. Out of this wrong to property, which threatened injury to nothing else, there has passed, we are told, to the plaintiff by derivation or succession a right of action for the invasion of an interest of another order, the right to bodily security. The

diversity of interests emphasizes the futility of the effort to build the plaintiff's right upon the basis of a wrong to someone else. * * * One who jostles one's neighbor in a crowd does not invade the rights of others standing at the outer fringe when the unintended contact casts a bomb upon the ground. The wrongdoer as to them is the man who carries the bomb, not the one who explodes it without suspicion of the danger. Life will have to be made over, and human nature transformed, before prevision so extravagant can be accepted as the norm of conduct, the customary standard to which behavior must conform.

* * *

The judgment of the Appellate Division and that of the Trial Term should be reversed, and the complaint dismissed, with costs in all courts.

CASE

8-4

Contributory Negligence
MOORE v. KITSMILLER
Court of Appeals of Texas, Twelfth District, Tyler, 2006
201 S.W.3d 147; review denied (2006)

Worthen, C. J.

In the spring of 2001, Kitsmiller purchased a house in Van Zandt County to use as rental property. In mid-June, he hired B&H Shaw Company, Inc. ("B&H") to install a replacement septic tank in the back yard. The septic tank was located about two or three feet from a concrete stoop at the back door of the garage. B&H mounded dirt over the septic tank and the lateral lines going out from it upon completion. Sometime after B&H installed the septic tank, Kitsmiller smoothed out the mounds of dirt over the septic tank and lateral lines using the box blade on his tractor. Kitsmiller then leased the property to Moore and his wife on July 27. Kitsmiller testified that he viewed the back yard about a week or ten days prior to leasing the property to the Moores and stated that the dirt around the septic system looked firm.

On August 7, the Moores moved in. On August 11, Moore and his wife ventured into the back yard for the first time, carrying some trash bags to a barrel. Moore testified that his wife led the way and he followed her about a foot and a half behind. Moore testified that at the time, his right arm was in a sling and a bag of trash was in his left hand. He stated that as he stepped off the stoop, he was unable to see the ground and could only see his wife and the bag of trash in his left arm. His wife testified that the ground looked flat as she walked toward the barrel. Moore testified that he had only taken a few steps off the stoop when his left leg sank into a hole, causing him to fall forward into his wife. As he tried to steady himself with his right foot, it hung and then sank, causing him to fall backward on his head and back. Moore testified that the injury to his back required surgery and affected his ability to earn a living.

Moore filed suit against Kitsmiller and B&H. He sought damages for past and future pain and suffering, past and future mental anguish, past and future physical impairment, and past and future loss of earning capacity. In their answers to Moore's suit, both Kitsmiller and B&H pleaded the affirmative defense of contributory negligence. [Citation.] B&H specifically pleaded that Moore was negligent for not having kept a proper lookout when stepping into the back yard and looking for obstructions, such as erosion or soft soil.

During the jury trial, Moore testified Kitsmiller should have notified him where the septic tank and lateral lines were located and that the dirt should have remained mounded over the tank and lines. On August 13, Moore asked Ken Martin to inspect the site of the fall (the "occurrence"). Martin is an on-site septic tank complaint investigator for both the Texas Commission on Environmental Quality and Van Zandt County. Martin testified that dirt should have been mounded over the septic tank and lateral lines, so that when the dirt settled, there would be no holes in the ground around the septic tank or lateral lines. However, there was no dirt mounded over the septic tank or lines when he inspected the site. Martin's photographs of the site also indicated that there were no mounds of dirt over the septic tank. Further, the photographs showed sunken ground around the septic tank, including, but not limited to, the area where Moore fell. Martin testified that it was common for sinkholes to develop around a septic tank. He also testified that he had observed situations where dirt around a septic tank or lateral line looked to be solid, but sank when a person stepped on it. Martin testified that the photographs showed an obvious depression around the septic tank. Bill Shaw, president of

B&H, testified that Moore should have been watching where he was going as he stepped into the back yard. Shaw stated that Martin's photographs indicated to him that the depressions in the ground around the septic tank were visible at the time of the occurrence.

The first question for the jury was whose negligence caused the occurrence. The jury responded that both Kitsmiller and Moore were negligent, but B&H was not. In the second question, the jury determined that Kitsmiller was 51% negligent and Moore was 49% negligent. In the third question, the jury determined that Moore was entitled to $210,000.00 in damages. On September 29, 2004, the trial court entered a judgment in favor of Moore and against Kitsmiller in the amount of $210,000.00 plus interest and costs.

On October 14, 2004, Kitsmiller asked that the trial court modify the judgment to $107,100.00 based upon Moore's contributory negligence. The trial court entered a modified final judgment on November 1, 2004 awarding Moore $107,100.00 plus interest and costs. On November 23, 2004, a partial satisfaction and release of judgment filed with the court showed that Kitsmiller had paid the amount awarded in the modified judgment to Moore. However, Moore reserved the right to appeal all issues involving his contributory negligence to this court. Moore then timely filed his notice of appeal.

* * *

* * * Moore contends the evidence is legally insufficient to support the judgment. Moore argues that his wife and Kitsmiller testified that the back yard was flat at the time of the occurrence. He contends that no one could have anticipated any danger from walking into the yard. Therefore, Moore argues that there is no evidence in the record to support the jury's determination that he was contributorily negligent.

Contributory negligence contemplates an injured person's failure to use ordinary care regarding his or her own safety. [Citation.] This affirmative defense requires proof that the plaintiff was negligent and that the plaintiff's negligence proximately caused his or her injuries. [Citation.] Negligence requires proof of proximate cause. [Citation.] Proximate cause requires proof of both cause in fact and foreseeability. [Citation.] The test for cause in fact is whether the negligent act or omission was a substantial factor in bringing about an injury without which the harm would not have occurred. [Citation.] Foreseeability requires that a person of ordinary intelligence should have anticipated the danger created by a negligent act or omission. [Citation.]

Because comparative responsibility involves measuring the party's comparative fault in causing the plaintiff's injuries, it necessitates a preliminary finding that the plaintiff was in fact contributorily negligent. [Citation.] The standards and tests for determining contributory negligence ordinarily are the same as those for determining negligence, and the rules of law applicable to the former are applicable to the latter. [Citation.] The burden of proof on the whole case is on the plaintiff. [Citation.] However, on special issues tendered by the defendant presenting an affirmative defense such as contributory negligence, the burden of proof is on the defendant to prove the defense by a preponderance of the evidence. [Citation.]

When attacking the legal sufficiency of an adverse finding on an issue on which the party did not have the burden of proof, that party must demonstrate there is no evidence to support the adverse finding. [Citation.] To evaluate the legal sufficiency of the evidence to support a finding, we must determine whether the proffered evidence as a whole rises to a level that would enable reasonable and fair minded people to differ in their conclusions. [Citation.] We sustain a no evidence issue only if there is no more than a scintilla of evidence proving the elements of the claim. [Citation.] In making this determination, we must view the evidence in the light most favorable to the verdict, crediting favorable evidence if reasonable jurors could and disregarding contrary evidence unless reasonable jurors could not. [Citation.] The trier of fact may draw reasonable and logical inferences from the evidence. [Citation.] It is within the province of the jury to draw one reasonable inference from the evidence although another inference could have been made. [Citation.]

* * *

Moore testified that when he stepped off the stoop into the back yard for the first time on August 11, 2001, he could only see his wife and the plastic bag of trash he was carrying in his left hand. The jury was allowed to draw an inference from this evidence that Moore was not watching where he was walking. An individual must keep a proper lookout where he is walking, and a jury is allowed to make a reasonable inference that failure to do so was the proximate cause of his injuries. [Citation.] It was reasonable for the jury to make an inference from Moore's testimony that his failure to keep a proper lookout where he was walking contributed to the occurrence.

Moore contends that the only reasonable inference the jury could have made was that, even if he had been watching where he was walking, he would not have been able to avoid stepping in the holes because they were not visible to the naked eye. The jury could have made that inference, but chose not to do so. Shaw's testimony that Martin's photographs showed the depressions could have been present at the time of the occurrence could have led the jury to believe that Moore's contention was not a reasonable inference. We conclude that the jury made a reasonable inference from the evidence in finding Moore contributorily negligent.

* * *

* * * [T]he judgment of the trial court is affirmed.

CASE
8-5

Abnormally Dangerous Activities
KLEIN v. PYRODYNE CORPORATION
Supreme Court of Washington, 1991
117 Wash.2d 1, 810 P.2d 917; as corrected, 817 P.2d 1359

Guy, J.

[Pyrodyne Corporation contracted to conduct the fireworks display at the Western Washington State Fairgrounds in Puyallup, Washington, on July 4, 1987. During the fireworks display, one of the five-inch mortars was knocked into a horizontal position. A shell inside ignited and discharged, flying five hundred feet parallel to the earth and exploding near the crowd of onlookers. Danny and Marion Klein were injured by the explosion. Mr. Klein suffered facial burns and serious injuries to his eyes. The parties provided conflicting explanations for the improper discharge, and because all the evidence had exploded, there was no means of proving the cause of the misfire. The Kleins brought suit against Pyrodyne under the theory of strict liability for participating in an abnormally dangerous activity.]

The Kleins contend that strict liability is the appropriate standard to determine the culpability of Pyrodyne because Pyrodyne was participating in an abnormally dangerous activity. * * *

The modern doctrine of strict liability for abnormally dangerous activities derives from *Rylands v. Fletcher*, [citation], in which the defendant's reservoir flooded mine shafts on the plaintiff's adjoining land. *Rylands v. Fletcher* has come to stand for the rule that "the defendant will be liable when he damages another by a thing or activity unduly dangerous and inappropriate to the place where it is maintained, in the light of the character of that place and its surroundings." [Citation.]

The basic principle of *Rylands v. Fletcher* has been accepted by the Restatement (Second) of Torts (1977). [Citation.] Section 519 of the Restatement provides that any party carrying on an "abnormally dangerous activity" is strictly liable for ensuing damages. The test for what constitutes such an activity is stated in section 520 of the Restatement. Both Restatement sections have been adopted by this court, and determination of whether an activity is an "abnormally dangerous activity" is a question of law. [Citations.]

Section 520 of the Restatement lists six factors that are to be considered in determining whether an activity is "abnormally dangerous." The factors are as follows: (a) existence of a high degree of risk of some harm to the person, land or chattels of others; (b) likelihood that the harm that results from it will be great; (c) inability to eliminate the risk by the exercise of reasonable care; (d) extent to which the activity is not a matter of common usage; (e) inappropriateness of the activity to the place where it is carried on; and (f) extent to which its value to the community is outweighed by its dangerous attributes.

Restatement (Second) of Torts § 520 (1977). As we previously recognized in [citation], the comments to section 520 explain how these factors should be evaluated:

> Any one of them is not necessarily sufficient of itself in a particular case, and ordinarily several of them will be required for strict liability. On the other hand, it is not necessary that each of them be present, especially if others weigh heavily. Because of the interplay of these various factors, it is not possible to reduce abnormally dangerous activities to any definition. The essential question is whether the risk created is so unusual, either because of its magnitude or because of the circumstances surrounding it, as to justify the imposition of strict liability for the harm that results from it, even though it is carried on with all reasonable care.

Restatement (Second) of Torts § 520, Comment f (1977). Examination of these factors persuades us that fireworks displays are abnormally dangerous activities justifying the imposition of strict liability.

We find that the factors stated in clauses (a), (b), and (c) are all present in the case of fireworks displays. Any time a person ignites aerial shells or rockets with the intention of sending them aloft to explode in the presence of large crowds of people, a high risk of serious personal injury or property damage is created. That risk arises because of the possibility that a shell or rocket will malfunction or be misdirected. Furthermore, no matter how much care pyrotechnicians exercise, they cannot entirely eliminate the high risk inherent in setting off powerful explosives such as fireworks near crowds.

* * *

The factor expressed in clause (d) concerns the extent to which the activity is not a matter "of common usage." The Restatement explains that "[a]n activity is a matter of common usage if it is customarily carried on by the great mass of mankind or by many people in the community." Restatement (Second) of Torts § 520, Comment i (1977). As examples of activities that are not matters of common usage, the Restatement comments offer driving a tank, blasting, the manufacture, storage, transportation, and use of high explosives, and drilling for oil. The deciding characteristic is that few persons engage in these activities. Likewise, relatively few persons conduct public fireworks displays. Therefore, presenting public fireworks displays is not a matter of common usage.

* * *

The factor stated in clause (e) requires analysis of the appropriateness of the activity to the place where it was carried on. In this case, the fireworks display was conducted at the Puyallup Fairgrounds. Although some locations—such as over water—may be safer, the Puyallup Fairgrounds is an appropriate place for a fireworks show because the audience can be seated at a reasonable distance from the display. Therefore, the clause (e) factor is not present in this case.

The factor stated in clause (f) requires analysis of the extent to which the value of fireworks to the community outweighs its dangerous attributes. We do not find that this factor is present here. This country has a long-standing tradition of fireworks on the 4th of July. That tradition suggests that we as a society have decided that the value of fireworks on the day celebrating our national independence and unity outweighs the risks of injuries and damage.

In sum, we find that setting off public fireworks displays satisfies four of the six conditions under the Restatement test; that is, it is an activity that is not "of common usage" and that presents an ineliminably high risk of serious bodily injury or property damage. We therefore hold that conducting public fireworks displays is an abnormally dangerous activity justifying the imposition of strict liability.

* * *

We hold that Pyrodyne Corporation is strictly liable for all damages suffered as a result of the July 1987 fireworks display. Detonating fireworks displays constitutes an abnormally dangerous activity warranting strict liability * * *. This establishes the standard of strict liability for pyrotechnicians. Therefore, we affirm the decision of the trial court.

C A S E 8-6

Keeping of Animals
PALUMBO v. NIKIRK

Supreme Court, Appellate Division, Second Department, New York, 2009
59 A.D.3d 691,874 N.Y.S.2d 222, 2009 N.Y. SLIP OP. 01454

Per Curiam

The plaintiff, a mail carrier, sustained injuries when he allegedly was bitten and attacked by a dog on the front steps of the defendants' house as he attempted to deliver the mail. The plaintiff, who crossed over the defendants' lawn and driveway from the house next door, and whose view of the dog was obstructed by a bush, did not see the dog or hear it bark until he opened the lid of the mailbox and was bitten. [The plaintiff brought an action to recover damages for personal injuries. The Supreme Court, Nassau County, granted the defendants' motion for summary judgment dismissing the complaint. The plaintiff appealed.]

To recover upon a theory of strict liability in tort for a dog bite or attack, a plaintiff must prove that the dog had vicious propensities and that the owner of the dog, or person in control of the premises where the dog was, knew or should have known of such propensities [citations]. "Vicious propensities

include the 'propensity to do any act that might endanger the safety of the persons and property of others in a given situation'" [citations].

Here, the defendants established their *prima facie* entitlement to judgment as a matter of law by presenting evidence that the dog had never bitten, jumped, or growled at anyone prior to the incident in question, nor had the dog exhibited any other aggressive or vicious behavior [citations]. In opposition, the plaintiff failed to come forward with any proof in evidentiary form that the dog had ever previously bitten anyone or exhibited any vicious propensities. Furthermore, the presence of a "Beware of Dog" sign on the premises, the breed of the dog, and the owner's testimony that the dog was always on a leash were insufficient to raise a triable issue of fact as to the dog's vicious propensities in the absence of any evidence that prior to this incident the dog exhibited any fierce or hostile tendencies [citations].

[Summary judgment is affirmed.]

Q U E S T I O N S

1. A statute requiring railroads to fence their tracks is construed as intended solely to prevent animals that stray onto the right-of-way from being hit by trains. B&A Railroad Company fails to fence its tracks. Two of Calvin's cows wander onto the track. Nellie is hit by a train. Elsie is poisoned by weeds growing beside the track. For which cow(s), if any, is B&A Railroad Company liable to Calvin? Why or why not?

2. Martha invites John to come to lunch. Though she knows that her private road is dangerous to travel, having been heavily eroded by recent rains, Martha doesn't warn John of the condition, reasonably believing that he will notice the deep ruts and exercise sufficient care. While John is driving over, his attention is diverted from the road by the screaming of his child, who has been stung by a bee. He fails to notice the condition of the road, hits

a rut, and skids into a tree. If John is not contributorily negligent, is Martha liable to John? Explain.

3. Nathan is run over by a car and left lying in the street. Sam, seeing Nathan's helpless state, places him in his car for the purpose of taking him to the hospital. Sam drives negligently into a ditch, causing additional injury to Nathan. Is Sam liable to Nathan? Discuss.

4. Led Foot drives his car carelessly into another car. The second car contains dynamite, a fact that Led had no way of knowing. The collision causes an explosion, which shatters a window of a building half a block away on another street. The flying glass inflicts serious cuts on Sally, who is working at a desk near the window. The explosion also harms Vic, who is walking on the sidewalk near the point of the collision. Toward whom is Led Foot negligent? Explain.

5. A statute requires all vessels traveling on the Great Lakes to provide lifeboats. One of Winston Steamship Company's boats is sent out of port without a lifeboat. Perry, a sailor, falls overboard in a storm so strong that had there been a lifeboat, it could not have been launched. Perry drowns. Is Winston liable to Perry's estate? Explain.

6. Lionel is negligently driving an automobile at excessive speed. Reginald's negligently driven car crosses the centerline of the highway and scrapes the side of Lionel's car, damaging its fenders. As a result, Lionel loses control of his car, which goes into the ditch. Lionel's car is wrecked, and Lionel suffers personal injuries. What, if anything, can Lionel recover? Explain.

7. Ellen, the owner of a baseball park, is under a duty to the entering public to provide a reasonably sufficient number of screened seats to protect those who desire such protection against the risk of being hit by batted balls. Ellen fails to do so.
   a. Frank, a customer entering the park, is unable to find a screened seat and, although fully aware of the risk, sits in an unscreened seat. Frank is struck and injured by a batted ball. Is Ellen liable? Explain.
   b. Gretchen, Frank's wife, has just arrived from Germany and is viewing baseball for the first time. Without asking any questions, she follows Frank to a seat. After the batted ball hits Frank, it caroms into Gretchen, injuring her. Is Ellen liable to Gretchen? Explain.

8. Negligent in failing to give warning of the approach of its train to a crossing, CC Railroad thereby endangers Larry, a blind man who is about to cross. Mildred, a bystander, in a reasonable effort to save Larry, rushes onto the track to push Larry out of danger. Although Mildred acts as carefully as possible, she is struck and injured by the train.
   a. Can Mildred recover from Larry? Why or why not?
   b. Can Mildred recover from CC Railroad? Why or why not?

9. Vance was served liquor while he was an intoxicated patron of the Clear Air Force Station Non-Commissioned Officers' Club. He later injured himself as a result of his intoxication. An Alaska State statute makes it a crime to give or to sell liquor to intoxicated persons. Vance has brought an action seeking damages for the injuries he suffered. Could Vance successfully argue that the United States was negligent *per se* by its employee's violation of the statute? Explain.

10. Timothy keeps a pet chimpanzee, which is thoroughly tamed and accustomed to playing with its owner's children. The chimpanzee escapes, despite every precaution to keep it upon its owner's premises. It approaches a group of children. Wanda, the mother of one of the children, erroneously thinking the chimpanzee is about to attack the children, rushes to her child's assistance. In her hurry and excitement, she stumbles and falls, breaking her leg. Can Wanda recover for her personal injuries? Explain.

CASE PROBLEMS

11. Hawkins slipped and fell on a puddle of water just inside the automatic door to the H. E. Butt Grocery Company's store. The water had been tracked into the store by customers and blown through the door by a strong wind. The store manager was aware of the puddle and had mopped it up several times earlier in the day. Still, no signs had been placed to warn store patrons of the danger. Hawkins brought an action to recover damages for injuries sustained in the fall. Was the store negligent in its conduct? Discuss.

12. Escola, a waitress, was injured when a bottle of soda exploded in her hand while she was putting it into the restaurant's cooler. The bottle came from a shipment that had remained under the counter for thirty-six hours after being delivered by the bottling company. The bottler had subjected the bottle to the method of testing for defects commonly used in the industry, and there is no evidence that Escola or anyone else did anything to damage the bottle between its delivery and the explosion. Escola brought an action against the bottler for damages. As she

is unable to show any specific acts of negligence on its part, she seeks to rely on the doctrine of *res ipsa loquitur*. Should she be able to recover on this theory? Explain.

13. Hunn injured herself when she slipped and fell on a loose plank while walking down some steps. The night before, while entering the hotel, she had noticed that the steps were dangerous, and although she knew from her earlier stays at the hotel that another exit was available, she chose that morning to leave via the dangerous steps. The hotel was aware of the hazard, as one of the other guests who had fallen that night had reported his accident to the desk clerk then on duty. Still, the hotel did not place cautionary signs on the steps to warn of the danger, and they were not roped off or otherwise excluded from use. Hunn brought an action against the hotel for injuries she sustained as a result of her fall. Should she recover? Explain.

14. Fredericks, a hotel owner, had a dog named "Sport" that he had trained as a watchdog. When Vincent Zarek, a guest at the hotel, leaned over to pet the dog, it bit him. Although Sport had never bitten anyone before, Fredericks was aware of the dog's violent tendencies and, therefore, did not allow it to roam around the hotel alone. Vincent brought an action for injuries sustained when the dog bit him. Is Fredericks liable for the actions of his dog? Explain.

15. Two thugs in an alley in Manhattan held up an unidentified man. When the thieves departed with his possessions, the man quickly gave chase. He had almost caught one when the thief managed to force his way into an empty taxicab stopped at a traffic light. The Peerless Transport Company owned the cab. The thief pointed his gun at the driver's head and ordered him to drive on. The driver started to follow the directions while closely pursued by a posse of good citizens, but then suddenly jammed on the brakes and jumped out of the car to safety. The thief also jumped out, but the car traveled on, injuring Mrs. Cordas and her two children. The Cordases then brought an action for damages, claiming that the cab driver was negligent in jumping to safety and leaving the moving vehicle uncontrolled. Was the cab driver negligent? Explain.

16. A foul ball struck Marie Uzdavines on the head while she was watching the Metropolitan Baseball Club ("The Mets") play the Philadelphia Phillies at the Mets' home stadium in New York. The ball came through a hole in a screen designed to protect spectators sitting behind home plate. The screen contained several holes that had been repaired with baling wire lighter in weight than the wire used in the original screen. Although the manager of the stadium makes no formal inspections of the screen, his employees do try to repair the holes as they find them. Weather conditions, rust deterioration, and baseballs hitting the screen are the chief causes of these holes. The owner of the stadium, the city of New York, leases the stadium to "The Mets" and replaces the entire screen every two years. Uzdavines sued The Mets for negligence under the doctrine of *res ipsa loquitur*. Is this an appropriate case for *res ipsa loquitur*? Explain.

17. Two-year-old David Allen was bitten by Joseph Whitehead's dog while he was playing on the porch at the Allen residence. Allen suffered facial cuts, a severed muscle in his left eye, a hole in his left ear, and scarring over his forehead. Through his father, David sued Whitehead, claiming that, as owner, Whitehead was responsible for his dog's actions. Whitehead admitted that (1) the dog was large, was mean looking, and frequently barked at neighbors; (2) the dog was allowed to roam wild; and (3) the dog frequently chased and barked at cars. He stated, however, that (1) the dog was friendly and often played with his and neighbors' children, (2) he had not received previous complaints about the dog, (3) the dog was neither aggressive nor threatening, and (4) the dog had never bitten anyone before this incident. Is Whitehead liable? Explain.

18. Larry VanEgdom, in an intoxicated state, bought alcoholic beverages from the Hudson Municipal Liquor Store in Hudson, South Dakota. An hour later, VanEgdom, while driving a car, struck and killed Guy William Ludwig, who was stopped on his motorcycle at a stop sign. Lela Walz, as special administrator of Ludwig's estate, brought an action against the city of Hudson, which operated the liquor store, for the wrongful death of Ludwig. Walz alleged that the store employee was negligent in selling intoxicating beverages to VanEgdom when he knew or could have observed that VanEgdom was drunk. Decision? Discuss.

19. The *MacGilvray Shiras* was a ship owned by the Kinsman Transit Company. During the winter months, when Lake Erie was frozen, the ship and others moored at docks on the Buffalo River. As oftentimes happened, one night an ice jam disintegrated upstream, sending large chunks of ice downstream. Chunks of ice began to pile up against the *Shiras*, which at that time was without power and manned only by a shipman. The ship broke loose when a negligently constructed "deadman" to which one mooring cable was attached pulled out of the ground. The "deadman" was operated by Continental Grain Company. The ship began moving down the S-shaped river stern first and struck another ship, the *Tewksbury*. The *Tewksbury* also broke loose from its mooring, and the two ships floated down the river together. Although the crew manning the Michigan Avenue Bridge downstream had been notified

of the runaway ships, they failed to raise the bridge in time to avoid a collision because of a mix-up in the shift changeover. As a result, both ships crashed into the bridge and were wedged against the bank of the river. The two vessels substantially dammed the flow of the river, causing ice and water to back up and flood installations as far as three miles upstream. The injured parties brought this action for damages against Kinsman, Continental, and the city of Buffalo. Who, if any, is liable? Explain.

20. Carolyn Falgout accompanied William Wardlaw as a social guest to Wardlaw's brother's camp. After both parties had consumed intoxicating beverages, Falgout walked onto a pier that was then only partially completed. Wardlaw had requested that she not go on the pier. Falgout said, "Don't tell me what to do" and proceeded to walk on the pier. Wardlaw then asked her not to walk past the completed portion of the pier. She ignored his warnings and walked to the pier's end. When returning to the shore, Falgout got her shoe caught between the boards. She fell, hanging by her foot, with her head and arms in the water. Wardlaw rescued Falgout, who had seriously injured her knee and leg. She sued Wardlaw for negligence. Decision?

21. Joseph Yania, a coal strip-mine owner, and Boyd Ross visited a coal strip-mining operation owned by John Bigan to discuss a business matter with Bigan. On Bigan's property, there were several cuts and trenches he had dug to remove the coal underneath. While Yania and Ross were there, Bigan asked the two men to help him pump water from one of these cuts in the earth. This particular cut contained water eight to ten feet in depth with sidewalls or embankments sixteen to eighteen feet in height. The two men agreed, and the process began with Ross and Bigan entering the cut and standing at the point where the pump was located. Yania stood at

the top of one of the cut's sidewalls. Apparently, Bigan taunted Yania into jumping into the water from the top of the sidewall—a height of sixteen to eighteen feet. As a result, Yania drowned. His widow brought a negligence action against Bigan. She claims that Bigan was negligent "(1) by urging, enticing, taunting, and inveigling Yania to jump into the water; (2) by failing to warn Yania of a dangerous condition on the land; and (3) by failing to go to Yania's rescue after he jumped into the water." Was Bigan negligent? Explain.

22. Old Island Fumigation, Inc., fumigated buildings A and B of a condominium complex using Vikane gas. Buildings A and B, together with building C, form a U shape; buildings B and C have between them an atrium and were thought to be separated by an impenetrable fire wall. Although Old Island evacuated occupants of buildings A and B before the fumigation, the company advised the occupants of building C that they could remain in their dwellings while the other buildings were treated. Several residents of building C became ill shortly after the Vikane gas was released into the adjacent buildings. The hospital admission forms indicate that the cause of their illnesses was sulfuryl fluoride poisoning. Sulfuryl fluoride is the active chemical ingredient of Vikane. Several months after this incident, an architect hired by the fumigation company discovered that the fire wall between buildings B and C was defective and contained a four-foot-by-eighteen-inch open space through which the gas had entered building C. The defect was only visible from a vantage point within the crawl space and had been missed by various building inspectors and by the fumigation company during an earlier inspection. The occupants of building C who had been injured by the Vikane fumes sued the fumigator. Explain whether the fumigator is strictly liable.

TAKING SIDES

Rebecca S. Dukat arrived at Mockingbird Lanes, a bowling alley in Omaha, Nebraska, at approximately 6:00 P.M. to bowl in her league game. The bowling alley's parking lot and adjacent sidewalk were covered with snow and ice. Dukat proceeded to walk into the bowling alley on the only sidewalk provided in and out of the building. She testified that she noticed the sidewalk was icy. After bowling three games and drinking three beers, Dukat left the bowling alley at approximately 9:00 P.M. She retraced her steps on the same sidewalk, which was still covered with ice and in a condition that, according to Frank Jameson, general manager of Mockingbird Lanes, was "unacceptable" if the bowling alley was open to customers. As Dukat proceeded along the

sidewalk to her car, she slipped, attempted to catch herself by reaching toward a car, and fell. She suffered a fracture of both bones in her left ankle as well as a ruptured ligament. Dukat sued Mockingbird Lanes, seeking damages for her for personal injuries. Mockingbird denied liability for Dukat's personal injuries.

a. What arguments would support Dukat's claim for her personal injuries?

b. What arguments would support Mockingbird's denial of liability for Dukat's personal injuries?

c. Which side should prevail? Explain.

Contracts

CH 9 INTRODUCTION TO CONTRACTS

CH 10 MUTUAL ASSENT

CH 11 CONDUCT INVALIDATING ASSENT

CH 12 CONSIDERATION

CH 13 ILLEGAL BARGAINS

CH 14 CONTRACTUAL CAPACITY

CH 15 CONTRACTS IN WRITING

CH 16 THIRD PARTIES TO CONTRACTS

CH 17 PERFORMANCE, BREACH, AND DISCHARGE

CH 18 CONTRACT REMEDIES

CHAPTER 9

Introduction to Contracts

After reading and studying this chapter, you should be able to:

- Distinguish between contracts that are covered by the Uniform Commercial Code and those covered by the common law.

- List the essential elements of a contract.

- Distinguish among (1) express and implied contracts; (2) unilateral and bilateral contracts; (3) valid, void, voidable, and unenforceable agreements; and (4) executed and executory contracts.

- Explain the doctrine of promissory estoppel.

- Explain how the three elements of enforceable quasi contract differ from the requirements of a contract.

It is impossible to overestimate the importance of contracts in the field of business. Every business, whether large or small, must enter into contracts with its employees, its suppliers, and its customers to conduct its business operations. Contract law is, therefore, an important subject for the business manager. Contract law is also basic to other fields of law treated in other parts of this book, such as agency, partnerships, corporations, sales of personal property, negotiable instruments, and secured transactions.

Even the most common transaction may involve a multitude of contracts. For example, in a typical contract for the sale of land, the seller promises to transfer title to the land and the buyer promises to pay an agreed-upon purchase price. In addition, the seller may promise to pay certain taxes or assessments; the buyer may promise to assume a mortgage on the property or may promise to pay the purchase price to a creditor of the seller. If attorneys represent the parties, they very likely do so on a contractual basis. If the seller deposits the proceeds of the sale in a bank, he enters into a contract with the bank. If the buyer leases the property, he enters into a contract with the tenant. When one of the parties leaves his car in a parking lot to attend to any of these matters, he assumes a contractual relationship with the proprietor of the lot. In short, nearly every business transaction is based upon contract and the expectations the agreed-upon promises create. Knowing the legal requirements for making binding contracts is, therefore, essential.

9-1 Development of the Law of Contracts

That law arises from social necessity is clearly true of the law of contracts. The vast and complicated institution of business can be conducted efficiently and successfully only upon the certainty that promises will be fulfilled. Business must be assured not only of supplies of raw materials or manufactured goods but also of labor, management, capital, and insurance. Common experience has shown that promises based solely on personal honesty or integrity do not have the reliability essential to business. This experience has driven the development of the law of contracts, which is the law of enforceable promises.

Contract law, like law as a whole, is not static. It has undergone—and is still undergoing—enormous changes. In the nineteenth century, virtually absolute autonomy in forming contracts was the rule. The law imposed contract liability only where the parties strictly complied with the required formalities. The same principle also dictated that once a contract was formed, it should be enforced according to its terms and that neither party should be lightly excused from performance.

During the twentieth century, many of the formalities of contract formation were relaxed, and as a result, the law generally recognizes contractual obligations whenever the parties clearly manifest an intent to be bound. In addition, an increasing number of promises are now enforced in certain circumstances, even though they do not comply strictly with the basic requirements of a contract. While in the past contract liability was absolute and escape from liability, once assumed, was rare, presently the law allows a party to be excused from contractual duties where fraud, duress, undue influence, mistake, unconscionability, or impossibility is present. The law has expanded the nineteenth century's narrow view of contract damages to grant equitable remedies and restitution as remedies for breach of contract. The older doctrine of privity of contract, which sharply restricted which parties could enforce contract rights, has given way to the current view that permits intended third-party beneficiaries to sue in their own right.

In brief, the twentieth century left its mark on contract law by limiting the absolute freedom of contract and, at the same time, by relaxing the requirements of contract formation. Accordingly, it is now considerably easier to get into a contract and correspondingly less difficult to get out of one.

9-1a COMMON LAW

Contracts are primarily governed by State common law. As mentioned in *Chapter 1*, the Restatements, prepared by the American Law Institute (ALI), present many important areas of the common law, including contracts. Although the Restatements are not law in themselves, they are highly persuasive in the courts. An orderly presentation of the common law of contracts is found in the Restatements of the Law of Contracts, valuable authoritative reference works extensively relied on and quoted in reported judicial opinions. The ALI adopted and promulgated the first Restatement on May 6, 1932. Between 1959 and 1981, the ALI adopted and promulgated a second edition of the Restatement of the Law of Contracts, which revised and superseded the first Restatement of the Law of Contracts. This book refers to the second Restatement of the Law of Contracts simply as the "Restatement."

There are two principal types of contracts: (1) business-to-business contracts (commercial contracts) and (2) business-to-consumer contracts (consumer contracts). The common law and the Restatement generally apply the same rules to both commercial and consumer contracts. (The Uniform Commercial Code's Article 2, discussed in the following paragraphs, for the most part also does not distinguish between sales of goods to consumers and sales between commercial parties.)

In 2012, the ALI began a new project: the Restatement of the Law of Consumer Contracts. This new project focuses on the rules of contract law that treat consumer contracts differently from commercial contracts. It includes regulatory rules that are prominently applied in consumer protection law. The project covers common law as well as statutory and regulatory law. It draws on the Restatement Second of Contracts, the Uniform Commercial Code, and court opinions in cases involving disputes between businesses and consumers. A draft of the entire project was presented for discussion at the ALI Annual Meeting in May 2017. In 2019, Section 1 (Definitions and Scope) was approved.

9-1b THE UNIFORM COMMERCIAL CODE

The sale of personal property forms a substantial portion of commercial activity. Article 2 of the Uniform Commercial Code (the Code, or UCC) governs sales in all States except Louisiana. A *sale* consists of the passing of title to goods from a seller to a buyer for a price. Section 2-106. A contract for sale includes both a present sale of goods and a contract to sell goods at a future time. Section 2-106. The Code essentially defines goods as movable personal property. Section 2-105(1). **Personal property** is any type of property other than an interest in real property (land). For example, the purchase of a television, automobile, or textbook is considered a sale of goods. All such transactions are governed by Article 2 of the Code, but in cases in which the Code has not specifically modified general contract law, the common law of contracts continues to apply. Section 1-103. In other words, the law of sales is a specialized part of the general law of contracts, and the law of contracts governs unless specifically displaced by the Code.

Amendments to Article 2 were promulgated in 2003 to accommodate electronic commerce and to reflect development of business practices, changes in other law, and interpretive difficulties of practical significance. Because no States had adopted them and prospects for enactment in the near future were bleak, the 2003 amendments to UCC Articles 2 and 2A were withdrawn in 2011. However, the 2001 Revisions to Article 1, which applies to all the articles of the Code, have been adopted by all States.

◆ **SEE FIGURE 9-1:** *Law Governing Contracts*

◆ *See Case 21-2*

9-1c TYPES OF CONTRACTS OUTSIDE THE CODE

General contract law governs all contracts outside the scope of the Code. Such contracts play a significant role in commercial activities. For example, the Code does not apply to employment contracts, service contracts, insurance contracts, contracts involving **real property** (land and anything attached to it, including buildings as well as any right, privilege, or power in the real property, including leases, mortgages, options, and easements), and contracts for the sale of intangibles such as patents and copyrights. These transactions continue to be governed by general contract law.

◆ *See Case 9-1*

9-1d INTERNATIONAL CONTRACTS

The legal issues inherent in domestic contracts also arise in international contracts. Moreover, certain additional issues, such as differences in language, customs, legal systems, and currency, are peculiar to international contracts. An international contract should specify its official language and define

FIGURE 9-1 Law Governing Contracts

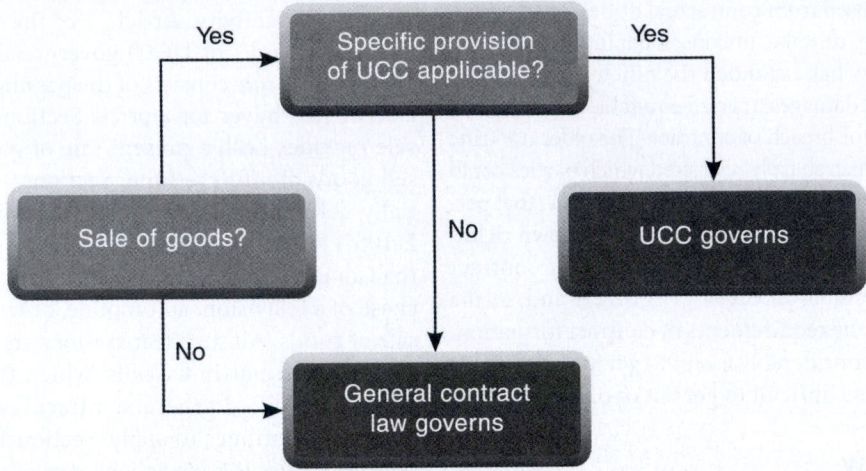

all of the significant legal terms it incorporates. In addition, it should specify the acceptable currency (or currencies) and payment method. The contract should include a choice of law clause designating what law will govern any breach or dispute regarding the contract and a choice of forum clause designating whether the parties will resolve disputes through one nation's court system or through third-party arbitration. (The United Nations Committee on International Trade Law and the International Chamber of Commerce have promulgated arbitration rules that have won broad international acceptance.) Finally, the contract should include a *force majeure* (unavoidable superior force) clause apportioning the liabilities and responsibilities of the parties in the event of an unforeseeable occurrence, such as a typhoon, tornado, flood, earthquake, nuclear disaster, or war, including civil war.

The United Nations Convention on Contracts for the International Sales of Goods (CISG), which has been ratified by the United States and at least ninety-three other countries, governs all contracts for the international sales of goods between parties located in different nations that have ratified the CISG. Because treaties are Federal law, the CISG supersedes the Uniform Commercial Code in any situation to which either could apply. The CISG includes provisions dealing with interpretation, trade usage, contract formation, obligations, remedies of sellers and buyers, and risk of loss. Parties to an international sales contract may, however, expressly exclude CISG governance from their contract. The CISG specifically excludes sales of (1) goods bought for personal, family, or household use; (2) ships or aircraft; and (3) electricity. In addition, it does not apply to contracts in which the primary obligation of the party furnishing the goods consists of supplying labor or services. The CISG is covered in *Chapters 21* through *25*.

9-2 Definition of a Contract

A **contract** is a binding agreement that the courts will enforce. Section 1 of the Restatement more precisely defines a contract as "a promise or a set of promises for the breach of which the law gives a remedy, or the performance of which the law in some way recognizes as a duty." The Restatement provides further insight by defining a *promise* as "a manifestation of the intention to act or refrain from acting in a specified way." Restatement, Section 2.

Those promises that meet all of the essential requirements of a binding contract are contractual and will be enforced. All other promises are not contractual, and usually no legal remedy is available for a **breach** (a failure to perform properly) of these promises. The remedies provided for breach of contract (discussed in *Chapter 18*) include compensatory damages, equitable remedies, reliance damages, and restitution. Thus, a promise may be contractual (and therefore binding) or noncontractual. In other words, all contracts are promises, but not all promises are contracts.

◆ **SEE FIGURE 9-2:** *Contractual and Noncontractual Promises*

◆ *See Case 9-2*

9-3 Requirements of a Contract

The four basic requirements of a contract are as follows:

1. **Mutual assent**. The parties to a contract must manifest by words or conduct that they have agreed to enter into a contract. The usual method of showing mutual assent is by offer and acceptance.

FIGURE 9-2 **Contractual and Noncontractual Promises**

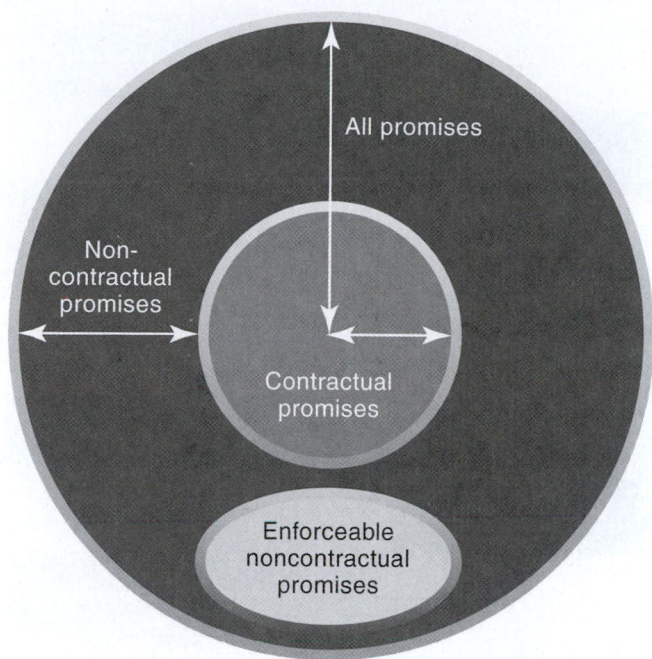

2. **Consideration**. Each party to a contract must intentionally exchange a legal benefit or incur a legal detriment as an inducement to the other party to make a return exchange.

3. **Legality of object**. The purpose of a contract must not be criminal, tortious, or otherwise against public policy.

4. **Capacity**. The parties to a contract must have contractual capacity. Certain persons, such as those adjudicated (judicially declared) incompetent, have no legal capacity to contract, whereas others, such as minors, incompetent persons, and intoxicated persons, have limited capacity to contract. All others have full contractual capacity.

In addition, though in some cases a contract must be evidenced by a writing to be enforceable, in most cases, an oral contract is binding and enforceable. If all of these essentials are present, the promise is contractual and legally binding. If any is absent, however, the promise is noncontractual. These requirements are considered separately in succeeding chapters.

◆ SEE FIGURE 9-3: *Validity of Agreements*

◆ *See Case 9-2*

9-4 Classification of Contracts

Contracts can be classified according to various characteristics, such as method of formation, content, and legal effect. The standard classifications are (1) express or implied contracts;

(2) bilateral or unilateral contracts; (3) valid, void, voidable, or unenforceable contracts; (4) executed or executory contracts; and (5) formal or informal contracts. These classifications are not mutually exclusive. For example, a contract may be express, bilateral, valid, executory, and informal.

9-4a EXPRESS AND IMPLIED CONTRACTS

Parties to a contract may indicate their assent either by express language or by conduct that implies such willingness. Thus, a contract may be (1) entirely oral, (2) partly oral and partly written, (3) entirely written, (4) partly oral or written and partly implied from the conduct of the parties, and (5) wholly implied from the conduct of the parties. The first three are known as express contracts; the last two, as implied contracts. Both express and implied contracts are genuine contracts, equally enforceable. The difference between them is merely the manner in which the parties manifest assent.

An **express contract** is therefore one in which the parties have manifested their agreement by oral or written language or both.

An **implied contract** is one that is inferred from the parties' conduct, not from spoken or written words. Implied contracts are also called implied in fact contracts. Thus, if Elizabeth orders and receives a meal in Bill's restaurant, a promise is implied on Elizabeth's part to pay Bill the price stated in the menu or, if none is stated, Bill's customary price. Likewise, when a passenger boards a bus, a wholly implied contract is

FIGURE 9-3   Validity of Agreements

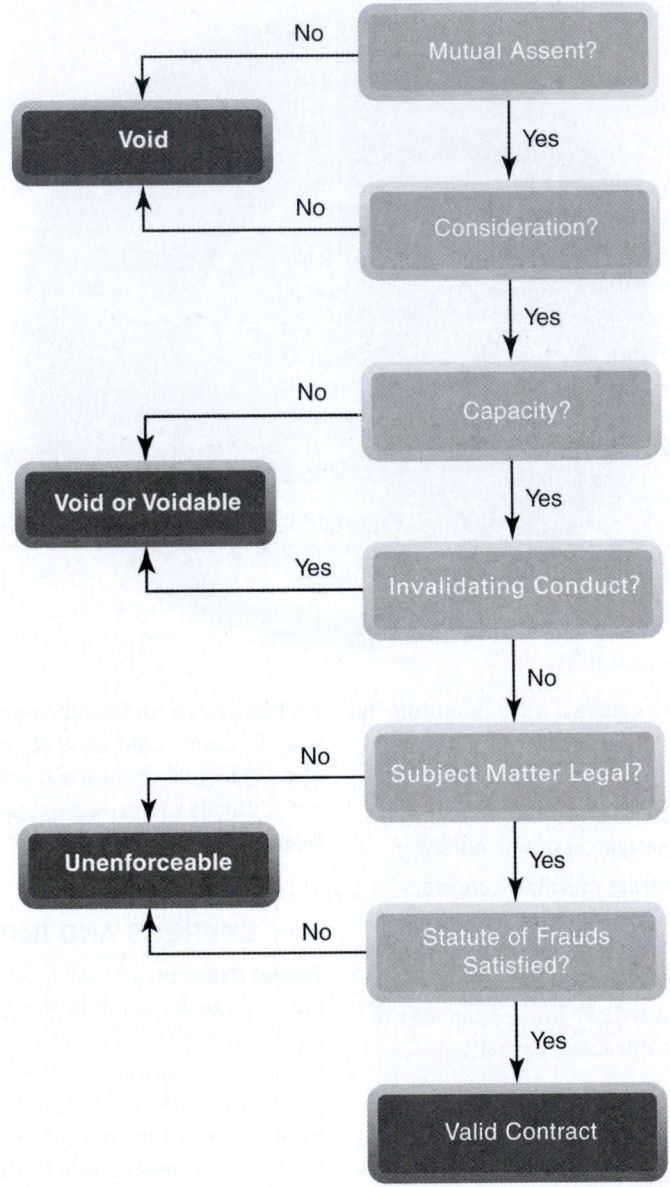

formed by which the passenger undertakes to pay the customary fare and the bus company undertakes to provide the passenger transportation.

◆ *See Case 9-1*

Practical Advice

Whenever possible, try to use written express contracts that specify all of the important terms rather than using implied in fact contracts.

9-4b BILATERAL AND UNILATERAL CONTRACTS

In the typical contractual transaction, each party makes at least one promise. For example, if Ali says to Ben, "If you promise to mow my lawn, I will pay you ten dollars" and Ben agrees to mow Ali's lawn, Ali and Ben have made mutual promises, each undertaking to do something in exchange for the promise of the other. When a contract comes into existence by the exchange of promises, each party is under a duty to the other. This kind of contract is called a **bilateral contract**, because each party is both a *promisor* (a person making a promise) and a *promisee* (the person to whom a promise is made).

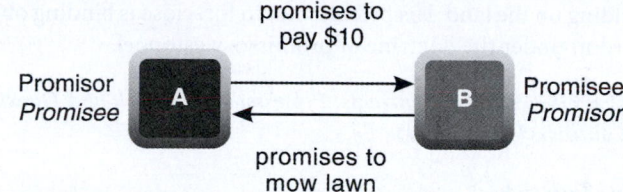

But suppose that only one of the parties makes a promise. Ali says to Ben, "If you will mow my lawn, I will pay you ten dollars." A contract will be formed when Ben has finished mowing the lawn and not before. At that time, Ali becomes contractually obligated to pay $10.00 to Ben. Ali's offer was in exchange for Ben's act of mowing the lawn, not for his promise to mow it. Because he never made a promise to mow the lawn, Ben was under no duty to mow it. This is a **unilateral contract** because only one of the parties made a promise.

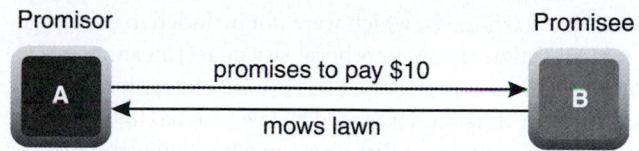

Thus, whereas a bilateral contract results from the exchange of a promise for a return promise, a unilateral contract results from the exchange of a promise either for an act or for a forbearance (refraining) from acting. If a contract is not clearly unilateral or bilateral, the courts presume that the parties intended a bilateral contract. Thus, in the previous example, if Ali says to Ben, "I will pay you ten dollars if you will mow my lawn" and Ben replies, "OK, I will mow your lawn," a bilateral contract is formed.

Practical Advice

Because it is uncertain whether the offeree in a unilateral contract will choose to perform, use bilateral contracts wherever possible.

9-4c VALID, VOID, VOIDABLE, AND UNENFORCEABLE CONTRACTS

By definition, a **valid contract** is one that meets all of the requirements of a binding contract. It is an enforceable promise or agreement.

A **void contract** is an agreement that does not meet all of the requirements of a binding contract. Thus, it is no contract at all; it is merely a promise or an agreement having no legal effect. An example of a void agreement is an agreement entered into by an adjudicated incompetent.

A voidable contract, on the other hand, is not wholly lacking in legal effect. A **voidable contract** is a contract, but because of the manner in which it was formed or a lack of capacity of a party to it, the law permits one or more of the parties to avoid the legal duties the contract creates. Restatement, Section 7. If the contract is avoided, both parties are relieved of their legal duties under the agreement. For instance, through intentional misrepresentation of a material fact (*fraud*), Thomas induces Regina to enter into a contract. Regina may, upon discovery of the fraud, notify Thomas that by reason of the misrepresentation, she will not perform her promise, and the law will support Regina. Though not void, the contract induced by fraud is voidable at the election of Regina, the defrauded party. Thomas, the fraudulent party, has no such election. If Regina elects to avoid the contract, Thomas will be released from his promise under the agreement, although he may be liable under tort law for damages for fraud.

A contract that is neither void nor voidable may, nonetheless, be unenforceable. An **unenforceable contract** is one for the breach of which the law provides no remedy. Restatement, Section 8. For example, a contract may be unenforceable because of a failure to satisfy the requirements of the Statute of Frauds, which requires certain kinds of contracts to be evidenced by a writing to be enforceable. Also, the running of the time within which a suit may be filed, as provided in the Statute of Limitations, bars the right to bring a lawsuit for breach of contract. After that period has run, the contract is referred to as unenforceable, rather than void or voidable.

Practical Advice

Be careful to avoid entering into void, voidable, and unenforceable contracts.

9-4d EXECUTED AND EXECUTORY CONTRACTS

The terms *executed* and *executory* pertain to the state of performance of a contract. A contract fully performed by all of the parties to it is an **executed contract**. Strictly, an executed contract is in the present tense no contract, as all duties under it have been performed; but it is useful to have a term for a completed contract. (The word *executed* is also used to mean "signed," as in to execute or sign a certain document.)

The term **executory**, which means "unperformed," applies to situations in which one or more promises by any party to the contract are as yet unperformed or where the contract is wholly unperformed by one or more of the parties. Thus, David and Carla make a contract under which David is to sell and deliver certain goods to Carla in ten days and Carla is to pay the agreed price in thirty days. Prior to the delivery of the goods by David on the tenth day, the contract is wholly executory. Upon David's delivery of the goods to Carla, the contract is executed as to David and executory as to Carla. When Carla duly pays for the goods, the contract is wholly executed and thereby completely fulfilled.

9-4e FORMAL AND INFORMAL CONTRACTS

A **formal contract** depends upon a particular form, or mode of expression, for its legal existence. For example, at common law, a promise under seal (a particular symbol that serves to authenticate an instrument) is enforceable without anything more. Another formal contract is a negotiable instrument, such as a check, which has certain legal attributes resulting solely from the special form in which it is made. A letter of credit (a promise to honor drafts or other demands for payment) is also a formal contract. Recognizances, or formal acknowledgments of indebtedness made in court, are another example of formal contracts. All other contracts, whether oral or written, are simple or **informal contracts**, as they do not depend upon formality for their legal validity.

9-5 Promissory Estoppel

As a general rule, promises are unenforceable if they do not meet all the requirements of a contract. Nevertheless, to avoid injustice, in certain circumstances, courts enforce noncontractual promises under the doctrine of promissory estoppel. A noncontractual promise is enforceable when it is made under circumstances that should lead the promisor reasonably to expect that the promise would induce the promisee to take definite and substantial action or forbearance in reliance on the promise and the promisee does take such action or forbearance. See *Figure 9-2*. Section 90 of the Restatement provides:

> A promise which the promisor should reasonably expect to induce action or forbearance on the part of the promisee or a third person and which does induce such action or forbearance is binding if injustice can be avoided only by enforcement of the promise. The remedy granted for breach may be limited as justice requires.

For example, Gordon promises Constance not to foreclose for a period of six months on a mortgage Gordon owns on Constance's land. Constance then expends $100,000 to construct a building on the land. His promise not to foreclose is binding on Gordon under the doctrine of promissory estoppel.

◆ SEE FIGURE 9-4: *Contracts, Promissory Estoppel, and Quasi Contracts (Restitution)*

◆ *See Case 9-3*

Practical Advice

Take care not to make promises on which others may detrimentally rely.

9-6 Quasi Contracts or Restitution

In addition to implied in fact contracts, there are implied in law, or quasi, contracts, which were not included in the foregoing classification of contracts because a quasi (meaning "as if") contract is not a contract at all but is based in restitution. **Restitution** is an obligation imposed by law to avoid injustice. The basic rule of restitution is that a person who is unjustly enriched at the expense of another is subject to liability in restitution, which usually requires the unjustly enriched person to restore the benefit received or pay money in an amount necessary to eliminate the unjust enrichment. In 2011, the ALI promulgated the Restatement (Third) of Restitution and Unjust Enrichment, which will be referred to as the "Restatement of Restitution."

Restitution is *not* a contract because it is based on neither an express nor an implied promise. Rather, restitution is an independent basis of liability, in addition to contract or tort liability. The comments to the Restatement of Restitution explain:

> Restitution is the law of nonconsensual and nonbargained benefits in the same way that torts is the law of nonconsensual and nonlicensed harms. Both subjects deal with the consequences of transactions in which the parties have not specified for themselves what the

FIGURE 9-4	Contracts, Promissory Estoppel, and Quasi Contracts (Restitution)		
	Contract	**Promissory Estoppel**	**Quasi Contract (Restitution)**
Type of Promise	Contractual	Noncontractual	None Void Unenforceable Invalidated
Requirements	All of the essential elements of a contract	Detrimental and justifiable reliance	Benefit conferred and knowingly accepted
Remedies	Equitable Compensatory Reliance Restitution	Promise enforced to the extent necessary to avoid injustice	Reasonable value of benefit conferred

consequences of their interaction should be…. [T]he law of restitution identifies those circumstances in which a person is liable for benefits received, measuring liability by the extent of the benefit.

For example, Anna by mistake delivers to Robert a plain, unaddressed envelope containing $100 intended for Claudia. Robert is under no contractual obligation to return it. However, Anna is permitted to recover the $100 from Robert. The law imposes a quasi-contractual obligation of restitution upon Robert to prevent his unjust enrichment at Anna's expense. The elements of such a recovery are (1) a benefit conferred upon the defendant (Robert) by the plaintiff (Anna), (2) an appreciation or knowledge by the defendant (Robert) of the benefit, and (3) acceptance or retention by the defendant (Robert) of the benefit under circumstances rendering inequitable the defendant's (Robert's) retention of the benefit without compensating the plaintiff for its value.

The law of restitution provides a remedy when the parties have entered into a void contract, an unenforceable contract, or a voidable contract that is avoided. In such a case, the law of restitution will determine the recovery permitted for any performance rendered by the parties under the invalid, unenforceable, or invalidated agreement. Restitution also provides a remedy for the breach of a contractual obligation as discussed in *Chapter 18*.

♦ **SEE FIGURE 9-4:** *Contracts, Promissory Estoppel, and Quasi Contracts (Restitution)*

♦ *See Case 9-4*

C H A P T E R   S U M M A R Y

DEVELOPMENT OF THE LAW OF CONTRACTS	**Common Law** most contracts are governed primarily by State common law, including contracts involving employment, services, insurance, real property (land and anything attached to it), patents, and copyrights **Uniform Commercial Code** (UCC) Article 2 of the UCC governs the sales of goods • *Sale* the transfer of title from seller to buyer • *Goods* tangible personal property (personal property is all property other than an interest in land) **International Contracts** involve additional issues beyond those in domestic contracts, such as differences in language, legal systems, and currency; the United Nations Convention on Contracts for the International Sales of Goods (CISG) governs all contracts for international sales of goods between parties located in different nations that have ratified the CISG
DEFINITION OF A CONTRACT	**Contract** binding agreement that the courts will enforce **Breach** failure to perform a contractual obligation properly
REQUIREMENTS OF A CONTRACT	**Mutual Assent** the parties to a contract must manifest by words or conduct that they have agreed to enter into a contract **Consideration** each party to a contract must intentionally exchange a legal benefit or incur a legal detriment as an inducement to the other party to make a return exchange **Legality of Object** the purpose of a contract must not be criminal, tortious, or otherwise against public policy **Capacity** the parties to a contract must have contractual capacity
CLASSIFICATION OF CONTRACTS	**Express and Implied Contracts** • *Express Contract* an agreement that is stated in words, either orally or in writing • *Implied in Fact Contract* a contract in which the agreement of the parties is inferred from their conduct

Bilateral and Unilateral Contracts

- *Bilateral Contract* a contract in which both parties exchange promises
- *Unilateral Contract* a contract in which only one party makes a promise

Valid, Void, Voidable, and Unenforceable Contracts

- *Valid Contract* one that meets all of the requirements of a binding contract
- *Void Contract* no contract at all; without legal effect
- *Voidable Contract* a contract capable of being made void
- *Unenforceable Contract* a contract for the breach of which the law provides no remedy

Executed and Executory Contracts

- *Executed Contract* a contract that has been fully performed by all of the parties
- *Executory Contract* a contract that has yet to be fully performed

Formal and Informal Contracts

- *Formal Contract* an agreement that is legally binding because of its particular form or mode of expression
- *Informal Contracts* all contracts other than formal contracts

---

PROMISSORY ESTOPPEL

Definition a doctrine enforcing some noncontractual promises

Requirements a promise made under circumstances that should lead the promisor reasonably to expect that the promise would induce the promisee to take definite and substantial action and the promisee does take such action

Remedy a court will enforce the promise to the extent necessary to avoid injustice

---

QUASI CONTRACTS OR RESTITUTION

Definition an obligation not based on a contract that is imposed to avoid injustice; also called an implied in law contract

Requirements a court will impose a quasi contract or restitution when (1) the plaintiff confers a benefit upon the defendant, (2) the defendant knows or appreciates the benefit, and (3) the defendant's retention of the benefit is inequitable

Remedy the plaintiff recovers the reasonable value of the benefit she conferred upon the defendant

---

C A S E S

CASE 9-1

Contracts Outside the Code/Express and Implied Contracts
FOX v. MOUNTAIN WEST ELECTRIC, INC.
Supreme Court of Idaho, 2002
137 Idaho 703, 52 P.3d 848 2002; rehearing denied, 2002

Walters, J.

Lockheed Martin Idaho Technical Company ("LMITCO") requested bids for a comprehensive fire alarm system in its twelve buildings located in Idaho Falls. At a prebid meeting, MWE [Mountain West Electric, Inc.] and Fox met and discussed working together on the project. MWE was in the business of installing electrical wiring, conduit and related hookups and attachments. Fox provided services in designing, drafting, testing and assisting in the installation of fire alarm systems, and in ordering specialty equipment necessary for such projects. The parties concluded that it would be more advantageous for them to work together on the project than for each of them to bid separately for the entire job, and they further agreed that Fox would work under MWE. The parties prepared a document defining each of their roles entitled "Scope and Responsibilities."

Fox prepared a bid for the materials and services that he would provide, which was incorporated into MWE's bid to LMITCO. MWE was the successful bidder and was awarded the LMITCO fixed price contract. In May 1996, Fox began performing various services at the direction of MWE's manager. During the course of the project, many changes and modifications to the LMITCO contract were made.

A written contract was presented to Fox by MWE on August 7, 1996. A dispute between MWE and Fox arose over the procedure for the compensation of the change orders. MWE proposed a flow-down procedure, whereby Fox would receive whatever compensation LMITCO decided to pay MWE. This was unacceptable to Fox. Fox suggested a bidding procedure to which MWE objected. On December 5, 1996, Fox met with MWE to discuss the contract. No compensation arrangement was agreed upon by the parties with respect to change orders. Fox left the project on December 9, 1996, after delivering the remaining equipment and materials to MWE. MWE contracted with Life Safety Systems ("LSS") to complete the LMITCO project.

Fox filed a complaint in July 1998 seeking monetary damages representing money due and owing for materials and services provided by Fox on behalf of MWE. MWE answered and counterclaimed seeking monetary damages resulting from the alleged breach of the parties' agreement by Fox.

Following a court trial, the district court found that an implied-in-fact contract existed between the parties based on the industry standard's flow-down method of compensation. The court found in favor of MWE … Fox appeals.

* * *

Implied-in-Fact Contract

* * *

This Court has recognized three types of contractual relationships:

> First is the express contract wherein the parties expressly agree regarding a transaction. Secondly, there is the implied in fact contract wherein there is no express agreement, but the conduct of the parties implies an agreement from which an obligation in contract exists. The third category is called an implied in law contract, or quasi contract. However, a contract implied in law is not a contract at all, but an obligation imposed by law for the purpose of bringing about justice and equity without reference to the intent or the agreement of the parties and, in some cases, in spite of an agreement between the parties. It is a noncontractual obligation that is to be treated procedurally as if it were a contract, and is often refered (sic) to as quasi contract, unjust enrichment, implied in law contract or restitution.

[Citation.]
"An implied in fact contract is defined as one where the terms and existence of the contract are manifested by the conduct of the parties with the request of one party and the performance by the other often being inferred from the circumstances attending the performance." [Citation.] The implied-in-fact contract is grounded in the parties' agreement and tacit understanding. [Citation.] * * *

[UCC §] 1-205(1) defines "course of dealing" as "a sequence of previous conduct between the parties to a particular transaction which is fairly to be regarded as establishing a common basis of understanding for interpreting their expressions and other conduct."

* * *

Although the procedure was the same for each change order, in that MWE would request a pricing from Fox for the work, which was then presented to LMITCO, each party treated the pricings submitted by Fox for the change orders in a different manner. This treatment is not sufficient to establish a meeting of the minds or to establish a course of dealing when there was no "common basis of understanding for interpreting [the parties'] expressions" under [UCC §] 1-205(1).

* * * After a review of the record, it appears that the district court's findings are supported by substantial and competent, albeit conflicting, evidence. This Court will not substitute its view of the facts for the view of the district court.

Using the district court's finding that pricings submitted by Fox were used by MWE as estimates for the change orders, the conclusion made by the district court that an implied-in-fact contract allowed for the reasonable compensation of Fox logically follows and is grounded in the law in Idaho. [Citation.]

This Court holds that the district court did not err in finding that there was an implied-in-fact contract using the industry standard's flow-down method of compensation for the change orders rather than a series of fixed price contracts between MWE and Fox.

Uniform Commercial Code

Fox contends that the district court erred by failing to consider previous drafts of the proposed contract between the parties to determine the terms of the parties' agreement. Fox argues the predominant factor of this transaction was the fire alarm system, not the methodology of how the system was installed, which would focus on the sale of goods and, therefore, the Uniform Commercial Code ("UCC") should govern. Fox argues that in using the UCC various terms were agreed upon by the parties in the prior agreement drafts, including terms for the timing of payments, payments to Fox's suppliers and prerequisites to termination.

MWE contends that the UCC should not be used, despite the fact that goods comprised one-half of the contract price, because the predominant factor at issue is services and not the sale of goods. MWE points out that the primary issue is the value of Fox's services under the change orders and the cost of obtaining replacement services after Fox left the job.

MWE further argues that the disagreement between the parties over material terms should prevent the court from using UCC gap fillers. Rather, MWE contends the intent and relationship of the parties should be used to resolve the conflict.

This Court in [citation], pointed out "in determining whether the UCC applies in such cases, a majority of courts look at the entire transaction to determine which aspect, the sale of goods or the sale of services, predominates." [Citation.] It is clear that if the underlying transaction to the contract involved the sale of goods, the UCC would apply. [Citation.] However, if the contract only involved services, the UCC would not apply. [Citation.] This Court has not directly articulated the standard to be used in mixed sales of goods and services, otherwise known as hybrid transactions.

The Court of Appeals in *Pittsley v. Houser*, [citation], focused on the applicability of the UCC to hybrid transactions. The court held that the trial court must look at the predominant factor of the transaction to determine if the UCC applies. [Citation.]

> The test for inclusion or exclusion is not whether they are mixed, but, granting that they are mixed, whether their predominant factor, their thrust, their purpose, reasonably stated, is the rendition of service, with goods incidentally involved (e.g., contract with artist for painting) or is a transaction of sale, with labor incidentally involved (e.g., installation of a water heater in a bathroom). This test essentially involves consideration of the contract in its entirety, applying the UCC to the entire contract or not at all.

[Citation.] This Court agrees with the Court of Appeals' analysis and holds that the predominant factor test should be used to determine whether the UCC applies to transactions involving the sale of both goods and services.

One aspect that the Court of Appeals noted in its opinion in *Pittsley*, in its determination that the predominant factor in that case was the sale of goods, was that the purchaser was more concerned with the goods and less concerned with the installation, either who would provide it or the nature of the work. MWE and Fox decided to work on this project together because of their differing expertise. MWE was in the business of installing electrical wiring, while Fox designed, tested and assisted in the installation of fire alarm systems, in addition to ordering specialty equipment for fire alarm projects.

The district court found that the contract at issue in this case contained both goods and services; however, the predominant factor was Fox's services. The district court found that the goods provided by Fox were merely incidental to the services he provided, and the UCC would provide no assistance in interpreting the parties' agreement.

This Court holds that the district court did not err in finding that the predominant factor of the underlying transaction was services and that the UCC did not apply.

* * *

This Court affirms the decision of the district court.

CASE 9-2	Definition and Requirements of a Contract **STEINBERG v. CHICAGO MEDICAL SCHOOL** Illinois Court of Appeals, 1976 41 Ill.App.3d 804, 354 N.E.2d 586	

Dempsey, J.

In December 1973 the plaintiff, Robert Steinberg, applied for admission to the defendant, the Chicago Medical School, as a first-year student for the academic year 1974–75 and paid an application fee of $15. The Chicago Medical School is a private, not-for-profit educational institution, incorporated in the State of Illinois. His application for admission was rejected and Steinberg filed a[n] * * * action against the school, claiming that it had failed to evaluate his application * * * according to the academic entrance criteria printed in the school's bulletin. Specifically, his complaint alleged that the school's decision to accept or reject a particular applicant for the first-year class was primarily based on such nonacademic considerations as the prospective student's familial relationship to members of the school's faculty and to members of its board of trustees, and the ability of the applicant or his family to pledge or make payment of large sums of money to the school. The complaint further alleged that, by using such unpublished criteria to evaluate

applicants, the school had breached the contract which Steinberg contended was created when the school accepted his application fee.

* * *

The defendant filed a motion to dismiss, arguing that the complaint failed to state a cause of action because no contract came into existence during its transaction with Steinberg inasmuch as the school's informational publication did not constitute a valid offer. The trial court sustained [ruled in favor of] the motion to dismiss and Steinberg appeals from this order.

* * *

A contract is an agreement between competent parties, based upon a consideration sufficient in law, to do or not do a particular thing. It is a promise or a set of promises for the breach of which the law gives a remedy, or the performance of which the law in some way recognizes as a duty. [Citation.] A contract's essential requirements are: competent parties, valid subject matter, legal consideration, mutuality of obligation and mutuality of agreement. Generally, parties may contract in any situation where there is no legal prohibition, since the law acts by restraint and not by conferring rights. [Citation.] However, it is basic contract law that in order for a contract to be binding the terms of the contract must be reasonably certain and definite. [Citation.]

A contract, in order to be legally binding, must be based on consideration. [Citation.] Consideration has been defined to consist of some right, interest, profit or benefit accruing to one party or some forbearance, disadvantage, detriment, loss or responsibility given, suffered, or undertaken by the other. [Citation.] Money is a valuable consideration and its transfer or payment or promises to pay it or the benefit from the right to its use, will support a contract.

In forming a contract, it is required that both parties assent to the same thing in the same sense [citation] and that their minds meet on the essential terms and conditions. [Citation.] Furthermore, the mutual consent essential to the formation of a contract must be gathered from the language employed by the parties or manifested by their words or acts. The intention of the parties gives character to the transaction, and if either party contracts in good faith he is entitled to the benefit of his contract no matter what may have been the secret purpose or intention of the other party. [Citation.]

Steinberg contends that the Chicago Medical School's informational brochure constituted an invitation to make an offer; that his subsequent application and the submission of his $15 fee to the school amounted to an offer; that the school's voluntary reception of his fee constituted an acceptance and because of these events a contract was created between the school and himself. He contends that the school was duty bound under the terms of the contract to evaluate his application according to its stated standards and that the deviation from these standards not only breached the contract, but amounted to an arbitrary selection which constituted a violation of due process and equal protection. He concludes that such a breach did in fact take place each and every time during the past ten years that the school evaluated applicants according to their relationship to the school's faculty members or members of its board of trustees, or in accordance with their ability to make or pledge large sums of money to the school. Finally, he asserts that he is a member and a proper representative of the class that has been damaged by the school's practice.

The school counters that no contract came into being because informational brochures, such as its bulletin, do not constitute offers, but are construed by the courts to be general proposals to consider, examine and negotiate. The school points out that this doctrine has been specifically applied in Illinois to university informational publications.

* * *

We agree with Steinberg's position. We believe that he and the school entered into an enforceable contract; that the school's obligation under the contract was stated in the school's bulletin in a definitive manner and that by accepting his application fee—a valuable consideration—the school bound itself to fulfill its promises. Steinberg accepted the school's promises in good faith and he was entitled to have his application judged according to the school's stated criteria.

* * *

[Reversed and remanded.]

CASE 9-3	Promissory Estoppel **BOUTON v. BYERS** Court of Appeals of Kansas, 2014 50 Kan.App.2d 35, 321 P.3d 780	

Atcheson, J.

This case revolves around a disputed million-dollar promise between father and daughter. * * * [Plaintiff Ellen Byers Bouton held a tenure-track teaching position at the Washburn University School of Law faculty and earned about $100,000 a year. In 2011, Bouton brought a promissory estoppel claim against defendant Walter Byers, her father, for breaching a promise she says he made to bequeath valuable ranchland to her—a promise that induced her to leave the Washburn University faculty in 2005 so she could help him manage his cattle business. Byers denied ever having made that promise to his daughter. In August 2006, Bouton signed the first of a series of employment contracts with Byers for her services in helping run the

ranching business under which she earned a small fraction of what she had been making as a law professor. After a series of disputes between father and daughter, in 2010 Bouton returned to the Washburn Law School faculty in a part-time teaching position without any possibility of tenure. In 2011 Byers sold the last of his land holdings—except for 10 acres—for $1.2 million. As a result, Byers no longer owned any land that Bouton might inherit. In November 2011, Byers signed a new trust that upon his death would distribute all of his assets to charitable foundations to provide college scholarships. Byers effectively disinherited Bouton.

On December 8, 2011, Bouton filed an action against Byers seeking damages on a promissory estoppel theory in an amount equal to what she would have earned had she continued at Washburn Law School in the full-time, tenure-track position that she had resigned in 2005. Bouton contended she gave up her teaching position to manage Byers' ranching operation in reliance on his promise that she would inherit land worth more than $1 million. Byers denied any liability to Bouton and filed a motion for summary judgment. The district court granted the motion, finding the evidence failed to show both a definite promise from Byers and reasonable reliance by Bouton. Bouton appealed.]

Promissory estoppel is an equitable doctrine designed to promote some measure of basic fairness when one party makes a representation or promise in a manner reasonably inducing another party to undertake some obligation or to incur some detriment as a result. The party assuming the obligation or detriment may bring an action for relief should the party making the representation or promise fail to follow through. The Kansas Supreme Court has recognized promissory estoppel to be applicable when: (1) a promisor reasonably expects a promisee to act in reliance on a promise; (2) the promisee, in turn, reasonably so acts; and (3) a court's refusal to enforce the promise would countenance a substantial injustice. [Citation.] * * *

Promissory estoppel and contract law are closely related and serve the same fundamental purposes by providing means to enforce one party's legitimate expectations based on the representations of another party. * * * A contract typically depends upon mutual promises that entail an exchange of bargained consideration. [Citation.] * * * Promissory estoppel commonly applies when a promise reasonably induces a predictable sort of action but without the more formal mutual consideration found in contracts. * * *

Kansas courts have explained that a party's *reasonable* reliance on a promise prompting a *reasonable* change in position effectively replaces the bargained for consideration of a formal contract, thereby creating what amounts to a contractual relationship. [Citations.] To the extent the promisee relies on equity to specifically enforce the promise or recover damages equivalent to the promised performance, the promise itself must define with sufficient particularity what the promisor was to do. [Citations.] The same required specificity governs contracts. [Citation.] * * *

* * *

The reasonableness of a party's actions, including reliance on statements of another party, typically reflects a fact question reserved for the factfinder. [Citations.] * * *

* * *

* * * Bouton contends she relied on the oral promise or representation Byers made in March 2005 that she would inherit

land worth more than $1 million so she should not worry about the financial impact of leaving the law school faculty. On the summary judgment record, Byers made that statement during a discussion with Bouton and her husband in which they specifically voiced concerns about her resigning that position to work exclusively on ranch business.

In that context, a factfinder could fairly conclude Byers not only might have expected Bouton to act on the promise but intended her to do so. * * *

* * * the district court held as a matter of law that Bouton's reliance on the March 2005 promise she attributed to Byers was unreasonable given her "education and the circumstances as a whole." * * * Our view is otherwise to the extent the record evidence as a whole would allow a factfinder to conclude Bouton reasonably relied on Byers' March 2005 promise that she would inherit property worth at least a $1 million, especially when that representation came in direct response to her trepidation about leaving a job that paid her well. * * *

* * *

The district court erred in granting summary judgment for the reasons it did.

Byers submits the remaining elements of promissory estoppel on which the district court did not rule support summary judgment. Byers identifies those elements as "substantial detriment" to the promisee and "injustice" resulting from a failure to enforce the promise. We disagree with Byers' assessment. The facts as Bouton portrays them show she left a lucrative job because of Byers' March 2005 promise to bequeath her land worth more than $1 million. And the evidence shows that once Bouton left the tenure-track teaching position, it was lost to her. Given the nature of the job, she could not later return to the law school faculty and simply pick up where she left off. Bouton's compensation for the ranch business came nowhere near her teaching income. All of that reasonably could be considered a substantial detriment to Bouton. In the same vein, we are unwilling to say that enforcement of Byers' March 2005 promise would be something less than just * * *.

* * *

The Restatement (Second) of Contracts §90 specifically states relief on a promissory estoppel claim should be tailored to effectuate fair or equitable results. Thus, "[t]he remedy granted for breach [of the promise] may be limited as justice requires." Restatement (Second) of Contracts §90. * * *

Both the Restatement (Second) of Contracts §90 and * * * case authority support a restitutionary award to Bouton if she can otherwise prove her promissory estoppel claim. * * *

Reversed and remanded for further proceedings.

CASE 9-4

Quasi Contracts
IN RE APA ASSESSMENT FEE LITIGATION
United States Court of Appeals, District of Columbia Circuit, 2014
766 F. 3d 39

Srinivasan, J.

The American Psychological Association (APA) is a national nonprofit organization representing clinical, research, and academic psychologists. APA members must pay annual association fees billed by the organization on its yearly "Membership Dues Statement." For certain members, the dues statement also includes a separate, "special assessment" fee. At all relevant times, the dues statement's instructions informed affected members that they "MUST PAY" the special assessment. Despite that mandatory language, the special assessment in fact was not a requirement of APA membership. Instead, it was an optional payment collected by the APA to fund the lobbying activities of a separate, APA affiliated organization.

After learning that there was no requirement to pay the special assessment to maintain APA membership, several members brought the present class action lawsuit seeking recovery of all special assessment fees paid. They alleged that the APA had intentionally misled members into believing that payment of the special assessment fee was a condition of membership, and that they would not have paid the fee had they known it was optional.

[The district court granted the defendants' motion to dismiss the unjust enrichment claim, explaining that unjust enrichment is an "equitable quasi-contract claim" that cannot proceed when an "actual contract exists between the parties" that "cover[s] the issue under dispute." The district court held that the APA bylaws and rules constituted such a contract, precluding any unjust enrichment claim related to membership fees. The plaintiffs appealed.]

Under D.C. law, "[u]njust enrichment occurs when: (1) the plaintiff conferred a benefit on the defendant; (2) the defendant retains the benefit; and (3) under the circumstances, the defendant's retention of the benefit is unjust." [Citations.] "In such a case, the recipient of the benefit has a duty to make restitution to the other person. . . ." [Citation.] * * *

Unjust enrichment is an equitable quasi-contract claim "based on a contract implied in law." [Citation.] Such a claim is a "[l]egal fiction" designed "to permit recovery by contractual remedy in cases where, in fact, there is no contract, but where circumstances are such that justice warrants a recovery as though there had been a promise." [Citation.] Unjust enrichment will not lie when "the parties have a contract governing an aspect of [their] relation," because "a court will not displace the terms of that contract and impose some other duties not chosen by the parties." [Citation.] That rule does not apply,

however, if the contract is invalid or does not cover the issue in dispute. [Citation.] * * *

Here, the district court considered plaintiffs' unjust enrichment claim to be precluded by an express contract—namely the APA bylaws and Association Rules, which "can be 'construed as a contractual agreement between the organization and its members.'" [Citation.] Urging us to accept that reasoning, defendants contend that the existence of an express membership contract between the parties precludes plaintiffs' unjust enrichment claim.

We reject that approach. According to defendants, plaintiffs' decision to pay the special assessment had no bearing on plaintiffs' rights or obligations as APA members under the bylaws and rules. Defendants in fact allow that nothing in the bylaws and rules "even *permits* APA to terminate membership based on nonpayment" of the special assessment. [Citation.] But if that is so, payment of the special assessment at no point formed any part of the explicit contractual arrangement between the APA and its members. It was instead an extra-contractual payment falling outside the "scope" of the governing contracts. [Citation.] The bylaws and rules then pose no obstacle to an unjust enrichment claim seeking to recover assessment fees paid. ***

Plaintiffs' claim, in fact, fits a standard pattern of unjust enrichment recovery. According to the complaint, defendants included misleading language on the dues statement in order to deceive plaintiffs into overpaying for APA membership. Plaintiffs seek recovery of the alleged overpayments. They thus base their claim on a theory of "[m]istaken payment of money not due"—"one of the core cases of restitution." [Citation.] The goal is "to bring the transfers between the parties into conformity with the true state of their contractual obligations." [Citation.] ***

Here, plaintiffs *** can seek to recover the "erroneously bill[ed]" special assessment fee, notwithstanding the existence of an express contract defining APA membership requirements. As the Restatement explains: "Payments resulting from a misunderstanding of the extent of … a contractual obligation present a characteristic issue of restitution." [Citations.] Defendants' basic position, that an unjust enrichment claim is precluded whenever it *relates* to the subject matter of an express contract, would eliminate not just plaintiffs' claim but the entire category of mistaken overpayments—"a characteristic issue of restitution." Restatement (Third) of Restitution & Unjust Enrichment § 6 cmt. c. We have little doubt that District of Columbia courts would reject such an approach.

* * *

Defendants argue next that their retention of the assessment fees is not "unjust." According to defendants, plaintiffs were fully aware that the special assessment funded the APAPO's advocacy activities, and plaintiffs allege no inadequacy in the organization's lobbying efforts. Because plaintiffs therefore received all the benefits they were promised in exchange for the assessment fees, defendants contend, it is "just" for defendants to retain the fees paid.

Defendants' argument erroneously assumes that the promise of APAPO advocacy activities induced plaintiffs to pay the special assessment in the first place. Plaintiffs, however, assert that they had no interest in APAPO lobbying. Rather, they paid the special assessment to attain (or retain) APA membership, and only because defendants intentionally misled them into believing that the assessment was a precondition to their doing so. In those circumstances, defendants' subsequent performance of APAPO lobbying activities cannot render "just" their retention of the assessment fees. ***

Defendants' final argument on the unjust enrichment claim is that it was not reasonable for plaintiffs to believe that payment of the special assessment was required for APA membership. As a threshold matter, defendants do not fully explain why plaintiffs' unjust enrichment claim would fail under D.C. law if plaintiffs had genuinely, but unreasonably, been misled by the dues statement's language. *Cf.* Restatement (Third) of Restitution & Unjust Enrichment § 6 cmt. a (2011) ("As in other cases of benefit conferred by mistake, the fact that the claimant may have acted negligently in making a mistaken payment is normally irrelevant to the analysis of the claim."). ***

* * *

Finally, defendants contend that plaintiffs had a duty to investigate further before concluding that the special assessment was required for APA membership. [Citation.] ***

For the reasons already explained, however, plaintiffs reasonably could have concluded that the meaning of the dues statement was clear, such that there was no reason to investigate further.

* * *

*** [W]e conclude that plaintiffs' unjust enrichment claim survives defendants' motion to dismiss.

QUESTIONS

1. Owen telephones an order to Hillary's store for certain goods, which Hillary delivers to Owen. Neither party says anything about the price or payment terms. What are the legal obligations of Owen and Hillary?

2. Minth is the owner of the Hiawatha Supper Club, which he leased for two years to Piekarski. During the period of the lease, Piekarski contracted with Puttkammer for the resurfacing of the access and service areas of the supper club. Puttkammer performed the work satisfactorily. Minth knew about the contract and the performance of the work. The work, including labor and materials, had a reasonable value of $2,540, but Puttkammer was never paid because Piekarski went bankrupt. Puttkammer brought an action against Minth to recover the amount owed to him by Piekarski. Will Puttkammer prevail? Explain.

3. Jonathan writes to Willa, stating "I'll pay you $150 if you reseed my lawn." Willa reseeds Jonathan's lawn as requested. Has a contract been formed? If so, what kind? Explain.

4. Calvin uses fraud to induce Maria to promise to pay money in return for goods he has delivered to her. Has a contract been formed? If so, what kind? What are the rights of Calvin and Maria?

5. Anna is about to buy a house on a hill. Prior to the purchase, she obtains a promise from Betty, the owner of the adjacent property, that Betty will not build any structure that would block Anna's view. In reliance on this promise Anna buys the house. Is Betty's promise binding? Why or why not?

CASE PROBLEMS

6. Mary Dobos was admitted to Boca Raton Community Hospital in serious condition with an abdominal aneurysm. The hospital called upon Nursing Care Services, Inc., to provide around-the-clock nursing services for Mrs. Dobos. She received two weeks of in-hospital care, forty-eight hours of postrelease care, and two weeks of at-home care. The total bill was $3,723.90. Mrs. Dobos refused to pay, and Nursing Care Services, Inc., brought an action to recover. Mrs. Dobos maintained that she was not obligated to render payment in that she never signed a written contract, nor did she orally agree to be liable for the services. The necessity for the services, reasonableness of the fee, and competency of the nurses were undisputed. After Mrs. Dobos admitted that she or

her daughter authorized the forty-eight hours of postrelease care, the trial court ordered compensation of $248 for that period. It did not allow payment of the balance, and Nursing Care Services, Inc., appealed. Decision? Explain.

7. St. Charles Drilling Co. contracted with Osterholt to install a well and water system that would produce a specified quantity of water. The water system failed to meet its warranted capacity, and Osterholt sued for breach of contract. Does the Uniform Commercial Code (UCC) apply to this contract? Explain.

8. Helvey brought suit against the Wabash County REMC (REMC) for breach of implied and express warranties. He alleged that REMC furnished electricity in excess of 135 volts to Helvey's home, damaging his 110-volt household appliances. This incident occurred more than four years before Helvey brought this suit. In defense, REMC pleads that the Uniform Commercial Code's (UCC's) Article 2 statute of limitations of four years has passed, thereby barring Helvey's suit. Helvey argues that providing electrical energy is not a transaction in goods under the UCC but rather a furnishing of services that would make applicable the general contract six-year statute of limitations. Is the contract governed by the UCC? Why or why not?

9. Jack Duran, president of Colorado Carpet Installation, Inc., began negotiations with Fred and Zuma Palermo for the sale and installation of carpeting, carpet padding, tile, and vinyl floor covering in their home. Duran drew up a written proposal that referred to Colorado Carpet as "the seller" and to the Palermos as "the customer." The proposal listed the quantity, unit cost, and total price of each item to be installed. The total price of the job was $4,777.75. Although labor was expressly included in this figure, Duran estimated the total labor cost at $926. Mrs. Palermo in writing accepted Duran's written proposal soon after he submitted it to her. After Colorado Carpet delivered the tile to the Palermo home, however, Mrs. Palermo had a disagreement with Colorado Carpet's tile man and arranged for another contractor to perform the job. Colorado Carpet brought an action against the Palermos for breach of contract. Does the Uniform Commercial Code apply to this contract? Explain.

10. On November 1, the Kansas City Post Office Employees Credit Union merged with the Kansas City Telephone Employees Credit Union to form the Communications Credit Union (Credit Union). Systems Design and Management Information (SDMI) develops computer software programs for credit unions, using Burroughs (now Unisys) hardware. SDMI and Burroughs together offered to sell to Credit Union both a software package, called the Generic System, and Burroughs hardware. Later in November, a demonstration of the software was held at SDMI's offices, and the Credit Union agreed to purchase the Generic System software. This agreement was oral. After Credit Union was converted to the SDMI Generic System, major problems with the system immediately became apparent, so SDMI filed suit against Credit Union to recover the outstanding contract price for the software. Credit Union counterclaimed for damages based upon breach of contract and negligent and fraudulent misrepresentation. Does the Uniform Commercial Code apply to this contract? Explain.

11. Insul-Mark is the marketing arm of Kor-It Sales, Inc. Kor-It manufactures roofing fasteners, and Insul-Mark distributes them nationwide. Kor-It contracted with Modern Materials, Inc., to have large volumes of screws coated with a rust-proofing agent. The contract specified that the coated screws must pass a standard industry test and that Kor-It would pay according to the pound and length of the screws coated. Kor-It had received numerous complaints from customers that the coated screws were rusting, and Modern Materials unsuccessfully attempted to remedy the problem. Kor-It terminated its relationship with Modern Materials and brought suit for the deficient coating. Modern Materials counterclaimed for the labor and materials it had furnished to Kor-It. The trial court held that the contract (a) was for performance of a service, (b) not governed by the UCC, (c) governed by the common law of contracts, and (d) therefore, barred by a two-year statute of limitations. Insul-Mark appealed. Decision? Explain.

12. In March, William Tackaberry, a real estate agent for Weichert Co. Realtors (Weichert), informed Thomas Ryan, a local developer, that he knew of property Ryan might be interested in purchasing. Ryan indicated he was interested in knowing more about the property. Tackaberry disclosed the property's identity and the seller's proposed price. Tackaberry also stated that the purchaser would have to pay Weichert a 10 percent commission. Tackaberry met with the property owner and gathered information concerning the property's current leases, income, expenses, and development plans. Tackaberry also collected tax and zoning documents relevant to the property. In a face-to-face meeting on April 4, Tackaberry gave Ryan the data he had gathered and presented Ryan with a letter calling for a 10 percent finder's fee to be paid to Weichert by Ryan upon "successfully completing and closing of title." Tackaberry arranged a meeting, held three days later, where Ryan contracted with the owner to buy the land. Ryan refused, however, to pay the 10 percent finder's fee to Weichert. Weichert sues Ryan

for the finder's fee. To what, if anything, is Weichert entitled to recover? Explain.

13. Max E. Pass, Jr., and his wife, Martha N. Pass, departed in an aircraft owned and operated by Mr. Pass from Plant City, Florida, bound for Clarksville, Tennessee. Somewhere over Alabama the couple encountered turbulence, and Mr. Pass lost control of the aircraft. The plane crashed killing both Mr. and Mrs. Pass. Approximately four and a half months prior to the flight in which he was killed, Mr. Pass had taken his airplane to Shelby Aviation, an aircraft service company, for inspection and service. In servicing the aircraft, Shelby Aviation replaced both rear wing attach point brackets on the plane. Three and one half years after the crash, Max E. Pass, Sr., father of Mr. Pass and administrator of his estate, and Shirley Williams, mother of Mrs. Pass and administratrix of her estate, filed suit against Shelby Aviation. The lawsuit alleged that the rear wing attach point brackets sold and installed by Shelby Aviation were defective because they lacked the bolts necessary to secure them properly to the airplane. The plaintiffs asserted claims against the defendant for breach of express and implied warranties under Article 2 of the Uniform Commercial Code (UCC), which governs the sale of goods. Shelby Aviation contended that the transaction with Mr. Pass had been primarily for the sale of services, rather than of goods, and that consequently Article 2 of the UCC did not cover the transaction. Does the UCC apply to this transaction? Explain.

14. Kasch and his brother owned M.W. Kasch Co. Kasch hired Skebba as a sales representative and over the years promoted him first to account manager; then to customer service manager, field sales manager, vice president of sales, senior vice president of sales and purchasing; and finally to vice president of sales. When M.W. Kasch Co. experienced serious financial problems in 2009, Skebba was approached by another company to leave Kasch and work there. When Skebba told Kasch he was accepting the new opportunity, Kasch asked what it would take to get him to stay. Skebba told Kasch that he needed security for his retirement and family and would stay if Kasch agreed to pay Skebba $250,000 if one of these three conditions occurred: (1) the company was sold, (2) Skebba was lawfully terminated, or (3) Skebba retired. Kasch agreed to this proposal and promised to have the agreement drawn up. Skebba turned down the job opportunity and stayed with Kasch from December 2009 through 2015 when the company assets were sold. Over the years, Skebba repeatedly but unsuccessfully asked Kasch for a written summary of this agreement. Eventually, Kasch sold the business, receiving $5.1 million dollars for his 51 percent share of the business. Upon the sale of the business, Skebba asked Kasch for the $250,000. Kasch refused and denied ever having made such an agreement. Instead, Kasch gave Skebba a severance agreement, which had been drafted by Kasch's lawyers in 2009. This agreement promised two years of salary continuation on the sale of the company, but only if Skebba was not hired by the successor company. The severance agreement also required a setoff against the salary continuation of any sums Skebba earned from any activity during the two years of the severance agreement. Skebba sued. Explain whether Skebba is entitled to recover.

15. Hannaford is a national grocery chain whose electronic payment processing system was breached by hackers as early as December 7, 2007. The hackers stole up to 4.2 million credit and debit card numbers, expiration dates, and security codes, but did not steal customer names. On February 27, 2008, Visa Inc. notified Hannaford that Hannaford's system had been breached. Hannaford discovered the means of access on March 8, 2008 and contained the breach on March 10, 2008. Hannaford gave notice to certain financial institutions on March 10, 2008. On March 17, 2008, "Hannaford publicly announced for the first time that between December 7, 2007 and March 10, 2008, the security of its information technology systems had been breached, leading to the theft of as many as 4.2 million debit card and credit card numbers belonging to individuals who had made purchases at more than 270 of its stores." It also announced, "that it had already received reports of approximately 1,800 cases of fraud resulting from the theft of those numbers." A number of affected customers sued Hannaford for breach of implied contract to recover losses arising from the unauthorized use of their credit and debit card data. Damages sought included the cost of replacement card fees when the issuing bank declined to issue a replacement card to them, fees for accounts overdrawn by fraudulent charges, fees for altering preauthorized payment arrangements, loss of accumulated reward points, inability to earn reward points during the transition to a new card, emotional distress, time and effort spent reversing unauthorized charges and protecting against further fraud, and the cost of purchasing identity theft/card protection insurance and credit monitoring services. Discuss the validity of their claim that Hannaford had breached an implied contract with its customers.

16. On May 5, Stewart Richardson (Seller) and Jasdip Properties SC, LLC (Buyer) entered into an agreement for the purchase of certain property in Georgetown, South Carolina, for $537,000. Buyer paid an initial earnest money deposit of $10,000, half of which Seller was entitled to retain in the event the sale was not concluded. The balance was due at the closing on or before July 28. Later, Seller granted Buyer extensions to the closing date in return for additional payments of $175,000 and $25,000, each to be applied to the purchase price. Without fault on his part, Buyer was unable to close in a timely fashion, and Seller rescinded the contract. Assuming that there is no breach of contract by either Seller or Buyer, explain what the rights of the parties are with respect to the money paid by Buyer.

TAKING SIDES

Richardson hired J. C. Flood Company, a plumbing contractor, to correct a stoppage in the sewer line of her house. The plumbing company's "snake" device, used to clear the line leading to the main sewer, became caught in the underground line. To release it, the company excavated a portion of the sewer line in Richardson's backyard. In the process, the company discovered numerous leaks in a rusty, defective water pipe that ran parallel with the sewer line. To meet public regulations, the water pipe, of a type no longer approved for such service, had to be replaced either then or later, when the yard would have to be excavated again. The plumbing company proceeded to repair the water pipe. Though Richardson inspected the company's work daily and did not express any objection to the extra work involved in replacing the water pipe, she refused to pay any part of the total bill after the company completed the entire operation. J. C. Flood Company then sued Richardson for the costs of labor and material it had furnished.

a. What arguments would support J. C. Flood's claim for the costs of labor and material it had furnished?

b. What arguments would support Richardson's refusal to pay the bill?

c. For what, if anything, should Richardson be liable? Explain.

Mutual Assent

CHAPTER OUTCOMES

After reading and studying this chapter, you should be able to:

- Explain the three essential elements of an offer.

- State the seven ways by which an offer may be terminated other than by acceptance.

- Compare the traditional and modern theories of definiteness of acceptance of an offer, as shown by the common law "mirror image" rule and by the rule of the Uniform Commercial Code.

- Describe the five situations limiting an offeror's right to revoke her offer.

- Explain the various rules that determine when an acceptance takes effect.

Although each of the requirements for forming a contract is essential to its existence, mutual assent is so basic that frequently a contract is referred to as the agreement between the parties. The Restatement, Section 3, provides this definition: "An agreement is a manifestation of mutual assent on the part of two or more parties." Enforcing the contract means enforcing the agreement; indeed, the agreement between the parties is the very core of the contract.

The manner in which parties usually show mutual assent is by **offer** and **acceptance**. One party makes a proposal (offer) by words or conduct to the other party, who agrees by words or conduct to the proposal (acceptance). A contractual agreement always involves either a promise exchanged for a promise *(bilateral contract)* or a promise exchanged for an act or forbearance to act *(unilateral contract)*, as manifested by what the parties communicate to each other.

An implied contract may be formed by conduct. Thus, though there may be no definite offer and acceptance, or definite acceptance of an offer, a contract exists if both parties have acted in a manner that manifests (indicates) a recognition by each of them of the existence of a contract. It may be impossible to determine the exact moment at which a contract was made.

To form the contract, the parties must manifest their agreement objectively. The important thing is what the parties indicate to each other by spoken or written words or by conduct. The law applies an **objective standard** and, therefore, is concerned only with the assent, agreement, or intention of a party

as it reasonably appears from his words or actions. The law of contracts is not concerned with what a party may have actually thought or the meaning that he intended to convey, even if his subjective understanding or intention differed from the meaning he objectively indicated by word or conduct. For example, if Leslie seemingly offers to sell to Sam her Chevrolet automobile but intends to offer and believes that she is offering her Ford automobile and Sam accepts the offer, reasonably believing it was for the Chevrolet, a contract has been formed for the sale of the Chevrolet. Subjectively, there is no agreement as to the subject matter, but objectively there is a manifestation of agreement, and the objective manifestation is binding.

The Uniform Commercial Code's (UCC or Code) treatment of mutual assent is covered in greater detail in *Chapter 21.*

OFFER

An offer is a definite proposal or undertaking made by one person to another that manifests a willingness to enter into a bargain. The person making the proposal is the **offeror**. The person to whom it is made is the **offeree**. Upon receipt, the offer confers on the offeree the power of acceptance, by which the offeree expresses her willingness to comply with the terms of the offer.

The communication of an offer to an offeree does not of itself confer any rights or impose any duties on either of the parties. The offeror, by making his offer, simply confers upon the offeree the power to create a contract by accepting the offer. Until the offeree exercises this power, the outstanding offer creates neither rights nor liabilities.

An offer may take several forms: (1) It may propose a promise for a promise. (This is an offer to enter into a bilateral contract.) An example is an offer to sell and deliver goods in thirty days in return for the promise to pay a stipulated amount upon delivery of the goods. If the offeree accepts this offer, the resulting contract consists of the parties' mutual promises, each made in exchange for the other. (2) An offer may be a promise for an act. (This is an offer to enter into a unilateral contract.) A common example is an offer of a reward for certain information or for the return of lost property. The offeree can accept such an offer only by the performance of the act requested. (3) An offer may be in the form of an act for a promise. (This is an offer to enter into an "inverted" unilateral contract.) For example, Maria offers the stated price to a clerk in a theater ticket office and asks for a ticket for a certain performance. The clerk can accept this offer of an act only by delivery of the requested ticket, which amounts, in effect, to the theater owner's promise to admit Maria to the designated performance.

10-1 Essentials of an Offer

An offer need not take any particular form to have legal validity. To be effective, however, it must (1) be communicated to the offeree, (2) manifest an intent to enter into a contract, and (3) be sufficiently definite and certain. If these essentials are present, an offer that has not terminated gives the offeree the power to form a contract by accepting the offer.

10-1a COMMUNICATION

To have the mutual assent required to form a contract, the offeree must have knowledge of the offer; he cannot agree to something of which he has no knowledge. Accordingly, the offeror must communicate the offer, in an intended manner, to the offeree.

For example, Andre signs a letter containing an offer to Bonnie and leaves it on top of the desk in his office. Later that day, Bonnie, without prearrangement, goes to Andre's office, discovers that Andre is away, notices the letter on his desk, reads it, and writes on it an acceptance which she dates and signs. No contract is formed because the offer never became effective; Andre never communicated it to Bonnie. If Andre had mailed the letter and it had gone astray in the mail, the offer would likewise never have become effective.

Not only must the offer be communicated to the offeree, but the communication must also be made or authorized by the offeror. For instance, if Joanne tells Karlene that she plans to offer Larry $600 for his piano and Karlene promptly informs Larry of this proposal, no offer has been made. There was no authorized communication of any offer by Joanne to Larry. By the same token, if Lance should offer to sell his diamond ring to Ed, an acceptance of this offer by Donnese would not be effective, because Lance made the offer to Ed, not to Donnese.

An offer need not be stated or communicated by words. Conduct from which a reasonable person may infer a proposal in return for either an act or a promise amounts to an offer.

An offer may be made to the general public. No person, however, can accept such an offer until and unless he has knowledge that the offer exists. For example, if a person, without knowing of an advertised reward for information leading to the return of a lost watch gives information that leads to its return, he is not entitled to the reward. His act was not an acceptance of the offer because he could not accept something of which he had no knowledge.

10-1b INTENT

To have legal effect, an offer must manifest an intent to enter into a contract. The intent of an offer is determined objectively from the words or conduct of the parties. The meaning of either party's manifestation is based upon what a reasonable person in the other party's position would have believed. The courts sometimes consider subjective intention in interpreting the parties' communications. (The interpretation of contracts is discussed in *Chapter 16*.)

Occasionally, a person exercises her sense of humor by speaking or writing words that—taken literally and without regard to context or surrounding circumstances—a promisee could construe as an offer. The promisor intends the promise as a joke, however, and the promisee as a reasonable person should understand it to be such. Therefore, it is not an offer. Because the person to whom it is made realizes or should realize that it is not made in earnest, it should not create a reasonable expectation in his mind. No contractual intent exists on the part of the promisor, and the promisee is or reasonably ought to be aware of that fact. If, however, the intended jest is so successful that the promisee as a reasonable person under all the circumstances believes that the joke is in fact an offer and so believing accepts, the objective standard applies and the parties have entered into a contract.

A promise made under obvious excitement or emotional strain is likewise not an offer. For example, Charlotte, after having her month-old Cadillac break down for the third time in two days, screams in disgust, "I will sell this car to anyone for $100!" Lisa hears Charlotte and hands her a one hundred-dollar bill. Under the circumstances, Charlotte's statement was not an offer if a reasonable person in Lisa's position would have recognized it merely as an overwrought, nonbinding utterance.

It is important to distinguish language that constitutes an offer from that which merely solicits or invites offers. Such proposals, although made in earnest, lack intent and are therefore not deemed offers. As a result, a purported acceptance does not bring about a contract but operates only as an offer to accept. These proposals include preliminary negotiations, advertisements, and auctions.

Practical Advice

Make sure that you indicate by words or conduct what agreement you wish to enter.

♦ *See Case 10-1*

PRELIMINARY NEGOTIATIONS If a communication creates in the mind of a reasonable person in the position of the offeree an expectation that his acceptance will conclude a contract, then the communication is an offer. If it does not, then the communication is a preliminary negotiation. Initial communications between potential parties to a contract often take the form of preliminary negotiations through which the parties either request or supply the terms of an offer that may or may not be given. A statement that may indicate a willingness to make an offer is not in itself an offer. If Terri writes to Susan, "Will you buy my automobile for $3,000?" and Susan replies "Yes," no contract exists. Terri has not made an offer to sell her automobile to Susan for $3,000. The offeror must manifest an intent to enter into a contract, not merely a willingness to enter into negotiation.

ADVERTISEMENTS Merchants desire to sell their merchandise and thus are interested in informing potential customers about the goods, the terms of sale, and the price. But if they make widespread promises to sell to each person on their mailing list, the number of acceptances and resulting contracts might conceivably exceed their ability to perform. Consequently, a merchant might refrain from making offers by merely announcing that he has goods for sale, describing the goods, and quoting prices. He is simply inviting his customers and, in the case of published advertisements, the public, to make offers to him to buy the goods. His advertisements, circulars, quotation sheets, and merchandise displays are *not* offers because (1) they do not contain a promise and (2) they leave unexpressed many terms that would be necessary to the making of a contract. Accordingly, his customers' responses are not acceptances because he has made no offer to sell.

Nonetheless, a seller is not free to advertise goods at one price and then raise the price once demand has been stimulated. Although, as far as contract law is concerned, the seller has made no offer, such conduct is prohibited by the Federal Trade Commission as well as by legislation in many States. (See *Chapter 41*.)

Moreover, in some circumstances, a public announcement or advertisement may constitute an offer if the advertisement or announcement contains a definite promise of something in exchange for something else and confers a power of acceptance upon a specified person or class of persons. The typical offer of a reward is an example of a definite offer, as was shown in *Lefkowitz v. Great Minneapolis Surplus Store, Inc.* In this case, the court held that a newspaper advertisement was an offer because it contained a promise of performance in definite terms in return for a requested act.

♦ *See Case 10-2*

AUCTION SALES The auctioneer at an auction sale does *not* make offers to sell the property that is being auctioned, but rather invites offers to buy. The classic statement by the auctioneer is, "How much am I offered?" The persons attending the auction may make progressively higher bids for the property, and each bid or statement of a price or a figure is an offer to buy at that figure. If the bid is accepted—this customarily is indicated by the fall of the hammer in the auctioneer's hand—a contract results. A bidder is free to withdraw his bid at any time prior to its acceptance. The auctioneer is likewise free to withdraw the goods from sale *unless* the sale is advertised or announced to be without reserve.

If the auction sale is advertised or announced in explicit terms to be **without reserve**, the auctioneer may not withdraw an article or lot put up for sale unless no bid is made within a reasonable time. Unless so advertised or announced, the sale is with reserve. A bidder at either type of sale may retract his bid at any time prior to acceptance by the auctioneer. Such retraction, however, does not revive any previous bid.

10-1c DEFINITENESS

The terms of a contract, all of which the offer usually contains, must be reasonably certain so as to provide a court with a basis for determining the existence of a breach and for giving an appropriate remedy. Restatement, Section 33. It is a fundamental policy that contracts should be made by the parties and not by the courts; accordingly, remedies for breach must have their basis in the parties' contract.

However, where the parties have intended to form a contract, the courts will attempt to find a basis for granting a remedy. Missing terms may be supplied by course of dealing, usage of trade, or inference. Thus, uncertainty as to incidental matters will seldom be fatal so long as the parties intended to form a contract. Nevertheless, the more terms the parties leave open, the less likely it is that they have intended to form a contract. Because of the great variety of contracts, the terms essential to all contracts cannot be stated. In most cases, however, material terms would include the parties, subject matter, price, quantity, quality, and time of performance.

OPEN TERMS With respect to agreements for the sale of goods, the Code provides standards by which omitted terms may be determined, provided the parties intended to enter into a binding contract. The Code provides missing terms in a number of instances, where, for example, the contract fails to specify the price, the time or place of delivery, or payment terms. Sections 2-204(3), 2-305, 2-308, 2-309, and 2-310. The Restatement, Section 34, has adopted an approach similar to the Code's in supplying terms the parties have omitted from their contract.

Under the Code, an offer for the purchase or sale of goods may leave open particulars of performance to be specified by one of the parties. Any such specification must be made in good faith and within limits set by commercial reasonableness. Section 2-311(1). **Good faith** is defined as honesty in fact and the observance of reasonable commercial standards of fair dealing under the 2001 Revised UCC Article 1, which has been adopted by all fifty States. Section 1-201(20). Commercial reasonableness is a standard determined with reference to the business judgment of reasonable persons familiar with the practices customary in the type of transaction involved and in terms of the facts and circumstances of the case.

If the price is to be fixed otherwise than by agreement and is not so fixed through the fault of one of the parties, the other party has an option to treat the contract as cancelled or to fix a reasonable price in good faith for the goods. However, where the parties intend not to be bound unless the price is fixed or agreed upon as provided in the agreement and it is not so fixed or agreed upon, the Code provides in accordance with the parties' intent that no contractual liability exists. In such case the seller must refund to the buyer any portion of the price she has received, and the buyer must return the goods to the seller or, if unable to do so, pay the reasonable value of the goods. Section 2-305(4).

♦ *See Case 12-4*

> ### *Practical Advice*
> *To make an offer that will result in an enforceable contract, make sure you include all the necessary terms.*

OUTPUT AND REQUIREMENTS CONTRACTS A buyer's agreement to purchase the entire output of a seller's factory for a stated period or a seller's agreement to supply a buyer with all his requirements for certain goods may appear to lack definiteness and mutuality of obligation. Such an agreement does not specify the exact quantity of goods; moreover, the seller may have some control over her output and the buyer over his requirements. Nonetheless, under the Code and the Restatement, such agreements are enforceable by the application of an objective standard based upon the good faith

of both parties. Thus, a seller who operated her factory for eight hours a day before entering an output agreement cannot operate her factory twenty-four hours a day and insist that the buyer take all of the output. Nor can the buyer expand his business abnormally and insist that the seller still supply all of his requirements.

10-2 Duration of Offers

An offer confers upon the offeree a power of acceptance, which continues until the offer terminates. The ways in which an offer may be terminated, *other than by acceptance*, are through (1) lapse of time, (2) revocation, (3) rejection, (4) counteroffer, (5) death or incompetency of the offeror or offeree, (6) destruction of the subject matter to which the offer relates, and (7) subsequent illegality of the type of contract the offer proposes.

10-2a LAPSE OF TIME

The offeror may specify the time within which the offer is to be accepted, just as he may specify any other term or condition in the offer. He may require that the offeree accept the offer immediately or within a **specified** period, such as a week or ten days. Unless otherwise terminated, the offer remains open for the specified period. Upon the expiration of that time, the offer no longer exists and cannot be accepted. Any subsequent purported acceptance will serve as a new offer.

If the offer states no time within which the offeree must accept, the offer will terminate after a **reasonable** time. Determining a "reasonable" period of time is a question of fact, depending on the nature of the contract proposed, the usages of business, and other circumstances of the case (including whether the offer was communicated by electronic means). Restatement, Section 41. For instance, an offer to sell a perishable good would be open for a far shorter time than an offer to sell undeveloped real estate.

> ### *Practical Advice*
> *Because of the uncertainty as to what is a "reasonable time," it is advisable to specify clearly the duration of offers you make.*

♦ *See Case 10-3*

10-2b REVOCATION

An offeror generally may withdraw an offer at any time before it has been accepted, even though he has definitely promised to keep it open for a stated time. To be effective, notice of revocation of the offer must actually reach the offeree before she has accepted. If the offeror originally promises that the offer will be open for thirty days but after five days wishes to terminate it, he may do so merely by giving the offeree notice that he is withdrawing the offer. Notice, which may be given by any means of communication, effectively terminates the offer when **received** by the offeree. Very few States, however, have adopted a rule that treats revocations the same as acceptances, thus making them effective upon dispatch. An offeror, however, may revoke an offer made to the general public only by giving to the revocation publicity equivalent to that given the offer.

Notice of revocation of an offer may be communicated indirectly to the offeree through reasonably reliable information from a third person that the offeror has disposed of the goods which he has offered for sale or has otherwise placed himself in a position which indicates an unwillingness or inability to perform the promise contained in the offer. Restatement, Section 43. For example, Jane offers to sell her portable television set to Bruce and tells Bruce that he has ten days in which to accept. One week later, Bruce observes the television set in Carl's house and is informed that Carl had purchased it from Jane. The next day Bruce sends Jane an acceptance of the offer. There is no contract, because Jane's offer was effectively revoked when Bruce learned of Jane's inability to sell the television set to him because she had sold it to Carl.

Certain limitations, however, restrict the offeror's power to revoke the offer at any time prior to its acceptance. These limitations apply to the following five situations.

10-2c OPTION CONTRACTS

An option is a contract by which the offeror is bound to hold open an offer for a specified period of time. It must comply with all of the requirements of a contract, including *consideration* being given to the offeror by the offeree. (Consideration is discussed in *Chapter 12*.) For example, if Ann, in return for the payment of $500 to her by Bobby, grants Bobby an option, exercisable at any time within thirty days, to buy Blackacre at a price of $80,000, Ann's offer is irrevocable. Ann is legally bound to keep the offer open for thirty days, and any communication by Ann to Bobby giving notice of withdrawal of the offer is ineffective. Bobby is not bound to accept the offer, but the option contract entitles him to thirty days in which to accept.

♦ *See Case 12-4*

FIRM OFFERS UNDER THE CODE The Code provides that a *merchant* is bound to keep an offer to buy or sell **goods** open for a stated period (or, if no time is stated, for a reasonable time) not exceeding three months if the merchant gives assurance in a **signed writing** that the offer will be held open. Section 2-205. The Code, therefore, makes a merchant's written promise not to revoke an offer for a stated period enforceable even though

no consideration is given to the offeror for that promise. A **merchant** is defined as a person (1) who is a dealer in goods of a given kind, (2) who by his occupation holds himself out as having knowledge or skill peculiar to the goods or practices involved, or (3) who employs an agent or broker whom he holds out as having such knowledge or skill. Section 2-104.

STATUTORY IRREVOCABILITY Certain offers, such as bids made to the State, municipality, or other government body for the construction of a building or some other public work, are made irrevocable by statute. Another example of statutory irrevocability is pre-incorporation stock subscription agreements, which are irrevocable for a period of six months under many State incorporation statutes. See Section 6.20 of the Revised Model Business Corporation Act.

IRREVOCABLE OFFERS OF UNILATERAL CONTRACTS Where an offer contemplates a unilateral contract (i.e., a promise for an act), injustice to the offeree may result if revocation is permitted after the offeree has started to perform the act requested in the offer and has substantially but not completely accomplished it. Traditionally, such an offer is not accepted and no contract is formed until the offeree has *completed* the requested act. By simply commencing performance, the offeree does not bind himself to complete performance; nor, historically, did he bind the offeror to keep the offer open. Thus, the offeror could revoke the offer at any time prior to the offeree's completion of performance. For example, Linda offers Tom $300 if Tom will climb to the top of the flagpole in the center of campus. Tom commences his ascent, and when he is five feet from the top, Linda yells to him, "I revoke."

The Restatement deals with this problem by providing that where the performance of the requested act necessarily requires the offeree to expend time and effort, the offeror is obligated not to revoke the offer for a reasonable time. This obligation arises when the offeree begins performance. If, however, the offeror does not know of the offeree's performance and has no adequate means of learning of it within a reasonable time, the offeree must exercise reasonable diligence to notify the offeror of the performance.

Practical Advice
When making an offer, be careful to make it irrevocable only if you so desire.

PROMISSORY ESTOPPEL As discussed in the previous chapter, a noncontractual promise may be enforced when it is made under circumstances that should lead the promisor reasonably to expect that the promise will induce the promisee to take action in reliance on it. This doctrine has been used in some cases to prevent an offeror from revoking an offer prior to its acceptance. The Restatement provides the following rule:

> An offer which the offeror should reasonably expect to induce action or forbearance of a substantial character on the part of the offeree before acceptance and which does induce such action or forbearance is binding as an option contract to the extent necessary to avoid injustice. Restatement, Section 87(2).

Thus, Ramanan Plumbing Co. submits a written offer for plumbing work to be used by Resolute Building Co. as part of Resolute's bid as a general contractor. Ramanan knows that Resolute is relying on Ramanan's bid, and in fact, Resolute submits Ramanan's name as the plumbing subcontractor in the bid. Ramanan's offer is irrevocable until Resolute has a reasonable opportunity to notify Ramanan that Resolute's bid has been accepted.

APPLYING THE LAW

Mutual Assent

FACTS Taylor and Arbuckle formed a partnership for the purpose of practicing pediatric medicine together. They found new medical office space to lease, and thereafter, among other things, they set about furnishing the waiting room in a way that children would find inviting. In addition to contracting with a mural painter, they decided to purchase a high-definition flat-panel television on which they could show children's programming. On a Monday, Taylor and Arbuckle visited a local retailer with a reputation for competitive pricing, called Today's Electronics. In addition to comparing the pictures on the various models on display, the doctors discussed the pros and cons of LCD (liquid crystal display) versus plasma with the store's owner, Patel.

While they were able to narrow their options down significantly, Taylor and Arbuckle nonetheless could not decide on the exact size set to purchase because they had not yet determined the configuration of the seating to be installed in the waiting room. Sensing that the doctors were considering shopping around, Patel offered them a sizeable discount: only $549 for the forty-inch LCD screen they had chosen or the fifty-inch plasma model they favored for only $799. As they were leaving the store, Patel gave the doctors his business card, on which he had jotted the model numbers and discount prices, his signature, and the notation "we assure you this offer is open through Sun., April 27."

Anxious to have the waiting room completed, Taylor and Arbuckle quickly agreed on a feasible seating arrangement for the waiting room, ordered the necessary furniture, and decided that the fifty-inch television would be too big. On Friday, April 25, Taylor returned to Today's Electronics. But before she could tell Patel that they had decided on the forty-inch LCD, Patel informed her that he could not honor the discounted prices because he no longer had in stock either model the doctors were considering.

ISSUE Is Patel free to revoke his offer notwithstanding having agreed to hold it open through the weekend?

RULE OF LAW The general rule is that an offeror may revoke, or withdraw, an offer anytime before it has been accepted. However, there are several limitations on an offeror's power to revoke an offer before acceptance. One of these is the Uniform Commercial Code's (UCC's) "merchant's firm offer" rule. Under the UCC, a merchant's offer to buy or sell goods is irrevocable for the stated period (or, if no period is stated, for a reasonable time) not exceeding three months, when he has signed a writing assuring the offeree that the offer will be kept open for that period. The Code defines a merchant as one who trades in the types of goods in question or who holds himself out, either personally or by way of an agent, to be knowledgeable regarding the goods or practices involved in the transaction.

APPLICATION The proposed contract between the doctors and Today's Electronics is governed by Article 2 of the Code because it involves a sale of goods, in this case a television set. Both Patel and Today's Electronics are considered merchants of televisions under the Code's definition, because Patel and his store regularly sell electronics, including television sets. Patel offered to sell to Taylor and Arbuckle either the forty-inch LCD television for $549 or the fifty-inch plasma for $799. By reducing his offer to a signed writing and by promising in that writing that the stated prices were assured to be open through Sun., April 27, Patel made a firm offer that he cannot revoke during that six-day period. Whether he still has either model in stock does not affect the irrevocability of the offer.

CONCLUSION Patel's offer is irrevocable through Sunday, April 27. Therefore Patel's attempt to revoke it is ineffective, and Taylor may still accept it.

10-2d REJECTION

An offeree is at liberty to accept or reject the offer as he sees fit. If the offeree decides not to accept it, he is not required to reject it formally but may simply wait until the offer terminates by the lapse of time. Through a **rejection** of an offer, the offeree manifests his unwillingness to accept. A communicated rejection terminates the power of acceptance. From the effective moment of rejection, which is the **receipt** of the rejection by the offeror, the offeree may no longer accept the offer. Rejection by the offeree may consist of express language or may be implied from language or from conduct.

10-2e COUNTEROFFER

A **counteroffer** is a counterproposal from the offeree to the offeror that indicates a willingness to contract but upon terms or conditions different from those contained in the offer. It is not an unequivocal acceptance of the original offer and, by indicating an unwillingness to agree to the terms of the offer, it operates as a rejection. It also operates as a new offer. For instance, assume that Jordan writes Chris a letter stating that he will sell to Chris a secondhand color television set for $300. Chris replies that she will pay Jordan $250 for the set. This is a counteroffer that, upon **receipt** by Jordan, terminates the original offer. Jordan may, if he wishes, accept the counteroffer and thereby create a contract for $250. If, on the other hand, Chris states in her reply that she wishes to consider the $300 offer but is willing to pay $250 at once for the set, she is making a counteroffer that does *not* terminate Jordan's original offer. In the first instance, after making the $250 counteroffer, Chris may not accept the $300 offer. In the second instance she may do so, as the manner in which she stated the counteroffer did not indicate an unwillingness to accept the original offer and Chris therefore did not terminate it. In addition, a mere inquiry about the possibility of obtaining different or new terms is not a counteroffer and does not terminate the offer.

Another common type of counteroffer is the **conditional** acceptance, which purports to accept the offer but expressly makes the acceptance conditional upon the offeror's assent to additional or different terms. Nonetheless, it is a counteroffer and terminates the original offer. The Code's treatment of acceptances containing terms that vary from the offer are discussed later in this chapter.

♦ *See Case 10-4*

Practical Advice

Consider whether you want to make a counterproposal that terminates the original offer or whether you merely wish to discuss alternative possibilities.

10-2f DEATH OR INCOMPETENCY

The death or incompetency of either the offeror or the offeree ordinarily terminates an offer. Upon his death or incompetency the offeror no longer has the legal capacity to enter into a contract; thus, all his outstanding offers are terminated. Death or incompetency of the offeree likewise terminates the offer, because an ordinary offer is not assignable (transferable) and may be accepted only by the person to whom it was made. When the offeree dies or ceases to have legal capability to enter into a contract, no one else has the power to accept the offer. Therefore, the offer terminates.

The death or incompetency of the offeror or offeree, however, does *not* terminate an offer contained in an option.

10-2g DESTRUCTION OF SUBJECT MATTER

Destruction of the specific subject matter of an offer terminates the offer. The impossibility of performance prevents a contract from being consummated and thus terminates all outstanding offers with respect to the destroyed property. Suppose that Martina, owning a Buick automobile, offers to sell the car to Worthy and allows Worthy five days in which to accept. Three days later, the car is destroyed by fire. On the following day, Worthy, without knowledge of the car's destruction, notifies Martina that he accepts her offer. There is no contract. Martina's offer was terminated by the destruction of the car.

10-2h SUBSEQUENT ILLEGALITY

One of the four essential requirements of a contract, as previously mentioned, is legality of purpose or subject matter. If performance of a valid contract is subsequently made illegal, the obligations of both parties under the contract are discharged. Illegality taking effect after the making of an offer but prior to acceptance has the same effect: the offer is legally terminated.

♦ SEE FIGURE 10-1: *Duration of Revocable Offers*

ACCEPTANCE OF OFFER

The acceptance of an offer is essential to the formation of a contract. Once an acceptance has been given, the contract is formed. An acceptance can be made only by an offeree. Acceptance of an offer for a bilateral contract requires some overt act by which the offeree manifests his assent to the terms of the offer, such as speaking, sending a letter, or using other explicit or implicit communication to the offeror. If the offer is for a unilateral contract, the offeree may refrain from acting as requested or may signify acceptance through performance of the requested act with the intention of accepting. For example, if Joy publishes an offer of a reward to anyone who returns the diamond ring which she has lost (a unilateral contract offer)

FIGURE 10-1 Duration of Revocable Offers

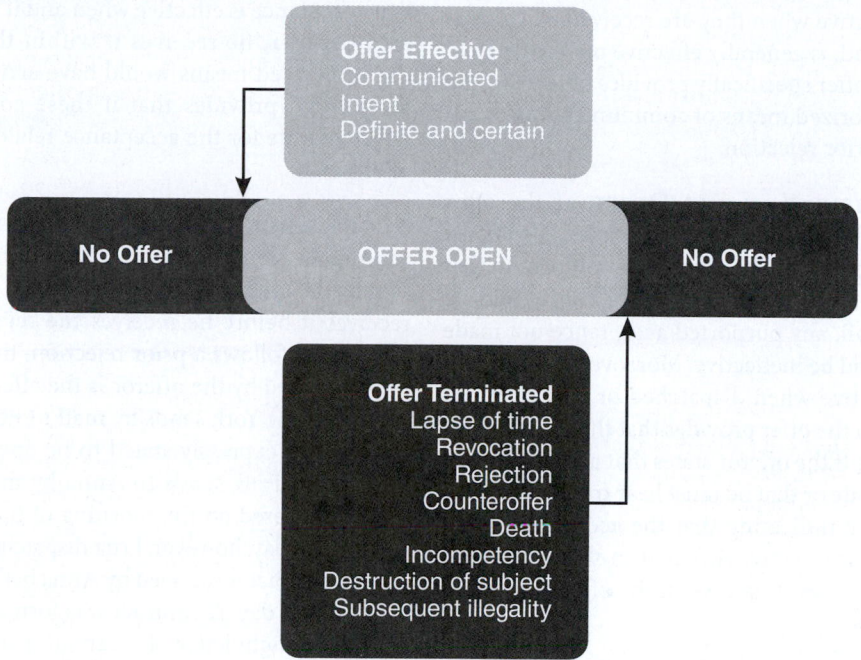

and Steven, with knowledge of the offer, finds and returns the ring to Joy, Steven has accepted the offer. If, however, Steven returns the ring to Joy but in doing so disclaims the reward and says that he does not accept the offer, there is no contract. Without the intention of accepting the offer, merely doing the act requested by the offeror is not sufficient to form a contract.

A late or defective acceptance does not create a contract. After the offer has expired, it cannot be validly accepted. A late or defective acceptance, however, does manifest the offeree's willingness to enter into a contract and therefore constitutes a new offer. To create a contract based upon this offer, the original offeror must accept the new offer by manifesting his assent.

10-3 Communication of Acceptance

10-3a GENERAL RULE

Because acceptance manifests the offeree's assent to the offer, the offeree must communicate this acceptance to the offeror. This is the rule as to all offers to enter into bilateral contracts. In the case of an offer to enter into a unilateral contract, however, notice of acceptance to the offeror is usually not required. If, however, the offeree in a unilateral contract has reason to know that the offeror has no adequate means of learning of the performance with reasonable promptness and certainty, then the offeree must make reasonable efforts to notify the offeror of acceptance or lose the right to enforce the contract. Restatement, Section 54.

10-3b SILENCE AS ACCEPTANCE

An offeree is generally under no legal duty to reply to an offer. Silence or inaction, therefore, does *not* indicate acceptance of the offer. By custom, usage, or course of dealing, however, silence or inaction by the offeree may operate as an acceptance.

Thus, the silence or inaction of an offeree who fails to reply to an offer operates as an acceptance and causes a contract to be formed. Through previous dealings, the offeree has given the offeror reason to understand that the offeree will accept all offers unless the offeree sends notice to the contrary. Another example of silence operating as an acceptance occurs when the prospective member of a mail-order club agrees that his failure to return a notification card rejecting offered goods will constitute his acceptance of the club's offer to sell the goods.

Furthermore, if an offeror sends unordered or unsolicited merchandise to a person stating that she may purchase the goods at a specified price and that the offer will be deemed to have been accepted unless the goods are returned within a stated period of time, the offer is one for an inverted unilateral contract (i.e., an act for a promise). This practice led to abuse, however, which has prompted the Federal government as well as most States to enact statutes which provide that in such cases, the offeree-recipient of the goods may keep them as a gift and is under no obligation either to return them or to pay for them.

◆ *See Case 10-5*

10-3c EFFECTIVE MOMENT

As previously discussed, an offer, a revocation, a rejection, and a counteroffer are effective when they are received. An acceptance, on the other hand, is generally effective upon **dispatch**. This is true unless the offer specifically provides otherwise, the offeree uses an unauthorized means of communication, or the acceptance follows a prior rejection.

STIPULATED PROVISIONS IN THE OFFER If the offer specifically stipulates the means of communication the offeree is to use, the acceptance, to be effective, must conform to that specification. Thus, if an offer states that acceptance must be made by registered mail, any purported acceptance not made by registered mail would be ineffective. Moreover, the rule that an acceptance is effective when dispatched or sent does not apply in cases in which the offer provides that the offeror must receive the acceptance. If the offeror states that a reply must be received by a certain date or that he must hear from the offeree or uses other language indicating that the acceptance must be received by him, the effective moment of the acceptance is when the offeror receives it, not when the offeree sends or dispatches it.

Practical Advice
Consider whether you should specify in your offers that acceptances are valid only upon receipt.

AUTHORIZED MEANS Historically, an authorized means of communication was the means the offeror expressly authorized in the offer, or, if none was authorized, it was the means the offeror used. For example, if in reply to an offer by mail, the offeree places in the mail a letter of acceptance properly stamped and addressed to the offeror, a contract is formed at the time and place that the offeree mails the letter. This assumes, of course, that the offer at that time was open and had not been terminated by any of the methods previously discussed. The reason for this rule is that the offeror, by using the mail, impliedly authorized the offeree to use the same method of communication. It is immaterial if the letter of acceptance goes astray in the mail and is never received.

The Restatement, Section 30, and the Code, Section 2-206(1)(a), both now provide that where the language in the offer or the circumstances do not otherwise indicate, an offer to make a contract shall be construed as authorizing acceptance in any **reasonable** manner. These provisions are intended to allow flexibility of response and the ability to keep pace with new modes of communication.

◆ SEE FIGURE 10-2: *Mutual Assent*

◆ *See Case 10-3*

UNAUTHORIZED MEANS When the offeree uses an unauthorized method of communication, the traditional rule is that acceptance is effective when and if received by the offeror, provided that he receives it within the time during which the authorized means would have arrived. The Restatement, Section 67, provides that if these conditions are met, the effective time for the acceptance relates back to the moment of dispatch.

ACCEPTANCE FOLLOWING A PRIOR REJECTION An acceptance sent after a prior rejection is not effective when sent by the offeree, but is only effective when and if the offeror receives it before he receives the rejection. Thus, when an acceptance follows a prior rejection, the first communication to be received by the offeror is the effective one. For example, Anna in New York sends by mail to Fritz in San Francisco an offer that is expressly stated to be open for ten days. On the fourth day, Fritz sends to Anna by mail a letter of rejection that is delivered on the morning of the seventh day. At noon on the fifth day, however, Fritz dispatches an overnight letter of acceptance that is received by Anna before the close of business on the sixth day. A contract was formed when Anna received Fritz's overnight letter of acceptance, as it was received before the letter of rejection.

◆ SEE FIGURE 10-3: *Offer and Acceptance*

10-4 Variant Acceptances

A variant acceptance—one that contains terms different from or additional to those in the offer—receives distinctly different treatment under the common law and the Code.

10-4a COMMON LAW

An acceptance must be *positive* and *unequivocal*. In that it may not change, add to, subtract from, or qualify in any way the provisions of the offer, it must be the **mirror image** of the offer. Any communication by the offeree that attempts to modify the offer is not an acceptance but is a counteroffer, which does not create a contract.

10-4b CODE

The Code modifies the common law "mirror image" rule, by which the acceptance cannot vary or deviate from the terms of the offer. This modification is necessitated by the realities of modern business practices. A vast number of business transactions use standardized business forms. For example, a merchant buyer sends to a merchant seller on the buyer's order form a purchase order for 1,000 dozen cotton shirts at $60.00 per dozen, with delivery by October 1 at the buyer's place of business. On the reverse side of this standard form

FIGURE 10-2 Mutual Assent

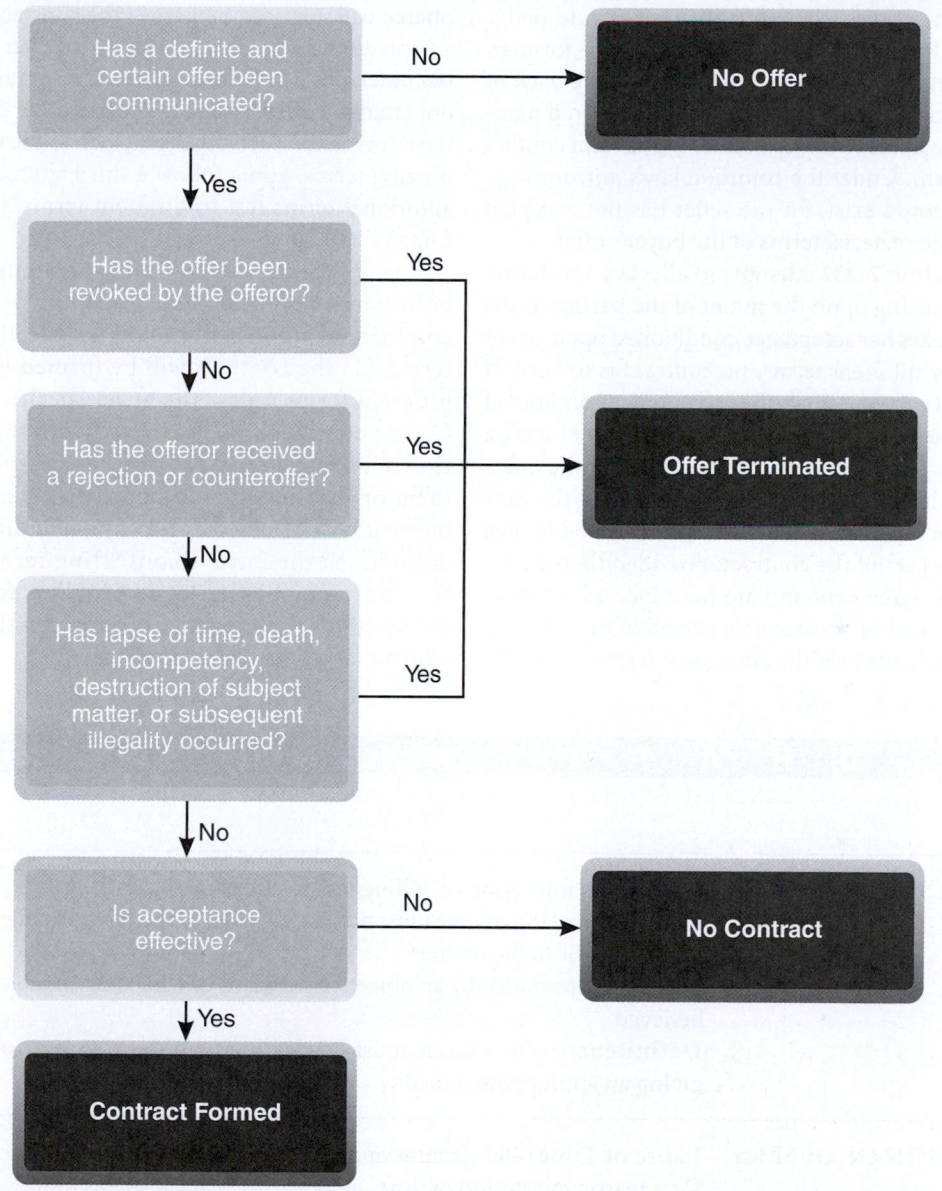

FIGURE 10-3 Offer and Acceptance

	Time Effective	Effect
Communications by Offeror		
Offer	Received by offeree	Creates power to form a contract
Revocation	Received by offeree	Terminates offer
Communications by Offeree		
Rejection	Received by offeror	Terminates offer
Counteroffer	Received by offeror	Terminates offer
Acceptance	Sent by offeree	Forms a contract
Acceptance after prior rejection	Received by offeror	If received before rejection, forms a contract

are twenty-five numbered paragraphs containing provisions generally favorable to the buyer. When the seller receives the buyer's order, he agrees to the quantity, price, and delivery terms and sends to the buyer on his acceptance form an unequivocal acceptance of the offer. However, on the back of his acceptance form, the seller has thirty-two numbered paragraphs generally favorable to himself and in significant conflict with the buyer's form. Under the common law's *mirror image* rule, no contract would exist, for the seller has not accepted unequivocally all the material terms of the buyer's offer.

The Code in Section 2-207 attempts to alleviate this **battle of the forms** by focusing upon the intent of the parties. If the offeree expressly makes her acceptance conditioned upon assent to the additional or different terms, no contract is formed. If the offeree does not expressly make her acceptance conditional upon the offeror's assent to the additional or different terms, a contract is formed. The issue then becomes whether the offeree's different or additional terms may become part of the contract. If both offeror and offeree are merchants, such *additional* terms may become part of the contract, provided they do not materially alter the agreement and are not objected to either in the offer itself or within a reasonable period of time. If both parties are not merchants or if the additional terms materially alter the offer, then the additional terms are merely construed as proposals to the contract. *Different* terms proposed by the offeree will not become part of the contract unless the offeror accepts them. The courts are divided over what terms a contract includes when those terms differ or conflict. Some courts hold that the offeror's terms govern; other courts, holding that the terms cancel each other out, look to the Code to provide the missing terms. Some follow a third alternative and apply the additional terms test to different terms. (See *Figure 21-4* in *Chapter 21*.)

To apply Section 2-207 to the previous example: because both parties are merchants and the acceptance was not conditional upon assent to the additional or different terms, (1) the contract will be formed without the seller's different terms unless the buyer specifically accepts them; (2) the contract will be formed without the seller's additional terms unless (a) the buyer specifically accepts them or (b) they do not materially alter the offer and the buyer does not object; and (3) depending upon the jurisdiction, (a) the buyer's conflicting terms are included in the contract, (b) the Code provides the missing terms, as the conflicting terms cancel each other out, or (c) the additional terms test is applied.

CHAPTER SUMMARY

OFFER

ESSENTIALS OF AN OFFER	**Definition** indication of willingness to enter into a contract **Communication** offeree must have knowledge of the offer, and the offer must be made by the offeror to the offeree **Intent** is determined by an objective standard of what a reasonable offeree would have believed **Definiteness** offer's terms must be clear enough to provide a court with a basis for giving an appropriate remedy
DURATION OF OFFERS	**Lapse of Time** offer remains open for the time period specified or, if no time is stated, for a reasonable period of time **Revocation** generally, an offer may be terminated at any time before it is accepted, subject to the following exceptions • *Option Contract* contract that binds offeror to keep an offer open for a specified time • *Firm Offer* a merchant's irrevocable offer to sell or buy goods in a signed writing ensures that the offer will not be terminated for up to three months • *Statutory Irrevocability* offer made irrevocable by statute • *Irrevocable Offer of Unilateral Contract* a unilateral offer may not be revoked for a reasonable time after performance is begun • *Promissory Estoppel* noncontractual promise that binds the promisor because she should reasonably expect that the promise will induce the promisee (offeree) to take action in reliance on it **Rejection** refusal to accept an offer terminates the power of acceptance

Counteroffer counterproposal to an offer that generally terminates the original offer
Death or Incompetency of either the offeror or the offeree terminates the offer
Destruction of Subject Matter of an offer terminates the offer
Subsequent Illegality of the purpose or subject matter of the offer terminates the offer

ACCEPTANCE OF OFFER

REQUIREMENTS	**Definition** positive and unequivocal expression of a willingness to enter into a contract on the terms of the offer **Mirror Image Rule** except as modified by the Code, an acceptance cannot deviate from the terms of the offer
COMMUNICATION OF ACCEPTANCE	**General Rule** acceptance effective upon dispatch unless the offer specifically provides otherwise or the offeree uses an unauthorized means of communication **Stipulated Provisions** the communication of acceptance must conform to the specification in the offer **Authorized Means** the Restatement and the Code provide that unless the offer provides otherwise, acceptance is authorized to be in any reasonable manner **Unauthorized Means** acceptance effective when received, provided that it is received within the time within which the authorized means would have arrived **Acceptance Following a Prior Rejection** first communication received by the offeror is effective **Defective Acceptance** does not create a contract but serves as a new offer

C A S E S

CASE 10-1

Objective Standard
CATAMOUNT SLATE PRODUCTS, INC. v. SHELDON
Supreme Court of Vermont, 2004
2003 VT 112, 845 A.2d 324

Skoglund, J.

Catamount Slate Products, Inc. and its principals the Reed family appeal from a Rutland Superior Court ruling enforcing what appellees characterize as a binding, mediated settlement agreement. The trial court concluded that, at the end of their September 5, 2000 mediation, the parties had reached a binding settlement agreement. Because the Reeds lacked the requisite intent to be bound to the settlement agreement in the absence of a writing, we hold that no binding agreement was reached. * * *

The Reeds own and operate Catamount Slate, a slate quarry and mill, on 122 acres in Fair Haven, Vermont. The appellees, the Sheldons, are also Fair Haven property owners and the Reeds' neighbors. Since 1997, the parties have been litigating the Reeds' right to operate their slate business and to use the access road leading to the quarry. In 2000, with several legal actions pending, the parties agreed to try to resolve their

disputes in a state-funded mediation with retired judge Arthur O'Dea serving as mediator.

Prior to the mediation, Judge O'Dea sent each party a Mediation Agreement outlining the rules governing the mediation. Paragraph nine of the Mediation Agreement stated that:

> [a]ll statements, admissions, confessions, acts, or exchanges . . . are acknowledged by the parties to be offers in negotiation of settlement and compromise, and as such inadmissible in evidence, and not binding upon either party unless reduced to a final agreement of settlement. Any final agreement of settlement must be in writing and signed by every party sought to be charged.

* * *

The mediation was held on September 5, 2000. Judge O'Dea began the session by reaffirming the statements made in the Mediation Agreement. After ten hours, the parties purportedly reached an agreement on all major issues. Judge O'Dea then orally summarized the terms of the resolution with the parties and counsel present. The attorneys took notes on the terms of the agreement with the understanding that they would prepare the necessary documents for signature in the coming days.

The resolution required the Reeds to pay the Sheldons $250 a month for the right to use the access road, while the Sheldons agreed to be coapplicants on Catamount Slate's pending Act 250 permit. Payments were to commence on October 1, 2000. The parties also agreed to a series of terms governing the operation of the slate quarry, including, among other things, hours of operation, number of truck trips permitted on the access road, the amount and frequency of blasting, and the location of seismic measurements. These terms were to be memorialized in two distinct documents, a Lease Agreement and a Settlement Agreement.

On September 7, 2000, two days after the mediation, the Sheldons' attorney, Emily Joselson, drafted a letter outlining the terms of the settlement and sent copies to James Leary, the Reeds' attorney, and Judge O'Dea. Within a week, Leary responded by letter concurring in some respects and outlining the issues on which the Reeds disagreed with Joselson's characterization of the settlement.

* * *

On October 1, 2000, the Reeds began paying the $250 monthly lease payments, but, since the settlement agreement was not final, the parties agreed that the money would go into an escrow account maintained by the Sheldons' counsel. The check was delivered to the Sheldons' attorney with a cover memo stating, "This check is forwarded to you with the understanding that the funds will be disbursed to your clients only after settlement agreement becomes final. Of course, if the settlement agreement does not come to fruition, then the funds must be returned to my clients." The parties continued to exchange letters actively negotiating the remaining details of the Lease and Settlement Agreements for the better part of the next five months. Although there were others along the way, by early 2001 the only remaining issues in dispute were the location of seismic measurements and the definition of "over blast."

In February 2001, while drafts were still being exchanged, Christine Stannard, the Reeds' daughter, saw a deed and map in the Fair Haven Town Clerk's Office which led her to believe that the disputed road was not owned by the Sheldons, but was a town highway. The Reeds then refused to proceed any further with negotiating the settlement agreement. A written settlement agreement was never signed by either party.

The Sheldons responded by filing a motion to enforce the settlement agreement. * * * The trial court granted the motion, finding that the attorneys' notes taken at the end of the mediation and the unsigned drafts of the Lease and Settlement Agreements sufficiently memorialized the agreement between the parties and thus constituted an enforceable settlement agreement. * * *

The question before us is whether the oral agreement reached at mediation, when combined with the unexecuted documents drafted subsequently, constituted a binding, enforceable settlement agreement. Parties are free to enter into a binding contract without memorializing their agreement in a fully executed document. See Restatement (Second) of Contracts § 4 (1981). In such an instance, the mere intention or discussion to commit their agreement to writing will not prevent the formation of a contract prior to the document's execution. [Citations.]

"On the other hand, if either party communicates an intent not to be bound until he achieves a fully executed document, no amount of negotiation or oral agreement to specific terms will result in the formation of a binding contract." [Citation.] The freedom to determine the exact moment in which an agreement becomes binding encourages the parties to negotiate as candidly as possible, secure in the knowledge that they will not be bound until the execution of what both parties consider to be a final, binding agreement.

We look to the intent of the parties to determine the moment of contract formation. [Citation.] Intent to be bound is a question of fact. [Citation.] "To discern that intent a court must look to the words and deeds [of the parties] which constitute objective signs in a given set of circumstances." [Citation.] In [citation], the Second Circuit articulated four factors to aid in determining whether the parties intended to be bound in the absence of a fully executed document. [Citation.] The court suggested that we "consider (1) whether there has been an express reservation of the right not to be bound in the absence of a writing; (2) whether there has been partial performance of the contract; (3) whether all of the terms of the alleged contract have been agreed upon; and (4) whether the agreement at issue is the type of contract that is usually committed to writing." [Citations.]

The language of the parties' correspondence and other documentary evidence presented reveals an intent by the mediation participants not to be bound prior to the execution of a final document. First, the Mediation Agreement Judge O'Dea sent to the parties prior to the mediation clearly contemplates that any settlement agreement emanating from the mediation would be binding only after being put in writing and signed. Paragraph nine of the Agreement expressly stated that statements made during mediation would not be "binding upon either party unless reduced to a final agreement of settlement" and that "any final agreement of settlement [would] be in writing and signed by every party sought to be charged." Further, Judge O'Dea reminded the parties of these ground rules at the outset of the mediation. The Reeds testified that they relied on these statements and assumed that, as indicated, they would not be bound until they signed a written agreement.

* * *

Even more compelling evidence of the Reeds' lack of intent to be bound in the absence of a writing is the statement in the cover letter accompanying the Reeds' $250 payments to the Sheldons' attorney saying, "This check is forwarded to you with the understanding that the funds will be disbursed to your clients only after settlement agreement becomes final. Of course, if the settlement agreement does not come to fruition, then the funds must be returned to my clients." This factor weighs in favor of finding that the Reeds expressed their right not to be bound until their agreement was reduced to a final writing and executed.

Because there was no evidence presented of partial performance of the settlement agreement, we next consider the third factor, whether there was anything left to negotiate. * * *

As stated by the Second Circuit in [citation], "the actual drafting of a written instrument will frequently reveal points of disagreement, ambiguity, or omission which must be worked out prior to execution. Details that are unnoticed or passed by in oral discussion will be pinned down when the understanding is reduced to writing." (internal quotations and citations omitted). [Citation.] This case is no exception. A review of the lengthy correspondence in this case makes clear that several points of disagreement and ambiguity arose during the drafting process. Beyond the location of seismic measurements and the definition of "over blast," correspondence indicates that the parties still had not reached agreement on the term and width of the lease, acceptable decibel levels and notice provisions for blasts, the definition of "truck trips," and whether all claims would be dismissed without prejudice after the execution of the agreement. Resolution of these issues was clearly important enough to forestall final execution until the language of the documents could be agreed upon. In such a case, where the parties intend to be bound only upon execution of a final document, for the court to determine that, despite continuing disagreement on substantive terms, the parties reached a binding, enforceable settlement agreement undermines their right to enter into the specific settlement agreement for which they contracted.

The fourth and final factor, whether the agreement at issue is the type of contract usually put into writing, also weighs in the Reeds' favor. Being a contract for an interest in land, the Lease Agreement is subject to the Statute of Frauds and thus generally must be in writing. * * *

* * *

In conclusion, three of the four factors indicate that the parties here did not intend to be bound until the execution of a final written document, and therefore we hold that the parties never entered into a binding settlement agreement. * * * Accordingly, the order enforcing the settlement is reversed and the case is remanded for further proceedings.

CASE 10-2

Invitations Seeking Offers
LEFKOWITZ v. GREAT MINNEAPOLIS SURPLUS STORE, INC.

Supreme Court of Minnesota, 1957
251 Minn. 188, 86 N.W.2d 689

Murphy, J.

This is an appeal from an order of * * * judgment award[ing] the plaintiff the sum of $138.50 as damages for breach of contract.

This case grows out of the alleged refusal of the defendant to sell to the plaintiff a certain fur piece which it had offered for sale in a newspaper advertisement. It appears from the record that on April 6, 1956, the defendant published the following advertisement in a Minneapolis newspaper:

SATURDAY 9 AM SHARP
3 BRAND NEW
FUR COATS Worth to $100.00
First Come
First Served
$1 EACH

On April 13, the defendant again published an advertisement in the same newspaper as follows:

SATURDAY 9 AM
2 BRAND NEW PASTEL
MINK 3-SKIN SCARFS
Selling for $89.50
Out they go
Saturday. Each ... $1.00
1 BLACK LAPIN [RABBIT] STOLE
Beautiful,
worth $139.50 ... $1.00
First Come
First Served

The record supports the findings of the court that on each of the Saturdays following the publication of the above-described ads the plaintiff was the first to present himself at the appropriate counter in the defendant's store and on each occasion demanded the coat and the stole so advertised and indicated his readiness to pay the sale price of $1. On both occasions, the defendant refused to sell the merchandise to the plaintiff, stating on the first occasion that by a "house rule" the offer was intended for women only and sales would not be made to men, and on the second visit that plaintiff knew defendant's house rules. * * *

The defendant contends that a newspaper advertisement offering items of merchandise for sale at a named price is a "unilateral offer" which may be withdrawn without notice. He relies upon authorities which hold that, where an advertiser publishes in a newspaper that he has a certain quantity or quality of goods which he wants to dispose of at certain prices and on certain terms, such advertisements are not offers which become contracts as soon as any person to whose notice they may come signifies his acceptance by notifying the other that he will take a certain quantity of them. Such advertisements have been construed as an invitation for an offer of sale on the terms stated, which offer, when received, may be accepted or rejected and which therefore does not become a contract of sale until accepted by the seller; and until a contract has been so made, the seller may modify or revoke such prices or terms. [Citations.] * * * On the facts before us we are concerned with whether the advertisement constituted an offer, and, if so, whether the plaintiff's conduct constituted an acceptance.

* * *

The test of whether a binding obligation may originate in advertisements addressed to the general public is "whether the facts show that some performance was promised in positive terms in return for something requested."

* * *

Whether in any individual instance a newspaper advertisement is an offer rather than an invitation to make an offer depends on the legal intention of the parties and the surrounding circumstances. [Citations.] We are of the view on the facts before us that the offer by the defendant of the sale * * * was clear, definite, and explicit, and left nothing open for negotiation. The plaintiff, having successfully managed to be the first one to appear at the seller's place of business to be served, as requested by the advertisement, and having offered the stated purchase price of the article, was entitled to performance on the part of the defendant. We think the trial court was correct in holding that there was in the conduct of the parties a sufficient mutuality of obligation to constitute a contract of sale.

* * *

Affirmed.

C A S E
10-3

Duration of Offers
SHERROD v. KIDD
Court of Appeals of Washington, Division 3, 2007
155 P.3d 976

Sweeney, C. J.
David and Elizabeth Kidd's dog bit Mikaila Sherrod. Mikaila through her guardian ad litem (GAL) made a claim for damages. On June 14, 2005, the Kidds offered to settle the claim for $31,837. On July 12, Mikaila through her GAL sued the Kidds. On July 20, the Kidds bumped their offer to $32,843.

The suit was subject to mandatory arbitration. The parties proceeded to arbitration on April 28, 2006. On May 5, the arbitrator awarded Mikaila $25,069.47. On May 9, the GAL wrote to the Kidds and purported to accept their last offer of $32,843, made the year before.

The GAL on Mikaila's behalf moved to enforce the settlement agreement. The court concluded the offer was properly accepted because it had not been withdrawn. And it entered judgment in the amount of the first written offer.

* * *

The Kidds contend that the trial court did not consider that implicit in its settlement offer was the GAL's forbearance in proceeding with the arbitration to its conclusion. The GAL argues that the offer was not conditioned upon the arbitration proceeding in any manner. And the offer provided no time limit for its acceptance. The GAL further claims that the consideration to create an enforceable agreement—her promise to dismiss her lawsuit—was the same when she accepted it as when it was offered. Her consideration included relinquishing her right to request a trial de novo.

An offer to form a contract is open only for a reasonable time, unless the offer specifically states how long it is open for acceptance. [Citations.] "[I]n the absence of an acceptance of an offer within a reasonable time (where no time limit is specified), there is no contract." [Citation.]

How much time is reasonable is usually a question of fact. [Citation.] But we can decide the limits of a reasonable time if the facts are undisputed. [Citation.] And here the essential facts are not disputed.

A reasonable time "is the time that a reasonable person in the exact position of the offeree would believe to be satisfactory to the offeror." [Citation.] "The purpose of the offeror, to be attained by the making and performance of the contract, will affect the time allowed for acceptance, if it is or should be known to the offeree. In such case there is no power to accept after it is too late to attain that purpose." [Citation.] A reasonable time for an offeree to accept an offer depends on the "nature of the contract and the character of the business in which the parties were engaged." [Citation.]

Implicit in an offer (and an acceptance) to settle a personal injury suit is the party's intent to avoid a less favorable result at the hands of a jury, a judge or, in this case, an arbitrator. The

defendant runs the risk that the award might be more than the offer. The plaintiff, of course, runs the risk that the award might be less than the offer. Both want to avoid that risk. And it is those risks that settlements avoid.

* * *

* * * Here, the value of this claim was set after arbitration. It was certainly subject to appeal but nonetheless set by a fact finder.

This offer expired when the arbitrator announced the award and was not subject to being accepted.

We reverse the decision of the trial judge to the contrary.

<table>
<tr><td>CASE
10-4</td><td>Counteroffer
THOR PROPERTIES v. WILLSPRING HOLDINGS LLC
Supreme Court, Appellate Division, First Department, New York, 2014
118 A.D.3d 505, 988 N.Y.S.2d 47</td><td></td></tr>
</table>

Sweeny, J. P.

[Plaintiff Thor Properties brought this action for breach of contract to compel specific performance by defendant Willspring Holdings to sell it a mixed-used building in Manhattan. On December 5, 2012, Thor emailed Willspring a letter of intent (LOI) offering to buy the property for $111 million under terms that included Willspring's transfer of the property free of liens. The December 5th LOI also provided that, unless Willspring countersigned and returned it by December 7, Thor's offer would "be deemed withdrawn in its entirety." On December 5, Willspring emailed Thor to reject its offer, noting that Thor's purchase price fell short of other bids. Willspring also refused to transfer the property free of liens because it demanded Thor assume the existing mortgage on the property. After more negotiations, on December 6 Willspring emailed Thor that Willspring expected a modified LOI to be issued under which Thor would (1) increase its offer to $115 million; (2) agree to assume the mortgage; (3) execute a long-form purchase agreement by December 11, 2012; and (4) close by the end of the year. Later on December 6, Thor emailed a second LOI, which increased the purchase price but did not commit to executing the purchase agreement by December 11 or closing in 2012, and still required Willspring to deliver the property free of liens. The new LOI also required Willspring's countersignature and delivery by December 7. Thereafter, Willspring responded by sending Thor a copy of its December 6th LOI, which Willspring had marked up by hand and signed. Willspring's response deleted Thor's requirement that the seller convey title free of liens and added the December 11 deadline for an executed purchase agreement. In addition, the response modified its demand for a closing by year's end by providing that the closing must occur within 30 days after the purchase

agreement was signed but also provided that "[time was of the essence]" for closing.

Minutes later, Willspring's principal emailed Thor that he was "pleased that we have been able to agree [to] terms." He cautioned, however, that if there were any "[renegotiating]" then Willspring would "walk away promptly." About one hour thereafter, however, Thor emailed Willspring that "[w]e will be getting our response to your proposed changes to the LOI shortly."

While the parties continued discussions on the evening of December 6, on the morning of December 7, Willspring's principal emailed Thor that "[p]er our conversation last night. I understand our changes to [the December 6th]

LOI are NOT acceptable to Thor as presented. Please send me a revised LOI with your suggested changes so I can have our attorney review them." Later on December 7, Thor sent Willspring a new or third LOI which changed the terms of the marked-up December 6th LOI by giving Thor a unilateral right to adjourn the closing date by 10 days, despite time being of the essence. The December 7th LOI sent by Thor also extended the deadline for a signed purchase agreement by two days but limited Thor's assumption of the mortgage to the only exception to Willspring's obligation to deliver the property free of liens. The December 7th LOI stated that it required Willspring's countersignature and return by that day. On the afternoon of December 7, Willspring's principal emailed Thor that the "LOI changes you have put forth [are] not what we agreed to" because "[w]e were very clear on the need to sign a contract early next week and to close by year end." The Willspring principal acknowledged that Thor's offer expired that day. On December 10, Thor emailed Willspring a copy of the December 6th LOI that Willspring had marked up and signed, which now bore Thor's initials by Willspring's handwritten changes purportedly to show Thor's acceptance of the agreement that it had previously sought to modify. Willspring, however, contracted to sell its property to a third party.

The Supreme Court, New York County granted Willspring's motion for summary judgment dismissing the complaint. Thor appealed.]

The record demonstrates that the parties never came to terms and instead proposed a series of offers and counteroffers to which they never mutually agreed. Moreover, Thor's belated attempt to form a binding contract on December 10 was a nullity. To enter into a contract, a party must clearly and unequivocally accept the offeror's terms [citations]. If instead the offeree responds by conditioning acceptance on new or modified terms, that response constitutes both a rejection and a counteroffer which extinguishes the initial offer [citation]. The counteroffer extinguishes the original offer, and thereafter the offeree cannot, as Thor attempted on December 10, unilaterally revive the offer by accepting it [citation].

While oral acceptance of a written offer can form a binding contract for the sale of real property [citation], the record does not support Thor's claim that it unequivocally accepted the counteroffer that Wellspring set forth in the mark-up of the December 6th LOI, before that counteroffer terminated. Thor's email that it would respond to Willspring's changes to the December 6th LOI indicates that Thor had not accepted those changes and intended further negotiation.

Moreover, Willspring's email on the morning of December 7 confirms that Thor had rejected Willspring's counteroffer. At the time, Thor did not claim that an agreement had been reached, but instead responded to Will-spring's email by submitting the December 7th LOI, which it described as another "offer." The December 7th LOI neither refers to the marked-up December 6th LOI as a binding agreement nor unconditionally accepts the counteroffer embodied in Willspring's handwritten changes.

Thor claims that on December 6 it orally accepted Willspring's changes to the December 6th LOI, but asked Willspring to consider some "slight modifications" that Thor would put into writing the next day. However, the changes in the December 7th LOI were not, as Thor claims, "immaterial," because they afforded Thor the unilateral right to adjourn the closing. If a real estate contract provides that the time of closing is of the essence, "performance on the specified date is a material element … and failure to perform on that date constitutes … a material breach" [citation]. By modifying a material term in Willspring's counteroffer, Thor rejected it and proposed a counteroffer that Willspring never accepted. Accordingly, the complaint for breach of contract was properly dismissed.

CASE 10-5

Silence as Acceptance
NORCIA v. SAMSUNG TELECOMMUNICATIONS AMERICA, LLC

United States Court of Appeals, Ninth Circuit, 2017
845 F. 3d 1279

Ikuta, J.

On May 23, 2013, [Daniel] Norcia entered a Verizon Wireless store in San Francisco, California, to purchase a Samsung Galaxy S4 phone. Norcia paid for the phone at the register, and a Verizon Wireless employee provided a receipt entitled "Customer Agreement" followed by the name and address of the Verizon Wireless store. The receipt stated the order location, Norcia's mobile number, the product identification number, and the contract end date. Under the heading "Items," the receipt stated "WAR6002 1 YR. MFG. WARRANTY." Under the heading "Agreement," the receipt included three provisions, including a statement (in all capital letters):

> I agree to the current Verizon Wireless Customer Agreement, including the calling plan, (with extended limited warranty/service contract, if applicable), and other terms and conditions for services and selected features I have agreed to purchase as reflected on the receipt, and which

have been presented to me by the sales representative and which I had the opportunity to review.

The receipt also stated (in all capital letters): "I understand that I am agreeing to…settlement of disputes by arbitration and other means instead of jury trials, and other important terms in the Customer Agreement." The Customer Agreement did not reference Samsung or any other party. Norcia signed the Customer Agreement, and Verizon Wireless emailed him a copy.

After signing the Customer Agreement, Norcia and a Verizon Wireless employee took the Galaxy S4 phone, still in its sealed Samsung box, to a table. The front of the product box stated "Samsung Galaxy S4." The back of the box stated: "Package Contains…Product Safety & Warranty Brochure." The Verizon Wireless employee opened the box, unpacked the phone and materials, and helped Norcia transfer his contacts from his old phone to the new phone. Norcia took the phone, the phone charger, and the headphones with him as he left the store, but he declined the offer by the Verizon Wireless employee to take the box and the rest of its contents.

The Samsung Galaxy S4 box contained, among other things, a "Product Safety & Warranty Information" brochure. The 101-page brochure consisted of two sections. Section 1 contained a wide range of health and safety information, while Section 2 contained Samsung's "Standard Limited Warranty" and "End User License Agreement for Software." The Standard Limited Warranty section explained the scope of Samsung's express warranty. In addition to explaining Samsung's obligations, the procedure for obtaining warranty service, and the limits of Samsung's liability, the warranty section included the following (in all capital letters):

> All disputes with Samsung arising in any way from this limited warranty or the sale, condition or performance of the products shall be resolved exclusively through final and binding arbitration, and not by a court or jury.

***

In February 2014, Norcia filed a class action complaint against Samsung, alleging that Samsung misrepresented the Galaxy S4's storage capacity and rigged the phone to operate at a higher speed when it was being tested. The complaint alleged that these deceptive acts constituted common law fraud and violated [several of California's Consumers Protection Laws. Citations.] The complaint sought certification of the case as a class action for all purchasers of the Galaxy S4 phone in California. Norcia did not bring any claims for breach of warranty.

Instead of filing an answer to the complaint, Samsung moved to compel arbitration by invoking the arbitration provision in the Product Safety & Warranty Information brochure. The district court denied Samsung's motion. It held that even though Norcia should be deemed to have received the Galaxy S4 box, including the Product Safety & Warranty Information brochure, the receipt of the brochure did not form an agreement to arbitrate non-warranty claims. Samsung timely appealed the district court's order.

***

"[A]rbitration is a matter of contract and a party cannot be required to submit to arbitration any dispute which he has not agreed so to submit." [Citations.] Therefore, to evaluate the district court's denial of Samsung's motion to compel arbitration, we must first determine "whether a valid agreement to arbitrate exists." [Citations.] ***

***

We first evaluate whether the Product Safety & Warranty Information brochure in the Galaxy S4 box created a binding contract between Norcia and Samsung to arbitrate the claims in Norcia's complaint. Although the brochure is in the form of an express consumer warranty from Samsung to Norcia, the arbitration provision states that arbitration is required not only for "[a]ll disputes with Samsung arising in any way from this limited warranty" but also for all disputes arising from "the sale, condition or performance of the products." Norcia's complaint involves a non-warranty dispute. Thus, our analysis is governed by contract law—not warranty law.

We begin with the basic principles of California contract law. Generally, under California law, "the essential elements for a contract are (1) '[p]arties capable of contracting;' (2) '[t]heir consent;' (3) '[a] lawful object;' and (4) '[s]ufficient cause or consideration.'" [Citation.] A party who is bound by a contract is bound by all its terms, whether or not the party was aware of them. "A party cannot avoid the terms of a contract on the ground that he or she failed to read it before signing." [Citation.]

***

As a general rule, "silence or inaction does not constitute acceptance of an offer." [Citations.] California courts have long held that "[a]n offer made to another, either orally or in writing, cannot be turned into an agreement because the person to whom it is made or sent makes no reply, even though the offer states that silence will be taken as consent, for the offer or cannot prescribe conditions of rejection so as to turn silence on the part of the offeree into acceptance." [Citations.]

There are exceptions to this rule, however. An offeree's silence may be deemed to be consent to a contract when the offeree has a duty to respond to an offer and fails to act in the face of this duty. [Citations.] ***

An offeree's silence may also be treated as consent to a contract when the party retains the benefit offered. [Citations.] ***

Even if there is an applicable exception to the general rule that silence does not constitute acceptance, courts have rejected the argument that an offeree's silence constitutes consent to a contract when the offeree reasonably did not know that an offer had been made. [Citations.] ***

*** There is no dispute that Norcia did not expressly assent to any agreement in the brochure. Nor did Norcia sign the brochure or otherwise act in a manner that would show "his intent to use his silence, or failure to opt out, as a means of accepting the arbitration agreement." [Citation.] Under California law, an offeree's inaction after receipt of an offer is generally insufficient to form a contract. [Citation.] Therefore, Samsung's offer to arbitrate all disputes with Norcia "cannot be turned into an agreement because the person to whom it is made or sent makes no reply, even though the offer states that silence will be taken as consent," unless an exception to this general rule applies.

Samsung fails to demonstrate the applicability of any exception to the general California rule that an offeree's silence does not constitute consent. ***

In the absence of an applicable exception, California's general rule for contract formation applies. Because Norcia did not give any "outward manifestations of consent [that] would lead a reasonable person to believe the offeree has assented to the agreement," [citation], no contract was formed between Norcia and Samsung, and Norcia is not bound by the arbitration provision contained in the brochure.

***

We next turn to Samsung's second argument, that Norcia agreed to arbitrate his claims by signing the Customer Agreement with Verizon Wireless. This argument is meritless.

The Customer Agreement is an agreement between Verizon Wireless and its customer. Samsung is not a signatory. While the agreement itself includes a number of terms governing the relationship between Norcia and Verizon Wireless, including an arbitration provision, nothing in the agreement references Samsung or any other party.

***

[We affirm the district court's denial of Samsung's motion.]

QUESTIONS

1. Ames, seeking business for his lawn maintenance firm, posted the following notice in the meeting room of the Antlers, a local lodge: "To the members of the Antlers— Special this month. I will resod your lawn for two dollars per square foot using Fairway brand sod. This offer expires July 15."

   The notice also included Ames's name, address, and signature and specified that the acceptance was to be in writing.

   Bates, a member of the Antlers, and Cramer, the janitor, read the notice and became interested. Bates wrote a letter to Ames saying he would accept the offer if Ames would use Putting Green brand sod. Ames received this letter July 14 and wrote to Bates saying he would not use Putting Green sod. Bates received Ames's letter on July 16 and promptly wrote Ames that he would accept Fairway sod. Cramer wrote to Ames on July 10, saying he accepted Ames's offer.

   By July 15, Ames had found more profitable ventures and refused to resod either lawn at the specified price. Bates and Cramer brought an appropriate action against Ames for breach of contract. Decisions as to the respective claims of Bates and Cramer? Discuss.

2. Garvey owned four speedboats named *Porpoise*, *Priscilla*, *Providence*, and *Prudence*. On April 2, Garvey made written offers to sell the four boats in the order named for $14,200 each to Caldwell, Meens, Smith, and Braxton, respectively, allowing ten days for acceptance. In which, if any, of the following four situations described was a contract formed? Explain.

   a. Five days later, Caldwell received notice from Garvey that he had contracted to sell *Porpoise* to Montgomery. The next day, April 8, Caldwell notified Garvey that he accepted Garvey's offer.

   b. On the third day, April 5, Meens mailed a rejection to Garvey which reached Garvey on the morning of the sixth day. But at 10:00 A.M. on the fourth day, Meens

   sent an acceptance by overnight letter to Garvey, who received it at noon on the fifth day.

   c. Smith, on April 3, replied that she was interested in buying *Providence* but declared the price asked appeared slightly excessive and wondered if, perhaps, Garvey would be willing to sell the boat for $13,900. Five days later, having received no reply from Garvey, Smith, by letter, accepted Garvey's offer and enclosed a certified check for $14,200.

   d. Braxton was accidentally killed in an automobile accident on April 9. The following day, the executor of Braxton's estate mailed an acceptance of Garvey's offer to Garvey.

3. Alpha Rolling Mill Corporation, by letter dated June 8, offered to sell Brooklyn Railroad Company two thousand to five thousand tons of fifty-pound iron rails upon certain specified terms, adding that, if the offer was accepted, Alpha Corporation would expect to be notified prior to June 20. Brooklyn Company, on June 16, by fax, referring to Alpha Corporation's offer of June 8, directed Alpha Corporation to enter an order for 1,200 tons of fifty-pound iron rails on the terms specified. The same day, June 16, Brooklyn Company, by letter to Alpha Corporation, confirmed the fax.

   On June 18, Alpha Corporation, by telephone, declined to fill the order. Brooklyn Company, on June 19, wrote Alpha Corporation: "Please enter an order for 2,000 tons of rails as per your letter of the eighth. Please forward written contract. Reply." In reply to Brooklyn Company's repeated inquiries regarding whether the order for two thousand tons of rails had been entered, Alpha denied the existence of any contract between Brooklyn Company and itself. Thereafter, Brooklyn Company sued Alpha Corporation for breach of contract. Decision? Discuss.

4. On April 8, Burchette received a telephone call from Bleluck, a truck dealer, who told Burchette that a new

model truck in which Burchette was interested would arrive in one week. Although Bleluck initially wanted $10,500, the conversation ended after Bleluck agreed to sell and Burchette agreed to purchase the truck for $10,000, with a $1,000 down payment and the balance upon delivery. The next day, Burchette sent Bleluck a check for $1,000, which Bleluck promptly cashed.

One week later, when Burchette called Bleluck and inquired about the truck, Bleluck informed Burchette he had several prospects looking at the truck and would not sell for less than $10,500. The following day, Bleluck sent Burchette a properly executed check for $1,000 with the following notation thereon: "Return of down payment on sale of truck." After notifying Bleluck that she will not cash the check, Burchette sues Bleluck for damages. Should Burchette prevail? Explain.

5. On November 15, I. Sellit, a manufacturer of crystalware, mailed to Benny Buyer a letter stating that Sellit would sell to Buyer one hundred crystal "A" goblets at $100 per goblet and that "the offer would remain open for fifteen (15) days." On November 18, Sellit, noticing the sudden rise in the price of crystal "A" goblets, decided to withdraw her offer to Buyer and so notified Buyer. Buyer chose to ignore Sellit's letter of revocation and gleefully watched as the price of crystal "A" goblets continued to skyrocket. On November 30, Buyer mailed to Sellit a letter accepting Sellit's offer to sell the goblets. The letter was received by Sellit on December 4. Buyer demands delivery of the goblets. Explain what the result is.

6. On May 1, Melforth Realty Company offered to sell Greenacre to Dallas, Inc., for $1 million. The offer was made by a letter sent by overnight delivery and stated that the offer would expire on May 15. Dallas decided to purchase the property and sent a letter by registered first-class mail to Melforth on May 10, accepting the offer. Due to unexplained delays in the postal service, Melforth did not receive the letter until May 22. Now, Melforth wishes to sell Greenacre to another buyer, who is offering $1.2 million for the tract of land. Has a contract resulted between Melforth and Dallas? Explain.

7. Rowe advertised in newspapers of wide circulation and otherwise made it known that she would pay $5,000 for a complete set consisting of ten volumes of certain rare books. Ford, not knowing of the offer, gave Rowe all but one volume of the set of rare books as a Christmas present. Ford later learned of the offer, obtained the one remaining book, tendered it to Rowe, and demanded the $5,000. Rowe refused to pay. Discuss whether Ford is entitled to the $5,000?

8. Scott, manufacturer of a carbonated beverage, entered into a contract with Otis, owner of a baseball park, whereby Otis rented to Scott a large signboard on top of the center field wall. The contract provided that Otis should letter the sign as Scott desired and would change the lettering from time to time within forty-eight hours after receipt of written request from Scott. As directed by Scott, the signboard originally stated in large letters that Scott would pay $1,000 to any ballplayer hitting a home run over the sign.

In the first game of the season, Hume, the best hitter in the league, hit one home run over the sign. Scott immediately served written notice on Otis instructing Otis to replace the offer on the signboard with an offer to pay $500 to every pitcher who pitched a no-hit game in the park. A week after receipt of Scott's letter, Otis had not changed the wording on the sign. On that day, Perry, a pitcher for a scheduled game, pitched a no-hit game while Todd, one of his teammates, hit a home run over Scott's sign. Scott refuses to pay any of the three players. Discuss what the rights of Scott, Hume, Perry, and Todd are.

9. Barnes accepted Clark's offer to sell to him a portion of Clark's coin collection. Clark forgot that his prized $20 gold piece at the time of the offer and acceptance was included in the portion that he offered to sell to Barnes. Clark did not intend to include the gold piece in the sale. Barnes, at the time of inspecting the offered portion of the collection and prior to accepting the offer, saw the gold piece. Is Barnes entitled to the $20 gold piece? Explain.

10. Small, admiring Jasper's watch, asked Jasper where and at what price he had purchased it. Jasper replied, "I bought it at West Watch Shop about two years ago for around $85, but I am not certain as to that." Small then said, "Those fellows at West are good people and always sell good watches. I'll buy that watch from you." Jasper replied, "It's a deal." The next morning Small telephoned Jasper and said he had changed his mind and did not wish to buy the watch. Jasper sued Small for breach of contract. In defense, Small has pleaded that he made no enforceable contract with Jasper (a) because the parties did not agree on the price to be paid for the watch and (b) because the parties did not agree on the place and time of delivery of the watch to Small. Are either or both of these defenses good? Explain.

11. Jeff says to Brenda, "I offer to sell you my PC for $900." Brenda replies, "If you do not hear otherwise from me by Thursday, I have accepted your offer." Jeff agrees and does not hear from Brenda by Thursday. Does a contract exist between Jeff and Brenda? Explain.

12. On November 19, Hoover Motor Express Company sent to Clements Paper Company a written offer to purchase

certain real estate. Sometime in December, Clements authorized Williams to accept. Williams, however, attempted to bargain with Hoover to obtain a better deal, specifically that Clements would retain easements on the property. In a telephone conversation on January 13 of the following year, Williams first told Hoover of his plan to obtain the easements. Hoover replied, "Well, I don't know if we are ready. We have not decided; we might not want to go through with it." On January 20, Clements sent a written acceptance of Hoover's offer. Hoover refused to buy, claiming it had revoked its offer through the January 13 phone conversation. Clements then brought suit to compel the sale or obtain damages. Did Hoover successfully revoke its offer? Explain.

13. Walker leased a small lot to Keith for ten years at $1,000 a month, with a right for Keith to extend the lease for another ten-year term under the same terms except as to rent. The renewal option provided:

> Rental will be fixed in such amount as shall actually be agreed upon by the lessors and the lessee with the monthly rental fixed on the comparative basis of rental values as of the date of the renewal with rental values at this time reflected by the comparative business conditions of the two periods.

Keith sought to exercise the renewal right and, when the parties were unable to agree on the rent, brought suit against Walker. Who prevails? Why?

C A S E   P R O B L E M S

14. The Brewers contracted to purchase Dower House from McAfee. Then, several weeks before the May 7 settlement date for the purchase of the house, the two parties began to negotiate for the sale of certain items of furniture in the house. On April 30, McAfee sent the Brewers a letter containing a list of the furnishings to be purchased at specified prices; a payment schedule, including a request for a $3,000 payment, due on acceptance; and a clause reading, "If the above is satisfactory, please sign and return one copy with the first payment."

On June 3, the Brewers sent a letter to McAfee stating that enclosed was a $3,000 check, that the original contract had been misplaced and could another be furnished, that they planned to move into Dower House on June 12, and that they wished the red desk to be included in the contract. McAfee then sent a letter dated June 8 to the Brewers, listing the items of furniture purchased.

The Brewers moved into Dower House in the middle of June. Soon after they moved in, they tried to contact McAfee at his office to tell him that there had been a misunderstanding relating to their purchase of the listed items. They then refused to pay him any more money, and he brought action to recover the balance outstanding. Will McAfee be able to collect the additional money from the Brewers? Why or why not?

15. The Thoelkes were owners of real property located in Orange County, which the Morrisons agreed to purchase. The Morrisons signed a contract for the sale of that property and mailed it to the Thoelkes in Texas on November 26. The next day the Thoelkes executed the contract and placed it in the mail addressed to the Morrisons' attorney in Florida. After the executed contract was mailed but before it was received in Florida,

the Thoelkes called the Morrisons' attorney in Florida and attempted to repudiate the contract. Does a contract exist between the Thoelkes and the Morrisons? Discuss.

16. Lucy and Zehmer met while having drinks in a restaurant. During the course of their conversation, Lucy apparently offered to buy Zehmer's 471.6-acre farm for $50,000 cash. Although Zehmer claims that he thought the offer was made in jest, he wrote the following on the back of a pad: "We hereby agree to sell to W. O. Lucy the Ferguson Farm complete for $50,000, title satisfactory to buyer." Zehmer then signed the writing and induced his wife Ida to do the same. She claims, however, that she signed only after Zehmer assured her that it was only a joke. Finally, Zehmer claims that he was "high as a Georgia pine" at the time but admits that he was not too drunk to make a valid contract. Decision? Explain.

17. Lee Calan Imports advertised a used Volvo station wagon for sale in the *Chicago Sun-Times*. As part of the information for the advertisement, Lee Calan Imports instructed the newspaper to print the price of the car as $1,795. However, due to a mistake made by the newspaper, without any fault on the part of Lee Calan Imports, the printed ad listed the price of the car as $1,095. After reading the ad and then examining the car, O'Brien told a Lee Calan Imports salesperson that he wanted to purchase the car for the advertised price of $1,095. Calan Imports refuses to sell the car to O'Brien for $1,095. Is there a contract? If so, for what price? Explain.

18. On May 20, cattle rancher Oliver visited his neighbor Southworth, telling him, "I know you're interested in buying the land I'm selling." Southworth replied, "Yes, I do want to buy that land, especially as it adjoins my property." Although the two men did not discuss the

price, Oliver told Southworth he would determine the value of the property and send that information to him so that Southworth would have "notice" of what Oliver "wanted for the land." On June 13, Southworth called Oliver to ask if he still planned to sell the land. Oliver answered, "Yes, and I should have the value of the land determined soon." On June 17, Oliver sent a letter to Southworth listing a price quotation of $324,000.

Southworth then responded to Oliver by letter on June 21, stating that he accepted Oliver's offer. However, on June 24, Oliver wrote back to Southworth, saying, "There has never been a firm offer to sell, and there is no enforceable contract between us." Oliver maintains that a price quotation alone is not an offer. Southworth claims a valid contract has been made. Who wins? Discuss.

19. On December 23, Wyman, a lawyer representing First National Bank & Trust (defendant), wrote to Zeller (plaintiff) stating that he had been instructed to offer a building to Zeller for sale at a price of $240,000. Zeller had previously expressed an interest in purchasing the building for $240,000. The letter also set forth details concerning interest rates and loan fees.

After receiving the letter, Zeller instructed his attorney, Jamma, to send Wyman a written counteroffer of $230,000 with interest and loan arrangements varying from the terms of the original offer. Jamma sent the written counteroffer as instructed on January 10. On the same day, Jamma telephoned Wyman and informed him of the counteroffer. Subsequently Jamma sent an acceptance of the original offer to Wyman. When Wyman refused to sell the property to him, Zeller brought an action to seek enforcement of the alleged contract. Decision? Explain.

20. First Development Corporation of Kentucky (FDCK) sought to purchase a fifteen-acre parcel of riverfront property owned by Martin Marietta. On May 9, FDCK made an offer to purchase the property for $300,000, which it submitted to Coldwell Banker, Martin Marietta's real estate agent. This offer was accompanied by an earnest money deposit evidenced by a $1,000 check payable to Coldwell Banker. The deposit was fully refundable if transfer of title to FDCK was not completed for any reason except FDCK's failure to perform. After this offer expired without being accepted, FDCK asked Don Gilmour, Coldwell Banker's account agent, to seek a counteroffer. In a letter to Gilmour dated September 7, Martin Marietta agreed to sell the property for $550,000. The counteroffer stated it was to remain open for thirty days. Gilmour informed Pollitt, president of FDCK, of the counteroffer by telephone on September 7 and sent

a copy of the letter to Pollitt, which was received on September 12.

Within days of the expiration of FDCK's original offer, Bill Harvey, president of Harmony Landing, a development company, initiated direct negotiations with Martin Marietta to purchase the riverfront parcel. These negotiations resulted in a contract being executed on September 21 or 22. During a September 21 phone call, Gilmour advised Pollitt of Harmony Landing's interest in buying the property, but Pollitt remained noncommittal during the conversation. Later that day, Pollitt, along with his partner and engineer, visited the property and discussed various studies and arrived at a decision to accept the September 7 offer from Martin Marietta. However, Pollitt did not convey this acceptance to Gilmour. Rather, he consulted his attorneys regarding a contract to accept Martin Marietta's offer.

After consulting with his attorneys, Pollitt prepared an acceptance of Martin Marietta's offer but did not put it in the mail. The next morning, Pollitt placed the acceptance in his office suite's mail depository. However, after being informed by Gilmour that Martin Marietta had accepted Harmony Landing's option on the river property, Pollitt retrieved the acceptance and personally delivered it to Gilmour at 4:15 P.M. The acceptance was returned to Pollitt, and he subsequently initiated this action for temporary and permanent injunction and specific performance. The district court ruled that the $1,000 check, payable to and in the possession of Coldwell Banker during the period of this controversy was, by operation of law, converted into consideration for a thirty-day irrevocable option in favor of FDCK to purchase the riverfront property in accordance with the terms of Martin Marietta's letter of September 7. Does a contract exist between Martin Marietta and FDCK? Explain.

21. On August 12, Mr. and Mrs. Mitchell, the owners of a small secondhand store, attended Alexander's Auction, where they bought a used safe for $50. The safe, part of the Sumstad estate, contained a locked inside compartment. Both the auctioneer and the Mitchells knew this fact. Soon after the auction, the Mitchells had the compartment opened by a locksmith, who discovered $32,207 inside. The Everett Police Department impounded the money. The city of Everett brought an action against the Sumstad estate and the Mitchells to determine the owner of the money. Who should receive the money? Why?

22. Irwin Schiff is a self-styled "tax rebel" who has made a career, and substantial profit, out of his tax protest activities. On February 7, Schiff appeared live on CBS News

Nightwatch, a late-night program with a viewer participation format. During the broadcast, Schiff repeated his assertion that nothing in the Internal Revenue Code stated that an individual was legally required to pay federal income tax. Schiff then challenged, "If anybody calls this show—I have the Code—and cites any section of this Code that says an individual is required to file a tax return, I will pay them $100,000." Call-in telephone numbers were periodically flashed on the screen. John Newman, an attorney, did not see Schiff's live appearance on *Nightwatch*. Newman did, however, see a two-minute videotaped segment, including Schiff's challenge, which was rebroadcast several hours later on the *CBS Morning News*. Newman researched the matter that same day and on the following day, February 9, placed a call using directory assistance to *CBS Morning News* stating that the call was performance of the consideration requested by Mr. Schiff in exchange for his promise to pay $100,000. When Schiff refused to pay, Newman sued. Should Newman prevail? Explain.

23. The Cornillies listed with a real estate agent a home for sale. Patrick and Anne Giannetti offered $155,000 for the home and submitted a deposit in the amount of $2,500. The Cornillies countered this offer with an offer to sell the house for $160,000. The Giannettis then inquired whether certain equipment and items of furniture could be included with the sale of the house. The Cornillies refused to include the questioned items in the sale. The Giannettis then accepted the $160,000 offer but changed the mortgage amount from $124,000 to $128,000. Is there a binding contract? Explain.

24. Kelly-Moore Paint Company, entered into a fifteen-year commercial lease with Osprey, for a property in Edmond, Oklahoma. The lease contained an option for two five-year renewals. The lease required that the Kelly-Moore give notice of its intent to renew at least six months prior to its expiration. It also provided that the renewal "may be delivered either personally or by depositing the same in United States mail, first class postage prepaid, registered or certified mail, return receipt requested." Upon expiration of the original fifteen-year lease, Kelly-Moore timely informed the Osprey by certified letter of its intent to extend the lease an additional five years. The first five-year extension was due to expire on August 31. On the last day of the six-month notification deadline, Kelly-Moore faxed a letter of renewal notice to Osprey's office at 5:28 P.M. In addition, Kelly-Moore sent a copy of the faxed renewal notice letter by Federal Express that same day. Osprey denies ever receiving the fax, but it admits receiving the Federal Express copy of the notice on the following business day. Osprey rejected the notice, asserting that it was late, and it filed an action to remove Kelley-Moore from the premises. Explain your decision.

TAKING SIDES

Cushing filed an application with the office of the Adjutant General of the State of New Hampshire for the use of the Portsmouth Armory to hold a dance on the evening of April 29. The application, made on behalf of the Portsmouth Area Clamshell Alliance, was received by the Adjutant General's office on or about March 30. On March 31, the Adjutant General mailed a signed contract after agreeing to rent the armory for the evening requested. The agreement required acceptance by the renter affixing his signature to the agreement and then returning the copy to the Adjutant General within five days after receipt. Cushing received the contract offer, signed it on behalf of the Alliance, and placed it in the outbox for mailing on April 3. At 6:30 on the evening of April 4, Cushing received a telephone call from the Adjutant General revoking the rental offer. Cushing stated during the conversation that he had already signed and mailed the contract. The Adjutant General sent a written confirmation of the withdrawal on April 5. On April 6, the Adjutant General's office received by mail from Cushing the signed contract dated April 3 and postmarked April 5.

a. What are the arguments that a binding contract exists?

b. What are the arguments that a contract does not exist or should not exist?

c. What is the proper outcome? Explain.

CHAPTER 11

Conduct Invalidating Assent

CHAPTER OUTCOMES

After reading and studying this chapter, you should be able to:

- Discuss the types of duress.

- Identify the situations giving rise to confidential relationship.

- Identify the types of fraud and the elements that must be shown to establish the existence of each.

- Define the two types of nonfraudulent misrepresentation.

- Explain the situations involving voidable mistakes.

The preceding chapter considered one of the essential requirements of a contract, namely, the objective manifestation of mutual assent by each party to the other. In addition to requiring that the offer and acceptance be satisfied, the law of contracts demands that the agreement be voluntary and knowing. If these requirements are not met, then the agreement is either voidable or void. This chapter deals with situations in which the consent manifested by one of the parties to the contract is not effective because it was not knowingly and voluntarily given. These situations are considered under the headings of duress, undue influence, fraud, nonfraudulent misrepresentation, and mistake.

11-1 Duress

A person should not be held to an agreement into which she has not entered voluntarily. Accordingly, the law will not enforce any contract induced by **duress,** which in general is any wrongful or unlawful act or threat that overcomes the free will of a party.

11-1a PHYSICAL COMPULSION

There are two basic types of duress. The first occurs when one party compels another to manifest assent to a contract through actual **physical force,** such as pointing a gun at a person or taking a person's hand and compelling him to sign a written contract. This type of duress, while extremely rare, renders the agreement **void,** and the party exerting the duress is liable in restitution as necessary to avoid unjust

enrichment. Restatement, Section 174(1); Restatement of Restitution, Section 14.

11-1b IMPROPER THREATS

The second type of duress involves the use of improper threats or acts, *including economic and social coercion,* to compel a person to enter into a contract. The threat may be explicit or may be inferred from words or conduct; in either case, it must leave the victim with no reasonable alternative. This type of duress makes the contract *voidable* at the option of the coerced party, and the party exerting the duress is liable in restitution as necessary to avoid unjust enrichment. (See *Chapter 18.*) Restatement, Section 175(2); Restatement of Restitution, Section 14.

For example, if Lance, a landlord, induces Tamara, an infirm, bedridden tenant, to enter into a new lease on the same apartment at a greatly increased rent by wrongfully threatening to terminate Tamara's lease and evict her, Tamara can escape or *avoid* the new lease by reason of the duress exerted upon her.

With respect to the second and more common type of duress, the fact that the act or threat would not affect a person of average strength and intelligence is not determinative if it places the particular person in fear and induces him to perform an action against his will. The test is *subjective,* and the question is, did the threat actually induce assent on the part of the person claiming to be the victim of duress? Threats that would suffice to induce assent by one person may not suffice to induce assent by another. All circumstances must be considered, including the age, background, and relationship of the parties. Restatement, Section 175. Indeed, as Comment c to this section of the Restatement states,

> Persons of a weak or cowardly nature are the very ones that need protection; the courageous can usually protect themselves. Timid and inexperienced persons are particularly subject to threats, and it does not lie in the mouths of the unscrupulous to excuse their imposition on such persons on the ground of their victims' infirmities.

Ordinarily, the acts or threats constituting duress are themselves crimes or torts. But this is not true in all cases. The acts need not be criminal or tortious to be *wrongful*; they merely need to be contrary to public policy or morally reprehensible. For example, if the threat involves a breach of a contractual duty of good faith and fair dealing or the use of the civil process in bad faith, it is improper.

Moreover, the courts have generally held that contracts induced by threats of criminal prosecution are voidable, regardless of whether the coerced party had committed an unlawful act. Likewise, threatening the criminal prosecution of a near relative, such as a son or husband, is duress, regardless of the guilt or innocence of the relative.

To be distinguished from such threats of prosecution are threats to resort to ordinary civil remedies to recover a debt due from another. Threatening to bring a civil suit against an individual to recover a debt is not wrongful. What is prohibited is threatening to bring a civil suit when bringing such a suit would be abuse of process.

Practical Advice

If you entered into a contract due to improper threats, consider whether you wish to void the contract. If you decide to do so, act promptly.

◆ *See Case 11-1*

11-2 Undue Influence

Undue influence is the unfair persuasion of a person by a party generally in a dominant position based upon a **confidential relationship**. The law very carefully scrutinizes contracts between those in a relationship of trust and confidence that is likely to permit one party to take unfair advantage of the other. Examples are the relationships of guardian-ward, trustee-beneficiary, principal-agent, spouses to each other, parent-child, attorney-client, physician-patient, and clergy-parishioner.

A transaction induced by undue influence on the part of the dominant party is *voidable*, and the dominant party is

liable in restitution as necessary to avoid unjust enrichment. (See *Chapter 18*.) Restatement of Restitution, Section 15. The ultimate question in undue influence cases is whether the dominant party induced the transaction by influencing a freely exercised and competent judgment or by dominating the mind, emotions, or both of a submissive party. The weakness or dependence of the person persuaded is a strong indicator of the fairness or unfairness of the persuasion. For example, Ronald, a person without business experience, has for years relied in business matters on the advice of Nancy, who is experienced in business; Nancy, without making any false representations of fad induces Ronald to enter into a contract with Nancy's confederate, George. The contract, however, is disadvantageous to Ronald, as both Nancy and George know. The transaction is voidable on the grounds of undue influence.

Undue influence, as previously mentioned, generally arises in the context of relationships in which one person is in a position of dominance or is likely to be. Where such relationship exists at the time of the transaction and it appears that the dominant party has gained at the other party's expense, the transaction is presumed to be voidable. For example, in a legally challenged contract between guardian and his ward, the law presumes that advantage was taken by the guardian. It is, therefore, incumbent upon the guardian to rebut this presumption. Important factors in determining whether a contract is fair are (1) whether the dominant party made full disclosure of all relevant information known to him, (2) whether the consideration was adequate, and (3) whether the dependent party received competent and independent advice before completing the transaction. Without limitation, in every situation in which confidential relationship exists, the dominant party is held to utmost good faith in his dealings with the other.

Practical Advice

If you are in a confidential relationship with another person when you enter into a contract with that person, make sure that (1) you fully disclose all relevant information about that transaction, (2) the contract is fair, and (3) the other part obtains independent advice about the transaction.

◆ *See Case 11-2*

11-3 Fraud

Another factor affecting the validity of consent given by contracting party is fraud, which prevents assent from being knowingly given. There are two distinct types of fraud: fraud in the execution and fraud in the inducement.

11-3a FRAUD IN THE EXECUTION

Fraud in the execution, which is extremely rare, consists of misrepresentation that deceives the defrauded person as to the very nature of the contract. Such fraud occurs when a person does not know, or does not have reasonable opportunity to know, the character or essence of a proposed contract because the other party misrepresents its character or essential terms. Fraud in the execution renders the transaction *void*.

For example, Abigail delivers a package to Boris, requests that Boris sign a receipt for it, holds out a simple printed form headed "Receipt," and indicates the line on which Boris is to sign. This line, which to Boris appears to be the bottom line of the receipt, is actually the signature line of a promissory note cleverly concealed underneath the receipt. Boris signs where directed without knowing that he is signing a note. This is fraud in the execution. The note is void and of no legal effect because Boris has not actually given his assent, even though his signature is genuine and appears to manifest his assent to the terms of the note. The nature of Abigail's fraud precluded consent to the signing of the note because it prevented Boris from reasonably knowing what he was signing.

11-3b FRAUD IN THE INDUCEMENT

Fraud in the inducement, generally referred to as fraud or deceit, is an intentional misrepresentation of material fact by one party to the other who consents to enter into a contract in justifiable reliance upon the misrepresentation. Fraud in the inducement renders the contract *voidable* by the defrauded party and makes the fraudulent party liable in restitution as necessary to avoid unjust enrichment. Restatement of Restitution, Section 13. For example, Ada, in offering to sell her dog to Ben, tells Ben that the dog won first prize in its class in a recent national dog show. In fact, the dog had not even been entered in the show. Nonetheless, Ada's statement induces Ben to accept the offer and pay a high price for the dog. A contract exists, but it is voidable by Ben because of Ada's fraud, which induced his assent.

The requisites for fraud in the inducement are as follows: a false representation

1. of a fact
2. that is material and
3. made with knowledge of its falsity and the intention to deceive (scienter) and
4. which is justifiably relied upon.

The Third Restatement of Torts: Liability for Economic Harm, Section 9, follows the same requirements. (The final portions of this new Restatement were approved in 2018. It updates coverage on torts that involve economic loss or pecuniary harm *not* resulting from physical harm or physical contact to a person or property.)

The remedies that may be available for fraud in the inducement include rescission, restitution, and damages, as discussed in *Chapter 18*.

FALSE REPRESENTATION A basic element of fraud is a false representation or misrepresentation (i.e., an assertion not in accord with the facts, made through positive statement or conduct that misleads). **Concealment** is an action intended or known to be likely to keep another from learning of a fact of which he otherwise would have learned. Active concealment is a form of misrepresentation that can form the basis for fraud, as where a seller puts heavy oil or grease in a car engine to conceal a knock. Truth may be suppressed by concealment as much as by misrepresentation.

Expressly denying knowledge of a fact, which a party knows to exist, is a misrepresentation if it leads the other party to believe that the facts do not exist or cannot be discovered. Moreover, a statement of misleading half-truth is considered the equivalent of a false representation.

As a general rule, **silence** or nondisclosure alone does *not* amount to fraud. A seller generally is not obligated to tell a purchaser everything he knows about the subject of a sale. Thus, it is not fraud when a buyer possesses advantageous information about the seller's property, of which he knows the seller to be ignorant, and does not disclose such information to the seller. Likewise, a buyer is under no duty to inform a seller of the greater value or other advantages of his property. Assume that Sid owns a farm that, as a farm, is worth $100,000. Brenda knows that there is oil under Sid's farm and knows that Sid is ignorant of this fact. Brenda, without disclosing this information to Sid, makes an offer to Sid to buy the farm for $100,000. Sid accepts the offer, and a contract is duly made. Sid, on later learning the facts, can do nothing about the matter, either at law or in equity. As one case puts it, "a purchaser is not bound by our laws to make the man he buys from as wise as himself."

Practical Advice

Consider bargaining with the other party to promise to give you full disclosure.

Although nondisclosure usually does not constitute a misrepresentation, in certain situations, it does. One such situation arises when (1) a person fails to disclose a fact known to him, (2) he knows that the disclosure of that fact would correct a mistake of the other party as to a basic assumption on which that party is making the contract, and (3) nondisclosure of the fact amounts to a failure to act in a good faith and in accordance with reasonable standards of fair dealing. Restatement, Section 161. Accordingly, if the property at issue in the contract possesses a substantial latent (hidden) defect, one that the buyer would not discover by an ordinary examination, the seller may be obliged to reveal it. Suppose, for example, that Judith owns a valuable horse, which Judith knows is suffering from a disease only a competent veterinary surgeon might detect. Judith offers to sell this horse to Curt but does not inform Curt about the condition of the horse. Curt makes a reasonable examination of the horse and, finding it in apparently normal condition, purchases it from Judith. Curt, on later discovering the disease in question, can have the sale set aside. Judith's silence, under the circumstances, was a misrepresentation.

Practical Advice

When entering into contract negotiations, first determine what duty of disclosure you owe to the other party.

In other situations, the law also imposes a duty of disclosure. For example, one may have a duty of disclosure because of prior representations, innocently made before entering into the contract, which are later discovered to be untrue. Another instance in which silence may constitute fraud is a transaction involving a fiduciary. A **fiduciary** is a person in a confidential relationship who owes a duty of trust, loyalty, and confidence to another. For example, an agent owes a fiduciary duty to his principal, as does a trustee to the beneficiary of a trust and a partner to her copartners. A fiduciary may not deal at *arm's length*, but rather owes a duty to make full disclosure of all relevant facts when entering into a transaction with the other party to the relationship. In contrast, in most everyday business or market transactions, the parties are said to deal at "arm's length," meaning that they deal with each other on equal terms.

The Third Restatement of Torts: Liability for Economic Harm, Section 13, is in accord and provides,

> A failure to disclose material information may result in liability if the actor has a duty to speak. Such a duty exists where (a) the actor has made a prior statement and knows that it will likely mislead another if not amended, even if it was not misleading when made; or (b) the actor is in a fiduciary or confidential relationship with another that obliges the actor to make disclosures; or (c) the actor knows that the other party to a transaction is mistaken about a basic assumption behind it, and that the other party, because of the relationship between them, the customs of the trade, or other circumstances, would reasonably expect disclosure of what the actor knows.

FACT The basic element of fraud is the misrepresentation of a material fact. A **fact** is an event that actually took place or

a thing that actually exists. Suppose that Dale induces Mike to purchase shares in a company unknown to Mike at a price of $100 per share by representing that she had paid $150 per share for them during the preceding year, when in fact she had paid only $50. This representation of a past event is a misrepresentation of fact.

Actionable fraud rarely can be based on what is merely a statement of **opinion**. A representation is one of opinion if it expresses only the uncertain belief of the representer as to the existence of a fact or his judgment as to quality, value, authenticity, or other matters of judgment.

The line between fact and opinion is not an easy one to draw and in close cases presents an issue for the jury. The solution will often turn on the superior knowledge of the person making the statement and the information available to the other party. Thus, if Dale said to Mike that the shares were "a good investment," she is merely stating her opinion, and in the usual case, Mike ought to regard it as no more than that. Other common examples of opinion are statements of value, such as "This is the best car for the money in town" or "This deluxe model will give you twice the wear of a cheaper model." Such exaggerations and commendations of articles offered for sale are to be expected from dealers, who are merely puffing their wares with sales talk. If, however, the representer is a professional advising a client, the courts are more likely to regard as actionable an untrue statement of opinion. When the person expressing the opinion is one who holds himself out as having expert knowledge, the tendency is to grant relief to those who have sustained loss through reasonable reliance upon the expert evaluation.

The Third Restatement of Torts: Liability for Economic Harm provides that a false statement of opinion results in liability only if (1) the parties are in a fiduciary or confidential relationship or (2) the perpetrator of the fraud holds himself out as having expertise or other knowledge not accessible to the defrauded party. Section 14.

Also to be distinguished from a representation of fact is a **prediction** of the future. Predictions, which are similar to opinions in that no one can know with certainty what will happen in the future, normally are not regarded as factual statements. Likewise, promissory statements ordinarily do not constitute a basis of fraud, as a breach of promise does not necessarily indicate that the promise was fraudulently made. A promise that the promisor at the time of making had no intention of keeping, however, is a misrepresentation of fact. Most courts take the position that a misrepresented state of mind "is as much a fact as the state of a person's digestion." *Edgington v. Fitzmaurice*, 29 Ch.D. 459 (1885). The Third Restatement of Torts: Liability for Economic Harm is in accord: "A statement of a speaker's intention to perform a promise is a fraudulent misrepresentation if the intention does not exist at the time the statement is made." Section 15.

If a dealer promises, "I will service this machine free for the next year" but at the time has no intention of doing so, his conduct is actionable if the other elements of fraud are present.

Historically, courts held that representations of **law** were not statements of fact but rather of opinion. The present trend is to recognize that a statement of law may have either the effect of a statement of fact or a statement of opinion. Restatement, Torts, Section 545. For example, a statement of law asserting that a particular statute has been enacted or repealed has the effect of a statement of fact. On the other hand, a statement as to the legal consequences of a particular set of facts is a statement of opinion. Nonetheless, such a statement may imply that the facts known to the maker are consistent with the legal conclusion stated. For example, an assertion that a company has the legal right to do business in a State may include the assurance that the company has taken all the steps required to be duly qualified. Moreover, a statement by one who is learned in the law, such as a practicing attorney, may be considered a statement of fact.

The Third Restatement of Torts: Liability for Economic Harm, Section 14, Comment c provides that false statements of law "subject their makers to liability if they imply untrue facts, or if the parties have a relationship that makes it reasonable for the plaintiff to rely on the defendant's opinions. They are not actionable if they amount to judgments based on facts available to both sides and on which the plaintiff can reasonably be expected to arrive at an independent view."

♦ *See Case 11-3*

MATERIALITY In addition to misrepresenting a fact, a misrepresentation also must be material. A misrepresentation is **material** if (1) it would be likely to induce a reasonable person to manifest his assent or (2) the maker knows that it would be likely to induce the recipient to do so. Restatement, Section 162. The Third Restatement of Torts: Liability for Economic Harm provides that a misrepresentation is material if a reasonable person would give weight to it in deciding whether to enter into the relevant transaction or if the fraudulent party knew that the defrauded party would give it weight (whether reasonably or not). Section 9, Comment d. In the sale of a racehorse, whether a certain jockey rode the horse in its most recent race may not be material, but its running time for the race probably would be. The Restatement of Contracts and the Restatement of Restitution provide that a contract justifiably induced by a misrepresentation is voidable if the misrepresentation is either fraudulent *or* material. Therefore, a fraudulent misrepresentation does not have to be material for the recipient to obtain rescission, but it must be material if she is to recover damages. Restatement, Section 164; Restatement,

Torts, Section 538; Third Restatement of Torts: Liability for Economic Harm, Section 9, Comment d.

♦ *See Case 11-4*

KNOWLEDGE OF FALSITY AND INTENTION TO DECEIVE To establish fraud, the misrepresentation must have been known by the one making it to be false and must have been made with an intent to deceive. This element of fraud is known as *scienter*. Knowledge of falsity can consist of (1) actual knowledge, (2) lack of belief in the statement's truthfulness, or (3) reckless indifference as to its truthfulness. The Third Restatement of Torts: Liability for Economic Harm similarly provides that scienter exists if the maker of a misrepresentation (1) knows or believes that the matter is not as represented, (2) knows that he does not have the confidence in the statement that he states or implies, or (3) knows that he does not have the basis for the statement that he states or implies. Section 10.

JUSTIFIABLE RELIANCE A person is not entitled to relief unless he has justifiably relied upon the misrepresentation. If the misrepresentation in no way influenced the complaining party's decision, he must abide by the terms of the contract. He is not deceived if he does not rely. Justifiable reliance requires that the misrepresentation contribute substantially to the misled party's decision to enter into the contract. If the complaining party knew or it was obvious that the defendant's representation was untrue, but he still entered into the contract, he has not justifiably relied. Moreover, where the misrepresentation is fraudulent, the party who relies on it is entitled to relief even though he does not investigate the statement or is contributorily negligent in relying on it. Restatement, Torts, Sections 540, 545A. Not knowing or discovering the facts before making a contract does not constitute unjustified reliance unless it amounts to a failure to act in good faith and in accordance with reasonable standards of fair dealing. Restatement, Section 172. Thus, most courts will not allow a person who concocts a deliberate and elaborate scheme to defraud—one that the defrauded party should readily detect—to argue that the defrauded party did not justifiably rely upon the misrepresentation.

Under the Third Restatement of Torts: Liability for Economic Harm, the defrauded party can recover for economic loss only if (1) the misrepresentation causes the loss, (2) the defrauded party relies on the misrepresentation, and (3) the reliance is justifiable. Section 11.

11-4 Nonfraudulent Misrepresentation

Nonfraudulent misrepresentation is a material, false statement that induces another to rely justifiably but is made without *scienter*.

Negligent misrepresentation is a false representation that is made without knowledge of its falsity *and* without due care in ascertaining its truthfulness. **Innocent misrepresentation** is a false representation made without knowledge of its falsity but with due care. To obtain relief for nonfraudulent misrepresentation, all of the other elements of fraud must be present *and* the misrepresentation must be material. The remedies that may be available for nonfraudulent misrepresentation are rescission, restitution, and damages. (See *Chapter 18.*)

♦ *See Case 11-5*

♦ **SEE FIGURE 11-1:** *Misrepresentation*

11-5 Mistake

A **mistake** is a belief that is not in accord with the facts. Where the mistaken facts relate to the basis of the parties' agreement, the law permits the adversely affected party to avoid or reform the contract under certain circumstances. But because permitting avoidance for mistake undermines the objective approach to mutual assent, the law has experienced considerable difficulty in specifying those circumstances that justify permitting the subjective matter of mistake to invalidate an otherwise objectively satisfactory agreement. As a result, establishing clear rules to govern the effect of mistake has proven elusive.

The Restatement and modern cases treat mistakes of law in existence at the time of making a contract no differently than mistakes of fact. For example, Susan contracts to sell a parcel of land to James with the mutual understanding that James will build an apartment house on the land. Both Susan and James believe that such a building is lawful. Unknown to them, however, the town in which the land is located had enacted an ordinance precluding such use of the land three days before they entered into the contract. This mistake of law, which the courts would treat as a mistake of fact, would lead to the consequences discussed in the following section.

11-5a MUTUAL MISTAKE

Mutual mistake occurs when *both* parties are mistaken as to the same set of facts. If the mistake relates to a basic assumption on which the contract is made and has a material effect on the agreed exchange, then it is **voidable** by the adversely affected party unless he bears the risk of the mistake. Restatement, Section 152. In addition, the adversely affected party is entitled to restitution as necessary to avoid unjust enrichment. Restatement of Restitution, Section 5.

Usually, market conditions and the financial situation of the parties are not considered basic assumptions. Thus, if Gail contracts to purchase Pete's automobile under the belief that she can sell it at a profit to Jesse, she is not excused from liability if she is mistaken in this belief. Nor can she rescind the agreement simply because she was mistaken as to her estimate of what the automobile was worth. These are the ordinary risks of business, and courts do not undertake to relieve against them. But suppose that the parties contract upon the assumption that the automobile is a 2008 Cadillac with fifteen thousand miles of use, when in fact the engine is that of a cheaper model and has been run in excess of fifty thousand miles. Here, a court would likely allow a rescission because of mutual mistake of a material fact. Another example of mutual mistake of fact was presented in a California case where a noted violinist purchased two violins from a collector for $8,000, the bill of sale reading, "I have on this date sold to Mr. Efrem Zimbalist one Joseph Guarnerius violin and one Stradivarius violin dated 1717." Actually, unknown to either party, neither violin was genuine. Taken together they were worth no more than $300.

FIGURE 11-1 Misrepresentation

	Fraudulent	Negligent	Innocent
False Statement of Fact	Yes	Yes	Yes
Materiality	Yes for damages No for rescission	Yes	Yes
Fault	With knowledge and intent (*scienter*)	Without due care	Without knowledge but with due care
Reliance	Yes	Yes	Yes
Injury	Yes for damages No for rescission	Yes for damages No for rescission	Yes for damages No for rescission
Remedies	Damages Rescission	Damages Rescission	Damages Rescission

The sale was voidable by the purchaser for mutual mistake. In a New Zealand case, the plaintiff purchased a "stud bull" at an auction. There were no express warranties as to "sex, condition, or otherwise." Actually, the bull was sterile. Rescission was allowed, with the court observing that it was a "bull in name only."

♦ *See Case 11-5*

11-5b UNILATERAL MISTAKE

Unilateral mistake occurs when only one of the parties is mistaken. Courts have been hesitant to grant relief for unilateral mistake even though it relates to a basic assumption on which the party entered into the contract and has a material effect on the agreed exchange. Nevertheless, relief will be granted in cases in which (1) the nonmistaken party knows, or reasonably should know, that such a mistake has been made (palpable unilateral mistake) or (2) the mistake was caused by the fault of the nonmistaken party. For example, suppose a building contractor makes a serious error in his computations and as a result submits a bid on a job that is one-half the amount it should be. If the other party knows that he made such an error, or reasonably should have known, she cannot, as a general rule, take advantage of the other's mistake by accepting the offer. In addition, many courts and the Restatement allow rescission in cases in which the effect of the unilateral mistake makes enforcement of the contract unconscionable. Section 153.

♦ *See Case 11-5*

APPLYING THE LAW   Conduct Invalidating Assent

FACTS Gillian bought a two-year-old used car from a luxury automobile dealer for $36,000. At the time of her purchase, the odometer and title documentation both indicated that the car had 21,445 miles on it. But after just a little more than a year, the engine failed, and Gillian had to take the car to a mechanic. The problem was the water pump, which needed to be replaced. Surprised that a water pump should fail in a car with so few miles on it, the mechanic more closely examined the odometer and determined that someone had cleverly tampered with it. According to the mechanic, the car probably had about sixty thousand miles on it when Gillian bought it. At the time Gillian bought the car, the retail value for the same vehicle with sixty thousand miles on it was approximately $30,000.

Gillian decided that under these conditions, she no longer wanted the car. She contacted the dealership, which strenuously denied having tampered with the odometer. In fact, the dealership's records reflect that it purchased Gillian's car at auction for $34,000, after a thorough inspection that revealed no mechanical deficiencies or alteration of the car's odometer.

ISSUE Is Gillian's contract voidable by her?

RULE OF LAW Innocent misrepresentation renders a contract voidable. Innocent misrepresentation is proven when the following elements are established: (1) a false representation, (2) of fact, (3) that is material, (4) made without knowledge of its falsity but with due care, and (5) the representation is justifiably relied upon.

APPLICATION Gillian can prove all five elements of innocent misrepresentation. First, the dealership's false representation was that the mileage on the car was 21,445, when the car actually had about sixty thousand miles on it. Second, the mileage of the car at the time of sale is an actual event, not an opinion or prediction. Third, as the mileage of a used car is probably the most critical determinant of its value, this misrepresentation was material to the parties' agreed sale price, inducing the formation of the contract. Indeed, while Gillian might still have purchased this car with sixty thousand miles on it, she most certainly would have done so only at a lower price. Fourth, it is highly unlikely that the dealership was aware of the incorrect odometer reading. We know this because it paid $34,000 for the car, which should have sold for something less than $30,000 in the wholesale market if the true mileage had been known. Moreover, the dealership appears to have conducted appropriate due diligence to support both its own purchase price and the price at which it offered the car to Gillian. The odometer tampering was cleverly concealed, so much so that neither the dealership's inspection before purchase nor Gillian's mechanic's initial inspection revealed it. Fifth, Gillian's reliance on the ostensible odometer reading is justified. The car was only two years old when she bought it, and 21,445 miles is within an average range of mileage for a used car of that age. Unless the car's physical condition or something in the title paperwork should have alerted her to an inconsistency between the stated mileage and the car's actual mileage, Gillian was entitled to rely on what appeared to be a correct odometer reading.

CONCLUSION Because all the elements of innocent misrepresentation can be shown, Gillian's contract is voidable by Gillian.

11-5c ASSUMPTION OF RISK OF MISTAKE

A party who has undertaken to bear the risk of a mistake will be unable to avoid the contract, even though the mistake (which may be either mutual or unilateral) otherwise would have permitted her to do so. This allocation of risk may occur by agreement of the parties. For instance, a ship at sea may be sold "lost or not lost." In such case, the buyer is liable whether the ship was lost or not lost at the time the contract was made. There is no mistake; instead, there is a conscious allocation of risk.

Conscious ignorance may serve to allocate the risk of mistake when the parties recognize that they have limited knowledge of the facts. For example, the Supreme Court of Wisconsin refused to set aside the sale of a stone for which the purchaser paid one dollar, but which was subsequently discovered to be an uncut diamond valued at $700. The parties did not know at the time of sale what the stone was and knew they did not know. Each consciously assumed the risk that the value might be more or less than the selling price.

Practical Advice

If you are unsure about the nature of a contract, consider allocating the risk of the uncertainties in your contract.

11-5d EFFECT OF FAULT UPON MISTAKE

The Restatement provides that a mistaken party's fault in not knowing or discovering a fact before making a contract does not prevent him from avoiding the contract "unless his fault amounts to a failure to act in good faith and in accordance with reasonable standards of fair dealing." Restatement, Section 157. This rule does not, however, apply to a failure to read a contract. As a general proposition, a party is held to what she signs. Her signature authenticates the writing, and she cannot repudiate that which she has voluntarily approved. Generally, one who assents to a writing is presumed to know its contents and cannot escape being bound by its terms merely by contending that she did not read them; her assent is deemed to cover unknown as well as known terms. Restatement, Section 157, Comment b.

11-5e MISTAKE IN MEANING OF TERMS

Somewhat related to mistakes of facts is the situation in which the parties misunderstand the meaning of each other's manifestations of mutual assent. A famous case involving this problem is *Raffles v. Wichelhaus*, 2 Hurlstone & Coltman 906 (1864), popularly known as the *"Peerless* Case." A contract of purchase was made for 125 bales of cotton to arrive on the *Peerless* from Bombay. It happened, however, that there were two ships by the name of *Peerless* sailing from Bombay, one in October and the other in December. The buyer had in mind the ship that sailed in October, whereas the seller reasonably believed the agreement referred to the *Peerless* sailing in December. Neither party was at fault, but both believed in good faith that a different ship was intended. The English court held that no contract existed. The Restatement, Section 20, is in accord.

There is no manifestation of mutual assent in cases in which the parties attach materially different meanings to their manifestations and neither party knows or has reason to know the meaning attached by the other. If blame can be ascribed to either party, however, that party will be held responsible. Thus, if the seller knew of two ships by the name of *Peerless* sailing from Bombay, then he would be at fault, and the contract would be for the ship sailing in October as the buyer expected. If neither party is to blame or both are to blame, there is no contract at all; that is, the agreement is void.

C H A P T E R   S U M M A R Y

DURESS	**Definition** wrongful or unlawful act or threat that overcomes the free will of a party **Physical Compulsion** coercion involving physical force renders the agreement void **Improper Threats** improper threats or acts, including economic and social coercion, render the contract voidable
UNDUE INFLUENCE	**Definition** taking unfair advantage of a person by reason of a dominant position based on a confidential relationship **Effect** renders the contract voidable
FRAUD	**Fraud in the Execution** a misrepresentation that deceives the other party as to the nature of a document, evidencing that the contract renders the agreement void

Fraud in the Inducement renders the agreement voidable if the following elements are present:

- *False Representation* positive statement or conduct that misleads
- *Fact* an event that occurred or a thing that actually exists
- *Materiality* misrepresentation that would be likely to induce a reasonable person to manifest her assent
- *Knowledge of Falsity and Intention to Deceive* called *scienter* and includes (1) actual knowledge, (2) lack of belief in the statement's truthfulness, or (3) reckless indifference to the statement's truthfulness
- *Justifiable Reliance* a defrauded party is reasonably influenced by the misrepresentation

NONFRAUDULENT MISREPRESENTATION	**Negligent Misrepresentation** misrepresentation made without knowledge of its falsity *and* without due care in ascertaining its truthfulness; renders the contract voidable **Innocent Misrepresentation** misrepresentation made without knowledge of its falsity but with due care; renders the contract voidable
MISTAKE	**Definition** an understanding that is not in accord with existing fact **Mutual Mistake** both parties have a common but erroneous belief forming the basis of the contract; renders the contract voidable by either party **Unilateral Mistake** courts are unlikely to grant relief unless the error is known or should be known by the nonmistaken party **Assumption of Risk** a party may assume the risk of a mistake **Effect of Fault upon Mistake** not a bar to avoidance unless the fault amounts to a failure to act in good faith

CASES

CASE 11-1

Duress
BERARDI v. MEADOWBROOK MALL COMPANY
Supreme Court of Appeals of West Virginia, 2002
212 W.Va. 377, 572 S.E.2d 900

Per Curiam

Jerry A. Berardi (hereinafter referred to as "Mr. Berardi"), Betty J. Berardi, and Bentley Corporation, plaintiffs below/appellants (hereinafter collectively referred to as "the Berardis"), seek reversal of a summary judgment granted to Meadowbrook Mall Company, an Ohio Limited Partnership, and the Cafaro Company (hereinafter referred to as "Cafaro Company"), an Ohio Corporation, defendants below/appellees (hereinafter collectively referred to as "Meadowbrook" or * * * "Cafaro Company"). * * *

Facts and Procedural History

Between 1985 and 1987, the Berardis leased space for three restaurants from Meadowbrook. In 1990, the Berardis were delinquent in their rent. Cafaro Company, an affiliate of Meadowbrook, sent a letter dated October 1, 1990, to Mr. Berardi citing the arrearages. The letter informed him that a lawsuit would be filed in Ohio requesting judgment for the total amount of the arrearages. The letter proposed that after filing the suits, a consent judgment would be forwarded to Mr. Berardi granting judgment for the full amount of arrearages. Once the consent judgment was signed by both parties and filed with the court, the letter pledged, no steps to enforce the judgment would be undertaken providing the Berardis continued to operate their three restaurants consistent with the then present payment arrangement. Mr. Berardi signed the letter on October 5, 1990. In April 1996, Meadow-brook caused to be filed in the Circuit Court of Harrison County, West Virginia, [the] * * * judgment of the Ohio lawsuits. * * * [Meadowbrook received a] lien on the Goff Building [which was owned by the Berardis, and which] impeded the refinancing [of the building by the Berardis].

Correspondence was exchanged between counsel for the parties. * * * The correspondence ultimately led, in June 1997, to the Berardis and Anthony Cafaro (an authorized agent for Meadowbrook) signing a "Settlement Agreement and Release" settling the 1990 Ohio judgments. In this document, the Berardis acknowledged the validity of the 1990 Ohio judgments and that the aggregate due under them, plus interest and leasehold charges, was $814,375.97. The Berardis agreed to pay Meadowbrook $150,000 on the date the Goff Building refinancing occurred, and also to pay Meadowbrook $100,000 plus 8.5% interest per year on the third anniversary of the initial $150,000 payment. These payments would discharge the Berardis from all other amounts due and owing. The payment of the initial $150,000 would also result in Meadowbrook releasing the lien against the Goff Building.

The agreement additionally recited:

Berardis hereby release and forever discharge Meadow-brook, its employees, agents, successors, and assigns from any and all claims, demands, damages, actions, and causes of action of any kind or nature that have arisen or may arise as a result of the leases, or Guaranties whether said claims are known or unknown, contingent, or liquidated, from the beginning of time to the effective date of the agreement. Berardis acknowledge there was no unethical behavior on behalf of Meadowbrook Mall Company, its employees, agents.

Nevertheless, on October 2, 2000, the Berardis filed a complaint against Meadowbrook alleging that Meadowbrook breached the October 1990 agreement by attempting to enforce the 1990 Ohio judgments, that Meadowbrook extorted by duress and coercion the 1997 agreement, and that Meadowbrook and other business entities had conspired to enter into extortionate agreements with their tenants. Meadowbrook filed a motion to dismiss under the 1997 settlement. * * * Meadowbrook sought summary judgment, which the circuit court granted. From this summary judgment, Berardi now appeals.
* * *

Discussion
* * *

"We begin our discussion of this issue by reiterating, at the outset, that settlements are highly regarded and scrupulously enforced, so long as they are legally sound." [Citation.] "The law favors and encourages the resolution of controversies by contracts of compromise and settlement rather than by litigation; and it is the policy of the law to uphold and enforce such contracts if they are fairly made and are not in contravention of some law or public policy." [Citations.] Those who seek to avoid a settlement "face a heavy burden" [citation] and "since * * * settlement agreements, when properly executed, are legal and binding, this Court will not set aside such agreements on allegations of duress * * * absent clear and convincing proof of such claims." [Citation.]

The Berardis contend the 1997 settlement is invalid as it was procured by "economic duress:"

The concept of "economic or business duress" may be generally stated as follows: Where the plaintiff is forced into a transaction as a result of unlawful threats or wrongful, oppressive, or unconscionable conduct on the part of the defendant which leaves the plaintiff no reasonable alternative but to acquiesce, the plaintiff may void the transaction and recover any economic loss.

[Citation.] In [citation], we emphasized that

[t]here appears to be general acknowledgment that duress is not shown because one party to the contract has driven a hard bargain or that market or other conditions now make the contract more difficult to perform by one of the parties or that financial circumstances may have caused one party to make concessions.

[Citation] "Duress is not readily accepted as an excuse" to avoid a contract. [Citation.] Thus, to establish economic duress, "in addition to their own * * * statements, the plaintiffs must produce objective evidence of their duress. The defense of economic duress does not turn only upon the subjective state of mind of the plaintiffs, but it must be reasonable in light of the objective facts presented." [Citation.]

Mr. Berardi is a sophisticated businessman who has operated a number of commercial enterprises. As of 1997, the Berardis had substantial assets and a considerable net worth. While economic duress may reach large business entities as well as the "proverbial little old lady in tennis shoes," [citation], when the parties are sophisticated business entities, releases should be voided only in "extreme and extraordinary cases." [Citation.] Indeed, "where an experienced businessman takes sufficient time, seeks the advice of counsel and understands the content of what he is signing he cannot claim the execution of the release was a product of duress." [Citation.] While the presence of counsel will not *per se* defeat a claim of economic duress, "a court must determine if the attorneys had an opportunity for meaningful input under the circumstances." [Citation.]
* * *

[N]o case can be found, we apprehend, where a party who, without force or intimidation and with full knowledge of all the facts of the case, accepts on account of an unliti-gated and controverted demand a sum less than what he claims and believes to be due him, and agrees to accept that sum in full satisfaction, has been permitted to avoid his act on the ground that this is duress.

[Citations.]

Moreover, the Berardis did not file their complaint until October 2, 2000. A party seeking to repudiate a release must act promptly in disavowing it once the putative duress ends or else the party will be deemed to have ratified the agreement. [Citations.] * * *

Finally, we do not believe that any relative economic inequal-ity between the Berardis and Meadowbrook sufficiently factor into the summary judgment calculation. We have recognized that, "in most commercial transactions it may be assumed that there is some inequality of bargaining power.* * * " [Citation.] Indeed, even when one sophisticated business entity enjoys "a decided economic advantage" over another such entity, eco-nomic duress is extremely circumscribed:

Because an element of economic duress is * * * present when many contracts are formed or releases given, the ability of a party to disown his obligations under a con-tract or release on that basis is reserved for extreme and extraordinary cases. Otherwise, the stronger party to a contract or release would routinely be at risk of having its rights under the contract or release challenged long after the instrument became effective.

[Citation.]

Given the facts, the law's disfavor of economic duress, its approbation of settlements, the sophisticated nature of the par-ties, and the extremely high evidentiary burden the Berardis must overcome, we harbor no substantial doubt nor do we believe the circuit court abused its discretion.

* * *

Conclusion

The judgment of the Circuit Court of Harrison County is affirmed.

CASE 11-2

Undue Influence
NEUGEBAUER v. NEUGEB AUER

Supreme Court of South Dakota, 2011
804 N.W.2d 450, 2011 S.D. 64

Zinter, J.

Harold and Pearl Neugebauer owned a 159-acre farm the par-ties called the "Home Place." The Hutchinson County farm included a house, garage, granary, machine sheds, barns, silos, and a dairy barn. During their marriage, Harold handled all of the legal and financial affairs of the farm and family. In 1980, Harold died, leaving Pearl as the sole owner of the Home Place and another farm property. Following Harold's death, Lincoln, the youngest of Harold and Pearl's seven children, began farm-ing both properties. Lincoln also resided with his mother on the Home Place.

In 1984, Lincoln and Dennis, one of Pearl's other sons, formed L & D Farms partnership for the purpose of managing the farming operation on Pearl's land. L & D Farms entered into a ten-year lease with Pearl that included an option to purchase the Home Place for $117,000, the appraised value in 1984. In 1985, Pearl moved from the farm to a home in Parkston. In 1989, Lincoln and Dennis dissolved L & D Farms without exer-cising the option to purchase.

After dissolution of the partnership, Lincoln farmed Pearl's land by himself. He paid annual rent, but Lincoln and Pearl never reduced their oral farm lease to writing. Pearl trusted Lincoln and left it to him to determine how much rent to pay. Pearl did, however, expect that Lincoln would be "fair." Pearl

never took any steps to determine if the $6,320 annual rent Lincoln was paying was fair.

On several occasions from 2004 to 2008, Lincoln privately consulted with attorney Keith Goehring about purchasing the Home Place. On December 3, 2008, Lincoln took Pearl to Goehring's office to discuss the purchase. Pearl, who only had an eighth-grade education, was almost eighty-four years old and was hard of hearing. Although Lincoln and Goehring discussed details of Lincoln's proposed purchase, Pearl said virtually nothing. She later testified that she could not keep up with the conversation and did not understand the terms discussed.

On December 17, 2008, * * * Pearl and Lincoln executed a contract for deed that had been drafted by Goehring. Goehring had been retained and his fees were paid by Lincoln. Neither Lincoln nor Goehring advised Pearl that Goehring represented only Lincoln, and neither suggested that Pearl could or should retain her own legal counsel.

There is no dispute that the fair market value of the Home Place was $697,000 in 2008 when the contract for deed was executed. Under the terms of the contract, Lincoln was to pay Pearl $117,000, the farm's 1984 appraised value. The contract price was to be paid over thirty years by making annual pay-ments of $6,902.98.

After executing the contract, Lincoln told Pearl not to tell the rest of her children about the agreement. Pearl later became suspicious that something may have been wrong with the contract. In January 2009, Pearl's children returned to Parkston for a funeral. For the first time, Pearl revealed the contract to the rest of her children, and they explained the contract to her. She began to cry and wanted the contract torn up. Pearl personally and through her children asked Lincoln to tear up the contract. Lincoln refused.

[Pearl then brought an action for rescission of the contract on the ground of undue influence. The trial court found that Lincoln had exerted undue influence and rescinded the contract. Lincoln appealed, claiming that the trial court erred in finding that the contract for deed was a product of undue influence.]

The elements [of undue influence] are: (1) a person susceptible to undue influence; (2) another's opportunity to exert undue influence on that person to effect a wrongful purpose; (3) another's disposition to do so for an improper purpose; and (4) a result clearly showing the effects of undue influence. [Citation.] The party alleging undue influence must prove these elements by a preponderance of the evidence. [Citation.]

Susceptibility to Undue Influence

Lincoln argues that no evidence supported the court's finding that Pearl was susceptible to undue influence. * * * Lincoln contends that in the absence of medical evidence of mental deficits, the court erred in finding that Pearl was susceptible to undue influence.

Concededly, "'physical and mental weakness is always material upon the question of undue influence.' Obviously, an aged and infirm person with impaired mental faculties would be more susceptible to influence than a mentally alert younger person in good health." [Citations.] But this Court has not required medical evidence to prove susceptibility to undue influence. * * *

In this case, there was substantial non-medical evidence demonstrating Pearl's susceptibility to undue influence. Pearl had an eighth-grade education, and she lacked experience in business and legal transactions. When she signed the contract for deed, Pearl was almost eighty-four and hard of hearing. Pearl and Dennis testified that she had relied on her deceased husband to take care of all their business and legal matters during their marriage. This dependency continued after Harold's death. Pearl testified that, with the exception of her checking account and monthly expenses, she often asked her children for help with business and financial affairs, which she did not understand. * * * We also note that Lincoln admitted Pearl had some mental impairment. He told [Pearl's daughter] Cheryl that Pearl was "slipping," meaning that Pearl would say something and a few minutes later repeat herself because she had forgotten what she had said. * * *

Opportunity to Exert Undue Influence

Lincoln contends that the court's finding of opportunity to exert undue influence was erroneous because Lincoln and Pearl had no confidential relationship and Pearl had the ability to seek independent advice between the two meetings with Goehring, but chose not to do so. * * *

In this case, Pearl testified that Lincoln was her son and someone with whom she had previously lived for many years: someone she trusted to "do right." Lincoln conceded that on the date Pearl signed the contract, he knew Pearl trusted him and had confidence that he would treat her fairly in his business dealings with her. This type of trust and confidence by a mother in her son was sufficient to prove opportunity.
* * *

Disposition to Exert Undue Influence

The court's finding that Lincoln had a disposition to exert undue influence for an improper purpose was also supported. Lincoln had substantial experience in farmland transactions and real estate appreciation. He collaborated with an attorney a number of times over four years to purchase the farm and draft the necessary documents. Yet Lincoln did not have the farm appraised as he had previously done when farming the property with his brother. Instead, Lincoln set the price at a value for which it had appraised twenty-four years earlier, a price that was one-sixth of its then current value. He also took no steps to ensure that his elderly mother understood the contract terms, including the fact that considering her age and the thirty-year amortization, she would likely never receive a substantial portion of the payments. Finally, neither Lincoln nor his attorney advised Pearl to seek legal representation. * * *

Lincoln's conduct after execution of the contract was also relevant to show disposition to exercise undue influence at the time the contract was executed. [Citation.] After this contract for deed was executed, Lincoln instructed Pearl not to tell her other children about the contract. * * *

The court finally observed that Lincoln historically took advantage of Pearl by paying her less than fair market rent under the oral lease. * * *
* * *

Result Showing Effects of Undue Influence

Finally, we see no clear error in the court finding a result clearly showing the effects of undue influence. By executing the contract for deed, Pearl sold her property for $580,000 less than its value. Not only was the contract price of $117,000 substantially below the market value of $697,000, the thirty-year payment term would have required Pearl to live to 114 years-of-age to receive the payments. * * *

We find no clear error in the circuit court's findings of fact. We affirm its conclusion that rescission was warranted. * * * The judgment of the circuit court is affirmed.

CASE 11-3

Fraud: Fact
MAROUN v. WYRELESS SYSTEMS, INC.

Supreme Court of Idaho, 2005
141 Idaho 604, 114 P.3d 974

Trout, J.

Tony Y. Maroun (Maroun) was employed by Amkor when he accepted an offer to work for Wyreless, a startup company. On November 20, 2000, a letter was sent from Bradley C. Robinson, president of Wyreless, to Maroun setting forth the terms of their employment agreement. The pertinent portions of the letter were as follows:

* * *

- Annual salary of $300,000.
- $300,000 bonus for successful organization of Wyreless Systems, Inc.
- 15% of the issued equity in Wyreless Systems, Inc.
- The equity and "organization bonus" will need to be tied to agreeable milestones (e.g., acquisition of Matricus, organization of management team, etc).
- Full medical benefits.
- Position of Chief Executive Officer, President and a position on the Board.
- Bonuses and incentives will need to be determined by the Board and you after the business plan has been agreed by all parties.

* * *

I would like you to have an understanding of the fund raising status. I was able to get a commitment from two investors today for a minimum of $250,000 for arrival into the WSI bank account early next week. I believe we will be able to raise an additional $350,000 during the following week. * * * If we are not successful in raising the required capital for the business the funds remaining in the account on May 1, 2001 will be release[d] to you and Jen Gadelman (sic) as compensation beyond salaries and expenses for your efforts in developing the business.

I anticipate a starting date of employment of December 1, 2000 or as soon you (sic) can reasonably and professional (sic) resolve your responsibilities with Amkor.

Thereafter, Maroun started working for Wyreless but his employment was terminated in February 2001. Maroun then filed suit (the Wyreless suit), alleging he had not received two salary payments totaling $23,077, had not received 15% of issued equity and had not received the remainder of the $600,000 in bank account funds, alleged to be a balance of

$429,145. * * * Maroun also claimed Wyreless' corporate shell should be set aside and the shareholders of Wyreless should be jointly and severally liable for any damages Wyreless caused to him. * * * After Maroun filed a motion for partial summary judgment against Wyreless on the basis that there was no dispute Maroun was owed $23,077 in unpaid wages, the parties stipulated to entry of a judgment in favor of Maroun in the amount of $23,077.

In the fall of 2002, * * * Wyreless filed a motion for summary judgment on the remaining portions of Maroun's wage claim, which included the claim for 15% of Wyreless shares and the alleged $429,145 balance of the Wyreless fund account. The district court granted the motion. * * * Maroun appealed.

* * *

Maroun argues the district court erred in granting summary judgment in favor of Robinson on the fraud claim. Fraud requires: (1) a statement or a representation of fact; (2) its falsity; (3) its materiality; (4) the speaker's knowledge of its falsity; (5) the speaker's intent that there be reliance; (6) the hearer's ignorance of the falsity of the statement; (7) reliance by the hearer; (8) justifiable reliance; and (9) resultant injury. [Citation.] In opposition to the defendants' motion for summary judgment, Maroun filed an affidavit that stated Robinson made the following representations to Maroun:

(1) That Wyreless was to be a corporation of considerable size, with initial net revenues in excess of several hundred million dollars.

(2) That Robinson would soon acquire one and one-half million dollars in personal assets, which Robinson would make available to personally guaranty payment of my compensation from Wyreless.

(3) That he would have no difficulty in obtaining the initial investments required to capitalize Wyreless as a large, world leading corporation with initial net revenues in excess of several hundred million dollars.

(4) That he had obtained firm commitments from several investors and that investment funds would be received in Wyreless' bank account in the near future.

"An action for fraud or misrepresentation will not lie for statements of future events." [Citation.] "[T]here is a general rule in [the] law of deceit that a representation consisting of [a] promise or a statement as to a future event will not serve as [a] basis for fraud. . ." [Citation.] Statements numbered one and two both address future events. Robinson allegedly stated

Wyreless "was to be" and that he "would soon acquire." "[T]he representation forming the basis of a claim for fraud must concern past or existing material facts." [Citation.] Neither of these statements constitutes a statement or a representation of past or existing fact. A "promise or statement that an act will be undertaken, however, is actionable, if it is proven that the speaker made the promise without intending to keep it." [Citation.] There is no indication in the record that Robinson did not intend to fulfill those representations to Maroun at the time he made the statements.

"Opinions or predictions about the anticipated profitability of a business are usually not actionable as fraud." [Citation.] Statement number three appears to be merely Robinson's opinion. As to statement number four, no evidence was submitted that Robinson had not received commitments at the time he made the statement to Maroun. Accordingly, the district court's grant of summary judgment against Maroun on the fraud claim is affirmed.

* * *

[The district court's ruling on this issue is affirmed.]

CASE 11-4

Fraud: Materiality
REED v. KING
California Court of Appeals, 1983
145 Cal.App.3d 261,193 Cal.Rptr. 130

Blease, J.

In the sale of a house, must the seller disclose it was the site of a multiple murder?

Dorris Reed purchased a house from Robert King. Neither King nor his real estate agents (the other named defendants) told Reed that a woman and her four children were murdered there 10 years earlier. However, it seems "truth will come to light; murder cannot be hid long." (*Shakespeare, Merchant of Venice,* act II, scene II.) Reed learned of the gruesome episode from a neighbor after the sale. She sues seeking rescission and damages. King and the real estate agent defendants successfully demurred to her first amended complaint for failure to state a cause of action. Reed appeals the ensuing judgment of dismissal. We will reverse the judgment.

* * * King and his real estate agent knew about the murders and knew the event materially affected the market value of the house when they listed it for sale. They represented to Reed the premises were in good condition and fit for an "elderly lady" living alone. They did not disclose the fact of the murders. At some point King asked a neighbor not to inform Reed of that event. Nonetheless, after Reed moved in neighbors informed her no one was interested in purchasing the house because of the stigma. Reed paid $76,000, but the house is only worth $65,000 because of its past.

* * *

Does Reed's pleading state a cause of action? Concealed within this question is the nettlesome problem of the duty of disclosure of blemishes on real property which are not physical defects or legal impairments to use.

Reed seeks to state a cause of action sounding in contract, i.e., rescission, or in tort, i.e., deceit. In either event her allegations must reveal a fraud. [Citation.] "The elements of actual fraud, whether as the basis of the remedy in contract or tort, may be stated as follows: There must be (1) a *false representation* or concealment of a material fact (or, in some cases, an opinion) susceptible of knowledge, (2) made with *knowledge* of its falsity or without sufficient knowledge on the subject to warrant a representation, (3) with the *intent* to induce the person to whom it is made to act upon it, and such person must (4) act in *reliance* upon the representation (5) to his *damage.*" (Original italics.) [Citation.]

The trial court perceived the defect in Reed's complaint to be a failure to allege concealment of a material fact. * * *

Concealment is a term of art which includes mere nondisclosure when a party has a duty to disclose. [Citation.] Rest.2d Contracts, § 161; Rest.2d Torts, § 551; Reed's complaint reveals only nondisclosure despite the allegation King asked a neighbor to hold his peace. There is no allegation the attempt at suppression was a cause in fact of Reed's ignorance. [Citations.] Accordingly, the critical question is: does the seller have a duty to disclose here? Resolution of this question depends on the materiality of the fact of the murders.

In general, a seller of real property has a duty to disclose: "where the seller knows of facts *materially* affecting the value or desirability of the property which are known or accessible only to him and also knows that such facts are not known to, or within the reach of the diligent attention and observation of the buyer, the seller is under a duty to disclose them to the buyer. [Citation.] This broad statement of duty has led one commentator to conclude: "The ancient maxim *caveat emptor* ('let the buyer beware') has little or no application to California real estate transactions." [Citation.]

Whether information "is of sufficient materiality to affect the value or desirability of the property * * * depends on the facts of the particular case." [Citation.] Materiality "is a question of law, and is part of the concept of right to rely or justifiable reliance." [Citation.] * * * Three considerations bear on this legal conclusion; the gravity of the harm inflicted by nondisclosure; the fairness of imposing a duty of discovery on the buyer as an alternative to compelling disclosure, and the impact on the stability of contracts if rescission is permitted.

Numerous cases have found nondisclosure of physical defects and legal impediments to use of real property are material. [Citation.] However, to our knowledge, no prior real estate sale case has faced an issue of nondisclosure of the kind presented here.

* * *

The murder of innocents is highly unusual in its potential for so disturbing buyers they may be unable to reside in a home where it has occurred. This fact may foreseeably deprive a buyer of the intended use of the purchase. Murder is not such a common occurrence that *buyers* should be charged with anticipating and discovering this disquieting possibility.

Accordingly, the fact is not one for which a duty of inquiry and discovery can sensibly be imposed upon the buyer. Reed alleges the fact of the murders has a quantifiable effect on the market value of the premises. We cannot say this allegation is inherently wrong and, in the pleading posture of the case, we assume it to be true. If information known or accessible only to the seller has a significant and measurable effect on market value and, as is alleged here, the seller is aware of this effect, we see no principled basis for making the duty to disclose turn upon the character of the information. Physical usefulness is not and never has been the sole criterion of valuation. * * *

Reputation and history can have a significant effect on the value of realty. "George Washington slept here" is worth something, however physically inconsequential that consideration may be. Ill repute or "bad will" conversely may depress the value of property. * * *

Whether Reed will be able to prove her allegation the decade-old multiple murder has a significant effect on market value we cannot determine. If she is able to do so by competent evidence she is entitled to a favorable ruling on the issues of materiality and duty to disclose. Her demonstration of objective tangible harm would still the concern that permitting her to go forward will open the floodgates to rescission on subjective and idiosyncratic grounds.

* * *

The judgment is reversed.

CASE 11-5

Mistake
BURNINGHAM v. WESTGATE RESORTS, LTD.
Court of Appeals of Utah, 2013
317 P.3d 445, 2013 UT.App. 244; rehearing denied February 6, 2014

Bench, Senior Judge

[In 2006, Jeff Burningham and Westgate Resorts, Ltd. (Westgate) entered into a real estate purchase contract (the REPC) in which Burningham agreed to purchase a Park City, Utah condominium unit from Westgate for $899,000. Pursuant to the REPC, Burningham made a 10 percent deposit of $89,900, which was to be retained by Westgate as liquidated damages if Burningham defaulted. As the 2007 closing date approached, real estate market conditions worsened, and Burningham refused to close. A dispute arose between the parties as to whether Burningham was entitled to a refund of the deposit, with Burningham alleging that Westgate had made misrepresentations to fraudulently induce him to enter into the REPC. In September 2010, the parties settled their dispute by executing a second contract (the Agreement) for the sale of the condominium unit, this time for the reduced purchase price of $462,500. The only deposit contemplated by the Agreement was the $89,900 that Burningham had previously paid. The Agreement purported to resolve all outstanding issues between the parties arising under the REPC and stated that it was "wholly integrated and shall supersede any and all previous and current understandings and agreements between the Buyer and Seller." Unlike the REPC, the Agreement contained a provision (Paragraph 38.1) granting Burningham the right to terminate the Agreement in his sole discretion by giving written notice to Westgate within seven days of the Agreement's effective date upon which timely notice Burningham would be entitled to repayment of his deposit. Burningham exercised this termination option by giving timely written notice to Westgate. However, Westgate refused to return Burningham's deposit, contending that neither party had intended to provide Burningham the unilateral right to cancel the Agreement and recover the full $89,900 originally deposited under the REPC. Burningham sued Westgate for the return of the deposit, and Westgate brought counterclaims arguing mutual mistake. The district court granted summary judgment in favor of Burningham for $89,900. Westgate appealed.]

* * * The district court concluded that, pursuant to paragraph 38.1 of the Agreement, Burningham timely terminated the Agreement and was entitled to a refund of his $89,900 deposit as a matter of law. Notwithstanding the language of paragraph 38.1, Westgate argues that extrinsic evidence—primarily the declaration of its sales agent [that the parties did not intend to include the provision of a full return of the deposit]—creates material questions of fact on its arguments of mutual mistake * * *.

* * * A mutual mistake of fact can provide the basis for equitable rescission or reformation of a contract even when the contract appears on its face to be a "complete and binding integrated agreement." [Citation.] "A mutual mistake occurs when both parties, at the time of contracting, share a misconception about a basic assumption or vital fact upon which they based their bargain." [Citation.] Westgate argues that its sales agent's declaration, viewed in light of the parties' course of conduct leading up to the Agreement, raises a fact question as to whether the inclusion of paragraph 38.1's refund language in the Agreement was a mutual mistake.

The sales agent's declaration summarizes, from Westgate's perspective, the events leading up to the execution of the Agreement. The declaration clearly provides evidence that *Westgate* did not intend for the $89,900 to be refundable, stating that "at no time did Westgate intend for the [$89,900] to be considered a refundable deposit under the [Agreement]." It also provides evidence of Westgate's subjective understanding that Burningham shared its intent, stating that the sales agent "understood these to be Burningham's intentions based on [the agent's] discussions and interactions with [Burningham] leading up to the [Agreement]."

What the sales agent's declaration does not do is provide evidence of *Burningham's* intent, as opposed to Westgate's understanding of that intent. The declaration does not provide the substance of any of the sales agent's "discussions and interactions" with Burningham that would provide evidence of Burningham's intent. Instead, the declaration relies on Burningham's silence, stating that "[a]t no time did Burningham indicate. . . that he intended the [$89,900] to be a refundable deposit under the [Agreement] or that he interpreted it to be the 'deposit' referenced in Paragraph 38.1 of the [Agreement]."

We agree with the district court that the sales agent's declaration "does not show that Mr. Burningham was also mistaken on [the deposit] issue." The declaration provides evidence only of unilateral mistake by Westgate, not the mutual mistake required to establish grounds for equitable rescission of the Agreement. We therefore conclude that the declaration did not raise a material question of fact on mutual mistake so as to preclude summary judgment.

* * *

The district court correctly concluded that Westgate's evidence demonstrated only a unilateral mistake by Westgate as to whether the $89,900 was refundable and did not raise a material fact question on mutual mistake as argued by Westgate. * * * For these reasons, we affirm the district court's entry of summary judgment in favor of Burningham, and we remand this matter to the district court for a determination of Burningham's reasonable attorney fees incurred on appeal.

QUESTIONS

1. Anita and Barry were negotiating, and Anita's attorney prepared a long and carefully drawn contract, which was given to Barry for examination. Five days later and prior to its execution, Barry's eyes became so infected that it was impossible for him to read. Ten days thereafter and during the continuance of the illness, Anita called upon Barry and urged him to sign the contract, telling him that time was running out. Barry signed the contract despite the fact he was unable to read it. In a subsequent action by Anita, Barry claimed that the contract was not binding upon him because it was impossible for him to read and he did not know what it contained prior to his signing it. Explain whether or not Barry should be held to the contract.

2. a. Johnson tells Davis that he paid $150,000 for his farm in 2016 and that he believes it is worth twice that at the present time. Relying upon these statements, Davis buys the farm from Johnson for $225,000. Johnson did pay $150,000 for the farm in 2016, but its value has increased only slightly, and it is presently not worth $300,000. On discovering this, Davis offers to reconvey the farm to Johnson and sues for the return of his $225,000. Result?

    b. Modify the facts in (a) by assuming that Johnson had paid $100,000 for the property in 2016. What is the result? Explain.

3. On September 1, Adams in Portland, Oregon, wrote a letter to Brown in New York City, offering to sell to Brown one thousand tons of chromite at $48 per ton, to be shipped by S.S. *Malabar* sailing from Portland, Oregon, to New York City via the Panama Canal. Upon receiving the letter on September 5, Brown immediately mailed to Adams a letter stating that she accepted the offer. There were two ships by the name of S.S. *Malabar* sailing from Portland to New York City via the Panama Canal, one sailing in October and the other sailing in December. At the time of mailing her letter of acceptance, Brown knew of both sailings and further knew that Adams knew only of the December sailing. Is there a contract? If so, to which S.S. *Malabar* does it relate?

4. Adler owes Panessi, a police captain, $5,000. Adler threatens that unless Panessi discharges him from the debt, Adler will disclose the fact that Panessi has on several occasions become highly intoxicated and has been seen in the company of certain disreputable persons. Panessi, induced by fear that such a disclosure would

cost him his position or in any event lead to social disgrace, gives Adler a release but subsequently sues to set it aside and recover on his claim. Will Adler be able to enforce the release? Why or why not?

5. Harris owned a farm that was worth about $600 per acre. By false representations of fact, Harris induced Pringle to buy the farm at $1,500 per acre. Shortly after taking possession of the farm, Pringle discovered oil under the land. Harris, on learning this, sues to have the sale set aside on the ground that it was voidable because of fraud. Result? Discuss.

6. On February 2, Phillips induced Miller to purchase from her fifty shares of stock in the XYZ Corporation for $10,000, representing that the actual book value of each share was $200. A certificate for fifty shares was delivered to Miller. On February 16, Miller discovered that the book value on February 2 was only $50 per share. Will Miller be successful in a lawsuit against Phillips? Why or why not?

7. Doris mistakenly accused Peter's son, Steven, of negligently burning down her barn. Peter believed that his son was guilty of the wrong and that he, Peter, was personally liable for the damage, as Steven was only fifteen years old. Upon demand made by Doris, Peter paid Doris $25,000 for the damage to her barn. After making this payment, Peter learned that his son had not caused the burning of Doris's barn and was in no way responsible for its burning. Peter then sued Doris to recover the $25,000 he had paid her. Explain whether or not he will succeed.

8. Jones, a farmer, found an odd-looking stone in his fields. He went to Smith, the town jeweler, and asked him what he thought it was. Smith said he did not know but thought it might be a ruby. Jones asked Smith what he would pay for it, and Smith said $200, whereupon Jones sold it to Smith for $200. The stone turned out to be an uncut diamond worth $3,000. Jones brought an action against Smith to recover the stone. On trial, it was proved that Smith actually did not know the stone was a diamond when he bought it, but he thought it might be a ruby. Can Jones void the sale? Explain.

9. Decedent Judith Johnson, a bedridden, lonely woman of eighty-six years, owned outright Greenacre, her ancestral estate. Ficky, her physician and friend, visited her weekly and was held in the highest regard by Johnson. Johnson was extremely fearful of suffering and depended upon Ficky to ease her anxiety and pain. Several months before her death, she deeded Greenacre to Ficky for $10,000. The fair market value of Greenacre at this time was $250,000. Johnson was survived by two children and six grandchildren. Johnson's children challenged the validity of the deed. Should the deed be declared invalid due to Ficky's undue influence? Explain.

CASE PROBLEMS

10. Dorothy and John Hufffschneider listed their house and lot for sale with C. B. Property. The the owners told C. B. that the size of the property was 6.8 acres. Dean Olson, a salesman for C. B., advertised the property in local newspapers as consisting of six acres. James and Jean Holcomb signed a contract to purchase the property through Olson after first inspecting the property with Olson and being assured by Olson that the property was at least 6.6 acres. The Holcombs never asked for or received a copy of the survey. In actuality, the lot was only 4.6 acres. The Holcombs now seek to rescind the contract. Decision?

11. In February, Gardner, a schoolteacher with no experience in running a tavern, entered into a contract to purchase for $40,000 the Punjab Tavern from Meiling. The contract was contingent upon Gardner's obtaining a five-year lease for the tavern's premises and a liquor license from the State. Prior to the formation of the contract, Meiling had made no representations to Gardner concerning the gross income of the tavern. Approximately three months after the contract was signed, Gardner and Meiling met with an inspector from the Oregon Liquor Control Commission (OLCC) to discuss transfer of the liquor license. Meiling reported to the agent, in Gardner's presence, that the tavern's gross income figures for February, March, and April were $5,710, $4,918, and $5,009, respectively. The OLCC granted the required license, the transaction was closed, and Gardner took possession on June 10. After discovering that the tavern's income was very low and that the tavern had very few female patrons, Gardner contacted Meiling's bookkeeping service and learned that the actual gross income for those three months had been approximately $1,400 to $2,000. Will a court grant Gardner rescission of the contract? Explain.

12. Christine Boyd was designated as the beneficiary of a life insurance policy issued by Aetna Life Insurance Company on the life of Christine's husband, Jimmie Boyd. The policy insured against Jimmie's permanent total disability and also provided for a death benefit to be paid on Jimmie's death. Several years after the policy was issued,

Jimmie and Christine separated. Jimmie began to travel extensively, and Christine therefore was unable to keep track of his whereabouts or his state of health. Jimmie, however, continued to pay the premiums on the policy until Christine tried to cash in the policy to alleviate her financial distress. A loan previously had been made on the policy, however, leaving its cash surrender value, and thus the amount that Christine received, at only $4.19. Shortly thereafter, Christine learned that Jimmie had been permanently and totally disabled before the surrender of the policy. Aetna also was unaware of Jimmie's condition, and Christine requested that the surrendered policy be reinstated and that the disability payments be made. Jimmie died soon thereafter, and Christine then requested that Aetna pay the death benefit. Decision?

13. Plaintiff, Gibson, entered into negotiation with W. S. May, president of Home Folks Mobile Home Plaza, Inc., to buy Home Plaza Corporation. Plaintiff visited the mobile home park on several occasions, at which time he noted the occupancy, visually inspected the sewer and water systems, and asked May numerous questions concerning the condition of the business. Plaintiff, however, never requested to see the books, nor did May try to conceal them. May admits making the following representations to the plaintiff: (a) the water and sewer systems were in good condition, and no major short-term expenditures would be needed; (b) the park realized a 40 percent profit on natural gas sold to tenants; and (c) usual park vacancy was 5 percent. In addition, May gave plaintiff the park's accountant-prepared income statement, which showed a net income of $38,220 for the past eight months. Based on these figures, plaintiff projected an annual net profit of $57,331.20. Upon being asked whether this figure accurately represented income of the business for the past three years, May stated by letter that indeed it did.

     Plaintiff purchased the park for $275,000. Shortly thereafter, plaintiff spent $5,384 repairing the well and septic systems. By the time plaintiff sold the park three years later, he had expended $7,531 on the wells and $8,125 on the septic systems. Furthermore, in the first year, park occupancy was nowhere near 95 percent. Even after raising rent and the charges for natural gas, plaintiff still operated at a deficit. Plaintiff sued defendant, alleging that May, on behalf of defendant, made false and fraudulent statements on which plaintiff relied when he purchased the park. Decision?

14. Columbia University brought suit against Jacobsen on two notes signed by him and his parents. The notes represented the balance of tuition he owed the University. Jacobsen counterclaimed for money damages due to Columbia's deceit or fraudulent misrepresentation. Jacobsen argues that Columbia fraudulently misrepresented that it would teach wisdom, truth, character, enlightenment, and similar virtues and qualities. He specifically cites as support the Columbia motto: *"in lumine tuo videbimus lumen"* ("In your light we shall see light"); the inscription over the college chapel: "Wisdom dwelleth in the heart of him that hath understanding"; and various excerpts from its brochures, catalogues, and a convocation address made by the University's president. Jacobsen, a senior who was not graduated because of poor scholastic standing, claims that the University's failure to meet its promises made through these quotations constituted fraudulent misrepresentation or deceit. Decision?

15. Frank Berryessa stole funds from his employer, the Eccles Hotel Company. His father, W. S. Berryessa, learned of his son's trouble and, thinking the amount involved was about $2,000, gave the hotel a promissory note for $2,186 to cover the shortage. In return, the hotel agreed not to publicize the incident or notify the bonding company. (A bonding company is an insurer that is paid a premium for agreeing to reimburse an employer for thefts by an employee.) Before this note became due, however, the hotel discovered that Frank had actually misappropriated $6,865. The hotel then notified its bonding company, Great American Indemnity Company, to collect the entire loss. W. S. Berryessa claims that the agent for Great American told him that unless he paid them $2,000 in cash and signed a note for the remaining $4,865, Frank would be prosecuted. Berryessa agreed, signed the note, and gave the agent a cashier's check for $1,500 and a personal check for $500. He requested that the agent not cash the personal check for about a month. Subsequently, Great American sued Berryessa on the note. He defends against the note on the grounds of duress and counterclaims for the return of the $1,500 and the cancellation of the uncashed $500 check. Who should prevail? Explain.

16. Jane Francois married Victor H. Francois. At the time of the marriage, Victor was a fifty-year-old bachelor living with his elderly mother, and Jane was a thirty-year-old, twice-divorced mother of two. Victor had a relatively secure financial portfolio; Jane, on the other hand, brought no money or property to the marriage.

     The marriage deteriorated quickly over the next couple of years, with disputes centered on financial matters. During this period, Jane systematically gained a joint interest in, and took control of, most of Victor's assets. Three years after they married, Jane contracted Harold Monoson, an attorney, to draw up divorce papers. Victor was unaware of Jane's decision until he was taken to Monoson's office, where Monoson presented for Victor's signature a "Property Settlement and Separation Agreement." Monoson told Victor that he would need an attorney, but Jane vetoed Victor's choice. Monoson then asked another lawyer, Gregory Ball, to come into the office. Ball read the agreement and strenuously advised Victor not to sign it because it would commit him to financial suicide. The agreement transferred most of Victor's remaining assets to Jane. Victor, however, signed it because Jane and Monoson persuaded him that it was the only way that his marriage could be saved. In October of the following year, Jane informed Victor that she had sold most of his former property and that she was leaving him permanently. Can Victor have the agreement set aside as a result of undue influence? Explain.

17. Iverson owned Iverson Motor Company, an enterprise engaged in the repair as well as the sale of Oldsmobile, Rambler, and International Harvester Scout automobiles. Forty percent of the business's sales volume and net earnings came from the Oldsmobile franchise. Whipp contracted to buy Iverson Motors, which Iverson said included the Oldsmobile franchise. After the sale, however, General Motors refused to transfer the franchise to Whipp. Whipp then returned the property to Iverson and brought this action seeking rescission of the contract. Should the contract be rescinded? Explain.

18. On February 10, Mrs. Sunderhaus purchased a diamond ring from Perel & Lowenstein for $6,990. She was told by the company's salesperson that the ring was worth its purchase price, and she also received at that time a written guarantee from the company attesting to the diamond's value, style, and trade-in value. When Mrs. Sunderhaus went to trade the ring for another, however, two jewelers gave the ring valuations of $3,000 and $3,500, respectively. Mrs. Sunderhaus knew little about the value of diamonds and claims to have relied on the oral representation of the Perel & Lowenstein's salesperson and the written representation as to the ring's value. She seeks rescission of the contract or damages in the amount of the sales price over the ring's value. Decision?

19. Division West Chinchilla Ranch advertised on television that a five-figure income could be earned by raising chinchillas with an investment of only $3.75 per animal per year and only thirty minutes of maintenance per day. The minimum investment was $2,150 for one male and six female chinchillas. Division West represented to plaintiffs that chinchilla ranching would be easy and that no experience was required to make ranching profitable. Plaintiffs, who had no experience raising chinchillas, each invested $2,150 or more to purchase Division's

chinchillas and supplies. After three years without earning a profit, plaintiffs sue Division for fraud. Do these facts sustain an action for fraud in the inducement? Why or why not?

20. William Schmalz entered into an employment contract with Hardy Salt Company. The contract granted Schmalz six months' severance pay for involuntary termination but none for voluntary separation or termination for cause. Schmalz was asked to resign from his employment. He was informed that if he did not resign, he would be fired for alleged misconduct. When Schmalz turned in his letter of resignation, he signed a release prohibiting him from suing his former employer as a consequence of his employment. Schmalz consulted an attorney before signing the release and upon signing it received $4,583 (one month's salary) in consideration. Schmalz then sued his former employer for the severance pay, claiming that he signed the release under duress. Is Schmalz correct in his assertion?

21. Treasure Salvors and the State of Florida entered into a series of four annual contracts governing the salvage of the *Nuestra Senora de Atocha*. The *Atocha* is a Spanish galleon that sank in 1622, carrying a treasure now worth well over $250 million. Both parties had contracted under the impression that the seabed on which the *Atocha* lay was land owned by Florida. Treasure Salvors agreed to relinquish 25 percent of the items recovered in return for the right to salvage on State lands. In accordance with these contracts, Treasure Salvors delivered to Florida its share of the salvaged artifacts. Subsequently, the U.S. Supreme Court held that the part of the continental shelf on which the *Atocha* was resting had *never* been owned by Florida. Treasure Salvors then brought suit to rescind the contracts and to recover the artifacts it had delivered to the State of Florida. Should Treasure Salvors prevail? Explain.

22. International Underwater Contractors, Inc. (IUC), entered into a written contract with New England Telephone and Telegraph Company (NET) to assemble and install certain conduits under the Mystic River for a lump sum price of $149,680. Delays caused by NET forced IUC's work to be performed in the winter months instead of during the summer as originally bid, and as a result, a major change had to be made in the system from that specified in the contract. NET repeatedly assured IUC that it would pay the cost if IUC would complete the work. The change cost IUC an additional $811,810.73; nevertheless, it signed a release settling the claim for a total sum of $575,000. IUC, which at the time was in financial trouble, now seeks to recover the balance due, arguing that the signed release is not binding

because it was signed under economic duress. Is IUC correct? Explain.

23. Conrad Schaneman was a Russian immigrant who could neither read nor write the English language. Conrad deeded (conveyed) a farm he owned to his eldest son, Laurence, for $23,500, which was the original purchase price of the property thirty years earlier. The value of the farm at the time of the conveyance was between $145,000 and $160,000. At the time he executed the deed, Conrad was an eighty-two-year-old invalid, was severely ill, and was completely dependent on others for his personal needs. He weighed between 325 and 350 pounds, had difficulty breathing, could not walk more than fifteen feet, and needed a special jackhoist to get in and out of the bathtub. Conrad enjoyed a long-standing, confidential relationship with Laurence, who was his principal adviser and handled Conrad's business affairs. Laurence also obtained a power of attorney from Conrad and made himself a joint owner of Conrad's bank account and $20,000 certificate of deposit. Conrad brought this suit to cancel the deed, claiming it was the result of Laurence's undue influence. The district court found that the deed was executed as a result of undue influence, set aside the deed, and granted title to Conrad. Laurence appealed. Decision?

24. At the time of her death, Olga Mestrovic was the owner of a large number of works of art created by her late husband, Ivan Mestrovic, an internationally known sculptor and artist whose works were displayed throughout Europe and the United States. By the terms of Olga's will, all the works of art created by her husband were to be sold and the proceeds distributed to members of the Mestrovic family. Also included in the estate of Olga Mestrovic was certain real property that 1st Source Bank (the Bank), as personal representative of the estate of Olga Mestrovic, agreed to sell to Terrence and Antoinette Wilkin. The agreement of purchase and sale made no mention of any works of art, although it did provide for the sale of such personal property as a dishwasher, drapes, and French doors stored in the attic. Immediately after closing on the real estate, the Wilkins complained to the Bank of the clutter left on the premises; the Bank gave the Wilkins the choice of cleaning the house themselves and keeping any personal property they desired, to which the Wilkins agreed. At the time these arrangements were made, neither the Bank nor the Wilkins suspected that any works of art remained on the premises. During cleanup, however, the Wilkins found eight drawings and a sculpture created by Ivan Mestrovic to which the Wilkins claimed ownership based upon their

agreement with the Bank that, if they cleaned the real property, they could keep such personal property as they desired. Who is entitled to ownership of the artwork?

25. Ronald D. Johnson is a former employee of International Business Machines Corporation (IBM). As part of a downsizing effort, IBM discharged Johnson. In exchange for an enhanced severance package, Johnson signed a written release and covenant not to sue IBM. IBM's downsizing plan provided that surplus personnel were eligible to receive benefits, including outplacement assistance, career counseling, job retraining, and an enhanced separation allowance. These employees were eligible, at IBM's discretion, to receive a separation allowance of two weeks' pay. However, employees who signed a release could be eligible for an enhanced severance allowance equal to one week's pay for each six months of accumulated service with a maximum of twenty-six weeks' pay. Surplus employees could also apply for alternate, generally lower-paying, manufacturing positions. Johnson opted for the release and received the maximum twenty-six weeks' pay. He then alleged, among other claims, that IBM subjected him to economic duress when he signed the release and covenant not to sue, and he sought to rescind both. What will Johnson need to show in order to prove his cause of action?

26. Vernon and Janene Lesher agreed to purchase an eighteen-acre parcel of real property from the Strids with the intention of using it to raise horses. In purchasing the property, the Leshers relied on their impression that at least four acres of the subject property had a right to irrigation from Slate Creek. The earnest money agreement to the contract provided:

> **D. Water Rights** are being conveyed to Buyer at the close of escrow. . . . Seller will provide Buyer with a written explanation of the operation of the irrigation system, water right certificates, and inventory of irrigation equipment included in sale.

The earnest money agreement also provided:

> **THE SUBJECT PROPERTY IS BEING SOLD "AS IS"** subject to the Buyer's approval of the tests and conditions as stated herein. Buyer declares that Buyer is not depending on any other statement of the Seller or licensees that is not incorporated by reference in this earnest money contract [Bold in original].

Before signing the earnest money agreement, the Strids presented to the Leshers a Water Resources Department water rights certificate and a map purporting to show an area of the subject property to be irrigated, which indicated that the property carried a four-acre water right. These documents were from eighteen years earlier. Both parties believed that the property carried the irrigation rights and that the Leshers needed such rights for their horse farm. The Leshers did not obtain the services of an attorney or a water rights examiner before purchasing the property.

After purchasing the property and before establishing a pasture, the Leshers learned that the property did not carry a four-acre water right. Explain whether the Leshers may rescind the contract.

TAKING SIDES

Mrs. Audrey E. Vokes, a widow of fifty-one years and without family, purchased fourteen separate dance courses from J. P. Davenport's Arthur Murray, Inc., School of Dance. The fourteen courses totaled in the aggregate 2,302 hours of dancing lessons at a cost to Mrs. Vokes of $31,090.45. Mrs. Vokes was induced continually to reapply for new courses by representations made by Mr. Davenport that her dancing ability was improving, that she was responding to instruction, that she had excellent potential, and that they were developing her into an accomplished dancer. In fact, she had no dancing ability or aptitude and had trouble "hearing the musical beat." Mrs. Vokes brought action to have the contracts set aside.

a. What are the arguments that the contracts should be set aside?

b. What are the arguments that the contracts should be enforced?

c. What is the proper outcome? Explain.

CHAPTER 12

Consideration

CHAPTER OUTCOMES

After reading and studying this chapter, you should be able to:

- Define *consideration* and explain what is meant by legal sufficiency.

- Describe illusory promises, output contracts, requirements contracts, exclusive dealing contracts, and conditional contracts.

- Explain whether preexisting public and contractual obligations satisfy the legal requirement of consideration.

- Explain the concept of bargained-for exchange and whether this element is present with past consideration and third-party beneficiaries.

- Discuss those contracts that are enforceable even though they are not supported by consideration.

onsideration is the primary—but not the only—basis for the enforcement of promises in our legal system. Consideration is the inducement to make a promise enforceable. The doctrine of consideration ensures that promises are enforced only in cases in which the parties have exchanged something of value in the eye of the law. Gratuitous (gift) promises, accordingly, are legally enforceable only under certain circumstances, which are discussed later in the chapter.

Consideration, or that which is exchanged for a promise, is present only when the parties intend an exchange. The consideration exchanged for the promise may be an act, a forbearance to act, or a promise to do either of these. In like manner, Section 71 of the Restatement defines consideration for a promise as (1) an act other than a promise; (2) a forbearance; (3) the creation, modification, or destruction of a legal relation; or (4) a return promise if any of these are bargained for and given in exchange for the promise.

Thus, consideration comprises two basic elements: (1) legal sufficiency (something of value) and (2) bargained-for exchange. Both must be present to satisfy the requirement of consideration. The consideration may be given to the promisor or to some other person; likewise, it may be given by the promisee or by some other person.

12-1 Legal Sufficiency

To be legally sufficient, the consideration exchanged for the promise must be either a legal detriment to the promisee or a legal benefit to the promisor. In other words, in return for the promise, the promisee must give up something of legal value or the promisor must receive something of legal value.

Legal detriment means (1) doing (or undertaking to do) that which the promisee was under no prior legal obligation to do or (2) refraining from doing (or the undertaking to refrain from doing) that which he was previously under no legal obligation to refrain from doing. On the other hand, **legal benefit** means the obtaining by the promisor of that which he had no prior legal right to obtain. Most, if not all, cases involving legal detriment to the promisee also will involve a legal benefit to the promisor. Nonetheless, the presence of either is sufficient.

12-1a ADEQUACY

Legal sufficiency has nothing to do with adequacy of consideration. Restatement, Section 79. The subject matter that the parties agree to exchange does not need to have the same or equal value; rather, the law will regard consideration as adequate if the parties have freely agreed to the exchange. The requirement of legally sufficient consideration, therefore, is not at all concerned with whether the bargain was good or bad or whether one party received disproportionately more or less than what he gave or promised in exchange. Such facts, however, may be relevant to the availability of certain defenses (such as fraud, duress, or undue influence) or certain remedies (such as specific performance). The requirement of legally sufficient consideration is simply (1) that the parties have agreed to an exchange and (2) that, with respect to each party, the subject matter exchanged, or promised in exchange, either imposed a legal detriment upon the promisee or conferred a legal benefit upon the promisor. If the purported consideration is clearly without value, however, such that the transaction is a sham, many courts would hold that consideration is lacking.

Practical Advice

Be sure you are satisfied with your agreed-upon exchange, because courts will not invalidate a contract for absence of adequate consideration.

12-1b UNILATERAL CONTRACTS

In a unilateral contract, a promise is exchanged for a completed act or a forbearance to act. Because only one promise exists, only one party, the **offeror,** makes a promise and is therefore the **promisor** while the other party, the **offeree,** is the person receiving the promise and thus is the **promisee.** For example, A promises to pay B $2,000 if B paints A's house. B paints A's house.

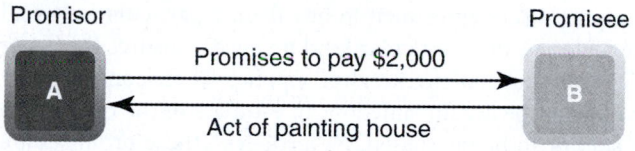

For A's promise to be binding, it must be supported by consideration consisting of either a legal detriment to B, the promisee (offeree), or a legal benefit to A, the promisor (offeror). B's having painted the house is a legal detriment to B, the promisee, because she was under no prior legal duty to paint A's house. Also, B's painting A's house is a legal benefit to A, the promisor, because A had no prior legal right to have his house painted by B.

A unilateral contract also may consist of a promise exchanged for a forbearance. To illustrate, A negligently injures B, for which B may recover damages in a tort action. A promises to pay B $5,000 if B forbears from bringing suit. B accepts by not filing suit.

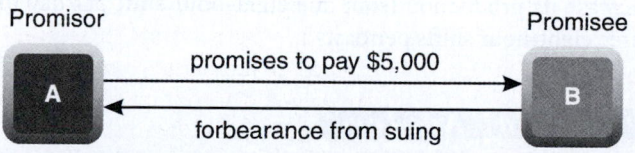

A's promise to pay B $5,000 is binding because it is supported by consideration: B, the promisee (offeree), has incurred a legal detriment by refraining from bringing suit, which he was under no prior legal obligation to refrain from doing. A, the promisor (offeror), has received a legal benefit because she had no prior legal right to B's forbearance from bringing suit.

12-1c BILATERAL CONTRACTS

In a bilateral contract, the parties exchange promises. Thus, each party is *both* a promisor and a promisee. For example, if A (the offeror) promises (offers) to purchase an automobile from B (the offeree) for $25,000 and B promises to sell the automobile to A for $25,000 (accepts the offer), the following relationship exists:

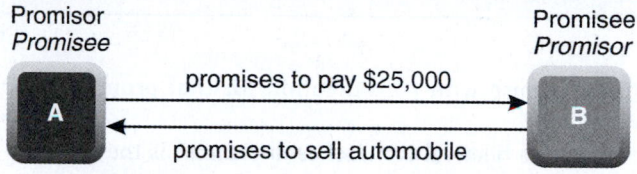

A's promise (the offer) to pay B $25,000 is binding and therefore enforceable by B, if that promise is supported by legal consideration from B (offeree), which may consist of either a legal detriment to B, the promisee, or a legal benefit to A, the promisor. B's promise to sell A the automobile is a legal detriment to B because he was under no prior legal duty to sell the automobile to A. Moreover, B's promise is also a legal benefit to A because A had no prior legal right to that automobile. Consequently, A's promise to pay $25,000 to B is supported by consideration and is enforceable.

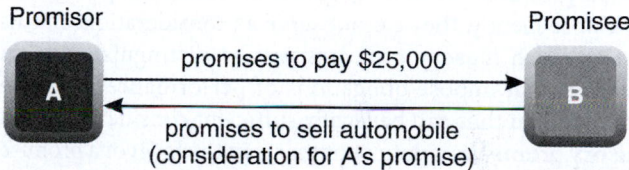

For **B's promise** (the acceptance) to sell the automobile to A to be binding, it likewise must be supported by consideration from A (offeror), which may be either a legal detriment to A, the promisee, or a legal benefit to B, the promisor. A's promise to pay B $25,000 is a legal detriment to A because he was under no prior legal duty to pay $25,000 to B. At the same time, A's promise is also a legal benefit to B because B had no prior legal right to the $25,000. Thus, B's promise to sell the automobile is supported by consideration and is enforceable.

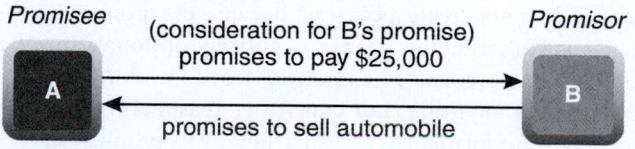

To summarize, for A's promise to B to be binding, B must support the promise with legally sufficient consideration, which requires that the promise A receives in exchange from B provide either a legal benefit to A (the promisor) or a legal detriment to B (the promisee). A, in turn, must support B's

FIGURE 12-1 Consideration in Unilateral and Bilateral Contracts

Type of Contract	Offer	Acceptance	Consideration
Unilateral	Promise by A	Performance of requested act or forbearance by B	*Promise* by A *Performance* of requested act or forbearance by B
Bilateral	Promise by A	Return promise by B to perform requested act or forbearance	*Promise* by A Return *promise* by B to perform requested act or forbearance

return promise with consideration for that promise to be binding on B.

Thus, in a bilateral contract each promise is the consideration for the other, a relationship that has been referred to as **mutuality of obligation.** A general consequence of mutuality of obligation is that each promisor in a bilateral contract must be bound, or neither is bound.

♦ SEE FIGURE 12-1: *Consideration in Unilateral and Bilateral Contracts*

12-1d ILLUSORY PROMISES

Words of promise that make the performance of the purported promisor entirely optional constitute no promise at all. Consequently, they cannot serve as consideration. In this section, such illusory promises will be distinguished from promises that impose obligations of performance upon the promisor and thus can be legally sufficient consideration. An **illusory promise** is a statement that is in the form of a promise but imposes no obligation upon the maker of the statement. An illusory promise is not consideration for a return promise. Thus, a statement committing the promisor to purchase such quantity of goods as she may "desire," "want," or "wish to buy" is an illusory promise because its performance is entirely optional. For example, if ExxonMobil, Inc., agrees to sell to Barnes Co. as many barrels of oil as Barnes shall choose at $40 per barrel, there would be no consideration: Barnes may wish or desire to buy none of the oil, yet in buying none, it would fulfill its promise. An agreement containing such a promise as that made by Barnes, although accepted by both parties, does not create a contract because the promise is illusory—performance by Barnes is entirely optional, and the offer places no constraint upon its freedom. Barnes is not bound to do anything, nor can Ames reasonably expect to receive any performance. Thus, Barnes, by its promise, suffers no legal detriment and confers no legal benefit. Consequently, Barnes's promise does not provide legally sufficient consideration for ExxonMobil's promise; thus, ExxonMobil's promise is not binding upon ExxonMobil.

♦ *See Case 12-1*

Practical Advice

Because an agreement under which one party may perform at his discretion is not a binding contract, be sure that you make a promise and receive a promise that is not optional.

OUTPUT AND REQUIREMENTS CONTRACTS A seller's agreement to sell her entire production to a particular purchaser is called an **output contract.** It affords the seller an ensured market for her product. Conversely, a **requirements contract,** or a purchaser's agreement to buy from a particular seller all the materials of a particular kind he needs, ensures the buyer of a ready source of inventory or supplies. These contracts may or may not be accompanied by an estimate of the quantity to be sold or to be purchased. Nevertheless, these promises are not illusory. The buyer under a requirements contract does not promise to buy as much as she desires to buy but, rather, to buy as much as she *needs*. Similarly, under an output contract, the seller promises to sell to the buyer the seller's entire production, not merely as much as the seller desires.

Furthermore, the Code, Section 2-306(1), imposes a good faith limitation upon the quantity to be sold or purchased under an output or requirements contract. Thus, a contract of this type involves such actual output or requirements as may occur in good faith, except that no quantity unreasonably disproportionate to any stated estimate or, in the absence of a stated estimate, to any normal prior output or requirements may be tendered or demanded. Therefore, after contracting to sell to Adler, Inc., its entire output, Benevito Company cannot increase its production from one eight-hour shift per day to three eight-hour shifts per day.

Practical Advice

If you use an output or requirements contract, be sure to act in good faith and do not take unfair advantage of the situation.

EXCLUSIVE DEALING CONTRACTS When a manufacturer of goods grants an exclusive right to a distributor to sell its products in a designated territory, unless otherwise agreed, the manufacturer is under an implied obligation to use its best efforts to supply the goods, and the distributor must use his best efforts to promote their sale. Uniform Commercial Code (UCC) Section 2-306(2). The obligations that arise upon acceptance of an **exclusive dealing agreement** are sufficient consideration to bind both parties to the contract.

CONDITIONAL PROMISES A conditional promise is a promise the performance of which depends upon the happening or nonhappening of an event not certain to occur (the condition). A conditional promise is sufficient consideration *unless* the promisor knows at the time of making the promise that the condition cannot occur. Restatement, Section 76.

Thus, if Debbie offers to pay John $8,000 for John's automobile, provided that Debbie receives such amount as an inheritance from the estate of her deceased uncle, and John accepts the offer, the duty of Debbie to pay $8,000 to John is *conditioned* upon her receiving $8,000 from her deceased uncle's estate. The consideration moving from John to Debbie is the promise to transfer title to the automobile. The consideration moving from Debbie to John is the promise of $8,000 subject to the condition.

12-1e PREEXISTING PUBLIC OBLIGATION

The law does not regard the performance of, or the promise to perform, a preexisting legal duty, public or private, as either a legal detriment to the party under the prior legal obligation or a benefit to the other party. A **public duty** does not arise out of a contract; rather, it is imposed upon members of society by force of the common law or by statute. As illustrated in the law of torts, public duty includes the duty not to commit an assault, battery, false imprisonment, or defamation. The criminal law also imposes numerous public duties. Thus, if Cleon promises to pay Spike, the village ruffian, $100 not to abuse him physically, Cleon's promise is unenforceable because both tort and criminal law impose on Spike a preexisting public obligation to refrain from so acting.

By virtue of their public office, public officials, such as the mayor of a city, members of a city council, police officers, and firefighters, are under a preexisting obligation to perform their duties.

12-1f PREEXISTING CONTRACTUAL OBLIGATION

The performance of, or the promise to perform, a **preexisting contractual duty**, a duty the terms of which are neither doubtful nor the subject of honest dispute, is also legally insufficient consideration because the doing of what one is legally bound to do is neither a detriment to the promisee nor a benefit to the promisor. For example, Leigh and Associates employs Jason for one year at a salary of $2,000 per month and at the end of six months promises Jason that, in addition to the salary, it will pay him $3,000 if he remains on the job for the remainder of the period originally agreed upon. Leigh's promise is not binding because Jason's promise does not constitute legally sufficient consideration. If Jason's duties were changed in nature or amount, however, Leigh's promise would be binding because Jason's new duties are a legal detriment.

◆ *See Case 12-2*

MODIFICATION OF A PREEXISTING CONTRACT A modification of a contract occurs when the parties to the contract mutually agree to change one or more of its terms. Under the common law, a modification of an existing contract must be supported by mutual consideration to be enforceable. In other words, the modification must be supported by some new consideration beyond that which is already owed (thus, there must be a separate and distinct modification contract). For example, Fred and Jodie agree that Fred shall put in a gravel driveway for Jodie at a cost of $2,000. Subsequently, Jodie agrees to pay an additional $1,000 if Fred will blacktop the driveway. Because Fred was not bound by the original contract to provide blacktopping, he would incur a legal detriment in doing so and is therefore entitled to the additional $1,000.

The Code has modified the common law rule for contract modification by providing that the parties can effectively modify a contract for the sale of goods without new consideration, though the Comments to this section make the modification subject to the requirement of good faith. Moreover, the Restatement has moved toward this position by providing that a modification of an executory contract is binding if it is fair and equitable in light of surrounding facts that the parties did not anticipate when the contract was made. Restatement, Section 89. A few States have followed the Code's rule by statutorily providing that the parties need provide no new consideration when modifying any contract. These States vary, however, as to whether the modification must be in writing and whether the original contract must be executory.

◆ **SEE FIGURE 12-2:** *Modification of a Preexisting Contract*

◆ *See Case 12-3*

Practical Advice

If you modify a contract governed by the common law, be sure to provide additional consideration to make the other party's new promise enforceable.

FIGURE 12-2 Modification of a Preexisting Contract

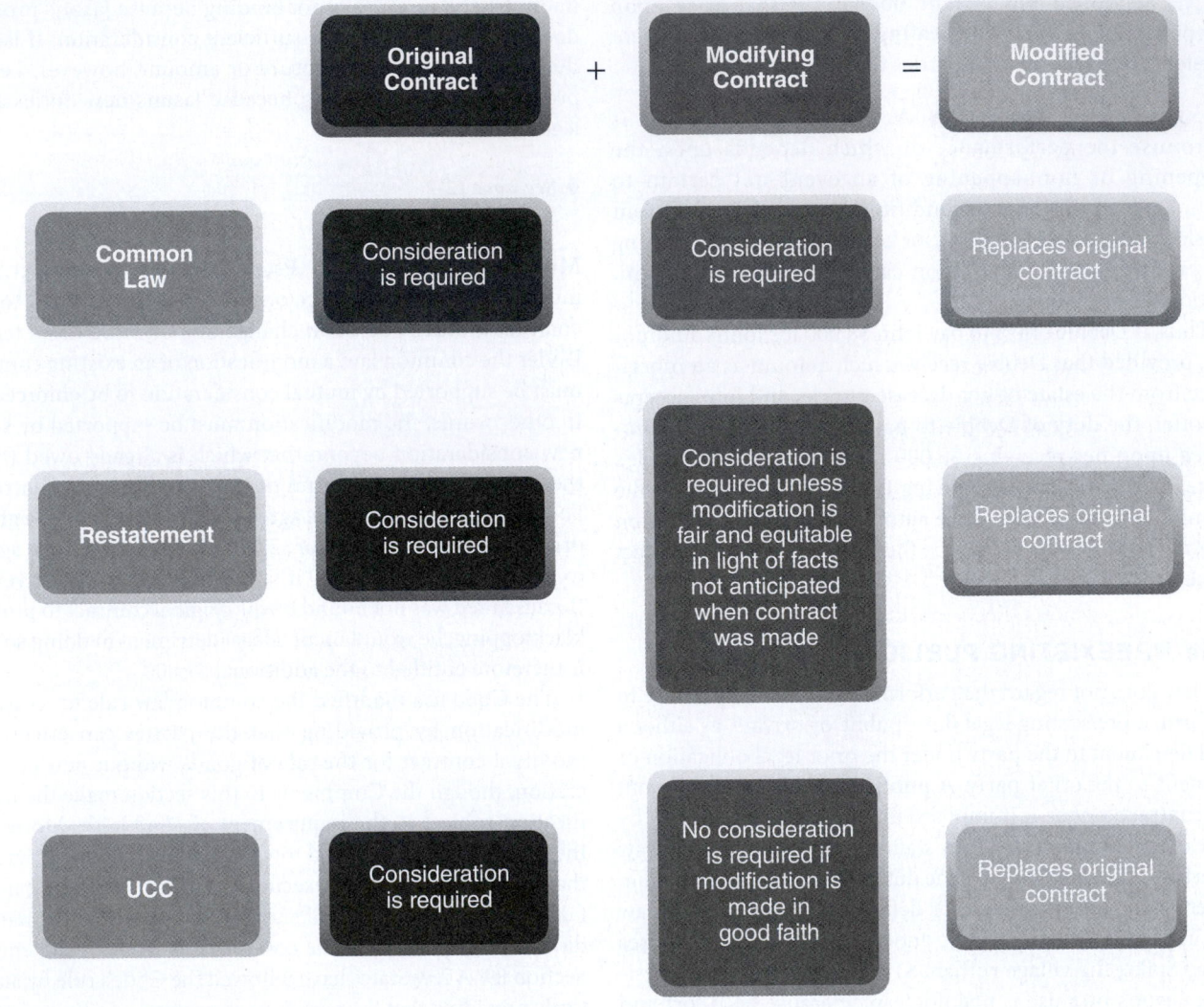

SUBSTITUTED CONTRACTS A substituted contract results when the parties to a contract mutually agree to rescind their original contract and enter into a new one. This situation involves separate contracts: the original contract, the agreement of rescission, and the substitute contract. Substituted contracts are perfectly valid, allowing the parties effectively to discharge the original contract and to impose obligations under the new one. The rescission is binding in that each party, by giving up his rights under the original contract, has provided consideration to the other, as long as each party still has rights under the original contract. Where the rescission and new agreement are simultaneous, the effect is the same as a contractual modification. The Restatement takes the position that the substitute contract is *not* binding unless it is

fair and equitable in view of circumstances the parties did not anticipate when they made the original contract. Section 89, Comment b.

SETTLEMENT OF A LIQUIDATED DEBT A **liquidated debt** is an obligation the existence and amount of which is undisputed. Under the common law, the partial payment of a sum of money in consideration of a promise to discharge a fully matured, undisputed debt is legally *insufficient* to support the promise of discharge. To illustrate, assume that Pamela owes Julie $100, and in consideration of Pamela's paying Julie $50, Julie agrees to discharge the debt. In a subsequent suit by Julie against Pamela to recover the remaining $50, at common law, Julie is entitled to judgment for $50 on the ground that Julie's promise of discharge is not binding because Pamela's payment of $50 was no legal detriment to the promisee, Pamela, as she was under a preexisting legal obligation to pay that much and more. Consequently, the consideration for Julie's promise of discharge was legally insufficient, and Julie is not bound on her promise. If, however, Julie had accepted from Pamela any new or different consideration, such as the sum of $40 and a fountain pen worth $10 or less, or even the fountain pen with no payment of money, in full satisfaction of the $100 debt, the consideration moving from Pamela would be legally sufficient inasmuch as Pamela was under no legal obligation to give a fountain pen to Julie. In this example, consideration would also exist if Julie had agreed to accept $50 before the debt became due, in full satisfaction of the debt. Pamela was under no legal obligation to pay any of the debt before its due date. Consequently, Pamela's early payment would represent a legal detriment to Pamela as well as a legal benefit to Julie. The law is not concerned with the amount of the discount, as that is simply a question of adequacy for the courts to decide. Likewise, Pamela's payment of a lesser amount on the due date at an agreed-upon different place of payment would be legally sufficient consideration. The Restatement requires that the new consideration "differs from what was required by the duty in a way which reflects more than a pretense of bargain." Section 73.

SETTLEMENT OF AN UNLIQUIDATED DEBT An **unliquidated debt** is an obligation disputed as to either its existence or its amount. A promise to settle a validly disputed claim in exchange for an agreed payment or other performance is supported by consideration. Where the dispute is based upon contentions that are nonmeritorious or not made in good faith, however, the debtor's surrender of such a claim is no legal detriment to the claimant. The Restatement adopts a different position by providing that the settlement of a claim that proves invalid is consideration if at the time of the settlement (1) the claimant honestly believed that the claim was valid or (2) the claim was in fact doubtful because of uncertainty as to the facts or the law. Section 74.

For example, in situations in which a person has requested professional services from an accountant or a lawyer and the parties reached no agreement with respect to the amount of the fee to be charged, the accountant or lawyer is entitled to receive from her client a reasonable fee for the services rendered. As no definite amount has been agreed upon, the client's obligation is uncertain; nevertheless, his legal obligation is to pay the reasonable worth of the services performed. When the accountant or lawyer sends the client a bill for services rendered, even though the amount stated in the bill is an estimate of the reasonable value of the services, the debt does not become undisputed until and unless the client agrees to pay the amount of the bill. If the client honestly disputes

the amount that is owed and tenders in full settlement an amount less than the bill, acceptance of the lesser amount by the creditor discharges the debt. Thus, if Ted sends to Betty, an accountant, a check for $120 in payment of his debt to Betty for services rendered, which services Ted considered worthless but for which Betty billed Ted $600, Betty's acceptance of the check releases Ted from any further liability. Ted has given up his right to dispute the billing further, while Betty has forfeited her right to further collection. Thus, there is mutuality of consideration.

> ### Practical Advice
> *If your contract is validly disputed, carefully consider whether to accept any payment marked "payment in full."*

12-2 Bargained-For Exchange

The central idea behind consideration is that the parties have intentionally entered into a bargained exchange with each other and have given to each other something in exchange for a promise or performance. "A performance or return promise is bargained for if it is sought by the promisor in exchange for his promise and is given by the promisee in exchange for that promise." Restatement, Section 71. Thus, a promise to give someone a birthday present is without consideration, as the promisor received nothing in exchange for his promise of a present.

> ### Practical Advice
> *Because a promise to make a gift is generally not legally enforceable, obtain delivery of something that shows your control or ownership of the item to make it an executed gift.*

12-2a PAST CONSIDERATION

Consideration is the inducement for a promise or performance. The element of bargained-for exchange is absent where a promise is given for a past transaction. Therefore, unbargained-for past events are not consideration, despite their designation as "past consideration." A promise made on account of something that the promisee has already done is not enforceable. For example, Noel gives emergency care to Tim's adult son while the son is ill. Tim subsequently promises to pay Noel for her services, but his promise is not binding because there is no bargained-for exchange.

◆ *See Case 12-4*

12-2b THIRD PARTIES

Consideration to support a promise may be given to a person other than the promisor if the promisor bargains for that exchange. For example, A promises to pay B $15 if B delivers a specified book to C.

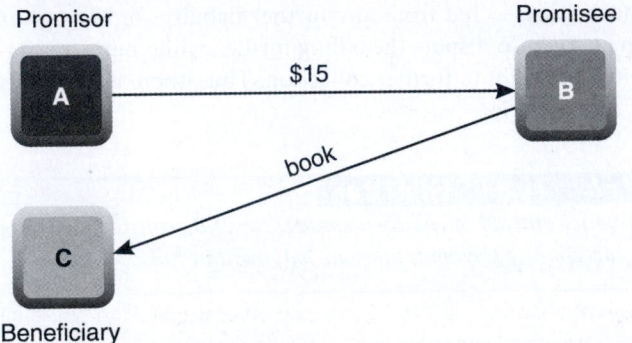

A's promise is binding because B incurred a legal detriment by delivering the book to C, as B was under no prior legal obligation to do so, and A had no prior legal right to have the book given to C. A and B have bargained for A to pay B $15 in return for B's delivering the book to C. A's promise to pay $15 is also consideration for B's promise to give the book to C.

Conversely, consideration may be given by some person other than the promisee. For example, A promises to pay B $25 in return for D's promise to give a radio to A.

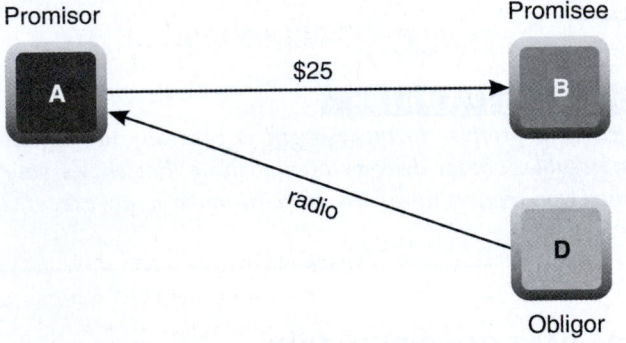

A's promise to pay $25 to B is consideration for D's promise to give a radio to A and vice versa.

12-3 Contracts without Consideration

Certain transactions are enforceable even though they are not supported by consideration. Such transactions include (1) promises to perform prior unenforceable obligations, (2) promises that induce detrimental reliance (promissory estoppel), (3) promises made under seal, and (4) promises made enforceable by statute.

12-3a PROMISES TO PERFORM PRIOR UNENFORCEABLE OBLIGATIONS

In certain circumstances, the courts will enforce new promises to perform an obligation that originally was not enforceable or has become unenforceable by operation of law. These situations include promises to pay debts barred by the statute of limitations, debts discharged in bankruptcy, and voidable obligations. In addition, as previously indicated, some courts will enforce promises to pay moral obligations.

PROMISE TO PAY DEBT BARRED BY THE STATUTE OF LIMITATIONS Every State has a statute of limitations, which provides that legal actions must be initiated within a prescribed period after the right to bring the action arose. Actions not commenced within the specified time period, which varies among the States and with the nature of the legal action, will be dismissed.

An exception to the past consideration rule extends to promises to pay all or part of a contractual or quasi-contractual debt barred by the statute of limitations. The new promise is binding according to its terms without consideration for a second statutory period. Any recovery under the new promise is limited to the terms contained in the new promise. Most States require that new promises falling under this rule, except those indicated by part payment, be in writing to be enforceable.

PROMISE TO PAY DEBT DISCHARGED IN BANKRUPTCY Another exception to the requirement that consideration be given in exchange for a promise to make it binding is a promise to pay a debt that has been discharged in bankruptcy. Restatement, Section 83. The Bankruptcy Act, however, imposes a number of requirements before a promise to pay a debt discharged in bankruptcy may be enforced. These requirements are discussed in *Chapter 38.*

VOIDABLE PROMISES Another promise that is enforceable without new consideration is a new promise to perform a voidable obligation that has not previously been avoided. Restatement, Section 85. The power of avoidance may be based on lack of capacity, fraud, misrepresentation, duress, undue influence, or mistake. For instance, a promise to perform an antecedent obligation made by a minor upon reaching the age of majority is enforceable without new consideration. To be enforceable, the promise itself must not be voidable. For example, if the new promise is made without knowledge of the original fraud or by a minor before reaching the age of majority, then the new promise is not enforceable.

MORAL OBLIGATION Under the common law, a promise made to satisfy a preexisting moral obligation is made for past consideration and therefore is unenforceable for lack of consideration. Instances involving such obligations include promises to pay for board and lodging previously furnished to a needy relative of the promisor, promises to pay debts owed by a relative, and an employer's promises to pay a completely disabled former employee a sum of money in addition to an award the employee has received under a workers' compensation statute. Although in many cases the moral obligation may be strong by reason of the particular facts and circumstances, no liability generally attaches to the promise.

The Restatement and a minority of States give considerable recognition to moral obligations as consideration. The Restatement provides that a promise made for "a benefit previously received by the promisor from the promisee is binding to the extent necessary to prevent injustice." Section 86. For instance, Tim's subsequent promise to Noel to reimburse her for the expenses she incurred in rendering emergency services to Tim's son is binding even though it is not supported by new consideration.

The Restatement also provides for enforcement of a moral obligation when a person promises to pay for a mistakenly conferred benefit. For example, Pam hires Elizabeth to pave her driveway, and Elizabeth mistakenly paves Chuck's driveway next door. Chuck subsequently promises to pay Pam $1,000 for the benefit conferred. Under the Restatement, Chuck's promise to pay the $1,000 is binding.

12-3b PROMISSORY ESTOPPEL

As discussed in *Chapter 9*, in certain circumstances in which detrimental reliance has occurred, the courts will enforce noncontractual promises under the doctrine of promissory estoppel. When applicable, the doctrine makes gratuitous promises enforceable to the extent necessary to avoid injustice. The doctrine applies when a promise that the promisor reasonably should expect to induce detrimental reliance does induce such action or forbearance.

Promissory estoppel does not mean that every gratuitous promise is binding simply because it is followed by a change of position on the part of the promisee. To create liability, the promisee must make the change of position in justifiable reliance on the promise. For example, Smith promises to Barclay not to foreclose on a mortgage Smith holds on Barclay's factory for a period of six months. In justifiable reliance on Smith's promise, Barclay expends $900,000 on expanding the factory. Smith's promise not to foreclose is binding on Smith under the doctrine of promissory estoppel.

The most common application of the doctrine of promissory estoppel is to charitable subscriptions. Numerous churches, memorials, college buildings, hospitals, and other structures used for religious, educational, and charitable purposes have been built with the assistance of contributions fulfilling pledges or promises to contribute to particular worthwhile causes. Although the pledgor regards herself as making a gift for a charitable purpose and gift promises generally are not enforceable, the courts tend to enforce charitable subscription promises. Numerous reasons and theories have been advanced in support of liability: The most accepted argues that the subscription has induced a change of position by the promisee (the church, school, or charitable organization) in reliance on the promise. The Restatement, moreover, has relaxed the reliance requirement for charitable subscriptions so that actual reliance need not be shown; the probability of reliance is sufficient.

♦ *See Case 12-4*

12-3c PROMISES MADE UNDER SEAL

Under the common law, when a person desired to bind himself by bond, deed, or solemn promise, he executed his promise under seal. He did not have to sign the document, his delivery of a document to which he had affixed his seal being sufficient. No consideration for his promise was necessary. In some States, the courts still hold a promise under seal to be binding without consideration.

Nevertheless, most States have abolished by statute the distinction between contracts under seal and written unsealed contracts. In these States, the seal is no longer recognized as a substitute for consideration. The Code has also adopted this position, specifically eliminating the use of seals in contracts for the sale of goods.

12-3d PROMISES MADE ENFORCEABLE BY STATUTE

Some gratuitous promises that otherwise would be unenforceable have been made binding by statute. Most significant among these are (1) contract modifications, (2) renunciations, and (3) irrevocable offers.

CONTRACT MODIFICATIONS As mentioned previously, the UCC has abandoned the common law rule requiring that a modification of an existing contract be supported by consideration to be valid. The Code provides that a contract for the sale of goods can be effectively modified without new consideration, provided the modification is made in good faith. Section 2-209.

RENUNCIATIONS Under the Revised UCC Article 1, a claim or right arising out of an alleged breach may be discharged in whole or in part without consideration by agreement of the aggrieved party in an authenticated record. This provision is subject to the obligation of good faith and, as with all sections of Article 1, applies to a transaction to the extent that it is governed by one of the other articles of the UCC. Section 1-304.

IRREVOCABLE OFFERS Under the Code, a *firm offer*, a written offer signed by a merchant offering or promising to keep open an offer to buy or sell goods, is not revocable for lack of consideration during the time stated, not to exceed three months, or if no time is stated, for a reasonable time. Section 2-205.

♦ **SEE FIGURE 12-3:** *Consideration*

FIGURE 12-3 Consideration

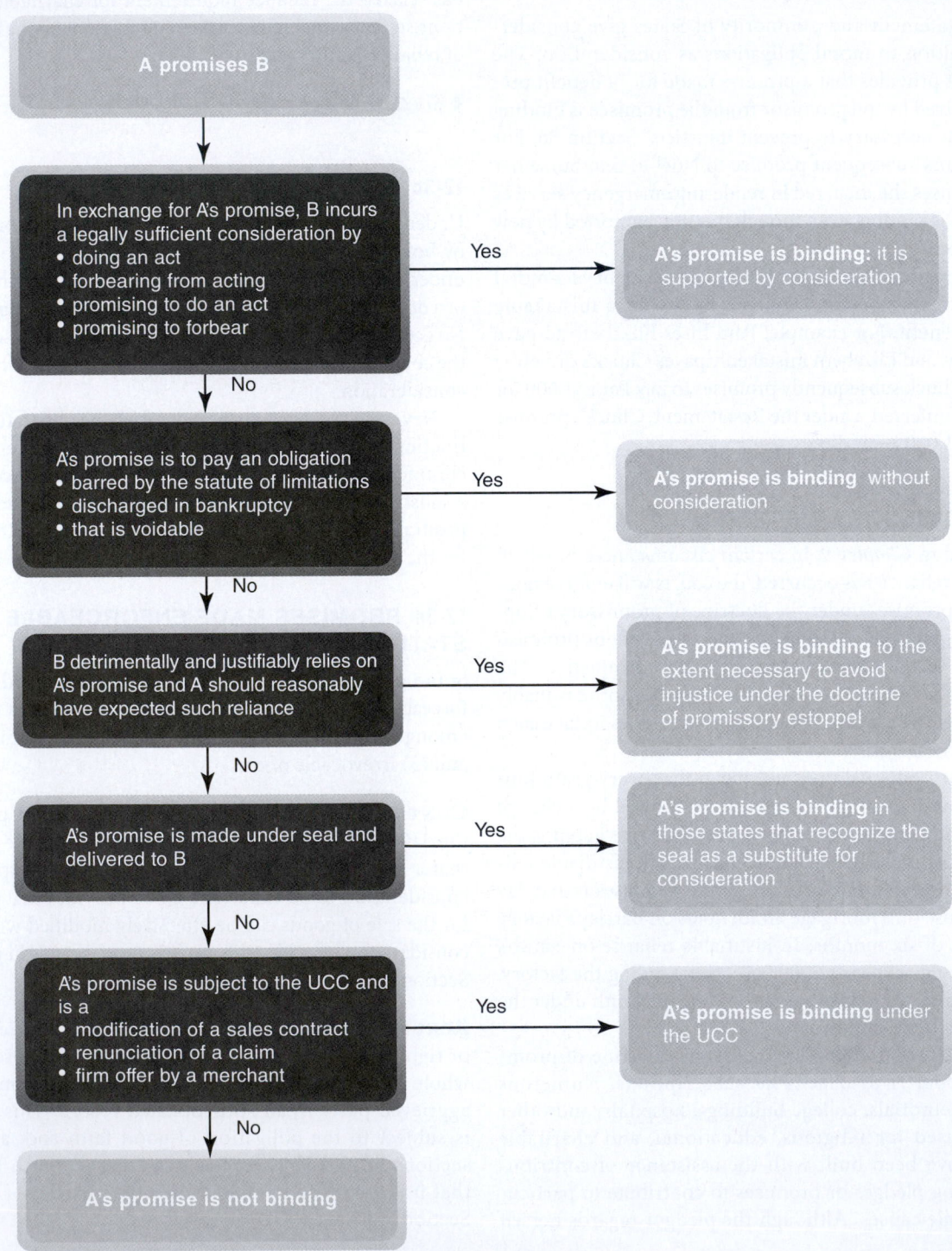

C H A P T E R   S U M M A R Y

CONSIDERATION	**Definition** the inducement to enter into a contract **Elements** legal sufficiency and bargained-for exchange

LEGAL SUFFICIENCY

Definition consists of either a benefit to the promisor or a detriment to the promisee
- *Legal Benefit* obtaining something to which one had no prior legal right
- *Legal Detriment* doing an act one is not legally obligated to do or not doing an act that one has a legal right to do

Adequacy not required where the parties have freely agreed to the exchange
Unilateral Contract a promise exchanged for an act or a forbearance to act
Bilateral Contract a promise exchanged for a promise
Illusory Promise promise that imposes no obligation on the promisor; the following promises are not illusory:
- *Output Contract* **agreement to sell all of one's production to a single buyer**
- *Requirements Contract* agreement to buy all of one's needs from a single producer
- *Exclusive Dealing Contract* grant to a franchisee or licensee by a manufacturer of the sole right to sell goods in a defined market
- *Conditional Promises* obligations that are contingent upon the occurrence of a stated event

Preexisting Public obligations public duties such as those imposed by tort or criminal law are neither a legal detriment nor a legal benefit
Preexisting Contractual Obligation performance of a preexisting contractual duty is not consideration
- *Modification of a Preexisting Contract* under the common law, a modification of a preexisting contract must be supported by mutual consideration; under the Code, a contract can be modified without new consideration
- *Substituted Contracts* the parties agree to rescind their original contract and to enter into a new one; rescission and new contract are supported by consideration
- *Settlement of an Undisputed Debt* payment of a lesser sum of money to discharge an undisputed debt (one whose existence or amount is not contested) does not constitute legally sufficient consideration
- *Settlement of a Disputed Debt* payment of a lesser sum of money to discharge a disputed debt (one whose existence or amount is contested) is legally sufficient consideration

BARGAINED-FOR EXCHANGE

Definition a mutually agreed-upon exchange
Past Consideration an act done before the contract is made is not consideration
Third Parties consideration to support a promise may be given to a person other than the promisor

CONTRACTS WITHOUT CONSIDERATION

Promises to Perform Prior unenforceable obligations
- *Promise to Pay Debt Barred by the Statute of Limitations* a new promise by the debtor to pay the debt renews the running of the statute for a second statutory period
- *Promise to Pay Debt Discharged in Bankruptcy* may be enforceable without consideration

Voidable Promises a new promise to perform a voidable obligation that has not been previously avoided is enforceable
- *Moral Obligation* a promise made to satisfy a preexisting moral obligation is generally unenforceable for lack of consideration

Promissory Estoppel doctrine that prohibits a party from denying her promise when the promisee takes action or forbearance to his detriment reasonably based upon the promise

Promises Made Under Seal where still recognized, the seal acts as a substitute for consideration
- **Promises Made Enforceable by Statute** some gratuitous promises have been made enforceable by statute; the Code makes enforceable (1) contract modifications, (2) renunciations, and (3) firm offers

C A S E S

<table>
<tr><td>C A S E

12-1</td><td>Illusory Promises
VANEGAS v. AMERICAN ENERGY SERVICES
Supreme Court of Texas, 2009
302 S.W.3d 299</td><td></td></tr>
</table>

Green, J.

In this case, we are asked to decide the enforceability of an employer's alleged promise to pay five percent of the proceeds of a sale or merger of the company to employees who are still employed at the time of the sale or merger. The employer, American Energy Services (AES), * * * was formed in the summer of 1996. AES hired the petitioners in this case (collectively, the employees) that same year. The employees allege that in an operational meeting in June 1997, they voiced concerns to John Carnett, a vice president of AES, about the continued viability of the company. The employees complained that the company required them to work long hours with antiquated equipment. The employees allege that, in an effort to provide an incentive for them to stay with the company, Carnett promised the employees, who were at-will and therefore free to leave the company at any time, that "in the event of sale or merger of AES, the original [eight] employees remaining with AES at that time would get 5% of the value of any sale or merger of AES." AES Acquisition, Inc. acquired AES in 2001. Seven of the eight original employees were still with AES at the time of the acquisition. Those remaining employees demanded their proceeds, and when the company refused to pay, the employees sued, claiming AES breached the oral agreement.

AES moved for summary judgment on [the ground] that the agreement was illusory and therefore not enforceable * * *. The employees responded that the promise represented a unilateral contract, and by remaining employed for the stated period, the employees performed, thereby making the promise enforceable. The trial court granted AES's motion for summary judgment, and the employees appealed. The court of appeals affirmed, holding that the alleged unilateral contract failed because it was not supported by at least one non-illusory promise, citing this Court's decision in *Light v. Centel Cellular Co. of Texas,* [citation]. The employees petitioned this Court for review, which we granted.

AES argues, and the court of appeals held, that our holdings in *Light* dictate the result in this case. [Citation.] In *Light,* we stated:

> Consideration for a promise, by either the employee or the employer in an at-will employment, cannot be dependent on a period of continued employment. Such a promise would be illusory because it fails to bind the promisor who always retains the option of discontinuing employment in lieu of performance. When illusory promises are all that support a purported bilateral contract, there is no contract.

* * *

Light involved an employee's challenge to a covenant not to compete. [Citation.] * * *

We revisited the issue of illusory promises in covenants not to compete in *Sheshunoff.* * * * We reaffirmed our previous holding in *Light* that covenants not to compete in bilateral contracts must be supported by "mutual non-illusory promises." [Citation.]

Citing our holdings in *Light* and *Sheshunoff*, the court of appeals [in this case] stated that "[a] unilateral contract may be formed when one of the parties makes only an illusory promise but the other party makes a non-illusory promise. The non-illusory promise can serve as the offer for a unilateral contract, which the promisor who made the illusory promise can accept by performance." [Citation.] We agree with that statement, but the court of appeals erroneously applied those holdings to the current case.

The issue turns on the distinction between bilateral and unilateral contracts. "A bilateral contract is one in which there are mutual promises between two parties to the contract, each party being both a promisor and a promisee." [Citations.] A unilateral contract, on the other hand, is "created by the promisor promising a benefit if the promisee performs. The contract becomes enforceable when the promisee performs." [Citation.] Both *Sheshunoff* and *Light* concerned *bilateral* contracts in which employers made promises in exchange for employees' promises not to compete with their companies after termination. [Citations.] The court of appeals' explanation of these cases—describing an exchange of promises where one party makes an illusory promise and the other a non-illusory promise—describes the attempted formation of a *bilateral* contract, not a unilateral contract. [Citation.] * * *

The court of appeals held that even if AES promised to pay the employees the five percent, that promise was illusory at the time it was made because the employees were at-will, and AES could have fired all of them prior to the acquisition. [Citation.] But whether the promise was illusory at the time it was made is irrelevant; what matters is whether the promise became enforceable by the time of the breach. [Citations.]

Almost all unilateral contracts begin as illusory promises. Take, for instance, the classic textbook example of a unilateral contract: "I will pay you $50 if you paint my house." The offer to pay the individual to paint the house can be withdrawn at any point prior to performance. But once the individual accepts the offer by performing, the promise to pay the $50 becomes binding. The employees allege that AES made an offer to split five percent of the proceeds of the sale or merger of the company among any remaining original employees. Assuming that allegation is true, the seven remaining employees accepted this offer by remaining employed for the requested period of time. [Citation.] At that point, AES's promise became binding. AES then breached its agreement with the employees when it refused to pay the employees their five percent share.

Furthermore, the court of appeals' holding would potentially jeopardize all pension plans, vacation leave, and other forms of compensation made to at-will employees that are based on a particular term of service. * * *

The fact that the employees were at-will and were already being compensated in the form of their salaries in exchange for remaining employed also does not make the promise to pay the bonus any less enforceable.

* * *

AES allegedly promised to pay any remaining original employees five percent of the proceeds when AES was sold. Assuming AES did make such an offer, the seven remaining employees accepted the offer by staying with AES until the sale. Regardless of whether the promise was illusory at the time it was made, the promise became enforceable upon the employees' performance. The court of appeals erred in holding otherwise. Accordingly, we reverse the court of appeals' judgment and remand the case to the trial court for further proceedings consistent with this opinion.

CASE 12-2

Preexisting Obligation
DENNEY v. REPPERT
Court of Appeals of Kentucky, 1968
432 S.W.2d 647

Myre, Special Commissioner

On June 12th or 13th, 1963, three armed men entered the First State Bank, Eubank, Kentucky, and with a display of arms and threats robbed the bank of over $30,000. Later in the day they were apprehended by State Policemen Garret Godby, Johnny Simms, and Tilford Reppert, placed under arrest, and the entire loot was recovered. Later all of the prisoners were convicted and Garret Godby, Johnny Simms, and Tilford Reppert appeared as witnesses at the trial.

The First State Bank of Eubank was a member of the Kentucky Bankers Association which provided and advertised

a reward of $500.00 for the arrest and conviction of each bank robber. Hence the outstanding reward for the three bank robbers was $1,500.00. Many became claimants for the reward and the Kentucky State Bankers Association, being unable to determine the merits of the claims for the reward, asked the circuit court to determine the merits of the various claims and to adjudge who was entitled to receive the reward or share in it. All of the claimants were made defendants in the action.

At the time of the robbery the claimants Murrell Denney, Joyce Buis, Rebecca McCollum, and Jewell Snyder were employees of the First State Bank of Eubank and came out of the grueling situation with great credit and glory. Each one of them deserves approbation and an accolade. They were vigilant in disclosing to the public and the peace officers the details of the crime, and in describing the culprits, and giving all the information that they possessed that would be useful in capturing the robbers. Undoubtedly, they performed a great service. It is in the evidence that the claimant Murrell Denney was conspicuous and energetic in his efforts to make known the robbery, to acquaint the officers as to the personal appearance of the criminals, and to give other pertinent facts.

The first question for determination is whether the employees of the robbed bank are eligible to receive or share in the reward. The great weight of authority answers in the negative. * * *

> To the general rule that, when a reward is offered to the general public for the performance of some specified act, such reward may be claimed by any person who performs such act, is the exception of agents, employees, and public officials who are acting within the scope of their employment or official duties. * * *

* * *

At the time of the robbery the claimants Murrell Denney, Joyce Buis, Rebecca McCollum, and Jewell Snyder were employees of the First State Bank of Eubank. They were under duty to protect and conserve the resources and moneys of the bank, and safeguard every interest of the institution furnishing them employment. Each of these employees exhibited great courage and cool bravery, in a time of stress and danger. The community and the county have recompensed them in commendation, admiration, and high praise, and the world looks on them as heroes. But in making known the robbery and assisting in acquainting the public and the officers with details of the crime and with identification of the robbers, they performed a duty to the bank and the public, for which they cannot claim a reward.

The claims of Corbin Reynolds, Julia Reynolds, Alvie Reynolds, and Gene Reynolds also must fail. According to their statements they gave valuable information to the arresting officers. However, they did not follow the procedure as set forth in the offer of reward in that they never filed a claim with the Kentucky Bankers Association. It is well established that a claimant of a reward must comply with the terms and conditions of the offer of reward. [Citation.]

State Policemen Garret Godby, Johnny Simms, and Tilford Reppert made the arrest of the bank robbers and captured the stolen money. All participated in the prosecution. At the time of the arrest, it was the duty of the state policemen to apprehend the criminals. Under the law they cannot claim or share in the reward and they are interposing no claim to it.

This leaves the defendant, Tilford Reppert, the sole eligible claimant. The record shows that at the time of the arrest he was a deputy sheriff in Rockcastle County, but the arrest and recovery of the stolen money took place in Pulaski County. He was out of his jurisdiction, and was thus under no legal duty to make the arrest, and is thus eligible to claim and receive the reward. In *Kentucky Bankers Ass'n et al. v. Cassady* [citation], it was said:

> It is * * * well established that a public officer with the authority of the law to make an arrest may accept an offer of reward or compensation for acts or services performed outside of his bailiwick or not within the scope of his official duties. * * *

* * *

It is manifest from the record that Tilford Reppert is the only claimant qualified and eligible to receive the reward.

Therefore, it is the judgment of the circuit court that he is entitled to receive payment of the $1,500.00 reward now deposited with the clerk of this court.

The judgment is affirmed.

CASE 12-3

Modification of a Preexisting Contract
NEW ENGLAND ROCK SERVICES, INC. v. EMPIRE PAVING, INC.

Appellate Court of Connecticut, 1999
53 Conn App. 771, 731 A.2d 784 *certiorari* denied, 250 Conn. 921, 738 A.2d 658

Schaller, J.

The defendants, Empire Paving, Inc. (Empire), and its bonding company, American Insurance Company, doing business as Fireman's Fund Insurance Company (Fireman's Fund), appeal from the judgment of the trial court awarding damages to the named plaintiff, New England Rock Services, Inc. (Rock Services), under a contract between the parties. The principal issue on appeal is whether the trial court improperly concluded that

an agreement made by the parties on December 9, 1995, modified an earlier contract executed by them on October 26, 1995. We affirm the judgment of the trial court.

The following facts are relevant to the disposition of this appeal. On October 26, 1995, Empire entered into a contract with Rock Services under which Rock Services would provide drilling and blasting services as a subcontractor on the Niles Hill Road sewer project on which Empire was the general contractor and the city of New London was the owner. Pursuant to the contract, Rock Services agreed to drill and blast a certain amount of rock encountered on the sewer project. In return, Rock Services was to be paid an agreed upon price of $29 per cubic yard with an estimated amount of 5000 cubic yards, or on a time and materials basis, whichever was less.

On October 31, 1995, Rock Services commenced work on the project. From the beginning, Rock Services experienced a number of problems with the project. The primary obstacle was the presence of a heavy concentration of water on the site. The water problem hindered Rock Services' ability to complete its work as anticipated. The trial court found that it was the custom and practice in the industry for the general contractor to control the water on the site and that, on this particular job, Empire failed to control the water on the site properly. In an effort to mitigate the water problem, Rock Services attempted to "load behind the drill," a process that allows a blaster to load the drilled hole with a charge immediately after the hole is drilled, before water has the opportunity to seep into the hole. The city fire marshal, however, refused to allow Rock Services to employ this method of drilling. Thereafter, in order to complete its work, Rock Services was compelled to use the more costly and time consuming method of casing the blasting hole, a process that requires the blaster to drive a plastic casing down into the drilled hole to prevent seepage.

In late November, 1995, Rock Services advised Empire that it would be unable to complete the work as anticipated because of the conditions at the site and requested that Empire agree to amend the contract to allow Rock Services to complete the project on a time and materials basis. On December 8, 1995, Empire signed a purchase order that modified the original agreement. The modification required Empire to pay for the blasting work on a time and materials basis for the remainder of the project. Rock Services, thereafter, completed its work on the project.

Upon completion of the work, Empire refused to pay Rock Services for the remaining balance due on the time and materials agreement in the amount of $58,686.63, and Rock Services instituted this action. The trial court concluded that the later purchase order was a valid and enforceable modification of the earlier contract. The trial court found that the parties intended the purchase order to modify the earlier agreement and that Empire's assent to the modification was not made under duress but, rather, was a calculated business decision. After finding Empire's withholding of the amount due to Rock Services wrongful, the trial court awarded Rock Services damages in the amount of $58,686.63, plus interest and costs. This appeal followed.

On appeal, Empire claims that the trial court improperly found that the later purchase order was a valid and enforceable modification of the earlier contract. Specifically, Empire claims that the later agreement lacked the requisite consideration to be a valid and enforceable modification of the earlier contract. We disagree.

* * *

In concluding that the modification was valid and enforceable, the trial court determined that the later agreement was supported by sufficient consideration. * * *

"The doctrine of consideration is fundamental in the law of contracts, the general rule being that in the absence of consideration an executory promise is unenforceable." [Citation.] While mutual promises may be sufficient consideration to bind parties to a modification; [citations] a promise to do that which one is already bound by his contract to do is not sufficient consideration to support an additional promise by the other party to the contract. [Citations.]

"A modification of an agreement must be supported by valid consideration and requires a party to do, or promise to do, something further than, or different from, that which he is already bound to do. [Citations.] It is an accepted principle of law in this state that when a party agrees to perform an obligation for another to whom that obligation is already owed, although for lesser remuneration, the second agreement does not constitute a valid, binding contract. [Citations.] The basis of the rule is generally made to rest upon the proposition that in such a situation he who promises the additional [work] receives nothing more than that to which he is already entitled and he to whom the promise is made gives nothing that he was not already under legal obligation to give. [Citations.]"

Our Supreme Court in [citation], however, articulated an exception to the preexisting duty rule: "'[W]here a contract must be performed under burdensome conditions not anticipated, and not within the contemplation of the parties at the time when the contract was made, and the promisee measures up to the right standard of honesty and fair dealing, and agrees, in view of the changed conditions, to pay what is then reasonable, just, and fair, such new contract is not without consideration within the meaning of that term, either in law or in equity.'" * * * "'What unforeseen difficulties and burdens will make a party's refusal to go forward with his contract equitable, so as to take the case out of the general rule and bring it within the exception, must depend upon the facts of each particular case. They must be substantial, unforeseen, and not within the contemplation of the parties when the contract was made. They need not be such as would legally justify the party in his refusal to perform his contract, unless promised extra pay, or to justify a court of equity in relieving him from the contract; for they are sufficient if they are of such a character as to render the party's demand for extra pay manifestly fair, so as to rebut all inference that he is seeking to be relieved from an unsatisfactory contract, or to take advantage of the necessities of the opposite party to coerce from him a promise for further compensation.

Inadequacy of the contract price which is the result of an error of judgment, and not of some excusable mistake of fact, is not sufficient." [Citation.] * * *

Empire argues strenuously that the water conditions on the site cannot qualify as a new circumstance that was not anticipated at the time the original contract was signed. * * *

Empire's argument, however, is misplaced. Rock Services does not argue that it was unaware of the water conditions on the site but, rather, that Empire's failure to control or remove

the water on the site constituted the new or changed circumstance. Rock Services argues that Empire's duty to control or remove the water on the job site arose in accordance with the custom and practice in the industry and, therefore, Empire's failure to control or remove the water on the site constituted a new circumstance that Rock Services did not anticipate at the time the original contract was signed.

* * *

The judgment is affirmed.

Past Condition/Promissory Estoppel
DILORENZO v. VALVE AND PRIMER CORPORATION
Appellate Court of Illinois, First District, Fifth Division, 2004
807 N.E.2d 673, 283 Ill.Dec. 68

Reid, J.

[DiLorenzo, a forty-year employee of Valve & Primer, was also an officer, director, and shareholder of one hundred shares of stock. DiLorenzo claims that in 1987 Valve & Primer offered him a ten-year stock option that would allow DiLorenzo to purchase an additional three hundred shares at the fixed price of $250 per share. DiLorenzo claims that in reliance on that employment agreement, he stayed in his job for over nine additional years and did not follow up on any of several recruitment offers from other companies. Valve & Primer claims the 1987 employment agreement between it and DiLorenzo did not contain a stock purchase agreement. The only purported proof of the agreement is an unsigned copy of board meeting minutes of which DiLorenzo had the only copy.

In January 1996, DiLorenzo entered into a semiretirement agreement with Valve & Primer, and he attempted to tender his remaining one hundred shares pursuant to a stock redemption agreement. Shortly thereafter, Valve & Primer fired DiLorenzo. DiLorenzo argued before the trial court that, even if the purported agreement was not found to be valid, it should be enforced on promissory estoppel grounds. Valve & Primer moved for summary judgment, which the trial court granted for lack of consideration. The trial court denied the promissory estoppel claim because of insufficient reliance. DiLorenzo appealed.]

We begin by addressing whether there was consideration for the stock options. "A stock option is the right to buy a share or shares of stock at a specified price or within a specified period." [Citation.] In order to evaluate the nature and scope of the stock options issued to DiLorenzo, we must assume, for purposes of this portion of our discussion, that DiLorenzo's corporate minutes are valid.

"A contract, to be valid, must contain offer, acceptance, and consideration; to be enforceable, the agreement must also be

sufficiently definite so that its terms are reasonably certain and able to be determined." [Citation.] "A contract is sufficiently definite and certain to be enforceable if the court is able from its terms and provisions to ascertain what the parties intended, under proper rules of construction and applicable principles of equity." [Citation.] "A contract may be enforced even though some contract terms may be missing or left to be agreed upon, but if essential terms are so uncertain that there is no basis for deciding whether the agreement has been kept or broken, there is no contract." [Citation.] A bonus promised to induce an employee to continue his employment is supported by adequate consideration if the employee is not already bound by contract to continue. [Citation.] Because we are assuming the validity of the document issuing the stock options, we now turn to whether the underlying option is supported by valid consideration so as to make it a proper contract.

"Consideration is defined as the bargained-for exchange of promises or performances and may consist of a promise, an act or a forbearance." [Citation.]

The general principles applicable to option contracts have been long established. An option contract has two elements, an offer to do something, or to forbear, which does not become a contract until accepted; and an agreement to leave the offer open for a specified time [citation], or for a reasonable time [citation]. An option contract must be supported by sufficient consideration; and if not, it is merely an offer which may be withdrawn at any time prior to a tender of compliance. [Citation.] If a consideration of "one dollar" or some other consideration is stated but which has, in fact, not been paid, the document is merely an offer which may be withdrawn at any time prior to a tender of compliance. The document will amount only to a continuing offer which may be withdrawn by the offer or at any time before acceptance.

[Citation.] The consideration to support an option consists of 'some right, interest, profit or benefit accruing to one party, or some forbearance, detriment, loss or responsibility given, suffered or undertaken by the other' [citation]; or otherwise stated, "Any act or promise which is of benefit to one party or disadvantage to the other * * *." [Citation.]

"The preexisting duty rule provides that where a party does what it is already legally obligated to do, there is no consideration because there has been no detriment." [Citation.]

Focusing on the lack of a detriment to the employee, the trial court found no valid consideration. Based upon our view of the discussion in [citation], the trial court was correct in concluding that the option contract is merely an offer which may be withdrawn at any time prior to a tender of compliance. DiLorenzo could have exercised the option the moment it was purportedly made, then immediately quit, thereby giving nothing to the employer. Though the exercise of the option would require the transfer of money for the stock, the option itself carries with it no detriment to DiLorenzo. Therefore, there was no consideration for the option.

* * *

We next address DiLorenzo's claim that he is entitled to the value of the shares of stock based upon the theory of promissory estoppel. DiLorenzo argues that the trial court misapplied the law in finding that there was insufficient reliance to support a claim for promissory estoppel. He claims that, once the trial court decided there was insufficient consideration to support the option contract, promissory estoppel should have been applied by the court to enforce the agreement as a matter of equity. DiLorenzo argues that he detrimentally relied upon Valve & Primer's promise in that he worked at Valve & Primer for an additional period in excess of nine years in reliance on the stock option agreement. * * *

Valve & Primer responds that the trial court was correct in finding insufficient reliance to support the promissory estoppel claim. Valve & Primer argues that DiLorenzo could not satisfy the detrimental reliance prong of the promissory estoppel elements. Though DiLorenzo claimed he did not act upon offers of employment he claims were made by other companies during the course of his employment with Valve & Primer, he presented to the trial court nothing but his own testimony in support of his claim. Valve & Primer argues that, since DiLorenzo essentially is claiming his stock option vested immediately, he cannot contend that he detrimentally relied upon the purported agreement in the corporate minutes by turning down those other opportunities. * * * For purposes of promissory estoppel, if DiLorenzo's allegations are taken as true, and the purported option vested immediately, it required nothing of him in order to be exercised other than the payment of $250 per share.

"Promissory estoppel arises when (1) an unambiguous promise was made, (2) the defendant relied on the promise, (3) the defendant's reliance on the promise was reasonable, and (4) the defendant suffered a detriment." [Citation.] Whether detrimental reliance has occurred is determined according to the specific facts of each case. [Citation.]

While we would accept that, under certain circumstances, it may be possible for a relinquishment of a job offer to constitute consideration sufficient to support a contract, this is not such a case. There is nothing in the language of the corporate minutes or any other source to be found in this record to suggest that Valve & Primer conditioned the alleged stock option on DiLorenzo's promise to remain in his employment. While the corporate minutes say the alleged grant of the stock option was intended to "retain and reward," it contains no mechanism making the retention mandatory. Since the corporate minutes lack a mandatory obligation on which DiLorenzo could have reasonably detrimentally relied, and he could have elected to buy the shares of stock immediately, DiLorenzo's decision to remain on the job for the additional period of over nine years must be viewed as a voluntary act. Under those circumstances, promissory estoppel would not apply. It was, therefore, not an abuse of discretion to grant Valve & Primer's motion for summary judgment on that issue.

* * *

Affirmed.

QUESTIONS

1. In consideration of $1,800 paid to him by Joyce, Hill gave Joyce a written option to purchase his house for $180,000 on or before April 1. Prior to April 1, Hill verbally agreed to extend the option until July 1. On May 18, Hill, known to Joyce, sold the house to Gray, who was ignorant of the unrecorded option. On May 20, Joyce sent an acceptance to Hill, who received it on May 25. Is there a contract between Joyce and Hill? Explain.

2. **a.** Ann owed $2,500 to Barry for services Barry rendered to Ann. The debt was due June 30, 2019. In March 2020, the debt was still unpaid. Barry was in urgent need of ready cash and told Ann that if she would pay $1,500 of the debt at once, Barry would release her from the balance. Ann paid $1,500 and stated to Barry that all claims had been paid in full. In August 2020, Barry demanded the unpaid balance and subsequently sued Ann for $1,000. Result?

b. Modify the facts in (a) by assuming that Barry gave Ann a written receipt stating that all claims had been paid in full. Result?

c. Modify the facts in (a) by assuming that Ann owed Barry the $2,500 on Ann's purchase of a motorcycle from Barry. Result?

3. a. Judy orally promises her daughter, Liza, that she will give her a tract of land for her home. Liza, as intended by Judy, gives up her homestead and takes possession of the land. Liza lives there for six months and starts construction of a home. Is Judy bound to convey the real estate? Why or why not?

b. Ralph, knowing that his son, Ed, desires to purchase a tract of land, promises to give him the $25,000 he needs for the purchase. Ed, relying on this promise, buys an option on the tract of land. Can Ralph rescind his promise? Why or why not?

4. George owed Keith $800 on a personal loan. Neither the amount of the debt nor George's liability to pay the $800 was disputed. Keith had also rendered services as a carpenter to George without any agreement as to the price to be paid. When the work was completed, an honest and reasonable difference of opinion developed between George and Keith with respect to the value of Keith's services. Upon receiving from Keith a bill of $600 for the carpentry services, George mailed in a properly stamped and addressed envelope his check for $800 to Keith. In an accompanying letter, George stated that the enclosed check was in full settlement of both claims. Keith indorsed and cashed the check. Thereafter, Keith unsuccessfully sought to collect from George an alleged unpaid balance of $600. May Keith recover the $600 from George? Explain.

5. The Snyder Mfg. Co., being a large user of coal, entered into separate contracts with several coal companies. In each contract, it was agreed that the coal company would supply coal during the entire year in such amounts as the manufacturing company might desire to order, at a price of $55 per ton. In February, the Snyder Company ordered one thousand tons of coal from Union Coal Company, one of the contracting parties. Union Coal Company delivered five hundred tons of the order and then notified Snyder Company that no more deliveries would be made and that it denied any obligation under the contract. In an action by Union Coal to collect $55 per ton for the five hundred tons of coal delivered, Snyder files a counterclaim, claiming damages of $1,500 for failure to deliver the additional five hundred tons of the order and damages of $4,000 for breach of agreement to deliver coal during the balance of the year. What contract, if any, exists between Snyder and Union?

6. On February 5, Devon entered into a written agreement with Gordon whereby Gordon agreed to drill a well on Devon's property for the sum of $5,000 and to complete the well on or before April 15. Before entering into the contract, Gordon made test borings and had satisfied himself as to the character of the subsurface. After two days of drilling, Gordon struck hard rock. On February 17, Gordon removed his equipment and advised Devon that the project had proved unprofitable and that he would not continue. On March 17, Devon went to Gordon and told Gordon that he would assume the risk of the enterprise and would pay Gordon $100 for each day required to drill the well, as compensation for labor, the use of Gordon's equipment, and Gordon's services in supervising the work, provided Gordon would furnish certain special equipment designed to cut through hard rock. Gordon said that the proposal was satisfactory. The work was continued by Gordon and completed in an additional fifty-eight days. Upon completion of the work, Devon failed to pay, and Gordon brought an action to recover $5,800. Devon answered that he had never become obligated to pay $100 a day and filed a counterclaim for damages in the amount of $500 for the month's delay based on an alleged breach of contract by Gordon. Decision?

7. Discuss and explain whether there is valid consideration for each of the following promises:

a. A and B entered into a contract for the purchase and sale of goods. A subsequently promised to pay a higher price for the goods when B refused to deliver at the contract price.

b. A promised in writing to pay a debt, which was due from B to C, on C's agreement to extend the time of payment for one year.

c. A orally promised to pay $150 to her son, B, solely in consideration of past services rendered to A by B, for which there had been no agreement or request to pay.

8. Alan purchased shoes from Barbara on open account. Barbara sent Alan a bill for $10,000. Alan wrote back that two hundred pairs of the shoes were defective and offered to pay $6,000 and give Barbara his promissory note for $1,000. Barbara accepted the offer, and Alan sent his check for $6,000 and his note, in accordance with the agreement. Barbara cashed the check, collected on the note, and one month later sued Alan for $3,000. Is Barbara bound by her acceptance of the offer?

9. Nancy owed Sharon $1,500, but Sharon did not initiate a lawsuit to collect the debt within the time prescribed by the statute of limitations. Nevertheless, Nancy promises Sharon that she will pay the barred debt. Thereafter,

Nancy refuses to pay. Sharon brings suit to collect on this new promise. Is Nancy's new promise binding? Explain.

10. Anthony lends money to Frank. Frank dies without having paid the loan. Frank's widow, Carol, promises Anthony to repay the loan. Upon Carol's refusal to pay the loan, Anthony brings suit against Carol for payment of the loan. Is Carol bound by her promise to pay the loan?

11. The parties entered into an oral contract in June, under which plaintiff agreed to construct a building for defendant on a time and materials basis, at a maximum cost of $56,146, plus sales tax and extras ordered by defendant. When the building was 90 percent completed, defendant told plaintiff he was unhappy with the whole job as "the thing just wasn't being run right." The parties then on October 17 signed a written agreement lowering the maximum cost to $52,000 plus sales tax. Plaintiff thereafter completed the building at a cost of $64,155. The maximum under the June oral agreement, plus extras and sales tax, totaled $61,040. Defendant contended that he was obligated to pay only the lower maximum fixed by the October 17 agreement. Decision?

CASE PROBLEMS

12. Taylor assaulted his wife, who then took refuge in Ms. Harrington's house. The next day, Mr. Taylor entered the house and began another assault on his wife, who knocked him down and, while he was lying on the floor, attempted to cut his head open or decapitate him with an ax. Harrington intervened to stop the bloodshed, and the ax, as it was descending, fell upon her hand, mutilating it badly, but sparing Taylor his life. Afterwards, Taylor orally promised to compensate Harrington for her injury. Is Taylor's promise enforceable? Explain.

13. Jonnel Enterprises, Inc., contracted to construct a student dormitory at Clarion State College. On May 6, Jonnel entered into a written agreement with Graham and Long as electrical contractors to perform the electrical work and to supply materials for the dormitory. The contract price was $70,544.66. Graham and Long claim that they believed the May 6 agreement obligated them to perform the electrical work on only one wing of the building, but that three or four days after work was started, a second wing of the building was found to be in need of wiring. At that time, Graham and Long informed Jonnel that they would not wire both wings of the building under the present contract, so a new contract was orally agreed upon by the parties. Under the new contract, Graham and Long were obligated to wire both wings and were to be paid only $65,000, but they were relieved of the obligations to supply entrances and a heating system. Graham and Long resumed their work, and Jonnel made seven of the eight progress payments called for. When Jonnel did not pay the final payment, Graham and Long brought this action. Jonnel claims that the May 6 contract is controlling. Is Jonnel correct in its assertion? Why or why not?

14. Baker entered into an oral agreement with Healey, the State distributor of Ballantine & Sons liquor products, that Ballantine would supply Baker with its products on demand and that Baker would have the exclusive agency for Ballantine within a certain area of Connecticut. Shortly thereafter the agreement was modified to give Baker the right to terminate at will. Eight months later, Ballantine & Sons revoked its agency. May Baker enforce the oral agreement? Explain.

15. PLM, Inc., entered into an oral agreement with Quaintance Associates, an executive "headhunter" service, for the recruitment of qualified candidates to be employed by PLM. As agreed, PLM's obligation to pay Quaintance did not depend on PLM's actually hiring a qualified candidate presented by Quaintance. After several months, Quaintance sent a letter to PLM, admitting that it had so far failed to produce a suitable candidate, but included a bill for $9,806.61, covering fees and expenses. PLM responded that Quaintance's services were worth only $6,060.48 and that payment of the lesser amount was the only fair way to handle the dispute. Accordingly, PLM enclosed a check for $6,060.48, writing on the back of the check "IN FULL PAYMENT OF ANY CLAIMS QUAINTANCE HAS AGAINST PLM, INC." Quaintance cashed the check and then sued PLM for the remaining $3,746.13. Decision?

16. Red Owl Stores told the Hoffman family that upon the payment of approximately $518,000, a grocery store franchise would be built for them in a new location. Upon the advice of Red Owl, the Hoffmans bought a small grocery store in their hometown in order to get management experience. After the Hoffmans operated at a profit for three months, Red Owl advised them to sell the small grocery, assuring them that Red Owl would find them a larger store elsewhere. Although selling at that point would cost them much profit, the Hoffmans followed Red Owl's directions. In addition, to raise the money required for the deal, the Hoffmans sold their bakery business in their hometown. The Hoffmans also

sold their house and moved to a new home in the city where their new store was to be located. Red Owl then informed the Hoffmans that it would take $624,100, not $518,000, to complete the deal. The family scrambled to find the additional funds. However, when told by Red Owl that it would now cost them $654,000 to get their new franchise, the Hoffmans decided to sue instead. Should Red Owl be held to its promises? Explain.

17. Plaintiff, Brenner, entered into a contract with the defendant, Little Red School House, Ltd., which stated that in return for a non-refundable tuition of $1,080, Brenner's son could attend defendant's school for a year. When Brenner's ex-wife refused to enroll their son, plaintiff sought and received a verbal promise of a refund. Defendant now refuses to refund plaintiff's money for lack of consideration. Did mutual consideration exist between the parties? Explain.

18. Ben Collins was a full professor with tenure at Wisconsin State University in 2015. In March 2015, Parsons College, in an attempt to lure Dr. Collins from Wisconsin State, offered him a written contract promising him the rank of full professor with tenure and a salary of $55,000 for the 2015–16 academic year. The contract further provided that the College would increase his salary by $2,000 each year for the next five years. In return, Collins was to teach two trimesters of the academic year beginning in October 2015. In addition, the contract stipulated, by reference to the College's faculty bylaws, that tenured professors could be dismissed only for just cause and after written charges were filed with the Professional Problems Committee. The two parties signed the contract, and Collins resigned his position at Wisconsin State.

In February 2017, the College tendered a different contract to Collins to cover the following year. This contract reduced his salary to $45,000 with no provision for annual increments, but left his rank of full professor intact. It also required that Collins waive any and all rights or claims existing under any previous employment contracts with the College. Collins refused to sign this new contract, and Parsons College soon notified him that he would not be employed the following year. The College did not give any grounds for his dismissal, nor did it file charges with the Professional Problems Committee. As a result, Collins was forced to take a teaching position at the University of North Dakota at a substantially reduced salary. He sued to recover the difference between the salary Parsons College promised to pay him until 2020 and the amount he earned. Decision? Will Collins prevail? Explain.

19. Rodney and Donna Mathis (Mathis) filed a wrongful death action against St. Alexis Hospital and several physicians, arising out of the death of their mother, Mary Mathis. Several weeks before trial, an expert consulted by Mathis notified the trial court and Mathis's counsel that, in his opinion, Mary Mathis's death was not proximately caused by the negligence of the physicians. Shortly thereafter, Mathis voluntarily dismissed the wrongful death action. Mathis and St. Alexis entered into a covenant-not-to-sue in which Mathis agreed not to pursue any claims against St. Alexis or its employees in terms of the medical care of Mary Mathis. St. Alexis, in return, agreed not to seek sanctions, including attorneys' fees and costs incurred in defense of the previously dismissed wrongful death action. Subsequently, Mathis filed a second wrongful death action against St. Alexis Hospital, among others. Mathis asked the court to rescind the covenant-not-to-sue, arguing that because St. Alexis was not entitled to sanctions in connection with the first wrongful death action, there was no consideration for the covenant-not-to-sue. Are they correct in this contention? Explain.

20. Harold Pearsall and Joe Alexander were friends for more than twenty-five years. About twice a week, they would get together after work and proceed to a liquor store, where they would purchase what the two liked to refer as a "package"—a half-pint of vodka, orange juice, two cups, and two lottery tickets. Occasionally these lottery tickets would yield modest rewards of two or three dollars, which the pair would then "plow back" into the purchase of additional tickets. On December 16, Pearsall and Alexander visited the liquor store twice, buying their normal "package" on both occasions. For the first package, Pearsall went into the store alone, and when he returned to the car, he said to Alexander, in reference to the tickets, "Are you in on it?" Alexander said, "Yes." When Pearsall asked him for his half of the purchase price, though, Alexander replied that he had no money. When they went to Alexander's home, Alexander snatched the tickets from Pearsall's hand and "scratched" them, only to find that they were both worthless. Later that same evening, Alexander returned to the liquor store and bought a second "package." This time, Pearsall snatched the tickets from Alexander and said that he would "scratch" them. Instead, he gave one to Alexander, and each man scratched one of the tickets. Alexander's was a $20,000 winner. Alexander cashed the ticket and refused to give Pearsall anything. Can Pearsall recover half of the proceeds from Alexander? Explain.

Anna Feinberg began working for the Pfeiffer Company in 1972 at age seventeen. By 2010, she had attained the position of bookkeeper, office manager, and assistant treasurer. In appreciation for her skill, dedication, and long years of service, the Pfeiffer board of directors resolved to increase Feinberg's monthly salary to $4,000 and to create a retirement plan for her. The plan allowed that Feinberg would be given the privilege of retiring from active duty at any time she chose and that she would receive retirement pay of $2,000 per month for life, although the Board expressed the hope that Feinberg would continue to serve the company for many years. Feinberg,

however, chose to retire two years later. The Pfeiffer Company paid Feinberg her retirement pay until 2020. The company thereafter discontinued payments.

a. What are the arguments that the company's promise to pay Feinberg $2,000 per month for life is enforceable?

b. What are the arguments that the company's promise is not enforceable?

c. What is the proper outcome? Explain.

CHAPTER 13

Illegal Bargains

CHAPTER OUTCOMES

After reading and studying this chapter, you should be able to:

- Explain the types of contracts that may violate a statute and distinguish between the two types of licensing statutes.

- Describe when a covenant not to compete will be enforced and identify the two situations in which these types of covenants most frequently arise.

- Explain when exculpatory agreements, agreements involving the commitment of a tort, and agreements involving public officials will be held to be illegal.

- Distinguish between procedural and substantive unconscionability.

- Explain the usual effects of illegality and the major exceptions to this rule.

An essential requirement of a binding promise or agreement is legality of objective. When the formation or performance of an agreement is criminal, tortious, or otherwise contrary to public policy, the agreement is illegal and unenforceable (as opposed to being void). The law does not provide a remedy for the breach of an unenforceable agreement and thus "leaves the parties where it finds them." It is preferable to use the term *illegal bargain* or *illegal agreement* rather than *illegal contract*, because the word *contract*, by definition, denotes a legal and enforceable agreement. The illegal bargain is made unenforceable (1) to discourage such undesirable conduct and (2) to preclude the inappropriate use of the judicial process in carrying out such socially undesirable bargains.

The Restatement avoids defining the term *illegal bargain*, instead focusing upon whether public policy should bar enforcement of the agreement. By relying upon the concept of public policy, the Restatement provides the courts with greater flexibility in determining the enforceability of questioned agreements by weighing the strength of legally recognized policies against the effect that declaring a particular bargain to be against public policy would have on the contracting parties and on the public.

This chapter discusses (1) agreements in violation of a statute, (2) agreements contrary to public policy, and (3) the effect of illegality upon agreements.

13-1 Violations of Statutes

The courts will not enforce an agreement declared illegal by statute. For example, wagering or gambling contracts are specifically declared unenforceable in most States. In addition,

an agreement to violate a statute prohibiting crimes, such as murder, robbery, embezzlement, forgery, and price fixing, is unenforceable. Likewise, an agreement that is induced by criminal conduct will not be enforced. For example, if Alice enters into an agreement with Brent Co. through the bribing of Brent Co.'s purchasing agent, the agreement would be unenforceable.

13-1a LICENSING STATUTES

Every jurisdiction has laws requiring a license for those who engage in certain trades, professions, or businesses. Common examples are licensing statutes that apply to lawyers, doctors, dentists, accountants, brokers, plumbers, and contractors. Some licensing statutes mandate schooling and/or examination, while others require only financial responsibility and/or good moral character. Whether or not a person may recover for services rendered if he has failed to comply with a licensing requirement depends upon the terms or type of licensing statute. This rule pertains only to the rights of the unlicensed party to enforce the obligations of the other party.

The statute itself may expressly provide that an unlicensed person engaged in a business or profession for which a license is required shall not recover for services rendered. Absent such statutory provision, the courts commonly distinguish between those statutes or ordinances that are regulatory in character and those that are enacted merely to raise revenue through the issuance of licenses. If the statute is regulatory, a person cannot recover for professional services unless he has the required license, as long as the public policy behind the regulatory purpose clearly outweighs the person's interest in being paid for his services. Restatement, Section 181. Some courts have gone further by balancing the penalty the unlicensed party suffers against the benefit the other party receives. In contrast, if the law is for revenue purposes only, agreements for such services are enforceable.

A **regulatory** license, including those issued under statutes prescribing standards for those wishing to practice law or medicine, is a measure designed to protect the public against unqualified persons. A **revenue** license, on the other hand, does not seek to protect against incompetent or unqualified practitioners but simply to furnish revenue. An example is a statute requiring a license of plumbers but not establishing standards of competence for those who seek to follow the trade. The courts regard such legislation as a taxing measure lacking any expression of legislative intent to preclude unlicensed plumbers from enforcing their business contracts.

Practical Advice

Obtain all necessary licenses before beginning to operate your business.

◆ *See Case 13-1*

13-1b GAMBLING STATUTES

In a wager, the parties stipulate that one shall win and the other lose depending upon the outcome of an event in which their sole "interest" arises from the possibility of such gain or loss. All States have legislation pertaining to gambling or wagering, and U.S. courts generally refuse to recognize the enforceability of a gambling agreement. Thus, if Arnold makes a bet with Bernice on the outcome of a ball game, the agreement is unenforceable by either party. Some States, however, now permit certain kinds of regulated gambling. Wagering conducted by government agencies, principally State-operated lotteries, has come to constitute an increasingly important source of public revenues.

To be distinguished from wagers are ordinary insurance contracts in which the insured, having an "insurable interest" (discussed in *Chapter 47*), pays a certain sum of money or premium in exchange for an insurance company's promise to pay a larger amount upon the occurrence of some event, such as a fire, which causes loss to the insured. Here, the agreement compensates for loss under an existing risk; it does not create an entirely new risk. In a wager, the parties contemplate gain through mere chance, whereas in an insurance contract, they seek to distribute possible loss. Furthermore, most games at fast-food restaurants and grocery store drawings have been upheld because the participants need not make a purchase to be eligible for the prize.

Practical Advice

Make sure that your promotions that offer prizes do not fall under State gambling statutes.

13-1c USURY STATUTES

A **usury statute** is a law establishing a maximum rate of permissible interest for which a lender and borrower of money may contract. Though, historically, every State had a usury law, a recent trend has been to limit or relax usury statutes. The maximum rates permitted vary greatly from State to State and among types of transactions. These statutes typically are general in their application, although certain specified types of transactions are exempted. For example, numerous States impose no limit on the rate of interest that may be charged on loans to corporations. Furthermore, some States permit the parties to contract for any rate of interest on loans made to individual proprietorships or partnerships for the purpose of carrying on a business. Moreover, there are not many protections remaining for typical consumer transactions, including those involving credit cards. (More than half of the States have no interest rate limits on credit card transactions. Furthermore, under Federal law, a national bank may charge the interest rate allowed in the State in which the bank is located to customers living anywhere in the United States, including States with more restrictive interest caps.)

In addition to the exceptions accorded certain designated types of borrowers, a number of States have exempted specific lenders. For example, the majority of the States have enacted installment loan laws, which permit eligible lenders a return on installment loans that is higher than the applicable general interest statute would permit. These specific lender usury statutes, which have all but eliminated general usury statutes, vary greatly but generally have included small consumer loans, corporate loans, loans by small lenders, real estate mortgages, and numerous other transactions.

For a transaction to be usurious, courts usually require evidence of the following factors: (1) a loan or forbearance (2) of money (3) which is repayable absolutely and in all events (4) for which an interest charge is exacted in excess of the interest rate allowed by law. Transactions that are really loans may not be clothed with the trappings of a sale for the purpose of avoiding the usury laws.

Practical Advice

When calculating interest, consider all charges, including service fees, that exceed the actual reasonable expense of making the loan.

The legal effect to be given a usurious loan varies from State to State. In a few States, the lender forfeits both principal and interest. In some jurisdictions, the lender can recover the principal but forfeits all interest. In other States, only that portion of interest exceeding the permitted maximum is forfeited. In several States, the amount forfeited is a multiple (double or treble) of the interest charged. Disposition of usurious interest already paid also varies. Some States do not allow any recovery of usurious interest paid; others allow recovery of such interest or a multiple of it.

♦ *See Case 13-2*

13-1d SUNDAY STATUTES

In the absence of a statutory prohibition, the common law does not prohibit entering into contracts on Sunday. Some States, however, have legislation, referred to as **Blue Laws**, modifying this common law rule and prohibiting certain types of commercial activity on Sunday. Even in a State that prohibits contracts on Sunday, a court nonetheless will enforce a subsequent weekday ratification of a loan made on Sunday or a promise to pay for goods sold and delivered on Sunday. In addition, Blue Laws usually do not apply to activities of "necessity" and "charity."

13-2 Violations of Public Policy

The reach of a statute may extend beyond its language. Sometimes, the courts, by analogy, use the statute and the policy it seeks to serve as a guide in determining the private contract rights of one harmed by a violation of the statute. In addition, the courts must frequently articulate the "public policy" of the State without significant help from statutory sources. This judicially declared public policy is very broad in scope, it often being said that agreements having "a tendency to be injurious to the public or the public good" are contrary to public policy. Thus, the term *public policy* eludes precise definition. Contracts raising questions of public policy include agreements that (1) restrain trade, (2) exempt or exculpate a party from liability for his own tortious conduct, (3) are unconscionable, (4) involve tortious conduct, (5) tend to corrupt public officials or impair the legislative process, (6) tend to obstruct the administration of justice, or (7) impair family relationships. This section focuses on the first five of these types of agreements.

13-2a COMMON LAW RESTRAINT OF TRADE

A **restraint of trade** is any contract or agreement that eliminates or tends to eliminate competition or otherwise obstructs trade or commerce. One type of restraint is a **covenant not to compete**, which is an agreement to refrain from entering into a competing trade, profession, or business.

An agreement to refrain from a particular trade, profession, or business is enforceable if (1) the purpose of the restraint is to protect a property interest of the promisee and (2) the restraint is no more extensive than is reasonably necessary to protect that interest. Restraints typically arise in two situations: the sale of a business and employment contracts.

SALE OF A BUSINESS As part of an agreement to sell a business, the seller frequently promises not to compete in that particular type of business in a *defined area* for a stated *time*. To protect the business's goodwill (an asset that the buyer has purchased), the buyer must be allowed to enforce such a covenant (promise) by the seller not to compete with the purchaser within reasonable limitations. Most litigation on this subject has involved the requirement that the restraint be no greater than is reasonably necessary. Whether the restraint is reasonable or not depends on the geographic area it covers, the time period for which it is to be effective, and the hardship it imposes on the promisor and the public.

For example, the promise of a person selling a service station business in Detroit not to enter the service station business in Michigan for the next twenty-five years is unreasonable, both as to area and time. The business interest to be protected would not include the entire State, so it is not necessary to the protection of the purchaser that the seller be prevented from engaging in the service station business in the entire State or perhaps, for that matter, in the entire city of Detroit. Limiting the area to the neighborhood in which the station is located or to a radius of a few miles probably would be adequate.

The same type of inquiry must be made about time limitations. In the sale of a service station, a twenty-five-year ban on competition from the seller would be unreasonable; a one-year ban probably would not. The court, in determining what is reasonable under particular circumstances, must consider each case on its own facts.

EMPLOYMENT CONTRACTS Salespeople, management personnel, and other employees frequently are required to sign employment contracts prohibiting them from competing with their employers during their time of employment and for some additional stated period after termination. The same is also frequently true among corporations or partnerships involving professionals, such as accountants, lawyers, investment brokers, stockbrokers, and doctors. Although the courts readily enforce a covenant not to compete during the period of employment, the promise not to compete after termination is subjected to an even stricter test of reasonableness than that applied to noncompetition promises included in a contract for the sale of a business. One reason for this is that the employer is in a stronger bargaining position than the employee.

A court order enjoining a former employee from competing in a described territory for a stated time is the usual method by which an employer seeks to enforce the employee's promise not to compete. Before granting such injunctions, the courts insist that the employer demonstrate that the restriction is *necessary* to protect his legitimate interests, such as trade secrets or customer lists. Because issuing the injunction may place the employee out of work, the courts must carefully balance the public policy favoring the employer's right to protect his business interests against the public policy favoring full opportunity for individuals to gain employment.

Thus, one court has held unreasonable a covenant in a contract requiring a travel agency employee, after termination of her employment, to refrain from engaging in a like business in any capacity in either of two named towns or within a sixty-mile radius of those towns for two years. There was no indication that the employee had enough influence over customers to cause them to move their business to her new agency, nor was it shown that any trade secrets were involved. *United Travel Service, Inc. v. Weber*, 108 Ill. App.2d 353, 247 N.E.2d 801 (1969). Instead of refusing to enforce an unreasonable covenant, some courts, considering the action justifiable under the circumstances of the case, will reform the agreement to make it reasonable and enforceable.

Due to the rapid evolution of business practices in the Internet industry, it has been argued that noncompete agreements for Internet company employees need their own rules. Courts have addressed the geographic scope of an Internet noncompetition agreement, upholding a one-year time restriction and a territorial clause that prevented the employee from taking another Internet-related job *anywhere* in the United States so long as the restrictions are consonant with the scope of the employee's duties. One of these courts stated, "Transactions involving the Internet, unlike traditional 'sales territory' cases, are not limited by state boundaries."

Practical Advice

If you include a covenant not to compete to protect your property interests, be careful to select a reasonable duration and geographic scope.

♦ *See Case 13-3*

13-2b EXCULPATORY CLAUSES

Some contracts contain an exculpatory clause that excuses one party from liability for her own tortious conduct. The courts generally agree that exculpatory clauses relieving a person from tort liability for harm caused intentionally or recklessly are unenforceable as violating public policy. On the other hand, exculpatory clauses that excuse a party from liability for harm caused by negligent conduct are scrutinized carefully by the courts, which often require that the clause be conspicuously placed in the contract and clearly written. Accordingly, an

exculpatory clause on the reverse side of a parking lot claim check, which attempts to relieve the parking lot operator of liability for negligently damaging the customer's automobile, generally will be held unenforceable as against public policy.

The Restatement provides that exculpatory clauses excusing negligent conduct are unenforceable on grounds of public policy if they exempt (1) an employer from liability to an employee, (2) a public service business (such as a common carrier) from liability to a customer, or (3) a person from liability to a party who is a member of a protected class. Restatement, Section 195. For example, a railroad company will not be permitted to avoid liability for the negligent operation or maintenance of its trains.

A similar rule applies to a contractual provision unreasonably exempting a party from the legal consequences of a misrepresentation. Restatement, Section 196. Such a term is unenforceable on the grounds of public policy with respect to both fraudulent and nonfraudulent misrepresentations.

Further, where the superior bargaining position of one party has enabled him to impose upon the other party such a provision, the courts are inclined to nullify the provision. Such a situation may arise in residential leases exempting a landlord from liability for his negligence. Moreover, an exculpatory clause may be unenforceable for unconscionability.

Practical Advice

Because many courts do not favor exculpatory clauses, carefully limit its applicability, make sure that it is clear and understandable, put it in writing, and have it signed.

♦ *See Cases 13-4 and 13-5*

13-2c UNCONSCIONABLE CONTRACTS

The court may scrutinize every contract of sale to determine whether it is, in its commercial setting, purpose, and effect, **unconscionable**. The court may refuse to enforce an unconscionable contract in its entirety or any part it finds to be unconscionable. Section 2-302 of the UCC provides:

If the court as a matter of law finds the contract or any clause of the contract to have been unconscionable at the time it was made the court may refuse to enforce the contract, or it may enforce the remainder of the contract without the unconscionable clause, or it may so limit the application of any unconscionable clause as to avoid any unconscionable result.

Similarly, Section 208 of the Restatement parallels this provision and provides:

If a contract or term thereof is unconscionable at the time the contract is made a court may refuse to enforce the contract, or may enforce the remainder of the contract without the unconscionable term, or may so limit the application of any unconscionable term as to avoid any unconscionable result.

Neither the Code nor the Restatement defines the word *unconscionable*; however, the *New Webster's Dictionary of the English Language* (Deluxe Encyclopedic Edition) defines the term as "contrary to the dictates of conscience; unscrupulous or unprincipled; exceeding that which is reasonable or customary; inordinate, unjustifiable."

The doctrine of unconscionability has been justified on the basis that it permits the courts to resolve issues of unfairness explicitly as regards that unfairness without recourse to formalistic rules or legal fictions. In policing contracts for fairness, the courts have again demonstrated their willingness to limit freedom of contract to protect the less advantaged from overreaching by dominant contracting parties. The doctrine of unconscionability has evolved through its application by the courts to include both procedural and substantive unconscionability.

Procedural unconscionability involves scrutiny for the presence of "bargaining naughtiness." In other words, was the negotiation process fair, or were there procedural irregularities, such as burying important terms of the agreement in fine print or obscuring the true meaning of the contract with impenetrable legal jargon?

Substantive unconscionability, which involves the actual terms of the contract, consists of oppressive or grossly unfair provisions, such as an exorbitant price or an unfair exclusion or limitation of contractual remedies. An all-too-common example is that involving a necessitous buyer in an unequal bargaining position with a seller, who consequently obtains an exorbitant price for his product or service. In one case, a court held unconscionable a price of $749 ($920 on time) for a vacuum cleaner that cost the seller $140. In another case, the buyers, welfare recipients, purchased by time payment contract a home freezer unit for $900 that, when added to time credit charges, credit life insurance, credit property insurance, and sales tax, amounted to $1,235. The purchase resulted from a visit to the buyer's home by a salesman representing Your Shop At Home Service, Inc.; the maximum retail value of the freezer unit at time of purchase was $300. The court held the contract unconscionable and reformed it by reducing the price to the total payment ($620) the buyers had managed to make.

Some courts hold that for a contract to be unenforceable, both substantive and procedural unconscionability must be present. Nevertheless, they need not exist to the same degree; the more oppressive one is, the less evidence of the other is required.

Practical Advice

When negotiating a contract, keep in mind that if your bargaining techniques or the contract terms are oppressive, a court may refuse to enforce the contract in part or in full.

Closely akin to the concept of unconscionability is the doctrine of contracts of adhesion. A standard-form contract prepared by one party, an **adhesion contract** generally involves the preparer's offering the other party the contract on a "take-it-or-leave-it" basis. Such contracts are not automatically unenforceable but are subject to greater scrutiny for procedural or substantive unconscionability.

◆ *See Case 13-4*

13-2d TORTIOUS CONDUCT

"A promise to commit a tort or to induce the commission of a tort is unenforceable on grounds of public policy." Restatement, Section 192. The courts will not permit contract law to violate the law of torts. Any agreement attempting to do so is considered contrary to public policy. For example, Andrew and Barlow Co. enter into an agreement under which Andrew promises Barlow that in return for $5,000, he will disparage the product of Barlow Co.'s competitor Cosmo, Inc., in order to provide Barlow Co. with a competitive advantage. Andrew's promise is to commit the tort of disparagement and is unenforceable as contrary to public policy.

13-2e CORRUPTING PUBLIC OFFICIALS

Agreements that may adversely affect the public interest through the corruption of public officials or the impairment of the legislative process are unenforceable. Examples include using improper means to influence legislation, to secure some official action, or to procure a government contract. Contracts to pay lobbyists for services to obtain or defeat official action by means of persuasive argument are to be distinguished from illegal influence-peddling agreements. (*Chapters 43* and *46* cover the Foreign Corrupt Practices Act, which prohibits any U.S. person—and certain foreign issuers of securities—from bribing foreign government or political officials to assist in obtaining or retaining business.)

For example, a bargain by a candidate for public office to make a certain appointment following his election is illegal. In addition, an agreement to pay a public officer something extra for performing his official duty, such as promising a bonus to a police officer for strictly enforcing the traffic laws on her beat, is illegal. The same is true of an agreement in which a citizen promises to perform, or to refrain from performing, duties imposed on her by citizenship. Thus, a promise by Carl to pay $50 to Rachel if she will register and vote is opposed to public policy and illegal.

13-3 Effect of Illegality

As a general rule, illegal contracts are unenforceable. In a few instances, however, one of the parties may be permitted to enforce all or part of the contract; whereas under other circumstances, the courts will allow one party to recover in restitution for his performance of the illegal contract.

13-3a GENERAL RULE: UNENFORCEABILITY

In most cases, when an agreement is illegal, neither party can successfully sue the other for breach or recover for any performance rendered. Whichever party is plaintiff is immaterial to the courts. As is frequently said in these cases, the court will leave the parties where it finds them.

13-3b EXCEPTIONS

The courts recognize several exceptions to the general rule regarding the effect of illegality on a contract and may, after considering the circumstances surrounding a particular contract, grant relief to one of the parties, though not to the other. The following sections will consider these exceptions.

Party Withdrawing before Performance A party to an illegal agreement may withdraw, prior to performance, from the transaction and recover whatever she has contributed, if the party has not engaged in serious misconduct. Restatement, Section 199. A common example is recovery of money left with a stakeholder pursuant to a wager before it is paid to the winner.

Party Protected by Statute Sometimes an agreement is illegal because it violates a statute designed to protect persons in the position of one of the parties. For example, State "Blue Sky Laws" prohibiting the sale of unregistered securities are designed primarily for the protection of investors. In such cases, even though there is an unlawful agreement, the statute usually expressly gives the purchaser the right to rescind the sale and recover the money paid.

Party Not Equally at Fault Where one of the parties is less at fault than the other, he will be allowed to recover payments made or property transferred. Restatement, Section 198. For example, this exception would apply where one party induces the other to enter into an illegal bargain through fraud, duress, or undue influence.

Excusable Ignorance An agreement that appears on its face to be entirely permissible, nevertheless, may be illegal by reason of facts and circumstances of which one of the parties is completely unaware. For example, a man and woman make mutual promises to marry, but unknown to the woman, the man is already married. This is an agreement to commit the crime of bigamy, and the marriage, if entered into, is void. In such case, the courts permit the party who is ignorant of the illegality to maintain a lawsuit against the other party for damages.

A party also may be excused for ignorance of relatively minor legislation. Restatement, Section 180. For instance, Jones and Old South Building Co. enter into a contract to build a factory that contains specifications in violation of the town's building ordinance. Jones did not know of the violation and had no reason to know. Old South's promise to build would not be rendered unenforceable on grounds of public policy, and Jones would have a claim against Old South for damages for breach of contract.

Partial Illegality A contract may be partly unlawful and partly lawful. The courts view such a contract in one of two ways. First, the partial illegality may be held to taint the entire contract with illegality, so that it is wholly unenforceable. Second, it may be possible to separate the illegal from the legal part, in which case the court will hold the illegal part unenforceable but will enforce the legal part. For example, if a contract contains an illegal covenant not to compete, the covenant will not be enforced, though the rest of the contract may be.

13-3c RESTITUTION

The Restatement of Restitution provides that a person who renders performance under an agreement that is illegal or otherwise unenforceable for reasons of public policy may obtain restitution from the other party, as necessary to prevent unjust enrichment, if the allowance of restitution will not defeat or frustrate the policy of the underlying prohibition. However, a claim in restitution is not allowed if it is foreclosed by the claimant's inequitable conduct. Section 32.

C H A P T E R   S U M M A R Y

VIOLATIONS OF STATUTES

General Rule the courts will not enforce agreements declared illegal by statute

Licensing Statutes require formal authorization to engage in certain trades, professions, or businesses
- *Regulatory License* licensing statute that is intended to protect the public against unqualified persons; an unlicensed person may not recover for services she has performed
- *Revenue License* licensing statute that seeks to raise money; an unlicensed person may recover for services he has performed

Gambling Statutes prohibit wagers, which are agreements that one party will win and the other party will lose depending upon the outcome of an event in which their only interest is the gain or loss

Usury Statutes establish a maximum rate of interest

Sunday Statutes prohibition of certain types of commercial activity on Sunday (also called Blue Laws)

VIOLATIONS OF PUBLIC POLICY	**Common Law Restraint of Trade** unreasonable restraints of trade are not enforceable

- *Sale of a Business* the promise by the seller of a business not to compete in that particular business in a reasonable geographic area for a reasonable period of time is enforceable
- *Employment Contracts* an employment contract prohibiting an employee from competing with his employer for a reasonable period following termination is enforceable provided the restriction is necessary to protect legitimate interests of the employer

Exculpatory Clauses the courts generally disapprove of contractual provisions excusing a party from liability for her own tortious conduct

Unconscionable Contracts unfair or unduly harsh agreements are not enforceable

- *Procedural Unconscionability* unfair or irregular bargaining
- *Substantive Unconscionability* oppressive or grossly unfair contractual terms

Tortious Conduct an agreement that requires a person to commit a tort is unenforceable

Corrupting Public Officials agreements that corrupt public officials are not enforceable

EFFECT OF ILLEGALITY	**Unenforceability** neither party may recover under an illegal agreement where both parties are *in pari delicto* (in equal fault)

Exceptions permit one party to recover payments

- *Party Withdrawing Before Performance*
- *Party Protected by Statute*
- *Party Not Equally at Fault*
- *Excusable Ignorance*
- *Partial Illegality*
- *Restitution*

C A S E S

CASE 13-1

Licensing Statutes

ALCOA CONCRETE & MASONRY v. STALKER BROS.

Court of Special Appeals of Maryland, 2010
993 A.2d 136, 191 MD. APP. 596

Rodowsky, J.

* * * At issue is whether a home improvement general contractor is contractually obligated to pay a subcontractor who was not licensed under * * *, either at the time of entering into the subcontract or when the subcontract was properly performed, but who was licensed when this suit was brought.

The subcontractor is the appellant, Alcoa Concrete and Masonry, Inc. (Alcoa or the Subcontractor). The general contractor is Stalker Brothers, Inc. (Stalker or the General Contractor), * * *. Alcoa initiated this action on September 30, 2008, in the Circuit Court for Montgomery County. Summary judgment was granted to the appellees [Stalker] * * *

The president of Alcoa affirmed that Alcoa and Stalker had done business from 2004 through 2007. In 2004, all of Alcoa's invoices were fully and timely paid. When payments in 2005 became less regular, Stalker promised to pay Alcoa when a building owned by the Brothers was sold, but full payment was not made. Alcoa continued to perform subcontract work for Stalker based on an agreement that the General Contractor would pay Alcoa $1,500 per week against invoices for past work and new work. In November 2006, Alcoa performed the cement and masonry work for Stalker on the "Cahill" job, in which Stalker represented there was sufficient profit to pay Alcoa for that subcontract and for the entire past due balance, but an indebtedness remained. In the summer of 2007, Stalker ceased paying Alcoa entirely. Alcoa claims $53,000 plus interest and attorney's fees. Appellees, through Donald Stalker's affidavit, assert that every subcontract performed by Alcoa for Stalker was "residential home improvement work" in Maryland, *i.e.*, done pursuant to a home improvement contract between the owner(s) of a residence and Stalker. Alcoa does not dispute that statement of fact.

Appellees moved for summary judgment on a number of grounds, but the circuit court granted the motion solely on the ground that the series of subcontracts were illegal and could not be enforced. The circuit court accepted appellees' argument that was based upon a venerable line of Maryland cases dealing with licensing and that is illustrated in the home improvement field principally by *Harry Berenter, Inc. v. Berman*, [citation]. In essence, these cases initially inquire whether the purpose of a business licensing statute is to raise revenue or to protect the public. If the purpose is the former, courts will enforce a contract for compensation for business activity that requires a license, even if made by an unlicensed person. But, if the purpose of the licensing requirement is to protect the public, then the Maryland cases relied upon by the appellees do not enforce contracts made by unlicensed persons who seek compensation for business activity for which a license is required.

* * *

Maryland appellate decisions have applied the revenue/regulation rule in a number of contexts. All of the cases under the Act have dealt with the contractor-owner relationship. The members of the public who were protected by the regulatory licensing requirement were the owners of the home. This Court recently again has held, applying *Harry Berenter*, that a contract between the owner of the improved premises and an unlicensed contractor would not be enforced. [Citation.] * * *

* * *

Our review fails to disclose any Maryland appellate decision directly answering whether the regulatory license rule applied in *Harry Berenter*, declaring unenforceable a home improvement contract between an owner and an unlicensed

contractor, applies to a subcontract between a licensed contractor and an unlicensed subcontractor. *Harry Berenter* does recognize that, pursuant to provisions of the Act * * *, the failure to comply with certain formal contractual requirements in a home improvement contract does not invalidate the contract. [Citation.]

* * *

The authors of *Corbin on Contracts*, after reviewing the revenue/regulatory rule, state:

Even when the purpose of a licensing statute is regulatory, courts do not always deny enforcement to the unlicensed party. The statute clearly may protect against fraud and incompetence. Yet, in very many cases the situation involves neither fraud nor incompetence. The unlicensed party may have rendered excellent service or delivered goods of the highest quality. The noncompliance with the statute may be nearly harmless. The real defrauder may be the defendant who will be enriched at the unlicensed party's expense by a court's refusal to enforce the contract. Although courts have yearned for a mechanically applicable rule, most have not made one in the present instance. Justice requires that the penalty should fit the crime. Justice and sound policy do not always require the enforcement of licensing statutes by large forfeitures going not to the state but to repudiating defendants.

In most cases, the statute itself does not require such forfeitures. The statute fixes its own penalties, usually a fine or imprisonment of a minor character with a degree of discretion in the court. The added penalty of unenforceability of bargains is a judicial creation. In many cases, the court may be wise to apply this additional penalty. When nonenforcement causes great and disproportionate hardship, a court must avoid nonenforcement.

* * *

After the decision in *Harry Berenter*, in which the Court relied in part on the Restatement of Contracts, the American Law Institute adopted Restatement (Second) of Contracts (1981). Section 178 states a more flexible approach to enforceability than the rigid revenue/regulatory dichotomy. Section 178 reads:

When a Term Is Unenforceable on Grounds of Public Policy

(1) A promise or other term of an agreement is unenforceable on grounds of public policy if legislation provides that it is unenforceable or the interest in its enforcement is clearly outweighed in the circumstances by a public policy against the enforcement of such terms.

(2) In weighing the interest in the enforcement of a term, account is taken of
  (a) the parties' justified expectations,
  (b) any forfeiture that would result if enforcement were denied, and
  (c) any special public interest in the enforcement of the particular term.

(3) In weighing a public policy against enforcement of a term, account is taken of
  (a) the strength of that policy as manifested by legislation or judicial decisions,
  (b) the likelihood that a refusal to enforce the term will further that policy.

(c) the seriousness of any misconduct involved and the extent to which it was deliberate, and

(d) the directness of the connection between that misconduct and the term.

We find no indication in the Act or in the Maryland cases that a policy of the Act is to protect general contractors from unlicensed subcontractors. Consequently, the fact that the Act is a regulatory measure does not bar Alcoa from recovering on its subcontracts.

* * *

Accordingly, we shall reverse the judgment of the Circuit Court for Montgomery County and remand this action for further proceedings, not inconsistent with this opinion.

CASE 13-2

Usury
BIBI v. ELFRINK
Supreme Court of Alaska, 2017
408 P.3d 809

Stowers, C. J.

Mariam Bibi and Javed Raja married and later bought a home in Anchorage with loans from IndyMac Bank, F.S.B. (IndyMac). IndyMac's loans were secured by deeds of trust on their home. The couple later received an additional loan of around $10,000 from Kevin Elfrink. The loan from Elfrink charged 10% interest but also included a funding fee of $4,000 rolled into the rest of the loan for payment over time rather than charged and paid at the outset. Over the course of six years, the couple made irregular payments, increased the loan balance three times until it exceeded $25,000, and eventually defaulted. Elfrink initiated foreclosure proceedings and then bought the house at his own foreclosure sale by credit-bidding all money he asserted was due to him under the modified promissory note, satisfying the couple's debt to him.

Following the foreclosure, Elfrink filed a complaint against Bibi and Raja for forcible entry and detainer to remove them from the home. Bibi moved out of her home but filed a counterclaim for usury, quiet title and possession, and surplus proceeds from the foreclosure sale. Raja confessed judgment to his removal from the home. As the lawsuit proceeded, IndyMac initiated a foreclosure on its senior deed of trust and Elfrink bought the house for a second time at IndyMac's foreclosure sale. The superior court ultimately denied Bibi's usury claim, determining that Bibi had no standing, her claim was time barred, and in any event, the loan did not violate Alaska's usury statute because the funding fee was not interest and the usury statute did not apply once the loan's principal rose over

$25,000. The superior court also denied Bibi's claim for title, ruling that the foreclosure statutes gave Elfrink clear title.

Bibi appeals. ***

Alaska's general usury statute applies to loans of $25,000 or less. [Citation.] The statute allows a borrower who has paid usurious interest to recover double the amount of interest she pays in excess of the statute's cap, [citation], but the borrower's total payments have to exceed the loan principal plus legal interest before she can recover. [Citation.]

Bibi argues she is entitled to recover under the usury statute. First, she argues that Elfrink's original loan was usurious because (1) when one treats the funding fee as disguised interest its initial interest rate exceeded the usury statute's cap and (2) the third loan modification's interest rate of 12% violated the usury statute on its face. Second, she argues that the three modifications to the original loan were each separate loans, so every loan was under $25,000 and thus subject to the interest cap. Third, she argues that adding the escrow payments and the proceeds from Elfrink's foreclosure sale, she paid the principal amount plus interest—both usurious and legal—on each loan, and at least one of these payments—the foreclosure sale proceeds—was within the statute of limitations. Accordingly, Bibi contends she satisfies the requirements for recovery under the usury statute and should prevail on her claim.

While we do not agree with all of Bibi's arguments, we conclude that Bibi is entitled to recover under the usury statute based on the following: (1) it was error to conclude that Bibi had no standing to bring her usury claim; (2) it was error to conclude the funding fee was not disguised interest; (3) the superior court correctly determined that the usury statute's cap on interest did not apply to most of the loan period, but it did apply before the loan's balance exceeded $25,000; (4) a borrower must make payments that exceed a usurious loan's principal plus lawful interest before she can recover under the usury statute; (5) it was error to conclude foreclosure sale proceeds do not constitute a payment for purposes of the usury statute; and (6) in light of the foreclosure sale it was error to conclude that Bibi's usury claim was time barred. We hold that Bibi may recover under the usury statute, and we provide instructions to guide the superior court in calculating her award on remand.

* * *

In March 2007, at the time of Elfrink's initial loan to Bibi and Raja, AS 45.45.010(b) established the maximum allowable interest rate for loans under $25,000 at 11.25 %. [Citation.] Under AS 45.45.020, "[a] person may not, directly or indirectly, receive in money, goods, or things in action, or in any other manner, a greater sum or value for the loan or use of money . . . than is prescribed in AS 45.45.010. "

The superior court found that Elfrink's original loan to Bibi and Raja was not usurious because the additional $4,000 fee Bibi was obligated to pay over the life of the loan was a "service fee or funding fee" rather than disguised interest. ***

Bibi argues Elfrink's funding fee is simply interest in disguise. While she concedes that the interest rate on the face of the deed of trust promissory note was 10%, she argues that when one looks at the underlying transaction, the interest rate was actually much higher. Her math is based on a principal of $10,597, the amount of money Bibi and Raja actually received from Elfrink, rather than $14,597, the amount received plus the $4,000 funding fee. Bibi argues that because she and Raja received $10,597 and were obligated to pay back $14,597 plus 10% interest through 24 monthly payments of $673.58, she paid over $16,000 ($673.58 x 24) for a $10,597 loan, which she argues yields an effective interest rate far exceeding 11.25%, the maximum allowable interest rate at the time. [Citation.]

* * *

Our precedent demonstrates that determining whether a fee is considered interest under Alaska's usury laws involves an application of law to fact that we review de novo, [citation], though factual questions underlie the determination. We have previously identified the set of factual questions germane to this determination. [Citation.] ***

Among the factual questions which we think are germane are the following: what charges, if any, the loan fee is designed to defray; whether the loan fee is a one-time charge or assessed throughout the life of the loan; whether the amount of the loan fee is dependent on the amount of the loan or the risk of the enterprise being financed; whether the loan fee and interest rate are charged on the entire committed amount no matter what the size and period of the balances outstanding; and what difference, if any, there is between [the bank's] internal accounting treatment of the loan fee and that of interest. *** [Citation.]

We also explained that "[i]f the loan fee is either substantially similar to interest in all material respects or unreasonably large, the loan fee, or a portion thereof, could well be treated as an interest charge in computing the effective interest rate for purposes of AS 45.45.010(b)." [Citation.]

* * *

These decisions establish two principles. First, while a loan transaction may facially comply with the cap on interest rates found in AS 45.45.010, it may nevertheless be charging an effective interest rate in violation of that cap because of disguised interest. [Citation.] Second, whether this is the case requires a court to determine if, given the facts regarding the substance of a given transaction, the transaction "come[s] within the broad terms of the Alaska usury law" [citation] or, stated alternatively, whether the service fee is "treated as an interest charge in computing the effective interest rate for purposes of AS 45.45.010(b)." [Citation.] This determination is an application of law to fact.

Here the superior court failed to consider some of the "factual questions . . . germane" to the funding fee issue we identified in [citation]. We find two questions particularly relevant to the issue before us. First, the court did not consider whether the funding fee was "a one-time charge or assessed throughout the life of the loan." [Citation.] The fee was rolled into the rest of the loan for payment over time rather than charged and paid at the outset. Thus it was assessed throughout the life of the loan, which favors concluding that it was interest. [Citation.] Second, the court did not consider whether the funding fee was unreasonably large. [Citation.] Elfrink claims his work investigating the [Bibi] business assets, meeting with Bibi and Raja, and making calls was worth $4,000, all to ensure that a loan for around $10,000 was sound. But the funding fee was over 37% of the value of the loan Bibi and Raja received. *** This establishes that the funding fee was unreasonably large. Lastly, given the language of AS 45.45.020, which defines interest as value "for the loan or use of money," Elfrink's own testimony that his funding fee is charged only if the loan is made, rather than regardless of whether it is made, places the funding fee squarely "within the broad terms of the Alaska usury law" [citation] because it is charged "for the loan or use of money," not for services. [Citation.]

* * *

We REVERSE the superior court's denial of Bibi's counterclaim for usury *** and REMAND for calculation of Bibi's usury award.

CASE
13-3

Restraint of Trade
PAYROLL ADVANCE, INC. v. YATES
Missouri Court of Appeals, 2008
270 S.W.3d 428

Barney, J.

Payroll Advance, Inc. ("Appellant") appeals from the judgment of the trial court entered in favor of Barbara Yates ("Respondent") on Appellant's petition for injunctive relief and breach of contract of an "Employment Agreement" ("the Employment Agreement") which contains a covenant not to compete. * * *

* * *

[T]he record reveals that Appellant, a foreign corporation, is licensed to transact business in the State of Missouri and has numerous locations throughout the state, including a branch located in Kennett, Missouri. [Footnote: Appellant is "a payday loan company. [It] gives loans to clients out in the community." As best we discern the record, loans are made for short periods of time at high rates of interest. Appellant's manager testified that a payday loan company such as Appellant's is not like a bank because banks "normally [do not do] short-term loans." She also distinguished Appellant's entity from a title loan company or a debt consolidation concern.] It is customary for each of Appellant's branch offices to employ a sole employee at each branch and that sole employee is typically referred to as the manager of that particular branch. In June of 1998, Respondent was hired as the manager of the branch office in Kennett. On November 19, 1999, as a condition of her continued employment, Appellant presented Respondent with the Employment Agreement which included * * *, a provision entitled "NON-COMPETE" ("the covenant not to compete"). This provision set out:

> [Respondent] agrees not to compete with [Appellant] as owner, manager, partner, stockholder, or employee in any business that is in competition with [Appellant] and within a 50 mile radius of [Appellant's] business for a period of two (2) years after termination of employment or [Respondent] quits or [Respondent] leaves employment of [Appellant].

Respondent was employed with Appellant from June of 1998 through November 8, 2007, when Respondent was apparently fired for cause.

Approximately thirty-two days after being terminated by Appellant, Respondent became employed with Check Please, one of the approximately fourteen other payday loan establishments in the area. At Check Please, Respondent performed basically the same duties such as office management and customer care as she had when employed with Appellant.

On February 7, 2008, Appellant filed its "First Amended Petition for Injunctive Relief and Breach of Contract." In this petition, Appellant brought Count I for injunctive relief to prevent Respondent from soliciting its clients for her new employer, and to stop her from using client information she purportedly obtained from her time with Appellant. Count II of the petition was for damages for breach of contract for violation of the covenant not to compete together with attorney fees and costs.

* * *

On February 14, 2008, the trial court entered its judgment which found "[n]o evidence exists that, following [Appellant's] termination of [Respondent's] ten year period of employment, [Respondent] removed any customer list or other documents from [Appellant's] place of business [or] ... made any personal or other contact with any previous or present customer of [Appellant's] business or intends to do so." The trial court further determined that if the covenant not to compete was enforced as requested, Respondent will be prohibited from engaging in employment with any payday loan business in at least 126 cities situated in Missouri, Arkansas and Tennessee ([p]resumably [Respondent] also would be prohibited from such employment within a 50-mile radius of [Appellant's] 17 other locations scattered throughout the State of Missouri. Further, [Respondent] arguably also would be prohibited from employment at a bank, savings and loan company, credit union, pawn shop or title-loan company within such geographical areas....)

Accordingly, in its discretion, the trial court found "the above result would be unreasonable under the facts and circumstances of the particular industry, agreement, and geographic location here involved." The trial court then ruled in favor of Respondent and against Appellant. The trial court also denied Respondent's request for attorney's fees and costs. This appeal followed.

* * *

"Generally, because covenants not to compete are considered to be restraints on trade, they are presumptively void and are enforceable only to the extent that they are demonstratively reasonable." [Citations.] "Noncompetition agreements are not favored in the law, and the party attempting to enforce a noncompetition agreement has the burden of demonstrating both the necessity to protect the claimant's legitimate interests and that the agreement is reasonable as to time and space." [Citation.]

There are at least four valid and conflicting concerns at issue in the law of non-compete agreements. First, the employer needs to be able to engage a highly trained workforce to be competitive and profitable, without fear that the employee will use the employer's business secrets against it or steal the employer's customers after leaving employment. Second, the employee must be mobile in order to provide for his or her family and to advance his or her career in an ever-changing marketplace. This mobility is dependent upon the ability of the employee to take his or her increasing skills and put them to work from one employer to the next. Third, the law favors the freedom of parties to value their respective interests in negotiated contracts. And, fourth, contracts in restraint of trade are unlawful.

[Citation.] "Missouri courts balance these concerns by enforcing non-compete agreements in certain limited circumstances." [Citation.] "Non-compete agreements are typically enforceable so long as they are reasonable. In practical terms, a non-compete agreement is reasonable if it is no more restrictive than is necessary to protect the legitimate interests of the employer." [Citation.] Furthermore, "[n]on-compete agreements are enforceable to the extent they can be narrowly tailored geographically and temporally." [Citation.] *** Lastly, it is not "necessary for the employer to show that actual damage has occurred, in order to obtain an injunction. The actual damage might be very hard to determine, and this is one reason for granting equitable relief." [Citation.]

Here, viewing the evidence in a light most favorable to the trial court's holding, [citation], it is clear the trial court took umbrage with the covenant's restrictive provisions and geographical limitations on Respondent's [Yates'] ability to find employment.

* * *

The question of reasonableness of a restraint is to be determined according to the facts of the particular case and hence requires a thorough consideration of all surrounding circumstances, including the subject matter of the contract, the purpose to be served, the situation of the parties, the extent of the restraint, and the specialization of the business.

* * *

Here, the covenant not to compete grandly declares that Respondent cannot "compete with Appellant [Payroll] as owner, manager, partner, stockholder, or employee *in any business* that is in competition with [Appellant] and within a 50 mile radius of [Appellant's] business. . . ." (Emphasis added.) There was evidence from Appellant's representative at trial that Appellant has seventeen branch offices in Missouri and still other locations in Arkansas. If this Court interprets the plain meaning of the covenant not compete as written, the covenant not to compete would prevent Respondent not only from working at a competing business within 50 miles of the branch office in Kennett, Missouri, but Respondent would also be barred from working in a competing business within 50 miles of *any* of Appellant's branch offices. Under this interpretation, Respondent would be greatly limited in the geographic area she could work.

Additionally, the covenant not to compete bars Respondent from working at "any business that is in competition with [Appellant]." Yet, it fails to set out with precision what is to be considered a competing business and certainly does not specify that it only applies to other payday loan businesses. In that Appellant is in the business of making loans, it could be inferred that in addition to barring Respondent's employment at a different payday loan establishment the covenant not to compete also bars her from being employed anywhere loans are made including banks, credit unions, savings and loan organizations, title-loan companies, pawn shops, and other financial organizations. Such a restraint on the geographic scope of Respondent's employment and upon her type of employment is unduly burdensome and unreasonable. [Citation.]

* * *

Appellant's second point relied on asserts the trial court erred in denying its petition because

[t]he trial court erroneously applied the law in failing to modify the covenant not to compete to a geographic scope it found to be reasonable in that the court found the geographic scope to be unreasonable for the payday loan industry but failed to modify the covenant not to compete to reflect a geographic scope that would be reasonable and enforceable.

* * * This Court "recognize[s] that an unreasonable restriction against competition in a contract may be modified and enforced to the extent that it is reasonable, regardless of the covenant's form of wording." * * *

Having reviewed the record in this matter, it appears the record is devoid of a request by Appellant for modification of the covenant not to compete either in its pleadings, at trial, or in its motion for new trial before the trial court. It is settled law that "'appellate courts are merely courts of review for trial court errors, and there can be no review of matter which has not been presented to or expressly decided by the trial court." [Citation.]

* * *

The judgment of the trial court is affirmed.

Exculpatory Clauses
ANDERSON v. McOSKAR ENTERPRISES, INC.
Court of Appeals of Minnesota, 2006
712 N.W.2d 796

Shumaker, J.

Respondent McOskar Enterprises, Inc. owns and operates a fitness and health club in Monticello known as "Curves for Women." [Plaintiff] Appellant Tammey J. Anderson joined the club on April 2, 2003.

As part of the registration requirements, Anderson read an "AGREEMENT AND RELEASE OF LIABILITY," initialed each of the three paragraphs in the document, and dated and signed it. The first paragraph purported to release Curves from liability for injuries Anderson might sustain in participating in club activities or using club equipment:

> In consideration of being allowed to participate in the activities and programs of Curves for Women® and to use its facilities, equipment and machinery in addition to the payment of any fee or charge, I do hereby waive, release and forever discharge Curves International Inc., Curves for Women®, and their officers, agents, employees, representatives, executors, and all others (Curves® representatives) from any and all responsibilities or liabilities from injuries or damages arriving [sic] out of or connected with my attendance at Curves for Women®, my participation in all activities, my use of equipment or machinery, or any act or omission, including negligence by Curves® representatives.

The second paragraph provided for Anderson's acknowledgment that fitness activities "involve a risk of injury" and her agreement "to expressly assume and accept any and all risks of injury or death." After completing the registration, Anderson began a workout, primarily with machines, under the supervision of a trainer. About 15 or 20 minutes later, having used four or five machines, Anderson developed a headache in the back of her head. She contends that she told the trainer, who suggested that the problem was likely just a previous lack of use of certain muscles and that Anderson would be fine.

Anderson continued her workout and developed pain in her neck, shoulder, and arm. She informed the trainer but continued to exercise until she completed the program for that session.

The pain persisted when Anderson returned home. She then sought medical attention, eventually had a course of physical therapy, and, in June 2003, underwent a cervical diskectomy. She then started this lawsuit for damages, alleging that Curves had been negligent in its acts or omissions during her workout at the club.

Curves moved for summary judgment on the ground that Anderson had released the club from liability for negligence. The district court agreed and granted the motion. Anderson challenges the court's ruling on appeal.

* * *

It is settled Minnesota law that, under certain circumstances, "parties to a contract may, without violation of public policy, protect themselves against liability resulting from their own negligence." [Citation.] The "public interest in freedom of contract is preserved by recognizing [release and exculpatory] clauses as valid." [Citation.]

Releases of liability are not favored by the law and are strictly construed against the benefited party. [Citation.] "If the clause is either ambiguous in scope or purports to release the benefited party from liability for intentional, willful or wanton acts, it will not be enforced." [Citation.] Furthermore, even if a release clause is unambiguous in scope and is limited only to negligence, courts must still ascertain whether its enforcement will contravene public policy. On this issue, a two-prong test is applied:

> Before enforcing an exculpatory clause, both prongs of the test are examined, to-wit: (1) whether there was a disparity of bargaining power between the parties (in terms of a compulsion to sign a contract containing an unacceptable provision and the lack of ability to negotiate elimination of the unacceptable provision) ... and (2) the types of services being offered or provided (taking into consideration whether it is a public or essential service).

[Citation.]

The two-prong test describes what is generally known as a "contract of adhesion," more particularly explained in *Schlobohm*:

> It is a contract generally not bargained for, but which is imposed on the public for *necessary* service on a "take it or leave it" basis. Even though a contract is on a printed form and offered on a "take it or leave it" basis, those facts alone do not cause it to be an adhesion contract. There must be a showing that the parties were greatly disparate in bargaining power, that there was no opportunity for negotiation *and* that the services could not be obtained elsewhere.

[Citation.]

* * *

* * * There is nothing in the Curves release that expressly exonerates the club from liability for any intentional, willful, or wanton act. Thus, we consider whether the release is ambiguous in scope.

* * *

Anderson argues that the release is ambiguous because it broadly exonerates Curves from liability for "any act or omission, including negligence..." * * *

* * *

The vice of ambiguous language is that it fails precisely and clearly to inform contracting parties of the meaning of their ostensible agreement. Because ambiguous language is susceptible of two or more reasonable meanings, each party might carry away from the agreement a different and perhaps contradictory understanding. In the context of a release in connection with an athletic, health, or fitness activity, the consumer surely is entitled to know precisely what liability is being exonerated. A release that is so vague, general, or broad as to fail to specifically designate the particular nature of the liability exonerated is not enforceable. [Citation.]

* * * It is clear from this release that Anderson agreed to exonerate Curves from liability for negligence, that being part of the express agreement that Anderson accepted and it is solely negligence of which Curves is accused.

The unmistakable intent of the parties to the Curves agreement is that Curves at least would not be held liable for acts of negligence. * * *

* * *

Even if a release is unambiguously confined to liability for negligence, it still will be unenforceable if it contravenes public policy. Anderson contends that the Curves contract is one of adhesion characterized by such a disparity in bargaining power that she was compelled to sign it without any ability to negotiate.

* * *

Even if there was a disparity of bargaining ability here—which has not been demonstrated—there was no showing that the services provided by Curves are necessary and unobtainable elsewhere. * * *

The Curves release did not contravene public policy, and we adopt the supreme court's conclusion in *Schlobohm*: "Here there is no special legal relationship and no overriding public interest which demand that this contract provision, voluntarily entered into by competent parties, should be rendered ineffectual." [Citation.]

* * *

The district court did not err in granting respondent's motion for summary judgment on the ground that appellant signed and agreed to a release of respondent's liability for negligence. We affirm.

CASE 13-5

Unconscionable Contracts/Exculpatory Clauses
BAGLEY v. MT. BACHELOR, INC.
Supreme Court of Oregon, 2014
356 Or. 543, 340 P.3d 27

Brewer, J.

[Bagley, a highly skilled and experienced snowboarder, purchased a season pass from Mt. Bachelor. Upon purchasing the season pass, plaintiff executed a written "release and indemnity agreement" that defendant required of all its patrons. That season pass agreement provided, in pertinent part:

> In consideration of the use of a Mt. Bachelor pass and/ or Mt. Bachelor's premises, I/we agree to release and indemnify Mt. Bachelor, Inc., its officers and directors, owners, agents, landowners, affiliated companies, and employees (hereinafter 'Mt. Bachelor, Inc.') from any and all claims for property damage, injury, or death which I/we may suffer or for which I/we may be liable to others, in any way connected with skiing, snowboarding, or snowriding. This release and indemnity agreement shall apply to any claim even if caused by negligence. The only claims not released are those based upon intentional misconduct.

* * *

> By my/our signature(s) below, I/we agree that this release and indemnity agreement will remain in full force and effect and I will be bound by its terms throughout this season and all subsequent seasons for which I/we renew this season pass.

* * *

On November 18, 2005, plaintiff began using the pass/lift ticket, which stated, in part:

> "Read this release agreement

> "In consideration for each lift ride, the ticket user releases and agrees to hold harmless and indemnify Mt. Bachelor, Inc., and its employees and agents from all claims for property damage, injury or death even if caused by negligence. The only claims not released are those based upon intentional misconduct."

Further, the following sign was posted at each of defendant's ski lift terminals:

"YOUR TICKET IS A RELEASE

"The back of your ticket contains a release of all claims against Mt. Bachelor, Inc. and its employees or agents. * * *"

Beginning on November 18, 2005, plaintiff used his season pass to ride defendant's lifts at least 119 times over the course of twenty-six days that he spent snow-boarding at the ski area. On February 16, 2006, while snowboarding over a human made jump in defendant's "air chamber" terrain park, plaintiff sustained serious injuries resulting in his permanent paralysis. Bagley sued Mt. Bachelor ski area for negligence in the design, construction, maintenance, and inspection of the jump. The trial court granted operator's motion for summary judgment, which was based on an affirmative defense of release.

In its summary judgment motion, defendant asserted that plaintiff "admittedly understood that he [had] entered into a release agreement and was snowboarding under its terms on the date of [the] accident." Defendant argued that the release conspicuously and unambiguously disclaimed its future liability for negligence, and that the release was neither unconscionable nor contrary to public policy under Oregon law, because "skiers and snowboarders voluntarily choose to ski and snowboard and ski resorts do not provide essential public services." In his cross-motion for partial summary judgment, plaintiff asserted that the release was unenforceable because it was contrary to public policy and was "both substantively and procedurally unconscionable." The trial court rejected plaintiff's public policy and unconscionability arguments, reasoning that "[s]now riding is not such an essential service which requires someone such as [p]laintiff to be forced to sign a release in order to obtain the service." Accordingly, the trial court granted summary judgment in defendant's favor and denied plaintiff's cross-motion for partial summary judgment.

The Court of Appeals affirmed.

The parties' dispute in this case involves a topic—the validity of exculpatory agreements—that this court has not comprehensively addressed in decades. Although the specific issue on review—the validity of an anticipatory release of a ski area operator's liability for negligence—is finite and particular, it has broader implications insofar as it lies at the intersection of two traditional common law domains—contract and tort—where, at least in part, the legislature has established statutory rights and duties that affect the reach of otherwise governing common law principles.

It is a truism that a contract validly made between competent parties is not to be set aside lightly. [Citations.] As this court has stated, however, "contract rights are [not] absolute; * * * [e]qually fundamental with the private right is that of the public to regulate it in the common interest." [Citation.]

That "common," or public, interest is embodied, in part, in the principles of tort law. As a leading treatise explains:

It is sometimes said that compensation for losses is the primary function of tort law * * * [but it] is perhaps more accurate to describe the primary function as one of determining when compensation is to be required.

* * *

One way in which courts have placed limits on the freedom of contract is by refusing to enforce agreements that are illegal. [Citations.]

In determining whether an agreement is illegal because it is contrary to public policy, "[t]he test is the evil tendency of the contract and not its actual injury to the public in a particular instance." [Citation.] The fact that the effect of a contract provision may be harsh as applied to one of the contracting parties does not mean that the agreement is, for that reason alone, contrary to public policy, particularly where "the contract in question was freely entered into between parties in equal bargaining positions and did not involve a contract of adhesion, such as some retail installment contracts and insurance policies." [Citation.]

* * * [C]ourts determine whether a contract is illegal by determining whether it violates public policy as expressed in relevant constitutional and statutory provisions and in case law, [citation], and by considering whether it is unconscionable. * * *

* * * [T]his court often has relied on public policy considerations to determine whether a contract or contract term is sufficiently unfair or oppressive to be deemed unconscionable. [Citations.]

* * *

Unconscionability may be procedural or substantive. Procedural unconscionability refers to the conditions of contract formation and focuses on two factors: oppression and surprise. [Citation.] Oppression exists when there is inequality in bargaining power between the parties, resulting in no real opportunity to negotiate the terms of the contract and the absence of meaningful choice. [Citations.] Surprise involves whether terms were hidden or obscure from the vantage of the party seeking to avoid them. [Citation.] Generally speaking, factors such as ambiguous contract wording and fine print are the hallmarks of surprise. In contrast, the existence of gross inequality of bargaining power, a take-it-or-leave-it bargaining stance, and the fact that a contract involves a consumer transaction, rather than a commercial bargain, can be evidence of oppression.

Substantive unconscionability, on the other hand, generally refers to the terms of the contract, rather than the circumstances of formation, and focuses on whether the substantive terms contravene the public interest or public policy. [Citation.] Both procedural and substantive deficiencies—frequently in combination—can preclude enforcement of a contract or contract term on unconscionability grounds. Restatement §208 comment a.

Identifying whether a contract is procedurally unconscionable requires consideration of evidence related to the specific circumstances surrounding the formation of the contract at issue. By contrast, the inquiry into substantive unconscionability can be more complicated. To discern whether, in the context of a particular transaction, substantive concerns relating to unfairness or oppression are sufficiently important to warrant interference with the parties' freedom to contract as they see fit, courts frequently look to legislation for relevant indicia of public policy. When relevant public policy is expressed in a statute, the issue is one of legislative intent. [Citation.] In that situation, the court must examine the statutory text and context to determine whether the legislature intended to invalidate the contract term at issue. [Citation.]

Frequently, however, the argument that a contract term is sufficiently unfair or oppressive as to be unenforceable is grounded in one or more factors that are not expressly codified; in such circumstances, the common law has a significant role to play. * * *

This court has considered whether enforcement of an anticipatory release would violate an uncodified public policy in only a few cases. * * * [This] court has not declared such releases to be *per se* invalid, but neither has it concluded that they are always enforceable. Instead, the court has followed a multi-factor approach:

> Agreements to exonerate a party from liability or to limit the extent of the party's liability for tortious conduct are not favorites of the courts but neither are they automatically voided. The treatment courts accord such agreements depends upon the subject and terms of the agreement and the relationship of the parties.
>
> [Citation.]

* * *

* * * [R]elevant procedural factors in the determination of whether enforcement of an anticipatory release would violate public policy or be unconscionable include whether the release was conspicuous and unambiguous; whether there was a substantial disparity in the parties' bargaining power; whether the contract was offered on a take-it-or-leave-it basis; and whether the contract involved a consumer transaction. Relevant substantive considerations include whether enforcement of the release would cause a harsh or inequitable result to befall the releasing party; whether the releasee serves an important public interest or function; and whether the release purported to disclaim liability for more serious misconduct than ordinary negligence. Nothing in our previous decisions suggests that any single factor takes precedence over the others or that the listed factors are exclusive. Rather, they indicate that a determination whether enforcement of an anticipatory release would violate public policy or be unconscionable must be based on the totality of the circumstances of a particular transaction. * * *

* * *

* * * [O]ur analysis leads to the conclusion that permitting defendant to exculpate itself from its own negligence would be unconscionable. * * * important procedural factors supporting that conclusion include the substantial disparity in the parties' bargaining power in the particular circumstances of this consumer transaction, and the fact that the release was offered to plaintiff and defendant's other customers on a take-it-or-leave-it basis.

There also are indications that the release is substantively unfair and oppressive. First, a harsh and inequitable result would follow if defendant were immunized from negligence liability, in light of (1) defendant's superior ability to guard against the risk of harm to its patrons arising from its own negligence in designing, creating, and maintaining its runs, slopes, jumps, and other facilities; and (2) defendant's superior ability to absorb and spread the costs associated with insuring against those risks. Second, because defendant's business premises are open to the general public virtually without restriction, large numbers of skiers and snowboarders regularly avail themselves of its facilities, and those patrons are subject to risks of harm from conditions on the premises of defendant's creation, the safety of those patrons is a matter of broad societal concern. The public interest, therefore, is affected by the performance of defendant's private duties toward them under business premises liability law.

In the ultimate step of our unconscionability analysis, we consider whether those procedural and substantive considerations outweigh defendant's interest in enforcing the release at issue here. *Restatement (Second) of Contracts* §178 comment b ("[A] decision as to enforceability is reached only after a careful balancing, in the light of all the circumstances, of the interest in the enforcement of the particular promise against the policy against the enforcement of such terms.") Defendant argues that, in light of the inherent risks of skiing, it is neither unfair nor oppressive for a ski area operator to insist on a release from liability for its own negligence. * * *

Defendant's arguments have some force. After all, skiing and snow boarding are activities whose allure and risks derive from a unique blend of factors that include natural features, artificial constructs, and human engagement. It may be difficult in such circumstances to untangle the causal forces that lead to an injury-producing accident. Moreover, defendant is correct that several relevant factors weigh in favor of enforcing the release. * * * [T]he release was conspicuous and unambiguous, defendant's alleged misconduct in this case was negligence, not more egregious conduct, and snow-boarding is not a necessity of life.

That said, the release is very broad; it applies on its face to a multitude of conditions and risks, many of which (such as riding on a chairlift) leave defendant's patrons vulnerable to risks of harm of defendant's creation. Accepting as true the allegations in plaintiff's complaint, defendant designed, created, and maintained artificial constructs, including the jump on which plaintiff was injured. Even in the context of expert snow-boarding in defendant's terrain park, defendant was in a better position than its invitees to guard against risks of harm created by its own conduct.

A final point deserves mention. It is axiomatic that public policy favors the deterrence of negligent conduct. * * * As the parties readily agree, the activities at issue in this case involve considerable risks to life and limb. Skiers and snowboarders have important legal inducements to exercise reasonable care for their own safety by virtue of their statutory assumption of the inherent risks of skiing. By contrast, without potential exposure to liability for their own negligence, ski area operators would lack a commensurate legal incentive to avoid creating unreasonable risks of harm to their business invitees. [Citation.] Where, as here, members of the public are invited to participate without restriction in risky activities on defendant's business premises (and many do), and where the risks of harm posed by operator negligence are appreciable, such an imbalance in legal incentives is not conducive to the public interest.

Because the factors favoring enforcement of the release are outweighed by the countervailing considerations that we have identified, we conclude that enforcement of the release at issue in this case would be unconscionable. And, because the release is unenforceable, genuine issues of fact exist that preclude summary judgment in defendant's favor.

The decision of the Court of Appeals is reversed. The judgment of the trial court is reversed and the case is remanded to that court for further proceedings.

QUESTIONS

1. Johnson and Wilson were the principal shareholders in Matthew Corporation, located in the city of Jonesville, Wisconsin. This corporation was engaged in the business of manufacturing paper novelties, which were sold over a wide area in the Midwest. The corporation was also in the business of binding books. Johnson purchased Wilson's shares of the Matthew Corporation, and in consideration thereof, Wilson agreed that for a period of two years he would not (a) manufacture or sell in Wisconsin any paper novelties of any kind that would compete with those sold by the Matthew Corporation or (b) engage in the bookbinding business in the city of Jonesville. Discuss the validity and effect, if any, of this agreement.

2. Wilkins, a resident of and licensed by the State of Texas as a certified public accountant (CPA), rendered service in his professional capacity in Louisiana to Coverton Cosmetics Company. He was not registered as a CPA in Louisiana. His service under his contract with the cosmetics company was not the only occasion on which he had practiced his profession in that State. The company denied liability and refused to pay him, relying upon a Louisiana statute declaring it unlawful for any person to perform or offer to perform services as a CPA for compensation until he has been registered by the designated agency of the State and holds an unrevoked registration card. Provision is made for issuance of a certificate as a CPA without examination to any applicant who holds a valid unrevoked certificate as a CPA under the laws of any other State. The statute provides further that rendition of services of the character performed by Wilkins, without registration, is a misdemeanor punishable by a fine or imprisonment in the county jail or both. Discuss whether Wilkins would be successful in an action against Coverton seeking to recover a fee in the amount of $1,500 as the reasonable value of his services.

3. Michael is interested in promoting the passage of a bill in the State legislature. He agrees with Christy, an attorney, to pay Christy for her services in drawing up the required bill, procuring its introduction in the legislature, and making an argument for its passage before the legislative committee to which it will be referred. Christy renders these services. Subsequently, upon Michael's refusal to pay her, Christy sues Michael for damage for breach of contract. Will Christy prevail? Explain.

4. Anthony promises to pay McCarthy $10,000 if McCarthy informs the public that Washington is a Communist. Washington is not a Communist and never has been. McCarthy successfully persuades the media to report that Washington is a Communist and now seeks to recover the $10,000 from Anthony, who refuses to pay. McCarthy initiates a lawsuit against Anthony. What result?

5. The Dear Corporation was engaged in the business of making and selling harvesting machines. It sold everything pertaining to its business to the ABC Company, agreeing "not again to go into the manufacture of harvesting machines anywhere in the United States." The seller, which has national and international goodwill in its business, now begins the manufacture of such machines contrary to its agreement. Should the court enjoin it? Explain.

6. Charles Leigh, engaged in the industrial laundry business in Central City, employed Tim Close, previously employed in the home laundry business, as a route salesperson on July 1. Leigh rents linens and industrial uniforms to commercial customers; the soiled linens and uniforms are picked up at regular intervals by route drivers and replaced with clean ones. Every employee is assigned a list of customers. The contract of employment stated that in consideration of being employed, upon termination of his employment, Close would not "directly or indirectly engage in the linen supply business or any competitive business within Central City, Illinois, for a period of one year from the date when his employment under this contract ceases." On May 10 of the following year, Leigh terminated Close's employment for valid reasons. Thereafter, Close accepted employment with Ajax Linen Service, a direct competitor of Leigh in Central City. He commenced soliciting former customers whom he had called on for Leigh and obtained some of them as customers for Ajax. Will Leigh be able to enforce the provisions of the contract? Why or why not?

7. On April 30, 2019, Barack and Donald entered into a bet on the outcome of the 2019 Kentucky Derby. On January 28, 2020, Barack, who bet on the winner, approached Donald, seeking to collect the $3,000 Donald had wagered. Donald paid Barack the $3,000 wager but now seeks to recover the funds from Barack. Result? Explain.

8. Carl, a salesman for Smith, comes to Benson's home and sells him a complete set of "gourmet cooking utensils" that are worth approximately $300. Benson, an eighty-year-old man living alone in a one-room efficiency apartment, signs a contract to buy the utensils for $1,450, plus a credit charge of $145, and to make payment in ten equal monthly installments. Three weeks after Carl leaves with the signed contract, Benson decides he cannot afford the cooking utensils and has no use for them. What can Benson do? Explain.

9. Consider the same facts as in Question 8, but assume that the price was $350. Benson, nevertheless, wishes to avoid the contract based on the allegation that Carl befriended and tricked him into the purchase. Discuss.

10. Adrian rents a bicycle from Barbara. The bicycle rental contract Adrian signed provides that Barbara is not liable for any injury to the renter caused by any defect in the bicycle or the negligence of Barbara. Injured when she is involved in an accident due to Barbara's improper maintenance of the bicycle, Adrian sues Barbara for her damages. Will Barbara be protected from liability by the provision in their contract? Explain.

11. Makayla was a Java programmer employed with Sun Microsystems in Palo Alto, California. Upon beginning employment, Makayla signed a contract that included a noncompete clause that prevented her, within three months of terminating her employment, from taking another Java programming position with any of five companies Sun listed as "direct competitors." Later that year, Makayla resigned and two months later accepted a position with Hewlett-Packard (HP) in Houston, Texas. HP was listed in Makayla's contract as a "direct competitor," but she argues that due to the significant geographic distance between both jobs, the contract is not enforceable. Explain whether the contract is enforceable.

CASE PROBLEMS

12. Merrill Lynch employed Post and Maney as account executives. Both men elected to be paid a salary and to participate in the firm's pension and profit-sharing plans rather than take a straight commission. Thirteen years later, Merrill Lynch terminated the employment of both Post and Maney. Both men began working for a competitor of Merrill Lynch. Merrill Lynch then informed them that all of their rights in the company-funded pension plan had been forfeited pursuant to a provision of the plan that permitted forfeiture in the event an employee directly or indirectly competed with the firm. Is Merrill Lynch correct in its assertion? Why or why not?

13. Tovar applied for the position of resident physician in Paxton Community Memorial Hospital. The hospital examined his background and licensing and assured him that he was qualified for the position. Relying upon the hospital's promise of permanent employment, Tovar resigned from his job and began work at the hospital. He was discharged two weeks later, however, because he did not hold a license to practice medicine in Illinois as required by State law. He had taken the examination but had never passed it. Tovar claims that the hospital promised him a position of permanent employment and that by discharging him, it breached their employment contract. Discuss.

14. Carolyn Murphy, a welfare recipient with very limited education and with four minor children, responded to an advertisement that offered the opportunity to purchase televisions without a deposit or credit history. She entered into a rent-to-own contract for a twenty-five-inch console color television set that required seventy-eight weekly payments of $16.00 (a total of $1,248,

which was two and one-half times the retail value of the set). Under the contract, the renter could terminate the agreement by returning the television and forfeiting any payments already made. After Murphy had paid $436 on the television, she read a newspaper article criticizing the lease plan. She stopped payment and sued the television company. The television company has attempted to take possession of the set. Decision? Explain.

15. Albert Bennett, an amateur cyclist, participated in a bicycle race conducted by the United States Cycling Federation. During the race, Bennett was hit by an automobile. He claims that employees of the Federation improperly allowed the car onto the course. The Federation claims that it cannot be held liable to Bennett because Bennett signed a release exculpating the Federation from responsibility for any personal injury resulting from his participation in the race. Is the exculpatory clause effective? Explain.

16. In February, Brady contracted to construct a house for Fulghum for $206,850. Brady began construction on March 13. Neither during the negotiation of this contract nor when he began performance was Brady licensed as a general contractor as required by North Carolina law. Brady was awarded his builder's license on October 22, having passed the examination on his second attempt. At that time, he had completed two-thirds of the work on Fulghum's house. Fulghum paid Brady $204,000. Brady brought suit, seeking an additional $2,850 on the original contract and $29,000 for "additions and changes" Fulghum requested during construction. Is Fulghum liable to Brady? Explain.

17. Robert McCart owned and operated an H&R Block tax preparation franchise. When Robert became a district manager for H&R Block, he was not allowed to continue operating a franchise. So in accordance with company policy, he signed over his franchise to his wife June. June signed the new franchise agreement, which included a covenant not to compete for a two-year period within a fifty-mile radius of the franchise territory should the H&R Block franchise be terminated, transferred, or otherwise disposed of. June and Robert were both aware of the terms of this agreement, but June chose to terminate her franchise agreement anyway. Shortly thereafter, June sent letters to H&R Block customers, criticizing H&R Block's fees and informing them that she and Robert would establish their own tax preparation services at the same address as the former franchise location. Each letter included a separate letter from Robert detailing the tax services to be offered by the McCarts' new business. Should H&R Block be able to obtain an injunction against June? Against Robert? Discuss.

18. Michelle Marvin and actor Lee Marvin began living together, holding themselves out to the general public as man and wife without actually being married. The two orally agreed that while they lived together, they would share equally any and all property and earnings accumulated as a result of their individual and combined efforts. In addition, Michelle promised to render her services as "companion, homemaker, housekeeper and cook" to Lee. Shortly thereafter, she gave up her lucrative career as an entertainer in order to devote her full time to being Lee's companion, homemaker, housekeeper, and cook. In return, he agreed to provide for all of her financial support and needs for the rest of her life. After living together for six years, Lee compelled Michelle to leave his household but continued to provide for her support. One year later, however, he refused to provide further support. Michelle sued to recover support payments and half of their accumulated property. Lee contended that their agreement was so closely related to the supposed "immoral" character of their relationship that its enforcement would violate public policy. The trial court granted Lee's motion for judgment on the pleadings. Decision?

19. Richard Brobston was hired by Insulation Corporation of America (ICA) in 2009 as a territory sales manager but was promoted to national account manager in 2013 and to general manager in 2017. In 2019, ICA was planning to acquire computer-assisted design (CAD) technology to upgrade its product line. Prior to acquiring this technology, ICA required that Brobston and certain other employees sign employment contracts that contained restrictive covenants or be terminated and changed their employment status to "at-will" employees. These restrictive covenants provided that in the event of Brobston's termination for any reason, Brobston would not reveal any of ICA's trade secrets or sales information and would not enter into direct competition with ICA within three hundred miles of Allentown, Pennsylvania, for a period of two years from the date of termination. The purported consideration for Brobston's agreement was a $2,000 increase in his base salary and proprietary information concerning the CAD system, customers, and pricing.

Brobston signed the proffered employment contract. In October 2019, Brobston became vice president of special products, which included responsibility for sales of the CAD system products as well as other products. Over the course of the next year, Brobston failed in several respects to perform his employment duties properly, and on August 13, 2020, ICA terminated Brobston's employment. In December 2020, Brobston was hired by a competitor of ICA who was aware of ICA's restrictive covenants. Can ICA enforce the employment agreement by enjoining Brobston from disclosing proprietary information about ICA and by restraining him from competing with ICA? If so, for what duration and over what geographic area? Explain.

20. Henrioulle, an unemployed widower with two children, received public assistance in the form of a rent subsidy. He entered into an apartment lease agreement with Marin Ventures that provided "INDEMNIFICATION: Owner shall not be liable for any damage or injury to the tenant, or any other person, or to any property, occurring on the premises, or any part thereof, and Tenant agrees to hold Owner harmless for any claims for damages no matter how caused." Henrioulle fractured his wrist when he tripped over a rock on a common stairway in the apartment building. At the time of the accident, the landlord had been having difficulty keeping the common areas of the apartment building clean. Will the exculpatory clause effectively bar Henrioulle from recovery? Explain.

21. Between 2015 and 2020, Williams purchased a number of household items on credit from Walker-Thomas Furniture Co., a retail furniture store. Walker-Thomas retained the right in its contracts to repossess an item if Williams defaulted on an installment payment. Each contract also provided that each installment payment by Williams would be credited *pro rata* to all outstanding accounts or bills owed to Walker-Thomas. As a result of this provision, an unpaid balance would remain on every item purchased until the entire balance due on all items, whenever purchased, was paid in full. Williams defaulted on a monthly installment payment in 2020, and Walker-Thomas sought to repossess all the items that Williams had purchased since 2015. Discuss.

22. Universal City Studios, Inc. (Universal), entered into a general contract with Turner Construction Company (Turner) for the construction of the Jurassic Park ride. Turner entered into a subcontract with Pacific Custom Pools, Inc. (PCP), for PCP to furnish and install all water treatment work for the project for the contract price of $959,131. PCP performed work on the project from April 2016 until June 2020 for which it was paid $897,719. PCP's contractor's license, however, was under suspension from October 12, 2019, to March 14, 2020. In addition, PCP's license had expired as of January 31, 2020, and it was not renewed until May 5, 2020. California Business and Professions Code Section 7031 provides that no contractor may bring an action to recover compensation for the performance of any work requiring a license unless he or she was "a duly licensed contractor at all times during the performance of that [work], regardless of the merits of the cause of action brought by the contractor." The purpose of this licensing law is to protect the public from incompetence and dishonesty in those who provide building and construction services. PCP brought suit against Universal and Turner, the defendants, for the remainder of the contract price. Explain who should prevail.

23. Octavio Sanchez worked as a delivery driver at a Domino's Pizza restaurant owned by Western Pizza. He drove his own car in making deliveries. His hourly wage ranged from the legal minimum wage to approximately $0.50 above minimum wage. Western Pizza reimbursed him at a fixed rate of $0.80 per delivery regardless of the number of miles driven or actual expenses incurred. Sanchez brought this class action against Western Pizza, alleging that the flat rate at which drivers were reimbursed for delivery expenses violated wage and hour laws and that the drivers were paid less than the legal minimum wage.

    Sanchez and Western Pizza are parties to an undated arbitration agreement. The agreement states that (1) the execution of the agreement "is not a mandatory condition of employment"; (2) any dispute that the parties are unable to resolve informally will be submitted to binding arbitration before an arbitrator approved by both parties and "selected from the then-current Employment Arbitration panel of the Dispute Eradication Services"; (3) the parties waive the right to a jury trial; (4) the arbitration fees will be borne by Western Pizza, and except as otherwise required by law, each party will bear its own attorney fees and costs; (5) small claims may be resolved by a summary small claims procedure; and (6) the parties waive the right to bring class arbitration. Should Sanchez be compelled to submit to arbitration to resolve his complaint? Explain.

24. Louis Dunnam borrowed $35,000 from Ken Burns and agreed to repay the principal plus $5,000 six months later. After Dunnam defaulted on the loan, Burns sued to recover. Dunnam defended by claiming the loan was usurious. Under the relevant state statute, for transactions between private persons, the maximum allowable rate of interest is 18 percent if the parties agree on a rate of interest and 6 percent if they do not. The statute further provides that persons who contract for or collect usurious interest are subject to penalties that may exceed the total value of the contract. Decision? Explain.

T A K I N G   S I D E S

EarthWeb provided online products and services to business professionals in the information technology (IT) industry. EarthWeb operated through a family of Websites offering information, products, and services for IT professionals to use for facilitating tasks and solving technology problems in a business setting. EarthWeb obtained this content primarily through licensing agreements with third parties. Schlack began his employment with EarthWeb in its New York City office. His title at EarthWeb was Vice President, Worldwide Content, and he was responsible for the content of all of EarthWeb's Websites. Schlack's employment contract stated that he was an employee at will and included a section titled "Limited Agreement Not To Compete." That section provided:

(c) For a period of twelve (12) months after the termination of Schlack's employment with EarthWeb, Schlack shall not, directly or indirectly:

  (1) work as an employee… or in any other… capacity for any person or entity that directly competes with EarthWeb. For the purpose of this section, the term "directly competing" is defined as a person or entity or division on an entity that is

  (i) an online service for Information Professionals whose primary business is to provide Information Technology Professionals with a directory of third party technology, software, and/or developer resources; and/or an online reference library, and or

  (ii) an online store, the primary purpose of which is to sell or distribute third party software or products used for Internet site or software development.

About one year later, Schlack tendered his letter of resignation to EarthWeb. Schlack revealed at this time that he had accepted a position with ITworld.com.

a. What arguments would support EarthWeb's enforcement of the covenant not to compete?

b. What arguments would support Schlack's argument that the covenant is not enforceable?

c. Which side should prevail? Explain.

CHAPTER 14

Contractual Capacity

CHAPTER OUTCOMES

After reading and studying this chapter, you should be able to:

- Explain how and when a minor may ratify a contract.

- Describe the liability of a minor who (1) disaffirms a contract or (2) misrepresents his age.

- Explain what a "necessary" is and how it affects the contracts of a minor.

- Distinguish between the legal capacity of a person under guardianship and a mentally incompetent person who is not under guardianship.

- Contrast the rule governing an intoxicated person's capacity to enter into a contract with the rules governing minors and incompetent persons.

A binding promise or agreement requires that the parties to the agreement have contractual capacity. Everyone is regarded as having such capacity unless the law for reasons of public policy holds that the individual lacks such capacity. This essential ingredient of a contract is discussed by considering those classes and conditions of persons who are legally limited in their capacity to contract: (1) minors, (2) incompetent persons, and (3) intoxicated persons.

14-1 Minors

Almost without exception, a minor's contract, whether executory or executed, is *voidable* unless the contract has been ratified. Restatement, Section 14. A **minor**, also called an infant, is a person who has not attained the age of legal majority. At common law, a minor was a person who was under twenty-one years of age. Today the age of majority has been changed in nearly all jurisdictions by statute, usually to age eighteen. Thus, the minor is in a favored position by having the option to disaffirm the contract or to enforce it. The adult party to the contract cannot avoid her contract with a minor. Even an "emancipated" minor, one who because of marriage or other reason is no longer subject to strict parental control, may avoid contractual liability in most jurisdictions. Consequently, businesspeople deal at their peril with minors and in situations of consequence generally require an adult to cosign or guarantee the performance of the contract. Nevertheless, most States recognize special categories of contracts that cannot be avoided (such as student loans and contracts for medical care) or that have a lower age for capacity (such as bank account, marriage, and insurance contracts).

14-1a LIABILITY ON CONTRACTS

A minor's contract is not entirely void and of no legal effect; rather, it is *voidable* at the minor's option. The exercise of this power of avoidance, called a **disaffirmance**, ordinarily releases the minor from any liability on the contract. On the other hand, after the minor becomes of age, she may choose to adopt or **ratify** the contract, in which case she surrenders her power of avoidance and becomes bound.

DISAFFIRMANCE As previously stated, a minor's contract is voidable at his or his guardian's option, conferring upon him a power to avoid liability. He, or in some jurisdictions his guardian, may, through words or conduct manifesting an intention not to abide by the contract, exercise the power to disaffirm.

A minor may disaffirm a contract at any time before reaching the age of majority. Moreover, a minor generally may disaffirm a contract within a reasonable time after coming of age as long as she has not already ratified the contract. A notable exception is that a minor cannot disaffirm a sale of land until *after* reaching her majority. In most States, determining a reasonable time depends upon such circumstances as the nature of the transaction, whether either party has caused the delay, and the extent to which either party has been injured by the delay. Some States, however, statutorily prescribe a time period, generally one year, in which the minor may disaffirm the contract.

Disaffirmance may be either *express* or *implied*. No particular form of words is essential so long as they show an intention not to be bound. This intention also may be manifested by acts or by conduct. For example, a minor agrees to sell property to Alice and then sells that property to Brian. The sale to Brian would constitute a disaffirmance of the contract with Alice.

RESTITUTION Disaffirmance of an executory contract releases the minor from any liability on the contractual obligation. In cases in which either or both of the parties have performed partially or fully, however, the issue of restitution arises. A minor who has disaffirmed a contract is entitled to restitution from the other party for any benefit the minor has conferred on the other party.

A troublesome yet important problem in this area pertains to the minor's duty to make restitution to the other party upon disaffirmance. The courts do not agree on this question. The majority hold that the minor must return any property he has received from the other party, provided he has it in his possession at the time of disaffirmance. Nothing more is required. Under this approach, if a minor disaffirms the purchase of an automobile and the vehicle has been wrecked, the minor need only return the wrecked vehicle. Other States require at least the payment of a reasonable amount for the use of the property or the amount of its depreciation while in the hands of the minor. Some States, either by statute or court ruling, recognize a duty upon the part of the minor to make restitution, that is, return an equivalent of what has been received in order to place the seller in approximately the same position she would have occupied had the sale not occurred.

The newly adopted Restatement of Restitution adopts the last position: if the other party has dealt with the minor in good faith on reasonable terms, rescission leaves the minor liable in restitution for benefits the minor received in the transaction. Section 16. The Restatement of Restitution provides the following example:

> Minor purchases a used car from Dealer, paying $5,000 cash and making no misrepresentation of age. Dealer acts in good faith, and the sale is on reasonable terms. Several months later, the car develops mechanical problems. Minor continues to drive the car without obtaining the necessary repairs; the car becomes inoperable; Minor repudiates the purchase. Minor is entitled to rescind the transaction on the ground of incapacity. In the two-way restoration consequent on rescission, Minor's claim is to $5,000 plus interest; Dealer recovers the car, with a credit (against Dealer's liability to Minor) equal to the car's depreciation in value while in Minor's possession.

Finally, can a minor disaffirm and recover property that his buyer has transferred to a good faith purchaser for value? Traditionally, the minor could avoid the contract and recover the property, despite the fact that the third person gave value for it and had no notice of the minority. Thus, in the case of the sale of real estate, a minor may rescind her deed of conveyance even against a good faith purchaser of the land who did not know of the minority. Regarding the sale of goods, however, this principle has been changed by Section 2-403 of the Uniform Commercial Code (UCC), which provides that a person with voidable title (e.g., the person buying goods from a minor) has power to transfer valid title to a good faith purchaser for value. For example, a minor sells his car to an individual who resells it to a used car dealership, a good faith purchaser for value. The used car dealer would acquire legal title even though he bought the car from a seller who had only voidable title.

Practical Advice

In all significant contracts entered into with a minor, have an adult cosign or guarantee the written agreement.

◆ *See Case 14-1*

RATIFICATION A minor has the option of ratifying a contract after reaching the age of majority. Ratification makes the contract binding *ah initio* (from the beginning). That is, the result is the same as if the contract had been valid and binding from its inception. Ratification, once effected, is final and cannot be withdrawn; furthermore, it must be in total, validating the entire contract. The minor can ratify the contract only as a whole, both as to burdens and benefits. He cannot, for example, ratify so as to retain the consideration received and escape payment or other performance on his part; nor can the minor retain part of the contract and disaffirm another part.

Note that a minor has *no* power to ratify a contract while still a minor. A ratification based on words or conduct occurring while the minor is still underage is no more effective than his original contractual promise. The ratification must take place after the individual has acquired contractual capacity by attaining his majority.

Ratification can occur in three ways: (1) through express language, (2) as implied from conduct, and (3) through failure to make a timely disaffirmance. Suppose that a minor makes a contract to buy property from an adult. The contract is voidable by the minor, and she can escape liability. But suppose that after reaching her majority, she promises to go through with the purchase. The minor has *expressly* ratified the contract she entered when she was a minor. Her promise is binding, and the adult can recover for breach if the minor fails to carry out the terms of the contract.

Ratification also may be *implied* from a person's conduct. Suppose that the minor, after attaining majority, uses the property involved in the contract, undertakes to sell it to someone else, or performs some other act showing an intention to affirm the contract. She may not thereafter disaffirm the contract but is bound by it. Perhaps the most common form of implied ratification occurs when a minor, after attaining majority, continues to use the property purchased as a minor. This use is obviously inconsistent with the nonexistence of a contract. Whether the contract is performed or still partly executory, the continued use of the property amounts to a ratification and prevents a disaffirmance by the minor. Simply keeping the goods for an unreasonable time after attaining majority has also been construed as a ratification.

◆ *See Case 14-2*

14-1b LIABILITY FOR NECESSARIES

Contractual incapacity does not excuse a minor from an obligation to pay for necessaries, those things that suitably and reasonably supply his personal needs, such as food, shelter, medicine, and clothing. Even here, however, the minor is liable not for the agreed price but for the *reasonable* value of the items furnished. Recovery is based on quasi contract. Thus, if a clothier sells a minor a suit that the minor needs, the clothier can successfully sue the minor. The clothier's recovery is limited, however, to the reasonable value of the suit, even if this amount is much less than the agreed-upon selling price.

Defining necessaries is a difficult problem. In general, the States regard as **necessary** those things that the minor needs to maintain himself in his particular station in life. Items necessary for subsistence and health—such as food, lodging, clothing, medicine, and medical services—are obviously included. But other less essential items, such as textbooks, school instruction, and legal advice, may be included as well. Further, many States enlarge the concept of necessaries to include articles of property and services that a minor needs to earn the money required to provide the necessities of life for himself and his dependents. Nevertheless, many States limit necessaries to items that are not provided to the minor. Thus, if a minor's guardian provides her with an adequate wardrobe, a blouse the minor purchased would not be considered a necessary. In addition, a minor is *not* liable for anything on the grounds that it is necessary unless it has been actually furnished to him and used or consumed by him. In other words, a minor may disaffirm his executory contracts for necessaries and refuse to accept the clothing, lodging, or other items or services.

Ordinarily, luxury items such as cameras, tape recorders, stereo equipment, television sets, and motorboats seldom qualify as necessaries. Whether automobiles and trucks are necessaries has caused considerable controversy, but some courts have recognized that under certain circumstances, an automobile may be necessary when the minor uses it for his business activities.

◆ *See Case 14-3*

14-1c LIABILITY FOR MISREPRESENTATION OF AGE

The States do not agree on whether a minor who has fraudulently misrepresented her age when entering into contract has the power to disaffirm. Suppose a contracting minor says that she is eighteen years of age (or another age if that is the age of attaining majority) and actually looks at least that age. By the prevailing view in this country, the minor may nevertheless disaffirm the contract. Some States, however, prohibit disaffirmance if a minor misrepresents her age and the adult party, in good faith, reasonably relied upon the misrepresentation. Other States not following the majority rule either (1) require the minor to restore the other party to the position she occupied before the making of the contract or (2) allow the defrauded party to recover damages against the minor in tort.

Practical Advice

In all significant contracts, if you have doubts about the age of your customers, have them prove that they are of legal age.

14-1d LIABILITY FOR TORT CONNECTED WITH CONTRACT

It is well settled that minors are generally liable for their torts. There is, however, a legal doctrine providing that if a tort and a contract are so "interwoven" that the court must enforce the contract to enforce the tort action, the minor is not liable in tort. Thus, if a minor rents an automobile from an adult, he enters into a contractual relationship obliging him to exercise reasonable care and diligence to protect the property from injury. By negligently damaging the automobile, he breaches that contractual undertaking. But his contractual immunity protects him from an action by the adult based on the contract. Can the adult nonetheless recover damages on a tort theory? By the majority view, he cannot. For, it is reasoned, a tort recovery would, in effect, be an enforcement of the contract and would defeat the protection that contract law affords the minor.

A different result arises, however, when the minor departs from the terms of the agreement, as by using a rental automobile for an unauthorized purpose and in so doing negligently causing damage to the automobile. In that event, most courts would hold that the tort is independent, and the adult can collect from the minor. Such a situation would not involve the breach of a contractual duty, but rather the commission of a tort while performing an activity completely beyond the scope of the rental agreement.

14-2 Incompetent Persons

This section discusses the contract status of mentally incompetent persons who are under court-appointed guardianship and those persons who have a mental incapacity but who have not been adjudicated as incompetent.

14-2a   PERSON UNDER GUARDIANSHIP

If a person is under guardianship by court order, her contracts are void and of no legal effect. Restatement, Section 13. A *guardian* is appointed by a court, generally under the terms of a statute, to control and preserve the property of a person (the **ward** or **adjudicated incompetent**) whose impaired capacity prevents her from managing her own property. Nevertheless, a party dealing with an individual under guardianship may be able to recover the fair value of any necessaries provided to the incompetent. Moreover, the contracts of the ward may be ratified by her guardian or by herself upon termination of the guardianship.

♦ *See Case 14-4*

14-2b   MENTAL ILLNESS OR DEFECT

A contract is a consensual transaction; therefore, for a contract to be valid, it is necessary that the parties have a certain level of mental capacity. If a person lacks such mental capacity (is mentally incompetent), he may avoid liability under the agreement (because the contract is **voidable**).

Under the traditional, cognitive ability test, a person is mentally incompetent if he is unable to comprehend the subject of the contract, its nature, and probable consequences. To avoid the contract, he need not be proved permanently mentally incompetent, but his mental defect must be something more than a weakness of intellect or a lack of average intelligence. In short, a person is competent unless he is unable to understand the nature and effect of his act in entering a contract. Restatement, Section 15. A mentally incompetent person may disaffirm the contract even if the other party did not know, or had no reason to know, of the incompetent's mental condition.

A second type of mental incompetence recognized by the Restatement of Contracts and some States is a mental condition that impairs a person's ability to act in a reasonable manner. Section 15. In other words, the person understands what he is doing but cannot control his behavior in order to act in a reasonable and rational way.

The newly adopted Restatement of Restitution provides that a transfer by a person lacking mental capacity is subject to rescission unless ratified. Upon disaffirmance by the mentally incompetent person, the other party to the contract is liable in restitution as necessary to avoid unjust enrichment. If the other party has dealt with the mentally incompetent person in good faith on reasonable terms, rescission leaves the mentally incompetent person liable in restitution for benefits the mentally incompetent person received in the transaction. Section 33.

Like minors and persons under guardianship, an incompetent person is liable for necessaries furnished him on the principle of quasi contract, the amount of recovery being the reasonable value of the goods or services. Moreover, an incompetent person may ratify or disaffirm his voidable contracts when he becomes competent or during a lucid period.

Practical Advice

If you have doubts about the capacity of the other party to a contract, have an individual with full legal capacity cosign the contract.

14-3 Intoxicated Persons

A person may avoid any contract that he enters into if the other party has reason to know that, because of intoxication, he is unable either to understand the nature and consequences of his actions or to act in a reasonable manner. Restatement, Section 16. Such contracts are voidable, although they may be ratified when the intoxicated person regains his capacity. Slight intoxication will not destroy one's contractual capacity, but neither is it essential that one be so drunk as to be totally without reason or understanding.

The effect of intoxication on contractual capacity is similar to that accorded contracts that are voidable because of the second type of incompetency, although the courts are even more strict with contracts a party enters while intoxicated, given the idea that the condition is voluntary. Most courts, therefore, require that the intoxicated person on regaining his capacity must act promptly to disaffirm and must generally offer to restore the consideration received. Individuals who are taking

FIGURE 14-1 Incapacity: Minors, Nonadjudicated Incompetents, and Intoxicated Persons

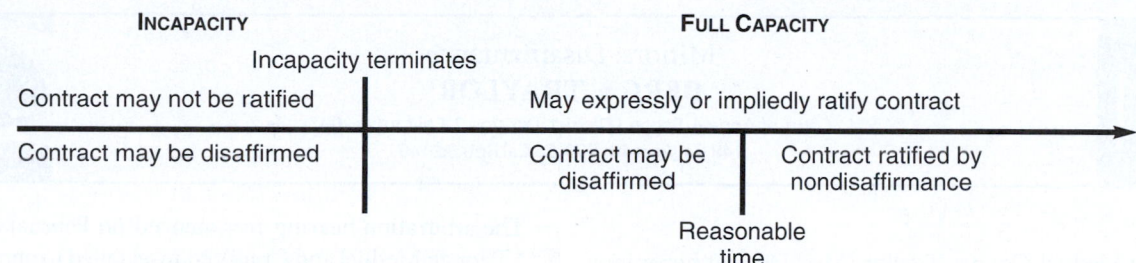

prescribed medication or who are involuntarily intoxicated are treated the same as those who are incompetent under the cognitive ability test. As with incompetent persons, intoxicated persons are liable in quasi contract for necessaries furnished them during their incapacity.

♦ **SEE FIGURE 14-1:** *Incapacity: Minors, Nonadjudicated Incompetents, and Intoxicated Persons*

♦ *See Case 14-4*

C H A P T E R   S U M M A R Y

MINORS	**Definition** persons who are under the age of majority (usually 18 years) **Liability on Contracts** a minor's contracts are voidable at the minor's option • *Disaffirmance* avoidance of the contract; may be done during minority and for a reasonable time after reaching majority • *Restitution* a minor who has disaffirmed a contract is entitled to restitution from the other party for any benefit the minor has conferred on the other party; the courts differ regarding the obligation of the minor to make restitution to the other party • *Ratification* affirmation of the entire contract; may be done upon reaching majority **Liability for Necessaries** a minor is liable for the reasonable value of necessary items (those that reasonably supply a person's needs) **Liability for Misrepresentation of Age** prevailing view is that a minor may disaffirm the contract **Liability for Tort Connected with Contract** a minor is not liable in tort if a tort and a contract are so intertwined that to enforce the tort the court must enforce the contract
INCOMPETENT AND INTOXICATED PERSONS	**Person Under Guardianship** a contract made by a mentally incompetent person placed under guardianship by court order is void **Mental Illness or Defect** a contract entered into by a nonadjudicated mentally incompetent person (one who is unable to understand the nature and consequences of his acts) is voidable **Intoxicated Persons** a contract entered into by an intoxicated person (one who cannot understand the nature and consequence of her actions) is voidable

C A S E S

Minors: Disaffirmance
BERG v. TRAYLOR
Court of Appeal, Second District, Division 2, California, 2007
148 Cal.App.4th 809, 56 Cal.Rptr.3d 140

Todd, J.

Appellants Meshiel Cooper Traylor (Meshiel) and her minor son Craig Lamar Traylor (Craig) appeal the judgment confirming an arbitration award in favor of Craig's former personal manager, respondent Sharyn Berg (Berg), for unpaid commissions under a contract between Berg, Meshiel and Craig and unrepaid loans from Berg. * * *

On January 18, 1999, Berg entered into a two-page "Artist's Manager's Agreement" (agreement) with Meshiel and Craig, who was then 10 years old. Meshiel signed the agreement and wrote Craig's name on the signature page where he was designated "Artist." Craig did not sign the agreement. Pursuant to the agreement, Berg was to act as Craig's exclusive personal manager in exchange for a commission of 15 percent of all gross monies or other consideration paid to him as an artist during the three-year term of the agreement, as well as income from merchandising or promotional efforts or offers of employment made during the term of the agreement, regardless of when Craig received such monies. The agreement expressly provided that any action Craig "may take in the future pertaining to disaffirmance of this agreement, whether successful or not," would not affect Meshiel's liability for any commissions due Berg. The agreement also provided that any disputes concerning payment or interpretation of the agreement would be determined by arbitration in accordance with the rules of Judicial Arbitration and Mediation Services, Inc. (JAMS).

On or about June 13, 2001, Craig obtained a recurring acting role on the Fox Television Network show "Malcolm in the Middle" (show). On September 11, 2001, four months prior to the expiration of the agreement, Meshiel sent a certified letter to Berg stating that while she and Craig appreciated her advice and guidance, they no longer needed her management services and could no longer afford to pay Berg her 15 percent commission because they owed a "huge amount" of taxes. On September 28, 2001, Berg responded, informing appellants that they were in breach of the agreement.

* * *

In 2004, Berg filed suit against Meshiel and Craig for breach of the agreement, breach of the implied covenant of good faith and fair dealing, breach of an oral loan agreement, conversion and declaratory relief. * * *

* * *

The arbitration hearing commenced on February 7, 2005. * * * Though Meshiel and Craig's counsel failed to appear at the hearing, Meshiel personally appeared with Craig's talent agent, Steven Rice. Craig did not appear. * * *

On February 11, 2005, the arbitrator issued his award, which was served on the parties on February 14, 2005. * * * The arbitrator awarded Berg commissions and interest of $154,714.15, repayment of personal loans and interest of $5,094, and attorney fees and costs of $13,762. He also awarded Berg $405,000 "for future earnings projected on a minimum of 6 years for national syndication earnings," and stated that this part of the award would "vest and become final, as monies earned after February 7, 2005, become due and payable." * * *

[The defendants then filed a petition with the State trial court to vacate the arbitration award. Following a hearing, the trial court entered a judgment in favor of Berg against Meshiel and Craig consistent with the arbitrator's award.]

* * *

Simply stated, one who provides a minor with goods and services does so at her own risk. [Citation.] The agreement here expressly contemplated this risk, requiring that Meshiel remain obligated for commissions due under the agreement regardless of whether Craig disaffirmed the agreement. Thus, we have no difficulty in reaching the conclusion that Craig is permitted to and did disaffirm the agreement and any obligations stemming therefrom, while Meshiel remains liable under the agreement and resulting judgment. Where our difficulty lies is in understanding how counsel, the arbitrator, and the trial court repeatedly and systematically ignored Craig's interests in this matter. From the time Meshiel signed the agreement, her interests were not aligned with Craig's. That no one—counsel, the arbitrator, or the trial court—recognized this conflict and sought appointment of a guardian *ad litem* for Craig is nothing short of stunning. It is the court's responsibility to protect the rights of a minor who is a litigant in court. [Citation.]

* * *

"As a general proposition, parental consent is required for the provision of services to minors for the simple reason that minors may disaffirm their own contracts to acquire such services." [Citation.] According to Family Code section 6700, "a minor may make a contract in the same manner as an adult, subject to the power of disaffirmance" * * * In turn, Family Code section 6710 states: "Except as otherwise provided by statute, a contract of a minor may be disaffirmed by the minor before majority or within a reasonable time afterwards or, in case of the minor's death within that period, by the minor's heirs or personal representative." Sound policy considerations support this provision:

> The law shields minors from their lack of judgment and experience and under certain conditions vests in them the right to disaffirm their contracts. Although in many instances such disaffirmance may be a hardship upon those who deal with an infant, the right to avoid his contracts is conferred by law upon a minor "for his protection against his own improvidence and the designs of others." It is the policy of the law to protect a minor against himself and his indiscretions and immaturity as well as against the machinations of other people and to discourage adults from contracting with an infant. Any loss occasioned by the disaffirmance of a minor's contract might have been avoided by declining to enter into the contract. [Citation.]

Berg offers two reasons why the plain language of Family Code section 6710 is inapplicable, neither of which we find persuasive. First, she argues that a minor may not disaffirm an agreement signed by a parent. * * * [This is not in accord with the law as stated in numerous cases.]

Second, Berg argues that Craig cannot disaffirm the agreement because it was for his and his family's necessities. Family Code section 6712 provides that a valid contract cannot be disaffirmed by a minor if all of the following requirements are met: the contract is to pay the reasonable value of things necessary for the support of the minor or the minor's family, the things have actually been furnished to the minor or the minor's family, and the contract is entered into by the minor when not under the care of a parent or guardian able to provide for the minor or the minor's family. These requirements are not met here. The agreement was not a contract to pay for the necessities of life for Craig or his family. While such necessities

have been held to include payment for lodging [citation] and even payment of attorneys' fees [citation], we cannot conclude that a contract to secure personal management services for the purpose of advancing Craig's acting career constitutes payment for the type of necessity contemplated by Family Code section 6712. Nor is there any evidence that Meshiel was unable to provide for the family in 1999 at the time of the agreement. As such, Family Code section 6712 does not bar the minor's disaffirmance of the contract.

No specific language is required to communicate an intent to disaffirm. "A contract (or conveyance) of a minor may be avoided by any act or declaration disclosing an unequivocal intent to repudiate its binding force and effect." [Citation.] Express notice to the other party is unnecessary. [Citation.] We find that the "Notice of Disaffirmance of Arbitration Award by Minor" filed on August 8, 2005 was sufficient to constitute a disaffirmance of the agreement by Craig. * * *

We find that Craig was entitled to and did disaffirm the agreement which, among other things, required him to arbitrate his disputes with Berg. On this basis alone, therefore, the judgment confirming the arbitration award must be reversed.

* * *

Appellants do not generally distinguish their arguments between mother and son, apparently assuming that if Craig disaffirms the agreement and judgment, Meshiel would be permitted to escape liability as well. But a disaffirmance of an agreement by a minor does not operate to terminate the contractual obligations of the parent who signed the agreement. [Citation.] The agreement Meshiel signed provided that Craig's disaffirmance would not serve to void or avoid Meshiel's obligations under the agreement and that Meshiel remained liable for commissions due Berg regardless of Craig's disaffirmance. Accordingly, we find no basis for Meshiel to avoid her independent obligations under the agreement.

The judgment is reversed as to Craig and affirmed as to Meshiel.

CASE 14-2

Minors: Ratification
IN RE THE SCORE BOARD, INC.
United States District Court, D. New Jersey, 1999
238 B.R. 585

Irenas, J.
During the Spring of 1996, Appellant Kobe Bryant ("Bryant"), then a seventeen-year old star high school basketball player, declared his intention to forego college and enter the 1996 lottery draft of the National Basketball Association. On May 8, 1996, The Score Board Inc. ("Debtor"), then a New Jersey based company in the business of licensing, manufacturing and

distributing sports and entertainment-related memorabilia, contacted Bryant's Agent, Arn Tellem ("Tellem" or "Agent") in anticipation of making a deal with Bryant.

* * *

In early July 1996, after the above [initial] negotiations, Debtor prepared and forwarded a signed written licensing agreement ("agreement") to Bryant. The agreement granted

Debtor the right to produce licensed products, such as trading cards, with Bryant's image. Bryant was obligated to make two personal appearances on behalf of Debtor and provide between a minimum of 15,000 and a maximum of 32,500 autographs. Bryant was to receive a $2.00 stipend for each autograph, after the first 7,500. Under the agreement, Bryant could receive a maximum of $75,000 for the autographs.

In addition to being compensated for the autographs, Bryant was entitled to receive base compensation of $10,000. Moreover, Debtor agreed to pay Bryant $5,000, of the $10,000, within ten days following receipt of the fully executed agreement. Finally, Bryant was entitled to a $5,000 bonus if he returned the agreement within six weeks.

Bryant rejected the above agreement, and on July 11, 1996, while still a minor, Bryant made a counter-offer ("counteroffer"), signed it and returned it to Debtor. The counter-offer made several changes to Debtor's agreement, including the number of autographs. Bryant also changed the number of prepaid autographs from 7,500 to 500.

Balser claimed that he signed the counter-offer and placed it into his files. The copy signed by Debtor was subsequently misplaced, however, and has never been produced by Debtor during these proceedings. Rather, Debtor has produced a copy signed only by Bryant.

On August 23, 1996, Bryant turned eighteen. Three days later, Bryant deposited a check for $10,000 into his account from Debtor.

On or about September 1, 1996, Bryant began performing his obligations under the agreement, including autograph signing sessions and public appearances. He subsequently performed his contractual duties for about a year and a half.

By late 1997, Bryant grew reluctant to sign any more autographs under the agreement and his Agent came to the conclusion that a fully executed contract did not exist. By this time, Tellem became concerned with Debtor's financial condition because it failed to make certain payments to several other players. Debtor claims that the true motivation for Bryant's reluctance stems from his perception that he was becoming a "star" player, and that his autograph was "worth" more than $2.00.

* * *

On March 17, 1998, Debtor sent Bryant a check for $1,130 as compensation for unpaid autographs. Bryant alleges that he was entitled to $10,130, not $1,130. The Bankruptcy Court found that Bryant was owed $10,130 and the check for $1,130 was based on a miscalculation.

On March 18, 1998, Debtor filed a voluntary Chapter 11 bankruptcy petition. On March 23, 1998, Tellem returned the $1,130 check upon learning of Debtor's financial trouble. Included with the check was a letter that questioned the validity of the agreement between Bryant and Debtor.

* * * On April 20, 1998, Tellem stated that no contract existed because the counter-offer was never signed by Debtor and there was never a meeting of the minds. Tellem added that the counter-offer expired and that Kobe Bryant withdrew from the counter-offer.

Subsequently, Debtor began to sell its assets, including numerous executory contracts with major athletes, including Bryant. Bryant argued that Debtor could not do this, because he believed that a contract never existed. In the alternative, if a contract was created, Bryant contended that it was voidable because it was entered into while he was a minor.

* * *

* * * On December 21, 1998, the Honorable Gloria M. Burns ruled in her memorandum opinion that Debtor accepted Bryant's counter-offer and, therefore, a valid contract existed between Bryant and Debtor. In the alternative, the Bankruptcy Court held that even if Bryant's counter-offer was not signed by Debtor, the parties' subsequent conduct demonstrated their acceptance of the contractual obligation by performance, thereby creating an enforceable contract. Judge Burns denied Bryant's claims of mutual mistake, infancy and his motion for stay relief.

* * *

On February 2, 1999, the Bankruptcy Court entered its final orders: (1) granting Debtor's motion to assume its executory contract with Bryant and assign it to Oxxford; and (2) overruling Bryant's objection to the sale.

* * *

Bryant challenges the Bankruptcy Court's finding that he ratified the agreement upon attaining majority. Contracts made during minority are voidable at the minor's election within a reasonable time after the minor attains the age of majority. [Citations]

The right to disaffirm a contract is subject to the infant's conduct which, upon reaching the age of majority, may amount to ratification. [Citation.] "Any conduct on the part of the former infant which evidences his decision that the transaction shall not be impeached is sufficient for this purpose." [Citation.]

On August 23, 1996, Bryant reached the age of majority, approximately six weeks after the execution of the agreement. On August 26, 1996, Bryant deposited the $10,000 check sent to him from Debtor. Bryant also performed his contractual duties by signing autographs.

The Bankruptcy Court did not presume ratification from inaction as Bryant asserts. It is clear that Bryant ratified the contract from the facts, because Bryant consciously performed his contractual duties.

Bryant asserts that he acted at the insistence of his Agent, who believed that he was obligated to perform by contract. Yet, neither Bryant nor his Agent disputed the existence of a contract until the March 23, 1998, letter by Tellem. That Bryant may have relied on his Agent is irrelevant to this Court's inquiry and is proper evidence only in a suit against the Agent. To the contrary, by admitting that he acted because he was under the belief that a contract existed, Bryant confirms the existence of the contract. Moreover, it was Bryant who deposited the check, signed the autographs, and made personal appearances.

* * *

For the above reasons, Bryant's appeal of the Bankruptcy Court's orders finding that a valid and enforceable contract exists is denied.

CASE 14-3

Minors: Liability for Necessaries
ZELNICK v. ADAMS
Supreme Court of Virginia, 2002
263 Va. 601, 561 S.E.2d 711

Lemons, J.

In this appeal, we consider whether a contract for legal services entered into on behalf of a minor is voidable upon a plea of infancy or subject to enforcement as an implied contract for necessaries and, if enforceable, the basis for determining value of services rendered.

Facts and Proceedings Below

Jonathan Ray Adams ("Jonathan") was born on April 5, 1980, the natural child of Mildred A. Adams ("Adams" or "mother") and Cecil D. Hylton, Jr. ("Hylton" or "father"). Jonathan's parents were never married to each other. On September 8, 1995, after highly contested litigation, an agreed order ("paternity order") was entered in Dade County, Florida, establishing Hylton's paternity of Jonathan.

Jonathan's grandfather, Cecil D. Hylton, Sr. ("Hylton Sr."), died testate [with a will] on August 25, 1989. His will established certain trusts and provided that the trustees had sole discretion to determine who qualified as "issue" under the will. * * *

The will created two separate trusts for Hylton Sr.'s grandchildren: the First Grandchildren's Charitable Trust and the Second Grandchildren's Charitable Trust ("the trusts"). Hylton Sr.'s grandchildren and great grandchildren would potentially receive distributions from the trusts in the years 2014 and 2021.

* * *

On July 11, 1996, Adams met with an attorney, Robert J. Zelnick ("Zelnick"), about protecting Jonathan's interest as a beneficiary of the trusts. She had received information leading her to believe that distributions were being made from the trusts to some of Hylton Sr.'s grandchildren. Adams told Zelnick that she contacted Jonathan's father about these alleged distributions, but she had not received a response from him. Adams explained that she had also contacted the law firm that had prepared Hylton Sr.'s will and the trustees, and no one would provide her any information about the distributions or whether the Estate would recognize Jonathan as a beneficiary. * * *

Adams explained that she could not afford to pay Zelnick's hourly fee and requested legal services on her son's behalf on a contingency fee basis. At the conclusion of the meeting, Zelnick told Adams that he was unsure whether he would take the case, but that he would investigate the matter.

Zelnick next spoke with Adams during a telephone conversation on July 18, 1996. He informed her that he had obtained a copy of the will and reviewed it, and that he was willing to accept the case "to help her have Jonathan declared a beneficiary of the estate." Adams went to Zelnick's office the next day, July 19, 1996, where Zelnick explained that the gross amount of the estate was very large. According to Zelnick, he "wanted to make sure that she had some understanding of the size of the estate before she entered into this agreement." * * * On July 19, 1996, Adams signed a retainer agreement ("the contract") for Zelnick's firm to represent Jonathan on a one-third contingency fee basis "in his claim against the estate of Cecil D. Hylton."

* * *

In May 1997, Zelnick filed a bill of complaint for declaratory judgment, accounting and other relief on Jonathan's behalf to have Jonathan recognized as the grandchild and "issue" of Hylton Sr. for the purposes of the will and trusts. * * * A consent decree was entered on January 23, 1998, which ordered that Jonathan was "declared to be the grandchild and issue of Cecil D. Hylton" and was "entitled to all bequests, devises, distributions and benefits under the Last Will and Testament of Cecil D. Hylton and the trusts created thereunder that inure to the benefit of the grandchildren and issue of Cecil D. Hylton."

In March 1998, Jonathan's father brought a bill of complaint for declaratory judgment against Adams and Zelnick, on Jonathan's behalf, to have the contract with Zelnick declared void. Upon reaching the age of majority, Jonathan filed a petition to intervene, wherein he disaffirmed the contract. * * *

On April 6, 2000, Jonathan filed a motion for summary judgment. He asserted that the contract was "void as a matter of law" because it was not a contract for necessaries. Jonathan argued that the 1997 suit was unnecessary due to the Florida paternity decree which conclusively established Hylton's paternity. He further argued that the 1997 suit was unnecessary because the trusts could not distribute any funds until the years 2014 and 2021 and the issue was not "ripe for determination." Finally, Jonathan claimed that the contingency fee agreement was unreasonable.

The trial court granted Jonathan's motion for summary judgment and ruled that the contingency fee agreement was void. The trial court held that the contract was not binding on Jonathan because he was "in his minority" when the contract was executed. Furthermore, according to the trial court, the doctrine of necessaries did not apply to the contract

"because the matter could have been adjudicated after the majority of [Jonathan], who was within a few years of his majority at the time that all of this came out."

Nonetheless, the trial court held that Zelnick was entitled to a fee under the theory of quantum meruit. * * * Zelnick testified that he spent approximately 150 to 200 hours on the case, and that in 1996–1997, his hourly rate was $200 an hour. * * *

The trial court entered judgment in favor of Zelnick in the amount of $60,000 * * * Both Zelnick and Jonathan have appealed the judgment of the trial court. * * *

Analysis
* * *

Under well and long-established Virginia law, a contract with an infant is not void, only voidable by the infant upon attaining the age of majority. [Citation.] This oft-cited rule is subject to the relief provided by the doctrine of necessaries which received thorough analysis in the case of *Bear's Adm'x v. Bear*, [citation].

In *Bear*, we explained that when a court is faced with a defense of infancy, the court has the initial duty to determine, as a matter of law, whether the "things supplied" to the infant under a contract may fall within the general class of necessaries. [Citation.] The court must further decide whether there is sufficient evidence to allow the finder of fact to determine whether the "things supplied" were in fact necessary in the instant case. If either of these preliminary inquiries is answered in the negative, the party who provided the goods or services to the infant under the disaffirmed contract cannot recover. If the preliminary inquiries are answered in the affirmative, then the finder of fact must decide, under all the circumstances, whether the "things supplied" were actually necessary to the "position and condition of the infant." If so, the party who provided the goods or services to the infant is entitled to the "reasonable value" of the things furnished. In contracts for necessaries, an infant is not bound on the express contract, but rather is bound under an implied contract to pay what the goods or services furnished were reasonably worth. [Citation.]

"[T]hings supplied," which fall into the class of necessaries, include "board, clothing and education." [Citation.] Things that are "necessary to [an infant's] subsistence and comfort, and to enable [an infant] to live according to his real position in society" are also considered part of the class of necessaries. [Citation.] * * *

Certainly, the provision of legal services may fall within the class of necessaries for which a contract by or on behalf of an infant may not be avoided or disaffirmed on the grounds of infancy. Generally, contracts for legal services related to prosecuting personal injury actions, and protecting an infant's personal liberty, security, or reputation are considered contracts for necessaries. [Citation.] "Whether attorney's services are to be considered necessaries or not depends on whether or not there is a necessity therefor. If such necessity exists, the infant may be bound. * * * If there is no necessity for services, there can be no recovery" for the services. [Citation.]

The Supreme Court of Appeals of West Virginia recently addressed this issue in a paternity action against the estate of an infant's father, brought by the infant's mother on the infant's behalf. [Citation.] The court held that contracts for legal services by infants should be regarded as contracts for necessaries in some instances because "if minors are not required to pay for legal representation, they will not be able to protect their various interests." [Citation.]

Other states have also broadened the definition of "necessaries" to include contracts for legal services for the protection of an infant's property rights. * * *

* * * The ultimate determination is an issue of fact. The trier of fact must conclude that "under all the circumstances, the things furnished were actually necessary to the position and condition of the infant * * * and whether the infant was already sufficiently supplied." [Citation.] If the contract does not fall within the "general classes of necessaries," the trial court must, as a matter of law, sustain the plea of infancy and permit the avoidance of the contract. Similarly, if the contract does fall within the "general classes of necessaries," but upon consideration of all of the circumstances, the trier of fact determines that the provision of the particular services or things was not actually necessary, the plea of infancy must be sustained. Where there is a successful avoidance of the contract, the trial court may not circumvent the successful plea of infancy by affording a recovery to the claimant on the theory of quantum meruit. However, if the plea of infancy is not sustained, the claimant is not entitled to enforcement of the express contract. Rather, as we have previously held, "even in contracts for necessaries, the infant is not bound on the express contract but on the implied contract to pay what they are reasonably worth." [Citation.]

* * *

Upon review of the record, we hold that the * * * reason stated by the trial court for holding that the necessaries doctrine did not apply, namely that the contract "was conducted while he was in his minority and he's not bound by that," is an error of law. We hold that a contract for legal services is within the "general classes of necessaries" that may defeat a plea of infancy. * * *

* * *

The trial court's determination that the necessaries doctrine did not apply was made upon motion for summary judgment filed by Jonathan. Nowhere in Jonathan's motion for summary judgment is the issue raised that the services were unnecessary at the time rendered. * * * Although Jonathan argues that the services were not necessary at all because he alleges that the Florida litigation resolved the question of his inclusion as a beneficiary under the will of Hylton Sr., the timing of the services was not even mentioned as an issue, much less as a reason for granting summary judgment. * * *

Because the trial court erred in its determination, on this record, on summary judgment, that the doctrine of necessaries did not apply, we will reverse the judgment of the trial court and remand for further proceedings, including the taking of evidence on the issue of the factual determination of necessity "under all of the circumstances." Consistent with this opinion, should the trial court upon remand hold that the doctrine of necessaries does not apply because the evidence adduced does not support the claim, the contract is avoided and no award shall be made.

Should the trial court upon remand hold that the evidence is sufficient to defeat Jonathan's plea of infancy, the trial court shall receive evidence of the reasonable value of the services rendered. * * *

Reversed and remanded.

CASE 14-4

Intoxicated Persons/Incompetent Persons
FIRST STATE BANK OF SINAI v. HYLAND
Supreme Court of South Dakota, 1987
399 N.W.2d 894

Henderson, J.

[Randy Hyland, unable to pay two promissory notes due September 19, 1981, negotiated with The First State Bank of Sinai (Bank) for an extension. The Bank agreed on the condition that Randy's father, Mervin, act as cosigner. Mervin, a good customer of the Bank, had executed and paid on time over sixty promissory notes within a seven-year period. Accordingly, the Bank drafted a new promissory note with an April 20, 1982, due date, which Randy took home for Mervin to sign. On April 20, 1982, the new note was unpaid. Randy, on May 5, 1982, brought the Bank a check signed by Mervin to cover the interest owed on the unpaid note and asked for another extension. The Bank agreed to a second extension, again on the condition that Mervin act as cosigner. Mervin, however, refused to sign the last note; and Randy subsequently declared bankruptcy. The Bank sued Mervin on December 19, 1982. Mervin responded that he was not liable since he had been incapacitated by liquor at the time he signed the note. He had been drinking heavily throughout this period, and in fact had been involuntarily committed to an alcoholism treatment hospital twice during the time of these events. In between commitments, however, Mervin had executed and paid his own promissory note with the Bank and had transacted business in connection with his farm. The trial court held that Mervin's contract as cosigner was void due to alcohol-related incapacity, and the Bank appealed.]

Historically, the void contract concept has been applied to nullify agreements made by mental incompetents who have

contracted * * * after a judicial determination of incapacity had been entered. [Citations.] * * *

Mervin had numerous and prolonged problems stemming from his inability to handle alcohol. However, he was not judicially declared incompetent during the note's signing. * * *

* * *

Contractual obligations incurred by intoxicated persons may be voidable. [Citation.] Voidable contracts (contracts other than those entered into following a judicial determination of incapacity * * *) may be rescinded by the previously disabled party. [Citation.] However, disaffirmance must be prompt, upon the recovery of the intoxicated party's mental abilities, and upon his notice of the agreement, if he had forgotten it. [Citation.] * * *

A voidable contract may also be ratified by the party who had contracted while disabled. Upon ratification, the contract becomes a fully valid legal obligation. [Citation.] Ratification can either be express or implied by conduct. [Citations.] In addition, failure of a party to disaffirm a contract over a period of time may, by itself, ripen into a ratification, especially if rescission will result in prejudice to the other party. [Citations.]

Mervin received both verbal notice from Randy and written notice from Bank on or about April 27, 1982, that the note was overdue. On May 5, 1982, Mervin paid the interest owing with a check which Randy delivered to Bank. This by itself could amount to ratification through conduct. If Mervin wished to avoid the contract, he should have then exercised his right of rescission. We find it impossible to believe that Mervin paid almost $900 in interest without, in his own mind, accepting responsibility for the note. His assertion that paying interest on the note relieved his obligation is equally untenable in light of his numerous past experiences with promissory notes.

* * *

We conclude that Mervin's obligation to Bank is not void. * * * Mervin's obligation on the note was voidable and his subsequent failure to disaffirm (lack of rescission) and his payment of interest (ratification) then transformed the voidable contract into one that is fully binding upon him. We reverse and remand.

QUESTIONS

1. Michael, a minor, operates a one-man automobile repair shop. Anderson, having heard of Michael's good work on other cars, takes her car to Michael's shop for a thorough engine overhaul. Michael, while overhauling Anderson's engine, carelessly fits an unsuitable piston ring on one of the pistons, with the result that Anderson's engine is seriously damaged. Michael offers to return the sum that Anderson paid him for his work but refuses to pay for the damage. Can Anderson recover from Michael in tort for the damage to her engine? Why or why not?

2. Explain the outcome of each of the following transactions.

    a. On March 20, Andy Small became seventeen years old, but he appeared to be at least twenty-one. On April 1, he moved into a rooming house in Chicago where he orally agreed to pay the landlady $300 a month for room and board, payable at the end of each month. On April 30, he refused to pay his landlady for his room and board for the month of April.

    b. On April 4, he went to Honest Hal's Carfeteria and signed a contract to buy a used car on credit with a small down payment. He made no representation as to his age, but Honest Hal represented the car to be in A-1 condition, which it subsequently turned out not to be. On April 25, he returned the car to Honest Hal and demanded a refund of his down payment.

    c. On April 7, Andy sold and conveyed to Adam Smith a parcel of real estate that he owned. On April 28, he demanded that Adam Smith reconvey the land although the purchase price, which Andy received in cash, had been spent in riotous living.

3. Jones, a minor, owned a 2019 automobile. She traded it to Stone for a 2020 car. Jones went on a three-week trip and found that the 2020 car was not as good as the 2019 car. She asked Stone to return the 2019 car but was told that it had been sold to Tate. Jones thereupon sued Tate for the return of the 2019 car. Is Jones entitled to regain ownership of the 2019 car? Explain.

4. On May 7, Roy, a minor, a resident of Smithton, purchased an automobile from Royal Motors, Inc., for $18,750 in cash. On the same day, he bought a motor scooter from Marks, also a minor, for $750 and paid him in full. On June 5, two days before attaining his majority, Roy disaffirmed the contracts and offered to return the car and the motor scooter to the respective sellers. Royal Motors and Marks each refused the offers. On June 16, Roy brought separate appropriate actions against Royal Motors and Marks to recover the purchase price of the car and the motor scooter. By agreement on July 30, Royal Motors accepted the automobile. Royal then filed a counterclaim against Roy for the reasonable rental value of the car between June 5 and July 30. The car was not damaged during this period. Royal knew that Roy lived twenty-five miles from his place of employment in Smithton and that he would probably drive the car, as he did, to provide himself transportation. Decision as to

    a. Roy's action against Royal Motors, Inc., and its counterclaim against Roy; and

    b. Roy's action against Marks?

5. On October 1, George Jones entered into a contract with Johnson Motor Company, a dealer in automobiles, to buy a used car for $10,850. He paid $1,100 down and, under the agreement, was to make monthly payments thereafter of $325 each. Jones was seventeen years old at the time he made the contract, but he represented to the company that he was twenty-one years old because he was afraid that if the company knew his real age, it would not sell the car to him. His appearance was that of a man of twenty-one years of age. After making the first payment on November 1, he failed to make any more payments. On December 15, the company repossessed the car under the terms provided in the contract. By that time, the car had been damaged and needed repairs. On December 20, George Jones became of age and at once disaffirmed the contract and demanded the return of the $1,425 he had paid on it. On refusal of the company to do so, George Jones brought an action to recover the $1,425, and the company set up a counterclaim for $1,500 for expenses it incurred in repairing the car. Who will prevail? Why?

6. Rebecca entered into a written contract to sell certain real estate to Mary, a minor, for $80,000, payable $4,000 on the execution of the contract and $800 on the first day of each month thereafter until paid. Mary paid the $4,000 down payment and eight monthly installments before attaining her majority. Thereafter, Mary made two additional monthly payments and caused the contract to be recorded in the county where the real estate was located. Mary was then advised by her attorney that the contract was voidable. After being so advised, Mary immediately tendered the contract to Rebecca, together with a deed reconveying all of Mary's interest in the property to Rebecca. Also, Mary demanded that Rebecca return the money she had paid under the contract. Rebecca refused the tender and declined to repay any portion of the money paid to her by Mary. Can Mary cancel the contract and recover the amount paid to Rebecca? Explain.

7. Anita sold and delivered an automobile to Marvin, a minor. Marvin, during his minority, returned the automobile to Anita, saying that he disaffirmed the sale. Anita accepted the automobile and said she would return the purchase price to Marvin the next day. Later in the day, Marvin changed his mind, took the automobile without Anita's knowledge, and sold it to Chris. Anita had not returned the purchase price when Marvin took the car. On what theory, if any, can Anita recover from Marvin? Explain.

8. Ira, who in 2017 had been found innocent of a criminal offense because of insanity, was released from a hospital for the criminally insane during the summer of 2018 and since that time has been a reputable and well-respected citizen and businessperson. On February 1, 2019, Ira and Shirley entered into a contract by which Ira would sell his farm to Shirley for $100,000. Ira now seeks to void the contract. Shirley insists that Ira is fully competent and has no right to avoid the contract. Who will prevail? Why?

9. Daniel, while under the influence of alcohol, agreed to sell his used automobile to Belinda for $13,000. The next morning, when Belinda went to Daniel's house with the $13,000 in cash, Daniel stated that he did not remember the transaction but that "a deal is a deal." One week after completing the sale, Daniel decides that he wishes to avoid the contract. What result?

CASE PROBLEMS

10. Langstraat, age seventeen, owned a motorcycle that he insured against liability with Midwest Mutual Insurance Company. He signed a notice of rejection attached to the policy indicating that he did not desire to purchase uninsured motorists' coverage from the insurance company. Later he was involved in an accident with another motorcycle owned and operated by a party who was uninsured. Langstraat now seeks to recover from the insurance company, asserting that his rejection was not a valid rejection because he is a minor. Can Langstraat recover from Midwest? Explain.

11. G.A.S. married his wife, S.I.S., on January 19, 2009. He began to suffer mental health problems in 2015, during which year he was hospitalized at the Delaware State Hospital for eight weeks. Similar illnesses occurred in 2017 and the early part of 2019, with G.A.S. suffering from such symptoms as paranoia and loss of a sense of reality. In early 2020, G.A.S. was still committed to the Delaware State Hospital, attending a regular job during the day and returning to the hospital at night. During this time, he entered into a separation agreement prepared by his wife's attorney.

G.A.S., however, never spoke with the attorney about the contents of the agreement, nor did he read it prior to signing. Moreover, G.A.S. was not independently represented by counsel when he executed this agreement. Can G.A.S. disaffirm the separation agreement? Explain.

12. A fifteen-year-old minor was employed by Midway Toyota, Inc. On August 18, 2018, the minor, while engaged in lifting heavy objects, injured his lower back. In October 2018, he underwent surgery to remove a herniated disk. Midway Toyota paid him the appropriate amount of temporary total disability payments ($53.36 per week) from August 18, 2018, through November 15, 2019. In February 2020, a final settlement was reached for 150 weeks of permanent partial disability benefits totaling $6,136.40. Tom Mazurek represented Midway Toyota in the negotiations leading to the agreement and negotiated directly with the minor and his mother, Hermione Parrent. The final settlement agreement was signed by the minor only. Mrs. Parrent, who was present at the time, did not object to the signing, but neither she nor anyone else of "legal guardian status" co-signed the agreement. The minor later sought to disaffirm the agreement and reopen his workers' compensation case. The workers' compensation court denied his petition, holding that Mrs. Parrent "participated fully in consideration of the offered final settlement and ... ratified and approved it on

behalf of her ward to the same legal effect as if she had actually signed [it]." The minor appealed. Decision?

13. Rose, a minor, bought a new Buick Riviera from Sheehan Buick. Seven months later, while still a minor, he attempted to disaffirm the purchase. Sheehan Buick refused to accept the return of the car or to refund the purchase price. Rose, at the time of the purchase, gave all the appearance of being of legal age. The car had been used by him to carry on his school, business, and social activities. Can Rose successfully disaffirm the contract? Why or why not?

14. L. D. Robertson bought a pickup truck from King and Julian, doing business as the Julian Pontiac Company. Robertson, at the time of purchase, was seventeen years old, living at home with his parents and driving his father's truck around the county to different construction jobs. According to the sales contract, he traded in a passenger car for the truck and was given $2,723 credit toward the truck's $6,743 purchase price, agreeing to pay the remainder in monthly installments. After he paid the first month's installment, the truck caught fire and was rendered useless. The insurance agent, upon finding that Robertson was a minor, refused to deal with him. Consequently, Robertson sued to exercise his right as a minor to rescind the contract and to recover the purchase price he had already paid ($2,723 credit for the car plus the one month's installment). The defendants argue that Robertson, even as a minor, cannot rescind the contract as it was for a necessary item. Are they correct? Explain.

15. Haydocy Pontiac sold Jennifer Lee a used automobile for $21,552, of which $20,402 was financed with a note and security agreement. At the time of the sale Lee, age twenty, represented to Haydocy that she was twenty-one years old, the age of majority, and capable of contracting. After receiving the car, Lee allowed John Roberts to take possession of it. Roberts took the car and has not returned. Lee has failed to make any further payments on the car. Haydocy has sued to recover on the note, but Lee disaffirms the contract, claiming that she was too young to enter into a valid contract. Can Haydocy recover the money from Lee? Explain.

16. Carol White ordered a $225 pair of contact lenses through an optometrist. White, an emancipated minor, paid $100 by check and agreed to pay the remaining $125 at a later time. The doctor ordered the lenses, incurring a debt of $110. After the lenses were ordered, White called to cancel her order and stopped payment on the $100 check. The lenses could be used by no one but White. The doctor sued White for the value of the lenses. Will the doctor be able to recover the money from White? Explain.

17. Williamson, her mortgage in default, was threatened with foreclosure on her home. She decided to sell the house. The Matthewses learned of this and contacted her about the matter. Williamson claims that she offered to sell her equity for $17,000 and that the Matthewses agreed to pay off the mortgage. The Matthewses contend that the asking price was $1,700. On September 27, the parties signed a contract of sale, which stated the purchase price to be $1,800 (an increase of $100 to account for furniture in the house) plus the unpaid balance of the mortgage. The parties met again on October 10 to sign the deed. Later that day, Williamson, concerned that she had not received her full $17,000 consideration, contacted an attorney. Can Williamson set aside the sale based upon inadequate consideration and mental weakness due to intoxication? Explain.

18. Halbman, a minor, purchased a used car from Lemke for $11,250. Under the terms of the contract, Halbman would pay $1,000 down and the balance in $125 weekly installments. Upon making the down payment, Halbman received possession of the car, but Lemke retained the title until the balance was paid. After Halbman had made his first four payments, a connecting rod in the car's engine broke. Lemke denied responsibility but offered to help Halbman repair it if Halbman would provide the parts. Halbman, however, placed the car in a garage where the repairs cost $637.40. Halbman never paid the repair bill.

Hoping to avoid any liability for the vehicle, Lemke transferred title to Halbman even though Halbman never paid the balance owed. Halbman returned the title with a letter disaffirming the contract and demanded return of the money paid. Lemke refused. Because the repair bill remained unpaid, the garage removed the car's engine and transmission and towed the body to Halbman's father's house. Vandalism during the period of storage rendered the car unsalvageable. Several times Halbman requested Lemke to remove the car. Lemke refused. Halbman sued Lemke for the return of his consideration, and Lemke countersued for the amount still owed on the contract. Decision?

19. On June 11, Chagnon bought a used Buick from Keser for $9,950. Chagnon, who was then a minor, obtained the contract by falsely advising Keser that he was over the age of majority. On September 25, two months and four days after reaching his majority, Chagnon disaffirmed the contract and, ten days later, returned the Buick to Keser. He then brought suit to recover the money he had paid for the automobile. Keser counterclaimed that he suffered damages as the direct result of Chagnon's false representation of his age. A trial was

brought to the court, sitting without a jury, all of which culminated in a judgment in favor of Chagnon against Keser in the sum of $6,557.80. This particular sum was arrived at by the trial court in the following manner: the trial court found that Chagnon initially purchased the Buick for the sum of $9,950 and that he was entitled to the return of his $9,950; and then, by way of setoff, the trial court subtracted from the $9,950 the sum of $3,392.20, apparently representing the difference between the purchase price paid for the vehicle and the reasonable value of the Buick on October 5, the date when the Buick was returned to Keser. Is this legally correct? Do you agree? Why or why not?

20. On April 29, Kirsten Fletcher and John E. Marshall III jointly signed a lease to rent an apartment for the term beginning on July 1 and ending on June 30 of the following year, for a monthly rent of $525 per month. At the time the lease was signed, Marshall was not yet eighteen years of age. Marshall turned eighteen on May 30. Two weeks later, the couple moved into the apartment. About two months later, Marshall moved out to attend college, but Fletcher remained. She paid the rent herself for the remaining ten months of the lease and then sought contribution for Marshall's share of the rent plus court costs in the amount of $2,500. Can Fletcher collect from Marshall? Why or why not?

21. Rogers was a nineteen-year-old (the age of majority then being twenty-one) high school graduate pursuing a civil engineering degree when he learned that his wife was expecting a child. As a result, he quit school and sought assistance from Gastonia Personnel Corporation in finding a job. Rogers signed a contract with the employment agency providing that he would pay the agency a service charge if it obtained suitable employment for him. The employment agency found him such a job, but Rogers refused to pay the service charge, asserting that he was a minor when he signed the contract. Gastonia sued to recover the agreed-upon service charge from Rogers. Should Rogers be liable under his contract? If so, for how much?

22. On September 29, just under two weeks before his eighteenth birthday, Bagley, a highly skilled and experienced snowboarder, purchased a season pass from the Mt. Bachelor ski resort. Upon purchasing the season pass, he executed a release agreement as required by Mt. Bachelor. The significant portions of the release agreement were also printed on the pass. Beginning on November 18, *after* his eighteenth birthday, Bagley used his season pass to ride Mt. Bachelor's lifts at least 119 times over the course of twenty-six days spent snowboarding at the ski area. However, on February 16 of the following year, while snowboarding over a manmade jump in Mt. Bachelor's "air chamber" terrain park, Bagley sustained serious injuries resulting in permanent paralysis. Bagley sued Mt. Bachelor for negligence, claiming that he had timely disaffirmed the release agreement by notifying Mt. Bachelor of the injury. Mt. Bachelor argued that Bagley had manifested his intent to ratify (a) by failing to disaffirm the voidable release agreement within a reasonable period of time after reaching the age of majority and (b) by accepting the benefits of that agreement. Explain whether Bagley has ratified the contract.

TAKING SIDES

Joseph Eugene Dodson, age sixteen, purchased a used pickup truck from Burns and Mary Shrader. The Shraders owned and operated Shrader's Auto Sales. Dodson paid $14,900 in cash for the truck. At the time of sale, the Shraders did not question Dodson's age, but thought he was eighteen or nineteen. Dodson made no misrepresentation concerning his age. Nine months after the date of purchase, the truck began to develop mechanical problems. A mechanic diagnosed the problem as a burnt valve but could not be certain. Dodson, who could not afford the repairs, continued to drive the truck until one month later,

when the engine "blew up." Dodson parked the vehicle in the front yard of his parents' home and contacted the Shraders to rescind the purchase of the truck and to request a full refund.

a. What arguments would support Dodson's termination of the contract?

b. What arguments would support Shrader's position that the contract is not voidable?

c. Which side should prevail? Explain.

CHAPTER 15

Contracts in Writing

CHAPTER OUTCOMES

After reading and studying this chapter, you should be able to:

- Explain the five types of contracts covered by the general contract statute of frauds and the contracts covered by the Uniform Commercial Code (UCC) statute of frauds provision.

- Describe the writings that are required to satisfy the general contract and the UCC statute of frauds provisions.

- Describe the other methods of complying with the general contract and the UCC statute of frauds provisions.

- Explain the parol evidence rule and the situations to which the rule does not apply.

- Discuss the rules that aid in the interpretation of a contract.

An **oral** contract, that is, one not written, is in every way as enforceable as a written contract unless otherwise provided by statute. Although most contracts are not required to be in writing to be enforceable, it is highly desirable that significant contracts be written. Written contracts avoid the numerous problems that proving the terms of oral contracts inevitably involves. The process of setting down the contractual terms in a written document also tends to clarify the terms and to reveal problems the parties might not otherwise foresee. Moreover, the terms of a written contract do not change over time, while the parties' recollections of the terms might.

When the parties do reduce their agreement to a complete and final written expression, the law (under the parol evidence rule) honors this document by not allowing the parties to introduce any evidence in a lawsuit that would alter, modify, or vary the terms of the written contract. Nevertheless, the parties may differ as to the proper or intended meaning of language contained in the written agreement where such language is ambiguous or susceptible to different interpretations. To ascertain the proper meaning requires an interpretation, or construction, of the contract. The rules of construction permit the parties to introduce evidence to resolve ambiguity and to show the meaning of the language employed and the sense in which both parties used it.

This chapter examines (1) the types of contracts that must be in writing to be enforceable, (2) the parol evidence rule, and (3) the rules of contractual interpretation.

STATUTE OF FRAUDS

Compliance with the statute of frauds requires a writing signed by the party to be charged (the party against whom the contract is to be enforced). The original statute became law in 1677, when the English Parliament adopted "An Act for Prevention of Frauds and Perjuries," commonly referred to as the statute of frauds. From the early days of U.S. history, practically every State had and continues to have a statute of frauds patterned upon the original English statute.

The statute of frauds has no relation whatever to any kind of fraud practiced in the making of contracts. The common law rules relating to such fraud are discussed in *Chapter 11.* The purpose of the statute is to prevent perjured testimony in court from creating fraud in the proof of certain oral contracts, which purpose the statute accomplishes by requiring that certain contracts be evidenced by a signed writing. On the other hand, the statute does not prevent the performance of oral contracts if the parties are willing to perform. In brief, the statute relates only to the proof or evidence of a contract. It has nothing to do with the circumstances surrounding the making of a contract or with a contract's validity.

Practical Advice

Significant contracts should be memorialized in a writing signed by both parties.

15-1 Contracts within the Statute of Frauds

Many more types of contracts are not subject to the statute of frauds than are subject to it. Most oral contracts, as previously indicated, are as enforceable and valid as a written contract. If, however, a given contract is subject to the statute of frauds, the contract is said to be **within** the statute; to be enforceable, it must comply with the statute's requirements. All other types of contracts are said to be "not within" or "outside" the statute and need not comply with its requirements to be enforceable.

The following kinds of contracts are within the original English statute and remain within most State statutes; compliance requires a writing signed by the party to be charged (the party against whom the contract is to be enforced).

A sixth type of contract within the statute applied to contracts for the sale of goods. Section 2–201 of the Uniform Commercial Code (UCC) now governs the enforceability of contracts of this kind.

1. Promises to answer for the duty of another
2. Promises of an executor or administrator to answer personally for a duty of the decedent whose funds he is administering
3. Agreements upon consideration of marriage
4. Agreements for the transfer of an interest in land
5. Agreements not to be performed within one year

The various provisions of the statute of frauds apply independently. Accordingly, a contract for the sale of an interest in land also may be a contract in consideration of marriage, a contract not to be performed in one year, *and* a contract for the sale of goods.

In addition to those contracts specified in the original statute, most States require that other contracts be evidenced by a writing as well; for example, a contract to make a will, to authorize an agent to sell or purchase real estate, or to pay a commission to a real estate broker. Moreover, the original Article 1 of the UCC requires that a contract for the sale of securities, contracts creating certain types of security interests, and contracts for the sale of other personal property for more than $5,000 also be in writing. However, the 2001 Revision to Article 1, adopted by all fifty States, has deleted this requirement.

15-1a ELECTRONIC RECORDS

One significant impediment to e-commerce has been the questionable enforceability of contracts entered into through electronic means such as the Internet or e-mail because of the writing requirements under contract and sales law (statute of frauds). In response, the **Uniform Electronic Transactions Act (UETA)** was promulgated by the Uniform Law Commission (ULC) in July 1999 and has been adopted by forty-eight States. As of March 2021, two States had not adopted the UETA (Illinois and New York), but each of these States has a statute recognizing electronic signatures. In 2021, legislation to adopt the UETA was introduced in Illinois. UETA applies only to transactions between parties each of which has agreed to conduct transactions by electronic means. It gives full effect to electronic contracts, encouraging their widespread use, and develops a uniform legal framework for their implementation. UETA protects electronic signatures and contracts from being denied enforcement because of the statute of frauds. Section 7 of UETA accomplishes this by providing the following:

1. A record or signature may not be denied legal effect or enforceability solely because it is in electronic form.
2. A contract may not be denied legal effect or enforceability solely because an electronic record was used in its formation.
3. If a law requires a record to be in writing, an electronic record satisfies the law.
4. If a law requires a signature, an electronic signature satisfies the law.

Section 14 of UETA further validates contracts formed by machines functioning as electronic agents for parties to a transaction: "A contract may be formed by the interaction of electronic agents of the parties, even if no individual was aware of or reviewed the electronic agents' actions or the resulting terms and agreements." The Act excludes from its coverage wills, codicils, and testamentary trusts as well as all Articles of the UCC except Articles 2 and 2A.

In addition, Congress in 2000 enacted the **Electronic Signatures in Global and National Commerce (E-Sign) Act**. The Act, which uses language very similar to that of UETA, makes electronic records and signatures valid and enforceable across the United States for many types of transactions in or affecting interstate or foreign commerce. E-Sign does not generally preempt UETA. E-Sign does not require any person to agree to use or accept electronic records or electronic signatures. The Act defines transactions quite broadly to include the sale, lease, exchange, and licensing of personal property and services, as well as the sale, lease, exchange, or other disposition of any interest in real property. E-Sign defines an electronic record as "a contract or other record created, generated, sent, communicated, received, or stored by electronic means." It defines an electronic signature as "an electronic sound, symbol, or process, attached to or logically associated with a contract or other record and executed or adopted by a person with the intent to sign the record." Like UETA, E-Sign ensures that Internet and e-mail agreements will not be unenforceable because of the statute of frauds. It does so by providing that

1. a signature, contract, or other record relating to such transaction may not be denied legal effect, validity, or enforceability solely because it is in electronic form; and

2. a contract relating to such transaction may not be denied legal effect, validity, or enforceability solely because an electronic signature or electronic record was used in its formation.

To protect consumers, E-Sign provides that they must consent *electronically* to conducting transactions with electronic records after being informed of the types of hardware and software required. Prior to consent, consumers must also receive a "clear and conspicuous" statement informing consumers of their right to (1) have the record provided on paper or in nonelectronic form; (2) after consenting to electronic records, receive paper copies of the electronic record; and (3) withdraw consent to receiving electronic records.

As defined by E-Sign, an electronic agent is a computer program or other automated means used independently to initiate an action or respond to electronic records or performances in whole or in part without review or action by an individual at the time of the action or response. The Act validates contracts or other records relating to a transaction in or affecting interstate or foreign commerce formed by electronic agents so long as the action of each electronic agent is legally attributable to the person to be bound.

E-Sign specifically excludes certain transactions, including (1) wills, codicils, and testamentary trusts; (2) adoptions, divorces, and other matters of family law; and (3) transactions governed by the UCC other than sales and leases of goods.

The United Nations Commission on International Trade Law (UNCITRAL) was established by the U.N. General Assembly to further the progressive harmonization and unification of the law of international trade. The Commission is composed of sixty member States elected by the General Assembly and is structured to be representative of the world's various geographic regions and its principal economic and legal systems. One of its primary functions is to develop conventions, model laws, and rules that are acceptable worldwide.

In 1996, the United Nations Commission on International Trade Law (UNCITRAL) adopted the Model Law on Electronic Commerce to facilitate the use of modern means of communications and storage of information. Legislation based on or influenced by it has been adopted in at least seventy-two nations, and in the United States, it has influenced the Uniform Electronic Transactions Act. In 2001, the UNCITRAL Model Law on Electronic Signatures was adopted to bring additional legal certainty regarding the use of electronic signatures.

Following a technology-neutral approach, the Act establishes a presumption that electronic signatures, which meet certain criteria of technical reliability, shall be treated as equivalent to handwritten signatures. Legislation based on or influenced by it has been adopted in at least thirty-three nations.

15-1b SURETYSHIP PROVISION

The **suretyship** provision applies to a contractual promise by a surety (*promisor*) to a **creditor** (*promisee*) to perform the duties or obligations of a third person (**principal debtor**) if the principal debtor does not perform. Thus, if a mother tells a merchant to extend $1,000 worth of credit to her son and says, "If he doesn't pay, I will," the promise must be in writing (or have a sufficient electronic record) to be enforceable. The factual situation can be reduced to the simple statement "If X doesn't pay, I will." The promise is said to be **collateral**, in that the promisor is not primarily liable. The mother does not promise to pay in any event; her promise is to pay only if the one primarily obligated, her son, defaults.

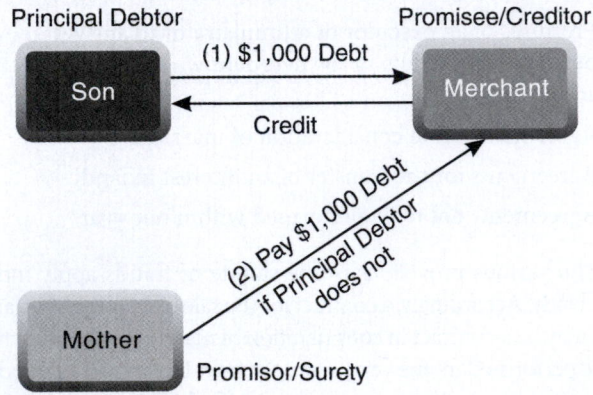

The rule applies only to cases involving three parties and two contracts. The primary contract, between the principal debtor and the creditor, creates the indebtedness. The collateral contract is made by the third person (surety) directly with the creditor, whereby the surety promises to pay the debt to the creditor in case the principal debtor fails to do so. For a complete discussion of suretyship, see *Chapter 37*.

ORIGINAL PROMISE If the promisor makes an **original promise** by undertaking to become primarily liable, then the statute of frauds does not apply. For example, a father tells a merchant to deliver certain items to his daughter and says, "I will pay $400 for them." The father is not promising to answer for the debt of another; rather, he is making the debt his own. It is to the father, and the father alone, that the merchant extends credit; only from the father may the creditor seek payment. The statute of frauds does not apply, and the promise may be oral.

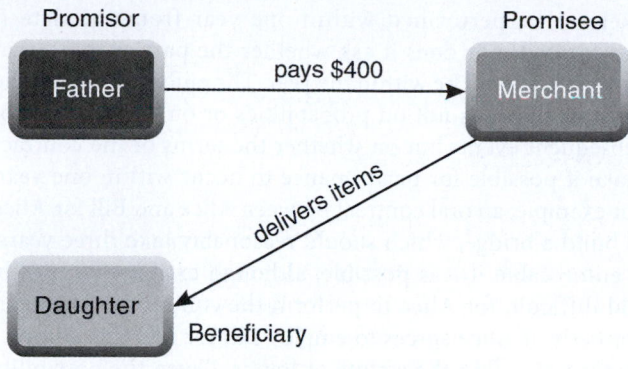

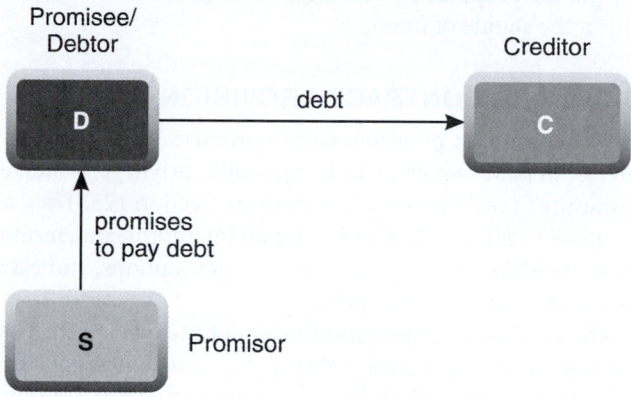

debt in return for valid consideration from D. Because S made the promise to the debtor (D), not the creditor, the promise may be oral. The promise is not a collateral promise to pay C if D fails to pay and thus is not a promise to discharge the obligation of another.

Practical Advice

When entering into a contract with two parties promising you that they will perform, make them both original promisors and avoid having a surety. In any event, if the contract is for a significant amount of money, have both parties sign a written agreement.

MAIN PURPOSE DOCTRINE The courts have developed an exception to the suretyship provision based on the purpose or object of the promisor, called the "main purpose doctrine" or "leading object rule." Where the object or purpose of the promisor is to obtain an economic benefit for himself, the promise is *not* within the statute. Restatement, Section 116. The expected benefit to the surety "must be such as to justify the conclusion that his main purpose in making the promise is to advance his own interest." Restatement, Section 116, Comment b. The fact that the surety received consideration for his promise or that he might receive a slight and indirect advantage is insufficient to bring the promise within the main purpose doctrine.

Suppose that a supply company has refused to furnish materials upon the credit of a building contractor. Facing a possible slowdown in the construction of his building, the owner of the land promises the supplier that if he will extend credit to the contractor, the owner will pay if the contractor does not. Here, the primary purpose of the promisor is to serve his own economic interest, even though the performance of the promise would discharge the duty of another. The intent to benefit the contractor is at most incidental, and courts will uphold oral promises of this type.

♦ *See Case 15-1*

PROMISE MADE TO DEBTOR The suretyship provision has been interpreted not to include promises made to a debtor. For example, D owes a debt to C. S promises D that she will pay D's

15-1c EXECUTOR-ADMINISTRATOR PROVISION

The executor-administrator provision applies to the contractual promises of an executor of a decedent's will, or to those of the administrator of his estate if the decedent dies without a will, to answer personally for a duty of the decedent. An **executor** or **administrator** is a person appointed by a court to carry on, subject to order of court, the administration of the estate of a deceased person. If the will of a decedent nominates a certain person as executor, the court customarily appoints that person. (For a more detailed discussion of executors and administrators, see *Chapter 50*.) If an executor or administrator promises to pay personally a debt of the decedent, the promise must be in writing—or in proper electronic form—to be enforceable. For example, Brian, who is Ann's son and executor of her will, recognizing that Ann's estate will not provide funds sufficient to pay all of her debts, orally promises Curtis, one of Ann's creditors, that he, Brian, will personally pay all of his mother's creditors in full in return for valid consideration from Curtis. Brian's oral promise is not enforceable. This provision does not apply to promises to pay debts of the deceased out of assets of the estate.

The executor-administrator provision is thus a specific application of the suretyship provision. Accordingly, the exceptions to the suretyship provision apply to this provision as well.

15-1d MARRIAGE PROVISION

The notable feature of the marriage provision is that it does *not* apply to mutual promises to marry. The provision applies only if a promise to marry is made in consideration for some promise other than a reciprocal promise to marry. Restatement, Section 124. If, for example, Greg and Betsy each orally promise and agree to marry each other, their agreement is not within the statute and is a binding contract between them. If, however, Greg promises to convey title to a certain farm to Betsy if she accepts his proposal of marriage, their agreement would fall within the statute of frauds.

15-1e LAND CONTRACT PROVISION

The land contract provision covers promises to transfer "any interest in land," which includes any right, privilege, power, or immunity in real property. Restatement, Section 125. Thus, all promises to transfer, buy, or pay for an interest in land, including ownership interests, leases, mortgages, options, and easements, are within the provision.

The land contract provision does not include contracts to transfer an interest in personal property. It also does not cover short-term leases, which by statute in most States are those for one year or less; contracts to build a building on a piece of land; contracts to do work on the land; or contracts to insure a building on the land.

The courts may enforce an oral contract for the transfer of an interest in land if the party seeking enforcement has so changed his position in reasonable reliance upon the contract that injustice can be prevented only by enforcing the contract. Restatement, Section 129. In applying this **part performance** exception, many States require that the transferee has paid a portion or all of the purchase price *and* either has taken possession of the real estate or has started to make valuable improvements on the land. For example, Aaron orally agrees to sell land to Barbara for $30,000. With Aaron's consent, Barbara takes possession of the land, pays Aaron $10,000, builds a house on the land, and occupies it. Several years later, Aaron repudiates the contract. The courts will enforce the contract against Aaron. On the other hand, the courts will not enforce the promise unless equity so demands.

An oral promise by a purchaser is also enforceable if the seller fully performs by conveying the property to the purchaser. As previously indicated, however, payment of part or all of the price is not sufficient in itself to remove the contract from the scope of the statute.

15-1f ONE-YEAR PROVISION

The statute of frauds requires all contracts that *cannot* be fully performed within one year of their making to be in writing or in proper electronic form. Restatement, Section 130.

THE POSSIBILITY TEST To determine whether a contract can be performed within a year, the courts ask whether it is *possible* to complete its performance within a year. The **possibility test** does not ask whether the agreement is likely to be performed within one year from the date it was formed; nor does it ask whether the parties think that performance will be within the year. The enforceability of the contract depends not on probabilities or on the actuality of subsequent events but on whether the terms of the contract make it possible for performance to occur within one year. For example, an oral contract between Alice and Bill for Alice to build a bridge, which should reasonably take three years, is enforceable if it is possible, although extremely unlikely and difficult, for Alice to perform the contract in one year. Similarly, if Alice agrees to employ Bill for life, this contract also is not within the statute of frauds. Given the possibility that Bill may die within the year (in which case the contract would be completely performed), the contract is therefore one that is *fully performable* within a year. Contracts of indefinite duration are likewise excluded from the provision. On the other hand, an oral contract to employ another person for thirteen months could not possibly be performed within a year and is unenforceable.

♦ *See Case 15-2*

COMPUTATION OF TIME The year runs from the time the agreement is made, not from the time when the performance is to begin. For example, on January 1, 2019, A orally hires B to work for eleven months starting on May 1, 2019. That contract will be fully performed on March 31, 2020, which is more than one year after January 1, 2019, the date the contract was made. Consequently, it is *within* the statute of frauds and unenforceable as it is oral.

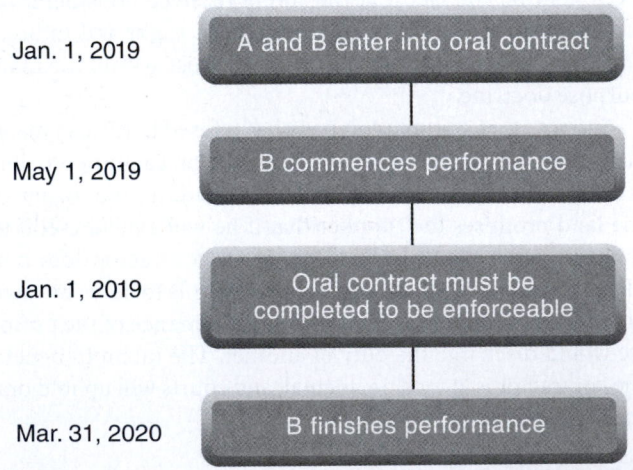

Jan. 1, 2019	A and B enter into oral contract
May 1, 2019	B commences performance
Jan. 1, 2019	Oral contract must be completed to be enforceable
Mar. 31, 2020	B finishes performance

Similarly, a contract for a year's performance, which is to begin three days after the date on which the contract is made, is within the statute and, if oral, is unenforceable. If, however, the performance is to begin the following day or, under the terms of the agreement, could have begun the following day, the contract is not within the statute and need not be in writing, as the one year's performance would be completed on the anniversary date of the making of the contract.

FULL PERFORMANCE BY ONE PARTY Where one party to a contract has fully performed, most courts hold that the promise of the other party is enforceable, even though by its terms the performance of the contract was not possible within the period of a year. Restatement, Section 130. For example, Vince borrows $4,800 from Julie, orally promising to pay Julie $4,800 in three annual installments of $1,600. Vince's promise is enforceable, notwithstanding the one-year provision, because Julie has fully performed by making the loan.

15-1g SALE OF GOODS

The original statute of frauds, which applied to contracts for the sale of goods, has been used as a prototype for the UCC Article 2 statute of frauds provision. Section 2–201 of the UCC provides that a contract for the sale of goods for the price of *$500 or more* is not enforceable unless there is some writing or record sufficient to indicate that the parties have made a contract for sale. **Goods**, as previously indicated, are defined as movable personal property. Section 2-105(1). The definition expressly includes growing crops and unborn animals.

ADMISSION The Code permits an oral contract for the sale of goods to be enforced against a party who in his pleading, testimony, or otherwise in court admits that a contract was made, but limits enforcement to the quantity of goods so admitted. Section 2–201(3)(b). The language "otherwise in court" may include pretrial deposition and written interrogatories of the defendant. Some courts now apply this exception to other statute of frauds provisions.

SPECIALLY MANUFACTURED GOODS The Code permits a seller to enforce an oral contract for goods specially manufactured for a buyer, but only if evidence indicates that the goods were made for the buyer and the seller can show that he made a *substantial beginning* of their manufacture prior to receiving any notice of repudiation. Section 2–201(3)(a). If goods manufactured on special order are nonetheless readily marketable in the ordinary course of the seller's business, this exception does not apply.

For example, if Jim brings an action against Robin alleging breach of an oral contract under which Robin agreed to purchase from Jim three million balloons with Robin's trademark imprinted on them at a price of $30,000, the action is not subject to the defense of the statute of frauds unless Robin can show (1) that the balloons are suitable for sale to other buyers, which is highly improbable in view of the trademark, or (2) that Jim received notice of repudiation before he had made a substantial start on the production of the balloons or had otherwise substantially committed himself to procuring them.

♦ *See Case 15-3*

DELIVERY OR PAYMENT AND ACCEPTANCE Prior to the Code, delivery and acceptance of part of the goods or payment of part of the price made the entire oral contract enforceable against the buyer who had received part delivery or against the seller who had received part payment. Under the Code, such "partial performance" validates the contract but only for the goods that have been accepted or for which payment has been accepted. Section 2–201(3)(c). To illustrate, Johnson orally agrees to buy one thousand watches from Barnes for $15,000. Barnes delivers three hundred watches to Johnson, who receives and accepts the watches. The oral contract is enforceable to the extent of three hundred watches ($4,500)—those received and accepted—but is unenforceable to the extent of seven hundred watches ($10,500).

♦ SEE FIGURE 15-1 *The Statute of Frauds*

FIGURE 15-1 The Statute of Frauds

Contracts within the Statute of Frauds	Exceptions
Suretyship—a promise to answer for the duty of another	• Main purpose rule • Original promise • Promise made to debtor
Executor-Administrator—a promise to answer personally for debt of decedent	• Main purpose rule • Original promise • Promise made to debtor
Agreements made upon consideration of marriage	• Mutual promises to marry
Agreements for the transfer of an interest in land	• Part performance plus detrimental reliance • Seller conveys property
Agreements not to be performed within one year	• Full performance by one party • Possibility of performance within one year
Sale of goods for $500 or more	• Admission • Specially manufactured goods • Delivery or payment acceptance

15-1h MODIFICATION OR RESCISSION OF CONTRACTS WITHIN THE STATUTE OF FRAUDS

Oral contracts modifying previously existing contracts are unenforceable if the resulting contract is within the statute of frauds. The reverse is also true: an oral modification of a prior contract is enforceable if the new contract is not within the statute. Thus, examples of unenforceable oral contractual modifications include an oral promise to guarantee additional duties of another, an oral agreement to substitute different land for that described in the original contract, and an oral agreement to extend an employee's contract for six months to a total of two years. On the other hand, an oral agreement to modify an employee's contract from two years to six months at a higher salary is not within the statute of frauds and is enforceable.

By extension, an oral rescission is effective and discharges all unperformed duties under the original contract. For example, Linda and Donald enter into a written contract of employment for a two-year term. Later they orally agree to rescind the contract. The oral agreement is effective, and the written contract is rescinded. Where, however, land has been transferred, an agreement to rescind the transaction constitutes a contract to retransfer the land and is within the statute of frauds.

Under the UCC, the decisive point is the contract price *after* the modification. Section 2–209(3). If the parties enter into an oral contract to sell for $450 a motorcycle to be delivered to the buyer and later, prior to delivery, orally agree that the seller shall paint the motorcycle and install new tires and that the buyer shall pay a price of $550, the modified contract is unenforceable. Conversely, if the parties have a written contract for the sale of two hundred bushels of wheat at a price of $4 per bushel and later orally agree to decrease the quantity to one hundred bushels at the same price per bushel, the agreement, as modified, is for a total price of $400 and thus is enforceable.

Practical Advice

When significantly modifying an existing common law contract, make sure that consideration is given and that the modification is in writing and signed by both parties.

15-2 Compliance with the Statute of Frauds

Even though a contract is within the statute of frauds, a sufficient *writing*, *memorandum*, or *record* may justify its enforcement. The writing or record need *not* (1) be in any specific form, (2) be an attempt by the parties to enter into a binding contract, or (3) represent their entire agreement; it need only comply with the requirements of the statute of frauds.

15-2a GENERAL CONTRACTS PROVISIONS

The English statute of frauds and most modern statutes of frauds require that the agreement be evidenced by a writing or record to be enforceable. The note, memorandum, or record, which may be formal or informal, must

1. specify the parties to the contract;
2. specify with reasonable certainty the subject matter and the essential terms of the unperformed promises; and
3. be signed by the party to be charged or by his agent.

The statute's purpose in requiring a writing or record is to ensure that the parties have entered into a contract. The writing or record, therefore, need not exist at the time of the litigation; showing that the memorandum once existed is sufficient.

The memorandum may be a receipt or a check. It may be such that the parties themselves view the memorandum as having no legal significance whatever, as, for example, a personal letter between the parties, an interdepartmental communication, an advertisement, or the record books of a business. The writing or record need not have been delivered to the party who seeks to take advantage of it, and it may even contain a repudiation of the oral agreement. For example, Adrian and Joseph enter into an oral agreement that Adrian will sell Blackacre to Joseph for $5,000. Adrian subsequently receives a better offer and sends Joseph a signed letter, which begins by reciting all the material terms of the oral agreement. The letter concludes, "Since my agreement to sell Blackacre to you for $5,000 was oral, I am not bound by my promise. I have since received a better offer and will accept that one." Adrian's letter constitutes a sufficient memorandum for Joseph to enforce Adrian's promise to sell Blackacre. It should be recognized that because Joseph did not sign the memorandum, the writing does not bind him. Thus, a contract may be enforceable against only one of the parties.

Practical Advice

To avoid becoming solely liable by signing a contract before the other party signs, include a provision to the effect that no party is bound to the contract until all parties sign the contract.

The "signature" may be initials or may even be typewritten or printed, so long as the party intended it to authenticate the writing or record. Furthermore, the signature need not be at the bottom of the page or at the customary place for a signature. The memorandum may consist of *several* papers or documents, none of which would be sufficient by itself. The several memoranda, however, must together satisfy all of the requirements of a writing or record to comply with the statute of frauds and must clearly indicate that they relate to the same transaction.

Restatement, Section 132. The latter requirement can be satisfied if (1) the writings are physically attached, (2) the writings refer to each other, or (3) an examination of the writings shows them to be in reference to each other.

♦ *See Case 15-4*

15-2b SALE OF GOODS

The statute of frauds provision under Article 2 is more liberal than under general contract law. For a sale of goods, Section 2–201 of the Code requires merely some writing or record

1. sufficient to indicate that a contract has been made between the parties,
2. specifying the quantity of goods to be sold, and
3. signed by the party against whom enforcement is sought or by her authorized agent or broker.

The writing or record is sufficient even if it omits or incorrectly states an agreed-upon term; however, where the quantity term is misstated, the contract can be enforced only to the extent of the quantity stated in the writing or record.

As with general contracts, several related documents may satisfy the writing or record requirement. Moreover, the signature again may be by initials or even typewritten or printed, so long as the party intended thereby to authenticate the writing or record.

In addition, the Code provides relief to a merchant who, within a reasonable time after entering into the oral contract, confirms the contract for the sale of goods by a letter or signed writing to the other party if he too is a merchant. As between **merchants**, the **written confirmation**, if sufficient against the sender, is also sufficient against the recipient unless he gives written notice of his objection within ten days after receiving the confirmation. Section 2–201(2). This means that if these requirements have been met, the recipient of the writing or record is in the same position he would have assumed by signing it; and the confirmation, therefore, is enforceable against him.

For example, Brown Co. and ATM Industries enter into an oral contract that provides that ATM will deliver twelve thousand shirts to Brown at $6 per shirt. Brown sends a letter to ATM acknowledging the agreement. The letter, containing the quantity term but not the price, is signed by Brown's president and is mailed to ATM's vice president for sales. Brown was bound by the contract once its authorized agent signs the letter; ATM cannot raise the defense of the statute of frauds if ATM does not object to the letter within ten days after receiving it.

Practical Advice

Merchants should examine written confirmations carefully and promptly to make certain that they are accurate.

15-3 Effect of Noncompliance

Under both the statute of frauds and the Code, the basic legal effect is the same: a contracting party has a defense to an action by the other party for enforcement of an *unenforceable* oral contract—that is, an oral contract that falls within the statute and does not comply with its requirements. For example, if Kirkland, a painter, and Riggsbee, a homeowner, make an oral contract under which Riggsbee is to give Kirkland a certain tract of land in return for the painting of Riggsbee's house, the contract is unenforceable under the statute of frauds. It is a contract for the sale of an interest in land. Either party can repudiate and has a defense to an action by the other to enforce the contract.

15-3a FULL PERFORMANCE

After *all* the promises of an oral contract have been performed by all the parties, the statute of frauds no longer applies. Accordingly, neither party can have the contract set aside on the grounds that it should have been in writing. The purpose of the statute is not to prohibit the performance of oral contracts but simply to exclude oral evidence of contracts within its provisions. Courts, in other words, will not "unscramble" a fully performed contract merely because it was not in writing or a proper record. In short, the statute applies to executory contracts only.

15-3b RESTITUTION

A party to a contract that is unenforceable because of the statute of frauds may have, nonetheless, acted in reliance upon the contract. In such a case, the party may recover in restitution the benefits he conferred upon the other in relying upon the unenforceable contract. Most courts require, however, that the party seeking restitution not be in default.

The Restatement of Restitution provides that a person who renders performance under an agreement that cannot be enforced by reason of the failure to satisfy the statute of frauds has a claim in restitution to prevent unjust enrichment. Section 31. In such a case, that party may recover in restitution the benefits he directly conferred on the other as the performance required or invited by the unenforceable contract.

Thus, if Matthew makes an oral contract to furnish services to Rachel that are not to be performed within a year and Rachel discharges Matthew after three months, Matthew may recover in restitution the value of the services rendered during the three months. Similarly, Lenny enters into an oral contract to sell land to Elaine, and Elaine pays a portion of the price as a down payment. Lenny subsequently repudiates the oral contract. Elaine may recover in restitution the portion of the price she paid.

15-3c PROMISSORY ESTOPPEL

A growing number of courts have used the doctrine of promissory estoppel to displace the requirement of a writing by enforcing oral contracts within the statute of frauds in cases in which the party seeking enforcement has reasonably and foreseeably relied upon a promise in such a way that injustice can be avoided only by enforcing the promise. Restatement, Section 139. This section is essentially identical to Section 90 of the Restatement, which, as discussed in *Chapter 12*, dispenses with the requirement of consideration, although the comments to Section 139 state that "the requirement of consideration is more easily displaced than the requirement of a writing." The remedy granted is limited, as justice requires, and depends upon such factors as the availability of other remedies; the foreseeability, reasonableness, and substantiality of the reliance; and the extent to which reliance corroborates evidence of the promise.

PAROL EVIDENCE RULE

A contract reduced to writing and signed by the parties is frequently the result of many conversations, conferences, proposals, counterproposals, letters, and memoranda and sometimes is the product of negotiations conducted, or partly conducted, by agents of the parties. Any given stage in the negotiations may have produced tentative agreements that were superseded (or regarded as such by one of the parties) by subsequent negotiations. Offers may have been made and withdrawn, either expressly or by implication, or forgotten in the give-and-take of negotiations. Ultimately, though, the parties prepare and sign a final draft of the written contract, which may or may not include all of the points that were discussed and agreed upon during the negotiations. By signing the agreement, however, the parties have declared it to be their contract; and the terms it contains represent the contract they have made. As a rule of substantive law, neither party is later permitted to show that the contract they made differs from the terms and provisions that appear in the written agreement. This rule, which also applies to wills and deeds, is called the parol evidence rule.

15-4 The Rule

When a contract is expressed in a writing that is intended to be the complete and final expression of the rights and duties of the parties, parol evidence of *prior* oral or written negotiations or agreements of the parties, or their *contemporaneous* oral agreements that vary or change the written contract, are not admissible. The word *parol* means literally "speech" or "words." The term **parol evidence** refers to any evidence, whether oral or in writing, which is outside the written contract and not incorporated into it either directly or by reference.

The parol evidence rule applies only to an *integrated* contract; that is, one contained in a certain writing or writings to which the parties have assented as the statement of the complete agreement or contract between them. When a contract is thus integrated, the courts will not permit parol evidence of any prior or contemporaneous agreement to vary, change, alter, or modify any of the terms or provisions of the written contract. Restatement, Section 213.

A writing may contain a **merger clause**, which states that the writing is intended to be the complete and final expression of the agreement between the parties. Most courts consider a merger clause to be conclusive proof of an integrated contract, while a few courts view a merger clause only as evidence of an integrated contract.

The reason for the parol evidence rule is that the parties, by reducing their entire agreement to writing, are regarded as having intended the writing that they signed to include the whole of their agreement. The terms and provisions contained in the writing are there because the parties intended them to be there. Conversely, any provision not in the writing is regarded as having been omitted because the parties intended that it should not be a part of their contract. In safeguarding the contract as made by the parties, the rule excluding evidence that would tend to change, alter, vary, or modify the terms of a written agreement applies to all integrated written contracts and deals with what terms are part of the contract. The rule differs from the statute of frauds, which governs what contracts must be evidenced by a writing to be enforceable.

Practical Advice

If your contract is intended to be the complete and final agreement, make sure that all terms are included and state your intention that the writing is complete and final. If you do not intend the writing to be complete or final, make sure that you so indicate in the writing itself.

♦ *See Case 15-5*

15-5 Situations to Which the Rule Does Not Apply

The parol evidence rule, in spite of its name, is neither an exclusionary rule of evidence nor a rule of construction or interpretation; rather, it is a rule of substantive law that defines the limits of a contract. Bearing this in mind, as well as the reason underlying the rule, it should be clear that the rule does **not** apply to any of the following:

1. A contract that is partly written and partly oral—that is, one in which the parties do not intend the writing to be their entire agreement.

2. A clerical or *typographical error* that obviously does not represent the agreement of the parties. Where, for example,

a written contract for the services of a skilled mining engineer provides that his rate of compensation is to be $7 per day, a court of equity would permit reformation (correction) of the contract to rectify the mistake upon a showing that both parties intended the rate to be $700 per day.

3. Evidence showing the lack of *contractual capacity* of one of the parties, such as proof of minority, intoxication, or mental incompetency. Such evidence would not tend to vary, change, or alter any of the terms of the written agreement, but rather would show that the written agreement was voidable or void.

4. A *defense* of fraud, misrepresentation, duress, undue influence, mistake, illegality, or unconscionability. Though evidence establishing any of these defenses would not purport to vary, change, or alter any of the terms of the written agreement, it would show such agreement to be voidable, void, or unenforceable.

5. A *condition precedent* to which the parties agreed orally at the time they executed the written agreement and to which they made the entire agreement subject. Again, such evidence does not tend to vary, alter, or change any of the terms of the agreement, but rather shows whether the entire written agreement, unchanged and unaltered, ever became effective. For example, if John signs a subscription agreement to buy stock in a corporation to be formed and delivers the agreement to Thompson with the mutual understanding that it is not to be binding unless the other persons financially responsible under it shall each agree to buy at least an equivalent amount of such stock, John is permitted to show by parol evidence this condition.

6. A *subsequent mutual rescission or modification* of the written contract. Parol evidence of a later agreement does not tend to show that the integrated writing did not represent the contract between the parties at the time it was made. Parties to an existing contract, whether written or oral, may agree to change the terms of their contract as they see fit, or to cancel it completely, if they so desire.

7. Parol evidence is admissible to explain *ambiguous* terms in the contract. To enforce a contract, it is necessary to understand its intended meaning. Nevertheless, such interpretation is not to alter, change, or vary the terms of the contract.

8. The rule does not prevent a party from proving the existence of a separate, distinct contract between the same parties.

15-6 Supplemental Evidence

Although a written agreement may not be contradicted by evidence of a prior agreement or of a contemporaneous agreement, under the Restatement, Section 216, and the Code, Section 2–202, a written contract may be explained or supplemented by

(1) course of dealing between the parties, (2) usage of trade, (3) course of performance, or (4) evidence of consistent additional terms, unless the parties intended the writing to be a complete and exclusive statement of their agreement.

A **course of dealing** is a sequence of previous conduct between the parties under an agreement that the court reasonably may regard as establishing a common basis of understanding for interpreting their expressions and other conduct.

A **usage of trade** is a practice or method of dealing, regularly observed and followed in a place, vocation, or trade.

Course of performance refers to the manner and extent to which the respective parties to a contract have accepted without objection successive tenders of performance by the other party.

The Restatement and the Code permit *supplemental consistent evidence* to be introduced into a court proceeding, but only if it does not contradict a term or terms of the original agreement and probably would not have been included in the original contract.

◆ **SEE FIGURE 15-2:** *Parol Evidence Rule*

INTERPRETATION OF CONTRACTS

Although the written words or language in which the parties embodied their agreement or contract may not be changed by parol evidence, the ascertainment (determination) of the meaning to be given the written language is outside the scope of the parol evidence rule. Though written words embody the terms of the contract, words are but symbols. If their meaning is unclear, the courts may clarify this meaning by applying rules of interpretation or construction and by using extrinsic (external) evidence, where necessary.

The Restatement, Section 200, defines **interpretation** as the ascertainment of the meaning of a promise or agreement or a term of the promise or agreement. Where the language in a contract is unambiguous, the courts will not accept extrinsic evidence tending to show a meaning different from that which the words clearly convey. Its function being to interpret and construe written contracts and documents, the court adopts rules of interpretation to apply a legal standard to the words contained in the agreement. The courts will attempt to interpret a contract in accordance with the intent of the parties. If the subjective intent of the parties fails to provide a clear interpretation, the courts will make an objective interpretation. Among the rules that aid interpretation are the following:

1. Words and other conduct are interpreted in the light of all the circumstances, and the principal purpose of the parties, if ascertainable, is given great weight.

2. A writing is interpreted as a whole, and all writings that are part of the same transaction are interpreted together.

FIGURE 15-2 Parol Evidence Rule

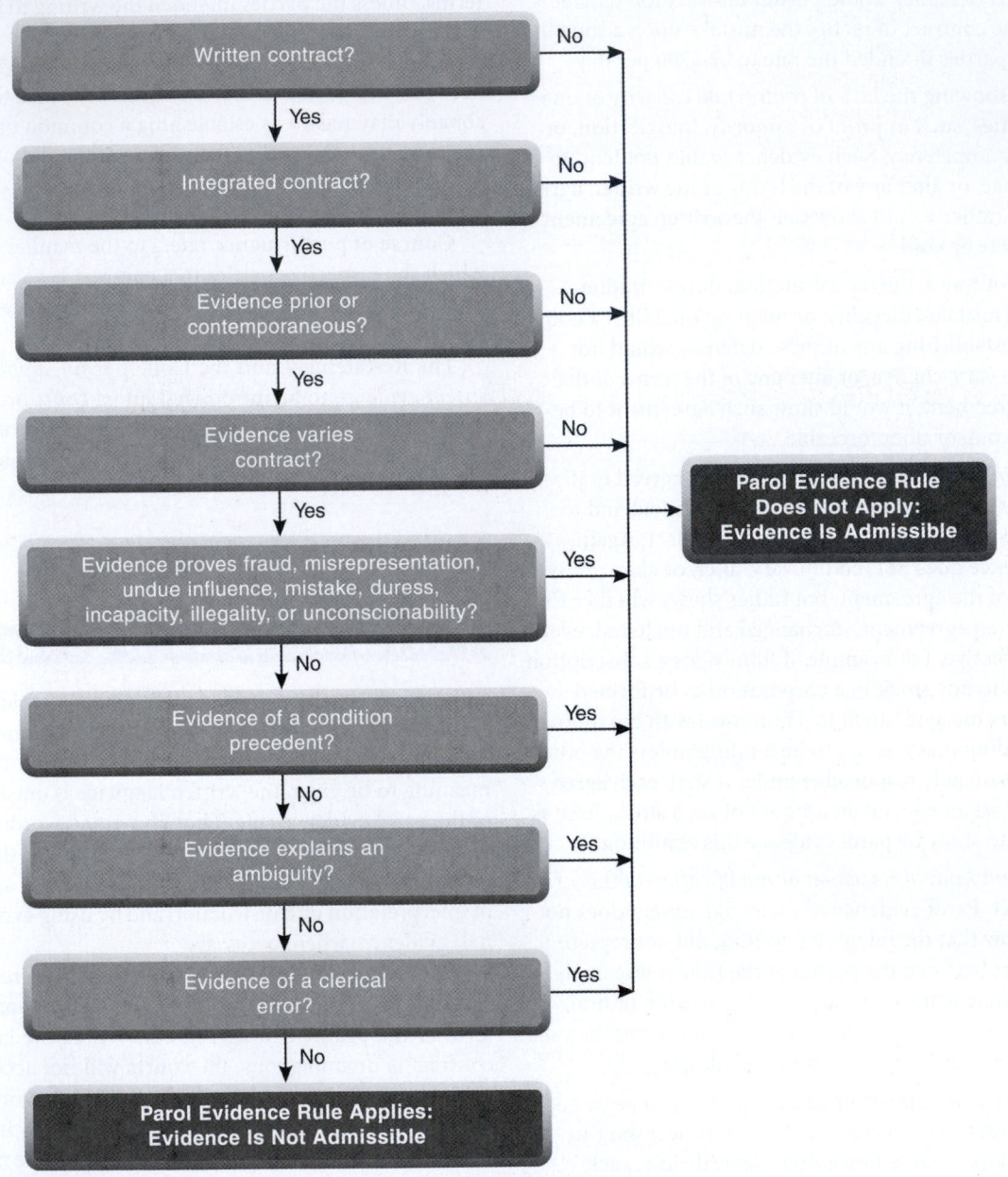

3. Unless a different intention is manifested, language that has a commonly accepted meaning is interpreted in accordance with that meaning.

4. Unless a different intention is manifested, technical terms and words of art are given their technical meanings.

5. Wherever reasonable, the manifestations of intention of the parties to a promise or agreement are interpreted as consistent with each other and with any relevant course of performance, course of dealing, or usage of trade.

6. An interpretation that gives a reasonable, lawful, and effective meaning to all the terms is preferred over an interpretation that leaves a part unreasonable, unlawful, or of no effect.

7. Specific terms and exact terms are given greater weight than general language.

8. Separately negotiated or added terms are given greater weight than standardized terms or other terms not separately negotiated.

9. Express terms, course of performance, course of dealing, and usage of trade are weighted in that order.

10. Where a term or promise has several possible meanings, it will be interpreted against the party who supplied the contract or the term. Restatement, Sections 201, 202, and 203.

11. Where written provisions are inconsistent with typed or printed provisions, the written provision is given preference. Likewise, typed provisions are given preferences to printed provisions.

12. If the amount payable is set forth in both figures and words and the amounts differ, the words control the figures.

It may be observed that, through the application of the parol evidence rule (where properly applicable) and the above rules of interpretation and construction, the law not only enforces a contract but, in so doing, exercises great care that the contract being enforced is the one the parties made and that the sense and meaning of the parties' intentions are carefully ascertained and given effect.

Practical Advice

Take care to ensure that your contracts are complete and understandable, especially if you drafted the contract.

C H A P T E R   S U M M A R Y

STATUTE OF FRAUDS

CONTRACTS WITHIN THE STATUTE OF FRAUDS

Rule contracts within the statute of frauds must be evidenced by a writing to be enforceable

Electronic Records full effect is given to electronic contracts and signatures

Suretyship Provision applies to promises to pay the debts of others

- *Promise Must Be Collateral* promisor must be secondarily, not primarily, liable; if the promisor makes an *original promise* by undertaking to become primarily liable, then the statute of frauds does *not* apply
- *Main Purpose Doctrine* if primary object is to provide an economic benefit to the surety, then the promise is not within the statute
- *Promise Made to Debtor* the suretyship provision does *not* apply to promises made to a debtor to pay the debtor's debt

Executor-Administrator Provision applies to promises to answer personally for duties of decedents

Marriage Provision applies to promises made in consideration of marriage but not to mutual promises to marry

Land Contract Provision applies to promises to transfer any rights, privileges, powers, or immunities in real property

One-Year Provision applies to contracts that cannot be performed within one year

- *The Possibility Test* the criterion is whether it is possible, not likely, for the agreement to be performed within one year
- *Computation of Time* the year runs from the time the agreement is made
- *Full Performance by One Party* makes the promise of the other party enforceable under majority view

Sale of Goods a contract for the sale of goods for the price of $500 or more must be evidenced by a writing or record to be enforceable

- *Admission* an admission in pleadings, testimony, or otherwise in court makes the contract enforceable for the quantity of goods admitted
- *Specially Manufactured Goods* an oral contract for specially manufactured goods is enforceable
- *Delivery or Payment and Acceptance* validates the contract only for the goods that have been accepted or for which payment has been accepted

Modification or Rescission of Contracts within the Statute of Frauds oral contracts modifying existing contracts are unenforceable if the resulting contract is within the statute of frauds

| METHODS OF COMPLIANCE | **General Contract Law** the writing(s) or record must |

General Contract Law the writing(s) or record must
- specify the parties to the contract
- specify the subject matter and essential terms
- be signed by the party to be charged or by her agent

Sale of Goods provides a general method of compliance for all parties and an additional one for merchants
- *Writing(s) or Record* must (1) be sufficient to indicate that a contract has been made between the parties, (2) be signed by the party against whom enforcement is sought or by her authorized agent, and (3) specify the quantity of goods to be sold
- *Written Confirmation* between merchants, a written confirmation that is sufficient against the sender is also sufficient against the recipient unless the recipient gives written notice of his objection within ten days

---

EFFECT OF NONCOMPLIANCE

Oral Contract within Statute of Frauds is unenforceable

Full Performance statute does not apply to executed contracts

Restitution is available in a quasi contract for benefits conferred in reliance on the oral contract

Promissory Estoppel oral contracts will be enforced in cases in which the party seeking enforcement has reasonably and justifiably relied on the promise and the court can avoid injustice only by enforcement

---

PAROL EVIDENCE RULE

Statement of Rule when parties express a contract in a writing that they intend to be the complete and final expression of their rights and duties, evidence of their prior oral or written negotiations or agreements of their contemporaneous oral agreements that vary or change the written contract are not admissible

Situations to Which the Rule Does Not Apply
- a contract that is not an integrated document
- correction of a typographical error
- showing that a contract was void or voidable
- showing whether a condition has in fact occurred
- showing a subsequent mutual rescission or modification of the contract

Supplemental Evidence may be admitted
- *Course of Dealing* previous conduct between the parties
- *Usage of Trade* practice engaged in by the trade or industry
- *Course of Performance* conduct between the parties concerning performance of the particular contract
- *Supplemental Consistent Evidence*

INTERPRETATION OF CONTRACTS

Definition the ascertainment of the meaning of a promise or agreement or a term of the promise or agreement

Rules of Interpretation include the following:
- all the circumstances are considered, and the principal purpose of the parties is given great weight
- a writing is interpreted as a whole

- commonly accepted meanings are used unless the parties manifest a different intention
- wherever possible, the intentions of the parties are interpreted as consistent with each other and with course of performance, course of dealing, or usage of trade
- an interpretation that gives a reasonable, lawful, and effective meaning to all the terms is preferred over an interpretation that leaves a part unreasonable, unlawful, or of no effect
- technical terms are given their technical meaning
- specific terms are given greater weight than general language
- separately negotiated terms are given greater weight than standardized terms or those not separately negotiated
- specific terms control general terms
- the order for interpretation is express terms, course of performance, course of dealing, and usage of trade
- where a term has several possible meanings, the term will be interpreted against the party who supplied the contract or term
- written provisions are given preference over typed or printed provisions, and typed provisions are given preference over printed provisions
- if an amount is set forth in both words and figures and they differ, words control figures

C A S E S

CASE 15-1

Suretyship/Main Purpose Rule
ROSEWOOD CARE CENTER, INC. v. CATERPILLAR, INC.
Supreme Court of Illinois, 2007
226 Ill.2d 559, 877 N.E.2d 1091, 315 Ill. Dec. 762

Burke, J.

[On January 3, 2002, Caterpillar contacted HSM Management Services (HSM), the management agent for Plaintiff, Rosewood Care Center, Inc. (Rosewood), a skilled nursing facility. Caterpillar requested that Rosewood admit Betty Jo Cook, an employee of Caterpillar, on a "managed care basis (fixed rate)." HSM advised Caterpillar that Rosewood would not admit Cook on those terms. Shortly thereafter, on January 10, Dr. Norma Just, Caterpillar's employee in charge of medical care relating to workers' compensation claims, contacted HSM. Just told HSM that Cook had sustained a work-related injury and was receiving medical care at Caterpillar's expense under the workers' compensation laws. Just requested that Cook be admitted to Rosewood for skilled nursing care and therapy and stated that the cost of Cook's care would be 100 percent covered and paid directly by Caterpillar to Rosewood with a zero deductible and no maximum limit. Just further advised HSM that Cook had been precertified for four weeks of care. Just asked that Rosewood send the bills for Cook's care to Caterpillar's workers' compensation division. On January 20, "Sue" from Dr. Just's office telephoned HSM and confirmed approval for Cook's transfer from the hospital to Rosewood. On January 30, Sue reconfirmed, via telephone, Caterpillar's authorization for Cook's care and treatment in accordance with the January 10 agreement, except that Sue now advised HSM that Cook was precertified for two weeks of care instead of the original four weeks. On January 30, Cook was admitted to Rosewood. Upon her admission, Cook signed a document entitled "Assignment of Insurance Benefits" as required by law. In this document, Cook assigned any insurance benefits she might receive to Rosewood and acknowledged her liability for any unpaid services. Caterpillar, through its health care management company, continued to orally "authorize" care for Cook and did so on February 8, February 25, March 11, March 21, April 8, April 18, May 16, and June 4. Cook remained at Rosewood until June 13, 2002. The total of Rosewood's charges for Cook's care amounted to $181,857. Caterpillar never objected to the bills being sent to it for Cook's care, nor did it ever advise Rosewood that treatment was not authorized. However, Caterpillar ultimately refused to pay for services rendered to Cook.

The plaintiff filed an action against Caterpillar seeking reimbursement for the services provided to Cook while she was a patient at Rosewood. In response, Caterpillar moved to dismiss the complaint, arguing that the alleged promise to pay for Cook's care was not enforceable because it was not in writing as required by the statute of frauds. The trial court granted Caterpillar's motion for summary judgment, and Rosewood appealed. The appellate court reversed and remanded.]

* * *

In general, the statute of frauds provides that a promise to pay the debt of another, i.e., a suretyship agreement, is unenforceable unless it is in writing. * * *

* * *

The plain object of the statute is to require higher and more certain evidence to charge a party, where he does not receive the substantial benefit of the transaction, and where another is primarily liable to pay the debt or discharge the duty; and thereby to afford greater security against the setting up of fraudulent demands, where the party sought to be charged is another than the real debtor, and whose debt or duty, on performance of the alleged contract by such third person, would be discharged. [Citation.]

* * *

II. "Main Purpose" or "Leading Object" Rule

* * * According to Rosewood, Caterpillar's promise falls outside the statute of frauds pursuant to the "main purpose" or "leading object" rule. Under this rule, when the "main purpose" or "leading object" of the promisor/surety is to subserve or advance its own pecuniary or business interests, the promise does not fall within the statute. [Citation.] As section 11 of the Restatement (Third) of Suretyship & Guaranty states:

A contract that all or part of the duty of the principal obligor to the obligee shall be satisfied by the secondary obligor is not within the Statute of Frauds as a promise to answer for the duty of another if the consideration for the promise is in fact or apparently desired by the secondary obligor mainly for its own economic benefit, rather than the benefit of the principal obligor. [Citation.]

The reason for the "main purpose" or "leading object" rule has been explained:

Where the secondary obligor's main purpose is its own pecuniary or business advantage, the gratuitous

or sentimental element often present in suretyship is eliminated, the likelihood of disproportion in the values exchanged between secondary obligor and obligee is reduced, and the commercial context commonly provides evidentiary safeguards. Thus, there is less need for cautionary or evidentiary formality than in other secondary obligations. [Citations.]

* * *

It is clear * * * that the "main purpose" or "leading object" rule, as set out in the Restatements, has been a part of Illinois law since 1873. We note that the majority of jurisdictions have adopted this rule as well. [Citations.]

Applying this rule in the case at bar, Caterpillar denies that the "main purpose" for its alleged promise to Rosewood was to promote its own interest. Caterpillar also denies that it received any benefit from the agreement. Alternatively, Caterpillar argues that we should remand this cause for further proceedings to determine the "main purpose" or "leading object" of its promise.

Whether the "main purpose" or "leading object" of the promisor is to promote a pecuniary or business advantage to it is generally a question for the trier of fact. [Citation.] * * * Here, a decision on what was Caterpillar's "main purpose" or "leading object" in making the promise cannot be made based on the allegations in the complaint. * * * The determination must be made by the trier of fact based on evidence to be presented by the parties. * * *

III. Whether a Suretyship Was Created in This Case

* * * Rosewood argues that no suretyship was created by Caterpillar's promise. According to Rosewood, Caterpillar contracted directly with Rosewood, became liable for its own commitment, and received benefits as a result.

A suretyship exists when one person undertakes an obligation of another person who is also under an obligation or duty to the creditor/obligee. [Citation.] Specifically, "[a] contract is not within the Statute of Frauds as a contract to answer for the duty of another unless the promisee is an obligee of the other's duty, the promisor is a surety for the other, and the promisee knows or has reason to know of the suretyship relation." [Citation.] * * *

* * *

The question of whether Caterpillar's promise was a suretyship or not, like the question regarding Caterpillar's "main purpose" or "leading object," cannot be determined on the basis of allegations in Rosewood's complaint. This question is a factual one to be made based on evidence to be presented by the parties. Accordingly, this issue must also be resolved by the circuit court on remand.

CASE 15-2

One-Year Provision
MACKAY v. FOUR RIVERS PACKING CO.
Supreme Court of Idaho, 2008
179 P.3d 1064

Jones, J.

Four Rivers operates an onion packing plant near Weiser, Idaho. Randy Smith, the general manager of Four Rivers, hired Stuart Mackay as a field man during the summer of 1999 to secure onion contracts from growers in the area. Four Rivers began experiencing financial difficulties in late 1999. All employees, including Mackay, were laid off at this time because one of the owners of Four Rivers filed suit to prevent the company from conducting business. When the lawsuit was resolved, Smith rehired Mackay as a field man. According to Mackay, Four Rivers offered him a long-term employment contract in March of 2000 to continue working as a field man up to the time of his retirement. Mackay claims he accepted the long-term offer of employment and advised Four Rivers that he may not retire for approximately ten years, at around age 62.

Four Rivers denies extending such an offer to Mackay. According to Four Rivers, the owners informed Randy Smith in 2000 that they did not know whether the company would be in business the next fall due to continuing financial difficulties. In 2001, Mackay asked Four Rivers for a written contract of employment. He refused to sign the agreement that was prepared because it gave Four Rivers the right to terminate his employment at will. Subsequent efforts to arrive at a written employment agreement were unsuccessful.

* * *

On March 7, 2003, Smith terminated Mackay's employment relationship without notice * * * [claiming that] Mackay's performance was not satisfactory because he was not meeting with growers with the frequency or regularity necessary to obtain the quantity of onions necessary to keep Four Rivers' packing plant operational on a full-time basis, resulting in the closure of the packing plant in February 2003. Four Rivers claims its employees, including Mackay, were laid off at this time as a result of the early closure. Mackay claims Four Rivers closed due to the price of onions at the time. Mackay applied for unemployment benefits in 2003, stating in his application that he was laid off due to company financial difficulties. Smith states he offered to rehire Mackay in a different position later that year, and Mackay declined.

Mackay filed a complaint on August 24, 2004, claiming Four Rivers breached his employment contract * * *. Four Rivers answered, alleging that Mackay was an "at will" employee. Further, it asserted an affirmative defense that a contract such as that claimed by Mackay is null, void, and unenforceable as violating Idaho Code §9–505 because the agreement could not be performed within one year of its making. Four Rivers moved for summary judgment in October 2006, and the district court granted its motion. The court concluded the alleged contract could not be performed by its terms within one year and would therefore be invalid in the state of Idaho. Thus, it granted summary judgment with regard to Mackay's breach of contract claim. * * * Plaintiff subsequently filed a motion for reconsideration, which the district court denied, resulting in this appeal.

* * *

The parties disagree regarding the proper application of Idaho's Statute of Frauds. According to Mackay, the longstanding rule in Idaho is that where an agreement depends upon a condition which may ripen within a year, even though it may not mature until much later, the agreement does not fall within the Statute. Since the alleged contract here contains a term that it will last until Mackay retires, and Mackay could have retired within the first year, the oral contract does not violate the Statute. * * *

Four Rivers denies entering into a long-term contract of employment, and * * * claims the contract violates [the] Idaho [Statute of Frauds] * * *

Idaho's Statute of Frauds provision * * * provides that "an agreement that by its terms is not to be performed within a year from the making thereof" is invalid, unless the same or some note or memorandum thereof, be in writing and subscribed by the party charged, or by his agent. [Citation.] * * * Under the prevailing interpretation, the enforceability of a contract under the one-year provision does not turn on the actual course of subsequent events, nor on the expectations of the parties as to the probabilities. [Citation.] Contracts of uncertain duration are simply excluded, and the provision covers only those contracts whose performance cannot possibly be completed within a year. [Citation.]

Leading treatises follow this general rule. It is well settled that the oral contracts invalidated by the Statute because they are not to be performed within a year include only those which *cannot* be performed within that period. [Citation.] A promise which is not likely to be performed within a year, and which in fact is not performed within a year, is not within the Statute, if at the time the contract is made there is a possibility in law and in fact that full performance such as the parties intended may be completed before the expiration of a year. [Citation.] The question is not what the probable, or expected, or actual, performance of the contract was, but whether the contract, according to the reasonable interpretation of its terms, required that it could not be performed within the year. [Citation.] Further, a promise which is performable at or until the happening of any specified contingency which may or may not occur within a year is not within the Statute. [Citation.]

Idaho cases are in accord. A contract which is capable of being performed and might have been fully performed and terminated within a year does not fall within the Statute. [Citation.] Where the termination of a contract is dependent upon the happening of a contingency which may occur within a year, although it may not happen until the expiration of a year, the contract is not within the Statute, since it may be performed within a year. [Citations.]

In this case, the district court applied the *Burton* decision and found that the alleged oral contract could not, by its terms, be completed within a year. In *Burton*, the plaintiff alleged there was an implied contract, which guaranteed her employment until she reached retirement, at age 65. * * *

This case differs. In this case, Mackay alleges the term of the contract is until retirement. * * * Unlike the contract in *Burton*, which specified "until age 65," the alleged contract term in this case is indefinite. Thus, the district court erred when it held *Burton* applied to preclude enforcement of the contract alleged in this case.

Rather, this case falls under the general rule cited in numerous Idaho cases and in the Restatement (Second) of Contracts. For the purposes of summary judgment, we must take as true Mackay's allegation that the contract was to last "until retirement." Since Mackay could have retired within one year under the terms of the alleged contract, this contract is outside Idaho's Statute of Frauds provision. * * * Since the event at issue here—Mackay's retirement—could possibly have occurred within one year, the Statute does not bar evidence of such contract.

* * *

We vacate the district court's order granting summary judgment against Mackay * * * and remand the case for further proceedings consistent with this opinion. * * *

CASE	Specially Manufactured Goods
15-3	**KALAS v. COOK** Appellate Court of Connecticut, 2002 70 Conn.App. 477, 800 A.2d 553, 47 UCC Rep.Serv.2d 1307

Peters, J.

Pursuant to a long-standing oral agreement, a print shop manufactured and delivered written materials designed by the buyer for the buyer's use and sale. After the buyer's death, the executor of her estate refused to pay for the last deliveries of these materials to the buyer. The principal issue in this appeal is whether the statute of frauds, as codified in the Uniform Commercial Code, [citation], bars enforcement of the oral agreement. * * * [W]e agree with the [trial] court's conclusion that, under the circumstances of this case, the seller is entitled to be paid.

The plaintiff, Barbara H. Kalas, owner of the print shop, filed a complaint against the defendant, Edward W. Cook, executor of the estate of the buyer, Adelma G. Simmons. The plaintiff alleged that the defendant, in breach of the obligations contained in an oral contract with Simmons for the sale of goods, had refused to pay for goods delivered to her. The defendant denied these allegations and interposed a number of special defenses, including a defense under the statute of frauds. * * *

The trial court held that the transaction between the plaintiff and the deceased was a sale of goods as that term is defined in [UCC] §2-105. That determination has not been challenged on

appeal. As a contract for the sale of goods, its enforcement was not precluded by the statute of frauds provision. * * * Accordingly, the court rendered a judgment in favor of the plaintiff in the amount of $24,599.38. The defendant has appealed.

The facts found by the trial court, which are currently uncontested, establish the background for the court's judgment. The plaintiff, doing business as Clinton Press of Tolland, operated a printing press and, for several decades, provided written materials, including books and pamphlets for Simmons. Simmons ordered these materials for use and sale at her farm, known as Caprilands Herb Farm (Caprilands). The defendant has not suggested that these materials could have been sold on the open market.

Due to limited space at Caprilands, the plaintiff and Simmons agreed that the written materials would remain stored at the plaintiff's print shop until Simmons decided that delivery was necessary. The materials were delivered either routinely, based on Simmons' ordinary need for materials, or upon her request for a special delivery. After each delivery, the plaintiff sent an invoice requesting payment by Simmons. These invoices were honored.

In 1991, the town of Tolland acquired the land on which the plaintiff resided. In early 1997, the plaintiff was notified that she would have to vacate the property by the end of that calendar year. Upon receiving that notice, the plaintiff decided to close her business. The plaintiff and Simmons agreed that the materials printed for Caprilands and stored at the plaintiff's print shop would be delivered on an accelerated basis. * * *

On December 3, 1997, after several months of deterioration of her physical health, Simmons died. * * * The plaintiff submitted a claim against the estate for $24,599.38 for unpaid deliveries to Caprilands. These deliveries took place from February 12, 1997 to December 11, 1997, with the last two deliveries occurring after Simmons' death.

* * *

On appeal, the defendant argues that the oral contract was invalid * * * because a writing was required by [UCC] §2–201. This argument is unpersuasive. * * *

* * *

* * * Contracts for the sale of goods * * * are governed by [UCC] §2–201. [Citations.]* * *

Under [UCC] §2–201, oral agreements for the sale of goods at a price of $500 or more are presumptively unenforceable. [Citations.] The applicable provisions in this case, however, are other subsections of [UCC] §2–201.

Under [UCC] §2–201 (3) (a), an oral contract for the sale of goods is enforceable if the goods in question are "specially manufactured." In determining whether the specially manufactured goods exception applies, courts generally apply a four part standard: "(1) the goods must be specially made for the buyer; (2) the goods must be unsuitable for sale to others in the ordinary course of the seller's business; (3) the seller must have substantially begun to have manufactured the goods or to

have a commitment for their procurement; and (4) the manufacture or commitment must have been commenced under circumstances reasonably indicating that the goods are for the buyer and prior to the seller's receipt of notification of contractual repudiation." [Citation.] In applying this standard, "courts have traditionally looked to the goods themselves. The term 'specially manufactured,' therefore, refers to the nature of the particular goods in question and not to whether the goods were made in an unusual, as opposed to the regular, business operation or manufacturing process of the seller." [Citations.]

Printed material, particularly that, as in this case, names the buyer, has been deemed by both state and federal courts to fall within the exception set out for specially manufactured goods. [Citations.]

It is inherent in the court's findings that the printed materials in the present case were specially manufactured goods. The materials were printed specifically for Caprilands. The materials included brochures and labels with the Caprilands name, as well as books that were written and designed by Simmons. The plaintiff testified that the books were printed, as Simmons had requested, in a rustic style with typed inserts and hand-drawn pictures. Therefore, none of these materials was suitable for sale to others. It is undisputed that, at the time of breach of the alleged contract, goods printed for Simmons already had been produced.

We conclude that, in light of the nature of the goods at issue * * * this case falls within the exception for specially manufactured goods. To be enforceable, the agreement for their production was, therefore, not required to be in writing under [UCC] §2–201 (3) (a). Accordingly, we affirm the judgment of the court. * * * [Citations.]

CASE 15-4

Compliance with the Statute of Frauds
DAHAN v. WEISS
Supreme Court, Appellate Division, Second Department, New York, 2014
120 A.D.3d 540, 991 N.Y.S.2d 119

Eng, P. J.

The defendant Michelle Weiss is the principal of the defendant Gateever, LLC. In August 2009, Gateever purchased seven properties in Far Rockaway, Queens, from the Alaska Group, Inc. The plaintiff [Sharon Dahan] alleges that he held a mortgage in the sum of $650,000 on the seven properties pursuant to an oral loan agreement with the Alaska Group. The plaintiff further claims that as part of the purchase price for the properties, the defendants orally agreed to assume the mortgage held by him and repay the debt within four months. The plaintiff demanded payment from the defendants. * * * [When the defendants refused to pay, the plaintiff brought this action.]

The defendants then moved to dismiss the complaint asserting that the plaintiff's claim to recover damages for breach of contract was barred by the statute of frauds. The plaintiff argued that handwritten statements from the closing and certain email messages, all of which had been attached to the complaint as exhibits, were sufficient evidence of a binding written agreement to satisfy the statute of frauds. The trial court denied the plaintiff's motion and granted the defendants' motion to dismiss. The plaintiff appealed.]

To satisfy the statute of frauds, a memorandum, subscribed [signed] by the party to be charged, must designate the parties, identify and describe the subject matter, and state all of the essential terms of a complete agreement, [citations]. A writing is not a sufficient memorandum unless the "full intention of the parties can be ascertained from it alone, without recourse to parol evidence" [citations]. However, "the statutorily required writing need not be contained in one single document, but rather may be furnished by 'piecing together other, related writings'" [citation].

* * * to the extent that the allegations set forth in the complaint can be liberally construed to allege the existence of an agreement by which the defendants were to repay the Alaska Group's debt to the plaintiff as part of the purchase price, it is * * * barred by the statute of frauds because an agreement to answer for the debt of another must be in writing [citation].

Contrary to the plaintiff's contention, the various writings attached to the complaint, taken together, were insufficient to memorialize the existence of an agreement by which the defendants were to repay the Alaska Group's debt to the plaintiff. Indeed, an email message dated September 1, 2009, indicated that Weiss was not willing to guarantee repayment of the plaintiff's $650,000 loan to the Alaska Group, and that the material terms of the agreement were not settled. The additional email messages submitted by the plaintiff also failed to express the full intention of the parties [citations]. The email messages, at best, showed that there were negotiations for an agreement [citation]. Accordingly, the [trial court] properly granted the defendants' * * * motion to dismiss the complaint. * * *

C A S E

15-5

Parol Evidence
JENKINS v. ECKERD CORPORATION
District Court of Appeal of Florida, First District, 2005
913 So.2d 43

Van Nortwick, J.

In January 1991, Sandhill and K & B Florida Corporation (K & B), a pharmaceutical retailer, entered into the subject lease (K & B Lease) providing for the rental of a parcel of real property located in the Gulf Breeze Shopping Center in Gulf Breeze, Florida. Shortly before the execution of the K & B Lease, Sandhill had leased space in the shopping center to Delchamps, Inc., a regional supermarket chain, as a so called "anchor" tenant in the shopping center. Article 2B of the K & B Lease referred to the Delchamps lease and provided, in pertinent part, as follows:

* * *

Lessor represents to Lessee that Lessor has entered into leases with the following named concerns: with Delchamps, Inc. (Delchamps) for a minimum of 45,000 square feet for supermarket grocery store and that Lessor will construct and offer for lease individual retail shops for a minimum of 21,000 square feet for various retail uses, all located and dimensioned shown on the attached Plot Plan, ... Lessor further represents that said Delchamps lease is for leasing and paying rent by Delchamps as designated hereinabove in the Shopping Center, all as shown on the Plot Plan, Exhibit "A", * * * *The continued leasing and payment of rent for their store in the Shopping Center by Delchamps is part of the consideration to induce Lessee to lease and pay rent for its store, as hereinafter described on the Leased Premises as a part of the Shopping Center. Accordingly, should Delchamps fail or cease to lease and pay rent for its store in the Shopping Center during the Lease Term as hereinafter*

set out, Lessee shall have the right and privilege of: (a) cancelling this Lease and of terminating all of its obligations hereunder at any time thereafter upon written notice by Lessee to Lessor, and such cancellation and termination shall be effective ninety (90) days after the mailing of such written notice; ... It is specifically understood that Lessor shall be obligated to immediately notify Lessee in writing should Delchamps fail or cease to lease and pay rent for such a store in the Shopping Center during the primary term of this Lease, but any failure of Lessor to notify Lessee thereof shall in no way deprive Lessee of its privilege of cancelling this Lease and terminating all of its obligation hereunder.

(Emphasis added [by court]).

Article 29A of the K & B Lease contained an integration clause which provided that "[t]his lease contains all of the agreements made between the parties hereto and may not be modified orally or in any manner other than by an agreement in writing signed by the parties hereto or their heirs, legal representatives, successors, transferees, or assigns." The Delchamps lease included an assignment provision which granted Delchamps "the right, at any time after the commencement of the term hereof, to assign this lease."

In August 1997, Rite Aid, Incorporated (Rite Aid), another drugstore operator, acquired K & B and continued to operate the drugstore in the shopping center under the K & B Lease as a Rite Aid store. In September 1997, Jitney Jungle Stores of America, Inc. (Jitney Jungle), another grocery store operator, acquired the capital stock of Delchamps and continued the operation of the Delchamps grocery store in the shopping center. In 1998, Eckerd acquired certain drugstore properties from Rite Aid, including the drugstore in the shopping center. The K & B Lease was assigned to Eckerd, which began operating an Eckerd drugstore in the leased premises. In October 1999, Jitney Jungle, and its affiliates, including Delchamps, filed for bankruptcy protection under Chapter 11 of the United States Bankruptcy Code. Thereafter, an order was entered in the bankruptcy proceeding approving Delchamps' assignment of its lease in the shopping center to Bruno's Supermarkets, Inc. (Bruno's). Since the assignment, Bruno's has occupied the leased premises under the assigned Delchamps lease and has operated a Bruno's grocery store there. Sandhill failed to provide notice to, or obtain consent from, Eckerd of this assignment.

* * * On June 22, 2001, Eckerd notified Sandhill that, because Delchamps had ceased to lease and pay rent for its store in the shopping center, pursuant to article 2B of the K & B Lease, Eckerd was cancelling its lease effective September 20, 2001. Eckerd continued to pay rent due under the lease through October 2001.

In December 2001, Sandhill filed suit against Eckerd for an alleged breach of the shopping center lease, * * *

At trial, Sandhill sought to introduce testimony relating to its negotiations of the K & B Lease to explain the parties' intent in drafting the allegedly ambiguous language of article 2B. [The district court prohibited the introduction of this evidence under the parol evidence rule.]

* * *

At the close of Sandhill's case, Eckerd moved for, and the trial court granted, a directed verdict in favor of Eckerd. * * *

The trial court also awarded Eckerd $16,026.04 in damages reflecting the amount of rent payments made by Eckerd for the period from September 20, 2001, to October 31, 2001. This appeal ensued.

* * *

It is a fundamental rule of contract interpretation that a contract which is clear, complete, and unambiguous does not require judicial construction. [Citations.]

* * *

In the case on appeal, the trial court concluded, and we agree, that article 2B of the K & B Lease clearly and unambiguously gave the lessee the option to cancel the lease if Delchamps ceased to lease and pay rent for the use of its store. As is clear from article 2B itself, the subject language was an inducement for the drugstore tenant to lease in the shopping center. * * *

* * *

Sandhill argues that the trial court erred in applying the parol evidence rule and refusing to allow the introduction

of extrinsic evidence in interpreting article 2B of the K & B Lease. Sandhill correctly acknowledges that, if a contract provision is "clear and unambiguous," a court may not consider extrinsic or "parol" evidence to change the plain meaning set forth in the contract. [Citation.] Sandhill contends that parol evidence was admissible below since the lease is incomplete and contains a latent ambiguity. [Citations.] A latent ambiguity arises when a contract on its face appears clear and unambiguous, but fails to specify the rights or duties of the parties in certain situations. [Citation.] Sandhill submits that, while the reference in article 2B of the K & B Lease to the Delchamps lease may be "unambiguous" when read literally, this reference was not "clear" or "complete" with regard to the operation of the lease should the Delchamps lease be assigned. We cannot agree.

The operation of the parol evidence rule encourages parties to embody their complete agreement in a written contract and fosters reliance upon the written contract. "The parol evidence rule serves as a shield to protect a valid, complete and unambiguous written instrument from any verbal assault that would contradict, add to, or subtract from it, or affect its construction." [Citation.] The parol evidence rule presumes that the written agreement that is sought to be modified or explained is an integrated agreement; that is, it represents the complete and exclusive instrument setting forth the parties' intended agreement. [Citation.] The concept of integration is based on a presumption that the parties to a written contract intended that writing "to be the sole expositor of their agreement." [Citation.] The terms of an integrated written contract can be varied by extrinsic evidence only to the extent that the terms are ambiguous and are given meaning by the extrinsic evidence. [Citation.]

Here, * * * the K & B Lease contains a so-called merger or integration clause. Although the existence of a merger clause does not *per se* establish that the integration of the agreement is total, [citation], a merger clause is a highly persuasive statement that the parties intended the agreement to be totally integrated and generally works to prevent a party from introducing parol evidence to vary or contradict the written terms. * * * Here, we find that the K & B Lease is an integrated agreement complete in all essential terms.

Further, Article 2B is not in the least unclear or incomplete. It contains no latent or patent ambiguity. Although article 2B does not mention assignment by Delchamps, it unambiguously grants the lessee the right to terminate the K & B Lease if Delchamps ceases to lease and pay rent for its store in the shopping center *for any reason*. * * * Accordingly, the trial court correctly ruled that it could not admit extrinsic evidence.

* * *

AFFIRMED.

QUESTIONS

1. Rafferty was the principal shareholder in Continental Corporation, and as a result, he received the lion's share of Continental's dividends. Continental Corporation was eager to close an important deal for iron ore products to use in its business. A written contract was on the desk of Stage Corporation for the sale of the iron ore to Continental. Stage Corporation, however, was cautious about signing the contract, and it did not sign until Rafferty called Stage Corporation on the telephone and stated that if Continental Corporation did not pay for the ore, he would. Business reversals struck Continental Corporation, and it failed. Stage Corporation sues Rafferty. What defense, if any, has Rafferty?

2. Green was the owner of a large department store. On Wednesday, January 26, he talked to Smith and said, "I will hire you as sales manager in my store for one year at a salary of $48,000; you are to begin work next Monday." Smith accepted and started work on Monday, January 31. At the end of three months, Green discharged Smith. On May 15, Smith brings an action against Green to recover the unpaid portion of the $28,000 salary. Is Smith's employment contract enforceable? Explain.

3. Rowe was admitted to the hospital, suffering from a critical illness. He was given emergency treatment and later underwent surgery. On at least four occasions, Rowe's two sons discussed with the hospital the payment for services it was to render. The first of these four conversations took place the day after Rowe was admitted. The sons informed the treating physician that their father had no financial means but that they themselves would pay for such services. During the other conversations, the sons authorized whatever treatment their father needed, assuring the hospital that they would pay for the services. After Rowe's discharge, the hospital brought this action against the sons to recover the unpaid bill for the services rendered to their father. Are the sons' promises to the hospital enforceable? Explain.

4. Ames, Bell, Cain, and Dole each orally ordered LCD (liquid crystal display) televisions from Marvel Electronics Company, which accepted the orders. Ames's television was to be encased in a specially designed ebony cabinet. Bell, Cain, and Dole ordered standard televisions described as "Alpha Omega Theatre." The price of Ames's television was $1,800, and the televisions ordered by Bell, Cain, and Dole were $700 each. Bell paid the company $75 to apply on his purchase; Ames, Cain, and Dole paid nothing. The next day, Marvel sent Ames, Bell, Cain, and Dole written confirmations captioned "Purchase Memorandum," numbered 12345, 12346, 12347, and 12348, respectively, containing the essential terms of the oral agreements. Each memorandum was sent in duplicate with the request that one copy be signed and returned to the company. None of the four purchasers returned a signed copy. Ames promptly called the company and repudiated the oral contract, which it received before beginning manufacture of the set for Ames or making commitments to carry out the contract. Cain sent the company a letter reading in part, "Referring to your Contract No. 12347, please be advised I have canceled this contract. Yours truly, (Signed) Cain." The four televisions were duly tendered by Marvel to Ames, Bell, Cain, and Dole, all of whom refused to accept delivery. Marvel brings four separate actions against Ames, Bell, Cain, and Dole for breach of contract. Decide liability for each claim. Explain.

5. Moriarty and Holmes enter into an oral contract by which Moriarty promises to sell and Holmes promises to buy Blackacre for $100,000. Moriarty repudiates the contract by writing a letter to Holmes in which she states accurately the terms of the bargain but adds "our agreement was oral. It, therefore, is not binding upon me, and I shall not carry it out." Thereafter, Holmes sues Moriarty for specific performance of the contract. Moriarty interposes the defense of the statute of frauds, arguing that the contract is within the statute and, hence, unenforceable. What result? Discuss.

6. On March 1, Lucas called Craig on the telephone and offered to pay him $190,000 for a house and lot that Craig owned. Craig accepted the offer immediately on the telephone. Later in the same day, Lucas told Annabelle that if she would marry him, he would convey to her the property he then owned, which was the subject of the earlier agreement. On March 2, Lucas called Penelope and offered her $25,000 if she would work for him for the year commencing March 15, and she agreed. Lucas and Annabelle were married on June 25. By this time, Craig had refused to convey the house to Lucas. Thereafter, Lucas renounced his promise to convey the property to Annabelle. Penelope, who had been working for Lucas, was discharged without cause on July 5; Annabelle left Lucas and instituted divorce proceedings.

   Explain what rights, if any, have—

   a. Lucas against Craig for his failure to convey the property.

   b. Annabelle against Lucas for failure to convey the house to her.

   c. Penelope against Lucas for discharging her before the end of the agreed term of employment.

7. Clay orally promises Trent to sell him five crops of pota-
    toes to be grown on Blackacre, a farm in Minnesota, and
    Trent promises to pay a stated price for them on delivery.
    Is the contract enforceable? Explain.

8. Grant leased an apartment to Epstein for the term May 1,
    at $750 a month "payable in advance on the first day of
    each and every month of said term." At the time the lease
    was signed, Epstein told Grant that he received his salary
    on the tenth of the month and that he would be unable to
    pay the rent before that date each month. Grant replied
    that would be satisfactory. On June 2, due to Epstein's not
    having paid the June rent, Grant sued Epstein for such
    rent. At the trial, Epstein offered to prove the oral agree-
    ment as to the date of payment each month. Is the oral
    evidence admissible? Why or why not?

9. Rachel bought a car from the Beautiful Used Car Agency
    under a written contract. She purchased the car in reli-
    ance on Beautiful's agent's oral representations that it had
    never been in a wreck and could be driven at least two
    thousand miles without adding oil. Thereafter, Rachel
    discovered that the car had, in fact, been previously
    wrecked and rebuilt, that it used excessive quantities of
    oil, and that Beautiful's agent was aware of these facts
    when the car was sold. Rachel brings an action to rescind
    the contract and recover the purchase price. Beautiful
    objects to the introduction of oral testimony concerning
    representations of its agent, contending that the written
    contract alone governed the rights of the parties. Explain
    whether Rachel should succeed.

10. In a contract drawn up by Booke Company, it agreed to
    sell and Yermack Contracting Company agreed to buy

    wood shingles at $950 per bunch. After the shingles were
    delivered and used, Booke Company billed Yermack
    Company at $950 per bunch of nine hundred shingles.
    Yermack Company refused to pay because it thought the
    contract meant $950 per bunch of one thousand shin-
    gles. Booke Company brought action to recover on the
    basis of $950 per bunch of nine hundred shingles. The
    evidence showed that there was no applicable custom or
    usage in the trade and that each party held its belief in
    good faith. Decision?

11. Halsey, a widower, was living without family or house-
    keeper in his house in Howell, New York. Burns and
    his wife claim that Halsey invited them to give up their
    house and business in Andover, New York, to live in his
    house and care for him. In return, they allege, he prom-
    ised them the house and its furniture upon his death.
    Acting upon this proposal, the Burnses left Andover,
    moved into Halsey's house, and cared for him until he
    died five months later. No deed, will, or memorandum
    exists to authenticate Halsey's promise. McCormick,
    the administrator of the estate, claims the oral promise
    is unenforceable under the statute of frauds. Explain
    whether McCormick is correct.

12. Amos orally agrees to hire Elizabeth for an eight-month
    trial period. Elizabeth performs the job magnificently,
    and after several weeks, Amos orally offers Elizabeth a
    six-month extension at a salary increase of 20 percent.
    Elizabeth accepts the offer. At the end of the eight-month
    trial period, Amos discharges Elizabeth, who brings suit
    against Amos for breach of contract. Is Amos liable?
    Why or why not?

CASE PROBLEMS

13. Ethel Greenberg acquired the ownership of the Carlyle
    Hotel on Miami Beach. Having had little experience in
    the hotel business, she asked Miller to participate in and
    counsel her operation of the hotel, which he did. He
    claims that because his efforts produced a substantial
    profit, Ethel made an oral agreement for the continuation
    of his services. Miller alleges that in return for his ser-
    vices, Ethel promised to marry him and to share the net
    income resulting from the operation of the hotel. Miller
    maintains that he rendered his services to Ethel in reli-
    ance upon her promises. The couple planned to wed in
    the fall, but Ethel, due to physical illness, decided not to
    marry. Miller sued for damages for Ethel's breach of their
    agreement. Is the oral contract enforceable? Discuss.

14. Dean was hired on February 12 as a sales manager of
    the Co-op Dairy for a minimum period of one year

    with the dairy agreeing to pay his moving expenses. By
    February 26, Dean had signed a lease, moved his family
    from Oklahoma to Arizona, and reported for work.
    After he worked for a few days, he was fired. Dean
    then brought this action against the dairy for his salary
    for the year, less what he was paid. The dairy argues
    that the statute of frauds bars enforcement of the oral
    contract because the contract was not to be performed
    within one year. Is the dairy correct in its assertion?
    Explain.

15. Alice solicited an offer from Robett Manufacturing
    Company to manufacture certain clothing that Alice
    intended to supply to the government. Alice contends
    that in a telephone conversation, Robett made an oral
    offer that she immediately accepted. She then received

the following letter from Robett, which, she claims, confirmed their agreement:

> Confirming our telephone conversation, we are pleased to offer the 3,500 shirts at $14.00 each and the trousers at $13.80 each with delivery approximately ninety days after receipt of order. We will try to cut this to sixty days if at all possible.
>
> This, of course, as quoted f.o.b. Atlanta and the order will not be subject to cancellation, domestic pack only. Thanking you for the opportunity to offer these garments, we are
>
> Very truly yours,
> Robett Manufacturing Co., Inc.
> Is the agreement enforceable against Robett? Why or why not?

16. David and Nancy Songer planned to travel outside the United States and wanted to acquire medical insurance prior to departure. They spoke with an agent of Continental who requested that Nancy Songer undergo a medical examination based on a statement that she had a heart murmur. She promptly complied, and the Songers later met with the agent to complete the application. David Songer signed the application and tendered a check for the first six months' premium. The Songers also claim that the agent stated that a "binder" was in effect such that policy coverage was available immediately. The agent subsequently denied making this statement, relying, instead, on a clause in the contract that required home office acceptance. The Songers left the United States and sixty days later inquired as to the status of their application. At approximately the same time, Continental denied the application and sent a refund to the Songers. Nancy Songer was then severely injured in an automobile accident. When Continental refused to honor the policy, the Songers claimed that the oral representation constituted part of the contract due to the vagueness of the policy "acceptance" language. Is the evidence regarding the oral representations admissible? Why or why not?

17. Yokel, a grower of soybeans, had sold soybeans to Campbell Grain and Seed Company and other grain companies in the past. Campbell entered into an oral contract with Yokel to purchase soybeans from him. Promptly after entering into the oral contract, Campbell signed and mailed to Yokel a written confirmation of the oral agreement. Yokel received the written confirmation but neither signed it nor objected to its content. Campbell now brings this action against Yokel for breach of contract upon Yokel's failure to deliver the soybeans. Should Yokel be considered a merchant and thus bound by Campbell's written confirmation? Explain.

18. Presti claims that he reached an oral agreement with Wilson by telephone in October 2016 to buy a horse for $60,000. Presti asserts that he sent Wilson a bill of sale and a postdated check, which Wilson retained. Presti also claims that Wilson told him that he wished not to consummate the transaction until January 1, 2017, for tax reasons. The check was neither deposited nor negotiated. Wilson denies that he ever agreed to sell the horse or that he received the check and bill of sale from Presti. Presti's claim is supported by a copy of his check stub and by the affidavit of his executive assistant, who says that he monitored the telephone call and prepared and mailed both the bill of sale and the check. Wilson argues that the statute of frauds governs this transaction, and because there was no writing, the contract claim is barred. Is Wilson correct? Explain.

19. After working for the Phelps Dodge Corporation under an oral contract for approximately twenty-three years, Louie E. Brown was suspended from work for unauthorized possession of company property. The next year, Phelps Dodge fired Brown after discovering that he was using company property without permission and building a trailer on company time. Brown sued Phelps Dodge for benefits under an unemployment benefit plan. According to the plan, "in order to be eligible for unemployment benefits, a laid-off employee must: (1) Have completed 2 or more years of continuous service with the company, and (2) Have been laid off from work because the company had determined that work was not available for him." The trial court held that the wording of the second condition was ambiguous and should be construed against Phelps Dodge, the party who chose the wording. A reading of the entire contract, however, indicates that the plan was not intended to apply to someone who was fired for cause. Explain what the correct interpretation of this contract is.

20. Katz offered to purchase land from Joiner, and after negotiating the terms, Joiner accepted. On October 13, over the telephone, both parties agreed to extend the time period for completing and mailing the written contract until October 20. Although the original paperwork deadline in the offer was October 14, Katz stated he had inserted that provision "for my purpose only." All other provisions of the contract remained unchanged. Accordingly, Joiner completed the contract and mailed it on October 20. Immediately after, however, Joiner sent Katz an overnight letter stating that "I have signed and returned contract, but have changed my mind. Do not wish to sell property." Joiner now claims an oral modification of a contract within the statute of frauds is unenforceable. Katz counters that the modification is not material and therefore does not affect the underlying contract. Explain who is correct.

21. When Mr. McClam died, he left the family farm, heavily mortgaged, to his wife and children. To save the farm from foreclosure, Mrs. McClam planned to use insurance proceeds and her savings to pay off the debts. She was unwilling to do so, however, unless she had full ownership of the property. Mrs. McClam wrote her daughter, stating that the daughter should deed over her interest in the family farm to her mother and promising that all the children would inherit the farm equally upon their mother's death. The letter further explained that if foreclosure occurred, each child would receive very little, but if they complied with their mother's plan, each would eventually receive a valuable property interest upon her death. Finally, the letter stated that all the other children had agreed to this plan. Consequently, the daughter also agreed. Years later, Mrs. McClam tries to convey the farm to her son Donald. The daughter challenges, arguing that the mother is contractually bound to convey the land equally to all of the children. Donald says this was an oral agreement to sell land and is unenforceable. The daughter argues that the letter satisfies the statute of frauds, making the contract enforceable. Who gets the farm? Explain.

22. Butler Brothers Building Company sublet all of the work in a highway construction contract to Ganley Brothers, Inc. Soon thereafter, Ganley brought this action against Butler for fraud in the inducement of the contract. The contract, however, provided: "The contractor [Ganley] has examined the said contracts…, knows all the requirements, and is not relying upon any statement made by the company in respect thereto." Can Ganley introduce into evidence the oral representations made by Butler? Why or why not?

23. Shane Quadri contacted Don Hoffman, an employee of Al J. Hoffman & Co. (Hoffman), to procure car insurance. Later, Quadri's car was stolen on October 25 or 26. Quadri contacted Hoffman, who arranged with Budget Rent-a-Car for a rental car for Quadri until his car was recovered. Hoffman authorized Budget Rent-a-Car to bill the Hoffman Agency. Later, when the stolen car was recovered, Hoffman telephoned Goodyear and arranged to have four new tires put on Quadri's car to replace those damaged during the theft. Budget and Goodyear sued Hoffman for payment of the car rental and tires. Is Hoffman liable on his oral promise to pay for the car rental and the four new tires? Why or why not?

24. Thomson Printing Company is a buyer and seller of used machinery. On April 10, the president of the company, James Thomson, went to the surplus machinery department of B.F. Goodrich Company in Akron, Ohio, to examine some used equipment that was for sale. Thomson discussed the sale, including a price of $9,000, with Ingram Meyers, a Goodrich employee and agent. Four days later, on April 14, Thomson sent a purchase order to confirm the oral contract for purchase of the machinery and a partial payment of $1,000 to Goodrich in Akron. The purchase order contained Thomson Printing's name, address, and telephone number, as well as certain information about the purchase, but did not specifically mention Meyers or the surplus equipment department. Goodrich sent copies of the documents to a number of its divisions, but Meyers never learned of the confirmation until weeks later, by which time the equipment had been sold to another party. Thomson Printing brought suit against Goodrich for breach of contract. Goodrich claimed that no contract had existed and that at any rate the alleged oral contract could not be enforced because of the statute of frauds. Is the contract enforceable? Why or why not?

25. On July 5, 2009, Richard Price signed a written employment contract as a new salesman with the Mercury Supply Company. The contract was of indefinite duration and could be terminated by either party for any reason upon fifteen days' notice. Between 2006 and 2014, Price was promoted several times. In 2014, Price was made vice president of sales. In September 2017, however, Price was told that his performance was not satisfactory and that if he did not improve, he would be fired. In February 2020, Price received notice of termination. Price claims that in 2014, he entered into a valid oral employment contract with Mercury Supply Company wherein he was made vice president of sales for life or until he should retire. Is the alleged oral contract barred by the one-year provision of the statute of frauds? Explain.

26. Plaintiffs leased commercial space from the defendant to open a florist shop. After the lease was executed, the plaintiffs learned that they could not place a freestanding sign along the highway to advertise their business because the Deschutes County Code allowed only one freestanding sign on the property, and the defendant already had one in place. The plaintiffs filed this action, alleging that defendant had breached the lease by failing to provide them with space in which they could erect a freestanding sign. Paragraph 16 of the lease provides as follows: "Tenant shall not erect or install any signs visible from outside the leased premises with out [sic] the previous written consent of the Landlord." Explain whether this evidence is admissible.

27. Jesse Carter and Jesse Thomas had an auto accident with a driver insured by Allstate. Carter and Thomas hired attorney Joseph Onwuteaka to represent them. Mr. Onwuteaka sent a demand letter for settlement of plaintiffs' claims to Allstate's adjustor, Ms. Gracie Weatherly. Mr. Onwuteaka claims Ms. Weatherly made, and he

orally accepted, settlement terms on behalf of the plaintiffs. When Allstate did not honor the agreements, Carter and Thomas filed a suit for breach of contract. Discuss the enforceability of the oral agreement.

28. Mary Iacono and Carolyn Lyons had been friends for almost thirty-five years. Mary suffers from advanced rheumatoid arthritis and is in a wheelchair. Carolyn invited Mary to join her on a trip to Las Vegas, Nevada, for which Carolyn paid. Mary contended she was invited to Las Vegas by Carolyn because Carolyn thought Mary was lucky. Sometime before the trip, Mary had a dream about winning on a Las Vegas slot machine. Mary's dream convinced her to go to Las Vegas, and she accepted Carolyn's offer to split "50-50" any gambling winnings. Carolyn provided Mary with money for gambling. Mary and Carolyn started to gamble, but after losing $47, Carolyn wanted to leave to see a show. Mary begged Carolyn to stay, and Carolyn agreed on the condition that Carolyn put the coins into the machines because doing so took Mary too long. Mary agreed and led Carolyn to a dollar slot machine that looked like the machine in her dream. The machine did not pay on the first try. Mary then said, "Just one more time," and Carolyn looked at Mary and said, "This one's for you, Puddin." They hit the jackpot, winning $1,908,064 to be paid over a period of twenty years. Carolyn refused to share the winnings with Mary. Is Mary entitled to one-half of the proceeds? Explain.

29. On February 9, George Jackson and his neighbors, Karen and Steve Devenyn, drafted and signed a document that purported to convey a seventy-nine-acre parcel of land owned by Jackson. By the terms of the agreement, Jackson wished to reserve a 1.3-acre portion of the parcel. Although the agreement contained a drawing and dimensions of the conveyance, it did not contain a specific description of the parcel. Jackson died on May 8, and his estate refused to honor the agreement. The Devenyns then filed a petition with the probate court to order a conveyance. Based on the parol evidence rule, the estate of Jackson objected to the admission of the witnesses' testimony that they could point out the specific area based on conversations with Jackson. Explain whether the oral evidence is admissible.

T A K I N G   S I D E S

Stuart Studio, an art studio, prepared a new catalog for the National School of Heavy Equipment, a school run by Gilbert and Donald Shaw. When the artwork was virtually finished, Gilbert Shaw requested Stuart Studio to purchase and supervise the printing of twenty-five thousand catalogs. Shaw told the art studio that payment of the printing costs would be made within ten days after billing and that if the "National School would not pay the full total, he would stand good for the entire bill." Shaw was chairman of the board of directors of the school, and he owned 100 percent of its voting stock and 49 percent of its nonvoting stock. The school became bankrupt, and Stuart Studio was unable to recover the sum from the school. Stuart Studio then brought an action against Shaw on the basis of his promise to pay the bill.

a. What are the arguments that Shaw is not liable on his promise?

b. What are the arguments that Shaw is liable on his promise?

c. Is Shaw obligated to pay the debt in question? Explain.

Third Parties to Contracts

CHAPTER OUTCOMES

After reading and studying this chapter, you should be able to:

- Distinguish between an assignment of rights and a delegation of duties.

- Identify (1) the requirements of an assignment of contract rights and (2) those rights that are not assignable.

- Identify those situations in which a delegation of duties is not permitted.

- Distinguish between an intended beneficiary and an incidental beneficiary.

- Explain when the rights of an intended beneficiary vest.

Whereas prior chapters considered contractual situations essentially involving only two parties, this chapter deals with the rights or duties of third parties, namely, persons who are not parties to the contract but who have a right to, or an obligation for, its performance. These rights and duties arise by (1) an assignment of the rights of a party to the contract, (2) a delegation of the duties of a party to the contract, or (3) the express terms of a contract entered into for the benefit of a third person. In an assignment or delegation, the third party's rights or duties arise after the contract is made, whereas in the third situation, the third-party beneficiary's rights arise at the time the contract was formed. We will consider these three situations in that order.

16-1 Assignment of Rights

Every contract creates both rights and duties. A person who owes a duty under a contract is an **obligor**, while a person to whom a contractual duty is owed is an **obligee**. For instance, Ann promises to sell to Bart an automobile for which Bart promises to pay $10,000 in monthly installments over the next three years. Ann's right under the contract is to receive payment from Bart, whereas Ann's duty is to deliver the automobile. Bart's right is to receive the automobile; his duty is to pay for it.

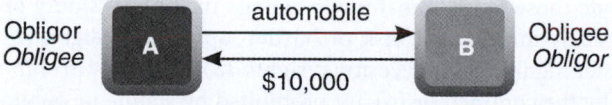

An **assignment of rights** is the voluntary transfer to a third party of the rights arising from the contract. In the previous example, if Ann were to transfer her right under the contract (the installment payments due from Bart) to Clark for $8,500 in cash, this would constitute a valid assignment of rights. In this case, Ann would be the **assignor,** Clark would be the **assignee,** and Bart would be the **obligor.**

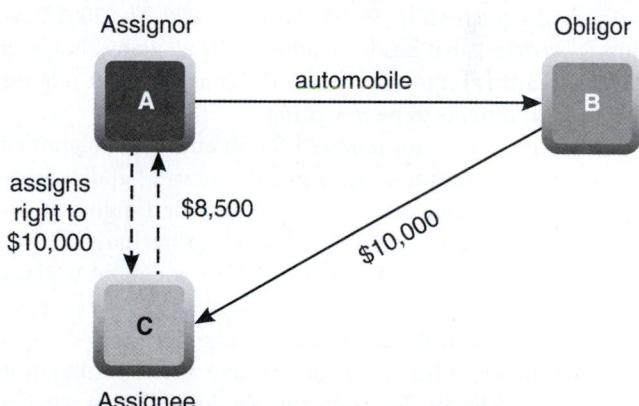

An effective assignment terminates the assignor's right to receive performance by the obligor. After an assignment, only the assignee has a right to the obligor's performance.

On the other hand, if Ann and Doris agree that Doris should deliver the automobile to Bart, this would constitute a delegation, not an assignment, of duties between Ann and Doris. A **delegation of duties** is a transfer to a third party of a contractual obligation. In this instance, Ann would be the **delegator,** Doris would be the **delegatee,** and Bart would be the **obligee.** Delegations of duties are discussed later in this chapter.

16-1a LAW GOVERNING ASSIGNMENTS

The law governing assignments arises principally from the common law of contracts, Article 2 of the Uniform Commercial Code (UCC), and Article 9 of the UCC. Article 2 applies to assignments of rights under a contract for the sale of goods. Article 9 covers all assignments made to secure the performance of an obligation *and* all assignments involving rights to payment for goods sold or leased or for services rendered.

16-1b REQUIREMENTS OF AN ASSIGNMENT

The Restatement defines an assignment of a right as a "manifestation of the assignor's intention to transfer it by virtue of which the assignor's right to performance by the obligor is extinguished in whole or in part and the assignee acquires a right to such performance." Section 317(1). No special form or particular words are necessary to create an assignment. Any words that fairly indicate an intention to make the assignee the owner of the right are sufficient. For instance, Eve delivers to Harold a writing addressed to Mary stating, "Pay Harold for his own use $1,000 out of the amount you owe me." This writing is a legally sufficient assignment. Restatement, Section 325, Illustration 1.

Unless otherwise provided by statute, an assignment may be oral. The original UCC imposed a writing requirement on all assignments greater than $5,000. Section 1-206. The 2001 Revision to Article 1 that has been adopted by all States, however, has deleted this requirement. In addition, Article 9 requires certain assignments to be in writing.

Consideration is not required for an effective assignment. Consequently, gratuitous assignments are valid and enforceable. By giving value for the assignment, the assignee manifests his assent to the assignment as part of the bargained-for exchange. On the other hand, when the assignment is gratuitous, the assignee's assent is not always required. Any assignee, however, who has not assented to an assignment, may disclaim the assignment within a reasonable time after learning of its existence and terms. Restatement, Section 327. No particular formality is required for the disclaimer, which renders the assignment inoperative from the beginning.

REVOCABILITY OF ASSIGNMENTS When the assignee gives consideration in exchange for an assignment, a contract exists between the assignor and the assignee. Consequently, the assignor may not revoke the assignment without the assignee's assent. A gratuitous assignment, in contrast, is revocable by the assignor and is terminated by her death, incapacity, or subsequent assignment of the right, unless she has made an effective delivery of the assignment to the assignee by

transferring a deed or other document evidencing the right, such as a stock certificate or savings passbook. Delivery also may consist of physically delivering a signed, written assignment of the contract right.

A gratuitous assignment is also rendered irrevocable if, prior to the attempted revocation, the donee-assignee receives payment of the claim from the obligor, obtains a judgment against the obligor, or obtains a new contract with the obligor. For example, Nancy owes Howard $50,000. Howard signs a written statement granting Paul a gratuitous assignment of his rights from Nancy but dies prior to delivering to Paul the signed, written assignment of the contract right. The assignment is terminated and therefore ineffective. On the other hand, had Howard delivered the signed, written assignment to Paul before he died, the assignment would have been effective and irrevocable.

Practical Advice

Be sure to make irrevocable assignments of only those rights you wish to transfer.

PARTIAL ASSIGNMENTS A partial assignment is a transfer of a portion of the contractual rights to one or more assignees. Although partial assignments were not enforceable at early common law, such assignments now are permitted and are enforceable. The obligor, however, may require all the parties entitled to the promised performance to litigate the matter in one action, thus ensuring that all parties are present and thereby avoiding the undue hardship of multiple lawsuits. For example, Jack owes Richard $2,500. Richard assigns $1,000 to Mildred. Neither Richard nor Mildred can maintain an action against Jack if Jack objects, unless the other is joined in the lawsuit against Jack.

16-1c RIGHTS THAT ARE ASSIGNABLE

As a general rule, most contract rights, including rights under an option contract, are assignable. The most common contractual right that may be assigned is the right to the payment of money, such as an account receivable or interest due or to be paid. The right to property other than money, such as goods and land, is also frequently assignable.

16-1d RIGHTS THAT ARE NOT ASSIGNABLE

To protect the obligor or the public interest, some contract rights are not assignable. These nonassignable contract rights include those that (1) materially change the obligor's duty or materially increase the risk or burden upon the obligor, (2) transfer highly personal contract rights, (3) are validly prohibited by the contract, or (4) are prohibited by statute or public policy. Restatement, Section 317(2).

ASSIGNMENTS THAT MATERIALLY INCREASE THE DUTY, RISK, OR BURDEN An assignment is ineffective when performance by the obligor to the assignee would differ materially from her performance to the assignor; that is, when the assignment would significantly change the nature or extent of the obligor's duty. Thus, an automobile liability insurance policy issued to Alex is not assignable by Alex to Betty. The risk assumed by the insurance company was liability for Alex's negligent operation of the automobile. Liability for operation of the same automobile by Betty would be a risk entirely different from the one that the insurance company had assumed. Similarly, Alex would not be allowed to assign to Cynthia, the owner of a twenty-five-room mansion, his contractual right to have Betty paint his small, two-bedroom house. Clearly, such an assignment would materially increase Betty's duty of performance. By comparison, the right to receive monthly payments under a contract may be assigned, for mailing the check to the assignee costs no more than mailing it to the assignor. Moreover, if a contract explicitly provides that it may be assigned, then rights under it are assignable even if the assignment would change the duty, risk, or burden of performance on the obligor. Restatement, Section 323(1).

ASSIGNMENTS OF PERSONAL RIGHTS When the rights under a contract are highly personal, in that they are limited to the person of the obligee, such rights are not assignable. An extreme example of such a contract is an agreement of two persons to marry one another. The prospective groom obviously cannot transfer to some third party the prospective bride's promise to marry him. A more typical example of a contract involving personal rights would be a contract between a teacher and a school. The teacher could not assign to another teacher her right to a faculty position. Similarly, a student who is awarded a scholarship cannot assign his right to some other person.

♦ *See Case 16-1*

EXPRESS PROHIBITION AGAINST ASSIGNMENT Contract terms prohibiting assignment of rights under the contract are strictly construed. Moreover, most courts interpret a general prohibition against assignments as a mere promise not to assign. As a consequence, the prohibition, if violated, gives the obligor a right to damages for breach of the terms forbidding assignment but does *not* render the assignment ineffective.

Section 322(1) of the Restatement provides that, unless circumstances indicate the contrary, a contract term prohibiting assignment of the contract bars only the delegation to the assignee (delegatee) of the assignor's (delegator's) duty of performance, not the assignment of rights. Thus, Abe and Bill contract for the sale of land by Bill to Abe for $300,000 and provide in their contract that Abe may not assign his rights

under it. Abe pays Bill $300,000 and thereby fully performs his obligations under the contract. Abe then assigns his rights to Cheryl, who is entitled to receive the land from Bill (the obligor) despite the contractual prohibition of assignment.

UCC Section 2-210(2) provides that a right to damages for breach of the whole contract or a right arising out of the assignor's due performance of his entire obligation can be assigned despite a contractual provision to the contrary. UCC Section 2-210(3) provides that unless circumstances indicate the contrary, a contract term prohibiting assignment of the contract bars only the delegation to the assignee (delegatee) of the assignor's (delegator's) duty of performance, not the assignment of rights. UCC Section 9-406 makes generally ineffective any term in a security agreement restricting the assignment of a security interest in any right to payment for goods sold or leased or for services rendered.

♦ *See Case 16-2*

Practical Advice

Consider including in your contract a provision prohibiting the assignment of any contractual rights without your written consent and making ineffective any such assignment.

ASSIGNMENTS PROHIBITED BY LAW Various Federal and State statutes, as well as public policy, prohibit or regulate the assignment of certain types of contract rights. For instance, assignments of future wages are subject to statutes, some of which prohibit such assignments altogether while others require them to be in writing and subject to certain restrictions. Moreover, an assignment that violates public policy will be unenforceable even in the absence of a prohibiting statute.

16-1e RIGHTS OF THE ASSIGNEE

OBTAINS RIGHTS OF ASSIGNOR The general rule is that an assignee **stands in the shoes** of the assignor. He acquires the rights of the assignor, but no new or additional rights, and takes the assigned rights with all of the defenses, defects, and infirmities to which they would be subject were the assignor to bring an action against the obligor. Thus, in an action brought by the assignee against the obligor, the obligor may plead fraud, duress, undue influence, failure of consideration, breach of contract, or any other defense against the assignor arising out of the original contract. The obligor also may assert rights of setoff or counterclaim arising against the assignor out of entirely separate matters, provided they arose prior to his receiving notice of the assignment.

The Code permits the buyer under a contract of sale to agree as part of the contract that he will not assert against an assignee any claim or defense that the buyer may have against the seller if the assignee takes the assignment for value, in good faith, and without notice of conflicting claims or of certain defenses. UCC Section 9-403. Such a provision in an agreement renders the seller's rights more marketable. The Federal Trade Commission, however, has invalidated such waiver of defense provisions in consumer credit transactions. (This rule is discussed more fully in *Chapter 27*.) Article 9 reflects this rule by essentially rendering waiver-of-defense clauses ineffective in consumer transactions. UCC Section 9-403(d). Most States also have statutes protecting buyers in consumer transactions by prohibiting waiver of defenses.

♦ *See Case 16-3*

NOTICE To be valid, notice of an assignment does not have to be given to the obligor. Nonetheless, giving such notice is advisable because an assignee will lose his rights against an obligor who pays the assignor without notice of the assignment: to compel an obligor to pay a claim a second time when she was not notified that a new party was entitled to payment would be unfair. For example, Donald owes Gary $1,000 due on September 1. Gary assigns the debt to Paula on August 1, but neither he nor Paula informs Donald. On September 1, Donald pays Gary. Donald is fully discharged from his obligation, whereas Gary is liable for $1,000 to Paula. On the other hand, if Paula had given notice of the assignment to Donald before September 1 and Donald had paid Gary nevertheless, Paula would then have the right to recover the $1,000 from either Donald or Gary.

Furthermore, notice cuts off any defenses based on subsequent agreements between the obligor and assignor. Moreover, as already indicated, notice precludes subsequent setoffs and counterclaims of the obligor that arise out of entirely separate matters.

Practical Advice
Upon receiving an assignment of a contractual right, promptly notify the obligor of the assignment.

16-1f IMPLIED WARRANTIES OF ASSIGNOR

An implied warranty is an obligation imposed by law upon the transfer of property or contract rights. In the absence of an express intention to the contrary, an assignor who receives value makes the following implied warranties to the assignee with respect to the assigned right:

1. that he will do nothing to defeat or impair the assignment;

2. that the assigned right actually exists and is subject to no limitations or defenses other than those stated or apparent at the time of the assignment;

3. that any writing evidencing the right delivered to the assignee or exhibited to him as an inducement to accept the assignment is genuine and what it purports to be; and

4. that the assignor has no knowledge of any fact that would impair the value of the assignment.

Thus, Eric has a right against Julia and assigns it for value to Gwen. Later, Eric gives Julia a release. Gwen may recover damages from Eric for breach of the first implied warranty.

16-1g EXPRESS WARRANTIES OF ASSIGNOR

An **express warranty** is an explicitly made contractual promise regarding property or contract rights transferred. The assignor is further bound by any express warranties he makes to the assignee with respect to the right assigned. The assignor does not, however, guarantee that the obligor will pay the assigned debt or otherwise perform, unless such a guarantee is explicitly stated.

Practical Advice
Consider obtaining from the assignor an express warranty stating that the contractual right is assignable and guaranteeing that the obligor will perform the assigned obligation.

16-1h SUCCESSIVE ASSIGNMENTS OF THE SAME RIGHT

The owner of a right could conceivably make successive assignments of the same claim to different persons. Assume that Barney owes Andrea $1,000. On June 1, Andrea for value assigns the debt to Carlos. Thereafter, on June 15, Andrea assigns it to David, who in good faith gives value and has no knowledge of the prior assignment by Andrea to Carlos. If the assignment is subject to Article 9, then that article's priority rules will control, as discussed in *Chapter 37*. Otherwise, the priority is determined by the common law. The majority rule in the United States is that the **first assignee in point of time** (here, Carlos) prevails over subsequent assignees. By comparison, in England and in a minority of the States, the first assignee to notify the obligor prevails.

The Restatement adopts a third view. A prior assignee is entitled to the assigned right and its proceeds to the exclusion of a subsequent assignee, *except* where the prior assignment is revocable or voidable by the assignor or where the subsequent assignee in good faith and without knowledge of the prior assignment gives value and obtains one of the following: (1) payment or satisfaction of the obligor's duty, (2) a judgment against the obligor, (3) a new contract with the obligor, or (4) possession of a writing of a type customarily accepted as a symbol or evidence of the right assigned. Restatement, Section 342.

16-2 Delegation of Duties

As indicated, contractual duties are *not* assignable, but their performance generally may be *delegated* to a third person. A **delegation of duties** is a transfer of a contractual obligation to a third party. For example, Anthony promises to sell Bella a new automobile, for which Bella promises to pay $10,000 by monthly installments over the next three years. If Anthony and Donald agree that Donald should deliver the automobile to Bella, this would not constitute an assignment but would be a delegation of duties between Anthony and Donald. In this instance, Anthony would be the **delegator**, Donald would be the **delegatee**, and Bella would be the **obligee**.

A delegation of duty does not extinguish the delegator's obligation to perform, because Anthony remains liable to Bella. When the delegatee accepts, or assumes, the delegated duty, both the delegator and delegatee are held liable to the obligee for performance of the contractual duty.

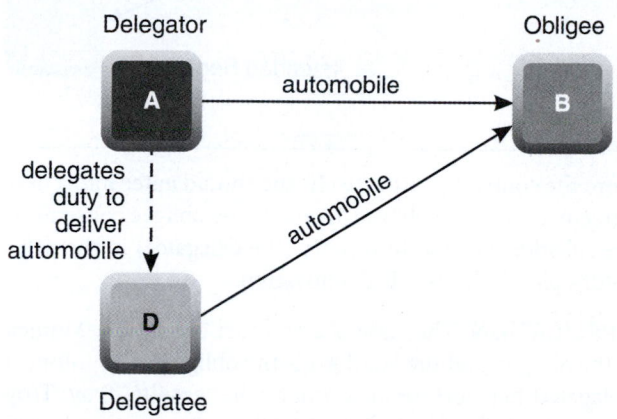

16-2a DELEGABLE DUTIES

Although contractual duties generally are delegable, a delegation will not be permitted if

1. the nature of the duties is personal in that the obligee has a substantial interest in having the delegator perform the contract;
2. the performance is expressly made nondelegable; or
3. the delegation is prohibited by statute or public policy.

Restatement, Section 318 and UCC Section 2-210. The courts will examine a delegation more closely than an assignment because a delegation compels the nondelegating party to the contract (the obligee) to receive performance from a party with whom she has not dealt.

For example, a schoolteacher may not delegate her performance to another teacher, even if the substitute is equally competent, because this is a contract that is personal in nature. In the frequently quoted words of an English case: "You have a

right to the benefit you contemplate from the character, credit and substance of the person with whom you contract." On the other hand, under a contract in which performance involves no peculiar or special skill and in which no personal trust or confidence is involved, the party may delegate the performance of his duty. For example, the duty to pay money, to deliver fungible goods such as corn, or to mow a lawn is usually delegable.

Practical Advice

When it is important that the other party to a contract personally perform his contractual obligations, consider including a term in the contract prohibiting any delegation of duties without written consent.

16-2b DUTIES OF THE PARTIES

Even when permitted, a delegation of a duty to a third person still leaves the delegator bound to perform. If the delegator desires to be discharged of the duty, she is allowed to enter into an agreement by which she obtains the consent of the obligee to substitute a third person (the delegatee) in her place. This is a **novation**, whereby the delegator is discharged and the third party becomes directly bound upon his promise to the obligee.

Though a delegation authorizes a third party to perform a duty for the delegator, a delegatee becomes liable for performance only if he assents to perform the delegated duties. Thus, if Frank owes a duty to Grace and Frank delegates that duty to Henry, Henry is not obligated to either Frank or Grace to perform the duty unless Henry agrees to do so. Nevertheless, if Henry promises either Frank (the delegator) or Grace (the obligee) that he will perform Frank's duty, Henry is said to have **assumed the delegated duty** and becomes liable to both Frank and Grace for nonperformance. Accordingly, when duties are both delegated and assumed, *both* the delegator and the delegatee are liable to the obligee for proper performance of the original contractual duty. The delegatee's promise to perform creates contract rights in the obligee who may bring an action against the delegatee as a third-party beneficiary of the contract between the delegator and the delegatee. (Third-party contracts are discussed later in this chapter.)

The question of whether a delegatee has assumed delegated duties frequently arises in the following ambiguous situation: Marty and Carol agree to an assignment of Marty's contract with Bob. The Code clearly resolves this ambiguity by providing that unless the language or circumstances indicate the contrary, an assignment of "the contract" or of "all my rights under the contract" or an assignment in similar general terms is an assignment of rights *and* a delegation of performance of the assignor's duties; its acceptance by the assignee constitutes a promise by her to perform those duties. Section 2-210(4). The Restatement, Section 328, has also adopted this position.

For example, Cooper Oil Co. has a contract to deliver oil to Halsey. Cooper Oil Co. delivers to Lowell Oil Co. a writing assigning to Lowell Oil Co. "all Cooper Oil Co.'s rights under the contract." Lowell Oil Co. is under a duty to Halsey to deliver the oil called for by the contract, and Cooper Oil Co. is liable to Halsey if Lowell Oil Co. does not perform. It should also be recalled that the Restatement and the Code provide that a clause prohibiting an assignment of "the contract" is to be construed as barring only the delegation to the assignee (delegatee) of the assignor's (delegator's) performance, unless the circumstances indicate the contrary.

◆ *See Case 16-4*

16-3 Third-Party Beneficiary Contracts

A contract in which a party (the **promisor**) promises to render a certain performance not to the other party (the **promisee**) but to a third person (the **beneficiary**) is called a third-party beneficiary contract. The third person is not a party to the contract but is merely a beneficiary of it. Such contracts may be divided into two types: (1) intended beneficiary and (2) incidental beneficiary. An **intended beneficiary** is intended by the two parties to the contract (the promisor and promisee) to receive a benefit from the performance of their agreement. Accordingly, the courts generally permit intended beneficiaries to enforce third-party contracts. For example, Abbott promises Baldwin to deliver an automobile to Carson if Baldwin promises to pay $10,000. Carson is the intended beneficiary.

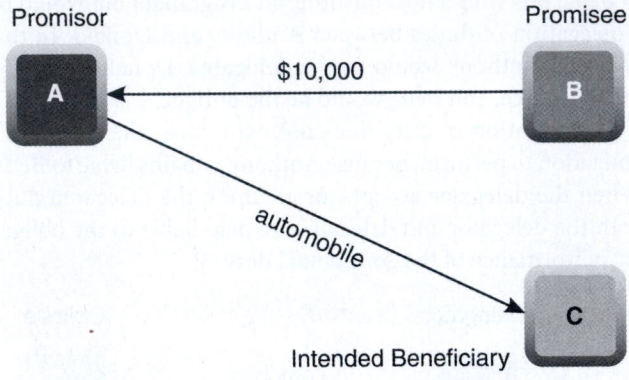

APPLYING THE LAW

Third Parties to Contracts

FACTS Monica signed a twelve-month lease with Grandridge Apartments in Grand City. But after only two months, she received a promotion that required her to move to Lakeville, three hundred miles away. Mindful of her lease obligation, she found an acquaintance, Troy, to rent the apartment for the remaining ten months. Troy promised Monica he would pay the rent directly to the landlord each month and would clean the place before moving out at the end of the lease term.

After moving in, Troy personally delivered a check for the rent to the landlord each month until four months later when he lost his job, at which point he stopped paying rent altogether. The landlord evicted Troy and, as he was unable to find another suitable tenant, he sued Monica for the rent owed on the remainder of the lease. Monica claimed the landlord should have sued Troy.

ISSUE Is Monica liable for the remaining lease payments?

RULE OF LAW Performance of a contract obligation generally may be delegated to a third person who is willing to assume the liability. However, such a delegation by the obligor does not extinguish the obligor/delegator's duty to perform the contract. If the delegator wishes to be discharged from the contract prospectively, she should enter into a new agreement with the obligee, in which the obligee consents to the substitution of a third party (the delegatee) in the delegator's place. This is called a novation.

APPLICATION The lease is a contract obligation. Monica is the obligor, and the landlord is the obligee. Here, Monica delegated her performance under the lease to Troy. Troy assumed liability for the lease payments by agreeing to pay the rent. However, even though a valid delegation has been made, Monica is not relieved of her duty to pay the rent. Instead, both Troy and Monica are now obligated to the landlord for the remaining lease term.

Had Monica entered into a novation with the landlord, only Troy would be liable for the remaining rent. But the facts do not support finding a novation. Troy made the rent payments directly to the landlord, who ultimately evicted Troy from the apartment. Therefore, the landlord was aware that Troy had taken possession of the apartment and that Troy may have taken on some responsibility for rent payments. At most, the landlord tacitly consented to the informal assignment and delegation of the lease to Troy. However, the landlord never agreed to substitute Troy for Monica and thereby to release Monica from her legal obligations under the lease.

CONCLUSION In a suit by the landlord, Monica is responsible for the remaining rent payments.

In an **incidental beneficiary** contract, the third party is not intended to receive a benefit under the contract. Accordingly, courts do not enforce the third party's right to the benefits of the contract. For example, Abbott promises to purchase and deliver to Baldwin an automobile for $10,000. In all probability, Abbott would acquire the automobile from Davis. Davis would be an incidental beneficiary and would have no enforceable rights against either Abbott or Baldwin.

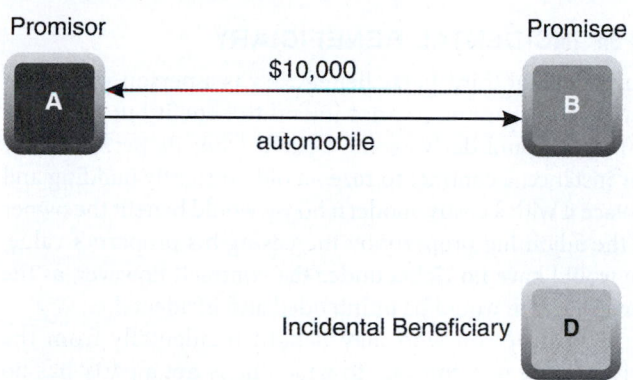

16-3a INTENDED BENEFICIARY

Unless otherwise agreed between the promisor and promisee, a beneficiary of a promise is an intended beneficiary if the parties intended this to be the result of their agreement. Restatement, Section 302. There are two types of intended beneficiaries: (1) donee beneficiaries and (2) creditor beneficiaries.

DONEE BENEFICIARY A third party is an intended donee beneficiary if the promisee's purpose in bargaining for and obtaining the agreement with the promisor is to make a gift of the promised performance to the beneficiary. The ordinary life insurance policy illustrates this type of contract. The insured (the promisee) makes a contract with an insurance company (the promisor) that promises, in consideration of premiums paid to it by the insured, to pay upon the death of the insured a stated sum of money to the named beneficiary, who is an intended donee beneficiary.

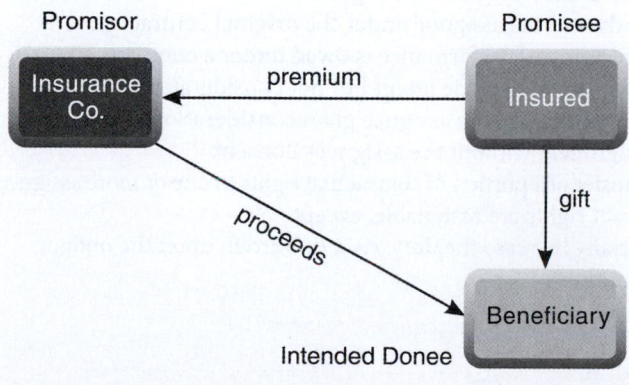

CREDITOR BENEFICIARY A third person is also an intended beneficiary if the promisee intends the performance of the promise to satisfy a legal duty he owes to the beneficiary, who is a creditor of the promisee. The contract involves consideration moving from the promisee to the promisor in exchange for the promisor's engaging to pay a debt or to discharge an obligation the promisee owes to the third person.

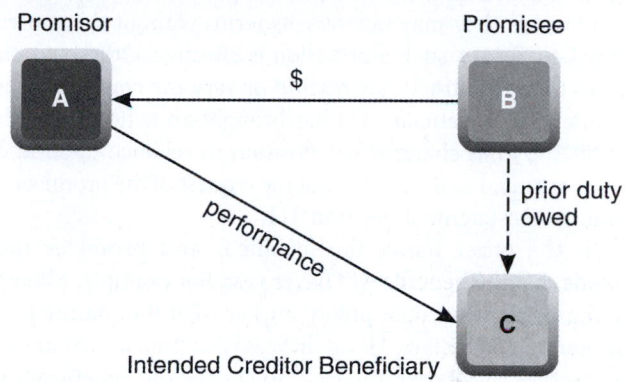

To illustrate, in a contract for the sale by Wesley of his business to Susan, Susan promises Wesley that she will pay all of his outstanding business debts, as listed in the contract. Here, Wesley's creditors are creditor beneficiaries. Similarly, in the classic *Lawrence v. Fox*, 20 N.Y. 268 (1859), Holly loaned Fox $300 in consideration for Fox's promise to pay that sum to Lawrence, a creditor of Holly. Fox failed to pay Lawrence, who sued Fox for the $300. The court held for Lawrence, who was permitted to recover as a third-party creditor beneficiary to the contract between Holly and Fox.

♦ *See Case 16-5*

RIGHTS OF INTENDED BENEFICIARY An intended *donee* beneficiary may enforce the contract only against the promisor. He cannot maintain an action against the promisee, as the promisee was under no legal obligation to him. An intended *creditor* beneficiary, however, may enforce the contract against either or both parties. If Willard owes Lola $500, and Julie contracts with Willard to pay this debt to Lola, Willard is not thereby relieved of his liability to Lola. If Julie breaks the contract, Lola, as a creditor beneficiary, may sue her. In addition, Lola may sue Willard as her debtor. If Lola should obtain judgments against both Julie and Willard, she is, of course, entitled to collect only one judgment. If Lola recovers against Willard, Willard has a right of reimbursement from Julie, the promisor. Restatement, Section 310.

VESTING OF RIGHTS A contract for the benefit of an intended beneficiary confers upon that beneficiary rights that she may enforce. Until these rights **vest** (take effect), however, the promisor and promisee may, by later agreement, vary or completely discharge them. The States vary considerably as to when vesting occurs. Some hold that vesting takes place immediately upon the making of the contract. In others, vesting occurs when the third party learns of the contract and assents to it. In another group of States, vesting requires the third party to change his position in reliance upon the promise made for his benefit. The Restatement has adopted the following position: if the contract between the promisor and promisee provides that they may not vary its terms without the consent of the beneficiary, such a provision is effective. Otherwise, the parties to the contract may rescind or vary the contract unless the intended beneficiary (1) has brought an action upon the promise, (2) has changed her position in reliance upon it, or (3) has assented to the promise at the request of the promisor or promisee. Restatement, Section 311.

On the other hand, the promisor and promisee may provide that the benefits will never vest. For example, Mildred purchases an insurance policy on her own life, naming her husband as beneficiary. Her policy, as such policies commonly do, reserves to Mildred the right to change the beneficiary or even to cancel the policy entirely.

Practical Advice

To avoid uncertainty, consider specifying in the contract whether there are any third-party beneficiaries and, if so, who they are, what their rights are, and when their rights vest.

Defenses Against Beneficiary In an action by the intended beneficiary of a third-party contract to enforce the promise, the promisor may assert any defense that would be available to her if the action had been brought by the promisee. The rights of the third party are based upon the promisor's contract with the promisee. Thus, the promisor may assert the absence of mutual assent or consideration, lack of capacity, fraud, mistake, and the like against the intended beneficiary. Once an intended beneficiary's rights have vested, however, the promisor may not assert the defense of contractual modification or rescission.

16-3b INCIDENTAL BENEFICIARY

An incidental third-party beneficiary is a person whom the parties to a contract did not intend to benefit but who nevertheless would derive some benefit from its performance. For instance, a contract to raze an old, unsightly building and replace it with a costly, modern house would benefit the owner of the adjoining property by increasing his property's value. He would have no rights under the contract, however, as the benefit to him would be unintended and incidental.

A third person who may benefit incidentally from the performance of a contract to which he is not a party has no rights under the contract. Neither the promisee nor the promisor intended that the third person benefit. Assume that for a stated consideration George promises Kathy that he will purchase and deliver to Kathy a brand-new Sony television of the latest model. Kathy pays in advance for the television. George does not deliver the television to Kathy. As an incidental beneficiary, Cosmos Appliances, Inc., the local exclusive Sony dealer, has no rights under the contract, although performance by George would produce a sale from which Cosmos would benefit.

CHAPTER SUMMARY

ASSIGNMENT OF RIGHTS **Definition of Assignment** voluntary transfer to a third party of the rights arising from a contract so that the assignor's right to performance is extinguished
- *Assignor* party making an assignment
- *Assignee* party to whom contract rights are assigned
- *Obligor* party owing a duty to the assignor under the original contract
- *Obligee* party to whom a duty of performance is owed under a contract

Requirements of an Assignment include intent but not consideration
- *Revocability of Assignment* when the assignee gives consideration, the assignor may not revoke the assignment without the assignee's consent
- *Partial Assignment* transfer of a portion of contractual rights to one or more assignees

Assignability most contract rights are assignable, except
- assignments that materially increase the duty, risk, or burden upon the obligor
- assignments of personal rights

- assignments expressly forbidden by the contract
- assignments prohibited by law

Rights of Assignee the assignee stands in the shoes of the assignor
- *Defenses of Obligor* may be asserted against the assignee
- *Notice* is not required but is advisable

Implied Warranty obligation imposed by law upon the assignor of a contract right

Express Warranty explicitly made contractual promise regarding contract rights transferred

Successive Assignments of the Same Right the majority rule is that the first assignee in point of time prevails over later assignees; minority rule is that the first assignee to notify the obligor prevails

DELEGATION OF DUTIES

Definition of Delegation transfer to a third party of a contractual obligation
- *Delegator* party delegating his duty to a third party
- *Delegatee* third party to whom the delegator's duty is delegated
- *Obligee* party to whom a duty of performance is owed by the delegator and delegatee

Delegable Duties most contract duties may be delegated, *except*
- duties that are personal
- duties that are expressly nondelegable
- duties whose delegation is prohibited by statute or public policy

Duties of the Parties
- *Delegation* delegator is still bound to perform original obligation
- *Novation* contract, to which the obligee is a party, substituting a new promisor for an existing promisor, who is consequently no longer liable on the original contract and is not liable as a delegator

THIRD-PARTY BENEFICIARY CONTRACTS

Definition a contract in which one party promises to render a performance to a third person (the beneficiary)

Intended Beneficiaries third parties intended by the two contracting parties to receive a benefit from their contract
- *Donee Beneficiary* a third party intended to receive a benefit from the contract as a gift
- *Creditor Beneficiary* a third person intended to receive a benefit from the agreement to satisfy a legal duty owed to her
- *Rights of Intended Beneficiary* an intended donee beneficiary may enforce the contract against the promisor; an intended creditor beneficiary may enforce the contract against either or both the promisor and the promisee
- *Vesting of Rights* if the beneficiary's rights vest, the promisor and promisee may not thereafter vary or discharge these vested rights
- *Defenses against Beneficiary* in an action by the intended beneficiary of a third-party contract to enforce the promise, the promisor may assert any defense that would be available to her if the action had been brought by the promisee

Incidental Beneficiary third party whom the two parties to the contract have no intention of benefiting by their contract and who acquires no rights under the contract

C A S E S

Rights That Are Not Assignable Personal Rights
IN RE MAGNESS
United States Court of Appeals, Sixth Circuit, 1992
972 F.2d 689

Joiner, J.

[The Dayton Country Club Company (the Club) offers many social activities to its members. The privilege to play golf at the Club, however, is reserved to a special membership category for which additional fees are charged. The Club chooses golfing memberships from a waiting list of members according to detailed rules, regulations, and procedures. Magness and Redman were golfing members of the Club. Upon their filing for bankruptcy, their trustee sought to assign by sale their golf rights to (1) other members on the waiting list, (2) other members not on the waiting list, or (3) the general public, provided the purchaser first acquired membership in the Club. The bankruptcy court found that the Club's rules governing golf membership were essentially anti-assignment provisions, and therefore, the estate could not assign rights contained in the membership agreement. On appeal to the district court, the bankruptcy court's ruling was affirmed. The district court added that this case was not a lease, but rather a "non-commercial dispute over the possession of a valuable membership in a recreational and social club."]

* * *

* * * [T]he contracts involve complex issues and multiple parties: the members of the club, in having an orderly procedure for the selection of full golfing members; the club itself, in demonstrating to all who would become members that there is a predictable and orderly method of filling vacancies in the golfing roster; and more particularly, persons on the waiting list who have deposited substantial sums of money based on

an expectation and a developed procedure that in due course they, in turn, would become full golfing members.

If the trustee is permitted to assume and assign the full golf membership, the club would be required to breach its agreement with the persons on the waiting list, each of whom has contractual rights with the club. It would require the club to accept performance from and render performance to a person other than the debtor. * * *

* * *

The contracts creating the complex relationships among the parties and others are not in any way commercial. They create personal relationships among individuals who play golf, who are waiting to play golf, who eat together, swim and play together. They are personal contracts and Ohio law does not permit the assignment of personal contracts. [Citation.]

So-called personal contracts, or contracts in which the personality of one of the parties is material, are not assignable. Whether the personality of one or both parties is material depends on the intention of the parties, as shown by the language which they have used, and upon the nature of the contract.

* * *

Therefore, we believe that the trustee's motion to assign the full golf membership should be denied. We reach this conclusion because the arrangements for filling vacancies proscribe assignment, the club did not consent to the assignment and sale, and applicable law excuses the club from accepting performance from or rendering performance to a person other than the debtor.

Express Prohibition of Assignment
ALDANA v. COLONIAL PALMS PLAZA, INC.
District Court of Appeal of Florida, Third District, 1991
591 So.2d 953; rehearing denied, 1992

Per Curiam

The appellant, Robert Aldana, appeals an adverse summary judgment in favor of appellee, Colonial Palms Plaza, Inc. and an order awarding Colonial Palms Plaza, Inc. attorney's fees pursuant to the offer of judgment rule. We reverse.

Colonial Palms Plaza, Inc. [Landlord], entered into a lease agreement with Abby's Cakes On Dixie, Inc. [Tenant] for

commercial space in a shopping center. The lease included a provision in which Landlord agreed to pay Tenant a construction allowance of up to $11,250 after Tenant satisfactorily completed certain improvements to the rented premises.

Prior to the completion of the improvements, Tenant assigned its right to receive the first $8,000 of the construction allowance to Robert Aldana [Assignee]. In return, Assignee loaned Tenant $8,000 to finance the construction. Assignee recorded the assignment and sent notice to the assignment by certified mail to Landlord.

When Tenant completed the improvements to the rented premises, Landlord ignored the assignment and paid Tenant the construction allowance. Assignee sued Landlord for the money due pursuant to the assignment. The trial court granted Landlord's motion for summary judgment.

The trial court also awarded Landlord attorney's fees pursuant to the offer of judgment rule, [citation], and costs pursuant to [citation].

Landlord relies on an anti-assignment clause in the lease agreement to argue that the assignment was void and unenforceable. The clause states in part:

> TENANT agrees not to assign, mortgage, pledge, or encumber this Lease, in whole or in part, or to sublet the whole or any part of the DEMISED PREMISES, or to permit the use of the whole or any part of the DEMISED PREMISES by any licensee or concessionaire, without first obtaining the prior, specific written consent of LANDLORD at LANDLORD'S sole discretion. * * * Any such assignment, encumbrance or subletting without such consent shall be void and shall at LANDLORD'S option constitute a default.

* * *

Assignee argues * * * that under ordinary contract principles, the lease provision at issue here does not prevent the assignment of the right to receive contractual payments. We agree.

So far as pertinent here, the lease provides that "TENANT agrees not to assign * * * this Lease, in whole or in part. * * *" Tenant did not assign the lease, but instead assigned a right to receive the construction allowance.

The law in this area is summarized in Restatement (Second) of Contracts, §322(1), as follows:

> Unless the circumstances indicate the contrary, a contract term prohibiting assignment of "the contract" bars only the delegation to an assignee of the performance by the assignor of a duty or condition.

As a rule of construction, in other words, a prohibition against assignment of the contract (or in this case, the lease) will prevent assignment of contractual duties, but does not prevent assignment of the right to receive payments due—unless the circumstances indicate the contrary. [Citations.]

Landlord was given notice of the assignment. Delivery of the notice of the assignment to the debtor fixes accountability of the debtor to the assignee. [Citation.] Therefore, Landlord was bound by the assignment. [Citation.] The trial court improperly granted final summary judgment in favor of Landlord and the judgment must be reversed. Consequently, the trial court's award of attorney's fees and costs to Landlord must also be reversed. The cause is remanded for further proceedings consistent herewith.

Reversed and remanded.

CASE 16-3

Rights of the Assignee
MOUNTAIN PEAKS FINANCIAL SERVICES, INC. v. ROTH-STEFFEN
Court of Appeals of Minnesota, 2010
778 N.W.2d 380

Bjorkman, J.

In May 1998, appellant Catherine Roth-Steffen graduated from law school with over $100,000 in school loans from more than a dozen lenders. Of this total, Roth-Steffen received $20,350 from the Missouri Higher Education Loan Authority (MOHELA) CASH Loan program through loans disbursed in 2005 and 2007. As of November 5, 1998, Roth-Steffen had incurred interest on these loans (MOHELA loan) in the amount of $3,043.28. Roth-Steffen listed the balance of $23,401.28 in a loan consolidation application she submitted in December 1998. She requested that the MOHELA loan not be consolidated with her other loans.

In February 2003, MOHELA assigned ownership of the MOHELA loan to Guarantee National Insurance Company (GNIC), which, in turn, assigned the loan for collection to respondent Mountain Peaks Financial Services, Inc. (Mountain Peaks). [Mountain Peaks commenced a collection action claiming that it holds the MOHELA loan and that it is entitled to judgment in the amount of the outstanding balance, $23,120.52, and additional interest at the rate of 2.54% from July 19, 2007. In response, Roth-Steffen asserted that the action is barred by Minnesota's six-year statute of limitations for collection on promissory notes. The district court granted summary judgment in favor of Mountain Peaks, determining that Mountain Peaks (1) owns Roth-Steffen's loan, (2) is a valid assignee of MOHELA's right, and (3) under the federal Higher Education Act is not to be subject to any state statutes of limitation.]

Enacted in 1965, the Higher Education Act was the first comprehensive government program designed to provide scholarships, grants, work-study funding, and loans for students to attend college [and graduate school]. [Citations.] Pursuant to the act, the federal government makes loans and guarantees loans made by private lenders. [Citation.] In 1991, in response to rising loan defaults and an unfavorable legal ruling, Congress adopted the Higher Education Technical Amendments. [Citation.]

The amendments eliminate all statutes of limitation on actions to recover on defaulted student loans for certain classes of lenders. [Citation.] These lenders are defined in section 1091a:

* * *

(B) a guaranty agency that has an agreement with the Secretary under section 1078(c) of this title that is seeking the repayment of the amount due from a borrower on a loan made under part B of this subchapter after such guaranty agency reimburses the previous holder of the loan for its loss on account of the default of the borrower; * * *

[Citation.] For convenience, we refer to the entities described in this statute as "named lenders."

Mountain Peaks argues that it is exempt from Minnesota's statutes of limitation because it is a valid assignee of MOHELA, a lender that has an agreement with the Secretary of Education under [section] 1091a(a)(2)(B). Roth-Steffen acknowledges that MOHELA is a named lender but argues that because Congress did not expressly identify assignees as named lenders, section 1091a does not preempt state statutes of limitation for claims asserted by assignees of named lenders.

* * *

Section 1091a does not, by its terms, extend its statutes-of-limitation exemption to assignees of named lenders. Nor does the statute expressly preclude application of the exemption to assignees. * * *

* * *

But courts interpreting federal statutes must also presume that Congress intended to preserve the common law * * *

The common law of most states, including Minnesota, has long recognized that "[a]n assignment operates to place the assignee in the shoes of the assignor, and provides the assignee with the same legal rights as the assignor had before assignment." [Citation]; *see generally* Restatement (Second) of Contracts § 317 (1981) (Assignment of a Right). Contractual rights and duties are generally assignable, including the rights to receive payment on debts, obtain nonmonetary performance, and recover damages. Restatement (Second) of Contracts § 316 (1981). But an assignor may not transfer rights that are personal, such as recovery for personal injuries or performance under contracts that involve personal trust or confidences. [Citation]; *see generally* Restatement (Second) of Contracts § 317 cmt. c. Under the common law, a contractual right to recover student-loan debt is assignable and does not fall within the personal-rights exclusion to the assignment rule.

* * *

* * * Because Congress legislated with a full knowledge of the common law of assignment, all contractual rights of the named lenders, including the protection from state statutes of limitations, should transfer to their assignees. * * *

We conclude that section 1091a of the Higher Education Act applies to assignees of named lenders. Mountain Peaks is an assignee of a named lender, therefore this action is not time-barred by any Minnesota statute of limitations.

CASE	Delegation of Duties	
16-4	**FEDERAL INS. CO. v. WINTERS** Supreme Court of Tennessee, 2011 354 S.W.3d 287	

Wade, J.

The defendant contractor [Winters Roofing Company] entered into a contract to replace a roof [on the home of Robert and Joanie Emerson]. When the newly installed roof developed leaks, [and without the knowledge of the Emersons,] the defendant hired an independent contractor [Bruce Jacobs] to make the necessary repairs. While performing the work, [Jacobs' use of a propane torch] caused a fire, resulting in an $871,069.73 insurance claim by the homeowners. [After paying the Emersons' claim, their insurer, Federal Insurance Company, acquired] the homeowners' rights and claims arising out of the fire[.] [T]he plaintiff insurance company sued the defendant * * * in contract. The

defendant filed a motion for summary judgment, asserting that because he had subcontracted the work, he could not be liable. The trial court granted the motion * * *. The Court of Appeals reversed, holding that the defendant had a non-delegable contractual duty to perform the roofing services in a careful, skillful, and workmanlike manner. This Court granted the defendant's application for permission to appeal in order to determine the propriety of the claim under the theory of contract.

In a breach of contract action, claimants must prove the existence of a valid and enforceable contract, a deficiency in the performance amounting to a breach, and damages caused by the breach. [Citation.] In addition to the explicit terms, contracts may be accompanied by implied duties, which can result in a breach. [Citations.] * * *

* * *

Here, the Plaintiff has alleged that the "[D]efendant breached its contractual *duties* by failing to complete the contract work... skillfully, carefully, diligently, [and] in a workmanlike manner." (Emphasis added). * * * In our view, the contract placed upon the Defendant the implied duty to skillfully, carefully, and diligently install and repair the Emersons' roof in a workmanlike manner.

The question that remains is whether the duty of the Defendant to replace the roof skillfully, carefully, diligently, and in a workmanlike manner could be delegated to a subcontractor. That is, may a contractor who has such a duty escape liability by subcontracting with a third party who breaches these implied responsibilities? * * *

The Restatement (Second) of Contracts specifically addresses this issue, explaining that "neither delegation of performance nor a contract to assume the duty [under a contract] . discharges any duty or liability of the delegating obligor." Restatement (Second) of Contracts §318(3) (1981). * * *

* * *

To be clear, this principle does not mean that the performance of service contracts cannot be delegated. Generally, a contractor may delegate the performance of the contract, in whole or in part, to a third party. Restatement (Second) of Contracts §318(1) (1981). The delegation of performance, however, does not relieve the contractor from the duties implicit in the original contract. [Citation.] Stated definitively, "'[o]ne who contracts to perform an undertaking is liable to his promise[e] for the [acts] of an independent contractor to whom he delegates performance." [Citation.]

* * *

Here, the Emersons contracted with the Defendant for the installation of a roof. * * * Because the Defendant had the implied duty under contract to install the roof carefully, skillfully, diligently, and in a workmanlike manner, and, further, because the delegation of the responsibility to perform the services did not operate to release him from liability, the Defendant, based on his contract with the Emersons, may be held liable for the damages caused by the acts of Jacobs, the subcontractor. * * *

* * * The judgment of the Court of Appeals is, therefore, affirmed, and the case is remanded for trial. * * *

| CASE 16-5 | Intended Beneficiary
FIRST BANK v. BRUMITT
Supreme Court of Texas, 2017
519 S.W.3d 95 |  |

Boyd, J.

This case arises from the unsuccessful sale of a Houston-area information-technology company Southway Systems, Inc. Richard Brumitt, who owned Southway, agreed to sell his stock to another Houston-area information-technology company, DTSG, Ltd. DTSG's owner and president, Don Oprea, initially wanted to purchase Brumitt's stock in two companies, Southway and NetStar Telecommunications. Seeking financing for the purchases, Oprea met with Tim Duffy, president of First Bank's division that handled federal Small Business Administration (SBA) loans. Oprea selected First Bank because he and DTSG already had an ongoing banking relationship with the bank. Shortly after their first meeting in September 2007, Duffy reviewed the companies' financial records and concluded that DTSG could have difficulty qualifying for the amount needed to purchase both of Brumitt's companies. Oprea and Brumitt then agreed that DTSG would acquire Southway but not NetStar.

At their first meeting, Oprea explained to Duffy that "a sense of urgency" existed and he needed to close on the loan by year's end because Brumitt was anxious to sell Southway and already had pending offers from other interested buyers.

Duffy told Oprea that they could close the loan by then because First Bank was a "preferred lender" and had "streamlined the [SBA-lending] process." Unfortunately, things did not go as planned. Over the next fourteen months, First Bank scheduled and postponed numerous closings. By November 2008, the loan still had not closed, and Oprea decided to seek financing elsewhere. Ultimately, Oprea never obtained a loan and DTSG never acquired Southway. By the time of trial in March 2013, Southway no longer had any employees and had essentially failed.

* * *

Oprea and DTSG sued First Bank in October 2009. Brumitt soon intervened as an additional plaintiff, alleging that he was a third-party-creditor beneficiary of the three "loan commitment letters executed by DTSG and First Bank." At trial in 2013, the jury found First Bank liable to both DTSG and Brumitt for breach of contract * * *. The trial court entered judgment based on the jury's verdict, awarding Brumitt $1,006,000 as breach-of-contract damages, * * *.

First Bank appealed. As to Brumitt's claims, the court of appeals affirmed the judgment on the breach of contract claim, expressly concluding that Brumitt was entitled to recover as a third-party beneficiary of the agreement between First Bank and DTSG. * * * [First Bank appealed.]

* * * Well-established principles govern our analysis of these issues. As a general rule, the benefits and burdens of a contract belong solely to the contracting parties, and "no person can sue upon a contract except he be a party to or in privity with it." [Citation.] An exception to this general rule permits a person who is not a party to the contract to sue for damages caused by its breach if the person qualifies as a third-party beneficiary. [Citation.] Absent a statutory or other legal rule to the contrary, a person's status as a third-party beneficiary depends solely on the contracting parties' intent. [Citation.] Specifically, a person seeking to establish third-party-beneficiary status must demonstrate that the contracting parties "intended to secure a benefit to that third party" and "entered into the contract directly for the third party's benefit." [Citations.] It is not enough that the third party would benefit—whether directly or indirectly—from the parties' performance, or that the parties knew that the third party would benefit. [Citations.] Nor does it matter that the third party intended or expected to benefit from the contract, for only the "intention of the contracting parties in this respect is of controlling importance." [Citation.] To create a third-party beneficiary, the contracting parties must have intended to grant the third party the right to be a "claimant" in the event of a breach. [Citation.]

To determine whether the contracting parties intended to directly benefit a third party and entered into the contract for that purpose, courts must look solely to the contract's language, construed as a whole. [Citations.] The contract must include "a clear and unequivocal expression of the contracting parties' intent to directly benefit a third party," and any implied intent to create a third-party beneficiary is insufficient. [Citations.] Courts may not presume the necessary intent. To the contrary, "we must begin with the presumption" that the parties contracted solely "for themselves," and only a clear expression of the intent to create a third-party beneficiary can overcome that presumption. [Citation.] If the contract's language leaves any doubt about the parties' intent, those "doubts must be resolved against conferring third-party beneficiary status." [Citation.] Although a contract may expressly provide that the parties do *not* intend to create a third-party beneficiary, [citation], the absence of such language is not determinative. "Instead, the controlling factor is the absence of any sufficiently clear and unequivocal language demonstrating" the necessary intent. [Citation.]

* * *

In his petition in intervention, Brumitt alleged that he is a third-party beneficiary of three "loan commitment letters executed by DTSG and First Bank." The first letter, which the parties signed in February 2008, stated that First Bank would provide a ten-year SBA loan to DTSG for $1,250,000,

and described the "loan purpose" as to "finance the purchase of existing business." The two-page letter described the loan rate, loan fees, repayment terms, collateral, and guarantors and listed seven "Conditions/Requirements," one of which was First Bank's "receipt and review of final purchase agreement." The second letter, which the parties signed in April 2008, reduced the loan amount to $800,000 and expressly identified Oprea as a guarantor, but was otherwise identical to the first. The third letter, signed in September 2008, increased the loan amount to $923,000 and identified different guarantors, but otherwise remained the same.

We agree with First Bank that these loan-commitment letters are unambiguous and did not clearly express the parties' intent to make Brumitt a third-party beneficiary. [Citation.] None of the three letters ever mentioned Brumitt or Southway or referred in any way to the seller from whom DTSG intended to purchase the "existing business." We could perhaps presume that Brumitt, as the seller of the existing business, would benefit from the sales transaction and thus from First Bank's agreement to finance that transaction, and we could also presume that both Oprea and Duffy knew that Brumitt would benefit. But such presumptions cannot support Brumitt's claim to be a third-party beneficiary. [Citation.] Contracts often benefit third parties, and the contracting parties are often aware that their performance under the contract will benefit third parties. Whether a third party may sue to enforce the parties' agreement, however, depends not on whether the third party will benefit or on whether the parties knew that the third party would benefit, but on whether the contracting parties "intended to secure a benefit to [a] third party" and "entered into the contract directly for the third party's benefit." [Citation.]

Here, the commitment letters' references to the loan's purpose—to finance DTSG's "purchase of [an] existing business"—and to the requirement of an acceptable "purchase agreement" indicate that DTSG and First Bank were aware that the seller would benefit from the loan agreement. But at most, they merely imply that the parties intended to confer some benefit to the business' seller, and any such implications are simply insufficient. [Citation.] Nothing in the loan-commitment letters "clearly," "fully," and "unequivocally" expresses the parties' intent to "contract directly for [Brumitt's] benefit" and thus to confer on Brumitt the right to be a "claimant" in the event of a breach. [Citations.] Relying on the agreement's plain and unambiguous language, we conclude that Brumitt is not a third-party beneficiary.

* * * In summary, we conclude that the agreement between First Bank and DTSG does not clearly and fully express the parties' intent to make Brumitt a third-party beneficiary, * * *. We thus reverse the court of appeals' judgment upholding First Bank's liability to Brumitt for breach of contract.

QUESTIONS

1. On December 1, Euphonia, a famous singer, contracted with Boito to sing at Boito's theater on December 31 for a fee of $45,000 to be paid immediately after the performance.

   a. Euphonia, for value received, assigns this fee to Carter.

   b. Euphonia, for value received, assigns this contract to sing to Dumont, an equally famous singer.

   c. Boito sells his theatre to Edmund and assigns his contract with Euphonia to Edmund. State the effect of each of these assignments.

2. The Smooth Paving Company entered into a paving contract with the city of Chicago. The contract contained the clause "contractor shall be liable for all damages to buildings resulting from the work performed." In the process of construction, one of the bulldozers of the Smooth Paving Company struck and broke a gas main, causing an explosion and a fire that destroyed the house of John Puff. Puff brought an action for breach of the paving contract against the Smooth Paving Company to recover damages for the loss of his house. Can Puff recover under this contract? Explain.

3. Anne, who was unemployed, registered with the Speedy Employment Agency. A contract was then made under which Anne, in consideration of such position as the Agency would obtain for her, agreed to pay the Agency one-half of her first month's salary. The contract also contained an assignment by Anne to the Agency of one-half of her first month's salary. Two weeks later, the Agency obtained a permanent position for Anne with the Bostwick Co. at a monthly salary of $1,900. The agency also notified Bostwick of the assignment by Anne. At the end of the first month, Bostwick paid Anne her salary in full. Anne then quit and disappeared. The Agency now sues Bostwick Co. for $950 under the assignment. Who will prevail? Explain.

4. Georgia purchased an option on Greenacre from Pamela for $10,000. The option contract contained a provision by which Georgia promised not to assign the option contract without Pamela's permission. Georgia, without Pamela's permission, assigns the contract to Michael. Michael seeks to exercise the option, and Pamela refuses to sell Greenacre to him. Must Pamela sell the land to Michael? Explain.

5. Julia contracts to sell to Hayden, an ice cream manufacturer, the amount of ice Hayden may need in his business for the ensuing three years to the extent of not more than 250 tons a week at a stated price per ton. Hayden makes a corresponding promise to Julia to buy such an amount of ice. Hayden sells his ice cream plant to Clark and assigns to Clark all of Hayden's rights under the contract with Julia. Upon learning of the sale, Julia refuses to furnish ice to Clark. Clark sues Julia for damages. Decision?

6. Brown enters into a written contract with Ideal Insurance Company under which, in consideration of her payment of the premiums, the insurance company promises to pay State College the face amount of the policy, $100,000, on Brown's death. Brown pays the premiums until her death. Thereafter, State College makes demand for the $100,000, which the insurance company refuses to pay upon the ground that State College was not a party to the contract. Can State College successfully enforce the contract? Why or why not?

7. Grant and Debbie enter into a contract binding Grant personally to do some delicate cabinetwork. Grant assigns his rights and delegates performance of his duties to Clarence.

   a. On being informed of this, Debbie agrees with Clarence, in consideration of Clarence's promise to do the work, that Debbie will accept Clarence's work, if properly done, instead of the performance promised by Grant. Later, without cause, Debbie refuses to allow Clarence to proceed with the work, though Clarence is ready to do so, and makes demand on Grant that Grant perform. Grant refuses.

   Can Clarence recover damages from Debbie?

   Can Debbie recover from Grant? Explain.

   b. Instead, assume that Debbie refuses to permit Clarence to do the work, employs another carpenter, and brings an action against Grant, claiming as damages the difference between the contract price and the cost to employ the other carpenter. Explain whether Debbie will prevail.

8. Rebecca owes Lewis $2,500 due on November 1. On August 15, Lewis assigns this right for value received to Julia, who gives notice on September 10 of the assignment to Rebecca. On August 25, Lewis assigns the same right to Wayne, who in good faith gives value and has no prior knowledge of the assignment by Lewis to Julia. Wayne gives Rebecca notice of the assignment on August 30. What are the rights and obligations of Rebecca, Lewis, Julia, and Wayne?

9. Lisa hired Jay in the spring, as she had for many years, to set out in beds the flowers Lisa had grown in her

greenhouses during the winter. The work was to be done in Lisa's absence for $300. Jay became ill the day after Lisa departed and requested his friend, Curtis, to set out the flowers, promising to pay Curtis $250 when Jay received his payment. Curtis agreed. Upon completion of the planting, an agent of Lisa's, who had authority to dispense the money, paid Jay, and Jay paid Curtis. Within two days, it became obvious that the planting was a disaster. Everything set out by Curtis died of water rot because he had operated Lisa's automatic watering system improperly.

May Lisa recover damages from Curtis? May she recover damages from Jay? If so, does Jay have an action against Curtis? Explain.

10. Caleb, operator of a window-washing business, dictated a letter to his secretary addressed to Apartments, Inc.,

stating, "I will wash the windows of your apartment buildings at $4.10 per window to be paid upon completion of the work." The secretary typed the letter, signed Caleb's name, and mailed it to Apartments, Inc. Apartments, Inc., replied, "Accept your offer."

Caleb wrote back, "I will wash them during the week commencing July 10 and direct you to pay the money you will owe me to my son, Bernie. I am giving it to him as a wedding present." Caleb sent a signed copy of the letter to Bernie.

Caleb washed the windows during the time stated and demanded payment to him of $8,200 (2,000 windows at $4.10 each), informing Apartments, Inc., that he had changed his mind about having the money paid to Bernie. What are the rights of the parties?

CASE PROBLEMS

11. McDonald's has an undeviating policy of retaining absolute control over who receives new franchises. McDonald's granted to Copeland a franchise in Omaha, Nebraska. In a separate letter, it also granted him a right of first refusal for future franchises to be developed in the Omaha–Council Bluffs area. Copeland then sold all rights in his six McDonald's franchises to Schupack. When McDonald's offered a new franchise in the Omaha area to someone other than Schupack, Schupack attempted to exercise the right of first refusal. McDonald's would not recognize the right in Schupack, claiming that it was personal to Copeland and, therefore, nonassignable without its consent. Schupack brought an action for specific performance, requiring McDonald's to accord him the right of first refusal. Is Schupack correct in his contention? Explain.

12. In 1952, the estate of George Bernard Shaw granted to Gabriel Pascal Enterprises, Limited, the exclusive rights to produce a musical play and a motion picture based on Shaw's play *Pygmalion*. The agreement contained a provision terminating the license if Gabriel Pascal Enterprises did not arrange for well-known composers, such as Lerner and Loewe, to write the musical and produce it within a specified time. George Pascal, owner of 98 percent of Gabriel Pascal Enterprises' stock, attempted to meet these requirements but died in July 1954 before negotiations had been completed. In February 1954, however, while the license had two years yet to run, Pascal sent a letter to Kingman, his executive secretary, granting to her certain percentages of his share of the profits from the expected stage and screen productions of *Pygmalion*. Subsequently, Pascal's estate arranged for

the writing and production of the highly successful *My Fair Lady*, based on Shaw's *Pygmalion*. Kingman then sued to enforce Pascal's gift assignment of the future royalties. Decision?

13. Northwest Airlines leased space in the terminal building at the Portland Airport from the Port of Portland. Crosetti entered into a contract with the Port to furnish janitorial services for the building, which required Crosetti to keep the floor clean, to indemnify the Port against loss due to claims or lawsuits based upon Crosetti's failure to perform, and to provide public liability insurance for the Port and Crosetti. A patron of the building who was injured by a fall caused by a foreign substance on the floor at Northwest's ticket counter brought suit for damages against Northwest, the Port, and Crosetti. Upon settlement of this suit, Northwest sued Crosetti to recover the amount of its contribution to the settlement and other expenses on the grounds that Northwest was a third-party beneficiary of Crosetti's contract with the Port to keep the floors clean and, therefore, within the protection of Crosetti's indemnification agreement. Will Northwest prevail? Why or why not?

14. Tompkins-Beckwith, as the contractor on a construction project, entered into a subcontract with a division of Air Metal Industries. Air Metal procured American Fire and Casualty Company to be surety on certain bonds in connection with contracts it was performing for Tompkins-Beckwith and others. As security for these bonds, on January 3, Air Metal executed an assignment to American Fire of all accounts receivable under the Tompkins-Beckwith subcontract. On November 26 of that year, Boulevard National Bank lent money to Air

Metal. To secure the loans, Air Metal purported to assign to the bank certain accounts receivable it had under its subcontract with Tompkins-Beckwith.

In June of the following year, Air Metal defaulted on various contracts bonded by American Fire. On July 1, American Fire served formal notice on Tompkins-Beckwith of Air Metal's assignment. Tompkins-Beckwith acknowledged the assignment and agreed to pay. In August, Boulevard National Bank notified Tompkins-Beckwith of its assignment. Tompkins-Beckwith refused to recognize the bank's claim and, instead, paid all remaining funds that had accrued to Air Metal to American Fire. The bank then sued to enforce its claim under Air Metal's assignment. Is the assignment effective? Why or why not?

15. The International Association of Machinists (the union) was the bargaining agent for the employees of Powder Power Tool Corporation. On August 24, the union and the corporation executed a collective bargaining agreement providing for retroactively increased wage rates for the corporation's employees effective as of April 1. Three employees who were working for Powder before and for several months after April 1 but who were not employed by the corporation when the agreement was executed on August 24, were paid to the time their employment terminated at the old wage scale. The three employees assigned their claims to Springer, who brought this action against the corporation for the extra wages. Decision? Explain.

16. In March, Adrian Saylor sold government bonds owned exclusively by him and with $6,450 of the proceeds opened a savings account in a bank in the name of "Mr. or Mrs. Adrian M. Saylor." In June of the following year, Saylor deposited the additional sum of $2,132 of his own money in the account. There were no other deposits and no withdrawals prior to Saylor's death a year later. Is the balance of the account on Saylor's death payable wholly to Adrian Saylor's estate, wholly to his widow, or half to each? Explain.

17. Linda King was found liable to Charlotte Clement as the result of an automobile accident. King, who was insolvent at the time, declared bankruptcy and directed her attorney, Prestwich, to list Clement as an unsecured creditor. The attorney failed to carry out this duty, and consequently King sued him for legal malpractice. When Clement pursued her judgment against King, she received a written assignment of King's legal malpractice claim against Prestwich. Clement has attempted to bring the claim, but Prestwich alleges that a claim for legal malpractice is not assignable. Decision? Explain.

18. Rensselaer Water Company contracted with the city of Rensselaer to provide water to the city for use in homes, public buildings, industry, and fire hydrants. During the term of the contract, a building caught fire. The fire spread to a nearby warehouse and destroyed it and its contents. The water company knew of the fire but failed to supply adequate water pressure at the fire hydrant to extinguish the fire. The warehouse owner sued the water company for failure to fulfill its contract with the city. Can the warehouse owner enforce the contract? Explain.

19. While under contract to play professional basketball for the Philadelphia 76ers, Billy Cunningham, an outstanding player, negotiated a three-year contract with the Carolina Cougars, another professional basketball team. The contract with the Cougars was to begin at the expiration of the contract with the 76ers. In addition to a signing bonus of $125,000, Cunningham was to receive under the new contract a salary of $100,000 for the first year, $110,000 for the second, and $120,000 for the third. The contract also stated that Cunningham "had special, exceptional and unique knowledge, skill and ability as a basketball player" and that Cunningham therefore agreed the Cougars could enjoin him from playing basketball for any other team for the term of the contract. In addition, the contract contained a clause prohibiting its assignment to another club without Cunningham's consent. In 1971, the ownership of the Cougars changed, and Cunningham's contract was assigned to Munchak Corporation, the new owners, without his consent. When Cunningham refused to play for the Cougars, Munchak Corporation sought to enjoin his playing for any other team. Cunningham asserts that his contract was not assignable. Was the contract assignable? Explain.

20. Pauline Brown was shot and seriously injured by an unknown assailant in the parking lot of National Supermarkets. Pauline and George Brown brought a negligence action against National; Sentry Security Agency; and T. G. Watkins, a security guard and Sentry employee. Sentry had a security contract with National. The Browns maintained that the defendants have a legal duty to protect National's customers both in the store and in the parking lot and that this duty was breached. The defendants denied this allegation. What will the Browns have to prove to prevail? Explain.

21. Members of Local 100, Transport Workers Union of America (TWU), engaged in an eleven-day mass transit strike that paralyzed the life and commerce of the city of New York. Plaintiffs are engaged in the practice of law as a profession, maintaining offices in Manhattan. Plaintiffs sue both individually and on behalf of all other professional and business entities (the class) that were damaged

as a consequence of the defendants' willful disruption of the service provided by the public transportation system of the City of New York. The law firm sought to recover as a third-party beneficiary of the collective bargaining agreement between the union and New York City. The agreement contains a no-strike clause and states that the TWU agreed to cooperate with the city to provide a safe, efficient, and dependable mass transit system. As a member of the public which depends on the public transit system and which employs dozens of persons who need the public transit system to get to and from work, plaintiffs argue that they are within the class of persons for whose benefit the TWU has promised to provide "dependable transportation service." Are the members of the class action suit entitled to recover? Explain.

22. On behalf of himself and other similarly situated options investors, Rick Lockwood sued defendant, Standard & Poor's Corporation (Standard & Poor's), for breach of contract. Lockwood alleged that he and other options investors suffered lost profits on certain options contracts because Standard & Poor's failed to correct a closing stock index value. Standard & Poor's compiles and publishes two composite stock indexes, the "S&P 100" and the "S&P 500" (collectively the S&P indexes).

The S&P indexes are weighted indexes of common stocks primarily listed for trading on the New York Stock Exchange (NYSE). Standard & Poor's licenses its S&P indexes to the Chicago Board Options Exchange (CBOE) to allow the trading of securities options contracts (S&P index options) based on the S&P indexes (the license agreement). S&P index options are settled by the Options Clearing Corporation (OCC). The exercise settlement values for S&P index options are the closing index values for the S&P 100 and S&P 500 stock market indexes as reported by Standard & Poor's to OCC following the close of trading on the day of exercise.

In his complaint, Lockwood alleged that at approximately 4:12 P.M. on Friday, December 15, the last trading day prior to expiration of the December S&P index options contracts, the NYSE erroneously reported a closing price for Ford Motor Company common stock. Ford Motor Company was one of the composite stocks in both the S&P 100 and S&P 500. At approximately 4:13 P.M., Standard & Poor's calculated and disseminated closing index values for the S&P 100 and S&P 500 stock market indexes based on the erroneous price for Ford stock. The NYSE reported a corrected closing price for Ford Motor at approximately 4:18 P.M. Standard & Poor's corrected the values of the S&P 100 and S&P 500 stock market indexes the following Monday, December 18. In the meantime, however, OCC automatically settled all expiring S&P index options according to the expiration date of Saturday, December 16. OCC used the uncorrected closing index values to settle all expiring S&P index options. Due to the error, Lockwood alleges that the S&P 100 index was overstated by 0.15 and he lost $105. Lockwood claimed investors in S&P 500 index options suffered similar losses. Lockwood filed a class action on behalf of "all holders of long put options and all sellers of short call options on the S&P 100 or S&P 500, which were settled based on the closing index values for December 15, as reported by Standard & Poor's," claiming that the options holders could recover in contract as third-party beneficiaries of the license agreement between Standard & Poor's and the CBOE. Are the members of the class action suit entitled to recover? Explain.

23. Potomac Electric Power Company (PEPCO) is an electric utility serving the metropolitan Washington, D.C., area. Panda-Brandywine, L.P. (Panda) is a "qualified facility" under the Public Utility Regulatory Policies Act of 1978. In August 1991, PEPCO and Panda entered into a power purchase agreement (PPA) calling for (1) the construction by Panda of a new 230-megawatt cogenerating power plant in Prince George's County, Maryland; (2) connection of the facility to PEPCO's high-voltage transmission system by transmission facilities to be built by Panda but later transferred without cost to PEPCO; and (3) upon commencement of the commercial operation of the plant, for PEPCO to purchase the power generated by that plant for a period of twenty-five years.

The plant was built at a cost of $215 million. The PPA is 113 pages in length, is single-spaced, and is both detailed and complex. It gave PEPCO substantial authority to review, influence, and, in some instances, determine important aspects of both the construction and operation of the Panda facility. Section 19.1 of the PPA provided that the agreement was not assignable and not delegable without the written consent of the other party, which consent could not be unreasonably withheld. In 1999, Maryland enacted legislation calling for the restructuring of the electric industry in an effort to promote competition in the generation and delivery of electricity. PEPCO's proposed restructuring involved a complete divestiture of its electric generating assets and its various PPAs, to be accomplished by an auction. The sale to the winning bidder was to be accomplished by an Asset Purchase and Sale Agreement (APSA) that included the PPA to which PEPCO and Panda were parties. Under the APSA, the buyer was authorized to take all actions that PEPCO could lawfully take under the PPA with Panda. On June 7, 2000, Southern Energy,

Inc. (SEI), was declared the winning bidder. On September 27, 2000, the Public Service Commission (PSC) entered an order declaring, among other things, that the provisions in the APSA did not constitute an assignment or transfer within the meaning of Section 19.1 of the Panda PPA, that PEPCO was not assigning "significant obligations and rights under the PPA," that Panda would not be harmed by the transaction, and that the APSA did not "fundamentally alter" the contract between Panda and PEPCO. The PSC thus concluded that Panda's consent to the proposed APSA was not required. Panda disagreed. Is Panda correct? Explain.

T A K I N G   S I D E S

Pizza of Gaithersburg and The Pizza Shops (Pizza Shops) contracted with Virginia Coffee Service (Virginia) to install vending machines in each of their restaurants. One year later, the Macke Company (a provider of vending machines) purchased Virginia's assets, and the vending machine contracts were assigned to Macke. Pizza Shops had dealt with Macke before but had chosen Virginia because they preferred the way it conducted its business. When Pizza Shops attempted to terminate their contracts for vending services, Macke brought suit for damages for breach of contract.

a. What arguments would support Pizza Shop's termination of the contracts?

b. What arguments would support Macke's suit for breach of contract?

c. Which side should prevail? Explain.

CHAPTER 17

Performance, Breach, and Discharge

CHAPTER OUTCOMES

After reading and studying this chapter, you should be able to:

- Distinguish among the various types of conditions.

- Distinguish between full performance and tender of performance.

- Explain the difference between material breach and substantial performance.

- Distinguish among a mutual rescission, a substituted contract, an accord and satisfaction, and a novation.

- Explain the ways discharge may be brought about by operation of law.

The subject of discharge of contracts concerns the termination of contractual duties. In earlier chapters we have seen how parties may become bound to a contract. It is also important to know how a person may become unbound from a contract. For although contractual promises are made for a purpose, and the parties reasonably expect this purpose to be fulfilled by performance, performance of a contractual duty is only one method of discharge.

Whatever causes a binding promise to cease to be binding constitutes a discharge of the contract. In general, there are four kinds of discharge: (1) performance by the parties, (2) material breach by one or both of the parties, (3) agreement of the parties, and (4) operation of law. Moreover, many contractual promises are not absolute promises to perform but rather are conditional; that is, they are dependent upon the happening or nonhappening of a specific event. After a discussion of conditions, the four kinds of discharge will be covered.

17-1 Conditions

A **condition** is an event whose happening or nonhappening affects a duty of performance under a contract. Some conditions must be satisfied before any duty to perform arises; others terminate the duty to perform; still others either limit or modify the duty to perform. A promisor inserts conditions into a contract for her protection and benefit. Furthermore, the more conditions to which a promise is subject, the less content the promise has. For example, a promise to pay

$8,000, provided such sum is realized from the sale of an automobile, provided the automobile is sold within sixty days, and provided the automobile, which has been stolen, can be found, is clearly different from, and worth considerably less than, an unconditional promise by the same promisor to pay $8,000.

A fundamental difference exists between the breach or nonperformance of a contractual promise and the failure or nonhappening of a condition. A breach of contract subjects the promisor to liability. It may or may not, depending upon its materiality, excuse nonperformance by the nonbreaching party of his duty under the contract. The happening or non-happening of a condition, on the other hand, either prevents a party from acquiring a right to performance by the other party or deprives him of such a right, but subjects neither party to any liability.

Conditions may be classified by *how* they are imposed: express conditions, implied-in-fact conditions, or implied-in-law conditions (also called constructive conditions). They also may be classified by *when* they affect a duty of performance: conditions concurrent, conditions precedent, or conditions subsequent. These two ways of classifying conditions are not mutually exclusive; for example, a condition may be constructive and concurrent or express and precedent.

Practical Advice

Consider using conditions to place the risk of the nonoccurrence of critical, uncertain events on the other party to the contract.

17-1a EXPRESS CONDITION

An **express condition** is explicitly set forth in language. No particular form of words is necessary to create an express condition, so long as the event to which the performance of the promise is made subject is clearly expressed. An express condition is usually preceded by such words as *provided that, on condition that, if, subject to, while, after, upon,* or *as soon as.*

The basic rule applied to express conditions is that they must be fully and literally performed before the conditional duty to perform arises. Where application of the full and literal performance test would result in a forfeiture, however, the courts usually apply to the completed portion of the condition a *substantial satisfaction* test, as discussed later in this chapter under the section titled "Substantial Performance."

SATISFACTION OF A CONTRACTING PARTY The parties to a contract may agree that performance by one of them will be to the satisfaction of the other, who will not be obligated to pay for such performance unless he is satisfied. This is an express condition to the duty to pay for the performance. Assume that tailor Melissa contracts to make a suit of clothes to Brent's satisfaction and that Brent promises to pay Melissa $850 for the suit if he is satisfied with it when completed. Melissa completes the suit using materials ordered by Brent. Though the suit fits Brent beautifully, he tells Melissa that he is not satisfied with it and refuses to accept or pay for it. If Brent's dissatisfaction is honest and in good faith, even if it is unreasonable, Melissa is not entitled to recover $850 or any amount from Brent by reason of the nonhappening of the express condition. Where satisfaction relates to a matter of personal taste, opinion, or judgment, the law applies the **subjective satisfaction** standard: if the promisor in good faith is dissatisfied, the condition has not occurred.

If the contract does not clearly indicate that satisfaction is subjective or if the performance contracted for relates to mechanical fitness or utility, the law assumes an **objective satisfaction** standard. For example, the objective standard would apply to the sale of a building or standard goods, such as steel, coal, or grain. In such cases, the question would not be whether the promisor was actually satisfied with the performance by the other party, but whether, as a reasonable person, he ought to be satisfied.

♦ *See Case 17-1*

Practical Advice

In your contracts based on satisfaction, specify which standard—subjective satisfaction or objective satisfaction—should apply to each contractual duty of performance.

SATISFACTION OF A THIRD PARTY A contract may condition the duty of one contracting party to accept and pay for the performance of the other contracting party upon the approval of a third party who is not a party to the contract. For example, building contracts commonly provide that before the owner is required to pay, the builder shall furnish a certificate of the architect stating that the building has been constructed according to the plans and specifications. Although the owner is paying for the building, not for the certificate, he must have both the building and the certificate before he is obligated to pay. The duty of payment was made expressly conditional upon the presentation of the certificate.

17-1b IMPLIED-IN-FACT CONDITIONS

Implied-in-fact conditions are similar to express conditions in that they must fully and literally occur and in that the parties understand them to be part of the agreement. They differ in that they are not stated in express language; rather, they are necessarily inferred from the terms of the contract, the nature of the transaction, or the conduct of the parties. Thus, if Fernando, for $1,750, contracts to paint Peggy's house any color Peggy desires, it is necessarily implied in fact that Peggy will inform Fernando of the desired color before Fernando begins to paint. The notification of choice of color is an implied-in-fact condition, an operative event that must occur before Fernando is subject to the duty of painting the house.

17-1c IMPLIED-IN-LAW CONDITIONS

An **implied-in-law condition**, or a **constructive condition**, is imposed by law to accomplish a just and fair result. It differs from an express condition and an implied-in-fact condition in two ways: (1) it is not contained in the language of the contract or necessarily inferred from the contract, and (2) it need only be substantially performed. For example, Melinda contracts to sell a certain tract of land to Kelly for $18,000, but the contract is silent as to the time of delivery of the deed and payment of the price. The law will imply that the respective performances are not independent of each other; consequently, the courts will treat the promises as mutually dependent and therefore will hold that a delivery or tender of the deed by Melinda to Kelly is a condition to Kelly's duty to pay the price. Conversely, Melinda's duty to deliver the deed to Kelly is conditioned upon the payment or tender of $18,000 by Kelly to Melinda. If the contract specifies a sale on credit, however, giving Kelly thirty days after delivery of the deed within which to pay the price, these conditions are not implied by law because the parties have expressly agreed to make their respective duties of performance independent of each other.

17-1d CONCURRENT CONDITIONS

Concurrent conditions occur when the mutual duties of performances are to take place simultaneously. As indicated previously in the discussion of implied-in-law conditions, in the absence of an agreement to the contrary, the law assumes that the respective performances under a contract are concurrent conditions.

17-1e CONDITIONS PRECEDENT

A **condition precedent** is an event that must occur before performance under a contract is due. For instance, if Gail is to deliver shoes to Mike on June 1, with Mike's duty to pay for the shoes on July 15, Gail's delivery of the shoes is a condition precedent to Mike's performance. Similarly, if Seymour promises to buy Edna's land for $50,000, provided Seymour can obtain financing in the amount of $40,000 at 10 percent interest or less for thirty years within sixty days of signing the contract, Seymour's obtaining the specified financing is a condition precedent to his duty. If the condition is satisfied, Seymour is bound to perform; if it is not, he is not so bound. Seymour, however, is under an implied-in-law duty to use his best efforts to obtain financing under these terms.

17-1f CONDITIONS SUBSEQUENT

A **condition subsequent** is an event that terminates an existing duty. For example, where goods are sold under terms of "sale or return," the buyer has the right to return the goods to the seller within a stated period but is under an immediate duty to pay the price unless she and the seller have agreed upon credit. A return of the goods, which operates as a condition subsequent, terminates the duty to pay the price. Conditions subsequent occur very infrequently in contract law, while conditions precedent are quite common.

17-2 Discharge by Performance

Discharge by performance is undoubtedly the most frequent method of discharging a contractual duty. If a promisor exactly performs his duty under the contract, he is no longer subject to that duty.

Every contract imposes upon each party a duty of good faith and fair dealing in its performance and its enforcement. Restatement, Section 205. As discussed in *Chapter 21*, the Uniform Commercial Code imposes a comparable duty. Section 1-203; Revised Section 1-304.

Tender is an offer by one party—who is ready, willing, and able to perform—to the other party to perform his obligation according to the terms of the contract. Under a bilateral contract, the refusal or rejection of a tender of performance may be treated as a repudiation that excuses or discharges the tendering party from further duty of performance under the contract. For example, on the due date of contractual performance, George arrives at Thelma's house prepared to do plumbing work under their contract. Thelma, however, refuses to allow George to enter the premises. George is therefore discharged from performing the contract and has a legal claim against Thelma for material breach.

If a debtor owes money on several accounts and tenders to his creditor less than the total amounts due, the debtor has the right to designate the account or debt to which the payment is to be applied, and the creditor must accept this direction. If the debtor does not direct the application of the payment, the creditor may apply it to any account owing to him by the debtor or distribute it among several such accounts.

17-3 Discharge by Breach

Breach of contract is the unexcused failure of a party to perform her promise. While breach of contract always gives rise to a cause of action for damages by the aggrieved (injured) party, it may have a more important effect: an uncured (uncorrected) *material* breach by one party operates as an excuse for nonperformance by the other party and discharges the aggrieved party from any further duty under the contract. If, on the other hand, the breach is not material, the aggrieved party is not discharged from the contract, although she may recover money damages. Under the Code, *any* deviation discharges the aggrieved party.

17-3a MATERIAL BREACH

An unjustified failure to perform *substantially* the obligations promised in a contract constitutes a **material breach.** The key is whether, despite the breach, the aggrieved party obtained substantially what he bargained for or whether the breach significantly impaired his rights under the contract. A material breach discharges the aggrieved party from his duty of performance. For instance, Esta orders a custom-made, tailored suit from Stuart to be made of wool, but Stuart instead makes the suit of cotton. Assuming that the labor component of this contract predominates and thus the contract is not considered a sale of goods, Stuart has materially breached the contract. Consequently, Esta not only is discharged from her duty to pay for the suit but may also recover money damages from Stuart due to his breach.

Although there are no clear-cut rules as to what constitutes a material breach, the Restatement, Section 241, lists a number of relevant factors:

In determining whether a failure to render or to offer performance is material, the following circumstances are significant:

(a) the extent to which the injured party will be deprived of the benefit which he reasonably expected;

(b) the extent to which the injured party can be adequately compensated for the part of that benefit of which he will be deprived;

(c) the extent to which the party failing to perform or to offer to perform will suffer forfeiture;

(d) the likelihood that the party failing to perform or to offer to perform will cure his failure, taking account of all the circumstances including any reasonable assurances;

(e) the extent to which the behavior of the party failing to perform or to offer to perform comports with standards of good faith and fair dealing.

An *intentional* breach of contract is generally held to be material. Moreover, a failure to perform a promise promptly is a material breach if **"time is of the essence,"** that is, if the parties have clearly indicated that a failure to perform by the stated time is material; otherwise, the aggrieved party may recover damages only for the loss caused by the delay.

Finally, the parties to a contract may, within limits, specify what breaches are to be considered material.

Practical Advice

If the timely performance of a contractual duty is important, use a "time-is-of-the-essence" clause to make failure to perform promptly a material breach.

PREVENTION OF PERFORMANCE One party's substantial interference with or **prevention of performance** by the other generally constitutes a material breach that discharges the other party to the contract. For instance, Craig prevents an architect from giving Maud a certificate that is a condition to Craig's liability to pay Maud a certain sum of money. Craig may not then use Maud's failure to produce a certificate as an excuse for his nonpayment. Likewise, if Harold has contracted to grow a certain crop for Rafael and Rafael plows the field and destroys the seedlings after Harold has planted the seed, his interference with Harold's performance discharges Harold from his duty under the contract. It does not, however, discharge Rafael from his duty under the contract.

PERFECT TENDER RULE The Code greatly alters the common law doctrine of material breach by adopting what is known as the **perfect tender rule**. This rule, which is discussed more fully in *Chapter 22*, essentially provides that *any* deviation from the promised performance in a sales contract under the Code constitutes a material breach of the contract and discharges the aggrieved party from his duty of performance. Thus, if a seller of camera accessories delivers to a buyer ninety-nine of the one hundred ordered pieces or ninety-nine correct accessories and one incorrect accessory, the buyer may rightfully reject the improper delivery.

17-3b SUBSTANTIAL PERFORMANCE

If a party substantially, but not completely, performs her obligations under a contract, the common law generally will allow her to obtain the other party's performance, less any damages caused by the partial performance. Thus, in the specially ordered suit illustration discussed in the previous section, if Stuart, the tailor, used the correct fabric but improperly used black buttons instead of blue, Stuart would be permitted to collect from Esta the contract price of the suit less the damage, if any, caused to Esta by the substitution of the wrongly colored buttons. The doctrine of substantial performance assumes particular importance in the construction industry in cases in which a structure is built on the aggrieved party's land. Consider the following: Kent Construction Co. builds a $300,000 house for Martha but deviates from the specifications, causing Martha $10,000 in damages. If this breach were considered material, then Martha would not have to pay for the house that is now on her land. This would clearly constitute an unjust forfeiture on Kent's part. Therefore, because Kent's performance is substantial, the courts would probably not deem the breach material. As a result, Kent would be able to collect $290,000 from Martha.

17-3c ANTICIPATORY REPUDIATION

A breach of contract, as discussed, is a failure to perform the terms of a contract. Although it is logically and physically impossible to fail to perform a duty before the date on which that performance is due, a party nonetheless may announce before the due date that she will not perform, or she may commit an act that makes her unable to perform. Either act repudiates the contract, which notifies the other party that a breach is imminent. Such repudiation before the performance date fixed by the contract is called an **anticipatory repudiation**. The courts, as shown in the leading case of *Hochster v. De La Tour*, view it as a breach that discharges the nonrepudiating party's duty to perform and permits her to bring suit immediately. Nonetheless, the nonbreaching party may wait until the time the performance is due to see whether the repudiator will retract his repudiation and perform his contractual duties. To be effective, the retraction must come to the attention of the injured party before she materially changes her position in reliance on the repudiation or before she indicates to the repudiator that she considers the repudiation to be final. If the retraction is effective and the repudiator does perform, then there is a discharge by performance; if he does not perform, there is a material breach.

♦ *See Case 17-2*

Practical Advice

If the other party to a contract commits an anticipatory breach, carefully consider whether it is better to sue immediately or to wait until the time performance is due.

17-3d UNAUTHORIZED MATERIAL ALTERATION OF WRITTEN CONTRACT

An unauthorized alteration or change of any of the material terms or provisions of a written contract or document is a discharge of the entire contract. To be a discharge, the alteration must be material and fraudulent and must be the act of a party to the contract or someone acting on his behalf. An alteration is material if it would vary any party's legal relations with the maker of the alteration or would adversely affect that party's legal relations with a third person. Restatement, Section 286. An unauthorized change in the terms of a written contract by a person who is not a party to the contract does not discharge the contract.

17-4 Discharge by Agreement of the Parties

The parties to a contract may by agreement discharge each other from performance under the contract. They may do this by rescission, substituted contract, accord and satisfaction, or novation.

17-4a MUTUAL RESCISSION

A **mutual rescission** is an agreement between the parties to terminate their respective duties under the contract. Literally a contract to end a contract, it must contain all the essentials of a contract. In rescinding an executory, bilateral contract, each party furnishes consideration in giving up his rights under the contract in exchange for the other party's relinquishment of his rights under the contract. Where one party has already fully performed, a mutual rescission may not be binding at common law because of lack of consideration.

APPLYING THE LAW Performance, Breach, and Discharge

FACTS Davis manages commercial real estate. In April, Davis contracted with Bidley to acquire and plant impatiens in the flowerbeds outside fourteen office properties that Davis manages. Bidley verbally agreed to buy and plant the impatiens by May 31, for a total of $10,000. Bidley purchased the necessary plants from Ackerman, who delivered them to Bidley on May 26. Bidley completed the planting at thirteen of the office buildings by May 29, but because another job took much longer than anticipated, Bidley was unable to finish planting the flowers outside the fourteenth office building until June 1. When he received Bidley's invoice, Davis refused to pay any of the $10,000.

ISSUE Has Bidley's committed a material breach of the contract so as to discharge Davis's performance under the contract?

RULE OF LAW Breach of contract is defined as a wrongful failure to perform. An uncured material breach discharges the aggrieved party's performance, serving as an excuse for the aggrieved party's nonperformance of his obligations under the contract. A breach is material if it significantly impairs the aggrieved party's contract rights. When a breach relates to timing of performance, failure to promptly perform a contract as promised is considered a material breach only if the parties have agreed that "time is of the essence," in other words, that the failure to perform on time is material. If, on the other hand, the aggrieved party does get substantially that for which he bargained, the breach is not material. In such a case, the aggrieved party is not discharged from the contract but has a right to collect damages for the injury sustained as a result of the breach.

APPLICATION Bidley failed to plant all of the flowers by May 31 as he promised. Therefore, he has breached the contract. However, Bidley's breach is not material. There is no indication that the parties agreed that time was of the essence or that there was any compelling reason the plants had to be in the ground by May 31. They simply agreed on May 31 as the date for performance.

Furthermore, Davis has gotten substantially that for which he bargained. In fact, as of May 31, Bidley had completed the planting at thirteen of the office buildings and had commenced the work at the fourteenth. One day later, the entire job was done. Given that Bidley's late performance did not significantly impair Davis's rights under the contract, the breach is not material. Therefore, Davis is entitled only to recover any damages he can prove were suffered as a result of Bidley's late performance.

CONCLUSION Bidley's breach is not material. Davis is not discharged from performance and must pay the $10,000 owed under the contract, less the value of any damages caused by the one-day delay in planting flowers at one office building.

17-4b SUBSTITUTED CONTRACT

A **substituted contract** is a new contract accepted by both parties in satisfaction of their duties under the original contract. Restatement, Section 279. A substituted contract immediately discharges the original duty and imposes new obligations. For example, the Restatement, Section 279, gives the following illustration:

> A and B make a contract under which A promises to build on a designated spot a building, for which B promises to pay $100,000. Later, before this contract is performed, A and B make a new contract under which A is to build on the same spot a different building, for which B is to pay $200,000. The new contract is a substituted contract, and the duties of A and B under the original contract are discharged.

17-4c ACCORD AND SATISFACTION

An **accord** is a contract by which an obligee promises to accept a stated performance in satisfaction of the obligor's existing contractual duty. Restatement, Section 281. The performance of the accord is called a **satisfaction**, and it discharges the original duty. Thus, if Ted owes Alan $500 and the parties agree that Ted shall paint Alan's house in satisfaction of the debt, the agreement is an accord. The debt, however, is not discharged until Ted performs the accord by painting Alan's house.

♦ *See Case 17-3*

17-4d NOVATION

A **novation** is a substituted contract that involves an agreement among *three* parties to substitute a new promisee for the existing promisee or to replace the existing promisor with a new one. Restatement, Section 280. A novation discharges the old obligation by creating a new contract in which there is either a new promisee or a new promisor. Thus, if Barbie owes Anson $500 and Anson, Barbie, and Cameron agree that Cameron will pay the debt and Barbie will be discharged, the novation is the substitution of the new promisor Cameron for Barbie. Alternatively, if the three parties agree that Barbie will pay $500 to Dontaya instead of to Anson, the novation is the substitution of a new promisee (Dontaya for Anson). In each instance, the debt Barbie owes to Anson is discharged.

17-5 Discharge by Operation of Law

This chapter has considered various ways by which contractual duties may be discharged. In all of these cases, the discharge resulted from the action of one or both of the parties to the contract. This section examines discharge brought about by the operation of law.

17-5a IMPOSSIBILITY

"Contract liability is strict liability … [and an] obligor is therefore liable for in damages breach of contract even if he is without fault and even if circumstances have made the contract more burdensome or less desirable than he had anticipated." Restatement, Introductory Note to *Chapter 11*. Historically, the common law excused a party from contractual duties for **objective impossibility**; that is, for situations in which no one could render the performance. If, by comparison, a particular contracting party is unable to perform because, for instance, of financial inability or lack of competence, this **subjective impossibility** does not excuse the promisor from liability for breach of contract. For example, the Christys entered into a written contract to purchase an apartment house from Pilkinton for $30,000. Pilkinton tendered a deed to the property and demanded payment of the unpaid balance of $29,000 due on the purchase price. Because of a decline in their used car business, the Christys, who did not possess and could not borrow the unpaid balance, asserted that it was impossible for them to perform their contract. The court held for Pilkinton, identifying a distinction between objective impossibility, which amounts to saying, "the thing cannot be done," and subjective impossibility—"I cannot do it." The latter, which is illustrated by a promisor's financial inability to pay, does not discharge the contractual duty. *Christy v. Pilkinton*, 224 Ark. 407, 273 S.W.2d 533 (1954).

The **death** or **incapacity** of a person who has contracted to render *personal services* discharges his contractual duty due to objective impossibility. Restatement, Section 262. For example, a singer unable to perform a contractual engagement because of a severe cold is excused from performance, as is a pianist or violinist who is unable to perform because of a hand injury.

DESTRUCTION OF SUBJECT MATTER Destruction of the subject matter or of the agreed-upon means of performance of a contract, without the fault of the promisor, is also excusable impossibility. "Subject matter" here means specific subject matter. Suppose that Alice contracts to sell to Gary five office chairs at an agreed price. Alice has one hundred of these chairs in stock, out of which she expects to deliver five to Gary. Before she can do so, fire destroys the entire stock of one hundred chairs. Though not at fault, Alice is not excused from performance. This was not a contract for the sale of specific goods; consequently, Alice could perform the contract by delivering to Gary any five chairs of the kind and grade specified in the contract. Her failure to do so will render her liable to Gary for breach of contract. Suppose, now, that Alice and Gary make a contract for Alice to manufacture these five chairs in her factory but that prior to their manufacture, fire destroys the factory. Again, Alice is not at fault. Although the chairs are available from other manufacturers, the destruction of the factory discharges Alice's duty to deliver the chairs.

Suppose further that Alice and Gary enter into a contract under which Alice is to sell to Gary the particular desk that she uses in her private office. This desk, and no other, is the specific subject matter of the contract. If, before the sale is completed, this desk is destroyed by fire without Alice's fault, it is then impossible for Alice to perform. The contract is therefore discharged.

Practical Advice

Use a clause in your contract specifying which events will excuse the nonperformance of the contract.

SUBSEQUENT ILLEGALITY If the performance of a contract that was legal when formed becomes illegal or impractical by reason of a subsequently enacted law, the duty of performance is discharged. Restatement, Section 264. For example, Jill contracts to sell and deliver to Fred ten cases of a certain whiskey each month for one year. A subsequent prohibition law makes the manufacture, transportation, or sale of intoxicating liquor unlawful. The contractual duties that Jill has yet to perform are discharged.

FRUSTRATION OF PURPOSE Under the doctrine of **frustration of purpose**, if after a contract is made, a party's principal purpose is substantially frustrated without his fault by the occurrence of an event the nonoccurrence of which was a basic assumption on which the contract was made, his remaining duties to render performance are discharged, unless the party has assumed the risk. Restatement, Second 265. This rule developed from the so-called coronation cases. When, upon the death of his mother, Queen Victoria, Edward VII became King of England, impressive coronation ceremonies were planned, including a procession along a designated route through certain streets in London. Owners and lessees of buildings along the route made contracts to permit the use of rooms with a view on the date scheduled for the procession. The King, however, became ill, and the procession did not take place. The purpose for using the rooms having failed, the rooms were not used. Numerous suits were filed, some by landowners seeking to hold the would-be viewers liable on their promises and some by the would-be viewers seeking to recover money they paid in advance for the rooms. The principle involved was novel, but from these cases evolved the **frustration of purpose doctrine**, under which a contract is discharged if supervening circumstances make impossible the fulfillment of the purpose that both parties had in mind, unless one of the parties has contractually assumed that risk.

COMMERCIAL IMPRACTICABILITY The Restatement, Section 261, and the Code, Section 2-615, have relaxed the traditional test of objective impossibility by providing that performance need not be actually or literally impossible, but that commercial impracticability will excuse nonperformance. This does not mean mere hardship or an unexpectedly increased cost of performance. A party will be discharged from performing his duty only when a supervening event not caused by his fault makes his performance impracticable. Moreover, the nonoccurrence of the subsequent event must have been a "basic assumption" both parties made when entering into the contract, neither party having assumed the risk that the event would occur. Commercial impracticability could include

> a severe shortage of raw materials or of supplies due to a contingency such as war, embargo, local crop failure, unforeseen shutdown of major sources of supply or the like, which either causes a marked increase in cost or altogether prevents the seller from securing supplies necessary to his performance. UCC Section 2-615, Comment 4.

♦ *See Case 17-4*

Practical Advice

Clearly state the basic assumptions of your contract and which risks are assumed by each of the parties.

AVAILABILITY OF RESTITUTION In cases in which impossibility, subsequent illegality, frustration, or impracticability apply, contract law permits the avoidance of a contract obligation. If the contract is wholly executory, discharge of the contract obligations resolves the legal issues. However, if the contract has been partially or wholly performed, the legal issues include both the enforceability of the contract and restitution. The Restatement of Restitution provides that a person who renders more advanced performance under a contract that is discharged for impossibility, subsequent illegality, frustration, or impracticability is entitled to restitution to prevent unjust enrichment of the other party. Section 34. Thus, for example, if the seller has performed prior to receiving payment, the seller would have a claim in restitution. On the other hand, if the buyer has paid part or all of the price in advance, the buyer would be entitled to restitution.

17-5b BANKRUPTCY

Bankruptcy is a discharge of a contractual duty by operation of law available to a debtor who, by compliance with the requirements of the Bankruptcy Code, obtains an order of discharge by the bankruptcy court. It is applicable only to obligations that the Code provides are dischargeable in bankruptcy. The subject of bankruptcy is covered in *Chapter 38.*

FIGURE 17-1 **Discharge of Contracts**

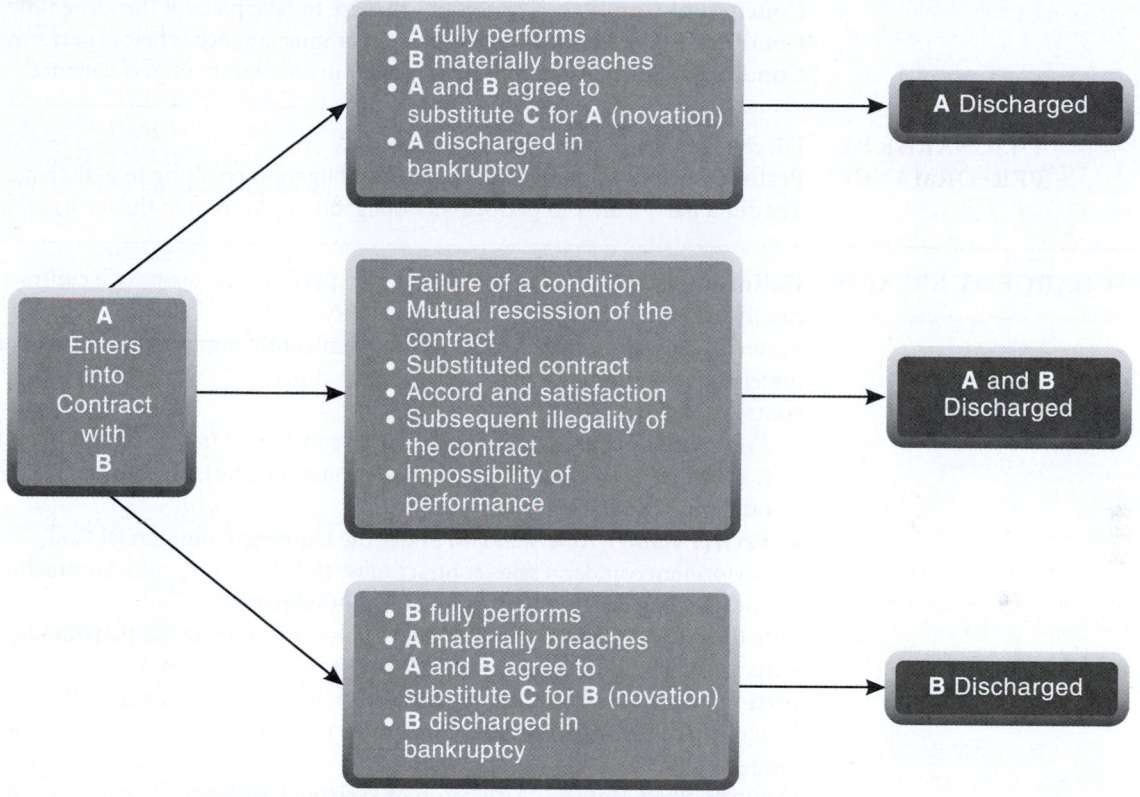

17-5c STATUTE OF LIMITATIONS

At common law, a plaintiff was not subject to any time limitation within which to bring an action. Now, however, all States have statutes providing such a limitation. The majority of courts hold that the running of the period of the statute of limitations does not operate to discharge the obligation, but only to bar the creditor's right to bring an action.

◆ **SEE FIGURE 17-1:** *Discharge of Contracts*

CHAPTER SUMMARY

CONDITIONS

Definition of a Condition an event whose happening or nonhappening affects a duty of performance

Express Condition contingency explicitly set forth in language

- *Satisfaction* express condition making performance contingent upon one party's approval of the other's performance
- *Subjective Satisfaction* approval based upon a party's honestly held opinion
- *Objective Satisfaction* approval based upon whether a reasonable person would be satisfied
- *Satisfaction of a Third Party* a contract may condition the duty of one contracting party to accept and pay for the performance of the other contracting party upon the approval of a third party who is not a party to the contract

Implied-in-Fact Conditions contingency understood by the parties to be part of the agreement, though not expressed

Implied-in-Law Conditions contingency not contained in the language of the contract but imposed by law; also called a constructive condition
Concurrent Conditions conditions that are to take place at the same time
Conditions Precedent an event that must or must not occur before performance is due
Conditions Subsequent an event that terminates a duty of performance

DISCHARGE BY PERFORMANCE

Discharge termination of a contractual duty
Performance fulfillment of a contractual obligation resulting in a discharge
Tender a party's offer to perform her obligation according to the terms of the contract

DISCHARGE BY BREACH

Definition of Breach a wrongful failure to perform the terms of a contract that gives rise to a right to damages by the injured party
Material Breach nonperformance that significantly impairs the injured party's rights under the contract and discharges the injured party from any further duty under the contract
- *Prevention of Performance* one party's substantial interference with or prevention of performance by the other; constitutes a material breach and discharges the other party to the contract
- *Perfect Tender Rule* standard under the Uniform Commercial Code that a seller's performance under a sales contract must strictly comply with contractual duties and that any deviation discharges the injured party

Substantial Performance performance that is incomplete but that does not defeat the purpose of the contract; does not discharge the injured party but entitles him to damages
Anticipatory Repudiation an inability or refusal to perform, before performance is due, that is treated as a breach, allowing the nonrepudiating party to bring suit immediately
Unauthorized Material Alteration of Written Contract an unauthorized and fraudulent alteration or change of a material term of a written contract by a party to the contract; discharges the entire contract

DISCHARGE BY AGREEMENT OF THE PARTIES

Mutual Rescission an agreement between the parties to terminate their respective duties under the contract
Substituted Contract a new contract accepted by both parties in satisfaction of the parties' duties under the original contract
Accord and Satisfaction substituted duty under a contract (accord) and the discharge of the prior contractual obligation by performance of the new duty (satisfaction)
Novation a substituted contract involving a new third-party promisor or promisee

DISCHARGE BY OPERATION OF LAW

Impossibility performance of contract cannot be done
- *Objective Impossibility* no promisor is able to perform; generally discharges the promisor
- *Subjective Impossibility* a particular promisor—but not all promisors—is unable to perform; does not discharge the promisor
- *Destruction of Subject Matter* will discharge contract if it occurs without the promisor's fault
- *Subsequent Illegality* if performance becomes illegal or impractical as a result of a change in the law, the duty of performance is discharged
- *Frustration of Purpose* if a party's principal purpose is substantially frustrated without that party's fault by the occurrence of an event whose nonoccurrence was a basic assumption on which the contract was made, the party's remaining duties to render performance are discharged, unless the party has assumed the risk

- **Commercial Impracticability** where performance can be accomplished only under unforeseen and unjust hardship, the contract is discharged under the Code and the Restatement
- **Availability of Restitution** a person who renders more advanced performance under a contract that is discharged for impossibility, subsequent illegality, frustration, or impracticability is entitled to restitution to prevent unjust enrichment of the other party

Bankruptcy discharge available to a debtor who obtains an order of discharge by the bankruptcy court

Statute of Limitations after the statute of limitations has run, the debt is not discharged, but the creditor cannot maintain an action against the debtor

C A S E S

CASE 17-1

Express Conditions: Satisfaction
SILVESTRI v. OPTUS SOFTWARE, INC.
Supreme Court of New Jersey, 2003
175 N.J. 113, 814 A.2d 602

LaVecchia, J.

This is a breach of contract action. Defendant Optus Software, Inc. ("Optus" or "the company"), a small computer software company, hired plaintiff Michael Silvestri as its Director of Support Services, responsible for supervising the provision of technical support services to the company's customers. Silvestri's two-year employment contract [commencing on January 4, 1999, at an annual salary of $70,000] contained a clause that reserved to the company the right to terminate his employment for failure to perform to the company's satisfaction (the "satisfaction clause").

Nine months into the contract, Silvestri was terminated under the satisfaction clause by the chief executive officer of Optus, Joseph Avellino. Silvestri filed this action, contending that the company's dissatisfaction was objectively unreasonable and that therefore his termination was a breach of the employment contract. The trial court granted summary judgment to the company. The Appellate Division reversed, however, holding that an employer must meet an objective standard for satisfaction in order to invoke a right to terminate pursuant to a satisfaction clause in an employment contract.

The question presented then is whether the employer's satisfaction is subject to an objective or subjective evaluation. We conclude that, absent language to the contrary, a subjective assessment of personal satisfaction applies and that the trial court's grant of summary judgment to the company was appropriate. * * *

* * * Silvestri was charged with supervision of the support services staff, responsibility for communication with resellers of the Optus computer software to end-users, and coordination of ongoing training for support staff and resellers of the company's products in order to maintain their proficiency in assisting end-users. * * *

[During the first six months of his employment, Silvestri enjoyed the full support of Joseph Avellino, the CEO of Optus. Avellino's attitude started to change during the summer months of 1999, when several clients and resellers communicated to Avellino their disappointment with the performance and attitude of the support services staff generally, and several complaints targeted Silvestri specifically. Avellino informed Silvestri of those criticisms. On September 17, 1999, Avellino terminated Silvestri under the satisfaction clause.]

* * *

Silvestri did not assert that there was any reason for his termination other than Avellino's genuine dissatisfaction with his performance. Rather, Silvestri challenged the reasonableness of that dissatisfaction. He portrayed Avellino as a meddling micro-manager who overreacted to any customer criticism and thus could not reasonably be satisfied. * * *

* * *

Agreements containing a promise to perform in a manner satisfactory to another, or to be bound to pay for satisfactory performance, are a common form of enforceable contract. [Citation.] Such "satisfaction" contracts are generally divided into two categories for purposes of review: (1) contracts that involve matters of personal taste, sensibility, judgment, or convenience; and (2) contracts that contain a requirement of satisfaction as to mechanical fitness, utility, or marketability. [Citation.] The standard for evaluating satisfaction depends on the type of contract. Satisfaction contracts of the first type are interpreted on a subjective basis, with satisfaction dependent on the personal, honest evaluation of the party to be satisfied. [Citation.] Absent language to the contrary, however, contracts of the second type-involving operative fitness or mechanical utility—are subject to an objective test of reasonableness, because in those cases the extent and quality of performance can be measured by objective tests. [Citation]; Restatement (Second) of Contracts §228; [citation].

A subjective standard typically is applied to satisfaction clauses in employment contracts because "there is greater reason and a greater tendency to interpret [the contract] as involving personal satisfaction," rather than the satisfaction of a hypothetical "reasonable" person. [Citations.] * * *

In the case of a high-level business manager, a subjective test is particularly appropriate to the flexibility needed by the owners and higher-level officers operating a competitive enterprise. [Citation.] When a manager has been hired to share responsibility for the success of a business entity, an employer is entitled to be highly personal and idiosyncratic in judging the employee's satisfactory performance in advancing the enterprise. [Citations.]

The subjective standard obliges the employer to act "honestly in accordance with his duty of good faith and fair dealing," [citation], but genuine dissatisfaction of the employer, honestly held, is sufficient for discharge. [Citations.]

Although broadly discretionary, a satisfaction-clause employment relationship is not to be confused with an employment-at-will relationship in which an employer is entitled to terminate an employee for any reason, or no reason, unless prohibited by law or public policy. [Citation.] In a satisfaction clause employment setting, there must be honest dissatisfaction with the employee's performance. * * * If * * * the employer's dissatisfaction is honest and genuine, even if idiosyncratic, its reasonableness is not subject to second guessing under a reasonable-person standard. * * *

* * *

We hold that a subjective test of performance governs the employer's resort to a satisfaction clause in an employment contract unless there is some language in the contract to suggest that the parties intended an objective standard. There is no such language here. * * *

Turning then to application of the subjective test in this setting, * * * we conclude that the entry of summary judgment in favor of defendants was appropriate. * * *

The judgment of the Appellate Division is reversed and the matter remanded for entry of summary judgment in favor of defendants.

C A S E	Anticipatory Breach	
17-2	**HOCHSTER v. DE LA TOUR** Queen's Bench of England, 1853 2 Ellis and Blackburn Reports 678	

Lord Campbell, C. J.

[On April 12, 1852, Hochster contracted with De La Tour to serve as a guide for De La Tour on his three-month trip to Europe, beginning on June 1 at an agreed-upon salary. On May 11, De La Tour notified Hochster that he would not need Hochster's services. He also refused to pay Hochster any compensation. Hochster brings this action to recover damages for breach of contract.]

On this motion * * * the question arises, Whether, if there be an agreement between A. and B., whereby B. engages to employ A. on and from a future day for a given period of time, to travel with him into a foreign country as a [guide], and to start with him in that capacity on that day, A. being to receive a monthly salary during the continuance of such service, B. may, before the day, refuse to perform the agreement and break and renounce it, so as to entitle A. before the day to commence an action against B. to recover damages for breach of the agreement; A. having been ready and willing to perform it, till it was broken and renounced by B.

* * *

If the plaintiff has no remedy for breach of the contract unless he treats the contract as in force, and acts upon it down to the 1st June, 1852, it follows that, till then, he must enter into no employment which will interfere with his promise "to start with the defendant on such travels on the day and year" and that he must then be properly equipped in all respects as a [guide] for a three months' tour on the continent of Europe. But it is surely much more rational, and more for the benefit of both parties, that, after the renunciation of the agreement by the defendant, the plaintiff should be at liberty to consider himself absolved from any future performance of it, retaining his right to sue for any damage he has suffered from the breach of it. Thus, instead of remaining idle and laying out money in preparations which must be useless, he is at liberty to seek service under another employer, which would go in mitigation of the damages to which he would otherwise be entitled for a breach of the contract. It seems strange that the defendant after renouncing the contract, and absolutely declaring that he will never act under it, should be permitted to object that faith is given to his assertion, and that an opportunity is not left to him of changing his mind. * * *

* * * The man who wrongfully renounces a contract into which he has deliberately entered cannot justly complain if he is immediately sued for a compensation in damage by the man whom he has injured: and it seems reasonable to allow an option to the injured party, either to sue immediately, or to wait till the time when the act was to be done, still holding it as prospectively binding for the exercise of this option, which may be advantageous to the innocent party, and cannot be prejudicial to the wrongdoer.

Judgment for plaintiff.

CASE 17-3

Accord and Satisfaction
MCDOWELL WELDING & PIPEFITTING, INC. v. UNITED STATES GYPSUM CO.
Supreme Court of Oregon, 2008
345 OR. 272, 193 P.3d 9

Kistler, J.

Defendant United States Gypsum (U.S. Gypsum) was constructing a new plant in Columbia County. Defendant B E & K Construction Co. (B E & K) was the general contractor on that project. B E & K subcontracted with plaintiff [McDowell Welding & Pipefitting, Inc.] to perform work on the project. During construction, defendants asked plaintiff to perform additional tasks, over and above plaintiff's contractual obligations, and defendants promised to pay plaintiff for doing so. After plaintiff completed its work on the project, the parties disagreed over the amount that defendants owed for the additional work that plaintiff had performed.

Plaintiff filed this action against defendants, alleging breach of contract and related claims. All of plaintiff's claims arose out of the modification to the construction contract. B E & K's answer included an affirmative defense [and counterclaim] captioned "Compromise and Settlement," alleging that plaintiff had agreed to settle its claims against defendants [for a total payment of $896,000.] * * *

B E & K filed a motion asking the trial court to bifurcate the proceedings and try its counterclaim before trying plaintiff's claims against it. * * * The trial court granted B E & K's motion.

After the trial court granted B E & K's motion, plaintiff filed a demand for a jury trial, which B E & K moved to strike. B E & K reasoned that, because its counterclaim was equitable, plaintiff had no right to a jury trial on the counterclaim. The trial court granted B E & K's motion to strike plaintiff's jury trial demand and, sitting as the trier of fact, found that plaintiff had accepted defendants' offer to settle its claims in return for defendants' promise to pay plaintiff $800,000. [Court's footnote: Although defendants alleged that they promised to pay plaintiff $896,000 in return for plaintiff's promise to release its claims against them, defendants proved and the trial court found that defendants had promised to pay only $800,000.]

Based on its resolution of defendants' counterclaim, the trial court entered a limited judgment directing defendants to tender $800,000 to the court clerk and directing plaintiff, after defendants tendered that sum, to execute releases of its claims against defendants. After the trial court entered the limited judgment, defendants tendered $800,000 to the court clerk and then moved for summary judgment on plaintiff's claims against them. The trial court granted defendants' motion and entered a general judgment that dismissed plaintiff's claims with prejudice. The plaintiff appealed, claiming a state constitutional right to a jury trial on the factual issues that the defendant's counterclaim had raised. A divided Court of Appeals affirmed the trial court's judgment. The Oregon Supreme Court allowed the plaintiff's petition for review.

As we discuss more fully below, a settlement agreement may take one of three forms: an executory accord, an accord and satisfaction, or a substituted contract. As we also discuss below, when the Oregon Constitution was adopted, only a court of equity would enforce an executory accord. The law courts would not enforce executory accords because they suspended the underlying obligation; they did not discharge it. By contrast, an accord and satisfaction and a substituted contract discharged the underlying obligation, albeit for different reasons, and both were enforceable in the law courts. It follows that the question whether the agreement that gave rise to defendants' counterclaim would have been cognizable in law or equity turns, at least initially, on whether it is an executory accord, an accord and satisfaction, or a substituted contract. We first describe the distinctions among those types of settlement agreements before considering which type of settlement agreement defendants alleged.

An executory accord is "an agreement for the future discharge of an existing claim by a substituted performance." [Citation.] Usually, an executory accord is a bilateral agreement; the debtor promises to pay an amount in return for the creditor's promise to release the underlying claim. When the parties enter into an executory accord, the underlying claim "is not [discharged] until the new agreement is performed.

The right to enforce the original claim is merely suspended, and is revived by the debtor's breach of the new agreement." [Citation.]

Because an executory accord does not discharge the underlying claim but merely suspends it, the law courts refused to allow it to be pleaded as a bar to the underlying claim. [Citations.] * * * Once the promised performance occurs, the accord has been executed or satisfied and the underlying claim is discharged, resulting in an accord and satisfaction. [Citation.] [Court's footnote: An accord and satisfaction may occur in one of two ways: "The two parties may first make an accord executory, that is, a contract for the future discharge of the existing claim by a substituted performance still to be rendered. When this executory contract is fully performed as agreed, there is said to be an accord and satisfaction, and the previously existing claim is discharged. It is quite possible, however, for the parties to make an accord and satisfaction without any preliminary accord executory or any other executory contract of any kind. [For example, a] debtor may offer the substituted performance in satisfaction of his debt and the creditor may receive it, without any binding promise being made by either party." [Citation.] Because an accord and satisfaction discharges the underlying claim, that defense is legal, not equitable. [Citation.]

Finally, the parties may enter into a substituted contract; that is, the parties may agree to substitute the new agreement for the underlying obligation. [Citation.] A substituted contract differs from an executory accord in that the parties intend that entering into the new agreement will immediately discharge the underlying obligation. [Citations.] A substituted contract discharges the underlying obligation and could be asserted as a bar to an action at law. [Citation.]

With that background in mind, we turn to the question whether defendants pleaded an executory accord, an accord and satisfaction, or a substituted contract. Here, defendants alleged that they agreed to pay plaintiff $896,000 in exchange for a release of plaintiff's claims against them. Defendants did not allege that they had paid plaintiff the promised sum—an allegation necessary for an accord and satisfaction. [Citations.] Nor did they allege that, by entering into the settlement agreement, they extinguished the underlying obligation—an allegation necessary to allege a substituted contract. [Citations.] Rather, defendants alleged that plaintiff agreed to release its claims only after defendants made the promised payment. In short, defendants alleged an executory accord.

* * *

[The Oregon constitutional right to a jury trial in civil cases does not extend to the defendants' counterclaim of an executory accord. We affirm the Court of Appeals decision on the plaintiff's jury trial claim but reverse its decision on a subsidiary issue regarding pre-judgment interest.]

CASE 17-4

Impossibility
NORTHERN CORP. v. CHUGACH ELECTRICAL ASSOCIATION
Supreme Court of Alaska, 1974
518 P.2d 76

Boochever, J.

[Northern Corporation entered into a contract with Chugach in August 1966 to repair and upgrade the upstream face of Cooper Lake Dam in Alaska. The contract required Northern to obtain rock from a quarry site at the opposite end of the lake and to transport the rock to the dam during the winter across the ice on the lake. In December 1966, Northern cleared the road on the ice to permit deeper freezing, but thereafter water overflowed on the ice, preventing the use of the road. Northern complained of the unsafe condition of the lake ice, but Chugach insisted on performance. In March 1967, one of Northern's loaded trucks broke through the ice and sank. Northern continued to encounter difficulties and ceased operations with the approval of Chugach. On January 8, 1968, Chugach notified Northern that it would be in default unless all rock was hauled by April 1. After two more trucks broke through the ice, causing the deaths of the drivers, Northern ceased operations and notified Chugach that it would make no more attempts to

haul across the lake. Northern advised Chugach it considered the contract terminated for impossibility of performance and commenced suit to recover the cost incurred in attempting to complete the contract.]

* * *

The focal question is whether the * * * contract was impossible of performance. The September 27, 1966 directive specified that the rock was to be transported "across Cooper Lake to the dam site when such lake is frozen to a sufficient depth to permit heavy vehicle traffic thereon," and * * * specified that the hauling to the dam site would be done during the winter of 1966-67. It is therefore clear that the parties contemplated that the rock would be transported across the frozen lake by truck. Northern's repeated efforts to perform the contract by this method during the winter of 1966-67 and subsequently in February 1968, culminating in the tragic loss of life, abundantly support the trial court's findings that the contract was impossible of performance by this method.

Chugach contends, however, that Northern was nevertheless bound to perform, and that it could have used means other than hauling by truck across the ice to transport the rock. The answer to Chugach's contention is that * * * the parties contemplated that the rock would be hauled by truck once the ice froze to a sufficient depth to support the weight of the vehicles. The specification of this particular method of performance presupposed the existence of ice frozen to the requisite depth. Since this expectation of the parties was never fulfilled, and since the provisions relating to the means of performance was clearly material, Northern's duty to perform was discharged by reason of impossibility.

There is an additional reason for our holding that Northern's duty to perform was discharged because of impossibility. It is true that in order for a defendant to prevail under the original common law doctrine of impossibility, he had to show that no one else could have performed the contract. However, this harsh rule has gradually been eroded, and the Restatement of Contracts has departed from the early common law rule by recognizing the principle of "commercial impracticability." Under this doctrine, a party is discharged from his contract obligations, even if it is technically possible to perform them, if the costs of performance would be so disproportionate to that reasonably contemplated by the parties as to make the contract totally impractical in a commercial sense. * * *

* * *

Removed from the strictures of the common law, "impossibility" in its modern context has become a coat of many colors, including among its hues the point argued here—namely, impossibility predicated upon "commercial impracticability." This concept—which finds expression both in case law . . . and in other authorities . . . is grounded upon the assumption that in legal contemplation something is impracticable when it can only be done at an excessive and unreasonable cost. * * *

. . . The doctrine ultimately represents the ever-shifting line, drawn by courts hopefully responsive to commercial practices and mores, at which the community's interest in having contracts enforced according to their terms is outweighed by the commercial senselessness of requiring performance. * * *

* * *

In the case before us the detailed opinion of the trial court clearly indicates that the appropriate standard was followed. There is ample evidence to support its findings that "[t]he ice haul method of transporting riprap ultimately selected was within the contemplation of the parties and was part of the basis of the agreement which ultimately resulted in amendment No. 1 in October 1966," and that that method was not commercially feasible within the financial parameters of the contract. We affirm the court's conclusion that the contract was impossible of performance.

QUESTIONS

1. A–1 Roofing Co. entered into a written contract with Jaffe to put a new roof on the latter's residence for $1,800, using a specified type of roofing, and to complete the job without unreasonable delay. A–1 undertook the work within a week thereafter, but when all the roofing material was at the site and the labor 50 percent completed, the premises were totally destroyed by fire caused by lightning. A–1 submitted a bill to Jaffe for $1,200 for materials furnished and labor performed up to the time of the destruction of the premises. Jaffe refused to pay the bill, and A–1 now seeks payment from Jaffe. Should A–1 prevail? Explain.

2. By contract dated January 5, Rebecca agreed to sell to Nancy, and Nancy agreed to buy from Rebecca, a certain parcel of land then zoned commercial. The specific intent of Nancy, which was known to Rebecca, was to erect a manufacturing plant on the land, and the contract stated that the agreement was conditioned upon Nancy's ability to construct such a plant upon the land. The closing date for the transaction was set for April 1.

On February 15, the city council rezoned the land from commercial to residential, which precluded the erection of the plant. As the closing date drew near, Nancy made it known to Rebecca that she did not intend to go through with the purchase because the land could no longer be used as intended. On April 1, Rebecca tendered the deed to Nancy, who refused to pay Rebecca the agreed purchase price. Rebecca brought an action against Nancy for breach of their contract. Can Rebecca enforce the contract? Why or why not?

3. The Perfection Produce Company entered into a written contract with Hiram Hodges for the purchase of three hundred tons of potatoes to be grown on Hodge's farm in Maine at a stipulated price per ton. Although the land would ordinarily produce one thousand tons and the planting and cultivation were properly done, Hodges was able to deliver only one hundred tons because an unprecedented drought caused a partial crop failure. Perfection accepted the one hundred tons but paid only 80 percent of the stipulated price per ton. Hodges sued the produce

company to recover the unpaid balance of the agreed price for the one hundred tons of potatoes accepted by Perfection. Perfection counterclaimed against Hodges for his failure to deliver the remaining two hundred tons. Who will prevail? Explain.

4. On November 23, Sylvia agreed to sell to Barnett her Buick automobile for $7,000, delivery and payment to be made on December 1. On November 26, Barnett informed Sylvia that he wished to rescind the contract and would pay Sylvia $350 if Sylvia agreed. She agreed and took the $350 cash. On December 1, Barnett tendered to Sylvia $6,650 and demanded that she deliver the automobile. Sylvia refused and Barnett initiated a lawsuit. May Barnett enforce the original contract? Explain.

5. Webster, Inc., dealt in automobile accessories at wholesale. Although he manufactured a few items in his own factory, among them windshield wipers, Webster purchased most of his inventory from a large number of other manufacturers. In January, Webster entered into a written contract to sell Hunter two thousand windshield wipers for $4,900, delivery to be made June 1. In April, Webster's factory burned to the ground, and Webster failed to make delivery on June 1. Hunter, forced to buy windshield wipers elsewhere at a higher price, is now trying to recover damages from Webster. Will Hunter be successful in its claim? Why or why not?

6. Erwick Construction Company contracted to build a house for Charles. The specifications called for the use of Karlene Pipe for all plumbing. Erwick, however, got a better price on Boynton Pipe and substituted the equally good Boynton Pipe for Karlene Pipe. Upon inspection, Charles discovered the change, and he now refuses to make the final payment. The contract price was for $200,000, and the final payment is $20,000. Erwick now brings suit seeking the $20,000. Will Erwick succeed in its claim? Explain.

7. Green owed White $3,500, which was due and payable on June 1. White owed Brown $3,500, which was due and payable on August 1. On May 25, White received a letter signed by Green stating, "If you will cancel my debt to you, in the amount of $3,500, I will pay, on the due date, the debt you owe Brown, in the amount of $3,500." On May 28, Green received a letter signed by White stating, "I received your letter and agree to the proposals recited therein. You may consider your debt to me canceled as of the date of this letter." On June 1, White, needing money to pay his income taxes, made a demand upon Green to pay him the $3,500 due on that date. Is Green obligated to pay the money demanded by White? Why or why not?

8. By written contract, Ames agreed to build a house on Bowen's lot for $165,000, commencing within ninety days of the date of the contract. Prior to the date for beginning construction, Ames informed Bowen that he was repudiating the contract and would not perform. Bowen refused to accept the repudiation and demanded fulfillment of the contract. Eighty days after the date of the contract, Bowen entered into a new contract with Curd for $162,000. The next day, without knowledge or notice of Bowen's contract with Curd, Ames began construction. Bowen ordered Ames from the premises and refused to allow him to continue. Will Ames be able to collect damages from Bowen? Explain.

9. Judy agreed in writing to work for Northern Enterprises, Inc., for three years as superintendent of Northern's manufacturing establishment and to devote herself entirely to the business, giving it her whole time, attention, and skill, for which she was to receive $72,000 per annum, in monthly installments of $6,000. Judy worked and was paid for the first twelve months, when, through no fault of her own or Northern's, she was arrested and imprisoned for one month. It became imperative for Northern to employ another, and it treated the contract with Judy as breached and abandoned, refusing to permit Judy to resume work upon her release from jail. Explain what rights, if any, Judy has under the contract?

10. The Park Plaza Hotel awarded its valet and laundry concession to Larson for a three-year term. The contract contained the following provision: "It is distinctly understood and agreed that the services to be rendered by Larson shall meet with the approval of the Park Plaza Hotel, which shall be the sole judge of the sufficiency and propriety of the services." After seven months, the hotel gave a month's notice to discontinue services based on the failure of the services to meet its approval. Larson brought an action against the hotel, alleging that its dissatisfaction was unreasonable. The hotel defended upon the ground that subjective or personal satisfaction may be the sole justification for termination of the contract. Who is correct? Explain.

11. Schlosser entered into an agreement to purchase a cooperative apartment from Flynn Company. The written agreement contained the following provision:

> This entire agreement is conditioned on Purchaser's being approved for occupancy by the board of directors of the Cooperative. In the event approval of the Purchaser shall be denied, this agreement shall thereafter be of no further force or effect.

When Schlosser unilaterally revoked her "offer," Flynn sued for breach of contract. Schlosser claims the approval provision was a condition precedent to the existence of a binding contract and, thus, she was free to revoke. Decision? Explain.

12. Jacobs, owner of a farm, entered into a contract with Earl Walker in which Walker agreed to paint the buildings on the farm. As authorized by Jacobs, Walker acquired the paint from Jones with the bill to be sent to Jacobs. Before the work was completed, Jacobs without good cause ordered Walker to stop. Walker made offers to complete the job, but Jacobs declined to permit Walker to fulfill his contract. Jacobs refused to pay Jones for the paint Walker had acquired for the job. Explain whether Jones and Walker will be successful in an action against Jacobs for breach of contract.

C A S E   P R O B L E M S

13. On August 20, Hildebrand entered into a written contract with the city of Douglasville whereby he was to serve as community development project engineer for three years at an "annual fee" of $19,000. This salary figure could be changed without affecting the other terms of the contract. One of the provisions for termination of the contract was written notice by either party to the other at any time at least ninety days prior to the intended date of termination. The contract listed a substantial number of services and duties Hildebrand was to perform for the city; among the lesser duties were (a) keeping the community development director (Hildebrand's supervisor) informed at all times of his whereabouts and how he could be contacted and (b) attending meetings at which his presence was requested. Two years later, on September 20, by which time Hildebrand's fee had risen to $1,915.83 per month, the city fired Hildebrand effective immediately, citing "certain material breaches . . . of the . . . agreement." The city specifically charged that he did not attend the necessary meetings although requested to do so and seldom if ever kept his supervisor informed of his whereabouts and how he could be contacted. Will Hildebrand prevail in a suit against the mayor and city for damages in the amount of $5,747.49 because of the city's failure to give him ninety days' notice prior to termination? Explain.

14. Walker & Co. contracted to provide a sign for Harrison to place above his dry-cleaning business. According to the contract, Harrison would lease the sign from Walker, making monthly payments for thirty-six months. In return, Walker agreed to maintain and service the sign at its own expense. Walker installed the sign in July, and Harrison made the first rental payment. Shortly thereafter, someone hit the sign with a tomato. Harrison also claims he discovered rust on its chrome and little spider webs in its corners. Harrison repeatedly called Walker for the maintenance work promised under the contract, but Walker did not respond immediately. Harrison then notified Walker that due to Walker's failure to perform the maintenance services, he held Walker in material breach of the contract. A week later, Walker sent out a crew, which did all of the requested maintenance services. Has Walker committed a material breach of contract? Explain.

15. Barta entered into a written contract to buy the K&K Pharmacy, located in the local shopping center. Included in the contract was a provision stating that "this Agreement shall be contingent upon Buyer's ability to obtain a new lease from Landlord for the premises presently occupied by Seller. In the event Buyer is unable to obtain a lease satisfactory to Buyer, this Agreement shall be null and void." Barta planned to sell "high traffic" grocery items such as bread, milk, and coffee to attract customers to his drugstore. A grocery store in the local shopping center, however, held the exclusive right to sell grocery items. Barta, therefore, could not obtain a leasing agreement meeting his approval. Barta refused to close the sale. In a suit by K&K Pharmacy against Barta for breach of contract, who will prevail? Explain.

16. Victor Packing Co. (Victor) contracted to supply Sun Maid Raisin Growers 1,800 tons of raisins from the current year's crop. After delivering 1,190 tons of raisins by August, Victor refused to supply any more. Although Victor had until the end of the crop season to ship the remaining 610 tons of raisins, Sun Maid treated Victor's repeated refusals to ship any more raisins as a repudiation of the contract. To prevent breaching its own contracts, Sun Maid went into the marketplace to "cover" and bought the raisins it needed. Unfortunately, between the time Victor refused delivery and Sun Maid entered the market, disastrous rains had caused the price of raisins to skyrocket. May Sun Maid recover from Victor the difference between the contract price and the market price before the end of the current crop year? Why or why not?

17. In May, Watts was awarded a construction contract, based on its low bid, by the Cullman County Commission. The contract provided that it would not become effective until approved by the State director of the Farmers Home Administration (now part of the U.S. Department of Agriculture Rural Development Office). In September, construction still had not been authorized, and Watts wrote to the County Commission requesting a

5 percent price increase to reflect seasonal and inflationary price increases. The County Commission countered with an offer of 3.5 percent. Watts then wrote the commission, insisting on a 5 percent increase and stating that if this was not agreeable, it was withdrawing its original bid. The commission obtained another company to perform the project and on October 14 informed Watts that it had accepted the withdrawal of the bid. Watts sued for breach of contract. Explain whether Watts will prevail.

18. K&G Construction Co. was the owner of and the general contractor for a housing subdivision project. Harris contracted with the company to do excavating and earth-moving work on the project. Certain provisions of the contract stated that (a) K&G was to make monthly progress payments to Harris, (b) no such payments were to be made until Harris obtained liability insurance, and (c) all of Harris's work on the project must be performed in a workmanlike manner. On August 9, a bulldozer operator, working for Harris, drove too close to one of K&G's houses, causing the collapse of a wall and other damage. When Harris and his insurance carrier denied liability and refused to pay for the damage, K&G refused to make the August monthly progress payment. Harris, nonetheless, continued to work on the project until mid-September, when the excavator ceased its operations due to K&G's refusal to make the progress payment. K&G had another excavator finish the job at an added cost of $1,450. It then sued Harris for the bulldozer damage, alleging negligence, and for the $1,450 damages for breach of contract. Harris claims that K&G defaulted first, having no legal right to refuse the August progress payment. Did K&G default first? Explain.

19. Mountain Restaurant Corporation (Mountain) leased commercial space in the ParkCenter Mall to operate a restaurant called Zac's Grill. The lease specified that the lessee shall "at all times have a nonexclusive and nonrevocable right, together with the other tenants and occupants of … the shopping center, to use the parking area … for itself, its customers and employees." Zac's Grill was to be a fast-food restaurant where tables were anticipated to "turn over" twice during lunch. Zac's operated successfully until parking close to the restaurant became restricted. Two other restaurants opened and began competing for parking spaces, and the parking lot would become full between 12:00 and 12:30 P.M. Parking, however, was always available at other areas of the mall. Business declined for Zac's, which fell behind on the rent due to ParkCenter until finally the restaurant closed. Mountain claims that it was discharged from its obligations under the lease because of material breach. Is Mountain correct? Explain.

20. In late 2017 or early 2018, the plaintiff, Lan England, agreed to sell 258,363 shares of stock to the defendant, Eugene Horbach, for $2.75 per share, for a total price of $710,498.25. Although the purchase money was to be paid in the first quarter of 2018, the defendant made periodic payments on the stock at least through September 2018. The parties met in May of 2019 to finalize the transaction. At this time, the plaintiff believed that the defendant owed at least $25,000 of the original purchase price. The defendant did not dispute that amount. The parties then reached a second agreement whereby the defendant agreed to pay to the plaintiff an additional $25,000 and to hold in trust 2 percent of the stock for the plaintiff. In return, the plaintiff agreed to transfer the stock and to forego his right to sue the defendant for breach of the original agreement.

In December 2020, the plaintiff made a demand for the 2 percent stock, but the defendant refused, contending that the 2 percent agreement was meant only to secure his payment of the additional $25,000. The plaintiff sued for breach of the 2 percent agreement. Prior to trial, the defendant discovered additional business records documenting that he had, before entering into the second agreement, actually overpaid the plaintiff for the purchase of the stock. The defendant asserts the plaintiff could not enforce the second agreement as an accord and satisfaction because (a) it was not supported by consideration and (b) it was based upon a mutual mistake that the defendant owed additional money on the original agreement. Is the defendant correct in his assertions? Explain.

21. An artist once produced a painting now called *The Plains of Meudon*. For a while, the parties in this case thought that the artist was Theodore Rousseau, a prominent member of the Barbizon school, and that the painting was quite valuable. With this idea in mind, the Kohlers consigned the painting to Leslie Hindman, Inc. (Hindman), an auction house. Among other things, the consignment agreement between the Kohlers and Hindman defined the scope of Hindman's authority as agent. First, Hindman was obliged to sell the painting according to the conditions of sale spelled out in the auction catalog. Those conditions provided that neither the consignors nor Hindman made any warranties of authenticity. Second, the consignment agreement gave Hindman extensive and exclusive discretionary authority to rescind sales if in its "sole discretion" it determined that the sale subjected the company or the Kohlers to any liability under a warranty of authenticity.

Despite having some doubts about its authenticity, Thune was still interested in the painting but wanted to have it authenticated before committing to its purchase. Unable to obtain an authoritative opinion about its authenticity before the auction, Leslie Hindman and Thune made a verbal agreement that Thune could return the painting within approximately thirty days of the auction if he was the successful bidder and if an expert then determined that Rousseau had not painted it. Neither Leslie Hindman nor anyone else at Hindman told the Kohlers about the questions concerning the painting or about the side agreement between Thune and Hindman. At the auction, Thune prevailed in the bidding with a high bid of $90,000, and he took possession of the painting without paying. He then sent it to an expert in Paris who decided that it was not a Rousseau. Thune returned the painting to Hindman within the agreed-upon period. Explain whether the Kohlers would be successful in a lawsuit against either Hindman, Inc., or Thune.

T A K I N G   S I D E S

Associated Builders, Inc., provided labor and materials to William M. Coggins and Benjamin W. Coggins, doing business as Ben & Bill's Chocolate Emporium, to complete a structure on Main Street in Bar Harbor, Maine. After a dispute arose regarding compensation, Associated and the Cogginses executed an agreement stating that there existed an outstanding balance of $70,000 and setting forth the following terms of repayment:

> It is agreed that, two payments will be made by the Cogginses to Associated Builders as follows: Twenty Five Thousand Dollars ($25,000.00) on or before June 1, 2019, and Twenty Five Thousand Dollars ($25,000.00) on or before June 1, 2020. No interest will be charged or paid providing payments are made as agreed. If the payments are not made as agreed, then interest shall accrue at 10 percent per annum figured from the date of default. It is further agreed that Associated Builders will forfeit the balance of Twenty Thousand Dollars and No Cents ($20,000.00) providing the above payments are made as agreed.

The Cogginses made their first payment in accordance with the agreement. The second payment, however, was delivered three days late on June 4, 2020. Claiming a breach of the contract, Associated contended that the remainder of the original balance of $20,000, plus interest and cost, were now due.

a. What arguments would support Associated's claim for $20,000?

b. What arguments would support the claim by the Cogginses that they were not liable for $20,000?

c. For what damages, if any, are the Cogginses liable? Explain.

CHAPTER 18

Contract Remedies

CHAPTER OUTCOMES

After reading and studying this chapter, you should be able to:

- Explain how compensatory damages and reliance damages are computed.

- Define (1) nominal damages, (2) incidental damages, (3) consequential damages, (4) foreseeability of damages, (5) punitive damages, (6) liquidated damages, and (7) mitigation of damages.

- Define the various types of equitable relief and explain when the courts will grant such relief.

- Explain how restitutionary damages are computed and identify the situations in which restitution is available as a contractual remedy.

- Explain the limitations on contractual remedies.

When one party to a contract breaches the contract by failing to perform his contractual duties, the law provides a remedy for the injured party. Although the primary objective of contract remedies is to compensate the injured party for the loss resulting from the breach, it is impossible for any remedy to equal the promised performance. To an injured party, a court can give as relief what it regards as an equivalent of the promised performance.

This chapter examines the most common judicial remedies available for breach of contract: (1) monetary damages, (2) the equitable remedies of specific performance and injunction, and (3) restitution. Sales of goods are governed by Article 2 of the Uniform Commercial Code (UCC), which provides specialized remedies that are discussed in *Chapter 25*.

18-1 Interests Protected by Contract Remedies

Contract remedies are available to protect one or more of the following interests of the injured party:

1. the **expectation interest**, which is his interest in having the benefit of his bargain by being put in a position as good as the one he would have occupied had the contract been performed;

2. the **reliance interest**, which is his interest in being reimbursed for loss caused by reliance on the contract by being put in a position as good as the one he would have been in had the contract not been made; or

3. the **restitution interest**, which is his interest in having restored to him any benefit that he has conferred on the other party. Restatement, Section 344.

The expectation interest is protected by the contract remedies of compensatory damages, specific performance, and injunction. The reliance interest is protected by the contractual remedy of reliance damages, while the restitution interest is protected by the contractual remedy of restitution.

Practical Advice
Consider including in your contracts a provision for the arbitration of contract disputes.

18-2 Monetary Damages

A judgment awarding monetary damages is the most frequently granted judicial remedy for breach of contract. Monetary damages, however, will be awarded only for losses that are foreseeable, established with reasonable certainty, and unavoidable. The equitable remedies discussed in this chapter are discretionary and are available only if monetary damages are inadequate.

Practical Advice
Consider including in your contracts a provision for the recovery of attorneys' fees in the event of breach of contract.

18-2a COMPENSATORY DAMAGES

The right to recover compensatory money damages for breach of contract is always available to the injured party. Restatement, Section 346. The purpose in allowing **compensatory damages** is to place the injured party in a position as good as the one she would have occupied had the other party performed under the contract. This involves compensating the injured party for the dollar value of the benefits she would have received had the contract been performed less any savings she experienced by not having to perform her own obligations under the contract. Because these damages are intended to protect the injured party's expectation interest, or the value she expected to derive from the contract, the amount of compensatory damages is generally computed as follows:

$$
\begin{array}{rl}
& \text{Loss of value} \\
- & \text{Loss or cost avoided by injured party} \\
+ & \text{Incidental damages} \\
+ & \text{Consequential damages} \\
\hline
= & \text{Compensatory damages}
\end{array}
$$

LOSS OF VALUE In general, loss of value is the *difference between the value of the promised performance* of the breaching party *and the value of the actual performance* rendered by the breaching party.

$$
\begin{array}{rl}
& \textbf{Value of promised performance} \\
- & \textbf{Value of actual performance} \\
\hline
= & \textbf{Loss of value}
\end{array}
$$

If the breaching party renders no performance at all, then the loss of value is the value of the promised performance. If defective or partial performance is rendered, the loss of value is the difference between the value that the full performance would have had and the value of the performance actually rendered. Thus, where there has been a breach of warranty, the injured party may recover the difference between the value the goods would have had, if they had been as warranted, and the value of the goods in the condition in which the buyer received them. To illustrate, Victor sells an automobile to Joan and expressly warrants that it will get forty-five miles per gallon, but the automobile gets only twenty miles per gallon. The automobile would have been worth $24,000 had it been as warranted, but it is worth only $20,000 as delivered. Joan would recover $4,000 in damages for loss of value.

In addition to loss of value, the injured party may also recover for all other losses actually suffered, subject to the limitation of foreseeability discussed in a subsequent section. These damages include incidental and consequential damages.

COST AVOIDED The recovery by the injured party, however, is reduced by any cost or loss she has avoided by not having to perform. For example, Clinton agrees to build a hotel for Debra for $11,250,000 by September 1. Clinton breaches by not completing construction until October 1. As a consequence, Debra loses revenues for one month in the amount of $400,000 but saves operating expenses of $60,000. She therefore may recover damages for $340,000. Similarly, in a contract in which the injured party has not fully performed, the injured party's recovery is reduced by the value to him of the performance he promised but did not render. For example, Clinton agrees to convey land to Debra in return for Debra's promise to work for Clinton for two years, but she repudiates the contract before Clinton has conveyed the land. Clinton's recovery for loss from Debra is reduced by the value to Clinton of the land.

INCIDENTAL DAMAGES **Incidental damages** are damages that arise directly out of the breach, such as costs incurred to acquire the nondelivered performance from some other source. For example, Agnes employs Benton for nine months for $40,000 to supervise construction of a factory, but fires him without cause after three weeks. Benton, who spends $850 in reasonable fees attempting to find comparable employment, may recover $850 in incidental damages, in addition to any other actual loss he may suffer.

CONSEQUENTIAL DAMAGES **Consequential damages** include lost profits and injury to person or property resulting from defective performance. Thus, if Tracy leases to Sean a defective machine that causes him $40,000 in property damage and $120,000 in personal injuries, Sean may recover, in addition to damages for loss of value and incidental damages, $160,000 as consequential damages.

> ### Practical Advice
> *If you are the provider of goods or services, consider including a contractual provision for the limitation or exclusion of consequential damages. If you are the purchaser of goods or services, avoid such limitations.*

18-2b NOMINAL DAMAGES

An action to recover damages for breach of contract may be maintained even though the plaintiff has not sustained or cannot prove any injury or loss resulting from the breach. Restatement, Section 346. In such a case, he will be permitted to recover **nominal damages**—a small sum fixed without regard to the amount of loss. For example, Edward contracts to sell and deliver goods to Florence for $1,000. Edward refuses to deliver the goods as agreed and so breaks the contract. Florence, however, is able to purchase goods of the same kind and quality elsewhere for $1,000 without incurring any incidental damages. As a result, although Edward has violated

Florence's rights under the contract, Florence has suffered no actual loss. Consequently, if Florence, as she may, should sue Edward for breach of contract, she would recover a judgment for nominal damages only. Nominal damages are also available where loss is actually sustained but cannot be proved with reasonable certainty.

18-2c RELIANCE DAMAGES

As an alternative to compensatory damages, a party injured by total breach or repudiation may seek reimbursement for foreseeable loss caused by his reliance upon the contract as measured by the cost or the value of the injured party's performance. The purpose of **reliance damages** is to place the injured party in a position as good as the position he would have held, had the contract *not been made*. The Restatement of Restitution provides that reliance damages for *cost* of performance include the injured party's uncompensated expenses incurred in preparing to perform, in actually performing, or in forgoing opportunities to enter into other contracts. Section 38. Recovery based on cost of performance, however, is reduced by any loss the breaching party can prove with reasonable certainty that the injured party would have suffered had the contract been performed. Alternatively, reliance damages may be the market *value* of the injured party's uncompensated contractual performance, not exceeding the contract price of such performance. Limiting damages for the value of performance to the contract price prevents injured parties from choosing reliance damages to escape from an unfavorable bargain. In addition to recovering the cost or value of her performance, the injured party may also recover for any other loss, including incidental or consequential loss, caused by the breach. Restatement of Restitution, Section 38.

An injured party may prefer damages for reliance to compensatory damages when he is unable to establish his lost profits with reasonable certainty. For example, Donald agrees to sell his retail store to Gary, who spends $750,000 acquiring inventory and fixtures. Donald then repudiates the contract, and Gary sells the inventory and fixtures for $735,000. Neither party can establish with reasonable certainty what profit Gary would have made; Gary, therefore, may recover from Donald as damages the loss of $15,000 he sustained on the sale of the inventory and fixtures plus any other costs he incurred in entering into the contract.

18-2d PUNITIVE DAMAGES

Punitive damages are monetary damages in addition to compensatory damages awarded to a plaintiff in certain situations involving willful, wanton, or malicious conduct. Their purpose is to punish the defendant and thus discourage him and others from similar wrongful conduct. The purpose of allowing contract damages, on the other hand, is to compensate the plaintiff

for the loss that he has sustained because of the defendant's breach of contract. Accordingly, the Restatement provides that punitive damages are *not* recoverable for a breach of contract unless the conduct constituting the breach is also a tort for which the plaintiff may recover punitive damages. Restatement, Section 355.

♦ *See Case 18-1*

18-2e LIQUIDATED DAMAGES

A contract may contain a **liquidated damages** provision by which the parties agree in advance to the damages to be paid in event of a breach. Such a provision will be enforced if it amounts to a reasonable forecast of the loss that may or does result from the breach. If, however, the sum agreed upon as liquidated damages bears no reasonable relationship to the amount of probable loss that may or does result from breach, it is unenforceable as a penalty. (A penalty is a contractual provision designed to deter a party from breaching her contract and to punish her for doing so.) Restatement, Section 356, Comment a states:

> The parties to a contract may effectively provide in advance the damages that are to be payable in the event of breach as long as the provision does not disregard the principle of compensation. The enforcement of such provisions for liquidated damages saves the time of courts, juries, parties and witnesses and reduces the expense of litigation. This is especially important if the amount in controversy is small. However, the parties to a contract are not free to provide a penalty for its breach. The central objective behind the system of contract remedies is compensatory, not punitive.

By examining the substance of the provision, the nature of the contract, and the extent of probable harm to the promisee that a breach may reasonably be expected to cause, the courts will determine whether the agreed amount is proper as liquidated damages or unenforceable as a penalty. If a liquidated damage provision is not enforceable, the injured party nevertheless is entitled to the ordinary remedies for breach of contract.

To illustrate, Reliable Construction Company contracts with Equerry to build a grandstand at Equerry's racecourse at a cost of $1,330,000, to have it completed by a certain date, and to pay Equerry, as liquidated damages, $5,000 per day for every day's delay beyond that date in completing the grandstand. The stipulated sum for delay is liquidated damages and not a penalty because the amount is reasonable. If, instead, the sum stipulated had been $40,000 per day, it obviously would have been unreasonable and therefore a penalty. Provisions for liquidated damages are sometimes found in contracts for the sale of a business, in which the seller agrees not to reenter the same business within a reasonable geographic area and time period. Actual damages resulting from the seller's breach of his agreement ordinarily would be difficult to ascertain, and the sum stipulated, if reasonable, would be enforced as liquidated damages.

♦ *See Case 18-2*

18-2f LIMITATIONS ON DAMAGES

To accomplish the basic purposes of contract remedies, the law imposes the limitations of foreseeability, certainty, and mitigation upon monetary damages. These limitations are intended to ensure that damages can be taken into account at the time of contracting, that damages are compensatory and not speculative, and that damages do not include loss that could have been avoided by reasonable efforts.

FORESEEABILITY OF DAMAGES A contracting party is generally expected to consider foreseeable risks when entering into the contract. Therefore, compensatory or reliance damages are recoverable only for loss that the party in breach had reason to foresee as a *probable* result of such breach when the contract was made; conversely, the breaching party is not liable for loss that was not foreseeable when the parties entered into the contract. The test of foreseeability is *objective*, based upon what the breaching party had reason to foresee. Loss may be deemed foreseeable as a probable result of a breach by following from the breach (1) in the ordinary course of events or (2) as a result of special circumstances, beyond the ordinary course of events, which the party in breach had reason to know. Restatement, Section 351(2). Moreover, "[a] court may limit damages for foreseeable loss by excluding recovery for loss of profits, by allowing recovery only for loss incurred in reliance, or otherwise if it concludes that in the circumstances justice so requires in order to avoid disproportionate compensation." Restatement, Section 351(3).

The leading case on the subject of foreseeability of damages is *Hadley* v. *Baxendale*, decided in England in 1854. In this case, the plaintiffs operated a flour mill at Gloucester. Their mill was compelled to cease operating because of a broken crankshaft attached to the steam engine that furnished power to the mill. It was necessary to send the broken shaft to a foundry located at Greenwich so that a new shaft could be made. The plaintiffs delivered the broken shaft to the defendants, who were common carriers, for immediate transportation from Gloucester to Greenwich, but did not inform the defendants that operation of the mill had ceased because of the nonfunctioning crankshaft. The defendants received the shaft, collected the freight charges in advance, and promised to deliver the shaft for repairs the following day. The defendants, however, did not make delivery as promised; as a result, the mill did not resume operations for several days, causing the plaintiffs to lose profitable sales. The defendants contended that the loss of profits was too remote, and therefore unforeseeable, to be recoverable. Nonetheless, the jury, in awarding damages to the plaintiffs, was permitted to take into consideration the loss of these profits. The appellate court reversed the decision and ordered a new trial on the ground that the plaintiffs had never communicated to the defendants the special circumstances that caused the loss of profits, namely, the continued stoppage of the mill while awaiting the return of the repaired crankshaft. A common carrier, the court reasoned, would not reasonably have foreseen that the plaintiffs' mill would be shut down as a result of delay in transporting the broken crankshaft.

On the other hand, if the defendants in *Hadley v. Baxendale* had been informed that the shaft was necessary for the operation of the mill, or otherwise had reason to know this fact, they would be liable for the plaintiffs' loss of profit during that period of the shutdown caused by their delay. Under these circumstances, the loss would be the "foreseeable" and "natural" result of the breach.

Should a plaintiff's expected profit be extraordinarily large, the general rule is that the breaching party will be liable for such special loss only if he had reason to know of it. In any event, the plaintiff may recover for any ordinary loss resulting from the breach. Thus, if Madeline breaches a contract with Jane, causing Jane, due to special circumstances, $10,000 in damages where ordinarily such a breach would result in only $6,000 in damages, Madeline would be liable to Jane for $6,000, not $10,000, provided that Madeline was unaware of the special circumstances causing Jane the unusually large loss.

CERTAINTY OF DAMAGES Damages are not recoverable for loss beyond an amount that the injured party can establish with reasonable certainty. Restatement, Section 352. If the injured party cannot prove a particular element of her loss with reasonable certainty, she nevertheless will be entitled to recover the portion of her loss that she can prove with reasonable certainty. The certainty requirement creates the greatest challenge for plaintiffs seeking to recover consequential damages for lost profits on related transactions. Plaintiffs attempting to prove lost profits caused by breach of a contract to produce a sporting event or to publish a new book experience similar difficulties.

MITIGATION OF DAMAGES Under the doctrine of mitigation of damages, the injured party may not recover damages for loss that he could have avoided with reasonable effort and without undue risk, burden, or humiliation. Restatement, Section 350. Thus, if James is under a contract to manufacture goods for Kathy and Kathy repudiates the contract after James has commenced performance, James will not be allowed to recover for losses he sustains by continuing to manufacture the goods if to do so would increase the amount of damages. The amount of loss that James reasonably could have avoided is deducted from the amount that otherwise would be recoverable as damages. On the other hand, if the goods were almost completed when Kathy repudiated the contract, completing the goods might mitigate the damages, because the finished goods may be resalable whereas the unfinished goods may not. UCC Section 2-704(2).

Similarly, if Harvey contracts to work for Olivia for one year for a weekly salary and is wrongfully discharged by Olivia after two months, Harvey must use reasonable efforts to mitigate his damages by seeking other employment. If, after such efforts, he cannot obtain other employment of the same general character, he is entitled to recover full pay for the contract period that he is unemployed. He is not obliged to accept a radically different type of employment or to accept work at a distant place. For example, a person employed as a schoolteacher or accountant who is wrongfully discharged is not obliged, in order to mitigate damages, to accept available employment as a chauffeur or truck driver. If Harvey does not seek other employment, then if Olivia proves with reasonable certainty that employment of the same general character was available, Harvey's damages are reduced by the amount he could have earned.

♦ *See Case 3-3*

Practical Advice

If the other party to the contract breaches, be sure to make reasonable efforts to avoid or mitigate damages.

18-3 Remedies in Equity

At times, damages based on the expectation interest, reliance interest, or restitution interest will not adequately compensate an injured party. In these cases, equitable relief in the form of specific performance or an injunction may be available to protect the injured party's interest.

The remedies of specific performance and an injunction are not a matter of right but instead rest in the discretion of the court. Consequently, they will not be granted where:

1. there is an adequate remedy at law;
2. it is impossible to enforce them, as where the seller has already conveyed the subject matter of the contract to an innocent third person;
3. the terms of the contract are unfair;
4. the consideration is grossly inadequate;
5. the contract is tainted with fraud, duress, undue influence, mistake, or unfair practices;
6. the terms of the contract are not sufficiently certain; or
7. the relief would cause unreasonable hardship.

A court may grant specific performance or an injunction despite a provision for liquidated damages. Restatement, Section 361. Moreover, a court will grant specific performance or an injunction even though a term of the contract prohibits equitable relief, if denying such relief would cause unreasonable hardship to the injured party. Restatement, Section 364(2).

Another equitable remedy is reformation, a process whereby the court "rewrites" or "corrects" a written contract to make it conform to the true agreement of the parties. The purpose of reformation is not to make a new contract for the parties but rather to express adequately the contract they have made for themselves. The remedy of reformation is granted when the parties agree on a contract but write it in a way that inaccurately reflects their actual agreement. For example, Acme Insurance Co. and Bell agree that for good consideration, Acme will issue an annuity paying $500 per month. Through a clerical error, the annuity policy is issued for $50 per month. A court of equity, upon satisfactory proof of the mistake, will reform the policy to provide for the correct amount—$500 per month. In addition, as discussed in *Chapter 13*, in cases in which a covenant not to compete is unreasonable, some courts will reform the agreement to make it reasonable and enforceable.

18-3a SPECIFIC PERFORMANCE

Specific performance is an equitable remedy that compels the defaulting party to perform her contractual obligations. Ordinarily, where a seller breaches her contract for the sale of **personal property**, the buyer has a sufficient remedy at law. If, however, the personal property contracted for is rare or unique, this remedy is inadequate. Examples of such property would include a famous painting or statue, an original manuscript or a rare edition of a book, a patent, a copyright, shares of stock in a closely held corporation, and an heirloom. Articles of this kind cannot be purchased elsewhere. Accordingly, should the seller breach her contract for the sale of any such article, money damages will not adequately compensate the buyer. Consequently, in these instances, the buyer may avail herself of the equitable remedy of specific performance.

Although courts of equity will grant specific performance for breach of contract for the sale of personal property only in exceptional circumstances, they will always grant specific performance for breach of contract for the sale of **real property**. The reason for this is that every parcel of land is considered unique. Consequently, if the seller refuses to convey title to the real estate contracted for, the buyer may seek the aid of a court of equity to compel the seller to convey the title. Most courts of equity will likewise compel the buyer in a real estate contract to perform at the suit of the seller. Courts of equity will not grant specific performance of contracts for personal services. In the first place, enforcing such a decree may be difficult if not impossible. In the second place, it is against the policy of the courts to force one person to work for or to serve another against his will, even though the person has contracted to do so, in that such enforcement would closely resemble involuntary servitude. For example, if Carmen, an accomplished concert pianist, agrees to appear at a certain time and place to play a specified program for Rudolf, a court would not issue a decree of specific performance upon her refusal to appear.

◆ *See Case 18-3*

18-3b INJUNCTIONS

An **injunction**, as used as a contract remedy, is a formal court order enjoining (commanding) a person to refrain from doing a specific act or to cease engaging in specified conduct. A court of equity, at its discretion, may grant an injunction against breach of a contractual duty where damages for a breach would be inadequate. For example, Clint enters into a written contract to give Janice the right of first refusal on a tract of land he owns. Clint, however, subsequently offers the land to Blake without first offering it to Janice. A court of equity may properly enjoin Clint from selling the land to Blake. Similarly, valid covenants not to compete may be enforced by an injunction.

An employee's promise of exclusive personal services may be enforced by an injunction against serving another employer as long as the probable result will not be to deprive the employee of other reasonable means of making a living. Restatement, Section 367. Suppose, for example, that Allan makes a contract with Marlene, a famous singer, under which Marlene agrees to sing at Allan's theater on certain dates for an agreed fee. Before the date of the first performance, Marlene makes a contract with Craig to sing for Craig at his theater on the same dates. Although, as already discussed, Allan cannot secure specific performance of his contract by Marlene, a court of equity will, on suit by Allan against Marlene, issue an injunction against her, ordering her not to sing for Craig.

In cases in which the services contracted for are not unusual or extraordinary, the injured party cannot obtain injunctive relief. His only remedy is an action at law for damages.

◆ *See Case 18-4*

18-4 Restitution

One remedy that may be available to a party to a contract is restitution. **Restitution** is the act of returning to the aggrieved party the consideration, or its value, which he gave to the other party. The purpose of restitution is to restore the injured party to the position he occupied before the contract was made. Therefore, the party seeking restitution must return what he has received from the other party.

Restitution is available in several contractual situations: (1) as an alternative remedy for a party injured by breach, (2) for a party in default, (3) for a party who may not enforce a contract because of the statute of frauds, and (4) for a party wishing to rescind (avoid) a voidable contract.

18-4a PARTY INJURED BY BREACH

The Restatement of Restitution provides that a party is entitled to restitution if the other party materially breaches the contract by nonperformance or repudiation. Section 37. For example, Benedict agrees to sell land to Beatrice for $60,000. After Beatrice makes a partial payment of $15,000, Benedict wrongfully refuses to transfer title. As an alternative to damages or specific performance, Beatrice may recover the $15,000 in restitution. The Restatement of Restitution provides, however, that restitution as a remedy for breach of contract is *not* available against a defendant whose defaulted obligation is exclusively an obligation to pay money. Section 37. Thus, restitution as an alternative contract remedy is available to a prepaying buyer but not to a credit seller.

18-4b PARTY IN DEFAULT

The Restatement of Restitution provides that a partly performing party whose material breach prevents a recovery on the contract has a claim in restitution against the recipient of performance, as necessary to prevent unjust enrichment. Section 36. Thus, if a party, after having partly performed, commits a breach by nonperformance or repudiation that discharges the other party's duty to perform, the party in default is entitled to restitution for any benefit she has conferred in excess of the loss she has caused by her breach. Restatement, Section 374. For example, Nathan agrees to sell land to Lilly for $160,000, and Lilly makes a partial payment of $15,000. Lilly then repudiates the contract. Nathan sells the land to Murray in good faith for $155,000. Lilly may recover from Nathan in restitution the part payment of the $15,000 less the $5,000 damages Nathan sustained because of Lilly's breach, which equals $10,000.

FIGURE 18-1 Contract Remedies

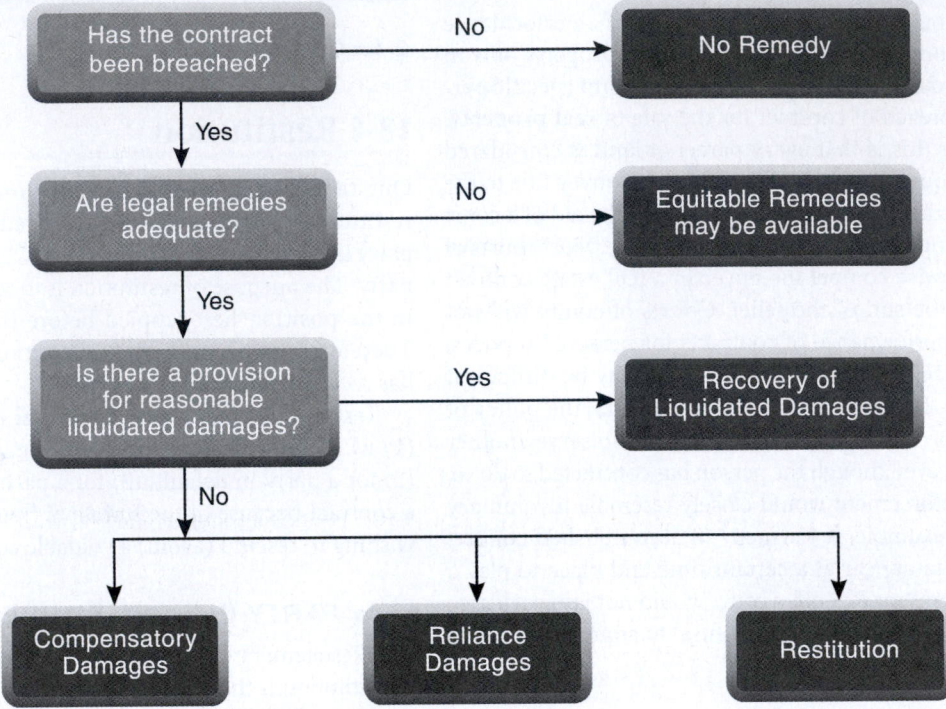

18-4c STATUTE OF FRAUDS

The Restatement of Restitution provides that a person who renders performance under an agreement that cannot be enforced by reason of the failure to satisfy the statute of frauds has a claim in restitution to prevent unjust enrichment. Section 31. In such a case, that party may recover in restitution the benefits she directly conferred upon the other as the performance required or invited by the unenforceable contract. Thus, if Wilton makes an oral contract to furnish services to Rochelle that are not to be performed within a year and Rochelle discharges Wilton after three months, Wilton may recover in restitution the value of the services he rendered during the three months. Similarly, Sanford enters into an oral contract to sell land to Betty, and Betty pays a portion of the price as a down payment. Sanford subsequently repudiates the oral contract. Betty may recover in restitution the portion of the price she paid.

18-4d VOIDABLE CONTRACTS

A party who has rescinded or avoided a contract for lack of capacity, duress, undue influence, fraud in the inducement, nonfraudulent misrepresentation, or mistake is entitled to restitution for any benefit he has conferred upon the other party. Restatement, Section 376. Generally, the party seeking restitution must return any benefit that he has received under the agreement; however, as discussed in *Chapter 14* (which deals

with contractual capacity), this is not always the case. Section 54 of the Restatement of Restitution provides:

Rescission requires a mutual restoration and accounting in which each party (a) restores property received from the other, to the extent such restoration is feasible, (b) accounts for additional benefits obtained at the expense of the other as a result of the transaction and its subsequent avoidance, as necessary to prevent unjust enrichment, and (c) compensates the other for loss from related expenditure as justice may require.

For example, Samuel fraudulently induces Jessica to sell land for $160,000. Samuel pays the purchase price, and Jessica conveys the land. Jessica then discovers the fraud. Jessica may disaffirm the contract and recover the land as restitution, but she must return the $160,000 purchase price to Samuel.

◆ See Figure 18-1: *Contract Remedies*

18-5 Limitations on Remedies

18-5a ELECTION OF REMEDIES

If a party injured by a breach of contract has more than one remedy available to him, his manifesting a choice of one of them, such as bringing suit, does not prevent him from seeking another remedy unless the remedies are inconsistent and the other party materially changes his position in reliance on the manifestation. Restatement, Section 378. For example, a party who seeks specific performance, an injunction, or restitution may be entitled to incidental damages for delay in performance. Damages for total *breach*, however, are inconsistent with the remedies of specific performance, injunction, and restitution. Likewise, the remedy of specific performance or an injunction is inconsistent with that of restitution.

With respect to contracts for the sale of goods, the Code rejects any doctrine of election of remedies. Thus, the remedies it provides are essentially cumulative, including all of the available remedies for breach. Whether one remedy precludes another depends on the facts of the individual case. UCC Section 2-703, Comment 1.

♦ *See Case 18-1*

18-5b LOSS OF POWER OF AVOIDANCE

A party with a power of avoidance for lack of capacity, duress, undue influence, fraud, misrepresentation, or mistake may lose that power if (1) she affirms the contract, (2) she delays unreasonably in exercising the power of disaffirmance, or (3) the rights of third parties intervene.

AFFIRMANCE A party who has the power to avoid a contract for lack of capacity, duress, undue influence, fraud in the inducement, nonfraudulent misrepresentation, or mistake will lose that power by affirming the contract. Affirmance occurs when the party, with full knowledge of the facts, either declares his intention to proceed with the contract or takes some other action from which such intention may reasonably be inferred. Thus, suppose that Pam was induced to purchase a ring from Sally through Sally's fraudulent misrepresentation. If, after learning the truth, Pam undertakes to sell the ring to Janet or does something that is consistent only with her ownership of the ring, she may no longer rescind the transaction with Sally. In the case of incapacity, duress, or undue influence, affirmance is effective only after the circumstances that made the contract voidable cease to exist. In the case of fraudulent misrepresentation, the defrauded party may affirm only after he knows of the misrepresentation. If the misrepresentation is nonfraudulent or a mistake is involved, the defrauded or mistaken party may affirm only after he knows or should have known of the misrepresentation or mistake.

DELAY The power of avoidance may be lost if the party who has the power does not rescind within a reasonable time after the circumstances that made the contract voidable have ceased to exist. Determining a reasonable time depends upon all the circumstances, including the extent to which the delay enables the party with the power of avoidance to speculate at the other party's risk. To illustrate, a defrauded purchaser of stock cannot wait unduly to see whether the market price or value of the stock appreciates sufficiently to justify retaining the stock.

RIGHTS OF THIRD PARTIES The intervening rights of third parties further limit the power of avoidance and the accompanying right to restitution. If A transfers property to B in a transaction that is voidable by A and B sells the property to C (a good faith purchaser for value) before A exercises her power of avoidance, A will lose the right to recover the property.

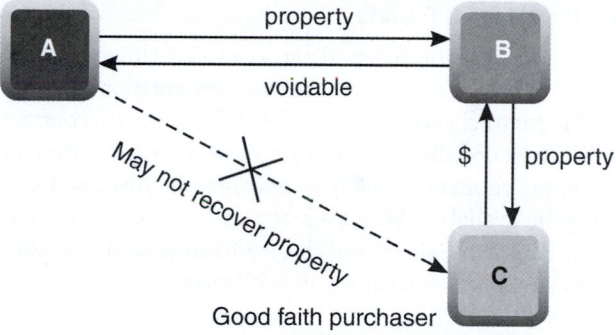

property

voidable

May not recover property

$ property

Good faith purchaser

Thus, if C, a third party who is a good faith purchaser, acquires an interest in the subject matter of the contract before A has elected to rescind, no rescission is permitted. Because the transaction is voidable, B acquires a voidable title to the property. Upon a sale of the property by B to C, who is a purchaser in good faith and for value, C obtains good title and is allowed to retain the property. As both A and C are innocent, the law will not disturb the title held by C, the good faith purchaser. In this case, as in all cases in which rescission is not available, A's only recourse is against B.

The one notable exception to this rule is the situation involving a sale, *other than a sale of goods*, by a minor who subsequently wishes to avoid the transaction, in which the property has been retransferred to a good faith purchaser. Under this special rule, a good faith purchaser is deprived of the protection generally provided such third parties. Therefore, the third party in a transaction not involving goods, real property being the primary example, is no more protected from the minor's disaffirmance than is the person dealing directly with the minor.

Practical Advice

If you have the power to avoid a contract, do not affirm the contract unless you are sure you wish to relinquish your right to rescind the contract.

18-6 Remedies for Misrepresentation

Misrepresentation that induces a party to enter into a contract may give rise to remedies under the law of restitution, contract law, and tort law. Although a deceived party may seek a remedy under tort law, contract law, and restitution, she may not be compensated more than once and may also be subject to election of remedies, discussed earlier. The Code liberalizes the common law by not restricting a defrauded party to an election of remedies; that is, the injured party may both rescind the contract by restoring the other party to the status quo and recover damages or obtain any other remedy available under the Code. UCC Section 2-721.

18-6a RESTITUTION

Under the law of restitution, a remedy for misrepresentation is rescission (avoidance) of the contract by the deceived party, though when appropriate, the courts also will require restitution. This remedy was discussed earlier in this chapter.

18-6b CONTRACT LAW

Under contract law the deceived party can elect either to affirm and enforce the contract despite the misrepresentation or to disaffirm the contract and seek rescission. Rescission as a contract remedy is functionally the same as rescission in restitution. In addition, the equitable remedy of reformation, discussed earlier, may be available. Moreover, if a misrepresentation satisfies the requirements of breach of warranty, compensatory damages, also discussed earlier, may be recovered.

18-6c TORT LAW

Under tort law, the deceived party may leave the contract in place and recover damages for the loss caused by the other party's misrepresentation. The availability and the measure of damages in tort for misrepresentation depend upon whether the misrepresentation is fraudulent or nonfraudulent.

DAMAGES IN TORT FOR FRAUD Fraud is an intentional misrepresentation of material fact by one party to the other, who consents to enter into a contract in justifiable reliance upon the misrepresentation. An intentionally defrauded party may recover general damages in a tort action. A minority of States allows an intentionally defrauded party to recover, under the **"out-of-pocket"** rule, general damages equal to the difference between the value of what she has received and the value of what she has given for it, along with such other monetary damages needed to restore the position the intentionally defrauded party would have occupied if the fraudulent party had not committed the fraud. (This measure of damages is comparable to a combination of reliance and consequential damages under contract law.) The great majority of States, however, under the **"benefit-of-the-bargain"** rule, permit the intentionally defrauded party to recover general damages that are equal to the difference between the value of what she has received and

the value of the fraudulent party's performance as represented. (This recovery is comparable to expectation damages under contract law.) The Second Restatement of Torts provides the intentionally defrauded party with the option of either out-of-pocket or benefit-of-the-bargain damages. Section 549. To illustrate, Emily intentionally misrepresents the capabilities of a printing press and thereby induces Melissa to purchase the machine for $20,000. The value of the press as delivered is $14,000, but if the machine had performed as represented, it would be worth $24,000. Under the out-of-pocket rule, Melissa would recover $6,000, whereas under the benefit-of-the-bargain rule, she would recover $10,000.

In addition to a recovery of general damages under one of the measures just discussed, consequential damages may be recovered to the extent they are proved with reasonable certainty and do not duplicate general damages. Moreover, where the fraud is gross, oppressive, or aggravated, punitive damages are permitted.

◆ *See Case 18-1*

DAMAGES IN TORT FOR NONFRAUDULENT MISREPRESENTATION With respect to damages in tort for nonfraudulent misrepresentation, the Second Restatement of Torts and the recent Third Restatement of Torts: Liability for Economic Harm diverge. When the misrepresentation is negligent, the Second Restatement of Torts permits the deceived party to recover general damages—under the out-of-pocket measure—and consequential damages. Second Restatement of Torts, Section 552B. Some States, however, permit the recovery of general damages under the benefit-of-the-bargain measure for negligent misrepresentation. Where the misrepresentation is innocent (neither fraudulent nor negligent), however, the Second Restatement of Torts limits damages to the out-of-pocket measure. Section 552C.

The Third Restatement of Torts: Liability for Economic Harm has changed the rules contained in Sections 552B and 552C of the Second Restatement of Torts. Section 3 of the Third Restatement of Torts: Liability for Economic Harm provides that there is no liability in tort for economic loss caused by negligence in the performance or negotiation of a contract between the parties. Thus, Section 3 eliminates the liability of sellers for negligent misrepresentations that cause buyers to enter into contracts with them. Comment d to Section 3 explains, "A seller's negligent misrepresentations are addressed sufficiently by the law of contract and restitution. Such misrepresentations may give the buyer a claim for breach of warranty, for rescission and incidental damages, or for breach of contract..."

For the same reasons, liability in tort for innocent misrepresentation is also not recognized.

MONETARY DAMAGES

Compensatory Damages contract damages placing the injured party in a position as good as the one he would have held had the other party performed; equals loss of value minus loss avoided by injured party plus incidental damages plus consequential damages

- *Loss of Value* value of promised performance minus value of actual performance
- *Cost Avoided* loss or costs the injured party avoids by not having to perform
- *Incidental Damages* damages arising directly out of a breach of contract
- *Consequential Damages* damages not arising directly out of a breach but arising as a foreseeable result of the breach

Nominal Damages a small sum awarded when a contract has been breached but the loss is negligible or unproved

Reliance Damages contract damages placing the injured party in as good a position as she would have been in had the contract not been made

Punitive Damages are generally *not* recoverable for breach of contract

Liquidated Damages reasonable damages agreed to in advance by the parties to a contract

Limitations on Damages

- *Foreseeability of Damages* potential loss that the party now in default had reason to know of when the contract was made
- *Certainty of Damages* damages are not recoverable beyond an amount that can be established with reasonable certainty
- *Mitigation of Damages* injured party may not recover damages for loss he could have avoided by reasonable effort

REMEDIES IN EQUITY

Availability only in cases in which there is no adequate remedy at law

Types

- **Specific Performance** court decree ordering breaching party to render promised performance
- **Injunction** court order prohibiting a party from doing a specific act
- **Reformation** court order correcting a written contract to conform with the original intent of the contracting parties

RESTITUTION

Definition of Restitution restoration of the injured party to the position she was in before the contract was made

Availability

- **Party Injured by Breach** if the other party totally breaches the contract by non-performance or repudiation
- **Party in Default** for any benefit conferred in excess of the loss caused by the breach of the party in default
- **Statute of Frauds** where a contract is unenforceable because of the statute of frauds, a party may recover the benefits conferred on the other party in performance of the contract
- **Voidable Contracts** a party who has rightfully avoided a contract is entitled to restitution for any benefit conferred on the other party but generally must return any benefit that he has received under the contract

LIMITATIONS ON REMEDIES

Election of Remedies if remedies are not inconsistent, a party injured by a breach of contract may seek more than one
Loss of Power of Avoidance a party with the power to avoid a contract may lose that power by
- affirming the contract
- delaying unreasonably in exercising the power of avoidance
- being subordinated to the intervening rights of third parties

REMEDIES FOR MISREPRESENTATION

Restitution the law of restitution allows rescission (avoidance) of the contract and, when appropriate, restitution
Contract Remedies include affirmation with damages, rescission, reformation, and warranty
Tort Damages depending on the State and the type of misrepresentation, tort damages may be either (1) benefit-of-the bargain damages (difference between the value of the fraudulent party's performance as represented and the value the defrauded party received) or (2) out-pocket damages (difference between the value given and the value received)

C A S E S

CASE	
18-1	Election of Remedies/Punitive Damages/Fraud **MERRITT v. CRAIG** Court of Special Appeals of Maryland, 2000 130 MdApp. 350, 746 A.2d 923; certiorari denied, 359 Md. 29, 753 A.2d 2

Davis, J.

In the fall of 1995, during their search for a new residence, appellants [Benjamin and Julie Merritt] inspected Craig's property located at Pergin Farm Road in Garrett County [Maryland]. After viewing the residence, appellants advised Craig that they were interested in purchasing the property; however, their offer was contingent upon a satisfactory home inspection. On November 5, 1995, appellants, their inspector, and appellee's husband Mark Craig conducted an inspection of the basement area of the residence, during which there was an examination of cistern and water supply pipes. The examination revealed that the cistern had been used to store a water supply reserve, but was not currently utilized.

The inspector advised appellants that the system he had observed was one which utilized a submersible pump in the well from which water flowed to a pressure tank in the basement. The pressure tank distributed water through the internal piping system of the house. There were also two water lines that entered into the basement area. One of the lines came from an 800-foot well that was located on the property, and the other line came from a well located on the adjacent property. The well located on the adjacent property supplied water to both appellants' residence and a guest house owned by Craig. The existence of the adjacent well was not disclosed to appellants.

On December 2, 1995, a contract of sale for the property was executed between appellants and Craig, along with a "Disclosure Statement" signed by Craig on June 9, 1994, and acknowledged

by appellants on November 2, 1995, affirming that there were no problems with the water supply to the dwelling. Between November 5, 1995 and June 1996, Craig caused the water line from the guest house to appellants' residence to be cut, and the cistern reactivated to store water from the existing well on appellants' lot. On May 18, 1996, Craig's husband advised Dennis Hannibal, one of the real estate agents involved in the deal, that he had spent $4,196.79 to upgrade the water system on appellants' property and to restore the cistern and remove appellants' house from the second well on Craig's guest house property. On June 14, 1996, appellants and Craig had settlement on the property. Later that afternoon, Craig's husband, without appellants' knowledge, excavated the inside wall of appellants' house and installed a cap to stop a leaking condition on the water line that he had previously cut.

Subsequently, appellants, while attempting to fill a water bed, noticed that the water supply in their well had depleted. On July 13, 1996, appellants met with Craig to discuss a solution to the water failure problem, believing that Craig was responsible for cutting a water line to their house. Appellants agreed with Craig to conduct a flow test to the existing well and contribute money for the construction of a new well. On October 29, 1996, the well was drilled and produced only one half gallon of water per minute. On December 13, appellants paid for the drilling of a second well on their property, but it failed to produce water. In January appellants contacted a plumber, Robert Warnick, who confirmed that the line from the guest house well to appellants' residence had been cut flush with the inside surface of the basement wall and cemented closed. Appellants continued to do further work on the house in an effort to cure the water problem.

On February 11, 1997, appellants brought suit against Craig and other appellees in the Circuit Court for Garrett County, seeking rescission of the deed to the property and contract of sale, along with compensatory and punitive damages. During the course of the trial, the judge dismissed appellants' claim for rescission on the ground that they had effectively waived their right to rescission. * * * At the close of trial, the jury returned a verdict in favor of appellants and awarded compensatory damages in the amount of $42,264.76. Appellants were also awarded punitive damages in the amount of $150,000. Subsequently, appellants filed a motion to alter or amend the judgment requesting the court to grant rescission of the contract of sale and the deed, which the circuit court denied on June 17, 1998.

* * *

* * * Under Maryland law, when a party to a contract discovers that he or she has been defrauded, the party defrauded has either "a right to retain the contract and collect damages for its breach, or a right to rescind the contract and recover his or her own expenditures," not both. [Citations.] "These rights [are] inconsistent and mutually exclusive, and the discovery put[s] the purchaser to a prompt election." [Citation.] "A plaintiff seeking rescission must demonstrate that he [or she] acted promptly after discovery of the ground for rescission," otherwise the right to rescind is waived. [Citations.] * * *

In the case *sub judice* [before the court], appellants claim that they were entitled to a rescission of the subject contract of sale and deed and incidental damages. Appellants also claim that they were entitled to compensatory and punitive damages arising from Craig's actions. Appellants, however, may not successfully rescind the contract while simultaneously recovering compensatory and punitive damages. Restitution is "a party's unilateral unmaking of a contract for a legally sufficient reason, such as the other party's material breach" and it in effect "restores the parties to their precontractual position." [Citation.] The restoration of the parties to their original position is incompatible with the circumstance when the complaining party is, at once, relieved of all obligations under the contract while simultaneously securing the windfall of compensatory and punitive damages beyond incidental expenses.

* * *

In sum, although whether appellants promptly repudiated the contract was not squarely before the court, we are not persuaded by appellees' assertion that appellants did not seek rescission in a timely fashion. We hold that, under the facts of this case, appellants must elect the form of relief, i.e., damages or rescission * * *

* * *

We hold that * * * the appellants are entitled to be awarded punitive damages resulting from Craig's actions. A "[p]laintiff seeking to recover punitive damages must allege in detail in the complaint the facts that indicate the entertainment by defendant of evil motive or intent." [Citation.] The Court of Appeals has held that "punitive damages may only be awarded in such cases where 'the plaintiff has established that the defendant's conduct was characterized by evil motive, intent to injure, ill will or fraud. * * *'" [Citation.] In cases of fraud that arise out of a contractual relationship, the plaintiff would have to establish actual malice to recover punitive damages. [Citation.] Finally, we have stated that "actual or express malice requires an intentional or willful act (or omission) … and 'has been characterized as the performance of an act without legal justification or excuse, but with an evil or rancorous motive influenced by hate, the purpose being to deliberately and willfully injure the plaintiff.'" [Citation.]

* * *

The jury believed that the representations made by Craig were undertaken with actual knowledge that the representations were false and with the intention to deceive appellants. * * * Moreover, the record reflects that the jury could reasonably infer Craig's intention to defraud appellants by her representation in the Disclosure Statement that there were no problems with the water supply, and by subsequently making substantial changes in the water system by cutting off a water line which supplied water to appellants' residence immediately after appellants' inspector examined the system. Therefore, we hold that the circuit court was not in error in finding facts from the record sufficient to support an award of punitive damages.

Craig also challenges the punitive damages award on the basis that the amount of the award was excessive. * * *

In the case at hand, the trial judge undertook the appropriate review of the jury's award. It is clear from the court's comments at the hearing that the court's decision not to disturb the jury's verdict was based on the evidence presented at trial and was not excessive. * * * Craig's conduct toward appellants was reprehensible and fully warranted punitive damages. Her conduct in willfully misrepresenting the condition of the water system in the Disclosure Statement, coupled with her actions and those of her husband in interfering and diverting the water flow subsequent to the inspection and sale of the property, constitute egregious conduct. As a result of Craig's conduct, appellants were forced to employ extreme water conservation practices due to an insufficient water supply and they attempted to ameliorate the problem by having two new wells drilled on the property which proved to be unproductive. Moreover, the lack of water supply to appellants' property clearly reduced its market value. * * *

* * *

* * * Consequently, should appellants seek compensatory and punitive damages on remand, appellants' actual knowledge, coupled with the intent to deceive, is a sufficient factual predicate for submission of punitive damages to the jury.

Judgment of the circuit court reversed; case remanded for further proceedings consistent with this opinion.

Liquidated Damages
ARROWHEAD SCHOOL DISTRICT NO. 75, PARK COUNTY, MONTANA, v. KLYAP
Supreme Court of Montana, 2003
318 Mont. 103, 79 P.3d 250

CASE 18-2

Nelson, J.

Arrowhead School District No. 75 (District) is located in Park County south of Livingston [Montana]. The District consists of one school, Arrowhead School (School).

For the 1997–98 school year, the School employed about eleven full-time teachers and several part-time teachers. During that school year, the School employed Klyap as a new teacher instructing math, language arts, and physical education for the sixth, seventh, and eighth grades. In addition, Klyap, through his own initiative, helped start a sports program and coached flag football, basketball, and volleyball.

* * * [T]he School offered Klyap a contract for the 1998–99 school year on or about June 15, 1998, which he accepted by signing on or about June 30, 1998. This contract provided for a $20,500 salary and included the liquidated damages clause at issue here. The clause calculated liquidated damages as a percentage of annual salary determined by the date of breach; a breach of contract after July 20, 1998, required payment of 20% of salary as damages. Klyap also signed a notice indicating he accepted responsibility for familiarizing himself with the information in the teacher's handbook which also included the liquidated damages clause.

* * *

* * * On August 12, [Klyap] informed the School that he would not be returning for the 1998–99 school year even though classes were scheduled to start on August 26. As a result of Klyap's decision not to teach at the School, the School sought to enforce the liquidated damages clause in Klyap's teaching contract for the stipulated amount of $4,100, 20% of the $20,500 salary. * * *

After Klyap resigned, the School attempted to find another teacher to take Klyap's place. Although at the time that Klyap was offered his contract the School had 80 potential applicants, only two viable applicants remained available. Right before classes started, the School was able to hire one of those applicants, a less experienced teacher, at a salary of $19,500.

* * * After a bench trial, the District Court determined the clause was enforceable * * * because the damages suffered by the School [were] impractical and extremely difficult to fix. Specifically, the court found the School suffered damages because it had to spend additional time setting up an interview committee, conducting interviews, training the new, less experienced teacher, and reorganizing the sports program.

The District Court also found that all these activities took away from the other school and administrative duties that had been scheduled for that time and that the new teacher missed all the staff development training earlier that year. Finally, the court found that such clauses are commonly used in Montana and that the School had routinely and equitably enforced the clause against other teachers. After concluding that the School took appropriate steps to mitigate its damages, the court awarded judgment in favor of the School in the amount of $4,100. * * *

* * *

The fundamental tenet of modern contract law is freedom of contract; parties are free to mutually agree to terms governing their private conduct as long as those terms do not conflict with public laws. [Citation.] This tenet presumes that parties are in the best position to make decisions in their own interest. Normally, in the course of contract interpretation by a court, the court simply gives effect to the agreement between the parties in order to enforce the private law of the contract. [Citation.] When one party breaches the contract, judicial enforcement of the contract ensures the nonbreaching party receives expectancy damages, compensation equal to what that party would receive if the contract were performed. [Citations.] By only awarding expectancy damages rather than additional damages intended to punish the breaching party for failure to perform the contract, court enforcement of private contracts supports the theory of efficient breach. In other words, if it is more efficient for a party to breach a contract and pay expectancy damages in order to enter a superior contract, courts will not interfere by requiring the breaching party to pay more than was due under their contract. [Citation.]

Liquidated damages are, in theory, an extension of these principles. Rather than wait until the occurrence of breach, the parties to a contract are free to agree in advance on a specific damage amount to be paid upon breach. [Citation.] This amount is intended to predetermine expectancy damages. Ideally, this predetermination is intended to make the agreement between the parties more efficient. Rather than requiring a post-breach inquiry into damages between the parties, the breaching party simply pays the nonbreaching party the stipulated amount. Further, in this way, liquidated damages clauses allow parties to estimate damages that are impractical or difficult to prove, as courts cannot enforce expectancy damages without sufficient proof.

* * *

In order to determine whether a clause should be declared a penalty, courts attempt to measure the reasonableness of a liquidated damages clause. * * * As indicated by * * * §356 of the RESTATEMENT (SECOND) OF CONTRACTS (1965) (hereinafter RESTATEMENT §356), the threshold indicator of reasonableness is whether the situation involves damages of a type that are impractical or extremely difficult to prove. * * *

According to RESTATEMENT §356 and other treatises, damages must be reasonable in relation to the damages the parties anticipated when the contract was executed or in relation to actual damages resulting from the breach. * * *

* * *

* * * Liquidated damages in a personal service contract induce performance by an employee by predetermining compensation to an employer if the employee leaves. However, the employer clearly prefers performance by the specific employee because that employee was chosen for hire. The preference for performance by a specific person is reflected in the rule that personal service contracts are not assignable. Further, because personal service contracts are not enforceable by specific performance, [citation], liquidated damages are an appropriate way for employers to protect their interests. * * *

* * *

After reviewing the facts of this case, we hold that while the 20% liquidated damages clause is definitely harsher than most, it is still within Klyap's reasonable expectations and is not unduly oppressive. First, as the School pointed out during testimony, at such a small school teachers are chosen in part depending on how their skills complement those of the other teachers. Therefore, finding someone who would provide services equivalent to Klyap at such a late date would be virtually impossible. This difficulty was born[e] out when only two applicants remained available and the School hired a teacher who was less experienced than Klyap. * * *

Second, besides the loss of equivalent services, the School lost time for preparation for other activities in order to attempt to find equivalent services. * * * Further, the new teacher missed all the staff development training earlier that year so individual training was required. And finally, because Klyap was essential to the sports program, the School had to spend additional time reorganizing the sports program as one sport had to be eliminated with Klyap's loss. * * *

* * *

Therefore, because as a teacher Klyap would know teachers are typically employed for an entire school year and would know how difficult it is to replace equivalent services at such a small rural school, it was within Klyap's reasonable expectations to agree to a contract with a 20% of salary liquidated damages provision for a departure so close to the start of the school year.

* * * Accordingly, we hold the District Court correctly determined that the liquidated damages provision was enforceable.

[Affirmed.]

| CASE 18-3 | Specific Performance **PRESTENBACH v. COLLINS** Supreme Court of Mississippi, 2014 159 So.3d 531 |  |

Dickinson, P. J.

[On September 15, 2011, Gerald Collins granted Garrett Prestenbach a one-year option to purchase approximately 150 acres of Collins's farm and pastureland for $500,000. Prestenbach agreed to make a $25,000 down payment on the property and finance the remaining $475,000 through a combination of a $225,000 USDA loan and $250,000 financing agreement with Collins.

The option contract included the following details: (1) a recital of $100 consideration; (2) a township-and-range description of the property; (3) a reference to the buyer's intent to obtain a USDA loan; (4) the total purchase price; and (5) a recital that the option was irrevocable for the first three months

and, after three months, the option could be revoked by giving ten days' written notice. The parties also agreed that Collins would allow the USDA to inspect the property before closing.

About a month after granting Prestenbach the option to purchase his land, another buyer offered to buy Collins's property immediately. Collins attempted to persuade Prestenbach to give up his option so he could sell to the other party, but Prestenbach refused and quickly recorded the option contract to prevent the sale.

By early December, relations between Collins and Prestenbach had deteriorated. On December 8, 2011, Collins's attorney sent Prestenbach a letter attempting to terminate the one-year option. Prestenbach responded on December 16, 2011, by hand-delivering a letter exercising his option to purchase. At that time, the USDA loan process was nearly complete, and on December 22, 2011, the USDA conditionally approved Prestenbach's loan.

Prestenbach tried to set a closing date for the loan, but Collins refused to move forward with the closing. Claiming that the option to purchase had been terminated, Collins denied the USDA's request to inspect the property. He then filed an action against Prestenbach to establish ownership of the property. In response, Prestenbach filed an answer and a counterclaim for specific performance, stating he was "ready, willing, and able" to close the deal. Both parties filed motions for summary judgment. The chancellor granted Collins's motion for summary judgment and denied Prestenbach's motion, finding that Prestenbach was not entitled to specific performance because, at the time he exercised his option, he could not pay the entire $500,000 purchase price. Prestenbach appealed.

The Court of Appeals affirmed the chancellor's judgment finding that Prestenbach was not entitled to "specific performance of [the] option contract," because when he exercised his option, he "indisputably lacked the financing to purchase the property." [Citation.] The Supreme Court of Mississippi then granted Prestenbach's writ of certiorari.]

The real-property option contract before us clearly provided how the option was to be exercised, and that a closing of the transaction would take place at some point following the exercise of the option. It further provided that "the purchase price shall be paid at the time of recording of [the] deed," and that taxes and other assessments would be prorated "as of the date of the closing of the transaction." So, while the contract required Prestenbach to pay the purchase price at "the closing of the transaction," nothing in the contract suggests that he was required to pay—or demonstrate his ability to pay—the purchase price prior to closing.

While an option contract is not a contract to sell, it morphs into a sales contract when the option holder exercises the option. [Citations.] When the option holder exercises the option "the option-giver has no choice but to sell when the option is accepted according to its terms." [Citation.] A valid and enforceable option contract requires: (1) an adequate description of the property, (2) consideration, and (3) a date when the option must be exercised. [Citation.] * * *

When the option holder exercises the option to purchase, the option holder "is entitled to specific performance of the optionor's duty to convey, so long as the holder is *willing* to pay the option price." [Citation.] If an option subject to financing does not specify when the sale must take place, "the court may decree a reasonable time [for performance]." [Citations.] And where the parties fail to include a closing date for the resulting sale, the closing date is "to be within a reasonable time from the date of exercising the option." [Citation.]

In this case, Collins and Prestenbach created a valid and enforceable option to purchase real property and Prestenbach timely exercised this option. When Prestenbach exercised his option to purchase, the option contract became an enforceable contract to sell and Prestenbach had the right to specifically enforce that contract. In the absence of a definite closing date in the option contract, it must be presumed that the parties intended that the sale would take place within a reasonable time after Prestenbach exercised his option to purchase. And Prestenbach was required to present himself at the closing with the purchase price as specified in the contract.

Absent language in the contract to the contrary, an option holder has no obligation or duty to show an ability to pay the entire sales price before the closing. Instead, by exercising the option, the option holder becomes bound to purchase the property at the closing, according to the terms of the contract. Prestenbach was entitled to set a closing date within a reasonable time following his exercise of the option. He attempted to do so, but Collins refused to cooperate. Thus, Prestenbach is entitled to specific performance, and the chancellor erred in denying Prestenbach's motion for summary judgment.

* * * We reverse the judgment of the Court of Appeals. * * *

CASE 18-4

Injunctions
MADISON SQUARE GARDEN CORP., ILL. v. CARNERA

United States Court of Appeals, Second Circuit, 1931
52 F.2d 47

Chase, J.
Suit by plaintiff, Madison Square Garden Corporation, against Primo Carnera, defendant. From an order granting an injunction against defendant, defendant appeals.

On January 13, 1931, the plaintiff and defendant by their duly authorized agents entered into the following agreement in writing:

1. Carnera agrees that he will render services as a boxer in his next contest (which contest, hereinafter called

the "First Contest," shall be with the winner of the proposed Schmeling-Stribling contest, or, if the same is drawn, shall be with Schmeling, and shall be deemed to be a contest for the heavyweight championship title; provided, however, that, in the event of the inability of the Garden to cause Schmeling or Stribling, as the case may be, to perform the terms of his agreement with the Garden calling for such contest, the Garden shall be without further liability to Carnera) exclusively under the auspices of the Garden, in the United States of America, or the Dominion of Canada, at such time, not, however, later than midnight of September 30, 1931, as the Garden may direct. * * *

9. Carnera shall not, pending the holding of the First Contest, render services as a boxer in any major boxing contest, without the written permission of the Garden in each case had and obtained. A major contest is understood to be one with Sharkey, Baer, Campolo, Godfrey, or like grade heavyweights, or heavyweights who shall have beaten any of the above subsequent to the date hereof. If in any boxing contest engaged in by Carnera prior to the holding of the First Contest, he shall lose the same, the Garden shall at its option, to be exercised by a two weeks' notice to Carnera in writing, be without further liability under the terms of this agreement to Carnera. Carnera shall not render services during the continuance of the option referred to in paragraph 8 hereof for any person, firm or corporation other than the Garden. Carnera shall, however, at all times be permitted to engage in sparring exhibitions in which no decision is rendered and in which the heavyweight championship title is not at stake, and in which Carnera boxes not more than four rounds with any one opponent. * * *

Thereafter the defendant, without the permission of the plaintiff, written or otherwise, made a contract to engage in a boxing contest with the Sharkey mentioned in paragraph 9 of the agreement above quoted, and by the terms thereof the contest was to take place before the first contest mentioned in the defendant's contract with the plaintiff was to be held.

The plaintiff then brought this suit to restrain the defendant from carrying out his contract to box Sharkey, and obtained the preliminary injunction order, from which this appeal was taken. Jurisdiction is based on diversity of citizenship and the required amount is involved.

The District Court has found on affidavits which adequately show it that the defendant's services are unique and extraordinary. A negative covenant in a contract for such personal services is enforceable by injunction where the damages for a breach are incapable of ascertainment. [Citations.]

The defendant points to what is claimed to be lack of consideration for his negative promise, in that the contract is inequitable and contains no agreement to employ him. It is true that there is no promise in so many words to employ the defendant to box in a contest with Stribling or Schmeling, but the agreement read as a whole binds the plaintiff to do just that, providing either Stribling or Schmeling becomes the contestant as the result of the match between them and can be induced to box the defendant. The defendant has agreed to "render services as a boxer" for the plaintiff exclusively, and the plaintiff has agreed to pay him a definite percentage of the gate receipts as his compensation for so doing. The promise to employ the defendant to enable him to earn the compensation agreed upon is implied to the same force and effect as though expressly stated. * * * [Citations.]

As we have seen, the contract is valid and enforceable. It contains a restrictive covenant which may be given effect. Whether a preliminary injunction shall be issued under such circumstances rests in the sound discretion of the court. [Citations.] The District Court, in its discretion, did issue the preliminary injunction and required the plaintiff as a condition upon its issuance to secure its own performance of the contract in suit with a bond for $25,000 and to give a bond in the sum of $35,000 to pay the defendant such damages as he may sustain by reason of the injunction. Such an order is clearly not an abuse of discretion. Order affirmed.

QUESTIONS

1. Edward, a candy manufacturer, contracted to buy one thousand barrels of sugar from Marcia. Marcia failed to deliver, and Edward was unable to buy any sugar in the market. As a direct consequence, he was unable to make candies to fulfill unusually lucrative contracts for the Christmas trade.
   a. What damages is Edward entitled to recover?
   b. Would it make any difference if Edward had told Marcia that he wanted the sugar to make candies for the Christmas trade and that he had accepted lucrative contracts for delivery for the Christmas trade? Explain.

2. Daniel agreed that he would erect an apartment building for Steven for $12 million and that Daniel would suffer a deduction of $12,000 per day for every day of delay. Daniel was twenty days late in finishing the job, losing ten days because of a strike and ten days because the material suppliers were late in furnishing materials.

Daniel claims that he is entitled to payment in full (a) because the agreement as to $12,000 a day is a penalty and (b) because Steven has not shown that he has sustained any damage. Discuss each contention and decide.

3. Sharon contracted with Jane, a shirtmaker, for one thousand shirts for men. Jane manufactured and delivered five hundred shirts, which were paid for by Sharon. At the same time, Sharon notified Jane that she could not use or dispose of the other five hundred shirts and directed Jane not to manufacture any more under the contract. Nevertheless, Jane proceeded to make up the other five hundred shirts and tendered them to Sharon. Sharon refused to accept the shirts, and Jane then sued for the purchase price. Is she entitled to the purchase price? If not, is she entitled to any damages? Explain.

4. Stuart contracts to act in a comedy for Charlotte and to comply with all theater regulations for four seasons. Charlotte promises to pay Stuart $1,800 for each performance and to allow Stuart one benefit performance each season. It is expressly agreed "Stuart shall not be employed in any other production for the period of the contract." During the first year of the contract, Stuart and Charlotte have a terrible quarrel. Thereafter, Stuart signs a contract to perform in Elaine's production and ceases performing for Charlotte. Charlotte seeks (a) to prevent Stuart from performing for Elaine and (b) to require Stuart to perform his contract with Charlotte. What result? Explain.

5. Louis leased a building to Pam for five years at a rental of $1,000 per month, Pam depositing $10,000 as security for performance of all her promises in the lease, which was to be retained by Louis in case of any breach on Pam's part. Pam defaulted in the payment of rent for the last two months of the lease. Louis refused to return any of the deposit, claiming it as liquidated damages. Pam sued Louis to recover $8,000 (the $10,000 deposit less the amount of rent due Louis for the last two months). What amount of damages should Pam be allowed to collect from Louis? Explain.

6. In which of the following situations is specific performance available as a remedy?

   a. Mary and Anne enter into a written agreement under which Mary agrees to sell and Anne agrees to buy for $100 per share one hundred shares of the three hundred shares outstanding of the capital stock of the Infinitesimal Steel Corporation, whose shares are not listed on any exchange and are closely held. Mary refuses to deliver when tendered the $10,000.

   b. Modifying (a), assume that the subject matter of the agreement is stock of the United States Steel Corporation, which is traded on the New York Stock Exchange.

   c. Modifying (a), assume that the subject matter of the agreement is undeveloped farmland of little commercial value.

7. On March 1, Joseph sold to Sandra fifty acres of land in Oregon, which Joseph at the time represented to be fine black loam, high, dry, and free of stumps. Sandra paid Joseph the agreed price of $140,000 and took from him a deed to the land. Subsequently discovering that the land was low, swampy, and not entirely free of stumps, Sandra nevertheless undertook to convert the greater part of the land into cranberry bogs. After one year of cranberry culture, Sandra became entirely dissatisfied, tendered the land back to Joseph, and demanded from Joseph the return of the $140,000. Upon Joseph's refusal to repay the money, Sandra brings an action against him to recover the $140,000. What judgment? Explain.

8. James contracts to make repairs to Betty's building in return for Betty's promise to pay $12,000 upon completion of the repairs. After partially completing the repairs, James is unable to continue. Betty refuses to pay James and hires another builder, who completes the repairs for $5,000. The building's value to Betty has increased by $10,000 as a result of the repairs by James, but Betty has lost $500 in rents because of the delay caused by James's breach. James sues Betty. How much, if any, may James recover in restitution from Betty?

9. Linda induced Sally to enter into a purchase of a home theater receiver by intentionally misrepresenting the power output to be seventy-five watts when in fact the unit delivered only forty watts. Sally paid $450 for the receiver. Receivers producing forty watts generally sell for $200, whereas receivers producing seventy-five watts generally sell for $550. Sally decides to keep the receiver and sue for damages. How much may Sally recover in damages from Linda?

10. Virginia induced Charles to sell his boat to her by misrepresentation of material fact upon which Charles reasonably relied. Virginia promptly sold the boat to Donald, who paid fair value for it and knew nothing concerning the transaction between Virginia and Charles. Upon discovering the misrepresentation, Charles seeks to recover the boat. What are Charles's rights against Virginia and Donald?

11. Felch was employed as a member of the faculty of Findlay College under a contract that permitted dismissal only for cause. He was dismissed by action of the President and Board of Trustees, which did not comply with a contractual provision for dismissal that requires a hearing. Felch requested the court to grant specific performance of the contract and require Findlay College to continue Felch as a member of the faculty and to pay him the salary agreed upon. Is Felch entitled to specific performance? Explain.

12. Copenhaver, the owner of a laundry business, contracted with Berryman, the owner of a large apartment complex, to allow Copenhaver to own and operate the laundry facilities within the apartment complex. Berryman subsequently terminated the five-year contract with Copenhaver with forty-seven months remaining. Within six months, Copenhaver placed the equipment into use in other locations and generated at least as much income as he would have earned at Berryman's apartment complex. He then filed suit, claiming that he was entitled to conduct the laundry operations for an additional forty-seven months and that through such operations he would have earned a profit of $13,886.58 after deducting Berryman's share of the gross receipts and other operating expenses. Decision? Explain.

13. Billy Williams Builders and Developers (Williams) entered into a contract with Hillerich under which Williams agreed to sell to Hillerich a certain lot and to construct on it a house according to submitted plans and specifications. The house built by Williams was defectively constructed. Hillerich brought suit for specific performance of the contract and for damages resulting from the defective construction and delay in performance. Williams argued that Hillerich was not entitled to have both specific performance and damages for breach of the contract because the remedies were inconsistent and Hillerich had to elect one or the other. Explain whether Williams is correct in this assertion.

14. Developers under a plan approved by the city of Rye had constructed six luxury cooperative apartment buildings and were to construct six more. To obtain certificates of occupancy for the six completed buildings, the developers were required to post a bond with the city to assure completion of the remaining buildings. The developers posted a $100,000 bond upon which the defendant, Public Service Mutual Insurance Company, as guarantor or surety, agreed to pay $200 for each day after the contractual deadline that the remaining buildings were not completed. After the contractual deadline, more than five hundred days passed without completion of the buildings. The city claims that its inspectors and employees will be required to devote more time to the project than anticipated because it has taken extra years to complete. It also claims that it will lose tax revenues for the years the buildings are not completed. Should the city prevail in its suit against the developers and the insurance company to recover $100,000 on the bond? Explain.

15. Kerr Steamship Company sent a telegram at a cost of $26.78 to the Philippines through the Radio Corporation of America. The telegram, which contained instructions in unintelligible code for loading cargo on one of Kerr's ships, was mislaid and never delivered. Consequently, the ship was improperly loaded, and the cargo was lost. Kerr sued the Radio Corporation for $6,675.29 in profits lost on the cargo because of the Radio Corporation's failure to deliver the telegram. Should Kerr be allowed to recover damages from Radio? Explain.

16. El Dorado Tire Company fired Bill Ballard, a sales executive. Ballard had a five-year contract with El Dorado but was fired after only two years of employment. Ballard sued El Dorado for breach of contract. El Dorado claimed that any damages due to breach of the contract should be mitigated because of Ballard's failure to seek other employment after he was fired. El Dorado did not provide any proof showing the availability of comparable employment. Explain whether El Dorado is correct in its contention.

17. California and Hawaiian Sugar Company (C and H) is an agricultural cooperative in the business of growing sugarcane in Hawaii and transporting the raw sugar to its refinery in California for processing. Because of the seasonal nature of the sugarcane crop, availability of ships to transport the raw sugar immediately after harvest is imperative. After losing the services of the shipping company it had previously used, C and H decided to build its own ship, a hybrid with two components, a tug and a barge. C and H contracted with Halter Marine to build the tug and with Sun Ship to build the barge. In finalizing the contract for construction of the barge, both C and H and Sun Ship were represented by senior management and by legal counsel. The resulting contract called for a liquidated damages payment of $17,000 per day that delivery of the completed barge was delayed. Deliveries of both the barge and the tug were significantly delayed. Sun Ship paid the $17,000 per day liquidated damages and then sued to recover it, claiming

that without the liquidated damages provision, C and H's legal remedy for money damages would have been significantly less than that paid by Sun Ship pursuant to the liquidated damages provision. Decision? Discuss.

18. Bettye Gregg offered to purchase a house from the seller. Though Gregg represented in writing that she had between $15,000 and $20,000 in equity in another home, which she would pay to the seller after she sold the other home, she knew that she did not have such equity. In reliance upon these intentionally fraudulent representations, the seller accepted Gregg's offer and the parties entered into a land contract. After taking occupancy, Gregg failed to make any of the contract payments. The seller's investigations then revealed the fraud. The seller then brought suit seeking rescission of the contract, return of the real estate, and restitution. Restitution was sought for the rental value for the five months of lost use of the property and the seller's out-of-pocket expenses made in reliance upon the bargain. Gregg contends that under the election of remedies doctrine, the seller cannot both rescind the contract and recover damages for its breach. Is Gregg correct? Explain.

19. Watson agreed to buy Ingram's house for $355,000. The contract provided that Watson was to deposit $15,000 as earnest money and that "in the event of default by the Buyer, earnest money shall be forfeited to Seller as liquidated damages, unless Seller elects to seek actual damages or specific performance." Because Watson did not timely comply with all of the terms of the contract, nine months after the Watson sale was to occur, Ingram sold the house to a third party for $355,000. Is Ingram entitled to Watson's $15,000 earnest money as liquidated damages? Explain.

20. Real Estate Analytics, LLC (REA), a limited liability company, became interested in Theodore Tee Vallas's 14.13-acre Lanikai Lane property located in Carlsbad, California. REA's primary goal in purchasing the property was to make a profit for its investors and the company. In March, REA and Vallas entered into a written agreement for Vallas to sell the property to REA. Under the agreement, the sales price was $8.5 million, with REA to pay an immediate $100,000 deposit and then pay $2.9 million at closing. In return, Vallas agreed to finance the remaining $5.5 million, with the unpaid balance to be paid over a five-year period. On June 14, Vallas cancelled the contract. The next day, REA brought a breach of contract action seeking specific performance. Explain whether REA is entitled to specific performance.

TAKING SIDES

Sanders agreed in writing to write, direct, and produce a motion picture on the subject of lithography (a method for printing using stone or metal) for the Tamarind Lithography Workshop. After the completion of this film, *Four Stones for Kanemitsu*, litigation arose concerning the parties' rights and obligations under their agreement. Tamarind and Sanders resolved this dispute by a written settlement agreement that provided for Tamarind to give Sanders a screen credit stating "A Film by Terry Sanders." Tamarind did not comply with this agreement and failed to include the agreed-upon screen credit for Sanders.

Sanders sued Tamarind seeking damages for breach of the settlement agreement and specific performance to compel Tamarind's compliance with its obligation to provide the screen credit.

a. What arguments would support the claim of Sanders for specific performance in addition to damages?

b. What arguments would support Tamarind's claim that Sanders was not entitled to specific performance in addition to damages?

c. Which side's arguments are most convincing? Explain.

Agency

CH 19 RELATIONSHIP OF PRINCIPAL AND AGENT

CH 20 RELATIONSHIP WITH THIRD PARTIES

CHAPTER 19

Relationship of Principal and Agent

CHAPTER OUTCOMES

After reading and studying this chapter, you should be able to:

- Distinguish among the following relationships: (1) agency, (2) employment, and (3) independent contractor.

- Explain the requirements for creating an agency relationship.

- Explain the duties owed by an agent to her principal.

- Explain the duties owed by a principal to his agent.

- Identify the ways in which an agency relationship may be terminated.

B y using agents, one person (the principal) may enter into any number of business transactions as though he had personally carried them out, thus multiplying and expanding his business activities. The law of agency, like the law of contracts, is basic to almost every other branch of business law. Practically every type of contract or business transaction can be created or conducted through an agent. Therefore, the place and importance of agency in the practical conduct and operation of business cannot be overemphasized.

This is particularly true in the case of partnerships, corporations, and other business associations. Partnership is founded on the agency of the partners. Each partner is an agent of the partnership and, as such, has the authority to represent and bind the partnership in all usual transactions of the partnership. A corporation, being an artificial legal entity, must act through the agency of its officers and employees. Limited liability companies act through the actions of their members, managers, or both. Thus, practically and legally, agency is an essential part of partnerships, corporations, and other business associations. In addition, sole proprietors also may employ agents in the operations of their business. Business, therefore, is conducted largely not by owners themselves but by their agents or representatives.

The law of agency divides broadly into two main and somewhat-overlapping parts: the internal and the external. An agent functions as an agent by dealing with third persons, thereby establishing legal relationships between the principal and those third persons. These relationships, which constitute the external part of agency law, are discussed in the next chapter. This chapter covers the internal relationship between

principal and agent, including the nature of agency, the creation of an agency, the duties of agent to principal, the duties of principal to agent, and the termination of agency.

Agency is governed primarily by State common law. An orderly presentation of this law was found in the Restatement (Second) of the Law of Agency, published in 1958 by the American Law Institute (ALI). Regarded as a valuable authoritative reference work, the Restatement is cited extensively and quoted in reported judicial opinions and by legal scholars. In 2006, the ALI published the Restatement of the Law Third, Agency, which replaced the ALI's Restatement Second of Agency. This chapter and the next chapter refers to the Third Restatement as the Restatement.

19-1 Nature of Agency

Agency is a consensual relationship in which one person (the agent) acts as a representative of or otherwise acts on behalf of another person (the principal) with power to affect the legal rights and duties of the principal. Moreover, the principal has a right to control the actions of the agent. Restatement, Section 1.01.

An agent, therefore, is one who represents another, the principal, in business dealings with a third person; the operation of agency therefore involves three persons: the principal, the agent, and a third person who deals with the agent. In dealing with a third person, the agent acts for and in the name and place of the principal, who, along with the third person, is, if properly entered into, a party to the transaction. When the agent is dealing with the third person, the principal, in legal effect, is present in the person of the agent; and the result of the agent's functioning is exactly the same as if the principal had dealt directly with the third person. If, moreover, the existence and identity of the principal are disclosed, the agent acts not as a party but simply as an intermediary.

Within the scope of the authority granted to her by her principal, the agent may negotiate the terms of contracts with others and bind her principal to such contracts. In addition, the negligence of an agent who is an employee in conducting the business of her principal exposes the principal to tort liability for injury and loss suffered by third persons. The old maxim "*qui facit per alium, faci tper se*" (he who acts through another, acts himself) accurately describes the relationship between principal and agent. The rights and liabilities of the parties where an agent enters into a contract with a third party or commits a tort against a third party are discussed in *Chapter 20*.

19-1a SCOPE OF AGENCY PURPOSES

As a general rule, a person may do through an agent whatever business activity he may accomplish personally. Conversely, whatever he cannot legally do himself, he cannot authorize another to do for him. Thus, a person may not validly authorize another to commit an illegal act or crime. Any such agreement is illegal and therefore unenforceable. Also, a person may not appoint an agent to perform acts that are so personal that their performance may not be delegated to another, as in the case of a contract for personal services. For example, Howard, a painter, contracts to paint a portrait of Doris. But Howard has one of his students execute the painting and tenders it to Doris. This is not a valid tender because the duty to paint Doris's portrait is not delegable.

19-1b OTHER LEGAL RELATIONSHIPS

Two other legal relationships overlap with agency: employer-employee and principal-independent contractor. In the **employment relationship** (historically referred to as the master-servant relationship), for the purposes of vicarious liability discussed in the next chapter, an employee is an agent whose principal controls or has the right to control the manner and means of the agent's performance of work. Restatement, Section 7.07(3). All employees are agents, even those employees not authorized to contract on behalf of the employer or otherwise to conduct business with third parties. Thus, an assembly-line worker in a factory is an agent of the company employing her since she is subject to the employer's control, thereby consenting to act "on behalf" of the principal, but she does not have the right to bind the principal in contracts with third parties.

Although all employees are agents, not all agents are employees. Agents who are not employees are generally referred to as **independent contractors**. (The Third Restatement does not use this term.) In these cases, although the principal has the right of control over the agent, the principal does not control the manner and means of the agent's performance. For instance, an attorney retained to handle a particular transaction would be an independent contractor-agent regarding that particular transaction because the attorney is hired by the principal to perform a service, but the manner of the attorney's performance is not controlled by the principal. Other examples are auctioneers, brokers, and factors.

Finally, not all independent contractors are agents because the person hiring the independent contractor has no right of control over the independent contractor. For example, a taxicab driver hired to carry a person to the airport is not an agent of that person. Likewise, if Pam hires Bill to build a stone wall around her property, Bill is an independent contractor who is not an agent.

In determining whether an agent is an employee, the courts consider numerous factors, including the following:

(a) the extent of control that the agent and the principal have agreed the principal may exercise—or has exercised in practice—over details of the work;

(b) whether the agent is engaged in a distinct occupation or business;

(c) whether the type of work done by the agent is customarily done under a principal's direction or without supervision;

(d) the skill required in the agent's occupation;

(e) whether the agent or the principal supplies the tools and other instrumentalities required for the work and the place in which to perform it;

(f) the length of time during which the agent is engaged by a principal;

(g) whether the agent is paid by the job or by the time worked;

(h) whether the agent's work is part of the principal's regular business;

(i) whether the principal and the agent believe that they are creating an employment relationship; and

(j) whether the principal is or is not in business.

Restatement, Section 7.07.

The distinction between employee and independent contractor has several important legal consequences. For example, as discussed in *Chapter 20*, a principal is liable for the torts committed by an employee within the scope of his employment but ordinarily is not liable for torts committed by an independent contractor. In addition, the obligations of a principal under numerous Federal and State statutes apply only to agents who are employees. These statutes cover such matters as labor relations, employment discrimination, disability, employee safety, workers' compensation, social security, minimum wage, and unemployment compensation. These and other statutory enactments affecting the employment relationship are discussed in *Chapter 24*.

♦ *See Case 19-1*

> ### Practical Advice
>
> *When appointing an agent, consider structuring the relationship as a principal and independent contractor.*

19-2 Creation of Agency

As stated earlier, agency is a consensual relationship that the principal and agent may form by contract *or* agreement. The Restatement defines an agency relationship as "the fiduciary relationship that arises when one person (a 'principal') manifests assent to another person (an 'agent') that the agent shall act on the principal's behalf and subject to the principal's control, and the agent manifests assent or otherwise consents so to act." Section 1.01. Thus, the agency relationship involves three basic elements: assent, control by the principal, and the agent's acting on behalf of the principal. A person can manifest assent or intention through written or spoken words or other conduct. Restatement, Section 1.03. Thus, whether an agency relationship has been created is determined by an *objective test*. If the principal requests another to act for him with respect to a matter and indicates that the other is to act without further communication and the other consents to act, the relation of principal and agent exists. For example, Paula writes to Austin, a factor whose business is purchasing goods for others, telling him to select described goods and ship them at once to Paula. Before answering Paula's letter, Austin does as directed, charging the goods to Paula. He is authorized to do this because an agency relationship exists between Paula and Austin.

The principal has the right to control the conduct of the agent with respect to the matters entrusted to the agent. Restatement, Section 1.01.

The principal's right to control continues throughout the duration of the agency relationship. The relationship of principal and agent is consensual and not necessarily contractual; therefore, it may exist without consideration. Restatement, Section 1.04(3). Even though the agency relationship is consensual, how the parties label the relationship does not determine whether it is an agency. Section 1.02. An agency created without an agent's right to compensation is a **gratuitous agency**. For example, Patti asks her friend Andrew to return for credit goods recently purchased from a store. If Andrew consents, a gratuitous agency has been created. The power of a gratuitous agent to affect the principal's relationships with third persons is the same as that of a paid agent, and his liabilities to and rights against third persons also are the same. Nonetheless, agency by contract, the most usual method of creating the relationship, must satisfy all the requirements of a contract.

In some circumstances, a person is held liable as a principal, even though no actual agency has been created, to protect third parties who justifiably rely on a reasonable belief that a person is an agent and who act on that belief to their detriment. Called **agency by estoppel**, apparent agency, or ostensible agency, this liability arises when (1) a person ("principal") intentionally or carelessly causes a third party to believe that another person (the "agent") has authority to act on the principal's behalf, (2) the principal has notice of the third party's belief and does not take reasonable steps to notify the third party, (3) the third party reasonably and in good faith relies on the appearances created by the principal, and (4) the third party justifiably and detrimentally changes her position in reliance on the agent's apparent authority. Restatement, Section 2.05. When these requirements are met, the principal is liable to the third party for the loss the third party suffered by changing her position. The doctrine is applicable when the person against whom estoppel is asserted has made no manifestation that an actor has authority as an agent but is responsible for the third party's belief that an actor is an agent and the third party has justifiably been induced by that belief to undergo a detrimental change in position. Restatement, Section 2.05.

♦ *See Case 19-2*

19-2a FORMALITIES

As a general rule, a contract of agency requires no particular formality. Usually the contract is express or inferred from the conduct of the principal. In some cases, however, the contract must be in writing. For example, the appointment of an agent for a period of more than a year comes within the one-year clause of the statute of frauds and thus must be in writing to be enforceable. In some States, the authority of an agent to sell land must be stated in a writing signed by the principal. Many States have "equal dignity" statutes providing that a principal must grant his agent in a written instrument the authority to enter into any contract required to be in writing. Restatement, Section 3.02. See *Chapter 15* for a discussion of State and Federal legislation giving electronic records and signatures the legal effect of traditional writings and signatures.

A **power of attorney** is an instrument that states an agent's authority. Restatement, Section 1.04(7). A power of attorney is a formal manifestation from principal to agent, who is known as "an attorney in fact," as well as to third parties that evidences the agent's appointment and the nature or extent of the agent's authority. Under a power of attorney, a principal may, for example, appoint an agent not only to execute a contract for the sale of the principal's real estate, but also to execute the deed conveying title to the real estate to the third party. A number of States have created an optional statutory short-form power of attorney based on the Uniform Statutory Form Power of Attorney Act. In 2006, a new Uniform Power of Attorney Act (UPOAA) was promulgated to replace the Uniform Statutory Form Power of Attorney Act. At least twenty-nine States have adopted the 2006 Act.

19-2b CAPACITY

The capacity of an individual to be a principal, and thus to act through an agent, depends upon the capacity of the principal to do the act herself. Restatement, Section 3.04(1). For example, contracts entered into by a minor or an incompetent not under a guardianship are voidable. Consequently, the appointment of an agent by a minor or an incompetent not under a guardianship and any resulting contracts are voidable, regardless of the agent's contractual capacity. The capacity of a person that is not an individual, such as a government or business association, is determined by the law governing that entity. Restatement, Section 3.04(2).

Almost all of the States have adopted the Uniform Durable Power of Attorney Act providing for a durable power of attorney under which an agent's power survives or is triggered by the principal's loss of mental competence. (In 2006, the new UPOAA was promulgated to replace the Uniform Durable Power of Attorney Act. At least twenty-nine States have adopted the 2006 Act. A power of attorney created under the UPOAA is durable unless it expressly provides that it is terminated by the incapacity of the principal.) A **durable power of attorney** is a written instrument that expresses the principal's intention that the agent's authority will not be affected by the principal's subsequent incapacity or that the agent's authority will become effective upon the principal's subsequent incapacity.

Any person able to act, including individuals, corporations, partnerships, and other associations, ordinarily has the capacity to act as an agent. Restatement, Section 3.05. Because the act of the agent is considered the act of the principal, the incapacity of an agent to bind himself by contract does not disqualify him from making a contract that is binding on his principal. The agent's liability, however, depends on the agent's capacity to contract. Thus, although the contract of agency may be voidable, an authorized contract between the principal and the third person who dealt with the agent is valid.

An "electronic agent" is a computer program or other automated means used independently to initiate an action or respond to electronic records or performances in whole or in part without review or action by an individual. Electronic agents are not persons and, therefore, are not considered agents. In 2000, Congress enacted the Electronic Signatures in Global and National Commerce (E-Sign). The Act makes electronic records and signatures valid and enforceable across the United States for many types of transactions in or affecting interstate or foreign commerce. The Act validates contracts or other records relating to a transaction in or affecting interstate or foreign commerce formed by electronic agents so long as the action of each electronic agent is legally attributable to the person to be bound. E-Sign specifically excludes certain transactions, including (1) wills, codicils, and testamentary trusts; (2) adoptions, divorces, and other matters of family law; and (3) the Uniform Commercial Code other than sales and leases of goods.

19-3 Duties of Agent to Principal

The duties of the agent to the principal are determined by the express and implied terms of any contract between the agent and the principal. Restatement, Section 8.07. In addition to these contractual duties, the agent is subject to various other duties imposed by law, unless the parties agree otherwise. Normally, a principal bases the selection of an agent on the agent's ability, skill, and integrity. Moreover, the principal not only authorizes and empowers the agent to bind her on contracts with third persons, but also frequently places the agent in possession of her money and other property. As a result, the agent is in a position, either through negligence or dishonesty, to injure the principal. Accordingly, an agent as a **fiduciary** (a person in a position of trust and confidence) owes his principal the duties of obedience, good conduct, diligence, and loyalty; the duty to inform; and the duty to provide an accounting. Moreover, the agent is subject to liability for loss caused to the principal by any breach of duty.

A gratuitous agent is subject to the same duty of loyalty that is imposed upon a paid agent and is liable to the principal for the harm he causes by his careless performance. Although the lack of consideration usually places a gratuitous agent under no duty to perform for the principal, such an agent may be liable to the principal for failing to perform a promise on which the principal has relied if the agent should have realized that his promise would induce reliance. Restatement, Section 8.07, Comment c.

Practical Advice

Recognize that even if you agree to serve as an agent without compensation, you owe a fiduciary duty to the principal and are liable to her for your negligence.

19-3a DUTY OF OBEDIENCE

The duty of obedience requires the agent to act in the principal's affairs only as actually authorized by the principal and to obey all lawful instructions and directions of the principal. Restatement, Section 8.09. If an agent exceeds her actual authority, she is subject to liability to the principal for loss caused to the principal. An agent is also liable to the principal for unauthorized acts that are the result of the agent's unreasonable interpretations of the principal's directions. An agent is not, however, under a duty to follow orders to perform illegal or tortious acts, such as misrepresenting the quality of his principal's goods or those of a competitor. Still, he may be subject to liability to his principal for breach of the duty of obedience (1) because he entered into an unauthorized contract for which his principal is liable, (2) because he has improperly delegated his authority, or (3) because he has committed a tort for which the principal is liable. Thus, an agent who sells on credit in violation of his principal's explicit instructions has breached the duty of obedience and is liable to the principal for any amounts the purchaser does not pay. Moreover, an agent who violates his duty of obedience materially breaches the agency contract and loses his right to compensation.

19-3b DUTY OF GOOD CONDUCT

An agent has a duty, within the scope of the agency relationship, to act reasonably and to avoid conduct that is likely to damage the principal's interests. Restatement, Section 8.10. This duty reflects the fact that the conduct of agents can have a significant effect on the principal's reputation. A breach of this duty makes the agent liable to the principal and subject to rightful discharge or termination.

19-3c DUTY OF DILIGENCE

Subject to any agreement with the principal, an agent has a duty to the principal to act with the care, competence, and diligence normally exercised by agents in similar circumstances. Special skills or knowledge possessed by an agent are circumstances to be taken into account in determining whether the agent acted with due care and diligence. Moreover, if the agent claims to possess special skill or knowledge, the agent has a duty to act with the care, competence, and diligence normally exercised by agents with such skill or knowledge. Restatement, Section 8.08. By failing to exercise the required care, competence, and diligence, she is liable to the principal for any resulting harm. For example, Peg appoints Alvin as her agent to sell goods in markets where the highest price can be obtained. Although by carefully obtaining information he could have obtained a higher price in a nearby market, Alvin sells goods in a glutted market, receiving only a low price. Consequently, he is liable to Peg for breach of the duty of diligence.

A gratuitous agent owes a standard of care that is reasonable to expect under the circumstances, which include the skill and experience that the agent possesses. Thus, providing a service gratuitously may subject an agent to duties of competence and diligence to the principal that do not differ from the duties owed by a compensated agent. Restatement, Section 8.08, Comment e.

19-3d DUTY TO INFORM

An agent has a duty to use reasonable effort to provide the principal with facts that the agent knows, has reason to know, or should know if (1) the agent knows, or has reason to know, that the principal would wish to have the facts or (2) the facts are material to the agent's duties to the principal. However, this duty does not apply to facts if providing them to the principal would violate a superior duty owed by the agent to another person. Restatement, Section 8.11. The rule of agency providing that notice to an agent is notice to his principal makes this duty imperative. Restatement, Section 5.02. An agent who breaches this duty is subject to liability to the principal for loss caused the principal by the agent's breach and may also be subject to termination of the agency relationship. Moreover, if the agent's breach of this duty constitutes a breach of the contract between the agent and the principal, the agent is also liable for breach of contract.

Examples of information that an agent is under a duty to communicate to his principal include the following: (1) that a customer of the principal has become insolvent, (2) that a debtor of the principal has become insolvent, (3) that a partner of a firm with which the principal has previously dealt and with which the principal or agent is about to deal has withdrawn from the firm, or (4) that property which the principal has authorized the agent to sell at a specified price can be sold at a higher price.

19-3e DUTY TO ACCOUNT

Subject to any agreement with the principal, an agent has a duty to keep and render accounts to the principal of money or other property received or paid out on the principal's account. Moreover, the agent may not mingle the principal's property with any other person's property and may not deal with the principal's property so that it appears to be the agent's property. Restatement, Section 8.12.

19-3f FIDUCIARY DUTY

A **fiduciary duty** arises out of a relationship of trust and confidence and requires the utmost loyalty and good faith. An agent has a fiduciary duty to act loyally for the principal's benefit in all matters connected with the agency relationship. Restatement, Section 8.01. This duty is imposed by law upon the agent and is also owed by an employee to his employer. The principal may agree that conduct by an agent that otherwise would constitute a breach of the fiduciary duty shall not constitute a breach of that duty provided that in obtaining the principal's consent, the agent (1) acts in good faith; (2) discloses all material facts that the agent knows, has reason to know, or should know would reasonably affect the principal's judgment; and (3) otherwise deals fairly with the principal. Restatement, Section 8.06.

An agent's fiduciary duty to a principal generally begins with the formation of the agency relationship and ends with its termination. Restatement, Section 8.01. However, as discussed later, an agent may be subject to duties after termination applicable to the agent's use of the principal's property and confidential information provided by the principal.

The fiduciary duty arises most frequently in the following situations involving principals and their agents although it is by no means limited to these situations.

CONFLICTS OF INTEREST An agent has a duty not to deal with the principal as, or on behalf of, an adverse party in a transaction connected with the agency relationship. Restatement, Section 8.03. An agent must act solely in the interest of his principal, not in his own interest or in the interest of another. In addition, an agent may not represent his principal in any transaction in which the agent has a personal interest. Nor may he act on behalf of adverse parties to a transaction without both principals' approval to the dual agency. An agent may take a position that conflicts with the interest of his principal only if the principal, with full knowledge of all of the facts, consents. For example, A, an agent of P who desires to purchase land, agrees with C, who represents B, a seller of land, that A and C will endeavor to effect a transaction between their principals and will pool their commissions. A and C have committed a breach of fiduciary duty to P and B.

SELF-DEALING An agent has a duty not to deal with the principal as an adverse party in a transaction connected with the agency relationship. Restatement, Section 8.03. The courts scrutinize transactions between an agent and her principal. Because the agent may not deal at arm's length with her principal, she thus owes her principal a duty of full disclosure of all relevant facts that affect the transaction. Moreover, the transaction must be fair. Thus, an agent who is employed to buy may not buy from himself without the principal's consent. Restatement, Section 8.06. For example, Penny employs Albert to purchase for her a site suitable for a shopping center. Albert owns such a site and sells it to Penny at the fair market value but does not disclose to Penny that he had owned the land. Penny may rescind the transaction even though Albert did not make a misrepresentation. An agent who is employed to sell may not become the purchaser, nor may he act as agent for the purchaser without the consent of the principal. The agent's loyalty must be undivided, and he must devote his actions exclusively to represent and promote the interests of his principal.

◆ *See Case 19-3*

DUTY NOT TO COMPETE During the agency relationship, an agent must not compete with his principal or act on behalf or otherwise assist any of the principal's competitors. Restatement, Section 8.04. After the agency terminates without breach by the agent, however, unless otherwise agreed, the agent may compete with his former principal. The courts will enforce by injunction a contractual agreement by the agent not to compete after the agency terminates if the restriction is reasonable as to time and place and is necessary to protect the principal's legitimate interest. Contractual agreements not to compete are discussed in *Chapter 13* where it is noted that such noncompete contracts may be subject to different standards for Internet companies and their employees.

◆ *See Case 13-2*

Practical Advice

If you are the principal, consider obtaining from your agents a reasonable covenant that they will not compete with you after the agency terminates.

MISAPPROPRIATION An agent may not use property of the principal for the agent's own purposes or for the benefit of a third party. Restatement, Section 8.05(1). Unless the principal consents, an agent who has possession of the principal's property has a duty to use it only on the principal's behalf even if the agent's use of the property does not cause harm to the principal. An agent is liable to the principal for any profit the agent made while using the principal's property or for the value of the agent's use of the principal's property. An agent's duties regarding the principal's property continue after the agency terminates, and a former agent has a duty to return any of the principal's property she still possesses.

CONFIDENTIAL INFORMATION An agent may not use or disclose confidential information obtained in the course of the agency for his own benefit or those of a third party. Restatement, Section 8.05(2). Confidential information is information that, if disclosed, would harm the principal's business or that has a value because it is not generally known. Such information includes unique business methods, trade secrets, business plans, personnel, nonpublic financial results, and customer lists. An agent, however, may reveal confidential information that the principal is committing or is about to commit a crime. Many statutes provided protection to employees who "whistle-blow."

Unless otherwise agreed, even after the agency terminates, the agent may not use or disclose to third persons confidential information. The agent, however, may utilize the generally known skills, knowledge, and information she acquired during the agency relationship.

DUTY TO ACCOUNT FOR FINANCIAL BENEFITS Unless otherwise agreed, an agent has a duty not to acquire any financial or other material benefits in connection with transactions conducted on behalf of the principal. Restatement, Section 8.02. Such benefits would include bribes, kickbacks, and gifts. Moreover, an agent may not profit secretly from any transaction subject to the agency. All material benefits, including secret profits, belong to the principal, to whom the agent must account. In addition, the principal may recover any damages caused by the agent's breach. Thus, if an agent, who is authorized to sell certain property of his principal for $1,000, sells it for $1,500, he may not secretly pocket the additional $500. Further, suppose Peabody employs real estate broker Anderson to sell his land for a commission of 6 percent of the sale price. Anderson, knowing that Peabody is willing to sell for $20,000, agrees secretly with a prospective buyer who is willing to pay $22,000 for the land that he will endeavor to obtain Peabody's consent to sell for $20,000, in which event the buyer will pay Anderson $1,000, or one-half of the amount that the buyer believes she is saving on the price. The broker has violated his fiduciary duty and must pay to Peabody the secret profit of $1,000. Furthermore, Anderson loses the right to any commission on the transaction.

PRINCIPAL'S REMEDIES An agent who violates his fiduciary duty is liable to his principal for breach of contract, in tort for losses caused and possibly punitive damages, and in restitution for profits he made or property he received in breach of the fiduciary duty. Moreover, he loses the right to compensation. The principal may avoid a transaction in which the agent breached his fiduciary duty, even though the principal suffered no loss. A breach of fiduciary duty also may constitute just cause for discharge of the agent. Restatement, Section 8.01, Comment d. The 2011 Restatement (Third) of Restitution and Unjust Enrichment provides that benefits derived from an agent's breach of her fiduciary duty may be recovered from a third party who acquires such benefits with notice of the agent's breach of her fiduciary duty.

Practical Advice

Do not agree to become an agent if you are not willing or able to fulfill all of the duties an agent owes, unless your agency contract clearly relieves you of those duties you find unacceptable.

19-4 Duties of Principal to Agent

Although both principal and agent have rights and duties arising out of the agency relationship, more emphasis is placed on the duties of the agent. This is necessarily so because of the nature of the agency relationship. First, the acts and services to be performed, both under the agency contract and as may be required by law, are to be performed mostly by the agent. Second, the agent is a fiduciary and as such is subject to the duties discussed earlier. Nonetheless, an agent has certain rights against the principal, both under the contract and by the operation of law. Correlative to these rights are certain duties, based in contract and tort law, which the principal owes to the agent.

♦ **SEE FIGURE 19-1:** *Duties of Principal and Agent*

19-4a CONTRACTUAL DUTIES

An agency relationship may exist in the absence of a contract between the principal and agent. However, many principals and agents do enter into contracts, in which case a principal has a duty to act in accordance with the express and implied terms of any contract between the principal and the agent. Restatement, Section 8.13. The contractual duties owed by a principal to an agent are the duties of compensation, reimbursement, and indemnification; each may be excluded or modified by agreement between the principal and agent. Although a gratuitous agent is not owed a duty of compensation, she is entitled to reimbursement and indemnification.

As with any party to a contract, a principal is under a duty to perform his part of the contract according to its terms. The most important duty of the principal, from the standpoint of the agent, is to compensate the agent as specified in the contract. It is also the duty of the principal not to terminate the agency wrongfully. Whether the principal must furnish the agent with the means of employment or the opportunity for work will depend upon the particular case. For example, a principal who employs an agent to sell his goods must supply the agent with conforming goods, whereas in other cases, the agent must create his own opportunity for work, as in the case of a broker employed to procure a buyer for his principal's house. How far, if at all, the principal must assist or cooperate with the agent will depend on the particular agency. Usually, cooperation on the part of the principal is more necessary in cases in which the agent's compensation is contingent upon the success of his efforts than in cases in which the agent is paid a fixed salary regularly over a period of permanent employment.

COMPENSATION A principal has a duty to compensate her agent unless the agent has agreed to serve gratuitously. If the agreement does not specify a definite compensation, a principal is under a duty to pay the reasonable value of the authorized services her agent has performed. Restatement, Section 8.13, Comment d. An agent loses the right to compensation by (1) breaching the duty of obedience, (2) breaching the duty of loyalty, or (3) willfully and deliberately breaching the agency contract. Furthermore, an agent whose compensation depends upon her accomplishing a specific result is entitled to the agreed compensation only if she achieves the result within the time specified or within a reasonable time, if no time is stated. A common example is a listing agreement between a seller and a real estate broker providing for a commission to the broker if he finds a buyer ready, willing, and able to buy the property

FIGURE 19-1 Duties of Principal and Agent

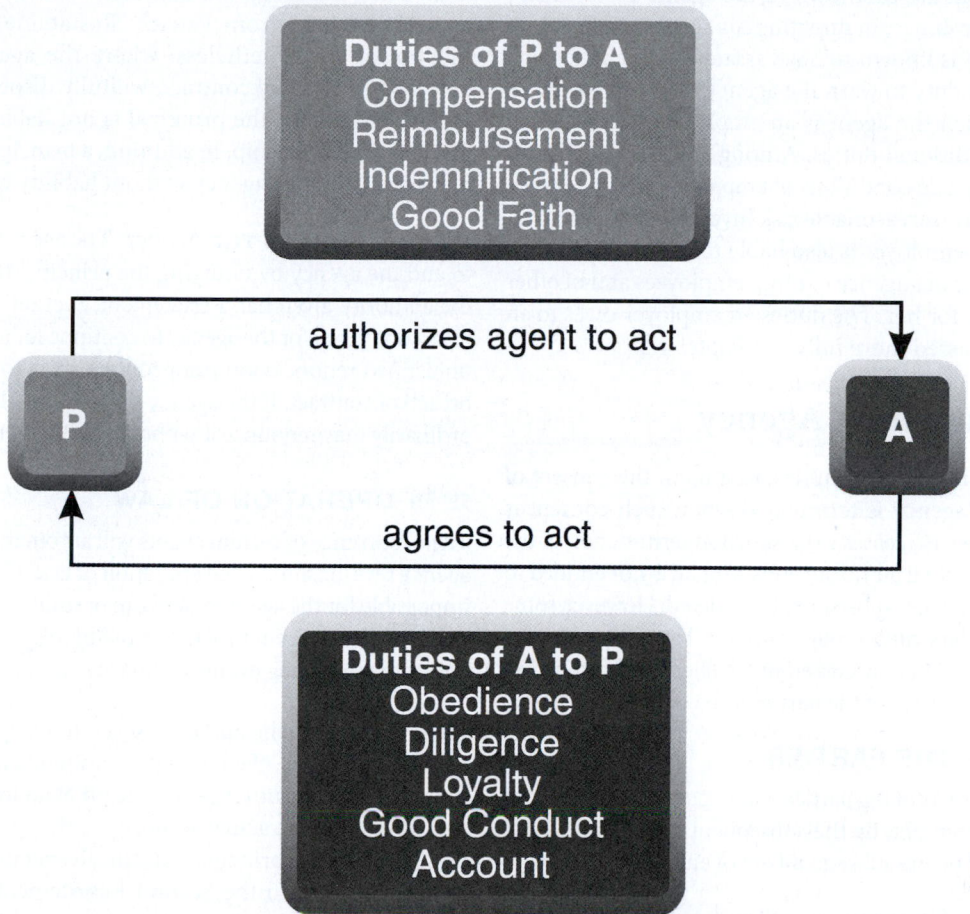

Duties of P to A
Compensation
Reimbursement
Indemnification
Good Faith

authorizes agent to act

P

A

agrees to act

Duties of A to P
Obedience
Diligence
Loyalty
Good Conduct
Account

on the terms specified in the agreement. A principal also has a duty to maintain and provide to the agent a true and complete account of the money or property due to her.

Practical Advice

Specify the compensation to be paid the agent; if none is to be paid, clearly state that the agency is intended to be gratuitous.

INDEMNIFICATION AND REIMBURSEMENT In general, a principal has an obligation to **indemnify** (compensate for a loss) an agent whenever the agent makes a payment or incurs an expense or other loss while acting as authorized on behalf of the principal. The contract between the principal and agent may specify the extent of this duty. In the absence of any contractual provisions, a principal has a duty to **reimburse** the agent when the agent makes a payment within the scope of the agent's actual authority. Restatement, Section 8.14. For example, an agent who reasonably and properly pays a

fire insurance premium for the protection of her principal's property is entitled to reimbursement for the payment.

A principal also has a duty to indemnify the agent when the agent suffers a loss that fairly should be borne by the principal in light of their relationship. Restatement, Section 8.14. For example, suppose that Perry, the principal, has in his possession goods belonging to Margot. Perry directs Alma, his agent, to sell these goods. Alma, believing Perry to be the owner, sells the goods to Turner. Margot then sues Alma for the conversion of her goods and recovers a judgment, which Alma pays to Margot. Alma is entitled to indemnification from Perry for her loss, including the amount she reasonably expended in defense of the action brought by Margot.

19-4b TORT AND OTHER DUTIES

A principal owes to any agent the same duties under tort law that the principal owes to all parties. Moreover, a principal has a duty to deal with the agent fairly and in good faith. This duty requires that the principal provide the agent with information about risks of physical harm or monetary loss that the principal knows, has reason to know, or should know are present in the agent's work but are unknown to the agent. Restatement, Section 8.15. For instance, in directing his agent to collect rent from a tenant who is known to have assaulted rent collectors, the principal has a duty to warn the agent of the risk involved.

In cases in which the agent is an employee, the principal owes the agent additional duties. Among these is the duty to provide reasonably safe conditions of employment and to warn the employee of any unreasonable risk involved in the employment. A negligent employer is also liable to her employees for injury caused by the negligence of other employees and of other agents doing work for her. The duties an employer owes to an employee are discussed more fully in *Chapter 42*.

19-5 Termination of Agency

Because the authority of an agent is based upon the consent of the principal, the agency is terminated when such consent is withdrawn or otherwise ceases to exist. Upon termination of the agency, the agent's actual authority ends, and he is not entitled to compensation for services subsequently rendered. However, some of the agent's fiduciary duties may continue. The termination of *apparent* authority will be discussed in *Chapter 20*. Termination may take place by the acts of the parties or by operation of law.

19-5a ACTS OF THE PARTIES

Termination by the acts of the parties may occur by the provisions of the original agreement, by the subsequent acts of both principal and agent, or by the subsequent act of either one of them.

LAPSE OF TIME An agent's actual authority terminates as agreed by the agent and the principal. Restatement, Section 3.09. Authority conferred upon an agent for a specified time terminates when that period expires. If no time is specified, authority terminates at the end of a reasonable period. Restatement, Section 3.09, Comment d. For example, Palmer authorizes Avery to sell a tract of land for him. After ten years pass without communication between Palmer and Avery, though Avery purports to have sold the tract, his authorization has terminated due to lapse of time.

MUTUAL AGREEMENT OF THE PARTIES The agency relationship is created by agreement and may be terminated at any time by mutual agreement of the principal and the agent. Restatement, Section 3.09(1).

REVOCATION OF AUTHORITY A principal may revoke an agent's authority at any time by notifying the agent. Restatement, Section 3.10. If, however, such revocation constitutes a breach of contract, the agent may recover damages from the principal. For example, Patrick, in consideration of Alice's agreement to advertise and give her best energies to the sale of Patrick's property, Blackacre, grants to Alice "a power of attorney, irrevocable for one year." Alice advertises and spends time trying to sell Blackacre. At the end of three months, Patrick informs Alice that he is revoking the power of attorney. Although her authority is terminated, Alice may recover damages from Patrick. Restatement, Section 3.10, Illustration 2. Nonetheless, where the agent has seriously breached the agency contract, willfully disobeyed, or violated the fiduciary duty, the principal is not liable for terminating the agency relationship. In addition, a principal ordinarily may revoke a gratuitous agency without liability to the agent.

RENUNCIATION BY THE AGENT The agent also has the power to end the agency by notifying the principal that she renounces the authority given her. Restatement, Section 3.10. If the parties have contracted for the agency to continue for a specified time, an unjustified renunciation prior to the expiration of that time is a breach of contract. If the agency is gratuitous, however, the agent ordinarily may renounce it without liability to the principal.

19-5b OPERATION OF LAW

The occurrence of certain events will automatically terminate an agency relationship by the operation of law. These events make it impossible for the agent to perform or unlikely that the principal would want the agent to act. As a matter of law, the occurrence of any of the following events ordinarily terminates agency.

DEATH Because the authority given to an agent by a principal is strictly personal, the death of an individual agent terminates the agent's actual authority. The death of an individual principal also terminates the actual authority of the agent when the agent has notice of the principal's death. Restatement, Section 3.07. This is contrary to the Second Restatement, which took the position that the principal's death terminated the agent's actual authority whether the agent had notice or not. Section 120. For example, Polk employs Allison to sell Polk's line of goods under a contract specifying Allison's commission and the one-year period for which the employment is to continue. Without Allison's knowledge, Polk dies. Under the Second Restatement, Allison no longer has authority to sell Polk's goods, even though the contract specified that she would be employed for one year. The death of Polk, the principal, terminated the authority of Allison the agent. Under the Third Restatement, on the other hand, Allison would continue to have actual authority until she received notice of Polk's death. A person has **notice** of a fact if the person knows the fact, has reason to know the fact, has received an effective notification of the fact, or should know the fact to fulfill a duty owed to another person. Restatement, Section 1.04(4). Moreover, the Uniform Durable Power of Attorney Act and the UPOAA allow the holder of *any* power of attorney, durable or otherwise, to exercise it on the death of the principal, if its exercise is in good faith and without knowledge of the principal's death.

When an agent or a principal is not an individual, the organizational statutes typically determine when authority terminates upon the cessation of the existence of that organization. (This is discussed further in *Parts 6* and *7* of this book.) When the organizational statute does not specify, the Restatement provides that the agent's actual authority terminates when the non-individual principal or agent ceases to exist or begins a process that will lead to the cessation of its existence. Restatement, Section 3.07.

INCAPACITY   Incapacity of the principal that occurs after the formation of the agency terminates the agent's actual authority when the agent has notice of the principal's incapacity. Restatement, Section 3.08. This is contrary to the Second Restatement, which took the position that the principal's incapacity terminated the agent's actual authority without notice to the agent. Section 122. To illustrate, Powell authorizes Anna to sell in the next ten months an apartment complex for not less than $2 million. Without Anna's knowledge, Powell is adjudicated incompetent two months later. Under the Second Restatement Anna's authority to sell the apartment complex is terminated. Under the Third Restatement, Anna would continue to have actual authority until she received notice of Powell's incapacity.

If an agent is appointed under a durable power of attorney, the authority of an agent survives, or is triggered by, the incapacity or disability of the principal. Moreover, the Uniform Durable Power of Attorney Act and the UPOAA allow the holder of a power of attorney that is *not* durable to exercise it on the incapacity of the principal, if its exercise is in good faith and without knowledge of the principal's incapacity.

♦ **See Case 19-4**

APPLYING THE LAW   Relationship of Principal and Agent

FACTS   After Thomson's husband died in 2011, she gave a power of attorney to her niece, Surani, who was an accountant. The written power of attorney granted Surani authority to manage all of Thomson's financial affairs and specified that Surani's authority was to remain unaffected by Thomson's subsequent incapacity. Accordingly, Surani provided a copy of the power of attorney to Thomson's bank, took possession of Thomson's checkbook, and began paying all of her aunt's expenses by drawing checks on Thomson's bank account.

In 2016, Surani was involved in an accident that diminished her mental capacity. As a result, she left her job as an accountant, but she was able to continue to pay Thomson's bills. In 2020, when Thomson was ninety-two, she was hospitalized for a severe illness and subsequently adjudicated to be incompetent. Nonetheless, Surani continued to write checks for Thomson's expenses from Thomson's checking account.

ISSUE   Was Surani's authority to issue checks from Thomson's account terminated as a matter of law—either by her own diminished capacity in 2016 or by the court's declaring Thomson incompetent in 2020?

RULE OF LAW   The general rule is that incapacity of the principal that occurs after the formation of the agency terminates the agent's actual authority. A durable power of attorney is a formal, written appointment of an agent that provides for the agent's authority to survive, or be triggered by, the principal's subsequent incapacity.

Because the act of the agent is considered the act of the principal, the incapacity of an agent to bind himself by contract does not disqualify him from making a contract that is binding on the principal. Thus, any person able to act ordinarily has the capacity to be an agent. Thus, if the contract is authorized, it is valid despite the agent's incapacity. However, if after the creation of the agency, the agent is rendered incapable of performing the acts authorized by the principal, the agency is terminated by operation of law.

APPLICATION   This case involves incapacity of both the principal, Thomson, and the agent, Surani, some years after the agency was created. The power of attorney Thomson granted to Surani by a written document in 2011 is a durable power of attorney because it expressly provided that Surani's authority to manage Thomson's financial affairs was to continue after Thomson lost her capacity to contract. Therefore, the fact that Thomson was adjudicated incompetent in 2020 did not terminate Surani's agency. Indeed, the point of a durable power of attorney is to empower the agent to act or continue to act on the principal's behalf after the principal's capacity is called into question.

Surani's capacity to perform the tasks required of the agency is a different question. The accident she suffered in 2016 reduced her mental capacity to some unspecified degree, but Surani was not adjudged incompetent. Instead, as a result of her disability, she either chose to or was required to leave her accounting practice. Nonetheless, she apparently was still capable of successfully handling Thomson's bills by issuing the necessary checks. Therefore, her accident did not terminate her authority to continue handling those expenses. This is true regardless of whether her diminished capacity may have operated to terminate other more sophisticated aspects of her written authority to "manage all of Thomson's financial affairs," such as making investment decisions, of which Surani may no longer have been capable after her accident.

CONCLUSION   Neither Surani's accident in 2016 nor Thomson's adjudicated incompetency in 2020 terminated Surani's agency, and she retained her authority to pay Thomson's bills by drawing checks on Thomson's bank account.

19-5c CHANGE IN CIRCUMSTANCES

An agent's actual authority terminates whenever the agent should reasonably conclude that the principal no longer would assent to the agent's taking action on the principal's behalf. Restatement, Section 3.09(2). Thus, Patricia authorizes Aaron to sell her eighty acres of farmland for $800 per acre. Subsequently, oil is discovered on nearby land, which causes Patricia's land to increase greatly in value. Because Aaron knows of this but Patricia does not, Aaron's authority to sell the land is terminated.

The Second Restatement specified a number of subsequent changes in circumstances that would terminate an agent's actual authority, including accomplishment of authorized act, bankruptcy of principal or agent, change in business conditions, loss or destruction of subject matter, disloyalty of agent, change in law, and outbreak of war. The Third Restatement takes a different approach by providing a basic rule that an agent acts with actual authority "when, *at the time of taking action* that has legal consequences for the principal, the agent reasonably believes, in accordance with the principal's manifestations to the agent, that the principal wishes the agent so to act." Section 2.01 (emphasis added). Thus, if circumstances have changed such that at the time the agent takes action it is not reasonable for the agent to believe that the principal at that time consents to the action being taken on the principal's behalf, then the agent lacks actual authority so to act even though she would have had actual authority prior to the change in circumstances.

19-5d IRREVOCABLE POWERS

A **power given as security** "is a power to affect the legal relations of its creator that is created in the form of a manifestation of actual authority and held for the benefit of the holder or a third person." Restatement, Section 3.12. A power given as security creates neither a relationship of agency nor actual authority, although the power enables its holder to affect the legal relations of the creator of the power. Restatement, Section 3.12, Comment b. The power arises from a manifestation of assent by its creator that the holder of the power may, for example, dispose of property or other interests of the creator. To illustrate: Pillsbury owns Blackacre, which is situated next to Whiteacre, on which Pillsbury operates a restaurant. To finance renovations and expansions, Pillsbury borrows money from Ashton. A written agreement between Pillsbury and Ashton provides that Ashton shall irrevocably have Pillsbury's authority to transfer ownership of Blackacre to Ashton in the event Pillsbury defaults on the loan. Ashton has a power given as security. Restatement, Section 3.12, Illustration 1.

The Restatement's definition includes, but is more extensive than, the rule in some States regarding an **agency coupled with an interest**, in which the holder (agent) has a security interest in the power conferred upon him by the creator (principal). For example, an agency coupled with an interest would arise in cases in which an agent has advanced funds on behalf of the principal and the agent's power to act is given as security for the loan.

Unless otherwise agreed, a power given as security may *not* be revoked. In addition, the incapacity of the creator or of the holder of the power does not terminate the power. Nor will the death of the creator terminate the power, unless the duty for which the power was given terminates with the death of the creator. Restatement, Section 3.13(2). A power given as security *is* terminated by an event that discharges the obligation secured by it or that makes execution of the power illegal or impossible. Restatement, Section 3.13(1). Thus, in the previous example, when the creator repays the loan, the power is terminated.

C H A P T E R   S U M M A R Y

NATURE OF AGENCY	**Definition of Agency** consensual relationship authorizing one party (the agent) to act on behalf of the other party (the principal) subject to the principal's control
	Scope of Agency Purposes generally, whatever business activity a person may accomplish personally he may do through an agent
	Other Legal Relationships
	• *Employment Relationship* one in which the employer has the right to control the manner and means of the employee's performance of work
	• *Independent Contractor* a person who contracts with another to do a particular job and who is not subject to the other's control over the manner and means of conducting the work

CREATION OF AGENCY	**Formalities** though agency is a consensual relationship that may be formed by contract or agreement between the principal and agent, agency may exist without consideration
	• *Requirements* no particular formality usually is required in a contract of agency, although appointments of agents for a period of more than one year must be in writing
	• *Power of Attorney* written, formal appointment of an agent
	Capacity
	• *Principal* if the principal is a minor or an incompetent not under a guardianship, his appointment of another to act as an agent is voidable, as are any resulting contracts with third parties
	• *Agent* any person able to act may act as an agent, as the act of the agent is considered the act of the principal
DUTIES OF AGENT TO PRINCIPAL	**Duty of Obedience** an agent must act in the principal's affairs only as actually authorized by the principal and must obey all lawful instructions and directions of the principal
	Duty of Good Conduct within the scope of the agency relationship, an agent must act reasonably and refrain from conduct that is likely to damage the principal's interests
	Duty of Diligence an agent must act with reasonable care, competence, and diligence in performing the work for which he is employed
	Duty to Inform an agent must use reasonable efforts to give the principal information material to the affairs entrusted to her
	Duty to Account an agent must maintain and provide the principal with an accurate account of money or other property that the agent has received or expended on behalf of the principal; an agent must not mingle the principal's property with any other person's property
	Fiduciary Duty an agent owes a duty of utmost loyalty and good faith to the principal; it includes:
	• *Conflicts of Interest*
	• *Self-Dealing*
	• *Duty Not to Compete*
	• *Misappropriation*
	• *Confidential Information*
	• *Duty to Account for Financial Benefits*
DUTIES OF PRINCIPAL TO AGENT	**Contractual Duties**
	• *Compensation* a principal must compensate the agent as specified in the contract or for the reasonable value of the services provided if no amount is specified
	• *Indemnification* the principal must pay the agent for losses the agent incurred while acting as directed by the principal
	• *Reimbursement* the principal must pay back to the agent authorized payments the agent has made on the principal's behalf
	Tort and Other Duties include (1) the duty to provide an employee with reasonably safe conditions of employment and (2) the duty to deal with the agent fairly and in good faith
TERMINATION OF AGENCY	**Acts of the Parties**
	• *Lapse of Time*
	• *Mutual Agreement of the Parties*
	• *Revocation of Authority*
	• *Renunciation by the Agent*

Operation of Law
- **Death** of either the principal or the agent
- **Incapacity** of either the principal or the agent
- **Change in Circumstances**

Irrevocable Powers a power given as security—including an agency coupled with an interest—is irrevocable

CASES

CASE	Other Legal Relationships: Employment versus Independent Contractors
19-1	**ALEXANDER v. FEDEX GROUND PACKAGE SYSTEM, INC.**
	United States Court of Appeals, Ninth Circuit, 2014
	765 F.3d 981

Fletcher, J.

As a central part of its business, FedEx Ground System, Inc. ("FedEx"), contracts with drivers to deliver packages to its customers. The drivers must wear FedEx uniforms, drive FedEx-approved vehicles, and groom themselves according to FedEx's appearance standards. FedEx tells its drivers what packages to deliver, on what days, and at what times. Although drivers may operate multiple delivery routes and hire third parties to help perform their work, they may do so only with FedEx's consent.

* * *

FedEx characterizes its drivers as independent contractors. FedEx's Operating Agreement ("OA") governs its relationship with the drivers. * * *

* * *

The OA requires FedEx drivers to pick up and deliver packages within their assigned "Primary Service Area[s]." Drivers must deliver packages every day that FedEx is open for business, and must deliver every package they are assigned each day. They must deliver each package within a specific window of time negotiated between FedEx and its customers. After each delivery, drivers must use an electronic scanner to send data about the delivery to FedEx. FedEx does not require drivers to follow specific delivery routes. However, FedEx tells its managers to design and recommend to its drivers routes that will "reduce travel time" and "minimize expenses and maximize earnings and service."

FedEx does not expressly dictate working hours, but it structures drivers' workloads to ensure that they work between 9.5 and 11 hours every working day. * * * Drivers are compensated according to a somewhat complex formula that includes per day and per-stop components. Drivers are expected to arrive at their delivery terminals each morning, and they are not supposed to leave the terminal until all of their packages are available for pick-up. * * *

* * *

FedEx trains its drivers on how best to perform their job and to interact with customers. * * * The OA requires drivers to conduct themselves "with integrity and honesty, in a professional manner, and with proper decorum at all times." They must "[f]oster the professional image and good reputation of FedEx."

A driver's managers may conduct up to four ride-along performance evaluations each year, "to verify that [the driver] is meeting the standards of customer service" required by the OA. * * *

Drivers must follow FedEx's "Safe Driving Standards." * * *

* * *

Drivers enter into the OA for an initial term of one, two, or three years. At the end of the initial term, the OA provides for automatic renewal for successive one-year terms if neither party provides notice of their intent not to renew. The OA may be terminated (1) by the parties' mutual agreement; (2) for cause, including a breach of any provision of the OA; (3) if FedEx stops doing business or reduces operations in all or part of the driver's service area; or (4) upon thirty days' written notice by the driver. The OA requires drivers to submit claims for wrongful termination to arbitration.

* * *

FedEx requires its drivers to provide their own vehicles. Vehicles must not only meet "all applicable federal, state and municipal laws and regulations," but also must be specifically approved by FedEx. The OA allows FedEx to dictate the "identifying colors, logos, numbers, marks and insignia" of the vehicles. All vehicles must be painted "FedEx white," a specific shade of Sherwin–Williams paint, or its equivalent. They must be marked with the FedEx logo, and "maintained in a clean and presentable fashion free of body damage and extraneous markings." FedEx requires vehicles to have specific dimensions, and all vehicles must also contain shelves with specific dimensions. * * *

* * *

FedEx offers a "Business Support Package," which provides drivers with uniforms, scanners, and other necessary equipment. FedEx deducts the cost of the equipment from drivers' pay. Purchase of the package is ostensibly optional, but more than 99 percent of drivers purchase it. * * *

[FedEx contends that its drivers are independent contractors under California law. Plaintiffs, a class of FedEx drivers in California, contend that they are employees and filed a class action asserting claims for employment expenses and unpaid wages on the ground that FedEx had improperly classified the drivers as independent contractors. The district court granted summary judgment to FedEx on the employment status issue. Plaintiffs appealed.]

* * *

California's right-to-control test requires courts to weigh a number of factors: "The principal test of an employment relationship is whether the person to whom service is rendered has the right to control the manner and means of accomplishing the result desired." *S.G. Borello & Sons, Inc. v. Department of Industrial Relations*, [citation]. California courts also consider "several 'secondary' indicia of the nature of a service relationship." *Id.* The right to terminate at will, without cause, is "[s]trong evidence in support of an employment relationship." [Citation.] Additional factors include:

(a) whether the one performing services is engaged in a distinct occupation or business; (b) the kind of occupation, with reference to whether, in the locality, the work is usually done under the direction of the principal or by a specialist without supervision; (c) the skill required in the particular occupation; (d) whether the principal or the worker supplies the instrumentalities, tools, and the place of work for the person doing the work; (e) the length of time for which the services are to be performed; (f) the method of payment, whether by the time or by the job; (g) whether or not the work is a part of the regular business of the principal; and (h) whether or not the parties believe they are creating the relationship of employer-employee.

[Citation.] These factors "[g]enerally . . . cannot be applied mechanically as separate tests; they are intertwined and their weight depends often on particular combinations." [Citation.]

FedEx argues that the OA creates an independent-contractor relationship. California law is clear that "[t]he label placed by the parties on their relationship is not dispositive, and subterfuges are not countenanced." [Citation.] What matters is what the contract, in actual effect, allows or requires. [Citation.] The OA and FedEx's policies and procedures unambiguously allow FedEx to exercise a great deal of control over the manner in which its drivers do their jobs. Therefore, this factor strongly favors plaintiffs.

First, FedEx can and does control the appearance of its drivers and their vehicles. * * *

* * *

Second, FedEx can and does control the times its drivers can work. * * *

Third, FedEx can and does control aspects of how and when drivers deliver their packages. * * *

* * *

In light of the powerful evidence of FedEx's right to control the manner in which drivers perform their work, none of the remaining right-to-control factors sufficiently favors FedEx to allow a holding that plaintiffs are independent contractors. [Citations.]

The first factor, the right to terminate at will, slightly favors FedEx. The OA contains an arbitration clause and does not give FedEx an unqualified right to terminate. Under California law, the right to discharge at will is "[s]trong evidence in support of an employment relationship," [citations].

* * *

The second factor, distinct occupation or business, favors plaintiffs. As the California Court of Appeal reasoned in [citation], "the work performed by the drivers is wholly integrated into FedEx's operation. The drivers look like FedEx employees, act like FedEx employees, [and] are paid like FedEx employees." [Citation.] "The customers are FedEx's customers, not the drivers' customers." [Citation.] While the drivers have opportunities to expand their businesses by taking on additional routes and hiring helpers, these opportunities themselves are only available subject to FedEx's business needs.

The third factor, whether the work is performed under the principal's direction, slightly favors plaintiffs. * * * although drivers retain freedom to determine several aspects of their day-to-day work, FedEx also closely supervises their work through various methods.

The fourth factor, the skill required in the occupation, also favors plaintiffs. FedEx drivers "need no experience to get the job in the first place and [the] only required skill is the ability to drive." [Citation.]

The fifth factor, the provision of tools and equipment, slightly favors FedEx. The drivers provide their own vehicles and are not required to get other equipment from FedEx. * * * Ultimately, the vast majority of drivers get their other equipment from FedEx. [Citation.] * * *

The sixth factor, length of time for performance of services, favors plaintiffs. Drivers enter into the OA for a term of one to three years. At the end of the initial term, the OA provides for automatic renewal for successive one-year terms if there is no notice of non-renewal by either party.

* * *

The seventh factor, method of payment, is neutral. FedEx pays its drivers according to a complicated scheme that * * * cannot easily be compared to either hourly payment (which favors employee status) or per job payment (which favors independent contractor status). * * *

The eighth factor, whether the work is part of the principal's regular business, favors plaintiffs. The work that the drivers perform, the pickup and delivery of packages, is "essential to FedEx's core business." [Citation.]

The final factor, the parties' beliefs, slightly favors FedEx. * * * the OA's statement of independent contractor status is evidence that the drivers believed that they were entering such a relationship. Ultimately, though, "neither [FedEx]'s nor the drivers' own perception of their relationship as one of independent contracting" is dispositive. [Citation.]

Viewing the evidence in the light most favorable to FedEx, the OA grants FedEx a broad right to control the manner in which its drivers perform their work. The most important factor of the right-to-control test thus strongly favors employee status.

* * *

We hold that plaintiffs are employees as a matter of law under California's right-to-control test. Accordingly, we reverse both the * * * grant of summary judgment to FedEx and [the] denial of plaintiffs' motion for partial summary judgment. We remand to the district court with instructions to enter summary judgment for plaintiffs on the question of employment status.

CASE 19-2

Creation of Agency
MILLER v. MCDONALD'S CORPORATION
Court of Appeals of Oregon, 1997
150 Or.App. 274, 945 P.2d 1107

Warren, J.

Plaintiff seeks damages from defendant McDonald's Corporation for injuries that she suffered when she bit into a heart-shaped sapphire stone while eating a Big Mac sandwich that she had purchased at a McDonald's restaurant in Tigard. The trial court granted summary judgment to defendant on the ground that it did not own or operate the restaurant; rather, the owner and operator was a nonparty, 3K Restaurants (3K), that held a franchise from defendant. Plaintiff appeals, and we reverse.

Most of the relevant facts are not in dispute. * * * 3K owned and operated the restaurant under a License Agreement (the Agreement) with defendant that required it to operate in a manner consistent with the "McDonald's System." The Agreement described that system as including proprietary rights in trade names, service marks and trade marks, as well as "designs and color schemes for restaurant buildings, signs, equipment layouts, formulas and specifications for certain food products, methods of inventory and operation control, bookkeeping and accounting, and manuals covering business practices and policies."

The manuals contain "detailed information relating to operation of the Restaurant," including food formulas and specifications, methods of inventory control, bookkeeping procedures, business practices, and other management, advertising, and personnel policies. 3K, as the licensee, agreed to adopt and exclusively use the formulas, methods, and policies contained in the manuals, including any subsequent modifications, and to use only advertising and promotional materials that defendant either provided or approved in advance in writing.

The Agreement described the way in which 3K was to operate the restaurant in considerable detail. It expressly required 3K to operate in compliance with defendant's prescribed standards, policies, practices, and procedures, including serving only food and beverage products that defendant designated. 3K had to follow defendant's specifications and blueprints for the equipment and layout of the restaurant, including adopting subsequent reasonable changes that defendant made, and to maintain the restaurant building in compliance with defendant's standards. 3K could not make any changes in the basic design of the building without defendant's approval.

The Agreement required 3K to keep the restaurant open during the hours that defendant prescribed, including maintaining adequate supplies and employing adequate personnel to operate at maximum capacity and efficiency during those hours. 3K also had to keep the restaurant similar in appearance to all other McDonald's restaurants. 3K's employees had to wear McDonald's uniforms, to have a neat and clean appearance, and to provide competent and courteous service. 3K could use only containers and other packaging that bore McDonald's trademarks. The ingredients for the foods and beverages had to meet defendant's standards, and 3K had to use "only those methods of food handling and preparation that [defendant] may designate from time to time." In order to obtain the franchise, 3K had to represent that the franchisee had worked at a McDonald's restaurant; the Agreement did not distinguish in this respect between a company-run or a franchised restaurant. The manuals gave further details that expanded on many of these requirements.

In order to ensure conformity with the standards described in the Agreement, defendant periodically sent field consultants to the restaurant to inspect its operations. 3K trained its employees in accordance with defendant's materials and recommendations and sent some of them to training programs that defendant administered. Failure to comply with the agreed standards could result in loss of the franchise.

Despite these detailed instructions, the Agreement provided that 3K was not an agent of defendant for any purpose. Rather, it was an independent contractor and was responsible for all obligations and liabilities, including claims based on injury, illness, or death, directly or indirectly resulting from the operation of the restaurant.

Plaintiff went to the restaurant under the assumption that defendant owned, controlled, and managed it. So far as she could tell, the restaurant's appearance was similar to that of other McDonald's restaurants that she had patronized. Nothing disclosed to her that any entity other than defendant was involved in its operation. The only signs that were visible and obvious to the public had the name "McDonald's," the employees wore uniforms with McDonald's insignia, and the menu was the same that plaintiff had seen in other McDonald's restaurants. The general appearance of the restaurant and the food products that it sold were similar to the restaurants and products that plaintiff had seen in national print and television advertising that defendant had run. To the best of plaintiff's knowledge, only McDonald's sells Big Mac hamburgers.

* * *

Under these facts, 3K would be directly liable for any injuries that plaintiff suffered as a result of the restaurant's negligence. The issue on summary judgment is whether there is evidence that would permit a jury to find defendant vicariously liable for those injuries because of its relationship with 3K. Plaintiff asserts two theories of vicarious liability, actual agency and apparent agency. We hold that there is sufficient evidence to raise a jury issue under both theories. We first discuss actual agency.

The kind of actual agency relationship that would make defendant vicariously liable for 3K's negligence requires that defendant have the right to control the method by which 3K performed its obligations under the Agreement. The common context for that test is a normal master-servant (or employer-employee) relationship. [Citations.] The relationship between two business entities is not precisely an employment relationship, but the Oregon Supreme Court, in common with most if not all other courts that have considered the issue, has applied the right to control test for vicarious liability in that context as well. [Citation.] We therefore apply that test to this case.

* * *

A number of other courts have applied the right to control test to a franchise relationship. The Delaware Supreme Court, in [citation], stated the test as it applies to that context:

If, in practical effect, the franchise agreement goes beyond the stage of setting standards, and allocates to the franchisor the right to exercise control over the daily operations of the franchise, an agency relationship exists. [Citation.]

* * *

* * * [W]e believe that a jury could find that defendant retained sufficient control over 3K's daily operations that an actual agency relationship existed. The Agreement did not simply set standards that 3K had to meet. Rather, it required 3K to use the precise methods that defendant established, both in the Agreement and in the detailed manuals that the Agreement incorporated. Those methods included the ways in which 3K was to handle and prepare food. Defendant enforced the use of those methods by regularly sending inspectors and by its retained power to cancel the Agreement. That evidence would support a finding that defendant had the right to control the way in which 3K performed at least food handling and preparation. In her complaint, plaintiff alleges that 3K's deficiencies in those functions resulted in the sapphire being in the Big Mac and thereby caused her injuries. * * *

Plaintiff next asserts that defendant is vicariously liable for 3K's alleged negligence because 3K was defendant's apparent agent. The relevant standard is in Restatement (Second) of Agency, §267, which we adopted in [citation]:

One who represents that another is his servant or other agent and thereby causes a third person justifiably to rely upon the care or skill of such apparent agent is subject to liability to the third person for harm caused by the lack of care or skill of the one appearing to be a servant or other agent as if he were such. [Citation.]

We have not applied §267 to a franchisor/franchisee situation, but courts in a number of other jurisdictions have done so in ways that we find instructive. In most cases the courts have found that there was a jury issue of apparent agency. The crucial issues are whether the putative principal held the third party out as an agent and whether the plaintiff relied on that holding out.

* * *

In this case * * * there is an issue of fact about whether defendant held 3K out as its agent. Everything about the appearance and operation of the Tigard McDonald's identified it with defendant and with the common image for all McDonald's restaurants that defendant has worked to create through national advertising, common signs and uniforms, common menus, common appearance, and common standards. The possible existence of a sign identifying 3K as the operator does not alter the conclusion that there is an issue of apparent agency for the jury. There are issues of fact of whether that sign was sufficiently visible to the public, in light of plaintiff's apparent failure to see it, and of whether one sign by itself is sufficient to remove the impression that defendant created through all of the other indicia of its control that it, and 3K under the requirements that defendant imposed, presented to the public.

Defendant does not seriously dispute that a jury could find that it held 3K out as its agent. Rather, it argues that there is insufficient evidence that plaintiff justifiably relied on that holding out. It argues that it is not sufficient for her to prove that she went to the Tigard McDonald's because it was a McDonald's restaurant. Rather, she also had to prove that she went to it because she believed that McDonald's Corporation operated both it and the other McDonald's restaurants that she had previously patronized. * * *

* * *

* * * [I]n this case plaintiff testified that she relied on the general reputation of McDonald's in patronizing the Tigard restaurant and in her expectation of the quality of the food and service that she would receive. Especially in light of defendant's efforts to create a public perception of a common McDonald's system at all McDonald's restaurants, whoever operated them, a jury could find that plaintiff's reliance was objectively reasonable. The trial court erred in granting summary judgment on the apparent agency theory.

Reversed and remanded.

CASE 19-3

Fiduciary Duty

DETROIT LIONS, INC. v. ARGOVITZ

United States District Court, Eastern District of Michigan, 1984
580 F.Supp. 542; affirmed, 767 F.2d 919

Demascio, J.

[Jerry Argovitz was employed as an agent of Billy Sims, a professional football player. Early in 1983, Argovitz informed Sims that he was awaiting the approval of his application for a U.S. Football League franchise in Houston. Sims was unaware, however, of Argovitz's extensive ownership interest in the new Houston Gamblers organization. Meanwhile, during the spring of 1983, Argovitz continued contract negotiations on behalf of Sims with the Detroit Lions of the National Football League. By June 22, Argovitz and the Lions were very close to an agreement, although Argovitz represented to Sims that the negotiations were not proceeding well. Argovitz then sought an offer for Sims's services from the Gamblers. The Gamblers offered Sims a $3.5 million, five-year deal. Argovitz told Sims that he thought the Lions would match this figure; however, he did not seek a final offer from the Lions and then present the terms of both packages to Sims. Sims, convinced that the Lions were not negotiating in good faith, signed with the Gamblers on July 1, 1983. On December 16, 1983, Sims signed a second contract with the Lions. The Lions and Sims brought an action against Argovitz, seeking to invalidate Sims's contract with the Gamblers on the ground that Argovitz breached his fiduciary duty when negotiating the contract with the Gamblers.]

* * *

The relationship between a principal and agent is fiduciary in nature, and as such imposes a duty of loyalty, good faith, and fair and honest dealing on the agent. [Citation.]

A fiduciary relationship arises not only from a formal principal-agent relationship, but also from informal relationships of trust and confidence. [Citations.]

In light of the express agency agreement, and the relationship between Sims and Argovitz, Argovitz clearly owed Sims the fiduciary duties of an agent at all times relevant to this lawsuit.

An agent's duty of loyalty requires that he not have a personal stake that conflicts with the principal's interest in a transaction in which he represents his principal. As stated in [citation]:

> (T)he principal is entitled to the best efforts and unbiased judgment of his agent. * * * (T)he law denies the right of an agent to assume any relationship that is antagonistic to his duty to his principal, and it has many times been held that the agent cannot be both buyer and seller at the same time nor connect his own interests with property involved in his dealings as an agent for another.

A fiduciary violates the prohibition against self-dealing not only by dealing with himself on his principal's behalf, but also by dealing on his principal's behalf with a third party in which he has an interest, such as a partnership in which he is a member. * * *

Where an agent has an interest adverse to that of his principal in a transaction in which he purports to act on behalf of his principal, the transaction is voidable by the principal unless the agent disclosed all material facts within the agent's knowledge that might affect the principal's judgment. [Citation.]

The mere fact that the contract is fair to the principal does not deny the principal the right to rescind the contract when it was negotiated by an agent in violation of the prohibition against self-dealing. * * *

Once it has been shown that an agent had an interest in a transaction involving his principal antagonistic to the principal's interest, fraud on the part of the agent is presumed. The burden of proof then rests upon the agent to show that his principal had full knowledge, not only of the fact that the agent was interested, but also of every material fact known to the agent which might affect the principal and that having such knowledge, the principal freely consented to the transaction.

It is not sufficient for the agent merely to inform the principal that he has an interest that conflicts with the principal's interest. Rather, he must inform the principal "of all facts that come to his knowledge that are or may be material or which might affect his principal's rights or interests or influence the action he takes." [Citation.]

Argovitz clearly had a personal interest in signing Sims with the Gamblers that was adverse to Sims' interest—he had an ownership interest in the Gamblers and thus would profit if the Gamblers were profitable, and would incur substantial personal liabilities should the Gamblers not be financially successful. Since this showing has been made, fraud on Argovitz's part is presumed, and the Gamblers' contract must be rescinded unless Argovitz has shown by a preponderance of the evidence that he informed Sims of every material fact that might have influenced Sims' decision whether or not to sign the Gamblers' contract.

We conclude that Argovitz has failed to show by a preponderance of the evidence either: (1) that he informed Sims of the [material] facts, or (2) that these facts would not have influenced Sims' decision whether to sign the Gamblers' contract. * * *

As a court sitting in equity, we conclude that recision is the appropriate remedy. We are dismayed by Argovitz's egregious conduct. The careless fashion in which Argovitz went about ascertaining the highest price for Sims' service convinces us of the wisdom of the maxim: no man can faithfully serve two masters whose interests are in conflict.

Judgment will be entered for the plaintiffs rescinding the Gamblers' contract with Sims.

CASE 19-4

Termination by Incapacity/Durable Power of Attorney
GADDY v. DOUGLASS
Court of Appeals of South Carolina, 2004
359 S.C. 329, 597 S.E.2d 12

Kittredge, J.
Ms. M was born in 1918 and grew up in Fairfield County [South Carolina]. She moved to Greenville, where she majored in sociology at Furman University and later worked for the South Carolina Department of Social Services. After retiring, Ms. M returned to Fairfield where she lived on her family farm with her brother, a dentist, until his death in the early 1980s. Ms. M never married.

Dr. Gaddy was Ms. M's physician and a close family friend. * * *

Conversely, Ms. M had little contact with many of her relatives, including Appellants [third cousins of Ms. M].

In 1988, * * * Ms. M then executed a durable general power of attorney (1988 durable power of attorney) designating Dr. Gaddy as her attorney-in-fact. * * *

* * * Concerns about Ms. M's progressively worsening mental condition prompted Dr. Gaddy to file the 1988 durable power of attorney in November 1995. Pursuant to the 1988 durable power of attorney, Dr. Gaddy began to act as Ms. M's attorney-in-fact and assumed control of her finances, farm, and health care. His responsibilities included paying her bills, tilling her garden, repairing fences, and hiring caregivers.

In March 1996, Dr. Gaddy discovered Ms. M had fallen in her home and fractured a vertebra. Ms. M was hospitalized for six weeks. During the hospitalization, Dr. Gaddy fumigated and cleaned her home, which had become flea-infested and unclean to the point where rat droppings were found in the house. Finding that Ms. M was not mentally competent to care for herself, he arranged for full-time caretakers to attend to her after she recovered from the injuries she sustained in her fall. He made improvements in her home, including replacing moth-eaten area rugs with new rugs and upgraded her kitchen to enable caretakers to prepare her meals. Dr. Gaddy also made plumbing repairs to the house, and took steps to adapt a bathroom to make it safer for caretakers to bathe Ms. M, who was incapable of doing so unassisted. During Ms. M's hospitalization, neither of the Appellants visited her in the hospital or sought to assist her in any manner.

Dr. Gaddy had Ms. M examined and evaluated by Dr. James E. Carnes, a neurologist, in December 1996. After examining

Ms. M, Dr. Carnes found that she suffered from dementia and confirmed she was unable to handle her affairs.

As Ms. M's Alzheimer's disease progressed and her faculties deteriorated, Dr. Gaddy managed her financial affairs, oversaw maintenance of her properties, and ensured that she received constant care including food, clothing, bathing, and housekeeping. * * *

Ms. M's long-standing distant relationship with some members of her family, including Appellants, changed in March of 1999.

On March 12, 1999, Appellants visited Ms. M, and with the help of disgruntled caretaker Lil Heller, took her to an appointment with Columbia attorney Douglas N. Truslow to "get rid of Dr. Gaddy." On the drive to Truslow's office, Heller had to remind Ms. M several times of their destination and purpose. At Truslow's office, Ms. M signed a document revoking the 1988 Will and the 1988 durable power of attorney. She also signed a new durable power of attorney (1999 durable power of attorney) naming Appellants as her attorneys-in-fact. Appellants failed to disclose Ms. M's dementia to Truslow. David Byrd, a witness to the execution of the March 12 documents, was likewise not informed of Ms. M's dementia.

Armed with the revocation of the 1988 power of attorney and recently executed power of attorney in their favor, Appellants prohibited Dr. Gaddy from contacting Ms. M. Dr. Gaddy was even threatened with arrest if he tried to visit Ms. M.

On March 15, 1999, three days after Ms. M purportedly revoked the 1988 documents and executed the 1999 durable power of attorney, Dr. Gaddy initiated the present action as her attorney-in-fact pursuant to the 1988 durable power of attorney. He alleged, among other things, that the purported revocation of the 1988 durable power of attorney and the execution of the 1999 durable power of attorney were invalid because "on March 12, 1999, the date on which Ms. M purportedly signed the 1999 power of attorney and the revocation, she was not mentally competent" due to "senile dementia of the Alzheimer's type." The action sought declaratory judgment to render the 1999 durable power of attorney invalid and declare the 1988 durable power of attorney valid.

* * *

Medical testimony was presented from five physicians who had examined Ms. M. * * * [They concluded that Ms. M. (1) was "unable to handle her financial affairs" and "would need help managing her daily activities," and (2) would not "ever have moments of lucidity" to "understand legal documents."]

* * *

The trial court concluded that Ms. M lacked contractual * * * capacity "from March 12, 1999 and continuously thereafter."

As a result, he invalidated the 1999 revocation of the 1988 durable power of attorney and * * * the 1999 durable power of attorney, and declared valid the 1988 durable power of attorney. Finally, he awarded Dr. Gaddy litigation expenses to be paid from Ms. M's assets.

Since 1986, the South Carolina Legislature has expressly authorized and sanctioned the use and efficacy of *durable* powers of attorneys. * * *

Upon the execution of a durable power of attorney, the attorney-in-fact retains authority to act on the principal's behalf notwithstanding the subsequent physical disability or mental incompetence of the principal. To honor this unmistakable legislative intent, it is incumbent on courts to uphold a durable power of attorney unless the principal retains contractual capacity to revoke the then existing durable power of attorney or to execute a new power of attorney. Otherwise, the very purpose of [the statute] would be undermined.

* * *

"In order to execute or revoke a valid power of attorney, the principal must possess contractual capacity." [Citation.] Contractual capacity is generally defined as a person's ability to understand in a meaningful way, at the time the contract is executed, the nature, scope and effect of the contract. [Citation.] Where, as here, the mental condition of the principal is of a chronic nature, evidence of the principal's prior or subsequent condition is admissible as bearing upon his or her condition at the time the contract is executed. [Citation.] * * *

Here, the credible medical * * * testimony presented compellingly indicates that Ms. M suffered from at least moderate to severe dementia caused by Alzheimer's Disease, a chronic and permanent organic disease, on March 12, 1999. We are firmly persuaded that Ms. M's dementia, chronic and progressive in nature, clearly rendered her incapable of possessing contractual capacity to revoke the 1988 durable power of attorney or execute the 1999 power of attorney. We find this conclusion inescapable based on the record before us.

* * *

The very idea of a durable power of attorney is to protect the principal should he or she become incapacitated. This case is precisely the type of situation for which the durable power of attorney is intended. On March 12, 1999, Ms. M, due to her chronic and severe dementia, lacked capacity to revoke the 1988 durable power of attorney and execute the 1999 power of attorney, and the evidence in this regard is overwhelming. In so holding, we return to Dr. Gaddy his fiduciary obligations to Ms. M, which he faithfully discharged prior to Appellants' regrettable involvement. The decision of the trial court is AFFIRMED IN PART AND VACATED IN PART.

1. Parker, the owner of certain unimproved real estate in Chicago, employed Adams, a real estate agent, to sell the property for a price of $250,000 or more and agreed to pay Adams a commission of 6 percent for making a sale. Adams negotiated with Turner, who was interested in the property and willing to pay as much as $280,000 for it. Adams made an agreement with Turner that if Adams could obtain Parker's signature to a contract to sell the property to Turner for $250,000, Turner would pay Adams a bonus of $10,000. Adams prepared, and Parker and Turner signed, a contract for the sale of the property to Turner for $250,000. Turner refuses to pay Adams the $10,000 as promised. Parker refuses to pay Adams the 6 percent commission. In an action by Adams against Parker and Turner, what judgment?

2. Perry employed Alice to sell a parcel of real estate at a fixed price without knowledge that David had previously employed Alice to purchase the same property for him. Perry gave Alice no discretion as to price or terms, and Alice entered into a contract of sale with David upon the exact terms authorized by Perry. After accepting a partial payment, Perry discovered that Alice was employed by David and brought an action to rescind. David resisted on the ground that Perry had suffered no damage for the reason that Alice had been given no discretion and the sale was made upon the exact basis authorized by Perry. Discuss whether Perry will prevail.

3. Packer owned and operated a fruit cannery in Southton, Illinois. He stored a substantial number of finished canned goods in a warehouse in East St. Louis, Illinois, owned and operated by Alden, in order to have goods readily available for the St. Louis market. On March 1, he had ten thousand cans of peaches and five thousand cans of apples in storage with Alden. On the day named, he borrowed $5,000 from Alden, giving Alden his promissory note for this amount due June 1 together with a letter authorizing Alden, in the event the note was not paid at maturity, to sell any or all of his goods in storage, pay the indebtedness, and account to him for any surplus. Packer died on June 2 without having paid the note. On June 8, Alden told Taylor, a wholesale food distributor, that he had for sale as agent of the owner ten thousand cans of peaches and five thousand cans of apples. Taylor said he would take the peaches and would decide later about the apples. A contract for the sale of ten thousand cans of peaches for $6,000 was thereupon signed "Alden, agent for Packer, seller; Taylor, buyer." Both Alden and Taylor knew of the death of Packer. Delivery of the peaches and payment were made on June 10. On June 11,

Alden and Taylor signed a similar contract covering the five thousand cans of apples, delivery and payment to be made June 30. On June 23, Packer's executor, having learned of these contracts, wrote Alden and Taylor stating that Alden had no authority to make the contracts, demanding that Taylor return the peaches, and directing Alden not to deliver the apples. Discuss the correctness of the contentions of Packer's executor.

4. Harvey Hilgendorf was a licensed real estate broker acting as the agent of the Hagues in the sale of eighty acres of farmland. The Hagues, however, terminated Hilgendorf's agency before the expiration of the listing contract when they encountered financial difficulties and decided to liquidate their entire holdings of land at one time. Hilgendorf brought this action for breach of the listing contract. The Hagues maintain that Hilgendorf's duty of loyalty required him to give up the listing contract. Are the Hagues correct in their assertion? Explain.

5. Palmer made a valid contract with Ames under which Ames was to sell Palmer's goods on commission from January 1 to June 30. Ames made satisfactory sales up to May 15 and was then about to close an unusually large order when Palmer suddenly and without notice revoked Ames's authority to sell. Can Ames continue to sell Palmer's goods during the unexpired term of her contract? Explain.

6. Piedmont Electric Co. gave a list of delinquent accounts to Alexander, an employee, with instructions to discontinue electric service to delinquent customers. Among those listed was Todd Hatchery, which was then in the process of hatching chickens in a large, electrically heated incubator. Todd Hatchery told Alexander that it did not consider its account delinquent, but Alexander nevertheless cut the wires leading to the hatchery. Subsequently, Todd Hatchery recovered a judgment of $5,000 in an action brought against Alexander for the loss resulting from the interruption of the incubation process. Alexander has paid the judgment and brings a cause of action against Piedmont Electric Co. What may he recover? Explain.

7. In October 2015, Black, the owner of the Grand Opera House, and Harvey entered into a written agreement leasing the Opera House to Harvey for five years at a rental of $300,000 per year. Harvey engaged Day as manager of the theater at a salary of $1,175 per week plus 10 percent of the profits. One of Day's duties was to determine the amount of money taken in each night and, after deducting expenses, to divide the profits between

Harvey and the manager of the particular attraction that was playing at the theater. In September 2020, Day went to Black and offered to rent the Opera House from Black at a rental of $375,000 per year, whereupon Black entered into a lease with Day for five years at this figure. When Harvey learned of and objected to this transaction, Day offered to assign the lease to him for $600,000 per year. Harvey refused and brought an appropriate action against Day. Should Harvey recover? If so, on what basis and to what relief is he entitled?

8. Timothy retains Cynthia, an attorney, to bring a lawsuit upon a valid claim against Vincent. Cynthia fails to make herself aware of recently enacted legislation that shortens the statute of limitations for this type of legal action, and consequently, she files the complaint after the statute of limitations has run. As a result, the lawsuit is dismissed. What rights, if any, does Timothy have against Cynthia?

9. Wilson engages Ruth to sell Wilson's antique walnut chest to Harold for $2,500. The next day, Ruth learns that Sandy is willing to pay $3,000 for Wilson's chest. Ruth nevertheless sells the chest to Harold. Wilson then discovers these facts. What are Wilson's rights, if any, against Ruth?

10. Morris, a salesperson for Acme, Inc., a manufacturer of household appliances, receives a commission on all sales made and no further compensation. He drives his own automobile, pays his own expenses, and calls on whom he pleases. While driving to make a call on a potential customer, Morris negligently collides with Hudson, who sues (a) Acme and (b) Morris. Who should be held liable?

CASE PROBLEMS

11. Sierra Pacific Industries purchased various areas of timber and six other pieces of real property, including a ten-acre parcel on which five duplexes and two single-family units were located. Sierra Pacific requested the assistance of Joseph Carter, a licensed real estate broker, in selling the non-timberland properties. It commissioned him to sell the property for an asking price of $850,000, of which Sierra Pacific would receive $800,000 and Carter would receive $50,000 as a commission. Unable to find a prospective buyer, Carter finally sold the property to his daughter and son-in-law for $850,000 and retained the $50,000 commission without informing Sierra Pacific of his relationship to the buyers. After learning of these facts, Sierra Pacific brought an action for breach of fiduciary duty against Carter. To what relief, if any, is Sierra Pacific entitled?

12. Murphy, while a guest at a motel operated by the Betsy-Len Motor Hotel Corporation, sustained injuries from a fall allegedly caused by negligence in maintaining the premises. At that time, Betsy-Len was under a license agreement with Holiday Inns, Inc. The license contained provisions permitting Holiday Inns to regulate the architectural style of the buildings as well as the type and style of the furnishings and equipment. The contract, however, did not grant Holiday Inns the power to control the day-to-day operations of Betsy-Len's motel, to fix customer rates, or to demand a share of the profits. Betsy-Len could hire and fire its employees, determine wages and working conditions, supervise the employee work routine, and discipline its employees. In return, Betsy-Len used the trade name "Holiday Inns" and paid a fee for use of the license and Holiday Inns's national advertising. Murphy sued Holiday Inns, claiming Betsy-Len was its agent. Is Murphy correct? Explain.

13. Tube Art was involved in moving a reader board sign to a new location. Tube Art's service manager and another employee went to the proposed site and took photographs and measurements. Later, a Tube Art employee laid out the exact size and location for the excavation by marking a four-by-four-foot square on the asphalt surface with yellow paint. The dimensions of the hole, including its depth of six feet, were indicated with spray paint inside the square. After the layout was painted on the asphalt, Tube Art engaged a backhoe operator, Richard F. Redford, to dig the hole. Redford began digging in the early evening hours at the location designated by Tube Art. At approximately 9:30 P.M., the bucket of Redford's backhoe struck a small natural gas pipeline. After examining the pipe and finding no indication of a break or leak, he concluded that the line was not in use and left the site. Shortly before 2:00 A.M. on the following day, an explosion and fire occurred in the building serviced by that gas pipeline. As a result, two people in the building were killed, and most of its contents were destroyed. Massey and his associates, as tenants of the building, brought an action against Tube Art and Richard Redford for the total destruction of their property. Will the plaintiff prevail? Explain.

14. Brian Hanson sustained a paralyzing injury while playing in a lacrosse match between Ohio State University and Ashland University. Hanson had interceded in a fight between one of his teammates and an Ashland player,

William Kynast. Hanson grabbed Kynast in a bear hug, but Kynast threw Hanson off his back. Hanson's head struck the ground, resulting in serious injuries. An ambulance was summoned, and after several delays Hanson was transported to a local hospital where he underwent surgery. Doctors determined that Hanson suffered a compression fracture of his sixth spinal vertebrae. Hanson, now an incomplete quadriplegic, subsequently filed suit against Ashland University, maintaining that because Kynast was acting as the agent of Ashland, the university was therefore liable for Kynast's alleged wrongful acts. Was Kynast an agent of Ashland? Why or why not?

15. Tony Wilson was a member of Troop 392 of the Boy Scouts of America (BSA) and of the St. Louis Area Council (Council). Tony went on a trip with the troop to Fort Leonard Wood, Missouri. Five adult volunteer leaders accompanied the troop. The troop stayed in a building that had thirty-foot aluminum pipes stacked next to it. At approximately 10:00 P.M., Tony and other scouts were outside the building, and the leaders were inside. Tony and two other scouts picked up a pipe and raised it so that it came into contact with 7,200-volt power lines that ran over the building. All three scouts were electrocuted, and Tony died.

His parents brought a suit for wrongful death against the Council, claiming that the volunteer leaders were agents or servants of the Council and that it was vicariously liable for their negligence. The Council filed a motion for summary judgment, arguing as follows: the BSA chartered local councils in certain areas, and councils in turn granted charters to local sponsors such as schools, churches, or civic organizations. Local councils did not administer the scouting program for the sponsor, did not select volunteers, did not prescribe training for volunteers, and did not direct or control the activities of troops. Troops were not required to get permission from local councils before participating in an activity. Are the troop leaders agents of the Council? Explain.

16. Hunter Farms contracted with Petrolia Grain & Feed Company, a Canadian company, to purchase a large supply of the farm herbicide Sencor from Petrolia for resale. Petrolia learned from the U.S. Customs Service that the import duty for the Sencor would be 5 percent but that the final rate could be determined only upon an inspection of the Sencor at the time of importation. Petrolia forwarded this information to Hunter. Meanwhile, Hunter employed F. W. Myers & Company, an import broker, to assist in moving the herbicide through customs. When customs later determined that certain chemicals in the herbicide, not listed on its label, would increase the customs duty from $30,000 to $128,000,

Myers paid the additional amount under protest and turned to Hunter for indemnification. Hunter refused to pay Myers, claiming that Myers breached its duty of care as an import broker in failing to inform Hunter that the 5 percent duty rate was subject to increase. Myers brought an action against Hunter, arguing that it was not employed to give advice to Hunter on matters of importation. Explain whether Myers had the duty to inform Hunter.

17. Danny Del Pilar sustained injuries when his car collided with a delivery van painted yellow—the widely recognized DHL color—and displaying the DHL name and logo. The truck was driven by a driver wearing a DHL uniform and laden with packages destined for DHL customers. The van was owned not by DHL, but by Johnny Boyd, a driver for Silver Ink, Inc., a local company that was responsible at the time for picking up, sorting, and delivering all DHL packages in metropolitan Jacksonville, Florida. Boyd, working for Silver Ink on the DHL contract, was shuttling DHL packages when the accident occurred. DHL's agreement with Silver Ink essentially delegated to Silver Ink the responsibility to service DHL customers in the Jacksonville area. The contract identified Silver Ink as an "independent contractor" and provided that "the manner and means by which Contractor performs the services shall be at Contractor's sole discretion and control and are Contractor's sole responsibility." The agreement also, however, recited an exhaustive and detailed list of procedures that Silver Ink employees were to follow in processing, picking up, and delivering packages and contained a provision under which Silver Ink was required to indemnify DHL in the event Silver Ink lost or damaged packages bound for DHL's customers. The agreement gave either party the power to terminate in the event of the other party's breach. Silver Ink employees were contractually required to "wear a DHL uniform." Silver Ink was required to submit to unannounced operational inspections and audits at DHL's sole discretion and was required to maintain a fleet of delivery vans operated in DHL livery, designed and placed on the vehicles in strict accordance with specifications established by DHL. Silver Ink's operational hub was co-located with DHL's Jacksonville facility, and DHL employees monitored and reviewed Silver Ink operations on a daily basis.

Danny Del Pilar sued DHL for his personal injuries arising from the auto accident. DHL argued that Silver Ink is an independent contractor for whose alleged negligence DHL is not vicariously liable. Explain whether Silver Ink is an independent contractor as a matter of law.

18. Sheree Demming—a real estate investor in the business of acquiring properties in the Bloomington, Indiana area for remodeling, renovation, leasing, and sale—engaged Cheryl Underwood's professional services as a realtor to buy and sell properties on multiple occasions between July 2015 and April 2020. In 2015, Demming became particularly interested in purchasing two properties owned by Marion and Frances Morris and managed by realtor Julie Costley. The properties, however, were not listed for sale. Underwood made an offer to Costley on Demming's behalf in the fall of 2015. After the offer was rejected, Underwood approached Costley every few months to inquire whether the properties were available for purchase. However, unknown to Demming, Underwood became interested in purchasing the properties for herself after she acquired a neighboring property in May 2019. In February 2020, Demming again instructed Underwood to inquire into the availability of the properties. Accordingly, Underwood asked Costley to contact Mrs. Morris, whose husband had recently died. Costley agreed to contact Mrs. Morris but expressed doubt as to Mrs. Morris's willingness to sell. The next day, Underwood told Demming that the properties were not for sale. A few days later, Costley contacted Mrs. Morris, who instructed Costley to request that anyone interested in purchasing the properties tender a written offer. When Costley informed Underwood that Mrs. Morris was willing to entertain an offer, Underwood did not relay this information to Demming. Instead, on March 30, 2020, Underwood and a partner purchased the property. Explain what rights, if any, Demming has against Underwood.

TAKING SIDES

Western Rivers Fly Fisher (Western) operates under license of the U.S. Forest Service as an "outfitter," a corporation in the business of arranging fishing expeditions on the Green River in Utah. Michael D. Petragallo is licensed by the Forest Service as a guide to conduct fishing expeditions but cannot do so by himself, because the Forest Service licenses only outfitters to float patrons down the Green River. Western and several other licensed outfitters contact Petragallo to guide clients on fishing trips. Because the Forest Service licenses only outfitters to sponsor fishing expeditions, every guide must display on the boat and vehicle he uses the insignia of the outfitter sponsoring the particular trip. Petragallo may agree or refuse to take individuals Western refers to him, and Western does not restrict him from guiding expeditions for other outfitters. Western pays Petragallo a certain sum per fishing trip and does not make any deductions from his compensation. Petragallo's responsibilities include transporting patrons to the Green River, using his own boat for fishing trips, providing food and overnight needs for patrons, assisting patrons in fly fishing, and transporting them from the river to their vehicles.

Robert McMaster contacted Western and arranged for a fishing trip for him and two others. Jaeger was a member of McMaster's fishing party. McMaster paid Western, which set the price for the trip, planned the itinerary for the McMaster party, rented fishing rods to them, and arranged for Petragallo to be their guide. When Petragallo met the McMaster party, he answered affirmatively when the plaintiff asked him if he worked for Western. Petragallo provided his own vehicle and boat and supplied the food, equipment, and gasoline for the trip. Both the vehicle and the boat had signs bearing Western's identification and logo. While driving the McMaster party back to town at the conclusion of the fishing trip, Petragallo lost control of his vehicle and got into an accident, injuring Jaeger.

a. What arguments could Jaeger make for claiming that Petragallo was an employee of Western?

b. What arguments could Western make for claiming that Petragallo was an independent contractor?

c. Which side should prevail?

CHAPTER 20

Relationship with Third Parties

CHAPTER OUTCOMES

After reading and studying this chapter, you should be able to:

- Distinguish among actual express authority, actual implied authority, and apparent authority.

- Explain the contractual liability of the principal, agent, and third party when the principal is (1) disclosed, (2) unidentified (partially disclosed), and (3) undisclosed.

- Explain how apparent authority is terminated and the differences between actual and constructive notice.

- Describe the tort liability of a principal for the (1) authorized acts of agents, (2) authorized acts of employees, and (3) unauthorized acts of independent contractors.

- Explain the criminal liability of a principal for the acts of agents.

The purpose of an agency relationship is to allow the principal to extend his business activities by authorizing agents to enter into contracts with third persons on the principal's behalf. Accordingly, it is important that the law balance the competing interests of principals and third persons. The principal wants to be liable only for those contracts he actually authorizes the agent to make for him. The third party, on the other hand, wishes the principal bound on all contracts that the agent negotiates on the principal's behalf. As this chapter discusses, the law has adopted an intermediate outcome: the principal and the third party are bound to those contracts the principal actually authorizes plus those the principal has apparently authorized.

While pursuing her principal's business, an agent may tortiously injure third parties, who then may seek to hold the principal personally liable. Under what circumstances should the principal be held liable? Similar questions arise concerning a principal's criminal liability for an agent's violation of the criminal law. The law of agency has established rules to determine when the principal is liable for the torts and crimes his agents commit. These rules are discussed in this chapter.

Finally, what liability to the third party should the agent incur, and what rights should she acquire against the third party? Usually, the agent has no liability for, or rights under, the contracts she makes on behalf of her principal. As discussed in this chapter, however, in some situations, the agent has contractually created obligations or rights or both.

RELATIONSHIP OF PRINCIPAL AND THIRD PERSONS

This section first considers the contract liability of the principal; then it examines the principal's potential tort liability.

20-1 Contract Liability of Principal

The power of an agent is his ability to change the legal status of his principal. An agent having either actual or apparent authority has the power to bind his principal. Thus, whenever an agent, acting within his authority, makes a contract for his principal, he creates new rights or liabilities for his principal, thereby changing his principal's legal status. This power of an agent to act for his principal in business transactions is the basis of agency.

A principal's contract liability also depends upon whether the principal is disclosed, unidentified, or undisclosed. The principal is a **disclosed principal** if, when an agent and a third party interact, the third party has notice that the agent is acting for a principal and has notice of the principal's identity. The principal is an **unidentified principal** if, when an agent and a third party interact, the third party has notice that the agent is acting for a principal but does not have notice of the principal's identity. (Some courts refer to an unidentified principal as a "partially disclosed principal.") An example is an auctioneer who sells on behalf of a seller who is not identified: the seller is an unidentified principal (or a partially disclosed principal) since it is understood that the auctioneer acts as an agent. The principal is an **undisclosed principal** if, when an agent and a third party interact, the third party has no notice that the agent is acting for a principal. Restatement, Section 1.04(2).

20-1a TYPES OF AUTHORITY

Authority is of two basic types: actual and apparent. **Actual authority** depends upon consent that the principal manifests to the agent. Section 2.01. It may be either express or implied. In either case, such authority is binding and confers upon the agent both the power and the right to create or affect the principal's legal relations with third persons. Actual express authority does not depend on the third party having knowledge of the manifestations or statements made by the principal to the agent.

Apparent authority is based upon acts or conduct of the principal that lead a third person to believe that the agent, or supposed agent, has actual authority, upon which belief the third person *justifiably* relies. Section 2.03. This manifestation, which confers upon the agent the power to create a legal relationship between the principal and a third party, may consist of words or actions of the principal as well as other facts and circumstances that induce the third person reasonably to rely upon the existence of an agency relationship.

ACTUAL EXPRESS AUTHORITY The express authority of an agent, found in the spoken or written words the principal communicates to the agent, is actual authority stated in language directing or instructing the agent to do something specific. "As commonly used, the term 'express authority' often means actual authority that a principal has stated in very specific or detailed language." Restatement, Section 2.01, Comment b. Thus, if Perkins, orally or in writing, requests his agent Abbott to sell Perkins's automobile for $6,500, Abbott's authority to sell the car for this sum is actual and express.

ACTUAL IMPLIED AUTHORITY Implied authority is not found in express or explicit words of the principal but is inferred from words or conduct that the principal manifests to the agent. An agent has implied authority to do that which she reasonably believes the principal wishes her to do, based on the agent's reasonable interpretation of the principal's manifestations to her and all other facts she knows or should know. Restatement, Section 2.02. Implied authority may arise from customs and usages of the principal's business. In addition, the authority granted to an agent to accomplish a particular purpose necessarily includes the implied authority to employ the means reasonably required to accomplish it. Restatement, Section 2.02. For example, Pearson authorizes Arlington to manage her eighty-two-unit apartment complex but says nothing about expenses. To manage the building, Arlington needs to employ a janitor, purchase fuel for heating, and arrange for ordinary maintenance.

Even though Pearson has not expressly granted him the authority to incur such expenses, Arlington may, because such expenses are necessary to proper apartment management, reasonably infer the authority to incur them from the express authority to manage the building. On the other hand, suppose Paige employs Arthur, a real estate broker, to find a purchaser for her residence at a stated price. Arthur has no authority to contract for its sale.

◆ **SEE FIGURE 20-1:** *Contract Liability of Disclosed Principal*

◆ *See Case 20-1*

> ## *Practical Advice*
>
> *As a principal, clearly and specifically communicate to your agents the extent of their actual authority. As a third party, be sure to check with the principal when there is any doubt as to the actual authority of an agent; this is a more certain approach than relying upon the possibility that you will be able to prove that the agent had apparent authority.*

APPARENT AUTHORITY Apparent authority is power arising from words or conduct of a disclosed or unidentified principal that, when manifested to third persons, reasonably induce them to rely upon the assumption that actual authority exists. Restatement, Section 2.03. Apparent authority depends upon the principal's manifestations to the third party; an agent's own statements about the agent's authority do not by themselves create apparent authority. Apparent authority confers upon the agent, or supposed agent, the power to bind the disclosed or unidentified principal in contracts with third persons and precludes the principal from denying the existence of actual authority. Thus, when authority is apparent but not actual, the disclosed or unidentified principal is nonetheless bound by the act of the agent. By exceeding his actual authority, however, the agent violates his duty of obedience and is liable to the principal for any loss the principal suffers as a result of the agent's acting beyond his actual authority.

Common ways in which apparent authority may arise include the following:

1. When a principal appoints an agent to a position in an organization, third parties may reasonably believe that the agent has the authority to do those acts customary of an agent in such a position. (Apparent authority for agents of various business associations is discussed in *Parts* 6 and 7.)

2. If a principal has given an agent general authority to engage in a transaction, subsequently imposed limitations or restrictions will not affect the agent's apparent authority to engage in that transaction until third parties are notified of the restrictions.

FIGURE 20-1 Contract Liability of Disclosed Principal

Agent Has Actual Authority

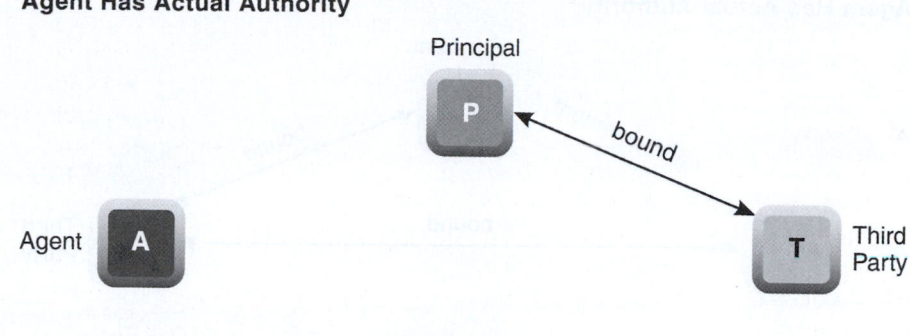

Agent Has Apparent Authority But Not Actual Authority

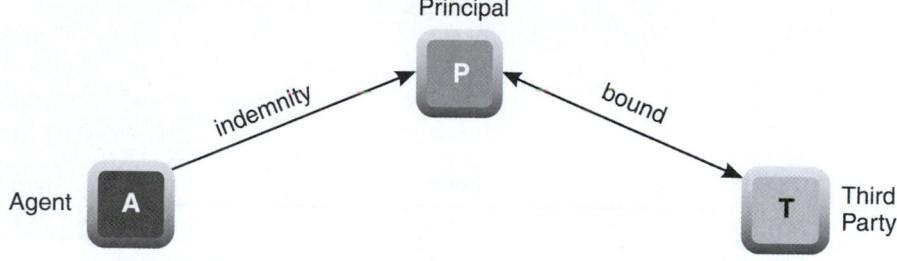

Agent Has No Actual or Apparent Authority

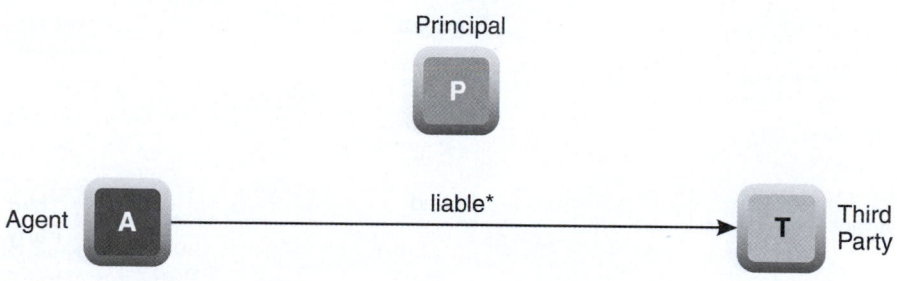

*Agent is liable for breach of implied warranty of authority or misrepresentation, as discussed later in this chapter.

3. The principal's acquiescence in prior similar transactions between the agent and a third party may create a basis for the third party reasonably to believe that the agent has apparent authority.

4. The agent shows the third party a document, such as a power of attorney, from the principal authorizing the agent to enter into such a transaction.

5. As discussed later, after many terminations of authority, an agent has lingering apparent authority until the third party has actual knowledge or receives notice of the termination.

For example, Peter writes a letter to Alice authorizing her to sell his automobile and sends a copy of the letter to Tomas, a prospective purchaser. On the following day, Peter writes a letter to Alice revoking the authority to sell the car but does not send a copy of the second letter to Tomas, who is not otherwise informed of the revocation. Although Alice has no actual authority to sell the car, she continues to have apparent authority with respect to Tomas. Or suppose that Arlene, in the presence of Polly, tells Thad that Arlene is Polly's agent to buy lumber. Although this statement is not true, Polly does not deny it, as she easily could. Thad, in reliance upon the statement, ships lumber to Polly on Arlene's order. Polly is obligated to pay for the lumber because Arlene had apparent authority to act on Polly's behalf. This apparent authority of Arlene exists only with respect to Thad. If Arlene were to give David an order for a shipment of lumber to Polly, David would be unable to hold Polly liable. Arlene would have had neither actual authority nor, as to David, apparent authority.

FIGURE 20-2   Contract Liability of Unidentified Principal

Agent Has Actual Authority

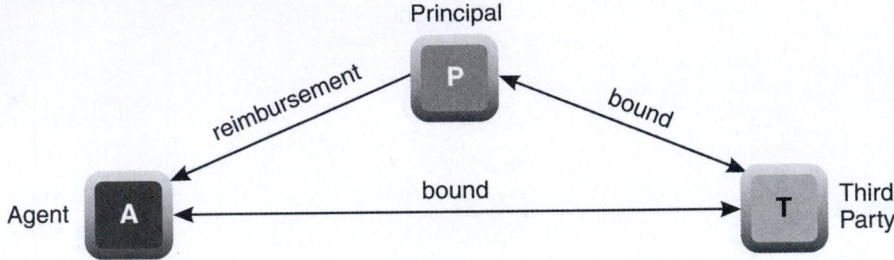

Agent Has Apparent Authority But Not Actual Authority

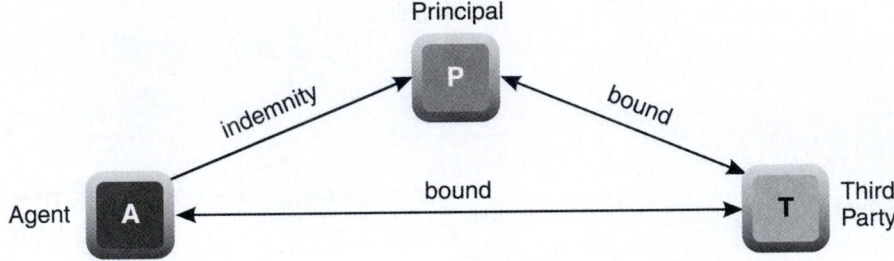

Agent Has No Actual or Apparent Authority

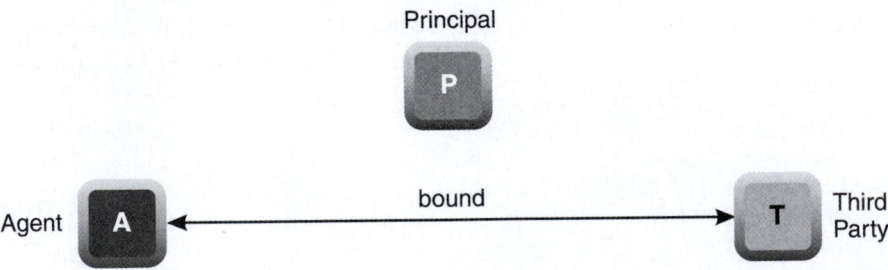

Because apparent authority is the power resulting from acts that appear to the third party to be authorized by the principal, apparent authority cannot exist where the principal is undisclosed. Nor can apparent authority exist where the third party knows that the agent has no actual authority.

◆ SEE FIGURE 20-2: *Contract Liability of Unidentified Principal*

◆ SEE FIGURE 20-3: *Contract Liability of Undisclosed Principal*

◆ *See Case 20-1*

Practical Advice

As a principal, be careful how you hold out your employees and agents because you may create apparent authority in them.

20-1b DELEGATION OF AUTHORITY

A subagent is a person appointed by an agent to perform functions that the agent has consented to perform on behalf of the agent's principal and for whose conduct the appointing agent is responsible to the principal. Restatement, Section 3.15(1). Because the appointment of an agent reflects the principal's confidence in and reliance upon the agent's personal skill, integrity, and other qualifications, an agent may appoint a subagent only if the agent has actual or apparent authority to do so. Restatement, Section 3.15(2).

If an agent is authorized to appoint subagents, the acts of the subagent are as binding on the principal as those performed by the agent. Restatement, Section 3.15, Comment b. As an agent of both the principal and the agent, the subagent owes a fiduciary duty to both. For example, P contracts with A, a real estate broker (agent), to sell P's house. P knows that A employs

FIGURE 20-3 Contract Liability of Undisclosed Principal

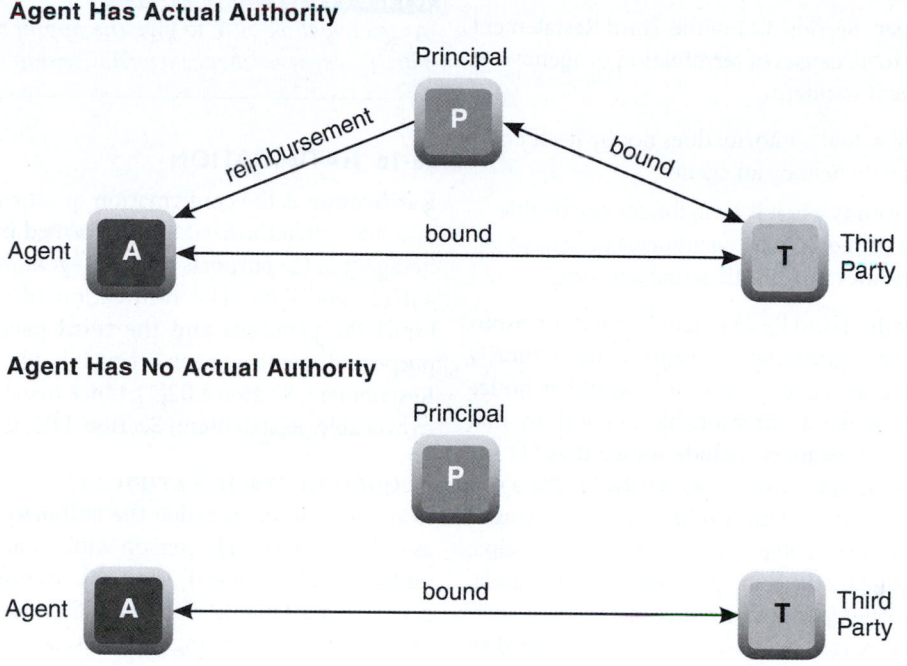

salespersons to show houses to prospective purchasers and to make representations about the property. The salespersons are A's employees and P's subagents.

If an agent having no authority to delegate her authority does so nevertheless, the acts of the subagent do not impose upon the principal any obligations or liability to third persons. Likewise, the principal acquires no rights against such third persons.

20-1c EFFECT OF TERMINATION OF AGENCY ON AUTHORITY

As discussed in *Chapter 19*, when an agency terminates, the agent's *actual authority* ceases. The Second and Third Restatements differ, however, regarding when an agent's *apparent authority* ceases.

SECOND RESTATEMENT In cases in which the performance of an authorized transaction becomes impossible, such as when the subject matter of the transaction is destroyed or the transaction is made illegal, the agent's *apparent authority* also expires and notice of such termination to third persons is *not* required. The bankruptcy of the principal terminates without notice the power of an agent to affect the principal's property, which has passed to the bankruptcy trustee.

When the termination is by the death or incapacity of the principal or agent, the Second Restatement provides that the agent's *apparent authority* also expires and notice of such

termination to third persons is not required. However, with respect to the death or incapacity of the principal, this rule has been legislatively changed in the great majority of States by the adoption of the Uniform Durable Power of Attorney Act or the Uniform Power of Attorney Act (UPOAA). Each Act provides that the death of a principal, who has executed a written power of attorney, whether or not it is durable, does not terminate the agency as to the attorney in fact (agent) or a third person who without actual knowledge of the principal's death acts in good faith under the power. Moreover, each Act provides that the incapacity of a principal, who has previously executed a written power of attorney that is *not* durable, does not terminate the agency as to the attorney in fact or a third person who without actual knowledge of the principal's incapacity acts in good faith under the power. If an agent is appointed under a durable power of attorney, the *actual* authority of an agent survives the incapacity of the principal.

In other cases, *apparent authority* continues until the third party has actual knowledge or receives actual notice, if that third party is one (1) with whom the agent had previously dealt on credit, (2) to whom the agent has been specially accredited, or (3) with whom the agent has begun to deal, as the principal should know. **Actual notice** requires a communication to the third party, either oral or written. If notice is given by mail, it is effective as actual notice upon delivery, not upon dispatch. All other third parties as to whom there was apparent authority must have actual knowledge or be given **constructive notice** through, for example, publication in a newspaper of general circulation in the area where the agency is regularly carried on.

THIRD RESTATEMENT Section 3.11 of the Third Restatement applies the same rule to *all* causes of termination of agency—it applies a reasonableness standard.

1. The termination of actual authority does not by itself end any apparent authority held by an agent.

2. Apparent authority ends when it is no longer reasonable for the third party with whom an agent deals to believe that the agent continues to act with actual authority.

The general rule of the Third Restatement is that it is reasonable for third parties to assume that an agent's actual authority continues ("lingers"), unless and until a third party has notice of circumstances that make it unreasonable to continue that assumption. These circumstances include notice that (1) the principal has revoked the agent's actual authority, (2) the agent has renounced it, or (3) circumstances otherwise have changed such that it is no longer reasonable to believe that the principal consents to the agent's act on the principal's behalf. Restatement, Section 3.11, Comment c. A person has **notice** of a fact if the person knows the fact, has reason to know the fact, has received an effective notification of the fact, or should know the fact to fulfill a duty owed to another person. Restatement, Section 1.04(4).

For example, if the principal tells a third party that the agent's authority has terminated, the former agent's lingering apparent authority with respect to that third party has terminated. Moreover, if a third party has notice of facts that call the agent's authority into question and these facts would prompt a reasonable person to make an inquiry of the principal before dealing with the agent, the agent no longer acts with apparent authority. In addition, suppose that a principal has furnished an agent with a power of attorney stating the extent, nature, and duration of the agent's actual authority. Before the stated expiration of the power of attorney, the principal terminates the agent's actual authority. At this time, the agent has a duty to return the power of attorney to the principal. If, however, the agent does not return the power of attorney to the principal, third parties to whom the agent shows the power of attorney would still be protected by apparent authority until the third parties have notice that actual authority had been terminated.

Consistent with this general rule—but contrary to the rule under the Second Restatement—a principal's death or loss of capacity does *not* automatically end the agent's apparent authority. In these instances, apparent authority terminates when the third party has (1) notice of the principal's death or (2) has notice that the principal's loss of capacity is permanent or that the principal has been adjudicated to lack capacity. Restatement, Sections 3.07 and 3.08. The Third Restatement's rule is consistent with the Uniform Durable Power of Attorney Act and the UPOAA.

◆ *See Case 20-2*

◆ *See Case 20-2*

Practical Advice

As principal, be sure to give the appropriate notice to third parties whenever an agency relationship terminates.

20-1d RATIFICATION

Ratification is the confirmation or affirmation by one person of a prior unauthorized act performed by another who (1) is his agent or (2) purports to be his agent. Restatement, Sections 4.01(1) and 4.03. The ratification of such act or contract binds the principal and the third party as if the agent or purported agent had been acting initially with actual authority. Restatement, Section 4.02(1). Once made, a valid ratification is irrevocable. Restatement, Section 4.02, Comment b.

REQUIREMENTS OF RATIFICATION Ratification may relate to acts that have exceeded the authority granted to an agent, as well as to acts that a person without any authority performs on behalf of an alleged principal. To effect a ratification, the principal must manifest an intent to do so with knowledge of all material facts concerning the transaction. Restatement, Section 4.06. The principal does not need to communicate this intent, which may be manifested by express language or implied from her conduct, such as accepting or retaining the benefits of a transaction. Thus, if Amanda, without authority, contracts in Penelope's name for the purchase of goods from Tate on credit and Penelope, having learned of Amanda's unauthorized act, accepts the goods from Tate, she thereby impliedly ratifies the contract and is bound on it. Furthermore, a principal may ratify an unauthorized action by failing to repudiate it once the principal knows the material facts about the agent's action. Restatement, Section 4.01, Comment f. If formalities are required for the authorization of an act, the same formalities apply to a ratification of that act. Restatement, Section 4.01, Comment e. In any event, the principal must ratify the entire act or contract. Restatement, Section 4.07.

Under the Third Restatement, a person may ratify an act if the actor acted *or* purported to act as an agent on the person's behalf. Restatement, Section 4.03. Under this section and a number of relatively recent cases, an undisclosed principal may ratify an agent's unauthorized act. This is *contrary* to the Second Restatement's rule, which requires that the actor must have indicated to the third person that he was acting on a principal's behalf. Thus, under the Second Restatement, there can be no ratification by an undisclosed principal. To illustrate: Archie, without any authority, contracts to sell to Tina an automobile belonging to Pierce. Archie states that the auto is his. Tina promises to pay $5,500 for the automobile. Pierce subsequently learns of the agreement and affirms. Under the Third Restatement, Pierce's affirmation of Archie's action *would* be a ratification because Archie had acted on behalf of Pierce. On the other hand, under the Second Restatement, it would *not* be a ratification because Archie did not indicate he was acting on behalf of a principal.

To be effective, ratification must occur before the third party gives notice of his withdrawal to the principal or agent. Restatement, Section 4.05(1). If the affirmance of a transaction occurs when the situation has so materially changed that it would be inequitable to subject the third party to liability, the third party may elect to avoid liability. Restatement, Section 4.05(2). For example, Alex has no authority but, purporting to act for Penny, contracts to sell Penny's house to Taylor. The next day, the house burns down. Penny then affirms. Taylor is not bound. Moreover, the power to ratify is terminated by the death or loss of capacity of the third party and by the lapse of a reasonable time. Restatement, Section 4.05, Comment b.

For ratification to be effective, the purported principal must have been in existence when the act was done. Restatement, Section 4.04(1)(a). For example, a promoter of a corporation not yet in existence may enter into contracts on behalf of the corporation. In the vast majority of States, however, the corporation cannot ratify these acts because the corporation did not exist when the contracts were made. Instead, the corporation may **adopt** the contract. Adoption differs from ratification because it is not retroactive and does not release the promoter from liability. See *Chapter 33*.

If a principal's lack of capacity entitles her to avoid transactions, the principal may also avoid any ratification made when under the incapacity. Restatement, Section 4.04(2). The principal, however, may ratify a contract that is voidable because of her incapacity when the incapacity no longer exists. Thus, after she reaches majority, a principal may ratify an unauthorized contract made on her behalf during her minority. She may also avoid any ratification made prior to attaining majority.

EFFECT OF RATIFICATION Ratification retroactively creates the effects of actual authority. Restatement, Section 4.02(1). Ratification is equivalent to prior authority, which means that the effect of ratification is substantially the same as if the agent or purported agent actually had been authorized when she performed the act. The respective rights, duties, and remedies of the principal and the third party are the same as if the agent had originally possessed actual authority. Both the principal and the agent are in the same position as they would have been if the principal had actually authorized the act originally. The agent is entitled to her due compensation and, moreover, is exonerated (freed) from liability to the principal for acting as his agent without authority or for exceeding her authority, as the case may be. Between the agent and the third party, the agent is released from any liability she may have to the third party by reason of her having induced the third party to enter into the contract without the principal's authority.

♦ *See Case 20-1*

20-1e FUNDAMENTAL RULES OF CONTRACTUAL LIABILITY

The following rules summarize the contractual relations between the principal and the third party:

1. A disclosed principal and the third party are parties to the contract if the agent acts within her actual or apparent authority in making the contract on the principal's behalf. Restatement, Section 6.01(1). See *Figure 20-1*.

2. An unidentified (partially disclosed) principal and the third party are parties to the contract if the agent acts within her actual or apparent authority in making the contract on the principal's behalf. Restatement, Section 6.02(1). See *Figure 20-2*.

3. An undisclosed principal and the third party are parties to the contract if the agent acts within her actual authority in making the contract on the principal's behalf unless the terms of the contract exclude the principal or his existence is fraudulently concealed. Restatement, Sections 6.03 and 6.11(4). See *Figure 20-3*.

4. No principal is a party to a contract with a third party if the agent acts without any authority in making the contract on the principal's behalf, unless the principal ratifies the contract. Restatement, Section 4.02. Under the Second Restatement, the principal must have been either disclosed or unidentified.

20-2 Tort Liability of Principal

In addition to being contractually liable to third persons, a principal may be liable in tort to third persons because of the acts of her agent. Tort liability may arise directly or indirectly (vicariously) from authorized or unauthorized acts of an agent. Also, a principal is liable for the unauthorized torts an agent commits in connection with a transaction that the purported principal, with full knowledge of the tort, subsequently ratifies. Restatement, Sections 4.01 and 7.04. Cases involving unauthorized but ratified torts are extremely rare. Of course, in all of these situations, the wrongdoing agent is personally liable to the injured persons because he committed the tort. Restatement, Section 7.01.

♦ **SEE FIGURE 20-4:** *Tort Liability*

20-2a DIRECT LIABILITY OF PRINCIPAL

A principal is liable for his own tortious conduct involving the use of agents. Such liability primarily arises in one of two ways. First, a principal is directly liable in damages for harm resulting from his directing an agent to commit a tort. Second, the principal is directly liable if he fails to exercise reasonable care in employing competent agents.

AUTHORIZED ACTS OF AGENT A principal who authorizes his agent to commit a tortious act with respect to the property or person of another is liable for the injury or loss that person sustains. This liability also extends to unauthorized tortious conduct that the principal subsequently ratifies. Restatement, Section 7.04(1). The authorized act is that of the principal. Thus, if Phillip directs his agent, Anthony, to enter upon Clark's land and cut timber, which neither Phillip nor Anthony has any right to do, the cutting of the timber is a trespass, and Phillip is liable to Clark. A principal may be subject to tort liability because of an agent's conduct even though the agent is not subject to liability. Restatement, Section 7.04(2). For example, Phillip instructs his agent, Anthony, to make certain representations as to Phillip's property, which Anthony is authorized to sell. Phillip knows these representations are

---

FIGURE 20-4   **Tort Liability**

Agent's Tort Authorized

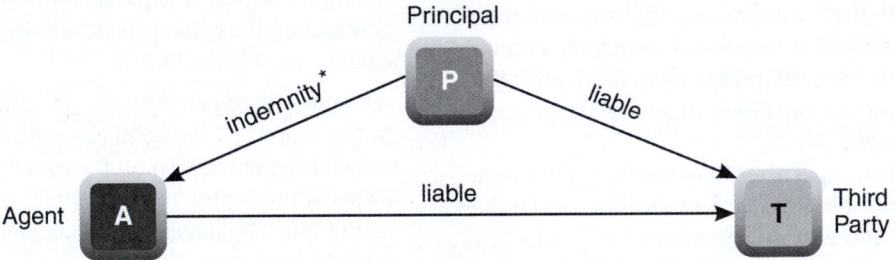

Employee's Tort Unauthorized But Within Scope of Employment

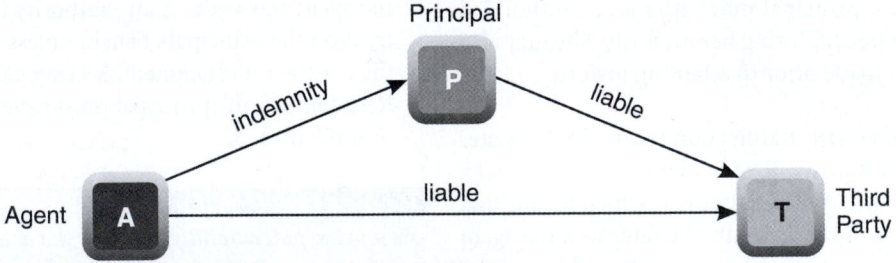

Employee's Tort Outside Authority and Scope of Employment or Independent Contractor's Tort Unauthorized

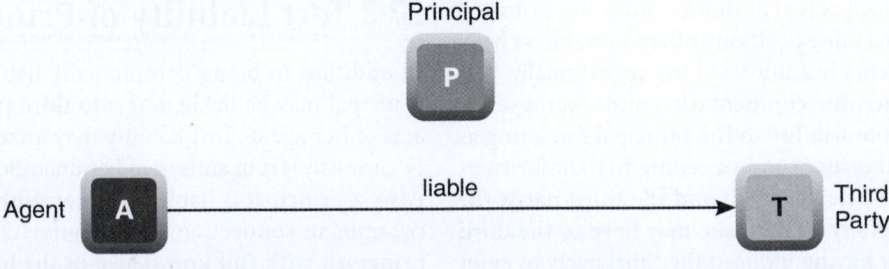

*If not illegal or known by A to be wrongful.

false, but Anthony does not know and has no reason or duty to know. Such representations by Anthony to Tammy, who buys the property in reliance on them, constitute a deceit for which Phillip is liable to Tammy. Anthony, however, would not be liable to Tammy.

UNAUTHORIZED ACTS OF AGENT A principal who negligently conducts activities through an employee or other agent is liable for harm resulting from such conduct. Restatement, Section 7.05(1). For example, a principal is liable if he negligently (1) selects agents, (2) retains agents, (3) trains agents, (4) supervises agents, or (5) otherwise controls agents.

The liability of a principal under this provision—called **negligent hiring**—arises when the principal does not exercise proper care in selecting an agent for the job to be done. For example, if Patricia lends to her employee, Art, a company car with which to run a business errand knowing that Art is incapable of driving the vehicle, Patricia would be liable for her own negligence to anyone injured through Art's unsafe driving. The negligent hiring doctrine also has been used to impose liability on a principal for intentional torts committed by an agent against customers of the principal or members of the public where the principal either knew or should have known that the agent was violent or aggressive.

♦ *See Case 20-3*

20-2b VICARIOUS LIABILITY OF PRINCIPAL FOR UNAUTHORIZED ACTS OF AGENT

The vicarious liability of a principal for the unauthorized torts of an agent depends primarily on whether the agent is an employee. In this context, an employee is an agent whose principal controls or has the right to control the manner and means of the agent's performance of work. Restatement, Section 7.07(3)(a). By comparison, if the principal does *not* control the manner and means of the agent's performance of the work, the agent is not an employee and is often referred to as an "independent contractor." The general rule is that a principal is not liable for physical harm caused by the tortious conduct of an agent who is an independent contractor if the principal did not intend or authorize the result or the manner of performance. Conversely, a principal is liable for an unauthorized tort committed by an employee acting within the scope of his employment. Restatement, Section 7.07(1).

RESPONDEAT SUPERIOR An employer is subject to vicarious liability for an unauthorized tort committed by his employee, even one that is in flagrant disobedience of his instructions, if the employee committed the tort within the scope of his employment. This form of employer liability without fault is based upon the doctrine of *respondeat superior* (let the superior respond). It does not matter how carefully the employer

selected the employee, if in fact the latter tortiously injures a third party while engaged in the scope of employment. Moreover, an *undisclosed* principal-employer is liable for the torts committed by her employee within the scope of employment. Furthermore, the principal is liable even if the work is performed gratuitously so long as the principal controls or has the right to control the manner and means of the agent's performance of work. Restatement, Section 7.07(3)(b).

The doctrine of *respondeat superior* is fundamental to the operation of tort law in the United States. The rationale for this doctrine is that a person who conducts his business activities through the use of employees should be liable for the employees' tortious conduct in carrying out those activities. The employer is more likely to insure against liability and is more likely to have the assets to satisfy a tort judgment than the employee. Moreover, *respondeat superior* creates an economic incentive for employers to exercise care in choosing, training, and supervising employees.

The liability of the principal under *respondeat superior* is vicarious or derivative and depends upon proof of wrongdoing by the employee *within the scope of his employment*. Restatement, Section 7.07. The employer's vicarious liability to the third party is in *addition* to the agent's liability to the third party. Frequently both principal and employee are joined as defendants in the same suit. Because the liability of the employer is based upon the employee's tortious conduct, if the employee is not held liable, the principal is not liable either. A principal who is held liable for her employee's tort has a right of **indemnification** against the employee, or the right to be reimbursed for the amount that she was required to pay as a result of the employee's wrongful act. Frequently, however, an employee is unable to reimburse his employer, who then must bear the brunt of the liability.

The wrongful act of the employee must be connected with his employment and within its scope if the principal is to be held liable for injuries or damage resulting to third persons. Section 7.07(2) of the Restatement provides a general rule for determining whether the conduct of an employee is within the scope of employment:

> An employee acts within the scope of employment when performing work assigned by the employer or engaging in a course of conduct subject to the employer's control. An employee's act is not within the scope of employment when it occurs within an independent course of conduct not intended by the employee to serve any purpose of the employer.

For example, Eugene, while delivering gasoline for Packer Oil Co., lights his pipe and negligently throws the blazing match into a pool of gasoline that has dripped onto the ground during the delivery. The gasoline ignites, burning Ray's filling station. Packer is subject to liability for the resulting harm because the negligence of the employee who delivered the gasoline relates directly to the manner in which he handled the goods in his custody. But if a chauffeur, while driving his employer's car on an errand for his employer, suddenly decides to shoot his pistol at pedestrians for target practice, the employer would not be liable to the pedestrians. This willful and intentional misconduct is not related to the performance of the services for which the chauffeur was employed, nor is it expectable by the employer.

To further illustrate, if Page employs Earl to deliver merchandise to Page's customers in a specified city and while driving a delivery truck to or from a place of delivery Earl negligently causes the truck to hit and injure Fred, Page is liable to Fred for the injuries he sustains. But if after making the scheduled deliveries Earl drives the truck to a neighboring city to visit a friend and while so doing negligently causes the truck to hit and injure Dottie, Page is not liable. In the latter case, Earl is said to be on a "frolic of his own." By using the truck to accomplish his own purposes, not those of his employer, he has deviated from serving any purpose of his employer.

A principal may be held liable for the intentional torts of his employee if the commission of the tort is so reasonably connected with the employment as to be within its scope. For example, a principal would be liable if his employee were to make fraudulent statements about the products she is selling, defame a competitor, or disparage the competitor's product.

AGENT ACTS WITH APPARENT AUTHORITY "A principal is subject to vicarious liability for a tort committed by an agent in dealing or communicating with a third party on or purportedly on behalf of the principal when actions taken by the agent with apparent authority constitute the tort or enable the agent to conceal its commission." Restatement, Section 7.08. This liability applies to (1) agents, whether or not they are employees, and (2) agents who are employees but whose tortious conduct is not within the scope of employment under *respondeat superior*. The torts to which this rule applies include fraudulent and negligent misrepresentations, defamation, wrongful institution of legal proceedings, and conversion of property. For example, Pillsbury engages Adams as an agent to sell some land. While negotiating with Trent, Adams states that a stream running through the property has not overflowed its banks during the past ten years. Adams knows that this is false. In reliance upon this false statement, Trent purchases the land. Pillsbury is liable to Trent for fraudulent misrepresentation.

TORTS OF INDEPENDENT CONTRACTOR As previously indicated, an independent contractor is not the employee of the person for whom he is performing work or rendering services. Hence, the doctrine of *respondeat superior* generally does not apply to torts committed by an independent contractor. For example, Parnell authorizes Bob, his broker, to sell land for

him. Parnell, Teresa, and Bob meet in Teresa's office, where Bob arranges the sale to Teresa. While Bob is preparing the deed for Parnell to sign, he negligently knocks over an inkstand and ruins a valuable rug belonging to Teresa. Bob, but not Parnell, is liable to Teresa. Similarly, Patty employs Igor, a roofer, as an independent contractor to repair her roof. Igor drops a hammer upon Wanda, a pedestrian walking by on the public sidewalk. Igor, but not Patty, is liable to Wanda.

Nonetheless, the principal may be *directly* liable if she fails to exercise reasonable care in selecting an independent contractor. For example, Melanie employs Gordon, whom she knows to be an alcoholic, as an independent contractor to repair her roof. Gordon attempts the repairs while heavily intoxicated and negligently drops a fifty-pound bundle of shingles upon Eric, a pedestrian walking on the sidewalk. Both Gordon and Melanie are liable to Eric.

Moreover, under some circumstances, a principal will be *vicariously* liable for torts committed by a carefully selected independent contractor. Certain duties imposed by law are nondelegable, and a person may not escape the consequences of their nonperformance by having entrusted them to another person, whether or not that person is an agent. Restatement, Section 7.06. For example, a landowner who permits an independent contractor to maintain a dangerous condition on his premises, such as an excavation neither surrounded by a guardrail nor lit at night, adjoining a public sidewalk is liable to a member of the public who is injured by falling into the excavation.

A principal is also vicariously liable for an independent contractor's conduct in carrying on an abnormally dangerous activity, such as using fire or high explosives or spraying crops.

> **Practical Advice**
>
> *As a principal, consider hiring an independent contractor to limit your potential tort liability.*

20-3 Criminal Liability of Principal

A principal is liable for the authorized criminal acts of his agents only if the principal directed, participated in, or approved of the acts. For example, if an agent, at his principal's direction or with his principal's knowledge, fixes prices with the principal's competitors, both the agent and the principal have criminally violated the antitrust laws. Otherwise, a principal ordinarily is not liable for the unauthorized criminal acts of his agents. One of the elements of a crime is mental fault, and this element is absent, so far as the criminal responsibility of the principal is concerned, in cases in which the principal did not authorize the agent's act.

An employer may, nevertheless, be subject to a criminal penalty for the act of an advisory or managerial person acting in the scope of employment. Moreover, an employer may be criminally liable under liability without fault statutes for certain unauthorized acts of an employee, whether the employee is managerial or not. These statutes, which usually are regulatory, do not require mental fault. For example, many States have statutes that punish "every person who by himself or his employee or agent sells anything at short weight," or "whoever sells liquor to a minor and any sale by an employee shall be deemed the act of the employer as well." Another example is a statute prohibiting the sale of unwholesome or adulterated food. See *Chapter 6* for a more detailed discussion of this topic.

RELATIONSHIP OF AGENT AND THIRD PERSONS

The function of an agent is to assist in the conduct of the principal's business by carrying out his orders. Generally, the agent acquires no rights against third parties and likewise incurs no liabilities to them. There are, however, several exceptions to this general proposition. In certain instances, an agent may become personally liable to the third party for contracts she made on behalf of her principal. In some of these situations, the agent also may acquire rights against the third party. In addition, an agent who commits a tort is personally liable to the injured third party. These circumstances involving the personal liability of an agent, as well as those in which an agent may acquire rights against third persons, are covered in this section.

20-4 Contract Liability of Agent

The agent normally is not a party to the contract he makes with a third person on behalf of a disclosed principal. An agent who exceeds his actual and apparent authority, however, may be personally liable to the third party. In addition, an agent acting for a disclosed principal may become liable if he expressly assumes liability on the contract. When an agent enters into a contract on behalf of an unidentified (partially disclosed) principal or an undisclosed principal, the agent becomes personally liable to the third party on the contract. Furthermore, an agent who knowingly enters into a contract on behalf of a nonexistent or completely incompetent principal is personally liable to the third party on that contract.

20-4a DISCLOSED PRINCIPAL

As explained, the principal is a disclosed principal if, when an agent and a third party interact, the third party has notice that the agent is acting for a principal and also has notice of the principal's identity. The liability of an agent acting for a disclosed principal depends on whether the agent acts within her authority in making the contract or otherwise assumes liability on the contract.

AUTHORIZED CONTRACTS When an agent acting with actual or apparent authority makes a contract with a third party on behalf of a disclosed principal, the agent is not a party to the contract unless she and the third party agree otherwise. Restatement, Section 6.01(2). The third person is on notice that he is transacting business with an agent who is acting for an identified principal and that the agent is not personally undertaking to perform the contract, but is simply negotiating on behalf of her principal. The resulting contract, if within the agent's actual authority, is between the third person and the principal, and the agent ordinarily incurs no liability on the contract to either party. Thus, Angela, who has actual authority to sell circuit boards manufactured by Pinter, writes to Toni, "On behalf of Pinter, I offer to sell you 5,000 circuit boards for $15,000." Toni accepts; consequently, a contract exists between Toni and Pinter. Angela is not a party to that contract and has no liability to Pinter or Toni. This is also true of unauthorized contracts that are subsequently ratified by the principal. If, however, the agent has apparent authority but no actual authority, he has no liability to the third party but is liable to the principal for any loss he causes by exceeding his actual authority.

♦ SEE FIGURE 20-1: *Contract Liability of Disclosed Principal*

Practical Advice
When signing contracts as an agent, be sure to indicate clearly your representative capacity.

UNAUTHORIZED CONTRACTS If an agent exceeds his actual *and* apparent authority, the principal is not bound. The fact that the principal is not bound does not, however, make the agent a party to the contract unless the agent had agreed to be a party to the contract. The agent's liability, if any, arises from express or implied representations about his authority that he makes to the third party. For example, an agent may give an **express warranty of authority** by stating that he has authority and that he will be personally liable to the third party if he does not in fact have the authority to bind his principal.

Moreover, a person who undertakes to make a contract on behalf of another gives an **implied warranty of authority** that he is in fact authorized to make the contract on behalf of the party whom he purports to represent. If the agent does not have authority to bind the principal, the agent is liable to the third party for damages unless the principal ratifies the contract or the third party knew that the agent was unauthorized. Restatement, Section 6.10. No implied warranty of authority exists, however, if the agent expressly states that the agent gives no warranty of authority or if the agent, acting in good faith, discloses to the third person all of the facts upon which his authority rests. For example, agent Larson has received an ambiguous letter of instruction from his principal, Dan. Larson shows it to Carol, stating that it represents all of the authority that he has to act, and both Larson and Carol rely upon its sufficiency. Larson has made no implied or express warranty of his authority to Carol.

The Restatement provides that breach of the implied warranty of authority subjects the agent to liability to the third party for damages caused by breach of that warranty, including loss of the benefit expected from performance by the principal. Restatement, Section 6.10. Some courts, however, limit the third party's recovery to the damage or loss the third party suffered and exclude the third party's expected gain from the contract.

If a purported agent **misrepresents** to a third person that he has authority to make a contract on behalf of a principal whom he has no power to bind, he is liable in a tort action to the third person for the loss she sustained in reliance upon the misrepresentation. If the third party knows, however, that the representation is false, then the agent is not liable.

AGENT ASSUMES LIABILITY An agent for a disclosed principal may agree to become liable on a contract between the principal and the third party (1) by making the contract in her own name, (2) by co-making the contract with the principal, or (3) by guaranteeing that the principal will perform the contract between the third party and the principal. In each situation, the agent's liability is separate unless the parties agree otherwise. Therefore, the third party may sue the agent separately without joining the principal and may obtain a judgment against either the principal or the agent or both. If the principal satisfies the judgment, the agent is discharged. If the agent pays the judgment, he usually will have a right of reimbursement from the principal. This right is based upon the principles of suretyship, discussed in *Chapter 37*.

20-4b UNIDENTIFIED PRINCIPAL

As discussed, the principal is an unidentified principal (partially disclosed principal) if, when an agent and a third party interact, the third party has notice that the agent is acting for a principal but does not have notice of the principal's identity. The use of an unidentified principal may be helpful when, for example, the third party might inflate the price of property he was selling if he knew the principal's identity. Partial disclosure also may occur inadvertently, when the agent fails through neglect to inform the third party of the principal's identity.

Unless otherwise agreed, when an agent makes a contract with actual or apparent authority on behalf of an unidentified principal, the agent is a party to the contract. Restatement, Section 6.02. For example, Ashley writes to Terrence offering to sell a rare painting on behalf of its owner, who wishes to remain unknown. Terrence accepts. Ashley is a party to the contract.

Whether the particular transaction is authorized or not, an agent for an unidentified principal is liable to the third party. If the agent is actually or apparently authorized to make the contract, then both the agent and the unidentified principal are liable. If the agent has no actual and no apparent authority, the agent is liable either as a party to the contract or for breach of the implied warranty of authority. Restatement, Section 6.02, Comment b. In any event, the agent is separately liable, and the third party may sue her individually without joining the principal and may obtain a judgment against either the principal or the agent or both. If the principal satisfies the judgment, the agent is also discharged. Restatement, Section 6.09. If the agent pays the judgment, the principal is discharged from liability to the third party, but the agent has the right to be reimbursed by the principal.

◆ **SEE FIGURE 20-2:** *Contract Liability of Unidentified Principal*

20-4c UNDISCLOSED PRINCIPAL

The principal is an undisclosed principal if, when an agent and a third party interact, the third party has no notice that the agent is acting for a principal. Thus, when an agent acts for an undisclosed principal, she appears to be acting on her own behalf and the third person with whom she is dealing has no knowledge that she is acting as an agent. The principal has instructed the agent to conceal not only the principal's identity but also the agency relationship. Such concealment can also occur if the agent simply neglects to disclose the existence and identity of her principal. Thus, the third person is dealing with the agent as though she were a principal.

The agent is personally liable upon a contract she enters into with a third person on behalf of an undisclosed principal. Restatement, Section 6.03(2). The agent is liable because the third person has relied upon the agent individually and has accepted the agent's personal undertaking to perform the contract. Obviously, where the principal is undisclosed, the third person does not know of the interest of anyone in the contract other than that of himself and the agent.

The Second Restatement and many cases hold that after the third person has learned of the identity of the undisclosed principal, he may obtain performance of the contract from either the principal or the agent, but not both, and his choice, once made, binds him irrevocably. Nevertheless, to avoid the possibility that evidence at trial will fail to establish the agency relationship, the third person may bring suit against both the principal and agent. In most States following this approach, this act of bringing suit and proceeding to trial against both is not an election, but before the entry of any judgment, the third person is compelled to make an election because he is not entitled to a judgment against both. A judgment against the agent by a third party who knows the identity of the previously undisclosed principal discharges the liability of the principal. In this case, the agent would have the right to be reimbursed by the principal. If, however, the third party obtains a judgment against the agent before learning the principal's identity, the principal is not discharged. Finally, the agent is discharged from liability if the third party gets a judgment against the principal.

The Third Restatement and a number of States have recently rejected the election rule, holding that a third party's rights against the principal are *additional* and not alternative to the third party's rights against the agent. Section 6.09 provides, "When an agent has made a contract with a third party on behalf of a principal, unless the contract provides otherwise, the liability, if any, of the principal or the agent to the third party is not discharged if the third party obtains a judgment against the other." However, the liability, if any, of the principal or the agent to the third party *is* discharged to the extent a judgment against the other is satisfied.

♦ **SEE FIGURE 20-3:** *Contract Liability of Undisclosed Principal*

♦ *See Case 20-4*

20-4d NONEXISTENT OR INCOMPETENT PRINCIPAL

Unless the third party agrees otherwise, if a person who purports to act as an agent knows or has reason to know that the person purportedly represented does not exist or completely lacks capacity to be a party to contract, the person purporting to act as agent will become a party to the contract. Restatement, Section 6.04. Complete lack of capacity to contract includes an individual person who has been adjudicated incompetent. An example of a nonexistent principal is a corporation or limited liability corporation (LLC) that has not yet been formed. Thus, a promoter of a corporation who enters into contracts with third persons in the name of a corporation yet to be organized is personally liable on such contracts. Not yet in existence, and therefore unable to authorize the contracts, the corporation is not liable. If, after coming into existence, the corporation affirmatively adopts a preincorporation contract made on its behalf, it, in addition to the promoter, becomes bound. If the corporation enters into a new contract with such a third person, however, the prior contract between the promoter and the third person is discharged, and the liability of the promoter is terminated. This is a novation.

♦ **SEE FIGURE 33-1:** *Promoter's Preincorporation Contracts Made in Corporation's Name*

An agent who makes a contract for a disclosed principal whose contracts are *voidable* for lack of contractual capacity is *not* liable to the third party. Restatement, Section 6.04, Comment b. There are two exceptions to this rule: (1) if the agent warrants or represents that the principal has capacity or (2) if the agent has reason to know of both the principal's lack of capacity and the third party's ignorance of that incapacity.

20-5 Tort of Liability of Agent

An agent is personally liable for his tortious acts that injure third persons, whether the principal authorizes such acts or not and whether or not the principal also may be liable. Restatement, Section 7.01. For example, an agent is personally liable if he converts the goods of a third person to his principal's use. An agent is also liable for making representations that he knows to be fraudulent to a third person who in reliance sustains a loss.

20-6 Rights of Agent Against Third Person

An agent who makes a contract with a third person on behalf of a disclosed principal usually has no right of action against the third person for breach of contract. Restatement, Section 6.01. The agent is not a party to the contract. An agent for a disclosed principal may sue on the contract, however, if it provides that the agent is a party to the contract. Furthermore, an agent for an undisclosed principal or an unidentified (partially disclosed) principal may maintain in her own name an action against the third person for breach of contract. Restatement, Sections 6.02 and 6.03.

C H A P T E R   S U M M A R Y

RELATIONSHIP OF PRINCIPAL AND THIRD PERSONS

| CONTRACT LIABILITY OF PRINCIPAL | **Types of Principals**
• *Disclosed Principal* principal whose existence and identity are known
• *Unidentified (Partially Disclosed) Principal* principal whose existence is known but whose identity is not known
• *Undisclosed Principal* principal whose existence and identity are not known |

Authority power of an agent to change the legal status of the principal
- *Actual Authority* power conferred upon the agent by actual consent manifested by the principal to the agent
- *Actual Express Authority* actual authority derived from written or spoken words of the principal communicated to the agent
- *Actual Implied Authority* actual authority inferred from words or conduct manifested to the agent by the principal
- *Apparent Authority* power conferred upon the agent by acts or conduct of the principal that reasonably lead a third party to believe that the agent has such power

Delegation of Authority is usually not permitted unless actually or apparently authorized by the principal; if the agent is authorized to appoint other subagents, the acts of these subagents are as binding on the principal as those of the agent

Effect of Termination of Agency on Authority ends *actual* authority
- *Second Restatement* if the termination is by operation of law, *apparent* authority also ends without notice to third parties; if the termination is by an act of the parties, *apparent* authority ends when third parties have actual knowledge or when appropriate notice is given to third parties: actual notice must be given to third parties with whom the agent has previously dealt on credit, has been specially accredited, or has begun to deal; all other third parties as to whom there was apparent authority need be given only constructive notice
- *Third Restatement* termination of actual authority does not by itself end any apparent authority held by an agent; *apparent* authority ends when it is no longer reasonable for the third party with whom an agent deals to believe that the agent continues to act with actual authority

Ratification affirmation by one person of a prior unauthorized act that another has done as her agent or as her purported agent

Fundamental Rules of Contractual Liability
- *Disclosed Principal* is contractually bound with the third party if the agent acts within her actual or apparent authority in making the contract on the principal's behalf
- *Partially Disclosed Principal* is contractually bound with the third party if the agent acts within her actual or apparent authority in making the contract on the principal's behalf
- *Undisclosed Principal* is contractually bound with the third party if the agent acts within her actual authority in making the contract on the principal's behalf

---

TORT LIABILITY OF PRINCIPAL

Direct Liability of Principal a principal is liable for his own tortious conduct involving the use of agents
- *Authorized Acts of Agent* a principal is liable for torts that she authorizes another to commit or that she ratifies
- *Unauthorized Acts of Agent* a principal is liable for failing to exercise reasonable care in employing agents whose unauthorized acts cause harm

Vicarious Liability of Principal for Unauthorized Acts of Agent
- *Respondeat Superior* an employer is liable for unauthorized torts committed by an employee in the scope of his employment
- *Agent Acts with Apparent Authority* a principal is liable for torts committed by an agent in dealing with third parties while acting within the agent's apparent authority
- *Independent Contractor* a principal is usually not liable for the unauthorized torts of an independent contractor

CRIMINAL LIABILITY OF PRINCIPAL	**Authorized Acts** the principal is liable if he directed, participated in, or approved the criminal acts of his agents **Unauthorized Acts** the principal may be liable either for a criminal act of a managerial person or under liability without fault statutes

RELATIONSHIP OF AGENT AND THIRD PERSONS

CONTRACT LIABILITY OF AGENT	**Disclosed Principal** • *Authorized Contracts* the agent is not normally a party to the contract she makes with a third person if she has actual or apparent authority or if the principal ratifies an unauthorized contract • *Unauthorized Contracts* if an agent exceeds her actual and apparent authority, the principal is not bound but the agent may be liable to the third party for breach of warranty or for misrepresentation • *Agent Assumes Liability* an agent may agree to become liable on a contract between the principal and the third party **Unidentified (Partially Disclosed) Principal** an agent who acts for a partially disclosed principal is a party to the contract with the third party unless otherwise agreed **Undisclosed Principal** an agent who acts for an undisclosed principal is personally liable on the contract to the third party **Nonexistent or Incompetent Principal** a person who purports to act as an agent for a principal whom the agent knows to be nonexistent or completely incompetent is personally liable on a contract entered into with a third person on behalf of such a principal
TORT LIABILITY OF AGENT	**Authorized Acts** the agent is liable to the third party for his own torts **Unauthorized Acts** the agent is liable to the third party for his own torts
RIGHTS OF AGENT AGAINST THIRD PERSON	**Disclosed Principal** the agent usually has no rights against the third party **Unidentified (Partially Disclosed) Principal** the agent may enforce the contract against the third party **Undisclosed Principal** the agent may enforce the contract against the third party

C A S E S

CASE 20-1

Types of Authority; Ratification:
SCHOENBERGER v. CHICAGO TRANSIT AUTHORITY
Appellate Court of Illinois, First District, First Division, 1980
84 Ill.App.3d 1132, 39 Ill.Dec. 941, 405 N.E.2d 1076

Campbell, J.

The plaintiff, James Schoenberger, brought a small claims action * * * in the * * * circuit court of Cook County against the defendant, Chicago Transit Authority (herein-after C.TA.) to recover contract damages. The trial court ruled in favor of the defendant and against the plaintiff. The plaintiff appeals from this judgment. At issue is whether the C.T.A. may be held liable under agency principles of a promise allegedly made by

an employee of the C.T.A. to the plaintiff at the time that he was hired to the effect that he would receive a $500 increase in salary within a specified period of time. We affirm.

Schoenberger was employed by the C.T.A. from August 16, 1976, to October, 1976, at a salary of $19,300. The facts surrounding his employment with the C.T.A. are controverted. The plaintiff's position at the trial was that he took the job with the C.T.A. at a salary of $19,300 upon the condition that he would receive a $500 salary increase, above and beyond any merit raises, within a year. Schoenberger testified at trial that, after filling out a job application and undergoing an initial interview with a C.T.A. Placement Department interviewer, he met several times with Frank ZuChristian, who was in charge of recruiting for the Data Center. At one of the meetings with ZuChristian, the Director of Data Center Operations, John Bonner, was present. At the third meeting held between ZuChristian and the plaintiff, ZuChristian informed the plaintiff that he desired to employ him at $19,800 and that he was making a recommendation to this effect. Schoenberger told ZuChristian that he would accept the offer. ZuChristian informed him that a formal offer would come from the Placement Department within a few days. However, when the offer was made, the salary was stated at $19,300. Schoenberger did not accept the offer immediately. Rather, he called ZuChristian for an explanation of the salary difference. After making inquiries, ZuChristian informed Schoenberger that a clerical error had been made and that it would take a number of weeks to have the necessary paperwork reapproved because several people were on vacation. To expedite matters, ZuChristian suggested Schoenberger take the job at the $19,300 figure and that he would see that the $500 would be made up to him at the April, October, 1976, or at the latest, the April, performance and salary review. The $500 increase was to be prospective and not retroactive in nature. John Hogan, the head of the Data Center, was aware of this promise, ZuChristian informed Schoenberger. Because the defendant was found to be ineligible for the October, 1976 performance evaluation and the April, 1976 review was cancelled, the April, 1977 evaluation was the first evaluation at which the issue of the salary increase was raised. When the increase was not given at that time, the plaintiff resigned and filed this suit.

* * *

The trial court, after hearing the evidence and reviewing the exhibits, ruled in favor of the defendant. The trial court ruled: (1) that it was inconceivable that the plaintiff thought ZuChristian had final authority in regard to employment contracts; and (2) that it was not shown that a commitment or promise was made to the plaintiff by an authorized agent of the C.T.A.

* * *

The main question before us is whether ZuChristian, acting as an agent of the C.T.A., orally contracted with Schoenberger for $500 in compensation in addition to his $19,300 salary. The authority of an agent may only come from the principal and it is therefore necessary to trace the source of an agent's authority to some word or act of the alleged principal. [Citations.] The authority to bind a principal will not be presumed, but rather, the person alleging authority must prove its source unless the act of the agent has been ratified.

[Citations.] Moreover, the authority must be founded upon some word or act of the principal, not on the acts or words of the agent. [Citations.]

* * * Both Hogan and Bonner, ZuChristian's superiors, testified that ZuChristian had no actual authority to either make an offer of a specific salary to Schoenberger or to make any promise of additional compensation. Furthermore, ZuChristian's testimony corroborated the testimony that he lacked the authority to make formal offers. From this evidence, it is clear that the trial court properly determined that ZuChristian lacked the actual authority to bind the C.T.A. for the additional $500 in compensation to Schoenberger.

Nor can it be said that the C.T.A. clothed ZuChristian with the apparent authority to make Schoenberger a promise of compensation over and above that formally offered by the Placement Department. The general rule to consider in determining whether an agent is acting within the apparent authority of his principal was stated in [citation] in this way:

> Apparent authority in an agent is such authority as the principal knowingly permits the agent to assume or which he holds his agent out as possessing—it is such authority as a reasonably prudent man, exercising diligence and discretion, in view of the principal's conduct, would naturally suppose the agent to possess.

* * *

Here, Schoenberger's initial contact with the C.T.A. was with the Placement Department where he filled out an application and had his first interview. There is no evidence that the C.T.A. did anything to permit ZuChristian to assume authority nor did they do anything to hold him out as having the authority to hire and set salaries. ZuChristian was not at a management level in the C.T.A. nor did his job title of Principal Communications Analyst suggest otherwise. The mere fact that he was allowed to interview prospective employees does not establish that the C.T.A. held him out as possessing the authority to hire employees or set salaries. Moreover, ZuChristian did inform Schoenberger that the formal offer of employment would be made by the Placement Department.

* * *

Our final inquiry concerns the plaintiff's contention that irrespective of ZuChristian's actual or apparent authority, the C.T.A. is bound by ZuChristian's promise because it ratified his acts. Ratification may be express or inferred and occurs where "the principal, with knowledge of the material facts of the unauthorized transaction, takes a position inconsistent with nonaffirmation of the transaction." [Citations.] Ratification is the equivalent to an original authorization and confirms that which was originally unauthorized. [Citation.] Ratification occurs where a principal attempts to seek or retain the benefits of the transaction. [Citations.]

Upon review of the evidence, we are not convinced that the C.T.A. acted to ratify ZuChristian's promise. * * *

* * *

For the reasons we have indicated, the judgment of the circuit court of Cook County granting judgment in favor of the defendant, C.T.A., is affirmed.

CASE 20-2

Effect of Termination of Agency on Authority
PARLATO v. EQUITABLE LIFE ASSURANCE SOCIETY OF THE UNITED STATES

Supreme Court of New York, Appellate Division, First Department, 2002
299 A.D.2d 108, 749 N.Y.S.2d 216

Friedman, J.

Plaintiffs [Parlato and Perry], who are sisters, were defrauded by Kenneth Soule, an agent of defendant Equitable Life Assurance Society of the United States (Equitable), beginning while Soule was employed by Equitable and continuing after Equitable terminated him in July 1992. Soule actually opened an Equitable account for one plaintiff, but he did not do so for the other, instead stealing all the funds that plaintiff entrusted to him. * * *

* * * Equitable hired Soule on or about April 1, 1990, as an agent authorized to sell Equitable financial products, such as insurance policies and annuities, to the public. Before becoming an Equitable agent, Soule from 1986 onward had been plaintiff Parlato's accountant and financial advisor. Parlato, a resident of Queens, began investing in Equitable financial products through Soule in May 1990, and Soule actually opened several Equitable accounts in Parlato's name while he was an Equitable agent. In the spring of 1992, however, Soule began criminally defrauding Parlato. Between March and May of 1992, Parlato, at Soule's urging, liquidated certain of her non-Equitable investments, and entrusted the proceeds to Soule for investment in Equitable financial products. Soule converted these funds, and all additional funds that Parlato subsequently entrusted to him, to his personal use.

In 1991, Soule began soliciting plaintiff Perry, Parlato's sister and a resident of Hawaii, to invest in Equitable products. In May 1992, Perry began entrusting funds to Soule to be used to open investment accounts for her at Equitable. Unlike Parlato, however, Perry alleges that Soule never opened any Equitable account for her, and that, from the start, he misappropriated every penny she ever entrusted to him. Thus, prior to the instant litigation, Perry was unknown to Equitable.

Equitable terminated Soule's employment in July 1992. Although Parlato allegedly still had an account with Equitable at that time, Equitable did not notify her of the termination. For approximately four years after his termination, Soule allegedly continued to represent himself to plaintiffs as an Equitable agent and to solicit their further investment in purported Equitable financial products. Plaintiffs do not allege, however, that they were exposed to any manifestations by Equitable of a continuing connection between Soule and Equitable after July 1992.

In August 1996, plaintiffs contacted Equitable to verify the status of their investments. At that time, Equitable informed plaintiffs that Soule had been terminated by Equitable in July 1992. This allegedly was the first time plaintiffs became aware that Soule's relationship with Equitable had been severed. Plaintiffs then alerted law enforcement authorities to Soule's misconduct. Ultimately, Soule pleaded guilty to a federal charge of mail fraud, and was sentenced to 27 months in prison and three years of supervised release, conditioned on his promise to make restitution in the amount of $416,000.

Plaintiffs commenced this action against Equitable in December 1999. Each plaintiff asserted a cause of action for fraud, based on the contention that she entrusted her money to Soule in reliance on the appearance of authority to act for Equitable with which the company had clothed him. [The trial court granted the defendant's motion to dismiss the complaint], and plaintiffs have appealed.

* * *

* * * [I]t is well established that a principal may be held liable in tort for the misuse by its agent of his apparent authority to defraud a third party who reasonably relies on the appearance of authority, even if the agent commits the fraud solely for his personal benefit, and to the detriment of the principal [citations]; Restatement [Second] of Agency §§ 261, 262, 265 [1]; [citations]. The reason for this rule is that the principal, by virtue of its ability to select its agents and to exercise control over them (see Restatement [Second] of Agency §1 [1]), is in a better position than third parties to prevent the perpetration of fraud by such agents through the misuse of their positions. Thus, the principal should not escape liability when an innocent third person suffers a loss as the result of an agent's abuse, for his own fraudulent purposes, of the third person's reasonable reliance on the apparent authority with which the principal has invested the agent. * * *

* * *

[The plaintiffs' claims based on frauds perpetrated during Soule's employment by Equitable are barred by the statute of limitations.]

* * * The final question before us, therefore, is whether, under these circumstances, Equitable's termination of Soule's employment in July 1992 had the effect, as a matter of law, of immediately cutting off his apparent authority to act for Equitable vis-à-vis the two plaintiffs. This question cannot be answered in the abstract. Rather, since the two plaintiffs are situated differently, the question must be addressed separately as to each plaintiff.

We hold that Parlato's claim, to the extent it is not time-barred, should not have been dismissed on a motion addressed to her pleading. The Court of Appeals has held that a third party who, like Parlato, is known by a principal to have previously dealt with the principal through the principal's authorized agent, is entitled to assume that the agent's authority continues until the third party receives notice the principal has revoked the agent's authority [citations]. The law of other states appears to be similar (see Restatement [Second] of Agency §§ 124A, 125, 127, 135, 136 [1], [2]; [citations]). In recognizing this duty of a principal to give notice of the revocation of an agent's authority, we are simply applying established principles.

In this case, Parlato alleges that Soule opened actual Equitable investment accounts for her while he was still an authorized agent of Equitable. If this is proven to be so, Parlato will be entitled to the benefit of the above-described rule permitting her, as a person known to have done business with Equitable through Soule in the past, to presume that Soule remained authorized to act for Equitable in the absence of either (1) notice that his authority had been revoked or (2) other circumstances that would have rendered it unreasonable to believe that Soule had authority to act for Equitable in the transactions he proposed [citation]; Restatement [Second] of Agency §125, Comment *b*; [citation]. Before any determination can be made as to whether it was reasonable for Parlato to believe that Soule had authority to act for Equitable in the transactions for which her claims are not time-barred, the particular facts of this case must be developed through discovery. Therefore, it was error to dismiss Parlato's claim on this pleading motion.

This brings us to the question of the viability of Perry's claim against Equitable. Perry alleges that Soule stole all of the money she entrusted to him, and that he never opened any Equitable account in her name. Thus, Perry's own allegations establish that Equitable had no way of notifying her of Soule's termination in July 1992. Under these circumstances, we hold that any apparent authority Soule may have had vis-à-vis Perry terminated along with his actual authority when his employment by Equitable came to an end.

Considerations of fairness, practicality and sound public policy lead us to this conclusion. Even in the case of a third party unknown to the principal, it seems fair to hold the principal responsible for the agent's misuse of his apparent authority while the principal-agent relationship continues to exist, bringing benefits to the principal and giving the principal a measure of control over the agent's conduct * * *. It seems unfair, however, to hold the principal responsible for torts its former agent commits after termination against an unknown third party, even if the former agent facilitates his wrongdoing by misrepresenting to the victim that the agency relationship is still in existence. Once the agent's employment has been terminated, the principal no longer has any power to control the agent's conduct. Moreover, the principal obviously cannot give notice of the agent's termination to a third party that is totally unknown to it. The law, of course, "does not require the impossible. . ." [Citation.] Further, allowing claims against a principal based on a former agent's post-termination torts against unknown third parties would subject the principal to potentially unlimited liability.

* * *

Finally, the amended complaint alleges that Equitable "made no effort to alert the public in general that Soule was no longer its agent." It is true that section 136 (3) of the Restatement (Second) of Agency (published in 1958) takes the position that, absent public notice (as by advertisement in a newspaper of general circulation) of revocation of an agent's authority in the area in which he formerly acted for the principal, apparent authority continues to exist after such revocation as to persons who previously knew of the agency and do not receive actual notice of the revocation, even if such persons never previously did business with the agent and thus are unknown to the principal. While this rule (hereinafter, the "public notice rule") finds support in a number of very old New York cases [citation], we do not regard the public notice rule as binding at this late date, at least under the particular facts alleged by plaintiffs. * * * Today, a person dealing with an individual known to have represented a company in the past can easily verify that the individual is still an agent for the company by contacting the company by telephone. Moreover, there is no reason to believe that the newspaper advertisements contemplated by the public notice rule would actually be read by customers such as plaintiffs in this action. This is particularly so in the case of plaintiff Perry, who, as a resident of Hawaii, would have been highly unlikely to come across a newspaper advertisement announcing Soule's termination in the New York area (see Restatement [Second] of Agency §136 [3] [a] [public notice rule is satisfied by publication "in a newspaper of general circulation in the place where the agency is regularly carried on"]). We therefore decline to ascribe legal significance to Equitable's alleged failure to give public notice of Soule's termination.

[Judgment modified in part and affirmed in part.]

CASE 20-3

Direct Liability of Principal: Negligent Hiring
CONNES v. MOLALLA TRANSPORT SYSTEM, INC.
Supreme Court of Colorado, 1992
831 P.2d 1316

Quinn, J.

[Terry Taylor was an employee of Molalla Transport. In hiring Taylor, Molalla followed its standard hiring procedure, which includes a personal interview with each applicant and requires the applicant to fill out an extensive job application form and to produce a current driver's license and a medical examiner's certificate. Molalla also contacts prior employers and other references about the applicant's qualifications and conducts an investigation of the applicant's driving record in the state where the applicant obtained the driver's license. Although applicants are asked whether they have been convicted of a crime, Molalla does not conduct an independent investigation to determine whether an applicant has been convicted of a crime. Approximately three months after Taylor began working for Molalla, he was assigned to transport freight from Kansas to Oregon. While traveling through Colorado, Taylor left the highway and drove by a hotel where Grace Connes was working as a night clerk. Observing that Connes was alone in the lobby, Taylor pulled his truck into the parking lot and entered the lobby. Once inside, Taylor sexually assaulted Connes at knifepoint. Although Taylor denied any prior criminal convictions on his application and during his interview, police and court records obtained since these events show that Taylor had been convicted of three felonies in Colorado and had been issued three citations for lewd conduct and another citation for simple assault in Seattle, Washington.

Connes sued Molalla on the theory of negligent hiring, claiming that Molalla knew or should have known that Taylor would come into contact with members of the public, that Molalla had a duty to hire and retain high-quality employees so as not to endanger members of the public, and that Molalla had breached its duty by failing to investigate fully and adequately Taylor's criminal background. The district court granted Molalla's motion for summary judgment. The Court of Appeals upheld the lower court's ruling, holding that Molalla had no legal duty to investigate the nonvehicular criminal record of its driver prior to hiring him as an employee. Connes appealed.]

* * *

The elements of a negligence claim consist of the existence of a legal duty by the defendant to the plaintiff, breach of that duty by the defendant, injury to the plaintiff, and a sufficient causal relationship between the defendant's breach and the plaintiffs injuries. [Citations.] A negligence claim will fail if it is predicated on circumstances for which the law imposes no duty of care upon the defendant. [Citations.] "A court's conclusion that a duty does or does not exist is 'an expression of the sum total of those considerations of policy which lead the law to say that the plaintiff is [or is not] entitled to protection.'" [Citations.]

The initial question in any negligence action, therefore, is whether the defendant owed a legal duty to protect the plaintiff against injury. The issue of legal duty is a question of law to be determined by the court. [Citations.]

A duty of reasonable care arises when there is a foreseeable risk of injury to others from a defendant's failure to take protective action to prevent the injury. [Citation.] While foreseeability is a prime factor in the duty calculus, a court also must weigh other factors, including the social utility of the defendant's conduct, the magnitude of the burden of guarding against the harm caused to the plaintiff, the practical consequences of placing such a burden on the defendant, and any additional elements disclosed by the particular circumstances of the case. [Citations.] "No one factor is controlling, and the question of whether a duty should be imposed in a particular case is essentially one of fairness under contemporary standards—whether reasonable persons would recognize a duty and agree that it exists." [Citation.]

The tort of negligent hiring is based on the principle that a person conducting an activity through employees is subject to liability for harm resulting from negligent conduct "in the employment of improper persons or instrumentalities in work involving risk of harm to others." Restatement (Second) of Agency §213(b)(1958). This principle of liability is not based on the rule of agency but rather on the law of torts. In [citation], the New Jersey Supreme Court offered the following distinction between the tort of negligent hiring and the agency doctrine of vicarious liability based on the rule of *respondeat superior*:

Thus, the tort of negligent hiring addresses the risk created by exposing members of the public to a potentially dangerous individual, while the doctrine of *respondeat superior* is based on the theory that the employee is the agent or is acting for the employer. Therefore the scope of employment limitation on liability which is part of the *respondeat superior* doctrine is not implicit in the wrong of negligent hiring.

Accordingly, the negligent hiring theory has been used to impose liability in cases where the employee commits an intentional tort, an action almost invariably outside the scope of employment, against the customer of a particular employer or other member of the public, where the employer either knew or should have known that the employee was violent or aggressive, or that the employee might engage in injurious conduct toward third persons.

Several jurisdictions, in addition to New Jersey, have recognized the tort of negligent hiring, * * * and we now join those jurisdictions in formally recognizing this cause of action.

In recognizing the tort of negligent hiring, we emphasize that an employer is not an insurer for violent acts committed by an employee against a third person. On the contrary, liability is predicated on the employer's hiring of a person under circumstances antecedently giving the employer reason to believe that the person, by reason of some attribute of character or prior conduct, would create an undue risk of harm to others in carrying out his or her employment responsibilities. See Restatement (Second) of Agency §213, comment d. The scope of the employer's duty in exercising reasonable care in a hiring decision will depend largely on the anticipated degree of contact which the employee will have with other persons in performing his or her employment duties.

Where the employment calls for minimum contact between the employee and other persons, there may be no reason for an employer to conduct any investigation of the applicant's background beyond obtaining past employment information and personal data during the initial interview. [Citation.] * * *

* * *

We endorse the proposition that where an employer hires a person for a job requiring frequent contact with members of the public, or involving close contact with particular persons as a result of a special relationship between such persons and the employer, the employer's duty of reasonable care is not satisfied by a mere review of personal data disclosed by the applicant on a job application form or during a personal interview. However, in the absence of circumstances antecedently giving the employer reason to believe that the job applicant, by reason of some attribute of character or prior conduct, would constitute an undue risk of harm to members of the public with whom the applicant will be in frequent contact or to particular persons standing in a special relationship to the employer and with whom the applicant will have close contact, we decline to impose upon the employer his duty to obtain and review official records of an applicant's criminal history. To impose such a requirement would mean that an employer would be obligated to seek out and evaluate official police and perhaps court records from every jurisdiction in which a job applicant had any significant contact. We have serious doubts whether such a task could be effectively achieved. Even if it could, there would remain the significant problem of interpreting the records and relating them in a practical way to the job in question. Accordingly, in the absence of circumstances antecedently giving the employer reason to believe that a job applicant, by reason of some attribute of character or prior conduct, would constitute an undue risk of harm to members of the public with whom the applicant will be in frequent contact or to particular persons who stand in a special relationship to the employer and with whom the applicant will be in close contact, the employer's duty of reasonable care does not extend to searching for and reviewing official records of a job applicant's criminal history.

In the instant case, we agree with the court of appeals' determination that Molalla had no duty to conduct an independent investigation into Taylor's non-vehicular criminal background before hiring him as a long-haul driver. Molalla had no reason to foresee that its hiring of Taylor under the circumstances of this case would create a risk that Taylor would sexually assault or otherwise endanger a member of the public by engaging in violent conduct. To be sure, Molalla had a duty to use reasonable care in hiring a safe driver who would not create a danger to the public in carrying out the duties of the job. Far from requiring frequent contact with members of the public or involving close contact with persons having a special relationship with the employer, Taylor's duties were restricted to the hauling of freight on interstate highways and, as such, involved only incidental contact with third persons having no special relationship to Molalla or to Taylor. After checking on Taylor's driving record and contacting some of his references, Molalla had no reason to believe that Taylor would not be a safe driver or a dependable employee. In addition, Molalla specifically instructed its drivers to stay on the interstate highways and, except for an emergency, to stop only in order to service the truck and to eat and to sleep. It further directed its drivers to sleep in the sleeping compartment behind the driver's seat of the truck at rest areas or truck stops located along the interstate highway system. Furthermore, Molalla required Taylor to fill out a job application and to submit to a personal interview. Taylor stated on the application form and at the interview that he had never been convicted of a crime. Nothing in the hiring process gave Molalla reason to foresee that Taylor would pose an unreasonable risk of harm to members of the public with whom he might have incidental contact during the performance of his duties.

* * * We accordingly hold that Molalla, in hiring Taylor as a long-haul truck driver, had no legal duty to conduct an

independent investigation into Taylor's non-vehicular criminal background in order to protect a member of the public, such as Connes, from a sexual assault committed by Taylor in the course of making a long-haul trip over the interstate highway system. The judgment of the court of appeals is affirmed.

CASE 20-4

Undisclosed Principal
A.E. ROBINSON OIL CO., INC. v. COUNTY FOREST PRODUCTS, INC.
Supreme Judicial Court of Maine, 2012
40 A.3d 20, 2012 ME 29, 77 UCC Rep.Serv.2d 59

Gorman, J.

Galen R. Porter Jr. is the sole shareholder in County Forest, a corporation that has existed since 1986. In 2004, Porter spoke with a vice president of A.E. Robinson at a charity golf event. Subsequently, the two orally agreed that A.E. Robinson would begin delivering fuel products to G.R. Porter & Sons, another corporation with which Porter was involved. In 2005, Porter began operating a fuel delivery business as Porter Cash Fuel but never registered that name with the Secretary of State. Porter testified that he intended to operate Porter Cash Fuel as a trade name of County Forest and not as a separate sole proprietorship. The record reveals that Porter ordered fuel and gas over the phone from A.E. Robinson in a series of transactions that continued for three years and eventually gave rise to this suit.

Several types of writings confirmed these oral agreements. Within two days after A.E. Robinson delivered its products, it mailed invoices directed to Porter Cash Fuel. A.E. Robinson also regularly sent Porter Cash Fuel statements of account. Further, an authorization for direct payment listed "Porter Cash Fuel" and bore two signatures, one of which belonged to Porter. None of the writings made any reference to County Forest and none indicated the corporate status of Porter Cash Fuel. All of A.E. Robinson's dealings were with Porter or with Porter Cash Fuel; it had no reason to believe it was dealing with County Forest.

Over the years of this business relationship, A.E. Robinson added terms to the bottom of its invoices asserting its entitlement to financing charges, collection costs, attorney fees, and court costs. Although Porter never expressly agreed to these terms, when Porter paid sporadically, some of the payments were applied to financing charges, and Porter never complained. Ultimately, the business relationship deteriorated, and A.E. Robinson refused to deliver any more products. A.E. Robinson sued County Forest and Porter seeking payment on the account. Following a non-jury trial, the court entered judgment

for A.E. Robinson jointly and severally against County Forest and Porter in the amount of the invoices plus financing charges and attorney fees. County Forest and Porter appeal from the entry of that judgment.

First, County Forest and Porter contend that the trial court erred in holding them jointly and severally liable for the debt. * * *

Porter became personally liable, as did County Forest, based on principles of agency. In his transactions with A.E. Robinson, Porter, through Porter Cash Fuel, was acting as an agent for an undisclosed principal—County Forest. The Restatement (Third) of Agency * * * states that "[w]hen an agent acting with actual authority makes a contract on behalf of an undisclosed principal . . . unless excluded by the contract, the principal is a party to the contract," as is the agent. Restatement (Third) of Agency §6.03 (2006). This rule is justified because "a third party's reasonable expectations will receive adequate protection only if an undisclosed principal is liable on a contract made on its behalf by an agent." *Id.* cmt. b. Notably, however, "[a]n undisclosed principal only becomes a party to a contract when an agent acts on the principal's behalf in making the contract." *Id.* cmt. c.

Here, Porter testified that he intended to operate Porter Cash Fuel as a trade name of County Forest. His brief to this Court reiterates that this was his intent. This testimony establishes that he was not operating Porter Cash Fuel as a separate sole proprietorship, which might have permitted County Forest to escape liability. Because Porter operated Porter Cash Fuel as an agent for County Forest without disclosing that County Forest was the principal, he and County Forest are parties to the contract. *See* Restatement (Third) of Agency §6.03. * * *

* * *

Judgment modified to remove the award of attorney fees. As modified, judgment affirmed.

QUESTIONS

1. Alice was Peter's traveling salesperson and was also authorized to collect accounts. Before the agreed termination of the agency, Peter wrongfully discharged Alice. Alice then called on Tom, an old customer, and collected an account from Tom. She also called on Laura, a new prospect, as Peter's agent, secured a large order, collected the price of the order, sent the order to Peter, and disappeared with the collections. Peter delivered the goods to Laura per the order.

   a. Explain what the result will be if Peter sues Tom for his account.

   b. Explain what the result will be if Peter sues Laura for the agreed price of the goods.

2. Paula instructed Alvin, her agent, to purchase a quantity of hides. Alvin ordered the hides from Ted in his own (Alvin's) name and delivered the hides to Paula. Ted, learning later that Paula was the principal, sends the bill to Paula, who refuses to pay Ted. Ted sues Paula and Alvin. What are Ted's rights against Paula and Alvin?

3. Stan sold goods to Bill in good faith, believing him to be a principal. Bill in fact was acting as agent for Nancy and was within the scope of his authority. The goods were charged to Bill, and on his refusal to pay, Stan sued Bill for the purchase price. While this action was pending, Stan learned of Bill's relationship with Nancy. Nevertheless, thirty days after learning of that relationship, Stan obtained judgment against Bill and had an execution issued that was never satisfied. Three months after rendition of the judgment, Stan sued Nancy for the purchase price of the goods. Is Nancy liable? Explain.

4. Green Grocery Company employed Jones as its manager. Jones was given authority by Green to purchase supplies and goods for resale and had conducted business for several years with Brown Distributing Company. Although her purchases previously had been limited to groceries, Jones contacted Brown and had it deliver a television set to her house, informing Brown the set was to be used in promotional advertising to increase Green's business. The advertising did not develop, and Jones disappeared from the area, taking the television set with her. Brown now seeks to recover the purchase price of the set from Green. Will Brown prevail? Explain.

5. Stone was the agent authorized to sell stock of the Turner Company at $10 per share and was authorized in case of sale to fill in the blanks in the certificates with the name of the purchaser, the number of shares, and the date of sale. He sold one hundred shares to Barrie, and without the knowledge or consent of the company and without reporting to the company, he endorsed the back of the certificate as follows:

   It is hereby agreed that Turner Company shall, at the end of three years after the date, repurchase the stock at $13 per share on thirty days' notice. Turner Company, by Stone.

   After three years, demand was made on Turner Company to repurchase. The company refused the demand and repudiated the agreement on the ground that the agent had no authority to make the agreement for repurchase. Is Turner Company liable to Barrie? Explain.

6. Helper, a delivery boy for Gunn, delivered two heavy packages of groceries to Reed's porch. As instructed by Gunn, Helper rang the bell to let Reed know the groceries had arrived. Mrs. Reed came to the door and asked Helper if he would deliver the groceries into the kitchen because the bags were heavy. Helper did so, and upon leaving, he observed Mrs. Reed having difficulty in moving a cabinet in the dining room. He undertook to assist her, but being more interested in watching Mrs. Reed than the cabinet, he failed to observe a small, valuable antique table, which he smashed into with the cabinet and destroyed. Does Reed have a cause of action against Gunn for the value of the destroyed antique? Why or why not?

7. Driver picked up Friend to accompany him on an out-of-town delivery for his employer, Speedy Service. A "No Riders" sign was prominently displayed on the windshield of the truck, and Driver violated specific instructions of his employer by permitting an unauthorized person to ride in the vehicle. While discussing a planned fishing trip with Friend, Driver ran a red light and collided with an automobile driven by Motorist. Both Friend and Motorist were injured. Is Speedy Service liable to either Friend or Motorist for the injuries they sustained? Explain.

8. Cook's Department Store advertises that it maintains in its store a barbershop managed by Hunter. Actually, Hunter is not an employee of the store but merely rents space in it. While shaving Jordon in the barbershop, Hunter negligently puts a deep gash into one of Jordon's ears, requiring ten stitches. Should Jordon be entitled to collect damages from Cook's Department Store? Why or why not?

9. The following contract was executed on August 22:

   Ray agrees to sell, and Shaw, the representative of Todd and acting on his behalf, agrees to buy 10,000 pounds of $0.32 \times 1\frac{5}{8}$ stainless steel strip type 410.

   (signed) Ray

   (signed) Shaw

On August 26, Ray informs Shaw and Todd that the contract was in reality signed by him as agent for Upson. What are the rights of Ray, Shaw, Todd, and Upson in the event of a breach of the contract? Explain.

10. Harris, owner of certain land known as Red Bank, mailed a letter to Byron, a real estate broker in City X, stating, "I have been thinking of selling Red Bank. I have never met you, but a friend has advised me that you are an industrious and honest real estate broker. I therefore employ you to find a purchaser for Red Bank at a price

of $350,000." Ten days after receiving the letter, Byron mailed the following reply to Harris:

> Acting pursuant to your recent letter requesting me to find a purchaser for Red Bank, this is to advise that I have sold the property to Sims for $350,000. I enclose your copy of the contract of sale signed by Sims. Your name was signed to the contract by me as your agent.

Is Harris obligated to convey Red Bank to Sims? Explain.

C A S E   P R O B L E M S

11. While crossing a public highway in the city, Joel was struck by a horse-drawn cart driven by Morison's agent. The agent was traveling between Burton Crescent Mews and Finchley on his employer's business and was not supposed to go into the city. Apparently, the agent was on a detour to visit a friend when the accident occurred. Joel brought this action against Morison for the injuries sustained as a result of the agent's negligence. Morison argues that he is not liable for his agent's negligence because the agent had strayed from his assigned path. Who is correct? Why?

12. Serges is the owner of a retail meat marketing business. Without authority, his managing agent borrowed $3,500 from David on Serges's behalf for use in Serges's business. Serges paid $200 on the alleged loan and on several other occasions told David that the full balance owed eventually would be paid. He then disclaimed liability on the debt, asserting that he had not authorized his agent to enter into the loan agreement. Should David succeed in an action to collect on the loan? Explain.

13. Sherwood negligently ran into the rear of Austen's car, which was stopped at a stoplight. As a result, Austen received bodily injuries and her car was damaged. Sherwood, arts editor for the *Mississippi Press Register*, was en route from a Louis Armstrong concert he had covered for the newspaper. When the accident occurred, he was on his way to spend the night at a friend's house. Austen sued Sherwood and—under the doctrine of *respondeat superior*—Sherwood's employer, the *Mississippi Press Register*. Who is liable? Explain.

14. Aretta J. Parkinson owned a two-hundred-acre farm in a State that requires written authority for an agent to sell land. Prior to her death on December 23, Parkinson deeded a one-eighth undivided interest in the farm to each of her eight children as tenants in common. On January 15 of the following year, one of the daughters,

Roma Funk, approached Barbara Bradshaw about selling the Parkinson farm to the Bradshaws. They orally agreed to a selling price of $800,000. After this meeting, Funk contacted Bryant Hansen, a real estate broker, to assist her in completing the transaction. Hansen prepared an earnest money agreement that was signed by the Bradshaws but by none of the Parkinson children. Hansen also prepared warranty deeds, which were signed by three of the children. Several of the children subsequently refused to convey their interests in the farm to the Bradshaws. Explain whether the Bradshaws can obtain specific performance of the oral contract of sale based on the defendants' ratification of the oral contract by their knowledge of and failure to repudiate it.

15. Raymond Zukaitis was a physician practicing medicine in Douglas County, Nebraska. Aetna issued a policy of professional liability insurance to Zukaitis through its agent, the Ed Larsen Insurance Agency. The policy covered the period from August 31, 2018, through August of the following year. On August 7, 2020, Dr. Zukaitis received a written notification of a claim for malpractice that occurred on September 27, 2018. Dr. Zukaitis notified the Ed Larsen Insurance Agency immediately and forwarded the written claim to them. The claim was then mistakenly referred to St. Paul Fire and Marine Insurance Company, the company that currently insured Dr. Zukaitis. Apparently without notice to Dr. Zukaitis, the agency contract between Larsen and Aetna had been canceled on August 1, 2019, and St. Paul had replaced Aetna as the insurance carrier. However, when St. Paul discovered it was not the carrier on the date of the alleged wrongdoing, it notified Aetna and withdrew from Dr. Zukaitis's defense. Aetna also refused to represent Dr. Zukaitis, contending that it was relieved of its obligation to Dr. Zukaitis because he had not notified Aetna immediately of the claim. Dr. Zukaitis then secured his

own attorney to defend against the malpractice claim and brought this action against Aetna to recover attorneys' fees and other expenses incurred in the defense. Should Dr. Zukaitis succeed? Explain.

16. Chris Zulliger was a chef at the Plaza Restaurant in the Snowbird Ski Resort in Utah. The restaurant is located at the base of a mountain. As a chef for the Plaza, Zulliger was instructed by his supervisor and the restaurant manager to make periodic trips to inspect the Mid-Gad Restaurant, which was located halfway up the mountain. Because skiing helped its employees to get to work, Snowbird preferred that its employees know how to ski and gave them ski passes as part of their compensation. Prior to beginning work at the Plaza, Zulliger went skiing. The restaurant manager asked Zulliger to stop at the Mid-Gad before beginning work that day, and Zulliger stopped at the Mid-Gad during his first run and inspected the kitchen. He then skied four runs before heading down the mountain to begin work. On the last run, Zulliger decided to take a route often taken by Snowbird employees. About midway down, Zulliger decided to jump off a crest on the side of an intermediate run. Because of the drop, a skier above the crest cannot see whether there are skiers below, and Zulliger ran into Margaret Clover, who was below the crest. The jump was well known to Snowbird; the resort's ski patrol often instructed people not to jump, and there was a sign instructing skiers to take it slow at that point. Clover sued Zulliger and, under the doctrine of *respondeat superior*, Snowbird, claiming that Zulliger had been acting within the scope of his employment. Who is liable? Explain.

17. Rubin was driving on one of the city's streets when he inadvertently obstructed the path of a taxicab, causing the cab to come into contact with his vehicle. Angered by Rubin's sudden blocking of his traffic lane, the taxi driver exited his cab, approached Rubin, and struck him about the head and shoulders with a metal pipe. Rubin filed suit against the cab driver to recover for bodily injuries resulting from the altercation. He also sued the Yellow Cab Company, asserting that the company was vicariously liable under the doctrine of *respondeat superior*. Is the Yellow Cab Company liable? Explain.

18. Van D. Costas, Inc. (Costas), entered into a contract to remodel the entrance of the Magic Moment Restaurant owned by Seascape Restaurants, Inc. Rosenberg, part owner and president of Seascape, signed the contract on a line under which was typed "Jeff Rosenberg, The Magic Moment." When a dispute arose over the performance and payment of the contract, Costas brought suit against Rosenberg for breach of contract. Rosenberg contended

that he had no personal liability for the contract and that only Seascape, the owner of the restaurant, was liable. Costas claimed that Rosenberg signed for an undisclosed principal and, therefore, was individually liable. Is Rosenberg liable on the contract? Explain.

19. Virginia and her husband, Ronnie Hulbert, were involved in an accident in Mobile County when their automobile collided with another automobile driven by Dr. Murray's nanny. The nanny's regular duties of employment included housekeeping, supervising the children, and taking the children places that they needed to go. At the time of the collision, the nanny was driving her own car and was following Dr. Murray and her family to Florida from Louisiana to accompany Dr. Murray's family on their vacation. One of Dr. Murray's daughters was in the automobile driven by the nanny. Virginia Hulbert sued Dr. Murray under the doctrine of *respondeat superior*, alleging that the nanny was acting within the scope of her employment when the automobile accident occurred. Should she be able to recover from Dr. Murray? Discuss.

20. Tommy Blair, Sr., was the sole owner and president of Tommy Blair, Inc., d/b/a Courtesy Autoplex. His son, Thomas Blair, Jr., was a management employee who supervised employees within the service department. On September 28, Tommie Lee Patterson entered into an agreement with Courtesy to trade his Camaro for a new GMC Jimmy. At the time of the trade, Patterson owed $12,402.82 on the Camaro. Despite this, he incorrectly informed Courtesy that he owed only $9,500.00 on the car. The transaction occurred at a time when Courtesy could not verify the payoff amount on the loan. Courtesy allowed Patterson to take possession of the Jimmy but did not transfer title. An agreement was also executed providing that (a) Courtesy would credit Patterson if he had overstated his outstanding indebtedness on the Camaro and (b) Patterson would pay the difference if he had understated that amount. The next day, Courtesy discovered the amount Patterson actually owed on the Camaro. When notified of this discrepancy, Patterson refused to pay the additional sum and refused to return the Jimmy. Courtesy subsequently tried unsuccessfully to repossess the truck on at least two occasions. On October 4, Thomas Blair, Jr., and another Courtesy employee encountered Patterson, who was driving the Jimmy, on a public road. At a stoplight, Thomas Blair, Jr., exited his car and knocked on the Jimmy's driver side window, demanding that Patterson get out of the vehicle. When Patterson refused, Thomas Blair, Jr., drew a pistol he was carrying and fired two shots in the front tire and two shots in the rear tire of the Jimmy. Ultimately, the

disabled truck was impounded and returned to Courtesy by the police. Thomas Blair, Jr., was convicted of wanton endangerment in the first degree, a felony. Patterson sued Thomas Blair, Jr., and Courtesy, claiming that Courtesy was vicariously liable for the tortious acts of its employee, Thomas Blair, Jr. Explain whether Courtesy is vicariously liable.

21. Frederick "Rick" Worrell conducted business as WRL Advertising. However, WRL Advertising was not a legal entity in its own right, but rather a trade name for Wingfield, Bennett & Baer, LLC, which is owned and operated by Worrell. Martha J. Musil, an employee of WRL Advertising, placed advertising orders with the Plain Dealer Publishing Company at the direction of her employer. Musil communicated to the Plain Dealer that she was working on behalf of WRL Advertising. WRL did not pay for all of the advertising, and the Plain Dealer sued Worrell and Musil. Shortly after the case was brought, Worrell filed for bankruptcy. Explain whether Musil is personally liable on the contracts.

T A K I N G   S I D E S

Sonenberg Company managed Westchester Manor Apartments through its on-site property manager, Judith. Manor Associates Limited Partnership, whose general partner is Westchester Manor, Ltd., owned the complex. The entry sign to the property did not reveal the owner's name but did disclose that Sonenberg managed the property. Judith contacted Redi-Floors and requested a proposal for installing carpet in several of the units. In preparing the proposal, Redi-Floors confirmed that Sonenberg was the managing company and that Judith was its on-site property manager. Sonenberg did not inform Redi-Floors of the owner's identity. Judith and her assistant orally ordered the carpet, and Redi-Floors installed the carpet. Redi-Floors sent invoices to the complex and received checks from "Westchester Manor Apartments."

Redi-Floor believed that Sonenberg owned the complex and did not learn of the true owner's identity until after the work had been completed when a dispute arose concerning the payment of some of its invoices.

a. What arguments would support Redi-Floors in recovering on the outstanding invoices from *both* Sonenberg and Manor Associates?

b. What arguments would limit Redi-Floors to recovering on the outstanding invoices from *either* Sonenberg or Manor Associates?

c. Explain what the outcome would be under (1) the Second Restatement and (2) the Third Restatement.

Sales

CH 21 INTRODUCTION TO SALES AND LEASES

CH 22 PERFORMANCE

CH 23 TRANSFER OF TITLE AND RISK OF LOSS

CH 24 PRODUCTS LIABILITY: WARRANTIES AND STRICT LIABILITY IN TORT

CH 25 SALES REMEDIES

Introduction to Sales and Leases

Sales are the most common and important of all commercial transactions. In an exchange economy such as ours, sales are the essential means by which the various units of production exchange their outputs, thereby providing the opportunity for specialization and enhanced productivity. An advanced, complex, industrialized economy with highly coordinated manufacturing and distribution systems requires a reliable mechanism for ensuring that *future* exchanges can be entered into today and fulfilled at a later time. Because practically everyone in our economy is a purchaser of both durable and consumable goods, the manufacture and distribution of goods involve numerous sales transactions. The law of sales establishes a framework in which these present and future exchanges may take place in a predictable, certain, and orderly fashion with a minimum of transaction costs.

Article 2 of the Code deals with transactions in sales and has been adopted in all of the States (except Louisiana) plus the District of Columbia and the Virgin Islands.

Leases of personal property are also of great economic significance. Leases range from a consumer renting an automobile or a lawn mower to a Fortune 500 corporation leasing heavy industrial machinery. Despite the frequent and widespread use of personal property leases, the law governing these transactions had been patched together from the common law of personal property, real estate leasing law, and Articles 2 and 9 of the UCC. Although containing several applicable provisions, the UCC did not directly relate to leases.

To fill this void, the drafters of the Code approved Article 2A—Leases in 1987 and subsequently amended Article 2A in 1990. An analogue of Article 2, the new Article adopts many of the rules contained in Article 2. Article 2A is an attempt to codify in one statute all the rules governing the leasing of personal property. South Dakota has enacted the 1987 version of Article 2A, while the District of Columbia and all the other states except Louisiana have adopted the 1990 version.

Amendments to UCC Articles 2 and 2A were promulgated in 2003 to accommodate electronic commerce and to reflect development of business practices, changes in other law, and interpretive difficulties of practical significance. Because no States had adopted them and prospects for enactment in the near future were bleak, the 2003 amendments to UCC Articles 2 and 2A were withdrawn in 2011. However, all States have adopted the 2001 Revisions to Article 1, which applies to all of the articles of the Code.

This part of the book covers sales and leases of goods. All of the chapters cover Article 2A in addition to Article 2 by stating the Article 2A section number wherever Article 2A's provision is identical to or essentially the same as the Article 2 provision. Where Article 2A significantly deviates from Article 2, both rules are discussed. This chapter discusses the nature and formation of sales and lease contracts as well as the fundamental principles of Article 2 and Article 2A.

NATURE OF SALES AND LEASES

The law of sales, which governs contracts involving the sale of goods, is a specialized branch of both the law of contracts (discussed previously in *Chapters 9–18*) and the law of personal

FIGURE 21-1 Law of Sales and Leases

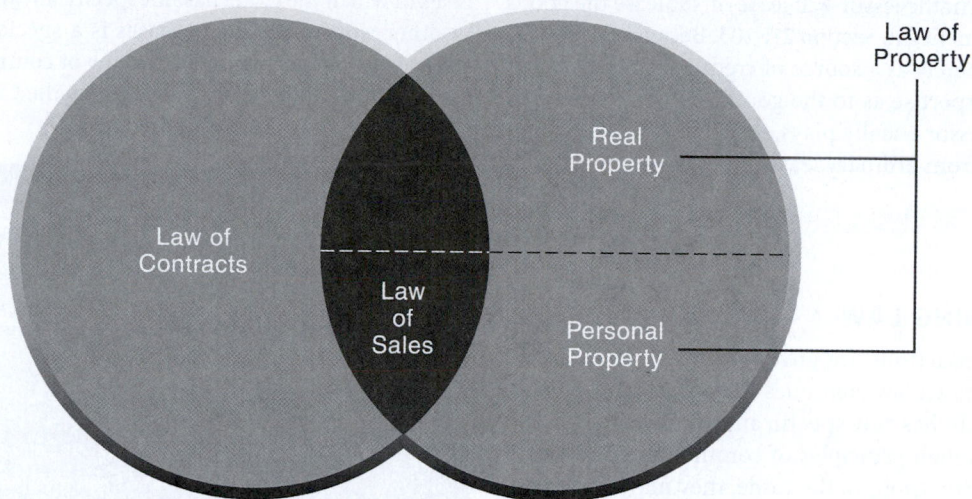

property (discussed later in *Chapter 47*). This section covers the definition of sales and lease contracts and the fundamentals of Article 2 and Article 2A.

♦ **SEE FIGURE 21-1:** *Law of Sales and Leases*

21-1 Definitions

21-1a GOODS

Goods essentially are defined as movable, tangible personal property. For example, the purchase of a bicycle, CD player, or this textbook is considered a sale of goods. "Goods" also include the unborn young of animals, growing crops, and, if removed by the seller, timber, minerals, or a building attached to real property. Section 2-105(1). Under Article 2A, minerals cannot be leased prior to their extraction. Section 2A-103(1)(h).

21-1b SALE

The Code defines a sale as the transfer of title to goods from seller to buyer for a price. Section 2-106. The price can be money, other goods, real estate, or services.

21-1c LEASE

Article 2A defines a lease of goods as a "transfer of the right to possession and use of goods for a term in return for consideration, but . . . retention or creation of a security interest is not a lease." Section 2A-103(1)(j). A transaction within this definition of a lease is governed by Article 2A, but if the transaction is a security interest disguised as a lease, it is governed by Article 9.

Categorizing a transaction as a lease has significant implications not only for the parties to the lease but also for third parties as well. If the transaction is deemed to be a lease, then the residual interest in the goods belongs to the lessor, who need not file publicly to protect this interest. On the other hand, if the transaction is a security interest, then the provisions of Article 9 regarding enforceability, perfection, priority, and remedies apply (see *Chapter 37*). UCC Section 1-201(37) and Revised Section 1-203 provide rules that govern the determination of whether a transaction in the form of a lease creates a security interest.

CONSUMER LEASES Article 2A affords special treatment for consumer leases. The definition of a consumer lease requires that (1) the transaction meet the definition of a lease under Article 2A; (2) the lessor be regularly engaged in the business of leasing *or* selling goods; (3) the lessee be an individual, not an organization; (4) the lessee take the lease interest primarily for a personal, family, or household purpose; and (5) the total payments under the lease do not exceed $25,000. Section 2A-103(1)(e). Although consumer protection for lease transactions is primarily left to other State and Federal law, Article 2A does contain a number of provisions that apply to consumer leases and that may *not* be varied by agreement of the parties.

FINANCE LEASES A finance lease is a special type of lease transaction generally involving three parties instead of two. Whereas in the typical lease situation the lessor also supplies the goods, in a finance lease arrangement, the lessor and the supplier are separate parties. The lessor's primary function in a finance lease is to provide financing to the lessee for a lease of goods provided by the supplier. For example, under a finance lease arrangement a manufacturer supplies goods pursuant to the lessee's instructions or specifications. The party functioning as the lessor will then either purchase those goods from the supplier or act as the prime lessee in leasing them from the supplier. In turn, the lessor will lease or sublease the goods to the lessee. Comment g to Section 2A-103. Because the finance lessor functions merely as a source of credit, she typically will have no special expertise as to the goods. Due to the limited role the finance lessor usually plays, Article 2A treats finance leases differently from ordinary leases.

♦ *See Case 21-1*

21-1d GOVERNING LAW

Though sales transactions are governed by Article 2 of the Code, general contract law continues to apply to sales in cases in which the Code has not specifically modified such law. Nevertheless, although principles of common law and equity may supplement provisions of the Code, they may not be used to supplant its provisions. Thus, the law of sales is a specialized part of the general law of contracts, and the law of contracts continues to govern unless specifically displaced by the Code.

General contract law also continues to govern all contracts outside the scope of the Code. Transactions not within the scope of Article 2 include employment contracts, service contracts, insurance contracts, contracts involving real property, and contracts for the sale of intangibles such as stocks, bonds, patents, and copyrights. For an illustration of the relationship between the law of sales and the general law of contracts, see *Figure 9-1*. In determining whether a contract containing both a sale of goods and a service is a UCC contract or a general contract, the majority of States follow the predominant purpose test. This test holds that if the predominant purpose of the whole transaction is a sale of goods, then Article 2 applies to the entire transaction. If, on the other hand, the predominant purpose is the nongood or service portion, then Article 2 does not apply at all. A few States apply Article 2 to the goods part of a transaction and general contract law to the nongoods or service part of the transaction.

♦ **SEE FIGURE 9-1 :** *Law Governing Contracts*

♦ *See Cases 21-2 and 9-1*

Although Article 2 governs sales, the drafters of the Article have invited the courts to extend Code principles to non-sale transactions in goods. To date, a number of courts have accepted this invitation and have applied Code provisions by analogy to other transactions in goods not expressly included within the Act, most frequently to leases and bailments. The Code has also greatly influenced the revision of the Restatement, Second, Contracts, which, as previously discussed, has great effect upon all contracts.

Although lease transactions are governed by Article 2A of the Code, general contract law continues to apply to leases in cases in which the Code has not specifically modified such law. In other words, the law of leases is a specialized part of the general law of contracts, and the law of contracts continues to govern unless specifically displaced by the Code.

CISG The United Nations Convention on Contracts for CISG the International Sale of Goods (CISG) which as of March 2020 has been ratified by the United States and ninety-two other countries, governs all contracts for the international sales of goods between parties located in different nations that have ratified the CISG. Because treaties are Federal law, the CISG supersedes the UCC in any situation to which either could apply. The CISG includes provisions dealing with interpretation, trade usage, contract formation, obligations and remedies of sellers and buyers, and risk of loss. Parties to an international sales contract may, however, expressly exclude CISG governance from their contract. The CISG specifically excludes sales of (1) goods bought for personal, family, or household use; (2) ships or aircraft; and (3) electricity. In addition, it does not apply to contracts in which the primary obligation of the party furnishing the goods consists of supplying labor or services.

Practical Advice

Because it is unclear which law will govern certain contracts, be careful to specify the particulars of your agreement in your written contract.

21-2 Fundamental Principles of Article 2 and Article 2A

The purpose of Article 2 is to modernize, clarify, simplify, and make uniform the law of sales. Furthermore, the Article is to be interpreted in accordance with these underlying principles and not according to some abstraction such as the passage of title. The Code

> is drawn to provide flexibility so that, since it is intended to be a semi-permanent piece of legislation, it will provide its own machinery for expansion of commercial practices. It is intended to make it possible for the law embodied in this Act to be developed by the courts in the light of unforeseen and new circumstances and practices. However, the proper construction of the Act requires that its interpretation and application be limited to its reason. Section 1-102, Comment 1; Revised Section 1-103, Comment 1.

CISG The CISG governs only the formation of the contract of sales and the rights and obligations of the seller and buyer arising from such contract. It does not cover the validity of the contract or any of its provisions. In addition, one of the purposes of the CISG is to promote uniformity of the law of sales.

This open-ended drafting includes the following fundamental concepts.

21-2a GOOD FAITH

All parties who enter into a contract or duty within the scope of the Code must perform their obligations in good faith. Revised UCC Article 1 **defines good** faith as "honesty in fact and the observance of reasonable commercial standards of fair dealing." Section 1-201(20). Commercial reasonableness is a standard determined in terms of the business judgment of reasonable persons familiar with the practices customary in the type of transaction involved and in terms of the facts and circumstances of the case. For instance, if the parties agree that the seller is to set the price term, the seller must establish the price in good faith.

CISG The CISG is also designed to promote the observation of good faith in international trade.

21-2b UNCONSCIONABILITY

The court may scrutinize every contract of sale to determine whether in its commercial setting, purpose, and effect it is unconscionable. The court may refuse to enforce an unconscionable contract or any part of it found to be unconscionable or may limit its application to prevent an unconscionable result. Section 2-302. Though the Code itself does not define *unconscionable*, the *New Webster's Dictionary* (Deluxe Encyclopedic Edition) defines the term as "contrary to the dictates of conscience; unscrupulous or unprincipled; exceeding that which is reasonable or customary; inordinate, unjustifiable."

The Code denies or limits enforcement of an unconscionable contract for the sale of goods to promote fairness and decency and to correct harshness or oppression in contracts resulting from inequality in the bargaining positions of the parties.

The doctrine of unconscionability has been justified on the basis that it permits the courts to resolve issues of unfairness explicitly on that basis without recourse to formalistic rules or legal fictions. In policing contracts for fairness, the courts have again demonstrated their willingness to limit freedom of contract to protect the less advantaged from overreaching by dominant contracting parties. Accordingly, most cases concerning unconscionability have involved low-income consumers.

The doctrine of unconscionability has evolved through its application by the courts to include both procedural and substantive unconscionability. **Procedural unconscionability** involves scrutiny for the presence of "bargaining naughtiness." In other words, was the negotiation process fair? Or were there procedural irregularities such as burying important terms of the agreement in fine print or obscuring the true meaning of the contract with impenetrable legal jargon?

In checking for **substantive unconscionability**, the court examines the actual terms of the contract for oppressive or grossly unfair provisions such as an exorbitant price or an unfair exclusion or limitation of contractual remedies. An all-too-common example places a necessitous buyer in an unequal bargaining position with a seller who consequently obtains an exorbitant price for his product or service. In one case, a price of $749 ($920 on time payments) for a vacuum cleaner that cost the seller $140 was held unconscionable. In another case, the buyers, welfare recipients, purchased by time payment contract a home freezer unit for $900 plus time credit charges, credit life insurance, credit property insurance, and sales tax for a total price of $1,235. The maximum retail value of the freezer unit at the time of purchase was $300. The court held the contract unconscionable and reformed it by changing the price to the total payment ($620) the buyers had managed to make. *Jones v. Star Credit Corp*, 59 Misc.2d 189, 298 N.Y.S.2d 264 (1969).

Practical Advice

Refrain from entering into contracts with provisions that are oppressively harsh or that were negotiated under unfair circumstances.

As to *all* leases, Article 2A provides that a court faced with an unconscionable contract or clause may refuse to enforce either the entire contract or just the unconscionable clause or may limit the application of the unconscionable clause to avoid an unconscionable result. This is similar to Article 2's treatment of unconscionable clauses in sales contracts. A lessee under a consumer lease, however, is provided with additional protection against unconscionability. In the case of a consumer lease, if a court as a matter of law finds that any part of the lease contract has been induced by unconscionable conduct, the court is expressly empowered to grant appropriate relief. Section 2A-108(2). The same is true when unconscionable conduct occurs in the collection of a claim arising from a consumer lease contract. The explicit availability of relief for consumers subjected to unconscionable conduct (procedural unconscionability)—in addition to a provision regarding unconscionable contracts (substantive unconscionability)—represents a departure from Article 2. An additional remedy that Article 2A provides for consumers is the award of attorneys' fees. If the court finds unconscionability with respect to a consumer lease, it shall award reasonable attorneys' fees to the lessee. Section 2A-108(4)(a).

♦ *See Cases 21-3 and 13-4*

21-2c EXPANSION OF COMMERCIAL PRACTICES

An underlying policy of the Code is "to permit the continued expansion of commercial practices through custom, usage and agreement of the parties." Section 1-102(2)(b), Revised Section 1-103(a)(2). In particular, the Code emphasizes the course of dealings and the usage of trade in interpreting agreements.

A **course of dealing** is a sequence of previous conduct between the parties that may fairly be regarded as establishing a common basis of understanding for interpreting their expressions and agreement. Section 1-205(1); Revised Section 1-303(b). For example, Plaza, a sugar company, enters into a written agreement with Brown, a grower of sugar beets, by which Brown agrees to raise and deliver and Plaza agrees to purchase specified quantities of beets during the coming season. No price is fixed. The agreement is on a standard form used by Plaza for Brown and many other growers in prior years. Plaza's practice is to pay all growers uniformly according to a formula based on Plaza's established accounting system. Unless otherwise agreed, the established pricing pattern is part of the agreement between Plaza and Brown as a course of dealing.

A **usage of trade** is a practice or method of dealing regularly observed and followed in a place, vocation, or trade. Section 1-205(2); Revised Section 1-303(c). To illustrate: Tamara contracts to sell Seth one thousand feet of San Domingo mahogany. By usage of dealers in mahogany, known to Tamara and Seth, good mahogany of a certain density is known as San Domingo mahogany, though it does not come from San Domingo. Unless otherwise agreed, the usage is part of the contract.

CISG The parties are bound by any usage or practices that they have agreed to or established between themselves. In addition, the parties are considered, unless otherwise agreed, to be bound by any usage of international trade that is widely known and regularly observed in the particular trade.

21-2d SALES BY AND BETWEEN MERCHANTS

The Code establishes separate rules that apply to transactions transpiring between merchants or involving a merchant as a party. A **merchant** is defined as a person who (1) is a dealer in the type of goods the transaction involves, (2) by his occupation holds himself out as having knowledge or skill peculiar to the goods or practices involved, or (3) employs an agent or broker whom he holds out as having such knowledge or skill. Section 2-104(1); Section 2A-103(3). These rules exact a higher standard of conduct from merchants because of their knowledge of trade and commerce and because merchants as a class generally set these standards for themselves. The most significant of these merchant rules are listed in *Figure 21-2*.

FIGURE 21-2 Selected Rules Applicable to Merchants

Section of UCC	Merchant Rules	Chapter in Text Where Discussed
2-103(1)(b), 2-103(3)	Good faith	21
2-201	Confirmation of oral contracts	15, 21
2-205, 2A-205	Firm offers	10, 21
2-207(2)	Battle of the forms	10, 21
2-312(3), 2A-211(2)	Warranty against infringement	24
2-314(1), 2A-212	Warranty of merchantability	24
2-327(1)(c)	Sales on approval	23
2-402(2)	Retention of possession of goods by seller	23
2-403(2), 2A-304(2), 2A-305(2)	Entrusting of goods	23
2-509(3), 2A-219(2)(c)	Risk of loss	23
2-603(1), 2A-511(1)	Duties after rightful rejection	22

♦ **SEE FIGURE 21-2:** *Selected Rules Applicable to Merchants*

21-2e LIBERAL ADMINISTRATION OF REMEDIES

Section 1-106 and Revised Section 1-305 of the Code provide that its remedies shall be liberally administered to place the aggrieved party in a position as good as the one she would have occupied had the defaulting party fully performed. The Code states clearly, however, that remedies are limited to compensation and do not include consequential or punitive damages, unless specifically provided by the Code. Nevertheless, the Code provides that even in cases in which it does not expressly provide a remedy for a right or obligation, the courts should provide an appropriate remedy. Remedies are discussed in *Chapter 25*.

21-2f FREEDOM OF CONTRACT

Most of the Code's provisions are not mandatory but permit the parties by agreement to vary or displace them altogether. The parties may not, however, disclaim by agreement the obligations of good faith, diligence, reasonableness, and care the Code prescribes, though they may by agreement determine the standards by which to measure the performance of these obligations, so long as such standards are not obviously unreasonable. Section 1-102(3); Revised Sections 1-103(a)(2) and 1-302. Through this approach, the Code not only maximizes freedom of contract but also permits the continued expansion of commercial practices through private agreement.

21-2g VALIDATION AND PRESERVATION OF SALES CONTRACTS

One of the requirements of commercial law is the establishment of rules that determine when an agreement is valid. The Code approaches this requirement by minimizing formal requisites and attempting to preserve agreements whenever the parties manifest an intent to enter into a contract.

FORMATION OF SALES AND LEASE CONTRACTS

The Code's basic approach to validation is to recognize contracts whenever the parties manifest such an intent. This is so whether or not the parties can identify a precise moment at which the contract was formed. Section 2-204(2); Section 2A-204(2).

As already noted, the law of sales and leases is a subset of the general law of contracts and is governed by general contract law unless particular provisions of the Code displace the general law. Although the Code leaves most issues of contract formation to general contract law, it has modified the general law of contract formation in several significant respects. These modifications serve to modernize contract law, to relax the validation requirements of contract formation, and to promote fairness.

21-3 Manifestation of Mutual Assent

For a contract to exist, there must be an objective manifestation of mutual assent: an offer and an acceptance. This section examines the UCC rules that affect offers and acceptances.

21-3a DEFINITENESS OF AN OFFER

At common law, the terms of a contract were required to be definite and complete. The Code has rejected the strict approach of the common law by recognizing an agreement as valid, despite missing terms, if there is any reasonably certain basis for granting a remedy. Accordingly, the Code provides that even a contract from which one or more terms have been omitted need not fail for indefiniteness. Section 2-204(3); Section 2A-204(3). The Code provides standards by which the courts may ascertain and supply omitted essential terms, provided the parties intended to enter into a binding agreement. Nevertheless, the more terms the parties leave open, the less likely their intent to enter into a binding contract. Article 2A generally does not provide the same gap-filling provisions.

CISG An offer to contract is sufficiently definite if it indicates the goods and fixes or makes provision, expressly or implicitly, for determining price and quality.

OPEN PRICE The parties may enter into a contract for the sale of goods even though they have reached no agreement on the price (i.e., left open the price term). Under the Code, the price is reasonable at the time for delivery where the agreement (1) says nothing as to price, (2) provides that the parties shall agree later as to the price and they fail to so agree, or (3) fixes the price in terms of some agreed market or other standard as set by a third person or agency and the price is not so set. Section 2-305(1). An agreement that the price is to be fixed by the seller or buyer means that it must be fixed in good faith.

OPEN DELIVERY Unless otherwise agreed, the place of delivery is the seller's place of business. Moreover, in the absence of specific instructions, the delivery must be made within a reasonable time and in a single delivery. Section 2-308.

OPEN QUANTITY: OUTPUT AND REQUIREMENT CONTRACTS A buyer's agreement to purchase a seller's entire output for a stated period or a seller's agreement to fulfill a buyer's need for certain goods used in her business operations may appear to lack definiteness and mutuality of obligation. In neither case do the parties specify the exact quantity of goods, and the seller and the buyer may have some control over their respective output and requirements. Nonetheless, such agreements are enforceable by the application of an objective standard based upon the good faith of both parties, and the quantities may not be disproportionate to any stated estimate or the prior output or requirements. Section 2-306(1). For example, the seller cannot operate his factory twenty-four hours a day and insist that the buyer take all of the output when the seller operated the factory only eight hours a day at the time the agreement was made. Nor can the buyer unilaterally triple the size of her business and insist that the seller supply all of her requirements.

♦ *See Case 21-3*

OTHER OPEN TERMS The Code further provides rules, where the parties do not agree, as to the terms of payment, the duration of the contract, and the particulars of performance. Sections 2-310, 2-309, 2-307, 2-311.

21-3b IRREVOCABLE OFFERS

An offeror generally may withdraw an offer at any time prior to its acceptance. To be effective, notice of revocation must reach the offeree before he has accepted the offer.

An **option** is a *contract* by which the offeror is bound to hold open an offer for a specified time. It must comply with all the requirements of a contract, including consideration. Option contracts apply to all types of contracts, including those for sales of goods.

The Code has made certain offers—called **firm offers**—irrevocable without any consideration being given for the promise to keep the offer open. The Code provides that a merchant who gives assurance in a signed writing that an offer will be held open is bound to keep the offer open for a maximum of three months. Section 2-205; Section 2A-205. The Code, therefore, makes a merchant's written promise not to revoke an offer for a stated time enforceable even though no consideration is given the merchant-offeror for that promise.

For example, Ben's Brewery approached Flora Flooring, Inc., to purchase tile for Ben's floor. Ben's employees would install the tile after it was delivered by Flora. On June 6, Flora sent Ben a written, signed offer to provide the tile according to Ben's specifications for $26,000 and promised that "the offer will remain open until July 17." Flora is bound by her firm offer to keep the offer open until July 17. The result would differ, however, if Flora had merely stated that the "offer terminates on July 17" or that "the offer will terminate if not accepted on or before July 17." In both of these instances, there is no assurance to keep the offer open: because it is not a firm offer, Flora could revoke it at any time prior to Ben's acceptance.

Any firm offer on a form supplied by the offeree must be separately signed by the offeror.

CISG An offer may not be revoked if it indicates that it is irrevocable; it need not be in writing.

21-3c VARIANT ACCEPTANCES

The realities of modern business practices have necessitated the modification by the Code of the common law's "**mirror image**" rule, by which the acceptance cannot vary or deviate from the

terms of the offer. A vast number of business transactions use standardized business forms, resulting in what has been termed the **battle of the forms**. For example, a merchant buyer sends to the merchant seller on the buyer's order form a purchase order for 1,000 dozen cotton shirts at $60 per dozen with delivery by October 1 at the buyer's place of business. On the reverse side of this standard form are twenty-five numbered paragraphs containing provisions generally favorable to the buyer. When the seller receives the buyer's order, he sends to the buyer an unequivocal acceptance of the offer on his acceptance form. Although the seller agrees to the buyer's quantity, price, and delivery terms, on the back of the form the seller utilizes in sending his unequivocal acceptance to the buyer are thirty-two numbered paragraphs generally favorable to the seller and in significant conflict with the buyer's form. Under the common law's "mirror image" rule, no contract would exist, for the seller has not in fact accepted unequivocally all of the material terms of the buyer's offer.

By comparison, Section 2-207 of the Code addresses variant acceptances by providing the following:

1. A definite and seasonable expression of acceptance or a written confirmation which is sent within a reasonable time operates as an acceptance even though it states terms additional to or different from those offered or agreed upon, unless acceptance is expressly made conditional on assent to the additional or different terms.

2. The additional terms are to be construed as proposals for addition to the contract. Between merchants such terms become part of the contract unless:

   (a) the offer expressly limits acceptance to the terms of the offer;

   (b) they materially alter it; or

   (c) notification of objection to them has already been given or is given within a reasonable time after notice of them is received.

3. Conduct by both parties which recognizes the existence of a contract is sufficient to establish a contract for sale although the writings of the parties do not otherwise establish a contract. In such case the terms of the particular contract consist of those terms on which the writings of the parties agree, together with any supplementary terms incorporated under any other provisions of this Act.

Thus, the Code attempts to settle the battle of the forms by focusing upon the intent of the parties. If the offeree expressly makes his acceptance conditioned upon the offeror's assent to the additional or different terms, no contract is formed. If the offeree does not expressly make his acceptance conditional upon such assent, a contract is formed. The issue then becomes whether the offeree's different or additional terms should become part of the contract. If both offeror and offeree are merchants, **additional** terms (terms the offeree proposed for the contract for the first time) will become part of the contract, provided they do not materially alter the agreement and are not objected to either in the offer itself or within a reasonable time. If either of the parties is not a merchant or if the additional terms materially alter the offer, then the terms are merely construed as proposals for addition to the contract. **Different** terms (terms that contradict terms of the offer) proposed by the offeree generally will not become part of the contract unless specifically accepted by the offeror. The courts are divided over what terms are included when the terms conflict. The majority of courts hold that the terms cancel each other out and look to the Code to provide the missing terms; other courts hold that the offeror's terms govern. Some States follow a third alternative and apply the additional terms test to different terms.

Applying Section 2-207 to the previous example: because both parties are merchants and the seller did not condition his acceptance upon the buyer's assent to the additional or different terms, (1) the contract will be formed without the *seller's different terms* unless the buyer specifically accepts them; (2) the contract will be formed without the *seller's additional terms* unless (a) the buyer specifically accepts or (b) the additional terms do not materially alter the offer and the buyer does not object to them; and (3) depending upon the jurisdiction, either (a) the conflicting (different) terms cancel each other out and the Code provides the missing terms or (b) the buyer's conflicting terms are included in the contract or (c) the additional terms test is applied.

CISG A reply to an offer that contains additions, limitations, or other modifications is a counteroffer that rejects the original offer. Nevertheless, a purported acceptance that contains additional or different terms acts as an acceptance if the terms do not materially alter the contract unless the offeror objects to the change. Changes in price, payment, quality, quantity, place and time of delivery, terms of delivery, liability of the parties, and settlement of a dispute are always considered to be material alterations.

Finally, subsection 3 of 2-207 deals with those situations in which the writings do not form a contract but the conduct of the parties recognizes the existence of one. For instance, Ernest makes an offer to Gwen, who replies with a conditional acceptance. Although no contract has been formed, Gwen ships the ordered goods and Ernest accepts the goods. Subsection 3 provides that in this instance, the contract consists of the written terms to which both parties agreed together with supplementary provisions of the Code.

♦ **SEE FIGURE 21-3:** *Battle of the Forms*

♦ *See Case 21-4*

Practical Advice

In negotiating a contract, try to be the offeror and consider providing in your offer that your terms control and that any new or different terms will be made part of the contract only if you specifically agree to them in a signed writing.

21-3d MANNER OF ACCEPTANCE

As with the common law, the offeror may specify the manner in which the offer must be accepted. If the offeror does not and the circumstances do not otherwise clearly indicate, an offer to make a contract invites acceptance in any manner and by any medium reasonable under the circumstances. Section 2-206(1)(a); Section 2A-206(1). The Code, therefore, allows flexibility of response and the ability to keep pace with new modes of communication.

An offer to buy goods for prompt or current shipment may be accepted either by a prompt promise to ship or by prompt shipment. Section 2-206(1)(b). Acceptance by performance requires notice within a reasonable time, or the offer may be treated as lapsed. Section 2-206(2); Section 2A-206(2).

21-3e AUCTIONS

The Code provides that if an auction sale is advertised or announced in explicit terms to be **without reserve**, the auctioneer may not withdraw the article put up for sale unless no bid is made within a reasonable time. Unless the sale is advertised as being without reserve, the sale is **with reserve**, and the auctioneer may withdraw the goods at any time until he announces completion of the sale. Whether the sale is with or without reserve, a bidder may retract his bid at any time prior to acceptance by the auctioneer. Such retraction does not, however, revive any previous bid. Section 2-328.

If the auctioneer knowingly receives a bid by or on behalf of the seller and notice has not been given that the seller reserves the right to bid at the auction sale, the bidder to whom the goods are sold can either avoid the sale or take the goods at the price of the last good faith bid.

CISG The CISG does not apply to sales by auctions.

21-4 Consideration

In several respects, the Code has relaxed the common law requirements regarding consideration. First, the Code has abandoned the common law rule requiring that a modification of an existing contract be supported by consideration to be valid. The Code provides that a contract for the sale of goods can be effectively modified without new consideration, provided the modification is made in good faith. Section 2-209(1); Section 2A-208(1).

FIGURE 21-3 Battle of the Forms

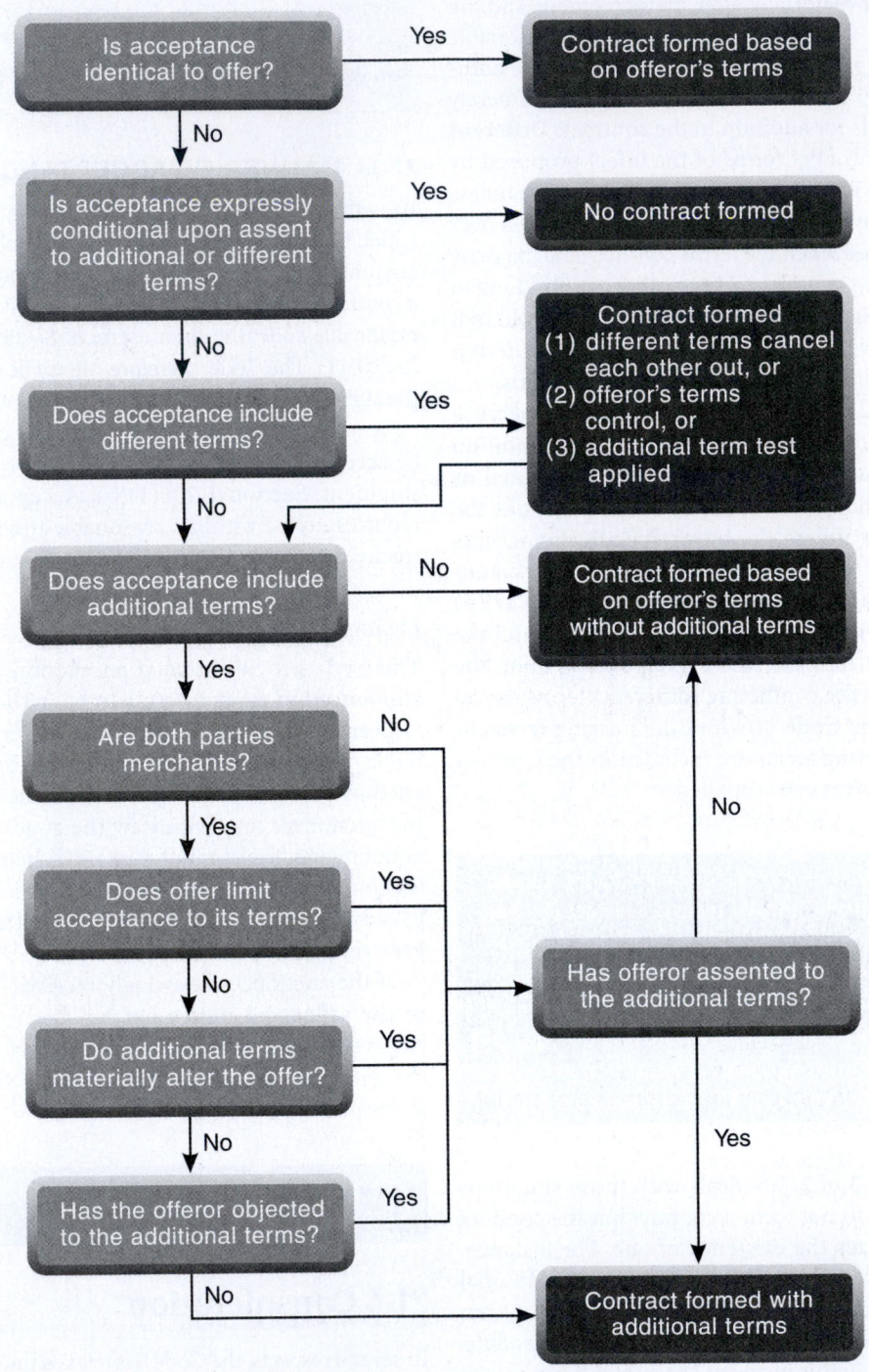

In addition, any claim of right arising out of an alleged breach of contract can be discharged in whole or in part without consideration by a written waiver or renunciation signed and delivered by the aggrieved party. Section 1-107. Under the Revised UCC Article 1, a claim or right arising out of an alleged breach may be discharged in whole or in part without consideration by agreement of the aggrieved party in an authenticated record. Section 1-306. Moreover, as previously noted, a firm offer is not revocable for lack of consideration.

CISG Consideration is not needed to modify a contract.

21-5 Form of the Contract

21-5a STATUTE OF FRAUDS

The original statute of frauds, which applied to contracts for the sale of goods, has been used as a prototype for the Article 2 statute of frauds provision. Section 2-201 of the Code provides that a contract for the sale of goods costing *$500 or more* is not enforceable unless there is some writing or record sufficient to evidence the existence of a contract between the parties ($1,000 or more for leases, Section 2A-201). As discussed in *Chapter 15*, forty-seven States have adopted the **Uniform Electronic Transactions Act (UETA)**, which gives full effect to contracts formed by electronic records and signatures. The Act applies to contracts governed by Articles 2 and 2A. In addition, Congress in 2000 enacted the **Electronic Signatures in Global and National Commerce (E-Sign)**. The Act, which uses language very similar to that of UETA, makes electronic records and signatures valid and enforceable across the United States for many types of transactions in or affecting interstate or foreign commerce. In 2001, the United Nations Commission on International Trade Law (UNCITRAL) adopted the Model Law on Electronic Signatures to bring additional legal certainty regarding the use of electronic signatures. Legislation based on or influenced by it has been adopted in at least thirty-three nations.

CISG A contract need not be evidenced by a writing, unless one of the parties has her place of business in a country that provides otherwise.

MODIFICATION OF CONTRACTS An agreement modifying a contract must be evidenced by a writing or record if the resulting contract is within the statute of frauds. Section 2-209(3). (Article 2A omits this provision.) Conversely, if a contract that was previously within the statute of frauds is modified so as to no longer fall within it, the modification is enforceable even if it is oral. Thus, if the parties enter into an oral contract to sell for $450 a dining room table to be delivered to the buyer and later, prior to delivery, orally agree that the seller shall stain the table and that the buyer shall pay a price of $550, the modified contract is unenforceable. In contrast, if the parties have a written contract for the sale of 150 bushels of wheat at a price of $4.50 per bushel and later, upon oral agreement, decrease the quantity to 100 bushels at the same price per bushel, the agreement, as modified, is enforceable.

A signed agreement that requires modifications or rescissions to be in a signed writing cannot be otherwise modified or rescinded. Section 2-209(2); Section 2A-208(2). If this requirement is on a form provided by a merchant, the other party must separately sign it unless the other party is a merchant.

WRITING(S) OR RECORD The statute of frauds compliance provisions under the Code are more liberal than the rules under general contract law. The Code requires merely some writing or record (1) sufficient to indicate that a contract has been made between the parties, (2) signed by the party against whom enforcement is sought or by her authorized agent or broker, that (3) includes a term specifying the quantity of goods the agreement involves. Whereas general contract law requires that a writing include all essential terms, even a writing or record that omits or incorrectly states a term agreed upon may be sufficient under the Code. This is consistent with other provisions of the Code stating that contracts may be enforced despite the omission of material terms. Nevertheless, the contract is enforceable only to the extent of the quantity set forth in the writing or record. Given proof that a contract was intended and a signed writing describing the goods, their quantity, and the names of the parties, under the Code, the court can supply omitted terms such as price and particulars of performance. Many courts have concluded, however, that the Code does not require a clear and precise quantity term in a requirements or output contract. Moreover, several related documents may satisfy the writing or record requirement.

Between merchants, if within a reasonable time a writing in confirmation of the contract is received, the **written merchant confirmation**, if sufficient against the sender, is also sufficient against the recipient unless he gives written notice of his objection within ten days after receiving the confirmation. Section 2-201(2). (Article 2A does not have a comparable rule.) This means that if these requirements have been met, the recipient of the writing or record is in the same position he would have assumed by signing it and the confirmation, therefore, is enforceable against him. For example, Brown Co. and ATM Industries enter into an oral contract providing that ATM will deliver 1,000 dozen shirts to Brown at $6 per shirt. The next day, Brown sends to ATM a letter signed by Brown's president confirming the agreement. The letter contains the quantity term but does not mention the price. Brown is bound by the contract when its authorized agent sends the letter, whereas ATM is bound by the oral contract ten days after receiving the letter, unless it objects in writing within that time. Therefore, it is essential that merchants examine their mail carefully and promptly to make certain that any written confirmations conform to their understanding of their outstanding contractual agreements. Where one or both of the parties is not a merchant, however, this rule does not apply.

EXCEPTIONS A contract that does not satisfy the writing requirement but is otherwise valid is enforceable in the following instances.

The Code permits an oral contract for the sale of goods to be enforced against a party who in his pleading, testimony, or otherwise in court **admits** that a contract was made, but limits enforcement to the quantity of goods so admitted. Section 2-201(3)(b); Section 2A-201(4)(b). This provision recognizes that the policy behind the statute of frauds does not apply when the party seeking to avoid the oral contract admits under oath the existence of the contract.

The Code also permits enforcement of an oral contract for goods **specially manufactured** for the buyer. Section 2-201(3)(a); Section 2A-201(4)(a). Nevertheless, if the goods, although manufactured on special order, are readily marketable in the ordinary course of the seller's business, the contract is not enforceable unless in writing.

Under the Code, delivery and acceptance of part of the goods or payment of part of the price and acceptance of the payment validates the contract only for the goods that have been **delivered and accepted** or for which **payment** has been **accepted**. Section 2-201(3)(c); Section 2A-201 (4)(c). To illustrate, Debra orally agrees to buy one thousand watches from Brian for $15,000. Brian delivers three hundred watches to Debra, who receives and accepts them. The oral contract is enforceable to the extent of three hundred watches ($4,500)—those received and accepted—but is unenforceable to the extent of seven hundred watches ($10,500).

21-5b PAROL EVIDENCE

Contractual terms that the parties set forth in a writing that they intend as a final expression of their agreement may not be contradicted by evidence of any prior agreement or of a contemporaneous agreement. Nevertheless, under the Code, the terms may be explained or supplemented by (1) course of dealing, usage of trade, or course of performance and (2) evidence of consistent additional terms, unless the writing was intended as the complete and exclusive statement of the terms of the agreement. Section 2-202; Section 2A-202.

For a comparison of general contract law and the law governing sales and leases of goods, see Figure 21-4.

CISG The CISG permits a court to consider all relevant circumstances of the agreement, including the negotiations, any course of performance between the parties, trade usages, and any subsequent conduct.

♦ SEE FIGURE 21-4: *Contract Law Compared with UCC Law of Sales and Leases*

FIGURE 21-4 Contract Law Compared with UCC Law of Sales and Leases

	Contract Law	**UCC Law of Sales and Leases**
Definiteness	Contract must include all material terms	Open terms permitted if parties intend to make contract (Sections 2-204; 2A-204)
Counteroffers	Acceptance must be a mirror image of offer Counteroffer and conditional acceptance are rejections	Battle of forms (Section 2-207) See *Figure 21-3*
Modification of Contract	Consideration is required	Consideration is not required (Sections 2-209; 2A-208)
Irrevocable Offers	Options	Options Firm offers up to three months binding without consideration (Sections 2-205; 2A-205)
Statute of Frauds	Writing must include all material terms	Writing must include quantity term Specially manufactured goods Confirmation by merchants Delivery or payment and acceptance Admissions (Sections 2-201; 2A-201 [except merchant confirmation])

NATURE OF SALES AND LEASES

DEFINITIONS **Goods** movable personal property

Sale transfer of title to goods from seller to buyer for a price

Lease a transfer of right to possession and use of goods in return for consideration

- *Consumer Leases* leases by a merchant to an individual who leases for personal, family, or household purposes for no more than $25,000
- *Finance Leases* special type of lease transaction generally involving three parties: the lessor, the supplier, and the lessee

Governing Law

- *Sales Transactions* governed by Article 2 of the Code, but where general contract law has not been specifically modified by the Code, general contract law continues to apply
- *Lease Transactions* governed by Article 2A of the Code, but where general contract law has not been specifically modified by the Code, general contract law continues to apply
- *Transactions Outside the Code* include employment contracts, service contracts, insurance contracts, contracts involving real property, and contracts for the sale of intangibles

FUNDAMENTAL PRINCIPLES
OF ARTICLE 2 AND
ARTICLE 2A

Purpose to modernize, clarify, simplify, and make uniform the law of sales and leases

Good Faith the Code requires all sales and lease contracts to be performed in good faith, which means honesty in fact and the observance of reasonable commercial standards of fair dealing

Unconscionability a court may refuse to enforce an unconscionable contract or any part of a contract found to be unconscionable

- *Procedural Unconscionability* unfairness of the bargaining process
- *Substantive Unconscionability* oppressive or grossly unfair contractual provisions

Expansion of Commercial Practices

- *Course of Dealing* a sequence of previous conduct between the parties establishing a common basis for interpreting their agreement
- *Usage of Trade* a practice or method of dealing regularly observed and followed in a place, vocation, or trade

Sales by and between Merchants the Code establishes separate rules that apply to transactions between merchants or involving a merchant (a dealer in goods or a person who by his occupation holds himself out as having knowledge or skill peculiar to the goods or practice involved or who employs an agent or broker whom he holds out as having such knowledge or skill)

Liberal Administration of Remedies

Freedom of Contract most provisions of the Code may be varied by agreement

Validation and Preservation of Sales Contract the Code reduces formal requisites to the bare minimum and attempts to preserve agreements whenever the parties manifest an intention to enter into a contract

FORMATION OF SALES AND LEASE CONTRACTS

MANIFESTATION OF MUTUAL ASSENT	**Definiteness of an Offer** the Code provides that a sales or lease contract does not fail for indefiniteness even though one or more terms may have been omitted; the Code provides standards by which missing essential terms may be supplied for sales of goods **Irrevocable Offers** • *Option* a contract to hold open an offer • *Firm Offer* a signed writing by a merchant to hold open an offer for the purchase or sale of goods for a maximum of three months **Variant Acceptances** the inclusion of different or additional terms in an acceptance is addressed by focusing on the intent of the parties **Manner of Acceptance** an acceptance can be made in any reasonable manner and is effective upon dispatch **Auction** auction sales are generally with reserve, permitting the auctioneer to withdraw the goods at any time prior to sale
CONSIDERATION	**Contractual Modifications** the Code provides that a contract for the sale or lease of goods may be modified without new consideration if the modification is made in good faith **Firm Offers** are not revocable for lack of consideration
FORM OF THE CONTRACT	**Statute of Frauds** sale of goods costing $500 or more (or lease of goods for $1,000 or more) must be evidenced by a signed writing to be enforceable • *Writing or Record* the Code requires some writing(s) or record sufficient to indicate that a contract has been made between the parties, signed by the party against whom enforcement is sought or by her authorized agent or broker, and including a term specifying the quantity of goods • *Alternative Methods of Compliance* written confirmation between merchants, admission, specially manufactured goods, and delivery or payment and acceptance **Parol Evidence** contractual terms that are set forth in a writing intended by the parties as a final expression of their agreement may not be contradicted by evidence of any prior agreement or of a contemporaneous oral agreement, but such terms may be explained or supplemented by course of dealing, usage of trade, course of performance, or consistent additional evidence

C A S E S

CASE 21-1

Finance Leases

CARTER v. TOKAI FINANCIAL SERVICES, INC.

Court of Appeals of Georgia, 1998
231 Ga.App. 755, 500 S.E.2d 638

Blackburn, J.

Tokai Financial Services, Inc. brought suit against Randy P. Carter for monies owed under Carter's guaranty of a telephone equipment lease agreement. The trial court granted summary judgment to Tokai, and Carter appeals. * * *

* * *

On January 3, 1996, Tokai's predecessor in interest, Mitel Financial, entered into a "Master Equipment Lease Agreement" (Agreement) with Applied Radiological Control, Inc.

(ARC) for the lease of certain telephone equipment valued at $42,000. Carter personally guaranteed ARC's obligations under the Agreement. ARC made four rental payments and then defaulted on its obligations as of June 1, 1996.

Thereafter, Tokai repossessed the telephone equipment and sold it for $5,900. * * * Tokai then brought this suit against Carter, and the trial court awarded Tokai $56,765.74.

* * * Carter contends the Agreement is a "finance agreement" rather than a true lease. * * *

As an initial matter, we note that Paragraph 13 of the Agreement states that each lease contemplated therein is a finance lease as defined by Article 2A of the UCC. "A 'finance lease' involves three parties—the lessee/business, the finance lessor, and the equipment supplier. The lessee/business selects the equipment and negotiates particularized modifications with the equipment supplier. Instead of purchasing the equipment from the supplier, the lessee/business has a finance lessor purchase the selected equipment, and then leases the equipment from the finance lessor." [Citation.]

Carter contends, nonetheless, that the true intent of the parties was to enter into a security agreement. "Whether a transaction creates a lease or security interest is determined by the facts of each case; however, a transaction creates a security interest if the consideration the lessee is to pay the lessor for the right to possession and use of the goods is an obligation for the term of the lease not subject to termination by the lessee, and (a) [t]he original term of the lease is equal to or greater than the remaining economic life of the goods, (b) [t]he lessee is bound to renew the lease for the remaining economic life of the goods or is bound to become the owner of the goods, (c) [t]he lessee has an option to renew the lease for the remaining economic life of the goods for no additional consideration or nominal additional consideration upon compliance with the lease agreement, or (d) [t]he lessee has an option to become the owner of the goods for no additional consideration or nominal additional consideration upon compliance with the lease agreement." [UCC]1-201(37).

Here, the Agreement's initial term was for five years, ARC was not required to renew the lease or purchase the telephone equipment at the end of the term, and ARC did not have the option to renew the lease or purchase the property at the end of the term for nominal consideration. Therefore, the Agreement does not fit within the definition of a secured transaction provided by [UCC]1-201(37).

Furthermore, "it is commonly held that the 'best test' for determining the intent of an agreement which provides for an option to buy is a comparison of the option price with the market value of the equipment at the time the option is to be exercised. Such a comparison shows whether the lessee is paying actual value acquiring the property at a substantially lower price. * * * If, upon compliance with the terms of the 'lease,' the lessee has an option to become the owner of the property for no additional or for a nominal consideration, the lease is deemed to be intended for security." [Citations.] ARC was given the option to purchase the telephone equipment in this case at the end of the lease term for its fair market value. "Additional consideration is not nominal if * * * when the option to become the owner of the goods is granted to the lessee the price is stated to be the fair market value of the goods determined at the time the option is to be performed." [UCC]§1-201(37)(x). Accordingly, the agreement in this case must be considered a true lease, not a secured transaction. As a result, the procedural safeguards of Article 9 of the UCC are inapplicable to the matter at hand, and Carter's claims under this enumeration must fail. [Citations.] * * *

"In Georgia, all lease contracts for 'goods,' including finance leases, first made or first effective on or after July 1, 1993, are governed by Article 2A of the Uniform Commercial Code." [Citations.] The Agreement was entered into by the parties on January 3, 1996; therefore, it is subject to Article 2A of the UCC. * * *

* * *

Judgment reversed.

CASE	Governing Law	
21-2	**PITTSLEY v. HOUSER**	
	Idaho Court of Appeals, 1994	
	875 P.2d 232	

Swanstrom, J.

[Jane Pittsley contracted with Donald Houser, who was doing business as Hilton Contract Co. (Hilton), to install carpet in her home. The total contract price was $4,402. From this sum, Hilton paid the installers $700 to put the carpet in Pittsley's home. Following installation, Pittsley complained to Hilton that the installation was defective in several respects. Hilton attempted to fix the installation but was unable to satisfy Pittsley. Eventually, Pittsley refused any further efforts to fix the carpet. She sued for rescission of the contract and return of the $3,500 she had previously paid on the contract plus incidental damages. Hilton counterclaimed for the balance due on the contract. The magistrate determined that the breach was not so material as to justify rescission of the contract and awarded Pittsley $250 in repair costs plus $150 in expenses. The magistrate also awarded Hilton the balance of $902 remaining on the contract. Pittsley appealed to the district court, which reversed and remanded the case to the magistrate for additional findings of fact and to apply the Uniform Commercial Code (UCC) to the transaction. Hilton appeals this ruling, asserting that application of the UCC is inappropriate because the only defects alleged were in the installation of the carpet, not in the carpet itself.]

* * *

The single question upon which this appeal depends is whether the UCC is applicable to the subject transaction. If the underlying transaction involved the sale of "goods," then the UCC would apply. If the transaction did not involve goods, but rather was for services, then application of the UCC would be erroneous.

Idaho Code §2-105(1) defines "goods" as "all things (including specially manufactured goods) which are movable at the time of identification to the contract for sale. . ." Although there is little dispute that carpets are "goods," the transaction in this case also involved installation, a service. Such hybrid transactions, involving both goods and services, raise difficult questions about the applicability of the UCC. Two lines of authority have emerged to deal with such situations.

The first line of authority, and the majority position, utilizes the "predominant factor" test. The Ninth Circuit, applying the Idaho Uniform Commercial Code to the subject transaction, restated the predominant factor test as:

> The test for inclusion or exclusion is not whether they are mixed, but, granting that they are mixed, whether their predominant factor, their thrust, their purpose, reasonably stated, is the rendition of service, with goods incidentally involved (e.g., contract with artist for painting) or is a transaction of sale, with labor incidentally involved (e.g., installation of a water heater in a bathroom).

[Citations.] This test essentially involves consideration of the contract in its entirety, applying the UCC to the entire contract or not at all.

The second line of authority, which Hilton urges us to adopt, allows the contract to be severed into different parts, applying the UCC to the goods involved in the contract, but not to the nongoods involved, including services as well as other nongoods assets and property. Thus, an action focusing on defects or problems with the goods themselves would be covered by the UCC, while a suit based on the service provided or some other nongoods aspect would not be covered by the UCC. * * *

We believe the predominant factor test is the more prudent rule. Severing contracts into various parts, attempting to label each as goods or nongoods and applying different law to each separate part clearly contravenes the UCC's declared purpose "to simplify, clarify and modernize the law governing commercial transactions." §1-102(2)(a). As the Supreme Court of Tennessee suggested in [citation], such a rule would, in many contexts, present "difficult and in some instances insurmountable problems of proof in segregating assets and determining their respective values at the time of the original contract and at the time of resale, in order to apply two different measures of damages."

Applying the predominant factor test to the case before us, we conclude that the UCC was applicable to the subject transaction. The record indicates that the contract between the parties called for "165 yds Masterpiece No. 2122—Installed" for a price of $4,319.50. There was an additional charge for removing the existing carpet. The record indicates that Hilton paid the installers $700 for the work done in laying Pittsley's carpet. It appears that Pittsley entered into this contract for the purpose of obtaining carpet of a certain quality and color. It does not appear that the installation, either who would provide it or the nature of the work, was a factor in inducing Pittsley to choose Hilton as the carpet supplier. On these facts, we conclude that the sale of the carpet was the predominant factor in the contract, with the installation being merely incidental to the purchase. Therefore, in failing to consider the UCC, the magistrate did not apply the correct legal principles to the facts as found. We must therefore vacate the judgment and remand for further findings of fact and application of the UCC to the subject transaction.

CASE
21-3

Unconscionability
COLEMAN, INC. v. NUFARM AMERICAS, INC.
United States District Court, North Dakota, 2010
693 F.Supp.2d 1055

Hovland, J.

The plaintiff, DJ Coleman, Inc. ("DJ Coleman"), is a farm corporation that is incorporated in the State of North Dakota and conducts farming operations in Burleigh County, North Dakota. DJ Coleman's principal, Clark Coleman, is responsible for DJ Coleman's commercial farming operations. Clark Coleman is a licensed pesticide purchaser and applicator. The defendant, Nufarm Americas, Inc. ("Nufarm"), is an Illinois corporation. Between May 10, 2007 and May 24, 2007, Clark Coleman planted different varietals of sunflowers. Clark

Coleman used preemergent chemicals, Mad Dog®, a generic glyphosate broad-spectrum herbicide, and Spartan®, a herbicide, prior to planting the sunflowers. Between June 21, 2007 and June 24, 2007, Clark Coleman sprayed his postemergent sunflower crops with a tank mix of Assert®, Scoil®, and Asana®. Nufarm is the manufacturer of Assert® and the wholesale distributor to United Agri Products, Inc. ("UAP"), the direct North Dakota retail seller to Clark Coleman. Clark Coleman did not contact Nufarm for approval before tank mixing Assert®, Scoil®, and Asana in 2007. DJ Coleman alleges that Assert caused severe damage to its 2007 sunflower crop by producing stunted and deformed heads, and seeks economic and non-economic damages.

* * *

Nufarm contends that the Assert label effectively limits any damages for breach of warranties to either the purchase price or the replacement of the product. Section 41-02-94 of the North Dakota Century Code permits the recovery of consequential damages for injury to property proximately resulting from any breach of warranty. However, Section 41-02-98 of the North Dakota Century Code, which is modeled after Section 2-719 of the Uniform Commercial Code, allows the parties to an agreement to limit the remedies available upon breach and to exclude consequential damages: * * * Consequential damages may be limited or excluded unless the limitation or exclusion is unconscionable. Limitation of consequential damages for injury to the person in the case of consumer goods is prima facie unconscionable but limitation of damages where the loss is commercial is not.

* * *

The doctrine of unconscionability permits a court to "'deny enforcement of a contract because of procedural abuses arising out of the contract's formation and substantive abuses relating to the terms of the contract.'" [Citation.] The determination of whether a contractual provision is unconscionable is a question of law. [Citation.] "The court is to look at the contract from the perspective of the time it was entered into, without the benefit of hindsight. The determination to be made is whether, under the circumstances presented in the particular commercial setting, the terms of the agreement are so onesided as to be unconscionable." [Citation.]

North Dakota law provides the Court with several options when a contract, or clause of a contract, is found to be unconscionable:

1. If the court as a matter of law finds the contract or any clause of the contract to have been unconscionable at the time it was made the court may refuse to enforce the contract, or it may enforce the remainder of the contract without the unconscionable clause, or it may so limit the application of any unconscionable clause as to avoid any unconscionable result.

2. When it is claimed or appears to the court that the contract or any clause thereof may be unconscionable the parties shall be afforded a reasonable opportunity to present evidence as to its commercial setting, purpose, and effect to aid the court in making the determination.

N.D.C.C. §41-02-19.

There is no North Dakota case that addresses whether a limitation of remedies provision is unconscionable for injury resulting from the application of agricultural chemicals. * * *

* * *

Courts from other jurisdictions vary on whether a limitation of remedies provision is unconscionable in the chemical agriculture business. * * *

In order to find that a provision is unconscionable, there must be a showing of both procedural and substantive unconscionability. "'The concept of unconscionability must necessarily be applied in a flexible manner, taking into consideration all of the facts and circumstances of a particular case.'" [Citation.]

(a) Procedural Unconscionability

"Procedural unconscionability focuses upon formation of the contract and fairness of the bargaining process, including factors such as inequality of bargaining power, oppression, and unfair surprise." [Citation.] Courts are more likely to find unconscionability in consumer transactions than in commercial transactions involving experienced parties [Citation.] "Courts' general skepticism of unconscionability claims in purely commercial transactions stems from the presumption that businessmen possess a greater degree of commercial understanding and substantially stronger economic bargaining power than the ordinary consumer." [Citation.] Nevertheless, the North Dakota Supreme Court has stated:

[G]eneralizations are always subject to exceptions and categorization is rarely an adequate substitution for analysis. With increasing frequency, courts have begun to recognize that experienced but legally unsophisticated businessmen may be unfairly surprised by unconscionable contract terms...and that even large business entities may have *relatively* little bargaining power, depending on the identity of the other contracting party and the commercial circumstances surrounding the agreement.

* * * It is undisputed that DJ Coleman had no bargaining power to alter the language of the limitation of remedies provision. The limitation of remedies provision contained on the Assert label was pre-printed and was not negotiated. There is a substantial inequality in bargaining power between DJ Coleman and Nufarm. DJ Coleman is a commercial farming operation located in North Dakota, and Nufarm is part of an enormous, highly diversified, and international conglomerate.

* * * [T]he facts of this case do not demonstrate an element of unfair surprise. Clark Coleman testified that he used Assert for ten years prior to 2007. Nonetheless, the evidence reveals that the parties had unequal bargaining power and there was no room for meaningful negotiation. The purchasers of herbicides, regardless of their experience, are not in a position to bargain for more favorable terms than those listed on the pre-printed label, nor are they in a position to test the effectiveness of a herbicide before purchasing it. The fact that Clark Coleman was an experienced farmer that had used Assert on sunflower crops for ten years should not control whether he is entitled to consequential damages for a breach of warranty. Accordingly, the Court finds that the limitation of remedies provision was procedurally unconscionable.

(b) Substantive Unconscionability

Substantive unconscionability focuses on the harshness or one-sidedness of the limitation of remedies provision. [Citation.] The Official Comment to Section 2-719 of the Uniform Commercial Code provides:

> However, it is of the very essence of a sales contact that at least minimum adequate remedies be available. If the parties intend to conclude a contract for sale within this Article they must accept the legal consequence that there be at least a fair quantum of remedy for breach of the obligations or duties outlined in the contract. Thus any clause purporting to modify or limit the remedial provisions of this Article in an unconscionable manner is subject to deletion and in that event the remedies made available by this Article are applicable as if the stricken clause had never existed.

The clause at issue here would limit DJ Coleman's remedy for a breach of an express warranty to the purchase price of Assert or the replacement of the product. The Court finds that the limitation of remedies provision is substantively unconscionable. "[T]he farmer is required to expend large sums of money before any defect [] is noticeable, and once a defect is found an entire year's crop might be worthless. Once the crop has failed, the farmer's only recourse is monetary compensation to cover his lost profit and expenditures; replacement and repair are not viable options." [Citation.] It is clear that the allocation of risk for defective herbicides is better shouldered by the manufacturer of the herbicide, rather than the consumer. The consumer does not have the ability or resources to test its use, but the manufacturer does. The Court finds that the limitation of remedies provision on the Assert label is unconscionable, both procedurally and substantively and, therefore, unenforceable. Accordingly, damages for a breach of express warranty of fitness for a particular purpose are not limited to the purchase price or replacement of the product.

* * *

* * * Summary judgment is granted on the Plaintiff's products liability, negligence, failure to warn, breach of implied warranties, and statutory violation * * * claims. Summary judgment is denied on the Plaintiff's breach of express warranties claim.

| CASE **21-4** | Variant Acceptances: Battle of the Forms
COMMERCE & INDUSTRY INSURANCE COMPANY
v. BAYER CORPORATION
Supreme Judicial Court of Massachusetts, 2001
433 Mass. 388, 742 N.E.2d 567, 44 UCC Rep.Serv.2d 50 |  |

Greaney, J.

We granted the application for direct appellate review of the defendant, Bayer Corporation (Bayer), to determine the enforceability of an arbitration provision appearing in the plaintiff's, Malden Mills Industries, Inc. (Malden Mills), orders purchasing materials from Bayer. In a written decision, a judge in the Superior Court concluded that the provision was not enforceable. * * * We affirm the order.

The background of the case is as follows. Malden Mills manufactures internationally-known apparel fabrics and other textiles. On December 11, 1995, an explosion and fire destroyed several Malden Mills's buildings at its manufacturing facility. Subsequently, Malden Mills and its property insurers, the plaintiffs Commerce and Industry Insurance Company and Federal Insurance Company, commenced suit in the Superior Court against numerous defendants, including Bayer. In their complaint, the plaintiffs allege, insofar as relevant here, that the cause of the fire was the ignition, by static electrical discharge, of nylon tow (also known as bulk nylon fiber), which was sold by Bayer (but manufactured by a French business entity) to Malden Mills. * * *

Malden Mills initiated purchases of nylon tow from Bayer either by sending its standard form purchase order to Bayer, or by placing a telephone order to Bayer, followed by a standard form purchase order. Each of Malden Mills's purchase orders contained, on the reverse side, as one of its "terms and conditions," an arbitration provision stating:

> Any controversy arising out of or relating to this contract shall be settled by arbitration in the City of New York or Boston as [Malden Mills] shall determine in accordance with the rules then obtaining of the American Arbitration Association or the General Arbitration Council of the Textile Industry, as [Malden Mills] shall determine.

Another "term and condition" appearing in paragraph one on the reverse side of each purchase order provides:

> This purchase order represents the entire agreement between both parties, not withstanding any Seller's order form, * * *, and this document cannot be modified except in writing and signed by an authorized representative of the buyer.

In response, Bayer transmitted Malden Mills's purchase orders to the manufacturer with instructions, in most instances, that the nylon tow was to be shipped directly to Malden Mills. Thereafter, Bayer prepared and sent Malden Mills an invoice. Each of the Bayer invoices contained the following language on its face, located at the bottom of the form in capital letters:

> TERMS AND CONDITIONS: NOTWITHSTANDING ANY CONTRARY OR INCONSISTENT CONDITIONS THAT MAY BE EMBODIED IN YOUR PURCHASE ORDER, YOUR ORDER IS ACCEPTED SUBJECT TO THE PRICES, TERMS AND CONDITIONS OF THE MUTUALLY EXECUTED CONTRACT BETWEEN US, OR, IF NO SUCH CONTRACT EXISTS, YOUR ORDER IS ACCEPTED SUBJECT TO OUR REGULAR SCHEDULED PRICE AND TERMS IN EFFECT AT TIME OF SHIPMENT AND SUBJECT TO THE TERMS AND CONDITIONS PRINTED ON THE REVERSE SIDE HEREOF.

The following "condition" appears in paragraph fourteen on the reverse side of each invoice:

> This document is not an Expression of Acceptance or a Confirmation document as contemplated in Section 2-207 of the Uniform Commercial Code. The acceptance of any order entered by [Malden Mills] is expressly conditioned on [Malden Mills's] assent to any additional or conflicting terms contained herein.

Malden Mills usually remitted payment to Bayer within thirty days of receiving an invoice.

Based on the arbitration provision in Malden Mills's purchase orders, Bayer demanded that Malden Mills arbitrate its claims against Bayer. After Malden Mills refused, Bayer moved to compel arbitration and to stay the litigation against it. The judge denied Bayer's motion, concluding, under §2-207 of * * * the Massachusetts enactment of the Uniform Commercial Code, that the parties' conduct, as opposed to their writings, established a contract. As to whether the arbitration provision was an enforceable term of the parties' contract, the judge concluded that subsection (3) of §2-207 governed, and, pursuant thereto, the arbitration provision was not enforceable because the parties had not agreed in their writings to arbitrate. * * *

This case presents a dispute arising from what has been styled a typical "battle of the forms" sale, in which a buyer and a seller each attempt to consummate a commercial transaction through the exchange of self-serving preprinted forms that clash, and contradict each other, on both material and minor terms. [Citation.] Here, Malden Mills's form, a purchase order, contains an arbitration provision, and Bayer's form, a seller's invoice, is silent on how the parties will resolve any disputes. Oddly enough, the buyer, Malden Mills, the party proposing the arbitration provision, and its insurers, now seek to avoid an arbitral forum.

Section 2-207 was enacted with the expectation of creating an orderly mechanism to resolve commercial disputes resulting from a "battle of the forms." The section has been characterized as "an amphibious tank that was originally designed to fight in the swamps, but was sent to fight in the desert." [Citation.] Section 2-207 sets forth rules and principles concerning contract formation and the procedures for determining the terms of a contract. As to contract formation, under §2-207, there are essentially three ways by which a contract may be formed. [Citation.] "First, if the parties exchange forms with divergent terms, yet the seller's invoice does not state that its acceptance is made 'expressly conditional' on the buyer's assent to any additional or different terms in the invoice, a contract is formed [under subsection (1) of §2-207]." "Second, if the seller does make its acceptance 'expressly conditional' on the buyer's assent to any additional or divergent terms in the seller's invoice, the invoice is merely a counteroffer, and a contract is formed [under subsection (1) of §2-207] only when the buyer expresses its affirmative acceptance of the seller's counteroffer." Third, "where for any reason the exchange of forms does not result in contract formation (e.g., the buyer 'expressly limits acceptance to the terms of [its offer]' under §2-207(2)(a), or the buyer does not accept the seller's counteroffer under the second clause of §2-207[1]), a contract nonetheless is formed [under subsection (3) of §2-207] if their subsequent conduct—for instance, the seller ships and the buyer accepts the goods—demonstrates that the parties believed that a binding agreement had been formed."

Bayer correctly concedes that its contract with Malden Mills resulted from the parties' conduct, and, thus, was formed pursuant to subsection (3) of §2-207. A contract never came into being under subsection (1) of §2-207 because (1) paragraph fourteen on the reverse side of Bayer's invoices expressly conditioned acceptance on Malden Mills's assent to "additional or different" terms, and (2) Malden Mills never expressed "affirmative acceptance" of any of Bayer's invoices. In addition, the exchange of forms between Malden Mills and Bayer did not result in a contract because Malden Mills, by means of language in paragraph one of its purchase orders, expressly limited Bayer's acceptance to the terms of Malden Mills's offers. [Citation.]

* * *

* * * Where a contract is formed by the parties' conduct (as opposed to writings), as is the case here, the terms of the contract are determined exclusively by subsection (3) of §2-207. [Citation.] Under subsection (3) of §2-207, "the terms of the particular contract consist of those terms on which the writings of the parties agree, together with any supplementary terms incorporated under any other provisions of this chapter." §2-207 (3). In this respect, one commentator has aptly referred to subsection (3) of §2-207 as the "fall-back" rule. [Citation.] Under this rule, the Code accepts "common terms but rejects all the rest." While this approach "serves to leave many matters uncovered," terms may be filled by "recourse to usages of trade or course of dealing under [§] 1-205 or, perhaps, the gap filling provisions of [§§] 2-300s." [Citation.]

* * *

Thus, the judge correctly concluded, under subsection (3) of §2-207, that the arbitration provision in Malden Mills's purchase orders did not become a term of the parties' contract. The arbitration provision was not common to both Malden Mills's purchase orders and Bayer's invoices. Bayer properly does not argue that any of the gap-filling provisions of [the UCC] apply. Because Bayer concedes that it never previously arbitrated a dispute with Malden Mills, we reject Bayer's claim that the parties' course of dealing requires us to enforce the arbitration provision.

* * *

Bayer may be right that the drafters of the Massachusetts version of the Code did not intend that §2-207 should provide "an avenue for a party to strike the terms of its own purchase documents." Bayer, however, cannot ignore the fact that the use of its own boilerplate invoices contributed to the result that Bayer now finds problematic. * * * The order denying the motion to compel arbitration and to stay litigation is affirmed.

QUESTIONS

1. Adams orders one thousand widgets at $5 per widget from International Widget to be delivered within sixty days. After the contract is consummated and signed, Adams requests that International deliver the widgets within thirty days rather than sixty days. International agrees. Is the contractual modification binding? Why or why not?

2. In Question 1, explain what effect, if any, would the following letter have? International Widget:

   > In accordance with our agreement of this date, you will deliver the one thousand previously ordered widgets within thirty days. Thank you for your cooperation in this matter. (signed) Adams

3. Browne & Assoc., a San Francisco company, orders from U.S. Electronics, a New York company, ten thousand electronic units. Browne & Assoc.'s order form provides that any dispute would be resolved by an arbitration panel located in San Francisco. U.S. Electronics executes and delivers to Browne & Assoc. its acknowledgment form, which accepts the order and contains the following provision: "All disputes will be resolved by the State courts of New York." A dispute arises concerning the workmanship of the parts, and Browne & Assoc. wishes the case to be arbitrated in San Francisco. What result? Explain.

4. Explain how the result in Question 3 might change if the U.S. Electronics form contained any of the following provisions:

   a. "The seller's acceptance of the purchase order to which this acknowledgment responds is expressly made conditional on the buyer's assent to any or different terms contained in this acknowledgment."

   b. "The seller's acceptance of the purchase order is subject to the terms and conditions on the face and reverse side hereof and which the buyer accepts by accepting the goods described herein."

   c. "The seller's terms govern this agreement—this acknowledgment merely constitutes a counteroffer."

5. Reinfort executed a written contract with Bylinski to purchase an assorted collection of shoes for $3,000. A week before the agreed shipment date, Bylinski called Reinfort and said, "We cannot deliver at $3,000; unless you agree to pay $4,000, we will cancel the order." After considerable discussion, Reinfort agreed to pay $4,000 if Bylinski would ship as agreed in the contract. After the shoes had been delivered and accepted by Reinfort, Reinfort refused to pay $4,000 and insisted on paying only $3,000. Is the contractual modification binding? Explain.

6. On November 23, Acorn, a dress manufacturer, mailed to Bowman a written and signed offer to sell one thousand sundresses at $50 per dress. The offer stated that it would "remain open for ten days" and that it could "not be withdrawn prior to that date."

Two days later, Acorn, noting a sudden increase in the price of sundresses, changed his mind. Acorn therefore sent Bowman a letter revoking the offer. The letter was sent on November 25 and received by Bowman on November 28.

Bowman chose to disregard the letter of November 25; instead, she happily continued to watch the price of sundresses rise. On December 1, Bowman sent a letter accepting the original offer. The letter, however, was not received by Acorn until December 9, due to a delay in the mails.

Bowman has demanded delivery of the goods according to the terms of the offer of November 23, but Acorn has refused. Does a contract exist between Acorn and Bowman? Explain.

7. Henry and Wilma, an elderly immigrant couple, agreed to purchase from Brown a refrigerator with fair market value of $450 for twenty-five monthly installments of $60 per month. Henry and Wilma now wish to void the contract, asserting that they did not realize the exorbitant price they were paying. Result?

8. Courts Distributors needed two hundred compact refrigerators on a rush basis. It contacted Eastinghouse Corporation, a manufacturer of refrigerators. Eastinghouse said it would take some time to quote a price on an order of that size. Courts replied, "Send the refrigerators immediately and bill us later." The refrigerators were delivered three days later and the invoice ten days after that. The price was $140,000. The Court believes that the wholesale market price of the refrigerators is only $120,000. Do the parties have a contract? If so, what is the price? Explain the result.

C A S E   P R O B L E M S

9. While adjusting a television antenna beside his mobile home and underneath a high-voltage electric transmission wire, Prince received an electric shock resulting in personal injury. He claims the high-voltage electric current jumped from the transmission wire to the antenna. The wire, which carried some 7,200 volts of electricity, did not serve his mobile home but ran directly above it. Prince sued the Navarro County Electric Co-Op, the owner and operator of the wire, for breach of implied warranty of merchantability under the Uniform Commercial Code. He contends that the Code's implied warranty of merchantability extends to the container of a product—in this instance the wiring—and that the escape of the current shows that the wiring was unfit for its purpose of transporting electricity. The electric company argues that the electricity passing through the transmission wire was not being sold to Prince and that, therefore, there was no sale of goods to Prince. Is the contract covered by the Code? Explain.

10. HMT, already in the business of marketing agricultural products, decided to try its hand at marketing potatoes for processing. Nine months before the potato harvest, HMT contracted to supply Bell Brand with one hundred thousand sacks of potatoes. At harvest time, Bell Brand would accept only sixty thousand sacks. HMT sues for breach of contract. Bell Brand argues that custom and usage in marketing potatoes for processing allows buyers to give *estimates* in contracts, not fixed quantities, because the contracts are established so far in advance. HMT responds that the quantity term in the contract was definite and unambiguous. Can custom and trade usage be used to interpret an unambiguous contract? Discuss.

11. Schreiner, a cotton farmer, agreed over the telephone to sell 150 bales of cotton to Loeb & Co. Schreiner had sold cotton to Loeb & Co. for the past five years. Written confirmation of the date, parties, price, and conditions was mailed to Schreiner, who did not respond to the confirmation in any way. Four months later, when the price of cotton had doubled, Loeb & Co. sought to enforce the contract. Explain whether the contract is enforceable.

12. American Sand & Gravel, Inc., agreed to sell sand to Clark at a special discount if at least 20,000 tons were ordered. The discount price was $0.45 per ton, compared with the normal price of $0.55 per ton. Clark ordered and received 1,600 tons of sand from American Sand & Gravel. Clark refused to pay more than $0.45 per ton. American Sand & Gravel sued for the remaining $0.10 per ton. Decision? Explain.

13. In September, Auburn Plastics (defendant) submitted price quotations to CBS (plaintiff) for the manufacture of eight cavity molds to be used in making parts for CBS's toys. Each quotation specified that the offer would not be binding unless accepted within fifteen days. Furthermore, CBS would be subject to an additional 30 percent charge for engineering services upon delivery of the molds. In December, CBS sent detailed purchase orders to Auburn Plastics for cavity molds. The purchase order forms stated that CBS reserved the right to remove the molds from Auburn Plastics without an additional or "withdrawal" charge. Auburn Plastics acknowledged the purchase order and stated that the sale would be subject

to all conditions contained in the price quotation. CBS paid Auburn for the molds, and Auburn began to fabricate toy parts from the molds for CBS. Later, Auburn announced a price increase, and CBS demanded delivery of the molds. Auburn refused to deliver the molds unless CBS paid the additional charge for engineering services. CBS claimed that the contract did not provide for a withdrawal charge. Who will prevail? Why?

14. Frank's Maintenance and Engineering, Inc., orally ordered steel tubing from C.A. Roberts Co. for use in the manufacture of motorcycle front fork tubes. Because these front fork tubes bear the bulk of the weight of a motorcycle, the steel used must be of high quality. Roberts Co. sent an acknowledgment with conditions of sale including one that limited consequential damages and restricted remedies available upon breach by requiring claims for defective equipment to be made promptly upon receipt. The conditions were located on the back of the acknowledgment. The legend "conditions of sale on reverse side" was stamped over so that on first appearance it read "No conditions of sale on reverse side." Roberts delivered the order in January. The steel had no visible defects; however, when Frank's Maintenance began using the steel in its manufacture in the summer, it discovered that the steel was pitted and cracked beyond repair. Frank's Maintenance informed Roberts Co. of the defects, revoked its acceptance of the steel, and sued for breach of warranty of merchantability. Is the limitation of rights enforceable? Why or why not?

15. Dorton, as a representative for The Carpet Mart, purchased carpets from Collins & Aikman that were supposedly manufactured of 100 percent Kodel polyester fiber but were, in fact, made of cheaper and inferior fibers. Dorton then brought suit for compensatory and punitive damages against Collins & Aikman for its fraud, deceit, and misrepresentation in the sale of the carpets. Collins & Aikman moved for a stay pending arbitration, claiming that Dorton was bound to an arbitration agreement printed on the reverse side of Collins & Aikman's printed sales acknowledgment form. A provision printed on the face of the acknowledgment form stated that its acceptance was "subject to all of the terms and conditions on the face and reverse side thereof, including arbitration, all of which are accepted by buyer." Is the arbitration clause enforceable? Why or why not?

16. Defendant, Gray Communications, desired to build a television tower. After a number of negotiation sessions conducted by telephone between the Defendant and Plaintiff, Kline Iron, the parties allegedly reached an oral agreement under which the Plaintiff would build a tower for the Defendant for a total price of $1,485,368. A few days later, Plaintiff sent a written document, referred to as a proposal, for execution by Defendant. The Proposal indicated that it had been prepared for immediate acceptance by Defendant and that prior to formal acceptance by Defendant it could be modified or withdrawn without notice. A few days later, without having executed the Proposal, Defendant advised Plaintiff that a competitor had provided a lower bid for construction of the tower. Defendant requested that Plaintiff explain its higher bid price, which Plaintiff failed to do. Defendant then advised Plaintiff by letter that it would not be retained to construct the tower. Plaintiff then commenced suit alleging breach of an oral contract, asserting that the oral agreement was enforceable because the common law of contracts, not the Uniform Commercial Code (UCC), governed the transaction and that under the common law a writing is not necessary to cover this type of transaction. Even if the transaction was subject to the UCC, Plaintiff alternatively argued, the contract was within the UCC "merchant's exception." Is the plaintiff correct in its assertions? Discuss.

17. Due to high gasoline prices, American Bakeries Company (ABC) considered converting its fleet of more than three thousand vehicles to a much less expensive propane fuel system. After negotiations with Empire Gas Corporation (Empire), ABC signed a contract for approximately three thousand converter units, "more or less depending upon requirements of Buyer," as well as agreeing to buy all propane to be used for four years from Empire. Without giving any reasons, however, ABC never ordered any converter units or propane from Empire, having apparently decided not to convert its vehicles. Empire brought suit against ABC for $3,254,963, representing lost profits on 2,242 converter units and the propane that would have been consumed during the contract period. Is ABC liable? Explain.

18. Emery Industries (Emery) contracted with Mechanicals, Inc. (Mechanicals), to install a pipe system to carry chemicals and fatty acids under high pressure and temperature. The system required stainless steel "stub ends" (used to connect pipe segments), which Mechanicals ordered from McJunkin Corporation (McJunkin). McJunkin in turn ordered the stub ends from the Alaskan Copper Companies, Inc. (Alaskan). McJunkin's purchase order required the seller to certify the goods and to relieve the buyer of liabilities that might arise from defective goods. After shipment of the goods to McJunkin, Alaskan sent written acknowledgment of the order, containing terms and conditions of sale different from those in McJunkin's purchase order. The acknowledgment provided a disclaimer of warranty and

a requirement for inspection of the goods within ten days of receipt. The acknowledgment also contained a requirement that the buyer accept all of the seller's terms.

The stub ends were delivered to Mechanicals in several shipments over a five-month period. Each shipment included a document reciting terms the same as those on Alaskan's initial acknowledgment. Apparently, McJunkin never objected to any of the terms contained in any of Alaskan's documents.

After the stub ends were installed, they were found to be defective. Mechanicals had to remove and replace them, causing Emery to close its plant for several days. McJunkin filed a complaint alleging that Mechanicals had failed to pay $26,141.88 owed on account for the stub ends McJunkin supplied. Mechanicals filed an answer and counterclaim against McJunkin, alleging $93,586.13 in damages resulting from the replacement and repair of the defective stub ends. McJunkin filed a third-party complaint against Alaskan, alleging that Alaskan was liable for any damages Mechanicals incurred as a result of the defective stub ends. Discuss.

19. Click2Boost, Inc. (C2B), entered into an Internet marketing agreement with the New York Times Company (NYT). Under the agreement, C2B was to solicit subscribers for home delivery of *The New York Times* newspaper by means of pop-up ads on websites with which C2B maintained "[m]arketing [a]lliances." According to C2B's description of the Internet marketing system it used in connection with the agreement, a person who clicked on the pop-up ad was invited to submit his or her zip code; if the zip code was suitable for home delivery of *The New York Times*, the person was prompted to provide additional information needed for a subscription; upon submission of this information, the C2B system displayed a confirmation of the subscription. The agreement required NYT to pay C2B a fee or commission for each home delivery subscription C2B submitted to NYT. Explain whether this contract is covered by the UCC.

20. Construction Associates (CA) was the successful bidder to construct a water supply line for the city of Breckenridge, Minnesota. CA purchased a large amount of polyvinyl chloride pipe manufactured by the Johns-Manville Sales Corporation (J-M) to construct the pipeline. CA, however, did not have any direct contact with J-M; instead, it purchased the pipe through an intermediate supply company. J-M shipped the pipe directly to the work site and included with each shipment an installation guide written for those who directed the installation of the pipe. On page 3 of the installation guide, J-M expressly warranted the pipe to be free from defects in workmanship and materials. In addition, J-M set forth a limitation of liability clause, which stated there would be no liability except for breach of the express warranty and that J-M would be responsible only for resupplying a like quantity of nondefective pipe. J-M stated that it would not be liable for any incidental, consequential, or other damages. Eventually the Breckenridge pipeline developed more than seventy leaks. The only way these leaks could be repaired was to remove the defective joints and replace them with stainless steel sleeves. After incurring more than $140,000 in repairs to the pipeline, CA sued J-M. In response, J-M claimed that the limitation of liability clause should be enforced, and, therefore, J-M is only responsible for resupplying a like quantity of nondefective pipe. Decision? Explain.

TAKING SIDES

Terminal Grain Corporation brought an action against Glen Freeman, a farmer, to recover damages for breach of an oral contract to deliver grain. According to Terminal Grain, Freeman orally agreed to two sales of wheat to Terminal Grain of four thousand bushels each at $6.21 a bushel and $6.41 a bushel, respectively. Dwayne Maher, merchandising manager of Terminal Grain, sent two written confirmations of the agreements to Freeman. Freeman never made any written objections to the confirmations. After the first transaction had occurred, the price of wheat rose to between $6.75 and $6.80 per bushel, and Freeman refused to deliver the remaining four thousand bushels at the agreed-upon price. Freeman denies entering into any agreement to sell the second four thousand bushels of wheat to Terminal Grain but admits that he received the two written confirmations sent by Maher.

(a) What arguments support considering Freeman to be a merchant who is bound by the written confirmations?

(b) What arguments support considering Freeman not to be a merchant seller and thus not bound by the written confirmations?

(c) What is the appropriate decision?

CHAPTER 22

Performance

After reading and studying this chapter, you should be able to:

- Explain the requirements of tender of delivery with respect to time, manner, and place of delivery.

- Explain the perfect tender rule and the three limitations on it.

- Explain when the buyer has the right to reject the goods and what obligations the buyer has upon rejection.

- Explain what constitutes acceptance by the buyer and the buyer's right to revoke acceptance.

- Describe the excuses for nonperformance and the Uniform Commercial Code's provisions for protecting the parties' expectations of performance by the other party.

P erformance is the process of discharging contractual obligations by carrying out those obligations according to the terms of the contract. The basic obligation of the seller in a contract for the sale of goods is to transfer and deliver goods that conform to the terms of the contract. The basic obligation of the buyer is to accept and pay for conforming goods in accordance with the contract. The basic obligation of the lessor is to transfer possession of the goods for the lease term, and that of the lessee is to pay the agreed rent. Section 2A-103(1)(j). Unless the parties have agreed otherwise, a tender (offer) of performance by one party is a condition to performance by the other party. A contract of sale also requires that each party not impair the other party's expectation of having the contract performed.

The obligations of the parties are determined by their contractual agreement. For example, the contract of sale may expressly provide that the seller must deliver the goods before receiving payment of the price or that the buyer must pay the price before receiving the goods. If the contract does not sufficiently cover the particulars of performance, these terms will be supplied by the Code, common law, course of dealing, usage of trade, and course of performance. (Article 2A provides only a few gap-fillers.) In all events, both parties to the sales contract must perform their contractual obligations in good faith.

This chapter examines the performance obligations of the seller and the buyer as well as the contractual obligations that apply to both of them.

22-1 Performance by the Seller

Tender of conforming goods by the seller entitles him to acceptance of them by the buyer and to payment of the contractually agreed-upon price. Nonetheless, the rights of the parties may be otherwise fixed by the terms of the contract. For example, if the seller has agreed to sell goods on sixty or ninety days' credit, he is required to perform his part of the contract before the buyer performs.

Tender of delivery requires that the seller put and hold goods that conform to the contract at the buyer's disposition and that he give the buyer reasonable notification to enable her to take delivery. Section 2-503. Tender must also be made at a reasonable time and be kept open for a reasonable period. For example, Roberto agrees to sell Barbara a home theater system composed of a speaker system (consisting of four identical, small speakers for the front and rear, a center channel speaker, and a subwoofer speaker), a Blu-ray disc player, and an audio-video receiver. Each component is specified by manufacturer and model number, and delivery is to be at Roberto's store. Roberto obtains the ordered equipment in accordance with the contractual specifications and notifies Barbara that she may pick up the system at her convenience. Roberto has now tendered and thus has performed his obligations under the sales contract: he holds goods that conform to the contract, he has reasonably placed them at the buyer's disposal, and he has notified the buyer of their readiness.

CISG According to the United Nations Convention on Contracts for the International Sales of Goods (CISG), the seller must deliver the goods, hand over any documents relating to them, and transfer the property in the goods, as specified by the contract and the CISG.

22-1a TIME AND MANNER OF TENDER

Tender must be at a *reasonable* time, and the goods tendered must be kept available for the period reasonably necessary to enable the buyer to take possession of them. Unless otherwise agreed, the buyer must furnish facilities reasonably suited to the receipt of the goods tendered by the seller. Section 2-503.

If the terms of the contract do not fix a definite time for delivery, the seller is allowed a reasonable time after entering into the contract within which to tender the goods to the buyer. Likewise, the buyer has a reasonable time within which to accept delivery. What length of time is reasonable depends upon the facts and circumstances of each case. If the goods can be delivered immediately, a reasonable time would be very short. Where the goods must be constructed or manufactured, however, "reasonable" would take into account the usual length of time required to make the goods.

A contract may not be performed piecemeal or in installments unless the parties specifically agree. If such performance is not so specified, all of the goods the contract specifies must be tendered in a single delivery, and payment is due on such tender.

CISG The seller must deliver the goods (1) if a date is fixed by or determinable from the contract on that date; (2) if a period of time is fixed by or determinable from the contract at any time within that period unless circumstances indicate that the buyer is to choose a date; or (3) in any other case, within a reasonable time after the conclusion of the contract.

22-1b PLACE OF TENDER

If the contract does not specify the place for delivery of the goods, the place for delivery is the *seller's place of business* or, if he has none, his residence. The seller must hold the goods for the buyer's disposition and notify her that the goods are being held for her to pick up. Section 2-308(a). If the contract is for the sale of identified goods that the parties know at the time of making the contract are located neither at the seller's place of business nor at his residence, the *location* of the goods is then the place for delivery. Section 2-308. For example, Jamal, a boat builder in Chicago, contracts to sell to Chris a certain yacht that both parties know is anchored at Milwaukee. The place of delivery would be Milwaukee. On the other hand, if the contract provides that Jamal shall overhaul the motor at his shipyard in Chicago, Jamal would have to return the yacht to Chicago, and the place of delivery would be Jamal's Chicago shipyard.

The parties frequently agree expressly upon the place of tender, typically by using one of various *delivery terms*. These terms specify whether the contract is a shipment or destination contract and determine the place where the seller must tender delivery of the goods.

CISG If the seller is not bound to deliver the goods at any other particular place and the contract of sale does not involve carriage of the goods, his obligation to deliver consists (1) if the contract relates to specific goods or unidentified goods to be drawn from a specific stock or to be manufactured or produced and at the time of the conclusion of the contract the parties knew that the goods were at or were to be manufactured or produced at a particular place, in placing the goods at the buyer's disposal at that place and (2) in other cases, in placing the goods at the buyer's disposal at the place where the seller had his place of business at the time of the conclusion of the contract.

SHIPMENT CONTRACTS The delivery terms *F.O.B. (free on board) place of shipment, F.A.S. (free alongside ship) port of shipment, C.I.F. (cost, insurance, and freight),* and *C.&F. (cost and freight)* are all "shipment contracts." Under a shipment contract, the seller is required or authorized to send the goods to the buyer, but the contract does not obligate her to deliver them at a particular destination. In these cases, the seller's tender of performance occurs at the point of shipment, provided the seller meets certain specified conditions designed to protect the interests of the absent buyer. A contract is assumed to be a shipment contract unless otherwise indicated.

Under the Uniform Commercial Code (UCC), the initials "F.O.B." and "F.A.S." are delivery terms, even though they are used only in connection with a stated price. Section 2-319(1)(a). A contract providing that the sale is **F.O.B. place of shipment** or **F.A.S. port of shipment** is a shipment contract. For example, Linda, whose place of business is in New York, enters into a contract with Holly, the buyer, who is located in San Francisco. The contract calls for delivery of the goods F.O.B. New York. This would be a shipment contract. Under a **C.I.F.** contract, in consideration for an agreed unit price for the goods, the seller agrees to pay all costs of transportation, insurance, and freight to the destination. The amount of the agreed unit price of the goods will, of course, reflect these costs. By comparison, under a **C.&F.** contract, the seller would pay "cost and freight." The unit price in such a contract is understandably less than in a C.I.F. contract as the C.&F. contract does not include the cost of insurance.

Under a shipment contract, the seller is required to (1) deliver the goods to a carrier, (2) make a contract for their transportation that is reasonable given the nature of the goods and other circumstances, (3) obtain and promptly deliver or tender to the buyer any document necessary to enable the buyer to obtain possession of the goods from the carrier, and (4) promptly notify the buyer of the shipment. Section 2-504. Failing either to make a proper contract for transportation or to notify the buyer of the shipment is a ground for rejection only if material loss or delay results. Section 2-504.

CISG If the seller is not bound to deliver the goods at any other particular place and if the contract of sale involves carriage of the goods, his obligation to deliver consists of handing the goods over to the first carrier for delivery to the buyer.

DESTINATION CONTRACTS The delivery terms *F.O.B. city of buyer, ex-ship,* and *no arrival, no sale* are destination contracts. Because a destination contract requires the seller to tender delivery of conforming goods at a specified destination, the seller must place the goods at the buyer's disposition and give the buyer reasonable notice to enable him to take delivery. In addition, if the destination contract involves documents of title, the seller must tender the necessary documents. Section 2-503.

When the contract provides that the sale is **F.O.B. place of destination**, the seller must at his own expense and risk transport the goods to that place and there tender delivery of them to the buyer. Section 2-319(1)(b). For example, if the buyer is in Boston and the seller is in Chicago, a contract providing F.O.B. Boston is a destination contract under which the seller must tender the goods at the designated place in Boston at his own expense and risk. A contract that provides for delivery "**ex-ship**," or from the ship, is also a destination contract, requiring the seller to unload the goods from the carrier at the named destination. Finally, where the contract contains the terms "**no arrival, no sale,**" the title and risk of loss do not pass to the buyer until the seller makes a tender of the goods after they arrive at their destination. The major significance of the "no arrival, no sale" term is that it excuses the seller from any liability to the buyer for the goods' failure to arrive, unless the seller has caused their nonarrival.

Practical Advice

In your sales contracts, clearly specify by use of the correct shipment term or specific language which party pays the shipping costs and where the seller must tender delivery of the goods.

GOODS HELD BY BAILEE Where goods are in the possession of a bailee and are to be delivered without being moved, in most instances, the seller may either tender to the buyer a document of title or obtain an acknowledgment by the bailee of the buyer's right to possess the goods. Section 2-503(4). This acknowledgment permits the buyer to obtain the goods directly from the bailee.

♦ **SEE FIGURE 22-1:** *Tender of Performance by the Seller*

22-1c PERFECT TENDER RULE

The Code imposes upon the seller the obligation to conform her tender of goods *exactly* to the requirements of the contract. The seller's tender cannot deviate in any way from the terms of the contract. Thus, a buyer may rightfully reject the delivery of 110 dozen shirts under an agreement calling for delivery of 100 dozen shirts. The size or extent of the breach does not affect the right to reject.

If the goods or the tender of delivery fail in any respect to conform to the contract, the buyer may (1) reject the whole lot, (2) accept the whole lot, or (3) accept any commercial unit or units and reject the rest. Section 2-601; Section 2A-509(1). A commercial unit means such a unit of goods as by commercial usage is a single unit and which, if divided, would be materially impaired in character or value. A **commercial unit** may be a single item (such as a machine), a set of articles (such as a suite of furniture or an assortment of sizes), a quantity (such as a bale, gross, or carload), or any other unit treated in use or in the relevant market as a whole. Section 2-105(6); Section 2A-103(1)(c).

CISG The CISG does not follow the perfect tender rule. The buyer may declare the contract avoided if the failure by the seller to perform any of his obligations under the contract or the CISG amounts to a fundamental breach of contract. A breach of contract committed by one of the parties is fundamental if it results in such detriment to the other party as substantially to deprive her of what she is entitled to expect under the contract, unless the party in breach did not foresee and a reasonable person of the same kind in the same circumstances would not have foreseen such a result.

The buyer's right to reject the goods upon the seller's failure to comply with the perfect tender rule is subject to three basic qualifications: (1) agreement between the parties limiting the buyer's right to reject nonconforming goods, (2) cure by the seller, and (3) the existence of an installment contract. In addition, as previously discussed, the perfect tender rule does not apply to a seller's breach of her obligation under a shipment contract to make a proper contract for transportation or to give proper notice of the shipment. A failure to perform either of these obligations is a ground for rejection only if material loss or delay results. Section 2-504.

FIGURE 22-1 Tender of Performance by the Seller

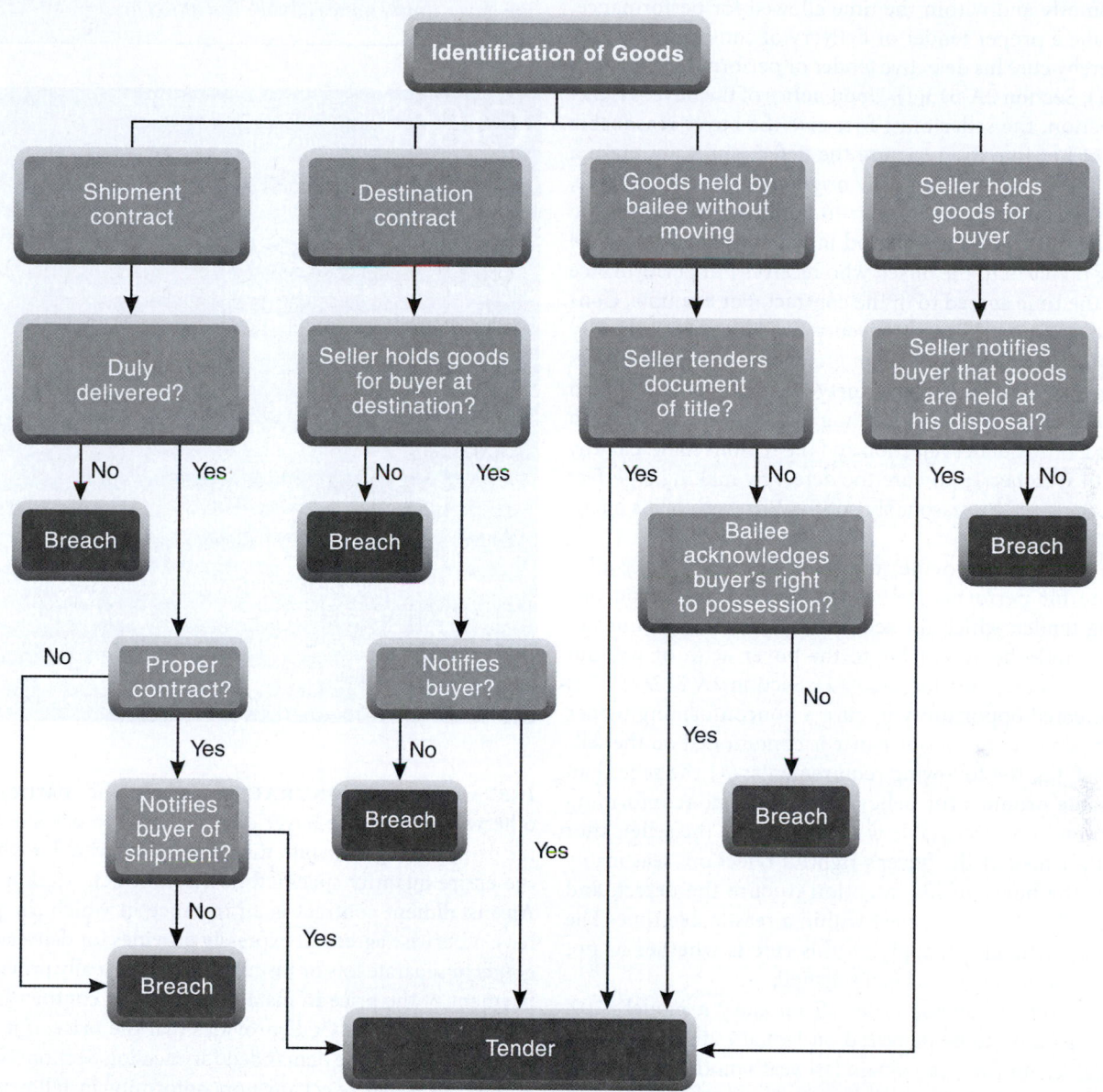

AGREEMENT BY THE PARTIES The parties may contractually agree to limit the operation of the perfect tender rule. For example, they may agree that the seller shall have the right to repair or replace any defective parts or goods. Such contractual limitations are discussed in *Chapter 25*.

Practical Advice
If you are the seller, consider using a contractual term to limit the operation of the perfect tender rule; if you are the buyer, carefully scrutinize such a limitation.

CURE BY THE SELLER The Code recognizes two situations in which a seller may cure or correct a nonconforming tender of goods. This relaxation of the seller's obligation to make a perfect tender gives the seller an opportunity to make either a second delivery or a substitute tender. Whereas the first opportunity for cure occurs when the time for performance under the contract has not expired, the second opportunity is available after the time for performance has expired, but only if the seller had reasonable grounds to believe that the nonconforming tender would be acceptable to the buyer, with or without monetary adjustment.

In cases in which the buyer refuses to accept a tender of goods that do not conform to the contract, the seller, by acting promptly and within the time allowed for performance, may make a proper tender or delivery of conforming goods and thereby cure his defective tender or performance. Section 2-508(1); Section 2A-513(1). Upon notice of the buyer's rightful rejection, the seller must first give the buyer reasonable notice of her intention to cure the defect and then make a proper tender according to the *original* contract. This rule, which predates the Code, is fair to both parties. It gives the seller the full contractual period in which to perform while causing no harm to the buyer, who receives full performance within the time agreed to in the contract. For example, Conroy is to deliver to Elizabeth twenty-five blue shirts and fifty white shirts by October 15. On October 1, Conroy delivers twenty-nine blue shirts and forty-six white shirts, which Elizabeth rejects as not conforming to the contract. Elizabeth notifies Conroy of her rejection and the reasons for it. Conroy has until October 15 to cure the defect by making a perfect tender, provided he seasonably notifies Elizabeth of his intention to do so.

The Code also provides the seller an opportunity after the time for performance has expired to cure a nonconforming tender, which the seller had reasonable grounds to believe would be acceptable to the buyer, with or without money allowance. Section 2-508(2); Section 2A-513(2). This Code-created opportunity to cure a nonconforming tender after the date set for performance is conditioned on the seller's satisfying the following requirements: (1) the seller had reasonable grounds for believing that the nonconforming tender would be acceptable to the buyer; (2) the seller, after being informed of the buyer's rightful rejection, seasonably notifies the buyer of his intention to cure the defect; and (3) the seller cures the defect within a reasonable time. The principal difficulty in applying this rule is whether or not the first requirement has been satisfied.

For example, Vanessa orders from Gary a model 110X S.C.A. television to be delivered on January 20. The 110X is unavailable, but Gary can obtain last year's model of the same television, a model 110, which lists for 5 percent less than the 110X. On January 20, Gary delivers to Vanessa the 110 at a discount price of 10 percent less than the contract price for the 110X. Vanessa rejects the substituted television set. Gary, who promptly notifies Vanessa that he will obtain and deliver a model 110X, will most likely have a reasonable time beyond the January 20 deadline in which to deliver the 110X television set to Vanessa, because under these facts, Gary appeared to have reasonable grounds to believe the model 110 would be acceptable with the money allowance.

♦ *See Case 22-1*

Practical Advice

If you want to exercise the seller's right to cure, be sure to give the buyer timely notice of your intent to cure.

CISG If the seller has delivered goods before the date for delivery, the seller may, up to the delivery date, cure any deficiency, provided that the exercise of this right does not cause the buyer unreasonable inconvenience or unreasonable expense. However, the buyer retains any right to claim damages as provided for in the CISG. If the seller does not perform on time, the buyer may fix an additional period of time of reasonable length for performance by the seller of his obligations. Unless the buyer has received notice from the seller that the seller will not perform within the period so fixed, the buyer may not, during that period, resort to any remedy for breach of contract. However, the buyer retains any right he may have to claim damages for delay in performance. If the seller does not deliver the goods within the additional period of time or declares that he will not deliver within the period so fixed, the buyer may declare the contract avoided.

The seller may, even after the date for delivery, cure a defective performance, if she can do so without unreasonable delay and without causing the buyer unreasonable inconvenience. However, the buyer retains any right to claim damages for delay in performance. If the seller requests the buyer to make known whether he will accept performance and the buyer does not comply with the request within a reasonable time, the seller may perform within the time indicated in his request.

INSTALLMENT CONTRACTS Unless the parties have otherwise agreed, the buyer does not have to pay any part of the price of the goods until the seller has delivered or tendered the entire quantity specified in the contract. Section 2-307. An installment contract is an instance in which the parties have otherwise agreed. It expressly provides for delivery of the goods in separate lots or installments and usually provides for payment of the price in installments. If the contract is silent about payment, the Code provides that the price, if it can be apportioned, may be demanded for each lot. Section 2-307.

The buyer may reject any nonconforming installment if the nonconformity *substantially* impairs the value of that installment and cannot be cured. Section 2-612(2); Section 2A-510(1). When, however, the installment substantially impairs the value of the installment but not the value of the entire contract, the buyer cannot reject the installment if the seller gives adequate assurance of the installment's cure. Section 2-612(2); Section 2A-510(1). Whenever the nonconformity or default with respect to one or more of the installments substantially impairs the value of the whole contract, however, the buyer can treat the breach as a breach of the *whole contract*. Section 2-612(3); Section 2A-510(2).

CISG When a contract calls for delivery of goods by installments, if the seller's failure to perform any of his obligations with respect to any installment constitutes a fundamental breach of contract with respect to that installment, the buyer may declare the contract avoided with respect to that installment. A buyer who declares the contract avoided with respect to any delivery may, at the same time, declare it avoided with respect to deliveries already made or to future deliveries if, by reason of their interdependence, those deliveries could not be used for the purpose contemplated by the parties at the time of the conclusion of the contract. If the seller's failure to perform any of his obligations with respect to any installment gives the buyer good grounds to conclude that a fundamental breach of contract will occur with respect to future installments, he may declare the contract avoided for the future, provided that he does so within a reasonable time.

22-2 Performance by the Buyer

The buyer is obligated to accept conforming goods and to pay for them according to the contract terms. Section 2-301; Section 2A-103(1)(j). Payment or tender of payment by the buyer, unless otherwise agreed, is a condition to the seller's duty to tender and to complete delivery. Section 2-507(1).

The buyer is not obliged to accept a tender or delivery of goods that does not conform to the contract. Upon determining that the tender or delivery is nonconforming, the buyer has three choices. He may (1) reject all of the goods, (2) accept all of the goods, or (3) accept any commercial unit or units of the goods and reject the rest. Section 2-601; Section 2A-509(1). The buyer must pay the contract rate for the commercial units he accepts.

CISG The buyer must pay the price for the goods and take delivery of them as required by the contract and the CISG.

♦ *See Case 22-2*

22-2a INSPECTION

Unless the parties otherwise agree, the buyer has a right to inspect the goods before payment or acceptance. Section 2-513(1). (Section 2A-515(1) provides for the right to inspect before acceptance.) This **inspection** enables him to ascertain whether the goods tendered or delivered conform to the contract. If the contract requires payment before acceptance (e.g., where the contract provides for shipment C.O.D. [collect on delivery]), payment must be made prior to inspection unless the nonconformity appears without inspection. Section 2-512. Payment, however, in such a case is not an acceptance of the goods and impairs neither the buyer's right to inspect nor any of his remedies.

The buyer, allowed a reasonable time in which to inspect the goods, may lose the right to reject or revoke acceptance of nonconforming goods by failing to inspect them in a timely manner. The expenses of inspection must be borne by the buyer but may be recovered from the seller if the goods do not conform and are rejected. Section 2-513(2); Section 2A-520(1).

Practical Advice

If you are the buyer, carefully inspect tendered goods before accepting them. If this is not feasible, inspect the goods as soon as possible.

CISG The buyer is not bound to pay the price until he has had an opportunity to examine the goods, unless the parties have agreed otherwise. The buyer must examine the goods within as short a period of time as is practicable in the circumstances. The buyer loses the right to rely on a lack of conformity of the goods if he does not give notice to the seller of the nonconformity within a reasonable time after he has discovered it or ought to have discovered it.

22-2b REJECTION

Rejection is a manifestation by the buyer of his unwillingness to become the owner of the goods. It must be made within a reasonable time after the goods have been tendered or delivered and is not effective unless the buyer seasonably notifies the seller. Section 2-602(1); Section 2A-509(2).

The rejection of tendered or delivered goods may be rightful or wrongful, depending on whether the goods conform to the contract. The buyer's rejection of nonconforming goods or tender is rightful under the perfect tender rule. Nonetheless, if the buyer refuses a tender of goods or rejects it as nonconforming without disclosing to the seller the nature of the defect, she may not assert such defect as an excuse for not accepting the goods or as a breach of contract by the seller if the defect is curable. Section 2-605(1); Section 2A-514(1).

After the buyer has rejected the goods, any attempt she makes to exercise ownership of the goods is wrongful as against the seller. (Because the lessor retains title in a lease, this does not apply to leases.) If the buyer has possession of the rejected goods but does not have a security interest in them, she is obliged to hold them with reasonable care for a time sufficient to permit the seller to remove them. Section 2-602(2)(b); Section 2A-512(1). The buyer who is not a merchant is under no further obligation with regard to goods rightfully rejected. Section 2-602(2); Section 2A-512(1)(c). If the seller gives no instructions within a reasonable time after notification of rejection, the buyer may (1) store the goods for the seller's account, (2) reship them to the seller, or (3) resell them for the seller's account. Such action is not an acceptance or conversion of the goods. Section 2-604; Section 2A-511(2). A *merchant* buyer of goods who has rightfully rejected them has additional duties: she is obligated to follow reasonable instructions from the seller with respect to the disposition of the goods in her possession or control when the seller has no agent or business at the place of rejection. Section 2-603(1); Section 2A-511(1). If the merchant buyer receives no instructions from the seller within a reasonable time after giving notice of the rejection, and the rejected goods are perishable or threaten to decline in value speedily, she is obligated to make reasonable efforts to sell them for the seller's account. Section 2-603(1); Section 2A-511(1).

When the buyer sells the rejected goods, she is entitled to reimbursement for the reasonable expenses of caring for and selling them and a reasonable selling commission not to exceed 10 percent of the gross proceeds. Section 2-603(2); Section 2A-511(2).

Practical Advice

If you have rejected nonconforming goods, be sure to notify the seller in a timely manner and do not exercise ownership of the rejected goods.

CISG

If the goods do not conform to the contract and the nonconformity constitutes a fundamental breach of contract, the buyer may require delivery of substitute goods. If the buyer has received the goods and intends to exercise any right under the contract or the CISG to reject them, she must take such steps to preserve them as are reasonable in the circumstances. She is entitled to retain them until she has been reimbursed her reasonable expenses by the seller.

♦ *See Case 22-2*

22-2c ACCEPTANCE

Acceptance of goods means a willingness by the buyer to become the owner of the goods tendered or delivered to him by the seller. Acceptance of the goods, which includes overt acts or conduct manifesting such willingness, precludes any subsequent rejection of the goods. Section 2-607(2); Section 2A-516(2). Acceptance may be indicated by express words, by the presumed intention of the buyer through his failure to act, or by conduct of the buyer that is inconsistent with the seller's ownership of the goods. More specifically, acceptance occurs when the buyer, after a reasonable opportunity to inspect the goods, (1) signifies to the seller that the goods conform to the contract, (2) signifies to the seller that he will take the

goods or retain them in spite of their nonconformity to the contract, or (3) fails to make an effective rejection of the goods. Section 2-606(1); Section 2A-515(1).

Acceptance, as previously noted, of any part of a commercial unit is acceptance of the entire unit. Section 2-606(2); Section 2A-515(2). Although the buyer must pay at the contract rate for those commercial units he accepts, he is entitled, after giving the seller timely notice of the breach, to recover from the seller or to deduct from the purchase price the amount of damages for nonconformity of the commercial units he has accepted and for nondelivery of the commercial units he has rejected. Sections 2-714 and 2-717; Sections 2A-516(1) and 2A-508(6) (except for finance leases in some situations). For example, Nancy agrees to deliver to Paul five hundred lightbulbs of 100 watts each for $300 and one thousand lightbulbs of 60 watts each for $500. Nancy delivers on time, but the shipment contains only four hundred of the 100-watt bulbs and eight hundred of the 60-watt bulbs. If Paul accepts the shipment, he must pay Nancy $240 for the 100-watt bulbs accepted and $400 for the 60-watt bulbs accepted, less the amount of damages Nancy's nonconforming delivery caused him.

When goods are rejected by the buyer, the burden is on the seller to establish their conformity to the contract, but the burden is on the buyer to establish any breach of contract (including warranty) with regard to goods accepted. Section 2-607(4); Section 2A-516(3)(c).

22-2d REVOCATION OF ACCEPTANCE

A buyer might accept defective goods either because discovering the defect by inspection was difficult or because the buyer reasonably assumed that the seller would correct the defect. In either instance, the buyer may revoke his acceptance of the goods if the uncorrected defect substantially impairs the value of the goods to him. With respect to the goods, **revocation of acceptance** gives the buyer rights and duties that are the same as if he had rejected them. Section 2-608(3); Section 2A-517(5).

More specifically, the buyer may revoke his acceptance of goods that do not conform to the contract when such nonconformity *substantially* impairs the value of the goods to him, provided that his acceptance was (1) premised on the reasonable assumption that the seller would cure the nonconformity and it was not seasonably cured or (2) made without discovery of the nonconformity and such acceptance was reasonably induced by the difficulty of discovery before acceptance or by the seller's assurances. Section 2-608(1); Section 2A-517(1).

Revocation of acceptance is not effective until notification is given to the seller. This must be done within a reasonable time after the buyer discovers or should have discovered the grounds for revocation and before the goods have undergone any substantial change not caused by their own defects. Section 2-608(2); Section 2A-517(4).

◆ *See Case 22-3*

◆ *See Case 22-3*

Practical Advice

If you have cause to revoke your acceptance of goods, be sure to notify the seller within a reasonable time after discovering the grounds for revocation.

22-2e OBLIGATION OF PAYMENT

The terms of the contract may expressly state the time and place at which the buyer is obligated to pay for the goods. If so, these terms are controlling. Thus, if the buyer has agreed to pay either the seller or a carrier for the goods in advance of delivery, his duty to pay is not conditioned upon performance or a tender of performance by the seller. Furthermore, where the sale is on credit, the buyer is not obligated to pay for the goods when he receives them, as the credit provision in the contract will control the time of payment. Unless the parties agree otherwise, payment is due at the time and place at which the buyer is to receive the goods, even though the place of shipment is the place of delivery. Section 2-310(a). This rule is understandable in view of the buyer's right, in the absence of agreement to the contrary, to inspect the goods before being obliged to pay for them.

Tender of payment in the ordinary course of business is sufficient when made by any means or in any manner current, such as a check, unless the seller demands cash and allows the buyer a reasonable time within which to obtain it. Payment by personal check is defeated as between seller and buyer, however, if the check is not paid when the seller attempts to cash it. Section 2-511(3).

Practical Advice

Specify in your sales contract the time and other terms of payment.

CISG Unless the buyer is bound to pay the price at any other specific time, he must pay it when the seller places either the goods or documents controlling their disposition at the buyer's disposal in accordance with the contract and the CISG. The seller may make such payment a condition for handing over the goods or documents. If the buyer is not bound to pay the price at any other particular place, he must pay it to the seller (1) at the seller's place of business or (2) if the payment is to be made against the handing over of the goods or of documents, at the place where the handing over takes place.

◆ **SEE FIGURE 22-2:** *Performance by the Buyer*

22-3 Obligations of Both Parties

Contracts for the sale of goods necessarily involve risks concerning future events that may or may not occur. In some instances, the parties explicitly allocate these risks; in most instances, they do not. The Code contains three sections that allocate these risks when the parties fail to do so. Each provision, when applicable, relieves the parties from the obligation of full performance under the sales contract. The first section deals with casualty to identified goods, the second with the nonhappening of presupposed conditions, and the third with substituted performance.

Related to the subject of whether the Code will excuse performance is the question of whether both parties are able and willing to perform. Should one party seem unwilling or unable, the Code allows the other party to seek reasonable assurance of the potentially defaulting party's willingness and ability to perform. In addition, if one of the parties clearly indicates an unwillingness or inability to perform, the Code protects the other party.

22-3a CASUALTY TO IDENTIFIED GOODS

If goods are destroyed before an offer to sell or buy them is accepted, the offer is terminated by general contract law. But what if the goods are destroyed after the sales contract is formed? The rules for the passage of risk of loss (as discussed in *Chapter 23*) apply with one exception: the contract is for goods that are identified when the contract was made, and the goods suffer damage without fault of either party *before* the risk of loss passes to the buyer. The outcome of this situation depends upon the degree of damage.

(1) If these goods are *totally* lost or damaged, the contract is avoided. Section 2-613(a); Section 2A-221(a). This means that each party is excused from his performance obligation under the contract: the seller is no longer obligated to deliver, and the buyer need not pay the price.

(2) In the case of a *partial* destruction or deterioration of the goods, the buyer may avoid the contract or may accept the goods with due allowance or deduction from the contract price sufficient to account for the deterioration or deficiency. Section 2-613(b); Section 2A-221(b) (except in a finance lease that is not a consumer lease). Thus, Adams agrees to sell to Taylor a specific lot of wheat containing one thousand bushels at a price of $4 per bushel. Without the fault of Adams or Taylor, fire destroys three hundred bushels of the wheat. Taylor does not have to take the remaining seven hundred bushels of wheat, but he has the option to do so upon paying $2,800, the price of seven hundred bushels.

On the other hand, if the destruction or damage to the goods, whether total or partial, occurs *after* risk of loss has passed to the buyer, the buyer has no option but must pay the entire contract price of the goods.

FIGURE 22-2 Performance by the Buyer

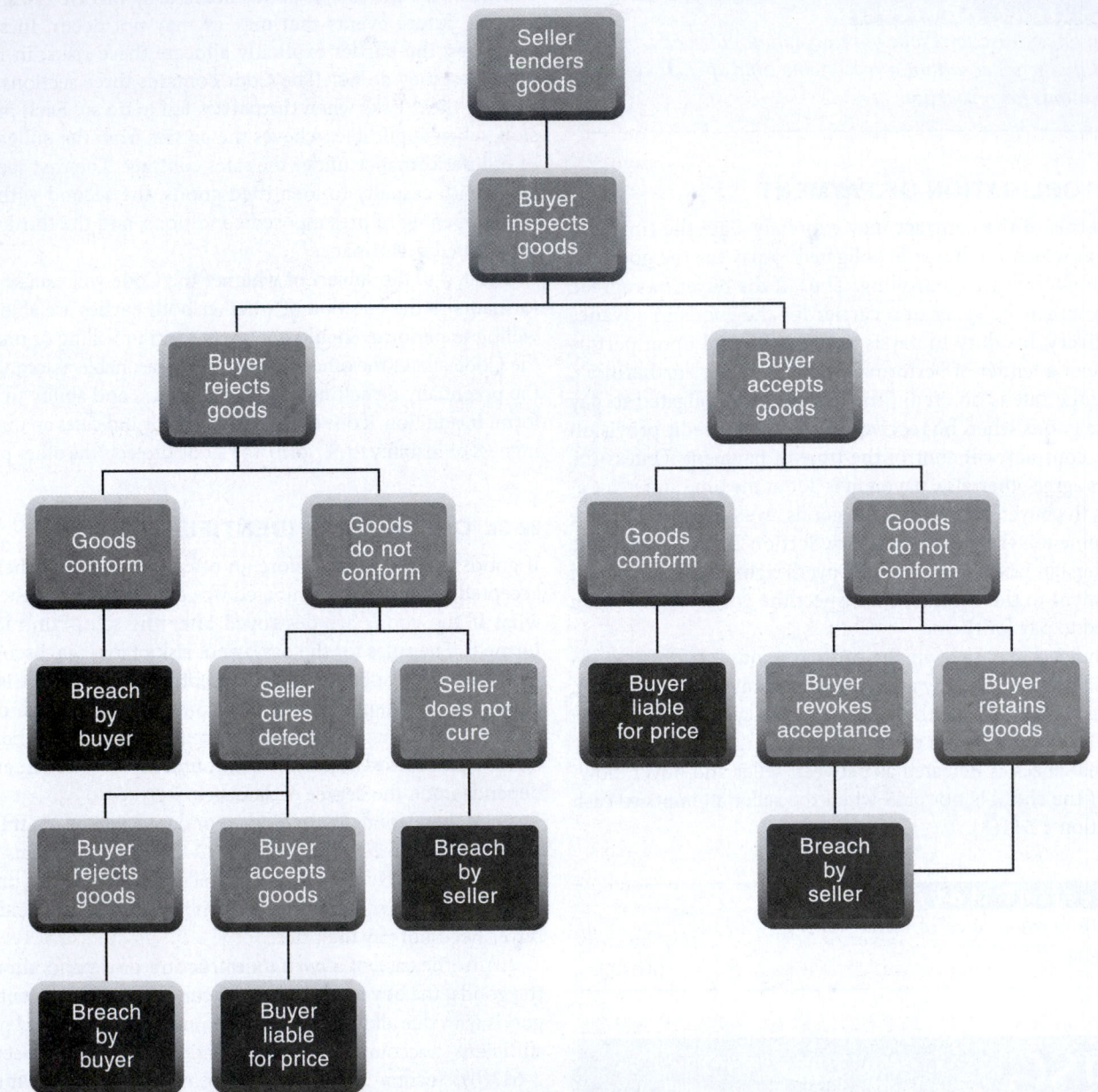

22-3b FAILURE OF PRESUPPOSED CONDITIONS

The seller is excused from the duty of performance on the nonoccurrence of presupposed conditions that were a basic assumption of the contract, unless the seller has expressly assumed the risk. Section 2-615(a); Section 2A-405(a). Although the nonhappening of presupposed conditions may relieve the seller of her contractual duty, if the contingency affects only a part of the seller's capacity to perform, the seller must, to the extent of her remaining capacity, allocate delivery and production in a fair and reasonable manner among her customers. Section 2-615(b); Section 2A-405(b).

Central to the Code's approach to impossibility is the concept of **commercial impracticability**, through which the Code will excuse performance that, while not actually or literally impossible, is commercially impracticable. This, however, requires more than mere hardship or increased cost of performance. For a party to be discharged, performance must be rendered impracticable as a result of an unforeseen supervening event not within the contemplation of the parties at the time of contracting. Moreover, the nonoccurrence of the event must have been a "basic assumption" that both parties made when entering into the contract.

Increased production cost alone does not excuse performance by the seller, nor does a collapse of the market for the goods excuse the buyer. But a party to a contract for the sale of programs for a scheduled but subsequently canceled yacht regatta, for the sale of tin horns for export which become subject to embargo, or for the production of goods at a designated factory that suffers extensive fire damage would be excused from performance on the basis of commercial impracticability.

♦ *See Case 17-4*

Practical Advice

Specify in your contract which events will excuse the nonperformance of the contract, the basic assumptions of your contract, and which risks are assumed by each of the parties.

CISG A party is not liable for a failure to perform any of her obligations if she proves that the failure was due to an impediment beyond her control and that she could not reasonably be expected to have taken the impediment into account at the time of contracting or to have avoided or overcome it or its consequences.

22-3c SUBSTITUTED PERFORMANCE

The Code provides that where neither party is at fault and the agreed manner of delivering the goods becomes commercially impracticable, as by the failure of loading or unloading facilities or the unavailability of an agreed type of carrier, a substituted manner of performance, if commercially reasonable, must be tendered and accepted. Section 2-614(1); Section 2A-404(1). Where a practical alternative or substitute exists, the Code excuses neither seller nor buyer on the ground that delivery in the express manner provided in the contract is impossible.

22-3d RIGHT TO ADEQUATE ASSURANCE OF PERFORMANCE

A contract of sale also requires that each party not impair the other party's expectation of having the contract performed. While the essential purpose of a contract is actual performance, an important feature of such performance is a secure and continuing sense that performance will occur when due. If after contracting but before the time for performance either the willingness or ability of a party to perform is put in doubt, the other party is threatened with the loss of a substantial part of what he has bargained for. Therefore, when reasonable grounds for insecurity arise regarding either party's performance, the other party may demand written assurance and suspend his own performance until he receives

that assurance. The failure to provide adequate assurance of performance within a reasonable time not exceeding thirty days constitutes a repudiation of the contract. Section 2-609; Section 2A-401.

CISG A party may suspend the performance of his obligations if, after the conclusion of the contract, it becomes apparent that the other party will not perform a substantial part of his obligations. A party suspending performance must immediately notify the other party of the suspension and must continue with performance if the other party provides adequate assurance of his performance.

22-3e RIGHT TO COOPERATION

Where one party's cooperation is necessary to the agreed performance but is not timely forthcoming, the other party is excused with regard to any resulting delay in her own performance. The nonbreaching party either may proceed to perform in any reasonable manner or, if the time for her performance has occurred, may treat the other's failure to cooperate as a breach. In either event, the nonbreaching party has access to any other remedies the Code may provide, as discussed in *Chapter 25*.

22-3f ANTICIPATORY REPUDIATION

While a repudiation is a clear indication by either party that he is unwilling or unable to perform his obligations under the contract, an **anticipatory repudiation** is a repudiation made *before* the time to perform occurs. It may occur by express communication or by the repudiating party's taking an action that makes performance impossible, such as selling unique goods to a third party. A repudiation also may result from a party's failure to give timely assurance of performance after a justifiable demand. If an anticipatory repudiation substantially impairs the value of the contract, the aggrieved party may (1) await performance for a commercially reasonable time or (2) resort to any remedy for breach. In either case, he may suspend his own performance. Section 2-610; Section 2A-402. The repudiating party may retract his anticipatory repudiation and thereby reinstate the contract unless the aggrieved party has canceled the contract, materially changed his position, or otherwise indicated that she considers the anticipatory repudiation final. Section 2-611; Section 2A-403.

CISG If prior to the date for performance of the contract it is clear that one of the parties will commit a fundamental breach of contract, the other party may declare the contract avoided.

♦ *See Case 22-4*

CHAPTER SUMMARY

PERFORMANCE BY THE SELLER

Tender of Delivery the seller makes available to the buyer goods conforming to the contract and so notifies the buyer
- *Buyer* is obligated to accept conforming goods
- *Seller* is entitled to receive payment of the contract price

Time and Manner of Tender tender must be made at a reasonable time and kept open for a reasonable period of time

Place of Tender if none is specified, place for delivery is the seller's place of business or, if he has no such place, his residence
- *Shipment Contracts* seller is required to tender delivery of the goods to a carrier for delivery to buyer; shipment terms include the following: *F.O.B. (free on board) place of shipment, F.A.S. (free alongside ship) port of shipment, C.I.F. (cost, insurance, and freight), C.&F. (cost and freight)*
- *Destination Contracts* seller is required to tender delivery of the goods at a named destination; destination terms include the following: *F.O.B. place of destination, ex-ship*, and *no arrival, no sale*
- *Goods Held by Bailee* seller must either tender to the buyer a document of title or obtain an acknowledgment from the bailee

Perfect Tender Rule the seller's tender of performance must conform exactly to the contract, subject to the following qualifications:
- *Agreement by the Parties* the parties may contractually limit the operation of the perfect tender rule
- *Cure by the Seller* when the time for performance under the contract has not expired or when the seller has shipped nonconforming goods in the belief that the nonconforming tender would be acceptable, a seller may cure or correct her nonconforming tender
- *Installment Contracts* when the contract calls for the goods to be delivered in separate lots, the buyer may reject a nonconforming installment if it substantially impairs the value of that installment and cannot be cured, but if nonconformity or default of one or more of the installments substantially impairs the value of the whole contract, the buyer can treat the breach as a breach of the whole contract

PERFORMANCE BY THE BUYER

Inspection unless otherwise agreed, the buyer has a reasonable time in which to inspect the goods before payment or acceptance to determine whether they conform

Rejection buyer's manifestation of unwillingness to become the owner of the goods; must be made within a reasonable time after the goods have been tendered or delivered and gives the buyer the right to (1) reject all of the goods, (2) accept all of the goods, or (3) accept any commercial unit(s) and reject the rest

Acceptance buyer's express or implied manifestation of willingness to become the owner of the goods

Revocation of Acceptance rescission of buyer's acceptance of the goods if nonconformity of the goods substantially impairs their value, provided that the acceptance was (1) premised on the assumption that the nonconformity would be cured by the seller and it was not or (2) the nonconformity was an undiscovered hidden defect

Obligation of Payment in the absence of an agreement, payment is due at the time and place the buyer is to receive the goods

OBLIGATIONS OF BOTH PARTIES

Casualty to Identified Goods if the contract is for goods that were identified when the contract was made and those goods are totally lost or damaged without fault of either party and before the risk of loss has passed to the buyer, the contract is avoided

Failure of Presupposed Conditions the seller is excused from the duty of performance on the nonoccurrence of presupposed conditions that were a basic assumption of the contract, unless the seller has expressly assumed the risk; performance that is impracticable as a result of an unforeseen supervening event is excused

Substituted Performance where neither party is at fault and the agreed manner of goods becomes commercially impracticable, a substituted manner of performance must be tendered and accepted

Right to Adequate Assurance of Performance when reasonable grounds for insecurity arise regarding either party's performance, the other party may demand written assurance and suspend his own performance until he receives that assurance

Right to Cooperation where one party's required cooperation is untimely, the other party is excused from any resulting delay in her own performance

Anticipatory Repudiation if either party clearly indicates an unwillingness or inability to perform before the performance is due, the other party may await performance for a reasonable time or resort to any remedy for breach

C A S E S

CASE 22-1

Cure by the Seller
WILSON v. SCAMPOLI
United States Court of Appeals, District of Columbia Circuit, 1967
228 A.2d 848

Myers, J.

This is an appeal from an order of the trial court granting rescission of a sales contract for a color television set and directing the return of the purchase price plus interest and costs.

Appellee [Wilson] purchased the set in question on November 4, 1965, paying the total purchase price in cash. The transaction was evidenced by a sales ticket showing the price paid and guaranteeing ninety days' free service and replacement of any defective tube and parts for a period of one year. Two days after purchase the set was delivered. * * * When the set was turned on, however, it did not function properly, the picture having a reddish tinge. Appellant's [Scampoli's] delivery man advised the buyer's daughter, Mrs. Kolley, that it was not his duty to tune in or adjust the color but that a service representative would shortly call at her house for that purpose. After the departure of the delivery men, Mrs. Kolley unplugged the set and did not use it.

On November 8, 1965, a service representative arrived, and after spending an hour in an effort to eliminate the red cast from the picture advised Mrs. Kolley that he would have to remove the chassis from the cabinet and take it to the shop as he could not determine the cause of the difficulty from his examination at the house. He also made a written memorandum of his service call, noting that the television "Needs Shop Work (Red Screen)." Mrs. Kolley refused to allow the chassis to be removed, asserting she did not want a "repaired" set but another "brand new" set. Later she demanded the return of the purchase price, although retaining the set. Appellant refused to refund the purchase price, but renewed his offer to adjust, repair, or if the set could not be made to function properly, to replace it. Ultimately, appellee instituted this suit against appellant seeking a refund of the purchase price. After a trial, the court ruled that "under the facts and circumstances the complaint is justified. Under the equity powers of the Court I will order the parties put back in their original status, let the $675 be returned, and the set returned to the defendant."

Appellant * * * contends the trial judge erred in holding that rescission here was appropriate. He argues that he was always willing to comply with the terms of the sale either by correcting the malfunction by minor repairs or, in the event the set could not be made thereby properly operative, by replacement; that as he was denied the opportunity to try to correct the difficulty, he did not breach the contract of sale or any warranty thereunder, expressed or implied.

[UCC §] 2-508 provides:

(1) Where any tender or delivery by the seller is rejected because non-conforming and the time for performance has not yet expired, the seller may seasonally notify the buyer of his intention to cure and may then within the contract time make a conforming delivery.

(2) Where the buyer rejects a non-conforming tender which the seller had reasonable grounds to believe would be acceptable with or without money allowance the seller may if he seasonally notifies the buyer have a further reasonable time to substitute a conforming tender.

A retail dealer would certainly expect and have reasonable grounds to believe that merchandise like color television sets, new and delivered as crated at the factory, would be acceptable as delivered and that, if defective in some way, he would have the right to substitute a conforming tender. The question then resolves itself to whether the dealer may conform his tender by adjustment or minor repair or whether he must conform by substituting brand new merchandise. The problem seems to be one of first impression. * * *

* * *

While these cases provide no mandate to require the buyer to accept patchwork goods or substantially repaired articles in lieu of flawless merchandise, they do indicate that minor repairs or reasonable adjustments are frequently the means by which an imperfect tender may be cured. In discussing the analogous question of defective title, it has been stated that:

The seller, then, should be able to cure [the defect] under subsection 2-508(2) in those cases in which he can do so without subjecting the buyer to any great inconvenience, risk, or loss. [Citations.]

Removal of a television chassis for a short period of time in order to determine the cause of color malfunction and ascertain the extent of adjustment or correction needed to effect full operational efficiency presents no great inconvenience to the buyer. In the instant case, [Appellant's] expert witness testified that this was not infrequently necessary with new televisions. Should the set be defective in workmanship or parts, the loss would be upon the manufacturer who warranted it free from mechanical defect. Here the adamant refusal of Mrs. Kolley * * * to allow inspection essential to the determination of the cause of the excessive red tinge to the picture defeated any effort by the seller to provide timely repair or even replacement of the set if the difficulty could not be corrected. The cause of the defect might have been minor and easily adjusted or it may have been substantial and required replacement by another new set—but the seller was never given an adequate opportunity to make a determination.

We do not hold that appellant has no liability to appellee, but as he was denied access and a reasonable opportunity to repair, appellee has not shown a breach of warranty entitling him either to a brand new set or to rescission. We therefore reverse the judgment of the trial court granting rescission and directing the return of the purchase price of the set.

Reversed.

CASE 22-2

Performance by the Buyer
FURLONG v. ALPHA CHI OMEGA SORORITY
Bowling Green County Municipal Court, 1993
73 Ohio Misc.2d 26, 657 N.E.2d 866

Bachman, J.

[Alpha Chi Omega (AXO) entered into an oral contract with Furlong to buy 168 "custom-designed" sweaters for the Midnight Masquerade III. The purchase price of $3,612 was to be paid as follows: $2,000 down payment when the contract was made and $1,612 upon delivery. During phone conversations with Furlong, Emily, the AXO social chairperson, described the design to be imprinted on the sweater. She also specified the colors to be used in the lettering (hunter green on top of maroon outlined in navy blue) and the color of the mask design (hunter green). Furlong promised to have a third party imprint the sweaters as specified. Furlong later sent to Emily a sweater with maroon letters to show her the color. He then

sent her a fax illustrating the sweater design with arrows indicating where each of the three colors was to appear. On the day before delivery was due, Argento, Furlong's supplier, requested design changes which Furlong approved without the consent of AXO. These changes included deleting the navy blue outline, reducing the number of colors from three to two, changing the maroon lettering to red, and changing the color of the masks from hunter green to red. Upon delivery, AXO gave a check to Furlong's agent for the balance of the purchase price. Later that day, Emily inspected the sweaters and screamed her dismay at the design changes. AXO immediately stopped payment on the check. Amy, the president of AXO, phoned Furlong, stating that the sweaters were not what AXO had ordered. She gave the specifics as to why the sweaters were not as ordered and offered to return them. Furlong refused but offered to reduce the unit price of the sweaters if AXO agreed to accept them. AXO refused this offer. Furlong then filed suit against AXO for the unpaid portion of the sweaters' purchase price ($1,612), and AXO counterclaimed for return of the down payment ($2,000).]

* * *

Furlong and Emily created an express warranty by * * * affirmation of fact (his initial phone calls); by sample (the maroon sweater); by description (the fax). This express warranty became part of the contract. Each of the three methods of showing the express warranty was not in conflict with the other two methods, and thus they are consistent and cumulative [UCC §2-317], and constitute the warranty.

The design was a "dickered" aspect of the individual bargain and went clearly to the essence of that bargain [UCC §2-313]. Thus, the express warranty was that the sweaters would be in accordance with the above design (including types of colors for the letters and the mask, and the number of colors for the same). Further, the express warranty became part of the contract. * * *

Furlong's obligation as the seller was to transfer and deliver the goods in accordance with the contract. AXO's obligation was to accept and pay in accordance with that contract. [UCC §2-301] * * *

* * *

The sweaters did not conform to the contract (specifically, the express warranty in the contract). Thus (in the words of the statute), the sweaters did "fail in any respect to conform to the contract." Actually, the sweaters failed in at least five respects [UCC §2-601]. * * * [t]hey were a nonconforming tender of goods [UCC §2-601].

* * *

AXO, as the buyer, had the right to inspect the boxes of sweaters before payment or acceptance [UCC §2-513]. AXO did so at a reasonable time and place, and in a reasonable manner, on the same day that Furlong had sent the sweaters and AXO had received them [UCC §2-513]. AXO's purpose of inspection had (in the words of the statute) "to do with the buyer's check-up on whether the seller's performance is in accordance with a contract previously made. * * *" (Official Comment 9 to UCC §2-513.)

* * *

According to the statute, "if the goods * * * fail in any respect to conform to the contract, the buyer may: (A) reject the whole * * * [.]" [UCC §2-601]. As concluded above, the sweaters were nonconforming goods. Therefore, Furlong breached the contract, and AXO had the right to reject the goods (sweaters).

* * *

One [section of the] statute provides: "Rejection of goods must be within a reasonable time after their delivery. * * * It is ineffective unless the buyer seasonably notifies the seller." [UCC §2-602(1)]. AXO did what this statute requires.

* * *

Thus, AXO never had an acceptance of the sweaters (as the term "acceptance" is legally defined) [UCC §2-606]. That is, AXO never did any of the following (per the statute): (1) signified to Furlong that the sweaters were conforming or that AXO would take or retain the sweaters in spite of their non-conformity; (2) failed to make an effective rejection of the sweaters; (3) did any act inconsistent with Furlong's ownership. [UCC §2-606.]

* * *

As concluded above, AXO rightfully rejected the sweaters, after having paid part of the purchase price: namely $2,000. AXO is entitled to cancel the contract and to recover the partial payment of the purchase price [UCC §2-711].

| CASE 22-3 | Revocation of Acceptance
WADDELL v. L.V.R.V. INC.
Supreme Court of Nevada, 2006
125 P.3d 1160 |  |

Gibbons, J.

L.V.R.V. Inc., D/B/A [doing business as] Wheeler's Las Vegas RV (Wheeler's) sold a 1996 Coachmen Santara motor home (the RV) to * * * Arthur R. Waddell and Roswitha M. Waddell (the Waddells). * * *

* * *

* * * Before they took possession of the RV, the Waddells requested that Wheeler's perform various repairs. The Waddells' request included a service on the RV's engine cooling system, new batteries, and alignment of the door frames. Wheeler's told Arthur Waddell that the repairs had been performed as requested. The Waddells took delivery of the RV on September 1, 1997.

The Waddells first noticed a problem with the RV's engine shortly after they took possession of it. They drove the RV from Las Vegas to Hemet, California. On the return trip, the RV's engine overheated while ascending a moderate grade to such a degree that Mr. Waddell had to pull over to the side of the road and wait for the engine to cool down.

When the Waddells returned from California, they took the RV back to Wheeler's for repairs. Despite Wheeler's attempts to repair the RV, the Waddells continually experienced more problems with the RV, including further episodes of engine overheating. Between September 1997 and March 1999, Wheeler's service department spent a total of seven months during different periods of time attempting to repair the RV.

On June 9, 2000, the Waddells filed a complaint in district court seeking both equitable relief and money damages. * * *

* * * The district court concluded that the RV's nonconformities substantially impaired its value to the Waddells. The district court allowed the Waddells to revoke their acceptance of the RV. * * *

* * *

[UCC §2-608(1)] provides that a buyer may revoke his acceptance if the item suffers from a "nonconformity [that] substantially impairs its value *to him*" and (a) the buyer accepted the goods on the understanding that the seller would cure the nonconformity or (b) the buyer was unaware of the nonconformity and the nonconformity was concealed by the difficulty of discovery or by the seller's assurances that the good was conforming.

* * *

The Supreme Court of Oregon has established a two-part test to determine whether a nonconformity, under the totality of the circumstances, substantially impairs the value of the goods to the buyer. The test has both an objective and a subjective prong:

Since [the statute] provides that the buyer may revoke acceptance of goods "whose nonconformity substantially impairs its value *to him*," the value of conforming goods to *the plaintiff* must first be determined. This is a subjective question in the sense that it calls for a consideration of the needs and circumstances of the plaintiff who seeks to revoke; not the needs and circumstances of an average buyer. The second inquiry is whether the nonconformity in fact substantially impairs the value of the goods to the buyer, having in mind his particular needs. This is an objective question in the sense that it calls for evidence of something more than plaintiff's assertion that the nonconformity impaired the value to him; it requires evidence from which it can be inferred

that plaintiff's needs were not met because of the nonconformity. [Citation.]

* * * [W]e adopt the Supreme Court of Oregon's two-part test for determining whether a nonconformity substantially affects the good's value to the buyer under [UCC §2-608(1)].

* * *

Mr. Waddell's testimony demonstrates that the RV's subjective value to the Waddells was based on their ability to spend two or three years driving the RV around the country. Thus, we must consider whether the RV's nonconformities substantially impaired the value of the RV based on the Waddells' particular needs.

Mr. Waddell testified that as a result of the RV's defects, he and his wife were unable to enjoy the RV as they had intended. Mr. Waddell further testified that the RV's engine would overheat within ten miles of embarking if the travel included any climbing. As a result of the overheating, the Waddells were forced to park on the side of the road and wait for the engine to cool down before continuing. Consequently, the RV spent a total of 213 days, or seven months and one day, at Wheeler's service department during the eighteen months immediately following the purchase. This testimony is sufficient to demonstrate an objective, substantial impairment of value.

* * *

Accordingly, we conclude that substantial evidence exists to support revocation of acceptance under [UCC §2-608(1)].

Wheeler's argues that the Waddells should not have been allowed to revoke their acceptance because they did not attempt to revoke within a reasonable time after purchasing the RV. We disagree.

Under [UCC §2-608(2)], "revocation of acceptance must occur within a reasonable time after the buyer discovers or should have discovered the ground for it and before any substantial change in condition of the goods which is not caused by their own defects." * * *

* * *

The seller of nonconforming goods must generally receive an opportunity to cure the nonconformity before the buyer may revoke his acceptance. * * *

Furthermore, the seller's attempts to cure do not count against the buyer regarding timely revocation. * * *

The Waddells gave Wheeler's several opportunities to repair the defects before revoking their acceptance. Because Wheeler's was unable to repair the defects after a total of seven months, the Waddells were entitled to say "that's all" and revoke their acceptance, notwithstanding Wheeler's good-faith attempts to repair the RV. * * *

Anticipatory Repudiation
DONALD R. HESSLER v. CRYSTAL LAKE CHRYSLER-PLYMOUTH, INC.

Appellate Court of Illinois, Second District, 2003
788 N.E.2d 405, 273 Ill.Dec 96, 50 UCC Rep.Serv.2d 330

Callum, J.

In February 1997, Chrysler Corporation introduced a new promotional vehicle called the Plymouth Prowler. However, the company did not reveal whether it would manufacture any of the vehicles. Plaintiff became aware of the vehicle and of its uncertain production, and, on February 4, 1997, contacted several dealerships to inquire about purchasing a Prowler.

On February 5, 1997, plaintiff met with Gary Rosenberg, co-owner of defendant-dealership and signed a "Retail Order for a Motor Vehicle" (hereinafter Agreement). The Agreement, which was filled out primarily by Rosenberg, stated that the order was for a 1997, V6, two-door, purple Plymouth Prowler. Moreover, it read:

> Customer to pay $5,000 00/100 over list price by manufacturer. Money refundable if can not [deliver] by 12/30/97. Dealer to keep car 2 weeks.

* * *

The order also noted that plaintiff had deposited $5,000 by check.

The Agreement contained a box labeled "TO BE DELIVERED ON OR ABOUT." Inside the box was written "ASAP" in a handwriting and ink different from that in the rest of the document. * * * Rosenberg stated that the term "ASAP" is used in his business "in lieu of a stock number. Just line it up in order. As soon as you can get it done, do it." * * *

Rosenberg testified that plaintiff was the first person to place an order for a Prowler. Further, Rosenberg was "pretty sure" that plaintiff's order was the first order on which he received a deposit.

* * *

Plaintiff testified that his next contact with Rosenberg was on May 11, 1997, when he called Rosenberg to discuss the Prowler's list price. They agreed that the information they had received was that the manufacturer's list price would be $39,000.

On May 23, 1997, Salvatore Palandri entered into a contract with defendant to purchase a 1997 Plymouth Prowler. His contract reflects a purchase price of "50,000 + tax + lic + doc" and a $10,000 deposit. It further states that Palandri would receive the "first one delivered to [the] dealership." * * *

[Plaintiff testified that on August 11, 1997, Rosenberg informed plaintiff that no Prowlers would be delivered to the Midwest and that he would be returning plaintiff's check. Defendant, according to the plaintiff, nevertheless, stated that should defendant receive a vehicle, it would be plaintiff's. Defendant denies having stated this.]

* * *

Plaintiff next testified that he attended a Chrysler customer appreciation event at Great America on September 19 and spoke to a company representative about the Prowler. Two days later, the representative sent him a fax that contained a tentative list of dealers who were to receive Prowlers. Defendant's name was on the list.

Plaintiff testified that he called Rosenberg on September 22 to notify him that his dealership was on a list of dealers due to receive Prowlers. Rosenberg informed plaintiff that he would not sell plaintiff a car because plaintiff had gone behind Rosenberg's back and that contacting Chrysler would cause Rosenberg problems. Rosenberg also stated that plaintiff was not the first person with whom he contracted to sell a Prowler. Plaintiff protested and Rosenberg informed him that he did not sign the contract and would not sell plaintiff the car. Based on this and previous conversations with Rosenberg, plaintiff did not believe that he would be able to purchase a Prowler from defendant.

* * *

Beginning on September 23, 1997, plaintiff contacted 38 Chrysler-Plymouth dealerships to inquire about purchasing a 1997 Prowler, but did not obtain one. Plaintiff had "serious doubts" about whether Rosenberg would deliver to him a Prowler.

On October 24, 1997, plaintiff attended a Prowler coming-out party at the Hard Rock Cafe and saw a purple Prowler in the parking lot with a sign in its window that had defendant's name written on it. On October 25, plaintiff went to defendant's showroom and saw a Prowler parked there. He found Rosenberg and informed him that he was there to pick up his car. Rosenberg stated that he was not going to sell plaintiff the car and that he did not want to do business with him. Later that day, plaintiff purchased a Prowler from another dealer for $77,706.

On October 27, 1997, defendant sold the only Prowler it received in that year to Palandri for a total sale price of $54,859, including his $10,000 deposit.

* * *

On April 23, 1998, plaintiff sued defendant for breach of contract. * * *

Following a bench trial, the court entered judgment for plaintiff and awarded him $29,853 in damages. It concluded that defendant breached the Agreement and that plaintiff properly covered by purchasing a replacement vehicle for $29,853 more than the contract price. * * * The trial court also concluded that defendant repudiated its contract in September and October of 1997 when Rosenberg told plaintiff that he would not sell him a car. It found plaintiff "ready, willing, and able to perform the contract." The court found that the price plaintiff paid for the car at another dealership was the best price he could receive for a Prowler after Rosenberg's refusal to sell to him a car.

* * *

Under the UCC, certain actions by a party to a contract may constitute an anticipatory repudiation of the contract if the actions are sufficiently clear manifestations of an intent not to perform under the contract. [UCC §] 2-610; [citation.]

* * *

Comment 1 to Section 2-610 provides, in relevant part:

Anticipatory repudiation centers upon an overt communication of intention or an action which renders performance impossible or demonstrates a clear determination not to continue with performance.

* * * When such a repudiation substantially impairs the value of the contract, the aggrieved party may at any time resort to his remedies for breach. * * * [UCC §] 2-610, Comment.

Comment 2 to Section 2-610 provides, in relevant part:

It is not necessary for repudiation that performance be made literally and utterly impossible. Repudiation can result from action which reasonably indicates a rejection of the continuing obligation. [UCC §] 2-610, Comment.

* * *

Upon learning that defendant was on a tentative list to receive a Prowler, plaintiff testified that he called Rosenberg to relate the information and that Rosenberg responded that plaintiff was not the first person to contract to purchase a Prowler. Rosenberg also stated that he would not do business with plaintiff. Further, Rosenberg's testimony about this conversation corroborated plaintiff's, in that Rosenberg stated that he told plaintiff that the vehicle was already "committed." The trial court also heard both plaintiff and Rosenberg testify that, when plaintiff went to defendant's showroom on October 25 and informed Rosenberg that he was there to pick up his car, Rosenberg told plaintiff that he did not want to do business with him.

We conclude that the trial court did not err in finding that defendant's foregoing actions reasonably indicated to plaintiff that defendant would not deliver to him a Prowler under the Agreement. * * *

* * * With respect to plaintiff's actions, Section 2-610(b) of the UCC provides that an aggrieved party may "resort to any remedy for breach" of the contract "even though he has notified the repudiating party that he would await the latter's performance." [UCC §] 2-610(b). One such remedy is to cover. [UCC §] 2-711(1)(a) (buyer may effect cover, upon seller's repudiation, whether or not buyer cancels the contract). The statute is clear that a buyer's willingness to proceed with performance under a contract does not excuse a repudiation. * * *

Defendant next asserts that, even if there was a repudiation in September or October of 1997, plaintiff did nothing to indicate that he thought this was the case. He took no self-help measures such as: terminating the contract; seeking to enjoin the sale to Palandri; requesting a retraction; or suspending his performance obligations. Again, we disagree. The UCC does not require a party to request assurances as a condition precedent to recovery. [Citation.]

For the foregoing reasons, we conclude that the trial court's finding of repudiation was not against the manifest weight of the evidence.

* * *

* * * [T]he judgment of the circuit court of McHenry County is affirmed.

QUESTIONS

1. Tammie contracted with Kristine to manufacture, sell, and deliver to Kristine and put in running order a certain machine. Once Tammie had set up the machine and put it in running order, however, Kristine found it unsatisfactory and notified Tammie that she rejected the machine. She continued to use it for three months but continually complained of its defective condition. At the end of the three months, she notified Tammie to come and get it. Has Kristine lost her right (a) to reject the machine? (b) to revoke acceptance of the machine? Explain.

2. Smith, having contracted to sell to Beyer thirty tons of described fertilizer, shipped to Beyer by carrier thirty tons of fertilizer, which he stated conformed to the contract. Nothing was stated in the contract as to time of payment, but Smith demanded payment as a condition of handing over the fertilizer to Beyer. Beyer refused to

pay unless he was given the opportunity to inspect the fertilizer. Who is correct? Explain.

3. Benny and Sheree entered into a contract for the sale of one hundred barrels of flour. No mention was made of any place of delivery. Thereafter, Sheree demanded that Benny deliver the flour at her place of business, and Benny demanded that Sheree come and take the flour from his place of business. Neither party acceded to the demand of the other. Has either one a right of action against the other? Explain.

4. Johnson, a manufacturer of air conditioning units, made a written contract with Maxwell to sell to Maxwell forty units at a price of $200 each and to deliver them at a certain apartment building owned by Maxwell for installation by Maxwell. Upon the arrival of Johnson's truck for delivery at the apartment building, Maxwell examined the units on the truck, counted only thirty units, and asked the driver if this was the total delivery. The driver replied that it was as far as he knew. Maxwell told the driver that she would not accept delivery of the units. The next day, Johnson telephoned Maxwell and inquired why delivery was refused. Maxwell stated that the units on the truck were not what she ordered—that she ordered forty units, that only thirty were tendered, and that she was going to buy air conditioning units elsewhere. In an action by Johnson against Maxwell for breach of contract, Maxwell defends upon the ground that the tender of thirty units was improper, as the contract called for delivery of forty units. Is this a valid defense? Explain.

5. Edwin sells a sofa to Jack for $800. Edwin and Jack both know that the sofa is in Edwin's warehouse, located approximately ten miles from Jack's home. The contract does not specify the place of delivery, and Jack insists that the place of delivery is either his house or Edwin's store. Is Jack correct? Why or why not?

6. On November 4, Kim contracted to sell to Lynn 500 sacks of flour at $4 each to be delivered to Lynn by December 12. On November 27, Kim shipped the flour. By December 5, when the shipment arrived, containing only 450 sacks, the market price of flour had fallen. Lynn

refused to accept delivery or to pay. Kim shipped 50 more sacks of flour, which arrived December 10. Lynn refused delivery. Kim resold the 500 sacks of flour for $3 per sack. Explain what Kim's rights are against Lynn.

7. Farley and Trudy enter into a written contract whereby Farley agrees to sell and Trudy agrees to buy six thousand bushels of wheat at $10.33 per bushel, deliverable at the rate of one thousand bushels a month commencing June 1, the price for each installment being payable ten days after delivery thereof. Although Farley delivered and received payment for the June installment, he defaulted by failing to deliver the July and August installments. By August 15, the market price of wheat had increased to $12 per bushel. Trudy thereupon entered into a contract with Albert to purchase five thousand bushels of wheat at $12 per bushel deliverable over the ensuing four months. In late September, the market price of wheat commenced to decline and by December 1 was $9.25 per bushel. Explain whether Trudy would succeed in a legal action against Farley for breach of contract.

8. Bain ordered from Marcum a carload of lumber, which he intended to use in the construction of small boats for the U.S. Navy pursuant to contract. The order specified that the lumber was to be free from knots, wormholes, and defects. The lumber was shipped, and immediately upon receipt, Bain looked in the door of the fully loaded car, ascertained that there was a full carload of lumber, and acknowledged to Marcum that the carload had been received. On the same day, Bain moved the car to his private siding and sent to Marcum full payment in accordance with the terms of the order.

A day later, the car was moved to the work area and unloaded in the presence of the Navy inspector, who refused to allow three-fourths of it to be used because of excessive knots and wormholes in the lumber. Bain then informed Marcum that he was rejecting the order and requested refund of the payment and directions on disposition of the lumber. Marcum replied that because Bain had accepted the order and unloaded it, he was not entitled to return of the purchase price. Who is correct? Explain.

CASE PROBLEMS

9. Plaintiff, a seller of milk, had for ten years bid on contracts to supply milk to defendant school district and had supplied milk to other school districts in the area. On June 15, plaintiff contracted to supply defendant's requirements of milk for the next school year at a price of $0.0759 per half pint. The price of raw milk delivered

from the farm had been for years controlled by the U.S. Department of Agriculture. On June 15, the department's administrator for the New York–New Jersey area had mandated a price for raw milk of $8.03 per hundredweight. By December, the mandated price had been raised to $9.31 per hundredweight, an increase of nearly

20 percent. If required to complete deliveries at the contract price, plaintiff would lose $7,350.55 on its contract with defendant and would face similar losses on contracts with two other school districts. Is the plaintiff correct in its assertion (a) that its performance had become impracticable through unforeseen events and (b) that it is entitled to relief from performance? Explain.

10. In April, F. W. Lang Company purchased an ice cream freezer and refrigeration compressor unit from Fleet for $2,160. Although the parties agreed to a written installment contract providing for an $850 down payment and eighteen installment payments, Lang made only one $200 payment upon receipt of the goods. One year later, Lang moved to a new location and took the equipment along without notifying Fleet. Two years after the sale, Lang disconnected the compressor from the freezer and used it to operate an air conditioner. Lang continued to use the compressor for that purpose until the sheriff seized the equipment and returned it to Fleet pursuant to a court order. Fleet then sold the equipment for $500 in what both parties conceded was a fair sale. Lang then brought an action charging that the equipment was defective and unusable for its intended purpose and sought to recover the down payment and expenses incurred in repairing the equipment. Fleet counterclaimed for the balance due under the installment contract less the proceeds from the sale. Who will prevail? Why?

11. Deborah McCullough bought a new car from Bill Swad Chrysler, Inc. The car was protected by both a limited warranty and an extended warranty. McCullough immediately encountered problems with the automobile's brakes, transmission, and air conditioning and discovered a number of cosmetic defects as well. She returned the car to Swad for repairs, but Swad did not fix the brakes properly or perform any of the cosmetic work. Moreover, new problems appeared with respect to the car's steering mechanism. McCullough returned the car twice more for repairs, but on each occasion, old problems persisted and new ones emerged. After the engine abruptly shut off on a short trip away from home and the brakes again failed on a more extensive excursion, McCullough presented Swad with a list of thirty-two of the car's defects and demanded their correction. When Swad failed to remedy more than a few of the problems, McCullough wrote a letter to Swad calling for rescission of the purchase agreement and a refund of the purchase price and offering to return the car upon receiving instructions from Swad regarding where to return it. Swad did not respond to the letter, and McCullough brought an action against Swad. She continued to operate the vehicle until the time of trial, some seventeen and one-half months (and

twenty-three thousand miles) later. Can McCullough rescind the agreement? Why or why not?

12. On March 17, Peckham bought a new car from Larsen Chevrolet for $16,400. During the first one and one-half months after the purchase, Peckham discovered that the car's hood was dented, its gas tank contained no baffles, its emergency brake was inoperable, the car did not have a jack or a spare tire, and neither the clock nor the speedometer worked. Larsen claimed that Peckham knew of the defects at the time of the purchase. Peckham, on the other hand, claimed that he did not know the extent of the defects and that despite his repeated efforts, the defects were not repaired until June 11. Then, on July 15, the car's dashboard caught fire, leaving the car's interior damaged and the car itself inoperable. Peckham then returned to Larsen Chevrolet and told Larsen that he had to repair the car at his own expense or that he, Peckham, would either rescind the contract or demand a new automobile. Peckham also claimed that at the end of their conversation, he notified Larsen Chevrolet that he was electing to rescind the contract and demanded the return of the purchase price. Larsen denied having received that oral notification. On October 12, Peckham sent a written notice of revocation of acceptance to Larsen. Discuss what the rights of the parties are.

13. Joc Oil bought a cargo of fuel oil for resale. The certificate from the foreign refinery stated that the sulfur content of the oil was 0.5 percent. Joc Oil entered into a written contract with Con Ed for the sale of this oil. The contract specified a sulfur content of 0.5 percent. Joc Oil knew, however, that Con Ed was authorized to buy and burn oil of up to 1 percent sulfur content and that Con Ed often bought and mixed oils of varying contents to stay within this limit. The oil under contract was delivered to Con Ed, but independent testing revealed a sulfur content of 0.92 percent. Con Ed promptly rejected the non-conforming shipment. Joc Oil immediately offered to substitute a conforming shipment of oil, although the time for performance had expired after the first shipment of oil. Con Ed refused to accept the substituted shipment. Joc Oil sues Con Ed for breach of contract. Explain which party should prevail.

14. The plaintiff, a German wine producer and exporter, contracted to ship 620 cases of wine to the defendant, a distributor in North Carolina. The contract was silent as to the shipment destination. During the next several months, the defendant called repeatedly to find out the status of the shipment. Later, without notifying the defendant, the plaintiff delivered the wine to a shipping line in Rotterdam, destined for Wilmington, North Carolina. The ship and the wine were lost at sea en route to Wilmington. When the defendant refused to pay on the contract, the plaintiff sued. Decision? Discuss.

15. Can-Key Industries, Inc., manufactured a turkey-hatching unit, which it sold to Industrial Leasing Corporation (ILC), which leased it to Rose-A-Linda Turkey Farms. ILC conditioned its obligation to pay on Rose-A-Linda's acceptance of the equipment. Rose-A-Linda twice notified Can-Key that the equipment was unacceptable and asked that it be removed. Over a period of fifteen months, Can-Key made several unsuccessful attempts to solve the problems with the equipment. During this time, Can-Key did not instruct Rose-A-Linda to refrain from using the equipment. Rose-A-Linda indicated its dissatisfaction with the equipment, and ILC refused to perform its obligations under the contract. Can-Key then brought suit against ILC for breach of contract. It argued that Rose-A-Linda accepted the equipment, as it used it for fifteen months. ILC countered that the equipment was unacceptable and asked that it be removed. It claimed that Can-Key refused and failed to instruct Rose-A-Linda to refrain from using the equipment. Therefore, ILC argued, Rose-A-Linda effectively rejected the turkey-hatching unit, relieving ILC of its contractual obligations. Who is correct? Explain.

16. Frederick Manufacturing Corp. ordered 500 dozen units of Import Traders' rubber pads for $2,580. The order indicated that the pads should be "as soft as possible." Import Traders delivered the rubber pads to Frederick Manufacturing on November 19. Frederick failed to inspect the goods upon delivery, even though the parties recognized that there might be a problem with the softness. Frederick finally complained about the nonconformity of the pads in April of the following year, when Import Traders requested the contract price for the goods. Can Import Traders recover the contract price from Frederick? Why or why not?

17. Moulton Cavity & Mold, Inc., agreed to manufacture twenty-six innersole molds to be purchased by Lyn-Flex. Moulton delivered the twenty-six molds to Lyn-Flex after Lyn-Flex allegedly approved the sample molds. However, Lyn-Flex rejected the molds, claiming that the molds did not satisfy the specifications exactly, and denied that it had ever approved the sample molds. Moulton then sued, contending that Lyn-Flex wrongfully rejected the molds. Lyn-Flex argued that the Code's perfect tender rule permitted its rejection of the imperfect molds, regardless of Moulton's substantial performance. Explain which party should prevail.

18. Neptune Research & Development, Inc. (the buyer), which manufactured solar-operated valves used in scientific instruments, saw advertised in a trade journal a hole-drilling machine with a very high degree of accuracy, manufactured and sold by Teknics Industrial Systems, Inc. (the seller). As the machine's specifications met the buyer's needs, the buyer contacted the seller in late March and ordered one of the machines to be delivered in mid-June. There was no "time-of-the-essence" clause in the contract.

Although the buyer made several calls to the seller throughout the month of June, the seller never delivered the machine and never gave the buyer any reasons for the nondelivery. By late August, the buyer desperately needed the machine. The buyer went to the seller's place of business to examine the machine and discovered that the still-unbuilt machine had been redesigned, omitting a particular feature that the buyer had wanted. Nonetheless, the buyer agreed to take the machine, and the seller promised that it would be ready on September 5. The seller also agreed to call the buyer on September 3 to give the buyer two days to arrange for transportation of the machine.

The seller failed to telephone the buyer on September 3 as agreed. On September 4, the buyer called the seller to find out the status of the machine and was told by the seller that "under no circumstances" could the seller have the machine ready by September 5. At this point, the buyer notified the seller that the order was canceled. One hour later, still on September 4, the seller called the buyer, retracted its earlier statement, and indicated that the machine would be ready by the agreed September 5 date. The buyer sued for the return of its $3,000 deposit. Should the buyer prevail? Explain.

19. ALPAC and Eagon are corporations that import and export raw logs. In April, Setsuo Kimura, ALPAC's president, and C. K. Ahn, Eagon's vice president, entered into a contract for ALPAC to ship about fifteen thousand cubic meters of logs between the end of July and the end of August. Eagon agreed to purchase them. Subsequently, the market for logs began to soften, making the contract less attractive to Eagon. ALPAC became concerned that Eagon would try to cancel the contract. Kimura and Ahn began a series of meetings and letters, apparently to assure ALPAC that Eagon would purchase the logs.

Eagon was troubled by the drop in timber prices and initially withheld approval of the shipment. Ahn sent numerous internal memoranda to the home office, indicating that it might not wish to complete the deal, but that accepting the logs was "inevitable" under the contract.

On August 23, Eagon received a fax from ALPAC suggesting a reduction in price and volume of the contract, but Eagon did not respond. Soon after, Kimura asked Ahn whether he intended to accept the logs; Ahn admitted that he was having trouble getting approval. On August 30, Ahn informed the home office that he would attempt to avoid accepting the logs but that it would be difficult and suggested holding ALPAC responsible for shipment delay. Kimura thereafter believed that Eagon would not accept the shipment and eventually canceled the vessel reserved to ship the logs, believing that Eagon was canceling the contract. The logs were not loaded or shipped by August 31, but Ahn and Kimura continued to discuss the contract. On September 7, Ahn told Kimura that he would try to convince the firm to accept the delivery and indicated that he did not want Kimura to sell the logs to another buyer. The same day, Ahn informed Eagon that it should consider accepting the shipment in September or October.

By September 27, ALPAC had not shipped the logs and sent a final letter to Eagon stating that because it failed to take delivery of the logs, it had breached the contract. Eagon responded to the letter, stating that there was "no contract" because ALPAC's breach (not shipping by the deadline) excused Eagon's performance. Explain whether either party breached the agreement.

20. In August, Bunge Corporation, a grain dealer, and Recker, a farmer, entered into a written contract under which Recker agreed to sell to Bunge ten thousand bushels of No. 2 yellow soybeans to be grown in the United States at $3.35 per bushel. Delivery of the grain was to be made at Bunge's place of business, Price's Landing, Missouri, during January of the following year. Nothing in the contract required Recker to grow the beans on his own land, to grow the beans himself, or to operate a farm. The contract also provided that Bunge could extend the time of delivery. Severe winter weather struck the southeastern Missouri area in the early part of January, making it impossible for Recker to harvest approximately 865 acres of his beans. Agents of Bunge visited Recker's farm in mid-January and observed that the beans were unharvestable. Shortly thereafter, Bunge directed a letter to Recker, calling attention to the fact that the 10,000 bushels of beans due under the contract had not been delivered. By the same communication, Bunge extended the time for delivery to March 31. From January 31 to March 31, the market price of beans increased by 10 percent. When delivery was not made by March 31, Bunge commenced an action to recover damages for breach of contract. Recker answered by admitting the failure to deliver but argued that he was excused from performance by the destruction of part of his crop. Explain which party should prevail.

21. Seller manufactures furnace-grade carbon black, a filler used in tires and other rubber and plastic products. Buyer was a longtime customer of Seller, purchasing three grades of carbon black for use in numerous rubber products it supplies to customers. Buyer and Seller entered into a supply agreement as of January 1, in which Seller agreed to supply all of Buyer's requirements for carbon black. When the demand for carbon black subsequently increased and its market price began to rise, Seller notified Buyer on April 14 of the following year that Seller was implementing a two-cents-per-pound base price increase to Buyer effective June 1. Buyer rejected Seller's request for a price increase and insisted that Seller provide adequate assurance that Seller would fill Buyer's orders under the contract. On April 26, Buyer sent Seller a purchase order for carbon black and requested that Seller confirm the order. When Seller failed to do so, Buyer sent several additional requests for confirmation, but Seller still did not confirm the order. Explain whether either party has breached the contract.

TAKING SIDES

On February 26, 2020, William Stem purchased a used BMW from Gary Braden for $26,600. Stem's primary purpose for buying the car was to use it to drive his child to school and various activities. Braden indicated to Stem that the car had not been wrecked and that it was in good condition. Stem thought the car had been driven only seventy thousand miles. Less than a week after the purchase, Stem discovered a disconnected plug that, when plugged in, caused the oil warning light to turn on. When Stem then took his car to a mechanic, the mechanic discovered that the front end was that of a 2010 BMW and the rear end was that of a 2006 BMW. Further investigation revealed that the front half had been driven one hundred and seventy thousand miles. On March 10, 2020, Stem sent a letter informing Braden that he refused the automobile and that he intended to rescind the sale. Braden refused. Stem then drove the automobile for seven months and nearly nine thousand miles before filing an action against Braden, seeking to revoke his acceptance and to obtain the return of the purchase price.

a. What arguments would support Stem's revocation of his acceptance and the return of the purchase price?

b. What arguments would support Braden's denial of Stem's claim?

c. Who should prevail? Explain.

CHAPTER 23

Transfer of Title and Risk of Loss

CHAPTER OUTCOMES

After reading and studying this chapter, you should be able to:

- Explain the relative importance of title under the common law and Article 2.

- Explain when the seller has a right or power to transfer title and when the transfer is void or voidable.

- Distinguish between a shipment contract and a destination contract and explain when title and risk of loss pass under each.

- Explain the rules covering (1) risk of loss in the absence of a breach and (2) risk of loss when there is a breach.

- Explain how bulk transfers concern creditors and how the Uniform Commercial Code attempts to regulate such transfers.

Historically, title governed nearly every aspect of the rights and duties of the buyer and seller arising out of a sales contract. To add greater precision and certainty to sales contracts, the Uniform Commercial Code (UCC or the Code) has abandoned the common law's reliance upon title. Instead, the Code approaches each legal issue arising out of a sales contract on its own merits and provides separate and specific rules to control the various transactional situations. This chapter covers the Code's approach to the transfer of title and other property rights, the passage of risk of loss, and the transfer of goods sold in bulk.

23-1 Transfer of Title

As previously stated, a sale of goods is defined as the transfer of title from the seller to the buyer for a price. Section 2-106. Transfer of title is, therefore, fundamental to a sale of goods. Title, however, cannot pass under a contract for sale until existing goods have been identified as those to which the contract refers. Section 2-401(1). Future goods (goods that are not both existing and identified) cannot constitute a present sale. Section 2-105. If the buyer rejects the goods, whether justifiably or not, title reverts to the seller. Section 2-401(4).

In a lease, title does not pass. Instead, the lessee obtains the right to possess and use the goods for a period of time in return for consideration. Section 2A-103(1)(j).

23-1a IDENTIFICATION

After formation of the contract, the seller normally takes steps to obtain, manufacture, prepare, or select goods with which to fulfill her obligation under the contract. At some stage in the process, the seller will have identified existing goods that she intends to ship, deliver, or hold for the buyer. Identification may be made by either the seller or the buyer and can be made at any time and in any manner agreed upon by the parties. In the absence of explicit agreement, **identification** takes place as provided in Section 2-501(1) (Section 2A-217 contains similar, but not identical, provisions):

1. upon the making of the contract if it is for goods already existing and identified;

2. if the contract is for all other future goods, when the seller ships, marks, or otherwise designates existing goods as those to which the contract refers; or

3. if the contract is (a) for crops to be grown within twelve months or at the time of the next normal harvest, when the crops are planted or start growing, or (b) for the offspring of animals to be born within twelve months, when the young animals are conceived.

To illustrate, suppose Barringer contracts to purchase a specific Buick automobile from Stevenson's car lot. Identification occurs as soon as the contract is entered into. If, however, Barringer agrees to purchase a television set from Stevenson, whose storeroom is filled with such televisions, identification will not occur until either Barringer or Stevenson selects a specific television to fulfill the contract.

Fungible goods are goods of which any unit, by nature, agreement, or usage of trade, is the equivalent of any other like unit. Section 1-201(b)(18). If the goods are fungible, identification of a share of undivided goods occurs when the contract is entered into. Thus, if Barringer agrees to purchase one thousand gallons of gasoline from Stevenson, who owns a five-thousand-gallon tank of gasoline, identification occurs as soon as the contract is formed.

INSURABLE INTEREST For a contract or policy of insurance to be valid, the insured must have an insurable interest in the subject matter (see *Chapter 47*). At common law, only a person with title or a lien (a legal claim of a creditor on property) could insure his interest in specific goods. The Code extends this right to a buyer's interest in goods that have been identified as goods to which the contract refers. Section 2-501(1); Section 2A-218(1). This **special property interest** of the buyer enables her to purchase insurance protection on goods that she does not presently own but she will own upon delivery by the seller.

So long as he has title to them or any security interest in them, the seller also has an insurable interest in the goods. Section 2-501(2). Nothing prevents both seller and buyer from simultaneously carrying insurance on goods in which they both have a property interest, whether it be title, a security interest, or a special property interest. In a lease, the lessor retains an insurable interest in the goods until an option to buy, if included in the lease, has been exercised by the lessee. Section 2A-218(3).

SECURITY INTEREST The Code defines a security interest as an interest in personal property or fixtures that ensures payment or performance of an obligation. Section 1-201(b)(35). Any reservation by the seller of title to goods delivered to the buyer is limited in effect to a reservation of a security interest. Section 2-401(1). As mentioned previously, the seller retains an insurable interest in goods for which he holds title or any security interest. Section 2-501(2). Security interests in goods are governed by Article 9 of the Code (discussed in *Chapter 37*).

23-1b PASSAGE OF TITLE

Title passes when the parties *intend* it to pass, provided the goods are in existence and have been identified. Where the parties have no explicit agreement as to transfer of title, the Code provides rules that determine when title passes to the buyer. Section 2-401.

PHYSICAL MOVEMENT OF THE GOODS When delivery is to be made by moving the goods, title passes at the time and place the seller completes his performance with reference to delivery of the goods. Section 2-401(2). When and where delivery occurs depends on whether the contract is a shipment contract or a destination contract.

A **shipment contract** requires or authorizes the seller to send the goods to the buyer but does not require the seller to deliver them at a particular destination. Under a shipment contract, title passes to the buyer at the time and place the seller *delivers* the goods to the carrier for shipment to the buyer.

A **destination contract** requires the seller to deliver the goods at a particular destination. Under a destination contract, title passes to the buyer upon *tender* of the goods at that destination. Tender, as discussed in *Chapter 22*, requires that the seller (1) put and hold conforming goods at the buyer's disposition, (2) give the buyer reasonable notice that the goods are available, and (3) keep the goods available for a reasonable time. Section 2-503.

NO MOVEMENT OF THE GOODS When delivery is to be made without moving the goods, unless otherwise agreed, title passes (1) upon delivery of a document of title, if the contract calls for delivery of such document (documents of title are documents that evidence a right to receive specified goods—they are discussed more fully in *Chapter 47*) or (2) at the time and place of contracting, if the goods at the time have been identified and no documents are to be delivered. Section 2-401(3). Where the goods are not identified at the time of contracting, title passes when the goods are identified.

For a summary of passage of title in the absence of an agreement by the parties, see *Figure 23-1*.

◆ *See Case 23-1*

◆ SEE FIGURE 23-1: *Passage of Title in Absence of Agreement by Parties*

23-1c POWER TO TRANSFER TITLE

It is important to understand under what circumstances a seller has the right or power to transfer title to a buyer. If the seller is the rightful owner of goods or is authorized to sell the goods for the rightful owner, then the seller has the **right** to transfer title. But when a seller is in possession of goods that he neither owns nor has authority to sell, then the sale is not rightful. In some situations, however, these unauthorized sellers may have the **power** to transfer good title to certain buyers. This section pertains to such sales by a person in possession of goods that he neither owns nor has authority to sell.

The fundamental rule of property law protecting existing ownership of goods is the starting point for any discussion of a sale of goods by a nonowner. A basic tenet of the law is that a purchaser of goods obtains such title as his transferor had or had power to transfer, and the Code expressly so states. Section 2-403; Sections 2A-304 and 2A-305. Likewise, the purchaser of a limited interest in goods acquires rights only to the extent of the interest that he purchased. By the same token, no one can transfer what he does not have. A purported sale by a thief or finder or ordinary bailee of goods does not transfer title to the purchaser.

The principal reason underlying the policy of the law in protecting existing ownership of goods is that a person should not be required to retain possession at all times of all the goods that he owns in order to maintain his ownership of them. Incidental to the ownership of goods is the owner's freedom to make a bailment of his goods as desired; the mere possession of goods by a bailee does not authorize the bailee to sell them.

A second policy, one concerning the protection of the good faith purchaser, conflicts with the policy protecting existing ownership of goods. Protecting the expectations of good faith transactions in goods is of paramount importance in trade and commerce. To encourage and make safe good faith acquisitions of goods, *bona fide* (good faith) purchasers for value must be protected under certain circumstances. A **good faith purchaser** is defined as one who acts honestly, gives value, and takes the goods without notice or knowledge of any defect in the title of his transferor.

VOID AND VOIDABLE TITLE TO GOODS A **void title** is no title. A person claiming ownership of goods by an agreement that is void obtains no title to the goods. Thus, a thief or a finder of goods or a person who acquires goods from someone under physical duress or under guardianship has no title to them and can transfer none.

A **voidable title** is one acquired under circumstances that permit the former owner to rescind the transfer and revest herself with title, as in the case of mistake, common duress, undue influence, fraud in the inducement, misrepresentation, mistake, or sale by a person without contractual capacity (other than an individual under guardianship). In these situations, the buyer has acquired legal title to the goods, which may be divested by action of the seller. If, however, before the seller has rescinded the transfer of title the buyer were to resell the goods to a good faith purchaser for value, the right of rescission in the seller is cut off, and the good faith purchaser for value acquires good title. The 2001 Revised UCC Article 1 defines **good faith** as "honesty in fact and the observance of reasonable commercial standards of fair dealing." Section 1-201(20). The Code defines value to include a consideration sufficient to support a simple contract. Section 1-204.

FIGURE 23-1   Passage of Title in Absence of Agreement by Parties

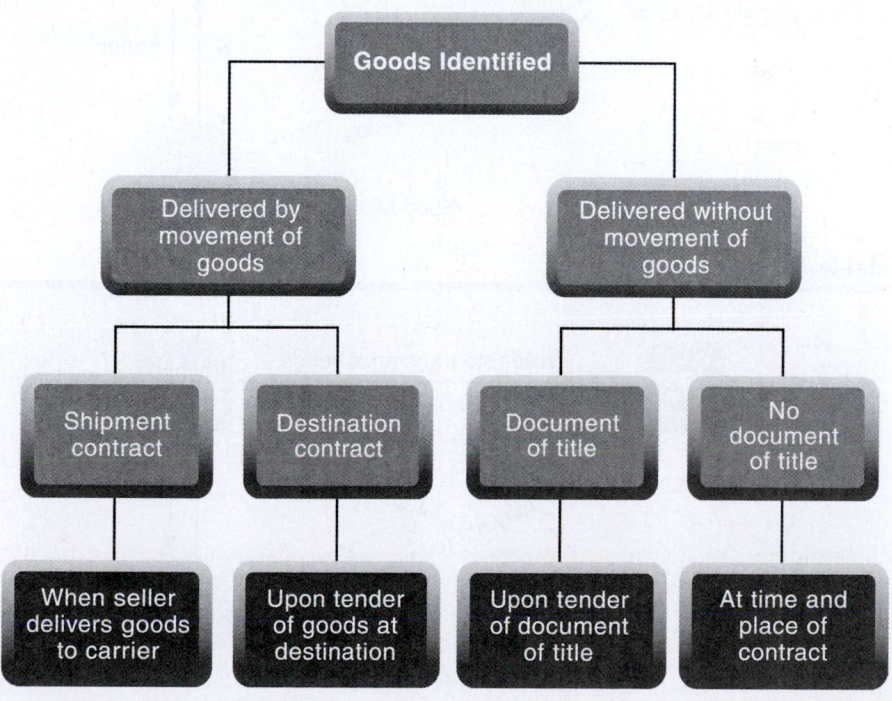

The distinction between a void and voidable title is, therefore, extremely important in determining the rights of good faith purchasers of goods. The good faith purchaser for value always believes that she is buying the goods from the owner or from one with authority to sell. Otherwise she would not be acting in good faith. In each situation, the party selling the goods appears to be the owner whether his title is valid, void, or voidable. Given a transaction involving two innocent persons—the true owner and the good faith purchaser for value, who have done nothing wrong—the law will not disturb the *legal title* but will rule in favor of the one who has it. Thus, where A transfers possession of goods to B under such circumstances that B acquires no title or a void title and B thereafter sells the goods to C, a good faith purchaser for value, B has nothing except possession to transfer to C. In a lawsuit between A and C involving the right to the goods, A will win because she has the legal title. C's only recourse is against B for breach of warranty of title, which will be discussed in *Chapter 24.*

If, however, B acquired voidable title from A and resold the goods to C, in a suit between A and C over the goods, C would win. In this case, B had title, although it was voidable, which she transferred to the good faith purchaser for value. The title thus acquired by C will be protected. The voidable title in B, which is title until it has been avoided, may not be avoided after transfer to a good faith purchaser. A's only recourse is against B for restitution or damages.

The Code has enlarged this common law doctrine by providing that a good faith purchaser for value obtains valid title from one possessing voidable title even if that person obtained voidable title by (1) fraud as to her identity, (2) exchange for a subsequently dishonored check, (3) an agreement that the transaction was to be a cash sale and the sale price has not been paid, or (4) criminal fraud punishable as larceny. Section 2-403(1); (Sections 2A-304 and 2A-305 are similar).

In addition, the Code has expanded the rights of good faith purchasers with respect to sales by **minors**. Although the common law permitted a minor seller of goods to disaffirm the sale and to recover the goods from a third person who had purchased them in good faith from the party who acquired the goods from the minor, the Code has changed this rule by no longer permitting a minor seller of goods to prevail over a good faith purchaser for value. Section 2-403.

◆ SEE FIGURE 23-2: *Void Title*

◆ SEE FIGURE 23-3: *Voidable Title*

◆ *See Case 23-2*

FIGURE 23-2 Void Title

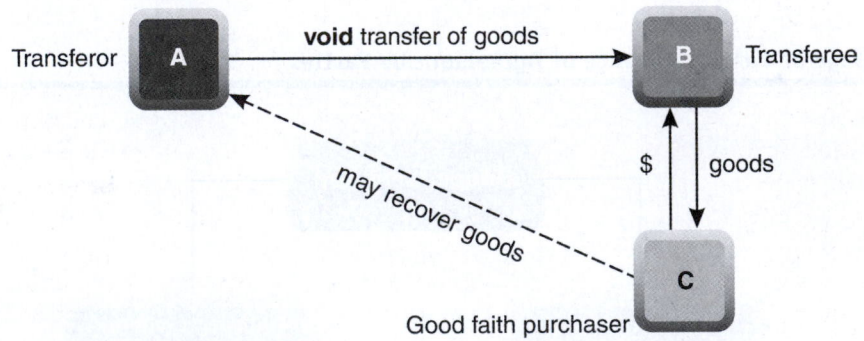

FIGURE 23-3 Voidable Title

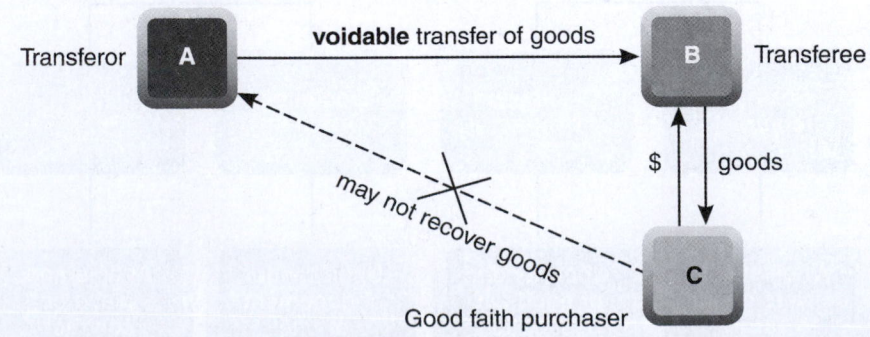

23-1d ENTRUSTING OF GOODS TO A MERCHANT

Frequently, an owner of goods entrusts (transfers possession of) the goods to a bailee for resale, repair, cleaning, or some other use. In some instances, the bailee violates this entrusting by selling the goods to a third party. Although the "true" owner has a right of recourse against the bailee for the value of the goods, what right, if any, should the true owner of the goods have against the third party? Once again, the law must balance the right of ownership against the rights of market transactions.

The Code takes the position of protecting a buyer of goods in the ordinary course of business from a merchant who deals in goods of the kind involved in the sale, where the owner has entrusted possession of the goods to the merchant. The Code defines **buyer in ordinary course of business** as a person who buys goods in good faith, without knowledge that the sale violates the rights of another person in the goods, and in the ordinary course of business from a person, other than a pawnbroker, in the business of selling goods of that kind. Section 1-201(b)(9). Because the merchant who deals in goods of that kind is cloaked with the appearance of ownership or apparent authority to sell, the Code seeks to protect the innocent third-party purchaser. Any such entrusting of possession bestows upon the merchant the power to transfer all rights of the entruster to a buyer in the ordinary course of business. Section 2-403(2); (Sections 2A-304(2) and 2A-305(2) are similar). For example, A brings her stereo for repair to B, who also sells both new and used stereo equipment. C purchases A's stereo from B in the ordinary course of business. The Code protects the rights of C and defeats the rights of A. A's only recourse is against B.

The Code, however, does not go so far as to protect the buyer in the ordinary course of business from a merchant to whom a thief, a finder, or a completely unauthorized person has entrusted the goods. It merely grants the buyer in the ordinary course of business the rights of the entruster.

Where a buyer of goods to whom title has passed leaves the seller in possession of the goods, the buyer has "entrusted the goods" to the seller. Section 2-403(3). If that seller is a merchant and resells and delivers the goods to another buyer in the ordinary course of business, this second buyer acquires good title to the goods. Thus, Marianne sells certain goods to Martin, who pays the price but allows possession to remain with Marianne. Marianne thereafter sells the same goods to Carla, a buyer in the ordinary course of business. Carla takes delivery of the goods. Martin does not have any rights against Carla or to the goods. Martin's only remedy is against Marianne.

♦ **SEE FIGURE 23-4:** *Entrusting of Goods to a Merchant*

♦ *See Case 23-3*

23-2 Risk of Loss

Risk of loss, as the term is used in the law of sales, addresses the question of allocation of loss between seller and buyer where the goods have been damaged, destroyed, or lost *without the fault* of either the seller or the buyer. If the loss is placed on the buyer, he is under a duty to pay the price for the goods even though they were damaged or he never received them. If loss is placed upon the seller, he has no right to recover the purchase price from the buyer and is usually liable to the buyer

FIGURE 23-4 Entrusting of Goods to a Merchant

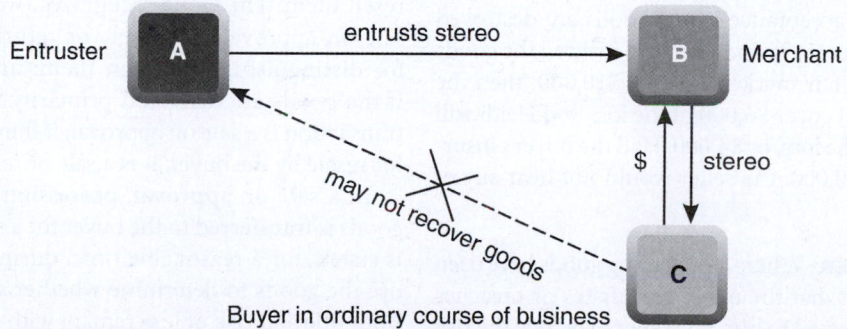

CISG Loss of or damage to the goods after the risk of loss has passed to the buyer does not discharge the buyer from his obligation to pay the purchase price.

for damages for nondelivery unless he tenders a performance in replacement of the lost or destroyed goods.

In determining which party carries the risk of loss, the Code provides definite rules for specific situations, a sharp departure from the common-law concept of risk of loss, which was determined by ownership of the goods and depended upon the transfer of title. The transactional approach under the Code is necessarily detailed and for this reason is probably more understandable and meaningful than the common law's reliance upon the abstract concept of title. The Code has adopted rules for determining the risk of loss in the absence of breach separate from those that apply where the sales contract has been breached.

Except in a finance lease, risk of loss is retained by the lessor and does not pass to the lessee. Section 2A-219(1). In a finance lease, risk of loss passes to the lessee, as discussed later in this chapter.

23-2a RISK OF LOSS IN CASES OF A BREACH

Where one party breaches the contract, the Code places the risk of loss on the breaching party. Nevertheless, where the nonbreaching party is in control of the goods, the Code places the risk of loss on him to the extent of his insurance coverage.

BREACH BY THE SELLER If the seller ships nonconforming goods to the buyer, the risk of loss remains on the seller until the buyer has accepted the goods or the seller has remedied the defect. Section 2-510(1); Section 2A-220(1)(a).

Where the buyer has accepted nonconforming goods, and thereafter by timely notice to the seller rightfully revokes his acceptance (discussed in *Chapter* 22), he may treat the risk of loss, to the extent of any deficiency in his effective insurance coverage, as resting from the beginning on the seller. Section 2-510(2); Section 2A-220(1)(b). For example, Heidi delivers to Gary nonconforming goods, which Gary accepts. Subsequently, Gary discovers a hidden defect in the goods and rightfully revokes his prior acceptance. If the goods are destroyed through no fault of either party and Gary has insured the goods for 60 percent of their fair market value of $10,000, then the insurance company will cover $6,000 of the loss and Heidi will bear the remainder of the loss, or $4,000. Had the buyer's insurance coverage been $10,000, the seller would not bear any of the loss.

BREACH BY THE BUYER Where conforming goods have been identified to a contract that the buyer repudiates or breaches before risk of loss has passed to him, the seller may treat the risk

of loss as resting on the buyer "for a commercially reasonable time" to the extent of any deficiency in the seller's effective insurance coverage. Section 2-510(3); Section 2A-220(2). For example, Susan agrees to sell forty thousand pounds of plastic resin to Bernie, F.O.B. (free on board) Bernie's factory, delivery by March 1. On February 1, Bernie wrongfully repudiates the contract by telephoning Susan and telling her that he does not want the resin. Susan immediately seeks another buyer, but before she is able to locate one, and within a commercially reasonable time, the resin is destroyed by a fire through no fault of Susan's. The fair market value of the resin is $35,000. Because Susan's insurance covers only $15,000 of the loss, Bernie is liable for $20,000.

23-2b RISK OF LOSS IN ABSENCE OF A BREACH

Where there is no breach of contract, the parties may by agreement allocate the risk of loss. Where there is no breach and the parties have not otherwise agreed, the Code places the risk of loss, for the most part, upon the party who is more likely to have greater control over the goods, is more likely to insure the goods, or is better able to prevent their loss.

AGREEMENT OF THE PARTIES The parties, by agreement, not only may shift the allocation of risk of loss but also may divide the risk between them. Section 2-303. Such agreement is controlling. Thus, the parties may agree, for example, that the seller shall retain the risk of loss even though the buyer is in possession of the goods or has title to them. Or the agreement may provide that the buyer bears 60 percent of the risk and the seller bears 40 percent.

Practical Advice

Specify in your contract of sale how risk of loss should be allocated.

TRIAL SALES Some sales are made with the understanding that the buyer can return the goods even though they conform to the contract. Such trial sales permit a buyer to try goods to determine whether she wishes to keep them or to try to resell them. The Code recognizes two types of trial sales—a sale on approval and a sale or return—and provides a test for distinguishing between them: unless otherwise agreed, if the goods are delivered primarily for the buyer's use, the transaction is a sale on approval; if they are delivered primarily for resale by the buyer, it is a sale or return. Section 2-326(1).

In a **sale on approval**, possession of, but not title to, the goods is transferred to the buyer for a stated time or, if no time is stated, for a reasonable time, during which the buyer may use the goods to determine whether she wishes to buy them. Both title and risk of loss remain with the *seller* until the buyer approves, or accepts, the goods. Section 2-327(1)(a). Until acceptance by the buyer, the sale is a bailment with an option to purchase.

Although use of the goods consistent with the purpose of approval is not acceptance, the buyer's failure to notify the seller within a reasonable time of her election to return the goods *is* an acceptance. The buyer also may manifest approval by exercising over the goods any dominion or control that is inconsistent with the seller's ownership. Upon approval, title and risk of loss passes to the buyer, who then becomes liable to the seller for the purchase price of the goods. If the buyer elects to return the goods and so notifies the seller, the return is at the seller's risk and expense.

In a **sale or return**, the goods are sold and delivered to the buyer with an option to return them to the seller. The risk of loss is on the *buyer*, who also has title until she revests it in the seller by returning the goods. The return of the goods is at the buyer's risk and expense.

A **consignment** is a delivery of possession of personal property to an agent for sale by the agent. Under the Code, a sale on consignment is regarded as a sale or return. Therefore, creditors of the consignee (the agent who receives the merchandise for sale) prevail over the consignor and may obtain possession of the consigned goods, provided the consignee maintains a place of business where he deals in goods of the kind involved under a name other than the name of the consignor. Nevertheless, under Section 2-326(3), the consignor will prevail if he (1) complies with applicable State law requiring a consignor's interest to be evidenced by a sign, (2) establishes that the consignee is generally known by his creditors to be substantially engaged in selling the goods of others, or (3) complies with the filing provisions of Article 9 (Secured Transactions). Section 2-326(3).

CONTRACTS INVOLVING CARRIERS Sales contracts frequently contain terms that indicate the agreement of the parties as to delivery by a carrier. These terms identify the contract as a shipment contract or a destination contract and, by implication, indicate when the risk of loss will pass. If the contract does not require the seller to deliver the goods to a particular destination but merely to the carrier (a **shipment contract**), risk of loss passes to the buyer upon *delivery* of the goods to the common carrier. If the seller is required to deliver them to a particular destination (a **destination contract**), risk of loss passes to the buyer at destination upon *tender* of the goods to the buyer. Section 2-509(1); Section 2A-219(2)(a).

Practical Advice

Select the shipment term that passes the risk of loss when you desire it to pass.

CISG If the sales contract involves the carriage of the goods and the seller is not obligated to hand them over at a particular destination, the risk of loss passes to the buyer when the goods are handed over to the first carrier. If the contract requires the seller to deliver the goods to a carrier at a particular destination, the risk of loss passes when the goods are handed over to the carrier at that place.

23-2c GOODS IN POSSESSION OF BAILEE

In some sales, the goods, at the time the contract is made, are held by a bailee and are to be delivered without being moved. For instance, a seller may contract with a buyer to sell grain that is located in a grain elevator and that the buyer intends to leave in the same elevator. In such situations, Sections 2-509(2) and 2A-219(2)(b) provide that the risk of loss passes to the buyer when one of the following occurs:

1. If a negotiable document of title [discussed in *Chapter 47*; Section 1-201(b)(16)] is involved, the risk of loss passes upon the buyer's receipt of the document.

2. If a nonnegotiable document of title is involved, the risk passes when the document is tendered to the buyer.

3. If no documents of title are employed, risk passes upon either (a) the seller's tender to the buyer of written directions to the bailee to deliver the goods to the buyer or (b) the bailee's acknowledgment of the buyer's right to possession of the goods.

In situations 2 and 3(a), if the buyer seasonably objects, the risk of loss remains upon the seller until the buyer has had a reasonable time to present the document or direction to the bailee.

CISG If the buyer is bound to take over the goods at a place other than the seller's place of business, the risk of loss passes when the buyer is aware of the fact that the goods are placed at her disposal at that location.

23-2d ALL OTHER SALES

If the buyer possesses the goods when the contract is formed, risk of loss passes to the buyer at that time. Section 2-509(3); Section 2A-219(2)(c).

All other sales not involving breach are covered by Section 2-509(3). This catchall provision applies when the buyer picks up the goods at the seller's place of business or when the seller delivers the goods using her own transportation. In these cases, risk of loss depends on whether or not the seller is a **merchant**. If the seller is a merchant, risk of loss passes to the buyer upon the buyer's *receipt* of the goods. If the seller is **not a merchant**, it passes on *tender* of the goods from the seller to the buyer. Section 2-509(3); Section 2A-219(2)(c). The policy behind this rule is that so long as the merchant seller is making delivery at her place of business or with her own vehicle, she continues to control the goods and can be expected to insure them. The buyer, on the other hand, has no control over the goods and is not likely to have insurance on them.

Suppose Belinda goes to Sidney's furniture store, selects a particular set of dining room furniture, and pays Sidney the agreed price of $1,800 for it upon Sidney's agreement to stain the set a darker color and deliver it. Sidney stains the furniture and notifies Belinda that he will deliver it the following day. That night, the furniture is accidentally destroyed by fire. Belinda can recover from Sidney the $1,800 payment. The risk of loss is on seller Sidney as he is a merchant and the goods were not received by Belinda, but were only tendered to her.

On the other hand, suppose Georgia, an accountant, prior to moving to a different city, contracts to sell her household furniture to Nina for $3,000. Though Georgia notifies Nina that the furniture is available for her to pick up, Nina delays picking up the furniture for several days. In the interim, the furniture is stolen from Georgia's residence without her fault. Georgia may recover from Nina the $3,000 purchase price. The risk of loss is on the buyer (Nina), as the seller is not a merchant and tender is sufficient to transfer the risk.

CISG If the sales contract does not involve the carriage of the goods, the risk of loss passes to the buyer when he takes over the goods or, if the buyer does not take over the goods in due time, from the time when the goods are placed at his disposal.

◆ **SEE FIGURE 23-5:** *Passage of Risk of Loss in Absence of Breach*

◆ *See Case 23-4*

23-3 Sales of Goods in Bulk

Because a debtor may secretly liquidate all or a major part of his tangible assets by a bulk sale and conceal or divert the proceeds of the sale without paying his creditors, creditors have an obvious interest in a merchant's bulk disposal of his merchandise made not in the ordinary course of business. The central purpose of bulk sales law is to deter two common forms of commercial fraud, namely, (1) when the merchant, owing debts, sells out his stock in trade to a friend for a low price, pays his creditors less than he owes them, and hopes to come back into the business "through the back door" sometime in the future and (2) when the merchant, owing debts, sells out his stock in trade to anyone for any price, pockets the proceeds, and disappears without paying his creditors.

Original Article 6 of the Code requires buyers in a bulk sale to provide notice to the seller's creditors and to maintain a list of the seller's creditors and a schedule of property obtained in a bulk sale for six months after the bulk sale takes place. If these procedures are not followed, the seller's creditors may void the sale.

In 1989, the Uniform Law Commission and the American Law Institute jointly issued a revision of Article 6. Revised UCC Article 6 provides States with two options: (1) Alternative A, which repeals Article 6 and (2) Alternative B, which replaces original Article 6 with a revised and updated Article 6 designed to afford better protection to creditors while minimizing the obstacles to good faith transactions. The ULC and ALI recommended repeal, and nearly every State has followed that recommendation.

FIGURE 23-5 Passage of Risk of Loss in Absence of Breach

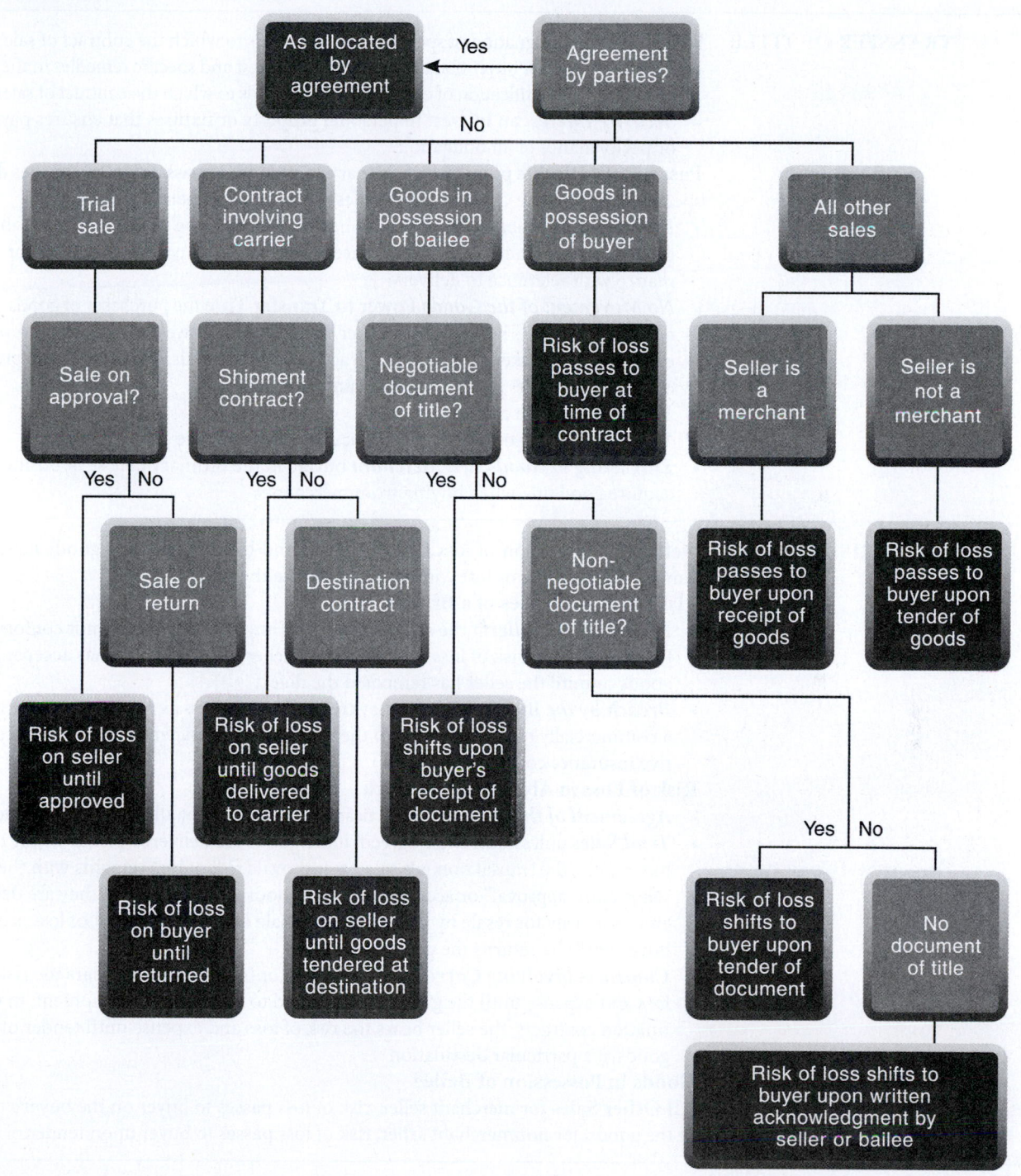

CHAPTER SUMMARY

TRANSFER OF TITLE

Identification designation of specific goods as goods to which the contract of sale refers
- *Insurable Interest* buyer obtains an insurable interest and specific remedies in the goods by the identification of existing goods as goods to which the contract of sale refers
- *Security Interest* an interest in personal property or fixtures that ensures payment or performance of an obligation

Passage of Title title passes when the parties intend it to pass; when the parties do not specifically agree, the Code provides rules to determine when title passes
- *Physical Movement of the Goods* when delivery is to be made by moving the goods, title passes at the time and place where the seller completes his performance with reference to delivery
- *No Movement of the Goods* **Power to Transfer Title** the purchaser of goods obtains such title as her transferor either has or had the power to transfer; however, to encourage and make secure good faith acquisitions of goods, it is necessary to protect certain third parties under certain circumstances
- *Void Title* no title can be transferred
- *Voidable Title* a good faith purchaser acquires good title
- *Entrusting of Goods to a Merchant* buyers in the ordinary course of business acquire good title when buying from merchants

RISK OF LOSS

Definition allocation of loss between seller and buyer where the goods have been damaged, destroyed, or lost without the fault of either party

Risk of Loss in Cases of a Breach
- *Breach by the Seller* if the seller ships to the buyer goods that do not conform to the contract, the risk of loss remains on the seller until the buyer has accepted the goods or until the seller has remedied the defect
- *Breach by the Buyer* the seller may treat the risk of loss as resting on the buyer for a commercially reasonable time to the extent of any deficiency in the seller's effective insurance coverage

Risk of Loss in Absence of a Breach
- *Agreement of the Parties* the parties may by agreement allocate the risk of loss
- *Trial Sales* unless otherwise agreed, if the goods are delivered primarily for the buyer's use, the transaction is a sale on approval (risk of loss remains with the seller until "approval" or acceptance of the goods by the buyer); if they are delivered primarily for resale by the buyer, it is a sale or return (the risk of loss is on the buyer until she returns the goods)
- *Contracts Involving Carriers* in shipment contracts, the seller bears the risk of loss and expense until the goods are delivered to the carrier for shipment; in destination contracts, the seller bears the risk of loss and expense until tender of the goods at a particular destination

Goods in Possession of Bailee

All Other Sales for merchant seller, risk of loss passes to buyer on the buyer's receipt of the goods; for nonmerchant seller, risk of loss passes to buyer upon tender of goods

SALES OF GOODS IN BULK

Definition a transfer of a major part of a merchant's inventory not made in the ordinary course of the seller's business

Revised Article 6—Alternative A repeals original Article 6; nearly every State has adopted this alternative

Revised Article 6—Alternative B updates Article 6 and makes a bulk sale ineffective against the seller's creditors unless specified requirements are met; only a few States have adopted this alternative

C A S E S

<table>
<tr><td>CASE
23-1</td><td> **Passage of Title: No Movement of the Goods**
DEITER v. COONS
Supreme Court of Idaho, 2017
394 P. 3d 87 </td><td></td></tr>
</table>

Eismann, J.

EISMANN, Justice.

Patty Anderson agreed to sell a 4-H steer for her eighteen-year-old granddaughter Danielle Bryant, who had purchased and raised the steer. Ms. Anderson placed an ad on Craigslist, and Joseph Deiter responded to the ad, but he only wanted to purchase one-half of the steer. He and Ms. Anderson communicated regarding various issues, and she ultimately prepared a handwritten contract ("Deiter Contract"), which they both signed. The contract provided:

> This is a contract iniated [sic] on Aug. 14, 2010 between Patty A. Anderson and Joseph and Melinda Deiter … Meridian, ID.

A deposit of $100.00 (check # 1178) has been received by Patty A. Anderson for ½ of a beef in (carcass weight). Once the beef has been killed and delivered to Don's Meat in Emmett, ID, the carcass weight will be known and Sharon Coons (owner of Don's Meat) will tell us what that weight is. At that time Joseph and Melinda Deiter will pay me (Patty Anderson) the amount of $2.25 lb for ½ the beef. When the meat has been cut + wrapped by Don's Meat Joseph and Melinda Deiter will pay Sharon Coons 45¢ lb for that service and will pick up their half of the beef.

Once Mr. Deiter had paid the $100.00 deposit and returned the signed contract, Ms. Anderson then had to find someone who was willing to purchase the other half of the steer before it was slaughtered. She placed another ad on Craigslist seeking a purchaser for the other half of the steer. A Mrs. Kirk responded to that ad, paid a $100.00 deposit, and signed a handwritten contract dated August 17, 2010, that had been prepared by Ms. Anderson.

Ms. Anderson contacted Donald Janak, who along with his wife own Janak, Inc., a mobile slaughtering business. He was asked to slaughter the steer on behalf of Mr. Deiter and Mrs. Kirk and to deliver the carcass to Don's Meats, which was a custom meat processing business that was owned and operated by Donald and Sharon Coons and their daughter Penny Coons. Mr. Janak and an employee of Janak, Inc., went to Ms. Anderson's property, where Ms. Anderson's ex-husband delivered possession of the steer to Mr. Janak. Mr. Janak and the employee slaughtered and skinned the steer, cut the carcass in half down the middle, and delivered the two halves of the

carcass to Don's Meats, where the meat was processed. Mr. Deiter's half of the carcass was processed first, and then Mrs. Kirk's half of the carcass was processed. Ms. Anderson paid Mr. Janak's fee. Mr. Deiter and Mrs. Kirk informed Don's Meats how they each wanted their respective halves of the carcass butchered and wrapped, and they each picked up their respective quantities of cut-and-wrapped meat from Don's Meats. Each package of meat was marked "Not for Sale." After eating the meat, the members of the Deiter family became ill due to becoming infected with E. coli bacteria.

On January 9, 2012, the Deiters filed this action against Ms. Anderson, Mr. Janak and his corporation, and the Coonses. Ms. Anderson filed a motion for summary judgment as to the claims against her, and, after briefing and argument, the district court granted her motion. The Deiters filed a motion for reconsideration, but the court denied their motion. The Coonses moved for summary judgment as to the claims against them and, after briefing and argument, the district court granted their motion. The Deiters settled with Mr. Janak and Janak, Inc., and they appealed the judgment in favor of Ms. Anderson and the Coonses.

* * *

In their complaint, the Deiters alleged various theories of liability against Ms. Anderson, but the only theory they argue on appeal is that she was negligent per se for violating the Federal Meat Inspection Act, specifically 21 U.S.C. § 610(c). They argued to the district court that she violated the act because she sold adulterated meat; the steer was slaughtered under insanitary conditions; and she did not sell, slaughter, or prepare the steer for her own use. * * *

* * *

In order to violate this provision, Ms. Anderson would have had to "sell, transport, offer for sale or transportation, or receive for transportation, [the described articles] in commerce." * * *

* * *

Ms. Anderson was not liable because under the Idaho Uniform Commercial Code, title to the steer passed to Mr. Deiter and Mrs. Kirk when possession was transferred to Mr. Janak. The Deiters contend that they did not purchase the steer; they only purchased the meat that was to be derived from the steer. They argue that the contract uses the word "beef," which means the meat from the steer, not the steer itself. The word "beef" can mean "the flesh of a cow, steer, or bull raised and killed for its meat" or "an adult cow, steer, or bull raised for its meat." Random House, Inc. http://www.dictionary.com/browse/beef (accessed: March 28, 2017). The Deiter Contract unambiguously used the word "beef" to mean an adult steer raised for meat.

The contract stated that Mr. Deiter purchased "1/2 of a beef in (carcass weight)." It was one-half of "*a* beef" that he contracted to purchase. (Emphasis added.) The use of the singular "a" indicates that he purchased one-half of an object. The contract then states, "Once the beef has been killed and delivered to Don's Meat in Emmett, ID, the carcass weight will be known..." Only something living could be killed. The steer was living, the meat later derived from the carcass was not living and could not be killed. The words "the beef" could only refer to the "beef" in the preceding sentence, which is the one-half of a beef that Mr. Deiter contracted to purchase. * * *

Idaho Code [UCC] section 2-401(2) provides, insofar as is relevant, "Unless otherwise explicitly agreed title passes to the buyer at the time and place at which the seller completes his performance with reference to the physical delivery of the goods. . . ." There was no explicit agreement that title to the steer would pass at any time other than when Ms. Anderson completed her performance with reference to the physical delivery of the steer. Therefore, title passed when she completed that performance.

Idaho Code section 2-308(a) states that unless otherwise agreed "the place for delivery of goods is the seller's place of business or if he has none his residence." It is undisputed that Mr. Janak went to Ms. Anderson's residence where the steer was being held to take possession of the steer so he could slaughter it. Upon taking possession of the steer, Mr. Janak and the employee slaughtered it and then delivered the steer carcass to Don's Meats.

Under the Deiter Contract, it is clear that the carcass was to be delivered to Don's Meats. The contract states, "Once the beef has been killed and delivered to Don's Meat in Emmett, ID, the carcass weight will be known and Sharon Coons (owner of Don's Meat) will tell us what that weight is." Ms. Anderson instructed Mr. Janak that after he had slaughtered the steer, he was to deliver the steer carcass to Don's Meats. Mr. Deiter and Mrs. Kirk became owners of the steer when Mr. Janak took possession of it. At that point Ms. Anderson had "complete[d] h[er] performance with reference to the physical delivery of the goods." [UCC section] 2-401(2).

"Under the Uniform Commercial Code, there are two types of sales contracts when a carrier is used to transport the goods sold: (1) 'shipment' contracts; and (2) 'destination' contracts." [Citation.] Idaho Code section 2-401 sets forth when title passes under shipment and destination contracts. It states:

(a) if the contract requires or authorizes the seller to send the goods to the buyer but does not require him to deliver them at destination, title passes to the buyer at the time and place of shipment; but

(b) if the contract requires delivery at destination, title passes on tender there.

* * *

Under the shipment contract, the seller delivers the goods to a third party to transport the goods to the place required under the contract, and title passes when the goods are delivered to the person who will transport them. "The effect of the [Uniform Commercial] Code is that in the 'shipment' contract, the most commonly used method, delivery to the carrier is delivery to the buyer." [Citation.] "'A delivery by direction of the buyer to a third person as intermediary to ship the goods is a good delivery to the buyer.'" [Citation.] Therefore, when Ms. Anderson delivered possession of the steer to Mr. Janak, who was then to slaughter it and transport the carcass to Don's Meats, title to the steer passed to Mr. Deiter and Mrs. Kirk.

"The 'shipment' contract is regarded as the normal one, and the 'destination' contract is regarded as the variant." [Citation.] If terms such as "F.O.B. the place of shipment" or "F.O.B. the place of destination" are not used in the contract "and there has been no specific agreement to the contrary, a contract for the transportation of goods by carrier will be presumed to be a 'shipment' contract." [Citation.] Thus, the Deiter Contract is a shipment contract if the contract did not have a specific agreement making it a destination contract.

Idaho Code section 2-503 deals with the manner of the seller's tender of delivery. Subsection (2) of the statute refers to delivery under a shipment contract, and subsection (3) deals with delivery under a destination contract. The Official Comment to the statute provides some explanation as to the difference between the two. It states:

5. For the purposes of subsections (2) and (3) there is omitted from this Article [Chapter] the rule under prior uniform legislation that a term requiring the seller to pay the freight or cost of the transportation to the buyer is equivalent to an agreement by the seller to deliver to the buyer or at an agreed destination. *This omission is with the specific intention of negating the rule,* for under this Article [Chapter] the "shipment" contract is regarded as the normal one and the "destination" contract is the variant type. The seller is not obligated to deliver at a named destination and bear the concurrent risk of loss until arrival, *unless he has specifically agreed so to deliver* or the commercial understanding of the terms used by the parties contemplates such delivery.

(Emphases added.)

As stated in the comment, the prior uniform law provided that a contractual provision requiring the seller to pay the cost of transporting the goods to the buyer made the contract a destination contract, but the current version of the Uniform Commercial Code was specifically intended to negate that rule. Thus, the facts that Ms. Anderson paid Mr. Janak's fee and had him deliver the steer carcass to Don's Meats did not make this contract a destination contract. Likewise, a provision as to where the goods are to be shipped does not make the contract a destination contract. ***

* * *

The Deiter Contract did not expressly require Ms. Anderson to deliver the steer or the steer carcass to any place. "The parties must explicitly agree to a destination contract; otherwise the contract will be considered a shipment contract." ***

Because the contract in this case was a shipment contract, title passed to Mr. Deiter and Mrs. Kirk at the time and place that Ms. Anderson completed her performance with reference to the physical delivery of the goods. [UCC] § 2-401(2). Once possession of the steer was delivered to Mr. Janak, there was nothing more for Ms. Anderson to do under the contract with respect to the physical delivery of the goods. She thereafter never had possession of the steer or its carcass. She had completed all that she was to do.

* * *

Finally, the Deiters argued in the district court that Ms. Anderson violated the Federal Meat Inspection Act because the steer was slaughtered under insanitary conditions. A carcass would be adulterated under the Act if the steer was slaughtered in insanitary conditions. 21 U.S. Code § 601(*l*) & (m)(4). However, she was not the owner of the steer when that occurred.

* * *

We affirm the judgment of the district court ***.

CASE 23-2

Void and Voidable Title to Goods: ROBINSON v. DURHAM

Alabama Court of Civil Appeals, 1988
537 So.2d 966

Wright, J.

Ronald Robinson, Wyman Robinson, and Friendly Discount Auto Sales (appellants) appeal from the granting of summary judgment in favor of appellee Mike Durham (Durham).

The facts material to this appeal and dispositive of this case are undisputed. Appellants, who are in car sales, purchased a 1968 Chevrolet Camaro. At the time of the purchase, a female transferred to the appellants tag receipts in her name and in the name of the previous owner. Wyman Robinson then registered the automobile in his name. In September 1986 Durham purchased the automobile from appellants, and all prior documentation was transferred to him. Shortly thereafter, the F.B.I. [Federal Bureau of Investigation] seized the automobile. The automobile had been reported stolen in Florida. It was subsequently returned to the original owner.

Durham filed a suit against appellants alleging fraud, breach of contract, and breach of warranty. Durham moved for summary judgment against appellants on all counts. The trial court granted Durham's motion on the count alleging that appellants made a statement to Durham as true without knowledge of its truth and on the issue of breach of warranty of title. Durham was awarded $5,200, the amount he paid for the car. Appellants appeal.

Appellants assert that the grant of summary judgment was in error because there was "a scintilla of evidence, if not substantial evidence" from which the trial court could have concluded that appellants held good title "or at least voidable title" on the automobile, thereby conveying actual title to Durham at the time of the purchase.

Appellants' argument is without merit. It is unequivocal that "a person who has stolen goods of another cannot pass title thereto to another, whether such other knew, or did not know, that the goods were stolen." [Citations.] A thief gets only void title and without more cannot pass any title to a subsequent purchaser, even a good faith purchaser. [Citation.] It is undisputed that the automobile had been stolen. Therefore, at the time of purchase appellants obtained no title. In other words, the title was void. Appellants could not convey good title to Durham; therefore, the subsequent sale to Durham constituted a breach of warranty of good title.

Relying on §2-403(1), [UCC], appellants contend that they at least acquired a voidable title when they purchased the automobile. Section 2-403 recognizes that a person with voidable title has power to transfer a good title to a good faith purchaser for value. Voidable title can only arise from a voluntary transfer, and the rightful owner must assent to the transfer. "A possessor of goods does not have voidable title unless the true owner has consented to the transfer of title to him." [Citation.] In this case the rightful owner did not consent or assent to the transfer of the automobile. Appellants obtained no title.

* * *

AFFIRMED. All the Judges concur.

Entrusting of Goods to a Merchant
HEINRICH v. TITUS-WILL SALES, INC.

Court of Appeals of Washington, Division 2, 1994
73 Wash. App. 147, 868 P.2d 169

Seinfeld, J.

[In 1989, Michael Heinrich retained James Wilson to purchase a new Ford pickup truck for him. Wilson had held himself out as a dealer/broker, but unbeknownst to Heinrich, Wilson had lost his vehicle dealer license. Wilson negotiated with Titus-Will Ford Sales, Inc. (Titus-Will), to purchase the truck for Heinrich. Titus-Will had dealt with Wilson as a dealer before but also did not know that he had lost his dealer license. All payments for the truck went through Wilson, and the purchase order indicated that the truck was being sold to Wilson as a dealer for resale. Wilson agreed to deliver the truck to Heinrich at Titus-Will on Saturday, October 21, 1989. Wilson delivered to a clerk at Titus-Will a postdated check for the balance of the purchase price, which the clerk accepted and, in return, delivered to Wilson a packet containing the keys to the truck, the owner's manual, an odometer disclosure statement, and the warranty card. The odometer statement showed that Wilson was the transferor, and Titus-Will did not fill out the warranty card, as the sale appeared to be dealer to dealer. Wilson's check, however, did not clear, and Titus-Will demanded the return of the truck. On November 6, Wilson picked up the truck from Heinrich, telling him he would have Titus-Will make certain repairs under the warranty, and returned the truck to Titus-Will. On November 9, 1989, Wilson admitted to Heinrich that he did not have funds to cover his check and that Titus-Will would not release the truck without payment. Heinrich then asked Titus-Will for the truck but was refused. Heinrich sued Titus-Will and Wilson, seeking return of the truck and damages for his loss of use. By pretrial arrangement, Heinrich regained possession of, but not clear title to, the truck. Heinrich also obtained a default order against Wilson. After a bench trial, the court awarded Heinrich title to the truck and $3,050 in damages for loss of its use. Titus-Will appeals.]

* * *

THE ENTRUSTMENT DOCTRINE

[UCC] 2-403(2) and (3) contain the entrustment provisions of the Uniform Commercial Code. * * *

To prevail under this statute, Heinrich must show (1) Titus-Will "entrusted" the truck to Wilson and, thus,

empowered Wilson subsequently to transfer all rights of Titus-Will in the truck to Heinrich; (2) Wilson was a merchant dealing in automobiles; and (3) Heinrich bought the truck from Wilson as a "buyer in ordinary course of business." [Citations.]

Three general policies support [§] 2-403(2), the UCC provision placing the risk of loss on the entruster. First, it protects the innocent buyer who, based on his observation of goods in the possession of a merchant of those goods, believes that the merchant has legal title to the goods and can, therefore, pass title in the goods to another. [Citation.] The statute carries forward the pre-Uniform Commercial Code law of estoppel under which an owner, who clothes a merchant with apparent ownership of or authority to sell goods, is estopped from denying such authority as against one buying the goods from the merchant in good faith. [Citations.]

Secondly, the entrustment clause reflects the idea that the entruster is in a better position than the innocent buyer to protect against the risk that an intermediary merchant will not pay for or not deliver the goods. [Citations.]

Thirdly, the entrustment clause facilitates the flow of commerce by allowing purchasers to rely on a merchant's apparent legal right to sell the goods. [Citations.] Without the safeguards of the entrustment provision, a prudent buyer would have to delay the finalization of any sizeable sales transaction for the time necessary to research the merchant's ownership rights to the goods.

Entrusting

The UCC definition of "entrusting," contained in 2-403(3), is broad. [Citation.] The statute declares that "any delivery and any acquiescence in retention of possession" constitutes entrustment. 2-403(3). A person can entrust goods to a merchant by a variety of methods, such as consigning them, creating a bailment, taking a security interest in inventory, leaving them with the merchant after purchase, and delivering them for purposes of repair. [Citations.] A sale can also constitute an entrustment when some aspect of the transaction remains incomplete. [Citations.]

Titus-Will properly concedes that it entrusted the truck to Wilson. However, it argues Wilson was not a merchant and

Heinrich was not a buyer in ordinary course. Further, Titus-Will contends that the timing of the entrusting deprived Wilson of the power to transfer its rights.

Merchant

Titus-Will argues that Wilson was not a merchant because he had no inventory. However, it is not necessary to possess an inventory to fit within the broad statutory definition of merchant. Article 2 of the UCC defines (in part) "merchant" as "a person who deals in goods of the kind or otherwise by his occupation holds himself out as having knowledge or skill peculiar to the practices or goods involved in the transaction." 2-104(1). Wilson was a merchant who dealt in automobiles; he held himself out as a dealer in automobiles and appeared to be a dealer in automobiles. Both parties treated him as one. Titus-Will processed all the documents as it would for a dealer and understood that Wilson was buying the truck for resale.

Titus-Will also argues that Wilson was not a merchant because he did not have a vehicle dealer license. However, the UCC does not require proper state licensing for merchant status. 2-104(1), 2-403(2). * * *

Buyer in Ordinary Course

There is also substantial evidence that Heinrich was a "buyer in ordinary course of business" although the trial court referred to him as a "good faith purchaser for value." A buyer in ordinary course of business is

> a person who in good faith and without knowledge that the sale to him is in violation of the ownership rights or security interest of a third party in the goods buys in ordinary course from a person in the business of selling goods of that kind[.]

1-201(9). "Buying" "includes receiving goods ... under a pre-existing contract for sale." 1-201(9). Good faith is "honesty in fact in the conduct or transaction concerned." 1-201(19).

The amount of the consideration is significant as evidence of good faith. [Citation.] Heinrich gave substantial value for the truck, more than Wilson agreed to pay Titus-Will. Nor did Heinrich know or have a basis to believe that Wilson's sale and delivery of the truck to him violated Titus-Will's ownership or security interest rights. There was no showing that Heinrich acted other than in good faith. * * * Wilson's illegal and fraudulent activity does not taint Heinrich's status

as a buyer under 2-403(2). When Heinrich accepted delivery after previously paying Wilson, Heinrich was "buying" as defined by 1-201(9).

Timing of Entrustment

Titus-Will also argues that the UCC entrustment provisions should not apply because it entrusted the truck to Wilson *after* Heinrich had completely paid Wilson. This is an issue of first impression in this jurisdiction.

Before the completion of the Wilson-Heinrich sales transaction, Titus-Will entrusted Wilson not only with the truck, but also with the signed odometer disclosure statement, the owner's manual, the warranty card, and the keys. By doing so, Titus-Will clothed Wilson with additional indicia of ownership and with the apparent authority to transfer an ownership interest in the truck. It also enabled Wilson to complete the sales transaction. 2-401(2) ("Unless otherwise explicitly agreed title passes to the buyer at the time and place at which the seller completes his performance with reference to the physical delivery of the goods"). In addition, the entrustment allowed Wilson to continue to deceive Heinrich from October 21, 1989, the date of delivery of possession, to November 9, 1989, when Wilson finally admitted the truth. We believe that under these circumstances, application of the entrustment doctrine, 2-403(2), furthers the policy of protecting the buyer who relies on the merchant's apparent legal ability to sell goods in the merchant's possession.

The second rationale for the entrustment doctrine also supports its application here. Titus-Will, in the business of selling cars, was in a better position than Heinrich to protect itself against another dealer/broker who might fail to pay for the goods. It could have insured against the loss, and it could have adopted preventive procedures.

* * * The third rationale for the entrustment doctrine focuses on the flow of commerce. Here we consider the potential impact on commercial transactions of requiring purchasers to research their dealer/broker's legal title before accepting possession of the goods. Although the record contains no evidence on this issue, it seems obvious that this requirement would inevitably cause some delay. [Citation.]

Requiring the entruster to retain the burden of risk, even when the entrustment occurs after a third party purchaser gives value, supports the policies underlying the entrustment doctrine. * * * The trial court did not err in applying the entrustment doctrine and granting replevin.

* * *

We affirm the trial court's judgment.

CASE 23-4

Risk of Loss: Seller Not a Merchant
MARTIN v. MELLAND'S INC.
Supreme Court of North Dakota, 1979
283 N.W.2d 76

Erickstad, C. J.

The narrow issue on this appeal is who should bear the loss of a truck and an attached haystack mover that was destroyed by fire while in the possession of the plaintiff, Israel Martin (Martin), but after certificate of title had been delivered to the defendant, Melland's Inc. (Melland's). The destroyed haymoving unit was to be used as a trade-in for a new haymoving unit that Martin ultimately purchased from Melland's. Martin appeals from a district court judgment dated September 28, 1978, that dismissed his action on the merits after it found that at the time of its destruction Martin was the owner of the unit pursuant to [UCC Section 2-401]. We hold that Section 2-401 is inapplicable to this case, but we affirm the district court judgment on the grounds that risk of loss had not passed to Melland's pursuant to [UCC Section 2-509].

On June 11, 1974, Martin entered into a written agreement with Melland's, a farm implement dealer, to purchase a truck and attached haystack mover for the total purchase price of $35,389. Martin was given a trade-in allowance of $17,389 on his old unit, leaving a balance owing of $18,000 plus sales tax of $720 or a total balance of $18,720. The agreement provided that Martin "mail or bring title" to the old unit to Melland's "this week." Martin mailed the certificate of title to Melland's pursuant to the agreement, but he was allowed to retain the use and possession of the old unit "until they had the new one ready." The new unit was not expected to be ready for two to three months because it required certain modifications. During this interim period, Melland's performed minor repairs to the trade-in unit on two occasions without charging Martin for the repairs.

Fire destroyed the truck and the haymoving unit in early August, 1974, while Martin was moving hay. The parties did not have any agreement regarding insurance or risk of loss on the unit and Martin's insurance on the trade-in unit had lapsed. Melland's refused Martin's demand for his new unit and Martin brought this suit. * * *

The district court found "that although the Plaintiff [Martin] executed the title to the ... [haymoving unit], he did not relinquish possession of the same and therefore the Plaintiff was the owner of said truck at the time the fire occurred pursuant to Section 2-401." [Martin appealed.]

* * *

* * * [T]he concept of title under the UCC is of decreased importance. * * *

* * *

No longer is the question of title of any importance in determining whether a buyer or seller bears the risk of loss. * * *

* * *

Thus, the question in this case is not answered by a determination of the location of title, but by the risk of loss provisions in [UCC §2-509]. Before addressing the risk of loss question in conjunction with [UCC §2-509], it is necessary to determine the posture of the parties with regard to the trade-in unit, i.e. who is the buyer and the seller and how are the responsibilities allocated. It is clear that a barter or trade-in is considered a sale and is therefore subject to the Uniform Commercial Code. [Citations.] It is also clear that the party who owns the trade-in is considered the seller. [UCC §2-304] provides that the "price can be made payable in money or otherwise. If it is payable in whole or in part in goods each party is a seller of the goods which he is to transfer." [Citations.]

Martin argues that he had already sold the trade-in unit to Melland's and, although he retained possession, he did so in the capacity of a bailee (apparently pursuant to [UCC §2-509(2)]). White and Summers in their hornbook on the Uniform Commercial Code argue that the seller who retains possession should not be considered bailee within Section 2-509.

* * *

The courts that have addressed this issue have agreed with White and Summers. [Citations.]

It is undisputed that the contract did not require or authorize shipment by carrier pursuant to Section [2-509(1)]; therefore, the residue section, subsection 3, is applicable:

> In any case not within subsection 1 or 2, the risk of loss passes to the buyer on his receipt of the goods if the seller is a merchant; otherwise the risk passes to the buyer on tender of delivery.

Martin admits that he is not a merchant; therefore, it is necessary to determine if Martin tendered delivery of the trade-in unit to Melland's. * * *

It is clear that the trade-in unit was not tendered to Melland's in this case. The parties agreed that Martin would keep the old unit "until they had the new one ready." * * *

* * *

We hold that Martin did not tender delivery of the trade-in truck and haystack mover to Melland's pursuant to [UCC §2-509]; consequently, Martin must bear the loss. We affirm the district court judgment.

QUESTIONS

1. Stein, a mechanic, and Beal, a life insurance agent, entered into a written contract for the sale of Stein's tractor to Beal for $6,800 cash. It was agreed that Stein would tune the motor on the tractor. Stein fulfilled this obligation and on the night of July 1 telephoned Beal that the tractor was ready to be picked up upon Beal's making payment. Beal responded, "I'll be there in the morning with the money." On the next morning, however, Beal was approached by an insurance prospect and decided to get the tractor at a later date. On the night of July 2, the tractor was destroyed by fire of unknown origin. Neither Stein nor Beal had any fire insurance. Who must bear the loss? Discuss.

2. Regan received a letter from Chase, the material portion of which stated: "Chase hereby places an order with you for fifty cases of Red Top Tomatoes, ship them C.O.D." Promptly upon receipt of the letter, Regan shipped the tomatoes to Chase. While en route, the railroad car carrying the tomatoes was wrecked. Upon Chase's refusal to pay for the tomatoes, Regan commenced an action to recover the purchase price. Chase defended on the ground that as the shipment was C.O.D., neither title to the tomatoes nor risk of loss passed until their delivery to Chase. Who has title? Who has risk of loss? Explain.

3. On May 10, the Apple Company, acting through one Brown, entered into a contract with Crane for the installation of a milking machine at Crane's farm. Following the enumeration of the articles to be furnished, together with the price of each article, the written contract provided: "This outfit is subject to thirty days' free trial and is to be installed about June 1." Within thirty days after installation, the entire outfit, excepting a double utility unit, was destroyed by fire through no fault of Crane. The Apple Company sued Crane to recover the value of the articles destroyed. Explain who bears the risk of loss.

4. Brown, located in Knoxville, contracted to buy sixty cases of Lovely Brand canned corn from Clark in Toledo at a contract price of $1,250. Pursuant to the contract, Clark selected and set aside sixty cases of Lovely Brand canned corn and tagged them "For Brown." The contract required Clark to ship the corn to Brown via T Railroad, F.O.B. Toledo. Before Clark delivered the corn to the railroad, the sixty cases were stolen from Clark's warehouse.

   a. Who is liable for the loss of the sixty cases of corn, Brown or Clark?

   b. Suppose Clark had delivered the corn to the railroad in Toledo. After the corn had been loaded on a freight car but before the train left the yard, the car was broken open and its contents, including the corn, stolen. As between Brown and Clark, who is liable for the loss? Why?

   c. Would your answer in Question (b) be the same if this was an F.O.B. Knoxville contract, all other facts remaining the same? Explain.

5. Gardner owned a quantity of corn, which was contained in a corncrib located on Gardner's farm. On March 12, Gardner wrote a letter to Bassett stating that he would sell to Bassett all of the corn in this crib, which he estimated at between nine hundred and one thousand bushels, for $3.90 per bushel. Bassett received this letter on March 13 and immediately wrote and mailed on the same day a letter to Gardner stating that he would buy the corn. The corncrib and its contents were accidentally destroyed by fire that broke out about 3 A.M. on March 14.

   a. What are the rights of the parties?

   b. What difference, if any, in result if Gardner were a merchant? Explain.

6. Franco, a New York dealer, purchased twenty-five barrels of specially graded and packed apples from a producer at Hood River, Oregon, under a contract that specified an agreed price on delivery at Franco's place of business in New York. The apples were shipped to Franco from Oregon but, through no fault of Franco, were totally destroyed before reaching New York. Does any liability rest on Franco? Explain.

7. Smith was approached by a man who introduced himself as Brown of Brown & Co. Brown was not known to Smith, but Smith asked Dun & Bradstreet for a credit report and obtained a very favorable report on Brown. He thereupon sold Brown some expensive gems and billed Brown & Co. "Brown" turned out to be a clever jewel thief, who later sold the gems to Brown & Co. for valuable consideration. Brown & Co. was unaware of "Brown's" transaction with Smith. Can Smith successfully sue Brown & Co. for either the return of the gems or the price as billed to Brown & Co.? Explain.

8. Charlotte, the owner of a new Cadillac automobile, agreed to loan the car to Ellen for the month of February while she (Charlotte) went to Florida for a winter vacation. It was understood that Ellen, who was a small-town Cadillac dealer, would merely place Charlotte's car in her showroom for exhibition and sales promotion purposes. While Charlotte was away, Ellen sold the car to Robert. Upon Charlotte's return from Florida, she sued to recover the car from Robert. Who has title to the automobile? Explain.

9. Brilles offered to sell his used automobile to Nevarro for $12,600 cash. Nevarro agreed to buy the car, gave Brilles a check for $12,600, and drove away in the car. The next day Nevarro sold the car for $13,000 to Hough, a *bona fide* purchaser. The $12,600 check was returned to Brilles by the bank in which he had deposited it because of insufficient funds in Nevarro's account. Brilles brings an action against Hough to recover the automobile. What judgment?

10. Yount told Lewis he wished to buy Lewis's automobile. He drove the car for about ten minutes, returned to Lewis, stated he wanted to take the automobile to show it to his wife, and then left with the automobile and never returned. Yount sold the automobile in another State to Turner and gave him a bill of sale. Can Lewis recover the automobile from Turner? Explain.

11. On February 7, Pillsbury purchased eight thousand bushels of wheat from Landis. The wheat was being stored at the Greensville Grain Company. Pillsbury also intended to store the wheat with Greensville. On February 10, the wheat was destroyed. Landis demands payment for the wheat from Pillsbury. Who prevails? Who has title? Who has the risk of loss? Explain.

12. Johnson, who owned a hardware store, was indebted to Hutchinson, one of her suppliers. Johnson sold her business to Lockhart, one of Johnson's previous competitors, who combined the inventory from Johnson's store with his own and moved them to a new, larger store. Hutchinson claims that Lockhart must pay Johnson's debt because the sale of the business had been made without complying with the requirements of the bulk sales law. Discuss whether Lockhart is obligated to pay Hutchison's debt to Johnson.

13. Seller had manufactured forty thousand pounds of plastic resin pellets specially for the buyer, who agreed to accept them at the rate of one thousand pounds per day upon his issuance of shipping instructions. Despite numerous requests by the seller, the buyer issued no such instructions. On August 18, the seller, after warehousing the goods for forty days, demanded by letter that the buyer issue instructions. The buyer agreed to issue them beginning August 20 but never did. On September 22, a fire destroyed the seller's plant containing the goods, which were not covered by insurance. Who bears the risk of loss? Explain.

14. McCoy, an Oklahoma cattle dealer, orally agreed with Chandler, a Texas cattle broker, to ship cattle to a New Mexico feedlot for delivery to Chandler. The agreement was for six lots of cattle valued at $119,000. After McCoy delivered the cattle, he presented invoices to Chandler that described the cattle and set forth the sales price. McCoy then demanded payment, which Chandler refused. Unknown to McCoy, Chandler had obtained a loan from First National Bank and pledged the subject cattle as collateral. The bank had no knowledge of any interest that McCoy may have had in the cattle. McCoy sued to recover the cattle. The bank counterclaimed that it had a perfected security interest in the cattle that was superior to any interest of McCoy's. Who has title to the cattle? Explain.

CASE PROBLEMS

15. Home Indemnity, an insurance company, paid one of its insureds after the theft of his car. The car reappeared in another State and was sold to Michael Schrier for $4,300 by a used car dealer. The dealer promised to give Mr. Schrier a certificate of title. One month later the car was seized by the police on behalf of Home Indemnity. Explain who is entitled to possession of the car.

16. Fred Lane, who sells boats, motors, and trailers, sold a boat, motor, and trailer to John Willis in exchange for a check for $6,285. The check was not honored when Lane attempted to use the funds. Willis subsequently left the boat, motor, and trailer with John Garrett, who sold the items to Jimmy Honeycutt for $2,500. Considering the boat's quality, Honeycutt was surprised at how inexpensive it was. He did not know where Garrett had obtained the boat, but he had dealt with Garrett before and described him as a "sly businessman." Garrett did not sell boats; normally, he sold fishing tackle and provisions. Honeycutt also received a forged certificate for the boat, on which he had observed Garrett forge the purported owner's signature. Can Lane compel Honeycutt to return the boat, motor, and trailer? Explain.

17. Mike Moses purchased a mobile home, including installation, from Gary Newman. Newman delivered the home to Moses's lot. Upon inspection of the home, Moses's fiancée found a broken window and water pipe. Moses also had not received keys to the front door. Before Newman corrected these problems, a windstorm destroyed the home. Who bears the risk for the loss of the home? Why?

18. United Road Machinery Company, a dealer in heavy road equipment (including truck scales supplied by

Thurman Scale Company), received a telephone call on July 21 from James Durham, an officer of Consolidated Coal Company, seeking to acquire truck scales for his coal mining operation. United and Consolidated entered into a twenty-four month lease-purchase arrangement. United then notified Thurman that Consolidated would take possession of the scales directly. United paid for the scales, and Consolidated took possession of them, but the latter never signed or returned the contract papers forwarded to it by United. Consolidated also never made any of the rental payments ($608/month) due under the lease. On September 20, Consolidated, through its officer Durham, sold the scales to Kentucky Mobile Homes for $8,500. Kentucky's president, Ethard Jasper, checked the county records prior to the purchase and found no lien or encumbrance on the title; likewise, he denied knowledge of the dispute between Consolidated and United. On September 22, Kentucky sold the scales to Clyde Jasper, individually, for $8,500. His search also failed to disclose any lien on the title to the scales, and he denied knowledge of the dispute between Consolidated and United. Can United recover the scales from Jasper? Explain.

19. James Norwood bought one hundred ninety heifers in Valentine, Nebraska, and then delivered them to Kevin Asbury in Missouri to care for them. Norwood and Asbury were merchants with regard to cattle. While in Asbury's care, one hundred fifty of the heifers were delivered to Max Hargrove. Hargrove in turn sold the heifers to B & W, Inc. Then B & W sold one hundred fifteen of the heifers to Steve Maulsby, who in turn sold the heifers to Kenneth Nordhues. Explain what Nordhues would have to prove to establish good title to the heifers.

20. Jordan Panel Systems, Inc., ordered custom-made windows from Windows, Inc. The purchase contract provided that the windows were to be shipped properly packaged for motor freight transit and "delivered to New York City." Windows constructed the windows according to Jordan's specifications and arranged to have them shipped to Jordan by a common carrier, Consolidated Freightways Corp. Windows delivered them to Consolidated intact and properly packaged. During the course of shipment, the goods sustained extensive damage. Much of the glass was broken, and many of the window frames were gouged and twisted. Jordan's president signed a delivery receipt noting that approximately two-thirds of the shipment was damaged due to "load shift." Jordan made a claim with Consolidated for damages it had sustained and also ordered a new shipment from Windows, which was delivered without incident. Jordan did not pay for either shipment of windows, and Windows brought suit. Jordan cross-claimed for incidental and consequential damages resulting from the damaged shipment. Decision? Explain.

TAKING SIDES

Harrison, a men's clothing retailer located in Westport, Connecticut, ordered merchandise from Ninth Street East, Ltd., a Los Angeles-based clothing manufacturer. Ninth Street delivered the merchandise to Denver-Chicago Trucking Company (Denver) in Los Angeles and then sent four invoices to Harrison that bore the notation "F.O.B. Los Angeles." Denver subsequently transferred the merchandise to a connecting carrier, Old Colony Transportation Company, for final delivery to Harrison's Westport store. When Old Colony tried to deliver the merchandise, Harrison's wife asked the truck driver to deliver the boxes inside the store, but the driver refused. The dispute remained unresolved, and the truck departed with Old Colony still in possession of the goods. By letter, Harrison then notified Ninth Street of the nondelivery, but Ninth Street was unable to locate the shipment. Ninth Street then sought to recover the contract purchase price from Harrison. Harrison refused, contending that risk of loss remained with Ninth Street because of its refusal to deliver the merchandise to Harrison's place of business.

a. What are the arguments that the risk of loss remained with Ninth Street?

b. What are the arguments that the risk of loss passed to Harrison?

c. What is the appropriate outcome?

CHAPTER 24

Products Liability: Warranties and Strict Liability in Tort

CHAPTER OUTCOMES

After reading and studying this chapter, you should be able to:

- Describe the types of warranties.

- Explain the various defenses that may be successfully raised to a warranty action.

- Describe the elements of an action based on strict liability in tort.

- Explain the obstacles to an action based on strict liability in tort.

- Compare strict liability in tort with the implied warranty of merchantability.

This chapter considers the liability of manufacturers and sellers of goods to buyers, users, consumers, and bystanders for damages caused by defective products. According to the U.S. Consumer Product Safety Commission, deaths, injuries, and property damage from consumer product incidents cost the United States more than $1 trillion annually. State case law has established products liability as a distinct field of law that combines and enforces rules and principles of contracts, sales, negligence, strict liability in tort, and statutory law.

One reason for the expansion of product liability law has been the modern method of distributing goods, in which retailers serve principally as a conduit of goods that are prepackaged in sealed containers and that are widely advertised by the manufacturer or distributor. This has resulted in the judicial extension of product liability coverage to include manufacturers and other parties within the chain of distribution. However, many States have statutorily revised their tort laws to make successful tort (including product liability) lawsuits more difficult to bring. These tort revisions include legislation dealing with joint and several liability, punitive damages, non-economic damages, and class actions. Repeated efforts to enact Federal product liability legislation have been unsuccessful.

The liability of manufacturers and other sellers of goods for a defective product, or for its failure to perform adequately, may be based upon one or more of the following: (1) negligence, (2) misrepresentation, (3) violation of statutory duty, (4) warranty, and (5) strict liability in tort. The first three causes of actions have been covered in *Chapters 8 and 11.*

Chapter 8 also covered traditional strict liability—where liability is imposed regardless of the defendant's negligence or intent to cause harm. In this chapter, we cover a specialized type of strict liability—strict liability in tort for products. This chapter also explores warranty liability.

WARRANTIES

A **warranty**, under the Uniform Commercial Code (UCC or the Code), creates a duty on the part of the seller that the goods she sells will conform to certain qualities, characteristics, or conditions. A seller, however, is not required to warrant the goods, and in general, she may, by appropriate words, disclaim, exclude, negate, or modify a specific warranty or even all warranties.

In bringing a warranty action, the buyer must prove that (1) a warranty existed, (2) the warranty has been breached, (3) the breach of the warranty proximately caused the loss suffered, and (4) notice of the breach was given to the seller. The seller has the burden of proving defenses based on the buyer's conduct. If the seller breaches his warranty, the buyer may reject or revoke acceptance of the goods. Moreover, whether he has

Practical Advice

Thoroughly test your products prior to releasing them into the channels of distribution to ensure that they are safe and properly designed. In addition, include all necessary warnings and instructions and be sure that they are clear and conspicuous.

accepted or rejected the goods, the buyer may recover a judgment against the seller for damages. Harm for which damages are recoverable includes personal injury, damage to property, and economic loss. Economic loss most commonly involves damages for loss of bargain and consequential damages for lost profits. (Damages for breach of warranty are discussed in the next chapter.) This section examines the various types of warranties as well as the obstacles to a cause of action for breach of warranty.

24-1 Types of Warranties

A warranty may arise out of the mere existence of a sale (a warranty of title), any affirmation of fact or promise made by the seller to the buyer (an express warranty), or the circumstances under which the sale is made (an implied warranty). In a contract for the sale of goods, it is possible to have all three types of warranties. All warranties are construed as consistent with each other and cumulative, unless such a construction is unreasonable. A purchaser, as discussed in previous chapters, means a person who takes by sale, lease, lien, security interest, gift, or any other voluntary transaction creating an interest in property. Article 1-201(b)(29), (30).

Article 2A carries over the warranty provisions of Article 2 with relatively minor revision to reflect differences in style, leasing terminology, or leasing practices. The creation of express warranties and, except for finance leases, the imposition of the implied warranties of merchantability and fitness for a particular purpose are virtually identical to their Article 2 analogues. Article 2 and Article 2A diverge somewhat in their treatment of the warranties of title and infringement as well as in their provisions for the exclusion and modification of warranties.

24-1a WARRANTY OF TITLE

Under the Code's warranty of title, the seller implicitly warrants that (1) the title conveyed is good and its transfer rightful and (2) the goods have no security interest or other lien (a claim on property by another for payment of debt) of which the buyer was not aware at the time of purchase. Section 2-312(1). In a lease, title does not transfer to the lessee. Accordingly, Article 2A's analogous provision protects the lessee's right to possession and use of the goods from the claims of other parties arising from an act or omission of the lessor. Section 2A-211(1).

For example, Iris acquires goods from Sherman in a transaction that is void and then sells the goods to Brenda. Sherman brings an action against Brenda and recovers the goods. Iris has breached the warranty of title because she did not have good title to the goods and her transfer of the goods to Brenda was not rightful. Accordingly, Iris is liable to Brenda for damages.

The Code does not label the warranty of title as an implied warranty, even though it arises from the sale and not from any particular words or conduct. Consequently, the Code's general disclaimer provision for implied warranties does not apply to a warranty of title, which instead is subject to its own disclaimer provision. Nevertheless, a seller of goods does implicitly warrant title to those goods.

A seller who is a merchant makes an additional warranty in sales of goods of the kind in which he regularly deals: that such goods shall be delivered free of the rightful claim of any third person that the goods infringe (use without authorization) upon any existing patent. Section 2-312(3); Section 2A-211(2).

24-1b EXPRESS WARRANTIES

An express warranty is an explicit undertaking by the seller with respect to the quality, description, condition, or functionality of the goods. The undertaking may consist of an affirmation of fact or a promise that relates to the goods, a description of the goods, or a sample or model of the goods. In each of these instances, the undertaking must become or be made part of the basis of the bargain for an express warranty to be created. The seller need not, however, have a specific intention to make a warranty or use formal words such as *warrant* or *guarantee*. Moreover, to be liable for breach of express warranty, it is not necessary that a seller know of the falsity of a statement she makes. Thus, a seller may be liable for breach of express warranty even if she is acting in good faith. For example, if John mistakenly asserts to Sam that a rope will easily support three hundred pounds and Sam is injured when the rope breaks while supporting only two hundred pounds, John is liable for breach of an express warranty.

CREATION The seller can create an express warranty either orally or in writing. One of the ways in which an express warranty can be created is through an **affirmation of fact** or a **promise** relating to the goods that becomes part of the basis of the bargain. Section 2-313(1)(a); Section 2A-210(1)(a). The statement can be in regard to the quality, condition, capacity, performability, or safety of the goods. For example, a statement made by a seller that an automobile will get forty-two miles to the gallon of gasoline or that a camera has automatic focus is an express warranty.

The Code further provides that a statement affirming the **value** of the goods or purporting merely to be the seller's **opinion** or recommendation of the goods does not create a warranty. Section 2-313(2); Section 2A-210(2). Such statements are not factual and do not deceive the ordinary buyer, who accepts them merely as opinions or as puffery (sales talk). For example, a statement by a salesperson that "this is one terrific deal" would likely be considered puffery. On the other hand, a statement that "this car gets thirty miles to the gallon" would be considered an express warranty, given its specificity.

A statement of value may be an express warranty, however, in cases in which the seller states the price at which the goods were purchased from a former owner or in which she gives market figures relating to sales of similar goods. As statements of events, not mere opinions, these are statements of facts, and the seller is liable for breach of warranty if they are untrue. Moreover, although a statement of opinion by the seller is not ordinarily a warranty, if the seller is an expert and gives her opinion as such, she may be liable for breach of warranty. Thus, if an art expert states that a certain painting is a genuine Rembrandt and this becomes part of the basis of the bargain, then the expert warrants the accuracy of her professional opinion.

Practical Advice

Make only those affirmations of fact or promises about the goods being sold that you wish to stand behind. Moreover, recognize that advertising claims and the statements made by salespeople can give rise to express warranties.

An express warranty also can be created by the use of a **description** of the goods that becomes part of the basis of the bargain. Section 2-313(1)(b); Section 2A-210(1)(b). Under such a warranty, the seller expressly warrants that the goods shall conform to the description. Examples include statements regarding a particular brand or type of goods, technical specifications, and blueprints.

The use of a **sample** or model is another means of creating an express warranty. Section 2-313(1)(c); Section 2A-210(1)(c). If a sample or model is part of the basis of the bargain, the seller expressly warrants that the entire lot of goods sold shall conform to the sample or model. A sample is a good drawn from the bulk of goods comprising the subject matter of the sale. A model, by comparison, is offered for inspection when the subject matter is not at hand; it is not drawn from the bulk. Section 2-313, Comment 6.

◆ *See Case 24-1*

CISG The seller must deliver goods that conform to the quality and description required by the contract. In addition, the goods must possess the qualities of any sample or model used by the seller.

BASIS OF BARGAIN The Code does not require that the buyer rely on the affirmations, promises, descriptions, samples, or models the seller makes or uses but only that they constitute a part of the basis of the bargain. If they are part of the buyer's assumption underlying the sale, then reliance by the buyer is presumed. Some courts merely require that the buyer know of the affirmation or promise for it to be presumed to be part of the basis of the bargain. Relaxing the reliance requirement more often forces sellers to live up to their express warranties than does a rule requiring reliance.

Because they may constitute part of the basis of the bargain just as much as statements in advertisements or catalogs would, statements or promises the seller makes to the buyer prior to the sale may be express warranties. Furthermore, under the Code, statements or promises made by the seller subsequent to the contract of sale may become express warranties even though no new consideration is given. Sections 2-209(1) and 2A-208(1) provide that an agreement modifying a sale or lease needs no consideration to be binding. Thus, a statement, promise, or assurance with respect to the goods that the seller makes to the buyer at the time of delivery may be considered a binding modification of the prior contract of sale and held to be an express warranty basic to the bargain.

◆ *See Case 24-2*

24-1c IMPLIED WARRANTIES

An implied warranty, unlike an express warranty, is not found in the language of the sales contract or in a specific affirmation or promise by the seller. Instead, an **implied warranty** is an obligation imposed by operation of law upon the transfer of property or contract rights. This warranty, which arises out of the circumstances under which the parties enter into their contract, depends on factors such as the type of contract or sale entered into, the seller's merchant or nonmerchant status, the conduct of the parties, and the applicability of other statutes.

MERCHANTABILITY Under the Code, a **merchant seller** impliedly warrants the merchantability of goods that are of the kind in which she deals. The implied warranty of **merchantability** provides that the goods are reasonably fit for the ordinary purposes for which they are used; pass without objection in the trade under the contract description; and are of fair, average quality. Section 2-314; Section 2A-212. Because the warranty arises as a matter of law, the buyer does not need to prove that she relied on the warranty or that the warranty formed a basis of the bargain. The warranty applies automatically unless disclaimed by the seller. The official Comments to the Code further provide that a contract for the sale of secondhand goods "involves only such obligation as is appropriate to such goods for that is their description."

The Code in Sections 2-314(3) and 2A-212(3) expressly provides that implied warranties may arise from course of dealing or usage of trade. Thus, where the seller of a new automobile failed to lubricate it before delivery to the buyer and the evidence established that it was the regular custom and usage of new car dealers to do so, the seller was held liable to the buyer for the resulting damages to the automobile in an action for breach of implied warranty.

CISG The seller must deliver goods, unless otherwise agreed, that are fit for the purposes for which goods of the same description ordinarily would be used.

♦ *See Case 24-2*

FITNESS FOR PARTICULAR PURPOSE Unlike the warranty of merchantability, the implied warranty of fitness for a particular purpose applies to *any* seller, whether he is a merchant or not. The **implied warranty of fitness for a particular purpose** arises if at the time of sale the seller had reason to know the buyer's particular purpose and the buyer was relying upon the seller's skill and judgment to select suitable goods. Section 2-315; Section 2A-213.

The implied warranty of fitness for a particular purpose does not require any specific statement by the seller. Rather, the warranty requires only that the seller know that the buyer is relying on the seller's expertise in selecting a product for the buyer's specific purpose. The buyer need not specifically inform the seller of her particular purpose; it is sufficient if the seller has reason to know it. On the other hand, the implied warranty of fitness for a particular purpose would not arise if the buyer were to insist on a particular product and the seller simply conveyed it to her because the buyer must be able to demonstrate that she relied on the seller's skill or judgment in selecting or furnishing suitable goods.

In contrast to the implied warranty of merchantability, the implied warranty of fitness for a particular purpose pertains to the *specific* purpose of the goods. A particular purpose may be a specific use or relate to a special situation in which the buyer intends to use the goods. Thus, if Miller has reason to know that Levine is purchasing a pair of shoes for mountain climbing and that Levine is relying upon Miller's judgment to furnish shoes suitable for this purpose, an implied warranty of fitness for a particular purpose would arise in this sale. If Miller sold Levine shoes suitable only for ordinary walking purposes, Miller would breach this implied warranty. Likewise, a buyer indicates to a seller that she needs a stamping machine to stamp ten thousand packages in an eight-hour period and that she

relies on the seller to select an appropriate machine. By selecting the machine, the seller impliedly warrants that the machine selected will stamp ten thousand packages in an eight-hour period.

Frequently, a seller's conduct may involve a breach of both the implied warranty of merchantability and the implied warranty of fitness for a particular purpose.

CISG The seller must deliver goods, unless otherwise agreed, that are fit for any particular purpose expressly or impliedly made known to the seller by the buyer, except in cases in which the buyer did not rely on the seller's skill and judgment or when it was unreasonable for the buyer to rely on the seller.

♦ *See Case 24-2*

24-2 Obstacles to Warranty Actions

A number of technical obstacles limit the effectiveness of warranty as a basis for recovery. These include disclaimers of warranties, limitations or modifications of warranties, privity, notice of breach, and the conduct of the plaintiff. These obstacles vary considerably from jurisdiction to jurisdiction.

24-2a DISCLAIMER OF WARRANTIES

To be effective, a **disclaimer** (negation) of a warranty must be positive, explicit, unequivocal, and conspicuous. The Code calls for a reasonable construction of words or conduct to disclaim or limit warranties. Section 2-316; Section 2A-214.

EXPRESS EXCLUSIONS In general, a seller cannot provide an **express warranty** and then disclaim it. A seller can avoid making an express warranty, however, by carefully refraining from making any promise or affirmation of fact relating to the goods, refraining from making a description of the goods, or refraining from using a sample or model. Section 2-313; Section 2A-210. A seller also may be able to negate an express warranty by *clear, specific, unambiguous* language. The Code, however, provides that words or conduct relevant to the creation of an express warranty and words or conduct negating a warranty shall be construed wherever reasonable as consistent with each other and that a negation or limitation is inoperative to the extent that such construction is unreasonable. Section 2-316; Section 2A-214. For example, a seller and a buyer enter into a written contract for the sale of a camera in which the seller warrants that the camera being sold is free of defects. This express warranty renders inoperative another provision in the contract that attempts to disclaim liability for any repairs necessitated by defects in the camera. The inconsistency between the two contractual provisions makes the disclaimer ineffective. Moreover, if the seller's disclaimer attempts to negate "all express warranties," this general disclaimer would be ineffective against the specific express warranty providing that the camera is free of defects. Finally, oral warranties made prior to the execution of a written agreement that contains an express disclaimer are subject to the parol evidence rule. Thus, as discussed in *Chapter 15*, if the parties intend the written contract to be the final and complete statement of the agreement between them, oral evidence of warranties that contradict the terms of the written contract is inadmissible.

A **warranty of title** may be excluded only by specific language or by certain circumstances, including judicial sales or sales by sheriffs, executors, or foreclosing lienors. Section 2-312(2); Section 2A-214(4). In the latter cases, the seller is manifestly offering to sell only such right or title as he or a third person might have in the goods, as it is apparent that the goods are not the property of the person selling them.

To exclude an **implied warranty of merchantability**, the language of disclaimer must mention merchantability and, in the case of a writing, must be *conspicuous*. Section 2-316(2). Article 2A requires that a disclaimer of an implied warranty of merchantability mention merchantability, be in writing, and be conspicuous. Section 2A-214(2). For example, Bart wishes to buy a used refrigerator from Ben's Used Appliances Store for $100. Given the low purchase price, Ben is unwilling to guarantee the refrigerator's performance. Bart agrees to buy it with no warranty protection. To exclude the warranty, Ben writes conspicuously on the contract, "This refrigerator carries no warranties, including no warranty of MERCHANTABIL-ITY." Ben has effectively disclaimed the implied warranty of merchantability. Some courts, however, do not require the disclaimer to be conspicuous in cases in which a *commercial* buyer has actual knowledge of the disclaimer. The Code's test for whether a provision is *conspicuous* is whether a reasonable person against whom the disclaimer is to operate ought to have noticed it. Section 1-201(b)(10). Article 1 provides that conspicuous terms include (1) a heading in capitals equal to or greater in size than the surrounding text; or in contrasting type, font, or color to the surrounding text of the same or lesser size; and (2) language in the body of a record or display in larger type than the surrounding text; or in contrasting type, font, or color to the surrounding text of the same size; or set off from surrounding text of the same size by symbols or other marks that call attention to the language. Section 1-201(b)(10). Whether a term is conspicuous is an issue for the court. Section 1-201, Comment.

To exclude or to modify an **implied warranty of fitness** for the particular purpose of the buyer, the disclaimer must be in *writing* and *conspicuous*. Section 2-316(2); Section 2A-214(2).

All implied warranties, unless the circumstances indicate otherwise, are excluded by expressions like *as is, with all faults,* or other language plainly calling the buyer's attention to the exclusion of warranties. Section 2-316(3)(a); Section 2A-214(3)(a). Most courts require the "as is" clause to be conspicuous. (At least thirteen States do not permit "as is" sales of consumer products.) Implied warranties also may be excluded by course of dealing, course of performance, or usage of trade. Section 2-316(3)(c); Section 2A-214(3)(c).

The courts will invalidate disclaimers they consider unconscionable. Sections 2-302 and 2A-108 of the Code, as discussed in *Chapter 21*, permit a court to limit the application of any contract or provision of a contract that it finds unconscionable.

◆ *See Case 24-3*

BUYER'S EXAMINATION OR REFUSAL TO EXAMINE If the buyer inspects the goods before entering into the contract, *implied warranties* do not apply to defects that are apparent upon examination. The particular buyer's skill and the normal method of examining goods in the circumstances determine what defects are excluded by examination. Section 2-316, Comment 8. Moreover, no implied warranty exists as to defects that an examination ought to have revealed not only where the buyer has examined the goods as fully as she desired but also where the buyer has *refused* to examine the goods. Section 2-316(3)(b); Section 2A-214(3)(b).

A mere failure or omission to examine the goods is not a refusal to examine them. It is not enough that the goods were available for inspection and the buyer did not see fit to inspect them. For the buyer to have "refused to examine the goods," the seller *must* first have demanded that the buyer examine them.

◆ *See Case 24-3*

CISG If at the time of entering into the sales contract the buyer knew or could not have been unaware of the lack of conformity, the seller is not liable for the warranty of particular purpose, ordinary purpose, or sale by sample or model.

FEDERAL LEGISLATION RELATING TO WARRANTIES OF CONSUMER GOODS To protect purchasers of consumer goods (defined as "tangible personal property normally used for personal, family, or household purposes"), Congress enacted the **Magnuson-Moss Warranty Act**. The purpose of the Act is to prevent deception and to make available to consumer purchasers adequate information with respect to warranties. Some courts have applied the Act to leases.

The Federal Trade Commission administers and enforces the Act. The commission's guidelines regarding the type of information a seller must set forth in warranties of consumer products are aimed at providing the consumer with clear and useful information. More significantly, the Act provides that a seller who makes a written warranty cannot disclaim *any* implied warranty. For a complete discussion of the Act, see *Chapter 41*.

Practical Advice

If you are a seller of consumer goods and wish to disclaim the implied warranties, make sure that you do not provide any written express warranties.

♦ **SEE FIGURE 24-1:** *Warranties*

24-2b LIMITATION OR MODIFICATION OF WARRANTIES

The Code permits a seller to *limit* or *modify* the buyer's remedies for breach of warranty. Section 2-719; Section 2A-503. One important exception to this right is the prohibition against "unconscionable" limitations or exclusions of consequential damages. Section 2-719(3); Section 2A-503(3). Specifically, the limitation of consequential damages for injury to the person in the case of consumer goods is *prima facie* unconscionable.

♦ *See Case 21-3*

In some cases, a seller may choose not to limit the buyer's rights to seek damages for breach of warranty but to impose time limits within which the warranty is effective. Except for instances of unconscionability, the Code permits such clauses; it does not, however, permit any attempt to shorten to less than one year the time period for filing an action for personal injury.

24-2c PRIVITY OF CONTRACT

Because of the association of warranties with contracts, a principle of law in the nineteenth century established that a plaintiff could not recover for breach of warranty unless he was in a

FIGURE 24-1 Warranties

Type of Warranty	How It Is Created	What Is Warranted	How It Is Disclaimed
Title (Section 2–312)/ Use and Possession (2A-211)	Seller contracts to sell goods	Good title Rightful transfer Not subject to lien	Specific language Circumstances giving buyer reason to know that seller does not claim title
Express (Section 2-313; Section 2A-210)	Affirmation of fact Promise Description Sample or model	Conform to affirmation Conform to promise Conform to description Conform to sample or model	Specific language (extremely difficult)
Merchantability (Section 2-314; Section 2A-212*)	Merchant sells goods	Fit for ordinary purpose Adequately contained, packaged, and labeled	Must mention "merchantability" If in writing, must be conspicuous; in lease, must be in writing and conspicuous As is sale Buyer examination Course of dealing, course of performance, usage of trade
Fitness for a Particular Purpose (Section 2-315; Section 2A-213*)	Seller knows buyer is relying upon seller to select goods suitable for buyer's particular purpose	Fit for particular purpose	No buzzwords necessary Must be in writing and conspicuous As is sale Buyer examination Course of dealing, course of performance, usage of trade

*Except in a finance lease.

contractual relationship with the defendant. This relationship is known as **privity** of contract.

Horizontal privity pertains to noncontracting parties who are injured by the defective goods; this group includes users, consumers, and bystanders who are not the contracting purchaser. Horizontal privity determines who benefits from a warranty and who, therefore, may sue for its breach.

The Code, however, relaxes the requirement of horizontal privity of contract by permitting recovery on a seller's warranty, at a minimum, to members of the buyer's family or household or to guests in his home. Section 2-318 of the Code provides three alternative sections from which the States may select. *Alternative A*, the least comprehensive and most widely adopted, provides that a seller's warranty, whether express or implied, extends to any natural person who is in the family or household of the buyer or who is a guest in his home if it is reasonable to expect that such person may use, consume, or be affected by the goods and who is injured in person by breach of the warranty. *Alternative B* extends Alternative A to any natural person who may reasonably be expected to use, consume, or be affected by the goods. *Alternative C* further expands the coverage of the section to any person, not just natural persons, and to property damage as well as personal injury. (A natural person would not include artificial entities such as corporations.) A seller may not exclude or limit the operation of this section for injury to a person. Section 2A-216 provides the same alternatives with slight modifications.

Nonetheless, the Code merely sets a minimum standard that the States may expand through case law. Most States have judicially accepted the Code's invitation to relax the requirements of horizontal privity and, for all practical purposes, have *eliminated* horizontal privity in warranty cases.

Vertical privity, in determining who is liable for breach of warranty, pertains to remote sellers within the chain of distribution, such as manufacturers and wholesalers, with whom the consumer purchaser has not entered into a contract. Although the Code adopts a neutral position regarding vertical privity, the courts in most States have eliminated the requirement of vertical privity in warranty actions.

24-2d NOTICE OF BREACH OF WARRANTY

When a buyer has accepted a tender of goods that are not as warranted by the seller, she is required to notify the seller of any breach of warranty within a reasonable time after she has discovered or should have discovered it. If the buyer fails to notify the seller of any breach within a reasonable time, she is barred from any remedy against the seller. Section 2-607(3)(a); Section 2A-516(3)(a). In determining whether notice was provided within a reasonable time, commercial standards apply to a merchant buyer, whereas standards designed to preserve a good faith consumer's right to his remedy apply to a retail consumer.

24-2e PLAINTIFF'S CONDUCT

Because warranty liability developed in the law of sales and contracts, in most States, contributory negligence of the buyer is no defense to an action against the seller for breach of warranty. In a number of States, however, comparative negligence statutes apply to warranty actions. (Comparative negligence is discussed more fully later in this chapter.)

If the buyer discovers a defect in the goods that may cause injury and then proceeds to make use of the goods, he will not be permitted to recover damages from the seller for loss or injuries caused by such use. This is not contributory negligence but voluntary assumption of a known risk.

STRICT PRODUCT LIABILITY IN TORT

The most far-reaching development in the field of products liability is that of strict liability in tort. All but a few States have now accepted the concept, which is embodied in **Section 402A** of the Restatement, Second, of Torts. In 1998, a new Restatement of the Law, Third, Torts: Products Liability (the Restatement Third) was promulgated. It is far more comprehensive than the second Restatement in dealing with the liability of commercial sellers and distributors of goods for harm caused by their products. (This revision is discussed more fully later in this chapter.)

Section 402A of the Restatement (Second) of Torts imposes **strict liability in tort** on merchant sellers for both personal injuries and property damage resulting from selling a product in a **defective condition, unreasonably dangerous** to the user or consumer. Section 402A applies even though "the seller has exercised all possible care in the preparation and sale of his product." Thus, negligence is not the basis of liability in strict liability cases. The essential distinction between the two doctrines is that actions in strict liability do not require the plaintiff to prove that the injury-producing defect resulted from any specific act of negligence of the seller. Strict liability actions focus on the product, not on the conduct of the manufacturer. Courts in strict liability cases are interested in the fact that a product defect arose—not in how it arose. Thus, even an "innocent" manufacturer–one who has not been negligent—may be liable if his product contains a defect that injures a consumer. Although liability for personal injuries caused by a product in an unreasonably dangerous defective condition is usually associated with sales of goods, such liability also exists with respect to **leases** and **bailments** of defective goods.

The reasons asserted in support of imposing strict liability in tort upon manufacturers and assemblers of products include the following: (1) consumers should be given maximum protection against dangerous defects in products; (2) manufacturers are in the best position to prevent or reduce the hazards to life and health in defective products; (3) manufacturers, who realize the most profit from the total sales of their goods, are best able to carry the financial burden of such liability by distributing it among the public as a cost of doing business; (4) manufacturers utilize wholesalers and retailers merely as conduits in the marketing of their products and should not be permitted to avoid liability simply because they have no contract with the user or consumer; and (5) because the manufacturer is liable to his purchaser who may be a wholesaler who in turn is liable to the retailer who in turn is liable to the ultimate purchaser, time and expense is saved by making liability direct rather than a series of lawsuits.

24-3 Requirements of Strict Liability

Section 402A imposes strict liability in tort on merchant sellers for both personal injuries and property damage that result from selling a product in a defective condition unreasonably dangerous to the user or consumer. Specifically, this section provides:

1. One who sells any product in a defective condition unreasonably dangerous to the user or consumer or to his property is subject to liability for physical harm thereby caused to the ultimate user or consumer, or to his property, if (a) the seller is engaged in the business of selling such a product, and (b) it is expected to and does reach the user or consumer without substantial change in the condition in which it is sold.

2. The rule stated in Subsection (1) applies although (a) the seller has exercised all possible care in the preparation and sale of his product, and (b) the user or consumer has not bought the product from or entered into any contractual relation with the seller.

Negligence, as previously stated, is not the basis of this liability; it applies even though "the seller has exercised all possible care in the preparation and sale of his product." The seller is not an insurer of the goods that he manufactures or sells, however, and the essential requirements for strict product liability are that (1) the defendant was engaged in the business of selling such a product, (2) the defendant sold the product in a defective condition, (3) the defective condition was one that made the product unreasonably dangerous to the user or consumer or to his property, (4) the defect in the product existed at the time it left the hands of the defendant, (5) the plaintiff sustained physical harm or property damage by use or consumption of the product, and (6) the defective condition was the proximate cause of such injury or damage.

This liability is imposed by tort law as a matter of public policy; it does not depend upon contract, either express or implied, and is not governed by the UCC. It does not require reliance by the injured user or consumer upon any statements made by the manufacturer or seller. The liability is not limited to persons in a buyer-seller relationship; thus, neither vertical nor horizontal privity is required. No notice of the defect is required to have been given by the injured user or consumer. The liability, furthermore, is generally not subject to disclaimer, exclusion, or modification by contractual agreement.

The majority of courts considering the question have held that Section 402A imposes liability for injury to person and damage to property (the economic loss doctrine) but not for commercial loss (such as loss of bargain or profits), which is recoverable in an action for breach of warranty. A minority of States have held, however, that commercial loss may be recovered in tort where the defect creates an unreasonable risk of personal injury or property damage, even though the only damage resulting is to the defective goods themselves.

24-3a MERCHANT SELLERS

Section 402A imposes liability only upon a person who is in the *business* of selling the product involved. It does *not* apply to an occasional seller, such as a person who trades in his used car or who sells his lawn mower to a neighbor. In this respect, the section is similar to the implied warranty of merchantability, which applies only to sales by a merchant with respect to goods of the type in which he deals. A growing number of jurisdictions recognize the applicability of strict liability in tort to merchant sellers of *used* goods.

24-3b DEFECTIVE CONDITION

In an action against a defendant manufacturer or other seller to recover damages under the rule of strict liability in tort based on Section 402A, the plaintiff must prove a defective condition in the product, but she is not required to prove how or why the product became defective. Under a strict liability approach, a manufacturer will be held liable even though it did not act negligently. For example, if the Quality Bottling Company, despite its having the most stringent quality control program in the industry and through no negligence of its own manufactures a bottle that explodes in the hands of a consumer, the company would be liable to the consumer under Section 402A. Whether or not Quality Bottling Company acted negligently is irrelevant. The plaintiff, however, must show that at the time she was injured, the condition of the product was not substantially changed from the condition in which the manufacturer or seller sold it.

In general, defects may arise through faulty manufacturing, faulty product design, or inadequate warning, labeling, packaging, or instructions. Some States, however, and the Restatement Third do not impose strict liability for a design defect or a failure to provide proper warnings or instructions.

♦ *See Case 24-4*

Manufacturing Defect A manufacturing defect occurs when the product is not properly made; that is, it fails to meet its own manufacturing specifications. For instance, suppose a chair is manufactured with legs designed to be attached by four screws and glue. If such a chair was produced without the required screws, this would constitute a manufacturing defect.

Design Defect A product contains a design defect when, despite its being produced as specified, the product is dangerous or hazardous because of inadequate design. Design defects can result from a number of causes, including poor engineering and poor choice of materials. An example of a design defect that received great notoriety was the Ford Pinto. A number of courts found the car to be inadequately designed because its fuel tank had been placed too close to its rear axle, causing the tank to rupture upon impact from the rear.

Section 402A provides no guidance in determining which injury-producing designs should give rise to strict liability and which should not. Consequently, the courts have adopted widely varying approaches in applying 402A to defective design cases. Nevertheless, virtually none of them has upheld a judgment in a strict liability case in which the defendant demonstrated that the "**state of the art**" was such that the manufacturer (1) neither knew nor could have known of a product hazard or (2), if he knew of the product hazard, could have designed a safer product given existing technology. Almost all courts evaluate the design of a product on the basis of the dangers that could have been known when the product was produced or sold.

In deciding design defect cases, courts identify any government safety standards applicable to the design involved in the product liability lawsuit. If such a standard exists and the manufacturer's failure to follow it caused the plaintiff's injury, the courts tend to impose liability automatically. On the other hand, a manufacturer's compliance with safety standards does not equal automatic relief from liability. If a plaintiff can demonstrate that a safer, cost-effective design was available to the manufacturer, the plaintiff can still prevail in a product liability lawsuit even though the manufacturer complied with a government safety standard.

Failure to Warn A seller is under a duty to provide adequate warning of possible danger, to provide appropriate directions for safe use, and to package the product safely. Warnings do not, however, always protect sellers from liability. A seller who could have designed or manufactured a product in a safe but cost-effective manner but who instead chooses to produce the product cheaply and to provide a warning of the product's hazards cannot escape liability simply through the warning. Warnings usually will avoid liability only if there are no cost-effective designs or manufacturing processes available to reduce a risk of injury.

The duty to give a warning arises out of a foreseeable danger of physical harm resulting from the normal or probable use of the product and out of the likelihood that, unless warned, the user or consumer will not ordinarily be aware of such danger or hazard. Section 402A imposes liability in failure-to-warn cases only in cases in which the seller "has knowledge, or by the application of reasonable, developed human skill and foresight should have knowledge, of the . . . danger." Comment j. In effect, the seller is held to the knowledge and skill of an expert in the field. Under strict liability principles, sellers are generally required to provide warnings against uses for which a product is not marketed, including certain instances of consumer misuse, if such uses are foreseeable by the manufacturer and the consumer is unlikely to recognize the hazard.

> **Practical Advice**
> *Warn consumers of your products of any significant danger, such as toxicity or flammability.*

◆ *See Cases 24-4 and 24-5*

24-3c UNREASONABLY DANGEROUS

Section 402A liability applies only if the defective product is **unreasonably dangerous** to the user or consumer. An unreasonably dangerous product is one that contains a danger beyond that which the ordinary consumer, who purchases the product with common knowledge of its characteristics, would contemplate. Thus,

> [G]ood whiskey is not unreasonably dangerous merely because it will make some people drunk, and is especially dangerous to alcoholics; but bad whiskey, containing a dangerous amount of fuel oil, is unreasonably dangerous. Good tobacco is not unreasonably dangerous merely because the effects of smoking may be harmful; but tobacco containing something like marijuana may be unreasonably dangerous. Good butter is not unreasonably dangerous merely because, if such be the case, it deposits cholesterol in the arteries and leads to heart attacks; but bad butter, contaminated with poisonous fish oil, is unreasonably dangerous. Comment i to Section 402A.

Most courts have left the question of reasonable consumer expectations to the jury.

◆ *See Case 24-6*

24-4 Obstacles to Recovery Under Second Restatement

Few of the obstacles to recovery in warranty cases present serious problems to plaintiffs in strict liability actions brought pursuant to Section 402A because this section was drafted largely to avoid such obstacles.

24-4a DISCLAIMERS AND NOTICE

Comment m to Section 402A provides that the basis of strict liability rests solely in tort and therefore is not subject to contractual defenses. The comment specifically states that strict product liability is not governed by the Code, that it is not affected by contractual limitations or disclaimers, and that it is not subject to any requirement that the injured party gives notice to the seller within a reasonable time. Nevertheless, most courts have allowed clear and specific disclaimers of Section 402A *liability in commercial* transactions between merchants of relatively equal economic power.

24-4b PRIVITY

With respect to horizontal privity, the majority of States hold that the strict liability in tort of manufacturers and other sellers extends not only to buyers, users, and consumers but also to injured bystanders. Some States, however, limit liability to foreseeable purchasers or users of the product.

In terms of vertical privity, strict liability in tort imposes liability on any seller who is engaged in the business of selling the product, including a wholesaler or distributor as well as the manufacturer and retailer. The rule of strict liability in tort also applies to the manufacturer of a defective component that has been incorporated into a larger product where the manufacturer of the finished product has made no essential change in the component.

24-4c PLAINTIFF'S CONDUCT

Many product liability defenses relate to the conduct of the plaintiff. The contention common to all of them is that the plaintiff's improper conduct so contributed to the plaintiff's injury that it would be unfair to blame the product or its seller.

CONTRIBUTORY NEGLIGENCE Contributory negligence is conduct on the part of the plaintiff that (1) falls below the standard to which he should conform for his own protection and (2) is the legal cause of the plaintiff's harm. Because strict liability is designed to assess liability without fault, Section 402A rejects contributory negligence as a defense. Thus, a seller cannot defend a strict liability lawsuit on the basis of a plaintiff's negligent failure to discover a defect or to guard against its possibility. But, as will be discussed, contributory negligence in the form of an assumption of the risk can bar recovery under Section 402A.

COMPARATIVE NEGLIGENCE The harshness of the contributory negligence doctrine has caused all but a few States to reject the all-or-nothing rule of contributory negligence and to substitute the doctrine of **comparative negligence**. Under comparative negligence, damages are apportioned between the parties in proportion to the degree of fault or negligence found against them.

Despite Section 402A's bar of contributory negligence in strict liability cases, some courts apply comparative negligence to strict liability cases. (Some courts use the term **comparative responsibility** rather than *comparative negligence*.) There are two basic types of comparative negligence or comparative responsibility. One is **pure comparative responsibility**, which simply reduces the plaintiff's recovery in proportion to her fault, whatever that may be. Thus, the recovery of a plaintiff found to be 80 percent at fault in causing an accident in which she suffered a $100,000 loss would be limited to 20 percent of her damages, or $20,000. By comparison, under **modified comparative responsibility**, the plaintiff recovers according to the general principles of comparative responsibility *unless* she is more than 50 percent responsible for her injuries, in which case she recovers nothing. The majority of comparative negligence States follow the modified comparative responsibility approach.

VOLUNTARY ASSUMPTION OF THE RISK Under the Second Restatement of Torts, assumption of risk is a defense in an action based on strict liability in tort. Basically, **assumption of risk** is the plaintiff's express or implied consent to encounter a known danger. The user or consumer who voluntarily uses goods in an unusual, inappropriate, or improper manner for which they were not intended, such use being, under the circumstances, unreasonable, assumes the risk of injuries that result from such use. Thus, a person who drives an automobile after realizing that the brakes are not working or an employee who attempts to remove a foreign object from a high-speed roller press without shutting off the power has assumed the risk of his own injury. In a comparative negligence or comparative responsibility State, assumption of the risk would either reduce or bar recovery, depending on the degree to which it contributed to the plaintiff's injury.

To establish such a defense, the defendant must show that (1) the plaintiff actually knew and appreciated the particular risk or danger the defect created, (2) the plaintiff voluntarily encountered the risk while realizing the danger, and (3) the plaintiff's decision to encounter the known risk was unreasonable.

The Third Restatement of Torts: Apportionment of Liability has abandoned the doctrine of implied voluntary assumption of risk in tort actions generally; it is no longer a defense that the plaintiff was aware of a risk and voluntarily confronted it. This new Restatement limits the defense of assumption of risk to express assumption of risk, which consists of a contract between the plaintiff and another person to absolve the other person from liability for future harm. Section 2.

MISUSE OR ABUSE OF THE PRODUCT Closely connected to voluntary assumption of the risk is the valid defense of misuse or abuse of the product by the injured party. **Misuse** or **abuse** occurs when the injured party knows or should know that he is using the product in a manner not contemplated by the seller. The major difference between misuse or abuse and assumption of the risk is that the former includes actions that the injured party does not know to be dangerous, whereas the latter does not. Instances of such misuse or abuse include standing on a rocking chair to change a light-bulb or using a lawn mower to trim hedges. The courts, however, have significantly limited this defense by requiring that the misuse or abuse not be foreseeable by the seller. If a use is foreseeable, then the seller must take measures to guard against it.

24-4d SUBSEQUENT ALTERATION

Section 402A provides that liability exists only if the product reaches "the user or consumer without substantial change in the condition in which it is sold." Accordingly, most, but not all, courts would not hold a manufacturer liable for a faulty oil pump if a car dealer were to remove the part and make significant changes in it prior to reinstalling it in an automobile.

24-4e STATUTE OF REPOSE

Numerous lawsuits have been brought against manufacturers many years after a product was first sold. In response, many States have adopted **statutes of repose**. These enactments limit the time period—typically to between six and twelve years—for which a manufacturer is liable for injury caused by a defective product. After the statutory period has elapsed, a manufacturer ceases to be liable for such harm.

24-4f LIMITATIONS ON DAMAGES

More than half of the States have limited the punitive damages that a plaintiff can collect in a product liability lawsuit. They have done this by a number of means, including the following:

1. Placing caps on the amount of damages that can be awarded, with caps ranging greatly but generally between $250,000 and $1 million;
2. Providing for the State to receive all or a portion of any punitive damages awarded with the State's share ranging from 35 percent to 100 percent to reduce the plaintiff's incentive to bring products liability suits;
3. Providing for bifurcated trials—that is, separate hearings to determine liability and punitive damages;

4. Increasing the plaintiff's burden of proof for recovery of punitive damages, with most states adopting the "clear and convincing" evidence standard; and
5. Requiring proportionality between compensatory and punitive damages by specifying an acceptable ratio between the two types of damages.

◆ SEE FIGURE 24-2: *Product Liability*

24-5 Restatement (Third) of Torts: Products Liability

The Restatement (Third) of Torts: Products Liability, which supersedes Section 402A of the Second Restatement of Torts, makes significant changes in product liability law. It is far more comprehensive than the Second Restatement in dealing with the liability of commercial sellers and distributors of goods for harm caused by their products. An increasing number of States have adopted some of the provisions of the new Restatement, but most States continue to follow Section 402A. The new Restatement expands Section 402A into an entire treatise of its own, comprising more than twenty sections. The Restatement Third does not use the term strict liability but instead defines separate liability standards for each type of defect. The new Restatement continues to cover anyone engaged in the business of selling or distributing a defective product if the defect causes harm to persons or property. Its major provision (Section 2) defines a product as defective "when, at the time of sale or distribution, it contains a manufacturing defect, is defective in design, or is defective because of inadequate instructions or warnings." Thus, Section 2 explicitly recognizes the three types of product defects discussed previously: manufacturing defects, design defects, and failure to warn. However, as will be discussed next, strict liability is imposed only on the first of these, while liability for inadequate design or warning is imposed only for foreseeable risks of harm that could have been avoided by the use of an alternative *reasonable* design, warning, or instruction.

24-5a MANUFACTURING DEFECT

Section 2(a) provides that "A product . . . contains a manufacturing defect when the product departs from its intended design even though all possible care was exercised in the preparation and marketing of the product." Therefore, sellers and distributors of products remain strictly liable for manufacturing defects, although a plaintiff may seek to recover based upon allegations and proof of negligent manufacture. In actions against the manufacturer, the plaintiff ordinarily must prove that the defect existed in the product when it left the manufacturer.

FIGURE 24-2   Product Liability

Type of Warranty	Warranty of Merchantability*	Strict Liability in Tort (§402A)
Condition of Goods Creating Liability	Not fit for ordinary purposes	Defective condition, unreasonably dangerous
Type of Transaction Covered	Sales and leases (except finance leases); some courts apply to bailments of goods	Sales, leases, and bailments of goods
Disclaimer	Must mention "merchantability" If in writing, must be conspicuous (lease must be in writing) Must not be unconscionable Sales subject to Magnuson-Moss Act/leases may be subject	Not possible in consumer transactions; may be permitted in commercial transactions
Notice to Seller	Required within reasonable time	Not required
Causation	Required	Required
Who May Sue	In some States, buyer and the buyer's family or guests in home; in other States, any person who may be expected to use, consume, or be affected by goods	Any user or consumer of product; also, in most States, any bystander
Compensable Harms	Personal injury, property damage, economic loss	Personal injury, property damage
Who May Be Sued	Seller or lessor who is a merchant with respect to the goods sold	Seller who is a merchant with respect to the goods sold

*The warranty of fitness for a particular purpose differs from the warranty of merchantability in the following respects: (1) the condition that triggers liability is the failure of the goods to perform according to the particular purpose described in the warranty, (2) a disclaimer need not mention "fitness for a particular purpose" but must be in writing, and (3) it applies to any seller.

24-5b   DESIGN DEFECT

Section 2(b) states:

> A product is defective in design when the foreseeable risks of harm posed by the product could have been reduced or avoided by the adoption of a reasonable alternative design by the seller or other distributor, or a predecessor in the commercial chain of distribution, and the omission of the reasonable alternative design renders the product not reasonably safe.

This rule pulls back from a strict liability standard and imposes a negligence-like standard by requiring that the defect be reasonably foreseeable and that it could have been avoided by a reasonable alternative design. The Comments explain that this standard involves resolving "whether a reasonable alternative design would, at a reasonable cost, have reduced the foreseeable risk of harm posed by the product and, if so, whether the omission of the alternative design by the seller … rendered the product not reasonably safe." The burden rests upon the plaintiff to demonstrate the existence of a reasonable alternative safer design that would have reduced the foreseeable risks of harm. However, consumer expectations do not constitute an independent standard for judging the defectiveness of product designs.

24-5c   FAILURE TO WARN

Section 2(c) provides:

> A product is defective because of inadequate instructions or warnings when the foreseeable risks of harm posed by the product could have been reduced or avoided by the provision of reasonable instructions or warnings by the seller or other distributor, or a predecessor in the commercial chain of distribution and the omission of the instructions or warnings renders the product not reasonably safe.

Commercial product sellers must provide reasonable instructions and warnings about risks of injury associated with their products. The omission of warnings sufficient to allow informed decisions by reasonably foreseeable users or consumers renders the product not reasonably safe at time of sale. A seller, however, is under a duty to warn only if it knew or should have known of the risks involved. Moreover, warning about risks is effective only if an alternative design to avoid the risk cannot reasonably be implemented. Whenever safer products can be reasonably designed at a reasonable cost, adopting the safer design is required rather than using a warning or instructions.

CHAPTER SUMMARY

WARRANTIES

TYPES OF WARRANTIES	**Definition of Warranty** an obligation of the seller to the buyer concerning title, quality, characteristics, or condition of goods
	Warranty of Title the obligation of a seller to convey the right to ownership without any lien (in a lease, the warranty protects the lessee's right to possess and use the goods)
	Express Warranty an affirmation of fact or promise about the goods or a description, including a sample, of the goods that becomes part of the basis of the bargain
	Implied Warranty a contractual obligation, arising out of certain circumstances of the sale, imposed by operation of law and not found in the language of the sales contract

- *Merchantability* warranty by a merchant seller that the goods are reasonably fit for the ordinary purpose for which they are manufactured or sold; pass without objection in the trade under the contract description; and are of fair, average quality
- *Fitness for Particular Purpose* warranty by any seller that goods are reasonably fit for a particular purpose if, at the time of contracting, the seller had reason to know the buyer's particular purpose and that the buyer was relying on the seller's skill and judgment to furnish suitable goods

OBSTACLES TO WARRANTY ACTIONS	**Disclaimers of Warranties** negations of warranties

- *Express Warranty* not usually possible to disclaim
- *Warranty of Title* may be excluded or modified by specific language or by certain circumstances, including judicial sale or a sale by a sheriff, executor, or foreclosing lienor
- *Implied Warranty of Merchantability* the disclaimer must mention "merchantability" and, in the case of a writing, must be conspicuous (in a lease, the disclaimer must be in writing)
- *Implied Warranty of Fitness for a Particular Purpose* the disclaimer must be in writing and conspicuous
- *Other Disclaimers of Implied Warranties* the implied warranties of merchantability and fitness for a particular purpose may also be disclaimed (1) by expressions like "as is," "with all faults," or other similar language; (2) by course of dealing, course of performance, or usage of trade; or (3) as to defects, an examination ought to have revealed where the buyer has examined the goods or where the buyer has refused to examine the goods
- *Federal Legislation Relating to Warranties of Consumer Goods* the Magnuson-Moss Warranty Act protects purchasers of consumer goods by providing that warranty information be clear and useful and that a seller who makes a written warranty cannot disclaim any implied warranty

Limitation or Modification of Warranties permitted as long as it is not unconscionable

Privity of Contract a contractual relationship between parties that was necessary at common law to maintain a lawsuit

- *Horizontal Privity* doctrine determining who benefits from a warranty and who therefore may bring a cause of action; the Code provides three alternatives
- *Vertical Privity* doctrine determining who in the chain of distribution is liable for a breach of warranty; the Code has not adopted a position on this

Notice of Breach if the buyer fails to notify the seller of any breach within a reasonable time, she is barred from any remedy against the seller

Plaintiff's Conduct

- *Contributory Negligence* is not a defense
- *Voluntary Assumption of the Risk* is a defense

STRICT PRODUCT LIABILITY IN TORT

REQUIREMENTS UNDER SECOND RESTATEMENT OF TORTS	**General Rule** imposes tort liability on merchant sellers for both personal injuries and property damage for selling a product in a defective condition unreasonably dangerous to the user or consumer **Merchant Sellers** applies only to a person who is in the business of selling the product involved **Defective Condition** • *Manufacturing Defect* by failing to meet its own manufacturing specifications, the product is not properly made • *Design Defect* the product, though made as designed, is dangerous because the design is inadequate • *Failure to Warn* failure to provide adequate warning of possible danger or to provide appropriate directions for use of a product **Unreasonably Dangerous** contains a danger beyond that which would be contemplated by the ordinary consumer
OBSTACLES TO RECOVERY UNDER SECOND RESTATEMENT	**Contractual Defenses** defenses such as privity, disclaimers, and notice generally do not apply to tort liability **Plaintiff's Conduct** • *Contributory Negligence* not a defense in the majority of States • *Comparative Negligence* most States have applied the rule of comparative negligence to strict liability in tort • *Voluntary Assumption of the Risk* express assumption of risk is a defense to an action based upon strict liability; some States apply implied assumption of risk to strict liability cases • *Misuse or Abuse of the Product* is a defense **Subsequent Alteration** liability exists only if the product reaches the user or consumer without substantial change in the condition in which it is sold **Statute of Repose** limits the time period for which a manufacturer is liable for injury caused by its product **Limitations on Damages** many States have limited the punitive damages that a plaintiff can collect in a product liability lawsuit
RESTATEMENT (THIRD) OF TORTS: PRODUCTS LIABILITY	**General Rule** one engaged in the business of selling products who sells a defective product is subject to liability for harm to persons or property caused by the defect **Defective Conditions** • *Manufacturing Defect* a seller is held to strict liability when the product departs from its intended design • *Design Defect* a product is defective when the foreseeable risks of harm posed by the product could have been reduced or avoided by the adoption of a reasonable alternative design • *Failure to Warn* a product is defective because of inadequate instructions or warnings when the foreseeable risks of harm posed by the product could have been reduced or avoided by the provision of reasonable instructions or warnings

C A S E S

CASE
24-1

Express Warranties:
BELDEN INC. v. AMERICAN ELECTRONIC COMPONENTS, INC.
Court of Appeals of Indiana, 2008
885 N.E.2d 751, 66 UCC Rep.Serv.2d 399

Barnes, J.

Belden, Inc., and Belden Wire & Cable Company (collectively "Belden") * * * manufactures wire, and [American Electronic Components, Inc.] AEC manufactures automobile sensors. Since 1989, AEC, in repeated transactions, has purchased wire from Belden to use in its sensors.

In 1996 and 1997, Belden sought to comply with AEC's quality control program and provided detailed information to AEC regarding the materials it used to manufacture its wire. In its assurances, Belden indicated that it would use insulation from Quantum Chemical Corp. ("Quantum"). In June 2003, however, Belden began using insulation supplied by Dow Chemical Company ("Dow"). The Dow insulation had different physical properties than the insulation provided by Quantum.

In October 2003, Belden sold AEC wire manufactured with the Dow insulation. AEC used this wire to make its sensors, and the insulation ultimately cracked. Chrysler had installed AEC's sensors containing the faulty wire in approximately 18,000 vehicles. Chrysler recalled 14,000 vehicles and repaired the remaining 4,000 prior to sale. Pursuant to an agreement with Chrysler, AEC is required to reimburse Chrysler for expenses associated with the recall.

In 2004, AEC filed a complaint against Belden seeking consequential damages for the changes in the insulation that resulted in the recall. In 2005, AEC filed a partial motion for summary judgment. In 2006, Belden responded and filed a cross-motion for summary judgment. * * * On July 6, 2007, the trial court entered an order granting AEC's motion for partial summary judgment and denying Belden's crossmotion. Belden now appeals.

* * *

"Where an agreement is entirely in writing, the question of whether express warranties were made is one for the court." [Citation.] More specifically, if all of the representations upon which the parties rely were in writing, the existence of express warranties is a question of law. [Citation.] Because the alleged warranty is based on written exchanges, whether the writings are sufficient to create an express warranty is a question of law appropriate for summary judgment.

* * *

Belden claims that these 1996 and 1997 communications did not amount to an express warranty for purposes of the October 2003 contract. Section 2-313 of the UCC provides:

(1) Express warranties by the seller are created as follows:

  (a) any affirmation of fact or promise made by the seller to the buyer which relates to the goods and becomes part of the basis of the bargain creates an express warranty that the goods shall conform to the affirmation or promise.

  (b) any description of the goods which is made part of the basis of the bargain creates an express warranty that the goods shall conform to the description.

  (c) any sample or model which is made part of the basis of the bargain creates an express warranty that the whole of the goods shall conform to the sample or model.

(2) It is not necessary to the creation of an express warranty that the seller use formal words such as "warrant" or "guarantee" or that he have a specific intention to make a warranty, but an affirmation merely of the value of the goods or a statement purporting to be merely the seller's opinion or commendation of the goods does not create a warranty.

"An express warranty requires some representation, term or statement as to how the product is warranted." [Citation.] There does not seem to be a dispute that in 1996 and 1997 Belden made express warranties regarding its wire. Instead, the issue is whether the 1996 and 1997 statements by Belden regarding certification created an express warranty that extended to the October 2003 contract.

Based on the designated evidence, we believe Belden's compliance with AEC's quality control program was essential to its contracts with AEC and was intended to extend to the parties' repeated contracts. First, Comment 7 to Section 2-313 provides in part, "The precise time when words of description or affirmation are made or samples are shown is not material. The sole question is whether the language or samples or models are fairly to be regarded as part of the contract." Thus, although Belden made its initial representations in 1996 and 1997, there is no indication that those representations were limited in time, that Belden subsequently disclaimed its compliance with AEC's quality control standards, or that AEC changed those standards. As the trial court observed, "it is illogical to believe that [AEC] intended to rely in this representation for only one (1) shipment of Wire and then to understand that Belden would follow whatever quality procedures it wanted as to future shipments."

Further, Comment 5 of Section 2-213 provides in part, "Past deliveries may set the description of quality, either expressly or impliedly by course of dealing. Of course, all descriptions by merchants must be read against the applicable trade usages with the general rules as to merchantability resolving any doubts." Belden claims that if the parties' course of dealing was insufficient to incorporate the limitation on damages into the parties' contract, then the course of dealing is also insufficient to establish an express warranty. We disagree. Irrespective of whether the course of dealing established that AEC assented to Belden's proposed limitation on damages, the parties' course of dealing established that Belden made an express warranty regarding its compliance with the quality control standards. The limitation on damages and the express warranty are unrelated issues—there is no correlation between the two.

A course of dealing is conduct "fairly to be regarded as establishing a common basis of understanding for interpreting their expressions and other conduct." §1-205(1). It is undisputed that Belden's wire complied with the AEC's quality control requirements for the parties' more than 100 transactions, until October 2003, when Belden switched from Quantum insulation to the Dow insulation without informing AEC of the changes. * * *

That Belden and AEC did not repeatedly or routinely "communicate" regarding Belden's continued use of Quantum insulation does not undermine the parties' course of dealing. The very point of a course of dealing is to allow the parties' prior actions to create a basis of common understanding. This is exactly what Belden's 1996 and 1997 assertions taken with its continued use of Quantum insulation did.

* * *

Affirmed.

CASE 24-2

Express Warranties/Implied Warranties

IN RE L.B. TRUCKING, INC.

United States Bankruptcy Court, D. Del, 1994
163 BR 709, 23 UCC Rep.Serv.2d 1092

Balick, J.

[Dudley B. Durham, Jr., and his wife, Barbara Durham, owned and operated a trucking company, L. B. Trucking, Inc., and a farm, Double-D Farms, Inc. In April 1983, Dudley Durham met with Richard Thomas of Southern States Cooperative—which is in the business of supplying various agricultural supplies to farmers—about arranging for the application of herbicides to the Durhams' fields.

At a subsequent meeting in early May, Durham met with Thomas to complete credit arrangements and to arrange the application of herbicides. Durham told Thomas, "I want it done the cheapest way, the best way it can be done." Thomas responded, "Will do." Thomas then outlined with some specificity the chemicals he proposed to use on the Durhams' fields. The plan included the use of a water-based carrier that was recommended by local experts, rather than a more expensive nitrogen solution. Durham had no experience or expertise on herbicidal chemicals and relied on Thomas's briefing on the various herbicide mixtures in choosing which ones to apply.

When the herbicides were actually to be applied, Southern States herbicide applicator, Gilbert McClements, received from Mr. Thomas instructions concerning which chemicals to apply and would mix the chemicals each day prior to spraying. Apparently, though, Mr. McClements used a nitrogen solution to prepare the herbicides and did not make extensive pre-spraying inspections of the grass and weeds in the fields to be

sprayed. When Durham noticed a significant number of weeds and grasses had survived the herbicidal treatment, he promptly notified Southern States. Southern States attempted to remedy the problem, but the harvest was dismal and far below the county average.

In 1983, the Durhams and both their businesses filed for bankruptcy. Southern States brought a claim against the consolidated bankruptcy estate to collect payment for the herbicides as well as application and other services provided. The trustee of the estate asserted counterclaims against Southern States for negligence and breach of warranties in the application of herbicides that caused severe damage to the Durhams' 1983 crop.]

1. Express Warranty

An express warranty may be created by a seller through: (1) any affirmation of fact or promise to the buyer relating to the goods which becomes the basis of the bargain so that the goods conform to the affirmation or promise; (2) any description of the goods which is made part of the basis of the bargain so that the whole of the goods conform to the sample of model. [UCC] §2-313(1)(a)-(c). The question of whether an express warranty has been made in a particular transaction is for the trier of fact. [Citation.] In the case at bar, there are no written express warranties claimed, but instead, oral statements made principally by the Middletown store manager, Thomas, to Durham which the Trustee contends were express warranties.

The relevant testimony concerning Thomas' statements to Durham reveal several oral express warranties concerning the herbicides and their application which Southern States plainly breached. First, Thomas stated that water would be the carrier for the herbicides, especially since Durham wanted the job done inexpensively. In its application, Southern States used the nitrogen solution regardless of the University of Delaware recommendations dissuading its use and despite the fact that it is more expensive than using water as a carrier. Southern States' reference to the common trade usage of nitrogen in 1983 is inapposite in an action for breach of express warranty because it is the affirmation or promise—not the custom or trade usage—which becomes the standard against which a breach is determined. In addition, Thomas' statements were more than "seller's talk" or puffing in that they were product-specific and not overly broad or vague. Second, Thomas also made statements regarding the effectiveness of the herbicides in removing weeds and grass so as to promote successful no-till farming. The purchase of herbicides is characteristically the subject of express warranties because the buyer of the product cannot determine its effectiveness prior to use and evaluate its effectiveness in a given situation. Here, Thomas' statements in early May of 1983 were part of the basis of the bargain upon which Durham relied when purchasing the herbicides. Beyond this, Thomas had superior knowledge about the herbicides as opposed to Durham who had little or none. Consequently, Thomas' selection of herbicidal recipes combined with his statements as to their effectiveness amounted to an express warranty that the respective mixtures would do the job adequately. Thomas made at least two express warranties which formed the basis of Durham's purchase of the chemicals and were ultimately breached. The liability for breach of express warranty is a strict liability. No defect need be shown other than breach of the warranty itself which is the proximate cause of the property damage. [Citations.] Accordingly, the court finds that Southern States breached its express warranty to Durham and, thus, is liable for the Durham's crop damage. * * *

2. IMPLIED WARRANTIES

There are two theories of recovery for breach of implied warranty under the Delaware UCC: breach of implied warranty of merchantability under [UCC] §2-314 and breach of implied warranty of fitness for a particular purpose under [UCC] §2-315. The implied warranty of fitness for a particular purpose may, to some degree, overlap a seller's express warranty. [Citations.] Unless there is a valid disclaimer, these implied warranties are implied in every sales transaction involving goods and run not only to those in contractual privity with the seller but to third party beneficiaries as well. [UCC] §2-318; [Citation]. Obviously, Durham was in direct privity with Southern States regarding the herbicides sale.

Turning first to the implied warranty of merchantability, there are five elements which the claimant must establish: (1) that a merchant sold goods, (2) which were not merchantable at the time of sale, (3) proximately causing by the defective nature of the goods, (4) injury and damages to the claimant or his property, and (5) notice to the seller of the injury. [Citation.] As to the element requiring the seller to be a merchant, there is no doubt that Southern States was a merchant. * * *

Addressing the second element concerning whether the herbicides were "merchantable," the goods must pass without objection in the trade under the contract description be fit for the ordinary purposes for which it was intended. [UCC] §2-314(2)(a) and (c). The facts show that Southern States sprayed (and in some instances resprayed) the various Durham farm tracts with herbicidal and other chemicals in order to increase the crop yields. Nevertheless, the farms' respective crop yields did not improve, but rather fell dramatically as the result of the chemical applications. Specifically, the herbicidal recipes were unfit for the ordinary purpose for which they were intended to be used, chemical agents that would kill weeds without damaging the primary crops. [Citation.] The chemicals did not operate for their ordinary purpose which was to promote no-till farming which is why Durham purchased them in the first place.

* * *

As for proximate cause and damages, the court finds that these elements have been met. * * *

Finally, the notice requirement for a breach of implied warranty of merchantability cause of action was plainly met. Durham notified Southern States as soon as he suspected that the herbicides were failing to work just a few weeks after their application. * * *

Southern States also breached the implied warranty that the herbicides were fit for their particular purpose. * * *

The breach of this warranty is the one most apparent on the facts. As indicated earlier, Durham relied on Thomas' skill and judgment in selecting suitable herbicides that would enable Durham to conduct no-till farming on his farms. The chemicals were mixed by Southern States' herbicide applicator, McClements, before each job based on a formula or recipe provided by Thomas or some other Southern States official. The herbicides did not effectively do their job of keeping the fields clear of weeds and the crops died. Though thoroughly familiar with till farming, Durham had no experience with the no-till farming method and, therefore, was not a "sophisticated purchaser" who might have been able to recognize mistakes made by Southern States' personnel. As a result, the herbicides' failure to do their intended task coupled with Durham's reliance on Southern States' judgment and skill in formulating, mixing, and applying the herbicidal chemicals breached the implied warranty of fitness. [Citations.] Accordingly, Southern States is found to be liable under [UCC] §2-315.

CASE 24-3

Disclaimer of Warranties

WOMCO, INC. v. NAVISTAR INTERNATIONAL CORPORATION

Court of Appeals of Texas, Twelfth District, Tyler, 2002
84 S.W.3d 272, 48 UCC Rep.Serv.2d 130

Griffith, J.

[In 1993, Womco, Inc., purchased through Price, a dealer, thirty 1993 International model 9300 tractor trucks manufactured by Navistar. Also in 1993, C. L. Hall purchased sixteen 1994 International model 9300 tractor trucks also manufactured by Navistar through Mahaney, another dealer. Almost immediately after the trucks were put into service, Womco and Hall (plaintiffs) each had problems with their trucks' engines overheating. As the problems occurred, plaintiffs took their trucks, which were still covered under warranty, to their dealerships for service related to the overheating problem. Although repeated attempts were made, the dealerships were unable to correct the problem. Subsequently it was discovered that the trucks' radiators were unusually small and were insufficient to cool the engine.

Womco and Hall filed suit against Navistar, Price, and Mahaney (defendants). The trial court granted the defendants' motion for summary judgment based on their affirmative defenses of disclaimer of warranty. Womco and Hall appealed.]

* * *

It is undisputed that Appellants' breach of implied warranty claims as to nine trucks are not barred by limitations. However, * * * Appellees contend that such implied warranties were disclaimed. The Texas Uniform Commercial Code allows sellers to disclaim both the implied warranty of merchantability as well as the implied warranty of fitness for particular purpose. [UCC] §2.316(b), [citation]. In order to disclaim an implied warranty of merchantability in a sales transaction, the disclaimer must mention the word "merchantability." The disclaimer may be oral or written, but if in writing, the disclaimer must be conspicuous. [Citation]; [UCC] §2.316(b). To disclaim an implied warranty of fitness for a particular purpose, the disclaimer must be in writing and must be conspicuous. [UCC] §2.316(b); [citation]. Whether a particular disclaimer is conspicuous is a question of law to be determined by the court. [Citation.] A term or clause is conspicuous if it is written so that a reasonable person against whom it is to operate ought to have noticed it. [UCC] §1.201(10) (Vernon Supp. 2002);

[citation]. Language is "conspicuous" if it is in larger type or other contrasting font or color. [Citation.] Conspicuousness is not required if the buyer has actual knowledge of the disclaimer. [Citation.]

* * *

Further, Appellants argue that Appellees were required to offer proof of the context of the purported disclaimers, contending that in order for a disclaimer of an implied warranty to be effective, the plaintiffs must have had an opportunity to examine it prior to consummation of the contract for sale. [Citation.] * * * In *Dickenson*, [citation], the court held that a disclaimer of an express warranty was ineffective where the buyer was not given the opportunity to read the warranty or warranties made until after the contract is signed. Although the instant case concerns a converse situation to *Dickenson*, the rationale applied by the *Dickenson* court is helpful. One of the underlying purposes of [UCC] Section 2.316 is to protect a buyer from surprise by permitting the exclusion of implied warranties. [UCC] §2.316, comment 1. We fail to see how Section [UCC] 2-316 can fulfill such a purpose unless a disclaimer is required to be communicated to the buyer before the contract of sale has been completed, unless the buyer afterward agrees to the disclaimer as a modification of the contract. [Citations.] * * *

In support of their motion for summary judgment, Appellees offered six disclaimers, all of which were deposition exhibits. None of these six disclaimers is probative as to the issue of whether the disclaimer was communicated prior to the completion of the contract of sale. * * * Therefore, we hold that since Appellant failed to conclusively prove that they were entitled to judgment as a matter of law on the disclaimer issue, summary judgment was not appropriate on that issue. * * *

* * *

Accordingly, the trial court's order granting summary judgment is *reversed* as to Appellants' claims for breach of warranty * * * and is *remanded* to the trial court for further proceedings. As to all other claims of Appellants, the trial court's order granting summary judgment is *affirmed*.

Strict Liability in Tort/Failure to Warn
O'NEIL v. CRANE CO.
Supreme Court of California, 2012
53 Cal.4th 335, 135 Cal.Rptr.3d 288, 266 P.3d 987

Corrigan, J.

Defendants Crane Co. (Crane) and Warren Pumps LLC (Warren) made valves and pumps used in Navy warships. They were sued here for a wrongful death allegedly caused by asbestos released from external insulation and internal gaskets and packing, all of which were made by third parties and added to the pumps and valves postsale. It is undisputed that defendants never manufactured or sold any of the asbestos-containing materials to which plaintiffs' decedent was exposed. Nevertheless, plaintiffs claim defendants should be held strictly liable * * * because it was foreseeable workers would be exposed to and harmed by the asbestos in replacement parts and products used in conjunction with their pumps and valves.

* * *

Following the close of evidence, Crane moved for nonsuit on all causes of action. * * *

The trial court granted the motions and dismissed all claims against Crane and Warren. * * * On appeal, this decision was reversed.

* * *

We granted review and now reverse.

* * *

Strict liability has been imposed for three types of product defects: manufacturing defects, design defects, and "'warning defects.'" [Citation.] The third category describes "products that are dangerous because they lack adequate warnings or instructions." [Citation.] A bedrock principle in strict liability law requires that "the plaintiff's injury must have been caused by a 'defect' in the [defendant's] product." [Citation.]

Plaintiffs argue defendants' products were defective because they included and were used in connection with asbestos-containing parts. They also contend defendants should be held strictly liable for failing to warn O'Neil about the potential health consequences of breathing asbestos dust released from the products used in connection with their pumps and valves. These claims lack merit. We conclude that defendants were not strictly liable for O'Neil's injuries because (a) any design defect in *defendants' products* was not a legal cause of injury to O'Neil, and (b) defendants had no duty to warn of risks arising from *other manufacturers'* products.

A. *No Liability Outside a Defective Product's Chain of Distribution*

From the outset, strict products liability in California has always been premised on harm caused by deficiencies in the defendant's own product. We first announced the rule in *Greenman v. Yuba Power Products, Inc.* (1963) (*Greenman*) [citation]: "A manufacturer is strictly liable in tort when an article *he places on the market* knowing that it is to be used without inspection for defects, proves to have a defect that causes injury to a human being." (Italics [in original].) We explained that "[t]he purpose of such liability is to insure that the costs of injuries resulting from defective products are borne by the manufacturers that put such products on the market rather than by the injured persons who are powerless to protect themselves." [Citation.] A year later, we extended strict liability to retailers, reasoning that, as an "integral part of the overall producing and marketing enterprise," they too should bear the cost of injuries from defective products. [Citations.]

Strict liability encompasses all injuries caused by a defective product, even those traceable to a defective component part that was supplied by another. [Citation.] However, the reach of strict liability is not limitless. We have never held that strict liability extends to harm from entirely distinct products that the consumer can be expected to use with, or in, the defendant's nondefective product. Instead, we have consistently adhered to the *Greenman* formulation requiring proof that the plaintiff suffered injury caused by a defect in the defendant's own product. [Citation.] Regardless of a defendant's position in the chain of distribution, "the basis for his liability remains that he has marketed or distributed a defective product" [citation], and that product caused the plaintiff's injury.

* * *

In this case, it is undisputed that O'Neil was exposed to *no* asbestos from a product made by defendants. Although he was exposed to potentially high levels of asbestos dust released from insulation the Navy had applied to the exterior of the pumps and valves, Crane and Warren did not manufacture or sell this external insulation. They did not mandate or advise that it be used with their products. O'Neil was also exposed to asbestos from the replacement gaskets and packing inside the pumps and valves. Yet, uncontroverted evidence established that these internal components were not the original parts supplied by Crane and Warren. They were replacement parts the Navy had purchased from other sources.

It is fundamental that the imposition of liability requires a showing that the plaintiff's injuries were caused by an act of the defendant or an instrumentality under the defendant's control. [Citation.] * * *

Nor does the record support plaintiffs' claim that defendants' products were defective because they were "designed to be used" with asbestos-containing components. The products were designed to meet the Navy's specifications. Moreover, there was no evidence that defendants' products *required* asbestos-containing gaskets or packing in order to function. Plaintiffs' assertion to the contrary is belied by evidence that defendants made some pumps and valves without asbestos-containing parts. As alternative insulating materials became available, the Navy could have chosen to replace worn gaskets and seals in defendants' products with parts that did not contain asbestos. Apart from the Navy's specifications, no evidence showed that the design of defendants' products required the use of asbestos components, and their mere compatibility for use with such components is not enough to render them defective.

* * *

B. *No Duty to Warn of Defects in Another Manufacturer's Product*

Plaintiffs also argue that defendants had a duty to warn O'Neil about the hazards of asbestos because the release of asbestos dust from surrounding products was a foreseeable consequence of maintenance work on defendants' pumps and valves.

"Generally speaking, manufacturers have a duty to warn consumers about the hazards inherent in their products. [Citation.] The requirement's purpose is to inform consumers about a product's hazards and faults of which they are unaware, so that they can refrain from using the product altogether or evade the danger by careful use. [Citation.] Typically, under California law, we hold manufacturers strictly liable for injuries caused by their failure to warn of dangers that were known to the scientific community at the time they manufactured and distributed their product. [Citations.]" [Citation.] However, we have never held that a manufacturer's duty to warn extends to hazards arising exclusively from *other* manufacturers' products. A line of Court of Appeal cases holds instead that the duty to warn is limited to risks arising from the manufacturer's own product.

* * *

So too here. Crane and Warren gave no warning about the dangers of asbestos in the gaskets and packing originally included in their products. However, O'Neil never encountered these original parts. His exposure to asbestos came from replacement gaskets and packing and external insulation added to defendants' products long after their installation on the [U.S. Navy vessel]. There is no dispute that these external and replacement products were made by other manufacturers. "[N]o case law. . . supports the idea that a manufacturer, after selling a completed product to a purchaser, remains under a duty to warn the purchaser of potentially defective additional pieces of equipment that the purchaser may or may not use to complement the product bought from the manufacturer." [Citation.]

Decisions from other jurisdictions are in accord. [Citations.] * * *

* * *

* * * California law does not impose a duty to warn about dangers arising entirely from another manufacturer's product, even if it is foreseeable that the products will be used together. Were it otherwise, manufacturers of the saws used to cut insulation would become the next targets of asbestos lawsuits. * * * Where the intended use of a product inevitably creates a hazardous situation, it is reasonable to expect the manufacturer to give warnings. Conversely, where the hazard arises entirely from another product, and the defendant's product does not create or contribute to that hazard, liability is not appropriate. We have not required manufacturers to warn about all foreseeable harms that might occur in the vicinity of their products. "From its inception, . . . strict liability has never been, and is not now, *absolute* liability. As has been repeatedly expressed, under strict liability the manufacturer does not thereby become the insurer of the safety of the product's user. [Citations.]" [Citation.]

We reaffirm that a product manufacturer generally may not be held strictly liable for harm caused by another manufacturer's product. The only exceptions to this rule arise when the defendant bears some direct responsibility for the harm, either because the defendant's own product contributed substantially to the harm or because the defendant participated substantially in creating a harmful combined use of the products. [Citation.]

The decision of the Court of Appeal is reversed, and the case is remanded for entry of a judgment of nonsuit in favor of defendants.

CASE 24-5

Failure to Warn
KELSO v. BAYER CORPORATION
United States Court of Appeals, Seventh Circuit, 2005
398 F.3d 640

Manion, J.
Ted Kelso sued Bayer Corporation for strict product liability, alleging that the warning Bayer provided on its Neo-Synephrine 12 Hour Extra Moisturizing Spray was defective. * * * Ted Kelso began using Neo-Synephrine 12 Hour Extra Moisturizing Spray in 1990. He used Neo-Synephrine continuously for

more than three years. After learning that his continued use of the product caused permanent nasal tissue damage requiring multiple sinus surgeries, he sued Bayer, the manufacturer of Neo-Synephrine, alleging Bayer failed to adequately warn him of the dangers associated with Neo-Synephrine.

Bayer moved for summary judgment, arguing that the warning it provided, as follows, was adequate, as a matter of law:

"Do not exceed recommended dosage."

* * *

"Stop use and ask a doctor if symptoms persist. Do not use this product for more than 3 days. Use only as directed. Frequent or prolonged use may cause nasal congestion to recur or worsen."

The district court agreed and granted Bayer summary judgment. Kelso appeals.

* * * Kelso argues that summary judgment was inappropriate because he presented sufficient evidence to recover in a product liability action against Bayer. "To recover in a product liability action, a plaintiff must plead and prove that the injury resulted from a condition of the product, that the condition was an unreasonably dangerous one, and that the condition existed at the time the product left the manufacturer's control." [Citation.] A product may be unreasonably dangerous because of a design defect, a manufacturing defect, "or a failure of a manufacturer to warn of a danger or instruct on the proper use of the product as to which the average consumer would not be aware." [Citation.]

Kelso claims the Neo-Synephrine was unreasonably dangerous because Bayer's warning was confusing as to whether or not the product could be used safely for more than three days, when such use was effective in relieving his congestion. * * * Kelso * * * interpreted the warning as meaning not to exceed three days use if the product failed to relieve the congestion;

he only needed to see a physician if the product did not work to relieve the congestion. Also, because the container included much more than three days' dosage, Kelso insists that he had good reason to believe that he could safely use Neo-Synephrine for more than three days.

However, Kelso's personal reaction to the warning is not the test. Whether a warning is sufficient "is determined using an objective standard, i.e., the awareness of an ordinary person." [Citation.] Here, the plain, clear and unambiguous language of the warning states, **"Do not use this product for more than 3 days."** Period. That the Neo-Synephrine container included doses sufficient to treat multiple users or multiple colds in no way takes away from the clear impact of the warning. Moreover, the warning clearly informs users to: **"Stop use and ask a physician if symptoms persist."** The warning was clear. Yet Kelso continued using the product well beyond the three days. It is unreasonable to create an ambiguity that excuses extended use when the warning against such use is unequivocal.

Kelso also argues that the warning was inadequate because it did not warn users that the product could also cause permanent nasal tissue damage and also had a risk of habituation (meaning that users would become dependent on the product, causing them to use the product for more than three days). However, under Illinois law, a manufacturer need not warn of all possible consequences of failing to follow a primary warning. [Citation.] Here, the primary warning told consumers **"not [to] use this product for more than 3 days."** That was sufficient under Illinois law. However, Bayer's warning went even further, informing consumers of the consequence of extended use, stating: **"[f]requent or prolonged use may cause nasal congestion to recur or worsen."** Although Kelso believes the warning should have provided him with more detailed information, Illinois law does not require more. [Citation.] Therefore, Kelso's defective warning claim fails.

| CASE 24-6 | Unreasonably Dangerous
GREENE v. BODDIE-NOELL ENTERPRISES, INC.
United States District Court, W.D. Virginia, 1997
966 F.Supp. 416 |  |

Jones, J.

In this products liability case, the plaintiff contends that she was badly burned by hot coffee purchased from the drive-through window of a fast food restaurant, when the coffee spilled on her after it had been handed to her by the driver of the vehicle. The defendant restaurant operator moves for summary judgment on the ground that the plaintiff cannot show a *prima facie* case of liability. I agree, and dismiss the case.

* * *

[Plaintiff, Katherine] Greene was a passenger in a car driven by her boyfriend, Chris Blevins, on the morning of December 31, 1994, when he purchased food and drink [coffees] from the drive-through window of the Hardee's restaurant in Wise, Virginia, operated by the defendant. * * * He immediately handed the food and beverages to Greene. The food was on a plate, and the beverages were in cups. Greene placed the plate on her lap and held a cup in each hand. According to Greene, the Styrofoam coffee cup was comfortable to hold, and had a lid on the top, although she did not notice whether the lid was fully attached.

Blevins drove out of the restaurant parking lot, and over a "bad dip" at the point at which the lot meets the road. When the front tires of the car went slowly across the dip, the coffee "splashed out" on Greene, burning her legs through her clothes. Blevins remembers Greene exclaiming, "the lid came off." She did not look at the cup until the coffee burned her, and does not know whether the cup was tilted in one direction or another when the coffee spilled out.

As soon as the coffee burned her, Greene threw the food and drink to the floor of the car, and in the process stepped on the coffee cup. When the cup was later retrieved from the floor of the car, the bottom of the cup was damaged, and the lid was at least partially off of the top of the cup.

After Greene was burned by the coffee, Blevins drove her to the emergency room of a local hospital, where she was treated. She missed eleven days of work, and suffered permanent scarring to her thighs.

Both Greene and Blevins testified that they had heard of the "McDonalds' coffee case" prior to this incident and Greene testified that while she was not a coffee drinker, she had been aware that if coffee spilled on her, it would burn her. After the accident, Greene gave a recorded statement to a representative of the defendant in which she stated, "I know the lid wasn't on there good. It came off too easy."

[Court's footnote: On August 17, 1994, a state court jury in Albuquerque, New Mexico, awarded 81-year-old Stella Liebeck $160,000 in compensatory damages and $2.7 million in punitive damages after she was burned by coffee purchased from a drive-through window at a McDonald's restaurant. The trial judge later reduced the punitive damages to $480,000, and the parties settled the case before an appeal. According to news reports, Mrs. Liebeck contended that for taste reasons, McDonald's served coffee about 20 degrees hotter than other fast-food restaurants and, in spite of numerous complaints, had made a conscious decision not to warn customers of the possibility of serious burns. The jury's verdict received worldwide attention. See Andrea Gerlin, A Matter of Degree: How a Jury Decided That One Coffee Spill Is Worth $2.9 Million, *Wall Street Journal*.]

* * *

To prove a case of liability in Virginia, a plaintiff must show that a product had a defect which rendered it unreasonably dangerous for ordinary or foreseeable use. [Citation.] In order to meet this burden, a plaintiff must offer proof that the product violated a prevailing safety standard, whether the standard comes from business, government or reasonable consumer expectation. [Citation.]

Here the plaintiff has offered no such proof. There is no evidence that either the heat of the coffee or the security of the coffee cup lid violated any applicable standard. Do other fast food restaurants serve coffee at a lower temperature, or with lids which will prevent spills even when passing over an obstruction in the road? Do customers expect cooler coffee, which may be less tasty, or cups which may be more secure, but harder to unfasten?

In fact, the plaintiff testified that she knew, and therefore expected, that the coffee would be hot enough to burn her if it spilled. While she also expressed the opinion that the cup lid was too loose, that testimony does not substitute for evidence of a generally applicable standard or consumer expectation, since "[the plaintiffs] subjective expectations are insufficient to establish what degree of protection * * * society expects from [the product]." [Citation.]

The plaintiff argues that the mere fact that she was burned shows that the product was dangerously defective, either by being too hot or by having a lid which came off unexpectedly. But it is settled in Virginia that the happening of an accident is not sufficient proof of liability, even in products cases. [Citation.] This is not like the case of a foreign substance being found in a soft drink bottle, where a presumption of negligence arises. [Citation.]

To be merchantable, a product need not be foolproof, or perfect. As one noted treatise has expressed, "[i]t is the lawyer's challenging job to define the term 'merchantability' in [the] case in some objective way so that the court or jury can make a determination whether that standard has been breached." [Citation.]

In the present case, there has been no showing that a reasonable seller of coffee would not conclude that the beverage must be sold hot enough to be palatable to consumers, even though it is hot enough to burn other parts of the body. A reasonable seller might also conclude that patrons desire coffee lids which prevent spillage in ordinary handling, but are not tight enough to avert a spill under other circumstances, such as when driving over a bump. It was the plaintiff's obligation to demonstrate that she had proof that the defendant breached a recognizable standard, and that such proof is sufficient to justify a verdict in her favor at trial. She has not done so, and accordingly the motion for summary judgment must be granted.

QUESTIONS

1. At the advent of the social season, Aunt Lavinia purchased a hula skirt in Sadie's dress shop. The salesclerk told her, "This superior garment will do things for a person." Aunt Lavinia's houseguest, her niece, Florabelle, asked and obtained her aunt's permission to wear the skirt to a masquerade ball. In the midst of the festivity, at which there was much dancing, drinking, and smoking, the long skirt brushed against a glimmering cigarette butt. Unknown to Aunt Lavinia and Florabelle, its wearer, the garment was made of a fine unwoven fiber that is highly flammable. It burst into flames, and Florabelle suffered severe burns. Aunt Lavinia notified Sadie of the accident and of Florabelle's intention to recover from Sadie. Can Florabelle recover damages from Sadie, the proprietor of the dress shop, and Exotic Clothes, Inc., the manufacturer from which Sadie purchased the skirt? Explain.

2. The Talent Company, manufacturer of a widely advertised and expensive perfume, sold a quantity of this product to Young, a retail druggist. Dentley and Bird visited Young's store and Dentley, desiring to make a gift to Bird, purchased from Young a bottle of this perfume, asking for it by its trade name. Young wrapped up the bottle and handed it directly to Bird. The perfume contained a foreign chemical that, upon the first use of the perfume by Bird, severely burned her face and caused a permanent facial disfigurement. What are the rights of Bird, if any, against Dentley, Young, and the Talent Company? Discuss.

3. John Doe purchased a bottle of "Bleach-All," a well-known brand, from Roe's combination service station and grocery store. When John used the "Bleach-All," his clothes deteriorated due to an error in mixing the chemicals during the detergent's manufacture. John brings an action against Roe to recover damages. Explain whether John will be successful in his lawsuit.

4. A route salesperson for Ideal Milk Company delivered a one-half-gallon glass jug of milk to Allen's home. The next day, when Allen grasped the milk container by its neck to take it out of his refrigerator, it shattered in his hand and caused serious injury. Allen paid Ideal on a monthly basis for the regular delivery of milk. Ideal's milk bottles each contained the legend "Property of Ideal—to be returned," and the route salesperson would pick up the empty bottles when he delivered milk. Can Allen recover damages from Ideal Milk Company? Why or why not?

5. While Butler and his wife, Wanda, were browsing through Sloan's used car lot, Butler told Sloan that he was looking for a safe but cheap family car. Sloan said, "That old Cadillac hearse ain't hurt at all, and I'll sell it to you for $6,950." Butler said, "I'll have to take your word for it because I don't know a thing about cars." Butler asked Sloan whether he would guarantee the car, and Sloan replied, "I don't guarantee used cars." Then Sloan added, "But I have checked that Caddy over, and it will run another 10,000 miles without needing any repairs." Butler replied, "It has to because I won't have an extra dime for any repairs." Butler made a down payment of $900 and signed a printed form contract furnished by Sloan, which contained a provision, "Seller does not warrant the condition or performance of any used automobile."

   As Butler drove the car out of Sloan's lot, the left rear wheel fell off, and Butler lost control of the vehicle. It veered over an embankment, causing serious injuries to Wanda. Explain what Sloan's liability is to Butler and Wanda?

6. John purchased for cash a Revenge automobile manufactured by Japanese Motors, Ltd., from an authorized franchised dealer in the United States. The dealer told John that the car had a "24-month, 24,000-mile warranty." Two days after John accepted delivery of the car, he received an eighty-page fine print manual that stated, among other things, on page 72:

   > The warranties herein are expressly in lieu of any other express or implied warranty, including any implied warranty of merchantability or fitness, and of any other obligation on the part of the company or the selling dealer.
   >
   > Japanese Motors, Ltd., and the selling dealer warrant to the owner each part of this vehicle to be free under use and service from defects in material and workmanship for a period of twenty-four months from the date of original retail delivery of first use, or until it has been driven for 24,000 miles, whichever first occurs.

   Within nine months after the purchase, John was forced to return the car for repairs to the dealer on thirty different occasions, and the car has been in the dealer's custody for more than seventy days during these nine months. The dealer has been forced to make major repairs to the engine, transmission, and steering assembly. The car is now in the custody of the dealer for further major repairs, and John has demanded that it keep the car and refund his entire purchase price. The dealer has refused on the ground that it has not breached its contract and is willing to continue repairing the car during the remainder of the "24-24" period. What are the rights and liabilities of the dealer and John? Discuss.

7. Fred Lyon of New York, while on vacation in California, rented a new model Home Run automobile from Hart's Drive-A-Car. The car was manufactured by the Dumars Motor Company and was purchased by Hart's from Jammer, Inc., an automobile importer. Lyon was driving the car on a street in San Jose when, due to a defect in the steering mechanism, it suddenly became impossible to steer. The speed of the car at the time was thirty miles per hour, but before Lyon could bring it to a stop, the car jumped a low curb and struck Peter Wolf, who was standing on the sidewalk, breaking both of his legs and causing other injuries. Explain what rights Wolf has against (a) Hart's Drive-A-Car, (b) Dumars Motor Company, (c) Jammer, and (d) Lyon.

8. The plaintiff brings this cause of action against a manufacturer for the loss of one leg below the hip. The leg was lost when caught in the gears of a screw auger machine sold and installed by the defendant. Shortly before the accident, the plaintiff's co-employees had removed a covering panel from the machine by use of sledgehammers and crowbars in order to do repair work. After finishing the repairs, they replaced the panel with a single piece of cardboard instead of restoring the equipment to its original condition. The plaintiff stepped on the cardboard in the course of his work and fell, catching his leg in the moving parts. Explain what causes of action the plaintiff may have against the defendant and what defenses the defendant could raise.

9. The plaintiff, while driving a van manufactured by the defendant, was struck in the rear by another motor vehicle. Upon impact, the plaintiff's head was jarred backward against the rear window of the cab, causing the plaintiff serious injury. The van was not equipped with a headrest, and none was required at the time. Should the plaintiff prevail on a cause of action based upon strict liability in tort? Why or why not?

10. The plaintiff, while dining at the defendant's restaurant, ordered a chicken potpie. While she was eating, she swallowed a sliver of chicken bone, which became lodged in her throat, causing her serious injury. The plaintiff brings a cause of action. Should she prevail? Why or why not?

11. Salem Supply Co. sells new and used gardening equipment. Ben Buyer purchased a slightly used riding lawn mower for $1,500. The price was considerably less than that of comparable used mowers. The sale was clearly indicated to be "as is." Two weeks after Ben purchased the mower, the police arrived at his house with Owen Owner, the true owner of the lawn mower, which had been stolen from his yard, and reclaimed the mower. What recourse, if any, does Ben have? Explain.

12. Seigel, a seventy-three-year-old man, was injured at one of Giant Food's retail food stores when a bottle of Coca-Cola exploded as he was placing a six-pack of Coke into his shopping cart. The explosion caused him to lose his balance and fall, injuring himself. Has Giant breached its implied warranty of merchantability to Seigel? Why or why not?

13. Guarino and two others (plaintiffs) died of gas asphyxiation and five others were injured when they entered a sewer tunnel without masks to answer the cries for help of their crew leader, Rooney. Rooney had left the sewer shaft and entered the tunnel to fix a water leakage problem. Having corrected the problem, Rooney was returning to the shaft when he apparently was overcome by gas because of a defect in his oxygen mask, which was manufactured by Mine Safety Appliance Company (defendant). Plaintiffs brought this action against the defendant for breach of warranty, and defendant raised the defense of plaintiffs' voluntary assumption of the risk. Explain who will prevail.

CASE PROBLEMS

14. Green Seed Company packaged, labeled, and marketed a quality tomato seed known as "Green's Pink Shipper" for commercial sale. Brown Seed Store, a retailer, purchased the seed from Green Seed and then sold it to Guy Jones, who was engaged in the business of growing tomato seedlings for sale to commercial tomato growers. Williams purchased the seedlings from Jones and then transplanted and raised them in accordance with accepted farming methods. The plants, however, produced not the promised "Pink Shipper" tomatoes but rather an inferior variety that spoiled in the field. Williams then brought an action against Green Seed for $900, claiming that his crop damage had been caused by Green Seed's breach of an express warranty. Green Seed argued in defense that its warranty did not extend to remote purchasers and that the company did not receive notice of the claimed breach of warranty. Who will prevail? Why?

15. Shell Oil Company leased to Flying Tiger Line a gasoline tank truck with a movable ladder for refueling certain types of aircraft. Under the terms of the lease, Flying Tiger was to maintain the equipment in safe operating order, but Shell was obligated to make most of the repairs at Flying Tiger's request. Four years after the lease was entered, Shell, at Flying Tiger's request, replaced the original ladder with a new one built by an undisclosed manufacturer. Both Flying Tiger and Shell inspected the new ladder. Two years later, however, Price, an aircraft mechanic employed by Flying Tiger, was seriously injured when the ladder's legs split while he was climbing onto an airplane wing. Explain what Price's rights are against Shell and Flying Tiger.

16. A gasoline-powered lawn mower that had been used earlier to cut grass was left unattended next to a water heater that had been manufactured by Sears. Expert testimony was presented to demonstrate that vapors from the mower's gas tank accumulated under the water heater and resulted in an explosion. Three-year-old Shawn Toups was injured as a result. Evidence was also presented negating any claim that Shawn had been handling the gasoline can located nearby or the lawn mower. He was not burned on the soles of his feet or the palms of his hands, and similarly, the gas can remained in an upright position even after the explosion. Is Sears liable to the Toups in strict product liability? Explain.

17. Mrs. Embs went into Stamper's Cash Market to buy soft drinks for her children. She removed five bottles from an upright soft drink cooler, placed them in a carton, and then turned to move away from the display when a bottle of 7Up in a carton at her feet exploded, cutting her leg. Apparently, several other bottles had exploded that same week. Stamper's Cash Market received its entire stock of 7Up from Arnold Lee Vice, the area distributor. Vice in turn received his entire stock of 7Up from Pepsi-Cola Bottling Co. Can Mrs. Embs recover damages from (a) Stamper, (b) Vice, or (c) Pepsi-Cola Bottling? Why or why not?

18. Catania wished to paint the exterior of his house. He went to Brown, a local paint store owner and asked him to recommend a paint for the job. Catania told Brown that the exterior walls were stucco and in a chalky, powdery condition. Brown suggested Pierce's shingle and shake paint. Brown then instructed Catania how to mix the paint and how to use a wire brush to prepare the surface. Five months later, the paint began to peel, flake, and blister. Catania brings an action against Brown. Decision?

19. Robinson, a truck driver for a moving company, decided to buy a used truck from the company. Branch, the owner, told Robinson that the truck was being repaired and that Robinson should wait and inspect the truck before signing the contract. Robinson, who had driven the truck before, felt that inspection was unnecessary. Again, Branch suggested Robinson wait to inspect the truck, and again Robinson declined. Branch then told Robinson he was buying the truck "as is." Robinson then signed the contract. After the truck broke down four times, Robinson sued. Discuss what defenses can Branch raise. Explain which party will be successful.s

20. Perfect Products manufactures balloons, which are then bought and resold by wholesale novelty distributors. Mego Corp. manufactures a doll called "Bubble Yum Baby." A balloon is inserted in the doll's mouth with a mouthpiece, and the doll's arm is pumped to inflate the balloon, simulating the blowing of a bubble. Mego Corp. used Perfect Products balloons in the dolls, bought through the independent distributors. Plaintiff's infant daughter died after swallowing a balloon removed from the doll. Is Perfect Products liable to plaintiff under a theory of strict liability? Explain.

21. Patient was injured when the footrest of an adjustable X-ray table collapsed, causing Patient to fall to the floor. G.E. manufactured the X-ray table and the footrest. At trial, evidence was introduced that G.E. had manufactured for several years another footrest model complete with safety latches. However, there was no evidence that the footrest involved was manufactured defectively. The action is based on a theory of strict liability. Who wins? Why?

22. Heckman, an employee of Clark Equipment Company, severely injured his left hand when he caught it in a power press that he was operating at work. The press was manufactured by Federal Press Company and sold to Clark. It could be operated either by hand controls that required the use of both hands away from the point of operation or by an optional foot pedal. When the foot pedal was used without a guard, nothing remained to keep the operator's hands from the point of operation. Federal Press did not provide safety appliances unless the customer requested them, but when it delivered the press to Clark with the optional pedal, it suggested that Clark install a guard. The press had a similar warning embossed on it. Clark did, in fact, purchase a guard for $100, but it was not mounted on the machine at the time of the injury, nor was it believed to be an effective safety device.

   Heckman argued that one type of guard, if installed, would have made the press safe in 95 percent of its customary uses. Federal, in turn, argued that the furnishing of guards was not customary in the industry, that the machine's many uses made it impracticable to design and install any one guard as standard equipment, that Clark's failure to obey Federal's warning was a superseding cause of the injury, and that state regulations placed responsibility for the safe operation of presses on employers and employees. The jury awarded Heckman $750,000, and Federal appealed. Decision?

23. Raymond and Sandra Duford purchased a wood-burning stove from Sears. The stove was manufactured by Preway, Inc. At trial, it was shown that Raymond had inadvertently installed the section of the chimney pipe that went through the roof upside down, and all parties agreed that such improper installation caused a fire that had destroyed the Dufords' house.

    At trial, the Dufords alleged, and Preway admitted, that there were no markings on the pipe indicating "which end was up." An expert for the Dufords then testified that the simple precaution of an embossed marking would have been satisfactory. Later, to the amazement of all the parties, a witness for Preway pointed out that the actual pipe in question had been marked with embossed letters. The pipe in fact had tiny letters spelling "UP" with two arrows pointed in the proper direction. Since no one on either side had noticed the letters except the one witness, the Dufords hastily changed their claim to that of inadequacy of the marking. Who will prevail? Why?

24. Vlases, a coal miner who had always raised small flocks of chickens, spent two years building a new two-story chicken coop large enough to house four thousand chickens. After its completion, he purchased two thousand two hundred one-day-old chicks from Montgomery Ward for the purpose of producing eggs for sale. He had selected them from Ward's catalog, which stated that these chicks, hybrid Leghorns, were noted for their excellent egg production. Vlases had equipped the coop with brand-new machinery and had taken further hygiene precautions for the chicks' health. Almost one month later, Vlases noticed that their feathers were beginning to fall off. A veterinarian's examination revealed signs of drug intoxication and hemorrhagic disease in a few of the chicks. Eight months later, it was determined that the chicks were suffering from visceral and ocular leucosis, or bird cancer, which reduced their egg-bearing capacity to zero. Avian leucosis may be transmitted either genetically or by unsanitary conditions. Subsequently, the disease infected the entire flock. Vlases then brought suit against Montgomery Ward for its breach of the implied warranties of merchantability and of fitness for a particular purpose. Ward claimed that there was no way to detect the disease in the one-day-old chicks, nor was

there medication available to prevent this disease from occurring. Is Montgomery Ward liable under a warranty and/or strict liability cause of action? Explain.

25. For more than forty years, Rose Cipollone smoked between one and two packs of cigarettes a day. Upon her death from lung cancer, Rose's husband, Antonio Cipollone, filed suit against Liggett Group, Inc., Lorillard, Inc., and Philip Morris, Inc., three of the leading firms in the tobacco industry, for the wrongful death of his wife. Many theories of liability and defenses were asserted in this decidedly complex and protracted litigation.

    One theory of liability claimed by Mr. Cipollone was breach of express warranty. It is uncontested that all three manufacturers ran multimedia ad campaigns that contained affirmations, promises, or innuendos that smoking cigarettes was safe. For example, ads for Chesterfield cigarettes boasted that a medical specialist could find no adverse health effects in subjects after six months of smoking. Chesterfields were also advertised as being manufactured with "electronic miracle" technology that made them "better and safer for you." Another ad stated that Chesterfield ingredients were tested and approved by scientists from leading universities. Another brand, L&M, publicly touted the "miracle tip" filter, claiming it was "just what the doctor ordered."

    At trial, the defendant tobacco companies were not permitted to try to prove that Mrs. Cipollone disbelieved or placed no reliance on the advertisements and their safety assurances. Did the defendants breach an express warranty to the plaintiff? Explain.

26. Trans-Aire International, Inc. (TAI) converts ordinary automotive vans into recreational vehicles. TAI had been installing carpet and ceiling fabrics in the converted vans with an adhesive made by the 3M Company. Unfortunately, during the hot summer months, the 3M adhesive would often fail to hold the carpet and fabrics in place.

    TAI contacted Northern Adhesive Company (Northern), seeking a "suitable" product to replace the 3M adhesive. Northern sent samples of several adhesives, commenting that hopefully one or more "might be applicable." Northern also informed TAI that one of the samples, Adhesive 7448, was a "match" for the 3M adhesive. After testing all the samples under cool plant conditions, TAI's chief engineer determined that Adhesive 7448 was better than the 3M adhesive. When TAI's president asked if the new adhesive should be tested under summer-like conditions, TAI's chief engineer responded that it was unnecessary to do so. The president then asked if Adhesive 7448 came with any warranties. A Northern representative stated that there were no warranties, except that the orders shipped would be identical to the sample.

After converting more than five hundred vans using Adhesive 7448, TAI became aware that high summer temperatures were causing the new adhesive to fail. Explain whether TAI should prevail against Northern in a suit claiming (a) breach of an implied warranty of fitness for a particular purpose, (b) breach of an implied warranty of merchantability, and (c) breach of express warranty.

27. The plaintiff's children purchased an Aero Cycle exercise bike for their mother to use in a weight-loss program. The Aero Cycle bike was manufactured by DP and purchased from Walmart. The first time the plaintiff, Judy Dunne, used the bike, she used it only for a few seconds. But the second time she used it, she pedaled for three or four rotations, after which the rear support strut failed and the bike collapsed under her. At the time of the accident, the plaintiff weighed between 450 and 500 pounds. She fell off the bike backward, struck her head on a nearby metal file cabinet, and was knocked unconscious. When the plaintiff regained consciousness, her mouth was bleeding and her neck, left shoulder, arm, leg, knee, and ankle were injured. The plaintiff was diagnosed as having a cervical strain and multiple contusions. She filed suit against Walmart and DP. Explain whether the plaintiff should prevail.

28. For sixteen years, Mrs. Dorothy Mae Palmer had been married to an insulator who worked with asbestos products. Mrs. Palmer was not exposed to asbestos dust in a factory setting; rather, she was exposed when her husband brought his work clothes home to be washed. Mrs. Palmer died of mesothelioma. This product liability suit was brought by Mrs. Palmer's daughters to recover for the alleged wrongful death of their mother. The daughters claim that Mrs. Palmer's mesothelioma was the result of exposure to asbestos-containing products manufactured by Owens Corning. The daughters claim that the asbestos products were defective and unreasonably dangerous and that Owens Corning was negligent in failing to warn of the dangers associated with its products. Explain whether the plaintiffs should prevail.

29. Raymond and Sandra Duford purchased a wood-burning stove from Sears. The stove was manufactured by Preway, Inc. At trial, it was shown that Raymond had inadvertently installed the section of the chimney pipe that went through the roof upside down, and all parties agreed that such improper installation caused a fire that had destroyed the Dufords' house.

At trial, the Dufords alleged, and Preway admitted, that there were no markings on the pipe indicating "which end should point up." An expert for the Dufords then testified that the simple precaution of an embossed marking would have been satisfactory. Later, a witness for Preway pointed out that the actual pipe in question had been marked with embossed letters. The pipe in fact had tiny letters spelling "UP," with two arrows pointed in the proper direction. Since no one on either side had noticed the letters except the one witness, the Dufords changed their claim to that of inadequate marking. Who will prevail? Why?

TAKING SIDES

Brian Felley purchased a used Ford Taurus from Thomas and Cheryl Singleton for $8,800. The car had one hundred and twenty-six thousand miles on it. After test driving the car, Felley discussed the condition of the car with Thomas Singleton, who informed Felley that the only thing known to be wrong with the car was that it had a noise in the right rear and that a grommet (a connector having to do with a strut) was bad or missing. Thomas told Felley that otherwise the car was in good condition. Nevertheless, Felley soon began experiencing problems with the car. On the second day that he owned the car, Felley noticed a problem with the clutch. Over the next few days, the clutch problem worsened and Felley was unable to shift the gears. Felley presented an invoice to Thomas showing that he paid $942.76 for the removal and repair of the car's clutch. In addition, the car developed serious brake problems within the first month that Felley owned it. Felley now contends that the Singletons breached their express warranty.

a. What arguments would support Felley's contention?

b. What arguments would support the claim by the Singletons that they had not given an express warranty?

c. What is the appropriate outcome? Explain.

CHAPTER 25

Sales Remedies

CHAPTER OUTCOMES

After reading and studying this chapter, you should be able to:

- Explain the goods-oriented remedies of the seller and the buyer.

- Explain the obligation-oriented remedies of the seller and the buyer.

- Explain the money-oriented damages of the seller and the buyer.

- Explain the "specific performance" remedies of the seller and the buyer.

- Describe the basic types of contractual provisions affecting remedies and the limitations that the Uniform Commercial Code imposes upon those provisions.

A contract for the sale of goods may require total performance at one time or part performance in stages, according to the agreement of the parties. At any stage, one of the parties may repudiate the contract, may become insolvent, or may breach the contract by failing to perform his obligations under it. In a sales contract, breach may consist of the seller's delivering defective goods, too few goods, the wrong goods, or no goods. The buyer may breach by not accepting conforming goods or by failing to pay for conforming goods that he has accepted. Breach may occur when the goods are in the possession of the seller, in the possession of a bailee, in transit to the buyer, or in the possession of the buyer.

Remedies, therefore, need to address not only the type of breach of contract but also the situation with respect to the goods. Consequently, the Uniform Commercial Code (UCC) provides distinct remedies for the seller and for the buyer, each specifically keyed to the factual situation.

In all events, the purpose of the Code is to put the aggrieved party in a position as good as the one he would have occupied had the other party fully performed. To accomplish this purpose, the Code has provided that its remedies should be liberally administered. Moreover, damages do not have to be "calculable with mathematical precision": they need only be proved with "whatever definiteness and accuracy the facts permit, but no more." Comment 1 to Section 1-106. The purpose of remedies under the Code is compensation; therefore, punitive damages generally are not available.

Finally, the Code has rejected the doctrine of election of remedies, essentially providing that remedies for breach are cumulative in nature. Whether one remedy bars another depends entirely on the facts of the individual case.

Practical Advice

Consider including in your contracts provisions for (1) the recovery of attorneys' fees in the event of breach of contract and (2) the arbitration of contract disputes.

CISG According to the United Nations Convention on Contracts for the International Sales of Goods (CISG), damages for breach of contract by one party consist of a sum equal to the loss, including loss of profit, suffered by the other party as a consequence of the breach. Such damages may not exceed the loss that the party in breach foresaw or should have foreseen at the time of the conclusion of the contract as a possible consequence of the breach of contract. The aggrieved party must take such measures as are reasonable in the circumstances to mitigate the loss, including loss of profit, resulting from the breach. If he fails to take such measures, the party in breach may claim a reduction in the damages in the amount by which the loss should have been mitigated.

25-1 Remedies of the Seller

A buyer's default in performing any of his contractual obligations deprives the seller of the rights for which he bargained. Such default may consist of any of the following acts: wrongfully rejecting the goods, wrongfully revoking acceptance of the goods, failing to make a payment due on or before delivery, or repudiating (indicating an intention not to perform) the contract in whole or in part. Section 2-703; Section 2A-523(1). The Code catalogs the seller's remedies for each of these defaults. Section 2-703. (Section 2A-523(1) contains a comparable set of remedies for the lessor.) These remedies allow the seller to—

1. withhold delivery of the goods;
2. stop delivery of the goods by a carrier or other bailee;
3. identify to the contract conforming goods not already identified;
4. resell the goods and recover damages;
5. recover damages for nonacceptance of the goods or repudiation of the contract;
6. recover the price;
7. recover incidental damages;
8. cancel the contract; and
9. reclaim the goods on the buyer's insolvency (Section 2-702).

Under Article 2A, a lessor also may recover compensation for any loss of or damage to the lessor's residual interest in the goods caused by the lessee's default. Section 2A-532.

The first three and the ninth remedies indexed above are *goods-oriented*—that is, they relate to the seller's exercising control over the goods. The fourth through seventh remedies are *money-oriented* because they provide the seller with the opportunity to recover monetary damages. The eighth remedy is *obligation-oriented* because it allows the seller to avoid his obligation under the contract.

Moreover, if the seller delivers goods on credit and the buyer fails to pay the price when due, the seller's sole remedy, unless the buyer is insolvent, is to sue for the unpaid price. If, however, the buyer received the goods on credit while insolvent, the seller may be able to reclaim the goods. The Code defines **insolvency** to include both its equity meaning and its bankruptcy meaning. Section 1-201(23); Revised Section 1-201(b)(23). The **equity** meaning of insolvency is the inability of a person to pay his debts in the ordinary course of business or as they become due. The **bankruptcy** meaning of insolvency is that total liabilities exceed the total value of all assets.

As noted previously, the Code's remedies are *cumulative*. Thus, by way of example, an aggrieved seller may (1) identify goods to the contract *and* (2) withhold delivery *and* (3) resell or recover damages for nonacceptance or recover the price *and* (4) recover incidental damages *and* (5) cancel the contract.

CISG If the buyer fails to perform any of her obligations under the contract or the CISG, the seller (1) may require the buyer to pay the price or (2) may fix an additional period of time of reasonable length for performance by the buyer of his obligations. Unless the seller has received notice from the buyer that she will not perform within the period so fixed, the seller may not, during that period, resort to any remedy for breach of contract. Moreover, if the buyer's breach is fundamental or the buyer fails to perform within the additional time granted by the seller, the seller may avoid the contract. In addition to these remedies, the seller also has the right to damages.

25-1a WITHHOLD DELIVERY OF THE GOODS

A seller may withhold delivery of goods to a buyer who has wrongfully rejected or revoked acceptance of the goods, who has failed to make a payment due on or before delivery, or who has repudiated the contract. Section 2-703; Section 2A-523(1). This right is essentially that of a seller to withhold or discontinue performance of her side of the contract because of the buyer's breach.

In cases in which the contract calls for installments, any breach of an installment that impairs the value of the *whole* contract will permit the seller to withhold the entire undelivered balance of the goods. In addition, upon discovery of the buyer's insolvency, the seller may refuse to deliver the goods except for cash, including payment for all goods previously delivered under the contract. Section 2-702. (Section 2A-525(1) is similar.)

25-1b STOP DELIVERY OF THE GOODS

An extension of the right to withhold delivery is the right of an aggrieved seller to stop the delivery of goods in transit to the buyer or in the possession of a bailee. A seller who discovers that the buyer is insolvent may stop *any* delivery. If the buyer is not insolvent but repudiates or otherwise breaches the contract, the seller may stop carload, truckload, planeload, or larger shipments. Section 2-705(1); Section 2A-526(1). To stop delivery, the seller must notify the carrier or other bailee soon enough for the bailee to prevent delivery of the goods. After this notification, the carrier or bailee must hold and deliver the goods according to the directions of the seller, who is liable to the carrier or bailee for any charges or damages incurred. If a negotiable document of title has been issued for the goods, the bailee need not obey a notification until the document is provided. Section 2-705(3).

The seller's right to stop delivery ceases when (1) the buyer receives the goods; (2) the bailee of the goods, except a carrier, acknowledges to the buyer that he holds them for the buyer; (3)

the carrier acknowledges to the buyer that he holds them for the buyer by reshipment or as warehouseman; or (4) a negotiable document of title covering the goods is negotiated to the buyer. Section 2-705(2); Section 2A-526(2) is similar.

25-1c IDENTIFY GOODS TO THE CONTRACT

Upon a breach of the contract by the buyer, the seller may proceed to identify to the contract conforming goods in her possession or control that were not so identified at the time she learned of the breach. Section 2-704(1); Section 2A-524(1). This enables the seller to exercise the remedy of resale of goods (discussed in the next section). Furthermore, the seller may resell any unfinished goods demonstrably intended to fulfill the particular contract. The seller may either complete the manufacture of unfinished goods and identify them to the contract or cease their manufacture and resell the unfinished goods for scrap or salvage value. Section 2-704(2); Section 2A-524(2). In so deciding, the seller must exercise reasonable commercial judgment to minimize her loss.

25-1d RESELL THE GOODS AND RECOVER DAMAGES

Under the same circumstances that permit the seller to withhold delivery of goods to the buyer (i.e., wrongful rejection or revocation, repudiation, or failure to make timely payment), the seller may resell the goods or the undelivered balance. If the resale is made in good faith and is commercially reasonable, the seller may recover from the buyer the difference between the contract price and the resale price, plus any incidental damages (discussed in a subsequent section), minus expenses saved because of the buyer's breach. Section 2-706(1). For example, Floyd agrees to sell goods to Beverly for a contract price of $80,000 due on delivery. Beverly wrongfully rejects the goods and refuses to pay Floyd anything. Floyd resells the goods in strict compliance with the Code for $60,000, incurring incidental damages for sales commissions of $5,000 but saving $2,000 in transportation costs. Floyd would recover from Beverly the difference between the contract price ($80,000) and the resale price ($60,000), plus incidental damages ($5,000), minus expenses saved ($2,000), which equals $23,000.

In a lease, the comparable recovery is the **difference between the present values** of the **old rent** due under the original lease and the **new rent** due under the new lease. More specifically, the lessor may recover (1) the accrued and unpaid rent as of the date of commencement of the new lease; (2) *plus* the present value as of that date of total rent for the then-remaining term of the original lease minus the present value, as of the same date, of the rent under the new lease applicable to a comparable time period; (3) *plus* any incidental damages; (4) *minus* expenses saved because of the lessee's breach. Section 2A-527(2).

The resale may be a public or private sale, and the goods may be sold as a unit or in parcels. The goods resold must be identified as those related to the contract, but where an anticipatory repudiation has occurred, for example, the goods need be neither in existence nor identified to the contract before the buyer's breach. Section 2-706(2).

When the resale is at a private sale, the seller must give the buyer reasonable notice of his intention to resell. Section 2-706(3). The seller or a broker may carry out a private sale by negotiations or solicitations. When the resale is at a public sale (such as an auction), only identified goods can be sold, except where a recognized market exists for a public sale of future goods of the kind involved. The public sale must be made at a usual place or market for public sale, if one is reasonably available, and the seller must give the buyer reasonable notice of the time and place of the resale unless the goods are perishable or threaten to decline in value speedily. Prospective bidders must be given an opportunity for reasonable inspection of the goods before the sale. Moreover, the seller may be a purchaser of the goods at the public sale. Section 2-706(4). In choosing between a public and private sale, the seller must observe relevant trade practices and usages and take into account the character of the goods.

The seller is not accountable to the buyer for any profit made on any resale of the goods. Section 2-706(6); Section 2A-527(5). Moreover, *a bona fide* purchaser at a resale takes the goods free of any rights of the original buyer, even if the seller has failed to comply with one or more of the requirements of the Code in making the resale. Section 2-706(5); Section 2A-524(4).

Failure to act in good faith and in a commercially reasonable manner deprives the seller of this remedy and relegates him to the remedy of recovering damages for nonacceptance or repudiation (discussed in the next section). Section 2-706, Comment 2; Section 2A-527(3).

CISG If the contract is avoided and the seller has resold the goods in a reasonable manner and within a reasonable time after avoidance, he may recover the difference between the contract price and the resale price. In addition, he may recover consequential damages.

25-1e RECOVER DAMAGES FOR NONACCEPTANCE OR REPUDIATION

In the event of the buyer's wrongful rejection or revocation, repudiation, or failure to make timely payment, the seller may recover damages from the buyer equal to the **difference between the unpaid contract price and the market price** at the time and place of tender of the goods, plus incidental damages, less expenses saved because of the buyer's breach. Section 2-708(1). This remedy is an alternative to the remedy of reselling the goods.

In a lease, the comparable recovery is the **difference between the present values** of the **old rent due** under the original lease and the **market rent**. Section 2A-528(1).

For example, Joan in Seattle agrees to sell goods to Nelson in Chicago for $20,000 F.O.B. (free on board) Chicago, with delivery by June 15. Nelson wrongfully rejects the goods. The market price would be ascertained as of June 15 in Chicago because F.O.B. Chicago is a destination contract in which the place of tender would be Chicago. The market price of the goods on June 15 in Chicago is $15,000. Joan, who incurred $1,000 in incidental expenses while saving $500 in expenses, would recover from Nelson the difference between the contract price ($20,000) and the market price ($15,000), plus incidental damages ($1,000), minus expenses saved ($500), which equals $5,500.

If the difference between the contract price and the market price will not place the seller in as good a position as performance would have, then the measure of damages is the **lost profit**; that is, the profit, including reasonable overhead, that the seller would have realized from full performance by the buyer, plus any incidental damages, minus expenses saved because of the buyer's breach. Section 2-708(2). For example, Green, an automobile dealer, enters into a contract to sell a large, fuel-inefficient luxury car to Holland for $22,000. The price of gasoline increases 20 percent, and Holland repudiates. The market value of the car is still $22,000, but because Green cannot sell as many cars as he can obtain, his sales volume has decreased by one as a result of Holland's breach. Therefore, Green would be permitted to recover the profits he lost on the sale to Holland (computed as the contract price minus what the car cost Green, plus an allocation of overhead), plus any incidental damages.

Article 2A has a comparable provision, except the profit is reduced to its present value as the lessor would have received it over the term of the lease. Section 2A-528(2).

Practical Advice

Carefully consider whether you are better off reselling the goods or seeking damages for nonacceptance or repudiation.

CISG If the contract is avoided and the seller has not made a resale, she may recover the difference between the contract price and the current price at the time of avoidance and at the place where delivery of the goods should have been made. In addition, she may recover consequential damages.

◆ *See Case 25-1*

25-1f RECOVER THE PRICE

The Code permits the seller to recover the price plus incidental damages in only three situations: (1) when the buyer has accepted the goods, (2) when conforming goods have been lost or damaged after the risk of loss has passed to the buyer, and (3) when the goods have been identified to the contract and there is no ready market available for their resale at a reasonable price. Section 2-709(1). For example, Kelly, in accordance with her agreement with Sally, prints ten thousand letterheads and envelopes with Sally's name and address on them. Sally wrongfully rejects the stationery, which Kelly is unable to resell at a reasonable price. Kelly is entitled to recover the price plus incidental damages from Sally.

Article 2A has a similar provision except that the lessor is entitled to (1) accrued and unpaid rent as of the date of the judgment, (2) the present value as of the judgment date of the rent for the then remaining lease term, and (3) incidental damages minus expenses saved. Section 2A-529(1).

A seller who sues for the price must hold for the buyer any goods identified to the contract that are still in her control. Section 2-709(2); Section 2A-529(2). If resale becomes possible, the seller may resell the goods at any time prior to the collection of the judgment, and the net proceeds of such resale must be credited to the buyer. Payment of the judgment entitles the buyer to any goods not resold. Section 2-709(2). In a lease, payment of the judgment entitles the lessee to the use and possession of the goods for the remaining lease term. Section 2A-529(4).

CISG The seller may require the buyer to pay the price, take delivery, or perform her other obligations, unless the seller has resorted to a remedy that is inconsistent with this requirement.

25-1g RECOVER INCIDENTAL DAMAGES

In addition to recovering damages for the difference between the contract price and the resale price, recovering damages for nonacceptance or repudiation, or recovering the price, the seller may in the same action recover her incidental damages to recoup expenses she reasonably incurred as a result of the buyer's breach. Section 2-710 defines a seller's **incidental damages** as follows:

Incidental damages to an aggrieved seller include any commercially reasonable charges, expenses or commissions incurred in stopping delivery, in the transportation, care and custody of goods after the buyer's breach, in connection with return or resale of the goods or otherwise resulting from the breach.

Section 2A-530 has an analogous definition.

Practical Advice

As an aggrieved seller, maintain good records regarding incidental damages you incurred.

25-1h CANCEL THE CONTRACT

Where the buyer wrongfully rejects or revokes acceptance of the goods, fails to make a payment due on or before delivery, or repudiates the contract in whole or in part, the seller may cancel the contract with respect to the goods directly affected. If the breach is of an installment contract and it substantially impairs the whole contract, the seller may cancel the entire contract. Section 2-703(f); Section 2A-523(1)(a).

The Code defines **cancellation** as one party's putting an end to the contract by reason of a breach by the other. Section 2-106(4); Section 2A-103(1)(b). The obligation of the canceling party for any future performance under the contract is discharged, although she retains any remedy for breach of the whole contract or any unperformed balance. Section 2-720; Section 2A-505(1). Thus, if the seller has the right to cancel, she may recover damages for breach without having to tender any further performance.

CISG The seller may declare the contract avoided if (1) the buyer commits a fundamental breach or (2) the buyer does not, within the additional period of time fixed by the seller, perform his obligation to pay the price or take delivery of the goods. Avoidance of the contract releases both parties from their obligations under it, subject to any damages that may be due. Avoidance does not affect any provision of the contract for the settlement of disputes or any other provision of the contract governing the rights and obligations of the parties consequent upon the avoidance of the contract. A party who has performed the contract either wholly or in part may claim restitution from the other party. If both parties are bound to make restitution, they must do so concurrently.

APPLYING THE LAW — Sales Remedies

FACTS TRAC is a wholesaler of computer hardware component parts. In late February, TRAC entered into a sales contract with Gemini, a small manufacturer of custom personal computers, for the sale of $10,000 worth of component parts. The written agreement required Gemini to pay $2,000 on April 15, another $3,000 on May 15, and the remaining $5,000 on June 15, with delivery of all components to Gemini's warehouse on or before May 30.

Gemini paid the $2,000 in March but was unable to make the second deposit payment of $3,000 on May 15. Soon thereafter, TRAC returned Gemini's $2,000 and notified Gemini in writing that it "considered the contract canceled" and "did not intend to perform any part of the February contract." The price of the component parts began to increase steadily in early March, and the goods can now be sold for 25 percent more.

ISSUE What are TRAC's rights and obligations under this sales contract?

RULE OF LAW A buyer who fails to make a payment due on or before delivery is in default. When faced with a buyer's default, the seller has goods-oriented, money-oriented, and obligation-oriented remedies available to it, all of which are cumulative to the extent they apply. Goods-oriented remedies include identifying the goods to the contract; withholding or stopping delivery of the goods; or if the buyer is insolvent, reclaiming the goods. The seller's money-oriented remedies involve recovery of (1) damages after a commercially reasonable resale, (2) damages for nonacceptance, or (3) the contract price and incidental and consequential damages. If the goods are resold at a profit to the seller, however, he need not account to the buyer for it. The seller's obligation-oriented remedy is cancellation, which discharges the seller from any further obligation under the contract.

APPLICATION Two of the four goods-oriented remedies are available to TRAC. It may both identify the goods to the contract, if it has not already done so, and withhold their delivery to Gemini. Neither of the other two goods-oriented remedies—stoppage in transit or reclamation—has any application here because the goods have not yet left TRAC's possession. Withholding delivery of the goods and identifying them to the contract enables TRAC to exercise its remedy of resale of the goods, which under current market conditions would yield a higher price than what Gemini had agreed to pay. As long as TRAC's incidental damages, or reasonable costs of such a sale, do not exceed the profit TRAC makes when it resells the goods, TRAC has suffered no damages. After returning Gemini's $2,000 deposit, TRAC has exercised its remaining Code remedy, the obligation-oriented remedy of cancellation. Cancellation effectively discharges TRAC of any further obligation to Gemini.

CONCLUSION TRAC may (1) withhold delivery of the goods to Gemini; (2) identify them to the contract; (3) resell them in a commercially reasonable manner, resulting here in a profit for which it is not accountable to Gemini; *and* (4) cancel the contract, resulting in a discharge of TRAC's performance under the contract.

25-1i RECLAIM THE GOODS ON THE BUYER'S INSOLVENCY

In addition to the right of an unpaid seller to withhold and stop delivery of the goods, he may reclaim them from an insolvent buyer by demand upon the buyer within ten days after the buyer has received the goods. Section 2-702(2). In cases in which, however, the buyer has committed fraud by misrepresenting her solvency to the seller in writing within three months prior to delivery of the goods, the ten-day limitation does not apply.

The seller's right to reclaim the goods is subject to the rights of a buyer in the ordinary course of business or to the rights of any other good faith purchaser. Furthermore, upon reclaiming the goods from an insolvent buyer, the seller is excluded from all other remedies with respect to those goods. Section 2-702(3).

A lessor retains title to the goods and therefore has the right to recover possession of them upon default by the lessee. Section 2A-525(2).

Practical Advice

If you wish to exercise the seller's rights of reclamation of goods sold, you will need to act quickly.

◆ SEE FIGURE 25-1: *Remedies of the Seller*

25-2 Remedies of the Buyer

Basically, a seller may default in three ways: he may repudiate, he may fail to deliver the goods, or he may deliver or tender goods that do not conform to the contract. Section 2-711; Section 2A-508. The Code provides remedies for each of these breaches. Some remedies are available for all three types; others are not. Moreover, the availability of some remedies depends on the buyer's actions. For example, if the seller tenders nonconforming goods, the buyer may reject or accept them. If the buyer rejects them, he can choose from a number of remedies. On the other hand, if the buyer accepts the nonconforming goods and does not justifiably revoke his acceptance, he limits himself to recovering damages.

In cases in which the seller fails to make delivery or repudiates or in which the buyer rightfully rejects or justifiably revokes acceptance, the buyer may, with respect to any goods involved or with respect to the whole if the breach goes to the whole contract, (1) cancel *and* (2) recover payments made. In addition, the buyer may (3) "cover" and obtain damages *or* (4) recover damages for nondelivery. In cases in which the seller fails to deliver or repudiates, the buyer, when appropriate, may also (5) recover identified goods if the seller is insolvent *or* (6) replevy the goods *or* (7) obtain specific performance. Moreover, upon rightful rejection or justifiable revocation of acceptance, the buyer (8) has a security interest in the goods. In cases in which the buyer has accepted goods and notified the seller of their

FIGURE 25-1 Remedies of the Seller

Buyer's Breach	Seller's Remedies		
	Obligation-Oriented	Goods-Oriented*	Money-Oriented**
Buyer Wrongfully Rejects Goods	Cancel	Withhold delivery of goods Stop delivery of goods in transit Identify conforming goods to the contract	Resell and recover damages Recover difference between unpaid contract and market prices or lost profits Recover price
Buyer Wrongfully Revokes Acceptance	Cancel	Withhold delivery of goods Stop delivery of goods in transit Identify conforming goods to the contract	Resell and recover damages Recover difference between unpaid contract and market prices or lost profits Recover price
Buyer Fails to Make Payment	Cancel	Withhold delivery of goods Stop delivery of goods in transit Identify conforming goods to the contract Reclaim goods upon buyer's insolvency	Resell and recover damages Recover difference between unpaid contract and market prices or lost profits Recover price
Buyer Repudiates	Cancel	Withhold delivery of goods Stop delivery of goods in transit Identify conforming goods to the contract	Resell and recover damages Recover difference between unpaid contract and market prices or lost profits Recover price

*In a lease, the lessor has the right to recover possession of the goods upon default by the lessee.
**In a lease, the lessor's recovery of damages for future rent payments is reduced to their present value.

nonconformity, the buyer may (9) recover damages for breach of warranty. Finally, in addition to the remedies listed above, the buyer may, when appropriate, (10) recover incidental damages and (11) recover consequential damages. Article 2A provides for essentially the same remedies for the lessee. Section 2A-508.

The first of these remedies is *obligation-oriented*, the second through fourth and ninth through eleventh are *money-oriented*, and the fifth through eighth are *goods-oriented*.

The buyer may deduct from the price due any damages resulting from any breach of contract by the seller. The buyer must, however, give notice to the seller of her intention to withhold such damages from payment of the price due. Section 2-717; Section 2A-508(6).

CISG If the seller fails to perform any of his obligations under the contract or the CISG, the buyer (1) may require the seller to perform his contractual obligations or (2) may fix an additional period of time of reasonable length for performance by the seller of his obligations. Unless the buyer has received notice from the seller that he will not perform within the period so fixed, the buyer may not, during that period, resort to any remedy for breach of contract. Moreover, if the seller's breach is fundamental or the seller fails to perform within the additional time granted by the buyer, the buyer may avoid the contract. In addition to these remedies, the buyer also has the right to damages. If the goods do not conform with the contract, the buyer may reduce the price in the same proportion as the value that the goods actually delivered had at the time of the delivery bears to the value that conforming goods would have had at that time.

25-2a CANCEL THE CONTRACT

In cases in which the seller fails to make delivery or repudiates the contract or in which the buyer rightfully rejects or justifiably revokes acceptance of goods tendered or delivered to him, the buyer may cancel the contract with respect to any goods involved, and if the breach by the seller concerns the whole contract, the buyer may cancel the entire contract. Section 2-711(1); Section 2A-508(1)(a). The buyer, who must give the seller notice of his cancellation, is excused from further performance or tender on his part. Section 2-106; Section 2A-505(1).

CISG The buyer may declare the contract avoided if (1) the seller commits a fundamental breach or (2) the seller does not deliver the goods within the additional period of time fixed by the buyer. Avoidance of the contract releases both parties from their obligations under it, subject to any damages that may be due. Avoidance does not affect any provision of the contract for the settlement of disputes or any other provision of the contract governing the rights and obligations of the parties consequent upon the avoidance of the contract. A party who has performed the contract either wholly or in part may claim restitution from the other party. If both parties are bound to make restitution, they must do so concurrently.

25-2b RECOVER PAYMENTS MADE

The buyer, upon the seller's breach, also may recover as much of the price as he has paid. Section 2-711(1). For example, Jonas and Sheila enter into a contract for a sale of goods for a contract price of $3,000, and Sheila, the buyer, has made a down payment of $600. Jonas delivers nonconforming goods to Sheila, who rightfully rejects them. Sheila may cancel the contract and recover the $600 plus whatever other damages she can prove. Under Article 2A, the lessee may recover so much of the rent and security as has been paid and is just under the circumstances. Section 2A-508(1)(b).

25-2c COVER

Upon the seller's breach, the buyer may protect himself by obtaining cover. Cover means that the buyer may in good faith and without unreasonable delay proceed to purchase needed goods or make a contract to purchase such goods in substitution for those due under the contract from the seller. Section 2-712(1). In a lease, the lessee may purchase or lease substitute goods. Section 2A-518(1).

On making a reasonable contract of cover, the buyer may recover from the seller the **difference between the cost of cover and the contract price**, plus any incidental and consequential damages (discussed in the following section), minus expenses saved because of the seller's breach. Section 2-712(2). For example, Doug, whose factory is in Oakland, agrees to sell goods to Velda, in Atlanta, for $22,000 F.O.B. Oakland. Doug fails to deliver, and Velda covers by purchasing substitute goods in Atlanta for $25,000, incurring $700 in sales commissions but suffering no other damages as a consequence of Doug's breach. Shipping costs from Oakland to Atlanta for the goods are $1,300. Velda would recover the difference between the cost of cover ($25,000) and the contract price ($22,000), plus incidental damages ($700 in sales commissions), plus consequential damages ($0 in this example), minus expenses saved ($1,300 in shipping costs that Velda need not pay under the contract of cover), which equals $2,400.

In a lease, the comparable recovery is the **difference between the present values** of the **new rent** due under the new lease and the **old rent** due under the original lease. Section 2A-518(2).

The buyer is not required to obtain cover, and his failure to do so does not bar him from any other remedy the Code provides. Section 2-712 (3); 2A-519(1). The buyer may not, however, recover consequential damages that he could have prevented by cover. Section 2-715(2)(a); Section 2A-520(2)(a).

CISG If the contract is avoided and the buyer has bought goods in replacement in a reasonable manner and within a reasonable time after avoidance, she may recover the difference between the contract price and the price paid in the substitute transaction. In addition, she may recover consequential damages.

◆ *See Case 25-2*

25-2d RECOVER DAMAGES FOR NONDELIVERY OR REPUDIATION

If the seller repudiates the contract or fails to deliver the goods or if the buyer rightfully rejects or justifiably revokes acceptance of the goods, the buyer is entitled to recover damages from the seller equal to the **difference between** the **market price** at the time when the buyer learned of the breach and the contract price, together with incidental and consequential damages, minus expenses saved because of the seller's breach. Section 2-713(1). This remedy is a complete alternative to the remedy of cover and, as such, is available only to the extent the buyer has not covered. As previously indicated, the buyer who elects this remedy may not recover consequential damages that she could have avoided by cover.

In a lease, the comparable recovery is the difference between the present values of the market rent and the old rent due under the original lease. Section 2A-519(1).

The market price is to be determined either as of the place for tender or, in the event the buyer has rightfully rejected the goods or has justifiably revoked his acceptance of them, as of the place of arrival. Section 2-713(2). For example, Janet, in Portland, agrees to sell goods to Laura, in Minneapolis, for $7,000 C.O.D. (collect on delivery), with delivery by November 15. Janet fails to deliver. As a consequence, Laura suffers incidental damages of $1,500 and consequential damages of $1,000. In the case of nondelivery or repudiation, market price is determined as of the place of tender. Because C.O.D. is a shipment contract, the place of tender would be the seller's city. Therefore, the market price must be the market price in Portland, the seller's city, on November 15, the date when Laura learned of the breach. At this time and place, the market price is $8,000. Laura would recover the difference between the market price ($8,000) and the contract price ($7,000), plus incidental damages ($1,500), plus consequential damages ($1,000), minus expenses saved ($0 in this example), which equals $3,500.

In the previous example, if Janet had instead delivered nonconforming goods that Laura rejected, then the market price would be determined at Laura's place of business in Minneapolis. If Janet had repudiated the contract on November 1 rather than November 15, then the market price would be determined as of November 1.

In a lease, market rent is to be determined as of the place for tender or, in cases of rejection after arrival or revocation of acceptance, as of the place of arrival. Section 2A-519(2).

Practical Advice
Carefully consider whether you are better off covering or seeking damages for nondelivery or repudiation.

CISG If the contract is avoided and the buyer has not made a replacement purchase, he may recover the difference between the contract price and the current price at the time of avoidance and at the place where delivery of the goods should have been made. In addition, he may recover consequential damages.

25-2e RECOVER IDENTIFIED GOODS ON THE SELLER'S INSOLVENCY

In cases in which existing goods are identified to the contract of sale, the buyer acquires a *special property interest* in the goods. Section 2-501. This special property interest exists even though the goods are nonconforming, and the buyer therefore has the right to return or reject them. Either the buyer or the seller may identify the goods to the contract.

The Code gives the buyer a right, which does not exist at common law, to recover from an insolvent seller the goods in which the buyer has a special property interest and for which he has paid part or all of the price. This right exists in cases in which the seller, who is in possession or control of the goods, becomes insolvent within ten days after receiving the first installment of the price. To exercise this right, the buyer must tender to the seller any unpaid portion of the price. If the special property interest exists by reason of an identification made by the buyer, he may recover the goods only if they conform to the contract for sale. Section 2-502; Section 2A-522.

25-2f SUE FOR REPLEVIN

Replevin is an action at law to recover from a defendant's possession specific goods that are being unlawfully withheld from the plaintiff. In cases in which the seller has repudiated or breached the contract, the buyer may maintain against the seller an action for replevin for goods that have been identified to the contract if the buyer after a reasonable effort is unable to effect cover for such goods. Section 2-716(3); Section 2A-521(3). Article 2 also provides the buyer with the right to replevin if the goods have been shipped under reservation of a security interest in the seller and satisfaction of this security interest has been made or tendered. Section 2-716(3).

25-2g SUE FOR SPECIFIC PERFORMANCE

Specific performance is an equitable remedy compelling the party in breach to perform the contract according to its terms. At common law, specific performance is available only if legal remedies are inadequate. For example, where the contract is for the purchase of a unique item, such as a work of art, a famous racehorse, or an heirloom, money damages may not be an adequate remedy. In such a case, a court of equity has the discretion to order the seller specifically to deliver to the buyer the goods described in the contract upon payment of the price.

The Code not only has continued the availability of specific performance but also has sought to encourage a more liberal attitude toward its use. Accordingly, it does not expressly require that the remedy at law be inadequate. Instead, the Code states that specific performance may be granted where "the goods are unique or in other proper circumstances." Section 2-716(1); Section 2A-521(1). As the Comment to Section 2-716 explains, the test of uniqueness under the Code must be made in view of the total situation that characterizes the contract.

CISG The buyer may require the seller to perform his contractual obligations. If the goods do not conform to the contract and the nonconformity constitutes a fundamental breach of contract, the buyer may require delivery of substitute goods. If the goods do not conform to the contract, the buyer may require the seller to remedy the lack of conformity by repair, unless this is unreasonable having regard to all the circumstances. Nevertheless, a court is not bound to enter a judgment for specific performance unless a court would do so under its own law in respect of similar contracts of sale not governed by the CISG.

25-2h ENFORCE A SECURITY INTEREST IN THE GOODS

A buyer who has rightfully rejected or justifiably revoked acceptance of goods that remain in his possession or control has a security interest in these goods to the extent of any payment of the price that he has made and for any expenses he reasonably has incurred in their inspection, receipt, transportation, care, and custody. The buyer may hold such goods and resell them in the same manner as an aggrieved seller may resell goods. Section 2-711(3); Section 2A-508(5). In the event of resale, the buyer is accountable to the seller for any amount of the net proceeds of the resale that exceeds the amount of his security interest. Section 2-706(6); Section 2A-527(5).

25-2i RECOVER DAMAGES FOR BREACH IN REGARD TO ACCEPTED GOODS

In cases in which the buyer has accepted nonconforming goods and has timely notified the seller of the breach of contract, the buyer is entitled to recover from the seller the damages resulting in the ordinary course of events from the seller's breach, as determined in any reasonable manner. Section 2-714(1); Section 2A-519(3). Where appropriate, the buyer may also recover incidental and consequential damages. Section 2-714(3); Section 2A-519(3). Nonconformity includes breaches of warranty as well

as any failure of the seller to perform according to her obligations under the contract. Thus, even if a seller cures a nonconforming tender, the buyer may recover under this section for any injury he suffered because the original tender was nonconforming.

In the event of breach of warranty, the measure of damages is the **difference** at the time and place of acceptance **between the value of the goods that have been accepted** and the **value** that the goods would have had if they had been **as warranted**, unless special circumstances show proximate damages of a different amount. Section 2-714(2). Article 2A has a comparable provision, except the recovery is for the **present value** of the difference between the value of the use of the goods accepted and the value if they had been as warranted for the lease term. Section 2A-519(4).

The contract price of the goods does not figure in this computation because the buyer is entitled to the benefit of his bargain, which is to receive goods that are as warranted. For example, Max agrees to sell goods to Stanley for $1,000. The value of the goods accepted is only $800; had they been as warranted, their value would have been $1,200. Stanley's damages for breach of warranty are $400, which he may deduct from any unpaid balance due on the purchase price upon notice to Max of his intention to do so. Section 2-717; Section 2A-508(6).

♦ *See Case 25-3*

25-2j RECOVER INCIDENTAL DAMAGES

In addition to remedies such as covering, recovering damages for nondelivery or repudiation, or recovering damages for breach in regard to accepted goods, including breach of warranty, the buyer may recover **incidental damages**. A buyer's incidental damages provide reimbursement for the buyer who incurs reasonable expenses in handling rightfully rejected goods or in effecting cover. Section 2-715(1) of the Code defines the buyer's incidental damages as follows:

> Incidental damages resulting from the seller's breach include expenses reasonably incurred in inspection, receipt, transportation and care and custody of goods rightfully rejected, any commercially reasonable charges, expenses or commissions in connection with effecting cover and any other reasonable expense incident to the delay or other breach.

Article 2A has an analogous definition. Section 2A-520(1).

For example, the buyer of a racehorse who justifiably revokes acceptance because the horse does not conform to the contract will be allowed to recover as incidental damages the cost of caring for the horse from the date the horse was delivered until the buyer returns it to the seller.

25-2k RECOVER CONSEQUENTIAL DAMAGES

In many cases, the buyer's remedies, previously discussed, will not fully compensate the aggrieved buyer for her losses. For example, nonconforming goods that are accepted may in some way damage or destroy the buyer's warehouse and its contents, or undelivered goods may have been the subject of a lucrative contract of resale, the profits from which are now lost. The Code responds to this problem by providing the buyer with the opportunity to recover **consequential damages** resulting from the seller's breach, including (1) any loss resulting from the buyer's requirements and needs of which the seller at the time of contracting had reason to know and which the buyer could not reasonably prevent by cover or otherwise and (2) injury to person or property proximately resulting from any breach of warranty. Section 2-715(2); Section 2A-520(2).

With respect to the first type of consequential damages, *particular* needs of the buyer usually must be made known to the seller, whereas *general* needs usually need not be. In the case of a buyer who is in the business of reselling goods, resale is one requirement of which the seller has reason to know. For example, Supreme Machine Co., a manufacturer, contracts to sell Allied Sales, Inc., a dealer in used machinery, a used machine that Allied plans to resell. When Supreme repudiates and Allied is unable to obtain a similar machine elsewhere, Allied's damages include the net profit that it would have made on resale of the machine. A buyer may not, however, recover consequential damages he could have prevented by cover. Section 2-715(2); Section 2A-520(2)(a). For instance, Supreme Machine Co. contracts for $10,000 to sell Capitol Manufacturing Co. a used machine to be delivered at Capitol's factory by June 1. Supreme repudiates the contract on May 1. By reasonable efforts, Capitol could buy a similar machine from United Machinery, Inc., for $11,000 in time for a June 1 delivery. Capitol fails to do so, thereby losing a $5,000 profit that it would have made from the resale of the machine. Though Capitol can recover $1,000 from Supreme, its damages do not include the loss of the $5,000 profit.

An example of the second type of consequential damages would be the following: Federal Machine Co. sells a machine to Southern Manufacturing Co., warranting its suitability for Southern's purpose. The machine is not suitable for Southern's purpose, however, and causes $10,000 in damage to Southern's property and $15,000 in personal injuries. Southern can recover the $25,000 consequential damages in addition to any other loss suffered.

Practical Advice

As the buyer, be sure to inform the other party to the contract of any "particular needs" beyond the ordinary course of events that could result from a breach of contract.

◆ See Figure 25-2: *Remedies of the Buyer*

25-3 Contractual Provisions Affecting Remedies

Within specified limits, the Code permits the parties to a sales contract to modify, exclude, or limit by agreement the remedies or damages that will be available for breach of that contract. Two basic types of contractual provisions affect remedies: (1) liquidation or limitation of damages and (2) modification or limitation of remedy.

25-3a LIQUIDATION OR LIMITATION OF DAMAGES

The parties may provide for liquidated damages in their contract by specifying the amount or measure of damages that either party may recover in the event of a breach by the other. The amount of such damages must be reasonable in light of the anticipated or actual loss resulting from a breach, the difficulties of proof of loss, and the inconvenience or lack of feasibility of otherwise obtaining an adequate remedy. A contractual provision fixing unreasonably large liquidated damages is void as a penalty. Section 2-718(1). An unreasonably small amount, on the other hand, might be stricken on the grounds of unconscionability. Comment 1 to Section 2-718.

To illustrate, Sterling Cabinetry Company contracts to build and install shelves and cabinets for an office building being constructed by Baron Construction Company. The contract price is $120,000, and the contract provides that Sterling would be liable for $100 per day for every day's delay beyond the completion date specified in the contract. The stipulated sum of $100 per day is reasonable and commensurate with the anticipated loss. Therefore, it is enforceable as liquidated damages. If, instead, the sum stipulated had been $5,000 per day, it would be unreasonably large and therefore would be void as a penalty.

Section 2A-504(1) authorizes liquidated damages payable by either party for default or any other act or omission. The amount of, or formula for, liquidated damages must be reasonable in light of the then-anticipated harm caused by default or other act or omission. Section 2A-504(1).

In cases in which the seller justifiably withholds delivery of the goods because of the buyer's breach and the buyer has made payments on the price, the buyer is entitled to restitution of the amount by which the sum of his payments exceeds the amount of liquidated damages to which the seller is entitled under the contract. In the absence of a provision for liquidated damages, the buyer may recover the difference between the amounts that he has paid on the price and 20 percent of the value of the total performance for which he is obligated under the contract, or $500, whichever is smaller. Section 2-718(2)(b). Article 2A has a comparable provision, except the $500 provision applies only to consumer leases. Section 2A-504(3)(b). The buyer's right to restitution is offset by the seller's right to recover other damages provided in the Code and by the value of any benefits the

FIGURE 25-2 Remedies of the Buyer

Seller's Breach	Buyer's Remedies		
	Obligation-Oriented	Goods-Oriented	Money-Oriented*
Buyer Rightfully Rejects Goods	Cancel	Have a security interest	Recover payments made Cover and recover damages Recover damages for nondelivery
Buyer Justifiably Revokes Acceptance	Cancel	Have a security interest	Recover payments made Cover and recover damages Recover damages for nondelivery
Seller Fails to Deliver	Cancel	Recover identified goods if seller is insolvent Replevy goods Obtain specific performance	Recover payments made Cover and recover damages Recover damages for nondelivery
Seller Repudiates	Cancel	Recover identified goods if seller is insolvent Replevy goods Obtain specific performance	Recover payments made Cover and recover damages Recover damages for nondelivery
Buyer Accepts Nonconforming Goods			Recover damages for breach of warranty

*In a lease, the lessee's recovery of damages for future rent payments is reduced to their present value.

buyer has received by reason of the contract. Section 2-718(3); Section 2A-504(4).

Thus, if a buyer, after depositing $1,500 with the seller on a $10,000 contract for goods, breaches the contract and the seller withholds delivery, in the absence of a provision for liquidated damages and in the absence of the seller's establishing greater actual damages resulting from the breach, the buyer is entitled to restitution of $1,000 ($1,500 minus $500). If the deposit was $250 on a $500 contract, the buyer would be entitled to $150 ($250 minus $100, which is 20 percent of the price).

Practical Advice

Both parties should consider including a contractual provision for reasonable liquidated damages, especially where damages would be difficult to prove.

◆ _See Case 25-4_

25-3b MODIFICATION OR LIMITATION OF REMEDY BY AGREEMENT

The contract between the seller and buyer may expressly provide for remedies in addition to or instead of those provided in the Code and may limit or change the measure of damages recoverable in the event of breach. Section 2-719(1); Section 2A-503(1). For instance, the contract may validly limit the buyer's remedy to a return of the goods and a refund of the price or to the replacement of nonconforming goods or parts.

A contractual remedy is deemed optional, however, unless the parties expressly agree that it is to be exclusive of other remedies, in which event it becomes the sole remedy. Section 2-719(1)(b); Section 2A-503(2). Moreover, in cases in which circumstances cause an exclusive or limited remedy to fail in its essential purpose, the parties may resort to the remedies provided by the Code. Section 2-719(2); Section 2A-503(2).

The contract may expressly limit or exclude consequential damages unless such limitation or exclusion would be unconscionable. Limitation of consequential damages for personal injuries resulting from breach of warranty in the sale of consumer goods is _prima facie_ unconscionable, whereas limitation of such damages for commercial loss is not. Section 2-719(3); Section 2A-503(3). For example, Ace Motors, Inc., sells a pickup truck to Brenda, a consumer. The contract of sale excludes liability for all consequential damages. The next day, the truck explodes, causing Brenda serious personal injury. Brenda would recover for her personal injuries unless Ace could prove that the exclusion of consequential damages was not unconscionable.

Practical Advice

If you are the seller, consider including a contractual provision for the limitation or exclusion of consequential damages. If you are the buyer, avoid such limitations.

◆ _See Case 25-3_

25-3c STATUTE OF LIMITATIONS

Any action for breach of a sales contract must be begun within four years after the cause of action has accrued. Section 2-725(1); Section 2A-506(1). The parties may reduce the period of limitation to not less than one year. Section 2-725(1); Section 2A-506(1). In a sale, they may not, however, extend the period. Article 2A does not include this limitation.

A cause of action accrues when the breach occurs without regard to the injured party's knowledge of the breach. Section 2-725(2). A breach of warranty occurs upon tender of delivery, except in cases in which the warranty extends to future performance. In that event, the cause of action occurs when the breach is or should have been discovered. In a lease, a cause of action for default accrues when the act or omission is discovered or should have been discovered by the aggrieved party, or when the default occurs, whichever is later. Section 2A-506(2).

CHAPTER SUMMARY

REMEDIES OF THE SELLER

Buyer's Default the seller's remedies are triggered by the buyer's actions in wrongfully rejecting or revoking acceptance of the goods, in failing to make payment due on or before delivery, or in repudiating the contract

Withhold Delivery of the Goods

Stop Delivery of the Goods if the buyer is insolvent (one who is unable to pay his debts as they become due or one whose total liabilities exceed his total assets), the seller may stop any delivery; if the buyer repudiates or otherwise breaches, the seller may stop carload, truckload, planeload, or larger shipments

Identify Goods

Resell the Goods and Recover Damages the seller *may* resell the goods concerned or the undelivered balance of the goods and recover the difference between the contract price and the resale price, together with any incidental damages, minus expenses saved
- *Type of Resale* may be public or private
- *Manner of Resale* must be made in good faith and in a commercially reasonable manner

Recover Damages for Nonacceptance or Repudiation
- *Market Price Differential* the seller may recover damages from the buyer measured by the difference between the unpaid contract price and the market price at the time and place of tender of the goods, plus incidental damages, minus expenses saved
- *Lost Profit* in the alternative, the seller may recover the lost profit, including reasonable overhead, plus incidental damages, minus expenses saved

Recover the Price the seller may recover the price—
- when the buyer has accepted the goods
- when the goods have been lost or damaged after the risk of loss has passed to the buyer
- when the goods have been identified to the contract and a ready market is not available for their resale

Recover Incidental Damages incidental damages include any commercially reasonable charges, expenses, or commissions directly resulting from the breach

Cancel the Contract

Reclaim the Goods on the Buyer's Insolvency an unpaid seller may reclaim goods from an insolvent buyer under certain circumstances

REMEDIES OF THE BUYER	**Seller's Default** the buyer's remedies arise in cases (1) in which the seller fails to make delivery or repudiates the contract or (2) in which the buyer rightfully rejects or justifiably revokes acceptance of goods tendered or delivered
	Cancel the Contract
	Recover Payments Made
	Cover the buyer may obtain cover by proceeding in good faith and without unreasonable delay to purchase substitute goods; the buyer may recover the difference between the cost of cover and the contract price, plus any incidental and consequential damages, minus expenses saved
	Recover Damages for Nondelivery or Repudiation the buyer may recover the difference between the market price at the time the buyer learned of the breach and the contract price, together with any incidental and consequential damages, minus expenses saved
	Recover Identified Goods on the Seller's Insolvency for which he has paid all or part of the price
	Sue for Replevin the buyer may recover goods identified to the contract if (1) the buyer is unable to obtain cover or (2) the goods have been shipped under reservation of a security interest in the seller
	Sue for Specific Performance the buyer may obtain specific performance in cases in which the goods are unique or in other proper circumstances
	Enforce a Security Interest in the Goods a buyer who has rightfully rejected or justifiably revoked acceptance of goods that remain in her possession has a security interest in these goods for any payments that she has made on their price and for any expenses she has reasonably incurred
	Recover Damages for Breach in Regard to Accepted Goods the buyer may recover damages resulting in the ordinary course of events from the seller's breach; in the case of breach of warranty, such recovery is the difference between the value the goods would have had if they had been as warranted and the value of the nonconforming goods that have been accepted
	Recover Incidental Damages the buyer may recover incidental damages, which include any commercially reasonable expenses connected with the delay or other breach
	Recover Consequential Damages the buyer may recover consequential damages resulting from the seller's breach, including (1) any loss resulting from the buyer's requirements and needs of which the seller at the time of contracting had reason to know and which the buyer could not reasonably prevent by cover or otherwise and (2) injury to person or property proximately resulting from any breach of warranty
CONTRACTUAL PROVISIONS AFFECTING REMEDIES	**Liquidation or Limitation of Damages** the parties may specify the amount or measure of damages that may be recovered in the event of a breach if the amount is reasonable
	Modification or Limitation of Remedy by Agreement the contract between the parties may expressly provide for remedies in addition to those in the Code, or it may limit or change the measure of damages recoverable for breach

C A S E S

Seller's Damages for Nonacceptance or Repudiation

PEACE RIVER SEED CO-OP. v. PROSEEDS MKTG.

Supreme Court of Oregon, 2014
355 Or. 44, 322 P. 3d 531

Balmer, C. J.

Peace River Seed Co-Operative ("plaintiff") is a Canadian company that buys grass seed from and sells grass seed for grass seed producers. Proseeds Marketing ("defendant") is an Oregon corporation that purchases grass seed from various sources to resell to end users. A broker prepared and the parties agreed to multiple contracts for defendant to purchase from plaintiff the total production of grass seed from a certain number of acres for a fixed price over a period of two years. The contracts incorporated the NORAMSEED Rules for the Trade of Seeds for Planting, which have been adopted by the American and Canadian Seed Trade Associations to govern the trade of seed. The NORAMSEED Rules provide that the UCC applies to transactions within the United States, and both parties have litigated this case under the UCC.

Under the contracts, defendant was to provide shipping and delivery instructions to plaintiff. During the contract period, however, the price of grass seed fell dramatically. Although defendant initially provided shipping instructions and plaintiff shipped conforming seed, defendant eventually refused to provide shipping instructions for delivery of additional seed under the contracts. After multiple requests for shipping instructions, and defendant's continued refusal to provide them, plaintiff cancelled the contracts. Over the next three years, plaintiff was able to sell at least some of the seed that defendant had agreed to purchase to other buyers.

[The plaintiff argued at trial that it was entitled to recover its market price damages. The trial court determined that the plaintiff was entitled to the lesser of its market price damages or its resale price damages, and the court ultimately awarded the plaintiff its resale price damages. The Court of Appeals reversed and remanded, determining that the plaintiff could recover its market price damages, even though it had resold some of the goods at issue.]

In this breach of contract case, we examine the availability of different remedies under the Uniform Commercial Code (UCC) for an aggrieved seller of goods after a buyer breaches a contract to purchase those goods. Specifically, we consider the relationship between ORS 72.7080(1) [UCC §2-708], which measures a seller's damages as the difference between the unpaid contract price and the *market* price at the time and place for tender, and ORS 72.7060 [UCC §2-706], which measures a seller's damages as the difference between the contract

price and the *resale* price. We examine those provisions to determine whether an aggrieved seller who has resold goods can recover a greater amount of damages using the market price measure of damages than the seller would recover using the resale price measure of damages.

* * *

* * * [W]e conclude that * * * the sellers' remedies provisions support a seller's right to recover either market price damages or resale price damages, even if market price damages lead to a larger recovery.

* * *

When a buyer breaches a contract for the sale of goods, ORS 72.7030 [UCC §2-703] provides a seller with an index of remedies * * *.

That section lists the seller's remedies, which, as relevant here, include resale price damages, ORS 72.7060, and market price damages, ORS 72.7080. Moreover, it lists those remedies without any limiting conjunction, such as "or," that might suggest that the remedies are mutually exclusive. In contrast, a similar index of a buyer's remedies after a seller's breach provides that the buyer may "(a) 'Cover' and have damages * * * *or* (b) Recover damages for nondelivery." ORS 72.7110(1) [UCC §2-711(1)] (emphasis added.) Thus, although the buyer's index of remedies suggests that a buyer who covers may be precluded from seeking market price damages, the seller's index of remedies does not contain a similar limitation if the seller chooses to resell. It follows that the text of ORS 72.7030 supports plaintiff's argument that a seller who has resold is not necessarily limited to its resale price damages under ORS 72.7060, but has the option of seeking to recover market price damages under ORS 72.7080.

* * *

* * * ORS 72.7060(1) states that "the seller *may* resell the goods concerned or the undelivered balance thereof," which suggests that an aggrieved seller is not required to resell. (Emphasis added.) [Citation.] Similarly, the text of ORS 72.7060 indicates that a seller who resells is not required to seek damages using the resale remedy. *See* ORS 72.7060(1) ("Where the resale is made in good faith and in a commercially reasonable manner the seller *may* recover the difference between the resale price and the contract price * * *." (Emphasis added.)). In fact, the unqualified text of ORS 72.7080(1) seems to suggest that market price is in fact the default measure of damages. See ORS 72.7080(1) ("Subject to * * * the provisions of ORS 72.7230 UCC §2-723] with respect to proof of market price, *the* measure of damages for nonacceptance or repudiation by the buyer is the difference between the market price at the time and place for tender and the unpaid contract price * * *." (Emphasis added.)). Thus, the text of the remedy provisions does not limit a seller who resells to its resale price damages.

* * *

The text of ORS 71.3050(1) [UCC §1-305] indicates that the drafters of the UCC intended a seller's remedies to be compensatory. [Citation.] The text of that section, however, also provides that the remedies in the UCC are to be "liberally administered." [Citations.]* * *

* * *

* * * [L]imiting an aggrieved seller to its resale price damages ignores the risk for which the parties bargained. When parties bargain for fixed price contracts, each party assumes the risk of market price fluctuations. The parties are willing to take that risk because of the benefits that they might receive: if the market price decreases, the seller benefits, and if the market price increases, the buyer benefits. In a fixed price contract, therefore, market price damages represent the risk for which both parties bargained. [Citation.] For those reasons, we conclude that a seller can recover market price damages, even if the seller resells some of the goods at above the market price at the time and place for tender.

* * *

In sum, when viewed in light of the bargained-for market risks and the UCC's rejection of the doctrine of election of remedies, the text, context, and legislative history of the sellers' remedy provisions demonstrate that an aggrieved seller can seek damages under either ORS 72.7080(1) or ORS 72.7060. That means that an aggrieved seller can seek damages under ORS 72.7080(1) even if the seller has resold the goods and market price damages exceed resale price damages.

* * *

The decision of the Court of Appeals is affirmed in [relevant] part and * * * the case is remanded to the circuit court.

CASE 25-2

Buyer's Remedy of Cover
BIGELOW-SANFORD, INC. v. GUNNY CORP.
United States Court of Appeals, Fifth Circuit, Unit B, 1981
649 F.2d 1060

Kravitch, J.

[The plaintiff, Bigelow-Sanford, Inc., contracted with defendant Gunny Corp. for the purchase of 100,000 linear yards of jute at $0.64 per yard. Gunny delivered 22,228 linear yards in January 1979. The February and March deliveries required under the contract were not made, though eight rolls (each roll containing 66.7 linear yards) were delivered in April. With 72,265 linear yards undelivered, Gunny told Bigelow-Sanford that no more would be delivered. In mid-March, Bigelow-Sanford turned to the jute spot market to replace the balance of the order at a price of $1.21 per linear yard. Since several other companies had also defaulted on their jute contracts with Bigelow-Sanford, the plaintiff purchased a total of 164,503 linear yards on the spot market. Plaintiff sues defendant to recover losses sustained as a result of the breach of contract.]

* * *

Gunny contends that appellee's [Bigelow-Sanford] alleged cover purchases should not have been used to measure damages in that they were not made in substitution for the contract purchases, were not made seasonably or in good faith and were not shown to be due to Gunny's breach. [W]e disagree. * * *

UCC §2-712 defines cover:

(1) After a breach * * * the buyer may "cover" by making in good faith and without unreasonable delay any reasonable purchase of or contract to purchase goods in substitution for those due from the seller.

(2) The buyer may recover from the seller as damages the difference between the cost of cover and the contract price together with any incidental or consequential damages * * *, but less expenses saved in consequence of the seller's breach.

(3) Failure of the buyer to effect cover within this section does not bar him from any other remedy.

* * *

Most importantly, "whether a plaintiff has made his cover purchases in a reasonable manner poses a classic jury issue." [Citation.] The district court thus acted properly in submitting the question of cover damages to the jury, which found that Gunny had breached, appellee had covered, and had done so in good faith without unreasonable delay by making reasonable purchases, and was therefore entitled to damages under §2-712. Gunny argues Bigelow is not entitled to such damages on the ground that it failed to make cover purchases without undue delay and that the jury should not have been permitted to average the cost of Bigelow's spot market purchases totalling 164,503 linear yards in order to arrive at the cost of cover for the 72,265 linear yards Gunny failed to deliver. Both arguments fail.

Gunny notified Bigelow in February that no more jute would be forthcoming. Bigelow made its first spot market purchases in mid-March. Given that it is within the jury's province to decide the reasonableness of the manner in which cover purchases were made, we believe the jury could reasonably decide such purchases, made one month after the date the jury assigned to Gunny's breach, were made without undue delay. The same is true with respect to Gunny's second argument: Bigelow's spot market purchases were made to replace several vendors'

shipments. Bigelow did not specifically allocate the spot market replacements to individual vendors' accounts, however, nor was there a requirement that they do so. The jury's method of averaging such costs and assigning them to Gunny in proportion to the amount of jute if [sic] failed to deliver would, therefore, seem not only fair but well within the jury's permissible bounds.

* * *

[Judgment for Bigelow is affirmed.]

CASE 25-3

Buyer's Damages for Breach in Regard to Accepted Goods/Limitation of Remedy by Agreement
MIDWEST HATCHERY v. DOORENBOS POULTRY

Court of Appeals of Iowa, 2010
783 N.W.2d 56

Zimmer, S.J.

Doorenbos Poultry, Inc., is a company that keeps chickens for egg production, and sells the eggs. The company conducts its business at two barn facilities in Sioux County [Iowa]. One of the barns can house 112,000 birds and the other has a capacity of 134,000.

The evidence presented at trial reveals that hens generally do not begin laying eggs until they are seventeen or eighteen weeks old. They reach their peak production at approximately twenty-six weeks and are generally most productive in laying eggs between the ages of twenty to eighty weeks old. At about eighty weeks, the chickens molt and go through a period where they are less productive. After that, they usually continue producing eggs until they are about 110 weeks old. The practice of Doorenbos Poultry has been to keep all chickens of a single age group through their productive life, and then simultaneously replace those birds with new chickens that are seventeen to eighteen weeks old. This practice maximizes production and continues some cash flow without interruption.

Midwest Hatchery & Poultry Farms, Inc. is a producer and seller of poultry products. Midwest sells hatch eggs, baby chicks, and started pullets, which are female hens that have reached the age of laying eggs. In the fall of 2006, Doorenbos Poultry entered into a written contract with Midwest, to purchase 112,000 pullets (young hens) of the Hy-Line W-36 variety, at eighteen weeks of age, to be delivered on December 28, 2006. The contract listed a price of $1.27 per pullet, plus the cost of feed from the time of hatching to the date of delivery. The contract provided, "Deliveries are subject to availability of the Products, availability of transportation, and availability due to demand from Seller's other customers."

The contract also provided, "If Seller breaches this Contract, at Seller's option, customer is entitled to either replacement or refund of the price paid by Customer."

Prior to the delivery date of December 28, 2006, Midwest notified Doorenbos Poultry it would be unable to deliver the chickens ordered on the date contemplated by the parties' contract. Doorenbos Poultry agreed to the delay, and cancelled arrangements to slaughter the approximately 110,000 chickens it had in one of its facilities at that time.

Over January 16, 17, and 18, 2007, Midwest delivered 115,581 pullets to Doorenbos Poultry. As the new chicks arrived, the old pullets were moved out. Scott Doorenbos, the president of Doorenbos Poultry, thought the new chickens looked small. Because of his concerns, he had two of the delivery trucks weighed before the pullets were unloaded. Doorenbos concluded the birds delivered were thirteen to fourteen weeks of age rather than eighteen weeks. Doorenbos testified he could not cancel the order and return the chickens because his former flock had already been removed. He explained that the barns in which the chickens are kept do not have heating. Because the buildings maintain their temperature from the body heat of the birds, Doorenbos believed the water lines in the barn would have frozen if he had not kept the pullets. Doorenbos testified the pullets delivered by Midwest did not start laying eggs until February 18, 2007. From the time the pullets were delivered and the existing flock was removed until the pullets reached their "laying" phase, Doorenbos Poultry incurred feeding and other maintenance costs for the pullets with no egg production to generate revenue.

* * * When this case was tried to the court in late September 2008, Doorenbos Poultry had kept the pullets delivered by Midwest in production through 117 weeks and was intending to keep them in production until at least 119 weeks.

On January 20, 2007, Midwest sent Doorenbos Poultry an invoice for $267,916.76, which represented $146,787.87 for the cost of 115,581 pullets, $112,460.31 for feed, and $8,668.58 for vaccine. Doorenbos Poultry did not pay for the birds Midwest delivered when it received the invoice. Door-enbos Poultry contacted Midwest within thirty days after the pullets were delivered and complained that it had not received chickens that were eighteen weeks old, as specified in the contract. Because it believed the chickens were younger than eighteen weeks, Doorenbos Poultry sought a reduction in the contract price. It stated it lost income while the chickens were not mature enough to lay eggs. Doorenbos Poultry did not seek to have any of the pullets replaced. * * *

* * * On August 19, 2007, Doorenbos Poultry sent Midwest a check for $184,135.18, which was what it believed should have been the cost for the younger pullets. Doorenbos Poultry never returned any chickens to Midwest.

[On September 14, 2007, Midwest filed an action for a money judgment alleging breach of contract. Doorenbos Poultry responded with a counterclaim alleging breach of contract by Midwest. The parties waived their right to a jury trial, and their case was tried to the court. In a decision filed January 9, 2009, the district court concluded that about 80 percent of the pullets were three weeks too young and about 20 percent were four weeks too young. The district court determined that (1) this action was governed by the Uniform Commercial Code (UCC); (2) because Doorenbos had accepted and kept the pullets, Midwest is entitled to the unpaid balance of the contract price; and therefore, (3) Doorenbos Poultry was liable for the full amount billed by Midwest Hatchery, meaning it still owed $83,781.58 for the pullets that had been delivered. The court also concluded that (1) Doorenbos Poultry's acceptance of the pullets did not preclude its breach of contract claim against Midwest; (2) Midwest had breached the contract by providing pullets that were not of the specified age; (3) the limitation of damages clause in the parties' contract failed in its essential purpose; and (4) Doorenbos Poultry had lost profits of $31,732.79 because it was not able to replace its existing flock with eighteen-week-old birds. The court set off the amount of the loss against the balance Doorenbos Poultry still owed Midwest and entered judgment against Doorenbos Poultry for $52,048.79 ($83,781.58 minus $31,732.79).

Doorenbos Poultry appealed the decision of the district court.]

* * *

Breach of Contract

* * *

* * * Under the UCC, section [2-607] provides, "The buyer must pay at the contract rate for any goods accepted." A buyer accepts goods when the buyer "take[s] or retain[s] them in spite of their nonconformity." [Section 2-606(1)(a).] A buyer also accepts goods if the buyer "does any act inconsistent with the seller's ownership." [Section 2-606(1)(c).]

* * * Under the UCC, if a buyer accepts goods, despite their nonconformity to the specifications of the contract, the buyer must pay the contract rate for the goods accepted. [Citation.]

We determine there is substantial evidence in the record to support the finding of the district court that Doorenbos Poultry accepted the chickens delivered by Midwest within the meaning of section [2-606], despite their nonconformity. * * *

* * *

Limitation of Remedies Provision

* * *

Before we begin our discussion of the limited remedy issue, we believe it is appropriate to express our agreement with the district court's conclusion that the acceptance of the non-conforming goods by Doorenbos Poultry did not preclude its counterclaim for breach of contract against Midwest. There is no dispute on appeal that Midwest breached the contract by providing nonconforming chickens. Section [2-607(2)] states, "acceptance does not of itself impair any other remedy provided by this Article for nonconformity."

* * *

Clearly, acceptance of the pullets does not preclude Doorenbos Poultry from asserting a claim based on breach of contract by Midwest. We now turn to the arguments concerning the limited remedies provision in the parties' contract.

Under the UCC, the parties to a contract may agree to limit the remedies available if the seller breaches the contract by providing nonconforming goods, as follows:

> [T]he agreement may provide for remedies in addition to or in substitution for those provided in this Article and may limit or alter the measure of damages recoverable under this Article, as by limiting the buyer's remedies to return of the goods and repayment of the price or to repair and replacement of nonconforming goods or parts.

[UCC Section 2-719(1)(a).] In this case, the parties' contract specifically provided, "If Seller breaches this Contract, at Seller's option, customer is entitled to either replacement or refund of the price paid by Customer."

Section [2-719(2)] provides, "Where circumstances cause an exclusive or limited remedy to fail of its essential purpose, remedy may be had as provided in this chapter." A remedy's essential purpose "is to give to a buyer what the seller promised him." [Citation.] The focus of analysis "is not whether the remedy compensates for all damage that occurred, but that the buyer is provided with the product as seller promised." [Citations.]

Where repair or replacement can give the buyer what is bargained for, a limitation of remedies does not fail of its essential purpose. [Citation.] In other circumstances, however, repair or replacement is not sufficient, and then a court may find the remedy failed of its essential purpose. [Citation.]

* * *

Upon our review of the record, we agree with the district court's ultimate conclusion that the limited remedy provision of the parties' contract failed of its essential purpose. The chickens were delivered over January 16, 17, and 18, 2007. Doorenbos Poultry notified Midwest that the pullets were not as specified in the contract within thirty days after delivery. We agree with the trial court's conclusion that the reference to a replacement or refund in the contract contemplates the entire sale with Midwest taking back the entire flock of birds.

At the time Scott Doorenbos informed Midwest that the pullets delivered were not eighteen weeks old, it is clear that Doorenbos Poultry was not interested in having the pullets replaced, and Midwest made no offer to replace them. When it was notified of the breach, we agree that Midwest could have exercised its option under the contract, taken back the entire flock, and either replaced the chickens with eighteen week old pullets or refunded the entire purchase price. The record supports the conclusion that this did not happen because, as the district court noted, it was plainly impractical.

It would have been extremely inefficient for both parties to replace the pullets Midwest had delivered. * * * In addition, it does not appear that either party was interested in the option of removal and refund.

* * *

Under the circumstance presented here, we conclude the district court did not err in concluding the limitation of remedies provision in the parties' contract failed in its essential purpose. We next consider Doorenbos Poultry's alternative claim that the trial court improperly calculated its damages.

Amount of Damages

Because the limitation of remedies provision failed in its essential purpose, a consideration of damages reverts to section [2-714(1)], which provides for the recovery of damages for "the loss resulting in the ordinary course of events from the seller's breach as determined in any manner which is reasonable." Thus, any manner that is reasonable may be used to determine a buyer's damages for nonconforming goods. [Citation.] Here, the district court found "a loss of profits would have been an expected loss resulting in the ordinary course of events from the nonconformity of the pullets delivered by Midwest under § [2-714(1)]."

Under section [2-714(2)], damages are measured by the difference between the value of the goods at the time of acceptance, and their value if they had been as specified in the contract, "unless special circumstances show proximate damages of a different amount." The court noted that neither party submitted any evidence as to the value of fourteen-or fifteen-week-old pullets and expressed skepticism that there would be any recognized value for pullets that were between fourteen and fifteen weeks old and did not have the ability to lay eggs. As a result, the court concluded the "special circumstances" provision of section [2-714(2)] should apply.

* * * After carefully considering the evidence presented, the district court concluded that eighty percent of the chickens were three weeks too young, and the feeding costs and lost revenues for those birds would have been sixty percent of the amount claimed by Doorenbos Poultry. Similarly, the court concluded that the feed costs and lost revenues for the chickens four weeks too young would have been eighty percent of the amount claimed by Doorenbos Poultry. The court calculated these prorated amounts and arrived at the total of $31,732.79 for the damages to be awarded Doorenbos Poultry on its counterclaim.

* * *

We affirm the decision of the district court. * * *

CASE 25-4

Liquidation of Damages

COASTAL LEASING CORPORATION v. T-BAR S CORPORATION

Court of Appeals of North Carolina, 1998
128 N.C. App. 379, 496 S.E.2d 795

Walker, J.

Plaintiff entered into a lease agreement (lease) with defendant T-Bar S Corporation (T-Bar) in May of 1992, whereby plaintiff agreed to lease certain cash register equipment (equipment) to T-Bar. Under the lease, T-Bar agreed to monthly rental payments of $289.13 each for a total of 48 months. Defendants George and Sharon Talbott (appellants) were the officers of

T-Bar and personally guaranteed payment of all amounts due under the lease.

After making 18 of the monthly payments, appellants and T-Bar defaulted on the lease in December of 1993. On 28 February 1994, plaintiff mailed a certified letter to appellants and T-Bar, return receipt requested, advising them that the lease was in default and, pursuant to the terms of the lease, plaintiff was accelerating the remaining payments due under the lease. They further advised appellants and T-Bar that if the entire amount due of $8,841.06 was not received within 7 days, plaintiff would seek to recover the balance due plus interest and reasonable attorneys' fees, as well as possession of the equipment. The record shows that appellants and T-Bar each received this letter on 1 March 1994.

On 10 March 1994, plaintiff mailed a certified letter and "Notice of Public Sale of Repossessed Leased Equipment" (notice of sale) to appellants and T-Bar at the same address, again return receipt requested. This letter advised appellants and T-Bar that plaintiff had taken possession of the equipment and was conducting a public sale pursuant to the terms of the lease. Although the date on the notice of sale stated that the sale was to be held on 23 March 1994, the sale was actually scheduled to be held on 25 March 1994. This letter and notice of sale were returned to plaintiffs "unclaimed" on 29 March 1994.

Plaintiffs conducted a public sale of the equipment on 25 March 1994 and no one appeared on behalf of appellants or T-Bar. There being no other bidders, plaintiff purchased the equipment at the sale for $2,000.00.

On 4 October 1994, plaintiff leased some of the same equipment to another company at a rate calculated to be $212.67 for 36 months. Plaintiff then filed this action on 6 October 1994 seeking to recover the balance due under the lease, minus the net proceeds from the 25 March 1994 public sale, plus interest and reasonable attorneys' fees. Appellants filed an answer and counterclaim on 27 July 1995. Plaintiff then filed a motion for summary judgment against appellants on 8 July 1996. * * *

After a hearing, the trial court entered summary judgment on 15 January 1997 in favor of plaintiff on its complaint and appellants' counterclaims and entered judgment against appellants for the sum of $7,223.56 plus interest and attorneys' fees of $1,083.54.

* * *

* * * Since both parties agree that the transaction at issue in this case is not a security interest, but rather is a lease, Article 2A controls. [Article 9 controls security interests and is discussed in *Chapter 37*.]

* * *

In their appeal, appellants contend that the trial court erred by granting summary judgment in favor of plaintiff because there exists a genuine issue of material fact as to whether: (1) the liquidated damages clause contained in Paragraph 13 of the lease is reasonable in light of the then-anticipated harm caused by default; * * *

As to appellants' first contention, the official commentary to Article 2A states that "in recognition of the diversity of the transactions to be governed [and] the sophistication of many of the parties to these transactions * * *, freedom of contract has been preserved." [UCC §] 2A-102 Official Comment. Also, under general contract principles, when the parties to a

transaction deal with each other at arms length and without the exercise by one of the parties of superior bargaining power, the parties will be bound by their agreement. [Citation.]

Article 2A recognizes that "[m]any leasing transactions are predicated on the parties' ability to agree to an appropriate amount of damages or formula for damages in the event of default or other act or omission." [UCC §] 2A-504 Official Comment. [UCC §] 2A-504 states, in pertinent part:

(1) Damages payable by either party for default, or any other act or omission * * * may be liquidated in the lease agreement but only at an amount or by a formula that is reasonable in light of the then-anticipated harm caused by the default or other act or omission.

[Citation.] This liquidated damages provision is more flexible than that provided by its statutory analogue under Article 2, [UCC §] 2-718. * * *

* * *

"The basic test of the reasonableness of an agreement liquidating damages is whether the stipulated amount or amount produced by the stipulated formula represents a reasonable forecast of the probable loss." [Citation.] However, "no court should strike down a reasonable liquidated damage agreement based on foresight that has proved on hindsight to have contained an inaccurate estimation of the probable loss. * * *" [Citation.] And, "the fact that there is a difference between the actual loss, as determined at or about the time of the default, and the anticipated loss or stipulated amount or formula, as stipulated at the time the lease contract was entered into * * *," does not necessarily mean that the liquidated damage agreement is unreasonable. [Citation.] This is so because "[t]he value of a lessor's interest in leased equipment depends upon 'the physical condition of the equipment and the market conditions at that time.'" [Citation.] Further, in determining whether a liquidated damages clause is reasonable:

[A] court should keep in mind that the clause was negotiated by the parties, who are familiar with the circumstances and practices with respect to the type of transaction involved, and the clause carries with it a consensual apportionment of the risks of the agreement that a court should be slow to overturn.

[Citation.]
In this case, Paragraph 13 of the lease (the liquidated damages clause) reads as follows:

13. REMEDIES If an event of default shall occur, Lessor may, at its option, at any time (a) declare the entire amount of unpaid rental for the balance of the term of this lease immediately due and payable, whereupon Lessee shall become obligated to pay to Lessor forthwith the total amount of the said rental for the balance of the

said term, and (b) without demand or legal process, enter into the premises where the equipment may be found and take possession of and remove the Equipment, without liability for suit, action or other proceeding, and all rights of Lessee in the Equipment so removed shall terminate absolutely. Lessee hereby waives notice of, or hearing with respect to, such retaking. Lessor may at its option, use, ship, store, repair or lease all Equipment so removed and sell or otherwise dispose of any such Equipment at a private or public sale. In the event Lessor takes possession of the Equipment, Lessor shall give Lessee credit for any sums received by Lessor from the sale or rental of the Equipment after deduction of the expenses of sale or rental and Lessor's residual interest in the Equipment.... Lessor and Lessee acknowledge the difficulty in establishing a value for the unexpired lease term and owing to such difficulty agree that the provisions of this paragraph represent an agreed measure of damages and are not to be deemed a forfeiture or penalty. * * *

After a careful review, we conclude the liquidated damages clause is a reasonable estimation of the then-anticipated damages in the event of default because it protects plaintiff's expectation interest. The liquidated damages clause places plaintiff in the position it would have occupied had the lease been fully performed by allowing it to accelerate the balance of the lease payments and repossess the equipment. Therefore, since there is no evidence that plaintiff exercised a superior bargaining position in the negotiation of the liquidated damages clause, no genuine issue of material fact exists as to its reasonableness, and the trial court did not err by enforcing its provisions.

Q U E S T I O N S

1. Mae contracted to sell one thousand bushels of wheat to Lloyd at $5 per bushel. Just before Mae was to deliver the wheat, Lloyd notified her that he would not receive or accept the wheat. Mae sold the wheat for $4.60 per bushel, the market price, and later sued Lloyd for the difference of $400. Lloyd claims he was not notified by Mae of the resale and, hence, is not liable. Is Lloyd correct? Why or why not?

2. On December 15, Judy wrote a letter to David stating that she would sell to David all of the mine-run coal that David might wish to buy during the next calendar year for use at David's factory, delivered at the factory at a price of $30 per ton. David immediately replied by letter to Judy, stating that he accepted the offer, that he would purchase all of his mine-run coal from Judy, and that he would need two hundred tons of coal during the first week in January. During the months of January, February, and March, Judy delivered to David a total of seven hundred tons of coal, for all of which David made payment to Judy at the rate of $30 per ton. On April 10, David ordered two hundred tons of mine-run coal from Judy, who replied to David on April 11 that she could not supply David with any more coal except at a price of $38 per ton delivered. David thereafter purchased elsewhere at the market price, namely $38 per ton, all of his factory's requirements of mine-run coal for the remainder of the year, amounting to a total of two thousand tons of coal. Can David now recover damages from Judy at the rate of $8 per ton for the coal thus purchased, amounting to $16,000? Why or why not?

3. On January 10, Betty, of Emanon, Missouri, visited the showrooms of the Forte Piano Company in St. Louis and selected a piano. A sales memorandum of the transaction signed by Betty and the salesperson of the Forte Piano Company read as follows: "Sold to Betty one new Andover piano, factory number 46832, price $3,300, to be shipped to the buyer at Emanon, Missouri, freight prepaid, before February 1. Prior to shipment, seller will stain the case a darker color in accordance with buyer's directions and will make the tone more brilliant." On January 15, Betty repudiated the contract by letter to the Forte Piano Company. The company subsequently stained the case, made the tone more brilliant, and offered to ship the piano to Betty on January 26. Betty persisted in her refusal to accept the piano. The Forte Piano Company sued Betty to recover the contract price. To what remedy, if any, is Forte entitled? Explain.

4. Sims contracted in writing to sell Blake one hundred electric motors at a price of $100 each, freight prepaid to Blake's warehouse. By the contract of sale, Sims expressly warranted that each motor would develop twenty-five-brake horsepower. The contract provided that the motors would be delivered in lots of twenty-five per week beginning January 2 and that Blake should pay for each lot of twenty-five motors as delivered but that Blake was to have right of inspection upon delivery. Immediately upon delivery of the first lot of twenty-five motors on January 2, Blake forwarded Sims a check for $2,500, but upon testing each of the twenty-five motors, Blake determined that none would develop more than fifteen-brake

horsepower. Discuss all of the remedies under the Uniform Commercial Code available to Blake.

5. Henry and Mary entered into a written contract whereby Henry agreed to sell and Mary agreed to buy a certain automobile for $8,500. Henry drove the car to Mary's residence and properly parked it on the street in front of her house, where he tendered it to Mary and requested payment of the price. Mary refused to take the car or pay the price. Henry informed Mary that he would hold her to the contract, but before Henry had time to enter the car and drive it away, a fire truck, answering a fire alarm and traveling at a high speed, crashed into the car and demolished it. Henry brings an action against Mary to recover the price of the car. Who is entitled to judgment? Would the result differ if Henry were a dealer in automobiles? Explain.

6. James sells and delivers to Gerald on June 1 certain goods and receives from Gerald at the time of delivery Gerald's check in the amount of $9,000 for the goods. The following day, Gerald is petitioned into bankruptcy, and the check is dishonored by Gerald's bank. On June 5, James serves notice upon Gerald and the trustee in bankruptcy that he reclaims the goods. The trustee is in possession of the goods and refuses to deliver them to James. What are the rights of the parties?

7. The ABC Company, located in Chicago, contracted to sell a carload of television sets to Dodd in St. Louis, Missouri, on sixty days' credit. ABC Company shipped the carload to Dodd. Upon arrival of the car at St. Louis, Dodd paid the freight charges and reshipped the car to Hines of Little Rock, Arkansas, to whom he had previously contracted to sell the television sets. While the car was in transit to Little Rock, Dodd went bankrupt. ABC Company was informed of this at once and immediately telephoned XYZ Railroad Company to withhold delivery of the television sets. Explain what the XYZ Railroad Company should do.

8. Robert in Chicago entered into a contract to sell certain machines to Terry in New York. The machines were to be manufactured by Robert and shipped F.O.B. Chicago not later than March 25. On March 24, when Robert is about to ship the machines, he receives a letter from Terry wrongfully repudiating the contract. The machines cannot readily be resold for a reasonable price because they are a special kind used only in Terry's manufacturing processes. Robert sues Terry to recover the agreed price of the machines. Discuss the rights of the parties.

9. Calvin purchased a log home construction kit manufactured by Boone Homes, Inc., from an authorized Boone dealer. The sales contract stated that Boone would repair or replace defective materials and that this was the exclusive remedy available against Boone. The dealer assembled the house, which was defective in several respects. The knotholes in the logs caused the walls and ceiling to leak. A support beam was too small and therefore cracked, causing the floor to crack also. These defects could not be completely cured by repair. Should Calvin prevail in a lawsuit against Boone for breach of warranty to recover damages for the loss in value? Explain.

10. Margaret contracted to buy a particular model Rolls-Royce from Paragon Motors, Inc. Only one hundred of these models are built each year. She paid a $30,000 deposit on the car, but Paragon sold the car to Gluck. What remedy, if any, does Margaret have against Paragon?

C A S E   P R O B L E M S

11. Technical Textile agreed by written contract to manufacture and sell 20,000 pounds of yarn to Jagger Brothers at a price of $2.15 per pound. After Technical had manufactured, delivered, and been paid for 3,723 pounds of yarn, Jagger Brothers by letter informed Technical that it was repudiating the contract and that it would refuse any further yarn deliveries. On August 12, the date of the letter, the market price of yarn was $1.90 per pound. The remaining 16,277 pounds were never manufactured. Technical sued Jagger Brothers for breach of contract. To what damages, if any, is Technical entitled? Explain.

12. Sherman Burrus, a job printer, purchased a printing press from the Itek Corporation for a price of $7,006.08.

Before making the purchase, Burrus was assured by an Itek salesperson, Mr. Nessel, that the press was appropriate for the type of printing Burrus was doing. Burrus encountered problems in operating the press almost continuously from the time he received it. Burrus, his employees, and Itek representatives spent many hours in an unsuccessful attempt to get the press to operate properly. Burrus requested that the press be replaced, but Itek refused. Burrus then brought an action against Itek for (a) damages for breach of the implied warranty of merchantability and (b) consequential damages for losses resulting from the press's defective operation. Burrus was able to prove that the actual value of the press was

$1,167 and, because of the defective press, that his output decreased and he sustained a great loss of paper. Itek contends that consequential damages are not recoverable in this case since Burrus elected to keep the press and continued to use it. How much should Burrus recover in damages for breach of warranty? Is he entitled to consequential damages? Why or why not?

13. A farmer made a contract in April to sell to a grain dealer forty thousand bushels of corn to be delivered in October. On June 3, the farmer unequivocally informed the grain dealer that he was not going to plant any corn, that he would not fulfill the contract, and that if the buyer had commitments to resell the corn, he should make other arrangements. The grain dealer waited in vain until October for performance of the repudiated contract. Then he bought corn at a greatly increased price on the market in order to fulfill commitments to his purchasers. To what damages, if any, is the grain dealer entitled? Explain.

14. Through information provided by S-2 Yachts, Inc., the plaintiff, Barr located a yacht to his liking at the Crow's Nest marina and yacht sales company. When Barr asked the price, he was told that, although the yacht normally sold for $102,000, Crow's Nest was willing to sell this particular one for only $80,000 to make room for a new model from the manufacturer, S-2 Yachts, Inc. Barr was assured that the yacht in question came with full manufacturer's warranties. Barr asked if the yacht was new and if anything was wrong with it. Crow's Nest told him that nothing was wrong with the yacht and that there were only twenty hours of use on the engines.

    Once the yacht had been delivered and Barr had taken it for a test run, he noticed several problems associated with saltwater damage, such as rusted screws, a rusted stove, and faulty electrical wiring. Barr was assured that Crow's Nest would pay for these repairs. However, as was later discovered, the yacht was in such a damaged condition that Barr experienced great personal hazard the two times that he used the boat. Examination by a marine expert revealed clearly that the boat had been sunk in saltwater prior to Barr's purchase. The engines were severely damaged, and there was significant structural and equipment damage as well. According to the expert, not only was the yacht not new, it was worth at most only one-half of the new value of $102,000. What should Barr be able to recover from S-2 Yachts and Crow's Nest?

15. Lee Oldsmobile sells Rolls-Royce automobiles. Mrs. Kaiden sent Lee a $25,000 deposit on a used Rolls-Royce with a purchase price of $155,500. Although Lee informed Mrs. Kaiden that the car would be delivered in November, the order form did not indicate the delivery date and contained a disclaimer for delay or failure to deliver due to circumstances beyond the dealer's control. On November 21, Mrs. Kaiden purchased another car from another dealer and canceled her car from Lee. When Lee attempted to deliver a Rolls-Royce to Mrs. Kaiden on November 29, Mrs. Kaiden refused to accept delivery. Lee later sold the car for $150,495. Mrs. Kaiden sued Lee for her $25,000 deposit plus interest. Lee counterclaims, based on the terms of the contract, for liquidated damages of $25,000 (the amount of the deposit) as a result of Mrs. Kaiden's breach of contract. What are the rights of the parties?

16. Servebest contracted to sell Emessee two hundred thousand pounds of 50 percent lean beef trimmings for $105,000. Upon a substantial fall in the market price, Emessee refused to pay the contract price and informed Servebest that the contract was canceled. Servebest sues Emessee for breach of contract, including (a) damages for the difference between the contract price and the resale price of the trimmings and (b) incidental damages. Decision?

17. Mrs. French was the highest bidder on eight antique guns at an auction held by Sotheby & Company. Mrs. French made a down payment on the guns but subsequently refused to accept the guns and refused to pay the remaining balance of $24,886.27 owed on them. Is Sotheby's entitled to collect the price of the guns from Mrs. French? Why or why not?

18. Teledyne Industries, Inc., entered into a contract with Teradyne, Inc., to purchase a T-347A transistor test system for the list and fair market price of $98,400 less a discount of $984. After the system was packed for shipment, Teledyne canceled the order, offering to purchase a Field Effects Transistor System for $65,000. Teradyne refused the offer and sold the T-347A to another purchaser pursuant to an order that was on hand prior to the cancellation. Can Teradyne recover from Teledyne for lost profits resulting from the breach of contract? Explain.

19. Wilson Trading Corp. agreed to sell David Ferguson a specified quantity of yarn for use in making sweaters. The written contract provided that notice of defects, to be effective, had to be received by Wilson before knitting or within ten days of receipt of the yarn. When the knitted sweaters were washed, the color of the yarn "shaded" (i.e., variations in color from piece to piece appeared). David Ferguson immediately notified Wilson of the problem and refused to pay for the yarn, claiming that the defect made the sweaters unmarketable. Wilson brought suit against Ferguson for the contract price. What result?

20. Bishop Logging Company is a large, family-owned logging contractor formed in the Lowcountry of South Carolina. Bishop Logging has traditionally harvested pine timber. However, Bishop Logging began investigating the feasibility of a fully mechanized hardwood swamp logging operation when its main customer, Stone Container Corporation, decided to expand hardwood production. In anticipating an increased demand for hardwood in conjunction with the operation of a new paper machine, Stone Container requested that Bishop Logging harvest and supply hardwood for processing at its mill. In South Carolina, most suitable hardwood is located deep in the swamplands. Because of the high accident risk in the swamp, Bishop Logging did not want to harvest hardwood by the conventional method of manual felling of trees. Because Bishop Logging had already been successful in its totally mechanized pine logging operation, it began a search for improved methods of hardwood swamp logging centered on mechanizing the process in order to reduce labor, minimize personal injury and insurance costs, and improve efficiency and productivity. Bishop Logging ultimately purchased several pieces of John Deere equipment to make up the system. The gross sales price of the machinery was $608,899. All the equipment came with a written John Deere "New Equipment Warranty," whereby John Deere agreed only to repair or replace the equipment during the warranty period and did not warrant the suitability of the equipment. In the "New Equipment Warranty," John Deere expressly provided the following: (a) John Deere's promise to repair or replace parts that were defective in material or workmanship; (b) a disclaimer of any express warranties or implied warranties of merchantability or fitness for a particular purpose; (c) an exclusion of all incidental or consequential damages; and (d) no authority for the dealer to make any representations, promises, modifications, or limitations of John Deere's written warranty. Hoping to sell more equipment if the Bishop Logging system was successful, however, John Deere agreed to assume part of the risk of the new enterprise by extending its standard equipment warranties notwithstanding the unusual use and modifications to the equipment. Soon after being placed in operation in the swamp, the machinery began to experience numerous mechanical problems. John Deere made more than $110,000 in warranty repairs on the equipment. However, Bishop Logging contended the swamp logging system failed to operate as represented by John Deere, and as a result, it suffered a substantial financial loss. What, if any, remedies is Bishop entitled to receive? Explain.

21. The plaintiff contracted with the defendant to deliver liquid nitrogen to the defendant's oil refinery production facility located in Belle Chasse, Louisiana. The defendant uses liquid nitrogen to ensure the safe operation of its plant. The contract was a "requirements" contract—deliveries were based on how much liquid nitrogen the defendant had in its tanks. As a result, the plaintiff typically made deliveries seven days a week and sometimes several times a day.

The defendant claims that the plaintiff repeatedly failed to deliver the liquid nitrogen on time, thereby dropping the liquid nitrogen to dangerously low levels and compromising the safety of the plant and its personnel. The contract provided that if the plaintiff failed to deliver the liquid nitrogen as required, the defendant's sole remedy would be to purchase the product from another supplier and charge the plaintiff for the additional expenses incurred. The defendant did not exercise this right because it claims it was unable to purchase nitrogen from other suppliers. However, on the only occasion the defendant actually tried to purchase nitrogen from another supplier, it was successful. The plaintiff sued the defendant for breach of contract, and the defendant counterclaimed. Explain the rights and remedies of the parties.

22. Appalachian is a coal hauling company in southern West Virginia. Appalachian purchased four new Mack trucks for off-road coal hauling. Appalachian purchased three of the trucks for $165,000 each and the fourth for $175,000. The trucks were sold to Appalachian by Worldwide, a franchised retail dealer for Mack. The express warranty made with regard to Appalachian's purchase of the four trucks validly disclaimed implied warranties and limited the express warranty to repairing or replacing defective parts. According to Appalachian, each of the four trucks failed to function properly due to a multitude of problems, which began immediately after the purchase. The trucks continually broke down, resulting in repeated instances of driving or towing the trucks back for repairs. The problems included not running, hard starting, transmission problems, overheating, leaking water pumps, hoods falling off, and cabs falling apart. Although Worldwide never declined to try to repair the trucks, the repairs were never successful and replacement vehicles were never provided. Appalachian brought an action for revocation of acceptance of the four trucks, a refund of the purchase price, incidental damages, and consequential damages. Decision? Explain.

23. Kenco buys mobile homes from the factory and sells them to the consumer. Sometimes, it contracts to sell a home that the factory has not yet built. It has a virtually

unlimited supply of product. On September 27, Kenco Homes, Inc., and Dale and Debi Williams signed a written contract for the Williamses to buy from Kenco a mobile home that had not yet been built. The price was $39,400, with $500 down. Subsequently, Dale Williams gave Kenco a $600 check so Kenco could order an appraisal of the land on which the mobile home would be located. Before Kenco could act, Dale Williams stopped payment on the check and repudiated the transaction.

His stated reason was that he "had found a better deal elsewhere." When Dale Williams repudiated, Kenco had not yet ordered the mobile home from the factory. After Dale Williams repudiated, Kenco simply did not place the order. As a result, Kenco's only out-of-pocket expense was a minor amount of office overhead. On November 1, Kenco sued the Williamses for lost profits in the amount of $11,133. Is Kenco entitled to recover its lost profits or just the $500 deposit? Explain.

TAKING SIDES

Daniel Martin and John Duke contracted with J & S Distributors, Inc., to purchase a KIS Magnum Speed printer for $17,000. The parties agreed that Martin and Duke would send one-half of the money as a deposit and would pay the balance upon delivery. They also agreed to the following provision:

In the event of non-payment of the balance of the purchase price reflected herein on due date and in the manner recorded or on such extended date which may be caused by late delivery on the part of [the seller], the Customer shall be liable for: (1) immediate payment of the full balance recorded herein; and (2) payment of interest at the rate of 12 percent per annum calculated on the balance due, when due, together with any attorney's fees, collection charges and other necessary expenses incurred by [the seller].

When the machine arrived five days late, Martin and Duke refused to accept it, stating that the company had purchased a substitute machine elsewhere. Martin and Duke requested the return of its deposit, but J & S refused. Martin and Duke sued J & S for the return of its deposit. J & S counter claimed for full performance of the contract, seeking an order that Martin and Duke accept delivery of the KIS machine and pay the entire balance of the contract.

a. What arguments would support the claim by Martin and Duke for the return of the deposit?

b. What arguments would support the claim by J & S for full performance of the contract?

c. Who should prevail? Explain.

5

Negotiable Instruments

CH 26 FORM AND CONTENT

CH 27 TRANSFER AND HOLDER IN DUE COURSE

CH 28 LIABILITY OF PARTIES

CH 29 BANK DEPOSITS, COLLECTIONS, AND FUNDS TRANSFERS

CHAPTER 26

Form and Content

CHAPTER OUTCOMES

After reading and studying this chapter, you should be able to:

- Describe the concept and importance of negotiability.

- Describe the types of negotiable instruments involving an order to pay.

- Describe the types of negotiable instruments involving a promise to pay.

- Explain the formal requirements that an instrument must meet to be negotiable.

- Explain the effect on negotiability of an instrument's (1) being undated, antedated, or postdated; (2) lack of completion; and (3) ambiguity.

Negotiable instruments, also referred to simply as instruments, include drafts, checks, promissory notes, and certificates of deposit. These instruments are widely used by individuals and businesses in paying for goods and services as well as in financing numerous types of transactions.

For a number of reasons, payment by noncash means is preferable in many transactions; approximately 85 percent of all payments in the United States are made by noncash means. According to the 2019 triennial Federal Reserve Payments Study, in the United States noncash payments totaled approximately 174 billion in number and $97 trillion in value. Noncash payments take two forms: paper (checks and drafts) and electronic (debit cards, credit cards, automated clearinghouse [ACH], prepaid cards, and online payment systems such as online banking and PayPal). In both number and value, electronic payments now greatly exceed paper payments. Ninety percent of electronic payments in value are ACH transfers.

The **financing** or credit function of negotiable instruments is indispensable. For example, promissory notes are used extensively in financing sales of goods. In addition, corporations fund their operating expenses or current assets by issuing commercial paper in the form of short-term promissory notes. In the United States in February 2020, more than $1.1 trillion of commercial paper was outstanding. Moreover, corporations obtain long-term financing by issuing long-term promissory notes (bonds). In the United States at the end of 2019, more than $10 trillion of corporate bonds were outstanding. Promissory notes are also used in financing sales of real estate, with more than $15.8 trillion of mortgage

debt outstanding in the United States at the end of September 2019. A certificate of deposit (CD) is a type of promissory note issued by a bank; CDs are used by many individuals as a type of deposit account that typically offers a higher rate of interest than a regular savings account.

Accordingly, the vital importance of negotiable instruments and electronic transfers as methods of payment and financing cannot be overstated. See *Figure 26-1* for a summary of how these instruments are commonly used and the chapters in this text that discuss them.

♦ **SEE FIGURE 26-1:** *Use of Negotiable Instruments*

In 1990, the American Law Institute and the Uniform Law Commission (also known as the National Conference of Commissioners on Uniform Laws) approved a Revised Article 3 to the Uniform Commercial Code (UCC). Named "Negotiable Instruments," the new Article maintains the basic scope and content of prior Article 3 (Commercial Paper). All States except New York have adopted the 1990 version of Article 3. In 2002, the American Law Institute and the Uniform Law Commission completed updates to Articles 3 and 4, and at least eleven States have adopted the 2002 version. This part of the text discusses the 1990 version of Revised Article 3.

26-1 Negotiability

Negotiability is a legal concept that makes written instruments more freely transferable and therefore a readily accepted form of payment in substitution for money.

FIGURE 26-1 Use of Negotiable Instruments

Instrument	Use	Chapter in Text
Check	Payment	26–29
Draft	Finance the movement of goods	26–28
Note	Commercial paper; business, personal, and real estate financing	26–28, 34, 37, 43, 49
Certificate of Deposit	Savings	26–28
Debit Card	Payment	29
Credit Card	Payment	29, 41
ACH	Payment	29
Prepaid Card	Payment	29

26-1a DEVELOPMENT OF LAW OF NEGOTIABLE INSTRUMENTS

The starting point for an understanding of negotiable instruments is recognizing that four or five centuries ago in England, a contract right to the payment of money was not assignable because a contractual promise ran to the promisee. The fact that performance could be rendered only to him constituted a hardship for the owner of the right because it prevented him from selling or disposing of it. Eventually, however, the law permitted recovery upon an assignment by the assignee against the obligor.

An innocent assignee bringing an action against the obligor was subject to all defenses available to the obligor. Such an action would result in the same outcome whether it was brought by the assignee or assignor. Thus, a contract right became assignable but not very marketable because merchants had little interest in buying paper that may be subject to a defense. This remains the law of **assignments**: the assignee stands in the shoes of his assignor. For a discussion of assignments, see *Chapter 16*.

With the flourishing of trade and commerce, it became essential to develop a more effective means of exchanging contractual rights for money. For example, a merchant who sold goods for cash might use the cash to buy more goods for resale. If he were to make a sale on credit in exchange for a promise to pay money, why should he not be permitted to sell that promise to someone else for cash with which to carry on his business? One difficulty was that the buyer of the goods gave the seller only a promise to pay money to him. The seller was the only person to whom performance or payment was promised. If, however, the seller obtained from the buyer a promise in writing to pay money to anyone in possession (a bearer) of the writing (the paper or instrument) or to anyone the seller (or payee in this case) designated, then the duty of performance would run directly to the holder (the bearer of the paper or to the person to whom the payee ordered payment to be made). This is one of the essential distinctions between negotiable and nonnegotiable instruments. Although a negotiable instrument has other formal requirements, this particular one eliminates the limitations of a promise to pay money only to a named promisee.

Moreover, if the promise to pay were not subject to all of the defenses available against the assignor, a transferee would not only be more willing to acquire the promise but also would pay more for it. Accordingly, the law of negotiable instruments developed the concept of the **holder in due course**, whereby certain good-faith transferees who gave value acquired the right to be paid, free of most of the defenses to which an assignee would be subject. By reason of this doctrine, a transferee of a negotiable instrument could acquire greater rights than his transferor, whereas an assignee would acquire only the rights of his assignor. With these basic innovations, negotiable instruments enabled merchants to sell their contractual rights more readily and thereby keep their capital working.

26-1b ASSIGNMENT COMPARED WITH NEGOTIATION

Negotiability invests negotiable instruments with a high degree of marketability and commercial utility. It allows negotiable instruments to be freely transferable and enforceable by a person with the rights of a holder in due course against any person obligated on the instrument, subject only to a limited number of defenses. To illustrate, assume that George sells and delivers goods to Elaine for $50,000 on sixty days' credit and that, a few days later, George assigns this account to Marsha. Unless Elaine is duly notified of this assignment, she may safely pay the $50,000 to George on the due date without incurring any liability to Marsha, the assignee. Assume next that the goods were defective and that Elaine, accordingly, has a defense against George to the extent of $20,000. Assume also that Marsha duly notified Elaine of the assignment. The result is that Marsha can

FIGURE 26-2 Order to Pay: Draft or Check

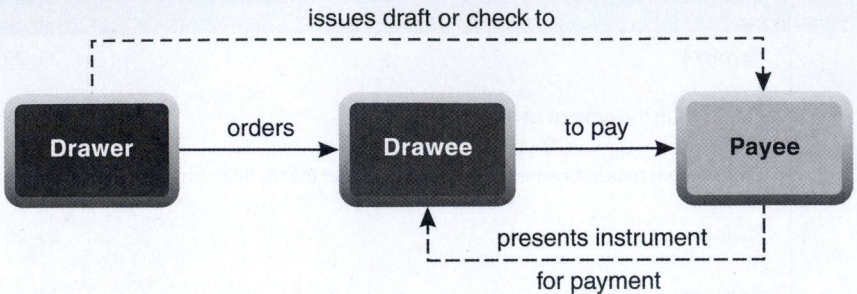

recover only $30,000, not $50,000, from Elaine because Elaine's defense against George is equally available against George's assignee, Marsha. In other words, an assignee of contractual rights merely "steps into the shoes" of her assignor and, hence, acquires only the same rights as her assignor—and no more.

Assume, instead, that upon the sale by George to Elaine, Elaine executes and delivers her negotiable note to George for $50,000 payable to George's order in sixty days and that, a short time later, George duly negotiates (transfers) the note to Marsha. In the first place, Marsha is not required to notify Elaine that she has acquired the note from George, because one who issues a negotiable instrument is held to know that the instrument may be negotiated and generally is obligated to pay the holder of the instrument, whoever that may be. In the second place, Elaine's defense is not available against Marsha if Marsha acquired the note in good faith and for value and had no knowledge of Elaine's defense against George and took it without reason to question its authenticity. Marsha, therefore, is entitled to hold Elaine for the full face amount of the note at maturity, namely, $50,000. In other words, Marsha, by the negotiation of the negotiable note to her, acquired rights greater than those George had, because, by keeping the note, George could have recovered only $30,000 on it because Elaine successfully could have asserted her defense in the amount of $20,000 against him.

To have the full benefit of negotiability, negotiable instruments not only must meet the requirements of negotiability but also must be acquired by a holder in due course. This chapter discusses the formal requirements instruments must satisfy to be negotiable. *Chapter 27* will deal with the manner in which a negotiable

instrument must be negotiated to preserve its advantages as well as the requisites and rights of a holder in due course. *Chapter 28* will examine the liability of all the parties to a negotiable instrument.

26-2 Types of Negotiable Instruments

There are four types of negotiable instruments: drafts, checks, notes, and certificates of deposit. Section 3-104. The first two contain **orders** or directions to pay money; the last two involve **promises** to pay money.

26-2a   DRAFTS

A **draft** involves three parties, each in a distinct capacity. One party, the **drawer**, *orders* a second party, the **drawee**, to pay a fixed amount of money to a third party, the **payee** (see *Figure 26-2*). Thus, the drawer "draws" the draft on the drawee. The drawee is ordinarily a person or an entity that either is in possession of money belonging to the drawer or owes money to him. A sample draft is reproduced as *Figure 26-3*. The same party may appear in more than one capacity; for instance, the drawer may also be the payee.

Drafts may be either "time" or "sight." A **time draft** is payable at a specified future date, whereas a **sight draft** is payable on demand (i.e., immediately upon presentation to the drawee). A form of time draft known as a trade acceptance is frequently used as a credit device in commercial transactions. A **trade acceptance** is a time draft, drawn by the seller (drawer) on the buyer (drawee), that names the seller or some third party as the payee.

♦ **SEE FIGURE 26-2:** *Order to Pay: Draft or Check*

FIGURE 26-3 Draft

Two years from date pay to the order of Perry Payee $50,000 Fifty Thousand . . . Dollars	St. Louis, Missouri May 1, 2021
To: DEBRA DRAWEE 50 Main St. Louisville, Kentucky	(Signed) Donald Drawer DONALD DRAWER

FIGURE 26-4 **Check**

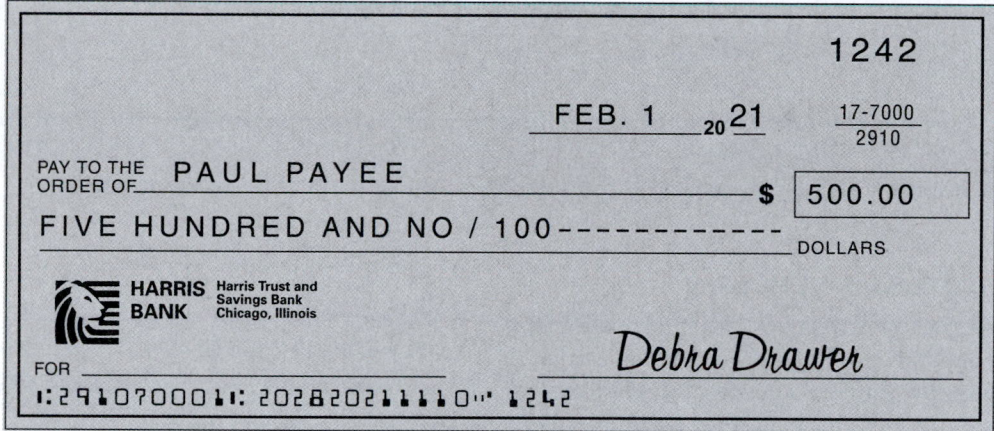

♦ **SEE FIGURE 26-3:** *Draft*

26-2b CHECKS

A check is a specialized form of draft, namely, an order to pay money drawn on a bank that is payable on demand (i.e., upon the payee's request for payment). Section 3-104(f). Once again, parties are involved in three distinct capacities: the *drawer*, who orders the *drawee*, a bank, to pay the *payee* on demand. Checks are by far the most widely used form of negotiable instruments. In 2018, the number of checks paid in the United States was approximately 14.5 billion with a value of approximately $26 trillion. A number of checks are converted into electronic payments that are processed through the ACH Network. In 2018, the percentage of checks converted to ACH-based electronic payment was 10 percent.

The Check Clearing for the 21st Century Act (also called Check 21 or the Check Truncation Act), which went into effect in late 2004, creates a new negotiable instrument called a substitute check or image replacement document (IRD). The law permits banks to truncate original checks, to process check information electronically, and to deliver substitute checks to banks that want to continue receiving paper checks. A substitute check would be the legal equivalent of the original check and would include all the information contained on the original check. The law does not require banks to accept checks in electronic form, nor does it require banks to use the new authority granted by the Act to create substitute checks. This type of instrument is more fully discussed in *Chapter 29*.

A **cashier's check** is a check drawn by a bank upon itself to the order of a named payee. Section 3-104(g).

♦ **SEE FIGURE 26-4:** *Check*

26-2c NOTES

A **promissory note** is an instrument involving two parties in two capacities. One party, the **maker**, promises to pay a second party, the payee, a stated sum of money, either on demand or at a stated future date (see *Figure 26-5*). The note may range from a simple "I promise to pay $X to the order of Y" form to more complex legal instruments such as installment notes, collateral notes, mortgage notes, and judgment notes. *Figure 26-6* is a note payable at a definite time—six months from the date of April 7, 2021—and thus is referred to as a **time note**. A note payable upon the request or demand of the payee or holder is a **demand note**.

♦ **SEE FIGURE 26-5:** *Promise to Pay: Promissory Note or Certificate of Deposit*

FIGURE 26-5 **Promise to Pay: Promissory Note or Certificate of Deposit**

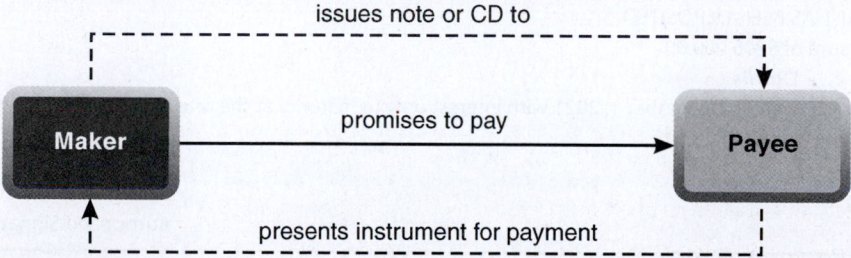

FIGURE 26-6 Note

| $10,000 | Albany, NY | April 7, 2021 |

Six months from date I promise to pay to the order of Pat Payee ten thousand dollars.

(signed) Matthew Maker

◆ **SEE FIGURE 26-6:** *Note*

26-2d CERTIFICATES OF DEPOSIT

A certificate of deposit, or CD as it is frequently called, is a specialized form of *promise* to pay money given by a *bank*. A **certificate of deposit** is a written acknowledgment by a bank of the receipt of money that it promises to repay. Section 3-104(j). The issuing party, the *maker*, which is always a bank, promises to pay a second party, the payee, who is named in the CD.

◆ **SEE FIGURE 26-7:** *Certificate of Deposit*

26-3 Formal Requirements of Negotiable Instruments

To perform its function in the business community effectively, a negotiable instrument must be able to pass freely from person to person. The fact that *negotiability* is wholly a matter of form makes such freedom possible. The instrument must contain within its "four corners" all the information required to determine whether it is negotiable. No reference to any other source is permitted. For this reason, a negotiable instrument is called a "courier without luggage." In addition, indorsements *cannot* create or destroy negotiability.

To be negotiable, the **instrument** must—

1. be in writing,
2. be signed,
3. contain a promise or order to pay,
4. be unconditional,
5. be for a fixed amount,
6. be for money,
7. contain no other undertaking or instruction,
8. be payable on demand or at a definite time, and
9. be payable to order or to bearer.

Section 3-104(a). If these requirements are not met, the undertaking is not a negotiable instrument, and the rights of the parties are governed by the law of contract (assignment).

Practical Advice

To increase the value of an undertaking, make sure that any document memorializing it qualifies as a negotiable instrument.

26-3a WRITING

The requirement that the instrument be in writing (Sections 3-103(a)(6), (9)) is broadly construed. Printing, typewriting, handwriting, or any other intentional tangible expression is sufficient to satisfy the requirement. Section 1-201; Revised Section 1-201. Most negotiable instruments, of course, are written on paper, but this is not required. For example, a check in one instance was reportedly written on the back of a cow and in another written on a coconut.

FIGURE 26-7 Certificate of Deposit

NEGOTIABLE CERTIFICATE OF DEPOSIT
The Mountain Bank
Mountain, N.Y.

No. 13900   June 1, 2021

THIS CERTIFIES THAT THERE HAS BEEN DEPOSITED
with the undersigned the sum of $200,000.00
Two hundred thousand......... Dollars
Payable to the order of Pablo Payee on December 1, 2021 with interest only to maturity at the rate of Two percent (2%) per annum upon surrender of this certificate properly indorsed.

The Mountain Bank
By (Signature) Malcolm Maker, Vice President
Authorized Signature

26-3b SIGNED

A note or certificate of deposit must be signed by the maker; a draft or check must be signed by the drawer. As in the case of a writing, extreme latitude is granted in determining what constitutes a **signature**, which is any symbol a party executes or adopts with the present *intention* to adopt or accept a writing. Section 1-201(39). Revised Article 1 changes the word *authenticate* to *adopt or accept.* Revised Section 1-201(b)(37). Moreover, it may consist of any word or mark used in place of a written signature, Section 3-401(b), such as initials, an X, or a thumbprint. It may be a trade name or an assumed name. Even the location of the signature on the document is unimportant. Normally, a maker or drawer signs in the lower right corner of the instrument, but this is not required. Negotiable instruments are frequently signed by an agent for her principal. For a discussion of the appropriate way in which an agent should sign a negotiable instrument, see *Chapter 28.*

26-3c PROMISE OR ORDER TO PAY

A negotiable instrument must contain either a promise to pay money, in the case of a note or certificate of deposit, or an order to pay, in the case of a draft or check.

PROMISE TO PAY A promise to pay is an undertaking and must be more than the mere acknowledgment or recognition of an existing obligation or debt. Section 3-103(a)(9). The so-called due bill or I.O.U. is not a promise but merely an acknowledgment of indebtedness. Accordingly, an instrument reciting "due Adam Brown $100" or "I.O.U., Adam Brown, $100" is not negotiable because it does not contain a promise to pay.

ORDER TO PAY An order to pay is an instruction to pay. It must be more than an authorization or request and must identify with reasonable certainty the person to be paid. Section 3-103(a)(6). The usual way to express an order is by use of the word *pay*: "*Pay* to the order of John Jones" or "*Pay* bearer." The addition of words of courtesy, such as "please pay" or "kindly *pay*," will not destroy the negotiability. Nonetheless, caution should be exercised in employing words that modify the prototypically correct "*Pay*." For example, the use of the words "I wish you would *pay*" has been held to destroy the negotiability of an instrument and to render its transfer a contractual assignment.

26-3d UNCONDITIONAL

The requirement that the promise or order be unconditional is to prevent the inclusion of any term that could reduce the promisor's obligation to pay. Conditions limiting a promise would diminish the payment and credit functions of negotiable instruments by necessitating costly and time-consuming

investigations to determine the degree of risk such conditions imposed. Moreover, if the holder (transferee) had to take an instrument subject to certain conditions, her risk factor would be substantial, and this would lead to limited transferability. Substitutes for money must be capable of rapid circulation at minimum risk.

A promise or order to pay is **unconditional** if it is absolute and not subject to any contingencies or qualifications. Thus, an instrument would not be negotiable if it stated that "ABC Corp. promises to pay $100,000 to the order of Johnson provided the helicopter sold meets all contractual specifications." On the other hand, suppose that upon delivering an instrument that provided "ABC Corp. promises to pay $100,000 to the order of Johnson," Meeker, the president of ABC, stated that the money would be paid only if the helicopter met all contractual specifications. The instrument would be negotiable because negotiability is determined solely by examining the instrument itself and is not affected by matters beyond the instrument's face.

A promise or order is unconditional unless it states that (1) there is an express condition to payment, (2) the promise or order is subject to or governed by another writing, or (3) rights or obligations concerning the order or promise are stated in another writing. A mere reference to another writing, however, does not make the promise or order conditional. Section 3-106(a).

An instrument is not made conditional by the fact that it is subject to implied or constructive conditions; the condition must be expressed to destroy negotiability. Section 3-106(a). Implications of law or fact are not to be considered in deciding whether an instrument is negotiable. Thus, a statement in an instrument that it is given for an executory promise does not imply that the instrument is conditioned upon performance of that promise.

REFERENCE TO OTHER AGREEMENTS The restriction against reference to another agreement is to enable any person to determine the right to payment provided by the instrument without having to look beyond its four corners. If such right is made subject to the terms of another agreement, the instrument is nonnegotiable. Section 3-106(a)(ii).

A distinction is to be made between a mere recital of the existence of a separate agreement (this does not destroy negotiability) and a recital that makes the instrument *subject* to the terms of another agreement (this does destroy negotiability).

A statement in a note such as "This note is given in partial payment for a television to be delivered two weeks from date in accordance with a contract of this date between the payee and the maker" does not impair negotiability. It merely describes the consideration and the transaction giving rise to the note. It does not place any restriction or condition on the maker's obligation to pay. The promise is not made subject to any other agreement.

Added words that would impair negotiability are "This note is subject to all terms of said contract." Such words make the promise to pay conditional upon the adequate performance of the television set in accordance with the terms of the contract and thus render the instrument nonnegotiable.

THE PARTICULAR FUND DOCTRINE Revised Article 3 provides that a promise or order is *not* made conditional because payment is to be made only out of a particular fund. Section 3-106(b)(ii).

26-3e FIXED AMOUNT

The purpose of the requirement of a fixed amount in money is to enable the person entitled to enforce the instrument to determine from the instrument itself the amount that he is entitled to receive.

The requirement that payment be of a "fixed amount" must be considered from the point of view of the person entitled to enforce the instrument, not the maker or drawer. The holder must be assured of a determinable minimum payment, although provisions of the instrument may increase the recovery under certain circumstances. Revised Article 3, however, applies the fixed amount requirement only to the *principal*. Section 3-112, Comment 1. Thus, the fixed amount portion does not apply to interest or to other charges, such as collection fees or attorneys' fees. Moreover, negotiability of an instrument is not affected by the inclusion or omission of a stated rate of interest. If the instrument does not state a rate of interest, it is payable without interest. Section 3-112(a). If the instrument states that it is payable "with interest" but does not specify a rate, the judgment rate of interest applies.

Most significantly, Revised Article 3 provides that "Interest may be stated in an instrument as a fixed or variable amount of money or it may be expressed as a fixed or variable rate or rates." Section 3-112(b). Moreover, determination of the rate of interest "may require reference to information not contained in the instrument." Section 3-112(b). Variable rate mortgages, therefore, may be negotiable; this result is consistent with the rule that the fixed amount requirement applies only to the principal.

A sum payable is a fixed amount even though it is payable (1) in installments, (2) with a fixed discount if paid before maturity, or (3) with a fixed addition if paid after maturity. This is because it is always possible to use the instrument itself to compute the amount due at any given time.

♦ *See Case 26-1*

26-3f MONEY

The term **money** means a medium of exchange currently authorized or adopted by a domestic or foreign government. Revised Section 1-201(b)(24). Consequently, even though local custom may make gold or diamonds a medium of exchange, an instrument payable in such commodities would be nonnegotiable because of the lack of government sanction of such media as legal tender. On the other hand, an instrument paying a fixed amount in Swiss francs, English pounds, Australian dollars, Japanese yen, Nigerian naira, or other foreign currency is negotiable. Section 3-107.

26-3g NO OTHER UNDERTAKING OR INSTRUCTION

A negotiable instrument must contain a promise or order to pay money, but it may not "state any other undertaking or instruction by the person promising or ordering payment to do any act in addition to the payment of money." Section 3-104(a)(3). Accordingly, an instrument containing an order or promise to do an act in addition to or in lieu of the payment of money is not negotiable. For example, a promise to pay $100 "and a ton of coal" would be nonnegotiable.

The Code sets out a list of terms and provisions that may be included in instruments without adversely affecting negotiability. Among these are (1) an undertaking or power to give, maintain, or protect collateral to secure payment; (2) an authorization or power to confess judgment (written authority by the debtor to allow the holder to enter judgment against the debtor in favor of the holder) on the instrument; (3) an authorization or power to sell or dispose of collateral upon default; and (4) a waiver of the benefit of any law intended for the advantage or protection of the obligor. It is important to note that the Code does not render any of these terms legal or effective; it merely provides that their inclusion will not affect negotiability.

Practical Advice

To preserve the negotiability of an instrument, avoid including any undertaking beyond the promise or order to pay.

26-3h PAYABLE ON DEMAND OR AT A DEFINITE TIME

A negotiable instrument must "be payable on demand or at a definite time." Section 3-104. This requirement, like the other formal requirements of negotiability, is designed to promote certainty in determining the present value of a negotiable instrument.

DEMAND "Payable upon demand" means that the money owed under the instrument must be paid upon the holder's request. **Demand paper** always has been considered sufficiently certain as to time of payment to satisfy the requirements of negotiability because it is the person entitled to enforce the instrument who makes the demand and who thus sets the time for payment. Any instrument in which no time for payment is stated—a check, for example—is payable on demand. An instrument also qualifies as being payable on demand if it is payable at sight or on presentment. Section 3-108(a).

♦ *See Case 26-2*

DEFINITE TIME Instruments payable at a definite time are called **time paper**. A promise or order is payable at a definite time if it is payable—

1. at a fixed date or dates,
2. at a definite period of time after sight or acceptance, or
3. at a time readily ascertainable at the time the promise or order is issued.

Section 3-108(b). An instrument is payable at a definite time if it is payable "on or before" a stated date. The person entitled to enforce the instrument is thus assured that she will have her money by the maturity date at the latest, although she may receive it sooner. This right of anticipation enables the obligor, at his option, to pay before the stated maturity date (*prepayment*) and thereby stop the further accrual of interest or, if interest rates have gone down, to refinance at a lower rate of interest. Nevertheless, it constitutes sufficient certainty so as not to impair negotiability. Section 3-108(b)(i).

Frequently, instruments are made payable at a fixed period after a stated date. For example, the instrument may be made payable "thirty days after date." This means it is payable thirty days after the date of issuance, which is recited on the instrument. Such an instrument is payable at a definite time, for its exact maturity date can be determined by simple math.

An undated instrument payable "thirty days after date" is not payable at a definite time, because the date of payment cannot be determined from its face. It is therefore nonnegotiable until it is completed.

An instrument that by its terms is otherwise payable only upon an act or event whose time of occurrence is uncertain is not payable at a definite time. An example would be a note providing for payment to the order "when X dies." However, as previously stated, a time that is readily ascertainable at the time the promise or order is issued is a definite time. Section 3-108(b). This seemingly would permit a note reading "payable on the day of the next presidential election." As long as the scheduled event is certain to happen, Revised Article 3 appears to be satisfied.

The clause "at a fixed period after sight" is frequently used in drafts. Because a fixed period after sight means a fixed period after acceptance, a simple mathematical calculation makes the maturity date certain, and the instrument is, therefore, negotiable.

An instrument payable at a fixed time subject to **acceleration** by the holder also satisfies the requirement of being payable at a definite time. Section 3-108(b)(ii). Indeed, such an instrument would seem to have a more certain maturity date than a demand instrument because it at least states a definite maturity date. In addition, the acceleration may be contingent upon the happening of some act or event.

Finally, a provision in an instrument granting the holder an option to extend the maturity of the instrument for a definite or indefinite period does not impair its negotiability. Section 3-108(b)(iii). In addition, a provision permitting the obligor of an instrument to extend the maturity date to a further definite time does not impair its negotiability. Section 3-108(b)(iv). For example, a provision in a note, payable one year from date, that the maker may extend the maturity date six months does not impair negotiability. If the obligor is given an option to extend the maturity of the instrument for an indefinite period, however, his promise is illusory, and there is no certainty regarding time of payment. Such an instrument is nonnegotiable. If the obligor's right to extend is limited to a definite time, the extension clause is no more indefinite than an acceleration clause with a time limitation.

In addition, extension may be made automatic upon or after a specified act or event, provided a definite time limit is stated. An example of such an extension clause is,

I promise to pay to the order of John Doe the sum of $2,000 on December 1, 2020, but it is agreed that if the crop of sections 25 and 26 of Twp. 145 is below eight bushels per acre for the 2020 season, this note shall be extended for one year.

AT A DEFINITE TIME AND ON DEMAND If the instrument, payable at a fixed date, *also* provides that it is payable on demand made before the fixed date, it is still a negotiable instrument. Revised Article 3 provides that the instrument is payable on demand until the fixed date and, if demand is not made prior to the specified date, becomes payable at a definite time on the fixed date. Section 3-108(c).

26-3i PAYABLE TO ORDER OR TO BEARER

A negotiable instrument must contain words indicating that the maker or drawer intends that it may pass into the hands of someone other than the payee. Although the "magic" **words of negotiability** typically are *to the order of* or *to bearer*, other clearly equivalent words also may fulfill this requirement. The use of synonyms, however, only invites trouble. Moreover, as noted above, indorsements cannot create or destroy negotiability, which must be determined from the "face" of the instrument. Words of negotiability must be present when the instrument is issued or first comes into possession of a holder. Section 3-104(a)(1).

Revised Article 3 provides that a *check* that meets all requirements of being a negotiable instrument except that it is not payable to bearer or order is nevertheless a negotiable instrument. Section 3-104(c). This rule does *not* apply to instruments other than checks.

PAYABLE TO ORDER An instrument is payable to order if it is payable (a) to the order of an identified person or (b) to an identified person or order. Section 3-109(b). If an instrument is payable to bearer, it cannot be payable to order; an instrument that is ambiguous as to this point is payable to bearer. Prior Article 3 provided that use of the word *assigns* met the requirement of words of negotiability; Revised Article 3, however, does not so provide.

Moreover, in every instance, the person to whose order the instrument is payable must be designated with reasonable certainty. Within this limitation, a broad range of payees is possible, including an individual, two or more payees, an office, an estate, a trust or fund, a partnership or unincorporated association, and a corporation.

This requirement should not be confused with the requirement that the instrument contain an order or promise to pay. An order to pay is an instruction to a third party to pay the instrument as drawn. The word *order* in terms of an "order instrument," on the other hand, pertains to the transferability of the instrument rather than to instructions directing a specific party to pay.

A writing, other than a *check*, that names a specified person without indicating that it is payable to order—for example, "Pay to Justin Matthew"—is not payable to order or to bearer. Such a writing is not a negotiable instrument and is not covered by Article 3. On the other hand, a check that meets all of the requirements of a negotiable instrument, except that it does not provide the words of negotiability, is still a negotiable instrument and falls within the purview of Article 3. Section 3-104(c). Thus, a check payable to Justin Matthew is a negotiable check.

PAYABLE TO BEARER Section 3-109(a) of the Code states that an instrument fulfills the requirements of being **payable to bearer** if it (1) states it is payable to bearer or the order of bearer, (2) does not state a payee, or (3) states it is payable to "cash" or to the order of "cash." Section 3-109(a). An instrument made payable both to order and to bearer, that is, "pay to the order of Mildred Courts or bearer," is payable to bearer. Section 3-109, Comment 2.

An instrument that does not state a payee is payable to bearer. Thus, if a drawer leaves blank the "pay to order of" line of a check or the maker of a note writes "pay to _____," the instrument is a negotiable bearer instrument. Section 3-109(a)(2).

◆ *See Case 26-3*

26-3j TERMS AND OMISSIONS AND THEIR EFFECT ON NEGOTIABILITY

The negotiability of an instrument may be questioned because of an omission of certain provisions or because of ambiguity. Problems may also arise in connection with the interpretation of an instrument, whether or not negotiability is called into question. Accordingly, the Code contains rules of construction that apply to every instrument.

DATING OF THE INSTRUMENT The negotiability of an instrument is not affected by the fact that it is antedated, or postdated. Section 3-113(a). If the instrument is undated, its date is the date of its issuance. If it is unissued, its date is the date it first comes into the possession of a holder. Section 3-113(b).

INCOMPLETE INSTRUMENTS Occasionally, a party will sign a paper that clearly is intended to become an instrument but that, either by intention or through oversight, is incomplete because of the omission of a necessary element such as a promise or order, a designated payee, an amount payable, or a time for payment. Section 3-115 provides that such an instrument is not negotiable until completed.

If, for example, an undated instrument is delivered on November 1, 2020, payable "thirty days after date," the payee has implied authority to fill in "November 1, 2020." Until he does so, however, the instrument is not negotiable because it is not payable at a definite time. If the payee completes the instrument by inserting an erroneous date, the rules as to material alteration, covered in *Chapter 28*, apply.

AMBIGUOUS INSTRUMENTS Rather than commit the parties to the use of parol evidence to establish the interpretation of an instrument, Article 3 establishes rules to resolve common ambiguities. This promotes negotiability by providing added certainty to the holder.

Where it is doubtful whether the instrument is a draft or note, the holder may treat it as either and present it for payment to the drawee or the person signing it. Section 3-104(e). For example, an instrument reading

> To X: On demand I promise to pay $500 to the order of Y.
>   Signed, Z

may be presented for payment to X as a draft or to Z as a note.

An instrument naming no drawee but stating

> On demand, pay $500 to the order of Y.
>   Signed, Z

although in the form of a draft, may be treated as a note and presented to Z for payment.

If a printed form of note or draft is used and the party signing it inserts handwritten or typewritten language that is inconsistent with the printed words, the handwritten words control the typewritten and the printed words and the typewritten words control the printed words. Section 3-114.

If the amount payable is set forth on the face of the instrument in both figures and words and the amounts differ, the words control the figures. It is presumed that the maker or drawer would be more careful with words. If the words are ambiguous, however, then the figures control. Section 3-114.

C H A P T E R S U M M A R Y

NEGOTIABILITY	**Rule** invests instruments with a high degree of marketability and commercial utility by conferring upon certain good faith transferees immunity from most defenses to the instrument **Formal Requirements** negotiability is wholly a matter of form, and all the requirements for negotiability must be met within the four corners of the instrument
TYPES OF NEGOTIABLE INSTRUMENTS	**Orders to Pay** • *Drafts* a draft involves three parties: the drawer orders the drawee to pay a fixed amount of money to the payee • *Checks* a specialized form of draft that is drawn on a bank and payable on demand; the drawer orders the drawee (bank) to pay the payee on demand (upon the request of the holder) **Promises to Pay** • *Note* a written promise by a maker (issuer) to pay a payee • *Certificates of Deposit* a specialized form of note that is given by a bank or thrift association
FORMAL REQUIREMENTS OF NEGOTIABLE INSTRUMENTS	**Writing** any intentional reduction to tangible form is sufficient **Signed** any symbol executed or adopted by a party with the present intention to adopt or accept a writing **Promise or Order to Pay** • *Promise to Pay* an undertaking to pay, which must be more than a mere acknowledgment or recognition of an existing debt • *Order to Pay* instruction to pay **Unconditional** an absolute promise to pay that is not subject to any contingencies • *Reference to Other Agreements* does not destroy negotiability unless the recital makes the instrument subject to or governed by the terms of another agreement • *The Particular Fund Doctrine* an order or promise to pay only out of a particular fund is not conditional and does not destroy negotiability **Fixed Amount** the holder must be assured of a determinable minimum principal payment, although provisions in the instrument may increase the amount of recovery under certain circumstances **Money** medium of exchange currently authorized or adopted by a domestic or foreign government **No Other Undertaking or Instruction** a promise or order to do an act in addition to the payment of money destroys negotiability **Payable on Demand or at a Definite Time** an instrument is demand paper if it must be paid upon request; an instrument is time paper if it is payable at a definite time **Payable to Order or to Bearer** a negotiable instrument must contain words indicating that the maker or drawer intends that it pass into the hands of someone other than the payee • *Payable to Order* payable to the "order of" (or other words which mean the same) a named person or anyone designated by that person • *Payable to Bearer* payable to the holder of the instrument; includes instruments (1) payable to bearer or the order of bearer, (2) that do not specify a payee, or (3) payable to "cash" or to order of "cash"

CASES

CASE
26-1

Formal Requirements of Negotiable Instruments
HERITAGE BANK v. BRUHA
Supreme Court of Nebraska, 2012
283 Neb. 263, 812 N.W.2d 260

Connolly, J.

[Jerome J. Bruha signed a promissory note on December 16, 2008, with Sherman County Bank. The note evidenced a promise to pay "the principal amount of Seventy-five Thousand & 00/100 ($75,000.00) or so much as may be outstanding, together with interest on the unpaid outstanding principal balance of each advance." The note stated that it "evidence[d] a revolving line of credit." The note contained a variable interest rate. The rate was subject to change every month and calculated on an index maintained by Sherman County Bank.

On this note, Bruha received advancements in the amount of $10,000 on December 16, 2008, $40,000 on December 17, and $1,000 on January 30, 2009. This totaled $51,000. Bruha then invested the money in accounts with a trading company, which allegedly shared management with Sherman County Bank.

There are a few typographical errors on the note. First, the maturity date on the note is February 1, 2008, which, read literally, means that the note would have matured about ten months before Bruha signed it. Other notes he had signed stated maturity dates of February 1, 2009. Second, in a section titled "COLLATERAL," the note reads: "Borrower acknowledges this Note is secured by an assignment of hedge account from Jerome Bruah [sic] to Sherman County Bank dated DATE [sic]." Thus, Bruha's name is misspelled and a line for a date is unfilled.

Sherman County Bank eventually failed, and the Federal Deposit Insurance Corporation (FDIC) was appointed as receiver. The FDIC then sold and assigned some of Sherman County Bank's assets to Heritage. These assets included the note signed by Bruha. Heritage sued Bruha to enforce the note.

In his answer, Bruha admitted that he signed the note but claims that he did not do it voluntarily. He claimed that Sherman County Bank had procured his signature "by fraud and/or misrepresentation." Bruha also claims that the typographical errors destroyed the negotiability of the promissory note. Moreover, Bruha claims that Sherman County Bank misled him into borrowing money that, in turn, he invested with a trading company that generated trade commissions through risky and speculative commodity trading. Bruha admitted that he had not paid the note but denied that he was obligated to do so.

The district court granted summary judgment to Heritage and awarded it $61,384.67 ($51,000 plus interest) on this note. The court disallowed Bruha's defenses because, under federal law, for certain defenses to be asserted against the FDIC or its assignees, the defenses must be evidenced in writing. The court found that there was no evidence in writing of a defense that would invalidate the note. The court also concluded that the FDIC had become a holder in due course and thus not subject to most defenses. Bruha appealed.]

The primary issues are whether either the holder-in-due-course rule of Nebraska's Uniform Commercial Code or federal banking law bars Bruha's defenses to the enforcement of the note.

* * *

Bruha argues that Heritage is not a holder in due course. Similarly, he argues that the FDIC was not a holder in due course when it held the note. A holder in due course is, with some exceptions, "immune to defenses, claims in recoupment, and claims of title that prior parties to commercial paper might assert. The holder in due course always enjoys certain pleading and proof advantages." So if Heritage were a holder in due course, it would enjoy an advantageous position in litigation with Bruha.

We conclude, however, that Heritage is not a holder in due course because the note was not "negotiable" and article 3 of the Uniform Commercial Code does not apply to this case.

Neb. U.C.C. §3-104(a) provides: "Except as provided in subsections (c) and (d), 'negotiable instrument' means an unconditional promise or order to pay a fixed amount of money, with or without interest or other charges described in the promise or order …." (Emphasis supplied.) Here, the note fails to meet the definition of a "negotiable instrument" because it was not a promise "to pay a fixed amount of money."

Although the Uniform Commercial Code allows notes to have a variable interest rate, under §3-104(a), the principal amount must be fixed. "A fixed amount is an absolute requisite to negotiability." This is because unless a purchaser can determine how much it will be paid under the instrument, it will be unable to determine a fair price to pay for it, which defeats the basic purpose for negotiable instruments.

We applied this principle in [citation], in which we stated that "[a] guaranty is not an agreement to pay a fixed amount and is therefore not a negotiable instrument subject to article 3 of the Nebraska Uniform Commercial Code." To meet the fixed amount requirement, the fixed amount generally must be determinable by reference to the instrument itself without any reference to any outside source. If reference to a separate instrument or extrinsic facts is needed to ascertain the principal due, the sum is not "certain" or fixed.

Here, the text of the note states that Bruha "promises to pay…the principal amount of Seventy-five Thousand & 00/100 Dollars ($75,000.00) or so much as may be outstanding…." Further, the note states that it "evidences a revolving line of credit" and that Bruha could request advances under the obligation up to $75,000. This fails the "fixed amount of money" requirement of §3-104(a); one looking at the instrument itself cannot tell how much Bruha has been advanced at any given time. So, the note is not negotiable. Stated simply, "[a] note given to secure a line of credit under which the amount of the obligation varies, depending on the extent to which the line of credit is used, is not negotiable…"

For a person to be a holder in due course, the instrument must be negotiable. Because the note was not a negotiable instrument, neither the FDIC nor Heritage could ever become a holder in due course of it under Nebraska law. And further, because this note is not a negotiable instrument, article 3 does not apply.

* * *

[The Supreme Court of Nebraska reversed the district court's finding that the holder-in-due-course rule of Nebraska's Uniform Commercial Code bars Bruha's defenses. The Supreme Court, however, concluded that Federal law bars Bruha's defenses and thus affirmed the district court's summary judgment in part. The Supreme Court also held that Bruha had failed to show how the typographical errors had invalidated the note. But because the Supreme Court found a minor error in the district court's calculation of interest, the Supreme Court remanded the case to the district court for correction.]

CASE 26-2

Demand
NATIONSBANK OF VIRGINIA, N.A. v. BARNES
Virginia Circuit Court, Twentieth Circuit, 1994
33 Va.Cir. 184, 24 UCC Rep.Serv.2d 782

Horne, J.

This matter is before the court on Plaintiff's Motion for Partial Summary Judgment. Defendants have filed a Grounds of Defense, asserting certain affirmative defenses to liability. Plaintiff argues that it is entitled to partial summary judgment. As discussed more fully below, Plaintiff's motion will be granted in part and denied in part. The court will address Defendant's affirmative defenses as they relate to each note specifically, and to both Notes in general.

* * *

The following facts are undisputed with respect to the 1991 Note which is the subject of Count II of the Motion for Judgment. Defendants Ad Barnes, Trustee, Ad Barnes and Elaine Barnes executed a * * * Note to Sovran Bank, N.A. on August 27, 1991, in the principal amount of $200,000. Plaintiff NationsBank is the successor by merger to Sovran and is now the holder of this Note. * * * By letter dated February 17, 1993, NationsBank made demand on the 1991 Note.

The factual question still in dispute concerning the 1991 Note is whether it is a demand note. Plaintiff argues that the language of the note is unambiguous and is clearly a demand note. Defendants argue that the detailed enumeration of events constituting default is inconsistent with a demand note. Thus,

a standard of good faith must be applied before a demand for accelerated repayment can be made.

[UCC] §1-203 establishes a general duty of good faith in every contract governed by the Commercial Code. Under any contract providing for accelerated payment at will, §1-208 states that the option is to be exercised only in the good faith belief that the prospect of payment or performance is impaired. However, the Official Comment to this section indicates that it is not applicable to a demand instrument.

[UCC] 3A-108(a) [UCC Revised §3-108(a)] states that a note is payable "on demand" if it says it is payable on demand or states no time for payment. In this case, the 1991 * * * Note is a standard form with different forms of repayment set out on the first page. The box marked payable "on demand" has been checked in this instance. There is no time set for repayment, only a provision requiring monthly payments of interest.

It is the court's opinion that the 1991 Note is unambiguous and is clearly a demand note. Thus, Plaintiff is under no obligation to show good faith before requesting payment on the note. Since demand has been made by Plaintiff, Defendants are liable. Thus, Plaintiff is entitled to summary judgment on the issue of liability under the 1991 Note.

Payable to Order or to Bearer
COOPERATIEVE CENTRALE RAIFFEISEN-BOERENLEENBANK
B.A. v. BAILEY
United States District Court, Central District California, 1989
710 F.Supp. 737

Rea, J.

This matter comes before the court on the motion of both parties to this action for partial summary adjudication and on plaintiff's motion for summary judgment. * * *

This is an action for collection on a promissory note brought by plaintiff, Cooperatieve Centrale Raiffeisen-Boerenleenbank, B.A. ("the Bank"), against the maker of the note, William Bailey, M.D. ("Bailey"). Bailey executed the note in December, 1982, in favor of "California Dreamstreet," a joint venture which solicited investments in a cattle-breeding operation. California Dreamstreet negotiated the note in 1986 to the Bank, which in turn filed this action on August 29, 1988.

The note states in relevant part:

DR. WILLIAM H. BAILEY * * * hereby promises to pay to the order to CALIFORNIA DREAMSTREET * * * the sum of Three Hundred Twenty Nine Thousand Eight Hundred ($329,800.00) Dollars. * * *

* * *

By this motion for partial summary adjudication, the parties seek to determine, as a threshold matter, whether the subject promissory note is a negotiable instrument. * * * [The parties] agree that the sole issue is whether the unusual language in the note obliging Bailey to "pay to the order *to* California Dreamstreet" (emphasis added) renders the note non-negotiable.

Whether an instrument is negotiable is a question of law to be determined solely from the face of the instrument, without reference to the intent of the parties. [Citation.] To be negotiable, an instrument must "be payable to order or bearer." Code §3-104(1)(d) [Revised §3-104(a)(i)]. "Payable to order" is further defined by Code §3-110(1), as follows:

(1) An instrument is payable to order when by its terms it is payable to the order or assigns of any person therein specified with reasonable certainty, or to him or his order, or when it is conspicuously designated on its face as "exchange" or the like and names a payee.

[Compare Revised §3-109(b).]

It is well established that a promissory note is nonnegotiable if it states only: "payable to (payee)," rather than "payable to the order of [payee]." [Citations.] Bailey claims that the instant note, which states "pay to the order to [payee]," falls between these two alternatives and should therefore be deemed non-negotiable.

The authorities are unhelpful. There is apparently no case on record in which a variance this small from the language of

the Code has been called into question. Both parties direct the Court's attention to Official UCC Comment 5 to Code §3-104, which states:

5. This Article omits the original Section 10, which provided that the instrument need not follow the language of the act if it "clearly indicates an intention to conform" to it. The provision has served no useful purpose, and it has been an encouragement to bad drafting and to liberality in holding questionable paper to be negotiable. The omission is not intended to mean that the instrument must follow the language of this section, or that one term may not be recognized as clearly the equivalent of another, as in the case of "I undertake" instead of "I promise," or "Pay to holder" instead of "Pay to bearer." It does mean that either the language of the section or a clear equivalent must be found, and that in doubtful cases the decision should be against negotiability.

In the court's opinion, the Comment fails to persuasively support either party's position. Rules of grammar belie the Bank's argument that the preposition "to" is an apt substitute for "of" since the resulting sentence, read literally, is not just ambiguous but incomplete. On the other hand, the Comment expressly disavows Bailey's argument that the Code drafters intended to set forth certain "magic words," the absence of which precludes negotiability.

What does emerge from the Comment is the need for certainty in determining negotiability. Though sensitive to this goal and to the potentially harsh result of such a finding, the court does not find the instant facts to present the kind of "doubtful" case which should be resolved against negotiability. In this context, the phrase "pay to the order to" can plausibly be construed only to mean "pay to the order of." While other explanations are possible, none are realistic. To hold otherwise would, in this court's opinion, set an overly technical standard that could unexpectedly frustrate legitimate expectations of negotiability in commercial transactions.

* * *

For all the above reasons, IT IS HEREBY ADJUDGED that the promissory note which is the subject of this action is a negotiable instrument. It is further Ordered that plaintiff's motion for summary judgment is denied without prejudice to its being renewed upon the completion of discovery.

1. State whether the following provisions impair or preclude negotiability, the instrument in each instance being otherwise in proper form. Answer each statement with either the word "Negotiable" or "Nonnegotiable" and explain why.

    a. A note for $2,000 payable in twenty monthly installments of $100 each that provides the following: "In case of death of maker, all payments not due at date of death are canceled."

    b. A note stating "This note is secured by a mortgage on personal property located at 351 Maple Street, Smithton, Illinois."

    c. A certificate of deposit reciting "June 6, 2020, John Jones has deposited in the Citizens Bank of Emanon, Illinois, Two Thousand Dollars, to the credit of himself, payable upon the return of this instrument properly indorsed, with interest at the rate of 2 percent per annum from date of issue upon ninety days' written notice. (Signed) Jill Crystal, President, Citizens Bank of Emanon."

    d. An instrument reciting "I.O.U., Mark Noble, $1,000.00."

    e. A note stating "In accordance with our contract of December 13, 2018, I promise to pay to the order of Sam Stone $100 on March 13, 2021."

    f. A draft drawn by Brown on the Acme Publishing Company for $500, payable to the order of the Sixth National Bank of Erehwon, directing the bank to "Charge this draft to my royalty account."

    g. A note executed by Pierre Janvier, a resident of Chicago, for $2,000, payable in Swiss francs.

    h. An undated note for $1,000 payable "six months after date."

    i. A note for $500 payable to the order of Ray Rodes six months after the death of Albert Olds.

    j. A note of $500 payable to the assigns of Levi Lee.

    k. A check made payable "to Ketisha Johnson."

2. State whether the following provisions in a note impair or preclude negotiability, the instrument in each instance being otherwise in proper form. Answer each statement with the word Negotiable or Nonnegotiable and explain why.

    a. A note signed by Henry Brown in the trade name of the Quality Store.

    b. A note for $850, payable to the order of TV Products Company, "If, but only if, the television set for which this note is given proves entirely satisfactory to me."

    c. A note executed by Adams, Burton, and Cady Company, a partnership, for $1,000, payable to the order of Davis, payable only out of the assets of the partnership.

    d. A note promising to pay $500 to the order of Leigh and to deliver ten tons of coal to Leigh.

    e. A note for $10,000 executed by Eaton payable to the order of the First National Bank of Emanon in which Eaton promises to give additional collateral if the bank deems itself insecure and demands additional security.

    f. A note reading, "I promise to pay to the order of Richard Roe $2,000 on January 31, 2021, but it is agreed that if the crop of Blackacre falls below ten bushels per acre for the 2020 season, this note shall be extended indefinitely."

    g. A note payable to the order of Ray Rogers fifty years from date but providing that payment shall be accelerated by the death of Silas Hughes to a point of time four months after his death.

    h. A note for $4,000 calling for payments of installments of $250 each and stating "In the event any installment hereof is not paid when due this note shall immediately become due at the holder's option."

    i. An instrument dated September 17, 2021, in the handwriting of John Henry Brown, which reads in full: "Sixty days after date, I, John Henry Brown, promise to pay to the order of William Jones $500."

    j. A note reciting "I promise to pay Ray Reed $100 on December 24, 2021."

3. On March 10, Tolliver Tolles, also known as Thomas Towle, delivered to Alonzo Craig and Abigail Craig the following instrument, written by him in pencil:

    For value received, I, Thomas Towle, promise to pay to the order of Alonzo Craig or Abigail Craig One Thousand Seventy-Five ($1,000.75) Dollars six months after my mother, Alma Tolles, dies with interest at the rate of 6 percent from date to maturity and after maturity at the rate of 6.75 percent. I hereby waive the benefit of all laws exempting real or personal property from levy or sale.

    Is this instrument negotiable? Explain.

4. Henry Hughes, who operates a department store, executed the following instrument:

    $2,600 Chicago, March 5, 2021

    On July 1, 2021, I promise to pay Daniel Dalziel, or order, the sum of Twenty-Six Hundred Dollars for the privilege of one framed advertising sign, size 24 × 36 inches, at one end of each of two hundred sixty buses of the New Omnibus Company for a term of three months from May 15, 2021.

(Signed) Henry Hughes

Is this instrument negotiable? Explain.

5. Paul agreed to lend Marsha $500. Thereupon Marsha made and delivered her note for $500 payable to Paul or order "ten days after my marriage." Shortly thereafter Marsha was married. Is the instrument negotiable? Explain.

6. For the balance due on the purchase of a tractor, Henry Brown executed and delivered to Jane Jones his promissory note containing the following language:

January 1, 2021, I promise to pay to the order of Jane Jones the sum of $7,000 to be paid only out of my checking account at the XYZ National Bank in Pinckard, Illinois, in two installments of $3,500 each, payable on May 1, 2021, and on July 1, 2021, provided that if I fail to pay the first installment on the due date, the entire sum shall become immediately due.

(Signed) Henry Brown

Is the note negotiable? Explain.

7. Sam Sharpe executed and delivered to Don Dole the following instrument:

Knoxville, Tennessee May 29, 2021

Thirty days after date I promise to pay Don Dole or order, Five Thousand Dollars. The holder of this instrument shall have the election to require the assignment and delivery to him of my 100 shares of Brookside Iron Works Corporation stock in lieu of the payment of Five Thousand Dollars in money.

(Signed) Sam Sharpe

Is this instrument negotiable? Explain.

8. Explain whether the following instrument is negotiable.

March 1, 2021

One month from date, I, James Jimson, hereby promise to pay Edmund Edwards: Six thousand, Seven hundred Fifty ($6,750.00) dollars, plus 4 3/4% interest. Payment for cutting machines to be delivered on March 15, 2021.

(Signed) James Jimson

9. The following instrument was given to Matthew Andrea:

Chapel Hill, N.C.

April 15, 2021

Ninety days after date pay to the order of Matthew Andrea, seven hundred and fifty dollars ($750). Value received and charge the trade account of Olympia Sales Corp., N.Y.

		Olympia Sales Corp.
To:	Citi Bank	by /s/ Carl Starr
	UN Plaza	President
	New York, N.Y.	

Explain what type of instrument this is and whether it is negotiable.

CASE PROBLEMS

10. Broadway Management Corporation obtained a judgment against Briggs. The note on which the judgment was based reads in part: "Ninety Days after date, I, we, or either of us, promise to pay to the order of Three Thousand Four Hundred Ninety Eight and 45/100 ____ Dollars." (The underlined words and symbols were typed in; the remainder was printed.) There are no blanks on the face of the instrument, any unused space having been filled in with hyphens. The note contains clauses permitting acceleration in the event the holder deems itself insecure and authorizes judgment "if this note is not paid at any stated or accelerated maturity." Explain whether the note is negotiable order paper.

11. Sandra and Thomas McGuire entered into a purchase and sale agreement for "Becca's Boutique" with Pascal and Rebecca Tursi. The agreement provided that the McGuires would buy the store for $75,000, with a down payment of $10,000 and the balance of $65,000 to be paid at closing on October 5, 2021. The settlement clause stated that the sale was contingent upon the McGuires' obtaining a Small Business Administration loan of $65,000. On September 4, 2021, Mrs. McGuire signed a promissory note in which the McGuires promised to pay to the order of the Tursis and the Green Mountain Inn the sum of $65,000. The note specified that interest payments of $541.66 would become due and payable on the fifth day of October, November, and December 2021. The entire balance of the note, with interest, would become due and payable at the option of the holder if any installment of interest was not paid according to that schedule.

The Tursis had for several months been negotiating with Parker Perry for the purchase of the Green Mountain Inn in Stowe, Vermont. On September 7, 2021, the Tursis delivered to Perry a $65,000 promissory note payable to the order of Green Mountain Inn, Inc. This note was secured by transfer to the Green Mountain Inn of the McGuires' note to the Tursis. Subsequently, Mrs. McGuire learned that her Small Business Administration loan had been disapproved. On December 5, 2021, the Tursis defaulted on their promissory note to the Green Mountain Inn. On June 11, 2021, PP, Inc., formerly Green Mountain Inn, Inc., brought an action against the McGuires to recover on the note held as security for the Tursis' promissory note. Discuss whether the instrument is negotiable.

12. On September 2, 2015, Levine executed a mortgage bond under which she promised to pay the Mykoffs a preexisting obligation of $54,000. On October 14, 2021, the Mykoffs transferred the mortgage to Bankers Trust Co., indorsing the instrument with the words "Pay to the Order of Bankers Trust Company Without Recourse." The Lincoln First Bank, N.A., brought this action asserting that the Mykoffs' mortgage is a nonnegotiable instrument because it is not payable to order or bearer; thus, it is subject to Lincoln's defense that the mortgage was not supported by consideration as an antecedent debt is not consideration. Is the instrument payable to order of bearer? Discuss.

13. Horne executed a $100,000 note in favor of R. C. Clark. On the back of the instrument was a restriction stating that the note could not be transferred, pledged, or otherwise assigned without Horne's written consent. As part of the same transaction between Horne and Clark, Horne gave Clark a separate letter authorizing Clark to pledge the note as collateral for a loan of $50,000 that Clark intended to secure from First State Bank. Clark did secure the loan and pledged the note, which was accompanied by Horne's letter authorizing Clark to use the note as collateral. First State contacted Horne and verified the agreement between Horne and Clark as to using the note as collateral. Clark defaulted on the loan. When First State later attempted to collect on the note, Horne refused to pay, arguing that the note was not negotiable as it could not be transferred without obtaining Horne's written consent. Is the instrument negotiable? Explain.

14. The Society National Bank (Society) agreed in a promissory note to lend U.S.A. Diversified Products, Inc. (USAD) up to $2 million in the form of an operating line of credit upon which USAD could make draws of varying amounts. The outstanding balance was to be paid on April 30 of the following year. USAD defaulted on the line of credit, and Society filed a complaint against USAD. Is the promissory note negotiable? Explain.

TAKING SIDES

Holly Hill Acres, Ltd., executed and delivered a promissory note and a purchase money mortgage to Rogers and Blythe. The note provided that it was secured by a mortgage on certain real estate and that the terms of that mortgage "are by this reference made a part hereof." Rogers and Blythe then assigned the note to Charter Bank, and the bank sought to foreclose on the note and mortgage. Holly Hill Acres refused to pay, claiming that the note was not negotiable and therefore subject to the defense that Holly Hill Acres had been defrauded by Rogers and Blythe.

a. Present the position that the note is a negotiable instrument.

b. What is the position that the note is nonnegotiable?

c. Is the note negotiable or nonnegotiable? Explain.

CHAPTER 27

Transfer and Holder in Due Course

CHAPTER OUTCOMES

After reading and studying this chapter, you should be able to:

- Distinguish among (1) transfer, (2) negotiation, and (3) assignment.

- Explain the requirements for becoming a holder in due course.

- Explain the shelter rule and when a payee can have the rights of a holder in due course.

- Explain the real defenses.

- Explain personal defenses.

The primary advantage of negotiable instruments is their ease of transferability. Nonetheless, although both negotiable instruments and nonnegotiable undertakings are transferable by assignment, only negotiable instruments can result in the transferee becoming a holder. This distinction is highly significant. If the transferee of a negotiable instrument is entitled to payment by the terms of the instrument, he is a holder of the instrument. Only holders may be holders in due course and thus may be entitled to greater rights in the instrument than the transferor may have possessed. These rights, discussed in the second part of this chapter, are the reason negotiable instruments move freely in the marketplace.

The unique and most significant aspect of negotiability is the concept of the holder in due course. Although a mere holder acquires a negotiable instrument subject to all claims and defenses to it, a holder in due course, *except in consumer credit transactions*, takes the instrument free of all claims of other parties and free of all defenses to the instrument except for a very limited number. The law has conferred this preferred position upon the holder in due course to encourage the free transferability of negotiable instruments by minimizing the risks assumed by an innocent purchaser of the instrument. The transferee of a negotiable instrument wants payment for it; he does not want to be subject to any dispute between the obligor and the obligee (generally the original payee).

TRANSFER

This part of the chapter discusses the methods by which negotiable instruments may be transferred.

27-1 Negotiation

Revised Article 1 of the Uniform Commercial Code (UCC or Code) broadly defines a **holder** as "the person in possession of a negotiable instrument that is payable either to bearer or to an identified person that is the person in possession." Section 1-201(b)(21). All fifty States have adopted Revised Article 1, which applies to all of the articles of the Code. **Negotiation** is the transfer of possession, whether voluntary or involuntary, by a person other than the issuer of a negotiable instrument in such a manner that the transferee becomes a holder. Section 3-201(a). An instrument is transferred when a person other than its issuer delivers it for the purpose of giving the recipient the right to enforce the instrument. Section 3-203(a). Accordingly, to qualify as a holder, a person must have possession of an instrument that runs to him. Thus, there are two ways in which a person can be a holder: (1) the instrument has been issued to that person, or (2) the instrument has been transferred to that person by negotiation.

The transfer of a nonnegotiable promise or order operates as an assignment, as does the transfer of a negotiable instrument by a means that does not render the transferee a holder.

FIGURE 27-1 Bearer Paper

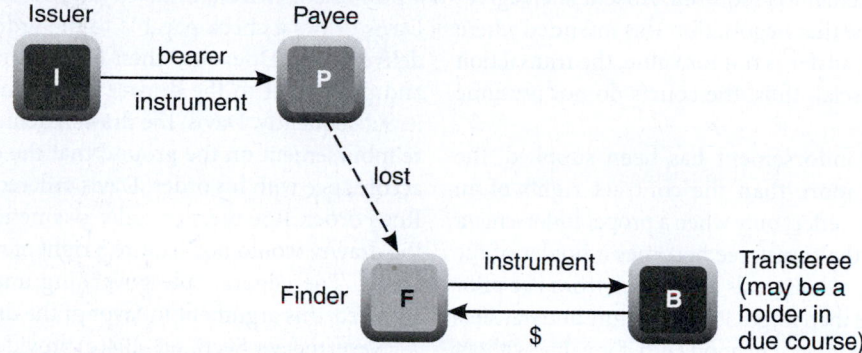

As discussed in *Chapter 16*, an **assignment** is the voluntary transfer to a third party of the rights arising from a contract.

Whether a transfer is by *assignment* or by *negotiation*, the transferee acquires the rights the transferor had. Section 3-203(b). The transfer need not be for value: if the instrument is transferred as a gift, the donee acquires all the rights of the donor. If the transferor was a holder in due course, the transferee acquires the rights of a holder in due course, which rights he in turn may transfer. This rule, sometimes referred to as the **shelter rule**, existed at common law and still exists under the UCC. The shelter rule is discussed more fully in the second part of this chapter.

The requirements for negotiation depend on whether the instrument is bearer paper or order paper.

27-1a NEGOTIATION OF BEARER PAPER

If an instrument is payable to bearer, it may be negotiated by transfer of possession alone. Section 3-201(b). Because bearer paper (an instrument payable to bearer) runs to whoever is in possession of it, a finder or a thief of bearer paper would be a holder even though he did not receive possession by voluntary transfer. Section 3-201(a). For example, Poe loses an instrument payable to bearer that Igor had issued to her. Frank finds it and sells and delivers it to Barbara, who thus receives it by negotiation and is a holder. Frank also qualified as a holder because he was in possession of bearer paper. As a holder, Frank had the power to negotiate the instrument, and Barbara, the transferee, may be a holder in due course if she meets the Code's requirements for such a holder (discussed later in this chapter). See *Figure 27-1* for an illustration of this example. Because a bearer instrument is transferred by mere *possession*, it is comparable to cash.

◆ **SEE FIGURE 27-1:** *Bearer Paper*

27-1b NEGOTIATION OF ORDER PAPER

If the instrument is order paper (an instrument payable to order), both (1) transfer of its *possession* and (2) its *indorsement* (signature) by the appropriate parties are necessary for the transferee to become a holder. Section 3-201(b). *Figure 27-2* compares the negotiation of bearer and order paper.

◆ **SEE FIGURE 27-2:** *Negotiation of Bearer and Order Paper*

Any transfer for *value* of an instrument not payable to bearer gives the transferee the specifically enforceable right to have the unqualified indorsement of the transferor, unless the parties agree otherwise. Section 3-203(c). The parties may agree that

FIGURE 27-2 Negotiation of Bearer and Order Paper

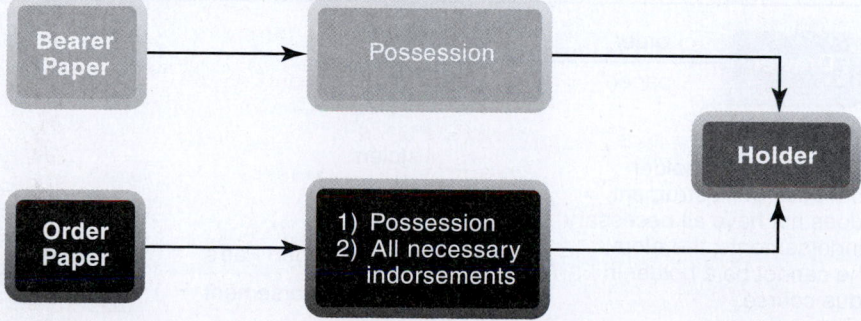

the transfer is to be an assignment rather than a negotiation, in which case no indorsement is required. Absent such agreement, the courts presume that negotiation was intended where value is given. When a transfer is not for value, the transaction is normally noncommercial; thus, the courts do not presume the intent to negotiate.

Until the necessary indorsement has been supplied, the transferee has nothing more than the contract rights of an assignee. Negotiation takes effect only when a proper indorsement is made, at which time the transferee becomes a holder of the instrument. Assume that a thief steals a paycheck from Poe prior to indorsement. The thief then forges Poe's signature and transfers the check to a grocer, who takes it in good faith, for value, without notice, and without reason to question its authenticity. Negotiation of an order instrument requires a valid indorsement by the person to whose order the instrument is payable, in this case, Poe. A forged indorsement is not valid. Consequently, the grocer had not taken the instrument with all necessary indorsements; therefore, he could not be a holder or a holder in due course. The grocer's only recourse would be to collect the amount of the check from the thief. *Figure 27-3* illustrates this example.

♦ **SEE FIGURE 27-3:** *Stolen Order Paper*

If a customer deposits a check or other instrument for collection without properly indorsing the item, the depository bank becomes a holder when it accepts the item for deposit if the depositor is a holder. Section 4-205(i). It no longer needs to supply the customer's indorsement.

♦ *See Case 27-1*

THE IMPOSTOR RULE Negotiation of an order instrument requires a valid indorsement by the person to whose order the instrument is payable. The impostor rule governing unauthorized signatures is an *exception* to this general rule. Usually, the impostor rule comes into play in situations involving a confidence man who impersonates a respected citizen and who deceives a third party into delivering a negotiable instrument to the impostor in the name of the respected citizen. For instance, John Doe, falsely representing himself as Richard Roe, a prominent citizen, induces Ray Davis to loan him $10,000. Davis draws a check payable to the order of Richard Roe and delivers it to Doe, who then forges Roe's name to the check and presents it to the drawee for payment. The drawee pays it. Subsequently, Davis, the drawer, denies the drawee's right of reimbursement on the ground that the drawee did not pay in accordance with his order: Davis ordered payment to Roe or to Roe's order. Roe did not order payment to anyone; therefore, the drawee would not acquire a right of reimbursement against Davis. The general rule governing unauthorized signatures supports this argument in favor of the drawer.

Nevertheless, Section 3-404(c) provides that the indorsement of the impostor (Doe) or of any other person in the name of the named payee is **effective** as the indorsement of the payee if the impostor has induced the maker or drawer (Davis) to issue the instrument to him or his confederate using the name of the payee (Roe). It is as if the named payee had indorsed the instrument. The reason for this rule is that the drawer or maker is to blame for failing to detect the impersonation by the impostor. Thus, in the previous example, the drawee would be able to debit the drawer's account. Moreover, Revised Article 3 extends the impostor rule to include an impostor who is impersonating an agent. Section 3-404(a). Thus, if an impostor impersonates Jones and induces the drawer to draw a check to the order of Jones, the impostor can negotiate the check. Moreover, under the Revision, if an impostor impersonates Jones, the president of Jones Corporation, and the check is to the order of Jones Corporation, the impostor can negotiate the check. Comment 1 to Section 3-404. If the person paying the instrument fails to exercise ordinary care, the issuer may recover from the payor to the extent the payor's negligence contributed to the loss. If the issuer is also negligent, comparative negligence would apply.

THE FICTITIOUS PAYEE RULE The rule just discussed also applies when a person who does not intend the payee to have an interest in the instrument signs as or on behalf of a maker or drawer. Section 3-404(b). In such a situation, any person's

---

FIGURE 27-3 **Stolen Order Paper**

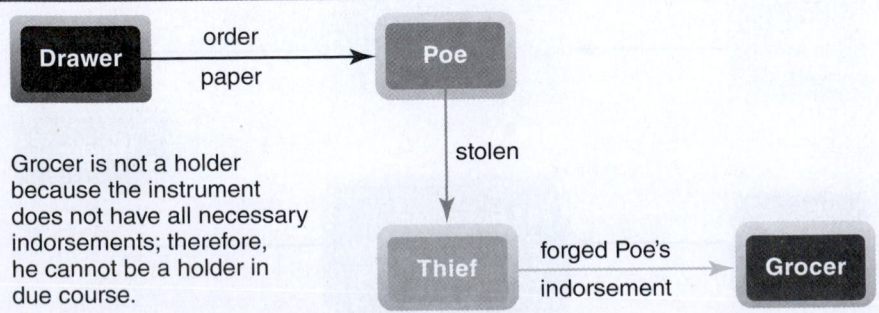

indorsement in the name of the named payee is *effective* if the person identified as the payee is a fictitious person. For instance, Palmer gives Albrecht, her employee, authority to write checks in order to pay Palmer's debts. Albrecht writes a check for $2,000 to Foushee, a fictitious payee, which Albrecht takes and indorses in Foushee's name to Albrecht. Albrecht cashes the check at Palmer's bank, which can debit Palmer's account because Albrecht's signature in Foushee's name is effective against Palmer. Palmer should bear the risk of her unscrupulous employees.

In a similar situation also involving a disloyal employee, a drawer's employee falsely tells the drawer that money is owed to Leon, and the drawer writes a check payable to the order of Leon and hands it to the agent for delivery to him. The agent forges Leon's name to the check and obtains payment from the drawee bank. The drawer then denies the bank's claim to reimbursement upon the grounds that (1) the bank did not comply with her order; (2) the drawer had ordered payment to Leon or order; (3) the drawee did not make payment either to Leon or as ordered by him, inasmuch as the forgery of Leon's signature is wholly inoperative; and (4) the drawee paid in accordance with the scheme of the faithless agent and not in compliance with the drawer's order. Under Section 3-405, an employer has liability on the instrument when one of its employees, who is entrusted with responsibility with respect to such an instrument, makes a fraudulent indorsement if (1) the instrument is payable to the employer and the employee forges the indorsement of the employer or (2) the instrument is issued by the employer and the employee forges the indorsement of the person identified as the payee. The previous example falls under the second part of the rule just stated. Accordingly, the employee's indorsement is effective as that of the unintended payee, and the drawee bank will be able to debit the drawer's (employer's) account.

Section 3-405 also applies to a situation (the first part of the rule) not involving a fictitious payee: a fraudulent indorsement made by an employee entrusted with responsibility with respect to an instrument payable to the employer. For example, an employee, whose job involves posting amounts of checks payable to her employer, steals some of the checks and forges her employer's indorsement. The indorsement is effective as the employer's indorsement because the employee's duties included processing checks for bookkeeping purposes.

Section 3-405 provides, however, that the employer may recover from the drawee bank to the extent the loss resulted from the bank's failure to exercise ordinary care. If the employer is also negligent, a rule of comparative negligence applies.

Practical Advice

Make sure that the payees of all your instruments are the appropriate parties and are being paid the appropriate amount.

27-1c NEGOTIATIONS SUBJECT TO RESCISSION

A negotiation conforming to the requirements discussed previously is effective to transfer the instrument even if it is

1. made by an infant, a corporation exceeding its powers, or a person without capacity; or
2. obtained by fraud, duress, or mistake; or
3. made in breach of a duty or as part of an illegal transaction. Section 3-202(a).

Thus, a negotiation is valid even though the transaction in which it occurs is voidable or even void. In all of these instances, the transferor loses all rights in the instrument until he regains possession of it. His right to do so, determined by state law, is valid against the immediate transferee and all subsequent holders, but not against a subsequent holder in due course or a person paying the instrument in good faith and without notice. Section 3-202(b).

27-2 Indorsements

An **indorsement** is

a signature, other than that of a signer as maker, drawer, or acceptor, that alone or accompanied by other words is made on an instrument for the purpose of (i) negotiating the instrument, (ii) restricting payment of the instrument, or (iii) incurring the indorser's liability on the instrument, but regardless of the intent of the signer, a signature and its accompanying words is an indorsement unless the accompanying words, terms of the instrument, place of the signature, or other circumstances unambiguously indicate that the signature was made for a purpose other than indorsement. Section 3-204(a).

An indorsement may be complex or simple. It may be dated and may indicate where it is made, but neither date nor place is required to be shown. The simplest type is merely the signature of the indorser. Because the indorser undertakes certain obligations, as explained later, an indorsement consisting of merely a signature may be said to be the shortest contract known to the law. A forged or otherwise unauthorized signature necessary to negotiation is inoperative and thus breaks the chain of title to the instrument. Section 3-403(a). The type of indorsement used in first negotiating an instrument affects its subsequent negotiation. Every indorsement is (1) either blank or special, (2) either restrictive or nonrestrictive, and (3) either qualified or unqualified. These categories are not mutually exclusive. Indeed, each indorsement may be placed within three of these six categories because all indorsements disclose three things: (1) the method to be employed in making subsequent negotiations (this depends upon whether the indorsement is blank or special), (2) the kind of interest that is being transferred (this depends upon whether the indorsement is restrictive or nonrestrictive), and (3) the liability of the indorser (this depends on whether the indorsement is qualified or unqualified). For instance, an indorser who merely signs her name on the back of an instrument is making a blank, nonrestrictive, unqualified indorsement.

Revised Article 3 identifies an additional type of indorsement—an anomalous indorsement. An anomalous indorsement is "an indorsement made by a person that is not the holder of the instrument." Section 3-205(d). The only effect of an anomalous indorsement is to make the signer liable on the instrument as an indorser. Such an indorsement does not affect the manner in which the instrument may be negotiated.

The effectiveness of an indorsement as well as the rights of the transferee and transferor depend on whether the indorsement meets certain formal requirements. This section will cover the different kinds of indorsements and the formal requirements of each.

Practical Advice

It is exceedingly important that you make your indorsements in the appropriate manner and at the appropriate time.

♦ **SEE FIGURE 27-4:** *Indorsements*

27-2a BLANK INDORSEMENTS

A **blank indorsement**, which specifies no indorsee, may consist solely of the signature of the indorser or an authorized agent. Such an indorsement converts order paper into bearer paper and leaves bearer paper as bearer paper. Thus, an instrument indorsed in blank may be negotiated by delivery alone without further indorsement. Hence, the holder should treat it with the same care as cash.

Practical Advice

Blank indorsements present a major risk and should be used judiciously.

27-2b SPECIAL INDORSEMENTS

A **special indorsement** specifically identifies the person to whom or to whose order the instrument is to be payable. Section 3-205(a). Thus, if Peter, the payee of a note, indorses it "Pay to the order of Andrea" or even "Pay Andrea," the indorsement is special because it names the transferee. Words of negotiability—"pay to order or bearer"—are *not* required in an indorsement. Thus, an indorsement reading "Pay Edward" is interpreted as meaning "Pay to the order of Edward." Any further negotiation of the instrument would require Edward's indorsement.

Moreover, a holder of an instrument with a blank indorsement may protect himself by converting the blank indorsement to a special indorsement by writing over the signature of the indorser words identifying the person to whom the instrument is payable. Section 3-205(c). For example, on the back of a negotiable instrument appears the blank indorsement "Sally Seller." Harry Holder, who receives the instrument from Seller, may convert this bearer instrument into order paper by inserting above Seller's signature "Pay Harry Holder" or other similar words.

27-2c RESTRICTIVE INDORSEMENTS

As the term implies, a **restrictive indorsement** attempts to restrict the rights of the indorsee in some fashion. It limits the purpose for which the proceeds of the instrument can be applied. Section 3-206. The Code discusses four types of indorsements as restrictive: conditional indorsements, indorsements prohibiting further transfer, indorsements for deposit or collection, and indorsements in trust. Section 3-206. Only the last two are effective. An **unrestrictive indorsement**, in contrast, does not attempt to restrict the rights of the indorsee.

INDORSEMENTS FOR DEPOSIT OR COLLECTION The most frequently used form of restrictive indorsement is that designed to place the instrument in the banking system for deposit or collection. Indorsements of this type, collectively referred to as "collection indorsements," include "for collection," "for deposit," and "pay any bank." Such an indorsement *effectively limits* further negotiation to those consistent with its limitation and binds (1) all nonbanking persons, (2) a depository bank that purchases the instrument or takes it for collection, and (3) a payor bank that is also the depository bank or that takes the instrument for immediate payment over the counter from a person other than a collecting bank. Section 3-206(c). Thus, a collection indorsement binds all parties except an intermediary bank (discussed in *Chapter 29*) or a payor bank that is not also the depository bank.

Practical Advice

Indorsements "for deposit only" protect you as the indorser and should be used whenever necessary.

♦ *See Case 27-2*

INDORSEMENTS IN TRUST Another common kind of restrictive indorsement is that in which the indorser creates a trust for the benefit of himself or others. If an instrument is indorsed "Pay Thelma in trust for Barbara," "Pay Thelma for Barbara," "Pay Thelma for account of Barbara," or "Pay Thelma as agent for Barbara," Thelma is a fiduciary, subject to liability for any breach of her obligation to Barbara. Trustees

FIGURE 27-4 Indorsements

Indorsement	Type of Indorsement	Interest Transferred	Liability of Indorser
1. "John Doe"	Blank	Nonrestrictive	Unqualified
2. "Pay to Richard Roe, John Doe"	Special	Nonrestrictive	Unqualified
3. "Without Recourse, John Doe"	Blank	Nonrestrictive	Qualified
4. "Pay to Richard Roe in trust for John Roe, without recourse, John Doe"	Special	Restrictive	Qualified
5. "For collection only, without recourse, John Doe"	Blank	Restrictive	Qualified
6. "Pay to XYZ Corp., on the condition that it delivers goods ordered this date, John Doe"	Special	Nonrestrictive	Unqualified

commonly and legitimately sell trust assets, and consequently, a trustee has power to negotiate an instrument. The first taker under an indorsement to her in trust (in this case Thelma) is under a duty to pay or apply, in a manner consistent with the indorsement, all the funds she receives. Thelma's immediate transferee may safely pay Thelma for the instrument if he does not have *notice* of any breach of fiduciary duty. Section 3-206(d)(1). Subsequent indorsements or transferees are not bound by such indorsement *unless* they *know* that the trustee negotiated the instrument for her own benefit or otherwise in breach of her fiduciary duty. Section 3-206(d)(2).

INDORSEMENTS WITH INEFFECTIVE RESTRICTIONS A conditional indorsement is one by which the indorser makes the rights of the indorsee subject to the happening or nonhappening of a specified event. Suppose Marcin makes a note payable to Parker's order. Parker indorses it "Pay Rodriguez, but only if the good ship Jolly Jack arrives in Chicago harbor by November 15, 2017." If Marcin had used this language in the instrument itself, it would be nonnegotiable because her promise to pay must be unconditional to satisfy the formal requisites of negotiability. Revised Article 3 makes such indorsements ineffective by providing that an indorsement stating a condition to the right of a holder to receive payment does not affect the right of the indorsee to enforce the instrument. Section 3-206(b). An indorsement may by its express terms attempt to prohibit further transfer by stating "Pay [name] only" or language to similar effect. Such an indorsement, or any other purporting to prohibit further transfer, is designed to restrict the rights of the indorsee. To remove any doubt as to the effect of such a provision, the Code provides that *no* indorsement limiting payment to a particular person or otherwise prohibiting further transfer is effective. Section 3-206(a). As a result, an indorsement that purports to *prohibit* further transfer of the instrument is given the same effect as an unrestricted indorsement.

27-2d UNQUALIFIED AND QUALIFIED INDORSEMENTS

In an **unqualified indorsement**, indorsers promise that they will pay the instrument according to its terms at the time of their indorsement to the holder or to any subsequent indorser who paid it. Section 3-415(a). In short, an unqualified indorser guarantees payment of the instrument if certain conditions are met.

An indorser may disclaim liability on the contract of indorsement, but only if the indorsement so declares and the disclaimer is written on the instrument. The customary manner of disclaiming an indorser's liability is to add the words *without recourse*, either before or after her signature. Section 3-415(b). A "without recourse" indorsement, called a **qualified indorsement**, does not, however, eliminate all of an indorser's liability. As discussed in *Chapter 28*, a qualified indorsement disclaims contract liability but does not entirely remove the warranty liability of the indorser. A qualified indorsement and delivery is a negotiation and transfers legal title to the indorsee, but the indorser does not guarantee payment of the instrument. Furthermore, a qualified indorsement does not destroy negotiability or prevent further negotiation of the instrument. For example, assume that an attorney receives a check payable to her order in payment of a client's claim. She may indorse the check to the client without recourse, thereby disclaiming liability as a guarantor of payment of the check. The qualified indorsement plus delivery would transfer title to the client.

27-2e FORMAL REQUIREMENTS OF INDORSEMENTS

PLACE OF INDORSEMENT An indorsement must be written on the instrument or on a paper, called an **allonge**, affixed to the instrument. Section 3-204(a). An allonge may be used even if the instrument contains sufficient space for the indorsement.

Customarily, indorsements are made on the back or reverse side of the instrument, starting at the top and continuing down. Under Federal Reserve Board guidelines, indorsements of checks must be in ink of an appropriate color, such as blue or black, and must be made within one-and-one-half inches of the trailing (left) edge of the back of the check. The remaining space is reserved for bank indorsements. (See *Figure 27-5* for the proper placement of indorsements.) Nevertheless, failure to comply with the guidelines does not destroy negotiability, and there are no penalties for violating the standard.

♦ **SEE FIGURE 27-5:** *Placement of Indorsement*

Occasionally, however, a signature may appear on an instrument in such a way that it is impossible to tell with certainty the nature of the liability the signer intended to undertake. In such an event, the Code specifies that the signer is to be treated as an indorser. Section 3-204(a). In keeping with the rule that a transferee must be able to determine her rights from the face of the instrument, the person who signed in an ambiguous capacity may not introduce parol evidence to establish that she intended to be something other than an indorser.

INCORRECT OR MISSPELLED INDORSEMENTS If an instrument is payable to a payee or an indorsee under a misspelled name or a name different from that of the holder, the holder may require the indorsement in the name stated or in the holder's correct name or both. Section 3-204(d). Nevertheless, the person paying or taking the instrument for value may require the indorser to sign both names.

FIGURE 27-5 Placement of Indorsement

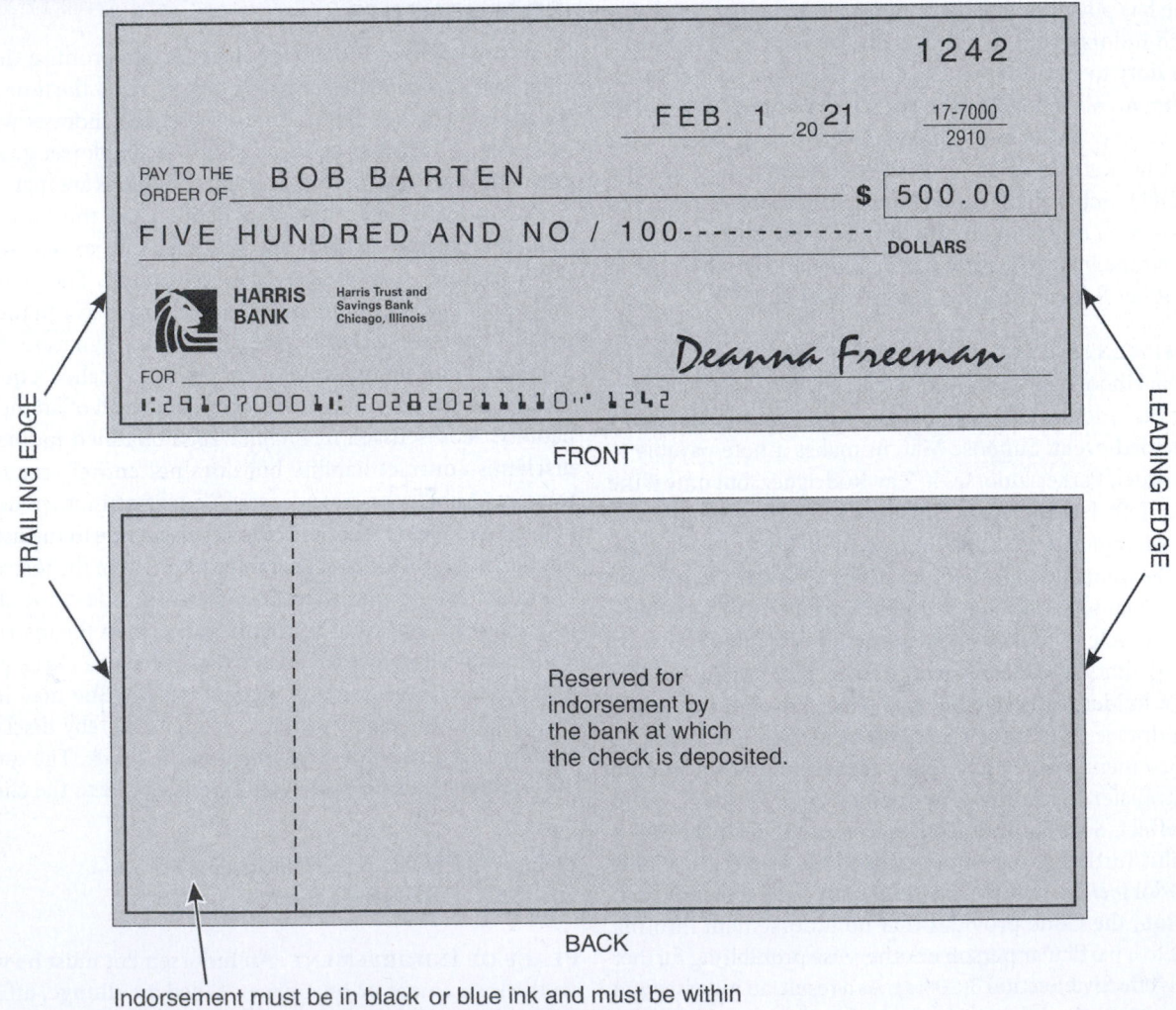

Indorsement must be in black or blue ink and must be within 1½ inches from the trailing edge so as not to interfere with indorsements from the bank.

APPLYING THE LAW

Transfer of Negotiable Instruments

FACTS On the evening of September 28, the last Friday of the month, Erica Dietz realized she had not yet made arrangements to deliver her October 1 rent payment to her landlord, Dr. Norman Toth. Though Erica's weekly aftertax earnings were $150 more than her $600 monthly rent, it was too late in the day to deposit her check and she knew she only had $212 in her checking account. Therefore, Erica indorsed her paycheck as follows: "Pay ONLY to Norman Toth, [signed] Erica Dietz" and placed it in the mail with a note asking Dr. Toth to apply the excess payment toward November's rent.

Dr. Toth's mail was stolen from his mailbox. The thief, Crawford, signed the words "Norman Toth" below Erica's indorsement on her paycheck and deposited it in Crawford's personal bank account at Farmers' Bank, along with several thousands of dollars worth of other checks he had stolen.

ISSUE Is Farmer's Bank a holder of Erica's paycheck?

RULE OF LAW A holder is a possessor of a negotiable instrument with all necessary indorsements. An indorsement is the signature—of a payee, a drawee, an accommodation party, or a holder—on an instrument. There are several classifications of indorsement: blank or special, restrictive or nonrestrictive, and qualified or unqualified. Special indorsements have two effects. First, they identify the person to whom or to whose order the instrument is thereafter payable, and second, they make the instrument order paper if it is not already. Hence negotiation of specially indorsed instruments requires delivery and the further indorsement of the named person.

Indorsements that purport to limit payment to a particular person or that prohibit further negotiation are ineffective in that regard. Instead they have the same effect as unrestricted indorsements. Forged indorsements are anomalous (made by a person who is not the holder of the instrument) and are effective only to make the forger liable on the instrument as an indorser. Forged indorsements break the chain of title to a negotiable instrument and so are not effective to negotiate it.

APPLICATION In effect, Erica's indorsement of her paycheck is a special, nonrestrictive, unqualified indorsement. By adding the words "Pay ONLY to Norman Toth" above her signature, she has simply identified Dr. Toth as the person to be paid and effectively renewed the check's status as order paper; any further negotiation of the check would require Dr. Toth's signature on it. However, Erica's attempt to restrict payment to Dr. Toth "ONLY" does not prevent further negotiation. If Dr. Toth had received the check, he could have negotiated the check simply by indorsing it and delivering it to another. But this is not what happened here.

Crawford's indorsement of Dr. Toth's name is a forgery, which operates not as Dr. Toth's signature but as Crawford's signature. Its only effect is to make Crawford liable on the instrument as an indorser. To effectively negotiate order paper, both indorsement and delivery are required. Crawford has delivered the instrument to Farmers' Bank. But Crawford's unauthorized indorsement on the stolen check breaks the chain of title and does not result in an effective negotiation to Farmer's Bank. Therefore, Crawford's transfer of the check to the Bank does not amount to a negotiation.

CONCLUSION Since a person in possession of a negotiable instrument can qualify as a holder only if the instrument has all necessary indorsements and Dr. Toth has not indorsed the check Erica specially indorsed to him, Farmers' Bank cannot qualify as a holder of Erica's paycheck.

HOLDER IN DUE COURSE

This part of the chapter discusses the requirements of becoming a holder in due course and the benefits conferred upon a holder in due course.

27-3 Requirements of a Holder in Due Course

To acquire the preferential rights of a holder in due course, a person either must meet the requirements of Section 3-302 or must "inherit" these rights under the shelter rule,

Section 3-203(b) (discussed later in this chapter). To satisfy the requirements of Section 3-302, a transferee must

1. be a holder of a negotiable instrument;
2. take it for value;
3. take it in good faith; and
4. take it without notice
   a. that it is overdue or has been dishonored, or
   b. that the instrument contains an unauthorized signature or an alteration, or
   c. that any person has any defense against or claim to it; and

FIGURE 27-6 Rights of Transferees

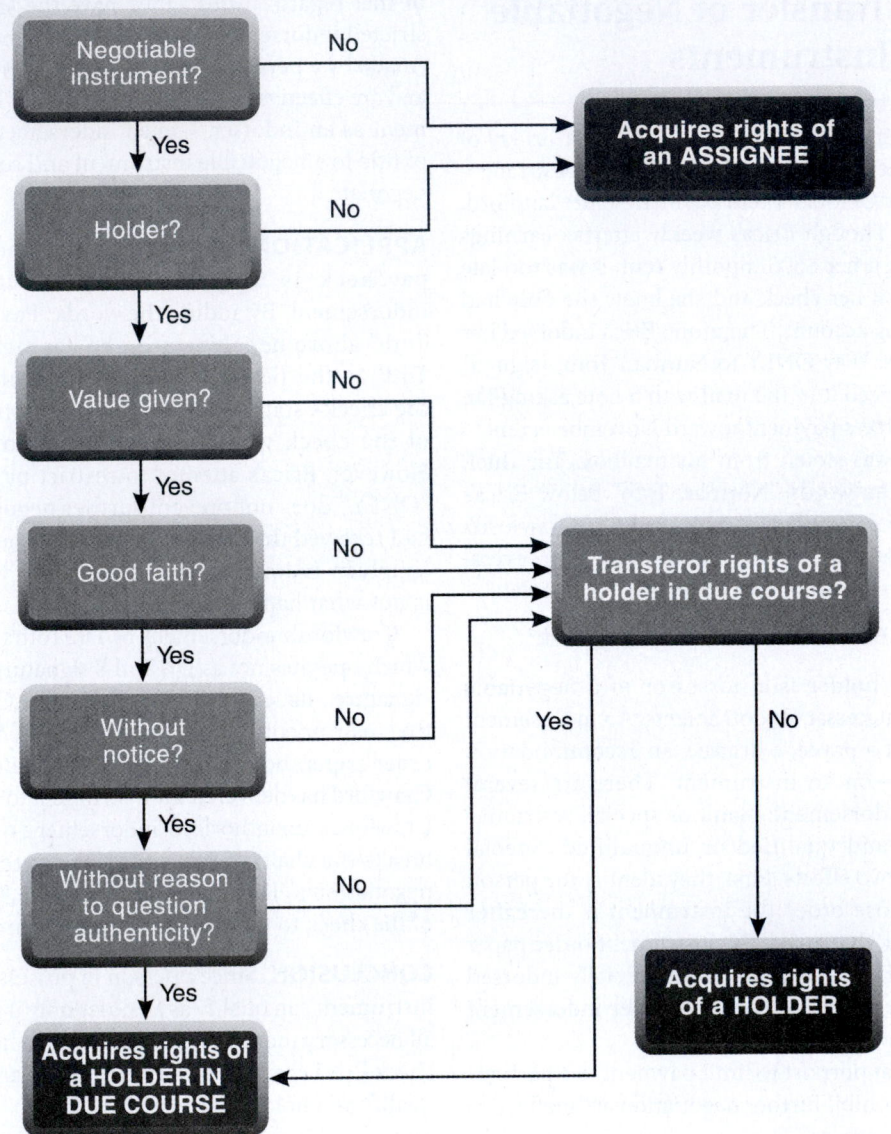

5. take it without reason to question its authenticity due to apparent evidence of forgery, alteration, incompleteness, or other irregularity.

Figure 27-6 illustrates the various requirements of becoming a holder in due course and the consequence of meeting or not meeting these requirements.

◆ **SEE FIGURE 27-6:** *Rights of Transferees*

27-3a HOLDER

To become a holder in due course, the transferee must first be a holder. A holder, as already discussed in this chapter, is "the person in possession of a negotiable instrument that is payable either to bearer or to an identified person that is the person in possession." Revised Section 1-201(b)(21). In other words, a holder is a person who has both possession of an instrument and all indorsements necessary to it.

◆ *See Case 27-3*

27-3b VALUE

The law requires a holder in due course to give value. An obvious case of the failure to do so is when the holder makes a gift of the instrument to a third person.

The concept of value in the law of negotiable instruments is not the same as that of consideration under the law of contracts. **Value**, for purposes of negotiable instruments, is defined as (1) the actual *performing* of the agreed promise (executory promises are excluded because they have not been performed), (2) the acquiring of a security interest or other lien in the instrument other than a judicial lien, (3) the taking of the instrument in payment of or as security for an antecedent debt, (4) the giving of a negotiable instrument, and (5) the giving of an irrevocable obligation to a third party. Section 3-303(a).

EXECUTORY PROMISE An executory promise, though clearly valid consideration to support a contract, is *not* the giving of value to support holder in due course status because such a promise has yet to be performed. A purchaser of a note or draft who has not yet given value may rescind the transaction if she learns of a defense to the instrument. A person who has given value, however, cannot do this; to recover value, she needs the protection accorded a holder in due course.

For example, Mike executes and delivers a $1,000 note payable to the order of Pat, who negotiates it to Henry, who promises to pay Pat for it a month later. During the month, Henry learns that Mike has a defense against Pat. Henry can rescind the agreement with Pat and return or tender the note back to her. Because this makes him whole, Henry has no need to cut off Mike's defense. Assume, on the other hand, that Henry has paid Pat for the note before he learns of Mike's defense. Because he may be unable to recover his money from Pat, Henry needs holder in due course protection, which permits him to recover on the instrument from Mike.

A holder therefore takes an instrument for value to the extent that the agreed promise of performance has been performed provided that performance was given prior to the holder's learning of any defense or claim to the instrument. Assume that in the previous example, Henry had agreed to pay Pat $900 for the note. If Henry had paid Pat $600, he could be a holder in due course to the extent of $666.67 (600/900 × $1,000), and if a defense were available, it would be valid against him only to the extent of the balance. Section 3-302(d). When Henry paid the $300 balance to Pat, he would become a holder in due course as to the full $1,000 face value of the note, provided payment was made prior to Henry's discovery of Mike's defense. If he made the $300 payment after discovering the defense or claim, Henry would be a holder in due course only to the extent of $666.67. A holder in due course, to give value, need pay only the amount he agreed to pay, not the face amount of the instrument.

The Code provides an exception to the executory promise rule in two situations: (1) the giving of a negotiable instrument and (2) the making of an irrevocable obligation to a third party. Section 3-303(a)(4), (5).

SECURITY INTEREST When an instrument is given as security for an obligation, the lender is regarded as having given value to the extent of his security interest. Sections 3-302(e) and 3-303(a). For example, Pedro is the holder of a $1,000 note payable to his order, executed by Monica and due in twelve months. Pedro uses the note as security for a $700 loan made to him by Larry. Larry has advanced $700; therefore, he has met the requirement of value to the extent of $700.

Likewise, a *bank* gives value when a depositor is allowed to withdraw funds against a deposited item. Sections 4-210 and 4-211. The provisional or temporary crediting of a depositor's account (discussed in *Chapter 29*) is not sufficient. If a number of checks have been deposited and some but not all of the funds have been withdrawn, the Code traces the deposit by following the "FIFO" (or "first-in, first-out") method of accounting.

ANTECEDENT DEBT Under general contract law, an antecedent debt (a preexisting obligation) is not consideration. Under Section 3-303(a)(3) of the Code, however, a holder gives value when she takes an instrument in payment of or as security for an antecedent debt. Thus, Martha makes and delivers a note for $1,000 to the order of Penny, who indorses the instrument and delivers it to Howard in payment of an outstanding debt of $970 that she owes him. Howard has given value.

27-3c GOOD FAITH

Revised Article 3 defines **good faith** as "honesty in fact and the observance of reasonable commercial standards of fair dealing." Section 3-103(4). Thus, Revised Article 3 adopts a definition of good faith that has both a subjective and objective component. (This is the same definition adopted by Revised Article 1.) The subjective component ("honesty in fact") measures good faith by what the purchaser knows or believes. The objective component ("the observance of reasonable commercial standards of fair dealing") is comparable to the definition of good faith applicable to *merchants* under Article 2 in that it includes the requirement of the observance of reasonable commercial standards of fairness. Buying an instrument at a discounted price, however, does not demonstrate lack of good faith.

♦ *See Case 27-4*

27-3d LACK OF NOTICE

To become a holder in due course, a holder must also take the instrument without notice that it is (1) overdue, (2) dishonored, (3) forged or altered, or (4) subject to any claim or defense. Notice of any of these matters should alert the purchaser that she may be buying a lawsuit and, consequently, may not be accorded the favored position of a holder in due course. Revised Article 1 defines *notice* as follows:

> [A] person has "notice" of a fact if the person: (1) has actual knowledge of it; (2) has received a notice or notification of it; or (3) from all the facts and circumstances known to the person at the time in question, has reason to know that it exists. Section 1-202(a).

Whereas the first two clauses of this definition impose a wholly subjective standard, the last clause provides a partially objective one: the presence of suspicious circumstances does not adversely affect the purchaser, unless he has reason to recognize them as suspicious. Because the applicable standard is "actual notice," "notice received," or "reason to know," constructive notice through public filing or recording is not of itself sufficient notice to prevent a person from being a holder in due course.

To be effective, notice must be received at a time and in a manner that the recipient will have a reasonable opportunity to act on it. Section 3-302(f).

NOTICE AN INSTRUMENT IS OVERDUE To be a holder in due course, the purchaser must take the instrument without notice that it is overdue. This requirement is based on the idea that overdue paper conveys a suspicion that something is wrong. **Time paper** is due on its stated due date if the stated date is a business day or, if not, on the next business day. It "becomes overdue on the day after the due date." Section 3-304(b)(2). Thus, if an instrument is payable on July 1, a purchaser cannot become a holder in due course by buying it on July 2, provided that July 1 was a business day. In addition, in the case of an installment note or of several notes issued as part of the same transaction with successive specified maturity dates, the purchaser has notice that an instrument is overdue if he has reason to know that any part of the principal amount is overdue or that there is an uncured default in payment of another instrument of the same series. Sections 3-302(a)(2) and 3-304(b).

   Demand paper is overdue for purposes of preventing a purchaser from becoming a holder in due course if the purchaser has notice that she is taking the instrument on a day after demand has been made or after it has been outstanding for an unreasonably long time. Section 3-304(a). The Code provides that for checks, a reasonable time is ninety days after its date. For all other demand instruments, the reasonable period of time varies, depending on the facts of the particular case. Thus, the particular situation, business custom, and other relevant factors must be considered in determining whether an instrument is overdue: no hard-and-fast rules are possible.

Acceleration clauses have caused problems. If an instrument's maturity date has been accelerated, the instrument becomes overdue on the day after the accelerated due date even though the holder may be unaware that it is past due. Section 3-304(b)(3).

NOTICE AN INSTRUMENT HAS BEEN DISHONORED Dishonor is the refusal to pay or accept an instrument when it becomes due. If a transferee has notice that an instrument has been dishonored, he cannot become a holder in due course. Section 3-302(a)(2)(iii). For example, a person who takes a check stamped "NSF" (not sufficient funds) or "no account" has notice of dishonor and will not be a holder in due course.

NOTICE OF A CLAIM OR DEFENSE A purchaser of an instrument cannot become a holder in due course if he purchases it with notice of "any claim to the instrument described in Section 3-306" or "a defense or claim in recoupment described in Section 3-305(a)." Section 3-302(a)(2). A **defense** protects a person from liability on an instrument, whereas a **claim** to an instrument asserts ownership to it.

Claims covered by Section 3-306 include "not only claims to ownership but also any other claim of a property or possessory right. It includes the claim to a lien or the claim of a person in rightful possession of an instrument who was wrongfully deprived of possession." Section 3-306, Comment. Claims to instruments may be made against thieves, finders, or possessors with void or voidable title. In many instances, both a defense and claim will be involved. For example, Donna is fraudulently induced to issue a check to Pablo. Donna has a claim to ownership of the instrument as well as a defense to Pablo's demand for payment.

Section 3-305(a), which is more fully discussed later in this chapter, provides that personal defenses are valid against a holder, while real defenses are effective against both holders and holders in due course. In addition, a person without the rights of a holder in due course is subject to an obligor's claim in recoupment "against the original payee of the instrument if the claim arose from the transaction that gave rise to the instrument." Section 3-305(a)(3). For example, Buyer gives Seller a negotiable note in exchange for Seller's promise to deliver certain goods. Seller delivers nonconforming goods that Buyer elects to accept. Buyer has a cause of action under Article 2 for breach of warranty under the contract, which "claim may be asserted against Seller, to reduce the amount owing on the note. It is not relevant whether Seller knew or had notice that Buyer had the warranty claim." Section 3-305, Comment 3. Buying an instrument at a discount or for a price less than face value does not mean that the buyer had notice of any defense or claim against the instrument. Nonetheless, a court may construe an unusually large discount as notice of a claim or defense.

27-3e WITHOUT REASON TO QUESTION ITS AUTHENTICITY

Revised Article 3 provides that a party may become a holder in due course only if the instrument issued or negotiated to the holder "does not bear such apparent evidence of forgery or alteration or is not otherwise so irregular or incomplete as to call into question its authenticity." Section 3-302(a)(1). According to the comments to this section, the term *authenticity* clarifies the idea that the irregularity or incompleteness must indicate that the instrument may not be what it purports to be. The Revision takes the position that persons who purchase such instruments do so at their own peril and should not be protected against defenses of the obligor or claims of prior owners. In addition, the Revision takes the position that it makes no difference if the holder does not have notice of such irregularity or incompleteness; it depends only on whether the instrument's defect is apparent and whether the taker should have reason to know of the problem.

27-4 Holder in Due Course Status

A holder who meets the requirements discussed in the previous section obtains the preferred position of holder in due course status. This section discusses whether a payee may become a holder in due course. It also addresses the rights of a transferee from a holder in due course under the shelter rule. Finally, it identifies those special circumstances that prevent a transferee from acquiring holder in due course status.

27-4a A PAYEE MAY BE A HOLDER IN DUE COURSE

A payee may be a holder in due course. Section 3-302, Comment 4. This does not mean that a payee automatically is a holder in due course, but that he *may* be one if he satisfies the requirements for such status. For example, if a seller delivers goods to a buyer and accepts a current check in payment, the seller will be a holder in due course if he acted in good faith and had no notice of defenses or claims and no reason to question its authenticity. The most common example occurs in cases in which the transaction involves three parties and the defense involves the parties other than the payee. For example, after purchasing goods from Punky, Robin fraudulently obtains a check from Clem payable to the order of Punky and forwards it to Punky. Punky takes it for value and without any knowledge that Robin had defrauded Clem into issuing the check. In such a case, the payee, Punky, is a holder in due course and takes the instrument free and clear of Clem's defense of fraud in the inducement.

27-4b THE SHELTER RULE

Through operation of the **shelter rule**, the transferee of an instrument acquires the *same* rights in the instrument as the transferor had. Section 3-203(b). Therefore, even a holder who does not comply fully with the requirements for being a holder in due course nevertheless acquires all the rights of a holder in due course if some previous holder of the instrument had been a

holder in due course. For example, Prosser induces Mundheim, by fraud in the inducement, to make a note payable to her order and then negotiates it to Henn, a holder in due course. After the note is overdue, Henn gives it to Corbin, who has notice of the fraud. Corbin is not a holder in due course, because he took the instrument when overdue, did not pay value, and had notice of Mundheim's defense. Nonetheless, through the operation of the shelter rule, Corbin acquires Henn's rights as a holder in due course, and Mundheim cannot successfully assert his defense against Corbin. The purpose of the shelter provision is not to benefit the transferee but to assure the holder in due course of a free market for the negotiable instrument he acquires.

> ### Practical Advice
> *If a negotiable instrument is to be transferred to you and you will not satisfy the requirements of a holder in due course, make sure that your transferor has the rights of a holder in due course.*

The shelter rule, however, provides that a transferee who has himself been a party to any fraud or illegality affecting the instrument cannot subsequently acquire the rights of a holder in due course. For example, Parker induces Miles, by fraud in the inducement, to make an instrument payable to the order of Parker, who subsequently negotiates the instrument to Henson, a holder in due course. If Parker later reacquires it from Henson, Parker will not succeed to Henson's rights as a holder in due course and will remain subject to the defense of fraud.

◆ *See Case 27-5*

27-5 The Preferred Position of a Holder in Due Course

In a *nonconsumer transaction*, a holder in due course takes the instrument (1) free from all *claims* on the part of any person and (2) free from all *defenses* of any party with whom he has not dealt, except for a limited number of defenses that are available against anyone, including a holder in due course. Such defenses that are available against all parties are referred to as **real defenses**. In contrast, defenses that may not be asserted against a holder in due course are referred to as **personal**, or **contractual, defenses**.

27-5a REAL DEFENSES

The real defenses available against *all* holders, including holders in due course, are

1. infancy, to the extent that it is a defense to a simple contract, Section 3-305(a)(1)(i);

2. any other incapacity, duress, or illegality of the transaction that renders the obligation void, Section 3-305(a)(1)(ii);

3. fraud in the execution, Section 3-305(a)(1)(iii);

4. discharge in insolvency proceedings, Section 3-305(a)(1)(iv);

5. any other discharge of which the holder has notice when he takes the instrument, Section 3-601(b);

6. unauthorized signature, Section 3-401(a); and

7. fraudulent alteration, Section 3-407(b), (c).

INFANCY All States have a firmly entrenched public policy of protecting minors from persons who might take advantage of them through contractual dealings. The Code does not state when minority (infancy) is available as a defense or the conditions under which it may be asserted. Rather, it provides that minority is a defense available against a holder in due course to the extent that it is a defense to a contract under the laws of the State involved. See *Chapter 14*.

VOID OBLIGATIONS When the obligation on an instrument originates in such a way that it is *void* or null under the law of the State involved, the Code authorizes the use of this defense against a holder in due course. This follows from the idea that when the party was never obligated, it is unreasonable to permit an event over which she has no control—negotiation to a holder in due course—to convert a nullity into a valid claim against her.

Incapacity, duress, and the illegality of a transaction are defenses that may render the obligation of a party either voidable or void, depending on the law of the State involved as applied to the facts of a given transaction. To the extent the obligation is rendered void (because of duress by physical force, because the party is a person under guardianship, or in some cases, because the contract is illegal), the defense may be asserted against a holder in due course. To the extent it is voidable, which is generally the case, the defense (other than minority, as discussed previously) is not effective against a holder in due course.

FRAUD IN THE EXECUTION Fraud in the execution of the instrument renders the instrument void and therefore is a defense valid against a holder in due course. The Code describes this type of fraud as misrepresentation that induced the party to sign the instrument with neither knowledge nor reasonable opportunity to learn of its character or its essential terms. For example, Frances is asked to sign a receipt and does so without realizing or having the opportunity of learning that her signature is going on a promissory note cleverly concealed under the receipt. Because her signature has been obtained by fraud in the execution, Frances would have a valid defense against a holder in due course.

DISCHARGE IN INSOLVENCY PROCEEDINGS If a party's obligation on an instrument is discharged in a proceeding for bankruptcy or for any other insolvency, he has a valid defense in any action brought against him on the instrument, including one brought by a holder in due course. Thus, a debtor, whose obligation on a negotiable instrument is discharged in an insolvency proceeding, is relieved of payment, even to a holder in due course.

DISCHARGE OF WHICH THE HOLDER HAS NOTICE Any holder, including a holder in due course, takes the instrument subject to *any* discharge of which she has notice at the time of taking. If only some, but not all, of the parties to the instrument have been discharged, the purchaser can still become a holder in due course. The discharged parties, however, have a real defense against a holder in due course who has notice of their discharge. For example, Harris, who is in possession of a negotiable instrument, strikes out the indorsement of Jones. The instrument is subsequently negotiated to Stephen, a holder in due course, against whom Jones has a real defense.

UNAUTHORIZED SIGNATURE A person's signature on an instrument is unauthorized when it is made without express, implied, or apparent authority. Because he has not made a contract, a person whose signature is unauthorized or forged cannot be held liable on the instrument in the absence of estoppel or ratification, even if the instrument is negotiated to a holder in due course. Similarly, if Joan's signature were forged on the back of an instrument, Joan could not be held as an indorser, because she has not made a contract. Thus, any unauthorized signature is totally invalid as that of the person whose name is signed unless she ratifies it or is precluded from denying it; the unauthorized signature operates only as the signature of the unauthorized signer. Section 3-403(a).

A person may be *estopped* or prevented from asserting a defense because his conduct in the matter has caused reliance by a third party to his loss or damage. Suppose Neal's son forges Neal's name to a check, which the drawee bank cashes. When the returned check reaches Neal, he learns of the forgery. Rather than subject his son to trouble, possibly including criminal prosecution, Neal says nothing. Thereafter, Neal's son continues to forge checks and to cash them at the drawee bank. Although the bank may be suspicious of the signature, the fact that Neal has not complained may induce it to believe that the signatures are proper. When he finally seeks to compel the bank to recredit his account for all the forged checks, Neal will not succeed: his conduct has estopped him from denying that his son had authority to sign his name.

A party is precluded from denying the validity of his signature if his **negligence** substantially contributes to the making of the unauthorized signature. The most obvious case is that of a drawer who uses a mechanized or other automatic signing device and is negligent in safeguarding it. In such an instance, the drawer would not be permitted to assert an unauthorized signature as a defense against a holder in due course. Section 3-406(c). Under Revised Article 3, if the person seeking to enforce the instrument is also negligent, then comparative negligence applies. Section 3-406(b).

An unauthorized signature may be **ratified** and thereby become valid so far as its effect as a signature. Section 3-403(a). Thus, Kathy forges Laura's indorsement on a promissory note and negotiates it to Allison. Laura subsequently ratifies Kathy's act. As a result, Kathy is no longer liable to Allison on the note, although Laura is. Nonetheless, Laura's ratification does *not* relieve Kathy from civil liability to Laura, nor does it in any way affect Kathy's criminal liability for the forgery.

FRAUDULENT ALTERATION An alteration is (1) an unauthorized change that modifies the obligation of any party to the instrument or (2) an unauthorized addition or change to an incomplete instrument concerning the obligation of a party.

An alteration that is fraudulently made discharges a party whose obligation is affected by the alteration except where that party assents or is precluded by his own negligence from raising the defense. Section 3-407(b). All other alterations do not discharge any party, and the instrument may be enforced according to its original terms. Section 3-407(b). Thus, if an instrument has been nonfraudulently altered, it may be enforced, but only to the extent of its original tenor (i.e., according to its initially written terms). See *Figure 27-7* illustrating the effects of alterations.

◆ **See Figure 27-7:** *Effects of Alterations*

A discharge under Section 3-407(b) for fraudulent alteration, however, is not effective against a holder in due course who took the instrument without notice of the alteration. Such a subsequent holder in due course may always enforce the instrument according to its original terms and, in the case of an incomplete instrument, may enforce it as completed. Section 3-407(c). (Under this section of the Code, a person taking the instrument for value, in good faith, and without notice of the alteration is accorded the same protection as a holder in due course.) The following examples demonstrate the operation of these rules (*Figure 27-8* illustrates these examples):

1. M executes and delivers a note to P for $2,000, which P subsequently indorses and transfers to A for $1,900. A intentionally and skillfully changes the figure on the note to $20,000 and then negotiates it to B, who takes it, in good faith, without notice of any wrongdoing and without reason to question its authenticity, for $19,000.

B is a holder in due course and, therefore, can collect the original amount of the note ($2,000) from M or P and the full amount ($20,000) from A, less any amount paid by the other parties.

2. Assume the facts in (1), except that B is not a holder in due course. M and P are both discharged by A's fraudulent alteration. B's only recourse is against A for the full amount ($20,000).

3. M issues his blank check to P, who is to complete it when the exact amount is determined. Though the correct amount is set at $2,000, P fraudulently fills in $4,000 and then negotiates the check to T. If T is a holder in due course, she can collect the amount as completed ($4,000) from either M or P. If T is not a holder in due course, however, she has no recourse against M but may recover the full amount ($4,000) from P.

4. Assume the facts in (3), except that P filled in the $4,000 amount in good faith. No party is discharged from liability on the instrument because the alteration was not fraudulent. If T is not a holder in due course, M is liable for the correct amount ($2,000). If T is a holder in due course, T is entitled to receive $4,000 from M because she can enforce an incomplete instrument as completed. Whether or not T is a holder in due course, T may recover $4,000 from P.

◆ **See Figure 27-8:** *Alteration*

27-5b PERSONAL DEFENSES

Defenses to an instrument may arise in many ways, either when the instrument is issued or later. In general, the numerous defenses to liability on a negotiable instrument, which are similar to those that may be raised in an action for breach of contract, are available against any holder of the instrument unless she has the rights of a holder in due course. Among the personal defenses are (1) lack of consideration; (2) failure of consideration; (3) breach of contract; (4) fraud in the inducement; (5) illegality that does not render the transaction void; (6) duress, undue influence, mistake, misrepresentation, or incapacity that does not render the transaction void; (7) setoff or counterclaim; (8) discharge of which the holder in due course does not have notice; (9) nondelivery of an instrument, whether complete or incomplete; (10) unauthorized completion of an incomplete instrument; (11) payment without obtaining surrender of the instrument; (12) theft of a bearer instrument or of an instrument payable to him; and (13) lack of authority of a corporate officer, agent, or partner as to the particular instrument, where such officer, agent, or partner had general authority to issue negotiable paper for his principal or firm.

FIGURE 27-7   Effects of Alterations

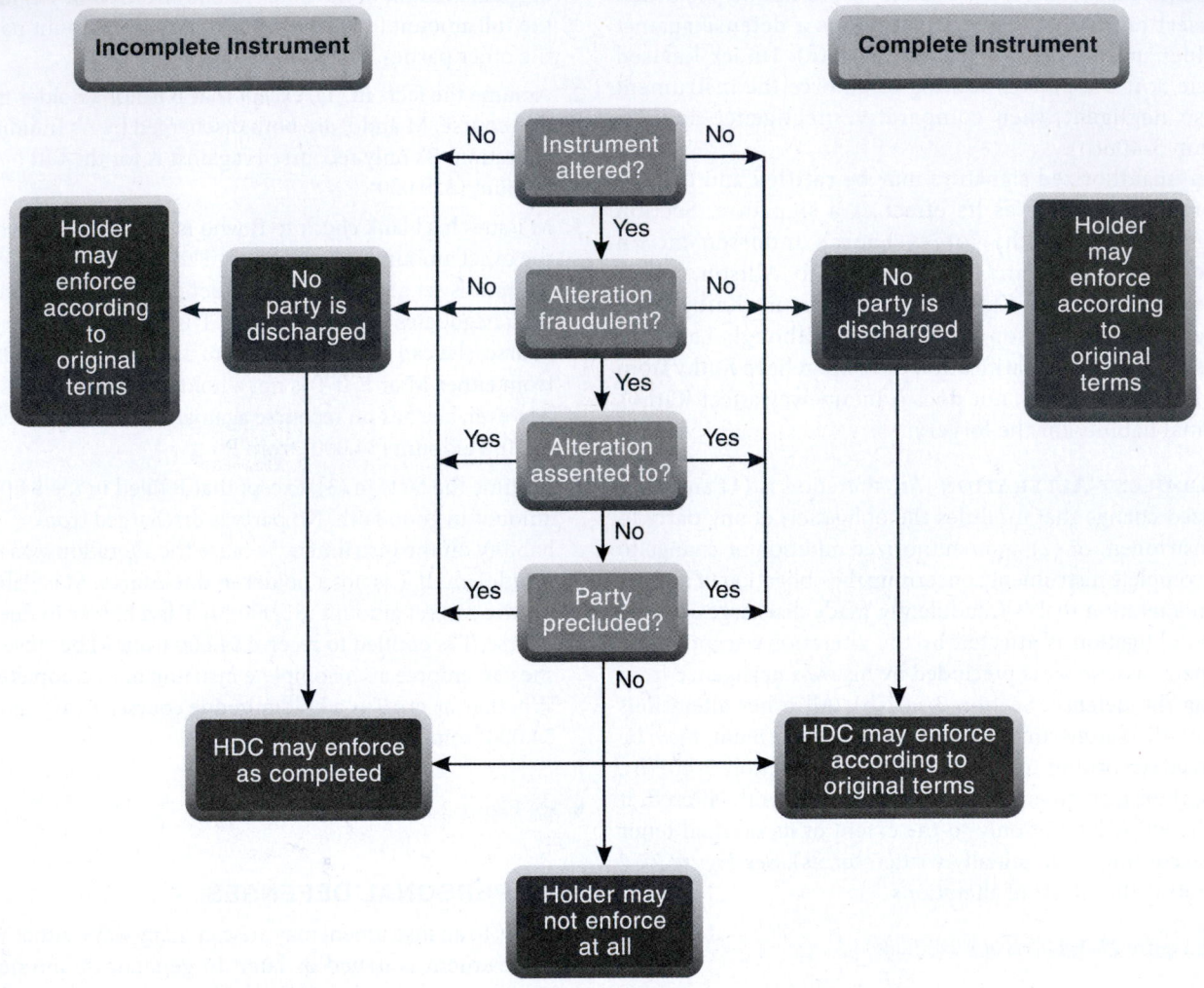

These situations are the most common examples, but others exist. Indeed, the Code does not attempt to detail defenses that may be cut off. It can be stated that a holder in due course takes the instrument free and clear of all claims and defenses, except those listed as real defenses. *Figure 27-9* depicts the availability of defenses against holders and holders in due course.

Practical Advice
When taking a negotiable instrument, make sure that you satisfy the requirements for becoming holder in due course.

◆ **SEE FIGURE 27-9:** *Availability of Defenses Against Holders and Holders in Due Course*

27-6 Limitations Upon Holder in Due Course Rights

The preferential position enjoyed by a holder in due course has been severely limited by a Federal Trade Commission (FTC) rule restricting the rights of a holder in due course of an instrument concerning a debt arising out of a **consumer credit contract**, which includes negotiable instruments. The rule, entitled "Preservation of Consumers' Claims and Defenses," applies to sellers and lessors of consumer goods, which are goods for personal, household, or family use. It also applies to lenders who advance money to finance a consumer's purchase of consumer goods or services. The rule is intended to prevent consumer purchase transactions from being financed in such a manner that the purchaser is legally obligated to make full payment of the price to a third party, even though the dealer from whom she

FIGURE 27-8   Alteration

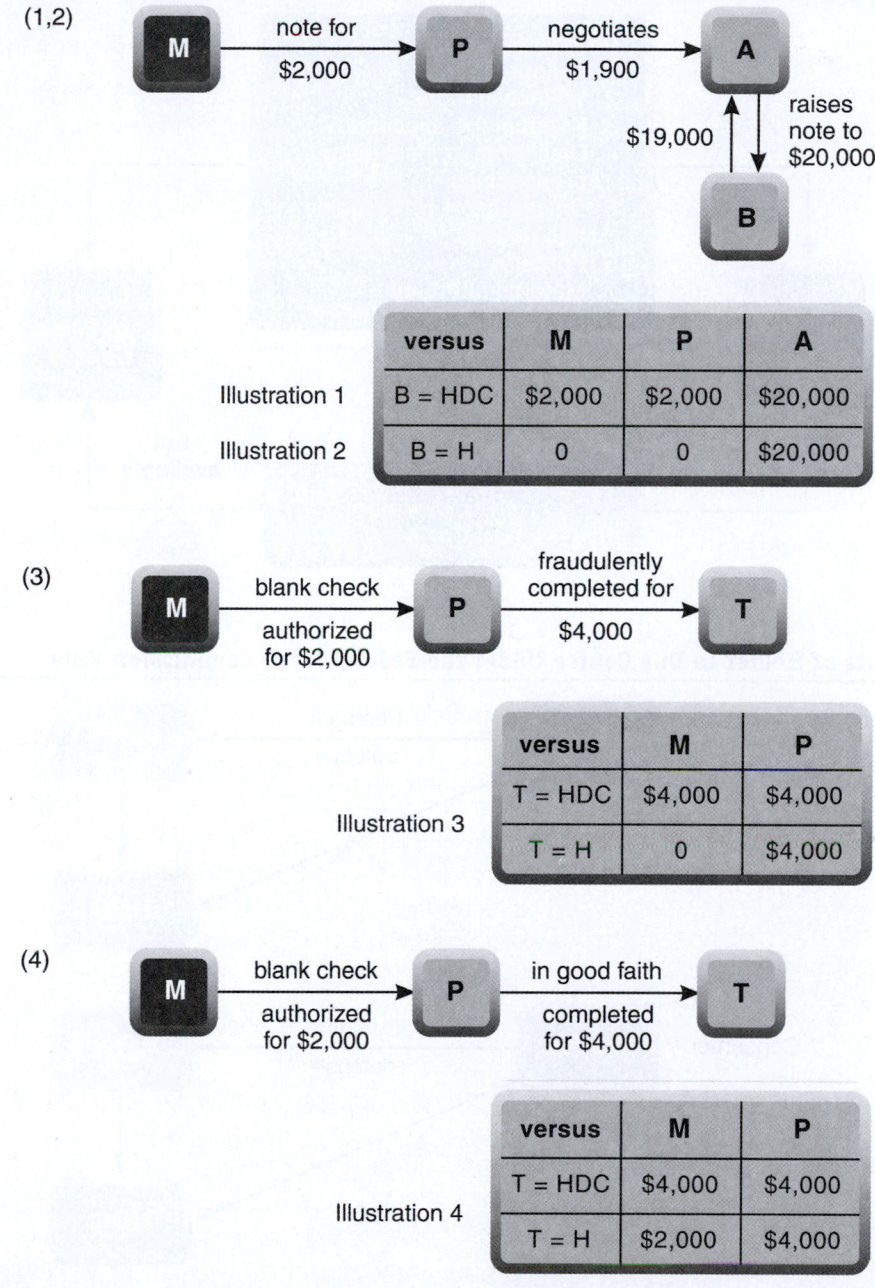

bought the goods committed fraud or the goods were defective. Such obligations arise when a purchaser executes and delivers to a seller a negotiable instrument that the seller negotiates to a holder in due course. The buyer's defense that the goods were defective or that the seller committed fraud, although valid against the seller, is not valid against the holder in due course. *Figure 27-10* illustrates the rights of holders in due course under the FTC rule.

♦ **See Figure 27-10:** *Rights of Holder in Due Course Under the Federal Trade Commission Rule*

To correct this situation, the FTC rule preserves claims and defenses of consumer buyers and borrowers against Availability of Defenses Against holders in due course. The rule states that no seller or creditor can take or receive a consumer credit

FIGURE 27-9 Availability of Defenses Against Holders and Holders in Due Course

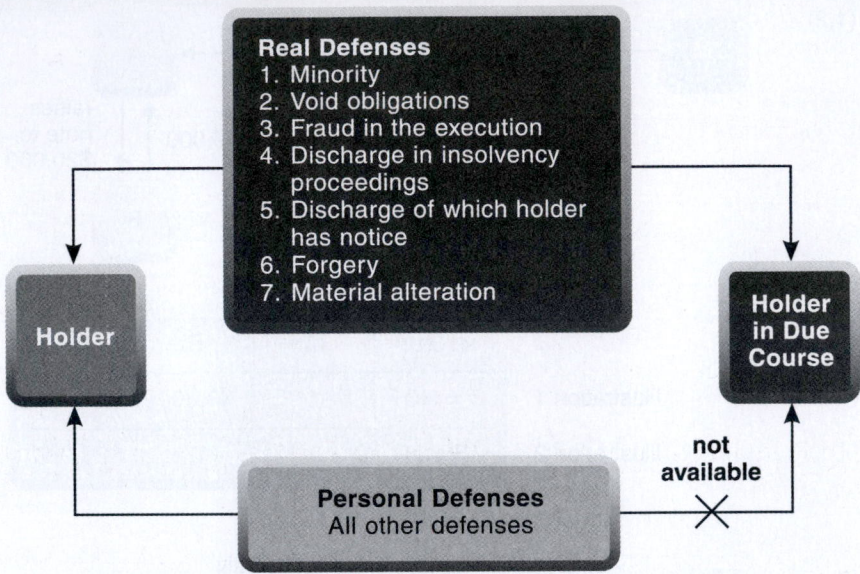

FIGURE 27-10 Rights of Holder in Due Course Under the Federal Trade Commission Rule

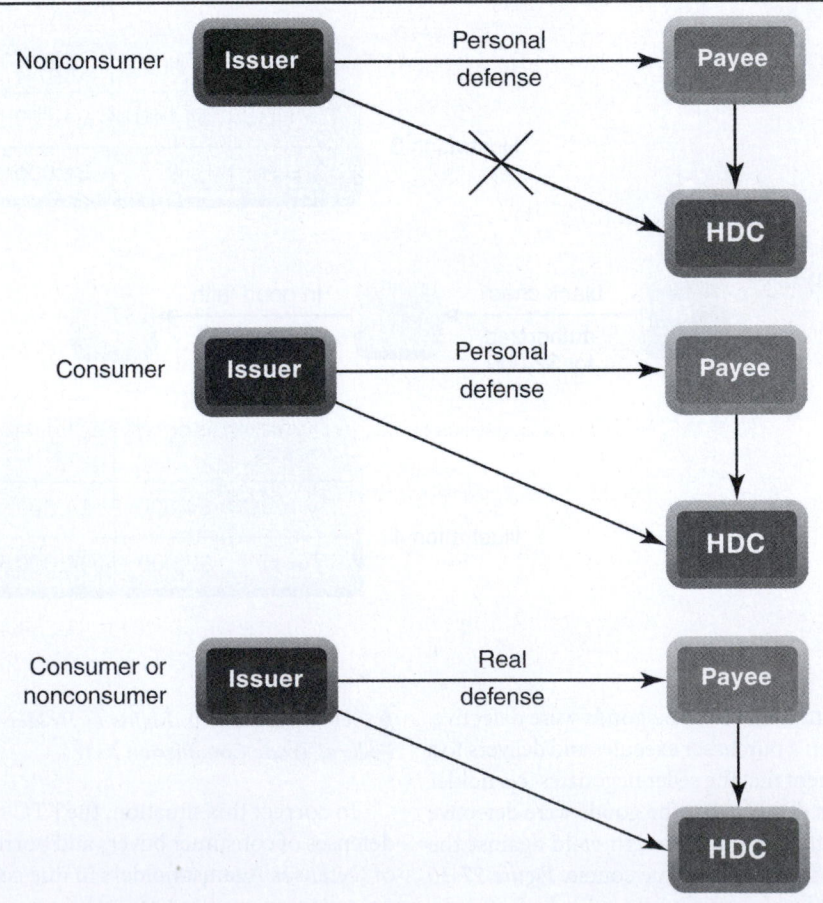

contract unless the contract contains the conspicuous provision shown below:

> NOTICE: ANY HOLDER OF THIS CONSUMER CREDIT CONTRACT IS SUBJECT TO ALL CLAIMS AND DEFENSES WHICH THE DEBTOR COULD ASSERT AGAINST THE SELLER OF THE GOODS OR SERVICES OBTAINED PURSUANT HERETO OR WITH THE PROCEEDS HEREOF. RECOVERY HEREUNDER BY THE DEBTOR SHALL NOT EXCEED AMOUNTS PAID BY THE DEBTOR HEREUNDER.

The purpose of this notice is to inform any holder in due course of a paper or negotiable instrument that he takes the instrument subject to all claims and defenses that the buyer could assert against the seller. The effect of the rule is to place the holder in due course in the position of an assignee.

Practical Advice

As a consumer, make sure that any negotiable instrument you give in a consumer credit transaction contains the notation required by the Federal Trade Commission. As a transferee of negotiable instruments arising from a consumer credit transaction, recognize that you are subject to all defenses.

CHAPTER SUMMARY

TRANSFER

NEGOTIATION	**Holder** possessor of an instrument with all necessary indorsements

Shelter Rule transferee gets rights of transferor

Negotiation of Bearer Paper transferred by mere possession

Negotiation of Order Paper transferred by possession and indorsement by all appropriate parties
* *The Impostor Rule* an indorsement of an impostor or of any other person in the name of the named payee is effective if the impostor has induced the maker or drawer to issue the instrument to him using the name of the payee
* *The Fictitious Payee Rule* an indorsement by any person in the name of the named payee is effective if an agent of the maker or drawer has supplied her with the name of the payee for fraudulent purposes

Negotiations Subject to Rescission negotiation is valid even though a transaction is void or voidable

---

INDORSEMENTS

Definition signature (on the instrument) of a payee, drawee, accommodation party, or holder

Blank Indorsement one specifying no indorsee and making the instrument bearer paper

Special Indorsement one identifying an indorsee to be paid and making the instrument order paper

Unrestrictive Indorsement one that does not attempt to restrict the rights of the indorsee

Restrictive Indorsement one attempting to limit the rights of the indorsee
* **Indorsements for Deposit or Collection** effectively limit further negotiation to those consistent with the indorsement
* *Indorsements in Trust* effectively require the indorsee to pay or apply all funds in accordance with the indorsement
* *Indorsements with Ineffective Restrictions* include conditional indorsements and indorsements attempting to prohibit further negotiation

Unqualified Indorsement one that imposes liability on the indorser

Qualified Indorsement without recourse, one that limits the indorser's liability

Formal Requirements of Indorsements
- *Place of Indorsement*
- *Incorrect or Misspelled Indorsement*

HOLDER IN DUE COURSE

REQUIREMENTS OF A HOLDER IN DUE COURSE	**Holder** possessor of a negotiable instrument that is payable either to bearer or to an identified person that is the person in possession **Value** differs from contractual consideration and consists of any of the following: • the timely performance of legal consideration (which excludes executory promises); • the acquisition of a security interest in or a lien on the instrument; • taking the instrument in payment of or as security for an antecedent debt; • the giving of a negotiable instrument; or • the giving of an irrevocable commitment to a third party **Good Faith** honesty in fact and the observance of reasonable commercial standards of fair dealing **Lack of Notice** • *Notice an Instrument Is Overdue* time paper is overdue after its stated date; demand paper is overdue after demand has been made or after it has been outstanding for an unreasonable period of time • *Notice an Instrument Has Been Dishonored* dishonor is the refusal to pay or accept an instrument when it becomes due • *Notice of Claim or Defense* a defense protects a person from liability while a claim is an assertion of ownership **Without Reason to Question Its Authenticity** instrument cannot bear such apparent evidence of forgery or alteration or otherwise be so irregular or incomplete as to call into question its authenticity
HOLDER IN DUE COURSE STATUS	**A Payee May Be a Holder in Due Course** the payee's rights as a holder in due course are limited to defenses of persons with whom he has not dealt **The Shelter Rule** the transferee of an instrument acquires the same rights that the transferor had in the instrument
THE PREFERRED POSITION OF A HOLDER IN DUE COURSE	**Real Defenses** real defenses are available against all holders, including holders in due course; such defenses are as follows: • *Infancy* • *Void Obligations* • *Fraud in the Execution* • *Discharge in Insolvency Proceedings* • *Discharge of Which the Holder Has Notice* • *Unauthorized Signature* • *Fraudulent Alteration* **Personal Defenses** all other defenses that might be asserted in the case of any action for breach of contract
LIMITATIONS UPON HOLDER IN DUE COURSE RIGHTS	The preferential position of a holder in due course has been severely limited by a Federal Trade Commission rule that applies to consumer credit contracts, under which a transferee of consumer credit contracts cannot take as a holder in due course.

C A S E S

Negotiation of Order Paper

CASE 27-1

THE HYATT CORPORATION v. PALM BEACH NATIONAL BANK

Court of Appeal of Florida, Third District, 2003
840 So.2d 300, 49 UCC Rep.Serv.2d 1039

Levy, J.

Appellant/defendant the Hyatt Corporation appeals the lower court's Summary Final Judgment in favor of appellee/plaintiff Palm Beach National Bank. * * * We affirm.

J&D Financial Corporation is a factoring company. Skyscraper Building Maintenance, LLC, had a contract with Hyatt to perform maintenance work for various Hyatt hotels in South Florida. Skyscraper entered into a factoring agreement with J&D. As part of the factoring agreement, J&D requested Hyatt to make checks payable for maintenance services to Skyscraper and J&D. Of the many checks issued by Hyatt to Skyscraper and J&D, two were negotiated by the bank but indorsed only by Skyscraper. They were made payable as follows:

1. Check No. 1-78671 for $22,531 payable to:
   J&D Financial Corp.
   Skyscraper Building Maint
   P.O. Box 610250
   North Miami, Florida 33261-0250

2. Check No. 1-75723 for $21,107 payable to:
   Skyscraper Building Maint
   J&D Financial Corp.
   P.O. Box 610250
   North Miami, Florida 33261-0250

Only one of the payees, Skyscraper, indorsed these two checks. The bank cashed the checks. According to J&D, it did not receive the benefit of these two payments.

J&D filed a complaint against Skyscraper and its principals on the guarantee, Hyatt and the bank. J&D sought damages against Skyscraper under the factoring agreement and separately against Hyatt and the bank for negotiation of the two checks. Hyatt answered and raised the bank's "fault" as an affirmative defense. * * * The bank, Hyatt and J&D then moved for summary judgment on the issue of whether the bank properly negotiated the checks. It was uncontested that the bank had a duty to negotiate the checks only on proper indorsement, and if it did not, it would be liable.

The bank argued that the checks were payable to J&D and Skyscraper alternatively, and thus the bank could properly negotiate the checks based upon the indorsement of either of the two payees. The bank further argued that the checks were drafted ambiguously as to whether they were payable alternatively or jointly, and thus under [UCC] Section [3-110(d)],

Florida Statutes, the checks would be construed as a matter of law to be payable alternatively.

Hyatt's position was that the checks were not ambiguous, were payable jointly and not alternatively, and thus under Section [3-110], the checks could only be negotiated by indorsement of both of the payees. J&D similarly argued that the checks were payable jointly. The trial court granted Summary Judgment in favor of the bank, finding that [UCC] Section [3-110(d)] precluded the bank's liability. Hyatt appealed. J&D filed a cross-appeal.

The issue on appeal is whether or not a check payable to
J&D Financial Corporation
Skyscraper Building Maintenance

(stacked payees) is payable jointly to both payees requiring the indorsement of both, or whether it is ambiguous regarding whether the check was drafted payable alternatively, so that the bank could negotiate the check when it was indorsed by only one of the two payees.

In 1990, Article 3 of the UCC was revised, and the language of UCC Section 3-116 was added to UCC section 3-110 and became subsection (d). Revised UCC Section 3-110(d), which added language to follow former 3-116(a) and (b), states, "If an instrument payable to two or more persons is ambiguous as to whether it is payable to the persons alternatively, the instrument is payable to the persons alternatively." The net effect of the amendment was to change the presumption. What was unambiguous before is now ambiguous.

Turning to our jurisdiction, Florida has adopted the statutory revision to UCC 3-110, * * *.

* * *

We conclude that based on the 1990 amendment to the Uniform Commercial Code, when a check lists two payees without the use of the word "and" or "or", the nature of the payee is ambiguous as to whether they are alternative payees or joint payees. Therefore, the UCC amendment prevails and they are to be treated as alternative payees, thus requiring only one of the payees' signatures. Consequently, the bank could negotiate the check when it was indorsed by only one of the two payees, thereby escaping liability.

* * *

* * * Thus, we hold that the trial court was correct in granting the Summary Final Judgment.

Affirmed.

Indorsements for Deposit or Collection
STATE OF QATAR v. FIRST AMERICAN BANK OF VIRGINIA
United States District Court, Eastern District of Virginia, 1995
885 F.Supp. 849

Ellis, J.

At issue in this sequel to *State of Qatar v. First American Bank of Virginia* ("Qatar I") is the meaning and legal significance of the phrase "for deposit only" following an indorsement on the back of a check. More specifically, the question presented is whether a depository bank complies with the restrictive indorsement "for deposit only" when it deposits a check bearing that restriction into *any* person's account, or whether that restriction requires a depository bank to deposit the check's proceeds only into the account of the named payee. For the reasons that follow, the court holds that the unqualified language "for deposit only" following an indorsement on the back of a check requires a depository bank to place the check's proceeds into the payee's account, and the bank violates that restrictive indorsement when it credits the check to any other account.

I

* * *

Plaintiffs are the State of Qatar and certain of its agencies (collectively, "Qatar"). From approximately 1986 to 1992, one of Qatar's employees, Bassam Salous, defrauded his employer by having checks drawn on Qatar's account in purported payment of false or duplicated invoices that he had created. Although all of the unauthorized checks were made payable to individuals and entities other than Salous, he nonetheless successfully deposited the checks into his own personal accounts with Defendant First American Bank of Virginia ("First American") and Central Fidelity Banks, Inc. (collectively, "the depository banks").

After Qatar discovered this fraudulent scheme in 1992, it brought suit against the depository banks for conversion. * * *

Only one category of checks remains in dispute. These checks all bear the forged indorsement of the payee named on the face of the check, followed by a stamped "for deposit only" restriction.

* * *

II

It is now established that First American may be liable to Qatar for handling a check's proceeds in violation of a restrictive indorsement. [Citation.] Under §3-205(c) of the pre-1993 Uniform Commercial Code ("UCC" or "Code") [Virginia adopted Revised Article 3 in 1993] restrictive indorsements are defined to "include the words 'for collection,' 'for deposit,' 'pay any bank,' or like terms signifying a purpose of deposit or collection." Thus, the UCC makes clear that the phrase "for deposit only" is, in fact, a restrictive indorsement. But the Code does not define "for deposit only" or specify what bank conduct would be inconsistent with that restriction. Nor does Virginia decisional law provide any guidance on this issue. As a result, reference to decisional law from other jurisdictions is appropriate.

Not surprisingly, most courts confronted with this issue have held that the restriction "for deposit only," without additional specification or directive, instructs depository banks to deposit the funds only into the payee's account. In addition, commentators on commercial law uniformly agree that the function of such a restriction is to ensure that the checks' proceeds be deposited into the payee's account.

This construction of "for deposit only" is commercially sensible and is adopted here. The clear purpose of the restriction is to avoid the hazards of indorsing a check in blank. Pursuant to former §3-204(2), a check indorsed in blank "becomes payable to bearer." It is, essentially, cash. Thus, a payee who indorses her check in blank runs the risk of having the check stolen and freely negotiated before the check reaches its intended destination. To protect against this vulnerability, the payee can add the restriction "for deposit only" to the indorsement, and the depository bank is required to handle the check in a manner consistent with that restriction. §3-206(3). And in so adding the restriction, the payee's intent plainly is to direct that the funds be deposited into her own account, not simply that the funds be deposited into some account. [Citation.] Any other construction of the phrase "for deposit only" is illogical and without commercial justification or utility. Indeed, it is virtually impossible to imagine a scenario in which a payee cared that her check be deposited, but was indifferent with respect to the particular account to which the funds would be credited.

* * *

Finally, it is worth noting that the new revisions to the negotiable instruments provisions of the UCC, [Revised Article 3], support the result reached here. Although these revisions are inapplicable to this case, the commentary following §3-206 states that the new subdivision dealing with "for deposit only" and like restrictions "continues previous law." §3-206 comment 3. Shortly thereafter, the commentary provides an example in which a check bears the words "for deposit only" above the indorsement. In those circumstances, the commentary states, the depository bank acts inconsistently with the restrictive indorsement where it deposits the check into an account other than that of the payee. Although the restriction in that example precedes the signature, whereas the restrictions on the checks at issue here follow the signature, this distinction is immaterial. The clear meaning of the restriction in both circumstances is that the funds should be placed into the payee's account.

Therefore, First American violated the restrictive indorsements in depositing into Bassam Salous' account checks made payable to others and restrictively indorsed "for deposit only." Pursuant to the holding in Qatar I, then, First American is liable to Qatar for conversion in the amount of the total face values of these checks.

CASE 27-3

Holder in Due Course/Holder
GEORG v. METRO FIXTURES CONTRACTORS, INC.
Supreme Court of Colorado, En Banc, 2008
178 P.3d 1209, 66 UCC Rep.Serv.2d 477

Hobbs, J.

We granted certiorari in this case to address an issue of first impression in Colorado regarding whether under [UCC] §1-201(b)(20) and [UCC] §3-302, Colorado's codification of the Uniform Commercial Code ("UCC"), a person can be a holder of a negotiable instrument entitled to holder in due course status under a theory of constructive possession of a negotiable instrument. The court of appeals partially reversed the trial court's grant of summary judgment in favor of Freestyle Sports Marketing, Inc. ("Freestyle"), ruling that Freestyle was not a holder in due course because it was not a holder who had actual possession of the negotiable instrument at issue in this action.

* * *

Freestyle employed Cassandra Demery as a bookkeeper for several years before it discovered that Demery had embezzled over $200,000 for personal use and had failed to pay, on Freestyle's behalf, approximately $240,000 in state and federal employment taxes. Freestyle terminated Demery's employment, demanded that she repay Freestyle, and threatened to notify the authorities if she did not.

After leaving Freestyle, Demery went to work as a bookkeeper at Metro Fixtures Contractors, Inc. ("Metro"), a company owned by her parents. Demery's bookkeeping position at Metro included balancing the accounting books, invoicing customers, and paying outstanding bills on behalf of the company. In her position as bookkeeper, Demery wrote a check from Metro's bank account and made it payable to Freestyle in the amount of $189,000. Demery wrote "for deposit only" on the back of the check as well as Freestyle's account number, filled out a deposit form, and deposited the check in Freestyle's bank account.

Demery then informed Clinton Georg, Freestyle's president, by phone, that she had obtained a loan from her family to repay Freestyle and had deposited the funds into Freestyle's account. After Demery's phone call, Georg called his bank and confirmed the deposit of the funds into Freestyle's account.

Georg subsequently used the deposited funds for payment of Freestyle's delinquent employment taxes.

After two years, Metro uncovered the transaction instigated by Demery and filed suit against Georg and Freestyle * * *. Metro alleged that it had not given Demery a loan or permission to write and deposit a check in the amount of $189,000 into Freestyle's bank account.

Freestyle moved for summary judgment, contending that it qualified as a holder in due course under [UCC] §3-302 and [UCC] §3-306. The trial court agreed that Freestyle was a holder in due course and granted the motion.

Metro appealed and the court of appeals partially reversed. The court of appeals held that Freestyle could not have been a holder in due course because it was not a holder with actual possession of the check. Freestyle then appealed to us arguing that it had constructive possession of the instrument when the check was deposited at its bank.

We hold, under the facts of this case, that Freestyle had constructive possession of the check and qualified as a holder in due course under [UCC] §3-302 and [UCC] §3-306 of Colorado's UCC.

* * *

If Freestyle is a holder in due course under [UCC] §3-306, it takes free of Metro's claims. [Citations.]

* * *

Holder in Due Course

* * *

A check is a negotiable instrument. [UCC] §3-104. The holder in due course doctrine is designed to encourage the transfer and usage of checks and facilitate the flow of capital. [Citation.] An entity may qualify as a holder in due course even if the instrument at issue may have passed through the hands of a thief. [Citation.] ("The holder in due course is one of the few purchasers in Anglo-Saxon jurisprudence who may derive a good title from a chain of title that includes a thief in its links.")

A holder in due course must meet five conditions: (1) be a holder; (2) of a negotiable instrument who took it; (3) for value; (4) in good faith; (5) without notice of certain problems with the instrument. [Citation.] To be a holder one must meet the two conditions in [UCC] §1-201(b)(20): (1) he or she must have possession (2) of an instrument drawn, issued, or indorsed to him or her. [Citation.] Possession is an element designed to prevent two or more claimants from qualifying as holders who could take free of the other party's claim of ownership. [Citation.] With rare exceptions, those claiming to be holders have physical ownership of the instrument in question. [Citation.]

An otherwise authorized signature on a negotiable instrument is not converted into an unauthorized forgery when an agent, authorized to sign negotiable instruments in his principal's name, abuses that authority by negotiating the instrument to a holder in due course for the agent's own personal benefit. [Citations.] [UCC] §3-402.

CONSTRUCTIVE POSSESSION

Section 4-201(a), states that a collecting bank "is an agent or sub-agent of the owner of the item." Further, the statute states, "This provision applies regardless of the form of indorsement or lack of indorsement…." [Citation.] A check payable to a party and deposited in that party's account makes the party the "owner" of the check under the UCC. [Citation.] Further, the White & Summers treatise on the UCC speaks to a collecting bank as an agent for the owner's possession:

> Sometimes the one claiming to be a holder in due course will not have possession of the instrument at the time of the suit. When a collecting bank holds the check, the solution is simple, for section 4-201 makes that bank the agent of the owner of the check. *Under traditional analysis, the agent's possession would be the owner's possession and thus the owner would have "possession."*

[Citation.] (emphasis added [by the court]).

Thus, there are circumstances wherein requiring actual physical possession of the instrument would be problematic and constructive possession applies. [Citation.] Nevertheless, a determination of constructive possession should occur only when delivery is clearly for an identifiable person under circumstances excluding any other party as a holder in due course. [Citation.]

Other jurisdictions have recognized constructive possession as qualifying under the UCC for holder in due course purposes. [Citations.] * * *

* * *

Application to This Case
In the case before us, Demery was Metro's agent, specifically its employee. As a bookkeeper for Metro, Demery's authority

included the power to write checks on Metro's behalf. Despite the fact that Metro did not specifically authorize Demery to write a check to Freestyle, Metro placed her in a position to do so. Subsequently, Demery informed Freestyle that she had obtained authority from Metro's owners, her parents, to issue the check and had directly deposited the funds into Freestyle's account. Freestyle verified with its bank the deposit of these funds into its account and then, relying on the availability of those funds, paid the delinquent taxes to the state and federal authorities.

The court of appeals held that Freestyle could not be a holder in due course because it lacked possession of the check. However, this is too narrow a reading of Section 3-302, which includes circumstances where the instrument does not bear apparent evidence of forgery and the person to whom the instrument is drawn took the instrument for value, in good faith, and without notice that it contained an unauthorized signature. * * *

The trial court found that Freestyle was a holder in due course based on the undisputed facts of this case. Demery delivered the check by depositing it into Freestyle's bank account. Section 1-201(b)(14) defines delivery with respect to an instrument as a voluntary transfer of possession. Two elements are required for delivery of an instrument: (1) intent of the transferor to transfer possession of an instrument, and (2) the actual transfer of the instrument. [Citation.]

However, Metro counters that the bank was not Freestyle's agent with respect to the collection of a "stolen instrument" because under the UCC, a collecting bank is only the agent for an owner of an instrument and, according to Metro, Freestyle did not own the check. But Metro's argument is contrary to prior Colorado law defining the term "owner" in relation to negotiable instruments such as checks. An otherwise authorized signature on a negotiable instrument is not converted into an unauthorized forgery when an agent, authorized to sign negotiable instruments in his principal's name, abuses that authority by negotiating the instrument to a holder in due course for the agent's own personal benefit. [Citation.] A check payable to a party and deposited in that party's account makes it the "owner" of the check under the UCC. [Citation.]

While Metro claims Freestyle was not a holder, it does not simultaneously argue that it was a competing holder. There is no other possible holder under the facts of this case. * * *

Freestyle was not only a holder under the facts of this case, it was a holder in due course. * * *

Freestyle argues that under section 3-303(a)(3), the instrument was issued as payment for Demery's outstanding debt to Freestyle. Metro does not contest that Demery embezzled funds from Freestyle and therefore owed Freestyle funds; rather, it asserts that it did not authorize Demery to issue the check. A pre-existing debt is sufficient consideration. [Citation.] Thus, Freestyle took the check for value.

Freestyle acted in good faith. Bad faith for the holder in due course standard means guilty knowledge or willful ignorance. [Citation.] Here, Freestyle lacked guilty knowledge or willful ignorance. The record contains no facts asserted by Metro that, if proven, would support a bad faith claim. * * *

Finally, Freestyle had no notice that Demery lacked authority to issue the check or that it was forged. The undisputed facts are that Demery was Metro's bookkeeper and had authority to issue the check. Metro simply insinuates that, because its employee stole from Freestyle, Freestyle should have been on notice that she was also stealing from Metro. However, Metro was in the best position to protect itself against Demery's action. * * *

Application of Colorado's UCC can result in loss to an innocent party in favor of a holder in due course. [Citation.] However, an important policy objective of the statute is to protect the party least able to protect himself or herself. [Citation.] "[W]here one of two innocent parties must suffer because of the wrongdoing of a third person, the loss must fall on the party who has by his conduct created the circumstances which enabled the third party to perpetuate the wrong." [Citation.]

Reasons to place the risk on the principal of an agent in commercial transactions include: (1) the increased incentive for a principal to exercise care in selecting agents; (2) the fact that the principal is in a better position to supervise the actions of the agent; and (3) the fact that the principal bears the fruit of a principal/agent relationship. [Citation.]

Applied to this case, Demery acted as a bookkeeper for Metro for several years. Metro was in the best position to have instituted internal procedures and mechanisms regarding the company's accounting. Attesting to its lack of internal procedure, Metro did not uncover the embezzlement until two years after Demery deposited the check into Freestyle's bank account. Freestyle was not in a position, as a third party, to dictate Metro's internal control procedures to prevent employee theft.

* * *

Having reviewed the holder in due course elements in light of the undisputed facts of the case, we determine that Freestyle was a holder with constructive possession of a negotiable instrument, which was given for value and taken in good faith without notice of a forgery or an unauthorized signature.

Accordingly, we reverse the judgment of the court of appeals and remand with directions that the court of appeals return this case to the district court for entry of judgment in favor of Freestyle.

CASE 27-4

Good Faith

ANY KIND CHECKS CASHED, INC. v. TALCOTT

Court of Appeal of Florida, Fourth District, 2002
830 So.2d 160, 48 U.C.C. Rep.Serv.2d 800, rehearing denied

Gross, J.

[In the mid-1990s, D. J. Rivera, a "financial adviser," sold ninety-three-year-old John G. Talcott, Jr., an investment for "somewhere in the amount of $75,000." The investment produced no returns. On December 7, 1999, Salvatore Guarino, a cohort of Rivera, established check-cashing privileges at Any Kind Checks Cashed, Inc. That day, he cashed a $450 check without incident. On January 10, 2000, Rivera telephoned Talcott and talked him into sending him a check for $10,000 made out to Guarino, which was to be used for travel expenses to obtain a return on the original $75,000 investment. Rivera received the check on January 11. On that same morning, Rivera spoke to Talcott and stated that the $10,000 was more than what was needed for travel. He said that $5,700 would meet the travel costs. Talcott called his bank and stopped payment on the $10,000 check.

In spite of what Rivera told Talcott, Guarino appeared at Any Kind's Stuart, Florida, office on January 11 and presented the $10,000 check to Nancy Michael. She was a supervisor at the company with the authority to approve checks over $2,000.

Guarino showed Michael his driver's license and the Federal Express envelope from Talcott in which he received the check. She asked him the purpose of the check, and he told her that he was a broker and that the maker of the check had sent it as an investment. She was unable to contact Talcott by telephone. Based on her experience, Michael believed the check was good. The Federal Express envelope was "very crucial" to her decision, because it indicated that the maker of the check had sent it to the payee trying to cash the check. After deducting the 5 percent fee, Michael cashed the check and gave Guarino $9,500.

On January 15, 2000, Rivera called Talcott and asked about the $5,700, again promising to send him a return on his investment. The same day, Talcott sent a check for $5,700. He assumed that Rivera knew that he had stopped payment on the $10,000 check. On January 17, 2000, Guarino went into the Stuart branch of the Any Kind store and presented the $5,700 check payable to him to the teller, Joanne Kochakian. He showed her the Federal Express envelope in which the check had come. Kochakian noticed that Michael had previously approved the $10,000 check. She called Michael, who was working at another location, and told her about Guarino's check. Any Kind had no written procedures that a supervisor was required to follow in deciding which checks over $2,000 to cash. Michael instructed the cashier not to cash the check until she contacted Talcott to obtain approval. On her first attempt, Kochakian received no answer. On the second call, Talcott approved cashing the $5,700 check. There was no discussion of the $10,000 check. Any Kind cashed the second check for Guarino and deducted a 3 percent fee.

On January 19, Rivera called Talcott to warn him that Guarino was a cheat and a thief. Talcott immediately called his bank and stopped payment on the $5,700 check. Talcott's daughter called Any Kind and told it of the stop payment on the $5,700 check.

Any Kind filed a two-count complaint against Guarino and Talcott, claiming that it was a holder in due course. Talcott's defense was that Any Kind was not a holder in due course and that his obligation on the checks was nullified because of Guarino's illegal acts.

The trial court entered final judgment in favor of Any Kind for only the $5,700 check. On the $10,000 check, the judge found for Talcott. The court held that the checkcashing store was not a holder in due course, because the procedures it followed with the $10,000 check did not comport with reasonable commercial standards of fair dealing. The court found that the circumstances surrounding the cashing of the $10,000 check were sufficient to put Any Kind on notice of potential defenses.]

Using the terminology of the Uniform Commercial Code, Talcott was the maker or "drawer" of the check, the person who signed the draft "as a person ordering payment." [UCC §3-103(3)(a)] By Federal Expressing the check to Guarino, Talcott issued the check to him. See [UCC §3-105(a)] (defining "issue" as "the first delivery of an instrument by the maker or drawer * * * for the purpose of giving rights on the instrument to any person"). Guarino indorsed the check and cashed it with Any Kind. See [UCC §3-204 (a)] (defining "indorsement"). Any Kind immediately made the funds available to Guarino, less its fee. Talcott stopped payment on the check with his bank, so the check was returned to Any Kind. See [UCC §4-403(a)] (regarding a customer's right to stop payment).

When Guarino negotiated the check with Any Kind, it became a holder of the check, making it a "person entitled to enforce" the instrument. See [UCC §§3-201(a), 3-203(b), 3-301(a)]. As the drawer of the check dishonored by his bank, Talcott's obligation was to pay the draft to a person entitled to enforce the draft "according to its terms at the time it was issued. * * *" [UCC §3-414(a)].

Unless Any Kind is a holder in due course, its right to enforce Talcott's obligation to pay the draft is subject to (1) all defenses Talcott could raise "if the person entitled to enforce the instrument were enforcing a right to payment under a simple contract," and (2) a claim of "recoupment" Talcott could raise against Guarino. [UCC §3-305(a) & (b)]. Because Talcott was fraudulently induced to issue the checks, this case turns on Any Kind's entitlement to holder in due course status.

* * *

The good faith requirement of the holder in due course doctrine "has been the source of an ancient and continuing dispute." [Citation]. On the one hand, should the courts apply a so-called objective test, and ask whether a reasonably prudent person, behaving the way the alleged holder in due course behaved, would have been acting in good faith? Or should the courts instead apply a subjective test and examine the person's actual behavior, however stupid and irrespective of the reaction a reasonably prudent person would have had in the same circumstance? The legal establishment has steered a crooked course through this debate. [Citations.]

* * *

Application of [old UCC's] "honesty in fact" standard to Any Kind's conduct in this case would clothe it with holder in due course status. It is undisputed that Any Kind's employees were pure of heart, that they acted without knowledge of Guarino's wrongdoing.

However, in 1992, the legislature adopted a new definition of "good faith" that applies to the [UCC §3-302] definition of a holder in due course: "'good faith' means honesty in fact and the observance of reasonable commercial standards of fair dealing." [Citation.] To the old, subjective good faith, "honesty in fact" standard, the legislature added an objective component—the "pure heart of the holder must now be accompanied by reasoning that assures conduct comporting with reasonable commercial standards of fair dealing." [Citation.] No longer may a holder of an instrument act with "a pure heart and an empty head and still obtain holder in due course status." [Citation.]

Comment 4 to section 3-103, Florida Statutes Annotated, attempts to shed light on how to interpret the new standard:

> Although fair dealing is a broad term that must be defined in context, it is clear that it is concerned with the fairness of conduct rather than the care with which an act is performed. Failure to exercise ordinary care in conducting a transaction is an entirely different concept than failure to deal fairly in conducting the transaction.

The Code does not define the term "fair dealing." * * *

Application of holder in due course status is the law's value judgment that certain holders are worthy of protection from certain types of claims. For example, it has been argued that application of the old subjective standard facilitated the transfer of checks in the stream of commerce; arguably one would be "more willing to accept the checks if * * * she knows * * * she can be a holder in due course of that instrument and take it free of defenses that might have existed between the buyer and the seller in the underlying transaction." [Citation.] In applying the new standard, "fairness" should be measured by taking a global view of the underlying transaction and all of its participants. A holder "must act in a way that is fair according to commercial standards that are themselves reasonable." [Citation.]

To apply the law requiring "good faith" under section 3-302(a), we adopt the analysis set forth by the Supreme Court of Maine:

> The fact finder must * * * determine, first, whether the conduct of the holder comported with industry or "commercial" standards applicable to the transaction and, second, whether those standards were reasonable standards intended to result in fair dealing. Each of those determinations must be made in the context of the specific transaction at hand. If the fact finder's conclusion on each point is "yes," the holder will be determined to have acted in good faith even if, in the individual transaction at issue, the result appears unreasonable. Thus a holder may be accorded holder in due course status where it acts pursuant to those reasonable commercial standards of fair dealing—even if it is negligent—but may lose that status, even where it complies with commercial standards, if those standards are not reasonably related to achieving fair dealing.

[Citation.]

* * *

Check cashing businesses occupy a special niche in the financial industry. They are part of the "alternative financial services" or "fringe banking" sector, a part of the market that "has become a major source of traditional banking services for low-income and working poor consumers, residents of minority neighborhoods, and people with blemished credit histories." [Citations.]

* * *

Against this backdrop, we cannot say that the trial court erred in finding that the $10,000 check was a red flag. The $10,000 personal check was not the typical check cashed at a check cashing outlet. The size of the check, in the context of the check cashing business, was a proper factor to consider under the objective standard of good faith in deciding whether Any Kind was a holder in due course. [Citation.]

Guarino was not the typical customer of a check cashing outlet. As the trial judge observed, because of the 5% fee charged, it is unusual for a small businessman such as a broker to conduct business through a check cashing store instead of through a traditional bank. Guarino did not have a history with Any Kind of cashing checks of similar size without incident. The need for speed in a business transaction is usually less acute than for someone cashing a paycheck or welfare check to pay for life's necessities. The need for speed in cashing a large business check is consistent with a drawer who, for whatever reason, might stop payment. Fair dealing in this case required that the $10,000 check be approached with a degree of caution.

* * *

To affirm the trial court is not to wreak havoc with the check cashing industry. Verification with the maker of a check will *not* be necessary to preserve holder in due course status in the vast majority of cases arising from check cashing outlets. This was neither the typical customer, nor the typical transaction of a check cashing outlet.

* * *

The legislature's addition of an objective standard of conduct may well have the effect of "slowing the 'wheels of commerce'" in some transactions. [Citation.] However, by adopting changes to the "good faith" standard in the holder in due course doctrine, the legislature "necessarily must have concluded that the addition of the objective requirement to the definition of 'good faith' serves an important goal. The paramount necessity of unquestioned negotiability has given way, at least in part to the desire for reasonable commercial fairness in negotiable transactions." [Citation.] In this case, reasonable commercial fairness required Any Kind to approach the $10,000 check with some caution and to verify it with the maker if it wanted to preserve its holder in due course status.

AFFIRMED.

CASE 27-5

The Shelter Rule
TRIFFIN v. CIGNA INSURANCE
Superior Court of New Jersey, Appellate Division, 1997
297 N.J. Super 199, 687 A.2d 1045, 31 UCC Rep.Serv.2d 1040

Dreier, J.

Plaintiff, Robert J. Triffin, appeals from a * * * summary judgment dismissing his complaint for payment of a draft of defendant Cigna Insurance Company transferred to plaintiff by a holder in due course after Cigna had stopped payment on the instrument.

* * * The defaulting defendant, James Mills, received a draft in the amount of $484.12, dated July 7, 1993 from one of Cigna's constituent companies, Atlantic Employers Insurance Company. The draft had been issued for workers' compensation benefits. Mills falsely indicated to the issuer that he had not received the draft due to a change in his address and

requested that payment be stopped and a new draft issued by defendant. The insurer complied and stopped payment on the initial draft. Mills nevertheless negotiated the initial draft to plaintiff's assignor, Sun Corp. t/a Sun's Market, before the stop payment notation was placed on the draft. All appear to agree that Sun Corp. was a holder in due course. Sun Corp. presented the draft for payment through depositary and collecting banks. The issuer's bank dishonored the draft in accordance with its customer's direction, stamped it "Stop Payment," and returned the draft to Sun Corp. There is no question that had Sun Corp. at that point pressed its claim against the insurer as the issuer of the instrument, Sun Corp. would have been entitled to a judgment because of its status as a holder in due course.

Thereafter, plaintiff, who apparently is in the business of purchasing dishonored instruments, obtained an assignment of Sun Corp.'s interests in this instrument and proceeded with this law suit. Plaintiff does not contend that he is a holder in due course of the instrument by virtue of it being negotiated to him for value, in good faith, without notice of dishonor, under the former holder in due course statute, UCC §3-302, nor under the present statute, §3-302a(2).

Such negotiation is, of course, only one way for a holder to claim the status of a holder in due course. There exists a second method by which one may become a holder in due course. The shelter provisions of former UCC (§3-201), which was in effect when plaintiff obtained his assignment of this instrument, state clearly that "[t]ransfer of an instrument vests in the transferee such rights as the transferor has therein * * *." Official Comment 3 to that section sets to rest any question of whether this section applies to the transfer by assignment of the rights of a holder in due course. The Comment reads: "A holder in due course may transfer his rights as such * * *. [The former Negotiable Instruments Law section's] policy is to assure the holder in due course a free market for the paper, and that policy is continued in this section." Example (a) following this comment could have been drawn from this case, but is even stronger because it adds an element of fraud and posits a gratuitous transfer rather than a purchase, as in our case:

(a) A [Mills] induces M [Cigna] by fraud to make an instrument payable to A. A negotiates it to B [Sun Corp.], who takes as a holder in due course. After the instrument is overdue B gives it to C [plaintiff], who has notice of the fraud. C succeeds to B's rights as a holder in due course, cutting off the defense.

If the 1995 amendments are to be given retroactive effect, the law governing the rights of a transferee who merely has accepted the transfer of the instrument is now found in Revised UCC [§3-203]. It restates the principle of the former Official Comment 3, example (a), as substantive law.

* * *

The Uniform Commercial Code Comment 2 to this [Revised] section similarly states:

Under subsection (b) a holder in due course that transfers an instrument transfers those rights as a holder in due course to the purchaser. The policy is to assure the holder in due course a free market for the instrument.

* * *

These sections could not be clearer. Plaintiff received by [negotiation] the right of a holder in due course to this instrument, which apparently had been presented and then dishonored because of defendant's stop payment order. * * *

The summary judgment appealed from is reversed, and the matter is remanded with directions to enter judgment in favor of plaintiff, with interest.

QUESTIONS

1. Roy Rand executed and delivered the following note to Sue Sims: "Chicago, Illinois, June 1, 2021; I promise to pay to Sue Sims or bearer, on or before July 1, 2021, the sum of $7,000. This note is given in consideration of Sims's transferring to the undersigned title to her 2013 Buick automobile. (signed) Roy Rand." Rand and Sims agreed that delivery of the car be deferred to July 1, 2021. On June 15, Sims sold and delivered the note, without indorsement, to Karl Kaye for $6,200. What rights, if any, has Kaye acquired? Explain.

2. Lavinia Lane received a check from Wilmore Enterprises, Inc., drawn on the Citizens Bank of Erehwon, in the sum of $10,000. Mrs. Lane indorsed the check "Mrs. Lavinia Lane for deposit only, Account of Lavinia Lane" and placed it in a "Bank by Mail" envelope addressed to the First National Bank of Emanon, where she maintained a checking account. She then placed the envelope over a tier of mailboxes in her apartment building along with other letters to be picked up by the postal carrier the next day.

    Flora Fain stole the check, went to the Bank of Omaha, where Mrs. Lane was unknown, represented herself to be Lavinia Lane, and cashed the check. Has Bank of Omaha taken the check by negotiation? Why or why not?

3. For each of the following indorsements indicate (a) the type of indorsement and whether the indorsement is (b) blank or special, (c) restrictive or nonrestrictive, and (d) qualified or unqualified:

    a. "Pay to Monsein without recourse."

    b. "Pay to Allinore for collection."

    c. "I hereby assign all my rights, title, and interest in this note to Fullilove in full."

    d. "Pay to the Southern Trust Company."

    e. "Pay to the order of the Farmers Bank of Nicholasville for deposit only."

4. Explain whether each of the following transactions results in a valid negotiation:

    a. Arnold gives a negotiable check payable to bearer to Betsy without indorsing it.

    b. Golden indorses a negotiable promissory note payable to the order of Golden, "Pay to Chambers and Rambis, (signed) Golden."

    c. Porter lost a negotiable check payable to his order. Kersey found it and indorsed the back of the check as follows: "Pay to Drexler, (signed) Kersey."

    d. Thomas indorsed a negotiable promissory note payable to the order of Thomas, "(signed) Thomas," and delivered it to Sally. Sally then wrote above Thomas's signature, "Pay to Sally."

    e. Margarita issued to Poncho a negotiable promissory note payable to the order of Poncho. Poncho indorsed the note "Pay to Randy only, (signed) Poncho" and sold it to Randy. Randy then sold the note to Stephanie after indorsing it "Pay to Stephanie, (signed) Randy."

5. Alpha issues a negotiable check to Beta payable to the order of Beta in payment of an obligation Alpha owed Beta. Beta delivers the check to Gamma without indorsing it in exchange for one hundred shares of General Motors stock owned by Gamma. How has Beta transferred the check? What rights, if any, does Gamma have against Beta? Explain.

6. Simon Sharpe executed and delivered to Ben Bates a negotiable promissory note payable to the order of Ben Bates for $500. Bates indorsed the note "Pay to Carl Cady upon his satisfactorily repairing the roof of my house, (signed) Ben Bates" and delivered it to Cady as a down payment on the contract price of the roofing job. Cady then indorsed the note and sold it to Timothy Tate for $450. What rights, if any, does Tate acquire in the promissory note?

7. Debbie Dean issued a check to Betty Brown payable to the order of Cathy Cain and Betty Brown. Betty indorsed the check, "Payable to Elizabeth East, (signed) Betty Brown." What rights, if any, does Elizabeth acquire in the check? Discuss.

8. Marcus issues a negotiable promissory note payable to the order of Parish for $3,000. Parish raises the amount to $13,000 and negotiates it to Hilda for $12,000.

    a. If Hilda is a holder in due course, how much can she recover from Marcus? How much from Parish? If Marcus's negligence substantially contributed to the making of the alteration, how much can Hilda recover from Marcus and Parish, respectively?

    b. If Hilda is not a holder in due course, how much can she recover from Marcus? How much from Parish? If Marcus's negligence substantially contributed to the making of the alteration, how much can Hilda recover from Marcus and Parish, respectively?

9. On December 2, 2021, Miles executed and delivered to Proctor a negotiable promissory note for $1,000, payable to Proctor or order, due March 2, 2022, with interest at 14 percent from maturity, in partial payment of a printing press. On January 3, 2022, Proctor, in need of ready cash, indorsed and sold the note to Hughes for $800. Hughes paid $600 in cash to Proctor on January 3 and agreed to pay the balance of $200 one week later, namely, on January 10. On January 6, Hughes learned that Miles claimed a breach of warranty by Proctor and, for this reason, intended to refuse to pay the note when it matured. On January 10, Hughes paid Proctor $200, in conformity with their agreement of January 3. Following Miles's refusal to pay the note on March 2, 2022, Hughes sues Miles for $1,000. Is Hughes a holder in due course? If so, for what amount? Explain.

10. Thornton fraudulently represented to Daye that he would obtain for her a new car to be used in Daye's business for $17,800 from Pennek Motor Company. Daye thereupon executed her personal check for $17,800 payable to the order of Pennek Motor Company and delivered the check to Thornton, who immediately delivered it to the motor company in payment of his own prior indebtedness. The motor company had no knowledge of the representations made by Thornton to Daye. Pennek Motor Company now brings an action on the check that was not paid against Daye, who defends on the ground of failure of consideration. Is Pennek subject to this defense? Explain.

11. Adams, who reads with difficulty, arranged to borrow $2,000 from Bell. Bell prepared a note, which Adams read laboriously. As Adams was about to sign it, Bell diverted Adams's attention and substituted the following paper, which was identical to the note Adams had read except that the amounts were different: "On June 1, 2021,

I promise to pay Ben Bell or order Twelve Thousand Dollars with interest from date at 16 percent. This note is secured by certificate No. 13 for one hundred shares of stock of Brookside Mills, Inc."

Adams did not detect the substitution, signed as maker, handed the note and stock certificate to Bell, and received from Bell $2,000. Bell indorsed and sold the paper to Fore, a holder in due course, who paid him $11,000. Fore presented the note at maturity to Adams, who refused to pay. What are Fore's rights, if any, against Adams?

12. On January 2, 2021, seventeen-year-old Martin paid $2,000 for a used motorboat to use in his fishing business, after Dealer's fraudulent misrepresentation of the condition of the boat. Martin signed an installment contract for $1,500, and gave Dealer the following instrument as down payment:

> Dated: _____ 2021
>
> I promise to pay to the order of Dealer, six months after date, the sum of $500 without interest. This is given as a down payment on an installment contract for a motorboat.
>
>   (signed) Martin

Dealer, on July 1, sold his business to Henry and included this note in the transaction. Dealer indorsed the note in blank and handed it to Henry, who left the note in his office safe. On July 10, Sharpie, an employee of Henry, without authority, stole the note and sold it to Bert for $300, indorsing the note "Sharpie." At the time, in Bert's presence, Sharpie filled in the date on the note as February 2, 2021. Bert demanded payment from Martin, who refused to pay. Explain what Bert's rights are against Martin.

13. McLaughlin borrowed $10,000 from Adler, who, apprehensive about McLaughlin's ability to pay, demanded security. McLaughlin indorsed and delivered to Adler a negotiable promissory note executed by Topping for $12,000 payable to McLaughlin's order in twelve equal monthly installments. The note did not contain an acceleration clause, but it recited that the consideration for the note was McLaughlin's promise to paint and shingle Topping's barn. At the time McLaughlin transferred the note to Adler, the first installment was overdue and unpaid. Adler was unaware that the installment had not been paid. Topping did not pay any of the installments on the note. When the last installment became due, Adler presented the note to Topping for payment. Topping refused upon the ground that McLaughlin had not painted or reshingled her barn. Explain what Adler's rights are, if any, against Topping on the note?

14. Adams, by fraudulent representations, induced Barton to purchase one hundred shares of the capital stock of the Evermore Oil Company. The shares were worthless. Barton executed and delivered to Adams a negotiable promissory note for $5,000, dated May 5, in full payment for the shares, due six months after date. On May 20, Adams indorsed and sold the note to Cooper for $4,800. On October 21, Barton, having learned that Cooper now held the note, notified Cooper of the fraud and stated he would not pay the note. On December 1, Cooper negotiated the note to Davis who, while not a party, had full knowledge of the fraud perpetrated on Barton. Upon refusal of Barton to pay the note, Davis sues Barton for $5,000. Is Davis a holder in due course, or if not, does he have the rights of a holder in due course? Explain.

15. Donna gives Peter a check for $3,000 in return for a desktop computer. The check is dated December 2. Peter transfers the check for value to Howard on December 14, and Howard deposits it in his bank on December 20. In the meantime, Donna has discovered that the computer is not what was promised and has stopped payment on the check. If Peter and Howard disappear, may the bank recover from Donna notwithstanding her defense of failure of consideration? What will be the bank's cause of action?

CASE PROBLEMS

16. The drawer, Commercial Credit Corporation (Corporation), issued two checks payable to Rauch Motor Company. Rauch indorsed the checks in blank, deposited them to its account in University National Bank, and received a corresponding amount of money. The Bank stamped "pay any bank" on the checks and initiated collection. However, the checks were dishonored and returned to the Bank with the notation "payment stopped." Rauch, through subsequent deposits, repaid the bank. Later, to compromise a lawsuit, the Bank executed a special two-page indorsement of the two checks to Lamson. Lamson then sued the Corporation for the face value of the checks, plus interest. The Corporation contends that Lamson was not a holder of the checks because the indorsement was not in conformity with the Uniform Commercial Code in that it was stapled to the checks. Is Lamson a holder? Why or why not?

17. While assistant treasurer of Travco Corporation, Frank Mitchell caused two checks, each payable to a fictitious company, to be drawn on Travco's account with Brown City Savings Bank. In each case, Mitchell indorsed the check in his own name and then cashed it at Citizens Federal Savings & Loan Association of Port Huron. Both checks were cleared through normal banking channels and charged against Travco's account with Brown City. Travco subsequently discovered the embezzlement, and after Citizens denied its demand for reimbursement, Travco brought a suit against Citizens. Is the indorsement effective? Explain.

18. Eldon's Super Fresh Stores, Inc., is a corporation engaged in the retail grocery business. William Drexler was the attorney for and the corporate secretary of Eldon's and was also the personal attorney of Eldon Prinzing, the corporation's president and sole shareholder. From January 2020 through January 2021, Drexler maintained an active stock trading account in his name with Merrill Lynch. Eldon's had no such account. On August 12, 2020, Drexler purchased one hundred shares of Clark Oil & Refining Company stock through his Merrill Lynch stockbroker. He paid for the stock with a check drawn by Eldon's, made payable to Merrill Lynch, and signed by Prinzing. On August 15, 2020, Merrill Lynch accepted the check as payment for Drexler's stock purchase. There was no communication between Eldon's and Merrill Lynch until November 2021, fifteen months after the issuance of the check. At that time, Eldon's asked Merrill Lynch about the whereabouts of the stock certificate and asserted a claim to its ownership. Does Merrill Lynch qualify as a holder in due course? Why or why not?

19. Walter Duester purchased a John Deere combine from St. Paul Equipment. John Deere Co. was the lender and secured party under the agreement. The combine was pledged as collateral. Duester defaulted on his debt, and the manager of St. Paul, Hansen, was instructed to repossess the combine. Hansen went to Duester's farm to accomplish this. Duester told him that he had received some payments for custom combining and would immediately purchase a cashier's check to pay the John Deere debt. Hansen followed Duester to the defendant, Boelus State Bank. Hansen remained outside, and Duester returned in a few minutes with a cashier's check in the amount of the balance of his indebtedness payable to John Deere. The check had been signed by an authorized bank employee. When John Deere, however, presented the check to the bank for payment shortly thereafter, the bank refused to pay, claiming that Duester acquired the cashier's check by theft. Is John Deere subject to this defense? Why or why not?

20. Stephens delivered one hundred eighty-four bushels of corn to Aubrey, for which he was to receive $478.23. Aubrey issued a check with $478.23 typewritten in numbers, and on the line customarily used to express the amount in words appeared "$100,478 and 23 cts" imprinted in red with a check-writing machine. Before Stephens cashed the check, someone crudely typed "100" in front of the typewritten $478.23. When Stephens presented this check to the State Bank of Salem, Anderson, the manager, questioned Stephens. Anderson knew that Stephens had just declared bankruptcy and was not accustomed to making such large deposits. Stephens told Anderson he had bought and sold a large quantity of corn at a great profit. Anderson accepted the explanation and applied the monies to nine promissory notes, an installment payment, and accrued interest owed by Stephens. Stephens also received $2,000 in cash, with the balance deposited in his checking account.

    Later that day, Anderson reexamined the check and discovered the suspicious appearance of the typewriting. He then contacted Aubrey, who said a check in that amount was suspicious, whereupon Anderson froze the transaction. When Aubrey stopped payment on the check, the bank sustained a $28,193.91 loss because Stephens could not be located. The bank then sued Aubrey for the loss. Explain who should bear the loss.

21. L&M Home Health Corporation (L&M) had a checking account with Wells Fargo Bank. L&M engaged Gentner and Company, Inc. (Gentner), to provide consulting services and paid Gentner for services rendered with a check drawn on its Wells Fargo account in the amount of $60,000, dated September 23, 2020. Eleven days later, on October 4, 2020, L&M orally instructed Wells Fargo to stop payment on the check. Eleven days after that, on October 15, 2020, Gentner presented the L&M check to Wells Fargo for payment. On the same date, the teller issued a cashier's check, payable to Gentner, in the amount of $60,000. On November 5, 2020, Wells Fargo placed a "stop payment order" on the cashier's check. On January 15, 2021, Gentner deposited the cashier's check at another bank, but it was not honored and was returned stamped "Payment Stopped." Gentner sues Wells Fargo for wrongful dishonor of the cashier's check. Is Gentner a holder in due course of the check? Discuss.

22. Stanley A. Erb became a vice president of the Shearson Lehman Brothers, Inc., branch office in Provo, Utah. That year, Erb was contacted by McKay Matthews, the controller for the Orem, Utah-based WordPerfect Corporation and its sister corporation, Utah Softcopy. At Matthews's request, Erb established and managed three separate investment accounts at Shearson. The

accounts were for the benefit of the WordPerfect and Utah Soft-copy corporations, and one account was for the WordPerfect principals, Allen Ashton, Bruce Bastian, and Willard Peterson. In March of that year, Erb personally accepted from Matthews a check drawn by Utah Soft-copy for $460,150.23 and payable to the order of "ABP Investments." At that time, there was no ABP investment account at Shearson, although the WordPerfect principals maintained accounts elsewhere in that name. Erb accepted the check, but rather than deposit it in one of the three authorized accounts, Erb opened a new account at Shearson in the name of "ABP Investments," apparently by forging the signature of Bruce Bastian on the new account documents. Over the next eleven months, Erb induced Shearson to draft thirty-seven checks on the ABP Investment account, payable to ABP Investments, by submitting falsified payment requests to Shearson's cashier. The checks were mailed to an Orem post office box unknown to WordPerfect and its principals. Erb would obtain the checks and indorse them in the name of ABP Investments. He took the checks to Wasatch Bank for deposit into his personal account. Wasatch accepted the deposits and later allowed Erb to withdraw $504,295.30, the entire amount, from the account. Shearson discovered Erb's activities after Erb had left Shearson after two years. Shearson brought a suit against Wasatch Bank. Discuss who should prevail.

23. Turman executed a deed of trust note for $107,500 payable to Ward's Home Improvement, Inc. (Ward's). The note was in consideration of a contract for Ward's to build a house on Turman's property. On the same day, Ward's executed an assignment of the note to Robert Pomerantz for which Pomerantz paid Ward's $95,000. Although the document uses the word *assignment*, no notation or indorsement was made on the note itself. Is Pomerantz a holder? Is Pomerantz a holder in due course? Explain.

24. Certain partners of the Finley Kumble law firm signed promissory notes that secured loans made to the law firm by the National Bank of Washington (NBW). When Finley Kumble subsequently declared bankruptcy and defaulted on the loans, NBW filed suit to collect on the notes. Then NBW itself became insolvent, and the Federal Deposit Insurance Corporation (FDIC) was appointed as receiver for NBW. The FDIC brought suit against the partners who had signed the note. Section 1823(e) of the Federal Deposit Insurance Act places the FDIC in the position of a holder in due course and thus bars all personal defenses against the FDIC claims. Twenty of the Finley partners claimed that they had signed the notes under the threat that their wages and standing in the firm would decrease if they refused to sign. Such a threat constituted economic duress, which, they contended, is not a personal defense but a real defense. Discuss who should prevail.

TAKING SIDES

Wilson was employed as the office manager of Palmer & Ray Dental Supply of Abilene, Inc. Soon after an auditor discovered a discrepancy in the company's inventory, Wilson confessed to cashing thirty-five checks that she was supposed to deposit on behalf of the company. Palmer & Ray Dental Supply used a rubber stamp to indorse checks. The stamp listed the company's name and address but did not read "for deposit only." The company's president, James Ray, authorized Wilson to indorse checks with this stamp. Wilson cashed all of the checks at First National Bank.

a. What are the arguments that First National Bank is liable to Palmer & Ray Dental Supply for converting the company's funds by giving Wilson cash instead of depositing the checks into the company's bank account?

b. What are the arguments that First National Bank is not liable to Palmer & Ray Dental Supply?

c. Explain who should prevail.

Liability of Parties

CHAPTER OUTCOMES

After reading and studying this chapter, you should be able to:

- Explain contractual liability, warranty liability, and liability of conversion.

- Explain the liability of makers, acceptors, drawers, drawees, indorsers, and accommodation parties.

- Discuss the condition precedents to the liability of secondary parties.

- Explain the methods by which liability on an instrument may be terminated.

- Compare the warranties on transfer with the warranties on presentment.

The preceding chapters discussed the requirements of negotiability, the transfer of negotiable instruments, and the preferred position of a holder in due course. When parties issue negotiable instruments, they do so with the expectation that they, either directly or indirectly, will satisfy their obligation under the instrument. Likewise, when a person accepts, indorses, or transfers an instrument, he incurs liability for the instrument under certain circumstances. This chapter examines the liability of parties arising out of negotiable instruments and the ways in which liability may be terminated.

Two types of potential liability are associated with negotiable instruments: contractual liability and warranty liability. The law imposes **contractual liability** on those who **sign**, or have a representative agent sign, a negotiable instrument. Because some parties to a negotiable instrument never sign it, they never assume contractual liability. Section 3-401(a).

Warranty liability, on the other hand, is not based on signature; thus, it may be imposed on both signers and nonsigners. **Warranty liability** applies (1) to persons who transfer an instrument and (2) to persons who obtain payment or acceptance of an instrument.

CONTRACTUAL LIABILITY

All parties whose signatures appear on a negotiable instrument incur certain contractual obligations, unless they disclaim liability. No person is liable on an instrument unless she signs it herself or has it signed by a person whose signature binds her. Once the person signs the instrument, the person has *prima facie* liability on the instrument. The *maker* of a promissory note and the *acceptor* of a draft assume primary, or unconditional, liability, subject to valid claims and defenses, to pay according to the terms of the instrument at the time they sign it or as completed according to the rules for incomplete instruments, discussed in *Chapter 27*. **Primary liability** means that a party is legally obligated to pay without the holder's having to resort first to another party. *Indorsers* of all instruments incur secondary, or conditional, liability if the instrument is not paid. **Secondary liability** means that a party is legally obligated to pay only after another party, who is expected to pay, fails to do so. The liability of drawers of drafts and checks is also conditional because it is generally contingent upon the drawee's dishonor of the instrument. A *drawee* has *no* liability on the instrument until he accepts it.

An **accommodation party** signs the instrument to lend her credit to another party to the instrument and is a direct beneficiary of the value received. Section 3-419(a). The liability of an accommodation party, who generally signs as a co-maker, or anomalous indorser, is determined by the capacity in which she signs. Section 3-419(b). If she signs as a maker, she incurs primary liability; if she signs as an anomalous indorser, she incurs secondary liability.

28-1 Signature

The word *signature*, as discussed in *Chapter 26*, is broadly defined to include any name, word, or mark, whether handwritten, typed, printed, or in any other form, made with the intention of authenticating an instrument. Sections 3-401(b); Revised Section 1-201(b)(37). The signature may be made by the individual herself or on her behalf by the individual's authorized agent.

28-1a AUTHORIZED SIGNATURES

A person is obligated by a signature on an instrument if the signature is her own or if an agent with authority signs the instrument. Authorized agents often execute negotiable instruments on behalf of their principals. The agent is not liable if she is authorized to execute the instrument and does so properly (e.g., "Prince, principal, by Adams, agent"). If these two conditions are met, then only the principal is liable on the instrument. (For a comprehensive discussion of the principal-agent relationship, see *Chapters 19* and *20*.)

Occasionally, however, the agent, although fully authorized, uses an inappropriate form of signature that may mislead holders or prospective holders as to the identity of the obligor. Although incorrect signatures by agents assume many forms, they can be conveniently sorted into three groups. In each of these instances, the intention of the original parties to the instrument is that the principal is to be liable on the instrument and the agent is not.

The first type occurs when an agent signs only his own name to an instrument, neither indicating that he is signing in a representative capacity nor stating the name of the principal. For example, Adams, the agent of Prince, makes a note on behalf of Prince but signs it "Adams." The signature does not indicate that Adams has signed in a representative capacity or that he has made the instrument on behalf of Prince. The second type of incorrect form occurs when an authorized agent indicates that he is signing in a representative capacity but does not disclose the name of his principal. For example, Adams, executing an instrument on behalf of Prince, merely signs it "Adams, agent." The third type of inappropriate signature occurs when an agent reveals both her name and her principal's name but does not indicate that she has signed in a representative capacity. For example, Adams, signing an instrument on behalf of Prince, signs it "Adams, Prince."

In all three situations, the agent is liable on the instrument only to a holder in due course without notice that Adams was not intended to be liable. Because Prince's liability on the instrument is determined by contract and agency law, Prince is liable to all holders. Under Article 3, if a representative (an agent) signs his name as the drawer of a *check* without indicating his representative status and the check is payable from an account of the represented person (the principal) who is identified on the check, the representative is not liable on the check if he is an authorized agent.

◆ *See Case 28-1*

28-1b UNAUTHORIZED SIGNATURES

An unauthorized signature, with two exceptions, is totally ineffective and does not bind anybody. Unauthorized signatures include both forgeries and signatures made by an agent without authority. Though generally not binding on the person whose name appears on the instrument, the unauthorized signature is binding upon the unauthorized signer, whether her own name appears on the instrument or not, to any person who in good faith pays or gives value for the instrument. Section 3-403(a). Thus, if Adams, without authority, signed Prince's name to an instrument, Adams, not Prince, would be liable on the instrument. The rule, therefore, is an exception to the principle that only those whose names appear on a negotiable instrument can be liable on it.

RATIFICATION OF UNAUTHORIZED SIGNATURE An unauthorized signature may be **ratified** by the person whose name appears on the instrument. Section 3-403(a). Although the ratification may relieve the actual signer from liability on the instrument, it does not of itself affect any rights the person ratifying the signature may have against the actual signer.

NEGLIGENCE CONTRIBUTING TO FORGED SIGNATURE Any person who by his **negligence** substantially contributes to the making of a forged signature may *not* assert the lack of authority as a defense against a holder in due course or a person who in good faith pays the instrument or takes it for value or for collection. Section 3-406. For example, Ingrid employs a signature stamp to sign her checks and carelessly leaves it accessible to third parties. Lisa discovers the stamp and uses it to write a number of checks without Ingrid's authorization. Norman, a person who takes the instrument for value and in good faith, will not be subject to Ingrid's defense of unauthorized signature and will be able to recover the amount of the check from Ingrid, due to Ingrid's negligence in storing the signature stamp. Nevertheless, if the person asserting the preclusion also fails to exercise reasonable care, Section 3-406(b) applies a comparative negligence standard.

28-2 Liability of Primary Parties

There is a primary party on every note: the *maker*. The maker's commitment is unconditional. Section 3-412. No one, however, is unconditionally liable on a draft or check as issued. A *drawee* is not liable on the instrument unless he accepts it. Section 3-408. If, however, the drawee accepts the draft, after which he is known as the *acceptor*, he becomes primarily liable on the instrument. **Acceptance** or, in the case of a check, certification is the drawee's signed promise to pay a draft as presented. Section 3-409(a), (d). Presentment (i.e., a demand for payment) is not a condition to the holder's right to recover from parties with primary liability.

28-2a MAKERS

The maker of a note is obligated to pay the instrument according to its terms at the time of issuance or, if the instrument is incomplete, according to its terms when completed, as discussed in *Chapter 27*. Section 3-412. The obligation of the maker is owed to a person entitled to enforce the instrument or to an indorser who paid the instrument.

Primary liability also applies to issuers of cashier's checks and to issuers of drafts drawn on the drawer (i.e., where the issuer is both the drawee and the drawer). Section 3-412.

28-2b ACCEPTORS

A drawee has no liability on the instrument until she accepts it, at which time she becomes an acceptor and, like a maker, primarily liable. The acceptor becomes liable on the draft according to its terms at the time of acceptance or as completed according to the rules for incomplete instruments as discussed in *Chapter 27*. Section 3-413(a). Nevertheless, if the acceptor does not state the amount accepted and the amount of the draft is later raised, a subsequent holder in due course can enforce the instrument against the acceptor according to the terms at the time the holder in due course took possession. Section 3-413(b). Thus, an acceptor should always indicate on the instrument the amount that she is accepting. The acceptor owes the obligation to pay to a person entitled to enforce the instrument or to the drawer or an indorser who paid the draft under drawer's or indorser's liability. Section 3-413(a).

An acceptance must be written on the draft. Section 3-409(a). Having met this requirement, it may take many forms. It may be printed on the face of the draft, ready for the drawee's signature. It may consist of a rubber stamp, with the signature of the drawee added. It may be the drawee's signature, preceded by a word or phrase such as "Accepted," "Certified," or "Good." It may consist of nothing more than the drawee's signature. Normally, but by no means necessarily, an acceptance is written vertically across the face of the draft. It must not, however, contain any words indicating an intent to refuse to honor the draft. Furthermore, no writing separate from the draft and no oral statement or conduct of the drawee will convert the drawee into an acceptor.

Checks, when accepted, are said to be certified. **Certification** is a special type of acceptance consisting of the drawee bank's promise to pay the check when subsequently presented for payment. Section 3-409(d).

The drawee bank has no obligation to certify a check, and its refusal to certify does not constitute dishonor of the instrument. If the drawee refuses to accept or pay the instrument, he may be liable to the drawer for breach of contract.

28-3 Liability of Secondary Parties

Parties with secondary (conditional) liability do not unconditionally promise to pay the instrument; rather, they engage to pay the instrument if the party expected to pay does not do so. The drawer is liable if the drawee dishonors the instrument. Indorsers (including the payee if he indorses) of an instrument are also conditionally liable; their liability is subject to the conditions of dishonor and notice of dishonor. If an instrument is *not* paid by the party expected to pay and the conditions precedent to the liability of a secondary party are satisfied, a secondary party is liable unless he has disclaimed his liability or he possesses a valid defense to the instrument.

28-3a DRAWERS

A drawer of a draft orders the drawee to pay the instrument and does not expect to pay the draft personally. The drawer is obligated to pay the draft only if the drawee fails to pay the instrument. The drawer of an *unaccepted draft* is obligated to pay the instrument upon its dishonor according to its terms at the time it was issued or, in the case of an incomplete instrument, according to the rules discussed in *Chapter 27*. The drawer's liability is contingent only upon dishonor and does not require notice of dishonor. The drawer's obligation on an unaccepted draft is owed to a person entitled to enforce the instrument or to an indorser who paid the instrument under indorser's liability.

If the draft has been accepted and the acceptor is not a bank, the obligation of the drawer to pay the instrument is then contingent upon both dishonor of the instrument and notice of dishonor; the drawer's liability in this instance is equivalent to that of an indorser. Sections 3-414(d), 3-503.

◆ *See Case 28-2*

28-3b INDORSERS

An indorser promises that upon dishonor of the instrument *and* notice of dishonor, she will pay the instrument according to the terms of the instrument at the time it was indorsed or, if an incomplete instrument when indorsed, according to its terms when completed, as discussed in *Chapter 27.* Sections 3-415, 3-503. Once again, this obligation is owed to a person entitled to enforce the instrument or to a subsequent indorser who paid the instrument under indorser's liability.

28-3c EFFECT OF ACCEPTANCE

Where a draft is accepted by a *bank*, the drawer and all prior indorsers are discharged. Sections 3-414(c), 3-415(d). The liability of indorsers subsequent to certification is not affected. When the bank accepts a draft, it should withhold from the drawer's account funds sufficient to pay the instrument. Because the bank is primarily liable on its acceptance and has the funds, whereas the drawer does not, the discharge is reasonable.

28-3d DISCLAIMER OF LIABILITY BY SECONDARY PARTIES

Both drawers and indorsers may disclaim their normal conditional liability by drawing or indorsing an instrument "**without recourse.**" Sections 3-414(e), 3-415(b). However, drawers of checks may not disclaim contractual liability. Section 3-414(e). The use of the qualifying words *without recourse* is understood to place purchasers on notice that they may not rely on the credit of the person using this language. A person drawing or indorsing an instrument in this manner does not incur the normal contractual liability of a drawer or indorser to pay the instrument, but he may nonetheless be liable for breach of warranty.

Practical Advice

If you take an instrument from another party, make sure that she unqualifiedly indorses the instrument to add her liability to it.

28-3e CONDITIONS PRECEDENT TO LIABILITY

A **condition precedent** is an event or events that must occur before liability arises. The condition precedent to the liability of the drawer of an *unaccepted* draft is dishonor. Conditions precedent to the liability of any indorser or the drawer of an *accepted* draft by a nonbank are dishonor and notice of dishonor. If the conditions to secondary liability are not met, a party's conditional obligation on the instrument is discharged, unless the conditions are excused.

DISHONOR Dishonor generally involves the refusal to pay an instrument when it is presented. **Presentment** is a demand made by or on behalf of a person entitled to enforce the instrument for (1) **payment** by the drawee or other party

obligated to pay the instrument or (2) **acceptance** by the drawee of a draft. Section 3-501(a). The return of any instrument for lack of necessary indorsements or for failure of the presentment to comply with the terms of the instrument, however, is not a dishonor. Section 3-501(b)(3).

What constitutes dishonor varies depending upon the type of instrument and whether presentment is required.

1. **Note:** A *demand note* is dishonored if the maker does not pay it on the day of presentment. Section 3-502(a)(1). If the note is payable at a *definite time* and (a) the terms of the note require presentment or (b) the note is payable at or through a bank, the note is dishonored if it is not paid on the date it is presented or its due date, whichever is later. Section 3-502(a)(2). All *other time notes* need not be presented and are dishonored if they are not paid on their due dates. Section 3-502(a)(3). Nevertheless, because makers are primarily liable on their notes, their liability is not affected by failure of proper presentment.

2. **Drafts:** An *unaccepted draft* (other than a check, discussed later) that is payable on *demand* is dishonored if presentment is made and it is not paid on the date presented. Section 3-502(b)(2). A *time draft* presented for *payment* is due on the due date or presentment date, whichever is later. Section 3-502(b)(3). A *time draft* presented for *acceptance* prior to its due date is dishonored if it is not accepted on the day presented. Section 3-502(b)(3). Refusal to accept a demand instrument is not a dishonor, although acceptance may be requested. Of course, if an instrument is payable at a certain time period after acceptance or sight, a refusal to accept the draft on the day presented is a dishonor. Section 3-502(b)(4).

   An accepted demand draft is dishonored if the acceptor (who is primarily liable on the instrument) does not pay it on the day presented for payment. Section 3-502(d)(1). An accepted time draft is dishonored if it is not paid on the due date for payment or on the presentment date, whichever is later. Section 3-502(d)(2).

   Drawers, with the exception of drafts accepted by a bank, are not discharged from liability by a delay in presentment. Once an instrument has been properly presented and dishonored, a drawer becomes liable to pay the instrument. As previously indicated, drawers and prior indorsers are discharged from liability when a draft is accepted by a bank. Sections 3-414, 3-415.

3. **Checks:** If a check is presented for payment directly to the payor/drawee bank for immediate payment, a refusal to pay the check on the day presented constitutes dishonor. Section 3-502(b)(2). In the more common situation of a check being presented through the normal collection process, a check is dishonored if the payor bank makes

timely return of the check, sends timely notice of dishonor or nonpayment, or becomes accountable for the amount of the check (until that payment has been made, the check is dishonored, Comment 4). Section 3-502(b)(1). As more fully explained in *Chapter 29*, under Article 4, a bank in most instances has a midnight deadline (before midnight of the next banking day) in which to decide whether to honor or dishonor an instrument. Thus, depending on the number of banks involved in the collection process, the time for dishonor can vary greatly.

Delay in presentment discharges an *indorser* only if the instrument is a check and it is not presented for payment or given to a depositary bank for collection within thirty days after the day the indorsement was made. Section 3-415(e). The same rule does not apply, however, to a drawer. If a person entitled to enforce a check fails to present a check within thirty days after its date, the drawer will be discharged only if the delay deprives the drawer of funds because of the suspension of payments by the drawee bank such as would result from a bank failure. Section 3-414(f). This discharge is quite unlikely because of Federal bank insurance but would be available when an account is not fully insured because it exceeds $100,000 or because the account does not qualify for deposit insurance. Section 3-414, Comment 6.

Practical Advice
Make sure that you timely and properly present any negotiable instrument that you possess for acceptance or payment.

NOTICE OF DISHONOR The obligation of an indorser of any instrument and of a drawer of a draft accepted by a nonbank is not enforceable unless the indorser or drawer is given notice of dishonor or the notice is otherwise excused. Sections 3-503(a), 3-415(c). Thus, lack of proper notice discharges the liability of an indorser; for this purpose, a drawer of a draft accepted by a party other than a bank is treated as an indorser. Notice of dishonor is *not* required to retain the liability of drawers of unaccepted drafts. In addition, as previously mentioned, a drawer is discharged when a draft is accepted by a *bank*. Section 3-414. In short, a drawer's liability usually is not contingent upon receiving notice of dishonor, whereas an indorser's liability is.

Notice of dishonor is normally given by the holder or by an indorser who has himself received notice. For example, Michael makes a note payable to the order of Phyllis; Phyllis indorses it to Arthur; Arthur indorses it to Bambi; and Bambi indorses it to Henry, the last holder. Henry presents it to Michael within a reasonable time, but Michael refuses to pay. Henry may give notice of dishonor to all secondary parties: Phyllis, Arthur, and Bambi. If he is satisfied that Bambi will pay him or if he

does not know how to contact Phyllis or Arthur, he may notify only Bambi, who then must see to it that Arthur or Phyllis is notified, or she will have no recourse. Bambi may notify either or both. If she notifies Arthur only, Arthur will have to see to it that Phyllis is notified, or Arthur will have no recourse. When properly given, notice benefits all parties who have rights on the instrument against the party notified. Section 3-503(b). Thus, Henry's notification to Phyllis operates as notice to Phyllis by both Arthur and Bambi. Likewise, if Henry notifies only Bambi and Bambi notifies Arthur and Phyllis, then Henry has the benefit of Bambi's notification of Arthur and Phyllis. Nonetheless, it would be advisable for Henry to give notice to all prior parties because Bambi may be insolvent and thus may not bother to notify Arthur or Phyllis.

If in the previous example Henry were to notify Phyllis alone, Arthur and Bambi would be discharged. Because she has no claim against Arthur or Bambi, who indorsed after she did, Phyllis would have no ground for complaint. It cannot matter to Phyllis that she is compelled to pay Henry rather than Arthur. Therefore, subsequent parties are permitted to skip intermediate indorsers if they want to discharge them and are willing to look solely to prior indorsers for recourse.

Any necessary notice must be given by a bank before midnight on the *next* banking day following the banking day on which it receives notice of dishonor. Any nonbank with respect to an instrument taken for collection must give notice within thirty days following the day on which it received notice. In all other situations, notice of dishonor must be within thirty days following the day on which dishonor occurred. Section 3-503(c). For instance, Donna draws a check on Youngstown Bank payable to the order of Pablo; Pablo indorses it to Andrea; Andrea deposits it to her account in Second Chicago National Bank; Second Chicago National Bank properly presents it to Youngstown Bank, the drawee; and Youngstown dishonors it because the drawer, Donna, has insufficient funds on deposit to cover it. Youngstown has until midnight of the following day to notify Second Chicago National, Andrea, or Pablo of the dishonor. Second Chicago National then has until midnight on the day after receipt of notice of dishonor to notify Andrea or Pablo. That is, if Second Chicago National received the notice of dishonor on Monday, it would have until midnight on Tuesday to notify Andrea or Pablo. If it failed to notify Andrea, it could not charge the item back to her. Andrea, in turn, has thirty days after receipt of notice of dishonor to notify Pablo. Donna, a drawer of an unaccepted draft, is not discharged from liability for failure to receive notice of dishonor.

Frequently, notice of dishonor is given by returning the unpaid instrument with an attached stamp, ticket, or memorandum stating that the item was not paid and requesting that the recipient make good on it. But because the purpose of notice is to give knowledge of dishonor and to inform the secondary party that he may be held liable on the instrument, any kind of notice which informs the recipient of his potential liability is sufficient. No formal requisites are imposed—notice may be given by any commercially reasonable means, including oral, written, or electronic communication. Section 3-503(b). An oral notice, while sufficient, is inadvisable because it may be difficult to prove. Notice of dishonor must reasonably identify the instrument. Section 3-503(b).

Practical Advice

Upon dishonor of any instrument that you have presented for payment or acceptance, give proper notice, wherever possible, to all prior parties.

PRESENTMENT AND NOTICE OF DISHONOR EXCUSED The Uniform Commercial Code excuses *presentment* for payment or acceptance if (1) the person entitled to enforce the instrument cannot with reasonable diligence present the instrument; (2) the maker or acceptor of the instrument has repudiated the obligation to pay, is dead, or is in insolvency proceedings; (3) the terms of the instrument do not require presentment to hold the indorsers or drawer liable; (4) the drawer or indorser has waived the right of presentment; (5) the drawer instructed the drawee not to pay or accept the draft; or (6) the drawee was not obligated to the drawer to pay the draft. Section 3-504(a).

Notice of dishonor is excused if the terms of the instrument do not require notice to hold the party liable or if notice has been waived by the party whose obligation is being enforced. Moreover, a waiver of presentment is also a waiver of notice of dishonor. Section 3-504(b). Finally, delay in giving notice of dishonor is excused if the delay is caused by circumstances beyond the control of the person giving notice and that person exercised reasonable diligence in giving notice after the cause of the delay ceased to exist. Section 3-504(c).

♦ **SEE FIGURE 28-1:** *Contractual Liability*

28-3f LIABILITY FOR CONVERSION

Conversion is a tort by which a person becomes liable in damages because of his wrongful control over the personal property of another. The law applicable to conversion of personal property applies to instruments. Section 3-420(a). An instrument is so converted if the instrument "is taken by transfer, other than by negotiation, from a person not entitled to enforce the instrument or a bank makes or obtains payment with respect to the instrument for a person *not* entitled to enforce the instrument or receive payment." Section 3-420(a) (emphasis added). Examples of conversion thus would include a drawee bank that pays an instrument containing a forged indorsement or a bank that pays an instrument containing only one of two required indorsements.

28-4 Termination of Liability

Eventually, every commercial transaction must end, terminating the potential liabilities of the parties to the instrument. *Discharge* means that an obligated individual is released from liability on the instrument due to either Article 3 or contract law. The Code specifies the various methods by and extent to which the liability of *any* party, primary or secondary, is discharged. The Code also specifies when the

FIGURE 28-1 Contractual Liability

Party	Instrument	Liability	Conditions
Maker	Note	Unconditional	None
Acceptor	Draft	Unconditional	None
Drawer	Unaccepted draft	Conditional	Dishonor
	Draft accepted by a nonbank	Conditional	Dishonor and notice
	Cashier's check	Unconditional	None
	Draft drawn on drawer	Unconditional	None
	Draft accepted by a bank	None	
	Draft (not check) drawn without recourse	None	
Indorser	Note or draft	Conditional	Dishonor and notice
	Draft subsequently accepted by a bank	None	
	Note or draft indorsed without recourse	None	
Drawee	Draft	None	

liability of *all* parties is discharged. No discharge of a party is effective against a subsequent holder in due course, however, unless she has notice of the discharge when she takes the instrument. Section 3-601(b). In addition, discharge of liability is not always final; liability under certain circumstances (e.g., coming into possession of a subsequent holder in due course) can be revived. Discharge applies to the individual and not the instrument, and discharge of individuals may occur at different points in time. Moreover, a person's liability may be discharged with regard to one party but not to another.

28-4a PAYMENT

The most obvious and common way for a party to discharge liability on an instrument is to pay a party entitled to enforce the instrument. Section 3-602. An instrument is paid to the extent that payment is made by or for a person obligated to pay the instrument and to a person entitled to enforce the instrument. Section 3-602(a). Subject to three exceptions, such payment results in a discharge even though it is made with knowledge of another person's claim to the instrument, unless such other person either supplies adequate indemnity or obtains an injunction in a proceeding to which the holder is made a party. It should be noted, however, that the discharge is only to the extent of the payment.

Practical Advice

The person making payment should take possession of the instrument or have it cancelled—marked "paid" or "cancelled"—so that it cannot pass to a subsequent holder in due course against whom his discharge would be ineffective.

28-4b TENDER OF PAYMENT

Any party liable on an instrument who makes proper tender of full payment to a person entitled to enforce the instrument when or after payment is due is discharged from liability for interest after the due date. Section 3-603(c). If her tender is refused, she is not discharged from liability for the face amount of the instrument or for any interest accrued until the time of tender. Moreover, if an instrument requires presentment and the obligor is ready and able to pay the instrument when it is due at the place of payment specified in the instrument, such readiness is the equivalent of tender. Section 3-603(c).

Occasionally a person entitled to enforce an instrument will refuse a tender of payment for reasons known only to himself. It may be that he believes his rights exceed the amount of the tender or that he desires to enforce payment against another party. In any event, his refusal of the tender wholly discharges to the extent of the amount of tender every party who has a right of recourse against the party making tender. Section 3-603(b).

28-4c CANCELLATION AND RENUNCIATION

Section 3-604 provides that a person entitled to enforce an instrument may discharge the liability of any party to an instrument by an intentional voluntary act, such as by canceling the instrument or the signature of the party or parties to be discharged, by mutilating or destroying the instrument, by obliterating a signature, or by adding words indicating a discharge. Section 3-604(a). A party entitled to enforce an instrument also may renounce his rights by a writing, signed and delivered, promising not to sue or otherwise renouncing rights against the party. Like other discharges, however, a written renunciation is of no effect against a subsequent holder in due course who takes without knowledge of the renunciation. Section 3-601(b).

Cancellation or renunciation is effective even without consideration.

LIABILITY BASED ON WARRANTY

Article 3 imposes two types of implied warranties: (1) transferor's warranties and (2) presenter's warranties. Sections 3-416 and 3-417. Although these warranties are effective whether or not the transferor or presenter signs the instrument, the extension of the transferor's warranty to subsequent holders does depend on whether one or the other has indorsed the instrument. Like other warranties, these may be disclaimed by agreement between immediate parties. In the case of an indorser, his disclaimer of transfer warranties and presentment warranties must appear in the indorsement itself and is effective, except with respect to checks. Sections 3-416(c), 3-417(e). Such disclaimers must be specific, such as "without warranty." The use of "without recourse" will disclaim only contract liability, not warranty liability.

28-5 Warranties on Transfer

Any person who transfers an instrument, whether by negotiation or assignment, and receives *consideration* makes certain **transferor's warranties.** Section 3-416. Any consideration sufficient to support a contract will support transfer warranties. If transfer is by delivery alone, warranties on transfer run only to the immediate transferee. If the transfer is made by indorsement, whether qualified or unqualified, the transfer warranty runs to "any subsequent transferee." *Transfer* means that the delivery of possession is voluntary. Sections 3-201(a), 1-201(14). The warranties of the transferor are as follows.

28-5a ENTITLEMENT TO ENFORCE

The first warranty that the Code imposes on a transferor is that the transferor is a person entitled to enforce the instrument. Section 3-416(a)(1). This warranty "is in effect a warranty that there are no unauthorized or missing indorsements that prevent the transferor from making the transferee a person entitled to enforce the instrument." Section 3-416, Comment 2. The following example illustrates this rule. Mitchell makes a note payable to the order of Penelope. A thief steals the note from Penelope, forges Penelope's indorsement, and sells the instrument to Aaron. Aaron is not entitled to enforce the instrument because the break in the indorsement chain prevents him from being a holder. If Aaron transfers the instrument to Judith for consideration, Judith can hold Aaron liable for breach of warranty. The warranty action is important to Judith because it enables her to hold Aaron liable, even if Aaron indorsed the note "without recourse."

28-5b AUTHENTIC AND AUTHORIZED SIGNATURES

The second warranty imposed by the Code is that all signatures are authentic and authorized. In the previous example, this warranty also would be breached. Section 3-416(a)(2). If, however, the signature of a maker, drawer, drawee, acceptor, or indorser not in the chain of title is unauthorized, there is a breach of this warranty but no breach of the warranty of entitlement to enforce.

28-5c NO ALTERATION

The third warranty is the warranty against alteration. Section 3-416(a)(3). Suppose that Maureen makes a note payable to the order of the payee in the amount of $100. The payee, without authority, alters the note so that it appears to be drawn for $1,000 and negotiates the instrument to Lois, who buys it without knowledge of the alteration. Lois, indorsing "without recourse," negotiates the instrument to Kyle for consideration. Kyle presents the instrument to Maureen, who refuses to pay more than $100 on it. Kyle can collect the difference from Lois, for although her qualified indorsement saves Lois from liability to Kyle on the indorsement contract, she is liable to him for breach of warranty. If Lois had not qualified her indorsement, Kyle would be able to recover against her on the basis of either warranty or the indorsement contract.

28-5d NO DEFENSES

The fourth transferor's warranty imposed by the Code is that the instrument is not subject to a defense or claim in recoupment of any party. Section 3-416(a)(4). A claim in recoupment, as discussed in *Chapter 27*, is a counterclaim that arose from the transaction that gave rise to the instrument. Suppose that Madeline, a minor and a resident of a State where minors' contracts for non-necessaries are voidable, makes a note payable to bearer in payment of a motorcycle. Pierce, the first holder, negotiates it to Iola by

mere delivery. Iola indorses it and negotiates it to Justin, who unqualifiedly indorses it to Hector. All negotiations are made for consideration. Because of Madeline's minority (a real defense), Hector cannot recover upon the instrument against Madeline. Hector therefore recovers against Justin or Iola on either the breach of warranty that no valid defenses exist to the instrument or the indorsement contract. Justin, if he is forced to pay Hector, can in turn recover against Iola on either a breach of warranty or the indorsement contract. Justin, however, cannot recover against Pierce. Pierce is not liable to Justin as an indorser because he did not indorse the instrument. Although Pierce, as a transferor, warrants that there are no defenses good against him, this warranty extends only to his immediate transferee, Iola. Therefore, Justin cannot hold Pierce liable. Iola, however, can recover from Pierce on a breach of warranty.

28-5e NO KNOWLEDGE OF INSOLVENCY

Any person who transfers a negotiable instrument warrants that he has no knowledge of any insolvency proceedings instituted with respect to the maker, acceptor, or drawer of an unaccepted instrument. Section 3-416(a)(5). Insolvency proceedings include bankruptcy and "any assignment for the benefit of creditors or other proceedings intended to liquidate or rehabilitate the estate of the person involved." Revised Section 1-201(22). Thus, if Marcia makes a note payable to bearer and the first holder, Taylor, negotiates it for consideration without indorsement to Ursula, who then negotiates it for consideration by qualified indorsement to Valerie, both Taylor and Ursula warrant that they do not know that Marcia is in bankruptcy. Valerie could not hold Taylor liable for breach of warranty, however, because Taylor's warranty runs only in favor of her immediate transferee, Ursula, because Taylor transferred the instrument without indorsement. If Valerie could hold Ursula liable on her warranty, Ursula could thereupon hold Taylor, her immediate transferor, liable.

♦ **SEE FIGURE 28-2:** *Liability on Transfer*

28-6 Warranties on Presentment

Any party who pays or accepts an instrument must do so in strict compliance with the orders that instrument contains. For example, the payment or acceptance must be made to a person entitled to receive payment or acceptance, the amount paid or accepted must be the correct amount, and the instrument must be genuine and unaltered. If the payment or acceptance is incorrect, the payor or acceptor potentially will incur a loss. In the case of a note, a maker who pays the wrong person will not be discharged from his obligation to pay the correct person. If the maker pays too much, the excess comes out of his pocket.

FIGURE 28-2 Liability on Transfer

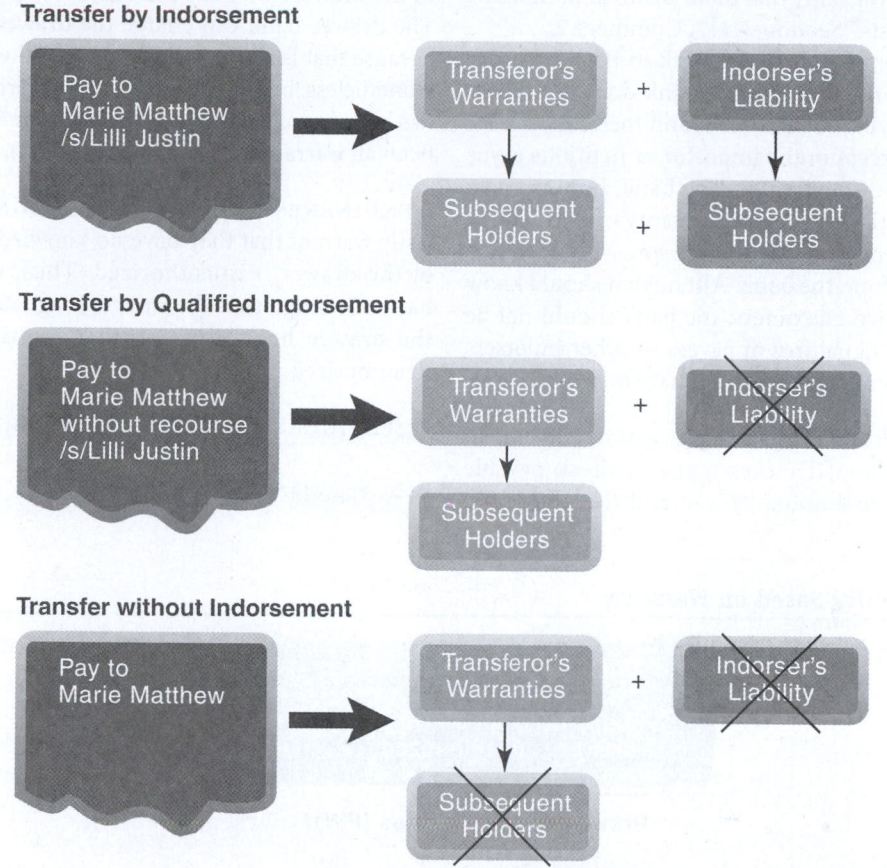

If a drawee pays the wrong person, he generally cannot charge the drawer's account; if he pays too much, he generally cannot charge the drawer's account for the excess. Indorsers who pay an instrument may make similar incorrect payments.

After paying or accepting an instrument to the wrong person, for the wrong amount, or in some other incorrect way, does the person who incorrectly paid or accepted have any recourse against the person who received the payment or acceptance? Section 3-418 addresses this critical question by providing that

> if an instrument has been paid or accepted by mistake … the person paying or accepting may recover the amount paid or revoke acceptance to the extent allowed by the law governing mistake and restitution. Section 3-418(b).

Nevertheless, this payment or acceptance is *final* and may not be asserted against a person who took the instrument in good faith and for value or who in good faith changed position in reliance on the payment or acceptance, unless there has been a breach of the implied **warranties on presentment**. Section 3-418(c). What warranties are given by presenters depends

upon who is the payor or acceptor. The greatest protection is given to drawees of unaccepted drafts, while all other payors receive significantly less protection.

28-6a DRAWEES OF UNACCEPTED DRAFTS

A drawee of an unaccepted draft (including uncertified checks), who pays or accepts in good faith, receives a presentment warranty from the person obtaining payment or acceptance and from all prior transferors of the draft. These parties warrant to the drawee making payment or accepting the draft in good faith that (1) the warrantor is a person entitled to enforce the draft, (2) the draft has not been altered, and (3) the warrantor has no knowledge that the drawer's signature is unauthorized. Section 3-417(a).

ENTITLED TO ENFORCE Presenters of unaccepted checks give the same warranty of entitlement to enforce to persons who pay or accept as is granted to transferees under the transferor's warranty. Thus, the presenter warrants that she is a person entitled to enforce the instrument. As explained, this warranty extends to the genuineness and completeness of the indorser's signatures but not to the signature of the drawer or maker. It is "in effect a warranty that there are no unauthorized or missing indorsements." Section 3-417, Comment 2.

For example, if Donnese draws a check to Peter or order and Peter's indorsement is forged, the bank does not follow Donnese's order in paying such an item and therefore cannot charge her account (except in the impostor or fictitious payee situations discussed in *Chapter 27*). The bank, however, can recover for breach of the presenter's warranty of entitlement to enforce the instrument from the person who obtained payment of the check from the bank. Although it should know the signatures of its own customers, the bank should not be expected to know the signatures of payees or other indorsers of checks; the bank, therefore, should not have to bear this loss.

No Alteration Presenters also give a warranty of no alteration. For example, if Dolores makes a check payable to Porter's order in the amount of $30 and the amount is fraudulently raised to $30,000, the drawee bank cannot charge to the drawer's account the $30,000 it pays out on the check. The drawee bank can charge the drawer's account only $30, because that is all the drawer ordered the drawee bank to pay. Nonetheless, because the presenter's warranty of no alteration has been breached, the drawee bank can collect the difference from all warrantors. Section 3-417(a)(2), (b).

Genuineness of Drawer's Signature Presenters lastly warrant that they have no knowledge that the signature of the drawer is unauthorized. Thus, unless the presenter has knowledge that the drawer's signature is unauthorized, the drawee bears the risk that the drawer's signature is unauthorized.

♦ SEE FIGURE 28-3: *Liability Based on Warranty*

♦ *See Case 28-3*

FIGURE 28-3 Liability Based on Warranty

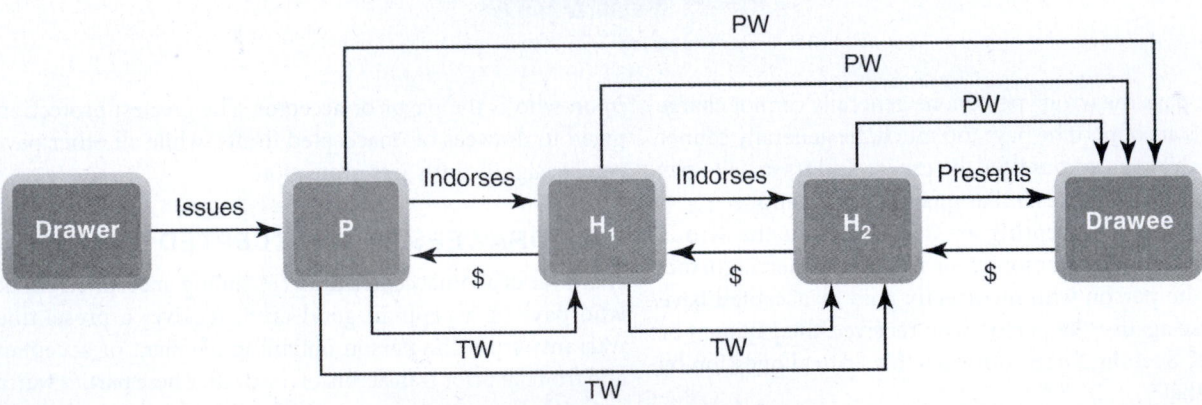

*For drawees of unaccepted drafts, all other payors receive only number 1—Entitled to enforce.

28-6b ALL OTHER PAYORS

In all instances other than a drawee of an unaccepted draft or uncertified check, the only presentment warranty that is given is that the warrantor is a person entitled to enforce the instrument or is authorized to obtain payment on behalf of the person entitled to enforce the instrument. Section 3-417(d). This warranty is given by the person obtaining payment and prior transferors and applies to the presentment of notes and accepted drafts for the benefit of any party obliged to pay the instrument, including an indorser. It also applies to presentment of dishonored drafts if made to the drawer or an indorser.

The warranties of no alteration and authenticity of the drawer's signature are not given to all other payors. These warranties are not necessary for makers and drawers because they should know their own signature and the terms of their instruments. Similarly, indorsers have already warranted the authenticity of signatures and that the instrument was not altered. Finally, acceptors should know the terms of the instrument when they accepted it; moreover, they did receive the full presentment warranties when they as a drawee accepted the draft upon presentment.

C H A P T E R   S U M M A R Y

CONTRACTUAL LIABILITY

GENERAL PRINCIPLES

Liability on the Instrument no person has contractual liability on an instrument unless her signature appears on it

Signature a signature may be made by the individual herself or by her authorized agent
- *Authorized Signatures* an agent who executes a negotiable instrument on behalf of his principal is not liable if the instrument is executed properly and as authorized
- *Unauthorized Signatures* include forgeries and signatures made by an agent without proper power; generally are not binding on the person whose name appears on the instrument but are binding on the unauthorized signer

LIABILITY OF PRIMARY PARTIES

Primary Liability absolute obligation to pay a negotiable instrument

Makers the maker guarantees that he will pay the note according to its original terms

Acceptors a drawee has no liability on the instrument until she accepts it; she then becomes primarily liable
- *Acceptance* a drawee's signed engagement to honor the instrument
- *Certification* acceptance of a check by a bank

LIABILITY OF SECONDARY PARTIES

Secondary (Conditional) Liability obligation to pay a negotiable instrument that is subject to conditions precedent

Drawers and Indorsers if the instrument is not paid by a primary party and if the conditions precedent to the liability of secondary parties are satisfied, indorsers and drawers are secondarily (conditionally) liable unless they have disclaimed their liability or have a valid defense to the instrument

Effect of Acceptance when a draft is accepted by a bank, the drawer and all prior indorsers are discharged from contractual liability

Disclaimer of Liability by Secondary Parties a drawer (except of a check) or indorser may disclaim liability by a qualified drawing or indorsing ("without recourse")

Conditions Precedent to Liability
- *Drawer* liability is generally only contingent upon dishonor and does not require notice
- *Indorser* liability is contingent upon dishonor and notice of dishonor

LIABILITY FOR CONVERSION

Tort Liability for conversion occurs when a person wrongfully controls the personal property of another and applies to instruments

Conversion of an Instrument includes the following: (1) when an instrument is paid on a forged indorsement or without an indorsement necessary for negotiation, (2) when a drawee refuses to return a draft that was presented for acceptance, (3) when any person refuses to return an instrument after he dishonors it, or (4) when a drawee takes the instrument and makes payment to a person not entitled to receive payment

TERMINATION OF LIABILITY	**Effect of Discharge** potential liability of parties to the instrument is terminated • *Discharge* • *Payment* • *Tender of Payment* • *Cancellation* • *Renunciation*

LIABILITY BASED ON WARRANTY

WARRANTIES ON TRANSFER	**Parties** • *Warrantor* any person who transfers an instrument and receives consideration gives the transferor's warranties • *Beneficiary* if the transfer is by delivery, the warranties run only to the immediate transferee; if the transfer is by indorsement, the warranties run to any subsequent holder who takes the instrument in good faith **Warranties** • *Entitled to Enforce* • *All Signatures Are Authentic and Authorized* • *No Alteration* • *No Defenses* • *No Knowledge of Insolvency*
WARRANTIES ON PRESENTMENT	**Parties** • *Warrantor* all people who obtain payment or acceptance of an instrument as well as all prior transferors give the presenter's warranties • *Beneficiary* the presenter's warranties run to any person who in good faith pays or accepts an instrument **Warranties** • *Entitled to Enforce* • *No Alteration* • *Genuineness of Drawer's Signature*

C A S E S

CASE 28-1

Authorized Signature
MARK LINE INDUSTRIES, INC. v. MURILLO MODULAR GROUP, LTD.

United States District Court, N.D. Indiana, South Bend Division, 2011
74 UCC Rep.Serv.2d 253, 2011 WL 1458496

Moody, J.

Plaintiffs Mark Line Industries, Inc., Mark Line Industries, Inc. of Pennsylvania, and Mark Line Industries of North Carolina, LLC (collectively "Mark Line") filed an amended complaint against defendants Murillo Modular Group, Ltd. ("MMG") and Salvador V. Murillo ("Murillo"). The complaint alleges that

defendants failed to pay the balances due on two promissory notes that they had given to Mark Line.

* * *

The first promissory note, dated September 18, 2009, was for $3,802,532.00. The terms of the note provided that it would mature on the date of whichever was sooner—November 15,

2009, or upon the date(s) when certain conditions were satisfied. Mark Line alleges that defendants did not pay the balance due by November 15, 2009.

The second note, also dated September 18, 2009, was for $743,297.50. The terms of this note also provided that it would mature on the date of whichever was sooner—November 15, 2009, or upon the date(s) when certain conditions were satisfied. Mark Line claims that defendants did not pay the balance by November 15, 2009. Mark Line alleges that it received a payment of $79,549.51 on this note on January 10, 2010. Of this payment, $14,175.47 was applied towards accrued interest and the remaining $65,374.04 was applied to reduce the remaining principal balance.

> Both notes include the following explanation for "Maker/Borrower": Maker/Borrower: Murillo Modular Group Ltd., Salvador Murillo and Nick Mackie, (collectively and severally the "Maker or Makers or Borrower" through Murillo Modular Group, Ltd.). The Makers/Borrowers shall be jointly and severally liable.

> At the end, both notes state:

> IN WITNESS WHEREOF, the Maker/Borrower understands that it is liable for all obligations arising under this Note and has caused the same to be signed and delivered as of the date first written above.

The form of signature then says "Murillo Modular Group, Ltd., Maker/Borrower." Murillo's signature appears above the signature block, "By: Salvador Murillo, Owner" on the first note and "By: Salvador Murillo, Partner" on the second note. Nick Mackie has also signed the first note as "owner" and the second note as "partner." The notes then say "Accepted: Mark Line" and are signed by "L. Michael Arnold, CEO."

[The parties have agreed to dismiss, without prejudice, the claim against Murillo for failure to pay the balance on the second promissory note. The defendants argue that the first promissory note for $3,802,532 shows only that Murillo signed the note in his representative capacity for MMG—not that he signed it in his individual capacity. They argue that Murillo is not individually liable because the "form of his signature shows unambiguously" that he signed as a representative of MMG.]

Mark Line's pleadings show two different plausible theories for Murillo's individual liability for the note. First, under [UCC 3-402(a)], Murillo may be liable on the promissory note as a matter of contract law. This part of the statute provides:

> If a person acting, or purporting to act, as a representative signs an instrument by signing either the name of the represented person or the name of the signer, the represented person is bound by the signature to the same extent the represented person would be bound if the signature were on a simple contract. If the represented

person is bound, the signature of the representative is the "authorized signature of the represented person" and the represented person is liable on the instrument, whether or not identified in the instrument.

[UCC 3-402(a).] So, for example, if Person A agreed to have Person B act as his representative as a matter of agency law, and Person B signed his own name or Person A's name to an instrument, Person A is bound to the instrument as a matter of contract law. This is because as the authorized representative of Person A, Person B's signature is an authorized signature of Person A.

The promissory note at issue states that MMG, Murillo, and Mackie are "collectively and severally the 'Maker or Makers or Borrower' through Murillo Modular Group, Ltd." The phrase "through Murillo Modular Group, Ltd." could mean that MMG was authorized to act on behalf of Murillo for this note, so that MMG was acting as Murillo's representative on the promissory note and Murillo was the represented person. In this way, Murillo could still be liable on the note even if he only signed in his representative capacity as the owner of MMG. It could be that MMG signed the note, through Murillo in his representative capacity, as Murillo's representative. Thus, the allegations paint a plausible story that MMG acted as the representative of Murillo under agency law, and by signing the note, it bound Murillo "to the same extent [he] would be bound if the signature were on a simple contract." [UCC 3-402(a).]

Second, Murillo may be liable on the note under [UCC 3-402(b)]. [UCC 3-401(a)] states that a person is not liable on an instrument unless he has signed the instrument or his agent or representative has signed the instrument. [UCC 3-402(b)(1)] provides that a representative signing his name to an instrument as an authorized signature of a represented person is not liable on an instrument if the "form of the signature shows unambiguously that the signature is made on behalf of the represented person." [UCC 3-402(b)(1).] If the form of signature "does not show unambiguously that the signature is made in a representative capacity," "the representative is liable on the instrument to a holder in due course that took the instrument without notice that the representative was not intended to be liable on the instrument." [UCC 3-402(b)(2).] As to any other person "the representative is liable on the instrument unless the representative proves that the original parties did not intend the representative to be liable on the instrument." [UCC 3-402(b)(2).]

In this case the form of signature is ambiguous. * * * The U.C.C. provides three examples of when the form of signature is ambiguous. One example of this is when the agent signs as an agent, but fails to identify the represented person. UCC §3-402 cmt. 2. That is similar to the situation as alleged here because the form of signature does not clearly identify MMG as the represented party. The note identifies MMG as the "Maker/

Borrower" in the form of signature. However, the note defines "Maker/Borrower" as MMG, Murillo, and Mackie "through Murillo Modular Group." It then says that the "Makers/Borrowers shall be jointly and severally liable." It could be argued that if MMG was the only Maker or Borrower, this definition would not make any sense because there would be no one for it to be jointly and severally liable with. Therefore the definition of "Maker/ Borrower" in the contract confuses the identity of the represented person and makes the form of signature ambiguous.

Further, the form of signature is also ambiguous because both Murillo and Mackie signed for MMG. As described above, the signature line on the promissory note * * * states: "Murillo Modular Group, Ltd., Maker/Borrower." Beneath that was "By: Salvador Murillo, Owner" with Murillo's alleged signature and "By: Nick Mackie, Owner" with Mackie's alleged signature. It could be argued that if they were signing only in their representative capacities for MMG, only one of them would have needed to sign the note. So this also causes some ambiguity in the form of signature.

In sum, at this point, Mark Line has plead plausible theories for Murillo's individual liability on the note * * *.

For the reasons give above, defendants Murillo Modular Group's and Murillo's motion to dismiss is DENIED. * * *

CASE 28-2

Drawer's Liability
DAVIS v. WATSON BROTHERS PLUMBING, INC.
Court of Civil Appeals of Texas, Dallas, 1981
615 S. W.2d 844

Akin, J.

Defendant was the drawer of a check for $152.38 payable to its employee Arnett Lee. Lee, in turn, endorsed the check over to plaintiff, who operated a liquor store. After Lee endorsed the check to plaintiff and after plaintiff had placed cash on the counter, Lee stated that he wanted to buy a six-pack of beer and a bottle of scotch. When plaintiff turned to obtain the requested merchandise, a thief grabbed approximately $110.00 of the $150.88 ($152.38 less a $1.50 check cashing fee) for which plaintiff cashed the check. Lee took the remainder of the $150.88, approximately $40.88, and notified defendant of the theft. Defendant issued Lee a second check for $152.38 and stopped payment on the first check. Plaintiff sued defendant based on the dishonor of the first check.

The county court rendered judgment for plaintiff for the $40.88 that Lee actually received from plaintiff [after the robbery]. Plaintiff, as appellant, asserts that since he proved that he was the holder of the check and since defendant failed to raise any valid defenses, defendant was liable to him for the full face value of the check, $152.38. We agree.

"Holder" is defined in *Tex. Bus. & Com. Code Ann.* [UCC] §1-201(20) as: "[A] *person who is in possession of* a document of title or *an instrument* or an investment security drawn, issued or *indorsed to him* or to his order or to bearer or *in blank.*" Under the undisputed facts, Lee, the payee endorsed the check in blank to plaintiff, who is now in possession of the check. Thus, as a matter of law, plaintiff is a "holder" under the code [UCC] §3-413(2), [Revised §3-414(b)] which sets forth the rights of a holder, [and] provides, in pertinent part, that: "The drawer engages that upon dishonor of the draft ... *he will pay the amount of the draft to the holder* or to any indorser who takes it up." Thus, the defendant is liable to the holder of the dishonored check unless the defendant has raised a valid defense against the holder.

* * *

Defendant here asserts that it may raise want or failure of consideration in the transaction between *plaintiff and Lee,* its payee, as a defense to plaintiff's enforcement of the instrument against it. We disagree.

[UCC] §3-408 [Revised §§3-303(b), 3-305] provides, in pertinent part that: "Want or failure of consideration is a defense against any person not having the rights of a holder in due course . . . ." The comments to §3-408 provide that: "'Consideration' refers to what the obligor has received for his obligation, and is Important only on the question of whether his obligation can be enforced against him." Thus, any holder can enforce the obligation of a draft against the drawer regardless of whether the holder gave anything in consideration for the draft to his endorser. The drawer can assert as a defense to enforcement of the draft want or failure of consideration only to the extent such defense lies against the payee of the draft. Thus, the fact that a holder remote to the drawer's transaction with the payee did not give full consideration for the draft is not a defense available to the drawer. [Citation.]

This is true because the drawer's sole obligation on the check is to pay it according to its tenor. Consequently, the fact that the transfer of the check by the payee to the transferee is without consideration is immaterial to the drawer's obligation and is not a defense available to the drawer against the holder. A similar conclusion was reached in [citation].

In that case the court held that a defendant maker was not the proper party to raise as a defense that the transfer of the note to the holder was void. Consequently, that court concluded that the maker could not assert the defense that the equitable ownership of the instrument was in someone other than the holder-plaintiff.

The rationale of this, and other decisions, reaching the same conclusion, is that the maker or drawer of an instrument admittedly owes the money and he should not be permitted to bring into the controversy equities of parties with which

he has no connection. [Citation.] Furthermore, if the drawer or maker is permitted to assert the defense of another party such as the payee, the judgment on that issue would not be binding on the third party claimant who is not a party to the suit. [Citation.] * * *

Because defendant here may not assert want or failure of consideration in the transaction between plaintiff and Lee, and because defendant has asserted no other defense against plaintiff, plaintiff is entitled to recover the full face value of the check under §3-413(b) [Revised §3-414] of the Texas Uniform Commercial Code. Accordingly, the judgment of the trial court is reversed and judgment is rendered that plaintiff recover judgment against defendant for $152.38 and all costs.

CASE 28-3

Warranties on Presentment

TRAVELERS INDEMNITY CO. v. STEDMAN

United States District Court, Eastern District of Pennsylvania, 1995
895 F.Supp. 742, 27 UCC Rep.Serv.2d 1347

Reed, J.

Currently pending before this court is the motion by defendant Main Line Federal Savings Bank ("Main Line") for judgment on the pleadings * * * or for partial summary judgment * * * on the crossclaim filed by codefendant Merrill, Lynch, Pierce, Fenner & Smith ("Merrill Lynch"). In dispute is the ultimate liability for pecuniary losses incurred by plaintiff The Travelers Indemnity Company ("Travelers") when defendants Main Line, as depositary and collecting bank, and Merrill Lynch, as drawee bank, honored seventeen checks unlawfully drawn on the account of the American Lung Association by codefendant Nancy Stedman. * * * In addition, Merrill Lynch advanced a claim for breach of presentment warranties against Main Line pursuant to [UCC] §3-417. The instant motion by Main Line seeks judgment in its favor with regard to twelve of the seventeen checks. Merrill Lynch concedes that Main Line is entitled to judgment on the pleadings with regard to the six checks that were neither deposited nor cashed at Main Line, but Merrill Lynch argues that Main Line is not entitled to judgment on the pleadings with regard to the other six checks at issue.

Factual Background and Procedural History

In November 1988, plaintiff Travelers issued a comprehensive crime insurance policy to the American Lung Association (the "ALA"), thereby insuring the ALA against financial losses due to employee fraud or dishonesty. Shortly thereafter, in October of

1989, the ALA hired defendant Nancy Stedman as the Director of Bureau Affairs. In her capacity as Director of Bureau Affairs, Stedman possessed the authority to draw checks on a Working Capital Management Account (the "WCMA"), an account established by the ALA with defendant Merrill Lynch for the sole purpose of paying the ALA's operating expenses. * * *

From approximately August 12, 1990 to March 13, 1992, Stedman embarked on a scheme of defalcation, misappropriating $129,624.23 of ALA funds from the WCMA. The ALA finally discovered the scheme in late April, 1992, and subsequently received compensation for its losses under the terms of its insurance policy with Travelers. Asserting its rights as the subrogee of the ALA, Travelers filed this civil action on July 9, 1993 against defendants Nancy Stedman, Merrill Lynch, and Main Line.

Merrill Lynch and Main Line agree that the seventeen checks misappropriated by Stedman can be divided into three groups based on the combination of forged or unauthorized [drawer] and payee signatures. Group One is comprised of six checks totalling $5,343.00, each bearing a forged cosignatory's signature, or [co-drawer's] signature, and forged indorsements. Main Line and Merrill Lynch agree that the Group One checks were neither deposited at nor cashed by defendant Main Line. * * * Group Two is comprised of six checks totalling $85,241.01, each payable to either "American Lung Association" or "American Lung Association/ Stedman." Each Group Two check bore two forged [drawer's] signatures and at least one forged indorsement. All Group Two checks were accepted for deposit into the personal checking account of Stedman by Main Line, and subsequently presented to and honored by Merrill Lynch. Finally, Group Three is comprised of five checks totalling $39,030.22, each payable to "American Lung Association" and bearing only a forged indorsement. * * * The Group Three checks are not the subject of the instant motion.

Discussion
* * *

Loss Allocation under the Uniform Commercial Code

Liability, or loss allocation, under the Uniform Commercial Code ("UCC") for honoring negotiable instruments containing forged or unauthorized signatures is governed by whether the forgery at issue is that of a [drawer's] signature or of the indorsement of a payee or holder. [Citations.] Generally, a drawee bank is strictly liable to its customer, the drawer, for payment over either a forged [drawer's] signature or a forged indorsement. [Citation.] * * * Moreover, when a drawee bank honors an instrument bearing a forged [drawer's] signature, that payment is final in favor of a holder in due course or one who has in good faith changed his position in reliance on the payment. UCC §3-418. As a result, where the only forgery is of the signature of the [drawer] and not of the indorsement, the negligence of a holder in taking the forged instrument will not allow a drawee bank to shift liability to a prior collecting or depositary bank, unless such negligence amounts to a lack of good faith, or unless the payee bank returns the instrument or sends notice of dishonor within the limited time provided by §4-301 of the UCC. [Citation.] But where the only forged signature is an indorsement, the drawee normally may pass liability back through the collection chain to the depositary or collecting bank, or to the forger herself if she is available, by a claim for breach of presentment warranties. [Citation.]

Regrettably, the drafters of the UCC failed to address the allocation of liability for honoring instruments containing *both* a forged [drawer's] signature and a forged indorsement, so called "double forgeries." [Citation.] Nor have the state courts of Pennsylvania addressed this issue. Based on a thorough examination of the rationales behind the allocation of liability in "single forgery" cases, however, the Court of Appeals for the Fifth Circuit concluded that double forgeries should be treated as though only containing forged [drawer's] signatures. [Citations.] * * * Therefore, this court concludes that under Pennsylvania's adoption of the UCC, checks containing both a forged [drawer's] signature and a forged indorsement should be treated, for loss allocation purposes, as though bearing only a forged [drawer's] signature. As a result, the negligence of a holder in taking a double forgery will not allow a drawee bank, such as Merrill Lynch, to shift liability to a prior collecting or depositary bank, such as Main Line, unless such negligence amounts to a lack of good faith, or unless the drawee bank returns the instrument or sends notice of dishonor within the limited time provided by §4-301 of the Pennsylvania adoption of the UCC. [Citation.]

* * *

Breach of Presentment Warranties

The final count of the crossclaim by Merrill Lynch is a claim for an alleged breach of presentment warranties under [UCC] §3-417. As the court illustrated above, the loss allocation rules of the UCC permit a payee bank to shift liability to a depositary bank via a claim for breach of presentment warranties if, and only if, the checks at issue contain only forged indorsements. Should the checks in fact also bear forged [drawer's] signatures, then a depositary or collecting bank is immunized from liability for having honored such checks unless the depositary or collecting bank failed to meet the requirements of the final payment rule codified in [UCC] §3-418. [Citation.] Moreover, checks bearing dual forgeries are treated as though containing only forged [drawer's] signatures. Thus, because it is uncontested that all Group Two checks bear forged [drawer's] signatures, liability for honoring these checks may only be assessed under the loss allocation rules relevant to checks bearing only forged [drawer's] signatures. See discussion supra part II.B. In other words, Merrill Lynch is precluded by the operation of law from asserting a claim for breach of presentment warranties under the loss allocation scheme of the UCC. As a matter of law, therefore, Merrill Lynch can prove no set of facts in support of this claim that would entitle it to the relief demanded, and this court will accordingly also grant judgment on the pleadings to Main Line on the claim for breach of presentment warranties as it relates to the Group Two checks.

QUESTIONS

1. $900.00 Smalltown, Illinois

    Maker, November 15, 2021

    The undersigned promises to pay to the order of John Doe Nine Hundred Dollars with interest from date of note. Payment to be made in five monthly installments of One Hundred Eighty Dollars, plus accrued interest beginning on December 1, 2021. In the event of default in the payment of any installment or interest on install-ment date, the holder of this instrument may declare the entire obligation due and owing and proceed forthwith to collect the balance due on this instrument.

    (Signed) Acton, agent

    On December 18, 2021, no payment having been made on the note, Doe indorsed and delivered the instrument to Todd to secure a preexisting debt in the amount of $800.

    On January 18, 2022, Todd brought an action against Acton and Phi Corporation, Acton's principal, to collect the full amount of the instrument with interest. Acton defended on the basis that he signed the instrument in a representative capacity and that Doe had failed to deliver the consideration for which the instrument had been issued. Phi Corporation defended on the basis that it did not sign the instrument and that its name does not appear on the instrument. For what amount, if any, are Acton and Phi Corporation liable? Explain.

2. While employed as a night security guard at the place of business of A. B. Cate Trucking Company, Fred Fain observed that the office safe had been left unlocked. It contained fifty payroll checks, which were ready for distribution to employees two days later. The checks had all been signed by the sole proprietor, Cate. Fain removed five of these checks and two blank checks that were also in the safe. Fain forged the indorsements of the payees on the five payroll checks and cashed them at local supermarkets. He then filled out one of the blank checks, making himself payee, and forged Cate's signature as drawer. After cashing that check at a supermarket, Fain departed by airplane to Jamaica. The supermarkets in good faith promptly presented the six checks for payment to the drawee bank, the Bank of Emanon, which paid each one. Shortly thereafter, Cate learned about the missing payroll checks and forgeries and demanded that the Bank of Emanon credit his account with the amount of the six checks. Must the Bank comply with Cate's demand? What are the Bank's rights, if any, against the supermarkets?

3. A negotiable promissory note executed and delivered by B to C passed in due course and was indorsed in blank by C, D, E, and F. G, the present holder, strikes out D's indorsement. What is the liability of D on her indorsement?

4. On June 15, 2016, Justin, for consideration, executed a negotiable promissory note for $10,000, payable to Renee on or before June 15, 2021. Justin subsequently suffered financial reverses. In January 2021, Renee on two occasions told Justin that she knew he was having a difficult time; that she, Renee, did not need the money; and that the debt should be considered completely cancelled with no other act or payment being required. These conversations were witnessed by three persons, including Larry. On March 15, 2021, Renee changed her mind and indorsed the note for value to Larry. The note was not paid by June 15, 2021, and Larry sued Justin for the amount of the note. Justin defended upon the ground that Renee had cancelled the debt and renounced all rights against Justin and that Larry had notice of this fact. Has the debt been properly cancelled? Explain.

5. Tate and Fitch were longtime friends. Tate was a man of considerable means; Fitch had encountered financial difficulties. To bolster his failing business, Fitch desired to borrow $6,000 from Farmers Bank of Erehwon. To accomplish this, he persuaded Tate to aid him in the making of a promissory note by which it would appear that Tate had the responsibility of maker, but with Fitch agreeing to pay the instrument when due. Accordingly, they executed the following instrument:

    December 1, 2021

    Thirty days after date and for value received, I promise to pay to the order of Frank Fitch the sum of $6,600.

    /s/ Timothy Tate

    On the back of the note, Fitch indorsed, "Pay to the order of Farmers Bank of Erehwon /s/ Frank Fitch" and delivered it to the bank in exchange for $6,000.

    a. If the note is not paid at maturity, may the bank, without first demanding payment by Fitch, recover in an action on the note against Tate? Why or why not?

    b. If Tate voluntarily pays the note to the bank, may he then recover on the note against Fitch, who appears as an indorser? Why or why not?

6. Alpha orally appointed Omega as his agent to find and purchase for him a 1930 Dodge automobile in good condition, and Omega located such a car. Its owner, Roe, agreed to sell and deliver the car on January 10, 2021, for $9,000. To evidence the purchase price, Omega mailed to Roe the following instrument:

> December 1, 2020 $9,000.00
> We promise to pay to the order of bearer Nine Thousand Dollars with interest from date of this instrument on or before January 10, 2021. This note is given in consideration of John Roe transferring title to and possession of his 1930 Dodge automobile.
>
> (Signed) Omega, agent

Smith stole the note from Roe's mailbox, indorsed Roe's name on the note, and promptly discounted it with Sunset Bank for $8,700. Not having received the note, Roe sold the car to a third party. On January 10, 2021, the bank, having discovered all the facts, demanded payment of the note from Alpha and Omega. Both refused payment.

a. What are Sunset Bank's rights with regard to Alpha and Omega?

b. What are Sunset Bank's rights with regard to Roe and Smith?

7. In payment of the purchase price of a used motorboat that had been fraudulently misrepresented, Young signed and delivered to Armstrong his negotiable note in the amount of $2,000 due October 1, with Selby as an accommodation co-maker. Young intended to use the boat for his fishing business. Armstrong indorsed the note in blank preparatory to discounting it. Tillman stole the note from Armstrong and delivered it to McGowan on July 1 in payment of a past-due debt in the amount of $600 that he owed to McGowan, with McGowan making up the difference by giving Tillman his check for $800 and an oral promise to pay Tillman an additional $600 on October 1.

When McGowan demanded payment of the note on December 1, both Young and Selby refused to pay because the note had not been presented for payment on its due date and because Armstrong had fraudulently misrepresented the motorboat for which the note had been executed.

What are McGowan's rights, if any, against Young, Selby, Tillman, and Armstrong?

8. On July 1, Anderson sold D'Aveni, a jeweler, a necklace containing imitation gems, which Anderson fraudulently represented to be diamonds. In payment for the necklace, D'Aveni executed and delivered to Anderson her promissory note for $25,000 dated July 1 and payable on December 1 to Anderson's order with interest at 6 percent per annum.

The note was thereafter successively indorsed in blank and delivered by Anderson to Bylinski; by Bylinski to Conrad; and by Conrad to Shearson, who became a holder in due course on August 10. On November 1, D'Aveni discovered Anderson's fraud and immediately notified Anderson, Bylinski, Conrad, and Shearson that she would not pay the note when it became due. Bylinski, a friend of Shearson, requested that Shearson release him from liability on the note, and Shearson, as a favor to Bylinski and for no other consideration, struck out Bylinski's indorsement.

On November 15, Shearson, who was solvent and had no creditors, indorsed the note to the order of Frederick, his father, and delivered it to Frederick as a gift. At the same time, Shearson told Frederick of D'Aveni's statement that D'Aveni would not pay the note when it became due. Frederick presented the note to D'Aveni for payment on December 1, but D'Aveni refused to pay. Thereafter, Frederick gave due notice of dishonor to Anderson, Bylinski, and Conrad.

What are Frederick's rights, if any, against Anderson, Bylinski, Conrad, and D'Aveni on the note?

9. Jack stole a check made out to the order of Bertha. Jack forged Bertha's name on the back and made the instrument payable to himself. Jack then transferred the check to Sun for cash by signing his name on the back of the check in Sun's presence. Sun was unaware of any of the facts surrounding the theft or forged indorsement and presented the check for payment. Central County Bank, the drawee bank, paid it. Who will bear the loss? Explain.

CASE PROBLEMS

10. R&A Concrete Contractors, Inc., executed a promissory note that identifies both R&A Concrete and Grover Roberts as its makers. On the reverse side of the note, the following appears: "X John Ament Sec. & Treas." National Bank of Georgia, the payee, now sues both R&A Concrete and Ament on the note. What rights does National Bank have against R&A and Ament?

11. On August 10, 2019, Theta Electronic Laboratories, Inc., executed a promissory note to George and Marguerite Thomson. Three other individuals, Gerald Exten, Emil

O'Neil, James Hane, and their wives also indorsed the note. The note was then transferred to Hane by the Thomsons on November 26, 2020. Although a default occurred at this time, it was not until April 2022, eighteen months later, that Hane gave notice of the dishonor and made a demand for payment on the Extens as indorsers. Are the Extens liable under their indorser's liability? Explain.

12. Attorney Eliot Disner tendered a check for $100,100 to Sidney and Lynne Cohen. In drawing the check, Disner was serving as an intermediary for his clients, Irvin and Dorothea Kipnes, who owed the money to the Cohens as part of a settlement agreement. The Kipneses had given Disner checks totaling $100,100, which he had deposited into his professional corporation's client trust account. After confirming with the Kipneses' bank that their account held sufficient funds, Disner wrote and delivered a trust account check for $100,100 to the Cohens' attorney, with this note: "Please find $100,100 in settlement (partial) of *Cohen v. Kipnes*, et al[.] Per our agreement, delivery to you constitutes timely delivery to your clients." Also typed on the check was a notation identifying the underlying lawsuit. Without Disner's knowledge, the Kipneses stopped payment on their checks, leaving insufficient funds in the trust account to cover the check to the Cohens. The trust account check therefore was not paid due to insufficient funds, the Kipneses declared bankruptcy, and the Cohens served Disner and his professional corporation with demand for payment. The Cohens sought the amount written on the check plus a $500 statutory penalty. Explain who should prevail and why.

13. Vincent Medina signed a check in the amount of $34,348 written on the account of First Delta Financial, a family corporation owned and controlled by Medina. His corporate title did not appear before his signature. He issued the check to James G. Wyche. The check was dishonored for insufficient funds. First Delta Financial is in bankruptcy. Wyche contends that Medina is personally liable because Medina signed the check without indicating his corporate capacity below his signature. Medina argues that he is not personally liable on account of having signed the check. Explain who should prevail.

TAKING SIDES

Saul sold goods to Bruce, warranting that the goods were of a specified quality. The goods were not of the quality warranted, however, and Saul knew this at the time of the sale. Bruce drew and delivered a check payable to Saul and drawn on Third National Bank in the amount of the purchase price. Bruce subsequently discovered the goods were faulty and stopped payment on the check. Third National refused to pay Saul on the check.

a. What are the arguments that Saul can recover (1) from Bruce and (2) from Third National?

b. What are the arguments that (1) Bruce should prevail? and (2) Third National should prevail?

c. Who should prevail? Why?

CHAPTER 29

Bank Deposits, Collections, and Funds Transfer

CHAPTER OUTCOMES

After reading and studying this chapter, you should be able to:

- Explain the various stages of and parties to the collection of a check.

- Explain the duties of collecting banks.

- Explain the relationship between a payor bank and its customers.

- Discuss consumer electronic funds transfer, the various types of electronic funds transfer, and the major provisions of the Electronic Funds Transfer Act.

- Explain wholesale fund transfers and how they operate.

In twenty-first-century society, most goods and services are bought and sold without a physical transfer of cash. In some sales, credit is extended by the seller or a third party. In other sales, a noncash payment is made either by *paper* (checks and drafts) or *electronically* (debit cards, credit cards, automated clearinghouse [ACH] transfers, and prepaid cards). But even credit sales ultimately must be settled—and when they are, payment is frequently made by check. When a check is issued, if the parties to the transaction happen to have accounts at the same bank, settlement of the check is easily accomplished. In the vast majority of checks, however, the parties have accounts at different banks. In those cases, the buyer's check must journey from the seller-payee's bank (the depositary bank), where the check is deposited by the seller for credit to his account, and then to the buyer-drawer's bank (the payor bank) for payment. In this collection process, the check frequently passes through one or more other banks (intermediary banks), each of which must accurately record its passing before it may be collected. The U.S. banking system has developed a network to handle the collection of checks and other instruments.

In recent years, payments by electronic funds transfer (EFTs) have increased at an astounding rate. The dollar amount of commercial payments made by wire transfer far exceeds the dollar amount made by checks or credit cards. In addition, EFTs have become increasingly popular with consumers. Consumer EFTs are covered by the Federal Electronic Fund Transfer Act (EFTA); nonconsumer (wholesale) electronic transfers are covered by Article 4A of the Uniform Commercial Code (UCC).

This chapter covers both the bank deposit-collection system and EFTs.

BANK DEPOSITS AND COLLECTIONS

Article 4 of the UCC, entitled "Bank Deposits and Collections," provides the principal rules governing the bank collection process. In 2002, the American Law Institute and the Uniform Law Commission completed updates to Article 4. At least eleven States have adopted the 2002 version. This part of the text discusses the pre-2002 Article 4.

The end result of the collection process is either the payment of the check or the dishonor (refusal to pay) of the check by the drawee bank. As items in the bank collection process are essentially those covered by Article 3, "Commercial Paper," and to a lesser extent by Article 8, "Investment Securities," these Articles often apply to a bank collection problem. In addition, Articles 3 and 4 are supplemented and, at times, preempted by Federal law: the Expedited Funds Availability Act and its implementing Federal Reserve Regulation (Regulation CC). This section covers the collection of an item through the banking system and the relationship between the payor bank and its customer.

29-1 Collection of Items

When a person deposits a check in his bank (the depositary bank), the bank credits his account by the amount of the check. This initial crediting is **provisional**. Normally, a bank does not permit a customer to draw funds against a provisional credit; by permitting its customer to thus draw, the bank will have given *value* and, provided it meets the other requirements, will be a holder in due course. Under the customer's contract with his bank, the bank is obligated to make a reasonable effort to obtain payment of all checks deposited for collection. When the amount of the check has been collected from the payor bank (the drawee), the credit becomes a **final credit**.

The Expedited Funds Availability Act has established maximum time periods for which a bank may hold (and thereby deny a customer access to the funds represented by) various types of instruments. Under the Act, (1) cash deposits, wire transfers, an ACH credit, government checks, the first $100 of a day's check deposits, cashier's checks, and checks deposited in one branch of a depository institution and drawn on the same or another branch of the same institution must clear by the next business day; (2) local checks must clear within one intervening business day; and (3) nonlocal checks must clear in no more than four intervening business days.

If the payor bank (the drawee bank) does not pay the check for some reason, such as a stop payment order or insufficient funds in the drawer's account, the depositary bank reverses the provisional credit to the account, debits his account for that amount, and returns the check to him with a statement of the reason for nonpayment. If, in the meantime, the customer has been permitted to draw against the provisional credit, the bank may recover the payment from him.

In some cases, the bank involved is both the depositary bank and the payor bank. In most cases, however, the depositary and payor banks are different, in which event the bank collection aspects of Article 4 come into play. Where the depositary and payor banks differ, it is necessary for the item to pass from one to the other, either directly through a clearinghouse or through one or more **intermediary banks** (banks, other than the depositary payor bank, that are involved in the collection process, such as one of the twelve Federal Reserve Banks). A **clearinghouse** is an association composed of banks or other payors whose members settle accounts with each other on a daily basis. Each member of the clearinghouse forwards all deposited checks drawn on other members and receives from the clearinghouse all checks drawn on it. Balances are adjusted and settled each day.

♦ SEE FIGURE 29-1: *Bank Collections*

29-1a COLLECTING BANKS

A **collecting bank** is any bank, other than the payor bank, handling an item for payment. In the usual situation where the depositary and payor banks are different, the depositary bank gives a provisional credit to its customer, transfers the item to the next bank in the chain, and receives a provisional

credit or "settlement" from it; the process repeats until the item reaches the payor bank, which gives a provisional settlement to its transferor. When the item is paid, all the provisional settlements given by the respective banks in the chain become final, and the particular transaction has been completed. Because this procedure simplifies bookkeeping by necessitating only one entry if the item is paid, no adjustment is necessary on the books of any of the banks involved.

If, however, the payor bank does not pay the check, it returns the item, and each intermediary or collecting bank reverses the provisional settlement or credit it previously gave to its forwarding bank. Ultimately, the depositary bank will charge (remove the provisional credit from) the account of the customer who deposited the item. The customer must then seek recovery from the indorsers or the drawer.

A collecting bank is an **agent** or subagent of the owner of the item until the settlement becomes final. Section 4-201(a). Unless otherwise provided, any credit given for the item initially is provisional. Once settled, the agency relationship changes to one of **debtor-creditor**. The effects of this agency rule are that the risk of loss remains with the owner and any chargebacks go to her, not to the collecting bank.

All collecting banks have certain responsibilities and duties in collecting checks and other items. These will now be discussed.

DUTY OF CARE A collecting bank must exercise ordinary care in handling an item transferred to it for collection. Section 4-202(a). The steps it takes in presenting an item or sending it for presentment are of particular importance. It must act within a reasonable time after receipt of the item and must choose a reasonable method of forwarding the item for presentment. It also is responsible for using care in routing and in selecting intermediary banks or other agents.

♦ *See Case 29-1*

DUTY TO ACT TIMELY Closely related to the collecting bank's duty of care is its duty to act in a timely manner. A collecting bank acts timely in any event if it takes proper action, such as forwarding or presenting an item before the "midnight deadline" following its receipt of the item, notice, or payment. If the bank adheres to this standard, the timeliness of its action cannot be challenged; should it, however, take a reasonably longer time, the bank bears the burden of proof in establishing timeliness. Section 4-202(b). The **midnight deadline** is the midnight of the banking day following the banking day on which the bank received the item or notice. Section 4-104(a)(10). Thus, if a bank receives a check on Monday, it must take proper action by midnight on the next banking day, or Tuesday. A banking day means the part of a day on which a bank is open to the public for carrying on substantially all of its banking functions. Section 4-104(a)(3). The midnight deadline presents a problem because

FIGURE 29-1 Bank Collections

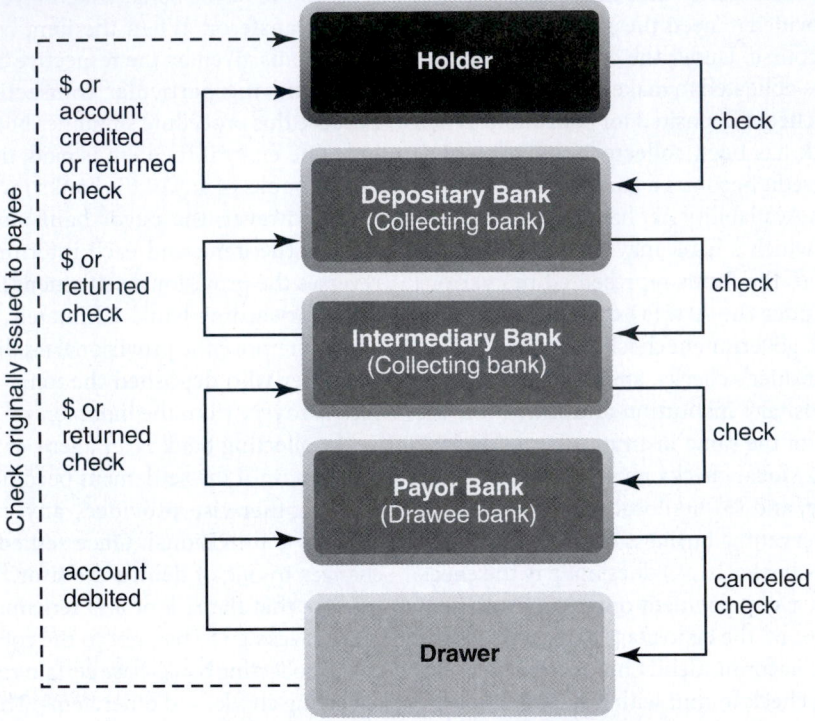

it takes time to process an item through a bank—whether it be the depositary, intermediary, or payor bank. If a day's transactions are to be completed without overtime work, the bank must either close early or fix an earlier cutoff time for the day's work. Accordingly, the Code provides that for the purpose of allowing time to process items, prove balances, and make the bookkeeping entries necessary to determine its position for the day, a bank may fix an afternoon hour of 2:00 P.M. or later as a cutoff point for handling money and items and for making entries on its books. Section 4-108. Items received after the cutoff hour fixed as the close of the banking day are considered to have been received at the opening of the next banking day, and the time for taking action and for determining the bank's midnight deadline begins to run from that point.

Recognizing that everyone involved will be greatly inconvenienced if an item is not paid, Section 4-109 provides that unless otherwise instructed, a collecting bank in a good faith effort to secure payment may, in the case of a specific item drawn on a payor other than a bank, waive, modify, or extend the time limits, but not in excess of two additional banking days. This extension may be made without the approval of the parties involved and without discharging drawers or indorsers. This section does not apply to checks and other drafts drawn on a bank. The Code also authorizes delay when communications or computer facilities are interrupted as a result of blizzard, flood, hurricane, or other disaster; the suspension of payments

by another bank; war; emergency conditions; failure of equipment; or other circumstances beyond the bank's control. Nevertheless, such delay will be excused only if the bank exercises such diligence as the circumstances require.

INDORSEMENTS An item restrictively indorsed with words such as "pay any bank" is locked into the bank collection system, and only a bank may acquire the rights of a holder. When forwarding an item for collection, a bank normally indorses the item "pay any bank," regardless of the type of indorsement, if any, that the item carried at the time of receipt. This protects the collecting bank by making it impossible for the item to stray from regular collection channels.

If the item had no indorsement when the depositary bank received it, the bank nonetheless becomes a holder of the item at the time it takes possession of the item for collection if the customer was a holder at the time of delivery to the bank and, if the bank satisfies the other requirements of a holder in due course, it will become a holder in due course in its own right. Section 4-205(1). In return, the bank warrants to the collecting banks, the payor, and the drawer that it has paid the amount of the item to the customer or deposited that amount to the customer's account. Section 4-205(2). This rule speeds up the collection process by eliminating the necessity of returning checks for indorsement when the depositary bank knows they came from its customers.

WARRANTIES Customers and collecting banks give substantially the same warranties as those given by parties under Article 3 upon presentment and transfer, which were discussed in *Chapter 28*. In addition, under Article 4, customers and collecting banks may give encoding warranties. Each collecting bank or customer who transfers an item and receives a settlement or other consideration warrants to his transferee and any subsequent collecting bank that (1) he is a person entitled to enforce the item, (2) *all* signatures are authentic and authorized, (3) the item has not been altered, (4) he is not subject to any defense or claim in recoupment, and (5) he has no knowledge of any insolvency proceeding involving the maker or acceptor or the drawer of an unaccepted draft. Section 4-207(a). Moreover, each customer or collecting bank who obtains payment or acceptance from a drawee on a draft as well as each prior transferor warrants to the drawee who pays or accepts the draft in good faith that (1) she is a person entitled to enforce the draft, (2) the item has not been altered, and (3) she has no knowledge that the signature of the drawer is unauthorized. Section 4-208.

Processing of checks is now done by Magnetic Ink Character Recognition (MICR). When a check is deposited, the depositary bank magnetically encodes the check with the amount of the check (all checks are pre-encoded with the drawer's account number and the designation of the drawee bank), after which the processing occurs automatically without further human involvement. Despite its efficiency, the magnetic encoding of checks has created several problems. The first is the problem a bank encounters when paying a postdated instrument prior to its date. The 2002 Revision changes prior law by providing that the drawee may debit the drawer's account, unless the drawer timely informs the drawee that the check is postdated. Section 4-401(c). A second difficulty arises when a depositing bank or its customer who encodes her own checks miscodes a check. The 2002 Revision provides that such an encoder **warrants** to any subsequent collecting bank and to the payor that information on a check is properly encoded. Section 4-209(a). If the customer does the encoding, the depositary bank also makes the warranty. Section 4-209(a).

FINAL PAYMENT The provisional settlements made in the collection chain are all directed toward final payment of the item by the payor bank. From this turnaround point in the collection process, the proceeds of the item begin their return flow, and provisional settlements become final. For example, a customer of the California Country State Bank may deposit a check drawn on the State of Maine Country National Bank. The check may then take a course such as follows: from the California Country State Bank to a correspondent bank in San Francisco, to the Federal Reserve Bank of San Francisco, to the Federal Reserve Bank of Boston, to the payor bank. Provisional settlements are made at each step. When the payor bank finally pays the item, the proceeds begin to flow back over the same course.

The critical question, then, is the point at which the payor bank has **paid** the item, as this not only commences the payment process but also affects questions of priority between the payment of an item and actions such as the filing of a stop payment order against it. Under the Code, *final payment* occurs when the payor bank first does any of the following: (1) pays an item in cash; (2) settles an item and does not have the right to revoke the settlement through statute, clearinghouse rule, or agreement; or (3) makes a provisional settlement and does not revoke it within the time and in the manner permitted by statute, clearinghouse rule, or agreement. Section 4-215(a).

29-1b PAYOR BANKS

The **payor** or drawee **bank**, under its contract of deposit with the drawer, agrees to pay to the payee or his order a check issued by the drawer, provided that the order is not countermanded and that there are sufficient funds in the drawer's account.

The tremendous increase in volume of bank collections has necessitated deferred posting procedures, whereby items are sorted and proved on the day of receipt but are not posted to customers' accounts or returned until the next banking day. The UCC not only approves such procedures but also establishes specific standards to govern their application to the actions of payor banks.

When a payor bank that is not also a depositary bank receives a demand item other than for immediate payment over the counter, it must either return the item or give its transferor a provisional settlement before **midnight** of the banking day on which the item is received. Otherwise, the bank becomes liable to its transferor for the amount of the item, unless it has a valid defense, such as breach of a presentment warranty. Section 4-302.

If the payor bank gives the provisional settlement as required, it has until the midnight deadline to return the item or, if the item is held for protest or is otherwise unavailable for return, to send written notice of dishonor or nonpayment. Section 4-301(a). After doing this, the bank is entitled to revoke the settlement and recover any payment it has made. Should it fail to return the item or send notice before its midnight deadline, the payor bank will be accountable for the amount of the item unless it has a valid defense for its inaction. If a check is for $2,500 or more, Federal law (Regulation CC) requires special notice of nonpayment—the paying bank must give notice to the depositary bank by 4:00 P.M. on the second business day following the banking day on which the check was presented to the paying bank. This regulation does not, however, relieve the paying bank of returning the check in compliance with Article 4.

A bank may dishonor an item and return it or send notice for innumerable reasons. The following situations are the most common: the drawer or maker may have no account or may have funds insufficient to cover the item, a signature on the item may be forged, or the drawer or maker may have stopped payment of the item.

If the funds in a customer's account are insufficient to pay all of the items that the bank receives on that account on any given day, the bank may charge them against the account in any order it deems convenient. The owner of the account from which the item was payable also has no basis for complaint when the bank pays one item rather than another. It is his responsibility to have enough funds on deposit to pay all of the items chargeable to his account at any time.

♦ *See Case 28-2*

29-2 Relationship between Payor Bank and its Customer

The relationship between a payor bank and its checking account customer is primarily the product of their contractual arrangement. Although the parties have relatively broad latitude in establishing the terms of their agreement and in altering the provisions of the Code, a bank may not validly (1) disclaim responsibility for its lack of good faith, (2) disclaim responsibility for its failure to exercise ordinary care, or (3) limit its damages for a breach comprising such lack or failure. Section 4-103(a). The parties by agreement, however, may determine the standards by which the bank's responsibility is to be measured, if these standards are not clearly unreasonable.

29-2a PAYMENT OF AN ITEM

A payor bank owes a duty to its customer, the drawer, to pay checks properly drawn by him on an account having funds sufficient to cover the items. A check or draft, however, is not an assignment of the drawer's funds that are in the drawee's possession. Moreover, as discussed in *Chapter 28*, the drawee is not liable on a check until it accepts the item. Section 408. Therefore, the *holder* of a check has no right to require the drawee bank to pay it, whether or not the drawer's account contains sufficient funds. But if a payor bank improperly refuses payment when presented with an item, it will incur a liability to the *customer* from whose account the item should have been paid. Section 4-402. If the customer has adequate funds on deposit and there is no other valid basis for the refusal to pay, the bank is liable to its customer for damages proximately caused by the *wrongful dishonor*. Liability is limited to actual damages proved and may include damages for arrest, prosecution, or other consequential damages. Section 4-402.

When a payor bank receives an item properly payable from a customer's account but the funds in the account are insufficient to pay it, the bank may (1) dishonor the item and

return it or (2) pay the item and charge its customer's account, even though the actions create an overdraft. Section 4-401(a). The item authorizes or directs the bank to make the payment and hence carries with it an enforceable implied promise to reimburse the bank. Furthermore, the customer may be liable to pay the bank a service charge for its handling of the overdraft or to pay interest on the amount of the overdraft. A customer, however, is not liable for an overdraft if the customer did not sign the item or benefit from the proceeds of the item. Section 4-401(b).

A payor bank is under no obligation to its customer to pay an uncertified check that is more than six months old. Section 4-404. This rule reflects the usual banking practice of consulting a depositor before paying a "stale" item (one more than six months old) on her account. The bank is not required to dishonor such an item, however; and if the bank makes payment in good faith, it may charge the amount of the item to its customers' account.

♦ *See Cases 29-2 and 28-2*

Practical Advice

Be sure to present checks you hold before they become stale.

29-2b SUBSTITUTE CHECK

The Check Clearing for the 21st Century Act (also called Check 21 or the Check Truncation Act) permits banks to truncate original checks, which means removing an original paper check from the check collection or return process and sending in lieu of it (1) a substitute check or, (2) *by agreement*, information relating to the original check (including data taken from the MICR line of the original check or an electronic image of the original check). The Act sets forth a statutory framework under which a substitute check is the legal equivalent of an original check for all purposes if the substitute check (1) accurately represents all of the information on the front and back of the original check as of the time the original check was truncated and (2) bears the legend "This is a legal copy of your check. You can use it the same way you would use the original check." The Act defines a **substitute check** as a paper reproduction of the original check that (1) contains an image of the front and back of the original; (2) bears an MICR containing all the information appearing on the MICR line of the original check; (3) conforms, in paper stock, dimension, and otherwise, with generally applicable industry standards for substitute checks; and (4) is suitable for automated processing in the same manner as the original. Thus, a substitute check is basically a copy of the original check that shows both the front and back of the original check.

The law does not require banks to accept checks in electronic form, nor does it require banks to use the new authority granted by the Act to create substitute checks. On the other hand, parties cannot refuse to accept a substitute check that meets the Act's requirements.

The Act permits banks to replace paper checks during the check collection process with either digital or paper substitutes. Thus, banks can employ digital images or image replacement documents (IRDs), which are documents that include the front, rear, and all MICR data in one image. However, the Act does not provide legal equivalence for electronic check or image presentment.

The ultimate objective of the Act is to make the collection process more efficient and much faster (transferring digital files within seconds rather than days) and to enhance fraud detection by accelerating return of dishonored checks.

29-2c STOP PAYMENT ORDERS

A check drawn on a bank is an order to pay a sum of money and an authorization to charge the amount to the drawer's account. The customer, or any person authorized to draw on the account, may countermand this order, however, by means of a **stop payment order**. Section 4-403. If the order does not come too late, the bank is bound by it. If the bank inadvertently pays a check over a valid stop order, it is *prima facie* liable to the customer, but only to the extent of the customer's loss resulting from the payment. The burden of establishing the fact and amount of loss is on the customer.

To be effective, a stop payment order must be received in time to provide the bank a reasonable opportunity to act on it. Section 4-403(a). An oral stop order is binding on the bank for only fourteen calendar days. Section 4-403(b). If the customer confirms an oral stop order in writing within the fourteen-day period, the order is effective for six months and may be renewed in writing for additional six-month periods.

> ### *Practical Advice*
>
> *If you wish to stop payment on a check, contact your bank as soon as possible and confirm an oral stop payment order in writing within fourteen days.*

The fact that a drawer has filed a stop payment order does not automatically relieve her of liability. If the bank honors the stop payment order and returns the check, the holder may bring an action against the drawer. If the holder qualifies as a holder in due course, personal defenses that the drawer might have to such an action would be of no avail.

◆ *See Case 29-2*

29-2d BANK'S RIGHT TO SUBROGATION ON IMPROPER PAYMENT

If a payor bank pays an item over a stop payment order, after an account has been closed, or otherwise in violation of its contract with the drawer or maker, the payor bank is subrogated to (obtains) the rights of (1) any holder in due course on the item against the drawer or maker, (2) the payee or any other holder against the drawer or maker, and (3) the drawer or maker against the payee or any other holder. Section 4-407. For instance, over the drawer's stop payment order, a bank pays a check presented to the bank by a holder in due course. The drawer's defense is that the check was obtained by fraud in the inducement. The drawee bank is subrogated to the rights of the holder in due course, who would not be subject to the drawer's personal defense, and thus can debit the drawer's account. Section 4-407(1). The same would be true if the presenter were the payee, against whom the drawer did not have a valid defense. Section 4-407(2).

29-2e DISCLOSURE REQUIREMENTS

Congress enacted the Truth in Savings Act, which requires all depositary institutions (including commercial banks, savings and loan associations, savings banks, and credit unions) to disclose in great detail to consumers the terms and conditions of their deposit accounts. The stated purpose of the Act is to allow consumers to make informed decisions regarding deposit accounts by mandating standardized disclosure of rates of interest and fees to facilitate meaningful comparison of different deposit products.

More specifically, the Act provides that the disclosures must be made in a clear and conspicuous writing and must be given to the consumer when an account is opened or service is provided. These disclosures must include the following: (1) the annual percentage yield (APY) and the percentage rate, (2) how variable rates are calculated and when the rates may be changed, (3) balance information (including how the balance is calculated), (4) when and how interest is calculated and credited, (5) the amount of fees that may be charged and how they are calculated, and (6) any limitation on the number or amount of withdrawals or deposits. In addition, the Act requires the depositary institution to disclose the following information with periodic statements it sends to its customers: (1) the APY earned, (2) any fees debited during the covered period, (3) the dollar amount of the interest earned during the covered period, and (4) the dates of the covered period.

29-2f CUSTOMER'S DEATH OR INCOMPETENCE

The general rule is that death or incompetence revokes all agency agreements. Furthermore, adjudication of incompetency by a court is regarded as notice to the world of that fact. Actual notice is not required. Section 4-405 of the Code modifies these stringent rules in several ways with respect to bank deposits and collections.

First, if either a payor or collecting bank does not know that a customer has been adjudicated incompetent, the existence of such incompetence at the time an item is issued or its collection is undertaken does not impair either bank's authority to accept, pay, or collect the item or to account for proceeds of its collection. The bank may pay the item without incurring any liability.

Second, neither death nor adjudication of incompetence of a customer revokes a payor or collecting bank's authority to accept, pay, or collect an item until the bank knows of the condition and has a reasonable opportunity to act on this knowledge.

Finally, even though a bank knows of the death of its customer, it may for ten days after the date of his death pay or certify checks drawn by the customer unless a person claiming an interest in the account, such as an heir, executor, or administrator, orders the bank to stop making such payments. Section 4-405(b).

29-2g CUSTOMER'S DUTIES

The Code imposes certain affirmative duties on bank customers and fixes time limits within which they must assert their rights. The duties arise and the time starts to run from the point at which the bank either sends or makes available to its customer a statement of account showing payment of items against the account. The statement of account will suffice provided it describes by item the number of the item, the amount, and the date of payment. The customer must exercise reasonable promptness in examining the bank statement or the items to determine whether any payment was unauthorized due to an *unauthorized signature* on or any *alteration* of an item. Section 4-406(c). Because the customer is not presumed to know the signatures of payees or indorsers, this duty of prompt and careful examination applies only to alterations and the customer's own signature, both of which he should be able to detect immediately. If he discovers an unauthorized signature or an alteration, he must notify the bank promptly. Section 4-406(c). A failure to fulfill these duties of prompt examination and notice precludes the customer from asserting against the bank his unauthorized signature or any alteration if the bank establishes that it suffered a loss by reason of such failure. Section 4-406(d).

Furthermore, the customer will lose his rights in a potentially more serious situation. Occasionally a forger, possibly an employee who has access to his employer's checkbook, carries out a series of transactions involving the account of the same individual. He may forge one or more checks each month until he is finally detected. The bank, noticing nothing suspicious, might pay one or more of the customer's checks bearing the

false signatures before the customer detects the forgery, months or even years later. Section 4-406(d) of the Code deals with these situations by stating that once the statement and items become available to him, the customer must examine them within a reasonable period—which in no event may exceed thirty calendar days and which may, under certain circumstances, be less—and notify the bank. Any instruments containing alterations or unauthorized signatures by the same wrongdoer that the bank pays during that period will be the bank's responsibility, but any paid thereafter but before the customer notifies the bank may not be asserted against it. This rule is based on the concept that the loss involved is directly traceable to the customer's negligence and that, as a result, he should stand the loss.

These rules depend, however, on the bank's exercising ordinary care in paying the items involved. If it does not and that failure by the bank substantially contributed to the loss, the loss will be allocated between the bank and the customer based on their comparative negligence. Section 4-406(e). But whether the bank exercised due care or not, the customer must in all events report any alteration or his unauthorized signature within one year from the time the statement or items are made available to him or be barred from asserting them against the bank. Section 4-406(f). Any *unauthorized indorsement* must be asserted within three years under the Article's general Statute of Limitations provisions. Section 4-111.

> ### Practical Advice
> *Promptly review your monthly bank statement to ensure that all checks and transactions were issued by you or your authorized agent and are for the correct amount.*

Consistent with modern automated methods for processing checks, Articles 3 and 4 provide that "ordinary care" does not require a bank to examine every check if the failure to do so does not vary unreasonably from general banking usage. Section 3-103(7).

◆ *See Case 29-3*

ELECTRONIC FUND TRANSFER

As mentioned, the use of negotiable instruments for payment has greatly reduced the use of *cash* in the United States. The advent and technological advances of interconnected computers have resulted in electronic fund transfer systems (EFTS) that have greatly reduced the use of *checks*. Financial institutions seek to substitute EFTS for checks for two principal reasons. The first is to eliminate the ever-increasing paperwork involved in processing the billions of checks issued annually.

The second is to eliminate the "float" that a drawer of a check currently enjoys by maintaining the use of his funds during the processing period between the time at which he issues the check and final payment.

The EFTA defines an EFT as "any transfer of funds, other than a transaction originated by check, draft, or similar paper instrument, which is initiated through an electronic terminal, telephonic instrument, or computer or magnetic tape so as to order, instruct or authorize a financial institution to debit or credit an account." For example, with an EFT, William in New York would be able to pay a debt he owes to Yvette in Illinois by entering into his computer an order to his bank to pay Yvette. The drawee bank would then instantly debit William's account and transfer the credit to Yvette's bank, where Yvette's account would immediately be credited in that amount.

The use of EFTs generated considerable confusion concerning the legal rights of customers and financial institutions. Congress provided a partial solution to the legal issues affecting consumer EFTs by enacting the EFTA, discussed below. Transactions not covered by the EFTA—primarily wholesale electronic transfers—are covered by Article 4A—Funds transfer of the UCC.

29-3 Types of Electronic Funds Transfer

Although new EFTs may appear in the coming years, six main types of EFTs are currently in use: (1) automated teller machines (ATMs), (2) point-of-sale systems (POS), (3) direct deposit and withdrawal of funds, (4) pay-by-phone systems, (5) online banking, and (6) wholesale EFTs.

29-3a AUTOMATED TELLER MACHINES

ATMs permit customers to conduct various transactions with their banks through the use of electronic terminals. After activating an ATM with a plastic identification card and a personal identification number, or PIN, a customer can deposit and withdraw funds from her account, transfer funds between accounts, obtain cash advances, and make payments on loan accounts.

29-3b POINT-OF-SALE SYSTEMS

POS permit consumers to transfer funds automatically from their bank accounts to a merchant. The POS machines, located within the merchant's store and activated by the consumer's identification card and code, instantaneously debit the consumer's account and credit the merchant's account.

29-3c DIRECT DEPOSITS AND WITHDRAWALS

Another type of EFT involves deposits, authorized in advance by a customer, that are made directly to his account. Examples include direct payroll deposits, deposits of Social Security

payments, and deposits of pension payments. Conversely, automatic withdrawals are preauthorized EFTs from the customer's account for regular payments to some party other than the financial institution at which the funds are deposited. Automatic withdrawals to pay insurance premiums, utility bills, or automobile loan payments are common examples of this type of EFT.

29-3d PAY-BY-PHONE SYSTEMS

Financial institutions provide a service that permits customers to pay bills by telephoning the bank's computer system and directing a transfer of funds to a designated third party. This service also permits customers to transfer funds between accounts.

29-3e ONLINE BANKING

Online banking enables the customer to execute many banking transactions via an Internet-connected computer. For instance, customers may view account balances, request transfers between accounts, and pay bills electronically.

29-3f WHOLESALE ELECTRONIC FUNDS TRANSFER

Wholesale EFTs, commonly called wholesale wire transfers, involve the movement of funds between financial institutions, between financial institutions and businesses, and between businesses. Wholesale EFTs amounting to almost $5 *trillion* are transferred this way *each business day* over the two major transfer systems—the Federal Reserve wire transfer network system (Fedwire) and the private New York Clearing House Interbank Payments System (CHIPS). In addition, a number of other private wholesale wire systems exist among the large banks. Limited aspects of wholesale wire transfers are governed by uniform rules promulgated by the Federal Reserve, CHIPS, and the National Automated Clearing House Association.

29-4 Consumer Funds transfer

Congress determined that the use of electronic systems to transfer funds provided the potential for substantial benefits to consumers. Existing consumer protection legislation failed to account for the unique characteristics of such systems, however, leaving the rights and obligations of consumers and financial institutions undefined. Accordingly, Congress enacted Title IX of the Consumer Protection Act, the EFTA, to "provide a basic framework establishing the rights, liabilities, and responsibilities of participants in electronic fund transfers" with primary emphasis on "the provision of individual consumer rights." Because the EFTA deals exclusively with the protection of **consumers**, it does not govern electronic transfers between financial institutions, between financial institutions and businesses, and between businesses. The Act is similar in many respects to the Fair Credit Billing Act (see *Chapter 41*), which applies to credit card transactions. The EFTA was administered by the Board of Governors of the Federal Reserve System, which is mandated to prescribe regulations to carry out the purposes of the Act. Pursuant to this congressional mandate, the Federal Reserve issued Regulation E. The Dodd-Frank Wall Street Reform and Consumer Protection Act of 2010 (Dodd-Frank Act) transferred administration of the EFTA to the Consumer Financial Protection Bureau (CFPB), an independent executive agency housed within the Federal Reserve. See *Chapter 41*.

The Dodd-Frank Act requires that the amount of any interchange transaction fee that an issuer may receive or charge with respect to an electronic debit transaction must be reasonable and proportional to the cost incurred by the issuer, as determined by the Federal Reserve. Debit cards issued by small banks and prepaid reloadable cards are exempt from this rule.

29-4a DISCLOSURE

The EFTA is primarily a disclosure statute and as such requires that the terms and conditions of EFTs involving a consumer's account be disclosed in readily understandable language at the time the consumer contracts for such services. Included among the required disclosure are the consumer's liability for unauthorized transfers, the kinds of EFTs allowed, the charges for transfers or for the right to make transfers, the consumer's right to stop payment of preauthorized EFTs, the consumer's right to receive documentation of EFTs, rules concerning disclosure of information to third parties, procedures for correcting account errors, and the financial institution's liability to the consumer under the Act.

In addition, the Dodd-Frank Act amended the EFTA to establish new standards for remittance transfers and authorized the CFPB to issue implementing regulations. A "remittance transfer" is an electronic transfer of money from a consumer in the United States to a person or business in a foreign country through persons or financial institutions that provide such transfers in the normal course of their business. Effective October 28, 2013, the CFPB amended Regulation E to protect consumers who make remittance transfers by generally requiring companies to disclose exact fees, taxes, and exchange rates to consumers before they pay for the remittance transfers, subject to a temporary exception permitting insured institutions to estimate certain pricing disclosures where exact information could not be determined for reasons beyond their control. In 2014, the CFPB extended the temporary exception by five years to expire on July 21, 2020. In May 2020, the Bureau issued a final rule amending the Remittance Rule.

29-4b DOCUMENTATION AND PERIODIC STATEMENTS

The Act requires the financial institution to provide the consumer with written documentation of each transfer made from an electronic terminal at the time of transfer—a receipt. The receipt must clearly state the amount involved, the date, the type of transfer, the identity of the account(s) involved, the identity of any third party involved, and the location of the terminal involved.

In addition, the financial institution must provide each consumer with a periodic statement for each account of the consumer that may be accessed by means of an EFT. The statement must describe the amount, date, and location for each transfer; the fee, if any, to be charged for the transaction; and an address and phone number for questions and information.

29-4c PREAUTHORIZED TRANSFERS

A preauthorized transfer from a consumer's account must be authorized in advance and in writing by the consumer, and a copy of the authorization must be provided to the consumer when the transfer is made. Up to three business days before the scheduled date of the transfer, a consumer may stop payment of a preauthorized EFT by notifying the financial institution orally or in writing, though the financial institution may require the consumer to provide written confirmation of an oral notification within fourteen days.

29-4d ERROR RESOLUTION

The consumer has sixty days after the financial institution sends a periodic statement in which to notify the institution of any errors appearing on that statement. The financial institution is required to investigate alleged errors within ten business days and to report its findings within three business days after completing the investigation. If the financial institution needs more than ten days to investigate, it may take up to forty-five days, provided it recredits the consumer's account for the amount alleged to be in error. The institution must correct an error within one business day after determining that the error has occurred. Failure to investigate in good faith makes the financial institution liable to the consumer for treble damages (three times the amount of provable damages).

29-4e CONSUMER LIABILITY

A consumer's liability for an unauthorized EFT is limited to a maximum of $50 if the consumer notifies the financial institution within two days after he learns of the loss or theft. If the consumer does not report the loss or theft within two days, he is liable for losses up to $500 but no more than $50 for the first two days. If the consumer fails to report the unauthorized use within sixty days of transmittal of a periodic statement, he is liable for losses resulting from any unauthorized EFT that appeared on the statement if the financial institution can show that the loss would not have occurred had the consumer reported the loss within sixty days; thus, there is unlimited liability on unauthorized transfers made after sixty days following the bank's sending the periodic statement.

29-4f LIABILITY OF FINANCIAL INSTITUTION

A financial institution is liable to a consumer for all damages proximately caused by its failure to make an EFT in accordance with the terms and conditions of an account, in the correct amount, or in a timely manner when properly instructed to do so by the consumer. There are, however, exceptions to such liability. The financial institution will not be liable if—

1. the consumer's account has insufficient funds through no fault of the financial institution,
2. the funds are subject to legal process,
3. the transfer would exceed an established credit limit,
4. an electronic terminal has insufficient cash, or
5. circumstances beyond the financial institution's control prevent the transfer.

The financial institution is also liable for failure to stop payment of a preauthorized transfer from a consumer's account when instructed to do so in accordance with the terms and conditions of the account.

29-5 Wholesale Funds transfer

The typical wholesale wire transfer involves sophisticated parties who seek great speed in transferring large sums of money. As mentioned, the dollar value of commercial or wholesale wire transfers over the two major transfer systems—Fedwire and CHIPS—is almost $5 trillion per business day.

Article 4A—Funds transfer is designed to provide a statutory framework for payment systems that are not covered by other Articles of the UCC or by the EFTA. All fifty States have adopted Article 4A. In general, "Article 4A governs a method of payment in which the person making payment (the 'originator') directly transfers an instruction to a bank to either make a payment to the person receiving the payment (the 'beneficiary') or to instruct some other bank to make payment to the beneficiary." Article 4A-102, Comment 1.

As discussed, on October 28, 2013, amended Regulation E went into effect governing consumer remittance transfers. Because these rules apply whether or not those remittance transfers are also EFTs as defined in the EFTA, neither the Federal rule nor Article 4A will apply to some aspects of remittance transfers. To address this regulatory gap, in 2012, the Uniform Law Commission proposed an amendment to Article 4A to allow Article 4A to apply to a funds transfer that also is a remittance transfer, so long as that remittance transfer is not an EFT as defined in the EFTA. As of June 2021, all States except Wyoming had adopted the 2012 Amendment to Article 4A.

Article 4A provides that the parties to a funds transfer generally may by agreement vary their rights and obligations. Moreover, funds-transfer system rules governing banks that use the system may be effective even if such rules conflict with Article 4A. Section 4A-501. Rights and obligations under Article 4A can also be changed by Federal regulations and operating circulars of Federal Reserve Banks. Section 4A-107.

29-5a SCOPE OF ARTICLE 4A

Article 4A, which covers wholesale funds transfer, defines a funds transfer as a

> series of transactions, beginning with the originator's payment order, made for the purpose of making payment to the beneficiary of the order. The term includes any payment order issued by the originator's bank or an intermediary bank intended to carry out the originator's payment order. A funds transfer is completed by acceptance by the beneficiary's bank of a payment order for the benefit of the beneficiary of the originator's payment order. Section 4A-104(a).

The Article, therefore, covers the transfers of credit that move from an originator to a beneficiary through the banking system. If any step in the process is governed by the EFTA, however, the entire transaction is excluded from the Article's coverage except for some remittance transfers in the forty-nine States adopting the 2012 Amendment of Article 4A. Section 4A-108.

The following examples illustrate the coverage of the Article:

1. Johnson Co. instructs its bank, First National Bank (FNB), to pay $2 million to West Co., also a customer of FNB. FNB executes the payment order by crediting West's account with $2 million and notifying West that the credit has been made and is available.
2. Assume the same facts as those in the first example except that West's bank is Central Bank (CB). FNB will execute the payment order of Johnson Co. by issuing to CB its own payment order instructing CB to credit the account of West.

3. Assume the facts presented in the second example with the added fact that FNB does not have a correspondent relationship with CB. In this instance, FNB will have to issue its payment order to Northern Bank (NB), a bank that does have a correspondent relationship with CB, and NB will then issue its payment order to CB.

PAYMENT ORDER **Payment order** is a sender's instruction to a receiving bank to pay, or to cause another bank to pay, a fixed or determinable amount of money to a beneficiary. Section 4A-103. The instruction may be communicated orally, electronically, or in writing. To be a payment order, the instruction must—

1. not contain a condition to payment other than the time of payment;
2. be sent to a receiving bank that is to be reimbursed either by debiting an account of the sender or by otherwise receiving payment from the sender; and
3. be transmitted by the sender directly to the receiving bank or indirectly through an agent, a funds-transfer system, or a communication system.

The payment order is issued when sent, and if more than one payment is to be made, each payment represents a separate payment order. Section 4A-104(b)(c). In the previous examples, one payment order is issued in the first example (from Johnson Co.), two in the second example (from Johnson Co. and from First National Bank), and three in the third example (from Johnson Co., from First National Bank, and from Northern Bank).

PARTIES The **originator** is either the sender of the payment order or, in a series of payment orders, the sender of the first payment order. Section 4A-104(c). A **sender** is the party who gives an instruction to the **receiving bank**, or the bank to which the sender's instruction is addressed. Section 4A-103(4). The receiving bank may be the **originator's bank**, an intermediary bank, or the **beneficiary's bank**. The originator's bank is either the bank that receives the original payment order or the originator if the originator is a bank. Section 4A-104(d). The beneficiary's bank, the last bank in the chain of a funds transfer, is the bank instructed in the payment order to credit the beneficiary's account. Section 4A-103(a)(3). The **beneficiary** is the person to be paid by the beneficiary bank. Section 4A-103(a)(2). An intermediary bank is any receiving bank, other than the originator's bank or the beneficiary's bank, that receives the payment order. Section 4A-104(b). Thus, in the above examples,

1. Johnson Co. is the *originator* in all three examples;
2. Johnson Co. is a *sender* in all three examples, FNB is a sender in examples 2 and 3, and NB is a sender in example 3;

3. FNB is the *receiving bank* of Johnson Co.'s payment order in all three examples; in example 2, CB is the receiving bank of FNB's payment order; and in example 3, CB is the receiving bank of NB's payment order and NB is the receiving bank of FNB's payment order;
4. FNB is the *originator's bank* in all three examples;
5. FNB is the *beneficiary's bank* in example 1; CB is the beneficiary's bank in examples 2 and 3;
6. West is the *beneficiary* in all three examples; and
7. NB is an *intermediary bank* in example 3.

See *Figure 29-2* for a summary of the parties in these three examples. In some instances, the originator and the beneficiary may be the same party. For example, a corporation may wish to transfer funds from one account to another account that is in the same or a different bank.

◆ **SEE FIGURE 29-2:** *Parties to a Funds Transfer*

EXCLUDED TRANSACTIONS As mentioned, Section 4A-108 provides that if any part of a funds transfer is governed by the EFTA, then the transfer is excluded from Article 4A coverage except for some remittance transfers in the forty-nine States adopting the 2012 Amendment of Article 4A. In addition, Article 4A covers only credit transactions; it therefore excludes debit transactions. If the person making the payment gives the instruction, the transfer is a credit transfer. If, however, the person receiving the payment gives the instruction, the transfer is a debit transfer. For example, a seller of goods obtains authority from the purchaser to debit the purchaser's account after the seller ships the goods. Article 4A does not cover this transaction because the instructions to make payment issue from the beneficiary (the seller), not from the party whose account is to be debited (the purchaser).

◆ **SEE FIGURE 29-3:** *Credit Transaction*

29-5b ACCEPTANCE

Rights and obligations arise as a result of a receiving bank's acceptance of a payment order. The effect of acceptance depends upon whether the payment order was issued to the beneficiary's bank or to a receiving bank other than the beneficiary's bank.

If a receiving bank is not the beneficiary's bank, the receiving bank does not subject itself to any liability until it accepts the instrument. Acceptance by a receiving bank other than the beneficiary's bank occurs when the receiving bank executes the sender's order. Section 4A-209(a). Such execution occurs when the receiving bank "issues a payment order intended to carry out" the sender's payment order. Section 4A-301(a).

FIGURE 29-2 Parties to a Funds Transfer

	Example 1	Example 2	Example 3
Originator	Johnson Co.	Johnson Co.	Johnson Co.
Sender(s)	Johnson Co.	Johnson Co. FNB	Johnson Co. FNB NB
Receiving Bank(s)	FNB	FNB CB	FNB CB NB
Originator's Bank	FNB	FNB	FNB
Beneficiary's Bank	FNB	CB	CB
Beneficiary	West	West	West
Intermediary Bank	—	—	NB

Note: CB = Central Bank; FNB = First National Bank; NB = Northern Bank.

When the receiving bank executes the sender's payment order, the bank is entitled to payment from the sender and can debit the sender's account. Section 4A-402(c).

The beneficiary's bank may accept an order in any of three ways, and acceptance occurs at the earliest of these events: (1) when the bank (a) pays the beneficiary or (b) notifies the beneficiary that the bank has received the order or has credited the beneficiary's account with the funds, (2) when the bank receives payment of the sender's order, or (3) the opening of the next funds-transfer business day of the bank after the payment date of the order if the order was not rejected and funds are available for payment. Section 4A-209(b).

If a beneficiary's bank accepts a payment order, the bank is obliged to pay the beneficiary the amount of the order. Section 4A-404(a). The bank's acceptance of the payment order does not, however, create any obligation to either the sender or the originator.

29-5c ERRONEOUS EXECUTION OF PAYMENT ORDERS

If a receiving bank mistakenly executes a payment order for an amount greater than the amount authorized, the bank is entitled to payment only in the amount of the sender's correct order. Section 4A-303(a). To the extent allowed by the law governing mistake and restitution, the receiving bank may then recover from the beneficiary of the erroneous order the amount in excess of the authorized amount. If the wrong beneficiary is paid, however, the bank that issued the erroneous payment order is entitled to payment neither from its sender nor from prior senders and has the burden of recovering the payment from the improper beneficiary. Section 4A-303(c).

29-5d UNAUTHORIZED PAYMENT ORDERS

If a bank wishing to prevent unauthorized transactions establishes commercially reasonable security measures, to which a customer agrees, and the bank properly follows the process it has established, the customer must pay an order even if it was unauthorized. Section 4A-202. The customer, however, can avoid liability by showing that the unauthorized order was not caused directly or indirectly by (1) a person with access to confidential security information who was acting for the customer or (2) a person who obtained such information from a source controlled by the customer. Section 4A-203.

FIGURE 29-3 Credit Transaction

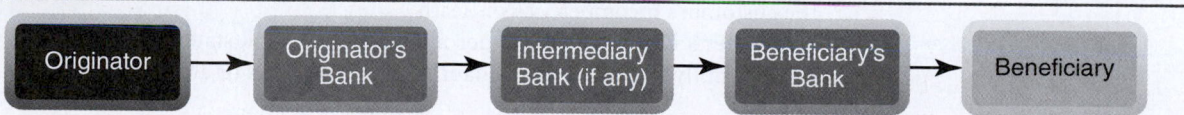

C H A P T E R   S U M M A R Y

BANK DEPOSITS AND COLLECTIONS

COLLECTION OF ITEMS	
	Depositary Bank the bank in which the payee or holder deposits a check for credit
	Provisional Credit tentative credit for the deposit of an instrument until final credit is given
	Final Credit payment of the instrument by the payor bank; if the payor bank (drawee) does not pay the check, the depositary bank reverses the provisional credit
	Intermediary Bank a bank, other than the depositary or payor bank, involved in the collection process
	Collecting Bank any bank (other than the payor bank) handling the item for payment
	• *Agency* a collecting bank is an agent or subagent of the owner of the check until the settlement becomes final
	• *Duty of Care* a collecting bank must exercise ordinary care in handling an item
	• *Duty to Act Timely* a collecting bank acts timely if it takes proper action before its midnight deadline (midnight of the next banking day)
	• *Indorsements* if an item is restrictively indorsed "for deposit only," only a bank may be a holder
	• *Warranties* customers and collecting banks give warranties on transfer, presentment, and encoding
	• *Final Payment* occurs when the payor bank does any of the following, whichever happens first: (1) pays an item in cash, (2) settles and does not have the right to revoke the settlement, or (3) makes a provisional settlement and does not properly revoke it
	Payor Bank under its contract with the drawer, the payor or drawee bank agrees to pay to the payee or his order checks that are issued by the drawer, provided the order is not countermanded by a stop payment order and provided there are sufficient funds in the drawer's account

RELATIONSHIP BETWEEN PAYOR BANK AND ITS CUSTOMER	
	Contractual Relationship the relationship between a payor bank and its checking account customer is primarily the product of their contractual arrangement
	Payment of an Item when a payor receives an item for which the funds in the account are insufficient, the bank may either dishonor the item and return it or pay the item and charge the customer's account even though an overdraft is created
	Substitute Check a paper reproduction of the original check that is the legal equivalent of an original check for all purposes
	Stop Payment Orders an oral stop payment order (a command from a drawer to a drawee not to pay an instrument) is binding for fourteen calendar days; a written order is effective for six months and may be renewed in writing
	Bank's Right to Subrogation on Improper Payment if a payor bank pays an item over a stop payment order or otherwise in violation of its contract, the payor bank is subrogated to (obtains) the rights of (1) any holder in due course on the item against the drawer or maker, (2) the payee or any other holder against the drawer or maker, and (3) the drawer or maker against the payee or any other holder
	Disclosure Requirement all depository institutions must disclose in great detail to their consumers the terms and conditions of their deposit account
	Customer's Death or Incompetence a bank may pay an item if it does not know of the customer's incompetency or death
	Customer's Duties the customer must examine bank statements and items carefully and promptly to discover any unauthorized signatures or alterations

ELECTRONIC FUNDS TRANSFER

NATURE AND TYPES OF ELEC-TRONIC FUNDS TRANSFER	**Definition** any transfer of funds, other than a transaction originated by check, draft, or similar paper instrument, which is initiated through an electronic terminal, telephonic instrument, or computer or magnetic tape so as to order, instruct, or authorize a financial institution to debit or credit an account

Purpose to eliminate the paperwork involved in processing checks and the "float" available to a drawer of a check

Types of Electronic Funds transfer
- *Automated Teller Machines*
- *Point-of-Sale Systems*
- *Direct Deposits and Withdrawals*
- *Pay-by-Phone Systems*
- *Online Banking*
- *Wholesale Electronic Funds transfer*

CONSUMER FUNDS TRANSFER	**Electronic Fund Transfer Act** provides a basic framework establishing the rights, liabilities, and responsibilities of participants in consumer electronic funds transfer

Financial Institution Responsibility liable to a consumer for all damages proximately caused by its failure to handle an electronic fund transfer transaction properly

WHOLESALE FUNDS TRANSFER	**Scope of Article 4A**

- *Wholesale Funds transfer* the movement of funds through the banking system; excludes all transactions governed by the Electronic Fund Transfer Act except for some remittance transfers
- *Payment Order* an instruction of sender to a receiving bank to pay, or to cause another bank to pay, a fixed amount of money to a beneficiary
- *Parties* include originator, sender, receiving bank, originator's bank, beneficiary's bank, beneficiary, and intermediary banks

Acceptance rights and obligations that arise as a result of a receiving bank's acceptance of a payment order

C A S E S

CASE 29-1

Duty of Care

DIXON, LAUKITIS AND DOWNING v. BUSEY BANK

Appellate Court of Illinois, Third District, 2013
2013 IL App 3d 120832, 993 N.E.2d 580, 373 Ill.Dec. 274

O'Brien, J.

[Plaintiff Dixon, Laukitis & Downing, P.C. (DLD) is a law firm that maintained its client trust account at defendant Busey Bank. On May 25, 2011, DLD deposited into its trust account a check from one of its clients in the amount of $350,000. The check was drawn on the account of Intact Insurance Company at Royal Bank of Canada in Toronto, Ontario. The check was marked "US Funds." On June 6, 2011, DLD transferred $210,000 from its trust account to the client who provided the

$350,000 check. On June 8, 2011, DLD transferred $60,000 from the trust account to the client. On June 10, 2011, the check was returned to Busey uncollected, and Busey notified DLD and charged back $350,000 to DLD's account the same day. DLD filed a negligence action against Busey, alleging that Busey breached a duty of ordinary care the bank owed DLD regarding a fraudulent check DLD deposited and drew against, which was later determined to be uncollectible. The trial court dismissed the complaint, and DLD appealed.]

* * * According to DLD, Busey owed it a duty of ordinary care under the common law and the UCC, breached its duty, and caused DLD damages. * * *

* * * Article 4 of the UCC governs bank deposits and collections. It sets forth a bank's general duty to exercise ordinary care and states that "action or non-action approved by this Article * * * is the exercise of ordinary care and, in the absence of special instructions, action or non-action consistent * * * with a general banking usage not disapproved by this Article, is prima facie the exercise of ordinary care." [Section 4-103(c)].

A bank that takes an item is a "Depository Bank" and a bank that handles an item for collection and is not a drawee of the draft is a "Collecting Bank." [Section 4-105]. A collecting bank acts as an agent of an item's owner until final settlement of the item and "any settlement given for the item is provisional." [Section 4-201(a)]. In addition, a collecting bank has a superior right over the item's owner to a setoff if an item does not settle. [Section 4-201(a)].

The UCC does not enumerate duties for a depository bank but section 4-202 sets forth the responsibilities for a collecting bank as follows:

(a) A collecting bank must exercise ordinary care in:
  (1) presenting an item or sending it for presentment;
  (2) sending notice of dishonor or nonpayment or returning an item other than a documentary draft to the bank's transferor after learning that the item has not been paid or accepted, as the case may be;
  (3) settling for an item when the bank receives final settlement; and
  (4) notifying its transferor of any loss or delay in transit within a reasonable time after discovery thereof.

(b) A collecting bank exercises ordinary care under subsection (a) by taking proper action before its midnight deadline following receipt of an item, notice, or settlement. [Section 4-202(a), (b)].

Section 4-214(a) provides that a collecting bank may charge back a customer's account when the bank makes provisional settlement but does not receive final payment on an item if the collecting bank gives notice to its customer by midnight of the next banking day. [Section 4-214(a)].

* * *

The account agreement [and the UCC] placed the risk of loss on DLD until final settlement of the $350,000 check. This provision applied whether Busey acted as a depository bank or a collecting bank. * * *

* * * Under section 4-202, a collecting bank exercises ordinary care when it presents an item, sends notice of dishonor, finally settles an item, or timely notifies the transferor of any delay by performing such actions before midnight following receipt, notice or settlement of an item. DLD seeks to add an additional duty of ordinary care under the common law to supplement these specific standards. Contrary to DLD's claims, the UCC displaces common law duties for a collecting bank. As the trial court noted, the UCC provides a comprehensive plan for the processing of checks. Where, like here, its specific provisions set forth standards regarding particular banking practices, they displace the ordinary care standard under the common law. In the amended complaint, DLD does not assert that Busey failed to timely perform any section 4-202 duties of a collecting bank, including notifying DLD before the midnight deadline that the check was dishonored.

* * *

As discussed above, the account holder agreement between DLD and Busey formed a contract, which incorporated the applicable UCC provisions and defined the parties' responsibilities. * * * Where, as here, the account agreement and UCC set forth Busey's duties and define ordinary care, there is no extracontractual relationship. * * * We find that the trial court properly dismissed the complaint * * *.

Affirmed.

CASE
29-2

Payment of an Item/Stop Payment Order
LEIBLING, P.C. v. MELLON PSFS (NJ) NATIONAL ASSOCIATION
Superior Court of New Jersey, Law Division, Special Civil Part, Camden County, 1998
710 A.2d 1067, 311 N.J. Super. 651, 35 UCC Rep.Serv.2d 590

Rand, J.

Facts

Mr. Scott D. Liebling, P.C. (hereinafter "Plaintiff") is an attorney at law. Plaintiff maintains an attorney trust account ("Account") at Mellon Bank (NJ) National Association ("Mellon") * * *. Mellon uses a computerized system to process checks for payment.

Plaintiff represented defendant Fredy Winda Ramos ("Ramos") in a personal injury action which resulted in a settlement. On or about May 19, 1995, plaintiff issued Check No. 1031 in the amount of $8,483.06 to Ramos representing her net proceeds from the settlement. Mellon honored that check on May 26, 1995. On or about May 24, 1995, plaintiff mistakenly issued another check, Check No. 1043, to Ramos in the same amount of $8,483.06. Realizing his error, on or about May 30, 1995, Plaintiff called Ramos in Puerto Rico and advised her that the Check No. 1043 was issued by mistake and instructed her to destroy the check. Thereafter, Plaintiff called Mellon and ordered an oral stop payment on the check.

On December 21, 1996, some nineteen months after plaintiff issued the Check No. 1043, Ramos cashed the check from Puerto Rico.

Plaintiff filed this complaint against both Ramos and Mellon. Ramos was served and defaulted. Plaintiff's complaint against Mellon alleges breach of duty of good faith, negligence, breach of fiduciary duty, payment of a stale check, and breach of contract as a result of Mellon honoring the second check, Check No. 1043.

* * *

* * * [T]he issue in the present case turns on whether Mellon acted in good faith when it honored plaintiff's check. Good faith under N.J. Uniform Commercial Code has been defined in [UCC] 3-103(a)(4) as "honesty in fact and the observance of reasonable commercial standards of fair dealing." * * *

* * *

* * * [P]laintiff's argument centers on the proposition that the bank's duty of good faith required it to inquire or consult with plaintiff before honoring a stale check that had a previous oral stop payment order on it. * * *

However, * * * "[t]he duty [of inquiry] is inconsistent with the provisions of subsection 4-403(2) on the expiration of the 'effectiveness' of stop orders. Such a duty is hardly practical

today." Moreover: "[t]o require that a payor bank check the date of every check received via the collection process would unreasonably increase the cost of processing every check written today."

* * *

Thus, in determining whether the defendant bank in the present action acted in good faith, the above cited material must be analyzed and applied. First, it appears clear that the Uniform Commercial Code acknowledges that computerized check processing systems are common and accepted banking procedures in the United States. [Citation.] Therefore, it cannot be said that defendant bank acted in bad faith by using a computerized system when it honored plaintiff's "stale" check. Furthermore, it appears that the test for good faith is a subjective test. Thus, based on all of the foregoing material, as long as the defendant bank used an adequate computer system for processing checks (here there is no proof to the contrary), it appears to have acted in good faith even though it did not consult the Plaintiff before it honored the "stale" check that had an expired oral stop-payment order on it * * *. [T]he obligation of a bank to stop payment on a check does not continue in perpetuity once the stop payment order expires.

The bank's conduct was fair and in accordance with reasonable commercial standards. Accordingly, it appears that the defendant bank is not liable and should prevail. A finding of no liability is entered for the defendant bank.

CASE 29-3	Customer's Duties

UNION PLANTERS BANK, NATIONAL ASSOCIATION v. ROGERS

Supreme Court of Mississippi, 2005
912 So.2d 116

Waller, J.

This appeal involves an issue of first impression in Mississippi—the interpretation of [UCC] 4-406 (Rev. 2002), which imposes duties on banks and their customers insofar as forgeries are concerned. The case arises from a series of forgeries made by one person on four checking accounts maintained by Helen Rogers at the Union Planters Bank. * * *

Facts

Neal D. and Helen K. Rogers maintained four checking accounts with the Union Planters Bank in Greenville,

Washington County, Mississippi. * * * The Rogers were both in their eighties when the events which gave rise to this lawsuit took place. After Neal became bedridden, Helen hired Jackie Reese to help her take care of Neal and to do chores and errands.

In September of 2000, Reese began writing checks on the Rogerses' four accounts and forged Helen's name on the signature line. Some of the checks were made out to "cash," some to "Helen K. Rogers," and some to "Jackie Reese." The following chart summarizes the forgeries to each account:

ACCOUNT NUMBER	BEGINNING	ENDING	NUMBER OF CHECKS	AMOUNT OF CHECKS
54282309	11/27/2000	6/18/2001	46	$ 16,635.00
0039289441	9/27/2000	1/25/2001	10	$ 2,701.00
6100110922	11/29/2000	8/13/2001	29	$ 9,297.00
6404000343	11/20/2000	8/16/2001	83	$ 29,765.00
TOTAL			168	$58,398.00

Neal died in late May of 2001. Shortly thereafter, the Rogerses' son, Neal, Jr., began helping Helen with financial matters. Together they discovered that many bank statements were missing and that there was not as much money in the accounts as they had thought. In June of 2001, they contacted Union Planters and asked for copies of the missing bank statements. In September of 2001, Helen was advised by Union Planters to contact the police due to forgeries made on her accounts. * * *

Subsequently, criminal charges were brought against Reese. In the meantime, Helen filed suit against Union Planters, alleging conversion (unlawful payment of forged checks) and negligence. After a trial, the jury awarded Helen $29,595 in damages, and the circuit court entered judgment accordingly. From this judgment, Union Planters appeals.

Discussion
* * *

The relationship between Rogers and Union Planters is governed by Article 4 of the Uniform Commercial Code, [citation]. [UCC] Section 4-406(a) & (c) provide that a bank customer has a duty to discover and report "unauthorized signatures"; i.e., forgeries. Section 4-406 of the UCC reflects an underlying policy decision that furthers the UCC's "objective of promoting certainty and predictability in commercial transactions." The UCC facilitates financial transactions, benefitting both consumers and financial institutions, by allocating responsibility among the parties according to whomever is best able to prevent a loss. Because the customer is more familiar with his own signature, and should know whether or not he authorized a particular withdrawal or check, he can prevent further unauthorized activity better than a financial institution which may process thousands of transactions in a single day. Section 4-406 acknowledges that the customer is best situated to detect unauthorized transactions on his own account by placing the burden on the customer to exercise reasonable care to discover and report such transactions. The customer's duty to exercise this care is triggered when the bank satisfies its burden to provide sufficient information to the customer. As a result, if the bank provides sufficient information, the customer bears the loss when he fails to detect and notify the bank about unauthorized transactions. [Citation.]

A. Union Planters' Duty to Provide Information under §4-406(a).

The court admitted into evidence copies of all Union Planters statements sent to Rogers during the relevant time period. Enclosed with the bank statements were either the cancelled checks themselves or copies of the checks relating to the period of time of each statement. The evidence shows that all bank statements and cancelled checks were sent, via United States Mail, postage prepaid, to all customers at their "designated address" each month. Rogers introduced no evidence to the contrary. We therefore find that the bank fulfilled its duty of making the statements available to Rogers and that the remaining provisions of §4-406 are applicable to the case at bar. * * *

In defense of her failure to inspect the bank statements, Rogers claims that she never received the bank statements and cancelled checks. Even if this allegation is true, it does not excuse Rogers from failing to fulfill her duties under §4-406(a) & (c) because the statute clearly states a bank discharges its duty in providing the necessary information to a customer when it "*sends ... to a customer a statement of account showing payment of items.*" §4-406(a) (emphasis added). [Citation.] The word "receive" is absent. The customer's duty to inspect and report does not arise when the statement is received, as Rogers claims; the customer's duty to inspect and report arises when the bank sends the statement to the customer's address. A reasonable person who has not received a monthly statement from the bank would promptly ask the bank for a copy of the statement. Here, Rogers claims that she did not receive numerous statements. We find that she failed to act reasonably when she failed to take any action to replace the missing statements.

B. Rogers' Duty to Report the Forgeries under §4-406(d).

A customer who has not promptly notified a bank of an irregularity may be precluded from bringing certain claims against the bank:

(d) If the bank proves that the customer failed, with respect to an item, to comply with the duties imposed on the customer by subsection (c), the customer is precluded from asserting against the bank:

(1) The customer's unauthorized signature... on the item, if the bank also proves that it suffered a loss by reason of the failure...

[UCC] §4-406(d)(1).

Also, when there is a series of forgeries, §4-406(d)(2) places additional duties on the customer:

(2) The customer's unauthorized signature...by the same wrongdoer on any other item paid in good faith by the bank if the payment was made before the bank received notice from the customer of the unauthorized signature... and after the customer had been afforded a reasonable period of time, not exceeding thirty (30) days, in which to examine the item or statement of account and notify the bank.

A bank may shorten the customer's thirty-day period for notifying the bank of a series of forgeries, and here, Union Planters shortened the thirty-day period to fifteen days. The statute states that a customer must report a series of forgeries within "a reasonable period of time, not *exceeding* thirty (30) days." "The 30-day period is an outside limit only. However 30 days is presumed to be reasonable and the bank bears the burden of proving otherwise." [Citation.]

* * *

Rogers is therefore precluded from making claims against Union Planters because (1) under §4-406(a), Union Planters provided the statements to Rogers, and (2) under §4-406(d)(2), Rogers failed to notify Union Planters of the forgeries within 15 and/or 30 days of the date she should have reasonably discovered the forgeries.

* * *

* * * [U]nder §4-406, Rogers is precluded from recovering amounts paid by Union Planters on any of the forged checks because she failed to timely detect and notify the bank of the unauthorized transactions and because she failed to show that Union Planters failed to use ordinary care in its processing of the forged checks. Therefore, we reverse the circuit court's judgment and render judgment here that Rogers take nothing and that the complaint and this action are finally dismissed with prejudice.

QUESTIONS

1. On November 9, Jane Jones writes a check for $5,000 payable to Ralph Rodgers in payment for goods to be received later in the month. Before the close of business on November 9, Jane notifies the bank by telephone to stop payment on the check. On December 19, Ralph gives the check to Bill Briggs for value and without notice. On December 20, Bill deposits the check in his account at Bank A. On December 21, Bank A sends the check to its correspondent, Bank B. On December 22, Bank B presents the check through the clearinghouse to Bank C. On December 23, Bank C presents the check to Bank P, the payor bank. On December 28, the payor bank makes payment of the check final. Is Jane Jones's stop payment order effective against the payor bank? Explain.

2. Howard Harrison, a longtime customer of Western Bank, operates a small department store, Harrison's Store. Because his store has few experienced employees, Harrison frequently travels throughout the United States on buying trips, although he also runs the financial operations of the business. On one of his buying trips, Harrison purchased two hundred sport shirts from Well-Made Shirt Company and paid for the transaction with a check on his store account with Western Bank in the amount of $3,000. Adams, an employee of Well-Made who deposits its checks in Security Bank, sloppily raised the amount of the check to $30,000 and indorsed the check, "Pay to the order of Adams from Pension Plan Benefits, Well-Made Shirt Company by Adams." He cashed the check and cannot be found. Western Bank processed the check, paid it, and sent it to Harrison's Store with the monthly statement. After briefly examining the statement, Harrison left on another buying trip for three weeks.

   a. Assuming the bank acted in good faith and the alteration is not discovered and reported to the bank until an audit conducted thirteen months after the statement was received by Harrison's Store, explain who must bear the loss on the raised check.

   b. Assume that Harrison, who was unable to examine his statement promptly because of his buying trips, left instructions with the bank to carefully examine and to notify him of any item over $5,000 to be charged to his account; assume further that the bank nevertheless paid the item in his absence. Who bears the loss if the alteration is discovered one month after the statement was received by Harrison's Store? If the alteration is discovered thirteen months later? Explain.

3. Tom Jones owed Bank of Cleveland $10,000 on a note due November 17, with 1 percent interest due the bank

for each day delinquent in payment. Jones issued a $10,000 check to Bank of Cleveland and deposited it in the night vault the evening of November 17. Several days later, he received a letter saying he owed one day's interest on the payment because of a one-day delinquency in payment. Jones refused because he said he had put the payment in the vault on November 17. Who is correct? Why?

4. Assume that Dinah draws a check on Oxford Bank, payable to the order of Pam; that Pam indorses it to Amy; that Amy deposits it to her account in Houston Bank; that Houston Bank presents it to Oxford Bank, the drawee; and that Oxford Bank dishonors it because of insufficient funds. Houston Bank receives notification of the dishonor on Monday but, because of an interruption of communication facilities, fails to notify Amy until Wednesday. What result? Explain.

5. Jones, a food wholesaler whose company has an account with City Bank in New York City, is traveling in California on business. He finds a particularly attractive offer and decides to buy a carload of oranges for delivery in New York. He gives Saltin, the seller, his company's check for $25,000 to pay for the purchase. Saltin deposits the check, with others he received that day, with his bank, the Carrboro Bank. Carrboro Bank sends the check to Downs Bank in Los Angeles, which in turn deposits it with the Los Angeles Federal Reserve Bank. The L.A. Fed sends the check, with others, to the N.Y. Fed, which forwards the check to City Bank, Jones's bank, for collection.

   a. Is City Bank a depository bank? A collecting bank? A payor bank?

   b. Is Carrboro Bank a depository bank? A collecting bank?

   c. Is the N.Y. Fed an intermediary bank?

   d. Is Downs Bank a collecting bank?

6. On April 1, Moore gave Pipkin a check properly drawn by Moore on Zebra Bank for $5,000 in payment of a painting to be framed and delivered the next day. Pipkin immediately indorsed the check and gave it to Yeager Bank as payment in full of his indebtedness to the bank on a note he previously had signed. Yeager Bank canceled the note and returned it to Pipkin.

   On April 2, upon learning that the painting had been destroyed in a fire at Pipkin's studio, Moore promptly went to Zebra Bank, signed a printed form of stop payment order, and gave it to the cashier. Zebra Bank refused payment on the check upon proper presentment by Yeager Bank.

   a. What are the rights of Yeager Bank against Zebra Bank?

   b. What are the rights of Yeager Bank against Moore?

   c. Assuming that Zebra Bank inadvertently paid the amount of the check to Yeager Bank and debited Moore's account, what are the rights of Moore against Zebra Bank?

7. As payment in advance for services to be performed, Acton signed and delivered the following instrument:

   December 1, 2021
   LAST NATIONAL BANK
   MONEYVILLE, STATE X
   Pay to the order of Olaf Owen $10,500.00
   Ten Thousand Five Hundred Dollars for services to be performed by Olaf Owen starting on December 6, 2021.

   (signed) Arthur Acton

   Owen requested and received Last National Bank's certification of the check even though Acton had only $9,000 on deposit. Owen indorsed the check in blank and delivered it to Dan Doty in payment of a preexisting debt.

   When Owen failed to appear for work, Acton issued a written stop payment order ordering the bank not to pay the check. Doty presented the check to Last National Bank for payment. The bank refused payment.

   What are the bank's rights and liabilities relating to the transactions described?

8. Jones drew a check for $1,000 on The First Bank and mailed it to the payee, Thrift, Inc. Caldwell stole the check from Thrift, Inc.; chemically erased the name of the payee; and inserted the name of Henderson as payee. Caldwell also increased the amount of the check to $10,000 and, by using the name of Henderson, negotiated the check to Willis. Willis then took the check to The First Bank; obtained its certification on the check; and negotiated the check to Griffin, who deposited the check in The Second National Bank for collection. The Second National Bank forwarded the check to the Detroit Trust Company for collection from The First Bank, which honored the check. Griffin exhausted her account in The Second National Bank, and the account was closed. Shortly thereafter, The First Bank learned that it had paid an altered check. What are the rights of each of the parties? Discuss.

9. Jason, who has extremely poor vision, went to an automated teller machine (ATM) to withdraw $200 on February 1. Joshua saw that Jason was having great difficulty reading the computer screen and offered to help. Joshua obtained Jason's personal identification number and secretly exchanged one of his old credit cards for Jason's ATM card. Between February 1 and February 15, Joshua

withdrew $1,600 from Jason's account. On February 15, Jason discovered that his ATM card was missing and immediately notified his bank. The bank closed Jason's ATM account on February 16, by which time Joshua had withdrawn another $150. What is Jason's liability, if any, for the unauthorized use of his account?

10. On July 21, Boehmer, a customer of Birmingham Trust, secured a loan from that bank for the principal sum of $5,500 to purchase a boat allegedly being built for him by A.C. Manufacturing Company, Inc. After Boehmer signed a promissory note, Birmingham Trust issued a cashier's check to Boehmer and A.C. Manufacturing Company as payees. The check was given to Boehmer, who then forged A.C. Manufacturing Company's indorsement and deposited the check in his own account at Central Bank. Central Bank credited Boehmer's account and then placed the legend "P.I.G.," meaning "Prior Indorsements Guaranteed," on the check. The check was presented to and paid by Birmingham Trust on July 22. When the loan became delinquent in March of the following year, Birmingham Trust contacted A.C. Manufacturing Company to learn the location of the boat. They were informed that it had never been purchased, and they soon after learned that Boehmer had died on January 24 of that year. Can Birmingham Trust obtain reimbursement from Central Bank under Central's warranty of prior indorsements? Explain.

11. Advanced Alloys, Inc., issued a check in the amount of $2,500 to Sergeant Steel Corporation. The check was presented for payment fourteen months later to the Chase Manhattan Bank, which made payment on the check and charged Advanced Alloy's account. Can Advanced Alloys recover the payment made on the check? Why or why not?

C A S E   P R O B L E M S

12. Laboratory Management deposited into its account at Pulaski Bank a check issued by Fairway Farms in the amount of $150,000. The date of deposit was February 5. Pulaski, the depositary bank, initiated the collection process immediately by forwarding the check to Worthen Bank on the sixth. Worthen sent the check on for collection to M Bank Dallas, and M Bank Dallas, still on February 6, delivered the check to M Bank Fort Worth. That same day, M Bank Fort Worth delivered the check to the Fort Worth Clearinghouse. Because TAB/West Side, the drawee/payor bank, was not a clearinghouse member, it had to rely on TAB/Fort Worth for further transmittal of the check. TASI, a processing center used by both TAB/Forth Worth and TAB/West Side, received the check on the sixth and processed it as a reject item because of insufficient funds. On the seventh, TAB/West Side determined to return the check unpaid. TASI gave M Bank Dallas telephone notice of the return on February 7 but physically misrouted the check. Because of this, M Bank Dallas did not physically receive the check until February 19. However, M Bank notified Worthen by telephone on the fifteenth of the dishonor and return of the check. Worthen received the check on the twenty-first and notified Pulaski by telephone on the twenty-second. Pulaski actually received the check from Worthen on the twenty-third. On February 22 and 23, Laboratory Management's checking account with Pulaski was $46,000. Pulaski did not freeze the account because it considered the return to be too late. The Laboratory Management account was finally frozen on April 30, when it had a balance of $1,400. Pulaski brings this suit against TAB/Fort Worth, TAB/Dallas, and TASI alleging their notice of dishonor was not timely relayed to Pulaski. Explain whether Pulaski is correct in its assertion.

13. On Tuesday, June 11, Siniscalchi issued a $200 check on the drawee, Valley Bank. On Saturday morning, June 15, the check was cashed. This transaction, as well as others taking place on that Saturday morning, was not recorded or processed through the bank's bookkeeping system until Monday, June 17. On that date, Siniscalchi arrived at the bank at 9:00 A.M. and asked to place a stop payment order on the check. A bank employee checked the bank records, which at that time indicated the instrument had not cleared the bank. At 9:45 A.M., she gave him a printed notice confirming his request to stop payment. Siniscalchi sought to recover the $200 paid on the check. Explain whether the stop payment order was effective.

14. Morvarid Kashanchi and her sister, Firoyeh Paydar, held a savings account with Texas Commerce Medical Bank. An unauthorized withdrawal of $4,900 from the account was allegedly made by means of a telephone conversation between some other unidentified individual and a bank employee. Paydar learned of the transfer of funds when she received her bank statement and notified the bank that the withdrawal was unauthorized. The bank, however, declined to recredit the account for the $4,900 transfer. Kashanchi brought an action against the bank, claiming that the bank had violated the Electronic Fund Transfer Act (EFTA). The bank defended by arguing that

the Act did not apply. Is the transaction governed by the EFTA? Explain.

15. Tally held a savings account with American Security Bank. On seven occasions, Tally's personal secretary, who received his bank statements and had custody of his passbook, forged Tally's name on withdrawal slips that she then presented to the bank. The secretary obtained $52,825 in this manner. Three years after the secretary's last fraudulent withdrawal, she confessed to Tally who promptly notified the bank of the issue. Can Tally recover the funds from American Security Bank? Explain.

16. For a period of sixteen months, Great Lakes Higher Education Corp. (Great Lakes), a not-for-profit student loan servicer, issued 224 student loan checks totaling $273,152.88. The checks were drawn against Great Lakes' account at First Wisconsin National Bank of Milwaukee (First Wisconsin). Each of the 224 checks was presented to Austin Bank of Chicago (Austin) without indorsement of the named payee. Austin Bank accepted each check for purposes of collection and without delay forwarded each check to First Wisconsin for that purpose. First Wisconsin paid Austin Bank the face amount of each check even though the indorsement signature of the payee was not on any of the checks. Has Austin Bank breached its warranty to First Wisconsin and Great Lakes due to the absence of proper indorsements? Explain.

17. Bank customer Aliaga Medical Center opened a checking account with Harris Bank. Aliaga issued a $50,000 check, which bore the notation "void after 90 days." More than ninety days after the check was issued, Harris honored the check. Aliaga now seeks reimbursement from Harris, claiming that the notation served as a stop payment order after the ninety days. Who will prevail? Why?

18. Ron Honeycutt was the president, treasurer, and sole stockholder of Sheldon, Inc. (Sheldon), which operated Sheldon's Lounge, a bar located in Baltimore City. Christine Honeycutt was, at one time, Ron Honeycutt's wife and held the position of vice president and secretary of Sheldon. Ron Honeycutt and Christine Honeycutt opened a business checking account with Maryland National Bank in the name of Sheldon's Lounge. At that time, Ron Honeycutt and Christine Honeycutt executed a signature card for the account, on which they checked off the box requiring only one signature to transact any business. Ron Honeycutt and Christine Honeycutt were the authorized signatories on the account.

Five days after Ron Honeycutt died, Christine Honeycutt withdrew funds in the amount of $13,066.48 from Sheldon's account. At the time of withdrawal, an employee of the bank retrieved and reviewed the signature card on file with the bank to verify Christine Honeycutt's authority to direct and conduct transactions on Sheldon's account. The bank did not inquire as to Christine Honeycutt's status with respect to Sheldon, nor did it inquire of anyone at Sheldon as to her status. At the time, the bank was unaware that Ron Honeycutt had died. A month later, Sheldon commenced an action against Christine Honeycutt and the bank, asserting claims for conversion, breach of contract, and negligence for permitting the allegedly unauthorized withdrawal. Explain whether the bank is liable.

TAKING SIDES

Mary Mansi claims that eighteen checks on her account contain forgeries but were nevertheless paid by her bank, Sterling National Bank. The checks bore signatures that, according to Mansi's handwriting expert, were apparently "written by another person who attempted to simulate her signature" and thus were not considered obvious forgeries. Sterling National Bank acknowledged that it did honor those eighteen checks, but nine of them were returned to the plaintiff more than one year prior to this action. In addition, Mansi had received bank statements and failed to examine them.

a. What are the arguments that the bank is liable to Mansi for wrongfully paying the checks?

b. What are the arguments that the bank is not liable to Mansi for paying the checks?

c. Who should prevail? Why?

Unincorporated Business Associations

CH 30 FORMATION AND INTERNAL
RELATIONS OF GENERAL
PARTNERSHIPS

CH 31 OPERATION AND DISSOLUTION
OF GENERAL PARTNERSHIPS

CH 32 LIMITED PARTNERSHIPS AND
LIMITED LIABILITY COMPANIES

Formation and Internal Relations of General Partnerships

CHAPTER OUTCOMES

After reading and studying this chapter, you should be able to:

- Explain the various types of business associations and the factors relevant to deciding which form to use.

- Explain the differences between a legal entity and a legal aggregate as well as those purposes for which a partnership is treated as a legal entity and those purposes for which it is treated as a legal aggregate.

- Distinguish between a partner's rights in specific partnership property and a partner's interest in the partnership.

- Explain the duties owed by a partner to her copartners.

- Describe the rights of partners.

A business enterprise may be operated or conducted as a sole proprietorship, an unincorporated business association (such as a general partnership, a limited partnership, a limited liability company, or a limited liability partnership), or a corporation. The choice of the most appropriate form cannot be determined in a general way but depends on the particular circumstances of the owners. We begin this chapter with a brief overview of the various types of business associations and the factors that are relevant to deciding which form to use. The rest of this chapter and the next chapter examine general partnerships. *Chapter 32* covers other types of unincorporated business associations. *Part 7* (*Chapters 33* through *36*) addresses corporations.

CHOOSING A BUSINESS ASSOCIATION

The owners of a business determine the form of business unit they wish to use based upon their specific circumstances. In the United States, the approximate relative proportions of the types of business entities are as follows: 73 percent are sole proprietorships, 16 percent are corporations, and 11 percent are unincorporated business associations. The approximate relative proportions of the types of unincorporated business associations are as follows: 67 percent are limited liability companies, 17 percent are general partnerships, 12 percent are limited partnerships, and 5 percent limited liability partnerships.

Unincorporated business associations are common in a number of areas. General partnerships, for example, are used

frequently in finance, insurance, accounting, real estate, law, and other service-related fields. Joint ventures have enjoyed popularity among major corporations planning to engage in cooperative research; in the exploitation of land and mineral rights; in the development, promotion, and sale of patents, trade names, and copyrights; and in manufacturing operations in foreign countries. Limited partnerships have been widely used for enterprises such as real estate investment and development, motion picture and theater productions, oil and gas ventures, and equipment leasing. All the States have authorized the formation of limited liability companies (LLC). This form of business organization has appealed to a rapidly growing number of businesses, including real estate ventures, high-technology enterprises, businesses in which transactions involve foreign investors, professional organizations, corporate joint ventures, start-up businesses, and venture capital projects. The number of limited liability companies now greatly exceeds the number of all types of partnerships combined.

First to be discussed are the most important factors to consider in choosing a form of business association. This is followed by a brief description of the various forms of business associations and how they differ with respect to these factors.

♦ SEE FIGURE 30-1: *General Partnership, Limited Partnership, Limited Liability Company, and Corporation*

Practical Advice
You should give considerable thought to choosing the best form of business association for you and your co-owners.

FIGURE 30-1	General Partnership, Limited Partnership, Limited Liability Company, and Corporation			
	General Partnership	**Limited Partnership**	**Limited Liability Company**	**Corporation**
Transferability	Financial interest may be assigned; Membership requires consent of all partners	Financial interest may be assigned, and assignee may become limited partner if all partners consent	Financial interest may be assigned; Membership requires consent of all members	Freely transferable unless shareholders agree otherwise
Liability	Partners have unlimited liability*	General partners have unlimited liability**; Limited partners have limited liability	All members have limited liability	Shareholders have limited liability
Control	By all partners	By general partners, not limited partners	By all members	By board of directors elected by shareholders
Continuity	RUPA: Usually unaffected by death, bankruptcy, or—in a term partnership— withdrawal of partner; UPA: Dissolved by death, bankruptcy, or withdrawal of partner	Dissolved by death, bankruptcy, or withdrawal of general partner; Unaffected by death, bankruptcy, or withdrawal of limited partner	In many States, death, bankruptcy, or withdrawal of member does not dissolve LLC	Unaffected by death, bankruptcy, or withdrawal of shareholder
Taxation	May elect that only partners are taxed	May elect that only partners are taxed	May elect that only members are taxed	Corporation taxed unless Subchapter S applies; Shareholders taxed

Note: RUPA = Revised Uniform Partnership Act; UPA = Uniform Partnership Act.

*In an LLP, the partners' liability is limited for some or all of the partnership's obligations.

**In an LLLP, the partners' liability is limited for some or all of the partnership's obligations.

30-1 Factors Affecting the Choice

In choosing the form in which to conduct business, the owners should consider a number of factors, including ease of formation, Federal and State income tax laws, external liability, management and control, transferability of ownership interests, and continuity. The relative importance of each factor will vary with the specific needs and objectives of the owners. In addition, for multinational enterprises (entities that transact business across national boundaries), a number of considerations determine which form of business organization is best to use in conducting international transactions. These factors include financing, tax consequences, legal restrictions imposed by the host country, and the degree to which the multinational enterprise wishes to control the business. Multinational enterprises are discussed in *Chapter 46*.

30-1a EASE OF FORMATION

Business associations differ as to the formalities and expenses of formation. Some can be created with no formality, while others require the filing of documents with the State.

30-1b TAXATION

Most business entities are not considered to be separate *taxable* entities, and taxation is on a "pass-through" basis. In these cases, the income of the business is conclusively presumed to have been distributed to the owners, who must pay taxes on that income. Losses receive comparable treatment and can be used to offset some of the owners' income. Passthrough tax treatment results in only the owners being taxed and thus avoids double taxation on the business income. In the United States, approximately 95 percent of all business entities are taxed on a pass-through basis.

In contrast, some business entities, most significantly certain corporations, are considered separate tax entities and are taxed directly. When such an entity distributes income to the owners, that income is taxed separately to the recipients. Thus, these funds are taxed twice: once to the entity and once to the owners. Unincorporated business entities can elect whether or not to be taxed as a separate entity. All businesses that have publicly traded ownership interests must be taxed as a separate entity.

30-1c EXTERNAL LIABILITY

External liability arises in a variety of ways, but the crucial and most commonly occurring are tort and contract liability. Owners of some business forms have unlimited liability for all of the obligations of the business. Thus, if the business does not have sufficient funds to pay its debts, every owner has personal liability to the creditors for the full amount of the debts. In brief, owners of interests in businesses with unlimited liability place their entire estates at risk. In some types of entities, the owners have unlimited liability for some but not all of the entity's obligations. Finally, in some types of business associations, the owners enjoy limited liability, which means their liability is limited to the extent of their capital contribution. It should be noted, however, that creditors often require that the owners of small businesses personally guarantee loans made to the businesses. Moreover, an owner of *any* type of business does not have limited liability for his own tortious conduct; the person is liable as an individual tortfeasor.

30-1d MANAGEMENT AND CONTROL

In some entities, the owners can fully share in the control of the business. In other types of business associations, the owners are restricted as to their right to take part in control.

30-1e TRANSFERABILITY

An ownership interest in a business consists of a financial interest, which is the right to share in the profits of the business, and a management interest, which is the right to participate in control of the business. In some types of business associations, the owners may freely transfer their financial interest but may not transfer their management interest without the consent of all of the other owners. In other types of business associations, the entire ownership interest is freely transferable.

30-1f CONTINUITY

Some business associations have low continuity, which means that the death, bankruptcy, or withdrawal of an owner results in the dissolution of the association. Other types have high continuity and are not affected by the death, bankruptcy, or withdrawal of owners.

30-2 Forms of Business Associations

This section contains a brief description of the various types of business associations and how they differ with respect to the factors just discussed. In addition, general partnerships, limited partnerships, LLCs, limited liability partnerships (LLPs), and corporations are discussed more extensively in this and the next part of the book.

30-2a SOLE PROPRIETORSHIP

A sole proprietorship is an unincorporated business consisting of one person who owns and completely controls the business. It is formed without any formality, and no documents need be filed. Moreover, if one person conducts a business and does not file with the State to form an LLC or a corporation, a sole proprietorship will result by default. A sole proprietorship is not a separate taxable entity, and only the sole proprietor is taxed. Sole proprietors have unlimited liability for the sole proprietorship's debts. The sole proprietor's interest in the business is freely transferable. The death of a sole proprietor dissolves the sole proprietorship.

30-2b GENERAL PARTNERSHIP

A general partnership is an unincorporated business association consisting of two or more persons who co-own a business for profit. It is formed without any formality, and no documents need be filed. Thus, if two or more people conduct a business and do not file with the State to form another type of business organization, a general partnership will result by default. A partnership may elect not to be a separate taxable entity, in which case only the partners are taxed. Partners have unlimited liability for the partnership's debts. Each partner has an equal right to control of the partnership. Partners may assign their financial interest in the partnership, but the assignee may become a member of the partnership only if all of the members consent. Under the Revised Partnership Act, the death or bankruptcy of a partner usually does not dissolve a partnership; the same is also true in a term partnership for the withdrawal of a partner.

30-2c JOINT VENTURE

A joint venture is an unincorporated business association composed of persons who combine their property, money, efforts, skill, and knowledge for the purpose of carrying out a particular business enterprise for profit. Usually, although not always, it is of short duration. A joint venture, therefore, differs from a partnership, which is formed to carry on a business over a considerable or indefinite period of time. Nonetheless, except for a few differences, the law of partnerships generally governs a joint venture. An example of a joint venture is a securities underwriting syndicate or a syndicate formed to acquire a certain tract of land for subdivision and resale. Other common examples involve joint research conducted by corporations, the exploitation of mineral rights, and manufacturing operations in foreign countries.

30-2d LIMITED PARTNERSHIP

A limited partnership is an unincorporated business association consisting of at least one general partner and at least one limited partner. It is formed by filing a certificate of limited partnership with the State. A limited partnership may elect not to be a separate taxable entity, in which case only the partners are taxed. Publicly traded limited partnerships, however, are subject to corporate income taxation. General partners have unlimited liability for the partnership's debts; limited partners have limited liability. Each general partner has an equal right to control of the partnership; limited partners have no right to participate in control. Partners may assign their financial interest in the partnership, but the assignee may become a limited partner only if all of the members consent. The death, bankruptcy, or withdrawal of a general partner dissolves a limited partnership; the limited partners have neither the right nor the power to dissolve the limited partnership.

30-2e LIMITED LIABILITY COMPANY

An LLC is an unincorporated business association that provides limited liability to all of its owners (members) and permits all of its members to participate in management of the business. It may elect not to be a separate taxable entity, in which case only the members are taxed. As already noted, publicly traded LLCs are subject to corporate income taxation. If an LLC has only one member, then it will be taxed as a sole proprietorship, unless separate entity tax treatment is elected. Thus, the LLC provides many of the advantages of a general partnership plus limited liability for all its members. Its benefits outweigh those of a limited partnership in that all members of an LLC not only enjoy limited liability but also may participate in management and control of the business. In most States, members may assign their financial interest in the LLC, but the assignee may become a member of the LLC only if all of the members consent or the LLC's operating agreement provides otherwise. In some States, the death, bankruptcy, or withdrawal of a member dissolves an LLC; in others, they do not. Every State has adopted an LLC statute.

30-2f LIMITED LIABILITY PARTNERSHIP

A registered LLP is a general partnership that, by making the statutorily required filing, limits the liability of its partners for some or all of the partnership's obligations. To become an LLP, a general partnership must file with the State an application containing specified information. All of the States have enacted LLP statutes. Except for the filing requirements and the partners' liability shield, the law governing LLPs is identical to the law governing general partnerships.

30-2g LIMITED LIABILITY LIMITED PARTNERSHIP

A limited liability limited partnership (LLLP) is a limited partnership in which the liability of the general partners has been limited to the same extent as in an LLP. A growing number of States authorize LLLPs, enabling the general partners in an LLLP to obtain the same degree of liability limitation that general partners can achieve in LLPs. Where available, a limited partnership may register as an LLLP without having to form a new organization, as would be the case in converting to an LLC.

30-2h CORPORATION

A corporation is a legal entity separate and distinct from its owners. It is formed by filing its articles of incorporation with the chosen State of incorporation. Some corporations are taxed as separate entities, and shareholders also are taxed on corporate earnings that are distributed to them. Most corporations, however, are eligible to elect to be taxed as Subchapter S corporations, which results in only the shareholders being taxed and thus avoids double taxation on corporate income. More than 70 percent of all corporations are taxed as Subchapter S corporations. The shareholders have limited liability for the corporation's obligations. The board of directors elected by the shareholders manages the corporation. Shares in a corporation are freely transferable. The death, bankruptcy, or withdrawal of a shareholder does not dissolve the corporation.

30-2i BUSINESS TRUSTS

The business trust, sometimes called a Massachusetts trust, was devised to avoid the burdens of corporate regulation, particularly the formerly widespread prohibition denying to corporations the power to own and deal in real estate. The business trust is used in the twenty-first century primarily for asset securitization ventures in which income-generating assets, such as mortgages, are pooled in a trust. Like an ordinary trust between natural persons, a business trust may be created by a voluntary agreement without any authorization or consent of the State. A business trust has three distinguishing characteristics: (1) the trust estate is devoted to the conduct of a business; (2) by the terms of the agreement, each beneficiary is entitled to a certificate evidencing his ownership of a beneficial interest in the trust, which he is free to sell or otherwise transfer; and (3) the trustees have the exclusive right to manage and control the business free from control of the beneficiaries. If the third condition is not met, the trust may fail; the beneficiaries, by participating in control, would become personally liable as partners for the obligations of the business.

The trustees are personally liable for the debts of the business unless, in entering into contractual relations with others, it is expressly stated or definitely understood between the parties that the obligation is incurred solely upon the responsibility of the trust estate. To escape personal liability on the contractual obligations of the business, the trustee must obtain the agreement or consent of the other contracting party to look solely to the assets of the trust. The personal liability of the trustees for their own torts or the torts of their agents and servants employed in the operation of the business stands on a different footing.

Although this liability cannot be avoided, the risk involved may be reduced substantially or eliminated altogether by insurance. In most jurisdictions, the beneficiaries of a business trust have no liability for obligations of the business trust.

FORMATION OF GENERAL PARTNERSHIPS

The form of business association known as partnership can be traced to ancient Babylonia, classical Greece, and the Roman Empire. It was also used in Europe and England during the Middle Ages. Eventually the English common law recognized partnerships. In the nineteenth century, partnerships were widely used in England and the United States, and the common law of partnership developed considerably during this period.

Partnerships are important in that they allow individuals with different expertise, backgrounds, resources, and interests to form a more competitive enterprise by combining their various skills. This part of the chapter covers the nature of general partnerships and how they are formed. It should be recalled that except for the filing requirements and the partners' liability shield, the law governing LLPs is identical to the law governing general partnerships. LLPs are discussed more fully in *Chapter 32*.

30-3 Nature of Partnership

In 1914, the Uniform Law Commission (ULC), which is also known as the National Conference of Commissioners on Uniform State Laws, promulgated the Uniform Partnership Act (UPA). Since then, it had been adopted in all States (except Louisiana) as well as by the District of Columbia, the Virgin Islands, and Guam.

In August 1986, the ULC and the UPA Revision Subcommittee of the Committee on Partnerships and Unincorporated Business Organizations of the American Bar Association's Section of Corporation, Banking, and Business Law decided to undertake a complete revision of the UPA. The revision was approved in 1997 and was amended in 2011 and 2013 as part of the Harmonization of Business Entity Acts project. These amendments harmonize the language in the 1997 Revised Act with the language of similar provisions in the other uniform unincorporated entity acts and make additional updates. At least forty-one States have adopted the 1997 Revised Act.

This chapter discusses the 1997 Revised Uniform Partnership Act, or RUPA. Where the RUPA has made significant changes, the original 1914 UPA also is discussed. (References to provisions of the RUPA state the section number only; references to the original UPA include the "UPA" designation.) The chapter summary reflects the RUPA.

Though fairly comprehensive, the RUPA and UPA do not cover all legal issues concerning partnerships. Accordingly, both the RUPA (Section 104) and the UPA (Section 5) provide that unless displaced by particular provisions of the Partnership Act, the principles of law and equity supplement the Partnership Act.

30-3a DEFINITION

The RUPA defines a **partnership** as "an association of two or more persons to carry on as co-owners a business for profit." Section 101(6). The RUPA broadly defines "person" to include "individuals, partnerships, corporations, joint ventures, business trusts, estates, trusts, and any other legal or commercial entity." Section 101(10). The comments indicate that this definition would include an LLC. Also defined by Section 101, a business includes every trade, occupation, and profession. The UPA has similar definitions. UPA Sections 2 and 6.

30-3b ENTITY THEORY

A **legal entity** is a unit capable of possessing legal rights and of being subject to legal duties. A legal entity may acquire, own, and dispose of property. It may enter into contracts, commit wrongs, sue, and be sued. For example, each business corporation is a legal entity having a legal existence separate from that of its shareholders.

A partnership was regarded by the common law as a legal aggregate, a group of individuals having no legal existence apart from that of its members. The Revised Act has greatly increased the extent to which partnerships are treated as entities. It applies aggregate treatment to very few aspects of partnerships, the most significant of which is that partners still have unlimited liability for the partnership's obligations. The UPA treats partnerships as legal entities for some purposes and as aggregates for others.

PARTNERSHIP AS A LEGAL ENTITY The RUPA Section 201 states: "A partnership is an entity distinct from its partners." The Revised Act embraces the entity treatment of partnerships, particularly in matters concerning title to partnership property, legal actions by and against the partnership, and continuity of existence. Examples of entity treatment include the following: (1) The assets of the firm are treated as those of the business and are considered to be distinct from the individual assets of the members. Section 203. (2) A partner is accountable as a fiduciary to the partnership. Section 404. (3) Every partner is considered an agent of the partnership. Section 301. (4) A partnership may sue and be sued in the name of the partnership. Section 307.

PARTNERSHIP AS A LEGAL AGGREGATE The Revised Act has retained the aggregate characteristic of a partner's unlimited liability for partnership obligations, unless the partnership has filed a statement of qualification to become an LLP. Section 306.

Thus, if Meg and Mike enter into a partnership that becomes insolvent, as does Meg, Mike is fully liable for the partnership's debts. Likewise, although a partner's interest in the partnership may be assigned, the assignee does not become a partner without the consent of all the partners. Sections 401(i), 502. Moreover, a partner's dissociation results in dissolution, although only in limited circumstances. Section 801.

Under the UPA, because a partnership is considered an aggregate for some purposes, it can neither sue nor be sued in the firm name unless a statute specifically allows such an action. In addition, a partnership generally lacks continuity of existence: whenever any partner ceases to be associated with the partnership, it is dissolved. UPA Section 29.

30-4 Formation of a Partnership

RUPA Section 202 provides that the association of two or more persons to carry on as co-owners a business for profit forms a partnership, whether or not the parties intend to form a partnership. The formation of a partnership is relatively simple and may be done consciously or unconsciously. A partnership may result from an oral or written agreement between the parties; from an informal arrangement; or from the conduct of the parties, who become partners by associating themselves in a business as co-owners. Consequently, if two or more individuals share the control and profits of a business, the law may deem them partners without regard to how they themselves characterize their relationship. Thus, associates frequently discover, to their chagrin, that they have inadvertently formed a partnership and have thereby subjected themselves to the duties and liabilities of partners. The legal existence of the relationship depends merely upon the parties' explicit or implicit agreement and their association in business as co-owners.

Practical Advice

Be careful that you do not unwittingly enter into a partnership; doing so will greatly increase your risk of personal liability.

30-4a PARTNERSHIP AGREEMENT

The RUPA defines a "partnership agreement" as "the agreement, whether written, oral, or implied, among the partners concerning the partnership, including amendments to the partnership agreement." Section 101(7). This definition does not include other agreements between some or all of the partners, such as a lease or a loan agreement.

Except as otherwise provided by the RUPA, the partnership agreement governs relations among the partners and between the partners and the partnership. Section 103. Thus, the RUPA gives almost total freedom to the partners to provide whatever provisions they agree upon in their partnership agreement.

In essence, RUPA is primarily a set of "default rules" that apply only when the partnership agreement does not address the issue. Nevertheless, the RUPA makes some duties mandatory; these cannot be waived or varied by the partnership agreement. Section 103(b).

To render their understanding more clear, definite, and complete, partners are advised, though not usually required, to put their partnership agreement in writing. A partnership agreement can provide almost any conceivable arrangement of capital investment, control sharing, and profit distribution that the partners desire. Unless the agreement provides otherwise, the partners may amend it only by unanimous consent. Any partnership agreement should include the following:

1. The firm name and the identity of the partners;
2. The nature and scope of the partnership business;
3. The duration of the partnership;
4. The capital contributions of each partner;
5. The division of profits and sharing of losses;
6. The managerial duties of each partner;
7. A provision for salaries, if desired;
8. Restrictions, if any, upon the authority of particular partners to bind the firm;
9. Any desired variations from the partnership statute's default provisions governing dissolution; and
10. A statement of the method or formula for determining the value of a partner's interest in the partnership.

STATUTE OF FRAUDS   Because the statute of frauds does not apply expressly to a contract for the formation of a partnership, usually no writing is required to create the relationship. A contract to form a partnership to continue for a period longer than one year is within the statute, however, as is a contract for the transfer of an interest in real estate to or by a partnership; consequently, both of these contracts require a writing in order to be enforceable.

FIRM NAME   In the interest of acquiring and retaining goodwill, a partnership should have a firm name. Although the name selected by the partners may not be identical or deceptively similar to the name of any other existing business concern, it may be the name of the partners or of any one of them, or the partners may decide to operate the business under a fictitious or assumed name, such as "Peachtree Restaurant," "Globe Theater," or "Paradise Laundry." A partnership may not use a name that would be likely to indicate to the public that it is a corporation. Nearly all of the States have enacted statutes that require any person or persons conducting business under an assumed or fictitious name to file in a designated public office a certificate setting forth the name under which the business is conducted and the real names and addresses of all persons conducting the business as partners or proprietors.

> ## Practical Advice
>
> *Partners should have a comprehensive written partnership agreement; doing so brings about a clearer and more reliable understanding of their respective rights and obligations in their relations as partners.*

30-4b TESTS OF PARTNERSHIP EXISTENCE

Partnerships can be formed without the slightest formality. Consequently, it is important that the law establish a test for determining whether or not a partnership has been formed. Two situations most often require this determination. The most common involves a creditor who has dealt only with one person but who wishes to hold another liable as well by asserting that the two were partners. Less frequently, a person seeks to share profits earned and property held by another by claiming that they are partners.

As mentioned, Section 202 of the UPA provides the operative rule for formation of a partnership: an association of two or more persons to carry on as co-owners a business for profit. Thus, three components are essential to the existence of a partnership: (1) an association of two or more persons, (2) conducting a business for profit, (3) which they co-own.

♦ **SEE FIGURE 30-2:** *Tests for Existence of a Partnership*

ASSOCIATION A partnership must consist of two or more persons who have agreed to become partners. Any natural person having *full capacity* may enter into a partnership. A corporation

is defined as a "person" by Section 101 of the RUPA and is, therefore, legally capable of entering into a partnership in those States whose incorporation statutes authorize a corporation to do so. Furthermore, as noted, a partnership, joint venture, business trust, estate, trust, and any other legal or commercial entity may be a member of a partnership. Section 101.

BUSINESS FOR PROFIT The RUPA provides that co-ownership does not in itself establish a partnership, even if the co-owners share profits made by the use of the property. Section 202(c). For a partnership to exist, there must be co-ownership of a business. Thus, passive co-ownership of property by itself, as distinguished from the carrying on of a business, does not establish a partnership. Moreover, to be a partnership, the business carried on by the association of two or more persons must be "for profit." This requirement excludes unincorporated nonprofit organizations from being partnerships. State common law and statutes govern such unincorporated nonprofit organizations. These laws, however, generally do not address the issues facing nonprofit associations in a systematic or integrated fashion. Consequently, in 1996, the ULC promulgated a Uniform Unincorporated Nonprofit Association Act (UUNAA) to reform the common law concerning unincorporated nonprofit associations in a limited number of major issues, including ownership of property, authority to sue and be sued, and the contract and tort liability of officers and members of the association. At least twelve States adopted the Act. In 2008, the Revised Uniform Unincorporated Nonprofit Association Act (RUUNAA)—a comprehensive revision of the UUNAA—was promulgated.

FIGURE 30-2   **Tests for Existence of a Partnership**

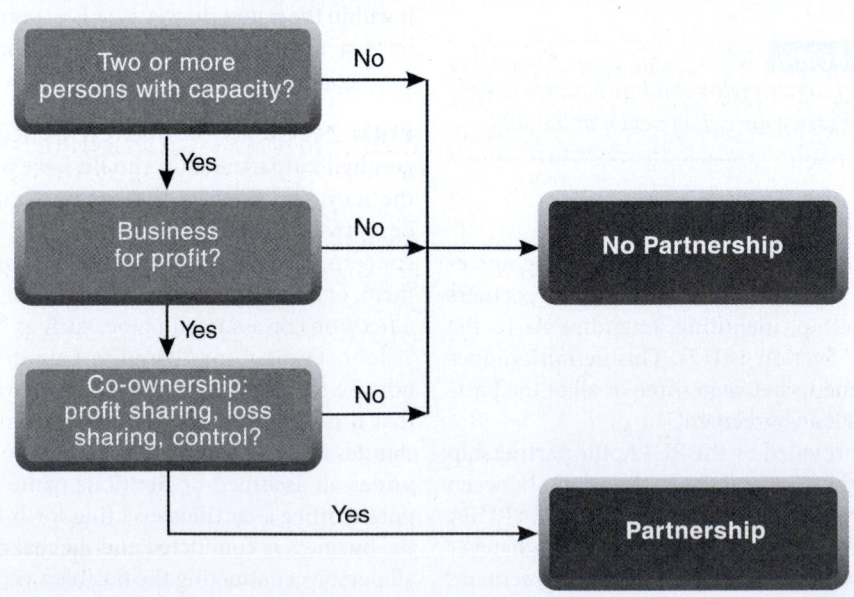

Atleast five States have adopted the 2008 RUUNAA. Technical amendments were made in 2011 to harmonize the language of the provisions of the 2008 RUUNAA with similar provisions in the other uniform unincorporated entity acts.

Nor does a partnership exist in situations in which persons associate for mutual financial gain on a temporary or limited basis involving a single transaction or a few isolated transactions: such persons are not engaged in the continuous series of commercial activities necessary to constitute a business. Co-ownership of the means or instrumentality of accomplishing a single business transaction or a limited series of transactions may result in a joint venture but not in a general partnership.

For example, Katherine and Edith have joint ownership of shares of the capital stock of a corporation, have a joint bank account, and have inherited or purchased real estate as joint tenants or tenants in common. They share the dividends paid on the stock, the interest on the bank account, and the net proceeds from the sale or lease of the real estate. Nevertheless, Katherine and Edith are not partners. Although they are co-owners and share profits, they are not engaged in carrying on a business; hence, no partnership exists. On the other hand, if Katherine and Edith continually bought and sold real estate over a period of time and conducted a business of trading in real estate, a partnership relation would exist between them, regardless of whether they considered themselves partners or not.

To illustrate further, Alec, Laura, and Shirley each inherit an undivided one-third interest in a hotel and, instead of selling the property, decide by an informal agreement to continue operating the hotel. The operation of a hotel is a business; as co-owners of a hotel business, Alec, Laura, and Shirley are partners and are subject to all of the rights, duties, and incidents arising from the partnership relation.

Co-Ownership Although the co-ownership of *property* used in a business is a condition neither necessary nor sufficient for the existence of a partnership, the co-ownership of a *business* is essential. In identifying business co-ownership, the two most important factors are the sharing of profits and the right to manage and control the business.

A person who receives a share of the profits from a business is presumed to be a partner in the business. This means that persons who share profits are deemed to be partners unless they can prove otherwise. Section 202(c)(3) of the RUPA, however, provides that the existence of a partnership relation shall not be presumed where such profits were received in payment:

1. of a debt, by installments or otherwise;
2. for services as an independent contractor or of wages or other compensation to an employee;
3. of rent;
4. of an annuity or other retirement or health benefit to a beneficiary, representative, or designee of a deceased or retired partner;
5. of interest or other charge on a loan, even if the amount of payment varies with the profits of the business; or
6. for the sale of the goodwill of a business or other property by installments or otherwise.

These transactions do not give rise to a presumption that the party is a partner because the law assumes that the creditor, employee, landlord, or other recipient of such profits is unlikely to be a co-owner. It is possible, nonetheless, to establish that such a person is a partner by proof of other facts and circumstances, such as the sharing of control.

The sharing of *gross returns*, in contrast to profits, does *not* of itself establish a partnership. Section 202(c)(2). This is so whether or not the persons sharing the gross returns have a joint or common right or interest in property from which the returns are derived. Thus, two brokers who share commissions are not necessarily partners, or even presumed to be. Similarly, an author who receives royalties (a share of gross receipts from the sales of a book) is not a partner with her publisher.

By itself, evidence as to participation in the *management* or **control** of a business is not conclusive proof of a partnership relation, but it is persuasive. Limited voice in the management and control of a business may be accorded to an employee, a landlord, or a creditor. On the other hand, an actual partner may choose to take no active part in the affairs of the firm and may, by agreement with his copartners, forgo all right to exercise any control over the ordinary affairs of the business. In any event, the right to participate in control is an important factor considered by the courts in conjunction with other factors, particularly with profit sharing.

♦ *See Case 30-1*

Practical Advice

If you receive a share of a partnership's profits in a capacity other than a partner, be sure to document your actual relationship and refrain from exercising such control that would be considered that of a partner or from holding yourself out as a partner.

30-4c PARTNERSHIP CAPITAL AND PROPERTY

The total money and property that the partners contribute and dedicate to use in the enterprise is the partnership capital. Partnership capital represents the partners' equity in the partnership. No minimum amount of capitalization is necessary before a partnership may commence business.

Partnership property is property acquired by a partnership. Section 203. Property acquired by the partnership is conclusively deemed to be partnership property. Property becomes partnership property if acquired in the name of the partnership, which includes a transfer to (1) the partnership in its name or (2) one or more partners in their capacity as partners in the partnership, if the name of the partnership is indicated in the instrument transferring title to the property. Section 204. Property also may be partnership property even if it is not acquired in the name of the partnership. Property is partnership property if acquired in the name of one or more of the partners with an indication in the instrument transferring title of either (1) their capacity as partners or (2) the existence of a partnership, even if the name of the partnership is not indicated. Section 204(a)(2).

Even if the instrument transferring title to one or more of the partners does not indicate their capacity as a partner or the existence of a partnership, the property nevertheless may be partnership property. Ultimately, the partners' intention controls whether property belongs to the partnership or to one or more of the partners in their individual capacities. The RUPA sets forth two rebuttable presumptions that apply when the partners have failed to express their intent. First, under Section 204(c), property purchased with partnership funds is presumed to be partnership property, without regard to the name in which title is held. The presumption applies not only when partnership cash or property is used for payment but also when partnership credit is used to obtain financing.

Second, under Section 204(d), property acquired in the name of one or more of the partners, without an indication of their capacity as partners and without use of partnership funds or credit, is presumed to be the partners' separate property, even if used for partnership purposes. In this last case, it is presumed that only the *use* of the property is contributed to the partnership.

As discussed later, who owns the property—an individual partner or the partnership—determines (1) who gets it upon dissolution of the partnership, (2) who shares in any loss or gain upon its sale, (3) who shares in income from it, and (4) who may sell it or transfer it by will.

A question may arise regarding whether property that was owned by a partner before formation of the partnership and was used in the partnership business is a capital contribution and hence an asset of the partnership. For example, a partner who owns a store building may contribute to the partnership the use of the building but not the building itself. The building is, therefore, not partnership property, and the amount of capital contributed by this partner is the reasonable value of the rental of the building.

The fact that legal title to property remains unchanged is not conclusive evidence that such property has not become a partnership asset. The intent of the partners controls the question of who owns the property. Without an express agreement, an intention to consider property as partnership property may be inferred from any of the following facts: (1) the property was improved with partnership funds; (2) the property was carried on the books of the partnership as an asset; (3) taxes, liens, or expenses, such as insurance or repairs, were paid by the partnership; (4) income or proceeds of the property were treated as partnership funds; or (5) the partners declared or admitted the property to be partnership property.

♦ *See Case 30-2*

Practical Advice

Make clear by a written agreement whether property previously owned by one partner but used by the partnership belongs to the partnership or to the partner.

RELATIONSHIPS AMONG PARTNERS

When parties enter into a partnership, the law imposes certain duties upon them and also grants them specific rights. Except as otherwise provided by the RUPA, the partnership agreement governs relations among the partners and between the partners and the partnership. Section 103. Thus, the RUPA gives almost total freedom to the partners to provide whatever provisions they agree upon in their partnership agreement. Nevertheless, the RUPA makes some duties mandatory; these cannot be waived or varied by the partnership agreement. Section 103(b).

Practical Advice

When forming a partnership, carefully consider which, if any, duties you wish to vary by agreement.

30-5 Duties Among Partners

The principal legal duties imposed upon partners in their relations with one another are (1) the fiduciary duty (the duty of loyalty), (2) the duty of obedience, and (3) the duty of care. In addition, each partner has a duty to inform his copartners and a duty to account to the partnership. (These additional duties are discussed later, in a section covering the rights of partners.) All of these duties correspond precisely with those duties owed by an agent to his principal and reflect the fact that much of the law of partnership is the law of agency.

30-5a FIDUCIARY DUTY

The fiduciary duty in a partnership is the duty of utmost loyalty, fairness, and good faith owed by partners to each other and to the partnership. The extent of the fiduciary duty or duty of loyalty has been most eloquently expressed by the often-quoted words of Judge (later Justice) Cardozo:

> Joint adventurers, like copartners, owe to one another, while the enterprise continues, the duty of the *finest loyalty*. Many forms of conduct permissible in a workaday world for those acting at arm's length, are forbidden to those bound by fiduciary ties. A trustee is held to something stricter than the morals of the market place. *Not honesty alone, but the punctilio of an honor the most sensitive, is then the standard of behavior.* As to this there has developed a tradition that is unbending and inveterate. Uncompromising rigidity has been the attitude of courts of equity when petitioned to undermine the rule of undivided loyalty by the "disintegrating erosion" of particular exceptions. Only thus has the level of conduct for fiduciaries been kept at a level higher than that trodden by the crowd. It will not consciously be lowered by any judgment of this court. *Meinhard v. Salmon*, 249 N.Y. 458, 459, 164 N.E. 545, 546 (1928) [emphasis added].

The RUPA's provision regarding the fiduciary duty is both comprehensive and exclusive. Section 404. "In that regard, it is structurally different from the UPA which touches only sparingly on a partner's duty of loyalty and leaves any further development of the fiduciary duties of partners to the common law of agency." Comment 1 to Section 404. The RUPA completely and exclusively states the components of the duty of loyalty by specifying that a partner has a duty not to appropriate partnership benefits without the consent of her partners, to refrain from selfdealing, and to refrain from competing with the partnership. Section 404(b). More specifically, Section 404(b) of the RUPA provides that a partner's duty of loyalty to the partnership and the other partners is limited to the following:

1. to account to the partnership and hold as trustee for it any property, profit, or benefit derived by the partner in the conduct and winding up of the partnership business or derived from a use by the partner of partnership property, including the appropriation of a partnership opportunity;
2. to refrain from dealing with the partnership in the conduct or winding up of the partnership business as, or on behalf of, a party having an interest adverse to the partnership; and
3. to refrain from competing with the partnership in the conduct of the partnership business before the dissolution of the partnership.

In addition, the Revised Act provides that a partner does not violate the duty of loyalty merely because the partner's conduct furthers the partner's own interest. Section 404(e).

For example, a partner committed a breach of fiduciary duty when he retained a secret discount on purchases of petroleum that he obtained through acquisition of a bulk plant, and the partnership was entitled to the entire amount of the discount.

Within the demands of the fiduciary duty, a partner cannot acquire for herself a partnership asset or opportunity without the consent of all the partners. Thus, a partner may not renew a partnership lease in her name alone. A partner cannot, without the permission of her partners, engage in any other business within the scope of the partnership enterprise. Should she participate in a competing or similar business, the disloyal partner not only must surrender any profit she has acquired from such business but also must compensate the existing partnership for any damage it may have suffered as a result of the competition. A partner, however, may enter into any business neither in competition with nor within the scope of the partnership's business. For example, a partner in a law firm may, without violating her fiduciary duty, act as an executor or administrator of an estate. Furthermore, she need not account for her fees in cases in which it cannot be shown that her service in this other capacity impaired her duty to the partnership (e.g., by monopolizing her attention).

The fiduciary duty does *not* extend to the formation of the partnership, when, according to the comments to RUPA Section 404, the parties are really negotiating at arm's length. The duty not to compete terminates upon dissociation, and the dissociated partner may immediately engage in a competitive business, without any further consent. Section 603(b)(2). The partner's other fiduciary duties continue only with regard to matters arising and events occurring before the partner's dissociation, unless the partner participates in winding up the partnership's business. Section 603(b)(3). Thus, upon a partner's dissociation, a partner may appropriate to his own benefit any *new* business opportunity coming to his attention after dissociation, even if the partnership continues, and a partner may deal with the partnership as an adversary with respect to *new* matters or events. A dissociated partner is not, however, free to use confidential partnership information after dissociation.

The Revised Act imposes a duty of good faith and fair dealing when a partner discharges duties to the partnership and the other partners under the RUPA or under the partnership agreement and exercises any rights. Section 404(d). The comments to this section state:

> The obligation of good faith and fair dealing is a contract concept, imposed on the partners because of the consensual nature of a partnership.... It is not characterized, in RUPA, as a fiduciary duty arising out of the partners' special relationship. Nor is it a separate and

independent obligation. It is an ancillary obligation that applies whenever a partner discharges a duty or exercises a right under the partnership agreement or the Act.

The partnership agreement may not eliminate the duty of loyalty or the obligation of good faith and fair dealing. However, the partnership agreement may identify specific types or categories of activities that do not violate the duty of loyalty, if not clearly unreasonable. In addition, the other partners may consent to a specific act or transaction that otherwise violates the duty of loyalty, if there has been full disclosure of all material facts regarding the act or transaction as well as the partner's conflict of interest. Similarly, the partnership agreement may prescribe the standards by which the performance of the obligation of good faith and fair dealing is to be measured, if the standards are not manifestly unreasonable. Section 103(b).

The fiduciary duty under the UPA differs in some respects from that of the RUPA. First, the partner's fiduciary duty under the UPA applies to the formation of the partnership. Second, it applies to the winding up of the partnership. The UPA states that every partner must account to the partnership for any benefit he receives and must hold as trustee for it any profits he derives without the consent of the other partners from any transaction connected with the formation, conduct, or liquidation of the partnership or from any use he makes of its property. UPA Section 21. A partner may not prefer himself over the firm, nor may he even deal at arm's length with his partners, to whom his duty is one of undivided and continuous loyalty. The fiduciary duty also applies to the purchase of a partner's interest from another partner. Each partner owes the highest duty of honesty and fair dealing to the other partners, including the obligation to disclose fully and accurately all material facts.

♦ *See Case 30-3*

Practical Advice

As a partner, be sure to make full disclosure of all material facts regarding the partnership and your relationship to your partners.

30-5b DUTY OF OBEDIENCE

A partner owes his partners a duty to act in obedience to the partnership agreement and to any business decisions properly made by the partnership. Any partner who violates this duty is liable individually to his partners for any resulting loss. For example, a partner who, in violation of a specific agreement not to extend credit to relatives, advances money from partnership funds and sells goods on credit to an insolvent relative would be held personally liable to his partners for the unpaid debt.

30-5c DUTY OF CARE

Whereas under the fiduciary duty a partner "is held to something stricter than the morals of the market place," he is held to something less than the skill of the marketplace. Each partner owes the partnership a duty of faithful service to the best of his ability. Nonetheless, he need not possess the degree of knowledge and skill of an ordinary paid agent. Under the Revised Act, a partner's duty of care to the partnership and the other partners in the conduct and winding up of the partnership business is limited to refraining from engaging in grossly negligent or reckless conduct, intentional misconduct, or a knowing violation of law. RUPA Section 404(c). For example, a partner assigned to keep the partnership books uses an overly complicated bookkeeping system and consequently produces numerous mistakes. Because these errors result simply from poor judgment, not an intent to defraud, and are not intended to and do not operate to the personal advantage of the negligent bookkeeping partner, she is *not* liable to her copartners for any resulting loss. The duty of care may not be eliminated entirely by agreement, but the standard may be reasonably reduced. Section 103(b)(4). The standard may be increased by agreement to one of ordinary care or an even higher standard of care. Comment 6 to RUPA Section 103.

30-6 Rights Among Partners

The law provides partners with certain rights, which include (1) their right to use and possess partnership property for partnership purposes, (2) their transferable interest in the partnership, (3) their right to share in distributions (part of their transferable interest), (4) their right to participate in management, (5) their right to choose associates, and (6) their enforcement rights.

30-6a RIGHTS IN SPECIFIC PARTNERSHIP PROPERTY

In adopting the entity theory, the Revised Act abolishes the UPA's concept of tenants in partnership: partnership property is owned by the partnership entity and not by the individual partners. Section 203. Moreover, RUPA Section 501 provides, "A partner is not a co-owner of partnership property and has no interest in partnership property which can be transferred, either voluntarily or involuntarily." A partner may use or possess partnership property only on behalf of the partnership. Section 401(g).

Under the UPA, a partner's ownership interest in any specific item of partnership property is that of a **tenant in partnership**. UPA Section 25. The UPA's tenancy in partnership reaches a similar entity result to the RUPA but states that result in aggregate terms. This type of ownership, which exists only in a partnership, has the following principal characteristics:

1. Each partner has a right equal to that of his copartners to possess partnership property for partnership purposes, but he has no right to possess it for any other purpose without his copartners' consent.

2. A partner may not make an individual assignment of his right in specific partnership property.

3. A partner's interest in specific partnership property is not subject to attachment or execution by his individual creditors. It is subject to attachment or execution only on a claim against the partnership.

4. Upon the death of a partner, his right in specific partnership property vests in the surviving partner or partners. Upon the death of the last surviving partner, his right in such property vests in his legal representative.

30-6b PARTNER'S TRANSFERABLE INTEREST IN THE PARTNERSHIP

Each partner has an **interest in the partnership**, which is defined as "all of a partner's interests in the partnership, including the partner's transferable interest and all management and other rights." Section 101(9). A **partner's transferable interest** is a more limited concept; it is the partner's share of the profits and losses of the partnership and the partner's right to receive distributions. This interest is personal property. Section 502. A partner's transferable interest is discussed here; a partner's management and other rights are discussed later in this chapter.

ASSIGNABILITY A partner may voluntarily transfer, in whole or in part, his transferable interest in the partnership. Section 503. The transfer does not by itself cause the partner's dissociation or a dissolution and winding up of the partnership business. (Dissolution is discussed in *Chapter 31*.) The transferee, however, is not entitled to (1) participate in the management or conduct of the partnership business, (2) require access to any information concerning partnership transactions, or (3) inspect or copy the partnership books or records. She is merely entitled to receive, in accordance with the terms of the assignment, any distributions to which the assigning partner would have been entitled under the partnership agreement before dissolution. After dissolution, the transferee is entitled to receive the net amount that would have been distributed to the transferring partner upon the winding up of the business. Moreover, the assignee may apply for a court-ordered dissolution. Section 801(6). The assigning partner remains a partner with all of a partner's rights and duties other than the transferred interest in distributions.

Under Section 601(4)(ii), however, the other partners by a unanimous vote may expel a partner who has transferred substantially all of his transferable partnership interest, other than as security for a loan. The partner may be expelled, nevertheless, upon *foreclosure* of the security interest.

Under Section 103(a), the partners may agree among themselves to restrict the right to transfer their partnership interests.

CREDITORS' RIGHTS A partner's transferable interest (the right to distributions from the partnership and the right to seek court-ordered dissolution of the partnership) is subject to the claims of that partner's creditors, who may obtain a **charging order** (a type of judicial lien) against the partner's transferable interest. Section 504. On application by a judgment creditor of a partner, a court may charge the transferable interest of the partner to satisfy the judgment. A charging order is also available to the judgment creditor of a *transferee* of a partnership interest. A charging order is the judgment creditor's exclusive remedy against a partner's transferable interest in the partnership. The court may appoint a receiver of the debtor's share of the distributions due or to become due. The court may order a foreclosure of the interest subject to the charging order at any time. The purchaser at the foreclosure sale has the rights of a transferee. At any time before foreclosure, an interest charged may be redeemed by (1) the partner who is the judgment debtor, (2) other partners with nonpartnership property, or (3) other partners with partnership property but only with the consent of all of the remaining partners.

The judgment creditor, the receiver, and the purchaser at foreclosure do not become a partner, and thus none of them is entitled to participate in the partnership's management or to have access to information. Furthermore, neither the charging order nor its sale upon foreclosure causes a dissolution, though the other partners may dissolve the partnership or redeem the charged interest. Section 601(4)(ii) provides that a partner may be expelled by a unanimous vote of the other partners upon foreclosure of a judicial lien charging a partner's interest.

◆ SEE FIGURE 30-3: *Partnership Property Compared with Partner's Interest*

30-6c RIGHT TO SHARE IN DISTRIBUTIONS

A **distribution** is a transfer of money or other partnership property from the partnership to a partner in the partner's capacity as a partner. Section 101(3). Distributions include a division of profits, a return of capital contributions, a repayment of a loan or advance made by a partner to the partnership, and a payment made to compensate a partner for services rendered to the partnership. The RUPA's rules regarding distribution are subject to contrary agreement of the partners. Section 103. A partner has no right to receive, and may not be required to accept, a distribution in kind. Section 402. The RUPA provides that each partner is deemed to have an account that is credited with the partner's contributions and share of the partnership

FIGURE 30-3 Partnership Property Compared with Partner's Interest

| | Partnership Property | | Partner's Interest |
	RUPA	UPA	
Definition	A partner is not a co-owner of partnership property	Tenant in partnership	Share of profits and surplus
Possession	For partnership purposes, not individual ones	For partnership purposes, not individual ones	Intangible, personal property right
Assignability	Partner has *no* interest in partnership property which can be transferred	If all other partners assign their rights in the property	Assignee does not become a partner
Attachment	Only for a claim against the partnership	Only for a claim against the partnership	By a charging order
Inheritance	Partner has *no* interest in partnership property which can be transferred	Goes to surviving partner(s)	Passes to the personal representative of deceased partner

Note: RUPA = Revised Uniform Partnership Act; UPA = Uniform Partnership Act.

profits and charged with distributions to the partner and the partner's share of partnership losses. Section 401.

RIGHT TO SHARE IN PROFITS Because a partnership is an association to carry on a business for profit, each partner is entitled, unless otherwise agreed, to a share of the profits. Absent an agreement to the contrary, however, a partner does not have a right to receive a current distribution of the profits credited to his account, the timing of the distribution of profits being a matter arising in the ordinary course of business to be decided by majority vote of the partners. In the absence of an agreement regarding the division of profits, the partners share the profits *equally*, regardless of the ratio of their financial contributions or the degree of their participation in management. Thus, under this default rule, partners share profits per capita and not in proportion to their capital contributions.

Conversely, each partner is chargeable with a share of any losses the partnership sustains. Section 401(b). A partner, however, is not obligated to contribute to partnership losses before his withdrawal or the liquidation of the partnership, unless the partners agree otherwise. The partners bear losses in a proportion *identical* to that in which they share profits. Section 401(b). The partnership agreement may, however, validly provide for bearing losses in a proportion different from that in which profits are shared.

For example, Alice, Belinda, and Carol form a partnership, with Alice contributing $10,000; Belinda, $20,000; and Carol, $30,000. They could agree that Alice would receive 20 percent of the profits and assume 30 percent of the losses, that Belinda would receive 30 percent of the profits and assume 50 percent of the losses, and that Carol would receive 50 percent of the profits and assume 20 percent of the losses. If their agreement is silent as to the sharing of profits and losses, however, each would have an equal one-third share of both profits and losses.

RIGHT TO RETURN OF CAPITAL Absent an agreement to the contrary, a partner does not have a right to receive a distribution of the capital contributions in his account before his withdrawal or the liquidation of the partnership.

Under the UPA after all the partnership's creditors have been paid, each partner is entitled to repayment of his capital contribution during the winding up of the firm. UPA Section 18(a). Unless otherwise agreed, a partner is not entitled to interest on his capital contribution; however, a delay in the return of his capital contribution entitles the partner to interest at the legal rate from the date when it should have been repaid. UPA Section 18(d).

RIGHT TO INDEMNIFICATION A partner who makes an advance beyond his agreed capital contribution is entitled to reimbursement from the partnership. Section 401(d). An advance is treated as a loan to the partnership that accrues interest. Section 401(e). In addition, the partnership must reimburse a partner for payments made and indemnify a partner for liabilities incurred by the partner in the ordinary course of the business of the partnership or for the protection of the partnership business or property. Section 401(c). Under the Revised Act, a loan from a partner to the partnership is treated the same as loans of a person not a partner, subject to other applicable law, such as fraudulent transfer law, the law of avoidable preferences under the Bankruptcy Act, and general debtor-creditor law. RUPA Section 404(f) and Comment 6.

♦ *See Case 31-4*

Under the UPA, a partner's claim as a creditor of the firm, though subordinate to the claims of nonpartner creditors, is superior to the partners' rights to the return of capital.

Practical Advice

If, as a partner, you advance money to your partnership, make it clear by a written agreement signed by all of the partners that your advance is to be treated as a loan, not as additional capital.

RIGHT TO COMPENSATION The RUPA provides that, unless otherwise agreed, *no* partner is entitled to payment for services performed for the partnership. Section 401(h). Even a partner who works disproportionately harder than the others to conduct the business is entitled to no salary but only to his share of the profits. A partner, however, by agreement among all of the partners, may receive a salary. Moreover, a partner is entitled to reasonable compensation for services rendered in winding up the business of the partnership. Section 401(h).

Practical Advice

If, as a partner, you expect to be compensated for services you render to the partnership, make that understanding clear by a written agreement signed by all of the partners.

30-6d RIGHT TO PARTICIPATE IN MANAGEMENT

Each of the partners, unless otherwise agreed, has *equal* rights in the management and conduct of the partnership business. Section 401(f). The majority governs the actions and decisions of the partnership with respect to matters in the ordinary course of partnership business. Section 401(j). *All* the partners must consent to any act outside the ordinary course of partnership business and to any amendment of the partnership agreement. Section 401(j). In their partnership agreement, the partners may provide for unequal voting rights. For example, Jones, Smith, and Williams form a partnership, agreeing that Jones will have two votes, Smith four votes, and Williams five votes. Large partnerships commonly concentrate most or all management authority in a committee of a few partners or even in just one partner. Classes of partners with different management rights also may be created. This practice is common in accounting and law firms, which may have two classes (e.g., junior and senior partners) or three classes (e.g., junior, senior, and managing partners).

30-6e RIGHT TO CHOOSE ASSOCIATES

No partner may be forced to accept as a partner any person of whom she does not approve. This is partly because of the fiduciary relationship between the partners and partly because each partner has a right to take part in the management of the business, to handle the partnership's

assets for partnership purposes, and to act as an agent of the partnership. An ill-chosen partner, through negligence, poor judgment, or dishonesty, may bring financial loss or ruin to her copartners. Because of this danger and because of the close relationship among the members, partnerships must necessarily be founded on mutual trust and confidence. All this finds expression in the term *delectus personae* (literally, "choice of the person"), which indicates the right one has to choose her partners. This principle is embodied in Section 401(i) of the RUPA, which provides: "A person may become a partner only with the consent of *all* of the partners." [Emphasis added.] It is because of *delectus personae* that a purchaser (assignee) of a partner's interest does not become a partner and is not entitled to participate in management. The partnership agreement may provide, however, for admission of a new partner by a less-than-unanimous vote.

Practical Advice

Consider whether your partnership agreement should permit the admission of partners by a less-than-unanimous vote, recognizing that by doing so you forfeit veto power over new members of the partnership.

30-6f ENFORCEMENT RIGHTS

As discussed, the partnership relationship creates a number of duties and rights among partners. Accordingly, partnership law provides partners and the partnership with the means to enforce these rights and duties.

RIGHT TO INFORMATION AND INSPECTION OF THE BOOKS The RUPA provides that if a partnership maintains books and records, they must be kept at its chief executive office. Section 403. A partnership must provide partners access to its books and records to inspect and copy them during ordinary business hours. Section 403(b). Former partners are given a similar right, although limited to the books and records pertaining to the period during which they were partners. A duly authorized agent on behalf of a partner may also exercise this right. A partnership may impose a reasonable charge, covering the costs of labor and material, for copies of documents furnished. The partnership agreement may not unreasonably restrict a partner's right of access to partnership books and records. Section 103(b)(2).

Each partner and the partnership must affirmatively disclose to a partner, *without demand*, any information concerning the partnership's business and affairs reasonably required for the proper exercise of the partner's rights and duties under the partnership agreement or the Act. Section 403(c)(1). (In addition, under some circumstances, a disclosure duty may arise from the obligation of good faith and fair dealing.) Moreover, on *demand*, each partner and the partnership must furnish to a partner any other information concerning the partnership's business and affairs, except to the extent the demand or the information demanded is unreasonable or otherwise improper under the circumstances. The rights to receive and demand information extend also to the legal representative of a deceased partner. They may, however, be waived or varied by agreement of the partners.

LEGAL ACTION Under the RUPA, a partner may maintain a direct suit against the partnership or another partner for legal or equitable relief, with or without an accounting as to partnership business, to enforce the partner's rights under the partnership agreement and the Revised Act. Section 405(b). Thus, under the RUPA, an accounting is not a prerequisite to the availability of the other remedies a partner may have against the partnership or the other partners. Since general partners are not passive investors, the RUPA does not authorize derivative actions. Reflecting the entity theory of partnership, the RUPA provides that the partnership itself may maintain an action against a partner for any breach of the partnership agreement or for the violation of any duty owed to the partnership, such as a breach of fiduciary duty. Section 405(a).

The UPA grants to each partner the right to an account whenever (1) his copartners wrongfully exclude him from the partnership business or possession of its property, (2) the partnership agreement so provides, (3) a partner makes a profit in violation of his fiduciary duty, or (4) other circumstances render it just and reasonable. UPA Section 22. If a partner does not receive or is dissatisfied with a requested account, she may bring an enforcement action, called an accounting. Designed to produce and evaluate all testimony relevant to the various claims of the partners, an accounting is an equitable proceeding for a comprehensive and effective settlement of partnership affairs.

C H A P T E R   S U M M A R Y

FORMATION OF GENERAL PARTNERSHIPS

NATURE OF PARTNERSHIP	**Definition** an association of two or more persons to carry on as co-owners a business for profit **Entity Theory** • *Partnership as a Legal Entity* an organization having a legal existence separate from that of its members; the Revised Act considers a partnership a legal entity for nearly all purposes • *Partnership as a Legal Aggregate* a group of individuals not having a legal existence separate from that of its members; the Revised Act considers a partnership a legal aggregate for few purposes
FORMATION OF A PARTNERSHIP	**Partnership Agreement** it is preferable, although not usually required, that the partners enter into a written partnership agreement **Tests of Existence** the formation of a partnership requires all of the following: • *Association* two or more persons with legal capacity who agree to become partners • *Business for Profit* • *Co-ownership* includes sharing of profits and control of the business **Partnership Capital** total money and property contributed by the partners for use by the partnership **Partnership Property** sum of all of the partnership's assets, including all property acquired by the partnership

RELATIONSHIPS AMONG PARTNERS

DUTIES AMONG PARTNERS	**Fiduciary Duty** duty of utmost loyalty, fairness, and good faith owed by partners to each other and to the partnership; includes duty not to appropriate partnership opportunities, not to compete, not to have conflicts of interest, and not to reveal confidential information **Duty of Obedience** duty to act in accordance with the partnership agreement and any business decisions properly made by the partners **Duty of Care** duty owed by partners to manage the partnership affairs without gross negligence, reckless conduct, intentional misconduct, or knowing violation of law
RIGHTS AMONG PARTNERS	**Rights in Specific Partnership Property** partners have the right to use and possess partnership property for partnership purposes **Partner's Interest in the Partnership** includes a (1) partner's transferable interest and (2) all management and other rights • *Transferable Interest in Partnership* the partner's share of the profits and losses of the partnership and the partner's right to receive distributions • *Assignability* a partner may sell or assign his transferable interest in the partnership; the new owner becomes entitled to the assigning partner's right to receive distributions but does not become a partner • *Creditors' Rights* a partner's transferable interest is subject to the claims of creditors, who may obtain a charging order (judicial lien) against the partner's transferable interest **Distributions** transfer of partnership property from the partnership to a partner • *Profits* each partner is entitled to an equal share of the profits unless otherwise agreed • *Capital* a partner does not have a right to receive a distribution of the capital contributions in his account before his withdrawal or the liquidation of the partnership • *Indemnification* if a partner makes an advance (loan) to the partnership, he is entitled to repayment of the advance plus interest; a partner is entitled to reimbursement for payments made and indemnification for liabilities incurred by the partner in the ordinary course of the business • *Compensation* unless otherwise agreed, no partner is entitled to payment for services rendered to the partnership **Management** each partner has equal rights in management of the partnership unless otherwise agreed **Choice of Associates** under the doctrine of *delectus personae*, no person can become a member of a partnership without the consent of all of the partners **Enforcement Rights** • *Information* each partner has the right (1) *without demand*, to any information concerning the partnership and reasonably required for the proper exercise of the partner's rights and duties and (2) *on demand*, to any other information concerning the partnership • *Legal Action* a partner may maintain a direct suit against the partnership or another partner for legal or equitable relief to enforce the partner's rights; the partnership itself may maintain an action against a partner for any breach of the partnership agreement or for the violation of any duty owed to the partnership

CASES

Test of the Partnership Existence
RE KEYTRONICS
Supreme Court of Nebraska, 2008
274 Neb. 936, 744 N.W.2d 425

McCormack, J.

[In 1999, King was doing business under the name of "Washco" as a sole proprietorship engaged in selling, installing, and servicing car wash systems and accessories. King offered to his customers the "QuikPay" system, a cashless vending system for car washes that used a memory chip key that interacted with a controller at the car wash. Either a cash value can be placed on the key or the car wash usage recorded on the key is billed monthly. Washco purchased QuikPay systems for resale from Datakey Electronics Inc. (Datakey), but it was becoming unprofitable for Datakey, partly because the keys for QuikPay could only be obtained from an attendant. According to Glen Jennings, president of Datakey, since most car washes are unattended, this reliance on the presence of the car wash owner or employee was limiting the product's market.

As QuikPay's largest distributor, King was aware that QuikPay's limitations made the product unattractive to many of his customers. King contacted Willson, an electronics technician and computer programmer, to see if Willson could develop a combined "key dispenser" and "revalue station" for the QuikPay system that would make the system self-service. King also asked Willson if he would design and install an interface between the QuikPay system and the car wash of one of King's customers. Designing such an interface was beyond King's technical expertise. Willson individually designed and installed at least four specific customer interfaces that allowed King to sell the QuikPay system to those customers, but Willson was never paid for his work.

According to King there was an oral agreement among himself, Willson, and Scott Gardeen (an employee of Datakey who was an original designer of QuikPay) to form a corporation whenever Willson developed the key dispenser-revalue station. The three parties met in the spring of 2002 to discuss the venture in which they would design and build the key dispenser-revalue station and sell it to Datakey. It was agreed that Willson would write the software and do the firmware, hardware, and any other electrical or software work; Gardeen would contribute his knowledge of the system and his contact with Datakey; and King would contribute financial resources and his experience and contacts as QuikPay's largest distributor. Together, Willson, King, and Gardeen came up with the name "Secure Data Systems" for their business. They discussed the

fact that the entity's initials, "SDS," were also the initials of their first names, Scott, Don, and Scott. By the summer, Willson had built a handheld revalue station for a meeting with Jennings. Jennings indicated that if a final, marketable key dispenser-revalue station were developed, Datakey would be interested in a business relationship with Secure Data Systems.

Around October 2002, Datakey decided to discontinue its QuikPay line and referred all of its customers to King for continued support of the system. By the beginning of 2003, King had deliberately separated his QuikPay sales, maintenance, and its future development from his Washco car wash business and had moved all QuikPay business to Secure Data Systems. Around the same time, Willson developed a website for Secure Data Systems with e-mail accounts for King and Willson.

By the spring of 2003, Willson's work for Secure Data Systems consisted primarily of dealing with QuikPay maintenance and repair issues, although he continued to try to finish the key dispenser-revalue station whenever he had time. Willson made changes in the QuikPay software to fix problems that customers wanted fixed.

In May 2003, King and Willson went together to an international car wash convention in Las Vegas, Nevada. King suggested to Willson that he make up Secure Data Systems business cards for King and Willson. The cards presented Willson as "System Designer & Engineer" and King as "Sales." The cards described Secure Data Systems as carrying the "QuikPay Product Line."

In correspondence with clients, King often referred to Willson as the person doing technical work for QuikPay. Willson also sent e-mails communicating directly with Quik-Pay clients on various issues. In an e-mail dated August 12, 2003, Willson described himself as the software and hardware designer with Secure Data Systems and he referred to King as his "partner." In October 2003, King sent an e-mail to a potential customer in which King referred to Willson as "the other half of Secure Data Systems."

Willson estimated that he had put at least 2,000 hours into QuikPay sales and maintenance and in developing the key dispenser-revalue station. When Willson was asked why he invested his time and expertise into QuikPay without any remuneration, he explained, "That was my contribution to the company. I mean that was my piece." Willson contacted a law firm to draw up papers to formalize the partnership.

These papers were never drafted. According to Willson, when he told King he was looking into creating a written agreement for their relationship, King "assured [him] that he was having his attorneys look at it." King and Willson had another meeting around the end of December and agreed to end their relationship and any joint QuikPay or key dispenser-revalue station activities. Approximately two weeks after this meeting, King called Willson and offered to compensate him for the time he had spent in maintaining or repairing QuikPay. Willson refused.

Willson brought an action for winding up and an accounting, alleging formation of a partnership. King denied they had formed a partnership. The trial court found that King and Willson had "pooled resources, money and labor" but found no partnership existed because there was no "specific agreement." Alternatively, the trial court found that because King did not commit his preexisting business to any specifically formed partnership, the scope of the partnership did not encompass any activity garnering profits. Willson appealed the trial court's order.]

This case is governed by the * * * revised Uniform Partnership Act. Section [202(a)] of the Act defines that a partnership is formed by "the association of two or more persons to carry on as co-owners a business for profit" and explains that this is true "whether or not the persons intend to form a partnership." [Citation.]

* * * [W]hether the business of QuikPay maintenance, or even the development of the never-produced key dispenser-revalue station, qualifies as a business "for profit" is not in issue. It is not essential that the business for which the association was formed ever actually be carried on, let alone that it earn a profit. Rather, a business qualifies under the "business for profit" element of [Section 202(a)] so long as the parties intended to carry on a business with the expectation of profits. [Citations.]

* * *

We first consider whether King and Willson formed an association. King correctly points out that inherent to the term "association" is the idea that the relationship between the "two or more persons" be intentional. [Citation.] King argues that no partnership was formed because he never intended to form a partnership relationship with Willson. * * *

But, as [Section 202(a)] explicitly states, the intent necessary to form an association does not refer to the intent to form a partnership per se. There is no requirement that the parties have a "specific agreement" in order to form a partnership. People do not become partners when they attain co-ownership of a business for profit through an involuntary act. [Citation.] But, if the parties' voluntary actions form a relationship in which they carry on as co-owners of a business for profit, then "they may inadvertently create a partnership despite their expressed subjective intention not to do so." [Citation.] Intent, in such cases, is still of prime concern, but it will be ascertained objectively, rather than subjectively, from all the evidence and circumstances. [Citation.]

* * *

In considering the parties' intent to form an association, it is generally considered relevant how the parties characterize their relationship or how they have previously referred to one another. [Citation.] The joint use of a business name is evidence of an association. [Citations.] This is especially true when the business name is composed of the parties' names or initials. [Citations.]

It is undisputed that King and Willson discussed the fact that Secure Data Systems had the initials of Scott, Don, and Scott. Granted, at its inception, Secure Data Systems was an association among three parties focused on the limited task of creating a key dispenser-revalue station. * * * King removed any QuikPay operations from his Washco business. He instead began to conduct all QuikPay business exclusively through Secure Data Systems. Willson was clearly associated with King in that venture.

* * * Business cards were created for King and Willson describing their respective positions in Secure Data Systems. King and Willson went as joint representatives of Secure Data Systems to a Las Vegas carwash convention. King and Willson worked together both in servicing the QuikPay line, assembling and repairing Datakey's old inventory, and developing the key dispenser-revalue station. Various e-mails to customers and to Datakey evidence their joint efforts in this regard. To King and to others, Willson referred to himself and King as partners. Specifically in regard to ventures involving the regular QuikPay system, King referred to Willson as "the other half of Secure Data Systems." We believe the evidence is clear that King and Willson formally associated to develop a key dispenser-revalue station and that further, this association expanded in scope to encompass all QuikPay operations.

* * * King claims that he started selling and maintaining QuikPay by himself and asserts that he maintained full control of that business line. According to King, Willson simply did what King asked him to—apparently for free.

Being "co-owners" of a business for profit does not refer to the co-ownership of property, [RUPA Section 202(c)(3)] but to the co-ownership of the business intended to garner profits. It is co-ownership that distinguishes partnerships from other commercial relationships such as creditor and debtor, employer and employee, franchisor and franchisee, and landlord and tenant. [Citation.] Co-ownership generally addresses whether the parties share the benefits, risks, and management of the enterprise such that (1) they subjectively view themselves as members of the business rather than as outsiders contracting with it and (2) they are in a better position than others dealing with the firm to monitor and obtain information about the business. [Citation.]

The objective indicia of co-ownership are commonly considered to be: (1) profit sharing, (2) control sharing, (3) loss sharing, (4) contribution, and (5) co-ownership of property. [Citation.] The five indicia of co-ownership are only that; they are not all necessary to establish a partnership relationship, and no single indicium of co-ownership is either necessary or sufficient to prove co-ownership. [Citation.]

* * * The record demonstrates that Willson contributed his time and expertise not only to the business of developing the key dispenser-revalue station, but also to the continued operations of the regular QuikPay product line. * * *

The continuing investment of one's labor without pay is generally considered a strong indicator of co-ownership. [Citations.] * * * Valid consideration for an ownership interest in a partnership may take the form of either property, capital, labor, or skill, and the law does not exalt one type of contribution over another. [Citations.]

In this case, Willson contributed his time and expertise without any compensation for approximately 1 year. Conservatively, Willson estimated his contribution as totaling over 2,000 hours. * * * that without Willson's technical assistance, King would have been unable to continue QuikPay's viability after Datakey abandoned the product. That King could have dealt with certain issues by hiring contractors or employees is irrelevant. He chose not to do so—presumably because the promise of the key dispenser-revalue station made a partnership relationship more worthwhile—and saved himself the expense of paying for this labor.

We also find that despite King's protestations to the contrary, the evidence shows that King and Willson shared control over QuikPay business. * * *

* * *

Willson also testified that he had an agreement with King to share profits, although King denies this. Of the five indicia of co-ownership, profit sharing is possibly the most important, and the presence of profit sharing is singled out in [Section 202(c)(3)] as creating a rebuttable presumption of a partnership. [Citations.] However, what is essential to a partnership is not that profits actually be distributed, but, instead, that there be an interest in the profits. [Citations.] Willson's testimony that they agreed to share in the profits of the business is, in light of all the evidence, simply more credible than King's statement that compensation "was never discussed." * * *

We do not find any evidence that King and Willson had an agreement for loss sharing. But we find this of little import, since purported partners, expecting profits, often do not have any explicit understanding regarding loss sharing. [Citation.] Likewise, although King and Willson admittedly do not own any joint property, in an informal relationship, the parties may intend co-ownership of property but fail to attend to the formalities of title. [Citation.] Moreover, in this case, it is unclear that there is much QuikPay "property" at all. * * *

We conclude that the objective, as well as subjective, indicia are sufficient to prove co-ownership of the business of selling, maintaining, and developing QuikPay. Having already concluded that there was an association for the same, we conclude that Willson proved that he and King had formed a partnership for the business of selling, maintaining, and developing QuikPay.

Reversed and remanded for further proceedings.

CASE
30-2

Partnership Property
THOMAS v. LLOYD
Missouri Court of Appeals, Southern District, Division One, 2000
17 S.W.3d 177

Shrum, J.

Plaintiffs husband of thirty years died in February 1988. In February 1989, Plaintiff met Defendant in Mobile, Alabama, while traveling. Their chance meeting quickly blossomed into a romantic relationship. When Plaintiff returned to her home in Maryland in late February 1989, Defendant accompanied her and they began living together.

Initially, Defendant told Plaintiff he worked for a major oil company, had been outside the country for the past three years, was independently wealthy, and was not married. As Plaintiff later learned, none of these statements was true. In truth, Defendant had recently been released from prison. He had multiple criminal convictions, including convictions for

counterfeiting and stealing. Further, Defendant's assets at the time were no more than $2,000, and he was legally married to Patricia Lloyd.

Evidence as to when Plaintiff learned of Defendant's deceptions was contradictory. The trial court found that Plaintiff first learned of Defendant's criminal history and lack of wealth soon after she returned to Maryland in February 1989. It found that Plaintiff discovered Defendant was not single "soon after her void marriage to Defendant." The parties' "void marriage" occurred July 10, 1989, in Canada.

Except for occasional vacations, Plaintiff and Defendant resided in Plaintiff's home in Maryland from late February 1989 through October 1990. During that period, Defendant made repairs and renovations to Plaintiffs house. In October 1990, Plaintiff sold her Maryland home in an "owner-finance" arrangement.

The parties then moved to Missouri. After looking at several farm properties, they bought a 600-acre farm in Crawford County, Missouri, for $150,000. The deed was dated March 8, 1991. The grantees named in the deed and the type of tenancy created were as follows: Plaintiff, a single person, and Defendant, a single person, as joint tenants with right of survivorship. The $150,000 purchase price was paid as follows: $100,000 cash downpayment and a $50,000 purchase money note that called for 120 monthly installments of $633.38.

After buying the farm, Plaintiff and Defendant bought cattle and farm machinery, then began operating a cattle business on the property. The parties also made improvements to the farm, including remodeling an old farm house in which they lived. In June 1992, they began construction on a 4,200 square-foot house. Later, the house was expanded to 6,500 square feet. By the time of trial, Plaintiffs expenditures for labor and materials on the home exceeded $201,000.

A progressive deterioration in the parties' relationship led to the filing of this multiple-count lawsuit in October 1995. [The trial court found that the subject real estate was not a partnership asset and ordered it be sold at public auction and the net sale proceeds to be distributed 98 percent to Plaintiff and 2 percent to Defendant. The Defendant appealed the trial court's refusal to classify farm real estate as a partnership asset.]

"The true method of determining whether, as between partners themselves, land standing in the names of individuals is to be treated as partnership property is to ascertain from the conduct of the parties and their course of dealing, the understanding and intention of the partners themselves, which, when ascertained, unquestionably should control." [Citations.] Whether real estate titled in the names of individual partners is partnership property is a question of fact and the burden of proof is on the one alleging that the ownership does not accord with the legal title. [Citation.]

In attempting to demonstrate that the parties intended for the real estate to be a partnership asset, Defendant points to the joint ownership of the farm and the fact that the parties operated the partnership cattle business on the farm as evidence that the two understood and intended for the farm to be a partnership asset. His reliance on those facts is misplaced, however. A joint purchase of real estate by two individuals does not, in and of itself, prove the land is a partnership asset. [Citation.] On the contrary, when land is conveyed to partnership members without any statement in the deed that the grantees hold the land as property of the firm, there is a presumption that title is in the individual grantees. [Citation.] * * * The mere use of land by a partnership does little to show the land is owned by the partnership. [Citation.] * * *

Defendant points to evidence that some real estate taxes and promissory note payments for the farm came from partnership funds. He argues such evidence indicates the parties intended the farm to be a partnership asset. We agree that such evidence is a factor to be considered, but it is not determinative of the issue, especially, when, as here, the partnership payment evidence is viewed in context. For instance, none of the $100,000 downpayment for the farm came from partnership funds. Instead, it all came from Plaintiff's separate funds. Plaintiff was never reimbursed by either the partnership or Defendant for her downpayment. Of eighty-four monthly farm note payments, only three were paid from the parties' joint account. Seventy-seven of the monthly farm note payments, a total of $48,770.26, were paid from Plaintiffs separate funds. Plaintiff also spent $201,927.87 of her separate money to build a new house on the farm. None of the house construction costs came from partnership funds. Of the seven years' worth of state and county real estate taxes that had been paid on the farm property, only one year was paid out of partnership funds. On the whole, the evidence is that Plaintiff invested over $350,000 of her own funds in this farm while less than $2,400 of partnership funds were used to pay the farm note and real estate taxes. Such minimal partnership expenditures is more indicative of the tendency of people—particularly in family or quasi-family businesses—to intermingle personal and partnership affairs, than it is an indication of the parties' intent to include the farm as a partnership asset. [Citation.]

Other evidence from which the parties' intent can be gleaned includes the following: (A) Plaintiff and Defendant signed as individuals on the $50,000 purchase money note and deed of trust securing the same, without a recital of partnership status; (B) neither party filed a partnership income tax return; (C) Plaintiff filed income tax returns as an individual; (D) Defendant never filed an income tax return after the farm was purchased; (E) Plaintiff wrote checks on her individual account for materials and labor for farm improvements; and (F) Plaintiff repeatedly testified she never intended nor agreed to a partnership with Defendant. We find these circumstances sufficient to support the implicit finding and judgment of the trial court that a partnership agreement did not exist regarding the land and it was not a partnership asset. * * *

The judgment of the trial court is affirmed.

Fiduciary Duty
ENEA v. THE SUPERIOR COURT OF MONTEREY COUNTY
Court of Appeal of California, Sixth Appellate District, 2005
132 Cal.App.4th 1559, 34 Cal.Rptr.3d 513

Rushing, P. J.

Defendants [William and Claudia Daniels] state that in 1980, they and other family members formed a general partnership known as 3-D. The partnership's sole asset was a building that had been converted from a residence into offices. Some portion of the property—apparently the greater part—has been rented since 1981 on a month-to-month basis by a law practice of which William Daniels is apparently the sole member. From time to time the property was rented on similar arrangements to others, including defendant Claudia Daniels. Plaintiff's counsel stipulated in the court below that "the partnership agreement has as its principal purpose the ownership, leasing and sale of the only partnership assets, which is the building." He also stipulated that the partnership agreement contained no provision that the property "[would] be leased for fair market value." Defendants also assert, as the trial court ultimately found, that there was no evidence of any agreement to maximize rental profits.

In 1993, plaintiff [Benny Enea], a client of William Daniels, purchased a one-third interest in the partnership from the latter's brother, John P. Daniels. * * * In 2001, however, plaintiff questioned William Daniels about the rents being paid for the property * * * "and in 2003, Plaintiff was 'dissociated' from the partnership."

On August 6, 2003, plaintiff brought this action "to determine partner's buyout price and for damages." Alleg[ing] that defendants had occupied the partnership property * * * [while] paying significantly less than fair rental value, "in breach of their fiduciary duty to plaintiff." In their answer, defendants denied all of these allegations except to admit that defendant Claudia Daniels had occupied a portion of the premises at one time.

* * *

[The trial court granted the defendants' motion for summary judgment, and the plaintiff appealed.]

* * *

Despite the numerous diversions offered by defendants, the case presents a very simple set of facts and issues. For present purposes it must be assumed that defendants in fact leased the property to themselves, or associated entities, at below-market rents. * * * Therefore the sole question presented is whether defendants were categorically entitled to lease partnership property to themselves, or associated entities (or for that matter, to anyone) at less than it could yield in the open market. * * * We are satisfied, however, that the answer is a resounding "No."

The defining characteristic of a partnership is the combination of two or more persons to jointly conduct business. [Citation.] It is hornbook law that in forming such an arrangement the partners obligate themselves to share risks and benefits and to carry out the enterprise with the highest good faith toward one another—in short, with the loyalty and care of a fiduciary. "Partnership is a fiduciary relationship, and partners are held to the standards and duties of a trustee in their dealings with each other." "'. . . [I]n all proceedings connected with the conduct of the partnership every partner is bound to act in the highest good faith to his copartner and may not obtain any advantage over him in the partnership affairs by the slightest misrepresentation, concealment, threat or adverse pressure of any kind.' [Citations.]" [Citation.] Or to put the point more succinctly, "Partnership is a fiduciary relationship, and partners may not take advantages for themselves at the expense of the partnership." [Citations.]

Here the facts as assumed by the parties and the trial court plainly depict defendants taking advantages for themselves from partnership property at the expense of the partnership. The advantage consisted of occupying partnership property at below-market rates, i.e., less than they would be required to pay to an independent landlord for equivalent premises. * * *

Defendants * * * persuaded the trial court that they had no duty to collect market rents in the absence of a contract expressly requiring them to do so. This argument turns partnership law on its head. Nowhere does the law declare that partners owe each other only those duties they explicitly assume by contract. On the contrary, the fiduciary duties at issue here are imposed by *law*, and their breach sounds in tort. * * *

* * *

[Accordingly, we direct the trial court to set aside its order and deny the motion.]

QUESTIONS

1. Lynn and Jack jointly own shares of stock of a corporation, have a joint bank account, and have purchased and own as tenants in common a piece of real estate. They share equally the dividends paid on the stock, the interest on the bank account, and the rent from the real estate. Without Lynn's knowledge, Jack makes a trip to inspect the real estate and, on his way, runs over Samuel. Samuel sues Lynn and Jack for his personal injuries, joining Lynn as defendant on the theory that Lynn was Jack's partner. Is Lynn a partner of Jack? Explain.

2. James and Suzanne engaged in the grocery business as partners. In one year, they earned considerable money, and at the end of the year, they invested a part of the profits in oil land, taking title to the land in their names as tenants in common. The investment was fortunate, for oil was discovered near the land, and its value increased many times. Is the oil land partnership property? Why or why not?

3. Sheila owned an old roadside building that she believed could be easily converted into an antique shop. She talked to her friend Barbara, an antique fancier, and they executed the following written agreement:
   a. Sheila would supply the building, all utilities, and $100,000 capital for purchasing antiques.
   b. Barbara would supply $30,000 for purchasing antiques, Sheila would repay her when the business terminated.
   c. Barbara would manage the shop, make all purchases, and receive a salary of $500 per week plus 5 percent of the gross receipts.
   d. Fifty percent of the net profits would go into the purchase of new stock. The balance of the net profits would go to Sheila.
   e. The business would operate under the name "Roadside Antiques."

   Business went poorly, and after one year, a debt of $40,000 is owed to Old Fashioned, Inc., the principal supplier of antiques purchased by Barbara in the name of Roadside Antiques. Old Fashioned sues Roadside Antiques, and Sheila and Barbara as partners. Decision? Explain.

4. Clark, who owned a vacant lot, and Bird, who was engaged in building houses, entered into an oral agreement by which Bird was to erect a house on the lot. Upon the sale of the house and lot, Bird was to have his money first. Clark was then to have the agreed value of the lot, and the profits were to be equally divided. Did a partnership exist? Why or why not?

5. Grant, Arthur, and David formed a partnership for the purpose of betting on boxing matches. Grant and Arthur would become friendly with various boxers and offer them bribes to lose certain bouts. David would then place large bets, using money contributed by all three, and would collect the winnings. After David had accumulated a large sum of money, Grant and Arthur demanded their share, but David refused to make any split. Can Grant and Arthur compel David to account for the profits of the partnership? Why or why not?

6. Teresa, Peter, and Walker were partners under a written agreement made in January that the partnership should continue for ten years. During the same year, Walker, being indebted to Smith, sold and conveyed his interest in the partnership to Smith. Teresa and Peter paid Smith $50,000 as Walker's share of the profits for that year but refused Smith permission to inspect the books or to come into the managing office of the partnership. Smith brings an action setting forth the above facts and asks for an account of partnership transactions and an order to inspect the books and to participate in the management of the partnership business.
   a. Does Walker's action dissolve the partnership?
   b. To what is Smith entitled with respect to (1) partnership profits, (2) inspection of partnership books, (3) an account of partnership transactions, and (4) participation in the partnership management?

7. Horn's Crane Service furnished supplies and services under a written contract to a partnership engaged in operating a quarry and rock-crushing business. Horn brought action against Prior and Cook, the individual members of the partnership, to recover a personal judgment against them for the partnership's liability under that contract. Horn has not sued the partnership itself, nor does he claim that the partnership property is insufficient to satisfy its debts. What result? Explain.

8. Cutler worked as a bartender for Bowen until they orally agreed that Bowen would have the authority and responsibility for the entire active management and operation of the tavern business known as the Havana Club. Each was to receive $300 per week plus half of the net profits. The business continued under this arrangement for four years until the building was taken over by the Salt Lake City Redevelopment Agency. The agency paid $30,000 to Bowen as compensation for disruption. The business, however, was terminated after Bowen and Cutler failed to find a new suitable location.

Cutler, alleging a partnership with Bowen, then brought this action against him to recover one-half of the $30,000. Bowen contends that he is entitled to the entire $30,000 because he was the sole owner of the business and that Cutler was merely his employee. Cutler argues that although Bowen owned the physical assets of the business, she, as a partner in the business, is entitled to one-half of the compensation that was paid for the business's goodwill and going-concern value. Who is correct? Explain.

9. In 2011, Gauldin and Corn entered into a partnership for the purpose of raising cattle and hogs. The two men were to share equally all costs, labor, losses, and profits. The business was started on land owned initially by Corn's parents but later acquired by Corn and his wife. No rent was ever requested or paid for use of the land. Partnership funds were used to bulldoze and clear the land, to repair and build fences, and to seed and fertilize the land. In 2015, at a cost of $2,487.50, a machine shed was built on the land. In 2020, a Cargill unit was built on the land at a cost of $8,000. When the partnership dissolved in 2021, Gauldin paid Corn $7,500 for the "removable" assets; however, the two had no agreement regarding the distribution of the barn and the Cargill unit. Is Gauldin entitled to one-half of the value of the two buildings? Explain.

10. Anita and Duncan had been partners for many years in a mercantile business. Their relationship deteriorated to the point at which Anita threatened to bring an action for an accounting and dissolution of the firm. Duncan then offered to buy Anita's interest in the partnership for $250,000. Anita refused the offer and told Duncan that she would take no less than $360,000. A short time later, James approached Duncan and informed him he had inside information that a proposed street change would greatly benefit the business and that he, James, would buy the entire business for $1 million or buy a one-half interest for $500,000. Duncan made a final offer of $350,000 to Anita for her interest. Anita accepted this offer, and the transaction was completed. Duncan then sold the one-half interest to James for $500,000. Several months later, Anita learned for the first time of the transaction between Duncan and James. What rights, if any, does Anita have against Duncan? Explain.

11. ABCD Company is a general partnership. It consists of Dianne, Greg, Knox, and Laura, whose capital contributions were as follows: Dianne = $5,000, Greg = $7,500, Knox = $10,000, and Laura = $5,000. The partnership agreement provided that the partnership would continue for three years and that no withdrawals of capital were to be made without the consent of all the partners. The agreement also provided that all advances would be entitled to interest at 10 percent per year. Six months after the partnership was formed, Dianne advanced $10,000 to the partnership. At the end of the first year, net profits totaled $11,000 before any moneys had been distributed to partners. Explain how the $11,000 should be allocated to Dianne, Greg, Knox, and Laura.

CASE PROBLEMS

12. Donald Petersen joined his father, William Petersen, in a chicken hatchery business William had previously operated as a sole proprietorship. When the partnership was formed, William contributed the assets of the proprietorship, which included cash, equipment, and inventory having a total value of $41,000. Donald contributed nothing. They agreed to share the profits equally. For fifteen years, Donald took over the operation of the hatchery with very little help from his father. When the business was terminated, William contended that he was entitled to the return of his capital investment of $41,000 before Donald could recover anything. Donald asserted that he is entitled to one-half the value of the business. Explain who is correct in his contention.

13. Smith, Jones, and Brown were creditors of White, who operated a grain elevator known as White's Elevator. Heavily in debt, White was about to fail when the three creditors agreed to take title to his elevator property and pay all the debts. It was also agreed that White should continue as manager of the business at a salary of $1,500 per month and that all profits of the business were to be paid to Smith, Jones, and Brown. It was further agreed that they could dispense with White's services at any time and that he was free to quit when he pleased. White accepted the proposition and continued to operate the business as before. The agreement worked successfully and for several years paid substantial profits, enough so that Smith, Jones, and Brown had received nearly all that they had originally advanced. Were Smith, Jones, and Brown partners? Explain.

14. Virginia, Georgia, Carolina, and Louis were partners doing business under the trade name of Morning Glory Nursery. Virginia owned a one-third interest, and Georgia, Carolina, and Louis owned two-ninths each. The partners acquired three tracts of land for the purpose of the partnership. Two of the tracts were acquired in

the names of the four partners, "trading and doing business as Morning Glory Nursery." The third tract was acquired in the names of the individuals, the trade name not appearing in the deed. This third tract was acquired by the partnership out of partnership funds and for partnership purposes. Who owns each of the three tracts? Explain.

15. Charles and L. W. Clement were brothers who formed a partnership that lasted forty years; then, Charles discovered that his brother, who kept the partnership's books, had made several substantial personal investments with funds improperly withdrawn from the partnership. He then brought an action in equity seeking dissolution of the partnership, appointment of a receiver, and an accounting. Should Charles succeed? Explain.

16. Michael, his mother, and his four siblings orally agreed that they would all play the lottery and that if any one of them should purchase a winning lottery ticket, all of them would share the money equally. Michael's mother purchased the sole winning ticket for the $6 million lottery prize and informed the lottery commission that, per the family agreement, a six-person partnership had won the prize. Each of the six family members took an equal one-sixth share of the lottery proceeds. Explain whether Michael's share of the lottery proceeds was income resulting from a partnership or instead was a gift from Michael's mother.

17. Anderson and Tallstrom are partners in Rancho Murieta Investors (RMI). Anderson owns 80 percent of RMI; Tallstrom owns the other 20 percent and is the managing partner of RMI. Hellman obtained judgments against Anderson in his individual capacity for more than $440,000. After various unsuccessful attempts to enforce the judgments, Hellman obtained an "Order Charging Debtor John B. Anderson's Partnership Interest" in RMI. Despite the charging order, Hellman has not received any monies in satisfaction of the judgments because RMI had not generated profits and was not expected to do so in the near future. Explain what Hellman's rights are with respect to the unsatisfied charging order.

TAKING SIDES

Chaiken entered into separate but nearly identical agreements with Strazella and Spitzer to operate a barbershop. Under the terms of the "partnership" agreements, Chaiken would provide barber chairs, supplies, and licenses, while the other two would provide tools of the trade. The agreements also stated that gross returns from the partnership were to be divided on a percentage basis among the three men and that Chaiken would decide all matters of partnership policy. Finally, the agreements stated hours of work and holidays for Strazella and Spitzer and required Chaiken to hold and distribute all receipts.

a. What are the arguments that Strazella and Spitzer are partners with Chaiken?

b. What are the arguments that Strazella and Spitzer are employees of Chaiken?

c. Explain which arguments should prevail.

CHAPTER 31

Operation and Dissolution of General Partnerships

CHAPTER OUTCOMES

After reading and studying this chapter, you should be able to:

- Explain the contract liability of a partnership and the partners.

- Explain the tort liability of a partnership and the partners.

- Distinguish between the liability of incoming partner for debts arising before his admission and those arising after admission.

- Identify the causes of dissolution of a partnership and the conditions under which partners have the right to continue the partnership after dissociation.

- Explain the effect of dissolution on the authority and liability of the partners and the order in which the assets of a partnership are distributed to creditors and partners.

The operation and management of a general partnership involve interactions among the partners as well as their interactions with third persons. The previous chapter covered the rights and duties of the partners among themselves. The first part of this chapter focuses on the relations among the partnership, the partners, and third persons who deal with the partnership. These relations are governed by the laws of agency, contracts, and torts as well as by the partnership statute. The second part of the chapter addresses the dissociation and dissolution of general partnerships.

RELATIONSHIP OF PARTNERSHIP AND PARTNERS WITH THIRD PARTIES

In the course of transacting business, the partnership and the partners also may acquire rights over and incur duties to third parties. For example, under the law of agency, a principal is liable upon contracts that his duly authorized agents make on his behalf and is liable in tort for the wrongful acts his employees commit in the course of their employment. Because much of the law of partnership is the law of agency, most problems arising between partners and third persons require the application of principles of agency law. The Revised Uniform Partnership Act (RUPA) makes this relationship explicit by stating that "[e]ach partner is an agent of the partnership for the purpose of its business." Section 301(1). In addition, the RUPA provides that unless displaced by particular provisions

of the RUPA, the principles of law and equity supplement the RUPA. Section 104. The law of agency is discussed in *Chapters 19* and *20*.

When a partnership becomes liable to a third party, each partner has **unlimited, personal liability** for that partnership obligation.

31-1 Contracts of Partnership

The act of every partner binds the partnership to transactions *within* the scope of the partnership business unless the partner does not have actual or apparent authority to so act. If the partnership is bound, then each general partner has unlimited, personal liability for that partnership obligation unless the partnership is a limited liability partnership (LLP) and the LLP statute shields contract obligations. Under the Revised Act, the partners are jointly and severally liable for all contract obligations of the partnership. Section 306(a). **Joint and several liability** means that all of the partners may be sued jointly in one action or that separate actions, leading to separate judgments, may be maintained against each of them. Judgments obtained are enforceable, however, against property of only the defendant or defendants named in the suit, and payment of any one of the judgments satisfies all of them. The Revised Act, in keeping with its entity treatment of partnerships, requires the judgment creditor to exhaust the partnership's assets before enforcing a judgment against the separate assets of a partner. Section 307(d).

The Uniform Partnership Act (UPA) provides that partners are jointly liable on all debts and contract obligations of the partnership. UPA Section 15(b). Under **joint liability**, a creditor must bring suit against all of the partners as a group, and the judgment must be against all of the obligors. Therefore, any suit in contract against the partners must name all of them as defendants.

◆ **SEE FIGURE 31-1:** *Contract Liability*

31-1a AUTHORITY TO BIND PARTNERSHIP

A partner may bind the partnership by her act if (1) she has actual authority, express or implied, to perform the act or (2) she has apparent authority to perform the act. If the act is not apparently for carrying on in the ordinary course the partnership business, then the partnership is bound only when

the partner has actual authority. In such a case, the third person dealing with the partner assumes the risk that such actual authority exists. Section 301(2). Where there is neither actual authority nor apparent authority, the partnership is bound only if it ratifies the act. Ratification is discussed in *Chapter 20*.

ACTUAL EXPRESS AUTHORITY The actual express authority of partners may be written or oral; it may be specifically set forth in the partnership agreement or in an additional agreement between the partners. In addition, it may arise from decisions made by a majority of the partners regarding ordinary matters connected with the partnership business. Section 401(j).

A partner who does not have actual authority from *all* of her partners may not bind the partnership by any act that does not apparently carry on in the ordinary course the partnership

FIGURE 31-1 Contract Liability

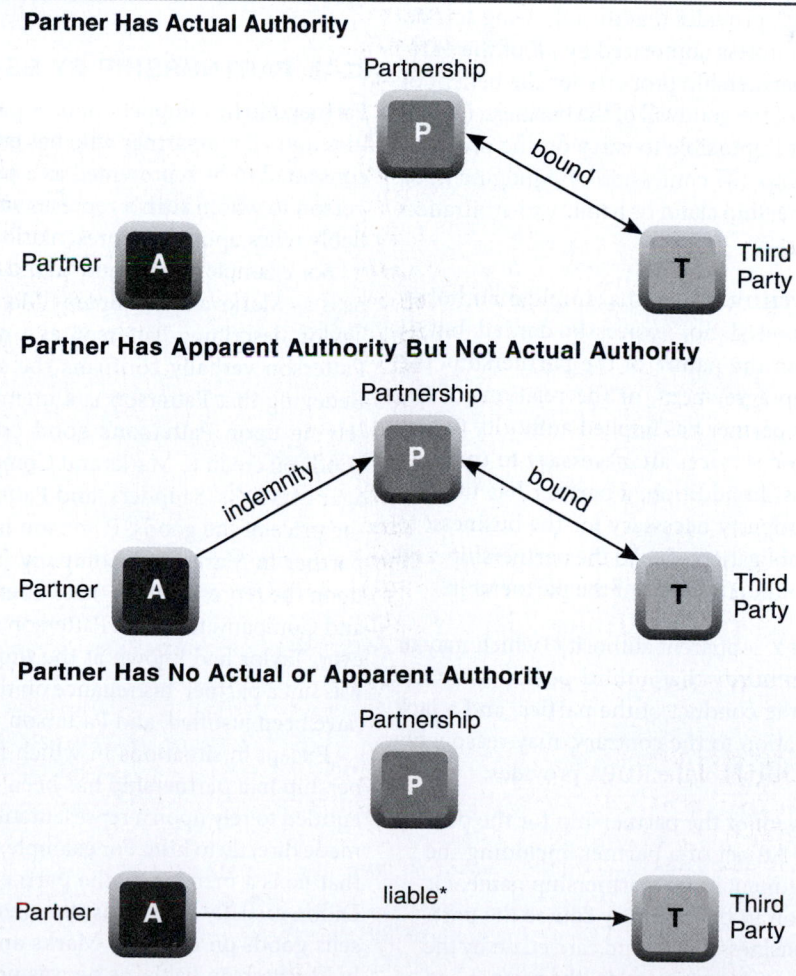

Partner Has Actual Authority

Partner Has Apparent Authority But Not Actual Authority

Partner Has No Actual or Apparent Authority

*Partner is liable for breach of implied warranty of authority or misrepresentation

business. Sections 301(2) and 401(j). Acts outside the ordinary course of the partnership business would include the following: (1) execution of contracts of guaranty or suretyship in the firm name, (2) sale of partnership property not held for sale in the usual course of business, and (3) payment of an individual partner's debts out of partnership assets.

The Revised Act also authorizes the optional, central filing of a statement of partnership authority specifying the names of the partners authorized to execute instruments transferring real property held in the name of the partnership. A statement also may limit the authority of a partner or partners to transfer real property. In addition, a statement may grant extraordinary authority to some or all of the partners or (2) limit their ordinary authority to enter into transactions on behalf of the partnership. A filed statement is effective for up to five years. Section 303. A partner or other person named as a partner may file a statement denying any fact asserted in a statement of partnership authority, including a denial of a person's status as a partner or of another person's authority as a partner. Section 304. A statement of denial is a limitation on authority.

Section 9(3) of the UPA provides that the following acts do not bind the partnership unless authorized by *all* of the partners: (1) assignment of partnership property for the benefit of its creditors, (2) disposal of the goodwill of the business, (3) any act which would make it impossible to carry on the ordinary business of the partnership, (4) confession of a judgment, or (5) submission of a partnership claim or liability to arbitration or reference.

ACTUAL IMPLIED AUTHORITY Actual implied authority is neither expressly granted nor expressly denied but is reasonably deduced from the nature of the partnership, the terms of the partnership agreement, or the relations of the partners. For example, a partner has implied authority to hire and fire employees whose services are necessary to carry on the partnership business. In addition, a partner has implied authority to purchase property necessary for the business, to receive performance of obligations due to the partnership, and to bring legal actions to enforce claims of the partnership.

APPARENT AUTHORITY Apparent authority (which may or may not be actual) is authority that a third person—in view of the circumstances—the conduct of the parties, and a lack of knowledge or notification to the contrary, may reasonably believe to exist. Section 301(1) of the RUPA provides:

Each partner is an agent of the partnership for the purpose of its business. An act of a partner, including the execution of an instrument in the partnership name, for apparently carrying on in the ordinary course the partnership business or business of the kind carried on by the partnership binds the partnership, unless the partner had

no authority to act for the partnership in the particular matter and the person with whom the partner was dealing knew or had received a notification that the partner lacked authority.

This section characterizes a partner as a general managerial agent having both actual and apparent authority within the scope of the firm's ordinary business. For example, a partner has apparent authority to indorse checks and notes, to make representations and warranties in selling goods, and to enter into contracts for advertising. A third person, however, may not rely upon apparent authority in any situation in which he already knows or has received notification that the partner does not have actual authority. A person knows a fact if the person has actual knowledge of it. A person receives a notification when the notification comes to the person's attention or is duly delivered at the person's place of business or at any other place held out by the person as a place for receiving communications. Section 102.

◆ *See Case 31-1*

31-1b PARTNERSHIP BY ESTOPPEL

Partnership by estoppel imposes partnership duties and liabilities upon a nonpartner who has either represented himself or consented to be represented as a partner. It extends to a third person to whom such a representation is made and who justifiably relies upon the representation. Section 308(a).

For example, Marks and Saunders are partners doing business as Marks and Company. Marks introduces Patterson to Taylor, describing Patterson as a member of the partnership. Patterson verbally confirms the statement made by Marks. Believing that Patterson is a member of the partnership and relying upon Patterson's good credit standing, Taylor sells goods on credit to Marks and Company. In an action by Taylor against Marks, Saunders, and Patterson as partners to recover the price of the goods, Patterson is liable although he is not a partner in Marks and Company. Taylor had justifiably relied upon the representation that Patterson was a partner in Marks and Company, to which Patterson actually consented. If, however, Taylor had known at the time of the sale that Patterson was not a partner, his reliance on the representation would not have been justified, and Patterson would not be liable.

Except in situations in which the representation of membership in a partnership has been made publicly, no person is entitled to rely upon a representation of partnership unless it is made directly to him. For example, Patterson falsely tells Dillon that he is a member of the partnership Marks and Company. Dillon casually relays this statement to Taylor, who in reliance sells goods on credit to Marks and Company. Taylor cannot hold Patterson liable, as he was not justified in relying on the representation made privately by Patterson to Dillon, which Patterson did not consent to have repeated to Taylor.

Where Patterson, however, knowingly consents to his name appearing publicly in the firm name or in a list of partners or to be used in public announcements or advertisements in a manner which indicates that he is a partner in the firm, Patterson is liable to any member of the public who relies on the purported partnership, whether or not Patterson is aware of being held out as a partner to such person. Section 308(a).

31-2 Torts and Crimes of Partnership

As discussed in *Chapter 20*, under the doctrine of *respondeat superior*, a partnership, like any employer, may be liable for an unauthorized tort committed by its employee if the employee committed the tort in the scope of his employment. With respect to a *partner's* conduct, the RUPA provides that a partnership is liable in tort for the loss or injury any partner causes by any wrongful act or omission, or other actionable conduct, while acting within the ordinary course of the partnership business or with the authority of the partnership. Section 305(a).

Tort liability of the partnership may include not only the negligence of the partners but also trespass, fraud, defamation, and breach of fiduciary duty, so long as the tort is committed in the course of partnership business. Moreover, though the fact that a tort is intentional does not necessarily remove it from the course of business, it is a factor to be considered. The Revised Act makes the partnership liable for no-fault torts by the addition of the phrase "or other actionable conduct." Comment to Section 305. A partnership is also liable if a partner in the course of the partnership's business or while acting with authority of the partnership commits a **breach of trust** by receiving money or property of a person not a partner and the partner misapplies the money or property. Section 305(b).

If the partnership is liable, each partner has **unlimited, personal liability** for the partnership obligation unless the partnership is an LLP. The liability of partners for a tort or breach of trust committed by any partner or by an employee of the firm in the course of partnership business is joint and several. Section 306. As mentioned earlier, the Revised Act requires the judgment creditor to exhaust the partnership's assets before enforcing a judgment against the separate assets of a partner. RUPA Section 307(d).

The partner who commits the tort or breach of trust is directly liable to the third party and must also **indemnify** the partnership for any damages it pays to the third party. Section 405(a).

A partner is not criminally liable for the crimes of her partners unless she authorized or participated in them. Nor is a partnership criminally liable for the crimes of individual partners or employees unless a statute imposes vicarious liability. Even under such a statute, a partnership usually is liable only in those States that have adopted the entity theory or if the statute itself expressly imposes liability upon partnerships. Otherwise, the vicarious liability statute renders the partners liable as individuals.

♦ **SEE FIGURE 31-2:** *Tort Liability*

FIGURE 31-2 **Tort Liability**

Tort Within Authority or Ordinary Course of Business

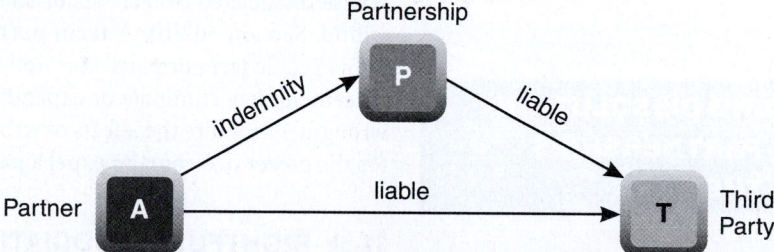

Tort Outside Authority and Ordinary Course of Business

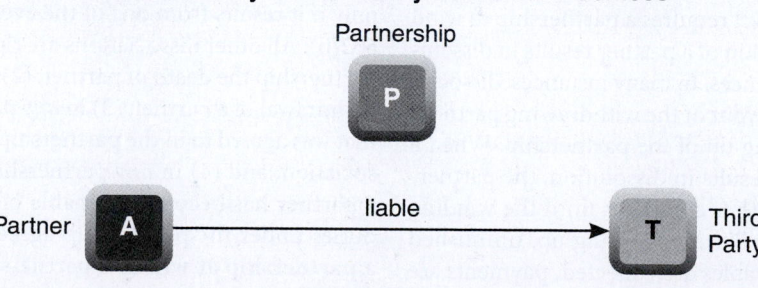

31-3 Notice to a Partner

A partner's knowledge, notice, or receipt of a notification of a fact relating to the partnership is effective immediately as knowledge by, notice to, or receipt of a notification by the partnership, except in the case of a fraud on the partnership committed by or with the consent of that partner. Section 102(f). A person has notice of a fact if the person (1) knows of it, (2) has received a notification of it, or (3) has reason to know it exists from all of the facts known to the person at the time in question. Section 102(b).

31-4 Liability of Incoming Partner

A person admitted as a partner into an existing partnership is *not* personally liable for any partnership obligations incurred before the person's admission as a partner. Section 306(b). This means that the liability of an incoming partner for **antecedent debts** and obligations of the firm is limited to his capital contribution. This restriction does not apply, of course, to **subsequent debts** (obligations arising after his admission into the partnership), for which obligations his liability is *unlimited*. For example, Nash is admitted to Higgins, Cooke, and Jackson Co., a partnership. Nash's capital contribution is $7,500, which she paid in cash upon her admission to the partnership. A year later, when liabilities of the firm exceed its assets by $40,000, the partnership is dissolved. Porter had lent the firm $15,000 eight months before Nash was admitted; Skinner lent the firm $20,000 two months after Nash was admitted. Nash has no liability to Porter *except* to the extent of her capital contribution, but she is *personally* liable to Skinner.

In an LLP, an incoming partner does not have personal liability for both antecedent debts *and* those subsequent debts that are shielded by that State's LLP statute.

♦ *See Case 31-2*

DISSOCIATION AND DISSOLUTION OF GENERAL PARTNERSHIPS UNDER THE RUPA

Dissociation occurs when a partner ceases to be associated in the carrying on of the business. Dissolution refers to those situations in which the Revised Act requires a partnership to wind up and terminate. A dissociation of a partner results in dissolution only in limited circumstances. In many instances, dissociation will result merely in a buyout of the withdrawing partner's interest rather than a winding up of the partnership. When a dissociation or other cause results in dissolution, the partnership *is not terminated* but rather continues until the winding up of its affairs is complete. During winding up, unfinished business is completed, receivables are collected, payments are made to creditors, and the remaining assets are distributed to the partners. Termination occurs when the process is finished.

31-5 Dissociation

Dissociation occurs when a partner ceases to be associated in the carrying on of the business. A number of events that were considered causes of dissociation or dissolution under the common law are no longer considered so under the RUPA. For example, the assignment of a partner's interest, a creditor's charging order on a partner's interest, and an accounting are not considered a dissociation or dissolution.

A partner has the *power* to dissociate at any time, rightfully or wrongfully, by expressing an intent to withdraw. Section 602(a). A partner does not, however, always have the *right* to dissociate. A partner who wrongfully dissociates is liable to the partnership for damages caused by the dissociation. Section 602(c). In addition, if the wrongful dissociation results in the dissolution of the partnership, the wrongfully dissociating partner is not entitled to participate in winding up the business.

31-5a WRONGFUL DISSOCIATIONS

A partner's dissociation is wrongful if it breaches an express provision of the partnership agreement. In addition, dissociation is wrongful in a *term partnership* if before the expiration of the term or the completion of the undertaking (1) the partner voluntarily withdraws by express will unless the withdrawal follows within ninety days after another partner's dissociation by death, bankruptcy, or wrongful dissociation; (2) the partner is expelled for misconduct by judicial determination; (3) the partner becomes a debtor in bankruptcy; or (4) the partner is an entity (other than a trust or estate) and is expelled or otherwise dissociated because its dissolution or termination was willful. Section 602(b). A **term partnership** is a partnership for a specific term or particular undertaking. The partnership agreement may eliminate or expand the dissociations that are wrongful or modify the effects of wrongful dissociation, except for the power of a court to expel a partner for misconduct.

31-5b RIGHTFUL DISSOCIATIONS

The RUPA provides that a partner's dissociation is wrongful only if it results from one of the events just discussed. Section 602(b). All other dissociations are rightful, including (1) in *any* partnership the death of partner, (2) in a *partnership at will* the withdrawal of a partner, (3) in *any* partnership an event occurs that was agreed to in the partnership agreement as causing dissociation, and (4) in *any* partnership a court determines that a partner has become incapable of performing the partner's duties under the partnership agreement. The RUPA defines a **partnership at will** as a partnership in which the partners have not agreed to remain partners until the expiration of a definite term or the completion of a particular undertaking. Section 101(8).

♦ *See Case 31-3*

31-5c EFFECTS OF DISSOCIATION

Upon a partner's dissociation, the partner's right to participate in the management and conduct of the partnership business terminates. Section 603(b). If, however, the dissociation results in a dissolution and winding up of the business, all of the partners who have not wrongfully dissociated may participate in winding up the business. Section 804(a). The duty not to compete terminates upon dissociation, and the dissociated partner may immediately engage in a competitive business, without any further consent. The partner's other fiduciary duties and duty of care continue only with regard to matters arising and events occurring before the partner's dissociation, unless the partner participates in winding up the partnership's business. For example, a partner who leaves a partnership providing consulting services may immediately compete with the firm for new clients but must exercise care in completing current transactions with clients and must account to the firm for any fees received from the old clients on account of those transactions.

31-6 Dissolution

Dissolution refers to those situations in which the Revised Act requires a partnership to wind up and terminate. In accordance with the Revised Act's emphasis on the entity treatment of partnerships, only a limited subset of dissociations requires the dissolution of a partnership. In addition, some events other than dissociation can bring about the dissolution of a partnership under RUPA. The following sections discuss the causes and effects of dissolution.

31-6a CAUSES OF DISSOLUTION

The basic rule under the RUPA is that a partnership is dissolved and its business must be wound up only if one of the events listed in Section 801 occurs. The events causing dissolution may be brought about by (1) an act of the partners (i.e., some dissociations), (2) operation of law, or (3) court order. The provisions of Section 801 that involve an act of the parties are default provisions: the partners may by agreement modify or eliminate these grounds. The partners may *not* vary or eliminate the grounds for dissolution based on operation of law or court order. Section 103.

DISSOLUTION BY ACT OF THE PARTNERS These causes of dissolution make up a subset of dissociations. In a **partnership at will**, a partner's giving notice of intent to withdraw will result

in dissolution of a partnership. Section 801. Thus, any member of a partnership at will has the right to force a liquidation of the partnership. (The death or bankruptcy of a partner does *not* dissolve a partnership at will.)

No partner by herself has the power to dissolve a term partnership. Section 801 provides for three ways in which a **term partnership** will be dissolved.

1. The term of the partnership expires or the undertaking is complete. If the partners continue a term partnership after the expiration of the term or completion of the undertaking, the partnership will be treated as a partnership at will. Section 406.

2. All of the partners expressly agree to dissolve. This reflects the principle that the partners can unanimously amend the partnership agreement.

3. A partner's dissociation caused by a partner's death or incapacity, bankruptcy or similar financial impairment, or wrongful dissociation will bring on a dissolution if within ninety days after dissociation at least half of the remaining partners express their will to wind up the partnership business. Thus, if a term partnership has eight partners and one of the partners wrongfully dissociates before the end of the term, the partnership will be dissolved only if four of the remaining seven partners vote in favor of liquidation.

In **all partnerships**, dissolution occurs upon the happening of an event that was specified in the partnership agreement as resulting in dissolution. The partners may, however, agree to continue the business.

DISSOLUTION BY OPERATION OF LAW A partnership is dissolved by operation of law if an event occurs that makes it unlawful to continue all or substantially all of the partnership's business. For example, a law prohibiting the production and sale of alcoholic beverages would dissolve a partnership formed to manufacture liquor. A cure of such illegality within ninety days after notice to the partnership of the event is effective retroactively. The partnership agreement cannot vary the requirement that an uncured illegal business must be dissolved and liquidated. Section 103(b)(8).

DISSOLUTION BY COURT ORDER On application by a **partner**, a court may order dissolution on grounds of another partner's misconduct or upon a finding that (1) the economic purpose of the partnership is likely to be unreasonably frustrated, (2) another partner has engaged in conduct relating to the partnership business that makes it not reasonably practicable to carry on the business in partnership with that partner, or (3) it is not otherwise reasonably practicable to carry on the partnership business in conformity with the partnership agreement. On application of a **transferee** of a partner's transferable interest or a purchaser at foreclosure of a charging order, a court may order dissolution if it determines that it is equitable to wind up the partnership business (1) at any time in a partnership at will or (2) after the term of a term partnership has expired. The partners may *not* by agreement vary or eliminate the court's power to wind up a partnership. Section 103(b)(8).

◆ *See Case 31-3*

31-6b EFFECTS OF DISSOLUTION

A partnership continues after dissolution only for the purpose of winding up its business. The partnership is terminated when the winding up of its business is completed. Section 802. The remaining partners have the right, however, to continue the business after dissolution if *all* of the partners, including any dissociating partner other than a wrongfully dissociating partner, waive the right to have the partnership's business wound up and the partnership terminated. Section 802(b). In that event, the partnership resumes carrying on its business as if dissolution had not occurred.

AUTHORITY Upon dissolution, the *actual authority* of a partner to act for the partnership terminates, except so far as is appropriate to wind up partnership business. Section 804. Actual authority to wind up includes the authority to complete existing contracts, to collect debts, to sell partnership assets, and to pay partnership obligations. A person winding up a partnership's business also has the authority to preserve the partnership business or property as a going concern for a reasonable time, bring and defend legal actions, settle and close the partnership's business, distribute the assets of the partnership pursuant to the RUPA, settle disputes by mediation or arbitration, and perform other necessary acts. Section 803(c).

With respect to apparent authority, the partnership is bound in a transaction not appropriate for winding up only if the partner's act would have bound the partnership before dissolution and the other party to the transaction did not have notice of the dissolution. Section 804(2). A person has notice of a fact if the person (1) knows of it, (2) has received a notification of it, or (3) has reason to know it exists from all of the facts known to the person at the time in question. Section 102(b). Moreover, RUPA Section 805 provides that after an event of dissolution, any partner who has not wrongfully dissociated may file a statement of dissolution on behalf of the partnership and that ninety days after the filing of the statement of dissolution nonpartners are deemed to have notice of the dissolution and the corresponding limitation on the authority of all partners. Thus, after ninety days, the statement of dissolution operates as constructive notice conclusively limiting the apparent authority of partners to transactions that are appropriate for winding up the business.

Practical Advice

Be sure to give the appropriate notice to third parties whenever a partnership dissolves.

LIABILITY Partners are liable for their share of partnership liabilities incurred after dissolution. Section 806(a). That includes not only obligations that are appropriate for winding up the business but also obligations that are inappropriate but within the partner's apparent authority. A partner, however, who, with knowledge of the dissolution nevertheless incurs a liability binding on the partnership by an act that is not appropriate for winding up the partnership business, is liable to the partnership for any damage caused to the partnership by the liability. Section 806(b).

31-6c WINDING UP

Whenever a dissolved partnership is not to be continued, the partnership must be liquidated. The process of liquidation, called **winding up**, involves completing unfinished business, collecting debts, taking inventory, reducing assets to cash, auditing the partnership books, paying creditors, and distributing the remaining assets to the partners. During this period, the fiduciary duties of the partners continue in effect except the duty not to compete.

PARTICIPATION IN WINDING UP After dissolution, a partner who has not wrongfully dissociated has the right to participate in winding up the partnership's business. Section 803(a). On application of any partner, partner's legal representative, or transferee, the court may order judicial supervision of the winding up if good cause is shown. Any partner winding up the partnership is entitled to reasonable compensation for services rendered in the winding up. Section 401(h).

DISTRIBUTION OF ASSETS After all the partnership assets have been collected and reduced to cash, they are distributed to creditors and the partners. When the partnership has been profitable, the order of distribution is not critical; however, when liabilities exceed assets, the order of distribution has great importance. In winding up a partnership's business, the "assets" of the partnership include all required contributions of partners. Section 807(a).

The RUPA provides that the partnership must apply its assets first to discharge the obligations of partners who are creditors on *parity* with other creditors, subject to any other laws, such as fraudulent conveyance laws and voidable transfers under the Bankruptcy Act. Second, any surplus must be applied to pay a liquidating distribution equal to the net amount distributable to partners in accordance with their right to distributions. Section 807. (This does not distinguish between amounts owing to partners for return of capital and amounts owing to partners for profits.) The partnership agreement may vary the

RUPA's rules for distributing the surplus among the partners. For example, it may distinguish between capital and operating losses, as the original UPA does.

Each partner is entitled to a settlement of all partnership accounts upon winding up. In settling accounts among the partners, profits and losses that result from the liquidation of the partnership assets must be credited and charged to the partners' accounts according to their respective shares of profits and losses. Then the partnership must make a final liquidating distribution to those partners with a positive account balance in an amount equal to any excess of the credits over the charges in the partner's account. Any partner with a negative account balance must contribute to the partnership an amount equal to any excess of the charges over the credits in the partner's account. Section 807(b). (In an LLP, a partner is *not* required to contribute for any partnership obligations for which that partner is not personally liable under the LLP statute's shield.)

Partners share proportionately in the shortfall caused by partners who fail to contribute their proportionate share. The partnership may enforce a partner's obligation to contribute. A partner is entitled to recover from the other partners any contributions in excess of that partner's share of the partnership's liabilities. After the settlement of accounts, each partner must contribute, in the proportion in which the partner shares partnership losses, the amount necessary to satisfy partnership obligations that were not known at the time of the settlement. The estate of a deceased partner is liable for the partner's obligation to contribute to the partnership.

MARSHALING OF ASSETS The Revised Act abolishes the marshaling of assets doctrine—which segregates and considers separately the assets and liabilities of the partnership and the respective assets and liabilities of the individual partners—and the dual priority rule. Section 807. (These are discussed later in this chapter.) Under the RUPA, like the UPA, partnership creditors are entitled to be satisfied first out of partnership assets. Unlike the UPA, the Revised Act provides that unsatisfied partnership creditors may recover any deficiency out of the individually owned assets of the partners on equal footing with the partners' creditors.

31-7 Dissociation without Dissolution

As mentioned, the RUPA uses the term *dissociation* instead of the UPA term *dissolution* to denote the change in the relationship caused by a partner's ceasing to be associated in the carrying on of the business. Under the RUPA, a dissociation of a partner results in dissolution only in limited circumstances, discussed previously. Thus, in many instances, dissociation will result merely in a buyout of the withdrawing partner's interest rather than a winding up of the partnership.

31-7a DISSOCIATIONS NOT CAUSING DISSOLUTION

In a **partnership at will**, a partner will be dissociated from the partnership without dissolution upon specified causes, including that partner's death, bankruptcy, or incapacity; the expulsion of that partner; or, in the case of an entity-partner, its termination. RUPA Sections 601 and 801. (As covered earlier, a partnership at will is *dissolved* upon notice of a partner's intent to withdraw.)

In a **term partnership**, if within ninety days after any specified cause of dissolution occurs fewer than half of the remaining partners express their will to wind up the partnership business, then the partnership will not dissolve. These causes include the following: a partner's dissociation by death, bankruptcy, or incapacity; the distribution by a trust-partner of its entire partnership interest; the termination of an entity-partner; or a partner's wrongful dissociation. (A wrongful dissociation includes a partner's voluntary withdrawal in violation of the partnership agreement and the judicial expulsion of a partner.) Section 801.

With three exceptions, the partners may by agreement modify or eliminate any of the grounds for dissolution. The three exceptions are (1) carrying on an illegal business, (2) a court-ordered dissolution on application of a partner, and (3) a court-ordered dissolution on application of a transferee of a partner's interest. Section 103. Moreover, at any time after the dissolution of a partnership and before the winding up of its business is completed, all of the partners, including any dissociating partner other than a wrongfully dissociating partner, may waive the right to have the partnership's business wound up and the partnership terminated. In that event, the partnership resumes carrying on its business as if dissolution had never occurred. Section 802(b).

31-7b CONTINUATION AFTER DISSOCIATION

If a partner is dissociated from a partnership without resulting in dissolution, the remaining partners have the right to continue the business. Creditors of the partnership remain creditors of the continued partnership. Moreover, the dissociated partner remains liable for partnership obligations incurred before dissociation. Section 703(a).

The partnership must purchase the dissociated partner's interest in the partnership. Section 701. The partnership agreement can vary these rights. Section 103. The buyout price of a dissociated partner's interest is the amount that would have been distributable to the dissociating partner in a winding up of the partnership if, on the date of dissociation, the assets of the partnership were sold at a price equal to the greater of liquidation value or going concern value without the dissociated partner. The partnership must offset against the buyout price all other amounts owing from the dissociated partner to the partnership, including damages for wrongful dissociation. RUPA Section 701. These rules, however, are merely default rules, and the partnership agreement may specify the method or formula for determining the buyout price and all of the other terms and conditions of the buyout right.

A partner in a term partnership who wrongfully dissociates before the expiration of a definite term or the completion of a particular undertaking is not entitled to payment of any portion of the buyout price until the expiration of the term or completion of the undertaking, unless the partner establishes to the satisfaction of the court that earlier payment will not cause undue hardship to the business of the partnership. Section 701(h).

A partnership must indemnify a dissociated partner whose interest is being purchased against all partnership liabilities, whether incurred before or after the dissociation, except liabilities incurred by an act of the dissociated partner after dissociation that binds the partnership, as discussed later.

◆ *See Case 31-4*

◆ **SEE FIGURE 31-3:** *Dissociation and Dissolution Under RUPA*

Practical Advice

Consider whether to include a provision in your partnership agreement specifying a method for valuing each partner's interest in the partnership.

31-7c DISSOCIATED PARTNER'S POWER TO BIND THE PARTNERSHIP

A dissociated partner has no actual authority to act for the partnership. Section 603(b)(1). With respect to apparent authority, Section 702 provides that for two years after a partner dissociates without resulting in a dissolution of the partnership business, the partnership is bound by an act of the dissociated partner which would have bound the partnership before dissociation but *only if* at the time of entering into the transaction the other party:

1. reasonably believed that the dissociated partner was then a partner;

2. did not have notice of the partner's dissociation; *and*

3. is not deemed to have had constructive notice from a filed statement of dissociation.

A dissociated partner is liable to the partnership for any damage caused to the partnership arising from an obligation improperly incurred by the dissociated partner after dissociation for which the partnership is liable. Section 702(b). The dissociated partner is also personally liable to the third party for the unauthorized obligation.

A person has *notice* of a fact if he knows or has reason to know it exists from all the facts that are known to him or he has received a notification of it. Section 102(b). The RUPA provides that ninety days after a statement of dissociation is filed, nonpartners are deemed to have constructive notice of the dissociation thereby conclusively terminating a dissociated partner's apparent authority. Section 704(c). Thus, under the RUPA, a partnership should notify all known creditors of a partner's dissociation and

file a statement of dissociation, which will conclusively limit a dissociated partner's continuing agency power to ninety days after filing. Conversely, third parties dealing with a partnership should check for partnership filings at least every ninety days.

31-7d DISSOCIATED PARTNER'S LIABILITY TO THIRD PERSONS

A partner's dissociation does not of itself discharge the partner's liability for a partnership obligation incurred before dissociation. Section 703(a). A dissociated partner is not liable for a partnership obligation incurred more than two years after dissociation. For partnership obligations incurred within two years after a partner dissociates without resulting in a dissolution of the partnership business, a dissociated partner is liable for a partnership obligation if, at the time of entering into the transaction, the other party (1) reasonably believed that the dissociated partner was then a partner, (2) did not have notice of the partner's dissociation, *and* (3) is not deemed to have had constructive notice from a filed statement of dissociation. Section 703(b).

By agreement with the partnership creditor and the partners continuing the business, a dissociated partner may be released from liability for a partnership obligation. Section 703(c). Moreover, a dissociated partner is released from liability for a partnership obligation if a partnership creditor, with notice of the partner's dissociation but without the partner's consent, agrees to a material alteration in the nature or time of payment of a partnership obligation. Section 703(d).

DISSOLUTION OF GENERAL PARTNERSHIPS UNDER THE UPA

The extinguishment of a partnership consists of three stages: (1) dissolution, (2) winding up or liquidation, and (3) termination. Dissolution occurs when the partners cease to carry on the business together. Upon dissolution, the partnership is not terminated, but rather it continues until the winding up of its affairs is complete. Termination occurs when the process of winding up is finished.

31-8 Dissolution

The UPA defines **dissolution** as the change in the relation of the partners caused by any partner's ceasing to be associated in the carrying on, as distinguished from the winding up, of the business. UPA Section 29.

31-8a CAUSES OF DISSOLUTION

Dissolution may be brought about by (1) an act of the partners, (2) operation of law, or (3) court order. UPA Section 31. Because a partnership is a personal relationship, a partner always has the power to dissolve it by his actions, but whether

FIGURE 31-3 Dissociation and Dissolution Under RUPA

Cause	Partnership at Will		Term Partnership	
	Dissociation	Dissolution	Dissociation	Dissolution
ACTS OF PARTNERS				
Assignment of partner's interest				
Accounting				
Withdrawal	•	•	•	*
Bankruptcy	•		•	*
Incapacity	•		•	*
Death	•		•	*
Expulsion of partner	•		•	
Expiration of term				•
Event specified in partnership agreement	•	•	•	•
Unanimous agreement to dissolve	•	•	•	•
OPERATION OF LAW				
Illegality		•		
COURT ORDER				
Judicial expulsion of partner	•		•	*
Judicial determination of partner's incapability to perform partnership duties	•		•	*
Judicial determination of economic frustration or impracticability		•		•
Application by transferee of partner's interest if equitable		•		

* Dissolution will occur if, within ninety days after dissociation, at least half the remaining partners express their will to wind up the partnership business.

he has the right to do so is determined by the partnership agreement. A partnership is dissolved by operation of law upon (1) the death of a partner, (2) the bankruptcy of a partner or of the partnership, or (3) the subsequent illegality of the partnership. A court-ordered dissolution may be sought by a partner, an assignee of a partner's interest, or a partner's personal creditor who has obtained a charging order against the partner's interest.

31-8b EFFECTS OF DISSOLUTION

On dissolution, the partnership is not terminated, but rather it continues until the winding up of its affairs is complete. UPA Section 30. Moreover, dissolution does not discharge the existing liability of any partner, though it does restrict her authority to act for the partnership.

Upon dissolution, the *actual authority* of a partner to act for the partnership terminates, except so far as may be necessary to wind up partnership affairs. UPA Section 33. Actual authority to wind up includes the authority to complete existing contracts, to collect debts, to sell partnership assets, and to pay partnership obligations.

Although actual authority terminates upon dissolution, *apparent authority* continues to bind the partnership for acts within the scope of the partnership business unless the third party is given notice of the dissolution. UPA Section 35.

31-9 Winding Up

Whenever a dissolved partnership is not to be continued, the partnership must be liquidated. The process of liquidation, called winding up, involves completing unfinished business, collecting debts, taking inventory, reducing assets to cash, auditing the partnership books, paying creditors, and distributing the remaining assets to the partners. During this period, the fiduciary duties of the partners continue in effect.

31-9a DISTRIBUTION OF ASSETS

Section 40 of the UPA sets forth the rules for settling accounts between the parties after dissolution. It states that the liabilities of a partnership are to be paid out of partnership assets in the following order: (1) amounts owing to nonpartner creditors, (2) amounts owing to partners other than for capital and profits (loans or advances), (3) amounts owing to partners for capital, and (4) amounts owing to partners for profits. The partners may by agreement among themselves change the internal priorities of distribution (numbers 2, 3, and 4) but not the preferred position of third parties (number 1). The UPA defines partnership assets to include all partnership property as well as the contributions necessary for the payment of all partnership liabilities, which consist of numbers 1, 2, and 3. UPA Section 40(a).

In addition, the UPA provides that in the absence of any contrary agreement, each partner shall share equally in the profits and surplus remaining after all liabilities (numbers 1, 2, and 3) are satisfied and must contribute toward the partnership's losses, capital or otherwise, according to his share in the profits. UPA Section 18(a). Thus, the proportion in which the partners bear losses depends not on their relative capital contributions but on their agreement. If no specific agreement exists, the partners bear losses in the same proportion in which they share profits.

31-9b MARSHALING OF ASSETS

The doctrine of marshaling of assets applies only in situations in which a court of equity is administering the assets of a partnership and of its members. **Marshaling of assets** means segregating and considering separately the assets and liabilities of the partnership and the respective assets and liabilities of the individual partners. Partnership creditors are entitled to be satisfied first out of partnership assets and may recover any deficiency out of the individually owned assets of the partners. This right is subordinate, however, to the rights of nonpartnership creditors to those assets. Conversely, the nonpartnership

creditors have first claim to the individually owned assets of their respective debtors, whereas their claims to partnership assets are subordinate to the claims of partnership creditors. This approach is called the "dual priority" rule.

Finally, the assets of an insolvent partner are distributed in the following order: (1) debts and liabilities owing to her nonpartnership creditors, (2) debts and liabilities owing to partnership creditors, and (3) contributions owing to other partners who have paid more than their respective share of the firm's liabilities to partnership creditors. UPA Section 40(i).

This rule, however, is no longer followed if the partnership is a debtor under the Bankruptcy Code. In a proceeding under the Federal bankruptcy law, a trustee is appointed to administer the estate of the debtor. If the partnership property is insufficient to pay all the claims against the partnership, the statute directs the trustee to seek recovery of the deficiency first from the general partners who are not bankrupt. The trustee may then seek recovery against the estates of bankrupt partners on the same basis as other creditors of the bankrupt partner. Bankruptcy Code, Section 723. This provision, although contrary to the UPA's doctrine of marshaling of assets, governs whenever partnership assets are being administered by a bankruptcy court.

31-10 Continuation after Dissolution

Dissolution produces one of two outcomes: either the partnership is liquidated or the remaining partners continue the partnership. Whereas liquidation sacrifices the value of a going concern, continuation of the partnership after dissolution avoids this loss. The UPA, nonetheless, gives each partner the right to have the partnership liquidated except in a few instances in which the remaining partners have the right to continue the partnership. UPA Section 37.

31-10a RIGHT TO CONTINUE PARTNERSHIP

After dissolution, the remaining partners have the right to continue the partnership when (1) the partnership has been dissolved in contravention of the partnership agreement, (2) a partner has been expelled in accordance with the partnership agreement, or (3) all the partners agree to continue the business.

31-10b RIGHTS OF CREDITORS

Any change in membership dissolves a partnership and forms a new one, despite the fact that the new combination may include a majority of the old partners. The creditors of the old partnership may pursue their claims against the new partnership and may proceed to hold all of the members of the dissolved partnership personally liable. UPA Section 41. If a withdrawing partner has made arrangements with those who continue the business whereby they assume and pay all debts and obligations of the firm, the partner is still liable to creditors whose claims arose before the dissolution. If compelled to pay such debts, the withdrawing partner nonetheless has a right of indemnity against her former partners, who agreed to pay the debts but failed to do so.

A retiring partner may be discharged from his existing liabilities by entering into a novation with the continuing partners and the creditors. A creditor must agree to a novation, although his consent may be inferred from his course of dealing with the partnership after dissolution. UPA Section 36(2). Whether such dealings with a continuing partnership constitute an implied novation is a factual question of intent.

A withdrawing partner may protect herself against liability upon contracts the firm enters subsequent to her withdrawal by giving notice that she is no longer a member of the firm. Otherwise, she will be liable for debts thus incurred to creditors who had no notice or knowledge of the partner's withdrawal. Persons who had extended credit to the partnership prior to its dissolution must receive actual notice, whereas constructive notice by newspaper publication will suffice for those who knew of the partnership but had not extended credit to it before its dissolution. UPA Section 35.

C H A P T E R   S U M M A R Y

RELATIONSHIP OF PARTNERSHIP AND PARTNERS WITH THIRD PARTIES

CONTRACTS OF PARTNERSHIP	**Partners' Liability** • *Personal Liability* if the partnership is contractually bound, each partner has joint and several unlimited, personal liability • *Joint and Several Liability* a creditor may sue the partners jointly as a group or separately as individuals **Authority to Bind Partnership** a partner who has actual authority (express or implied) or apparent authority may bind the partnership • *Actual Express Authority* authority set forth in the partnership agreement, in additional agreements among the partners, or in decisions made by a majority of the partners regarding the ordinary business of the partnership • *Actual Implied Authority* authority that is reasonably deduced from the nature of the partnership, the terms of the partnership agreement, or the relations of the partners • *Apparent Authority* an act of a partner for apparently carrying on in the ordinary course the partnership business or business of the kind carried on by the partnership binds the partnership, so long as that third person has no knowledge or notice of the lack of actual authority **Partnership by Estoppel** imposes partnership duties and liabilities on a nonpartner who has either represented himself or consented to be represented as a partner
TORTS AND CRIMES OF PARTNERSHIP	**Torts** the partnership is liable for loss or injury caused by any wrongful act or omission or other actionable conduct of any partner while acting within the ordinary course of the business or with the authority of her copartners; the partners are jointly and severally liable **Breach of Trust** the partnership is liable if a partner in the course of the partnership's business or while acting with authority of the partnership breaches a trust by misapplying money or property entrusted by a third person; the partners are jointly and severally liable **Crimes** a partner is not criminally liable for the crimes of her partners unless she authorized or participated in them
NOTICE TO A PARTNER	**Binds Partnership** a partnership is bound by a partner's knowledge, notice, or receipt of a notification of a fact relating to the partnership **Notice** a person has notice of a fact if the person (1) knows of it, (2) has received a notification of it, or (3) has reason to know it exists from all of the facts known to the person at the time in question

| LIABILITY OF INCOMING PARTNER | **Antecedent Debts** the liability of an incoming partner for antecedent debts of the partnership is limited to her capital contribution |
| | **Subsequent Debts** the liability of an incoming partner for subsequent debts of the partnership is unlimited |

DISSOCIATION AND DISSOLUTION OF GENERAL PARTNERSHIPS UNDER THE RUPA

DISSOCIATION	**Definition of Dissociation** change in the relation of partners caused by any partner's ceasing to be associated in carrying on of the business
	• *Term Partnership* partnership for a specific term or particular undertaking
	• *Partnership at Will* partnership in which the partners have not agreed to remain partners until the expiration of a definite term or the completion of a particular undertaking
	Wrongful Dissociation a dissociation that breaches an express provision of the partnership agreement or in a term partnership if before the expiration of the term or the completion of the undertaking (1) the partner voluntarily withdraws by express will, (2) the partner is judicially expelled for misconduct, (3) the partner becomes a debtor in bankruptcy, or (4) the partner is an entity (other than a trust or estate) and is expelled or otherwise dissociated because its dissolution or termination was willful
	Rightful Dissociation all other dissociations are rightful, including the death of a partner in *any* partnership and the withdrawal of a partner in a *partnership at will*
	Effects of Dissociation terminates the dissociating partner's right to participate in the management of the partnership business and duties to partnership

DISSOLUTION	**Definition of Dissolution** refers to those situations in which the Revised Act requires a partnership to wind up and terminate
	Causes of Dissolution
	• *Dissolution by Act of the Partners* in a **partnership at will:** withdrawal of a partner; in a **term partnership:** (1) the term ends, (2) all partners expressly agree to dissolve, or (3) a partner's dissociation is caused by a partner's death or incapacity, bankruptcy or similar financial impairment, or wrongful dissociation if within ninety days after dissociation at least half of the remaining partners express their will to wind up the partnership business; in **any partnership:** an event occurs that was specified in the partnership agreement as resulting in dissolution
	• *Dissolution by Operation of Law* a partnership is dissolved by operation of law upon the subsequent illegality of the partnership business
	• *Dissolution by Court Order* a court will order dissolution of a partnership under certain conditions
	Effects of Dissolution upon dissolution, a partnership is not terminated but continues until the winding up is completed
	• *Authority* a partner's actual authority to act for the partnership terminates, except so far as may be appropriate to wind up partnership affairs; apparent authority continues unless notice of the dissolution is given to a third party
	• *Liability* dissolution does not in itself discharge the existing liability of any partner; partners are liable for their share of partnership liabilities incurred after dissolution
	Winding Up completing unfinished business, collecting debts, and distributing assets to creditors and partners; also called liquidation
	• *Winding Up Required* a dissolved partnership must be wound up and terminated when the winding up of its business is completed unless all of the partners, including any rightfully dissociating partner, waive the right to have the partnership's business wound up and the partnership terminated

- *Participation in Winding Up* any partner who has not wrongfully dissociated may participate in winding up the partnership's business
- *Distribution of Assets* the assets of the partnership include all required contributions of partners; the liabilities of a partnership are to be paid out of partnership assets in the following order: (1) amounts owing to nonpartner and partner creditors and (2) amounts owing to partners on their partners' accounts
- *Partnership Creditors* are entitled to be first satisfied out of partnership assets
- *Nonpartnership Creditors* share on equal footing with unsatisfied partnership creditors in the individually owned assets of their respective debtor-partners

---

DISSOCIATION WITHOUT DISSOLUTION

Dissociations Not Causing Dissolution
- *Partnership at Will* a partner's death, bankruptcy, or incapacity, the expulsion of a partner, or the termination of an entity-partner results in a dissociation of that partner but does not result in a dissolution
- *Term Partnership* if within ninety days after any of the following causes of dissolution occurs fewer than half of the remaining partners express their will to wind up the partnership business, then the partnership will not dissolve: a partner's dissociation by death, bankruptcy, or incapacity; the distribution by a trust-partner of its entire partnership interest, the termination of an entity-partner; or a partner's wrongful dissociation

Continuation after Dissociation the remaining partners have the right to continue the partnership with a mandatory buyout of the dissociating partner; the creditors of the partnership have claims against the continued partnership

Dissociated Partner's Power to Bind the Partnership a dissociated partner's actual authority to act for the partnership terminates; apparent authority continues for two years unless notice of the dissolution is given to a third party

Dissociated Partner's Liability to Third Persons a partner's dissociation does not of itself discharge the partner's liability for a partnership obligation incurred before dissociation; a dissociated partner is liable for a partnership obligation incurred within two years after a partner dissociates unless notice of the dissolution is given to a third party

---

C A S E S

CASE 31-1

Authority to Bind Partnership

RNR INVESTMENTS LIMITED PARTNERSHIP v. PEOPLES FIRST COMMUNITY BANK

Court of Appeal of Florida, First District, 2002
812 So.2d 561

Van Nortwick, J.

RNR is a Florida limited partnership formed * * * to purchase vacant land in Destin, Florida, and to construct a house on the land for resale. Bernard Roeger was RNR's general partner and Heinz Rapp, Claus North, and S.E. Waltz, Inc., were limited partners. The agreement of limited partnership provides for various restrictions on the authority of the general partner. Paragraph 4.1 of the agreement required the general partner to prepare a budget covering the cost of acquisition and construction of the project (defined as the "Approved Budget"). * * *

Paragraph 4.3 restricted the general partner's ability to borrow, spend partnership funds and encumber partnership assets, if not specifically provided for in the Approved Budget. Finally, with respect to the development of the partnership project, paragraph 2.2(b) provided:

The General Partner shall not incur debts, liabilities or obligations of the Partnership which will cause any line item in the Approved Budget to be exceeded by more than ten percent (10%) or which will cause the aggregate

Approved Budget to be exceed by more than five percent (5%) unless the General Partner shall receive the prior written consent of the Limited Partner.

In June 1998, RNR, through its general partner, entered into a construction loan agreement, note and mortgage in the principal amount of $990,000. From June 25, 1998 through Mar. 13, 2000, the bank disbursed the aggregate sum of $952,699, by transfers into RNR's bank account. All draws were approved by an architect, who certified that the work had progressed as indicated and that the quality of the work was in accordance with the construction contract. No representative of RNR objected to any draw of funds or asserted that the amounts disbursed were not associated with the construction of the house.

RNR defaulted under the terms of the note and mortgage by failing to make payments due in July 2000 and all monthly payments due thereafter. The Bank filed a complaint seeking foreclosure. RNR filed an answer and affirmative defenses. In its first affirmative defense, RNR alleged that the Bank had failed to review the limitations on the general partner's authority in RNR's limited partnership agreement. RNR asserted that the Bank had negligently failed to investigate and to realize that the general partner had no authority to execute notes, a mortgage and a construction loan agreement and was estopped from foreclosing. The Bank filed a motion for summary judgment * * *.

* * *

RNR asserts that a copy of the limited partnership agreement was maintained at its offices. Nevertheless, the record contains no copy of an Approved Budget of the partnership or any evidence that would show that a copy of RNR's partnership agreement or any partnership budget was given to the Bank or that any notice of the general partner's restricted authority was provided to the Bank.

* * * [T]he trial court entered a summary final judgment of foreclosure in favor of the Bank. * * *

* * *

* * * Section 301(1), [citation], a part of the Florida Revised Uniform Partnership Act (FRUPA), provides:

Each partner is an agent of the partnership for the purpose of its business. An act of a partner, including the execution of an instrument in the partnership name, for apparently carrying on in the ordinary scope of partnership business or business of the kind carried on by the partnership, in the geographic area in which the partnership operates, binds the partnership unless the partner had no authority to act for the partnership in the particular manner and the person with whom the partner was dealing knew or had received notification that the partner lacked authority.

[Court's footnote: RNR mistakenly argues that section 301(1) has no application to a limited partnership because that section is part of the Florida Revised Uniform Partnership Act, not the Florida Revised Uniform Limited Partnership Act. Section 620.186 (comparable to Revised Uniform Limited Partnership Act Section 1105), however, provides, as follows: "In any case not provided for in this act, the provisions of the Uniform Partnership Act or the Revised Uniform Partnership Act of 1995, as applicable, and the rules of law and equity shall govern."]

Thus, even if a general partner's actual authority is restricted by the terms of the partnership agreement, the general partner possesses the apparent authority to bind the partnership in the ordinary course of partnership business or in the business of the kind carried on by the partnership, unless the third party "knew or had received a notification that the partner lacked authority." [Citation.] "Knowledge" and "notice" under FRUPA are defined in section 102. That section provides that "[a] person knows a fact if the person has actual knowledge of the fact." [Citation.] Further, a third party has notice of a fact if that party "(a) knows of the fact; (b) has received notification of the fact; or (c) has reason to know the fact exists from all other facts known to the person at the time in question." [FRUPA] §102(2). Finally, under [FRUPA] section 303 a partnership may file a statement of partnership authority setting forth any restrictions in a general partner's authority.

* * *

"Absent actual knowledge, third parties have no duty to inspect the partnership agreement or inquire otherwise to ascertain the extent of a partner's actual authority in the ordinary course of business * * * even if they have some reason to question it." [Citation.] The apparent authority provisions of section 301(1), reflect a policy by the drafters that "the risk of loss from partner misconduct more appropriately belongs on the partnership than on third parties who do not knowingly participate in or take advantage of the misconduct." * * * [Citation.]

Under section 301(1), the determination of whether a partner is acting with authority to bind the partnership involves a two-step analysis. The first step is to determine whether the partner purporting to bind the partnership apparently is carrying on the partnership business in the usual way or a business of the kind carried on by the partnership. An affirmative answer on this step ends the inquiry, unless it is shown that the person with whom the partner is dealing actually knew or had received a notification that the partner lacked authority. [Citation.] Here, it is undisputed that, in entering into the loan, the general partner was carrying on the business of RNR in the usual way. The dispositive question in this appeal is whether there are issues of material fact as to whether the Bank had actual knowledge or notice of restrictions on the general partner's authority.

RNR argues that, as a result of the restrictions on the general partner's authority in the partnership agreement, the Bank had constructive knowledge of the restrictions and was obligated to inquire as to the general partner's specific authority to bind RNR in the construction loan. We cannot agree. Under section 301, the Bank could rely on the general partner's apparent authority, unless it had actual knowledge or notice of restrictions on that authority. While the RNR partners may have agreed upon restrictions that would limit the general partner to borrowing no more than $650,000 on behalf of the partnership, RNR does not contend and nothing

before us would show that the Bank had actual knowledge or notice of any restrictions on the general partner's authority. Here, the partnership could have protected itself by filing a statement pursuant to section 303 or by providing notice to the Bank of the specific restrictions on the authority of the general partner.

* * *

Because there is no disputed issue of fact concerning whether the Bank had actual knowledge or notice of restrictions on the general partner's authority to borrow, summary judgment was proper.

Affirmed.

| CASE 31-2 | Liability of Incoming Partner
CONKLIN FARM v. LEIBOWITZ
Supreme Court of New Jersey, 1995
140 N.J.417, 658 A.2d 1257 |  |

Garibaldi, J.

This appeal addresses whether an incoming partner is personally liable for interest that accrues on a partnership debt that arose before the incoming partner's admission. Under section 17 of New Jersey's Uniform Partnership Law, [citation] (the Act), an incoming partner is liable for preexisting debt only to the extent of partnership property; the incoming partner is not personally liable for preexisting debt. The parties to this appeal differ over whether the interest on a preexisting debt that accrues after the incoming partner's admission is new debt or part of the preexisting debt.

In December 1986, Paula Hertzberg, Elliot Leibowitz, and Joel Leibowitz formed, under the Act, a general partnership, LongView Estates (LongView), to acquire from plaintiff Conklin Farm (Conklin) approximately 100 acres of land in the Township of Montville. Paula Hertzberg owned forty percent of LongView; Elliot and Joel Leibowitz owned thirty percent each. They intended to build a residential condominium complex on the property.

On the same day that Paula Hertzberg, Elliot Leibowitz, and Joel Leibowitz formed LongView, LongView executed a promissory note in favor of Conklin for $9 million. The three LongView partners signed the note as partners, and also guaranteed the note personally. The note represented a portion of the purchase price for the land, and was secured by a mortgage on the land. The note provided for monthly payments of interest only—to accrue at eight and a quarter percent annually for the first year and nine percent thereafter—with the principal and any unpaid interest due on January15, 1992. * * * The final payment on January 15, 1992, was to include any unpaid interest and the principal amount of $9 million. * * *

* * *

On March 15, 1990, Joel Leibowitz assigned his thirty percent interest in LongView to his wife, defendant Doris Leibowitz, who "agreed to be bound by all the terms and conditions of the Partnership Agreement dated December 22, 1986." Seventeen months later, on August 30, 1991, Doris assigned the interest back to her husband. During those seventeen months, the entire principal of the Conklin note of $9 million was outstanding, and interest accrued at an annual rate of nine percent.

LongView's condominium project failed, and LongView defaulted on * * * the Conklin note. * * * In March 1991, LongView filed a petition for bankruptcy under Chapter 11 of the Bankruptcy Code. * * * Eventually, Paula Hertzberg, Elliot Leibowitz, and Joel Leibowitz filed for personal bankruptcy protection, and all three were discharged of any personal liability on the Conklin [note].

II

Conklin looked to Doris Leibowitz for payment of thirty percent of the interest that accrued on the Conklin note over the seventeen months during which she had held her husband's interest. Conklin sued her in November 1991, claiming that she was *personally* liable for $547,000: thirty percent of the interest that accrued during the seventeen months, plus interest and costs. [Court's footnote: As the opinion below noted, "It is unclear from this record why plaintiff sought only thirty percent of the interest from defendant." [Citation.] If the interest at issue is indeed new debt, Doris Leibowitz is personally liable for 100% of it under [the Partnership Act]].

* * *

* * * [T]he sole issue became whether Doris Leibowitz, as an incoming partner, was personally liable for the interest that had accrued on the preexisting debt while she had been a partner. The trial court held that the interest was part of the preexisting debt, not new debt. The trial court found that [section 17 of New Jersey's Uniform Partnership Law] therefore limited Doris Leibowitz's liability to her interest in partnership property, which, of course, was by then worthless. Holding that Doris Leibowitz was thus not personally liable for the interest, the court granted her motion for summary judgment.

Conklin filed a Notice of Appeal. * * * The Appellate Division reversed. [Citation.] Ruling that the interest on preexisting debt is new debt, the Appellate Division held that Doris Leibowitz was personally liable for the interest that accrued on the note while she was a partner of LongView.

We granted Doris Leibowitz's petition for certification, [citation], and now reverse.

III

We find that the plain language of section 17 of New Jersey's Uniform Partnership Law and its legislative history compel the conclusion that Doris Leibowitz, as an incoming partner, is liable for debt to Conklin only to the extent of her interest in partnership assets. Under [section 15(b) of New Jersey's Uniform Partnership Law] each partner is personally liable for the debts and obligations of a partnership. [Section 17 of New Jersey's Uniform Partnership Law] defines the liability of new partners entering an existing partnership. That statute provides:

A person admitted as a partner into an existing partnership is liable for all the obligations of the partnership arising before his admission as though he had been a partner when such obligations were incurred, except *that this liability shall be satisfied only out of partnership property.* (Emphasis added).

Under this statute, although the original partners are personally liable for preexisting debt, the incoming partner's liability for preexisting debt is limited to partnership property.

* * *

Thus, section 17 of the Uniform Partnership Act * * * made incoming partners personally liable for preexisting debts, but only to the extent of their investment in the partnership. * * *

* * *

IV

The Conklin note was executed by the partnership prior to Doris Leibowitz's having any interest in LongView. She did not sign or guarantee payment of that note. Thus, the issue appears resolved by the clear language of [section 17]: Because the note was a preexisting debt, and because Doris Leibowitz was an incoming partner, she is not personally liable for the debt. The parties agree that the principal of the note was preexisting debt. However, while Doris Leibowitz argues that the interest that accrued while she was a partner was part of that preexisting debt, Conklin argues that it was new debt that arose each month as it became due. Thus, according to Conklin, Doris Leibowitz is personally liable for the interest that accrued while she was a partner. We disagree.

* * *

V

Conklin argues that just as a rent obligation arises for current use of property, an interest obligation arises for current use of principal. The Appellate Division described the analogy as a "sound approach," and agreed that "interest is current rent for money and also should be treated as new debt." [Citation.] We disagree, and we find the rent analogy faulty.

Contractual interest is created by the contract, and is therefore inseparable from the contractual debt. In [citation], we described contractual interest as "an integral part of the debt itself." Indeed, contractual interest does not exist absent provision for it in the debt-creating instrument. * * * The interest obligation cannot be a separate debt from the principal obligation because, independent of the contract establishing the principal obligation, there is no obligation to pay interest.

* * *

Because there is no obligation to pay interest independent of the promissory note, Conklin's rent analogy fails. Since the obligation to pay interest arises only as a result of the original loan instrument, interest, unlike rent, cannot be "new" debt. * * *

* * *

Moreover, there is no prejudice to Conklin in the fact that it may look to only the original partners for payment of the preexisting debt and interest. In executing the note, Conklin considered the personal credit of only Paula Hertzberg, Elliot Leibowitz, and Joel Leibowitz, all of whom guaranteed the loan. Conklin did not rely on the personal credit of Doris Leibowitz. When lenders loan money, they rely on the financial statements of the general partners, and not of some future, unknown general partner. * * *

VI

We find that contractual interest is not new debt. * * * Accordingly, LongView's obligation to pay interest arose when it executed the Conklin note, before Doris Leibowitz became a partner. Hence, the interest on the note was preexisting debt under [section 17], and Doris Leibowitz is not personally liable for its payment.

The judgment of the Appellate Division is reversed.

CASE 31-3

Dissolution
ROBERTSON v. JACOBS CATTLE CO.
Supreme Court of Nebraska, 2013
830 N.W.2d 191, 285 Neb. 859

Stephan, J.

[Jacobs Cattle Company is an at-will family partnership whose current partners are Ardith, Duane, Carolyn, Patricia, James, and Dennis. Under the terms of the partnership agreement, Ardith has general management authority (1) to conduct day-to-day business on behalf of the partnership and (2) to bind the partnership, but a vote of six partners has authority to override a decision made by Ardith. Ardith and Dennis each have two votes; Patricia, James, Duane, and Carolyn each have one vote. Ardith and Dennis together have a capital interest in the partnership of approximately 78 percent.

The partnership owns approximately 1,525 acres of agricultural land in Valley County, Nebraska. A real estate appraiser valued the land as of September 20, 2011, at $5,135,000. The partnership rented its land to others, including Patricia, James, Dennis, Duane, and Carolyn, although James did not sign a lease. At least some of the land was rented for less than its fair rental value.

Since June 19, 1997, the partnership has not returned a profit and there have been no distributions of net profits to the partners. There were no partnership meetings after January 2005, after which Ardith replaced the partnership's attorney and accountant, who were the last accountant and attorney agreeable to all of the partners. None of the tenants had paid their rent for 2004. In March 2005, Dennis and Patricia were involved in a physical altercation. As a result, Dennis pled no contest to criminal assault charges. On April 28, Patricia and James were served with a notice to quit the leased premises for nonpayment of rent. Around the same time, Duane was also notified that he needed to quit the premises he was leasing due to nonpayment of rent. Duane eventually paid his rent, but on May 4, the partnership sued Patricia and James for rents due for the years 2003 and 2004. Ardith alone made the decision to file the lawsuit. On August 11, a court entered judgment against Patricia for unpaid rent. The court did not enter judgment against James because his name was not on the lease. The land that the partnership had leased to Patricia was later rented to Dennis.

In July 2007, Patricia, James, Duane, and Carolyn (appellants) filed a complaint against the partnership, Ardith, and Dennis (collectively appellees), seeking a dissolution and winding up of the partnership under the Uniform Partnership Act of 1998 (1998 UPA). Appellees filed an answer alleging that dissociation of appellants, not dissolution of the partnership, was the proper remedy.

After conducting a bench trial, the district court concluded that appellants did not prove the occurrence of events authorizing dissolution under §67-439(5) because (1) nothing had occurred to interfere with the partnership's ability to buy, own, and rent land; (2) no partners took steps to override decisions made by Ardith; and (3) Ardith had not acted beyond the partner restrictions specified in the partnership agreement. The court reasoned that nothing had occurred to make the partnership agreement difficult or impossible with which to comply, and it dismissed appellants' dissolution claims.

However, the court found that appellants' failure to pay rent in a timely manner supported appellees' request that appellants be dissociated from the partnership under §67-431(5)(a) and (c). The court reasoned that because the primary purpose of the partnership was to rent land, appellants' delinquency in paying rent materially and adversely affected the partnership business and made it not practicable for the partnership to carry on with appellants as partners. The court thus ordered dissociation of appellants by judicial expulsion pursuant to §67-431(5)(a) and (c) and ordered the partnership to purchase appellants' interests in the partnership.]

The 1998 UPA replaced the original Uniform Partnership Act, [citations], and brought about significant changes in partnership law. Prior law required an at-will partnership to dissolve upon any partner's expressed will to dissolve the partnership. [Citations.] RUPA, on which the 1998 UPA is based, sought to avoid mandatory dissolution of partnerships by making a partnership a distinct entity from its partners. [Citation.] * * *

* * *

The statutory provisions governing dissociation and dissolution are similar but not identical. Dissolution of a partnership is governed by §67-439, which provides that "[a] partnership is dissolved, and its business must be wound up, only upon the occurrence of any of the following events," which include

(5) On application by a partner, a judicial determination that:

(a) The economic purpose of the partnership is likely to be unreasonably frustrated;

(b) Another partner has engaged in conduct relating to the partnership business which makes it not reasonably practicable to carry on the business in partnership with that partner; or

(c) It is not otherwise reasonably practicable to carry on the partnership business in conformity with the partnership agreement[.]

The district court concluded that none of these circumstances existed because (1) nothing had occurred which would frustrate the partnership's ability to buy, sell, or own land, and (2) Ardith, as managing partner, had authority on behalf of the partnership to take the actions with which appellants disagreed.

Dissociation is a new concept introduced by RUPA "to denote the change in the relationship caused by a partner's ceasing to be associated in the carrying on of the business." [Citation.] Under RUPA, "the dissociation of a partner does not necessarily cause a dissolution and winding up of the business of the partnership." [Citation.] Section 67-431 lists events which may trigger a partner's dissociation, including

(5) On application by the partnership or another partner, the partner's expulsion by judicial determination because:

(a) The partner engaged in wrongful conduct that adversely and materially affected the partnership business;

(b) The partner willfully or persistently committed a material breach of the partnership agreement or of a duty owed to the partnership or the other partners under section 67-424; or

(c) The partner engaged in conduct relating to the partnership business which makes it not reasonably practicable to carry on the business in partnership with the partner.

In this case, the district court concluded that the grounds for dissociation stated in §67-431(5)(a) and (c) were met by the failure of appellants to pay timely rent for the land leased from the partnership.

With these principles in mind, we first consider appellants' argument that the district court erred in determining that there were grounds to dissociate them from the partnership. Given that the sole business of the partnership was to own farmland which it leased to others, we have no difficulty concluding that the failure of appellants who executed leases to pay timely rents constituted wrongful conduct that adversely and materially affected the partnership business and made it not reasonably practical to carry on the partnership business with the existing partners. * * *

Next, we consider whether the district court erred in concluding that appellants failed to establish grounds for dissolution of the partnership. Appellees argue the district court correctly decided this issue because no wrongdoing on the part of Ardith or Dennis has been proved. But even appellees acknowledge that "much acrimony exists between and among the parties." [Citation.] At oral argument, appellees' counsel conceded that there were unspecified grounds for dissolution of the partnership, but argued that dissociation was nevertheless the appropriate remedy. We perceive this concession as agreement that the somewhat autocratic manner in which Ardith conducted the affairs of the partnership in recent years, even if not in violation of the partnership agreement, would constitute grounds for dissolution under §67-439(5)(b), i.e., "conduct relating to the partnership business which makes it not reasonably practicable to carry on the business in partnership with that partner." We find no other possible grounds for dissolution. * * * such conduct is also grounds for dissociation under §67-431(5)(c), and the record supports the district court's determination that appellants engaged in such conduct. Thus, we conclude that there are grounds for dissolution of the partnership under §67-439(5)(b) and dissociation of appellants under §67-431(5)(a) and (c).

Under the RUPA model upon which our statutes are based, the dissociation of a partner does not necessarily cause a dissolution and winding up of the partnership's business. [Citations.] Generally, the partnership must be dissolved and its business wound up only upon the occurrence of one of the events listed in §801 of RUPA, upon which Nebraska's §67-439 is based. [Citation.]

The question we must resolve is whether dissolution is mandatory where the conduct of multiple partners constitutes grounds for dissolution under §67-439(5)(b) and also constitutes grounds for dissociation pursuant to §67-431(5)(c).

* * *

* * * Construing the dissolution remedy as mandatory in this circumstance would be contrary to the entity theory of partnership embodied in RUPA. * * * a main purpose of RUPA is "to prevent mandatory dissolution" of a partnership. Accordingly, we hold that where a court determines that the conduct of one or more partners constitutes grounds for dissociation by judicial expulsion under §67-431(5)(c) and dissolution under §67-439(5)(b), and there are no other grounds for dissolution, the court may in its discretion order either dissociation by expulsion of one or more partners or dissolution of the partnership.

We conclude that dissociation by judicial expulsion of appellants is an appropriate remedy under the facts of this case. * * * Ardith and Dennis have a capital interest in the partnership of approximately 78 percent. Pursuant to the partnership agreement, Ardith has general management authority to conduct the day-today business on behalf of the partnership. We agree with the finding of the district court that there is no apparent reason why the partnership cannot continue to exist and function in accordance with the partnership agreement with Ardith and Dennis as its sole partners.

[Judgment dissociating appellants from the partnership by judicial expulsion and declining to dissolve the partnership affirmed.]

CASE
31-4

Continuation after Dissociation
WARNICK v. WARNICK
Supreme Court of Wyoming, 2003
2003 WY 113, 76 P.3d 316

Golden, J.

In August 1978, Wilbur and Dee Warnick and their son Randall Warnick contracted to purchase a ranch in Sheridan County for an agreed price of $335,000, with $90,000 down plus $245,000 in installments over ten years at 8% interest. In April 1979, they formed Warnick Ranches general partnership to operate the ranch and complete the installment purchase agreement. The partnership agreement recited that the initial capital contributions of the partners totaled $60,000, paid 36% by Wilbur, 30% by Dee, and 34% by Randall.

The partnership leased out the ranch property for the first two years. Wilbur and Dee Warnick then moved onto the ranch in 1981, living there and working the ranch up to the present time. Randall lived and worked on the ranch during the 1981 and 1982 summer haying seasons and again from 1991 to 1998.

The partners over the years each contributed additional funds to the operation of the ranch and received cash distributions from the partnership. After 1983, Randall contributed very little new money and almost all of the additional funds to pay off the mortgage came from Wilbur and Dee Warnick. Wilbur also left in the partnership account two $12,000 cash distributions that were otherwise payable to him. The net cash contributions of the partners through 1999, considering the initial contributions, payments to or on behalf of the partnership, draws not taken and distributions from the partnership were:

Wilbur $170,112.60 (51%)
Dee 138,834.63 (41%)
Randall 25,406.28 (8%)

In 1998, Randall Warnick began having discussions with his brother about the possibility of selling his interest in Warnick Ranches. When Randall mentioned this to his father, a dispute arose between them concerning the percentage of the partnership that Randall owned. Finally, on April 14, 1999, Randall's attorney sent a letter to Warnick Ranches which stated:

I have been asked to contact you regarding [Randall's] desire to either sell his interest in the ranch to a third party, to the partnership, or to liquidate the partnership under Paragraph 12 of the partnership agreement.

* * * It would appear that it would be in the best interests of all to amicably agree to a selling price of his interest either to a third party or to the partnership as provided in the partnership agreement.

On August 11, 1999, Warnick Ranches responded in writing, treating the letter from Randall's attorney as the expressed will of a partner to dissociate. The partnership's response included a tender offer for Randall's share, as provided under [RUPA] §701(e) and (g) in the case of a dissociating partner. Randall in turn exercised his right under [RUPA] §701(j) to reject the tender and bring an action against the partnership to determine his interest in the partnership, including a buyout price if he is determined to be dissociated from the partnership.

* * * The parties stipulated to facts regarding the cash flows into and out of the partnership accounts, as well as the partnership tax returns for each year from 1979 through 1999. * * *

The district court, in granting Randall Warnick's motion for summary judgment, found that dissociation of Randall as a partner was the appropriate remedy and that the schedule of ownership recited in the partnership agreement, absent evidence of any other written agreement, controls the partners' percentage upon dissolution or dissociation. The court awarded judgment to Randall Warnick for the amount of his cash contributions, plus 34% of the partnership assets' increase in value above all partners' cash contributions. As a result of that calculation, $230,819.14, or 25.24%, of the undisputed value of the partnership was awarded to Randall, without provision of interest for any partner in the calculation.

* * *

Resolution of this matter relies almost entirely on application of the Wyoming Revised Uniform Partnership Act ("RUPA"), [citation]. * * * RUPA states in pertinent part:

[A] partnership agreement governs relations among the partners and between the partners and the partnership. To the extent the partnership agreement does not otherwise provide, this chapter governs relations among the partners and between the partners and the partnership.

[RUPA] §103(a). "The Revised Act is, therefore, largely a series of 'default rules' that govern the relations among partners in situations they have not addressed in a partnership agreement." [Citations.]

During the existence of the partnership, each partner has authority to act on behalf of the partnership, [RUPA] §§301, 401(f), and "all partners are liable jointly and severally for all obligations of the partnership unless otherwise agreed by the claimant or provided by law." [RUPA] §306(a). "A partner may lend money to and transact other business with the partnership," [RUPA] §404(f), and "[a] partnership shall repay a partner who, in aid of the partnership, makes a payment or advance beyond the amount of capital the partner agreed to contribute." [RUPA] §401(d). Such a payment or advance by a partner constitutes a loan to the partnership which accrues interest from the date of the payment or advance. [RUPA] §401(e).

The provisions of the Warnick Ranches Partnership Agreement addressing the above subjects are paragraphs six and nine, which state:

> 6. CAPITAL CONTRIBUTION. The parties hereto hereby agree to contribute the personal property listed on Exhibit "A" attached hereto to the Partnership to be used in the Partnership business. By unanimous agreement of all Partners, additional contributions may be made to, or withdrawals may be made from, the capital of the Partnership.

* * *

> 9. ACCOUNTING. On December 31 of each year, the accounts of the Partnership business will be closed for the year. As of that date, the Partnership income and expenses will be totaled and the difference shall be divided among the Partners on any basis which is mutually agreed upon by all Partners, giving due consideration to services rendered during the year by each Partner, drawings during the year by each Partner and the amount of capital invested by each Partner during such year.

The partnership agreement is entirely silent as to how cash advances or payments on behalf of the business are to be treated. The partners knew that additional cash would be needed to make the mortgage payments on the ranch, and perhaps assumed that paragraph six of their agreement would cover the additional funds when they would unanimously agree to adjust the capital accounts when a partner paid more money into the operation.

It is, however, undisputed that the partners never entered into a unanimous agreement to amend their partnership agreement or to reflect additional capital contributions. It is also undisputed that the advances by the partners were not anywhere documented as a loan to the partnership rather than capital contributions. The district court found these facts dispositive in granting Randall Warnick's summary judgment motion. The court specifically found that there was no documentation to support a conclusion that the payments by the elder Warnicks were a loan, so they could not be treated as a loan.

The district court's decision, however, misapplies the clear provisions of the Revised Uniform Partnership Act. RUPA operates automatically if a partnership agreement does not have contrary provisions. * * * In this sense, RUPA operates

like the Uniform Probate Code, which fills in the blanks of an estate plan for those who die intestate or with a will that does not address a contingency that has occurred.

The district court's calculations in this case treat the mortgage payments as neither capital contributions nor advances, but as something else not contemplated by RUPA. The partnership agreement at paragraph ten and RUPA at [RUPA] §401(k) are consistent in requiring that the partners must unanimously consent to any amendments of the partnership agreement. Advances are not addressed in the agreement, so we must turn to RUPA's default provisions in that regard. [Citation.] Nothing in RUPA requires advances to the partnership or payment of partnership debts by partners to be memorialized in writing as a loan. In fact, the act addresses payments and advances in several places without requiring a writing or unanimous partner approval:

- [RUPA] §401(c) requires the partnership to reimburse a partner for payments made by the partner in the ordinary and proper conduct of the business of the partnership or for the preservation of its business or property;

- [RUPA] §401(d) requires the partnership to reimburse a partner for a payment or advance to the partnership beyond the amount of capital the partner agreed to contribute;

- [RUPA] §401(e) provides that a partner's cash payment on behalf of the partnership automatically constitutes a loan which accrues interest from the date of the payment;

Read [together], these provisions of the act evidence a presumption that additional amounts paid by a partner, over and above the capital contributions recited in the partnership agreement or agreed to, are presumed to be loans to the partnership, with interest payable from the date of the advance. RUPA is unequivocal on this point. The drafters' comment to §401(d) states: "Subsection (d) is based on UPA Section 18(c). It makes explicit that the partnership must reimburse a partner for an advance of funds beyond the amount of the partner's agreed capital contribution, thereby treating the advance as a loan." [Citation.]

Warnick Ranches partnership was formed "for the purpose of managing and operating a farming and ranching business" on property that was subject to a mortgage at the time the partnership was formed. It was entirely foreseeable that additional cash would be needed to meet the mortgage payments, as in fact happened. * * * The silence of the partnership agreement on [the duty to make capital contributions beyond the partnership agreement], combined with the statutory presumption in favor of advances over capital contributions, leads necessarily to the conclusion that a partner's payment of the Warnick Ranch mortgage, without the unanimous consent required for additional capital contributions, would be an advance and a loan to the partnership.

* * *

We turn then to the consequences of this dispute. RUPA, with the goal of avoiding unnecessary dissolutions of partnerships, contains a significant change from prior partnership law. Again in the words of the drafters:

RUPA dramatically changes the law governing partnership breakups and dissolution. An entirely new concept, "dissociation," is used in lieu of the UPA term "dissolution" to denote the change in the relationship caused by a partner's ceasing to be associated in the carrying on of the business. * * *

Under RUPA, unlike the UPA, the dissociation of a partner does not necessarily cause a dissolution and winding up of the business of the partnership. Section 801 identifies the situations in which the dissociation of a partner causes a winding up of the business. Section 701 provides that in all other situations there is a buyout of the partner's interest in the partnership, rather than a windup of the partnership business. In those other situations, the partnership entity continues, unaffected by the partner's dissociation.

[Revised] Uniform Partnership Act §601, cmt. 1, [citation].

The Warnick Ranch Partnership Agreement is again silent as to dissociation, addressing only liquidation. RUPA states hat a partner has the power to dissociate at any time by express will, [RUPA] §602(a), and that:

(a) A partner is dissociated from a partnership upon:

(i) Receipt by the partnership of notice of the partner's express will to withdraw as a partner or upon any later date specified in the notice; * * *

* * *

Under these circumstances, the record supports the district court's conclusion that there was no genuine issue as to the material fact that a dissociation occurred. Considering the April 1999 letter from Randall's attorney to the partnership, in the context of deposition testimony regarding allegations of physical violence and misappropriation of partnership funds, we determine that the date of the letter is the date of dissociation.

However, the court erred in its calculation of the judgment. RUPA states that a dissociated partner's interest in the partnership shall be purchased by the partnership for a buyout price. [RUPA] §§603(a), 701(a), (b). The buyout price is equal to the amount that would have been distributable to the dissociating partner under [RUPA] §808(b) if, on the date of the dissociation, the partnership's assets had been sold. [RUPA] §701(b). However, §808(a) provides that partnership assets must first be applied to discharge partnership liabilities to creditors, including partners who are creditors. As noted above, as each partner advanced funds to pay the mortgage or other partnership expenses, that partner became a creditor of the partnership or the amount advanced, and is entitled to interest on each amount from the date of the advance. In calculating Randall's buyout price, it is therefore necessary to first calculate the amount that the partnership owes to each partner for advances to the partnership, with interest accrued rom the date of each advance at the rate specified in [RUPA] §104(b).

Next, there is the matter of two $12,000 draws, or "guaranteed payments," that Wilbur Warnick was entitled to in 1998 and 1999, but actually left in the partnership account and did not receive. The guaranteed payment arrangement was at Randall's request and agreed among the partners in order to provide Randall an income and to avoid the partnership showing a taxable profit. Randall received his draw as agreed in 1998 and 1999 but Wilbur did not, even though he reported it as personal income and paid taxes on it. At the time he became entitled to the "guaranteed payment," the $12,000 was Wilbur's personal money and his leaving it with the partnership was the functional equivalent of another advance to the partnership. [RUPA] §401(d); [citation]. Upon remand, therefore, in calculating the buyout price for Randall Warnick's share, it is necessary to first calculate the amount the partnership owes Wilbur Warnick for the two $12,000 draws he left with the partnership, with interest from the date he was entitled to the payments.

* * *

A partnership agreement governs relations among general partners and between partners and their partnership. To the extent the agreement is silent or ambiguous, the Revised Uniform Partnership Act provisions apply. Review of the entire record leads us to conclude that there is no genuine issue regarding the fact that a partner dissociation occurred, and that the Plaintiff is entitled to a judgment as a matter of law for the buyout price of his interest. However, the district court's calculation of the dissociated partner's buyout price is reversed and the case remanded for a calculation of that price after repayment of partner advances as loans, in accord with the statute and this decision.

QUESTIONS

1. Albert, Betty, and Carol own and operate the Roy Lumber Company. Each contributed one-third of the capital, and they share equally in the profits and losses. Their partnership agreement provides that two partners must authorize all purchases over $2,500 in advance and that only Albert is authorized to draw checks. Unknown to Albert or Carol, Betty purchases on the firm's account a $5,500 diamond bracelet and a $5,000 forklift and orders $5,000 worth of logs, all from Doug, who operates a jewelry store and is engaged in various activities connected with the lumber business. Before Betty made these purchases, Albert told Doug that Betty is not the log buyer. Albert refuses to pay Doug for Betty's purchases. Doug calls at the mill to collect, and Albert again refuses to pay him. Doug calls Albert an unprintable name, and Albert then punches Doug in the nose, knocking him out. While Doug is lying unconscious on the ground, an employee of Roy Lumber Company negligently drops a log on Doug's leg, breaking three bones. The firm and the three partners are completely solvent.

   What are the rights of Doug against Roy Lumber Company, Albert, Betty, and Carol? Explain.

2. Paula, Fred, and Stephanie agree that Paula and Fred will form and conduct a partnership business and that Stephanie will become a partner in two years. Stephanie agrees to lend the firm $50,000 and take 10 percent of the profits in lieu of interest. Without Stephanie's knowledge, Paula and Fred tell Harold that Stephanie is a partner, and Harold, relying on Stephanie's sound financial status, gives the firm credit. The firm later becomes insolvent, and Harold seeks to hold Stephanie liable as a partner. Should Harold succeed? Explain.

3. Simmons, Hoffman, and Murray were partners doing business under the firm name of Simmons & Co. The firm borrowed money from a bank and gave the bank the firm's note for the loan. In addition, each partner guaranteed the note individually. The firm became insolvent, and a receiver was appointed. The bank claims that it has a right to file its claim as a firm debt and that it has a right to participate in the distribution of the assets of the individual partners before partnership creditors receive any payment from such assets.

   a. Explain the principle involved in this case.

   b. Is the bank correct? Why or why not?

4. Anthony and Karen were partners doing business as the Petite Garment Company. Leroy owned a dye plant that did much of the processing for the company. Anthony and Karen decided to offer Leroy an interest in their company, in consideration for which Leroy would contribute his dye plant to the partnership. Leroy accepted the offer and was duly admitted as a partner. At the time he was admitted as a partner, Leroy did not know that the partnership was on the verge of insolvency. About three months after Leroy was admitted to the partnership, a textile firm obtained a judgment against the partnership in the amount of $50,000. This debt represented an unpaid balance that had existed before Leroy was admitted as a partner.

   The textile firm brought an action to subject the partnership property, including the dye plant, to the satisfaction of its judgment. The complaint also requested that in the event the judgment was unsatisfied by sale of the partnership property, Leroy's home be sold and the proceeds applied to the balance of the judgment. Anthony and Karen own nothing but their interest in the partnership property.

   Explain what the result should be (a) with regard to the dye plant and (b) with regard to Leroy's home.

5. Jones and Ray formed a partnership on January 1, known as JR Construction Co., to engage in the construction business, each partner owning a one-half interest. On February 10, while conducting partnership business, Jones negligently injured Ware, who brought an action against Jones, Ray, and JR Construction Co. and obtained judgment for $250,000 against them on March 1. On April 15, Muir joined the partnership by contributing $100,000 cash, and by agreement, each partner was entitled to a one-third interest. In July, the partners agreed to purchase new construction equipment for the partnership, and Muir was authorized to obtain a loan from XYZ Bank in the partnership name for $200,000 to finance the purchase. On July 10, Muir signed a $200,000 note on behalf of the partnership, and the equipment was purchased. In November, the partnership was in financial difficulty, its total assets amounting to $50,000. The note was in default, with a balance of $150,000 owing to XYZ Bank. Muir has substantial resources, while Jones and Ray each individually have assets of $20,000.

   What is the extent of Muir's personal liability and the personal liability of Jones and Ray as to (a) the judgment obtained by Ware and (b) the debt owing to XYZ Bank?

6. Lauren, Matthew, and Susan form a partnership, with Lauren contributing $100,000, Matthew contributing $50,000, and Susan contributing her time and skill. Nothing is said regarding the division of profits. The firm later dissolves. No distributions to partners have

been made since the partnership was formed. The partnership sells its assets for a loss of $90,000. After payment of all firm debts, $60,000 is left. Lauren claims that she is entitled to the entire $60,000. Matthew contends that the distribution should be $40,000 to Lauren and $20,000 to Matthew. Susan claims the $60,000 should be divided equally among the partners. Who is correct? Explain.

7. Adams, a consulting engineer, entered into a partnership with three others for the practice of their profession. The only written partnership agreement is a brief document specifying that Adams is entitled to 55 percent of the profits and the others to 15 percent each. The venture is a total failure. Creditors are pressing for payment, and some have filed suit. The partners cannot agree on a course of action.

   Explain how many of the partners must agree to achieve each of the following objectives:

   a. To add Jones, also an engineer, as a partner, Jones being willing to contribute a substantial amount of new capital.

   b. To sell a vacant lot held in the partnership name, which had been acquired as a future office site for the partnership.

   c. To move the partnership's offices to less expensive quarters.

   d. To demand a formal accounting.

   e. To dissolve the partnership.

   f. To agree to submit certain disputed claims to arbitration, which Adams believes will prove less expensive than litigation.

   g. To sell all of the partnership's personal property, with Adams having what he believes to be a good offer for the property from a newly formed engineering firm.

   h. To alter the respective interests of the parties in the profits and losses by decreasing Adams's share to 40 percent and increasing the others' shares accordingly.

   i. To assign all the partnership's assets to a bank in trust for the benefit of creditors, hoping to work out satisfactory arrangements without filing for bankruptcy.

8. Charles and Jack orally agreed to become partners in a tool and die business. Charles, who had experience in tool and die work, was to operate the business. Jack was to take no active part but was to contribute the entire $500,000 capitalization. Charles worked ten hours a day at the plant, for which he was paid nothing. Nevertheless, despite Charles's best efforts, the business failed. The $500,000 capital was depleted, and the partnership owed $500,000 in debts. Prior to the failure of the partnership business, Jack became personally insolvent; consequently, the creditors of the partnership collected the entire $500,000 indebtedness from Charles, who was forced to sell his home and farm to satisfy the indebtedness. Jack later regained his financial responsibility, and Charles brought an appropriate action against Jack for (a) one-half of the $500,000 he had paid to partnership creditors and (b) one-half of $80,000, the reasonable value of Charles's services during the operation of the partnership. Who will prevail and why?

9. Glenn refuses an invitation to become a partner of Dorothy and Cynthia in a retail grocery business. Nevertheless, Dorothy inserts an advertisement in the local newspaper representing Glenn as their partner. Glenn takes no steps to deny the existence of a partnership between them. Ron, who extended credit to the firm, seeks to hold Glenn liable as a partner. Is Glenn liable? Explain.

10. Hanover leased a portion of his farm to Brown and Black, doing business as the Colorite Hatchery. Brown went upon the premises to remove certain chicken sheds that he and Black had placed there for hatchery purposes. Thinking that Brown intended to remove certain other sheds, which were Hanover's property, Hanover accosted Brown, who willfully struck Hanover and knocked him down. Brown then ran to the Colorite truck, which he had previously loaded with chicken coops, and drove back to the hatchery. On the way, he picked up George, who was hitchhiking to the city to look for a job. Brown was driving at seventy miles an hour down the highway. At an open intersection with another highway, Brown in his hurry ran a stop sign, striking another vehicle. The collision caused severe injuries to George. Immediately thereafter, the partnership was dissolved, and Brown was insolvent. Hanover and George each bring separate actions against Black as copartner for the alleged tort committed by Brown against each. What judgments as to each? Discuss.

11. Martin, Mark, and Marvin formed a retail clothing partnership named M Clothiers and conducted a business for many years, buying most of their clothing from Hill, a wholesaler. On January 15, Marvin retired from the business, but Martin and Mark decided to continue it. As part of the retirement agreement, Martin and Mark agreed in writing with Marvin that Marvin would not be responsible for any of the partnership debts, either past or future. On January 15, the partnership published a notice of Marvin's retirement in a newspaper of general circulation where the partnership carried on its business.

Before January 15, Hill was a creditor of M Clothiers to the extent of $10,000, and on January 30, he extended additional credit of $5,000. Hill was not advised and did not in fact know of Marvin's retirement and the change of the partnership. On January 30, Ray, a competitor of Hill, extended credit for the first time to M Clothiers in the amount of $3,000. Ray also was not advised and did not in fact know of Marvin's retirement and the change of the partnership.

On February 1, Martin and Mark departed for parts unknown, leaving no partnership assets with which to pay the described debts. Explain what Marvin's liability is, if any, (a) to Hill and (b) to Ray.

12. Ben, Dan, and Lilli were partners sharing profits in proportions of one-fourth, one-third, and five-twelfths, respectively. Their business failed, and the firm was dissolved. At the time of dissolution, no financial adjustments between the partners were necessary with reference to their respective partners' accounts, but the firm's liabilities to creditors exceeded its assets by $24,000. Without contributing any amount toward the payment of the liabilities, Dan moved to a destination unknown. Ben and Lilli are financially responsible. How much must each contribute? Discuss.

13. Ames, Bell, and Cole were equal partners in the ABC Construction Company. Their written partnership agreement provided that the partnership would dissolve upon the death of any partner. Cole died on June 30, and his widow, Cora Cole, qualified as executor of his will. Ames and Bell wound up the business of the partnership, and on December 31, they completed the sale of all of the partnership's assets. After paying all partnership debts, they distributed the balance equally among themselves and Mrs. Cole as executor.

Subsequently, Mrs. Cole learned that Ames and Bell had made and withdrawn a net profit of $200,000 from July 1 to December 31. The profit was made through new contracts using the partnership name and assets. Ames and Bell had concealed such contracts and profit from Mrs. Cole, and she learned about them from other sources. Immediately after acquiring this information, Mrs. Cole made demand upon Ames and Bell for one-third of the profit of $200,000. They rejected her demand. Explain what are the rights and remedies, if any, of Cora Cole as executor.

14. The articles of partnership of the firm of Wilson and Company provide the following:

William Smith to contribute $50,000; to receive interest thereon at 13 percent per annum and to devote such time as he may be able to give; to receive 30 percent of the profits.

John Jones to contribute $50,000; to receive interest on same at 13 percent per annum; to give all of his time to the business and to receive 30 percent of the profits.

Henry Wilson to contribute all of his time to the business and to receive 20 percent of the profits.

James Brown to contribute all of his time to the business and to receive 20 percent of the profits.

There is no provision for sharing losses. After six years of operation, the firm is dissolved and wound up. No distributions to partners have been made since the partnership was formed. The partnership assets are sold for $400,000 with a loss of $198,000. Liabilities to creditors total $420,000. Explain what are the rights and liabilities of the respective parties.

15. Adam, Stanley, and Rosalind formed a partnership in State X to distribute beer and wine. Their agreement provided that the partnership would continue until December 31, 2024. Which of the following events would cause the ABC partnership to dissolve? If so, when would the partnership be dissolved? Discuss.

a. Rosalind assigns her interest in the partnership to Mary on April 1, 2022.

b. Stanley dies on June 1, 2024.

c. Adam withdraws from the partnership on September 15, 2023.

d. A creditor of Stanley obtains a charging order against Stanley's interest on October 9, 2021.

e. In 2022, the legislature of State X enacts a statute making the sale or distribution of alcoholic beverages illegal.

f. Stanley has a formal accounting of partnership affairs on September 19, 2023.

16. Phillips and Harris are partners in a used car business. Under their oral partnership, each has an equal voice in the conduct and management of the business. Because of their irregular business hours, the two further agreed that they could use any partnership vehicle as desired. This use includes transportation to and from work, even though the vehicles are for sale at all times. Harris conducted partnership business both at the used car lot and from his home. He was on call by Phillips or customers at his home, and he went back to the lot two or three times after going home. While driving a partnership vehicle home from the used car lot, Harris negligently hit a car driven by Cook, who brought this action against Harris and Phillips individually and as copartners for his injuries. Who is liable? Explain.

17. Voeller, the managing partner of the Pay-Out Drive-In Theater, signed a contract to sell to Hodge a small parcel of land belonging to the partnership. Except for the last twenty feet, which were necessary for the theater's driveway, the parcel was not used in theater operations. The agreement stated that it was between Hodge and the partnership, with Voeller signing for the partnership. Voeller claims that he told Hodge before signing that a plot plan would have to be approved by the other partners before the sale. Hodge denies this and sues for specific performance, claiming that Voeller had actual and apparent authority to bind the partnership. The partners argue that Voeller had no such authority and that Hodge knew this. Who is correct? Explain.

18. L. G. and S. L. Patel, husband and wife, owned and operated the City Center Motel in Eureka. On April 16, Rajeshkumar, the son of L. G. and S. L., formed a partnership with his parents and became owner of 35 percent of the City Center Motel. The partnership agreement required that Rajeshkumar approve any sale of the motel. Record title to the motel was not changed, however, to reflect his interest. On April 21, L. G. and S. L. listed their motel for sale with a real estate broker. On May 2, P. V. and Kirit Patel made an offer on the motel, which L. G. and S. L. accepted. Neither the broker nor the purchasers knew of the son's interest in the motel. When L. G. and S. L. notified Rajeshkumar of their plans, to their surprise, he refused to sell his 35 percent of the motel. On May 4, L. G. and S. L. notified P. V. and Kirit that they wished to withdraw their acceptance. They offered to pay $10,000 in damages and to give the purchasers a right of first refusal for five years. Rather than accept the offer, on May 29, P. V. and Kirit filed an action for

specific performance and incidental damages. L. G., S. L., and Rajeshkumar responded that the contract could not lawfully be enforced. Discuss who will prevail and why.

19. Davis and Shipman founded a partnership under the name of Shipman & Davis Lumber Company. Four years later, the partnership was dissolved by written agreement. Notice of the dissolution was published in a newspaper of general circulation in Merced County, where the business was conducted. No actual notice of dissolution was given to firms that previously had extended credit to the partnership. By the dissolution agreement, Shipman, who was to continue the business, was to pay all of the partnership's debts. He continued the business as a sole proprietorship for a short time until he formed a successor corporation, Shipman Lumber Servaes Co. After the partnership's dissolution, two firms that previously had done business with the partnership extended credit to Shipman for certain repair work and merchandise. The partnership also had a balance due to Valley Company for a prior purchase. Five months later, two checks were drawn by Shipman Lumber Servaes Co. and accepted by Valley as partial payment on this debt. Credit Bureaus of Merced County, as assignee of these three accounts, sued the partnership as well as Shipman and Davis individually. Does the dissolution of the partnership relieve Davis of personal liability for the accounts? Explain.

20. In August, Victoria Air Conditioning, Inc. (VAC), entered into a subcontract for insulation services with Southwest Texas Mechanical Insulation Company (SWT), a partnership comprising Charlie Jupe and Tommy Nabors. In February of the following year, Jupe and Nabors dissolved the partnership, but VAC did not receive notice of the dissolution at that time. Sometime later, insulation was removed from Nabors's premises to Jupe's possession and Jupe continued the insulation project with VAC. From then on, Nabors had no more involvement with SWT. One month later, Nabors informed VAC's project manager, Von Behrenfeld, that Nabors was no longer associated with SWT, had formed his own insulation company, and was interested in bidding on new jobs. Subsequently, SWT failed to perform the subcontract and Jupe could not be found. VAC brought suit for breach of contract against SWT, Jupe, and Nabors. Nabors claims that several letters and change orders introduced by both parties show that VAC knew of the dissolution and impliedly agreed to discharge Nabors from liability. These documents indicated that VAC had dealt with Jupe but not with Nabors after

the dissolution. VAC denies that the course of dealings between VAC and Jupe was the type from which an agreement to discharge Nabors could be inferred. Who is correct? Explain.

21. Horizon is a large, publicly traded provider of both nursing homes and management for nursing homes. It wanted to expand into Osceola County, Florida. Southern Oaks was already operating in Osceola County; it owned the Southern Oaks Health Care Center and had a Certificate of Need issued by the Florida Agency for Health Care Administration for a new one-hundred-and-twenty-bed facility in Kissimmee. Horizon and Southern Oaks decided to form a partnership to own the proposed Kissimmee facility, which was ultimately named Royal Oaks, and agreed that Horizon would manage both the Southern Oaks facility and the new Royal Oaks facility. To that end, Southern Oaks and Horizon entered into twenty-year partnership and management contracts. The partnership agreements provided that "irreconcilable differences" was a permissible reason for dissolving the partnership. Three years later, Southern Oaks filed suit, alleging that Horizon breached its obligations under two different partnership agreements and that Horizon had breached the various management contracts. The court ordered that the partnerships be dissolved, finding that the partners were incapable of continuing to operate in business together. Explain whether Southern Oaks is entitled to receive a damage award for the loss of the partnerships' remaining seventeen years' worth of future profits.

TAKING SIDES

Stroud and Freeman are general partners in Stroud's Food Center, a grocery store. Nothing in the articles of partnership restricts the power or authority of either partner to act in respect to the ordinary business of the Food Center. In November, however, Stroud informed National Biscuit that he would not be personally responsible for any more bread sold to the partnership. Then, in the following February, at the request of Freeman, National Biscuit sold and delivered more bread to the Food Center.

a. What are the arguments that Stroud is not liable to National Biscuit for the value of the bread delivered to the Food Center?

b. What are the arguments that Stroud is liable to National Biscuit for the value of the bread delivered to the Food Center?

c. Explain which arguments should prevail.

CHAPTER 32

Limited Partnerships and Limited Liability Companies

CHAPTER OUTCOMES

After reading and studying this chapter, you should be able to:

- Distinguish between a general partnership and a limited partnership.
- Identify those activities in which a limited partner may engage without forfeiting limited liability.
- Distinguish between a limited partnership and a limited liability company.
- Distinguish between a member-managed limited liability company and a manager-managed limited liability company.
- Distinguish between a limited liability partnership and a limited liability limited partnership.

This chapter considers other types of unincorporated business associations: limited partnerships, limited liability companies, limited liability partnerships, and limited liability limited partnerships. These organizations have developed to meet special business and investment needs. Consequently, each has characteristics that make it appropriate for certain purposes.

32-1 Limited Partnerships

The limited partnership has proved to be an attractive vehicle for a variety of investments because of its tax advantages and the limited liability it confers upon limited partners. Unlike general partnerships, limited partnerships are statutory creations. Before 1976, the governing statute in all States except Louisiana was the Uniform Limited Partnership Act (ULPA), which was promulgated in 1916. At that time, most limited partnerships were small and had only a few limited partners. But over time, limited partnerships became much larger, typically involving a small number of major investors and a relatively large group of widely distributed investors who purchase limited partnership interests. This type of organization has evolved to attract substantial amounts of investment capital. As a result, limited partnerships have been used to muster the sizable investments necessary in areas such as real estate, oil and gas, motion pictures, professional sports, and research and development. The large-scale and multistate operations of the modern limited partnership, however, have severely burdened the framework established by the ULPA.

These shortcomings prompted the Uniform Law Commission (ULC) to develop a Revised Uniform Limited Partnership Act (RULPA), which was promulgated in 1976. According to its preface, the RULPA is "intended to modernize the prior uniform law while retaining the special character of limited partnerships as compared with corporations." In 1985, the ULC revised the RULPA "for the purpose of more effectively modernizing, improving and establishing uniformity in the law of limited partnerships." The 1985 Act is substantially similar to the 1976 RULPA, preserving the philosophy of the older Act and making almost no change in its basic structure. All of the States except Louisiana had adopted either the 1976 Act or the 1985 Act with a large majority of these States adopting the 1985 version.

In 2001, the ULC promulgated a new revision of the 1985 Revised Uniform Limited Partnership Act (the 2001 ReRULPA). The new Act has been drafted to reflect that limited liability partnerships and limited liability companies can meet many of the needs formerly met by limited partnerships. Accordingly, the 2001 ReRULPA adopts as default rules provisions that strongly favor incumbent, strong, centralized management and treat limited partners as passive investors with little control over or right to exit the limited partnership. To date, at least twenty-three States have adopted the 2001 ReRULPA. (In 2011 and 2013, the 2001 ReRULPA was amended as part of the Harmonization of Business Entity Acts project. These amendments brought the language in the 2001 ReRULPA into agreement with the language of similar provisions in the other uniform and model unincorporated entity acts.)

In its coverage of limited partnerships, this chapter primarily discusses the 1985 RULPA. The ULPA, the 1976 RULPA, and the 1985 RULPA are supplemented by the Uniform Partnership Act, which applies to limited partnerships in any case for which the Limited Partnership Act does not provide. In addition, this chapter notes provisions of the 2001 ReRULPA that significantly differ from the 1985 RULPA. Unlike the 1985 RULPA, the 2001 ReRULPA is a stand-alone statute and is not linked to the Uniform Partnership Act. Nevertheless, the 2001 ReRULPA incorporates many provisions from the Revised Uniform Partnership Act and some provisions from the Uniform Limited Liability Company Act.

The chapter summary and all figures in this chapter pertaining to limited partnerships reflect the 1985 RULPA.

♦ SEE FIGURE 30-1: *General Partnership, Limited Partnership, Limited Liability Company, and Corporation*

In addition, limited partnership interests are almost always considered to be securities, and their sale is therefore subject to State and Federal securities regulation, as discussed in *Chapter 43.*

32-1a DEFINITION

A **limited partnership** is a partnership formed by two or more persons under the laws of a State and having one or more general partners and one or more limited partners. Section 101(7). A *person* includes a natural person, partnership, limited partnership, trust, estate, association, or corporation. Section 101(11). A limited partnership differs from a general partnership in several respects, three of which are fundamental:

1. a statute providing for the formation of limited partnerships must be in effect;
2. the limited partnership must substantially comply with the requirements of that statute; and
3. the liability of a limited partner for partnership debts or obligations is limited to the extent of the capital he has contributed or has agreed to contribute.

32-1b FORMATION

Although the formation of a general partnership calls for no special procedures, the formation of a limited partnership requires substantial compliance with the limited partnership statute. Failure to so comply may result in the limited partners' not obtaining limited liability.

FILING OF CERTIFICATE Section 201 of the RULPA provides that two or more persons desiring to form a limited partnership shall file in the office of the Secretary of State of the State in which the limited partnership is to have its principal office a signed certificate of limited partnership. The certificate must include the following information:

1. the name of the limited partnership;
2. the address of the office and the name and address of the agent for service of process;
3. the name and the business address of each general partner;
4. the latest date upon which the limited partnership is to dissolve; and
5. any other matters the general partners decide to include in the certificate.

The certificate of limited partnership must be amended if a new general partner is admitted, a general partner withdraws, or a general partner becomes aware that any statement in the certificate was or has become false. Section 202. In addition, the certificate may be amended at any time for any other purpose the general partners deem proper. As discussed later, false statements in a certificate or amendment that cause loss to third parties who rely on the statements may result in liability for the general partners.

The 2001 ReRULPA permits a limited partnership to have perpetual duration unless otherwise provided in the partnership agreement. Section 110(c).

NAME The inclusion of the surname of a limited partner in the partnership name is prohibited unless it is also the name of a general partner or unless the business had operated under that name before the admission of the limited partner. A limited partner who knowingly permits his name to be used in violation of this provision is liable to any creditor who did not know that he was a limited partner. Section 303(d). In addition, a limited partnership cannot use a name that is the same as, or deceptively similar to, the name of any corporation or other limited partnership. Section 102. Finally, the name of the limited partnership must contain the unabbreviated words "limited partnership."

The 2001 ReRULPA permits a limited partnership to use the name of a limited partner. Section 114(a).

CONTRIBUTIONS The contribution of a partner may be cash, property, services rendered, or a promissory note or other obligation to contribute cash or property or to perform services. Section 501. A promise by a limited partner to contribute to the limited partnership is not enforceable unless it is in a signed writing. Should a partner fail to make a required capital contribution described in a signed writing, the limited partnership may hold her liable to contribute the cash value of the stated contribution.

DEFECTIVE FORMATION A limited partnership is formed when a certificate of limited partnership that substantially complies with the requirements of the statute is filed. Therefore, the formation is defective if no certificate is filed or if the certificate filed does not substantially meet the statutory requirements. In either case, the limited liability of limited partners is jeopardized. The RULPA provides that a person who has contributed to the capital of a business (an "equity participant"), erroneously and in good faith believing that he has become a limited partner in a limited partnership, is not liable as a general partner, provided that on ascertaining the mistake he either (1) withdraws from the business and renounces future profits or (2) files a certificate or an amendment curing the defect. Section 304. The equity participant will be liable, however, to any third party who transacted business with the enterprise before the withdrawal or amendment and who in good faith believed that the equity participant was a general partner at the time of the transaction.

The 1985 RULPA does not require that the limited partners be named in the certificate. This greatly reduces the risk that an inadvertent omission of such information will expose a limited partner to liability.

Practical Advice

To obtain limited liability as a limited partner, make sure that the limited partnership has been properly organized.

FOREIGN LIMITED PARTNERSHIPS A limited partnership is considered "foreign" in any State other than the one in which it was formed. The laws of the State in which a foreign limited partnership is organized govern its organization, its internal affairs, and the liability of its limited partners. Section 901. In addition, the RULPA requires all foreign limited partnerships to register with the Secretary of State before transacting any business in a State. Section 902. Any foreign limited partnership transacting business without so registering may not bring enforcement actions in the State's courts until it registers, although it may defend itself in the State's courts. Section 907.

32-1c RIGHTS

Because limited partnerships are organized pursuant to statute, the rights of the parties are usually set forth in the certificate of limited partnership and the limited partnership agreement. Unless otherwise agreed or provided in the Act, a general partner of a limited partnership has all the rights and powers of a partner in a partnership without limited partners. Section 403. A general partner also may be a limited partner; as such, he shares in profits, losses, and distributions both as a general partner and as a limited one. Section 404.

Practical Advice

When forming a limited partnership, carefully specify the rights and duties of the general and limited partners but be sure to adhere to the statutory limitations on the powers of limited partners.

CONTROL The general partners of a limited partnership have almost exclusive control and management of the limited partnership. A limited partner, on the other hand, is not permitted to share in this management or control; if he does, he may forfeit his limited liability. A limited partner who participates in the control of the business is liable only to those persons who transact business with the limited partnership reasonably believing, based upon the limited partner's conduct, that the limited partner is a general partner. Section 303(a). Under the 2001 ReRULPA, a limited partner *cannot* be held liable for the partnership debts even if the limited partner participates in the management and control of the limited partnership. Section 303(a).

In addition, Section 303(b) of the RULPA provides a "safe harbor" by enumerating activities that a limited partner may perform without being deemed to have taken part in control of the business. They are the following:

1. being a contractor for, or an agent or employee of, the limited partnership or of a general partner or being an officer, director, or shareholder of a general partner that is a corporation;

2. consulting with and advising a general partner with respect to the business of the limited partnership;

3. acting as surety for the limited partnership;

4. bringing a derivative action in the right of the limited partnership;

5. requesting or attending a meeting of partners;

6. voting on one or more of the following matters:
    (a) the dissolution and winding up of the limited partnership;
    (b) the sale, exchange, lease, mortgage, pledge, or other transfer of all or substantially all of the assets of the limited partnership;
    (c) the incurrence of indebtedness by the limited partnership other than in the ordinary course of its business;
    (d) a change in the nature of the business;
    (e) the admission or removal of a general partner;
    (f) the admission or removal of a limited partner;
    (g) a transaction involving an actual or potential conflict of interest between a general partner and the limited partnership or the limited partners;
    (h) an amendment to the partnership agreement or certificate of limited partnership; or
    (i) other matters related to the business of the limited partnership which the partnership agreement states in writing may be subject to the approval or disapproval of limited partners;

7. winding up the limited partnership; or

8. exercising any other right or power permitted to limited partners under the Act.

♦ *See Case 32-1*

Practical Advice

As a limited partner, exercise care not to take part in the control of the limited partnership beyond that which is legally permitted.

VOTING RIGHTS The partnership agreement may grant to all or a specified group of general or limited partners the right to vote on any matter. Sections 302 and 405. If, however, the agreement grants limited partners voting powers beyond the safe harbor of Section 303, a court may hold that the limited partners have participated in control of the business. The RULPA does not require that limited partners have the right to vote on matters as a class separate from the general partners, although the partnership agreement may provide such a right.

CHOICE OF ASSOCIATES After the formation of a limited partnership, the admission of additional limited partners requires the written consent of all partners, unless the partnership agreement provides otherwise. Section 301. The admission of the new limited partner is not effective until the records of the limited partnership have been amended to reflect that fact. Regarding the admission of additional general partners, the written partnership agreement determines the procedure for authorizing their admission. The written consent of all partners is required only if the partnership agreement fails to deal with this issue. Section 401.

WITHDRAWAL A general partner may withdraw from a limited partnership at any time by giving written notice to the other partners. Section 602. If the withdrawal violates the partnership agreement, the limited partnership may recover damages from the withdrawing general partner. A limited partner may withdraw as provided in the written partnership agreement. If the agreement does not specify when a limited partner may withdraw or a definite time for the limited partnership's dissolution, a limited partner may withdraw upon giving at least six months' prior written notice to each general partner. Section 603. However, limited partnership agreements typically specify a term, thus eliminating a limited partner's right to withdraw. The 2001 ReRULPA provides that a limited partner does *not* have a right to dissociate as a limited partner before the termination of the limited partnership except as provided by the partnership agreement or an event listed in the 2001 ReRULPA. Sections 601(a), 601(b).

Upon withdrawal, a withdrawing partner is entitled to receive any distribution to which she is entitled under the partnership agreement, subject to the restrictions on the amounts discussed in the section on distributions. If the partnership agreement makes no provision, the partner is entitled to receive the fair value of her interest in the limited partnership as of the date of withdrawal, based upon her right to share in distributions from the limited partnership. Section 604. The 2001 ReRULPA does *not* provide for a payout to a withdrawing partner but instead provides that any transferable interest owned by the withdrawing partner immediately before dissociation is owned by the withdrawing partner solely as a transferee. Sections 602(3) and 605(a)(4).

ASSIGNMENT OF PARTNERSHIP INTEREST A partnership interest is a partner's share of the profits and losses of a limited partnership and the right to receive distributions of partnership assets. Section 101(10). A partnership interest is personal property. Section 701. Unless otherwise provided in the partnership agreement, a partner may assign his partnership interest. An assignment does not dissolve the limited partnership. The assignee, who does not become a partner, may exercise none of the rights of a partner: the assignment entitles the assignee only to receive, to the extent of the assignment, the assigning partner's share of distributions. Except as otherwise provided in the partnership agreement, a partner ceases to be a partner upon assignment of all his partnership interest. Section 702.

An assignee of a partnership interest, including an assignee of a general partner, however, may become a *limited* partner if all the other partners consent or if the assigning partner, having such power provided in the partnership agreement, grants the assignee this right. Section 704. An assignee who becomes a limited partner is liable for the obligation of his assignor to make or return contributions, except for those liabilities unknown to the assignee at the time he became a limited partner. Section 704(b). Upon the death of a partner, her executor or administrator has all the rights of the partner for the purpose of settling her estate, including any power the deceased partner had to make her assignee a substituted limited partner. Section 705.

A creditor of a partner may obtain a charging order against a partner's interest in the partnership. To the extent of the charging order, the creditor has the rights of an assignee of the partnership interest. Section 703.

PROFIT AND LOSS SHARING Profits and losses are allocated among the partners as provided in the partnership agreement. If the agreement makes no such provision in writing, then the profits and losses are allocated on the basis of the value of the contributions each partner actually has made. Section 503. Nonetheless, limited partners usually are not liable for losses beyond their capital contribution. Section 303(a).

DISTRIBUTIONS The partners share distributions of cash or other assets of the limited partnership as provided in writing in the partnership agreement. The RULPA allows partners to share in distributions in a proportion different from that in which they share in profits. If the partnership agreement does not provide for allocation in writing, then distributions are based on the value of contributions each partner actually made. Section 504.

Unless otherwise provided in writing, a partner has no right to demand a distribution in any form other than cash. Once a partner becomes entitled to a distribution, he has the status of a creditor with respect to that distribution. Section 606. A partner may not receive a distribution from a limited partnership unless the assets remaining after the distribution are sufficient to pay all partnership liabilities other than liabilities to partners on account of their partnership interests. Section 607.

Loans Both general and limited partners may be secured or unsecured creditors of the partnership with the same rights as a person who is not a partner, subject to applicable State and Federal bankruptcy and fraudulent conveyance statutes. Section 107.

Information The partnership must continuously maintain within the State an office at which it keeps basic organizational and financial records. Section 105. Each partner has the right to inspect and copy any of the partnership records. Each limited partner may obtain from the general partners upon reasonable demand (1) complete and accurate information regarding the business and financial condition of the limited partnership; (2) copies of the limited partnership's Federal, State, and local income tax returns for each year; and (3) any other reasonable information regarding the affairs of the limited partnership. Section 305.

Derivative Actions A limited partner has the right to bring an action on behalf of a limited partnership to recover a judgment in its favor if the general partners having authority to bring the action have refused to do so. Section 1001. The Act also establishes standing and pleading requirements similar to those imposed in shareholder's derivative actions and permits the court to award reasonable expenses, including attorneys' fees, to a successful plaintiff. Section 1002.

32-1d DUTIES AND LIABILITIES

The duties and liabilities of general partners in a limited partnership are quite different from those of limited partners. A general partner is subject to all the duties and restrictions of a partner in a partnership without limited partners, whereas a limited partner is subject to few, if any, duties and enjoys limited liability.

Duties A *general partner* of a limited partnership owes a fiduciary duty to her general and limited partners. The existence of this duty is extremely important to the limited partners because of their circumscribed role in the control and management of the business enterprise. Conversely, whether a limited partner owes a fiduciary duty either to his general partners or to the limited partnership remains unclear. The very limited judicial authority on this question seems to indicate that the limited partner does not. The 2001 ReRULPA specifies that a limited partner does not owe fiduciary duties "solely by reason of being a limited partner." Section 305(b).

The RULPA does not distinguish between the duty of care owed by a general partner to a general partnership and that owed by a general partner to a limited partnership. Thus, although a general partner owes her partners a duty not to be grossly negligent (as discussed in *Chapter 30*), some courts have imposed upon general partners a higher duty of care toward *limited partners*. On the other hand, a limited partner owes no duty of care to a limited partnership as long as she remains a limited partner.

◆ *See Case 32-2*

Liabilities One of the most appealing features of a limited partnership is the limited personal liability it offers limited partners. **Limited liability** means that a limited partner has liability for partnership obligations only to the extent of the capital that the limited partner contributed or agreed to contribute to the limited partnership (i.e., the amount invested in the company or agreed to be invested). Accordingly, a limited partner who has paid her contribution in full has no further liability to the limited partnership or its creditors. Thus, if a limited partner buys a 25 percent share of a limited partnership for $50,000 and does not forfeit her limited liability, her liability is limited to the $50,000 she contributed, even if the limited partnership suffers losses of $500,000. This protection is subject to three conditions discussed earlier:

1. that the partnership has substantially complied in good faith with the requirement that a certificate of limited partnership be filed;
2. that the surname of the limited partner does not appear in the partnership name; and
3. that the limited partner does not participate in control of the business.

The 2001 ReRULPA eliminates the second and third conditions. Under the 2001 ReRULPA, a limited partner cannot be held liable for the partnership debts even if the limited partner participates in the management and control of the limited partnership. Section 303(a). In addition, the 2001 ReRULPA permits a limited partnership to use the name of a limited partner. Section 114(a).

In addition, if the certificate contains a false statement, anyone who suffers loss by reliance on that statement may hold liable any party to the certificate who knew the statement to be false when the certificate was executed. Section 207. As long as the limited partner abides by these conditions, his liability for any and all obligations of the partnership is limited to his capital contribution.

At the same time, the general partners of a limited partnership have unlimited external liability, unless the limited partnership is a limited liability limited partnership, discussed later in this chapter. Also, any general partner who knew or

FIGURE 32-1 Comparison of General and Limited Partners

	General Partner	Limited Partner
Control	Has all the rights and powers of a partner in a partnership without limited partners	Has no right to take part in management or control
Liability	Unlimited	Limited, unless partner takes part in control or partner's name is used
Agency	Is an agent of the partnership	Is not an agent of the partnership
Fiduciary Duty	Yes	No
Duty of Care	Yes	No

should have known that the limited partnership certificate contained a false statement is liable to anyone who suffers loss by reliance on that statement. Moreover, a general partner is liable if he knows or should know that a statement has become false and he does not amend the certificate within a reasonable time. Accordingly, it has become a common practice for limited partnerships to be formed with a corporation or other limited liability entity as the sole general partner.

Any partner to whom any part of her contribution has been returned without violation of the partnership agreement or of the limited partnership act is liable for one year to the limited partnership, to the extent necessary to pay creditors who extended credit during the period the partnership held the contribution. Section 608. In contrast, any partner to whom any part of her contribution was returned in violation of the partnership agreement or the limited partnership act is liable to the limited partnership for six years for the amount of the contribution wrongfully returned.

Under the 2001 ReRULPA, a person that receives a distribution knowing that the distribution violates the Act is personally liable to the limited partnership to the extent that the distribution received by the person exceeded the amount that could have been properly paid under the Act. Section 505(a). The limited partnership must bring an action to enforce this right within two years after the distribution. Section 505(d).

♦ **SEE FIGURE 32-1:** *Comparison of General and Limited Partners*

Practical Advice

Consider using a corporation as the sole general partner; then no natural person will be subject to unlimited, personal liability.

32-1e DISSOLUTION

As with a general partnership, extinguishing a limited partnership involves three steps: (1) dissolution, (2) winding up or liquidation, and (3) termination. The causes of dissolution

and the priorities for distributing the assets, however, differ somewhat from those in a general partnership.

CAUSES In a limited partnership, the limited partners have no right or power to dissolve the partnership, except by court decree. The death or bankruptcy of a limited partner does not dissolve the partnership. Section 801 of the RULPA specifies those events that will trigger a dissolution, after which the affairs of the partnership must be liquidated:

1. the expiration of the time period specified in the certificate;

2. the happening of events specified in writing in the partnership agreement;

3. the unanimous written consent of all the partners;

4. the withdrawal of a general partner unless either

   (a) there is at least one other general partner and the written provisions of the partnership agreement permit the remaining general partners to continue the business, or

   (b) within ninety days all partners agree in writing to continue the business; or

5. a decree of judicial dissolution, which may be granted whenever it is not reasonably practicable to carry on the business in conformity with the partnership agreement.

A general partner's withdrawal occurs upon his retirement, assignment of all his general partnership interest, removal, bankruptcy, death, or adjudication of incompetency.

The 2001 ReRULPA changed the requirement of unanimous consent in RULPA Section 801 to "the affirmative vote or consent of all general partners and of limited partners owning a majority of the rights to receive distributions as limited partners at the time the vote or consent is to be effective." Section 801(a)(2).

A certificate of cancellation must be filed when the limited partnership dissolves and winding up commences. Section 203. Under the 2001 ReRULPA, a limited partnership *may* amend its certificate of limited partnership to state that the partnership is dissolved and *may* file a statement of termination indicating that winding up has been completed and the limited partnership is terminated. Section 801(b)(2).

WINDING UP Unless otherwise provided in the partnership agreement, the general partners who have not wrongfully dissolved the limited partnership may wind up its affairs. Section 803. The limited partners may wind up the limited partnership if all the general partners have wrongfully dissolved the partnership. But any partner, his legal representative, or his assignee may obtain a winding up by court order if cause is shown.

DISTRIBUTION OF ASSETS Section 804 sets forth the priorities in distributing the assets of a limited partnership:

1. to creditors, including partners who are creditors, except with respect to liabilities for distributions;

2. to partners and ex-partners in satisfaction of liabilities for unpaid distributions;

3. to partners for the return of their contributions, except as otherwise agreed; and

4. to partners for their partnership interests in the proportions in which they share in distributions, except as otherwise agreed.

General partners and limited partners rank equally unless the partnership agreement provides otherwise.

32-2 Limited Liability Companies

A limited liability company (LLC) is another form of unincorporated business association. Prior to 1990, only two States had statutes permitting LLCs. By 1996, all States had enacted LLC statutes. Since then, many States have amended or revised their LLC statutes. Until 1995, there was no uniform statute on which States might base their LLC legislation, and since its promulgation, eight States have adopted the Uniform Limited Liability Company Act (ULLCA), which was amended in 1996. In 2006, the Revised ULLCA was completed and at least twenty-one States have adopted it. (In 2011 and 2013, the 2006 Revised ULLCA was amended as part of the Harmonization of Business Entity Acts project. These amendments coordinate the language in the 2006 Revised ULLCA with the language of similar provisions in the other uniform and model unincorporated entity acts.)

Therefore, LLC statutes vary from State to State with respect to such matters as LLC management, admission and withdrawal of members, power of members and managers to bind the LLC, duties imposed on managers and members, and the LLC's right to merge with other business entities. Nevertheless, the LLC statutes generally share certain characteristics.

A **limited liability company** is a noncorporate business organization that provides limited liability to *all* of its owners (members) and permits all of its members to participate in

management of the business. It may elect not to be a separate taxable entity, in which case only the members are taxed. (Publicly traded LLCs, however, are subject to corporate income taxation.) If an LLC has only one member, then it will be taxed as a sole proprietorship, unless separate entity tax treatment is elected. Thus, the LLC provides many of the advantages of a general partnership plus limited liability for all its members. Its benefits outweigh those of a limited partnership in that all members of an LLC not only enjoy limited liability but also may participate in management and control of the business. LLCs have become the most popular and widely used unincorporated business form. The most frequent use of LLCs has been in real estate transactions, professional services, construction, finance, and retail. Ownership interests in an LLC may be considered to be securities, especially interests in those LLCs operated by managers. If a particular LLC interest is considered a security, its sale will be subject to State and Federal securities regulation, as discussed in *Chapter 43*.

A **low-profit limited liability company** (L3C) is a new variation of the limited liability company. An L3C is a for-profit company with a socially beneficial purpose as its primary objective. (A comparable type of corporation is the *benefit corporation*, discussed in *Chapter 33*.) Legislation authorizing the formation of L3Cs has been enacted in at least eleven States.

♦ **SEE FIGURE 30-1:** *General Partnership, Limited Partnership, Limited Liability Company, and Corporation*

32-2a FORMATION

The formation of an LLC requires substantial compliance with a State's LLC statute. All States permit an LLC to have only one member. Once formed, an LLC is a separate legal entity that is distinct from its members, who are normally not liable for its debts and obligations. An LLC can contract in its own name and is generally permitted to carry on any lawful purpose, although some statutes restrict the permissible activities of LLCs.

MEMBERS LLC statutes permit members to include individuals, corporations, general partnerships, limited partnerships, limited liability companies, trusts, estates, and other associations. LLC statutes differ concerning the procedure for adding members after an LLC has been formed.

FILING The LLC statutes generally require the central public filing of articles of organization in a designated State office. The States vary regarding the information they require the articles to include, but all require at least the following: (1) the name of the firm, (2) the address of the principal place of business or registered office, and (3) the name and address of the agent for service of process. The articles may also include any provision consistent with law for regulating internal LLC matters.

Most LLC statutes provide that the acceptance for filing is conclusive evidence that the LLC has been properly formed, except against the State in an involuntary dissolution or certificate revocation proceeding. Most LLC statutes require the articles to state whether the LLC will be managed by managers. Most States provide that LLCs have perpetual existence unless the members agree otherwise. The articles of organization may be amended by filing articles of amendment. In most States, LLCs must file annual reports with the State.

NAME LLC statutes generally require the name of the LLC to include the words *limited liability company* or the abbreviation LLC. The name of each LLC must be distinguishable from other firms doing business within the State.

CONTRIBUTION In most States, the contribution of a member to an LLC may be cash, property, services rendered, a promissory note, or other obligation to contribute cash or property or to perform services. Most LLC statutes require both a written agreement to make a contribution and a written record of contributions. Members are liable to the LLC for failing to make an agreed contribution.

OPERATING AGREEMENT The members of most LLCs adopt an **operating agreement**, which is the basic contract among the members governing the affairs of an LLC and stating the various rights and duties of the members and any managers. The operating agreement is subordinate to Federal and State law. LLC statutes generally do not require the operating agreement to be in writing, although some statutes permit modification of certain statutory rules to be only by written provision in an operating agreement. Unless the operating agreement provides otherwise, the members may amend it only by unanimous consent.

FOREIGN LIMITED LIABILITY COMPANIES An LLC is considered "foreign" in any State other than that in which it was formed. LLC statutes provide that the laws of the State in which a foreign LLC is organized govern its organization, its internal affairs, and the liability of its members and managers. Foreign LLCs, however, generally are not permitted to transact business that domestic LLCs may not transact. Foreign LLCs must register with the Secretary of State before transacting any business in a State. Any foreign LLC transacting business without so registering may not bring enforcement actions in the State's courts until it registers, although it may defend itself in the State's courts. Moreover, States generally impose fines and penalties on unregistered foreign LLCs that transact business in the State.

Practical Advice

To obtain limited liability as a member of a limited liability company, make sure that the LLC has been properly organized.

32-2b RIGHTS OF MEMBERS

A member has no property interest in property owned by the LLC. On the other hand, a member does have an interest in the LLC, which is personal property. A member's interest in the LLC includes two components:

1. the **financial interest**, which is the right to share profits and losses and to receive distributions, and
2. the **management interest**, which consists of all other rights granted to a member by the LLC operating agreement and the LLC statute. The management interest typically includes the right to manage, vote, obtain information, and bring enforcement actions.

PROFIT AND LOSS SHARING The LLC's operating agreement determines how the partners allocate the profits and losses. If the LLC's operating agreement makes no such provision, in most States, the profits and losses are allocated on the basis of the value of the members' contributions. A few States follow the partnership model under which profits are divided equally. Section 405.

DISTRIBUTIONS LLC statutes do not provide LLC members the right to distributions before withdrawal from the LLC. Therefore, the members share distributions of cash or other assets of an LLC as provided in the operating agreement. If the LLC's operating agreement does not allocate distributions, in most States, they are made on the basis of the contributions each member made. All LLC statutes impose liability on members who receive wrongful distributions; some statutes also impose liability on members and managers who approved the wrongful distributions. The statutes vary in defining what constitutes a wrongful distribution, but most make a distribution wrongful if the LLC is insolvent or if the distribution would make the LLC insolvent. In most States, members are liable whether or not they knew that the distribution was wrongful.

WITHDRAWAL Some statutes permit a member to withdraw and demand payment of her interest upon giving the notice specified in the statute or the LLC's operating agreement. Some of the statutes permit the operating agreement to deny members the right to withdraw from the LLC.

MANAGEMENT Nearly all LLC statutes provide that in the absence of a contrary agreement, each member has equal rights in the management of the LLC. All LLC statutes permit LLCs to be managed by one or more managers who may, but need not, be members. LLC statutes generally provide that the members select the managers. In a member-managed LLC, the members have actual and apparent authority to bind the LLC. In a manager-managed LLC, the managers have this authority, while the members have no actual or apparent authority to bind the manager-managed LLC. Most statutes require a publicly filed document to elect a manager-managed structure; a few statutes permit the operating agreement to make that election.

FIGURE 32-2 Comparison of Member-Managed and Manager-Managed LLCs

	Member of Member-Managed LLC Manager of Manager-Managed LLC	Member of Manager-Managed LLC
Control	Full	None
Liability	Limited	Limited
Agency	Is an agent of the LLC	Is not an agent of the LLC
Fiduciary Duty	Yes	No
Duty of Care	Yes	No

Note: LLC = limited liability company.

◆ *See Case 32-3*

VOTING Most of the LLC statutes specify the voting rights of members, subject to a contrary provision in an LLC's operating agreement. In most States, the default rule for voting follows a corporate approach (voting is based on the financial interests of members), while a few States take a partnership approach (each member has equal voting rights). Typically, members have the right to vote on proposals to (1) adopt or amend the operating agreement, (2) admit any person as a member, (3) sell all or substantially all of the LLC's assets prior to dissolution, and (4) merge the LLC with another LLC or other business entity. Some LLC statutes authorize voting by proxy. A proxy is a member's authorization to an agent to vote for the member.

INFORMATION The LLC must keep basic organizational and financial records. Each member has the right to inspect and copy the LLC records.

DERIVATIVE ACTIONS A member has the right to bring an action on behalf of an LLC to recover a judgment in its favor if the managers or members with authority to bring the action have refused to do so.

ASSIGNMENT OF LLC INTEREST Unless otherwise provided in the LLC's operating agreement, a member may assign his financial interest in the LLC. An assignment does not dissolve the LLC. The assignment only entitles the assignee to receive, to the extent of the assignment, the assigning member's share of distributions. A judgment creditor of a member may obtain a charging order against the member's financial interest in the LLC. The charging order gives the creditor the same rights as an assignee to the extent of the interest charged.

The assignee does not become a member and may not exercise any management rights of a member. However, an assignee of a financial interest in an LLC may acquire the other rights by being admitted as a member of the company by all the remaining members. (Some States allow admission by majority vote.) In most States, this unanimous acceptance rule is now a default rule, and the operating agreement may eliminate or modify it.

32-2c DUTIES

As with general partnerships and limited partnerships, the duties of care and loyalty also apply to LLCs. In most States, the LLC statute expressly imposes these duties. In other States, the common law imposes these duties. Many statutes also expressly impose an obligation of good faith and fair dealing. Who has these duties in an LLC depends upon whether the LLC is a manager-managed LLC (analogous to a limited partnership) or a member-managed LLC (analogous to a partnership).

MANAGER-MANAGED LLCS All LLC statutes either permit or require LLCs to be managed by one or more managers selected by the members. Most LLC statutes impose upon the managers of an LLC a duty of care. In some States, this is a duty to refrain from grossly negligent, reckless, or intentional tortious conduct; in other States, it is a duty to act in good faith and as a prudent person would in similar circumstances. Managers also have a fiduciary duty, although the statutes vary in how they specify that duty. Usually, members of manager-managed LLCs have no duties to the LLC or its members by reason of being a member.

MEMBER-MANAGED LLCS Members of member-managed LLCs have the same duties of care and loyalty that managers have in manager-managed LLCs.

◆ *See Case 32-4*

◆ **SEE FIGURE 32-2:** *Comparison of Member-Managed and Manager-Managed LLCs*

Practical Advice

Recognize that your rights and duties as a member of a limited liability company depend on whether the LLC is member managed or manager managed.

32-2d LIABILITIES

One of the most appealing features of an LLC is the limited personal liability it offers to all its members and managers. LLC statutes typically provide that no member or manager of an LLC shall be obligated personally for any debt, obligation, or liability of the LLC solely by reason of being a member or acting as a manager of the LLC. The limitation on liability, however, will not affect the liability of a member or manager who committed the wrongful act. A member or manager is also personally liable for any LLC obligations guaranteed by the member or manager. The general rule that members and managers are not personally liable for the LLC's obligations is subject to a number of exceptions.

1. Because persons are always individually liable for their own torts, a member or manager who committed the tort giving rise to the liability is personally liable for that LLC obligation.

2. A member or manager is personally liable for any LLC obligations guaranteed by the member or manager.

3. LLC statutes generally state that persons who assume to act as an LLC prior to formation or without authority to do so are jointly and severally liable for all debts and liabilities.

4. As mentioned previously, a member who fails to make an agreed contribution is liable to the LLC for the unpaid amount.

5. Under the doctrine of *piercing the corporate veil*, members may be held personally liable for the LLC's debts, obligations, or liabilities under certain circumstances. (This doctrine is covered more fully in *Chapter 33*.) Courts pierce the corporate (company) veil and hold LLC members personally liable for LLC obligations in cases in which the members (a) have not conducted the business on a company basis by failing to observe company formalities, (b) have not provided the LLC an adequate financial basis for the business, or (c) have used the LLC to defraud.

6. A member who receives a distribution or return of her contribution in violation of the LLC's operating agreement or the LLC statute is liable to the LLC for the amount of the contribution wrongfully returned.

♦ *See Case 32-5*

32-2e DISSOLUTION

Ending an LLC involves three steps: (1) dissolution, (2) winding up or liquidation, and (3) termination. LLC statutes require a public filing in connection with dissolution. For example, after winding up the company, some LLC statutes provide for the filing of articles of dissolution stating (1) the name of the company, (2) the date of the dissolution, and (3) that the company's business has been wound up and the legal existence of the company has been terminated. Other statutes require either (1) a public filing of the intent to dissolve at the time of dissolution or (2) filings at both the time of dissolution and after winding up.

CAUSES Most LLC statutes no longer require that LLCs dissolve at the end of a stated term. Moreover, LLC statutes either (1) provide that a member's dissociation does *not* cause dissolution or (2) permit the remaining members, by either unanimous or majority vote, to avoid dissolution upon a member's disassociation. LLC statutes generally provide that an LLC will automatically dissolve upon the following:

1. the expiring of the LLC's agreed duration, if any, or the happening of any of the events specified in the articles;

2. the written consent of all the members; or

3. a decree of judicial dissolution typically on the grounds that "it is not reasonably practicable to carry on the LLC's activities in conformity with the articles of organization and the operating agreement" or, under some statutes, the members or managers have acted illegally, fraudulently, or oppressively.

LLC statutes require a public filing in connection with dissolution. For example, after winding up the company, the ULLCA and some LLC statutes provide for the filing of articles of termination stating (1) the name of the company, (2) the date of the dissolution, and (3) that the company's business has been wound up and the legal existence of the company has been terminated. Other statutes require either (1) a public filing of the intent to dissolve at the time of dissolution or (2) filings at both the time of dissolution and after winding up.

♦ *See Case 32-6*

DISSOCIATION Dissociation means that a member has ceased to be associated with the company through voluntary withdrawal, death, incompetence, expulsion, or bankruptcy. Some LLC states have eliminated a member's dissociation as a mandatory cause of dissolution. Other LLC statutes permit the remaining members, by either unanimous or majority vote, to avoid dissolution upon a member's disassociation.

WINDING UP An LLC continues after dissolution only for the purpose of winding up its business, which involves completing unfinished business, collecting debts, disposing of inventory, reducing assets to cash, paying creditors, and distributing the remaining assets to the members. During this period, the fiduciary duties of members and managers continue.

AUTHORITY Upon dissolution, the *actual authority* of a member or manager to act for the LLC terminates, except so far as is appropriate to wind up LLC business. Actual authority to wind up includes the authority to complete existing contracts, to collect debts, to sell LLC assets, and to pay LLC obligations. In addition, some statutes expressly provide that after dissolution, members and managers continue to have *apparent authority* to bind the company they had prior to dissolution provided that the third party did not have notice of the dissolution.

DISTRIBUTION OF ASSETS Most statutes provide default rules for distributing the assets of an LLC as follows:

1. to creditors, including members and managers who are creditors, except with respect to liabilities or distributions;
2. to members and former members in satisfaction of liabilities for unpaid distributions, except as otherwise agreed;
3. to members for the return of their contributions, except as otherwise agreed; and
4. to members for their LLC interests in the proportions in which members share in distributions, except as otherwise agreed.

APPLYING THE LAW — Limited Partnerships and Limited Liability Companies

FACTS Rustin was a member of a limited liability company (LLC) called Global Trade, LLC, which refurbished and exported used construction equipment to foreign buyers. When Rustin and his wife divorced, they entered into a property settlement agreement, which divided up their assets and liabilities in a mutually acceptable manner. As part of this contract, Rustin assigned his membership in Global Trade to his ex-wife, Fanning. Rustin's divorce lawyer notified Global Trade of the assignment to Fanning and provided a copy of the court order approving the property settlement to Global Trade's manager. The LLC's operating agreement is silent with respect to transfers of a member's interest.

Fanning subsequently declared herself a member of Global Trade. As such, she requested detailed information about a proposed merger of Global Trade with one of its primary suppliers and demanded permission to attend a meeting of Global Trade's members, at which they anticipated discussing and voting on the proposed merger. Global Trade's members declined to give her the requested information and denied her access to the meeting at which they approved the merger.

ISSUE Did Rustin's assignment to Fanning make her a member of the LLC?

RULE OF LAW Members of an LLC own an interest in the entity, which is personal property. A member's interest in the LLC consists of two components: a financial interest and a management interest. The financial interest is a right to share profits and to receive distributions only. The management interest is the bundle of remaining member rights, including the right to manage, right to be informed, and right to vote. Members may assign their financial interest unless the operating agreement provides otherwise. On the other hand, members may assign their management interest *only* if the operating agreement expressly provides members that right. Otherwise, an assignee of an interest in an LLC will become a member only if the remaining members consent to admit her.

APPLICATION As a member of Global Trade, LLC, Rustin had two distinct membership interests—the financial interest and the management interest. Because of the nature of LLCs, both of these membership rights are necessarily shaped and constrained by the terms of the relevant operating agreement and state LLC statute. In this case, the operating agreement said nothing about transfers of members' interests. Therefore, by default, Rustin's assignment is only of his financial interest.

This result is reinforced by the fact that, with notice of Rustin's assignment to her, the members denied Fanning access to their meeting. An assignee of a financial interest in an LLC, like Fanning, can acquire a management interest if the other members of the LLC consent to her membership. Here, it is unclear whether the members formally voted on the question of whether Fanning should be admitted to the LLC. Nonetheless, because they denied her request for information and excluded her from the merger meeting, it is apparent that they are unwilling to consent to her admission as a member.

CONCLUSION Fanning did not become a member of Global Trade, LLC, by virtue of Rustin's assignment. Instead, she gained only the right to Rustin's share of distributions from the LLC.

PROTECTION OF CREDITORS Many LLC statutes establish procedures to safeguard the interests of the LLC's creditors. Such procedures typically include the required mailing of notice of dissolution to known creditors, a general publication of notice, and the preservation of claims against the LLC for a specified time.

32-2f MERGERS AND CONVERSIONS

Most LLC statutes expressly provide for mergers. A merger of two or more entities is the combination of all of their assets. One of the entities, known as the **surviving entity**, receives title to all the assets. The other party or parties to the merger, known as the merged entity or entities, is merged into the surviving entity and ceases to exist as a separate entity. Thus, if Alpha LLC and Beta LLC combine into the Alpha LLC, Alpha is the surviving LLC and Beta is the merged LLC.

The LLC statutes vary with respect to the voting rights of the members regarding approval of a merger. Some provide for a majority or unanimous vote; others leave it to the operating agreement. Some statutes require the filing of articles of merger; others require a merged LLC to file articles of dissolution. Upon the required filing, the merger is effective, and the separate existence of each merged entity terminates. All property and assets owned by each of the merged entities vests in the surviving entity, and all debts, liabilities, and other obligations of each merged entity become the obligations of the surviving entity.

Many LLC statutes provide for the conversion of another business entity into an LLC. LLC statutes and other business association statutes also provide for an LLC to be converted into another business entity. The converted entity remains the same entity that existed before the conversion.

32-3 Other Types of Unincorporated Business Associations

32-3a LIMITED LIABILITY PARTNERSHIPS

All of the States have enacted statutes enabling the formation of limited liability partnerships (LLPs). Until 1997, there was no uniform LLP statute, so the enabling statutes vary from State to State. In 1997, the Revised Uniform Partnership Act (RUPA) was amended to add provisions enabling general partnerships to elect to become LLPs, and more than thirty States have adopted this version of the RUPA. A registered **limited liability partnership** is a general partnership that, by making the statutorily required filing, limits the liability of its partners for some or all of the partnership's obligations.

FORMALITIES To become an LLP, a general partnership must file with the Secretary of State an application containing specified information. The RUPA requires the partnership to file a statement of qualification. RUPA Section 1001(c). Most of the statutes require only a majority of the partners to authorize registration as an LLP; others require unanimous approval. The RUPA requires unanimity unless the partnership agreement provides otherwise. RUPA Section 1001(b). Some statutes require renewal of registrations annually, other statutes require periodic reports, and a few require no renewal. The RUPA requires filing annual reports. RUPA Section 1003. Some statutes require a new filing after any change in membership of the partnership, but a few of the statutes do not. The RUPA does not.

DESIGNATION All statutes require LLPs to designate themselves as such. Most statutes require the name of the LLP to include the words *limited liability partnership* or *registered limited liability partnership* (or the abbreviation LLP or RLLP). Most statutes provide that the laws of the jurisdiction under which a foreign LLP is registered shall govern its organization, internal affairs, and the liability and authority of its partners. Many, but not all, of the statutes require a foreign LLP to register or obtain a certificate of authenticity. The RUPA requires a foreign LLP to qualify and file annual reports. RUPA Sections 1102 and 1003.

LIABILITY LIMITATION LLP statutes have taken three different approaches to limiting the liability of partners for the partnership's obligations. The earliest statutes limited liability for negligent acts only; they retained unlimited liability for all other obligations. The next generation of statutes extended limited liability to any partnership tort or contract obligation that arose from negligence, malpractice, wrongful acts, or misconduct committed by any partner, employee, or agent of the partnership. Unlimited liability remained for ordinary contract obligations, such as those owed to suppliers, lenders, and landlords. The first two generations of LLP statutes are called "partial shield" statutes. Many of the more recent statutes (called "full shield" statutes) have provided limited liability for all debts and obligations of the partnership, including Section 306(c) of the RUPA. Most States have now adopted full shield statutes although some States still provide only a partial shield.

The statutes, however, generally provide that the limitation on liability will not affect the liability of (1) a partner who committed the wrongful act giving rise to the liability and (2) a partner who supervised the partner, employee, or agent of the partnership who committed the wrongful act. A partner is also personally liable for any partnership obligations guaranteed by the partner. The statutes also provide that the limitations on liability will apply only to claims that arise while the partnership was a registered LLP. Accordingly, partners would

FIGURE 32-3 Liability Limitations in LLPs

LLP Statutes	Limited Liability	Unlimited Liability
First Generation	Negligent acts	• All other obligations • Wrongful partner • Supervising partner
Second Generation	Tort and contract obligations arising from wrongful acts	• All other obligations • Wrongful partner • Supervising partner
Third Generation	All obligations	• Wrongful partner • Supervising partner

Note: LLP = limited liability partnership.

have unlimited liability for obligations that arose either before registration or after registration lapses.

♦ **SEE FIGURE 32-3:** *Liability Limitations in LLPs*

Practical Advice

Professionals should consider registering their partnerships as limited liability partnerships or organizing their firms as LLPs.

32-3b LIMITED LIABILITY LIMITED PARTNERSHIPS

A **limited liability limited partnership (LLLP)** is a limited partnership in which the liability of the general partners has been limited to the same extent as in an LLP. Some States have statutes expressly providing for LLLPs. In other States, by operation of the provision in the RULPA that a general partner in a limited partnership assumes the liabilities of a general partner in a general partnership, the LLP statute may provide limited liability to general partners in a limited partnership that registers as an LLLP under the LLP statute. Where authorized, the general partners in an LLLP will obtain the same degree of

liability limitation that general partners can achieve in LLPs. Where available, a limited partnership may register as an LLLP without having to form a new organization, as would be the case in converting to an LLC.

The 2001 ReRULPA, which has been adopted by at least twenty-three States, provides that an LLLP "means a limited partnership whose certificate of limited partnership states that the limited partnership is a limited liability limited partnership." Section 102(10). The 2001 ReRULPA provides a full shield for general partners in LLLPs:

> A debt, obligation, or other liability of a limited partnership incurred while the partnership is a limited liability limited partnership is solely the debt, obligation, or other liability of the limited liability limited partnership. A general partner is not personally liable … for a debt, obligation, or other liability of the limited liability limited partnership solely solely by reason of being or acting as a general partner.

Section 404(c). Moreover, under the 2001 ReRULPA, a *limited* partner cannot be held liable for the partnership debts even if he participates in the management and control of the limited partnership. Section 303(a).

C H A P T E R   S U M M A R Y

LIMITED PARTNERSHIPS **Definition of a Limited Partnership** a partnership formed by two or more persons under the laws of a State and having one or more general partners and one or more limited partners **Formation** a limited partnership can be formed only by substantial compliance with a State-limited partnership statute

- *Filing of Certificate* two or more persons must file a signed certificate of limited partnership

- *Name* inclusion of a limited partner's surname in the partnership name in most instances will result in the loss of the limited partner's limited liability
- *Contributions* may be cash, property, or services or may be a promise to contribute cash, property, or services
- *Defective Formation* if no certificate is filed or if the one filed does not substantially meet the statutory requirements, the formation is defective and the limited liability of the limited partners is jeopardized
- *Foreign Limited Partnerships* a limited partnership is considered "foreign" in any State other than that in which it was formed

Rights a general partner in a limited partnership has all the rights and powers of a partner in a general partnership

- *Control* the general partners have almost exclusive control and management of the limited partnerships; a limited partner who participates in the control of the limited partnership may lose limited liability
- *Voting Rights* the partnership agreement may grant to all or a specified group of general or limited partners the right to vote on any matter
- *Choice of Associates* no person may be added as a general partner or a limited partner without the consent of all partners
- *Withdrawal* a general partner may withdraw from a limited partnership at any time by giving written notice to the other partners; a limited partner may withdraw as provided in the limited partnership certificate
- *Assignment of Partnership Interest* unless otherwise provided in the partnership agreement, a partner may assign his partnership interest; an assignee may become a substituted limited partner if all other partners consent
- *Profit and Loss Sharing* profits and losses are allocated among the partners as provided in the partnership agreement; if the partnership agreement has no such provision, then profits and losses are allocated on the basis of the contributions each partner actually made
- *Distributions* the partners share distributions of cash or other assets of a limited partnership as provided in the partnership agreement
- *Loans* both general and limited partners may be secured or unsecured creditors of the partnership
- *Information* each partner has the right to inspect and copy the partnership records
- *Derivative Actions* a limited partner may sue on behalf of a limited partnership if the general partners refuse to bring the action

Duties and Liabilities

- *Duties* general partners owe a duty of care and loyalty (fiduciary duty) to the general partners, the limited partners, and the limited partnership; limited partners do not
- *Liabilities* the general partners have unlimited liability; the limited partners have limited liability (liability for partnership obligations only to the extent of the capital that they contributed or agreed to contribute)

Dissolution

- *Causes* the limited partners have neither the right nor the power to dissolve the partnership, except by decree of the court; the following events trigger a dissolution: (1) the expiration of the time period; (2) the withdrawal of a general partner, unless all partners agree to continue the business; or (3) a decree of judicial dissolution
- *Winding Up* unless otherwise provided in the partnership agreement, the general partners who have not wrongfully dissolved the partnership may wind up its affairs

- *Distribution of Assets* the priorities for distribution are as follows: (1) creditors, including partners who are creditors; (2) partners and ex-partners in satisfaction of liabilities for unpaid distributions; (3) partners for the return of contributions, except as otherwise agreed; and (4) partners for their partnership interests in the proportions in which they share in distributions, except as otherwise agreed

---

LIMITED LIABILITY COMPANIES

Definition a limited liability company (LLC) is a noncorporate business organization that provides limited liability to all of its owners (members) and permits all of its members to participate in management of the business

Formation the formation of an LLC requires substantial compliance with a State's LLC statute

- *Members* LLC statutes permit members to include individuals, corporations, general partnerships, limited partnerships, limited liability companies, trusts, estates, and other associations
- *Filing* LLC statutes generally require the central filing of articles of organization in a designated State office
- *Name* LLC statutes generally require the name of the LLC to include the words limited liability company or the abbreviation LLC
- *Contribution* the contribution of a member to an LLC may be cash, property, services rendered, or a promissory note or other obligation to contribute cash or property or to perform services
- *Operating Agreement* the basic contract governing the affairs of an LLC and stating the various rights and duties of the members
- *Foreign Limited Liability Companies* an LLC is considered "foreign" in any State other than that in which it was formed

Rights of Members a member's interest in the LLC includes the financial interest (the right to distributions) and the management interest (which consists of all other rights granted to a member by the LLC operating agreement and the LLC statute)

- *Profit and Loss Sharing* the LLC's operating agreement determines how the partners allocate the profits and losses; if the LLC's operating agreement makes no such provision, in most States, the profits and losses are allocated on the basis of the value of the members' contributions
- *Distributions* the members share distributions of cash or other assets of an LLC as provided in the operating agreement; if the LLC's operating agreement does not allocate distributions, in most States, they are made on the basis of the contributions each member made
- *Withdrawal* a member may withdraw and demand payment of her interest upon giving the notice specified in the statute or the LLC's operating agreement
- *Management* in the absence of a contrary agreement, each member has equal rights in the management of the LLC, but LLCs may be managed by one or more managers who may be members
- *Voting* LLC statutes usually specify the voting rights of members, subject to a contrary provision in an LLC's operating agreement
- *Information* LLCs must keep basic organizational and financial records; each member has the right to inspect and copy the LLC records
- *Derivative Actions* a member has the right to bring an action on behalf of an LLC to recover a judgment in its favor if the managers or members with authority to bring the action have refused to do so
- *Assignment of LLC Interest* unless otherwise provided in the LLC's operating agreement, a member may assign his financial interest in the LLC; an assignee of a financial interest in an LLC may acquire the other rights by being admitted as a member of the company if all the remaining members consent or the operating agreement so provides

Duties

- *Manager-Managed LLCs* the managers of a manager-managed LLC have a duty of care and loyalty; usually, members of a manager-managed LLC have no duties to the LLC or its members by reason of being members
- *Member-Managed LLCs* members of member-managed LLCs have the same duties of care and loyalty that managers have in manager-managed LLCs

Liabilities subject to certain exceptions, no member or manager of an LLC is obligated personally for any debt, obligation, or liability of the LLC solely by reason of being a member or acting as a manager of the LLC

Dissolution

- *Causes* an LLC will automatically dissolve upon (1) in some States, the dissociation of a member if the remaining members do *not* choose to continue the LLC, (2) the expiration of the LLC's agreed duration or the happening of any of the events specified in the articles, (3) the written consent of all the members, or (4) a decree of judicial dissolution
- *Dissociation* means that a member has ceased to be associated with the company through voluntary withdrawal, death, incompetence, expulsion, or bankruptcy
- *Winding Up* completing unfinished business, collecting debts, and distributing assets to creditors and members; also called liquidation
- *Authority* the actual authority of a member or manager to act for the LLC terminates, except so far as may be appropriate to wind up LLC affairs; apparent authority continues unless notice of the dissolution is given to a third party
- *Distribution of Assets* the default rules for distributing the assets of an LLC are (1) to creditors, including members and managers who are creditors, except with respect to liabilities for distributions; (2) to members and former members in satisfaction of liabilities for unpaid distributions, except as otherwise agreed; (3) to members for the return of their contributions, except as otherwise agreed; and (4) to members for their LLC interests in the proportions in which members share in distributions, except as otherwise agreed
- *Protection of Creditors* many LLC statutes establish procedures to safeguard the interests of the LLC's creditors, including (1) mailing notice of dissolution to known creditors, (2) publishing of notice, and (3) preserving claims against the LLC for a specified time

Mergers

- *Definition* the combination of the assets of two or more business entities into one of the entities
- *Effect* the surviving entity receives title to all of the assets of the merged entities and assumes all of their liabilities; the merged entities cease to exist

---

OTHER TYPES OF UNINCORPORATED BUSINESS ASSOCIATIONS

Limited Liability Partnership (LLP) a general partnership that, by making the statutorily required filing, limits the liability of its partners for some or all of the partnership's obligations

- *Formalities* most statutes require only a majority of the partners to authorize registration as an LLP; others require unanimous approval
- *Designation* the name of the LLP must include the words *limited liability partnership* or *registered limited liability partnership* or the abbreviation LLP
- *Liability Limitation* some statutes limit liability only for negligent acts; others limit liability to any partnership tort or contract obligation that arose from negligence, malpractice, wrongful acts, or misconduct committed by any partner, employee, or agent of the partnership; most provide limited liability for all debts and obligations of the partnership

Limited Liability Limited Partnership (LLLP) a limited partnership in which the liability of the general partners has been limited (1) to the same extent as in an LLP or (2) completely as under the 2001 ReRULPA

C A S E S

<table>
<tr><td>CASE
32-1</td><td>Control in Limited Partnerships
ALZADO v. BLINDER, ROBINSON & CO., INC.
Supreme Court of Colorado, 1988
752 P.2d 544</td><td></td></tr>
</table>

Kirshbaum, J.

[In 1979, Lyle Alzado, a former professional football player, and two business associates formed Combat Promotions, Inc., to promote an eight-round exhibition boxing match in Denver, Colorado, between Alzado and Muhammad Ali, a former world champion boxer.] Ali had agreed to engage in the match on the condition that prior to the event his attorneys would receive an irrevocable letter of credit guaranteeing payment of $250,000 to Ali.

Combat Promotions, Inc. initially encountered difficulties in obtaining the letter of credit. Ultimately, however, Meyer Blinder (Blinder), President of Blinder-Robinson, expressed an interest in the event. Blinder anticipated that his company's participation would result in a positive public relations image for its recently opened Denver office. Blinder-Robinson ultimately agreed to provide the $250,000 letter of credit.

Blinder-Robinson insisted on several conditions to protect its investment. It required the formation of a limited partnership with specific provisions governing repayment to Blinder-Robinson of any sums drawn against the letter of credit. It also required Alzado's personal secured guarantee to reimburse Blinder-Robinson for any losses it might suffer. Alzado and Combat Promotions, Inc. accepted these conditions.

On June 25, 1979, an agreement was executed by Combat Promotions, Inc. and Blinder-Robinson creating a limited partnership, Combat Associates. Under the terms of the agreement, Combat Promotions, Inc. was the general partner and Blinder-Robinson was the sole limited partner. Blinder-Robinson contributed a $250,000 letter of credit to Combat Associates, and the partnership agreement provided expressly that the letter of credit was to be paid off as a partnership expense.

On the same day, June 25, 1979, Alzado executed a separate guaranty agreement with Blinder-Robinson. This agreement provided that if Ali drew the letter of credit, Alzado personally would reimburse Blinder-Robinson for any amount Blinder-Robinson was unable to recover from Combat Associates under the terms of the limited partnership agreement. As security for his agreement, Alzado placed a general warranty deed to his residence, an assignment of an investment account and a confession of judgment in escrow for the benefit of Blinder-Robinson. Thereafter, a separate agreement was apparently executed by Alzado and Combat Associates

providing that Alzado would receive $100,000 in compensation for the exhibition match but subordinating any payment of that sum to the payment of expenses of the match, including, if drawn, the letter of credit.

Approximately one week before the date of the match, Alzado announced that he might not participate because he feared he might lose the assets he had pledged as security for the guaranty agreement. Alzado informed Blinder of this concern, and the two met the next day in Blinder-Robinson's Denver office. Tinter, Kauffman and Ali's representative, Greg Campbell, were also present. Subsequently, on July 14, 1979, the event occurred as scheduled.

Few tickets were sold, and the match proved to be a financial debacle. Ali drew the letter of credit and collected the $250,000 to which he was entitled. Combat Associates paid Blinder-Robinson only $65,000; it did not pay anything to Alzado or, apparently, to other creditors.

In January of 1980, Blinder-Robinson filed this civil action seeking $185,000 in damages plus costs and attorney fees from Alzado pursuant to the terms of the June 25, 1979, guaranty agreement. Alzado denied any liability to Blinder-Robinson and * * * also filed two counterclaims against Blinder-Robinson. The first alleged that because of its conduct Blinder-Robinson must be deemed a general partner of Combat Associates and, therefore, liable to Alzado under the agreement between Alzado and the partnership for Alzado's participation in the match. * * * [The jury returned a verdict of $92,500 in favor of Alzado on this counterclaim. The court of appeals reversed.]

* * *

Alzado next contends that the Court of Appeals erred in concluding that Blinder-Robinson's conduct in promoting the match did not constitute sufficient control of Combat Associates to justify the conclusion that the company must be deemed a general rather than a limited partner. We disagree.

A limited partner may become liable to partnership creditors as a general partner if the limited partner assumes control of partnership business. [Citations]; *see also* [RULPA] §303, which provides that a limited partner does not participate in the control of partnership business solely by doing one or more of the following:

(a) Being a contractor for or an agent or employee of the limited partnership or of a general partner;

(b) Being an officer, director, or shareholder of a corporate general partner;

(c) Consulting with and advising a general partner with respect to the business of the limited partnership;

* * *

* * * Any determination of whether a limited partner's conduct amounts to control over the business affairs of the partnership must be determined by consideration of several factors, including the purpose of the partnership, the administrative activities undertaken, the manner in which the entity actually functioned, and the nature and frequency of the limited partner's purported activities.

* * * The record here reflects that Blinder-Robinson used its Denver office as a ticket outlet, gave two parties to promote the exhibition match and provided a meeting room for many of Combat Associates' meetings. Blinder personally appeared on a television talk show and gave television interviews to promote the match. Blinder-Robinson made no investment, accounting or other financial decisions for the partnership; all such fiscal decisions were made by officers or employees of Combat Promotions, Inc., the general partner. The evidence established at most that Blinder-Robinson engaged in a few promotional activities. It does not establish that it took part in the management or control of the business affairs of the partnership. Accordingly, we agree with the Court of Appeals that the trial court erred in denying Blinder-Robinson's motion for judgment notwithstanding the verdict with respect to Alzado's first counterclaim.

* * *

We * * * affirm the judgment of the Court of Appeals insofar as it reverses the judgments entered at trial in favor of Alzado on his first counterclaim against Blinder-Robinson.

CASE 32-2

Duties of General Partner in Limited Partnerships
WYLER v. FEUER
California Court of Appeal, Second District, Division 2, 1978
85 Cal.App.3d 392, 149 Cal.Rptr. 626

Fleming, J.

Defendants Cy Feuer and Ernest Martin, associated as Feuer and Martin Productions, Inc. (FMPI), have been successful producers of Broadway musical comedies since 1948. Their first motion picture, "Cabaret," produced by Feuer in conjunction with Allied Artists and American Broadcasting Company, received eight Academy Awards in 1973. Plaintiff Wyler is president and largest shareholder of Tool Research and Engineering Corporation, a New York Stock Exchange Company based in Beverly Hills. Prior to 1972 Wyler had had no experience in the entertainment industry.

[In 1972, FMPI bought the motion picture and television rights to Simone Berteaut's best-selling books about her life with her half-sister Edith Piaf. To finance a movie based on this novel, FMPI sought a substantial private investment from Wyler. In July 1973, Wyler signed a final limited partnership agreement with FMPI. The agreement stated that Wyler would provide, interest free, 100 percent financing for the proposed $1.6 million project, in return for a certain portion of the profits, not to exceed 50 percent. In addition, FMPI would obtain $850,000 in production financing by September 30, 1973. The contract specifically provided that FMPI's failure to raise this amount by September 30, 1973, "shall not be deemed a breach of this agreement" and that Wyler's sole remedy would be a reduction in the producer's fee.]

Despite their acclaimed success in "Cabaret," defendants at the time of execution of the limited partnership agreement were experiencing difficulties in obtaining distributor commitments and knew it would be unlikely they could obtain any production financing by the September 30 deadline. Their difficulties arose from their overestimation of the attractiveness of the Piaf subject-matter, from the unknown leading actress, and from the scheduling of photography during the summer months when most Europeans go on vacation.

Filming of the motion picture began July 23 and ended October 9. By that time Wyler had advanced $1.25 million and defendants had failed to obtain any production financing. The completed cost of the picture was $1,512,000.

Early in October, Feuer met Wyler in Paris and requested an extension of the deadline for production financing to December 30, so that defendants could take advantage of distributor negotiations in process and recoup their profit percentage and their producer's fee. Wyler said he had already financed the picture and refused to extend the deadline, thereby maintaining his profit percentage at 50 percent.

[A year after its release in 1974, the motion picture proved less than an overwhelming success—costing $1.5 million but making only $478,000 in total receipts. From the receipts, Wyler received $313,500 for his investment. FMPI had failed to obtain an amount even close to the $850,000 required for production financing. Wyler then sued Feuer, Martin, and FMPI for mismanagement of the business of the limited partnership and to recover his $1.5 million as damages.]

A limited partnership affords a vehicle for capital investment whereby the limited partner restricts his liability to the amount of his investment in return for surrender of any right to manage and control the partnership business. [Citation.] In a limited partnership the general partner manages and controls the partnership business. [Citation.] In exercising his management functions the general partner comes under a fiduciary duty of good faith and fair dealing toward other members of the partnership. [Citations.]

These characteristics—limited investor liability, delegation of authority to management, and fiduciary duty owed by management to investors—are similar to those existing in corporate investment, where it has long been the rule that directors are not liable to stockholders for mistakes made in the exercise of honest business judgment [citations], or for losses incurred in the good faith performance of their duties when they have used such care as an ordinarily prudent person would use. [Citation.] By this standard a general partner may not be held liable for mistakes made or losses incurred in the good faith exercise of reasonable business judgment.

According all due inferences to plaintiff's evidence, as we do on review of a nonsuit, we agree with the trial court that plaintiff did not produce sufficient evidence to hold defendants liable for bad business management. Plaintiff's evidence showed that the Piaf picture did not make money, was not sought after by distributors, and did not live up to its producers' expectations. The same could be said of the majority of motion pictures made since the invention of cinematography. No evidence showed that defendants' decisions and efforts failed to conform to the general duty of care demanded of an ordinarily prudent person in like position under similar circumstances. The good faith business judgment and management of a general partner need only satisfy the standard of care demanded of an ordinarily prudent person, and will not be scrutinized by the courts with the cold clarity of hindsight.

[Judgment for Feuer, Martin, and FMPI affirmed.]

CASE 32-3

Management of Limited Liability Companies
MONTANA FOOD, LLC v. TODOSIJEVIC
Supreme Court of Wyoming, 2015
2015 WY 26, 344 P.3d 751

Kite, J.

[Montana Food,] LLC is a limited liability company organized under the laws of the State of Wyoming and listing its principal place of business in Laramie County, Wyoming. During 2010, Mr. Todosijevic and Mr. Vukov, who are residents of Belgrade, Serbia, each held a 50% membership interest in the LLC. The LLC organized several subsidiaries in Belgrade, including Delbin Investments, MD, LTD (Delbin). The LLC and its subsidiaries invested in buildings located in Belgrade with an eye toward developing them.

The LLC's articles of organization provided that the LLC was manager-managed and named Maksim Stajcer, who was not a member of the LLC, as the manager. The articles of organization also provided that after the initial capital contribution of $10,000, "[a]dditional contributions shall be made at such times and in such amounts as may be agreed upon by the Members as provided in the Operating Agreement." In late 2010, Mr. Vukov became concerned that he was the only member making additional contributions. He retained counsel in Serbia to investigate. The investigation apparently showed that Mr. Vukov had contributed 1,260,600 Euros while Mr. Todosijevic had made no additional contributions. Mr. Vukov issued a notice of meeting indicating that he wished to address the issue of capital contributions by the members as provided in the articles of organization and propose that any member who did not contribute to the LLC's capital would be

subject to a reduction of his ownership interest. Mr. Todosijevic claimed he did not receive the notice. In any event, he did not attend. At the meeting, Mr. Vukov adopted and approved resolutions showing his capital contribution of 1,260,600 Euros, increasing his ownership interest to 99.72% and reducing Mr. Todosijevic's interest to 0.28%. Thereafter, Mr. Vukov amended the articles of organization by naming himself and his wife as the new managers of the LLC.

[In 2011, Mr. Todosijevic filed an action against Mr. Vukov and the LLC, claiming, among other things, that Mr. Vukov did not have the authority to adjust the members' ownership interests. The district court granted Mr. Todosijevic's motion for summary judgment. The LLC appealed.]

The narrow issue before us is whether Mr. Vukov on behalf of the LLC had the contractual or statutory authority to adjust the members' capital contributions. In deciding that issue, we must determine whether provisions of Wyoming's current LLC Act are controlling or whether provisions of the earlier Act apply. [Section 17-29-1103 of the current Act provides that four sections of the former Act applied at the time this action arose, including the management provision.]

The effective date of the current Act was July 1, 2010. The LLC we are concerned with here was organized in June of 2007. Therefore, we look to the former provisions * * * for guidance. We begin with §17-15-116:

§17-15-116. Management.

Management of the limited liability company shall be vested in its members, which unless otherwise provided in the operating agreement, shall be in proportion to their contribution to the capital of the limited liability company, *as adjusted from time to time to properly reflect any additional contributions or withdrawals* by the members; *however, if provision is made for it in the articles of organization, management of the limited liability company may be vested in a manager* or managers who shall be elected by the members in the manner prescribed by the operating agreement of the limited liability company. If the articles of organization provide for the management of the limited liability company by a manager or manage[r]s, *unless the operating agreement expressly dispenses with or substitutes for the requirement of annual elections, the manager or managers shall be elected annually by the members* in the manner provided in the operating agreements. The manager or managers, or persons appointed by the manager or managers, shall also hold the offices and have the responsibilities accorded to them by the members and set out in the operating agreement of the limited liability company.

(Emphasis added.)

In the present case, the articles of organization received by the Wyoming Secretary of State on June 1, 2007, provided as follows:

IX: Management:

The Company is to be managed by a manager. The name and address of the manager who is to serve as manager until the first annual meeting of Members or until its successor or successors is or are elected and qualify, and who shall have authority to act and bind the Company upon his individual signature, is:

Maksim Stajcer, CPA S.A. 76 Dean Street Belize City Belize, C. America

The LLC operating agreement, also dated June 1, 2007, provided:

3.1 MANAGEMENT OF THE BUSINESS. The name and place of residence of each Manager is attached as Exhibit 1 of this Agreement. By a vote of Member(s) holding a majority of capital interests in the Company, as set forth in Exhibit 2 as amended from time to time, shall elect so many Managers as the Members determine, but no fewer than one.

Exhibit 1 to the operating agreement stated that by a majority vote of the members, Maksim Stajcer was elected to serve as manager of the LLC until removed by a majority vote of the members or his voluntary resignation. There is no evidence in the record that Mr. Stajcer had been removed or voluntarily resigned prior to Mr. Vukov's unilateral amendment of the articles of organization in 2011. * * *

* * *

The next question for our determination is whether, in a manager-managed LLC, a member has the authority to adjust the members' ownership interests. Again, we begin by considering which version of Wyoming's LLC Act applies. Section 17-29-1103 * * * states that four sections of the former Act applied at the time this action arose * * *. None of those provisions address the authority of a member of a manager-managed LLC to adjust ownership interests. We, therefore, look to the new Act to resolve the issue.

Section 17-29-407(c) * * * addresses LLC management. Subsection (c)(i) provides that in a manager-managed LLC, unless the articles of organization or the operating agreement provide otherwise, any matter relating to the activities of the company is decided exclusively by the manager. Subsection (c)(iv)(C) further provides that the consent of all members is required to undertake any act outside the ordinary course of the company's activities. Pursuant to the plain language of subsection (c)(i), unless the articles of organization and operating agreement provide otherwise, Mr. Vukov, as a member of the LLC, did not have the authority to decide matters relating to company activities. Pursuant to subsection (c)(iv)(C), Mr. Vukov also had no authority to take action outside the ordinary course of the LLC's activities without Mr. Todosijevic's consent unless the organizational documents provide otherwise.

The articles of organization at issue here provided that the manager "shall have the authority to act for and bind the Company upon his individual signature." The operating agreement further provided:

* * * Members that are not Managers shall take no part whatever in the control, management, direction, or operation of the Company's affairs and shall have no power to bind the Company.

* * *

Pursuant to these provisions, LLC members were not authorized to control, manage, direct or operate LLC affairs; rather, the manager was to control ordinary LLC operations. The manager was not authorized, however, to change members' ownership interests. Nothing in the articles of organization or operating agreement gave anyone the authority to change ownership interests. We conclude, as the district court did, that changing ownership interests was action outside the ordinary course of the LLC's activities. Applying the clear language of §17-29-407(c)(iv)(C), the consent of all members was required. The district court correctly concluded Mr. Vukov did not have the statutory or contractual authority to unilaterally change the members' ownership interests.

Duties in Limited Liability Companies
GRIFFIN v. JONES
United States District Court, W.D. Kentucky, Paducah Division, 2016
170 F.Supp.3d 956

Russell, Senior Judge

[Charles] Jones is a businessman from Murray, Kentucky who has spent his career in the education market. Jones founded his first business, Integrated Computer Solutions, Inc. ("ICS") in 1993. ICS sold computers and information technology services to schools.

In February, 2008, Jones met David Griffin, a wealthy cotton farmer, at the Peabody Hotel in Memphis, Tennessee. The pair discussed several business ideas, ultimately agreeing to start a venture to buy and sell college textbooks. Jones would provide day-to-day management. Griffin would supply financing, initially investing $100,000. They formed a new entity, Blackrock Investments, LLC ("Blackrock"), in March, 2008. Jones and Griffin each owned 50% of Blackrock.

Blackrock created a subsidiary, SE Book Company, LLC ("SE Book") which was used to purchase a "long-standing textbook wholesaler based in Murray with established customer relationships and distribution channels" and "established sources for textbooks, including bi-annual book buybacks from college students." Among SE Book's customers were companies which rented, rather than sold, textbooks to college students. These companies were tapping a new market: college students shopping online. Jones observed that these companies "enjoyed substantial demand" but "faced difficulties obtaining supply." "Textbook publishers guarded their distribution channels" and were reluctant to sell to rental companies, who they viewed as competitors. Jones recognized that SE Book had a "competitive advantage" over these companies because it had an established supply source for textbooks. Jones approached Griffin about moving into the textbook rental market. In March, 2009, the pair formed College Book Rental Company, LLC ("College Book Rental"). Also in 2009, Griffin purchased a 50% share of ICS from a third party for $2 million.

Shortly after both SE Book and College Book Rental were formed they signed a management agreement with CA Jones Management. CA Jones Management provided "accounting, banking, human resources, computer and legal services" for the companies. All employees who worked at SE Book and College Book Rental were actually employed by CA Jones Management and "leased" to SE Book and College Book Rental. CA Jones Management charged SE Book and College Book Rental a monthly management fee for its services. While Griffin and Jones co-owned SE Book and College Book Rental, Jones was the sole owner of CA Jones Management.

College Book Rental was "very successful in a short period of time," with gross profit of $6.3 million in 2010 and $19.4 million in 2011. In September, 2011, John Farris of Commonwealth Economics prepared a valuation of SE Book and College Book Rental that valued the companies between $191 million and $319 million.

Despite this apparent success, Griffin and Jones had an escalating dispute over the health and management of the businesses. Griffin claims that Jones regularly informed him that the companies would soon be profitable but needed immediate financing to pay operating expenses and purchase inventory. From 2009 to 2011 Griffin made over 100 transfers of money totaling over $28 million. Griffin alleges that, unbeknownst to him, Jones was using the management agreement between CA Jones Management and the co-owned companies to siphon money out of the co-owned companies. * * * Griffin claims he invested approximately $28 million in reliance upon Jones's representations that the companies would become profitable. Griffin also guaranteed various bank loans, later paying $19.5 million to satisfy these debts. Griffin also paid $20 million to settle a claim from a vendor, Baker & Taylor. In total, Griffin claims he has lost approximately $75 million as a result of his business relationship with Jones.

Conversely, Jones alleges that beginning in 2010 "Griffin began demanding that he be given an increased ownership interest" in SE Book and College Book Rental because of his additional investments. "In response, I reminded him of our agreement, reached years earlier, that I was responsible for operating the businesses and he was responsible for providing the necessary financial support to operate the businesses." Jones alleges that Griffin demanded and received $1.7 million in September 2011 and $1.07 million in December, 2011. Transferring this money to Griffin "substantially impaired operations and expansion efforts." * * * Jones further contends that in July 2012, Griffin persuaded Security Bank to declare its loan to CBR in default, with Griffin paying the loan personally in exchange for the Bank's cooperation in urging Jones to resign his management position with CBR. Griffin also allegedly convinced Planters Bank to withdraw from an agreement restructuring SE Book's loans to pressure the company into bankruptcy. Jones claims SE Book and College Book Rental would have been worth $1 billion were in not for Griffin's actions.

In February, 2012, Griffin filed a lawsuit against Jones in this Court seeking the appointment of a receiver for the companies. In August, 2012, the parties agreed upon the appointment of Myles MacDonald of KraftCPAs Turnaround & Restructuring Group, PLLC. Griffin then dismissed that lawsuit without prejudice. [Citation.] Griffin alleges that MacDonald immediately "discovered substantial, unjustified transfers of funds" among the companies and to entities solely owned by Jones. MacDonald also found that ICS had not collected more than $5 million in accounts receivables because Jones instructed customers to instead pay a Jones-controlled company. Jones also "secretly established and controlled additional companies which were in direct competition" with the jointly owned companies, including a new business which sold textbooks online. MacDonald also "discovered massive discrepancies in the inventory records" with thousands of textbooks missing.

The mystery of the missing textbooks was solved in September, 2012, when McGraw Hill and other publishers filed a lawsuit claiming that Jones, College Book Rental, SE Book, and a web of other entities related to Jones had engaged in a massive "textbook chop shop" scheme. [Citation.] The companies purchased "steeply discounted U.S. Edition textbooks, specially priced for distribution in developing companies" and "International Edition" textbooks from "nontraditional suppliers." [Citation.] Employees were instructed to remove copyright pages, replace ISBN numbers, and remove any markings indicating the textbooks were non-standard with hot irons, dremels, and slicers. * * * Jones then purchased a printing business to create high quality look-alike textbook covers. To provide a front for their claim that books were being distributed internationally, Jones formed four entities in the Dominican Republic. [Citation.] Jones admitted to copyright infringement and Jones, along with the entities he controlled, settled for $900,000. Griffin alleges he had no knowledge of this scheme. The publishers' case against Griffin is still ongoing.

The *McGraw-Hill* case is but one of a multitude of lawsuits involving Jones and Griffin. This Court previously noted eight lawsuits in Kentucky state and federal courts alone. [Citation.] Bankruptcy petitions, either voluntary or involuntary, have been filed for College Book Rental, ICS, SE Book, Blackrock, and Jones. Griffin claims he has secured judgment in excess of $16 million against Jones "in two other matters ***."

[In a lawsuit brought by David Griffin against Charles Jones, the defendant counterclaimed that Griffin breached his fiduciary duties. Griffin filed a motion for summary judgment dismissing the defendant Charles Jones's counterclaim. Jones has also filed a motion for summary judgment in his favor on the counterclaim.]

The Kentucky Supreme Court has explained that generally, a fiduciary relationship is "one founded on trust or confidence reposed by one person in the integrity and fidelity of another." [Citation.] The relationship must also involve "an undertaking in which a duty is created in one person to act primarily for another's benefit in matters connected with such undertaking." [Citation.] To prevail upon a claim for breach of fiduciary duty, a plaintiff must demonstrate: (1) that the defendant owes a fiduciary duty to the plaintiff; (2) that the defendant breached

that duty; and (3) that the plaintiff suffered damages as a result of the breach. [Citation.] * * *

* * * Griffin argues that he did not owe a fiduciary duty to Jones. * * * The Court will address whether Griffin owed Jones a fiduciary duty for (i) ICS, (ii) Blackrock, (iii) SE Book, and (iv) College Book Rental.

Integrated Computer Solutions

Integrated Computer Solutions, Inc. is a Kentucky corporation that was incorporated in 1993. Jones is the CEO of ICS. His wife, Sarah Jones, is the Secretary. Stuart Bain was previously a Vice President. In 2008, Bain sold his 50% stake in ICS to Griffin for $2 million. Griffin is a stockholder in ICS but has never been an officer or director of ICS.

In Kentucky, a stockholder does not owe a fiduciary duty. [Citation.] Other states have held that a stockholder may owe a fiduciary duty in the special case of closely-held corporations. [Citation.] Kentucky has not adopted this rule.

[Citations.]

* * *

Blackrock

Blackrock is a Kentucky limited liability company. Griffin and Jones each own 50% of Blackrock. Blackrock was originally organized on March 27, 2008 as member-managed limited liability company. On January 20, 2009, it was converted to a manager-managed limited liability company. Jones is the manager. Griffin is a member.

"Under Kentucky law, fiduciary duties are generally concomitant with the responsibility for management of the LLC." [Citations.] A Kentucky LLC can be managed either by its members or by a manager. [Citation.] If an LLC is member-managed, then the members have fiduciary duties. Conversely, if the LLC is manager-managed, then the manager owes fiduciary duties, but the members do not.

[Citations.]

Griffin is a member of Blackrock, a manager-managed LLC. Jones is the manager of Blackrock. Therefore, as a matter of Kentucky law, Griffin does not owe a fiduciary duty to Jones as a member of Blackrock.

* * *

SE Book

SE Book is a Kentucky limited liability company that was organized on May 27, 2008. Neither Griffin nor Jones have an ownership interest in SE Books. Instead, SE Book is owned by Blackrock. SE Book was originally organized as a member-managed limited liability company with Blackrock as the sole member. On February 17, 2009, it was converted to a manager-managed limited liability company. Jones is the manager.

Griffin does not owe Jones a fiduciary duty arising out of SE Book because Griffin is not a manager of SE Book.

College Book Rental

College Book Rental is a Wyoming limited liability company. The sole member of College Book Rental is the BR Trust. College Book Rental is manager-managed. Jones is the manager.

Wyoming law imposes fiduciary duties of loyalty and care upon a member in a member-managed limited liability company. [Citation.] If the limited liability company is manager-managed, then non-managing members are expressly exempted from these fiduciary duties. [Citation.]

Griffin is neither a manager nor a member of College Book Rental. Accordingly, Griffin does not owe Jones a fiduciary duty arising out of College Book Rental.

* * *

CONCLUSION

The Court finds that, as a matter of law, Griffin is entitled to summary judgment on Jones's counterclaim. Jones has failed to establish that Griffin owed Jones a fiduciary duty.

CASE 32-5

Liabilities in Limited Liability Companies
ESTATE OF COUNTRYMAN V. FARMERS COOP. ASS'N
Supreme Court of Iowa, 2004
679 N.W.2d 598

Cady, J.

In the afternoon of September 6, 1999, an explosion leveled the home of Jerry Usovsky (Usovsky) in Richland, Iowa. Tragically, seven people who had gathered in the home to celebrate the Labor Day holiday died from the explosion. Six others were injured, some seriously. The likely cause of the explosion was stray propane gas. The survivors and executors of the estates of those who died eventually filed a lawsuit seeking monetary damages against a host of defendants. The legal theories of recovery included negligence, breach of warranty, and strict liability. The defendants included Iowa Double Circle, L.C. (Double Circle) and Farmers Cooperative Association of Keota (Keota).

Double Circle is an Iowa limited liability company. It is a supplier of propane, and delivered propane to Usovsky's home prior to the explosion. Keota is one of two members in Double Circle. It owns a ninety-five percent interest in the company. The other member is Farmland Industries, Inc. (Farmland Industries), a regional cooperative. Keota and Farmland Industries formed Double Circle in 1996 from an existing operation.

Keota is a farm cooperative that provides a variety of farm products and services to area farmers. It is a member of Farmland Industries and is managed by Dave Hopscheidt (Hopscheidt). The executive committee of Keota's board of directors serves as the board of directors of Double Circle, along with a representative of Farmland Industries. Keota provides managerial services to Double Circle, pursuant to a management agreement between Keota and Double Circle. Keota's duties under the agreement include "human resource and safety management." Hopscheidt oversees the daily operations of both Keota and Double Circle. However, Keota and Double Circle operate as separate entities and maintain separate finances. Keota moved for summary judgment. * * *

The plaintiffs resisted the motion by pointing to allegations in their petition indicating Keota participated in the claims of wrongdoing through the management decisions it made in consumer safety matters. For example, plaintiffs claimed Keota, through Hopscheidt, was negligent in failing to provide proper warnings to propane users, including the failure to warn users to install a gas detector, and to properly design the odorant added to the propane. * * *

The district court granted summary judgment for Keota. It found plaintiffs failed to produce any facts to show that Keota engaged in conduct separate from its duties as director or manager of Double Circle. Consequently, it concluded Keota was protected as a matter of law from personal liability for claims of wrongful conduct attributable to Double Circle. * * *

* * *

Plaintiffs filed their notice of appeal from the summary judgment. * * * They claimed the district court erred by finding that Keota was insulated from liability as a matter of law. * * *

* * *

The limited liability company, "LLC" as it is now known, is a hybrid business entity that is considered to have the attributes of a partnership for federal income tax purposes and the limited liability protections of a corporation. [Citation.] As such, it provides for the operational advantages of a partnership by allowing the owners, called members, to participate in the management of the business. [Citation.] Yet, the members and managers are protected from liability in the same manner shareholders, officers, and directors of a corporation are protected. [Citation.]

The LLC * * * has now been adopted by statute in every state in the nation. [Citation.] Iowa joined the trend in 1992 with the passage of the Iowa Limited Liability Company Act (ILLCA). [Citation.] The ILLCA, among other features, permits the owners or members to centralize management in one or more managers or reserve all management powers to themselves. [Citations.]

Although the tax treatment of an LLC has been largely resolved, the contours of the limited liability of an LLC are less certain. [Citation.] Only a few courts have specifically addressed the issue of tort liability. * * *

* * *

The[se] rules of liability derived from [the ILLCA] have been summarized as follows:

Sections * * * of the Act generally provide that a member or manager of a limited liability company is not personally liable for acts or debts of the company solely by reason of being a member or manager, except in the following situations: (1) the ILLCA expressly provides for the person's liability; (2) the articles of organization provide for the person's liability; (3) the person has agreed in writing to be personally liable; (4) the person participates in tortious conduct; or (5) a shareholder of a corporation would be personally liable in the same situation, except that the failure to hold meetings and related formalities shall not be considered.

[Citation.]

* * * While liability of members and managers is limited, the statute clearly imposes liability when they participate in tortious conduct. [Citation.] This approach is compatible with the longstanding approach to liability in corporate settings, where, under general agency principles, corporate officers and directors can be liable for their torts even when committed in their capacity as an officer.

[Citations.] * * *.

Keota suggests that liability of an LLC member or manager for tortious conduct is limited to conduct committed outside the member or manager role. Yet, this approach is contrary to the corporate model and agency principles upon which the liability of LLC members and managers is based, and cannot be found in the language of the statute. We acknowledge that the "participation in tortious conduct" standard would not impose tort liability on a manager for merely performing a general administrative duty. [Citations.] There must be some participation. [Citation.] The participation standard is consistent with the principle that members or managers are not liable based only on their status as members or managers. [Citation.] Instead, liability is derived from individual activities. Yet, a manager who takes part in the commission of a tort is liable even when the manager acts on behalf of a corporation. [Citation.] The ILLCA does not insulate a manager from liability for participation in tortious conduct merely because the conduct occurs within the scope and role as a manager. * * * The limit on liability created for members and managers of LLCs in [citation] means members and managers are not liable for company torts "solely by reason of being a member or manager" of an LLC. [Citation.] The phrase "solely by reason of" refers to liability based upon membership or management status. It does not distinguish between conduct of a member or manager that may be separate and independent from the member or management role. Thus, it is not inconsistent to protect a member or manager from vicarious liability, while imposing liability when the member or manager participates in a tort. Liability of members of an LLC is limited, but not to the extent claimed by Keota.

* * *

We conclude that Keota is not protected from liability if it participated in tortious conduct in performing its duties as manager of Double Circle. Consequently, the district court improperly granted summary judgment based on the limited liability provisions of [citation]. A trial is necessary to develop the facts relating to allegations of Keota's participation in the alleged torts.

We reverse the summary judgment ruling of the district court on the issue of liability under [citation], and remand for further proceedings.

| CASE 32-6 | Judicial Dissolution of Limited Liability Companies
IN THE MATTER OF 1545 OCEAN AVE., LLC
Appellate Division of the Supreme Court of New York, Second Department, 2010
72 A.D.3d 121, 893 N.Y.S.2d 590 |  |

Austin, J.

[1545 LLC was formed in November 2006 by its two members Crown Royal Ventures, LLC (Crown Royal) and Ocean Suffolk Properties, LLC (Ocean Suffolk) that executed an operating agreement that provided for two managers: Walter T. Van Houten (Van Houten), who was a member of Ocean Suffolk, and John J. King, who was a member of Crown Royal. Each member of 1545 LLC contributed 50 percent of the capital, which was used to purchase premises known as 1545 Ocean Avenue in Bohemia, New York, on January 5, 2007. 1545 LLC was formed to purchase the property, rehabilitate an existing building, and build a second building for commercial rental. Van Houten, who owns his own construction company, Van Houten Construction (VHC), was permitted to submit bids for the project, subject to the approval of the managers.

Article 4.1 of the operating agreement provides that "[a]t any time when there is more than one Manager, any one Manager may take any action permitted under the Agreement, unless the approval of more than one of the Managers is expressly required pursuant to the [operating agreement] or the [Limited Liability Company Law]."

Article 4.12 of the operating agreement entitled, "Regular Meetings," does not require meetings of the managers with any particular regularity. Meetings may be called without notice as the managers may "from time to time determine."

The managers disagreed about various aspects of the construction work performed on the LLC property by VHC, which billed 1545 LLC the sum of $97,322.27 for this work. King claims that he agreed 1545 LLC would pay VHC's invoice on the condition that VHC would no longer unilaterally do work on the site. Notwithstanding King's demand, VHC continued working on the site. Despite his earlier protests, King did nothing to stop it. The managers also disagreed about which company to hire to perform environmental remediation work on the site.

King contended that thereafter tensions between King and Van Houten escalated and that Van Houten refused to meet on a regular basis, proclaiming himself to be a "cowboy" and would "just get it done." Nevertheless, King acknowledged that the construction work undertaken by VHC was "awesome." By April 2007, King announced that he wanted to withdraw his investment from 1545 LLC. He proposed to have all vendors so notified, telling them that Van Houten was taking over the management of 1545 LLC. As a result, Van Houten viewed King as having resigned as a manager of 1545 LLC.

Ultimately, King sought to have Ocean Suffolk buy out Crown Royal's membership in 1545 LLC or, alternatively, to have Crown Royal buy out Ocean Suffolk. Despite discussions regarding competing proposals for the buyout of the interest of each member by the other member, no satisfactory resolution was realized. During this period of disagreements, VHC continued to work unilaterally on the site so that the project was within weeks of completion when Crown Royal filed a petition to dissolve 1545 LLC. The sole ground for dissolution cited by Crown Royal was deadlock between the managing members arising from Van Houten's alleged violations of various provisions of article 4 of the operating agreement. The trial court granted the petition of Crown Royal to dissolve 1545 Ocean Avenue, LLC. Ocean Suffolk appealed.]

Limited Liability Company Law §702 provides for judicial dissolution as follows:

> On application by or for a member, the supreme court in the judicial district in which the office of the limited liability company is located may decree dissolution of a limited liability company *whenever it is not reasonably practicable to carry on the business* in conformity with the articles of organization or operating agreement (emphasis added).

* * *

* * * Limited Liability Company Law §702 is clear that * * * the court must first examine the limited liability company's operating agreement, [citation], to determine, in light of the circumstances presented, whether it is or is not "reasonably practicable" for the limited liability company to continue to carry on its business in conformity with the operating agreement [citation]. * * *

* * * Where an operating agreement, such as that of 1545 LLC, does not address certain topics, a limited liability company is bound by the default requirements set forth in the Limited Liability Company Law [citations].

The operating agreement of 1545 LLC does not contain any specific provisions relating to dissolution. * * *

Crown Royal argues for dissolution based on the parties' failure to hold regular meetings, failure to achieve quorums, and deadlock. The operating agreement, however, does not require regular meetings or quorums [citation]. It only provides, in article 4.12, for meetings to be held at such times as the managers may "from time to time determine." The record demonstrates that the managers, King and Van Houten, communicated with each other on a regular basis without the formality of a noticed meeting which appears to conform with the spirit and letter of the operating agreement and the continued ability of 1545 LLC to function in that context.

King and Van Houten did not always agree as to the construction work to be performed on the 1545 LLC property. King claims that this forced the parties into a "deadlock." "Deadlock" is a basis, in and of itself, for judicial dissolution under Business Corporation Law §1104. However, no such independent ground for dissolution is available under Limited Liability Company Law §702. Instead, the court must consider the managers' disagreement in light of the operating agreement and the continued ability of 1545 LLC to function in that context.

It has been suggested that judicial dissolution is only available when the petitioning member can show that the limited liability company is unable to function as intended or that it is failing financially [citation]. Neither circumstance is demonstrated by the petitioner here. On the contrary, the purpose of 1545 LLC was feasibly and reasonably being met.

* * *

* * * Thus, the only basis for dissolution can be if 1545 LLC cannot effectively operate under the operating agreement to meet and achieve the purpose for which it was created. In this case, that is the development of the property which purpose, despite the disagreements between the managing members, was being met. As the Delaware Chancery Court noted in *Matter of Arrow Inv. Advisors, LLC,*

The court will not dissolve an LLC merely because the LLC has not experienced a smooth glide to profitability or because events have not turned out exactly as the LLC's owners originally envisioned; such events are, of course, common in the risk-laden process of birthing new entities in the hope that they will become mature, profitable ventures. In part because a hair-trigger dissolution standard would ignore this market reality and thwart the expectations of reasonable investors that entities will not be judicially terminated simply because of some market turbulence, dissolution is reserved for situations in which the LLC's management has become so dysfunctional or its business purpose so thwarted that it is no longer practicable to operate the business, such as in the case of a voting deadlock or where the defined purpose of the entity has become impossible to fulfill * * * [citation].

Here, the operating agreement avoids the possibility of "deadlock" by permitting each managing member to operate unilaterally in furtherance of 1545 LLC's purpose.

After careful examination of the various factors considered in applying the "not reasonably practicable" standard, we hold that for dissolution of a limited liability company pursuant to Limited Liability Company Law §702, the petitioning member must establish, in the context of the terms of the operating agreement or articles of incorporation, that (1) the management of the entity is unable or unwilling to reasonably permit or promote the stated purpose of the entity to be realized or achieved, or (2) continuing the entity is financially unfeasible.

Dissolution is a drastic remedy [citation]. * * * [T]he petitioner has failed to meet the standard for dissolution enunciated here * * *.

[Order of the trial court is reversed, the petition is denied, and the proceeding is dismissed.]

QUESTIONS

1. John Palmer and Henry Morrison formed the limited partnership of Palmer & Morrison for the management of the Huntington Hotel and filed an appropriate certificate in compliance with the limited partnership statute. The limited partnership agreement provided that Palmer would contribute $400,000 and be a general partner and that Morrison would contribute $300,000 and be a limited partner. Palmer was to manage the dining and cocktail rooms, and Morrison was to manage the rest of the hotel. Nanette, a popular French singer, who knew nothing of the limited partnership's affairs, appeared for four weeks in the Blue Room at the hotel and was not paid her fee of $8,000. Subsequently, the limited partnership became insolvent. Nanette sued Palmer and Morrison for $8,000.

   a. For how much, if anything, are Palmer and Morrison liable? Explain.

   b. If Palmer and Morrison had formed a limited liability limited partnership, for how much, if anything, would Palmer and Morrison be liable? Explain.

   c. If Palmer and Morrison had formed a limited liability company with each as a member, for how much, if anything, would Palmer and Morrison be liable? Explain.

   d. If Palmer and Morrison had formed a limited liability partnership with each as a general partner, for how much, if anything, would Palmer and Morrison be liable? Explain.

2. A limited partnership was formed consisting of Webster as general partner and Stevens and Stewart as the limited partners. The limited partnership was organized in strict compliance with the limited partnership statute. Stevens was employed by the partnership as a purchasing agent. Stewart personally guaranteed a loan made to the partnership. Both Stevens and Stewart consulted with Webster with respect to partnership business, voted on a change in the nature of the partnership business, and disapproved an amendment to the partnership agreement proposed by Webster. The partnership experienced serious financial difficulties, and its creditors seek to hold Webster, Stevens, and Stewart personally liable for the debts of the partnership. Discuss who, if anyone, is personally liable.

3. Fox, Dodge, and Gilbey agreed to become limited partners in Palatine Ventures, a limited partnership. In a signed writing, each agreed to contribute $20,000. Fox's contribution consisted entirely of cash, Dodge contributed $12,000 in cash and gave the partnership her promissory note for $8,000, and Gilbey's contribution was his promise to perform two hundred hours of legal services for the partnership.

   a. Discuss what liability, if any, Fox, Dodge, and Gilbey have to the partnership by way of capital contribution.

   b. If Palatine Ventures had been formed as a limited liability company (LLC) with Fox, Dodge, and Gilbey as members, discuss what liability, if any, Fox, Dodge, and Gilbey would have to the LLC by way of capital contribution.

4. Madison and Tilson agree to form a limited partnership with Madison as general partner and Tilson as the limited partner, each to contribute $12,500 as capital. No papers are

ever filed, and after ten months, the enterprise fails, its liabilities exceeding its assets by $30,000. Creditors of the partnership seek to hold Madison and Tilson personally liable for the $30,000. Explain whether the creditors will prevail.

5. Kraft is a limited partner of Johnson Enterprises, a limited partnership. As provided in the limited partnership agreement, Kraft decided to leave the partnership and demanded that her capital contribution of $20,000 be returned. At this time, the partnership assets were $150,000 and liabilities to all creditors totaled $140,000. The partnership returned to Kraft her capital contribution of$20,000.

   a. Explain what liability, if any, Kraft has to the creditors of Johnson Enterprises.

   b. If Johnson Enterprises had been formed as a limited liability company, explain what liability, if any, Kraft would have to the creditors of Johnson Enterprises.

6. Gordon is the only limited partner in Bushmill Ventures, a limited partnership whose general partners are Daniels and McKenna. Gordon contributed $10,000 for his limited partnership interest and loaned the partnership $7,500. Daniels and McKenna each contributed $5,000 by way of capital. After a year, the partnership is dissolved, at which time it owes $12,500 to its only creditor, Dickel, and has assets of $30,000.

   a. Explain how these assets should be distributed.

   b. Explain how these assets should be distributed if Bushmill Ventures had been formed as a limited liability company with Gordon, Daniels, and McKenna as members.

7. Discuss when a limited partner does or does not have the following rights or powers: (a) to assign his interest in the limited partnership, (b) to receive repayment of loans made to the partnership on a *pro rata* basis with general creditors, (c) to manage the affairs of the limited partnership, (d) to receive his share of the profits before the general partners receive their shares of the profits, and (e) to dissolve the partnership upon his withdrawing from the partnership.

8. Discuss when a member of a limited liability company does or does not have the following rights or powers: (a) to assign her interest in the LLC, (b) to receive repayment of loans made to the LLC on a *pro rata* basis with general creditors, (c) to manage the affairs of the LLC, and (d) to dissolve the LLC upon her withdrawing from the LLC.

9. Albert, Betty, and Carol own and operate the Roy Lumber Company, a limited liability partnership (LLP). Each contributed one-third of the capital, and they share equally in the profits and losses. Their LLP agreement provides that all purchases exceeding $2,500 must be authorized in advance by two partners and that only Albert is authorized to draw checks. Unknown to Albert or Carol, Betty purchases on the firm's account a $5,500 diamond bracelet and a $5,000 forklift and orders $5,000 worth of logs, all from Doug, who operates a jewelry store and is engaged in various activities connected with the lumber business. Before Betty made these purchases, Albert told Doug that Betty is not the log buyer. Albert refuses to pay Doug for Betty's purchases. Doug calls at the mill to collect, and Albert again refuses to pay him. Doug calls Albert an unprintable name, and Albert then punches Doug in the nose, knocking him out. While Doug is lying unconscious on the ground, an employee of Roy Lumber Company negligently drops a log on Doug's leg, breaking three bones. The firm and the three partners are completely solvent.

   Discuss what the rights of Doug are against Roy Lumber Company, Albert, Betty, and Carol.

CASE PROBLEMS

10. In January, Dr. Vidricksen contributed $250,000 to become a limited partner in a Chevrolet car agency business with Thom, the general partner. Articles of limited partnership were drawn up, but no effort was made to comply with the State's statutory requirement of recording the certificate of limited partnership. In March, Vidricksen learned that because of the failure to file, he might not have formed a limited partnership. At this time, the business developed financial difficulties and went into bankruptcy on September 1. Eight days later, Vidricksen filed a renunciation of the business's profits. Is Dr. Vidricksen a general partner? Why or why not?

11. Dale Fullerton was chairman of the board of Enviro-search and the sole stockholder in Westover Hills Management. James Anderson was president of AGFC. Fullerton and Anderson agreed to form a limited partnership to purchase certain property from WYORCO, a joint venture of which Fullerton was a member. The parties intended to form a

limited partnership with Westover Hills Management as the sole general partner and AGFC and Envirosearch as limited partners. The certificate filed with the Wyoming Secretary of State, however, listed all three companies as both general and limited partners of Westover Hills Ltd. Anderson and Fullerton later became aware of this error and filed an amended certificate of limited partnership, which correctly named Envirosearch and AGFC as limited partners only. Subsequently, Westover Hills Ltd. became insolvent. What is the liability of Envirosearch and AGFC to creditors of the limited partnership? Discuss.

12. Namvar Taghipour, Danesh Rahemi, and Edgar Jerez formed a limited liability company to purchase and develop a parcel of real estate. The LLC's articles of organization designated Jerez as the LLC's manager. In addition, the written operating agreement among the members of the LLC provided, "No loans may be contracted on behalf of the [LLC] . . . unless authorized by a resolution of the members." On the next day, the LLC acquired the intended real estate. Two years later, Jerez, without the knowledge or consent of the LLC's other members, entered into a loan agreement on behalf of the LLC with Mount Olympus. According to the loan agreement, Mount Olympus lent the LLC $25,000, and as security for the loan, Jerez executed and delivered a trust deed on the LLC's real estate. Mount Olympus then disbursed $20,000 to Jerez and retained the $5,000 balance to cover various fees. In making the loan, Mount Olympus did not investigate Jerez's authority to enter into the loan agreement beyond determining that Jerez was the manager of the LLC. Jerez absconded with the $20,000. The LLC never made payments on the loan, since it was unaware of the loan. Mount Olympus then foreclosed on the LLC's property, giving notice of the default and pending foreclosure sale to only Jerez. Explain whether the foreclosure was valid.

13. Carolinian is a closely held, manager-managed limited liability company organized under the laws of South Carolina. Carolinian owns and manages various hotel and rental properties in South Carolina. In February 2018, the Levys obtained a judgment against Patel, a member of Carolinian, in the amount of $2.5 million. Thereafter, the Levys obtained a charging order in the circuit court, which constituted a lien against Patel's distributional interest in Carolinian. Subsequently, the Levys filed a petition to foreclose the charging lien, and the foreclosure sale was held in April 2020. The Levys were the successful bidders, purchasing Patel's distributional interest for $215,000. Carolinian was represented at the foreclosure sale by its registered agent and its attorney, who unsuccessfully bid $190,000 on Carolinian's behalf. Carolinian's Operating Agreement provides that a member's financial rights can be redeemed at any time up until foreclosure sale. But neither Carolinian nor any of the remaining members redeemed Patel's interest prior to the foreclosure sale, and the Levys did not thereafter seek to be admitted as members of Carolinian.

Following the foreclosure sale, Carolinian asserted it was entitled to purchase Patel's distributional interest from the Levys pursuant to Article 11 of the Operating Agreement, which provides that if a member attempts to transfer all or a portion of his membership share without obtaining the other members' consent, such member is deemed to have offered to the LLC all of his membership share. Carolinian contended that since the Levys failed to obtain the consent required under Section 11.1 of the Operating Agreement, their distributional interest was deemed to have been offered to Carolinian, and Carolinian was entitled to purchase that interest under Section 11.2. The Levys objected to Carolinian's attempt to force them to sell their interest, arguing they were not subject to the terms of Article 11 of the Operating Agreement. Explain who should prevail.

On April 5, Handy contracted to purchase land with the intent of forming a limited liability company (LLC) with Ginsburg and McKinley for the purpose of building a residential community on the property. On April 21, they learned from Coastal, an environmental consulting firm they had hired, that the property contained federally protected wetlands. The presence of wetlands adversely affected the property's value and development potential. Handy, Ginsburg, and McKinley abandoned construction plans and instead decided to sell the property. To advertise and promote that sale, they placed on the property a sign that stated the property had "Excellent Development Potential." Unaware of the existence of wetlands, Pepsi acquired an option to purchase the property from Handy on August 5. At that time, Willow Creek had not yet been formed and Handy had not yet purchased the property. On August 18, Handy, Ginsburg, and McKinley formed Willow Creek Estates,

LLC. During the option period, Pepsi hired a soil-engineering consultant to conduct an environmental investigation of the property. In Handy's written answers to specific questions from the consultant about the property, Handy did not disclose that the property contained wetlands or that Coastal had already performed a written preliminary wetlands determination the month before. On September 4, Willow Creek, LLC, took title to the property. Four months later Willow Creek, LLC, sold the property to Pepsi for more than twice the amount of its purchase price and did not disclose the existence of wetlands on the property. After Pepsi learned that the property contained wetlands, it brought an action for fraud against Willow Creek, Handy, Ginsburg, and McKinley.

a. What are the arguments that Handy, Ginsburg, and McKinley are not individually liable to Pepsi for fraud?

b. What are the arguments that Handy, Ginsburg, and McKinley are individually liable to Pepsi for fraud?

c. Explain who should prevail.

Corporations

CH 33 NATURE, FORMATION, AND
POWERS

CH 34 FINANCIAL STRUCTURE

CH 35 MANAGEMENT STRUCTURE

CH 36 FUNDAMENTAL CHANGES

CHAPTER 33

Nature, Formation, and Powers

CHAPTER OUTCOMES

After reading and studying this chapter, you should be able to:

- Identify the principal attributes and classifications of corporations.

- Explain how a corporation is formed and the role, liability, and duties of promoters.

- Distinguish between the statutory and common law approaches to defective formation of a corporation.

- Explain how the doctrine of piercing the corporate veil applies to closely held corporations and parent-subsidiary corporations.

- Explain the sources of corporate powers and the legal consequences of a corporation's exceeding its powers.

A corporation is an entity created by law whose existence is distinct from that of the individuals whose initiative, property, and management enable it to function. In the opinion of the Supreme Court in *Dartmouth College v. Woodward*, 17 U.S. (4 Wheat.) 518, 4 L.Ed. 629 (1819), Chief Justice Marshall stated:

> A corporation is an artificial being, invisible, intangible, and existing only in contemplation of law. Being the mere creature of law, it possesses only those properties which the charter of its creation confers upon it, either expressly or as incidental to its very existence. These are such as are supposed best calculated to effect the object for which it was created. Among the most important are immortality, and, if the expression may be allowed, individuality; properties by which a perpetual succession of many persons are considered as the same, so that they may act as a single individual. A corporation manages its own affairs, and holds property without the hazardous and endless necessity of perpetual conveyances for the purpose of transmitting it from hand to hand.

The corporation is the dominant form of business organization in the United States, accounting for 77 percent of the gross revenues of all business entities. Approximately 6 million domestic corporations, with annual revenues approaching $30 trillion, are currently doing business in the United States. Approximately 50 percent of American households own stock directly or indirectly through institutional investors, such as mutual funds, pension funds, banks, and insurance companies. Corporations have achieved this dominance because their attributes of limited liability, free transferability of shares, and continuity have attracted great numbers of widespread investors. Moreover, the centralized management of corporations has facilitated the development of large organizations that employ great quantities of invested capital, thereby utilizing economies of scale.

Use of the corporation as an instrument of commercial enterprise has made possible the vast concentrations of wealth and capital that have largely transformed this country's economy from an agrarian to an industrial one. Due to its size, power, and impact, the business corporation is a key institution not only in the American economy but also in the world power structure.

In 1946, a committee of the American Bar Association, after careful study and research, submitted a draft of a Model Business Corporation Act (MBCA). The MBCA has been amended frequently since then. Although the provisions of the Act do not become law until enacted by a State, its influence has been widespread, and a majority of the States adopted it in whole or in part.

In 1984, the Committee on Corporate Laws of the Section of Corporation, Banking, and Business Law of the American Bar Association approved a Revised Model Business Corporation Act (RMBCA). More than thirty States have adopted the RMBCA in whole or in substantial part. Moreover, many other States have adopted selected provisions of the RMBCA. However, Delaware and seven of the ten most populous States have *not* adopted either the MBCA or the RMBCA. The RMBCA as amended is used throughout the chapters on corporations in this text and is referred to as the Revised Act or the RMBCA.

In 2009, a number of sections of the RMBCA were amended to update the Act's electronic technology provisions to bring them into alignment with the Uniform Electronic Transmissions Act (UETA) and the Federal Electronic Signatures in Global and National Commerce Act (E-Sign), both of which are discussed in Chapter 15.

Since 1984, the Corporate Laws Committee of the American Bar Association has continued to revise various provisions of the RMBCA. In 2010, the Committee began a thorough review and revision of the 1984 Revised Act, resulting in the adoption and publication of the 2016 Revision of the Model Business Corporation Act (referred to here as the 2016 Revision or 2016 RMBCA). The 2016 Revision is based on the 1984 RMBCA and incorporates the amendments to the 1984 RMBCA that had been separately published. At least five States have adopted the 2016 Revision. Significant changes contained in the 2016 Revision are discussed in this chapter and in *Chapters 34–36*.

NATURE OF CORPORATIONS

To understand corporations, it is helpful to examine their common attributes and their various types. Both of these topics are discussed in this section.

33-1 Corporate Attributes

The principal attributes of a corporation are as follows: (1) it is a legal entity; (2) it owes its existence to a State, which also regulates it; (3) it provides limited liability to its shareholders; (4) its shares of stock are freely transferable; (5) its existence may be perpetual; (6) its management is centralized; and it is considered, for some purposes, (7) a person and (8) a citizen.

♦ SEE FIGURE 30-1: *General Partnership, Limited Partnership, Limited Liability Company, and Corporation*

33-1a LEGAL ENTITY

A corporation is a legal entity separate from its shareholders, with rights and liabilities entirely distinct from theirs. It may sue or be sued by, as well as contract with, any other party, including any one of its shareholders. A transfer of stock in the corporation from one individual to another has no effect upon the legal existence of the corporation. Title to corporate property belongs not to the shareholders, but to the corporation. Even where a single individual owns all of the stock of a corporation, the existence of the shareholder is distinct from that of the corporation.

33-1b CREATURE OF THE STATE

A corporation may be formed only by substantial compliance with a State incorporation statute. Every State has a general incorporation statute authorizing the Secretary of State to issue a certificate of incorporation upon compliance with its provisions.

A corporation's articles of incorporation and the provisions of the statute under which it is formed constitute a contract between it and the State. Article I, Section 10, of the U.S. Constitution provides that no State shall pass any law "impairing the obligation of contracts," and this prohibition applies to contracts between a State and a corporation. See *Chapter 4*.

To avoid the impact of this provision, incorporation statutes reserve to the State the power to establish such regulations, provisions, and limitations as it deems advisable and to amend or repeal the statute at its pleasure. Section 1.02. This reservation is a material part of the contract between the State and a corporation formed under the statute; consequently, because the contract expressly permits them, amendments or modifications regulating or altering the structure of the corporation do not impair the obligation of contract.

33-1c LIMITED LIABILITY

A corporation is a legal entity and therefore is liable out of its own assets for its debts. Generally, the shareholders have **limited liability** for the corporation's debts—their liability does not extend beyond the amount of their investment—although, as discussed later in this chapter, under certain circumstances, a shareholder may be personally liable. The limitation on liability, however, will not affect the liability of a shareholder who committed the wrongful act. A shareholder is also liable for any corporate obligations personally guaranteed by the individual member or manager.

33-1d FREE TRANSFERABILITY OF CORPORATE SHARES

In the absence of contractual restrictions, shares in a corporation may be freely transferred by way of sale, gift, or pledge. The ability to transfer shares is a valuable right and may enhance their market value. Article 8 of the Uniform Commercial Code, Investment Securities, governs transfers of shares of stock.

33-1e PERPETUAL EXISTENCE

A corporation's existence is perpetual unless otherwise stated in its articles of incorporation. Section 3.02. Consequently, the death, withdrawal, or addition of a shareholder, a director, or an officer does not terminate the existence of a corporation. A corporation's existence will terminate upon its dissolution or merger into another business.

33-1f CENTRALIZED MANAGEMENT

The shareholders of a corporation elect a board of directors to manage the business of the corporation. The board in turn appoints officers to run the day-to-day operations of the business. As neither the directors nor the officers (collectively referred to as *management*) need be shareholders, it is entirely possible, and in large corporations quite typical, for ownership and management to be separate. The management structure of corporations is discussed in *Chapter 35*.

33-1g AS A PERSON

Whether a corporation is a "person" within the meaning of a constitution or statute is a matter of construction based upon the intent of the lawmakers in using the word. For example, a corporation is considered a person within the provision in the Fifth and Fourteenth Amendments to the U.S. Constitution that no "person" shall be "deprived of life, liberty, or property without due process of law" and in the provision in the Fourteenth Amendment that no State shall "deny to any person within its jurisdiction the equal protection of the laws." A corporation also enjoys the right of a person to be secure against unreasonable searches and seizures, as provided for in the Fourth Amendment. On the other hand, a corporation is not considered to be a person within the Fifth Amendment's clause that protects a "person" against self-incrimination.

33-1h AS A CITIZEN

A corporation is considered a citizen for some purposes but not for others. A corporation is not deemed to be a citizen as the term is used in the Fourteenth Amendment, which provides, "No State shall make or enforce any law which shall abridge the privileges or immunities of citizens of the United States."

A corporation is, however, regarded as a citizen of the State of its incorporation and of the State in which it has its principal office for the purpose of identifying diversity of citizenship between the parties to a lawsuit and thereby providing a basis for Federal court jurisdiction.

33-2 Classification of Corporations

Corporations may be classified as public or private, profit or nonprofit, domestic or foreign, publicly held or closely held, Subchapter S, and professional. As will be seen, these classifications are not mutually exclusive. For example, a corporation may be a closely held, professional, private, profit, domestic corporation.

33-2a PUBLIC OR PRIVATE

A **public corporation** is one that is created to administer a unit of local civil government, such as a county, city, town, village, school district, or park district, or one created by the United States to conduct public business, such as the Tennessee Valley Authority or the Federal Deposit Insurance Corporation. A public corporation usually is created by specific legislation, which determines the corporation's purpose and powers. Many public corporations are also referred to as municipal corporations.

A **private corporation** is founded by and composed of private persons for private purposes and has no government duties. A private corporation may be for profit or nonprofit.

33-2b PROFIT OR NONPROFIT

A **profit corporation** is one founded for the purpose of operating a business for profit from which payments are made to the corporation's shareholders in the form of dividends.

Although a **nonprofit** (or not-for-profit) **corporation** may make a profit, the profit may not be distributed to members, directors, or officers but must be used exclusively for the charitable, educational, or scientific purpose for which the corporation was organized. Examples of nonprofit corporations include private schools, library clubs, athletic clubs, fraternities, sororities, and hospitals. Most States have special incorporation statutes governing nonprofit corporations, most of which are patterned after the Model Nonprofit Corporation Act.

A **benefit corporation**, also called a **public benefit corporation** or **B-corporation**, is a type of for-profit corporate entity whose legally defined goals include having a positive impact on society and the environment in addition to making a profit. Benefit corporations are authorized in at least thirty-seven States, and four other States have introduced enacting legislation. A benefit corporation is subject in all respects to the provisions of the for-profit incorporation statute, except to the extent the benefit incorporation statute imposes additional or different requirements. The purposes of a benefit corporation include creating a general public benefit and operating in a responsible and sustainable manner. For example, the Delaware public benefit corporation statute defines public benefit to mean "a positive effect (or reduction of negative effects) on 1 or more categories of persons, entities, communities or interests (other than stockholders in their capacities as stockholders) including, but not limited to, effects of an artistic, charitable, cultural, economic, educational, environmental, literary, medical, religious, scientific or technological nature." A benefit corporation must be managed in a manner that balances the stockholders' financial interests, the best interests of those materially affected by the corporation's conduct, and the public benefits identified in the corporation's articles of incorporation. A benefit corporation must periodically report on its promotion of the public benefit and of the best interests of those materially affected by the corporation's conduct.

33-2c DOMESTIC OR FOREIGN

A corporation is a **domestic corporation** in the State in which it is incorporated. It is a **foreign corporation** in every other State or jurisdiction. A corporation may not do business, except for acts in interstate commerce, in a State other than the State of its incorporation without the permission and authorization of the other State. Every State, however, provides for the issuance of certificates of authority that allow foreign corporations to do business within its borders and for the taxation of such foreign businesses. Obtaining a certificate (called "qualifying") usually involves filing certain information with the Secretary of State, paying prescribed fees, and designating a resident agent. Doing or transacting business within a particular State makes the corporation subject to local litigation, regulation, and taxation.

DOING BUSINESS The Revised Act does not attempt to fully define what constitutes the transaction of business. Instead, the Act provides a definition by exclusion by listing activities that do *not* constitute the transaction of business. Section 15.01. Generally, any conduct more regular, systematic, or extensive than that described in this section constitutes the transaction of business and requires a corporation to obtain a certificate of authority. Conduct typically requiring a certificate of authority includes maintaining an office to conduct local intrastate business, selling personal property not in interstate commerce, entering into contracts relating to local business or sales, and owning or using real estate for general corporate purposes. Section 15.01, Comment.

The Revised Act, as stated, provides a *nonexclusive* list of "safe harbors," that is, activities in which a foreign corporation may engage without being considered to have transacted intrastate business. The list includes the following:

1. maintaining bank accounts;
2. selling through independent contractors;
3. soliciting or obtaining orders, whether by mail or through employees or agents or otherwise, if such orders require acceptance outside the State before they become contracts;
4. owning, without more, real or personal property;
5. conducting an isolated transaction that is completed within thirty days and that is not one of a number of repeated transactions of like nature; and
6. transacting business in interstate commerce.

♦ *See Case 33-1*

SCOPE OF REGULATION It is a common and accepted principle that local courts will not interfere with the internal affairs of a foreign corporation. To this end, the Revised Act states that "this Act does not authorize this state to regulate the organization or internal affairs of a foreign corporation." Section 15.05(c). Nevertheless, subjecting foreign corporations to reasonable regulation need not violate due process or constitute a burden on interstate commerce. A few States—most notably California and New York—regulate some of the internal affairs of foreign corporations that conduct a majority of their business in those States.

SANCTIONS A foreign corporation that transacts business without having first qualified may be subject to a number of penalties. Statutes in many States provide that an unlicensed foreign corporation doing business in a State shall not be entitled to maintain a suit in the State's courts until such corporation obtains a certificate of authority to transact business in that State. Failure to obtain such a certificate does not, however, impair the validity of a contract entered into by the corporation or prevent such corporation from defending any action or proceeding brought against it in the State. Section 15.02. In addition, most States impose fines upon an unqualified corporation, while a few States also impose fines upon the corporation's officers and directors as well as hold them personally liable on contracts made within the State.

33-2d PUBLICLY HELD OR CLOSELY HELD

A **publicly held corporation** is one whose shares are owned by a large number of people and are widely traded. There is no accepted minimum number of shareholders, but any corporation required to register under the Federal Securities and Exchange Act of 1934 is considered to be publicly held. In addition, corporations that have issued securities subject to a registered public distribution under the Federal Securities Act of 1933 usually are also considered publicly held. The Federal securities laws are discussed in Chapter 43. To distinguish publicly held corporations from other corporations, the Revised Act was amended to define the term *public corporation* as "a corporation that has shares listed on a national securities exchange or regularly traded in a market maintained by one or more members of a national securities association." Section 1.40(18A). This definition was deleted in the 2016 RMBCA.

A **corporation** is described as **closely held** or **close** when its outstanding shares of stock are held by a small number of persons who often are family, relatives, or friends. In most closely held corporations, the shareholders are active in the management and control of the business. Accordingly, they are concerned about the identities of their fellow shareholders, a concern that frequently leads shareholders to restrict the transfer of shares to prevent "outsiders" from obtaining stock in a closely held corporation. See the discussion of *Galler v. Galler* in Chapter 35. Although a vast majority of corporations in the United States are closely held, they account for only a small fraction of corporate revenues and assets.

In most States, closely held corporations are subject to the general incorporation statute that governs all corporations. The Revised Act includes a number of liberalizing provisions for closely held corporations. In addition, about twenty States have enacted special legislation to accommodate the needs of such corporations, and a Statutory Close Corporation Supplement to the Model and Revised Acts was promulgated. The Supplement applies only to those eligible corporations that elect statutory close corporation status. To be eligible, a corporation must have fewer than fifty shareholders. A corporation may voluntarily terminate statutory close corporation status. Other provisions of the Supplement are discussed in this and other chapters.

In 1991, the Revised Act was amended to authorize shareholders in closely held corporations to adopt unanimous shareholders' agreements that depart from the statutory norms by altering (1) the governance of the corporation, (2) the allocation of the economic return from the business, and (3) other aspects of the relationship among shareholders, directors, and the corporation. Section 7.32. Such a shareholder agreement is valid for ten years unless the agreement provides otherwise but terminates automatically if the corporation's shares become publicly traded. (The 2016 Revision eliminated the requirement that a shareholders' agreement automatically ceases to be effective when the corporation becomes a public corporation.) Shareholder agreements validated by Section 7.32 bind only the shareholders and the corporation; they do not bind the State, creditors, or other third parties. The provisions of Section 7.32 are discussed in this and other chapters.

Practical Advice

If you take a minority interest in a closely held corporation, attempt to provide adequate protection for your rights in the corporation's articles of incorporation and bylaws as well as in shareholder agreements.

33-2e SUBCHAPTER S CORPORATION

Subchapter S of the Internal Revenue Code permits a corporation meeting specified requirements to elect to be taxed essentially as though it were a partnership. More than 70 percent of all corporations in the United States are taxed as Chapter S corporations, although they account for only 40 percent of total corporate net income. Under subchapter S, a corporation's income is taxed only once at the individual shareholder level. The requirements for a corporation to elect

subchapter S treatment are (1) it must be a domestic corporation; (2) it must have no more than one hundred shareholders; (3) each shareholder must be an individual, or an estate, or certain types of trusts; (4) no shareholder may be a nonresident alien; and (5) it may have only one class of stock, although classes of common stock differing only in voting rights are permitted.

33-2f PROFESSIONAL CORPORATIONS

All of the States have professional association or corporation statutes that permit duly licensed individuals to practice their professions within the corporate form. Some statutes apply to all professions licensed to practice within the State, while others apply only to specified professions. There is a Model Professional Corporation Supplement to the MBCA.

FORMATION OF A CORPORATION

The formation of a corporation under a general incorporation statute requires the action of various groups, individuals, and State officials. The procedure to organize a corporation begins with the promotion of the proposed corporation by its organizers, also known as promoters, who procure offers by interested persons, known as subscribers, to buy stock in the corporation, once created, and who prepare the necessary incorporation papers. The incorporators then execute the articles of incorporation and file them with the Secretary of State, who issues the certificate of incorporation. Finally, an organizational meeting is held.

33-3 Organizing the Corporation

33-3a PROMOTERS

A **promoter** is a person who brings about the "birth" of a corporation by arranging for capital and financing; assembling the necessary assets, equipment, licenses, personnel, leases, and services; and attending to the actual legal formation of the corporation. Upon incorporation, the promoter's organizational task is finished.

PROMOTERS' CONTRACTS In addition to procuring subscriptions and preparing the incorporation papers, promoters often enter into contracts in anticipation of the creation of the corporation. The contracts may be ordinary agreements necessary for the eventual operation of the business, such as leases, purchase orders, employment contracts, sales contracts, or franchises. If the promoter executes these contracts in her own name and there is no further action, the promoter is liable on such contracts;

FIGURE 33-1 Promoter's Preincorporation Contracts Made in the Corporation's Name

Corporation Does NOT Adopt Preincorporation Contract

Corporation Does Adopt Preincorporation Contract

Corporation, Promoter, and Third Party Enter into a Novation or Preincorporation Contract Provides That Adoption Will Terminate Promoter's Liability

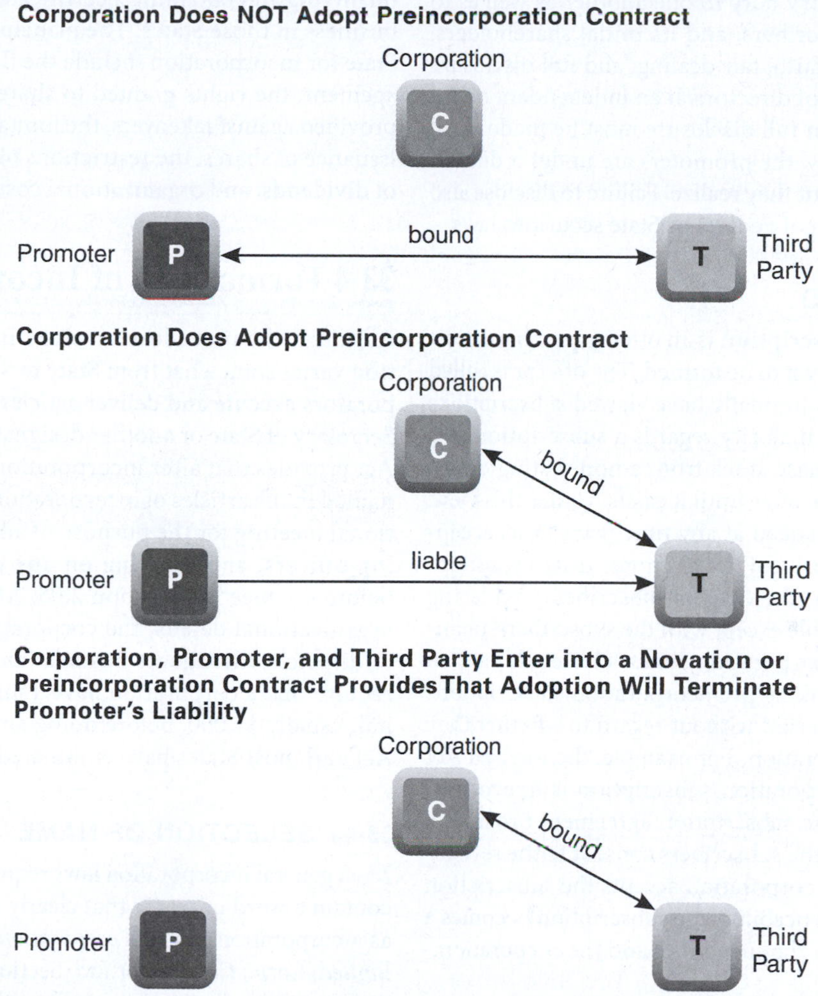

the corporation, when created, is not liable. Moreover, a preincorporation contract made by a promoter in the name of the corporation and on its behalf does not bind the corporation. The promoter, in executing such contracts, may do so in the corporate name even if incorporation has yet to occur. Before its formation, a corporation has no capacity to enter into contracts or to employ agents or representatives. After its formation, it is not liable at common law upon any prior contract, even one made in its name, unless it adopts the contract expressly, impliedly, or by knowingly accepting benefits under it.

A promoter who enters into a preincorporation contract in the name of the corporation usually remains liable on that contract even if the corporation adopts it. This liability results from the rule of agency law stating that to be able to ratify a contract, a principal must be in existence at the time the contract is made. A promoter will be relieved of liability, however, if the contract provides that adoption shall terminate the promoter's liability or if the promoter, the third party, and the corporation enter into a novation substituting the corporation for the promoter.

♦ SEE FIGURE 33-1: *Promoter's Preincorporation Contracts Made in the Corporation's Name*

♦ *See Case 33-2*

Practical Advice

As a promoter, obtain the agreement of the third party that the corporation's adoption of a preincorporation contract will terminate your liability; as a third party, carefully consider whether you should agree to such a provision.

PROMOTERS' FIDUCIARY DUTY The promoters of a corporation owe a fiduciary duty to one another as well as to the corporation, its subscribers, and its initial shareholders. This duty requires good faith, fair dealing, and full disclosure to an independent board of directors. If an independent board has not been elected, then full disclosure must be made to all shareholders. Accordingly, the promoters are under a duty to account for any *secret* profit they realize. Failure to disclose also may constitute a violation of Federal or State securities laws.

33-3b SUBSCRIBERS

A **preincorporation subscription** is an offer to purchase capital stock in a corporation yet to be formed. The offeror is called a "subscriber." Courts traditionally have viewed subscriptions in one of two ways. The majority regards a subscription as a continuing offer to purchase stock from a nonexistent entity, incapable of accepting the offer until it exists. Under this view, a subscription may be revoked at any time prior to its acceptance. In contrast, a minority of jurisdictions treats a subscription as a contract among the various subscribers, rendering the subscription irrevocable except with the subscribers' unanimous consent. Most incorporation statutes have adopted an intermediate position making preincorporation subscriptions irrevocable for a stated period without regard to whether they are supported by consideration. For example, the Revised Act provides that a preincorporation subscription is irrevocable for six months, unless the subscription agreement provides a different period or all of the subscribers consent to the revocation. Section 6.20. If the corporation accepts the subscription during the period of irrevocability, the subscription becomes a contract binding on both the subscriber and the corporation.

Practical Advice

As a preincorporation subscriber, consider how long you are willing to have your subscription be irrevocable.

A **postincorporation subscription** is a subscription agreement entered into after incorporation. It is treated as a contract between the subscriber and the corporation. RMBCA Section 6.20(e). Unlike preincorporation subscriptions, the subscriber may withdraw her offer to enter into a postincorporation subscription at any time before the corporation accepts it. She cannot, however, withdraw the offer after the corporation has accepted it as the acceptance forms a contract.

33-3c SELECTION OF STATE FOR INCORPORATION

A corporation is usually incorporated in the State in which it intends to be located and to transact all or the principal part of its business. Nevertheless, a corporation may be formed in one State and have its principal place of business and conduct all or most of its operations in another State or States by duly qualifying and obtaining a certificate of authority to transact business in those States. The principal criteria in selecting a State for incorporation include the flexibility accorded management, the rights granted to shareholders, the protection provided against takeovers, the limitations imposed upon the issuance of shares, the restrictions placed upon the payment of dividends, and organizational costs such as fees and taxes.

33-4 Formalities of Incorporation

Although the procedure involved in organizing a corporation varies somewhat from State to State, typically the incorporators execute and deliver articles of incorporation to the Secretary of State or another designated official. The Revised Act provides that after incorporation, the board of directors named in the articles of incorporation shall hold an organizational meeting for the purpose of adopting bylaws, appointing officers, and carrying on any other business brought before the meeting. Section 2.05. After completion of these organizational details, the corporation's officers and board of directors manage its business and affairs. Several States require that a corporation have a minimum amount of capital, usually $1,000, before doing any business. The Revised Act and most States have eliminated this requirement.

33-4a SELECTION OF NAME

Most general incorporation laws require that a corporate name contain a word or words that clearly identify the organization as a corporation, such as *corporation, company, incorporated, limited, Corp., Co., Inc., or Ltd.* Section 4.01. Furthermore, the name must be distinguishable from the name of any domestic corporation or any foreign corporation authorized to do business within the State. Section 4.01.

33-4b INCORPORATORS

The **incorporators** are the persons who sign the articles of incorporation, which are filed with the Secretary of State of the State of incorporation. Although they perform a necessary function, in many States, their services as incorporators are perfunctory and short-lived, ending with the organizational meeting. Furthermore, modern statutes have greatly relaxed the qualifications of incorporators and also have reduced the number required. The Revised Act and all States provide that only one person need act as the incorporator or incorporators, though more may do so. Section 2.01. The Revised Act and most States permit artificial entities to serve as incorporators. For example, the Revised Act defines a person to include individuals and entities, with an entity defined to include domestic and foreign corporations, not-for-profit corporations, profit

FIGURE 33-2 Comparison of Articles of Incorporation and Bylaws

	Articles of Incorporation	Bylaws
Filing	Publicly	Not publicly
Amendment	Requires board and shareholder approval	Requires only board approval
Availability	Must include certain mandatory provisions; may include optional provisions although some optional provisions may be elected only in the articles of incorporation	Must include certain provisions unless they are included in the articles of incorporation
Validity	May include any provision not inconsistent with law	May include any provision not inconsistent with law and the articles of incorporation

and not-for-profit unincorporated associations, business trusts, estates, partnerships, and trusts. Section 1.40.

33-4c ARTICLES OF INCORPORATION

The articles of incorporation, also called the **charter**, is generally a rather simple document that under the Revised Act must include the name of the corporation, the number of authorized shares, the street address of the registered office and the name of the registered agent, and the name and address of each incorporator. Section 2.02(a). The Act also permits the articles of incorporation to include optional information such as the identities of the corporation's initial directors, corporate purposes, procedures for managing internal affairs, powers of the corporation, the par value of shares, and any provision required or permitted to be set forth in the bylaws. Some optional provisions may be elected *only* in the articles of incorporation, including cumulative voting, supermajority voting requirements, preemptive rights, and limitations on the personal liability of directors for breach of their duty of care.

To form a corporation, the articles of incorporation, once it is drawn up, must be executed and filed with the Secretary of State. The articles of incorporation then become the basic governing document of the corporation, so long as its provisions are consistent with State and Federal law.

33-4d ORGANIZATIONAL MEETING

The Revised Act and most States require that an organizational meeting be held to adopt the new corporation's bylaws, appoint officers, and carry on any other business brought before it. If the articles of incorporation do not name the corporation's initial directors, the incorporators hold the organizational meeting to elect directors, after which either the incorporators or the directors complete the organization of the corporation. Section 2.05. Additional business that may be brought before the meeting typically includes authorization to issue shares of stock, approval of preincorporation contracts made

by promoters, selection of a bank, and approval of a corporate seal and the form of stock certificates.

33-4e BYLAWS

The **bylaws** of a corporation are the rules and regulations that govern its internal management. Because bylaws are necessary to the organization of the corporation, their adoption is one of the first items of business at the organizational meeting held promptly after incorporation. Under the Revised Act, either the incorporators or the board of directors may adopt the bylaws. Section 2.06.

The bylaws may contain any provision that is not inconsistent with law or the articles of incorporation. Section 2.06. In contrast to the articles of incorporation, the bylaws do not have to be publicly filed. Under the Revised Act, the shareholders may amend or repeal the bylaws, as may the board of directors, unless (1) the articles of incorporation or other sections of the RMBCA reserve that power exclusively to the shareholders in whole or in part or (2) the shareholders in amending, repealing, or adopting a bylaw expressly provide that the board of directors may not amend, repeal, or reinstate that bylaw. Section 10.20.

The Statutory Close Corporation Supplement (Section 22) permits close corporations to avoid the adoption of bylaws by including either in a shareholder agreement or in the articles of incorporation all information required to be included in corporate bylaws.

♦ **SEE FIGURE 33-2:** *Comparison of Articles of Incorporation and Bylaws*

Practical Advice

When you have the choice of placing a provision in either the articles of incorporation or the bylaws, carefully consider the advantages and disadvantages of each. You may prefer the articles of incorporation for provisions that protect your interests because articles of incorporation provisions prevail over bylaws provisions and are more difficult to amend.

**RECOGNITION OR DISREGARD
OF CORPORATENESS**

Business associates choose to incorporate to obtain one or more corporate attributes—primarily limited liability and perpetual existence. Because a corporation is a creature of the State, such attributes are recognized when the enterprise complies with the State's requirements for incorporation. Although the formal procedures are relatively simple, errors or omissions sometimes occur. In some cases, the mistakes may be trivial, such as incorrectly stating an incorporator's address; in other instances, the error may be more significant, such as a complete failure to file the articles of incorporation. The consequences of procedural noncompliance depend upon the seriousness of the error. Conversely, even when a corporation has been formed in strict compliance with the incorporation statute, a court may disregard the corporateness of the enterprise if justice requires. This section addresses these two complementary issues.

33-5 Defective Incorporation

Although modern incorporation statutes have greatly simplified incorporation procedures, defective incorporations do occur. The possible consequences of a defective incorporation include the following: (1) the State brings an action against the association for involuntary dissolution, (2) the associates are held personally liable to a third party, (3) the association asserts that it is not liable on an obligation, or (4) a third party asserts that it is not liable to the association. Corporate statutes addressing this issue have taken an approach considerably different from that of the common law.

33-5a COMMON LAW APPROACH

Under the common law, a defectively formed corporation was, under certain circumstances, accorded corporate attributes. The courts developed a set of doctrines granting corporateness to *de jure* (of right) corporations, *de facto* (of fact) corporations, and corporations by estoppel but denying corporateness to corporations that were too defectively formed.

CORPORATION *DE JURE* A corporation *de jure* is one that has been formed in substantial compliance with the incorporation statute and the required organizational procedure. Once such a corporation is formed, its existence may not be challenged by anyone, even by the State in a direct proceeding for this purpose.

CORPORATION *DE FACTO* Though it fails to comply substantially with the incorporation statute (and therefore is not *de jure*), a corporation *de facto* nevertheless is recognized for most purposes as a corporation. A failure to form a *de jure*

corporation may result in the formation of a *de facto* corporation if the following requirements are met: (1) the existence of a general corporation statute, (2) a *bona fide* attempt to comply with that law in organizing a corporation under the statute, and (3) the actual exercise of corporate power by conducting business in the belief that a corporation has been formed. If the corporation sues to collect a debt, the fact that the corporation is not *de jure* is not a defense. Furthermore, the existence of the *de facto* corporation can be challenged only by the State, though not even the State can question its existence collaterally (in a proceeding involving some other issue). The State must bring an independent suit against the corporation for this express purpose, known as an action of *quo warranto* ("by what right").

CORPORATION BY ESTOPPEL The doctrine of corporation by estoppel is distinct from that of corporation *de facto*. Estoppel does not create a corporation. It operates only to prevent a person or persons under the facts and circumstances of a particular case from questioning a corporation's existence or its capacity to act or to own property. Corporation by estoppel requires a holding out by a purported corporation or its associates and reliance by a third party. In addition, application of the doctrine depends on equitable considerations. A person who has dealt with a defectively organized corporation may be precluded or estopped from denying its corporate existence where the necessary elements of holding out and reliance are present. The doctrine can be applied not only to third parties but also to the purported corporation and to the associates who held themselves out as a corporation.

DEFECTIVE CORPORATION If the associates who purported to form a corporation so fail to comply with the requirements of the incorporation statute that neither a *de jure* nor a *de facto* corporation is formed and the circumstances do not justify applying the corporation by estoppel doctrine, the courts generally deny the associates the benefits of incorporation. This results in some or all of the associates being held unlimitedly liable for the obligations of the business.

33-5b STATUTORY APPROACH

While the common law approach to defective incorporation is cumbersome both in theory and in application, incorporation statutes now address the issue more simply. All States provide that corporate existence begins either upon the filing of the articles of incorporation or their acceptance by the Secretary of State. Moreover, the Revised Act and most States provide that the *filing* or acceptance of the articles of incorporation by the Secretary of State is conclusive proof that the incorporators have satisfied all conditions precedent to incorporation, except in a proceeding brought by the State. Section 2.03(b). This applies even if the articles of incorporation contain mistakes or omissions.

With respect to the attribute of limited liability, the original Model Act and a few States provide that "[a]ll persons who assume to act as a corporation without authority so to do shall be jointly and severally liable for all debts and liabilities incurred or arising as a result thereof." Section 146. The Revised Act, however, imposes liability *only* on persons who purport to act as or on behalf of a corporation, knowing that there was no incorporation. Section 2.04.

Consider the following two illustrations: First, Smith had been shown executed articles of incorporation some months before he invested in the corporation and became an officer and director. He was also told by the corporation's attorney that the articles had been filed; however, because of confusion in the attorney's office, the filing had not in fact occurred. Under the Revised Act and many court decisions, Smith would not be held personally liable for the obligations of the defective corporation. Second, Jones represents that a corporation exists and enters into a contract in the corporate name when she knows that no corporation has been formed because no attempt has been made to file articles of incorporation. Jones would be held liable for the obligations of the defective corporation under the Model Act, the Revised Act, and most court decisions involving similar situations. RMBCA Section 2.04 and Comment.

The 2016 RMBCA provides a statutory ratification procedure for corporate actions that may not have been properly authorized and shares that may have been improperly issued. It also provides for retroactive validity of subsequent actions taken in reliance on the validity of the defective action that is ratified. Corporate actions include any action taken by or on behalf of the corporation by the incorporator, the board of directors, a committee of the board of directors, an officer or agent of the corporation, or the shareholders.

♦ *See Case 33-3*

Practical Advice

To obtain limited liability as a shareholder in a corporation, make sure that the corporation has been properly organized before becoming a shareholder.

33-6 Piercing the Corporate Veil

If substantial compliance with the incorporation statute results in a *de jure* or *de facto* corporation, the courts generally will recognize corporateness and its attendant attributes, including limited liability. Nonetheless, the courts will disregard the corporate entity when it is used to defeat public convenience, commit a wrongdoing, protect fraud, or circumvent the law. Going behind the corporate entity to confront those seeking to insulate themselves from personal accountability and the consequences of their wrongdoing is known as piercing the corporate veil. Courts will pierce the corporate veil where they deem such action necessary to remedy wrongdoing. However, there is no commonly accepted test used by the courts. They have done so most frequently in regard to closely held corporations and parent-subsidiary relationships. It should be noted that piercing the corporate veil is the exception, and in most cases, courts uphold the separateness of corporations.

33-6a CLOSELY HELD CORPORATIONS

The joint and active management by all the shareholders of closely held corporations frequently results in a tendency to forgo corporate formalities, such as holding meetings of the board and shareholders, while the small size of close corporations often renders creditors unable to fully satisfy their claims against the corporation. Such frustrated creditors often ask the court to disregard an organization's "corporateness" and to impose personal liability for the corporate obligations upon the shareholders. Courts have responded by piercing the corporate veil in cases in which the shareholders (1) have not conducted the business on a corporate basis, (2) have not provided an adequate financial basis for the business, or (3) have used the corporation to defraud. For example, *in D.I Felsenthal Co. v. Northern Assurance Co.* 284 Ill. 343,120 N.E. 268 (1918), Felsenthal Company sued the Northern Assurance Company to collect on its fire insurance policy. Northern claimed that it was not liable under the policy because Felsenthal's property had been destroyed by a fire instigated by Fox, the president, director, creditor, and principal shareholder of Felsenthal. The court ruled in favor of Northern Assurance because the instigator of the fire, Fox, was the beneficial owner of almost all of Felsenthal's stock as well as the corporation's president and director. Under those circumstances, the corporation could not recover because to allow such a recovery would allow a wrongdoer to benefit from his own illegal act. The corporate form could not be used in this case to protect Fox and to aid him in his plan to defraud the insurance company.

Conducting the business on a corporate basis involves separately maintaining the corporation's funds and the shareholders' funds, maintaining separate financial records, holding regular directors' meetings, and generally observing corporate formalities. Adequate capitalization requires that the shareholders invest capital or purchase liability insurance sufficient to meet the reasonably anticipated requirements of the enterprise.

Practical Advice

If you form a closely held corporation, be sure to adhere to the required corporate formalities and adequately capitalize the corporation.

The Revised Act validates unanimous shareholder agreements by which the shareholders may relax traditional corporate formalities. Section 7.32. The Revised Act further provides that the existence or performance of an agreement authorized by Section 7.32

> shall not be grounds for imposing personal liability on any shareholder for the acts or the debts of the corporation even if the agreement or its performance treats the corporation as if it were a partnership or results in failure to observe the corporate formalities otherwise applicable to the matters governed by the agreement.

Thus, this section narrows the grounds for imposing personal liability on shareholders for the liabilities of a corporation for acts or omissions authorized by a shareholder agreement validated by Section 7.32.

The Statutory Close Corporation Supplement validates several arrangements whereby the shareholders may relax traditional corporate formalities. Section 25 of the Supplement provides: "The failure of a statutory close corporation to observe the usual corporate formalities or requirements relating to the exercise of its corporate powers or management of its business and affairs is not a ground for imposing personal liability on the shareholders for liabilities of the corporation." Courts may still pierce the corporate veil of a statutory close corporation if the same circumstances would justify imposing personal liability on the shareholders of a general business corporation. The Supplement simply prevents a court from piercing the corporate veil just because the corporation is a statutory close corporation.

33-6b PARENT-SUBSIDIARY CORPORATIONS

A corporation wishing to risk only a portion of its assets in a particular enterprise may choose to form a **subsidiary corporation**. A subsidiary corporation is one in which another corporation, the **parent corporation**, owns at least a majority of the shares and over which the other corporation therefore has control. Courts may pierce the corporate veil and hold the parent liable for the debts of its subsidiary if any of the following criteria are met:

1. both corporations are not adequately capitalized, *or*
2. the formalities of separate corporate procedures are not observed, *or*
3. each corporation is not held out to the public as a separate enterprise, *or*
4. the funds of the two corporations are commingled, *or*
5. the parent corporation completely dominates the subsidiary solely to advance its own interests.

So long as a parent and a subsidiary avoid these pitfalls, the courts generally will recognize the subsidiary as a separate entity, even if the parent owns all the subsidiary's stock and the two corporations share facilities, employees, directors, and officers.

◆ *See Case 33-4*

CORPORATE POWERS

Because a corporation derives its existence and all of it powers from its State of incorporation, it possesses only those powers that the State confers on it. These powers consist of those expressly set forth in the statute unless limited by the articles of incorporation.

33-7 Sources of Corporate Powers

33-7a STATUTORY POWERS

Typical of the general corporate powers granted by incorporation statutes are those provided by Section 3.02 of the Revised Act, which include the following:

1. to have perpetual succession;
2. to sue and be sued in the corporate name;
3. to have a corporate seal;
4. to make and amend bylaws for managing the business and regulating the affairs of the corporation;
5. to acquire, own, improve, use, and dispose of real or personal property;
6. to own, vote, and dispose of shares or other interests in, or obligations of, any other entity;
7. to make contracts and guarantees; incur liabilities; borrow money; issue notes, bonds, and other obligations; and secure any corporate obligations;
8. to lend money, invest and reinvest funds, and receive and hold real and personal property as security for repayment;
9. to be a promoter, partner, member, associate, or manager of any partnership, joint venture, trust, or other entity;
10. to conduct business, locate offices, and exercise the powers granted by the Act within or without the State of incorporation;
11. to elect directors and appoint officers, employees, and agents; define their duties; fix their compensation; and lend them money and credit;
12. to pay pensions and establish pension plans, pension trusts, profit-sharing plans, share bonus plans, share option

plans, and benefit or incentive plans for any or all current or former directors, officers, employees, and agents;

13. to make donations for the public welfare or for charitable, scientific, or educational purposes;

14. to transact any lawful business that will aid government policy; and

15. to make payments or donations or do any other act, not inconsistent with law, that furthers the business and affairs of the corporation.

In most States, this list is not exclusive. Moreover, the Revised Act also grants to all corporations the same powers as individuals have to do all things necessary or convenient to carry out their business and affairs. Section 3.02.

33-7b PURPOSES

All State incorporation statutes provide that a corporation may be formed for any lawful purposes. The Revised Act permits a corporation's articles of incorporation to state a more limited purpose. Many State statutes, but not the RMBCA, require that the articles of incorporation specify the corporation's purposes although they usually permit a general statement that the corporation is formed to engage in any lawful purpose.

33-8 *Ultra Vires* Acts

Because a corporation has authority to act only within its powers, any action or contract that is not within the scope and type of acts which the corporation is legally empowered to perform is *ultra vires*. The doctrine of *ultra vires* is less significant today because modern statutes permit incorporation for any lawful purpose, and most articles of incorporation do not limit corporate powers. Consequently, far fewer acts are *ultra vires*.

33-8a EFFECT OF *ULTRA VIRES* ACTS

Traditionally, *ultra vires* contracts were unenforceable as null and void. Under the modern approach, courts allow the *ultra vires* defense in cases in which the contract is wholly executory on both sides. A corporation having received full performance from the other party to the contract is not permitted to escape liability by a plea of *ultra vires*. Conversely, the defense of *ultra vires* is unavailable to a corporation suing for breach of a contract that has been fully performed on its side.

Almost all statutes have abolished the defense of *ultra vires* in an action by or against a corporation. The Revised Act provides that "the validity of corporate action may not be challenged on the ground that the corporation lacks or lacked the power to act." Section 3.04. This section extends beyond contract actions to encompass any corporate action, including conveyances of property. Thus, under this section, persons dealing with a corporation need not examine its articles of incorporation for limitations upon its purposes or powers. The section does not, however, validate illegal corporate actions.

33-8b REMEDIES FOR *ULTRA VIRES* ACTS

Although *ultra vires* under modern statutes may no longer be used as a shield against liability, corporate activities that are *ultra vires* may be redressed in any of three ways, as provided by Section 3.04(b) of the Revised Act:

1. in a proceeding by a shareholder against the corporation to enjoin the unauthorized act, if such an injunction is equitable and if all affected persons are parties to the proceeding, and the court may award damages for losses suffered by the corporation or another party because of enjoining the unauthorized act;

2. in a proceeding by the corporation, or a shareholder derivatively (in a representative capacity), against the incumbent or former directors or officers for exceeding their authority; or

3. in a proceeding by the Attorney General of the State of incorporation to dissolve the corporation or to enjoin it from transacting unauthorized business.

33-9 Liability for Torts and Crimes

A corporation is liable for the torts its agents commit in the course of their employment. The doctrine of *ultra vires*, even in those jurisdictions where it is permitted as a defense, does not apply to wrongdoing by the corporation. The doctrine of *respondeat superior* imposes full liability upon a corporation for the torts its agents and employees commit during the course of their employment. For example, Robert, a truck driver employed by the Webster Corporation, negligently runs over Pamela, a pedestrian, while on a business errand. Both Robert and the Webster Corporation are liable to Pamela in her action to recover damages for the injuries she sustained. A corporation also may be found liable for fraud, false imprisonment, malicious prosecution, libel, and other torts, though some States hold the corporation liable for *punitive* damages only if it authorized or ratified the agent's act.

Historically, corporations were not held criminally liable because, under the traditional view, a corporation could not possess the criminal intent requisite to committing a crime. Dramatic growth in the size and importance of corporations has changed this view. Under the modern approach, a corporation may be liable for violating statutes that impose liability without fault. In addition, a corporation may be liable for an offense perpetrated by a high corporate officer or by its board of directors. Punishment of a corporation for crimes is necessarily by fine, not imprisonment.

CHAPTER SUMMARY

NATURE OF CORPORATIONS

CORPORATE ATTRIBUTES

Legal Entity a corporation is an entity apart from its shareholders, with entirely distinct rights and liabilities

Creature of the State a corporation may be formed only by substantial compliance with a State incorporation statute

Limited Liability a shareholder's liability is limited to the amount invested in the business enterprise

Free Transferability of Corporate Shares unless otherwise specified in the articles of incorporation

Perpetual Existence unless the articles of incorporation provide otherwise

Centralized Management shareholders of a corporation elect the board of directors to manage its business affairs; the board appoints officers to run the day-to-day operations of the business

As a Person a corporation is considered a person for some but not all purposes

As a Citizen a corporation is considered a citizen for some but not all purposes

CLASSIFICATION OF CORPORATIONS

Public or Private
- *Public Corporation* one created to administer a unit of local civil government or one created by the United States to conduct public business
- *Private Corporation* one founded by and composed of private persons for private purposes; has no government duties

Profit or Nonprofit
- *Profit Corporation* one founded to operate a business for profit
- *Nonprofit Corporation* one whose profits must be used exclusively for charitable, educational, or scientific purposes

Domestic or Foreign
- *Domestic Corporation* one created under the laws of a given State
- *Foreign Corporation* one created under the laws of any other State or jurisdiction; it must obtain a certificate of authority from each State in which it does intrastate business

Publicly Held or Closely Held
- *Publicly Held Corporation* one whose shares are owned by a large number of people and are widely traded
- *Closely Held Corporation* one that is owned by few shareholders and whose shares are not actively traded

Subchapter S Corporation eligible corporation electing to be taxed as a partnership under the Internal Revenue Code

Professional Corporations corporate form under which duly licensed individuals may practice their professions

FORMATION OF A CORPORATION

ORGANIZING THE CORPORATION

Promoter person who takes the preliminary steps to organize a corporation
- *Promoters' Contracts* promoters remain liable on preincorporation contracts made in the name of the corporation unless the contract provides otherwise or unless a novation is effected
- *Promoters' Fiduciary Duty* promoters owe a fiduciary duty among themselves and to the corporation, its subscribers, and its initial shareholders

Subscribers persons who agree to purchase the initial stock in a corporation
- *Preincorporation Subscription* an offer to purchase capital stock in a corporation yet to be formed which under many incorporation statutes is irrevocable for a specified time period
- *Postincorporation Subscription* a subscription agreement entered into after incorporation; an offer to enter into such a subscription is revocable at any time before the corporation accepts it

FORMALITIES OF INCORPORATION	**Selection of Name** the name must clearly designate the entity as a corporation **Incorporators** the persons who sign the articles of incorporation **Articles of Incorporation** the charter or basic organizational document of a corporation **Organizational Meeting** the first meeting, held to adopt the bylaws and appoint officers **Bylaws** rules governing a corporation's internal management

RECOGNITION OR DISREGARD OF CORPORATENESS

DEFECTIVE INCORPORATION	**Common Law Approach** • *Corporation de Jure* one formed in substantial compliance with the incorporation statute and having all corporate attributes • *Corporation de Facto* one not formed in compliance with the statute but recognized for most purposes as a corporation • *Corporation by Estoppel* prevents a person from raising the question of a corporation's existence • *Defective Corporation* the associates are denied the benefits of incorporation **Statutory Approach** the filing or acceptance of the articles of incorporation is generally conclusive proof of proper incorporation • *Revised Model Business Corporation Act (RMBCA)* liability is imposed only on persons who act on behalf of a defectively formed corporation knowing that there was no incorporation • *Model Business Corporation Act (MBCA)* unlimited personal liability is imposed on all persons who act on behalf of a defectively formed corporation
PIERCING THE CORPORATE VEIL	**General Rule** the courts may disregard the corporate entity when it is used to defeat public convenience, commit a wrongdoing, protect fraud, or circumvent the law **Application** most frequently applied to • *Closely Held Corporations* • *Parent-Subsidiary Corporations*

CORPORATE POWERS

SOURCES OF CORPORATE POWERS	**Statutory Powers** typically include perpetual existence, right to hold property in the corporate name, and all powers necessary or convenient to effect the corporation's purposes **Purposes** a corporation may be formed for any lawful purposes unless its articles of incorporation state a more limited purpose
ULTRA VIRES ACTS	**Definition of *Ultra Vires* Acts** any action or contract that goes beyond a corporation's express and implied powers **Effect of *Ultra Vires* Acts** under RMBCA, *ultra vires* acts and conveyances are not invalid **Remedies for *Ultra Vires* Acts** the RMBCA provides three possible remedies
LIABILITY FOR TORTS AND CRIMES	**Torts** under the doctrine of *respondeat superior*, a corporation is liable for torts committed by its employees within the course of their employment **Crimes** a corporation may be criminally liable for violations of statutes imposing liability without fault or for an offense perpetrated by a high corporate officer or its board of directors

CASE

33-1

Foreign Corporation
DRAKE MFG. CO., INC. v. POLYFLOW, INC.
Superior Court of Pennsylvania, 2015
109 A.3d 250, 2015 PA Super 16

Jenkins, J.

In late 2007, Drake, a Delaware corporation, entered an agreement to sell "couplings" to Polyflow, which the agreement defined as "products designed by Polyflex for use as termination fittings in Polyflex's Thermoflex Tubing." The agreement provided that Drake would ship the couplings from Drake's plant in Sheffield, Pennsylvania to Polyflow. The record includes approximately 75 bills from Drake to Polyflow for couplings between August 2008 and April 2009. These bills indicate that Drake shipped most of the couplings from its plant in Sheffield, Pennsylvania to Polyflow's business establishment in Oaks, Pennsylvania. Other bills during the same time period indicate that Drake shipped equipment known as "portable swaging machines" to Polyflow. * * *

On June 10, 2009, Drake filed a civil complaint for breach of contract alleging Polyflow's failure to pay Drake * * *.

* * *

* * * Polyflow did not dispute its failure to pay Drake or contend that Drake failed to perform its duties under the 2007 agreement. Polyflow's only defense was that Drake lacked capacity to sue Polyflow due to Drake's failure to obtain a certificate of authority from the Department of State authorizing Drake to do business in Pennsylvania as a foreign corporation. Drake did not possess a certificate of authority at the time of trial. Indeed, Drake did not even apply for a certificate of authority until the day of trial.

At the close of Drake's case, Polyflow moved for a compulsory nonsuit due to Drake's lack of capacity to sue, i.e., its failure to submit a certificate of authority from the Department of State into evidence. The court denied Polyflow's motion for nonsuit. Polyflow did not present any further evidence, and the court announced its verdict in favor of Drake in the amount of $291,766.61.

On March 5, 2014, Polyflow filed timely post-trial motions seeking judgment * * * due to Drake's failure to submit a certificate of authority into evidence. On March 17, 2014, the Department of State issued Drake a certificate of authority to do business in Pennsylvania as a foreign corporation. On April 17, 2014, almost two months after the verdict, Drake submitted its certificate of authority as an exhibit to its response to Polyflow's post-trial motions. On May 23, 2014, relying on the delinquent certificate of authority, the trial court denied

Polyflow's post-trial motions. Polyflow thereupon * * * filed a timely notice of appeal.

* * *

We turn to whether Polyflow was entitled to judgment * * * due to Drake's failure to submit a certificate of authority. * * *

* * *

Section 4121 [of the Corporations and Unincorporated Associations Code ("Code")] provides: "A foreign business corporation, before doing business in this Commonwealth, shall procure a certificate of authority to do so from the Department of State,* * *" [Citation.]

While the Code does not expressly define "doing business", section 4122(a) identifies activities which do *not* constitute "doing business", either individually or collectively. * * *

* * *

* * * The Committee Comment to section 4122 explains:

> [Section 4122] does not attempt to formulate an inclusive definition of what constitutes the transaction of business. Rather, the concept is defined in a negative fashion by subsection (a), which states that certain activities do not constitute the transaction of business. In general terms, *any conduct more regular, systematic, or extensive than that described in subsection (a) constitutes the transaction of business and requires the corporation to obtain a certificate of authority*. Typical conduct requiring a certificate of authority includes *maintaining an office to conduct local intrastate business, selling personal property not in interstate commerce*, entering into contracts relating to local business or sales, and owning or using real estate for general corporate purposes.

* * *

A corporation is not "doing business" *solely because* it resorts to the courts of this Commonwealth to recover an indebtedness, enforce an obligation, recover possession of personal property, obtain the appointment of a receiver, intervene in a pending proceeding, bring a petition to compel arbitration, file an appeal bond, or pursue appellate remedies.

* * *

The concept of "doing business" involves regular, repeated, and continuing business contacts of a local nature. A single agreement or isolated transaction does not constitute the doing of business if there is no intention to repeat the transaction or engage in similar transactions. * * *

[Citation,] (emphasis added).

Lastly, section 4141(a) provides in relevant part that "[a] nonqualified foreign business corporation doing business in this Commonwealth * * * shall not be permitted to maintain any action or proceeding in any court of this Commonwealth until the corporation has obtained a certificate of authority." [Citation.] A foreign corporation may comply with this requirement by obtaining a certificate of authority "during the course of a lawsuit." [Citation.]

* * *

* * * [T]he evidence demonstrates that Drake failed to submit a certificate of authority into evidence prior to the verdict in violation of * * * §4121(a). Therefore, the trial court should not have permitted Drake to prosecute its action. [Citation.]

The trial court contends that Drake is exempt from the certificate of authority requirement because it merely commenced suit in Pennsylvania to collect a debt, conduct that does not constitute "doing business" under section 4122(a) * * *. Drake did much more, however, than file suit or attempt to collect a debt. Drake maintains an office in Pennsylvania to conduct local business, conduct which "[typically] require[s] a certificate of authority." [Citation.] Drake also entered into a contract with Polyflow, and, on dozens of occasions over an eight month period, shipped couplings and portable swaging machines to Polyflow's place of business in Pennsylvania—far more than the "isolated transaction" exempted under section 4122(a)(10) * * *. [Citation.] In short, Drake's conduct was "more regular, systematic, [and] extensive than that described in section 4122(a), [thus] constitute[ing] the transaction of business and requir[ing] [Drake] to obtain a certificate of authority." [Citation.]

* * *

The trial court thus erred by denying Polyflow's [posttrial] motion for judgment * * *.

CASE 33-2

Promoters' Contracts
COOPERS & LYBRAND v. FOX
Colorado Court of Appeals, Div. IV, 1988
758 P.2d 683

Kelly, C. J.

In an action based on breach of express and implied contracts, the plaintiff, Coopers & Lybrand (Coopers), appeals the judgment of the trial court in favor of the defendant, Garry J. Fox (Fox). Coopers contends that the trial court erred in ruling that Fox, a corporate promoter, could not be held liable on a pre-incorporation contract in the absence of an agreement that he would be so liable, and that Coopers had, and failed to sustain, the burden of proving any such agreement. We reverse.

On November 3, 1981, Fox met with a representative of Coopers, a national accounting firm, to request a tax opinion and other accounting services. Fox informed Coopers at this meeting that he was acting on behalf of a corporation he was in the process of forming, G. Fox and Partners, Inc. Coopers accepted the "engagement" with the knowledge that the corporation was not yet in existence.

G. Fox and Partners, Inc., was incorporated on December 4, 1981. Coopers completed its work by mid-December and billed "Mr. Garry R. (sic) Fox, Fox and Partners, Inc." in the amount of $10,827. When neither Fox nor G. Fox and Partners, Inc., paid the bill, Coopers sued Garry Fox, individually, for breach of express and implied contracts based on a theory of promoter liability.

Fox argued at trial that, although Coopers knew the corporation was not in existence when he engaged the firm's services, it either expressly or impliedly agreed to look solely to the corporation for payment. Coopers argued that its client was Garry Fox, not the corporation. The parties stipulated that Coopers had done the work, and Coopers presented uncontroverted testimony that the fee was fair and reasonable.

The trial court failed to make written findings of fact and conclusions of law. However, in its bench findings at the end of trial, the court found that there was no agreement, either express or implied, that would obligate Fox, individually, to pay Coopers' fee, in effect, because Coopers had failed to prove the existence of any such agreement. The court entered judgment in favor of Fox.

As a preliminary matter, we reject Fox's argument that he was acting only as an agent for the future corporation. One cannot act as the agent of a nonexistent principal. [Citation.]

On the contrary, the uncontroverted facts place Fox squarely within the definition of a promoter. A promoter is one who, alone or with others, undertakes to form a corporation and to procure for it the rights, instrumentalities, and capital to enable it to conduct business. [Citations.]

When Fox first approached Coopers, he was in the process of forming G. Fox and Partners, Inc. He engaged Coopers' services for the future corporation's benefit. In addition, though not dispositive on the issue of his status as a promoter, Fox became the president, a director, and the principal shareholder of the corporation, which he funded, only nominally, with a $100 contribution. Under these circumstances, Fox cannot deny his role as a promoter.

Coopers asserts that the trial court erred in finding that Fox was under no obligation to pay Coopers' fee in the absence of an agreement that he would be personally liable. We agree.

As a general rule, promoters are personally liable for the contracts they make, though made on behalf of a corporation to be formed. [Citation.] The well-recognized exception to the general rule of promoter liability is that if the contracting party knows the corporation is not in existence but nevertheless agrees to look solely to the corporation and not to the promoter for payment, then the promoter incurs no personal liability. [Citations.] In the absence of an express agreement, the existence of an agreement to release the promoter from liability may be shown by circumstances making it reasonably certain that the parties intended to and did enter into the agreement. [Citations.]

Here, the trial court found there was no agreement, either express or implied, regarding Fox's liability. Thus, in the absence of an agreement releasing him from liability, Fox is liable.

Coopers also contends that the trial court erred in ruling, in effect, that Coopers had the burden of proving any agreement regarding Fox's personal liability for payment of the fee. We agree.

Release of the promoter depends on the intent of the parties. As the proponent of an alleged agreement to release the promoter from liability, the promoter has the burden of proving the release agreement. [Citations.]

Fox seeks to bring himself within the exception to the general rule of promoter liability. However, as the proponent of the exception, he must bear the burden of proving the existence of the alleged agreement releasing him from liability. The trial court found that there was no agreement regarding Fox's liability. Thus, Fox failed to sustain his burden of proof, and the trial court erred in granting judgment in his favor.

It is undisputed that the defendant, Garry J. Fox, engaged Coopers' services, that G. Fox and Partners, Inc., was not in existence at that time, that Coopers performed the work, and that the fee was reasonable. The only dispute, as the trial court found, is whether Garry Fox is liable for payment of the fee. We conclude that Fox is liable, as a matter of law, under the doctrine of promoter liability.

Accordingly, the judgment is reversed, and the cause is remanded with directions to enter judgment in favor of Coopers & Lybrand in the amount of $10,827, plus interest to be determined by the trial court pursuant to [citation].

CASE 33-3
Recognition of Corporateness
HARRIS v. LOONEY
Court of Appeals of Arkansas, 1993
43 Ark.App. 127, 862 S.W.2d 282

Pittman, J.

On February 1, 1988, appellant, Robert L. Harris, sold his business and its assets to J & R Construction. The articles of incorporation for J & R Construction were signed by the incorporators on February 1, 1988, but were not filed with the Secretary of State's office until February 3, 1988. In 1991, J & R Construction defaulted on its contract and promissory note, and appellant sued the incorporators of J & R Construction, Joe Alexander and appellees, Avanell Looney and Rita Alexander, for judgment jointly and severally on the corporation's debt of $49,696.21. In his amended complaint, appellant alleged that the incorporators were jointly and severally liable for the debt of J & R Construction because its articles of incorporation had not been filed with the Secretary of State's Office at the time Joe Alexander, on behalf of the corporation, entered into the contract with appellant. After a bench trial, the circuit court held that Joe Alexander was personally liable for the debts of J & R Construction because he was the contracting party who

dealt on behalf of the corporation. The court refused, however, to hold appellees, Avanell Looney and Rita Alexander, liable, because neither of them had acted for or on behalf of the corporation pursuant to Ark. Code Ann. §4-27-204.

On appeal, appellant contends that the trial court erred in not holding appellees jointly and severally liable, along with Joe Alexander. It was undisputed that the contract and promissory note were signed by Joe Alexander on behalf of J & R Construction and that J & R Construction had not yet been incorporated when the contract was executed. [Court's footnote: Arkansas Code Annotated §4-27-203, which provides that, "[u]nless a delayed effective date is specified, the corporation's existence begins when the articles of incorporation are filed."] Appellant concludes that, because Arkansas law imposes joint and several liability on those purporting to act as or on behalf of a corporation knowing there is no incorporation, the trial court erred in not also awarding him judgment against appellees.

In support of his argument, appellant cites [citation], where the supreme court held that:

> [W]here an incorporator signs a contract or agreement in the name of the corporation before the corporation is actually formed and the other party to the agreement believes at the time of the signing that the corporation is already formed, then the incorporators are responsible as a partnership for the obligations contained in the contract or agreement, including damages resulting from any breach of the contract on their part. * * *

[Citations.] These cases, however, were decided before the Arkansas General Assembly had specifically addressed the issue of liability of individuals for preincorporation debt.

* * * Section 204 of [the Arkansas Business Corporation] Act, [citation], concerns liability for pre-incorporation transactions and is identical to Section 2.04 of the Revised Model Business Corporation Act. It states: "All persons purporting to act as or on behalf of a corporation, knowing there was no incorporation under this Act, are jointly and severally liable for all liabilities created while so acting." The official comment to §2.04 of the Revised Model Business Corporation Act explains:

> * * * Incorporation under modern statutes is so simple and inexpensive that a strong argument may be made that nothing short of filing articles of incorporation should create the privilege of limited liability. A number of situations have arisen, however, in which the protection of limited liability arguably should be recognized even though the simple incorporation process established by modern statutes has not been completed. * * *

* * * [I]t seemed appropriate to impose liability only on persons who act as or on behalf of corporations "knowing" that no corporation exists.

* * * The Act requires that, in order to find liability under §4-27-204, there must be a finding that the persons sought to be charged acted as or on behalf of the corporation and knew there was no incorporation under the Act.

The evidence showed that the contract to purchase appellant's business and the promissory note were signed only by Joe Alexander on behalf of the corporation. The only evidence introduced to support appellant's allegation that appellees were acting on behalf of the corporation was Joe Alexander's and Avanell Looney's statements that they were present when the contract with appellant was signed; however, these statements were disputed by appellant and his wife. Appellant testified that he, his wife, Kathryn Harris, and Joe Alexander were present when the documents were signed to purchase his business and he did not remember appellee Avanell Looney being present. Kathryn Harris testified that appellees were not present when the contract was signed.

The trial court denied appellant judgment against appellees because he found appellees had not acted for or on behalf of J & R Construction as required by §4-27-204. The findings of fact of a trial judge sitting as the fact finder will not be disturbed on appeal unless the findings are clearly erroneous or clearly against the preponderance of the evidence, giving due regard to the opportunity of the trial court to assess the credibility of the witnesses. [Citation.] From our review of the records, we cannot say that the trial court's finding in this case is clearly against the preponderance of the evidence, and we find no error in the court's refusal to award appellant judgment against appellees.

Affirmed.

CASE 33-4

Disregard of Corporateness: Parent-Subsidiary Corporations
INTER-TEL TECHNOLOGIES, INC. v. LINN STATION PROPERTIES, LLC
Supreme Court of Kentucky, 2012
360 S.W.3D 152

Abramson, J.

[Integrated Telecom Services Corp. (ITS) was acquired by and became a wholly owned subsidiary of Inter-Tel Technologies, Inc. (Technologies), which in turn is a wholly owned subsidiary of Inter-Tel, Inc. (Inter-Tel). Inter-Tel designs, manufactures, sells, and services telecommunications systems through its subsidiaries and affiliates. Technologies is the retail division of Inter-Tel. ITS was the company's first retail branch in Kentucky, selling Inter-Tel's telecommunications products from an office building it leased from Linn Station Properties, LLC (Linn Station).

After ITS was acquired by Technologies, ITS was not permitted to maintain a bank account, hold any funds, or pay any bills.

All of ITS's regional offices were transformed from independent dealers of communications equipment into direct sales "branches" of Inter-Tel. ITS employees became employees of Inter-Tel and were paid by Inter-Tel from its headquarters in Arizona. When a customer purchased a telecommunications system from ITS, the payment went directly into a depository account controlled by Inter-Tel. Inter-Tel paid all the vendors who provided ITS with goods and services. All of ITS's inventory was provided by another Inter-Tel subsidiary. Inter-Tel paid ITS's rent for the Linn Station Road property from the time Technologies acquired ITS until ITS abandoned the premises in 2002. Further, Inter-Tel and Technologies were the named insureds listed on the property damage insurance for ITS's premises on Linn Station Road.

ITS did not hold an annual board of directors or shareholders meeting from 1999 through 2002. Nor did Technologies hold an annual board of directors or shareholders meeting from 1998 through 2002. During the four-year period from 1999 through 2002, ITS and Technologies had identical boards of directors; each ITS and Technologies director served as an officer of Inter-Tel; the President and CEO of Inter-Tel served on the boards of ITS, Technologies, and Inter-Tel; and all of ITS's officers served as officers of both Technologies and Inter-Tel. Although all Inter-Tel business conducted in Kentucky since 2001 was performed by ITS in its own name, Inter-Tel, Technologies, and another Inter-Tel subsidiary filed sales and use tax returns with Kentucky in 2001, 2002, and 2003.

On June 19, 2002, Linn Station filed suit against ITS, seeking damages for failure to repair and maintain the premises and for unpaid rent. ITS failed to respond, and on August 12, 2002, a default judgment was entered against ITS for $332,900 plus interest. After repeated, unsuccessful attempts to satisfy the judgment against ITS, on June 20, 2003, Linn Station sued ITS, Technologies, and Inter-Tel to pierce the corporate veil and establish Inter-Tel and Technologies' liability for the judgment against ITS. The trial court granted summary judgment to Linn Station, and the Court of Appeals affirmed, finding it appropriate to pierce the corporate veil where the evidence showed ITS was merely an instrumentality or alter ego of Technologies and Inter-Tel, operated by them to achieve tax benefits and to avoid various liabilities. Technologies and Inter-Tel appealed.]

Piercing the corporate veil is an equitable doctrine invoked by courts to allow a creditor recourse against the shareholders of a corporation. In short, the limited liability which is the hallmark of a corporation is disregarded and the debt of the pierced entity becomes enforceable against those who have exercised dominion over the corporation to the point that it has no real separate existence. A successful veilpiercing claim requires both this element of domination and circumstances in which continued recognition of the corporation as a separate entity would sanction a fraud or promote injustice. The leading Kentucky case on piercing, *White v. Winchester Land Development Corp.*, [citation], like decisions from courts across the country, refers to this two-part test as the "alter ego" test. In recent years, courts and commentators have recognized piercing by using various tests and formulations, most commonly the "alter ego" and "instrumentality" tests, and by identifying common characteristics of corporations which have forfeited the right to separate legal existence. * * * This case requires us to consider this important doctrine in the context of an increasingly common scenario, a creditor's attempt to collect on debt incurred by a wholly-owned subsidiary where the subsidiary has been deprived of all income and rendered asset-less by the acts of its parent (and in this case also grandparent) corporation. * * *

The instrumentality theory requires the co-existence of three elements: "(1) that the corporation was a mere instrumentality of the shareholder; (2) that the shareholder exercised control over the corporation in such a way as to defraud or to harm the plaintiff; and (3) that a refusal to disregard the corporate entity would subject the plaintiff to unjust loss." * * *

* * *

* * * The Seventh Circuit Court of Appeals, when applying Illinois law, uses the two-part alter ego test and considers the following factors under the first prong of that test:

(1) inadequate capitalization; (2) failure to issue stock; (3) failure to observe corporate formalities; (4) nonpayment of dividends; (5) insolvency of the debtor corporation; (6) nonfunctioning of the other officers or directors; (7) absence of corporate records; (8) commingling of funds; (9) diversion of assets from the corporation by or to a stockholder or other person or entity to the detriment of creditors; (10) failure to maintain arm's-length relationships among related entities; and (11) whether, in fact, the corporation is a mere facade for the operation of the dominant stockholders.

[Citations.] * * *

* * *

* * * The alter ego test * * * expressly refers to "promoting injustice" and, indeed, piercing should not be limited to instances where all the elements of a common law fraud claim can be established. [Citations.] * * * We agree * * *, however, that the injustice must be something beyond the mere inability to collect a debt from the corporation.

* * *

The trial court and Court of Appeals were correct in concluding the undisputed facts of this case justified piercing ITS's corporate veil. ITS lost all semblance of separate corporate existence and through the joint acts of Technologies and Inter-Tel was rendered income-less and asset-less. Their diversion of ITS's corporate income and transfer of ITS's corporate assets for their own benefit provides the extra "injustice" * * *, something more than simply a creditor's inability to collect a debt from ITS. In brief, the alter ego test is satisfied and numerous of the equities factors are present. * * *

* * *

* * * The equitable doctrine of veil piercing cannot be thwarted by having two entities, rather than one, dominate the subsidiary and dividing the conduct between the two so that each can point the finger to some extent at the other. Technologies was 100% owned and controlled by Inter-Tel and the two corporations acted completely in concert in dominating ITS and extracting anything of value from ITS. It is entirely appropriate for this Court to look at the larger picture of the

conduct of Inter-Tel and Technologies as opposed to only the individual actions of the parent entity. To do otherwise would render the equitable piercing doctrine hopelessly inadequate, if not meaningless in some cases, based on the sheer number of business entities involved. * * *

* * *

ITS had grossly inadequate capital for day-to-day operations because it had no funds at all, literally nothing of its own. * * *

* * *

The transfers of any and all operating capital that ITS previously possessed to Inter-Tel resulted in an undercapitalization at the times relevant to this litigation, regardless of the initial capitalization when ITS was independently incorporated years before the Inter-Tel group purchased it.

Inter-Tel paid the employees' salaries and other expenses of ITS. ITS had no assets of its own, only those it was allowed to use by Technologies or Inter-Tel. ITS simply had no independent financial existence. * * * Both Technologies and Inter-Tel used the Linn Station lease premises and any other assets previously held by ITS solely for the benefit of Inter-Tel, not for ITS's benefit. Certainly the ITS officers

and directors failed to act in that corporation's best interest because they allowed it to be stripped of its income and assets by Technologies and Inter-Tel, acting in the interest of Inter-Tel to the detriment of any other entity. Finally, the formal legal requirements of ITS were not observed. There were no shareholder or director meetings in 1999, 2000, 2001, and 2002 and * * * there was such unity of ownership and interest that ITS's separateness from Technologies and Inter-Tel ceased to exist.

* * *

Courts should not pierce corporate veils lightly but neither should they hesitate in those cases where the circumstances are extreme enough to justify disregard of an allegedly separate corporate entity. This case is clearly within the boundaries of proper application of the equitable doctrine and thus we conclude that the trial court and Court of Appeals did not err in piercing ITS's veil to hold Inter-Tel and Technologies responsible for ITS's debt to Linn Station.

[The decision of the Court of Appeals is affirmed, and case is remanded to the trial court for entry of judgment against Inter-Tel and Technologies.]

QUESTIONS

1. After part of the shares of a proposed corporation had been successfully subscribed, one of the promoters hired a carpenter to repair a building that was to be conveyed to the proposed corporation. The promoters subsequently secured subscriptions to the balance of the shares and completed the organization, but the corporation, finding the building to be unsuitable for its purposes, declined to use the building or pay the carpenter. The carpenter brought suit against the corporation and the promoter for the amount the promoter agreed would be paid to him. Who, if anyone, is liable? Explain.

2. C. A. Nimocks was a promoter engaged in organizing the Times Printing Company. On September 12, on behalf of the proposed corporation, he made a written contract with McArthur for her services as comptroller for a one-year period beginning October 1. The Times Printing Company was incorporated October 16, and on that date, McArthur commenced her duties as comptroller. Neither the board of directors nor any officer took formal action on her employment, but all the shareholders, directors, and officers knew of the contract made by Nimocks. On December 1, McArthur was discharged without cause.

   a. Does she have a cause of action against the Times Printing Company? Explain.

   b. Does she have a cause of action against Nimocks? Explain.

3. Todd and Elaine purchased for $300,000 a building that was used for manufacturing pianos. Then as promoters, they formed a new corporation and resold the building to the new corporation for $500,000 worth of stock. After discovering the actual purchase price paid by the promoters, the other shareholders desire to have $200,000 of the common stock canceled. Can they succeed in this action? Why or why not?

4. Wayne signed a subscription agreement to purchase one hundred shares of stock of the proposed ABC Company, at a price of $18 per share in a State that has adopted the Revised Act. Two weeks later, the company was incorporated. A certificate was duly tendered to Wayne, but he refused to accept it. He was notified of all shareholders' meetings, but he never attended. A dividend check was sent to him, but he returned it. ABC Company brings a legal action against Wayne to recover $1,800. He defends upon the ground that his subscription agreement was an unaccepted offer and that he had done nothing to ratify it and was therefore not liable upon it. Is he correct? Explain.

5. Julian, Cornelia, and Sheila petitioned for a corporate certificate of incorporation for the purpose of conducting a retail shoe business. They met all of the statutory provisions, with the exception of having their articles of incorporation recorded. This was simply an oversight on

their part, and they felt that they had fully complied with the law. They operated the business for three years, after which time it became insolvent. The creditors desire to hold the members personally and individually liable. May they do so? Explain.

6. Arthur, Barbara, Carl, and Debra decided to form a corporation for bottling and selling apple cider. Arthur, Barbara, and Carl were to operate the business, and Debra was to supply the necessary capital but was to have no voice in the management. They went to Jane, a lawyer, who agreed to organize a corporation for them under the name A-B-C Inc., and paid her funds sufficient to accomplish the incorporation. Jane promised that the corporation would definitely be formed by May 3. On April 27, Arthur telephoned Jane to inquire how the incorporation was progressing, and Jane said she had drafted the articles of incorporation and would send them to the Secretary of State that very day. She assured Arthur that incorporation would occur before May 3.

   On May 4, relying on Jane's assurance, Arthur, with the approval of Barbara and Carl, entered into a written contract with Grower for the latter's entire apple crop. The contract was executed by Arthur on behalf of "A-B-C Inc." Grower delivered the apples as agreed. Unknown to Arthur, Barbara, Carl, Debra, or Grower, the articles of incorporation were never filed, through Jane's negligence. The business subsequently failed.

   Explain what Grower's rights are, if any, against Arthur, Barbara, Carl, and Debra as individuals.

7. The Pyro Corporation has outstanding twenty thousand shares of common stock, of which nineteen thousand are owned by Peter B. Arson; five hundred shares are owned by Elizabeth Arson, his wife; and five hundred shares are owned by Joseph Q. Arson, his brother. These three individuals are the officers and directors of the corporation. The Pyro Corporation obtained a $750,000 fire insurance policy to cover a certain building it owned. Thereafter, Peter B. Arson set fire to the building, and it was totally destroyed. Can the corporation recover from the fire insurance company on the $750,000 fire insurance policy? Why or why not?

8. A corporation formed for the purpose of manufacturing, buying, selling, and dealing in drugs, chemicals, and similar products contracted to purchase, under authority of its board of directors, the land and building it occupied as a factory and store. Collins, a shareholder, sues in equity to restrain the corporation from completing the contract, claiming that as the certificate of incorporation contained no provision authorizing the corporation to purchase real estate, the contract was *ultra vires*. Can Collins prevent the contract from being executed? Why or why not?

9. Amalgamated Corporation, organized under the laws of State S, sends several traveling salespersons into State M to solicit orders, which are accepted only at the home office of Amalgamated Corporation in State S. Riley, a resident of State M, places an order which is accepted by Amalgamated Corporation in State S. The Corporation Act of State M provides that "no foreign corporation transacting business in this state without a certificate of authority shall be permitted to maintain an action in any court of this state until such corporation shall have obtained a certificate of authority." Riley fails to pay for the goods, and when Amalgamated Corporation sues Riley in a court of State M, Riley defends on the ground that Amalgamated Corporation does not possess a certificate of authority from State M. Discuss what the result should be.

CASE PROBLEMS

10. Dr. North, a surgeon practicing in Georgia, engaged an Arizona professional corporation consisting of twenty lawyers to represent him in a dispute with a Georgia hospital. West, a member of the law firm, flew to Atlanta and hired local counsel with Dr. North's approval. West represented Dr. North in two hearings before the hospital and in one court proceeding, also negotiating a compromise between Dr. North and the hospital. The total bill for the law firm's travel costs and professional services was $21,000, but Dr. North refused to pay $6,000 of it. When the law firm brought an action against Dr. North for the balance owed, he argued that the action should be dismissed because the law firm failed to register as a foreign corporation in accordance with the Georgia Corporation Statute. Will the law firm be prevented from collecting on the contract? Explain.

11. An Arkansas statute provides that if any foreign corporation authorized to do business in the State should remove to the Federal court any suit brought against it by an Arkansas citizen or initiate any suit in the Federal court against a local citizen, without the consent of the other party, Arkansas's Secretary of State should revoke all authority of the corporation to do business in the State. The Burke Construction Company, a Missouri corporation authorized to do business in Arkansas, has brought a suit in Federal court and has removed to a

Federal court a State suit brought against it. Burke now seeks to enjoin the Secretary of State from revoking its authority to do business in Arkansas. Should the injunction be issued? Explain.

12. Little Switzerland Brewing Company was incorporated on January 28. On February 18, Ellison and Oxley were made directors of the company after they purchased some stock. Then on September 25, Ellison and Oxley signed stock subscription agreements to purchase five thousand shares each. Under the agreement, they both issued a note that indicated that they would pay for the stock "at their discretion." Two years later in March, the board of directors passed a resolution canceling the stock subscription agreements of Ellison and Oxley. The creditors of Little Switzerland brought suit against Ellison and Oxley to recover the money owed under the subscription agreements. Are Ellison and Oxley liable? Why or why not?

13. Oahe Enterprises was formed by the efforts of Emmick, who acted as a promoter and contributed shares of Colonial Manors, Inc. (CM), stock in exchange for stock in Oahe. The CM stock had been valued by CM's directors for internal stock option purposes at $19 per share. One month prior to Emmick's incorporation of Oahe Enterprises, however, CM's board reduced the stock value to $9.50 per share. Although Emmick knew of this reduction before the meeting to form Oahe Enterprises, he did not disclose this information to the Morrises, the other shareholders of the new corporation. Can Oahe Enterprises recover the shortfall? Explain.

14. Healthwin-Midtown Convalescent Hospital, Inc. (Health-win), was incorporated in California for the purpose of operating a health-care facility. For three years thereafter, it participated as a provider of services under the Federal Medicare Act and received periodic payments from the U.S. Department of Health, Education and Welfare. Undisputed audits revealed that a series of overpayments had been made to Healthwin. The United States brought an action to recover this sum from the defendants, Healthwin and Israel Zide. Zide was a member of the board of directors of Healthwin, the administrator of its health-care facility, its president, and owner of 50 percent of its stock. Only Zide could sign the corporation's checks without prior approval of another corporate officer. Board meetings were not regularly held. In addition, Zide had a 50 percent interest in a partnership that owned both the realty in which Healthwin's health-care facility was located and the furnishings used at that facility. Healthwin consistently had outstanding liabilities in excess of $150,000, and its initial capitalization was only $10,000. Zide exercised control over Healthwin, causing its finances to become inextricably intertwined with both his personal finances and his other business holdings. The United States contends that the corporate veil should be pierced and that Zide should be held personally liable for the Medicare overpayments made to Healthwin. Is the United States correct in its assertion? Why or why not?

15. MPL Leasing Corporation is a California corporation that provides financing plans to dealers of Saxon Business Products. MPL invited Jay Johnson, a Saxon dealer in Alabama, to attend a sales seminar in Atlanta. MPL and Johnson entered into an agreement under which Johnson was to lease Saxon copiers with an option to buy. MPL shipped the equipment into Alabama and filed a financing statement with the Secretary of State. When Johnson became delinquent with his payments to MPL, MPL brought an action against Johnson in an Alabama court. Johnson moved to dismiss the action, claiming that MPL was not qualified to conduct business in Alabama and was thus barred from enforcing its contract with Johnson in an Alabama court. Alabama law prevents foreign corporations not qualified to do business in Alabama from enforcing their intrastate contracts in the Alabama court system. Is Johnson correct? Explain.

16. In April, Cranson was asked to invest in a new business corporation that was about to be created. He agreed to purchase stock and to become an officer and director. After his attorney advised him that the corporation had been formed under the laws of Maryland, Cranson paid for and received a stock certificate evidencing his ownership of shares. The business of the new venture was conducted as if it were a corporation. Cranson was elected president, and he conducted all of his corporate actions, including those with IBM, as an officer of the corporation. At no time did he assume any personal obligation or pledge his individual credit to IBM. As a result of an oversight of the attorney, of which Cranson was unaware, the certificate of incorporation, which had been signed and acknowledged prior to May 1, was not filed until November 24. Between May 1 and November 8, the "corporation" purchased eight computers from IBM. The corporation made only partial payment. Can IBM hold Cranson personally liable for the balance due? Explain.

17. Berger was planning to produce a fashion show in Las Vegas. In April 1965, Berger entered into a written licensing agreement with CBS Films, Inc., a wholly owned subsidiary of CBS, for presentation of the show. In 1966, Stewart Cowley decided to produce a fashion show similar to Berger's and entered into a contract with CBS. CBS broadcast Cowley's show but not Berger's, and Berger brought an action against CBS to recover

damages for breach of his contract with CBS Films. Berger claimed that CBS was liable because CBS Films was not operated as a separate entity and that the court should disregard the parent-subsidiary form. In support of this claim, Berger showed that the directors of CBS Films were employees of CBS, that CBS's organizational chart included CBS Films, and that all lines of employee authority from CBS Films passed through CBS employees to the CBS chairman of the board. CBS, in turn, argued that Berger had failed to justify piercing the corporate veil and disregarding the corporate identity of CBS Films in order to hold CBS liable. Decision? Discuss.

18. Frank McAnarney and Joseph Lemon entered into an agreement to promote a corporation to engage in the manufacture of farm implements. Before the corporation was organized, McAnarney and Lemon solicited subscriptions to the stock of the corporation and presented a written agreement for the subscribers to sign. The agreement provided that the subscribers would pay $100 per share for stock in the corporation in consideration of McAnarney and Lemon's agreement to organize the corporation and advance the preincorporation expenses. Thomas Jordan signed the agreement, making application for one hundred shares of stock. After the articles of incorporation were filed with the Secretary of State but before the certificate of incorporation was issued to the corporation, Jordan died. The administrator of Jordan's estate notified McAnarney and Lemon that the estate would not honor Jordan's subscription.

    After the formation of the corporation, Franklin Adams signed a subscription agreement making application for one hundred shares of stock. Before the corporation accepted the subscription, Adams informed the corporation that he was canceling it.

    a. Can the corporation enforce Jordan's stock subscription against Jordan's estate? Explain.

    b. Can the corporation enforce Adams's stock subscription? Explain.

19. Green & Freedman Baking Company (Green & Freedman) was a corporation that produced and sold baked goods. It was owned by the Elmans. The terms of a collective bargaining agreement required Green & Freedman Baking Company to make periodic payments on behalf of its unionized drivers to the New England Teamsters and Baking Industry Health Benefits and Insurance Fund (Health Fund). After sixty years of operation, Green & Freedman experienced financial difficulties and ceased to make the agreed-upon contributions. The Elmans mixed their own finances with those of Green & Freedman's. The Elmans, through their domination of Green & Freedman, caused the corporation to make payments to themselves and their relatives at a time when the corporation was known to be failing and could be expected to default or was already in default on its obligations to the Health Fund. It then transferred all remaining assets to a successor entity named Boston Bakers, Inc. (Boston Bakers). Boston Bakers operated essentially the same business as Green & Freedman until its demise two years later. The Health Fund sued Green & Freedman, Boston Bakers, and the two corporations' principals, Richard Elman and Stanley Elman, to recover the payments owed by Green & Freedman with interest, costs, and penalties. There was no evidence of financial self-dealing in the case of Boston Bakers. Both corporate defendants conceded liability for the delinquent contributions owed by Green & Freedman to the Health Fund. The suit against the Elmans was based on piercing the corporate veil with respect to Green & Freedman and Boston Bakers. The Elmans, however, denied they were personally liable for these corporate debts. Are the Elmans liable? Explain.

20. Ronald Nadler was a resident of Maryland and the CEO of Glenmar Cinestate, Inc., a Maryland corporation, as well as its principal stockholder. Glenmar leased certain space in the Westridge Square Shopping Center, located in Frederick, Maryland, and in Cranberry Mall, located in Westminster, Maryland. Tiller Construction Corporation and Nadler entered into two contracts for the construction of movie theaters at these locations, one calling for Tiller to do "the work" for Nadler at Westridge for $637,000 and the other for Tiller to do "the work" for Nadler at Cranberry for $688,800. Ronald Nadler requested that Tiller send all bills to Glenmar, the lessee at both shopping malls, but agreed to be personally liable to Tiller for the payment of both contracts. All inventory was bought and paid for locally, and Tiller paid sales tax in Maryland. Although there was no formal office in the state, Tiller leased a motel room for a considerable period of time, posted a sign at the job site, and maintained a Maryland telephone number listed in directory assistance. In addition, Tiller engaged in fairly pervasive management functions, and the value of the projects comprised a substantial part of Tiller's revenues during the period. At the time of the suit, there was a net balance due for the Cranberry project in the amount of $229,799.46 and on the Westridge project for the sum of $264,273.85. Nadler refused to pay both balances even though he had approved all work and the work had been performed in a timely, good, and workmanlike manner. Tiller Construction Corporation sued Ronald Nadler and Glenmar Cinestate, Inc., for breach of contract.

Nadler filed a motion to dismiss based on Maryland's business corporation statute, which prohibits a foreign corporation that conducts intrastate business in Maryland from maintaining a suit in Maryland courts if the corporation fails to register or qualify under Maryland law. Nadler asserted that Tiller was a New York corporation that had never qualified to transact business in the state of Maryland. Tiller conceded that the corporation had not qualified to do business in Maryland but argued that Tiller was not required to qualify because its activities did not constitute, in the contemplation of the statute, doing business in the state as Tiller just had occasional business in Maryland. Discuss whether Tiller could bring suit in Maryland.

21. Harold Lang Jewelers, Inc. (Lang), a Florida corporation, through its single employee, had sold and consigned merchandise to jewelry stores in western North Carolina for almost thirty years. Lang's employee came frequently to North Carolina for the purpose of transacting business. When the employee came to North Carolina, he always brought jewelry with him for delivery. When he visited jewelry stores in the State, he would either (a) make a direct sale on the spot without any confirmation from any other person or (b) consign the jewelry, also without any further confirmation or approval from any other person. When the employee took orders, he either shipped the ordered items to the business in North Carolina or personally delivered the merchandise. He also took returns of merchandise from customers. Lang filed suit against Johnson, alleging that Johnson owed Lang $160,322.90 plus interest for jewelry sold or consigned. Johnson asserted as one of its defenses that Lang could not sue in a North Carolina court because Lang had failed to obtain a certificate of authority to transact business in the State. Explain whether the court should dismiss Lang's action.

TAKING SIDES

In May, Parr and Presba, while in the course of negotiations with Barker (a salesperson for Quaker Hill) to purchase plants and flowers, undertook to organize a corporation to be named the Denver Memorial Nursery, Inc. On May 14 and 16, Parr signed two orders on behalf of Denver Memorial Nursery, Inc., which, to the knowledge of Quaker Hill, was not yet formed; that fact was noted in the contract. A down payment in the amount of $1,000 was made to Quaker Hill. The corporation was not formed before the parties entered into the contract because Quaker Hill had insisted that the deal be concluded at once since the growing season was rapidly passing. Under the contract, the balance of the purchase price was not due until the end of the year. The plants and flowers were shipped immediately and arrived on May 26. The Denver Memorial Nursery, Inc., was never formed. Quaker Hill seeks to recover the unpaid balance of the purchase price from Parr and Presba.

a. What are the arguments that Parr and Presba are personally liable for the unpaid balance?

b. What are the arguments that Parr and Presba are not personally liable for the unpaid balance?

c. Explain who should prevail.

CHAPTER 34

Financial Structure

After reading and studying this chapter, you should be able to:

- Distinguish between equity and debt securities.
- Describe the principal kinds of debt securities.
- Describe the principal kinds of equity securities.
- Explain what type and amount of consideration a corporation may validly receive for the shares it issues.
- Explain the legal restrictions imposed upon dividends and other distributions.

apital is necessary for any business to function. Two principal sources for corporate financing involve debt and equity investment securities. While equity securities represent an ownership interest in the corporation and include both common and preferred stock, corporations finance most of their operations through debt securities. Debt securities, which include notes and bonds, do not represent an ownership interest in the corporation but rather create a debtor–creditor relationship between the corporation and the bondholder. The third principal way in which a corporation may meet its financial needs is through retained earnings.

All States have statutes regulating the issuance and sale of corporate shares and other securities. Popularly known as **blue-sky laws**, these statutes typically have provisions prohibiting fraud in the sale of securities. In addition, a number of States require the registration of securities, and some States also regulate brokers, dealers, and others who engage in the securities business.

In 1933, Congress passed the first Federal statute for the regulation of securities offered for sale and sold through the use of the mails or otherwise in interstate commerce. The statute requires a corporation to disclose certain information about a proposed security in a registration statement and in its **prospectus** (an offer a corporation makes to interest people in buying securities). Although the Securities and Exchange Commission (SEC) does not examine the merits of the proposed security and although registration does not guarantee the accuracy of the facts presented in the registration statement or prospectus, the law does prohibit

false and misleading statements under penalty of fine or imprisonment or both.

Under certain conditions, a corporation may receive an exemption from the requirement of registration under the blue-sky laws of most States and the Securities Act of 1933. If no exemption is available, a corporation offering for sale or selling its shares of stock or other securities, as well as any person selling such securities, is subject to court injunction, possible criminal prosecution, and civil liability in damages to the persons to whom securities are sold in violation of the regulatory statute. A discussion of Federal regulation of securities appears in *Chapter 43*.

An investor has the right to transfer her investment securities by sale, gift, or pledge. The right to transfer is a valuable one, and easy transferability augments the value and marketability of investment securities. The availability of a ready market for any security affords liquidity and makes the security both attractive to investors and useful as collateral. The Uniform Commercial Code (UCC), Article 8, Investment Securities, contains the statutory rules applicable to transfers of investment securities; these rules are similar to those in Article 3, which concern negotiable instruments. In 1994, a revision to Article 8 was promulgated, and all of the States have adopted the revision. The Federal securities laws also regulate several aspects of the transfer of investment securities, as discussed in *Chapter 43*.

This chapter discusses debt and equity securities as well as the payment of dividends and other distributions to shareholders.

DEBT SECURITIES

Corporations frequently find it advantageous to use debt as a source of funds. **Debt securities** (also called **bonds**) generally involve the corporation's promise to repay the principal amount of a loan at a stated time and to pay interest, usually at a fixed rate, while the debt is outstanding. Thus, a debt security creates a debtor–creditor relationship between the corporation and the holder of the security. In addition to bonds, a corporation may finance its operations through other forms of debt, such as credit extended by its suppliers and shortterm commercial paper. Some State statutes, but not the Revised Act, permit the articles of incorporation to confer voting rights on debt security holders; a few States allow other shareholder rights to be conferred on bondholders.

Practical Advice

When raising capital for a corporation, carefully consider the ratio between debt and equity financing, recognizing that this ratio varies considerably with the type and life cycle of a corporation.

34-1 Authority to Issue Debt Securities

The Revised Act provides that every corporation has the power "to make contracts and guarantees, incur liabilities, borrow money, issue its notes, bonds, and other obligations (which may be convertible into or include the option to purchase other securities of the corporation), and secure any of its obligations by mortgage or pledge of any of its property, franchises, or income." Section 3.02. The board of directors may issue bonds without the authorization or consent of the shareholders.

34-2 Types of Debt Securities

Debt securities can be classified into various types according to their characteristics. The variants and combinations possible within each type are limited only by a corporation's ingenuity. Debt securities are typically issued under an **indenture** or debt agreement, which specifies in great detail the terms of the loan. The Federal Trust Indenture Act of 1939 applies to indentures covering bonds issued for $10 million or more.

In addition, a high-yield bond (non-investment-grade bond or junk bond is a bond that is rated below investment grade at the time of purchase. These bonds have a greater risk of default than investment-grade bonds but typically pay higher yields than investment-grade bonds to make them attractive to investors.

Independent credit rating agencies analyze the companies and municipalities that issue bonds and assign ratings to reflect the creditworthiness of the issuer. Credit rating agencies that are registered as such with the SEC are known as Nationally

Recognized Statistical Rating Organizations (NRSROs). There are nine firms currently registered as NRSROs: A.M. Best Rating Services, Inc.; DBRS, Inc.; Egan-Jones Ratings Company; Fitch Ratings, Inc.; HR Ratings de México, S.A. de C.V.; Japan Credit Rating Agency, Ltd.; Kroll Bond Rating Agency, Inc.; Moody's Investors Service, Inc.; and S & P Global Ratings. In 2006, Congress passed the Credit Rating Agency Reform Act requiring the SEC to establish clear guidelines for determining which credit rating agencies qualify as NRSROs. The Dodd-Frank Wall Street Reform and Consumer Protection Act of 2010 (see *Chapter 35*) imposed additional requirements on NRSROs to enhance their accountability and transparency.

♦ *See Case 34-1*

34-2a UNSECURED BONDS

Unsecured bonds, usually called **debentures**, have only the obligation of the corporation behind them. Debenture holders are thus unsecured creditors and rank equally with other general creditors. To protect the unsecured bondholders, indentures frequently impose limitations on the corporation's borrowing, its payment of dividends, and its redemption and reacquisition of its own shares. They also may require the corporation to maintain specified minimum reserves.

34-2b SECURED BONDS

A secured creditor is one whose claim not only is enforceable against the general assets of the corporation but also is a lien upon specific property. Thus, **secured** or mortgage **bonds** provide the security of specific corporate property in addition to the general obligation of the corporation. After resorting to the specified security, the holder of secured bonds becomes a general creditor for any unpaid amount of the debt.

34-2c INCOME BONDS

Traditionally, debt securities bear a fixed interest rate that is payable without regard to the financial condition of the corporation. **Income bonds**, on the other hand, condition the payment of interest to some extent upon corporate earnings. This provision lessens the burden of the debt upon the issuer during periods of financial adversity. **Participating bonds** call for a stated percentage of return regardless of earnings, with additional payments dependent upon earnings.

34-2d CONVERTIBLE BONDS

Convertible bonds may be exchanged, usually at the option of the holder, for other securities of the corporation at a specified ratio. For example, a convertible bond may provide that the bondholder shall have the right for a specified time to exchange each bond for twenty shares of common stock.

34-2e CALLABLE BONDS

Callable bonds are subject to a redemption provision that permits the corporation to redeem or call (pay off) all or part of the issue before maturity at a specified redemption price. This provision enables the corporation to reduce fixed costs, to improve its credit rating, to refinance at a lower interest rate, to free mortgaged property, or to reduce its proportion of debt.

Practical Advice

If you purchase callable bonds, recognize that if interest rates decline, the corporation is likely to exercise its redemption privilege.

EQUITY SECURITIES

An **equity security** is a source of capital creating an ownership interest in the corporation. The holders of equity security, as owners of the corporation, occupy a position financially riskier than that of creditors; they, more than any other class of investor, bear the impact of changes in the corporation's fortunes and general economic conditions.

Though **shares** of equity securities describe a proportionate proprietary interest in a corporate enterprise, they do not in any way vest their owner with title to any of the corporation's property. Shares do, however, confer on their owner a threefold interest in the corporation: (1) the right to participate in control, (2) the right to participate in the earnings of the corporation, and (3) the right to participate in the residual assets of the corporation upon dissolution. The shareholder's interest is usually evidenced by a certificate of ownership and is recorded by the corporation.

34-3 Issuance of Shares

The State of incorporation regulates the issuance of shares by determining the type of shares that may be issued, the kinds and amount of consideration for which shares may be issued, and the rights of shareholders to purchase a proportionate part of additionally issued shares. Moreover, the Federal government and each State in which the shares are issued or sold regulate the issuance and sale of shares.

34-3a AUTHORITY TO ISSUE SHARES

The initial number of shares to be issued is determined by the promoters or incorporators and is generally governed by practical business considerations and financial needs. A corporation is limited, however, to selling only the number of shares that has been authorized in its articles of incorporation. Section 6.03. Unauthorized shares of stock that a corporation

purportedly issues are void. The rights of parties entitled to these overissued shares are governed by Article 8 of the UCC, which provides that the corporation must either obtain an identical security, if it is reasonably available, for the person entitled to the security or pay that person the price he (or the last purchaser for value) paid for it, with interest from the date of that person's demand. UCC Section 8-210.

The 2016 RMBCA provides a statutory ratification procedure for shares that may have been improperly issued. Upon the effectiveness of the ratification, the overissued shares are valid shares as of the date the shares were *originally* issued.

Once the number of shares that the corporation is authorized to issue has been specified in the charter, it cannot be increased or decreased without amending the articles of incorporation. This means that the shareholders, who must approve any amendment to the articles of incorporation, have residual authority over increases in the amount of authorized capital stock. Consequently, articles of incorporation commonly specify more shares than are to be issued initially.

Practical Advice

When drafting the articles of incorporation, you should authorize shares in addition to those that are to be issued immediately unless the State-imposed fees based on the number of authorized shares are prohibitive.

34-3b PREEMPTIVE RIGHTS

A shareholder's proportionate interest in a corporation can be changed by either a disproportionate issuance of additional shares or a disproportionate reacquisition of outstanding shares. In either transaction, management owes both the shareholder and the corporation a fiduciary duty. Moreover, when additional shares are issued, a shareholder may have the **preemptive right** to purchase a proportionate part of the new issue. Preemptive rights are used far more frequently in closely held corporations than in publicly traded corporations. Without such rights, a shareholder may be unable to prevent a dilution of his ownership interest in the corporation. For example, Leonard owns two hundred shares of stock of the Fordham Company, which has a total of one thousand shares outstanding. The company decides to increase its capital stock by issuing one thousand additional shares of stock. If Leonard has preemptive rights, he and every other shareholder will be offered one share of the newly issued stock for every share they own. If he accepts the offer and buys the stock, he will have four hundred shares out of a total of two thousand outstanding, and his relative interest in the corporation will be unchanged. Without preemptive rights, however, he would have only two hundred out of the two thousand shares outstanding; instead of owning 20 percent of the stock, he would own 10 percent.

Most statutes expressly authorize articles of incorporation to deny or limit preemptive rights to the issuance of additionally authorized shares. In about half of the States, preemptive rights exist unless denied by the charter (**opt-out**); in about half of the States, they do not exist unless the charter so provides (**opt-in**).

Certain shares are not subject to preemptive rights. In some States, preemptive rights do not apply to the reissue of previously issued shares. In addition, preemptive rights generally do not apply to shares issued for noncash consideration or shares issued in connection with a merger or consolidation. Moreover, preemptive rights do not apply to the issuance of unissued shares that were originally authorized if the shares represent part of the initial capitalization.

The Revised Act adopts the opt-in approach: preemptive rights are nonexistent unless the charter provides for them. Section 6.30. If the charter simply states that "the corporation elects to have preemptive rights," then the shareholders have a preemptive right to acquire proportional amounts of the corporation's unissued shares, but they have no preemptive rights with respect to (1) shares issued as compensation to directors, officers, and employees; (2) shares issued within six months of incorporation; and (3) shares issued for consideration other than money. In addition, holders of nonvoting preferred stock have no preemptive rights with respect to *any* class of shares, and holders of voting common shares have no preemptive rights with respect to preferred stock unless the preferred stock is convertible into common stock. Section 6.30(b). The articles of incorporation may expressly modify any or all of these limitations.

Practical Advice

To protect your share of ownership from dilution, when organizing a close corporation, you should consider including in the charter a carefully drafted provision for preemptive rights. You should recognize, however, that preemptive rights will protect you only if you can afford to purchase a proportionate part of a new issue of shares.

34-3c AMOUNT OF CONSIDERATION FOR SHARES

The board of directors usually determines the price for which the corporation will issue shares, although the charter may reserve this power to the shareholders. Section 6.21. Shares are deemed fully paid and nonassessable when the corporation receives the consideration for which the board of directors authorized their issuance. Section 6.21(d). The amount of that consideration depends upon the kind of shares being issued.

PAR VALUE STOCK In some States, a corporation must specify in the articles of incorporation either a par value for its shares or that the shares are no par. Par value shares may be issued for any amount, not less than par, set by the board of directors or shareholders. The par value of a share of stock can be an arbitrary value selected by the corporation and may or may not reflect either the actual value of the share or the actual price paid to the corporation. It indicates only the *minimum price* that the corporation must receive for the share. The par value of stock must be stated in the articles of incorporation. The consideration received constitutes *stated-capital* to the extent of the par value of the shares; any consideration in excess of par value constitutes *capital surplus*. It is common practice to authorize *low* or *nominal* par shares, such as $1 per share, and issue these shares at a considerably higher price, thereby providing ample capital surplus. By doing so, the corporation, in some jurisdictions, obtains greater flexibility in declaring subsequent distributions to shareholders.

The Revised Act, the 1980 amendments to the Model Business Corporation Act (MBCA), and at least twenty-eight States have eliminated the concepts of par value, stated capital, and capital surplus. Under these statutes, all shares may be issued for such consideration as authorized by the board of directors or, if the charter so provides, the shareholders. Section 6.21. A corporation, however, may elect to issue shares with par value. Section 2.02(b).

NO PAR VALUE STOCK Shares without par value may be issued for any amount set by the board of directors or shareholders. Under incorporation statutes recognizing par value, stated value, and capital surplus, the entire consideration the corporation receives for such stock constitutes stated capital unless the board of directors allocates a portion of the consideration to capital surplus. MBCA Section 21, repealed in 1980. (As noted above, the Revised Act and the 1980 amendments to the MBCA eliminated the concepts of par value, stated capital, and capital surplus.) The directors are free to allocate any or all of the consideration received, unless the no par stock has a liquidation preference. In that event, only the consideration in excess of the amount of liquidation preference may be allocated to capital surplus. No par shares provide the directors with great latitude in establishing capital surplus, which can, in some jurisdictions, provide greater flexibility in declaring subsequent distributions to shareholders.

Practical Advice

Because a number of States grant more favorable tax treatment to par value stock, often it is more cost-effective to issue low par value stock. This approach provides nearly the same flexibility as no par stock but with lower taxes.

TREASURY STOCK Treasury stock consists of shares that the corporation has issued and subsequently reacquired. Treasury shares are issued *but not* outstanding, in contrast to shares owned by shareholders, which are issued *and* outstanding. A corporation may sell treasury shares for any amount the board of directors determines, even if the shares have a par value that is more than the sale price. Treasury shares provide neither voting rights nor preemptive rights; furthermore, no dividend may be paid upon them.

The Revised Act advances the 1980 amendments to the MBCA, which eliminated the concept of treasury shares. Under the Revised Act, all shares reacquired by a corporation constitute authorized but unissued shares, unless the articles of incorporation prohibit reissue, in which event the authorized shares are reduced by the number of shares reacquired. Section 6.31.

◆ **SEE FIGURE 34-1:** *Issuance of Shares*

34-3d PAYMENT FOR SHARES

Two major issues arise regarding payment for shares. First, what type of consideration may the corporation validly accept in payment for shares? Second, who shall determine the value to be placed upon the consideration the corporation receives in payment for shares?

TYPE OF CONSIDERATION In terms of the issuance of capital stock, consideration receives a more limited definition than it does under contract law. In about twenty-five States, cash, property, and services actually rendered to the corporation are generally acceptable as valid consideration, but promissory notes and promises regarding the performance of future services are not. Some States permit shares to be issued for preincorporation services; other States do not.

The Revised Act greatly liberalized these rules by specifically validating for the issuance of shares consideration consisting of any tangible or intangible property or *benefit* to the corporation, including cash, services performed, *contracts for future services*, and *promissory notes*. Section 6.21(b). To guard against possible abuse, the corporation may place the shares in escrow or otherwise restrict their transfer until the services are performed, the note is paid, or the benefits are received. If the services are not performed, the note is not paid, or the benefits are not received, the shares escrowed or restricted may be canceled. Section 6.21(e). Moreover, the Revised Act requires that corporations annually inform their shareholders in writing of all shares issued during the previous year for promissory notes or promises of future services. Section 16.21.

| FIGURE 34-1 | Issuance of Shares |

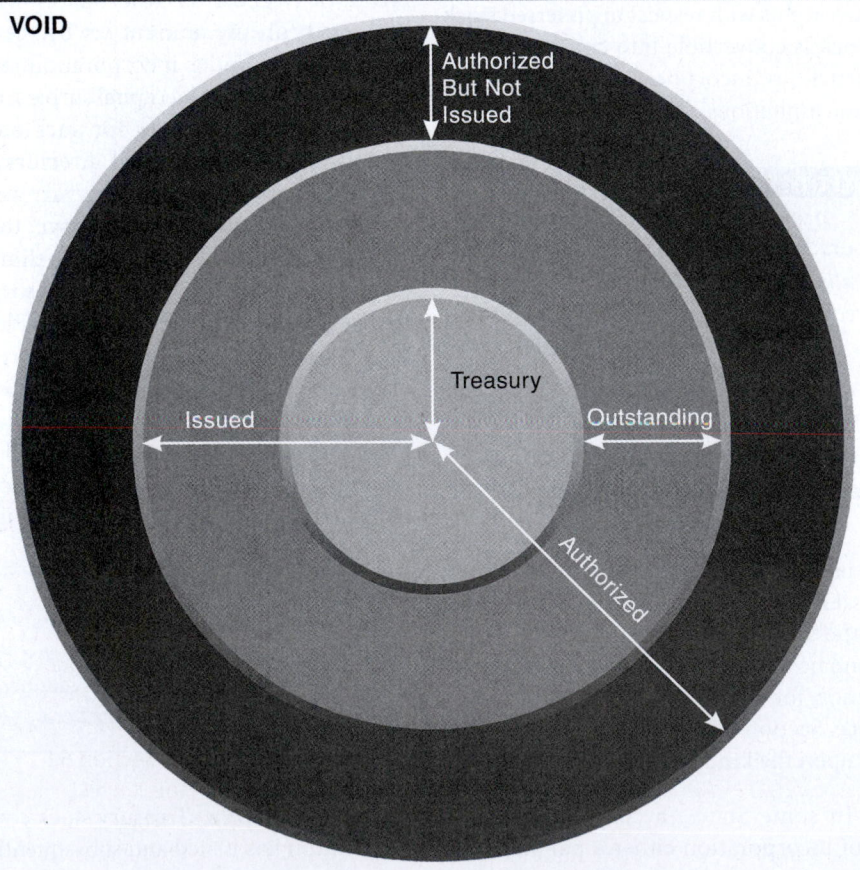

VALUATION OF CONSIDERATION Determining the value to be placed on the consideration that stock purchasers will exchange for shares is the responsibility of the directors. Many jurisdictions hold that this valuation is a matter of opinion and that in the absence of fraud in the transaction, the judgment of the board of directors as to the value of the consideration actually or to be received for shares shall be conclusive. For example, assume that the directors of Elite Corporation authorize the issuance of two thousand shares of common stock for $10 per share to Kramer for property that the directors purportedly value at $20,000. The valuation is fraudulent, however, and the property is actually worth only $10,000. Kramer is liable to Elite Corporation and its creditors for $10,000. If, on the other hand, the directors had made the valuation without fraud and in good faith, Kramer would not be liable, even though the property is actually worth less than $20,000.

Under the Revised Act, the directors simply determine whether or not the consideration received (or to be received) for shares is *adequate*. Their determination is "conclusive insofar as the adequacy of consideration for the issuance of shares relates to whether the shares are validly issued, fully paid, and nonassessable." Section 6.21(c). Under the Revised Act, the articles of incorporation may reserve to the shareholders the powers granted to the board regarding the issuance of shares. Section 6.21(a).

Practical Advice

To protect the value of your shares from dilution, when organizing a close corporation, you should consider including in the charter a carefully drafted provision reserving to the shareholders the power to determine the value of consideration received for the issuance of additional shares.

34-3e LIABILITY FOR SHARES

A purchaser of shares has no liability to the corporation or its creditors with respect to the shares except to pay the corporation either the consideration for which the shares were authorized to be issued or the consideration specified in the preincorporation stock subscription. Section 6.22(a). When the corporation receives that consideration, the shares are fully paid and nonassessable. Section 6.21(d). A transferee who acquires these shares in good faith and without knowledge or notice that the full consideration had not been paid is not personally liable to the corporation or its creditors for the unpaid portion of the consideration.

34-4 Classes of Shares

Corporations are generally authorized by statute to issue different classes of stock, which may vary with respect to their rights to dividends, their voting rights, and their right to share in the assets of the corporation upon liquidation. The usual classifications of stock are common and preferred shares. Although the Revised Act has eliminated the terms *preferred* and *common*, it permits the issuance of shares with different preferences, limitations, and relative rights. Section 6.01. As amended in 2002, the Revised Act permits the creation of classes or series of shares with terms that vary among holders of the same class or series, so long as the variations are explicitly set forth in the articles of incorporation. The Revised Act, however, explicitly requires that the charter authorize "(1) one or more classes or series of shares that together have unlimited voting rights, and (2) one or more classes or series of shares (which may be the same class, classes, or series as those with voting rights) that together are entitled to receive the net assets of the corporation upon dissolution." Section 6.01(b). In most States, however, even nonvoting shares may vote on certain mergers, share exchanges, and other fundamental changes which affect that class of shares as a class. See *Chapter 36*.

34-4a COMMON STOCK

Common stock does not have any special contract rights or preferences. Often the only class of stock outstanding, it generally represents the greatest proportion of the corporation's capital structure and bears the greatest risk of loss should the enterprise fail.

Common stock may be divided into one or more classes bearing designations, limitations, or relative rights stated in the articles of incorporation. Section 6.01. The Revised Act and some States permit common stock to be redeemable or convertible. Section 6.01(c)(2). The articles also may limit or deny the voting rights of classes of common shares, but at least one or more classes of shares must together have unlimited voting rights. Section 6.01(b). For example, Class A common may be entitled to three times the dividends per share to which Class B common is entitled. Or Class A common may be entitled to elect six directors while Class B common elects three directors. Or Class A common may have two votes per share while Class B common has no votes per share.

34-4b PREFERRED STOCK

Stock generally is considered preferred stock if it has contractual rights superior to those of common stock with regard to dividends, assets upon liquidation, or both. (Most preferred stock has both dividend and liquidation preferences.) Other special rights or privileges generally do not remove stock from the common stock classification. The articles of incorporation must provide for the contractual rights and preferences of an issue of preferred stock. Section 6.01(c).

Notwithstanding the special rights and preferences that distinguish preferred from common stock, both represent a contribution of capital. Preferred stock is no more a debt than common, and until a dividend is declared, the holder of preferred shares is not a creditor of the corporation. Furthermore, the rights of preferred shareholders are subordinate to the rights of the corporation's creditors.

DIVIDEND PREFERENCES Though the holders of an issue of preferred stock with a dividend preference will receive full dividends before any dividend may be paid to holders of common stock, no dividend is payable upon any class of stock, common or preferred, unless such dividend has been declared by the board of directors. The dividend preference may be described in terms of dollars per share ("$3 preferred") or as a percentage of par value ("10 percent preferred").

Preferred stock may provide that dividends are cumulative, noncumulative, or cumulative to the extent earned. For **cumulative** stock, if the board does not declare regular dividends on the preferred stock, such omitted dividends cumulate, and no dividend may be declared on common stock until all dividend arrearages on the preferred stock are declared and paid. For **noncumulative** stock, regular dividends do not cumulate upon the board's failure to declare them, and all rights to a dividend for the period omitted are gone forever. Accordingly, noncumulative stock has a priority over common only during a fiscal period in which a dividend on common stock is declared. Unless the charter expressly makes the dividends on preferred stock noncumulative, the courts generally hold them to be cumulative. **Cumulative-to-the-extent-earned** stock cumulates unpaid dividends only to the extent that funds were legally available to pay such dividends during that fiscal period.

Preferred stock also may be participating, although generally it is not. **Participating preferred** shares are entitled to their original dividend, and after the common shares receive a specified amount, the participating preferred stock shares with the common stock in any additional dividends. The manner in which preferred stock participates in dividends with common stock must be specified in the articles of incorporation. For example, a class of participating preferred stock could be entitled to share at the same rate with the common stock in any additional distribution of earnings for a given year *after* provision has been made for paying the prior preferred dividend and for paying dividends on the common at a rate equal to the fixed rate of the preferred.

LIQUIDATION PREFERENCES After a corporation has been dissolved, its assets liquidated, and the claims of its creditors satisfied, the remaining assets are distributed *pro rata* among the shareholders according to their priority as provided in the articles of incorporation. In the event that a class of stock with a dividend preference does not expressly provide for a preference of any kind upon dissolution and liquidation, its holders share *pro rata* with the common shareholders.

When the articles provide a liquidation preference, preferred stock has priority over common stock to the extent the articles state. In addition, if specified, preferred shares may participate beyond the liquidation preference in a stated ratio with other classes of shares. Such shares are said to be participating preferred with reference to liquidation. Preferred shares not so specified do not participate beyond the liquidation preference.

ADDITIONAL RIGHTS AND LIMITATIONS Preferred stock may have additional rights, designations, and limitations. For instance, it may be expressly denied voting rights if the incorporation statute so permits, or it may be redeemable by the corporation or convertible into shares of another class. Sections 6.01(c) and 7.21(a). Preferred stock is typically non-voting.

Practical Advice

When organizing a corporation, consider issuing common stock to the original shareholders and preferred stock to subsequent investors.

34-4c STOCK OPTIONS

A corporation may issue **stock options** entitling their holders to purchase from the corporation shares of a specified class or classes. A **stock warrant** is a type of stock option that typically has a longer term and is freely transferable. A **stock right** is a short-term warrant. The board of directors determines the terms upon which stock rights, options, or warrants are issued; their form and content; and the consideration for which the shares are to be issued. Section 6.24. Stock options or warrants are used in incentive compensation plans for directors, officers, and employees. Corporations also use them in raising capital to make one class of securities more attractive by including in it the right to purchase shares in another class immediately or at a later date.

♦ **SEE FIGURE 34-2:** *Debt and Equity Securities*

DIVIDENDS AND OTHER DISTRIBUTIONS

The board of directors, in its discretion, determines when and in what amount to declare distributions and dividends. The corporation's working capital requirements, shareholder expectations, tax consequences, and other factors influence the board as it creates distribution policy. In addition, the conditions under which the earnings of a business may be paid out in the form of dividends or other distributions of corporate assets will depend upon the contractual rights of those who hold the particular shares involved or shares having superior rights, provisions in the charter and bylaws of the corporation, and provisions of the State incorporation statute that are designed to protect creditors and shareholders from the dissipation of corporate assets. Creditors receive more significant protection under contractual restrictions typically included in their loan agreements, as well as under State fraudulent conveyance laws and Federal bankruptcy law.

FIGURE 34-2 Debt and Equity Securities

	Debt	Equity	
		Preferred	**Common**
Ownership Interest	No	Yes	Yes
Obligation to Repay Principal	Yes	No	No
Fixed Maturity	Yes	No	No
Obligation to Pay Income	Yes	No	No
Preference on Income	Yes	Yes	No
Preference on Liquidation	Yes	Yes	No
Voting Rights	Some States	Yes, unless denied	Yes, unless denied
Redeemable	Yes	Yes	In some States
Convertible	Yes	Yes	In some States

34-5 Types of Dividends and Other Distributions

The Revised Act defines a **distribution** as

> a direct or indirect transfer of money or other property (except its own shares) or incurrence of indebtedness by a corporation to or for the benefit of its shareholders in respect of any of its shares. A distribution may be in the form of a declaration or payment of a dividend; a purchase, redemption, or other acquisition of shares; a distribution of indebtedness; or otherwise. Section 1.40(6).

The comments to this section explain that the term *indirect* is intended to include any other transaction the substance of which is clearly the same as that of a typical dividend or share repurchase, without regard to how the transaction is labeled or structured. Stock dividends and stock splits, which are not included in this definition, will also be covered in this section.

The Revised Act validates in close corporations unanimous shareholder agreements by which the shareholders may relax traditional corporate formalities. Section 7.32. This section, for example, expressly authorizes shareholder agreements that permit making distributions not in proportion to share ownership.

34-5a CASH DIVIDENDS

The most customary type of dividend is a cash dividend, declared and paid at regular intervals from legally available funds. These dividends may vary in amount, depending upon the policy of the board of directors and the earnings of the enterprise.

34-5b PROPERTY DIVIDENDS

Although dividends are almost always paid in cash, shareholders occasionally receive a property dividend, a distribution of earnings in the form of property. On one occasion, a distillery declared and paid a dividend in bonded whiskey.

34-5c STOCK DIVIDENDS

A stock or share dividend is a proportional distribution of additional shares of the capital stock of a corporation to its shareholders. The practical and legal significance of a stock dividend differs greatly from that of a dividend payable in cash or property. Following the payment of a stock dividend, the assets of the corporation are no less than they were before, and the shareholder's relative interest in the net worth of the corporation is no greater than it was before, except possibly where the dividend is paid in shares of a different class. His shares will each represent a smaller proportionate interest in the corporation's assets, but by reason of the increase in the number of shares, his total investment will remain the same. Accordingly, a stock dividend is *not* considered a distribution. Under incorporation statutes recognizing par value and stated capital, a stock dividend results in the transfer from surplus to stated capital of an amount equal to the par value of the stock dividend.

34-5d STOCK SPLITS

In a stock split, the corporation simply breaks each of the issued and outstanding shares into a greater number of shares, each representing a proportionately smaller interest in the corporation. Under incorporation statutes recognizing par value and stated capital, the par value of the shares to be split is divided among the new shares. The usual purpose of a stock split is to lower the price per share to a more marketable price and thus increase the number of potential shareholders. Like a stock dividend, a stock split is not a distribution; unlike a stock dividend, a split entails no transfer of surplus to stated capital.

34-5e LIQUIDATING DIVIDENDS

Although dividends ordinarily are identified with the distribution of profits, a distribution of capital assets to shareholders is referred to as a liquidating dividend in some jurisdictions. Incorporation statutes usually require that the shareholder be informed when a distribution is a liquidating dividend.

34-5f REDEMPTION OF SHARES

Redemption is the repurchase by the corporation of its own shares, usually at its own option. The Model Act and the statutes of many States permit corporations to redeem preferred shares but not common stock; the Revised Act, in contrast, does not prohibit redeemable common stock. The articles of incorporation must expressly provide for the power of redemption.

34-5g ACQUISITION OF SHARES

A corporation may acquire its own shares. Such shares, unless canceled, are referred to as treasury shares. Under the Revised Act, such shares are considered authorized but unissued. Section 6.31. As with redemption, the acquisition of shares constitutes a distribution to shareholders and has an effect similar to a dividend.

34-6 Legal Restrictions on Dividends and Other Distributions

Several legal restrictions limit the amount of distributions a board of directors may declare. Though all States have statutes restricting the funds that are legally available for dividends and other distributions of corporate assets, lender-imposed contractual restrictions often limit the declaration of dividends and distributions even more stringently.

States restrict the payment of dividends and other distributions to protect creditors. All States impose the **equity insolvency test**, which prohibits the payment of any dividend or other distribution when the corporation either is insolvent or would become so through the payment of the dividend or distribution. **Insolvent** in the equity sense indicates the inability of a corporation to pay its debts as they become due in the usual course of business. In addition, almost all States impose further restrictions regarding the funds that

are legally available to pay dividends and other distributions. These additional restrictions are based upon the corporation's assets or balance sheet, whereas the equity insolvency test is based upon the corporation's cash flow.

34-6a DEFINITIONS

The legal, asset-based restrictions upon the payment of dividends or other distributions involve the concepts of earned surplus, surplus, net assets, stated capital, and capital surplus.

Earned surplus consists of the corporation's undistributed net profits, income, gains, and losses, computed from its date of incorporation.

Surplus is the amount by which the net assets of a corporation exceed its stated capital.

Net assets equal the amount by which the total assets of a corporation exceed its total debts.

Stated capital is the sum of the consideration the corporation has received for its issued stock, excepting the consideration properly allocated to capital surplus but including any amount transferred to stated capital when a stock dividend is declared. In the case of par value shares, the amount of stated capital is the total par value of all the issued shares. In the case of no par stock, it is the consideration the corporation has received for all the no par shares that it has issued, except that amount allocated to capital surplus or paid-in surplus.

Capital surplus means the entire surplus of a corporation other than its earned surplus. It may result from an allocation of part of the consideration received for no par shares, from any consideration in excess of par value received for par shares, or from a higher reappraisal of certain corporate assets.

♦ SEE FIGURE 34-3: *Key Concepts in Legal Restrictions upon Distributions*

34-6b LEGAL RESTRICTIONS ON CASH DIVIDENDS

Each State imposes an equity insolvency test on the payment of dividends. The States differ regarding the asset-based or balance sheet test they apply. Some apply the earned surplus test, others use the surplus test, and the Revised Act adopts a net assets test.

EARNED SURPLUS TEST Unreserved and unrestricted earned surplus is available for dividends in all jurisdictions. Many States permit dividends to be paid *only* from earned surplus; corporations in these jurisdictions may not pay dividends out of capital surplus or stated capital. In addition, the corporation may not pay dividends if it is or would be rendered insolvent in the equity sense by the payment. The MBCA used this test until 1980.

FIGURE 34-3 Key Concepts in Legal Restrictions upon Distributions

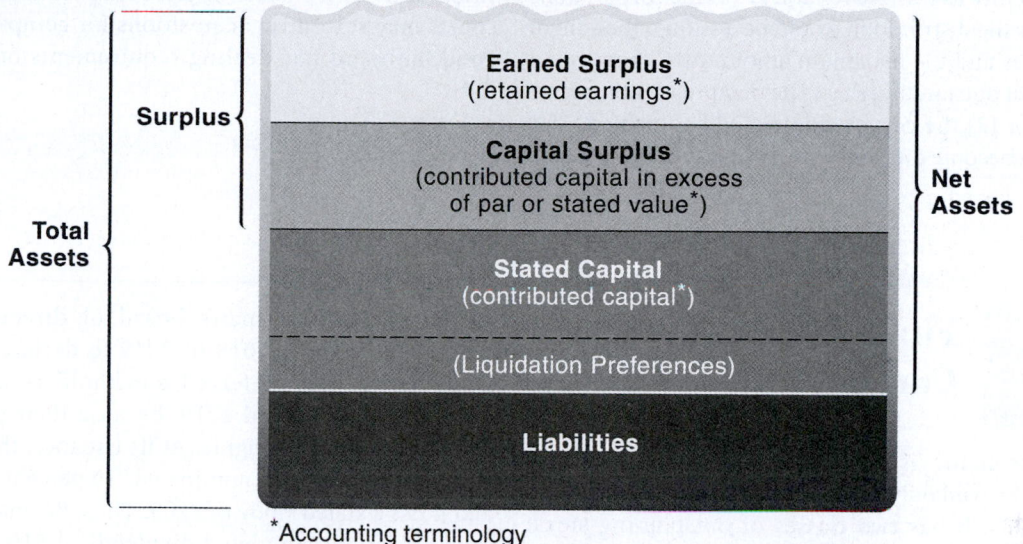

*Accounting terminology

SURPLUS TEST A number of less restrictive States permit dividends to be paid out of any surplus—earned or capital. Some of these States express this test by prohibiting dividends that impair stated capital. Moreover, dividends may not be paid if the corporation is or would be rendered insolvent in the equity sense by the payment.

NET ASSETS TEST The MBCA, as amended in 1980, and the Revised Act have adopted a net assets test. Section 6.40 of the Revised Act as amended states:

(c) No distribution may be made if, after giving it effect:
(1) the corporation would not be able to pay its debts as they become due in the usual course of business; or
(2) the corporation's total assets would be less than the sum of its total liabilities plus (unless the articles of incorporation permit otherwise) the amount that would be needed, if the corporation were to be dissolved at the time of the distribution, to satisfy the preferential rights upon dissolution of shareholders whose preferential rights are superior to those receiving the distribution.

34-6c LEGAL RESTRICTIONS ON LIQUIDATING DISTRIBUTIONS

Even those States that do not permit cash dividends to be paid from capital surplus usually will permit distributions, or dividends, in partial liquidation from that source. Before 1980, the Model Act had such a provision. A distribution paid out of such surplus is a return to the shareholders of part of their investment.

The corporation may make no such distribution, however, when it is insolvent or when the distribution would render it so. Distributions from capital surplus are also restricted to protect the liquidation preference and cumulative dividend arrearages of preferred shareholders. Unless provided for in the articles of incorporation, a liquidating dividend must be authorized not only by the board of directors but also by the affirmative vote of the holders of a majority of the outstanding shares of stock of each class.

Because the Revised Act does not distinguish between cash and liquidating dividends, it therefore imposes upon liquidating dividends the same limitations it imposes upon cash dividends, discussed above. Section 6.40.

34-6d LEGAL RESTRICTIONS ON REDEMPTION AND ACQUISITION OF SHARES

To protect creditors and holders of other classes of shares, most States place statutory restrictions upon redemption. A corporation may not redeem or purchase its redeemable shares when insolvent or when such redemption or purchase would render it insolvent or would reduce its net assets below the aggregate amount payable upon shares having prior or equal rights to the assets of the corporation upon involuntary dissolution.

A corporation may purchase its own shares only out of earned surplus or, if the articles of incorporation permit or if the shareholders approve, out of capital surplus. As with redemption, the corporation may make no purchase of shares when insolvent or when such purchase would make it insolvent.

The Revised Act permits a corporation to purchase, redeem, or otherwise acquire its own shares unless (1) the corporation's total assets after the distribution would be less than the sum of its total liabilities and the maximum amount that then would be payable for all outstanding shares having preferential rights in liquidation or (2) the corporation would be unable to pay its debts as they become due in the usual course of its business. Section 6.40.

Additional restrictions may apply to a corporation's acquisition of its own shares. In close corporations, for example, courts may scrutinize acquisitions for compliance with the good faith and fair dealing requirements of the fiduciary duty.

♦ *See Cases 34-2 and 35-3*

APPLYING THE LAW

Financial Structure of Corporations

FACTS Borman, Inc., is incorporated in a state that permits dividends to be paid only from unreserved and unrestricted earned surplus. It has two classes of outstanding stock: one hundred thousand shares of common stock and four thousand shares of 10 percent cumulative preferred stock with a stated value of $100. In each of 2018, 2019, and 2020, Borman had enough unreserved and unrestricted surplus earnings to pay $100,000 in dividends. However, in 2018 and 2019, the board declared no dividend. In 2020, the board declared a dividend of $10 per share on the preferred and $0.75 per share on the common stock.

ISSUE To what dividend payments are Borman's stockholders entitled?

RULE OF LAW The most common type of distribution is a cash dividend, which is payable from legally available funds. In all jurisdictions, unreserved and unrestricted earned surplus is available for payment of dividends, but in Borman's State, dividends may be paid *only* from unreserved and unrestricted earned surplus. The board of directors has the discretion, but not the obligation, to declare distributions to shareholders. However, the actual amount and timing of a corporation's dividend payments depends on such factors as its working capital requirements, shareholder expectations, and tax consequences.

Corporations are statutorily authorized to issue different classes of stock, which vary in their rights to vote, to dividends, and to payments upon liquidation. The usual stock classifications are common and preferred. Common stock does not have any special contract rights or preferences. Preferred stock has a preference over common stock with respect to payment of dividends and/or with respect to distributions upon liquidation. If preferred stock has a cumulative dividend preference, no dividends may be paid to common stockholders until any current *as well as* accumulated dividends on that preferred stock have been declared and paid.

APPLICATION Borman's board of directors had no obligation in either 2018 or 2019 to declare a dividend. Nonetheless, the preferred stockholders accumulated dividends in 2018 and 2019, because their stock carries cumulative dividend rights. At its issuance, this particular preferred stock was denominated "10 percent cumulative," and it has a stated value of $100. Thus, Borman's preferred stockholders accumulated dividends of $10 per share in each of 2018 and 2019, despite the fact Borman's board did not declare a dividend. This means that before the 2020 dividend declaration, the preferred stockholders were already owed $20 per share. Before a dividend for the common stock can be declared and paid in 2020, this $80,000 ($20 × 4,000 shares) arrearage must be paid to the preferred stockholders. Since the earned surplus available for distribution in 2020 is only $100,000, that year's preferred stock dividend and accumulated arrearages—totaling $120,000—cannot be paid in full. If the board declares and pays this $100,000 to the preferred shareholders, the $20,000 remaining unpaid to them carries forward as an arrearage.

Because there is still an arrearage owed to preferred stockholders, the declaration of a dividend on the common stock was improper, and the common stockholders will receive no dividend payment in 2020. Unlike preferred stockholders, owners of common stock are entitled to dividends only when declared by the board of directors—and then only after dividend arrearages and any current dividend preferences on the preferred stock are declared and paid.

CONCLUSION The preferred dividend declaration of $10 per share on the preferred stock is proper. If the board chooses to pay out the remainder of the legally available funds as dividends, the preferred stockholders are entitled to that remainder resulting in a distribution to them of $25 per share. The remaining $5 per share not paid to the preferred stockholders would accumulate. Common stockholders are entitled to nothing; moreover, they will not be paid any dividend in the future until any arrearages and then-current dividends owed to the preferred stockholders have been paid in full.

34-7 Declaration and Payment of Distributions

The declaration of dividends and other distributions is within the discretion of the board of directors and may not be delegated. If the charter clearly and expressly provides for mandatory dividends, however, the board must comply with the provision. Nonetheless, such provisions are extremely infrequent, and shareholders cannot usurp the board's power in any other way, although it is in their power to elect a new board. Moreover, the board cannot discriminate in its declaration of dividends among shareholders of the same class.

34-7a SHAREHOLDERS' RIGHT TO COMPEL A DIVIDEND

Should the directors fail to declare a dividend, a shareholder may bring a suit in equity against them and the corporation to seek a mandatory injunction requiring the directors to declare a dividend. Courts of equity are reluctant to order an injunction of this kind, which involves substituting the business judgment of the court for that of the directors elected by the shareholders. Where the evidence shows noncorporate motives or personal animosity as the basis for a refusal to declare dividends, however, a court may require the directors to distribute an apparently reasonable portion of the earnings. This is not a frequent occurrence; *Dodge v. Ford Motor Co.* is a landmark example.

With respect to the directors' discretion regarding the declaration of dividends, a preferred shareholder having prior rights with respect to dividends occupies a position identical to that of a holder of common shares. In the absence of special contractual or statutory rights, the holder of preferred shares, like the holder of common ones, must abide by the directors' decision.

◆ *See Case 34-3*

34-7b EFFECT OF DECLARATION OF A DISTRIBUTION

Once lawfully and properly declared, a cash distribution is considered a debt the corporation owes to the shareholders. It follows from this debtor–creditor relationship that, once declared, a distribution cannot be rescinded without the shareholders' consent. A stock dividend, however, may be revoked unless actually distributed.

34-8 Liability for Improper Dividends and Distributions

The Revised Act imposes personal liability upon the directors of a corporation who vote for or assent to the declaration of a dividend or other distribution of corporate assets contrary to the incorporation statute or the articles of incorporation. Section 8.33(a). The measure of damages is the amount of the dividend or distribution in excess of the amount that the corporation lawfully may have paid.

A **director** is not liable if she acted in accordance with the relevant standard of conduct: in good faith, with reasonable care, and in a manner she reasonably believed to be in the best interests of the corporation. Sections 8.30 and 8.33. (This standard of conduct will be discussed in the next chapter.) In discharging this duty, a director is entitled to rely in good faith upon financial statements presented by the corporation's officers, public accountants, or finance committee. Such statements must be prepared on the basis of "accounting practices and principles that are reasonable in the circumstances or on a fair valuation or other method that is reasonable in the circumstances." Section 6.40(d). According to the Comments to this section, generally accepted accounting principles are *always* reasonable in the circumstances; other accounting principles *may* be acceptable under a general standard of reasonableness.

A **shareholder's** obligation to repay an illegally declared dividend depends upon a variety of factors, which may include the good or bad faith in which the shareholder accepted the dividend, his knowledge of the facts, the solvency or insolvency of the corporation, and, in some instances, special statutory provisions. Statutory liability on the part of directors does not relieve shareholders of the duty to make repayment.

A shareholder who receives illegal dividends with knowledge of their illegality is under a duty to refund them. Section 8.33(b). Where the corporation is insolvent, the shareholder may retain not even a dividend he received in good faith, as the assets of an insolvent corporation are regarded as a trust fund for its creditors. Where an unsuspecting shareholder receives an illegal dividend from a solvent corporation, however, the majority rule is that the corporation cannot compel a refund.

◆ SEE FIGURE 34-4: *Liability for Improper Distributions*

FIGURE 34-4 Liability for Improper Distributions

	Corporation Solvent	Corporation Insolvent
Nonbreaching Director	No	No
Breaching Director	Yes	Yes
Knowing Shareholder	Yes	Yes
Innocent Shareholder	No	Yes

C H A P T E R   S U M M A R Y

DEBT SECURITIES

AUTHORITY TO ISSUE DEBT SECURITIES	**Definitions** • *Debt Security* source of capital creating no ownership interest and involving the corporation's promise to repay funds lent to it • *Bond* a debt security **Rule** each corporation has the power to issue debt securities as determined by the board of directors
TYPES OF DEBT SECURITIES	**Unsecured Bonds** called debentures; have only the obligation of the corporation behind them **Secured Bonds** are claims against a corporation's general assets as well as liens on specific property **Income Bonds** condition to some extent the payment of interest on corporate earnings **Participating Bonds** call for a stated percentage of return regardless of earnings, with additional payments dependent upon earnings **Convertible Bonds** may be exchanged for other securities **Callable Bonds** bonds subject to redemption

EQUITY SECURITIES

ISSUANCE OF SHARES	**Definitions** • *Equity Security* source of capital creating an ownership interest in the corporation • *Share* a proportionate ownership interest in a corporation • *Treasury Stock* shares reacquired by a corporation **Authority to Issue Shares** only those shares authorized in the articles of incorporation may be issued **Preemptive Rights** right to purchase a *pro rata* share of new stock offerings **Amount of Consideration for Shares** shares are deemed fully paid and nonassessable when a corporation receives the consideration for which the board of directors authorized the issuance of the shares, which in the case of par value stock must be at least par **Payment for Newly Issued Shares** may be cash, property, and services actually rendered, as determined by the board of directors; under the Revised Act, promises to contribute cash, property, or services are also permitted
CLASSES OF SHARES	**Common Stock** stock not having any special contract rights **Preferred Stock** stock having contractual rights superior to those of common stock • *Dividend Preferences* must receive full dividends before any dividend may be paid on common stock • *Liquidation Preferences* priority over common stock in corporate assets upon liquidation **Stock Options** contractual right to purchase stock from a corporation

DIVIDENDS AND OTHER DISTRIBUTIONS

TYPES OF DIVIDENDS AND OTHER DISTRIBUTIONS	**Distributions** transfers of property by a corporation to any of its shareholders in respect of its shares **Cash Dividends** the most common type of distribution **Property Dividends** distribution in the form of property **Stock Dividends** a proportional distribution of additional shares of stock **Stock Splits** each of the outstanding shares is broken into a greater number of shares **Liquidating Dividends** a distribution of capital assets to shareholders **Redemption of Shares** a corporation's exercise of the right to purchase its own shares **Acquisition of Shares** a corporation's repurchase of its own shares
LEGAL RESTRICTIONS ON DIVIDENDS AND OTHER DISTRIBUTIONS	**Legal Restrictions on Cash Dividends** dividends may be paid only if the cash flow and applicable balance sheet tests are satisfied • *Cash Flow Test* a corporation must not be or become insolvent (unable to pay its debts as they become due in the usual course of business) • *Balance Sheet Test* varies among the States and includes the earned surplus test (available in all States), the surplus test, and the net assets test (used by the Model and Revised Acts) **Legal Restrictions on Liquidating Distributions** States usually permit distribution in partial liquidation from capital surplus unless the company is insolvent **Legal Restrictions on Redemptions of Shares** in most States, a corporation may not redeem shares when insolvent or when such redemption would render it insolvent **Legal Restrictions on Acquisition of Shares** restrictions similar to those on cash dividends usually apply
DECLARATION AND PAYMENT OF DISTRIBUTIONS	**Shareholders' Right to Compel a Distribution** the declaration of distributions is within the discretion of the board of directors, and only rarely will a court substitute its business judgment for that of the board's **Effect of Declaration of a Distribution** once properly declared, a distribution is considered a debt the corporation owes to the shareholders
LIABILITY FOR IMPROPER DIVIDENDS AND DISTRIBUTIONS	**Directors** the directors who assent to an improper dividend are liable for the unlawful amount of the dividend **Shareholders** a shareholder must return illegal dividends if he knew of the illegality, if the dividend resulted from his fraud, or if the corporation is insolvent

C A S E S

CASE
34-1

Debt Securities
METROPOLITAN LIFE INSURANCE COMPANY v. RJR NABISCO, INC.

United States District Court, S.D. New York, 1989
716 F.Supp. 1504

Walker, J.

Introduction

The corporate parties to this action are among the country's most sophisticated financial institutions, as familiar with the Wall Street investment community and the securities market as American consumers are with the Oreo cookies and Winston cigarettes made by defendant RJR Nabisco, Inc. (sometimes "the company" or "RJR Nabisco"). The present action traces its origins to October 20, 1988, when F. Ross Johnson, then the

Chief Executive Officer of RJR Nabisco, proposed a $17 billion leveraged buy-out ("LBO") of the company's shareholders, at $75 per share. (Court's footnote: "A leveraged buy-out occurs when a group of investors, usually including members of a company's management team, buy the company under financial arrangements that include little equity and significant new debt. The necessary debt financing typically includes mortgages or high risk/high yield bonds, popularly known as "junk bonds." Additionally, a portion of this debt is generally secured by the company's assets. Some of the acquired company's assets are usually sold after the transaction is completed in order to reduce the debt incurred in the acquisition." [See *Chapter 36.*]) Within a few days, a bidding war developed among the investment group led by Johnson and the investment firm of Kohlberg Kravis Roberts & Co. ("KKR"), and others. On December 1, 1988, a special committee of RJR Nabisco directors, established by the company specifically to consider the competing proposals, recommended that the company accept the KKR proposal, a $24 billion LBO that called for the purchase of the company's outstanding stock at roughly $109 per share.

* * *

Plaintiffs * * * allege, in short, that RJR Nabisco's actions have drastically impaired the value of bonds previously issued to plaintiffs by, in effect, misappropriating the value of those bonds to help finance the LBO and to distribute an enormous windfall to the company's shareholders. As a result, plaintiffs argue, they have unfairly suffered a multimillion dollar loss in the value of their bonds.

* * *

Although the numbers involved in this case are large, and the financing necessary to complete the LBO unprecedented, the legal principles nonetheless remain discrete and familiar. Yet while the instant motions thus primarily require the Court to evaluate and apply traditional rules of equity and contract interpretation, plaintiffs do raise issues of first impression in the context of an LBO. At the heart of the present motions lies plaintiffs' claim that RJR Nabisco violated a restrictive covenant—not an explicit covenant found within the four corners of the relevant bond indentures, but rather an *implied* covenant of good faith and fair dealing—not to incur the debt necessary to facilitate the LBO and thereby betray what plaintiffs claim was the fundamental basis of their bargain with the company. The company, plaintiffs assert, consistently reassured its bondholders that it had a "mandate" from its Board of Directors to maintain RJR Nabisco's preferred credit rating. Plaintiffs ask this Court first to imply a covenant of good faith and fair dealing that would prevent the recent transaction, then to hold that this covenant has been breached, and finally to require RJR Nabisco to redeem their bonds.

RJR Nabisco defends the LBO by pointing to express provisions in the bond indentures that * * * permit mergers and the assumption of additional debt. These provisions, as well as others that could have been included but were not, were known to the market and to plaintiffs, sophisticated investors who freely bought the bonds and were equally free to sell them at any time. Any attempt by this Court to create contractual terms *post hoc*, defendants contend, not only finds no basis in the controlling law and undisputed facts of this case, but also would constitute an impermissible invasion into the free and open operation of the marketplace.

For the reasons set forth below, this Court agrees with defendants. There being no express covenant between the parties that would restrict the incurrence of new debt, and no perceived direction to that end from covenants that are express, this Court will not imply a covenant to prevent the recent LBO and thereby create an indenture term that, while bargained for in other contexts, was not bargained for here and was not even within the mutual contemplation of the parties.

Background
* * *

The Parties

Metropolitan Life Insurance Co. ("MetLife"), incorporated in New York, is a life insurance company that provides pension benefits for 42 million individuals. According to its most recent annual report, MetLife's assets exceed $88 billion and its debt securities holdings exceed $49 billion. [Citation.] MetLife alleges that it owns $340,542,000 in principal amount of six separate RJR Nabisco debt issues, bonds allegedly purchased between July 1975 and July 1988. Some bonds become due as early as this year; others will not become due until 2017. The bonds bear interest rates of anywhere from 8 to 10.25 percent. MetLife also owned 186,000 shares of RJR Nabisco common stock at the time this suit was filed. [Citation.]

Jefferson-Pilot Life Insurance Co. ("Jefferson-Pilot") is a North Carolina company that has more than $3 billion in total assets, $1.5 billion of which are invested in debt securities. Jefferson-Pilot alleges that it owns $9.34 million in principal amount of three separate RJR Nabisco debt issues, allegedly purchased between June 1978 and June 1988. Those bonds, bearing interest rates of anywhere from 8.45 to 10.75 percent, become due in 1993 and 1998. [Citation.]

RJR Nabisco, a Delaware corporation, is a consumer products holding company that owns some of the country's best known product lines, including LifeSavers candy, Oreo cookies, and Winston cigarettes. The company was formed in 1985, when R.J. Reynolds Industries, Inc. ("R.J. Reynolds") merged with Nabisco Brands, Inc. ("Nabisco Brands"). In 1979, and thus before the R.J. Reynolds-Nabisco Brands merger, R.J. Reynolds acquired the Del Monte Corporation ("Del Monte"), which distributes canned fruits and vegetables. From January 1987 until February codefendant Johnson served as the company's CEO. KKR, a private investment firm, organizes funds through which investors provide pools of equity to finance LBOs. [Citation.]

The Indentures

The bonds implicated by this suit are governed by long, detailed indentures, which in turn are governed by New York contract law. No one disputes that the holders of public bond issues, like plaintiffs here, often enter the market after the indentures have been negotiated and memorialized. Thus, those indentures are often not the product of face-to-face negotiations between the ultimate holders and the issuing company. What remains equally true, however, is that underwriters ordinarily negotiate the terms of the indentures with the issuers. Since the underwriters must then sell or place the bonds, they necessarily negotiate in part with the interests of the buyers in mind. Moreover, these indentures were not secret agreements foisted upon unwitting participants in the bond market. No successive holder is required to accept or to continue to hold the bonds, governed by their accompanying indentures; indeed, plaintiffs readily admit that they could have sold their bonds right up until the announcement of the LBO. [Citation.] Instead, sophisticated investors like plaintiffs are well aware of the indenture terms and, presumably, review them carefully before lending hundreds of millions of dollars to any company.

* * *

Further, as plaintiffs themselves note, the contracts at issue "[do] not impose debt limits, since debt is assumed to be used for productive purposes." [Citation.]

Discussion

* * *

The indentures at issue clearly address the eventuality of a merger. They impose certain related restrictions not at issue in this suit, but no restriction that would prevent the recent RJR Nabisco merger transaction. * * *

* * *

In contracts like bond indentures, "an implied covenant . . . derives its substance directly from the language of the Indenture, and 'cannot give the holders of Debentures any rights inconsistent with those set out in the Indenture.' *[Where] plaintiffs' contractual rights [have not been] violated, there can have been no breach of an implied covenant.*" [Citation.] (emphasis added).

* * *

It is not necessary to decide that indentures like those at issue could never support a finding of additional benefits, under different circumstances with different parties. Rather, for present purposes, it is sufficient to conclude what obligation is not covered, either explicitly or implicitly, by these contracts held by these plaintiffs. Accordingly, this Court holds that the "fruits" of these indentures do not include an implied restrictive covenant that would prevent the incurrence of new debt to facilitate the recent LBO. To hold otherwise would permit these plaintiffs to straight-jacket the company in order to guarantee their investment. These plaintiffs do not invoke an implied covenant of good faith to protect a legitimate, mutually contemplated benefit of the indentures; rather, they seek to have this Court create an additional benefit for which they did not bargain.

* * *

The sort of unbounded and one-sided elasticity urged by plaintiffs would interfere with and destabilize the market. * * * The Court has no reason to believe that the market, in evaluating bonds such as those at issue here, did not discount for the possibility that any company, even one the size of RJR Nabisco, might engage in an LBO heavily financed by debt. That the bonds did not lose any of their value until the October 20, 1988 announcement of a possible RJR Nabisco LBO only suggests that the market had theretofore evaluated the risks of such a transaction as slight.

* * *

[Judgment for defendant on count of breach of implied covenant.]

CASE 34-2

Legal Restrictions on Acquisition of Shares
COX ENTERPRISES, INC. v. PENSION BENEFIT GUARANTY CORPORATION

United States Court of Appeals, Eleventh Circuit, 2012
666 F.3D 697

COX, J.

Marc L. Davidson, Julia Davidson Truilo, Robert Truilo (the "Davidson Directors"), and the Pension Benefit Guaranty Corporation ("PBGC") appeal following the district court's order to distribute all of News-Journal Corporation's ("News-Journal") assets to Cox Enterprises, Inc. ("Cox"), a long-time shareholder of the closely-held News-Journal. * * *

Cox, a minority shareholder of News-Journal, filed suit in May of 2004 seeking relief for misuse of corporate funds and waste of corporate assets. This suit triggered Florida's election-to-purchase statute, Fla. Stat. §607.1436. News-Journal elected to pursue the option created by the statute to repurchase Cox's shares. Because the parties could not agree on the fair market value of Cox's shares, the statute required that the district court determine their value. The court set the value of Cox's shares at $129.2 million and directed the terms of payment in a September 27, 2006 order. * * *

Following the dictates of the election-to-purchase statute, the repurchase order dismissed Cox's original complaint for waste of corporate assets. * * *

[Between the valuation of Cox's shares and the court-ordered date for payment, News-Journal's ability to pay diminished significantly. In response, the district court appointed a receiver to manage News-Journal and prepare it for sale. After the sale of News-Journal's assets, the receiver solicited claims from News-Journal's various creditors. The district court disposed of these competing claims for News-Journal's limited assets by ordering the distribution of all the assets to Cox as payment for its shares. PBGC and the Davidson Directors appealed this order, contending that to distribute News-Journal's assets to Cox (a single News-Journal shareholder) pursuant to the repurchase order would render News-Journal insolvent and that the distributions-to-shareholders provision of the Florida business corporation statute forbids this payment.]

* * *

The [Florida] election-to-purchase statute allows a corporation or other shareholders to avoid dissolution by purchasing the shares of the petitioning shareholder who initiated a dissolution proceeding. After a corporation has elected to repurchase all of the shares owned by the petitioning shareholder, the parties may agree upon the value of the shares. [Citation.] If the parties cannot agree on the value, then the court must determine the "fair value" and enter an order detailing the terms for the repurchase fixed by the court. * * *

* * *

The statute, however, places an important condition on these payments. * * * [P]ayments made pursuant to a repurchase order must comply with Fla. Stat. §607.06401, which governs the distribution of corporate assets to shareholders.

This distributions-to-shareholders statute creates a scheme focused on the corporation's solvency to evaluate the propriety of distributions to shareholders. It provides in part:

No distribution may be made if, after giving it effect: (a) The corporation would not be able to pay its debts as they become due in the usual course of business; or (b) The corporation's total assets would be less than the sum of its total liabilities plus (unless the articles of incorporation permit otherwise) * * * the preferential rights upon dissolution of shareholders whose preferential rights are superior to those receiving the distribution.

[Citation.] Section 607.06401, by placing restrictions on the distribution of corporate assets, maintains the fundamental tenet of corporate law that creditors' claims on corporate assets are superior to claims of shareholders. To achieve this, a distribution of corporate assets to a shareholder must not result in the violation of one of these insolvency tests contained in Fla. Stat. §607.06401(3). The statute also explains when to measure the effect of a distribution * * *. It requires:

Except as provided in subsection (8), the effect of a distribution under subsection (3) is measured: (a) In the case of distribution by purchase, redemption, or other acquisition of the corporation's shares, as of the earlier of:

1. The date money or other property is transferred or debt incurred by the corporation, or
2. The date the shareholder ceases to be a shareholder with respect to the acquired shares.

Fla. Stat. §607.06401(6) (emphasis added). The exception contained in §607.06401(8) contains a different timing provision. It provides, "If the indebtedness is issued as a distribution, each payment of principal or interest is treated as a distribution, the effect of which is measured *on the date the payment is actually made*." Fla. Stat. §607.06401(8) (emphasis added). Thus any payment made pursuant to a repurchase order must satisfy the insolvency test of the distributions-to-shareholders statute judged at the time dictated by the distributions-to-shareholders statute.

* * *

We hold that any payment to Cox based on the district court's September 2006 repurchase order must comply with the condition of §607.1436(8) that the payment satisfy Florida's distributions-to-shareholders statute. This requires that we consider the application of that statute to this case.

As mentioned previously, Florida's distributions-to-shareholders statute forbids distributions by the corporation to shareholders if those distributions would render the corporation insolvent. The parties here dispute when the court should evaluate News-Journal's insolvency. Cox asserts that News-Journal's solvency should be measured as of September 2006 based on §607.06401(6), which states that the effect of a distribution is generally measured on the date the corporation incurs a debt or the date a shareholder ceases to be a shareholder. [Citation.] PBGC suggests that §607.06401(8) requires solvency be measured on the date of payment. As we have already highlighted, §607.06401(6) applies "[e]xcept as provided in subsection (8)." If subsection (8) applies in this case, then PBGC correctly recognizes that the effect of a distribution to Cox is measured on the date of payment.

Section 607.06401(8) provides, "If the indebtedness is issued as a distribution, each payment of principal or interest is treated as a distribution, the effect of which is measured on the date the payment is actually made." Fla. Stat. §607.06401(8). * * * Thus, on remand, the district court must consider whether a payment to Cox would comply with the insolvency test of the distributions-to-shareholders statute at the time of payment to Cox. * * * If on remand the district court finds a distribution to Cox would violate this section, News-Journal's other creditors should receive payment before any distribution is made to Cox.

* * *

We conclude that the district court misinterpreted Fla. Stat. §607.1436 and in so doing erred in its order for the distribution of News-Journal's assets. The district court's order dated August 13, 2010 is VACATED in its entirety. * * *

CASE 34-3

Declaration of Dividends
DODGE v. FORD MOTOR CO.
Supreme Court of Michigan, 1919
204 Mich. 459, 170 N.W. 668

Ostrander, J.

[Action in equity by John F. and Horace E. Dodge, plaintiffs, against the Ford Motor Company and its directors to compel the declaration of dividends and for an injunction restraining a contemplated expansion of the business. The complaint was filed in November 1916. Since 1909, the capital stock of the company has been $2,000,000, divided into 20,000 shares of a par value of $100 each, of which plaintiffs held 2,000. As of the close of business on July 31, 1916, the end of the company's fiscal year, the surplus above capital was $111,960,907.53 and the assets included cash on hand of $52,550,771.92.

For a number of years, the company had regularly paid quarterly dividends equal to 60 percent annually on the capital stock of $2,000,000. In addition, from December 1911 to October 1915, inclusive, eleven special dividends totaling $41,000,000 had been paid, and in November 1916, after this action was commenced, a special dividend of $2,000,000 was paid.

Plaintiffs' complaint alleged that Henry Ford, president of the company and a member of its board of directors, had declared it to be the settled policy of the company not to pay any special dividends in the future but to put back into the business all future earnings in excess of the regular quarterly dividend. Plaintiffs sought an injunction restraining the carrying out of the alleged declared policy of Henry Ford and a decree requiring the directors to pay a dividend of at least 75 percent of the accumulated cash surplus.

In December 1917, the trial court entered a decree requiring the directors to declare and pay a dividend of $19,275,385.96 and enjoining the corporation from using its funds for a proposed smelting plant and certain other planned projects. From this decree, defendants have appealed.]

* * *

The case for plaintiffs must rest upon the claim, and the proof in support of it, that the proposed expansion of the business of the corporation involving the further use of profits as capital, ought to be enjoined because inimical to the best interests of the company and its shareholders, and upon the further claim that in any event the withholding of the special dividend

asked for by plaintiffs is arbitrary action of the directors requiring judicial interference.

The rule which will govern courts in deciding these questions is not in dispute. * * * In [citation], it is stated:

> Profits earned by a corporation may be divided among its shareholders; but it is not a violation of the charter if they are allowed to accumulate and remain invested in the company's business. The managing agents of a corporation are impliedly invested with a discretionary power with regard to the time and manner of distributing its profits. They may apply profits in payment of floating or funded debts, or in development of the company's business; and so long as they do not abuse their discretionary powers, or violate the company's charter, the courts cannot interfere. But it is clear that the agents of a corporation, and even the majority, cannot arbitrarily withhold profits earned by the company, or apply them to any use which is not authorized by the company's charter. The nominal capital of a company does not necessarily limit the scope of its operations; a corporation may borrow money for the purpose of enlarging its business, and in many instances it may use profits for the same purpose. * * *

When plaintiffs made their complaint and demand for further dividends the Ford Motor Company had concluded its most prosperous year of business. The demand for its cars at the price of the preceding year continued. It could make and could market in the year beginning August 1, 1916, more than 500,000 cars. Sales of parts and repairs would necessarily increase. The cost of materials was likely to advance, and perhaps the price of labor, but it reasonably might have expected a profit for the year of upwards of $60,000,000. It had assets of more than $132,000,000, a surplus of almost $112,000,000, and its cash on hand and municipal bonds were nearly $54,000,000. Its total liabilities, including capital stock, was a little over $20,000,000. It had declared no special dividend during the business year except the October, 1915, dividend. It had been the practice, under similar circumstances, to declare larger dividends. Considering only these facts, a refusal to declare and pay further dividends appears to be not an exercise of discretion on the part of the directors, but an arbitrary refusal to do what the circumstances required to be done. These facts and others call upon the directors to justify their action, or failure or refusal to act. In justification, the defendants have offered testimony tending to prove, and which does prove, the following facts. It had been the policy of the corporation for a considerable time to annually reduce the selling price of cars, while keeping up, or improving their quality. As early as in June 1915 a general plan for the expansion of the productive capacity of the concern by a practical duplication of its plant had been talked over by the executive officers and directors and agreed upon, not all of the details having been settled and no formal action of directors having been taken. The erection of a smelter was considered, and engineering and other data in connection therewith secured. In consequence, it was determined not to reduce the selling price of cars for the year beginning August 1, 1915, but to maintain the price and to accumulate a large surplus to pay for the proposed expansion of plant and equipment, and perhaps to build a plant for smelting ore. It is hoped, by Mr. Ford, that eventually 1,000,000 cars will be annually produced. The contemplated changes will permit the increased output.

The plan, as affecting the profits of the business for the year beginning August 1, 1916, and thereafter, calls for a reduction in the selling price of cars. * * * In short, the plan does not call for and is not intended to produce immediately a more profitable business but a less profitable one; not only less profitable than formerly but less profitable than it is admitted it might be made. The apparent immediate effect will be to diminish the value of shares and the return to shareholders.

It is the contention of plaintiffs that the apparent effect of the plan is intended to be the continued and continuing effect of it and that it is deliberately proposed, not of record and not by official corporate declaration, but nevertheless proposed, to continue the corporation henceforth as a semieleemosynary institution and not as a business institution. In support of this contention they point to the attitude and to the expressions of Mr. Henry Ford.

Mr. Henry Ford is the dominant force in the business of the Ford Motor Company. No plan of operations could be adopted unless he consented, and no board of directors can be elected whom he does not favor. One of the directors of the company has no stock. One share was assigned to him to qualify him for the position, but it is not claimed that he owns it. A business, one of the largest in the world, and one of the most profitable, has been built up. It employs many men, at good pay.

"My ambition," said Mr. Ford, "is to employ still more men, to spread the benefits of this industrial system to the greatest possible number, to help them build up their lives and their homes. To do this we are putting the greatest share of our profits back in the business." * * *

The record, and especially the testimony of Mr. Ford, convinces that he has to some extent the attitude towards shareholders of one who has dispensed and distributed to them large gains and that they should be content to take what he chooses to give. His testimony creates the impression, also, that he thinks the Ford Motor Company has made too much money, has had too large profits, and that although large profits might still be earned, a sharing of them with the public, by reducing the price of the output of the company, ought to be undertaken. We have no doubt that certain sentiments, philanthropic and altruistic, creditable to Mr. Ford, had large influence in determining the policy to be pursued by the Ford Motor Company— the policy which has been herein referred to. * * *

These cases, after all, like all others in which the subject is treated, turn finally upon the point, the question, whether it appears that the directors were not acting for the best interest of the corporation. * * * The difference between an incidental humanitarian expenditure of corporate funds for the benefit of the employees, like the building of a hospital for their use and the employment of agencies for the betterment of their condition, and a general purpose and plan to benefit mankind at the expense of others, is obvious. * * * A business corporation is organized and carried on primarily for the profit of the stockholders. The powers of the directors are to be employed for that end. The discretion of directors is to be exercised in the choice of means to attain that end and does not extend to a change in the end itself, to the reduction of profits or to the nondistribution of profits among stockholders in order to devote them to other purposes. * * *

We are not, however, persuaded that we should interfere with the proposed expansion of the business of the Ford Motor Company. In view of the fact that the selling price of products may be increased at any time, the ultimate results of the larger business cannot be certainly estimated. The judges are not business experts. It is recognized that plans must often be made for a long future, for expected competition, for a continuing as well as an immediately profitable venture. The experience of the Ford Motor Company is evidence of capable management of its affairs. * * *

Defendants say, and it is true, that a considerable cash balance must be at all times carried by such a concern. But, as has been stated, there was a large daily, weekly, monthly, receipt of cash. The output was practically continuous and was continuously, and within a few days, turned into cash. Moreover, the contemplated expenditures were not to be immediately made. The large sum appropriated for the smelter plant was payable over a considerable period of time. So that, without going further, it would appear that, accepting and approving the plan of the directors, it was their duty to distribute on or near the first of August, 1916, a very large sum of money to stockholders. * * *

The decree of the court below fixing and determining the specific amount to be distributed to stockholders is affirmed. In other respects, except as to the allowance of costs, the said decree is reversed.

QUESTIONS

1. Olympic National Agencies was organized with an authorized capitalization of preferred stock and common stock. The articles of incorporation provided for a 7 percent annual dividend for the preferred stock. The articles further stated that the preferred stock would be given priority interests in the corporation's assets up to the par value of the stock. Subsequently, the shareholders voted to dissolve Olympic. Olympic's assets greatly exceeded its liabilities. The liquidating trustee petitioned the court for instructions on the respective rights of the shareholders in the assets of the corporation upon dissolution. The court ordered the trustee to distribute the corporate assets remaining after the preference of the preferred stock is satisfied to the common and preferred stockholders on a *pro rata* basis. Was the court correct in rendering this decision? Explain.

2. The XYZ Corporation was duly organized on July 10. Its certificate of incorporation provides for total authorized capital of $1 million, consisting of ten thousand shares of common stock with a par value of $100 per share. The corporation issues for cash a total of five hundred certificates, numbered 1 to 500 inclusive, representing various amounts of shares in the names of various individuals. The shares were all paid for in advance, so the certificates are all dated and mailed on the same day. The five hundred certificates of stock represent a total of ten thousand five hundred shares. Certificate 499 for three hundred shares was issued to Jane Smith. Certificate 500 for two hundred fifty shares was issued to William Jones. Is the validity of the stock thus issued in any way questionable? Explain. What are the rights of Smith and Jones? Explain.

3. Doris subscribed for two hundred shares of 12 percent cumulative, participating, redeemable, convertible, preferred shares of the Ritz Hotel Company with a par value of $100 per share. The subscription agreement provided that she was to receive a bonus of one share of common stock of $100 par value for each share of preferred stock. Doris fully paid her subscription agreement of $20,000 and received the two hundred shares of preferred stock and the bonus stock of two hundred shares of the par value common. The Ritz Hotel Company later becomes insolvent. Ronald, the receiver of the corporation, brings suit for $20,000, the par value of the common stock. What judgment? Discuss.

4. The Hyperion Company has an authorized capital stock of one thousand shares with a par value of $100 per share, of which nine hundred shares, all fully paid, were outstanding. Having an ample surplus, the Hyperion Company purchased from its shareholders one hundred shares at par. Subsequently, the Hyperion Company, needing additional working capital, issued two hundred shares to Alexander at $80 per share. Two years later, the Hyperion Company was forced into bankruptcy. Explain how much, if any, the trustee in bankruptcy may recover from Alexander.

5. For five years, Henry and James had been engaged as partners in building houses. They owned the equipment necessary to conduct the business and had an excellent reputation. In March, Joyce, who had previously been in the same kind of business, proposed that Henry, James, and Joyce form a corporation for the purpose of constructing medium-priced houses. They engaged attorney Portia, who did all the work required to incorporate the business under the name of Libra Corp.

   The certificate of incorporation authorized one thousand shares of $100 par value stock. At the organizational meeting of the incorporators, Henry, James, and Joyce were elected directors, and Libra Corp. issued a total of six hundred fifty shares for its stock. Henry and James each received two hundred shares in consideration of transferring to Libra Corp. the equipment and goodwill of their partnership, which had a combined value of more than $40,000. Joyce received two hundred shares in consideration for promising to work for Libra Corp. in the future, and Portia received fifty shares as compensation for the legal services she rendered in forming Libra Corp.

   Later that year, Libra Corp. suffered several financial setbacks and in December ceased operations. Explain what rights, if any, Libra Corp. has against Henry, James, Joyce, and Portia in connection with the original issuance of its shares.

6. Paul Bunyan is the owner of noncumulative 8 percent preferred stock in the Broadview Corporation, which had no earnings or profits in 2019. In 2020, the corporation had large profits and a surplus from which it might properly have declared dividends. The directors refused to do so, however, instead using the surplus to purchase goods necessary for the corporation's expanding business. The corporation earned a small profit in 2021. The directors at the end of 2021 declared a 10 percent dividend on the common stock and an 8 percent dividend on the preferred stock without paying preferred dividends for 2020.

   a. Is Bunyan entitled to dividends for 2019? For 2020? Explain.

   b. Is Bunyan entitled to a dividend of 10 percent rather than 8 percent in 2021? Explain.

7. Alpha Corporation has outstanding four hundred shares of $100 par value common stock, which has been issued and sold at $105 per share for a total of $42,000. Alpha is incorporated in State X, which has adopted the earned surplus test for all distributions. At a time when the assets of the corporation amount to $65,000 and the liabilities to creditors total $10,000, the directors learn that Rachel, who holds one hundred of the four hundred shares of stock, is planning to sell her shares on the open market for $10,500. Believing that this will not be in the best interest of the corporation, the directors enter into an agreement with Rachel to buy the shares from her for $10,500. About six months later, when the assets of the corporation have decreased to $50,000 and its liabilities, not including its liability to Rachel, have increased to $20,000, the directors use $10,000 to pay a dividend to all of the shareholders. The corporation later becomes insolvent.

   a. Does Rachel have any liability to the corporation or its creditors in connection with the reacquisition by the corporation of the one hundred shares? Explain.

   b. Was the payment of the $10,000 dividend proper? Why or why not?

8. Almega Corporation, organized under the laws of State S, has outstanding twenty thousand shares of $100 par value nonvoting preferred stock calling for noncumulative dividends of $5 per year; ten thousand shares of voting preferred stock with $50 par value, calling for cumulative dividends of $2.50 per year; and ten thousand shares of no par common stock. State S has adopted the earned surplus test for all distributions. As of the end of 2016, the corporation had no earned surplus. In 2017, the corporation had net earnings of $170,000; in 2018, $135,000; in 2019, $60,000; in 2020, $210,000; and in 2021, $120,000. The board of directors passed over all dividends during the four years from 2017 through 2020, because the company needed working capital for expansion purposes. In 2021, however, the directors declared on the noncumulative preferred shares a dividend of $5 per share, on the cumulative preferred stock a dividend of $12.50 per share, and on the common stock a dividend of $30 per share. The board submitted its declaration to the voting shareholders, and they ratified it. Before the dividends were paid, Payne, the record holder of five hundred shares of the noncumulative preferred stock, brought an appropriate action to restrain any payment to the cumulative preferred or common shareholders until the company paid to noncumulative preferred shareholders a full dividend for the period from 2017 to 2020. Decision? What is the maximum lawful dividend that may be paid to the owner of each share of common stock? Explain.

9. Sayre learned that Adams, Boone, and Chase were planning to form a corporation for the purpose of manufacturing and marketing a line of novelties to wholesale outlets. Sayre had patented a self-locking gas tank cap but lacked the financial backing to market it profitably. He negotiated with Adams, Boone, and Chase, who agreed to purchase the patent rights for $5,000 in cash and two hundred shares of $100 par value preferred stock in a corporation to be formed.

   The corporation was formed and Sayre's stock issued to him, but the corporation has refused to make the cash payment. It has also refused to declare dividends, although the business has been very profitable because of Sayre's patent and has a substantial earned surplus with a large cash balance on hand. It is selling the remainder of the originally authorized issue of preferred shares, ignoring Sayre's demand to purchase a proportionate number of these shares. What are Sayre's rights, if any? Discuss.

CASE PROBLEMS

10. Wood, the receiver of Stanton Oil Company, sued Stanton's shareholders to recover dividends paid to them for three years, claiming that at the time these dividends were declared, Stanton was in fact insolvent. Wood did not allege that the present creditors were also creditors when the dividends were paid. Were the dividends wrongfully paid? Explain.

11. International Distributing Export Company (I.D.E.) was organized as a corporation on September 7, 2014, under the laws of New York and commenced business on November 1, 2014. I.D.E. formerly had been in existence as a sole proprietorship. On October 31, 2014, the newly organized corporation had liabilities of $64,084. Its only assets, in the sum of $33,042, were those of the former sole proprietorship. The corporation, however, set up an asset on its balance sheet in the amount of $32,000 for goodwill. As a result of this entry, I.D.E. had a surplus at the end of each of its fiscal years from 2015 until 2020. Cano, a shareholder, received $7,144 in dividends from I.D.E. during the period from 2016 to 2021. May Fried, the trustee in bankruptcy of I.D.E., recover the amount of these dividends from Cano on the basis that they had been paid when I.D.E. was insolvent or when its capital was impaired? Explain.

12. GM Sub Corporation (GM Sub), a subsidiary of Grand Metropolitan Limited, acquired all outstanding shares of Liggett Group, Inc., a Delaware corporation. Rothschild International Corporation (Rothschild) was the owner of 650 shares of the 7 percent cumulative preferred stock of Liggett Group, Inc. According to Liggett's certificate of incorporation, the holders of the 7 percent preferred were to receive $100 per share "in the event of any liquidation of the assets of the Corporation." GM Sub had offered $70 per share for the 7 percent preferred, $158.63 for another class of preferred stock, and $69 for each common stock share. Liggett's board of directors approved the offer as fair and recommended acceptance by Liggett's shareholders. As a result, 39.8 percent of the 7 percent preferred shares was sold to GM Sub. In addition, GM Sub acquired 75.9 percent of the other preferred stock and 87.4 percent of the common stock. The acquisition of the overwhelming majority of these classes of stock—coupled with the fact that the 7 percent preferred shareholders could not vote as a class on the merger proposal—gave GM Sub sufficient voting power to approve a follow-up merger. As a result, all remaining shareholders other than GM Sub were eliminated in return for payment of cash for their shares. These shareholders received the same consideration ($70 per share) offered in the tender offer.

Rothschild brought suit against Liggett and Grand Metropolitan, charging each with a breach of its duty of fair dealing owed to the 7 percent preferred shareholders. Rothschild based both claims on the contention that the merger was a liquidation of Liggett insofar as the rights of the 7 percent preferred stockholders were concerned and that those preferred shareholders therefore were entitled to the liquidation preference of $100 per share, not $70 per share. Are the preferred shareholders entitled to a liquidation preference? Why or why not?

13. Smith's Food & Drug Centers, Inc. (SFD), is a Delaware corporation that owns and operates a chain of supermarkets in the southwestern United States. Jeffrey P. Smith, SFD's chief executive officer, and his family hold common and preferred stock constituting 62.1 percent voting control of SFD. On January 29, SFD entered into a merger agreement with the Yucaipa Companies that would involve a recapitalization of SFD and the repurchase by SFD of up to 50 percent of its common stock. SFD was also to repurchase 3 million shares of preferred stock from Jeffrey Smith and his family. In an April 25 proxy statement, the SFD board released a pro forma balance sheet showing that the merger and self-tender offer would result in a deficit to surplus on SFD's books of more than $100 million. SFD

hired the investment firm of Houlihan Lokey Howard & Zukin (Houlihan) to examine the transactions, and it rendered a favorable solvency opinion based on a revaluation of corporate assets. On May 17, in reliance on the Houlihan opinion, SFD's board of directors determined that there existed sufficient surplus to consummate the transactions. On May 23, SFD's stockholders voted to approve the transactions, which closed on that day. The self-tender offer was oversubscribed, so SFD repurchased fully 50 percent of its shares at the offering price of $36 per share. A group of shareholders challenged the transaction alleging that the corporation's repurchase of shares violated the statutory prohibition against the impairment of capital. They argued that (a) the negative net worth that appeared on SFD's books following the repurchase constitutes conclusive evidence of capital impairment and (b) the SFD board was not entitled to rely on a solvency opinion based on a revaluation of corporate assets. Explain who should prevail.

14. In addition to a class of common stock, Peabody Coal Company had outstanding a class of cumulative 5 percent preferred shares with a par value of $25 with the following contractual rights as stated in the corporation's articles of incorporation:

Preferences on Liquidation In the event of any liquidation, dissolution or winding up of the Company (whether voluntary or involuntary), the holders of the 5% Preferred Shares then outstanding shall, to the extent of the full par value of their shares and unpaid cumulative dividends accrued thereon be entitled to priority of payment out of the Companys assets over the holders of the Common Shares then outstanding. After such payment to the holders of the 5% Preferred Shares, the remaining assets shall be distributed pro rata to the holders of the Common Shares then outstanding.

Redemption The Company, upon the sole authority of its Board of Directors, may at any time redeem and retire all or any part of the 5% Preferred Shares at any time outstanding by paying or setting aside for payment for each share so called for redemption the sum of $26.00 plus a sum equal to the amount of all dividends accrued or in arrears thereon at the redemption date.

Peabody entered into negotiations for its sale to the Kennecott Copper Company. In order to complete the transaction, Peabody submitted to its shareholders a resolution for the approval of the sale to Kennecott and the adoption of a plan of complete liquidation. The proposed dissolution plan would (a) entitle the preferred shareholders to a preferential liquidating dividend of

$25 par value per share plus any unpaid cumulative dividends accrued and (b) pay the remainder of the assets on a *pro rata* basis to the holders of the common stock of Peabody. The resolution was approved by the common and preferred shares voting as a single class. Preferred shareholders have challenged the plan of liquidation, claiming that the corporation should have redeemed the preferred stock and then liquidated the corporation, thus entitling each preferred share to a $26 redemption payment along with accrued dividends. Explain whether the preferred shareholders should succeed.

T A K I N G   S I D E S

A closely held corporation sought to repurchase 25 percent of its outstanding shares from one of its shareholders. The corporation and the shareholder agreed that the corporation would purchase all of the shareholder's stock at a price of $500,000, payable $100,000 immediately in cash and the balance in four consecutive annual installments. The State's incorporation statute provides, "A corporation may purchase its own shares only out of earned surplus but the corporation may make no purchase of shares when it is insolvent or when such purchase would make it insolvent." At the time of the repurchase of the shares, the corporation had an earned surplus of $250,000.

a. What are the arguments that the repurchase of shares satisfied the incorporation statute?

b. What are the arguments that the repurchase of the shares did not satisfy the incorporation statute?

c. Which argument should prevail?

CHAPTER 35

Management Structure

CHAPTER OUTCOMES

After reading and studying this chapter, you should be able to:

- Compare the actual governance of closely held corporations, the actual governance of publicly held corporations, and the statutory model of corporate governance.

- Explain the role of shareholders in the management of a corporation.

- Explain the role of the board of directors in the management of a corporation.

- Explain the role of officers in the management of a corporation.

- Explain management's duties of loyalty, obedience, and diligence.

The corporate management structure, as required by State incorporation statutes, is pyramidal. At the base of the pyramid are the *shareholders*, who are the residual owners of the corporation. Basic to their role in controlling the corporation is the right to elect representatives to manage the ordinary business matters of the corporation and the right to approve all extraordinary matters.

The *board of directors*, as the shareholders' elected representatives, are delegated the power to manage the business of the corporation. Directors exercise dominion and control over the corporation, hold positions of trust and confidence, and determine questions of operating policy. Because they are not expected to devote their time completely to the affairs of the corporation, directors have broad authority to delegate power to agents and to *officers* who hold their offices at the will of the board and who, in turn, hire and fire all necessary operating personnel and run the day-to-day affairs of the corporation.

♦ **SEE FIGURE 35-1:** *Management Structure of Corporations: The Statutory Model*

CORPORATE GOVERNANCE

The statutory model of corporate management, although required by most States, accurately describes the actual governance of only a few corporations. A great majority of corporations are closely held; they have a small number of stockholders and no ready market for their shares, and most of the shareholders actively participate in the management of the business. Typically, the shareholders of a closely held corporation are also its directors and officers.

Although the statutory model and the actual governance of closely held corporations diverge, in most States, **closely held corporations** must adhere to the general corporate statutory model. One of the greatest burdens conventional general business corporation statutes impose on closely held corporations is a set of rigid corporate formalities. Although these formalities may be necessary and desirable in publicly held corporations, where management and ownership are separate, in a closely held corporation, where the owners are usually the managers, many of these formalities are unnecessary and meaningless. Consequently, shareholders in closely held corporations tend to disregard corporate formalities, sometimes forfeiting their limited liability as a result. In response to this problem, the 1969 Amendments to the Model Business Corporation Act (MBCA), which the Revised Act carried over and expanded, included several liberalizing provisions for closely held corporations. Moreover, about twenty States have enacted special legislation to accommodate the needs of closely held corporations. These statutes vary considerably, but they are all optional and must be specifically elected by eligible corporations. Eligibility is generally based on the corporation having fewer than a specified maximum number of shareholders. These special close corporation statutes permit operation without a board of directors and authorize broad use of shareholder agreements, including their use in place of bylaws. Some prohibit courts from denying limited liability simply because an electing corporation engages in informal conduct.

As noted in *Chapter 33*, a Statutory Close Corporation Supplement (the Supplement) to the Model and Revised Acts has been promulgated. The Supplement relaxes the most nonessential corporate formalities by permitting operation without a board of directors, authorizing broad use of shareholder agreements (including their use in place of bylaws), making annual meetings optional, and authorizing one person to execute documents in more than one capacity. Most important, it prevents courts from denying limited liability simply because the corporation is a statutory close corporation. The general incorporation statute applies to closely held corporations except to the extent that it is inconsistent with the Supplement.

The Revised Act was amended to authorize shareholders in closely held corporations to adopt unanimous shareholders' agreements that depart from the statutory norms. Section 7.32. This section requires that the agreement is set forth either (1) in the articles of incorporation or bylaws and approved by all persons who are shareholders at the time of the agreement or (2) in a written agreement that is signed by all persons who are shareholders at the time of the agreement and is made known to the corporation. Section 7.32(b). Any limits on the duration of the shareholder agreement must be explicitly set forth in the agreement. The section *specifically* validates a number of provisions, including those (1) eliminating or restricting the powers of the board of directors, (2) establishing who shall be directors or officers, (3) specifying how directors or officers will be selected or removed, (4) governing the exercise or division of voting power by or between the shareholders and directors, (5) permitting the use of weighted voting rights or director proxies, and (6) transferring the authority of the board of directors to one or more shareholders or other persons. The section also *generally* authorizes any provision that governs the exercise of the corporate powers or the management of the business and affairs of the corporation or the relationship among the shareholders, the directors, and the corporation, or among any of them, so long as it is not contrary to public policy. There are limits, however, and a shareholder agreement that provides that the directors of the corporation have no duties of care or loyalty to the corporation or the shareholders would be beyond the authorization of Section 7.32. To the extent that an agreement authorized by this section limits the discretion or powers of the board of directors, it relieves the directors of liability while imposing that liability upon the person or persons in whom such discretion or powers are vested.

In sharp contrast is the large **publicly held corporation** with a vast market for its shares. These shares typically are widely dispersed, and very few are owned by management. Approximately two-thirds are held by institutional investors, such as insurance companies, banks, pension and retirement funds, mutual funds, hedge funds, and university endowments. Institutional investor ownership is even more significant in the largest corporations: institutional investors own approximately three-fourths of the outstanding shares of the one thousand largest U.S. corporations. The remaining shares are owned directly by individual investors Whereas a great majority of institutional investors exercise their right to vote their shares, most individual investors do not. Nonetheless, virtually all shareholders who vote for the directors do so through the use of a **proxy**—an authorization by a shareholder to an agent (usually the chief executive officer [CEO] of the corporation) to vote his shares The majority of shareholders who return their proxies vote as management advises. As a result, the nominating committee of the board of directors actually determines the board's membership.

Thus, the five hundred to one thousand largest publicly held corporations—which own the great bulk of the industrial wealth of the United States—are controlled by a small group of corporate officers. This great concentration of control over wealth, and the power that results from it, raises social, policy, and ethical issues concerning the governance of these corporations and the accountability of their management. The actions (or inactions) of these powerful corporations greatly affect the national economy, employment policies, the health and safety of the workplace and the environment, product quality, and the effects of overseas operations.

Accordingly, the accountability of management is a critical issue. In particular, what obligations should the large publicly held corporation and its management have to (1) the corporation's shareholders, (2) its employees, (3) its customers, (4) its suppliers, (5) the communities in which the corporation is located, and (6) the rest of society? These critical questions remain mostly unanswered. Some corporate statutes now provide that the board of directors, committees of the board, individual directors, and individual officers *may*, in determining the corporation's best interests, consider the effects of any action upon employees, suppliers, creditors, and customers of the corporation; the communities in which the corporation maintains offices or other establishments; the economy of the State and nation; societal considerations; and all other pertinent factors.

In response to the business scandals involving companies such as Enron, WorldCom, Global Crossing, Adelphia, and Arthur Andersen, in 2002, Congress passed the Sarbanes-Oxley Act, which is further discussed in *Chapter 43*, Securities Regulation, as well as in *Chapters 6* and *44*. The legislation seeks to prevent these types of scandals by increasing corporate responsibility, adding new financial disclosure requirements, creating new criminal offenses, increasing the penalties for existing federal crimes, and creating a five-person Accounting Oversight Board with authority to review and discipline auditors. Several provisions of the Act impose governance requirements on publicly held corporations and are discussed in this chapter.

FIGURE 35-1 **Management Structure of Corporations: The Statutory Model**

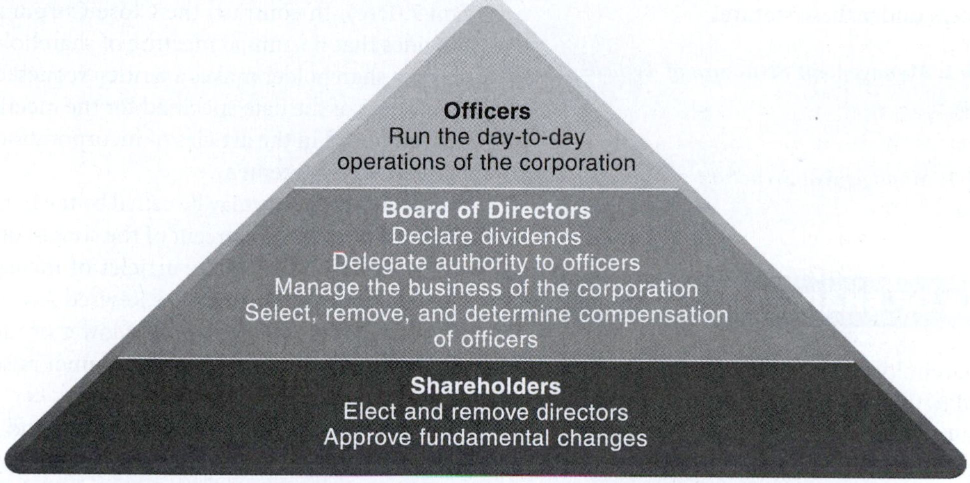

Officers
Run the day-to-day
operations of the corporation

Board of Directors
Declare dividends
Delegate authority to officers
Manage the business of the corporation
Select, remove, and determine compensation
of officers

Shareholders
Elect and remove directors
Approve fundamental changes

FIGURE 35-2 **Management Structure of Typical Closely Held Corporation**

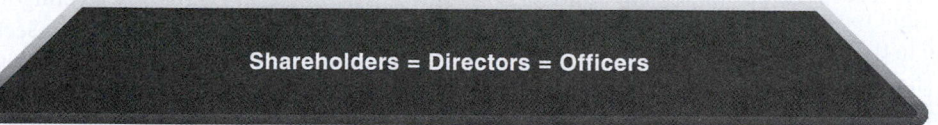

Shareholders = Directors = Officers

FIGURE 35-3 **Management Structure of Typical Publicly Held Corporation**

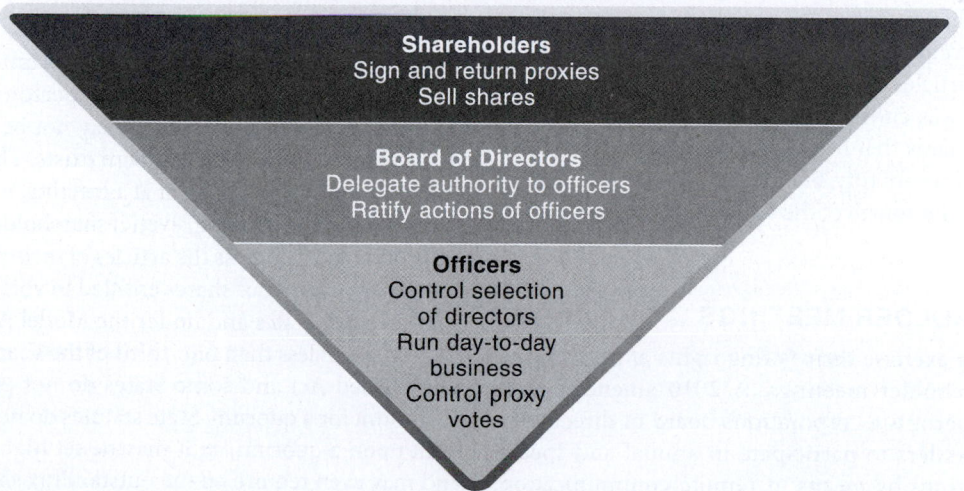

Shareholders
Sign and return proxies
Sell shares

Board of Directors
Delegate authority to officers
Ratify actions of officers

Officers
Control selection
of directors
Run day-to-day
business
Control proxy
votes

In July 2010, President Obama signed into law the Dodd-Frank Wall Street Reform and Consumer Protection Act (Dodd-Frank Act), the most significant change to U.S. financial regulation since the New Deal. One of the many stand-alone statutes included in the Dodd-Frank Act is the Investor Protection and Securities Reform Act of 2010, which imposes new corporate governance rules on publicly held companies. These corporate governance provisions of the Dodd-Frank Act are discussed in this chapter, *Chapter 36*, and *Chapter 43*.

The structure and governance of corporations must adhere to incorporation statute requirements. Therefore, this chapter discusses the rights, duties, and liabilities of share-holders, directors, and officers under these statutes.

♦ SEE FIGURE 35-2: *Management Structure of Typical Closely Held Corporation*

♦ SEE FIGURE 35-3: *Management Structure of Typical Publicly Held Corporation*

ROLE OF SHAREHOLDERS

The role of the shareholders in managing the corporation is generally restricted to the election of directors, the approval of certain extraordinary matters, the approval of corporate transactions that are void or voidable unless ratified, and the right to bring suits to enforce these rights.

35-1 Voting Rights of Shareholders

The shareholder's right to vote is fundamental both to the corporate concept and to the corporation's management structure. In most States, a shareholder is entitled to one vote for each share of stock that she owns, unless the articles of incorporation provide otherwise. In addition, incorporation statutes generally permit the issuance of one or more classes of nonvoting stock, so long as at least one class of shares has voting rights. Section 6.01. The articles of incorporation may provide for more or less than one vote for any share. For example, in *Providence & Worcester Co. v. Baker*, 378 A.2d 121 (Del. 1977), the court upheld articles of incorporation which provided that each shareholder was entitled to one vote per share for each of fifty or fewer shares that he owned and one vote for every twenty shares in excess of fifty, but no shareholder was entitled to vote more than one-fourth of the whole number of outstanding shares.

35-1a SHAREHOLDER MEETINGS

Shareholders may exercise their voting rights at both annual and special shareholder meetings. A 2010 amendment to the Revised Act permits a corporation's board of directors to authorize shareholders to participate in annual and special shareholder meetings by means of remote communication, such as over the Internet or through telephone conference calls. **Annual meetings** are required and must be held at a time fixed by the bylaws. Section 7.01. If the annual shareholder meeting is not held within the earlier of six months after the end of the corporation's fiscal year or fifteen months after its last annual meeting, any shareholder may petition and obtain a court order

requiring such meeting to be held. Section 7.03. The Revised Act further provides that the failure to hold an annual meeting does not affect the validity of any corporate action. Section 7.01(c). In contrast, the Close Corporation Supplement provides that no annual meeting of shareholders need be held unless a shareholder makes a written request at least thirty days in advance of the date specified for the meeting. The date may be established in the articles of incorporation, the bylaws, or a shareholders' agreement.

Special meetings may be called by the board of directors, by holders of at least 10 percent of the shares, or by other persons authorized to do so in the articles of incorporation. Section 7.02. As amended in 1996, the Revised Act permits a corporation's articles of incorporation to lower or raise the 10 percent requirement, but the corporation cannot raise the requirement to more than 25 percent of the shares.

Written notice, stating the date, time, and place of the meeting and, in the case of a special meeting, the purposes for which it is called, must be given in advance of the meeting. Section 7.05. Notice, however, may be waived in writing by any shareholder entitled to notice. Section 7.06.

A number of States and the Revised Act permit shareholders to conduct business without a meeting if they consent unanimously in writing to the action taken. Section 7.04. Some States have further relaxed the formalities of shareholder action by permitting shareholders to act without a meeting simply by obtaining the written consent of the number of shares required to act on the matter. In 2006, the Revised Act was amended to permit these types of provisions in a corporation's articles of incorporation.

35-1b QUORUM AND VOTING

To effectuate corporate business, a quorum of shares must be represented at the meeting, either in person or by proxy. Unissued shares and treasury stock may not be voted or counted in determining whether a quorum exists. The majority view is that once a quorum is present at a meeting, it is deemed present for the rest of the meeting, even if shareholders withdraw in an effort to break it. Unless the articles of incorporation otherwise provide, a majority of shares entitled to vote constitutes a quorum. In most States and under the Model Act, a quorum may not consist of less than one-third of the shares entitled to vote; the Revised Act and some States do not provide a statutory minimum for a quorum. State statutes do not impose an upper limit upon a quorum, so it may be set higher than a majority and may even require *all* the outstanding shares.

Most States require shareholder actions to be approved by a majority of shares represented at the meeting and entitled to vote if a quorum exists. The Revised Act and some States, however, provide a different rule: if a quorum exists, a shareholder action (other than the election of directors) is approved if the votes cast for the action exceed the votes cast against it.

Section 7.25(c). Moreover, virtually all States permit the articles of incorporation to increase the percentage of shares required to take any action that is subject to shareholder approval. Section 7.27. A provision that increases voting requirements is commonly called a "supermajority provision." Close corporations frequently have used supermajority shareholder voting requirements to protect minority shareholders from oppression by the majority, while some publicly held corporations have used them to defend against hostile takeover bids.

Practical Advice

If you are forming a close corporation and will hold a minority interest in it, consider including in the articles of incorporation supermajority quorum and voting provisions for shareholder decisions to ensure that you will have veto power over specified managerial issues.

35-1c ELECTION OF DIRECTORS

The shareholders elect directors each year at the annual meeting of the shareholders. Most States provide that where a corporation's board consists of nine or more directors, the articles of incorporation or bylaws may provide for a **classification** or staggering of directors, that is, a division into two or three classes to be as nearly equal in number as possible and to serve for staggered terms. Under the Revised Act as amended, there is no minimum-size board required. Section 8.06. If the directors are divided into two classes, the members of each class are elected once a year in alternate years for a two-year term; if divided into three classes, they are elected for three-year terms. This permits one-half of the board to be elected every two years or one-third to be elected every three years, thus lending continuity to the board's membership. Moreover, where there are two or more classes of shares, each class may elect a specified number of directors, if the articles of incorporation so provide. The Revised Act, Section 8.04.

A 2010 amendment to the Revised Act expressly authorizes bylaws that contain one or both of the following requirements: (1) that if the corporation solicits proxies with respect to an election of directors the corporation include individuals nominated by shareholders for election as directors in its proxy statement and proxy cards and (2) that the corporation reimburse the expenses incurred by a shareholder in soliciting proxies in connection with the election of directors. The bylaws may provide procedures and conditions for the exercise of each of these rights. Section 2.06(c).

STRAIGHT VOTING Normally, each shareholder has one vote for each share owned, and under the Revised Act and many State statutes, directors are elected by a *plurality* of the votes. Section 7.28(a). In other States, directors are elected by a

majority of the votes. The articles of incorporation may increase the percentage of shares required for the election of directors. Thus, under straight voting, shareholders owning a majority of the voting shares can always elect the entire board of directors.

CUMULATIVE VOTING In certain States, shareholders have the right of cumulative voting when electing directors. In most of these States and under the Revised Act, cumulative voting is permissive, not mandatory. Section 7.28(b). **Cumulative voting** entitles the shareholders to multiply the number of votes they are entitled to cast by the number of directors for whom they are entitled to vote and to cast the product for a single candidate or distribute the product among two or more candidates. Cumulative voting permits a minority shareholder, or a group of minority shareholders acting together, to obtain minority representation on the board if they own a certain minimum number of shares. In the absence of cumulative voting, the holder or holders of 51 percent of the voting shares can elect all of the members of the board.

The formula for determining how many shares a minority shareholder with cumulative voting rights must own, or have proxies to vote, to secure representation on the board is as follows:

$$X = \frac{ac}{b+1} + 1$$

where

a = number of shares voting

b = number of directors to be elected

c = number of directors desired to be elected

X = number of shares necessary to elect the number of directors desired to be elected

For example, Gray Corporation has two shareholders, Stephanie with sixty-four shares and Thomas with thirty-six shares. The board of directors of Gray Corporation consists of three directors. Under "straight" or noncumulative voting, Stephanie could cast sixty-four votes for each of her three candidates, and Thomas could cast thirty-six votes for his three candidates. As a result, all three of Stephanie's candidates would be elected. On the other hand, if cumulative voting were in force, Thomas could elect one director:

$$X = \frac{ac}{b+1} + 1$$

$$X = \frac{100(1)}{3+1} + 1 = 26 \text{ shares}$$

This result indicates that Thomas would need at least twenty-six shares to elect one director. Because Thomas has the right to vote thirty-six shares, he would be able to elect one director. Stephanie, of course, with her sixty-four shares, could elect the remaining two directors.

The effect of cumulative voting for directors may be diluted by classification, by staggered elections, or by a reduction in the size of the board. For example, if nine directors are each elected annually, only 11 percent of the shares are needed to elect one director; if the nine directors' elections are staggered and three are elected annually, 26 percent of the shares are required to elect one director.

Practical Advice

If you are forming a close corporation and will hold a minority interest in it, consider including a provision for cumulative voting in the articles of incorporation to ensure yourself a position on the board of directors.

35-1d REMOVAL OF DIRECTORS

By a majority vote, shareholders may remove any director or the entire board of directors, with or without cause, in a meeting called for that purpose. In the case of a corporation having cumulative voting, however, a director may be removed only if the number of votes opposing his removal would be insufficient to elect him. Section 8.08(c). Removal of directors is discussed more fully later in this chapter.

35-1e APPROVAL OF FUNDAMENTAL CHANGES

The board of directors manages the ordinary business affairs of the corporation. Extraordinary matters involving fundamental changes in the corporation require shareholder approval; such matters include amendments to the articles of incorporation, a sale or lease of all or substantially all of the corporate assets not in the regular course of business, most mergers, consolidations, compulsory share exchanges, and dissolution. Fundamental changes are discussed in *Chapter 36*.

35-1f CONCENTRATIONS OF VOTING POWER

Certain devices enable groups of shareholders to combine their voting power for purposes such as obtaining or maintaining control or maximizing the impact of cumulative voting. The most important methods of concentrating voting power are proxies, voting trusts, and shareholder voting agreements.

♦ **SEE FIGURE 35-4:** *Concentrations of Voting Power*

PROXIES A shareholder may vote either in person or by written proxy. Section 7.22(a). As mentioned earlier, a proxy is simply a shareholder's authorization to an agent to vote his shares at a particular meeting or on a particular question. Generally, proxies must be in writing to be effective; furthermore, statutes typically limit the duration of proxies to no more than eleven months, unless the proxy specifically provides otherwise.

Section 7.22(c). Some States limit all proxy appointments to a period of eleven months. Because a proxy is the appointment of an agent, it is revocable, as all agencies are, unless conspicuously stated to be irrevocable *and* coupled with an interest, such as shares held as collateral. Section 7.22(d). The solicitation of proxies by publicly held corporations is also regulated by the Securities Exchange Act of 1934, as discussed in *Chapter 43*.

As discussed, in large publicly held corporations, virtually all shareholders who vote for the directors do so through the use of proxies. Because the majority of shareholders who return their proxies vote as management advises, the nominating committee of the board of directors almost always determines the board's membership. In 2010, the Revised Model Business Corporation Act (RMBCA) was amended to authorize the directors or shareholders of corporations to establish procedures in the corporate bylaws that require one or both of the following: (1) the corporation to include in the corporation's proxy statement one or more individuals nominated by a shareholder in addition to individuals nominated by the board of directors and (2) the corporation to reimburse shareholders for reasonable expenses incurred in soliciting proxies in an election of directors. Section 2.06(c).

Moreover, the Dodd-Frank Act authorizes the Securities and Exchange Commission (SEC) to issue rules requiring that a publicly held company's proxy solicitation include nominations for the board of directors submitted by shareholders. The SEC has issued a new such rule. See *Chapter 43*.

VOTING TRUSTS Voting trusts, which are designed to concentrate corporate control in one or more persons, have been used in both publicly held and closely held corporations. A voting trust is a device by which one or more shareholders separate the voting rights of their shares from the ownership of those shares. Under a voting trust, one or more shareholders confer on a trustee the right to vote or otherwise act for them by signing a written agreement setting out the provisions of the trust and transferring their shares to the trustee. Section 7.30(a). In most States, voting trusts are permitted by statute but usually are limited in duration to ten years. The Revised Act and many States permit all or some of the parties to a voting trust to extend it for an additional term of up to ten years by signing an extension agreement and obtaining the voting trustee's written consent. Section 7.30(c). The extension runs from the time the first shareholder signs the agreement but binds only those shareholders who consent to it.

SHAREHOLDER VOTING AGREEMENTS In most jurisdictions, shareholders may agree in writing to vote in a specified manner for the election or removal of directors or on any other matter subject to shareholder approval. Section 7.31(a). The Revised Act and some State statutes expressly provide that shareholder voting agreements are enforceable by a decree of specific performance. Section 7.31(b). Unlike voting

FIGURE 35-4 Concentrations of Voting Power

	Proxy	Voting Trust	Shareholder Agreement
Definition	Authorization of an agent to vote shares	Conferral of voting rights on trustee	Agreement among shareholders on voting of shares
Formalities	Signed writing delivered to corporation	Signed writing delivered to corporation	Signed writing
Duration	Eleven months, unless otherwise agreed	Ten years; may be extended	No limit
Revocability	Yes, unless coupled with an interest	No	Only by unanimous agreement
Prevalence	Publicly held	Publicly and closely held	Closely held

trusts, shareholder voting agreements are usually not limited in duration. Shareholder voting agreements are used frequently in closely held corporations, especially in conjunction with restrictions on the transfer of shares, to provide each shareholder with greater control and *delectus personae* (the right to choose those who will become shareholders).

Galler v. Galler, 32 Ill.2d 16, 203 N.E.2d 577 (1964), provides a well-known example of the effect a shareholder agreement may have within a close corporation. In 1927, two brothers, Benjamin and Isadore Galler, incorporated the Galler Drug Co., a wholesale drug business they had operated as equal partners since 1919. The company continued to grow, and in 1955, the two brothers and their wives, Emma and Rose Galler, entered into a written shareholder agreement to leave the corporation in equal control of each family after the death of either brother. Specifically, the agreement provided that the corporation would continue to provide income for the support and maintenance of their immediate families and that the parties would vote for directors so as to give the estate and heirs of a deceased shareholder the same representation as before. Benjamin died in 1957, and shortly thereafter his widow, Emma, requested that Isadore, the surviving brother, comply with the terms of the agreement. When he refused, instead proposing that certain changes be made in the agreement, Emma brought an action seeking specific performance of the agreement. Isadore and his wife, Rose, defended on the ground that the shareholder agreement was against public policy and the State's corporation law. The court decided in favor of Emma Galler, explaining that a close corporation is one in which the stock is held in a few hands and is rarely traded. In contrast to a shareholder in a public corporation, who may easily trade his shares on the open market when he disagrees with management over corporate policy, the shareholder of a closely held corporation often has no ready market in which to sell his shares should he wish to do so. Moreover, the shareholder in a closely held corporation often has most of his capital invested in the corporation and, therefore,

views himself not only as an investor but also as a participant in the management of the business. Without a shareholder agreement subject to specific performance by the courts, the minority shareholder might find himself at the mercy of the controlling majority shareholder. In short, the detailed shareholder voting agreement is the only sound means by which the minority shareholder can protect himself. Therefore, the court concluded, because the agreement was reasonable in its scope and purpose of providing continuing support for the Galler brothers' families, it should be enforced.

Practical Advice

If you are forming a close corporation and will hold a minority interest in it, consider using a detailed shareholder agreement to provide fair treatment for all of the shareholders.

35-1g RESTRICTIONS ON TRANSFER OF SHARES

In the absence of a specific agreement, shares of stock are freely transferable. Although free transferability of shares is usually considered an advantage of the corporate form, in some situations, the shareholders may prefer to restrict the transfer of shares. In closely held corporations, for example, stock transfer restrictions are used to control who may become shareholders, thereby achieving the corporate equivalent of *delectus personae* (choice of the person). They are also used to maintain statutory close corporation status or S Corporation status by restricting the number of persons who may become shareholders. In publicly held corporations, restrictions on the transfer of shares are used to preserve exemptions under State and Federal securities laws. (These are discussed in *Chapter 43*.)

Most incorporation statutes have no provisions governing share transfer restrictions. The common law validates such restrictions if they are adopted for a lawful purpose and do not unreasonably restrain or prohibit transferability. In addition, the Uniform Commercial Code provides that an otherwise valid share transfer restriction is ineffective against a person without actual knowledge of it unless the restriction is conspicuously noted on the share certificate. Section 8-204.

The Revised Act and the statutes of several States permit the articles of incorporation, bylaws, or a shareholder agreement to impose transfer restrictions but require that the restriction be noted conspicuously on the stock certificate. The Revised Act authorizes restrictions for any reasonable purpose, including maintaining statutory close corporation status and preserving exemptions under Federal and State securities law. Section 6.27.

Practical Advice

To achieve delectus personae (choice of person) when organizing a close corporation, you should consider including in the articles of incorporation a carefully drafted provision restricting the transfer of shares. If you do so, be sure to note such share transfer restriction on the share certificates.

35-2 Enforcement Rights of Shareholders

To protect a shareholder's interests in the corporation, the law provides shareholders with certain enforcement rights, including the right to obtain information, the right to sue the corporation directly or to sue on the corporation's behalf, and the right to dissent.

35-2a RIGHT TO INSPECT BOOKS AND RECORDS

Most States have enacted statutory provisions granting shareholders the right to inspect for a *proper purpose* books and records in person or through an agent and to make extracts from them. The right generally covers all records relevant to the shareholder's legitimate interest. The Revised Act extends the right to copy records to include, if reasonable, the right to receive copies made by photographic, xerographic, or other means. Section 16.03. The Act provides that every shareholder is entitled to examine *specified* corporate records upon prior signed written request if the demand is made in good faith, for a proper purpose, and during regular business hours at the corporation's principal office. Section 16.02. Many States, however, limit this right to shareholders who own a minimum number of shares or to those who have been shareholders for a specified minimum time. For example, the original MBCA requires that a shareholder either must own 5 percent of the outstanding shares or must have owned his shares for at least six months; a court, however, may order an inspection even when neither condition is met. In 2016, the Revised Act was amended to require corporations, upon the written request of a shareholder, to make financial statements available to the shareholders.

A **proper purpose** for inspection is one that is reasonably relevant to a shareholder's interest in the corporation. Proper purposes include determining the financial condition of the corporation, the value of shares, the existence of mismanagement or improper transactions, or the names of other shareholders in order to communicate with them about corporate affairs. The right of inspection is subject to abuse and will be denied a shareholder who is seeking information for an improper purpose. Examples of improper purposes include obtaining proprietary information for use by a competing company or obtaining a list of shareholders in order to offer it for sale.

The Revised Act requires that a voting list of shareholders be prepared and that it be made available to shareholders upon request. Section 7.20. In addition, unlike many States, the Act requires every corporation to prepare and submit to its shareholders annual financial statements. Section 16.20.

♦ *See Case 35-1*

35-2b SHAREHOLDER SUITS

The ultimate recourse of a shareholder, short of selling her shares, is to bring suit against or on behalf of the corporation. Shareholder suits are essentially of two kinds: direct suits or derivative suits.

♦ **SEE FIGURE 35-5:** *Shareholder Suits*

DIRECT SUITS A shareholder may bring a direct suit to enforce a claim that he has *against* the corporation, based upon his ownership of shares. Any recovery in a direct suit goes to the shareholder plaintiff. Examples of direct suits include shareholder actions to compel payment of dividends properly declared, to enforce the right to inspect corporate records, to enforce the right to vote, to protect preemptive rights, and to compel dissolution. Shareholders also may bring a class suit or class action. A **class suit** is a direct suit in which one or more shareholders purport to represent a class of shareholders to recover for injuries to the entire class. Such a suit is a direct suit because the representative claims that all similarly situated shareholders were injured by an act that did not injure the corporation.

DERIVATIVE SUITS A derivative suit is a cause of action brought by one or more shareholders *on behalf* of the corporation to enforce a right belonging to the corporation. Shareholders may bring such an action when the board of directors refuses to so act on the corporation's behalf. Recovery usually goes to the corporation's treasury so that all shareholders can benefit proportionately. Examples of derivative suits are actions to recover damages from management for an *ultra vires* act, to recover damages for a managerial breach of duty, and to recover improper dividends. In such situations, the board

FIGURE 35-5 Shareholder Suits

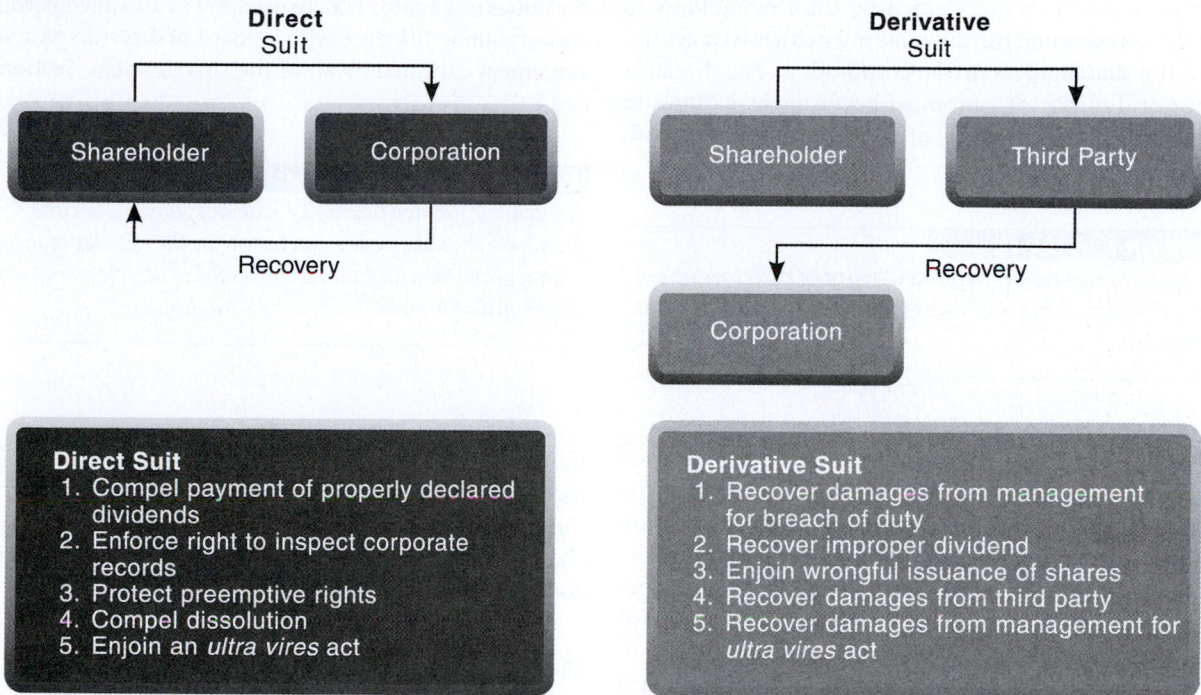

Direct
Suit

Shareholder → Corporation

Recovery (Corporation → Shareholder)

Derivative
Suit

Shareholder   Third Party

Recovery

Corporation

Direct Suit
1. Compel payment of properly declared dividends
2. Enforce right to inspect corporate records
3. Protect preemptive rights
4. Compel dissolution
5. Enjoin an *ultra vires* act

Derivative Suit
1. Recover damages from management for breach of duty
2. Recover improper dividend
3. Enjoin wrongful issuance of shares
4. Recover damages from third party
5. Recover damages from management for *ultra vires* act

of directors may well be hesitant to bring suit against the corporation's officers or directors. Consequently, a shareholder derivative suit is the only recourse.

In most States, a shareholder must have owned his shares at the time the complained-of transaction occurred in order to bring a derivative suit. Section 7.41. In addition, under the Revised Act and some State statutes, the shareholder must first make demand upon the board of directors to enforce the corporate right. Section 7.42. In a number of States and under the Revised Act, demand is excused in limited situations. The Revised Act requires dismissal of a derivative suit if qualified (disinterested) directors determine, in good faith after conducting a reasonable inquiry, that maintenance of the derivative suit is not in the best interests of the corporation. The statutes of some States require a plaintiff to give security for reasonable expenses, including attorneys' fees, if his holdings of shares are not of a specified size or value. The Revised Act does not have this requirement.

◆ *see Cases 35-1 and 35-2*

35-2c SHAREHOLDER'S RIGHT TO DISSENT

A shareholder has the right to dissent from certain corporate actions that require shareholder approval. These actions include most mergers, consolidations, compulsory share

exchanges, and a sale or exchange of all or substantially all the assets of the corporation not in the usual and regular course of business. The shareholder's right to dissent is discussed in *Chapter 36*.

ROLE OF DIRECTORS AND OFFICERS

Management of a corporation is vested by statute in its board of directors, which determines general corporate policy and appoints officers to execute that policy and to administer day-to-day corporate operations. Both the directors and the officers owe certain duties to the corporate entity as well as to the corporation's shareholders and are liable for breaching these duties.

The following sections discuss the roles of corporate directors and officers. In some instances, controlling shareholders, or those owning a number of shares sufficient to allow them effective control over the corporation, are held to duties the same as those of directors and officers; this is discussed later in this chapter. Moreover, in close corporations, many courts impose upon *all* the shareholders a fiduciary duty similar to that imposed upon partners.

◆ *See Case 35-3*

35-3 Function of the Board of Directors

Although the directors are elected by the shareholders to manage the corporation, the directors are neither trustees nor agents of the shareholders or the corporation. The directors are, however, fiduciaries who must perform their duties in good faith, in the best interests of the corporation, and with due care.

Practical Advice

Do not agree to serve on a corporate board of directors unless you have sufficient time and energy to meet the requirements of the position.

The Revised Act and the statutes of many States provide that "[a]ll corporate powers shall be exercised by or under the authority of, and the business and affairs of the corporation managed under the direction of, its board of directors, subject to any limitation set forth in the articles of incorporation." Section 8.01(b). In some corporations, the members of the board all are actively involved in the management of the business. In these cases, the corporate powers are exercised *by* the board of directors. On the other hand, in publicly held corporations, most board members are unlikely to be actively involved in management. Here, the corporate powers are exercised *under* the authority of the board, which formulates major management policy and monitors management's performance but does not involve itself in day-to-day management.

In publicly held corporations, the directors who are also officers or employees of the corporation are inside directors while the directors who are not officers or employees are **outside directors**. Outside directors who have no business contacts with the corporation are **unaffiliated directors**; outside directors who do have such contacts with the corporation—such as investment bankers, lawyers, and suppliers—are **affiliated directors**. Historically, the boards of many publicly held corporations consisted mainly or entirely of inside directors. During the past two decades, however, the number and influence of outside directors have increased substantially, and now boards of the great majority of publicly held corporations consist primarily of outside directors.

Under the Dodd-Frank Act, the SEC must issue rules requiring publicly held companies to disclose in annual proxy statements the reasons the company has chosen to separate or combine the positions of chairman of the board of directors and CEO.

In those States with special close corporation statutes, electing corporations can operate without a board of directors. Moreover, under the Revised Act as originally enacted, a corporation having fifty or fewer shareholders may dispense with

or limit the authority of a board of directors by describing in its articles of incorporation those who will perform some or all of the duties of a board. The Revised Act as amended permits any corporation to dispense with a board of directors by a written agreement executed by all of the shareholders. Sections 7.32 and 8.01.

Practical Advice

To achieve greater flexibility when organizing a close corporation, you should consider including in the articles of incorporation a provision eliminating the board of directors and assigning the board's duties to designated shareholders.

Under incorporation statutes, the board has the responsibility for determining corporate policy in a number of areas, including (1) selecting and removing officers, (2) determining the corporation's capital structure, (3) initiating fundamental changes, (4) declaring dividends, and (5) setting management compensation.

35-3a SELECTION AND REMOVAL OF OFFICERS

In most States, the board of directors is responsible for choosing the corporation's officers and may remove any officer at any time. Sections 8.40 and 8.43. Officers are corporate agents who are delegated their responsibilities by the board of directors.

35-3b CAPITAL STRUCTURE

The board of directors determines the capital structure and financial policy of the corporation. For example, the board of directors has the power to—

1. fix the selling price of newly issued shares unless the articles reserve this power to the shareholders;

2. determine the value of the consideration the corporation will receive in payment for the shares it issues;

3. purchase, redeem, or otherwise acquire shares of the corporation's equity securities;

4. borrow money; issue notes, bonds, and other obligations; and secure any of the corporation's obligations by mortgage or pledge of any or all of the corporation's property; and

5. sell, lease, or exchange assets of the corporation in the usual and regular course of business.

35-3c FUNDAMENTAL CHANGES

The board of directors has the power to amend or repeal the bylaws, unless the articles of incorporation reserve this power exclusively to the shareholders. Section 10.20. In a few States, directors may not repeal or amend bylaws adopted by the shareholders. In addition, the board initiates certain actions that require shareholder approval. For instance, the board initiates proceedings to amend the articles of incorporation; to effect a merger, consolidation, compulsory share exchange, or the sale or lease of all or substantially all of the assets of the corporation other than in the usual and regular course of business; and to dissolve the corporation.

35-3d DIVIDENDS

The board of directors declares the amount and type of dividends, subject to restrictions in the State incorporation statute, the articles of incorporation, and corporate loan and preferred stock agreements. Section 6.40. The board also fixes a record date for the purpose of determining the shareholders who are entitled to receive dividends. Section 6.40(b).

35-3e MANAGEMENT COMPENSATION

The board of directors usually determines the compensation of officers. Moreover, a number of States allow the board to fix the compensation of its members. Section 8.11. In addition to fixed salaries, executive compensation may include (1) cash bonuses, (2) share bonuses, (3) share options, (4) share purchase plans, (5) insurance benefits, (6) deferred compensation, (7) retirement plans, and (8) a variety of other fringe benefits.

The Dodd-Frank Act requires that at least once every three years, publicly held companies include a provision in certain proxy statements for a nonbinding shareholder vote on the compensation of executives. In a separate resolution, shareholders determine whether this "say on pay" vote should be held every one, two, or three years.

Under the Sarbanes-Oxley Act, if a publicly held company is required to issue an accounting restatement due to a material violation of securities law, the CEO and the chief financial officer must forfeit certain bonuses and compensation received, as well as any profit realized from the sale of the company's securities, during the twelve-month period following the original issuance of the noncomplying financial document.

These "clawback" requirements of the Sarbanes-Oxley Act have been greatly expanded by the Dodd-Frank Act. Under the Dodd-Frank Act, the SEC must issue rules directing the national securities exchanges to require each listed company to disclose and implement a policy regarding any incentive-based compensation that is based on financial information that must be reported under the securities laws. In the event that a company is required to prepare an accounting restatement due to the material noncompliance with any financial reporting requirement under the securities laws, the company must recover from any current or former executive officers who received excess incentive-based compensation (including stock options awarded as compensation) during the three-year period preceding the date on which the company is required to prepare an accounting restatement. The amount of the recovery is the incentive-based compensation in excess of what would have been paid to the CEO under the accounting restatement.

35-4 Election and Tenure of Directors

The incorporation statute, articles of incorporation, and bylaws determine the qualifications essential for those who would be directors of the corporation. They also determine the election, number, tenure, and compensation of directors. Only individuals may serve as directors. Section 8.03(a).

35-4a ELECTION, NUMBER, AND TENURE OF DIRECTORS

The initial board of directors generally is named in the articles of incorporation and serves until the first meeting of the shareholders at which directors are elected. Section 8.05(a). Thereafter, directors are elected at annual meetings of the shareholders and hold office for one year unless their terms are staggered. If the shares represented at a meeting in person or by proxy are insufficient to constitute a quorum, however, or if the shareholders are deadlocked and unable to elect a new board, the incumbent directors continue in office as "holdover" directors until their successors are duly elected and qualified. Section 8.05(e). Although State statutes traditionally required each corporation to have three or more directors, most States permit the board to consist of one or more members. Section 8.03(a). Moreover, the number of directors may be increased or decreased, within statutory limits, by amendment to the bylaws or articles of incorporation.

35-4b VACANCIES AND REMOVAL OF DIRECTORS

The Revised Act provides that a vacancy in the board may be filled either by the shareholders or by the affirmative vote of a majority of the remaining directors, even if they constitute less than a quorum of the board. Section 8.10(a). When shareholders fill a vacant office that was held by a director elected by a class of shares, only the holders of that class of shares have the right to vote to fill that vacancy. The term of a director elected to fill a vacancy expires at the next shareholders' meeting at which directors are elected. Section 8.05(d).

Some States have no statutory provision for the removal of directors, although a common-law rule permits removal for cause by action of the shareholders. The Revised Act and an increasing number of other statutes permit the shareholders to remove one or more directors or the entire board, with or without cause, at a special meeting called for that purpose, subject to cumulative voting rights, if applicable. Section 8.08. Nevertheless, the Revised Act permits the articles of incorporation to provide that directors may be removed only for cause. Section 8.08(a). As amended in 2001, the Revised Act authorizes judicial removal of a director in an action brought by the corporation or derivatively by a shareholder if the court finds that (1) the director engaged in fraudulent conduct, grossly abused the position of director, or intentionally inflicted harm on the corporation and (2) considering the director's conduct and the inadequacy of other remedies, removal is in the best interests of the corporation. Section 8.09.

35-4c COMPENSATION OF DIRECTORS

Traditionally, directors did not receive salaries for their directorial services, although they usually collected a fee or honorarium for attendance at meetings. The Revised Act and many incorporation statutes now specifically authorize the board of directors to fix the compensation of directors unless there is a contrary provision in the articles of incorporation or bylaws. Section 8.11.

35-5 Exercise of Directors' Functions

Although they are powerless to bind the corporation when acting individually, directors can exert this power when acting as a board. Nevertheless, the board may act only through a meeting of the directors or with the written, unanimously signed consent of the directors if written consent without a meeting is authorized by the statute and not contrary to the articles of incorporation or bylaws. Section 8.21.

Meetings either are held at a regular time and place fixed in the bylaws or are called at special times. Notice of meetings must be given as prescribed in the bylaws. A director's attendance at any meeting is a waiver of such notice, unless the director attends only to object to the holding of the meeting or to the transacting of business at it and does not vote for or assent to action taken at the meeting. Section 8.23(b). Waiver of notice also may be given in a signed writing. Most modern statutes provide that meetings of the board may be held either in or outside the State of incorporation. Section 8.20(a).

35-5a QUORUM AND VOTING

A majority of board members constitutes a quorum (the minimum number of members that must be present at a meeting in order to transact business). Although most States do not permit a quorum to be set at less than a majority, the Revised Act and some States allow the articles of incorporation or the bylaws to authorize a quorum consisting of as few as one-third of a board's members. Section 8.24(b). In contrast, however, in all States, the articles of incorporation or bylaws may require a number greater than a simple majority. Section 8.24(a). If a quorum is present at any meeting, the act of a majority of

the directors in attendance is the act of the board, unless the articles of incorporation or bylaws require the act of a greater number. Section 8.24(c).

Closely held corporations sometimes impose supermajority or unanimous quorum requirements. In addition, they may require a supermajority or unanimous vote of the board for some or all matters. The use of either or both of these provisions, however, creates the possibility of deadlock at the director level.

> ### *Practical Advice*
>
> *If you are forming a close corporation and will hold a minority interest in it, consider including in the articles of incorporation supermajority quorum and voting provisions for voting by the board of directors to ensure that you will have control over specified managerial issues.*

By requiring a quorum to be present when "a vote is taken," the Revised Act makes it clear that the board may act only when a quorum is present. Section 8.24(c) and Comment 2. This rule is in contrast to the rule governing shareholder meetings: once obtained, a quorum of shareholders cannot be broken by the withdrawal of shareholders. Many State statutes, however, do not have this provision. In any event, directors may not vote by proxy, although most States permit directors to participate in meetings through teleconference. See Section 8.20.

A director who is present at a board meeting at which action on any corporate matter is taken is deemed to have assented to such action unless, in addition to dissenting or abstaining from it, he (1) has his dissent or abstention entered in the minutes of the meeting, (2) files his written dissent or abstention to such action with the presiding officer before the meeting adjourns, or (3) delivers his written dissent or abstention to the corporation immediately after adjournment. Section 8.24(d).

35-5b ACTION TAKEN WITHOUT A MEETING

The Revised Act and most States provide that unless the articles of incorporation or bylaws provide otherwise, any action the statute requires or permits to be taken at a meeting of the board may be taken without a meeting if consent in writing is signed by all of the directors. Section 8.21. Such consent has the same effect as a unanimous vote.

35-5c DELEGATION OF BOARD POWERS

Unless otherwise provided by the articles of incorporation or bylaws, the board of directors may, by majority vote of the full board, appoint one or more committees, all of whose members must be directors. Section 8.25. Many State statutes, however, permit the board to form committees only if the articles of incorporation expressly authorizes such action; furthermore, the Revised Act and many States require that the creation of a committee and appointment of members to it must be approved by the greater of (1) a majority of all the directors in office when the action is taken or (2) the number of directors required by the articles of incorporation or bylaws to take action. Section 8.25(b). The Revised Act as amended and some statutes permit with certain exceptions a committee to have as few as one member, whereas the statutes of many States require that a committee consist of at least two directors.

Committees may exercise all of the authority of the board, except with regard to certain matters specified in the incorporation statute, such as declaring dividends and other distributions, filling vacancies in the board or in any of its committees, amending the bylaws, or proposing actions that require approval by shareholders. Section 8.25(e). Delegating authority to a committee does not relieve any board member of his duties to the corporation. Commonly used committees include executive committees, audit committees (to recommend and oversee independent public accountants), compensation committees, finance committees, nominating committees, and investment committees.

The Sarbanes-Oxley Act confers on the audit committee of every publicly held corporation direct responsibility for the appointment, compensation, and oversight of the work of the public accounting firm employed by the company to perform audit services. Moreover, the public accounting firm must report directly to the audit committee, and the lead auditor must rotate every five years. Each member of the audit committee must be independent, and at least one member must qualify as a financial expert. The Act requires that the company provide appropriate funding for the audit committee to compensate the auditors, independent counsel, and other advisers. The audit committee is responsible for resolving disagreements between management and the auditor regarding the company's financial reporting. The audit committee must establish procedures for addressing complaints regarding accounting, internal accounting controls, or auditing matters.

As required by the Dodd-Frank Act, the SEC has issued rules directing the national securities exchanges to require that each member of a listed company's compensation committee be an independent member of the board of directors. The SEC has approved the exchanges' rules implementing this requirement.

35-5d DIRECTORS' INSPECTION RIGHTS

A director has the right to inspect corporate books, records, and documents at any reasonable time to the extent reasonably related to the performance of the director's duties as a director. This right is considerably broader than a shareholder's right to inspect. Nevertheless, it is subject to limitations.

35-6 Officers

The board of directors appoints the officers of a corporation to hold the offices provided in the bylaws, which set forth the respective duties of each officer. Statutes generally require as a minimum that the officers consist of a president, one or more vice presidents as prescribed by the bylaws, a secretary, and a treasurer. A person may hold more than one office, with the exception that the same person may not hold the office of president and secretary at the same time.

The Revised Act and other modern statutes permit every corporation to designate whatever officers it wants. Although the Act specifies no particular number of officers, one of them must be delegated responsibility for preparing the minutes of directors' and shareholders' meetings and authenticating corporate records. The Revised Act permits the same individual to hold *all* of the offices of a corporation. Section 8.40(d).

35-6a SELECTION AND REMOVAL OF OFFICERS

Most State statutes provide that officers be appointed by the board of directors and that they serve at the pleasure of the board. In 2005, the Revised Act was amended to provide that an officer may appoint one or more officers if authorized by the bylaws or the board of directors. Section 8.40(b). The board may remove officers with or without cause. Section 8.43(b). In addition, an officer who was appointed by another officer may be removed by that officer, unless the bylaws or the board of directors provide otherwise. Section 8.43(b). Of course, if the officer has an employment contract that is valid for a specified time, removing the officer without cause before that time expires would constitute a breach of the employment contract. The board also determines the compensation of officers.

35-6b ROLE OF OFFICERS

The officers are, like the directors, fiduciaries of the corporation. On the other hand, unlike the directors, they are agents of the corporation. The roles of officers are set forth in the corporate bylaws. In 2005, the Revised Act was amended to emphasize the responsibility of officers to inform others in the corporation of matters that come to their attention, including any material violation of law involving the corporation or material breach of duty by an officer, employee, or agent of the corporation. Section 8.42.

35-6c AUTHORITY OF OFFICERS

The Revised Act provides that each officer has the authority provided in the bylaws or prescribed by the board of directors, to the extent that such prescribed authority is consistent with the bylaws. Section 8.41. Like that of other agents, the authority of an officer to bind the corporation may be (1) actual express, (2) actual implied, or (3) apparent.

ACTUAL EXPRESS AUTHORITY Actual express authority results when the corporation manifests its assent to the officer that the officer should act on its behalf. Actual express authority arises from the incorporation statute, the articles of incorporation, the bylaws, and resolutions of the board of directors. The last represent the principal source of such authority. The Revised Act further provides that the board of directors may authorize an officer to prescribe the duties of other officers. Section 8.41. This provision empowers officers to delegate authority to subordinates.

ACTUAL IMPLIED AUTHORITY Officers, as agents of the corporation, have actual implied authority to do what is reasonably necessary to perform their actual, delegated authority. In addition, a common question is whether officers possess implied authority merely by virtue of their positions. The courts have been circumspect in granting such implied or inherent authority. Traditionally, the courts tended to hold that the president had no implied authority by virtue of his office, although more recent decisions tend to recognize his authority to bind the corporation in ordinary business transactions. Any act requiring board approval, such as issuing stock, however, is clearly beyond the implied authority of the president or any other officer. In most jurisdictions, implied authority of position does not extend to any officer other than the president.

APPARENT AUTHORITY Apparent authority arises from acts of the corporation that lead third parties to believe reasonably and in good faith that an officer has the required authority. Apparent authority might arise when a third party relies on the fact that an officer has exercised the same authority in the past with the consent of the board of directors.

RATIFICATION A corporation may ratify the unauthorized acts of its officers. Equivalent to the corporation's having granted the officer prior authority, ratification relates back to the original transaction and may be either express or implied from the corporation's acceptance of contractual benefits with full knowledge of the facts.

Practical Advice

When signing contracts in your capacity as an officer for a corporation, be sure to indicate your representative status.

35-7 Duties of Directors and Officers

Generally, directors and officers owe the duties of obedience, diligence, and loyalty to the corporation. These duties are for the most part judicially imposed. State and Federal statutes supplement the common law by imposing liability upon directors and officers for specific acts, but the common law remains the most significant source of duties.

A corporation may not recover damages from its directors and officers for losses resulting from their poor business judgment or honest mistakes of judgment. Directors and officers are not insurers of business success. They are required only to be obedient, reasonably diligent, and completely loyal. In 1999, an amendment to the Revised Act was adopted refining the Act's standards of conduct and liability for directors.

35-7a DUTY OF OBEDIENCE

Directors and officers must act within their respective authority. For any loss the corporation suffers because of their unauthorized acts, they are in some jurisdictions held strictly liable; in others, they are held liable only if they exceeded their authority intentionally or negligently.

35-7b DUTY OF DILIGENCE

In discharging their duties, directors and officers must exercise ordinary care and prudence. Some States interpret this standard to mean that directors and officers must exercise "the same degree of care and prudence that [those] promoted by self-interest generally exercise in their own affairs." *Hun v. Cary*, 82 N.Y. 65 (1880). The great majority of States and the Revised Act, however, hold that the test requires a director or officer to discharge her duties—

1. in good faith;
2. with the care an ordinarily prudent person in a like position would exercise under similar circumstances; and
3. in a manner she reasonably believes to be in the best interests of the corporation.

Sections 8.30 and 8.42. A director or officer who has performed the duties of his office in compliance with these requirements is liable neither for any action he has taken as a director or officer nor for any failure to act. Sections 8.30(d) and 8.42(d).

So long as the directors and officers act in good faith and with due care, the courts will not substitute their judgment for that of the board or officer—the so-called **business judgment** rule. Directors and officers, nonetheless, will be held liable for bad faith or negligent conduct. Moreover, they may be liable for failing to act. In one instance, a bank director, who in the five-and-one-half years he had been on the board had never attended a board meeting or made any examination of the books and records, was held liable for losses resulting from the unsupervised acts of the president and cashier, who had made various improper loans and had permitted large overdrafts.

In 1999, an amendment to the Revised Act was adopted refining the Act's standards of conduct and liability for directors. It substituted a different duty of care standard for the second point in the preceding list (prudent person): when becoming informed in connection with their decisionmaking function or devoting attention to their oversight function, directors shall discharge their duties with the care that a person in a like position would reasonably believe appropriate under similar circumstances. Section 8.30(b) as amended. While some aspects of a director's role will be performed individually, such as preparing for meetings, this reformulation explicitly recognizes that directors perform most of their functions as a unit.

RELIANCE UPON OTHERS Directors and officers are, nevertheless, permitted to entrust important work to others, and if they have selected employees with care, they are not personally liable for the negligent acts or willful wrongs of those selected. A reasonable amount of supervision is required, however, and an officer or director who knew or should have known or suspected that an employee was incurring losses through carelessness, theft, or embezzlement will be held liable for such losses.

A director also may rely in good faith upon *information* provided him by officers and employees of the corporation; legal counsel, public accountants, or other persons as to matters the director reasonably believes are within the person's professional or expert competence; and a committee of the board of directors of which the director is not a member if the director reasonably believes the committee merits confidence. Section 8.30 of the Revised Act. A director is not acting in good faith if he has knowledge concerning the matter in question that makes reliance unwarranted. The 1999 amendments to the Revised Act added a provision entitling a director to rely on the *performance* of board functions properly delegated by the board to officers, employees, or a committee of the board of directors of which the director is not a member unless the director has knowledge that makes reliance unwarranted. Section 8.30(c) as amended.

An officer is also entitled to rely upon this information, but this right may, in many circumstances, be more limited than a director's right to so rely because of the officer's greater familiarity with the corporation's affairs. Section 8.42 and Comment.

BUSINESS JUDGMENT RULE Directors and officers are continually called upon to make decisions that require balancing benefits and risks to the corporation. Although hindsight may reveal that some of these decisions were less than optimal, the business judgment rule precludes imposing liability upon the directors or officers for honest mistakes of judgment if they make an informed decision (1) with due care, (2) in good faith without any conflict of interests, and (3) with a rational basis for believing the decision was in the best interests of the corporation. (With respect to *directors*, the 1999 amendments to the Revised Act added a new Section 8.31 codifying much of the business judgment rule and providing guidance as to its application.) Moreover, when a director or officer fails to satisfy this standard of conduct, it must be shown that her action (or inaction) is the proximate cause of damage to the corporation.

Hasty or ill-advised action also can render directors liable. The Supreme Court of Delaware has held directors liable for approving the terms of a cash-out merger because the directors did not adequately inform themselves of the company's intrinsic value and were grossly negligent in approving the terms of the merger upon two hours' consideration and without prior notice. *Smith v. Van Gorkom*, 488 A.2d 858 (1985).

◆ *See Case 35-4*

35-7c DUTY OF LOYALTY

The officers and directors of a corporation owe a duty of loyalty (a **fiduciary duty**) to the corporation and to its shareholders. The essence of a fiduciary duty is the subordination of self-interest to the interest of the person or persons to whom the duty is owed. It requires officers and directors to be constantly loyal to the corporation, which they both serve and control.

An officer or director is required to disclose fully to the corporation any financial interest that he may have in any contract or transaction to which the corporation is a party. (This is a corollary to the rule that forbids fiduciaries from making secret profits.) He must eschew self-interest in his business conduct, and he may not advance his personal interests at the corporation's expense. Moreover, he may not represent conflicting interests; his duty is one of strict allegiance to the corporation.

The remedy for breach of fiduciary duty is a suit in equity by the corporation, or more often a derivative suit instituted by a shareholder, to require the fiduciary to pay to the corporation the profits that he obtained through breach of his fiduciary duty. It need not be shown that the corporation could otherwise have made the profits that the fiduciary has realized. The object of the rule is to discourage breaches of duty by taking from the fiduciary all of the profits he has made. Though enforcing the rule may result in a windfall to the corporation, this is incidental to the rule's deterrent objective. Whenever a director or officer breaches his fiduciary duty, he forfeits his right to compensation during the period he engaged in the breach.

CONFLICT OF INTEREST A contract or other transaction between an officer or a director and the corporation inherently involves a conflict of interest. Contracts between officers and the corporation are covered under the law of agency. (See *Chapter 19.*) Early on, the common law viewed all director-corporation transactions as automatically void or voidable but eventually regarded this rule as unreasonable because it would prevent directors from entering into contracts beneficial to the corporation. Now, therefore, if such a contract is honest and fair, the courts will uphold it. In the case of contracts between corporations having an interlocking directorate (corporations whose boards of directors share one or more members), the courts subject the contracts to scrutiny and will set them aside unless the transaction is shown to have been entirely fair and entered in good faith.

Most States and the original version of the Revised Act address these related problems by providing that such transactions are neither void nor voidable if, after full disclosure, they are approved by either the board of disinterested directors or the shareholders or if they are fair and reasonable to the corporation.

The Revised Act was amended in 1988 and 2005 to adopt a more specific approach to a director's conflict-of-interest transactions, which it defines as transactions between a corporation (or a subsidiary of it or an entity controlled by it) and one of the corporation's directors, a close relative of the director, or a person to whom the director owes a fiduciary duty. Section 8.60. The amended Revised Act establishes more clearly prescribed safe harbors to validate conflict-of-interest transactions. Section 8.61. The amended Revised Act provides two alternative safe harbors, each of which is available before or after the transaction: approval by "qualified" (disinterested) directors or approval by the shareholders. In either case, the interested director must make full disclosure to the approving group. Full disclosure requires the director to disclose both the existence of the conflicting interest and all material facts known to her regarding the subject matter of the transaction.

If neither of the safe harbor provisions is satisfied, then the transaction is subject to appropriate judicial action unless the transaction is fair to the corporation. The comments to Section 8.61 explain that fairness requires that (1) the terms of the transaction, including the price, are fair; (2) the transaction benefits the corporation; and (3) the course of dealing or process of the transaction is fair.

LOANS TO DIRECTORS AND OFFICERS The Model Act and some States permit a corporation to lend money to its directors only with its shareholders' authorization for each loan. The statutes in most States permit such loans on either a general or limited basis. The Revised Act initially permitted such loans if each was approved (1) by a majority of disinterested shareholders or (2) by the board of directors after its determination that the loan would benefit the corporation. Section 8.32. The 1988 amendments to the Revised Act deleted this section, instead subjecting director loans to the procedure that applies to a director's conflict-of-interest transactions.

The Sarbanes-Oxley Act prohibits any publicly held corporation from making personal loans to its directors or its executive officers, although it does provide certain limited exceptions.

CORPORATE OPPORTUNITY Directors and officers may not usurp any corporate opportunity that in all fairness should belong to the corporation. A corporate opportunity is one in which the corporation has a right, property interest, or expectancy; whether or not such an opportunity exists depends on the facts and circumstances of each case.

A corporate opportunity should be promptly offered to the corporation, which, in turn, should promptly accept or reject it. Rejection may be based on one or more of several factors, such as the corporation's lack of interest in the opportunity, its financial inability to acquire the opportunity, legal restrictions on its ability to accept the opportunity, or a third party's unwillingness to deal with the corporation. Section 8.70 was added to the Revised Act in 2005 to deal with business opportunities and to provide safe-harbor protection for directors considering involvement with a business opportunity that might be considered a corporate opportunity. In 2014 and 2016, the Revised Act was amended to permit corporations to include in their articles of incorporation a provision that limits or eliminates the duty of a director or an officer to present a business opportunity to the corporation.

For instance, a party proposes a business arrangement to a corporation through its vice president, who personally accepts the arrangement without offering it to the corporation. The vice president has usurped a corporate opportunity. On the other hand, a corporate opportunity generally would not include one that the corporation was unable to accept or one that the corporation expressly rejected by a vote of disinterested directors after full disclosure. In both of these instances, a director or officer is free to take personal advantage of the opportunity.

◆ *See Case 35-5*

TRANSACTIONS IN SHARES The issuance of shares at favorable prices to management by excluding other shareholders normally will constitute a violation of the fiduciary duty. So might the issuance of shares to a director at a fair price if the purpose of the issuance is to perpetuate corporate control rather than to raise capital or to serve some other interest of the corporation.

Officers and directors have access to inside advance information, unavailable to the public, which may affect the future market value of the corporation's shares. Federal statutes have attempted to deal with this trading advantage by prohibiting officers and directors from purchasing or selling shares of their corporation's stock without adequately disclosing all material facts in their possession that may affect the stock's actual or potential value. See *Chapter 43* for a discussion of these matters.

Although the imposition of liability upon officers and directors for secret, profitable use of inside information has been inconsistent under State law, the trend is toward holding them liable for breach of fiduciary duty to shareholders from whom they purchase stock without disclosing facts that give the stock added potential value. They are also held liable to the corporation for profits realized upon a sale of the stock when undisclosed conditions of the corporation make a substantial decline in value practically inevitable.

DUTY NOT TO COMPETE As fiduciaries, directors and officers owe to the corporation the duty of undivided loyalty, which means they may not compete with the corporation. A director or officer who breaches his fiduciary duty by competing with the corporation is liable for the damages he thus causes to the corporation. Although directors and officers may engage in their own business interests, courts will closely scrutinize any interest that competes with the corporation's business. Moreover, an officer or director (1) may not use corporate personnel, facilities, or funds for her own benefit and (2) may not disclose trade secrets of the corporation to others.

35-7d INDEMNIFICATION OF DIRECTORS AND OFFICERS

Directors and officers incur personal liability for breaching any of the duties they owe to the corporation and its shareholders. Under many modern incorporation statutes, a corporation *may* indemnify a director or officer for liability incurred if he acted in good faith and in a manner he reasonably believed to be in the best interests of the corporation, so long as he has not been adjudged negligent or liable for misconduct. The Revised Act provides for *mandatory* indemnification of directors and officers for reasonable expenses they incur in the wholly successful defense of any proceeding brought against them because they are or were directors or officers. Sections 8.52 and 8.56. These provisions, however, may be limited by the articles of incorporation. In addition, a corporation may

purchase insurance to indemnify officers and directors for liability arising out of their corporate activities, including liabilities against which the corporation is not empowered to indemnify directly. Section 8.57.

Practical Advice

Before agreeing to serve on a corporate board of directors, make sure that the company has sufficient director's liability insurance and determine what the policy covers.

35-7e LIABILITY LIMITATION STATUTES

Virtually all States have enacted legislation limiting the liability of directors. Most of these States, including Delaware, have authorized corporations—with shareholder approval—to limit or eliminate the liability of directors for some breaches of duty. (A few States permit shareholders to limit the liability of officers.) The Delaware statute provides that the articles of incorporation may contain a provision eliminating or limiting the personal liability of a director to the corporation or its stockholders for monetary damages for breach of fiduciary duty as a director, provided that such provision does not eliminate or limit the liability of a director (1) for any breach of the director's duty of loyalty to the corporation or its stockholders, (2) for acts or omissions not in good faith or involving intentional misconduct or a knowing violation of law, (3) for liability for unlawful dividend payments or redemptions, or (4) for any transaction from which the director derived an improper personal benefit.

A few States have directly limited personal liability for directors, subject to certain exceptions, without requiring an amendment to the articles of incorporation. Other States adopt a third approach by limiting the amount of money damages that may be assessed against a director or officer.

The Revised Act was amended in 1990 to authorize the articles of incorporation to include a provision eliminating or limiting—with certain exceptions—the liability of a director to the corporation or its shareholders for any action that he, as a director, has taken or has failed to take. The exceptions, for which liability would be unaffected, are (1) the amount of any financial benefit the director receives to which he is not entitled, such as a bribe, a kickback, or profits from a usurped corporate opportunity; (2) an intentional infliction of harm on the corporation or the shareholders; (3) liability under Section 8.33 for unlawful distributions; and (4) an intentional violation of the criminal law. Section 2.02(b)(4).

C H A P T E R   S U M M A R Y

ROLE OF SHAREHOLDERS

VOTING RIGHTS OF SHAREHOLDERS	**Management Structure of Corporations** see *Figures 35-1, 35-2,* and *35-3* for illustrations of the statutory model of corporate governance, the structure of the typical closely held corporation, and the structure of the typical publicly held corporation, respectively

Shareholder Meetings shareholders may exercise their voting rights at both annual and special shareholder meetings

Quorum minimum number necessary to be present at a meeting to transact business

Election of Directors the shareholders elect the board at the annual meeting of the corporation

- *Straight Voting* directors are elected by a plurality of votes
- *Cumulative Voting* entitles shareholders to multiply the number of votes they are entitled to cast by the number of directors for whom they are entitled to vote and to cast the product for a single candidate or to distribute the product among two or more candidates

Removal of Directors the shareholders may by majority vote remove directors with or without cause, subject to cumulative voting rights

Approval of Fundamental Changes shareholder approval is required for amendments to the articles of incorporation, most acquisitions, and dissolution

Concentrations of Voting Power

- *Proxy* authorization to vote another's shares at a shareholder meeting
- *Voting Trust* transfer of corporate shares' voting rights to a trustee
- *Shareholder Voting Agreement* used to provide shareholders with greater control over the election and removal of directors and other matters
- *Restrictions on Transfer of Shares* must be reasonable and conspicuously noted on stock certificate

ENFORCEMENT RIGHTS OF SHAREHOLDERS	**Right to Inspect Books and Records** if the demand is made in good faith and for a proper purpose

Shareholder Suits

- *Direct Suits* brought by a shareholder or a class of shareholders against the corporation based upon the ownership of shares
- *Derivative Suits* brought by a shareholder on behalf of the corporation to enforce a right belonging to the corporation

Shareholder's Right to Dissent a shareholder has the right to dissent from certain corporate actions that require shareholder approval

ROLE OF DIRECTORS AND OFFICERS

FUNCTION OF THE BOARD OF DIRECTORS	**Selection and Removal of Officers Capital Structure**

Fundamental Changes the directors have the power to make, amend, or repeal the bylaws, unless this power is exclusively reserved to the shareholders

Dividends directors declare the amount and type of dividends

Management Compensation the board of directors usually determines the compensation of officers and, in a number of States, the compensation of directors

Election and Tenure of Directors directors are elected at annual meetings of the shareholders and hold office for one year unless their terms are staggered

Vacancies in the Board may be filled by the vote of a majority of the remaining directors

Removal of Directors the Revised Act (1) permits the shareholders to remove one or more directors with or without cause and (2) authorizes judicial removal of directors for cause

EXERCISE OF DIRECTORS' FUNCTIONS	**Meeting** directors have the power to bind the corporation only when acting as a board
	Action Taken Without a Meeting permitted if a consent in writing is signed by all of the directors
	Delegation of Board Powers committees may be appointed to perform some but not all of the board's functions
	Directors' Inspection Rights directors have the right to inspect corporate books and records
OFFICERS	**Selection and Removal of Officers** the board of directors appoints and removes the officers
	Role of Officers officers are agents of the corporation
	Authority of Officers
	• *Actual Express Authority* arises from the incorporation statute, the articles of incorporation, the bylaws, and resolutions of the directors
	• *Actual Implied Authority* authority to do what is reasonably necessary to perform actual authority
	• *Apparent Authority* acts of the principal that lead a third party to believe reasonably and in good faith that an officer has the required authority
	• *Ratification* a corporation may ratify the unauthorized acts of its officers
DUTIES OF DIRECTORS AND OFFICERS	**Duty of Obedience** must act within respective authority
	Duty of Diligence must exercise ordinary care and prudence
	Duty of Loyalty requires undeviating loyalty to the corporation
	Business Judgment Rule precludes imposing liability on directors and officers for honest mistakes in judgment if they act with due care, in good faith, and in a manner reasonably believed to be in the best interests of the corporation
	Indemnification a corporation may indemnify a director or officer for liability incurred if he acted in good faith and was not adjudged negligent or liable for misconduct
	Liability Limitation Statutes many States authorize corporations—with shareholder approval—to limit or eliminate the liability of directors for some breaches of duty

C A S E S

CASE 35-1

Right to Inspect Books and Records
KING v. VERIFONE HOLDINGS, INC

Supreme Court of Delaware, 2011
12 A.3d 1140

Jacobs, J.

VeriFone, a Delaware corporation whose principal place of business is in San Jose, California, designs, markets, and services electronic payment transaction systems. On November 1, 2006, VeriFone acquired the Israeli-based Lipman Electronic Engineering Ltd. ("Lipman"), which was then the world's

fourth-largest point-of-sale terminal maker. That acquisition made VeriFone the world's largest provider of electronic payment solutions and services.

On December 3, 2007, VeriFone publicly announced that it would restate its reported earnings and net income for the prior three fiscal quarters. Both sets of numbers had been materially overstated due to accounting and valuation errors made while Lipman's inventory systems were being integrated with Veri-Fone's. After that restatement announcement, VeriFone's stock price dropped over 45% * * *.

[Charles R.] King beneficially owns 3000 VeriFone shares, of which he has held at least 500 since December 11, 2006. On December 14, 2007, King filed a stockholder derivative action on behalf of VeriFone against certain of its officers and members of its board of directors ("Board") in the California Federal Court, * * * claiming that various VeriFone officers and directors had committed breaches of fiduciary duty and corporate waste. Specifically, King alleged that VeriFone's officers and Board had: (a) made materially false financial statements to the SEC and the public; (b) abdicated their fiduciary duties by allowing VeriFone to operate with material weaknesses in its internal controls over financial reporting, while representing publicly that the company had effective internal controls; and (c) allowed eight VeriFone directors and/or officers, while possessing material insider information, to sell over 12.4 million of their VeriFone shares for a $462 million dollar profit.

VeriFone moved to dismiss * * * for failure to make a presuit demand upon its Board, as required by Federal Rule of Civil Procedure (FRCP) 23.1(b)(3). On May 26, 2009, the California Federal Court granted VeriFone's motion, holding that King's consolidated complaint failed to allege particularized facts that would excuse a pre-suit demand. That dismissal was without prejudice. In granting leave to amend the complaint, the California Federal Court suggested that King first "engage in further investigation to assert additional particularized facts" by filing a Section 220 action in Delaware. * * *

On June 9, 2009, King submitted to VeriFone a written demand to inspect specified categories of documents. The parties were able to resolve all of King's requests except one—the Audit Committee Report ("Audit Report"), which contained the results of an internal investigation of VeriFone's accounting and financial controls that had been conducted after the December 3, 2007 restatement announcement.

[Unable to resolve the dispute through mediation, on November 6, 2009, King filed a Section 220 action in the Delaware Court of Chancery for an order permitting him to inspect the Audit Report and any documents relied upon in its preparation. VeriFone moved to dismiss the Section 220 complaint, claiming that King had "initiated this litigation backwards" by first filing his derivative suit in California. The Court of Chancery agreed and dismissed King's action, holding that King lacked a "proper purpose" for inspection, as Section 220 requires. The Chancellor reasoned that because King had "elected" to file his California derivative action before conducting a pre-suit investigation (including resort to the Section 220 process), King was precluded from using the Delaware courts to obtain discovery that was unnecessary or unavailable in his Federalderivative action. King appealed.]

The sole issue on this appeal is whether a stockholder-plaintiff who has brought a stockholder's derivative action without first prosecuting an action to inspect books and records under [Section] 220 is, for that reason alone, legally precluded from prosecuting a later-filed Section 220 proceeding. * * *

* * *

Section 220 expressly grants a stockholder of a Delaware corporation the right to inspect that corporation's books and records. [Citation.] That right is not absolute, however, because to obtain inspection relief the stockholder must demonstrate a proper purpose for making such a demand. [Citation.] A "proper purpose" is defined as "a purpose reasonably related to such person's interest as a stockholder." [Citation.] To cite one example, investigating corporate mis-management—the purpose stated by King—is a proper purpose for seeking a Section 220 books and records inspection. [Citation.]

Delaware courts have strongly encouraged stockholder-plaintiffs to utilize Section 220 before filing a derivative action * * *. By first prosecuting a Section 220 action to inspect books and records, the stockholder-plaintiff may be able to uncover particularized facts that would establish demand excusal in a subsequent derivative suit. [Citation.]

A failure to proceed in that specific sequence, however, although ill-advised, has not heretofore been regarded as fatal. * * *

* * *

Although we reject the result reached by the Court of Chancery, and the brightline rule that drove it, we are sensitive to the policy concerns that animated both. We agree with the * * * Chancellor that it is wasteful of the court's and the litigants' resources to have a regime that could require a corporation to litigate repeatedly the issue of demand futility. Undoubtedly the preclusion rule adopted by the Court of Chancery was intended as a needed prophylactic cure. In our view, however, a rule that would automatically bar a stockholder-plaintiff from bringing a Section 220 action *solely* because that plaintiff previously filed a plenary derivative suit, is a remedy that is overbroad and unsupported by the text of, and the policy underlying, Section 220. * * *

* * *

* * * For the Court of Chancery in a Section 220 proceeding to establish and impose a preclusive judge-made rule that finds no support either in the language or its underlying policy of Section 220, or in Delaware case law, was error.

For the reasons stated above, the judgment of the Court of Chancery is reversed.

CASE 35-2

Shareholder Suits
NICHOLS v. HEALTHSOUTH CORPORATION
Supreme Court of Alabama, 2018
281 So.3d 350

Mendheim, J.

Nichols, Deavours, Akers, Dryden, and Evans (* * * "the employee shareholders") at one time were all HealthSouth employees and holders of HealthSouth stock. [HealthSouth [now Encompass Health] is incorporated in Delaware.] On March 28, 2003, the employee shareholders sued HealthSouth, [officers] Richard Scrushy, Weston Smith, [and] William Owens, and the accounting firm Ernst & Young, alleging fraud and negligence. The action was delayed for 11 years for a variety of reasons, including a stay imposed until related criminal prosecutions were completed and a stay imposed pending the resolution of federal and state class actions.

In their original complaint—and in several subsequent amended complaints—the employee shareholders alleged that HealthSouth and several of its executive officers [mentioned above had]

> published financial statements of Healthsouth from 1987 forward. Those representations were made … with the intent that investors such as [the employee shareholders] would rely upon them in making decisions to buy, sell, or hold HealthSouth stock. [The employee shareholders] relied upon the false statements about HealthSouth's financial condition in making those decisions. As a result of that reliance, [the employee shareholders] suffered damage[].

* * *

* * * [T]he employee shareholders filed their eighth amended complaint on November 25, 2014, and * * * alleged that "ultimately their decisions to buy and hold HealthSouth stock were made in reliance upon the personal reassurances of Richard Scrushy [founder, former chairman and former CEO of HealthSouth] himself" and that this constituted a direct fraud upon them that did not affect other HealthSouth stockholders.

* * *

On May 26, 2016, the trial court entered an order dismissing the employee shareholders' complaint for failure to comply with the procedures for filing a derivative suit. The trial court stated

> while Scrushy is alleged to have committed fraud against these plaintiffs, in truth he committed fraud against all shareholders of his company. As alleged in the plaintiffs' various complaints, Scrushy and other executives devised a scheme of hiding the company's true financial

condition from everyone. The fraud was global in nature, and all shareholders ultimately suffered as a result.

The court therefore agrees with HealthSouth that under Delaware law, a shareholder may not pursue a direct claim based on the diminution in stock value that all other shareholders suffered. * * *

[The shareholder employees filed a timely appeal.]

This Court previously has stated that "the determination whether the shareholders' claims are derivative or direct must … be made in accordance with" the law of the state of incorporation. [Citations.] This is also known as the "internal affairs doctrine."

* * *

* * * The trial court was correct in concluding that Delaware law applied to the issue whether the employee shareholders' claims are derivative or direct in nature. The trial court, however, erred in concluding that Delaware law categorizes the present action as derivative in nature.

The trial court relied upon *Tooley v. Donaldson, Lufkin & Jenrette, Inc.*, [citation], in concluding that the focus in determining whether a claim is derivative or direct is "the nature of the plaintiff's claimed injury, not on the nature of the wrongdoing." The *Tooley* court stated: "[The] issue [whether a stockholder's claim is derivative or direct] must turn solely on the following questions: (1) who suffered the alleged harm (the corporation or the suing stockholders, individually); and (2) who would receive the benefit of any recovery or other remedy (the corporation or the stockholders, individually)?" [Citation.] As the trial court noted, the Tooley court went on to explain:

> [A] court should look to the nature of the wrong and to whom the relief should go. The stockholder's claimed direct injury must be independent of any alleged injury to the corporation. The stockholder must demonstrate that the duty breached was owed to the stockholder and that he or she can prevail without showing an injury to the corporation. [Citation.]

If *Tooley* was the only guidance we had for Delaware law on this issue, we would agree with the trial court's conclusion. But, two days after the trial court issued its final order, the Delaware Supreme Court decided *Citigroup Inc. v. AHW Investment Partnership*, [citation], in which it clarified when the Tooley test should be applied. ***

* * *

The Delaware Supreme Court * * * proceeded to dispel the notion that its test in *Tooley* initially should be used to examine whether such a claim is derivative or direct in nature.

The familiar two-pronged test we articulated in *Tooley v. Donaldson, Lufkin & Jenrette, Inc.*, is not relevant to the analysis of whether the holder claims at issue here are direct or derivative. Rather, *Tooley* and its progeny deal with the narrow issue of whether a claim for breach of fiduciary duty or otherwise to enforce the corporation's own rights must be asserted derivatively or directly. Before evaluating a claim under *Tooley*, "a more important initial question has to be answered: does the plaintiff seek to bring a claim belonging to her personally or one belonging to the corporation itself?" [Citation.] Because the holder claims at issue here belong to the holding stockholders under the state laws that govern the claims, and are not fiduciary duty claims or claims otherwise belonging to the corporation, *Tooley* does not affect our answer to this certified question.

[Citation.] The court later restated its holding this way: "[T]he Holder Claims are direct claims because they belong to the holders and are ones that only the holders can assert, not claims that could plausibly belong to the issuer corporation, Citigroup." [Citation.]

* * *

In sum, in *Citigroup*, the Delaware Supreme Court concluded that the plaintiffs' claims were direct claims because the plaintiffs personally held the stock and made the decision to continue to hold it allegedly based on misleading information from Citigroup. The court stated that the same principle held for purchaser claims because for such a claim the stock purchaser makes a personal decision to buy stock based on allegedly false information. The court emphasized that the plaintiffs did not base their claims on something related to internal corporate affairs such as fiduciary duties. Finally, the court declined to analyze the type of injury the plaintiffs sustained in assessing whether their claims were direct or derivative.

Citigroup is directly on point because the employee shareholders have asserted purchaser and holder claims in their eighth amended complaint. That is, they allege that they purchased additional stock in HealthSouth and continued to hold stock they already owned because of specific fraudulent misrepresentations from Richard Scrushy to them about the financial condition of HealthSouth. They do not allege that Scrushy was a fiduciary who owed them a heightened duty; they do not allege that HealthSouth itself owed a special duty to its shareholders when it issued stock. The employee shareholders simply allege common-law fraud claims based on direct, personal misrepresentations. As the employee shareholders contended in their brief: "[T]he claims of appellants could not have been brought by the corporation. The corporation itself was not induced to do anything by the fraudulent statements of its CEO." [Citation.] Under *Citigroup*, because the rights allegedly infringed upon— the right to choose to purchase and to hold HealthSouth stock— personally belonged to the employee shareholders and not to the corporation, the claims are direct in nature. [Citations.]

Based on the foregoing, we conclude that the employee shareholders' claims are direct rather than derivative and that, therefore, the trial court erred in dismissing the employee shareholders' claims * * *.

* * *

* * * The employee shareholders were not required to comply with the procedures * * * for filing a derivative action because, under Delaware law, their claims are direct in nature. Accordingly, the judgment of the trial court is due to be reversed and the cause is remanded for further proceedings.

CASE 35-3

Duties of Controlling Shareholders

DONAHUE v. RODD ELECTROTYPE CO., INC.

Massachusetts Supreme Court, 1974
367 Mass. 578, 328 N.E.2d 505

Tauro, C. J.

The plaintiff, Euphemia Donahue, a minority stockholder in the Rodd Electrotype Company of New England, Inc. (Rodd Electrotype), a Massachusetts corporation, brings this suit against the directors of Rodd Electrotype, Charles H. Rodd, Frederick I. Rodd and Mr. Harold E. Magnuson, against Harry C. Rodd, a former director, officer, and controlling stockholder of Rodd Electrotype and against Rodd Electrotype (hereinafter called defendants).

The plaintiff seeks to rescind Rodd Electrotype's purchase of Harry Rodd's shares in Rodd Electrotype and to compel Harry Rodd "to repay to the corporation the purchase price of said shares, $36,000, together with interest from the date of purchase." The plaintiff alleges that the defendants caused the corporation to purchase the shares in violation of their fiduciary duty to her, a minority stockholder of Rodd Electrotype.

* * * We deem a close corporation to be typified by: (1) a small number of stockholders; (2) no ready market for the

corporate stock; and (3) substantial majority stockholder participation in the management, direction and operations of the corporation.

As thus defined, the close corporation bears striking resemblance to a partnership. Commentators and courts have noted that the close corporation is often little more than an "incorporated" or "chartered" partnership. * * * Just as in a partnership, the relationship among the stockholders must be one of trust, confidence and absolute loyalty if the enterprise is to succeed. Close corporations with substantial assets and with more numerous stockholders are no different from smaller close corporations in this regard. All participants rely on the fidelity and abilities of those stockholders who hold office. Disloyalty and self-seeking conduct on the part of any stockholder will engender bickering, corporate stalemates, and, perhaps, efforts to achieve dissolution. * * *

Although the corporate form provides * * * advantages for the stockholders (limited liability, perpetuity, and so forth), it also supplies an opportunity for the majority stockholders to oppress or disadvantage minority stockholders. The minority is vulnerable to a variety of oppressive devices, termed "freeze-outs," which the majority may employ. [Citation.] An authoritative study of such "freeze-outs" enumerates some of the possibilities: "The squeezers [those who employ the freeze-out techniques] may refuse to declare dividends; they may drain off the corporation's earnings in the form of exorbitant salaries and bonuses to the majority shareholder-officers and perhaps to their relatives, or in the form of high rent by the corporation for property leased from majority shareholders; ... they may deprive minority shareholders of corporate offices and of employment by the company; they may cause the corporation to sell its assets at an inadequate price to the majority shareholders." ... [Citation.] In particular, the power of the board of directors, controlled by the majority, to declare or withhold dividends and to deny the minority employment is easily converted to a device to disadvantage minority stockholders.

The minority can, of course, initiate suit against the majority and their directors. Self-serving conduct by directors is proscribed by the director's fiduciary obligation to the corporation. [Citation.] However, in practice, the plaintiff will find difficulty in challenging dividend or employment policies. Such policies are considered to be within the judgment of the directors. This court has said: "The courts prefer not to interfere ... with the sound financial management of the corporation by its directors, but declare as a general rule that the declaration of dividends rests within the sound discretion of the directors, refusing to interfere with their determination unless a plain abuse of discretion is made to appear." * * *

Thus, when these types of "freeze-outs" are attempted by the majority stockholders, the minority stockholders, cut off from all corporation-related revenues, must either suffer their losses or seek a buyer for their shares. Many minority stockholders will be unwilling or unable to wait for an alteration in majority policy. Typically, the minority stockholder in a close corporation has a substantial percentage of his personal assets invested in the corporation. [Citation.] The stockholder may have anticipated that his salary from his position with the corporation would be his livelihood. Thus, he cannot afford to wait passively. He must liquidate his investment in the close corporation in order to reinvest the funds in income-producing enterprises.

* * * In a large public corporation, the oppressed or dissident minority stockholder could sell his stock in order to extricate some of his invested capital. By definition, this market is not available for shares in the close corporation. In a partnership, a partner who feels abused by his fellow partners may cause dissolution by his "express will ... at any time" [citation] and recover his share of partnership assets and accumulated profits. * * * To secure dissolution of the ordinary close corporation subject to [citation], the stockholder, in the absence of corporate deadlock, must own at least fifty percent of the shares [citation] or have the advantage of a favorable provision in the articles of organization [citation]. The minority stockholder, by definition lacking fifty percent of the corporate shares, can never "authorize" the corporation to file a petition for dissolution under [citation], by his own vote. He will seldom have at his disposal the requisite favorable provision in the articles of organization.

Thus, in a close corporation, the minority stockholders may be trapped in a disadvantageous situation. No outsider would knowingly assume the position of the disadvantaged minority. The outsider would have the same difficulties. To cut losses, the minority stockholder may be compelled to deal with the majority. This is the capstone of the majority plan. Majority "freeze-out" schemes which withhold dividends are designed to compel the minority to relinquish stock at inadequate prices. * * * When the minority stockholder agrees to sell out at less than fair value, the majority has won.

Because of the fundamental resemblance of the close corporation to the partnership, the trust and confidence which are essential to this scale and manner of enterprise, and the inherent danger to minority interests in the close corporation, we hold that stockholders in the close corporation owe one another substantially the same fiduciary duty in the operation of the enterprise that partners owe to one another. In our previous decisions, we have defined the standard of duty owed by partners to one another as the "utmost good faith and loyalty." [Citations.] Stockholders in close corporations must discharge their management and stockholder responsibilities in conformity with this strict good faith standard. They may not act out of avarice, expediency or self-interest in derogation of their duty of loyalty to the other stockholders and to the corporation.

We contrast this strict good faith standard with the somewhat less stringent standard of fiduciary duty to which directors and stockholders of all corporations must adhere in the discharge of their corporate responsibilities. Corporate directors are held to a good faith and inherent fairness standard of conduct [citation] and are not "permitted to serve two masters whose interests are antagonistic." [Citation.] "Their paramount duty is to the corporation, and their personal pecuniary interests are subordinate to that duty." [Citation.]

The more rigorous duty of partners and participants in a joint adventure, here extended to stockholders in a close corporation, was described by then Chief Judge Cardozo of the New York Court of Appeals in [citation]: "Joint adventurers, like co-partners, owe to one another, while the enterprise continues, the duty of the finest loyalty. Many forms of conduct permissible in a workaday world for those acting at arm's length, are forbidden to those bound by fiduciary ties. … Not honesty alone, but the punctilio of an honor the most sensitive, is then the standard of behavior."

* * *

Under settled Massachusetts law, a domestic corporation, unless forbidden by statute, has the power to purchase its own shares. When the corporation reacquiring its own stock is a close corporation, the purchase is subject to the additional requirement, in the light of our holding in this opinion, that the stockholders, who, as directors or controlling stockholders, caused the corporation to enter into the stock purchase agreement, must have acted with the utmost good faith and loyalty to the other stockholders.

To meet this test, if the stockholder whose shares were purchased was a member of the controlling group, the controlling stockholders must cause the corporation to offer each stockholder an equal opportunity to sell a ratable number of his shares to the corporation at an identical price. * * *

* * * If the close corporation purchases shares only from a member of the controlling group, the controlling stockholder can convert his shares into cash at a time when none of the other stockholders can. Consistent with its strict fiduciary duty, the controlling group may not utilize its control of the corporation to establish an exclusive market in previously unmarketable shares from which the minority stockholders are excluded. * * *

The purchase also distributes corporate assets to the stockholder whose shares were purchased. Unless an equal opportunity is given to all stockholders, the purchase of shares from a member of the controlling group operates as a *preferential* distribution of assets. * * *

The rule of equal opportunity in stock purchases by close corporations provides equal access to these benefits for all stockholders. We hold that, in any case in which the controlling stockholders have exercised their power over the corporation to deny the minority such equal opportunity, the minority shall be entitled to appropriate relief. * * *

On its face, then, the purchase of Harry Rodd's shares by the corporation is a breach of the duty which the controlling stockholders, the Rodds, owed to the minority stockholders, the plaintiff and her son. * * *

Because of the foregoing, we hold that the plaintiff is entitled to relief.

CASE 35-4	Duty of Diligence **BREHM v. EISNER** Supreme Court of Delaware, 2000 746 A.2d 244	

Veasey, C. J.

[On October 1, 1995, Disney hired as its president Michael S Ovitz, who was a longtime friend of Disney Chairman and CEO Michael Eisner. At the time, Ovitz was an important talent broker in Hollywood. Although he lacked experience managing a diversified public company, other companies with entertainment operations had been interested in hiring him for high-level executive positions. The employment agreement approved by the board of directors then in office (Old Board) had an initial term of five years and required that Ovitz "devote his full time and best efforts exclusively to the Company," with exceptions for volunteer work, service on the board of another company, and management of his passive investments. In return, Disney agreed to give Ovitz a base salary of $1 million

per year, a discretionary bonus, and two sets of stock options (the "A" options and the "B" options) that collectively would enable Ovitz to purchase 5 million shares of Disney common stock. The "A" options were scheduled to vest in three annual increments of 1 million shares each, beginning at the end of the third full year of employment and continuing for the following two years. The agreement specifically provided that the "A" options would vest immediately if Disney granted Ovitz a non-fault termination of the employment agreement. The "B" options, consisting of 2 million shares, were scheduled to vest annually starting the year after the last "A" option would vest and were conditioned on Ovitz and Disney first having agreed to extend his employment beyond the five-year term of the employment agreement. In addition, Ovitz would forfeit the "B" options if his initial employment term of five years ended prematurely for any reason, even if from a non-fault termination.

The employment agreement provided three ways for Ovitz employment to end. He might serve his five years, and Disney might decide against offering him a new contract. If so, Disney would owe Ovitz a $10 million termination payment. Before the end of the initial term, Disney could terminate Ovitz for "good cause" only if Ovitz committed gross negligence or malfeasance or if Ovitz resigned voluntarily. Disney would owe Ovitz no additional compensation if it terminated him for "good cause." Termination without cause (non-fault termination) would entitle Ovitz to the present value of his salary payments remaining under the agreement, a $10 million severance payment, an additional $7.5 million for each fiscal year remaining under the agreement, and the immediate vesting of the first 3 million stock options (the "A" Options).

Soon after Ovitz began work, problems surfaced and the situation continued to deteriorate during the first year of his employment. The deteriorating situation led Ovitz to begin seeking alternative employment and expressing his desire to leave the Company. On December 11, 1996, Eisner and Ovitz agreed to arrange for Ovitz to leave Disney on the non-fault basis provided for in the 1995 employment agreement. The board of directors then in office (New Board) approved this by authorizing a "non-fault termination" agreement with cash payments to Ovitz of almost $39 million and the immediate vesting of 3 million stock options with a value of $101 million.

Shareholders brought a derivative suit alleging that (a) the Old Board had breached its fiduciary duty in approving an extravagant and wasteful employment agreement of Michael S. Ovitz as president of Disney and (b) the New Board had breached its fiduciary duty in agreeing to an extravagant and wasteful "non-fault" termination of the Ovitz employment agreement. The plaintiffs alleged that the Old Board had failed to inform itself properly about the total costs and incentives of the Ovitz employment agreement, especially the severance package, and failed to realize that the contract gave Ovitz an incentive to find a way to exit the Company via a non-fault termination as soon as possible because doing so would permit him to earn more than he could by fulfilling his contract. They alleged that the corporate compensation expert, Graef Crystal, who had advised Old Board in connection with its decision to approve the Ovitz employment agreement, stated two years later that the Old Board failed to consider the incentives and the total cost of the severance provisions. The defendants moved to dismiss, and the Court of Chancery granted the motion. The shareholders appealed.]

This is potentially a very troubling case on the merits. On the one hand, it appears from the Complaint that: (a) the compensation and termination payout for Ovitz were exceedingly lucrative, if not luxurious, compared to Ovitz'

value to the Company; and (b) the processes of the boards of directors in dealing with the approval and termination of the Ovitz Employment Agreement were casual, if not sloppy and perfunctory. [T]he processes of the Old Board and the New Board were hardly paradigms of good corporate governance practices. Moreover, the sheer size of the payout to Ovitz, as alleged, pushes the envelope of judicial respect for the business judgment of directors in making compensation decisions. Therefore, both as to the processes of the two Boards and the waste test, this is a close case.

* * *

This is a case about whether there should be personal liability of the directors of a Delaware corporation to the corporation for lack of due care in the decisionmaking process and for waste of corporate assets. This case is not about the failure of the directors to establish and carry out ideal corporate governance practices.

All good corporate governance practices include compliance with statutory law and case law establishing fiduciary duties. But the law of corporate fiduciary duties and remedies for violation of those duties are distinct from the aspirational goals of ideal corporate governance practices. Aspirational ideals of good corporate governance practices for boards of directors that go beyond the minimal legal requirements of the corporation law are highly desirable, often tend to benefit stockholders, sometimes reduce litigation and can usually help directors avoid liability. But they are not required by the corporation law and do not define standards of liability. [Citation.]

The inquiry here is not whether we would disdain the composition, behavior and decisions of Disney's Old Board or New Board as alleged in the Complaint if we were Disney stockholders. In the absence of a legislative mandate, [citation], that determination is not for the courts. That decision is for the stockholders to make in voting for directors, urging other stockholders to reform or oust the board, or in making individual buy-sell decisions involving Disney securities. The sole issue that this Court must determine is whether the particularized facts alleged in this Complaint provide a reason to believe that the conduct of the Old Board in 1995 and the New Board in 1996 constituted a violation of their fiduciary duties.

Plaintiffs claim that the Court of Chancery erred when it concluded that a board of directors is "not required to be informed of every fact, but rather is required to be reasonably informed." [Citation.] * * * The "reasonably informed" language used by the Court of Chancery here may have been a shorthand attempt to paraphrase the Delaware jurisprudence that, in making business decisions, directors must consider all material information reasonably available, and that the directors' process is actionable only if grossly negligent. [Citation.] The question is whether the trial court's formulation is consistent with our objective test of reasonableness, the test of materiality and concepts of gross negligence. We agree with the Court of

Chancery that the standard for judging the informational component of the directors' decisionmaking does not mean that the Board must be informed of every fact. The Board is responsible for considering only material facts that are reasonably available, not those that are immaterial or out of the Board's reasonable reach. [Citation.]

Certainly in this case the economic exposure of the corporation to the payout scenarios of the Ovitz contract was material, particularly given its large size, for purposes of the directors' decisionmaking process. [Court's footnote: The term "material" is used in this context to mean relevant and of a magnitude to be important to directors in carrying out their fiduciary duty of care in decisionmaking.] And those dollar exposure numbers were reasonably available because the logical inference from plaintiffs' allegations is that Crystal or the New Board could have calculated the numbers. Thus, the objective tests of reasonable availability and materiality were satisfied by this Complaint. But that is not the end of the inquiry for liability purposes.

* * *

* * * The Complaint, fairly construed, admits that the directors were advised by Crystal as an expert and that they relied on his expertise. Accordingly, the question here is whether the directors are to be "fully protected" (i.e., not held liable) on the basis that they relied in good faith on a qualified expert [citation]. * * *

* * * Plaintiffs must rebut the presumption that the directors properly exercised their business judgment, including their good faith reliance on Crystal's expertise. * * *

* * * [T]he complaint must allege particularized facts (not conclusions) that, if proved, would show, for example, that: (a) the directors did not in fact rely on the expert; (b) their reliance was not in good faith; (c) they did not reasonably believe that the expert's advice was within the expert's professional competence; (d) the expert was not selected with reasonable care by or on behalf of the corporation, and the faulty selection process was attributable to the directors; (e) the subject matter (in this case the cost calculation) that was material and reasonably available was so obvious that the board's failure to consider it was grossly negligent regardless of the expert's advice or lack of advice; or (f) that the decision of the Board was so unconscionable as to constitute waste or fraud. This Complaint includes no particular allegations of this nature, and therefore it was subject to dismissal as drafted.

* * *

We conclude that * * * the Complaint * * * as drafted, fails to create a reasonable doubt that the Old Board's decision in approving the Ovitz Employment Agreement was protected by the business judgment rule. * * *

* * *

Plaintiffs' principal theory is that the 1995 Ovitz Employment Agreement was a "wasteful transaction for Disney ab initio" because it was structured to "incentivize" Ovitz to seek an early non-fault termination. The Court of Chancery correctly dismissed this theory as failing to meet the stringent requirements of the waste test, i.e., "'an exchange that is so one sided that no business person of ordinary, sound judgment could conclude that the corporation has received adequate consideration.'" Moreover, the Court concluded that a board's decision on executive compensation is entitled to great deference. It is the essence of business judgment for a board to determine if "a 'particular individual warrant[s] large amounts of money, whether in the form of current salary or severance provisions.'" [Citation.]

* * *

* * * Irrationality is the outer limit of the business judgment rule. Irrationality may be the functional equivalent of the waste test or it may tend to show that the decision is not made in good faith, which is a key ingredient of the business judgment rule. [Court's footnote: The business judgment rule has been well formulated by Aronson and other cases. ("It is a presumption that in making a business decision the directors * * * acted on an informed basis, in good faith and in the honest belief that the action taken was in the best interests of the corporation.") Thus, directors' decisions will be respected by courts unless the directors are interested or lack independence relative to the decision, do not act in good faith, act in a manner that cannot be attributed to a rational business purpose or reach their decision by a grossly negligent process that includes the failure to consider all material facts reasonably available.]

The plaintiffs contend in this Court that Ovitz resigned or committed acts of gross negligence or malfeasance that constituted grounds to terminate him for cause. In either event, they argue that the Company had no obligation to Ovitz and that the directors wasted the Company's assets by causing it to make an unnecessary and enormous payout of cash and stock options when it permitted Ovitz to terminate his employment on a "non-fault" basis. We have concluded, however, that the Complaint currently before us does not set forth particularized facts that he resigned or unarguably breached his Employment Agreement.

* * *

Construed most favorably to plaintiffs, the facts in the Complaint (disregarding conclusory allegations) show that Ovitz' performance as president was disappointing at best, that Eisner admitted it had been a mistake to hire him, that Ovitz lacked commitment to the Company, that he performed services for his old company, and that he negotiated for other jobs (some very lucrative) while being required under the contract to devote his full time and energy to Disney.

All this shows is that the Board had arguable grounds to fire Ovitz for cause. But what is alleged is only an argument—perhaps a good one—that Ovitz' conduct constituted gross negligence or malfeasance. * * *

The Complaint, in sum, contends that the Board committed waste by agreeing to the very lucrative payout to Ovitz under the non-fault termination provision because it had no obligation to him, thus taking the Board's decision outside the protection of the business judgment rule. Construed most favorably to plaintiffs, the Complaint contends that, by reason of the New Board's available arguments of resignation and good cause, it had the leverage to negotiate Ovitz down to a more reasonable payout than that guaranteed by his Employment Agreement. But the Complaint fails on its face to meet the waste test because it does not allege with particularity facts tending to show that no reasonable business person would have made the decision that the New Board made under these circumstances.

* * *

To rule otherwise would invite courts to become superdirectors, measuring matters of degree in business decisionmaking and executive compensation. Such a rule would run counter to the foundation of our jurisprudence.

* * *

One can understand why Disney stockholders would be upset with such an extraordinarily lucrative compensation agreement and termination payout awarded a company president who served for only a little over a year and who underperformed to the extent alleged. That said, there is a very large—though not insurmountable—burden on stockholders who believe they should pursue the remedy of a derivative suit instead of selling their stock or seeking to reform or oust these directors from office.

[Dismissal affirmed in part and reversed in part, and case remanded.]

CASE 35-5

Duty of Loyalty
BEAM v. STEWART
Court of Chancery of Delaware, New Castle, 2003
833 A.2d 961; affirmed, 845 A.2d 1040

Chandler, Chancellor

Monica A. Beam, a shareholder of Martha Stewart Living Omnimedia, Inc. ("MSO"), brings this derivative action against the defendants, all current directors and a former director of MSO, and against MSO as a nominal defendant. * * *

Plaintiff Monica A. Beam is a shareholder of MSO and has been since August 2001. Derivative plaintiff and nominal defendant MSO is a Delaware corporation that operates in the publishing, television, merchandising, and internet industries marketing products bearing the "Martha Stewart" brand name.

Defendant Martha Stewart ("Stewart") is a director of the company and its founder, chairman, chief executive officer, and by far its majority shareholder. * * * [S]he controls roughly 94.4% of the shareholder vote. Stewart, a former stockbroker, has in the past twenty years become a household icon, known for her advice and expertise on virtually all aspects of cooking, decorating, entertaining, and household affairs generally.

* * *

The market for MSO products is uniquely tied to the personal image and reputation of its founder, Stewart. MSO retains "an exclusive, worldwide, perpetual royalty-free license to use [Stewart's] name, likeness, image, voice and signature for its products and services." In its initial public offering prospectus, MSO recognized that impairment of Stewart's services to the company, including the tarnishing of her public reputation,

would have a material adverse effect on its business. The prospectus distinguished Stewart's importance to MSO's business success from that of other executives of the company noting that, "Martha Stewart remains the personification of our brands as well as our senior executive and primary creative force." In fact, under the terms of her employment agreement, Stewart may be terminated for gross misconduct or felony conviction that results in harm to MSO's business or reputation but is permitted discretion over the management of her personal, financial, and legal affairs to the extent that Stewart's management of her own life does not compromise her ability to serve the company.

Stewart's alleged misadventures with ImClone arise in part out of a longstanding personal friendship with Samuel D. Waksal ("Waksal"). Waksal is the former chief executive officer of ImClone as well as a former suitor of Stewart's daughter. More pertinently, * * * Waksal and Stewart have provided one another with reciprocal investment advice and assistance, and they share a stockbroker, Peter E. Bacanovic ("Bacanovic") of Merrill Lynch. Bacanovic, coincidentally, is a former employee of ImClone. * * * The speculative value of ImClone stock was tied quite directly to the likely success of its application for FDA approval to market the cancer treatment drug Erbitux. On December 26, Waksal received information that the FDA was rejecting the application to market Erbitux. The following day, December 27, he tried to sell his own shares and tipped his father and daughter to do the same. Stewart also sold her shares on December 27. * * * After the close of trading on December 28, ImClone publicly announced the rejection of its application to market Erbitux. The following day the trading price closed slightly more than 20% lower than the closing price on the date that Stewart had sold her shares. By mid-2002, this convergence of events had attracted the interest of the *New York Times* and other news agencies, federal prosecutors, and a committee of the United States House of Representatives. Stewart's publicized attempts to quell any suspicion were ineffective at best because they were undermined by additional information as it came to light and by the other parties' accounts of the events. Ultimately Stewart's prompt efforts to turn away unwanted media and investigative attention failed. Stewart eventually had to discontinue her regular guest appearances on CBS' *The Early Show* because of questioning during the show about her sale of ImClone shares. After barely two months of such adverse publicity, MSO's stock price had declined by slightly more than 65%. * * *

In January 2002, Stewart and the Martha Stewart Family Partnership sold 3,000,000 shares of Class A stock to [an investor group]. "ValueAct." * * *

* * *

* * * [T]he amended complaint alleges that the director defendants * * * breached their fiduciary duties by failing to ensure that Stewart would not conduct her personal, financial, and legal affairs in a manner that would harm the Company, its intellectual property, or its business. The "duty to monitor" has been litigated in other circumstances, generally where directors were alleged to have been negligent in monitoring the activities of the corporation, activities that led to corporate liability. Plaintiff's allegation, however, that the Board has a duty to monitor the personal affairs of an officer or director is quite novel. That the Company is "closely identified" with Stewart is conceded, but it does not necessarily follow that the Board is required to monitor, much less control, the way Stewart handles her *personal* financial and legal affairs.

* * *

* * * Regardless of Stewart's importance to MSO, she is not the corporation. And it is unreasonable to impose a duty upon the Board to monitor Stewart's personal affairs because such a requirement is neither legitimate nor feasible. * * *

* * * [This count] is dismissed for failure to state a claim.

* * * [T]he amended complaint alleges that Stewart * * * breached [her] fiduciary duty of loyalty, usurping a corporate opportunity by selling large blocks of MSO stock to ValueAct. * * * The basic requirements for establishing usurpation of a corporate opportunity were articulated by the Delaware Supreme Court in *Broz v. Cellular Information Systems, Inc.*:

[A] corporate officer or director may not take a business opportunity for his own if: (1) the corporation is financially able to exploit the opportunity; (2) the opportunity

is within the corporation's line of business; (3) the corporation has an interest or expectancy in the opportunity; and (4) by taking the opportunity for his own, the corporate fiduciary will thereby be placed in a position [inimical] to his duties to the corporation.

In this analysis, no single factor is dispositive. Instead the Court must balance all factors as they apply to a particular case. For purposes of the present motion, I assume that the sales of stock to ValueAct could be considered to be a "business opportunity." I now address each of the four factors articulated in *Broz*.

The amended complaint asserts that MSO was able to exploit this opportunity because the Company's certificate of incorporation had sufficient authorized, yet unissued, shares of Class A common stock to cover the sale to ValueAct. Defendants do not deny that the Company could have sold previously unissued shares to ValueAct. I therefore conclude that the first factor has been met.

An opportunity is within a corporation's line of business if it is "an activity as to which [the corporation] has fundamental knowledge, practical experience and ability to pursue." * * *

* * * MSO is a consumer products company, not an investment company. Simply stated, selling stock is not the same line of business as selling advice to homemakers. * * * For the foregoing reasons, * * * the sale of stock by Stewart * * * was not within MSO's line of business.

A corporation has an interest or expectancy in an opportunity if there is "some tie between that property and the nature of the corporate business." * * * Here, plaintiff does not allege any facts that would imply that MSO was in need of additional capital, seeking additional capital, or even remotely interested in finding new investors. * * *

* * *

"[T]he corporate opportunity doctrine is implicated only in cases where the fiduciary's seizure of an opportunity results in a conflict between the fiduciary's duties to the corporation and the self-interest of the director as actualized by the exploitation of the opportunity." Given that * * * MSO had no interest or expectancy in the issuance of new stock to ValueAct, I fail to see, based on the allegations before me, how Stewart['s] * * * sales placed [her] in a position inimical to [her] duties to the Company. * * *

Additionally, Delaware courts have recognized a policy that allows officers and directors of corporations to buy and sell shares of that corporation at will so long as they act in good faith. * * *

* * *

On balancing the four factors, I conclude that plaintiff has failed to plead facts sufficient to state a claim that Stewart * * * usurped a corporate opportunity for [herself] in violation of [her] fiduciary duty of loyalty to MSO. [This count] is dismissed in its entirety * * * for failure to state a claim upon which relief can be granted.

QUESTIONS

1. Brown, the president and director of a corporation engaged in owning and operating a chain of motels, was advised upon what seemed to be good authority that a superhighway was to be constructed through the town of X, which would be a most desirable location for a motel. Brown presented these facts to the board of directors of the motel corporation and recommended that the corporation build a motel in the town of X at the location described. The board of directors agreed, and the new motel was constructed. The superhighway plans were changed, however, after the motel was constructed, and the highway was never built. Later, a packinghouse was built on property adjoining the motel, and the corporation sustained a considerable loss as a result. The shareholders brought an appropriate action against Brown, charging that his proposal had caused a substantial loss to the corporation and seeking recovery of that loss from Brown. What result? Explain.

2. A, B, C, D, and E constituted the board of directors of the X Corporation. While D and E were out of town, A, B, and C held a special meeting of the board. Just as the meeting began, C became ill. He then gave a proxy to A and went home. A resolution was then adopted directing and authorizing X Corporation's purchase of an adjoining piece of land owned by S as a site for an additional factory building. As was known by S, the purchase required approval by the board of directors. A and B voted for the resolution, and A, as C's proxy, cast C's vote in favor of the resolution. X Corporation then made a contract with S for the purchase of the land. After the return of D and E, another special meeting of the board was held with all five directors present. A resolution was then unanimously adopted to cancel the contract with S. So notified, may S recover damages for breach of contract from X Corporation? Explain.

3. Bernard Koch was president of United Corporation, a closely held corporation. Koch, James Trent, and Henry Phillips made up the three-person board of directors. At a meeting of the board, Trent was elected president, replacing Koch. At the same meeting, Trent attempted to have the salary of the president increased. He was unable to obtain board approval of the increase because, although Phillips voted for the increase, Koch voted against it. Trent was disqualified from voting by the corporation's articles of incorporation. As a result, the directors, by a two-to-one vote, amended the bylaws to provide for the appointment of an executive committee composed of three reputable businesspersons to pass upon and fix all matters of salary for employees of the corporation. Subsequently, the executive committee, consisting of Jane Jones, James Black, and William Johnson, increased the salary of the president. Will Koch succeed in an appropriate action against the corporation, Trent, and Phillips to enjoin them from paying compensation to the president above that amount fixed by the board of directors? Explain.

4. Zenith Steel Company operates a prosperous business. In January, Zenith's chief executive officer (CEO) and president, Roe, who is also a member of the board, was voted a $1 million bonus by the board of directors for the valuable services he provided to the company during the previous year. Roe receives an annual salary of $850,000 from the company. Black, Inc., a minority shareholder in Zenith Steel Company, brings an appropriate action to enjoin the company from paying the $1 million bonus. Explain whether Black will succeed in its attempt.

5. Raphael, a minority shareholder of the Sample Corporation, claims that the following sales are void and should be annulled. Explain whether Raphael is correct.

   a. Smith, a director of the Sample Corporation, sells a piece of vacant land to the Sample Corporation for $500,000. The land cost him $200,000.

   b. Jones, a shareholder of the Sample Corporation, sells a used truck to the Sample Corporation for $8,400, although the truck is worth $6,000.

6. The X Corporation manufactures machine tools. The five directors of X Corporation are Black, White, Brown, Green, and Crimson. At a duly called meeting of the board of directors of X Corporation in January, all five directors were present. A contract for the purchase of $10 million worth of steel from the D Company, of which Black, White, and Brown are directors, was discussed and approved by a unanimous vote. The board also discussed at length entering into negotiations for the purchase of Q Corporation, which allegedly was about to be sold for around $150 million. By a 3-2 vote, it was decided not to open such negotiations. Three months later, Green purchased Q Corporation for $150 million. Shortly thereafter, a new board of directors for X Corporation took office. X Corporation now brings actions to rescind its contract with D Company and to compel Green to assign to X Corporation his contract for the purchase of Q Corporation. Explain whether X Corporation should succeed on each action.

7. Gore had been the owner of 1 percent of the outstanding shares of the Webster Company, a corporation since its organization ten years ago. Ratliff, the president of the

company, was the owner of 70 percent of the outstanding shares. Ratliff used the shareholders' list to submit to the shareholders an offer of $50 per share for their stock. Gore, upon receiving the offer, called Ratliff and told him that the offer was inadequate and advised that she was willing to offer $60 per share and for that purpose demanded a shareholders' list. Ratliff knew that Gore was willing and able to supply the funds necessary to purchase the stock, but he nevertheless refused to supply the list to Gore. Furthermore, he did not offer to transmit Gore's offer to the shareholders of record. Gore then brought an action to compel the corporation to make the shareholders' list available to her. Will Gore be able to obtain a copy of the shareholders' list? Why or why not?

8. Mitchell, Nelson, Olsen, and Parker, experts in manufacturing baubles, each owned fifteen out of one hundred authorized shares of Baubles, Inc., a corporation in a State with an incorporation statute that does not permit cumulative voting. On July 7, 2014, the corporation sold forty shares to Quentin, an investor, for $1.5 million, which it used to purchase a factory building for $1.5 million. On July 8, 2014, Mitchell, Nelson, Olsen, and Parker contracted as follows:

> All parties will act jointly in exercising voting rights as shareholders. In the event of a failure to agree, the question shall be submitted to George Yost, whose decision shall be binding upon all parties.

> Until a meeting of shareholders on April 17, 2021, when a dispute arose, all parties to the contract had voted consistently and regularly for Nelson, Olsen, and Parker as directors. At that meeting, Yost considered the dispute and decided and directed that Mitchell, Nelson, Olsen, and

Parker vote their shares for the latter three as directors. Nelson, Olsen, and Parker so voted. Mitchell and Quentin voted for themselves and Mrs. Quentin as directors.

   a. Is the contract of July 8, 2014, valid? If so, what is its effect?

   b. Who were elected directors of Baubles, Inc., at the meeting of its shareholders on April 17, 2021? Explain.

9. Acme Corporation's articles of incorporation require cumulative voting for the election of its directors. The board of directors of Acme Corporation consists of nine directors, each elected annually.

   a. Smith owns 24 percent of the outstanding shares of Acme Corporation. Explain how many directors he can elect with his votes.

   b. If Acme Corporation were to classify its board into three classes, each consisting of three directors elected every three years, explain how many directors Smith would be able to elect.

10. A bylaw of Betma Corporation provides that no shareholder can sell his shares unless he first offers them for sale to the corporation or its directors. The bylaw also states that this restriction shall be printed or stamped upon each stock certificate and shall bind all present or future owners or holders. Betma Corporation did not comply with this latter provision. Shaw, having knowledge of the bylaw restriction, nevertheless purchased twenty shares of the corporation's stock from Rice without having Rice first offer them for sale to the corporation or its directors. When Betma Corporation refused to effectuate a transfer of the shares to her, Shaw sued to compel a transfer and the issuance of a new certificate to her. What result? Explain.

CASE PROBLEMS

11. Neese, trustee in bankruptcy for First Trust Company, brings a suit against the directors of the company for losses the company sustained as a result of the directors' failure to use due care and diligence in the discharge of their duties. The specific acts of negligence alleged are (a) failure to give as much time and attention to the affairs of the company as its business interests required; (b) abdication of their control of the corporation by turning its management entirely over to its president, Brown; (c) failure to keep informed as to the affairs, condition, and management of the corporation; (d) failure to take action to direct or control the corporation's affairs; (e) permission of large, open, unsecured loans to affiliated but financially unsound companies that were owned and controlled by Brown; (f) failure to examine financial

reports that would have shown illegal diversions and waste of the corporation's funds; and (g) failure to supervise properly the corporation's officers and directors. Explain which, if any, of these allegations could constitute a breach of the duty of diligence.

12. Minority shareholders of Midwest Technical Institute Development Corporation, a closed-end investment company owning assets consisting principally of securities of companies in technological fields, brought a shareholder derivative suit against officers and directors of Midwest, seeking to recover on Midwest's behalf profits that the officers and directors realized through dealings in stock held in Midwest's portfolio in breach of their fiduciary duty. Approximately three years after commencement of the action, a new corporation,

Midtex, was organized to acquire Midwest's assets. May the shareholders now add Midtex as a party defendant to their suit? Why or why not?

13. Riffe, while serving as an officer of Wilshire Oil Company, received a secret commission for work he did on behalf of a competing corporation. Can Wilshire Oil recover these secret profits and, in addition, recover the compensation paid to Riffe by Wilshire Oil during the period that he acted on behalf of the competitor? Explain.

14. Muller, a shareholder of SCM, brought an action against SCM over his unsuccessful negotiations to purchase some of SCM's assets overseas. He then formed a shareholder committee to challenge the position of SCM's management in that suit. To conduct a proxy battle for management control at the next election of directors, the committee sought to obtain the list of shareholders who would be eligible to vote. At the time, however, no member of the committee had owned stock in SCM for the six-month period required to gain access to such information. Then Lopez, a former SCM executive and a shareholder for more than one year, joined the committee and demanded to be allowed to inspect the minutes of SCM shareholder proceedings and to gain access to the current shareholder list. His stated reason for making the demand was to solicit proxies in support of those the committee had nominated for positions as directors. Lopez brought this action after SCM rejected this demand. Will Lopez succeed? Explain.

15. Pritchard & Baird was a reinsurance broker. A reinsurance broker arranges contracts between insurance companies so that companies that have sold large policies may sell participations in these policies to other companies in order to share the risks. Charles Pritchard, who died in December 2018, controlled Pritchard & Baird for many years. Prior to his death, he brought his two sons, Charles Jr. and William, into the business. The pair assumed an increasingly dominant role in the affairs of the business during the elder Charles's later years. Starting in 2015, Charles Jr. and William began to withdraw from the corporate account ever-increasing sums that were designated as "loans" on the balance sheet. These "loans," however, represented a significant misappropriation of funds belonging to the corporation's clients. By late 2020, Charles Jr. and William had plunged the corporation into hopeless bankruptcy. A total of $12,333,514.47 in "loans" had accumulated by October of that year. Mrs. Lillian Pritchard, the widow of the elder Charles, was a member of the corporation's board of directors until her resignation on December 3, 2020, the day before the corporation filed for bankruptcy. Francis, as trustee in the bankruptcy proceeding, brought suit against United Jersey Bank, the

administrator of the estate of Charles Sr. He also charged that Lillian Pritchard, as a director of the corporation, was personally liable for the misappropriated funds on the basis of negligence in discharging her duties as director. Is Francis correct? Why or why not?

16. Donald J. Richardson, Grove L. Cook, and Wayne Weaver were stockholders of Major Oil. They brought a direct action, individually and on behalf of all other stockholders of Major, against certain directors and other officers of the corporation. The complaint stated twelve causes of action. The first eight causes alleged some misappropriation of Major's assets by the defendants and sought to require the defendants to return the assets to Major. Three of the remaining four causes alleged breaches of fiduciary duty implicit in those fraudulent acts and sought compensatory or punitive damages for the injury that resulted. The final cause sought the appointment of a receiver. Richardson, Cook, and Weaver moved for an order certifying the suit as a class action. Decision? Explain.

17. Klinicki and Lundgren, both furloughed Pan Am pilots stationed in West Germany, decided to start their own charter airline company. They formed Berlinair, Inc., a closely held Oregon corporation. Lundgren was president and a director in charge of developing the business. Klinicki was vice president and a director in charge of operations and maintenance. Klinicki, Lundgren, and Lelco, Inc. (Lundgren's family business), each owned one-third of the stock. Klinicki and Lundgren, as representatives of Berlinair, met with BFR, a consortium of Berlin travel agents, to negotiate a lucrative air transportation contract. When Lundgren learned of the likelihood of actually obtaining the BFR contract, he formed his own solely owned company, Air Berlin Charter Company (ABC). Although he continued to negotiate for the BFR contract, he did so on behalf of ABC, not Berlinair. Eventually BFR awarded the contract to ABC. Klinicki commenced a derivative action on behalf of Berlinair and a suit against Lundgren individually for usurping a corporate opportunity of Berlinair. Lundgren claimed that Berlinair was not financially able to undertake the BFR contract and therefore no usurpation of corporate opportunity could occur. Who is correct? Explain.

18. Horton owned one hundred twelve shares of common stock in Compaq Computer Corporation, a Delaware corporation. Horton and seventy-eight other parties sued Compaq, fifteen of its advisers, and certain management personnel, alleging that Compaq and its codefendants had (1) violated the Texas Security Act and the Texas Deceptive Trade Practices Consumer Protection Act and (2) committed fraud and breached their fiduciary duty. All these claims arise from the contention that Compaq misled the public regarding the true value of its stock

at a time when members of management were selling their own shares. Horton delivered a letter demanding to inspect Compaq's stock ledger and related information. The demand letter stated that the purpose of the request was to enable Horton to communicate with other Compaq shareholders to inform them of the pending shareholders' suit and to ascertain whether any of them would desire to become associated with that suit or bring similar actions against Compaq and assume a pro rata share of the litigation expenses. Compaq refused the demand, stating that the purpose described in the letter was not a "proper purpose" for inspecting corporate books and records. Explain who should prevail and why.

19. The Brazilian Equity Fund, Inc., is a nondiversified, publicly traded, closed-end investment company incorporated under the laws of Maryland. As a closed-end fund, it has a fixed number of outstanding shares, so that investors who wish to acquire shares in the Fund ordinarily must purchase them from a shareholder rather than, as in open-end funds, directly from the Fund itself. Shares in closed-end funds are traded in the same manner as are shares of corporate stock. Shares in the Fund are listed and traded on the New York Stock Exchange. The number of outstanding shares in the Fund is "fixed" because this number does not change on a daily basis. Although closed-end funds do not sell their shares to the public in the ordinary course of their business, there are methods available to them to raise new capital after their initial public offering. One such device is a "rights offering," by which a fund offers shareholders the opportunity to purchase newly issued shares. Rights so offered may be transferable, allowing the current shareholder to sell them in the open market, or nontransferable, requiring the current shareholder to use them herself or lose their value when the rights expire.

On June 6, the Fund announced that it would issue one nontransferable "right" per outstanding share to every shareholder, and that every three rights would enable the shareholder to purchase one new share in the Fund. The subscription price per share was set at 90 percent of the lesser of (1) the average of the last reported sales price of a share of the Fund's common stock on the New York Stock Exchange on August 16, the date on which the rights expired, and the four business days preceding and (2) the per-share net asset value at the close of business on August 16.

At the close of business on August 16, the closing market price for the Fund's shares was $12.38, and the Fund's per-share net asset value was $17.24. The Fund's shareholders purchased 70.3 percent of the new shares available at a subscription price set at $11.09 per share, 90 percent of the average closing price for the Fund on that and the preceding four days. Through the rights offering, the Fund raised $20.6 million in new capital.

A shareholder brought a class action against the Fund's directors, senior officers, and investment advisor asserting that this sort of rights offering is coercive because it penalized shareholders who did not participate by diluting the value of old shares. The plaintiff's complaint included three direct class-action claims on behalf of all shareholders alleging that the defendants breached their duties of loyalty and care at common law. It asserted that these breaches of duty resulted in four kinds of injury to shareholders: (1) loss of share value resulting from the underwriting and other transaction costs associated with the rights offering; (2) downward pressure on share prices resulting from the supply of new shares; (3) downward pressure on share prices resulting from the offering of shares at a discount; and (4) injury resulting from coercion, in that "shareholders were forced to either invest additional monies in the Fund or suffer a substantial dilution."

Explain (1) which of these claims are direct claims and (2) which of these claims are derivative claims.

TAKING SIDES

Sinclair Oil Corporation organized a subsidiary, Sinclair Venezuelan Oil Company (Sinven), for the purpose of operating in Venezuela. Sinclair owned about 97 percent of Sinven's stock. Sinclair nominates all members of Sinven's board of directors, and none of the directors were independent of Sinclair. A minority shareholder of Sinven brought a derivative action on behalf of Sinven against Sinclair, seeking to recover damages sustained by Sinven. The derivative suit alleged that Sinclair had caused Sinven to pay out such excessive dividends that the industrial development of Sinven was effectively prevented.

a. What are the arguments that the transactions between Sinclair and Sinven should be subjected to judicial scrutiny and upheld only if Sinclair shows them to have been entirely fair and entered in good faith?

b. What are the arguments that the transactions between Sinclair and Sinven should be subjected to the business judgment rule and overturned only if Sinven shows that Sinclair had *not* acted with due care, in good faith, and in a manner reasonably believed to be in the best interests of Sinven?

c. Explain which standard should apply.

CHAPTER 36

Fundamental Changes

CHAPTER OUTCOMES

After reading and studying this chapter, you should be able to:

- Explain the procedure for amending the articles of incorporation and which amendments give rise to the appraisal remedy.

- Identify which combinations do not require shareholder approval and which give dissenting shareholders an appraisal remedy.

- Distinguish between a tender offer and a compulsory share exchange.

- Compare a cash-out combination and a management buyout.

- Identify the ways by which voluntary and involuntary dissolution may occur.

Certain extraordinary changes exert such a fundamental effect on a corporation by altering the corporation's basic structure that they fall outside the authority of the board of directors and require shareholder approval. Such fundamental changes include amendments to the articles of incorporation, mergers, consolidations, compulsory share exchanges, dissolution, conversions, domestications, and dispositions of all or substantially all of the corporation's assets, other than those in the regular course of business. Although each of these actions is authorized by State incorporation statutes, which impose specific procedural requirements, they are also subject to equitable limitations imposed by the courts. In 1999, substantial revisions were made to the Revised Act's treatment of fundamental changes.

Because shareholder approval for fundamental changes usually does not need to be unanimous, such changes frequently will be approved despite opposition by minority shareholders. Shareholder approval means a majority (or some other specified fraction) of *all votes entitled* to be cast, rather than a majority (or other fraction) of votes represented at a shareholders' meeting at which a quorum is present. The 1999 amendments to the Revised Act, however, significantly changed this voting rule: fundamental changes need only be approved by a plurality of the shares cast (that is, the votes cast for the action exceed the votes cast against the action) at a meeting at which a quorum consisting of at least a majority of the votes entitled to be cast on the action. In some instances, minority shareholders have the right to dissent and to recover the fair value of their shares if they follow the prescribed procedure for doing so. This right is called the appraisal remedy.

The legal aspects of fundamental changes are discussed in this chapter.

36-1 Amendments to the Articles of Incorporation

Shareholders do not have a vested property right resulting from any provision in the articles of incorporation. Section 10.01(b). Accordingly, incorporation statutes grant the authority to amend corporate articles of incorporation if specified procedures are followed. The amended articles of incorporation, however, may contain only those provisions that the articles of incorporation might lawfully contain at the time of the amendment. Section 10.01(a).

36-1a APPROVAL BY DIRECTORS AND SHAREHOLDERS

Under the Revised Act and most statutes, the typical procedure for amending the articles of incorporation requires the board of directors to adopt a resolution setting forth the proposed amendment, which must then be approved by a majority vote of the shareholders entitled to vote, although some older statutes require a two-thirds shareholder vote. Moreover, a class of shares is entitled to vote as a class on certain proposed amendments, whether the articles of incorporation provide such entitlement or not. In some States, shareholders may approve amendments to the articles of incorporation without a prior board of directors' resolution.

After the shareholders approve the amendment, the corporation executes articles of amendment and delivers them to the Secretary of State for filing. Section 10.06. The amendment does not affect the existing rights of nonshareholders. Section 10.09.

Under Section 13.02(a)(4) of the Revised Act, dissenting shareholders may obtain the appraisal remedy only if an amendment materially and adversely affects their rights by—

1. altering or abolishing a preferential right of the shares;

2. creating, altering, or abolishing a right involving the redemption of the shares;

3. altering or abolishing a preemptive right of the holder of the shares;

4. excluding or limiting the shareholder's right to vote on any matter or to cumulate his votes; or

5. reducing to a fraction of a share the number of shares the shareholder owns, if the fractional share is to be acquired for cash.

The 1999 amendments to the Revised Act eliminate the appraisal remedy for all amendments to the articles of incorporation except for reverse stock splits that result in cashing out some of the shares of a class or series. Section 13.02(a)(4). However, the 1999 amendments permit appraisal rights to be made available for amendments to the articles of incorporation to the extent provided by the articles of incorporation, the bylaws, or a resolution of the board of directors. Section 13.02(a)(5).

Under the Revised Act, the shareholder approval required for an amendment depends upon the nature of the amendment. An amendment that would give rise to dissenters' rights must be approved by a majority of all votes entitled to be cast on the amendment, unless the act, the articles of incorporation, or the board of directors requires a greater vote. All other amendments must be approved by a majority of all votes cast on the amendment at a meeting where a quorum exists, unless the act, the articles of incorporation, or the board of directors requires a greater vote. Sections 10.03, 7.25. Under the 1999 amendments to the Revised Act, amendments to the articles of incorporation need be approved by only a plurality of the shares cast at a meeting at which exists a quorum consisting of at least a majority of the votes entitled to be cast on the amendment.

Practical Advice

If you are forming a close corporation and will hold a minority interest in it, consider including in the articles of incorporation provisions for supermajority quorum and voting for amendments to the articles of incorporation to ensure that you will have veto power.

36-1b APPROVAL BY DIRECTORS

The Revised Act permits the board of directors to adopt certain amendments without shareholder action, unless the articles of incorporation provide otherwise. Section 10.02. These amendments include (1) extending the duration of the corporation if it was incorporated when limited duration was required by law, (2) changing each issued and unissued authorized share of an outstanding class into a greater number of whole shares if the corporation has only one class of shares, and (3) making minor name changes.

36-2 Combinations

Acquiring all or substantially all of the assets of another corporation or corporations may be both desirable and profitable. A corporation may accomplish this through (1) purchase or lease of other corporations' assets, (2) purchase of a controlling stock interest in other corporations, (3) merger with other corporations, or (4) consolidation with other corporations. The incorporation statutes in a number of States and the 1999 amendments to the Revised Act contain provisions authorizing a corporation to merge or convert into another type of business organization, referred to as an **eligible entity**, which means (1) a domestic or foreign unincorporated entity, such as a limited partnership, a limited liability company, or a limited liability partnership or (2) a domestic or foreign nonprofit corporation. Section 9.30.

In 2007, the Uniform Law Commission promulgated the Model Entity Transactions Act (META), which provides a comprehensive statutory framework for four kinds of transactions among different kinds of business organizations: a merger of one entity with another entity of the same or different kind; a conversion of an entity to another kind of entity; an interest exchange between two entities of the same or different kind, so that one of them acquires control over the other but the two entities do not merge; and the domestication in one State of an entity originally organized in another State. Amended in 2011 and 2013, META has been adopted in at least eight States.

Any method of combination that involves the issuance of shares, proxy solicitations, or tender offers may be subject to Federal securities regulation, as discussed in *Chapter 43*. Moreover, a combination that is potentially detrimental to competition may be subject to Federal antitrust laws, as discussed in *Chapter 40*.

In July 2010, President Obama signed into law the Dodd-Frank Wall Street Reform and Consumer Protection Act (Dodd-Frank Act), the most significant change to U.S. financial regulation since the New Deal. One of the many stand-alone statutes included in the Dodd-Frank Act is the Investor Protection and Securities Reform Act of 2010, which imposes new corporate governance rules on publicly held companies.

(This statute is also discussed in *Chapters 34, 35, 43,* and *46.*) One of these provisions of the Dodd-Frank Act applies to proxy solicitations asking shareholders to approve an acquisition, merger, consolidation, or proposed sale or other disposition of all or substantially all of the assets of a publicly held company issuer. In these proxy solicitations, publicly held companies must disclose, and provide shareholders with a nonbinding vote to approve, any type of compensation that is based on or relates to these specified combinations.

36-2a PURCHASE OR LEASE OF ALL OR SUBSTANTIALLY ALL OF THE ASSETS

When one corporation purchases, leases, exchanges, or otherwise acquires all or substantially all of the assets of another corporation, the legal personality of neither corporation changes. The purchaser or lessee corporation simply acquires ownership or control of additional physical assets. The selling or lessor corporation, in exchange for its physical properties, receives cash, other property, or a stipulated rental. Having altered only the form or extent of its assets, each corporation continues its separate existence.

Generally, a corporation that purchases the assets of another corporation does not assume the other's liabilities unless (1) the purchaser expressly or impliedly agrees to assume the seller's liabilities; (2) the transaction amounts to a consolidation or merger of the two corporations; (3) the purchaser is a mere continuation of the seller; or (4) the sale is for the fraudulent purpose of avoiding the liabilities of the seller. Some courts recognize a fifth exception (called the "product line" exception), which imposes strict tort liability upon the purchaser for defects in products manufactured and distributed by the seller corporation when the purchaser corporation continues the product line.

Practical Advice

Recognize that under some circumstances, courts will treat the purchase of all the assets of a corporation as a de facto merger and make the purchaser liable for the debts of the seller.

DISPOSITION OF ASSETS NOT REQUIRING SHAREHOLDER APPROVAL Unless the articles of incorporation otherwise provide, no shareholder approval is required for (1) a sale, lease, exchange, or other disposition of all or substantially all of a corporation's assets in the disposing corporation's usual and regular course of business; (2) a mortgage or pledge of any or all of a corporation's property and assets, whether or not in the usual or regular course of business; and (3) a transfer of any or all of a corporation's assets to a wholly owned subsidiary. Section 12.01.

DISPOSITION OF ASSETS REQUIRING SHAREHOLDER APPROVAL Shareholder approval is necessary for a sale, lease, exchange, or other disposition of all or substantially all of its assets not in the corporation's usual and regular course of business. The 1999 amendments to the Revised Act clarify and adopt an objective test for determining when shareholder approval is required: if the disposition would leave the corporation without a significant business activity. The amendments provide a safe harbor by specifying that a corporation is conclusively deemed to have retained a significant business activity if it retains a business activity that represents at least (1) 25 percent of total assets and (2) either 25 percent of income or 25 percent of revenues from continuing operations.

The disposing corporation, by liquidating its assets, or placing its physical assets beyond its control, has significantly changed its position and perhaps its ability to carry on the type of business contemplated in its articles of incorporation. For this reason, such a disposition must be approved not only by action of the directors but also by the affirmative vote of the holders of a majority of the corporation's shares entitled to vote at a shareholders' meeting called for this purpose. Section 12.02. Under the 1999 amendments to the Revised Act, a disposition of all or substantially all of a corporation's assets that is not in the usual and regular course of business must be approved by a plurality of the shares cast at a meeting at which exists a quorum consisting of at least a majority of the votes entitled to be cast on the issue. In most States, dissenting shareholders of the disposing corporation are given an appraisal remedy. The Revised Act provides this appraisal right except when shareholders will receive in cash the corporation's net assets within one year after the shareholders' approval of the disposition. Section 13.02(a)(3). In addition, the 1999 amendments to the Revised Act permit additional appraisal rights to be made available for dispositions to the extent provided by the articles of incorporation, the bylaws, or a resolution of the board of directors. Section 13.02(a)(5).

36-2b PURCHASE OF SHARES

An alternative to purchasing another corporation's assets is to purchase its stock. When one corporation acquires all of, or a controlling interest in, the stock of another corporation, the legal existence of neither corporation changes. The acquiring corporation acts through its board of directors, whereas the corporation that becomes a subsidiary does not act at all, because the decision to sell stock is made not by the corporation but by its individual shareholders. The capital structure of the subsidiary remains unchanged, and that of the parent is usually not altered unless financing the acquisition of the stock necessitates a change in capital. Because the action of neither corporation requires formal shareholder approval, there is no appraisal remedy.

SALE OF CONTROL When a controlling interest is owned by one or a few shareholders, a privately negotiated transaction is possible, though the courts require that these sales be made with due care. The controlling shareholders must make a reasonable investigation so as not to transfer control to purchasers who wrongfully plan to steal or "loot" the corporation's assets or to act against its best interests. In addition, purchasers frequently are willing to pay a premium for a block of shares that conveys control. Although historically some courts required that this so-called control premium inure to the benefit of the corporation, virtually all courts now permit the controlling shareholders to retain the full amount of the control premium.

TENDER OFFER When a controlling interest is not held by one or a few shareholders, the acquisition of a corporation through the purchase of shares may take the form of a tender offer. A tender offer is a general invitation to all the shareholders of a target company to tender their shares for sale at a specified price. The offer may be for all of the target company's shares or for just a controlling interest. Tender offers for publicly held companies, which are subject to Federal securities regulation, are discussed in *Chapter 43*.

36-2c COMPULSORY SHARE EXCHANGE

The Revised Act and some State statutes provide different procedures for which a corporation to acquire shares through a **compulsory share exchange**, a transaction by which the corporation becomes the owner of *all* the outstanding shares of one or more classes of another corporation by an exchange that is compulsory on all owners of the acquired shares. Section 11.02. The Revised Act has been amended to authorize corporations to acquire all of the eligible interests of one or more classes or series of interests of an eligible entity. Section 11.03. The corporation may acquire the shares with its or any other corporation's shares, obligations, or other securities or for cash or other property. For example, if A corporation acquires all of the outstanding shares of B corporation through a compulsory exchange, then B becomes a wholly owned subsidiary of A. A compulsory share exchange affects the separate existence of neither corporate party to the transaction. Although they produce results similar to mergers, as discussed in the following section, compulsory share exchanges are used instead of mergers where preserving the existence of the acquired corporation is essential or desirable, as, for example, in the formation of holding company systems for insurance companies and banks.

A compulsory share exchange requires approval from the board of directors of each corporation and from a majority of the shareholders of the corporation whose shares are being acquired. Sections 11.02 and 11.03. (Under the 1999 amendments to the Revised Act, a share exchange need be approved by only a plurality of the shares cast at a meeting at which exists a quorum consisting of at least a majority of the votes entitled to be cast on the share exchange.) Each included class of shares must vote separately on the exchange. The shareholders of the acquiring corporation need not approve the transaction. Once the shareholders of the corporation whose shares are to be acquired have adopted and approved a compulsory share exchange plan, it is binding on all who hold shares of the class to be acquired. Dissenting shareholders of the corporation whose shares are acquired are given an appraisal remedy. Section 13.02(a)(2). In addition, the 1999 amendments to the Revised Act permit additional appraisal rights to be made available for share exchanges to the extent provided by the articles of incorporation, the bylaws, or a resolution of the board of directors. Section 13.02(a)(5).

36-2d MERGER

A **merger** of two or more corporations is the combination of all of their assets. (The Revised Act has been amended to authorize corporations to merge with any eligible entity.) One of the corporations, known as the **surviving corporation**, receives title to the combined assets. The other party or parties to the merger, known as the **merged corporation** or corporations, are merged into the surviving corporation and cease their separate existence. Thus, if A Corporation and B Corporation combine into the A Corporation, A is the surviving corporation and B is the merged corporation. Under the Revised Act and most statutes, the shareholders of the merged corporation may receive stock or other securities issued by the surviving corporation or other consideration *including cash*, as provided in the merger agreement. Moreover, the surviving corporation assumes all debts and other liabilities of the merged corporation. Section 11.06.

A merger requires the approval of each corporation's board of directors, as well as the affirmative vote of the holders of a majority of the shares of each corporation that are entitled to vote. Sections 11.01 and 11.03. Under the 1999 amendments to the Revised Act, a merger need be approved by a plurality of the shares cast at a meeting at which exists a quorum consisting of at least a majority of the votes entitled to be cast on the merger. A dissenting shareholder of any corporate party to the merger has an appraisal remedy if shareholder approval is required and the shareholder is entitled to vote on the merger. Section 13.02(a)(1). The 1999 amendments to the Revised Act eliminated the appraisal rights of shareholders in the surviving corporation. However, the 1999 amendments permit additional appraisal rights to be made available for mergers to the extent provided by the articles of incorporation, the bylaws, or a resolution of the board of directors. Many States and the 1999 amendments to the Revised Act permit the vote of the shareholders of the surviving corporation to be eliminated when a merger increases the number of outstanding shares by no more than 20 percent. In 2016, the Revised Act was amended to permit the vote of the shareholders of the surviving corporation to be eliminated in additional circumstances, unless the articles of incorporation provide otherwise.

In a **short-form merger**, a corporation that owns a statutorily specified percentage of the outstanding shares of each class of a subsidiary may merge the subsidiary into itself without approval by the shareholders of either corporation. The Revised Act and most States specify 90 percent. Section 11.04. Obtaining approval from the subsidiary's shareholders or from the subsidiary's board of directors is unnecessary because the parent's 90 percent ownership ensures approval of the merger plan. All the merger requires is a resolution by the board of directors of the parent corporation. The Revised Act has been amended to extend the short-form merger provisions to include (1) eligible entities, (2) a merger between subsidiaries, and (3) a merger of a parent into a subsidiary.

The dissenting shareholders of the subsidiary have the right to obtain payment from the parent for their shares. Section 13.02(a)(1). The shareholders of the parent do not have this appraisal remedy because the transaction has not materially changed their rights. Instead of indirectly owning 90 percent of the subsidiary's assets, the parent now directly owns 100 percent of the same assets.

36-2e CONSOLIDATION

A consolidation of two or more corporations is the combination of all of their assets, the title to which is taken by a newly created corporation known as the **consolidated corporation**. Each constituent corporation ceases to exist, and all of its debts and liabilities are assumed by the new corporation. The shareholders of the constituent corporations receive stock or other securities, not necessarily of the same class, issued to them by the new corporation or other consideration provided in the plan of consolidation. A consolidation requires the approval of each corporation's board of directors, as well as the affirmative vote of the holders of a majority of the shares of each corporation that are entitled to vote. Dissenting shareholders have an appraisal remedy.

The Revised Act has deleted all references to consolidations, as explained by the comment to Section 11.01: "In modern corporate practice consolidation transactions are obsolete since it is nearly always advantageous for one of the parties in the transaction to be the surviving corporation."

36-2f DOMESTICATION AND CONVERSION

The Revised Act was amended in 2002 to provide for domestication and conversion into other entities without a merger. The **domestication** procedures permit a corporation to change its State of incorporation, thus allowing a domestic business corporation to become a foreign business corporation or a foreign business corporation to become a domestic business corporation. The **conversion** procedures permit a domestic business corporation to become a domestic or foreign partnership, LLC, or other eligible entity and permit a domestic or foreign partnership, LLC, or other eligible entity to become a domestic business corporation. In both of these transactions, a domestic business corporation must be present immediately before or after the transaction. Dissenting shareholders have an appraisal remedy in (1) a conversion of a corporation to an unincorporated entity or to nonprofit status and (2) some domestications.

36-2g GOING PRIVATE TRANSACTIONS

Corporate combinations are sometimes used to take a publicly held corporation private to eliminate minority interests, to reduce the burdens of certain provisions of the Federal securities laws, or both. One method of going private is for the corporation or its majority shareholder to acquire the corporation's shares through purchases on the open market or through a tender offer for the shares. Other methods include a cash-out combination, a merger with or sale of assets to a corporation controlled by the majority shareholder. If the majority shareholder is a corporation, it may arrange a cash-out combination with itself or, if it owns enough shares, use a short-form merger. In recent years, a new type of going private transaction—a management buyout—has become much more frequent. This section examines cash-out combinations and management buyouts.

CASH-OUT COMBINATIONS Cash-out combinations are used to eliminate minority shareholders by forcing them to accept cash or property for their shares. A cash-out combination often follows the acquisition, by a person, group, or company, of a large interest in a target company (T) through a tender offer. The tender offeror (TO) then seeks to eliminate all other shareholders, thereby achieving complete control of T. To do so, TO might form a new corporation (Corporation N) and take 100 percent of its stock. A cash-out merger of T into N is then arranged, with all the shareholders of T other than TO to receive cash for their shares. Because TO owns all the stock of N and a controlling interest in T, the shareholders of both companies will approve the merger. Alternatively, TO could purchase for cash or notes the assets of T, leaving the minority shareholders with only an interest in the proceeds of the sale. The use of cash-out combinations has raised questions concerning their purpose and their fairness to minority shareholders. Some States require that cash-out combinations have a valid business purpose and that they be fair to all concerned. Fairness, in this context, includes both fair dealing (which involves the procedural aspects of the transaction) and fair price (which involves the financial considerations of the merger). Other States require only the transaction to be fair.

◆ *See Case 36-1*

MANAGEMENT BUYOUT A management buyout is a transaction by which existing management increases its ownership of a corporation while eliminating the entity's public shareholders. The typical procedure is as follows. The management of an existing company (Corporation A) forms a new corporation (Corporation B) in which the management owns some of the stock and institutional investors own the rest. Corporation B issues bonds to institutional investors to raise cash, with which it purchases the assets or stock of Corporation A. The assets of Corporation A are used as security for the bonds issued by Corporation B. (Because of the extensive use of borrowed funds, a management buyout is commonly called a **leveraged buyout** [LBO].) The result of this transaction is twofold: the public shareholders of Corporation A no longer have any proprietary interest in the assets of Corporation A, and management's equity interest in Corporation B is greater than its interest was in Corporation A.

A critical issue is the fairness of the management buyout to the shareholders of Corporation A. The transaction inherently presents a potential conflict of interest to those in management, who owe a fiduciary duty to represent the interests of the shareholders of Corporation A. As substantial shareholders of Corporation B, however, those in management are apt to have personal and probably adverse financial interests in the transaction.

36-2h DISSENTING SHAREHOLDERS

The shareholder's right to dissent, a statutory right to obtain payment for shares, is accorded to shareholders who object to certain fundamental changes in the corporation. The Revised Act, as amended, provides this right when (1) the proposed corporate action as approved by the majority will result in a fundamental change in the shares affected by the action and (2) uncertainty about the fair value of the affected shares raises questions about the fairness of the terms of the proposed corporate action. The Introductory Comment to Chapter 13 of the Revised Act explains the purpose of dissenters' rights:

> Chapter 13 deals with the tension between the desire of the corporate leadership to be able to enter new fields, acquire new enterprises, and rearrange investor rights and the desire of investors to adhere to the rights and the risks on the basis of which they invested. Most contemporary corporation codes in the United States attempt to resolve this tension through a combination of two devices. On the one hand, the majority is given an almost unlimited power to change the nature and shape of the enterprise and the rights of its members. On the other hand, the members who dissent from these changes are given a right to withdraw their investment at a fair value.

TRANSACTIONS GIVING RISE TO DISSENTERS' RIGHTS States vary considerably with respect to which transactions give rise to dissenters' rights. Some include transactions not covered by the Revised Act, and other States omit transactions included in the Revised Act.

The Revised Act grants dissenters' rights to dissenting shareholders of (1) a corporation selling or leasing all or substantially all of its property or assets not in the usual or regular course of business, except when shareholders will receive in cash the corporation's net assets within one year after the shareholders' approval of the sale or lease; (2) each corporate party to a merger, except in a short-form merger, where only the dissenting shareholders of the subsidiary have dissenters' rights; (3) a corporation that is a party to a plan of compulsory share exchange in which their corporation is to be the one acquired; (4) any amendment to the articles of incorporation that materially and adversely affects a dissenter's rights regarding her shares; (5) conversion of a corporation to an unincorporated entity or to nonprofit status; (6) some domestications; and (7) any other corporate action taken pursuant to a shareholder vote with respect to which the articles of incorporation, the bylaws, or a resolution of the board of directors provides that shareholders shall have a right to dissent and obtain payment for their shares. Section 13.02.

The 1999 amendments to the Revised Act narrowed the scope of the appraisal remedy by making the following changes: (1) It eliminated the appraisal remedy for all amendments to the articles of incorporation except for reverse stock splits that result in cashing out some of the shares of a class or series. (2) In a merger, only shareholders whose shares have been exchanged have dissenters' rights.

Many States have a stock market exception to the appraisal remedy. Under these statutes, a shareholder has no right to dissent if an established market, such as the New York Stock Exchange, exists for the shares. The original Revised Act does not contain this exception, but the 1999 and 2006 amendments to the Revised Act have added such an exception for publicly traded shares meeting specified criteria.

PROCEDURE The corporation must notify the shareholders of the existence of dissenters' rights before taking the vote on the corporate action. As amended in 2006, the Revised Act requires specific financial disclosure to shareholders. A dissenting shareholder who strictly complies with the provisions of the statute is entitled to receive the fair value of his shares. Unless he makes written demand within the prescribed time, however, the dissenting shareholder is not entitled to payment for his shares.

APPRAISAL REMEDY A dissenting shareholder who complies with all applicable requirements is entitled to an appraisal remedy, which is payment by the corporation of the **fair value** of his shares, plus accrued interest. The fair value is the value immediately preceding the effectuation of the corporate action to which the dissenter objects, excluding any appreciation or depreciation that occurs in anticipation of such corporate action, unless such exclusion would be inequitable. The 1999 amendments to the Revised Act provide that fair value is to be determined "using customary and current valuation concepts and techniques generally employed for similar businesses in the context of the transaction requiring appraisal without discounting for lack of marketability or minority status except, if appropriate, for amendments to the articles."

♦ *See Case 36-2*

> ### *Practical Advice*
> *If you wish to dissent and obtain your appraisal remedy, be sure to follow all of the required procedures and do so in a timely manner.*

A shareholder who has a right to obtain payment for his shares does not have the right to attack the validity of the corporate action that gives rise to his right to obtain payment or to have the action set aside or rescinded, except when the corporate action is unlawful or procured by fraud, material misrepresentation, or omission of a material fact. Section 13.40(b)(2). Where the corporate action is not unlawful or fraudulent, the appraisal remedy is usually exclusive, and the shareholder may not challenge the action. Some States, however, make the appraisal remedy exclusive in all cases; others make it nonexclusive in certain cases.

36-3 Dissolution

Although a corporation may have perpetual existence, its life may be terminated in a number of ways. Incorporation statutes usually provide for both voluntary dissolution and involuntary dissolution. Dissolution does not in itself terminate the corporation's existence but does require that the corporation wind up its affairs and liquidate its assets.

36-3a VOLUNTARY DISSOLUTION

Voluntary dissolution may be brought about through a board resolution approved by the affirmative vote of the holders of a majority of the corporation's shares entitled to vote at a shareholders' meeting duly called for this purpose. Section 14.02. (Under the 1999 amendments to the Revised Act, a dissolution need be approved by only a plurality of the shares cast at a meeting at which exists a quorum consisting of at least a majority of the votes entitled to be cast on the dissolution.) Although shareholders who object to dissolution usually have no right to dissent and recover the fair value of their shares, the Revised Act grants dissenters' rights in connection with a disposition of

all or substantially all of a corporation's assets not made in the usual or regular course of business, including a sale in dissolution. Nevertheless, the Act excludes such rights in sales by court order and sales for cash on terms requiring that all or substantially all of the net proceeds be distributed to the shareholders within one year. Section 13.02(a)(3). In addition, in many States, but not the Revised Act, dissolution without action by the directors may be effected by unanimous consent of the shareholders.

The Revised Act authorizes shareholders in closely held corporations to adopt unanimous shareholders' agreements requiring dissolution of the corporation at the request of one or more shareholders or upon the occurrence of a specified event or contingency.

The Statutory Close Corporation Supplement gives the shareholders, if they elect such a right in the articles of incorporation, the power to dissolve the corporation. Unless the articles of incorporation specify otherwise, an amendment to include, modify, or delete a power to dissolve must be approved by all of the shareholders. The power to dissolve may be conferred upon any shareholder or holders of a specified number or percentage of shares of any class and may be exercised either at will or upon the occurrence of a specified event or contingency.

♦ **See Figure 36-1:** *Fundamental Changes under the RMBCA*

> ### *Practical Advice*
> *To achieve increased protection when organizing a close corporation, you should consider including in the articles of incorporation a provision giving each shareholder the power to dissolve the corporation.*

36-3b INVOLUNTARY DISSOLUTION

A corporation may be involuntarily dissolved by administrative dissolution or by judicial dissolution.

ADMINISTRATIVE DISSOLUTION The Secretary of State may commence an administrative proceeding to dissolve a corporation if (1) the corporation does not pay any franchise tax or penalty within sixty days after it is due; (2) the corporation does not deliver its annual report to the Secretary of State within sixty days after it is due; (3) the corporation is without a registered agent or registered office in the State for sixty days or more; (4) the corporation does not notify the Secretary of State within sixty days that it has changed its registered agent or registered office, that its registered agent has resigned, or that it has discontinued its registered office; or (5) the corporation's period of duration stated in its articles of incorporation expires. Section 14.20.

JUDICIAL DISSOLUTION The State, a shareholder, or a creditor may bring a proceeding seeking judicial dissolution. A court may dissolve a corporation in a proceeding brought by the Attorney General if it is proved that the corporation obtained its articles of incorporation through fraud or has continued to exceed or abuse the authority conferred upon it by law. Section 14.30(1).

A court may dissolve a corporation in a proceeding brought by a shareholder if it is established that (1) the directors are deadlocked in the management of the corporate affairs, the shareholders are unable to break the deadlock, and the corporation is threatened with or suffering irreparable injury; (2) the acts of the directors or those in control of the corporation are illegal, oppressive, or fraudulent; (3) the corporate assets are being misapplied or wasted; or (4) the shareholders are deadlocked and have failed to elect directors for at least two consecutive annual meetings. Section 14.30(2). (The 2006 amendments to the Revised Act made these grounds inapplicable to certain publicly held corporations that meet specified market capitalizations and whose shares are traded in particular types of markets.) The Revised Act as amended in 1990 provides a closely held corporation or its remaining shareholders a limited right to purchase at fair value the shares of a shareholder who has brought a proceeding for involuntary dissolution. Section 14.34.

A creditor may bring a court action for dissolution if the creditor can show that the corporation has become unable to pay its debts and obligations as they mature in the regular course of its business and that either (1) the creditor has reduced its claim to a judgment and an execution issued on it has been returned unsatisfied or (2) the corporation has admitted in writing that the claim of the creditor is due and owing. Section 14.30(3).

♦ *See Case 36-3*

FIGURE 36-1 Fundamental Changes under the RMBCA

Change	Board of Directors Resolution Required	Shareholder Approval Required	Shareholder's Appraisal Remedy Available
A amends its articles of incorporation	A: Yes	A: Yes	A: No (usually)
B disposes of its assets in usual and regular course of business to A	B: Yes	B: No	B: No
B disposes of its assets not in usual and regular course of business to A	B: Yes	B: Yes	B: Yes
A voluntarily purchases shares of B	A: Yes B: No	A: No B: No, individual shareholders decide	A: No B: No
A acquires shares of B through a compulsory exchange	A: Yes B: Yes	A: No B: Yes	A: No B: Yes
A and B merge into A	A: Yes B: Yes	A: Yes B: Yes	A: Yes* B: Yes
A merges its 90 percent subsidiary B into A	A: Yes B: No	A: No B: No	A: No B: Yes
A and B consolidate into C	A: Yes B: Yes	A: Yes B: Yes	A: Yes B: Yes
A converts into another entity	A: Yes	A: Yes	A: Yes, if A becomes an unincorporated entity or a nonprofit corporation
A domesticates	A: Yes	A: Yes	A: Yes, in some domestications
A voluntarily dissolves	A: Yes	A: Yes	A: No (usually)

*Under the 1999 amendments, shareholders of A have *no* appraisal remedy.

Note: RMBCA = Revised Model Business Corporation Act.

36-3c LIQUIDATION

Dissolution, as mentioned, requires that the corporation devote itself to winding up its affairs and liquidating its assets. After dissolution, the corporation must cease carrying on its business except as is necessary to wind up. Section 14.05. When a corporation is dissolved, its assets are liquidated and used first to pay the expenses of liquidation and its creditors according to their respective contract or lien rights. Any remainder is distributed proportionately to shareholders according to their respective contract rights; stock with a liquidation preference has priority over common stock. Voluntary liquidation is carried out by the board of directors, who serve as trustees; a court-appointed receiver may conduct involuntary liquidation. Section 14.32.

36-3d PROTECTION OF CREDITORS

The statutory provisions governing dissolution and liquidation usually prescribe procedures to safeguard the interests of the corporation's creditors. Such procedures typically include a required mailing of notice of dissolution to known creditors, a general publication of notice, and the preservation of claims against the corporation for a specified time. The Revised Act specifies five years; it was amended in 2000 to shorten the period to three years. Section 14.07.

CHAPTER SUMMARY

AMENDMENTS TO ARTICLES OF INCORPORATION	**Authority to Amend** incorporation statutes permit the articles of incorporation to be amended **Procedure** the board of directors adopts a resolution that must be approved by the shareholders
COMBINATIONS	**Purchase or Lease of All or Substantially All of the Assets** results in no change in the legal personality of either corporation • *Disposition of Assets in Regular Course of Business* approval by the selling corporation's board of directors is required, but shareholder authorization is not • *Disposition of Assets in Other Than in Regular Course of Business* approval by the board of directors and shareholders of selling corporation is required **Purchase of Shares** a transaction by which one corporation acquires all of or a controlling interest in the stock of another corporation; no change occurs in the legal existence of either corporation, and no formal shareholder approval of either corporation is required **Compulsory Share Exchange** a transaction by which a corporation becomes the owner of all of the outstanding shares of one or more classes of stock of another corporation by an exchange that is compulsory on all owners of the acquired shares; the board of directors of each corporation and the shareholders of the corporation whose shares are being acquired must approve **Merger** the combination of the assets of two or more corporations into one of the corporations • *Procedure* requires approval by the board of directors and shareholders of each corporation • *Short-Form Merger* a corporation that owns at least 90 percent of the outstanding shares of a subsidiary may merge the subsidiary into itself without approval by the shareholders of either corporation • *Effect* the surviving corporation receives title to all of the assets of the merged corporation and assumes all of its liabilities; the merged corporation ceases to exist **Consolidation** the combination of two or more corporations into a new corporation • *Procedure* requires approval of the board of directors and shareholders of each corporation • *Effect* each constituent corporation ceases to exist; the new corporation assumes all of the constituents' debts and liabilities **Domestication** Revised Act permits a corporation to change its State of incorporation **Conversion** Revised Act permits (1) a domestic business corporation to become a domestic or foreign partnership, LLC, or other eligible entity and (2) a domestic

or foreign partnership, LLC, or other eligible entity to become a domestic business corporation

Going Private Transactions a combination that makes a publicly held corporation a private one; includes cash-out combinations and management buyouts

Dissenting Shareholder one who opposes a fundamental change and has the right to receive the fair value of her shares

- *Availability* dissenters' rights arise in (1) mergers, (2) consolidations, (3) sales or leases of all or substantially all of the assets of a corporation not in the regular course of business, (4) compulsory share exchanges, (5) certain amendments to the articles of incorporation, (6) some conversions, and (7) some domestications
- *Appraisal Remedy* the right to receive the fair value of one's shares (the value of shares immediately before the corporate action to which the dissenter objects takes place, excluding any appreciation or depreciation in anticipation of such corporate action unless such exclusion would be inequitable)

DISSOLUTION   **Voluntary Dissolution** may be brought about by a resolution of the board of directors that is approved by the shareholders

Involuntary Dissolution may occur by administrative or judicial action taken (1) by the Attorney General, (2) by shareholders under certain circumstances, or (3) by a creditor on a showing that the corporation has become unable to pay its debts and obligations as they mature in the regular course of its business

Liquidation when a corporation is dissolved, its assets are liquidated and used first to pay its liquidation expenses and its creditors according to their respective contract or lien rights; any remainder is proportionately distributed to shareholders according to their respective contract rights

C A S E S

CASE 36-1

Cash-Out Combinations
ALPERT v. 28 WILLIAMS ST. CORP.
New York Court of Appeals, 1984
63 N.Y.2d 557, 483 N.Y.S.2d 667, 473 N.E.2d 19

Cooke, C. J.

The subject of contention in this litigation is a valuable 17-story office building, located at 79 Madison Avenue in Manhattan [New York]. In dispute is the propriety of a complex series of transactions that had the net effect of permitting defendants, who were outside investors, to gain ownership of the property and to eliminate the ownership interests of plaintiffs, who were minority shareholders of the corporation that formerly owned the building. This was achieved through what is commonly known as a "two-step" merger: (1) an outside investor purchases control of the majority shares of the target corporation by tender offer or through private negotiations; (2) this newly acquired control is used to arrange for the target and a second corporation controlled by the outside investor to merge, with one condition being the "freeze-out" of the minority

shareholders of the target corporation by the forced cancellation of their shares, generally through a cash purchase. This accomplishes the investor's original goal of complete ownership of the target corporation.

Since 1955, the office building was owned by 79 Realty Corporation (Realty Corporation), which had no other substantial assets. About two-thirds of Realty Corporation's outstanding shares were held by two couples, the Kimmelmans and the Zauderers, who were also the company's sole directors and officers. Plaintiffs owned 26% of the outstanding shares. The remaining shares were owned by persons who are not parties to this litigation.

Defendants, a consortium of investors, formed a limited partnership, known as Madison 28 Associates (Madison Associates), for the purpose of purchasing the building. * * *

Madison Associates formed a separate, wholly owned company, 28 Williams Street Corporation (Williams Street), to act as the nominal purchaser and owner of the Kimmelman and Zauderer interests. * * *

[T]he partners of Madison Associates approved a plan to merge Realty Corporation with Williams Street, Realty Corporation being the surviving corporation. Together with a notice for a shareholders' meeting to vote on the proposed merger, a statement of intent was sent to all shareholders of Realty Corporation, explaining the procedural and financial aspects of the merger, as well as defendants' conflict of interest and the intended exclusion of the minority shareholders from the newly constituted Realty Corporation through a cash buyout. Defendants also disclosed that they planned to dissolve Realty Corporation after the merger and thereafter to operate the business as a partnership. The merger plan did not require approval by any of the minority shareholders.

The merger proposed by the directors was approved at the shareholders meeting, held on November 7, 1980. As a result, the office building was owned by the "new" Realty Corporation, which, in turn, was wholly owned by Madison Associates. In accordance with the merger plan, Realty Corporation was dissolved within a month of the merger and its principal asset, title to the building, devolved to Madison Associates.

* * *

The plaintiffs instituted this action * * * [seeking] rescission of the merger.

The propriety of the merger was contested on several grounds. It was contended that the merger was unlawful because its sole purpose was to personally benefit the partners of Madison Associates and that the alleged purposes had no legitimate business benefit inuring to the corporation. Plaintiffs argue that the "business judgment" of the directors in assigning various purposes for the merger was indelibly tainted by a conflict of interest because they were committed to the merger prior to becoming directors and were on both sides of the merger transaction when consummated. Further, they assert that essential financial information was not disclosed and that the value offered for the minority's shares was understated and determined in an unfair manner.

* * *

On this appeal, the principal task facing this court is to prescribe a standard for evaluating the validity of a corporate transaction that forcibly eliminates minority shareholders by means of a two-step merger. It is concluded that the analysis employed by the courts below was correct: the majority shareholders' exclusion of minority interests through a two-step merger does not violate the former's fiduciary obligations so long as the transaction viewed as a whole is fair to the minority shareholders and is justified by an independent corporate business purpose. Accordingly, this court now affirms.

* * *

In New York, two or more domestic corporations are authorized to "merge into a single corporation which shall be one of the constituent corporations," known as the "surviving corporation" [citation]. The statute does not delineate substantive justifications for mergers, but only requires compliance with certain procedures: the adoption by the boards of each corporation of a plan of merger setting forth, among other things, the terms and conditions of the merger; a statement of any changes in the certificate of incorporation of the surviving corporation; the submission of the plan to a vote of shareholders pursuant to notice to all shareholders; and adoption of the plan by a vote of two-thirds of the shareholders entitled to vote on it [citation].

Generally, the remedy of a shareholder dissenting from a merger and the offered "cash-out" price is to obtain the fair value of his or her stock through an appraisal proceeding [citation]. This protects the minority shareholder from being forced to sell at unfair values imposed by those dominating the corporation while allowing the majority to proceed with its desired merger [citations]. The pursuit of an appraisal proceeding generally constitutes the dissenting stockholder's exclusive remedy [citations]. An exception exists, however, when the merger is unlawful or fraudulent as to that shareholder, in which event an action for equitable relief is authorized [citations]. Thus, technical compliance with the Business Corporation Law's requirements alone will not necessarily exempt a merger from further judicial review.

* * *

* * * In reviewing a freeze-out merger, the essence of the judicial inquiry is to determine whether the transaction, viewed as a whole, was "fair" as to all concerned. This concept has two principal components: the majority shareholders must have followed "a course of fair dealing toward minority holders" * * * and they must also have offered a fair price for the minority's stock. * * *

* * *

Fair dealing is also concerned with the procedural fairness of the transaction, such as its timing, initiation, structure, financing, development, disclosure to the independent directors and shareholders, and how the necessary approvals were obtained. * * * [Citations.] Basically, the courts must look for complete and candid disclosure of all the material facts and circumstances of the proposed merger known to the majority or directors, including their dual roles and events leading up to the merger proposal. * * * [Citations.]

The fairness of the transaction cannot be determined without considering the component of the financial remuneration offered the dissenting shareholders. * * *

In determining whether there was a fair price, the court need not ascertain the precise "fair value" of the shares as it would be determined in an appraisal proceeding. It should be noted, however, that the factors used in an appraisal proceeding are relevant here. * * * [Citations.] This would include but would not be limited to net asset value, book value, earnings, market value, and investment value * * *. Elements of future value arising from the accomplishment or expectation of the merger which are known or susceptible of proof as of the date of the merger and not the product of speculation may also be considered.

* * *

In the context of a freeze-out merger, variant treatment of the minority shareholders—i.e., causing their removal—will be justified when related to the advancement of a general corporate interest. The benefit need not be great, but it must be for the corporation. For example, if the sole purpose of the merger is reduction of the number of profit sharers—in contrast to increasing the corporation's capital or profits, or improving its management structure—there will exist no "independent corporate interest" [citation]. All of these purposes ultimately seek to increase the individual wealth of the remaining shareholders. What distinguishes a proper corporate purpose from an improper one is that, with the former, removal of the minority shareholders furthers the objective of conferring some general gain upon the corporation. Only then will the fiduciary duty of good and prudent management of the corporation serve to override the concurrent duty to treat all shareholders fairly [citation]. We further note that a finding that there was an independent corporate purpose for the action taken by the majority will not be defeated merely by the fact that the corporate objective could have been accomplished in another way, or by the fact that the action chosen was not the best way to achieve the bona fide business objective.

In sum, in entertaining an equitable action to review a freeze-out merger, a court should view the transaction as a whole to determine whether it was tainted with fraud, illegality, or self-dealing, whether the minority shareholders were dealt with fairly, and whether there exists any independent corporate purpose for the merger.

* * *

Without passing on all of the business purposes cited by [the trial court] as underlying the merger, it is sufficient to note that at least one justified the exclusion of plaintiff's interests: attracting additional capital to effect needed repairs of the building. There is proof that there was a good-faith belief that additional, outside capital was required. Moreover, this record supports the conclusion that this capital would not have been available through the merger had not plaintiffs' interest in the corporation been eliminated. Thus, the approval of the merger, which would extinguish plaintiffs' stock, was supported by a bona fide business purpose to advance this general corporate interest of obtaining increased capital.

Accordingly, the order of the Appellate Division should be affirmed.

CASE 36-2

Appraisal Remedy
SHAWNEE TELECOM RESOURCES, INC. v. BROWN
Supreme Court of Kentucky, 2011
354 S.W.3d 542

Abramson, J.

[In December 2003, Shawnee Technology, Inc. (Shawnee Tech), a Kentucky corporation, merged into Appellant Shawnee Telecom Resources, Inc. (Shawnee Tel), also a Kentucky corporation. The merger plan provided that one of Shawnee Tech's shareholders, Kathy Brown, would receive cash for her shares instead of shares in the new company, a so-called cash-out merger authorized by the Kentucky Business Corporation Act. Under that statute's dissenters' rights provisions, Brown demanded from Shawnee Tech the "fair value" for her shares. Disputing the amount of Brown's entitlement, Shawnee Tech brought an action in a Kentucky trial court for an appraisal of Brown's interest in the company.

The trial court referred the appraisal to the Master Commissioner, who heard testimony from both parties' experts concerning the value of the business and the value of Brown's shares. To arrive at the value of Brown's shares, Shawnee's expert discounted his estimate of the company's total value by 25 percent to account for the fact that shares of a closely held corporation do not enjoy a ready market and thus would sell for less than the more easily traded shares of a publicly held company. Thus discounted, the total value of the company's shares was $969,750, and the value of Brown's 24 percent interest was $232,740. Brown's expert, on the other hand, arrived at a value for Brown's interest of at least $576,232.

The Commissioner was not entirely satisfied with either expert's analysis. Instead, the Commissioner, borrowing from both experts' analyses, found a capitalized earnings value of $2,304,178 and a net asset value of $1,343,860. The Commissioner did, however, discount the capitalized earnings value for lack of marketability. Although he acknowledged that the current version of the Model Business Corporations Act (MBCA) precludes marketability discounts, the Commissioner nevertheless ruled that such discounts are allowed under

Kentucky's version of the MBCA. The Commissioner then averaged the two values, giving the net asset value twice the weight of the capitalized earnings value, and arrived at a value for Brown's 24 percent interest of $353,633.

The trial court adopted the Commissioner's report without change, and both parties appealed. The Court of Appeals agreed with Brown and held that marketability discounts are inappropriate in fair-value proceedings under the dissenters' rights statute and should not have been applied in this case. Agreeing with Brown as well that in this case the net asset valuation amounted to an impermissible market value determination, the Court of Appeals reversed the trial court's judgment and remanded for a determination of the fair value of Brown's shares without reference to the company's net asset value and without any discount for lack of marketability. Shawnee appealed.]

At common law, [citation], prior to the advent of corporation statutes, unanimous shareholder consent was required to effect fundamental changes in the corporation. The minority's veto power enabled it to create a nuisance value for its shares, so to counteract such abuses the early corporation statutes provided that even fundamental changes could be effected by majority, rather than unanimous, vote. [Citation.] To compensate minority shareholders for the loss of their veto, every state adopted in some form a statute that gave them instead, in the event of a wide variety of fundamental corporate changes, a right to withdraw their investment for its value as determined by a judicial appraisal. [Citation.] The purpose of the appraisal remedy was twofold. It was meant to provide a sort of liquidity for the shares of investors who found themselves trapped in an altered corporate investment of which they no longer approved, and it was meant to protect minority shareholders from majority overreaching. [Citation.]

* * *

* * * Indeed, the remedy is now invoked primarily in situations not where the minority shareholder wants out, but where he or she is being forced out. * * *

Dissenters' rights statutes, as noted above, exist in some form in every state, and in the vast majority of the states protection is accorded by an appraisal remedy pursuant to which the dissenting shareholder is entitled to the "fair value" of his or her shares. * * * [U]nder [the Kentucky statute which is based on the Model Business Corporation Act], "fair value" for dissenters' rights purposes is simply defined as "the value of the shares immediately before the effectuation of the corporate action to which the dissenter objects, excluding any appreciation or depreciation in anticipation of the corporate action unless exclusion would be inequitable." [Citation.] * * *

* * *

As long as liquidity seemed the purpose of the appraisal remedy, courts often understood "fair value" to mean essentially fair market value and understood their task as identifying a sort of quasi-market price for the dissenting shareholder's particular shares. [Citation.] Since a block of shares that does not convey a controlling interest in the company would ordinarily sell for less than a block that did, in arriving at this hypothetical market price, courts sometimes applied a discount for lack of control, a so-called minority discount. [Citation.] Similarly, since shares of a private corporation generally sell for less, other things being equal, than shares of a public company for which there is a ready market, when appraising shares of a private company courts sometimes applied a discount for lack of liquidity, a so-called marketability discount. [Citation.] Because these discounts apply to share value, as opposed to the value of the company as a whole, they are referred to as shareholder-level discounts and are contrasted with so called entity-level discounts, discounts meant to account for factors that affect the value of the going concern, such as a company's reliance on one or a few key managers or dependence upon a limited customer or supplier base. [Citation.]

As the appraisal remedy came more clearly to focus on the anti-oppression as opposed to the liquidity purpose, courts increasingly construed "fair value" for that purpose not as the hypothetical price of the dissenting shareholder's shares, but rather as the shareholder's proportionate interest in the company as a going concern. Since the price of the particular dissenter's shares was not being estimated, the shareholder-level discounts used to arrive at that price came to be regarded as inapplicable. * * *

* * *

* * * [T]he vast majority of states to consider the appraisal remedy for ousted minority shareholders have * * * held that "fair value" in this context means the shareholder's proportionate interest in the company as a whole valued as a going concern according to accepted business practices. [Citation.] Because an award of anything less than a fully proportionate share would have the effect of transferring a portion of the minority interest to the majority, and because it is the company being valued and not the minority shares themselves as a commodity, shareholder-level discounts for lack of control or lack of marketability have also widely been disallowed. [Citations.]

Recognizing and endorsing the trend against such discounts, in 1994 the American Law Institute's Principles of Corporate Governance recommended that in dissenters' rights appraisal proceedings "fair value" should be the value of the shareholder's "proportionate interest in the corporation, without any discount for minority status or, absent extraordinary circumstances, lack of marketability. . . [F]air value should be determined using the customary valuation concepts and techniques generally employed in the relevant securities and financial markets for similar businesses in the context of the transaction giving rise to appraisal." Principles of Corporate Governance: Analysis and Recommendations §7.22(a) (ALI 1994). In 1999 the American Bar Association's Committee on Corporate Laws followed suit and revised the Model Business Corporation Act's definition of "fair value" to provide that value was to be determined "using customary and current valuation concepts and techniques generally employed for similar businesses in the context of the transaction requiring appraisal; and . . . without discounting for lack of marketability or minority status except, if appropriate, for amendments to the articles pursuant to section 13.02(a)(5)." *Model Business Corporation Act* §13.01(4)(ii)(iii) (2006).

As of 2010, ten states had adopted the 1999 Model Act revision, [citation], but even in states, like Kentucky, that continue to use the 1984 version of the Model Act, "fair value" has been construed as the dissenting shareholder's pro rata share of the company as a whole, without shareholder-level discounts for lack of control or lack of marketability. [Citations.] These Courts have found no legislative significance in the failure of their legislatures to adopt the 1999 revision; have emphasized the statute's use of "fair value" as distinct from "fair market value" as indicating an express rejection of a market value standard; and have endorsed the * * * view that if the appraisal remedy is to be effective, as the legislature must have intended, then shareholder-level discounts should not be applied.

* * *

* * * [We] find a broad consensus among courts, commentators, and the drafters of the Model Act that "fair value" in this context is best understood, not as a hypothetical price at which the dissenting shareholder might sell his or her particular shares, but rather as the dissenter's proportionate interest in the company as a going concern. Arrived at only in the long course of many cases balancing the interest of the corporate majority in controlling their investment with the interest of the minority in fair treatment, this understanding reflects a reasonable balance of those competing interests. It does so by helping to insure that the majority's freedom to eliminate minority shareholders is not employed to transfer a portion of the minority interest to the majority, a result fully in keeping, we believe, with the General Assembly's intent. Because a hypothetical market price for the dissenter's particular shares as a commodity is thus not the value being sought, market adjustments to arrive at such a price, such as discounts for lack of control or lack of marketability, are inappropriate. This principled conclusion accounts for the broad consensus of courts writing in this area. * * *

* * * Although appraisers and courts remain free to consider market, income, and asset approaches to valuation and may employ a weighted average of the results of those approaches if the evidence supports such averaging, there is no suggestion in the statutes that the General Assembly meant to require that approach. We have no hesitation in understanding instead a legislative intent that the value of the going concern be determined by any valuation technique generally recognized in the business and financial community and shown to be relevant to the circumstances of the particular company at issue. We hold, in sum, that in a[n] * * * appraisal proceeding the dissenting shareholder is entitled to the fair value of his or her shares as measured by the proportionate interest those shares represent in the value of the company as a going concern, a value determined in accord with generally accepted valuation concepts and techniques and without shareholder-level discounts for lack of control or lack of marketability.

* * *

Accordingly, for the reasons stated, we reverse in part and affirm in part the decision of the Court of Appeals and remand this matter to the trial court for further proceedings consistent with this Opinion.

CASE 36-3

Involuntary Judicial Dissolution
COOKE v. FRESH EXPRESS FOODS CORPORATION, INC.
Court of Appeals of Oregon, 2000
169 Or.App. 101, 7 P.3d 717

Armstrong, J.

Terry J. Cooke (plaintiff) is the former husband of defendant, Joni Quicker (Joni); defendant Allen John Quicker (John) is Joni's father. In the early 1980s John and Joni began a business distributing fresh produce. Plaintiff soon left his job and began working with John and Joni full time. The business was originally a partnership, with John having a half interest and Joni and plaintiff together having the other half interest. The business grew throughout the 1980s. In June 1990 John, Joni, and plaintiff incorporated the business as Fresh Express Foods Corporation, Inc. (Fresh Express). John received 50 percent of the stock, and Joni and plaintiff each received 25 percent. John was the president of the corporation, Joni was the vice-president, and plaintiff was the secretary and treasurer. They also constituted the three members of the board of directors.

Fresh Express was the primary source of income for all three parties. Part of that income came from their salaries, but substantial additional amounts came as loans that the corporation made to them for various purposes, including paying their individual taxes on their portions of the corporation's retained earnings. Because Fresh Express elected to be a subchapter S corporation, which for tax purposes does not pay taxes itself but passes its income through to its shareholders, plaintiff and defendants were liable for taxes on those retained earnings whether or not the corporation actually distributed them. Without the loans, they would have had no corporate money to pay the taxes on that corporate income.

Joni and plaintiff separated at about the time of the incorporation. The tension between them increased significantly beginning in June 1993 when, after starting a relationship with a Fresh Express employee, plaintiff filed for dissolution of the marriage.

Plaintiff managed the company's delivery system, which included supervising the operation of its trucks. In December 1993, while plaintiff was on vacation, John discovered a notice on plaintiff's desk from the Public Utilities Commission (PUC) that showed deficiencies resulting in a fine of $6,000 and additional penalties of $4,000. Plaintiff had not paid those amounts, and that failure threatened Fresh Express with the loss of its PUC authority to operate. When plaintiff returned from vacation, John, acting as president of the company, gave plaintiff a written notice of termination that included the statement that "Fresh Express Foods Corporation has suffered monetary loss associated with [plaintiff's] position and this constitutes a Breach of Fiduciary Responsibility to the Corporation." It did not refer to a threatened loss of PUC operating authority. After the termination, plaintiff received his unpaid wages and two weeks' severance pay. Before the termination, the corporation distributed money to all of its shareholders that it treated as shareholder loans. It continued to make those distributions to John and Joni, but it did not make them to plaintiff after his termination. Although plaintiff remained a corporate officer and director for almost two years, he was never again informed of or consulted about corporate business.

The court entered a judgment dissolving plaintiff's and Joni's marriage in August 1994, awarding Joni approximately $27,000. Because the corporation had never issued any stock certificates, Joni was unable to use plaintiff's ownership interest in the corporation to satisfy the court judgment. In order to provide Joni a stock certificate to garnish, John called a directors' meeting for November 2, 1995, for the purpose of electing officers. At the meeting John and Joni first reelected John as president and Joni as vice-president; then they also elected Joni as secretary and treasurer. Plaintiff abstained from all three votes. A few days later Joni issued a stock certificate to plaintiff. Instead of sending the certificate to plaintiff, she immediately delivered it to the sheriff under a writ of garnishment on her judgment against plaintiff.

In September 1996, defendants called a special shareholders' meeting, at which they reduced the number of directors to two, over plaintiff's dissenting vote, and elected John and Joni to those positions. During an informal discussion, plaintiff asked John's attorney if the company intended to pay the considerable amount of money it owed to him. After consulting with John, the

attorney responded that John had decided not to make any more distributions to shareholders at that time. After the shareholders' meeting ended and plaintiff left the room at their request, John and Joni held a directors' meeting at which they first removed plaintiff "from all of his positions as an officer, employee and agent of the corporation." John and Joni then agreed, despite the attorney's statement to plaintiff, to distribute the corporation's entire accumulated adjustment account to the shareholders by using it to reduce the outstanding shareholder loans. Finally, they agreed to purchase automobiles for John and Joni, and to increase John's salary from $54,000 per year to $120,000.

[The plaintiff brought suit against the corporation, John, and Joni. The trial court found that John would not have terminated Joni for a comparable error. It concluded that the purpose for firing plaintiff was to exclude him from participating in the corporate business or receiving any benefits from the corporation. The court found that the reason for the exclusion was the breakdown of the marriage and the animosities that followed. The trial court found that the defendants had acted oppressively toward plaintiff in the management and control of defendant Fresh Express. As a remedy, the court ordered defendants to purchase plaintiff's interest in Fresh Express at a price set by the court. The defendants appealed.]

Plaintiff argues that these actions together constituted a course of oppressive conduct and that defendants breached their fiduciary duties to him by freezing him out of all participation in the corporation and depriving him of all of the benefits of being a stockholder. ORS 60.661(2)(b) provides that a court may dissolve a corporation when the directors or those in control "have acted, are acting or will act in a manner that is illegal, oppressive, or fraudulent[.]" Although there is not, and probably cannot be, a definitive definition of oppressive conduct under the statute, at least in a closely held corporation conduct that violates the majority's fiduciary duties to the minority is likely to be oppressive. [Citations.] Cases that discuss either oppressive conduct or the majority's fiduciary duties are, thus, relevant to this question.

A number of cases make it clear that when

the majority shareholders of a closely held corporation use their control over the corporation to their own advantage and exclude the minority from the benefits of participating in the corporation, [in the absence of] a legitimate business purpose, the actions constitute a breach of their fiduciary duties of loyalty, good faith and fair dealing.

[Citation.] A finding that the majority shareholders have engaged in oppressive conduct under ORS 60.661 permits the court either to order a dissolution of the corporation or to award lesser appropriate relief, including requiring the majority to buy out the minority's interest at a price that the court fixes. [Citation.] Because many things can constitute oppressive conduct or a breach of fiduciary duties, what matters is not so much matching the specific facts of one case to those of another but examining the pattern and intent of the majority and the effect on the minority of those specific facts. [Citation.]

The facts of this case show a classic squeeze-out. * * * Defendants withheld dividends and other benefits from plaintiff while preserving benefits for themselves.

* * * [W]itholding dividends can be especially devastating in an S corporation as all corporate income is passed through to the shareholders for tax purposes and shareholders are required to pay taxes on that income, but if no dividends are declared, the shareholders will have no cash from the enterprise with which to pay those taxes.

[Citation.] * * * In addition, the "abrupt removal of a minority shareholder from positions of employment and management can be a devastatingly effective squeeze-out technique." [Citation.] Finally, majority shareholders may siphon off corporate wealth by causing a corporation to pay the majority shareholders excessively high compensation, not only in salaries but in generous expense accounts and other fringe benefits. * * *

The existence of one or more of these characteristic signs of oppression does not necessarily mean that the majority has acted oppressively within the meaning of ORS 60.661(2)(b). Courts give significant deference to the majority's judgment in the business decisions that it makes, at least if the decisions appear to be genuine business decisions. * * * The court must evaluate the majority's actions, keeping in mind that, even if some actions may be individually justifiable, the actions in total may show a pattern of oppression that requires the court to provide a remedy to the minority.

* * *

Finally, * * * defendants acted to ensure that they would permanently receive all benefits of the corporation. They began by replacing plaintiff as a director and reducing the number of directors to two. Although that was not necessarily improper in itself, their first actions as the sole directors of Fresh Express showed their purpose to exclude plaintiff from any share in the corporation other than his tax liabilities. They first removed defendant from any office or agency with the corporation and then took a number of actions to direct all corporate income to themselves. Despite having told plaintiff that there would be no corporate distributions, defendants distributed the entire retained earnings through a paper transaction that ensured that the corporate books would show no source for making any cash distribution to plaintiff. They then more than doubled John's salary, with the result that he received his income from the corporation as an expense that would reduce its profits rather than as a distribution of profits. Finally, they had the corporation pay for their recently purchased automobiles, again adding to the corporation's expenses and reducing its profits for their benefit.

* * *

In summary, we conclude that defendants consistently acted to further their individual interests, not the interests of the corporation, and without regard to their fiduciary duties to plaintiff. They did so either knowing or intending that their actions would harm plaintiff, among other ways by excluding him from any benefits of his ownership of one quarter of the corporate stock. They thereby violated their fiduciary duties to him and engaged in oppressive conduct.

Under ORS 60.661, the trial court had the authority to choose a remedy for defendants' actions; we agree with it that requiring defendants to purchase plaintiff's shares is the preferable option. A purchase will disentangle the parties' affairs while keeping the corporation a going concern; dissolution would not benefit anyone, and plaintiff did not seek it at trial. * * *

* * *

* * * [B]ecause defendants must purchase plaintiffs shares as a remedy for their misconduct, and the price for plaintiff's shares is therefore based on their fair value rather than their fair market value, either a minority or marketability discount would be inappropriate. [Citation.]

Affirmed.

QUESTIONS

1. The stock in Hotel Management, Inc., a hotel management corporation, was divided equally between two families. For several years, the two families had been unable to agree on or cooperate in the management of the corporation. As a result, no meeting of shareholders or directors had been held for five years. There had been no withdrawal of profits for five years, and last year the hotel operated at a loss. Although the corporation was not insolvent, such a state was imminent because the business was poorly managed and its properties were in need of repair. As a result, the owners of half the stock brought an action in equity for dissolution of the corporation. Will they succeed? Explain.

2. **a.** When may a corporation sell, lease, exchange, mortgage, or pledge all or substantially all of its assets in the usual and regular course of its business?

   b. When may a corporation sell, lease, exchange, mortgage, or pledge all or substantially all of its assets other than in the usual and regular course of its business?

   c. What are the rights of a shareholder who dissents from a proposed sale or exchange of all or substantially all of the assets of a corporation other than in the usual and regular course of its business?

3. The Cutler Company was duly merged into the Stone Company. Yetta, a shareholder of the former Cutler Company, having paid only one-half of her subscription, is now sued by the Stone Company for the balance of the subscription. Yetta, who took no part in the merger proceedings, denies liability on the ground that, inasmuch as the Cutler Company no longer exists, all her rights and obligations in connection with the Cutler Company have been terminated. Explain whether she is correct.

4. Smith, while in the course of his employment with the Bee Corporation, negligently ran the company's truck into Williams, injuring him severely. Subsequently, the Bee Corporation and the Sea Corporation consolidated, forming the SeaBee Corporation. Williams filed suit against the SeaBee Corporation for damages, and the SeaBee Corporation asserted the defense that the injuries Williams sustained were not caused by any of SeaBee's employees, that SeaBee did not even exist at the time of the injury, and that the SeaBee Corporation was, therefore, not liable. What decision? Explain.

5. The Johnson Company, a corporation organized under the laws of State X, after proper authorization by the shareholders, sold its entire assets to the Samson Company, also a State X corporation. Ellen, an unpaid creditor of the Johnson Company, sues the Samson Company upon her claim. Is Samson liable? Explain.

6. Zenith Steel Company operates a prosperous business. The board of directors voted to spend $20 million of the company's surplus funds to purchase a majority of the stock of two other companies—the Green Insurance Company and the Blue Trust Company. The Green Insurance Company is a thriving business whose stock is an excellent investment at the price at which it will be sold to Zenith Steel Company. The principal reasons for Zenith's purchase of the Green Insurance stock are to invest surplus funds and to diversify its business. The Blue Trust Company owns a controlling interest in Zenith Steel Company. The Blue Trust Company is subject to special governmental controls. The main purpose for Zenith's purchase of the Blue Trust Company stock is to enable the present management and directors of Zenith Steel Company to perpetuate their management of the company. Jones, a minority shareholder in Zenith Steel Company, brings an appropriate action to enjoin the purchase by Zenith Steel Company of the stock of either the Green Insurance Company or the Blue Trust Company. What decision as to each purchase? Explain.

7. Mildred, Deborah, and Bob each own one-third of the stock of Nova Corporation. On Friday, Mildred received an offer to merge Nova into Buyer Corporation. Mildred, who agreed to call a shareholders' meeting to discuss the offer on the following Tuesday, telephoned Deborah and Bob and informed them of the offer and the scheduled meeting. Deborah agreed to attend. Bob, however, was unable to attend because he was leaving on a trip on Saturday and asked if the three of them could meet on Friday night instead. Mildred and Deborah agreed. The three shareholders met informally Friday night and agreed to accept the offer only if they received preferred stock of Buyer Corporation for their shares. Bob then left on his trip. On Tuesday, at the time and place appointed by Mildred, Mildred and Deborah convened the shareholders' meeting. After discussion, they concluded that the preferred stock payment limitation was unwise and passed a formal resolution to accept Buyer Corporation's offer without any such condition. Bob files suit to enjoin Mildred, Deborah, and the Nova Corporation from implementing this resolution. Explain whether the injunction should be issued.

C A S E P R O B L E M S

8. Tretter alleged that his exposure over the years to asbestos products manufactured by Philip Carey Manufacturing Corporation caused him to contract asbestosis. Tretter brought an action against Rapid American Corporation, which was the surviving corporation of a merger between Philip Carey and Rapid American. Rapid American denied liability, claiming that immediately after the merger, it had transferred its asbestos operations to a newly formed subsidiary corporation. Can Rapid avoid liability by such transfer? Explain.

9. All Steel Pipe and Tube is a closely held corporation engaged in the business of selling steel pipes and tubes. Leo and Scott Callier are its two equal shareholders. Scott, Leo's uncle, is one of the company's two directors and is president of the corporation. Scott is the general manager. Scott's father and Leo's grandfather, Felix, is

the other director. Over the years, Scott and Leo have had differences of opinion regarding the operation of the business. Nevertheless, despite their deteriorating relationship, the company has flourished. When negotiations aimed at Leo's redemption of Scott's shares began, however, the parties could not reach an agreement. The discussion then turned to voluntary dissolution and liquidation of the corporation, but still no agreement could be reached. Finally, Leo fired Scott and began to wind down All Steel's business and to form a new corporation, Callier Steel Pipe and Tube. Leo then brought an action seeking a dissolution and liquidation of All Steel. Should the court order dissolution? Explain.

10. The shareholders of Endicott Johnson who had dissented from a proposed merger of Endicott with McDonough Corporation brought a proceeding to fix the fair value of their stock. At issue was the proper weight to be given to the market price of the stock in fixing its fair value. The shareholders argued that the market value should not be considered because McDonough controlled 70 percent of Endicott's stock and the stock had been delisted from the New York Stock Exchange. Are the shareholders correct? Explain.

11. Ray fell from a defective ladder while working for his employer. Ray brought suit in strict tort liability against the Alad Corporation (Alad II), which neither manufactured nor sold the ladder to Ray's employer. Prior to the accident, Alad II succeeded to the business of the ladder's manufacturer, the now-dissolved "Alad Corporation" (Alad I), through a purchase of Alad I's assets for an adequate cash consideration. Alad II acquired Alad I's plant, equipment, inventory, trade name, and goodwill and continued to manufacture the same line of ladders under the "Alad" name, using the same equipment, designs, and personnel. In addition, Alad II solicited through the same sales representatives with no outward indication of any change in the ownership of the business. The parties had no agreement, however, concerning Alad II's assumption of Alad I's tort liabilities. Decision? Discuss.

12. Kemp & Beatley was a company incorporated under the laws of New York. Eight shareholders held the corporation's outstanding one thousand five hundred shares of stock. Petitioners Dissin and Gardstein together owned 20.33 percent of the stock, and each had been a longtime employee of the corporation. Kemp & Beatley had a long-standing practice of awarding compensation bonuses based upon stock ownership. However, when the policy was changed in 2019 to compensation based on service to the corporation, not on stock ownership, Dissin resigned. The company terminated Gardstein in 2020. Dissin and Gardstein brought a suit in 2021, seeking involuntary dissolution of the corporation and alleging that the corporation's board of directors had acted in a "fraudulent and oppressive" manner toward them, rendering their stock virtually worthless and frustrating their "reasonable expectations" regarding this business venture. What result? Explain.

13. In early 1984, Royal Dutch Petroleum Company (Royal Dutch), through various subsidiaries, controlled approximately 70 percent of the outstanding common shares of Shell Oil Co. (Shell). On January 24, 1984, Royal Dutch announced its intention to merge Shell into SPNV Holdings, Inc. (Holdings), which is now Shell Petroleum, Inc., by offering the minority shareholders $55 per share. Shell's board of directors, however, rejected the offer as inadequate. Royal Dutch then withdrew the merger proposal and initiated a tender offer at $58 per share. As a result of the tender offer, Holdings' ownership interest increased to 94.6 percent of Shell's outstanding stock. Holdings then initiated a short-form merger. Under the terms of the merger, Shell's minority stockholders were to receive $58 per share. However, if before July 1, 1985, a shareholder waived his right to seek an appraisal, he would receive an extra $2 per share. In conjunction with the short-form merger, Holdings distributed several documents to the minority, including a document entitled "Certain Information About Shell" (CIAS).

The CIAS included a table of discounted future net cash flows (DCF) for Shell's oil and gas reserves. However, due to a computer programming error, the DCF failed to account for the cash flows from approximately 295 million barrel equivalents of U.S. proved oil and gas reserves. Shell's failure to include the reserves in its calculations resulted in an understatement of its DCF of approximately $993 million to $1.1 billion, or $3 to $3.45 per share. Moreover, as a result of the error, Shell stated in the CIAS that there had been a slight decline in the value of its oil and gas reserves from 1984 to 1985. When properly calculated, the value of the reserves had actually increased over that time period.

Shell's minority shareholders sued in the Court of Chancery, asserting that the error in the DCF along with other alleged disclosure violations constituted a breach of Holdings' fiduciary "duty of candor." Was the error in the DCF material and misleading? Explain.

14. McLoon, Morse Bros., and T-M Oil Companies were closely held companies entirely owned by members of the Pescosolido family, under the leadership of Carl Pescosolido, Sr. His sons, Carl Jr. and Richard, each held shares in McLoon, Morse Bros., and T-M. Together, their shares constituted 50 percent of the McLoon and

Morse Bros. common stock and 14.3 percent of the T-M common stock. Carl Sr. proposed to merge all of the family-held companies into Lido Inc., over which he would exercise sole voting control. Carl Jr. and Richard dissented in writing to the proposed merger. The parties executed a merger agreement in which the dissenters expressly preserved their statutory appraisal rights. The dissenters individually wrote to each of the three companies of which they were shareholders and requested payment for their shares. Lido responded by offering each dissenter an amount that both dissenters rejected. The dissenters filed a suit for valuation of their stock in all three companies. The referee held that the fair value of each dissenter's stock was his proportionate share of the full value of each company, as determined from the expert testimony. The fair value thus determined was 2.6 times the amount that Lido had offered. Explain whether the court should accept the referee's report.

TAKING SIDES

Wilcox, chief executive officer and chairman of the board of directors, owned 60 percent of the shares of Sterling Corporation. When the market price of Sterling's shares was $22 per share, Wilcox sold all of his shares in Sterling to Conrad for $29 per share. The minority shareholders of Sterling brought suit against Wilcox, demanding a pro rata share of the amount Wilcox received in excess of the market price.

a. What are the arguments to support the minority shareholders' claim for a pro rata share of the amount Wilcox received in excess of the market price?

b. What are the arguments to reject the minority shareholders' claim for a pro rata share of the amount Wilcox received in excess of the market price?

c. Which side should prevail?

Debtor and Creditor Relations

CH 37 SECURED TRANSACTIONS AND SURETYSHIP

CH 38 BANKRUPTCY

CHAPTER 37

Secured Transactions and Suretyship

CHAPTER OUTCOMES

After reading and studying this chapter, you should be able to:

- Explain the various types of collateral.

- Explain the purposes, methods, and requirements of attachment and perfection.

- Discuss the priorities among the various parties who may have competing interests in collateral and the rights and remedies of the parties to a security agreement after default by the debtor.

- Explain the requirements for the formation of a suretyship relationship.

- Explain the rights of a creditor against a surety and the rights of a surety, including those of a cosurety.

"Neither a borrower nor a lender be"—Shakespeare's well-known line in Hamlet—reflects an earlier view of debt, for today borrowed funds are both essential and honorable under our economic system. In fact, the absence of loans would severely restrict the availability of goods and services and would greatly limit consumers in the quantities they would be able to purchase.

The public policy and social issues created by today's enormous use of debt center on certain tenets; among them are the following:

1. The means by which debt is created and transferred should be as simple and as inexpensive as possible.

2. The risks to lenders should be minimized.

3. Lenders should have a way to collect unpaid debts.

A lender typically incurs two basic collection risks: the borrower may be unwilling to repay the loan even though he is able to, or the borrower may prove to be unable to repay the loan. In addition to the remedies dealing with the first of these risks, the law has developed several devices to maximize the likelihood of repayment. These devices, which are discussed in this chapter, include consensual security interests (also called secured transactions) and suretyships.

In addition, debtors of all sorts—wage earners, sole proprietorships, partnerships, unincorporated associations, and corporations—sometimes accumulate debts far in excess of their assets or suffer financial reverses that make it impossible for them to meet their obligations. In such an event, it is an important policy of the law to treat all creditors fairly and

equitably and to provide the debtor with relief from these debts so that he may continue to contribute to society. These are the two basic purposes of the Federal bankruptcy law, which are discussed briefly in this chapter and will be discussed more fully in *Chapter 38.*

SECURED TRANSACTIONS IN PERSONAL PROPERTY

An obligation or debt can exist without security if the creditor deems adequate the integrity, reputation, and net worth of the debtor. Often, however, businesses or individuals cannot obtain credit without giving adequate security, or in some cases, even if the borrower can obtain an unsecured loan, he can negotiate more favorable terms by giving security.

Transactions involving security in personal property are governed by Article 9 of the Uniform Commercial Code (UCC). Article 9 was substantially revised in 1998, and the 1998 revisions have been adopted in all States. In 2010, Article 9 was amended to respond to filing issues and address other matters that have arisen in practice with the 1998 Revisions of Article 9. All States have adopted the 2010 Amendments. This chapter covers Article 9 as revised in 1998 and 2010.

Article 9 provides a simple and unified structure within which a tremendous variety of secured financing transactions can take place with less cost and with greater certainty. Moreover, the article's flexibility and simplified formalities allow new forms of secured financing to fit comfortably under its provisions. In addition, Article 9 now recognizes and provides coverage for electronic commerce.

37-1 Essentials of Secured Transactions

Article 9 governs a secured transaction in personal property in which the debtor *consents* to provide a security interest in personal property to secure the payment of a debt. A security interest in property cannot exist apart from the debt it secures, and discharging the debt in any manner terminates the security interest in the property. Article 9 also applies to the *sales* of certain types of collateral (accounts, chattel paper, payment intangibles, and promissory notes). Article 9 does *not* apply to nonconsensual security interests that arise by operation of law, such as mechanics' or landlords' liens, although it does cover nonpossessory statutory agricultural liens.

A common type of consensual secured transaction covered by Article 9 occurs when a person wanting to buy goods has neither the cash nor a sufficient credit standing to obtain the goods on open credit, and the seller, to secure payment of all or part of the price, obtains a security interest in the goods. Alternatively, the buyer may borrow the purchase price from a third party and pay the seller in cash. The third-party lender may then take a security interest in the goods to secure repayment of the loan.

Every consensual secured transaction involves a debtor, a secured party, collateral, a security agreement, and a security interest. Some Article 9 definitions follow:

A **security interest** is "an interest in personal property or fixtures which secures payment or performance of an obligation." Section 9-406(d) 1-201.

A **security agreement** is an agreement that creates or provides for a security interest. Section 9-102(a)(73).

Collateral is the property subject to a security interest or agricultural lien. Section 9-102(a)(12).

A **secured party** is the person in whose favor a security interest in the collateral is created or provided for under a security agreement. Section 9-102(a)(72). The definition of a secured party includes lenders, credit sellers, consignors, purchasers of certain types of collateral (accounts, chattel paper,

payment intangibles, or promissory notes), and other specified persons.

A **debtor** is a person (1) having an interest in the collateral other than a security interest or lien, whether or not the person is an obligor; (2) a seller of accounts, chattel paper, payment intangibles, or promissory notes; or (3) a consignee. Section 9-102(a)(28).

An **obligor** is a person who, with respect to an obligation secured by a security interest in or an agricultural lien on the collateral, (1) owes payment or other performance, (2) has provided property other than the collateral to secure payment or performance, or (3) is otherwise accountable for payment or performance. Section 9-102(a)(59).

A **secondary obligor** is usually a guarantor or surety of the debt. Section 9-102(a)(71).

A **purchase money security interest** (PMSI) is created in goods when a seller retains a security interest in the goods sold on credit by a security agreement. Similarly, a third-party lender who advances funds to enable the debtor to purchase goods has a PMSI in goods if she has a security agreement and the debtor in fact uses the funds to purchase the goods.

In most secured transactions, the debtor is an obligor with respect to the obligation secured by the security interest. Thus, a security interest is created when an automobile dealer sells and delivers a car to an individual (the *debtor*) under a retail installment contract (a *security agreement*) that provides that the dealer (the *secured party*) obtains a *security interest* (a PMSI) in the car (the *collateral*) until the price is paid.

◆ See Figure 37-1: *Fundamental Rights of Secured Party and Debtor*

37-2 Classification of Collateral

Although most of the provisions of Article 9 apply to all kinds of personal property, some provisions state special rules that apply only to particular kinds of collateral. Under the UCC, collateral is classified according to its nature and its use. The classifications according to nature are (1) goods, (2) indispensable paper, and (3) intangibles.

FIGURE 37-1 Fundamental Rights of Secured Party and Debtor

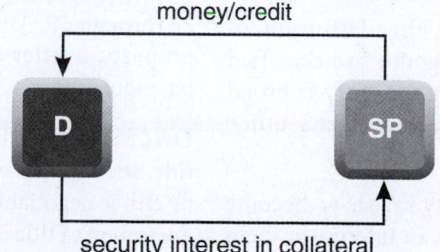

37-2a GOODS

Goods are all things that are movable when a security interest attaches and include fixtures; standing timber to be cut; the unborn young of animals; crops grown, growing, or to be grown; and manufactured homes. Section 9-102(a)(44). Goods also include computer programs embedded in goods if the software becomes part of the goods. (When software maintains its separate state, it is considered a general intangible.) Goods are further classified according to their use.

Goods are subdivided into (1) consumer goods, (2) farm products, (3) inventory, (4) equipment, (5) fixtures, and (6) accessions. Depending on its primary use or purpose, the same item of goods may fall into different classifications. For example, a refrigerator purchased by a physician to store medicines in his office is classified as equipment, while the same refrigerator would be classified as consumer goods if the physician purchased it for home use. In the hands of a refrigerator dealer or manufacturer, the refrigerator would be classified as inventory. If goods are used for multiple purposes, such as by a physician in both her office and her home, their classification is dependent upon their predominant use.

CONSUMER GOODS Goods used or bought primarily for personal, family, or household purposes are consumer goods. Section 9-102(a)(23).

FARM PRODUCTS The UCC defines farm products as goods, other than standing timber, which are part of a farming operation and which are crops grown, growing, or to be grown, including crops produced on trees, vines, and bushes, and aquatic goods. In addition, farm products include livestock, born or unborn, including aquatic goods such as fish raised on a fish farm as well as supplies used or produced in a farming operation. Section 9-102(a)(34). Thus, farm products would include wheat growing on the farmer's land; the farmer's pigs, cows, and hens; and the hens' eggs. When such products become the possessions of a person not engaged in farming operations, they cease to be farm products.

INVENTORY The term *inventory* includes nonfarm product goods (1) that are held for sale, held for lease, or to be furnished under a service contract or (2) that consist of raw materials, work in process, or materials used or consumed in a business. Section 9-102(a)(33). Thus, a retailer's or a wholesaler's merchandise, as well as a manufacturer's raw materials, are inventory.

EQUIPMENT Goods not included in the definition of inventory, farm products, or consumer goods are classified as equipment. Section 9-102(a)(33). This category is broad enough to include a lawyer's library, a physician's office furniture, or a factory's machinery.

FIXTURES Goods and personal property that have become so related to particular *real property* that an interest in them arises under real estate law are called fixtures. Section 9-102(a)(41). Thus, State law other than the UCC determines whether and when goods become fixtures. In general terms, fixtures are goods so firmly affixed to real estate that they are considered part of such real estate. Examples are furnaces, central airconditioning units, and plumbing fixtures. See *Chapter 47* for a further discussion of fixtures. A security interest in fixtures may arise under Article 9, and under certain circumstances, a perfected security interest in fixtures will have priority over a conflicting security interest or mortgage in the real property to which the goods are attached.

ACCESSION Goods installed in or firmly affixed to *personal property* are accessions if the identity of the original goods is not lost. Section 9-102(a)(1). Thus, a new engine placed in an old car automobile is an accession.

37-2b INDISPENSABLE PAPER

Four kinds of collateral involve rights evidenced by indispensable paper: (1) chattel paper,(2) instruments,(3) documents, and (4) investment property.

CHATTEL PAPER Chattel paper is a record or records that evidence both a monetary obligation and a security interest in or a lease of specific goods. Section 9-102(a)(11). A record is information inscribed on a tangible medium (written on paper) or stored in an electronic or other medium and retrievable in perceivable form (electronically stored). Section 9-102(a)(69). Thus, chattel paper can be either tangible chattel paper or electronic chattel paper.

For example, Dealer sells goods on credit to Buyer who uses the goods as equipment. Dealer retains a PMSI in the goods. Dealer then borrows against (or sells) the security agreement of Buyer along with Dealer's security interest in the collateral. The collateral provided by Dealer to his lender in this type of transaction (consisting of the security agreement and the security interest) is chattel paper.

INSTRUMENTS The definition of an instrument includes negotiable instruments (drafts, checks, promissory notes, and certificate of deposits) as well as any other writing that evidences a right to payment of money that is transferable by delivery with any necessary indorsement or assignment and that is not of itself a security agreement or lease. Section 9-102(a)(47). Negotiable instruments are covered in *Chapters 26* through *29*. An instrument does not include an investment property, a letter of credit, or writings evidencing a right to payment from a credit or charge card.

DOCUMENTS The term *document* includes documents of title, such as bills of lading and warehouse receipts, which may be either negotiable or nonnegotiable. Section 9-102(a)(30). A document of title is negotiable if by its terms the goods it covers are deliverable to the bearer or to the order of a named person. Any other document is nonnegotiable. Documents of title are covered in *Chapter 47*.

INVESTMENT PROPERTY The term *investment property* means an investment security, such as stocks and bonds, as well as securities accounts, commodity contracts, and commodity accounts. Section 9-102(a)(49). A **certificated security** is an investment security that is represented by a certificate. Section 8-102(a)(4). An **uncertificated security** is not represented by a certificate. Section 8-102(a)(18). A **security entitlement** means the rights and property interests of a person who holds securities or other financial assets through a securities intermediary such as a bank, broker, or clearinghouse, which in the ordinary course of business maintains security accounts for others. A security entitlement thus includes both the rights against the securities intermediary and an interest in the property held by the securities intermediary. Section 8-102(7), (14), (17).

37-2c INTANGIBLES

The UCC also recognizes two kinds of collateral that are neither goods nor indispensable paper, namely, accounts and general intangibles. These types of intangible collateral are not evidenced by any indispensable paper, such as a stock certificate or a negotiable bill of lading.

ACCOUNTS The term *account* includes the right to monetary payment, whether or not such right has been earned by performance, for (1) goods sold, leased, licensed, or otherwise disposed of or (2) services rendered. Section 9-102(a)(2). Accounts include credit card receivables and health-care-insurance receivables. Section 9-102(a)(2). An example of an account is a business's accounts receivable.

GENERAL INTANGIBLES The term *general intangibles* applies to any personal property *other than* goods; accounts; chattel paper; commercial tort claims; deposit accounts; documents; instruments; investment property; letter-of-credit rights; money; and oil, gas, and other minerals before extraction. Section 9-102(a)(42). Included in the definition are software, goodwill, literary rights, and interests in patents, trademarks, and copyrights to the extent they are not regulated by Federal statute. Also included is a payment intangible, which is a general intangible under which the account debtor's principal obligation is the payment of money. Section 9-102(a)(61).

37-2d OTHER KINDS OF COLLATERAL

Proceeds include whatever is received upon the sale, lease, license, exchange, or other disposition of collateral; whatever is collected on, or distributed on account of, collateral; or other rights arising out of collateral. Section 9-102(a)(64).

For example, an automobile dealer grants a security interest in its inventory to the automobile manufacturer that sold the inventory. When the dealer sells a car to Henry and receives from Henry a used car and the remainder of the purchase price in a monetary payment, both the used car and the money are proceeds from the sale of the new car. Unless otherwise agreed, a security agreement gives the secured party (the manufacturer in this example) the rights to proceeds. Section 9-203(f).

Additional types of collateral include timber to be cut, minerals, motor vehicles, mobile goods (goods used in more than one jurisdiction), and money. Article 9 also includes the following kinds of collateral: commercial tort claim, letter-of-credit rights, and deposit accounts (a demand, savings, time, or similar account maintained with a bank). In consumer transactions, however, deposit accounts may not be taken as *original* collateral. Section 9-109(d)(13).

37-3 Attachment

Attachment is the UCC's term to describe the creation of a security interest that is enforceable against the *debtor*. Attachment is also a prerequisite to rendering a security interest enforceable against third parties, though in some instances, attachment in itself is sufficient to create such enforceability. Perfection, which provides the greatest enforceability against third parties who assert competing interests in the collateral, is discussed in the next section.

Until a security interest "attaches," it is *ineffective* against the debtor. Under Section 9-203, the security interest created by a security agreement attaches to the described collateral once the following events have occurred:

1. the secured party has given value;
2. the debtor has acquired rights in the collateral or has the power to transfer such rights to a secured party; and
3. the debtor and secured party have an agreement, which in most instances must be authenticated by the debtor, although in some cases, alternative evidence, such as possession by the secured party pursuant to agreement, will suffice.

The parties may, however, by explicit agreement postpone the time of attachment. Section 9-203(a).

37-3a VALUE

The term **value** is broadly defined and includes consideration under contract law, a binding commitment to extend credit, and an antecedent debt. Revised Section 1-204. For example, Buyer purchases equipment from Seller on credit. When Buyer fails to make timely payment, Seller and Buyer enter into a security agreement that grants Seller a security interest in the equipment. By entering into the agreement, Seller has given value, even though he relies upon an antecedent debt—the original transfer of goods to Buyer—instead of providing new consideration. Moreover, Seller is not limited to acquiring a security interest in the equipment he sold to Buyer but also may obtain a security interest in other personal property of Buyer.

37-3b DEBTOR'S RIGHTS IN COLLATERAL

The elusive concept of the debtor's rights in collateral is not specifically defined by the UCC. As a general rule, the debtor is deemed to have **rights in collateral** that she owns or is in possession of as well as in those items that she is in the process of acquiring from the seller. Section 9-203(b)(2). For example, if Adrien borrows money from Richard and grants him a security interest in corporate stock that she owns, then Adrien had rights in the collateral before entering into the secured transaction. Likewise, if Sally sells goods to Benjamin on credit and he provides Sally a security interest in the goods, Benjamin will acquire rights in the collateral upon identification of the goods to the contract. In addition, Section 9-203(b)(2) adds the words "or the power to transfer rights in the collateral to a secured party." The comments to this section state "[h]owever, in accordance with basic personal property conveyancing principles, the baseline rule is that a security interest attaches only to whatever rights a debtor may have, broad or limited as those rights may be." Comment 6.

♦ *See Case 37-1*

SECURITY AGREEMENT A security interest cannot attach unless an agreement (contract) between the debtor and creditor creates or provides the creditor with a security interest in the debtor's collateral. Sections 9-203, 9-102(a)(73). With certain exceptions (discussed in the following section), the agreement must (1) be authenticated by the debtor and (2) contain a reasonable description of the collateral. Section 9-203(b)(3)(A). In addition, if the collateral is timber to be cut, the agreement must contain a reasonable description of the land concerned. A description of personal or real property is sufficient if it reasonably identifies what is described. Section 9-108(a). A description of personal property may identify the collateral by specific listing, category, or in most cases a type of collateral defined in the UCC (e.g., inventory or farm equipment). Section 9-108(b). The description, however, may not be a super-generic description, such as "all my personal property." Section 9-108(c).

The UCC provides the parties with a great deal of freedom to draft the security agreement, although this freedom is limited by good faith, diligence, reasonableness, and care. Revised Section 1-302. Moreover, security agreements frequently contain a provision for acceleration at the secured party's option of all payments upon the default in any payment by the debtor,

the debtor's bankruptcy or insolvency, or the debtor's failure to meet other requirements of the agreement. Sometimes security agreements require the debtor to furnish additional collateral if the secured party becomes insecure about the prospects of future payments.

AUTHENTICATING RECORD In most instances, there must be a record of the security agreement authenticated by the debtor. Section 9-203(b)(3)(A). Authentication can occur in one of two ways. First, the debtor can sign a written security agreement. Section 9-102(a)(7)(A). A writing can include any printing, typewriting, or other intentional reduction to tangible form. Section 1-201. To sign includes using any symbol executed or adopted with present intention to adopt or accept a writing. Revised Section 1-201(b)(37).

Second, in recognition of e-commerce and electronic security agreements, Article 9 as amended provides that a debtor can authenticate a security agreement by executing or otherwise adopting a symbol, or by encrypting or similarly processing a record in whole or in part, with the present intent of the authenticating party to adopt or accept the record. Section 9-102(a)(7)(B). As already mentioned, a record means information (1) on a tangible medium or (2) that is stored in an *electronic* or other medium and is retrievable in perceivable form. According to the UCC "[e]xamples of current technologies commercially used to communicate or store information include, but are not limited to, magnetic media, optical discs, digital voice messaging systems, electronic mail, audio tapes, and photographic media, as well as paper. 'Record' is an inclusive term that includes all of these methods." Section 9-102, Comment 9. It does not, however, include any oral or other communication that is not stored or preserved.

AUTHENTICATING RECORD NOT REQUIRED Under the UCC, a record of a security agreement is not mandated in some situations. A record of a security agreement is not required when some types of collateral are pledged or are in the possession of the secured party pursuant to an agreement. Sections 9-203(b)(3)(B), 9-310(b)(6), 9-313. This rule applies to a security interest in negotiable documents, goods, instruments, money, and tangible chattel paper. A **pledge** is the delivery of personal property to a creditor as security for the payment of a debt. A pledge requires that the secured party (the pledgee) and the debtor agree to the pledge of the collateral and that the collateral be *delivered* to the pledgee. Other situations in which a secured party does not need a record authenticated by the debtor include the following: (1) the collateral is a certificated security in registered form that has been delivered to the secured party, Section 9-203(b)(3)(C), or(2) the collateral is a deposit account, electronic chattel paper, investment property, or letter-of-credit rights and the secured party has control over the collateral. Section 9-203(b)(3)(D). Control is discussed later.

CONSUMER GOODS Federal regulation prohibits a credit seller or lender from obtaining a consumer's grant of a nonpossessory security interest in household goods. This rule does not apply to PMSIs or to pledges. Rather, it prevents a lender or seller from obtaining a nonpurchase money security interest covering the consumer's household goods, which are defined to include clothing, furniture, appliances, kitchenware, personal effects, wedding rings, one radio, and one television. (These hard-to-sell items are also referred to as "junk" collateral.) The definition of household goods specifically excludes works of art, other electronic entertainment equipment, antiques, and jewelry.

AFTER-ACQUIRED PROPERTY Article 9 states "[A] security agreement may create or provide for a security interest in after-acquired collateral." Section 9-204(a). After-acquired property is property that the debtor presently does not own or have rights to but may acquire at some time. For example, an after-acquired property clause in a security agreement may include all present and subsequently acquired inventory, accounts, or equipment of the debtor. This clause would provide the secured party with a valid security interest not only in the typewriter, desk, and file cabinet that the debtor currently owns but also in a personal computer she purchases later. Article 9 therefore accepts the concept of a "continuing general lien," or a *floating lien*, though the UCC limits the operation of an after-acquired property clause against consumers by providing that no such interest can be claimed as additional security in consumer goods, except accessions, if the goods are acquired more than ten days after the secured party gives value. Section 9-204(b)(1). As discussed later, the 2010 Amendments provide added protection for a secured party having a security interest in after-acquired property when its debtor relocates to another State or merges with another entity.

FUTURE ADVANCES The obligations covered by a security agreement may include future advances. Section 9-204(c). Frequently, a debtor obtains a line of credit from a creditor for advances to be made at some later time. For instance, a manufacturer may provide a retailer with a $60,000 line of credit, only $20,000 of which the retailer initially uses. Nevertheless, the manufacturer and the retailer may enter a security agreement granting to the manufacturer a security interest in the retailer's inventory that covers not only the initial $20,000 advance but also any future advances.

37-4 Perfection

To be effective against third parties who assert competing interests in the collateral (including other creditors of the debtor, the debtor's trustee in bankruptcy, and transferees of the debtor), the security interest must be perfected. **Perfection** of a security interest occurs when it has attached *and* when all the applicable steps required for perfection have been satisfied. Section 9-308(a). If these steps precede attachment, the security interest is perfected at the time it attaches. Once a security interest becomes perfected, it "may still be or become subordinate to other interests . . . [h]owever, in general, after perfection the secured party is protected against creditors and transferees of the debtor and, in particular, against any representative of creditors in insolvency proceedings instituted by or against the debtor." Section 9-308, Comment 2. Thus, in most instances, a perfected secured party will prevail over a subsequent perfected security interest, a subsequent lien creditor or a representative of creditors (e.g., a trustee in bankruptcy), and subsequent buyers of the collateral.

Depending on the type of collateral, a security interest may be perfected:

1. by the secured party filing a financing statement in the designated public office;
2. by the secured party taking or retaining possession of the collateral;
3. automatically, on the attachment of the security interest;
4. temporarily, for a period specified by the UCC; or
5. by the secured party taking control of the collateral.

A security interest or agricultural lien is perfected continuously if it is originally perfected by one method and is later perfected by another if there is no period when it was unperfected. Section 9-308(c).

Many States have adopted certificate of title statutes for automobiles, trailers, mobile homes, boats, and farm tractors. A **certificate of title** is an official representation of ownership. In these States, Article 9's filing requirements do not apply to perfecting a security interest in such collateral except when the collateral is inventory held by a dealer for sale. Section 9-311(a), (d).

♦ **See Figure 37-2:** *Requisites for Enforceability of Security Interests*

Practical Advice

As a creditor, make sure that you properly perfect any security interest that you acquire.

37-4a FILING A FINANCING STATEMENT

Filing a financing statement is the most common method of perfecting a security interest under Article 9. Filing is *required* to perfect a security interest in general intangibles and accounts except for assignments of isolated accounts. Filing *may* be used

FIGURE 37-2   Requisites for Enforceability of Security Interests

Attachment	Perfection

A. Value given by secured party
B. Debtor has rights in collateral
C. Agreement
    1. record authenticated by debtor (except for most pledges)
    2. providing a security interest
    3. in described collateral
	A. Secured party files a financing statement
	B. Secured party takes possession
	C. Automatically
	D. Temporarily, or
	E. Control

to perfect a security interest in any other kind of collateral, with the general *exception* of deposit accounts, letter-of-credit rights, and money. Section 9-312(b). A financing statement may be filed before or after the security interest attaches. The form of the **financing statement**, which is filed to give public notice of the security interest, may vary from State to State.

WHAT TO FILE   Article 9 uses a system of "notice filing," which indicates merely that a person may have a security interest in the collateral. Article 9 also authorizes and encourages filing financing statements electronically. Though it need not be highly detailed, the financing statement must include the name of the debtor, the name of the secured party or a representative of the secured party, and an indication of the collateral covered by the financing statement. Section 9-502(a). If the financing statement substantially complies with these requirements, minor errors that do not seriously mislead will not render the financing statement ineffective. Section 9-506(a). Significantly, Article 9 no longer requires the debtor's signature on the financing statement to facilitate **paperless or electronic filing**. Section 9-502, Comment 3. Since a signature is not required, Article 9 attempts to deter unauthorized filings by imposing statutory damages of $500 in addition to damages for any loss caused. Section 9-625(b), (e)(3).

Financing statements are indexed under the debtor's name, so it is particularly important that the financing statement provide the debtor's name. Section 9-503 provides rules for what names must appear for registered organizations (such as corporations, limited partnerships, and limited liability companies), trusts, and other organizations. If the organization does not have a name, the names of the partners, members, associates, or other persons comprising the debtor must appear on the financing statement. Section 9-503(a)(4). A financing statement that includes only the trade name is insufficient. Section 9-503(c). A financing statement that does not comply with these requirements is considered to be seriously misleading. Section 9-506(b).

The description of the collateral is sufficient if it meets the requirements for a security agreement discussed earlier or if it indicates that the financing statement covers all assets or all personal property. Section 9-504(1), (2). Thus, the use of super-generic descriptions is permitted in financing statements but is *not* permitted in security agreements. In real-property-related filings (collateral involving fixtures, timber to be cut, or minerals to be extracted), a description of the real property must be included sufficient to reasonably identify the real property. Section 9-502(b).

The 2010 Amendments provide greater guidance as to the name of an individual debtor to be provided on a financing statement. As amended, Section 9-503 offers two alternative provisions:

- Alternative A provides that if the debtor holds an unexpired driver's license issued by the State where the financing statement is filed, the debtor's name as it appears on the driver's license is the name required to be used on the financing statement. If the debtor does not have such a driver's license, either the debtor's actual name or the debtor's surname and first personal name may be used on the financing statement.

- Alternative B provides that the debtor's driver's license name, the debtor's actual name, or the debtor's surname and first personal name may be used on the financing statement.

The 2010 Amendments further improve the filing system for financing statements. More detailed guidance is provided for the debtor's name on a financing statement when the debtor is a corporation, limited liability company, or limited partnership as well as when the collateral is held in trust or in a decedent's estate. Moreover, some nonessential information that was provided on financing statements is no longer required. Section 9-503.

DURATION OF FILING   A financing statement is generally effective for five years from the date of filing. Section 9-515(a). A continuation statement filed by the secured party within six months prior to expiration will extend the effectiveness of the filing for another five years. Section 9-515(d), (e). If the financing statement lapses, the security interest is no longer perfected unless it is perfected by another method. Section 9-515(c).

In many States, security interests in motor vehicles and other specified collateral must be perfected by making a notation on the certificate of title rather than by filing a financing statement. Nevertheless, as previously indicated, certificate of title laws do not apply if the collateral is held as inventory for sale by a dealer.

PLACE OF FILING Article 9 greatly simplifies the place or places of filing: except for real-estate-related collateral financing, statements must be filed in a central location designated by the State. Section 9-501(a)(2). With respect to real-estate-related collateral, the financing statement is to be filed in the office designated for the filing or recording of mortgages on the related real property, which is usually local. Section 9-501(a)(1). If the debtor is an individual, the financing statement is to be filed in the State of the individual's principal residence; for a registered organization, the place of filing is the State where the debtor is organized.

SUBSEQUENT CHANGE OF DEBTOR'S LOCATION After a secured party has filed a financing statement properly, the debtor may change the place of his residence or business or the location or use of the collateral and thus render the information in the filing incorrect. A change in the use of the collateral or a move within the State (intrastate) does not impair the effectiveness of the original filing. If the debtor moves to another State after the initial filing, the security interest remains perfected until the earliest of (1) the time the security interest would have terminated in the State in which perfection occurred, (2) four months after the debtor moved to the new State, or (3) the expiration of one year after the debtor transfers the collateral to a person, who becomes the debtor, in another State. Section 9-316(a). The 2010 Amendments also address perfection issues related to after-acquired property when a debtor moves to a new State. Under the 2010 Amendments, this four-month period of perfection applies to security interests that attach to collateral acquired *after* the debtor moves. Thus, a filed financing statement that would have been effective to perfect a security interest in the collateral if the debtor had not changed its location is effective to perfect a security interest in collateral acquired within four months after the debtor relocates. Section 9-316(h).

37-4b POSSESSION

Possession by the secured party perfects a security interest in goods (e.g., those in the possession of pawnbrokers), instruments, money, negotiable documents, or tangible chattel paper. Section 9-313(a). Moreover, a secured party may perfect a security interest in a certificated security by taking delivery of it. Sections 8-301 and 9-313(a). Possession is *not* available, however, as a means of perfecting a security interest in accounts, general intangibles, commercial tort claims, deposit accounts, other types of investment property, letter-of-credit rights, or oil, gas, and other minerals before extraction. Section 9-313, Comment 2.

A **pledge**, which is a possessory security interest, is the delivery of personal property to a creditor, or to a third party acting as an agent or bailee for the creditor, as security for the payment of a debt. No pledge occurs in cases in which the debtor retains possession of the collateral. In making a pledge, the debtor is not legally required to sign a written security agreement; an oral agreement granting the secured party a security interest is sufficient. In any situation not involving a pledge, however, the UCC requires an authenticated record of the security agreement. Section 9-203(b)(3)(B).

One type of pledge is the field warehouse. This common arrangement for financing inventory allows the debtor access to the pledged goods and provides the secured party with control over the pledged property at the same time. In this arrangement, a professional warehouseman generally establishes a warehouse on the debtor's premises—usually by enclosing a portion of those premises and posting appropriate signs—to store the debtor's unsold inventory. The warehouseman then typically issues nonnegotiable receipts for the goods to the secured party, who may then authorize the warehouseman to release a portion of the goods to the debtor as the goods are sold, at a specified quantity per week, or at any rate on which the parties agree. Thus, the secured party legally possesses the goods while allowing the debtor easy access to her inventory.

> *Practical Advice*
>
> *Field warehousing is a useful way for a creditor to perfect her security interest while providing the debtor with easy access to his inventory.*

37-4c AUTOMATIC PERFECTION

In some situations, a security interest is automatically perfected on attachment. The most important situation to which automatic perfection applies is a PMSI in consumer goods. A partial or isolated assignment of accounts that transfers a less-than-significant portion of the assignor's outstanding accounts is also automatically perfected. Sections 9-309(2), 9-310(b)(2).

A PMSI in consumer goods, with the exception of motor vehicles, is perfected automatically upon attachment; filing a financing statement is unnecessary. Sections 9-309(1), 9-310(b)(2). For example, Doris purchases a refrigerator from Carol on credit for Doris's personal, family, or household use. Doris takes possession of the refrigerator and then grants Carol a security interest in the refrigerator pursuant to a written security agreement. Upon Doris's granting Carol the security interest, Carol's security interest attaches and is automatically perfected. The same would be true if Doris purchased the refrigerator for cash but borrowed the money from Logan, to whom Doris granted a security interest in the refrigerator pursuant to a written security agreement. Logan's security interest would attach and would be automatically perfected when she received the security agreement from Doris. Nevertheless, because an automatically perfected PMSI in consumer goods protects the secured party less fully than a filed PMSI, secured parties frequently file a financing statement, rather than rely solely on automatic perfection.

♦ *See Case 37-2*

37-4d TEMPORARY PERFECTION

Security interests in certain types of collateral are automatically, but only temporarily, perfected. Section 9-312(e) provides that a security interest in a certificated security, negotiable document, or instrument is perfected upon attachment for a period of twenty days. This provision, however, is applicable only to the extent that the security interest arises for new value given under an authenticated security agreement. Section 9-312(e). A perfected security interest in a certificated security or an instrument also remains perfected for twenty days if the secured party delivers the security certificate or instrument to the debtor for the purpose of (1) sale or exchange or (2) presentation, collection, enforcement, renewal, or registration of transfer. Section 9-312(g). After the temporary period expires, the security interest becomes unperfected unless it is perfected by other means. Section 9-312(h).

37-4e PERFECTION BY CONTROL

A security interest in investment property, deposit accounts (not including consumer deposit accounts), electronic chattel paper, and letter-of-credit rights may be perfected by control of the collateral. Section 9-314. A security interest in deposit accounts and letter-of-credit rights may be perfected *only* by control. What constitutes control varies with the type of collateral involved. For example, control of a commercial deposit account (e.g., a checking account) is acquired if (1) the secured party is the bank with which the checking account is maintained or (2) the debtor, secured party, and bank agree in an authenticated record that the bank will comply with the secured party's instructions. Section 9-104. The rules for control for other collateral are somewhat different as provided in the following sections: investment property (Section 9-106), electronic chattel paper (Section 9-105), and letter-of-credit rights (Section 9-107).

♦ *See Figure 37-3: Methods of Perfecting Security Interests*

37-5 Priorities Among Competing Interests

As previously noted, a security interest must be perfected to be most effective against the debtor's other creditors, her trustee in bankruptcy, and her transferees. Nonetheless, perfection of a security interest does *not* provide the secured party with a **priority** over *all* third parties with an interest in the collateral. On the other hand, even an unperfected but attached security interest has priority over a limited number of third parties and is enforceable against the debtor. Article 9 establishes a complex set of rules that determine the relative priorities among these parties.

37-5a AGAINST UNSECURED CREDITORS

Once a security interest *attaches*, it has priority over claims of other creditors who do not have a security interest or a lien. This priority does not depend upon perfection. If a security interest does not attach, the creditor is merely an unsecured or general creditor of the debtor.

37-5b AGAINST OTHER SECURED CREDITORS

The rights of a secured creditor against other secured creditors depend upon the security interests perfected, when they are perfected, and the type of collateral. Notwithstanding the rules of priority, a secured party entitled to priority may subordinate her interest to that of another secured creditor. The parties may do this by agreement, and nothing need be filed.

PERFECTED VERSUS UNPERFECTED A creditor with a perfected security interest or agricultural lien has superior rights in the collateral over a creditor with an unperfected security interest or agricultural lien, whether or not the unperfected security interest has attached. Section 9-322(a)(2).

PERFECTED VERSUS PERFECTED Two parties each having a perfected security interest or agricultural lien rank according to priority in *time of filing or perfection*. This general rule is stated in Section 9-322(a)(1), which provides:

> Conflicting perfected security interests and agricultural liens rank according to priority in time of filing or perfection. Priority dates from the earlier of the time a filing covering the collateral is first made or the security interest or agricultural lien is first perfected, if there is no period thereafter when there is neither filing nor perfection.

This rule favors filing, as it can occur prior to attachment and thus grant priority from a time that may precede perfection. Generally, the original time for filing or perfection of a security interest in collateral is also the time of filing or perfection for a security interest in proceeds from that collateral. Section 9-322(b)(1).

FIGURE 37-3 Methods of Perfecting Security Interests

Collateral	Applicable Method of Perfection: Filing	Possession	Automatic	Temporary (for twenty days)	Control
Goods					
Consumer goods	•	•	PMSI		
Farm products	•	•			
Inventory	•	•			
Equipment	•	•			
Fixtures	•	•			
Indispensable Paper					
Chattel paper	•	Tangible			Electronic
Instruments	•	•		•	
Documents	Negotiable	Negotiable		Negotiable	
Investment property	•	Certificated		Certificated	•
Intangibles					
Accounts	•		Isolated assignment		
General intangibles	•				
Deposit Accounts					Commercial
Letter of Credit Accounts					•
Money		•			

Note: PMSI = purchase money security interest.

Practical Advice

If perfecting by filing, file your financing statement as soon as possible.

Practical Advice

Before accepting personal property as collateral, check the public records to ensure that there are no prior filings against that property.

For example, Debter Store and Leynder Bank enter into a loan agreement (assume there is no binding commitment to extend credit) under the terms of which Leynder agrees to lend $5,000 on the security of Debter's existing store equipment. A security agreement is executed and a financing statement is filed, but no funds are advanced. One week later, Debter enters into a loan agreement with Reserve Bank, and Reserve agrees to lend $5,000 on the security of the same store equipment. The funds are advanced, a security agreement is executed, and a financing statement is filed. One week later, Leynder Bank advances the agreed sum of $5,000. Debter Store defaults on both loans. Between Leynder Bank and Reserve Bank, Leynder has priority, because priority among security interests perfected by filing is determined by the order in which they were filed. Reserve Bank should have checked the financing statements on file. Had it done so, it would have discovered that Leynder Bank claimed a security interest in the equipment. Conversely, after filing its financing statement, with no prior secured party of record, Leynder had no need to check the files before advancing funds to Debter Store in accordance with its loan commitment.

To further illustrate, assume that Marc grants a security interest in a Chagall painting to Miro Bank and that the bank advances funds to Marc in accordance with the loan agreement. A financing statement is filed. Later, Marc wants more money and goes to Brague, an art dealer, who advances funds to Marc upon a pledge of the painting. Marc defaults on both loans. As between Miro and Brague, Miro has priority because its financing statement was filed before Brague's perfection by possession. By checking the financing statement on file, Brague would have discovered that Miro had a prior security interest in the painting.

There are several exceptions to the general rules just discussed:

1. **A PMSI in noninventory goods** (except livestock) takes priority over a conflicting security interest if the PMSI is perfected when the debtor receives possession of the collateral *or* within twenty days of receiving possession.

Section 9-324(a). Thus, the secured party has a twenty-day grace period in which to perfect.

For example, Dawkins Manufacturing Co. enters into a loan contract with Larkin Bank, which loans money to Dawkins on the security (as provided in the security agreement) of Dawkins's existing and future equipment and files a financing statement stating that the collateral is "all equipment presently owned and subsequently acquired" by Dawkins. At a later date, Dawkins buys new equipment from Parker Supply Co., paying 25 percent of the purchase price, with Parker retaining a security interest (as provided in the security agreement) in the equipment to secure the remaining balance. If Parker files a financing statement within ten days of Dawkins's obtaining possession of the equipment, Parker's PMSI in the new equipment purchased from Parker has priority over Larkin's interest. If, however, Parker files one day beyond the statutory grace period, Parker's interest is subordinate to Larkin's.

2. A **PMSI in inventory** has priority over earlier-filed security interests in inventory if the following requirements are met. The purchase money security holder must perfect his interest in the inventory at the time the debtor receives the inventory and send an authenticated notification to the holder of a conflicting security interest. The holder of the conflicting security interest must receive the notification within five years before the debtor receives possession of the inventory, and the notification must state that the person sending the notification has or will acquire a PMSI in the debtor's inventory and must describe the inventory. Section 9-324(b).

For example, Dodger Store and Lyons Bank enter into a loan agreement in which Lyons agrees to finance Dodger's entire inventory of stoves, refrigerators, and other kitchen appliances. A security agreement is executed, a financing statement is filed, and Lyons advances funds to Dodger. Subsequently, Dodger enters into an agreement under which Rodger Stove Co. will supply Dodger with stoves, retaining a PMSI in this inventory. Rodger will have priority as to the inventory it supplies to Dodger, provided that Rodger files a financing statement by the time Dodger receives the goods and notifies Lyons that it is going to engage in this purchase money financing of the described stoves. If Rodger fails either to give the required notice or to file timely a financing statement, Lyons will have priority over Rodger as to the stoves Rodger supplies to Dodger. As noted, the UCC adopts a system of notice filing, and secured parties who fail to check the financing statements on file proceed at their peril.

3. A **security interest perfected by control** in deposit accounts, letter-of-credit rights, or investment property has priority over a conflicting perfected security interest held by a secured party who does not have control. Sections 9-327(1), 9-328(1), 9-329(1). If both conflicting security interests are perfected by control, they rank according to priority in time of obtaining control.

UNPERFECTED VERSUS UNPERFECTED If conflicting security interests and agricultural liens are unperfected, then the first to attach or become effective has priority. Section 9-322(a)(3). If neither attaches or becomes effective, all of the creditors are general, unsecured creditors.

37-5c AGAINST BUYERS

A security interest or agricultural lien continues even in collateral that is sold, leased, licensed, exchanged, or otherwise disposed of unless the secured party authorizes the sale. Section 9-315. Thus, following a sale, lease, license, exchange, or other disposition of collateral, a secured party who did not authorize the transaction does not have to file a new financing statement to continue her perfected interest. The security interest also attaches to any identifiable proceeds from the sale, including proceeds in consumer deposit accounts. Sections 9-315(a)(2), 9-109(d)(13).

In many instances, however, buyers of collateral sold without the secured party's authorization take it free of an **unperfected** security interest. A buyer of goods, tangible chattel paper, documents, instruments, or certificated securities who gives value and receives delivery of the collateral without knowledge of the security interest *before* it is perfected takes free of the security interest. Section 9-317(b). Similarly, a buyer of accounts, electronic chattel paper, general intangibles, or investment property other than certificated securities takes free of a security interest if the buyer gives value without knowledge of the security interest and does so *before* it is perfected. Section 9-317(d). Thus, with respect to all of these types of collateral, an unperfected security interest prevails over a buyer who does *not* give value or has *knowledge* of the security interest.

In addition, in some instances, purchasers take the collateral free of a **perfected** security interest. The most significant of these instances are as follows:

BUYERS IN THE ORDINARY COURSE OF BUSINESS A buyer in the ordinary course of business takes collateral (other than farm products) free of any security interest created by *the buyer's* seller, even if the security interest is perfected and the buyer *knows* of its existence. Section 9-320(a). A buyer in the ordinary course of business is a person that buys goods in good faith, without knowledge that the sale violates the rights of another person in the goods, and in the ordinary course from a person, other than a pawnbroker, in the business of selling goods of that kind. Revised Section 1-201(b)(9). Thus, this rule applies primarily to purchasers of inventory. For example, a consumer who purchases a sofa from a furniture dealer and the dealer who purchases the sofa from another dealer are both buyers in the ordinary course of business. On the other hand, a person who purchases a sofa from a dentist who used the sofa in his waiting room or from an individual who used the sofa in his home is not a buyer in the ordinary course of business.

To illustrate further, a person who in the ordinary course of business buys an automobile from an automobile dealership will take free and clear of a security interest created by the dealer from whom she purchased the car. That same buyer in the ordinary course of business will not, however, take clear of a security interest created by any person who owned the automobile prior to the dealer.

BUYERS OF FARM PRODUCTS Buyers in the ordinary course of business of **farm products**, although not protected by Section 9-320, may be protected by the Federal Food Security Act. This Act defines a buyer in the ordinary course of business as "a person who, in the ordinary course of business, buys farm products from a person engaged in farming operations who is in the business of selling farm products." The Act provides that such a buyer shall take free of most security interests created by the seller, even if the security interest is perfected and the buyer knows of its existence.

BUYERS OF CONSUMER GOODS In the case of consumer goods, a buyer who buys without knowledge of a security interest, for value, and primarily for personal, family, or household purposes takes the goods free of any PMSI *automatically* perfected but takes the goods subject to a security interest perfected by filing. Section 9-320(b). For example, Ann purchases on credit a refrigerator from Sean for use in her home and grants Sean a security interest in the refrigerator. Sean does not file a financing statement but has a security interest perfected by attachment. Ann subsequently sells the refrigerator to her neighbor, Juwan, for use in his home. Juwan does not know of Sean's security interest and therefore takes the refrigerator free of that interest. If Sean had filed a financing statement, however, his security interest would continue in the collateral, even in Juwan's hands.

BUYERS OF OTHER COLLATERAL To the extent provided by UCC Articles 3, 7, and 8, a secured party who has a perfected security interest in a negotiable instrument, a negotiable document of title, or a security has a *subordinate* interest to a purchaser of (1) the instrument who has the rights of a holder in due course, (2) the document of title to whom it has been duly negotiated, or (3) the security who is a protected purchaser. Section 9-331. In addition, in certain instances, a secured party who has a perfected security interest in chattel paper also may have subordinate rights to a purchaser of such collateral. Section 9-330.

37-5d AGAINST LIEN CREDITORS

A lien creditor is a creditor who has acquired a lien in the property by judicial decree ("attachment garnishment, or the like"), an assignee for the benefit of creditors, a receiver in equity, or a **trustee in bankruptcy**. Section 9-102(a)(52). (A trustee in bankruptcy is a representative of an estate in bankruptcy who is responsible for collecting, liquidating, and distributing the debtor's assets.) Whereas a perfected security interest or agricultural lien has priority over lien creditors who acquire their liens after perfection, an unperfected security interest or agricultural lien is subordinate to the rights of one who becomes a lien creditor before (1) its perfection or (2) a financing statement covering the collateral is filed and (a) the debtor has authenticated a properly drawn security agreement; (b) if the collateral is a certificated security, the certificate has been delivered to the secured party; or (c) if the collateral is an uncertificated security, it is in possession of the secured party. Section 9-317(a)(2). If a secured party files with respect to a *PMSI* within twenty days after the debtor receives possession of the collateral, however, the secured party takes priority over the rights of a lien creditor that arise between the time the security interest attaches and the time of filing. Section 9-317(e). Nonetheless, a lien securing claims arising from services or materials furnished in the ordinary course of a person's business with respect to goods (an artisan's or mechanic's lien) has priority over a security interest in the goods unless the lien is created by a statute that expressly provides otherwise. Section 9-333.

37-5e AGAINST TRUSTEE IN BANKRUPTCY

The Bankruptcy Code empowers a trustee in bankruptcy to invalidate secured claims in certain instances. It also imposes some limitations on the rights of secured parties. This section examines the power of a trustee in bankruptcy to take priority over an unperfected security interest and avoid preferential transfers.

PRIORITY OVER UNPERFECTED SECURITY INTEREST A trustee in bankruptcy may invalidate any security interest that is voidable by a creditor who obtained a judicial lien on the date the bankruptcy petition was filed. Bankruptcy Code, Section 544. Under Article 9 and the Bankruptcy Code, the trustee, as a hypothetical lien creditor, has priority over a creditor whose security interest was not perfected when the bankruptcy petition was filed. A creditor with a PMSI interest who files within the UCC's statutory grace period of twenty days after the debtor receives the collateral will defeat the trustee, even if the bankruptcy petition is filed before the creditor perfects and after the security interest is created. For example, David borrowed $5,000 from Cynthia on September 1 and gave her a security interest in the equipment he purchased with the borrowed funds. On October 3, before Cynthia perfected her security interest, David filed for bankruptcy. The trustee in bankruptcy can invalidate Cynthia's security interest because it was unperfected when the bankruptcy petition was filed. If, however, David had filed for bankruptcy on September 8 and Cynthia had perfected the security interest within the UCC's statutory grace period of twenty days, Cynthia would prevail.

AVOIDANCE OF PREFERENTIAL TRANSFERS Section 547 of the Bankruptcy Code provides that a trustee in bankruptcy may invalidate any transfer of property—including the granting of a security interest—from the debtor, provided that the transfer (1) was to or for the benefit of a creditor; (2) was made on account of an antecedent debt; (3) was made when the debtor was insolvent; (4) was made on the date of or within ninety days before the filing of the bankruptcy petition or, if made to an insider, was made within one year before the date of the filing; and (5) enabled the transferee to receive more than he would have received in bankruptcy. (An insider includes a relative or general partner of a debtor, as well as a partnership in which the debtor is a general partner or a corporation of which the debtor is a director, officer, or person in control.) In determining whether the debtor is insolvent, the Bankruptcy Code establishes a rebuttable presumption of insolvency for the ninety days prior to the filing of the bankruptcy petition. To avoid a transfer to an insider that occurred more than one year before bankruptcy, the trustee must prove that the debtor was insolvent when the transfer was made. If a security interest is invalidated as a preferential transfer, the creditor may still make a claim for the unpaid debt, but the creditor's claim is unsecured.

To illustrate the operation of this rule, consider the following. On May 1, Debra bought and received merchandise from Stuart and gave him a security interest in the goods for the unpaid price of $20,000. On June 5, Stuart filed a financing statement. On August 1, Debra filed a petition for bankruptcy. The trustee in bankruptcy may avoid the perfected security interest as a preferential transfer because (1) the transfer of the perfected security interest on June 5 was to benefit a creditor (Stuart), (2) the transfer was on account of an antecedent debt (the $20,000 owed from the sale of the merchandise), (3) the debtor was insolvent at the time (the Bankruptcy Code presumes that the debtor is insolvent for the ninety days preceding the date the bankruptcy petition was filed—August 1), (4) the transfer was made within ninety days of bankruptcy (June 5 is less than ninety days before August 1), and (5) the transfer enabled the creditor to receive more than he would have received in bankruptcy (Stuart would have a secured claim on which he would recover more than he would on an unsecured claim).

Nevertheless, not all transfers made within ninety days of bankruptcy are voidable. As amended in 2005, the Bankruptcy Code makes exceptions for certain prebankruptcy transfers. If the creditor gives the debtor new value which the debtor uses to acquire property in which he grants the creditor a security interest, the resulting PMSI is not voidable if the creditor perfects it within thirty days after the debtor receives possession of the property. For example, if within ninety days of the filing of the petition the debtor purchases a refrigerator on credit and grants the seller or lender a PMSI in the refrigerator, the transfer of that interest is not voidable if the secured party perfects within thirty days after the debtor receives possession of the property.

◆ See Figure 37-4: *Priorities*

37-6 Default

Because the UCC does not define or specify what constitutes default, general contract law or the agreement between the parties will determine when a default occurs. After default, the security agreement and the applicable provisions of the UCC govern the rights and remedies of the parties. In general, the secured party may reduce his claim to judgment, foreclose, or otherwise enforce the claim, security interest, or agricultural lien by any available judicial procedure. Section 9-601(a)(1). If the collateral consists of documents, the secured party may proceed against the documents or the goods they cover. Section 9-601(a)(2). These rights and remedies of the creditor are cumulative. Section 9-601(c).

Practical Advice

Provide in your security agreement which events place the debtor in default and what remedies the creditor will have in the event of default.

Unless the debtor has waived his rights in the collateral after default, he has a right of redemption (to free the collateral of the security interest by fulfilling all obligations securing the collateral and paying reasonable expenses and attorneys' fees) at any time before the secured party has collected the collateral, has disposed of the collateral, has entered a contract to dispose of it, or has discharged the obligation by accepting the collateral. Section 9-623.

37-6a REPOSSESSION

Unless the parties have agreed otherwise, the secured party may take possession of the collateral on default. If it can be done without a breach of the peace, such taking may occur without judicial process. Section 9-609. The UCC leaves the term *breach of the peace* for the courts to define. Some States have defined such a breach to require either the use of violence or the threat of violence, while others require merely an entry without consent. Most States require permission for entry to a residence or garage. On the other hand, the courts do permit the repossession of motor vehicles from driveways or streets. Some courts, however, do not permit a creditor to repossess if the debtor has orally protested the repossession.

FIGURE 37-4 Priorities

Versus	Unsecured Creditor	Creditor with Unperfected Security Interests	Creditor with Perfected Security Interest	Creditor with Perfected Money Security Interest
Unsecured Creditor	=	↑	↑	↑
Creditor with Unperfected Security Interest	←	first to attach	↑	↑
Creditor with Perfected Security Interest	←	←	first to file or perfect	↑ if PMSI perfected within grace period
Creditor with Perfected PMSI	←	←	first to file or perfect	↑ if PMSI gives notice and perfects by time debtor gets possession
Buyer in Ordinary Course of Business	←	←	← if created by immediate seller	←
Consumer Buyer of Consumer Goods	←	←	↑	← if not filed
Lien Creditor (including trustee in bankruptcy)	←	←	first in time	first in time but PMSI has grace period
Trustee in Bankruptcy— Voidable Preferences	←	←	↑ if secured party perfects within grace period	↑ if PMSI perfects within grace period

Note: PMSI = purchase money security interest.

After default, instead of removing the collateral, the secured party may render it unusable and leave it on the debtor's premises until disposing of it. It also may be done without judicial process if accomplished without a breach of peace. Section 9-609.

♦ *See Case 37-3*

37-6b SALE OF COLLATERAL

The secured party may sell, lease, license, or otherwise dispose of any collateral in its existing condition at the time of default or following any commercially reasonable preparation or processing. Section 9-610(a). A secured party's disposition of the collateral after default (1) transfers to a transferee for value all of the debtor's rights in the collateral, (2) discharges the security interest under which the disposition occurred, and (3) discharges any subordinate security interests and liens. Section 9-617(a).

The collateral may be disposed of at public sale (auction) or private sale, so long as all aspects of the disposition, including its method, manner, time, place, and other terms, are "commercially reasonable." Section 9-610(b). The secured party may buy at a public sale and at a private sale if the collateral is customarily sold in a recognized market or is the subject of widely distributed standard price quotations. Section 9-610(c). The collateral,

if it is commercially reasonable, may be disposed of by one or more contracts or as a unit or in parcels. Section 9-610(b). The UCC favors private sales since they generally garner a higher price for the collateral. Section 9-610, Comment 2. The fact that the secured party could have received a greater amount is not of itself sufficient to establish that the sale was not made in a commercially reasonable manner. Section 9-627(a). Unless the collateral is perishable or threatens to decline speedily in value or is of a type customarily sold on a recognized market, the secured party must send a reasonable authenticated notification of disposition to the debtor, any secondary obligor (surety or guarantor) and, except in the case of consumer goods, other parties who have sent an authenticated notice of a claim or any secured party or lien holder who has filed a financing statement at least ten days before the notification date. Section 9-611.

Section 9-615(a) provides that the proceeds from the sale of the collateral are to be applied in the following order:

1. paying the reasonable expenses of retaking and disposing of the collateral,
2. paying the debt owed to the secured party,
3. paying any subordinate interests in the collateral, and
4. paying a secured party that is a consignor.

The debtor is entitled to any *surplus* and is liable for any *deficiency*, except in the case of a sale of accounts, chattel paper, payment intangibles, or promissory notes for which he is neither entitled nor liable unless the security agreement so provides. Section 9-615(d)(e). If the goods are consumer goods, the secured party must give the debtor an explanation of how the surplus or deficiency was calculated. Section 9-616.

37-6c ACCEPTANCE OF COLLATERAL

Acceptance of collateral (strict foreclosure) is a way for a secured party to acquire the debtor's interests without the need for a sale or other disposition. The secured party may, after default and repossession if the debtor consents in a record authenticated after default, keep the collateral in full or partial satisfaction of the obligation. Section 9-620(a)(1)(c). In addition, the secured party may accept the collateral in *full* satisfaction of the obligation if she sends an unconditional proposal to the debtor to accept the collateral in full satisfaction of the obligation and she does not receive a notice of objection authenticated by the debtor within twenty days. Section 9-620(c)(2). If there is an objection, however, the secured party must dispose of the collateral as provided in the UCC. Section 9-620. Silence is not consent to a *partial* satisfaction of the obligation. The debtor's consent, however, will not permit the secured party to accept the collateral in satisfaction of the obligation if a person holding a junior interest (secured party or lien holder) lodges a proper objection to the proposal. Section 9-620(a)(2), Comment 3.

In the case of *consumer goods*, if the debtor has paid 60 percent or more of the obligation, the secured party who has taken possession of the collateral must dispose of it by sale within ninety days after repossession unless the debtor and all secondary obligors have agreed in a record authenticated after default to a longer period of time. Section 9-620(e), (f). Additionally, with a consumer debt, the secured party may not accept collateral in *partial* satisfaction of the obligation it secures. Section 9-620(g).

The acceptance of collateral in full or partial satisfaction discharges the obligation to the extent consented to by the debtor, transfers all of the debtor's rights to the secured party, and terminates all subordinate interests in the collateral. Section 9-622.

SURETYSHIP

In many business transactions, especially those involving the extension of credit, the creditor will require that someone in addition to the principal debtor promise to fulfill the obligation. This **secondary obligor**, generally known as a surety, is obligated to perform all or part of the underlying obligation of the principal debtor if the principal debtor fails to perform.

In a contract involving a minor, a surety commonly acts as a party with full contractual capacity who can be held responsible for the obligations arising from the contract. Sureties are often used in addition to security interests to further reduce the risks involved in the extension of credit and are used instead of security interests when security is unavailable or when the use of a secured transaction is too expensive or inconvenient. Employers frequently use sureties to protect against losses caused by employees' embezzlement, and property owners use sureties to bond the performance of contracts for the construction of commercial buildings. Similarly, statutes commonly require that contracts for work to be done for government entities have the added protection of a surety.

Suretyship is governed primarily by State common law. A comprehensive presentation of this law is found in the Restatement of the Law Third, Suretyship and Guaranty, published in 1996 by the American Law Institute. Regarded as a valuable authoritative reference work, it is cited extensively and quoted in reported judicial opinions. The rest of this chapter refers to the Restatement of the Law Third, Suretyship and Guaranty as the Restatement.

37-7 Nature and Formation

A secondary obligor (**surety**) promises to perform an underlying obligation owed to one person (called the **creditor**) by another (the **principal debtor**) on the principal debtor's *failure* to perform the obligation. Section 1. Thus, the suretyship relationship involves three parties—the principal debtor, the creditor, and the surety—and three relationships, as illustrated in *Figure 37-5*.

1. *Relationship between the principal debtor and the creditor.* The creditor's rights against the principal debtor are determined by the underlying contract between them. The creditor also may take action on any collateral that the creditor or the surety holds to secure the principal debtor's performance.

2. *Relationship between the surety and the creditor.* Based on the suretyship contract, the creditor may proceed against the surety if the principal debtor defaults.

3. *Relationship between the surety and the principal debtor.* Based on the law of suretyship, a surety has rights against the principal debtor, including exoneration, reimbursement, and subrogation (see *Figure 37-5*). These rights of sureties, which may be modified by agreement, are discussed later in this chapter.

◆ See Figure 37-5: *Suretyship Relationship*

FIGURE 37-5 Suretyship Relationship

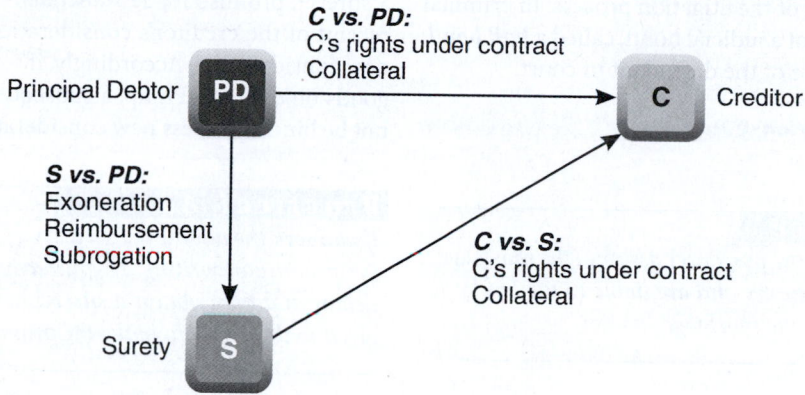

37-7a **TYPES OF SURETIES**

The Restatement provides that if the secondary obligor is identified as a **guarantor**, the creditor may hold the guarantor liable as soon as the principal debtor defaults. The creditor need not proceed first against the principal debtor. In contrast, a secondary obligor who is identified as a **guarantor of collection** is liable only when the creditor exhausts his legal remedies against the principal debtor. Section 15. Thus, a conditional guarantor of collection is liable if the creditor first obtains, but is unable to collect, a judgment against the principal debtor. A secondary obligor who is identified as a **surety** is jointly and severally liable with the principal debtor to perform the obligation set forth in the contract. Two or more secondary obligors bound for the same debt of a principal debtor are **cosureties**.

Although a distinction exists between a surety and a guarantor, these two secondary obligors are governed by the Restatement. Section 1, Comment c. For convenience, and because the rights and duties of a surety and a guarantor are almost indistinguishable, the term *surety* will be used to include both of these secondary obligors.

37-7b **PARTICULAR KINDS OF SURETYSHIPS**

Creditors frequently use a suretyship arrangement to reduce the risk of default by their debtors. For example, Philco Developers, a closely held corporation, applies to Caldwell Bank, a lending institution, for a loan. After scrutinizing Philco's assets and financial prospects, the lender refuses to extend credit unless Simpson, Philco's sole shareholder, promises to repay the loan if Philco does not. Simpson agrees, and Caldwell Bank makes the loan. Simpson's undertaking is that of a surety. Similarly, Philco Developers wishes to purchase goods on credit from Bird Enterprises, the seller, who agrees to extend credit only if Philco Developers obtains an acceptable surety. Simpson agrees to pay Bird Enterprises for the goods if Philco Developers does

not. Simpson is a surety. In each of these examples, the surety's promise gives the creditor recourse for payment against two persons—the principal debtor and the surety—instead of one, thereby reducing the creditor's risk of loss.

Another common suretyship relation arises when an owner of property subject to a mortgage sells the property to a purchaser who *assumes the mortgage*. Although by assuming the obligation the purchaser becomes the principal debtor and therefore personally obligated to pay the seller's debt to the lender, the seller nevertheless remains liable to the lender and is a surety on the obligation the purchaser has assumed (see *Figure 37-6*).

However, a purchaser who does *not* assume the mortgage but simply takes the property subject to the mortgage, is *not* personally liable for the mortgage, nor is he a surety for the mortgage obligation. In this case, the purchaser's potential loss is limited to the value of the property, for although the mortgagee creditor may foreclose against the property, she may not hold the purchaser personally liable for the debt.

In addition, there are numerous specialized kinds of suretyship, the most important of which are (1) fidelity, (2) performance, (3) official, and (4) judicial. A surety undertakes a *fidelity bond* to protect an employer against employee dishonesty. *Performance bonds* guarantee the performance of the terms and conditions of a contract. These bonds are used frequently in the construction industry to protect an owner from losses that may result from a contractor's failure to complete the construction in accordance with the construction contract. Statutes of the United States and of most States require performance bonds for construction contracts with government entities. *Official bonds* arise from statutes requiring public officers to furnish bonds for the faithful performance of their duties. Such bonds obligate a surety for all losses an officer causes through negligence or through nonperformance of her duties. *Judicial bonds*, including attachment bonds, injunction bonds, and appeal bonds, represent a guaranty that the party required to furnish the bond will fulfill all of her obligations in connection with an aspect of the litigation process. In criminal proceedings, the purpose of a judicial bond, called a **bail bond**, is to ensure the appearance of the defendant in court.

♦ See Figure 37-6: *Assumption of Mortgage*

Practical Advice

If you sell your house and the purchaser assumes the mortgage, recognize that you are a surety and are liable to the lender if the purchaser defaults on the mortgage.

37-7c FORMATION

The suretyship relationship is contractual and must satisfy all the usual elements of a contract. Section 7. No particular words are required to constitute a contract of suretyship or guaranty.

As discussed in *Chapter 15*, under the statute of frauds, the contractual promise of a surety to the creditor must be in writing to be enforceable. This requirement, which applies only to secondary or collateral promises, is subject to the exception known as the *main purpose doctrine*. Under this doctrine, if the leading object (main purpose) of the promisor (surety) is to obtain an economic benefit that he did not previously enjoy, the promise is *not* within the statute of frauds.

The promise of a surety is *not* binding without consideration. Because the surety generally makes her promise to induce the creditor to confer a benefit upon the principal debtor, the same consideration that supports the principal debtor's promise usually supports the surety's promise as well. Section 9. Thus, if Constance lends money to Philip upon Sally's promise to act as a surety, Constance's extension of credit is

the consideration to support not only Philip's promise to repay the loan but also Sally's suretyship undertaking. In contrast, a surety's promise made *subsequent* to the principal debtor's receipt of the creditor's consideration must be supported by new consideration. Accordingly, if Constance has already sold goods on credit to Philip, a subsequent guaranty by Sally will not be binding unless new consideration is given.

Practical Advice

If you seek the additional security of a surety, obtain the surety's promise in writing. If you have already lent money to a debtor and then obtain a surety, new consideration must be given to the surety to make the promise binding.

37-8 Duties of Surety

Upon default by the principal debtor, the creditor may proceed against the surety to enforce the surety's undertaking. A surety or guarantor usually has *no* right to compel the creditor to collect from the principal debtor or to take action on collateral provided by the principal debtor. Sections 15 and 51. Nor is the creditor required to give the surety notice of the principal debtor's default unless the contract of suretyship provides otherwise. A guarantor of collection, on the other hand, has no liability until the creditor exhausts his legal remedies of collection against the principal debtor, including taking action on collateral provided by the principal debtor.

Up to the amount of each surety's undertaking, cosureties are *jointly and severally* liable for the principal debtor's default. The creditor may proceed against any or all of the cosureties and collect from any of them the amount that the surety has agreed to guarantee, up to and including the entire amount of the principal debtor's obligation. Section 52.

FIGURE 37-6 Assumption of Mortgage

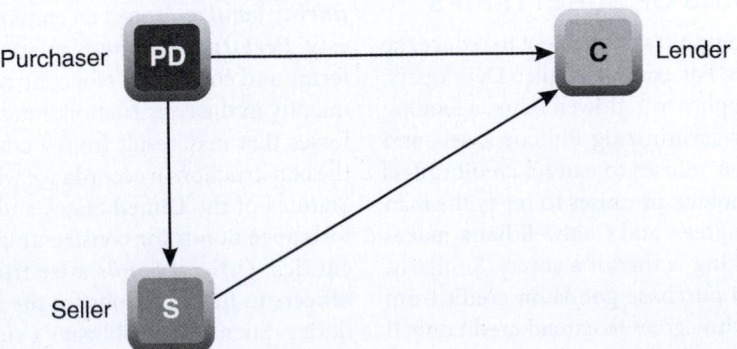

37-9 Rights of Surety

Upon the principal debtor's default, the surety has a number of rights against the principal debtor, third parties, and cosureties. These rights include (1) exoneration, (2) reimbursement, (3) subrogation, and (4) contribution. Section 18. These rights may, by agreement, be augmented, modified, or limited. Section 6.

37-9a EXONERATION

The ordinary expectation in a suretyship relation is that the principal debtor will perform the obligation and the surety will not be required to perform. Therefore, the surety has the right to require that her principal debtor perform the underlying obligation when that obligation is due. Section 21. This right of the surety against the principal debtor, called the right of **exoneration**, is enforceable at equity. If the principal debtor fails to pay the creditor when the debt is due, the surety may obtain a decree ordering the principal debtor to pay the creditor. The remedy of exoneration against the principal debtor does not, however, impair the creditor's right to proceed against the surety. Unless otherwise agreed, collateral supplied by the principal debtor to secure the duty to reimburse the surety also secures the principal debtor's duty of exoneration to the surety to perform the underlying obligation. Section 25.

A surety also has a right of exoneration against his cosureties. When the principal debtor's obligation becomes due, each surety owes every other cosurety the duty to pay her proportionate share of the principal debtor's obligation to the creditor. Accordingly, a surety may bring an action in equity to obtain an order requiring his cosureties to pay their share of the debt to the creditor.

37-9b REIMBURSEMENT

When, on the default of the principal debtor, a surety pays the creditor, the surety has the right of **reimbursement** (repayment) against the principal debtor. Section 22. This right arises, however, only when the surety actually has made payment and then applies only to the extent of the payment. Thus, a surety who advantageously negotiates a defaulted obligation down to a compromise figure less than the original sum may recover from the principal debtor only the sum he actually paid, not the sum before negotiation. When collateral secures the obligations of the principal debtor to the surety, if the principal debtor fails to perform the duty of reimbursement, the surety can enforce her rights against the collateral. Section 25, Comment a.

37-9c SUBROGATION

On payment of the principal debtor's *entire* obligation, the surety "steps into the shoes" of the creditor. Called **subrogation**, this confers on the surety all the rights the creditor has with respect to the underlying obligation as though the obligation had not been satisfied. Section 27. These include the creditor's rights:

1. against the principal debtor, including the creditor's priorities with respect to those rights;

2. in collateral of the principal debtor, including the creditor's priorities with respect to that collateral;

3. against third parties, such as co-makers, who are also obligated on the principal debtor's obligation; and

4. against cosureties. Section 28.

37-9d CONTRIBUTION

A surety who pays her principal debtor's obligation may require her cosureties to pay her their proportionate shares of the obligation she has paid. This right of **contribution** arises when a surety has paid more than her proportionate share of a debt, even if the cosureties originally were unaware of each other or were bound on separate instruments. They need only be sureties for the same principal debtor and the same obligation. The right and extent of contribution is determined by contractual agreement among the cosureties. If no agreement exists, sureties obligated for equal amounts share equally; where they are obligated for varying amounts, the proportion of the debt that each surety must contribute is determined by proration according to each surety's undertaking. Section 57. For example, if X, Y, and Z are cosureties for PD to C in the amounts of $5,000, $10,000, and $15,000, respectively, which totals $30,000, then X's contributive share is one-sixth ($5,000/$30,000), Y's share is one-third ($10,000/$30,000), and Z's share is one-half ($15,000/$30,000).

37-10 Defenses of Surety and Principal Debtor

The obligations the principal debtor and the surety owe to the creditor arise out of contracts. Accordingly, those in surety relationships can assert the usual contractual defenses, such as those resulting from (1) the nonexistence of the principal debtor's obligation, (2) a discharge of the principal debtor's obligation, (3) a modification of the principal debtor's contract, or (4) a variation of the surety's risk. Some of these defenses are available only to the principal debtor, some only to the surety, and others to both parties.

♦ See Figure 37-7: *Defenses of Surety and Principal Debtor*

37-10a PERSONAL DEFENSES OF PRINCIPAL DEBTOR

The defenses available only to a principal debtor are known as the personal defenses of the principal debtor. For example, the principal debtor's **incapacity** due to infancy or mental incompetency may serve as a defense for the principal debtor but not for the surety. If, however, the principal debtor disaffirms the contract *and* returns the consideration he received from the creditor, the surety is discharged from his liability to the extent the value of the consideration equals the principal debtor's underlying obligation. Section 34. A discharge of the principal debtor's obligation in bankruptcy does not discharge the surety's liability to the creditor on that obligation. The principal obligor may assert a claim against the creditor unrelated to the underlying obligation to the extent permitted under the law governing setoffs. Subject to several exceptions discussed later, the surety may *not* use as a setoff any unrelated claim that the principal debtor has against the creditor.

37-10b PERSONAL DEFENSES OF SURETY

Those defenses that only the surety may assert are called **personal defenses of surety**. They include defenses based on the surety's contract and those resulting from actions of the creditor after the formation of the surety's contract.

SURETY'S CONTRACT The surety may use as a defense his own incapacity, noncompliance with the *statute of frauds*, or the absence of mutual assent or consideration to support his obligation. *Fraud* (fraudulent or material misrepresentation) or *duress* practiced by the creditor on the surety is also a defense. Although as a general rule the creditor's nondisclosure of material facts to the surety is not fraud, there are two important exceptions. First, if a prospective surety requests information, the creditor must disclose it; the concealment of material facts will constitute fraud. Second, a creditor who (1) knows facts unknown to the surety that materially increase the surety's risk beyond that which the surety intends to assume and (2) has reason to believe that the facts are unknown to the surety is under a duty to disclose this information; nondisclosure is considered fraud. Section 12. Fraud on the part of the principal debtor may *not* be asserted against the creditor if the creditor is unaware of such fraud. Similarly, duress exerted by the principal debtor on the surety is not a defense against the creditor.

A surety is not liable if an intended cosurety, as named in the contract instrument, does not sign. A surety who has a claim against the creditor that is unrelated to the transaction giving rise to the surety's obligation may *set off* that claim against the surety's obligation. Section 36.

◆ *See Case 37-4*

VARIATION OF THE SURETY'S RISK If after the surety enters into the secondary obligation the creditor does an act that changes the risks that the surety assumed, there is the potential for a loss to the surety. In most cases, unless the surety agrees otherwise, the Restatement discharges the surety to the extent that such acts would cause the surety to suffer a loss; in some cases, the discharge is total.

If the principal debtor and the creditor agree to a *modification* (other than an extension of time or a release) of the underlying obligation, the surety is discharged *if* the modification creates a substituted contract or imposes risks on the surety fundamentally different from the surety's original undertaking. If the modification is not a substitute contract and does not fundamentally change the surety's risk, the surety is discharged to the extent that the modification would otherwise cause the surety a loss. Section 41. The Restatement provides the following example of a fundamental change:

> P and O make a contract pursuant to which P promises to construct an office building on a designated site for $1,500,000. S issues payment and performance bonds with respect to the contract. Later, before the contract is performed, P and O agree to change the contract to provide that P will construct a factory on the site for $2,000,000. The change is so fundamental as to amount to a substituted contract. Therefore, S is discharged from its payment and performance bonds.

Unless the terms of the extension provide otherwise, if the creditor grants the principal debtor an *extension* of the time for performance of the underlying obligation, (1) the extension also extends the time for performance of the principal debtor's duties of exoneration and reimbursement owed by the principal obligor to the secondary obligor and (2) the surety is discharged to the extent that the extension would otherwise cause the surety a loss and (3) the surety is entitled to have the extension apply to the time for performance of the surety's obligation. Section 40.

On the other hand, if the terms of the extension expressly preserve the surety's recourse against the principal debtor as though no extension had been granted, the Restatement provides that the surety is *not* discharged unless the creditor's extension otherwise causes the surety to suffer a loss. Section 38. If the creditor releases or impairs the value of collateral, the surety is discharged to the extent of the reduction in the value of the collateral. Section 42. More generally, whenever the creditor brings about an impairment of the surety's recourse against the principal debtor, the surety is discharged from his duties to the creditor to the extent necessary to avoid this loss. An *impairment of recourse* includes an act by the creditor that increases the risk that the surety will be called upon to perform or that the surety will be unable

FIGURE 37-7 Defenses of Surety and Principal Debtor

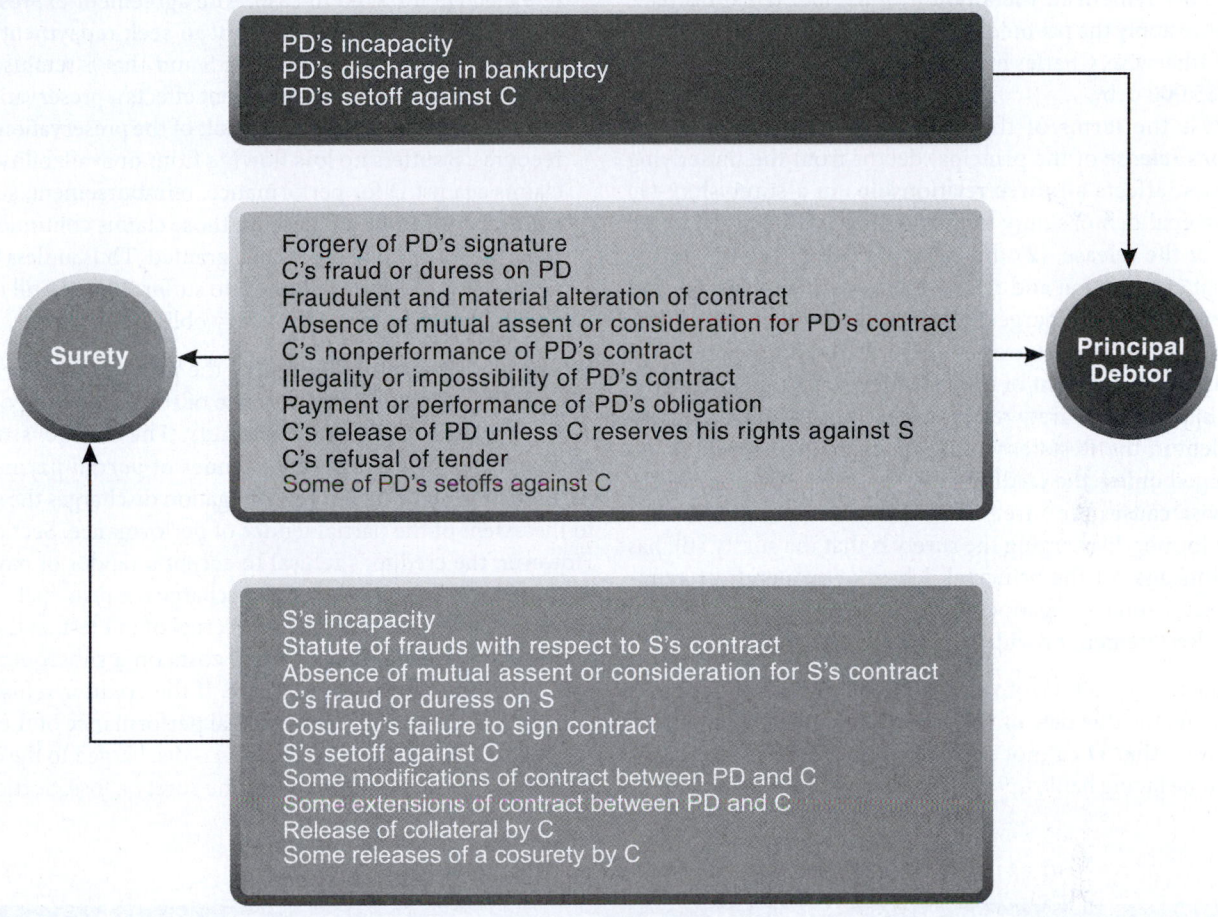

PD's incapacity
PD's discharge in bankruptcy
PD's setoff against C

Surety

Forgery of PD's signature
C's fraud or duress on PD
Fraudulent and material alteration of contract
Absence of mutual assent or consideration for PD's contract
C's nonperformance of PD's contract
Illegality or impossibility of PD's contract
Payment or performance of PD's obligation
C's release of PD unless C reserves his rights against S
C's refusal of tender
Some of PD's setoffs against C

Principal Debtor

S's incapacity
Statute of frauds with respect to S's contract
Absence of mutual assent or consideration for S's contract
C's fraud or duress on S
Cosurety's failure to sign contract
S's setoff against C
Some modifications of contract between PD and C
Some extensions of contract between PD and C
Release of collateral by C
Some releases of a cosurety by C

to recover from the principal debtor. Section 44. Similarly, if the creditor releases a cosurety, the other cosureties are discharged to the extent of the released surety's contributive share. Section 54.

37-10c DEFENSES OF BOTH SURETY AND PRINCIPAL DEBTOR

The surety may raise any defense of the principal obligor to the underlying obligation except the personal defenses of (1) the primary debtor's discharge of the underlying obligation in bankruptcy and (2) the unenforceability of the underlying obligation due to the principal debtor's lack of capacity. Section 34. The surety may use as a setoff any unrelated claim that the principal debtor has against the creditor if (1) the creditor does not contest the principal debtor's claim asserted by the surety, (2) the principal debtor is made a party to the action, *or* (3) the principal debtor consents to the use of her claim by surety. Section 35.

Examples of defenses available to both the surety and the principal debtor include the following. If the principal debtor's signature on an instrument is *forged* or if the creditor has exerted *fraud* or *duress* on the principal debtor, neither the principal debtor nor the surety is liable. Likewise, if the creditor has fraudulently and *materially altered* the contract instrument, both the principal debtor and the surety are discharged.

The absence of mutual assent or consideration to support the principal debtor's obligation is a defense for both the principal debtor and the surety. In addition, both may assert as defenses the *illegality* and the *impossibility* of performance of the principal debtor's contract.

Full *performance* of the underlying obligation by the principal debtor discharges both the principal debtor and the surety. Section 46, Comment b. If the principal debtor owes several debts to the creditor and makes a payment to the creditor without specifying the debt to which the payment should apply, the creditor is free to apply it to any one of them. For example,

Pam owes Charles two debts, one for $5,000 and another for $10,000. Susan is a surety on the $10,000 debt. Pam sends Charles a payment in the amount of $3,500. If Pam directs Charles to apply the payment to the $10,000 debt, Charles must do so. Otherwise, Charles may, if he pleases, apply the payment to the $5,000 debt.

Unless the terms of the release provide otherwise, the creditor's **release** of the principal debtor from the underlying obligation affects all three relationships in a suretyship: (1) the principal debtor's duty to the creditor is discharged to the extent of the release, (2) the principal debtor's duties to the surety of exoneration and reimbursement are discharged, and (3) the surety is discharged. Section 39. On the other hand, if the release expressly provides that the creditor retains the right to seek repayment of the remainder of the debt from the surety *and* that the surety retains her recourse against the principal debtor, the Restatement provides that the surety is *not* discharged unless the creditor's release of the principal debtor otherwise causes the surety to suffer a loss. Section 38. The reason for not discharging the surety is that the surety still has her rights against the principal debtor of exoneration, reimbursement, and subrogation.

The Restatement provides the following example:

D borrows $1,000 from C. S guarantees D's obligation to C. As the due date of the debt approaches, it becomes obvious that D cannot repay the debt in full and may soon be facing bankruptcy. C, in order to collect as much as possible from D and lessen the need to collect from S, agrees to release D from the repayment obligation in exchange for $100 in cash. The agreement expressly provides that C retains the right to seek repayment of the remainder of the debt from S and that S retains its recourse against D. The agreement effects a preservation of S's recourse against D. As a result of the preservation of recourse, S suffers no loss flowing from unavailability of claims against D for performance, reimbursement, subrogation, or restitution because those claims continue as though the release had not been granted. Thus, unless C's release of D otherwise caused S to suffer a loss, S will not be discharged from its secondary obligation.

The creditor's refusal to accept the principal debtor's **tender** of *full* payment or performance of the underlying obligation completely discharges the surety. The creditor's refusal to accept the principal debtor's tender of *partial* payment or performance of the underlying obligation discharges the surety to the extent of the partial tender of performance. Section 46. However, the creditor's refusal to accept a tender of payment by the principal debtor does not discharge the principal debtor. Rather, such refusal stops further accrual of interest on the debt and deprives the creditor of court costs on a subsequent suit by him to recover the amount due. If the creditor refuses the surety's tender of complete or partial performance of the surety's obligation, the surety's obligation is discharged to the extent that refusal of such tender causes the surety a loss. Section 46.

C H A P T E R　S U M M A R Y

SECURED TRANSACTIONS IN PERSONAL PROPERTY

ESSENTIALS OF SECURED TRANSACTIONS	**Definition of Secured Transaction** an agreement by which one party obtains a security interest in the personal property of another to secure the payment of a debt

- **Debtor** person who has an interest in the collateral other than a security interest; typically is the person obligated on the debt secured by the security interest
- **Secured Party** person in whose favor a security interest in the collateral is created or provided for under the security agreement
- **Collateral** property subject to a security interest
- **Security Agreement** agreement that creates or provides for a security interest
- **Security Interest** right in personal property that secures payment or performance of an obligation
- **Purchase Money Security Interest** security interest in goods purchased; interest is retained either by the seller of the goods or by a lender who advances the purchase price

Fundamental Rights of Debtor
- To redeem collateral by payment of the debt
- To possess general rights of ownership

Fundamental Rights of Secured Party
- To recover amount of debt
- To have collateral applied to payment of debt upon default

CLASSIFICATION OF COLLATERAL	**Goods** things that are movable when a security interest attaches

Goods things that are movable when a security interest attaches
- *Consumer Goods* goods bought or used primarily for personal, family, or household purposes
- *Farm Products* goods that are part of a farming operation, including crops, including livestock, or supplies used or produced in farming
- *Inventory* includes nonfarm product goods that (1) are held for sale, are held for lease, or are to be furnished under a service contract or (2) consist of raw materials, work in process, or materials used or consumed in a business
- *Equipment* goods not included in the definition of consumer goods, inventory, or farm products
- *Fixtures* goods that are so related to real property that they are considered part of the real estate
- *Accession* goods installed in or firmly affixed to personal property

Indispensable Paper
- *Chattel Paper* tangible or electronic record that evidences both a debt and a security interest in specific goods
- *Instruments* negotiable instruments or any other writing that evidences a right to payment of money that is transferable by delivery with any necessary indorsement
- *Documents* documents of title
- *Investment Property* investment security (stocks and bonds), security accounts, commodity contracts, and commodity accounts

Intangibles
- *Account* right to payment for (1) goods sold, leased, licensed, or otherwise disposed of or (2) services rendered
- *General Intangibles* catchall category of collateral not otherwise covered; includes software, goodwill, literary rights, and interests in patents, trademarks, and copyrights

Other Types of Collateral
- *Proceeds* whatever is received upon sale, lease, license, exchange, or other disposition of collateral; the secured party, unless the security agreement states otherwise, has rights to the proceeds
- *Deposit Accounts* a demand, savings, time, or similar account maintained with a bank

---

ATTACHMENT

Definition security interest that is enforceable against the debtor

Value consideration under contract law, a binding commitment to extend credit, or an antecedent debt

Debtor's Rights in Collateral a debtor is deemed to have rights in personal property the debtor owns, possesses, is in the process of acquiring, or has the power to transfer rights to a secured party

Security Agreement agreement between debtor and creditor creating a security interest; must be in a record authenticated by the debtor, unless, in the case of most types of collateral, the secured party has possession of the collateral, and must contain a reasonable description of the collateral
- *Consumer Goods* Federal regulation prohibits a credit seller or lender from obtaining a consumer's grant of a nonpossessory security interest in household goods
- *After-Acquired Property* a security agreement may cover property the debtor may acquire in the future
- *Future Advances* a security agreement may include future advances

PERFECTION	**Definition** attachment plus any steps required for perfection **Effect** enforceable against most third parties
METHODS OF PERFECTING	**Filing a Financing Statement** may be used for all collateral except deposit accounts, letter-of-credit rights, and money • *Financing Statement* document filed to provide notice of a security interest • *Duration* filing is effective for five years but may be continued by filing a continuation statement • *Place of Filing* statements, except for real-estate-related collateral, must be filed in a central location designated by the State • *Subsequent Change of Debtor's Location* **Possession** by the secured party (a pledge); may be used for goods, instruments, money, negotiable documents, tangible chattel paper, or certificated securities **Automatic Perfection** perfection upon attachment; applies to a purchase money security interest in consumer goods and isolated assignments of accounts **Temporary Perfection** a security interest in certificated securities, instruments, and negotiable documents is automatically perfected for twenty days **Control** may be used to perfect a security interest in electronic chattel paper, investment property, nonconsumer deposit accounts, and letter-of-credit rights
PRIORITIES AMONG COMPETING INTERESTS	**Priority Rules** See *Figure 37-4* for a summary of the priority rules
DEFAULT	**Repossession of Collateral** the secured party may take possession of the collateral on default without judicial process if it can be done without a breach of the peace **Sale of Collateral** the secured party may sell, lease, license, or otherwise dispose of any collateral **Acceptance of Collateral** the secured party, unless the debtor objects, may retain the collateral in full or partial satisfaction of the obligation (with the exception of the compulsory disposition of some consumer goods)

SURETYSHIP

NATURE AND FORMATION	**Definition of Surety (Secondary Obligor)** a person who is obligated to perform an underlying obligation owed by the principal debtor to the creditor upon the principal debtor's failure to perform • *Principal Debtor* the party primarily liable on the obligation • *Guarantor* secondary obligor liable to a creditor immediately upon the default of a principal debtor • *Guarantor of Collection* secondary obligor liable to a creditor only after the creditor has exhausted the legal remedies against the principal debtor • *Surety* secondary obligor jointly and severally liable with the principal debtor to perform the underlying obligation • *Cosurety* each of two or more secondary obligors who are liable for the same debt of the principal debtor **Particular Kinds of Suretyships** • *Party Assuming a Mortgage* • *Fidelity Bonds* • *Performance Bonds*

- *Official Bonds*
- *Judicial Bonds*

Formation the promise of the surety must satisfy all the elements of a contract and must be in writing

DUTIES OF SURETY	**Duty of Surety** upon default by the principal debtor, the creditor may proceed against the surety to enforce the surety's undertaking **Duty of Cosurety** up to the amount of each surety's undertaking, cosureties are *jointly and severally* liable for the principal debtor's default
RIGHTS OF SURETY	**Exoneration** the right of a surety to be relieved of his obligation to the creditor by having the principal debtor perform the underlying obligation **Reimbursement** the right of a surety who has paid the creditor to be repaid by the principal debtor **Subrogation** the right of a surety who has paid the creditor to assume all the rights the creditor has with respect to the underlying obligation **Contribution** the right to payment from each cosurety of her proportionate share of the amount paid to the creditor
DEFENSES OF SURETY AND PRINCIPAL DEBTOR	**Personal Defenses of Principal Debtor** defenses available only to the principal debtor, including her incapacity, discharge in bankruptcy, and some setoffs **Personal Defenses of Surety** defenses available only to the surety, including her own incapacity, the statute of frauds, contract defenses to her suretyship undertaking, setoff, some modifications of the contract between the creditor and the principal debtor, and the creditor's release of collateral or a cosurety **Defenses of Both Surety and Principal Debtor** include contract defenses to the contract between the creditor and the principal debtor except for the principal debtor's discharge in bankruptcy and incapacity

C A S E S

CASE 37-1

Security Agreement
BORDER STATE BANK OF GREENBUSH v. BAGLEY LIVESTOCK EXCHANGE, INC.
Court of Appeals of Minnesota, 2004
690 N.W.2d 326

Lansing, J.

Bert Johnson, doing business as Johnson Farms, and Hal Anderson entered into an oral cattle-sharing contract in December 1997. Approximately one month later, they memorialized the oral contract in written form. Under the written instrument, Anderson agreed to care for and breed cattle owned by Johnson and Johnson would receive a "guaranteed" percentage of the annual calf crop. The contract further provided that the cattle Johnson placed with Anderson were "considered to be owned by Johnson Farms and any offspring is to be sold under Johnson Farms' name." The contract required Johnson Farms and Anderson mutually to agree when the calves would be sold

and within thirty days of receiving money for the sale, Johnson Farms to pay the "remainder" to Anderson "for his keeping of [the] cattle."

In the fall of 1998 and 1999, calves bred under the contract were sold under the provisions of the written contract. Anderson testified that in October 1999, Johnson asked him to care for additional cattle on the same terms. Anderson initially declined, explaining to Johnson that he was ending his cattle business because of adverse personal circumstances. Anderson said that his father had died, his mother was in a nursing home, his partner, Linda Peterson, was caring for an ill family member, he had no additional help at his farm, he had insufficient feed for the cattle, and he had not planted hay for the coming winter. Nevertheless, according to Anderson, they continued to discuss their cattle-sharing contract, and he eventually agreed to continue based on certain modifications: (1) the share percentage would be a straight 40/60 split, without Johnson's "guaranteed" percentage; (2) Johnson would provide feed, including beet tailings; (3) Johnson would provide additional pasture; and (4) the agreement would include approximately 500 cattle, instead of the original 151 cattle.

Johnson testified that he discussed the cattle-sharing agreement with Anderson in October 1999 and that he agreed to send Anderson beet tailings, which were free to him, so long as Anderson paid the cost of shipping. Johnson also testified that he and Anderson agreed that approximately 500 cattle would be cared for under the cattle-sharing agreement, rather than the original 151 cattle. But Johnson denied that he had agreed to provide feed, other than the beet tailings, and denied that he had agreed to change the provision that "guaranteed" that his percentage of the calf crop would be calculated on the initial number of cows regardless of whether each produced a calf that survived.

In March 2000, Anderson negotiated with Border State Bank for loans totaling $155,528. To secure these loans, Anderson granted Border State Bank a security interest in, among other things, all of Anderson's "rights, title and interest" in all "livestock" then owned or thereafter acquired.

After the modification of the cattle-sharing contract, Johnson made a number of shipments of beet tailings to Anderson. When Johnson stopped the shipments, he sent checks totaling $55,000 to Anderson for the purchase of feed. In November 2000, Anderson encountered difficulty caring for the cattle due to heavy rainfall and lack of feed. The cattle were reclaimed by Johnson, but the calves remained with Anderson for sale. At trial, Anderson testified that some of the cattle that Johnson reclaimed were actually Anderson's cattle or were cattle that belonged to Evonne Stephens, another person with whom Anderson had a cattle-sharing contract.

In December 2000, 289 calves that had remained with Anderson were sold at Bagley Livestock Exchange. The livestock exchange knew of Border State's security interest in Anderson's livestock but, after discussing the agreement with Johnson, determined the security interest did not attach to the calves. The livestock exchange issued a check to Johnson Farms in the amount of $119,403. Thereafter, Johnson gave Anderson a check for $19,404, representing Anderson's share of the sale proceeds, less $55,000 that Johnson claimed as repayment for money advanced to Anderson to purchase feed.

Border State Bank sued Bagley Livestock Exchange and Johnson, contending that they had converted Border State Bank's perfected security interest in the calves sold in December 2000. * * * Anderson served a counterclaim against Johnson, asserting breach of contract.

These claims were tried to a jury in September 2003. Following Border State Bank's case-in-chief, Johnson and Bagley Livestock Exchange moved for a directed verdict. The district court granted the motion, finding that, under the cattle-sharing agreement, Johnson did not "grant" Anderson an "ownership interest" in the calves. Border State Bank appeals from the directed verdict on its conversion claim.

Following the directed verdict, Anderson presented evidence on his breach-of-contract counterclaim against Johnson, and the counterclaim was submitted to the jury. In response to special-verdict questions, the jury determined that the written contract between Anderson and Johnson had been modified, Johnson breached the contract, and Johnson's breach directly caused damages to Anderson in the amount of $92,360. * * * Johnson appeals * * *.

* * *

Article 9 of the Uniform Commercial Code, incorporated into Minnesota law, provides that a security interest attaches to collateral, and is enforceable against the debtor or third parties, when (1) value has been given; (2) the debtor "has rights in the collateral or the power to transfer rights"; and (3) the debtor has signed a security agreement that contains a description of the collateral. [UCC] 9-203(b). To perfect the security interest, both the security agreement and financing statement must contain an adequate description of the collateral. [Citation.] We liberally construe descriptions in the security agreement and financing statement because their essential purpose is to provide notice, not to definitively describe each item of collateral. [Citation.]

The parties do not dispute that Anderson signed a security agreement and that value was given. The security agreement stated that the collateral included, in part, "all livestock owned or hereafter acquired" and Anderson's "rights, title and interest" in such livestock. The financing statements covered "all livestock," whether "now owned or hereafter acquired, together with the proceeds from the sale thereof." The parties also do not dispute the validity of these descriptions or the assertion that "livestock" includes cattle and calves. What is disputed is whether the bank's security interest attached to the 289 calves sold in December 2000 under Anderson and Johnson's cattle-sharing agreement. [Citation.]

* * * The district court stated on the record that the cattle-sharing contract had not "granted" Anderson an "ownership interest" in the calves, specifically finding that "the modifications testified to by Mr. Anderson in the light most favorable to Border State Bank do not modify the terms of the agreement such that an ownership interest is granted." Based on the arguments presented, the district court apparently determined that, for Border State Bank's security interest to attach, Johnson would have had to grant Anderson an interest equivalent to ownership.

The provisions of the Uniform Commercial Code's Article 9, incorporated into Minnesota law, refer to "rights in the collateral," not solely the "ownership" of the collateral. [UCC] § 9-203(b)(2) (stating security interest may attach to collateral if "the debtor has rights in the collateral or the power to transfer rights in the collateral"). Rights in the collateral, as the term is used in Article 9, include full ownership and limited rights that fall short of full ownership. [UCC] § 9-203 U.C.C. cmt., para. 6. [Citations.] Simply stated, the UCC "does not require that collateral be owned by the debtor." [Citation.]

* * * For purposes of the UCC, "sufficient rights" arise with far less than full ownership. [Citation.] Ownership or title is not the relevant concern under Article 9; "the issue is whether the debtor has acquired sufficient rights in the collateral so that the security interest would attach." [Citation.] The "rights in the collateral" language is a "gateway through which one looks to other law to determine the extent of the debtor's rights." [Citation.] Thus, "[a]ll or some of owner's rights can be transferred by way of sale, lease, or license [and a] person with transferable rights can grant an enforceable security interest in those rights." [Citation.] A "security interest will attach to the collateral only to the extent of the debtor's rights in the collateral"; mere possession of the collateral is insufficient to support an attachment, but the debtor need not have full ownership. [Citation.] * * *

The district court did not analyze the modified cattlesharing contract to determine the nature of Anderson's rights in the calves or whether Anderson's interests or rights were sufficient to permit attachment of a security interest. We conclude that the standard relied on by the district court is inconsistent with Minnesota law. The application of the incorrect standard prematurely terminated the analysis of the cattle-sharing agreement, which is necessary to determine whether Anderson's rights in the collateral were sufficient for the bank's security interest to attach. * * * Because the district court applied a standard of ownership that is inconsistent with Minnesota law, its finding that the security interest did not attach was influenced by an error of law.

* * *

* * * On remand, the district court shall consider the cattle-sharing agreement to determine whether Anderson had "rights" in the calves, to which the bank's security interest attached.

| CASE
37-2 | Automatic Perfection
KIMBRELL'S OF SANFORD, INC. v. KPS, INC.
Court of Appeals of North Carolina, 1994
113 N.C.App 830, 440 S.E.2d 329 |  |

McCrodden, J.

This action arises out of plaintiff's attempt to recover from defendant KPS, Inc. a VCR which plaintiff had sold to defendant Burns and which Burns had immediately pawned at the Kendale Pawn Shop. Plaintiff filed a complaint in small claims court, and the magistrate, after a hearing on 17 February 1992, entered judgment denying plaintiff recovery of the VCR. Plaintiff appealed to the district court. Judge William A. Christian, sitting without a jury, entered judgment denying plaintiff recovery and dismissing the action. From this judgment, plaintiff appeals.

Plaintiff offers one argument raising the issue of whether it was entitled to recover from defendant pawn shop a VCR plaintiff had sold to defendant Burns under a purchase money security agreement. * * *

Plaintiff argues that the judgment denying it recovery of the VCR contravened Article 9 of the Uniform Commercial Code, [citation]. We agree.

At the time defendant Burns purchased the VCR from plaintiff, he signed a purchase money security agreement, thereby granting plaintiff a purchase money security interest in the VCR. [UCC] § 9-107 [Revised § 9-103]. Since a VCR is a consumer good, [UCC] § 9-109(1) [Revised § 9-102(a) (23)], plaintiff did not have to file a financing statement in order to perfect its purchase money security interest in the VCR. [UCC] § 9-302(1)(d) [Revised § 9-309]. Defendant Burns failed to make any further payments for the VCR and defaulted on the security agreement. Therefore, plaintiff was entitled to recover possession of the VCR when it filed its action in small claims court. [UCC] § 9-501 [Revised § 9-601], 9-503 [Revised § 9-609]. Accordingly, we hold that the trial court erred in dismissing plaintiff's claim to recover possession of the VCR.

* * *

For the foregoing reasons, we reverse the judgment of the trial court and remand for entry of judgment in favor of plaintiff.

Reversed.

CASE 37-3

Repossession
CHAPA v. TRACIERS & ASSOCIATES

Court of Appeals of Texas, Houston (14th Dist.), 2008
267 S.W.3d 386, 66 UCC Rep.Serv.2d 451

Guzman, J.

In this appeal, we must determine whether appellants, the parents of two young children, have legally cognizable claims for mental anguish allegedly sustained when a repossession agent towed their vehicle out of sight before he realized their children were inside. The parents filed suit against the financing company, the repossession company it hired, and the repossession agent who towed the vehicle. They asserted claims for mental anguish and its physical manifestations under (a) [UCC] section 9.609 * * *

Ford Motor Credit Corp. ("FMCC") hired Traciers & Associates ("Traciers") to repossess a white 2002 Ford Expedition owned by Marissa Chapa, who was in default on the associated promissory note. Traciers assigned the job to its field manager, Paul Chambers, and gave him an address where the vehicle could be found. FMCC, Traciers, and Chambers were unaware that the address was that of Marissa's brother, Carlos Chapa. Coincidentally, Carlos and his wife Maria Chapa also had purchased a white Ford Expedition financed by FMCC. Their vehicle, however, was a 2003 model, and the Chapas were not in default.

On the night of February 6, 2003, Chambers went to the address and observed a white Ford Expedition. The license number of the vehicle did not match that of the vehicle he was told to repossess, and he did not see the vehicle's vehicle identification number ("VIN"), which was obscured. Chambers returned early the next morning and still could not see the Expedition's VIN. He returned to his own vehicle, which was parked two houses away.

Unseen by Chambers, Maria Chapa left the house and helped her two sons, ages ten and six, into the Expedition for the trip to school. Her mother-in-law's vehicle was parked behind her, so Maria backed her mother-in-law's vehicle into the street, then backed her Expedition out of the driveway and parked on the street. She left the keys to her truck in the ignition with the motor running while she parked her mother-in-law's car back in the driveway and reentered the house to return her mother-in-law's keys.

After Chambers saw Maria park the Expedition on the street and return to the house, it took him only thirty seconds to back his tow truck to the Expedition, hook it to his truck, and drive away. Chambers did not leave his own vehicle to perform this operation, and it is undisputed that he did not know the Chapa children were inside. When Maria emerged from the house, the Expedition, with her children, was gone. Maria began screaming, telephoned 911, and called her husband at work to tell him the children were gone.

Meanwhile, on an adjacent street, Chambers noticed that the Expedition's wheels were turning, indicating to him that the vehicle's engine was running. He stopped the tow truck and heard a sound from the Expedition. Looking inside, he discovered the two Chapa children. After he persuaded one of the boys to unlock the vehicle, Chambers drove the Expedition back to the Chapas' house. He returned the keys to Maria, who was outside her house, crying. By the time emergency personnel and Carlos Chapa arrived, the children were back home and Chambers had left the scene.

Maria testified that the incident caused her to have an anxiety attack, including chest pain and numbness in her arm. She states she has continued to experience panic attacks and has been diagnosed with an anxiety disorder. In addition, both Carlos and Maria have been diagnosed with post-traumatic stress disorder.

* * *

The Chapas first argue that the trial court erred in granting summary judgment against them on their claim that appellees are liable under [UCC] section 9.609. This statute provides in pertinent part:

(a) After default, a secured party:
  (1) may take possession of the collateral;
(b) A secured party may proceed under Subsection (a)
  (2) without judicial process, if it proceeds without breach of the peace. [Citation.]

The Chapas correctly point out that this statute imposes a duty on secured creditors to take precautions for public safety when repossessing property. [Citation.] Thus, the creditor who elects to pursue nonjudicial repossession assumes the risk that a breach of the peace might occur. [Citation.] A secured creditor "remains liable for breaches of the peace committed by its independent contractor." [Citation.] Thus, a creditor cannot escape liability by hiring an independent contractor to repossess secured property.

The Chapas assert that FMCC and Traciers, who employed Chambers as a repossession agent, are liable for any physical or mental injuries sustained by Carlos and Maria as a result of Chambers's breach of the peace. But this argument presupposes that a breach of peace occurred. * * *

* * *

Most frequently, the expression "breach of the peace" as used in the Uniform Commercial Code "connotes conduct that incites or is likely to incite immediate public turbulence, or that leads to or is likely to lead to an immediate loss of public order and tranquility." [Citations.] ("[S]ecured creditor, in exercising privilege to enter upon premises of another to repossess collateral, may not perpetrate '[a]ny act or action manifesting force or violence, or naturally calculated to provide a breach of peace'") [Citations.] ("[A]lthough actual violence is not required to find 'breach of the peace,' within meaning of self-help repossession statute, disturbance or violence must be reasonably likely, and not merely a remote possibility."); [Citation.] (no breach of peace when vehicle repossessed from public street while debtor inside house). In addition, "[b]reach of the peace... refers to conduct at or near and/or incident to seizure of property." [Citations.] ("[E]ven in attempted repossession of a chattel off a street, parking lot or unenclosed space, if repossession is verbally or otherwise contested at actual time of and in immediate vicinity of attempted repossession by defaulting party or other person in control of chattel, secured party must desist and pursue his remedy in court.")

Here, there is no evidence that Chambers proceeded with the attempted repossession over an objection communicated to him at, near, or incident to the seizure of the property. To the contrary, Chambers immediately "desisted" repossession efforts and peaceably returned the vehicle and the children when he learned of their presence. Moreover, Chambers actively avoided confrontation. By removing an apparently unoccupied vehicle from a public street when the driver was not present, he reduced the likelihood of violence or other public disturbance.

In sum, the Chapas have not identified and we have not found any case in which the repossession of a vehicle from a public street, without objection or confrontation, has been held to constitute a breach of the peace. [Citation,] (deputy sheriff did not breach the peace when he repossessed debtor's truck because, even if he violated traffic regulation when he drove away, he did so before debtor had an opportunity to confront him); [Citation,] (no breach of the peace occurred when repossession from parking lot was not verbally or otherwise contested). We therefore conclude that Chambers's conduct did not violate a duty imposed by [UCC] section 9.609.

* * *

We therefore affirm the judgment of the trial court.

CASE	Nature and Formation/Personal Defenses of Surety
37-4	**AMERICAN MANUFACTURING MUTUAL INSURANCE COMPANY v. TISON HOG MARKET, INC.** United States Court of Appeals, Eleventh Circuit, 1999 182 F.3d 1284; *certiorari* denied, 531 U.S.819, 121 S.Ct. 59, 148 L.Ed.2d 26 (2000)

Cox, J.

[Every livestock dealer must execute and maintain a reasonable bond to secure the performance of its obligations. Thurston Paulk, doing business as Paulk Livestock Company (Paulk Livestock), and Coffee County Stockyard, Incorporated (Coffee County Livestock), both livestock dealers, applied to plaintiff American Manufacturing Mutual Insurance Company (American) to serve as a surety and issue bonds for them to meet their legal requirements. The applications for both bonds contained agreements to indemnify American for any losses that it might incur as a result of their issuance. The principal *debtor* on the first bond was Thurston Paulk, doing business as Paulk Livestock. The application was signed by Thurston Paulk in his role as the sole proprietor of Paulk Livestock. The indemnification agreement contained the purported signatures of Thurston Paulk and Betty Paulk. The principal *debtor* on the second bond was Coffee County Livestock. This application contained the signature of Thurston Paulk in his role as president of Coffee County Livestock and contained the purported signatures of Thurston Paulk, Betty Paulk, and Ashley Paulk.

After the bonds were issued, Paulk Livestock and Coffee County Livestock purchased numerous hogs from defendants Tison Hog Market, Inc.; Gainesville Livestock Market, Inc.; Townsend Livestock Market; South Carolina Farm Bureau Marketing Association; and Georgia Farm Bureau Marketing Association, Inc. When the defendant hog sellers did not receive payment for the hogs, they made claims against American on the surety bonds for the purchase money they were owed. American conducted an investigation and learned that the bonds' indemnification agreements contained forged signatures of Ashley Paulk and Betty Paulk. American claimed that it would not have issued the bonds had it known that Betty and Ashley Paulk had not agreed to indemnify it, and it declared the bonds rescinded and returned all the premiums.

American then brought an action seeking a declaratory judgment relieving it from liability to the defendants on the ground that the bonds were void under Georgia insurance law due to the fraudulent and material misrepresentations of the bonds' principals. American argued that the principals had forged the signatures of Betty and Ashley Paulk on the indemnification agreements. The district court granted American's motion for summary judgment.]

It is well established under the common law of suretyship that "fraud or misrepresentation practiced by the principal alone on the surety, without any knowledge or participation on the part of the creditor or obligee, in inducing the surety to enter into the suretyship contract will not affect the liability of the surety." [Citations.] From a practical standpoint, this common law treatment of a principal's fraud is the only one that makes sense. A creditor does business with a principal in reliance upon the existence of a bond. The bond provides security for the creditor because normally the creditor would have no way of knowing whether the principal is insolvent or otherwise an unreliable party with which to engage in business. [Citation.] If the creditor's ability to recover on a bond was dependent on the accuracy of the principal's representations to the surety, then the value of the bond to the creditor would be greatly lessened because the creditor would have no way of knowing what representations were made in the procurement of the bond. More importantly for the case at bar, this common law approach * * * enables a livestock seller to deal freely with livestock dealers knowing that the required bond will protect them in the event of a default even if the principal hid facts from the surety when obtaining the bond. * * *

* * *

Instead of applying * * * insurance law, however, the district court should have applied Georgia surety law. The surety bonds in this case are surety contracts that are not governed exclusively by the insurance law of Georgia. * * *

The Georgia Code contains an entirely separate title that applies to suretyship contracts. [Citation.] The chapter defines a contract of suretyship as one "whereby a person obligates himself to pay the debt of another in consideration of a benefit flowing to the surety . . ." [citation]. This is the commonly understood definition of a surety relationship and describes the situation that we have in the case at bar. The Georgia Code does not contain a statement as to the effect of a principal's fraud on a surety's liability to the creditor. Georgia courts, however, have applied the common law and held that a surety is still liable to a creditor even if the principal commits fraud so long as the creditor does not participate in the fraud. [Citation.] * * *

* * *

* * * Applying the common law to the case at bar, there is no evidence that the defendants participated in any fraud. The fraud was committed solely by the principals. Under these circumstances, American is not relieved of liability on the bonds.

* * *

For the foregoing reasons, the district court's judgment is vacated, and we remand this case for further proceedings consistent with this opinion.

QUESTIONS

1. Victor sells to Bonnie a refrigerator for $600 payable in monthly installments of $30 for twenty months. Bonnie signs a security agreement granting Victor a security interest in the refrigerator. The refrigerator is installed in the kitchen of Bonnie's apartment. There is no filing of any financing statement. Assume that after Bonnie has made the first three monthly payments:

   a. Bonnie moves from her apartment and sells the refrigerator in place to the new occupant for $350 cash. What are the rights of Victor?

   b. Bonnie is adjudicated bankrupt, and her trustee in bankruptcy claims the refrigerator. What are the rights of the parties?

2. On January 2, Burt asked Logan to loan him money "against my diamond ring." Logan agreed to do so. To guard against intervening liens, Logan received permission to file a financing statement, and Burt and Logan signed a security agreement giving Logan an interest in the ring. Burt also signed a financing statement, which Logan properly filed on January 3. On January 4, Burt borrowed money from Tillo, pledging his ring to secure the debt. Tillo took possession of the ring and paid Burt the money on the same day. The next day, January 5,

Logan loaned Burt the money under the assumption that Burt still had the ring. Who has priority, Logan or Tillo? Explain.

3. Joanna takes a security interest in the equipment in Jason Store and files a financing statement claiming "equipment and all after acquired equipment." Berkeley later sells Jason Store a cash register, taking a security interest in the register, and (a) files nine days after Jason receives the register or (b) files twenty-five days after Jason receives the register. If Jason fails to pay both Joanna and Berkeley and they foreclose their security interests, who has priority on the cash register? Explain.

4. Finley Motor Company sells an automobile to Sara and retains a security interest in it. The automobile is insured, and Finley is named beneficiary. Three days after the automobile is totally destroyed in an accident, Sara files a petition in bankruptcy. As between Finley and Sara's trustee in bankruptcy, who is entitled to the insurance proceeds? Explain.

5. On September 5, Wanda, a widow who occasionally teaches piano and organ in her home, purchased an electric organ from Murphy's music store for $4,800, trading in her old organ for $1,200 and promising in writing

to pay the balance at $120 per month and granting to Murphy a security interest in the property in terms consistent with and incorporating provisions of the Uniform Commercial Code. A financing statement covering the transaction was also properly filled out and signed, and Murphy properly filed it. After Wanda failed to make the December or January payments, Murphy went to her home to collect the payments or take the organ. Finding no one home and the door unlocked, he went in and took the organ. Two hours later, Tia, a third party and the present occupant of the house, who had purchased the organ for her own use, stormed into Murphy's store, demanding the return of the organ. She showed Murphy a bill of sale from Wanda to her, dated December 15, that listed the organ and other furnishings in the house.

   a. What are the rights of Murphy, Tia, and Wanda?

   b. Would your answer change if Murphy had not filed a financing statement? Explain why or why not.

   c. Would your answer change if the organ had been used principally to give lessons? Explain.

6. On May 1, Lincoln lends Donaldson $200,000 and receives from Donaldson his agreement to pay this amount in two years and takes a security interest in the machinery and equipment in Donaldson's factory. A proper financing statement is filed with respect to the security agreement. On August 1, upon Lincoln's request, Donaldson executes an addendum to the security agreement covering after-acquired machinery and equipment in Donaldson's factory. A second financing statement covering the addendum is filed. In September, Donaldson acquires $50,000 worth of new equipment from Thompson, which Donaldson installs in his factory. In December, Carter, a judgment creditor of Donaldson, causes an attachment to issue against the new equipment. What are the rights of Lincoln, Donaldson, Carter, and Thompson? What can the parties do to best protect themselves?

7. Anita bought a television set from Bertrum for her personal use. Bertrum, who was out of security agreement forms, showed Anita a form he had executed with Nathan, another consumer. Anita and Bertrum orally agreed to the terms of the form. Anita subsequently defaulted on payment, and Bertrum sought to repossess the television.

   a. Explain who would prevail.

   b. Explain whether the result would differ if Bertrum had filed a financing statement.

   c. Explain whether the result would differ if Anita had subsequently sent Bertrum an e-mail that met all the requirements of an effective security agreement.

8. Aaron bought a television set for personal use from Penny. Aaron properly signed a security agreement and paid Penny $125 down, as their agreement required. Penny did not file, and subsequently Aaron sold the television for $800 to Clark, his neighbor, for use in Clark's hotel lobby.

   a. When Aaron fails to make the January and February payments, may Penny repossess the television from Clark? Explain.

   b. What if instead of Aaron's selling the television set to Clark a judgment creditor levied (sought possession) on the television? Explain who would prevail.

   c. What if Clark intended to use the television set in his home? Explain who would prevail.

9. Jones bought a used car from the A-Herts Car Rental System, which regularly sold its used equipment at the end of its fiscal year. First National Bank of Roxboro had previously obtained a perfected security interest in the car based upon its financing of A-Herts's automobiles. Upon A-Herts's failure to pay, First National is seeking to repossess the car from Jones. Does First National have an enforceable security interest in the car against Jones? Explain.

10. Allen, Barker, and Cooper are cosureties on a $750,000 loan by Durham National Bank to Kingston Manufacturing Co., Inc. The maximum liability of the sureties is as follows: Allen, $750,000; Barker, $300,000; and Cooper, $150,000. If Kingston defaults on the entire $750,000 loan, what are the liabilities of Allen, Barker, and Cooper? Discuss.

11. Peter Diamond owed Carter $500,000 secured by a first mortgage on Diamond's plant and land. Stephens was a surety on this obligation in the amount of $250,000. After Diamond defaulted on the debt, Carter demanded and received payment of $250,000 from Stephens. Carter then foreclosed upon the mortgage and sold the property for $375,000. What rights, if any, does Stephens have in the proceeds from the sale of the property? Explain.

12. Paula Daniels purchased an automobile from Carey on credit. At the time of the sale, Scott agreed to be a surety for Paula, who is sixteen years old. The automobile's odometer stated fifty-two thousand miles, but Carey had turned it back from seventy-two thousand miles. Paula refuses to make any payments due on the car. Carey proceeds against Paula and Scott. Discuss what defenses, if any, are available to (a) Paula and (b) Scott.

13. Stafford Surety Co. agreed to act as the conditional guarantor of collection on a debt owed by Preston Decker to Cole. Stafford was paid a premium by Preston to serve as surety. Preston defaults on the obligation. Explain what Cole's rights are against Stafford Surety Co.

14. Campbell loaned Perry Dixon $7,000, which was secured by a possessory security interest in stock owned by Perry. The stock had a market value of $4,000. In addition, Campbell insisted that Perry obtain a surety. For a premium, Sutton Surety Co. agreed to act as a surety for the full amount of the loan. Prior to the due date of the loan, Perry convinced Campbell to return the stock because its value had increased and he wished to sell it to realize the gain. Campbell released the stock, and Perry subsequently defaulted. Is Sutton released from his liability? Why or why not?

15. Pamela Darden owed Clark $5,000 on an unsecured loan. On May 1, Pamela approached Clark for an additional loan of $3,000. Clark agreed to make the loan only if Pamela could obtain a surety. On May 5, Simpson agreed to be a surety on the $3,000 loan, which was granted that day. Both loans were due on October 1. On June 15, Pamela sent $1,000 to Clark but did not provide any instructions.

    a. What are Clark's rights?

    b. What are Simpson's rights?

16. Patrick Dillon applied for a $10,000 loan from Carlton Savings & Loan. Carlton required him to obtain a surety. Patrick approached Sinclair Surety Co., which insisted that Patrick provide it with a financial statement. Patrick did so, but the statement was materially false. In reliance upon the financial statement and in return for a premium, Sinclair agreed to act as surety. Upon Sinclair's commitment to act as surety, Carlton loaned Patrick the $10,000. After one payment of $400, Patrick defaulted. He then filed a voluntary petition in bankruptcy. Does Sinclair have any valid defense against Carlton? Explain.

17. On June 1, Smith contracted with Martin doing business as Martin Publishing Company to distribute Martin's newspapers and to account for the proceeds. As part of the contract, Smith agreed to furnish Martin a bond in the amount of $10,000 guaranteeing the payment of the proceeds. At the time the contract was executed and the credit extended, the bond was not furnished, and no mention was made as to the prospective sureties. On July 1, Smith signed the bond with Black and Blue signing as sureties. The bond recited the awarding of the contract for distribution of the newspapers as consideration for the bond.

    On December 1, payment was due from Smith to Martin for the sum of $3,600 under the distributor's contract. Demand for payment was made, but Smith failed to make payment. As a result, Martin brought an appropriate action against Black and Blue to recover the $3,600. What result? Explain.

18. Diggitt Construction Company was the low bidder on a well-digging job for the Village of Drytown. On April 15, Diggitt signed a contract with Drytown for the job at a price of $40,000. At the same time, pursuant to the notice of bidding, Diggitt prevailed upon Ace Surety Company to execute a performance bond indemnifying Drytown on the contract. On May 1, after Diggitt had put in three days on the job, the president of the company refigured his bid and realized that if his company were to complete the job, it would lose $10,000. Accordingly, Diggitt notified Drytown that it was canceling the contract, effective immediately. What are the rights and duties of Ace Surety Company?

C A S E   P R O B L E M S

19. National Cash Register Company (NCR), a manufacturer of cash registers, entered into a sales contract for a cash register with Edmund Carroll. On November 18, Firestone and Company made a loan to Carroll, who conveyed certain property to Firestone as collateral under a security agreement. The property outlined in the security agreement included "[a]ll contents of luncheonette including equipment such as . . . 'twenty-five different listed items,' . . . together with all property and articles now, and which may hereafter be, used . with, [or] added . to . any of the foregoing described property." A similarly detailed description of the property conveyed as collateral appeared in Firestone's financing statement, but the financing statement made no mention of property to be acquired thereafter, and neither document made a specific reference to a cash register. NCR delivered the cash register to Carroll in Canton between November 19 and November 25 and filed a financing statement with the town clerk of Canton on December 20 and with the Secretary of State on December 21. Carroll subsequently defaulted both on the contract with NCR and on the security agreement with Firestone. Firestone took possession of the cash register and sold it at auction. Discuss whether Firestone has a security interest in the cash register.

20. National Acceptance Company loaned Ultra Precision Industries $692,000 and to secure repayment of the loan Ultra executed a chattel mortgage security agreement on National's behalf on March 7, 2015. National perfected the security interest by timely filing a financing

statement. Although the security interest covered specifically described equipment of Ultra, both the security agreement and the financing statement contained an after-acquired property clause that did not refer to any specific equipment.

Later in 2015 and in 2016, Ultra placed three separate orders for machines from Wolf Machinery Company. In each case, it was agreed that after the machines had been shipped to Ultra and installed, Ultra would be given an opportunity to test them in operation for a reasonable period. If the machines passed inspection, Wolf would then provide financing that was satisfactory to Ultra. In all three cases, financing was arranged with Community Bank (Bank) and accepted, and a security interest was given in the machines. Furthermore, in each case, a security agreement was entered into, and the secured parties filed a financing statement within ten days. Ultra became bankrupt on October 7, 2018. National claimed that its security interest in the after-acquired machines should take priority over those of Wolf and Bank because their interests were not perfected by timely filed financing statements. Discuss who has priority in the disputed collateral.

21. Elizabeth Tilleraas received three student loans totaling $3,500 under the Federal Insured Student Loan Program (FISLP) of the Higher Education Act. These loans were secured by three promissory notes executed in favour of Dakota National Bank & Trust Co., Fargo, North Dakota. Under the terms of these student loans, periodic payments were required beginning twelve months after Tilleraas ceased to carry at least one-half of a full-time academic workload at an eligible institution. Her student status terminated on January 28, 2018, and the first installment payment thus became due January 28, 2019. She never made a payment on any of her loans. Under the provisions of the FISLP, the United States assured the lender bank repayment in the event of any failure to pay by the borrower. The first payment due on the loans was in "default" on July 27, 2019, 180 days after the failure to make the first installment payment. On December 17, 2020, Dakota National Bank & Trust sent notice of its election under the provisions of the loan to accelerate the maturity of the note. The bank demanded payment in full by December 27, 2020. It then filed FISLP insurance claims against the United States on May 6, 2021, and assigned the three Tilleraas notes to the United States on May 10, 2021. The government, in turn, paid the bank's claim in full on July 5, 2021. The government subsequently filed suit against Tilleraas. Discuss whether the United States will prevail.

22. New West Fruit Corporation (New West) and Coastal Berry Corporation are both brokers of fresh

strawberries. In the second half of 2019, New West's predecessor, Monc's Consolidated Produce, Inc., loaned money and strawberry plants to a group of strawberry growers known as Cooperativa La Paz (La Paz). In September 2019, Monc's and La Paz signed a "Sales and Marketing Agreement" to allow Monc's the exclusive right to market the strawberries grown by La Paz during the 2020–2021 season. The agreement did not mention the advances of money or plants but did give Monc's a security interest in all crops and proceeds on specified property in the 2020–2021 season. The financing statement was properly signed and filed. Monc's closed down in January 2021, and its assets were assigned to New West. In April, New West learned that La Paz had agreed to market its 2021 crop through Coastal Berry. New West immediately arranged a meeting to advise the Coastal Berry officers of its contract with the growers. New West requested that Coastal Berry either pay New West the amounts owed by the growers or allow New West to market the berries to recover the money. Coastal Berry did not respond. After Coastal Berry began marketing the berries, New West sent letters demanding payment of the proceeds. In August 2021, New West filed suit against Coastal Berry, La Paz, the individual growers, and a berry-freezing company that its security interest was valid and that it had duly notified Coastal Berry both through the financing statement on file and through the letters it had sent to Coastal Berry directly. Coastal Berry claimed that the security agreement was not effective because it did not specifically identify the debt (money and plants) being secured. Discuss.

23. Standridge purchased a Chevrolet automobile from Billy Deavers, an agent of Walker Motor Company. According to the sales contract, the balance due after the trade-in allowance was $282.50, to be paid in twelve weekly installments. Standridge claims that he was unable to make the second payment and that Billy Deavers orally agreed that he could make two payments the next week. The day after the double payment was due, Standridge still had not paid. That day, Ronnie Deavers, Billy's brother, went to Standridge's place of employment to repossess the car, which the Walker Motor contract permitted. Rather than consenting to the repossession, Standridge drove the car to the Walker Motor Company's place of business and tendered the overdue payments. The Deaverses refused to accept the late payment and instead demanded the entire unpaid balance. Standridge could not pay it. The Deaverses then blocked Standridge's car with another car and told him he could just "walk his ... home." Standridge brought suit, seeking damages for the Deavers's wrongful repossession of his

car. The Deaverses deny that they granted Standridge permission to make a double payment, that Standridge tendered the double payment, and that they rejected it. They claim that he made no payment and that, therefore, they were entitled to repossess the car. Discuss whether the car was properly repossessed.

24. In July 2020, Edward Slater purchased a new Galaxy boat primarily for personal purposes. To finance the purchase, Slater obtained a loan from Howell State Bank, agreeing to repay the loan in ninety-six monthly installments of $151.41. The Galaxy boat was purchased in the State of New Jersey, and Howell State Bank filed a copy of the Financing Statement Agreement in the office of the Secretary of State of New Jersey. Subsequently, the boat was moved to the State of New York. Explain whether Howell has a perfected security interest in the boat.

T A K I N G   S I D E S

James Koontz agreed to purchase a Plymouth Sundance from Chrysler Credit Corporation (Chrysler) in exchange for sixty payments of $185.92. Koontz soon thereafter defaulted, and Chrysler notified Koontz that unless he made the payments, it would repossess the vehicle. Koontz responded by notifying Chrysler that he would make every effort to make up missed payments, that he did not want the car repossessed, and that Chrysler was not to enter his private property to repossess the vehicle. A few weeks later, Chrysler sent the M & M Agency to repossess the vehicle. When he heard the repossession in progress, Koontz, dressed only in his underwear, came outside and yelled, "Don't take it!" The repossessor ignored him and took the car anyway. Koontz did not physically challenge or threaten the repossessor.

a. Discuss the arguments that Chrysler legally repossessed the automobile.

b. Discuss the arguments that Chrysler illegally repossessed the automobile.

c. Who should prevail? Explain.

CHAPTER 38

Bankruptcy

After reading and studying this chapter, you should be able to:

- Explain (1) the requirements for voluntary and involuntary bankruptcy cases, (2) the priorities of creditors' claims, (3) the debtor's exemptions, and (4) the debts that are not dischargeable in bankruptcy.

- Explain the duties of a trustee and his rights (1) as a lien creditor, (2) to avoid preferential transfers, (3) to avoid fraudulent transfers, and (4) to avoid statutory liens.

- Explain the procedure followed in distributing the debtor's estate under Chapter 7.

- Compare the adjustment of debt proceedings under Chapters 11 and 13.

- Discuss the nonbankruptcy compromises between debtors and creditors.

A debt is an obligation to pay money owed by a debtor to a creditor. Debts are created daily by countless purchasers of goods at the consumer level; by retailers of goods in buying merchandise from a manufacturer, wholesaler, or distributor; by borrowers of funds from various lending institutions; and through the issuance and sale of bonds and other types of debt securities. Multitudes of business transactions are entered into daily on a credit basis. Commercial activity would be restricted greatly if credit were not readily obtainable or if needed funds were unavailable for lending.

Fortunately, most debts are paid when due, thus justifying the extension of credit and encouraging its continuation. Although defaults may create credit and collection problems, the total amount in default normally represents a very small percentage of the total amount of outstanding indebtedness. Nevertheless, financial crises and business misfortune confront both individuals and businesses. Both may accumulate debts that exceed their total assets. Conversely, their assets may exceed their total indebtedness but be in such nonliquid form that these debtors are unable to pay their debts as they become due. For businesses as well as individuals, relief from overly burdensome debt and from the threat of impending lawsuits by creditors is frequently necessary for economic survival.

The conflict between creditor rights and debtor relief has engendered various solutions, such as voluntary adjustments and compromises requiring installment payments to creditors over a period of time during which they agree to withhold legal action. Other voluntary methods include compositions and assignments of assets by a debtor to a trustee or assignee for the benefit of creditors, who sometimes also file for equity receiverships or insolvency proceedings in a State court, pursuant to statute. Nonetheless, the most adaptable and frequently employed method of debtor relief—one that also affords protection to creditors—is a proceeding in a Federal court under Federal bankruptcy law.

FEDERAL BANKRUPTCY LAW

The most important method of protecting creditor rights and granting debtor relief is Federal bankruptcy law, which is largely statutory and involves court supervision. U.S. bankruptcy law serves a dual purpose: (1) to effect a quick, equitable distribution of the debtor's property among her creditors and (2) to discharge the debtor from her debts, enabling her to rehabilitate herself and start afresh. Other purposes are to provide uniform treatment of similarly situated creditors, preserve existing business relations, and stabilize commercial usages.

The Constitution of the United States provides that "the Congress shall have power . . . to establish . . . uniform Laws on the subject of Bankruptcies throughout the United States." Article I, Section 8, clause 4. Federal bankruptcy law has generally superseded State insolvency laws.

The U.S. Bankruptcy Abuse Prevention and Consumer Protection Act of 2005 (2005 Act) contains the most extensive amendments to Federal bankruptcy law since 1978. The U.S. Bankruptcy Code consists of eight odd-numbered chapters and one even-numbered chapter. Chapters 7, 9, 11, 12, and 13 provide five different types of proceedings; Chapters 1, 3, and 5 apply to all of those proceedings unless otherwise specified. **Straight**, or ordinary, **bankruptcy** (Chapter 7) provides for the liquidation of the debtor's property, whereas the other proceedings provide for the **reorganization** and adjustment of the debtor's debts and, in the case of a business debtor, the continuance of the debtor's business. In reorganization cases, the creditors usually look to the debtor's future earnings, whereas in liquidation cases, the creditors look to the debtor's property at the commencement of the bankruptcy proceeding. Chapters 7, 11, 12, and 13 have provisions governing conversion of a case under that chapter to another chapter. The 2005 Act added Chapter 15 to the Bankruptcy Code for cross-border insolvency cases. Chapter 1 and certain sections of Chapters 3 and 5 apply to proceedings under Chapter 15.

1. Chapter 7 applies to *all* debtors, except for railroads, insurance companies, banks, savings and loan associations, homestead associations, licensed small business investment companies, and credit unions. (In recent years, 62 to 70 percent of bankruptcies have been filed under Chapter 7.) Moreover, Chapter 7 has special provisions for liquidating the estates of stockbrokers and commodity brokers.

2. Chapter 11 applies to railroads and any person who may be a debtor under Chapter 7 (except a stockbroker or a commodity broker). (Less than 1 percent of bankruptcies are filed under Chapter 11.)

3. Chapter 9 applies only to municipalities that are generally authorized to be debtors under that chapter, that are insolvent, and that desire to effect plans to adjust their debts.

4. Chapter 12 applies to individuals, or individuals and their spouses, who are engaged in farming if 50 percent of their gross income is from farming, their aggregate debts do not exceed $4,411,400, and at least 50 percent of their debts arise out of farming operations. (Less than one-tenth of 1 percent of bankruptcies are filed under Chapter 12.) Corporations or partnerships also may qualify for Chapter 12. The 2005 Act made Chapter 12 permanent and extended its coverage to certain family fishermen if 50 percent of their gross income is from commercial fishing, their aggregate debts do not exceed $2,044,225, and at least 80 percent of their debts arise out of commercial fishing operations. The process under Chapter 12 is very similar to that of Chapter 13.

5. Chapter 13 applies to individuals with regular income who owe liquidated unsecured debts of less than $419,275 and secured debts of less than $1,257,850. (In recent years, 29 to 37 percent of bankruptcies have been filed under Chapter 13.)

6. Chapter 15 covers cross-border (transnational) insolvencies and incorporates the Model Law on Cross-Border Insolvency, promulgated by the United Nations Commission on International Trade Law (UNCITRAL). These changes are intended to make cross-border filings easier to accomplish and provide greater predictability. Chapter 15 encourages cooperation between the United States and foreign countries with respect to transnational insolvency cases. This text will not further cover Chapters 9, 12, and 15.

The 1994 amendments to the Bankruptcy Code require that every three years, beginning in 1998, the U.S. Judicial Conference adjust for inflation the dollar amounts of certain provisions, including eligibility for Chapters 12 and 13, requirements for filing involuntary cases, priorities, exemptions, and exceptions to discharge. Section 104. The dollar amounts in this chapter reflect the adjustment that was effective on April 1, 2019.

The Bankruptcy Code grants to U.S. district courts original and exclusive jurisdiction over all bankruptcy cases and original, but not exclusive, jurisdiction over civil proceedings arising under bankruptcy cases. The district court must, however, abstain from related matters that, except for their relationship to a bankruptcy, could not have been brought in a Federal court. The district court in which a bankruptcy case is commenced has exclusive jurisdiction over all of the debtor's property. In addition, within each Federal district court, the Bankruptcy Code establishes a bankruptcy court staffed by bankruptcy judges. Bankruptcy courts are authorized to hear certain matters specified by the Bankruptcy Code and to enter appropriate orders and judgments subject to review by the district court or, where established, by a panel of three bankruptcy judges. The Federal Circuit Court of Appeals has jurisdiction over appeals from the district court or panel. In all other matters, unless the parties agree otherwise, only the district court may issue final order or judgment based on proposed findings of fact and conclusions of law submitted to the court by the bankruptcy judge.

The U.S. trustees are government officials appointed by the U.S. Attorney General with administrative responsibilities in bankruptcy cases in almost all of the districts. (In North Carolina and Alabama, bankruptcy administrators perform similar functions that U.S. trustees perform in the other States.) The U.S. trustee program is administered by the Department of Justice, while the bankruptcy administrator program is administered by the Administrative Office of the United States Courts.

For example, the U.S. trustee selects bankruptcy trustees and, in Chapter 11 proceedings, appoints the members of the unsecured creditors' committee. The 2005 Act gives the U.S. trustees added responsibilities in a number of areas.

38-1 Case Administration—Chapter 3

Chapter 3 of the Bankruptcy Code contains provisions dealing with the commencement of a case in bankruptcy, the meetings of creditors, the officers who administer the case, and the administrative powers of those officers.

38-1a   COMMENCEMENT OF THE CASE

The filing of a voluntary or involuntary petition commences a bankruptcy case, thereby beginning the jurisdiction of the bankruptcy court and the operation of the bankruptcy laws.

VOLUNTARY PETITIONS More than 99 percent of all bankruptcy petitions are filed voluntarily. Any person eligible to be a debtor under a given bankruptcy proceeding may file a voluntary petition under that chapter and need *not* be insolvent to do so. Commencing a voluntary case by filing a petition constitutes an automatic **order for relief**. The petition must include a list of all creditors (secured and unsecured), a list of all property the debtor owns, a list of property that the debtor claims to be exempt, and a statement of the debtor's affairs.

The 2005 Act added a requirement that all individual debtors receive credit counseling from an approved nonprofit budget and credit counseling agency within the 180-day period *before* filing the petition. This requirement does not apply to a debtor who (1) is exempted by the court or (2) resides in a district for which the U.S. trustee or the bankruptcy administrator determines that approved nonprofit budget and credit counseling agencies are not reasonably able to provide adequate services to the additional individuals who would seek required credit counseling. The role of the credit counseling agencies is to analyze the client's current financial condition, the factors that caused the financial distress, and how the client can develop a plan to respond to these problems. Section 109(h).

INVOLUNTARY PETITIONS An involuntary petition in bankruptcy may be filed only under Chapter 7 (liquidation) or Chapter 11 (reorganization). It may be filed (1) by three or more creditors who have undisputed unsecured claims that total $16,750 or more or (2) if the debtor has fewer than twelve creditors, by one or more creditors whose total unsecured claims equal $16,750 or more. Section 303(b). An involuntary petition may not be filed against a farmer or against a banking, insurance, or nonprofit corporation. Section 303(a).

Like a voluntary petition, the filing of an involuntary petition commences a case, but unlike a voluntary petition, it does *not* operate as an order for relief. The debtor has the right to answer. If the debtor does not timely contest the involuntary petition, the court will enter an order for relief against the debtor. If the debtor timely opposes the petition, however, the court may enter an order of relief only (1) if the debtor is generally not paying his undisputed debts as they become due or (2) if, within 120 days before the filing of the petition, a custodian assignee or general receiver was appointed or took possession of substantially all of the debtor's property. Section 303(h).

If the court orders relief, the debtor must provide the court with schedules the same as those provided by a voluntary petitioner.

38-1b   DISMISSAL

The court may dismiss a Chapter 7 case for cause after notice and a hearing. Section 707(a). In a case filed by an individual debtor whose debts are primarily consumer debts, the court may dismiss the case or, with the debtor's consent, convert the case to one under Chapter 11 or 13 if the court finds that granting relief would be an abuse of the provisions of Chapter 7. Section 707(b). A court can find abuse in one of two ways: (1) on general grounds based on whether the debtor filed the petition in bad faith or the totality of the circumstances of the debtor's financial situation demonstrates abuse or (2) on an unrebutted presumption of abuse based on the means test established by the 2005 Act. The means test is discussed later in this chapter.

Under Chapter 11, the court may dismiss a case for cause after notice and a hearing. Section 1112(b). Under Chapter 13, the debtor has an absolute right to have his case dismissed. Under Chapter 13, if a motion to dismiss is filed by an interested party other than the debtor, the court may dismiss the case only for cause after notice and a hearing.

38-1c   AUTOMATIC STAYS

The filing of a voluntary or involuntary petition operates as a stay (i.e., restraint against) all creditors beginning or continuing to recover claims against the debtor, or creating, perfecting, or enforcing liens against property of the debtor. Section 362. This stay applies to both secured and unsecured creditors, although a secured creditor may petition the court to terminate the stay as to her security upon showing that she lacks adequate protection in the secured property. An automatic stay ends when the bankruptcy case is closed or dismissed or when the debtor receives a discharge.

Practical Advice

If you file a bankruptcy petition, you are protected from creditors pursuing their claims against you except through the bankruptcy proceeding; this may be advantageous in that it requires all claims to be heard in one court at one time.

38-1d   TRUSTEES

In a bankruptcy proceeding, the trustee represents the debtor's estate and has the capacity to sue and be sued on behalf of the estate. In proceedings under Chapter 7, trustees are selected by a vote of the creditors. The 1994 amendments allow the creditors to elect a trustee in a Chapter 11 proceeding if the court orders the appointment of a trustee for cause. In Chapter 13, the trustee is appointed. Under Chapter 7, the trustee is responsible for collecting, liquidating, and distributing the debtor's estate. Her duties and powers in fulfilling these responsibilities include the following: (1) to collect the property of the estate;

(2) to challenge certain transfers of property of the estate; (3) to use, sell, or lease property of the estate; (4) to deposit or invest money of the estate; (5) to employ attorneys, accountants, appraisers, or auctioneers; (6) to assume or reject any executory contract or unexpired lease of the debtor; (7) to object to creditors' claims that are improper; and (8) to oppose, if advisable, the debtor's discharge. Trustees under Chapters 11 and 13 perform some but not all of the duties of a Chapter 7 trustee.

38-1e MEETINGS OF CREDITORS

Within a reasonable time after relief is ordered, a meeting of creditors must be held. The court may not attend this meeting. The debtor must appear and submit to an examination by creditors and the trustee with respect to his financial situation. In a proceeding under Chapter 7, qualified creditors at this meeting elect a permanent trustee.

38-2 Creditors, the Debtor, and the Estate—Chapter 5

38-2a CREDITORS

The Bankruptcy Code defines a **creditor** as any entity having a claim against the debtor that arose at the time of or before the order for relief. A **claim** means a "right to payment whether or not such right is reduced to judgment, liquidated, unliquidated, fixed, contingent, matured, unmatured, disputed, undisputed, legal, equitable, secured, or unsecured." Section 101(5).

PROOF OF CLAIMS Creditors wishing to participate in the distribution of the debtor's estate may file a proof of claim. If a creditor does not do so in a timely manner, then the debtor or trustee may file a proof of such claim. Section 501. The debtor thereby may prevent a claim from becoming nondischargeable. Filed claims are allowed unless a party in interest objects. If an objection is made, the court determines, after a hearing, the amount and validity of the claim. The court may not allow any claim that (1) is unenforceable against the debtor or his property, (2) is for unmatured interest, or (3) is for **insider** or attorney services in excess of the reasonable value of such services. Section 502. An insider includes a relative or general partner of a debtor as well as a partnership in which the debtor is a general partner or a corporation of which the debtor is a director, officer, or person in control. Section 101(31).

Practical Advice

If you are a debtor in a bankruptcy proceeding, file a proof of claim for any creditor who does not file on her own. Such a filing may enable you to receive a discharge from that claim.

SECURED AND UNSECURED CLAIMS A lien is a charge or interest in property to secure payment of a debt or performance of an obligation and must be satisfied before the property is available to satisfy the claims of unsecured creditors. An allowed claim of a creditor who has a lien on property of the estate is a **secured claim** to the extent of the value of the creditor's interest in the property. The creditor's claim is an **unsecured claim** to the extent of the difference between the value of his secured interest and the allowed amount of his claim. Thus, if Andrew has an allowed claim of $5,000 against the estate of debtor Barbara and has a security interest in property of the estate that is valued at $3,000, Andrew has a secured claim in the amount of $3,000 and an unsecured claim for $2,000.

A lien or secured claim can arise by agreement, judicial proceeding, common law, or statute. Consensual security interests in personal property are governed by Article 9 of the Uniform Commercial Code (UCC) and are discussed in *Chapter 37*. Consensual security interests in real property, called mortgages or deeds of trust, are covered in *Chapter 49*. A judicial lien is obtained by a judgment, a levy, or some other legal or equitable process. The common law grants to certain creditors, including innkeepers and common carriers, a possessory lien on property of their debtors that is in the creditor's possession or on the creditor's premises. Finally, a number of Federal and State statutes grant liens to specified creditors.

PRIORITY OF CLAIMS After secured claims have been satisfied, the remaining assets are distributed among creditors with unsecured claims. Certain classes of unsecured claims, however, have a **priority**, which means that they must be paid in full before any distribution is made to claims of lesser rank. Each claimant within a priority class shares *pro rata* if the assets are not sufficient to satisfy all claims in that class. The claims having a priority, and the order of their priority, as provided in Section 507, are as follows:

1. *Domestic support obligations* (debts owed to a spouse, former spouse, or child of the debtor in the nature of alimony, maintenance, or support) subject to the expenses of a trustee in administering assets that otherwise can be used to pay support obligation.

2. *Expenses of administration* of the debtor's estate, including the filing fees paid by creditors in involuntary cases; the expenses of creditors in recovering concealed assets for the benefit of the bankrupt's estate; the trustee's necessary expenses; and reasonable compensation to receivers, trustees, and their attorneys, as allowed by the court.

3. *Unsecured claims of "gap" creditors*. These are claims in an involuntary case arising in the ordinary course of the debtor's business after the commencement of the case but before the earlier of either the appointment of the trustee or the entering of the order for relief.

4. Allowed, unsecured claims up to $13,650 for *wages, salaries, or commissions* earned within 180 days before the filing of the petition or before the date on which the debtor's business ceases, whichever comes first.

5. Allowed, unsecured claims for contributions to *employee benefit plans* arising from services rendered within 180 days before the filing of the petition or the cessation of the debtor's business, whichever occurs first, but limited to $13,650 multiplied by the number of employees covered by the plan, less the aggregate amount paid to such employees under number 3.

6. Allowed, unsecured claims up to $6,725 for *grain* or *fish producers* against a storage facility.

7. Allowed, unsecured claims up to $3,025 for *consumer deposits*; that is, moneys deposited in connection with the purchase, lease, or rental of property or the purchase of services for personal, family, or household use.

8. Specified income, property, employment, or excise *taxes* owed to governmental units.

9. Allowed claims for death or personal injuries resulting from the debtor's operation of a motor vehicle or vessel while legally intoxicated from using alcohol, a drug, or other substance.

After creditors with secured claims and creditors with claims having a priority have been satisfied, creditors with allowed, unsecured claims share proportionately in any remaining assets.

SUBORDINATION OF CLAIMS A subordination agreement is enforceable under the Bankruptcy Code to the same extent that it is enforceable under nonbankruptcy law. Section 510. In addition to statutory and contract priorities, the bankruptcy court can, at its discretion in proper cases, apply equitable priorities. Section 510. The court accomplishes this through the doctrine of subordination of claims, whereby, assuming two claims of equal statutory priority, the court declares that one claim must be paid in full before the other claim can be paid anything. Subordination is applied in cases in which allowing a claim in full would be unfair and inequitable to other creditors. (Allowing the inflated salary claims of officers in a closely held corporation would be an example.) In such cases, the court does not disallow the claim but merely orders that it be paid after all other claims are paid in full. For example, the claim of a parent corporation against its bankrupt subsidiary may be subordinated to the claims of other creditors of the subsidiary if the parent has so mismanaged the subsidiary to the detriment of its innocent creditors that this unconscionable conduct precludes the parent from seeking the aid of a bankruptcy court.

38-2b DEBTORS

As indicated, the purpose of the Bankruptcy Code is to bring about an equitable distribution of the debtor's assets and to provide him a discharge. Accordingly, the Code explicitly subjects the debtor to specified duties while exempting some of his property and discharging most of his debts.

DEBTOR'S DUTIES Under the Bankruptcy Code, the debtor must file a list of creditors, a schedule of assets and liabilities, a schedule of current income and expenditures, and a statement of her financial affairs. In any case in which a trustee is serving, the debtor must cooperate with the trustee and surrender to the trustee all property of the estate and all records relating to such property.

DEBTOR'S EXEMPTIONS Section 522 of the Bankruptcy Code exempts specified property of an individual debtor from bankruptcy proceedings, including the following:

1. up to $25,150 in equity in property used as a residence or burial plot;

2. up to $4,000 in equity in one motor vehicle;

3. up to $625 for any particular item, and not to exceed $13,400 in aggregate value, of household furnishings, household goods, wearing apparel, appliances, books, animals, crops, or musical instruments that are primarily for personal, family, or household use;

4. up to $1,700 in jewelry;

5. any property up to $1,325 plus up to $12,575 of any unused amount of the first exemption;

6. up to $2,525 in implements, professional books, or tools of the debtor's trade;

7. unmatured life insurance contracts owned by the debtor, other than a credit life insurance contract;

8. professionally prescribed health aids;

9. social security, veteran's, and disability benefits;

10. unemployment compensation;

11. alimony and support payments, including child support;

12. payments from pension, profit-sharing, and annuity plans;

13. tax-exempt retirement funds; and

14. payments from an award under a crime victim's reparation law, a wrongful death award, and up to $25,150, not including compensation for pain and suffering or for actual pecuniary loss, from a personal injury award.

In addition, the debtor may avoid judicial liens on any exempt property and nonpossessory, nonpurchase money security interests on certain household goods, tools of the trade, and professionally prescribed health aids.

The debtor has the option of using either the exemptions provided by the Bankruptcy Code or those available under State law. Nevertheless, a State may by specific legislative action limit its citizens to the exemptions provided by State law. Approximately two-thirds of the States have enacted such "opt out" legislation. The 2005 Act specifies that a debtor's exemption is governed by the law of the State where the debtor was domiciled for 730 days immediately before filing. If the debtor did not maintain a domicile in a single State for the 730-day period, then the governing law is of the State where the debtor was domiciled for 180 days immediately preceding the 730-day period (or for a longer portion of such 180-day period than in any other State).

Whether or not Federal or State exemptions apply, the 2005 Act provides that tax-exempt retirement accounts are exempt. Individual retirement accounts (IRAs) are subject to a $1,362,800 cap periodically adjusted for inflation. Nevertheless, the 2005 Act makes exempt property liable for nondischargeable domestic support obligations.

The 2005 Act also imposes limits on the use of State homestead exemptions. First, to the extent that the homestead was obtained through fraudulent conversion of nonexempt assets during the ten-year period before filing the petition, the exemption is reduced by that amount. Second, regardless of the level of the State exemption, a debtor may only exempt up to $170,350 of an interest in a homestead that was acquired during the 1,215-day period prior to the filing, but this limitation does not apply to any equity that has been transferred from the debtor's principal residence acquired more than 1,215 days before filing to the debtor's current principal residence if both residences are located in the same State. Third, a debtor may not exempt more than $170,350 if (1) the debtor has been convicted of a felony, which under the circumstances demonstrates that the filing of the case was an abuse of the Bankruptcy Code; or (2) the debtor owes a debt arising from (a) any violation of State or Federal securities laws; (b) fraud, deceit, or manipulation in a fiduciary capacity or in connection with the purchase or sale of securities registered under the Securities Exchange Act of 1934; or (c) any criminal act, intentional tort, or willful or reckless misconduct that caused serious physical injury or death to another individual in the preceding five years. The $170,350 limitation is to be adjusted periodically for inflation.

Practical Advice

If you intend to enter bankruptcy, determine what property is exempt from the debtor's estate in your State and take appropriate action.

DISCHARGE A discharge relieves the debtor from liability for certain specified debts called **dischargeable debts**. All other debts are nondischargeable under the Code. A discharge of a debt voids any judgment obtained at any time with respect to that debt and operates as a permanent injunction against commencing or continuing any action to recover that debt. Section 524. A discharge does not, however, affect a secured creditor to the extent of his security. The timing of discharge and which debts are discharged in bankruptcy vary depending on the type of case a debtor files, as discussed later in this chapter.

No private employer may terminate the employment of, or discriminate with respect to employment against, an individual who is or has been a debtor under the Bankruptcy Code solely because such debtor (1) is or has been such a debtor, (2) has been insolvent before the commencement of a case or during the case, or (3) has not paid a debt that is dischargeable in a case under the Bankruptcy Code. Section 525(b).

A reaffirmation agreement between a debtor and a creditor permitting the creditor to enforce a discharged debt is enforceable to the extent State law permits but only if (1) the agreement was made before the discharge has been granted; (2) the debtor received the required disclosures, which must be written, clear, and conspicuous, at or before the time at which the debtor signed the agreement; (3) the agreement has been filed with the court, accompanied, if applicable, by a declaration or an affidavit of the attorney who represented the debtor during the course of negotiating the agreement, which states that such agreement represents a fully informed and voluntary agreement by the debtor and imposes no undue hardship on her; (4) the debtor has not rescinded the agreement at any time prior to discharge or within sixty days after the agreement is filed with the court, whichever occurs later; (5) the court has informed a debtor who is an individual that he is not required to enter into such an agreement and has explained the legal effect of the agreement; and (6) in a case concerning an individual who was not represented by an attorney during the course of negotiating the agreement, the court has approved such agreement as imposing no undue hardship on the debtor and being in her best interests. Section 524.

Section 523 provides that certain debts of an individual are not dischargeable in bankruptcy: the debtor will continue to be liable for these types of debts to the extent that they are not paid in the bankruptcy proceeding. This section applies to individuals receiving discharges under Chapters 7 and 11 and, as discussed later in this chapter, the "hardship discharge" provision of Chapter 13. (The 2005 Act makes *most* of these apply to the standard discharge provision of Chapter 13.) The nondischargeable debts include the following:

1. certain taxes and customs duties and debt incurred to pay such taxes or customs duties;
2. legal liabilities for obtaining money, property, or services by false pretenses, false representations, or actual fraud;
3. legal liability for willful and malicious injuries to the person or property of another;

4. domestic support obligations and property settlements arising from divorce or separation proceedings; (i.e., alimony and child support);

5. debts not scheduled, unless the creditor knew of the bankruptcy;

6. debts the debtor created by fraud or defalcation while acting in a fiduciary capacity, embezzlement, or larceny;

7. student loans unless excluding the debt from discharge would impose undue hardship;

8. debts that were or could have been listed in a previous bankruptcy in which the debtor waived or was denied a discharge;

9. consumer debts for luxury goods or services in excess of $725 per creditor, if incurred by an individual debtor on or within ninety days before the order for relief, are presumed to be nondischargeable;

10. cash advances aggregating more than $1,000 obtained by an individual debtor under an open-ended credit plan within seventy days before the order for relief are presumed to be nondischargeable;

11. liability for death or personal injury based upon the debtor's operation of a motor vehicle, vessel, or aircraft while legally intoxicated;

12. fines, penalties, or forfeitures owed to a governmental entity; and

13. certain debts incurred for violations of securities fraud law. (This provision was added by the Sarbanes-Oxley Act.)

The following example illustrates the operation of discharge: Donaldson files a petition in bankruptcy. Donaldson owes Anders $1,500, Boynton $2,500, and Conroy $3,000. Assume that Anders's claim is not dischargeable in bankruptcy, whereas Boynton's and Conroy's claims are. Anders receives $180 from the liquidation of Donaldson's bankruptcy estate, Boynton receives $300, and Conroy receives $360. If Donaldson receives a bankruptcy discharge, Boynton and Conroy will be precluded from pursuing Donaldson for the remainder of their claims ($2,200 and $2,640, respectively). Anders, on the other hand, because his debt is not dischargeable, may pursue Donaldson for the remaining $1,320, subject to the applicable statute of limitations. If Donaldson does not receive a discharge, Anders, Boynton, and Conroy may all pursue Donaldson for the unpaid portions of their claims.

♦ *See Case 38-1*

38-2c THE ESTATE

The commencement of a bankruptcy case creates an estate, which is treated as a separate legal entity, distinct from the debtor. The estate consists of all legal and equitable interests of the debtor in nonexempt property as of the commencement of the case. The estate also includes property that the debtor acquires within 180 days after the filing of the petition by inheritance, by a property settlement, by a divorce decree, or as a beneficiary of a life insurance policy. In addition, the estate includes proceeds, rents, and profits from property of the estate and any interest in property that the estate acquires after the case commences. Section 541. The 2005 Act *excludes* from the estate savings for postsecondary education through education IRAs and 529 plans if certain criteria are met. Finally, the estate includes property that the trustee recovers under her powers (1) as a lien creditor, (2) to avoid voidable preferences, (3) to avoid fraudulent transfers, and (4) to avoid statutory liens. While in a Chapter 7 case the estate does not include earnings from services an *individual* debtor performs after the case commences, in a Chapter 11 or Chapter 13 case, it does include wages an *individual* debtor earns and property she acquires after the case commences.

TRUSTEE AS LIEN CREDITOR The trustee has, as of the commencement of the case, the rights and powers of any creditor with a judicial lien against the debtor or an execution that is returned unsatisfied, whether or not such a creditor exists. Section 544(a). The trustee is made an ideal creditor possessing every right and power that the State confers by law upon its most favored creditor who has acquired a lien through legal or equitable proceedings. By assuming the rights and powers of a purely hypothetical lien creditor, the trustee has no need to locate an actual existing lien creditor.

Thus, under the UCC and the Bankruptcy Code, the trustee, as a hypothetical lien creditor, has priority over a creditor with a security interest that was not perfected when the bankruptcy petition was filed. A creditor with a purchase money security interest who files within the grace period allowed under State law, which in most States is twenty days after the debtor receives the collateral, however, will defeat the trustee, even if the creditor gap-files the petition before perfecting and after the security interest is created. For example, Donald borrows $5,000 from Cathy on September 1 and gives her a security interest in the equipment he purchases with the borrowed funds. On October 3, before Cathy perfects her security interest, Donald files for bankruptcy. The trustee in bankruptcy can invalidate Cathy's security interest because it was unperfected when the bankruptcy petition was filed. Cathy would be able to assert a claim only as an unsecured creditor. If, however, Donald had filed for bankruptcy on September 18 and Cathy had perfected the security interest on September 19, Cathy would prevail because she perfected her purchase money security interest within twenty days after Donald received the equipment.

VOIDABLE PREFERENCES The Bankruptcy Code invalidates certain preferential transfers from the debtor to favored creditors before the date of bankruptcy. A creditor who has received a transfer invalidated as preferential still may make a claim for the unpaid debt, but the property he received under the preferential transfer becomes a part of the debtor's estate to be shared by all creditors. Under Section 547, the trustee may recover any transfer of the debtor's property:

1. to or for the benefit of a creditor;

2. for or on account of an antecedent debt the debtor owed before such transfer was made;

3. made while the debtor was insolvent;

4. made on or within ninety days before the date of the filing of the petition or, if the creditor was an "insider" (as previously defined), made within one year of the date of the filing of the petition; *and*

5. that enables such creditor to receive more than he would have received under Chapter 7.

A **transfer** is any mode, direct or indirect, voluntary or involuntary, of disposing of property or an interest in property, including the retention of title as a security interest. Section 101(54). The debtor is presumed to have been insolvent on and during the ninety days immediately preceding the date on which the petition was filed. **Insolvency** is a financial condition of a debtor such that the sum of her debts exceeds the sum of all her property at fair valuation.

For example, on March 3, David borrows $15,000 from Carla, promising to repay the loan on April 3. David repays Carla on April 3 as he promised. Then on June 1, David files a petition in bankruptcy. His assets are sufficient to pay general creditors only forty cents on the dollar. David's repayment of the loan is a voidable preference, which the trustee may recover from Carla. The transfer (repayment) on April 3 (1) was to a creditor (Carla), (2) was on account of an antecedent debt (the $15,000 loan made on March 3), (3) was made while the debtor was insolvent (a debtor is presumed insolvent for the ninety days preceding the filing of the bankruptcy petition—June 1), (4) was made within ninety days of bankruptcy (April 3 is less than ninety days before June 1), and (5) enabled the creditor to receive more than she would have received under Chapter 7 (Carla received $15,000; she would have received $0.40 \times $15,000 = $6,000 in bankruptcy). After returning the property to the trustee, Carla would have an unsecured claim of $15,000 against David's estate in bankruptcy, for which she would receive $6,000.

To illustrate further, consider the following example. On May 1, Debra buys and receives merchandise from Stuart and gives him a security interest in the goods for the unpaid price of $20,000. On May 25, Stuart files a financing statement. On August 1, Debra files a petition for bankruptcy. The trustee in bankruptcy may avoid the perfected security interest as a preferential transfer because (1) the transfer of the perfected

security interest on May 25 was to benefit a creditor (Stuart), (2) it was on account of an antecedent debt (the $20,000 owed from the sale of the merchandise), (3) the debtor was insolvent at the time (the debtor's insolvency is presumed for the ninety days preceding the filing of the bankruptcy petition—August 1), (4) the transfer was made within ninety days of bankruptcy (May 25 is less than ninety days before August 1), and (5) the transfer enabled the creditor to receive more than he would have received in bankruptcy (on his secured claim, Stuart would recover more than he would on an unsecured claim).

Nevertheless, not all transfers made within ninety days of bankruptcy are voidable. The Bankruptcy Code makes exceptions for certain prebankruptcy transfers, including the following:

1. *Exchanges for new value.* If, for example, within ninety days before the petition is filed the debtor purchases an automobile for $9,000, this transfer of property (i.e., the $9,000) is not voidable because it was not made for an antecedent debt but rather as a substantially contemporaneous exchange for new value.

2. *Enabling security interests.* If the creditor gives the debtor new value which the debtor uses to acquire property in which he grants the creditor a security interest, the security interest is not voidable if the creditor perfects it within thirty days after the debtor receives possession of the property. For example, if within ninety days of the filing of the petition the debtor purchases a refrigerator on credit and grants the seller or lender a security interest in the refrigerator, the transfer of that interest is not voidable if the secured party perfects within thirty days after the debtor receives possession of the property.

3. *Payments in ordinary course.* The trustee may *not* avoid a transfer in payment of a debt incurred in the ordinary course of business or financial affairs of the debtor and the transferee and either (a) made in the ordinary course of business or financial affairs of the debtor and transferee or (b) made according to ordinary business terms.

4. *Consumer debts.* This exception provides that if the debtor is an individual whose debts are primarily consumer debts, the trustee may not avoid any transfer of property valued at less than $600.

5. *Nonconsumer debts.* In a case filed by a debtor whose debts are not primarily consumer debts, the trustee may not avoid any transfer of property valued at less than $6,825.

6. *Domestic support obligations.* The trustee may not avoid any transfer that is a *bona fide* payment of a debt for a domestic support obligation. Section 547(c).

FRAUDULENT TRANSFERS The trustee may avoid fraudulent transfers made on or within two years before the date of the filing of the petition. Section 548. One type of fraudulent transfer consists of the debtor's transferring property with the actual intent to hinder, delay, or defraud any of her creditors. Another type of fraudulent transfer involves the debtor's transfer of property for less than a reasonably equivalent consideration when she is insolvent or when the transfer would render her so. For example, Dale, who is in debt, transfers title to her house to Tony, her father, without any payment by Tony to Dale and with the understanding that when the house is no longer in danger of seizure by creditors, Tony will reconvey it to Dale. The transfer of the house by Dale to Tony is a fraudulent transfer. The 2005 Act specifies that a fraudulent transfer includes a payment to an insider under an employment contract that is not in the ordinary course of business. A 1998 amendment to the Bankruptcy Code provides that a transfer of a charitable contribution to a qualified religious or charitable entity or organization will not be considered a fraudulent transfer if the amount of that contribution does not exceed 15 percent of the gross annual income of the debtor for the year in which the transfer is made. Transfers that exceed 15 percent are protected if they are "consistent with the practices of the debtor in making charitable contributions."

In addition, the trustee may avoid transfers of the debtor's property if the transfer is voidable under State law by a creditor with an allowable, unsecured claim. Section 544(b). This section empowers a trustee to avoid transfers that violate State fraudulent conveyance statutes, which create a right of action for any creditor against any debtor and against any other person who has received property from the debtor in a fraudulent transfer. A fraudulent transfer occurs when a debtor transfers property (1) to hinder, delay, or defraud a creditor or (2) under certain conditions, to another person without receiving reasonably equivalent value in return. These statutes generally provide a three- to six-year limitations period, which the trustee can utilize under Section 544(b). At least forty-five States have adopted the Uniform Voidable Transactions Act (formerly the Uniform Fraudulent Transfer Act), which has a four-year statute of limitations. The 2014 amendments to the Act have been adopted by at least twenty-two States.

♦ *See Case 38-1*

STATUTORY LIENS A statutory lien arises solely by force of a statute and does not include a security interest or judicial lien. Section 101(53). The trustee may avoid a statutory lien on property of the debtor if the lien (1) first becomes effective when the debtor becomes insolvent, (2) is not perfected or enforceable on the date of the commencement of the case against a *bona fide* purchaser, or (3) is for rent. Section 545.

38-3 Liquidation—Chapter 7

To accomplish its dual goals of equitably distributing the debtor's property and providing the debtor with a fresh start, the Bankruptcy Code has established two approaches: liquidation and adjustment of debts. Chapter 7 uses liquidation, whereas Chapters 11 and 13, discussed later in the chapter, take the second approach—that of adjusting debts. Liquidation is a court-supervised procedure in which a trustee sells the debtor's nonexempt assets and distributes the proceeds to creditors in accordance with the provisions of the Bankruptcy Code. In Chapter 7 cases, an individual debtor usually receives a discharge that releases the debtor from personal liability for some of her debts. However, the right to a discharge is not absolute: some types of debts are not discharged, and a discharge in bankruptcy does not extinguish a lien on property. In a Chapter 7 case, an individual debtor's principal objective is to maximize the exempt property she retains and to obtain a discharge that includes as many debts as possible.

38-3a PROCEEDINGS

Proceedings under Chapter 7 apply to all debtors except railroads, insurance companies, banks, savings and loan associations, homestead associations, and credit unions. A petition commencing a case under Chapter 7 may be either voluntary or involuntary. After the order for relief, an interim trustee is appointed to serve until the creditors select a permanent trustee. If the creditors do not elect a trustee, the interim trustee becomes the permanent trustee. Under Chapter 7, the trustee collects and reduces to money the property of the estate in a manner that maximizes the return to the debtor's unsecured creditors. The trustee accomplishes this by selling the debtor's (1) nonexempt property if it has no liens or security interests, (2) nonexempt property with liens or security interests if it is worth more than the lien or security interest, and (3) exempt property if it is worth more than the exemption. In addition, the trustee attempts to recover money or property under the trustee's powers to avoid certain transfers, as discussed earlier; accounts for all property received; investigates the financial affairs of the debtor; examines and, if appropriate, challenges proofs of claim; opposes, if advisable, the discharge of the debtor; and makes a final report of the administration of the estate. A notable example of a trustee's efforts to maximize the return to the debtor's unsecured creditors is in the case involving Bernard L. Madoff's Ponzi scheme that defrauded customers of approximately $20 billion. As of June 18, 2021, more than $14 billion either had been recovered in actual receipts of funds or agreements to repay funds.

The creditors may also elect a committee of not fewer than three and not more than eleven unsecured creditors to consult with the trustee, to make recommendations to him, and to submit questions to the court.

38-3b CONVERSION

The debtor may convert a case under Chapter 7 to Chapter 11 or 13, provided the case has not previously been converted to Chapter 7. Any waiver of this right is unenforceable. Moreover, on request of a party in interest and after notice and a hearing, the court may convert a case under Chapter 7 to Chapter 11. The court also may convert a case under Chapter 7 to Chapter 13, but this can occur only upon the debtor's request. Any conversion to another chapter can only occur if the debtor also may be a debtor under that chapter. Section 706.

38-3c DISMISSAL

The court may dismiss a Chapter 7 case for cause after notice and a hearing. In a case filed by an individual debtor whose debts are primarily consumer debts, the court may dismiss a case or, with the debtor's consent, convert the case to one under Chapter 11 or 13 if the court finds that granting relief would be an abuse of the provisions of Chapter 7. A court can find abuse (1) on general grounds based on whether the debtor filed the petition in bad faith or the totality of the circumstances of the debtor's financial situation demonstrates abuse or (2) on an unrebutted presumption of abuse based on a new means test established by the 2005 Act.

Under the **means test**, abuse is presumed (i.e., the debtor is not eligible for Chapter 7 unless the debtor can prove special circumstances) for an individual debtor whose net current monthly income is greater than the State median income *and* if (1) the debtor has available net income (income after deducting allowed expenses) for repayment to creditors over five years totaling at least $13,650 or (2) the available net income for repayment to creditors over five years is between $8,175 and $13,650 and such available net income is at least 25 percent of nonpriority unsecured claims. Section 707. The means test can be explained by the following scenarios:

1. If the debtor's net current monthly income is less than or equal to the State median income, no presumption of abuse arises.

2. If the debtor's net current monthly income is greater than the State median income *and* the debtor's current monthly income less allowed expenses is less than $136.25 per month, no presumption of abuse arises.

3. If the debtor's net current monthly income is greater than the State median income *and* the debtor's current monthly income less allowed expenses is at least $136.25 per month, a presumption of abuse arises *if* the current monthly income less allowed expenses is sufficient to pay 25 percent of the debtor's nonpriority unsecured claims over sixty months.

4. If the debtor's net current monthly income is greater than the State median income *and* the debtor's current monthly

income less allowed expenses is at least $227.50 per month, a presumption of abuse arises without regard to the amount of nonpriority unsecured claims.

For example, Debra's net current monthly income is greater than the State median income. After deducting allowed expenses, her monthly income is $150, which places her in the third situation. If her nonpriority unsecured claims are $35,000, a presumption of abuse will arise because $150 multiplied by sixty equals $9,000, which is greater than 25 percent of $35,000, which equals $8,750. On the other hand, Debra would be eligible to file under Chapter 7 if her nonpriority unsecured claims are $36,100, because $150 multiplied by sixty equals $9,000, which is less than 25 percent of $36,100, which equals $9,025.

38-3d DISTRIBUTION OF THE ESTATE

After the trustee has collected all the assets of the debtor's estate, she distributes them to the creditors and, if any assets remain, to the debtor, in the following order:

1. Secured creditors are paid on their security interests.

2. Creditors entitled to a priority are paid in the order provided.

3. Unsecured creditors who filed their claims on time (or tardily if they did not have notice or actual knowledge of the bankruptcy) are paid.

4. Unsecured creditors who filed their claims late are paid.

5. Claims for fines and multiple, exemplary, or punitive damages are paid.

6. Interest at the legal rate from the date of the filing of the petition is paid to all of these claimants.

7. Whatever property remains is distributed to the debtor.

Claims of the same rank are paid *pro rata*. For example, Donley has filed a petition for a Chapter 7 proceeding. The total value of Donley's estate after paying the expenses of administration is $25,000. Evans, who is owed $15,000, has a security interest in property valued at $10,000. Fishel has an unsecured claim of $6,000, which is entitled to a priority of $2,000. The United States has a claim for income taxes of $4,000. Green has an unsecured claim of $9,000 that was filed on time. Hiller has an unsecured claim of $12,000 that was filed on time. Jerdee has a claim of $8,000 that was filed late. The distribution would be as follows:

1. Evans receives $11,500.

2. Fishel receives $3,200.

3. United States receives $4,000.

4. Green receives $2,700.

5. Hiller receives $3,600.

6. Jerdee receives $0.

FIGURE 38-1 Collection and Distribution of the Debtor's Estate

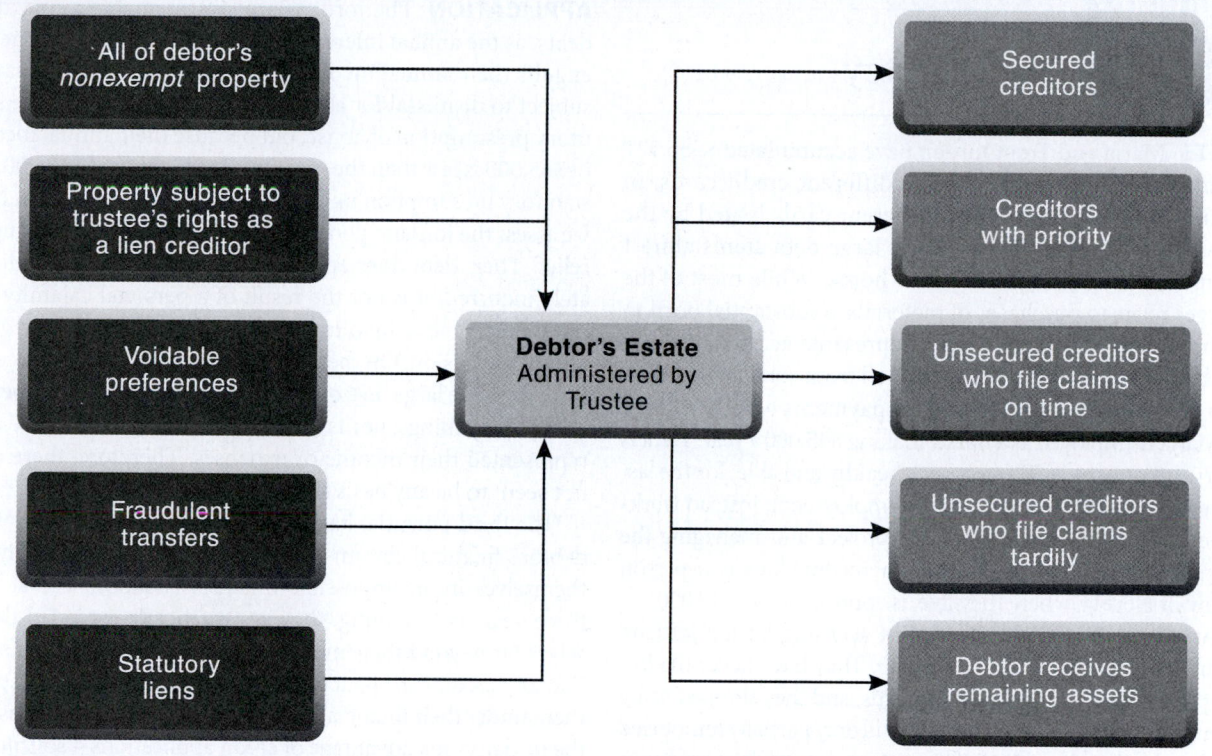

To analyze this distribution: Evans receives $10,000 as a secured creditor and has an unsecured claim of $5,000. Fishel receives $2,000 on the portion of his claim entitled to a priority and has an unsecured claim of $4,000. The United States has a priority of $4,000. After paying $10,000 to Evans, $2,000 to Fishel, and $4,000 to the United States, $9,000 remains ($25,000 − $10,000 − $2,000 − $4,000) to be distributed *pro rata* to unsecured creditors who filed on time. Their claims total $30,000 (Evans = $5,000, Fishel = $4,000, Green = $9,000, and Hiller = $12,000). Therefore, each will receive $9,000/$30,000, or thirty cents on the dollar. Accordingly, Evans receives an additional $1,500, Fishel receives an additional $1,200, Green receives $2,700, and Hiller receives $3,600. Because the assets were insufficient to pay all unsecured claimants who filed on time, Jerdee, who filed tardily, receives nothing. If, however, Jerdee's late filing resulted from Donley's failure to schedule Jerdee's claim, then Donley's debts to Jerdee would not be discharged unless Jerdee knew or had notice of the bankruptcy.

♦ **SEE FIGURE 38-1:** *Collection and Distribution of the Debtor's Estate*

38-3e DISCHARGE

A discharge under Chapter 7 relieves the debtor of all dischargeable debts that arose before the date of the order for relief. The discharge does not include those debts that are not dischargeable. The debtor will continue to be liable for non-dischargeable debts to the extent that they are not paid in a Chapter 7 case. After distribution of the estate, the court will grant the debtor a discharge unless the debtor:

1. is not an individual (partnerships and corporations may *not* receive a discharge under Chapter 7);

2. has destroyed, falsified, concealed, or failed to keep records and account books;

3. has knowingly and fraudulently made a false oath or account, presented or used a false claim, or given or received bribes;

4. has transferred, removed, destroyed, or concealed any (a) of his property with intent to hinder, delay, or defraud his creditors within twelve months preceding the filing of the bankruptcy petition, or (b) property of the estate after the date of filing of the petition;

5. has within eight years prior to bankruptcy been granted a discharge under Chapter 7 or 11. A debtor also will be denied a discharge under Chapter 7 if she received a discharge under Chapter 13 within the past six years, unless payments under that chapter's plan totaled at least (1) 100 percent of the allowed unsecured claims or (2) 70 percent of such claims, the plan was proposed in good faith, and the payments represented the debtor's best effort;

APPLYING THE LAW

Bankruptcy

FACTS Maria and Trent Jordan have accumulated $356,327 in unsecured debt on fifty-nine different credit cards, in several cases on six or seven different cards issued by the same financial institutions. Their large debt stems almost exclusively from remodeling their home. While most of the charges relate to purchases of materials, a substantial portion of the total credit card balance represents accrued interest and large cash advances they obtained from some of the cards to enable them to make minimum payments on other cards.

Maria is employed as a nurse, making $45,000 a year. Trent is a carpenter by trade. Though he is healthy and able, for the last three years he has not had outside employment, instead working exclusively on the remodeling project and managing the couple's finances. The median annual income for a two-person family in Florida, where they live, is approximately $47,000.

At this point, the annual interest accruing on the Jordans' credit card balances is about $36,000. They have never made a late payment on any of the credit cards, and they stopped using them six months ago. Their home is still only partially remodeled and is valued at about $115,000, with an outstanding mortgage of approximately $102,000. When the remodeling is complete, the home will be worth in excess of $350,000. However, given its partially completed state, the Jordans' current equity in the house is far less than Florida's homestead exemption. They own two modest automobiles that are subject to purchase money security interests, and they have no other assets of any value.

Earlier this year, the Jordans filed a petition for Chapter 7 bankruptcy relief. The U.S. trustee has now filed a motion to dismiss their case for abuse.

ISSUE Will the Jordans' petition in bankruptcy be dismissed?

RULE OF LAW If the court finds that granting relief to an individual debtor with primarily consumer debts would be an abuse of Chapter 7's provisions, the court may dismiss the debtor's bankruptcy case after notice and a hearing. Abuse may be established in one of three situations. First, the debtor may be unable to rebut a statutory presumption of abuse based on the means test established by the Bankruptcy Abuse Prevention and Consumer Protection Act of 2005 (2005 Act). The statutory presumption of abuse, however, does not arise in a case in which the debtor's income is less than the applicable state median income figure. Second, the court may dismiss the debtor's case for abuse if the filing was made in bad faith. Finally, the court might dismiss the bankruptcy case if the totality of the circumstances of the debtor's financial situation reflects abuse.

APPLICATION The Jordans are clearly unable to pay their debts, as the annual interest on their credit cards alone nearly engulfs their annual income. Nonetheless, their case may be subject to dismissal for abuse. The first possibility is the statutory presumption of abuse, but because their annual income of $45,000 is less than the state median income of $47,000, the statutory presumption under the 2005 Act does not arise. Next we assess the Jordans' good or bad faith in seeking bankruptcy relief. Their debt does appear to be voluntarily and deliberately incurred; it is not the result of a personal calamity like uninsured illness, involuntary loss of employment, or gambling compulsion. On the other hand, there is no evidence the Jordans made large "eve of bankruptcy" purchases or repeated bankruptcy filings, nor is there any indication they have misrepresented their income or expenses. Therefore, there does not seem to be any basis for a finding of bad faith.

The third potential basis for dismissal is the totality of the debtor's financial circumstances. The Jordans have clearly put themselves in an impossible financial situation. For at least three years before filing, they systematically extended themselves far beyond their means. While it belies common sense that any credit card issuer would continue to extend credit to them under their financial circumstances, the fact remains that the Jordans took advantage of credit applications—solicited or unsolicited—to request and obtain fifty-nine different credit card accounts, carefully sustaining only the short-term obligations of each while somehow running up total unsecured debt of eight times their annual income.

A court could certainly find that these debtors are using bankruptcy as part of a scheme to avoid obligations they never intended to satisfy. They appear to have made no significant attempt to address their enormous financial obligation. Indeed, it appears as though Mr. Jordan's management of the couple's finances may have become something of a complex game, using a combination of meager income and new cards with available cash advances to placate the demands of growing balances on older cards. Moreover, the couple has sought bankruptcy protection at a time when their remodeling project is still incomplete and their home's potential equity is still unavailable to satisfy the unsecured creditors. While Chapter 7 bankruptcy is a solution for the honest debtor who is hopelessly indebted, bankruptcy for the Jordans instead seems to be just the final step of a calculated process to avoid meaningful financial responsibility.

CONCLUSION A finding of substantial abuse due to the "totality of the debtor's financial circumstances" is within the discretion of the court. Here, it is likely that a court would dismiss the Jordans' bankruptcy case based on a finding that their intentional, irresponsible choices constitute abuse.

6. refused to obey any lawful order of the court or to answer any question approved by the court;

7. has failed to explain satisfactorily, in terms of meeting his liabilities, any loss or deficiency of assets; or

8. has executed a written waiver of discharge approved by the court. Section 727.

The 2005 Act denies a discharge to an individual debtor who fails to complete a personal financial management course. This provision, however, does not apply if the debtor resides in a district for which the U.S. trustee or the bankruptcy administrator has determined that the approved instructional courses are not adequate to service the additional individuals who would be required to complete these instructional courses.

On the request of the trustee or a creditor and after notice and a hearing, the court may revoke within one year a discharge the debtor obtained through fraud or other specified misconduct.

38-4 Reorganization—Chapter 11

Reorganization is the process of correcting or eliminating factors responsible for the distress of a business enterprise to achieve the purposes of reorganization: (1) to preserve both the enterprise and its value as a going concern and (2) to pay creditors over time. Chapter 11 of the Bankruptcy Code governs reorganization of eligible debtors, including individuals, partnerships, and corporations, and permits the restructuring of their finances. A number of large corporations have made use of Chapter 11, including WorldCom, Enron, Kmart, Texaco, A.H. Robins, Johns-Manville, Allied Stores, Global Crossing, Pacific Gas and Electric, CIT Group, Conseco, Lehman Brothers, American Airlines, MF Global, Washington Mutual, Circuit City, Linens 'n Things, General Motors, and Chrysler. The main objective of a reorganization proceeding is to develop and carry out a fair, equitable, and feasible plan of reorganization. The Bankruptcy Code provides three ways for a debtor under Chapter 11 to exit the bankruptcy case: (1) confirmation of a plan of reorganization, (2) conversion to a Chapter 7 liquidation, or (3) dismissal of the case.

Chapter 11 is typically used to reorganize a business, which may be a limited liability entity (such as a corporation, limited liability company, or limited liability partnership), a sole proprietorship, or a general partnership. When a limited liability entity is a debtor in a Chapter 11 bankruptcy case, the personal assets of the equity owners are not at risk beyond the value of their investment in the entity. A bankruptcy case involving a sole proprietorship includes both the business and personal assets of the owner-debtor. When a general partnership is a debtor in a bankruptcy case, if the partnership property is insufficient to pay all the claims against the partnership, the

Bankruptcy Code directs the trustee to seek recovery of the shortfall first from the general partners who are not bankrupt and then against the estates of bankrupt partners on the same basis as other creditors of the bankrupt partners.

After a plan has been prepared and filed, a hearing held before the court determines whether or not it will be confirmed. Chapter 11 permits but does not require a sale of assets. Rather, it contemplates that the debtor will keep its assets and use them to generate earnings that will pay creditors under the terms of the plan confirmed by the court.

The 1994, 2005, and 2019 amendments provide for streamlined and more flexible procedures in a small business case, which is any case under Chapter 11 filed by a small business debtor. The amendments define the term *small business debtor* to include persons engaged in commercial or business activities whose aggregate, noncontingent, liquidated debts do not exceed $2,725,625 (subject to periodic adjustments for inflation) provided that 50 percent or more of the debt must arise from the commercial or business activities of the debtor. However, the following persons are excluded from being a small business debtor: (1) a person whose primary activity is the business of owning single asset real estate and (2) any debtor that is a corporation subject to the reporting requirements under the Securities Exchange Act of 1934. In a small business case, the U.S. trustee has additional oversight duties, and the debtor has additional reporting requirements, although the plan process can be simpler and the time periods and deadlines are different. In addition, under the 2019 amendments, no committee of unsecured creditors is appointed unless the bankruptcy court orders otherwise.

The **Small Business Reorganization Act of 2019** (SBRA)—which became effective on February 19, 2020—creates new *optional* bankruptcy procedures for small business debtors filing for reorganization under Chapter 11. The purpose of SBRA is "to streamline the process by which small business debtors reorganize and rehabilitate their financial affairs." The SBRA applies in cases in which a small business debtor **elects** its application. (In the absence of an election, the provisions of Chapter 11 that govern a small business debtor discussed in the previous paragraph would apply.) The SBRA provides for the appointment of a trustee and permits a debtor to operate its business as a debtor in possession during the reorganization. In addition, the SBRA provides that a committee of creditors will not be appointed unless ordered by the bankruptcy court for cause. Under the SRBA, only a debtor is allowed to file a reorganization plan, but the debtor must file within ninety days of the petition date, except with permission of the bankruptcy court for cause. The bankruptcy court may approve a reorganization plan for a small business debtor over the objections of the creditors if the plan (1) does not discriminate unfairly and (2) is fair and equitable towards each class of claims or interests that is impaired under, and has not accepted, the plan.

38-4a PROCEEDINGS

Any person who may be a debtor under Chapter 7 (except stockbrokers and commodity brokers) and railroads may be a debtor under Chapter 11. Petitions may be voluntary or involuntary.

After a Chapter 11 petition has been filed, an estate is created comprising all property of the debtor, and an automatic stay against creditors goes into effect. The debtor remains in possession and control of the property of the estate until the debtor's plan of reorganization is confirmed, the debtor's case is dismissed or converted to Chapter 7, or a Chapter 11 trustee is appointed. The court will order the appointment of a trustee *only* for *cause* (including fraud, dishonesty, incompetence, or gross mismanagement of the debtor's affairs) or if the appointment is in the interests of creditors or equity security holders. Section 1104. The 1994 amendments allow the creditors to elect the trustee. If the court does not order the appointment of a trustee upon the request of a party in interest, the court will order the appointment of an examiner to investigate allegations of fraud, dishonesty, incompetence, misconduct, or mismanagement if (1) such appointment is in the interests of creditors or equity security holders or (2) the debtor's fixed, liquidated, unsecured debts exceed $5 million.

The duties of a trustee in a case under Chapter 11 include the following:

1. to be accountable for all property received;
2. to examine proofs of claim;
3. to furnish information to all parties in interest;
4. to provide the court and taxing authorities with financial reports of the debtor's business operations;
5. to make a final report and account of the administration of the estate;
6. to investigate the financial condition of the debtor and determine the desirability of continuing the debtor's business; and
7. to file a plan, to file a report explaining why there will be no plan, or to recommend that the case be converted to Chapter 7.

At any time before confirmation of a plan, the court may terminate the trustee's appointment and restore the debtor to possession and management of the property of the estate and operation of the debtor's business. Section 1105.

As soon as practicable after the order for relief, a committee of unsecured creditors is appointed. This committee usually consists of persons holding the seven largest unsecured claims against the debtor. In addition, the court may order the appointment of additional committees of creditors or of equity security holders to ensure adequate representation. Section 1102. The committee may, with the court's approval, employ attorneys, accountants, and other agents to represent or perform services for the committee. The committee may consult with the debtor or trustee concerning the administration of the case; investigate the debtor's acts, conduct, assets, liabilities, and financial condition; participate in formulating a reorganization plan; and request the appointment of a trustee. Section 1103.

When a trustee has not been appointed, which is usually the case, the debtor in possession performs many of the functions and duties of a trustee, with the principal exception of investigating the debtor. Section 1107.

The Bankruptcy Code (Section 1113) deals with the rejection of collective bargaining agreements. Subsection (b)(1) provides that subsequent to filing and prior to seeking such rejection, the trustee or debtor-in-possession must propose the labor contract modifications that are necessary to enable the debtor to reorganize and that will provide for the fair and equitable treatment of all parties concerned. Subsection (b)(2) requires that good faith meetings to reach a mutually satisfactory agreement be held between management and the union. Subsection (c) authorizes the court to approve rejection of the collective bargaining agreement only if the court finds that the proposal for rejection was made in accordance with these conditions, that the union refused the proposal without good cause, and that the balance of equities clearly favors rejection.

38-4b CONVERSION OR DISMISSAL

The debtor may convert a case under Chapter 11 to Chapter 7 *unless* (1) the debtor is not a debtor in possession, (2) the case originally was commenced as an involuntary case under Chapter 11, or (3) the case was converted to Chapter 11 other than at the debtor's request. On request of a party in interest, and after notice and a hearing, the court may convert *for cause* a case under Chapter 11 to Chapter 7 or dismiss a case under Chapter 11, whichever is in the best interests of creditors and the estate, unless the court determines that the appointment of a trustee is in the best interests of creditors and the estate. The court may convert a case under Chapter 11 to Chapter 13 if the debtor requests such conversion and the debtor has not been discharged under Chapter 11.

Usually a dismissal of a Chapter 11 case revests the property in the entity in which that property was vested immediately before the commencement of the case. However, the Bankruptcy Code permits the bankruptcy court, for cause, to alter a Chapter 11 dismissal's ordinary revesting of the estate's property. A dismissal that does so is often referred to as a **structured dismissal**, which has been defined by the American Bankruptcy Institute as a "hybrid dismissal and confirmation order . . . that . . . typically dismisses the case while, among other things, approving certain distributions to creditors." In a 2017 case, the U.S. Supreme Court held that in Chapter 11 cases, including structured dismissal cases, a bankruptcy court cannot confirm a plan that contains distributions that violate the priority rules over the objection of an impaired creditor class. *Czyzewski v. Jevic Holding Corp.*, 580 U.S. ____.

♦ SEE FIGURE 38-2: *Comparison of Bankruptcy Proceedings*

38-4c PLAN OF REORGANIZATION

The debtor may file a plan at any time and has the exclusive right to file a plan during the 120 days after the order for relief, unless a trustee has been appointed. Other parties in interest, including the trustee, if one has been appointed, or a creditors' committee, may file a plan if (1) a trustee has been appointed, (2) the debtor has not filed a plan before 120 days after the order for relief, *or* (3) the debtor has not filed a plan that has been accepted before 180 days after the order for relief. Section 1121. On request of an interested party and after notice and a hearing, the court may for cause reduce or increase the 120-day or 180-day periods. The 2005 Act provides, however, that the 120-day period may not be extended beyond eighteen months and the 180-day period may not be extended beyond twenty months. After the exclusivity period has expired, a creditor or the trustee may file a competing plan.

A plan of reorganization must divide creditors' claims and shareholders' interests into classes, specify how each class will be treated, deal with claims within each class equally, and provide adequate means for implementing the plan. After a plan has been filed, the plan and a written disclosure statement approved by the court as containing adequate information must be transmitted to each holder of a claim before seeking acceptance or rejection of the plan. Adequate information is that which would enable a hypothetical, reasonable investor to make an informed judgment about the plan. Section 1125.

38-4d ACCEPTANCE OF PLAN

Each class of claims and interests has the opportunity to accept or reject the proposed plan. To be accepted by a class of claims, a plan must be accepted by creditors that hold at least two-thirds in amount and more than one-half in number of the allowed claims of such class that actually voted on the plan. Acceptance of a plan by a class of interests, such as shareholders, requires acceptance by holders of at least two-thirds in

amount of the allowed interests of such class that actually voted on the plan.

A class that is not impaired under a plan is conclusively presumed to have accepted the plan. Basically, a class is unimpaired if the plan leaves unaltered the legal, equitable, and contractual rights to which the holder of such claim or interest is entitled. Section 1124. A class that will receive no distribution under a plan is deemed not to have accepted the plan.

38-4e CONFIRMATION OF PLAN

Before a plan is binding on any parties, the court, after notice and a hearing, must confirm such plan. To be confirmed, the plan must meet all the requirements of Section 1129 of the Bankruptcy Code. The most important of these requirements are the following.

GOOD FAITH The plan must have been proposed in good faith and not by any means forbidden by law. Section 1129(a)(3).

FEASIBILITY The court must find that confirmation of the plan is not likely to be followed by the debtor's liquidation or by its need for further financial reorganization. Section 1129(a)(11).

CASH PAYMENTS Unless the claim holder agrees otherwise, certain priority creditors must have their allowed claims paid in full in cash immediately or, in some instances, on a deferred basis. Section 1129(a)(9). These priority claims include the expenses of administration, gap creditors, claims for wages and salaries, and employee benefits and consumer deposits.

In the case of a debtor who is an individual, the 2005 Act requires that the plan provide for payments to be made out of the debtor's future earnings from personal services or other future income. It also imposes an additional requirement for confirmation if an unsecured creditor objects to confirmation of the plan: the value of property distributed on account of that claim must not be less than (1) the amount of that claim or (2) the debtor's projected disposable income to be received during the longer of (a) the five-year period beginning on the first payment due date or (b) the plan's term. Section 1129(a)(15).

ACCEPTANCE BY CREDITORS To be confirmed, the plan must be accepted by at least *one* class of claims, and with respect to *each* class, each holder must either accept the plan or receive not less than the amount he would have received under Chapter 7. In addition, each class must accept the plan or be unimpaired by it. Nonetheless, under certain circumstances, the court may confirm a plan that is not accepted by all impaired classes, upon determining that the plan does not discriminate unfairly and that it is fair and equitable. Section 1129(b)(1). Under these circumstances, a class of claims or interests may, despite objections by that class, be subjected to the provisions of a plan.

"Fair and equitable" with respect to secured creditors requires that they (1) retain their security interest and receive deferred cash payments, the present value of which is at least equal to their claims; (2) receive a lien on the proceeds of the sale of their collateral if the collateral is sold free and clear of their lien; or (3) realize the "indubitable equivalent" of their claims. Fair and equitable with respect to unsecured creditors means that such creditors are to receive property of value equivalent to the full amount of their claim or that no junior claim or interest is to receive anything. With respect to a class of interests, a plan is fair and equitable if the holders receive full value or if no junior interest receives anything at all.

♦ *See Case 38-2*

38-4f EFFECT OF CONFIRMATION

Once confirmed, the plan governs the debtor's performance obligations. The plan binds the debtor and any creditor, equity security holder, or general partner of the debtor. Upon the entry of a final decree closing the proceedings, a debtor that is *not* an individual is discharged from all of its debts and liabilities that arose before the date the plan was confirmed, except as otherwise provided in the plan, the order of confirmation, or the Bankruptcy Code. Section 1141. Unlike under Chapter 7, under Chapter 11, partnerships and corporations may receive a discharge unless the plan calls for the liquidation of the business entity's property and termination of its business. The 2005 Act excludes from the discharge of any corporate debtor any debt (1) owed to the government as a result of fraud or (2) arising from a fraudulent tax return or willful evasion of taxes.

An *individual* debtor is not discharged until all plan payments have been made. However, if the debtor fails to make all payments, the court may, after a hearing, grant a "hardship discharge" if the value of property actually distributed is not less than what the creditors would have received under Chapter 7 and modification of the plan is not practicable. A discharge under Chapter 11 does not discharge an *individual* debtor from debts that are not dischargeable under Section 523.

If a confirmation order is obtained through fraud, the court can revoke the confirmation order or discharge at any time before 180 days after the date of the confirmation order. Section 1144.

38-5 Adjustment of Debts of Individuals—Chapter 13

The purpose of Chapter 13 of the Bankruptcy Code is to permit an individual debtor with regular income to file a repayment plan that, if confirmed by the court, will discharge him from almost all of his debts upon completion of the payments under the plan. If, as occurs in many cases, the debtor does not make the required payments under the plan, the case will be converted to Chapter 7 or dismissed.

38-5a PROCEEDINGS

Chapter 13 provides a procedure for adjusting the debts of an individual with regular income who owes liquidated, unsecured debts of less than $419,275 and secured debts of less than $1,257,850. Chapter 13 also may be used by debtors who do not qualify for Chapter 7 relief under the means test. Sole proprietorships meeting these debt limitations are also eligible; partnerships and corporations are not eligible. Only a voluntary petition may initiate a case under Chapter 13, and a trustee is appointed in every Chapter 13 case. Among other duties, the trustee collects payments from the debtor and makes distributions to creditors. Property of the estate in Chapter 13 includes not only the nonexempt property the debtor owned at the time of her bankruptcy petition but also wages the debtor earned and property the debtor acquired *after* the Chapter 13 filing. Section 1306.

38-5b CONVERSION OR DISMISSAL

The debtor may convert a case under Chapter 13 to Chapter 7. On request of the debtor, if the case has not been previously converted from Chapter 7 or Chapter 11, the court shall dismiss a case under Chapter 13. On request of a party in interest or the U.S. trustee and after notice and a hearing, the court may convert a case under Chapter 13 to Chapter 7 *or* may dismiss a case under Chapter 13, whichever is in the best interests of creditors and the estate, for cause, including (1) unreasonable delay by the debtor, (2) failure of the debtor to file a plan timely, (3) denial of confirmation of a plan, or (4) material default by the debtor with respect to a term of a confirmed plan. Before the confirmation of a plan, on request of a party in interest or the U.S. trustee and after notice and a hearing, the court may convert a case under Chapter 13 to Chapter 11. Nonetheless, a case may *not* be converted to another chapter unless the debtor may be a debtor under that chapter. Section 1307.

♦ *See Case 38-3*

38-5c THE PLAN

The debtor files the plan and may modify it at any time before confirmation. The plan must meet three requirements under Section 1322:

1. It must require the debtor to submit all or any portion of her future earnings or income, as is necessary for the execution of the plan, to the trustee's supervision and control.

2. It must provide for full payment on a deferred basis of all claims entitled to a priority unless a holder of a claim agrees to a different treatment of such claim.

3. If the plan classifies claims, it must provide the same treatment for each claim in the same class.

In addition, the plan may modify the rights of unsecured and secured creditors, except those secured only by a security interest in the debtor's principal residence. The plan also may provide for payments on any unsecured claim to be made concurrently with payments on any secured claim. If the debtor's net current monthly income is equal to or greater than the State median income, the plan may not provide for payments over a period longer than five years. If the debtor's net current monthly income is less than the State median income, the plan may not provide for payments over a period longer than three years, unless the court approves, for cause, a longer period not to exceed five years.

38-5d CONFIRMATION OF PLAN

To be confirmed by the court, the plan must meet certain requirements. Section 1325. First, the filing of the case must have been in good faith, and the plan must comply with applicable law and be proposed in good faith. Second, the present value of the property to be distributed to unsecured creditors must not be less than the amount they would receive under Chapter 7. Third, the secured creditors must accept the plan, the plan must provide that the debtor will surrender the collateral to the secured creditors, or the plan must permit the secured creditors to retain their security interest and the present value of the property to be distributed to them is not less than the allowed amount of their claim. Fourth, the debtor must be able to make all payments and comply with the plan. Fifth, if the trustee or the holder of an unsecured claim objects to the plan's confirmation, then the plan must either provide for payments the present value of which is not less than the amount of that claim or provide that all of the debtor's disposable income for three years be paid to unsecured creditors under the plan. If, however, the debtor's net current monthly income is equal to or greater than the State median income, the debtor's disposable income for not less than five years must be committed to pay unsecured creditors. For purposes of this provision, *disposable income* means current monthly income received by the debtor that is not reasonably necessary for the maintenance or support of the debtor or a dependent of the debtor, for domestic support obligations, or, if the debtor is engaged in business, for the payment of expenditures necessary for continuing, preserving, and operating the business. Sixth, if a debtor is required by judicial or administrative order or statute to pay a domestic support obligation, then the debtor must pay all such obligations that became payable after the filing.

◆ *See Case 38-4*

38-5e EFFECT OF CONFIRMATION

The provisions of a confirmed plan bind the debtor and all of her creditors. The confirmation of a plan vests in the debtor all property of the estate free and clear of any creditor's claim or interest for which the plan provides, except as otherwise provided in the plan or in the order confirming the plan. Section 1327. A plan may be modified after confirmation at the request of the debtor, the trustee, or a holder of an unsecured claim. The modification may increase or decrease the amount of payments on claims of a particular class or extend or reduce the time for such payments. Section 1329.

38-5f DISCHARGE

Before the 2005 Act, the discharge under Chapter 13 was considerably more extensive than that granted under Chapter 7. The 2005 Act, however, made the discharge of debts under Chapter 13 less extensive than it was previously. As a result, Chapter 13 discharges only a few types of debts that are not also discharged under Chapter 7.

After a debtor completes all payments under the plan and of certain postpetition domestic support obligations, the court will grant him a discharge of all debts provided for by the plan, with the exception of nondischargeable debts for (1) unfiled, late-filed, and fraudulent tax returns; (2) legal liabilities resulting from obtaining money, property, or services by false pretenses, false representations, or actual fraud; (3) legal liability for willful *or* malicious conduct that caused personal injury to an individual; (4) domestic support obligations; (5) debts not scheduled unless the creditor knew of the bankruptcy; (6) debts the debtor created by fraud or embezzlement while acting in a fiduciary capacity; (7) most student loans; (8) consumer debts for luxury goods or services in excess of $725 per creditor if incurred by an individual debtor on or within ninety days before the order for relief; (9) cash advances aggregating more than $1,000 obtained by an individual debtor under an open-ended credit plan within seventy days before the order for relief; (10) liability for death or personal injury based upon the debtor's operation of a motor vehicle, vessel, or aircraft while legally intoxicated; (11) restitution or criminal fine included in a sentence for a criminal conviction; and (12) certain long-term obligations on which payments extend beyond the term of the plan.

Even if the debtor fails to make all payments, the court may, after a hearing, grant a "hardship discharge" if the debtor's failure is due to circumstances for which the debtor is not justly accountable, the value of property actually distributed is not less than what the creditors would have received under Chapter 7, and modification of the plan is impracticable. Section 1328(b). This discharge is subject, however, to the same exceptions for nondischargeable debts as a discharge under Chapter 7.

FIGURE 38-2 **Comparison of Bankruptcy Proceedings**

	Chapter 7	Chapter 11	Chapter 12	Chapter 13
Objective	Liquidation	Reorganization	Adjustment	Adjustment
Eligible Debtors	Most debtors	Most debtors, including railroads	Family farmer who meets certain debt limitations	Individual with regular income who meets certain debt limitations
Type of Petition	Voluntary or involuntary	Voluntary or involuntary	Voluntary	Voluntary
Trustee	Usually selected by creditors; otherwise appointed	Only if court orders appointment for cause; creditors then may select trustee	Appointed	Appointed

The 2005 Act denies a discharge under Chapter 13 to a debtor who has received a discharge (1) in a prior Chapter 7 or Chapter 11 case filed during the four-year period preceding the filing of the current Chapter 13 case or (2) in a prior Chapter 13 case filed during the two-year period preceding the date of filing the current Chapter 13 case. It also denies a discharge to a debtor who fails to complete a personal financial management course. This provision, however, does not apply if the debtor resides in a district for which the U.S. trustee or the bankruptcy administrator has determined that the approved instructional courses are not adequate to serve the additional individuals who would be required to complete these required instructional courses. Sections 1328(f), (g).

◆ SEE FIGURE 38-2: *Comparison of Bankruptcy Proceedings*

CREDITORS' RIGHTS AND DEBTOR'S RELIEF OUTSIDE OF BANKRUPTCY

The rights and remedies of debtors and creditors outside of bankruptcy are governed mainly by State law. Because of the expense and notoriety associated with bankruptcy, resolving claims outside a bankruptcy proceeding is often in the best interests of both debtor and creditor. Accordingly, bankruptcy usually is considered a last resort.

The rights and remedies of creditors outside bankruptcy are varied. The first part of this section examines the basic right of all creditors to pursue their overdue claims to judgment and to satisfy that judgment out of property belonging to the debtor. Other rights and remedies are discussed elsewhere in this book. The rights under Article 2 of the UCC of an unpaid credit seller to reclaim the goods sold are covered in *Chapter 25*. The right of a secured creditor to enforce a security interest in personal property is the subject of *Chapter 37*. Likewise, the right of a creditor to foreclose a mortgage on real property is discussed in *Chapter 49*. In addition, the right of a creditor to proceed against a surety on the debt is addressed in *Chapter 37*.

At the same time, the law attempts to protect debtors against overreaching by creditors. This goal has been pursued by a number of means. States have enacted usury laws, as discussed in *Chapter 13*. The Federal Trade Commission has limited the rights of a holder in due course against consumer debtors, as explained in *Chapter 27*. Congress has prohibited abusive, deceptive, and unfair debt collection practices employed by debt collection agencies, as discussed in *Chapter 41*. That chapter also covers other legal protection offered to *consumer* debtors. The second part of this section describes the various forms of nonbankruptcy compromises that provide relief to debtors who have become overextended and who are unable to pay all of their creditors.

38-6 Creditors' Rights

When a debtor fails to pay a debt, the creditor may file suit to collect the debt owed. The objective is to obtain a judgment against the debtor and ultimately to collect on that judgment.

38-6a PREJUDGMENT REMEDIES

Because litigation takes time, a creditor attempting to collect on a claim through the judicial process will almost always experience delay in obtaining judgment. To prevent the debtor from meanwhile disposing of his assets, the creditor may use, when available, certain prejudgment remedies. The most important of these is **attachment**, the process of seizing property through a writ, summons, or other judicial order, and bringing the property into the custody of the court to secure satisfaction of the judgment ultimately to be entered in the action. At common law, the main objective of attachment was to coerce the defendant debtor into appearing in court; today the writ of attachment is statutory and is used primarily to seize the debtor's property in the event a judgment is rendered. Most States limit attachment to specified grounds and provide the debtor an opportunity for a hearing before a judge prior to the issuance of a writ of execution. Generally, attachment is limited to situations in which (1) the defendant cannot be personally served, (2) the claim is based upon fraud or the equivalent, or (3) the defendant has transferred or is likely to transfer his property. In addition, the plaintiff generally must post a bond to compensate the defendant for loss should the plaintiff not prevail in the cause of action.

Similar in purpose is the remedy of prejudgment **garnishment**, which is a statutory proceeding directed at a third person who owes a debt to the debtor or who has property belonging to the debtor. Garnishment is most commonly used against the employer of the debtor and the bank in which the debtor has a savings or checking account. Property garnished remains in the hands of the third party pending the outcome of the suit. For example, Calvin brings an action against Daisy to collect a debt that is past due. Alvin has property belonging to Daisy. Calvin might garnish this property so that if he is successful in his action against Daisy, his judgment could be satisfied out of that property held by Alvin. If Alvin no longer had the property when Calvin obtained judgment, Calvin could recover from Alvin.

38-6b POSTJUDGMENT REMEDIES

If the debtor still has not paid the claim, the creditor may proceed to trial and try to obtain a court judgment against the debtor. Though necessary, obtaining a judgment is only the first step in collecting the debt. If the debtor does not voluntarily pay the judgment, the creditor will have to take additional steps to collect on it. These steps are called "post judgment remedies."

First, the judgment creditor will have the court clerk issue a **writ of execution** demanding payment of the judgment, which is served by the sheriff upon the defendant/debtor. Upon return of the writ "unsatisfied" (unpaid), the judgment creditor may post bond or other security and order a levy on and sale of specified nonexempt property belonging to the defendant/debtor, which is then seized by the sheriff, advertised for sale, and sold at public sale under the writ of execution.

The writ of execution is limited to nonexempt property of the debtor. All States restrict creditors from recourse to certain property, the type and amount of which varies greatly from State to State.

If the proceeds of the sale do not produce funds sufficient to pay the judgment, the creditor may institute a **supplementary proceeding** in an attempt to locate money or other property belonging to the defendant. He also may proceed by **garnishment** against the debtor's employer or against a bank in which the debtor has an account. As discussed in *Chapter 41*, State and Federal statutes contain exemption provisions that limit the amount of wages subject to garnishment.

38-7 Debtor's Relief

The creditor's pursuit of a judgment on which she can collect and the debtor's quest for relief inherently give rise to conflicts among (1) the right of diligent creditors to pursue their claims to judgment and to satisfy their judgments by sale of property of the debtor, (2) the right of unsecured creditors who have refrained from suing the debtor, and (3) the social policy of affording relief to a debtor who has contracted debts beyond his ability to pay and who therefore may bear a lifetime burden.

Various nonbankruptcy compromises provide relief to debtors. Certain compromises, such as those offered by credit agencies and adjustment bureaus, are relatively informal. Some, such as compositions and assignments, are founded in common law and involve simple contract and trust principles; others, such as statutory assignments, are statutory. Some, such as equity receiverships, involve the intervention of a court and its officers, while others do not.

38-7a COMPOSITIONS

A common law or nonstatutory **composition** (or "workout") is an ordinary contract or agreement between the debtor and two or more of her creditors, under which the creditors receive pro *rata* a part of their claims and the debtor is discharged from the balance of the claims. A composition is the State law analogue of Chapter 11 of the Bankruptcy Act. As a contract, it requires contractual formalities, such as offer, acceptance, and consideration. For example, debtor D, owing debts of $5,000 to A, $2,000 to B, and $1,000 to C, offers to settle these claims by paying a total of $4,000 to A, B, and C. If A, B, and C accept the offer, a composition results, with A receiving $2,500, B $1,000, and C $500. The consideration for the promise of A to forgive the balance of his claim consists of the promises of B and C to forgive the balance of their claims. By avoiding a race among themselves to obtain the debtor's limited assets, all the creditors benefit.

Note, however, that the debtor in a composition is discharged from liability only regarding the claims of those creditors who voluntarily consent to the composition. If in the previous illustration C had refused to accept the offer of composition and had refused to take the $500, he could attempt to collect his full $1,000 claim. Likewise, if D owed additional debts to X, Y, and Z, these creditors would not be bound by the agreement between D and A, B, and C. Another disadvantage of the composition is the fact that any creditor can attach the assets of the debtor during the negotiation period that usually precedes the execution of the composition agreement. For instance, once D advised A, B, and C that he was offering to compose the claims, any one of the creditors could seize D's property.

A variation of the composition is an extension agreement, developed by the debtor and two or more of her creditors, that provides an extended period of time for payment of her debts either in full or proportionately reduced.

38-7b ASSIGNMENTS FOR BENEFIT OF CREDITORS

A common law or nonstatutory assignment for the benefit of creditors, sometimes called a general assignment, is a voluntary transfer by the debtor of his property to a trustee who applies the property to the payment of all the debtor's debts. For instance, debtor D transfers title to his property to trustee T, who converts the property into money and pays it to all of the creditors on a *pro rata* basis. An assignment for the benefit of creditors is a State law analogue of Chapter 7 of the Bankruptcy Act.

In most States, statutes now govern assignments for the benefit of creditors. These statutes typically require recording the assignment, filing schedules of assets and liabilities, and providing notice to the creditors. Almost all of the statutes require that all creditors be treated equally except those with liens or statutorily created priorities.

The advantages of an assignment over a composition are that it protects the debtor's assets from attachment and execution and that it halts diligent creditors in their race to attach. An assignment does not require the creditors' consent, and payment by the trustee of part of the claims does not discharge the debtor from the balance of them. Thus, in the previous example, even after T pays A $2,500, B $1,000, and C $500 (and makes appropriate payments to all other creditors), A, B, and C and the other creditors still may attempt to collect the balance of their claims. Moreover, an assignment for the benefit of creditors is a ground for sustaining an involuntary petition for bankruptcy.

Because assignments benefit creditors by protecting the debtor's assets from attachment, some statutory enactments have endeavored to combine the idea of the assignment with a corresponding benefit that would discharge the debtor from the balance of his debts. But because the U.S. Constitution prohibits a State from impairing the contractual obligation between private citizens, it is impossible for a State to force all creditors to discharge a debtor upon a *pro rata* distribution of assets, although, as previously discussed, the Federal government *does* have such power and exercises it in the Bankruptcy Code. Accordingly, the States generally have enacted assignment statutes permitting the debtor to obtain *voluntary* releases of the balance of claims from creditors who accept partial payments, thus combining the advantages of common law compositions and assignments.

38-7c EQUITY RECEIVERSHIPS

One of the oldest remedies in equity is the appointment of a receiver by the court. The receiver is a disinterested person who collects and preserves the debtor's assets and income and disposes of them at the direction of the court which appointed her. The court may instruct her (1) to liquidate the assets by public or private sale, (2) to operate the business as a going concern temporarily, or (3) to conserve the assets until final disposition of the matter before the court.

The court will appoint a receiver upon the petition (1) of a secured creditor seeking foreclosure of his security, (2) of a judgment creditor who has exhausted legal remedies to satisfy the judgment, or (3) of a shareholder of a corporate debtor whose assets will likely be dissipated by fraud or mismanagement. The appointment of a receiver always rests within the sound discretion of the court. Insolvency, in the equity sense of inability by the debtor to pay his debts as they mature, is one of the factors the court considers in appointing a receiver.

C H A P T E R   S U M M A R Y

FEDERAL BANKRUPTCY LAW

CASE ADMINISTRATION—CHAPTER 3	**Commencement of the Case** the filing of a voluntary or involuntary petition begins jurisdiction of the bankruptcy court • *Voluntary Petitions* available to any eligible debtor even if solvent • *Involuntary Petitions* may be filed only under Chapter 7 or Chapter 11 if the debtor is generally not paying his debts as they become due **Dismissal** the court may dismiss a case for cause after notice and a hearing; under Chapter 13, the debtor has an absolute right to have his case dismissed **Automatic Stay** prevents attempts by creditors to recover claims against the debtor **Trustee** responsible for collecting, liquidating, and distributing the debtor's estate **Meeting of Creditors** debtor must appear and submit to an examination of her financial situation

CREDITORS, THE DEBTOR, AND THE ESTATE—CHAPTER 5	**Creditor** any entity that has a claim against the debtor • **Claim** a right to payment • **Lien** charge or interest in property to secure payment of a debt or performance of an obligation • **Secured Claim** claim with a lien on property of the debtor • **Unsecured Claim** portion of a claim that exceeds the value of any property securing that claim • **Priority of Claims** the right of certain claims to be paid before claims of lesser rank **Debtors** • **Debtor's Duties** the debtor must file specified information, cooperate with the trustee, and surrender all property of the estate • **Debtor's Exemptions** determined by State or Federal law, depending upon the State • **Discharge** relief from liability for all debts except those the Bankruptcy Code specifies as not dischargeable **The Estate** all legal and equitable interests of the debtor in nonexempt property and those assets a trustee recovers from transferees under the following powers • **Trustee as Lien Creditor** trustee gains the rights and powers of creditor with judicial lien (an interest in property, obtained by court action, to secure payment of a debt) • **Voidable Preferences** Bankruptcy Code invalidates certain preferential transfers made before the date of bankruptcy from the debtor to favored creditors • **Fraudulent Transfers** trustee may avoid (1) fraudulent transfers made on or within two years before the date of bankruptcy and (2) transfers of the debtor's property if the transfer is voidable under State law by a creditor with an allowable, unsecured claim • **Statutory Liens** trustee may avoid statutory liens which first become effective on insolvency, are not perfected at commencement of case, or are for rent
LIQUIDATION—CHAPTER 7	**Purpose** to distribute equitably the debtor's nonexempt assets and usually to discharge all dischargeable debts of the debtor **Proceedings** apply to most debtors **Conversion** a Chapter 7 case may be voluntarily converted to Chapter 11 or Chapter 13; a Chapter 7 case may be involuntarily converted by the court to Chapter 11 **Dismissal** the court may dismiss a case on general grounds *and* in a case filed by an individual debtor based on a means test **Distribution of the Estate** in the following order: (1) secured creditors, (2) creditors entitled to a priority, (3) unsecured creditors, and (4) the debtor **Discharge** of dischargeable debts granted by the court unless the debtor has committed an offense under the Bankruptcy Code or has received a discharge (1) within eight years under Chapter 7 or Chapter 11 or (2) subject to exceptions within six years under Chapter 13
REORGANIZATION—CHAPTER 11	**Purpose** to preserve a distressed enterprise's value as a going concern and to pay creditors over time **Proceedings** debtor usually remains in possession of the property of the estate **Conversion or Dismissal** a Chapter 11 case may be voluntarily or involuntarily dismissed or converted to Chapter 7; a Chapter 11 case may be voluntarily converted to Chapter 13 **Acceptance of Plan** requires a specified proportion of creditors to approve the plan **Confirmation of Plan** requires (1) good faith, (2) feasibility, (3) cash payments to certain priority creditors, and (4) usually acceptance by creditors **Effect of Confirmation** binds the debtor and creditors and discharges the debtor
ADJUSTMENT OF DEBTS OF INDIVIDUALS—CHAPTER 13	**Purpose** to permit an individual debtor with regular income to file a repayment plan that will discharge her from most debts

Conversion or Dismissal a Chapter 13 case may be voluntarily or involuntarily dismissed or converted to Chapter 7 or Chapter 11

Confirmation of Plan requires (1) good faith; (2) that the present value of property distributed to unsecured creditors not be less than the amount that would be paid them under Chapter 7; (3) that secured creditors accept the plan, keep their collateral, or retain their security interest and that the present value of the property to be distributed to them is not less than the allowed amount of their claim; and (4) that the debtor be able to make all payments and comply with the plan

Discharge after a debtor completes all payments under the plan except for specified nondischargeable debts

CREDITORS' RIGHTS AND DEBTOR'S RELIEF OUTSIDE OF BANKRUPTCY

CREDITORS' RIGHTS

Prejudgment Remedies include attachment and garnishment

Postjudgment Remedies include writ of execution and garnishment

DEBTOR'S RELIEF

Compositions agreement between debtor and two or more of her creditors that each will take a portion of his claim as full payment

Assignment for Benefit of Creditors voluntary transfer by the debtor of his property to a trustee, who applies the property to the payment of all the debtor's debts

Equity Receivership receiver is a disinterested person appointed by the court to collect and preserve the debtor's assets and income and to dispose of them at the direction of the court

C A S E S

CASE 38-1

Discharge/Fraudulent Transfers

HUSKY INTERNATIONAL ELECTRONICS, INC., v. RITZ

Supreme Court of the United States, 2016
578 U.S. ____, 136 S.Ct. 1581, 194 L.Ed.2d 655

Sotomayor, J.

The Bankruptcy Code prohibits debtors from discharging debts "obtained by. . . false pretenses, a false representation, or actual fraud." 11 U. S. C. §523(a)(2)(A). The Fifth Circuit held that a debt is "obtained by. . . actual fraud" only if the debtor's fraud involves a false representation to a creditor. That ruling deepened an existing split among the Circuits over whether "actual fraud" requires a false representation or whether it encompasses other traditional forms of fraud that can be accomplished without a false representation, such as a fraudulent conveyance of property made to evade payment to creditors. We granted certiorari to resolve that split and now reverse.

Husky International Electronics, Inc., is a Colorado-based supplier of components used in electronic devices. Between 2003 and 2007, Husky sold its products to Chrysalis Manufacturing Corp., and Chrysalis incurred a debt to Husky of $163,999.38. During the same period, respondent Daniel Lee Ritz, Jr., served as a director of Chrysalis and owned at least 30% of Chrysalis' common stock.

All parties agree that between 2006 and 2007, Ritz drained Chrysalis of assets it could have used to pay its debts to creditors like Husky by transferring large sums of Chrysalis' funds to other entities Ritz controlled. For instance—and Ritz' actions were by no means limited to these examples—Ritz transferred $52,600 to CapNet Risk Management, Inc., a company he owned in full; $121,831 to CapNet Securities Corp., a company in which he owned an 85% interest; and $99,386.90 to Dynalyst Manufacturing Corp., a company in which he owned a 25% interest.

In May 2009, Husky filed a lawsuit against Ritz seeking to hold him personally responsible for Chrysalis' $163,999.38 debt. Husky argued that Ritz' intercompany transfer scheme was "actual fraud" for purposes of a Texas law that allows creditors to hold shareholders responsible for corporate debt. [Citation.] In December 2009, Ritz filed for Chapter 7 bankruptcy in the United States Bankruptcy Court for the Southern District of Texas. Husky then initiated an adversarial proceeding in Ritz' bankruptcy case again seeking to hold Ritz personally liable for Chrysalis' debt. Husky also contended that Ritz could not discharge that debt in bankruptcy because the same intercompany-transfer scheme constituted "actual fraud" under 11 U. S. C. §523(a)(2)(A)'s exemption to discharge.

The District Court held that Ritz was personally liable for the debt under Texas law, but that the debt was not "obtained by . . . actual fraud" under §523(a)(2)(A) and could be discharged in his bankruptcy.

The Fifth Circuit affirmed. It did not address whether Ritz was responsible for Chrysalis' debt under Texas law because it agreed with the District Court that Ritz did not commit "actual fraud" under §523(a)(2)(A). Before the Fifth Circuit, Husky argued that Ritz' asset-transfer scheme was effectuated through a series of fraudulent conveyances—or transfers intended to obstruct the collection of debt. And, Husky said, such transfers are a recognizable form of "actual fraud." The Fifth Circuit disagreed, holding that a necessary element of "actual fraud" is a misrepresentation from the debtor to the creditor, as when a person applying for credit adds an extra zero to her income or falsifies her employment history. [Citation.] In transferring Chrysalis' assets, Ritz may have hindered Husky's ability to recover its debt, but the Fifth Circuit found that he did not make any false representations to Husky regarding those assets or the transfers and therefore did not commit "actual fraud."

We reverse. The term "actual fraud" in §523(a)(2)(A) encompasses forms of fraud, like fraudulent conveyance schemes, that can be effected without a false representation.

Before 1978, the Bankruptcy Code prohibited debtors from discharging debts obtained by "false pretenses or false representations." [Citation.] In the Bankruptcy Reform Act of 1978, Congress added "actual fraud" to that list. [Citation.] The prohibition now reads: "A discharge under [Chapters 7, 11, 12, or 13] of this title does not discharge an individual debtor from any debt . . . for money, property, services, or an extension, renewal, or refinancing of credit, to the extent obtained by . . . false pretenses, a false representation, or actual fraud." §523(a)(2)(A).

When "'Congress acts to amend a statute, we presume it intends its amendment to have real and substantial effect.'" [Citation.] It is therefore sensible to start with the presumption that Congress did not intend "actual fraud" to mean the same thing as "a false representation," as the Fifth Circuit's holding suggests.* * *

This Court has historically construed the terms in §523(a)(2)(A) to contain the "elements that the common law has defined them to include." [Citation.] "Actual fraud" has two parts: actual and fraud. The word "actual" has a simple meaning in the context of common-law fraud: It denotes any fraud that "involv[es] moral turpitude or intentional wrong." [Citation.] "Actual" fraud stands in contrast to "implied" fraud or fraud "in law," which describe acts of deception that "may exist without the imputation of bad faith or immorality." [Citation.] * * *

* * *

Equally important, the common law also indicates that fraudulent conveyances, although a "fraud," do not require a misrepresentation from a debtor to a creditor. As a basic point, fraudulent conveyances are not an inducement-based fraud. Fraudulent conveyances typically involve "a transfer to a close relative, a secret transfer, a transfer of title without transfer of possession, or grossly inadequate consideration." [Citations.] In such cases, the fraudulent conduct is not in dishonestly inducing a creditor to extend a debt. It is in the acts of concealment and hindrance. In the fraudulent-conveyance context, therefore, the opportunities for a false representation from the debtor to the creditor are limited. The debtor may have the opportunity to put forward a false representation if the creditor inquires into the whereabouts of the debtor's assets, but that could hardly be considered a defining feature of this kind of fraud.

Relatedly, * * * both the debtor and the recipient of the conveyed assets were liable for fraud even though the recipient of a fraudulent conveyance of course made no representation, true or false, to the debtor's creditor. * * * That principle also underscores the point that a false representation has never been a required element of "actual fraud," and we decline to adopt it as one today.

* * *

* * * Because we must give the phrase "actual fraud" in §523(a)(2)(A) the meaning it has long held, we interpret "actual fraud" to encompass fraudulent conveyance schemes, even when those schemes do not involve a false representation. We therefore reverse the judgment of the Fifth Circuit and remand the case for further proceedings consistent with this opinion.

Confirmation of Chapter 11 Plan
RADLAX GATEWAY HOTEL, LLC v. AMALGAMATED BANK

Supreme Court of the United States, 2012
566 U.S. 639, 132 S.Ct. 2065, 182 L.Ed.2d 967

Scalia, J.

[In 2007, RadLAX Gateway Hotel, LLC and RadLAX Gateway Deck, LLC (debtors) purchased the Radisson Hotel at Los Angeles International Airport, together with an adjacent lot on which the debtors planned to build a parking structure. To finance the purchase, the renovation of the hotel, and construction of the parking structure, the debtors obtained a $142 million loan from Longview Ultra Construction Loan Investment Fund, for which Amalgamated Bank (creditor or Bank) served as trustee. The lenders obtained a blanket lien on all of the debtors' assets to secure the loan.

Within two years, the debtors had run out of funds and were forced to stop construction. By August 2009, they owed more than $120 million on the loan, with over $1 million in interest accruing every month and no prospect for obtaining additional funds to complete the project. Both debtors filed voluntary petitions under Chapter 11 of the Bankruptcy Code.

Pursuant to Section 1129(b)(2)(A) of the Bankruptcy Code, the debtors sought to confirm a "cramdown" bankruptcy plan over the Bank's objection. That plan proposed selling substantially all of the debtors' property at an auction and using the sale proceeds to repay the Bank. Under the debtors' proposed auction procedures, however, the Bank would not be permitted to bid for the property using the debt it was owed to offset the purchase price, a practice known as "credit-bidding." Instead, the Bank would be forced to bid cash. The Bankruptcy Court denied the debtors' request, concluding that the auction procedures did not comply with the Bankruptcy Code's requirements for cramdown plans. The Seventh Circuit affirmed, holding that Section 1129(b)(2)(A) does not permit debtors to sell an encumbered asset free and clear of a lien without permitting the lienholder to credit-bid.]

A Chapter 11 bankruptcy is implemented according to a "plan," typically proposed by the debtor, which divides claims against the debtor into separate "classes" and specifies the treatment each class will receive. Generally, a bankruptcy court may confirm a Chapter 11 plan only if each class of creditors affected by the plan consents. Section 1129(b) creates an exception to that general rule, permitting confirmation of nonconsensual plans—commonly known as "cramdown" plans—if "the plan does not discriminate unfairly, and is fair and equitable, with respect to each class of claims or interests that is impaired under, and has not accepted, the plan." Section 1129(b)(2)(A) * * * establishes criteria for determining whether a cramdown plan is "fair and equitable" with respect to secured claims like the Bank's.

* * *

A Chapter 11 plan confirmed over the objection of a "class of secured claims" must meet one of three requirements in order to be deemed "fair and equitable" with respect to the nonconsenting creditor's claim. The plan must provide:

(i)(I) that the holders of such claims retain the liens securing such claims, whether the property subject to such liens is retained by the debtor or transferred to another entity, to the extent of the allowed amount of such claims; and (II) that each holder of a claim of such class receive on account of such claim deferred cash payments totaling at least the allowed amount of such claim, of a value, as of the effective date of the plan, of at least the value of such holder's interest in the estate's interest in such property;

(ii) for the sale, subject to section 363(k) of this title, of any property that is subject to the liens securing such claims, free and clear of such liens, with such liens to attach to the proceeds of such sale, and the treatment of such liens on proceeds under clause (i) or (iii) of this subparagraph; or

(iii) for the realization by such holders of the indubitable equivalent of such claims." 11 U.C. §1129(b)(2)(A).

Under clause (i), the secured creditor retains its lien on the property and receives deferred cash payments. Under clause (ii), the property is sold free and clear of the lien, "subject to section 363(k)," and the creditor receives a lien on the proceeds of the sale. Section 363(k), in turn, provides that "unless the court for cause orders otherwise the holder of such claim may bid at such sale, and, if the holder of such claim purchases such property, such holder may offset such claim against the purchase price of such property"—*i.e.*, the creditor may credit-bid at the sale, up to the amount of its claim. Finally, under clause (iii), the plan provides the secured creditor with the "indubitable equivalent" of its claim.

The debtors in this case have proposed to sell their property free and clear of the Bank's liens, and to repay the Bank using the sale proceeds—precisely, it would seem, the disposition contemplated by clause (ii). Yet since the debtors' proposed auction procedures do not permit the Bank to credit-bid, the proposed sale cannot satisfy the requirements of clause (ii). Recognizing this problem, the debtors instead seek plan confirmation pursuant to clause (iii), which—unlike clause (ii)—does not expressly foreclose the possibility of a sale without credit-bidding. According to the debtors, their plan can satisfy clause (iii) by ultimately providing the Bank with the "indubitable equivalent" of its secured claim, in the form of cash generated by the auction.

We find the debtors' reading of §1129(b)(2)(A)—under which clause (iii) permits precisely what clause (ii) proscribes—to be hyperliteral and contrary to common sense. * * *

* * *

Here, clause (ii) is a detailed provision that spells out the requirements for selling collateral free of liens, while clause (iii) is a broadly worded provision that says nothing about such a sale. The general/specific canon explains that the "general language" of clause (iii), "although broad enough to include it, will not be held to apply to a matter specifically dealt with" in clause (ii). [Citation.]

* * * The structure here suggests * * * that (i) is the rule for plans under which the creditor's lien remains on the property, (ii) is the rule for plans under which the property is sold free and clear of the creditor's lien, and (iii) is a residual provision covering dispositions under all other plans—for example, one under which the creditor receives the property itself, the "indubitable equivalent" of its secured claim. Thus, debtors may not sell their property free of liens under §1129(b)(2)(A) without allowing lienholders to credit-bid, as required by clause (ii).

* * *

* * * Because the RadLAX debtors may not obtain confirmation of a Chapter 11 cramdown plan that provides for the sale of collateral free and clear of the Bank's lien, but does not permit the Bank to credit-bid at the sale, we affirm the judgment of the Court of Appeals.

Conversion of Chapter 13 Case
HARRIS v. VIEGELAHN

Supreme Court of the United States, 2015
575 U.S. 510, 135 S.Ct. 1829, 191 L.Ed.2d 783

Ginsburg, J.

In February 2010, petitioner Charles Harris III filed a Chapter 13 bankruptcy petition. At the time of filing, Harris was indebted to multiple creditors, and had fallen $3,700 behind on payments to Chase Manhattan, his home mortgage lender.

Harris' court-confirmed Chapter 13 plan provided that he would immediately resume making monthly mortgage payments to Chase. The plan further provided that $530 per month would be withheld from Harris' postpetition wages and remitted to the Chapter 13 trustee, respondent Mary Viegelahn. Viegelahn, in turn, would distribute $352 per month to Chase to pay down Harris' outstanding mortgage debt. She would also distribute $75.34 per month to Harris' only other secured lender, a consumer-electronics store. Once those secured creditors were paid in full, Viegelahn was to begin distributing funds to Harris' unsecured creditors.

Implementation of the plan was short lived. Harris again fell behind on his mortgage payments, and in November 2010, Chase received permission from the Bankruptcy Court to foreclose on Harris' home. Following the foreclosure, Viegelahn continued to receive $530 per month from Harris' wages, but stopped making the payments earmarked for Chase. As a result, funds formerly reserved for Chase accumulated in Viegelahn's possession.

On November 22, 2011, Harris exercised his statutory right to convert his Chapter 13 case to one under Chapter 7. By that time, Harris' postpetition wages accumulated by Viegelahn amounted to $5,519.22. On December 1, 2011—ten days after Harris' conversion—Viegelahn disposed of those funds by giving $1,200 to Harris' counsel, paying herself a $267.79 fee, and distributing the remaining money to the consumer-electronics store and six of Harris' unsecured creditors.

Asserting that Viegelahn lacked authority to disburse funds to creditors once the case was converted to Chapter 7, Harris moved the Bankruptcy Court for an order directing refund of the accumulated wages Viegelahn had given to his creditors. The Bankruptcy Court granted Harris' motion, and the District Court affirmed.

[The Fifth Circuit reversed, holding that despite a Chapter 13 debtor's conversion to Chapter 7, a former Chapter 13 trustee must distribute a debtor's accumulated postpetition wages to his creditors. The U.S. Supreme Court granted *certiorari*.]

* * *

This case concerns the disposition of wages earned by a debtor *after* he petitions for bankruptcy. The treatment of postpetition wages generally depends on whether the debtor is proceeding under Chapter 13 of the Bankruptcy Code (in which the debtor retains assets, often his home, during bankruptcy subject to a court-approved plan for the payment of his debts) or Chapter 7 (in which the debtor's assets are immediately liquidated and the proceeds distributed to creditors). In a Chapter 13 proceeding, post-petition wages are "[p]roperty of the estate," [citation], and may be collected by the Chapter 13 trustee for distribution to creditors, [citation]. In a Chapter 7 proceeding, those earnings are not estate property; instead, they belong to the debtor. [Citation.] The Code permits the debtor to convert a Chapter 13 proceeding to one under Chapter 7 "at any time," [citation]; upon such conversion, the service of the Chapter 13 trustee terminates, [citation].

When a debtor initially filing under Chapter 13 exercises his right to convert to Chapter 7, who is entitled to postpetition wages still in the hands of the Chapter 13 trustee? Not the Chapter 7 estate when the conversion is in good faith, all agree. May the trustee distribute the accumulated wage payments to creditors as the Chapter 13 plan required, or must she remit them to the debtor? That is the question this case presents. We hold that, under the governing provisions of the Bankruptcy Code, a debtor who converts to Chapter 7 is entitled to return of any postpetition wages not yet distributed by the Chapter 13 trustee.

* * *

Chapter 7 allows a debtor to make a clean break from his financial past, but at a steep price: prompt liquidation of the debtor's assets. When a debtor files a Chapter 7 petition, his assets, with specified exemptions, are immediately transferred to a bankruptcy estate. [Citation.] A Chapter 7 trustee is then charged with selling the property in the estate, [citation], and distributing the proceeds to the debtor's creditors, [citation]. Crucially, however, a Chapter 7 estate does not include the wages a debtor earns or the assets he acquires *after* the bankruptcy filing. [Citation.] Thus, while a Chapter 7 debtor must forfeit virtually all his prepetition property, he is able to make a "fresh start" by shielding from creditors his postpetition earnings and acquisitions.

Chapter 13 works differently. A wholly voluntary alternative to Chapter 7, Chapter 13 allows a debtor to retain his property if he proposes, and gains court confirmation of, a plan to repay his debts over a three- to five-year period. [Citations.] Payments under a Chapter 13 plan are usually made from a debtor's "future earnings or other future income." [Citations.]

Accordingly, the Chapter 13 estate from which creditors may be paid includes both the debtor's property at the time of his bankruptcy petition, and any wages and property acquired after filing. [Citation.] A Chapter 13 trustee is often charged with collecting a portion of a debtor's wages through payroll deduction, and with distributing the withheld wages to creditors.

* * *

Many debtors, however, fail to complete a Chapter 13 plan successfully. [Citation.] Recognizing that reality, Congress accorded debtors a nonwaivable right to convert a Chapter 13 case to one under Chapter 7 "at any time." [Citation.] ***

Conversion from Chapter 13 to Chapter 7 does not commence a new bankruptcy case. The existing case continues along another track, Chapter 7 instead of Chapter 13, without "effect[ing] a change in the date of the filing of the petition." [Citation.] Conversion, however, immediately "terminates the service" of the Chapter 13 trustee, replacing her with a Chapter 7 trustee. [Citation.]

* * *

Section 348(f) [of the Bankruptcy Code], all agree, makes one thing clear: A debtor's postpetition wages, including undisbursed funds in the hands of a trustee, ordinarily do not become part of the Chapter 7 estate created by conversion. Absent a bad-faith conversion, §348(f) limits a converted Chapter 7 estate to property belonging to the debtor "as of the date" the original Chapter 13 petition was filed. Postpetition wages, by definition, do not fit that bill.

* * *

By excluding postpetition wages from the converted Chapter 7 estate, §348(f)(1)(A) removes those earnings from the pool of assets that may be liquidated and distributed to creditors. Allowing a terminated Chapter 13 trustee to disburse the very same earnings to the very same creditors is incompatible with that statutory design. * * *

* * *

[Judgment of the Fifth Circuit is reversed.]

CASE
38-4

Confirmation of Chapter 13 Plan
HAMILTON v. LANNING
Supreme Court of the United States, 2010
560 U.S. 505, 130 S.Ct. 2464, 177 L.Ed.2d 23

Alito, J.

Chapter 13 of the Bankruptcy Code provides bankruptcy protection to "individual[s] with regular income" whose debts fall within statutory limits. [Citation.] Unlike debtors who file under Chapter 7 and must liquidate their non-exempt assets in order to pay creditors, [citation], Chapter 13 debtors are permitted to keep their property, but they must agree to a court-approved plan under which they pay creditors out of their future income, [citation]. A bankruptcy trustee oversees the filing and execution of a Chapter 13 debtor's plan. [Citations.]

Section 1325 of the [Bankruptcy Code] specifies circumstances under which a bankruptcy court "shall" and "may not" confirm a plan. §1325(a), (b). If an unsecured creditor or the bankruptcy trustee objects to confirmation, §1325(b)(1) requires the debtor either to pay unsecured creditors in full or to pay all "projected disposable income" to be received by the debtor over the duration of the plan.

We granted certiorari to decide how a bankruptcy court should calculate a debtor's "projected disposable income." Some lower courts have taken what the parties term the "mechanical approach," while most have adopted what has been called the "forward-looking approach." We hold that the "forward-looking approach" is correct.

I

* * * Before the enactment of the Bankruptcy Abuse Prevention and Consumer Protection Act of 2005 (BAPCPA), [citation], the Bankruptcy Code (Code) loosely defined "disposable income" as "income which is received by the debtor and which is not reasonably necessary to be expended" for the "maintenance or support of the debtor," for qualifying charitable contributions, or for business expenditures. §1325(b)(2)(A), (B).

The Code did not define the term "projected disposable income," and in most cases, bankruptcy courts used a mechanical approach in calculating projected disposable income. That is, they first multiplied monthly income by the number of months in the plan and then determined what portion of the result was "excess" or "disposable." [Citation.]

In exceptional cases, however, bankruptcy courts took into account foreseeable changes in a debtor's income or expenses. [Citations.]

BAPCPA left the term "projected disposable income" undefined but specified in some detail how "disposable income" is to be calculated. "Disposable income" is now defined as "current monthly income received by the debtor" less "amounts reasonably necessary to be expended" for the debtor's maintenance and support, for qualifying charitable contributions, and for business expenditures. [Citation.] "Current monthly income," in turn, is calculated by averaging the debtor's monthly income during what the parties refer to as the 6-month look-back period, which generally consists of the six full months preceding the filing of the bankruptcy petition. [Citation.] The phrase "amounts reasonably necessary to be expended" in §1325(b)(2) is also newly defined. For a debtor whose income is below the median for his or her State, the phrase includes the full amount needed for "maintenance or support," [citation], but for a debtor with income that exceeds the state median, only certain specified expenses are included, [citations.]

II

Respondent had $36,793.36 in unsecured debt when she filed for Chapter 13 bankruptcy protection in October 2006. In the six months before her filing, she received a one-time buyout from her former employer, and this payment greatly inflated her gross income for April 2006 (to $11,990.03) and for May 2006 (to $15,356.42). [Citation.] As a result of these payments, respondent's current monthly income, as averaged from April through October 2006, was $5,343.70—a figure that exceeds the median income for a family of one in Kansas. [Citation.] Respondent's monthly expenses, calculated pursuant to [citation] were $4,228.71. [Citation.] She reported a monthly "disposable income" of $1,114.98 on Form 22C. [Citation.]

On the form used for reporting monthly income (Schedule I), she reported income from her new job of $1,922 per month—which is below the state median. [Citations.] On the form used for reporting monthly expenses (Schedule J), she reported actual monthly expenses of $1,772.97. [Citation.] Subtracting the Schedule J figure from the Schedule I figure resulted in monthly disposable income of $149.03.

Respondent filed a plan that would have required her to pay $144 per month for 36 months. [Citation.] Petitioner, a private Chapter 13 trustee, objected to confirmation of the plan because the amount respondent proposed to pay was less than the full amount of the claims against her, [citation], and because, in petitioner's view, respondent was not committing all of her "projected disposable income" to the repayment of creditors, [citation]. According to petitioner, the proper way to calculate projected disposable income was simply to multiply disposable income, as calculated on Form 22C, by the number of months in the commitment period. Employing this mechanical approach, petitioner calculated that creditors would be paid in full if respondent made monthly payments of $756 for a period of 60 months. [Citation.] There is no dispute that respondent's actual income was insufficient to make payments in that amount. [Citation.]

The Bankruptcy Court endorsed respondent's proposed monthly payment of $144 but required a 60-month plan period. [Citation.] The court agreed with the majority view

that the word "projected" in §1325(b)(1)(B) requires courts "to consider at confirmation the debtor's *actual* income as it was reported on Schedule I." [Citation] (emphasis added [by court]). This conclusion was warranted by the text of §1325(b)(1), the Bankruptcy Court reasoned, and was necessary to avoid the absurd result of denying bankruptcy protection to individuals with deteriorating finances in the six months before filing. [Citation.]

Petitioner appealed to the Tenth Circuit Bankruptcy Appellate Panel, which affirmed. [Citation.] * * *

The Tenth Circuit affirmed. * * *

This petition followed, and we granted certiorari. [Citation.]

III

The parties differ sharply in their interpretation of §1325's reference to "projected disposable income." Petitioner, advocating the mechanical approach, contends that "projected disposable income" means past average monthly disposable income multiplied by the number of months in a debtor's plan. Respondent, who favors the forward-looking approach, agrees that the method outlined by petitioner should be determinative in most cases, but she argues that in exceptional cases, where significant changes in a debtor's financial circumstances are known or virtually certain, a bankruptcy court has discretion to make an appropriate adjustment. Respondent has the stronger argument.

First, respondent's argument is supported by the ordinary meaning of the term "projected." "When terms used in a statute are undefined, we give them their ordinary meaning." [Citation.] Here, the term "projected" is not defined, and in ordinary usage future occurrences are not "projected" based on the assumption that the past will necessarily repeat itself. For example, projections concerning a company's future sales or the future cash flow from a license take into account anticipated events that may change past trends. * * * While a projection takes past events into account, adjustments are often made based on other factors that may affect the final outcome. [Citation.]

Second, the word "projected" appears in many federal statutes, yet Congress rarely has used it to mean simple multiplication. * * *

By contrast, we need look no further than the Bankruptcy Code to see that when Congress wishes to mandate simple multiplication, it does so unambiguously—most commonly by using the term "multiplied." [Citations.]

Third, pre-BAPCPA case law points in favor of the "forward-looking" approach. * * *

Pre-BAPCPA bankruptcy practice is telling because we "'will not read the Bankruptcy Code to erode past bankruptcy practice absent a clear indication that Congress intended such a departure.'" [Citation.] Congress did not amend the term "projected disposable income" in 2005, and pre-BAPCPA bankruptcy practice reflected a widely acknowledged and well-documented view that courts may take into account known or virtually certain changes to debtors' income or expenses when projecting disposable income. In light of this historical practice, we would expect that, had Congress intended for "projected" to carry a specialized—and indeed, unusual—meaning in Chapter 13, Congress would have said so expressly. [Citation.]

* * *

In cases in which a debtor's disposable income during the 6-month look-back period is either substantially lower or higher than the debtor's disposable income during the plan period, the mechanical approach would produce senseless results that we do not think Congress intended. In cases in which the debtor's disposable income is higher during the plan period, the mechanical approach would deny creditors payments that the debtor could easily make. And where, as in the present case, the debtor's disposable income during the plan period is substantially lower, the mechanical approach would deny the protection of Chapter 13 to debtors who meet the chapter's main eligibility requirements. Here, for example, respondent is an "individual whose income is sufficiently stable and regular" to allow her "to make payments under a plan," §101(30), and her debts fall below the limits set out in §109(e). But if the mechanical approach were used, she could not file a confirmable plan. Under §1325(a)(6), a plan cannot be confirmed unless "the debtor will be able to make all payments under the plan and comply with the plan." And as petitioner concedes, respondent could not possibly make the payments that the mechanical approach prescribes.

* * *

IV

* * * Consistent with the text of §1325 and pre-BAPCPA practice, we hold that when a bankruptcy court calculates a debtor's projected disposable income, the court may account for changes in the debtor's income or expenses that are known or virtually certain at the time of confirmation. We therefore affirm the decision of the Court of Appeals.

QUESTIONS

1. **a.** Benson goes into bankruptcy. His estate is not sufficient to pay all taxes owed. Explain whether Benson's taxes are discharged by the proceedings.

    b. Benson obtained property from Anderson on credit by representing that he was solvent when in fact he knew he was insolvent. Explain whether Benson's debt to Anderson is discharged by Benson's discharge in bankruptcy.

2. Bradley goes into bankruptcy under Chapter 7 owing $25,000 as wages to his four employees. There is enough in his estate to pay all costs of administration and enough to pay his employees, but nothing will be left for general creditors. Do the employees take all the estate? If so, under what conditions? If the general creditors received nothing, would these debts be discharged? Explain.

3. Jessica sold goods to Stacy for $2,500 and retained a security interest in them. Two months later, Stacy filed a voluntary petition in bankruptcy under Chapter 7. At this time, Stacy still owed Jessica $2,000 for the purchase price of the goods, the value of which was $1,500.

    a. May the trustee invalidate Jessica's security interest? If so, under what provision?

    b. If the security interest is invalidated, what is Jessica's status in the bankruptcy proceeding?

    c. If the security interest is *not* invalidated, what is Jessica's status in the bankruptcy proceeding?

4. A debtor went through bankruptcy under Chapter 7 and received his discharge. Explain which of the following debts were completely discharged and which will remain as future debts against him.

    a. A claim of $9,000 for wages earned within five months immediately prior to bankruptcy.

    b. A judgment of $3,000 against the debtor for breach of contract.

    c. $1,000 for domestic support obligations.

    d. A judgment of $4,000 for injuries received because of the debtor's negligent operation of an automobile.

5. Rosinoff and his wife, who were business partners, entered bankruptcy. A creditor, Baldwin, objected to their discharge in bankruptcy on the grounds that

    a. the partners had obtained credit from Baldwin on the basis of a false financial statement;

    b. the partners had failed to keep books of account and records from which their financial condition could be ascertained; and

    c. Rosinoff had falsely sworn that he had taken $70 from the partnership account when the amount he took was actually $700.

    Were the debtors entitled to a discharge? Why or why not?

6. Ross Corporation is a debtor in a reorganization proceeding under Chapter 11 of the Bankruptcy Code. By fair and proper valuation, its assets are worth $100,000. The indebtedness of the corporation is $105,000, and it has outstanding $100 par value preferred stock in the amount of $20,000 and $30 par value common stock in the amount of $75,000. The plan of reorganization submitted by the trustees would give nothing to the common shareholders and would issue new bonds in the face amount of $5,000 to the creditors and new common stock in the ratio of 84 percent to the creditors and 16 percent to the preferred shareholders. Should this plan be confirmed? Explain.

7. Alex is a wage earner with a regular income. He has unsecured debts of $42,000 and secured debts owing to Betty, Connie, David, and Eunice totaling $120,000. Eunice's debt is secured only by a mortgage on Alex's house. Alex files a petition under Chapter 13 and a plan providing payment as follows: (a) 60 percent of all taxes owed; (b) 35 percent of all unsecured debts; and (c) $100,000 in total to Betty, Connie, David, and Eunice. Should the court confirm the plan? If not, explain how the plan must be modified or what other conditions must be satisfied.

8. John Bunker has assets of $130,000 and liabilities of $185,000 owed to nine creditors. Nonetheless, his cash flow is positive, and he is making payment on all of his obligations as they become due. I. M. Flintheart, who is owed $22,000 by Bunker, files an involuntary petition in bankruptcy under Chapter 7 against Bunker. Bunker contests the petition. What result? Explain.

9. Karen has filed a voluntary petition for a Chapter 7 proceeding. The total value of her estate is $35,000. Ben, who is owed $18,000, has a security interest in property valued at $12,000. Lauren has an unsecured claim of $9,000, which is entitled to a priority of $2,000. The United States has a claim for income taxes of $7,000. Steve has an unsecured claim of $10,000 that was filed on time. Sarah has an unsecured claim of $17,000 that was filed on time. Wally has a claim of $14,000 that he filed late, even though he was aware of the bankruptcy proceedings. Explain what each of the creditors should receive in a distribution under Chapter 7.

C A S E   P R O B L E M S

10. Landmark at Plaza Park, Ltd., filed a plan of reorganization under Chapter 11 of the Bankruptcy Code. Landmark is a limited partnership whose only substantial asset is a two-hundred-unit garden apartment complex. City Federal holds the first mortgage on the property in the face amount of $2,250,000. The mortgage is due and payable six years from now.

    Landmark has proposed a plan of reorganization under which the property now in possession of City Federal would be returned. Landmark will then deliver a nonrecourse note, payable in three years, in the face amount of $2,705,820.31 to City Federal in substitution of all of the partnership's existing liabilities. On the sixteenth month through the thirty-sixth month after the effective date of the plan, Landmark will make monthly interest payments computed on a property value of $2,260,000 at a rate 3 percent above the original mortgage rate but 2.5 percent below the market rate for loans of similar risk. Finally, the note will be secured by the existing mortgage. Landmark's theory is that the note will be paid off at the end of thirty-six months by a combination of refinancing and accumulation of cash from the project. The key is Landmark's proposal to obtain a new first mortgage in three years in the face amount of $2,400,000.

    City Federal is a first mortgagee without recourse that has been collecting rents pursuant to a rent assignment agreement since the default on the mortgage eleven months ago. City Federal is impaired by the plan and has rejected the plan. May it complete its foreclosure action? Explain.

11. Freelin Conn filed a voluntary petition under Chapter 7 of the Bankruptcy Code on September 30, 2021. Conn listed BancOhio National Bank as having a claim incurred in October 2020 in the amount of $4,000 secured by an eight-year-old automobile. The car is listed as having a market value of $3,500. During the period from June 30, 2021, to September 30, 2021, Conn made three payments totaling $439.17 to BancOhio. May the trustee in bankruptcy set aside those three payments as voidable preferences? Explain.

12. David files a bankruptcy petition under Chapter 13. After the claims of secured and priority creditors have been satisfied, David's remaining bankruptcy estate has a value of $100,000. David's creditors with allowed unsecured claims are owed $250,000 in total. Chris, an unsecured creditor, is owed $13,500. David's Chapter 13 plan proposes to pay Chris $150 per month for three years. Should the bankruptcy court confirm David's plan? Explain.

13. Yolanda Christophe filed a bankruptcy petition under Chapter 13. Her scheduled debts consist of $11,100 of secured debt, $9,300 owed on an unsecured student loan, and $6,960 of other unsecured debt. Christophe asserts that the student loan is nondischargeable, and that assertion has not been questioned. Christophe's proposed amended Chapter 13 Plan calls for fifty-six monthly payments of $440 a month. The questioned provision in that Plan is the division of the unsecured creditors into two classes. The general unsecured creditors would receive 32 percent, while the separately classified student loan creditor would receive 100 percent. Should this plan be confirmed? Why or why not?

14. On December 17, ZZZZ Best Co., Inc. (the debtor) borrowed $7 million from Union Bank (the bank). On July 8 of the following year, the debtor filed a voluntary petition for bankruptcy under Chapter 7. During the preceding ninety days, the debtor had made interest payments of $100,000 to the bank on the loan. The trustee of the debtor's estate files a complaint against the bank to recover those payments as a voidable preference. The bank argues that the payments were not voidable because they came within the ordinary course of business exception. The trustee maintains that the exception applies only to short-term, not long-term, debt. Who is correct? Explain.

15. A landlord owned several residential properties, one of which was subject to a local rent control ordinance. The local rent control administrator determined that the landlord had been charging rents above the levels permitted by the ordinance and ordered him to refund the wrongfully collected rents to the affected tenants. The landlord did not comply with the order. The landlord subsequently filed for relief under Chapter 7 of the Bankruptcy Code, seeking to discharge his debts. The tenants filed an adversary proceeding against the landlord in the bankruptcy court, arguing that the debt owed to them arose from rent payments obtained by "actual fraud" and that the debt was therefore nondischargeable under §523(a)(2)(A) of the Bankruptcy Code. They also sought treble damages and attorneys' fees and costs pursuant to the State Consumer Fraud Act. The bankruptcy court ruled in favor of the tenants, finding that the landlord had committed "actual fraud" within the meaning of §523(a)(2)(A) and that his conduct violated State law.

The court therefore awarded the tenants treble damages totaling $94,147.50. Does the Bankruptcy Code bar the discharge of treble damages awarded on account of the debtor's fraud? Explain.

16. Krieger is a 53-year-old woman who has not held a job in more than twenty-five years. Prior to that period, she did not earn more than $12,000 a year in her working career. Krieger is living with her mother, age seventy-five, in a rural community where few jobs are available. Between the two of them, she and her mother receive only a few hundred dollars from governmental programs every month. Krieger is too poor to move in search of better employment prospects elsewhere. Her car needs repairs, and she lacks Internet access, both of which hamper a search for work. Having no assets or income, Krieger filed for, and is entitled to receive, a discharge in bankruptcy. Her largest creditor—Educational Credit Management, which acts on behalf of some Federal loan guarantors—seeks to exclude Krieger's student loans from the discharge. Explain whether Krieger should be discharged from her educational loans.

17. Robert Marrama filed a voluntary bankruptcy petition under Chapter 7. In the filing, Marrama made a number of statements about his principal asset, a house in Maine, which were misleading or inaccurate. He reported that he was the sole beneficiary of the trust that owned the property, and he listed its value as zero. He also denied that he had transferred any property other than in the ordinary course of business during the year preceding the filing of his petition. In fact, the Maine property had substantial value, and seven months prior to filing his petition, Marrama had transferred it into the newly created trust for no consideration. Marrama later admitted that the purpose of the transfer was to protect the property from his creditors. The trustee stated that he intended to recover the Maine property as an asset of the estate. Thereafter, Marrama sought to convert to Chapter 13, claiming that he had an absolute right to convert his case. Both the trustee and Marrama's principal creditor objected, contending that the request to convert was made in bad faith. Explain whether Marrama should be permitted to convert the case to Chapter 13.

Leonard and Arlene Warner sold the Warner Manufacturing Company to Elliott and Carol Archer for $610,000. A few months later, the Archers sued the Warners in a State court for fraud connected with the sale. The parties settled the lawsuit for $300,000. The Warners paid the Archers $200,000 and executed a promissory note for the remaining $100,000. After the Warners failed to make the first payment on the $100,000 promissory note, the Archers sued for the payment in State court. The Warners then filed for bankruptcy under Chapter 7 of the Bankruptcy Code. The Archers claimed that the $100,000 debt was nondischargeable because it was for "money obtained by fraud." Arlene Warner claimed that the $100,000 debt was dischargeable in bankruptcy because it was a new debt for money promised in a settlement contract and thus was not a debt for money obtained by fraud.

a. What are the arguments that the debt is dischargeable in bankruptcy?

b. What are the arguments that the debt is *not* dischargeable in bankruptcy?

c. Explain whether the debt is dischargeable in bankruptcy.

Regulation of Business

CH 39 PROTECTION OF INTELLECTUAL PROPERTY

CH 40 ANTITRUST

CH 41 CONSUMER PROTECTION

CH 42 EMPLOYMENT LAW

CH 43 SECURITIES REGULATION

CH 44 ACCOUNTANTS' LEGAL LIABILITY

CH 45 ENVIRONMENTAL LAW

CH 46 INTERNATIONAL BUSINESS LAW

CHAPTER 39

Protection of Intellectual Property

CHAPTER OUTCOMES

After reading and studying this chapter, you should be able to:

- Explain what trade secrets protect and how they may be infringed.

- Distinguish among the various types of trade symbols.

- Explain the extent to which trade names are protected.

- Explain what copyrights protect and the remedies for infringement.

- Explain what patents protect and the remedies for infringement.

I ntellectual property (IP) is an economically significant type of intangible personal property that includes trade secrets, trade symbols, copyrights, and patents. These interests are protected from infringement, or unauthorized use, by others. Such protection is essential to the conduct of business. For example, a business would be far less willing to invest considerable resources in research and development if the resulting discoveries, inventions, and processes were not protected by patents and trade secrets. Similarly, a company would not be secure in devoting time and money to marketing its products and services without laws that protect its trade symbols and trade names. Moreover, without copyright protection, the publishing, entertainment, and computer software industries would be vulnerable to piracy, both by corporate competitors and by the general public. This chapter discusses the law protecting (1) trade secrets; (2) trade symbols, including trademarks, service marks, certification marks, collective marks, and trade names; (3) copyrights; and (4) patents.

The U.S. laws protecting intellectual property do not apply to transactions in other countries. Generally, the owner of an intellectual property right must comply with each country's requirements to obtain from that country whatever protection is available. The requirements vary substantially from country to country, as does the degree of protection. The United States, however, belongs to multinational treaties that try to coordinate the application of member nations' intellectual property laws. The Trade-Related Aspects of Intellectual Property Rights (TRIPS) portion of the World Trade Organization (WTO) Agreement states how the range of intellectual property should be protected when trade is involved. The

World Intellectual Property Organization (WIPO), one of the specialized agencies of the United Nations, attempts to promote—through cooperation among nations—the protection of intellectual property throughout the world. WIPO administers twenty-six international treaties dealing with intellectual property protection and includes at least 193 nations as member states.

39-1 Trade Secrets

Every business has secret information. Such information may include customer lists or contracts with suppliers and customers; it also may comprise formulas, processes, and production methods that are vital to the successful operation of the business. A business may disclose a trade secret in confidence to an employee with the understanding that the employee will not reveal the information to others. To the extent the owner of the information obtains a patent on it, it is no longer a trade secret but is protected by patent law. Some businesses, however, choose not to obtain a patent because it provides protection for only a limited time, whereas trade secret law protects a trade secret as long as it is kept secret. Moreover, if the courts invalidate a patent, the information will have been disclosed to competitors without the owner of the information obtaining any benefit.

Unlike other types of intellectual property, which are primarily protected under Federal law, trade secrets historically have been protected by State law. The Uniform Trade Secrets Act (UTSA), promulgated in 1979 and amended in 1985, has been adopted in some variation by at least forty-eight States but differences nevertheless exist among the specific State trade secret laws. At the Federal level, the Economic Espionage Act of 1996 makes it a Federal criminal offense to misappropriate a trade secret that has an interstate or foreign connection. To provide greater uniformity, the recently enacted Defend Trade Secrets Act of 2016 amends the Economic Espionage Act to provide a Federal civil remedy for the misappropriation of trade secrets that have an interstate or foreign connection, thus bringing the rights of owners of trade secrets into alignment with those rights conferred on owners of other forms of intellectual property, including trademarks, copyrights, and patents.

39-1a STATE PROTECTION OF TRADE SECRETS

DEFINITION A **trade secret** is commercially valuable information that is guarded from disclosure and is not general knowledge. The UTSA defines a trade secret as

information, including a formula, pattern, compilation, program, device, method, technique, or process, that:
(i) derives independent economic value, actual or potential, from not being generally known to, and not being readily ascertainable by proper means by, other persons who can obtain economic value from its disclosure or use, and
(ii) is the subject of efforts that are reasonable under the circumstances to maintain its secrecy.

A famous example of a trade secret is the formula for Coca-Cola.

MISAPPROPRIATION The misappropriation of a trade secret is the wrongful use of a trade secret. A person misappropriates a trade secret of another (1) by knowingly acquiring it through improper means or (2) by disclosing or using it without consent if her knowledge of the trade secret came under circumstances giving rise to a duty to maintain secrecy or came from a person who used improper means or who owed the owner of the trade secret a duty to maintain secrecy. Trade secrets most frequently are misappropriated in two ways: (1) an employee wrongfully uses or discloses such information, or (2) a competitor wrongfully obtains it.

An employee is under a duty of loyalty to his employer, which, among other responsibilities, obligates the employee not to disclose trade secrets to competitors. It is wrongful, in turn, for a competitor to obtain vital secret trade information from an employee through bribery or other means. Besides breaching the duty of loyalty, the faithless employee who divulges secret trade information also commits a tort. In the absence of a contract restriction, an employee is under no duty upon termination of his employment to refrain either from competing with a former employer or from working for a competitor

of that employer; however, he may not use trade secrets or disclose them to third persons. The employee is entitled, nevertheless, to use the skill, knowledge, and general information he acquired during the previous employment relationship.

Another improper method of acquiring trade secrets is industrial espionage conducted through methods such as electronic surveillance or spying. Improper means of acquiring another person's trade secrets also include theft, bribery, fraud, unauthorized interception of communications, and inducement or knowing participation in a breach of confidence. In the broadest sense, discovering another's trade secrets by any means other than independent research or personal inspection of the publicly available finished product is improper unless the other party voluntarily discloses the secret or fails to take reasonable precautions to protect its secrecy.

Practical Advice
Before disclosing a trade secret to another, require that person to sign a nondisclosure agreement.

REMEDIES The remedies for misappropriation of trade secrets are damages and, where appropriate, injunctive relief. Damages are awarded in the amount of either the pecuniary loss to the plaintiff caused by the misappropriation or the pecuniary gain to the defendant, whichever is greater. A court will grant an injunction to prevent a continuing or threatened misappropriation of a trade secret for as long as is necessary to protect the plaintiff from any harm attributable to the misappropriation and to deprive the defendant of any economic advantage attributable to the misappropriation.

♦ *See Case 39-1*

39-1b FEDERAL PROTECTION OF TRADE SECRETS

CRIMINAL PENALTIES As amended in 2012 and 2016, the Economic Espionage Act of 1996 prohibits the theft of trade secrets, as well as attempts and conspiracies to steal trade secrets, if the trade secret is related to a product or service used in or intended for use in interstate or foreign commerce. The Act imposes criminal penalties for violations and authorizes the U.S. Attorney General to bring a civil action to obtain appropriate injunctive relief against any violation of the Act. The statute defines trade secrets to mean

all forms and types of financial, business, scientific, technical, economic, or engineering information, including patterns, plans, compilations, program devices, formulas, designs, prototypes, methods, techniques, processes, procedures, programs, or codes, whether tangible or intangible, and whether or how stored, compiled, or memorialized physically, electronically, graphically, photographically, or in writing if (A) the owner thereof has taken reasonable measures to keep such information secret; and (B) the information derives independent economic value, actual or potential, from not being generally known to, and not being readily ascertainable through proper means by, another person who can obtain economic value from the disclosure or use of the information.

The Act broadly defines theft to include all types of intentional conversion of trade secrets, including the following:

1. stealing, obtaining by fraud, or concealing such information;

2. without authorization copying, duplicating, sketching, drawing, photographing, downloading, uploading, photocopying, mailing, or conveying such information; and

3. purchasing or possessing a trade secret with knowledge that it had been stolen.

The Act punishes individuals who knowingly violate the Act with fines, imprisonment for up to ten years, or both. Organizations that knowingly violate the Act are subject to fines of up to the greater of $5 million or three times the value of the stolen trade secret to the organization.

The Act imposes more severe penalties on persons who knowingly violate the Act intending or knowing that the offense will benefit any foreign government, foreign instrumentality, or foreign agent. Such individuals may be fined up to $5 million, imprisoned for up to fifteen years, or both; such organizations are subject to fines of not more than the greater of $10 million or three times the value of the stolen trade secret to the organization violating the Act.

CIVIL REMEDIES In May 2016, the **Defend Trade Secrets Act (DTSA)** became effective. The DTSA amends the Economic Espionage Act to allow the owner of a trade secret that is misappropriated to bring a civil action in Federal court if the trade secret is related to a product or service used in, or intended for use in, interstate or foreign commerce. State trade secret laws are *not* preempted by the DTSA. Like the UTSA, the DTSA defines trade secrets as information that derives independent economic value from not being generally known and which the owner has taken reasonable measures to keep secret. The DTSA provides for equitable remedies and the award of damages for the misappropriation of a trade secret. Under extraordinary circumstances, where necessary to preserve evidence or prevent dissemination of a trade secret, the DTSA also provides for expedited relief in the form of a seizure of property from a party accused of misappropriation.

The DTSA defines **misappropriation** identically in all relevant respects to the UTSA: (1) the *acquisition* of a trade secret of another by a person who knows or has reason to know that the trade secret was acquired by improper means or (2) the *disclosure* or *use* of a trade secret of another by a person who (a) used *improper means* to acquire knowledge of the trade secret or (b) at the time of disclosure or use knew or had reason to know that the knowledge of the trade secret was acquired by *improper means* or derived from a person who owed a duty to maintain the secrecy of the trade secret. The DTSA definition of **improper means** is identical to that in the UTSA and includes theft, bribery, misrepresentation, breach or inducement of a breach of a duty to maintain secrecy, or espionage through electronic or other means. Improper means does *not* include reverse engineering, independent derivation, or any other lawful means of acquisition.

The remedies available under the DTSA are similar to those under the UTSA and include injunctive relief and damages. A Federal court may issue an **injunction** to prevent any actual or threatened misappropriation, provided the order does not prevent a person from entering into an employment relationship. Moreover, any conditions placed by a Federal court on employment must be based on evidence of threatened misappropriation and not merely on the information the person knows. A Federal court may award **damages** for misappropriation for actual loss and any unjust enrichment, or—in lieu of damages measured by any other method—a reasonable royalty. If a trade secret is willfully and maliciously misappropriated, a Federal court may award exemplary (punitive) damages in an amount not more than two times the amount of compensatory damages.

39-2 Trade Symbols

One of the earliest forms of unfair competition was the fraudulent marketing of one person's goods as those of another. Still common, this unlawful practice is sometimes referred to as "passing off" or "palming off." Basically, the process of "cashing in" on the goodwill, good name, and reputation of a competitor and of his products, this fraudulent marketing deceives the public and deprives honest businesses of trade. Section 43(a) of the Federal Trademark Act (the Lanham Act) prohibits a person from using a false designation of origin in connection with any goods or services in interstate commerce. This section also prohibits a person from making a false or misleading description or representation of fact which misrepresents the nature, characteristics, qualities, or geographic origin of her own goods, services, or commercial activities. In 1988, this section was amended to prohibit misrepresentations of *another* person's goods, services, or commercial activities. As a result, Section 43(a) also forbids "reverse palming off," by which a producer misrepresents someone else's goods as his own. Accordingly, James would violate Section 43(a) by passing off his product as Sally's or by reverse passing off Sally's product as his. A violator of Section 43(a) is liable in a civil action to any person who is, or is likely to be, injured by the violation. The remedies are (1) injunctive relief, (2) an accounting for profits, (3) damages, (4) destruction of infringing articles, (5) costs, and (6) attorneys' fees in exceptional cases.

The Lanham Act also established Federal registration of trade symbols and protection against misuse or infringement by injunctive relief and a right of action for damages against the infringer. A form of passing off one's goods or services as those of the owner of the mark, an infringement deceives the public and constitutes unfair competition. Thus, trade symbol infringement law protects consumers from being misled by the use of infringing trade symbols as well as producers from unfair practices by competitors.

International treaties protecting trademarks are the Paris Convention for the Protection of Industrial Property (at least 177 nations), the Arrangement of Nice Concerning the International Classification of Goods and Services (at least 88 nations), the Madrid Protocol of 1989 (at least 108 nations), the 1973 Vienna Trademark Agreement (at least 35 nations), and the Trademark Law Treaty of 1994 (at least 54 nations).

39-2a TYPES OF TRADE SYMBOLS

The Lanham Act recognizes four types of trade symbols or **marks**. A **trademark** is a distinctive symbol, word, name, device, letter, number, design, picture, or combination in any arrangement that a person adopts or uses to identify goods that he manufactures or sells and to distinguish them from those manufactured or sold by others. Examples of trademarks include the Starbucks mermaid, the rainbow apple logo of Apple, and the twin golden arches of McDonald's . A trademark can also consist of goods' "trade dress," which is the appearance or image of goods as presented to prospective purchasers. Trade dress includes the distinctive but nonfunctional design of packaging, labels, containers, and the product itself or its features. Examples include the Campbell Soup label and the shape of the Coca-Cola bottle. Internet domain names that are used to identify and distinguish the goods or services of one person from the goods or services of others and to indicate the source of the goods and services may be registered as trademarks. To qualify, an applicant must show that it offers services via the internet and that it uses the internet domain name as a source identifier.

Some trademarks are embodied in sounds, scents, and other formats that cannot be represented by a drawing. Examples of distinctive sound marks are MGM's lion's roar, NBC's chimes, the Harlem Globetrotters' theme song "Sweet Georgia Brown," Intel's chimes, and Lucasfilm's THX logo theme. In 2018, Hasbro, Inc., registered the nonvisual Play-Doh scent as a trademark, described as "a scent of a sweet, slightly musky, vanilla fragrance, with slight overtones of cherry, combined with the smell of a salted, wheat-based dough."

Similar in function to the trademark, which identifies tangible goods and products, a **service mark** is used to identify and distinguish one person's services from those of others. For example, the titles, character names, and other distinctive features of radio and television shows may be registered as service marks. Service marks may also consist of trade dress such as the decor or shape of buildings in which services are provided. Examples include the Hard Rock Cafe's distinctive music decor and McDonald's yellow arches.

A **certification mark** is used upon or in connection with goods or services to certify their regional or other origin, composition, mode of manufacture, quality, accuracy, or other characteristics or to certify that members of a union or other organization performed the work or labor in such goods or services. The marks "Good Housekeeping Seal of Approval" and "Underwriter's Laboratory" are examples of certification marks. The owner of the certification mark does not produce or provide the goods or services with which the mark is used.

A **collective mark** is a distinctive mark or symbol used to indicate either that the producer or provider is a member of a trade union, trade association, fraternal society, or other organization or that members of a collective group produce the goods or services. As in the case of a certification mark, the owner of a collective mark is not the producer or provider but rather is the group of which the producer or provider is a member. An example of a collective mark is the union mark attached to a product to indicate its manufacture by a unionized company.

39-2b REGISTRATION

To be protected by the Lanham Act, a mark must be distinctive enough to identify clearly the origin of goods or services. A trade symbol may satisfy the distinctiveness requirement in either of two ways. First, it may be **inherently distinctive** if prospective purchasers are likely to associate it with the product or service it designates because of the nature of the designation and the context in which it is used. Fanciful, arbitrary, or suggestive marks satisfy the distinctiveness requirement. In contrast, a descriptive or geographic designation is *not* inherently distinctive. Such a designation is one that is likely to be perceived by prospective purchasers as merely descriptive of the nature, qualities, or other characteristics of the goods or service with which it is used. Thus, the word *Apple* cannot be a trademark for apples, although it may be a trademark for computers.

Descriptive or geographic designations, however, may satisfy the distinctiveness requirement through the second method: acquiring distinctiveness through a **"secondary meaning."** A designation acquires a secondary meaning when a substantial number of prospective purchasers associate the designation with the product or service it identifies. The trademark office may accept proof of substantially exclusive and continuous use of a mark for five years as *prima facie* evidence of secondary meaning.

A **generic name** is one that is understood by prospective purchasers to denominate the general category, type, or class of goods or services with which it is used. A user cannot acquire rights in a generic name as a trade symbol. Moreover, a trade symbol will lose its eligibility for protection if prospective purchasers come to perceive a trade symbol primarily as a generic name for the category, type, or class of goods or services with which it is used. Under the Lanham Act, the test for when this has occurred is "the primary significance of the registered mark to the relevant public rather than purchaser motivation." Examples of marks that have lost protection because they became generic include "aspirin," "thermos," and "cellophane."

A trademark may not consist of the flag, coat of arms, or other insignia of the United States or of any State, municipality, or foreign nation. In addition, a mark will not be registered if it so resembles a registered or previously used mark that it would be likely to cause confusion, mistake, or deceit.

The Lanham Act denied registration to marks that (1) are immoral, deceptive, or scandalous or (2) "disparage … persons, living or dead, institutions, beliefs, or national symbols, or bring them into contempt, or disrepute." However, the U.S. Supreme Court has recently invalidated all of these bars to registration as unconstitutional in violation of the First Amendment. *Matal v. Tam*, 582 U.S. _____ (2017); *Iancu v. Brunetti*, 588 U.S. _____ (2019).

To obtain Federal protection, which has a ten-year term with unlimited ten-year renewals, the mark must be registered with the U.S. Patent and Trademark Office (USPTO). An applicant must either (1) have actually used the mark in commerce or (2) demonstrate a *bona fide* intent to use the mark in commerce and actually use it within six months, which period may be extended. For a trademark registration to remain valid, an Affidavit of Use must be filed (1) between the fifth and sixth year following registration and (2) within the year before the end of every ten-year period after the date of registration.

Federal registration is not required to establish rights in a mark, nor is it required to begin using a mark. Registration, however, provides numerous advantages. It gives nationwide constructive notice of the mark to all later users. It permits the registrant to use the Federal courts to enforce the mark and constitutes *prima facie* evidence of the registrant's exclusive right to use the mark. This right becomes incontestable, subject to certain specified limitations, after five years. Finally, registration provides the registrant with Customs Bureau protection against imports that threaten to infringe upon the mark. A U.S. trade symbol registration provides protection only in the United States. However, in 2002, Congress enacted legislation implementing the Madrid Protocol, a procedural agreement allowing U.S. trademark owners to file for registration in at least 108 members by filing a single application.

To retain trademark protection, the owner of a mark must not abandon it by failing to make *bona fide* use of it in the ordinary course of trade. Abandonment occurs when an owner does not use a mark and no longer intends to use it. Three years of nonuse raises a presumption of abandonment, which the owner may rebut by proving her intent to resume use.

Anyone who claims rights in a mark may use the ™ (trademark) or ˢᴹ (service mark) designation, even if the mark is not registered. Only owners of registered marks may use the symbol ®.

◆ *See Case 39-2*

39-2c INFRINGEMENT

Infringement of a mark occurs when a person without authorization uses an identical or substantially indistinguishable mark that is *likely* to cause confusion, to cause mistake, or to deceive. The intent to confuse is not required, nor is proof of actual confusion, although likelihood of confusion may be inferred from either. In a case involving consumer confusion, infringement occurs if an appreciable number of ordinarily prudent purchasers are *likely* to be misled or confused as to the source of the goods or services. In deciding whether infringement has occurred, the courts consider various factors, including the strength of the mark, the intent of the unauthorized user, the degree of similarity between the two marks, the relation between the two products or services the marks identify, and the marketing channels through which the goods or services are purchased.

The Federal Trademark Dilution Act of 1995 amended the Lanham Act to protect famous marks from dilution of their distinctive quality. The term *dilution* means the lessening of the capacity of a famous mark to identify and distinguish goods or services even if (1) there is no competition between the owner of the famous mark and the other party using the mark or (2) the other party's use of the mark does not result in the likelihood of confusion, mistake, or deception. Examples of dilution include DuPont shoes, Toyota aspirin, and Rolex cameras. In determining whether a mark is distinctive and famous, a court may consider factors such as (1) the degree of inherent or acquired distinctiveness of the mark; (2) the degree of recognition of the mark; (3) the duration and extent of the use, advertising, and publicity of the mark; (4) the geographical extent of the trading area in which the mark is used; and (5) the channels of trade for the goods or services with which the mark is used. The amendment exempts fair use of a famous mark in comparative commercial advertising, noncommercial use of a mark, and mention of a famous mark in news reporting.

The Trademark Cyberpiracy Prevention Act of 1999 amended the Lanham Act to protect the owner of a trademark or service mark from any person who, with a bad faith intent to profit from the mark, registers, traffics in, or uses a domain name which, at the time of its registration, (1) is identical or confusingly similar to a distinctive mark or (2) is dilutive of a famous mark or (3) is a protected trademark, word, or name. The Act specifies factors a court may consider in determining bad faith intent but prohibits such a determination if the defendant believed, with reasonable grounds, that the use of the domain name was fair or otherwise lawful. It further authorizes a court to order cancellation of the domain name or its transfer to the owner of the mark. In addition to injunctive relief, the Act makes available remedies that include recovery of the defendant's profits, actual damages, attorneys' fees, and court costs. It also provides for statutory damages in an amount of at least $1,000 and up to $100,000 per domain name. The Act shields a registrar, registry, or other registration authority from liability for damages for the registration or maintenance of a domain name for another, unless there is a showing of bad faith intent to profit from such registration or maintenance of the domain name registration.

39-2d REMEDIES

The Lanham Act provides several remedies for infringement: (1) injunctive relief, (2) an accounting for profits, (3) damages, (4) destruction of infringing articles, (5) attorneys' fees in exceptional cases, and (6) costs. In assessing profits, the plaintiff has to prove only the gross sales made by the defendant; the defendant has the burden of proving any costs to be deducted in determining profits. If the court finds that the amount of recovery based on profits is either inadequate or excessive, the court may, in its discretion, award an amount it determines to be just. In assessing damages, the court may award up to three times the actual damages, according to the circumstances of the case. When an infringement is knowing and intentional, the court in the absence of extenuating circumstances shall award attorneys' fees plus the greater of treble profits or treble damages. In an action brought under the Federal Trademark Dilution Act of 1995, the owner of the famous mark can obtain only injunctive relief unless the person against whom the injunction is sought willfully intended to trade on the owner's reputation or to cause dilution of the famous mark. If willful intent is proven, the owner of the famous mark also may obtain the other remedies discussed.

When a person intentionally traffics in goods or services known to bear a counterfeit mark, both civil and criminal remedies are available. In addition, goods bearing the counterfeit mark may be seized and destroyed. A **counterfeit mark** is a spurious mark that is identical with, or substantially indistinguishable from, a registered mark and the use of which is likely to cause confusion, to cause mistake, or to deceive. In assessing damages for trademark counterfeiting, the court shall, unless it finds extenuating circumstances, enter judgment for three times the defendant's profits or the plaintiff's damages, whichever is greater, plus reasonable attorneys' fees. Instead of actual damages and profits, the plaintiff may elect to receive an award of statutory damages, in an amount the court considers just, between $1,000 and $200,000 per counterfeit mark or, if the use of the counterfeit mark was willful, not more than $2 million per counterfeit mark. Criminal sanctions include a fine of up to $2 million, imprisonment of up to ten years, or both. For a repeat offense, the limits are $5 million and twenty years, respectively. For a nonindividual offender, such as a corporation, the fine may be up to $5 million for a first offense and up to $15 million for a repeat offense.

39-3 Trade Names

A **trade name** is any name used to identify a business, vocation, or occupation. Descriptive and generic words, and personal and generic names, although not proper trademarks, may become protected as trade names upon acquiring a special significance in the trade. A name acquires such significance, frequently referred to as a "secondary meaning," through its continuing and extended use in connection with specific goods or services, whereby the acquired meaning eclipses the primary meaning of the name in the minds of a substantial number of purchasers or users of the goods or services. Although they are not eligible for Federal registration under the Lanham Act, trade names are protected, and a person who palms off her goods or services by using the trade name of another is liable in damages and also may be enjoined from doing so.

39-4 Copyrights

Copyright is a form of protection provided by Federal law to authors of original works, which, under Section 102 of the Copyright Act, include literary, musical, and dramatic works; pantomimes; choreographic works; pictorial, graphic, and sculptural works; motion picture and other audiovisual works; sound recordings; and architectural works. This listing is illustrative, not exhaustive, as the Act extends copyright protection to "original works of authorship fixed in any tangible medium of expression, now known or later developed." Section 102(a). Moreover, in 1980, the Copyright Act was amended to extend copyright protection to computer programs. Furthermore, the Semiconductor Chip Protection Act of 1984 extended protection for ten years to safeguard mask works embodied in a semiconductor chip product.

On March 1, 1989, the United States joined the Berne Convention, an international treaty protecting copyrighted works adopted by at least 179 nations. Other treaties covering copyrights are the 1952 Universal Copyright Convention (at least 100 nations), the World Intellectual Property Organization (WIPO) Copyright Treaty of 1996 (at least 110 nations) and the WIPO Performances and Phonograms Treaty of 1996 (at least 109 nations). The Marrakesh Treaty of 2013 administered by WIPO creates a set of mandatory limitations and exceptions for the benefit of the blind, visually impaired, and otherwise print disabled. It has been adopted by the United States and at least 79 other nations.

In 1998, Congress enacted the Digital Millennium Copyright Act (DMCA), which amended the Copyright Act to implement the WIPO Copyright Treaty and the WIPO Performances and Phonograms Treaty by extending U.S. copyright protection to works required to be protected under these two treaties. The WIPO treaties called for adequate legal protection and effective legal remedies against the circumvention of effective technological measures that are used by copyright owners to prevent unauthorized exercise of their copyrights. The DMCA contains three principal anticircumvention provisions. The first provision prohibits circumventing a technological protection measure put in place by a copyright owner to control *access* to a copyrighted work. Under the DMCA, "to circumvent a technological measure" means "to descramble a scrambled work, to decrypt an encrypted work, or otherwise to avoid, bypass, remove, deactivate, or impair a technological measure, without the authority of the copyright owner." The second provision prohibits creating or making available technologies developed or advertised to defeat technological protections against unauthorized *access* to a copyrighted work. The third provision prohibits creating or making available technologies developed or advertised to defeat technological protections against unauthorized copying or other infringements of the exclusive rights of the copyright owner in a copyrighted work. Thus, the first two prohibitions deal with access controls while the third prohibition deals with copy controls. They make it illegal, for example, to create or distribute a computer program that can break the access or copy protection security code on an electronic book or a DVD movie.

In 2018, Congress enacted the Music Modernization Act (MMA) to update copyright law by creating a new compulsory licensing system for digital music services that transmit sound recordings. The MMA also provides Federal protection to sound recordings fixed before February 15, 1972, which were previously covered only by State law. It further authorizes royalties for producers, mixers, and sound engineers that made a creative contribution to a sound recording.

In no case does the copyright protection accorded an original work of authorship extend to any idea, procedure, process, system, method of operation, concept, principle, or discovery, regardless of the form in which it is described, explained, illustrated, or embodied in such work. Section 102(b). Copyright protection encompasses only an *original expression* of an idea. For example, the idea of interfamily feuding cannot be copyrighted, but a particular expression of that idea in the form of a novel, drama, movie, or opera may be copyrighted.

39-4a REGISTRATION

Copyright applications are filed with the Register of Copyrights in Washington, D.C. In recent years, the Copyright Office has issued more than 500,000 copyright registrations each year. Although copyright registration is not required, because copyright protection begins automatically as soon as the work is fixed in a tangible medium, registration is advisable, nonetheless, because it is a condition of certain remedies (statutory damages and attorneys' fees) for copyright infringement. When a work is published, it is advisable, though no longer required, to place a copyright notice on all publicly distributed copies so as to notify users about the copyright claim. If proper notice appears on the published copies to which a defendant in a copyright infringement case had access, then the defendant will be unable to mitigate actual or statutory damages by asserting a defense of innocent infringement. Section 401. Innocent infringement occurs when the infringer did not realize that the work was protected.

Practical Advice

You should register your copyrights and place a copyright notice on all publicly distributed copies. Notice consists of three elements: (1) the symbol © or the word Copyright *or the abbreviation* Copr.; *(2) the year of first publication of the work; and (3) the name of the owner of the copyright in the work.*

39-4b RIGHTS

As amended in 1998 by the Sonny Bono Copyright Extension Act, in most instances, copyright protection subsists for the duration of the author's life plus an additional seventy years. Section 106 of the Copyright Act gives the owner of a copyright the exclusive right to

1. reproduce the copyrighted work in copies or recordings;
2. prepare derivative works based upon the copyrighted work;
3. distribute copies or recordings of the copyrighted work to the public by sale or other transfer of ownership or by rental, lease, or lending;
4. perform the copyrighted work publicly, in the case of literary, musical, dramatic, choreographic, pantomime, motion picture, and other audiovisual works; and
5. display the copyrighted work publicly, in the case of literary, musical, dramatic, and choreographic works, pantomimes, and pictorial, graphic, or sculptural works, including the individual images of a motion picture or other audiovisual work.

These broad rights are subject, however, to several limitations, the most important of which are "compulsory licenses," "fair use," and the "first sale doctrine." **Compulsory licenses** permit certain limited uses of copyrighted material upon the payment of specified royalties and compliance with statutory conditions. Section 107 codifies the common law doctrine of **fair use** by providing that the fair use of a copyrighted work for purposes such as criticism, comment, news reporting, teaching (including multiple copies for classroom use), scholarship, or research is not an infringement of copyright. In determining whether the use made of a work in any particular case is fair, the courts consider the following factors: (1) the purpose and character of the use, including whether such use is of a commercial nature or is for nonprofit educational purposes; (2) the nature of the copyrighted work; (3) the amount and substantiality of the portion used in relation to the copyrighted work as a whole; and (4) the effect of the use upon the potential market for or value of the copyrighted work.

The **first sale doctrine** limits the copyright owner's exclusive right of distribution by allowing the owner of a particular lawfully made copy of a work to sell or otherwise dispose of possession of that copy without authority of the copyright owner. Section 109. In 1990, amendments to Section 109 created an exception to the first sale doctrine by prohibiting the rental, lease, or commercial lending of sound recordings and computer programs for direct or indirect commercial advantage unless authorized by the copyright owner.

◆ *See Case 39-3*

39-4c OWNERSHIP

The author of a creative work owns the entire copyright. Although the actual creator of a work is usually the author, in two situations under the doctrine of **works for hire**, she is not considered the author. Section 101. First, if an employee prepares a work within the scope of her employment, her employer is considered to be the author of the work. Second, if a work is specially ordered or commissioned for certain purposes specified in the copyright statute *and* the parties expressly agree in writing that the work shall be considered a work for hire, the person commissioning the work is deemed to be the author. The kinds of works subject to becoming works for hire by commission include contributions to collective works; parts of motion pictures or other audiovisual works; translations; supplementary works such as prefaces, illustrations, or after words; compilations; instructional texts; and tests. In a work made for hire, the copyright lasts for a term of 95 years from the year of its first publication, or a term of 120 years from the year of its creation, whichever expires first.

The ownership of a copyright may be transferred in whole or in part by conveyance, will, or intestate succession. Section 201. A transfer of copyright ownership, other than by operation of law, is not valid, however, unless it is memorialized in a note or memorandum signed by the owner of the rights conveyed or by the owner's duly authorized agent. Section 204. An author may terminate any transfer of copyright ownership, other than that of a work for hire, during the five-year period beginning thirty-five years after the transfer was granted. Section 203.

Ownership of a copyright or of any of the exclusive rights under a copyright is distinct from the ownership of any material object that embodies the work. Transferring the ownership of any material object, including the copy or recording in which the work was first fixed, does not in itself convey any rights in the copyrighted work embodied in the object, nor in the absence of an agreement does the transfer of copyright ownership or of any exclusive rights under a copyright convey property rights in any material object. Section 202. Thus, the purchase of this textbook neither affects the publisher's copyright nor authorizes the purchaser to make and sell copies of the book. Under the first sale doctrine, however, the purchaser may rent, lend, or resell the book. Section 109.

39-4d INFRINGEMENT AND REMEDIES

The Copyright Act entitles a copyright owner to institute a civil action in a Federal district court for infringement of the owner's exclusive rights under the Act. In addition, the **Copyright Alternative in Small-Claims Enforcement Act of 2019** (the CASE Act) established a Copyright Claims Board (CCB) in the Copyright Office to hear copyright infringement disputes. Damages awarded by the CCB are capped at $30,000. Participation in CCB proceedings is voluntary with an opt-out procedure for defendants to have the dispute heard in a Federal district court. If the parties agree to have their dispute heard by the CCB, they give up the right to be heard in a Federal district court and the right to a jury trial.

Infringement occurs whenever somebody exercises, without authorization, the rights exclusively reserved for the copyright owner. Infringement need not be intentional. To prove infringement, the plaintiff need only establish that he owns the copyright and that the defendant violated one or more of the plaintiffs exclusive rights under the copyright. Proof of infringement usually consists of showing that the allegedly infringing work is substantially similar to the copyrighted work and that the alleged infringer had access to the copyrighted work. The DMCA amended the Copyright Act to create limitations on the liability of online providers for copyright infringement when engaging in certain activities.

For the owner to sue for infringement, the copyright must be registered with the Copyright Office, unless the work is a Berne Convention work whose country of origin is not the United States. For an infringement occurring after registration, the following remedies are available: (1) injunction; (2) the impoundment and, possibly, destruction of infringing articles; (3) actual damages, plus profits made by the infringer that are additional to those damages, *or* statutory damages of at least $750 but no more than $30,000 ($150,000 if the infringement is willful), according to what the court determines to be just; (4) in the court's discretion, costs including reasonable attorneys' fees to the prevailing party; and (5) criminal penalties of a fine and/or up to one year's imprisonment for willful infringement for purposes of commercial advantage or private financial gain.

In 1997, Congress enacted the No Electronic Theft Act (NET Act) to close a loophole in the Copyright Act, which permitted infringers to pirate copyrighted works willfully and knowingly so long as they did not do so for profit. The NET Act amended Federal copyright law to define "financial gain" to include the receipt of anything of value, including the receipt of other copyrighted works. The NET Act also clarified that when internet users or any other individuals distribute copyrighted works broadly, even if they do not intend to profit personally, they have violated the Copyright Act. The Act accomplished this by imposing penalties for willfully infringing a copyright (1) for purposes of commercial advantage or private financial gain or (2) by reproducing or distributing, including by electronic means, during any 180-day period one or more copies of one or more copyrighted works with a total retail value of more than $1,000. It also extended the statute of limitations for criminal copyright infringement from three to five years. Finally, it increased criminal penalties for certain copyright violations. Imprisonment for up to five years (ten years for subsequent offenses) may be imposed for willful infringement if at least ten copies with a total retail value of more than $2,500 in a 180-day period are reproduced or distributed.

The Family Entertainment and Copyright Act of 2005 established criminal penalties for willful copyright infringement by the distribution of a computer program, musical work, motion picture or other audiovisual work, or sound recording being prepared for commercial distribution by making it available on a computer network accessible to members of the public if the person knew or should have known that the work was intended for commercial distribution. In essence, it prohibits (1) bootlegging of copyrighted audio and video material or (2) recording a cinema-released film on videotape from the audience (the primary way bootleggers make illegal copies of recently released movies). The bill does, however, allow for the sale and use of technology that can skip content of films to edit out language, violence, or sex. The criminal penalties are a fine and/or imprisonment for up to three years (six years for subsequent offenses), but if the infringement was for purposes of commercial advantage or private financial gain, then imprisonment may be imposed for up to five years (ten years for subsequent offenses).

The Anti-counterfeiting Amendments Act of 2004 prohibits knowingly trafficking in (1) a counterfeit or illicit label of a copy of a computer program, motion picture (or other audiovisual work), literary work, or pictorial, graphic, or sculptural work, a phonorecord, a work of visual art, or documentation or packaging or (2) counterfeit documentation or packaging. Violators are subject to fines and/or imprisonment of up to five years. In addition, a copyright owner who is injured, or threatened with injury, may bring a civil action to obtain (1) an injunction, (2) impoundment and possible destruction of infringing articles, (3) reasonable attorneys' fees and costs, and (4) actual damages and any additional profits of the violator or statutory damages of at least $2,500 but no more than $25,000. Moreover, the court may increase an award of damages by three times the amount that would otherwise be awarded for a violation occurring within three years after a final judgment was entered for a previous violation.

39-5 Patents

The U.S. Constitution grants Congress the power "to promote the Progress of Science and useful Arts, by securing for limited Times to … Inventors the exclusive Right to their … Discoveries." Through a **patent**, the Federal government grants an inventor a monopolistic right to make, use, or sell an invention to the absolute exclusion of others for the period of the patent. The patent owner may also profit by selling the patent or by licensing others to use the patent on a royalty basis. The patent may not be renewed, however: upon expiration, the invention enters the "public domain," and anyone may use it.

Moreover, under the **patent exhaustion doctrine**, when a patent owner sells one of its products, the patent owner can no longer control that item through the patent laws. Accordingly, the purchaser and all subsequent owners are free to use or resell the product just like any other item of personal property, without being subject to a patent infringement lawsuit. This doctrine is analogous to the first sale doctrine in copyright law. The U.S. Supreme Court applied the exhaustion doctrine to a case in which Lexmark sold laser toner cartridges at a discount domestically and internationally. In exchange for the lower price, customers signed a contract agreeing to use the cartridge only once and to refrain from transferring the empty cartridge to anyone but Lexmark. The Supreme Court held that a patent owner's decision to sell a product exhausts all its patent rights in that item, regardless of any restrictions the patent owner purports to impose or the location of the sale. *Impression Products, Inc. v. Lexmark International, Inc.*, 581 U. S. _____ (2017).

On September 16, 2011, President Obama signed into law the Leahy-Smith America Invents Act, which represents the most significant reform of the Patent Act since 1952. Most of its provisions apply to any patent issued on or after September 16, 2012. The legislation is intended to establish a more efficient patent system that will improve patent quality and limit unnecessary litigation costs. Subject to some exceptions, the America Invents Act provides that the United States will no longer award a patent to the first person to create an invention but instead will award the patent to the first inventor to file an application for the invention. Converting from a "first to invent" to a "first inventor to file" patent registration system is intended to simplify the application system and to harmonize the U.S. patent system with systems commonly used in other countries with which the United States conducts trade. The "first inventor to file" provision went into effect on March 16, 2013. In recent years, more than 300,000 U.S. patents have been issued each year, and approximately 52 percent of them have been issued to foreign residents.

39-5a PATENTABILITY

The Patent Act specifies those inventions that may be patented as **utility patents**. Section 101 provides:

> Whoever invents or discovers any new and useful process, machine, manufacture, or composition of matter, or any new and useful improvement thereof, may obtain a patent therefor, subject to the conditions and requirements of this title.

Thus, naturally occurring substances are not patentable, as the invention must be made or modified by humans. For example, the discovery of a bacterium with useful properties is not patentable, whereas the manufacture of a genetically engineered bacterium is. By the same token, laws of nature, principles, bookkeeping systems, fundamental truths, methods of calculation, and ideas are not patentable. Accordingly, as Chief Justice Burger noted in *Diamond, Commissioner of Patents and Trademarks v. Chakrabarty*, "Einstein could not patent his law that $E = mc^2$, nor could Newton have patented the law of gravity." Similarly, isolated computer programs are not patentable, although, as mentioned previously, they may be copyrighted. In recent years, approximately 91 percent of U.S. patents issued have been utility patents.

To be patentable as a utility patent, the process, machine, manufacture, or composition of matter must meet three criteria:

1. *Novelty.* The invention must not conflict with a prior pending application or a previously issued patent;
2. *Utility.* The invention must possess specific and substantial usefulness, which must be affirmatively disclosed by the application; and
3. *Nonobviousness.* The invention, in light of the prior art, must not be obvious to a person skilled in such prior art.

In addition to utility patents, the Patent Act provides for plant patents and design patents. A **plant patent** protects the exclusive right to reproduce a new and distinctive variety of an asexually reproducing plant. Asexually propagated plants are those that are reproduced by means other than from seeds, such as by the rooting of cuttings as well as by layering, budding, or grafting. Plant patents require (1) novelty, (2) distinctiveness, and (3) nonobviousness. In recent years, fewer than four-tenths of 1 percent of patents issued have been plant patents.

A **design patent** protects a new, original, ornamental design for an article of manufacture. A design patent protects only the appearance of an article—not its structural or functional features. Design patents require (1) novelty, (2) ornamentality, and (3) nonobviousness. In recent years, approximately 9 percent of patents issued have been design patents.

Utility and plant patents have a term that begins on the date of the patent's grant and ends twenty years from the date of application, subject to extensions for statutorily specified delays. Design patents have a term of fourteen years from the date of grant.

♦ *See Case 39-4*

39-5b ISSUANCE OF PATENTS

The USPTO issues a patent upon the basis of a patent application containing a *specification*, which describes how the invention works, and *claims*, which describe the features that make the invention patentable. Prior to the 2011 America Invents Act, the applicant must have been the inventor. Under the America Invents Act, a person to whom the inventor has assigned, or is under an obligation to assign, the invention may file a patent application. Before granting a patent, the USPTO thoroughly examines the prior art (the information available to the public at the time of the application) and determines whether the submitted invention is nonobvious and has novelty and utility (or distinctiveness or ornamentality in the case of plant or design patents). An application for a patent is confidential, and the USPTO will not divulge its contents. This confidentiality ends, however, upon the granting of the patent. Unlike rights under a copyright, no monopoly rights arise until the USPTO actually issues a patent. Therefore, anyone is free to make, use, and sell an invention for which a patent application is filed until the patent has been granted.

The rights granted by a U.S. patent extend only to the United States. A person desiring a patent in another country must apply for a patent in that country. The Patent Cooperation Treaty, adhered to by the United States and at least 152 other countries, facilitates the filing of applications for patents on the same invention in member countries by providing for centralized filing procedures and a standardized application format. Other treaties for patent protection are the Paris Convention for the Protection of Industrial Property (at least 177 nations) and the Patent Law Treaty (PLT) of 2000 (at least 43 nations).

Congress previously amended the Patent Act to require the publication of certain utility and plant patent applications eighteen months after filing even if the patent has not yet been granted. This requirement applies only to those patent applications that are filed in other countries that require publication after eighteen months or under the Patent Cooperation Treaty. An applicant may obtain a reasonable royalty from a third party who between publication and issuance of the patent infringes it, provided the third party had actual notice of the published application. An applicant whose application is rejected may apply for reexamination. If the application is again rejected, the applicant may appeal to the USPTO's Patent Trial and Appeal Board (previously called the Board of Patent Appeals and Interferences) and from there to the Federal courts.

Under the America Invents Act, any person other than the patent owner may file a petition for **inter partes** review to request cancellation of one or more claims of a patent on the grounds that the claim fails the novelty or nonobviousness standards for patentability. If a petition is filed, the patent owner has the right to file a preliminary response explaining why *inter partes* review should not be instituted. Once *inter partes* review is instituted, the U.S. Patent Trial and Appeal Board must decide the patentability of all of the challenged claims. The petitioner has the burden of proving unpatentability by a preponderance of the evidence. A party dissatisfied with the Board's decision may seek judicial review in the Court of Appeals for the Federal Circuit. In a 7–2 decision, the U.S. Supreme Court upheld the constitutionality of the *inter partes* review. *Oil States Energy Services, LLC v. Greene's Energy Group, LLC*, 584 U. S. _____ (2018).

39-5c INFRINGEMENT

Anyone who, without permission, makes, uses, or sells a patented invention is a **direct infringer**, whereas a person who actively encourages another to make, use, offer to sell, or sell a patented invention without permission is an **indirect infringer**. A **contributory infringer** is one who knowingly sells or offers to sell a part or component of a patented invention, unless the component is a staple or commodity or is suitable for a substantial noninfringing use. While good faith and ignorance are defenses to contributory infringement, they are not defenses to direct infringement. To recover damages, a patent owner must give (1) actual notice to an infringer or (2) constructive notice by marking a patented article with the word *Patent* and the number of the patent. The America Invents Act permits patent holders to "virtually mark" a product by providing the address of a publicly available website that associates the patented article with the number of the patent.

The rights under a patent do not extend beyond the first sale; that is, the purchaser of a patented item is permitted to use or resell that item. The right to use a purchased item includes the right to repair it so long as the repair does not constitute reconstruction, which would infringe upon the patent holder's exclusive right to make the invention.

Practical Advice

Give notice of your patented articles by fixing on them the word patent *or the abbreviation* pat.*, together with (1) the number of the patent or (2) a reference to an internet address.*

39-5d REMEDIES

If a patent is infringed, the patent owner may sue for relief in Federal court. The remedies for infringement under the Patent Act are (1) injunctive relief; (2) damages adequate to compensate the plaintiff but "in no event less than a reasonable royalty for the use made of the invention by the infringer"; (3) treble damages, when appropriate; (4) attorneys' fees in exceptional cases, such as those that involve knowing infringement; and (5) costs.

♦ **SEE FIGURE 39-1** *Intellectual Property*

FIGURE 39-1 **Intellectual Property**

	Trade Secrets	Trade Symbols	Copyright	Patents
What Is Protected	Information	Mark	Work of authorship	Invention
Rights Protected	Use or sell	Use or sell	Reproduce, prepare derivative works, distribute, perform, or display	Make, use, or sell
Duration	Until disclosed	Until abandoned	Usually author's life plus seventy years	For utility and plant patents, twenty years from application; For design patents, fourteen years from grant
Federally Protected	Yes*	Yes	Yes	Yes
Requirements for Protection	Valuable secret	Distinctive	Original and fixed	Novel, useful, and nonobvious

*Trade secrets are also protected under State law.

C H A P T E R   S U M M A R Y

TRADE SECRETS

Definition commercially valuable, secret information
Protection under State and Federal law, the owner of a trade secret may obtain damages or injunctive relief when the trade secret is misappropriated (wrongfully used) by an employee or a competitor; under Federal law, criminal penalties are imposed for the theft of trade secrets

TRADE SYMBOLS

Types of Trade Symbols
- *Trademark* distinctive symbol, word, or design that is used to identify the manufacturer
- *Service Mark* distinctive symbol, word, or design that is used to identify a provider's services
- *Certification Mark* distinctive symbol, word, or design used with goods or services to certify specific characteristics
- *Collective Mark* distinctive symbol used to indicate membership in an organization

Registration to be registered and thus protected by the Lanham Act, a mark must be distinctive
Infringement occurs when a person without authorization uses a substantially indistinguishable mark that is likely to cause confusion, mistake, or deception
Remedies the Lanham Act provides the following remedies for infringement: injunctive relief, profits, damages, destruction of infringing articles, costs, and attorneys' fees in exceptional cases

TRADE NAMES

Definition any name used to identify a business, vocation, or occupation
Protection may not be registered under the Lanham Act, but infringement is prohibited
Remedies damages and injunctions are available if infringement occurs

COPYRIGHTS

Definition exclusive right, usually for the author's life plus seventy years, to original works of authorship
Registration is not required but provides additional remedies for infringement
Rights copyright protection provides the exclusive right to (1) reproduce the copyrighted work, (2) prepare derivative works based on the work, (3) distribute copies of the work, and (4) perform or display the work publicly

Ownership the author of the copyrighted work is usually the owner of the copyright, which may be transferred in whole or in part

Infringement occurs when someone exercises the copyright owner's rights without authorization

Remedies if infringement occurs after registration, the following remedies are available: (1) injunction, (2) impoundment and possible destruction of infringing articles, (3) actual damages plus profits or statutory damages, (4) costs, and (5) criminal penalties

---

PATENTS

Definition the exclusive right to an invention for twenty years from the date of application for utility and plant patents; fourteen years from grant for design patents

Patentability to be patentable, the invention must be (1) novel, (2) useful, and (3) not obvious

Issuance of Patents patents are issued upon application to and after examination by the U.S. Patent and Trademark Office

Infringement occurs when anyone without permission makes, uses, or sells a patented invention

Remedies for infringement of a patent are (1) injunctive relief; (2) damages; (3) treble damages, where appropriate; (4) attorneys' fees; and (5) costs

---

C A S E S

CASE 39-1

Trade Secrets
ED NOWOGROSKI INSURANCE, INC. v. RUCKER
Supreme Court of Washington, En Banc, 1999
137 Wash.2d 427, 971 P.2d 936

Guy, C. J.

This case is a trade secrets misappropriation action brought under the Uniform Trade Secrets Act, [citation], by an employer against former employees. The employer, Ed Nowogroski Insurance, Inc. (Nowogroski Inc.), owned by the Rupp family, sued its former employees, Michael Rucker, Darwin Rieck and Jerry Kiser, for soliciting its clients using confidential information. The employees had worked for Nowogroski Inc. as insurance salesmen and servicers of insurance business. Nowogroski Inc. also sued Potter, Leonard and Cahan, Inc., a rival insurance agency, for which employees Rucker, Rieck and Kiser commenced work when they terminated their employment with Nowogroski Inc.

Following * * * trial, the trial court found that the employees had misappropriated Nowogroski Inc.'s trade secrets by retaining and using confidential client lists and other information. However, it awarded no damages for one employee's solicitation of clients through the use of memorized client information. None of the factual findings has been challenged in this Court.

* * *

Nowogroski Inc. appealed, arguing that the trial court erred in holding that prior Washington cases prohibiting an ex-employee from using memorized, confidential client information to solicit his former employer's customers were abrogated by the Uniform Trade Secrets Act. Nowogroski Inc. argued that the form of information which constituted a trade secret is irrelevant. Nowogroski Inc. also argued that the employees should be liable for misappropriation of a trade secret whether the information that constituted the protected information was written or memorized.

* * *

The Court of Appeals held that there was no legal distinction between written and memorized information under the Washington Uniform Trade Secrets Act. * * * The Court of Appeals affirmed the trial court's award of damages based on 0.5 percent of commission * * *.

We granted the employees and their new employer's petition for review. * * * The Petitioners challenge only the Court of Appeals' conclusion that both memorized confidential information, as well as written information, may be protected under the Uniform Trade Secrets Act if it otherwise qualifies as a trade secret under the Act. * * *

* * *

As a general rule, an employee who has not signed an agreement not to compete is free, upon leaving employment, to engage in competitive employment. In so doing, the former employee may freely use general knowledge, skills, and experience acquired under his or her former employer. However, the former employee, even in the absence of an enforceable covenant not to compete, remains under a duty not to use or disclose, to the detriment of the former employer, trade secrets acquired in the course of previous employment. Where the former employee seeks to use the trade secrets of the former employer in order to obtain a competitive advantage, then competitive activity can be enjoined or result in an award of damages. [Citation.]

Once a common law concept, trade secret protection is now governed by statutes in most states, including Washington. [Citation.] * * * The [Uniform Trade Secrets] Act codifies the basic principles of common law trade secret protection. [Citation.] A purpose of trade secrets law is to maintain and promote standards of commercial ethics and fair dealing in protecting those secrets. [Citation.]

* * *

* * * A plaintiff seeking damages for misappropriation of a trade secret under the Uniform Trade Secrets Act has the burden of proving that legally protectable secrets exist. [Citation.]

In this case, the trial court found that the insurance information, including the customer lists: (1) derived independent economic value from not being known or readily ascertainable by proper means by other persons who can obtain economic value from its disclosure or use, and (2) that the plaintiff's efforts to keep the customer files secret by educating its staff and by providing employment manuals and employment agreements had been reasonable.

* * *

The nature of the employment relationship imposes a duty on employees and former employees not to use or disclose the employer's trade secrets. [Citation.] The Petitioners in the present case do not argue that the trial court erred in concluding that they "misappropriated" a trade secret; rather, they argue that information in the memory of the employee about a customer list is not a trade secret.

A customer list is one of the types of information which can be a protected trade secret if it meets the criteria of the Trade Secrets Act. [Citations.]

* * *

Briefly expressed, whether a customer list is protected as a trade secret depends on three factual inquiries: (1) whether the list is a compilation of information; (2) whether it is valuable because unknown to others; and (3) whether the owner has made reasonable attempts to keep the information secret. There is no dispute in this case that the customer names, expiration dates, coverage information and related information is a compilation of information. The trial court found that the customer list and associated information derived independent economic value from not being known, or readily ascertainable by proper means, by other persons who can obtain economic

value from its disclosure or use and that Nowogroski Inc. undertook reasonable steps to protect its secrecy.

The question before us is whether the fact that the customer information was in one of the employee's memory allows him to use with impunity the information which was otherwise a trade secret under our statute. * * *

* * *

The Uniform Trade Secrets Act does not distinguish between written and memorized information. The Act does not require a plaintiff to prove actual theft or conversion of physical documents embodying the trade secret information to prove misappropriation. [Citations.] The Washington Uniform Trade Secrets Act defines a "trade secret" to include compilations of information which have certain characteristics without regard to the form that such information might take. The definition of "misappropriation" includes unauthorized "disclosure or use." [Citation.] As the Court of Appeals noted, two types of information mentioned in the Uniform Trade Secrets Act as examples of trade secrets include "method" and "technique;" these do not imply the requirement of written documents. [Citation.]

* * *

* * * If an employee was privy to a secret formula of a manufacturing company, which was valuable and kept secret, it should not cease to be a trade secret if an employee committed it to memory. [Citation.] While customer lists may or may not be trade secrets depending on the facts of the case, we conclude that trade secret protection does not depend on whether the list is taken in written form or memorized.

The form of information, whether written or memorized, is immaterial under the trade secrets statute; the Uniform Trade Secrets Act makes no distinction about the form of trade secrets. Whether the information is on a CD, a blueprint, a film, a recording, a hard paper copy or memorized by the employee, the inquiry is whether it meets the definition of a trade secret under the Act and whether it was misappropriated. Absent a contract to the contrary, an employee is free to compete against his or her former employer, and a former employee may use general knowledge, skills and experience acquired during the prior employment in competing with a former employer. However, an employee may not use or disclose trade secrets belonging to the former employer to actively solicit customers from a confidential customer list. In this case, the former employees actively solicited customers from the employer's customer lists, which the trial court found to be of independent value because unknown and subject to reasonable efforts to keep secret. The weight of modern authority is that the manner of taking a trade secret is irrelevant. Hence, we conclude the Court of Appeals was correct in holding that there is no legal distinction between written and memorized information under the Uniform Trade Secrets Act and in remanding for a recalculation of damages. We affirm.

Trademarks
WAL-MART STORES, INC. v. SAMARA BROTHERS, INC.
Supreme Court of the United States, 2000
529 U.S. 205, 120 S.Ct. 1339, 146 L.Ed.2d 182

Scalia, J.

In this case, we decide under what circumstances a product's design is distinctive, and therefore protectible, in an action for infringement of unregistered trade dress under §43(a) of the Trademark Act of 1946 (Lanham Act), [citation].

Respondent Samara Brothers, Inc., designs and manufactures children's clothing. Its primary product is a line of spring/summer one-piece seersucker outfits decorated with appliques of hearts, flowers, fruits, and the like. A number of chain stores, including JCPenney, sell this line of clothing under contract with Samara.

Petitioner Wal-Mart Stores, Inc., is one of the nation's best known retailers, selling among other things children's clothing. In 1995, Wal-Mart contracted with one of its suppliers, Judy-Philippine, Inc., to manufacture a line of children's outfits for sale in the 1996 spring/summer season. Wal-Mart sent Judy-Philippine photographs of a number of garments from Samara's line, on which Judy-Philippine's garments were to be based; Judy-Philippine duly copied, with only minor modifications, 16 of Samara's garments, many of which contained copyrighted elements. In 1996, Wal-Mart briskly sold the so-called knockoffs, generating more than $1.15 million in gross profits.

In June 1996, a buyer for JCPenney called a representative at Samara to complain that she had seen Samara garments on sale at Wal-Mart for a lower price than JCPenney was allowed to charge under its contract with Samara. The Samara representative told the buyer that Samara did not supply its clothing to Wal-Mart. Their suspicions aroused, however, Samara officials launched an investigation, which disclosed that Wal-Mart and several other major retailers—Kmart, Caldor, Hills, and Goody's—were selling the knockoffs of Samara's outfits produced by Judy-Philippine.

After sending cease-and-desist letters, Samara brought this action in the United States District Court for the Southern District of New York against Wal-Mart, Judy-Philippine, Kmart, Caldor, Hills, and Goody's for copyright infringement under federal law, consumer fraud and unfair competition under New York law, and—most relevant for our purposes—infringement of unregistered trade dress under §43(a) of the Lanham Act, [citation]. All of the defendants except Wal-Mart settled before trial.

After a weeklong trial, the jury found in favor of Samara on all of its claims. Wal-Mart then renewed a motion for judgment as a matter of law, claiming * * * that there was insufficient evidence to support a conclusion that Samara's clothing designs could be legally protected as distinctive trade dress for purposes of §43(a). The District Court denied the motion, [citation], and awarded Samara damages, interest, costs, and fees totaling almost $1.6 million, together with injunctive relief, [citation]. The Second Circuit affirmed the denial of the motion for judgment as a matter of law, [citation], and we granted certiorari, [citation].

The Lanham Act provides for the registration of trademarks, which it defines in §45 to include "any word, name, symbol, or device, or any combination thereof [used or intended to be used] to identify and distinguish [a producer's] goods ... from those manufactured or sold by others and to indicate the source of the goods ..." [Citation.] Registration of a mark under the Act, [citation], enables the owner to sue an infringer under [citation]; it also entitles the owner to a presumption that its mark is valid, [citation], and ordinarily renders the registered mark incontestable after five years of continuous use, [citation]. In addition to protecting registered marks, the Lanham Act, in §43(a), gives a producer a cause of action for the use by any person of "any word, term, name, symbol, or device, or any combination thereof ... which ... is likely to cause confusion ... as to the origin, sponsorship, or approval of his or her goods. ..." [Citation.] It is the latter provision that is at issue in this case.

The breadth of the definition of marks registrable under [the Act], and of the confusion-producing elements recited as actionable by §43(a), has been held to embrace not just word marks, such as "Nike," and symbol marks, such as Nike's "swoosh" symbol, but also "trade dress"—a category that originally included only the packaging, or "dressing," of a product, but in recent years has been expanded by many courts of appeals to encompass the design of a product. [Citations.] These courts have assumed, often without discussion, that trade dress constitutes a "symbol" or "device" for purposes of the relevant sections, and we conclude likewise. * * *

The text of §43(a) provides little guidance as to the circumstances under which unregistered trade dress may be protected. It does require that a producer show that the allegedly infringing feature is not "functional," [citation], and is likely to cause confusion with the product for which protection is sought, [citation]. Nothing in §43(a) explicitly requires a producer to show that its trade dress is distinctive, but courts have universally imposed that requirement, since without distinctiveness the trade dress would not "cause confusion * * * as to the origin, sponsorship, or approval of [the] goods," as the section requires. Distinctiveness is, moreover, an explicit prerequisite for registration of trade dress * * *. [Citation.]

In evaluating the distinctiveness of a mark * * *, courts have held that a mark can be distinctive in one of two ways. First, a mark is inherently distinctive if "[its] intrinsic nature serves to identify a particular source." [Citation.] In the context of word marks, courts have applied the now-classic test originally formulated by Judge Friendly, in which word marks that are "arbitrary" ("Camel" cigarettes), "fanciful" ("Kodak" film), or "suggestive" ("Tide" laundry detergent) are held to be inherently distinctive. [Citation.] Second, a mark has acquired distinctiveness, even if it is not inherently distinctive, if it has developed secondary meaning, which occurs when, "in the minds of the public, the primary significance of a [mark] is to identify the source of the product rather than the product itself." [Citation.]

The judicial differentiation between marks that are inherently distinctive and those that have developed secondary meaning has solid foundation in the statute itself. [The Act] requires that registration be granted to any trademark "by which the goods of the applicant may be distinguished from the goods of others"—subject to various limited exceptions. [Citation.] * * *

Indeed, with respect to at least one category of mark—colors—we have held that no mark can ever be inherently distinctive. * * * We held that a color could be protected as a trademark, but only upon a showing of secondary meaning. * * *

It seems to us that design, like color, is not inherently distinctive. The attribution of inherent distinctiveness to certain categories of word marks and product packaging derives from the fact that the very purpose of attaching a particular word to a product, or encasing it in a distinctive packaging, is most often to identify the source of the product. Although the words and packaging can serve subsidiary functions—a suggestive word mark (such as "Tide" for laundry detergent), for instance, may invoke positive connotations in the consumer's mind, and a garish form of packaging (such as Tide's squat, brightly decorated plastic bottles for its liquid laundry detergent) may attract an otherwise indifferent consumer's attention on a crowded store shelf—their predominant function remains source identification. Consumers are therefore predisposed to regard those symbols as indication of the producer, which is why such symbols "almost automatically tell a customer that they refer to a brand," [citation], and "immediately * * * signal a brand or a product 'source,'" [citation]. And where it is not reasonable to assume consumer predisposition to take an affixed word or packaging as indication of source—where, for example, the affixed word is descriptive of the product ("Tasty" bread) or of a geographic origin ("Georgia" peaches)—inherent distinctiveness will not be found. That is why the statute generally excludes, from those word marks that can be registered as inherently distinctive, words that are "merely descriptive" of the goods, [citation], or "primarily geographically descriptive of them," [citation]. In the case of product design, as in the case of color, we think consumer predisposition to equate the feature with the source does not exist. Consumers are aware of the reality that, almost invariably, even the most unusual of product designs—such as a cocktail shaker shaped like a penguin—is intended not to identify the source, but to render the product itself more useful or more appealing.

* * *

* * * To the extent there are close cases, we believe that courts should err on the side of caution and classify ambiguous trade dress as product design, thereby requiring secondary meaning. The very closeness will suggest the existence of relatively small utility in adopting an inherentdistinctiveness principle, and relatively great consumer benefit in requiring a demonstration of secondary meaning. * * *

We hold that, in an action for infringement of unregistered trade dress under §43(a) of the Lanham Act, a product's design is distinctive, and therefore protectible, only upon a showing of secondary meaning. The judgment of the Second Circuit is reversed, and the case is remanded for further proceedings consistent with this opinion.

CASE 39-3

Copyright
KIRTSAENG v. JOHN WILEY & SONS, INC.
Supreme Court of the United States, 2013
568 U.S. 519, 133 S.Ct. 1351, 185 L.Ed.2d 392

Breyer, J.
[The business of respondent, John Wiley & Sons, Inc., includes publishing academic textbooks. Wiley often assigns to its wholly owned foreign subsidiary, Wiley Asia, rights to publish, print, and sell a foreign edition of Wiley's English language textbooks abroad. Each copy of a Wiley Asia foreign edition will likely contain language making clear that the copy is to be sold only in a particular country or geographical region outside the United States. Thus, there are two essentially equivalent versions of a Wiley textbook, each version manufactured and sold with Wiley's permission: (1) a U.S. version printed and sold in the United States and (2) a foreign version manufactured and sold abroad. Wiley makes certain that copies of the foreign version state that they are not to be taken without permission into the United States.

Petitioner, Supap Kirtsaeng, a citizen of Thailand, moved to the United States in 1997 to study mathematics at Cornell University. He paid for his education with the help of a Thai Government scholarship which required him to teach in Thailand for ten years on his return. Kirtsaeng successfully completed his undergraduate courses at Cornell; successfully completed a Ph.D. program in mathematics at the University of Southern California; and then, as promised, returned to Thailand to teach. While he was studying in the United States, Kirtsaeng asked his friends and family in Thailand to buy copies of foreign edition English language textbooks at Thai bookstores, where they sold at low prices, and mail them to him in the United States. Kirtsaeng would then sell them, reimburse his family and friends, and keep the profit.

In 2008, Wiley brought this Federal lawsuit against Kirtsaeng for copyright infringement. Wiley claimed that Kirtsaeng's unauthorized importation of its English language books and his later resale of those books amounted to an infringement of Wiley's exclusive right to distribute under the Copyright Act's as well as the Act's related import prohibition. Kirtsaeng replied that the books he had acquired were "lawfully made" and that he had acquired them legitimately. Thus, in his view, the Copyright Act's "first sale" doctrine permitted him to resell or otherwise dispose of the books without the copyright owner's further permission.

The District Court held that Kirtsaeng could not assert the "first sale" defense because that doctrine does not apply to "foreign-manufactured goods," even if made abroad with the copyright owner's permission. The jury then found that Kirtsaeng had willfully infringed Wiley's American copyrights by selling and importing without authorization copies of eight of Wiley's copyrighted titles and assessed statutory damages of $600,000 ($75,000 per work). On appeal, the Second Circuit affirmed, concluding that the "first sale" doctrine does not apply to copies of American copyrighted works manufactured abroad.]

Section 106 of the Copyright Act grants "the owner of copyright under this title" certain "exclusive rights," including the right "to distribute copies ... of the copyrighted work to the public by sale or other transfer of ownership." [Citation.] These rights are qualified, however, by the application of various limitations set forth in the next several sections of the Act, §§107 through 122. Those sections, typically entitled "Limitations on exclusive rights," include, for example, the principle of "fair use" (§107), permission for limited library archival reproduction, (§108), and the doctrine at issue here, the "first sale" doctrine (§109).

Section 109(a) sets forth the "first sale" doctrine as follows:

"Notwithstanding the provisions of section 106(3) [the section that grants the owner exclusive distribution rights], the owner of a particular copy or phonorecord *lawfully made under this title* ... is entitled, without the authority of the copyright owner, to sell or otherwise

dispose of the possession of that copy or phonorecord." (Emphasis added.)

Thus, even though §106(3) forbids distribution of a copy of, say, the copyrighted novel Herzog without the copyright owner's permission, §109(a) adds that, once a copy of Herzog has been lawfully sold (or its ownership otherwise lawfully transferred), the buyer of *that copy* and subsequent owners are free to dispose of it as they wish. In copyright jargon, the "first sale" has "exhausted" the copyright owner's §106(3) exclusive distribution right.

What, however, if the copy of Herzog was printed abroad and then initially sold with the copyright owner's permission? Does the "first sale" doctrine still apply? * * *

To put the matter technically, an "importation" provision, §602(a)(1), says that

"[i]mportation into the United States, without the authority of the owner of copyright under this title, of copies ... of a work that have been acquired outside the United States is an infringement of the exclusive right to distribute copies ... *under section 106 ...*" [Citation] (emphasis added [by Court]).

Thus §602(a)(1) makes clear that importing a copy without permission violates the owner's exclusive distribution right. But in doing so, §602(a)(1) refers explicitly to the *§106(3)* exclusive distribution right. As we have just said, §106 is by its terms "[s]ubject to" the various doctrines and principles contained in §§107 through 122, including §109(a)'s "first sale" limitation. * * *

* * *

* * * [W]e ask whether the "first sale" doctrine applies to protect a buyer or other lawful owner of a copy (of a copyrighted work) lawfully manufactured abroad. Can that buyer bring that copy into the United States (and sell it or give it away) without obtaining permission to do so from the copyright owner? * * *

In our view, the answers to these questions are, yes. We hold that the "first sale" doctrine applies to copies of a copyrighted work lawfully made abroad.

* * *

[The Court reasoned that §109(a)'s language, its context, and the common law history of the "first sale" doctrine, taken together, favor an interpretation that imposes no geographical restrictions. The language of §109(a) read literally favors a non-geographical interpretation, namely, that "lawfully made under this title" means made "in accordance with" or "in compliance with" the Copyright Act. The language of §109(a) says nothing about geography.]

* * *

The American Library Association tells us that library collections contain at least 200 million books published abroad (presumably, many were first published in one of the nearly 180 copyright-treaty nations and enjoy American copyright protection under [citation]); that many others were first published in the United States but printed abroad because of lower costs; and that a geographical interpretation will likely require the libraries to obtain permission (or at least create significant uncertainty) before circulating or otherwise distributing these books. [Citations.]

* * *

Technology companies tell us that "automobiles, microwaves, calculators, mobile phones, tablets, and personal computers" contain copyrightable software programs or packaging. [Citations.] Many of these items are made abroad with the American copyright holder's permission and then sold and imported (with that permission) to the United States. [Citation.] A geographical interpretation would prevent the resale of, say, a car, without the permission of the holder of each copyright on each piece of copyrighted automobile software. * * * Without that permission a foreign car owner could not sell his or her used car.

Retailers tell us that over $2.3 trillion worth of foreign goods were imported in 2011. [Citation.] American retailers buy many of these goods after a first sale abroad. [Citation.] And, many of these items bear, carry, or contain copyrighted "packaging, logos, labels, and product inserts and instructions for [the use of] everyday packaged goods from floor cleaners and health and beauty products to breakfast cereals." [Citation.] The retailers add that American sales of more traditional copyrighted works, "such as books, recorded music, motion pictures, and magazines" likely amount to over $220 billion. [Citations.] A geographical interpretation would subject many, if not all, of them to the disruptive impact of the threat of infringement suits. [Citation.]

* * *

Thus, we believe that the practical problems * * * are too serious, too extensive, and too likely to come about for us to dismiss them as insignificant—particularly in light of the ever-growing importance of foreign trade to America. [Citation.] See The World Bank, Imports of goods and services (% of GDP) (imports in 2011 18% of U.S. gross domestic product compared to 11% in 1980), [citation]. The upshot is that copyright-related consequences along with language, context, and interpretive canons argue strongly against a geographical interpretation of §109(a).

* * *

For these reasons we conclude that the considerations supporting Kirtsaeng's nongeographical interpretation of the words "lawfully made under this title" are the more persuasive. The judgment of the Court of Appeals is reversed, and the case is remanded for further proceedings consistent with this opinion.

CASE
39-4

Patents

ASSOCIATION FOR MOLECULAR PATHOLOGY v. MYRIAD GENETICS, INC.

Supreme Court of the United States, 2013
569 U.S. 576, 133 S.Ct. 2107, 186 L.Ed.2d 124

Thomas, J.
Respondent Myriad Genetics, Inc. (Myriad), discovered the precise location and sequence of two human genes, mutations of which can substantially increase the risks of breast and ovarian cancer. Myriad obtained a number of patents based upon its discovery. This case involves claims from three of them and requires us to resolve whether a naturally occurring segment of deoxyribonucleic acid (DNA) is patent eligible under [Section 101 of the Patent Act] by virtue of its isolation from the rest of the human genome. We also address the patent eligibility of synthetically created DNA known as complementary DNA (cDNA), which contains the same protein-coding information found in a segment of natural DNA but omits portions within the DNA segment that do not code for proteins. For the reasons that follow, we hold that a naturally occurring DNA segment is a product of nature and not patent eligible merely because it has been isolated, but that cDNA is patent eligible because it is not naturally occurring. We, therefore, affirm in part and reverse in part the decision of the United States Court of Appeals for the Federal Circuit.

* * *

DNA's informational sequences and the processes * * * occur naturally within cells. Scientists can, however, extract DNA from cells using well known laboratory methods. These methods allow scientists to isolate specific segments of DNA—for instance, a particular gene or part of a gene—which can then be further studied, manipulated, or used. It is also possible to create DNA synthetically through processes similarly well known in the field of genetics. * * * This synthetic DNA created in the laboratory * * * is known as complementary DNA (cDNA).

Changes in the genetic sequence are called mutations. Mutations can be as small as the alteration of a single nucleotide [a molecule that forms the building block for DNA]—a change affecting only one letter in the genetic code. Such small-scale changes can produce an entirely different amino acid or can end protein production altogether. Large changes, involving the deletion, rearrangement, or duplication of hundreds or even millions of nucleotides, can result in the elimination, misplacement, or duplication of entire genes. Some mutations are harmless, but others can cause disease or increase the risk of disease. As a result, the study of genetics can lead to valuable medical breakthroughs.

This case involves patents filed by Myriad after it made one such medical breakthrough. Myriad discovered the precise location and sequence of what are now known as the BRCA1 and BRCA2 genes. Mutations in these genes can dramatically increase an individual's risk of developing breast and ovarian cancer. The average American woman has a 12- to 13-percent risk of developing breast cancer, but for women with certain genetic mutations, the risk can range between 50 and 80 percent for breast cancer and between 20 and 50 percent for ovarian cancer. Before Myriad's discovery of the BRCA1 and BRCA2 genes, scientists knew that heredity played a role in establishing a woman's risk of developing breast and ovarian cancer, but they did not know which genes were associated with those cancers.

Myriad identified the exact location of the BRCA1 and BRCA2 genes on chromosomes 17 and 13. * * * Knowledge of the location of the BRCA1 and BRCA2 genes allowed Myriad to determine their typical nucleotide sequence. That information, in turn, enabled Myriad to develop medical tests that are useful for detecting mutations in a patient's BRCA1 and BRCA2 genes and thereby assessing whether the patient has an increased risk of cancer.

Once it found the location and sequence of the BRCA1 and BRCA2 genes, Myriad sought and obtained a number of patents. * * *

* * *

Myriad's patents would, if valid, give it the exclusive right to isolate an individual's BRCA1 and BRCA2 genes * * * The patents would also give Myriad the exclusive right to synthetically create BRCA cDNA. In Myriad's view, manipulating BRCA DNA in either of these fashions triggers its "right to exclude others from making" its patented composition of matter under the Patent Act. [Citation.]

* * * Some years later, [petitioners including medical patients, advocacy groups, and doctors] filed this lawsuit seeking a declaration that Myriad's patents are invalid * * * The District Court then granted summary judgment to petitioners on the composition claims at issue in this case based on its conclusion that Myriad's claims, including claims related to cDNA, were invalid because they covered products of nature. [Citation.] [The Federal Circuit initially reversed, but on remand the Federal Circuit found both isolated DNA and cDNA patent eligible.]

* * *

Section 101 of the Patent Act provides:

"Whoever invents or discovers any new and useful…composition of matter, or any new and useful improvement thereof, may obtain a patent therefor, subject to the conditions and requirements of this title." [Citation.]

We have "long held that this provision contains an important implicit exception[:] Laws of nature, natural phenomena, and abstract ideas are not patentable." [Citation.] Rather, "'they are the basic tools of scientific and technological work'" that lie beyond the domain of patent protection. [Citation.] As the Court has explained, without this exception, there would be considerable danger that the grant of patents would "tie up" the use of such tools and thereby "inhibit future innovation premised upon them." [Citation.] This would be at odds with the very point of patents, which exist to promote creation. [Citation.]

The rule against patents on naturally occurring things is not without limits, however, for "all inventions at some level embody, use, reflect, rest upon, or apply laws of nature, natural phenomena, or abstract ideas," and "too broad an interpretation of this exclusionary principle could eviscerate patent law." [Citation.] As we have recognized before, patent protection strikes a delicate balance between creating "incentives that lead to creation, invention, and discovery" and "imped[ing] the flow of information that might permit, indeed spur, invention." [Citation.] We must apply this well-established standard to determine whether Myriad's patents claim any "new and useful … composition of matter," §101, or instead claim naturally occurring phenomena.

It is undisputed that Myriad did not create or alter any of the genetic information encoded in the BRCA1 and BRCA2 genes. The location and order of the nucleotides existed in nature before Myriad found them. Nor did Myriad create or alter the genetic structure of DNA. Instead, Myriad's principal contribution was uncovering the precise location and genetic sequence of the BRCA1 and BRCA2 genes within chromosomes 17 and 13. The question is whether this renders the genes patentable.

Myriad recognizes that our decision in [*Diamond* v. *Chakrabarty*] is central to this inquiry. * * * The *Chakrabarty* bacterium was new "with markedly different characteristics from any found in nature," [citation], due to the additional plasmids and resultant "capacity for degrading oil." [Citation.] In this case, by contrast, Myriad did not create anything. To be sure, it found an important and useful gene, but separating that gene from its surrounding genetic material is not an act of invention.

Groundbreaking, innovative, or even brilliant discovery does not by itself satisfy the §101 inquiry. * * * Myriad found the location of the BRCA1 and BRCA2 genes, but that discovery, by itself, does not render the BRCA genes "new … composition[s] of matter," §101, that are patent eligible.

* * * Nor are Myriad's claims saved by the fact that isolating DNA from the human genome severs chemical bonds and thereby creates a nonnaturally occurring molecule. * * *

* * *

cDNA does not present the same obstacles to patentability as naturally occurring, isolated DNA segments. As already explained, creation of a cDNA sequence * * * results in a * * * molecule that is not naturally occurring. Petitioners concede that cDNA differs from natural DNA in that "the non-coding regions have been removed." [Citation.] They nevertheless argue that cDNA is not patent eligible because "[t]he nucleotide sequence of cDNA is dictated by nature, not by the lab technician." [Citation.] That may be so, but the lab technician unquestionably creates something new when cDNA is made. cDNA retains the naturally occurring exons of DNA, but it is distinct from the DNA from which it was derived. As a result, cDNA is not a "product of nature" and is patent eligible under §101, except insofar as very short series of DNA may * * * be indistinguishable from natural DNA.

* * *

For the foregoing reasons, the judgment of the Federal Circuit is affirmed in part and reversed in part.

Q U E S T I O N S

1. Keller, a professor of legal studies at Rhodes University, is a diligent instructor. Late one night while reading a newly published, copyrighted treatise of 1,800 pages written by Gilbert, he came across a three-page section discussing the subject matter he intended to cover in class the next day. Keller considered the treatment to be illuminating and therefore photocopied the three pages and distributed the copies to his class. One of Keller's students is a second cousin of Gilbert, the author of the treatise, and she showed Gilbert the copies. May Gilbert recover from Keller for copyright infringement? Explain.

2. A conceived a secret process for the continuous freeze-drying of foodstuffs and related products and constructed a small pilot plant that practiced the process. A, however, lacked the financing necessary to develop the commercial potential of the process and, in hopes of obtaining a contract for its development and the payment of royalties, disclosed it in confidence to B, a coffee manufacturer, who signed an agreement not to disclose it to anyone else. At the same time, A signed an agreement not to disclose the process to any other person as long as A and B were considering a contract for its development. Upon A's disclosure of the process, B became extremely interested and offered to pay A the sum of $1,750,000 if, upon further development, the process proved to be commercially feasible. While negotiations between A and B were in progress, C, a competitor of B, learned of the process and requested a disclosure from A, who informed C that the process could not be disclosed to anyone unless negotiations with B were broken off. C offered to pay A $2,500,000 for the process, provided it met certain defined objective performance criteria. A contract was prepared and executed between A and C on this basis, without any prior disclosure of the process to C. Upon the making of this contract, A rejected B's offer. The process was thereupon disclosed to C, and demonstration runs of the pilot plant in the presence of C's representatives were conducted under varying conditions. After three weeks of conducting experimental demonstrations, compiling data, and analyzing results, C informed A that the process did not meet the performance criteria in the contract and that for this reason C was rejecting the process. Two years later, C placed on the market freeze-dried coffee that resembled in color, appearance, and texture the product of A's pilot plant. What are the rights of the parties? Discuss.

3. B, a chemist, was employed by A, a manufacturer, to work on a secret process for A's product under an exclusive three-year contract. A employed C, a salesperson, on a week-to-week basis. B and C resigned their employment with A and accepted employment in their respective capacities with D, a rival manufacturer. C began soliciting patronage from A's former customers, whose names he had memorized. What are the rights of the parties in (a) a suit by A to enjoin B from working for D and (b) a suit by A to enjoin C from soliciting A's customers? Explain.

4. Conrad and Darby were competitors in the business of dehairing raw cashmere, the fleece of certain Asiatic goats. Dehairing is the process of separating the commercially valuable soft down from the matted mass of raw fleece, which contains long coarse guard hairs and other impurities. Machinery for this process is not readily available on the open market. Each company in the business designed and built its own machinery and kept the nature of its process secret. Conrad contracted with Lawton, the owner of a small machine shop, to build and install new improved dehairing machinery of increased efficiency for which Conrad furnished designs, drawings, and instructions. Lawton, who knew

that the machinery design was confidential, agreed that he would manufacture the machinery exclusively for Conrad and that he would not reproduce the machinery or any of its essential parts for anyone else. Darby purchased from Lawton a copy of the dehairing machinery that Conrad had specially designed. What rights, if any, does Conrad have against (a) Lawton and (b) Darby? Explain.

5. Jones, having filed locally an affidavit required under the assumed name statute, has been operating and advertising his exclusive toy store for twenty years in Centerville, Illinois. His advertising has consisted of large signs on his premises reading "The Toy Mart." Lewis, after operating a store in Chicago under the name of "The Chicago Toy Mart," relocated in Centerville, Illinois, and erected a large sign reading "TOY MART" with the word "Centerville" written underneath in substantially smaller letters. Thereafter, Jones's sales declined, and many of his customers patronized Lewis's store, thinking it to be a branch of Jones's business. Discuss the rights of the parties.

6. Ryan Corporation manufactures and sells a variety of household cleaning products in interstate commerce. On national television, Ryan falsely advertises that its laundry liquid is biodegradable. Has Ryan violated the Lanham Act? Explain.

7. Gibbons, Inc., and Marvin Corporation are manufacturers who sell a variety of household cleaning products in interstate commerce. On national television, Gibbons states that its laundry liquid is biodegradable and that Marvin's is not. In fact, both products are biodegradable. Has Gibbons violated the Lanham Act? Explain.

8. George McCoy of Florida has been manufacturing and distributing a cheesecake for more than five years, labeling his product with a picture of a cheesecake, which serves as a background for a Florida bathing beauty and under which is written the slogan "McCoy All Spice Florida Cheese Cake." George McCoy has not registered his trademark. Subsequently, Leo McCoy of California begins manufacturing a similar product on the West Coast using a label similar in appearance to that of George McCoy, containing a picture of a Hollywood star and the words "McCoy's All Spice Cheese Cake." Leo McCoy begins marketing his products in the eastern United States, using labels with the word *Florida* added, as in George McCoy's label. Leo McCoy has registered his product under the Federal Trademark Act. To what relief, if any, is George McCoy entitled? Discuss.

C A S E   P R O B L E M S

9. Sony Corporation manufactured and sold home video recorders, specifically Betamax videotape recorders (VTRs). Universal City Studios, Inc. (Universal), owned the copyrights on some programs aired on commercially sponsored television. Individual Betamax owners frequently used the device to record some of Universal's copyrighted television programs for their own noncommercial use. Universal brought suit, claiming that the sale of the Betamax VTRs to the general public violated its rights under the Copyright Act. It sought no relief against any Betamax consumer. Instead, Universal sued Sony for contributory infringement of its copyrights, seeking money damages, an equitable accounting of profits, and an injunction against the manufacture and sale of Betamax VTRs. Explain whether Universal will prevail in its action.

10. The Coca-Cola Company manufactures a carbonated beverage, Coke, made from coca leaves and cola nuts. The Koke Company of America introduced into the beverage market a similar product named Koke. The Coca-Cola Company brought a trademark infringement action against Koke. Coca-Cola claimed unfair competition within the beverage business due to Koke's imitation of the Coca-Cola product and Koke's attempt to reap the benefit of consumer identification with the Coke name. Should Coca-Cola succeed? Explain.

11. Vuitton, a French corporation, manufactures high-quality handbags, luggage, and accessories. Crown Handbags, a New York corporation, manufactures and distributes ladies' handbags. Vuitton handbags are sold exclusively in expensive department stores, and distribution is strictly controlled to maintain a certain retail selling price. The Vuitton bags bear a registered trademark and a distinctive design. Crown's handbags appear identical to the Vuitton bags but are of inferior quality. May Vuitton recover from Crown for manufacturing counterfeit handbags and selling them at a discount? Explain.

12. T.G.I. Friday's, a New York corporation and registered service mark, entered into an exclusive licensing agreement with Tiffany & Co. that allowed Tiffany to open a Friday's restaurant in Jackson, Mississippi. International Restaurant Group, operated by the owners of Tiffany, applied for a license to open a Friday's in Baton Rouge, Louisiana, but was refused. In Baton Rouge, International then opened another restaurant, called E.L. Saturday's, or Ever Lovin' Saturday's, which had the

same type of menu and decor as Friday's. Friday's sues International for trademark infringement. Explain who will prevail.

13. As part of its business, Kinko's Graphics Corporation (Kinko's) copied excerpts from books, compiled them in "packets," and sold the packets to college students. Kinko's did this without permission from the owners of the copyrights to the books and without paying copyright fees or royalties. Kinko's has more than two hundred stores nationwide and reported $15 million in assets and $3 million in profits for 1989. Basic Books, Harper & Row, John Wiley & Sons, and others (plaintiffs) sued Kinko's for violation of the Copyright Act of 1976. Plaintiffs owned copyrights to the works copied and sold by Kinko's and derived substantial income from royalties. They argued that Kinko's had infringed on their copyrights by copying excerpts from their books and selling the copies to college students for profit. Kinko's admitted that it had copied excerpts without permission and had sold them in packets to students, but it contended that its actions constituted a fair use of the works in question under the Copyright Act. What result? Explain.

14. In 1967, a Chicago brewer, Meister Brau, Inc., began making and selling a reduced-calorie, reduced-carbohydrate beer under the name "LITE." Late in 1968, that company filed applications to register "LITE" as a trademark in the U.S. Patent Office, which ultimately approved three registrations of labels containing the name "LITE" for "beer with no available carbohydrates." In 1972, Meister Brau sold its interest in the "LITE" trademarks and the accompanying goodwill to Miller Brewing Company. Miller decided to expand its marketing of beer under the brand "LITE." It developed a modified recipe, which resulted in a beer lower in calories than Miller's regular beer but not without available carbohydrates. The label was revised, and one of the registrations was amended to show "LITE" printed rather than in script. In addition, Miller undertook an extensive advertising campaign. From 1973 through 1976, Miller expanded its annual sales of "LITE" from 50 thousand barrels to 4 million barrels and increased its annual advertising expenditures from $500,000 to more than $12 million.

Beginning in early 1975, a number of other brewers, including G. Heileman Brewing Company, introduced reduced-calorie beers labeled or described as "light." In response, Miller began filing trademark infringement actions against competitors to enjoin the use of the word *light*. Should Miller be granted the injunction? Explain.

15. B. C. Ziegler and Company (Ziegler) was a securities company located in West Bend. It had established an internal procedure by which its customer lists were treated confidentially. This procedure included burning or shredding any paper to be disposed of that contained a customer name or information. Nonetheless, in late 1985, Ziegler delivered a number of boxes of unshredded scrap paper to Lynn's Waste Paper Company for disposal. One of Lynn's employees, Ehren, who had been in the securities business and had worked for two of Ziegler's competitors, noticed the information contained in the delivery from Ziegler and purchased six boxes of the Ziegler wastepaper for $16.75 from Lynn's. Shortly thereafter, Ehren and his daughter sorted through the information and ultimately obtained 11,600 envelopes of information on Ziegler's customers, including names, account summaries, and other information. Ehren sold this information to Thorson, a broker in competition with Ziegler. Thorson then sent a mailing to the Ziegler customers to solicit security sales for his firm and obtained an abnormally high response rate as a result. Ziegler, with the help of the West Bend Police Department, traced the dissemination of this information to Ehren and sought from the court a permanent injunction against Ehren using or disclosing the information regarding Ziegler's clients. What result? Explain.

16. Since the 1950s, Qualitex Company has used a special shade of green-gold color on the pads that it makes and sells to dry cleaning firms for use on dry cleaning presses. In 1989, Jacobson Products (a Qualitex rival) began to sell its own press pads to dry cleaning firms, and it colored those pads a similar green-gold. In 1991, Qualitex registered the special green-gold color on press pads with the Patent and Trademark Office as a trademark. Qualitex sued Jacobson for trademark infringement. Jacobson argues that the Lanham Act does not permit registering "color alone" as a trademark. Explain whether a trademark violation has been committed.

17. Napster, Inc. (Napster), facilitates the transmission of MP3 files (a digital format for the storage of audio recordings) between and among its users. Through a process commonly called "peer-to-peer" file sharing, Napster allows its users to (a) make MP3 music files stored on individual computer hard drives available for copying by other Napster users, (b) search for MP3 music files stored on other users' computers, and (c) transfer exact copies of the contents of other users' MP3 files from one computer to another via the internet. These functions are made possible by Napster's Music-Share software, available free of charge from Napster's internet site, and Napster's network servers and server-side software. The plaintiffs include A&M Records, Geffen Records, Sony Music Entertainment, MCA Records, Atlantic Recording Corporation, Motown Record Company, and Capitol Records.

The plaintiffs are engaged in the commercial recording, distribution, and sale of copyrighted musical compositions and sound recordings. The plaintiffs allege that Napster is a contributory and vicarious copyright infringer. Explain whether Napster should be enjoined "from engaging in, or facilitating others in copying, downloading, uploading, transmitting, or distributing plaintiffs' copyrighted musical compositions and sound recordings, protected by either Federal or State law, without express permission of the rights owner."

18. Bernard L. Bilski and Rand A. Warsaw sought patent protection for a claimed invention that explains how buyers and sellers of commodities in the energy market can protect, or hedge, against the risk of price changes. Claim 1 describes a series of steps instructing how to hedge risk. Claim 4 puts the concept articulated in claim 1 into a simple mathematical formula. The remaining claims explain how claims 1 and 4 can be applied to allow energy suppliers and consumers to minimize the risks resulting from fluctuations in market demand for energy. Bilski and Warsaw sought to patent both the concept of hedging risk and the application of that concept to energy markets. Explain whether a patent for this invention should be granted.

T A K I N G S I D E S

Southwire Company and Essex Group, Inc., are direct competitors in the cable and wire industry. Southwire's logistics system is a warehouse organizational system with components extending from architectural layout features to customized equipment and modified computer software. Southwire's logistics system was designed primarily over a three-year period, with a development cost exceeding $2 million, by a project team headed by Richard McMichael. In addition to self-testing and a trial-and-error learning process, development of Southwire's logistics system also included modifications based on observation of logistics systems in other industries and the adaptation of commercially available components. The selection and arrangement of components and equipment in the new logistics system is unique to the Southwire logistics system. The new logistics system has resulted in substantial efficiencies to Southwire, with annual savings of $12 million.

Because Southwire and its competitors produce basically identical goods for sale, the marketing advantage gained by the important efficiencies that have resulted from the new logistics system has proved especially valuable for Southwire. Essex hired McMichael, and Southwire brought suit against its former employee, McMichael, and his new employer, Essex, to enjoin McMichael from disclosing to Essex any Southwire trade secrets, particularly trade secrets involving Southwire's logistics system.

a. What are the arguments in favor of the court *not* issuing the injunction?

b. What are the arguments in favor of the court issuing the injunction?

c. Explain whether the court should issue the injunction.

CHAPTER 40

Antitrust

After reading and studying this chapter, you should be able to:

- Explain horizontal restraints of trade.

- Explain vertical restraints of trade.

- Explain monopolization, attempts to monopolize, and conspiracies to monopolies.

- Explain the Clayton Act and its rules governing (1) tying contracts, (2) exclusive dealing, (3) horizontal mergers, (4) vertical mergers, and (5) conglomerate mergers.

- Describe (1) the Robinson-Patman Act and the various defenses to it and (2) the Federal Trade Commission Act.

The economic community is best served by free competition in trade and industry. It is in the public interest that quality, price, and service in an open, competitive market for goods and services be determining factors in the business rivalry for the customer's dollar. Nevertheless, in lieu of competing, businesses would prefer to eliminate their rivals and consequently gain a position from which they could dictate both the price of their goods and the quantity they produce. Although to eliminate competition by producing a better product is the goal of a business, some businesses try to effect this elimination through illegitimate means, such as fixing prices and allocating exclusive territories to certain competitors within an industry. The law of antitrust prohibits such activities and attempts to ensure free and fair competition in the marketplace.

The common law has traditionally favored competition and has held agreements and contracts in restraint of trade illegal and unenforceable. In addition, several States enacted antitrust statutes during the 1800s. The latter half of the nineteenth century, however, disclosed concentrations of economic power in the form of "trusts" and "combinations" that were too powerful and widespread to be effectively curbed by State action. In 1890, this awesome growth of corporate power prompted Congress to enact the Sherman Antitrust Act, which was the first Federal statute in this field. Since then, Congress has enacted other antitrust statutes, including the Clayton Act, the Robinson-Patman Act, and the Federal Trade Commission Act. These statutes prohibit anticompetitive practices and seek to prevent unreasonable concentrations of economic power that stifle or weaken competition. In addition to these Federal statutes, most States have antitrust laws that are enforced by State attorneys general or private plaintiffs.

40-1 Sherman Act

Section 1 of the Sherman Act prohibits contracts, combinations, and conspiracies that restrain trade, while Section 2 prohibits monopolies and attempts to monopolize. Failure to comply with either section is a criminal felony and subjects the offender to fine or imprisonment or both. As amended by the Antitrust Criminal Penalty Enhancement and Reform Act of 2004, the Sherman Act subjects individual offenders to imprisonment of up to ten years and fines up to $1 million, while corporate offenders are subject to fines of up to $100 million per violation. Moreover, under the Federal Alternative Fines Act, the maximum fine may be increased to twice the amount the conspirators gained from the illegal acts or twice the money lost by the victims of the crime, if either of those amounts is over $100 million. In addition, the Sherman Act empowers the Federal district courts to issue injunctions restraining violations, and anyone injured by a violation is entitled to recover in a civil action treble damages (i.e., three times the amount of the actual loss sustained). In addition, State Attorneys General may bring suit for treble damages on behalf of citizens of their States. The U.S. Department of Justice (DOJ) and the Federal Trade Commission (FTC) have the duty to bring appropriate enforcement proceedings other than treble damage actions.

Practical Advice

Be advised that a violation of the Sherman Antitrust Act carries both criminal penalties and civil liability including treble damages.

The DOJ has expanded its enforcement policy regarding the Sherman Act to cover conduct by foreign companies that harms U.S. exports. Under this policy, the DOJ examines conduct to determine whether it would violate the law if it occurred within the borders of the United States. The DOJ has indicated that it will focus primarily on boycotts and cartels that injure the export of U.S. products and services. See *Figure 40-1* for the DOJ Antitrust Division's listing of Sherman Act violations resulting in corporate fines of $300 million or more.

◆ **SEE FIGURE 40-1:** *Sherman Act Violations Yielding a Corporate Fine of $300 Million or More*

40-1a RESTRAINT OF TRADE

Section 1 of the Sherman Act provides that "[e]very contract, combination in the form of trust or otherwise, or conspiracy, in restraint of trade or commerce among the several states, or with foreign nations is hereby declared to be illegal." Because the language of the section is so broad, judicial interpretation has played a significant role in establishing the elements that constitute a violation.

STANDARDS As noted, Section 1 prohibits every contract, combination, or conspiracy in restraint of trade. Taken literally, this prohibition would invalidate every unperformed contract. For example, under a strict interpretation of the section, a contract in which a seller agrees to supply a buyer with one thousand pounds of grapes, no one but the seller would be permitted to fulfill the buyer's need for those one thousand pounds of grapes, and the seller would not be allowed to sell those grapes to any other buyer. This agreement would therefore restrain trade. To avoid such a broad and impractical application, the courts have interpreted this section to invalidate only *unreasonable* restraints of trade:

The true test of legality is whether the restraint imposed is such as merely regulates and perhaps thereby promotes competition or whether it is such as may suppress or even destroy competition. To determine that question the courts must ordinarily consider the facts peculiar to the business to which the restraint is applied; its

FIGURE 40-1 Sherman Act Violations Yielding a Corporate Fine of $300 Million or More

Defendant (FY)/	Product	Fine ($ Millions)	Geographic Scope	Country
Citicorp (2017)	Foreign Currency Exchange	$925	International	United States
Barclays, PLC (2017)	Foreign Currency Exchange	$650	International	United Kingdom of Great Britain and Northern Ireland
JPMorgan Chase & Co. (2017)	Foreign Currency Exchange	$550	International	United States
AU Optronics Corporation of Taiwan (2012)	Liquid Crystal Display (LCD) Panels	$500	International	Taiwan
F. Hoffmann-La Roche, Ltd. (1999)	Vitamins	$500	International	Switzerland
Yazaki Corporation (2012)	Automobile Parts	$470	International	Japan
Bridgestone Corporation (2014)	Anti-vibration Rubber Products for Automobiles	$425	International	Japan
LG Display Co., Ltd LG Display America (2009)	Liquid Crystal Display (LCD) Panels	$400	International	Korea
Royal Bank of Scotland (2017)	Foreign Currency Exchange	$395	International	Scotland (United Kingdom)
Société Air France and Koninklijke Luchtvaart Maatschappij, N.V. (2008)	Air Transportation (Cargo)	$350	International	France (Société Air France) The Netherlands (KLM)
Korean Air Lines Co., Ltd. (2007)	Air Transportation (Cargo & Passenger)	$300	International	Korea
British Airways PLC (2007)	Air Transportation (Cargo & Passenger)	$300	International	United Kingdom
Samsung Electronics Company, Ltd. Samsung Semiconductor, Inc. (2006)	DRAM	$300	International	Korea

Source: Department of Justice, "Sherman Act Violations Yielding a Corporate Fine of $10 Million or More," as of March 4, 2020, https://www.justice.gov/atr/page/file/991706.

condition before and after the restraint was imposed; the nature of the restraint and its effect, actual or probable. The history of the restraint, the evil believed to exist, the reason for adopting the particular remedy, the purpose or end sought to be attained, are all relevant facts. This is not because a good intention will save an otherwise objectionable regulation or the reverse, but because knowledge of intent may help the court to interpret facts and to predict consequences. *Chicago Board of Trade v. United States*, 246 U.S. 231 (1918).

This flexible standard, known as the **rule of reason test**, requires the courts, in determining whether a challenged practice unreasonably restricts competition, to consider a variety of factors, including the makeup of the relevant industry, the defendants' positions within that industry, the ability of the defendants' competitors to respond to the challenged practice, and the defendants' purpose in adopting the restraint. After reviewing the various factors, a court determines whether the challenged restraint unreasonably restricts competition. By requiring courts to balance the anticompetitive effects of every questioned restraint against its procompetitive effects, this standard places a substantial burden upon the judicial system. The U.S. Supreme Court addressed this problem by declaring certain categories of restraints to be unreasonable by their very nature, that is, **illegal *per se***:

> [T]here are certain agreements or practices which because of their pernicious effect on competition and lack of any redeeming virtue are conclusively presumed to be unreasonable and therefore illegal without elaborate inquiry as to the precise harm they have caused or the business excuse for their use. This principle of *per se* unreasonableness not only makes the type of restraints which are proscribed by the Sherman Act more certain to the benefit of everyone concerned, but it also avoids the necessity for an incredibly complicated and prolonged economic investigation into the entire history of the industry involved, as well as related industries, in an effort to determine at large whether a particular restraint has been unreasonable—an inquiry so often wholly fruitless when undertaken. *Northern Pacific Railway Co. v. United States*, 356 U.S. 1 (1958).

Characterizing a type of restraint as *per se* illegal therefore has a significant effect on the prosecution of an antitrust suit. In such a case, the plaintiff need only show that the type of restraint occurred; she does not need to prove that the restraint limited competition. Furthermore, the defendants may not defend on the basis that the restraint is reasonable. Additionally, as noted in *Northern Pacific Railway*, the court is not required to conduct extensive, and often difficult, economic analysis.

More recently a third intermediate test has been frequently used when the *per se* approach is not appropriate for the situation but the challenged conduct has obvious anticompetitive effects. Under this "quick look" rule of reason analysis, the courts will apply an **abbreviated rule of reason standard** rather than use the extensive analysis required by a full-blown rule of reason test. However, the extensiveness of the legal analysis required under the quick look test will vary based upon the circumstances, details, and logic of the restraint being reviewed.

◆ *See Case 40-1*

Practical Advice

Recognize that certain types of conduct, due to their pernicious effect on competition and their lack of any redeeming virtue, are conclusively presumed to be unreasonable and therefore are illegal per se.

HORIZONTAL AND VERTICAL RESTRAINTS A restraint of trade may be classified as either horizontal or vertical. A **horizontal restraint** involves collaboration among competitors at the same level in the chain of distribution. For example, an agreement among manufacturers, among wholesalers, or among retailers is horizontal.

On the other hand, an agreement made by parties that are not in direct competition at the same level of distribution is a **vertical restraint**. Thus, an agreement between a manufacturer and a wholesaler is vertical.

Although the distinction between horizontal and vertical restraints can become blurred, it often determines whether a restraint is illegal *per se* or should be judged by the rule of reason test. For instance, horizontal market allocations are illegal *per se*, whereas vertical market allocations are subject to the rule of reason test.

CONCERTED ACTION Section 1 does not prohibit unilateral conduct; rather, it forbids **concerted action**. Thus, one person or business by itself cannot violate the section. An organization has the "right to deal, or refuse to deal, with whomever it likes, as long as it does so independently." *Monsanto Co. v. Spray-Rite Service Corporation*, 465 U.S. 752 (1984). For example, if a manufacturer announces its resale prices in advance and refuses to deal with those who disagree with the pricing, there is no violation of Section 1 because the manufacturer has acted alone. On the other hand, if a manufacturer and its retailers together agree that the manufacturer will sell only to those retailers who agree to sell at a specified price, there may be a violation of Section 1.

For purposes of the concerted action requirement, a firm and its employees are viewed as one entity. The same rule is also true for a corporation and its wholly owned subsidiaries; thus, the Sherman Act is not violated when a parent and its wholly owned subsidiary agree to a restraint in trade. *Copperwald Corp. v. Independence Tube Corp.*, 467 U.S. 752 (1984). The Supreme Court has yet to decide, however, whether a parent and its partially owned subsidiary may violate Section 1.

The concerted action requirement may be established by an express agreement. Not surprisingly, however, an express agreement often is nonexistent, leaving the court to infer an agreement between the parties from circumstantial evidence:

No formal agreement is necessary to constitute an unlawful conspiracy. Often crimes are a matter of inference deduced from the acts of the person accused and done in pursuance of a criminal purpose. Where the conspiracy is proved, as here, from the evidence of the action taken in concert by the parties to it, it is all the more convincing proof of an intent to exercise the power of exclusion acquired through the conspiracy. The essential combination or conspiracy in violation of the Sherman Act may be found in a course of dealings or other circumstances as well as in any exchange of words … Where the circumstances are such as to warrant a jury in finding that the conspirators had a unity of purpose or a common design and understanding, or a meeting of minds in an unlawful arrangement, the conclusion that a conspiracy is established is justified. *American Tobacco Co. v. United States*, 328 U.S. 781 (1946).

Nonetheless, similar patterns of conduct among competitors, called **conscious parallelism**, are not sufficient in themselves to suggest a conspiracy in violation of Section 1. Actual conspiracy requires an additional factor, such as complex action that, to benefit the competitors, requires the participation of each or indications of a traditional conspiracy, such as identical sealed bids from each competitor.

Joint ventures, which are discussed in *Chapter 30*, are a form of business association organized to carry out a particular business enterprise. Competitors frequently will pool their resources to share costs and to eliminate wasteful redundancy.

The validity under antitrust law of a joint venture generally depends on the competitors' primary purpose in forming it. A joint venture that was not formed to fix prices or divide markets will be judged under the rule of reason. However, because uncertainty about the legality of joint ventures seemed to discourage their use for joint research and development, Congress passed the National Cooperative Research Act to facilitate such applications. The Act provides that joint ventures in the research and development of new technology are to be judged under the rule of reason test and that treble damages do not apply to ventures formed in violation of Section 1 if those forming the venture have notified the Justice Department and the FTC of their intent to form the joint venture.

◆ *See Case 40-1*

PRICE FIXING Price fixing is an agreement with the purpose or effect of inhibiting price competition; such an agreement may attempt to raise, depress, fix, peg, or stabilize prices. Price fixing is the primary and most serious example of a *per se* violation under the Sherman Act. As held in *United States v. Socony-Vacuum Oil Co.*, 310 U.S. 150 (1940), all *horizontal* price-fixing agreements are illegal *per se*. This prohibition not only covers any agreement between sellers to establish the *maximum* prices at which certain commodities or services will be offered for sale but also encompasses agreements establishing *minimum* prices as well as other terms that affect prices to consumers, such as shipping fees, warranties, discount programs, and financing rates.

The U.S. Supreme Court has condemned not only agreements among horizontal competitors that directly fix prices but also agreements whose effect on price is indirect. For example, in *Catalano, Inc. v. Target Sales, Inc.*, 446 U.S. 643 (1980), the Court held that an agreement among beer wholesalers to eliminate interest-free short-term credit on sales to beer retailers was illegal *per se*. The Court viewed the credit terms "as an inseparable part of price" and concluded that the agreement to eliminate interest-free short-term credit was equivalent to an agreement to eliminate discounts and was thus an agreement to fix prices.

In a 2007 case, *Leegin Creative Leather Products, Inc. v. PSKS, Inc.*, 551 U.S. 877, the U.S. Supreme Court ruled that vertical price restraints (vertical minimum resale price maintenance agreements) are to be judged by the rule of reason. This decision overruled a 1911 U.S. Supreme Court decision that established the rule that it is *per se* illegal under Section 1 of the Sherman Act for a manufacturer to agree with its retailers to set the minimum price the retailer can charge for the manufacturer's goods. Although many States harmonize their antitrust laws with Federal antitrust law, some States specifically prohibit vertical price fixing and at least one State's supreme court has held that minimum, vertical price fixing is illegal *per se* under that State's antitrust laws.

◆ *See Case 40-2*

MARKET ALLOCATIONS Direct price fixing is not the only way to control prices. Another method involves **market allocation**, whereby competitors agree not to compete with each other in specific markets, which may be defined by geographic area, customer type, or product class. All *horizontal* agreements to divide markets have been declared illegal *per se*, because they confer upon the firm remaining in the market a monopolistic control over price. Thus, if Sony and Samsung, both manufacturers of televisions, agree that Sony shall have the exclusive right to sell televisions in Illinois and Iowa and that Samsung shall have the exclusive right in Minnesota and Wisconsin, Sony and Samsung have committed a *per se* violation of Section 1 of the Sherman Act. Likewise, if Sony and Samsung agree that Sony shall have the exclusive right to sell televisions to Walmart and that Samsung shall sell exclusively to Target or that Sony shall have the exclusive right to manufacture forty-three-inch televisions while Samsung alone manufactures fifty-inch sets, they are also in *per se* violation of Section 1 of the Sherman Antitrust Act. Horizontal market allocations may be found not only on the manufacturing level but also on the wholesale or retail level.

No longer illegal *per se*, *vertical* territorial and customer restrictions are now judged by the rule of reason. This change in approach resulted from the U.S. Supreme Court decision in Continental T.V., Inc. v. GTE Sylvania, Inc., 433 U.S. 36 (1977), that mandated the lower Federal courts to balance the positive effect of vertical market restrictions upon interbrand competition against the negative effects upon intrabrand competition. Consequently, in some situations, vertical market restrictions will be found legitimate if, on balance, they do not inhibit competition in the relevant market.

The DOJ has issued a "market structure screen," under which the DOJ will not challenge restraints by a firm having less than 10 percent of the relevant market or a "Vertical Restraint Index" (a measure of relative market share), indicating that neither collusion nor exclusion is possible. The concept of relevant market is discussed later in the section on monopolization.

BOYCOTTS As noted, Section 1 of the Sherman Act applies not to unilateral action but only to agreements or combinations. Accordingly, a seller's refusal to deal with any particular buyer does not violate the Act, and a manufacturer thus can refuse to sell to a retailer who persists in selling below the manufacturer's suggested retail price. On the other hand, when two or more firms agree not to deal with a third party, their agreement constitutes a **concerted refusal to deal**, or a group boycott, which may violate Section 1 of the Sherman Act. Such a boycott may be clearly anticompetitive, eliminating competition or reducing market entry.

Some group boycotts are illegal *per se*, while others are subject to the rule of reason. Group boycotts designed to eliminate a competitor or to force that competitor to meet a group standard are illegal *per se* if the group has market power. On the other hand, cooperative arrangements "designed to increase economic efficiency and render markets more, rather than less, competitive" are subject to the rule of reason.

Finally, most courts hold that the *per se* rule of illegality for concerted refusals to deal extends only to horizontal boycotts, not to vertical refusals to deal. Most courts have held that a rule of reason test should govern all nonprice vertical restraints, including concerted refusals to deal.

When attending trade association meetings or other conferences with competitors, be extremely careful not to discuss pricing, refusals to deal with certain customers, and territorial emphases.

TYING ARRANGEMENTS A tying arrangement occurs when the seller of a product, service, or intangible (the "tying" product) conditions its sale on the buyer's purchasing a second product, service, or intangible (the "tied" product) from the seller. For example, assume that Xerox, a major manufacturer of photocopying equipment, were to require that all purchasers of its photocopiers also purchase from Xerox all of the paper they would use with the copiers. Xerox thereby would tie the sale of its photocopier—the *tying* product—to the sale of paper—the *tied* product.

Because tying arrangements limit buyers' freedom of choice and may exclude competitors, the law closely scrutinizes such agreements. An illegal tying arrangement exists in situations in which a seller exploits its economic power in one market to expand its empire into another market. When the seller has considerable economic power in the tying product and more than an insubstantial amount of interstate commerce is affected in the tied product, the tying arrangement will be *per se* illegal. The courts may establish a seller's economic power by showing that (1) the seller occupied a dominant position in the tying market, (2) the seller's product enjoys an advantage not shared by its competitors in the tying market, or (3) a substantial number of customers have accepted the tying arrangement and the sole explanation for their willingness to comply is the seller's economic power in the tying market. If the seller lacks economic power, the tying arrangement is judged by the rule of reason test.

◆ **SEE FIGURE 40-2:** *Restraints of Trade Under the Sherman Act*

◆ *See Case 40-3*

40-1b MONOPOLIES

Economic analysis indicates that a monopolist will use its power to limit production and increase prices. Accordingly, a monopolistic market will produce fewer goods than a competitive market would and will sell those goods at higher prices. To address the problem of monopolization, Section 2 of the Sherman Act prohibits monopolies and all attempts or conspiracies to monopolize. Thus, Section 2 prohibits both agreements among businesses and, unlike Section 1, unilateral conduct by one firm.

MONOPOLIZATION Although the language of Section 2 appears to prohibit without exception *all* monopolization,

FIGURE 40-2 Restraints of Trade under the Sherman Act

Type of Restraint	Standard	
	Per Se Illegal	Rule of Reason
Price Fixing	Horizontal	Vertical
Market Allocations	Horizontal	Vertical
Group Boycotts or Refusals to Deal	Horizontal Vertical (Minority)	Vertical (Majority)
Tying Arrangements	If seller has economic power in tying product and affects a substantial amount of interstate commerce in the tied product	If seller lacks economic power in tying product

the courts have required that in addition to merely possessing market power, a firm must have either attained the monopoly power unfairly or abused that power, once attained. Possession of monopoly power is not in itself considered a violation of Section 2 because a firm may have obtained such power through its skills in developing, marketing, and selling products; that is, through the very competitive conduct that the antitrust laws are designed to promote.

Because it is extremely rare to find an unregulated industry with only one firm, determining the presence of monopoly power involves defining the degree of market dominance that constitutes such power. Monopoly power is the ability to control prices or to exclude competitors from the marketplace. In grappling with this question of power, the courts have developed a number of criteria, but the prevalent test is market share. A market share greater than 75 percent generally indicates monopoly power, whereas a share less than 50 percent does not. A share between 50 percent and 75 percent share is inconclusive.

Market share is a firm's fractional share of the total relevant product and geographic markets, but defining these relevant markets is often a difficult and subjective task for the courts. The relevant *product market* includes products that are substitutable for the firm's product on the basis of price, quality, and elasticity. For example, although brick and wood siding are both used on building exteriors, they would not likely be considered part of the same product market. On the other hand, Coca-Cola and Pepsi are both soft drinks and would be considered part of the same product market.

The relevant *geographic market* is that territory in which the firm makes sales of its products or services. This may be at the local, regional, or national level. For instance, the relevant geographic market for the manufacture and sale of aluminum might be national, whereas that of a taxicab operating company would be local. The scope of a geographic market depends upon factors such as transportation costs, the type of product or services, and the location of competitors and customers.

If sufficient monopoly power has been proved, the law then must show that the firm has engaged in **unfair conduct**.

The courts, however, have yet to agree upon what constitutes such conduct. One judicial approach is to place upon a firm possessing monopoly power the burden of proving that it acquired such power passively or that the power was "thrust" upon it. An alternative view is that monopoly power, when coupled with conduct designed to exclude competitors, violates Section 2. A third approach requires monopoly power plus some type of predatory practice, such as pricing below marginal costs. For example, one case that adopted the third approach held that a firm does not violate Section 2 of the Sherman Act if it attained its market share through either (1) research, technical innovation, or a superior product or (2) ordinary marketing methods available to all. *Telex Corp. v. IBM*, 510 F.2d 894 (10th Cir. 1975).

The U.S. Supreme Court decision in *Aspen Skiing Co. v. Aspen Highlands Skiing Corp.*, 472 U.S. 585 (1985), appears to combine these approaches. The Court held that "[i]f a firm has been attempting to exclude rivals on some basis other than efficiency, it is fair to characterize its behavior as predatory."

To date, however, the U.S. Supreme Court has yet to define the exact conduct, beyond the mere possession of monopoly power, that violates Section 2. To do so, the Court must resolve the complex and conflicting policies this most basic question regarding monopolies involves. On the one hand, condemning fairly acquired monopoly power—that acquired "merely by virtue of superior skill, foresight, and industry"—penalizes firms that compete effectively. On the other hand, permitting firms with monopoly power to continue provides them the opportunity to lower output and raise prices, thereby injuring consumers.

♦ *See Case 40-3*

ATTEMPTS TO MONOPOLIZE Section 2 also prohibits attempts to monopolize. As with monopolization, the courts have had difficulty developing a standard that distinguishes undesirable conduct likely to engender a monopoly from healthy competitive conduct. The standard test applied by the courts requires proof of a specific intent to monopolize plus a dangerous probability of success; however, this test neither defines an "intent" nor provides a standard of power by which to measure "success." Recent cases suggest that the greater the measure of market power a firm acquires, the less flagrant must its conduct be to constitute an attempt. These cases do not, however, specify any threshold level of market power.

CONSPIRACIES TO MONOPOLIZE Section 2 also condemns conspiracies to monopolize. Few cases involve this offense alone, as any conspiracy to monopolize would also constitute a combination in restraint of trade in violation of Section 1.

40-2 Clayton Act

In 1914, Congress strengthened the Sherman Act by adopting the Clayton Act, which was expressly designed "to supplement existing laws against unlawful restraints and monopolies." The Act is intended to stop trade practices before they become restraints of trade or monopolies forbidden by the Sherman Act. The Clayton Act provides only for civil actions, not for criminal penalties. Private parties may bring civil actions in Federal court for treble damages and attorneys' fees. In addition, the DOJ and the FTC are authorized to bring civil actions, including proceedings in equity, to prevent and restrict violations of the Act.

The substantive provisions of the Clayton Act deal with price discrimination, tying contracts, exclusive dealing, mergers, and interlocking directorates. Section 2, which deals with price discrimination, was amended and rewritten by the Robinson-Patman Act, which is discussed later in this chapter. In addition, the Clayton Act exempts labor, agricultural, and horticultural organizations from all antitrust laws.

40-2a TYING CONTRACTS AND EXCLUSIVE DEALING

Section 3 of the Clayton Act prohibits tying arrangements and exclusive dealing, selling, or leasing arrangements that prevent purchasers from dealing with the seller's competitors and which *may* substantially lessen competition or *tend* to create a monopoly. This section is intended to attack incipient anticompetitive practices before they ripen into violations of Section 1 or 2 of the Sherman Act. Unlike the Sherman Act, however, Section 3 applies only to practices involving commodities, not to those that involve services, intangibles, or land.

Tying arrangements, discussed earlier in the sections covering the Sherman Act, have been labeled by the Supreme Court as serving "hardly any purpose beyond the suppression of competition." Although the Court at one time indicated that different standards applied under the Sherman Act and the Clayton Act, recent lower court cases suggest that the same rules now govern both types of actions.

Exclusive dealing arrangements are agreements by which the seller or lessor of a product conditions the agreement upon the buyer's or lessor's promise not to deal in the goods of a competitor. For example, a manufacturer of razors might require retailers wishing to sell its line of shaving equipment to agree not to carry competing merchandise. Such conduct, although treated more leniently than tying arrangements, violates Section 3 if it tends to create a monopoly or may substantially lessen competition. The courts regard exclusive dealing arrangements more tolerantly because such arrangements may be procompetitive to the extent that they benefit buyers and thus, indirectly, ultimate consumers by ensuring supplies, deterring price increases, and enabling long-term planning on the basis of known costs.

40-2b MERGERS

In the United States, corporate mergers have played a significant role in reshaping both the structure of corporations and our economic system. Mergers are horizontal, vertical, or conglomerate, depending upon the relationship between the acquirer and the acquired company. A **horizontal merger** involves the acquisition by a company of all or part of the stock or assets of a competing company. For example, if Apple were to acquire Dell, this would be a horizontal merger. A vertical merger is a company's acquisition of one of its customers or suppliers. A vertical merger is a *forward* merger if the acquiring company purchases a customer, such as the purchase of Walgreens by Procter & Gamble Company. A vertical merger is a *backward* merger if the acquiring company purchases a supplier—for example, if Best Buy were to purchase Whirlpool Corporation. The third type of merger, the **conglomerate merger**, is a catchall category that covers all acquisitions not involving a competitor, customer, or supplier. 2015 was the biggest year ever for global mergers with approximately $4.7 trillion in reported mergers and acquisitions. Since then, the amount has declined to $4.1 trillion dollars in 2018 and $3.7 trillion in 2019.

Section 7 of the Clayton Act prohibits a corporation from merging or acquiring stock or assets of another corporation where such action would lessen competition substantially or would tend to create a monopoly.

Section 7 of the Clayton Act was intended to arrest the anticompetitive effects of market power in their incipiency. The core question is whether a merger may substantially lessen competition, and necessarily requires a prediction of the merger's impact on competition, present and future. The section can deal only with probabilities, not with certainties. And there is certainly no requirement that the anticompetitive power manifest itself in anticompetitive action before §7 can be called into play. If the enforcement of §7 turned on the existence of actual anticompetitive practices, the congressional policy of thwarting such practices in their incipiency would be frustrated. *F.T.C. v. Procter & Gamble Co*, 386 U.S. 568 (1967).

The Hart-Scott-Rodino Act of 1976 amended the Clayton Act to establish the federal premerger notification program, which provides the DOJ and the FTC with information about large mergers and acquisitions before they occur. The parties may not close their merger until the specified waiting period has passed, unless the government grants early termination of the waiting period. Currently, the law regarding horizontal, vertical, and conglomerate mergers is in a state of flux, particularly with respect to the last two.

The principal objective of the antitrust law governing mergers is to maintain competition. Accordingly, horizontal mergers are scrutinized most stringently. Factors that the courts consider in reviewing the legality of a horizontal merger include the market share of each of the merging firms, the degree of industry concentration, the number of firms in the industry, entry barriers, market trends, the strength of other competitors in the industry, the character and history of the merging firms, market demand, and the extent of industry price competition. The leading Supreme Court cases on horizontal mergers date from the 1960s and early 1970s. Since then, lower Federal courts, the DOJ, and the FTC have emphasized antitrust law's goal of promoting economic efficiency. Accordingly, while the Supreme Court cases remain the law of the land, lower court decisions reflect a greater willingness to tolerate industry concentrations. Nevertheless, the government continues to prosecute, and the courts continue to condemn, horizontal mergers that are likely to hurt consumers. Though vertical mergers are far less likely to be challenged, the DOJ and the FTC have attacked vertical mergers that threatened to raise entry barriers in the industry or to foreclose other firms in the acquiring firm's industry from competitively significant customers or suppliers. While the Supreme Court has not decided a vertical merger case since 1972, recent decisions indicate that at least some lower courts have been willing to condemn only those vertical mergers that clearly show anticompetitive effects.

Finally, conglomerate mergers have been challenged only (1) where one of the merging firms would be highly likely to enter the market of the other firm or (2) where the merged company would be disproportionately large as compared with the largest competitors in its industry.

The DOJ and the FTC have both indicated that they will be concerned primarily with horizontal mergers in highly or moderately concentrated industries and that they question the benefits of challenging vertical and conglomerate mergers. Both the DOJ and the FTC have justified this policy on the basis that the latter two types of mergers are necessary to transfer assets to their most productive use and that any challenge to such mergers would impose costs on consumers without corresponding benefits.

Antitrust law, as currently applied, focuses on the size of the merged firm in relation to the relevant market, not on the resulting entity's absolute size. In 1992 (subsequently revised in 1997 and 2010), the DOJ and the FTC jointly issued new Horizontal Merger Guidelines to replace their earlier and separate guidelines (originally issued in 1968). In doing so, the two agencies sought to prevent market power that results in "a transfer of wealth from buyers to sellers or a misallocation of resources." The guidelines are designed to provide an analytical framework to judge the impact of potential mergers.

The 2010 guidelines are intended to identify harmful mergers while avoiding unnecessary interference with those mergers that are economically beneficial or likely will have no competitive effect on the market. "These guidelines are intended to assist the business community … by increasing the transparency of the analytical process." The 2010 guidelines clarify that "merger analysis does not use a single methodology but rather is a fact-specific process through which the agencies employ a variety of tools to analyze the evidence to determine whether a merger may substantially lessen competition." In addition, the 2010 rules explain (1) what sources of evidence and categories of evidence the agencies have found to be informative, (2) that market definition is not an end in itself or a necessary starting point of merger analysis, and (3) that market concentration is a useful tool to the extent it illuminates the merger's likely competitive effects. The 2010 guidelines add a new section dealing with mergers of powerful buyers and mergers between competing buyers.

The 1992, 1997, and 2010 guidelines, like their earlier counterparts, quantify market concentration through the Herfindahl-Hirschman Index (HHI) and measure a horizontal merger's impact on the index. This concentration index is calculated by summing the squares of the individual market shares of all firms in the market. An industry with only one firm would have an HHI of $10,000 (100^2)$. With two firms of equal size, the index would be $5,000 (50^2 + 50^2)$; with five firms of equal size, the result would be $2,000 (20^2 + 20^2 + 20^2 + 20^2 + 20^2)$. The increase a merger would cause in the index is calculated by doubling the product of the merging firms' market shares. For example, the merger of two firms with market shares of 5 percent and 10 percent respectively would increase the index by 100 ($5 \times 10 \times 2 = 100$).

The 2010 guidelines classify an HHI of less than 1,500 as an unconcentrated market, an HHI between 1,500 and 2,500 as a moderately concentrated market, and an HHI above 2,500 as a highly concentrated market. The 2010 guidelines indicate that the FTC and DOJ employ the following general standards for the relevant markets they have defined:

Small Change in Concentration: Mergers involving an increase in the HHI of less than 100 points are unlikely to have adverse competitive effects and ordinarily require no further analysis.

Unconcentrated Markets: Mergers resulting in unconcentrated markets are unlikely to have adverse competitive effects and ordinarily require no further analysis.

Moderately Concentrated Markets: Mergers resulting in moderately concentrated markets that involve an increase in the HHI of more than 100 points potentially raise significant competitive concerns and often warrant scrutiny.

Highly Concentrated Markets: Mergers resulting in highly concentrated markets that involve an increase in the HHI of between 100 points and 200 points potentially raise significant competitive concerns and often warrant scrutiny. Mergers resulting in highly concentrated markets that involve an increase in the HHI of more than 200 points will be presumed to be likely to enhance market power. The presumption may be rebutted by persuasive evidence showing that the merger is unlikely to enhance market power.

The 2010 guidelines explain that the purpose of these thresholds is to provide one way to identify some mergers unlikely to raise competitive concerns and some others for which it is particularly important to examine whether other competitive factors confirm, reinforce, or counteract the potentially harmful effects of increased concentration. The higher the post-merger HHI and the increase in the HHI, the greater the Agencies' potential competitive concerns and the greater the likelihood that the Agencies will request additional information to conduct their analysis.

On June 30, 2020, the DOJ and the FTC issued new guidelines that outline the principal analytical techniques, practices, and enforcement policies of the agencies with respect to vertical mergers within a supply chain. These guidelines describe the framework applied by the DOJ and the FTC to determine whether a vertical merger decreases competition and harms consumers by distinguishing anticompetitive from procompetitive (and competitively neutral) vertical mergers. The guidelines discuss how a vertical merger could diminish competition by allowing the newly integrated company to (1) raise its rivals' costs, (2) cause its rivals to lose significant sales in the relevant market or compete less aggressively, (3) increase its rivals access to competitive information, or (4) block its rivals' access to the supply of a crucial part or product altogether—a practice known as foreclosure. The guidelines note that among the types of adverse effects on competition are (1) adverse unilateral effects that may be imposed by

the merged firm as a result of the merger and (2) adverse coordinated effects that diminish competition by enabling or encouraging coordinated interaction among firms in the relevant market.

In 1987, the National Association of Attorneys General, composed of the Attorneys General of the fifty States and five U.S. territories and protectorates, promulgated its own set of guidelines for horizontal mergers. Intended to apply to enforcement actions brought by the State Attorneys General under Federal and State antitrust statutes, the State guidelines place a greater emphasis on preventing transfers of wealth from consumers to producers than do the Federal guidelines. Accordingly, the State Attorneys General would be more likely to challenge certain mergers than would the Federal government.

♦ *See Case 40-4*

Practical Advice
When considering potential merger targets, make sure to take into consideration the Herfindahl-Hirschman Index and the impact of the merger on the Index.

40-3 Robinson-Patman Act

Section 2 of the Clayton Act originally prohibited only sellers from differentially pricing their products to injure local or regional competitors. In 1936, in an attempt to limit the power of large purchasers, Congress amended Section 2 of the Clayton Act by adopting the Robinson-Patman Act, which further prohibited **price discrimination** in interstate commerce involving commodities of like grade and quality. Thus, the Act prohibits buyers from inducing and sellers from granting discrimination in prices. To constitute a violation, the price discrimination must substantially lessen competition or tend to create a monopoly.

Under this Act, a seller of goods may not grant discounts to buyers, including allowances for advertisements, counter displays, and samples, unless the seller offers the same discounts to all other purchasers on proportionately equal terms. The Act also prohibits other types of discounts, rebates, and allowances and makes it unlawful to sell goods at unreasonably low prices for the purpose of destroying competition or eliminating a competitor. Furthermore, the Act makes it unlawful for a person knowingly to "induce or receive" an illegal discrimination in price, thus imposing liability on the buyer as well as the seller. Violation of the Robinson-Patman Act, with limited exceptions, is civil, not criminal, in nature. The Act does permit price differentials that are justified by proof of either a cost savings to the seller or a good-faith price reduction to meet the lawful price of a competitor.

40-3a PRIMARY-LINE INJURY

In enacting Section 2 of the Clayton Act in 1914, Congress was concerned with sellers who sought to harm or eliminate their competitors through price discrimination. Injuries accruing to a seller's competitors are called "primary-line" injuries. Because the Act forbids price discrimination only where such discrimination may substantially lessen competition or tend to create a monopoly, the plaintiff in a Robinson-Patman primary-line injury case must either show that the defendant, with the intent to harm competition, has engaged in predatory pricing or present a detailed market analysis that demonstrates how the defendant's price discrimination actually harmed competition. To prove predatory intent, a plaintiff may rely either on direct evidence of such intent or, more commonly, on inferences drawn from the defendant's conduct, such as a significant period of below-cost or unprofitable pricing. A predatory pricing scheme also may be challenged under the Sherman Act.

40-3b SECONDARY- AND TERTIARY-LINE INJURY

In amending Section 2 of the Clayton Act in 1936 through the adoption of the Robinson-Patman Act, Congress was concerned primarily with small buyers, who were harmed by the discounts that sellers granted to large buyers. Injuries accruing to some buyers because of the lower prices granted to other buyers are called "secondary-line" injuries. To prove the required harm to competition, a plaintiff in a secondary-line injury case must either show substantial and sustained price differentials in a market or offer a detailed market analysis that demonstrates actual harm to competition. Because courts have been willing in secondary-line injury cases to infer harm to competition from a sustained and substantial price differential, proving a secondary-line injury generally is easier than proving a primary-line injury.

Tertiary-line injury occurs when the recipient of a favored price passes the benefits of the lower price on to the next level of distribution. Purchasers from other secondary-line sellers are injured in that they do not receive the benefits of the lower price; these purchasers may recover damages from the original discriminating seller.

40-3c COST JUSTIFICATION

If a seller can show that it costs less to sell a product to a particular buyer, the seller may lawfully pass along the cost savings. Section 2(a) provides that the Act does not "prevent differentials which make only due allowance for differences in the cost of manufacture, sale, or delivery resulting from the differing methods or quantities in which … commodities are … sold or delivered." For example, if Retailer A orders goods from Seller X by the carload, whereas Retailer B orders in small quantities, Seller X, who delivers F.O.B. (free on board) buyer's warehouse, may pass along the transportation savings to Retailer A. Nonetheless, although it is possible to pass along transportation savings, it is extremely difficult to pass along alleged savings in manufacturing or distribution because of the complexity involved in calculating and proving such savings. Therefore, sellers rarely rely upon the defense of cost justification.

40-3d MEETING COMPETITION

A seller may lower his price in a good-faith attempt to meet competition. To illustrate:

1. Manufacturer X sells its motor oil to retail outlets for $0.65 per can. Manufacturer Y approaches A, one of Manufacturer X's customers, and offers to sell a comparable type of motor oil for $0.60 per can. Manufacturer X will be permitted to lower its price to A to $0.60 per can and need not lower its price to its other retail customers—B, C, and D. Manufacturer X, however, may not lower its price to A to $0.55 unless it also offers this lower price to B, C, and D.

2. To allow A to meet the lower price that A's competitor, N, charges when selling Manufacturer Y's oil, Manufacturer X will not be permitted to lower its price to A without also lowering its price to B, C, and D. A seller may beat its competitor's price, however, if it does not know the competitor's price, cannot reasonably determine the competitor's price, and acts reasonably in setting its own price.

♦ SEE FIGURE 40-3: *Meeting Competition Defense*

40-4 Federal Trade Commission Act

In 1914, through the enactment of the Federal Trade Commission Act, Congress created the FTC and charged it with the duty to prevent "unfair methods of competition in commerce, and unfair or deceptive acts or practices in commerce." To this end, the five-member commission is empowered to conduct appropriate investigations and hearings and to issue against violators "cease-and-desist" orders

FIGURE 40-3 Meeting Competition Defense

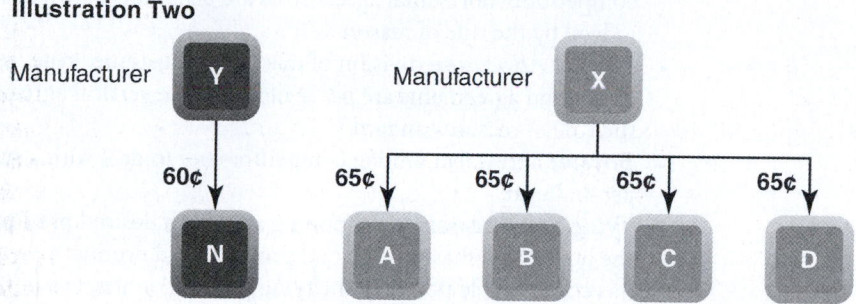

Illustration One

Manufacturer Y

Manufacturer X

60¢

65¢ 65¢ 65¢ 65¢

A B C D

Result: Manufacturer **X** may lower its price to A to 60¢ without lowering its price to B, C, and D.

Illustration Two

Manufacturer Y

Manufacturer X

60¢

65¢ 65¢ 65¢ 65¢

N A B C D

Result: Manufacturer **X** may *not* lower its price to A to 60¢ without lowering its price to B, C, and D.

enforceable in the Federal courts. Its broad power has been described by the U.S. Supreme Court:

> The "unfair methods of competition," which are condemned by ... the Act, are not confined to those that were illegal at common law or that were condemned by the Sherman Act.... It is also clear that the Federal Trade Commission Act was designed to supplement and bolster the Sherman Act and the Clayton Act ... *to stop in their incipiency acts and practices which, when full blown, would violate those Acts.* F.T.C. v. Motion Picture Advertising Service Co., 344 U.S. 392 (1953). (Emphasis supplied.)

Complaints may be instituted by the commission, which, after a hearing, "has wide latitude for judgment and the courts will not interfere except where the remedy selected has no reasonable relation to the unlawful practices found to exist." The FTC most frequently enters a cease-and-desist order having the effect of an injunction. The FTC Act imposes a civil monetary penalty of not more than $43,280, as adjusted annually for inflation in January 2020, on any person who violates a final cease-and-desist order of the FTC. Each day of noncompliance with a cease-and-desist order is considered a separate offense. In addition, the FTC may order other relief, such as affirmative disclosure, corrective advertising, and the granting of patent licenses on a reasonable royalty basis. Appeals may be taken from orders of the commission to the U.S. Courts of Appeals, which have exclusive jurisdiction to enforce, set aside, or modify orders of the commission.

In performing its duties, the FTC investigates not only possible violations of the antitrust laws but also unfair methods of competition, such as false and misleading advertisements, false or inadequate product labeling, the passing or palming off of goods as those of a competitor, lotteries, gambling schemes, discriminatory rebate or discount offers, false disparagement of a competitor's goods, false or misleading descriptive names of products, the use of false testimonials, and other unfair trade practices. For a more detailed discussion of the FTC and its powers, see *Chapter 41*.

SHERMAN ANTITRUST ACT

Restraint of Trade Section 1 prohibits contracts, combinations, and conspiracies that restrain trade

- *Rule of Reason* standard that balances the anticompetitive effects against the procompetitive effects of the restraint
- *Per se* **Violations** conclusively presumed unreasonable and therefore illegal
- *Quick Look Standard* a modified or abbreviated rule of reason standard
- *Horizontal Restraints* agreements among competitors
- *Vertical Restraints* agreements among parties at different levels in the chain of distribution

Application of Section 1

- *Price Fixing* an agreement with the purpose or effect of inhibiting price competition; horizontal agreements are *per se* illegal, while vertical price fixing is judged by the rule of reason
- *Market Allocation* division of markets by customer type, geography, or products; horizontal agreements are *per se* illegal, while vertical agreements are judged by the rule of reason standard
- *Boycott* agreement among competitors not to deal with a supplier or customer; *per se* illegal
- *Tying Arrangement* conditioning a sale of a desired product (tying product) on the buyer's purchasing a second product (tied product); *per se* illegal if the seller has considerable power in the tying product or affects a not-insubstantial amount of interstate commerce in the tied product

Monopolies Section 2 prohibits monopolization, attempts to monopolize, and conspiracies to monopolize

- *Monopolization* requires market power (ability to control price or exclude others from the marketplace) plus either the unfair attainment of the power or the abuse of such power
- *Attempt to Monopolize* specific intent to monopolize, plus a dangerous probability of success
- *Conspiracies to Monopolize*

Sanctions

- *Civil Liability* injured parties may recover treble damages (three times actual loss)
- *Criminal Penalties*

CLAYTON ACT

Tying Arrangement prohibited if it tends to create a monopoly or may substantially lessen competition

Exclusive Dealing arrangement by which a party has sole right to a market; prohibited if it tends to create a monopoly or may substantially lessen competition

Merger prohibited if it tends to create a monopoly or may substantially lessen competition

- *Horizontal Merger* one company's acquisition of a competing company
- *Vertical Merger* a company's acquisition of one of its suppliers or customers
- *Conglomerate Merger* the acquisition of a company that is not a competitor, customer, or supplier

Sanctions civil actions may be brought for treble damages and injunctions

| ROBINSON-PATMAN ACT | **Price Discrimination** the Act prohibits buyers from inducing or sellers from giving different prices to buyers of commodities of similar grade and quality
Injury plaintiff may prove injury to competitors of the seller (primary-line injury), to competitors of other buyers (secondary-line injury), or to purchasers from other secondary-line sellers (tertiary-line injury)
Defenses (1) cost justification, (2) meeting competition, and (3) functional discounts
Sanctions civil (treble damages); criminal in limited situations |
| FEDERAL TRADE COMMISSION ACT | **Purpose** to prevent unfair methods of competition and unfair or deceptive practices
Sanctions actions may be brought by the Federal Trade Commission, not by private individuals |

C A S E S

CASE 40-1

Restraint of Trade/Concerted Action

AMERICAN NEEDLE, INC. v. NATIONAL FOOTBALL LEAGUE

Supreme Court of the United States, 2010
560 U.S. 183, 130 S.Ct. 2201, 176 L.Ed.2d 947

Stevens, J.

[Originally organized in 1920, the National Football League (NFL) is an unincorporated association that encompasses 32 separately owned professional football teams. Each team has its own name, colors, and logo and owns related intellectual property. Prior to 1963, the teams made their own arrangements for licensing their intellectual property and marketing trademarked items such as caps and jerseys. In 1963, the teams formed National Football League Properties (NFLP) to develop, license, and market their intellectual property. Most, but not all, of the substantial revenues generated by NFLP have either been given to charity or shared equally among the teams. However, the teams are able to and have at times sought to withdraw from this arrangement.

Between 1963 and 2000, NFLP granted nonexclusive licenses to a number of vendors, permitting them to manufacture and sell apparel bearing team insignias. American Needle, Inc., was one of those licensees. In December 2000, the teams voted to authorize NFLP to grant exclusive licenses, and NFLP granted Reebok International Ltd. an exclusive ten-year license to manufacture and sell trade-marked headwear for all thirty-two teams. It thereafter declined to renew American Needle's nonexclusive license.

American Needle filed this action in the Northern District of Illinois, alleging that the agreements between the NFL, its teams, NFLP, and Reebok violated Sections 1 and 2 of the Sherman Act. In their answer to the complaint, the defendants asserted that the teams, NFL, and NFLP were incapable of conspiring within the meaning of Section 1 "because they are a single economic enterprise, at least with respect to the conduct challenged." The District Court granted summary judgment for the NFL on this question. The Court of Appeals for the Seventh Circuit affirmed.]

As the case comes to us, we have only a narrow issue to decide: whether the NFL respondents are capable of engaging in a "contract, combination..., or conspiracy" as defined by §1 of the Sherman Act, [citation], or, as we have sometimes phrased it, whether the alleged activity by the NFL respondents "must be viewed as that of a single enterprise for purposes of §1." [Citation.]

* * *

We have long held that concerted action under §1 does not turn simply on whether the parties involved are legally distinct entities. Instead, we have eschewed such formalistic distinctions in favor of a functional consideration of how the parties involved in the alleged anticompetitive conduct actually operate. * * *

Conversely, there is not necessarily concerted action simply because more than one legally distinct entity is involved. * * *

* * *

* * * The key is whether the alleged "contract, combination..., or conspiracy" is concerted action—that is, whether it joins together separate decisionmakers. The relevant inquiry, therefore, is whether there is a "contract, combination... or conspiracy" amongst "separate economic actors pursuing separate economic interests," [citation], such that the agreement "deprives the marketplace of independent centers of decisionmaking," [citation], and therefore of "diversity of entrepreneurial interests," [citations]. * * *

The NFL teams do not possess either the unitary decision-making quality or the single aggregation of economic power characteristic of independent action. Each of the teams is a substantial, independently owned, and independently managed business. "[T]heir general corporate actions are guided or determined" by "separate corporate consciousnesses," and "[t]heir objectives are" not "common." [Citations.] The teams compete with one another, not only on the playing field, but to attract fans, for gate receipts and for contracts with managerial and playing personnel. [Citations.]

Directly relevant to this case, the teams compete in the market for intellectual property. To a firm making hats, the Saints and the Colts are two potentially competing suppliers of valuable trademarks. When each NFL team licenses its intellectual property, it is not pursuing the "common interests of the whole" league but is instead pursuing interests of each "corporation itself," [citation]; teams are acting as "separate economic actors pursuing separate economic interests," and each team therefore is a potential "independent cente[r] of decisionmaking," [citation]. Decisions by NFL teams to license their separately owned trademarks collectively and to only one vendor are decisions that "depriv[e] the marketplace of independent centers of decisionmaking," [citation], and therefore of actual or potential competition. [Citation.] * * *

* * *

* * * Although NFL teams have common interests such as promoting the NFL brand, they are still separate, profit-maximizing entities, and their interests in licensing team trademarks are not necessarily aligned. [Citations.]

* * *

The question whether NFLP decisions can constitute concerted activity covered by §1 is closer than whether decisions made directly by the 32 teams are covered by §1. This is so both because NFLP is a separate corporation with its own management and because the record indicates that most of the revenues generated by NFLP are shared by the teams on an equal basis. Nevertheless, we think it clear that for the same reasons the 32 teams' conduct is covered by §1, NFLP's actions also are subject to §1, at least with regards to its marketing of property owned by the separate teams. NFLP's licensing decisions are made by the 32 potential competitors, and each of them actually owns its share of the jointly managed assets. [Citation.] Apart from their agreement to cooperate in exploiting those assets, including their decisions as the NFLP, there would be nothing to prevent each of the teams from making its own market decisions relating to purchases of apparel and headwear, to the sale of such items, and to the granting of licenses to use its trademarks.

* * * Thirty-two teams operating independently through the vehicle of the NFLP are not like the components of a single firm that act to maximize the firm's profits. The teams remain separately controlled, potential competitors with economic interests that are distinct from NFLP's financial well-being. [Citation.] Unlike typical decisions by corporate shareholders, NFLP licensing decisions effectively require the assent of more than a mere majority of shareholders. And each team's decision reflects not only an interest in NFLP's profits but also an interest in the team's individual profits. [Citation.] The 32 teams capture individual economic benefits separate and apart from NFLP profits as a result of the decisions they make for the NFLP. NFLP's decisions thus affect each team's profits from licensing its own intellectual property. "Although the business interests of" the teams "will *often* coincide with those of the" NFLP "as an entity in itself, that commonality of interest exists in every cartel." [Citation.] In making the relevant licensing decisions, NFLP is therefore "an instrumentality" of the teams. [Citation.]

If the fact that potential competitors shared in profits or losses from a venture meant that the venture was immune from §1, then any cartel "could evade the antitrust law simply by creating a 'joint venture' to serve as the exclusive seller of their competing products." [Citations.] However, competitors "cannot simply get around" antitrust liability by acting "through a third-party intermediary or 'joint venture.'" [Citation.]

* * * The fact that NFL teams share an interest in making the entire league successful and profitable, and that they must cooperate in the production and scheduling of games, provides a perfectly sensible justification for making a host of collective decisions. But the conduct at issue in this case is still concerted activity under the Sherman Act that is subject to §1 analysis.

When "restraints on competition are essential if the product is to be available at all," *per se* rules of illegality are inapplicable, and instead the restraint must be judged according to the flexible Rule of Reason. [Citations.] And depending upon the concerted activity in question, the Rule of Reason may not require a detailed analysis; it "can sometimes be applied in the twinkling of an eye." [Citation.]

Other features of the NFL may also save agreements amongst the teams. We have recognized, for example, "that the interest in maintaining a competitive balance" among "athletic teams is legitimate and important." [Citation.] While that same interest applies to the teams in the NFL, it does not justify treating them as a single entity for §1 purposes when it comes to the marketing of the teams' individually owned intellectual property. It is, however, unquestionably an interest that may well justify a variety of collective decisions made by the teams. What role it properly plays in applying the Rule of Reason to the allegations in this case is a matter to be considered on remand.

Accordingly, the judgment of the Court of Appeals is reversed, and the case is remanded for further proceedings consistent with this opinion.

CASE 40-2	Price Fixing
	LEEGIN CREATIVE LEATHER PRODUCTS, INC. v. PSKS, INC.
	Supreme Court of the United States, 2007
	551 U.S. 877, 127 S.Ct. 2705, 168 L.Ed.2d 623

Kennedy, J.

Petitioner, Leegin Creative Leather Products, Inc. (Leegin), designs, manufactures, and distributes leather goods and accessories. In 1991, Leegin began to sell belts under the brand name "Brighton." The Brighton brand has now expanded into a variety of women's fashion accessories. It is sold across the United States in over 5,000 retail establishments, for the most part independent, small boutiques and specialty stores. Leegin's president, Jerry Kohl, also has an interest in about 70 stores that sell Brighton products. Leegin asserts that, at least for its products, small retailers treat customers better, provide customers more services, and make their shopping experience more satisfactory than do larger, often impersonal retailers. Kohl explained: "[W]e want the consumers to get a different experience than they get in Sam's Club or in Wal-Mart. And you can't get that kind of experience or support or customer service from a store like Wal-Mart."

Respondent, PSKS, Inc. (PSKS), operates Kay's Kloset, a women's apparel store in Lewisville, Texas. Kay's Kloset buys from about 75 different manufacturers and at one time sold the Brighton brand. It first started purchasing Brighton goods from Leegin in 1995. Once it began selling the brand, the store promoted Brighton. For example, it ran Brighton advertisements and had Brighton days in the store. Kay's Kloset became the destination retailer in the area to buy Brighton products. Brighton was the store's most important brand and once accounted for 40 to 50 percent of its profits.

In 1997, Leegin instituted the "Brighton Retail Pricing and Promotion Policy." Following the policy, Leegin refused to sell to retailers that discounted Brighton goods below suggested prices. The policy contained an exception for products not selling well that the retailer did not plan on reordering. In the letter to retailers establishing the policy, Leegin stated:

> * * * We, at Leegin, choose to break away from the pack by selling [at] specialty stores; specialty stores that can offer the customer great quality merchandise, superb service, and support the Brighton product 365 days a year on a consistent basis. * * *

Leegin adopted the policy to give its retailers sufficient margins to provide customers the service central to its distribution strategy. It also expressed concern that discounting harmed Brighton's brand image and reputation.

A year after instituting the pricing policy Leegin introduced a marketing strategy known as the "Heart Store Program." It offered retailers incentives to become Heart Stores, and, in exchange, retailers pledged, among other things, to sell at Leegin's suggested prices. Kay's Kloset became a Heart Store soon after Leegin created the program. After a Leegin employee visited the store and found it unattractive, the parties appear to have agreed that Kay's Kloset would not be a Heart Store beyond 1998. Despite losing this status, Kay's Kloset continued to increase its Brighton sales.

In December 2002, Leegin discovered Kay's Kloset had been marking down Brighton's entire line by 20 percent. Kay's Kloset contended it placed Brighton products on sale to compete with nearby retailers who also were undercutting Leegin's suggested prices. Leegin, nonetheless, requested that Kay's Kloset cease discounting. Its request refused, Leegin stopped selling to the store. The loss of the Brighton brand had a considerable negative impact on the store's revenue from sales.

PSKS sued Leegin in the United States District Court for the Eastern District of Texas. It alleged, among other claims, that Leegin had violated the antitrust laws by "enter[ing] into agreements with retailers to charge only those prices fixed by Leegin." Leegin planned to introduce expert testimony describing the procompetitive effects of its pricing policy. The District Court excluded the testimony, relying on the *per se* rule established by *Dr. Miles*. [In *Dr. Miles Medical Co. v. John D. Park & Sons Co.* (1911), the U.S. Supreme Court established the rule that it is *per se* illegal under the Sherman Act for a manufacturer to agree with its distributor to set the minimum price the distributor can charge for the manufacturer's goods.] * * * The jury agreed with PSKS and awarded it $1.2 million. Pursuant to [statute], the District Court trebled the damages and reimbursed PSKS for its attorney's fees and costs. It entered judgment against Leegin in the amount of $3,975,000.80.

The Court of Appeals for the Fifth Circuit affirmed. * * * We granted certiorari to determine whether vertical minimum resale price maintenance agreements should continue to be treated as *per se* unlawful.

* * *

The rule of reason is the accepted standard for testing whether a practice restrains trade in violation of §1. [Citation.] "Under this rule, the fact finder weighs all of the circumstances of a case in deciding whether a restrictive practice should be prohibited as imposing an unreasonable restraint on competition." [Citation.] Appropriate factors to take into account include "specific information about the relevant business" and "the restraint's history, nature, and effect."

[Citation.] Whether the businesses involved have market power is a further, significant consideration. [Citations.] In its design and function the rule distinguishes between restraints with anticompetitive effect that are harmful to the consumer and restraints stimulating competition that are in the consumer's best interest.

The rule of reason does not govern all restraints. Some types "are deemed unlawful *per se*." [Citation.] The *per se* rule, treating categories of restraints as necessarily illegal, eliminates the need to study the reasonableness of an individual restraint in light of the real market forces at work, [citation]; and, it must be acknowledged, the *per se* rule can give clear guidance for certain conduct. Restraints that are *per se* unlawful include horizontal agreements among competitors to fix prices, [citation], or to divide markets [citation].

Resort to *per se* rules is confined to restraints, like those mentioned, "that would always or almost always tend to restrict competition and decrease output." [Citation.] To justify a *per se* prohibition a restraint must have "manifestly anticompetitive" effects, [citation], and "lack … any redeeming virtue," [citation].

As a consequence, the per se rule is appropriate only after courts have had considerable experience with the type of restraint at issue, [citation], and only if courts can predict with confidence that it would be invalidated in all or almost all instances under the rule of reason, [citation]. It should come as no surprise, then, that "we have expressed reluctance to adopt *per se* rules with regard to restraints imposed in the context of business relationships where the economic impact of certain practices is not immediately obvious." [Citations.] And, as we have stated, a "departure from the rule-of-reason standard must be based upon demonstrable economic effect rather than … upon formalistic line drawing." [Citation.]

The Court has interpreted *Dr. Miles Medical Co. v. John D. Park & Sons Co.*, [citation], as establishing a *per se* rule against a vertical agreement between a manufacturer and its distributor to set minimum resale prices. * * *

* * *

The reasons upon which *Dr. Miles* relied do not justify a *per se* rule. As a consequence, it is necessary to examine, in the first instance, the economic effects of vertical agreements to fix minimum resale prices, and to determine whether the *per se* rule is nonetheless appropriate. [Citation.]

* * *

* * * The justifications for vertical price restraints are similar to those for other vertical restraints. [Citation.] Minimum resale price maintenance can stimulate interbrand competition—the competition among manufacturers selling different brands of the same type of product—by reducing intrabrand competition—the competition among retailers selling the same brand. The promotion of interbrand competition is important because "the primary purpose of the antitrust laws is to protect [this type of] competition." [Citation.] A single manufacturer's use of vertical price restraints tends to eliminate intrabrand price competition; this in turn encourages retailers to invest in tangible or intangible services or promotional efforts that aid the manufacturer's position as against rival manufacturers. Resale price maintenance also has the potential to give consumers more options so that they can choose among low-price, low-service brands; high-price, high-service brands; and brands that fall in between.

Absent vertical price restraints, the retail services that enhance interbrand competition might be underprovided. This is because discounting retailers can free ride on retailers who furnish services and then capture some of the increased demand those services generate. [Citation.] Consumers might learn, for example, about the benefits of a manufacturer's product from a retailer that invests in fine showrooms, offers product demonstrations, or hires and trains knowledgeable employees. [Citation.] Or consumers might decide to buy the product because they see it in a retail establishment that has a reputation for selling high-quality merchandise. [Citation.] If the consumer can then buy the product from a retailer that discounts because it has not spent capital providing services or developing a quality reputation, the high-service retailer will lose sales to the discounter, forcing it to cut back its services to a level lower than consumers would otherwise prefer. Minimum resale price maintenance alleviates the problem because it prevents the discounter from undercutting the service provider. With price competition decreased, the manufacturer's retailers compete among themselves over services.

Resale price maintenance, in addition, can increase interbrand competition by facilitating market entry for new firms and brands. "[N]ew manufacturers and manufacturers entering new markets can use the restrictions in order to induce competent and aggressive retailers to make the kind of investment of capital and labor that is often required in the distribution of products unknown to the consumer." [Citations.] New products and new brands are essential to a dynamic economy, and if markets can be penetrated by using resale price maintenance there is a procompetitive effect.

Resale price maintenance can also increase interbrand competition by encouraging retailer services that would not be provided even absent free riding. It may be difficult and inefficient for a manufacturer to make and enforce a contract with a retailer specifying the different services the retailer must perform. Offering the retailer a guaranteed margin and threatening termination if it does not live up to expectations may be the most efficient way to expand the manufacturer's market share by inducing the retailer's performance and allowing it to use its own initiative and experience in providing valuable services. [Citations.]

While vertical agreements setting minimum resale prices can have procompetitive justifications, they may have anticompetitive effects in other cases; and unlawful price fixing, designed solely to obtain monopoly profits, is an ever present temptation. Resale price maintenance may, for example, facilitate a manufacturer cartel. [Citation.] * * *

Vertical price restraints also "might be used to organize cartels at the retailer level." [Citation.] A group of retailers might collude to fix prices to consumers and then compel a manufacturer to aid the unlawful arrangement with resale price maintenance. In that instance the manufacturer does not establish the practice to stimulate services or to promote its brand but to give inefficient retailers higher profits. Retailers with better distribution systems and lower cost structures would be prevented from charging lower prices by the agreement. [Citations.]

A horizontal cartel among competing manufacturers or competing retailers that decreases output or reduces competition in order to increase price is, and ought to be, *per se* unlawful. * * *

Resale price maintenance, furthermore, can be abused by a powerful manufacturer or retailer. A dominant retailer, for example, might request resale price maintenance to forestall innovation in distribution that decreases costs. A manufacturer might consider it has little choice but to accommodate the retailer's demands for vertical price restraints if the manufacturer believes it needs access to the retailer's distribution network. * * *

Notwithstanding the risks of unlawful conduct, it cannot be stated with any degree of confidence that resale price maintenance "always or almost always tend[s] to restrict competition and decrease output." [Citation.] Vertical agreements establishing minimum resale prices can have either procompetitive or anticompetitive effects, depending upon the circumstances in which they are formed. And although the empirical evidence on the topic is limited, it does not suggest efficient uses of the agreements are infrequent or hypothetical. [Citations.] As the rule would proscribe a significant amount of pro-competitive conduct, these agreements appear ill suited for *per se* condemnation.

* * *

Resale price maintenance, it is true, does have economic dangers. If the rule of reason were to apply to vertical price restraints, courts would have to be diligent in eliminating their anticompetitive uses from the market. * * *

* * *

The rule of reason is designed and used to eliminate anticompetitive transactions from the market. This standard principle applies to vertical price restraints. * * *

For all of the foregoing reasons, we think that were the Court considering the issue as an original matter, the rule of reason, not a *per se* rule of unlawfulness, would be the appropriate standard to judge vertical price restraints.

* * *

The judgment of the Court of Appeals is reversed, and the case is remanded for proceedings consistent with this opinion.

CASE 40-3

Tying Arrangements/Monopoly

EASTMAN KODAK CO. v. IMAGE TECHNICAL SERVICES, INC.

Supreme Court of the United States, 1992
504 U.S. 451, 112 S.Ct. 2072, 119 L.Ed.2d 265

Blackmun, J.

Kodak manufactures and sells complex business machines—as relevant here, high-volume photocopier and micrographics equipment. Kodak equipment is unique; micro-graphic software programs that operate on Kodak machines, for example, are not compatible with competitors' machines. Kodak parts are not compatible with other manufacturers' equipment, and vice versa. Kodak equipment, although expensive when new, has little resale value.

Kodak provides service and parts for its machines to its customers. It provides some of the parts itself; the rest are made to order for Kodak by independent original-equipment manufacturers (OEMs). Kodak does not sell a complete system of original equipment, lifetime service, and lifetime parts for a single price. Instead, Kodak provides service after the initial warranty period either through annual service contracts, which include all necessary parts, or on a per-call basis. It charges, through negotiations and bidding, different prices for equipment, service, and parts for different customers. Kodak provides 80% to 95% of the service for Kodak machines.

Beginning in the early 1980s, ISOs [independent service organizations] began repairing and servicing Kodak equipment. They also sold parts and reconditioned and sold used Kodak equipment. Their customers were federal, state, and local government agencies, banks, insurance companies, industrial enterprises, and providers of specialized copy and microfilming services. ISOs provide service at a price substantially lower than Kodak does. Some customers found that the ISO service was of higher quality.

Some of the ISOs' customers purchase their own parts and hire ISOs only for service. Others choose ISOs to supply both service and parts. ISOs keep an inventory of parts, purchased from Kodak or other sources, primarily the OEMs.

In 1985 and 1986, Kodak implemented a policy of selling replacement parts for micrographic and copying machines only to buyers of Kodak equipment who use Kodak service or repair their own machines.

As part of the same policy, Kodak sought to limit ISO access to other sources of Kodak parts. Kodak and the OEMs agreed that the OEMs would not sell parts that fit Kodak equipment to anyone other than Kodak. Kodak also pressured Kodak equipment owners and independent parts distributors not to sell Kodak parts to ISOs. In addition, Kodak took steps to restrict the availability of used machines.

Kodak intended, through these policies, to make it more difficult for ISOs to sell service for Kodak machines. It succeeded. ISOs were unable to obtain parts from reliable sources, and many were forced out of business, while others lost substantial revenue. Customers were forced to switch to Kodak service even though they preferred ISO service.

In 1987, the [18] ISOs filed the present action in the District Court, alleging, inter alia, that Kodak had unlawfully tied the sale of service for Kodak machines to the sale of parts, in violation of §1 of the Sherman Act, and had unlawfully monopolized and attempted to monopolize the sale of service for Kodak machines, in violation of §2 of that Act.

* * *

A tying arrangement is "an agreement by a party to sell one product but only on the condition that the buyer also purchases a different (or tied) product, or at least agrees that he will not purchase that product from any other supplier." [Citation.] Such an arrangement violates §1 of the Sherman Act if the seller has "appreciable economic power" in the tying product market and if the arrangement affects a substantial volume of commerce in the tied market. [Citation.]

Kodak did not dispute that its arrangement affects a substantial volume of interstate commerce. It, however, did challenge whether its activities constituted a "tying arrangement" and whether Kodak exercised "appreciable economic power" in the tying market. We consider these issues in turn.

For the respondents to defeat a motion for summary judgment on their claim of a tying arrangement, a reasonable trier of fact must be able to find, first, that service and parts are two distinct products and, second, that Kodak has tied the sale of the two products.

For service and parts to be considered two distinct products, there must be sufficient consumer demand so that it is efficient for a firm to provide service separately from parts. [Citation.] Evidence in the record indicates that service and parts have been sold separately in the past and still are sold separately to self-service equipment owners. Indeed, the development of the entire high-technology service industry is evidence of the efficiency of a separate market for service.

Kodak insists that because there is no demand for parts separate from service, there cannot be separate markets for service and parts. By that logic, we would be forced to conclude that there can never be separate markets, for example, for cameras and film, computers and software, or automobiles and tires. That is an assumption we are unwilling to make.

* * *

Having found sufficient evidence of a tying arrangement, we consider the other necessary feature of an illegal tying arrangement: appreciable economic power in the tying market. Market power is the power "to force a purchaser to do something that he would not do in a competitive market." [Citation.] It has been defined as "the ability of a single seller to raise price and restrict output." [Citations.] The existence of such power ordinarily is inferred from the seller's possession of a predominant share of the market. [Citations.]

* * *

The extent to which one market prevents exploitation of another market depends on the extent to which consumers will change their consumption of one product in response to a price change in another, i.e., the "cross-elasticity of demand." See *Du Pont*, [citations]. Kodak's proposed rule rests on a factual assumption about the cross-elasticity of demand in the equipment and after-markets: "If Kodak raised its parts or service prices above competitive levels, potential customers would simply stop buying Kodak equipment. Perhaps Kodak would be able to increase short term profits through such a strategy, but at a devastating cost to its long term interests." Kodak argues that the Court should accept, as a matter of law, this "basic economic realit[y]," that competition in the equipment market necessarily prevents market power in the aftermarkets.

* * *

We conclude * * * that Kodak has failed to demonstrate that respondents' inference of market power in the service and parts markets is unreasonable, and that, consequently, Kodak is entitled to summary judgment. It is clearly reasonable to infer that Kodak has market power to raise prices and drive out competition in the aftermarkets, since respondents offer direct evidence that Kodak did so. It is also plausible, as discussed above, to infer that Kodak chose to gain immediate profits by exerting that market power where locked-in customers, high information costs, and discriminatory pricing limited and perhaps eliminated any long-term loss. Viewing the evidence in the light most favorable to respondents, their allegations of market power "mak[e] * * * economic sense." [Citation.]

* * *

We need not decide whether Kodak's behavior has any procompetitive effects and, if so, whether they outweigh the anticompetitive effects. We note only that Kodak's service and parts policy is simply not one that appears always or almost always to enhance competition, and therefore to warrant a legal presumption without any evidence of its actual economic impact. In this case, when we weigh the risk of deterring procompetitive behavior by proceeding to trial against the risk that illegal behavior go unpunished, the balance tips against summary judgment. [Citations.]

* * * We therefore affirm the denial of summary judgment on respondents' §1 claim.

* * *

Respondents also claim that they have presented genuine issues for trial as to whether Kodak has monopolized or attempted to monopolize the service and parts markets in violation of §2 of the Sherman Act. "The offense of monopoly under §2 of the Sherman Act has two elements: (1) the possession of monopoly power in the relevant market and (2) the willful acquisition or maintenance of that power as distinguished from growth or development as a consequence of a superior product, business acumen, or historic accident." [Citation.]

The existence of the first element, possession of monopoly power, is easily resolved. As has been noted, respondents have presented a triable claim that service and parts are separate markets, and that Kodak has the "power to control prices or exclude competition" in service and parts. *Du Pont*, [citation]. Monopoly power under §2 requires, of course, something greater than market power under §1. [Citation.] Respondents' evidence that Kodak controls nearly 100% of the parts market and 80% to 95% of the service market, with no readily available substitutes, is, however, sufficient to survive summary judgment under the more stringent monopoly standard of §2. [Citations.]

Kodak also contends that, as a matter of law, a single brand of a product or service can never be a relevant market under the Sherman Act. We disagree. The relevant market for antitrust purposes is determined by the choices available to Kodak equipment owners. [Citation.] Because service and parts for Kodak equipment are not interchangeable with other manufacturers' service and parts, the relevant market from the Kodak equipment owner's perspective is composed of only those companies that service Kodak machines. See *Du Pont*, [citation] (the "market is composed of products that have reasonable interchangeability"). This Court's prior cases support the proposition that in some instances one brand of a product can constitute a separate market. [Citations.]

The second element of a §2 claim is the use of monopoly power "to foreclose competition, to gain a competitive advantage, or to destroy a competitor." [Citation.] If Kodak adopted its parts and service policies as part of a scheme of willful acquisition or maintenance of monopoly power, it will have violated §2. [Citations.]

As recounted at length above, respondents have presented evidence that Kodak took exclusionary action to maintain its parts monopoly and used its control over parts to strengthen its monopoly share of the Kodak service market. Liability turns, then, on whether "valid business reasons" can explain Kodak's actions. [Citations.] * * *

* * *

In the end, of course, Kodak's arguments may prove to be correct. It may be that its parts, service, and equipment are components of one unified market, or that the equipment market does discipline the aftermarkets so that all three are priced competitively overall, or that any anticompetitive effects of Kodak's behavior are outweighed by its competitive effects. But we cannot reach these conclusions as a matter of law on a record this sparse. Accordingly, the judgment of the Court of Appeals denying summary judgment is affirmed.

CASE 40-4

Horizontal Merger
HOSPITAL CORPORATION OF AMERICA v. FTC
United States Court of Appeals, Seventh Circuit, 1986
807 F.2d 1381

Posner, J.

Hospital Corporation of America, the largest proprietary hospital chain in the United States, asks us to set aside the decision by the Federal Trade Commission that it violated section 7 of the Clayton Act, [citation], by the acquisition in 1981 and 1982 of two corporations, Hospital Affiliates International, Inc. and Health Care Corporation. Before these acquisitions (which cost Hospital Corporation almost $700 million), Hospital Corporation had owned one hospital in Chattanooga,

Tennessee. The acquisitions gave it ownership of two more. In addition, pursuant to the terms of the acquisitions it assumed contracts, both with four-year terms, that Hospital Affiliates International had made to manage two other Chattanooga-area hospitals. So after the acquisitions Hospital Corporation owned or managed 5 of the 11 hospitals in the area. Later one of the management contracts was cancelled; and one of the lesser issues raised by Hospital Corporation, which we might as well dispose of right now, is whether the Commission should have disregarded the assumption of that contract. We agree with the Commission that it was not required to take account of a post-acquisition transaction that may have been made to improve Hospital Corporation's litigating position. The contract was cancelled after the Commission began investigating Hospital Corporation's acquisition of Hospital Affiliates, and while the initiative in cancelling was taken by the managed hospital, Hospital Corporation reacted with unaccustomed mildness by allowing the hospital to withdraw from the contract. For it had sued three other hospitals that tried to get out of their management contracts—only none of these hospitals was in a market where Hospital Corporation's acquisition of Hospital Affiliates was likely to be challenged. Post-acquisition evidence that is subject to manipulation by the party seeking to use it is entitled to little or no weight. [Citation.] * * *

If all the hospitals brought under common ownership or control by the two challenged acquisitions are treated as a single entity, the acquisitions raised Hospital Corporation's market share in the Chattanooga area from 14 percent to 26 percent. This made it the second largest provider of hospital services in a highly concentrated market where the four largest firms together had a 91 percent market share compared to 79 percent before the acquisitions. These are the FTC's figures, and Hospital Corporation thinks they are slightly too high * * * but the discrepancy is too slight to make a legal difference. Nor would expressing the market shares in terms of the Herfindahl index alter the impression of a highly concentrated market.

* * *

The Commission may have made its task harder (and opinion longer) than strictly necessary, however, by studiously avoiding reliance on any of the [U.S.] Supreme Court's section 7 decisions from the 1960s except [citation], which took an explicitly economic approach to the interpretation of the statute. The other decisions in that decade * * * seemed, taken as a group, to establish the illegality of any nontrivial acquisition of a competitor, whether or not the acquisition was likely either to bring about or shore up collusive or oligopoly pricing. The elimination of a significant rival was thought by itself to infringe the complex of social and economic values conceived by a majority of the Court to inform the statutory words "may * * * substantially * * * lessen competition."

None of these decisions has been overruled. * * *

The most important developments that cast doubt on the continued vitality of such [1960s] cases as [citations] are found in other cases, where the Supreme Court, echoed by the lower courts, has said repeatedly that the economic concept of competition, rather than any desire to preserve rivals as such, is the lodestar that shall guide the contemporary application of the antitrust laws, not excluding the Clayton Act * * * . Applied to cases brought under section 7, this principle requires the district court (in this case, the Commission) to make a judgment whether the challenged acquisition is likely to hurt

consumers, as by making it easier for the firms in the market to collude, expressly or tacitly, and thereby force price above or farther above the competitive level. So it was prudent for the Commission, rather than resting on the very strict merger decisions of the 1960s, to inquire into the probability of harm to consumers. * * *

When an economic approach is taken in a section 7 case, the ultimate issue is whether the challenged acquisition is likely to facilitate collusion. In this perspective the acquisition of a competitor has no economic significance in itself; the worry is that it may enable the acquiring firm to cooperate (or cooperate better) with other leading competitors on reducing or limiting output, thereby pushing up the market price * * *. There is plenty of evidence to support the Commission's prediction of adverse competitive effect in this case;

* * *

The acquisitions reduced the number of competing hospitals in the Chattanooga market from 11 to 7. * * *

The reduction in the number of competitors is significant in assessing the competitive vitality of the Chattanooga hospital market. The fewer competitors there are in a market, the easier it is for them to coordinate their pricing without committing detectable violations of section 1 of the Sherman Act, which forbids price fixing. This would not be very important if the four competitors eliminated by the acquisitions in this case had been insignificant, but they were not; they accounted in the aggregate for 12 percent of the sales of the market. As a result of the acquisitions the four largest firms came to control virtually the whole market, and the problem of coordination was therefore reduced to one of coordination among these four.

Moreover, both the ability of the remaining firms to expand their output should the big four reduce their own output in order to raise the market price (and, by expanding, to offset the leading firms' restriction of their own output), and the ability of outsiders to come in and build completely new hospitals, are reduced by Tennessee's certificate-of-need law. Any addition to hospital capacity must be approved by a state agency. * * *

* * *

In showing that the challenged acquisitions gave four firms control over an entire market so that they would have little reason to fear a competitive reaction if they raised prices above the competitive level, the Commission went far to justify its prediction of probable anticompetitive effects. Maybe it need have gone no further. [Citations.] But it did. First it pointed out that the demand for hospital services by patients and their doctors is highly inelastic under competitive conditions. This is not only because people place a high value on their safety and comfort and because many of their treatment decisions are made for them by their doctor, who doesn't pay their hospital bills; it is also because most hospital bills are paid largely by insurance companies or the federal government rather than by the patient. The less elastic the demand for a good or service is, the greater are the profits that providers can make by raising price through collusion. * * *

Second, there is a tradition, well documented in the Commission's opinion, of cooperation between competing hospitals in Chattanooga * * *. But a market in which competitors are unusually disposed to cooperate is a market prone to collusion. * * *

Third, hospitals are under great pressure from the federal government and the insurance companies to cut costs. One way of resisting this pressure is by presenting a united front in negotiations with the third-party payors * * *. The fewer the independent competitors in a hospital market, the easier they will find it, by presenting an unbroken phalanx of

representations and requests, to frustrate efforts to control hospital costs. This too is a form of collusion that the antitrust laws seek to discourage * * *.

All these considerations, taken together, supported * * * the Commission's conclusion that the challenged acquisitions are likely to foster collusive practices, harmful to consumers, in the Chattanooga hospital market. Section 7 does not require proof that a merger or other acquisition has caused higher prices in the affected market. All that is necessary is that the merger create an appreciable danger of such consequences in the future. A predictive judgment, necessarily probabilistic and judgmental rather than demonstrable [citation].

* * *

The Commission's order is affirmed and enforced.

QUESTIONS

1. Discuss the validity and effect of each of the following:

    a. A, B, and C, manufacturers of stereos, orally agree that due to the disastrous, cutthroat competition in the market, they will establish a reasonable price to charge their purchasers.

    b. D, E, F, and G, newspaper publishers, agree not to charge their customers more than $0.30 per newspaper.

    c. H, a distiller of liquor, and I, H's retail distributor, agree that I should charge a price of $5 per bottle.

2. Discuss the validity of the following:

    a. A territorial allocation agreement between two manufacturers of the same type of products, whereby neither will sell its products in the area allocated to the other.

    b. An agreement between manufacturer and distributor not to sell a dealer a particular product or parts necessary for repair of the product.

3. Universal Video sells 40 percent of the video recording equipment in the United States. One-half of Universal's sales is to Giant Retailer, a company that possesses 50 percent of the retail market. Giant seeks either (a) to obtain an exclusive dealing arrangement with Universal or (b) to acquire Universal. Advise Giant as to the validity of its alternatives.

4. Z sells cameras to A, B, C, and D for $110 per camera. Y, one of Z's competitors, sells a comparable camera to A for $101.50. Z, in response to this competitive pressure from Y, lowers its price to A to $101.50. B, C, and D insist that Z lower its price to them to $101.50, but Z refuses. B, C, and D sue Z for unlawful price discrimination. Decision? Would your answer differ if Z reduced its price to A to $100? Explain.

5. Discount is a discount appliance chain store that continually sells goods at a price below manufacturers' suggested retail prices. A, B, and C, the three largest manufacturers of appliances, agree that unless Discount ceases its discount pricing, they will no longer sell to Discount. Discount refuses, and A, B, and C refuse to sell to Discount. Discount contends that A, B, and C are in violation of antitrust law. Explain whether Discount is correct.

6. Magnum Company produces 77 percent of the coal utilized in the United States. Coal provides 25 percent of all of the energy used in the United States. In a suit brought by the United States against Magnum for violation of the antitrust laws, what result? Explain.

7. Justin Manufacturing Company sells high-fashion clothing under the prestigious "Justin" label. The company has a firm policy that it will not deal with any company that sells below its suggested retail price. Justin is informed by one of its customers, XYZ, that its competitor, Duplex, is selling the "Justin" line at a great discount. Justin now demands that Duplex comply with the agreement not to sell the "Justin" line below the suggested retail price. Discuss the implications of this situation.

8. Jay Corporation, the largest manufacturer of bicycles in the United States, with 40 percent of the market, has recently entered into an agreement with Retail Bike, the largest retailer of bicycles in the United States, with 37 percent of the market, under which Jay will furnish its bicycles only to Retail and Retail will sell only Jay's bicycles. The government is now questioning this agreement. Discuss.

9. Whirlpool Corporation manufactured vacuum cleaners under both its own name and under the Kenmore name. Oreck exclusively distributed the vacuum cleaners sold under the Whirlpool name. Sears, Roebuck & Co. exclusively distributed the Kenmore vacuum cleaners. Oreck alleged that its exclusive distributorship agreement with Whirlpool was not renewed because of the existence of an unlawful conspiracy between Whirlpool and Sears. Oreck further contended that a per se rule was applicable because the agreement was (a) price fixing or (b) a group boycott or (c) both. Is Oreck correct? Why or why not?

10. Indian Coffee of Pittsburgh, Pennsylvania, marketed vacuum-packed coffee under the Breakfast Cheer brand name in the Pittsburgh and Cleveland, Ohio, areas. That same year, Folgers Coffee, a leading coffee seller, began selling coffee in Pittsburgh. To make inroads into the new territory, Folgers sold its coffee at greatly reduced prices. At first, Indian Coffee met Folgers' prices, but could not continue operating at such a reduced price and was forced out of the market. Indian Coffee brings an antitrust action. Explain whether Folgers has violated the Sherman Antitrust Law.

CASE PROBLEMS

11. Von's Grocery, a large retail grocery chain in Los Angeles, sought to acquire Shopping Bag Food Stores, a direct competitor. At the time of the proposed merger, Von's sales ranked third in the Los Angeles area and Shopping Bag's ranked sixth. Both chains were increasing their number of stores. The merger would have resulted in the creation of the second largest grocery chain in Los Angeles, with total sales in excess of $170 million. Prior to the proposed merger, the number of owners operating single stores declined from 5,365 to 3,590 over a thirteen-year period. During this same period, the number of chains with two or more stores rose from 96 to 150. The United States brought suit against Von's to prevent the merger, claiming that the proposed merger violated Section 7 of the Clayton Act in that it could result in the substantial lessening of competition or could tend to create a monopoly. What result? Explain.

12. Boise Cascade Corporation is a wholesaler and retailer of office products. The FTC issued a complaint charging that Boise had violated the Robinson-Patman Act by receiving a wholesaler's discount from certain suppliers on products that Boise resold at retail, in competition with other retailers that could not obtain wholesale discounts. Has the Robinson-Patman Act been violated? Explain.

13. Great Atlantic and Pacific Tea Company desired to achieve cost savings by switching to the sale of "private label" milk. A&P asked Borden Company, its longtime supplier of "brand label" milk, to submit a bid to supply certain of A&P's private label dairy products. A&P was not satisfied with Borden's bid, however, and it solicited other offers. Bowman Dairy, a competitor of Borden's, submitted a lower bid. At this point, A&P contacted Borden and asked it to rebid on the private label contract. A&P included a warning that Borden would have to lower its original bid substantially to undercut Bowman's

bid. Borden offered a bid that doubled A&P's potential annual cost savings. A&P accepted Borden's bid. The FTC then brought an action, charging that A&P had violated the Robinson-Patman Act by knowingly inducing or receiving illegal price discrimination from Borden. Discuss whether the FTC is correct in its allegations.

14. Clorox is the nation's leading manufacturer of household liquid bleach (accounting for 49 percent—$40 million—of sales annually) and is the only brand sold nationally. Clorox and its next largest competitor, Purex, hold 65 percent of national sales, and the top four bleach manufacturers control 80 percent of sales. As all bleach is chemically identical, Clorox spends more than $5 million each year in advertising to attract and keep customers.

 Procter & Gamble is the dominant national manufacturer of household cleaning products, with yearly sales of $1.1 billion. As with bleach, advertising is vital in the household cleaning products industry. Procter & Gamble spends more than $127 million in advertising and promotions annually. Procter & Gamble decided to diversify into the bleach business, as its household cleaning products and bleach are both low-cost, high-turnover consumer goods; are dependent on mass advertising; and are sold to the same customers at the same stores through the same merchandising methods. Procter & Gamble decided to merge with Clorox, rather than start its own bleach division, to secure the dominant position in the bleach market immediately. Should the FTC take action against this merger, and if so, what decision? Explain.

15. The National Collegiate Athletic Association (NCAA) adopted a plan for televising college football games to reduce the adverse effect of television coverage on spectator attendance. The plan limited the total number

of televised intercollegiate football games and limited the number of games any one school could televise. No member of the NCAA was permitted to sell any television rights except in accordance with the plan. As part of the plan, the NCAA had agreements with the American Broadcasting Company (ABC) and the Columbia Broadcasting System (CBS) to pay to each school at least a specified minimum price for televising football games. Several member universities now join to bring suit against the NCAA, claiming the new plan is a horizontal price fixing agreement and output limitation and as such is illegal *per se*. The NCAA counters that the existence of the product, college football, depends upon member compliance with restrictions and regulations. According to the NCAA, its restrictions, including the television plan, have a procompetitive effect. Is the television plan valid? Explain.

16. The National Society of Professional Engineers (Society) had an ethics rule that prohibited member engineers from disclosing or discussing price and fee information with customers until after the customer had hired a particular engineer. This rule against competitive bidding was designed to maintain high standards in the field of engineering. The Society felt that competitive pressure to offer engineering services at the lowest possible price would encourage engineers to design and specify inefficient, unsafe, and unnecessarily expensive structures and construction methods. According to the Society, awarding engineering contracts to the lowest bidder, regardless of quality, would be dangerous to the public health, safety, and welfare. The Society emphasizes that the rule is not an agreement to fix prices. Rather, it claims the rule was drafted by experienced, highly trained professional engineers to prevent public harm and is therefore reasonable. Does the rule unreasonably restrain trade and thus violate Section 1 of the Sherman Act? Why or why not?

17. During a period of a few years, intense price competition characterized both the retail and the wholesale oil markets. At times, prices in the wholesale market fell below the manufacturer's cost. One cause of the volatile situation was the supply of "distress gasoline" placed on the market by seventeen independent refiners. These independent refiners had no retail sales outlets and little storage capacity, so they were forced to sell their product at "distress prices." In spite of their unprofitable operations, they could not afford to shut down, for if they did so, they would be apt to lose both their oil connections in the field and their regular customers.

In an attempt to remedy this problem, the major oil companies entered into an informal agreement whereby each selected as its "dancing partner" one or more independent refiners having distress gasoline. The major oil company would then assume responsibility for purchasing the independent's distress supply at the "fair going market price." As a result, the market price of oil rose for two consecutive years, and the spot market became stable. Have the companies engaged in horizontal price fixing in violation of the Sherman Act? Why or why not?

18. As part of a corporate plan to stimulate sagging television sales, GTE Sylvania began to phase out its wholesale distributors and began to sell its television sets directly to a smaller and more select group of franchised retailers. To this end, Sylvania limited the number of franchises granted for any given area and required each franchisee to sell Sylvania products only from the location or locations at which it was franchised. A franchise did not constitute an exclusive territory, and Sylvania retained sole discretion to increase the number of retailers in an area in light of the success or failure of existing retailers. The strategy apparently was successful, as Sylvania's national market share increased from less than 2 percent to 5 percent.

In the course of carrying out its plan, Sylvania franchised Young Brothers as a television retailer at a San Francisco location one mile from that of Continental T.V., Inc., one of Sylvania's most successful franchisees. A course of feuding began between Sylvania and Continental that reached a head when Continental requested permission to open a store in Sacramento and Sylvania refused. Continental opened the Sacramento store anyway and began shipping merchandise there from its San Jose warehouse. Shortly thereafter, Sylvania terminated Continental's franchise. Is the franchise location restriction a *per se* violation of the Sherman Act? Explain.

19. In 1923, DuPont was granted the exclusive right to make and sell cellophane in North America. In 1927, the company introduced a moisture-proof brand of cellophane that was ideal for various wrapping needs. Although more expensive than most competing wrapping, it offered a desired combination of transparency, strength, and cost. Except for its permeability to gases, however, cellophane had no qualities that a number of competing materials did not possess as well. Cellophane sales increased dramatically, and by 1950, DuPont produced almost 75 percent of the cellophane sold in the United States. Nevertheless, sales of the material constituted less than 20 percent of the sales of "flexible packaging materials."

The United States brought an action, contending that by so dominating cellophane production, DuPont had monopolized a part of trade or commerce in violation of the Sherman Act. DuPont argued that it had not monopolized because it did not have the power to control the price of cellophane or to exclude competitors from the market for flexible wrapping materials. Who is correct? Explain.

20. Ed O'Bannon, a highly talented former basketball player at UCLA, alleges an antitrust violation based on the premise that current and former NCAA men's basketball and Division I-A football players should be allowed to sell the rights to their name, image, and likeness to the NCAA, its licensing division, and outside entities including television and other media networks. The NCAA does not permit this activity, contending that such activity would destroy the system of amateurism. The plaintiffs (O'Bannon and "all others similarly situated") argue that "the NCAA has unreasonably and illegally restrained trade in order to commercially exploit former student-athletes subject to its control, with such exploitation affecting those individuals well into their post-collegiate lives." Explain who should prevail.

TAKING SIDES

The California Dental Association (CDA) is a voluntary nonprofit association of local dental societies to which some nineteen thousand dentists belong, about three-quarters of those practicing in the state. The CDA lobbies on behalf of its members' interests and conducts marketing and public relations campaigns for their benefit. The dentists who belong to the CDA through these associations agree to abide by a Code of Ethics (Code), which includes a regulation limiting their right to advertise. Responsibility for enforcing the Code rests in the first instance with the local dental societies. Applicants who refuse to withdraw or revise objectionable advertisements may be denied membership, and members are subject to censure, suspension, or expulsion from the CDA.

The FTC brought a complaint against the CDA, alleging that it applied its Code so as to restrict truthful, nondeceptive advertising and therefore violated Section 5 of the FTC Act. The FTC alleged that the CDA unreasonably restricted price advertising—particularly discounted fees—and advertising relating to the quality of dental services.

a. What are the arguments that the *per se* standard applies to this case?

b. What are the arguments that a rule of reason standard applies to this case?

c. Which standard should apply to this case? Explain.

Consumer Protection

- Describe the role of the Federal Trade Commission (FTC) and the major enforcement sanctions that it may use.

- Describe the role and workings of (1) the Consumer Product Safety Commission (CPSC) and (2) the Consumer Financial Protection Bureau (CFPB).

- Explain the principal provisions of the Magnuson-Moss Warranty Act and the differences between a full and a limited warranty.

- Describe what information a creditor must provide a consumer before the consumer incurs the obligation.

- Outline the major remedies that are available to a creditor.

Consumer transactions have increased enormously since World War II. As of the end of 2019, total consumer indebtedness was more than $14 trillion, which was composed of consumer credit card debt of almost $1 trillion, automobile debt of $1.3 trillion, student debt of $1.5 trillion, and total consumer mortgage debt of $10 trillion. Although the definition varies, a consumer transaction generally involves goods, credit, services, or land acquired for personal, household, or family purposes. Historically, consumers were subject to the rule of *caveat emptor*—let the buyer beware. In recent years, however, the law has largely abandoned this principle and now provides consumers greater protection. Most of this protection takes the form of statutory enactments at both the State and Federal levels, and a number of government agencies are charged with enforcing these statutes. This enforcement varies enormously. In some cases, only government agencies may exercise enforcement rights, which they impose through criminal penalties, civil penalties, injunctions, and cease-and-desist orders. In other cases, in addition to the government's enforcement rights, consumers may privately seek the rescission of contracts and damages for harm resulting from violations of consumer protection laws. Finally, under certain consumer protection statutes such as State "lemon laws," consumers alone may exercise enforcement rights. This chapter examines State and Federal consumer protection agencies and consumer protection statutes.

41-1 State and Federal Consumer Protection Agencies

Through the enactment of laws and regulations, legislatures and administrative bodies at the Federal, State, and local levels all actively seek to shield consumers from an enormous range of harm. The most common abuses in consumer transactions involve the extension of credit, deceptive trade practices, unsafe products, and unfair pricing.

41-1a STATE AND LOCAL CONSUMER PROTECTION AGENCIES

The many consumer protection agencies at the State and local levels typically deal with fraudulent and deceptive trade practices and fraudulent sales practices, such as false statements about a product's value or quality. In most jurisdictions, consumer protection agencies also help to resolve consumer complaints about defective goods or poor service.

Most State Attorneys General play an active role in consumer protection by enforcing laws against consumer fraud through judicially imposed injunctions and restitution. In recent years, as the Federal government's role in consumer protection has diminished in response to the deregulatory movement, the States correspondingly have expanded their role. The National Association of Attorneys General (NAAG) has been active in coordinating lawsuits among the States. Under NAAG's guidance, several States often will simultaneously file lawsuits against a company that has been engaging in fraudulent acts involving more than one State.

In some instances, however, States have not coordinated their efforts and, as a consequence, have acted inconsistently with respect to consumer protection, especially in health and safety matters. This lack of coordination can present serious problems for companies that sell large numbers of products in interstate commerce.

41-1b THE FEDERAL TRADE COMMISSION

At the Federal level, the most significant consumer protection agency is the Federal Trade Commission (FTC). Established in 1914, the FTC has two major functions: (1) under its mandate to prevent "unfair methods of competition in commerce," it and the Antitrust Division of the Department of Justice are responsible for antitrust enforcement at the Federal level (the FTC's role in antitrust enforcement is discussed in *Chapter 40*), and (2) under its mandate to prevent "unfair and deceptive" trade practices, it is responsible for stopping fraudulent sales techniques.

In addressing unfair and deceptive trade practices, the five-member commission (no more than three of these members may be from the same political party) has the power to issue substantive industry-wide "trade regulation rules" and to conduct appropriate investigations and hearings. Among the rules it has issued so far are those regulating used car sales, franchising and business opportunity ventures, funeral home services, and the issuance of consumer credit, as well as those requiring a "cooling-off" period for door-to-door sales (discussed later in this chapter).

When considering a deceptive trade practice, the agency often may seek a **cease-and-desist** order rather than issue a substantive industry-wide trade regulation rule. A cease-and-desist order directs a party to stop a certain practice or face punishment such as a fine. In a typical situation, the FTC staff discovers a potentially deceptive practice, investigates the matter, and files a complaint against the alleged offender (usually referred to as the respondent). After a hearing in front of an administrative law judge (ALJ) to determine whether a violation of the law has occurred, the FTC obtains a cease-and-desist order if the ALJ finds that one is necessary. The respondent may appeal to the FTC commissioners to reverse or modify the order. Appeals from orders issued by the commissioners go to the U.S. Courts of Appeals, which have exclusive jurisdiction to enforce, set aside, or modify orders of the commission.

STANDARDS Though the FTC Act does not define the words *unfair* or *deceptive*, the Commission issued three policy statements. The first, which addresses the meaning of unfairness, provides the following:

> To justify a finding of unfairness the injury must satisfy three tests. It must be substantial; it must not be outweighed by any countervailing benefits to consumers or competition that the practice produces; and it must be an injury that consumers themselves could not reasonably have avoided. The standard, therefore, applies a cost-benefit analysis to the issue of unfairness.

The second policy statement deals with the meaning of **deception**—the basis of most FTC consumer protection actions. It provides that "the Commission will find deception if there is a misrepresentation, omission, or practice that is likely to mislead the consumer acting reasonably in the circumstances, to the consumer's detriment." Thus, the Commission will find an act or practice deceptive if it meets a three-prong test:

> First, there must be a representation, omission, or practice that is likely to mislead the consumer. Second, we examine the practice from the perspective of a consumer acting reasonably in the circumstances. Third, the representation, omission, or practice must be a "material" one. The basic question is whether the act or practice is likely to affect the consumer's conduct or decision with regard to a product or service. If so, the practice is material, and consumer injury is likely because consumers are likely to have chosen differently but for the deception.

Deception may occur through either false representation or material omission. Examples of deceptive practices have included advertising that a certain product will save consumers 25 percent on their automotive motor oil, when the product simply replaced a quart of oil in the engine (which normally contains four quarts of oil) and was, in fact, more expensive than the oil it replaced; placing marbles in a bowl of vegetable soup to displace the vegetables from the bottom of the bowl and therefore make the soup appear thicker; and claiming that one drug provides greater pain relief than another, when the evidence was insufficient to prove the claim to the medical community. On the other hand, the FTC will not take action against puffery (sales talk composed of general bragging or overstatement that makes no specific factual representation) if the consumer would recognize it as puffery and not be deceived. For example, a statement by a salesperson that "this is one terrific deal" would likely be considered puffery.

To ensure that the FTC's guidance for online advertisers stays current with changes in digital media and internet searches, in 2013, the FTC sent letters to search engine companies to update guidance published in 2002 on distinguishing paid search results and other forms of advertising from natural search results. The letters note that in recent years, paid search results have become less distinguishable as advertising, and the FTC is urging the search industry to make sure the distinction is clear. Failing to distinguish advertising clearly and prominently from natural search results could be a deceptive practice.

Deception can also occur through a failure to disclose important product information if such disclosure is necessary to correct a false and material expectation created in the consumer's mind by the product or by the circumstances of sale. For example, the FTC has insisted that the failure to disclose a product's country of origin constitutes a deceptive omission, based on the agency's view that consumers assume the United States to be the country of origin of a product bearing no other country's name.

The third policy statement issued by the commission involves **ad substantiation**. This policy requires advertisers to have a reasonable basis for their claims at the time they make such claims. Moreover, in determining the reasonableness of a claim, the commission places great weight upon the cost and benefits of substantiation.

◆ *See Case 41-1*

REMEDIES In addition to the remedies already discussed, the FTC has employed three other potent remedies: (1) affirmative disclosure, (2) corrective advertising, and (3) multiple product orders.

Affirmative disclosure, a remedy frequently employed by the FTC, requires an offender to provide certain information in its advertisement to prevent the ad from being considered deceptive.

Corrective advertising goes beyond affirmative disclosure by requiring an advertiser who has made a deceptive claim to disclose in future advertisements that such prior claims were in fact untrue. The theory behind this remedy is that the effects of a previous deception will continue until expressly corrected.

A **multiple product order** requires a deceptive advertiser to cease and desist from any future deception not only in regard to the product in question but also in regard to all products sold by the company. This remedy is particularly useful in dealing with companies that have violated the law repeatedly.

In addition to these traditional remedies, the FTC has turned to direct court action in lieu of administrative proceedings. The FTC has the power to seek in a Federal district court a preliminary injunction, pending completion of administrative proceedings, whenever the agency had reason to believe that a person was violating FTC laws or rules. First used to stop mergers, this authority is now often invoked in consumer protection cases. The same provision also grants the agency authority to seek a permanent injunction "in proper cases" without a prior administrative finding that FTC law has been violated. In addition, the FTC may bring an action in a U.S. district court to have a civil monetary penalty imposed for a knowing violation of any rule respecting unfair or deceptive acts or practices of up to $43,280, as adjusted annually for inflation in January 2020.

41-1c THE CONSUMER PRODUCT SAFETY COMMISSION

In 1972, Congress enacted the Consumer Product Safety Act (CPSA), which established an independent Federal regulatory agency, the Consumer Product Safety Commission (CPSC). The purposes of the CPSA were fourfold:

1. to protect the public against unreasonable risks of injury associated with consumer products;

2. to assist consumers in evaluating the comparative safety of consumer products;

3. to develop uniform safety standards for consumer products and to minimize conflicting State and local regulations; and

4. to promote research and investigation into the causes and prevention of product-related deaths, illnesses, and injuries.

According to the CPSC, deaths, injuries, and property damage from consumer product incidents cost the United States more than $1 trillion annually. Consisting of five commissioners, no more than three of whom can be from the same political party, the CPSC has authority to set safety standards for consumer products; ban unsafe products; issue administrative "recall" orders to compel repair, replacement, or refunds for products found to present substantial hazards; and seek court orders requiring the recall of "imminently hazardous" products. In addition, Congress requires businesses under CPSC jurisdiction to notify the agency of any information indicating that their products contain defects that "could create" substantial product hazards. By triggering investigations that may lead to product recalls, these reports play a major role in the agency's regulatory activities. While the CPSC has jurisdiction over more than 15,000 kinds of consumer products, it does not have jurisdiction over some categories of products, including automobiles and other on-road vehicles, tires, boats, alcohol, tobacco, firearms, food, drugs, cosmetics, pesticides, and medical devices.

The CPSC also enforces four statutes previously enforced by other agencies. These acts, commonly referred to as the "transferred acts," are the Federal Hazardous Substances Act, the Flammable Fabrics Act, the Poison Prevention Packaging

Act, and the Refrigerator Safety Act. Whenever the CPSC can regulate a product under one of these specific acts, rather than under the more general CPSA, the agency is directed to do so unless it finds specifically that regulating the product under the CPSA is in the public interest. Thus, many CPSC regulations, such as those for toys, children's flammable sleepwear, and hazard warnings on household chemical products, arise under the transferred acts rather than under the CPSA.

When first established, the CPSC promulgated a number of **mandatory safety standards**; manufacturers either must follow these rules, which regulate product design, packaging, and warning labels, or face legal sanctions. To save time and money, the agency began to rely on the industry to establish **voluntary safety standards**—rules for which noncompliance does not violate the law—reserving mandatory standards for those instances in which voluntary standards proved inadequate. In 1981, Congress enacted legislation requiring the CPSC to rely on voluntary standards "whenever compliance with such voluntary standards would eliminate or adequately reduce the risk of injury addressed and there is substantial compliance with such voluntary standards." Although the 1981 amendments do not bar the CPSC from writing mandatory standards, the CPSC has promulgated few such standards since the law was amended.

In 2008, Congress enacted the Consumer Product Safety Improvement Act (CPSIA). To provide the public with immediate access to safety information about consumer products, one of the CPSIA's provisions requires the CPSC to create a searchable public database of reports of harm related to the use of products within the CPSC's jurisdiction. Members of the public can search the CPSC's Publicly Available Consumer Product Safety Information Database for safety information about products. Product manufacturers that are identified in a report may submit comments to be displayed in the database along with the report. Information about product recalls is also available in the database.

41-1d CONSUMER FINANCIAL PROTECTION BUREAU

In July 2010, President Obama signed into law the Dodd-Frank Wall Street Reform and Consumer Protection Act (Dodd-Frank Act), the most significant change to U.S. financial regulation since the New Deal. The Dodd-Frank Act establishes the Consumer Financial Protection Bureau (CFPB), an independent executive agency, which began operation in 2011, housed within the Federal Reserve, to regulate the offering and provision of consumer financial products or services under the existing Federal consumer financial laws, most of which are discussed in this chapter. The primary goal of the CFPB is to ensure that all consumers have access to markets for consumer financial products and services and that markets for consumer financial services and products are fair, transparent, and competitive. The CFPB replaced the current Federal consumer financial regulatory system, which had been split among seven different agencies: Office of the Comptroller of the Currency, Office of Thrift Supervision, Federal Deposit Insurance Corporation, Federal Reserve, National Credit Union Administration, Department of Housing and Urban Development (HUD), and the FTC.

The CFPB has broad rulemaking, supervisory, and enforcement authority over persons engaged in offering or providing a consumer financial product or service. A **consumer financial product or service** is a financial product or service that is "offered or provided for use primarily for personal, family, or household purposes." Financial products and services include the following: extending credit and servicing loans; engaging in deposit-taking activities; transmitting or exchanging funds; providing most real estate settlement services; providing stored value or payment instruments; providing check-cashing, check collection, or check guaranty services; providing consumer credit reports; and collecting debt related to any consumer financial product or service. The Act excludes certain activities and parties from the CFPB's authority, including auto dealers, real estate brokerage activities, sellers of nonfinancial goods and services, legal practitioners, employee benefit plans, and persons regulated by the U.S. Securities and Exchange Commission (SEC), the U.S. Commodity Futures Trading Commission, or a State Securities Commission.

The CFPB may impose civil penalties for violations of a law, rule, or final order or condition imposed in writing by the CFPB in the following amounts as adjusted annually for inflation in January 2020: (1) up to $5,883 per day for any violation, (2) up to $29,416 per day for reckless violations, and (3) up $1,176,638 per day for knowing violations. Civil penalties are paid into the CFPB Civil Penalty Fund established by the Dodd-Frank Act. In 2013, the CFPB issued a rule creating a process for allocating money from the Fund to compensate victims harmed by a person or company that was fined in an enforcement action brought by the CFPB.

The Trump administration maintained a more restricted view of the CFPB's mission. In April 2018, the acting CFPB director declared that while the CFPB will continue to execute the Dodd-Frank Act, it will no longer go beyond its statutory mandate. The acting director also requested that Congress make four changes to the Dodd-Frank Act: (1) fund the bureau through Congressional appropriations, (2) require legislative approval of major bureau rules, (3) ensure that the director answers to the President in the exercise of executive authority, and (4) create an independent inspector general for the bureau. To date, Congress has not acted on these requests. Moreover, the acting director sought to delay the payday rule finalized in October 2017 under the previous CFPB director. The payday rule applies to loans that require consumers to repay all or most of the debt at once. Under the payday rule, lenders must conduct a full-payment test to determine that borrowers can afford to repay their loans without re-borrowing. In 2018, a U.S. district court denied the request by the acting CFPB director to delay the payday rule's compliance date. In 2019, the CFPB delayed the compliance date for the mandatory underwriting provisions in the payday rule to November 19, 2020.

On June 29, 2020, the U.S. Supreme Court ruled that the single-director leadership structure of the CFPB violated the separation of powers under the U.S. Constitution. The Court held that the "CFPB Director's removal protection is severable from the other statutory provisions bearing on the CFPB's authority. The agency may therefore continue to operate, but its Director, in light of our decision, must be removable by the President at will." *Seila Law LLC v. Consumer Financial Protection Bureau*, 591 U.S.___ .

41-1e OTHER FEDERAL CONSUMER PROTECTION AGENCIES

Congress established the **National Highway Traffic Safety Administration (NHTSA)** to reduce the number of deaths and injuries resulting from automobile accidents. Highway crashes in 2019 in the United States killed more than 38,800 people and inflicted injury on more than 4.4 million others. It is estimated that the cost of deaths, injuries, property damage, and societal costs attributed to automobile crashes in 2019 totaled $871 billion.

Under authority similar to that of the CPSC, the NHTSA sets motor vehicle safety standards that promote crash prevention (e.g., rules for safer tires and brakes) and crashworthiness (e.g., interior padding, safety belts, and collapsible steering columns). As with the CPSC, manufacturers are required to report possible safety defects, and the agency may seek a recall if it determines that a particular automobile model presents a sufficiently great hazard. In 2018, the number of vehicles recalled dropped to 29.3 million from a high of 53.2 million in 2016. In addition, NHTSA is charged with establishing theft-resistance regulations and fuel economy standards for motor vehicles. The NHTSA also is authorized to provide grants-in-aid for State highway safety programs and to conduct research on improving highway safety.

The **Food and Drug Administration (FDA)** is the oldest Federal consumer protection agency, dating back to 1906. The FDA enforces the Food, Drug and Cosmetic Act, enacted in 1938, which authorizes the agency to regulate "adulterated and misbranded" products. The FDA, an agency of the U.S. Department of Health and Human Services, is responsible for protecting and promoting public health through the regulation and supervision of food safety, tobacco products, dietary supplements, prescription and over-the-counter pharmaceutical drugs, vaccines, biopharmaceuticals, blood transfusions, medical devices, electromagnetic radiation emitting devices, veterinary products, and cosmetics. The FDA uses two basic methods of enforcement: it sets standards for products or requires their premarket approval. The products most often subject to premarket approval are drugs. Since 1976, the agency also has had the authority to require the premarket approval of medical devices such as pacemakers and intrauterine devices; the number of such devices required to undergo this approval process is large and increasing.

The **Federal Communications Commission (FCC)**, an independent U.S. government agency overseen by Congress, regulates interstate communications by radio, television, wire, satellite, and cable. On February 26, 2015, the FCC issued its Open Internet rules to protect and maintain open, uninhibited access to legal online content by prohibiting broadband internet access providers from blocking or slowing the delivery of internet content. The new rules impose so-called "net neutrality" on both fixed and mobile broadband service providers by regulating them as utilities. In 2016, this rule was upheld in a divided decision of a three-judge panel at the U.S. Court of Appeals for the District of Columbia Circuit. In June 2018, the FCC repealed the Open Internet Order.

Although the FTC, CFPB, CPSC, NHTSA, FDA, and FDA, and FCC are perhaps the best-known Federal consumer protection agencies, numerous other agencies also play important roles in this area. For example, the U.S. Postal Service (USPS) brings many cases every year to close down mail fraud operations and the SEC protects consumers against fraud in the sale of securities. (The SEC is discussed in *Chapter 43*.) In addition, many other agencies assist consumers with specific types of problems that fall within the agency's scope.

The Gramm-Leach-Bliley Financial Modernization Act (GLBA) contains provisions to protect consumers' personal financial information held by financial institutions and originally gave authority to eight Federal agencies and the States to administer and enforce its provisions. In 2011, the Dodd-Frank Act transferred GLBA privacy notice rulemaking authority from some of these agencies to the CFPB. The authority to promulgate the GLBA privacy rules is vested for (1) depository institutions and many nondepository institutions in the CFPB; (2) securities and futures-related companies in the SEC and the Commodity Futures Trading Commission, respectively; and (3) certain motor vehicle dealers in the FTC.

The GLBA requires financial institutions to give their customers privacy notices that explain the financial institution's information collection and sharing practices. Customers then have the right to limit sharing some of their personal financial information. Also, financial institutions and other companies that receive personal financial information from a financial institution may be limited in their ability to use that information.

41-2 Consumer Purchases

Whenever a consumer purchases a product or obtains a service, certain rights and obligations arise. The extent to which these rights and obligations apply to all contracts is discussed more fully in *Chapters 9* through *18*; the extent to which they apply to a sale of goods under the Uniform Commercial Code (UCC) is discussed in *Chapters 21* through *25*. Although a number of consumer protection laws have been enacted in recent years, they still leave large areas of a consumer's rights and duties to State contract law. In particular, Article 2 of the UCC provides the basic rules governing when a contract for the sale of goods is formed, what constitutes a breach of contract, and what rights an innocent party has against a party who commits a breach. While many consumer protection laws provide for rights the UCC does not address, they still use its principles as building blocks. For example, the Magnuson-Moss Warranty Act builds upon the perceived inadequacy of the UCC in permitting sellers to disclaim or modify warranties. Similarly, many States have passed so-called lemon laws to provide additional contract cancellation rights to dissatisfied automobile purchasers. In 2012, the American Law Institute began a new project: the Restatement of the Law of Consumer Contracts. This new project focuses on the rules of contract law that treat consumer contracts differently from commercial contracts. It includes regulatory rules that are prominently applied in consumer protection law. The project covers common law as well as statutory and regulatory law. It draws on the Restatement Second of Contracts, the Uniform Commercial Code, and court opinions in cases involving disputes between businesses and consumers. A draft of the entire project was presented for discussion at the ALI Annual Meeting in May 2017. In 2019, Section 1 (Definitions and Scope) was approved by the membership.

The **Consumer Review Fairness Act of 2016 (CFRA)** invalidates non-disparagement clauses in certain standardized form contracts and makes it unlawful for a person to offer or enter into a form contract containing a non-negotiable, non-disparagement clause. Violations of this prohibition are enforced by the FTC and State attorneys general. Thus, the CRFA protects consumers' assessments of products, services, and customer services. This protection applies to written reviews as well as social media posts, oral appraisals, videos, and photography. The CFRA, however, does not limit the ability of a person or business to file a civil action against a consumer for defamation, libel, slander, or any other cause of action under State law.

The CFRA prohibits companies from entering into form contracts with customers that include any of the following terms:

1. Restrictions on consumers' ability to review company products, services or conduct
2. Penalties or fees for giving reviews
3. Requirements that customers relinquish copyright when writing reviews
4. A clause that transfers intellectual property rights from the consumer to the business.

41-2a FEDERAL WARRANTY PROTECTION

A warranty creates a duty on the part of the seller to ensure that the goods or services she sells will conform to certain qualities, characteristics, or conditions. A seller, however, is not required to warrant what she sells, and in general, she may, by appropriate words, disclaim (exclude) or modify a particular warranty or all warranties. Because a seller's power to disclaim or modify is so flexible, consumer protection laws have been enacted to ensure that consumers understand the warranty protection provided them.

To protect buyers and to prevent deception in selling, Congress enacted the **Magnuson-Moss Warranty Act**, which requires sellers of consumer products to provide adequate information about written warranties. The FTC administers and enforces the Act, which was enacted to alleviate certain reported warranty problems: (1) most warranties were not understandable; (2) most warrantors disclaimed implied warranties; (3) most warranties were unfair; and (4) in some instances, the warrantors did not live up to their warranties. Through the Magnuson-Moss Warranty Act, Congress attempted to make consumer product warranties more comprehensible and to facilitate the satisfactory enforcement of consumer remedies. To accomplish these purposes, the Act provides for the following:

1. clear and understandable disclosure of the warranty that is to be offered,
2. a description of the warranty as either "full" or "limited,"
3. a prohibition against disclaiming implied warranties if a written warranty is given, and
4. an optional informal settlement mechanism.

The Act applies to consumer products with **written warranties**. A consumer product is any item of tangible personal property that is normally used for family, household, or personal use and is distributed in commerce. The Act does not protect commercial purchasers, who are considered sufficiently knowledgeable, in terms of contracting, to protect themselves; better able to retain attorneys for their ongoing protection; and able to spread the cost of their injuries in the marketplace.

PRESALE DISCLOSURE The Act contains presale disclosure provisions, which are calculated to avert confusion and deception and to enable purchasers to make educated product comparisons. A warrantor must, "to the extent required by the rules of the [Federal Trade] Commission, fully and conspicuously disclose in simple and readily understood language the terms and conditions of such warranty." When it implemented this requirement, the FTC adopted a rule requiring that the text of a warranty be accessible to the consumer. Under that rule, the warranty could be attached to the package, placed on a visible sign, or maintained in a binder. In 1986, the FTC relaxed the rule by permitting stores simply to make warranties available to consumers upon request. Retailers using this option, however, must post signs informing the consumer that the warranties are available. Separate rules apply to mail order, catalog, and door-to-door sales.

LABELING REQUIREMENTS The second major part of the Act provides for labeling requirements by first dividing written warranties into two categories—limited and full—one of which, for any product costing more than $10, must be designated on the written warranty itself. The purpose of this provision is to enable the consumer to make an initial comparison of her legal rights under certain warranties. The Act provides that under a **full warranty**, the warrantor must agree to repair the product to conform with the warranty, without charge; no limitation may be placed on the duration of any implied warranty; the consumer must be given the option of a refund or replacement if repair is unsuccessful; and consequential damages may be excluded only if the warranty conspicuously notes their exclusion. A **limited warranty** is any warranty not designated as full.

LIMITATIONS ON DISCLAIMERS Most significantly, the Act provides that a written warranty, whether full or limited, cannot disclaim any implied warranty. This provision strikes at the heart of the problems plaguing warranty protection, for, as revealed in an earlier presidential task force report, most written warranties provided limited protection but in return nullified the more valuable implied warranties. Hence, consumers believed—often mistakenly—that the warranties they received and the warranty registration cards they promptly returned to the manufacturer were to their benefit. The Act, on the other hand, provides that a full warranty must not disclaim, modify, or limit any implied warranty and that a limited warranty cannot disclaim or modify any implied warranty but can limit its duration to that of the written warranty, provided that such limitation is reasonable, conscionable, and conspicuously displayed. Some States, however, do not allow limitations in the duration of implied warranties.

Practical Advice

As a consumer, check to see if the product you are purchasing is covered by a full or limited warranty. If the warranty is limited, ascertain the coverage and terms of the warranty.

For example, GE sells consumer goods to Barry for $150 and provides a written warranty regarding the quality of the goods. GE must designate the warranty as full or limited, depending on its characteristics, and cannot disclaim or modify any

implied warranty. On the other hand, if GE had not provided Barry with a written warranty, the Magnuson-Moss Warranty Act would not apply, and GE could then disclaim any and all implied warranties.

♦ **SEE FIGURE 41-1:** *Magnuson-Moss Warranty Act*

41-2b STATE "LEMON LAWS"

With the enactment of the Magnuson-Moss Warranty Act, many consumers assumed that automobile manufacturers would feel compelled to offer full warranties to buyers of new cars, thereby giving such buyers the option to obtain a refund or replacement without charge for a defective automobile or defective parts. Automobile sellers, however, opted for limited warranties. In response, virtually all of the State legislatures enacted "**lemon laws**" that attempt to provide new car purchasers with rights that are similar to full warranties under the Magnuson-Moss Warranty Act. Some States have broadened their laws to cover used cars; some also cover motorcycles. There are many different lemon laws, but most define a *lemon* as a car that continues to have a defect that substantially impairs its use, value, or safety, even after the manufacturer has made reasonable attempts to correct the problem. In most States, the opportunity to repair a defect is considered sufficient if the manufacturer made four unsuccessful attempts to fix the problem or the car was out of service for more than thirty days during the year it was sold. If a consumer can prove that her car is a lemon, most lemon laws require the manufacturer either to replace the car or to refund its retail price, less an allowance for the consumer's use of the car. In addition, most lemon laws provide that the consumer may recover attorneys' fees and expenses if the case goes to litigation.

41-2c CONSUMER RIGHT OF RESCISSION

In most cases, a consumer is legally obligated once he has signed a contract. In many States, however, a consumer has by statute a brief time—generally two or three days—during which he may **rescind** an otherwise-binding credit obligation if the sale was solicited in his home. Moreover, the FTC has promulgated a trade regulation applicable to door-to-door sales, leases, or rentals of goods and services for $25 or more, whether the sale is for cash or on credit. The regulation permits a consumer to rescind a contract within three days of signing. To make the rule effective, the FTC requires sellers to provide a buyer with written notice of her cancellation rights. If the buyer properly cancels, she must make available to the seller, in a condition substantially as good as that in which they were received, any goods the seller has delivered. The seller in turn must, within ten business days of receiving notice of rescission, return any money paid or any negotiable instrument (such as a personal check or a promissory note) executed by the buyer and cancel

FIGURE 41-1 Magnuson-Moss Warranty Act

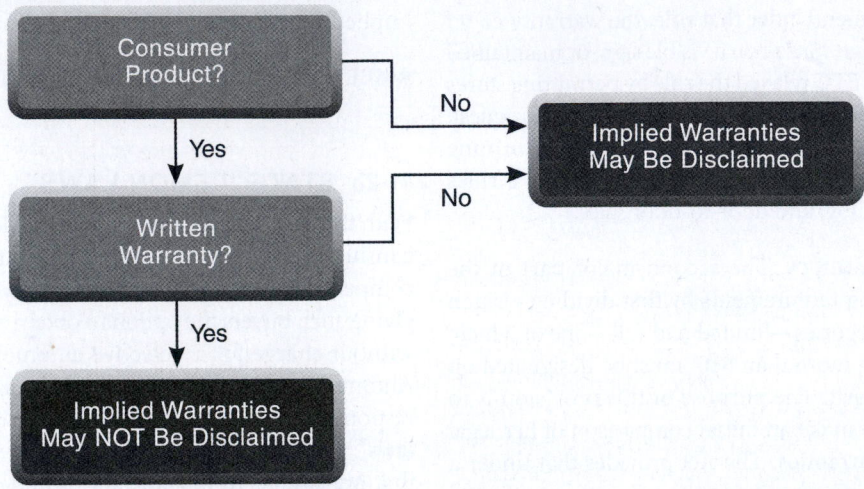

any security interest arising out of the transaction. If the seller fails to comply, the FTC will consider the noncompliance to be a violation of the Federal Trade Commission Act and will seek appropriate sanctions, such as a cease-and-desist order and civil penalties. To the extent that State laws on door-to-door sales are directly inconsistent with the FTC rule (e.g., if a State provides only two days for rescission), they are unenforceable.

The right of rescission also exists under the **Federal Consumer Credit Protection Act** (discussed more fully later), which allows a consumer three days during which he may withdraw from any credit obligation secured by a mortgage on his home, unless the extension of credit was made to acquire the dwelling. This right of rescission exists whether the contract was the result of a door-to-door sale or not. If the consumer rescinds, the creditor has twenty days to return any money or property he has received from the consumer.

The **Interstate Land Sales Full Disclosure Act (ILSA)** applies to sales or leases of one hundred or more lots of unimproved land as part of a common promotional plan in interstate commerce. The Act requires a developer to file with HUD a detailed "statement of record" containing specified information about the subdivision and the developer before offering the lots for sale or lease. The Dodd-Frank Act transferred from HUD regulatory authority over the ILSA to the Consumer Financial Protection Bureau. The developer must provide a property report, which is a condensed version of the statement of record, to each prospective purchaser or lessee. The Act provides that a purchaser or lessee may revoke any contract or agreement for sale or lease at her option within seven days of signing the contract and that the contract must clearly provide this right. A purchaser or lessee who does not receive a property report before signing a contract may revoke the contract within two years from the date of signing.

◆ SEE FIGURE 41-2: *Consumer Rescission Rights*

Practical Advice

As a consumer, recognize that in certain situations, you have a period of time in which you may rescind your contract.

FIGURE 41-2 Consumer Rescission Rights

Law	Rescission Period	Door-to-Door Solicitation Required?	Credit or Cash
State "Cooling-Off" Laws	Varies	Yes	Varies
Federal Trade Commission Trade Regulation	Within three days of signing the contract	Yes	Both
Consumer Credit Protection Act (CCPA)	Within three days of signing the contract	No	Credit only
Interstate Land Sales Full Disclosure Act	Within seven days of signing the contract	No	Both

41-3 Consumer Credit Transactions

A **consumer credit transaction** is customarily defined as any credit transaction involving subject matter to be used by one of the parties for personal, household, or family purposes. The following are illustrative: Atkins borrows $600 from a bank to pay a dentist bill or to take a vacation; Bevins buys a refrigerator for her home from a department store and agrees to pay the purchase price in twelve equal monthly installments; Carpenter has an oil company credit card that he uses to purchase gasoline and tires for his family car.

Regulation of consumer credit has increased considerably because of the dramatic expansion of consumer credit since World War II and the numerous abuses in credit transactions, including misleading credit disclosures, unfair marketing practices, and oppressive collection methods. In 1968, in response to concerns about consumer credit, Congress passed the **Federal Consumer Credit Protection Act (FCCPA)**, which requires creditors to disclose finance charges (including interest and other charges) and credit extension charges and sets limits on garnishment proceedings. Since 1968, Congress has added additional titles to this law, including the following laws: (1) the Truth-in-Lending Act (TILA) (including the Fair Credit Billing Act and the Consumer Leasing Act), (2) the Restriction on Garnishment, (3) the Fair Credit Reporting Act, (4) the Equal Credit Opportunity Act, (5) the Fair Debt Collection Practices Act, and (6) the Electronic Fund Transfer Act. Also in 1968, the National Conference of Commissioners on Uniform State Laws (now known as the Uniform Law Commission) promulgated the **Uniform Consumer Credit Code (UCCC)**, which integrated into one recommended law the regulation of all consumer credit transactions—loans and purchases on credit. Though the UCCC has been adopted in only eleven States, its impact on the development of consumer credit has extended well beyond their borders.

41-3a ACCESS TO THE MARKET

The **Equal Credit Opportunity Act (ECOA)** prohibits all businesses that regularly extend credit from discriminating against any applicant for credit on the basis of race, color, sex, marital status, religion, national origin, age, or receipt of public assistance. When originally enacted, the ECOA gave the Federal Reserve Board (Fed) responsibility for prescribing the implementing regulation. The Fed issued **Regulation B** to implement the ECOA. The Dodd-Frank Act transferred rulemaking authority under the ECOA to the Consumer Financial Protection Bureau.

Under the ECOA, a creditor has thirty days after receiving a credit application to notify the applicant of action taken, and the creditor must give specific reasons for a denial of credit. Several Federal agencies administer and enforce the ECOA, under the overall enforcement authority of the FTC. Credit applicants aggrieved by a violation of the ECOA may recover actual and punitive damages plus attorneys' fees. Failure to comply with Regulation B can subject a financial institution to civil liability for actual and punitive damages in individual or class action suits. Liability for punitive damages can be (1) $10,000 in individual actions and (2) the lesser of $500,000 or 1 percent of the creditor's net worth in class action suits.

The **Home Mortgage Disclosure Act (HMDA)** was enacted by Congress along with the **Community Reinvestment Act (CRA)** to emphasize to financial institutions the importance of their reinvesting funds in the communities that they serve. Through the HMDA, Congress outlawed geographic discrimination, or *redlining*, the process by which financial institutions refuse to provide reasonable home-financing terms to qualified applicants whose homes are located in geographic areas of declining value. In addition, the HMDA requires public disclosure of the financial institution's geographic pattern of mortgage lending. The CRA, by comparison, was intended to encourage financial institutions to meet the credit needs of their local communities. Amendments to the HMDA and the CRA in 1989 expanded the disclosure and reporting requirements for all mortgage lenders and mandated that Federal regulating agencies evaluate and rate CRA performance reports.

In 2008, Congress enacted the **Troubled Asset Relief Program**, commonly referred to as TARP. TARP is a program of the U.S. government that purchased assets and equity from financial institutions to strengthen the U.S. financial sector. By the end of 2014, the U.S. Treasury sold its last holdings. TARP recovered funds totaling $441.7 billion from $426.4 billion invested, earning a $15.3 billion profit.

41-3b DISCLOSURE REQUIREMENTS

Title One of the FCCPA, also known as the **Truth-in-Lending Act (TILA)**, as amended by the Dodd-Frank Act, has superseded State disclosure requirements relating to credit terms for both consumer loans and credit sales less than $58,300, as adjusted annually for inflation in January 2020. The Act does not cover credit transactions for business, commercial, or agricultural purposes. Creditors in every State not specifically exempted by the Fed must comply with Federal disclosure standards. The board exempts only those States that have disclosure requirements substantially the same as the Federal requirements and that ensure enforcement of their requirements. The FCCPA does not, however, excuse creditors from compliance with State requirements not covered by, or more stringent than, the FCCPA requirements, so long as the State-required disclosure is not inconsistent with the FCCPA. The Bankruptcy Abuse Prevention and Consumer Protection Act of 2005, discussed in *Chapter 38*, made a number of amendments to the TILA.

Before a consumer formally incurs a contractual obligation for credit, both State and Federal statutes require a creditor to present to the consumer a written statement containing certain information about contract terms. Generally, the required disclosure concerns the cost of credit, such as interest, sales charges, finder's fees, mortgage guarantee insurance, or any mandatory credit life insurance. An important requirement in the TILA is that sales finance charges and interest rates must be quoted in terms of an **annual percentage rate (APR)** and must be calculated on a uniform basis. Congress required disclosure of this information to encourage consumers to compare credit terms, to increase competition among financial institutions, and to facilitate economic stability. Enforcement and interpretation of the TILA was assigned to several agencies, the two most important being the FTC and the Fed, which issued **Regulation Z** to carry out this responsibility. However, in 2011, these functions were transferred to the CFPB.

Practical Advice

As a lender, make sure that you disclose the annual percentage rate (including all appropriate costs) and all other required information prior to closing the loan.

The **Fair Credit and Charge Card Disclosure Act** of 1988 adds to the TILA a new section requiring all credit and charge card applications and solicitations to include extensive disclosures whose requirements depend upon the type of card involved and whether the application or solicitation is by mail, telephone, or other means.

CREDIT ACCOUNTS　Under the TILA, a creditor must inform consumers who open revolving or open-end credit accounts about how the finance charge is computed and when it is charged, what other charges may be imposed, and whether the creditor retains or acquires a security interest. Moreover, in 2000, the Fed published a rule requiring marketing material to display clearly a table that shows the APR and other important information such as the annual fee. The Bankruptcy Act of 2005 further requires a disclosure of any low or discounted introductory rates, how long these rates will apply, and the rates that will take effect upon the termination of the introductory rate. It further requires billing statements to disclose all late payment charges and the date that the payment is due. To be included in the billing statement is a warning that making only the minimum payment will increase the amount of interest that must be paid and the time it takes to repay the balance. In addition, the billing statement must include an example to show the consumer how long it will take to pay off a stated balance at a specified interest rate if she makes only the minimum required payment.

An **open-end** credit account is one that permits the debtor to enter into a series of credit transactions that he may pay off either in installments or in a lump sum. Examples of this type of credit include most department store credit cards, most gasoline credit cards, VISA cards, and Master Cards. With this type of credit, the creditor is also required to provide a statement of account for each billing period.

If a solicitation for a credit card appears on the internet or other interactive computer service, the provider must clearly and conspicuously disclose all information required by the TILA. These disclosures must be readily accessible to the consumer and be current.

Closed-end credit is credit extended for a specified time, during which the debtor generally makes periodic payments in an amount and at a time agreed upon in advance. Examples of this type of credit include most automobile financing agreements, most real estate mortgages, and numerous other major purchases. For nonrevolving or closed-end credit accounts, the creditor must provide the consumer with information about the total amount financed; the cash price; the number, amount, and due date of installments; delinquency charges; and a description of the security, if any.

◆ *See Case 41-2*

ARMs　The Fed has amended Regulation Z to deal with variable or adjustable rate mortgages (ARMs). The *ARM disclosure rules* apply to any loan that is (1) a closed-end consumer transaction, (2) secured by the consumer's principal residence, (3) longer than one year in duration, and (4) subject to interest rate variation. This coverage excludes open-end lines of credit secured by the consumer's principal dwelling. A creditor must make the disclosures when he furnishes an application to a prospective borrower or before the creditor receives payment of a nonrefundable fee, whichever occurs first. The ARM disclosure rules require that the creditor provide the consumer with a consumer handbook on ARMs and a loan program disclosure statement covering the terms of each ARM that the creditor offers.

HOME EQUITY LOANS　A home equity loan is a loan for a fixed amount of money that is secured by the consumer's home. A home equity line of credit (HELOC) is a revolving line of credit using the consumer's home as collateral for the loan. Under a line of credit, payments are owed only on the amount actually borrowed, not the full amount available. To regulate the disclosures and advertising of these loans, Congress enacted the **Home Equity Loan Consumer Protection Act (HELCPA)**. HELCPA amends the TILA to require that lenders provide a disclosure statement and consumer pamphlet at (or, in some limited instances, within three days of) the time they provide an application to a prospective consumer borrower. HELCPA applies to all open-end credit plans for consumer loans that are secured by the consumer's principal dwelling. Unlike other Truth-in-Lending statutes, HELCPA defines a principal dwelling to include second or vacation homes. The disclosure statement must include a statement that (1) a default on the loan may result in the consumer's loss of the dwelling; (2) certain conditions must be met, such as a time by which an application must be submitted to obtain the specified terms; and (3) the creditor, under certain circumstances, may terminate the plan and accelerate the outstanding balance, prohibit the further extension of credit, reduce the plan's credit limit, or impose fees upon the termination of the account. In addition, if the plan contains a fixed interest rate, the creditor must disclose each APR imposed. If the plan involves an ARM, it must include how the rate is computed, the manner in which rates will be changed, the initial rate and how it was determined, the maximum rate change that may occur in any one year, the maximum rate that can be charged under the plan, the earliest time at which the maximum interest can be reached, and an itemization of all fees imposed by the plan.

Regulation Z provides the consumer with the right to rescind such a plan until midnight of the third day following the opening of the plan, until delivery of a notice of the right to rescind, or until delivery of all material disclosures, whichever comes last. When the loan amount exceeds the fair market value of the house, the Bankruptcy Act of 2005 requires the lender to inform a consumer that the amount in excess of the fair market value is not tax deductible for Federal income tax purposes.

BILLING ERRORS The **Fair Credit Billing Act** went into effect to relieve some of the problems and abuses associated with credit card billing errors. The Act establishes procedures for the consumer to follow in making complaints about specified billing errors and requires the creditor to explain or correct such errors. Billing errors include (1) credit extensions that were never made or were not made in the amount indicated on the billing statement, (2) undelivered or unaccepted goods or services, (3) incorrect recording of payments or credits, and (4) accounting or computational errors. Until the creditor responds to the complaint, it may not take any action to collect the disputed amount, restrict the use of an open-ended credit account because the

disputed amount is unpaid, or report the disputed amount as delinquent.

SETTLEMENT CHARGES Congress enacted the **Real Estate Settlement Procedures Act (RESPA)** to provide consumers who purchase a home with greater and more timely information on the nature and costs of the settlement process and to protect them from unnecessarily high settlement charges. RESPA, which applies to all Federally related mortgage loans, requires advance disclosure to homebuyers and sellers of all settlement costs, including attorneys' fees, credit reports, title insurance, and, if relevant, an initial escrow account statement. Nearly all first mortgage loans fall within the scope of the Act. RESPA prohibits kickbacks and referral fees and limits the amount homebuyers must place in escrow accounts to insure payment of real estate taxes and insurance. RESPA was amended in 1990 by the National Affordable Housing Act of 1990 to require an annual analysis of escrow accounts. RESPA was administered and enforced by the Secretary of HUD until 21, 2011, when these functions were transferred to the CFPB.

In 2013, the CFPB amended Regulation X (issued under the RESPA) and Regulation Z (issued under the TILA) to implement provisions of the Dodd-Frank Act regarding mortgage loan servicing. Effective in 2014, the new rules implement laws to protect consumers from detrimental actions by mortgage loan servicers and to provide consumers with better tools and information when dealing with mortgage loan servicers. In addition, effective in 2015, the CFPB amended Regulation X and Regulation Z to combine certain disclosures that consumers receive in connection with applying for and closing a mortgage loan.

♦ *See Case 41-3*

MORTGAGE DISCLOSURE IMPROVEMENT ACT Enacted in 2008 as an amendment to the TILA, the Mortgage Disclosure Improvement Act (MDIA) seeks to ensure that consumers receive cost disclosures earlier in the mortgage process. The MDIA requires creditors to provide good-faith estimates of mortgage loan costs ("early disclosures") within three business days after receiving a consumer's application for a mortgage loan and before any fees are collected from the consumer, other than a reasonable fee for obtaining the consumer's credit history. In addition, the Fed issued rules implementing the MDIA's requirements that (1) creditors wait seven business days after they provide the early disclosures before closing the loan and (2) creditors provide new disclosures with a revised APR, and wait an additional three business days before closing the loan, if a change occurs that makes the APR in the early disclosures inaccurate beyond a specified tolerance. In 2018, the CFPB amended Regulation Z to address when a creditor may compare charges paid by or imposed on the consumer to amounts disclosed on a Closing Disclosure, instead of a Loan Estimate, to determine if an estimated closing cost was disclosed in good faith.

MORTGAGE REFORM AND ANTI-PREDATORY LENDING ACT One of the many stand-alone statutes included in the Dodd-Frank Act is the Mortgage Reform and Anti-Predatory Lending Act of 2010. It sets minimum underwriting standards for mortgages by requiring lenders to verify reasonably and in good faith that consumer-borrowers have a reasonable ability to repay the loan at the time the mortgage is granted. It also prohibits mandatory arbitration clauses and prepayment penalties for ARMs.

41-3c CONTRACT TERMS

Consumer credit is marketed on a mass basis. Frequently, contract documents are printed forms containing blank spaces to accommodate the contractual details the creditor usually will negotiate at the time she extends credit. Standardization and uniformity of contract terms facilitate the transfer of the creditor's rights (in most situations, those of a seller) to a third party, usually a bank or finance company.

Almost all the States impose statutory ceilings on the amount that creditors may charge for the extension of consumer credit. Statutes regulating rates also specify what other charges may be made. For example, charges for insurance, official fees, and taxes usually are not considered part of the finance charge, whereas charges incidental to the extension of credit, such as a service charge or a commission for extending credit, usually are. Any charge that does not qualify as an authorized additional charge is treated as part of the finance charge and is subject to the statutory rate ceiling. Other special permitted charges include delinquency and default charges, charges incurred in connection with storing and repairing repossessed goods for sale, reasonable fees for a lawyer who is not a salaried employee of the creditor, and court costs.

Most statutes require a creditor to permit the debtor to pay her obligation in full at any time prior to the maturity date of the final installment. If the interest charge for the loan period was computed in advance and added to the principal of the loan, a debtor who prepays in full is entitled to a refund of the unearned interest already paid.

In the past, certain purchases involving consumer goods were financed in such a manner that the consumer was legally obligated to make full payment of the price to a third party, even though the dealer from whom she bought the goods had committed fraud or the goods were defective. This occurred when the purchaser executed and delivered to the seller a negotiable promissory note which the seller negotiated to a holder in due course, a third party who purchased

the note for value, in good faith, and without notice of its being overdue or of any defenses or claims to it. Though valid against the seller, the buyer's defense that the goods were defective or that the seller had committed fraud was not valid against a holder in due course of the note. To preserve the claims and defenses of consumer buyers and borrowers and to make such claims and defenses available against holders in due course, the FTC adopted a rule that limits the rights of a holder in due course of an instrument that evidences a debt arising out of a consumer credit contract. The rule applies to sellers and lessors of goods. A discussion of the rule is in *Chapter 27*.

A similar rule applies to credit card issuers under the Fair Credit Billing Act. The Act preserves a consumer's defenses against the issuer (provided the consumer has made a good faith attempt to resolve the dispute with the seller), but only if (1) the seller is controlled by the card issuer or is under common control with the issuer, (2) the issuer has included the seller's promotional literature in the monthly billing statements sent to the card holder, or (3) the sale involves more than $50 and the consumer's billing address is in the same State as, or within one hundred miles of, the seller's place of business.

41-3d CONSUMER CREDIT CARD FRAUD

Consumer credit card fraud—including stolen credit cards or card numbers, identity theft, skimming, and phishing—has become an increasingly serious problem. Worldwide credit card and debit card fraud resulted in losses amounting to $31.67 billion in 2019, up from $21.84 billion in 2015. Card issuers and merchants in 2015 incurred 62 percent and 38 percent of those losses, respectively.

The **Credit Card Fraud Act** prohibits the following practices: (1) possessing unauthorized cards; (2) counterfeiting or altering credit cards; (3) using account numbers alone; and (4) using cards obtained from a third party with his consent, even if the third party conspires to report the cards as stolen. It also imposes stiffer criminal penalties for violation.

In addition, the FCCPA, discussed previously, protects the credit card holder from loss by limiting to $50 the card holder's liability for another's unauthorized use of the holder's card. The card issuer may collect up to that amount for unauthorized use only if (1) the holder has accepted the card, (2) the issuer has furnished adequate notice of potential liability to the card holder, (3) the issuer has provided the card holder with a statement describing the means by which the holder may notify the card issuer of the loss or theft of the credit card, (4) the unauthorized use occurs before the card holder has notified the card issuer of the loss or theft, and (5) the card issuer has provided a method by which the person using the card can be identified as the person authorized to use the card.

41-3e FAIR CREDIT REPORTAGE

Because creditors usually grant consumers credit only after investigating their creditworthiness, it is essential that the information on which creditors base such decisions is accurate and current. To this end, Congress enacted the **Fair Credit Reporting Act (FRCA)**, which sets guidelines for credit reports used to secure employment, insurance, and credit. The Act prohibits consumer reporting agencies from including inaccurate or obsolete information in consumer reports (most information is obsolete after seven years; bankruptcy information becomes obsolete after ten years) and requires consumer reporting agencies to give consumers written, advance notice before making investigative reports. Consumers may request and receive from any consumer reporting agency information regarding (1) the nature and substance of all information on the consumer in the agency's files, (2) the sources of the information, and (3) the names of all recipients to whom the agency has furnished the information for employment purposes within the preceding two years and for other purposes within the preceding six months.

Practical Advice

The consumer may request information regarding the nature and substance of all information in the consumer reporting agency's files, the source of the information, and the names of all who received the consumer reports furnished for employment purposes within the preceding two years and for other purposes within the preceding six months.

If the consumer believes that the information in the file is inaccurate or incomplete, and so notifies the agency, the agency must then reinvestigate the matter within a reasonable period of time unless the complaint is frivolous or irrelevant. If reinvestigation proves that the information is inaccurate, it must be promptly deleted. If the dispute remains unresolved after reinvestigation, the consumer may submit a brief statement setting forth the nature of the dispute, which the agency must incorporate into the report.

Congress has amended the Act to restrict the use of credit reports by employers. An employer must now notify the job applicant or current employee that a report may be used and must obtain the applicant's consent prior to requesting an individual's credit report from a credit bureau. In addition, prior to taking an adverse action (refusal to hire, reassignment or termination, or denial of a promotion) against the applicant or employee, the employer must provide the individual with a "pre-adverse action disclosure," which must contain the credit report and a copy of the FTC's "A Summary of Your Rights Under the Fair Credit Reporting Act."

A recent amendment to the FCRA requires each of the nationwide consumer reporting companies to provide upon an individual's request a free copy of her credit report once every twelve months. In 2013, the responsibility of interpreting and enforcing requirements under the FCRA shifted from the FTC to the CFPB.

The Economic Growth, Regulatory Relief, and Consumer Protection Act of 2018 amended the FCRA to (1) require consumer reporting agencies to provide consumers with free credit freezes and free removal of credit freezes and (2) increase the length of time consumer reporting agencies must include a fraud alert in a consumer's file. A **credit freeze** on a consumer credit report prohibits a consumer reporting agency from releasing information in a credit report without the consumer's express authorization. The credit freeze is designed to prevent credit, loans, and services from being approved in a consumer's name without the consumer's consent. When a consumer requests a temporary removal of a security freeze, the consumer reporting agency must remove the credit freeze for the period of time specified by the consumer. A credit freeze, however, does not apply to consumer credit reports used for (1) insurance underwriting and (2) employment, tenant, or background screening.

41-3f CREDIT CARD BILL OF RIGHTS

In 2009, President Obama signed into law the **Credit Card Accountability, Responsibility, and Disclosure Act** (also known as the Credit Card Bill of Rights or CARD). The 2009 Act amends the TILA to establish fair and transparent practices relating to credit cards. The Act delegated regulation to the Fed. (As of 2011, administration of CARD was transferred to the CFPB.) The Fed issued regulations in three stages, the latest in 2010. These regulations include the following:

1. Credit card issuers generally cannot raise interest rates, or any fees, during the first year an account is open, except when a variable rate changes, a promotional rate ends, or a required minimum payment is more than sixty days late.

2. After the first year, forty-five days' advance notice is required to (a) raise the interest rate on future purchases; (b) make certain changes in terms, such as increased annual fees, cash advance fees, and late fees; and (c) increase the minimum payment.

3. If a credit card issuer lawfully imposes a rate increase on a customer, the rate must be restored to the prior rate if the customer pays the minimum balance on time for the next six months.

4. Credit card issuers are prohibited from giving credit cards to a full-time college student under twenty-one years of age unless that student can prove that she has the means to pay or a parent or guardian cosigns for the card.

5. Credit card issuers may not raise the credit limit on accounts held by a college student under twenty-one and a cosigner without written permission from the cosigner.

6. Credit card agreements must be posted online, and no fees can be charged to make a payment online, by phone, mail, or any other means.

7. Credit card issuers must mail account statements twenty-one days prior to the payment due date.

8. Credit card issuers must apply excess payments received to the balance with the highest interest rate first.

9. If the credit card issuer receives payment by 5:00 P.M. on the due date, the payment must be considered on time.

10. Credit card issuers must obtain the customer's permission before allowing the customer to spend more than the credit limit.

11. Card holders cannot be charged overlimit fees unless they give express permission ("opt in") to the card issuer to approve transactions that exceed their credit limits.

12. First-year fees required to open a credit card account cannot total more than 25 percent of the initial credit limit. This restriction applies to annual fees, application fees, and processing fees, but not to penalty fees, such as penalties for late payments.

13. If the account is closed or canceled by the consumer, the closed account will not be considered in default and the card issuer cannot require immediate repayment of the entire balance. Issuers also cannot charge monthly maintenance fees on closed accounts.

14. Penalty fees, such as late fees and overlimit fees, must be "reasonable and proportional to the omission or violation" of the card agreement.

15. Gift cards or certificates may not expire sooner than five years after issuance.

16. Ads that make promotional offers for free credit reports must state that free credit reports are available under Federal law at AnnualCreditReport.com. The disclosure must read: "You have the right to a free credit report from AnnualCreditReport.com or 877-322-8228, the ONLY authorized source under federal law."

41-4 Creditors' Remedies

A primary concern of creditors involves their rights should a debtor default or become tardy in payment. When the credit charge is precomputed, the creditor may impose a delinquency charge for late payments, subject to statutory limits for such charges. If instead of being delinquent the consumer defaults, the creditor may declare the entire balance of the debt immediately due and payable and may sue on the debt.

The other courses of action to which the creditor may turn depend upon his security. Security provisions included in consumer credit contracts may require a cosigner, an assignment of wages, a security interest in the goods sold, a security interest in other real or personal property of the debtor, and a confession of judgment clause (i.e., an agreement by the debtor giving the creditor the authority to enter judgment against the debtor).

41-4a WAGE ASSIGNMENTS AND GARNISHMENT

Wage assignments are prohibited by some States. In most States and under the FCCPA, a limitation is imposed on the amount that may be deducted from an individual's wages during any pay period. In addition, the FCCPA prohibits an employer from discharging an employee solely because of a creditor's exercise of an assignment of wages in connection with any one debt.

Even in cases in which wage assignments are prohibited, the creditor may still reach a consumer's wages through garnishment. But garnishment is available only in a court proceeding to enforce the collection of a judgment. The FCCPA and State statutes contain exemption provisions which limit the amount of wages subject to garnishment.

41-4b SECURITY INTERESTS IN GOODS

In the case of credit sales, the seller may retain a security interest in the goods sold. Many States impose restrictions on other security the creditor may obtain. Where the debt is secured by property as collateral, the creditor, upon default by the debtor, may take possession of the property and, subject to the provisions of the UCC, either retain it in full satisfaction of the debt or sell it and, if the proceeds are less than the outstanding debt, sue the debtor for the balance and obtain a deficiency judgment. The UCC provides that where a buyer of goods has paid 60 percent of the purchase price or 60 percent of a loan secured by consumer goods, the secured creditor may not retain the property in full satisfaction but must sell the goods and pay to the buyer that part of the sale proceeds in excess of the balance due. In addition, Federal regulation prohibits a credit seller or lender from obtaining a consumer's grant of a nonpossessory security interest in household goods. Household goods include clothing, furniture, appliances, kitchenware, personal effects, one radio, and one television; such goods specifically exclude works of art, other electronic entertainment equipment, antiques, and jewelry. This rule, which does not apply to purchase money security interests or to pledges, prevents a lender or seller from obtaining a nonpurchase money security interest covering the consumer's household goods. Secured transactions are discussed in *Chapter 37*.

41-4c DEBT COLLECTION PRACTICES

Abuses by some collection agencies led Congress to pass the **Fair Debt Collection Practices Act (FDCPA)**, which makes abusive, deceptive, and unfair practices by debt collectors in collecting consumer debts illegal. As of 2011, *administration* of the FDCPA was transferred from the FTC to the CFPB. Both the CFPB and the FTC have law *enforcement* powers under the FDCPA. The FDCPA does not apply to creditors who use their own names in trying to collect debts themselves. Rather, it applies only to those who collect debts for others. This does not mean that creditors are free to use improper methods to collect debts. Most States have laws or common law decisions that prohibit unfair debt collection practices. Moreover, the Dodd-Frank Act and Section 5 of the FTC Act prohibit creditors from engaging in unfair, deceptive, or abusive practices in their own collection activity.

The FDCPA bars, except in certain narrow circumstances, debt collectors from communicating with third parties about a consumer's debt. The FDCPA does permit debt collectors to contact a third party to ascertain the location of the consumer, but it prohibits them from disclosing that they are debt collectors and from stating that the consumer owes any debt.

The FDCPA forbids other abusive collection practices, including (1) communication with the consumer at unusual or inconvenient hours; (2) communication with the consumer if he is represented by an attorney; (3) harassing, oppressive, or abusive conduct, such as threats of violence or the use of obscene language; (4) false, deceptive, or misleading representations, such as false claims that the debt collector is an attorney or a government official or that the consumer has committed a crime; or(5) other unfair or unconscionable means to collect or attempt to collect a debt, such as a false threat of a lawsuit.

The FDCPA requires a debt collector, within five days of the initial communication with a consumer, to provide the consumer with a written notice that includes (1) the amount of the debt, (2) the name of the current creditor, and (3) a statement informing the consumer that she can request verification of the alleged debt.

The FDCPA gives consumers one extremely powerful right in dealing with debt collectors. If a consumer notifies a debt collector in writing that the consumer refuses to pay a debt or that the consumer wishes the debt collector to cease further communication with the consumer, the debt collector must stop further communication except to notify the consumer that the creditor or collector may invoke specified remedies such as filing a lawsuit to collect the debt. Consumers have the right to seek damages from debt collectors for violations of the FDCPA. In addition, the FTC and the CFPB have authority for administrative enforcement of the FDCPA's provisions.

Practical Advice

As a creditor, carefully refrain from harassing or abusing a debtor and make sure that all contacts with the debtor strictly comply with all laws and regulations.

◆ *See Case 41-4*

CHAPTER SUMMARY

FEDERAL TRADE COMMISSION	**Purpose** to prevent unfair methods of competition and unfair or deceptive acts or practices **Standards** • *Unfairness* requires injury to be (1) substantial, (2) not outweighed by any countervailing benefit, and (3) unavoidable by reasonable consumer action • *Deception* misrepresentation, omission, or practice that is likely to mislead the consumer acting reasonably in the circumstances • *Ad Substantiation* requires advertisers to have a reasonable basis for their claims **Remedies** • *Cease-and-Desist Order* command to stop doing the act in question • *Civil Monetary Penalties* may be imposed for a knowing violation of any rule respecting unfair or deceptive acts or practices • *Affirmative Disclosure* requires an advertiser to include certain information in its ad so that the ad is not deceptive • *Corrective Advertising* requires an advertiser to disclose that previous ads were deceptive • *Multiple Product Order* requires an advertiser to cease and desist from deceptive statements regarding all products it sells

CONSUMER HEALTH, SAFETY, AND FINANCIAL PROTECTION	**Consumer Product Safety Act** Federal statute enacted to • *Protect Public against Unsafe Products* • *Assist Consumers in Evaluating Products* • *Develop Uniform Safety Standards* • *Promote Safety Research* **Consumer Financial Protection Bureau (CFPB)** an independent executive agency housed within the Federal Reserve with broad rulemaking, supervisory, and enforcement authority over persons engaged in offering or providing a consumer financial product or service **Other Federal Consumer Protection Agencies**
CONSUMER PURCHASES	**Federal Warranty Protection** applies to sellers of consumer goods who give written warranties • *Presale Disclosure* requires terms of warranty to be simple and readily understood and to be made available before the sale • *Labeling Requirement* requires warrantor to inform consumers of their legal rights under a warranty (full or limited) • *Disclaimer Limitation* prohibits a written warranty from disclaiming any implied warranty **State "Lemon Laws"** State laws that attempt to provide new car purchasers with rights similar to full warranties under the Magnuson-Moss Warranty Act **Consumer Right of Rescission** in certain instances, a consumer is granted a brief period of time during which she may rescind (cancel) an otherwise-binding obligation
CONSUMER CREDIT TRANSACTIONS	**Definition** any credit transaction involving goods, services, or land for personal, household, or family purposes **Access to the Market** discrimination in extending credit on the basis of race, color, gender, marital status, religion, national origin, or age is prohibited **Truth-in-Lending Act** requires creditor to provide certain information about contract terms, including annual percentage rate (APR), to the consumer before he formally incurs the obligation **Contract Terms** statutory, administrative, and judicial limitations have been imposed on consumer obligations **Consumer Credit Card Fraud Act** prohibits certain fraudulent practices and limits a card holder's liability for unauthorized use of a credit card to $50 **Fair Credit Reportage** consumer credit reports are prohibited from containing inaccurate or obsolete information **Credit Card Bill of Rights (CARD)** The 2009 Act amends the Truth-in-Lending Act to establish fair and transparent practices relating to credit cards
CREDITORS' REMEDIES	**Wage Assignments and Garnishment** most States limit the amount that may be deducted from an individual's wages through either assignment or garnishment **Security Interests in Goods** seller may retain a security interest in goods sold or other collateral of the buyer, although some restrictions are imposed **Debt Collection Practices** abusive, deceptive, and unfair practices by debt collectors in collecting consumer debts are prohibited by the Fair Debt Collection Practices Act

C A S E S

FTC
STANDARDS FTC v. WYNDHAM WORLDWIDE CORP.
United States Court of Appeals, Third Circuit, 2015
799 F. 3d 236

Ambro, J.

The Federal Trade Commission Act prohibits "unfair or deceptive acts or practices in or affecting commerce." 15 U.S.C. §45(a). In 2005 the Federal Trade Commission began bringing administrative actions * * * against companies with allegedly deficient cybersecurity that failed to protect consumer data against hackers. The vast majority of these cases have ended in settlement.

On three occasions in 2008 and 2009, hackers successfully accessed Wyndham Worldwide Corporation's computer systems. In total, they stole personal and financial information for [over 619,000] consumers leading to over $10.6 million dollars in fraudulent charges. The FTC filed suit in federal District Court, alleging that Wyndham's conduct was an unfair practice and that its privacy policy was deceptive. The District Court denied Wyndham's motion to dismiss, and we granted interlocutory appeal on two issues: whether the FTC has authority to regulate cybersecurity under the unfairness prong of §45(a); and, if so, whether Wyndham had fair notice its specific cybersecurity practices could fall short of that provision. * * *

Wyndham Worldwide is a hospitality company that franchises and manages hotels and sells timeshares through three subsidiaries. Wyndham licensed its brand name to approximately 90 independently owned hotels. Each Wyndham-branded hotel has a property management system that processes consumer information that includes names, home addresses, email addresses, telephone numbers, payment card account numbers, expiration dates, and security codes. Wyndham "manage[s]" these systems and requires the hotels to "purchase and configure" them to its own specifications. It also operates a computer network in Phoenix, Arizona, that connects its data center with the property management systems of each of the Wyndham-branded hotels.

The FTC alleges that, at least since April 2008, Wyndham engaged in unfair cybersecurity practices that, "taken together, unreasonably and unnecessarily exposed consumers' personal data to unauthorized access and theft." [Citation.] This claim is fleshed out as follows.

1. The company allowed Wyndham-branded hotels to store payment card information in clear readable text.
2. Wyndham allowed the use of easily guessed passwords to access the property management systems. For example,

to gain "remote access to at least one hotel's system," which was developed by Micros Systems, Inc., the user ID and password were both "micros."

3. Wyndham failed to use "readily available security measures"—such as firewalls—to "limit access between [the] hotels' property management systems, ... corporate network, and the Internet."
4. Wyndham allowed hotel property management systems to connect to its network without taking appropriate cybersecurity precautions. * * *
5. Wyndham failed to "adequately restrict" the access of third-party vendors to its network and the servers of Wyndham-branded hotels. * * *
6. It failed to employ "reasonable measures to detect and prevent unauthorized access" to its computer network or to "conduct security investigations."
7. It did not follow "proper incident response procedures." The hackers used similar methods in each attack, and yet Wyndham failed to monitor its network for malware used in the previous intrusions.

* * *

The Federal Trade Commission Act of 1914 prohibited "unfair methods of competition in commerce." [Citation.] * * * Congress designed the term as a "flexible concept with evolving content," [citation] and "intentionally left [its] development ... to the Commission," [Citation.]

* * *

For the next few decades, the FTC interpreted the unfair-practices prong primarily through agency adjudication. But in 1964 it issued a "Statement of Basis and Purpose" * * * which explained [the] factors [that] governed unfairness determinations: * * *

In 1994, Congress codified [this FTC rule] at 15 U.S.C. §45(n): The Commission shall have no authority under this section... to declare unlawful an act or practice on the grounds that such act or practice is unfair unless the act or practice causes or is likely to cause substantial injury to consumers which is not reasonably avoidable by consumers themselves and not outweighed by countervailing benefits to consumers or to competition. In determining whether an act or practice is unfair, the

Commission may consider established public policies as evidence to be considered with all other evidence. Such public policy considerations may not serve as a primary basis for such determination.

* * *

Wyndham argues (for the first time on appeal) that the three requirements of 15 U.S.C. §45(n) are necessary but insufficient conditions of an unfair practice and that the plain meaning of the word "unfair" imposes independent requirements that are not met here. Arguably, §45(n) may not identify all of the requirements for an unfairness claim. (While the provision forbids the FTC from declaring an act unfair "unless" the act satisfies the three specified requirements, it does not answer whether these are the *only* requirements for a finding of unfairness.) * * *

* * *

Continuing on, Wyndham asserts that a business "does not treat its customers in an 'unfair' manner when the business *itself* is victimized by criminals." It offers no reasoning or authority for this principle, and we can think of none ourselves. Although unfairness claims "usually involve actual and completed harms," [citation.], "they may also be brought on the basis of likely rather than actual injury," [citation.]. And the FTC Act expressly contemplates the possibility that conduct can be unfair before actual injury occurs. 15 U.S.C. §45(n) ("[An unfair act or practice] causes or is *likely to cause* substantial injury"). More importantly, that a company's conduct was not *the most* proximate cause of an injury generally does not immunize liability from foreseeable harms. [Citation.] * * * For good reason, Wyndham does not argue that the cybersecurity intrusions were unforeseeable. That would be particularly implausible as to the second and third attacks.

Finally, Wyndham posits a *reductio ad absurdum*, arguing that if the FTC's unfairness authority extends to Wyndham's conduct, then the FTC also has the authority to "regulate the locks on hotel room doors, ... to require every store in the land to post an armed guard at the door," and to sue supermarkets that are "sloppy about sweeping up banana peels," * * * The argument is alarmist to say the least. And it invites the tart retort that, were Wyndham a supermarket, leaving so many banana peels all over the place that 619,000 customers fall hardly suggests it should be immune from liability under §45(a).

We are therefore not persuaded by Wyndham's arguments that the alleged conduct falls outside the plain meaning of "unfair."

* * *

Having rejected Wyndham's arguments that its conduct cannot be unfair, we assume for the remainder of this opinion that it was.

* * *

Wyndham argues it was entitled to "ascertainable certainty" of the FTC's interpretation of what specific cybersecurity practices are required by §45(a). Yet it has contended repeatedly—no less than seven separate occasions in *this* case— that there is no FTC rule or adjudication about cybersecurity that merits deference here. The necessary implication, one that Wyndham itself has explicitly drawn on two occasions noted below, is that federal courts are to interpret §45(a) in the first instance to decide whether Wyndham's conduct was unfair.

* * *

Wyndham's position is unmistakable: the FTC has not yet declared that cybersecurity practices can be unfair; there is no relevant FTC rule, adjudication or document that merits deference; and the FTC is asking the federal courts to interpret §45(a) in the first instance to decide whether it prohibits the alleged conduct here. The implication of this position is similarly clear: if the federal courts are to decide whether Wyndham's conduct was unfair in the first instance under the statute without deferring to any FTC interpretation, then this case involves ordinary judicial interpretation of a civil statute, and the ascertainable certainty standard does not apply. The relevant question is not whether Wyndham had fair notice of the *FTC's interpretation* of the statute, but whether Wyndham had fair notice of what the *statute itself* requires.

* * *

We thus conclude that Wyndham was not entitled to know with ascertainable certainty the FTC's interpretation of what cybersecurity practices are required by §45(a). Instead, the relevant question in this appeal is whether Wyndham had fair notice that its conduct could fall within the meaning of the statute. If later proceedings in this case develop such that the proper resolution is to defer to an agency interpretation that gives rise to Wyndham's liability, we leave to that time a fuller exploration of the level of notice required. For now, however, it is enough to say that we accept Wyndham's forceful contention that we are interpreting the FTC Act (as the District Court did). As a necessary consequence, Wyndham is only entitled to notice of the meaning of the statute and not to the agency's interpretation of the statute.

* * *

Having decided that Wyndham is entitled to notice of the meaning of the statute, we next consider whether the case should be dismissed based on fair notice principles. We do not read Wyndham's briefs as arguing the company lacked fair notice that cybersecurity practices can, as a general matter, form the basis of an unfair practice under §45(a). Wyndham argues instead it lacked notice of what *specific* cybersecurity practices are necessary to avoid liability. We have little trouble rejecting this claim.

To begin with, Wyndham's briefing focuses on the FTC's failure to give notice of its interpretation of the statute and does not meaningfully argue that the statute itself fails fair notice principles. * * *

* * *

Wyndham's * * * challenge falls well short given the allegations in the FTC's complaint. As the FTC points out in its brief, the complaint does not allege that Wyndham used *weak* firewalls, IP address restrictions, encryption software, and passwords. Rather, it alleges that Wyndham failed to use *any* firewall at critical network points, [citation], did not restrict specific IP addresses *at all*, [citation], did not use *any* encryption for certain customer files, [citation], and did not require some users to change their default or factory-setting passwords *at all*, [citation]. Wyndham did not respond to this argument in its reply brief.

Wyndham's * * * challenge is even weaker given it was hacked not one or two, but three, times. At least after the second attack, it should have been painfully clear to Wyndham that a court could find its conduct failed the cost-benefit analysis. That said, we leave for another day whether Wyndham's alleged cybersecurity practices do in fact fail, an issue the parties did not brief. We merely note that certainly after the second time Wyndham was hacked, it was on notice of the possibility that a court *could* find that its practices fail the cost-benefit analysis.

* * *

Before the attacks, the FTC also filed complaints and entered into consent decrees in administrative cases raising unfairness claims based on inadequate corporate cybersecurity. The agency published these materials on its website and provided notice of proposed consent orders in the Federal Register. * * *

* * *

The three requirements in §45(n) may be necessary rather than sufficient conditions of an unfair practice, but we are not persuaded that any other requirements proposed by Wyndham pose a serious challenge to the FTC's claim here. Furthermore, Wyndham repeatedly argued there is no FTC interpretation of §45(a) or (n) to which the federal courts must defer in this case, and, as a result, the courts must interpret the meaning of the statute as it applies to Wyndham's conduct in the first instance. Thus, Wyndham cannot argue it was entitled to know with ascertainable certainty the cybersecurity standards by which the FTC expected it to conform. Instead, the company can only claim that it lacked fair notice of the meaning of the statute itself—a theory it did not meaningfully raise and that we strongly suspect would be unpersuasive under the facts of this case.

We thus affirm the District Court's decision.

CASE 41-2

Disclosure Requirements
HOUSEHOLD CREDIT SERVICES, INC. v. PFENNIG
Supreme Court of the United States, 2004
541 U.S. 232, 124 S.Ct. 1741, 158 L.Ed.2d 450

Thomas, J.

[Sharon Pfennig holds a credit card initially issued by Household Credit Services, Inc., but in which MBNA America Bank, N.A., now holds an interest through the acquisition of Household's credit card operation. Although the terms of Pfennig's credit card agreement set her credit limit at $2,000, Pfennig was able to make charges exceeding that limit, subject to a $29 "over-limit fee" for each month in which her balance exceeded $2,000.

On August 24, 1999, Pfennig filed a complaint in the U.S. District Court for the Southern District of Ohio on behalf of a purported nationwide class of all consumers who were charged over-limit fees by Household or MBNA (defendants). Pfennig alleged that defendants allowed her and the other members of the class to exceed their credit limits, thereby subjecting them to over-limit fees. Pfennig claims the defendants violated the Truth-in-Lending Act (TILA) by failing to classify the over-limit fees as "finance charges" and thereby "misrepresented the true cost of credit." Defendants moved to dismiss the complaint on the ground that Regulation Z specifically excludes over-limit fees from the definition of "finance charge." The district court granted petitioners' motion to dismiss. On appeal, Pfennig argued, and the Court of Appeals agreed, that Regulation Z's explicit exclusion of over-limit fees from the definition of "finance charge" conflicts with the TILA.]

TILA itself does not explicitly address whether over-limit fees are included within the definition of "finance charge." Congress defined "finance charge" as "all charges, payable directly or indirectly by the person to whom the credit is extended, and imposed directly or indirectly by the creditor as an incident to the extension of credit." §1605(a). * * * Because petitioners would not have imposed the over-limit fee had they not "granted [respondent's] request for additional credit, which resulted in her exceeding her credit limit," the Court of Appeals held that the over-limit fee in this case fell squarely within §1605(a)'s definition of "finance charge." * * *

The Court of Appeals' characterization of the transaction in this case, however, is not supported even by the facts as set forth in respondent's complaint. Respondent alleged in her complaint that the over-limit fee is imposed for each month in which her balance exceeds the original credit limit. If this were true, however, the over-limit fee would be imposed not as a direct result of an extension of credit for a purchase that caused respondent to exceed her $2,000 limit, but rather as a result of the fact that her charges exceeded her $2,000 limit at the time respondent's monthly charges were officially calculated. Because over-limit fees, regardless of a creditor's particular billing practices, are imposed only when a consumer exceeds his credit limit, it is perfectly reasonable to characterize an over-limit fee not as a charge imposed for obtaining an extension of credit over a consumer's credit limit, but rather as a penalty for violating the credit agreement.

* * *

Moreover, an examination of TILA's related provisions, as well as the full text of §1605 itself, casts doubt on the Court of Appeals' interpretation of the statute. A consumer holding an open-end credit plan may incur two types of charges—finance charges and "other charges which may be imposed as part of the plan." [Citation]. TILA does not make clear which charges fall into each category. But TILA's recognition of at least two categories of charges does make clear that Congress did not contemplate that *all* charges made in connection with an open-end credit plan would be considered "finance charges." And where TILA does explicitly address over-limit fees, it defines them as fees imposed "in connection with an extension of credit," rather than "incident to the extension of credit," §1605(a). * * *

* * *

Regulation Z's exclusion of over-limit fees from the term "finance charge" is in no way manifestly contrary to §1605. Regulation Z defines the term "finance charge" as "the cost of consumer credit." [Citation]. * * *

* * * Because over-limit fees, which are imposed only when a consumer breaches the terms of his credit agreement, can reasonably be characterized as a penalty for defaulting on the credit agreement, the Board's decision to exclude them from the term "finance charge" is surely reasonable.

* * *

* * * The judgment of the Court of Appeals is therefore reversed.

CASE 41-3

RESPA
FREEMAN v. QUICKEN LOANS, INC.
Supreme Court of the United States, 2012
566 U.S. 624, 132 S.Ct. 2034, 182 L.Ed.2d 955

Scalia, J.

[The Freemans, Bennetts, and Smiths (petitioners) are three married couples who obtained mortgage loans from respondent Quicken Loans, Inc. In 2008, they filed separate actions alleging that the respondent had violated a provision of the Real Estate Settlement Procedures Act (RESPA) by charging them fees for which no services were provided. In particular, the Freemans and Bennetts allege that they were charged loan discount fees of $980 and $1,100, respectively, but that the respondent did not give them lower interest rates in return. The Smiths' allegations focus on a $575 loan "processing fee" and a "loan origination" fee of more than $5,100. The District Court granted summary judgment in favor of respondent because the petitioners did not allege any splitting of fees. A divided panel of the United States Court of Appeals for the Fifth Circuit affirmed. The U.S. Supreme Court granted *certiorari.*]

Enacted in 1974, RESPA regulates the market for real estate "settlement services," a term defined by statute to include "any service provided in connection with a real estate settlement," such as "title searches, ... title insurance, services rendered by an attorney, the preparation of documents, property surveys, the rendering of credit reports or appraisals, ... services rendered by a real estate agent or broker, the origination of a federally related mortgage loan ..., and the handling of the processing, and closing or settlement." [Citation.] Among RESPA's consumer-protection provisions is [citation], which directly furthers Congress's stated goal of "eliminating] ... kickbacks or referral fees that tend to increase unnecessarily the costs of certain settlement services," [citation.]

* * *

[Section 2607], subsection (b), adds the following:

No person shall give and no person shall accept any portion, split, or percentage of any charge made or received for the rendering of a real estate settlement service in connection with a transaction involving a federally related mortgage loan other than for services actually performed.

These substantive provisions are enforceable through * * * actions for damages brought by consumers of settlement services against "[a]ny person or persons who violate the prohibitions or limitations" of §2607, with recovery set at an amount equal to three times the charge paid by the plaintiff for the settlement service at issue. §2607(d)(2).

* * *

The question in this case pertains to the scope of §2607(b), which as we have said provides that "[n]o person shall give and no person shall accept any portion, split, or percentage of any charge made or received for the rendering of a real estate settlement service . . . other than for services actually performed." The dispute between the parties boils down to whether this provision prohibits the collection of an unearned charge by a single settlement-service provider—what we might call an undivided unearned fee—or whether it covers only transactions in which a provider shares a part of a settlement-service charge with one or more other persons who did nothing to earn that part.

* * *

By providing that no person "shall give" or "shall accept" a "portion, split, or percentage" of a "charge" that has been "made or received," "other than for services actually performed," §2607(b) clearly describes two distinct exchanges. First, a "charge" is "made" to or "received" from a consumer by a settlement-service provider. That provider then "give[s]," and another person "accept[s]," a "portion, split, or percentage" of the charge. Congress's use of different sets of verbs, with distinct tenses, to distinguish between the consumer-provider transaction (the "charge" that is "made or received") and the fee-sharing transaction (the "portion, split, or percentage" that is "give[n]" or "accept[ed]") would be pointless if, as petitioners contend, the two transactions could be collapsed into one.

Petitioners try to merge the two stages by arguing that a settlement-service provider can "make" a charge (stage one) and then "accept" (stage two) the portion of the charge consisting of 100 percent. But then is not the provider also "receiv[ing]"

the charge at the same time he is "accept[ing]" the portion of it? And who "give[s]" the portion of the charge consisting of 100 percent? The same provider who "accept[s]" it? This reading does not avoid collapsing the sequential relationship of the two stages, and it would simply destroy the tandem character of activities that the text envisions at stage two (*i.e.*, a giving and accepting).

Petitioners seek to avoid this consequence, at stage two at least, by saying that the *consumer* is the person who "give[s]" a "portion, split, or percentage" of the charge to the provider who "accept[s]" it. [Citation.] But since under this statute it is (so to speak) as accursed to give as to receive, this would make lawbreakers of consumers—the very class for whose benefit §2607(b) was enacted, [citation.]

* * *

The phrase "portion, split, or percentage" reinforces the conclusion that §2607(b) does not cover a situation in which a settlement-service provider retains the entirety of a fee received from a consumer. It is certainly true that "portion" or "percentage" *can* be used to include the entirety, or 100 percent. [Citations.] But that is not the normal meaning of "portion" when one speaks of "giv[ing]" or "accept[ing]" a portion of the whole, as dictionary definitions uniformly show. * * * As for "percentage," that word *can* include 100 percent—or even 300 percent—when it refers to merely a ratable measure ("unemployment claims were up 300 percent"). But, like "portion," it normally means less than all when referring to a "percentage" of a specific whole ("he demanded a percentage of the profits"). And it is normal usage that, in the absence of contrary indication, governs our interpretation of texts. [Citation.]

In the present statute, that meaning is confirmed by the "commonsense canon of *noscitur a sociis*—which counsels that a word is given more precise content by the neighboring words with which it is associated." [Citation.] For "portion" and "percentage" do not stand in isolation, but are part of a phrase in which they are joined together by the intervening word "split"—which, as petitioners acknowledge, [citation], cannot possibly mean the entirety. We think it clear that, in employing the phrase "portion, split, or percentage," Congress sought to invoke the words' common "core of meaning," [citation], which is to say, a part of a whole. * * *

* * *

In order to establish a violation of §2607(b), a plaintiff must demonstrate that a charge for settlement services was divided between two or more persons. Because petitioners do not contend that respondent split the challenged charges with anyone else, summary judgment was properly granted in favor of respondent. We therefore affirm the judgment of the Court of Appeals.

CASE
41-4

Debt Collection Practices
JERMAN v. CARLISLE, MCNELLIE, RINI, KRAMER & ULRICH LPA

Supreme Court of the United States, 2010
559 U.S. 573, 130 S.Ct. 1605, 176 L.Ed.2d 519

Sotomayor, J.

The Fair Debt Collection Practices Act (FDCPA or Act) imposes civil liability on "debt collector[s]" for certain prohibited debt collection practices. Section 813(c) of the Act, [citation], provides that a debt collector is not liable in an action brought under the Act if she can show "the violation was not intentional and resulted from a bona fide error notwithstanding the maintenance of procedures reasonably adapted to avoid any such error." * * *

I

A

Congress enacted the FDCPA in 1977, [citation], to eliminate abusive debt collection practices, to ensure that debt collectors who abstain from such practices are not competitively disadvantaged, and to promote consistent state action to protect consumers. [Citation.] The Act regulates interactions between consumer debtors and "debt collector[s]," defined to include any person who "regularly collects ... debts owed or due or asserted to be owed or due another." [Citation]. Among other things, the Act prohibits debt collectors from making false representations as to a debt's character, amount, or legal status, [citation]; communicating with consumers at an "unusual time or place" likely to be inconvenient to the consumer, [citation]; or using obscene or profane language or violence or the threat thereof. [Citations.]

The Act is enforced through administrative action and private lawsuits. With some exceptions not relevant here, violations of the FDCPA are deemed to be unfair or deceptive acts or practices under the Federal Trade Commission Act (FTC Act), [citation], and are enforced by the Federal Trade Commission (FTC). [Citation.] As a result, a debt collector who acts with "actual knowledge or knowledge fairly implied on the basis of objective circumstances that such act is [prohibited under the FDCPA]" is subject to civil penalties of up to $16,000 per day. [Citation.]

The FDCPA also provides that "any debt collector who fails to comply with any provision of th[e] [Act] with respect to any person is liable to such person." [Citation.] Successful plaintiffs are entitled to "actual damage[s]," plus costs and "a reasonable attorney's fee as determined by the court." [Citation.] A court may also award "additional damages," subject to a statutory cap

of $1,000 for individual actions, or, for class actions, "the lesser of $500,000 or 1 per centum of the net worth of the debt collector." [Citation.] In awarding additional damages, the court must consider "the frequency and persistence of [the debt collector's] noncompliance," "the nature of such noncompliance," and "the extent to which such noncompliance was intentional." [Citation.]

The Act contains two exceptions to provisions imposing liability on debt collectors. Section 1692k(c), at issue here, provides that

> [a] debt collector may not be held liable in any action brought under [the FDCPA] if the debt collector shows by a preponderance of evidence that the violation was not intentional and resulted from a bona fide error notwithstanding the maintenance of procedures reasonably adapted to avoid any such error.

The Act also states that none of its provisions imposing liability shall apply to "any act done or omitted in good faith in conformity with any advisory opinion of the [Federal Trade] Commission." [Citation.]

B

Respondents in this case are a law firm, Carlisle, McNellie, Rini, Kramer & Ulrich, L. P. A., and one of its attorneys, Adrienne S. Foster (collectively Carlisle). In April 2006, Carlisle filed a complaint in Ohio state court on behalf of a client, Countrywide Home Loans, Inc. Carlisle sought foreclosure of a mortgage held by Countrywide in real property owned by petitioner Karen L. Jerman. The complaint included a "Notice," later served on Jerman, stating that the mortgage debt would be assumed to be valid unless Jerman disputed it in writing. Jerman's lawyer sent a letter disputing the debt, and Carlisle sought verification from Countrywide. When Countrywide acknowledged that Jerman had, in fact, already paid the debt in full, Carlisle withdrew the foreclosure lawsuit. Jerman then filed her own lawsuit seeking class certification and damages under the FDCPA, contending that Carlisle violated §1692g by stating that her debt would be assumed valid unless she disputed it in writing. While acknowledging a division of authority on the question, the District Court held that Carlisle had violated §1692g by requiring Jerman to dispute the debt in writing. [Citation.] The court ultimately granted summary judgment to Carlisle, however, concluding that §1692k(c) shielded it from liability because the violation was not intentional, resulted from a bona fide error, and occurred despite the maintenance of procedures reasonably adapted to avoid any such error. [Citation.] The Court of Appeals for the Sixth Circuit affirmed. * * * [T]he court observed that Congress has amended the FDCPA several times since 1977 without excluding mistakes of law from §1692k(c). [Citation.]

We granted *certiorari*. * * *

II

A

The parties disagree about whether a "violation" resulting from a debt collector's misinterpretation of the legal requirements of the FDCPA can ever be "not intentional" under §1692k(c). Jerman contends that when a debt collector intentionally commits the act giving rise to the violation (here, sending a notice that included the "in writing" language), a misunderstanding about what the Act requires cannot render the violation "not intentional," given the general rule that mistake or ignorance of law is no defense. Carlisle * * *, in contrast, argue[s] that nothing in the statutory text excludes legal errors from the category of "bona fide error[s]" covered by §1692k(c) and note that the Act refers not to an unintentional "act" but rather an unintentional "violation." The latter term, they contend, evinces Congress' intent to impose liability only when a party knows its conduct is unlawful. Carlisle urges us, therefore, to read §1692k(c) to encompass "all types of error," including mistakes of law. [Citation.]

We decline to adopt the expansive reading of §1692k(c) that Carlisle proposes. We have long recognized the "common maxim, familiar to all minds, that ignorance of the law will not excuse any person, either civilly or criminally." [Citations.]

* * *

We draw additional support for the conclusion that bona fide errors in §1692k(c) do not include mistaken interpretations of the FDCPA, from the requirement that a debt collector maintain "procedures reasonably adapted to avoid any such error." * * * In that light, the statutory phrase is more naturally read to apply to processes that have mechanical or other such "regular orderly" steps to avoid mistakes—for instance, the kind of internal controls a debt collector might adopt to ensure its employees do not communicate with consumers at the wrong time of day, §1692c(a)(1), or make false representations as to the amount of a debt, §1692e(2). * * * But legal reasoning is not a mechanical or strictly linear process. For this reason, we find force in the suggestion by the Government (as *amicus curiae* supporting Jerman) that the broad statutory requirement of procedures reasonably

designed to avoid "any" bona fide error indicates that the relevant procedures are ones that help to avoid errors like clerical or factual mistakes. Such procedures are more likely to avoid error than those applicable to legal reasoning, particularly in the context of a comprehensive and complex federal statute such as the FDCPA that imposes open ended prohibitions on, *inter alia*, "false, deceptive," §1692e, or "unfair" practices, §1692f. Even if the text of §1692k(c), read in isolation, leaves room for doubt, the context and history of the FDCPA provide further reinforcement for construing that provision not to shield violations resulting from misinterpretations of the requirements of the Act. [Citation.] In our view, the Court of Appeals' reading is at odds with the role Congress evidently contemplated for the FTC in resolving ambiguities in the Act. Debt collectors would rarely need to consult the FTC if §1692k(c) were read to offer immunity for good-faith reliance on advice from private counsel. Indeed, debt collectors might have an affirmative incentive not to seek an advisory opinion to resolve ambiguity in the law, as receipt of such advice would prevent them from claiming good-faith immunity for violations and would potentially trigger civil penalties for knowing violations under the FTC Act. More importantly, the existence of a separate provision that, by its plain terms, is more obviously tailored to the concern at issue (excusing civil liability when the Act's prohibitions are uncertain) weighs against stretching the language of the bona fide error defense to accommodate Carlisle's expansive reading.

* * *

B

Carlisle, its *amici*, and the dissent raise the additional concern that our reading will have unworkable practical consequences for debt collecting lawyers. [Citations.] Carlisle claims the FDCPA's private enforcement provisions have fostered a "cottage industry" of professional plaintiffs who sue debt collectors for trivial violations of the Act. [Citation.] If debt collecting attorneys can be held personally liable for their reasonable misinterpretations of the requirements of the Act, Carlisle and its *amici* foresee a flood of lawsuits against creditors' lawyers by plaintiffs (and their attorneys) seeking damages and attorney's fees. The threat of such liability, in the dissent's view, creates an irreconcilable conflict between an attorney's personal financial interest and her ethical obligation of zealous advocacy on behalf of a client: An attorney uncertain about what the FDCPA requires must choose between, on the one hand, exposing herself to liability and, on the other, resolving the legal ambiguity against her client's interest or advising the client to settle—even where there is substantial legal authority for a position favoring the client. [Citation.]

We do not believe our holding today portends such grave consequences. For one, the FDCPA contains several provisions that expressly guard against abusive lawsuits, thereby mitigating the financial risk to creditors' attorneys. When an alleged violation is trivial, the "actual damage[s]" sustained, §1692k(a)(1), will likely be *de minimis* or even zero. The Act sets a cap on "additional" damages, §1692k(a)(2), and vests courts with discretion to adjust such damages where a violation is based on a good faith error, §1692k(b). * * *

* * *

To the extent the FDCPA imposes some constraints on a lawyer's advocacy on behalf of a client, it is hardly unique in our law. * * *

* * * For the reasons discussed above, the judgment of the United States Court of Appeals for the Sixth Circuit is reversed, and the case is remanded for further proceedings consistent with this opinion.

QUESTIONS

1. The Federal Trade Commission (FTC) brings a deceptive trade practice action against Beneficial Finance Company based on Beneficial's use of its "instant tax refund" slogan. The FTC argues that Beneficial's advertising a tax refund loan or instant tax refund is deceptive in that the loan is not in any way connected with a tax refund but is merely Beneficial's everyday loan based on the applicant's creditworthiness. Is this an unfair or deceptive trade practice? Explain.

2. Barnes borrows $10,000 from Linda for one year, agreeing to pay Linda $2,000 in interest on the loan and to repay the loan in twelve monthly installments of $1,000. The contract which Linda provides and Barnes signs specifies that the annual percentage rate is 20 percent. Does this contract violate the Federal Consumer Credit Protection Act? Why or why not?

3. A consumer entered into an agreement with Rent-It Corporation for the rental of a television set at a charge of $17 per week. The agreement also provides that if the renter chooses to rent the set for seventy-eight consecutive weeks, title would be transferred. The consumer now contends that the agreement was really a sales agreement, not a lease, and therefore is a credit sale subject to the Truth-in-Lending Act. Explain whether the consumer is correct.

4. Central Adjustment Bureau allegedly threatened Consumer with a lawsuit, service at his office, and attachment and sale of his property to collect a debt when it did not intend to take such actions and when it did not have the authority to commence litigation. On some notices sent to Consumer, Central failed to disclose that it was attempting to collect a debt. In addition, Consumer claims that Central sent notices demanding payment that purported to be from attorneys but that were in fact written, signed, and sent by Central. Has Central violated the Fair Debt Collection Act? Explain.

5. The Giant Development Company undertakes a massive real estate venture to sell 9,000 one-acre unimproved lots in Utah. The company advertises the project nationally. Arrington, a resident of New York, learns of the opportunity and requests information about the project. The company provides Arrington with a small advertising brochure that is devoid of information about the developer and the land. The brochure consists of vague descriptions of the joys of homeownership and nothing else. Arrington purchases a lot. Two weeks after entering into the agreement, Arrington wishes to rescind the contract. Will Arrington prevail? Explain.

6. Jane Jones, a married woman, applies for a credit card from Exxon but is refused credit. Jane is bewildered as to why she was turned down. Explain what her legal rights are in this situation.

7. On a beautiful Saturday in October, Francie decides to take the twenty-mile ride from her home in New Jersey into New York City to do some shopping. Francie finds that Brown's Retail Sales, Inc., has a terrific sale on televisions and decides to surprise her husband with a new high-definition television. She purchases the set from Brown's on her VISA card for $1,450. When the set is delivered, Francie discovers that it does not work. Brown's refuses to repair or replace it or to credit Francie's account. Francie therefore refuses to pay VISA for the television. VISA brings a suit against Francie. Will VISA prevail? Why or why not?

8. Frank finds Thomas's wallet, which contains numerous credit cards and Thomas's identification. By using Thomas's identification and VISA card, Frank goes on a shopping spree and runs up $5,000 in charges. Thomas does not discover that he has lost his wallet until the following day, when he promptly notifies his VISA bank. Explain how much VISA can collect from Thomas.

9. Robert applies to Northern National Bank for a loan. Prior to granting the loan, Northern requests that Callis Credit Agency provide it with a credit report on Robert. Callis reports that three years earlier, Robert had embezzled money from his employer. Based on this report, Northern rejects Robert's loan application.

    a. Robert demands to know why, but Northern refuses to divulge the information, arguing that it is privileged. Is Robert entitled to the information? Explain.

    b. Assume that Robert obtains the information and alleges that it is inaccurate. Explain what recourse Robert has.

C A S E   P R O B L E M S

10. Colgate-Palmolive Co. produced a television advertisement that dramatically demonstrated the effectiveness of its Rapid Shave shaving cream. The ad purported to show the shaving cream being used to shave sandpaper. But because actual sandpaper appeared on television to be regular colored paper, Colgate substituted a sheet of Plexiglas with sand sprinkled on it. The FTC brought an action against Colgate, claiming that Colgate's ad was deceptive. Colgate defended on the ground that the consumer was merely being shown a representation of the actual test. Explain whether Colgate has engaged in an unfair or deceptive trade practice.

11. Several manufacturers introduced into the American market products known as all-terrain vehicles (ATVs). ATVs are motorized bikes that sit on three or four low-pressure balloon tires and are meant to be driven off paved roads. Almost immediately, the Consumer Product Safety Commission (CPSC) began receiving reports of deaths and serious injuries. As the number of injuries and deaths increased, the CPSC began investigating ATV hazards. According to CPSC staff, children under the age of sixteen accounted for roughly half the deaths and injuries associated with this product. What type of rule, if any, may the CPSC issue for ATVs? Explain.

12. Sears formulated a plan to increase sales of its top-of-the-line "Lady Kenmore" brand dishwasher; it sought to change the Lady Kenmore's image without reengineering or making any mechanical improvements in the dishwasher itself. To accomplish this, Sears undertook a four-year, $8 million advertising campaign that claimed that the Lady Kenmore completely eliminated the need to prerinse and prescrape dishes. As a result of this campaign, sales rose by more than 300 percent. The "no scraping, no prerinsing" claim was not true, however, and Sears had no reasonable basis for asserting the claim. In addition, the owner's manual that customers received after they purchased the dishwasher contradicted the claim.

    After a thorough investigation, the Federal Trade Commission (FTC) filed a complaint against Sears, alleging that the advertisements were false and misleading. The final FTC order required Sears to stop making the no prescraping, no prerinsing claim. The order also prevented Sears from (1) making any "performance claims" for "major home appliances" without first establishing a reasonable basis consisting of substantiating tests or other evidence; (2) misrepresenting any test, survey, or demonstration regarding "major home appliances"; and (3) making any advertising statements not consistent with statements in postpurchase materials supplied to purchasers of "major home appliances." Sears contends the order is too broad, as it covers appliances other than dishwashers and includes "performance claims" as well. Explain whether Sears is correct.

13. Onondaga Bureau of Medical Economics (OBME), a collection agency for physicians, sent plaintiff Seabrook a letter demanding payment for a $198 physician's bill. In addition to demanding payment, the letter stated that legal action resulting in a garnishment of his wages could be commenced against the plaintiff. Does OBME's letter violate the Fair Debt Collection Practices Act in that it (a) does not give Seabrook the required notice or (b) threatened legal action against him? Explain.

14. William Thompson was denied credit based on an inaccurate credit report compiled by the San Antonio Retail Merchant's Association. The Association confused Thompson's credit history with that of another William Thompson and failed to use social security numbers to distinguish the two men. The second Mr. Thompson had a poor credit history. Thompson made numerous attempts to have the Association correct its mistake, but the error was never corrected. Has the Association violated the Fair Credit Reporting Act? Explain.

15. Thompson Medical Company manufactures and sells Aspercreme, a topical analgesic. Aspercreme is a pain reliever that contains no aspirin. Thompson's advertisements strongly suggest that Aspercreme is related to aspirin, however, by claiming that it provides "the strong relief of aspirin right where you hurt." Is Thompson's advertisement for Aspercreme false and misleading? Explain.

16. Mary Smith bought a car from Doug Chapman under an installment sales contract. Smith carried the insurance on the car, as required by the contract. Shortly after Smith purchased the car, it was wrecked in an accident. Smith's insurance company paid Chapman the installments still owed on the car as well as Smith's equity in the car. Smith requested a new car from Chapman under an installment plan that was the same as the one under which she purchased the first car. Chapman refused, claiming that the contract for the first car allowed him to retain the equity amount as security interest and that Smith understood this as a term of the contract. The provision relating to the security interest appeared on the back of the contract, although the Truth-in-Lending Act required it to be on the front side. The front side had a notice referring to provisions on the back side. Explain whether Chapman's contract violates the Truth-in-Lending Act.

17. The Federal Trade Commission (FTC) ordered Warner-Lambert to cease and desist from advertising that its product, Listerine antiseptic mouthwash, prevents, cures, or alleviates the common cold and sore throats. The order further required Warner-Lambert to disclose in future advertisements that "[c]ontrary to prior advertising, Listerine will not help prevent colds or sore throats or lessen their severity." Warner-Lambert contended that even if its past advertising claims were false, the corrective advertising portion of the order exceeded the FTC's statutory power. The FTC claimed that corrective advertising was necessary in light of Warner-Lambert's one hundred years of false claims and the resulting persistence of erroneous consumer beliefs. Explain whether the FTC is correct.

18. Lenvil Miller owed $2,501.61 to the Star Bank of Cincinnati. Star Bank referred collection of Miller's account to Payco-General American Credits, Inc. (Payco), a debt collection agency. Payco sent Miller a collection form. Across the top of the form was the caption "DEMAND FOR PAYMENT" in large, red, boldface type. The middle of the page stated "THIS IS A DEMAND FOR IMMEDIATE FULL PAYMENT OF YOUR DEBT," also in large, red, boldface type. That statement was followed in bold by "YOUR SERIOUSLY PAST DUE ACCOUNT HAS BEEN GIVEN TO US FOR IMMEDIATE ACTION. YOU HAVE HAD AMPLE TIME TO PAY YOUR DEBT, BUT YOU HAVE NOT. IF THERE IS A VALID REASON, PHONE US AT [.] TODAY. IF NOT, PAY US—NOW." The word NOW covered the bottom third of the form. At the very bottom in the smallest type to appear on the form was the statement "NOTICE: SEE REVERSE SIDE FOR IMPORTANT INFORMATION." The notice was printed in white against a red background. On the reverse side were four paragraphs in gray ink. The last three paragraphs contained the validation notice required by the Fair Debt Collection Practices Act (FDCPA) to inform the consumer how to obtain verification of the debt.

Miller sued Payco on the ground that the validation notice did not comply with the FDCPA. Miller argued that even though the validation notice contained all the necessary information, it violated the FDCPA because it contradicted other parts of the collection letter, was overshadowed by the demands for payment, and was not effectively conveyed to the consumer. Discuss whether Payco has violated the FDCPA.

19. Greg Henson sold his Chevrolet Camaro Z-28 to his brother, Jeff Henson. To purchase the car, Jeff secured a loan with Cosco Federal Credit Union (Cosco). Soon thereafter, the car was stolen and Jeff stopped making payments on his loan from Cosco. At the time, Cosco was unsure whether Greg retained an interest in the car, so Cosco sued both Jeff and Greg for possession of the car. The trial court rendered a default judgment against Jeff and ruled that Greg no longer had any interest in the car. The court further entered a deficiency judgment against Jeff in the amount of $4,076. The clerk erroneously noted in the judgment docket that the money judgment had been rendered against Greg as well as against Jeff although the official record of judgments and orders correctly reflected that only Jeff was affected by the money judgment. Two credit agencies, CSC Credit Services (CSC) and Trans Union Corporation (Trans Union), relied on the state court judgment docket and indicated in Greg's credit report that he owed the money judgment. Greg and his wife, Mary Henson, allege that they then "contacted Trans [Union] twice, in writing, to correct this horrible injustice." When Trans Union did not respond, the Hensons brought an action alleging violations of the Federal Credit Reporting Act (FCRA). Explain whether the Hensons should prevail.

20. Pantron Corporation and Hal Z. Lederman market a product known as the Helsinki Formula. This product supposedly arrests hair loss and stimulates hair regrowth in baldness sufferers. The formula consists of a conditioner and a shampoo, and it sells at a list price of $49.95 for a three-month supply. The ingredients that allegedly cause the advertised effects are polysorbate 60

and polysorbate 80. Pantron offers a full money-back guarantee for those who are not satisfied with the product. The Federal Trade Commission (FTC) challenged both Pantron's claims that the formula arrested hair loss and promoted growth of new hair as unfair and deceptive trade practices. The FTC presented a variety of evidence that tended to show that the Helsinki Formula had no effectiveness other than its placebo effect (achieving results due solely to belief that the product will work). The FTC introduced expert testimony of a dermatologist and two other experts who denied there was any scientific evidence that the Helsinki Formula would be in any way useful in treating hair loss. Finally, the FTC introduced evidence of two studies that had determined that polysorbate-based products were ineffective in stopping hair loss and promoting regrowth. In response, Pantron introduced evidence that users of the Helsinki Formula were satisfied that it was effective. It offered testimony of eighteen users who had experienced hair regrowth or a reduction in hair loss after using the formula. It also introduced evidence of a "consumer satisfaction survey" it had conducted. Pantron further provided evidence that more than half of its orders come from repeat purchasers, that it had received very few written complaints, and that very few of Pantron's customers (less than 3 percent) had redeemed the money-back guarantee. Pantron finally introduced several clinical studies of its own, none performed in the United States or under U.S. standards for scientific studies. The evidence from these studies did show effectiveness, but the studies were not random, blind-reviewed studies and thus did not take into account the placebo effect. Discuss.

21. Lavon Phillips became engaged to marry Sarah Grendahl and moved in with her. Sarah's mother, Mary, became suspicious that Phillips was not telling the truth about his past, particularly about whether he was an attorney and where he had worked. She also was confused about who his ex-wives and girlfriends were and where they lived. She did some preliminary investigation herself, but she felt that she was hampered by not being able to use a computer, so she contacted Kevin Fitzgerald, a family friend who worked for McDowell, a private investigation agency. She asked Fitzgerald to do a "background check" on Phillips. Fitzgerald searched public records in Minnesota and Alabama, where Phillips had lived earlier and discovered one suit against Phillips for delinquent child support in Alabama, a suit to establish child support for two children in Minnesota,

and one misdemeanor conviction for writing dishonored checks. Fitzgerald then supplied the social security information to Econ Control (a business which furnishes credit reports, Finder's Reports, and credit scoring for credit companies and for private investigators) and asked for "Finder's Reports" on Phillips. Fitzgerald testified that he believed that Finder's Reports were not consumer reports and therefore they were not subject to the Federal Credit Reporting Act (FCRA). William Porter, president of Econ Control, stated that he believed a "Finder's Report" could be obtained without authorization of the person who was the subject of the report because the Finder's Report contained no information on credit history or creditworthiness. Econ Control then obtained a consumer report on Phillips from Computer Science Corporation and passed it on to McDowell. Fitzgerald met with Mary Grendahl and gave her the results of his investigation, including the Finder's Report. Did this investigation violate the Fair Credit Reporting Act? Explain.

22. Ian Eisenberg and Chris Hebard formed Electronic Publishing Ventures, LLC (EPV) and its four subsidiaries: Cyberspace.com, LLC; Essex Enterprises, LLC; Surfnet Services, LLC; and Splashnet.net, LLC. Two offshore entities, French Dreams Investments, N.V. (collectively *EFO* and owned by Eisenberg) and Coto Settlement (controlled by *Hebard*) owned EPV in equal parts. EPV's four subsidiaries mailed approximately 4.4 million solicitations offering internet access to individuals and small businesses. The solicitations included a check, usually for $3.50, attached to a form resembling an invoice designed to be detached from the check by tearing at the perforated line. The check was addressed to the recipient. and the recipient's phone number appeared on the "re" line. The back of the check and invoice contained small-print disclosures revealing that cashing or depositing the check would constitute agreement to pay a monthly fee for internet access, but the front of the check and the invoice contained no such disclosures. The mailing explained in small print that a monthly fee would be billed to the customer's local phone bill after the check was cashed or deposited. At least 225,000 small businesses and individuals cashed or deposited the solicitation checks. The EPV subsidiaries used a billing aggregation service to place charges for $19.95 or $29.95 a month on the small businesses' and individuals' ordinary telephone bills. internet usage records show, however, that less than 1 percent of the 225,000 individuals and

businesses billed for internet service actually logged on to the service.

Eisenberg and Hebard were aware that the solicitation had misled some consumers. The companies received complaints from recipients of the solicitations, which indicated that some customers had

deposited the solicitation check without realizing that they had contracted for internet services. The Federal Trade Commission alleges that the solicitations were deceptive in violation of Section 5 of the Federal Trade Commission Act. Explain whether the FTC is correct.

TAKING SIDES

Kevin Miller bought a house in Atlanta in 2016 and took out a mortgage. He lived in the house until 2019, when he accepted a job in Chicago; from then on, he rented the house. He received a letter demanding payment from a law firm on behalf of the mortgage company in 2021. By this time, Miller was renting the property to strangers and thus was making a business use of the property. Miller claimed that the law firm had violated the Fair Debt Collection Practices Act. The law firm replied that

the letter is outside the scope of the Act because it was trying to collect a business debt rather than a consumer debt.

a. What are the arguments that the debt is a consumer debt?

b. What are the arguments that the debt is a business debt?

c. Which arguments would prevail? Explain.

CHAPTER 42

Employment Law

CHAPTER OUTCOMES

After reading and studying this chapter, you should be able to:

- Explain the major labor law statutes.

- Explain the major laws prohibiting employment discrimination.

- Discuss the defenses available to employers under the various laws prohibiting discrimination in employment.

- Explain the doctrine of employment at will and the laws protecting employee privacy.

- Explain (1) the Occupational Safety and Health Administration (OSHA) and the Occupational Safety and Health Act, (2) workers' compensation, (3) unemployment compensation, (4) social security, (5) the Fair Labor Standards Act, (6) the Worker Adjustment and Retraining Notification Act, and (7) the Family and Medical Leave Act.

Though in general the common law governs the relationship between employer and employee in terms of tort and contract duties (rules that are part of the law of agency; see *Chapter 19*), this common law has been supplemented—and in some instances replaced—by statutory enactments, principally at the Federal level. In fact, government regulation now affects the balance and working relationship between employers and employees in three areas. First, the general framework in which management and labor negotiate the terms of employment is regulated by Federal statutes designed to promote both labor-management harmony and the welfare of society at large. Second, Federal law prohibits employment discrimination based upon race, sex, religion, age, disability, or national origin. Finally, Congress, in response to the changing nature of American industry and the tremendous number of industrial accidents, has mandated that employers provide their employees with a safe and healthy work environment. Moreover, all of the States have adopted workers' compensation acts to provide compensation to employees injured during the course of employment.

This chapter focuses on the three major categories of government regulation of the employment relationship: (1) labor law, (2) employment discrimination law, and (3) employee protection.

42-1 Labor Law

Traditionally, labor law opposed concerted activities by workers (such as strikes, picketing, and refusals to deal) to obtain higher wages and better working conditions. At various times, such activities were found to constitute criminal conspiracy, tortious conduct, and violation of antitrust law. As subjecting union workers to criminal sanctions became publicly unpopular, employers began to resort to civil remedies in an attempt to halt unionization. The primary tool in this campaign was the injunction. Eventually, public pressure opposing such action forced Congress to intervene.

42-1a NORRIS-LA GUARDIA ACT

Congress enacted the **Norris-La Guardia Act** (also known as the Anti-Injunction Bill) in 1932 in response to the growing criticism of the use of injunctions in peaceful labor disputes. The Act withdrew from the Federal courts the power to issue injunctions in nonviolent labor disputes. Section 1. The term **labor dispute** was broadly defined to include any controversy concerning terms or conditions of employment or union representation, regardless of whether the parties stood in an employer-employee relationship or not. Section 13(c). More significantly, the Act declared it to be U.S. policy that labor was to have full freedom to form unions without employer interference. Section 2. Accordingly, the Act prohibited the so-called yellow dog contracts through which employers coerced their employees into promising that they would not join a union.

42-1b NATIONAL LABOR RELATIONS ACT

Enacted in 1935, the **National Labor Relations Act (NLRA)**, or the *Wagner Act*, embodied the Federal government's effort to support collective bargaining and unionization. The Act provides that "the right to self-organization, to form, join or assist labor organizations, to bargain collectively through representatives of their own choosing, and to engage in concerted activities for the purpose of collective bargaining or other mutual aid or protection" is, for workers, a Federally protected right. Thus, the Act gave employees the right to union representation when negotiating employment terms with their employers. Section 7.

The Act also sought to enforce the collective bargaining right by prohibiting certain employer conduct deemed to constitute **unfair labor practices**. Under the Act, the following employer activities are unfair labor practices: (1) to interfere with the employees' rights to unionize and bargain collectively, (2) to dominate the union, (3) to discriminate against union members, (4) to discriminate against an employee who has filed charges or testified under the NLRA, and (5) to refuse to bargain in good faith with duly established employee representatives. Section 8(a).

Moreover, the Act established the **National Labor Relations Board (NLRB)** to monitor and administer these employee rights. The NLRB is empowered to order employers to remedy their unfair labor practices and to supervise elections by secret ballot so that employees can freely select a representative organization.

Practical Advice

Treat all employees with appropriate respect and dignity.

42-1c LABOR-MANAGEMENT RELATIONS ACT

Following the passage of the NLRA, union membership and labor unrest increased tremendously in the United States. In response to this trend, Congress passed the **Labor-Management Relations Act** (the **LMRA**, or **Taft-Hartley Act**) in 1947. The Act prohibits certain unfair union practices and separates the NLRB's prosecutorial and adjudicative functions. More specifically, the Act amended the NLRA by declaring the following seven *union* activities to be **unfair labor practices**: (1) coercing an employee to join a union, (2) causing an employer to discharge or discriminate against a nonunion employee, (3) refusing to bargain in good faith, (4) levying excessive or discriminatory dues or fees, (5) causing an employer to pay for work not performed ("featherbedding"), (6) picketing an employer to require it to recognize an uncertified union, and (7) engaging in secondary activities. NLRA Section 8(b). A **secondary activity** is a boycott, strike, or picketing of an employer with whom a union has no labor dispute to persuade the employer to cease doing business with the company that is the target of the labor dispute. For example, assume that a union is engaged in a labor dispute with Adams Company. To coerce Adams into resolving the dispute in the union's favor,

the union organizes a strike against Brookings Company, with which the union has no labor dispute. The union agrees to cease striking Brookings Company if Brookings agrees to cease doing business with Adams. The strike against Brookings Company is a secondary activity prohibited as an unfair labor practice.

In addition to prohibiting unfair union practices, the Act also fosters *employer* free speech by declaring that no employer unfair labor practice could be based on any statement of opinion or argument that contains no threat of reprisal. NLRA Section 8(c).

The LMRA also prohibits the closed shop, although it permits union shops if such are not prohibited by a State right-to-work law. A **closed shop** contract requires the employer to hire only union members. A **union shop** contract permits the employer to hire nonunion members but requires them to become union members within a specified time and to remain members in good standing as a condition of employment. Although a State may prohibit union shop contracts through a **right-to-work law**, most States permit the existence of union shops.

Finally, the Act reinstates the availability of civil injunctions in labor disputes, if requested of the NLRB to prevent an unfair labor practice. The Act also empowers the president of the United States to obtain an injunction for an eighty-day cooling-off period for a strike that is likely to endanger the national health or safety.

In a 5–4 decision, the U.S. Supreme court ruled that an Illinois law requiring *public* employees who choose not to join a union to "pay their proportionate share of the costs of the collective bargaining process, contract administration and pursuing matters affecting wages, hours and other conditions of employment" violates the First Amendment. *Janus v. State, County, and Municipal Employees*, 585 U. S. _____ (2018). A number of States have laws similar to the Illinois law. Some States, however, have passed laws to help shield unions from the full impact of the *Janus* decision. For example, New York enacted legislation that provides that unions are not required to extend full benefits to workers who are not dues-paying members of the union.

◆ **SEE FIGURE 42-1:** *Unfair Labor Practices*

42-1d LABOR-MANAGEMENT REPORTING AND DISCLOSURE ACT

The **Labor-Management Reporting and Disclosure Act**, also known as the **Landrum-Griffin Act**, is aimed at eliminating corruption in labor unions. The Act attempts to eradicate corruption through an elaborate reporting system and a union "bill of rights" designed to make unions more democratic. Section 101. The latter provides union members with the right to nominate candidates for union offices, to vote in elections,

FIGURE 42-1 Unfair Labor Practices

Unfair Employer Practices	Unfair Union Practices
Interfering with right to unionize	Coercing an employee to join the union
Refusing to bargain in good faith	Refusing to bargain in good faith
Discriminating against union members	Causing an employer to discriminate against a nonunion employee
Dominating the union	Featherbedding
Discriminating against an employee	Picketing an employer to require recognition of an uncertified union
	Engaging in secondary activity
	Levying excessive or discriminatory dues

to attend membership meetings, to participate in union business, to express themselves freely at union meetings and conventions, and to be accorded a full and fair hearing before the union takes any disciplinary action against them.

42-2 Employment Discrimination Law

A number of Federal statutes prohibit discrimination in employment on the basis of race, sex, religion, national origin, age, disability, and genetic information. The cornerstone of Federal employment is Title VII of the 1964 Civil Rights Act, but other statutes and regulations also are significant, including two subsequently enacted discrimination laws: the Civil Rights Act of 1991 and the Americans with Disabilities Act of 1990 (ADA). In addition, most States have enacted similar laws prohibiting discrimination based on race, sex, religion, national origin, disability, and genetic information. The Civil Rights Act of 1991 extended the coverage of both Title VII and the ADA to include U.S. citizens working for U.S.-owned or U.S.-controlled companies in foreign countries.

The **Equal Employment Opportunity Commission** (EEOC) is the enforcement agency for Federal laws that makes it illegal to discriminate against a job applicant or an employee because of race, sex, religion, national origin, age, disability, and genetic information. The EEOC is empowered (1) to file legal actions in its own name or to intervene in actions filed by third parties, (2) to attempt to resolve alleged violations through informal means prior to bringing suit, (3) to investigate all charges of discrimination, and (4) to issue guidelines and regulations concerning enforcement policy.

♦ See Case 42-1

42-2a EQUAL PAY ACT

The **Equal Pay Act** prohibits an employer from discriminating between employees on the basis of sex by paying unequal wages for the same work. The Act forbids an employer from paying wages at a rate less than the rate at which he pays wages to employees of the opposite sex for *equal work* at the same establishment. Most courts define *equal work* to mean "substantially equal" rather than identical. The burden of proof is on the claimant to make a *prima facie* showing that the employer pays unequal wages for work requiring equal skill, effort, and responsibility under similar working conditions. Once the employee has demonstrated that the employer pays members of the opposite sex unequal wages for equal work, the burden shifts to the employer to prove that the pay differential is based on the following:

1. a seniority system,
2. a merit system,
3. a system that measures earnings by quantity or quality of production, or
4. any factor except sex.

Remedies include recovering back pay, awarding liquidated damages (an additional amount equal to back pay), and enjoining the employer from further unlawful conduct. Although the Department of Labor was the Federal agency originally designated by the statute to interpret and enforce the Act, these functions subsequently were transferred to the EEOC.

42-2b CIVIL RIGHTS ACT OF 1964

Title VII of the **Civil Rights Act of 1964** prohibits **employment discrimination** on the basis of race, color, sex, religion, or national origin in hiring, firing, compensating, promoting, training, and other employment-related processes. Harassment based on any of these characteristics is also prohibited. The definition of *religion* includes all aspects of religious observance and practice, and the statute provides that an employer must make reasonable efforts to accommodate an employee's religious belief. In 2015, the EEOC ruled "an allegation of discrimination on the basis of sexual orientation is necessarily an allegation of sex discrimination under Title VII." The Act applies to employers engaged in an industry affecting commerce and having fifteen or more employees. The Act also covers Federal, State, and local governments, as well as labor organizations with fifteen or more members. The Act contains an antiretaliation provision that forbids an employer from discriminating against an employee who has brought a claim or proceeding under Title VII or who has testified, assisted, or participated in such action.

On June 15, 2020, in a 6–3 decision, the U.S. Supreme Court ruled that Title VII of the Civil Rights Act of 1964 protects gay, lesbian, and transgender people from discrimination in employment. "In Title VII, Congress adopted broad language making it illegal for an employer to rely on an employee's sex when deciding to fire that employee. We do not hesitate to recognize today a necessary consequence of that legislative choice: An employer who fires an individual merely for being gay or transgender defies the law." *Bostock v. Clayton County*, 590 U.S. ___ (2020).

◆ *See Cases 42-2 and 42-3*

When Congress passed the **Pregnancy Discrimination Act**, it extended the benefits of Title VII to pregnant women. Under the Act, an employer cannot refuse to hire a pregnant woman, fire her, or force her to take maternity leave unless the employer can establish a *bona fide* occupational qualification defense (discussed later in this chapter). The Act, which protects the job reinstatement rights of women returning from maternity leave, requires employers to treat pregnancy like any other temporary disability.

◆ **SEE FIGURE 42-2:** *Charges Filed with the EEOC from 2012 to 2019*

Practical Advice

Issue a strong company policy against all types of prohibited discrimination and ensure that all business decisions comply with your policy.

PROVING DISCRIMINATION Each of the following constitutes discriminatory conduct prohibited by the Act:

1. **Disparate Treatment**. An individual shows that an employer used a prohibited criterion in making an employment decision by treating some people less favorably than others. Liability is based on proving that the employer's decision was motivated by the protected characteristic or trait. *Raytheon Co. v. Hernandez*, 537 U.S. 1187 (2003). The Supreme Court held in *McDonnell Douglas Corp. v. Green*, 411 U.S. 792 (1973), that a *prima facie* case of discrimination would be shown if the plaintiff (a) is within a protected class, (b) applied for an open position, (c) was qualified for the position, (d) and was denied the job and (e) the employer continued to try to fill the position from a pool of applicants with the complainant's qualifications

or gave it to someone with similar qualifications from a different class. Once the plaintiff establishes a *prima facie* case, the burden of proof shifts to the defendant to "articulate legitimate and nondiscriminatory reasons for the plaintiff's rejection." If the defendant so rebuts, the plaintiff then has the opportunity to demonstrate that the employer's stated reason was merely a pretext.

If the employer's decision was based on a "mixed motive" (the employer used both lawful and unlawful reasons in making its decision) the courts employ a shifting burden-of-proof standard. First, the plaintiff must prove by a preponderance of the evidence that the employer used the protected characteristic as a motivating factor. The defendant, however, can limit the remedies available to the plaintiff by proving by a preponderance of the evidence that the defendant would have made the same decision even without the forbidden motivating factor. If the defendant sustains its burden of proof, under the Civil Rights Act of 1991, the remedies are limited to declaratory relief, certain types of injunctive relief, and attorneys' fees and costs.

2. **Present Effects of Past Discrimination**. An employer engages in conduct that on its face is "neutral," that is, non-discriminatory, but that actually perpetuates past discriminatory practices. For example, it has been held illegal for a union that had previously limited its membership to whites to adopt a requirement that new members be related to or recommended by existing members. *Local 53 of International Association of Heat and Frost Insulators and Asbestos Workers v. Vogler*, 407 F.2d 1047 (5th Cir. 1969).

3. **Disparate Impact**. This occurs when an employer adopts "neutral" rules that adversely affect a protected class and that are not justified as being necessary to the business. *Raytheon Co. v. Hernandez*, 537 U.S. 1187 (2003). Despite the employee's proof of disparate impact, the employer may prevail if it can demonstrate that the challenged practice is "job related for the position in question and consistent with business necessity." *Wards Cove Packing Co. v. Antonio*, 490 U.S. 642, 109 S.Ct. 2115 (1989). Thus, all requirements that might have a disparate impact upon women, such as height and weight requirements, must be shown to be job related. Nevertheless, under the **Civil Rights Act of 1991**, even if the employer can demonstrate the business necessity of the questioned practice, the complainant will still prevail if she shows that a nondiscriminatory alternative practice exists.

◆ *See Case 42-4*

In an 8–1 decision in 2015, the U.S. Supreme Court held that in disparate-treatment claims, an employer may not make an applicant's religious practice, confirmed or otherwise, a factor

FIGURE 42-2 Charges Filed with the EEOC from 2012 to 2019

Category	Number of Charges							
	2012	2013	2014	2015	2016	2017	2018	2019
Race	33,512	33,068	31,073	31,027	32,309	28,528	24,600	23,976
Sex	30,356	27,687	26,027	26,396	26,934	25,605	24,655	23,532
National Origin	10,883	10,642	9,579	9,438	9,840	8,299	7,106	7,009
Religion	3,811	3,721	3,549	3,502	3,825	3,436	2,859	2,725
Color	2,662	3,146	2,756	2,833	3,102	3,240	3,166	3,415
Retaliation	31,208	31,478	30,771	31,893	33,082	32,023	39,469	39,110
Age	22,857	21,396	20,588	20,144	20,857	18,376	16,911	15,573
Disability	26,379	25,957	25,369	26,968	28,073	26,838	24,605	24,238
Equal Pay Act	1,082	1,019	938	973	1,075	996	1,066	1,117
Genetic Information	280	333	333	257	238	206	220	209
Total Charges	99,412	93,727	88,778	89,385	91,503	84,254	76,418	72,675

Source: EEOC, "Enforcement & Litigation Statistics," http://www.eeoc.gov/eeoc/statistics/enforcement/charges.cfm.

in employment decisions. In this case, a practicing Muslim woman was denied employment because she wore a headscarf pursuant to her religious obligations. Despite the fact that the employer's policy was neutral, barring all head coverings, the Court held that federal law gives faith-related expression "favored treatment, affirmatively obligating employers" to accommodate religious practice that they could accommodate without undue hardship. *EEOC v. Abercrombie & Fitch Stores, Inc.*, 575 U.S. ____. In another case decided in 2015, the U.S. Supreme Court ruled that the Fair Housing Act prohibits seemingly neutral practices that harm minorities, even without proof of intentional discrimination. *Texas Department of Housing and Community Affairs v. Inclusive Communities Project 576 U.S. ____.*

DEFENSES The Act provides several basic defenses: (1) a *bona fide* seniority or merit system, (2) a professionally developed ability test, (3) a compensation system based on performance results, and (4) a *bona fide* occupational qualification (BFOQ). The BFOQ defense does not apply to discrimination based on race. A fifth defense, business necessity, is available in a disparate impact case. In addition, a defendant can reduce damages in a "mixed-motive" case by showing that it would have discharged the plaintiff for legal reasons.

REMEDIES Remedies for violation of the Act include enjoining the employer from engaging in the unlawful behavior, appropriate affirmative action, and reinstatement of employees to their rightful place (which may include promotion) and award of back pay from a date not more than two years prior to the filing of the charge with the EEOC. First employed by Executive Order, as discussed in the following section, **affirmative action** generally means the active recruitment of minority applicants, although courts also have used the remedy to impose numerical hiring ratios (quotas) and hiring goals based on race and sex. The EEOC has defined affirmative action in employment as "actions appropriate to overcome the effects of past or present practices, policies, or other barriers to equal employment opportunity."

Prior to 1991, only victims of racial discrimination could recover compensatory and punitive damages from the courts. Today, however, under the Civil Rights Act of 1991, *all* victims of *intentional* discrimination—whether based on race, sex, religion, national origin, or disability—can recover compensatory and punitive damages, except in cases involving disparate impact. In cases not involving race, the Act limits the amount of recoverable damages according to the number of persons the defendant employs. Companies with 15 to 100 employees are required to pay no more than $50,000; companies with 101 to 200 employees, no more than $100,000; those with 201 to 500 employees, no more than $200,000; and those with 501 or more employees, no more than $300,000. Either party may demand a jury trial. Victims of racial discrimination are still entitled to recover unlimited compensatory and punitive damages.

REVERSE DISCRIMINATION A major controversy has arisen over the use of reverse discrimination in achieving affirmative action. In this context, **reverse discrimination** refers to affirmative action that directs an employer to remedy the underrepresentation of a given race or sex in a traditionally segregated job by considering an individual's race or gender when hiring or promoting. An example would be an employer who discriminates against white males to increase the proportion of females or members of a racial minority in a company's workforce.

Due to the absence of State action, challenges to affirmative action plans adopted by private employers—those that are not government units at the local, State, or Federal level—are tested under Title VII of the Civil Rights Act of 1964, not under the Equal Protection Clause of the U.S. Constitution. In Johnson v. Transportation Agency, 480 U.S. 616 (1987), also an action under Title VII, the Supreme Court upheld the employer's right to promote a female employee rather than a white male employee who had scored higher on a qualifying examination.

When a State or local government adopts an affirmative action plan that is challenged as constituting illegal reverse discrimination, the plan is subject to strict scrutiny under the **Equal Protection Clause** of the Fourteenth Amendment. Under the strict scrutiny test, the subject classification must (1) be justified by a compelling government interest and (2) be the least intrusive means available. (For a fuller discussion of the Equal Protection Clause and the standards of review, see *Chapter 4.*)

With regard to racial discrimination, the U.S. Supreme Court has placed significant constraints upon the ability of governments to create programs favoring minorities over whites: benign and invidious discrimination are both held to the standard under which the government must show a compelling interest that is as narrowly tailored as feasible. Following this decision, the EEOC issued a statement which provided that "affirmative action is lawful only when it is designed to respond to a demonstrated and serious imbalance in the workforce, is flexible, time-limited, applies only to qualified workers, and respects the rights of non-minorities and men."

Practical Advice

In attempting to promote equal opportunity, respect the rights of nonminority applicants and employees.

SEXUAL HARASSMENT The EEOC has defined sexual harassment as follows:

Unwelcome sexual advances, requests for sexual favors, and other verbal or physical conduct of a sexual nature constitute sexual harassment when

1. submission to such conduct is made either explicitly or implicitly a term or condition of an individual's employment,

2. submission to or rejection of such conduct by an individual is used as the basis for employment decisions affecting such individual, or

3. such conduct has the purpose or effect of reasonably interfering with an individual's work performance or creating an intimidating, hostile or offensive working environment.

The courts, including the Supreme Court, have held that sexual harassment may constitute illegal sexual discrimination in violation of Title VII. Moreover, an employer will be held liable for sexual harassment committed by one of its employees if it does not take reasonable action when it knows or should have known of the harassment. When the employee engaging in sexual harassment is an agent of the employer or holds a supervisory position over the victim, the employer may be liable without knowledge or reason to know.

The U.S. Supreme Court has also held that sex discrimination consisting of same-sex harassment is actionable under Title VII.

Practical Advice

Issue a strong company policy against sexual harassment and thoroughly investigate any charge of a violation of such policy.

♦ *See Cases 42-3 and 42-5*

COMPARABLE WORTH Industrial statistics indicate that women earn significantly less money than men do. Because the Equal Pay Act requires equal pay for equal work only, it does not apply to different jobs even if they are comparable. Thus, that statute provides no remedy for women who have been systematically undervalued and underpaid in "traditional" occupations, such as secretary, teacher, or nurse. As a result, women have sought redress under Title VII by arguing that the failure to pay **comparable worth** is discrimination on the basis of sex. The concept of comparable worth provides that employers should measure the relative values of different jobs through a job evaluation rating system that is free of any potential sex bias. Theoretically, the consistent application of objective criteria (including factors such as skill, effort, working conditions, responsibility, and mental demands) across job categories will ensure fair payment for all employees. For example, if under such a system the jobs of truck driver and nurse were evaluated at the same level, then workers in both jobs would receive the same pay.

The U.S. Supreme Court has held that a claim of discriminatory under-compensation based on sex may be brought under Title VII, even in cases in which the plaintiffs were performing jobs different from those of their opposite-sex counterparts. As the Court noted, however, the case involved a situation in which the defendant intentionally discriminated in wages and the defendant, not the courts, had compared the jobs in terms of value. *County of Washington v. Gunther*, 452 U.S. 161 (1981). The Court also held that the four defenses available under the Equal Pay Act would apply to a Title VII claim. Since *Gunther*, the concept of comparable worth has met with limited success in the courts. Nonetheless, a number of States have adopted legislation requiring public and private employers to pay equally for comparable work.

42-2c EXECUTIVE ORDER

In 1965, President Johnson issued an Executive Order that prohibits discrimination by Federal contractors on the basis of race, color, sex, religion, or national origin in employment on any work the contractor performs during the period of the Federal contract. Federal contractors are also required to implement affirmative action in recruiting. The Secretary of Labor, **Office of Federal Contract Compliance Programs (OFCCP)**, enforces compliance with the program.

The program applies to all contractors (and all of their subcontractors in excess of $10,000) who enter into a Federal contract to be performed in the United States. Compliance with the affirmative action requirement differs for construction and nonconstruction contractors. All **nonconstruction** contractors with fifty or more employees or with contracts for more than $50,000 must have a written affirmative action plan to be in compliance. The plan must include a workforce analysis; planned corrective action, if necessary, with specific goals and timetables; and procedures for auditing and reporting. The Director of the OFCCP periodically issues goals and timetables for each segment of the construction industry for each region of the country. As a condition precedent to bidding on a Federal contract, a contractor must agree to make a good faith effort to achieve current published goals.

42-2d AGE DISCRIMINATION IN EMPLOYMENT ACT OF 1967

The **Age Discrimination in Employment Act (ADEA)** prohibits discrimination in hiring, firing, compensating, or other employment-related processes on the basis of age when the employee or applicant is more than forty years old. The Act applies to private employers having twenty or more employees and to all government units regardless of size. The Act also prohibits the mandatory retirement of most employees, no matter what their age, though it provides employers a limited exception regarding *bona fide* executives and high policymaking employees. In 2004, the U.S. Supreme Court held that the ADEA does not prevent an employer from favoring an older employee over a younger employee.

In 2009, the U.S. Supreme Court held that the ADEA's text does not authorize an alleged mixed-motives age discrimination claim that would result in a shifting burden-of-proof standard as previously discussed. Accordingly,

> a plaintiff bringing a disparate-treatment claim pursuant to the ADEA must prove, by a preponderance of the evidence, that age was the "but-for" cause of the challenged adverse employment action. The burden of persuasion does not shift to the employer to show that it would have taken the action regardless of age, even when

a plaintiff has produced some evidence that age was one motivating factor in that decision. *Gross v. FBL Financial Services, Inc.*, 557 U.S. 167.

The major statutory defenses include (1) a BFOQ; (2) a *bona fide* seniority system; and (3) any other reasonable action, including the voluntary retirement of an individual. Remedies include back pay, injunctive relief, affirmative action, and liquidated damages equal to the amount of the award for "willful" violations. Furthermore, an ADEA claimant is entitled to a jury trial.

42-2e DISABILITY LAW

The **Rehabilitation Act** attempts to assist the handicapped in obtaining rehabilitation training, access to public facilities, and employment. The Act requires Federal contractors and Federal agencies to take affirmative action to hire qualified handicapped persons. It also prohibits discrimination on the basis of handicap in Federal programs and programs receiving Federal financial assistance.

A **handicapped person** is defined in the Rehabilitation Act as an individual who (1) has a physical or mental impairment that substantially affects one or more of her major life activities, (2) has a history of major life activity impairment, *or* (3) is regarded as having such an impairment. Major life activities include such functions as caring for oneself, seeing, speaking, or walking. Alcohol and drug abuses are not considered handicapping conditions for the purposes of this statute.

The **ADA** forbids an employer from discriminating against any person with a disability with regard to "hiring or discharge … employee compensation, advancement, job training and other terms, conditions and privileges of employment." In addition, businesses must make special accommodations, such as installing wheelchair-accessible bathrooms, for handicapped workers and customers unless the cost is unduly burdensome. An employer may use qualification standards, tests, or selection criteria that screen out handicapped workers if these measures are job related and consistent with business necessity and if no reasonable accommodation is possible. The ADA applies to employers with fifteen or more employees. Remedies for violation of the ADA are those generally allowed under Title VII and include injunctive relief; reinstatement; back pay; and for intentional discrimination, compensatory and punitive damages (capped according to company size by the Civil Rights Act of 1991).

In 2008, President George W. Bush signed into law the ADA Amendments Act of 2008 (ADAAA). This gave broader protections for disabled workers and "turn[ed] back the clock" on court rulings that Congress deemed too restrictive. The ADAAA includes a list of *major life activities*, including "caring for oneself, performing manual tasks, seeing, hearing, eating, sleeping, walking, standing, lifting, bending, speaking, breathing, learning, reading, concentrating, thinking, communicating, and working," as well as the operation of several specified "major bodily functions." The ADAAA overturned a 1999 U.S. Supreme Court case that held that an employee was not disabled if the impairment could be corrected by mitigating measures; the ADAAA specifically provides that such impairment must be determined without considering such ameliorative measures. Another judicially imposed restriction overturned by the ADAAA is the interpretation that an impairment that substantially limits one major life activity must also limit others to be considered a disability.

In addition, the **Vietnam Veterans Readjustment Act** requires firms having $10,000 or more in Federal contracts to take affirmative action regarding handicapped veterans and Vietnam era veterans.

Practical Advice

Make reasonable accommodation for individuals with disabilities.

♦ SEE FIGURE 42-3: *Federal Employment Discrimination Laws*

♦ *See Case 42-6*

42-2f GENETIC INFORMATION DISCRIMINATION

The **Genetic Information Nondiscrimination Act** of 2008 (GINA) forbids discrimination on the basis of genetic information with respect to any aspect of employment, including hiring, firing, pay, job assignments, promotions, layoffs, training, fringe benefits, or any other term or condition of employment. The Act explicitly states that disparate impact on the basis of genetic information does not establish a cause of action. Under GINA, it is also illegal to (1) harass a person because of his or her genetic information and (2) retaliate against an applicant or employee because the person complained about discrimination, filed a charge of genetic discrimination, or participated in an employment discrimination investigation or lawsuit. Genetic information includes information about an individual's genetic tests and the genetic tests of an individual's family members, as well as information about any disease, disorder, or condition of an individual's family members (i.e., an individual's family medical history). Remedies for violation

FIGURE 42-3 Federal Employment Discrimination Laws

	Protected Characteristics	Prohibited Conduct	Defenses	Remedies
Equal Pay Act	Gender	Wages	Seniority Merit Quality or quantity measures Any factor other than sex	Back pay Injunction Liquidated damages Attorneys' fees
Title VII of Civil Rights Act	Race Color Gender Religion National origin	Terms, conditions, or privileges of employment	Seniority Ability test BFOQ (except for race) Business necessity (disparate impact only)	Back pay Injunction Reinstatement Compensatory and punitive damages for intentional discrimination • unlimited for race • limited for all others Attorneys' fees
Age Discrimination in Employment Act	Age	Terms, conditions, or privileges of employment	Seniority BFOQ Any other reasonable act	Back pay Injunction Reinstatement Liquidated damages for willful violation Attorneys' fees
Americans with Disabilities Act	Disability	Terms, conditions, or privileges of employment	Undue hardship Job-related criteria and business necessity Risk to public health and safety	Back pay Injunction Reinstatement Compensatory and punitive damages for intentional discrimination (limited) Attorneys' fees

Note: BFOQ = *bona fide* occupational qualification.

of GINA are generally allowed under Title VII and include injunctive relief; reinstatement; back pay; and for intentional discrimination, compensatory and punitive damages (capped according to company size by the Civil Rights Act of 1991). The EEOC enforces GINA's provisions dealing with genetic discrimination in employment.

42-3 Employee Protection

Employees are accorded a number of job-related protections. These include a limited right not to be unfairly dismissed, a right to a safe and healthy workplace, compensation for injuries sustained in the workplace, and some financial security upon retirement or loss of employment. This section discusses (1) employee termination at will, (2) occupational safety and health, (3) employee privacy, (4) workers' compensation, (5) Social Security and unemployment insurance, (6) the Fair Labor Standards Act (FLSA), (7) employee notice of termination or layoff, and (8) family and health leave.

42-3a EMPLOYEE TERMINATION AT WILL

Under the common law, a contract of employment is terminable at will by either party unless the employment is for other than a definite term or the employee is represented by a labor union. Accordingly, under the common law, employers may "dismiss their employees at will for good cause, for no cause or even for cause morally wrong, without being thereby guilty of legal wrong." In recent years, however, the courts have delineated a growing number of judicial exceptions to the rule, based on implied contract, tort, and public policy. A number of Federal and State statutes enacted in the last sixty years further limit the rule, which also may be restricted by contractual agreement between employer and employee. In particular, most collective bargaining agreements negotiated through union representatives contain a provision prohibiting dismissal "without cause."

STATUTORY LIMITATIONS In 1934, as previously discussed, Congress enacted the NLRA, which provided employees with the right to unionize free of intimidation or coercion from their employers, including freedom from dismissal for engaging in union activities. Since the enactment of the NLRA, additional Federal legislation, such as the ADEA, ADA, Employee Retirement Income Security Act, and FLSA, has limited the employer's right to discharge. These statutes fall into three categories: (1) those protecting certain employees from discriminatory discharge, (2) those protecting certain employees in their exercise of statutory rights, and (3) those protecting certain employees from discharge without cause.

At the State level, statutes protect workers from discriminatory discharge for filing workers' compensation claims. Also, many State statutes parallel Federal legislation. Some States have adopted statutes similar to the NLRA, and many States prohibit discrimination in employment on the basis of factors such as race, creed, nationality, sex, or age. In addition, some States have statutes prohibiting employers from discharging employees or taking other punitive actions to influence voting or, in some States, political activity.

JUDICIAL LIMITATIONS Judicial limitations on the employment-at-will doctrine have been based on contract law, tort law, and public policy. Cases founded in contract theory have relied on arguments contending, among other things, (1) that the dismissal was improper because the employee had detrimentally relied on the employer's promise of work for a reasonable time; (2) that the employment was not at will because of implied-in-fact promises of employment for a specific duration, which meant that the employer could not terminate the employee without just cause; (3) that the employment contract implied or provided expressly that the employee would not be dismissed so long as he satisfactorily performed his work; (4) that the employer had assured the employee that he would not be dismissed except for cause; or (5) that upon entering into the employment contract, the employee gave consideration over and above the performance of services to support a promise of job security.

Some courts have circumvented the common law at-will doctrine under implied contract theories by finding that employment contracts contain an implied promise to deal in good faith, including a duty on the part of the employer to terminate only in good faith. These cases provide a remedy for an employee whose discharge was motivated by bad faith, malice, or retaliation.

Courts have also created exceptions to the employment-at-will doctrine by imposing tort obligations on employers, particularly the torts of intentional infliction of emotional distress and of interference with employment relations.

A majority of States now consider a discharge as wrongful if it violates a statutory or other established public policy. In general, this public policy exception renders a discharge wrongful if it involves a dismissal for (1) refusing to violate a statute, (2) exercising a statutory right, (3) performing a statutory obligation, or (4) reporting an alleged violation of a statute that is of public interest ("whistle-blowing").

♦ *See Case 42-7*

42-3b OCCUPATIONAL SAFETY AND HEALTH ACT

Congress enacted the **Occupational Safety and Health Act** to ensure, as much as possible, a safe and healthful working environment for every worker. The Act established the *Occupational Safety and Health Administration* (OSHA) to develop standards, conduct inspections, monitor compliance, and institute enforcement actions against those who are not in compliance.

Upon each employer engaged in a business affecting interstate commerce, the Act imposes a general duty to provide a work environment that is "free from recognized hazards that are causing or likely to cause death or serious physical harm to his employees." Section 119. In addition to this general duty, the employer must comply with specific OSHA-promulgated safety rules. The Act also requires employees to comply with all OSHA rules and regulations. Finally, the Act prohibits any employer from discharging or discriminating against an employee who exercises her rights under the Act. Section 11(c)(1).

Enforcing the Act generally involves OSHA inspections and citations of employers, as appropriate, for (1) breach of the general duty obligation; (2) breach of specific safety and health standards; or (3) failure to keep records, make reports, or post notices required by the Act.

When a violation is discovered, the offending employer receives a written citation, a proposed penalty, and a date by which the employer must remedy the breach. A citation may be contested, in which case the Occupational Safety and Health Review Commission assigns an administrative law judge to hold a hearing. The commission, at its discretion, may grant review of an administrative law judge's decision; review is not a matter of right. If no such review occurs, the judge's decision becomes the final order of the commission thirty days after its receipt by the aggrieved party, who then may appeal the order to the appropriate U.S. Circuit Court of Appeals.

Penalties for violations are both civil and criminal. In cases involving civil penalties, serious violations require that a penalty be proposed; in contrast, for nonserious violations, penalties are discretionary and rarely proposed. The Act further empowers the Secretary of Labor to obtain temporary restraining orders when regular OSHA procedures are insufficient to halt imminently hazardous or deadly business operations.

One stated purpose of the Act is to encourage State participation in regulating safety and health. The Act therefore permits a State to regulate the safety and health of the work environment within its borders, provided that OSHA approves the plan. The Act sets minimum acceptable standards for the States to impose, but it does not require that a State plan be identical to OSHA guidelines. More than half of the States regulate workplace health and safety through State-promulgated plans.

Practical Advice
Ensure your workers a safe and healthy work environment.

42-3c EMPLOYEE PRIVACY

Over the past two decades, employee privacy has become a major issue. The fundamental right to privacy is a product of common law protection, discussed in *Chapter 7*. Thus, employee protection from unwanted searches, electronic monitoring and other forms of surveillance, and disclosure of confidential records is safeguarded by the tort of invasion of privacy, which actually consists of four different torts: (1) unreasonable intrusion into the seclusion of another, (2) unreasonable public disclosure of private facts, (3) unreasonable publicity that places another in a false light, and (4) appropriation of a person's name or likeness. In addition, the Federal government and some States have legislatively supplemented the common law in certain areas.

DRUG AND ALCOHOL TESTING Although no Federal legislation deals comprehensively with drug and alcohol tests, legislation in a number of States either prohibits such tests altogether or prescribes certain scientific and procedural standards for conducting them. In the absence of a State statute, *private* sector employees have little or no protection from such tests. The NLRB has held, however, that drug and alcohol testing in a union setting is a mandatory subject of collective bargaining.

The U.S. Supreme Court has ruled that the employer of a *public* sector employee whose position involved public health or safety or national security could subject the employee to a drug or alcohol test without either first obtaining a search warrant or having reasonable grounds to believe the individual had engaged in any wrongdoing. Based on Supreme Court and lower court decisions, it appears that a government employer may use (1) random or universal testing where the public health or safety or national security is involved and (2) selective drug testing when there is sufficient cause to believe an employee has a drug problem.

LIE DETECTOR TESTS The **Federal Employee Polygraph Protection Act** prohibits private employers from requiring employees or prospective employees to undergo a lie detector test, inquiring about the results of such a test, or using the results of such a test or the refusal to be thus tested as grounds for an adverse employment decision. The Act exempts government employers and, in certain situations, Energy Department contractors or persons providing consulting services for Federal intelligence agencies. In addition, security firms and manufacturers of controlled substances may use a polygraph to test prospective employees. Moreover, an employer, as part of an ongoing investigation of economic loss or injury to its business, may utilize a polygraph test. Nevertheless, the use of the test must meet the following requirements: (1) it must be designed to investigate a specific incident or activity, not to document a chronic problem; (2) the employee to be tested must have had access to the property that is the subject of the investigation; and (3) the employer must have reason to suspect the particular employee.

Employees and prospective employees tested under any of these exemptions cannot be terminated, disciplined, or denied employment solely as a result of the test. The Act further provides that those subjected to a polygraph test (1) cannot be asked intrusive or degrading questions regarding topics such as their religious beliefs, opinions as to racial matters, political views, or sexual preferences or behaviors; (2) must be given the right to review all questions before the test and to terminate the test at any time; and (3) must receive a complete copy of the test results.

Practical Advice

Be careful to respect the privacy of employees.

42-3d WORKERS' COMPENSATION

At common law, the basis of most actions by an injured employee against his employer was the employer's failure to use reasonable care under the circumstances to ensure the employee's safety. In such an action, however, the employer could make use of several well-established defenses, including the fellow servant rule, contributory negligence on the part of the employee, and the doctrine of assumption of risk by the employee. By establishing any of these defenses, the employer was not liable to the injured employee.

The **fellow servant rule** relieved an employer from liability for injuries an employee sustained through the negligence of a fellow employee. Under the common law defense of **contributory negligence**, if an employer established that an employee's negligence contributed to the injury he sustained in the course of his employment, in many jurisdictions, the employee could not recover damages from the employer. Additionally, at common law, an employer was not liable to an employee for harm or injury caused by the unsafe condition of the premises if the employee, with knowledge of the facts and an understanding of the risks involved, voluntarily entered into or continued in the employment. This was regarded as a **voluntary assumption of risk** by the employee.

To provide speedier and more certain relief to injured employees, all States have adopted statutes providing for workers' compensation. (Several States, however, exempt specified employers from such statutes.) Workers' compensation statutes create commissions or boards that determine whether an injured employee is entitled to receive compensation and, if so, how much. The basis of recovery under workers' compensation is strict liability: the employee does not have to prove that the employer was negligent. The common law defenses discussed previously are not available to employers in proceedings under these statutes. Such defenses are abolished. The only requirement is that the employee be injured and that the injury arises out of and in the course of his employment. The amounts recoverable are fixed by statute for each type of injury and are lower than the amounts a court or jury would probably award in an action at common law. The courts, therefore, do not have jurisdiction over such cases, except to review decisions of the board or commission; even then, the courts may determine only whether such decisions are in accordance with the statute. If a third party causes the injury, however, the employee may bring a tort action against that third party.

Early workers' compensation laws did not provide coverage for occupational disease, and most courts held that occupational injury did not include disease. Today, virtually all States provide general compensation coverage for occupational diseases, although the coverage varies greatly from State to State.

42-3e SOCIAL SECURITY AND UNEMPLOYMENT INSURANCE

Social Security was enacted in 1935 in an attempt to provide limited retirement and death benefits to certain employees. Since then, the benefits have increased greatly; the Federal Social Security system, which has expanded to cover almost all employees, now contains four major benefit programs: (1) Old-Age and Survivors Insurance (OASI) (providing retirement and survivor benefits), (2) Disability Insurance (DI), (3) Hospitalization Insurance (Medicare), and (4) Supplemental Security Income (SSI).

The system is financed by contributions (taxes) paid by employers, employees, and self-employed individuals. Employees and employers pay matching contributions. These contributions are calculated by multiplying the Social Security tax (a fixed percentage) times the employee's wages up to a specified maximum. Both the base tax rate and the maximum dollar amount are subject to change by Congress. It is the employer's responsibility to withhold the employee's contribution and to forward the full amount of the tax to the Internal Revenue Service. Contributions made by the employee are not tax deductible by the employee, whereas those made by the employer are tax deductible. Self-employed persons are also required to report their taxable income and to pay the combined employer and employee amount of Social Security tax.

The Federal **unemployment insurance** system was initially created by Title IX of the Social Security Act of 1935. Subsequently, Title IX was supplemented by the Federal Unemployment Tax Act and by numerous other Federal statutes. This complex system depends upon cooperation between State and Federal entities. Federal law provides the general guidelines, standards, and requirements for the program, while the States administer the program through their employment laws. The system is funded by employer taxes: Federal taxes generally pay the administrative costs of the program, and State contributions pay for the actual benefits. Due to the impact of the coronavirus pandemic, as of May 14, 2020, first-time claims for unemployment compensation over the previous two months exceeded 36 million.

Under the Federal Unemployment Tax Act, unemployment compensation is provided to workers who have lost their jobs, usually through no fault of their own. The Act is meant to help workers who are temporarily out of work and who need to support themselves while they search for jobs. Unemployed workers usually receive weekly payments in an amount based on each State's particular formula. Employees who voluntarily quit without good cause, who have been dismissed for misconduct, or who fail to look for or who refuse suitable work are not eligible for unemployment benefits.

42-3f FAIR LABOR STANDARDS ACT

The **Fair Labor Standards Act (FLSA)** regulates the employment of child labor outside of agriculture. The Act prohibits the employment of anyone under fourteen years of age in all nonfarm work except newspaper delivery and acting. Fourteen-and fifteen-year-olds may work for a limited number of hours outside of school hours under specific conditions in certain nonhazardous occupations. Sixteen-and seventeen-year-olds may work in any nonhazardous job, while persons eighteen years old or older may work in any job, whether it is hazardous or not. The Secretary of Labor determines which occupations are considered hazardous.

In addition, the FLSA imposes wage and hour requirements upon covered employers. With certain exceptions, the Act provides for a minimum hourly wage and overtime pay of time-and-a-half for hours worked in excess of forty hours per week; those workers exempted from both the FLSA's minimum wage and overtime provisions include professionals, managers, and outside salespersons.

In a 2018 case alleging violations of the FLSA, the U.S. Supreme Court addressed the question: "Should employees and employers be allowed to agree that any disputes between them will be resolved through one-on-one arbitration? Or should employees always be permitted to bring their claims in class or collective actions, no matter what they agreed with their employers?" In a 5–4 decision potentially affecting approximately 25 million nonunionized,

private-sector employees, the Court held that employers may enforce employment agreements that require employees to settle employment disputes through individual arbitration rather than in class or collective actions. *Epic Systems Corp. v. Lewis*, 584 U. S. ____ (2018).

42-3g WORKER ADJUSTMENT AND RETRAINING NOTIFICATION ACT

The **Worker Adjustment and Retraining Notification Act (WARN)** requires an employer to provide sixty days' advance notice of a plant closing or mass layoff. A "plant closing" is defined as the permanent or temporary shutting down of a single site or units within a site if the shutdown results in fifty or more employees losing employment during any thirty-day period. A "mass layoff" is defined as a loss of employment during a thirty-day period either for five hundred employees or for at least one-third of the employees at a given site, if that one-third equals or exceeds fifty employees. WARN requires that notification be given to specified State and local officials as well as to the affected employees or their union representatives. The Act, which reduces the notification period with regard to failing companies and emergency situations, applies to employers with a total of one hundred or more employees who in the aggregate work at least two thousand hours per week, not including overtime.

42-3h FAMILY AND MEDICAL LEAVE ACT

The **Family and Medical Leave Act** requires employers with fifty or more employees and governments at the Federal, State, and local levels to grant eligible employees up to twelve weeks of leave during any twelve-month period for the birth of a child; adopting or gaining foster care of a child; or the care of a spouse, child, or parent who suffers from a serious health condition. A "serious health condition" is defined as an "illness, injury, impairment or physical or mental condition" that involves inpatient medical care at a hospital, hospice, or residential care facility or continuing medical treatment by a health care provider. Employees are eligible for such leave if they have been employed by their present employer for at least twelve months and have worked at least 1,250 hours for their employer during the twelve months preceding the leave request. The requested leave may be paid, unpaid, or a combination of both.

LABOR LAW

Purpose to provide the general framework in which management and labor negotiate terms of employment

Norris-La Guardia Act established as U.S. policy the full freedom of labor to form labor unions without employer interference and withdrew from the Federal courts the power to issue injunctions in nonviolent labor disputes (any controversy concerning terms or conditions of employment or union representation)

National Labor Relations Act
- *Right to Unionize* declares it a Federally protected right of employees to unionize and to bargain collectively
- *Prohibits Unfair Employer Practices* the Act identifies five unfair labor practices by an employer
- *National Labor Relations Board* created to administer these rights

Labor-Management Relations Act
- *Prohibits Unfair Union Practices* the Act identifies seven unfair labor practices by a union
- *Prohibits Closed Shops* agreements that mandate that employers can hire only union members
- *Allows Union Shops* an employer can hire nonunion members, but the employee must join the union

Labor-Management Reporting and Disclosure Act aimed at eliminating corruption in labor unions

EMPLOYMENT DISCRIMINATION LAW

Equal Employment Opportunity Commission enforcement agency for Federal laws that make it illegal to discriminate against a job applicant or an employee because of the person's race, color, religion, sex, national origin, age, disability, or genetic information

Equal Pay Act prohibits an employer from discriminating between employees on the basis of gender by paying unequal wages for the same work

Civil Rights Act of 1964 prohibits employment discrimination on the basis of race, color, gender, religion, or national origin
- *Pregnancy Discrimination Act* extends the benefits of the Civil Rights Act to pregnant women
- *Affirmative Action* the active recruitment of a designated group of applicants
- *Discrimination* prohibited by the Act; includes (1) using proscribed criteria to produce disparate treatment, (2) engaging in nondiscriminatory conduct that perpetuates past discrimination, and (3) adopting neutral roles that have a disparate impact
- *Reverse Discrimination* affirmative action that directs an employer to consider an individual's race or gender when hiring or promoting for the purpose of remedying underrepresentation of that race or gender in traditionally segregated jobs
- *Defenses* four defenses are provided by the Act (1) a bona fide seniority or merit system, (2) a professionally developed ability test, (3) a compensation system based on performance results, and (4) a bona fide occupational qualification
- *Remedies* remedies for violation of the Act include injunctions, affirmative action, reinstatement, back pay, and compensatory and punitive damages
- *Sexual Harassment* an illegal form of sexual discrimination that includes unwelcome sexual advances, requests for sexual favors, and other verbal or physical conduct of a sexual nature

- *Comparable Worth* equal pay for jobs that are of equal value to the employer

Executive Order prohibits discrimination by Federal contractors on the basis of race, color, gender, religion, or national origin on any work the contractors perform during the period of the Federal contract

Age Discrimination in Employment Act of 1967 prohibits discrimination on the basis of age in hiring, firing, or compensating

Disability Law several Federal acts, including the Americans with Disabilities Act, provide assistance to the disabled in obtaining rehabilitation training, access to public facilities, and employment

Genetic Information Nondiscrimination Act forbids discrimination on the basis of genetic information with respect to any aspect of employment

---

EMPLOYEE PROTECTION

Employee Termination at Will under the common law, a contract of employment for other than a definite term is terminable at will by either party

- *Statutory Limitations* have been enacted by the Federal government and some States
- *Judicial Limitations* based on contract law, tort law, or public policy
- *Limitations Imposed by Union Contract*

Occupational Safety and Health Act enacted to assure workers of a safe and healthful work environment

Employee Privacy

- *Drug and Alcohol Testing* some States either prohibit such tests or prescribe certain scientific and procedural safeguards
- *Lie Detector Tests* Federal statute prohibits private employers from requiring employees or prospective employees to take such tests

Workers' Compensation compensation awarded to an employee who is injured in the course of his employment

Social Security measures by which the government provides economic assistance to disabled or retired employees and their dependents

Unemployment Compensation compensation awarded to workers who have lost their jobs and cannot find other employment

Fair Labor Standards Act regulates the employment of child labor outside of agriculture

Worker Adjustment and Retraining Notification Act Federal statute that requires an employer to provide sixty days' advance notice of a plant closing or mass layoff

Family and Medical Leave Act requires some employers to grant eligible employees leave for serious health conditions or certain other events

---

C A S E S

CASE 42-1

Employment Discrimination

ZARDA v. ALTITUDE EXPRESS, INC.

United States Court of Appeals, Second Circuit 2018
883 F.3d 100

Katzmann, C.J.

In the summer of 2010, Donald Zarda, a gay man, worked as a sky-diving instructor at Altitude Express. As part of his job, he regularly participated in tandem skydives, strapped hip-to-hip and shoulder-to-shoulder with clients. In an environment where close physical proximity was common, Zarda's co-workers routinely referenced sexual orientation or made sexual jokes around clients, and Zarda sometimes told female clients about his sexual orientation to assuage any concern they might have about being strapped to a man for a tandem skydive. That June, Zarda told a female client with whom he was preparing for a tandem skydive that he was gay "and ha[d] an ex-husband to prove it." * * * Although he later said this disclosure was intended simply to preempt any discomfort the client may have felt in being strapped to the body of an unfamiliar man, the client alleged that Zarda inappropriately touched her and disclosed his sexual orientation to excuse his behavior. After the jump was successfully completed, the client told her boyfriend about Zarda's alleged behavior and reference to his sexual orientation; the boyfriend in turn told Zarda's boss, who fired shortly Zarda thereafter. Zarda denied inappropriately touching the client and insisted he was fired solely because of his reference to his sexual orientation.

One month later, Zarda filed a discrimination charge with the EEOC concerning his termination. Zarda claimed that "in addition to being discriminated against because of [his] sexual orientation, [he] was also discriminated against because of [his] gender." [Citation.] In particular, he claimed that "[a]ll of the men at [his workplace] made light of the intimate nature of being strapped to a member of the opposite sex," but that he was fired because he "honestly referred to [his] sexual orientation and did not conform to the straight male macho stereotype." [Citation.]

In September 2010, Zarda brought a lawsuit in federal court alleging, inter alia, sex stereotyping in violation of Title VII and sexual orientation discrimination in violation of New York law. Defendants moved for summary judgment arguing that Zarda's Title VII claim should be dismissed because, although "Plaintiff testifie[d] repeatedly that he believe[d] the reason he was terminated [was] because of his sexual orientation … [,] under Title VII, a gender stereotype cannot be predicated on sexual orientation." [Citation.] In March 2014, the district court granted summary judgment to the defendants on the Title VII claim. As relevant here, the district court concluded that, although there was sufficient evidence to permit plaintiff to proceed with his claim for sexual orientation discrimination under New York law, plaintiff had failed to establish a prima facie case of gender stereotyping discrimination under Title VII.

* * *

[Zarda appealed. After a panel of the U.S. Court of Appeals for the Second Circuit ruled against Zarda, the Second Circuit convened a rehearing en banc.]

* * *

Although it is well-settled that gender stereotyping violates Title VII's prohibition on discrimination "because of … sex," we have previously held that sexual orientation discrimination claims, including claims that being gay or lesbian constitutes nonconformity with a gender stereotype, are not cognizable under Title VII. See *Simonton v. Runyon*, [citation]; see also *Dawson v. Bumble & Bumble*, [citation].

At the time *Simonton* and *Dawson* were decided, and for many years since, this view was consistent with the consensus among our sister circuits and the position of the Equal Employment Opportunity Commission * * *. [Citations.] Since then, two circuits have revisited the question of whether claims of sexual orientation discrimination are viable under Title VII. In March 2017, a divided panel of the Eleventh Circuit declined to recognize such a claim, * * *. One month later, the Seventh Circuit, sitting en banc, took "a fresh look at [its] position in light of developments at the Supreme Court extending over two decades" and held that "discrimination on the basis of sexual orientation is a form of sex discrimination." [Citation.] * * *

***

"In passing Title VII, Congress made the simple but momentous announcement that sex, race, religion, and national origin are not relevant to the selection, evaluation, or compensation of employees." [Citation.] * * *

In deciding whether Title VII prohibits sexual orientation discrimination, we are guided, as always, by the text and, in particular, by the phrase "because of … sex." * * * As defined by Title VII, an employer has engaged in "impermissible consideration of … sex … in employment practices" when "sex … was a motivating factor for any employment practice," irrespective of whether the employer was also motivated by "other factors." [Citation]. Accordingly, the critical inquiry for a court assessing whether an employment practice is "because of … sex" is whether sex was "a motivating factor." [Citation.]

Recognizing that Congress intended to make sex "irrelevant" to employment decisions, [citation], the Supreme Court has held that Title VII prohibits not just discrimination based on sex itself, but also discrimination based on traits that are a function of sex, such as life expectancy, [citation], and non-conformity with gender norms, [citation]. * * *

With this understanding in mind, the question before us is whether an employee's sex is necessarily a motivating factor in discrimination based on sexual orientation. If it is, then sexual orientation discrimination is properly understood as "a subset of actions taken on the basis of sex." [Citation.]

We now conclude that sexual orientation discrimination is motivated, at least in part, by sex and is thus a subset of sex discrimination. Looking first to the text of Title VII, the most natural reading of the statute's prohibition on discrimination "because of … sex" is that it extends to sexual orientation discrimination because sex is necessarily a factor in sexual orientation. This statutory reading is reinforced by considering the question from the perspective of sex stereotyping because sexual orientation discrimination is predicated on assumptions about how persons of a certain sex can or should be, which is an impermissible basis for adverse employment actions. * * *

We begin by considering the nature of sexual orientation discrimination. The term "sexual orientation" refers to "[a] person's predisposition or inclination toward sexual activity or behavior with other males or females" and is commonly categorized as "heterosexuality, homosexuality, or bisexuality." [Citation.] * * *

* * *

* * * Stated differently, because Congress could not anticipate the full spectrum of employment discrimination that would be directed at the protected categories, it falls to courts to give effect to the broad language that Congress used. [Citation] ("Title VII is a broad remedial measure, designed 'to assure equality of employment opportunities,'" [citation]

The Supreme Court gave voice to this principle of construction when it held that Title VII barred male-on-male sexual harassment, which "was assuredly not the principal evil Congress was concerned with when it enacted Title VII," * * *.

* * *

A plaintiff alleging disparate treatment based on sex in violation of Title VII must show two things: (1) that he was "discriminate[d] against … with respect to his compensation, terms, conditions, or privileges of employment," and (2) that the employer discriminated "because of … sex." [Citation.] * * *

* * * To determine whether a trait operates as a proxy for sex, we ask whether the employee would have been treated differently "but for" his or her sex. In the context of sexual orientation, a woman who is subject to an adverse employment action because she is attracted to women would have been treated differently if she had been a man who was attracted to women. We can therefore conclude that sexual orientation is a function of sex and, by extension, sexual orientation discrimination is a subset of sex discrimination.

* * *

The conclusion that sexual orientation discrimination is a subset of sex discrimination is further reinforced by viewing this issue through the lens of associational discrimination. Consistent with the nature of sexual orientation, in most contexts where an employer discriminates based on sexual orientation, the employer's decision is predicated on opposition to romantic association between particular sexes. For example, when an employer fires a gay man based on the belief that men should not be attracted to other men, the employer discriminates based on the employee's own sex. [Citation.]

* * *

* * * If an employer disapproves of close friendships among persons of opposite sexes and fires a female employee because she has male friends, the employee has been discriminated against because of her own sex. "Once we accept this premise, it makes little sense to carve out same-sex [romantic] relationships as an association to which these protections do not apply." [Citation.] Applying the reasoning of [citation], if a male employee married to a man is terminated because his employer disapproves of same-sex marriage, the employee has suffered associational discrimination based on his own sex because "the fact that the employee is a man instead of a woman motivated the employer's discrimination against him." [Citation.]

* * *

In sum, we see no principled basis for recognizing a violation of Title VII for associational discrimination based on race but not on sex. Accordingly, we hold that sexual orientation discrimination, which is based on an employer's opposition to association between particular sexes and thereby discriminates against an employee based on their own sex, constitutes discrimination "because of … sex." Therefore, it is no less repugnant to Title VII than anti-miscegenation policies.

* * *

Since 1964, the legal framework for evaluating Title VII claims has evolved substantially. Under [citation], traits that operate as a proxy for sex are an impermissible basis for disparate treatment of men and women. Under [citation], discrimination on the basis of sex stereotypes is prohibited. Under [citation], * * * it is unlawful to discriminate on the basis of an employee's association with persons of another race. Applying these precedents to sexual orientation discrimination, it is clear that there is "no justification in the statutory language … for a categorical rule excluding" such claims from the reach of Title VII. [Citations.]

Title VII's prohibition on sex discrimination applies to any practice in which sex is a motivating factor. [Citation.] As explained above, sexual orientation discrimination is a subset of sex discrimination because sexual orientation is defined by one's sex in relation to the sex of those to whom one is attracted, making it impossible for an employer to discriminate on the basis of sexual orientation without taking sex into account. Sexual orientation discrimination is also based on assumptions or stereotypes about how members of a particular gender should be, including to whom they should be attracted. Finally, sexual orientation discrimination is associational discrimination because an adverse employment action that is motivated by the employer's opposition to association between members of particular sexes discriminates against an employee on the basis of sex. Each of these three perspectives is sufficient to support this Court's conclusion and together they amply demonstrate that sexual orientation discrimination is a form of sex discrimination.

* * *

Zarda has alleged that, by "honestly referr[ing] to his sexual orientation," he failed to "conform to the straight male macho stereotype." For this reason, he has alleged a claim of discrimination of the kind we now hold cognizable under Title VII. * * * Thus, we hold that Zarda is entitled to bring a Title VII claim for discrimination based on sexual orientation.

* * *

Based on the foregoing, we VACATE the district court's judgment on the Title VII claim and REMAND for further proceedings consistent with this opinion. We AFFIRM the judgment of the district court in all other respects.

Civil Rights Act of 1964
BURLINGTON N. & S. F. R. CO. v. WHITE
Supreme Court of the United States, 2006
548 U.S. 53, 126 S.Ct. 2405, 165 L.Ed.2d 345

Breyer, J.

[Sheila White (White) was hired by Burlington Northern & Santa Fe Railway Company (Burlington) in June 1997 as a "track laborer," a job that involves removing and replacing track components, transporting track material, cutting brush, and clearing litter and cargo spillage from the right-of-way. White's primary responsibility soon became operating a forklift; however, she also performed some of the track laborer tasks. White was the only woman working in the Maintenance of Way department. In September 1997, White reported to Burlington officials that Bill Joiner (Joiner), her immediate supervisor, had repeatedly told her that women should not be working in the Maintenance of Way department and also had made insulting and inappropriate remarks to her in front of other colleagues. After Burlington conducted an internal investigation, Joiner was suspended for ten days and required to attend sexual harassment training. Marvin Brown, a Burlington manager, then reassigned White to standard track laborer tasks and completely removed her from forklift duty. Brown explained that the reassignment reflected coworker's complaints that in fairness, a "more senior man" should have the "less arduous and cleaner job" of forklift operator.

On October 10, White filed a complaint with the Equal Employment Opportunity Commission (EEOC). She claimed that the reassignment of her duties amounted to unlawful gender-based discrimination and retaliation for her having earlier complained about Joiner. In early December, White filed a second retaliation charge with the Commission, claiming that Brown had placed her under surveillance and was monitoring her daily activities. A few days later, White and her immediate supervisor, Percy Sharkey, had a disagreement. Sharkey told Brown that White had been insubordinate. Brown suspended White without pay, prompting White to initiate internal grievance procedures that eventually led Burlington to conclude White had not been insubordinate. White was reinstated with thirty-seven days' back pay for the time she was suspended. Based on the suspension, she then filed another EEOC charge for retaliation.

White filed a Title VII action against Burlington in federal court. A jury found in White's favor, awarding her $43,500 in damages for her claims of unlawful retaliation. Burlington appealed, arguing White did not suffer any harm from these acts of retaliation since she received back pay. The Sixth Circuit affirmed the district court's judgment for White. The U.S. Supreme Court granted *certiorari*.]

The anti-discrimination provision seeks a workplace where individuals are not discriminated against because of their racial, ethnic, religious, or gender-based status. [Citation.] The anti-retaliation provision seeks to secure that primary objective by preventing an employer from interfering (through retaliation) with an employee's efforts to secure or advance enforcement of the Act's basic guarantees. The substantive provision seeks to prevent injury to individuals based on who they are, *i.e.*, their status. The anti-retaliation provision seeks to prevent harm to individuals based on what they do, *i.e.*, their conduct.

To secure the first objective, Congress did not need to prohibit anything other than employment-related discrimination. The substantive provision's basic objective of "equality of employment opportunities" and the elimination of practices that tend to bring about "stratified job environments," [citation], would be achieved were all employment-related discrimination miraculously eliminated.

But one cannot secure the second objective by focusing only upon employer actions and harm that concern employment and the workplace. Were all such actions and harms eliminated, the anti-retaliation provision's objective would not be achieved. An employer can effectively retaliate against an employee by taking actions not directly related to his employment or by causing him harm *outside* the workplace. [Citations.] A provision limited to employment-related actions would not deter the many forms that effective retaliation can take. Hence, such a limited construction would fail to fully achieve the anti-retaliation provision's "primary purpose," namely, "[m]aintaining unfettered access to statutory remedial mechanisms." [Citation.]

Thus, purpose reinforces what language already indicates, namely, that the anti-retaliation provision, unlike the substantive provision, is not limited to discriminatory actions that affect the terms and conditions of employment. [Citation.]

* * *

* * * [W]e conclude that Title **VII's** substantive provision and its anti-retaliation provision are not coterminous. The scope of the anti-retaliation provision extends beyond workplace-related or employment-related retaliatory acts and harm. * * *

The anti-retaliation provision protects an individual not from all retaliation, but from retaliation that produces an injury or harm. * * * In our view, a plaintiff must show that a reasonable employee would have found the challenged action materially adverse, "which in this context means it well might have 'dissuaded a reasonable worker from making or supporting a charge of discrimination.'" [Citation.]

* * * The anti-retaliation provision seeks to prevent employer interference with "unfettered access" to Title VII's remedial mechanisms. [Citation.] It does so by prohibiting employer actions that are likely "to deter victims of discrimination from complaining to the EEOC," the courts, and their employers. [Citation.] And normally petty slights, minor annoyances, and simple lack of good manners will not create such deterrence. [Citation.]

We refer to reactions of a *reasonable* employee because we believe that the provision's standard for judging harm must be objective. An objective standard is judicially administrable. It avoids the uncertainties and unfair discrepancies that can plague a judicial effort to determine a plaintiff's unusual subjective feelings. * * *

We phrase the standard in general terms because the significance of any given act of retaliation will often depend upon the particular circumstances. Context matters. * * *

* * *

Applying this standard to the facts of this case, we believe that there was a sufficient evidentiary basis to support the jury's verdict on White's retaliation claim. [Citation.] The jury found that two of Burlington's actions amounted to retaliation: the reassignment of White from forklift duty to standard track laborer tasks and the 37-day suspension without pay.

* * * Our holding today makes clear that the jury was not required to find that the challenged actions were related to the terms or conditions of employment. And insofar as the jury also found that the actions were "materially adverse," its findings are adequately supported. * * *

To be sure, reassignment of job duties is not automatically actionable. Whether a particular reassignment is materially adverse depends upon the circumstances of the particular case, and "should be judged from the perspective of a reasonable person in the plaintiff's position, considering 'all the circumstances.'" [Citation.] But here, the jury had before it considerable evidence that the track labor duties were "by all accounts more arduous and dirtier"; that the "forklift operator position required more qualifications, which is an indication of prestige"; and that "the forklift operator position was objectively considered a better job and the male employees resented White for occupying it." [Citation.] Based on this record, a jury could reasonably conclude that the reassignment of responsibilities would have been materially adverse to a reasonable employee.

* * *

* * * White did receive backpay. But White and her family had to live for 37 days without income. They did not know during that time whether or when White could return to work. Many reasonable employees would find a month without a paycheck to be a serious hardship. And White described to the jury the physical and emotional hardship that 37 days of having "no income, no money" in fact caused. [Citation.] Indeed, she obtained medical treatment for her emotional distress. A reasonable employee facing the choice between retaining her job (and paycheck) and filing a discrimination complaint might well choose the former. That is to say, an indefinite suspension without pay could well act as a deterrent, even if the suspended employee eventually received backpay. [Citation.] Thus, the jury's conclusion that the 37-day suspension without pay was materially adverse was a reasonable one.

CASE
42-3

Discrimination
VANCE v. BALL STATE UNIVERSITY
Supreme Court of the United States, 2013
570 U.S. 421, 133 S. Ct. 2434, 186 L. Ed. 2d 565

Alito, J.

In this case, we decide a question left open in *Burlington Industries, Inc. v. Ellerth*, [citation], and *Faragher v. Boca Raton*, [citation, see Case 42-4], namely, who qualifies as a "supervisor" in a case in which an employee asserts a Title VII claim for workplace harassment?

Under Title VII, an employer's liability for such harassment may depend on the status of the harasser. If the harassing employee is the victim's co-worker, the employer is liable only if it was negligent in controlling working conditions. In cases in which the harasser is a "supervisor," however, different rules apply. If the supervisor's harassment culminates in a tangible employment action, the employer is strictly liable.

But if no tangible employment action is taken, the employer may escape liability by establishing, as an affirmative defense, that (1) the employer exercised reasonable care to prevent and correct any harassing behavior and (2) that the plaintiff unreasonably failed to take advantage of the preventive or corrective opportunities that the employer provided. [Citation.] Under this framework, therefore, it matters whether a harasser is a "supervisor" or simply a co-worker.

We hold that an employee is a "supervisor" for purposes of vicarious liability under Title VII if he or she is empowered by the employer to take tangible employment actions against the victim, and we therefore affirm the judgment of the Seventh Circuit.

I

Maetta Vance, an African-American woman, began working for Ball State University (BSU) in 1989 as a substitute server in the University Banquet and Catering division of Dining Services. In 1991, BSU promoted Vance to a part-time catering assistant position, and in 2007 she applied and was selected for a position as a full-time catering assistant. Over the course of her employment with BSU, Vance lodged numerous complaints of racial discrimination and retaliation, but most of those incidents are not at issue here. For present purposes, the only relevant incidents concern Vance's interactions with a fellow BSU employee, Saundra Davis. During the time in question, Davis, a white woman, was employed as a catering specialist in the Banquet and Catering division. The parties vigorously dispute the precise nature and scope of Davis' duties, but they agree that Davis did not have the power to hire, fire, demote, promote, transfer, or discipline Vance. * * * In late 2005 and early 2006, Vance filed internal complaints with BSU and charges with the Equal Employment Opportunity Commission (EEOC), alleging racial harassment and discrimination, and many of these complaints and charges pertained to Davis. [Citation.] Vance complained that Davis "gave her a hard time at work by glaring at her, slamming pots and pans around her, and intimidating her." She alleged that she was "left alone in the kitchen with Davis, who smiled at her"; that Davis "blocked" her on an elevator and "stood there with her cart smiling"; and that Davis often gave her "weird" looks. [Citation.]

Vance's workplace strife persisted despite BSU's attempts to address the problem. As a result, Vance filed this lawsuit in 2006 in the United States District Court for the Southern District of Indiana, claiming, among other things, that she had been subjected to a racially hostile work environment in violation of Title VII. In her complaint, she alleged that Davis was her supervisor and that BSU was liable for Davis' creation of a racially hostile work environment. [Citation.]

Both parties moved for summary judgment, and the District Court entered summary judgment in favor of BSU. The court explained that BSU could not be held vicariously liable for Davis' alleged racial harassment because Davis could not "hire, fire, demote, promote, transfer, or discipline" Vance and, as a result, was not Vance's supervisor under the Seventh Circuit's interpretation of that concept. [Citation.] The court further held that BSU could not be liable in negligence because it responded reasonably to the incidents of which it was aware. [Citation.]

The Seventh Circuit affirmed. * * *

II

A

Title VII of the Civil Rights Act of 1964 makes it "an unlawful employment practice for an employer ... to discriminate against any individual with respect to his compensation, terms, conditions, or privileges of employment, because of such individual's race, color, religion, sex, or national origin." [Citation.] This provision obviously prohibits discrimination with respect to employment decisions that have direct economic consequences, such as termination, demotion, and pay cuts. But not long after Title VII was enacted, the lower courts held that Title VII also reaches the creation or perpetuation of a discriminatory work environment.

* * * [T]he lower courts generally held that an employer was liable for a racially hostile work environment if the employer was negligent, i.e., if the employer knew or reasonably should have known about the harassment but failed to take remedial action. [Citation.]

When the issue eventually reached this Court, we agreed that Title VII prohibits the creation of a hostile work environment. [Citation.] In such cases, we have held, the plaintiff must show that the work environment was so pervaded by discrimination that the terms and conditions of employment were altered. [Citation.]

B

* * * [W]e have held that an employer is directly liable for an employee's unlawful harassment if the employer was negligent with respect to the offensive behavior. [Citation.] Courts have generally applied this rule to evaluate employer liability when a co-worker harasses the plaintiff.

In Ellerth and Faragher, however, we held that different rules apply where the harassing employee is the plaintiff's "supervisor." In those instances, an employer may be vicariously liable for its employees' creation of a hostile work environment. And in identifying the situations in which such vicarious liability is appropriate, we looked to the Restatement of Agency for guidance.

Under the Restatement, "masters" are generally not liable for the torts of their "servants" when the torts are committed outside the scope of the servants' employment. [Citation.] And because racial and sexual harassment are unlikely to fall within the scope of a servant's duties, application of this rule would generally preclude employer liability for employee harassment. [Citations.] But in Ellerth and Faragher, we held that a provision of the Restatement provided the basis for an exception. Section 219(2)(d) of that Restatement recognizes an exception to the general rule just noted for situations in which the servant was "aided in accomplishing the tort by the existence of the agency relation." [Citation.]

Adapting this concept to the Title VII context Ellerth and Faragher identified two situations in which the aided in-the-accomplishment rule warrants employer liability even in the absence of negligence, and both of these situations involve harassment by a "supervisor" as opposed to a co-worker. First, the Court held that an employer is vicariously liable "when a supervisor takes a tangible employment action," *Ellerth*, [citation]; *Faragher*, [citation]—i.e., "a significant change in employment status, such as hiring, firing, failing to promote, reassignment with significantly different responsibilities, or a decision causing a significant change in benefits." [Citation.] * * *

Second, *Ellerth* and *Faragher* held that, even when a supervisor's harassment does not culminate in a tangible employment action, the employer can be vicariously liable for the supervisor's creation of a hostile work environment if the employer is unable to establish an affirmative defense. [See Case 42-5.] * * *

* * *

C

Under *Ellerth* and *Faragher* it is obviously important whether an alleged harasser is a "supervisor" or merely a co-worker, and the lower courts have disagreed about the meaning of the concept of a supervisor in this context. * * *

* * *

III

We hold that an employer may be vicariously liable for an employee's unlawful harassment only when the employer has empowered that employee to take tangible employment actions against the victim, *i.e.*, to effect a "significant change in employment status, such as hiring, firing, failing to promote, reassignment with significantly different responsibilities, or a decision causing a significant change in benefits." [Citation.] * * *

* * *

* * * "Supervisor" is not a term used by Congress in Title VII. Rather, the term was adopted by this Court in *Ellerth* and *Faragher* as a label for the class of employees whose misconduct may give rise to vicarious employer liability. Accordingly, the way to understand the meaning of the term "supervisor" for present purposes is to consider the interpretation that best fits within the highly structured framework that those cases adopted.

* * *

[In those cases] this Court simply was not presented with the question of the degree of authority that an employee must have in order to be classified as a supervisor. * * *

* * *

C

Although our holdings in *Ellerth* and *Faragher* do not resolve the question now before us, we believe that the answer to that question is implicit in the characteristics of the framework that we adopted.

To begin, there is no hint in either *Ellerth* and *Faragher* that the Court contemplated anything other than a unitary category of supervisors, namely, those possessing the authority to effect a tangible change in a victim's terms or conditions of employment. The [citations] framework draws a sharp line between co-workers and supervisors. Co-workers, the Court noted, "can inflict psychological injuries" by creating a hostile work environment, but they "cannot dock another's pay, nor can one co-worker demote another." [Citation.] Only a supervisor has the power to cause "direct economic harm" by taking a tangible employment action. [Citation.] "Tangible employment actions fall within the special province of the supervisor. The supervisor has been empowered by the company *as a distinct class* of agent to make economic decisions affecting other employees under his or her control.... Tangible employment actions are the means by which the supervisor brings the official power of the enterprise to bear on subordinates." [Citation.] The strong implication of this passage is that the authority to take tangible employment actions is the defining characteristic of a supervisor, not simply a characteristic of a subset of an ill-defined class of employees who qualify as supervisors.

The way in which we framed the question presented in *Ellerth* as supervisors supports this understanding. As noted, the *Ellerth/Faragher* framework sets out two circumstances in which an employer may be vicariously liable for a supervisor's harassment. The first situation (which results in strict liability) exists when a supervisor actually takes a tangible employment action based on, for example, a subordinate's refusal to accede to sexual demands. The second situation (which results in vicarious liability if the employer cannot make out the requisite affirmative defense) is present when no such tangible action is taken. * * * [T]he Court couched the question at issue in the following terms: "whether an employer has vicarious liability when a supervisor creates a hostile work environment by making explicit threats to alter a subordinate's terms or conditions of employment, based on sex, but does not fulfill the threat." [Citation.] This statement plainly ties the second situation to a supervisor's authority to inflict direct economic injury. It is because a supervisor has that authority—and its potential use hangs as a threat over the victim—that vicarious liability (subject to the affirmative defense) is justified.

* * *

Under the definition of "supervisor" that we adopt today, the question of supervisor status, when contested, can very often be resolved as a matter of law before trial. The elimination of this issue from the trial will focus the efforts of the parties, who will be able to present their cases in a way that conforms to the framework that the jury will apply. The plaintiff will know whether he or she must prove that the employer was negligent or whether the employer will have the burden of proving the elements of the *Ellerth/Faragher* affirmative defense. Perhaps even more important, the work of the jury, which is inevitably complicated in employment discrimination cases, will be simplified. The jurors can be given preliminary instructions that allow them to understand, as the evidence comes in, how each item of proof fits into the framework that they will ultimately be required to apply. And even where the issue of supervisor status cannot be eliminated from the trial (because there are genuine factual disputes about an alleged harasser's authority to take tangible employment actions), this preliminary question is relatively straightforward.

* * *

IV
* * *

In any event, the dissent is wrong in claiming that our holding would preclude employer liability in other cases with facts similar to these. Assuming that a harasser is not a supervisor, a plaintiff could still prevail by showing that his or her employer was negligent in failing to prevent harassment from taking place. Evidence that an employer did not monitor the workplace, failed to respond to complaints, failed to provide a system for registering complaints, or effectively discouraged complaints from being filed would be relevant. Thus, it is not true, as the dissent asserts, that our holding "relieves scores of employers of responsibility" for the behavior of workers they employ. [Citation.]

* * *

Turning to the "specific facts" of petitioner's and Davis' working relationship, there is simply no evidence that Davis directed petitioner's day-to-day activities. The record indicates that Bill Kimes (the general manager of the Catering Division) and the chef assigned petitioner's daily tasks, which were given to her on "prep lists." The fact that Davis sometimes may have handed prep lists to petitioner, is insufficient to confer supervisor status, [citations].

* * *

We hold that an employee is a "supervisor" for purposes of vicarious liability under Title VII if he or she is empowered by the employer to take tangible employment actions against the victim. Because there is no evidence that BSU empowered Davis to take any tangible employment actions against Vance, the judgment of the Seventh Circuit is affirmed.

CASE
42-4

Proving Discrimination
RICCI v. DESTEFANO
Supreme Court of the United States, 2009
567 U.S. 557, 129 S.Ct. 2658, 174 L.Ed.2d 490

Kennedy, J.

In 2003, 118 New Haven firefighters took examinations to qualify for promotion to the rank of lieutenant or captain. Promotion examinations in New Haven (or City) were infrequent, so the stakes were high. The results would determine which firefighters would be considered for promotions during the next two years, and the order in which they would be considered. Many firefighters studied for months, at considerable personal and financial cost.

When the examination results showed that white candidates had outperformed minority candidates, the mayor and other local politicians opened a public debate that turned rancorous. Some firefighters argued the tests should be discarded because the results showed the tests to be discriminatory. They threatened a discrimination lawsuit if the City made promotions based on the tests. Other firefighters said the exams were neutral and fair. And they, in turn, threatened a discrimination lawsuit if the City, relying on the statistical racial disparity, ignored the test results and denied promotions to the candidates who had performed well. In the end the City took the side of those who protested the test results. It threw out the examinations.

Certain white and Hispanic firefighters who likely would have been promoted based on their good test performance sued the City and some of its officials. * * * The suit alleges that, by discarding the test results, the City and the named officials discriminated against the plaintiffs based on their race, in violation of both Title VII of the Civil Rights Act of 1964, [citation], and the Equal Protection Clause of the Fourteenth Amendment. The City and the officials defended their actions, arguing that if they had certified the results, they could have faced liability under Title VII for adopting a practice that had a disparate impact on the minority firefighters. The District Court granted summary judgment for the defendants, and the Court of Appeals affirmed.

We conclude that race-based action like the City's in this case is impermissible under Title VII unless the employer can demonstrate a strong basis in evidence that, had it not taken the action, it would have been liable under the disparate-impact statute. The respondents, we further determine, cannot meet that threshold standard. * * *

* * *

Title VII of the Civil Rights Act of 1964, [citation], prohibits employment discrimination on the basis of race, color, religion, sex, or national origin. Title VII prohibits both intentional discrimination (known as "disparate treatment") as well as, in some cases, practices that are not intended to discriminate but in fact have a disproportionately adverse effect on minorities (known as "disparate impact"). As enacted in 1964, Title VII's principal nondiscrimination provision held employers liable only for disparate treatment. That section retains its original wording today. It makes it unlawful for an employer "to fail or refuse to hire or to discharge any individual, or otherwise to discriminate against any individual with respect to his compensation, terms, conditions, or privileges of employment, because of such individual's race, color, religion, sex, or national origin." [Citation.] Disparate-treatment cases present "the most easily understood type of discrimination," [citation] and occur where an employer has "treated [a] particular person less favorably than others because of" a protected trait. [Citation.] A disparate-treatment plaintiff must establish "that the defendant had a discriminatory intent or motive" for taking a job-related action. [Citation.]

The Civil Rights Act of 1964 did not include an express prohibition on policies or practices that produce a disparate impact. But in *Griggs v. Duke Power Co.*, [citation], the Court interpreted the Act to prohibit, in some cases, employers' facially neutral practices that, in fact, are "discriminatory in operation." [Citation.] The *Griggs* Court stated that the "touchstone" for disparate impact liability is the lack of "business necessity": "If an employment practice which operates to exclude [minorities] cannot be shown to be related to job performance, the practice is prohibited." [Citations.]

Twenty years after *Griggs*, the Civil Rights Act of 1991, [citation], was enacted. The Act included a provision codifying the prohibition on disparate-impact discrimination. * * * Under the disparate-impact statute, a plaintiff establishes a prima facie violation by showing that an employer uses "a particular employment practice that causes a disparate impact on the basis of race, color, religion, sex, or national origin." [Citation.] An employer may defend against liability by demonstrating that the practice is "job related for the position in question and consistent with business necessity." [Citation.] Even if the employer meets that burden, however, a plaintiff may still succeed by showing that the employer refuses to adopt an available alternative employment practice that has less disparate impact and serves the employer's legitimate needs. [Citation.]

We consider, therefore, whether the purpose to avoid disparate-impact liability excuses what otherwise would be prohibited disparate-treatment discrimination. Courts often confront cases in which statutes and principles point in different directions. Our task is to provide guidance to employers and courts for situations when these two prohibitions could be in conflict absent a rule to reconcile them. In providing this guidance our decision must be consistent with the important purpose of Title VII—that the workplace be an environment free of discrimination, where race is not a barrier to opportunity.

* * *

[This] Court has held that certain government actions to remedy past racial discrimination—actions that are themselves based on race—are constitutional only where there is a "'strong basis in evidence'" that the remedial actions were necessary. [Citations.]

* * *

* * * Congress has imposed liability on employers for unintentional discrimination in order to rid the workplace of "practices that are fair in form, but discriminatory in operation." *Griggs*, [citation.]. But it has also prohibited employers from taking adverse employment actions "because of" race. [Citation.] Applying the strong-basis-in-evidence standard to Title VII gives effect to both the disparate-treatment and disparate-impact provisions, allowing violations of one in the name of compliance with the other only in certain, narrow circumstances. The standard leaves ample room for employers' voluntary compliance efforts, which are essential to the statutory scheme and to Congress's efforts to eradicate workplace discrimination. [Citation.] And the standard appropriately constrains employers' discretion in making race-based decisions: It limits that discretion to cases in which there is a strong basis in evidence of disparate-impact liability, but it is not so restrictive that it allows employers to act only when there is a provable, actual violation.

Resolving the statutory conflict in this way allows the disparate-impact prohibition to work in a manner that is consistent with other provisions of Title VII, including the prohibition on adjusting employment-related test scores on the basis of race. [Citation.] Examinations like those administered by the City create legitimate expectations on the part of those who took the tests. As is the case with any promotion exam, some of the firefighters here invested substantial time, money, and personal commitment in preparing for the tests. Employment tests can be an important part of a neutral selection system that safeguards against the very racial animosities Title VII was intended to prevent. Here, however, the firefighters saw their efforts invalidated by the City in sole reliance upon race-based statistics.

If an employer cannot rescore a test based on the candidates' race, [citation], then it follows *a fortiori* that it may not take the greater step of discarding the test altogether to achieve a more desirable racial distribution of promotion-eligible candidates—absent a strong basis in evidence that the test was deficient and that discarding the results is necessary to avoid violating the disparate impact provision. Restricting an employer's ability to discard test results (and thereby discriminate against qualified candidates on the basis of their race) also is in keeping with Title VII's express protection of bona fide promotional examinations. [Citations.]

For the foregoing reasons, we adopt the strong-basis-in evidence standard as a matter of statutory construction to resolve any conflict between the disparate-treatment and disparate-impact provisions of Title VII.

* * *

* * * We hold only that, under Title VII, before an employer can engage in intentional discrimination for the asserted purpose of avoiding or remedying an unintentional disparate impact, the employer must have a strong basis in evidence to believe it will be subject to disparate-impact liability if it fails to take the race-conscious, discriminatory action.

CASE 42-5

Sexual Harassment
FARAGHER v. CITY OF BOCA RATON
Supreme Court of the United States, 1998
524 U.S. 775, 118 S.Ct. 2275, 141 L.Ed.2d 662

Souter, J.

This case calls for identification of the circumstances under which an employer may be held liable under Title VII of the Civil Rights Act of 1964, [citation], for the acts of a supervisory employee whose sexual harassment of subordinates has created a hostile work environment amounting to employment discrimination. We hold that an employer is vicariously liable for actionable discrimination caused by a supervisor, but subject to an affirmative defense looking to the reasonableness of the employer's conduct as well as that of a plaintiff victim.

I

Between 1985 and 1990, while attending college, petitioner Beth Ann Faragher worked part time and during the summers as an ocean lifeguard for the Marine Safety Section of the Parks and Recreation Department of respondent, the City of Boca Raton, Florida (City). During this period, Faragher's immediate supervisors were Bill Terry, David Silverman, and Robert Gordon. In June 1990, Faragher resigned.

* * *

In February 1986, the City adopted a sexual harassment policy, which it stated in a memorandum from the City Manager addressed to all employees. [Citation.] In May 1990, the City revised the policy and reissued a statement of it. Although the City may actually have circulated the memos and statements to some employees, it completely failed to disseminate its policy among employees of the Marine Safety Section, with the result that Terry, Silverman, Gordon, and many lifeguards were unaware of it. [Citation.]

From time to time over the course of Faragher's tenure at the Marine Safety Section, between 4 and 6 of the 40 to 50 lifeguards were women. During that 5-year period, Terry repeatedly touched the bodies of female employees without invitation, [citation], would put his arm around Faragher, with his hand on her buttocks, [citation], and once made contact with another female lifeguard in a motion of sexual simulation, [citation]. He made crudely demeaning references to women generally, and once commented disparagingly on Faragher's shape, [citation]. During a job interview with a woman he hired as a lifeguard, Terry said that the female lifeguards had sex with their male counterparts and asked whether she would do the same. [Citation.]

Silverman behaved in similar ways. He once tackled Faragher and remarked that, but for a physical characteristic he found unattractive, he would readily have had sexual relations with her. [Citation.] Another time, he pantomimed an act of oral sex. [Citation.] Within ear-shot of the female lifeguards, Silverman made frequent, vulgar references to women and sexual matters, commented on the bodies of female lifeguards and beachgoers, and at least twice told female lifeguards that he would like to engage in sex with them. [Citation.]

Faragher did not complain to higher management about Terry or Silverman. Although she spoke of their behavior to Gordon, she did not regard these discussions as formal complaints to a supervisor but as conversations with a person she held in high esteem. [Citation.] Other female lifeguards had similarly informal talks with Gordon, but because Gordon did not feel that it was his place to do so, he did not report these complaints to Terry, his own supervisor, or to any other city official. [Citation.] Gordon responded to the complaints of one lifeguard by saying that "the City just [doesn't] care." [Citation.]

In April 1990, however, two months before Faragher's resignation, Nancy Ewanchew, a former lifeguard, wrote to Richard Bender, the City's Personnel Director, complaining that Terry and Silverman had harassed her and other female lifeguards. Following investigation of this complaint, the City found that Terry and Silverman had behaved improperly, reprimanded them, and required them to choose between a suspension without pay or the forfeiture of annual leave. [Citation.]

On the basis of these findings, the District Court concluded that the conduct of Terry and Silverman was discriminatory harassment sufficiently serious to alter the conditions of

Faragher's employment and constitute an abusive working environment. [Citation.] The District Court then ruled that there were three justifications for holding the City liable for the harassment of its supervisory employees. First, the court noted that the harassment was pervasive enough to support an inference that the City had "knowledge, or constructive knowledge" of it. [Citation.] Next, it ruled that the City was liable under traditional agency principles because Terry and Silverman were acting as its agents when they committed the harassing acts. [Citation.] Finally, the court observed that Gordon's knowledge of the harassment, combined with his inaction, "provides a further basis for imputing liability on [sic] the City." [Citation.] The District Court then awarded Faragher one dollar in nominal damages on her Title VII claim. [Citation.]

A panel of the Court of Appeals for the Eleventh Circuit reversed the judgment against the City. [Citation.] Although the panel had "no trouble concluding that Terry's and Silverman's conduct … was severe and pervasive enough to create an objectively abusive work environment," [citation], it overturned the District Court's conclusion that the City was liable. The panel ruled that Terry and Silverman were not acting within the scope of their employment when they engaged in the harassment, that they were not aided in their actions by the agency relationship, [citation], and that the City had no constructive knowledge of the harassment by virtue of its pervasiveness or Gordon's actual knowledge, [citation].

In a 7-to-5 decision, the full Court of Appeals, sitting en banc, adopted the panel's conclusion. [Citation.] * * *

* * *

II

118 S.Ct. 2275A

Thus, in *Meritor* we held that sexual harassment so "severe or pervasive" as to "alter the conditions of [the victim's] employment and create an abusive working environment" violates Title VII. [Citation.]

* * *

So, in *Harris*, we explained that in order to be actionable under the statute, a sexually objectionable environment must be both objectively and subjectively offensive, one that a reasonable person would find hostile or abusive, and one that the victim in fact did perceive to be so. [Citation.] We directed courts to determine whether an environment is sufficiently hostile or abusive by "looking at all the circumstances," including the "frequency of the discriminatory conduct; its severity; whether it is physically threatening or humiliating, or a mere offensive utterance; and whether it unreasonably interferes with an employee's work performance." [Citation.] Most recently, we explained that Title VII does not prohibit "genuine but innocuous differences in the ways men and women routinely interact with members of the same sex and of the opposite sex." *Oncale*, [citation]. A recurring point in these opinions is that "simple teasing," [citation], "off hand comments, and isolated incidents (unless extremely serious) will not amount to discriminatory changes in the "terms and conditions of employment."

These standards for judging hostility are sufficiently demanding to ensure that Title VII does not become a "general civility code." [Citation.] Properly applied, they will filter out complaints attacking "the ordinary tribulations of the workplace, such as the sporadic use of abusive language, gender-related jokes, and occasional teasing." [Citations.]

While indicating the substantive contours of the hostile environments forbidden by Title VII, our cases have established few definite rules for determining when an employer will be liable for a discriminatory environment that is otherwise actionably abusive. * * * There have, for example, been myriad cases in which District Courts and Courts of Appeals have held employers liable on account of actual knowledge by the employer, or high-echelon officials of an employer organization, of sufficiently harassing action by subordinates, which the employer or its informed officers have done nothing to stop. * * *

* * *

B

* * *

In order to accommodate the principle of vicarious liability for harm caused by misuse of supervisory authority, as well as Title VII's equally basic policies of encouraging forethought by employers and saving action by objecting employees, we adopt the following holding in this case and in *Burlington Industries, Inc. v. Ellerth*, [citation], also decided today. An employer is subject to vicarious liability to a victimized employee for an actionable hostile environment created by a supervisor with immediate (or successively higher) authority over the employee. When no tangible employment action is taken, a defending employer may raise an affirmative defense to liability or damages, subject to proof by a preponderance of the evidence, see [citation]. The defense comprises two necessary elements: (a) that the employer exercised reasonable care to prevent and correct promptly any sexually harassing behavior, and (b) that the plaintiff employee unreasonably failed to take advantage of any preventive or corrective opportunities provided by the employer or to avoid harm otherwise. While proof that an employer had promulgated an antiharassment policy with complaint procedure is not necessary in every instance as a matter of law, the need for a stated policy suitable to the employment circumstances may appropriately be addressed in any case when litigating the first element of the defense. And while proof that an employee failed to fulfill the corresponding obligation of reasonable care to avoid harm is not limited to showing an unreasonable failure to use any complaint procedure provided by the employer, a demonstration of such failure will normally suffice to satisfy the employer's burden under the second element of the defense. No affirmative defense is available, however, when the supervisor's harassment culminates in a tangible employment action, such as discharge, demotion, or undesirable reassignment. [Citation.]

Applying these rules here, we believe that the judgment of the Court of Appeals must be reversed. The District Court found that the degree of hostility in the work environment rose to the actionable level and was attributable to Silverman and Terry. It is undisputed that these supervisors "were granted virtually unchecked authority" over their subordinates, "directly control[ing] and supervise[ing] all aspects of [Faragher's] day-to-day activities." [Citation.] It is also clear that Faragher and her colleagues were "completely isolated from the City's higher management." [Citation.] The City did not seek review of these findings.

While the City would have an opportunity to raise an affirmative defense if there were any serious prospect of its presenting one, it appears from the record that any such avenue is closed. The District Court found that the City had entirely failed to disseminate its policy against sexual harassment among the beach employees and that its officials made no attempt to keep track of the conduct of supervisors like Terry and Silverman. The record also makes clear that the City's policy did not include any assurance that the harassing supervisors could be bypassed in registering complaints. Under such circumstances, we hold as a matter of law that the City could not be found to have exercised reasonable care to prevent the supervisors' harassing conduct. Unlike the employer of a small workforce, who might expect that sufficient care to prevent tortious behavior could be exercised informally, those responsible for city operations could not reasonably have thought that precautions against hostile environments in any one of many departments in far-flung locations could be effective without communicating some formal policy against harassment, with a sensible complaint procedure.

III

The Court of Appeals also rejected the possibility that it could hold the City liable for the reason that it knew of the harassment vicariously through the knowledge of its supervisors. We have no occasion to consider whether this was error, however. We are satisfied that liability on the ground of vicarious knowledge could not be determined without further factfinding on remand, whereas the reversal necessary on the theory of supervisory harassment renders any remand for consideration of imputed knowledge entirely unjustifiable (as would be any consideration of negligence as an alternative to a theory of vicarious liability here).

IV

The judgment of the Court of Appeals for the Eleventh Circuit is reversed, and the case is remanded for reinstatement of the judgment of the District Court.

<table>
<tr><td>CASE
42-6</td><td>Discrimination Based on Disability
YOUNG v. UNITED PARCEL SERVICE, INC.
Supreme Court of the United States, 2015
575 U.S. _____ , 135 S.Ct. 1338, 191 L.Ed.2d 279</td><td></td></tr>
</table>

Breyer, J.

The Pregnancy Discrimination Act makes clear that Title VII's prohibition against sex discrimination applies to discrimination based on pregnancy. It also says that employers must treat "women affected by pregnancy … the same for all employment-related purposes … as other persons not so affected but similar in their ability or in-ability to work." [Citation.] We must decide how this latter provision applies in the context of an employer's policy that accommodates many, but not all, workers with nonpregnancy-related disabilities.

In our view, the Act requires courts to consider the extent to which an employer's policy treats pregnant workers less favorably than it treats nonpregnant workers similar in their ability or inability to work. And here—as in all cases in which an individual plaintiff seeks to show disparate treatment through indirect evidence—it requires courts to consider any legitimate, nondiscriminatory, nonpretextual justification for these differences in treatment. [Citation.] Ultimately the court must determine whether the nature of the employer's policy and the way in which it burdens pregnant women shows that the employer has engaged in intentional discrimination. The Court of Appeals here affirmed a grant of summary judgment in favor of the employer. * * *

We begin with a summary of the facts. The petitioner, Peggy Young, worked as a part-time driver for the respondent, United Parcel Service (UPS). Her responsibilities included pickup and delivery of packages that had arrived by air carrier the previous night. In 2006, after suffering several miscarriages, she became pregnant. Her doctor told her that she should not lift more than 20 pounds during the first 20 weeks of her pregnancy or more than 10 pounds thereafter. UPS required drivers like Young to be able to lift parcels weighing up to 70 pounds (and up to 150 pounds with assistance). UPS told Young she could not work while under a lifting restriction. Young consequently stayed home without pay during most of the time she was pregnant and eventually lost her employee medical coverage.

Young subsequently brought this federal lawsuit. We focus here on her claim that UPS acted unlawfully in refusing to accommodate her pregnancy-related lifting restriction. Young said that her co-workers were willing to help her with heavy packages. She also said that UPS accommodated other drivers who were "similar in their … inability to work." She accordingly concluded that UPS must accommodate her as well.

UPS responded that the "other persons" whom it had accommodated were (1) drivers who had become disabled on the job, (2) those who had lost their Department of Transportation (DOT) certifications, and (3) those who suffered from a disability covered by the Americans with Disabilities Act of 1990 (ADA), [citation.] UPS said that, since Young did not fall within any of those categories, it had not discriminated against Young on the basis of pregnancy but had treated her just as it treated all "other" relevant "persons."

Title VII of the Civil Rights Act of 1964 forbids a covered employer to "discriminate against any individual with respect to … terms, conditions, or privileges of employment, because of such individual's … sex." [Citation.] In 1978, Congress enacted the Pregnancy Discrimination Act, [citation], which added new language to Title VII's definitions subsection. The first clause of the 1978 Act specifies that Title VII's "ter[m] 'because of sex' … include[s] … because of or on the basis of pregnancy, childbirth, or related medical conditions." [Citation.] The second clause says that

"women affected by pregnancy, childbirth, or related medical conditions shall be treated the same for all employment-related purposes … as other persons not so affected but similar in their ability or inability to work.…" [Citation.]

This case requires us to consider the application of the second clause to a "disparate-treatment" claim—a claim that an employer intentionally treated a complainant less favorably than employees with the "complainant's qualifications" but outside the complainant's protected class. [Citation.] We have said that "[l]iability in a disparate-treatment case depends on whether the protected trait actually motivated the employer's decision." [Citation.] We have also made clear that a plaintiff can prove disparate treatment either (1) by direct evidence that a workplace policy, practice, or decision relies expressly on a protected characteristic, or (2) by using the burden-shifting framework [Citation.].

In *McDonnell Douglas*, we considered a claim of discriminatory hiring. We said that, to prove disparate treatment, an individual plaintiff must "carry the initial burden" of "establishing a prima facie case" of discrimination by showing

"(i) that he belongs to a … minority; (ii) that he applied and was qualified for a job for which the employer was seeking applicants; (iii) that, despite his qualifications, he was rejected; and (iv) that, after his rejection, the position remained open and the employer continued to seek applicants from persons of complainant's qualifications." [Citation.]

If a plaintiff makes this showing, then the employer must have an opportunity "to articulate some legitimate, nondiscriminatory reason for" treating employees outside the protected class better than employees within the protected class. [Citation.] If the employer articulates such a reason, the plaintiff then has "an opportunity to prove by a preponderance of the evidence that the legitimate reasons offered by the defendant [*i.e.*, the employer] were not its true reasons, but were a pretext for discrimination." [Citation.]

We note that employment discrimination law also creates what is called a "disparate-impact" claim. In evaluating a disparate-impact claim, courts focus on the *effects* of an employment practice, determining whether they are unlawful irrespective of motivation or intent. [Citation.] But Young has not alleged a disparate-impact claim.

* * *

The [UPS] manager * * * determined that Young did not qualify for a temporary alternative work assignment. [Citation.]

* * *

When Young later asked UPS' Capital Division Manager to accommodate her disability, he replied that, while she was pregnant, she was "too much of a liability" and could "not come back" until she "was no longer pregnant." [Citation.]

* * *

Young returned to work as a driver in June 2007, about two months after her baby was born. [Citation.]

As direct evidence of intentional discrimination, Young relied, in significant part, on the statement of the Capital Division Manager * * *. As evidence that she had made out a prima facie case under *McDonnell Douglas*, Young relied, in significant part, on evidence showing that UPS would accommodate workers injured on the job, those suffering from ADA disabilities, and those who had lost their DOT certifications. That evidence, she said, showed that UPS had a light-duty-for-injury policy with respect to numerous "other persons," but not with respect to pregnant workers.

Young introduced further evidence indicating that UPS had accommodated several individuals when they suffered disabilities that created work restrictions similar to hers. * * *

We note that statutory changes made after the time of Young's pregnancy may limit the future significance of our interpretation of the Act. In 2008, Congress expanded the definition of "disability" under the ADA to make clear that "physical or mental impairment[s] that substantially limi[t]" an individual's ability to lift, stand, or bend are ADA-covered disabilities. ADA Amendments Act of 2008. As interpreted by the EEOC, the new statutory definition requires employers to accommodate employees whose temporary lifting restrictions originate off the job. * * *

The parties disagree about the interpretation of the Pregnancy Discrimination Act's second clause * * * [T]he meaning of the second clause is less clear; it adds: "[W]omen affected by pregnancy, childbirth, or related medical conditions shall be treated the same for all employment-related purposes … as *other persons* not so affected but *similar in their ability or inability to work*." [Citation.] Does this clause mean that courts must compare workers only in respect to the work limitations that they suffer? Does it mean that courts must ignore all other similarities or differences between pregnant and nonpregnant workers? Or does it mean that courts, when deciding who the relevant "other persons" are, may consider other similarities and differences as well? If so, which ones?

* * *

* * * disparate-treatment law normally permits an employer to implement policies that are not intended to harm members of a protected class, even if their implementation sometimes harms those members, as long as the employer has a legitimate, nondiscriminatory, nonpretextual reason for doing so [Citation.] There is no reason to believe Congress intended its language in the Pregnancy Discrimination Act to embody a significant deviation from this approach. * * *

Before Congress passed the Pregnancy Discrimination Act, the EEOC issued guidance stating that "[d]isabilities caused or contributed to by pregnancy … are, for all job-related purposes, temporary disabilities" and that "the availability of … benefits and privileges … shall be applied to disability due to pregnancy or childbirth on the same terms and conditions as they are applied to other temporary disabilities." [Citation.] Indeed, as early as 1972, EEOC guidelines provided: "Disabilities caused or contributed to by pregnancy … are, for all job-related purposes, temporary disabilities and should be treated as such under any health or temporary disability insurance or sick leave plan available in connection with employment." [Citation.]* * *

More recently—in July 2014—the EEOC promulgated an additional guideline apparently designed to address this ambiguity. That guideline says that "[a]n employer may not refuse to treat a pregnant worker the same as other employees who are similar in their ability or inability to work by relying on a policy that makes distinctions based on the source of an employee's limitations (e.g., a policy of providing light duty only to workers injured on the job)." [Citation.] The EEOC also provided an example of disparate treatment that would violate the Act:

> "An employer has a policy or practice of providing light duty, subject to availability, for any employee who cannot perform one or more job duties for up to 90 days due to injury, illness, or a condition that would be a disability under the ADA. An employee requests a light duty assignment for a 20-pound lifting restriction related to her pregnancy. The employer denies the light duty request."

The EEOC further added that "an employer may not deny light duty to a pregnant employee based on a policy that limits light duty to employees with on-the-job injuries."

* * *

* * * The EEOC promulgated its 2014 guidelines only recently, after this Court had granted certiorari in this case. In these circumstances, it is fair to say that the EEOC's current guidelines take a position about which the EEOC's previous guidelines were silent. And that position is inconsistent with positions for which the Government has long advocated. * * * Without further explanation, we cannot rely significantly on the EEOC's determination.

* * *

In our view, an individual pregnant worker who seeks to show disparate treatment through indirect evidence may do so through application of the *McDonnell Douglas* framework. That framework requires a plaintiff to make out a prima facie case of discrimination. But it is "not intended to be an inflexible rule." [Citation.] Rather, an individual plaintiff may establish a prima facie case by "showing actions taken by the employer from which one can infer, if such actions remain unexplained, that it is more likely than not that such actions were based on a discriminatory criterion illegal under" Title VII. [Citation.] In particular, making this showing is not as burdensome as succeeding on "an ultimate finding of fact as to" a discriminatory employment action. [Citation.] Neither does it require the plaintiff to show that those whom the employer favored and those whom the employer disfavored were similar in all but the protected ways. [Citation.]

Thus, a plaintiff alleging that the denial of an accommodation constituted disparate treatment under the Pregnancy Discrimination Act's second clause may make out a prima facie case by showing, as in *McDonnell Douglas*, that she belongs to the protected class, that she sought accommodation, that the employer did not accommodate her, and that the employer did accommodate others "similar in their ability or inability to work."

The employer may then seek to justify its refusal to accommodate the plaintiff by relying on "legitimate, nondiscriminatory" reasons for denying her accommodation. [Citation.] But, consistent with the Act's basic objective, that reason normally cannot consist simply of a claim that it is more expensive or less convenient to add pregnant women to the category of those ("similar in their ability or inability to work") whom the employer accommodates. * * *

If the employer offers an apparently "legitimate, nondiscriminatory" reason for its actions, the plaintiff may in turn show that the employer's proffered reasons are in fact pretextual. We believe that the plaintiff may reach a jury on this issue by providing sufficient evidence that the employer's policies impose a significant burden on pregnant workers, and that the employer's "legitimate, nondiscriminatory" reasons are not sufficiently strong to justify the burden, but rather—when considered along with the burden imposed—give rise to an inference of intentional discrimination.

* * *

Under this interpretation of the Act, the judgment of the Fourth Circuit must be vacated. A party is entitled to summary judgment if there is "no genuine dispute as to any material fact and the movant is entitled to judgment as a matter of law." [Citation.] We have already outlined the evidence Young introduced. [Citation.]. Viewing the record in the light most favorable to Young, there is a genuine dispute as to whether UPS provided more favorable treatment to at least some employees whose situation cannot reasonably be distinguished from Young's. In other words, Young created a genuine dispute of material fact as to the fourth prong of the *McDonnell Douglas* analysis.

* * *

We do not determine whether Young created a genuine issue of material fact as to whether UPS' reasons for having treated Young less favorably than it treated these other nonpregnant employees were pretextual. We leave a final determination of that question for the Fourth Circuit to make on remand, in light of the interpretation of the Pregnancy Discrimination Act that we have set out above.

* * *

For the reasons above, we vacate the judgment of the Fourth Circuit and remand the case for further proceedings consistent with this opinion.

CASE
42-7

Termination at Will
JASPER v. H. NIZAM, INC.
Supreme Court of Iowa, 2009
764 N.W.2d 751

Cady, J.
This case arose when Kimberly Jasper was terminated from her employment as the director of a child care facility in Johnston, Iowa, called Kid University. The center was owned by H. Nizam, Inc. Mohsin Hussain was the president of the corporation. Zakia Hussain was the vice president. The Hussains were married. Mohsin Hussain was a special education teacher for the Des Moines School District and was not involved in the day-to-day operation of the center.

Jasper began her employment as director of the center in late August 2003. She was paid an hourly wage. There was no specific term of employment. A few weeks after Jasper started her employment, she and her husband agreed to rent a home owned by the Hussains. The Jaspers had moved to Des Moines from Arizona and were looking for housing at the time. Jasper learned the Hussain house was available to rent when she and Hussain went to the house to retrieve some equipment to use at the day care center that was stored in the house. The house had four bedrooms and two bathrooms, but had sustained

substantial water damage and was in a general state of disrepair. The agreed monthly rent was $10, plus utilities, and the Jaspers were required to make all repairs to the house at their own expense.

Within a short time after Jasper started her employment, Hussain told her the center was not making enough money to justify the size of the staff. He also encouraged Jasper to attract more children to the center. Jasper responded by telling Hussain that any staff cuts would place the center in jeopardy of violating state regulations governing the minimum ratios between staff and children. [Citation.] Hussain was generally aware of the staffing requirements imposed by state regulations through his contact with a consultant and compliance official from the Iowa Department of Human Services. The consultant dealt with licensing and regulatory compliance of child care facilities. She would periodically stop by the center to determine if the facility was being operated in compliance with all regulations. Hussain had also hired a private consultant prior to employing Jasper. The private consultant also informed Hussain of the necessity to comply with the state ratio requirements. Within a month after Jasper started her employment, Hussain was again told of the staffing ratios at a meeting with both consultants and Jasper.

The staff-to-child ratio became a frequent subject of conversation, and friction, between Hussain and Jasper. Hussain was persistent in his desire to reduce staff to decrease expenses, and Jasper was adamant that the current staff was necessary to meet the minimum staffing ratios under the state regulations. During one meeting with the Hussains and Jasper in early November, staff reductions were again discussed. Jasper claimed Zakia Hussain said, "What [the department of human services consultant] doesn't know won't hurt her." Hussain made no response to the statement. In fact, Hussain never specifically told Jasper to violate or ignore the staffing regulations.

At a meeting between Hussain and Jasper later in November, Hussain proposed that Jasper and her assistant director begin to work as staff in the classrooms occupied by the children as a means to cut staff and reduce expenses. Jasper objected to the plan as unreasonable. She believed it would prevent her from performing her duties as director of the center and risk placing the center in violation of the ratio regulations.

On December 1, 2003, Hussain terminated Jasper from her employment with Kid University shortly after she arrived for work at the center in the morning. She was handed a written letter listing the reasons for the termination and was escorted outside the building. A confrontation followed after she was told she could not return to the building to remove her children from the day-care center, and police were called.

Hussain also brought a forcible entry and detainer action against the Jaspers for failing to pay the December rent. Jasper and her family subsequently moved from the house, and she obtained new employment with another child care facility in April 2004.

Jasper brought a wrongful discharge action against the corporation and Hussain individually. She claimed Hussain terminated her employment because she refused to violate the staff-to-child ratios, in violation of public policy of this state. She sought damages for lost earnings, emotional pain and suffering, and punitive damages. She also sought damages relating to the termination of the rental agreement and for unreimbursed expenses relating to improvements made to the center. At trial, Jasper presented testimony that the center violated the staff-to-child ratios shortly after she was terminated. This violation occurred when one staff member was left in a classroom to supervise five or more children between the ages of one and two years old. The regulations promulgated by the department of human services required one staff member for every four children under the age of two. However, the district court refused to permit Jasper to present evidence that a second day care facility owned by

Hussain had been cited by the state for violating the staff-to-child ratios.

* * *

The jury returned a verdict for Jasper against the corporation and Hussain individually, based solely on the tort of wrongful discharge in violation of public policy. The jury awarded Jasper lost wages of $26,915 and past pain and suffering of $100,000. It awarded her $39,507.25 for expenses relating to the house and additional services and expenses. The district court refused to submit the punitive-damage claim to the jury.

* * *

Jasper appealed, * * * . The court of appeals determined a clear public policy existed in Iowa that child care centers be adequately staffed. It also found Jasper presented substantial evidence to support a finding that she refused to reduce staff below the minimum ratios and that this conduct was the cause of her termination. The court of appeals then determined the district court did not err in finding the $100,000 award for emotional distress was excessive and in setting aside the award of $39,507.25 for additional services and housing expenses.

* * *

We adhere to the common-law employment-at-will doctrine in Iowa. [Citation.] However, we joined the parade of other states twenty years ago in adopting the public-policy exception to the employment-at-will doctrine. [Citation.] In doing so, we recognized a cause of action in Iowa for wrongful discharge from employment when the reasons for the discharge contravene public policy. [Citation.] Since the adoption of this exception, we have identified and explained the elements of the cause of action. [Citation.] These elements are: (1) existence of a clearly defined public policy that protects employee activity; (2) the public policy would be jeopardized by the discharge from employment; (3) the employee engaged in the protected activity, and this conduct was the reason for the employee's discharge; and (4) there was no overriding business justification for the termination. [Citation.]

This case primarily focuses on the public-policy element of the tort and ultimately requires us to decide if the source of public policy can be derived from administrative regulations. Yet, the case also requires us to consider the parameters of the public-policy element and to dig into the element to unearth and identify the often difficult distinction between a claim based on public policy and a claim based on a private dispute between an employer and employee. In this way, we must also consider the element of the tort that requires the employee to establish that the discharge was caused by the employee's participation in an activity protected by public policy.

Sources of Public Policy

The concept of public policy generally captures the communal conscience and common sense of our state in matters of public health, safety, morals, and general welfare. [Citation.] Although public policy can be an elusive concept, once recognized, it becomes a benchmark in the application of our legal principles. [Citation.] * * * Thus, the public-policy exception to the employment-at-will doctrine carries forward a hallmark concept of this state; that the rights of each individual in a civilized society are ultimately "limited by the rights of others and of the public at large" and that the delicate balance between these rights is what helps hold us together as a society. [Citations.] When a contract violates public policy, including a contract of employment, the entire community is damaged.

In each case we have decided since adopting the public-policy exception to the employment-at-will doctrine, we have relied on a statute as a source of public policy to support the tort. * * * In fact, consistent with other states, our wrongful-discharge cases that have found a violation of public policy can generally be aligned into four categories of statutorily protected activities: (1) exercising a statutory right or privilege, [citations]; (2) refusing to commit an unlawful act, [citations]; (3) performing a statutory obligation [citation]; and (4) reporting a statutory violation, [citations].

Our adherence in our prior cases to identifying statutes as a source of public policy is consistent with our earlier pronouncement that the tort of wrongful discharge should exist in Iowa only as a narrow exception to the employment-at-will doctrine. [Citations.] The use of statutes as a source of public policy also helps provide the essential notice to employers and employees of conduct that can lead to dismissal, as well as conduct that can lead to tort liability. [Citation.] The public-policy exception was adopted merely to place a limitation on an employer's discretion to discharge an employee when the public policy is so clear and well-defined that it should be understood and accepted in our society as a benchmark. [Citation.] * * *

While we have justifiably relied on statutes, we have not closed the door to using other sources as a means to derive public policy to support the tort. We have repeatedly observed that our constitution is a proper source of public policy. [Citation.] Moreover, we have recognized that other jurisdictions have used administrative regulations as a source of public policy, yet we have not had the occasion to decide the issue until today. [Citations.]

* * *

In deciding whether administrative regulations may be used as an additional source of public policy to support the tort of wrongful discharge, we generally observe a strong fundamental congruence between statutes and administrative regulations. Administrative agencies have become an important component of our modern world of governance as a means for our legislature to better deal with the array of complex and technical problems it faces. [Citation.] Thus, our legislature often delegates its rule-making authority to administrative agencies as a means to better accomplish its objectives in dealing with these problems. [Citation.] The administrative regulations ultimately adopted are necessarily tied to the broad directives of the legislature and effectuate the intent of the enabling legislation. [Citation.] Administrative regulations have the force and effect of a statute. [Citation.] Moreover, the regulations are required to be consistent with the underlying broader statutory enactment. [Citation.] These observations reveal that administrative regulations can be an important part of a broader statutory scheme to advance legislative goals. They can reflect the objectives and goals of the legislature in the same way as a statute. Consequently, the justification for relying on statutes as a source of public policy can equally apply to administrative regulations. * * * Consequently, we are satisfied that administrative regulations can be used as a source of public policy to support the tort of wrongful discharge when adopted pursuant to a delegation of authority in a statute that seeks to further a public policy. We also recognize this position is consistent with most jurisdictions that have considered the question. [Citations.]

* * *

Public Policy Derived from Administrative Rules Governing Staff Ratios of Child Care Facilities

Our legislature has chosen to regulate child care facilities under chapter 237A of the Code. The regulatory agency is the department of human services. [Citation.] Specifically, this statute authorizes the department to "adopt rules setting minimum standards to provide quality child care in the operation and maintenance" of child care facilities. [Citation.] The legislature specifically authorized the department to adopt rules regulating "[t]he number … of personnel necessary to assure the health, safety, and welfare of children in the facilities." [Citation.]

* * *

From the beginning of our adoption of the public-policy exception, we have emphasized that the public policy must be both well recognized and clearly expressed. * * *

* * *

In this case, the legislature clearly delegated authority to the department of human services to promulgate specific rules concerning the proper staff-to-child ratios as a means "to assure the health, safety, and welfare of children" in child care facilities. [Citation.] Without question, the protection of children is a matter of fundamental public interest. [Citations.] These factors satisfy the goal that the regulation affect the public interest.

* * *

We conclude the particular administrative rule at issue in this case supports a clear and well-defined public policy that gives rise to the tort of wrongful discharge. The ratios were implemented at the specific direction of the legislature to protect the health, safety, and welfare of those children in Iowa who attend day care facilities. Additionally, the legislature intended for the ratios to be an important component of the larger public policy to protect children and, in turn, established a basic, important component of the operation of a day care center in Iowa. These factors transform the ratios into a public policy and satisfy the element of the tort that a clear and well-defined public policy that relates to public health, safety, or welfare be identified.

Employee Participation in the Protected Activity as a Cause of the Discharge

In addition to the existence of a public policy to create a protected activity, the tort of wrongful discharge requires proof that the discharge was a result of the employee's participation in the protected activity. * * *

* * *

We readily recognize the tort of wrongful discharge is not intended to interfere with legitimate business decisions of an employer. Yet, staffing a child care facility below the minimum requirements established by an administrative rule is not a legitimate business concern.

In this case, there was sufficient circumstantial evidence that Kid University wanted Jasper to reduce staff below the minimum state requirements. * * *

This same evidence supports a finding by the jury that Jasper was discharged because she refused to violate the state requirements.

* * *

We affirm the district court in part and reverse in part. We remand for a new trial in accordance with this opinion.

QUESTIONS

1. Gooddecade manufactures and sells automobile parts throughout the eastern United States. Among its fulltime employees are 220 fourteen-and fifteen-year-olds. These teenagers are employed throughout the company and are paid an hourly wage rate of $5 per hour. Discuss the legality of this arrangement.

2. Janet, a twenty-year-old woman, applied for a position driving a truck for Federal Trucking, Inc. Janet, who is 5′4″ tall and weighs 135 pounds, was denied the job because the company requires that all employees be at least 5′6″ tall and weigh at least 150 pounds. Federal justifies this requirement on the basis that its drivers frequently are forced to move heavy loads when making pickups and deliveries. Janet brings a cause of action. Has Federal Trucking violated the Civil Rights Act? Explain.

3. N.I.S. promoted John, a forty-two-year-old employee, to a foreman's position while passing over James, a fifty-eight-year-old employee. N.I.S. told James that he was too old for the job and that the company preferred to have a younger man in the position. Discuss whether James will succeed if he brings a cause of action.

4. Anthony was employed as a forklift operator for Blackburn Construction Company. While on the job, Anthony operated the forklift in a careless manner and in direct violation of Blackburn's procedure manual. As a result, he caused himself severe injury. Blackburn denies liability based on Anthony's (a) gross negligence, disobedience of the procedure manual, and written waiver of liability. Can Anthony recover for his injury? Explain.

5. Hazelwood School District, located in Sleepy Hollow Township, is being sued by several teachers who applied for teaching positions within the school district but were rejected. The plaintiffs, who are all African American, produce the following evidence:

   a. 1.8 percent of the Hazelwood School District's certified teachers are African American, whereas 15.4 percent of the certified teachers in Sleepy Hollow Township are African American; and

   b. the hiring decisions by Hazelwood School District are based solely on subjective criteria.

   Will the plaintiffs prevail? Explain.

6. T.W.E., a large manufacturer, prohibited its employees from distributing union leaflets to other employees while on the company's property. Richard, an employee of T.W.E., disregarded the prohibition and passed out the leaflets before his work shift began. T.W.E. discharged Richard for his actions. Has T.W.E. committed an unfair labor practice? Explain.

7. Erwick was dismissed from her job at the C & T Steel Company because she was "an unsatisfactory employee." At the time, Erwick was active in an effort to organize a union at C & T. Is the dismissal valid? Why or why not?

8. Johnson, president of the First National Bank of A, believes that it is appropriate to employ only female tellers. Hence, First National refuses to employ Ken Baker as a teller but does offer him a maintenance position at the same salary. Baker brings a cause of action against First National Bank. Is First National illegally discriminating based on gender? Why or why not?

9. Section 103 of the Federal Public Works Employment Act establishes the MBE (Minority Business Enterprise) program and requires that, absent a waiver by the Secretary of Commerce, 10 percent of all Federal grants given by the Economic Development Administration must be used to purchase services or supplies from businesses owned and controlled by U.S. citizens belonging to one of six minority groups: African American, Spanish-speaking, Asian, Native American, Eskimo, and Aleut. White owners of businesses contend that the Act constitutes illegal reverse discrimination. Discuss.

C A S E   P R O B L E M S

10. Worth H. Percivil, a mechanical engineer, was employed by General Motors (GM) for twenty-six years until he was discharged. At the time his employment was terminated, Percivil was head of GM's Mechanical Development department. Percivil sued GM for wrongful discharge. He contends that he was discharged as a result of a conspiracy among his fellow executives to force him out of his employment because of his age; because he had legitimately complained about certain deceptive practices of GM; because he had refused to give the government false information although urged to do so by his superiors; and because he had, on the contrary, undertaken to correct certain alleged misrepresentations made to the government. GM claims that Percivil's employment was terminable at the will of GM for any reason and with or without cause, provided that the discharge was not prohibited by statute. Has Percivil been wrongly discharged? Why or why not?

11. Samsoc brought an action against the Sailors' Union alleging that the Union had induced and encouraged employees of Moore Dry Dock Company to engage in a strike or concerted refusal in the course of their employment to perform services for Moore in connection with the conversion into a bulk gypsum carrier of the *SS Pho-pho*, a vessel owned by Samsoc. The object was to force Moore to cease doing business with Samsoc and thus force Samsoc to resolve its dispute with the respondent. Has an unfair labor practice been committed? Explain.

12. The defendant, Berger Transfer and Storage, operated a national moving and transfer business employing approximately forty persons. In May and June, Local 705 of the International Brotherhood of Teamsters spoke with a number of Berger employees, obtaining twenty-eight cards signed in support of the union. The management of Berger, unwilling to work with the union, attempted to prevent it from representing Berger employees. The company first assigned all work to those with high seniority, in effect temporarily laying off low-seniority employees. The management then threatened to lay off permanently those with low seniority and threatened all employees with a total shutdown of the plant. The management interrogated several employees about their union involvement and attempted to extract information about other employees' activities. When the union presented the company the signed cards and recognition agreement, Berger refused to acknowledge the union's existence or its right to bargain on behalf of the employees. The union then called a strike, with employees picketing the Berger warehouse. During the picketing, the company threatened to terminate the picketers if they did not return to work. Later, one manager on two occasions recklessly drove a truck through the picket line, striking employees. Finally, the company contacted several of the employees and offered them the "grievance procedures and job security" the union would provide. The employees refused the offer. On June 15, the strike ended, with most of the picketers returning to work. Local 705 filed a complaint with the National Labor Relations Board, alleging that Berger had committed unfair labor practices in violation of the National Labor Relations Act. Will the Local 705 succeed? Explain.

13. The City of Richmond, Virginia, adopted a Minority Business Utilization Plan requiring prime contractors awarded city construction contracts to subcontract at least 30 percent of the dollar amount of each contract to one or more Minority Business Enterprises (MBEs). The Plan defined an MBE to include a business from anywhere in the country that is at least 51 percent owned and controlled by African American, Spanish-speaking, Asian, Native American, Eskimo, or Aleut citizens. Although the Plan declared that it was "remedial" in nature, it was adopted after a public hearing at which no direct evidence was presented that the City had discriminated on the basis of race in granting contracts or that its prime contractors had discriminated against minority subcontractors. The evidence introduced in support of the Plan included a statistical study indicating that although the City's population was 50 percent African American, less than 1 percent of its prime construction

contracts had been awarded to minority businesses in recent years. Additional evidence showed that a variety of local contractors' trade associations had virtually no MBE members. J. A. Crosen Co., the sole bidder on a city contract, was denied a waiver and lost its contract because of the Plan. Discuss the legality of the plan.

14. Burdine, a female, was hired by the Texas Department of Community Affairs as a clerk in the Public Service Careers (PSC) Division. The PSC provides training and employment opportunities for unskilled workers. At the time she was hired, Burdine already had several years' experience in employment training. She was soon promoted, and later, when her supervisor resigned, she performed additional duties that usually had been assigned to the supervisor. Burdine applied for the position of supervisor, but the position remained unfilled for six months until a male employee from another division was brought in to fill it. Burdine alleges discrimination violating Title VII of the 1964 Civil Rights Act. The defendant, Texas Department of Community Affairs, responds that nondiscriminatory evaluation criteria were used to choose the new supervisor. To comply with Title VII, must the Texas Department of Community Affairs hire Burdine as supervisor if she and the male candidate are equally qualified? Explain.

15. Wise was fired from her job at the Mead Corporation after she was involved in a fight with a coworker. On four other unrelated occasions, fights occurred between male co-workers. Only one of the males was fired, but this was after his second fight, in which he seriously injured another employee. There is no dispute that Wise was qualified and performed her duties adequately. Wise successfully establishes a *prima facie* case of discrimination; however, defendant Mead Corporation meets its burden to "articulate legitimate and nondiscriminatory reasons" for firing Wise. Can she prevail? Explain.

16. The United Steelworkers of America and Kaiser Aluminum entered into a master collective bargaining agreement covering terms and conditions of employment at fifteen Kaiser plants. The agreement contained an affirmative action plan designed to eliminate conspicuous racial imbalances in Kaiser's then almost exclusively white craftwork forces. African American craft-hiring goals were set for each Kaiser plant equal to the percentage of African Americans in the respective local labor forces. To meet these goals, on-the-job training programs were established to teach unskilled production workers— African Americans and whites—the skills necessary to become craftworkers. The plan reserved for African American employees 50 percent of the openings in these newly created in-plant training programs.

Pursuant to the national agreement, Kaiser altered its craft-hiring practice in its Gramercy, Louisiana, plant by establishing a program to train its production workers to fill craft openings. Selection of craft trainees was made on the basis of seniority. At least 50 percent of the new trainees were to be African American until the percentage of African American skilled craft workers in the Gramercy plant approximated the percentage of African Americans in the local labor force. During this affirmative action plan's first year of operation, thirteen craft trainees (seven African American, six white) were selected from Gramercy's productions workforce. The most senior African American selected had less seniority than several white production workers who were denied admission to the program. Does the affirmative action plan wrongfully discriminate against white employees and therefore violate the Civil Rights Act of 1964? Justify your decision.

17. At Whirlpool's manufacturing plant in Ohio, overhead conveyors transported household appliance components throughout the plant. A wire mesh screen was positioned below the conveyors to catch falling components and debris. Maintenance employees frequently had to stand on the screens to clean them. Whirlpool began installing heavier wire because several employees had fallen partly through the old screens, and one had fallen completely through to the plant floor. At this time, the company warned workers to walk only on the frames beneath the wire but not on the wire itself. Before the heavier wire had been completely installed, a worker fell to his death through the old screen. A short time after this incident, Deemer and Cornwell, two plant employees, met with the plant safety director to discuss the mesh, to voice their concerns, and to obtain the name, address, and telephone number of the local Occupational Safety and Health Administration representative. The next day, the two employees refused to clean a portion of the old screen. They were then ordered to punch out for the remainder of the shift without pay and also received written reprimands, which were placed in their employment files. Does Whirlpool's actions against Deemer and Cornwell constitute discrimination in violation of the Occupational Safety and Health Act? Explain.

18. John Novosel was employed by Nationwide Insurance Company for fifteen years. Novosel had been a model employee and, at the time of discharge, was a district claims manager and a candidate for the position of division claims manager. During Novosel's fifteenth year of employment, Nationwide circulated a memorandum requesting the participation of all employees in an effort to lobby the Pennsylvania state legislature for the passage

of a certain bill before the body. Novosel, who had privately indicated his disagreement with Nationwide's political views, refused to lend his support to the lobby, and his employment with Nationwide was terminated. Novosel brought two separate claims against Nationwide, arguing, first, that his discharge for refusing to lobby the state legislature on behalf of Nationwide constituted the tort of wrongful discharge in that it was arbitrary, malicious, and contrary to public policy. Novosel also contended that Nationwide breached an implied contract guaranteeing continued employment so long as his job performance was satisfactory. What decision as to each claim? Explain.

19. During the years prior to the passage of the Civil Rights Act of 1964, Duke Power openly discriminated against African Americans by allowing them to work only in the labor department of the plant's five departments. The highest-paying job in the labor department paid less than the lowest-paying jobs in the other four "operating" departments in which only whites were employed. In 1955, the company began requiring a high school education for initial assignment to any department except labor. However, when Duke Power stopped restricting African Americans to the labor department in 1965, it made completion of high school a prerequisite to transfer from labor to any other department. White employees hired before the high school education requirement was adopted continued to perform satisfactorily and to achieve promotions in the "operating" departments.

   In 1965, the company also began requiring new employees in the departments other than labor to register satisfactory scores on two professionally prepared aptitude tests, in addition to having a high school education. In September 1965, Duke Power began to permit employees to qualify for transfer to another department from labor by passing either of two tests, neither of which was directed or intended to measure the ability to learn to perform a particular job or category of jobs. Griggs brought suit against Duke Power, claiming that the high school education and testing requirements were discriminatory and therefore prohibited by the Civil Rights Act of 1964. Is Griggs correct? Why or why not?

20. Michelle Vinson was an employee of Meritor Savings Bank for approximately four years. Beginning as a teller-trainee, she ultimately advanced to the position of assistant branch manager. Her promotions were based solely upon merit. Sidney Taylor, a vice president of the bank and manager of the branch office in which Vinson worked, was Vinson's supervisor throughout her employment with the bank. After the bank fired Vinson for her abusive use of sick leave, Vinson brought an action against Taylor and the bank, alleging that during her employment, she had "constantly been subjected to sexual harassment" by Taylor in violation of Title VII of the Civil Rights Act of 1964. Vinson stated that Taylor repeatedly demanded sexual favors from her, fondled her in front of other employees, and forcibly raped her on a number of occasions. Taylor and the bank categorically denied Vinson's allegations. Does the conduct constitute sexual harassment? Explain.

21. Plaintiff, Beth Lyons, a staff attorney for the Legal Aid Society (Legal Aid) brought suit against her employer, alleging that Legal Aid violated the Americans with Disabilities Act (ADA) and the Rehabilitation Act by failing to provide her with a parking space near her office. Plaintiff worked for defendant in its lower Manhattan office.

   Lyon's disability was the result of being struck and nearly killed by an automobile. For six years from the date of the accident, Lyons was on disability leave from Legal Aid; she underwent multiple reconstructive surgeries and received "constant" physical therapy. Since the accident, Lyons has been able to walk only by using walking devices, including walkers, canes, and crutches. Since returning to work, Lyons has performed her job duties successfully. Nevertheless, her condition severely limits her ability to walk long distances either at one time or during the course of a day.

   Before returning to work, Lyons asked Legal Aid to accommodate her disability by providing her a parking space near her office and the courts in which she would practice. She stated that this would be necessary because she is unable to take public transportation from her home in New Jersey to the Legal Aid office in Manhattan because such "commuting would require her to walk distances, climb stairs, and on occasion to remain standing for extended periods of time," thereby "overtax[ing] her limited physical capabilities." Lyons's physician advised Legal Aid by letter that such a parking space was "necessary to enable [Lyons] to return to work." Legal Aid informed Lyons that it would not pay for a parking space for her. Accordingly, Lyons has spent $300 to $520 a month, representing 15 percent to 26 percent of her monthly net salary, for a parking space adjacent to her office building. Are the accommodations requested by Lyons unreasonable? Why or why not?

22. The Steamship Clerks Union has approximately 124 members, 80 of whom are classified as active. Members serve as steamship clerks who, during the loading and unloading of vessels in the port of Boston, check

cargo against inventory lists provided by shippers and consignees. The work is not taxing; it requires little in the way of particular skills. On October 1, 1980, the Union formally adopted the membership sponsorship policy (the MSP), which provided that any applicant for membership in the Union (other than an injured longshoreman) had to be sponsored by an existing member for his application to be considered. The record reveals, without contradiction, that (a) the Union had no African American or Hispanic members when it adopted the MSP; (b) blacks and Hispanics constituted from 8 percent to 27 percent of the relevant labor pool in the Boston area; (c) the Union welcomed at least thirty new members between 1980 and 1986 and then closed the membership rolls; (d) all "sponsored" applicants during this period and, hence, all the new members were Caucasian; and (e) every recruit was related to (usually the son or brother of) a Union member.

After conducting an investigation and instituting administrative proceedings, the Equal Employment Opportunity Commission (EEOC) brought suit, alleging that the Union had discriminated against African Americans and Hispanics by means of the MSP. Explain whether or not the EEOC will prevail.

23. Johnson Controls implemented a policy that women who are pregnant or who are capable of bearing children would not be placed in jobs involving lead exposure. In April 1984, employees filed a class action lawsuit challenging Johnson Controls' fetal-protection policy as sex discrimination that violated Title VII of the Civil Rights Act of 1964. Among the individual plaintiffs were Mary Craig, who had chosen to be sterilized to avoid losing her job; Elsie Nason, a fifty-year-old divorcee, who had suffered a loss in compensation when she was transferred out of a job that exposed her to lead; and Donald Penney, who had been denied a request for a leave of absence for the purpose of lowering his lead level because he intended to become a father. Discuss whether the plaintiffs have a valid cause of action.

24. Ella Williams began working at Toyota's automobile manufacturing plant in Georgetown, Kentucky, in August 2010. She was placed on an engine fabrication assembly line, where her duties included work with pneumatic tools. Use of these tools eventually caused pain in her hands, wrists, and arms. She sought treatment at Toyota's in-house medical service, where she was diagnosed with bilateral carpal tunnel syndrome and bilateral tendinitis. Williams consulted a personal physician who placed her on permanent

work restrictions that precluded her from lifting more than 20 pounds or from "frequently lifting or carrying of objects weighing up to 10 pounds," engaging in "constant repetitive … flexion or extension of [her] wrists or elbows," performing "overhead work," or using "vibratory or pneumatic tools." In light of these restrictions, for the next two years, Toyota assigned Williams to various modified duty jobs. Nonetheless, Williams missed some work for medical leave and eventually filed a claim under the Kentucky Workers' Compensation Act. The parties settled this claim, and Williams returned to work.

Upon her return, Toyota placed Williams on a team in Quality Control Inspection Operations (QCIO). QCIO is responsible for four tasks: (1) "assembly paint," (2) "paint second inspection," (3) "shell body audit," and (4) "ED surface repair." Williams was initially placed on a team that performed only the first two of these tasks, and for a couple of years, she rotated on a weekly basis between them. Williams was physically capable of performing both of these jobs, and her performance was satisfactory.

During the fall of 2016, Toyota announced that it wanted QCIO employees to be able to rotate through all four of the QCIO processes. Williams therefore received training for the shell body audit job, in which team members apply a highlight oil to the hood, fender, doors, rear quarter panel, and trunk of passing cars at a rate of approximately one car per minute. The highlight oil has the viscosity of salad oil, and employees spread it on cars with a sponge attached to a block of wood. After they wipe each car with the oil, the employees visually inspect it for flaws. Wiping the cars required respondent to hold her hands and arms up around shoulder height for several hours at a time.

A short while after the shell body audit job was added to Williams's rotations, she began to experience pain in her neck and shoulders. However, she could still brush her teeth, wash her face, bathe, tend her flower garden, fix breakfast, do laundry, and pick up around the house. Williams requested that Toyota accommodate her medical conditions by allowing her to return to doing only her original two jobs in QCIO, which Williams claimed she could still perform without difficulty. Toyota refused. Subsequently Williams was terminated. Williams sued Toyota for failing to provide her with a reasonable accommodation as required by the Americans with Disabilities Act (ADA). Explain whether Williams has a successful cause of action against Toyota.

T A K I N G   S I D E S

Mark Hunger was the safety director at Grand Central Sanitation. On September 7, Hunger "became aware" that hazardous materials consisting of blasting caps were being deposited into garbage containers at Shu-Deb, Inc. Grand Central collected garbage from these containers and dumped it at a dump site. Hunger knew that Grand Central was not licensed to dispose of hazardous materials and believed that it would violate State and/or Federal law if the company transported or disposed of hazardous materials. Hunger also became concerned about the safety of company employees from the danger of transporting blasting caps. On September 9, Hunger informed Grand Central's owner and vice president, Gary Perin, of the information he received about the blasting caps. On September 12, Hunger, accompanied by Pennsylvania state police and agents of the Federal Bureau of Alcohol, Tobacco, and Firearms, went to search the contents of Shu-Deb's containers. However, the garbage had already been collected, so Hunger and the police located the garbage truck that had collected the garbage and searched it. No hazardous materials were found in the truck. On October 4, Hunger was terminated because of the incident. Hunger sued Grand Central for wrongful termination.

a. What are the arguments that Hunger was wrongfully terminated?

b. What are the arguments that Hunger was legally terminated?

c. Will Hunger prevail? Explain.

CHAPTER 43

Securities Regulation

CHAPTER OUTCOMES

After reading and studying this chapter, you should be able to:

- Explain the disclosure requirements of the 1933 Act, including which securities and transactions are exempt from these disclosure requirements.

- Explain the potential civil liabilities under the 1933 Act.

- List which provisions of the 1934 Act apply only to publicly held companies and which apply to all companies.

- Explain the disclosure requirements of the 1934 Act.

- Explain the potential civil liabilities under the 1934 Act.

The primary purpose of Federal securities regulation is to foster public confidence in the securities market by preventing fraudulent practices in the sale of securities. Federal securities law consists principally of two statutes: the **Securities Act of 1933**, which focuses on the issuance of securities, and the **Securities Exchange Act of 1934**, which deals mainly with trading in issued securities. These "secondary" transactions greatly exceed in number and dollar value the original offerings by issuers.

The 1933 Act has two basic objectives: (1) to provide investors with material information concerning securities offered for sale to the public and (2) to prohibit misrepresentation, deceit, and other fraudulent acts and unfair practices in the sale of securities, whether or not they are required to be registered.

The 1934 Act extends protection to investors trading in securities that already have been issued and are outstanding. The 1934 Act also imposes disclosure requirements on publicly held corporations as well as regulates tender offers and proxy solicitations.

Both statutes are administered by the **Securities and Exchange Commission** (SEC), an independent, quasi-judicial agency consisting of five commissioners. The responsibilities of the SEC include interpreting and enforcing Federal securities laws; issuing new rules and amending existing rules; and coordinating U.S. securities regulation with Federal, State, and foreign authorities. In 1996, Congress enacted legislation requiring the SEC, when making rules under either of the securities statutes, to consider, in addition to the protection of investors, whether its action will promote efficiency, competition, and capital formation.

When enforcing Federal securities laws, depending upon the type of sanction the SEC is seeking, the SEC can bring a civil case in Federal court, bring an administrative case within the SEC before an administrative law judge, or recommend that the U.S. Department of Justice (DOJ) bring a **criminal prosecution**. The SEC can bring a **civil action** in a U.S. District Court seeking an injunction, civil monetary penalties, or disgorgement (the return of illegal profits). The maximum amount of civil monetary penalties must be adjusted for inflation annually. The court may also bar or suspend an individual from serving as a corporate officer or director. A person who violates the court's order may be found in contempt and be subject to additional fines or imprisonment. The SEC may bring an **administrative action** seeking a cease-and-desist orders, civil monetary penalties, and disgorgement, as well as orders censuring, suspending, or expelling broker-dealers, investment advisers, and investment companies.

The SEC has recognized that the "use of electronic media also enhances the efficiency of the securities markets by allowing for the rapid dissemination of information to investors and financial markets in a more cost-efficient, widespread, and equitable manner than traditional paper-based methods." The SEC has provided interpretative guidance for the use of electronic media for the delivery of information required by the Federal securities laws. The SEC defined *electronic media* to include audiotapes, videotapes, facsimiles, CD-ROM, electronic mail, bulletin boards, internet websites, and computer networks. Basically, electronic delivery must provide notice, access, and evidence of delivery comparable to that provided by paper delivery.

The SEC has established the EDGAR (Electronic Data Gathering, Analysis, and Retrieval) computer system, which performs automated collection, validation, indexing, acceptance, and dissemination of reports required to be filed with the SEC. Its primary purpose is to increase the efficiency and fairness of the securities market for the benefit of investors, corporations, and the economy by speeding up the receipt, acceptance, dissemination, and analysis of corporate information filed with the SEC. The SEC now requires all public domestic companies to make their filings on EDGAR, except filings exempted for hardship. EDGAR filings are posted at the SEC's website twenty-four hours after the date of filing.

Since enacting the 1933 and 1934 Acts, Congress has amended them a number of times.

1. Congress enacted the **Private Securities Litigation Reform Act of 1995** (1995 Reform Act), which amends both the 1933 Act and the 1934 Act. One of its provisions grants authority to the SEC to bring civil actions for specified violations of the 1934 Act against aiders and abettors (those who knowingly provide substantial assistance to a person who violates the statute. The 1995 Reform Act also sought to prevent abuses in private securities fraud lawsuits brought by investors.

2. To prevent certain State private securities class action lawsuits alleging fraud from being used to frustrate the objectives of the 1995 Reform Act, Congress enacted the **Securities Litigation Uniform Standards Act of 1998**. The 1998 Act sets national standards for securities class action lawsuits involving nationally traded securities, while preserving the appropriate enforcement powers of State securities regulators and leaving unchanged the current treatment of individual lawsuits. The 1998 Act amends both the 1933 Act and the 1934 Act by prohibiting any private class action suit in State or Federal court by any private party based upon State statutory or common law alleging (1) an untrue statement or omission in connection with the purchase or sale of a covered security or (2) the defendant's use of any manipulative or deceptive device in connection with such a transaction.

3. In response to the business scandals involving companies such as Enron, WorldCom, Global Crossing, Adelphia, and Arthur Andersen, in 2002, Congress passed the **Sarbanes-Oxley Act**, which amends the 1933 and 1934 Acts in a number of significant respects. The Sarbanes-Oxley Act allows the SEC to add civil monetary penalties to a disgorgement fund for the benefit of victims of violations of the 1933 Act or the 1934 Act. Other

provisions of the Sarbanes-Oxley Act are discussed later in this chapter, as well as in *Chapters 6, 35,* and *44.*

4. In 2010, Congress enacted the **Dodd-Frank Wall Street Reform and Consumer Protection Act** (Dodd-Frank Act), the most significant change to U.S. financial regulation since the New Deal. The Dodd-Frank Act imposes new corporate governance and investor protection rules on publicly held companies and are discussed in this chapter as well as in *Chapters 34, 35, 36,* and *46.* The Dodd-Frank Act has extended the SEC's authority to bring civil actions for specified violations of the 1934 Act against aiders and abettors authority in two ways: (1) it empowers the SEC to bring enforcement actions under the 1933 Act against aiders and abettors, and (2) it amends the 1933 and 1934 Acts to allow *recklessness* as well as knowledge to satisfy the mental state required for the SEC to bring aiding and abetting cases. In addition, the Dodd-Frank Act requires the SEC to make an award to eligible whistleblowers who voluntarily provide original information that leads to a successful enforcement action in which the SEC imposes monetary sanctions in excess of $1 million. The amount of the award must be between 10 percent and 30 percent of funds collected as monetary sanctions, as determined by the SEC.

5. To increase U.S. job creation and economic growth by improving access to the public capital markets for emerging growth companies, Congress enacted the **Jumpstart Our Business Startups Act of 2012** (JOBS Act). As discussed later in this chapter, the JOBS Act amends both the 1933 Act and the 1934 Act to provide reduced disclosure requirements for emerging growth companies (defined as companies with total annual gross revenues of less than $1.07 billion, as of April 2017 and adjusted for inflation every five years, during their last completed fiscal year) and to expand the availability of exemptions from registering securities under the 1933 Act.

In addition to the Federal laws regulating the sale of securities, each State has its own laws regulating such sales within its borders. Commonly called Blue Sky laws, these statutes all contain provisions prohibiting fraud in the sale of securities. In addition, most States require the registration of securities and regulate brokers and dealers. The Uniform Securities Act of 1956 has been adopted at one time or another, in whole or in part, by thirty-seven jurisdictions, whereas the Revised Uniform Securities Act of 1985 has been adopted in only a few States. Both Acts, however, have been preempted in part by the National Securities Markets Improvement Act of 1996 and the Securities Litigation Uniform Standards Act of 1998. In 2002, the Uniform Law Commission promulgated a new Uniform Securities Act, which has been adopted by at least twenty States. The 2002 Uniform Securities Act seeks to give States regulatory and enforcement authority that minimizes duplication of regulatory resources and that blends with Federal regulation and enforcement.

Any person who sells securities must comply with the Federal securities laws as well as with the securities laws of each State in which the securities are offered. However, in 1996, Congress enacted the National Securities Markets Improvements Act, preempting State regulation of many offerings of securities. Because the State securities laws vary greatly, this chapter discusses only the 1933 Act and the 1934 Act.

SECURITIES ACT OF 1933

The 1933 Act, also called the "Truth in Securities Act," requires that a registration statement be filed with the SEC and that it become effective before any securities may be offered for sale to the public, unless either the securities or the transaction in which they are offered is exempt from registration. Effective on March 15, 2021, the SEC amended its rules to harmonize and simplify the exemptions from registration. Foreign issuers that issue securities in the United States also must register them under the 1933 Act unless an exemption is available to them. The purpose of registration is to disclose financial and other significant information about the issuer, those who control it, and the securities being offered for sale, so that potential investors may appraise the merits of the securities. The 1933 Act also requires that potential investors be furnished with a **prospectus** (a document offering the securities for sale) containing the important data set forth in the registration statement. The 1933 Act prohibits deceit, misrepresentations, and other fraud in *all* sales of securities involving interstate commerce or the mails, even if the securities are exempt from the registration and disclosure requirements of the 1933 Act. Civil and criminal liability may be imposed for violations of the 1933 Act.

The National Securities Markets Improvements Act of 1996 broadly authorized the SEC to issue regulations or rules exempting any person, security, or transaction from any of the provisions of the 1933 Act or the SEC's rules promulgated under that Act. This authorization extends so far as such exemption is necessary or appropriate in the public interest and is consistent with the protection of investors.

There are two methods available for a company to offer securities for sale to the public. In an **initial public offering** (IPO), shares are underwritten by an intermediary (underwriter) and sold to the public. In a **direct listing**, a company sells its shares on a securities exchange without hiring an intermediary. On December 22, 2020, the SEC approved the New York Stock Exchange's proposed rule change allowing companies to sell shares directly to investors under a new **primary direct floor listing**. The new rule requires that a company meet certain listing requirements regarding the company's market value and establishes specific auction requirements for the initial sales. The new rule also requires that all primary direct floor listings be registered under the 1933 Act and thus subject to the liability and disclosure requirements of the 1933 Act for registered offerings.

43-1 Definition of a Security

Section 2(1) of the 1933 Act defines a security as

any note, stock, treasury stock, bond, debenture, evidence of indebtedness, certificate of interest or participation in any profit-sharing agreement, collateral-trust certificate, preorganization certificate or subscription, transferable share, investment contract, voting-trust certificate, certificate of deposit for a security, fractional undivided interest in oil, gas, or other mineral rights, any put, call, straddle, option, or privilege on any security … or, in general, any interest or instrument commonly known as a "security," or any certificate of interest or participation in, temporary or interim certificate for, receipt for, guarantee of, or warrant or right to subscribe to or purchase, any of the foregoing.

This definition broadly incorporates the many types of instruments that fall within the concept of a security. Furthermore, the courts generally have interpreted the statutory definition to include nontraditional forms of investments. In *Landreth Timber Co. v. Landreth*, 471 U.S. 681 (1985), the Supreme Court adopted a two-tier analysis of what constitutes a security. Under this analysis, the Court will presumptively treat as a security a financial instrument designated as a note, stock, bond, or other instrument specifically named in the Act.

On the other hand, if a financial transaction lacks the traditional characteristics of an instrument specifically named in the 1933 Act, the Court has used a three-part test, derived from *Securities and Exchange Commission v. W.J. Howey* Co., 328 U.S. 293 (1946), to determine whether that financial transaction constitutes an **investment contract** and thus a security. Under the *Howey* test, a financial instrument or transaction constitutes an investment contract if it involves (1) an investment in a common venture (2) premised on a reasonable expectation of profit (3) to be derived from the entrepreneurial or managerial efforts of others. Thus, limited partnership interests are usually considered securities because limited partners may not participate in management or control of the limited partnership. On the other hand, general partnership interests are usually held not to be securities because general partners have the right to participate in management of the general partnership. Similarly, interests in limited liability companies (LLCs) are considered securities when the members do not take part in management (manager-managed LLCs) but are not deemed securities when the members exercise control of the company (member-managed LLCs). In certain circumstances, investments in citrus groves, whiskey warehouse receipts, real estate condominiums, cattle, franchises, and pyramid schemes have been held to be securities under the *Howey* test.

♦ *See Case 43-1*

Practical Advice

Because securities are so broadly defined, if you plan to sell any type of financial investment, be sure to obtain legal counsel to assist you in complying with the requirements of the securities laws.

43-2 Registration of Securities

The 1933 Act prohibits the offer or sale of any security through the use of the mails or any means of interstate commerce unless a registration statement for the securities being offered is in effect or the issuer secures an exemption from registration. Section 5. The purpose of registration is to adequately and accurately disclose financial and other information on which investors may make informed judgments about the merits of the securities. Registration does not, however, insure investors against loss—the SEC does not judge the financial merits of any security. Moreover, the SEC does not guarantee the accuracy of the information presented in a registration statement. However, investors who purchase securities and suffer losses have remedies if they can prove that there was incomplete or inaccurate disclosure of material information.

Practical Advice

When deciding whether to invest in a publicly offered security, keep in mind that the SEC does not pass on the merits of the securities, nor does it guarantee the accuracy of the statements made in the registration statement or prospectus.

43-2a DISCLOSURE REQUIREMENTS

In general, registration (Form S-1) calls for disclosure of such information as (1) a description of the registrant's properties, business, and competition; (2) a description of the significant provisions of the security to be offered for sale and its relationship to the registrant's other capital securities; (3) information about the management of the registrant; and (4) financial statements certified by independent public accountants. In 1992, the SEC imposed new disclosure requirements regarding compensation paid to senior executives and

directors. In 2006, the SEC amended these rules to mandate clearer and more complete disclosure of compensation paid to directors, the chief executive officer (CEO), the chief financial officer (CFO), and the three other highest-paid executive officers. The registration statement must be signed by the issuer, its CEO, its CFO, its chief accounting officer, and a majority of its board of directors.

A registration statement and the prospectus become public immediately on filing with the SEC, and if they are filed by a U.S. issuer, investors can access them using EDGAR. The effective date of a registration statement is the twentieth day after filing, although the commission, at its discretion, may advance the effective date or require an amendment to the filing, which will begin a new twenty-day period. After the effective date, the issuer may make sales, provided the purchaser has received a final prospectus. The SEC has also adopted rules to provide for an "access equals delivery" prospectus delivery model: the final prospectus delivery obligations are satisfied without printing and actually delivering final prospectuses if the issuer timely filed a final prospectus with the SEC.

In 1998, the SEC issued a rule requiring issuers to write and design the cover page, summary, and risk factors section of their prospectuses in plain English. In these sections, issuers must use short sentences; definite, concrete, everyday language; tabular presentation of complex information; no legal or business jargon; and no multiple negatives. Issuers will also have to design these sections to make them inviting to the reader and free from legalese and repetition that blur important information.

43-2b INTEGRATED DISCLOSURE

The disclosure system under the 1933 Act developed independently of that required by the 1934 Act, which is discussed later in this chapter. As a result, issuers subject to both statutes were compelled to provide duplicative or overlapping disclosure. In an effort to reduce or eliminate unnecessary duplication of corporate reporting, the SEC in 1982 adopted an integrated system that provides for different levels of disclosure, depending on the issuer's reporting history and market following. All issuers may use the detailed form (S-1) described previously. The SEC has amended these rules to recognize four categories of issuers: nonreporting issuers, unseasoned issuers, seasoned issuers, and well-known seasoned issuers.

1. A nonreporting issuer is an issuer that is not required to file reports under the 1934 Act. Such an issuer must use Form S-1.

2. An unseasoned issuer is an issuer that has reported continuously under the 1934 Act for at least three years. Such an issuer must use Form S-1 but is permitted to

disclose less detailed information and to incorporate some information by reference to reports filed under the 1934 Act.

3. A seasoned issuer is an issuer that has filed continuously under the 1934 Act for at least one year and has a minimum market value of publicly held voting and nonvoting stock of $75 million. Such an issuer is permitted to use Form S-3, thus disclosing even less detail in the 1933 Act registration and incorporating even more information by reference to 1934 Act reports. An issuer that does not meet the $75 million "public float" requirement can use Form S-3 if it (a) has a class of common equity securities listed and registered on a national securities exchange, (b) has a class of securities registered under the 1934 Act, (c) has filed continuously under the 1934 Act for at least one year, and (d) does not sell more than the equivalent of one-third of its public float in primary offerings over any period of twelve calendar months. "Public float" means the value of a company's outstanding shares that is in the hands of public investors, as opposed to company officers, directors, or controlling-interest investors.

4. A well-known seasoned issuer is an issuer that has filed continuously under the 1934 Act for at least one year and has either (a) a minimum worldwide market value of its outstanding publicly held voting and nonvoting stock of $700 million or (b) $1 billion of nonconvertible debt or preferred stock that has been issued for cash in a registered offering within the preceding three years. A well-known seasoned issuer is also eligible to use Form S-3.

In 1992, the SEC established an integrated registration and reporting system for small business issuers. These rules are intended to facilitate access to the public financial markets for start-up and developing companies and to reduce costs for small business issuers wishing to have their securities traded in public markets. In 2008, the SEC replaced the term "small business issuer" with "smaller reporting company," extended the benefits of small business issuer regulations to a greater number of companies, and simplified the scaled disclosure and reporting requirements. As amended in 2018, the rules generally define a **smaller reporting company** as a noninvestment company with (1) a public float of less than $250 million (2) annual revenues of less than $100 million and either no public float or a public float of less than $700 million. The scaled disclosure requirements for smaller reporting companies permit less extensive narrative disclosure and audited financial statements for two fiscal years, in contrast to other reporting companies, which must provide audited financial statements for three fiscal years.

43-2c SHELF REGISTRATIONS

As amended in 2005, the SEC's shelf registration regulations permit seasoned and well-known seasoned issuers to register unlimited amounts of securities that are to be offered and sold "off the shelf" on a delayed or continuous basis in the future. This is a departure from the requirement that an issuer must file a registration for *every* new distribution of nonexempt securities. The information in the original registration must be kept accurate and current, and the issuer must reasonably expect that the securities will be sold within three years of the effective date of the registration. Well-known seasoned issuers are eligible for a more streamlined shelf-registration process and automatic effectiveness of shelf-registration statements upon filing. Shelf registrations allow issuers to respond more quickly to market conditions such as changes in stock prices and interest rates.

43-2d COMMUNICATIONS

The SEC's 2005 revisions greatly liberalize the rules regarding written communications before and during registered securities offerings. These rules create a new type of written communication, called a "free-writing prospectus," which is any written offer, including electronic communications, other than a statutory prospectus. The flexibility provided under the new rules depends upon the characteristics of the issuer, including the type of issuer, the issuer's history of reporting, and the issuer's market capitalization.

1. Well-known seasoned issuers may engage at any time in oral and written communications, including a free-writing prospectus, subject to certain conditions.

2. All reporting issuers (unseasoned issuers, seasoned issuers, and well-known seasoned issuers) may at any time continue to publish regularly released factual business information and forward-looking information (predictions).

3. Nonreporting issuers may at any time continue to publish factual business information that is regularly released and intended for use by persons other than in their capacity as investors or potential investors.

4. Communications by issuers more than thirty days before filing a registration statement are permitted so long as they do not refer to a securities offering that is the subject of a registration statement.

5. All issuers may use a free-writing prospectus after the filing of the registration statement, subject to certain conditions.

6. As of 2019, all issuers may engage in oral or written communications with potential investors that are qualified

institutional buyers or institutional accredited investors to determine whether such investors might have an interest in a contemplated registered securities offering, either prior to or following the date of filing of a registration statement.

43-2e EMERGING GROWTH COMPANIES

The JOBS Act defines an **emerging growth company (EGC)** as a domestic or foreign issuer with total annual gross revenues of less than $1.07 billion (as of April 2017 and adjusted for inflation every five years) during its most recently completed fiscal year *if* that issuer did not first sell common equity securities in an initial public offering (IPO) on or before December 8, 2011. An issuer continues to be deemed to be an EGC until the earliest of the following: (1) it has annual gross revenues of $1.07 billion, as adjusted for inflation in April 2017, or more; (2) five years after its IPO; (3) the date on which the issuer has, or had during the previous three-year period, issued more than $1 billion in nonconvertible debt; and (4) the date on which it is deemed to be a "large accelerated filer" pursuant to SEC rules.

The JOBS Act reduces the financial reporting requirements, and therefore the cost, in connection with an EGC's IPO. In particular, EGCs are permitted to include less extensive narrative disclosure than required of other reporting companies and to provide audited financial statements for two fiscal years instead of the three fiscal years required of other reporting companies.

The JOBS Act also authorizes an EGC, before its IPO date, to submit to the SEC a draft registration statement for *confidential nonpublic review* by SEC staff before the public filing, provided that the initial confidential submission is publicly filed with the SEC no later than twenty-one days before the issuer conducts a "road show." (A "road show" is an offer that contains a presentation regarding an offering by one or more members of the issuer's management and includes discussion of the issuer, its management, and/or the securities being offered.) In addition, prior to the filing of a registration statement to determine whether such investors might have an interest in a contemplated securities offering, EGCs may engage in oral or written communications with potential investors that are qualified institutional buyers or *institutional* accredited investors. The JOBS Act also liberalizes the use of research reports on EGCs.

43-3 Exempt Securities

The 1933 Act exempts a number of specific securities from its registration requirements. Because these exemptions apply to the securities themselves, the securities also may be resold without registration.

43-3a SHORT-TERM COMMERCIAL PAPER

The Act exempts any note, draft, or bankers' acceptance (a draft accepted by a bank) issued for working capital that has a maturity of not more than nine months when issued. Section 3(a)(3). This exemption is not available, however, if the proceeds are to be used for permanent purposes, such as the acquisition of a plant, or if the paper is of a type not ordinarily purchased by the general public.

43-3b OTHER EXEMPT SECURITIES

The 1933 Act also exempts the following kinds of securities from registration:

1. securities issued or guaranteed by domestic government organizations, such as municipal bonds;
2. securities of domestic banks and savings and loan associations;
3. securities of not-for-profit, charitable organizations;
4. certain securities issued by Federally regulated common carriers; and
5. insurance policies and annuity contracts issued by State-regulated insurance companies.

43-4 Exempt Transactions for Issuers

In addition to exempting specific types of securities, the 1933 Act also exempts *issuers* from the registration requirements for certain kinds of transactions. These exempt transactions for issuers include (1) private placements (Rule 506), (2) limited offers not exceeding $10 million (Rule 504), and (3) limited offers not exceeding $5 million solely to accredited investors (Section 4(a)(5)). Except for some issuances under Rule 504, these exemptions from registration apply only to the transaction in which the securities are issued; therefore, any resale must be made by registration, unless the resale qualifies as an exempt transaction. Moreover, these transactions are *not* exempt from the anti-fraud, civil liability, or other provisions of the Federal securities laws.

The JOBS Act added Section 4(a)(6) providing a new crowdfunding exemption from registration that allows eligible, domestic, nonpublic issuers to raise up to $1.07 million (as of April 2017 and periodically adjusted for inflation every five years) in any twelve-month period.

In addition, the 1933 Act provides a number of securities exemptions that are in effect transaction exemptions. These include intrastate issues, exchanges between an issuer and its security holders, and reorganization securities issued and exchanged with court or other government approval. Moreover, the Bankruptcy Act exempts securities issued by a debtor if they are offered under a reorganization plan in exchange for a claim or interest in the debtor. Bankruptcy Act, Section 1145(a). These exemptions apply only to the original

FIGURE 43-1 **Registration and Exemptions under the 1933 Act**

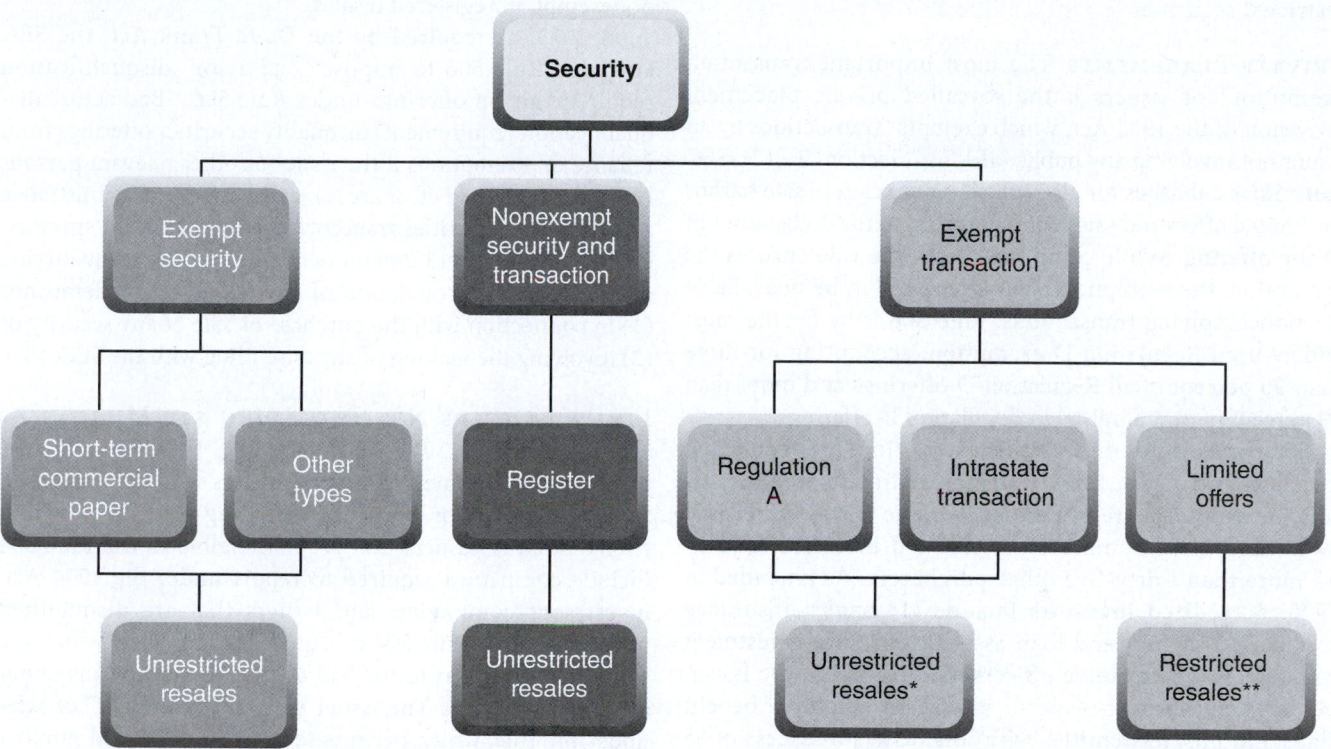

*Under the intrastate exemption, resales to nonresidents may only be made after six months from the date of the sale.
**Except some issuances under Rule 504.

issuance; resales may be made only by registration unless the resale qualifies as an exempt transaction.

Another transaction exemption is Regulation A, which permits an issuer to sell a limited amount of securities in an unregistered public offering if certain conditions are met. Unlike other transaction exemptions, Regulation A places no restrictions upon the resale of securities issued under it.

♦ **SEE FIGURE 43-1:** *Registration and Exemptions Under the 1933 Act*

Practical Advice

If you plan to issue securities, carefully explore the possibility of using a transaction that is exempt from registration.

43-4a LIMITED OFFERS

The 1933 Act exempts, or authorizes the SEC to exempt, transactions that do not require the protection of registration because they either involve a small amount of money or are made in a limited manner. Sections 3(b) and 4(a)(2).

Promulgated in 1982 to simplify and clarify these transaction exemptions, Regulation D originally contained three separate exemptions (Rules 504, 505, and 506), each involving limited offers, but Rule 505 was repealed in 2017. An exemption for limited offers made solely to accredited investors is a companion provision of the 1933 Act to the exemptions under Regulation D. Section 4(a)(5). Each of these three exemptions requires the issuer to file a Form D with the SEC online within fifteen days after the first sale of securities in the offering.

Securities sold pursuant to these exemptions (with the exception of some sold pursuant to Rule 504) are considered restricted securities and may be resold only by registration or in another transaction exempt from registration. An issuer who uses these exemptions must take reasonable care to prevent nonexempt, unregistered resales of restricted securities. Reasonable care includes, but is not limited to, the following: (1) making a reasonable inquiry to determine whether the purchaser is acquiring the securities for herself or for other persons, (2) providing written disclosure prior to the sale to each purchaser that the securities have not been registered and therefore cannot be resold unless they are registered or unless an exemption from registration is available, and (3) placing a legend on the securities certificate stating that the securities have not been registered and that they are restricted securities.

PRIVATE PLACEMENTS The most important transaction exemption for issuers is the so-called private placement provision of the 1933 Act, which exempts "transactions by an issuer not involving any public offering." Section 4(a)(2). SEC **Rule 506** establishes for all issuers a nonexclusive safe harbor for limited offers and sales without regard to the dollar amount of the offering. While compliance with the rule ensures the exemption, the exemption is not presumed to be unavailable for noncomplying transactions. Rule 506 is by far the most widely used Regulation D exemption, accounting for more than 90 percent of all Regulation D offerings and more than 99 percent of capital raised in Regulation D offerings.

Securities sold under this exemption are restricted securities and may be resold only by registration or in a transaction exempt from registration. The issue may be purchased by an unlimited number of "accredited investors" and by no more than thirty-five other purchasers. As amended in 2020, **accredited investors** include (1) banks, insurance companies, savings and loan associations, and investment companies, (2) executive officers or directors of the issuer, (3) registered broker-dealers, (4) certain employee benefit plans and business entities with total assets in excess of $5 million, (5) any natural person whose individual net worth, or joint net worth with that person's spouse or *spousal equivalent*, exceeds $1 million (not including the value of the person's primary residence), (6) any natural person who had an individual income in excess of $200,000 in each of the two most recent years, or joint income with that person's spouse or *spousal equivalent* in excess of $300,000 in each of those years, and has a reasonable expectation of reaching the same income level in the current year, and (7) any natural person holding in good standing one or more professional certifications or designations or credentials from an accredited educational institution that the SEC has designated as qualifying an individual for *accredited investor* status.

Before a sale involving any nonaccredited investors, such purchasers must receive specified information about the issuer, its business, and the securities being offered. If the sale involves only accredited investors, such disclosure is not mandatory. The issuer must reasonably believe that each purchaser who is not an accredited investor has sufficient knowledge regarding and experience in financial and business matters to evaluate capably the merits and risks of the investment or has the services of a representative possessing such knowledge and experience. General advertising or solicitation is not permitted unless, as provided by the JOBS Act and a 2013 amendment to Rule 506, sales are made exclusively to accredited investors and the issuer takes reasonable steps to verify that such purchasers

are accredited investors. The issuer must notify the SEC of sales made under the exemption and must take precautions against nonexempt, unregistered resales.

In 2013, as required by the Dodd-Frank Act, the SEC amended Rule 506 to impose "bad actor" disqualification requirements on offerings under Rule 506. "Bad actor" disqualification requirements disqualify securities offerings from reliance on exemptions if the issuer or other relevant persons have been convicted of, or are subject to court or administrative sanctions for, securities fraud or other violations of specified laws. Under the 2013 amendment to Rule 506, disqualifying conduct includes conviction of any felony or misdemeanor (1) in connection with the purchase or sale of any security or (2) involving the making of any false filing with the SEC.

LIMITED OFFERS NOT EXCEEDING $10 MILLION As amended in 1999 2017, and 2021, SEC **Rule 504** provides private, noninvestment company issuers with an exemption from registration for issues not exceeding $10 million within twelve months. Issuers that are *not* eligible to use Rule 504 include companies required to report under the 1934 Act, investment companies, and issuers that are disqualified under amended Rule 504's disqualification rules, which are substantially similar to the bad actor disqualifications under amended Rule 506. The issuer is to notify the SEC of sales under the rule, which permits sales to an unlimited number of investors and does not require the issuer to furnish any information to them.

If the issuance meets certain conditions, Rule 504 permits general solicitations, and acquired shares are freely transferable. The conditions are that the issuance is either (1) registered under State law requiring public filing and delivery of a disclosure document to investors before sale or (2) exempted under State law permitting general solicitation and advertising so long as sales are made only to accredited investors.

If the issuance does not meet these conditions, general solicitation and advertising are not permitted. Moreover, the securities issued are restricted, and the issuer must take precautions against nonexempt, unregistered resales.

LIMITED OFFERS SOLELY TO ACCREDITED INVESTORS Section 4(a)(5) of the 1933 Act exempts from registration offers and sales of securities solely to accredited investors if the total offering price is less than $5 million. General advertising or public solicitation is not permitted. As with Rules 506, an unlimited number of accredited investors may purchase the issue; however, unlike these rules, Section 4(a)(5) allows no unaccredited investors to purchase. No information is required to be furnished to the purchasers. Securities sold under this exemption are restricted securities and may be resold only by registration or in a transaction exempt from registration. The issuer must notify the SEC of sales made under the exemption and must take precautions against nonexempt, unregistered resales.

43-4b CROWDFUNDING EXEMPTION

Crowdfunding is the use of the internet or other means to raise money—typically in small amounts—from a large number of contributors to support a wide range of ideas and ventures. The JOBS Act establishes a regulatory structure for startups and small businesses to raise capital through securities offerings using the internet or other means through crowdfunding. The Act adds Section 4(a)(6) to the 1933 Act requiring the SEC to adopt rules to implement a new **crowdfunding exemption** from registration that will allow eligible, domestic, non-public issuers to raise annually up to $5 million (as of March 2021 and adjusted for inflation every five years). This crowdfunding exemption permits the sale of limited amounts of stock to a large number of individuals, whether accredited or not, through brokers or a new category of intermediaries, funding portals. A funding portal is a crowdfunding intermediary that is registered with the SEC and is a member of a registered national securities association. FINRA (Financial Industry Regulatory Authority) is currently the only such registered national securities association and, as of July 2021, it regulated more than sixty-five registered funding portals.

The issuer must file with the SEC and disclose to investors certain basic information, including a description of the company's business, risk factors, the company's financial statements, the target offering amount, and the intended use of the funds raised through the offering. Investors' annual combined investments in securities sold under this exemption are limited based on an income and net worth test. The purchaser may not transfer securities issued pursuant to this exemption for one year after purchase except for transfers to the issuer or accredited investors or as part of an offering registered with the SEC. The JOBS Act adds a new private right of action for a purchaser of a security in an exempted crowdfunding transaction for negligence-based liability for oral or written communications containing material misrepresentations or omissions made in the offering or sale of a security in that transaction. The suit may be brought against the "issuer," which is defined broadly to include any director, partner, principal executive officer, principal financial officer, and certain other officers, as well as any person who offers and sells securities on behalf of the issuer.

Effective in 2016, the SEC adopted **Regulation Crowdfunding** to implement the crowdfunding exemption provided by the JOBS Act. Regulation Crowdfunding prescribes rules governing the offer and sale of securities and provides a framework for the regulation of registered funding portals and broker-dealers that issuers are required to use as intermediaries in the offer and sale of securities in reliance on Section 4(a)(6). Regulation

Crowdfunding permits individuals to invest in securities-based crowdfunding transactions subject to certain thresholds, limits the amount of money an issuer can raise under the crowdfunding exemption, requires issuers to disclose certain information about their offers, and creates a regulatory framework for the intermediaries that facilitate the crowdfunding transactions. The following summarizes the key provisions of Regulation Crowdfunding. (The dollar amounts are as of March 2021 and are adjusted for inflation every five years.)

1. An issuer is permitted to raise a maximum aggregate amount of $5 million through crowdfunding offerings in a twelve-month period. Any amounts raised pursuant to other 1933 Act exemptions during that period do *not* count toward the $5 million limit.

2. The investment limitations for investors were amended effective March 15, 2021. Accredited investors are no longer subject to any investment limitations. For nonaccredited investors, the aggregate amount of securities sold to that investor during the 12-month period preceding the date of the crowdfunding transaction, including the securities sold to that investor in the crowdfunding transaction, may not exceed: (a) the greater of $2,200 or 5 percent of the greater of the investor's annual income or net worth, if either the investor's annual income or net worth is less than $107,000 or (b) 10 percent of the greater of the investor's annual income or net worth, not to exceed an amount sold of $107,000, if both the investor's annual income and net worth are equal to or more than $107,000.

3. Issuers that are *not* eligible to use the Regulation Crowdfunding exemption include non-U.S. companies, companies that already are 1934 Act reporting companies, certain investment companies, companies that are disqualified under Regulation Crowdfunding's disqualification rules that are similar to the bad actor disqualifications under amended Rule 506, companies that have failed to comply with the annual reporting requirements under Regulation Crowdfunding during the two years immediately preceding the filing of the offering statement, and companies that have no specific business plan or have indicated their business plan is to engage in a merger or acquisition with an unidentified company or companies.

4. Issuers must file certain information, including financial information, with the SEC via EDGAR and provide this information to investors and the relevant intermediary facilitating the crowdfunding offering. The information required to be disclosed includes the names of officers and directors as well as owners of 20 percent or more of the issuer; a description of the issuer's business and the use of proceeds from the offering; the price to the public of the

securities or the method for determining the price, the target offering amount, the deadline to reach the target offering amount, and whether the issuer will accept investments in excess of the target offering amount; a discussion of the issuer's financial condition; and specified financial statements of the issuer. As amended in 2021, before filing the offering statement with the SEC, issuers may "test the waters" by soliciting interest in a potential offering from the general public.

5. Offerings must be conducted exclusively through a platform operated by a registered broker or a funding portal, which is a new type of SEC registrant.

6. Securities cannot be resold for a period of one-year subject to certain limited exceptions, including resales to the issuer, to an accredited investor, as part of a registered offering, and to a family member of the purchaser.

7. An issuer's advertising notice that includes the terms of the offering can include no more than (a) a statement that the issuer is conducting an offering, the name of the intermediary through which the offering is being conducted, and a link directing the investor to the intermediary's platform; (b) the terms of the offering including the amount of securities offered, the nature of the securities, the price of the securities, and the closing date of the offering period; and (c) specified factual information about the company's legal identity and its business location.

8. Holders of securities sold pursuant to this exemption do not count toward the threshold that requires an issuer to register its securities with the SEC under Section 12 of the 1934 Act (discussed later) if the issuer (a) is current in its annual reporting obligation, (b) retains the services of a registered transfer agent, and (c) has less than $25 million in assets.

43-4c REGULATION A

Regulation A permits U.S. and Canadian issuers to offer up to $75 million of securities in any twelve-month period without registering them, subject to eligibility, disclosure, and reporting requirements. Regulation A establishes two tiers of offerings: Tier 1, for offerings of up to $20 million, and Tier 2, for offerings of up to $75 million. The following requirements apply to both Tier 1 and Tier 2 offerings. For offerings of up to $20 million, issuers may elect whether to proceed under Tier 1 or Tier 2.

1. As amended in 2019, Regulation A is available to U.S. and Canadian issuers except certain investment companies. (Prior to 2019, issuers required to report under the 1934 Act were not eligible.) Regulation A offerings are subject to "bad actor" disqualification rules that are substantially the same as the provisions in amended Rule 506.

2. Under Regulation A, securities may be offered and sold publicly with no prohibition on general solicitation and general advertising. Offerees and purchasers must be provided an offering circular, which includes a simplified form of narrative disclosure about the issuer and its business. An offering statement with specified disclosure must be filed electronically with the SEC on EDGAR. All issuers under Regulation A must file balance sheets and other required financial statements for the last two completed fiscal years. The SEC must qualify offering statements before sales may be made. Issuers may submit to the SEC a draft offering statement for confidential nonpublic review by SEC staff before the public filing. Moreover, Regulation A permits issuers to "test the waters" with, or solicit interest in a potential offering from, the general public either before or after the filing of the offering statement. Issuers must file summary information after the termination or completion of a Regulation A offering.

3. Securities sold under Regulation A are not restricted securities and therefore are not subject to the limitations on resale that apply to securities sold in private offerings.

4. Because Regulation A offerings are exempt from the registration requirements of the 1933 Act, the liability provisions of Section 11 of the 1933 Act, discussed later, do not apply. However, the civil liability provision in section 12(a)(2) and the antifraud liability provision in Section 17, discussed later in this chapter, apply to Regulation A offerings.

TIER 1 Tier 1 of Regulation A imposes (1) no restrictions regarding the number or qualifications of investors who may purchase securities and (2) no ongoing reporting requirements. Tier 1 offerings remain subject to the registration and qualification requirements of State Blue Sky securities laws.

TIER 2 Tier 2 of Regulation A imposes additional reporting requirements that include providing audited financial statements in the offering statement and filing annual, semiannual, and current event reports with the SEC electronically on EDGAR. The amount of securities that a nonaccredited investor can purchase in a Tier 2 offering is limited to no more than 10 percent of the greater of the investor's annual income or net worth, unless the securities are listed on a national securities exchange. These investment limitations, however, do not apply to investors who qualify as accredited investors under Regulation D. Regulation A as it applies to Tier 2 issuers preempts the registration and qualification requirements of State Blue Sky securities laws.

43-4d INTRASTATE ISSUES

The 1933 Act also exempts from registration any security that is part of an issue offered and sold only to persons resident within a single State where the issuer of such security is resident and doing business. Section 3(a)(11). This exemption is intended to apply to local issues representing local financing carried out by local persons through local investments.

RULE 147 SEC Rule 147, as amended in 2017, provides a nonexclusive safe harbor for securing the intrastate exemption. While compliance with the rule ensures the exemption, the exemption is not presumed to be unavailable for noncomplying transactions. Rule 147 as amended imposes the following requirements.

1. The issuer is resident within the State in which the issuance occurs, which means that the issuer is incorporated or organized and has its principal place of business in that State.

2. The issuer is doing business in that State, which means that the issuer satisfies at least one of the following: it derives at least 80 percent of its gross revenues from that State, at least 80 percent of its assets are located in that State, at least 80 percent of its net proceeds from the issue are used in that State, *or* a majority of the issuer's employees are based in that State.

3. All of the *offerees* and purchasers are residents of that State, or the issuer has a reasonable belief that all of the offerees and purchasers are residents of that State.

4. For a period of six months from the date of the sale by the issuer of a security under this exemption, any resale of such security is made *only* to residents of that State.

5. The issuer takes precautions against interstate sales. Such precautions include (a) placing on the security certificate a prominent legend stating that the securities have not been registered and that resales can be made only to residents of that State for six months from the date of sale and (b) obtaining a written statement of residence from each purchaser.

RULE 147A Effective in 2017, the SEC adopted a new intrastate exemption. Called Rule 147A, the new rule is substantially identical to Rule 147 as amended except that it allows issuers (1) to make offers accessible to out-of-State residents, so long as sales are limited to in-State residents and (2) to be incorporated or organized outside of the State of issuance provided (a) the issuer is resident in the State of issuance by having its principal place of business in that State and (b) the issuer is doing business in that State. For example, a company incorporated in Delaware has its principal place of business in Virginia and is doing business in Virginia. It may use new Rule 147A to sell securities to residents of Virginia. Moreover, unlike Rule 147, new Rule 147A permits issuers to engage in general solicitation and general advertising of their offerings, using any form of mass media, including unrestricted, publicly-available websites, so long as sales of securities so offered are made only to residents of the State in which the issuer is resident and doing business.

♦ SEE FIGURE 43-2: *Exempt Transactions for Issuers Under the 1933 Act*

43-5 Exempt Transactions for Nonissuers

The 1933 Act requires registration for any sale by any person (including nonissuers) of any nonexempt security unless a statutory exemption can be found for the transaction. The Act, however, provides a transaction exemption for any person other than an issuer, underwriter, or dealer. Section 4(a)(1). In addition, the Act exempts most transactions by dealers and brokers. Sections 4(a)(3) and 4(a)(4). These three provisions exempt from the registration requirements of the 1933 Act most secondary transactions; that is, the numerous resales that occur on an exchange or in the over-the-counter market. Nevertheless, these exemptions do not extend to some situations involving resales by nonissuers, in particular to (1) resales of restricted securities acquired under Regulation D (Rules 506 or 504) or Sections 4(a)(5) and (2) sales of restricted or nonrestricted securities by affiliates. Such sales must be made pursuant to registration, Rule 144, or Regulation A, subject to the limited exception provided to some issuances by Rule 504. An **affiliate** is a person who controls, is controlled by, or is under common control with the issuer. **Control** is the direct or indirect possession of the power to direct the management and policies of a person through ownership of securities, by contract, or otherwise. Rule 405.

Practical Advice

If you acquire restricted securities, do not resell them until you either register them—which is rarely feasible—or comply with an exemption for nonissuers.

43-5a RULE 144

Rule 144 of the SEC sets forth conditions that, if met by an affiliate or any person selling restricted securities, exempt her from registering those securities. As amended in 2008, the rule imposes less strict requirements on resales of securities of issuers that are subject to the reporting requirements of the 1934 Act than on resales of securities of nonreporting issuers.

FIGURE 43-2   Exempt Transactions for Issuers Under the 1933 Act

Exemption	Price Limitation	Information Required	Limitations on Purchasers	Resales
Regulation A Tier 1	$20 million	Offering circular	None	Unrestricted
Regulation A Tier 2	$75 million	Offering circular; Annual audited financial statements	Amounts purchased are limited for nonaccredited investors	Unrestricted
Intrastate Rule 147	None	None	Intrastate only	Only to residents before six months
Intrastate Rule 147A	None	None	Intrastate only	Only to residents before six months
Rule 506	None	Material information to nonaccredited purchasers	Unlimited accredited; Thirty-five sophisticated nonaccredited	Restricted
Rule 504	$10 million	None	None	Restricted*
Limited Offers Solely to Accredited Investors	$5 million	None	Only accredited	Restricted
Crowdfunding	$5 million	Specified basic information	Unlimited in number; Amount purchased limited for a nonaccredited purchaser based on that purchaser's net worth and income	Restricted

*Unrestricted if under State law the issuance is either (1) registered or(2) exempted with sales only to accredited investors.

NONREPORTING ISSUERS In the case of an affiliate selling *restricted* securities amended Rule 144 requires that there be adequate current public information about the issuer, that the affiliate selling under the rule have owned the restricted securities for at least one year, that she sell them only in limited amounts in unsolicited brokers' transactions, and that notice of the sale be provided to the SEC. An affiliate selling *nonrestricted* securities is subject to the same requirements except that the one-year holding period does not apply.

A person who is *not* an affiliate of the issuer when the restricted securities are sold and who has owned the restricted securities for at least one year may sell them in unlimited amounts and is not subject to any of the other requirements of Rule 144.

REPORTING ISSUERS Amended Rule 144 requires for an affiliate selling *restricted* securities that there be adequate current public information about the issuer, that the affiliate selling under the rule have owned the restricted securities for at least six months, that she sell them only in limited amounts in unsolicited brokers' transactions, and that notice of the sale be provided to the SEC. An affiliate selling *nonrestricted* securities is subject to the same requirements except for the one-year holding period.

If there is adequate current public information about the issuer, a person who is *not* an affiliate of the issuer when the *restricted* securities are sold and has owned the restricted securities for at least six months may sell them in unlimited amounts and is not subject to any of the other requirements of Rule 144. After one year, the nonaffiliate selling *restricted* securities need not comply with the current information requirement of Rule 144.

43-5b RULE 144A

While Rule 144 permits sales of restricted securities, the requirements of the rule have hampered the liquidity of privately placed securities. To improve the liquidity of such securities, in 1990, the SEC adopted Rule 144A, which provides an additional nonexclusive safe harbor from registration for resales of certain restricted securities. Only securities that at the time of issue are not of the same class as securities listed on a national securities exchange or quoted in a U.S. automated interdealer quotation system ("nonfungible securities") may be sold under Rule 144A. Such nonfungible securities may be sold only to a qualified institutional buyer, defined generally as an institution that in the aggregate owns and invests on a discretionary basis at least $100 million in securities. In 2013, the SEC amended Rule 144A to provide that securities may be *offered* pursuant to Rule 144A to persons other than qualified institutional buyers, provided that the securities are *sold* only to persons that the seller reasonably believes are qualified institutional buyers. Rule 144A also requires the seller of the nonfungible securities to take reasonable steps to ensure that the buyer knows that the seller is relying on Rule 144A. In addition, special requirements apply to securities issued by foreign companies. Securities acquired pursuant to Rule 144A are restricted securities.

43-5c REGULATION A

Regulation A also provides an exemption for nonissuers. Sales by selling stockholders that are affiliates of the issuer may not exceed (1) $6 million (of the $20 million overall limit) in Tier 1 offerings or (2) $22.5 million (of the $75 million overall limit) in Tier 2 offerings. These limits do not apply to secondary sales by nonaffiliates of an issuer. However, sales by affiliates and nonaffiliates in an issuer's initial Regulation A offering, and in any subsequently qualified Regulation A offering within twelve months thereafter, are limited to 30 percent of the aggregate offering price.

43-6 Liability

To implement the statutory objectives of providing full disclosure and preventing fraud in the sale of securities, the 1933 Act imposes a number of sanctions for noncompliance with its requirements. These sanctions include administrative remedies by the SEC, civil liability to injured investors, and criminal penalties.

Congress authorized both Federal and State courts to exercise jurisdiction over private suits brought under the 1933 Act. Unlike most instances of concurrent jurisdiction, Congress barred the removal of these actions from State to Federal court. So, if a plaintiff brings a 1933 Act suit in a State court, the defendant may not remove the case to a Federal court. In a unanimous 2018 decision, the U.S. Supreme Court held that under the Securities Litigation Uniform Standards Act of 1998, discussed earlier, (1) State courts have jurisdiction over class actions alleging violations of only the 1933 Act and (2) defendants are not permitted to remove such actions from State court to Federal court. *Cyan, Inc. v. Beaver County Employees Retirement Fund*, 583 U. S. _____.

The 1995 Reform Act provides "forward-looking" statements (predictions) a "safe harbor" under the 1933 Act from civil liability based on an untrue statement of material fact or an omission of a material fact necessary to make the statement not misleading. The safe harbor applies only to issuers required to report under the 1934 Act. The safe harbor eliminates civil liability if a forward-looking statement is (1) immaterial, (2) made without actual knowledge that it was false or misleading, or (3) identified as a forward-looking statement and is accompanied by meaningful cautionary statements identifying important factors that could cause actual results to differ materially from those predicted. "Forward-looking statements" include projections of revenues, income, earnings per share, capital expenditures, dividends, or capital structure; management's plans and objectives for future operations; and statements of future economic performance. The safe harbor provision, however, does not cover statements made in connection with an IPO, a tender offer, a going private transaction, or offerings by a partnership or an LLC.

43-6a UNREGISTERED SALES

Section 12(a)(1) of the 1933 Act imposes express civil liability for the sale of an unregistered security that is required to be registered, the sale of a registered security without delivery of a prospectus, the sale of a security by use of an outdated prospectus, or the offer of a sale prior to the filing of the registration statement. Liability is strict or absolute because there are no defenses. The person who purchases a security sold in violation of this provision has the right to tender it back to the seller and recover the purchase price. If the purchaser no longer owns the security, he may recover monetary damages from the seller.

43-6b FALSE REGISTRATION STATEMENTS

When securities have been sold subject to a registration statement, Section 11of the 1933 Act imposes express liability upon those who have included any untrue statement in the registration statement or who omit from the statement any material fact. Material matters are those to which a reasonable investor would be substantially likely to attach importance in determining whether to purchase the security registered. SEC Rule 405. Usually, proof of reliance upon the misstatement or omission is not required. The section imposes liability upon (1) the issuer; (2) all persons who signed the registration statement, including the principal executive officer, principal financial officer, and principal accounting officer; (3) every person who was a director or partner; (4) every accountant, engineer, appraiser, or expert who prepared or certified any part of the registration statement; and (5) all underwriters. These persons generally are jointly and severally liable for the amount paid for the security, less either its value at the time of suit or the price for which it was sold, to any person who acquires the security without knowledge of the untruth or omission. A defendant is not liable for any or the entire amount otherwise recoverable under Section 11 that the defendant proves was caused by something other than the defective disclosure. The court may award attorneys' fees against any party who brings suit or asserts a defense without merit.

An expert is liable only for misstatements or omissions in the portion of the registration that he prepared or certified. Moreover, any defendant, other than the issuer (who has strict liability), may assert the affirmative defense of due diligence. This due diligence defense generally requires the defendant to show that she had reasonable grounds to believe, and did believe, that there were no untrue statements or material omissions. In some instances, due diligence requires a reasonable investigation to determine grounds for belief. The standard of reasonableness for such investigation and such grounds is that required of a prudent person in the management of his own property. Section 11(c).

♦ *See Case 43-2*

43-6c ANTIFRAUD PROVISIONS

The 1933 Act contains two general antifraud provisions: Section 12(a)(2) and Section 17(a). In addition, Rule 10b-5 of the 1934 Act applies to the issuance or sale of all securities, even those exempted by the 1933 Act. Rule 10b-5 is discussed later in this chapter.

SECTION 12(A)(2) Section 12(a)(2) imposes express liability upon any person who offers or sells a security by means of a prospectus or oral communication that contains an untrue statement of material fact or omits a material fact. That liability extends only to the immediate purchaser, provided she did not know of the untruth or omission. The seller may avoid liability by proving that he did not know and in the exercise of reasonable care could not have known of the untrue statement or omission. The seller is liable to the purchaser for the amount paid upon tender of the security. If the purchaser no longer owns the security, she may recover damages from the seller. A defendant is not liable for any portion of or the entire amount otherwise recoverable under Section 12(a)(2) that the defendant proves was caused by something other than the defective disclosure.

SECTION 17(A) Section 17(a) makes it unlawful for any person in the offer or sale of any securities, whether registered or not, to do any of the following when using any means of transportation or communication in interstate commerce or the mails:

1. employ any device, scheme, or artifice to defraud;

2. obtain money or property by means of any untrue statement of a material fact or any statement that omits a material fact, without which the information is misleading; or

3. engage in any transaction, practice, or course of business that operates or would operate as a fraud or deceit upon the purchaser.

There is considerable doubt whether the courts may imply a private right of action for persons injured by violations of this section. The Supreme Court has reserved this question, and most lower courts have denied the existence of a private remedy. The SEC, however, may bring enforcement actions under Section 17(a).

43-6d CIVIL SANCTIONS

The SEC can bring a civil action in a U.S. District Court seeking an injunction, civil monetary penalties, or disgorgement (the return of illegal profits). The maximum amount of civil monetary penalties must be adjusted for inflation annually. The court may also bar or suspend an individual from serving as a corporate officer or director. A person who violates the court's order may be found in contempt and be subject to additional fines or imprisonment. The SEC may bring an administrative action seeking a cease-and-desist order; civil monetary penalties; disgorgement; and orders censuring, suspending, or expelling broker-dealers, investment advisers, and investment companies.

For almost all violations of the1933 Act, the SEC may bring a **civil action** in a U.S. district court seeking a civil monetary penalty of up to $975,230 (as adjusted annually for inflation in January 2021) to be paid by the person who committed the violation. Section 20(d). In any **administrative** cease-and-desist **action** under 1933 Act, the SEC may impose a civil monetary penalty of up to $863,145 (as adjusted annually for inflation in January 2021) on a person for a violation of any provision of the 1933 Act if the civil monetary penalty is in the public interest. Section 8A(g).

43-6e CRIMINAL SANCTIONS

The 1933 Act imposes criminal sanctions upon any person who willfully violates any of its provisions or the rules and regulations the SEC promulgates pursuant to the 1933 Act. Section 24. Conviction may carry a fine of not more than $10,000 or imprisonment of not more than five years or both. Moreover, under the Federal Alternative Fines Act, if any person derives pecuniary gain from the offense or if the offense results in pecuniary loss to a person other than the defendant, the defendant may be fined up to the greater of twice the gross gain or twice the gross loss.

♦ **SEE FIGURE 43-3:** *Registration and Liability Provisions of the 1933 Act*

SECURITIES EXCHANGE ACT OF 1934

The Securities Exchange Act of 1934 deals principally with the secondary distribution (resale) of securities. The definition of a security in the 1934 Act is substantially the same as the definition in the 1933 Act. The 1934 Act seeks to ensure fair and orderly securities markets by prohibiting fraudulent and manipulative practices and by establishing rules for market operations. As amended by the JOBS Act, the 1934 Act requires

FIGURE 43-3 Registration and Liability Provisions of the 1933 Act

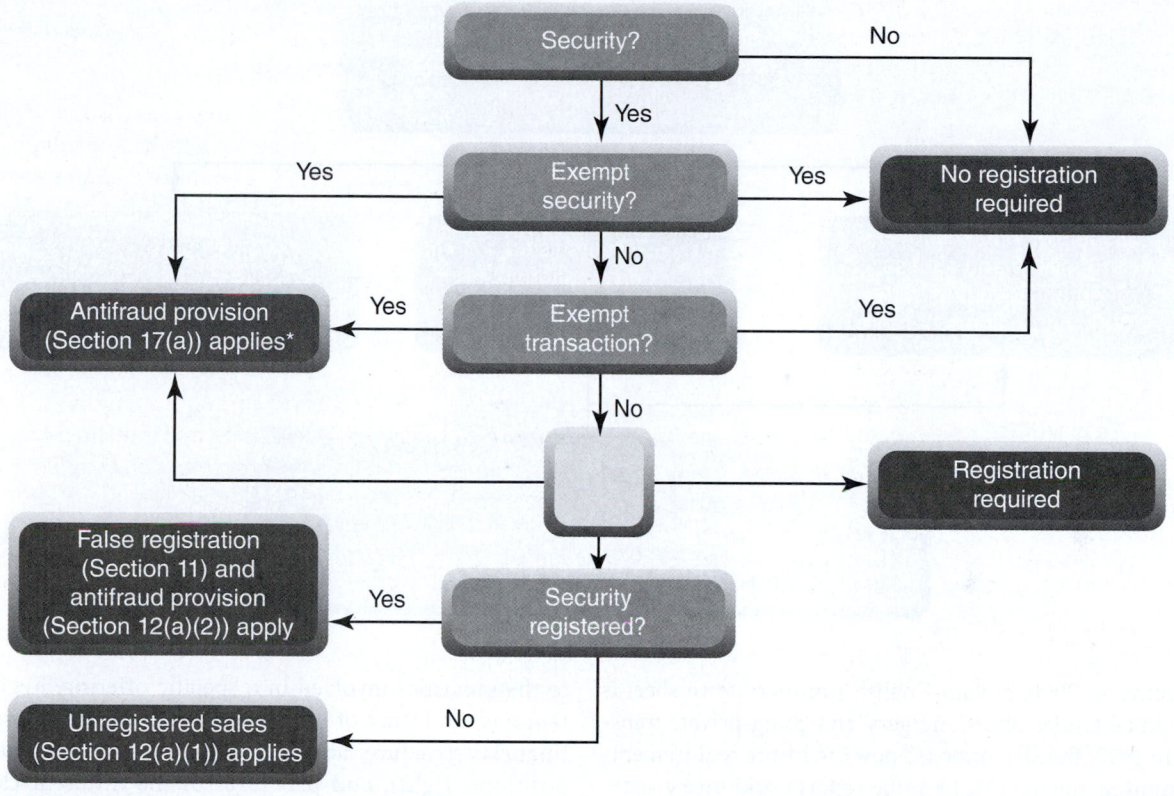

*Section 12(a)(2) may apply to some of these issuances.

registration of all securities listed on national exchanges, as well as equity securities of companies (1) whose total assets exceed $10 million and (2) whose equity securities include a class of equity securities held by either (a) two thousand or more persons or (b) five hundred or more persons who are not accredited investors. In 2016, the SEC issued rules implementing the JOBS Act amendments to the 1934 Act registration requirements. Foreign issuers whose securities are sold in the secondary market in the United States must register under the 1934 Act unless the issuers are exempt. Issuers who must register such securities are also subject to the 1934 Act's periodic reporting requirements, short-swing profits provision, tender offer provisions, and proxy solicitation provisions, as well as the internal control and recordkeeping requirements of the Foreign Corrupt Practices Act. In addition, issuers of securities, whether registered under the 1934 Act or not, must comply with the antifraud and antibribery provisions of the Act.

◆ *See Case 43-1*

◆ *SEE FIGURE 43-4: Applicability of the 1934 Act*

The National Securities Markets Improvements Act of 1996 broadly authorized the SEC to issue regulations, rules, or orders exempting any person, security, or transaction from any of the provisions of the 1934 Act or the SEC's rules promulgated under that Act. This authorization extends so far as such exemption is necessary or appropriate in the public interest and is consistent with the protection of investors. This exemptive authority does not, however, extend to the regulation of government securities broker-dealers.

43-7 Disclosure

The 1934 Act imposes significant disclosure requirements upon reporting companies. These include the filing of securities registrations, periodic reports, disclosure statements for proxy solicitations, and disclosure statements for tender offers, as well as compliance with the accounting requirements imposed by the Foreign Corrupt Practices Act. As part of its integrated registration and reporting system for small business issuers, in 1992, the SEC developed a new series of forms for qualifying issuers to use for registration and periodic reporting under the 1934

FIGURE 43-4   Applicability of the 1934 Act

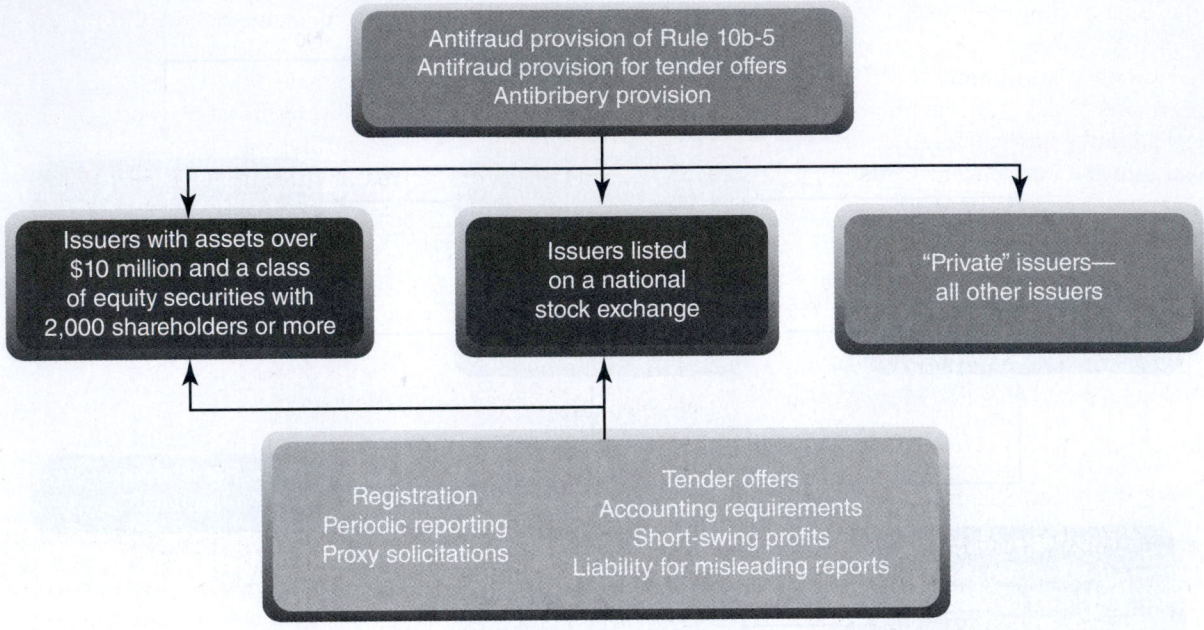

Act. Effective in 2000, a plain-English summary term sheet is required in all tender offers, mergers, and going-private transactions. In 1992, the SEC imposed new disclosure requirements for registration statements, periodic reports, and proxy statements that contain information regarding the compensation paid to senior executives and directors. As noted, in 2006, the SEC amended these rules to mandate clearer and more complete disclosure of compensation paid to directors, the CEO, the CFO, and the three other highest-paid executive officers. The issuer must disclose executive compensation over the past three years, including salary, bonus, a dollar value for stock and option awards, amount of compensation under nonequity incentive plans, annual change in present value of accumulated pension benefits and above-market earnings on nonqualified deferred compensation, and all other compensation including perquisites. Similar disclosure is required for director compensation for the last fiscal year. As mandated by the Dodd-Frank Act, in 2015, the SEC issued a rule requiring most public companies regularly to disclose the ratio of a CEO's compensation to the median compensation of the company's employees.

◆ **SEE FIGURE 43-5:** *Disclosure Under the 1934 Act*

43-7a REGISTRATION REQUIREMENTS FOR SECURITIES

The 1934 Act requires all regulated publicly held companies to register with the SEC. Section 12. These one-time registrations apply to an entire class of securities. Thus, they differ from registrations under the Securities Act of 1933, which relate only to the securities involved in a specific offering. Registration requires disclosure of information such as the organization, financial structure, and nature of the business; the terms, positions, rights, and privileges of the different classes of outstanding securities; the names of the directors, officers, and underwriters and of each security holder owning more than 10 percent of any class of nonexempt equity security; bonus and profit-sharing arrangements; and balance sheets and profit-and-loss statements for the three preceding fiscal years.

43-7b PERIODIC REPORTING REQUIREMENTS

Following registration, an issuer must file specified annual (10-K) and periodic (10-Q and 8-K) reports to update the information contained in the original registration. Also subject to the periodic reporting requirements are issuers who have filed a 1933 Act registration statement with respect to any security. Section 15. This duty is suspended, however, in any subsequent year during which the securities registered under the 1933 Act are held by fewer than three hundred persons.

The SEC has adopted rules under the Sarbanes-Oxley Act requiring an issuer's CEO and CFO to *certify* the financial and other information contained in the issuer's annual and quarterly reports. Moreover, the Act requires that each periodic report shall be *accompanied* by a written statement by the CEO and CFO of the issuer certifying that the periodic report fully complies with the requirements of the 1934 Act and that information contained in the periodic report fairly presents, in all material respects, the financial condition and results of operations of the issuer. A CEO or CFO who certifies while *knowing* that the report does not comply with the Act is subject to a fine of not more than $1 million or imprisonment of not more than ten years or both. A CEO or CFO who *willfully* certifies a statement knowing it does not comply with the Act shall be fined not more than $5 million or be imprisoned not more than twenty years or both.

The Sarbanes-Oxley Act requires that issuers disclose in plain English to the public on a rapid and current basis such additional information concerning material changes in the financial condition or operations of the issuer as the SEC determines is necessary or useful for the protection of investors and in the public interest.

The 1934 Act, as amended by the Dodd-Frank Act, requires that each director, each officer, and any person who owns more than 10 percent of a registered equity security file reports with the SEC within ten days after he or she becomes such beneficial

owner, director, or officer or within such shorter time as the SEC may establish by rule. The 1934 Act also requires that each director, each officer, and any person who owns more than 10 percent of a registered equity security file reports with the SEC for any month during which changes in his ownership of such equity securities have occurred before the end of the second business day following the day on which the transaction was executed, unless the SEC establishes a different deadline. The 1934 Act also requires that these filings reporting changes in ownership be made electronically on EDGAR, that the SEC make them publicly available on its website, and that the issuers make them available on their corporate websites if they have them.

Effective in 2010, the SEC adopted new requirements to improve the disclosure shareholders of public companies receive regarding compensation and corporate governance.

FIGURE 43-5 Disclosure Under the 1934 Act

	Initial Registration	Periodic Reporting	Insider Reporting	Proxy Statement	Tender Offer
Registrant	Issuer if regulated, publicly held company	Issuer if regulated, publicly held company	Statutory insiders (directors, officers, and principal stockholders)	Issuer and other persons soliciting proxies	5 percent stockholder, tender offeror, or issuer
Information	Nature of business; Financial structure; Directors and executive officers; Financial statements	Annual, quarterly, or current report updating information in initial registration	Initial statement of beneficial ownership of equity securities; Changes in beneficial ownership	Details of solicitation; Legal terms of proxy; Annual report (if directors to be elected)	Identity and background; Terms of transaction; Source of funds; Intentions
Filing Date	Within 120 days after becoming a reporting company	Annual: within 90 days* after year's end; Quarterly: within 45 days** after quarter's end; Current: within 4 days after any material change	Within 10 days of becoming a statutory insider; Within 2 days after a change in ownership takes place	10 days before final proxy statement is distributed	5 percent stockholder: within 10 days after acquiring more than 5 percent of a class of registered securities; Tender offeror: before tender offer is made; Issuer: before offer to repurchase
Purpose of Disclosure	Adequate and accurate disclosure of material facts regarding securities listed on a national exchange or traded publicly over the counter	Update information contained in initial registration	Prevent unfair use of information that may have been obtained by a statutory insider	Full disclosure of material information; Facilitation of shareholder proposals	Adequate and accurate disclosure of material facts; Opportunity to reach uncoerced decision

*Certain issuers must file within sixty or seventy-five days.
**Certain issuers must file within forty days.

These new rules require disclosure of (1) the qualifications of directors and nominees for director and the reasons why that person should serve as a director of the issuer; (2) any directorships held by each director and nominee at any time during the past five years at any public company or registered investment company; (3) the consideration of diversity in the process by which candidates for director are considered for nomination by an issuer's nominating committee; (4) an issuer's board leadership structure and the board's role in the oversight of risk; (5) the aggregate grant date fair value of stock awards and option awards granted in the fiscal year computed in accordance with Financial Accounting Standards Board Accounting Standards; and (6) the issuer's compensation policies or practices as they relate to risk management and risk-taking incentives that can affect the issuer's risk and management of that risk, to the extent that risks arising from an issuer's compensation policies and practices for employees are reasonably likely to have a material adverse effect on the issuer.

Practical Advice

If you are a director, are an officer, or own more than 10 percent of a registered security, be sure to report to the SEC any sales or purchases you make of the company's equity securities.

43-7c PROXY SOLICITATIONS

A **proxy** is a writing signed by a shareholder authorizing a named person to vote his shares of stock at a specified shareholders' meeting. To ensure that shareholders have adequate information with which to vote and an opportunity to participate effectively at shareholder meetings, the 1934 Act regulates the proxy solicitation process. The 1934 Act makes it unlawful for any person to solicit any proxy with respect to any registered security "in contravention of such rules and regulations as the Commission may prescribe." Section 14. **Solicitation** includes any request for a proxy, any request not to execute a proxy, or any request to revoke a proxy. The SEC has issued comprehensive and detailed rules prescribing the solicitation process and the disclosure of information about the issuer.

PROXY STATEMENTS Rule 14a-3 prohibits the solicitation of a proxy unless each person solicited has been furnished with a written proxy statement containing specified information. An issuer making solicitations must furnish security holders with a *proxy statement* describing all material facts concerning the matters being submitted to their vote, together with a *proxy form* on which the security holders can indicate their approval or disapproval of each proposal to be presented. Even a company that submits a matter to a shareholder vote rather than solicits proxies must provide its shareholders with information substantially equivalent to what would appear in a proxy statement. With few exceptions, the issuer must file preliminary copies of a proxy statement and proxy form with the SEC at least ten days prior to the first date they are to be sent. In addition, in an election of directors, solicitations of proxies by a person other than the issuer are subject to similar disclosure requirements. The issuer in such an election also must include an annual report with the proxy statement. Effective in 2010, the SEC requires in proxy materials relating to the election of directors that the issuer disclose the qualifications of nominees for director and the reasons why that person should serve as a director of the issuer. The same information is required in the proxy materials prepared with respect to nominees for director nominated by others. Moreover, the Dodd-Frank Act authorizes the SEC to issue rules requiring that an issuer's proxy solicitation include nominations for the board of directors submitted by shareholders. Under the Dodd-Frank Act, the SEC must issue rules requiring issuers to disclose in annual proxy statements the reasons why the issuer has chosen to separate or combine the positions of chairman of the board of directors and CEO.

The Dodd-Frank Act contains several provisions regarding executive compensation. First, at least once every three years, issuers must include a provision in certain proxy statements for a nonbinding shareholder vote on the compensation of executives. In a separate resolution, shareholders determine whether this "say on pay" vote should be held every one, two, or three years. Second, the SEC must issue rules requiring issuers to describe clearly in annual proxy statements information that shows the relationship between executive compensation actually paid and the financial performance of the issuer, taking into account any change in the value of the shares of stock and dividends of the issuer and any distributions. (In 2015, the SEC proposed rules implementing this Dodd-Frank Act mandate but had not issued a final rule by the time this book went to press.) Third, the SEC must issue rules requiring the disclosure of (1) the median of the annual total compensation of all issuer's employees except the CEO, (2) the annual total compensation of the CEO, and (3) the ratio of the amount described in (1) to the amount described in (2). The JOBS Act exempts EGCs from the requirement for separate shareholder approval of executive compensation, including golden parachute compensation.

In 2007, the SEC amended its proxy rules to provide an alternative method for issuers and other persons to furnish proxy materials to shareholders: posting them on a website and providing shareholders with notice of the availability of the proxy materials. Issuers must make paper or e-mail copies of the proxy materials available without charge to shareholders on request.

SHAREHOLDER PROPOSALS Where management makes a solicitation, any security holder entitled to vote has the opportunity to communicate with other security holders. Upon written request, the corporation must mail the communication at the security holder's expense or, at its option, promptly furnish to that security holder a current list of security holders.

If an eligible security holder entitled to vote submits a timely and appropriate proposal for action at a forthcoming meeting, management must include the proposal in its proxy statement and provide security holders with an opportunity to vote for or against it. To be eligible, the holder must own the lesser of 1 percent or $2,000 in market value of the security for at least one year prior to submitting the proposal. If management opposes the proposal, it must include in its proxy materials a statement by the security holder in support of the proposal. The aggregate length of the proposal and the supporting statement may not exceed five hundred words. A security holder is limited to submitting one proposal to an issuer each year.

Management may omit a proposal if, among other things, (1) under State law it is not a proper subject for shareholder action, (2) it would require the company to violate any law, (3) it is beyond the issuer's power or authority to effectuate, (4) it relates to the conduct of the ordinary business operations of the issuer, or (5) it relates to a nomination or an election for membership on the issuer's board of directors or to a procedure for such nomination or election. However, in 2010, the SEC amended the last exclusion by providing shareholders, under certain circumstances, the power to include in an issuer's proxy materials a shareholder proposal to establish in the issuer's governing documents a procedure for the inclusion in the proxy materials of director nominees selected by a shareholder or group of shareholders. Such a proposal must be consistent with the following new rule. In 2011, the U.S. Court of Appeals for the District of Columbia invalidated this new proxy access provision based on the court's conclusion that the SEC had violated the Administrative Procedure Act by failing adequately to assess the economic effects of the new rule as required by the 1934 Act. The SEC decided not to seek a rehearing or review by the U.S. Supreme Court of this court decision. Unaffected by this court decision is a companion SEC rule adopted in 2010 permitting eligible shareholders to require companies to include shareholder proposals regarding proxy access procedures in company proxy materials. Under this new rule, companies will no longer be able to exclude a proposal seeking to establish a procedure in a company's governing documents for the inclusion of one or more shareholder nominees for director in the company's proxy materials.

43-7d TENDER OFFERS

A **tender offer** is a general invitation by a buyer (bidder) to the shareholders of a target company to tender their shares for sale at a specified price for a specified time. In 1968, Congress enacted the Williams Act, which amended the 1934 Act to extend reporting and disclosure requirements to tender offers and other block acquisitions. The purpose of the Williams Act is to provide public shareholders with full disclosure by both the bidder and the target company so that the shareholders may make an informed decision.

DISCLOSURE REQUIREMENTS The 1934 Act imposes disclosure requirements in three situations: (1) when a person or group acquires more than 5 percent of a class of voting securities registered under the 1934 Act, (2) when a person makes a tender offer for more than 5 percent of a class of registered equity securities, or (3) when the issuer makes an offer to repurchase its own registered shares. Although each situation is governed by different rules, the disclosure required is substantially the same. A statement must be filed with the SEC containing (1) the acquisitor's background; (2) the source of the funds used to acquire the securities; (3) the purpose of the acquisition, including any plans to liquidate the company or to make major changes in the corporate structure; (4) the number of shares owned; (5) the terms of the transaction; and (6) any relevant contracts, arrangements, or understandings. Sections 13(d) and 14(d). This disclosure is also required of anyone soliciting shareholders to accept or reject a tender offer. A copy of the statement must be furnished to each offeree and sent to the issuer. The target company has ten days in which to respond to the bidder's tender offer by (1) recommending acceptance or rejection, (2) expressing no opinion and remaining neutral or stating that it is unable to take a position. The target company's response must include the reasons for the position taken.

REQUIRED PRACTICES A tender offer by either a third party or the issuer is subject to the following rules. The initial tender offer must be kept open for at least twenty business days and for at least ten days after any change in terms. Shareholders who tender their shares may withdraw them at any time during the offering period. The tender offer must be open to all holders of the class of shares subject to the offer, and all shares tendered must be purchased for the same price; thus, if an offering price is increased, both those who have tendered and those who have yet to tender will receive the benefit of the increase. A tender offeror who offers to purchase less than all of the outstanding securities of the target must accept, on a *pro rata* basis, securities tendered during the offer. During the tender offer, the bidder may buy shares of the target only through that tender offer. In a tender offer for all outstanding shares of a class, a tender offeror may provide a subsequent offering period of three to twenty days after completion of a tender offer, during which time security holders can tender shares without withdrawal rights.

DEFENSIVE TACTICS When confronted by an uninvited takeover bid—or by a potential, uninvited bid-management of the target company may decide either to oppose the bid or seek to prevent it. The defensive tactics management employs to prevent or defend against undesired tender offers have developed (and are still evolving) into a highly ingenious, and metaphorically named, set of maneuvers, some of which require considerable planning and several of which are of questionable legality.

STATE REGULATION More than forty States have enacted statutes regulating tender offers. Although they vary greatly, most of these statutes tend to protect a target company from an unwanted tender offer. Some empower the State to review the merits of an offer or the adequacy of disclosure. Many impose waiting periods before the tender offer becomes effective. The State statutes generally require disclosures more detailed than those the Williams Act requires, and many of them exempt tender offers supported by the target company's management. A number of States have adopted fair price statutes, which require the acquisitor to pay to all shareholders the highest price paid to any shareholder. Some States have enacted business combination statutes prohibiting transactions with an acquisitor for a specified time after change in control, unless disinterested shareholders approve.

43-7e FOREIGN CORRUPT PRACTICES ACT

In 1977, Congress enacted the Foreign Corrupt Practices Act (FCPA) as an amendment to the 1934 Act. Amended in 1988 and 1998, the Act (1) imposes internal control requirements upon issuers with securities registered under the 1934 Act and (2) prohibits all U.S. persons, and certain foreign issuers of securities, from bribing foreign governmental or political officials, as discussed later in this chapter.

The accounting requirements of the FCPA reflect the ideas that accurate recordkeeping is essential to managerial responsibility and that investors should be able to rely on the financial reports they receive. Accordingly, the accounting requirements were enacted (1) to assure that an issuer's books accurately reflect financial transactions, (2) to protect the integrity of independent audits of financial statements, and (3) to promote the reliability of financial information required by the 1934 Act.

The FCPA requires every issuer that has a class of registered securities to

1. make and keep books, records, and accounts which, in reasonable detail, accurately and fairly reflect the transactions and disposition of the assets of the issuer; and
2. devise and maintain a system of internal controls to assure that transactions are executed as authorized and recorded in conformity with generally accepted accounting principles, thereby establishing accountability with regard to assets and assuring that access to those assets is permitted only with management's authorization. Section 13(b).

43-8 Liability

To implement its objectives, the 1934 Act imposes a number of sanctions for noncompliance with its disclosure and antifraud requirements. These sanctions include civil monetary liability to injured investors and issuers, civil monetary penalties, and criminal penalties. Unlike the 1933 Act, all private suits under the 1934 Act must be brought in Federal court.

The 1995 Reform Act contains several provisions that affect civil liability under the 1934 Act. First, the 1995 Reform Act imposes on a plaintiff in any private action under the 1934 Act the burden of proving that the defendant's alleged violation of the 1934 Act caused the loss for which the plaintiff seeks to recover damages. Second, the 1995 Reform Act imposes a limit on the amount of damages a plaintiff can recover in any private action under the 1934 Act based on a material misstatement or omission in which she seeks to establish damages by reference to the market price of a security. The plaintiff may not recover damages in excess of the difference between the purchase or sale price she paid or received for the security and the mean trading price of that security during the ninety-day period beginning on the date when the information correcting the misstatement or omission is disseminated to the market. Third, the 1995 Reform Act provides a "safe harbor" under the 1934 Act from civil liability based on an untrue statement of material fact or an omission of a material fact necessary to make the statement not misleading. The safe harbor applies to issuers required to report under the 1934 Act and who make "forward-looking" statements (predictions) if the statements meet specified requirements. The requirements of the safe harbor and the transactions to which it does not apply were discussed earlier in this chapter.

43-8a MISLEADING STATEMENTS IN REPORTS

Section 18 of the 1934 Act imposes express civil liability upon any person who makes or causes to be made any false or misleading statement with respect to any material fact in any application, report, document, or registration filed with the SEC under the 1934 Act. Any person who purchased or sold a security in reliance upon a false or misleading statement without knowing that it was false or misleading may recover under Section 18. Nevertheless, a person who made such a statement or who caused one to be made is not liable if she proves that she acted in good faith and had no knowledge that such statement was false or misleading. The court may award attorneys' fees against either the plaintiff or the defendant.

43-8b SHORT-SWING PROFITS

Section 16(b) of the 1934 Act imposes express liability upon insiders—directors, officers, and any person owning more than 10 percent of the stock of a corporation listed on a national stock exchange or registered with the SEC—for all profits resulting from their "short-swing" trading in such stock. If any insider sells such stock within six months from the date of its purchase or purchases such stock within six months from the date of a sale of the stock, the corporation is entitled to recover any and all profit the insider realizes from these transactions. The "profit" recoverable is calculated by matching the highest sale price against the lowest purchase price within the relevant six-month period. Losses cannot be offset against profits. Suit to recover such profit may be brought by the issuer or by the owner of any security of the issuer in the name and on behalf of the issuer if the issuer fails or refuses to bring such suit within sixty days of the owner's request.

43-8c ANTIFRAUD PROVISION

Section 10(b) of the 1934 Act and SEC Rule 10b-5 make it unlawful for any person to do any of the following when using the mails or facilities of interstate commerce in connection with the purchase or sale of any security:

1. employ any device, scheme, or artifice to defraud;

2. make any untrue statement of a material fact;

3. omit to state a material fact necessary to make the statements made not misleading; or

4. engage in any act, practice, or course of business that operates or would operate as a fraud or deceit upon any person.

Rule 10b-5 applies to any purchase or sale of any security, whether it is registered under the 1934 Act or not, whether it is publicly traded or closely held, whether it is listed on an exchange or sold over the counter, or whether it is part of an initial issuance or a secondary distribution. There are *no* exemptions. The implied liability under Rule 10b-5 applies to purchaser as well as seller misconduct and allows both defrauded sellers and buyers to recover.

REQUISITES OF RULE 10B-5   Recovery of damages under Rule 10b-5 requires proof of (1) a misstatement or omission (2) that is material, (3) made with *scienter*, (4) relied upon (5) in connection with the purchase or sale of a security and (6) that causes economic loss. This rule differs from common law fraud in that Rule 10b-5 imposes an affirmative duty of disclosure. A misstatement or omission is **material** if there is a substantial likelihood that a reasonable investor would consider it important in deciding whether to purchase or sell the security. Examples of material facts include substantial changes in dividends or earnings, significant misstatements of asset value, and the fact that the issuer is about to become a target of a tender offer. In an action for damages under Rule 10b-5, it must be shown that the violation was committed with *scienter*, or intentional misconduct. Negligence is not sufficient. Although the Supreme Court has yet to decide whether reckless conduct is sufficient to satisfy the requirement of *scienter*, the vast majority of circuit and district courts have held recklessness to be sufficient.

Direct reliance may be difficult to prove in a 10b-5 action because the buyer and seller usually do not negotiate their deal face to face. Recognizing the special nature of securities market transactions, the Supreme Court adopted the fraud-on-the-market theory, which establishes a rebuttable presumption of reliance based on the premise that the market price of a stock reflects any misstatement or omission and that the fraudulently affected market price has injured the plaintiff. Thus, a person who bought or sold a corporation's shares on a securities exchange after the issuance of a materially misleading statement by the corporation may invoke a rebuttable presumption that, in trading, he relied on the integrity of the price set by the market.

Remedies for violations of Rule 10b-5 include rescission, damages, and injunctions. The courts are divided over the measure of damages to impose.

♦ *See Case 43-3*

INSIDER TRADING   Rule 10b-5 applies to sales or purchases of securities made by an "insider" who possesses material information that is not available to the general public. An insider who fails to disclose the material, nonpublic information before trading on the information will be liable under Rule 10b-5 unless he waits for the information to become public. Under SEC Rule 10b5-1, a purchase or sale of an issuer's security is based on material nonpublic information about that security or issuer if the person making the purchase or sale was *aware* of the information when the person entered into the transaction. **Insiders**, for the purpose of Rule 10b-5, include directors, officers, employees, and agents of the security issuer, as well as those with whom the issuer has entrusted information solely for corporate purposes, such as underwriters, accountants, lawyers, and consultants. In some instances, the rule also precludes persons who receive material, nonpublic information from insiders—tippees—from trading on that information. A tippee who knows or should know that an insider has breached his fiduciary duty to the shareholders by disclosing inside information to the tippee is under a duty not to trade on such information.

♦ **SEE FIGURE 43-6:** *Parties Forbidden to Trade on Inside Information*

The U.S. Supreme Court has upheld the misappropriation theory as an additional and complementary basis for imposing liability for insider trading. *United States v. O'Hagan*, 521 U.S. 642 (1997). Under this theory, a person may be held liable for

FIGURE 43-6 **Parties Forbidden to Trade on Inside Information**

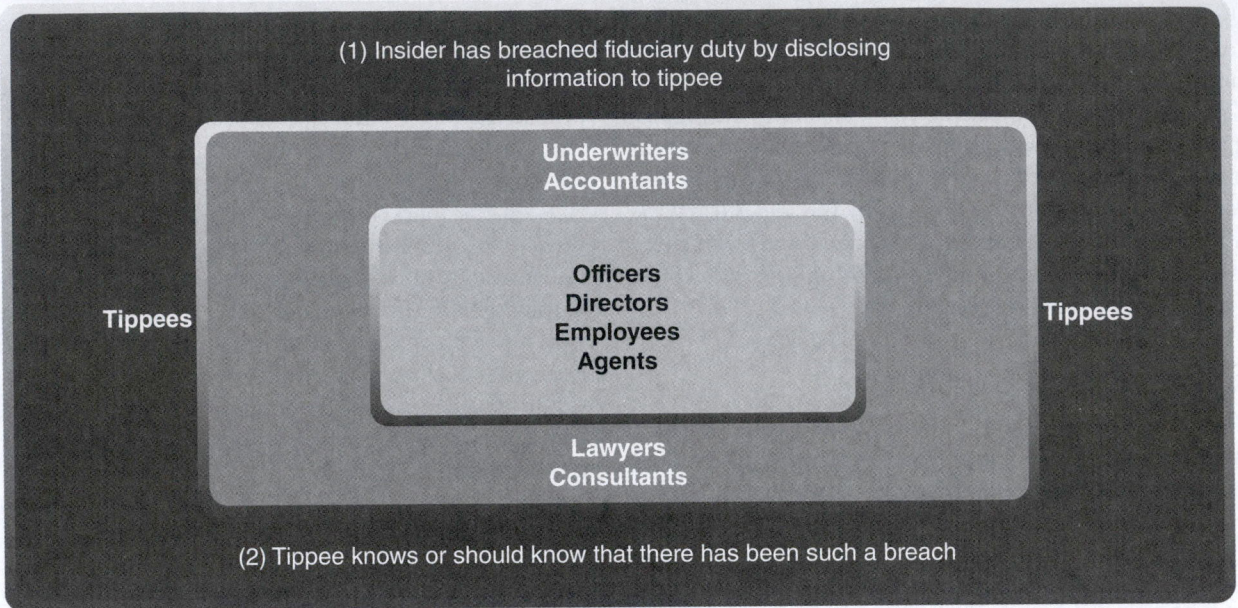

insider trading under Rule 10b-5 if she trades in securities for personal profit using confidential information misappropriated in breach of a fiduciary duty to the source of the information. This liability applies even though the source of information is not the issuer of the securities that were traded. SEC Rule 10b5-2 adopts the misappropriation theory of liability: A violation of Section 10(b) includes the purchase or sale of a security of an issuer on the basis of material nonpublic information about that security or issuer in breach of trust or confidence that is owed to the issuer, the shareholders of that issuer, or *any other person who is the source of the material nonpublic information*. Under SEC Rule 10b5-2, a person has a duty of trust or confidence for purposes of the misappropriation theory of liability when (1) a person agrees to maintain information in confidence; (2) two people have a history, pattern, or practice of sharing confidences such that the recipient of the information knows or reasonably should know that the person communicating the material nonpublic information expects that the recipient will maintain its confidentiality; *or* (3) a person receives or obtains material nonpublic information from his or her spouse, parent, child, or sibling.

◆ *See Case 43-4*

The **Stop Trading on Congressional Knowledge Act of 2012** prohibits the purchase or sale of securities of any issuer by a person in possession of material nonpublic information regarding pending or prospective legislative action relating to the issuer of the securities if the information was obtained

(1) by reason of being a member or employee of Congress or (2) knowingly from a member or employee of Congress. The Act also prohibits the purchase or sale of securities of any issuer by a person in possession of material nonpublic information derived from Federal employment and relating to the issuer of the securities if the information was obtained (1) by reason of being a Federal employee or (2) knowingly from a Federal employee.

Under SEC **Regulation FD** (for "fair disclosure"), regulated issuers who disclose material nonpublic information to specified persons (primarily securities market professionals such as analysts and mutual fund managers) must make public disclosure of that information. If the selective disclosure was intentional or reckless, the issuer must make public disclosure simultaneously; for a nonintentional disclosure, the issuer must make public disclosure promptly, usually within twenty-four hours. In 2013, the SEC issued a report (1) confirming that Regulation FD applies to social media and other emerging means of communication used by public companies the same way it applies to company websites and (2) clarifying that issuers can use social media outlets like Facebook and Twitter to announce key information in compliance with Regulation FD so long as investors have been alerted about which social media will be used to disseminate such information. With a few exceptions, Regulation FD does not apply to disclosures made in connection with a securities offering registered under the 1933 Act. The SEC can enforce this rule by bringing an administrative action seeking a cease-and-desist order or a civil action seeking an injunction and/or civil monetary penalties.

Although both Section 16(b) of the 1934 Act and Rule 10b-5 address the problem of insider trading and both may apply to the same transaction, they differ in several respects. First, Section 16(b) applies only to transactions involving registered equity securities; Rule 10b-5 applies to all securities. Second, the definition of *insider* under Rule 10b-5 extends beyond directors, officers, and owners of more than 10 percent of a company's stock, whereas the definition under Section 16(b) is limited to these persons. Third, Section 16(b) does not require that the insider possess material, nonpublic information; liability is strict. Rule 10b-5 applies to insider trading only where such information is not disclosed. Fourth, Section 16(b) applies only to transactions occurring within six months of each other; Rule 10b-5 has no such limitation. Fifth, under Rule 10b-5, injured investors may recover damages on their own behalf; under Section 16(b), although shareholders may bring suit, any recovery is on behalf of the corporation.

43-8d EXPRESS INSIDER TRADING LIABILITY

Section 20A of the 1934 Act imposes express civil liability upon any person who violates the Act by purchasing or selling a security while in possession of material, nonpublic information. Any person who contemporaneously sold or purchased securities of the same class as those improperly traded may bring a private action against the traders to recover damages for the violation. The total amount of damages may not exceed the profit gained or loss avoided by the violation, diminished by any amount the violator disgorges to the SEC pursuant to a court order. The action must be brought within five years after the date of the last transaction that is the subject of the violation. Tippers are jointly and severally liable with tippees who commit a violation by trading on the inside information.

43-8e CIVIL MONETARY PENALTIES FOR INSIDER TRADING

In addition to the remedies discussed previously, the SEC is authorized to bring an action in a U.S. district court to have a civil monetary penalty imposed upon any person who purchases or sells a security while in possession of material, nonpublic information. Liability also extends to any person who by communicating material, nonpublic information aids and abets another in committing such a violation. Liability also may be imposed on any person who directly or indirectly controlled a person who ultimately committed a violation if the controlling person knew or recklessly disregarded the fact that the controlled person was likely to commit a violation and consequently failed to take appropriate steps to prevent the transgression. Under this provision, law firms, accounting firms, issuers, financial printers, news media, and others must implement policies to prevent insider trading. The violating transaction must be on or through the facilities of a national securities exchange or from or through a broker or dealer. Purchases that are part of a public offering by an issuer of securities are not subject to this provision.

The civil monetary penalty for a person who trades on inside information is determined by the court in light of the facts and circumstances but may not exceed three times the profit gained or loss avoided as a result of the unlawful purchase or sale. The maximum amount that may be imposed upon a controlling person is the greater of $2,166,279 (as adjusted annually for inflation in Jnauary 2021) or three times the profit gained or loss avoided as a result of the controlled person's violation. If that violation consists of tipping inside information, the court measures the controller's liability by the profit gained or loss avoided by the person to whom the controlled person directed the tip. For the purpose of this provision, "profit gained" or "loss avoided" is "the difference between the purchase or sale price of the security and the value of that security as measured by the trading price of the security a reasonable period after public dissemination of the nonpublic information."

Civil monetary penalties for insider trading are payable into the U.S. Treasury. An action to recover a penalty must be brought within five years after the date of the purchase or sale. The SEC is authorized to award bounties of up to 10 percent of a recovered penalty to informants who provide information leading to the imposition of the penalty. However, the Dodd-Frank Act has expanded whistleblower awards: the SEC now must award eligible whistle-blowers who voluntarily provide original information that leads to *any* successful enforcement action in which the SEC imposes monetary sanctions in excess of $1 million. The amount of the award must be between 10 percent and 30 percent of funds collected as monetary sanctions, as determined by the SEC.

Practical Advice

If you confidentially acquire any nonpublic information about a company, do not trade in that company's securities until that information has become public.

43-8f MISLEADING PROXY STATEMENTS

Any person who distributes a materially false or misleading proxy statement may be liable to a shareholder who relies upon the statement in purchasing or selling a security and thereby suffers a loss. In this context, a misstatement or omission is material if there is a substantial likelihood that a reasonable shareholder would consider it important in deciding how to vote. A number of courts have held that negligence is sufficient for an action under the proxy rule's antifraud provisions. In addition, when the proxy disclosure or filing requirement has been violated, a court may, if appropriate, enjoin a shareholder meeting or any action taken at that meeting. Other remedies are rescission, damages, and attorneys' fees. Since a proxy statement is filed with the SEC, a materially false or misleading proxy statement may also give rise to liability under Section 18, discussed earlier.

In addition, Rule 10b-5 also applies to misstatements in proxy statements. Moreover, most proxy statements used with mergers and sales of assets are also considered 1933 registration statements subject to civil liability under Section 11 of the 1933 Act.

43-8g FRAUDULENT TENDER OFFERS

It is unlawful for any person in connection with any tender offer to (1) make any untrue statement of material fact; (2) omit to state any material fact; or (3) engage in any fraudulent, deceptive, or manipulative practices. Section 14(e). This provision applies even if the target company is not subject to the 1934 Act's reporting requirements. Insider trading during a tender offer is prohibited by Rule 14e-3, which has been upheld by the U.S. Supreme Court in *United States v. O'Hagan*, discussed previously.

Some courts have implied civil liability for violations of Section 14(e). Because relatively few cases have involved such violations, however, the requirements for such an action are not entirely clear. At present, a target company may seek an injunction, and a shareholder of the target may be able to recover damages or obtain rescission. Furthermore, it appears likely that the courts will require *scienter*.

♦ *See Case 43-5*

♦ **SEE FIGURE 43-7:** *Civil Liability Under the 1933 and 1934 Acts*

43-8h ANTIBRIBERY PROVISION OF FCPA

The FCPA generally prohibits a U.S. person, and certain foreign issuers of securities, from paying bribes to foreign officials to assist in obtaining or retaining business. Since 1998, the antibribery provisions also apply to foreign firms and persons who take any act in furtherance of such a corrupt payment while in the United States.

The FCPA makes it unlawful for any U.S. person, and certain foreign issuers of securities, or any of its officers, directors, employees, or agents to offer or give anything of value directly or indirectly to any foreign official, political party, or political official for the purpose of (1) influencing any act or decision of that person or party in his or its official capacity, (2) inducing an act or omission in violation of his or its lawful duty, or (3) inducing such person or party to use his or its influence to affect a decision of a foreign government to assist the person in obtaining or retaining business. An offer or promise to make a prohibited payment is a violation even if the offer is not accepted or the promise is not performed. The 1988 amendments to the Act explicitly excluded routine government actions not involving the official's discretion, such as obtaining permits or processing applications. They also added

an affirmative defense for payments that are lawful under the written laws or regulations of the foreign official's country.

Violations can result in fines of up to $2 million for corporations and other business entities; individuals may be fined a maximum of $100,000 or be imprisoned for up to five years or both. Section 32(c). Moreover, under the Federal Alternative Fines Act, the actual fine may be up to twice the benefit that the person sought to obtain by making the corrupt payment. Fines imposed upon individuals may not be paid directly or indirectly by the corporation or other business entity on whose behalf the individuals acted. In addition, the courts may impose civil monetary penalties of up to $21,663, as adjusted annually for inflation in January 2021.

In 1997, the United States signed the Organisation for Economic Co-operation and Development Convention on Combating Bribery of Foreign Public Officials in International Business Transactions (OECD Convention). The OECD Convention has been adopted by at least forty-four nations. In 1998, Congress enacted the International Anti-Bribery and Fair Competition Act of 1998 to conform the FCPA to the OECD Convention. The 1998 Act expands the FCPA to include (1) payments made to "secure any improper advantage" from foreign officials, (2) all foreign persons who commit an act in furtherance of a foreign bribe while in the United States, and (3) officials of public international organizations within the definition of a "foreign official." A public international organization is defined as either an organization designated by executive order pursuant to the International Organizations Immunities Act or any other international organization designated by executive order of the president.

43-8i CIVIL SANCTIONS

The SEC can bring a civil action in a U.S. District Court seeking an injunction, civil monetary penalties, or disgorgement (the return of illegal profits). The maximum amount of civil monetary penalties must be adjusted for inflation annually. The court may also bar or suspend an individual from serving as a corporate officer or director. A person who violates the court's order may be found in contempt and be subject to additional fines or imprisonment. The SEC may bring an administrative action seeking cease-and-desist orders; civil monetary penalties; disgorgement; and orders censuring, suspending, or expelling broker-dealers, investment advisers, and investment companies. For almost all violations of the 1934 Act, the SEC may bring a **civil action** in a U.S. district court seeking a civil monetary penalty of up to $975,230 (as adjusted annually for inflation in January 2021) to be paid by the person who committed the violation. Section 21(d)(3). In any **administrative** cease-and-desist **action** under 1934 Act, the SEC may impose a civil monetary penalty of up to $863,145 (as adjusted annually for inflation in January 2021) on a person for a violation of any provision of the 1934 Act if the civil monetary penalty is in the public interest. Section 21B(b).

FIGURE 43-7 Civil Liability Under the 1933 and 1934 Acts

Provision	Conduct	Plaintiffs	Defendants	Standard of Culpability	Reliance Required	Type of Liability	Remedies
Section 12(a)(1) 1933 Act	Unregistered sale or sale without prospectus	Purchasers from a violator	Sellers in violation	Strict liability	No	Express	Rescission Damages
Section 11 1933 Act	Registration statement containing material misstatement or omission	Purchasers of registered security	Issuer; Directors; Signers; Underwriters; Experts	Strict liability for issuer; Negligence for others	No	Express	Damages Attorneys' fees
Section 12(a)(2) 1933 Act	Material misstatement or omission	Purchasers from a violator	Sellers in violation	Negligence	No	Express	Rescission Damages
Section 18 1934 Act	False or misleading statements in a document filed with SEC	Purchasers or sellers	Persons making filing in violation	Knowledge or bad faith	Yes	Express	Damages Attorneys' fees
Section 16(b) 1934 Act	Short-swing profit by insider	Issuer; Shareholder of issuer	Directors; Officers; 10 percent shareholders	Strict liability	No	Express	Damages
Rule 10b-5 1934 Act	Deception or material misstatement or omission	Purchasers or sellers	Purchasers or sellers in violation	*Scienter*	Yes	Implied	Rescission Damages Injunction
Section 20A 1934 Act	Insider trading	Contemporaneous purchasers or sellers	Inside traders	*Scienter*	No	Express	Damages
Section 14(a) 1934 Act	Materially false or misleading proxy solicitation	Shareholders	Persons making proxy solicitation in violation	Negligence (probably)	Probably	Implied	Rescission Damages Injunction Attorneys' fees
Section 14(e) 1934 Act	Tender offer with deception or manipulation or material misstatement or material omission	Target company; Shareholders of target	Persons making tender offer in violation	*Scienter* (probably)	Probably	Implied	Rescission Damages Injunction

Note: SEC = Securities and Exchange Commission.

43-8j CRIMINAL SANCTIONS

Section 32 of the 1934 Act imposes criminal sanctions on any person who willfully violates any provision of the Act (except the antibribery provision) or the rules and regulations the SEC promulgates pursuant to the Act. As amended by the Sarbanes-Oxley Act, for individuals, conviction may carry a fine of not more than $5 million or imprisonment for not more than twenty years or both, with one exception: a person who proves she had no knowledge of the rule or regulation is not subject to imprisonment. If the person, however, is not a natural person (e.g., a corporation), a fine not exceeding $25 million may be imposed. Moreover, under the Federal Alternative Fines Act, if any person derives pecuniary gain from the offense or if the offense results in pecuniary loss to a person other than the defendant, the defendant may be fined up to the greater of twice the gross gain or twice the gross loss.

C H A P T E R   S U M M A R Y

SECURITIES ACT OF 1933

DEFINITION OF A SECURITY
Security includes any note, stock, bond, preorganization subscription, and investment contract
Investment Contract any investment of money or property made in expectation of receiving a financial return solely from the efforts of others

REGISTRATION OF SECURITIES
Disclosure Requirements disclosure of accurate material information required in all public offerings of nonexempt securities unless offering is an exempt transaction
Integrated Disclosure and Shelf Registrations permitted for certain qualified issuers
Emerging Growth Companies have reduced disclosure requirements and expanded permissible communications

EXEMPT SECURITIES
Definition securities not subject to the registration requirements of the 1933 Act
Types exempt securities include short-term commercial paper, municipal bonds, and certain insurance policies and annuity contracts

EXEMPT TRANSACTIONS FOR ISSUERS
Definition issuance of securities not subject to the registration requirements of the 1933 Act
Types exempt transactions for issuers include limited offers under Regulation D and Section 4(a)(5), crowdfunding, Regulation A, and intrastate issues

EXEMPT TRANSACTIONS FOR NONISSUERS
Definition resales by persons other than the issuer that are exempted from the registration requirements of the 1933 Act
Types exempt transactions for nonissuers include Rule 144 for reporting and nonreporting issuers, Regulation A, and Rule 144A

LIABILITY
Unregistered Sales Section 12(a)(1) imposes absolute civil liability as there are no defenses
False Registration Statements Section 11 imposes liability on the issuer, all persons who signed the statement, every director or partner, experts who prepared or certified any part of the statement, and all underwriters; defendants other than the issuer may assert the defense of due diligence
Antifraud Provisions Section 12(a)(2) imposes liability upon the seller to the immediate purchaser, provided the purchaser did not know of the untruth or omission, but the seller is not liable if he did not know and in the exercise of reasonable care could not have known of the untrue statement or omission; Section 17(a) broadly prohibits fraud in the sale of securities
Civil Sanctions the SEC may bring civil and administrative actions to impose injunctions, civil monetary penalties, and disgorgement for violations of the 1933 Act
Criminal Sanctions willful violations are subject to a fine of not more than $10,000 and/or imprisonment of not more than five years

SECURITIES EXCHANGE ACT OF 1934

DISCLOSURE **Registration and Periodic Reporting Requirements** apply to all regulated publicly held companies and include one-time registration as well as annual, quarterly, and monthly reports

Proxy Solicitations
- *Definition of a Proxy* a signed writing by a shareholder authorizing a named person to vote her stock at a specified meeting of shareholders
- *Proxy Statements* proxy disclosure statements are required when proxies are solicited or an issuer submits a matter to a shareholder vote

Tender Offers
- *Definition of a Tender Offer* a general invitation to shareholders to purchase their shares at a specified price for a specified time
- *Disclosure Requirements* a statement disclosing specified information must be filed with the Securities and Exchange Commission and furnished to each offeree

Foreign Corrupt Practices Act imposes internal control requirements on issuers with securities registered under the 1934 Act

LIABILITY **Misleading Statements in Reports** Section 18 imposes civil liability for any false or misleading statement made in a registration or report filed with the Securities and Exchange Commission

Short-Swing Profits Section 16(b) imposes liability on certain insiders (directors, officers, and shareholders owning more than 10 percent of the stock of a corporation) for all profits made on sales and purchases within six months of each other, with any recovery going to the issuer

Antifraud Provision Rule 10b-5 makes it unlawful to (1) employ any device, scheme, or artifice to defraud; (2) make any untrue statement of a material fact; (3) omit to state a material fact; or (4) engage in any act that operates as a fraud
- *Requisites of Rule 10b-5* recovery requires (1) a misstatement or omission, (2) materiality, (3) *scienter* (intentional and knowing conduct), (4) reliance, (5) connection with the purchase or sale of a security, and (6) economic loss
- *Insider Trading* "insiders" are liable under Rule 10b-5 for failing to disclose material, nonpublic information before trading on the information

Express Insider Trading Liability is imposed on any person who sells or buys a security while in possession of inside information

Civil Monetary Penalties for Inside Trading may be imposed on inside traders in an amount up to three times the gains they made or losses they avoided

Misleading Proxy Statements any person who distributes a false or misleading proxy statement is liable to injured investors

Fraudulent Tender Offers Section 14(e) imposes civil liability for false and material statements or omissions or fraudulent, deceptive, or manipulative practices in connection with any tender offer

Antibribery Provision of FCPA prohibited bribery can result in civil monetary penalties, fines, and imprisonment

Civil Sanctions the SEC may bring civil and administrative actions to impose injunctions, civil monetary penalties, and disgorgement for violations of the 1934 Act

Criminal Sanctions individuals who willfully violate the 1934 Act are subject to a fine of not more than $5 million and/or imprisonment of not more than twenty years

C A S E S

Definition of a Security
SEC v. EDWARDS
Supreme Court of the United States, 2004
540 U.S. 389, 124 S.Ct. 892, 157 L.Ed.2d 813

O'Connor, J.

"Opportunity doesn't always knock … sometimes it rings." [Citation.] And sometimes it hangs up. So it did for the 10,000 people who invested a total of $300 million in the payphone sale-and-leaseback arrangements touted by respondent under that slogan. The Securities and Exchange Commission (SEC) argues that the arrangements were investment contracts, and thus were subject to regulation under the federal securities laws. In this case, we must decide whether a moneymaking scheme is excluded from the term "investment contract" simply because the scheme offered a contractual entitlement to a fixed, rather than a variable, return.

I

Respondent Charles Edwards was the chairman, chief executive officer, and sole shareholder of ETS Payphones, Inc. (ETS). ETS, acting partly through a subsidiary also controlled by respondent, sold payphones to the public via independent distributors. The payphones were offered packaged with a site lease, a 5-year leaseback and management agreement, and a buyback agreement. All but a tiny fraction of purchasers chose this package, although other management options were offered. The purchase price for the payphone packages was approximately $7,000. Under the leaseback and management agreement, purchasers received $82 per month, a 14% annual return. Purchasers were not involved in the day-today operation of the payphones they owned. ETS selected the site for the phone, installed the equipment, arranged for connection and long-distance service, collected coin revenues, and maintained and repaired the phones. Under the buyback agreement, ETS promised to refund the full purchase price of the package at the end of the lease or within 180 days of a purchaser's request.

In its marketing materials and on its website, ETS trumpeted the "incomparable pay phone" as "an exciting business opportunity," in which recent deregulation had "open[ed] the door for profits for individual pay phone owners and operators." According to ETS, "[v]ery few business opportunities can offer the potential for ongoing revenue generation that is available in today's pay telephone industry." [Citation.]

The payphones did not generate enough revenue for ETS to make the payments required by the leaseback agreements,

so the company depended on funds from new investors to meet its obligations. In September 2000, ETS filed for bankruptcy protection. The SEC brought this civil enforcement action the same month. It alleged that respondent and ETS had violated the registration requirements of §§5(a) and (c) of the Securities Act of 1933, [citation], the antifraud provisions of both §17(a) of the Securities Act of 1933, [citation], and §10(b) of the Securities Exchange Act of 1934, [citation], and Rule 10b-5 thereunder, [citation]. The District Court concluded that the payphone sale-and-leaseback arrangement was an investment contract within the meaning of, and therefore was subject to, the federal securities laws. [Citation.] The Court of Appeals reversed. [Citation.] It held that respondent's scheme was not an investment contract, on two grounds. First, it read this Court's opinions to require that an investment contract offer either capital appreciation or a participation in the earnings of the enterprise, and thus to exclude schemes, such as respondent's, offering a fixed rate of return. [Citation.] Second, it held that our opinions' requirement that the return on the investment be "derived solely from the efforts of others" was not satisfied when the purchasers had a contractual entitlement to the return. [Citation.] We conclude that it erred on both grounds.

II

"Congress' purpose in enacting the securities laws was to regulate *investments*, in whatever form they are made and by whatever name they are called." [Citation.] To that end, it enacted a broad definition of "security," sufficient "to encompass virtually any instrument that might be sold as an investment." [Citation.] * * * [The 1993 Act and the 1934 Act] define "security" to include "any note, stock, treasury stock, security future, bond, debenture, … investment contract, … [or any] instrument commonly known as a 'security.'" "Investment contract" is not itself defined.

The test for whether a particular scheme is an investment contract was established in our decision in *SEC v. W. J. Howey Co*, [citation]. We look to "whether the scheme involves an investment of money in a common enterprise with profits to come solely from the efforts of others." [Citation.] This definition "embodies a flexible rather than a static principle, one that is capable of adaptation to meet the countless and variable schemes devised by those who seek the use of the money of others on the promise of profits." [Citation.]

* * * Thus, when we held that "profits" must "come solely from the efforts of others," we were speaking of the profits that investors seek on their investment, not the profits of the scheme in which they invest. We used "profits" in the sense of income or return, to include, for example, dividends, other periodic payments, or the increased value of the investment.

There is no reason to distinguish between promises of fixed returns and promises of variable returns for purposes of the test, so understood. In both cases, the investing public is attracted by representations of investment income, as purchasers were in this case by ETS' invitation to "watch the profits add up." [Citation.] Moreover, investments pitched as low-risk (such as those offering a "guaranteed" fixed return) are particularly attractive to individuals more vulnerable to investment fraud, including older and less sophisticated investors. [Citation.] * * *

* * *

We hold that an investment scheme promising a fixed rate of return can be an "investment contract" and thus a "security" subject to the federal securities laws. The judgment of the United States Court of Appeals for the Eleventh Circuit is reversed, and the case is remanded for further proceedings consistent with this opinion.

CASE 43-2

Liability for False Registration Statements
OMNICARE, INC. v. LABORERS DISTRICT COUNCIL CONSTRUCTION INDUSTRY PENSION FUND
Supreme Court of the United States, 2015
575 U.S. 175, 135 S.Ct. 1318, 191 L.Ed.2d 253

Kagan, J.

Before a company may sell securities in interstate commerce, it must file a registration statement with the Securities and Exchange Commission (SEC). If that document either "contain[s] an untrue statement of a material fact" or "omit[s] to state a material fact … necessary to make the statements therein not misleading," a purchaser of the stock may sue for damages. [Citation.] This case requires us to decide how each of those phrases applies to statements of opinion.

The Securities Act of 1933, [citation], protects investors by ensuring that companies issuing securities (known as "issuers") make a "full and fair disclosure of information" relevant to a public offering. [Citation.] * * *

Section 11 of the Act promotes compliance with these disclosure provisions by giving purchasers a right of action against an issuer or designated individuals (directors, partners, underwriters, and so forth) for material misstatements or omissions in registration statements. * * * Section 11 thus creates two ways to hold issuers liable for the contents of a registration statement—one focusing on what the statement says and the other on what it leaves out. Either way, the buyer need not prove (as he must to establish certain other securities offenses) that the defendant acted with any intent to deceive or defraud. [Citation.]

This case arises out of a registration statement that * * * Omnicare filed in connection with a public offering of common stock. Omnicare is the nation's largest provider of pharmacy services for residents of nursing homes. Its registration statement contained (along with all mandated disclosures) analysis of the effects of various federal and state laws on its business model, including its acceptance of rebates from pharmaceutical manufacturers. [Citation.] Of significance here, two sentences in the registration statement expressed Omnicare's view of its compliance with legal requirements:

> We believe our contract arrangements with other healthcare providers, our pharmaceutical suppliers and our pharmacy practices are in compliance with applicable federal and state laws. [Citation.]

> We believe that our contracts with pharmaceutical manufacturers are legally and economically valid arrangements that bring value to the healthcare system and the patients that we serve. [Citation.]

Accompanying those legal opinions were some caveats. On the same page as the first statement above, Omnicare mentioned several state-initiated "enforcement actions against pharmaceutical manufacturers" for offering payments to pharmacies that dispensed their products; it then cautioned that the laws relating to that practice might "be interpreted in the future in a manner inconsistent with our interpretation and application." [Citation.] And adjacent to the second statement, Omnicare noted that the Federal Government had expressed "significant concerns" about some manufacturers' rebates to pharmacies and warned that business might suffer "if these price concessions were no longer provided." [Citation.]

* * * pension funds that purchased Omnicare stock in the public offering (hereinafter Funds), brought suit alleging that the company's two opinion statements about legal compliance give rise to liability under §11. Citing lawsuits that the Federal Government later pressed against Omnicare, the Funds' complaint maintained that the company's receipt of payments from drug manufacturers violated anti-kickback laws. [Citation.]

Accordingly, the complaint asserted, Omnicare made "materially false" representations about legal compliance. [Citation.] And so too, the complaint continued, the company "omitted to state [material] facts necessary" to make its representations not misleading. [Citation.] The Funds claimed that none of Omnicare's officers and directors "possessed reasonable grounds" for thinking that the opinions offered were truthful and complete. [Citation.] * * *

The District Court granted Omnicare's motion to dismiss * * * [because] the Funds' complaint failed to [claim] that "the company's officers knew they were violating the law." [Citation.] The Court of Appeals for the Sixth Circuit reversed. [Citation.] It acknowledged that the two statements highlighted in the Funds' complaint expressed Omnicare's "opinion" of legal compliance * * * But even so, the court held, the Funds had to allege only that the stated belief was "objectively false"; they did not need to contend that anyone at Omnicare "disbelieved [the opinion] at the time it was expressed." [Citation.]

We granted certiorari, [citation], to consider how §11 pertains to statements of opinion. * * *

The Sixth Circuit held, and the Funds now urge, that a statement of opinion that is ultimately found incorrect—even if believed at the time made—may count as an "untrue statement of a material fact." * * * But that argument wrongly conflates facts and opinions. A fact is "a thing done or existing" or "[a]n actual happening." Webster's New International Dictionary 782 (1927). An opinion is "a belief[,] a view," or a "sentiment which the mind forms of persons or things." [Citation.] Most important, a statement of fact ("the coffee is hot") expresses certainty about a thing, whereas a statement of opinion ("I think the coffee is hot") does not. * * * And Congress effectively incorporated just that distinction in §11's first part by exposing issuers to liability not for "untrue statement[s]" full stop (which would have included ones of opinion), but only for "untrue statement[s] of ... *fact.*" [Citation.]

* * *

That still leaves some room for §11's false-statement provision to apply to expressions of opinion. As even Omnicare acknowledges, every such statement explicitly affirms one fact: that the speaker actually holds the stated belief. [Citations.] For that reason, [a] statement about product quality ("I believe our TVs have the highest resolution available on the market") would be an untrue statement of fact—namely, the fact of her own belief—if she knew that her company's TVs only placed second. And so too the statement about legal compliance ("I believe our marketing practices are lawful") would falsely describe her own state of mind if she thought her company was breaking the law. * * *

In addition, some sentences that begin with opinion words like "I believe" contain embedded statements of fact * * *. [Citation.] Suppose the CEO * * * said: "I believe our TVs have the highest resolution available because we use a patented technology to which our competitors do not have access." That statement may be read to affirm not only the speaker's state of mind, as described above, but also an underlying fact: that the company uses a patented technology. [Citation.] Accordingly, liability under §11's false-statement provision would follow (once again, assuming materiality) not only if the speaker did not hold the belief she professed but also if the supporting fact she supplied were untrue.

But the Funds cannot avail themselves of either of those ways of demonstrating liability. The two sentences to which the Funds object are pure statements of opinion: To simplify their content only a bit, Omnicare said in each that "we believe we are obeying the law." And the Funds do not contest that Omnicare's opinion was honestly held. * * * What the Funds instead claim is that Omnicare's belief turned out to be wrong—that whatever the company thought, it was in fact violating anti-kickback laws. But that allegation alone will not give rise to liability under §11's first clause because, as we have shown, a sincere statement of pure opinion is not an "untrue statement of material fact," regardless whether an investor can ultimately prove the belief wrong. That clause, limited as it is to factual statements, does not allow investors to second-guess inherently subjective and uncertain assessments. * * *

That conclusion, however, does not end this case because the Funds also rely on §11's omissions provision, alleging that Omnicare "omitted to state facts necessary" to make its opinion on legal compliance "not misleading." [Citation.] As all parties accept, whether a statement is "misleading" depends on the perspective of a reasonable investor: The inquiry (like the one into materiality) is objective. [Citation.] We therefore must consider when, if ever, the omission of a fact can make a statement of opinion like Omnicare's, even if literally accurate, misleading to an ordinary investor.

* * *

* * * [A] reasonable investor may, depending on the circumstances, understand an opinion statement to convey facts about how the speaker has formed the opinion—or, otherwise put, about the speaker's basis for holding that view. And if the real facts are otherwise, but not provided, the opinion statement will mislead its audience. * * * An opinion statement, however, is not necessarily misleading when an issuer knows, but fails to disclose, some fact cutting the other way. Reasonable investors understand that opinions sometimes rest on a weighing of competing facts; indeed, the presence of such facts is one reason why an issuer may frame a statement as an opinion, thus conveying uncertainty. * * *

* * * The reasonable investor understands a statement of opinion in its full context, and §11 creates liability only for the omission of material facts that cannot be squared with such a fair reading.

* * *

* * * Congress adopted §11 to ensure that issuers "tell[ ] the whole truth" to investors. [Citation.] For that reason, literal accuracy is not enough: An issuer must as well desist from misleading investors by saying one thing and holding back another. * * *

* * *

* * * The decision Congress made, for the reasons we have indicated, was to extend §11 liability to all statements rendered misleading by omission. * * * Section 11's omissions clause, as applied to statements of both opinion and fact, necessarily brings the reasonable person into the analysis, and asks what she would naturally understand a statement to convey beyond its literal meaning. And for expressions of opinion, that means considering the foundation she would expect an issuer to have before making the statement. * * *

* * * As we have explained, an investor cannot state a claim by alleging only that an opinion was wrong; the complaint must as well call into question the issuer's basis for offering the opinion. [Citation.] * * * To be specific: The investor must identify particular (and material) facts going to the basis for the issuer's opinion—facts about the inquiry the issuer did or did not conduct or the knowledge it did or did not have—whose omission makes the opinion statement at issue misleading to a reasonable person reading the statement fairly and in context. [Citation.] That is no small task for an investor.

[The judgment of the Court of Appeals is vacated, and the case is remanded for further proceedings.]

CASE 43-3	Rule 10b-5 **MATRIXX INITIATIVES, INC. v. SIRACUSANO** Supreme Court of the United States, 2011 563 U.S. 4, 131 S.Ct. 1309, 179 L.Ed.2d 398	

Sotomayor, J.

[Matrixx develops, manufactures, and markets over-the-counter pharmaceutical products. Its core brand of products is called Zicam. All of the products sold under the Zicam name are used to treat the common cold and associated symptoms. At the time of the events in question, one of Matrixx's products was Zicam Cold Remedy, which came in several forms including nasal spray and gel. The active ingredient in Zicam Cold Remedy was zinc gluconate. Respondents allege that Zicam Cold Remedy accounted for approximately 70 percent of Matrixx's sales.

Respondents initiated this securities fraud class action against Matrixx on behalf of individuals who purchased Matrixx securities between October 22, 2003, and February 6, 2004. The action arises principally out of statements that Matrixx made during that period relating to revenues and product safety. Respondents claim that Matrixx's statements were misleading in light of reports that Matrixx had received, but did not disclose, about consumers who had lost their sense of smell (a condition called anosmia) after using Zicam Cold Remedy nasal spray or gel.

On January 30, 2004, Dow Jones Newswires reported that the Food and Drug Administration (FDA) was "looking into complaints that an over-the-counter common-cold medicine manufactured by a unit of Matrixx Initiatives, Inc. (MTXX) may be causing some users to lose their sense of smell" in light of at least three product liability lawsuits. Matrixx's stock fell from $13.55 to $11.97 per share after the report. In response, on February 2, Matrixx issued a press release:

All Zicam products are manufactured and marketed according to FDA guidelines for homeopathic medicine. Our primary concern is the health and safety of our customers and the distribution of factual information about our products. Matrixx believes statements alleging that intranasal Zicam products caused anosmia (loss of smell) are completely unfounded and misleading.

In no clinical trial of intranasal zinc gluconate gel products has there been a single report of lost or diminished olfactory function (sense of smell). Rather, the safety and efficacy of zinc gluconate for the treatment of symptoms related to the common cold have been well established in two double-blind, placebo-controlled, randomized clinical trials. In fact, in neither study were there any reports of anosmia related to the use of this compound. The overall incidence of adverse events associated with zinc gluconate was extremely low, with no statistically significant difference between the adverse event rates for the treated and placebo subsets. * * *

The day after Matrixx issued this press release, its stock price rebounded to $13.40 per share.

On February 19, 2004, Matrixx filed a Form 8-K with the SEC stating that it had "convened a two-day meeting of physicians and scientists to review current information on smell disorders" and that "[i]n the opinion of the panel, there is insufficient scientific evidence at this time to determine if zinc gluconate, when used as recommended, affects a person's ability to smell."

Respondents claimed that Matrixx violated §10(b) of the Securities Exchange Act and SEC Rule 10b-5 by making untrue statements of fact and failing to disclose material facts necessary to make the statements not misleading in an effort to maintain artificially high prices for Matrixx securities. Matrixx moved to dismiss respondents' complaint. The District Court granted the motion to dismiss, holding that the respondents had not alleged a statistically significant correlation between the use of Zicam and anosmia so as to make failure to publicly disclose complaints and a medical study a material omission. The District Court also agreed that the respondents had not stated with particularity facts giving rise to a strong inference of scienter. The Court of Appeals reversed, holding that the District Court had erred in requiring an allegation of statistical significance to establish materiality. It concluded that the complaint adequately alleged "information regarding the possible link between Zicam and anosmia" that would have been significant to a reasonable investor. With respect to scienter, the Court of Appeals concluded that "[w]ithholding reports of adverse effects of and lawsuits concerning the product responsible for the company's remarkable sales increase is 'an extreme departure from the standards of ordinary care,'" giving rise to a strong inference of scienter.]

Section 10(b) of the Securities Exchange Act makes it unlawful for any person to "use or employ, in connection with the purchase or sale of any security … any manipulative or deceptive device or contrivance in contravention of such rules and regulations as the Commission may prescribe as necessary or appropriate in the public interest or for the protection of investors." [Citation.] SEC Rule 10b-5 implements this provision by making it unlawful to, among other things, "make any untrue statement of a material fact or to omit to state a material fact necessary in order to make the statements made, in the light of the circumstances under which they were made, not misleading." [Citation.] We have implied a private cause of action from the text and purpose of §10(b). [Citation.]

To prevail on their claim that Matrixx made material misrepresentations or omissions in violation of §10(b) and Rule 10b-5, respondents must prove "(1) a material misrepresentation or omission by the defendant; (2) scienter; (3) a connection between the misrepresentation or omission and the purchase or sale of a security; (4) reliance upon the misrepresentation or omission; (5) economic loss; and (6) loss causation." [Citation.] * * *

* * *

To prevail on a §10(b) claim, a plaintiff must show that the defendant made a statement that was "*misleading* as to a

material fact." *Basic [Inc. v. Levinson*, citation.] In *Basic*, we held that this materiality requirement is satisfied when there is "'a substantial likelihood that the disclosure of the omitted fact would have been viewed by the reasonable investor as having significantly altered the "total mix" of information made available.'" [Citation.] * * *

* * *

Given that medical professionals and regulators act on the basis of evidence of causation that is not statistically significant, it stands to reason that in certain cases reasonable investors would as well. * * *As a result, assessing the materiality of adverse event reports is a "fact-specific" inquiry, [citation], that requires consideration of the source, content, and context of the reports. This is not to say that statistical significance (or the lack thereof) is irrelevant—only that it is not dispositive of every case.

Application of *Basic*'s "total mix" standard does not mean that pharmaceutical manufacturers must disclose all reports of adverse events. * * * The fact that a user of a drug has suffered an adverse event, standing alone, does not mean that the drug caused that event. [Citation.] The question remains whether a *reasonable* investor would have viewed the nondisclosed information "'as having *significantly* altered the "total mix" of information made available.'" For the reasons just stated, the mere existence of reports of adverse events—which says nothing in and of itself about whether the drug is causing the adverse events—will not satisfy this standard. [Citation.] Something more is needed, but that something more is not limited to statistical significance and can come from "the source, content, and context of the reports," [citation]. This contextual inquiry may reveal in some cases that reasonable investors would have viewed reports of adverse events as material even though the reports did not provide statistically significant evidence of a causal link.

Moreover, it bears emphasis that §10(b) and Rule 10b-5(b) do not create an affirmative duty to disclose any and all material information. Disclosure is required under these provisions only when necessary "to make … statements made, in the light of the circumstances under which they were made, not misleading." [Citations.] Even with respect to information that a reasonable investor might consider material, companies can control what they have to disclose under these provisions by controlling what they say to the market.

Applying *Basic*'s "total mix" standard in this case, we conclude that respondents have adequately pleaded materiality. * * *

* * *

We believe that these allegations suffice to "raise a reasonable expectation that discovery will reveal evidence" satisfying the materiality requirement, [citation], and to "allo[w] the court to draw the reasonable inference that the defendant is liable for the misconduct alleged," [citation]. The information provided to Matrixx by medical experts revealed a plausible causal relationship between Zicam Cold Remedy and anosmia. Consumers likely would have viewed the risk associated with Zicam (possible loss of smell) as substantially outweighing the benefit of using the product (alleviating cold symptoms), particularly in light of the existence of many alternative products on the market. Importantly, Zicam Cold Remedy allegedly accounted for 70 percent of Matrixx's sales. Viewing the allegations of the complaint as a whole, the complaint alleges facts suggesting a significant risk to the commercial viability of Matrixx's leading product.

It is substantially likely that a reasonable investor would have viewed this information "'as having significantly altered the "total mix" of information made available.'" *Basic*, [citation]. Matrixx told the market that revenues were going to rise 50 and then 80 percent. Assuming the complaint's allegations to be true, however, Matrixx had information indicating a significant risk to its leading revenue-generating product. Matrixx also stated that reports indicating that Zicam caused anosmia were "'completely unfounded and misleading'" and that "'the safety and efficacy of zinc gluconate for the treatment of symptoms related to the common cold have been well established.'" [Citation.] Importantly, however, Matrixx had evidence of a biological link between Zicam's key ingredient and anosmia, and it had not conducted any studies of its own to disprove that link. In fact, as Matrixx later revealed, the scientific evidence at that time was "'insufficient … to determine if zinc gluconate, when used as recommended, affects a person's ability to smell.'" [Citation.]

Assuming the facts to be true, these were material facts "necessary in order to make the statements made, in the light of the circumstances under which they were made, not misleading." [Rule 10b-5.] * * *

Matrixx also argues that respondents failed to allege facts plausibly suggesting that it acted with the required level of scienter. "To establish liability under §10(b) and Rule 10b-5, a private plaintiff must prove that the defendant acted with scienter, 'a mental state embracing intent to deceive, manipulate, or defraud.'" [Citation.] We have not decided whether recklessness suffices to fulfill the scienter requirement. [Citation.] Because Matrixx does not challenge the Court of Appeals' holding that the scienter requirement may be satisfied by a showing of "deliberate recklessness," [citation], we assume, without deciding, that the standard applied by the Court of Appeals is sufficient to establish scienter.

For the reasons stated, the judgment of the Court of Appeals for the Ninth Circuit is Affirmed.

CASE 43-4

Insider Trading
SALMAN v. UNITED STATES
Supreme Court of the United States, 2016
580 U.S. ___, 137 S.Ct. 420, 196 L.Ed.2d 351

Alito, J.

[Bassam Salman was indicted for federal securities-fraud crimes for trading on inside information he received from a friend and in-law, Michael Kara, who, in turn, received the information from his brother, Maher Kara, a former investment banker at Citigroup who dealt with highly confidential information about mergers and acquisitions. Maher shared inside information about pending mergers and acquisitions with his brother Michael to benefit him and expected him to trade on it. Maher and Michael enjoyed a very close relationship, and Michael was the best man at Maher's wedding to Bassam Salman's sister. Without Maher's knowledge, Michael fed the information to others, including Salman, who knew that the information was from Maher. Salman made over $1.5 million in profits that he split with another relative who executed trades via a brokerage account on Salman's behalf.

Salman was indicted on one count of conspiracy to commit securities fraud and four counts of securities fraud. Facing charges of their own, both Maher and Michael pleaded guilty and testified at Salman's trial. Salman was convicted on all counts. He was sentenced to 36 months of imprisonment, three years of supervised release, and $730,000 in restitution. After his motion for a new trial was denied, Salman appealed to the Ninth Circuit. While Salman's appeal to the Ninth Circuit was pending, the Second Circuit decided that a fact-finder could not infer a personal benefit to the tipper from a gift of confidential information to a trading relative or friend, unless there is "proof of a meaningfully close personal relationship" between tipper and tippee "that generates an exchange that is objective, consequential, and represents at least a potential gain of a pecuniary or similarly valuable nature." The Ninth Circuit declined to follow the Second Circuit case, holding that a jury may infer that the tipper breached a duty because he made a gift of confidential information to a trading relative. The U.S. Supreme Court granted *certiorari*.]

Section 10(b) of the Securities Exchange Act of 1934 and the Securities and Exchange Commission's Rule 10b-5 prohibit undisclosed trading on inside corporate information by individuals who are under a duty of trust and confidence that prohibits them from secretly using such information for their personal advantage. [Citations.] Individuals under this duty may face criminal and civil liability for trading on inside information (unless they make appropriate disclosures ahead of time).

These persons also may not tip inside information to others for trading. The tippee acquires the tipper's duty to disclose or abstain from trading if the tippee knows the information was disclosed in breach of the tipper's duty, and the tippee may commit securities fraud by trading in disregard of that knowledge. In *Dirks v. SEC*, [citation], this Court explained that a tippee's liability for trading on inside information hinges on whether the tipper breached a fiduciary duty by disclosing the information. A tipper breaches such a fiduciary duty, we held, when the tipper discloses the inside information for a personal benefit. And, we went on to say, a jury can infer a personal benefit—and thus a breach of the tipper's duty—where the tipper receives something of value in exchange for the tip or "makes a gift of confidential information to a trading relative or friend." [Citation.]

* * *

We adhere to Dirks, which easily resolves the narrow issue presented here.

In Dirks, we explained that a tippee is exposed to liability for trading on inside information only if the tippee participates in a breach of the tipper's fiduciary duty. Whether the tipper breached that duty depends "in large part on the purpose of the disclosure" to the tippee. [Citation.] "[T]he test," we explained, "is whether the insider personally will benefit, directly or indirectly, from his disclosure." [Citation.] Thus, the disclosure of confidential information without personal benefit is not enough. In determining whether a tipper derived a personal benefit, we instructed courts to "focus on objective criteria, i.e., whether the insider receives a direct or indirect

personal benefit from the disclosure, such as a pecuniary gain or a reputational benefit that will translate into future earnings." [Citation.] This personal benefit can "often" be inferred "from objective facts and circumstances," we explained, such as "a relationship between the insider and the recipient that suggests a quid pro quo from the latter, or an intention to benefit the particular recipient." [Citation.] In particular, we held that "[t]he elements of fiduciary duty and exploitation of nonpublic information also exist when an insider makes a gift of confidential information to a trading relative or friend." [Citation].

* * *

Our discussion of gift giving resolves this case. Maher, the tipper, provided inside information to a close relative, his brother Michael. Dirks makes clear that a tipper breaches a fiduciary duty by making a gift of confidential information to "a trading relative," and that rule is sufficient to resolve the case at hand. As Salman's counsel acknowledged at oral argument, Maher would have breached his duty had he personally traded on the information here himself then given the proceeds as a gift to his brother. [Citation.] It is obvious that Maher would personally benefit in that situation. But Maher effectively achieved the same result by disclosing the information to Michael, and allowing him to trade on it. * * * Here, by disclosing confidential information as a gift to his brother with the expectation that he would trade on it, Maher breached his duty of trust and confidence to Citigroup and its clients—a duty Salman acquired, and breached himself, by trading on the information with full knowledge that it had been improperly disclosed.

To the extent the Second Circuit held that the tipper must also receive something of a "pecuniary or similarly valuable nature" in exchange for a gift to family or friends, [citation], we agree with the Ninth Circuit that this requirement is inconsistent with Dirks.

[The judgment of the Ninth Circuit is affirmed.]

CASE
43-5

Fraudulent Tender Offers
SCHREIBER v. BURLINGTON NORTHERN, INC.
Supreme Court of the United States, 1985
472 U.S. 1, 105 S.Ct. 2458, 86 L.Ed.2d 1

Burger, C. J.
On December 21, 1982, Burlington Northern, Inc., made a hostile tender offer for El Paso Gas Co. Through a wholly owned subsidiary, Burlington proposed to purchase 25.1 million El Paso shares at $24 per share. Burlington reserved the right to terminate the offer if any of several specified events occurred. El Paso management initially opposed the takeover, but its shareholders responded favorably, fully subscribing the offer by the December 30, 1982 deadline.

Burlington did not accept those tendered shares; instead, after negotiations with El Paso management, Burlington announced on January 10, 1983, the terms of a new and friendly takeover agreement. Pursuant to the new agreement, Burlington undertook, *inter alia*, to (1) rescind the December tender offer, (2) purchase 4,166,667 shares from El Paso at $24 per share, (3) substitute a new tender offer for only 21 million shares at $24 per share, (4) provide procedural protections against a squeeze-out merger of the remaining El Paso shareholders, and

(5) recognize "golden parachute" contracts between El Paso and four of its senior officers. By February 8, more than 40 million shares were tendered in response to Burlington's January offer, and the takeover was completed.

The rescission of the first tender offer caused a diminished payment to those shareholders who had tendered during the first offer. The January offer was greatly oversubscribed and consequently those shareholders who retendered were subject to substantial proration. Petitioner Barbara Schreiber filed suit on behalf of herself and similarly situated shareholders, alleging that Burlington, El Paso, and members of El Paso's board violated §14(e)'s prohibition of "fraudulent, deceptive or manipulative acts or practices … in connection with any tender offer." [Citation.] She claimed that Burlington's withdrawal of the December tender offer coupled with the substitution of the January tender offer was a "manipulative" distortion of the market for El Paso stock. Schreiber also alleged that Burlington violated §14(e) by failing in the January offer to disclose the "golden parachutes" offered to four of El Paso's managers. She claims that this January non-disclosure was a deceptive act forbidden by §14(e).

The District Court dismissed the suit for failure to state a claim. * * *

* * *

We are asked in this case to interpret §14(e) of the Securities Exchange Act, [citation]. The starting point is the language of the statute. Section 14(e) provides:

It shall be unlawful for any person to make any untrue statement of a material fact or omit to state any material fact necessary in order to make the statements made, in the light of the circumstances under which they are made, not misleading, or to engage in any fraudulent, deceptive or manipulative acts or practices, in connection with any tender offer or request or invitation for tenders, or any solicitation of security holders in opposition to or in favor of any such offer, request, or invitation. The Commission shall, for the purposes of this subsection, by rules and regulations define, and prescribe means reasonably designed to prevent, such acts and practices as are fraudulent, deceptive, or manipulative. [Citation.]

* * * Petitioner reads the phrase "fraudulent, deceptive or manipulative acts or practices" to include acts which, although fully disclosed, "artificially" affect the price of the takeover target's stock. Petitioner's interpretation relies on the belief that §14(e) is directed at purposes broader than providing full and true information to investors.

Petitioner's reading of the term "manipulative" conflicts with the normal meaning of the term. We have held in the context of an alleged violation of §10(b) of the Securities Exchange Act:

Use of the word "manipulative" is especially significant. It is and was virtually a term of art when used in connection with the securities markets. It connotes intentional or willful conduct *designed to deceive or defraud investors by controlling or artificially affecting the price of securities.* *Ernst & Ernst v. Hochfelder* [see *Chapter 44*].

* * *

The meaning the Court has given the term "manipulative" is consistent with the use of the term at common law, and with its traditional dictionary definition.

* * *

Our conclusion that "manipulative" acts under §14(e) require misrepresentation or nondisclosure is buttressed by the purpose and legislative history of the provision. Section 14(e) was originally added to the Securities Exchange Act as part of the Williams Act, [citation]. "The purpose of the Williams Act is to insure that public shareholders who are confronted by a cash tender offer for their stock will not be required to respond without adequate information." [Citation.]

* * *

Nowhere in the legislative history is there the slightest suggestion that §14(e) serves any purpose other than disclosure, or that the term "manipulative" should be read as an invitation to the courts to oversee the substantive fairness of tender offers; the quality of any offer is a matter for the marketplace.

* * *

We hold that the term "manipulative" as used in §14(e) requires misrepresentation or nondisclosure. It connotes "conduct designed to deceive or defraud investors by controlling or artificially affecting the price of securities." *Ernst & Ernst v. Hochfelder* [see *Chapter 44*]. Without misrepresentation or nondisclosure, §14(e) has not been violated.

Applying that definition to this case, we hold that the actions of respondents were not manipulative. The amended complaint fails to allege that the cancellation of the first tender offer was accompanied by any misrepresentation, nondisclosure or deception. The District Court correctly found, "All activity of the defendants that could have conceivably affected the price of El Paso shares was done openly." [Citation.]

* * *

The judgment of the Court of Appeals is affirmed.

QUESTIONS

1. Acme Realty, a real estate development company, is a limited partnership organized in Georgia. It is planning to develop a two-hundred-acre parcel of land for a regional shopping center and needs to raise $1,250,000. As part of its financing, Acme plans to offer $1,250,000 worth of limited partnership interests to about one hundred prospective investors in the southeastern United States. It anticipates that about forty to fifty private investors will purchase the limited partnership interests.

   a. Must Acme register this offering? Why or why not?

   b. If Acme must register but fails to do so, what are the legal consequences?

2. Bigelow Corporation has total assets of $850,000; sales of $1,350,000; and one class of common stock with 375 shareholders and a class of preferred stock with 250 shareholders, both of which are traded over the counter. Explain which provisions of the Securities Exchange Act of 1934 apply to Bigelow Corporation.

3. Capricorn, Inc., is planning to "go public" by offering its common stock, which previously had been owned by only three shareholders. The company intends to limit the number of purchasers to twenty-five persons residing in the State of its incorporation. All of Capricorn's business and all of its assets are located in its State of incorporation. Based upon these facts, explain what exemptions from registration, if any, are available to Capricorn, and what conditions would each of these available exemptions impose upon the terms of the offer.

4. The boards of directors of DuMont Corp. and Epsot, Inc., agreed to enter into a friendly merger, with DuMont to be the surviving entity. The stock of both corporations was listed on a national stock exchange. In connection with the merger, both corporations distributed to their shareholders proxy statements seeking approval of the proposed merger. The shareholders of both corporations voted to approve the merger. About three weeks after the merger was consummated, the price of DuMont stock fell from $25 to $13 as a result of the discovery that Epsot had entered into several unprofitable long-term contracts two months before the merger had been proposed. The contracts will result in substantial losses from Epsot's operations for at least the next four years. The existence and effect of these contracts, although known to both corporations at the time of the proposed merger, were not disclosed in the proxy statements of either corporation. Can the shareholders of DuMont recover in a suit against DuMont under the 1934 Act? Explain.

5. Farthing is a director and vice president of Garp, Inc., whose common stock is listed on the New York Stock Exchange. Farthing engaged in the following transactions in the same calendar year: on January 1, Farthing sold five hundred shares at $30 per share; on January 15, she purchased three hundred shares at $30 per share; on February 1, she purchased two hundred shares at $45 per share; on March 1, she purchased three hundred shares at $60 per share; on March 15, she sold two hundred shares at $55 per share; and on April 1, she sold one hundred shares at $40 per share. Howell brings suit on behalf of Garp, alleging that Farthing has violated the Securities Exchange Act of 1934. Farthing defends on the ground that she lost money on the transactions in question. Is Farthing liable? If so, under which provisions and for what amount of money? Explain.

6. Intercontinental Widgets, Inc., had applied for a patent for a new state-of-the-art widget, which, if patented, would significantly increase the value of Intercontinental's shares. On September 1, the U.S. Patent and Trademark Office notified Jackson, the attorney for Intercontinental, that the patent application had been approved. After informing Kingsley, the president of Intercontinental, of the good news, Jackson called his broker and purchased one thousand shares of Intercontinental at $18 per share. He also told his partner, Lucas, who immediately proceeded to purchase five hundred shares at $19 per share. Lucas then called his brother-in-law, Mammon, and told him the news. On September 3, Mammon bought four thousand shares at $21 per share. On September 4, Kingsley issued a press release that accurately reported that a patent had been granted to Intercontinental. The next day Intercontinental's stock soared to $38 per share. A class action suit is brought against Jackson, Lucas, Mammon, and Intercontinental for violations of Rule 10b-5. Who, if anyone, is liable? Discuss.

7. Nova, Inc., sought to sell a new issue of common stock. It registered the issue with the SEC but included false information in both the registration statement and the prospectus. The issue was underwritten by Omega & Sons and was sold in its entirety by Periwinkle, Ramses, and Sheffield, Inc., a securities broker-dealer. Telford, who was unaware of the falsity of this information, purchased five hundred shares at $6 per share. Three months later, the falsity of the information contained in the prospectus was made public, and the price of the shares fell to $1 per share. The following week, Telford brought suit against

Nova, Inc., Omega & Sons, and Periwinkle, Ramses and Sheffield, Inc., under the Securities Act of 1933.

a. Who, if anyone, is liable under the Act? If liable, under which provisions?

b. What defenses, if any, are available to the various defendants?

8. Tanaka, a director and officer of Deep Hole Oil Company, telephoned Romani for the purpose of buying two hundred shares of Deep Hole Company stock owned by Romani. During the period of negotiations, Tanaka concealed his identity and did not disclose the fact that earlier in the day he had received a report of two rich oil strikes on the oil company's property. Romani sold his two hundred shares to Tanaka for $10 per share. Taking into consideration the new strikes, the fair value of the stock was approximately $20 per share. Romani sues Tanaka to recover damages. Is Tanaka liable? If so, under which provisions and for what amount of money?

9. Venable Corporation has 750,000 shares of common stock outstanding, which are owned by 2,640 shareholders. The assets of Venable Corporation are valued at more than $10 million. In March, Underhill began purchasing shares of Venable's common stock in the open market. By April, he had acquired 40,000 shares at prices ranging from $12 to $14. Upon discovering Underhill's activities in late April, the directors of Venable had the corporation purchase the 40,000 shares from Underhill for $18 per share. Explain which provisions of the 1934 Act, if any, have been violated.

C A S E   P R O B L E M S

10. Dirks was an officer of a New York broker-dealer firm that specialized in providing investment analysis of insurance company securities to institutional investors. On March 6, Dirks received information from Ronald Secrist, a former officer of Equity Funding of America. Secrist alleged that the assets of Equity Funding, a diversified corporation primarily engaged in selling life insurance and mutual funds, were vastly overstated as the result of fraudulent corporate practices. Dirks decided to investigate the allegations. He visited Equity Funding's headquarters in Los Angeles and interviewed several officers and employees of the corporation. The senior management denied any wrongdoing, but certain corporation employees corroborated the charges of fraud. Neither Dirks nor his firm owned or traded any Equity Funding stock, but throughout his investigation he openly discussed the information he had obtained with a number of clients and investors. Some of these persons sold their holdings of Equity Funding securities, including five investment advisers who liquidated holdings of more than $16 million.

While Dirks was in Los Angeles, he was in touch regularly with William Blundell, The *Wall Street Journal's* Los Angeles bureau chief. Dirks urged Blundell to write a story on the fraud allegations. Blundell did not believe, however, that such a massive fraud could go undetected and declined to write the story. He feared that publishing such damaging hearsay might be libelous.

During the two-week period in which Dirks pursued his investigation and spread word of Secrist s charges, the price of Equity Funding stock fell from $26 per share to less than $15 per share. This led the New York Stock Exchange to halt trading on March 27. Shortly thereafter, California insurance authorities impounded Equity Funding's records and uncovered evidence of the fraud.

Only then did the Securities and Exchange Commission (SEC) file a complaint against Equity Funding.

The SEC began an investigation into Dirks's role in the exposure of the fraud. After a hearing by an administrative law judge, the SEC found that Dirks had aided and abetted violations of Section 10(b) of the Securities Exchange Act of 1934 and SEC Rule 10b-5 by repeating the allegations of fraud to members of the investment community who later sold their Equity Funding stock. Has Dirks violated Section 10(b) and Rule 10b-5? Explain.

11. Texas Gulf Sulphur Company (TGS) was a corporation engaged in exploring for and mining certain minerals. A particular tract of Canadian land looked very promising as a source of desired minerals, and TGS drilled a test hole on November 8. Because the core sample of the hole contained minerals of amazing quality, TGS began to acquire surrounding tracts of land. Stevens, the president of TGS, instructed all on-site personnel to keep the find a secret. Because subsequent test drillings were performed, the amount of activity surrounding the drilling gave rise to rumors regarding the size and quality of the find. To counteract these rumors, Stevens authorized a press release denying the validity of the rumors and describing them as excessively optimistic. The release was issued on April 12 of the following year, though drilling continued through April 15. In the meantime, several officers, directors, and employees had purchased or accepted options to purchase additional TGS stock on the basis of the information concerning the drilling. They also recommended similar purchases to outsiders without divulging the inside information to the public. At 10:00 A.M. on April 16, an accurate report on the find was finally released to the American financial press. The SEC brought an action against TGS and several of its officers, directors, and

employees to enjoin conduct alleged to violate Section 10(b) of the Securities Act of 1934 and to compel rescission by the individual defendants of securities transactions assertedly conducted in violation of Rule 10b-5. Have any of the defendants violated Section 10(b)? Explain.

12. W. J. Howey Company and Howey-in-the-Hills Service, Inc., were Florida corporations under direct common control and management. Howey Company owned large tracts of citrus acreage in Florida. The service company cultivated, harvested, and marketed the crops. For several years, Howey Company offered one-half of its planted acreage to the public to help it "finance additional development." Each prospective customer was offered both a land sales contract and a service contract with Howey-in-the-Hills after being told that it was not feasible to invest in the grove without a service arrangement. Upon payment of the purchase price, the land was conveyed by warranty deed. The service company was given full discretion over cultivating and marketing the crop. The purchaser had no right of entry to market the crop. The service company also was accountable only for an allocation of the net profits after the companies pooled the produce. The purchasers were predominantly nonresident businesspersons attracted by the expectation of substantial profits. Contending that this arrangement was an investment contract within the coverage of the Securities Act of 1933, the Securities and Exchange Commission (SEC) brought an action against the two companies to restrain them from using the mails and instrumentalities of interstate commerce in the offer and sale of unregistered and nonexempt securities. Explain whether the SEC should succeed.

13. Between December 4 and December 17, John Malone, a director and large shareholder of Discovery Communications, Inc., engaged in sales of Discovery's "Series C" stock totaling 953,506 shares and purchases of Discovery's "Series A" stock totaling 632,700 shares. Discovery's Series A stock and Series C stock are different equity securities; are separately registered; and are traded separately on the NASDAQ stock exchange under the ticker symbols DISCA and DISCK, respectively. The principal difference between the two securities is that Series A stock comes with voting rights whereas Series C stock does not confer any voting rights. Series A stock and Series C stock are not convertible into each other. A shareholder brought a shareholder suit seeking disgorgement of the profits that Malone realized from these transactions. Explain whether the plaintiff should succeed.

14. James O'Hagan was a partner in the law firm of Dorsey & Whitney in Minneapolis, Minnesota. In July 1988, Grand Metropolitan PLC, a company based in London, England, retained Dorsey & Whitney as local counsel to represent Grand Met regarding a potential tender offer for the common stock of the Pillsbury Company, headquartered in Minneapolis. Both Grand Met and Dorsey & Whitney took precautions to protect the confidentiality of Grand Met's tender offer plans. O'Hagan did no work on the Grand Met representation. On August 18, 1988, O'Hagan began purchasing call options for Pillsbury stock. Each option gave him the right to purchase one hundred shares of Pillsbury stock by a specified date in September 1988. Later in August and in September, O'Hagan made additional purchases of Pillsbury call options. By the end of September, he owned two thousand five hundred unexpired Pillsbury options, apparently more than any other individual investor. In September 1988, O'Hagan also purchased some five thousand shares of Pillsbury common stock, at a price just under $39 per share. When Grand Met announced its tender offer in October, the price of Pillsbury stock rose to nearly $60 per share. O'Hagan then sold his Pillsbury call options and common stock, making a profit of more than $4.3 million. Explain whether O'Hagan violated the Federal securities laws.

TAKING SIDES

Basic, Inc., was a publicly traded company. Combustion Engineering, Inc., and Basic began discussions concerning the possibility of a merger of the two companies. During the next two years, Basic made three public statements denying that it was engaged in merger negotiations. In December of the second year, Basic publicly announced its approval of Combustion's offer for all its outstanding shares. Former owners of Basic stock who sold their shares after Basic publicly denied that it was engaged in merger negotiations brought a class action suit against Basic and its directors for having released false or misleading information in violation of Section 10(b) of the 1934 Act and Rule 10b-5. The plaintiffs claimed that they were injured by selling their shares at prices that were artificially depressed as a consequence of Basic's misleading public statements. The defendants claimed that the plaintiffs had not proven that the plaintiffs had, in fact, relied upon the misleading statements in selling their stock.

a. What are the arguments that the plaintiffs have satisfied the reliance requirement of Section 10(b) of the 1934 Act and Rule 10b-5?

b. What are the arguments that the plaintiffs have not satisfied the reliance requirement of Section 10(b) of the 1934 Act and Rule 10b-5?

c. Which side should prevail?

CHAPTER 44

Accountants' Legal Liability

After reading and studying this chapter, you should be able to:

- Describe the contract liability of an accountant to her client.

- Describe for what and to whom an accountant has tort liability.

- Discuss the ownership of working papers and the privilege attached to client information.

- Discuss the potential civil and criminal liability of an accountant under the 1933 Securities Act.

- Discuss the potential civil and criminal liability of an accountant under the 1934 Securities Act.

An accountant is subject to potential civil liability arising from the professional services he provides to his clients and third parties. This legal liability is imposed both by the common law at the State level and by securities laws at the Federal level. In addition, an accountant may violate Federal or State criminal law through the performance of his professional activities. This chapter deals with accountants' legal liability under both State and Federal law.

44-1 Common Law

An accountant's legal responsibility under State law may be based upon (1) contract law, (2) tort law, or (3) criminal law. In addition, the common law provides accountants with certain rights and privileges, in particular, the ownership of their working papers and, in some States, a limited accountant-client privilege.

44-1a CONTRACT LIABILITY

The employment contract between an accountant and her client is subject to the general principles of contract law. For the contract to be binding, therefore, it must meet all of the requirements of a common law contract, including offer and acceptance, capacity, consideration, legality, and a writing if, as is often the case, the agreement falls within the one-year provision of the statute of frauds.

Upon entering into a contract (frequently referred to as an *engagement* letter), the accountant is bound to perform all the duties she **explicitly** agrees to provide under the contract. For

example, if an accountant agrees to complete her audit of a client by October 15 so that the client may release its annual report on time, the accountant is under a contractual obligation to do so. Likewise, an accountant who contractually promises to conduct an audit to detect possible embezzlement is under a contractual obligation to provide for her client an expanded audit *beyond* Generally Accepted Auditing Standards (GAAS).

By entering into a contract, an accountant also **implicitly** agrees to perform the contract in a competent and professional manner. His agreement to render professional services holds an accountant to those standards that are generally accepted by the accounting profession, such as GAAS and Generally Accepted Accounting Practices (GAAP). Although accountants need not ensure the absolute accuracy of their work, they must exercise the care of reasonably skilled professionals.

Practical Advice

As an auditor, always exercise due diligence when auditing a client's financial statements. Moreover, be sure to issue the appropriate opinion.

An accountant who breaches his contract incurs liability not only to his client but also to certain third-party contract beneficiaries. A **third-party beneficiary** is a noncontracting party whom the contracting parties *intend* to be the recipient of the primary benefit under the contract. For example, Otis Manufacturing Co. hires Adler, an accountant, to prepare a financial statement for Otis to use in obtaining a loan from Citibank. Citibank is a third-party beneficiary of the contract between Otis and Adler. Another example of a potential third party is an investor considering the purchase of part or all of a particular company. For a more detailed discussion of third-party beneficiaries, see *Chapter 16*.

Pursuant to general contract principles, an accountant who *materially breaches* his contract is entitled to no compensation (i.e., the client is discharged from his obligations under the contract because of the material breach). Thus, if an accountant does not perform an audit on time when time is of the essence or completes only 60 percent of the audit, she has committed a material breach. On the other hand, an accountant who *substantially performs* his contractual duties is generally entitled to be compensated for the contractually agreed-upon fee, less any damages or loss his nonmaterial breach has caused the client. (See *Chapter 18*.)

Practical Advice

In your engagement letter, clearly specify the terms of your contract and the parties for whom the financial statements are being prepared.

44-1b TORT LIABILITY

In performing his professional services, an accountant may incur tort liability to his client or third parties for negligence or fraud. A tort, as discussed in *Chapter 7* (intentional torts, including fraud) and *Chapter 8* (negligence), is a private or civil wrong or injury, other than a breach of contract, for which the courts will provide a remedy in the form of an action for damages.

NEGLIGENCE An accountant is negligent if she does not exercise the degree of care a reasonably competent accountant would exercise under the circumstances. For example, Arthur, an accountant, is engaged to audit the books of Zebra Corporation. During the course of Arthur's investigation, Olivia, an officer of Zebra, notifies Arthur that she suspects that Terrence, Zebra's treasurer, is engaged in a scheme to embezzle from the corporation. Previously informed that Olivia and Terrence are on bad terms with each other, Arthur does not pursue the matter. Terrence is, in fact, engaged in a common embezzlement scheme. Arthur is negligent for failing to conduct a reasonable investigation of the alleged defalcation. Nonetheless, an accountant is *not* liable for honest inaccuracies or errors of judgment so long as she exercised reasonable care in performing her duties. Moreover, as mentioned, an accountant need *not* guarantee the accuracy of her reports, provided she acted in a reasonably competent and professional manner.

Most courts do not permit an accountant to raise the defense of the plaintiff's contributory (or comparative) negligence. Nevertheless, a few courts do permit the defense of contributory or comparative negligence despite the fact that they recognize "that professional malpractice actions pose peculiar problems and that the comparison of fault between a layperson and a professional should be approached with caution." *Halla Nursery, Inc. v. Baumann-Furrie & Co.*, 454 N.W.2d 905 (Minn. 1990).

Historically, an accountant's liability for negligence extended only to the client and to third-party beneficiaries. Under this view, privity of contract was a requirement for a cause of action based upon negligence. This approach was established by the landmark case *Ultramares Corporation v. Touche*, 255 N.Y. 170, 170 N.E. 441 (1931).

In recent years, the courts apply three different tests to determine accountants' liability for negligence to third parties. Several States follow the Ultramares test, which has evolved into a **primary-benefit test**, explained in Credit Alliance Corp. v. Arthur Andersen & Co., 65 N.Y.2d 536 (1985), as follows:

> Before accountants may be held liable in negligence to noncontractual parties who rely to their detriment on inaccurate financial reports, certain prerequisites must be satisfied: (1) the accountants must have been aware that the financial reports were to be used for a particular purpose or purposes (2) in the furtherance of which a known party or parties was intended to rely, and (3) there must have been some conduct on the part of the accountants linking them to that party or parties, which evinces the accountants' understanding of that party or parties' reliance.

A majority of the States has adopted a **foreseen users** or **foreseen class of users** test. This approach, which also has been adopted by the Second Restatement of Torts and the Restatement Third, Torts: Liability for Economic Harm, expands the class of protected individuals to include those the accountant knew would use the work product *or* those who use the accountant's work for a purpose for which the accountant knew the work would be used. For instance, an accountant knows that her client will use a work product to try to obtain a loan from a particular bank. Even if the client uses the audited financial statements to obtain a loan from a different bank, the auditor would be liable to that second bank for any negligent misrepresentations in the financial statements. This class of protected individuals does not, however, include potential investors and the general public.

Some courts have extended liability to benefit an even broader group: reasonably **foreseeable plaintiffs**, including those who are neither known to the accountant nor are members of a class of intended recipients. A few States have adopted this test, which requires only that the accountant reasonably foresee that such individuals might use the financial statements. The rationale behind the foreseeability standard of the law of negligence is that a tortfeasor should be fully liable for all reasonably foreseeable consequences of her conduct.

◆ **SEE FIGURE 44-1:** *Accountants' Liability to Third Parties for Negligent Misrepresentation*

◆ *See Case 44-1*

FIGURE 44-1 **Accountants' Liability to Third Parties for Negligent Misrepresentation**

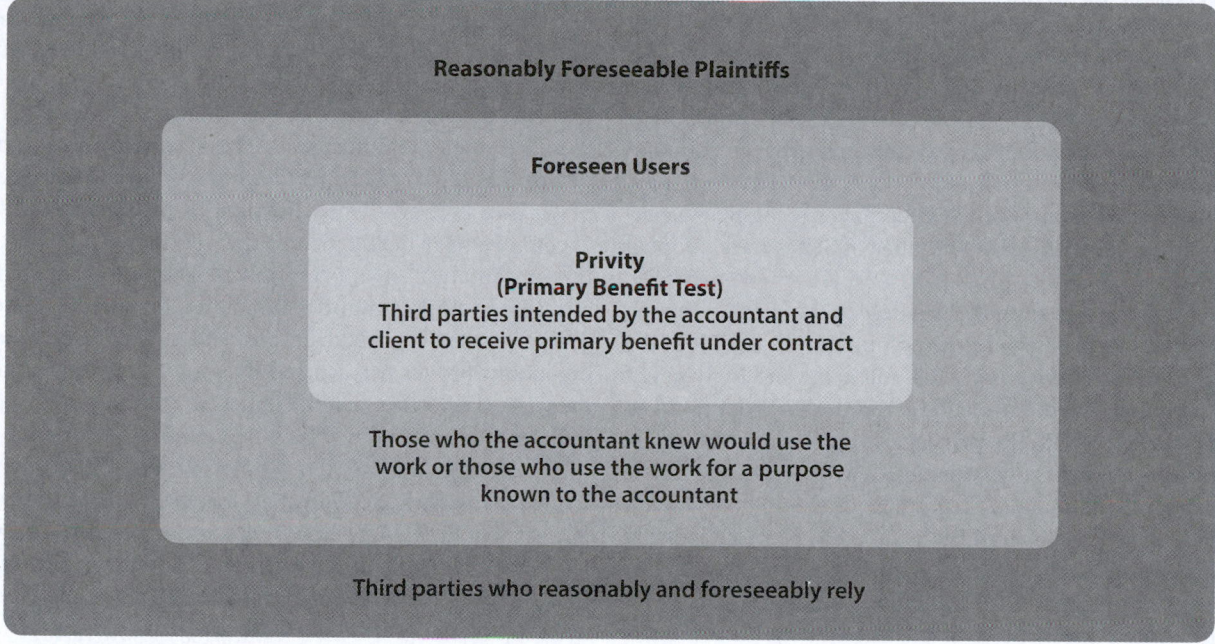

FRAUD An accountant who commits a fraudulent act is liable to any person whom the accountant reasonably should have foreseen would be injured through justifiable reliance on the misrepresentation. The requisite elements of fraud, which are more fully discussed in *Chapter 11*, are (1) a false representation, (2) of fact, (3) that is material, and (4) is made with knowledge of its falsity and with the intention to deceive, (5) is justifiably relied upon, and (6) causes injury to the plaintiff. An accountant who commits fraud may be held liable for both compensatory and punitive damages.

Accountants also have been subject to civil lawsuits based on the Racketeer Influenced and Corrupt Organizations Act (RICO). For a discussion of this Act, see *Chapter 6*.

44-1c CRIMINAL LIABILITY

An accountant's potential criminal liability in rendering professional services is based primarily on the Federal law of securities regulation (discussed later) and taxation. Nonetheless, an accountant would violate State criminal law if she knowingly and willfully certified false documents, altered or tampered with accounting records, used false financial reports, gave false testimony under oath, or committed forgery.

Criminal sanctions may be imposed under the Internal Revenue Code for knowingly preparing false or fraudulent tax returns or documents used in connection with a tax return. Such liability also extends to willfully assisting or advising a client or others to prepare a false return. Penalties for tax fraud may be a fine not to exceed $250,000 ($500,000 for a corporation) or three years' imprisonment or both. Moreover, under the Federal Alternative Fines Act, if any person derives pecuniary gain from the offense or if the offense results in pecuniary loss to a person other than the defendant, the defendant may be fined up to the greater of twice the gross gain or twice the gross loss.

44-1d CLIENT INFORMATION

In providing services for his client, an accountant necessarily obtains information concerning the client's business affairs. Two legal issues concerning this client information involve (1) the ownership of the working papers generated by the accountant and (2) the question of whether or not client information is privileged.

WORKING PAPERS Audit working papers include an auditor's records of the procedures she followed, the tests she performed, the information she obtained, and the conclusions she reached in connection with an audit. All relevant information pertaining to the examination should be included in the working papers. Because an accountant is held to be the owner of his working papers, he need not surrender them to his client. Nevertheless, the accountant may not disclose the contents of these papers unless either (1) the client consents or (2) a court orders the disclosure.

ACCOUNTANT-CLIENT PRIVILEGE Because information considered to be privileged may not be admitted into evidence over the objection of the person possessing the privilege, an accountant must endeavor to maintain confidentiality regarding her communications with her client. The question of a possible accountant-client privilege frequently arises in tax disputes, criminal prosecution, and civil litigation.

Neither the common law nor Federal law recognizes a general privilege. Nevertheless, a number of States have adopted statutes granting some form of accountant-client privilege. Most of these statutes grant the privilege to the client, although a few extend the privilege to the accountant. In addition, the Internal Revenue Service (IRS) Restructuring and Reform Act grants accountants who are authorized under Federal law to practice before the IRS the privilege of confidentiality for tax advice given to their client-taxpayers with respect to Internal Revenue Code matters. Regardless of whether or not the privilege exists, it is generally considered to be professionally unethical for an accountant to disclose confidential communications from a client unless the disclosure is in accordance with (1) American Institute of Certified Public Accountants (AICPA) or GAAS requirements, (2) a court order, or (3) the client's request.

44-2 Federal Securities Law

Accountants may be both civilly and criminally liable under provisions of the Securities Act of 1933 and the Securities Exchange Act of 1934. (*Chapter 43* contains a more comprehensive discussion of the securities laws.) This liability is more extensive and has fewer limitations than liability under the common law. SEC regulations require that auditors be qualified and independent of their audit clients both in fact and in appearance. Accordingly, Rule 2-01 of SEC Regulation S-X imposes restrictions on financial, employment, and business relationships between an accountant and an audit client and restrictions on an accountant providing certain nonaudit services to an audit client.

44-2a SECURITIES ACT OF 1933

Accountants are subject to express civil liability under Section 11 if the financial statements they prepare or certify for inclusion in a registration statement contain any untrue statement or omit any material fact. This liability extends to anyone who acquires the security without knowledge of the untruth or omission. Not only does such liability require no proof of privity between the accountant and the purchasers, but proof of reliance upon the financial statements is also usually not required under Section 11. An accountant will not be liable, however, if he can prove his "due diligence defense." **Due diligence** requires that the accountant had, after reasonable investigation, reasonable ground to believe and did believe at the time the registration statement became effective that the financial statements were true, complete, and accurate. The standard of reasonableness is that required of a prudent person in the management of her own property. Thus, Section 11 imposes liability upon accountants for negligence in the conduct of an audit or in the presentation of information in financial statements. In addition, an accountant is not liable for any or the entire amount otherwise recoverable under Section 11 that the defendant proves was caused by something other than the defective disclosure. In addition, an accountant who *willfully* violates this section may be held criminally liable for a fine of not more than $10,000 or imprisonment of not more than five years or both. Section 24. Moreover, under the Federal Alternative Fines Act, if any person derives pecuniary gain from the offense or if the offense results in pecuniary loss to a person other than the defendant, the defendant may be fined up to the greater of twice the gross gain or twice the gross loss.

44-2b SECURITIES EXCHANGE ACT OF 1934

CIVIL LIABILITY Section 18 imposes express civil liability upon an accountant who makes or causes to be made any false or misleading statement with respect to any material fact in any application, report, document, or registration filed with the SEC under the 1934 Act. Liability extends to any person who purchased or sold a security in reliance upon that statement without knowing that it was false or misleading. An accountant is not liable, however, if she proves that she acted in good faith and had no knowledge that such statement was false or misleading. Thus, an accountant is not liable for false or misleading statements resulting from good faith negligence.

Accountants also may be held civilly liable for violations of **Rule 10b-5**. Rule 10b-5, as discussed in *Chapter 43*, Rule 10b-5 is extremely broad in that it applies to both oral and written misstatements or omissions of material fact and to all securities. An accountant may be liable for a violation of the rule to those who rely upon the misstatement or omission of material fact when purchasing or selling a security. Nevertheless, liability is imposed only if the accountant acted with *scienter*, or intentional or knowing conduct. Therefore, accountants are not liable under Rule 10b-5 for mere negligence, although most courts have held that reckless disregard of the truth is sufficient.

APPLYING THE LAW

Accountants' Legal Liability

FACTS For years, Eldon Jacobsen LLP prepared, certified, and audited the financial records of a large publicly traded telecom company called TeleNon. In 2021, TeleNon acquired a smaller telecom company known as TDT. When accounting for the TDT acquisition, TeleNon allocated a large portion of the purchase price to goodwill, which the company reported on its 2021 Form 10K would thereafter be amortized on a straight-line basis over forty years. Eldon Jacobsen certified that this treatment was in accordance with generally accepted accounting principles (GAAP) and generally accepted auditing standards (GAAS) and, accordingly, that the company's financial statements fairly represented TeleNon's financial position in all material respects. Eldon Jacobsen assigned the forty-year useful life to TDT's goodwill based on its detailed review of GAAP and GAAS, on the fact that most other telecom companies did so at the time, and on the fact that the Securities and Exchange Commission (SEC) did not object to a letter Eldon Jacobsen sent in early 2021 detailing the reasons behind its proposed choice of a forty-year depreciation period.

Subsequently, an internal audit of TeleNon's capital expenditure accounting revealed that a fifteen-year amortization period was more appropriate than forty. This and some other changes in accounting treatment led to a fairly massive restatement of TeleNon's 2021 financials. Unfortunately, TeleNon had issued some debt in 2021. The registration statement filed in connection with that bond offering included the financials certified by Eldon Jacobsen. A year after TeleNon's accounting restatement, purchasers of the bonds sued Eldon Jacobsen and others, alleging among other things that the registration statement misrepresented TeleNon's true financial picture by understating its expenses.

ISSUE Has Eldon Jacobsen violated Section 11 of the 1933 Securities Act?

RULE OF LAW If the financial statements prepared or certified by an accounting firm for inclusion in a registration statement contain any untrue statement or omit any material fact, the accounting firm may be subject to civil liability under Section 11 of the 1933 Act. Anyone who purchases the security without knowledge of the falsehood can bring a civil suit for damages, whether or not the purchaser relied on the misstatement in the registration statement. The accounting firm, however, has a due diligence defense available to it. Proof of due diligence requires the accountants to have conducted a reasonable investigation and, therefore, to have had reasonable grounds to believe, and to have in fact believed at the time the registration became effective, that the financial statements they prepared or certified were true, accurate, and complete. In essence, this amounts to a negligence standard, requiring the accountants to show they had an objectively reasonable basis for their accounting decisions.

APPLICATION An accounting firm has responsibility under Section 11 of the 1933 Act for the accuracy of the financial statements it certifies. If TeleNon's and Eldon Jacobsen's choice of a forty-year useful life for goodwill in the 2021 good financials was not in conformity with GAAP and GAAS as understood at that time, the financial statements and Eldon Jacobsen's certification thereof were inaccurate. Therefore, unless Eldon Jacobsen can prove due diligence, it will be held liable to the bondholders. To do so, first the firm must be able to show that it conducted a reasonable investigation before choosing the depreciation period. It appears here that, at a minimum, Eldon Jacobsen specifically researched GAAP and GAAS relative to the depreciation of goodwill, that it studied the convention then in use by "most other" telecom companies, and that its sought the SEC's input into its choice of this intangible asset's useful life. This seems to be an objectively reasonable approach, especially if there is expert testimony that this is the extent to which a reasonably skilled accountant would go in assessing the appropriate depreciation period under these circumstances.

Furthermore, the firm must be able to show that it had reasonable grounds to believe, and in fact did believe, that the financials were accurate, true, and correct as of the effective date of the registration statement. With no evidence of fraudulent intent present, it is reasonable to assume that the firm was convinced it was in compliance with GAAP and GAAS by virtue of its own research, the trend in the industry, and the Commission's failure to object to its letter setting forth the basis for choosing the forty-year depreciation period. Presumably, the Eldon Jacobsen accountants who were on the engagement will testify that they in fact believed their choice to be supported by and in conformity with GAAP and GAAS, as interpreted in 2021 when the registration statement became effective.

CONCLUSION Eldon Jacobsen can prove the due diligence defense in connection with its preparation of TeleNon's 2021 financial statements and its certification for inclusion in the registration statement attendant to the bond offering. Therefore, Eldon Jacobsen will not be held liable to the bondholders who are suing under Section 11 of the 33 Act.

Practical Advice

Recognize that civil liability for accountants under the federal securities laws extends to a greater range of misconduct and third parties than under common law.

♦ SEE FIGURE 44-2: *Accountants' Liability Under Federal Securities Law*

♦ See Case 44-2

CRIMINAL LIABILITY Accountants may also be held criminally liable for any willful violation of Section 18 or Rule 10b-5. As amended by the Sarbanes-Oxley Act, conviction may carry a fine of not more than $5 million or imprisonment for not more than twenty years or both. An accounting firm may be fined up to $25 million. Section 32. Moreover, under the Federal Alternative Fines Act, if any person derives pecuniary gain from the offense or if the offense results in pecuniary loss to a person other than the defendant, the defendant may be fined not more than the greater of twice the gross gain or twice the gross loss.

AUDIT REQUIREMENTS The **Private Securities Litigation Reform Act of 1995 (Reform Act)** imposed a significant set of obligations upon independent public accountants who audit financial statements required by the 1934 Act. The Reform Act authorizes the SEC to adopt rules that modify or supplement the practices or procedures followed by auditors in the conduct of an audit. Moreover, the Act requires auditors to establish procedures capable of detecting material illegal acts, identifying material related to party transactions, and evaluating whether there is a substantial doubt about the issuer's ability to continue as a going concern during the next fiscal year.

If the auditor becomes aware of information indicating an illegal act, the auditor must determine whether an illegal act occurred and the illegal act's possible effect on the issuer's financial statements. Then the auditor must inform the issuer's management about any illegal activity and make sure that the audit committee or the board of directors is adequately informed. If the auditor concludes that (1) the illegal act has a material effect on the issuer's financial statements, (2) neither senior management nor the board has taken timely and appropriate remedial actions, *and* (3) the failure to take remedial action is reasonably expected to warrant departure from a standard auditor report or warrant resignation from the auditor's engagement, then the auditor promptly must report these conclusions to the issuer's board. Within one day of receiving such report, the issuer must notify the SEC and furnish the auditor with a copy of that notice. If the auditor does not receive such notice, then the auditor must either resign or furnish the SEC with the auditor's report to the board. If the auditor resigns, the auditor must furnish the SEC with a copy of the auditor's report.

The Reform Act provides that an auditor shall not be held liable in a private action for any finding, conclusion, or statement expressed in the report the Act requires the auditor to make to the SEC. The SEC can impose civil penalties against an auditor who willfully violates the Reform Act by failing to resign or to furnish a report to the SEC.

44-2c SARBANES-OXLEY ACT

In response to the business scandals involving companies such as Enron, WorldCom, Global Crossing, and the accounting firm of Arthur Andersen, in 2002, Congress passed the Sarbanes-Oxley Act (SOX), which amends the securities acts in a number of significant respects to protect investors by improving the accuracy and reliability of corporate disclosures. SOX provides for the establishment of the five-member Public Company Accounting Oversight Board (the Board) to oversee the audit of public companies to further the public interest in the preparation of informative, accurate, and independent audit reports for public companies. The SEC has oversight and

FIGURE 44-2 Accountants' Liability under Federal Securities Law

	Section 11 (1933 Act)	Section 18 (1934 Act)	Rule 10b-5 (1934 Act)
Conduct	Registration statement containing material misstatement or omission	False or misleading statements in a document filed with SEC	Deception or material misstatement or opinion
Fault	Negligence	Knowledge or bad faith	*Scienter*
Plaintiff's Knowledge Is a Defense	Yes	Yes	Yes
Reliance Required	No	Yes	Yes
Privity Required	No	No	No

Note: SEC = Securities and Exchange Commission.

enforcement authority over the Board. The Board enforces SOX, the Federal securities laws, the SEC's rules, the Board's rules, and professional accounting standards. The duties of the Board include (1) registering public accounting firms that prepare audit reports for issuers; (2) overseeing the audit of public companies; (3) establishing audit report standards and rules; and (4) inspecting, investigating, and enforcing compliance on the part of registered public accounting firms and their associated persons. SOX directs the Board to establish or modify the auditing and related attestation standards, quality control standards, and ethics standards used by registered public accounting firms to prepare and issue audit reports. The willful violation of any Board rule is treated as a willful violation of the 1934 Act. Moreover, the Board can impose sanctions in its disciplinary proceedings, including the permanent revocation of an accounting firm's registration, a permanent ban on a person's associating with any registered firm, and monetary penalties of $21,543,299 for an accounting firm and $1,077,165 for a natural person, as adjusted annually for inflation in 2021.

To make auditors more independent from their clients, the Act prohibits accounting firms from performing eight specified non-audit services for audit clients, including bookkeeping or other services related to the accounting records or financial statements, financial information systems design and implementation, appraisal or valuation services, fairness opinions, management functions or human resources, and actuarial services. Accounting firms may perform other nonaudit services not expressly forbidden by the Act if the company's audit committee grants prior approval and the approval by the audit committee is disclosed to investors in periodic reports. The lead audit partner having primary responsibility for the audit and the audit partner responsible for reviewing the audit must rotate at least every five years.

Auditors must report directly to the company's audit committee and make timely disclosure of accounting issues concerning (1) critical accounting policies and practices used in the audit, (2) alternative treatments and their ramifications within generally accepted accounting principles that have been discussed with management officials and the treatment preferred by the auditor, and (3) other material written communications between the auditor and management.

CHAPTER SUMMARY

COMMON LAW

Contract Liability the employment contract between an accountant and her client is subject to the general principles of contract law

- *Explicit Duties* the accountant is bound to perform all the duties she expressly agrees to provide
- *Implicit Duties* the accountant impliedly agrees to perform the contract in a competent and professional manner
- *Beneficiaries* contract liability extends to the client or contracting party and to third-party beneficiaries (noncontracting parties intended by the contracting parties to receive the primary benefit under the contract)
- *Breach of Contract* general contract law principles apply

Tort Liability a tort is a private or civil wrong or injury other than a breach of contract

- *Negligence* an accountant is liable for failing to exercise the degree of care a reasonably competent accountant would exercise under the circumstances; most courts have extended an accountant's liability for negligence beyond the client and third-party beneficiaries to foreseen third parties
- *Fraud* an accountant who commits a fraudulent act is liable for both compensatory and punitive damages to any person who he should have reasonably foreseen would be injured; a fraudulent act is a false representation of fact that is material, is made with knowledge of its falsity and with the intention to deceive, and is justifiably relied on

Criminal Liability State law imposes criminal liability on accountants for willfully certifying false documents, altering or tampering with accounting records, using false financial reports, giving false testimony, and committing forgery

Client Information

- *Working Papers* an accountant is considered the owner of his working papers but may not disclose their contents unless the client agrees or a court orders the disclosure

- *Accountant-Client Privilege* not recognized generally by the common law or Federal law, although some States have adopted statutes granting some form of privilege; accountants authorized to practice before the Internal Revenue Service have privilege for tax advice given to their client-taxpayers with respect to Internal Revenue Code matters

| **FEDERAL SECURITIES LAW** | **1933 Act** |

1933 Act

- *Civil Liability* Section 11 imposes express civil liability upon accountants if the financial statements they prepare or certify for a registration statement contain any untrue statement or omit any material fact, unless the accountant proves her due diligence defense, which requires that the accountant had, after reasonable investigation, reasonable grounds to believe and did believe that the financial statements were true, complete, and accurate
- *Criminal Liability* a willful violator of Section 11 is subject to fines of not more than $10,000 and/or imprisonment of not more than five years

1934 Act

- *Section 18* imposes express civil liability on an accountant who knowingly makes any false or misleading statement about any material fact in any report, document, or registration filed with the Securities and Exchange Commission
- *Rule 10b-5* an accountant is civilly liable under this rule if he acts with *scienter* in making oral or written misstatements or omissions of material fact in connection with the purchase or sale of a security
- *Criminal Liability* a willful violator of either Section 18 or Rule 10b-5 is subject to fines of not more than $5 million and/or imprisonment of not more than twenty years
- *Audit Requirements* auditors must establish procedures capable of detecting material illegal acts, identifying material related to party transactions, and evaluating whether there is a substantial doubt about the issuer's ability to continue as a going concern during the next fiscal year
- **Sarbanes-Oxley Act** establishes a new regulatory body to oversee public company auditors, makes auditors more independent from their clients, and places direct responsibility for the audit relationship on audit committees

---

C A S E S

CASE

44-1

Tort Liability

MURPHY v. BDO SEIDMAN, LLP

Court of Appeal, Second District, 2003
113 Cal.App.4th 687, 6 Cal.Rptr.3d 770

Rubin, J.

In November 1995, respondent accounting firm Logan, Throop & Company (Logan) prepared a financial statement for World Interactive Networks, Inc. (WIN), a non-publicly traded corporation, for the period ending in August 1995. The statement misrepresented the value of various WIN assets, claiming they were worth $145 million when in fact they amounted to only $30 million. Logan also claimed the financial statement complied with generally accepted accounting principles (GAAP)

when it did not. In February 1996, Logan repeated essentially the same misrepresentations in its auditors' report of WIN's 1995 balance sheet.

The same month that Logan released its auditors' report, respondent accounting firm BDO Seidman, LLP (Seidman), issued WIN's audited financial statement for 1995. In the statement, Seidman misrepresented the value of WIN's assets, claiming they were worth slightly more than $121 million, when they were truly worth only $6.9 million. In addition,

Seidman misrepresented WIN's shareholder equity as $88 million, when the company was worthless. Several months later, Seidman repeated essentially the same misrepresentations when it released its review of WIN's quarterly balance sheet for the period ending March 1996.

Struthers Industries, Inc. (Struthers), was a publicly traded corporation. In 1995, WIN and Struthers agreed to a reverse merger, subject to shareholder approval, in which WIN would sell its assets to Struthers in return for Struthers stock, following which Struthers would become WIN's subsidiary. While the proposed merger was pending, Seidman prepared a pro forma financial statement of Struthers and WIN as a combined entity, which substantially repeated, from Seidman's earlier audit of WIN, the same false asset values and misrepresentations about complying with GAAP. In January 1997, Seidman sent the pro forma statement to the Securities and Exchange Commission. The SEC told Struthers the pro forma statement did not comply with GAAP because it did not properly account for the inherent uncertainty of the proposed merger. Seidman did not tell appellants, all of whom either owned or later bought WIN or Struthers stock, about the SEC's rejection of Seidman's accounting for the proposed merger.

In March 1998, WIN and Struthers filed for bankruptcy, and appellants, who allege they relied on Seidman's and Logan's financial statements to buy stock in the companies, lost their investments. Consequently, appellants sued both accounting firms, alleging causes of action for negligent and intentional misrepresentation. * * *

Respondents demurred to the complaint * * * arguing it failed for a number of reasons to state a cause of action and pleaded fraud with insufficient detail. The court adopted respondents' arguments and sustained [the] demurrers without leave to amend. * * * The court entered judgment for respondents. This appeal followed.

* * *

Respondents' Duty to Appellants

* * *

In *Bily v. Arthur Young & Co.* [citation], our Supreme Court formulated a hierarchy of duty for accountants who prepare inaccurate financial statements. Casting an ever-widening circle of obligation, *Bily* established that the more egregious the misstatement, the broader the duty: For *ordinary negligence*, an auditor owes a duty only to its client. As *Bily* explained, "[A]n auditor's liability for general negligence in the conduct of an audit of its client financial statements is confined to the client, i.e., the person who contracts for or engages the audit services. Other persons may not recover on a pure negligence theory." [Citation.]

- For *negligent misrepresentation*, the duty expands to specifically intended beneficiaries of the report who are substantially likely to receive the misinformation. *Bily*

defined such beneficiaries as "persons who, although not clients, may reasonably come to receive and rely on an audit report and whose existence constitutes a risk of audit reporting that may fairly be imposed on the auditor. Such persons are specifically intended beneficiaries of the audit report who are known to the auditor and for whose benefit it renders the audit report." [Citation.] Liability arises toward such plaintiffs when the representation was made "with the intent to induce plaintiff, or a particular class of persons to which plaintiff belongs, to act in reliance upon the representation in a specific transaction, or a specific type of transaction, that defendant intended to influence. Defendant is deemed to have intended to influence [its client's] transaction with plaintiff whenever defendant knows with *substantial certainty* that plaintiff, or the particular class of persons to which plaintiff belongs, will rely on the representation in the course of the transaction." [Citations.]

- For *intentional misrepresentation*, the duty expands yet further to include anyone whom the auditor should have reasonably foreseen would rely on the misrepresentations. *Bily* explained, "The representation must have been made with the intent to defraud plaintiff, or a particular class of persons to which plaintiff belongs, whom defendant intended or *reasonably should have foreseen* would rely upon the representation. One who makes a representation with intent to defraud the public or a particular class of persons is deemed to have intended to defraud every individual in that category who is actually misled thereby." [Citation.]

Bily can * * * be briefly summarized as follows: (1) ordinary negligence—*no duty* to third parties; (2) negligent misrepresentation—duty to third parties who would be known with *substantial certainty* to rely on the misrepresentation; and (3) intentional misrepresentation—duty to third parties who could be *reasonably foreseen* to rely on the misrepresentation.

* * *

1. *Appellants Allege the Duty for Negligent Misrepresentation.* The complaint alleges WIN and Struthers hired respondents to prepare various financial statements that appellants relied upon in buying WIN or Struthers stock and in approving their merger. The complaint also alleges respondents knew WIN or Struthers would distribute the statements to existing and potential shareholders for such purposes. * * * Such an allegation, and similar allegations targeted at Logan, satisfy *Bily's* criteria for negligent misrepresentation: respondents knew with substantial certainty that potential investors such as appellants would rely on the misstatements. [Citation.] The complaint therefore states a cause of action for negligent misrepresentation.

2. *Appellants Allege the Duty for Intentional Misrepresentation.* The complaint alleges respondents either intentionally or recklessly misstated the value of WIN's assets and shareholder equity. It further alleges respondents should have foreseen that current and future investors in WIN and Struthers would rely on the misstated values in deciding whether to invest in those companies and to approve their merger. * * * The complaint therefore states a cause of action for intentional misrepresentation.

3. *Appellants Who Bought Struthers Stock Allege Causes of Action.* Some appellants bought only Struthers stock. Respondents note that Struthers hired Seidman, but not Logan, to prepare its financial statements. According to respondents, Struthers appellants therefore cannot state a cause of action against Logan because Struthers was not Logan's client and thus owed no duty to Struthers' shareholders for any misstatements.

Bily imposes on respondents a duty to more than just their clients. Respondents owed a duty to anyone whom they (1) should have reasonably foreseen would rely on their intentional misrepresentations, or (2) knew with substantial certainty would rely on their negligent misrepresentations. [Citation.] The complaint alleges respondents knew the proposed merger of WIN and Struthers would induce investors in Struthers to rely on financial statements about WIN in anticipation of the two companies becoming one. In addition, the complaint alleges respondents knew Struthers investors would rely on WIN's financial statements in deciding whether to approve the merger itself. The complaint therefore alleges a duty from respondents to Struthers' shareholders, making respondents liable to those shareholders for their misrepresentations.

Reliance

1. *Sufficient Detail.* Logan contends the complaint does not describe appellants' reliance on Logan's alleged misrepresentations with enough detail. According to Logan, appellants must identify the "when, where, and how" of their reliance. Our review finds most appellants describe their reliance on WIN's inflated assets with enough specificity, often including the precise date they bought stock in the company and the amount paid, to permit respondents to prepare a defense. * * *

2. *Forbearance Is Reliance.* A number of appellants, whom we identify in Appendix 2, bought WIN or Struthers stock before Logan and Seidman issued their first reports, and thereafter relied on respondents' rosy misstatements in deciding not to sell their stock. * * * After briefing ended in this appeal, our Supreme Court held in [citation] that holding stock can be actionable reliance. * * *

3. *"Grapevine" Plaintiffs.* Some appellants did not read or otherwise directly rely on the Logan or Seidman financial statements. Instead, they relied on what others told them the statements said. Respondents argue such indirect reliance by those appellants, whom they call "grapevine plaintiffs," does not constitute legal reliance and is thus not actionable.

The law is otherwise. Indirect reliance is actionable if Logan or Seidman had reason to know others would convey their misrepresentations to appellants. Under *Bily*, respondents are liable for (1) negligent misrepresentation if they knew it was substantially certain that appellants would receive the misstatements and (2) intentional misrepresentation if it was reasonably foreseeable appellants would receive the statements. Thus, nothing in *Bily*'s formulation of negligent or intentional misrepresentation precludes indirect reliance. * * * Respondents' contention is well-taken, however, as to certain appellants who do not expressly allege relying on any Logan or Seidman misstatement, whether directly or indirectly. Because they do not allege reliance, the trial court properly dismissed them for failing to state a claim for negligent or intentional misrepresentation. * * *

* * *

The trial court's judgment is reversed in part and affirmed in part. * * *

CASE 44-2

Liability under the 1934 Act: Rule 10b-5
ERNST & ERNST v. HOCHFELDER
Supreme Court of the United States, 1976
425 U.S. 185, 96 S.Ct. 1375, 47 L.Ed.2d 668

Powell, J.

The issue in this case is whether an action for civil damages may lie under §10(b) of the Securities Exchange Act of 1934 (1934 Act), * * *, and Securities and Exchange Commission Rule 10b-5, * * * in the absence of an allegation of intent to deceive, manipulate, or defraud on the part of the defendant.

Petitioner, Ernst & Ernst, is an accounting firm. From 1946 through 1967 it was retained by First Securities Company of Chicago (First Securities), a small brokerage firm and member of the Midwest Stock Exchange and of the National Association of Securities Dealers, to perform periodic audits of the firm's books and records. In connection with these audits Ernst

& Ernst prepared for filing with the Securities and Exchange Commission (Commission) the annual reports required of First Securities under §17(a) of the 1934 Act. It also prepared for First Securities responses to the financial questionnaires of the Midwest Stock Exchange (Exchange).

Respondents were customers of First Securities who invested in a fraudulent securities scheme perpetrated by Leston B. Nay, president of the firm and owner of 92% of its stock. * * *

This fraud came to light in 1968 when Nay committed suicide, leaving a note that described First Securities as bankrupt and the escrow accounts as "spurious." Respondents subsequently filed this action for damages against Ernst & Ernst in the United States District Court for the Northern District of Illinois under §10(b) of the 1934 Act. The complaint charged that Nay's escrow scheme violated §10(b) and Commission Rule 10b-5, and that Ernst & Ernst had "aided and abetted" Nay's violations by its "failure" to conduct proper audits of First Securities. As revealed through discovery, respondents' cause of action rested on a theory of negligent nonfeasance. The premise was that Ernst & Ernst had failed to utilize "appropriate auditing procedures" in its audits of First Securities, thereby failing to discover internal practices of the firm said to prevent an effective audit. * * *

Federal regulation of transactions in securities emerged as part of the aftermath of the market crash in 1929. The Securities Act of 1933 (1933 Act), [citation] was designed to provide investors with full disclosure of material information concerning public offerings of securities in commerce, to protect investors against fraud and, through the imposition of specified civil liabilities, to promote ethical standards of honesty and fair dealing. [Citation.] The 1934 Act was intended principally to protect investors against manipulation of stock prices through regulation of transactions upon securities exchanges and in over-the-counter markets, and to impose regular reporting requirements on companies whose stock is listed on national securities exchanges. [Citation.] Although the Acts contain numerous carefully drawn express civil remedies and criminal penalties, Congress recognized that efficient regulation of securities trading could not be accomplished under a rigid statutory program. As part of the 1934 Act Congress created the Commission, which is provided with an arsenal of flexible enforcement powers. [Citations.]

Section 10 of the 1934 Act makes it "unlawful for any person ... (b) [t]o use or employ, in connection with the purchase or sale of any security ... any manipulative or deceptive device or contrivance in contravention of such rules and regulations as the Commission may prescribe as necessary or appropriate in the public interest or for the protection of investors." [Citation.] In 1942, acting pursuant to the power conferred by §10(b), the Commission promulgated Rule 10b-5.

* * *

Although §10(b) does not by its terms create an express civil remedy for its violation, and there is no indication that Congress, or the Commission when adopting Rule 10b-5, contemplated such a remedy, the existence of a private cause of action for violations of the statute and the Rule is now well established. [Citation.] During the 30-year period since a private cause of action was first implied under §10(b) and Rule 10b-5, a substantial body of case law and commentary has developed as to its elements. Courts and commentators long have differed with regard to whether scienter is a necessary element of such a cause of action, or whether negligent conduct alone is sufficient. * * *

* * *

Although the extensive legislative history of the 1934 Act is bereft of any explicit explanation of Congress' intent, we think the relevant portions of that history support our conclusion that §10(b) was addressed to practices that involve some element of scienter and cannot be read to impose liability for negligent conduct alone.

* * *

The Commission argues that Congress has been explicit in requiring willful conduct when that was the standard of fault intended. * * *

The structure of the Acts does not support the Commission's argument. In each instance that Congress created express civil liability in favor of purchasers or sellers of securities it clearly specified whether recovery was to be premised on knowing or intentional conduct, negligence, or entirely innocent mistake. [Citations.] For example, §11 of the 1933 Act unambiguously creates a private action for damages when a registration statement includes untrue statements of material facts or fails to state material facts necessary to make the statements therein not misleading. Within the limits specified by §11(e), the issuer of the securities is held absolutely liable for any damages resulting from such misstatement or omission. But experts such as accountants who have prepared portions of the registration statement are accorded a "due diligence" defense. In effect, this is a negligence standard. An expert may avoid civil liability with respect to the portions of the registration statement for which he was responsible by showing that "after reasonable investigation" he had "reasonable ground[s] to believe" that the statements for which he was responsible were true and there was no omission of a material fact. §11(b)(3)(B)(i). See, e.g., *Escott v. BarChris Const. Corp.* [citation, see Case 43-2]. The express recognition of a cause of action premised on negligent behavior in §11 stands in sharp contrast to the language of §10(b), and significantly undercuts the Commission's argument.

We also consider it significant that each of the express civil remedies in the 1933 Act allowing recovery for negligent conduct, see §§11, 12(2), 15, [citations] is subject to significant procedural restrictions not applicable under §10(b). * * *

* * *

We have addressed, to this point, primarily the language and history of §10(b). The Commission contends, however, that subsections (b) and (c) of Rule 10b-5 are cast in language which—if standing alone—could encompass both intentional and negligent behavior. These subsections respectively provide that it is unlawful "[t]o make any untrue statement of a material fact or to omit to state a material fact necessary in order to make the statements made, in the light of the circumstances under which they were made, not misleading…" and "[t]o engage in any act, practice, or course of business which operates or would operate as a fraud or deceit upon any person…." Viewed in isolation the language of subsection (b), and arguably that of subsection (c), could be read as proscribing, respectively, any type of material misstatement or omission, and any course of conduct, that has the effect of defrauding investors, whether the wrongdoing was intentional or not.

We note first that such a reading cannot be harmonized with the administrative history of the Rule, a history making clear that when the Commission adopted the Rule it was intended to apply only to activities that involved scienter. More importantly, Rule 10b-5 was adopted pursuant to authority granted the Commission under §10(b). The rulemaking power granted to an administrative agency charged with the administration of a federal statute is not the power to make law. Rather, it is "'the power to adopt regulations to carry into effect the will of Congress as expressed by the statute.'" [Citations.] * * * When a statute speaks so specifically in terms of manipulation and deception, and of implementing devices and contrivances—the commonly understood terminology of intentional wrongdoing—and when its history reflects no more expansive intent, we are quite unwilling to extend the scope of the statute to negligent conduct.

* * *

The judgment of the Court of Appeals is reversed.

QUESTIONS

1. Baldwin Corporation made a public offering of $25 million of convertible debentures and registered the offering with the SEC. The registration statement contained financial statements certified by Adams and Allen, Certified Public Accountants. The financial statements overstated Baldwin's net income and assets by 20 percent and understated the company's liability by 15 percent. Because Adams and Allen did not carefully follow Generally Accepted Accounting Standards, it failed to detect these inaccuracies, the discovery of which has caused the bond prices to drop from their original selling price of $1,000 per bond to $720. Can Conrad, who purchased $10,000 of the debentures, collect from Adams and Allen for his damages? Explain.

2. Ingram is a Certified Public Accountant (CPA) employed by Jordan, Keller and Lane, CPAs, to audit Martin Enterprises, Inc., a fast-growing service firm that went public two years ago. The financial statements Ingram audited were included in a proxy statement proposing a merger with several other firms. The proxy statement was filed with the Securities and Exchange Commission and included several inaccuracies. First, approximately $1 million, or more than 20 percent, of the previous year's "net sales originally reported" had proven nonexistent by the time the proxy statement was filed and had been written off on Martin's own books. This was not disclosed in the proxy statement, in violation of Accounting Board Opinion Number 9. Second, Martin's net sales for the current year were stated as $11.3 million when in fact they were less than $10.5 million. Third, Martin's net profits for the current year were reported as $700,000, when the firm actually had no earnings at all.

    a. What civil liability, if any, does Ingram have?

    b. What criminal liability, if any, does Ingram have?

3. Girard & Company, Certified Public Accountants, audited the financial statements included in the annual report submitted by PMG Enterprises, Inc., to the Securities and Exchange Commission (SEC). The audit failed to detect numerous false and misleading statements contained in the financial statements.

    a. Investors who subsequently purchased PMG stock have brought suit against Girard under Section 18 of the 1934 Act. What defenses, if any, are available to Girard?

    b. The SEC has initiated criminal proceedings under the 1934 Act against Girard. What must be proven for Girard to be held criminally liable?

4. Dryden, a certified public accountant, audited the books of Elixir, Inc., and certified incorrect financial statements in a form that was filed with the Securities and Exchange Commission. Shortly thereafter, Elixer, Inc., went bankrupt. Investigation into the bankruptcy disclosed that through an intricate and clever embezzlement scheme Kraft, the president of Elixir, had siphoned off substantial sums of money that now support Kraft in a luxurious lifestyle in South America. Investors who purchased shares of Elixir have brought suit against Dryden under Rule 10b-5. At trial, Dryden produces evidence demonstrating that his failure to discover the embezzlement

resulted merely from negligence on his part and that he had no knowledge of the fraudulent conduct. Is Dryden liable under the Securities Exchange Act of 1934? Why or why not?

5. Johnson Enterprises, Inc., contracted with the accounting firm of P, A & E to perform an audit of Johnson. The accounting firm performed its duty in a nonnegligent, competent manner but failed to discover a novel embezzlement scheme perpetrated by Johnson's treasurer. Shortly thereafter, Johnson's treasurer disappeared with $75,000 of the company's money. Johnson now refuses to pay P, A & E its $20,000 audit fee and is seeking to recover $75,000 from P, A & E.

   a. What are the rights and liabilities of P, A & E and Johnson? Explain.

   b. Would your answer to (a) differ if the scheme were a common embezzlement scheme that Generally Accepted Accounting Standards should have disclosed? Explain.

6. The accounting firm of T, W & S was engaged to perform an audit of Progate Manufacturing Company. During the course of the audit, T, W & S discovered that the company had overvalued its inventory by carrying the inventory on its books at the previous year's prices, which were significantly higher than current prices. When T, W & S approached Progate's president, Lehman, about the improper valuation of inventory, Lehman became enraged and told T, W & S that unless the firm accepted the valuation, Progate would sue T, W & S. Although T, W & S knew that Progate's suit was frivolous

and unfounded, it wished to avoid the negative publicity that would arise from any suit brought against it. Therefore, on the assumption that the overvaluation would not harm anybody, T, W & S accepted Progate's inflated valuation of inventory. Progate subsequently went bankrupt, and T, W & S is now being sued by (1) First National Bank, a bank that relied upon T, W & S's statement to loan money to Progate; and (2) Thomas, an investor who purchased 20 percent of Progate's stock after receiving T, W & S's statement. Explain what are the rights and liabilities of First National Bank, Thomas, and T, W & S.

7. J, B & J, Certified Public Accountants, has audited the Highcredit Corporation for the past five years. Recently, the Securities and Exchange Commission (SEC) has commenced an investigation of Highcredit for possible violations of Federal securities law. The SEC has subpoenaed all of J, B & J's working papers pertinent to the audit of Highcredit. Highcredit insists that J, B & J not turn over the documents to the SEC. What action should J, B & J take? Explain.

8. On February 1, the Gazette Corporation hired Susan Sharp to conduct an audit of its books and to prepare financial statements for the corporation's annual meeting on July 1. Sharp made every reasonable attempt to comply with the deadline but could not finish the report on time due to delays in receiving needed information from Gazette. Gazette now refuses to pay Sharp for her audit and is threatening to bring a cause of action against Sharp. What course of action should Sharp pursue? Discuss.

C A S E   P R O B L E M S

9. John P. Butler Accountancy Corporation agreed to audit the financial statements of Westside Mortgage, Inc., a mortgage company that arranged financing for real property, for the year ending December 31, 2019. On March 22, 2020, after completing the audit, Butler issued unqualified audited financial statements listing Westside's corporate net worth as $175,036. The primary asset on the balance sheet was a $100,000 note receivable that had, in reality, been rendered worthless in August 2018 when the trust deed on real property securing the note was wiped out by a prior foreclosure of a superior deed of trust. The note constituted 57 percent of Westside's net worth and was thus material to an accurate representation of Westside's financial position. In October 2020, International Mortgage Company (IMC) approached Westside for the purpose of buying and selling loans on

the secondary market. IMC signed an agreement with Westside in December after reviewing Westside's audited financial statements. In June 2021, Westside issued a $475,293 promissory note to IMC, on which it ultimately defaulted. IMC brought an action against Westside, its owners, principals, and Butler. IMC alleged negligence and negligent misrepresentation against Butler in auditing and issuing without qualification the defective financial statements on which IMC relied in deciding to do business with Westside. Butler claimed that it owed no duty of care to IMC, a third party that was not specifically known to Butler as an intended recipient of the audited financial statements. Is Butler correct? Explain.

10. Equisure, Inc., was required to file audited financial statements when it applied to have its stock listed on the American Stock Exchange (AmEx). It retained an

accounting firm, defendant Stirtz Bernards Boyden Surdel & Larter, P.A. (Stirtz). Stirtz issued a favorable interim audit report that Equisure used to gain listing on the stock exchange. Subsequently, Equisure retained Stirtz to audit the financial statements required for Equisure's Form 10 filing with the U.S. Securities and Exchange Commission (SEC). Stirtz's auditor knew that the audit was for the SEC reports. Stirtz issued a "clean" audit opinion, which, with the audited financial statements, was included in Equisure's SEC filing and made available to the public. NorAm Investment Services, Inc., also known as Equity Securities Trading Company, Inc. (NorAm), a securities broker, began lending margin credit to purchasers of Equisure stock. These purchasers advanced only a portion of the purchase price; NorAm extended credit (a margin loan) for the balance and held the stock as collateral for the loan, charging interest on the balance. When NorAm had loaned approximately $900,000 in margin credit, its president, Nathan Newman, reviewed Stirtz's audit report and the audited financial statements. Based on his review, NorAm extended more than $1.6

million of additional margin credit for the purchase of Equisure shares. When AmEx stopped trading Equisure stock due to allegations of insider trading and possible stock manipulation, the stock became worthless. NorAm was left without collateral for more than $2.5 million in margin loans. Stirtz resigned as auditor of Equisure and warned that its audit report might be misleading and should no longer be relied upon. NorAm sued Stirtz for negligent misrepresentation and negligence. Explain whether or not NorAm will prevail.

11. Holtz Rubenstein Reminick, CPAs, audited year-end financial statements of Quality Food Brands, Inc., and related companies. Signature Bank, relying upon the audited financial reports prepared by Holtz Rubenstein Reminick, extended a term note to Quality in the principal sum of $10 million. Quality subsequently filed a petition under Chapter 7 of the U.S. Bankruptcy Code, and Signature Bank only then learned of various false and misleading statements contained in the audited financial reports. Explain whether Signature Bank can recover damages for negligent misrepresentation.

T A K I N G   S I D E S

Arthur Young & Co., a firm of certified public accountants, was the independent auditor for Amerada Hess Corporation. During its review of Amerada's financial statements as required by Federal securities laws, Young confirmed Amerada's statement of its contingent tax liabilities and prepared tax accrual work papers. These work papers, which pertained to Young's evaluation of Amerada's reserves for contingent tax liabilities, included discussions of questionable positions Amerada might have taken on its tax returns. The Internal Revenue Service (IRS) initiated a criminal investigation of Amerada's tax returns when, during a routine audit, it discovered questionable payments made by Amerada from a "special disbursement

account." The IRS summoned Young to make available all its information relating to Amerada, including the tax accrual work papers. Amerada instructed Young not to obey the summons. The IRS then brought an action against Young to enforce the administrative summons.

a. What are the arguments that Young must turn over the work papers?

b. What are the arguments that the work papers are protected from government summons?

c. Who should prevail? Explain.

CHAPTER 45

Environmental Law

CHAPTER OUTCOMES

After reading and studying this chapter, you should be able to:

- Explain the common law actions for environmental damage and the difficulties in prevailing in such actions.

- Explain the major substantive provisions of the National Environmental Policy Act.

- Explain the regulatory scheme of the Clean Air Act.

- Explain the regulation of both point and nonpoint sources of pollution by the Clean Water Act.

- Explain (1) the Federal Insecticide, Fungicide and Rodenticide Act; (2) the Toxic Substances Control Act; (3) the Resource Conservation and Recovery Act; (4) the Superfund; and (5) the various United Nations Conventions on Climate Change.

A s technology has advanced and people have become more urbanized, their effect on the environment has increased. Our air has become dirtier; our waters have become more polluted. Although individuals and environmental groups have brought private actions against some polluters, the common law has proved unable to control environmental damage. Because of this inadequacy, the Federal and State governments have enacted a variety of statutes designed to promote environmental concerns and prevent environmental harm. Although in recent years certain industrial countries such as the United States have made significant progress in controlling pollutants, such is not the case worldwide. Moreover, even as we have enjoyed some success in controlling some pollutants, a new generation of environmental problems has arisen. One of the more recent environmental issues is the regulation of high-volume horizontal hydraulic fracturing (fracking) for oil and gas. In this chapter, we discuss both common law causes of action for environmental damage and Federal regulation of the environment.

COMMON LAW ACTIONS FOR ENVIRONMENTAL DAMAGE

Private tort actions may be used to recover for harm to the environment. For example, if Alice's land is polluted by the mill next door, Alice may sue the mill in tort for the damage to her land. In suing to recover for environmental damage, plaintiffs generally have relied on the theories of nuisance, trespass, and strict liability.

45-1 Nuisance

The term *nuisance* encompasses two distinct types of wrong: private nuisance and public nuisance. A private nuisance involves an interference with a person's use and enjoyment of his land, while a public nuisance is an act that interferes with a public right.

45-1a PRIVATE NUISANCE

To establish a private nuisance, a plaintiff must show that the defendant has substantially and unreasonably interfered with the use and enjoyment of the plaintiff's land. In an action for damages, the plaintiff need not prove that the defendant's conduct was unreasonable, only that the interference was unreasonable. Thus, assuming all other requirements are met, the question in a private nuisance suit for damages is whether the defendant should pay for the harm it caused the plaintiff, even if the defendant's action was not unreasonable. For example, in one case, an electric utility using a coal-burning electric generator which employed the latest scientific methods for reducing emissions was held liable for the harm it caused its neighbor's alfalfa crops, even though the utility was performing the socially useful function of creating electric power.

Although a plaintiff need not prove the defendant's conduct is unreasonable to recover in a private nuisance action for damages, such reasonableness is an issue when the plaintiff sues for an injunction. In determining whether an injunction against a nuisance is appropriate, a court will "balance the equities" by considering a number of factors, including the gravity of the harm to the plaintiff, the social value of the defendant's activity that is causing the harm, the feasibility and costs of avoiding the harm, and the public interest, if any.

The need to balance the equities has meant that courts often deny injunctions when the defendant is engaged in a socially useful activity. Additionally, injunctions are frequently denied because the defendant successfully raises an equitable defense. Consequently, private nuisance actions have been of limited value in controlling environmental damage.

45-1b PUBLIC NUISANCE

To be treated as a public nuisance, an activity must somehow interfere with the health, safety, or comfort of the public. For example, the actions of an industrial plant in polluting a stream will be treated as a private nuisance if such actions inconvenience only the owners of land downstream but will be treated as a public nuisance if they kill the stream's marine life. Generally, only a public representative, such as the attorney general, may sue to stop a public nuisance. If, however, the nuisance inflicts upon an individual some unique harm that the general populace does not suffer, that individual may also sue to halt the nuisance. Out of concern about the economic impact of closing an industrial operation, public representatives frequently are unwilling to sue to abate a public nuisance. Consequently, because these representatives often will not, and private parties may not, sue, relatively few public nuisance actions have been brought against polluters.

45-2 Trespass to Land

To establish trespass to land, a plaintiff must show an invasion that interferes with the plaintiff's right of exclusive possession of the property and that is the direct result of an action by the defendant. For example, entering or throwing trash on someone else's land without permission constitutes a trespass. Trespass differs from private nuisance in that trespass requires an interference with the plaintiff's possession of the land. Thus, sending smoke or gas onto another's property may constitute a private nuisance but does not constitute a trespass.

Trespass often is difficult to establish in actions for environmental damage, either because the plaintiff is not in possession of the property or because the injury does not stem from an invasion of the property. Trespass actions have thus been of limited benefit in halting environmental damage. For a more complete discussion of trespass, see *Chapter 7*.

45-3 Strict Liability for Abnormally Dangerous Activities

While they generally base tort liability on fault, the courts may hold **strictly liable**, that is, liable without fault, a person engaged in an abnormally dangerous activity. To establish such strict liability, a plaintiff must show that the defendant is carrying on an unduly dangerous activity in an inappropriate location and that the plaintiff has suffered damage because of this activity. For example, a person who operates an oil refinery in a densely populated area may be held strictly liable for any damage the refinery causes. The requirement that the activity engaged in be (1) ultrahazardous and (2) inappropriate for its locale has limited the number of strict liability actions brought against polluters.

45-4 Problems Common to Private Causes of Action

In addition to the shortcomings of each tort theory discussed previously, using a private cause of action to control environmental damage presents its own problems. The costs associated with private litigation (including the payment of one's own legal fees) are high, and although overall the environmental damage may be considerable, the extent of any particular injury may not warrant pursuing a private lawsuit. Furthermore, tort actions generally do not provide relief for aesthetic, as opposed to physical, injury. Additionally, in many tort actions, a significant issue of causation arises. For example, if a landowner lives near several plants, each of which emits pollution and none of which, by itself, would cause the amount of damage the landowner's property has suffered, the landowner may have difficulty recovering from any of the plant owners. Finally, even if a private plaintiff is successful, her recovery may be limited to monetary damages, leaving the defendant free to continue to pollute.

FEDERAL REGULATION OF THE ENVIRONMENT

Because private causes of action have proved inadequate to recompense and prevent environmental damage, the Federal, State, and some local governments have enacted statutes designed to protect the environment. In this chapter, we will consider some of the more important Federal environmental laws. In addition, the Environmental Protection Agency (EPA) has encouraged companies to conduct voluntary environmental audits. One of the key issues surrounding such self-audits is whether these audits are discoverable by State or Federal prosecutors. As a regulatory agency, the EPA is authorized to write regulations that implement the environmental protection laws and that are mandatory requirements applicable to individuals, businesses, state or local governments, non-profit institutions, and others. At the time this textbook is going to press, recently issued EPA regulations are in a state of rapid change. According to the *Washington Post*, the Trump administration "worked to scale back or abolish more than 200 environmental protections … completing more than 170 of them." As of June 25, 2021, the Biden administration had added twenty-two new protections and overturned thirty-six of the Trump administration's environmental regulations. The Biden administration has identified many more of the Trump administration's environmental rollbacks for reversal. Given the future uncertainty of the Trump administration's environmental regulations, this chapter will not cover them.

45-5 The National Environmental Policy Act

Congress enacted the **National Environmental Policy Act (NEPA)** to establish environmental protection as a goal of Federal policy. The NEPA's declaration of national environmental policy states the following:

> The Congress, recognizing the profound impact of man's activity on the interrelations of all components of the natural environment, particularly the profound influences of population growth, high-density urbanization, industrial expansion, resource exploitation, and new and expanding technological advances, and recognizing further the critical importance of restoring and maintaining environmental quality to the overall welfare and development of man, declares that it is the continuing policy of the Federal Government, in cooperation with State and local governments … to use all practicable means and measures … in a manner calculated to foster and promote the general welfare, to create and maintain conditions under which man and nature can exist in productive harmony, and fulfill the social, economic and other requirements of present and future generations of Americans.

Thus, NEPA imposes the responsibility for maintaining the environment on all Federal agencies. It is the responsibility of the Federal government to consider the environmental consequences of all of its actions and to administer all of its programs in an environmentally sound manner.

The NEPA has two major substantive sections, one creating the Council on Environmental Quality (CEQ) and the other requiring that each Federal agency, when recommending or

reporting on proposals for legislation or other major Federal action, prepare an **environmental impact statement (EIS)** if the legislation or Federal action will have a significant environmental effect.

45-5a THE COUNCIL ON ENVIRONMENTAL QUALITY

The CEQ, a three-member advisory group, is not a separate administrative agency but rather is part of the Executive Office of the President; as such, it makes recommendations to the President on environmental matters and prepares annual reports on the condition of the environment. Although not expressly authorized to do so by statute, the CEQ, acting under a series of executive orders, has issued regulations regarding the content and preparation of EISs. The Federal courts generally have deferred to these regulations.

45-5b ENVIRONMENTAL IMPACT STATEMENTS

Unlike most Federal environmental statutes, the NEPA does not focus on a particular type of environmental damage or harmful substance but instead expresses the Federal government's continuing concern with protection of the environment. The NEPA's promotion of environmental considerations is effected through the EIS requirement. An EIS is required if the proposed action (1) is Federal, (2) is considered "major," and (3) has a significant environmental impact.

PROCEDURE FOR PREPARING AN EIS When proposing legislation or considering a major Federal action, the CEQ regulations require that a Federal agency initially make an "environmental assessment," which is a short analysis of the need for an EIS. If the agency decides that no EIS is required, it must make this decision available to the public. If, on the other hand, the agency concludes that an EIS is required, the agency must engage in "scoping," which consists of consulting other relevant Federal agencies and the public to determine the significant issues the EIS will address and the statement's appropriate scope. After scoping, the agency prepares a draft EIS, for which there is a comment period. After the comment period ends and revisions, if necessary, are made, a final EIS is published.

SCOPE OF EIS REQUIREMENT The EIS requirement of the NEPA applies to a broad range of projects: [T]here is "Federal action" within the meaning of the statute not only when an agency proposes to build a facility itself, but also whenever an agency makes a decision which permits action by other parties which will affect the quality of the environment. NEPA's impact statement procedure has been held to apply where a Federal agency approves a lease of land to private parties, grants licenses and permits to private parties, or approves and funds state highway projects. In each of these instances, the Federal agency took action affecting the environment in the sense that the agency made a decision which permitted some other party—private or governmental—to take action affecting the environment.

The NEPA's EIS requirement applies not only to a broad range of projects but also to a broad range of environmental effects. The NEPA has been held to apply not only to the natural environment but also to the urban environment, including impact on crime, esthetics, and socio-economics.

> The Act [NEPA] must be construed to include protection of the quality of life for city residents. Noise, traffic, overburdened mass transportation systems, crime, congestion and even availability of drugs all affect the urban "environment" and are surely results of the "profound influences of high-density urbanization [and] industrial expansion."

While effects on health, including psychological health, are considered environmental effects under the NEPA, the Supreme Court has held that an effect is environmental only if it has a reasonably close causal relation to an impact on the physical environment.

CONTENT OF AN EIS The NEPA requires that an EIS describe in detail the environmental impact of a proposed action, any adverse environmental effects which could not be avoided if the proposal were implemented, alternatives to the proposed action, the relationship between local short-term uses of the environment and the maintenance and enhancement of long-term productivity, and any irreversible and irretrievable commitments of resources the proposed action would involve if it were implemented. Impact statements provide a basis for evaluating the benefits of a proposed project in light of its environmental risks and for comparing its environmental risks with those of alternatives. The Supreme Court has held that a Federal agency is required to consider all *reasonable* alternatives in its EIS (a rule of reason standard). One reasonable alternative that always must be considered is doing nothing.

NATURE OF EIS REQUIREMENT Whether the NEPA was solely procedural or whether it had a substantive component was initially unclear. The Supreme Court resolved the issue by holding that the NEPA's requirements are primarily procedural and that the NEPA does not require that the relevant Federal agency attempt to mitigate the adverse effects of a proposed Federal action. Rather, the NEPA attempts to prohibit uninformed decisions, not unwise agency actions.

45-6 The Clean Air Act

Initially, the Federal government's role in controlling air pollution was quite limited. The States had primary responsibility for air pollution control, and the Federal government merely supervised their efforts and offered technical and financial assistance. When State efforts proved inadequate to alleviate the problem, Congress enacted the Clean Air Act Amendments of 1970, greatly expanding the Federal role in antipollution efforts. Major revisions to the Clean Air Act were enacted in 1977 and 1990. In 2011, the EPA issued the Second Prospective Report that looked at the results of the Clean Air Act from 1990 to 2020. According to this study, the direct benefits from the 1990 Clean Air Act Amendments are estimated to reach *almost* $2 trillion for the year 2020 and to prevent 230,000 early deaths. Direct costs of implementation are estimated at $65 billion.

The Clean Air Act establishes two regulatory schemes, one for existing sources and one for new stationary sources. The States retain primary responsibility for regulating existing stationary sources and motor vehicles then in use (i.e., in use when the Act, or its subsequently enacted amendments, took effect), whereas the Federal government regulates new sources, new vehicles, and hazardous air pollutants.

Under the Clean Air Act, the EPA may impose civil penalties, which are adjusted annually for inflation; in January 2021, the maximum penalty was $48,762 per day of violation. Criminal penalties, which depend on the type of violation, vary greatly, providing for a maximum fine of $1 million per violation and/or fifteen years' imprisonment for a knowing violation that endangers a person. For repeat convictions, the Act doubles the maximum punishments. Moreover, under the Federal Alternative Fines Act, if any person derives pecuniary gain from the offense or the offense results in pecuniary loss to a person other than the defendant, the defendant may be fined up to the greater of twice the gross gain or twice the gross loss.

45-6a EXISTING STATIONARY SOURCES AND MOTOR VEHICLES THEN IN USE

Because the States had not managed to control air pollution adequately, the 1970 amendments provided that, with respect to existing stationary sources and motor vehicles then in use, the Federal government would set national air quality standards that the States would be primarily responsible for achieving.

◆ *See Case 45-1*

NATIONAL AMBIENT AIR QUALITY STANDARDS Under the Act, the EPA administrator is required to establish **national ambient air quality standards (NAAQSs)** for air pollutants that endanger the public health and welfare. The EPA administrator must establish "primary" standards to protect the public health, allowing for an adequate safety margin, and "secondary" standards to protect elements relating to the public welfare, such as animals, crops, and structures. The NAAQS for a particular pollutant specifies the concentration of that pollutant that will be allowed in the outside air over designated periods of time.

The EPA administrator established quality standards for seven major classes of pollutants—carbon monoxide, particulates, sulfur dioxide, nitrogen dioxide, hydrocarbons, ozone, and lead. The hydrocarbon NAAQS was subsequently withdrawn because it was no longer necessary. The 1990 amendments to the Act sought to hasten attainment of the standards and provided that the EPA must establish new standards for major pollutants every five years. The amendments also imposed tighter standards with regard to ozone pollution.

STATE IMPLEMENTATION PLANS Once the EPA promulgates a new NAAQS, each State must submit to the agency a **State implementation plan (SIP)** detailing how the State will implement and maintain the NAAQS within the State. If the State adopted the SIP after public hearings and the SIP meets certain statutory conditions, the EPA is required to approve it. Foremost among the statutory conditions is the requirement that under the SIP, the State will attain primary standards as soon as practicable but in any case within three years after the EPA approves the SIP. If the EPA determines that under an SIP a State will not attain an NAAQS within the designated time and the State fails to make the necessary amendments, the EPA is authorized to make amendments that will be binding on the State.

Under the 1990 amendments, the EPA also must decide whether a SIP is complete. If it is not, the EPA may treat the plan as a nullity in whole or in part. If it is complete, the EPA must approve or disapprove the plan within a year. Once the EPA approves a SIP, the plan is regarded as both State and Federal law, enforceable by either its State of implementation or the Federal government.

PREVENTION OF SIGNIFICANT DETERIORATION AREAS Soon after enactment of the Act, an issue arose as to whether air that was cleaner than required by an applicable NAAQS would be allowed to deteriorate to the NAAQS level. This issue was significant because much of the United States, particularly land in the Southwest, had air whose quality was higher than that required by applicable standards. Responding to this issue, Congress, in the 1977 amendments to the Act, established a policy to prevent the quality of such air from deteriorating. To effectuate this policy, Congress established rules for areas whose air quality was higher than the applicable NAAQS required it to be or for which information was insufficient to determine the air quality (so-called **prevention of significant deterioration [PSD] areas**). Because the rules classified an area on a pollutant-by-pollutant basis, a particular area might be a PSD area with respect to one pollutant and an

area that had not met the applicable NAAQS with respect to another pollutant.

In PSD areas, only limited increases in air pollution are allowed. Before a major stationary source in a PSD area may be constructed or modified, the owner or operator of the source must receive a permit from the applicable State regulator. To receive a permit, the owner or operator must demonstrate that the source will not increase pollution beyond permitted levels and must show that the source will utilize the best control technology available. These rules were modified in January 2011 to cover additional construction projects.

NONATTAINMENT AREAS The 1977 and 1990 amendments also established special rules for areas that did not meet applicable NAAQSs, so-called **nonattainment areas**. Before a major stationary source may be constructed or modified in a nonattainment area, the owner/operator of the source must receive a permit from the applicable State regulator. To receive a permit, the owner/operator must show that the source will comply with the lowest achievable emission rate, which is the more stringent of either the most stringent emission limitation contained in any SIP or the most stringent emission limitation actually achieved. Additionally, total emissions from existing stationary sources and the proposed new or modified source together must be less than the total emissions allowed from existing sources at the time the permit is sought. Thus, to obtain a permit in a nonattainment area, an owner/operator must in some way reduce total emissions from all sources (existing and new or modified).

Under the 1990 amendments, the reduction required varies with the severity of the area's nonattainment problem. One way to reduce total emissions from all sources is to pay the owner/operator of another source to reduce its emissions by either installing more advanced emission control technology or closing its source. Alternatively, an owner/operator may reduce its own total emissions by altering the mix of emission controls at its plant. Under the EPA's "**bubble concept**," an entire plant is viewed as one source; consequently, the permit process applies only if total emissions from the plant increase. If, instead, the EPA treated each unit at a plant as a separate source, the owner/operator would be required to obtain a permit whenever it made a change to one unit. The bubble concept thus enables an owner/operator to bypass the permit process in some instances. Though environmental groups challenged the concept on this basis, the Supreme Court upheld the bubble concept, finding the regulation to be a reasonable exercise of the EPA's discretion.

Practical Advice

When considering where to locate a facility that will emit pollution, carefully scrutinize pollution levels in those locations.

45-6b NEW SOURCE STANDARDS

The scheme of the Federal NAAQS and State SIPs applies to existing stationary sources and to motor vehicles then in use. In contrast, the Clean Air Act authorizes the Federal government to establish national emission standards for new stationary sources, new vehicles, and hazardous air pollutants.

NEW STATIONARY SOURCES The Act requires the EPA administrator to establish performance standards for stationary sources that are constructed or modified after the publication of applicable regulations. The standard of performance must "reflect the degree of emission limitation and percentage reduction achievable through application of the best technological system of continuous emission reduction which has been adequately demonstrated." As *Case 45-1* indicates, the standard governing new sources is more stringent than the standard governing existing sources; accordingly, from industry's perspective, it is better to be considered an existing source than a new or modified one.

◆ *See Case 45-1*

NEW VEHICLES The Clean Air Act requires the EPA administrator to establish emission standards for new motor vehicles and new motor vehicle engines. The Act also requires the use of reformulated automotive fuels to reduce ozone and carbon monoxide pollution. The reformulated gasoline must contain more oxygen and less volatile organic compounds.

HAZARDOUS AIR POLLUTANTS The Act authorizes the EPA administrator to establish national emission standards for hazardous or toxic air pollutants, defined as "air pollutant[s] ... caus[ing], or contribut[ing] to, air pollution which may reasonably be anticipated to result in an increase in mortality or an increase in serious irreversible, or incapacitating reversible, illness." The standard must be set at a level that "provides an ample margin of safety to protect the public health."

ACID RAIN The 1990 amendments attempt to halt environmental destruction caused by acid rain, precipitation that contains high levels of sulfuric or nitric acid. Because sulfur dioxide (which forms sulfuric acid in the atmosphere and comes back as acid rain) is released into the atmosphere primarily by electric utilities, the 1990 amendments regulate such utilities by allotting them emission allowances with regard to the amount of sulfur dioxide they may release into the atmosphere, based upon past emissions and fuel consumption. The amendments establish an allowance schedule that should

significantly reduce emissions of sulfur dioxide and nitrous oxides. The amendments also permit each utility to bank or sell its emission allowances.

GREENHOUSE GASES In 2007, the U.S. Supreme Court held that the Clean Air Act's sweeping definition of "air pollutant" includes greenhouse gases; therefore, the EPA has statutory authority to regulate such gases from new motor vehicles. *Massachusetts v. Environmental Protection Agency*, 549 U.S. 497. Effective in 2011, the EPA-promulgated greenhouse gas emission standards for new passenger cars, light-duty trucks, and medium-duty passenger vehicles. In addition, the EPA issued regulations subjecting stationary sources to PSD permitting based on their potential to emit greenhouse gases. This regulation was challenged, and the U.S. Supreme Court largely upheld the EPA's authority to regulate greenhouse gas emissions from stationary sources. The Supreme Court held that the EPA may continue to treat greenhouse gases as a pollutant subject to regulation for purposes of requiring permits for power plants and other large stationary pollution sources that would need permits based on their emission of conventional pollutants. *Utility Air Regulatory Group v. EPA*, 573 U.S. 302, (2014).

45-7 The Clean Water Act

As with air pollution control, the primary responsibility for controlling water pollution fell initially to the States. When their efforts proved inadequate, Congress fundamentally revised the nation's water pollution laws in its 1972 amendments to the Federal Water Pollution Control Act (subsequently renamed the Clean Water Act). Substantially amended again in 1977, 1981, and 1987, the Act attempts comprehensively to restore and maintain the chemical, physical, and biological integrity of the nation's waters.

The EPA may impose civil penalties, as adjusted annually for inflation in January 2021, of up to $48,762 per day for each violation. Criminal penalties for knowing violations are not less than $5,000 or more than $50,000 per day of violation and/or three years' imprisonment. For repeat convictions, the maximum punishments are doubled. Moreover, under the Federal Alternative Fines Act, if any person derives pecuniary gain from the offense or if the offense results in pecuniary loss to a person other than the defendant, the defendant may be fined up to the greater of twice the gross gain or twice the gross loss.

Like the Clean Air Act, the Clean Water Act establishes different schemes for existing sources and new sources. Additionally, the Act provides different programs for point and nonpoint sources of pollution. A **point source** is "any discernible, confined and discrete conveyance from which pollutants are or may be discharged." A **nonpoint source**, in contrast, is a land use that causes pollution, such as a pesticide runoff from farming operations.

The scope of the Act is extremely broad, applying not only to all navigable waters in the United States but also to tributaries of navigable waters, interstate waters and their tributaries, the use of non-navigable intrastate waters if their misuse could affect interstate commerce, and freshwater wetlands.

♦ *See Case 5-3*

A recent and expensive case involving violations of the Clean Water Act arose from the Deepwater Horizon oil-drilling rig that burned and sank in April 2010, spilling oil into the Gulf of Mexico. It was the largest-ever U.S. offshore oil spill. British Petroleum (BP) chartered the rig from Transocean, its owner. Transocean pleaded guilty in Federal district court to violating the Clean Water Act for its role and was sentenced to pay a $400 million criminal fine and $1 billion in civil penalties. In addition, BP settled a class-action suit brought by businesses and individuals damaged by the oil spill. In settling, BP agreed to create a $20 billion compensation fund, but the settlement does not have a cap. Claims stopped being accepted as of June 8, 2015. A Federal judge who ruled on the Clean Water Act suit in September 2014 found that BP was primarily responsible for the oil spill as a result of its deliberate misconduct and gross negligence. In 2015, five Gulf Coast States (Alabama, Florida, Louisiana, Mississippi, and Texas) and the Federal government reached a settlement requiring BP to pay $18.7 billion over eighteen years. Under the agreement, BP will pay the Federal government a civil penalty of $5.5 billion under the Clean Water Act. Moreover, in a criminal action for manslaughter charges stemming from the Deepwater Horizon explosion but not based on the Clean Water Act, BP pleaded guilty in Federal court and agreed to pay $4.5 billion in criminal penalties. Thus, BP agreed to pay $18 billion in penalties in addition to the $28 billion already paid out in claims and cleanup costs. In March 2014, the EPA ended its ban on BP obtaining government contracts.

45-7a POINT SOURCES

The Act mandates that the EPA administrator establish effluent limitations for categories of existing point sources. An **effluent limitation** is a technology-based standard that limits the amount of a pollutant that a point source may discharge into a body of water. The Act effectuates such limitations through the **National Pollutant Discharge Elimination System (NPDES)**, a permit system.

EFFLUENT LIMITATIONS Under the 1972 amendments, effluent limitations for existing point sources, other than publicly owned treatment works, required application of the **best practicable control technology (BPT)** currently available by 1977 and application of the **best available technology (BAT)** economically achievable by 1983. According to the EPA, BPT is "the average of the best existing performance by well-operated plants within each industrial category or subcategory," while BAT is "the very best control and treatment measures that have been or are capable of being achieved." Somewhat different standards apply to publicly owned treatment works.

THE NATIONAL POLLUTANT DISCHARGE ELIMINATION SYSTEM The National Pollutant Discharge Elimination System (NPDES), the permit system through which effluent limitations are to be achieved, requires that any person responsible for the discharge from a point source of a pollutant into U.S. waters must obtain a discharge permit from the EPA, the Army Corps of Engineers, or, in some circumstances, the relevant State. An NPDES permit incorporates the applicable effluent limitations and establishes a schedule for compliance. The holder of an NPDES permit is required to notify the appropriate authority if the holder will not meet its obligations under the permit. A discharge not in compliance with a permit is unlawful. With limited exceptions, new permits for existing facilities cannot be less stringent than current permits.

In April 2019, the EPA issued an Interpretative Statement clarifying the application of the NPDES permitting requirements to groundwater. The EPA concluded that releases of pollutants to groundwater are categorically excluded from the CWA's permitting requirements. In April 2020, the U.S. Supreme Court rejected the EPA's interpretation, holding that the CWA "requires a permit when there is a direct discharge from a point source into navigable waters or when there is the *functional equivalent of a direct discharge*.... That is, an addition falls within the statutory requirement that it be "from any point source" when a point source directly deposits pollutants into navigable waters, or when the discharge reaches the same result through roughly similar means. Time and distance are obviously important. Where a pipe ends a few feet from navigable waters and the pipe emits pollutants that travel those few feet through groundwater (or over the beach), the permitting requirement clearly applies. If the pipe ends 50 miles from navigable waters and the pipe emits pollutants that travel with groundwater, mix with much other material, and end up in navigable waters only many years later, the permitting requirements likely do not apply." *County of Maui v. Hawaii Wildlife Fund*, 590 U. S. _____ (2020).

♦ *See Case 45-2*

THE 1977 AMENDMENTS Recognizing that the application deadlines it had set in the 1972 amendments would not be met, Congress extended and modified the deadlines in 1977. The 1977 amendments to the Clean Water Act divided pollutants into three categories—toxic, conventional, and non-conventional (any pollutants that are neither toxic nor conventional)—and established different deadlines and standards for each category. For conventional pollutants, a new standard, **best conventional pollution control technology (BCT)**, was to be achieved.

45-7b NONPOINT SOURCE POLLUTION

Controlling nonpoint source pollution—such as agricultural and urban runoff—is inherently more difficult than controlling point source pollution. According to the EPA,

> There is no effective way as yet, other than land use control, by which you can intercept that runoff and control it in a way that you do a point source. We have not yet developed technology to deal with that kind of a problem. We need to find ways to deal with it, because a great quantity of pollutants [are] discharged by runoff, not only from agriculture but from construction sites, from streets, from parking lots, and so on, and we have to be concerned with developing controls for them.

Although Congress tried to address the problem of nonpoint source pollution in the 1972 amendments, little effective control of nonsource pollution occurred before 1987. The 1987 amendments require States to identify State waters that will not meet the Act's requirements without the management of nonpoint sources of pollution and to institute "best management practices" to control such sources. The EPA must approve each State's management plan.

45-7c NEW SOURCE PERFORMANCE STANDARDS

The Act requires the EPA administrator to establish Federal performance standards for new sources. A performance standard should "reflect the greatest degree of effluent reduction achievable through application of the best available demonstrated control technology." The preferred standard for new sources is one "permitting no discharge of pollutants." Violation of a standard by an owner/operator of a new source is unlawful.

45-8 Hazardous Substances

Technological advances have enabled human beings to produce numerous artificial substances, some of which have proven extremely hazardous to health. As the potential and actual harm from these latter substances became clear, Congress responded by enacting various hazardous substances-related statutes. In this section, we will consider some of the most important Federal statutes governing hazardous substances: the Federal Insecticide, Fungicide, and Rodenticide Act (FIFRA); the Toxic Substances Control Act (TSCA); the Resource Conservation and Recovery Act (RCRA); the Comprehensive Environmental Response, Compensation, and Liability Act (CERCLA, or the Superfund); and the Superfund Amendments and Reauthorization Act of 1986 (SARA).

45-8a THE FEDERAL INSECTICIDE, FUNGICIDE, AND RODENTICIDE ACT (FIFRA)

The Federal government began regulating pesticides in 1910 and greatly expanded its control over such substances in 1947 with the passage of the Federal Insecticide, Fungicide, and Rodenticide Act (FIFRA). Concern about pesticides increased dramatically after the publication in 1962 of *Silent Spring*, by Rachel Carson, and Congress has amended the FIFRA several times.

The FIFRA requires that a pesticide be registered with the EPA before any person in any State may distribute it. Such registration is legal only if the pesticide's composition warrants the claims its manufacturer proposes for it, the pesticide will perform its intended function without "unreasonable adverse effects on the environment," the pesticide generally will not cause unreasonably adverse environmental effects when used in accordance with widespread and commonly recognized practice, and the pesticide complies with FIFRA labeling requirements. The FIFRA defines "unreasonable adverse effects on the environment" as any unreasonable risk to humans or the environment, taking into account the economic, social, and environmental costs and benefits of the use of any pesticide. Thus, unlike many environmental statutes, the FIFRA expressly requires the EPA to consider the costs of the action it takes under the statute.

If a pesticide is registered and subsequent data reveal additional hazards, the EPA may cancel the registration after an administrative hearing. The 1988 amendments placed upon industry the cost of disposing of canceled pesticides. Cancellation proceedings typically take years, both because of the numerous stages of the administrative process and because of the required use of a scientific advisory committee. While the cancellation process is in progress, the pesticide may be manufactured and sold. If additional hazard is imminent, however, the product's registration may be suspended until the cancellation proceeding is completed. Once its registration has been suspended, the pesticide may not be manufactured or distributed.

Until recently, the FIFRA did not adequately address the problem of old pesticides that had been registered under earlier and less strict standards. Concerned that these pesticides did not meet current standards, Congress in 1988 amended the FIFRA to require the reregistration of pesticides registered before 1984. U.S. exports are not subject to most of the Act's requirements, though an exported pesticide not registered under the FIFRA must bear a label stating "Not Registered for Use in the United States of America."

To establish a more consistent, protective regulatory scheme, in 1996, Congress enacted the Food Quality Protection Act (FQPA), which amended FIFRA and the Federal Food, Drug, and Cosmetic Act. The FQPA imposed stricter safety standards, especially for infants and children, and a complete reassessment of all existing pesticide tolerances.

The EPA may impose civil penalties, as adjusted annually for inflation in January 2021, of up to $20,528 for each offense. Maximum criminal penalties for knowing violations are a $50,000 fine and/or one year's imprisonment. Moreover, under the Federal Alternative Fines Act, if any person derives pecuniary gain from the offense or if the offense results in pecuniary loss to a person other than the defendant, the defendant may be fined up to the greater of twice the gross gain or twice the gross loss.

45-8b THE TOXIC SUBSTANCES CONTROL ACT

Congress passed the **Toxic Substances Control Act (TSCA)** in 1976 in an effort to provide a comprehensive scheme for regulating toxic substances. The TSCA contains provisions on the manufacture of new chemicals, the testing of suspect chemicals, the regulation of chemicals that present an unreasonable risk of injury to health and the environment, and the inventorying of all chemicals.

Under the Act, a manufacturer must notify the EPA before it manufactures a new chemical or makes a significant new use of an existing chemical. If the EPA administrator concludes that the information submitted is insufficient to permit a reasoned evaluation of the health and environmental effects of the chemical and the chemical may present an unreasonable risk of injury to health or the environment, the administrator may limit or prohibit the chemical's manufacture or distribution.

The Act authorizes the EPA to require the testing of any substance, whether existing or new, if (1) the manufacture or distribution of the substance may present an unreasonable risk of injury to health or the environment, (2) the data on the effects of the substance on health and the environment are insufficient, and (3) testing is necessary to develop such data.

Because of the many substances that might be subject to testing under the statutory standard, the TSCA mandates that the EPA establish a priority list for testing that contains no more than fifty substances at any time. This list is established by a committee whose members come from eight specified agencies.

Once the EPA determines, either through its testing program or through the premanufacturing notice process, that a substance "presents or will present an unreasonable risk of injury to health or the environment," the agency may restrict or prohibit use of the substance.

If the EPA administrator believes that a substance presents an imminent hazard, he is authorized to bring an action in Federal district court for seizure of the substance or other appropriate relief. The statute defines an "imminently hazardous chemical substance or mixture" as one that presents an unreasonable risk of serious or widespread injury to health or the environment.

The TSCA requires the EPA to compile and keep current a list of each chemical substance manufactured or processed in the United States. The EPA's initial inventory of existing chemicals listed approximately fifty-five thousand substances. A chemical not listed on the inventory is subject to premanufacture review, even if it was in fact previously manufactured. Although not explicitly required to do so by the TSCA, the EPA reviews the substances on the inventory to determine their safety.

The EPA may impose civil penalties, as adjusted annually for inflation in January 2021, of up to $41,056 per day for a violation of the TSCA. Maximum criminal penalties for knowing violations are $25,000 fines for each day of violation and/or one year's imprisonment. Moreover, under the Federal Alternative Fines Act, if any person derives pecuniary gain from the offense or if the offense results in pecuniary loss to a person other than the defendant, the defendant may be fined up to the greater of twice the gross gain or twice the gross loss.

In 2007, the European Union (EU) enacted a new law Registration, Evaluation and Authorization of Chemicals (REACH), which requires companies producing more than specified quantities of chemicals to investigate the potential hazards to human health and the environment. This differs from TSCA in that it applies to all chemicals commercially available in the EU. REACH requires EU manufacturers and importers to gather information on the properties of their substances, which will help them manage them safely, and to register the information in a central database. The European Chemicals Agency will act as the central point in the REACH system: it will run the databases necessary to operate the system, coordinate the in-depth evaluation of suspicious chemicals, and run a public database in which consumers and professionals can find hazard information. REACH also calls for the progressive substitution of the most dangerous chemicals when suitable alternatives have been identified.

In 2016, the Frank R. Lautenberg Chemical Safety for the 21st Century Act, which amended the TSCA, was signed into law. The Act requires review of all commercial chemicals, as well as chemicals new to the market, using a risk assessment. In addition, the law provides for increased public transparency for chemical information and a consistent source of funding for the EPA to carry out the responsibilities under the law.

45-8c THE RESOURCE CONSERVATION AND RECOVERY ACT

In 1976, Congress enacted the **Resource Conservation and Recovery Act (RCRA)** to provide a comprehensive scheme for the treatment of solid waste, particularly hazardous waste. The statute provides that the States are primarily responsible for nonhazardous waste, while the EPA regulates all phases of hazardous waste: generation, transportation, and disposal. Under the Act, the Federal government must establish criteria for identifying hazardous waste, taking into account factors that include toxicity, persistence, degradability, flammability, and corrosiveness.

The Act prescribes for generators (entities that produce hazardous waste) standards concerning recordkeeping, labeling, the use of appropriate containers, and reporting. The statute requires the EPA to establish a **manifest system** to be used by generators. A manifest is a form on which the generator must specify the quantity, composition, origin, routing, and destination of hazardous waste. On the manifest, the generator also must certify that the volume and toxicity of the waste have been reduced to the greatest degree economically practicable and that the method of treatment, storage, and disposal minimizes the threat to health and the environment.

Transporters must maintain records and properly label the waste they transport. Furthermore, they must comply with manifests and may transport hazardous waste only to facilities holding an RCRA hazardous waste facility permit.

Owners/operators of hazardous waste treatment, storage, and disposal sites must maintain records and comply with generator manifests. Facilities for hazardous waste treatment, storage, and disposal must obtain an RCRA hazardous waste facility permit. To obtain a permit, a facility must comply with relevant EPA standards. Failure to comply may subject the owner/operator to civil or criminal penalties.

Practical Advice

Make sure that you maintain proper records, apply proper labels, and obtain all necessary permits for the generation, transportation, and disposal of all hazardous waste material.

The Act authorizes the EPA administrator to sue in Federal court for an injunction if the administrator has evidence that "the past or present handling, storage, treatment, transportation or disposal of any solid waste or hazardous waste may present an imminent and substantial endangerment to health or the environment." Moreover, the EPA may impose civil penalties, as adjusted annually for inflation in January 2021, of up to $61,820 per day of violation. Maximum criminal penalties for knowing violations are $50,000 for each day of violation and/or five years' imprisonment. When a knowing violation endangers a person, the maximum criminal penalty is a $1 million fine and/or fifteen years' imprisonment. Moreover, under the Federal Alternative Fines Act, if any person derives pecuniary gain from the offense or if the offense results in pecuniary loss to a person other than the defendant, the defendant may be fined up to the greater of twice the gross gain or twice the gross loss.

45-8d THE SUPERFUND

Although the RCRA regulates current and future generation, transportation, and disposal of hazardous waste, the Act provides only limited authority for the cleanup of abandoned or inactive hazardous waste sites. To fill this gap and to respond to the serious environmental and health risks posed by industrial pollution, Congress in 1980 enacted the Comprehensive Environmental Response, Compensation, and Liability Act (CERCLA, or the Superfund). CERCLA was also designed to have the polluter bear the expense of the cleanup. By 1986, the EPA, working under the Act, had spent $1.6 billion and had begun the cleanup of only eight sites. This record and other problems with the initial legislation prompted Congress to amend the CERCLA by enacting the Superfund Amendments and Reauthorization Act (SARA). The EPA has cleaned up more than a thousand National Priorities List sites, but funds in the Superfund are nearly exhausted.

Under CERCLA, when the EPA determines that an environmental cleanup is necessary at a contaminated site, the agency has four options: (1) enter into a settlement with potentially responsible parties (PRPs); (2) conduct the cleanup with Superfund money and then file suit to obtain reimbursement from the PRPs; (3) file an abatement action in a Federal district court to compel the PRPs to conduct the cleanup; or (4) issue a unilateral administrative order instructing the PRPs to clean the site.

CERCLA requires the Federal government to establish a National Contingency Plan (NCP) prescribing procedures and standards for responding to hazardous substance releases. The NCP specifies criteria for determining the priority of sites to be cleaned. The plan also identifies, on at least an annual basis, the sites that most require immediate cleanup. As adjusted annually for inflation in January 2021, the EPA may impose a civil penalty of up to $59,017 per day of violation; for repeat violations, the penalty may reach up to $177,053 per day of violation.

CERCLA establishes a trust fund to pay for hazardous waste removal and other remedial actions. The trust fund is financed in part by a surtax on businesses with annual incomes over $2 million, a tax on petroleum, and a tax on chemical feedstocks. An additional part of the trust fund comes from money recovered from persons responsible for the release of hazardous substances. These parties include the owners and operators of a hazardous waste disposal facility from which there has been a release, as well as any generator of hazardous wastes that were disposed of at that facility.

Because CERCLA initially imposed liability on all owners of contaminated property, some parties were held liable even though they had acquired the land either involuntarily or without knowledge of the hazardous wastes stored there. For example, after foreclosing on a mortgage of $335,000 and taking title to a piece of property, a bank was held liable for Superfund costs of more than $555,000. Responding to the inequity of such situations, Congress in SARA established a new defense to CERCLA liability for "innocent landowners." To qualify as an innocent landowner, one "must have undertaken, at the time of acquisition, all appropriate inquiry into the previous ownership and uses of the property consistent with good commercial or customary practice in an effort to minimize liability." In addition, under the Superfund Recycling Act of 1999, recyclers are exempt from liability to third parties, although they remain liable in suits brought by the Federal or State governments.

In 2002, President Bush signed into law the Small Business Liability Relief and Brownfields Revitalization Act. The purpose of the Act is to promote the purchase, development, and use of brownfields (industrially polluted property which are not sufficiently contaminated as to be classified as a priority by either the EPA or state environmental agencies). The Act attempts to accomplish this purpose by providing protection from liability under CERCLA to any purchaser of contaminated property, to owners and developers who clean up property under state voluntary cleanup programs, and to owners of property that has become contaminated by migrating pollutants.

♦ SEE FIGURE 45-1: *Major Federal Environmental Statutes*

FIGURE 45-1 Major Federal Environmental Statutes

Act	Major Purpose	Maximum Civil Penalty[a]	Maximum Criminal Penalty[b]
National Environmental Policy Act (NEPA)	• Establish environmental protection as a major national goal • Mandate environmental impact statements be prepared prior to Federal action having a significant environmental effect	None	None
Clean Air Act	• Control and reduce air pollution • Establish National Ambient Air Quality Standards	$48,762 per day of violation	$1,000,000 fine per violation and/or fifteen years' imprisonment[c]
Clean Water Act	• Protect against water pollution • Establish effluent limitations	$37,500 per day of violation	$50,000 per day of violation and/or three years' imprisonment[c]
Federal Insecticide, Fungicide, and Rodenticide Act (FIFRA)	• Regulate the sale and distribution of pesticides • Prevent pesticides having an unreasonably adverse effect on the environment	$20,528 per offense of pesticides	$50,000 fine and/or one year's imprisonment
Toxic Substances Control Act (TSCA)	• Regulate toxic substances • Prevent unreasonable risk of injury to health and the environment from toxic substances	$41,056 per day of violation	$25,000 fine per day of violation and/or one year's imprisonment
Resource Conservation and Recovery Act (RCRA)	• Regulate the disposal of solid waste • Establish standards to protect human health and the environment from hazardous wastes	$61,820 per day of violation	$1,000,000 fine and/or fifteen years' imprisonment
Comprehensive Environmental Response, Compensation, and Liability Act (CERCLA, or the Superfund) and Superfund Amendments and Reauthorization Act (SARA)	• Establish a national contingency plan for responding to releases of hazardous substances • Establish a trust fund to pay for removal of hazardous waste and other remedial actions	$59,017 per day of violation; $177,053 for repeat violations	None

[a]As adjusted for inflation in January 2021.
[b]Under the Federal Alternative Fines Act, if any person derives pecuniary gain from the offense, or if the offense results in pecuniary loss to a person other than the defendant, the defendant may be fined up to the greater of twice the gross gain or twice the gross loss.
[c]Doubled for repeat convictions.

45-9 International Protection of the Ozone Layer

In 1987, the United States and twenty-three other countries entered into the Montreal Protocol on Substances that Deplete the Ozone Layer, a treaty designed to prevent pollution that harms the ozone layer. At least 197 parties have ratified the treaty. The treaty requires all signatories to reduce their production and consumption of all chemicals, in particular chlorofluorocarbons (CFCs, more commonly called Freon), which deplete the ozone layer. Although having excessive ozone in the air we breathe can be hazardous, the ozone layer in the stratosphere helps to protect the earth from harmful ultraviolet radiation.

CFCs, halocarbons, carbon dioxide, methane, and nitrous oxide are extremely potent "greenhouse gases," which trap heat and thereby warm the earth. Human activities, however, have increased the release of greenhouse gases, resulting in the serious threat of global warming. If this occurs, the levels of the seas will rise and the climate will change over most of the earth, causing severe flooding and disruptions of agricultural production.

To combat this predicted climate change, 165 nations in 1992 negotiated an international treaty on global warming at the **United Nations Framework Convention on Climate Change (UNFCCC)** in Rio de Janeiro. The Convention sets an overall framework for intergovernmental efforts to address the challenge posed by climate change. The treaty's ultimate objective is to stabilize the "greenhouse gas concentration in the atmosphere at a level that would prevent dangerous anthropogenic [human-induced] interference with the climate system." Nearly 200 countries eventually ratified the treaty, which went into effect in 1994. The UNFCCC calls for all signatory countries to develop and update national inventories of all greenhouse gases not otherwise covered by the Montreal Protocol.

At a subsequent UNFCCC conference of parties, held in Kyoto, Japan, in December 1997, the participating nations adopted the **Kyoto Protocol**, which is an international agreement linked to UNFCCC establishing a set of binding greenhouse gas emission targets for industrial nations. The Kyoto Protocol entered into force in February 2005. The Protocol's first commitment period started in 2008 and ended in 2012. At least 192 countries have ratified the Kyoto Protocol.

The United States is the only signatory to the Kyoto Protocol not to ratify the protocol.

On December 8, 2012, the Doha Amendment to the Kyoto Protocol was adopted. The Amendment includes a second commitment period from 2013 through 2020 and a revised list of greenhouse gases to be reported on by the parties in the second commitment period.

In 2005, the United States and six Asia-Pacific nations (Australia, Canada, China, India, Japan, and the Republic of Korea) announced a pact—the Asia-Pacific Partnership on Clean Development—which was designed to meet goals for energy security, national air pollution reduction, and climate change in ways that promote sustainable economic growth and poverty reduction. As of 2011, the Partnership formally concluded, although a number of individual projects continue.

In December 2015, at the Paris Climate Change Conference, officially known as the 21st Conference of the Parties (COP 21 or CMP 11) to the United Nations Framework Convention on Climate Change (UNFCCC), 197 parties adopted the first-ever universal, legally binding global climate agreement. The **Paris Agreement** entered into force in November 2016 when it was ratified by 55 parties, which together represented at least 55 percent of global greenhouse emissions. As of February 2021, almost all of the 197 parties had ratified the convention. The agreement sets out a global action plan to put the world on track to avoid climate change by limiting global warming to below 2°C compared to previous industrial levels. The agreement further calls for zero net anthropogenic greenhouse gas emissions to be reached during the second half of the 21st century. In November 2019, the United States submitted to the United Nations formal notification of its withdrawal from the Paris Agreement. The withdrawal took effect on November 4, 2020. However, on January 20, 2021, the United States again accepted the Paris Agreement effective February 19, 2021. On January 20, 2021, President Biden's first day in office, the President issued the following executive order:

I, Joseph R. Biden Jr., President of the United States of America, having seen and considered the Paris Agreement, done at Paris on December 12, 2015, do hereby accept the said Agreement and every article and clause thereof on behalf of the United States of America.

C H A P T E R   S U M M A R Y

COMMON LAW ACTIONS FOR ENVIRONMENTAL DAMAGE

NUISANCE	**Private Nuisance** substantial and unreasonable interference with the use and enjoyment of a person's land **Public Nuisance** interference with the health, safety, or comfort of the public
OTHER COMMON LAW ACTIONS	**Trespass** an invasion of land that interferes with the right of exclusive possession of the property **Strict Liability for Abnormally Dangerous Activities** liability without fault for an individual who engages in an unduly dangerous activity in an inappropriate location

FEDERAL REGULATION OF THE ENVIRONMENT

NATIONAL ENVIRONMENTAL POLICY ACT (NEPA)	**Purpose** to establish environmental protection as a goal of Federal policy **Council on Environmental Quality** three-member advisory group in the Executive Office of the President that makes recommendations to the President on environmental matters **Environmental Impact Statement (EIS)** a detailed statement concerning the environmental impact of a proposed Federal action • *Scope* NEPA applies to a broad range of activities, including direct action by a Federal agency as well as any action by a Federal agency that permits action by other parties that will affect the quality of the environment • *Content* the EIS must contain, among other items, a detailed statement of the environmental impact of the proposed action, any adverse environmental effects that cannot be avoided, and alternative proposals
CLEAN AIR ACT	**Purpose** to control and reduce air pollution **Existing Sources** • *National Ambient Air Quality Standards (NAAQSs)* the Environmental Protection Agency (EPA) administrator must establish NAAQSs for air pollutants that endanger the public health and welfare • *New Stationary Sources* owner/operator must employ the best technological system of continuous emission reduction that has been adequately demonstrated **New Sources** • *New Vehicles* extensive emission standards are established • *Hazardous Air Pollutants* to protect the public health, the EPA administrator must establish for hazardous air pollutants standards that provide ample safety margins • *Acid Rain* standards are established to protect against acid rain (precipitation that contains high levels of sulfuric or nitric acid) • *Greenhouse Gases* air pollutant includes greenhouse gases and, therefore, the EPA has statutory authority to regulate such gases
CLEAN WATER ACT	**Purpose** protect against water pollution **Point Sources Act** establishes the National Pollutant Discharge Elimination System (NPDES), a permit system, to control the amounts of pollutants that may be discharged by point sources into U.S. waters **Nonpoint Sources Act** requires the States to use best management practices to control water runoff from agricultural and urban areas

HAZARDOUS SUBSTANCES	**FIFRA** the Federal Insecticide, Fungicide, and Rodenticide Act regulates the sale and distribution of pesticides
	TSCA the Toxic Substances Control Act provides a comprehensive scheme for regulation of toxic substances
	RCRA the Resource Conservation and Recovery Act provides a comprehensive scheme for treatment of solid waste, particularly hazardous waste
	Superfund the Comprehensive Environmental Response, Compensation, and Liability Act (CERCLA) establishes (1) a national contingency plan for responding to releases of hazardous substances and (2) a trust fund to pay for removal and cleanup of hazardous waste
INTERNATIONAL PROTECTION OF THE OZONE LAYER	**Montreal Protocol** treaty by which countries agreed to cut production of chlorofluorocarbons (CFCs)
	United Nations Framework Convention on Climate Change (UNFCCC) treaty sets an overall framework for intergovernmental efforts to address the challenge posed by climate change with the objective of preventing dangerous human interference of the climate system
	Kyoto Protocol international agreement linked to UNFCCC establishing a set of binding greenhouse gas emission targets for developed nations
	Paris Agreement the first-ever universal, legally binding global climate agreement

CASES

CASE 45-1

Clean Air Act
ENVIRONMENTAL PROTECTION AGENCY v. EME HOMER CITY GENERATION, L. P.

Supreme Court of the United States, 2014
572 U.S. 489, 134 S.Ct. 1584, 188 L.Ed.2d 775

Ginsburg, J.

These cases concern the efforts of Congress and the Environmental Protection Agency (EPA or Agency) to cope with a complex problem: air pollution emitted in one State, but causing harm in other States. Left unregulated, the emitting or upwind State reaps the benefits of the economic activity causing the pollution without bearing all the costs. [Citation.] Conversely, downwind States to which the pollution travels are unable to achieve clean air because of the influx of out-of-state pollution they lack authority to control the problem. [Citation.]

Congress included a Good Neighbor Provision in the Clean Air Act (Act or CAA). That provision, in its current phrasing, instructs States to prohibit in-states sources "from emitting any air pollutant in amounts which will ... contribute significantly" to downwind States' "nonattainment ..., or interfere with maintenance," of any EPA-promulgated national air quality standard. [Citation.] Interpreting the Good Neighbor Provision, EPA adopted the Cross-State Air Pollution Rule (commonly and hereinafter called the Transport Rule). The rule calls for consideration of costs, among other factors, when determining the emission reductions an upwind State must make to improve air quality in polluted downwind areas. The Court of Appeals for the D.C. Circuit vacated the rule in its entirety. * * * [The U.S. Supreme Court granted certiorari.]

* * *

Air pollution is transient, heedless of state boundaries. Air pollution is transient, heedless of state boundaries. Pollutants generated by upwind sources are often transported by air currents, sometimes over hundreds of miles, to downwind States. As the pollution travels out of State, upwind States are relieved of the associated costs. Those costs are borne instead by the downwind States, whose ability to achieve and maintain satisfactory air quality is hampered by the steady stream of infiltrating pollution.

For several reasons, curtailing interstate air pollution poses a complex challenge for environmental regulators. First, identifying the upwind origin of downwind air pollution is no easy endeavor. Most upwind States propel pollutants to more than one downwind State, many downwind States receive pollution from multiple upwind States, and some States qualify as both upwind and downwind. [Citation.] The overlapping and interwoven linkages between upwind and downwind States with which EPA had to contend number in the thousands.

Further complicating the problem, pollutants do not emerge from the smokestacks of an upwind State and uniformly migrate downwind. Some pollutants stay within upwind States' borders, the wind carries others to downwind States, and some subset of that group drifts to States without air quality problems. * * * In crafting a solution to the problem of interstate air pollution, regulators must account for the vagaries of the wind.

Finally, upwind pollutants that find their way downwind are not left unaltered by the journey. Rather, as the gases emitted by upwind polluters are carried downwind, they are transformed, through various chemical processes, into altogether different pollutants. The offending gases at issue in these cases—nitrogen oxide (NOX) and sulfur dioxide (SO$_2$)—often develop into ozone and fine particulate matter (PM2.5) by the time they reach the atmospheres of downwind [citation] that must be reduced to enable downwind States to keep their levels of ozone and PM2.5 in check.

* * *

Under the Transport Rule, EPA employed a "two-step approach" to determine when upwind States "contribute[d] significantly to nonattainment," [citation], and therefore in "amounts" that had to be eliminated. At step one, called the "screening" analysis, the Agency excluded as de minimis any upwind State that contributed less than one percent of the three NAAQS to any downwind State "receptor," a location at which EPA measures air quality. * * *

The remaining States were subjected to a second inquiry, which EPA called the "control" analysis. At this stage, the Agency sought to generate a cost-effective allocation of emission reductions among those upwind States "screened in" at step one.

The control analysis proceeded this way. EPA first calculated, for each upwind State, the quantity of emissions the State could eliminate at each of several cost thresholds. [Citation.] Cost for these purposes is measured as cost per ton of emissions prevented, for instance, by installing scrubbers on power plant smokestacks. EPA estimated, for example, the amount each upwind State's NOX emissions would fall if all pollution sources within each State employed every control measure available at a cost of $500 per ton or less. [Citation.]

The Agency then repeated that analysis at ascending cost thresholds. [Citation.]

Armed with this information, EPA conducted complex modeling to establish the combined effect the upwind reductions projected at each cost threshold would have on air quality in downwind States. [Citation.] The Agency then identified "significant cost threshold[s]," points in its model where a "noticeable change occurred in downwind air quality, such as … where large upwind emission reductions become available because a certain type of emissions control strategy becomes cost-effective." [Citation.] For example, reductions of NOX sufficient to resolve or significantly curb downwind * * *

Finally, EPA translated the cost thresholds it had selected into amounts of emissions upwind States would be required to eliminate. For each regulated upwind State, EPA created an annual emissions "budget." These budgets represented the quantity of pollution an upwind State would produce in a given year if its in-state sources implemented all pollution controls available at the chosen cost thresholds. [Citation.] If EPA's projected improvements to downwind air quality were to be realized, an upwind State's emissions could not exceed the level this budget allocated to it, subject to certain adjustments not relevant here.

Taken together, the screening and control inquiries defined EPA's understanding of which upwind emissions were within the Good Neighbor Provision's ambit. In short, under the Transport Rule, an upwind State "contribute[d] significantly" to downwind nonattainment to the extent its exported pollution both (1) produced one percent or more of an NAAQS in at least one downwind State (step one) and (2) could be eliminated cost-effectively, as determined by EPA (step two). [Citation.]

* * *

[The Act supports the EPA's position. Once the EPA has found a SIP inadequate, the EPA has a statutory duty to correct the deficiency. The Good Neighbor Provision delegates authority to the EPA to reduce upwind pollution, but only in "amounts" that push a downwind state's pollution concentrations above the relevant NAAQS. However, the nonattainment of downwind states results from the collective and interwoven contributions of multiple upwind states. Using costs in the Transport Rule calculus makes good sense. Eliminating those amounts that can cost-effectively be reduced is an efficient and equitable solution to the allocation problem the Good Neighbor Provision requires the EPA to address.]

For the reasons stated, the judgment of the United States Court of Appeals for the D.C. Circuit is reversed, and the cases are remanded for further proceedings consistent with this opinion.

CASE
45-2

Clean Water Act: NPDES
SOUTH FLORIDA WATER MANAGEMENT DISTRICT v. MICCOSUKEE TRIBE OF INDIANS

Supreme Court of the United States, 2004
541 U.S. 95, 124 S.Ct. 1537, 158 L.Ed.2d 264

O'Connor, J.

Petitioner South Florida Water Management District operates a pumping facility that transfers water from a canal into a reservoir a short distance away. Respondents Miccosukee Tribe of Indians and the Friends of the Everglades brought a citizen suit under the Clean Water Act contending that the pumping facility is required to obtain a discharge permit under the National Pollutant Discharge Elimination System. The District Court agreed and granted summary judgment to respondents. A panel of the United States Court of Appeals for the Eleventh Circuit affirmed. Both the District Court and the Eleventh Circuit rested their holdings on the predicate determination that the canal and reservoir are two distinct water bodies. For the reasons explained below, we vacate and remand for further development of the factual record as to the accuracy of that determination.

The Central and South Florida Flood Control Project (Project) consists of a vast array of levees, canals, pumps, and water impoundment areas in the land between south Florida's coastal hills and the Everglades. Historically, that land was itself part of the Everglades, and its surface and groundwater flowed south in a uniform and unchanneled sheet. Starting in the early 1900's, however, the State began to build canals to drain the wetlands and make them suitable for cultivation. These canals proved to be a source of trouble; they lowered the water table, allowing salt water to intrude upon coastal wells, and they proved incapable of controlling flooding. Congress established the Project in 1948 to address these problems. It gave the United States Army Corps of Engineers the task of constructing a comprehensive network of levees, water storage areas, pumps, and canal improvements that would serve several simultaneous purposes, including flood protection, water conservation, and drainage. These improvements fundamentally altered the hydrology of the Everglades, changing the natural sheet flow of ground and surface water. The local sponsor and day-to-day operator of the Project is the South Florida Water Management District (District).

Five discrete elements of the Project are at issue in this case. One is a canal called "C—11." C—11 collects groundwater and rainwater from a 104 square-mile area in south central Broward County. The area drained by C—11 * * * is home to 136,000 people. At the western terminus of C—11 is the second Project element at issue here: a large pump station known as "S—9." When the water level in C—11 rises above a set level, S—9 begins operating and pumps water out of the canal. The water does not travel far. Sixty feet away, the pump station

empties the water into a large undeveloped wetland area called "WCA—3," the third element of the Project we consider here. WCA—3 is the largest of several "water conservation areas" that are remnants of the original South Florida Everglades. The District impounds water in these areas to conserve fresh water that might otherwise flow directly to the ocean, and to preserve wetlands habitat. [Citation.]

Using pump stations like S—9, the District maintains the water table in WCA—3 at a level significantly higher than that in the developed lands drained by the C—11 canal to the east. Absent human intervention, that water would simply flow back east, where it would rejoin the waters of the canal and flood the populated areas of the C—11 basin. That return flow is prevented, or, more accurately, slowed by levees that hold back the surface waters of WCA—3. Two of those levees, L—33 and L—37, are the final two elements of the Project at issue here. The combined effect of L—33 and L—37, C—11, and S—9 is artificially to separate the C—11 basin from WCA—3; left to nature, the two areas would be a single wetland covered in an undifferentiated body of surface and groundwater flowing slowly southward.

As the above description illustrates, the Project has wrought large-scale hydrologic and environmental change in South Florida, some deliberate and some accidental. Its most obvious environmental impact has been the conversion of what were once wetlands into areas suitable for human use. But the Project also has affected those areas that remain wetland ecosystems.

Rain on the western side of the L—33 and L—37 levees falls into the wetland ecosystem of WCA—3. Rain on the eastern side of the levees, on the other hand, falls on agricultural, urban, and residential land. Before it enters the C—11 canal, whether directly as surface runoff or indirectly as groundwater, that rainwater absorbs contaminants produced by human activities. The water in C—11 therefore differs chemically from that in WCA—3. Of particular interest here, C—11 water contains elevated levels of phosphorous, which is found in fertilizers used by farmers in the C—11 basin. When water from C—11 is pumped across the levees, the phosphorous it contains alters the balance of WCA—3's ecosystem (which is naturally low in phosphorous) and stimulates the growth of algae and plants foreign to the Everglades ecosystem.

[Plaintiffs Miccosukee Tribe of Indians and the Friends of the Everglades brought a citizen suit under the Clean Water Act contending that the pumping facility is required to obtain a discharge permit under the National Pollutant Discharge

Elimination System (NPDES). The district court agreed and granted summary judgment to the plaintiffs. The U.S. Court of Appeals for the Eleventh Circuit affirmed. Both the district court and the Eleventh Circuit rested their holdings on the predicate determination that the canal and reservoir are two distinct water bodies.]

* * *

Congress enacted the Clean Water Act (Act) in 1972. Its stated objective was "to restore and maintain the chemical, physical, and biological integrity of the Nation's waters." [Citation.] To serve those ends, the Act prohibits "the discharge of any pollutant by any person" unless done in compliance with some provision of the Act. [Citation.] The provision relevant to this case, [citation], establishes the National Pollutant Discharge Elimination System, or "NPDES." Generally speaking, the NPDES requires dischargers to obtain permits that place limits on the type and quantity of pollutants that can be released into the Nation's waters. The Act defines the phrase "'discharge of a pollutant'" to mean "any addition of any pollutant to navigable waters from any point source." [Citation.] A "'point source,'" in turn, is defined as "any discernible, confined and discrete conveyance," such as a pipe, ditch, channel, or tunnel, "from which pollutants are or may be discharged." [Citation.]

According to the Tribe, the District cannot operate S—9 without an NPDES permit because the pump station moves phosphorous-laden water from C—11 into WCA—3. The District does not dispute that phosphorous is a pollutant, or that C—11 and WCA—3 are "navigable waters" within the meaning of the Act. The question, it contends, is whether the operation of the S—9 pump constitutes the "discharge of [a] pollutant" within the meaning of the Act.

* * *

The District and the Federal Government * * * advance three separate arguments, any of which would, if accepted, lead to the conclusion that the S—9 pump station does not require a point source discharge permit under the NPDES program. Two of these arguments involve the application of disputed contentions of law to agreed-upon facts, while the third involves the application of agreed-upon law to disputed facts. For reasons explained below, we decline at this time to resolve all of the parties' legal disagreements, and instead remand for further proceedings regarding their factual dispute.

* * *

* * * For purposes of determining whether there has been "any addition of any pollutant to navigable waters from any point source," * * *, the Government contends that all the water bodies that fall within the Act's definition of "'navigable waters'" (i.e., all "the waters of the United States, including the territorial seas") should be viewed unitarily for purposes of NPDES permitting requirements. Because the Act requires NPDES permits only when there is an addition of a pollutant

"to navigable waters," the Government's approach would lead to the conclusion that such permits are not required when water from one navigable water body is discharged, unaltered, into another navigable water body. That would be true even if one water body were polluted and the other pristine, and the two would not otherwise mix. [Citation.] Under this "unitary waters" approach, the S—9 pump station would not need an NPDES permit.

* * *

In the courts below, as here, the District contended that the C—11 canal and WCA—3 impoundment area are not distinct water bodies at all, but instead are two hydrologically indistinguishable parts of a single water body. The Government agrees with the District on this point, claiming that because the C—11 canal and WCA—3 "share a unique, intimately related, hydrological association," they "can appropriately be viewed, for purposes of Section 402 of the Clean Water Act, as parts of a single body of water." [Citation.] The Tribe does not dispute that if C—11 and WCA—3 are simply two parts of the same water body, pumping water from one into the other cannot constitute an "addition" of pollutants. * * *

The record does contain information supporting the District's view of the facts. Although C—11 and WCA—3 are divided from one another by the L—33 and L—37 levees, that line appears to be an uncertain one. Because Everglades soil is extremely porous, water flows easily between ground and surface waters, so much so that "[g]round and surface waters are essentially the same thing." C—11 and WCA—3, of course, share a common underlying aquifer. Moreover, the L—33 and L—37 levees continually leak, allowing water to escape from WCA—3. This means not only that any boundary between C—11 and WCA—3 is indistinct, but also that there is some significant mingling of the two waters; the record reveals that even without use of the S—9 pump station, water travels as both seepage and groundwater flow between the water conservation area and the C—11 basin. * * *

We do not decide here whether the District Court's test is adequate for determining whether C—11 and WCA—3 are distinct. Instead, we hold only that the District Court applied its test prematurely. * * * The record before us leads us to believe that some factual issues remain unresolved. The District Court certainly was correct to characterize the flow through the S—9 pump station as a non-natural one, propelled as it is by diesel-fired motors against the pull of gravity. And it also appears true that if S—9 were shut down, the water in the C—11 canal might for a brief time flow east, rather than west, as it now does. But the effects of shutting down the pump might extend beyond that. The limited record before us suggests that if S—9 were shut down, the area drained by C—11 would flood quite quickly. [Citation.] That flooding might mean that C—11 would no longer be a "distinct body of navigable water," [citation] but part of a larger water body extending over WCA—3 and the C—11 basin. It also might call into question the Eleventh Circuit's conclusion that S—9 is the cause in fact of phosphorous addition to WCA—3. Nothing in the record suggests that the District Court considered these issues when it granted summary judgment. * * *

We find that further development of the record is necessary to resolve the dispute over the validity of the distinction between C—11 and WCA—3. * * * Accordingly, the judgment of the United States Court of Appeals for the Eleventh Circuit is vacated, and the case is remanded for further proceedings consistent with this opinion.

QUESTIONS

1. Atlantic Cement operated a large cement plant. Neighboring landowners sued for damages and an injunction, claiming that their properties were injured by the dirt, smoke, and vibrations coming from the plant. The lower court found that the plant constituted a nuisance and granted temporary damages but refused to grant an injunction because the benefits of operating the plant outweighed the harm to the plaintiffs' properties. The landowners appealed. Does the plant constitute a nuisance? Should it be shut down? Explain.

2. Seindenberg and Hutchinson (the site owners) leased a four-acre tract of land (the Bluff Road site) to a chemical manufacturing corporation (COCC). While the lease initially was for the sole purpose of allowing COCC to store raw materials and finished products in a warehouse on the land, COCC later expanded its business to include the brokering and recycling of chemical waste generated by third parties. COCC's owners subsequently formed a new corporation, South Carolina Recycling and Disposal, Inc. (SCRDI), for the purpose of taking over COCC's

waste-handling business. The site owners accepted rent from SCRDI. The waste stored at Bluff Road contained many chemical substances that Federal law defines as hazardous. Subsequently, the Environmental Protection Agency concluded that the site was a major fire hazard. The Federal government contracted with a third party to perform a partial cleanup of the site. South Carolina completed the cleanup. The Federal government and South Carolina sued SCRDI, COCC, the site owners, and three third-party generators as responsible parties under the Resource Conservation and Recovery Act and Comprehensive Environmental Response, Compensation, and Liability Act. Explain whether the United States and South Carolina will prevail.

3. The State of Y submits a plan under the Clean Air Act to attain national ambient air quality standards. Can the Environmental Protection Agency administrator deny approval of the State plan because it is (a) less stringent or (b) more stringent than the agency believes is feasible? Explain.

CASE PROBLEMS

4. Kennecott Copper Corp. challenged an Environmental Protection Agency (EPA) order that rejected a portion of the State of Nevada's implementation plan dealing with the control of stationary sources of sulfur dioxide (SO_2). All of the SO_2 emissions come from a single source—the Kennecott copper smelter at McGill. The EPA bases its decision on the belief that the Clean Air Act National Ambient Air Quality Standards (NAAQS) must be met by continuous emission limitations to the maximum extent possible and that the Act permits the intermittent use of emission controls only when continuous controls are not economically feasible. Kennecott contends that the EPA must approve any State implementation plan

that will attain and maintain an NAAQS within the statutory time period. Who will prevail? Why or why not?

5. The Environmental Protection Agency (EPA) administrator issued an order suspending the registration of the pesticides heptachlor and chlordane under the Federal Insecticide, Fungicide, and Rodenticide Act (FIFRA). Velsicol Chemical Corp., the sole manufacturer of these pesticides, brings an action contending that the evidence does not support the administrator's contention that the continued use of these chemicals poses an imminent hazard to human health. Velsicol and the U.S. Department of Agriculture (USDA) contend (a) that the EPA's laboratory tests on mice and rats do not

"conclusively" show that either chemical is carcinogenic, (b) that mice are too prone to tumors to be reliable test subjects, and (c) that human exposure to these chemicals is insufficient to create a risk. Nonetheless, human epidemiology studies on both chemicals provide no basis for concluding that either pesticide is safe. The administrator based part of his claim on residues of these chemicals found in soil, air, and the aquatic ecosystem over long periods of time and on the presence of these chemicals in the human diet and human tissue. Does FIFRA apply in this situation? Explain.

6. The U.S. Department of the Interior filed an environmental impact statement (EIS) with regard to its proposal to lease approximately eighty tracts of submerged land, primarily located off the coast of Louisiana, for oil and gas exploration. Adjacent to the proposed area is the greatest estuarine coastal marsh in the United States. This marsh provides rich nutrients for the Gulf of Mexico, the most productive fishing region of the country. The EIS focused primarily on oil pollution and its negative environmental effect. Three conservation groups contend that the EIS is insufficient in that it does not properly discuss alternatives. The government contends that (a) it need only provide a detailed statement of the alternatives, not a discussion of their environmental impact, and (b) the only alternatives the NEPA requires it to discuss are those which can be adopted and implemented by the agency issuing the impact statement. Is the government correct in its contentions? Why or why not?

7. Chemical Manufacturers Association (CMA) and four companies that manufacture chemicals challenged a test rule promulgated by the Environmental Protection Agency (EPA) under the Toxic Substances Control Act (TSCA). The plaintiffs asserted that the EPA must find that the existence of an unreasonable risk of injury to health is more probable than not before it may issue a test rule under the Act. In response, the EPA claimed that it may issue a test rule under the TSCA if the agency determines that there is a substantial probability of an unreasonable risk of injury to health. The test rule required toxicological testing to determine the health effects of the chemical, 2-ethylhexanoic acid, and imposed on exporters of this chemical a duty to file certain notices with the EPA. Explain what standard should be applied.

8. National-Southwire Aluminum Company (NSA) owns and operates a plant that emits fluoride. When its wet scrubbers were turned off as part of its regular maintenance program, NSA discovered no appreciable change in ambient fluoride levels. Because of the expense of operating the scrubbers and its belief that using the scrubbers did not significantly affect ambient fluoride levels, NSA desired to turn the scrubbers off permanently. Accordingly, NSA sought a determination from the Environmental Protection Agency (EPA) that turning off the scrubbers would not constitute a modification requiring the application of new source performance standards to the plant. Turning off the scrubbers would result in an increase of more than 1,100 tons per year of fluoride emissions with no decrease in the emission of any other pollutant. This increase was nearly four hundred times the level the EPA had established as inconsequential. The EPA determined that turning off the scrubbers would constitute a "new source" modification. Accordingly, NSA was required either to leave the scrubbers on or to install new pollutant control equipment. Is the EPA correct in its assertion? Explain.

9. The city of Fayetteville, Arkansas, received a National Pollutant Discharge Elimination System permit from the Environmental Protection Agency (EPA) for the discharge of sewage into a stream that ultimately reaches the Illinois River, twenty-two miles upstream from the Oklahoma border. The EPA permit limited the effluent discharge to comply with Oklahoma water quality standards, but the EPA stated that those standards would be violated only if the discharge would cause an actual, detectable violation of Oklahoma standards. Oklahoma appealed the permit, arguing that the permit violated Oklahoma water quality standards, which allow no degradation of water quality. Explain whether the permit should be granted.

10. On October 20, 1999, a group of nineteen private organizations filed a rulemaking petition asking the Environmental Protection Agency (EPA) to regulate greenhouse gas emissions from new motor vehicles under the Clean Air Act. Fifteen months after the petition's submission, the EPA requested public comment on all the issues raised in the petition, adding a "particular" request for comments on "any scientific, technical, legal, economic or other aspect of these issues that may be relevant to EPA's consideration of this petition." The EPA received more than fifty thousand comments over the next five months. On September 8, 2003, the EPA entered an order denying the rulemaking petition. The agency gave two reasons for its decision: (1) that contrary to the opinions of its former general counsels, the Clean Air Act does not authorize the EPA to issue mandatory regulations to address global climate change and (2) that even if the agency had the authority to set greenhouse gas emission standards, it would be unwise to do so at this time. In concluding

that it lacked statutory authority over greenhouse gases, the EPA observed that Congress "was well aware of the global climate change issue when it last comprehensively amended the [Clean Air Act] in 1990," yet it declined to adopt a proposed amendment establishing binding emissions limitations. Calling global warming "the most pressing environmental challenge of our time," twelve states, local governments, and private organizations alleged that the EPA had abdicated its responsibility under the Clean Air Act to regulate the emissions of four greenhouse gases, including carbon dioxide, and challenged the decision. Explain who is correct.

T A K I N G   S I D E S

When considering an application for a special use permit to develop and operate a ski resort at Sandy Butte, a mountain in Washington that is part of a national forest, the Forest Service prepared an environmental impact statement (EIS). The EIS recommended the issuance of a special use permit for what was to be a sixteen-lift ski area, and the forest service issued the permit as recommended. Four organizations sued, claiming that the EIS was inadequate. The lower court held that the EIS was adequate, but the Court of Appeals reversed, concluding that the National Environmental Policy Act required that actions be taken to mitigate the adverse effects of a major Federal action and that the EIS contain a detailed mitigation plan.

a. What are the arguments that the EIS should take a hard look only at the relevant environmental consequences?

b. What are the arguments that the EIS should propose actions that mitigate the relevant environmental consequences?

c. What else should the EIS include in this situation?

CHAPTER 46

International Business Law

CHAPTER OUTCOMES

After reading and studying this chapter, you should be able to:

- Describe the purposes and major features of regional trade communities (especially the European Union and United States-Mexico-Canada Agreement [USMCA]) and the World Trade Organization (General Agreement on Tariffs and Trade [GATT]).

- Explain sovereign immunity, the act of state doctrine, expropriation, and confiscation.

- Explain the legal controls imposed on the flow of trade, labor, and capital across national borders.

- Explain the international dimensions of antitrust law, securities regulation, and the protection of intellectual property.

- Describe the forms in which a multinational enterprise may conduct its business in a foreign country.

I n the twenty-first century, every aspect of business, including business law, requires some understanding of international business practices. Since World War II, the global economy has become increasingly interconnected. Many U.S. corporations now have investments or manufacturing facilities in other countries, while an increasing number of foreign corporations are conducting business operations in the United States. Furthermore, whether a domestic corporation exports goods or not, it competes with imports from many other countries. For example, U.S. firms face competition from Japanese electronics and automobiles, Chinese electronics and textiles, Korean automobiles and electronics, French wines and fashions, German machinery, and Indian software programmers and call centers. To compete effectively, U.S. firms need to be aware of international business practices and developments.

Laws vary greatly from country to country: what one nation requires by law, another may forbid. To complicate matters, there is no single authority in international law that can compel countries to act. When the laws of two or more nations conflict or when one party has violated an agreement and the other party wishes to enforce it or recover damages, establishing who will adjudicate the matter, which laws will be applied, what remedies will be available, or where the matter will be decided often is very confusing. Nonetheless, given the growing impact of the global economy, a basic understanding of international business law is essential.

46-1 The International Environment

International law deals with the conduct and relations between nation-states and international organizations, as well as some of their relations with persons. Unlike domestic law, international law generally cannot be enforced. Nevertheless, although international courts do not have compulsory jurisdiction to resolve international disputes, they do have authority to resolve an international dispute if the parties to the dispute *accept* the court's jurisdiction over the matter. Furthermore, a sovereign nation that has adopted an international law will enforce that law to the same extent as all of its domestic laws. This section of the chapter examines some of the sources and institutions of international law.

46-1a INTERNATIONAL COURT OF JUSTICE

The United Nations (U.N.), with at least 193 member states, has a judiciary branch called the International Court of Justice (ICJ). The ICJ consists of fifteen judges, no two of whom may be from the same sovereign state, elected for nine-year terms by a majority of both the U.N. General Assembly and the U.N. Security Council. The usefulness of the ICJ is limited, however, because only nations (not private individuals or corporations) may be parties to an action before the court. Furthermore, the ICJ has contentious jurisdiction only over nation-parties that agree both to allow the ICJ to decide the case and to be bound by its decision. Moreover, because the ICJ cannot enforce its rulings, countries displeased with an ICJ decision may simply ignore it. Consequently, few nations submit their disputes to the ICJ.

The ICJ also has advisory jurisdiction if requested by a U.N. organ or specialized U.N. agency. Neither sovereign states nor individuals may request an advisory opinion. These opinions are nonbinding, and the U.N. agency requesting the opinion usually decides by vote whether to follow it.

46-1b REGIONAL TRADE COMMUNITIES

Of much greater significance are international organizations, conferences, and treaties that focus on business and trade regulation. Regional trade communities, such as the European Union (EU), promote common trade policies among member nations. Other important regional trade communities include the Regional Comprehensive Economic Partnership (RCEP), the Comprehensive and Progressive Agreement for Trans-Pacific Partnership (CPTPP), the Central American Common Market (CACM), the Caribbean Community (CARICOM), the Association of Southeast Asian Nations (ASEAN), the Andean Common Market (ANCOM), the Common Market for Eastern and Southern Africa (COMESA), the Asian Pacific Economic Cooperation (APEC), *Mercado Comun del Cono Sur* (Latin American Trading Group, MERCO-SUR), the Gulf Cooperation Council (GCC), *Alianza del Pacífico* (Pacific Alliance), and the Economic Community of West African States (ECOWAS).

EUROPEAN UNION The European Community (EC), the predecessor to the European Union, was formed in 1967 through a merger between the European Economic Community (better known as the Common Market), the European Coal and Steel Community, and the European Atomic Energy Community (Euratom). In 1993, the Treaty on European Union (popularly called the Maastricht Treaty) took effect. It changed the name of the EC to the European Union (EU) and stated the EU's objectives to include (1) promoting economic and social progress by creating an area without internal borders and by establishing an economic and monetary union (the euro), (2) asserting its identity on the international scene by implementing a common foreign and security policy, (3) strengthening the protection of the rights and interests of citizens of its member states, and (4) developing close cooperation on justice and home affairs.

The **euro** (€) is the single currency currently shared by nineteen of the EU's members, which collectively are known as the Eurozone. The **Schengen Area** is a zone without internal borders within which citizens, many non-EU nationals, business people, and tourists can freely circulate without being subjected to border checks. It now encompasses twenty-two EU countries and four associated non-EU countries.

Until 2004, the EU had fifteen members: Austria, Belgium, Denmark, Finland, France, Germany, Greece, Ireland, Italy, Luxembourg, the Netherlands, Portugal, Spain, Sweden, and the United Kingdom. In 2004, the European Union admitted ten eastern and southern European countries: Cyprus, the Czech Republic, Estonia, Hungary, Latvia, Lithuania, Malta, Poland, the Slovak Republic, and Slovenia. In 2007, Bulgaria and Romania became full EU members, bringing the total number of members to twenty-seven. Croatia became the EU's twenty-eighth member in 2013. The United Kingdom withdrew from the European Union on January 31, 2020, bringing the number of members to twenty-seven. Five countries are candidates for EU membership: Albania, Montenegro, North Macedonia, Serbia, and Turkey. The EU's total population is approximately 450 million (7 percent of the world's population) while the EU's trade with the rest of the world accounts for approximately 15 percent of global trade exports and imports. With the United Kingdom's exit, the EU's economy—measured in terms of the goods and services it produces—is approximately 80 percent of the economy of the United States.

USMCA In 2020, the United States-Mexico-Canada Agreement (USMCA) was ratified by all three countries and went into effect. The USMCA updates the North American Free Trade Agreement (NAFTA) of 1994, which established a free trade area among the United States, Canada, and Mexico. The USMCA includes major changes in NAFTA regarding automobiles, labor and environmental standards, intellectual property protections, and digital trade provisions. Significant provisions of USMCA include the following:

1. **Automobiles**. Automobiles must have 75 percent of their components manufactured in North America to qualify for zero tariffs. This is an increase from 62.5 percent under NAFTA.

2. **Labor**. Forty to 45 percent of automobile parts must be made by workers who earn at least $16 an hour by 2023.

3. **Intellectual Property**. USMCA extends the fifty years of protection for copyrights in NAFTA to seventy years and strengthens protection of trade secrets.

4. **Sunset Provision**. The USMCA will end after sixteen years unless each country agrees to continue the USMCA for a new sixteen-year term.

46-1c INTERNATIONAL TREATIES

A **treaty** is an agreement between or among independent nations. As discussed in *Chapter 1*, the U.S. Constitution authorizes the President to enter into treaties with the advice and consent of the Senate "providing two-thirds of the Senators present concur." The Constitution provides that all valid treaties are "the law of the land," having the legal force of a Federal statute.

Nations have entered into bilateral and multilateral treaties to facilitate and regulate trade and to protect their national interests. In addition, treaties have been used to serve as constitutions of international organizations, to establish general international law, to transfer territory, to settle disputes, to secure human rights, and to protect investments. The Treaty Section of the Office of Legal Affairs within the United Nations Secretariat is responsible for registering and publishing treaties and agreements among member nations. Since its inception in 1946, the U.N. Secretariat has registered and published more than 30,000 treaties that expressly or indirectly concern international business.

WORLD TRADE ORGANIZATION (WTO) The WTO is the only global international organization dealing with the rules of trade among nations. Probably the most important multilateral trade treaty is the General Agreement on Tariffs and Trade (GATT), which the WTO replaced as an international organization. The WTO officially commenced on January 1, 1995 and has at least 164 members accounting for more than 98 percent of world trade. (More than twenty countries are observers and are seeking membership.) Its basic purpose is to facilitate the flow of trade by establishing agreements on potential trade barriers such as import quotas, customs, export regulations, antidumping restrictions (the prohibition against selling goods for less than their fair market value), subsidies, and import fees. The WTO administers trade agreements, acts as a forum for trade negotiations, handles trade disputes, monitors national trade policies, and provides technical assistance and training for developing countries.

Under GATT's **most-favored nation provision**, all signatories must treat each other as favorably as they treat any other country. Thus, any privilege, immunity, or favor given to one country must be given to all. Nevertheless, nations may give preferential treatment to developing nations and may enter into free trade areas with one or more other nations. A free trade area permits countries to discriminate in favor of their free trade partners, provided that the agreement covers substantially all trade among the partners. A second important principle adopted by GATT is that the protection accorded domestic industries should take the form of a customs tariff, rather than other more trade-inhibiting measures.

The most recent set of accords, adopted in 1994, included multilateral trade agreements on such matters as agricultural products, textiles and clothing, technical barriers to trade, trade-related investment measures, customs valuation, subsidies and countervailing measures, trade in services, antidumping measures, and protection of intellectual property rights. It also created the Dispute Settlement Body and increased the scope of GATT's dispute resolution process.

UNITED NATIONS CONVENTION ON THE LAW OF THE SEA (UNCLOS) The United Nations Convention on the Law of the Sea (UNCLOS) establishes a comprehensive set of rules governing all uses of the oceans and their resources. UNCLOS also provides the framework for further development of specific areas of the law of the sea. UNCLOS entered into force in 1994 and has been ratified by at least 168 nations.

UNCLOS governs all aspects of the ocean, including economic and commercial activities, transfer of technology, environmental control, scientific research, and the settlement of disputes relating to ocean matters. A key feature of UNCLOS is that coastal nations have (1) sovereignty over their territorial sea up to a limit not to exceed twelve nautical miles, (2) sovereign rights in a 200-nautical mile exclusive economic zone (EEZ) with respect to natural resources and certain economic activities, and (3) sovereign rights to the continental shelf (the national area of the seabed) for exploring and exploiting it. The shelf can extend at least 200 nautical miles from the shore, and more under specified circumstances, but coastal nations share with the international community part of the revenue derived from exploiting resources from any part of their shelf beyond 200 miles.

Disputes can be submitted to the International Tribunal for the Law of the Sea established under UNCLOS, to the International Court of Justice, or to arbitration. The Tribunal also has exclusive jurisdiction over deep seabed mining disputes.

46-2 Jurisdiction Over Actions of Foreign Governments

This section focuses on the power, and the limits on that power, of a sovereign nation to exercise jurisdiction over a foreign nation or to take over property owned by foreign citizens. More specifically, it examines state immunities (the principle of sovereign immunity and the act of state doctrine) and the power of a state to take foreign investment property.

46-2a SOVEREIGN IMMUNITY

One of the oldest concepts in international law is that each nation has absolute authority over the events occurring within its territory. It also has been long recognized, however, that to maintain international relations and trade, a host country must refrain from imposing its laws on a foreign sovereign nation present within its borders. This absolute immunity from the courts of a host country is known as **sovereign immunity**. Originally, all acts of a foreign sovereign nation within a host country were considered immune from the host country's laws. In modern times, however, international law distinguishes between the public and commercial acts of a foreign nation. Only public acts, such as those concerning diplomatic activity, internal administration, or armed forces, will be granted sovereign immunity. When engaging in trade or commercial activities, a foreign nation subjects itself to the jurisdiction of the host country's courts with respect to disputes arising out of those commercial activities and its commercial property may be levied upon for the satisfaction of judgments rendered against it in connection with its commercial activities.

In 1976, Congress enacted the Foreign Sovereign Immunities Act to establish the circumstances under which the United States would extend immunity to foreign nations. Under the Act as amended, a "foreign state shall be immune from the jurisdiction of the courts of the United States and of the States" unless one of several statutorily defined exceptions applies. The most significant of the Act's exceptions is the "commercial" exception which applies if the suit is based upon (1) a commercial activity conducted in the United States by the foreign state, (2) an act that the foreign state performed in the United States in connection with a commercial activity it carried on elsewhere, or (3) a commercial activity performed outside the territory of the United States that directly affects the United States. The Act defines a commercial activity as "either a regular course of commercial conduct or a particular commercial transaction or act. The commercial character of an activity shall be determined by reference to the nature of the course of conduct or particular transaction or act, rather than by reference to its purpose."

If an activity is one that a private party could normally carry on, it is commercial and a foreign government engaging in that activity is not immune. On the other hand, if the activity is one that only governments can undertake, it is noncommercial under the Act. Examples of commercial activities include a contract by a foreign government to buy provisions or equipment for its armed forces; a contract by a foreign government to construct or repair a government building; and a sale of a service or a product by a foreign government or its leasing of property, borrowing of money, or investing in a security of a U.S. corporation. Examples of public (noncommercial) activities to which sovereign immunity would extend include nationalizing a corporation, determining limitations upon the use of natural resources, and granting licenses to export a natural resource.

The International Organizations Immunities Act of 1945 grants international organizations such as the United Nations, the International Monetary Fund, the World Bank, and the World Health Organization the "same immunity from suit … as is enjoyed by foreign governments." In 2018, the U.S. Supreme Court held that the Foreign Sovereign Immunities Act governs the immunity of international organizations. *Jam v. International Finance Corp.*, 586 U.S. ____.

♦ *See Case 46-1*

46-2b ACT OF STATE DOCTRINE

The act of state doctrine provides that a nation's judicial branch should not question the validity of the actions a foreign government takes within its own borders. In 1897,

the U.S. Supreme Court described the act of state doctrine in terms that still remain valid: "Every sovereign State is bound to respect the independence of every other sovereign State, and the courts of one country will not sit in judgment on the acts of the government of another done within its own territory."

In the United States, there are several possible exceptions to the act of state doctrine. Some courts hold (1) that a sovereign may waive its right to raise the act of state defense and (2) that the doctrine may be inapplicable to commercial activities of a foreign sovereign. In addition, by Federal statute, the courts will not apply the act of state doctrine to claims to property based on the assertion that a foreign state confiscated the property in violation of the principles of international law, unless the President of the United States determines that the doctrine should be applied in a particular case.

46-2c TAKING OF FOREIGN INVESTMENT PROPERTY

Investing in foreign states involves the risk that the host nation's government may take the investment property. An **expropriation** or nationalization occurs when a government seizes foreign-owned property or assets for a public purpose and pays the owner just compensation for what is taken. In contrast, **confiscation** occurs when a government offers no payment (or a highly inadequate payment) in exchange for seized property or seizes it for a nonpublic purpose. Confiscations violate generally observed principles of international law, whereas expropriations do not. In either case, few remedies are available to injured parties.

One precaution that U.S. firms can take is to obtain insurance from a private insurer or from the Overseas Private Investment Corporation (OPIC), an independent U.S. government agency. OPIC was established to facilitate the participation of U.S. private capital and skills in the economic and social development of developing countries and countries in transition from nonmarket to market economies. In 2018, Congress enacted the Better Utilization of Investments Leading to Development (BUILD) Act combining the capabilities of OPIC and the Development Credit Authority into the U.S. International Development Finance Corporation (DFC). The DFC offers coverage of up to $1 billion against losses due to currency inconvertibility, expropriation, and political violence including terrorism. The DFC also offers reinsurance to increase underwriting capacity.

Practical Advice

If you invest in foreign states, consider obtaining expropriation insurance from a private insurer or from the U.S. International Development Finance Corporation (DFC), an agency of the U.S. government.

The World Bank established the Multilateral Investment Guarantee Agency (MIGA) to encourage increased investment in developing nations. The MIGA has at least 182 member countries. MIGA's mission is to promote foreign direct investment into developing countries to help support economic growth, reduce poverty, and improve people's lives. It does this by providing political risk insurance (guarantees) to the private sector for such noncommercial risks as deprivation of ownership or control by governmental actions, breach of contract by a government where there is no judicial recourse, and loss from military action or civil disturbance.

46-3 Transacting Business Abroad

Transacting business abroad may involve activities such as selling goods, information, or services; investing capital; or arranging for the movement of labor. Because these transactions may affect the national security, economy, foreign policy, and interests of both the exporting and importing countries, nations have imposed measures to restrict or encourage such transactions. This section examines the legal controls imposed upon the flow of trade, labor, and capital across national borders.

46-3a FLOW OF TRADE

Advances in modern technology, communication, transportation, and production methods have greatly increased the flow of goods across national boundaries. The governments within each country thereby face a dilemma. On the one hand, they wish to protect and stimulate domestic industry. On the other hand, they want to provide their citizens with the best quality goods at the lowest possible prices and to encourage exports from their own countries.

Governments have used a variety of trade barriers to protect domestic businesses and to achieve other social and political goals. A frequently applied device is the **tariff**, which is a duty or tax imposed on goods moving into or out of a country. Tariffs raise the price of imported goods, prompting some consumers to purchase less expensive, domestically produced items. Governments can also use **nontariff barriers** to give local industries a competitive advantage. Examples of nontariff barriers include unilateral or bilateral import quotas; import bans; overly restrictive safety, health, or manufacturing standards; environmental laws; complicated and time-consuming customs procedures; and subsidies to local industry.

Dumping is the sale of exported goods from one country to another country at less than normal value. Under the WTO's Antidumping Code, "normal value" is the price that would be charged for the same or a similar product in the ordinary course of trade for domestic consumption in the exporting country. Dumping violates the GATT "if it causes or threatens material injury to an established industry in the territory of a contracting party or materially retards the establishment of a domestic industry."

Governments also control the flow of goods out of their countries by imposing quotas, tariffs, or total prohibitions. **Export controls** or restrictions usually result from important policy considerations, such as national defense, foreign policy, or the protection of scarce national resources. For example, the United States passed the Export Administration Act of 1979, which restricts the flow of technologically advanced goods and data from the United States to other countries. The Act expired in 2001, but Presidents have extended control over exports by invoking their emergency powers under the International Emergency Economic Powers Act. In 2018, the Export Administration Act was repealed by the Export Controls Act, which established a permanent statutory basis for the control of dual-use exports licensed by the Department of Commerce. Dual-use items are commodities, software, and technologies that have civilian and military applications. Nonetheless, to assist domestic businesses, countries generally encourage exports through the use of **export incentives** and **export subsidies**.

Practical Advice

If you export goods, be sure to determine whether you must obtain an export license from the U.S. government and what import barriers, such as tariffs, you must satisfy in the countries to which you are sending the goods.

46-3b FLOW OF LABOR

The flow of labor across national borders generates policy questions involving the employment needs of local workers. Each country has immigration policies and regulations. Almost all countries require that foreigners obtain valid passports before entering their borders; citizens, in turn, usually must have passports to leave or reenter the country. In addition, a country may issue foreign citizens visas that permit them to enter the country for identified purposes or for specific periods of time. For example, the U.S. Citizenship and Immigration Services (USCIS), a component of the Department of Homeland Security, oversees lawful immigration to the United States.

46-3c FLOW OF CAPITAL

Multinational businesses frequently need to transfer funds to, and receive money from, operations in other countries. Because there is no international currency, nations have sought to ease the flow of capital among themselves. In 1945, the International Monetary Fund (IMF) was established to promote international monetary cooperation, to facilitate the expansion and balanced growth of international trade, to assist in the elimination of foreign exchange restrictions that hamper such growth, and to shorten the duration and lessen the disequilibrium in the international balance of payments between the members of the fund. Currently, at least 189 countries are members of the IMF.

Many nations have laws regulating foreign investment. Restrictions on the establishment of foreign investment tend to limit the amount of equity and the amount of control allowed foreign investors. They may also restrict the way in which the investment is created, such as limiting or prohibiting investment by acquiring an existing locally owned business. At least 154 nations have signed the Convention on the Settlement of Investment Disputes Between States and Nationals of Other States. The Convention created the International Centre for the Settlement of Investment Disputes, which offers conciliation and arbitration for investment disputes among governments and foreign investors to promote increased flows of international investment.

Nations also have joined to form international and regional banks to facilitate the flow of capital and trade. Such banks include the International Bank for Reconstruction and Development (part of the World Bank), the African Development Bank, the Asian Development Bank, the European Investment Bank, and the Inter-American Development Bank.

46-3d INTERNATIONAL CONTRACTS

The legal issues inherent in domestic commercial contracts also arise in international contracts. Moreover, certain additional issues, such as differences in language, customs, legal systems, and currency, are peculiar to international contracts. Such a contract should specify its official language and define all of the significant legal terms it incorporates. In addition, it should specify the acceptable currency (or currencies) and payment method. The contract should include a choice of law clause designating what law will govern any breach or dispute regarding the contract and a choice of forum clause designating whether the parties will resolve disputes through one nation's court system or through third-party arbitration. (The United Nations Committee on International Trade Law and the International Chamber of Commerce have promulgated arbitration rules that have won broad international acceptance.) Finally, the contract should include a *force majeure* (unavoidable superior force) clause apportioning the liabilities and responsibilities of the parties in the event of an unforeseeable occurrence, such as a typhoon, tornado, flood, earthquake, war, or nuclear disaster.

The United Nations Commission on International Trade Law (UNCITRAL) was established by the U.N. General Assembly to further the progressive harmonization and unification of the law of international trade. The Commission is composed of sixty member states elected by the General Assembly and is structured to be representative of the world's various geographic regions and its principal economic and legal systems. One of its primary functions is to develop conventions, model laws, and rules that are acceptable worldwide.

One example is the United Nations Convention on Contracts for the International Sales of Goods (CISG) (discussed in the following section and in *Chapters 21* through *25*) and the arbitration rules mentioned earlier. Another is the UNCITRAL Model Law on Electronic Commerce, adopted in 1996, which is intended to facilitate the use of modern means of communications and storage of information. Legislation based on it has been adopted by at least seventy-two nations. In the United States, it has influenced the Uniform Electronic Transactions Act, which was promulgated by the Uniform Law Commission (ULC) in 1999 and has been adopted by at least forty-eight States (see *Chapter 15*). In 2001, the UNCITRAL Model Law on Electronic Signatures was adopted to bring additional legal certainty regarding the use of electronic signatures. Following a technology-neutral approach, the Act establishes a presumption that electronic signatures, which meet certain criteria of technical reliability, shall be treated as equivalent to hand-written signatures. Legislation based on it has been adopted in at least thirty-three nations.

Practical Advice

When you enter into international contracts, be sure that your contracts include provisions for payment, including acceptable currencies, choice of law, choice of forum, and force majeure.

CISG The United Nations Convention on Contracts for the International Sales of Goods (CISG), which has been ratified by the United States and at least ninety-three other countries, governs all contracts for the international sale of goods between parties located in different nations that have ratified the CISG. Because treaties are Federal law, the CISG supersedes the Uniform Commercial Code in any situation to which either could apply. The CISG includes provisions dealing with interpretation, trade usage, contract formation, obligations and remedies of sellers and buyers, and risk of loss. Parties to an international sales contract may, however, expressly exclude CISG governance from their contract. The CISG specifically excludes sales of (1) goods bought for personal, family, or household use; (2) ships or aircraft; and (3) electricity. In addition, it does not apply to contracts in which the primary obligation of the party furnishing the goods consists of supplying labor or services. The CISG is discussed in *Chapters 21* through *25*.

LETTERS OF CREDIT International trade involves a number of risks not usually encountered in domestic trade, particularly the threat of government controls over the export or import of goods and currency. The most effective means of managing these risks—as well as the ordinary trade risks of nonperformance by seller and buyer—is the irrevocable documentary letter of credit. Most international letters of credit are governed by the Uniform Customs and Practices for Documentary Credits, a document drafted by commercial law experts from many countries and adopted by the International Chamber of Commerce. A **letter of credit** is a promise by a buyer's bank to pay the seller, provided certain conditions are met. The letter of credit transaction involves three or four different parties and three underlying contracts. To illustrate: a U.S. business wishes to sell computers to a Belgian company. The U.S. and Belgian firms enter into a sales agreement that includes details such as the number of computers, the features they will have, and the date they will be shipped. The buyer then enters into a second contract with a local bank, called an *issuer*, committing the bank to pay the agreed price upon receiving specified documents. These documents normally include a bill of lading (proving that the seller has delivered the goods for shipment), a commercial invoice listing the purchase terms, proof of insurance, and a customs certificate indicating that customs officials have cleared the goods for export. The buyer's bank's commitment to pay is the irrevocable letter of credit. Typically, a correspondent or paying bank located in the seller's country makes payment to the seller. Here, the Belgian issuing bank arranges to pay the U.S. correspondent bank the agreed sum of money in exchange for the documents. The issuer then sends the U.S. computer firm the letter of credit. When the U.S. firm obtains all the necessary documents, it presents them to the U.S. correspondent bank, which verifies the documents, pays the computer company in U.S. dollars, and sends the documents to the Belgian issuing bank. Upon receiving the required documents, the issuing bank pays the correspondent bank and then presents the documents to the buyer. In our example, the Belgian buyer pays the issuing bank in Belgian francs for the letter of credit when the buyer receives the specified documents from the bank.

46-3e ANTITRUST LAWS

Section 1 of the Sherman Act provides that U.S. antitrust laws shall have a broad, extraterritorial reach. As discussed in *Chapter 40*, contracts, combinations, or conspiracies that restrain trade with foreign nations, as well as among the domestic States, are deemed illegal. Therefore, agreements among competitors to increase the cost of imports, as well as arrangements to exclude imports from U.S. domestic markets in exchange for agreements not to compete in other countries, clearly violate U.S. antitrust laws. The antitrust provisions are also designed to protect U.S. exports from privately imposed restrictions seeking to exclude U.S. competitors from foreign markets. Amendments to the Sherman Act and the Federal Trade Commission Act limit their application to unfair methods of competition that have a direct, substantial, and reasonably foreseeable effect on U.S. domestic commerce, U.S. import commerce, or U.S. export commerce. The U.S. Supreme Court has held that where price-fixing conduct significantly and adversely affects customers outside and inside the United States but the foreign injury is separate from the domestic injury, the Sherman Act does not apply to a claim based solely on the foreign injury. *Hoffmann-La Roche Ltd v. Empagran S.A.*, 542 U.S. 155 (2004).

The International Antitrust Enforcement Assistance Act of 1994 authorizes the Justice Department (DOJ) and the Federal Trade Commission (FTC) to enter into mutual assistance agreements with foreign antitrust authorities. Under such agreements, U.S. and foreign authorities may share, subject to certain restrictions, evidence of antitrust violations and provide each other with investigatory assistance. In 1995, the DOJ and the FTC issued the Antitrust Enforcement Guidelines for International Operations for businesses engaged in international operations. The guidelines address such topics as subject matter jurisdiction over conduct and entities outside the United States, mutual assistance in international antitrust enforcement, and the effects of foreign governmental involvement on the antitrust liability of private entities.

46-3f SECURITIES REGULATION

The securities markets have become increasingly internationalized, thereby raising questions regarding which country's law governs a particular transaction in securities. (U.S. Federal securities laws are discussed in *Chapter 43*.) Foreign issuers who issue securities in the United States must register them under the 1933 Act unless an exemption is available. Foreign issuers whose securities are sold in the secondary market in the United States must register under the 1934 Act unless the issuer is exempt. Some nonexempt foreign issuers may avoid registration under the 1934 Act by providing the Securities and Exchange Commission (SEC) with copies of all information material to investors that they have made public in their home country. Regulation S provides a safe harbor from the 1993 Act registration requirements for offshore sales of equity securities of U.S. issuers.

The antifraud provisions of the U.S. securities laws apply to securities sold by the use of any means or instrumentality of interstate commerce. In determining the extraterritorial application of these provisions, the lower courts had generally found jurisdiction in cases in which there was either *conduct* or *effects* in the United States relating to a violation of the Federal securities laws. In the 2010 case of *Morrison v. National Australia Bank Ltd.* (see Case 46-2), the U.S. Supreme Court rejected these cases, holding that Section 10(b) and Rule 10b-5 of the Securities Exchange Act of 1934 do not apply extraterritorially but *only* reach the use of a manipulative or deceptive device or contrivance in connection with (1) the purchase or sale of a security listed on a U.S. stock exchange or (2) the purchase or sale of any other security in the United States. The Supreme Court held that Section 10(b) and Rule 10b-5 do not provide a cause of action to foreign plaintiffs suing foreign or U.S. defendants for misconduct in connection with securities traded on foreign exchanges.

The Dodd-Frank Wall Street Reform and Consumer Protection Act of 2010 (Dodd-Frank Act), discussed in *Chapter 43*, extends the reach of the antifraud provisions of the 1933 and 1934 Acts with respect to actions brought by the U.S. Justice Department and the SEC. In such actions, jurisdiction would include "(1) conduct within the United States that constitutes significant steps in furtherance of the violation, even if the violation is committed by a foreign adviser and involves only foreign investors; or (2) conduct occurring outside the United States that has a foreseeable substantial effect within the United States." The Dodd-Frank Act also requires the SEC to study the extent to which private rights of action under the antifraud provisions of the 1934 Act should be governed by these new standards. On April 11, 2012, the SEC delivered to Congress its "Study on the Cross-Border Scope of the Private Right of Action Under Section 10(b) of the Securities Exchange Act of 1934," which provides several options but no specific recommendations. To date, Congress has not taken any action. Thus, the Dodd-Frank Act restores to the SEC and the Department of Justice—but not private litigants—the right to bring proceedings to enforce the antifraud provisions of the U.S. securities laws in cases with an extraterritorial component.

The International Organization of Securities Commissions has a membership of more than two hundred national securities agencies and exchanges, which regulate more than 95 percent of the world's securities markets. The member agencies have agreed (1) to cooperate to promote high standards of regulation to maintain just, efficient, and sound markets; (2) to exchange information to promote the development of domestic markets; (3) to work together to establish standards and effective surveillance of international securities transactions; and (4) to provide support to promote the integrity of the markets by a rigorous application of the standards and by effective enforcement against offenses.

♦ *See Case 46-2*

46-3g PROTECTION OF INTELLECTUAL PROPERTY

The U.S. laws protecting intellectual property (discussed in *Chapter 39*) for the most part do not apply to transactions in other countries. Generally, the owner of an intellectual property right must comply with each country's requirements to obtain from that country whatever protection is available. The requirements vary substantially from country to country, as does the degree of protection. Nevertheless, to a limited extent, U.S. intellectual property laws apply to certain conduct outside the United States depending upon the type of intellectual property. The Economic Espionage Act, as amended by the Defend Trade Secrets Act, applies to misappropriations of **trade secrets** even if the conduct occurs outside the United States if either (1) the offender is a U.S. citizen or organization or (2) an act in furtherance of the offense was committed in the United States. With respect to **trademarks**, the U.S. Supreme Court has held that the Lanham Act provides relief to a U.S. corporation against acts of trademark infringement consummated outside the United States by a citizen and resident of the United States who purchases parts in the United States and some of whose products, sold abroad, enter the United States where they may reflect adversely on the U.S. corporation's trade reputation. Under the Berne Convention, a U.S. **copyright** is given the same protection in each of the other treaty members as the member grants to the works of its own nationals. Moreover, the U.S. Copyright Act provides that importing a copy without permission violates the copyright owner's exclusive distribution right. See *Kirtsaeng v. John Wiley & Sons, Inc.*, in *Chapter 39*. Under the Patent Act, a company can be liable for **patent** infringement if it ships components of a patented invention overseas to be assembled there. A patent owner who proves infringement under this provision is entitled to recover damages. In a 7–2 decision, the U.S. Supreme Court held that these provisions allow the patent owner to recover for lost foreign profits. *WesternGeco LLC v. ION Geophysical Corp.*, 585 U. S. _____ (2018).

Moreover, the United States belongs to multinational treaties that try to coordinate the application of member nations' intellectual property laws.

The Trade-Related Aspects of Intellectual Property Rights (TRIPS) portion of the WTO Agreement states how the range of intellectual property should be protected when trade is involved. The WIPO, one of the specialized agencies of the United Nations, attempts to promote—through cooperation among nations—the protection of intellectual property throughout the world. WIPO administers twenty-six international treaties dealing with intellectual property protection and includes at least 193 states as members.

1. **Patents**. The principal treaties for patent protection are the Paris Convention for the Protection of Industrial Property (at least 177 nations), the Patent Cooperation Treaty (at least 152 nations), and the Patent Law Treaty (PLT) of 2000, which seeks to harmonize and streamline formal procedures in national and regional patent

applications and patents. The PLT is in force in at least forty-three nations.

2. **Trademarks**. International treaties protecting trademarks are the Paris Convention for the Protection of Industrial Property (at least 177 nations), the Arrangement of Nice Concerning the International Classification of Goods and Services (at least eighty-eight nations), the Madrid Protocol of 1989 (at least 108 nations), the 1973 Vienna Trademark Agreement (at least thirty-five nations), and the Trademark Law Treaty of 1994 (at least fifty-four nations). In 2002 Congress enacted legislation implementing the Madrid Protocol, a procedural agreement allowing U.S. trademark owners to file for registration in any number of more than ninety member countries by filing a single application in English and paying a single fee. The Trademark Law Treaty of 1994 seeks to streamline national and regional trademark registration procedures.

3. **Copyrights**. The principal treaties covering copyrights are the 1952 Universal Copyright Convention, revised in 1971, and the Berne Convention for the Protection of Literary and Artistic Works of 1886 (at least 179 nations). The World Intellectual Property Organization (WIPO) Copyright Treaty of 1996 is a special agreement under the Berne Convention, signed by at least 110 nations, which extended copyright protection to computer programs and compilations of data and granted new rights corresponding to new forms for works in the digital environment. The WIPO Performances and Phonograms Treaty of 1996, signed by at least 109 nations, deals with the rights of performers and producers of phonograms (the fixation of sounds other than in audiovisual works). The Marrakesh Treaty of 2013 administered by WIPO creates a set of mandatory limitations and exceptions for the benefit of the blind, visually impaired, and otherwise print disabled. It has been adopted by the United States and at least 79 other nations.

46-3h FOREIGN CORRUPT PRACTICES ACT

In 1977, Congress enacted the Foreign Corrupt Practices Act (FCPA) prohibiting any U.S. person, and certain foreign issuers of securities, from bribing foreign government or political officials to assist in obtaining or retaining business. Since 1998, the antibribery provisions also apply to foreign firms and persons who take any act in furtherance of such a corrupt payment while in the United States. The FCPA makes it unlawful for any U.S. person, and certain foreign issuers of securities, or any of its officers, directors, employees, or agents to offer or give anything of value directly or indirectly to any foreign official, political party, or political official for the purpose of (1) influencing any act or decision of that person or party in his or its official capacity, (2) inducing an act or omission in violation of his or its lawful duty, or (3) inducing such person or party to use his or its influence to affect a decision of a foreign government to assist the person in obtaining or retaining business. An offer or promise to make a prohibited payment is a violation even if the offer is not accepted or the promise is not performed. The 1988 amendments to the FCPA explicitly excluded routine government actions not involving the discretion of the official, such as obtaining permits or processing applications. This exclusion does *not* cover any decision by a foreign official whether, or on what terms, to award new business or to continue business with a particular party. The amendments also added an affirmative defense for payments that are lawful under the written laws or regulations of the foreign official's country.

Violations can result in fines of up to $2 million for corporations and other business entities; individuals may be fined a maximum of $100,000 or imprisoned up to five years or both. Section 32(c). Moreover, under the Alternative Fines Act, the actual fine may be up to twice the benefit that the person sought to obtain by making the corrupt payment. Fines imposed upon individuals may not be paid directly or indirectly by the corporation or other business entity on whose behalf the individuals acted. In addition, the courts may impose civil penalties of up to $21,663, as adjusted annually for inflation in March 2021.

In 1997, the United States signed the Organisation for Economic Co-operation and Development Convention on Combating Bribery of Foreign Public Officials in International Business Transactions (OECD Convention). The OECD Convention has been adopted by at least forty-four nations. In 1998, Congress enacted the International Anti-Bribery and Fair Competition Act of 1998 to conform the FCPA to the OECD Convention. The 1998 Act expands the FCPA to include (1) payments made to "secure any improper advantage" from foreign officials, (2) all foreign persons who commit an act in furtherance of a foreign bribe while in the United States, and (3) officials of public international organizations within the definition of a "foreign official." A public international organization is defined as either an organization designated by executive order pursuant to the International Organizations Immunities Act or any other international organization designated by executive order of the President.

The International Organization for Standardization (ISO) is an independent, nongovernmental international organization with a membership of at least 165 national standards bodies. In 2016, ISO issued the first-ever global standard for antibribery compliance programs. It specifies requirements and provides guidance for establishing, implementing, maintaining, reviewing, and improving an antibribery management system.

Practical Advice

Take care to instruct your employees and agents not to bribe foreign officials, political parties, or political officials. Moreover, train them to distinguish between bribes, which are prohibited, and nondiscretionary facilitating payments, which are permitted.

46-3i EMPLOYMENT DISCRIMINATION

Title VII of the Civil Rights Act of 1964, the Americans with Disabilities Act, and the Age Discrimination in Employment Act, discussed in *Chapter 42*, apply to U.S. citizens employed abroad by U.S. employers or by foreign companies controlled by U.S. employers. Employers, however, are not required to comply with these employment discrimination laws if compliance would violate the law of the foreign country in which the workplace is located.

46-3j BANKRUPTCY

Enacted in 2005, Chapter 15 of the U.S. Bankruptcy Code covers cross-border (transnational) insolvencies and incorporates the Model Law on Cross-Border Insolvency, promulgated by the United Nations Commission on International Trade Law (UNCITRAL). The UNCITRAL Model Law has also been adopted in at least forty-eight other countries including Australia, Canada, Great Britain, Israel, Japan, Korea, Mexico, Singapore, and New Zealand.

The purpose of Chapter 15 is to provide effective mechanisms for dealing with cases of cross-border insolvency; that is, cases with debtors, assets, claimants, and other parties of interest involving more than one country. Chapter 15 specifies five objectives: (1) cooperation of the courts, trustees, and debtors in the United States with the courts and other competent authorities of foreign countries involved in cross-border insolvency cases; (2) greater legal certainty for trade and investment; (3) fair and efficient administration of cross-border insolvencies that protects the interests of all creditors and other interested entities, including the debtor; (4) protection and maximization of the value of the debtor's assets; and (5) facilitation of the rescue of financially troubled businesses, thereby protecting investment and preserving employment.

Chapter 15 allows proceedings for a foreign debtor or other related parties to access U.S. Bankruptcy Courts. Generally, a Chapter 15 case is ancillary (secondary) to a primary proceeding brought in another country, typically the debtor's home country. As an alternative, in some circumstances, the debtor or a creditor may commence a Chapter 7 or Chapter 11 case in the United States.

46-4 Forms of Multinational Enterprises

The term *multinational enterprise* (MNE) refers to any business that engages in transactions involving the movement of goods, information, money, people, or services across national borders. Such an enterprise may conduct its business in any of several forms: direct sales, foreign agents, distributorships, licensing, joint ventures, and wholly owned subsidiaries. A number of considerations determine the form of business organization that would be best for conducting international transactions. These factors include financing, tax consequences, legal restrictions imposed by the host country, and the degree to which the MNE wishes to control the business.

46-4a DIRECT EXPORT SALES

Under a direct export sale, the seller contracts directly with the buyer in the other country. This is the simplest and least involved MNE.

46-4b FOREIGN AGENTS

An agency relationship often is used by MNEs seeking limited involvement in an international market. The principal firm will appoint a local agent, who may be empowered to enter into contracts in the agent's country on behalf of the principal or who may be authorized only to solicit and take orders. The agent generally does not take title to the merchandise.

46-4c DISTRIBUTORSHIPS

A commonly used form of MNE is the distributorship, in which a producer of goods appoints a foreign distributor. Unlike an agent, a distributor takes title to the merchandise it receives; consequently, the distributor, not the producer, bears many of the risks connected with commercial sales. By its very format, the distributorship is especially susceptible to antitrust violations. Therefore, both the producer and the distributor must take special care to ensure that the arrangement does not violate the antitrust laws of their respective governments.

46-4d LICENSING

An MNE wishing to exploit an intellectual property right, such as a patent, a trademark, a trade secret, or an unpatented but innovative production technology, may choose to sell the right to use such property to a foreign company rather than enter the foreign market itself. The sale of such rights, called licensing, is one of the major means by which technology and information are transferred among nations. Normally, the foreign firm will pay royalties in exchange for the information, technology, or patent. Franchising is a form of licensing in which the owner of intellectual property grants permission to a foreign business under carefully specified conditions.

46-4e JOINT VENTURES

In a joint venture, two or more independent businesses from different countries agree to coordinate their efforts to achieve a common result. The sharing of profits and liabilities, as well as the delegation of responsibilities, is fixed by contract. One advantage of the joint venture is that each company can be assigned responsibility for that which it does best. To promote local ownership of investments, a number of developing nations and regional groups have enacted legislation that prohibits foreign businesses from owning more than 49 percent of any business enterprise in those countries. In addition, each country may require that its citizens make up a majority of the management of an enterprise.

46-4f WHOLLY OWNED SUBSIDIARIES

By far, wholly owned subsidiaries require the most active participation by a parent firm. Nevertheless, creating a foreign wholly owned subsidiary corporation can offer a business numerous advantages, most significantly, the ability to retain authority and control over all phases of operation. This is especially attractive to businesses wishing to safeguard their technology.

CHAPTER SUMMARY

THE INTERNATIONAL ENVIRONMENT	**International Law** includes law that deals with the conduct and relations of nation states and international organizations as well as some of their relations with persons; such law is enforceable by the courts of a nation that has adopted the international law as domestic law **International Court of Justice** judicial branch of the United Nations having voluntary jurisdiction over nations **Regional Trade Communities** international organizations, conferences, and treaties focusing on business and trade regulation; the European Union (EU) and the United States-Mexico-Canada Agreement (USMCA) are the most prominent of these **International Treaties** agreements between or among independent nations, such as the General Agreement on Tariffs and Trade (GATT), now called the World Trade Organization (WTO), and the United Nations Convention on the Law of the Sea (UNCLOS) • *World Trade Organization (WTO)* global international organization dealing with the rules of trade among nations • *United Nations Convention on the Law of the Sea (UNCLOS)* establishes a comprehensive set of rules governing all uses of the oceans and their resources
JURISDICTION OVER ACTIONS OF FOREIGN GOVERNMENTS	**Sovereign Immunity** foreign country's freedom from a host country's laws **Act of State Doctrine** rule that a court should not question the validity of actions taken by a foreign government in its own country **Taking of Foreign Investment Property** • *Expropriation* governmental taking of foreign-owned property for a public purpose and with payment of just compensation • *Confiscation* governmental taking of foreign-owned property without payment (or for a highly inadequate payment) or for a nonpublic purpose
TRANSACTING BUSINESS ABROAD	**Flow of Trade** controlled by trade barriers on imports and exports • *Tariff* duty or tax imposed on goods moving into or out of a country • *Nontariff Barriers* include quotas, bans, safety standards, and subsidies **Flow of Labor** controlled through passport, visa, and immigration regulations **Flow of Capital** the International Monetary Fund facilitates the expansion and balanced growth of international trade, assists in eliminating foreign exchange restrictions, and smooths the international balance of payments

International Contracts involve additional issues beyond those in domestic contracts, such as differences in language, legal systems, and currency

- *CISG* United Nations Convention on Contracts for the International Sales of Goods governs all contracts for international sales of goods between parties located in different nations that have ratified the CISG
- *Letter of Credit* bank's promise to pay the seller, provided certain conditions are met; used to manage the payment risks in international trade

Antitrust Laws U.S. antitrust laws apply to unfair methods of competition that have a direct, substantial, and reasonably foreseeable effect on the domestic, import, or export commerce of the United States

Securities Regulation foreign issuers who issue securities, or whose securities are sold in the secondary market, in the United States must register them unless an exemption is available

Protection of Intellectual Property the owner of an intellectual property right must comply with each country's requirement to obtain from that country whatever protection is available

Foreign Corrupt Practices Act prohibits all U.S. persons, and certain foreign issuers of securities, from bribing foreign government or political officials to assist in obtaining or retaining business

Employment Discrimination Title VII of the Civil Rights Act of 1964, the Americans with Disabilities Act, and the Age Discrimination in Employment Act apply to U.S. citizens employed in foreign countries by U.S.-owned or U.S.-controlled companies

Bankruptcy Chapter 15 of the U.S. Bankruptcy Code provides mechanisms for dealing with cases of cross-border insolvency; that is, cases with debtors, assets, claimants, or other parties of interest involving more than one country

---

FORMS OF MULTINATIONAL ENTERPRISES (MNE)

Definition any business that engages in transactions involving the movement of goods, information, money, people, or services across national borders

Forms of MNE the choice of form depends on a number of factors, including financing considerations, tax consequences, and degree of control

- *Direct Export Sales* seller contracts directly with the buyer in the other country
- *Foreign Agents* a local agent in the host country is used to provide limited involvement for an MNE
- *Distributorship* MNE sells to a foreign distributor who takes title to the merchandise
- *Licensing* MNE sells a foreign company the right to use technology or information
- *Joint Ventures* two independent businesses from different countries share profits, liabilities, and duties
- *Wholly Owned Subsidiary* enables an MNE to retain control and authority over all phases of operation

CASES

Sovereign Immunity
OBB PERSONENVERKEHR AG v. SACHS

Supreme Court of the United States, 2015
577 U.S. 27, 136 S.Ct. 390, 193 L. Ed. 2d 269

Roberts, C. J.

The Foreign Sovereign Immunities Act shields foreign states and their agencies from suit in United States courts unless the suit falls within one of the Act's specifically enumerated exceptions. This case concerns the scope of the commercial activity exception, which withdraws sovereign immunity in any case "in which the action is based upon a commercial activity carried on in the United States by [a] foreign state." 28 U.S.C. §1605(a)(2).

[Plaintiff] Carol Sachs is a resident of California who purchased in the United States a Eurail pass for rail travel in Europe. She suffered traumatic personal injuries when she fell onto the tracks at the Innsbruck, Austria, train station while attempting to board a train operated by the Austrian state-owned railway. She sued the railway in Federal District Court, arguing that her suit was not barred by sovereign immunity because it is "based upon" the railway's sale of the pass to her in the United States. * * *

[Defendant] OBB Personenverkehr AG (OBB) operates a railway that carries nearly 235 million passengers each year on routes within Austria and to and from points beyond Austria's frontiers. OBB is wholly owned by OBB Holding Group, a joint-stock company created by the Republic of Austria. OBB Holding Group in turn is wholly owned by the Austrian Federal Ministry of Transport, Innovation, and Technology. [Citation.]

OBB—along with 29 other railways throughout Europe—is a member of the Eurail Group, an association responsible for the marketing and management of the Eurail pass program. [Citation.] Eurail passes allow their holders unlimited passage for a set period of time on participating Eurail Group railways. They are available only to non-Europeans, who may purchase them both directly from the Eurail Group and indirectly through a worldwide network of travel agents. [Citation.]

Carol Sachs is a resident of Berkeley, California. In March 2007, she purchased a Eurail pass over the Internet from The Rail Pass Experts, a Massachusetts-based travel agent. The following month, Sachs arrived at the Innsbruck train station, planning to use her Eurail pass to ride an OBB train to Prague. As she attempted to board the train, Sachs fell from the platform onto the tracks. OBB's moving train crushed her legs, both of which had to be amputated above the knee. [Citation.]

Sachs sued OBB in the United States District Court for the Northern District of California, asserting five causes of action: (1) negligence; (2) strict liability for design defects in the train and platform; (3) strict liability for failure to warn of those design defects; (4) breach of an implied warranty of merchantability for providing a train and platform unsafe for their intended uses; and (5) breach of an implied warranty of fitness for providing a train and platform unfit for their intended uses. [Citation.] OBB claimed sovereign immunity and moved to dismiss the suit for lack of subject matter jurisdiction. [Citation.]

The Foreign Sovereign Immunities Act "provides the sole basis for obtaining jurisdiction over a foreign state in the courts of this country." [Citation.] The Act defines "foreign state" to include a state "agency or instrumentality," 28 U.S.C. §1603(a), and both parties agree that OBB qualifies as a "foreign state" for purposes of the Act. OBB is therefore "presumptively immune from the jurisdiction of United States courts" unless one of the Act's express exceptions to sovereign immunity applies. [Citation.] Sachs argues that her suit falls within the Act's commercial activity exception, which provides in part that a foreign state does not enjoy immunity when "the action is based upon a commercial activity carried on in the United States by the foreign state." §1605(a)(2).

The District Court concluded that Sachs's suit did not fall within §1605(a)(2) and therefore granted OBB's motion to dismiss. [Citation.] A divided panel of the United States Court of Appeals for the Ninth Circuit affirmed. [Citation.] The full court ordered rehearing en banc and, with three judges dissenting, reversed the panel decision. [Citation.]

* * *

[The full court found that the sale of the Eurail pass in the United States formed an essential element of each of Sachs's claims and thus concluded that each claim was "based upon a commercial activity carried on in the United States" by OBB.]

We granted certiorari. [Citation.]

OBB contends that the sale of the Eurail pass is not attributable to the railway, reasoning that the Foreign Sovereign Immunities Act does not allow attribution through principles found in the common law of agency. OBB also argues that even if such attribution were allowed under the Act, Sachs's suit is not "based upon" the sale of the Eurail pass for purposes of §1605(a)(2). We agree with OBB on the second point and therefore do not reach the first.

The Act itself does not elaborate on the phrase "based upon." Our decision in *Saudi Arabia v. Nelson*, [citation], however, provides sufficient guidance to resolve this case. In *Nelson*, a husband and wife brought suit against Saudi Arabia and its state-owned hospital, seeking damages for intentional and negligent torts stemming from the husband's allegedly wrongful arrest, imprisonment, and torture by Saudi police while he was employed at a hospital in Saudi Arabia. [Citation.] The Saudi defendants claimed sovereign immunity under the Act, arguing * * * that §1605(a)(2) was inapplicable because the suit was "based upon" sovereign acts—the exercise of Saudi police authority—and not upon commercial activity. [Citation.] The Nelsons countered that their suit was "based upon" the defendants' commercial activities in "recruit[ing] Scott Nelson for work at the hospital, sign[ing] an employment contract with him, and subsequently employ[ing] him." [Citation.] We rejected the Nelsons' arguments.

The Act's "based upon" inquiry, we reasoned, first requires a court to "identify[] the particular conduct on which the [plaintiff's] action is 'based.'" [Citation.] Considering dictionary definitions and lower court decisions, we explained that a court should identify that "particular conduct" by looking to the "basis" or "foundation" for a claim, [citation], "those elements … that, if proven, would entitle a plaintiff to relief," [citation], and "the 'gravamen of the complaint,'" [citation]. Under that analysis, we found that the commercial activities, while they "led to the conduct that eventually injured the Nelsons," were not the particular conduct upon which their suit was based. The suit was instead based upon the Saudi sovereign acts that actually injured them. [Citation.] The Nelsons' suit therefore did not fit within §1605(a)(2). [Citation.]

The Ninth Circuit held that Sachs's claims were "based upon" the sale of the Eurail pass because the sale of the pass provided "*an element*" of each of her claims. [Citation.] Under *Nelson*, however, the mere fact that the sale of the Eurail pass would establish a single element of a claim is insufficient to demonstrate that the claim is "based upon" that sale for purposes of §1605(a)(2).

The Ninth Circuit apparently derived its one-element test from an overreading of one part of one sentence in *Nelson*, in which we observed that "the phrase ['based upon'] is read most naturally to mean those elements of a claim that, if proven, would entitle a plaintiff to relief under his theory of the case." [Citation.] We do not see how that mention of elements—plural—could be considered an endorsement of a *one*-element test, nor how the particular element the Ninth Circuit singled out for each of Sachs's claims could be construed to entitle her to relief.

* * *

* * * the conduct constituting the gravamen of Sachs's suit plainly occurred abroad. All of her claims turn on the same tragic episode in Austria, allegedly caused by wrongful conduct and dangerous conditions in Austria, which led to injuries suffered in Austria.

Sachs maintains that some of those claims are not limited to negligent conduct or unsafe conditions in Austria, but rather involve at least some wrongful action in the United States. Her strict liability claim for failure to warn, for example, alleges that OBB should have alerted her to the dangerous conditions at the Innsbruck train station when OBB sold the Eurail pass to her *in the United States*. Under any theory of the case that Sachs presents, however, there is nothing wrongful about the sale of the Eurail pass standing alone. Without the existence of the unsafe boarding conditions in Innsbruck, there would have been nothing to warn Sachs about when she bought the Eurail pass. However Sachs frames her suit, the incident in Innsbruck remains at its foundation.

* * *

We therefore conclude that Sachs has failed to demonstrate that her suit falls within the commercial activity exception in §1605(a)(2). OBB has sovereign immunity under the Act, and accordingly the courts of the United States lack jurisdiction over the suit.

The judgment of the United States Court of Appeals for the Ninth Circuit is reversed.

CASE
46-2

Securities Regulation
MORRISON v. NATIONAL AUSTRALIA BANK LTD.
Supreme Court of the United States, 2010
561 U.S. 130 S.Ct. 2869, 177 L.Ed.2d 535

Scalia, J.
[Respondent National Australia Bank Limited (National) was the largest bank in Australia. Its ordinary shares (common stock) are not traded on any exchange in the United States. National's American Depositary Receipts (ADRs), which represent the right to receive a specified number of National's ordinary

shares, however, are listed on the New York Stock Exchange. In February 1998, National bought respondent HomeSide Lending, Inc., a mortgage servicing company headquartered in Florida. HomeSide's business was to receive fees for servicing mortgages. The rights to receive those fees, so-called mortgage servicing rights, can provide a valuable income stream. How valuable each of the rights is depends, in part, on the likelihood that the mortgage to which it applies will be fully repaid before it is due, terminating the need for servicing. HomeSide calculated the present value of its mortgage servicing rights by using valuation models designed to take this likelihood into account. It recorded the value of its assets, and the numbers appeared in National's financial statements. From 1998 until 2001, National's annual reports and other public documents touted the success of HomeSide's business, and senior executives of National and HomeSide did the same in public statements. But on July 5, 2001, National announced that it was writing down the value of HomeSide's assets by $450 million and then again on September 3 by an additional $1.75 billion. The prices of both ordinary shares and ADRs declined.

Petitioners Russell Leslie Owen and Brian and Geraldine Silverlock, all Australians, purchased National's ordinary shares in 2000 and 2001, before the write-downs. They sued National, HomeSide, National's CEO, and three HomeSide executives in the United States District Court for alleged violations of Sections 10(b) and 20(a) of the Securities and Exchange Act of 1934. According to the complaint, Home-Side and three of its executive officers had manipulated HomeSide's financial models to make the rates of early repayment unrealistically low in order to cause the mortgage servicing rights to appear more valuable than they really were. The complaint also alleges that National and its CEO were aware of this deception by July 2000 but did nothing about it. Respondents moved to dismiss for lack of subject matter jurisdiction * * * and for failure to state a claim on which relief can be granted * * *. The District Court granted the motion to dismiss for lack of subject matter jurisdiction. The Court of Appeals for the Second Circuit affirmed on similar grounds. The U.S. Supreme Court granted *certiorari*.] Before addressing the question presented, we must correct a threshold error in the Second Circuit's analysis. It considered the extraterritorial reach of §10(b) to raise a question of subject-matter jurisdiction, wherefore it affirmed the District Court's dismissal * * *. [Citation.]

* * *

* * * The District Court here had [subject-matter] jurisdiction * * * to adjudicate the question whether §10(b) applies to National's conduct.

* * * Since nothing in the analysis of the courts below turned on the mistake, * * * we proceed to address whether petitioners' allegations state a claim.

It is a "longstanding principle of American law 'that legislation of Congress, unless a contrary intent appears, is meant to apply only within the territorial jurisdiction of the United States.'" [Citation.] * * * When a statute gives no clear indication of an extraterritorial application, it has none.

* * *

Rule 10b-5, the regulation under which petitioners have brought suit, was promulgated under §10(b), and "does not extend beyond conduct encompassed by §10(b)'s prohibition."

[Citation.] Therefore, if §10(b) is not extraterritorial, neither is Rule 10b-5.

On its face, §10(b) contains nothing to suggest it applies abroad. * * *

* * *

In short, there is no affirmative indication in the Exchange Act that §10(b) applies extraterritorially, and we therefore conclude that it does not.

Petitioners argue that the conclusion that §10(b) does not apply extraterritorially does not resolve this case. They contend that they seek no more than domestic application anyway, since Florida is where HomeSide and its senior executives engaged in the deceptive conduct of manipulating HomeSide's financial models; their complaint also alleged that Race and Hughes made misleading public statements there. * * *

* * * [W]e think that the focus of the Exchange Act is not upon the place where the deception originated, but upon purchases and sales of securities in the United States. Section 10(b) does not punish deceptive conduct, but only deceptive conduct "in connection with the purchase or sale of any security registered on a national securities exchange or any security not so registered." [Citations.] Those purchase-and-sale transactions are the objects of the statute's solicitude. It is those transactions that the statute seeks to "regulate," [citation]; it is parties or prospective parties to those transactions that the statute seeks to "protec[t]," [citation]. [Citation.] And it is in our view only transactions in securities listed on domestic exchanges, and domestic transactions in other securities, to which §10(b) applies.

* * *

* * * The probability of incompatibility with the applicable laws of other countries is so obvious that if Congress intended such foreign application "it would have addressed the subject of conflicts with foreign laws and procedures." [Citation.] Like the United States, foreign countries regulate their domestic securities exchanges and securities transactions occurring within their territorial jurisdiction. And the regulation of other countries often differs from ours as to what constitutes fraud, what disclosures must be made, what damages are recoverable, what discovery is available in litigation, what individual actions may be joined in a single suit, what attorney's fees are recoverable, and many other matters. * * *

* * *

Section 10(b) reaches the use of a manipulative or deceptive device or contrivance only in connection with the purchase or sale of a security listed on an American stock exchange, and the purchase or sale of any other security in the United States. This case involves no securities listed on a domestic exchange, and all aspects of the purchases complained of by those petitioners who still have live claims occurred outside the United States. Petitioners have therefore failed to state a claim on which relief can be granted. We affirm the dismissal of petitioners' complaint on this ground.

QUESTIONS

1. Three banks that are wholly owned by the Republic of Costa Rica had issued promissory notes, payable in U.S. dollars in New York City. The notes are now in default due solely to actions of the Costa Rican government, which had suspended all payments of external debt because of escalating economic problems. Efforts by Costa Rica to curb foreign debt payment difficulties conflicted with U.S. policy for debt resolution procedure as conducted under the auspices of the International Monetary Fund. A syndicate of U.S. banks brought suit to recover on the promissory notes. The three Costa Rican banks assert the act of state doctrine as a defense. Should the doctrine apply? Explain.

2. Six U.S. manufacturers of broad-spectrum antibiotics derived a large percentage of their sales from overseas markets, including India, Iran, the Philippines, Spain, the Republic of Korea, Germany, Colombia, and Kuwait. The manufacturers agreed to a common plan of marketing, whereby territories were divided and prices for products were set. The members of the plan also agreed not to grant foreign producers licenses to the manufacturing technology of any of their "big money" drugs. May the above foreign countries recover treble damages for violation of the U.S. antitrust laws? Why or why not?

3. After reading attractive brochures advertising a package tour of the Dominican Republic, a U.S. family decided to purchase tickets for the family vacation plan. The tour was a product of four different business entities, two domestic (U.S.) and two foreign. Sheraton Hotels & Inns, World Corporation, was to provide food and lodging; Dominicana Airlines, wholly owned by the government of the Dominican Republic, which routinely flew into Miami International Airport and sold tickets within the United States, was to provide round-trip air transportation and "tourist cards" necessary for entry into the Dominican Republic; and two U.S. firms organized and sold the tour. Problems for the family began when their Dominicana flight landed in the Dominican Republic and immigration officials denied them entry. Forced to leave, the family was shuttled first to Puerto Rico and then to Haiti, where they had to secure their own passage back to the United States at additional expense. The family brings suit for battery, false imprisonment, breach of warranty, and breach of contract against all four business entities. The Dominicana Airlines asserts the act of state doctrine as a defense. Explain whether this defense applies in this situation.

4. A privately owned business in a developing country determines that current computer technology could solve many of the problems faced by its country's private and public sectors. This business, however, lacks the capital resources necessary for research and development to acquire such computer technology, even if trained personnel were available. Furthermore, despite a sense of patriotism, the business concludes that its national government could not efficiently or effectively handle such a development project. What business forms are available to this business for acquiring sophisticated computer technology? Discuss the advantages and problems inherent in the various options?

5. King Faisal II of Iraq was killed on July 14, 1958, in the midst of a revolution in that country that led to the establishment of a republic subsequently recognized by the U.S. government. On July 19, 1958, the new republic issued a decree that all property of the former ruling dynasty, regardless of location, should be confiscated. Subsequently, the Republic of Iraq brought suit in the United States to obtain possession of money and stocks deposited in the deceased king's U.S. bank account in New York City. Explain whether Iraq will be able to collect the funds.

6. A business entity incorporated under the laws of one of the European Union (EU) member nations contracts with the government of a developing nation to form a joint venture for the mining and refining of a scarce raw material used by several industrial nations in the manufacture of highly sensitive weapons systems. The contract calls for the EU-based corporation to invest money and technology that will be used to build permanent refinery plants that eventually will revert to the developing nation. The developing nation also reserves the right to set quotas on sales of this scarce resource and to choose the destination of exports. Due to political conflicts, the developing nation refuses to allow any exports of the scarce material to the United States. This causes a sharp price increase in exports to the United States by other suppliers. The United States asserts antitrust violations against the EU-based corporation for the effects produced within the United States. Should the United States succeed? Explain.

CASE PROBLEMS

7. A Panamanian corporation lends money to a Turkish enterprise, which issues a promissory note. The loan contract specifies that payment on the interest and principal shall be made to the Chemical Bank of New York City, where both parties maintain accounts. The loan contract contains no choice of law designation, but the Panamanian and Turkish companies have referred to the Chemical Bank in New York as their "legal address." As a result of a contractual performance dispute, the Turkish company suspends payments on the loan. The Panamanian corporation then brings suit in the United States to recover the balance of the payments due. Explain what possible options for choice of law apply?

8. New England Petroleum Corporation (NEPCO), a New York corporation, was in the business of selling fuel oil in the United States. PETCO, a refinery incorporated in the Bahamas, was a wholly owned subsidiary of NEPCO. In 1968, PETCO entered into a long-term contract to purchase crude oil from Chevron Oil Trading (COT), which held 50 percent of an oil concession in Libya. In 1973, Libya nationalized COT and several other foreign-owned oil concessions, thereby forcing COT to terminate its contract with PETCO. To secure needed oil supplies, PETCO entered into a new contract with National Oil Corporation (NOC), which was wholly owned by the Libyan government. This contract was at a substantially higher price than the original contract with COT. The following month, Libya declared an oil embargo on exports to the United States, the Netherlands, and the Bahamas. Accordingly, NOC canceled its contracts with PETCO. After oil prices rose dramatically, NOC accepted bids for new contracts to replace the ones inactivated by the embargo. NEPCO brought suit in a U.S. district court against the Libyan government and NOC, alleging breach of contract. Does the district court have jurisdiction? Explain.

9. Nigeria, experiencing an economic boom due to exports of high-grade oil, embarked on an infrastructure development plan. Accordingly, Nigeria entered into at least 109 contracts with 68 suppliers for the purchase of cement at a price of almost $1 billion. Among the contracting suppliers were four U.S. corporations, including Texas Trading & Milling Corporation. Nigeria misjudged the cement market (having anticipated only a 20 percent fulfillment rate) and was forced to repudiate most of the contracts. Texas Trading & Milling Corporation and three other American companies

brought suit, alleging anticipatory breach of contract. Nigeria claimed immunity under the Foreign Sovereign Immunities Act. Is Nigeria's claim correct? Explain.

10. Prior to 1918, a Russian corporation had deposited sums of money with August Belmont, a private banker doing business in New York City. In 1918, the Soviet government nationalized the corporation and appropriated all of the corporation's property and assets, including the deposit account with Belmont. The deposit became the property of the Soviet government until 1933, when it was released and assigned to the U.S. government as part of an international compact between the United States and the former Soviet Union. The purpose of this arrangement was to bring about a final settlement of the claims and counterclaims between the two countries. The United States brought an action to recover the deposit from Belmont. Belmont resists, arguing that the act of nationalization by the Soviets was a confiscation prohibited by the Fifth Amendment to the U.S. Constitution and was also a violation of New York public policy. Explain who will prevail.

11. A Federal grand jury handed down an indictment naming as a defendant Nippon Paper Industries Co., Ltd. (NPI), a Japanese manufacturer of facsimile paper. The indictment alleged that five years earlier, NPI and certain unnamed coconspirators held a number of meetings in Japan, which culminated in an agreement to fix the price of thermal fax paper throughout North America. NPI and other manufacturers who were involved in the scheme purportedly accomplished their objective by selling the paper in Japan to unaffiliated trading houses on the condition that the latter charge specified (inflated) prices for the paper when they resold it in North America. The trading houses then shipped and sold the paper to their subsidiaries in the United States, which in turn sold it to U.S. consumers at inflated prices. The indictment further states that to ensure the success of the venture, NPI monitored the paper trail and confirmed that the prices charged to end users were those that it had arranged. The indictment maintains that these activities had a substantial adverse effect on commerce in the United States and unreasonably restrained trade in violation of the Sherman Act. Does the Sherman Act apply to this conduct? Explain.

12. American Rice, Inc. ("ARI"), is a Houston-based company that exports rice to foreign countries, including Haiti. Rice Corporation of Haiti ("RCH"), a wholly

owned subsidiary of ARI, was incorporated in Haiti to represent ARI's interests and deal with third parties there. As an aspect of Haiti's standard importation procedure, its customs officials assess duties based on the quantity and value of rice imported into the country. Haiti also requires businesses that deliver rice there to remit an advance deposit against Haitian sales taxes, based on the value of that rice, for which deposit a credit is eventually allowed on Haitian sales tax returns when filed. The United States indicted David Kay and Douglas Murphy, both officers of ARI, for violation of the Foreign Corrupt Practices Act (FCPA). The indictment detailed how Kay and Murphy allegedly orchestrated the bribing of Haitian customs officials to accept false bills of lading and other documentation that intentionally understated by one-third the quantity of rice shipped to Haiti, thereby significantly reducing ARI's customs duties and sales taxes. The defendants argue that bribes paid to obtain favorable tax treatment are not payments made to "obtain or retain business" within the FCPA and thus are not within the scope of that statute's proscription of foreign bribery. Does the FCPA apply to this conduct? Explain.

TAKING SIDES

The Commercial Office of Spain hired Enrique Segni to develop a market for Spanish wines in the U.S. Midwest. The Commercial Office is an arm of the Spanish government. Seven months later, Segni was fired, whereupon he filed a lawsuit in a U.S. district court charging that the Commercial Office had breached the contract and seeking payment for the remainder of the contract term as damages. The Commercial Office moved for dismissal, claiming immunity from suit under the terms of the Foreign Sovereign Immunities Act (FSIA).

a. What are the arguments that Spain is immune from suit under the FSIA?

b. What are the arguments that Spain is *not* immune from suit under the FSIA?

c. Explain which party should prevail.

Property

CH 47 INTRODUCTION TO PROPERTY,
PROPERTY INSURANCE,
BAILMENTS, AND DOCUMENTS
OF TITLE

CH 48 INTERESTS IN REAL PROPERTY

CH 49 TRANSFER AND CONTROL
OF REAL PROPERTY

CH 50 TRUSTS AND DECEDENTS'
ESTATES

CHAPTER 47

Introduction to Property, Property Insurance, Bailments, and Documents of Title

CHAPTER OUTCOMES

After reading and studying this chapter, you should be able to:

- Define (1) tangible and intangible property, (2) real and personal property, and (3) a fixture.

- Explain (1) the ways to transfer title to personal property; (2) the three elements of a valid gift; and (3) the difference in the law's treatment of abandoned property, lost property, and mislaid property.

- With respect to property insurance, explain (1) the different types of fires, (2) insurance clauses,

(3) other insurance clauses, (4) insurable interest, (5) valued and open policies, and (6) the defenses of misrepresentation, breach of warranty, concealment, waiver, and estoppel.

- Explain (1) the essential elements of a bailment and (2) the rights and duties of the bailor and bailee.

- Explain (1) what a document of title is and (2) the various types of documents of title.

Although many U.S. rules of property stem directly from English law, in the United States, property occupies a unique status because of the protection expressly granted it by the U.S. Constitution and by most State constitutions as well. The Fifth Amendment to the Federal Constitution provides that "No person shall be … deprived of life, liberty, or property, without due process of law; nor shall private property be taken for public use, without just compensation." The Fourteenth Amendment contains a similar requirement: "No State shall … deprive any person of life, liberty, or property, without due process of law." Under the police power, however, this protection afforded to property owners is subject to regulation for the public good.

The first part of this chapter provides a general introduction to the law governing real and personal property. The second part of this chapter deals specifically with personal property; the third part covers property insurance. The fourth part of the chapter covers bailments,

and the last part of the chapter discusses documents of title.

INTRODUCTION TO PROPERTY AND PERSONAL PROPERTY

Property is a legally protected interest or group of interests. It is valuable only because our law provides that certain consequences follow from the ownership of it. The right to use property, to sell it, and to control to whom it shall pass on the death of the owner are all included within the term *property*. Thus, a person who speaks of "owning property" may have one of two ideas in mind: (1) the *physical thing itself*, as when a homeowner says, "I just bought a piece of property in Oakland," meaning complete ownership of a physically identifiable parcel of land, or (2) a *right or interest* in a physical object (e.g., with respect to land, a tenant under a lease has a property interest in the leased land, although he does not own the land).

47-1 Kinds of Property

Property may be classified as (1) tangible or intangible and (2) real or personal, but these classifications are not mutually exclusive.

47-1a TANGIBLE AND INTANGIBLE

Tangible property is a legally protected interest in *physical* objects such as a farm, a chair, and a household pet. **Intangible property**, in contrast, is a legally protected interest in things that do not exist in a physical form. For example, the rights represented by a stock certificate, a promissory note, and a deed granting Jones a right-of-way over Smith's land are intangible property. Each represents certain rights that defy reduction to physical possession but have a legal reality in that the courts will protect them.

The same item may be the object of both tangible and intangible property rights. Suppose Ann purchases a book published by Brown & Sons. On the first page is the statement "Copyright 2021 by Brown & Sons." Ann owns the volume she has purchased. She has the right to exclusive physical possession and use of that particular copy. It is tangible property of which she is the owner. Brown & Sons, however, has the exclusive right to publish copies of the book, a right granted to the publisher by the copyright laws. The courts will protect this intangible property of Brown & Sons, as well as Ann's tangible property right to her particular volume.

47-1b REAL AND PERSONAL

The most significant practical distinction between types of property is the classification into real and personal property. To define this distinction simply, land and all interests in it are **real property** (also called realty), and every other thing or interest identified as property is **personal property** (also called chattel). This easy description encompasses most property, with the exception of certain physical objects that are personal property under most circumstances but that may, because of their attachment to land or their use in connection with land, become a form of real property called fixtures.

47-1c FIXTURES

As noted, a **fixture** is an article or piece of property that was formerly treated as personal property but has been attached in such a manner to land or a building that it is now designated as real property even though it retains its original identity. The intent of the parties to convert the property to real property from personal property is usually shown by the permanent manner of affixation or the adaptation of the affixed object to the property. For example, building materials are clearly personal property; however, when worked into a building as its construction progresses, such materials become real property, as buildings are a part of the land they occupy. Thus, clay in its natural state is, of course, real property; when made into bricks, it becomes personal property; and if the bricks are then built into the wall of a house, the "clay" once again becomes real property.

Although doing so may be difficult, determining whether various items are personal property or real property may be the only way to settle certain conflicting ownership claims. Unless otherwise provided by agreement, personal property remains the property of the person who placed it on the real estate. On the other hand, property that has been affixed so as to become a fixture (an actual part of the real estate) becomes the property of the real estate owner.

In determining whether personal property has become a fixture, the intention of the parties, as expressed in their agreement, will control the settlement of conflicting claims. In the absence of an agreement, the following factors are relevant in determining whether any particular item is a fixture:

1. the physical relationship of the item to the land or building;
2. the intention of the person who attached the item to the land or building;
3. the purpose the item serves in relation to the land or building and in relation to the person who brought it there; and
4. the interest of that person in the land or building at the time of the item's attachment.

Although physical attachment is significant, a more important test is whether the item can be removed without causing material injury to the land or building on the land. If it cannot be so removed, the item is generally held to have become part of the realty.

Practical Advice

Specify in your contracts for the sale of real estate which fixtures stay with the property and which fixtures may be removed by the seller.

By comparison, the test of purpose or use applies only if the item (1) is affixed to the realty in some way but (2) can be removed without material injury to the realty. In such a situation, if the use or purpose of the item is peculiar to a particular owner or occupant of the premises, the courts will tend to let him remove the item when he leaves. Accordingly, in the law of landlord and tenant, the tenant may remove trade fixtures (i.e., items used in connection with a trade but not intended to become part of the realty), provided that she

FIGURE 47-1 Kinds of Property

	Personal	Real
Tangible	Goods	Land Buildings Fixtures
Intangible	Negotiable instruments Stock certificates Contract rights Copyrights Patents	Leases Easements Mortgages

can accomplish this without material injury to the realty. On the other hand, doors may be removed without injury to the structure; yet, because they are necessary to the ordinary use of the building and are not peculiar to the use of the occupant, they are considered to be fixtures and thus part of the real property.

Practical Advice

When placing on leased real property a permanently affixed structure, such as a billboard, provide in your lease agreement with the owner of the land terms specifying who owns the structure and whether you have the right to remove it upon termination of the lease.

♦ SEE FIGURE 47-1: *Kinds of Property*

♦ See Case 47-1

47-2 Transfer of Title to Personal Property

The transfer of title to real property typically is a formal affair. In contrast, title to personal property may be acquired and transferred with relative ease and little formality. Such facility with regard to the transfer of personal property is essential within a society whose trade and industry are based principally on transactions in personal property, which must be sold with minimal delay.

Accordingly, the law concerning personal property has been largely codified. The Uniform Commercial Code (UCC or the Code) includes the law of sales of goods (Article 2), as well as the law governing the transfer and negotiation of negotiable instruments (Article 3) and of investment securities (Article 8). Nonetheless, the Code does not cover a number of issues (addressed in this chapter) involving the ownership and transfer of title to personal property. In addition, personal property may be, and often is, acquired by producing the item, rather than by selling or transferring it.

47-2a BY SALE

By definition, a sale of *tangible* personal property (goods) is transfer of title to specified existing goods for a consideration known as the price. Title passes when the parties intend it to pass, and transfer of possession is not required for a transfer of title. For a discussion of transfer of title, see *Chapter 21*.

Sales of *intangible* personal property also involve the transfer of title. Many of these sales also are governed by UCC provisions, while some, such as sales of copyrights and patents, are governed by specialized Federal legislation.

47-2b BY GIFT

A gift is a transfer of title to property from one person to another without consideration. This lack of consideration is the basic distinction between a gift and a sale. Because a gift involves no consideration or compensation, it must be completed by delivery of the gift to be effective. A gratuitous promise to make a gift is not binding. In addition, there must be intent on the part of the maker (the **donor**) of the gift to make a present transfer, and there must be acceptance by the recipient (the **donee**) of the gift.

DELIVERY Delivery is essential to a valid gift. The term *delivery* has a very special meaning that includes, but is not limited to, the manual transfer of the item to the donee. A donor may effect an irrevocable delivery by, for example, turning an item over to a third person with instructions to give it to the donee. Frequently, an item, because of its size, location, or intangibility, is incapable of immediate manual delivery. In such cases, an irrevocable gift may be effected through the delivery of something that symbolizes dominion over the item. This is referred to as **constructive delivery**. For example, if Joanne declares that she gives an antique desk and all its contents to Barry and hands Barry the key to the desk, in many states a valid gift has been made.

Practical Advice

As a donee of a gift, attempt to receive actual or constructive delivery of the item as quickly as possible.

INTENT The law also provides clearly that the donor must intend to make a gift of the property. Thus, if Jack leaves a packet of stocks and bonds with Joan, her acquiring good title to them depends on whether Jack intended to make a gift of them or simply intended to place them in Joan's hands for safekeeping. A voluntary, uncompensated delivery made with the intent to give the recipient title constitutes a gift when the donee accepts the delivery. If these conditions are met, the donor has no further claim to the property.

Gifts, therefore, cannot be conditional. There is, however, one major exception to this rule: an engagement gift given in anticipation of marriage. If the marriage does not take place, the donor usually can recover the gift unless the donor broke the engagement without justification. But the courts will not apply the exception when a marriage is called off due to the death of one of the engaged parties.

ACCEPTANCE The final requirement of a valid gift is acceptance by the donee. In most instances, of course, the donee will accept the gift gratefully. Accordingly, the law usually presumes that the donee has accepted. But certain circumstances may render acceptance objectionable, such as when a gift would impose a burden upon the donee. In such cases, the law will not require the recipient to accept an unwanted gift. For example, a donee may prudently reject a gift of an elephant or a wrecked car in need of extensive repairs.

CLASSIFICATION Gifts may be either *inter vivos* or *causa mortis*. An *inter vivos* gift is a gift made by a donor during her lifetime. A gift *causa mortis* is a gift made by a donor in contemplation of her imminent death. A gift *causa mortis* is a conditional gift, contingent upon (1) the donor's death as she anticipated, (2) the donor's not revoking the gift prior to her death, and (3) the donee's surviving the donor.

◆ *See Case 47-2*

47-2c BY WILL OR DESCENT

Title to personal property frequently is acquired by inheritance from a person who dies, either with or without a will. This method of acquiring title is discussed in *Chapter 50*.

47-2d BY ACCESSION

Accession, in its strict sense, means the right of the owner of property to any increase in it, whether natural or human-made. For example, the owner of a cow acquires title by accession to any calves born to that cow.

47-2e BY CONFUSION

Confusion arises when identical goods belonging to different people become so *commingled* (mixed) that the owners cannot identify their own property except as part of a mass of like goods. For example, Hereford cattle belonging to Benton become mixed with Hereford cattle belonging to Armstrong, and neither can specifically identify his herd as a result or grain owned by Courts is combined inseparably with similar grain owned by Reichel. Confusion may result from accident, mistake, willful act, or agreement of the parties. If the goods can be apportioned, each owner who can prove his proportion of the whole is entitled to receive his share. If, however, the confusion results from the willful and wrongful act of one of the parties, he will lose his entire interest if unable to prove his share. Frequently, problems arise not because the owners cannot prove their original interests but because there is not enough left to distribute a full share to each. In such cases, if the confusion was due to mistake, accident, or agreement, each owner will bear the loss in proportion to his share. If the confusion resulted from an intentional and unauthorized act, the wrongdoer will first bear any loss.

47-2f BY POSSESSION

Sometimes a person may acquire title to movable personal property by taking possession of it. If the property has been intentionally **abandoned** (intentionally disposed of), a finder is entitled to the property. Moreover, under the general rule, a *finder* is entitled to lost (unintentionally left) **property** against everyone except the true *owner*. Suppose Zenner, the owner of an apartment complex, leases a kitchenette apartment to Terrell. One night, Waters, Terrell's mother-in-law, is invited to sleep in the convertible bed in the living room. In the course of preparing the bed, Waters finds an emerald ring caught on the springs under the mattress. She turns the ring over to the police, but diligent inquiry fails to ascertain the true owner. As the finder, Waters will be entitled to the ring.

A different rule applies when the lost property is in the ground. Here, the owner of the land has a claim superior to that of the finder. For example, Josephs employs Kasarda to excavate a lateral sewer. Kasarda uncovers ancient Native American artifacts. Josephs, not Kasarda, has the superior claim.

A further exception to the rule gives the finder first claim against all but the true owner. If property is intentionally placed somewhere by the owner, who then unintentionally leaves it, it becomes **mislaid property**. Most courts hold that if property has been mislaid, not lost, then the owner of the premises, not the finder, has first claim if the true owner is not discovered. This doctrine is frequently invoked in cases involving items found in restaurants or on trains, buses, or airplanes.

Another category of property is the **treasure trove**, which consists of coins or currency concealed by the owner. To be classified as treasure trove, the property must have been hidden or concealed for such a length of time that the owner is probably dead or undiscoverable. Treasure trove belongs to the finder as against all but the true owner.

Many States now have statutes that provide a means of vesting title to lost property in the finder where a prescribed search for the owner proves fruitless.

PROPERTY INSURANCE

Insurance covers a vast range of contracts, each of which distributes risk among a large number of members (the insureds) through an insurance company (the insurer). Insurance is a contractual undertaking by the insurer to pay a sum of money or give something of value to the insured or a beneficiary upon the happening of a contingency or fortuitous event that is beyond the control of the contracting parties.

Insurance coverage of one form or another affects every commercial activity. Through insurance, a business can safeguard its tangible assets against almost any form of damage or destruction, whether resulting from natural causes or from the accidental or improper actions of people. Insurance may also protect a business from tort liability, including assertions involving strict liability, negligence, or the intentional acts of its representatives. A business may procure credit insurance to guard against losses from poor credit risks and fidelity bonds to secure it against losses incurred through employee defalcations. If a business hires a famous pianist, it may insure the latter's hands; if it decides to present an outdoor concert, it may insure against the possibility of rain. A business may purchase life insurance on its key executives to reimburse it for financial losses arising from their deaths, or it may purchase such life insurance payable to the families of executives as part of their compensation. An additional, increasingly important use of insurance is to carry out pension commitments arising from agreements with employees. Nonetheless, the remaining sections of this chapter will focus on the insurance of property.

The McCarran-Ferguson Act, enacted by Congress in 1945, left insurance regulation to the States. Statutes in each State regulate domestic insurance companies and establish standards for foreign (out-of-state) insurance companies wishing to do business within the State. Most State legislation relates to the incorporation, licensing, supervision, and liquidation of insurers and to the licensing and supervision of agents and brokers.

Because the insurance relationship arises from a contract of insurance between the insurer and the insured, the law of insurance is a branch of contract law. For this reason, the doctrines of offer and acceptance, consideration, and other rules applicable to contracts in general are equally applicable to insurance contracts. Beyond that, however, insurance law, like the law of sales, bailments, negotiable instruments,

or other specialized types of contracts, contains numerous modifications of fundamental contract law, which are examined in the following sections.

47-3 Fire and Property Insurance

Fire and property insurance protects the owner (or another person with an insurable interest, such as a secured creditor or mortgagee) of real or personal property against loss resulting from damage to or destruction of the property by fire and certain related perils. Most fire insurance policies also cover damage caused by lightning, explosion, earthquake, water, wind, rain, collision, and riot.

Fire insurance policies are standardized in the United States, either by statute or by order of the State insurance departments, but their coverage is frequently enlarged through an "endorsement" or "rider" to include other perils or to benefit the insured in ways the provisions in the standard form do not. These policies normally are written for periods of one or three years.

Practical Advice

Maintain, off the premises, a detailed inventory of your insured property in case you must file a claim for loss.

47-3a TYPES OF FIRE COVERED

Fire insurance policies usually are held to cover damage from "hostile" fires, but they do not cover losses caused by "friendly" fires. A **friendly fire** is one contained in its intended location (e.g., a fire in a fireplace, furnace, or stove). A **hostile fire** is any other fire—all fires outside their intended or usual locales. Thus, a friendly fire becomes hostile if it escapes from its usual confines.

A standard insurance policy therefore will not cover heat or soot damage to a fireplace resulting from its continual use or damage done to personal property accidentally thrown into a stove. Damages caused by smoke, soot, water, and heat from a hostile fire are covered by the standard fire insurance policy, whereas such damages caused by a friendly fire generally are not. Moreover, most policies do not cover recovery for business interruption, unless they contain endorsements specifically covering such loss.

47-3b CO-INSURANCE CLAUSES

Co-insurance is an arrangement common in property insurance to share the risk between insurer and insured. **Co-insurance** is a reduction in benefits for underinsuring the value of the property based on a percentage stated in the insurance policy and the amount underinsured. For example, under the typical 80 percent co-insurance clause, the insured may recover the full amount of loss, not to exceed the face amount of the policy, provided the policy is for an amount not less than 80 percent of the property's insurable value. If the policy is for less than 80 percent, the insured recovers that proportion of the loss that the amount of the policy bears, up to 80 percent of the insurable value. The formula for recovery is as follows:

$$\text{Recovery} = \frac{\text{Face Value of Policy}}{\text{Fair Market Value of Property} \times \text{Co-insurance \%}} \times \text{Loss}$$

Thus, if the co-insurance percentage is 80 percent, the value of the property is $100,000, and the policy is for $80,000 or more, the insured is fully protected against loss not to exceed the policy amount. If the policy amount is less than 80 percent of the property value, however, the insured receives only the proportion of the loss amount as determined in the previous formula. Thus, in the previous example, if the fire policy was for $60,000 and the property was 50 percent destroyed, the loss would be $50,000, of which the insurer would pay $37,500, which is $60,000/($100,000 × 80%) of $50,000. On a total loss, the recovery could not, of course, exceed the face amount of the policy. Some States do not favor co-insurance clauses and strictly construe the applicable statute against their validity. In addition, property insurance is not held to be co-insurance unless the policy specifically so provides.

Practical Advice

When purchasing property insurance, determine whether there is a co-insurance clause and, if so, what the co-insurance percentage is.

47-3c OTHER INSURANCE CLAUSES

Recovery under property insurance policies typically is also limited by **other insurance clauses**, which generally require that liability be distributed *pro rata* among the various insurers. For example, Alexander insures his $120,000 building with Hamilton Insurance Co. for $60,000 and Jefferson Insurance Co. for $90,000. Alexander's building is partially destroyed by fire, causing Alexander $20,000 in damages. Alexander will collect two-fifths ($60,000/$150,000) of his damages from Hamilton ($8,000) and three-fifths ($90,000/$150,000) from Jefferson ($12,000).

47-3d TYPES OF POLICIES

Property insurance may be either a valued policy or an open policy. A **valued policy** is one providing for the full value of the property, upon which value the insured and the insurer specifically agree at the time the policy is issued. Should total loss occur, the insurer must pay this amount, not the actual or fair market value of the property. By comparison, no agreement in an **open policy** specifies the property's value; instead, the insurer pays the fair market value of the property calculated immediately prior to its loss. Thus, if Latrisha insures her building for $650,000 and at the time of its loss the property is valued at $600,000, under an open policy, Latrisha would recover $600,000, while under a valued policy, she would recover $650,000. If she insured the building for $700,000 and it was valued at that amount just prior to being blown apart by a tornado, under both types of policies, Latrisha would recover $700,000. Insurance of property under a marine policy (insurance covering marine vessels and cargo) is generally considered to be valued, whereas nonmarine property insurance is presumed to be unvalued or open.

47-4 Nature of Insurance Contracts

The basic principles of **contract** law apply to insurance policies. Furthermore, because insurance companies engage in a large volume of business over wide areas, they tend to standardize their policies. In some States, standardization is required by statute. This usually means that the insured must accept a given policy or do without the desired insurance.

47-4a OFFER AND ACCEPTANCE

No matter how many stories tell of insurance agents aggressively soliciting would-be insureds to take out policies, the applicant usually makes the offer, and the contract is created when the insurance company accepts that offer. The company may condition its acceptance—upon payment of the premium, for instance. It also may write a policy that differs from the application, thereby making a counteroffer that the applicant may or may not choose to accept.

In fire and casualty insurance, agents often have authority to make the insurance effective immediately, when needed, by means of a **binder**, which is a temporary, preliminary insurance contract that is legally binding until the completion of the formal insurance contract. Should a loss occur before the company actually issues a policy, the binder will be effective on the same terms and conditions the policy would have had if it had been issued.

In general, insurance contracts have not been held to be subject to the statute of frauds; thus, courts have held oral contracts for insurance to be enforceable. As a practical matter, however, oral contracts for insurance are very infrequent.

47-4b INSURABLE INTEREST

The concept of insurable interest has been developed over many years, primarily to eliminate gambling and to lessen the moral hazard. If a person could obtain an enforceable fire insurance policy on property that he did not own or in which he had no interest, he would be in a position to profit unfairly by the destruction of such property. An insurable interest is a relationship a person has with respect to certain property such that the happening of a possible, specific, damage-causing contingency would result in direct loss or injury to her. The purpose of insurance is protection against the risk of loss that would result from such a happening, not the realization of gain or profit.

Whether sole or concurrent, ownership obviously creates an insurable interest in property. Moreover, a right deriving from a contract concerning the property also gives rise to an insurable interest. For instance, shareholders in a closely held corporation have been held to have an insurable interest in the corporation's property to the extent of their interest. Likewise, lessees of property have insurable interests, as do holders of security interests, such as mortgagees or sellers with a purchase money security interest. Most courts have gone beyond the requirement of a legally recognized interest and apply a factual expectancy test. Under this test, the determinative question is whether the insured will obtain a benefit from the continued existence of the property or suffer a loss from its destruction. Thus, an individual who buys and insures a stolen automobile without knowledge that the automobile is stolen has an insurable interest in the automobile.

The insurable interest must exist at the time the property *loss* occurs, although some courts speak in terms of having the insurable interest at the time of insuring *and* at the time of loss. Property insurance policies are freely assignable after, but not before, a loss occurs.

Practical Advice

When purchasing property insurance, make sure you have an insurable interest in the property and terminate the policy once you cease to have an insurable interest.

47-4c PREMIUMS

Premiums are the consideration paid for an insurance policy. Property insurance policies are written only for periods lasting a few years at most. Long, continued liability on this type of policy is the exception rather than the rule. State law regulates the rates that may be charged for fire and various kinds of casualty insurance. The regulatory authorities are under a duty to require that the companies' rates be reasonable, not unfairly discriminatory, and neither excessively high nor inordinately low.

47-4d DEFENSES OF THE INSURER

An insurer may assert the ordinary defenses available to any contract. In addition, the terms of the insurance contract may provide specific defenses, such as the subject matter of the policy, types of perils covered, amount of coverage, and period of coverage. Moreover, the insurer may assert the closely related defenses of misrepresentation, breach of warranty, and concealment.

MISREPRESENTATION A representation is a statement made by or on behalf of an applicant for insurance to induce an insurer to enter into a contract. The representation is not a part of the insurance contract, but if the application containing the representation is incorporated by reference into the contract, the representation becomes a warranty. For a **misrepresentation** to have legal consequences, it must be material, the insurer must have justifiably relied on it as an inducement to enter into the contract, and it must either have been substantially false when the insured made it or have become so, to the insured's knowledge, before the contract was created. The principal remedy of the insurer on discovery of the material misrepresentation is rescission of the contract. To rescind the contract, the insurer must tender to the insured all premiums that have been paid, unless the misrepresentation was fraudulent. To be effective, rescission must be made as soon as possible after discovery of the misrepresentation.

BREACH OF WARRANTY Warranties are of great importance in insurance contracts because they operate as conditions that must exist before the contract is effective or before the insurer's promise to pay is enforceable. If such is the case, the insurer does not merely have a defense against payment of the policy but can void the policy.

Failure of the condition to exist or to occur relieves the insurer from any obligation to perform its promise. Broadly speaking, a condition is simply an event whose happening or failure to happen either precedes the existence of a legal relationship or terminates one previously existing. Conditions are either precedent or subsequent. For example, payment of the premium is a condition precedent to the enforcement of the insurer's promise, as is the happening of the insured event. A condition subsequent is an operative event the happening of which terminates an existing, matured legal obligation. A provision in a policy to the effect that the insured shall not be liable unless suit is brought within twelve months from the date on which the loss occurs is an example of a condition subsequent.

To be a warranty, the provision must be expressly included in the insurance contract or clearly incorporated by reference. Usually, the policy statements that the insurer considers to be express warranties are characterized by words such as *warrant,* on *condition that*, *provided that*, or words of similar import. Other statements important to the risk assumed, such as the address of a building in a case in which personal property at a particular location is insured against fire, are sometimes held to be informal warranties.

Generally, it is becoming more difficult for an insurer to avoid liability on a policy when an insured breaches a warranty. For example, a number of States now require a breach to be material before the insurer may avoid liability.

CONCEALMENT Concealment is the failure of an applicant for insurance to disclose material facts that the insurer does not know. The nondisclosure normally must be fraudulent as well as material to invalidate the policy, the applicant must have had reason to believe the fact was material, and its disclosure must have affected the insurer's acceptance of the risk. The principal remedy of the insurer on discovery of concealment is rescission of the contract.

47-4e WAIVER AND ESTOPPEL

In certain instances, an insurer who normally would be entitled to deny liability under a policy because of a misrepresentation, breach of condition, or concealment is "estopped" from taking advantage of the defense or is said to have "waived" the right to rely on it because of other facts.

The terms *waiver* and *estoppel* are used interchangeably, although by definition, they are not synonymous. As generally defined, **waiver** is the intentional relinquishment of a known right, and **estoppel** means that a person is prevented by his own conduct from asserting a position inconsistent with such conduct, on which another person has justifiably relied.

Because a corporation such as an insurance company can act only through agents, situations involving waiver invariably are based on an agent's conduct. The higher the agent's position in the company's organization, the more likely his conduct is to bind the company, as an agent acting within the scope of his authority binds his principal. Insureds have the right to rely on representations made by the insurer's employees, and when such representations reasonably induce or cause the insured to change her position or prevent her from causing a condition to occur, the insurer may not assert as a defense the condition's failure to occur, whether the term applied to her situation be waiver or estoppel. Companies have tried with little success to limit the authority of local selling agents to bind the company through waiver or estoppel.

47-4f TERMINATION

Most insurance contracts are performed according to their terms, and due **performance** terminates the insurer's obligation. Normally, the insurer pays the principal sum due and the contract is thereby performed and discharged.

Cancellation by mutual consent is another way of terminating an insurance contract. Cancellation by the insurer alone means that the insurer remains liable, according to the terms of the policy, until such time as the cancellation is effective. To cancel a policy, the insurer must tender the unearned portion of the premium to the insured.

BAILMENTS AND DOCUMENTS OF TITLE

47-5 Bailments

A **bailment** is the relationship created when one person (the bailor) transfers the possession of personal property by delivery, without transfer of title, to another (the bailee) for the accomplishment of a certain purpose, after which the bailee is to return the property to the bailor or dispose of it according to the bailor's directions. One of the most common occurrences in everyday life, bailments are of great commercial importance. Bailments include the transportation, storage, repair, and rental of goods, which together involve billions of dollars in transactions each year. The following are common examples of bailments: keeping a car in a public garage; leaving a car, a watch, or any other article to be repaired; renting a car or truck; checking a hat or coat at a theater or restaurant; leaving clothes to be laundered; delivering jewelry, stocks, bonds, or other valuables to secure the payment of a debt; storing goods in a warehouse; and shipping goods by public or private transportation. The benefit of a bailment may, by its terms, accrue solely to the bailor, solely to the bailee, or to both parties. A bailment may be with or without compensation. On these bases, bailments are classified as follows:

1. *Bailments for the bailor's sole benefit* include the gratuitous custody of personal property and the gratuitous services that involve custody of personal property, such as repairs or transportation. For example, if Sherry stores, repairs, or transports Tim's goods without compensation, this is a bailment for the sole benefit of the bailor, Tim.

2. *Bailments for the bailee's sole benefit* are usually limited to the gratuitous loan of personal property for use by the bailee, as where Tim, without compensation, lends his car, lawn mower, or book to Sherry for her use.

3. *Bailments for the mutual benefit* of both parties include ordinary commercial bailments, such as the delivery of goods to a person for repair, jewels to a pawnbroker, or an automobile to a parking lot attendant.

♦ *See Case 47-3*

47-5a ESSENTIAL ELEMENTS OF A BAILMENT

The basic elements of a bailment are (1) the delivery of possession from a bailor to a bailee; (2) the delivery of personal property, not real property; (3) possession without ownership by the bailee for a determinable period; and (4) an absolute duty on the bailee to return the property to the bailor or to dispose of it according to the bailor's directions.

In most cases, two simple elements determine the existence of a bailment: (1) a separation of ownership and possession of the property (possession without ownership) and (2) a duty on the party in possession to redeliver the identical property to the owner or to dispose of it according to the owner's directions. Since a bailment need not be a contract, consideration is not required. A bailment may be created by operation of law from the facts of a particular situation; thus, a bailment may be **implied** or **constructive**.

DELIVERY OF POSSESSION Possession by a bailee involves (1) the bailee's power to control the personal property and (2) either the bailee's intention to control the property or her awareness that the rightful possessor has given up physical control of it. Thus, for example, when a restaurant customer hangs his hat or coat on a hook furnished for that purpose, the hat or coat is within an area under the restaurant owner's physical control. But the restaurant owner is not a bailee of the hat or coat unless he clearly signifies an intention to exercise control over the hat or coat. On the other hand, when a clerk in a store helps a customer to remove his coat to try on a new one, the owner of the store usually is held to have become a bailee of the old coat through the clerk, her employee. Here, the clerk has signified an intention to control the coat by taking it from the customer, and a bailment results.

PERSONAL PROPERTY The bailment relationship can exist only with respect to personal property. The delivery of possession of real property by the owner to another is covered by real property law. Bailed property need not be tangible. Intangible property, such as the rights represented by promissory notes, corporate bonds, shares of stock, documents of title, and life insurance policies that are evidenced by written instruments and are thus capable of delivery, may be and frequently are the subject matter of bailments.

POSSESSION FOR A DETERMINABLE TIME To establish a bailment relationship, the person receiving possession must be under a duty to return the personal property and must not obtain title to it. If the identical property transferred is to be returned, even in an altered form, the transaction is a bailment; however, if other property of equal value or the money value of the original property may be returned, a transfer of title has occurred and the transaction is a sale.

RESTORATION OF POSSESSION TO THE BAILOR The bailee is legally obligated to restore the property to the bailor's possession when the bailment period ends. Normally, the bailee is required to return the identical goods bailed, although their condition may be changed because of the work that the bailee was required to perform on them. An exception to this rule concerns **fungible goods**, such as grain, which, for all practical purposes, consist of particles that are the equivalent of every other particle and are expected to be mingled with other like goods during a bailment. Given such goods, a bailee obviously cannot be required to return the identical goods bailed. His obligation is simply to return goods of the same quality and quantity.

A bailee has a duty to return the property to the right person. Her mistake in delivering property to the wrong person does not excuse her, even when the bailor's negligence induces the mistake. A bailee who, through mistake or intention, misdelivers the property to a third person who has no right to its possession is guilty of conversion and is liable to the bailor.

47-5b RIGHTS AND DUTIES OF BAILOR AND BAILEE

The bailment relationship creates rights and duties on the part of the bailor and the bailee. The bailee is under a duty to exercise due care for the safety of the property and to return it to the right person; conversely, the bailee has the exclusive right to possess the property for the term of the bailment. In addition, depending on the nature of the transaction, a bailee may have the right to limit his liability, as well as to receive compensation and reimbursement of expenses. The bailor, in turn, has certain duties with respect to the condition of the bailed goods.

BAILEE'S DUTY TO EXERCISE DUE CARE The bailee must exercise due care not to permit injury to or destruction of the property by the bailee or by third parties. The degree of care depends on the nature of the bailment relationship and the character of the property. In the context of a **commercial bailment**, from which the parties derive a mutual benefit, the law requires the bailee to exercise the care that a reasonably prudent person would exercise under the same circumstances. When the bailment benefits the bailee alone (Tim's borrowing Michael's truck without payment would be an example), the law requires more-than-reasonable care of the bailee. On the other hand, in cases in which the bailee accepts the property for the bailor's sole benefit, the law requires a lesser degree of care. Nevertheless, the amount of care required to satisfy any of the standards will vary with the character of the property.

When the property is lost, damaged, or destroyed while in the bailee's possession, it is often impossible for the bailor to obtain enough information to show that the loss or damage was due to the bailee's failure to exercise required care. The law aids the bailor in this respect by *presuming* that the bailee was at fault. The bailor is merely required to show that certain property was delivered by way of bailment and that the bailee either has failed to return it or has returned it in a damaged condition. The burden is then on the bailee to prove that he exercised the degree of care required.

♦ **SEE FIGURE 47-2:** *Duties in a Bailment*

♦ *See Case 47-3*

BAILEE'S ABSOLUTE LIABILITY TO RETURN PROPERTY As discussed, the bailee is free from liability if she exercised the degree of care required of her under the particular bailment while the property was within her control. This general rule has certain important exceptions that impose an absolute duty on the bailee to return the property undamaged to the proper person.

When the bailee has an obligation by express agreement with the bailor or by custom to insure the property against certain risks but fails to do so and the property is destroyed or damaged through such risks, she is liable for the damage or nondelivery, even if she has exercised due care.

When the bailee uses the bailed property in a manner not authorized by the bailor or by the character of the bailment and during the course of such use the property is damaged or destroyed without fault on the bailee's part, the bailee is nonetheless absolutely (strictly) liable for the damage or destruction. The wrongful use by the bailee automatically terminates her lawful possession: she becomes a trespasser as to the property and, as such, is absolutely liable for whatever harm befalls it.

Practical Advice

As a bailee, exercise appropriate care to protect the safety of the property and to return it to its true owner.

BAILEE'S RIGHT TO LIMIT LIABILITY Certain bailees—namely, common carriers, public warehousers, and innkeepers—may limit their liability for breach of their duties to the bailor only as provided by statute. Other bailees, however, may vary their duties and liabilities by contract with the bailor. When liability may be limited by contract, the law requires that any such limitation be properly brought to the bailor's attention before he bails the property. This is especially true in the case of "professional bailees," such as repair garages, who make it their business to act as bailees and who deal with the public on a uniform rather than an individual basis. Thus, a variation or limitation in writing, contained, for example, in a claim check or stub given to the bailor or posted on the walls of the bailee's place of business, ordinarily will *not* bind the bailor unless (1) the bailee draws the bailor's attention to the writing, (2) the bailee informs the bailor that it contains a limitation or variation of liability, and (3) the limitation is not the result of unequal bargaining power. Some States do not permit professional bailees (who commonly include warehousers, garagers, and parking lot owners) to disclaim liability for their own negligence.

Practical Advice

When dealing with bailees, be alert as to whether they are attempting to limit their liability, and if they are, carefully consider whether you are comfortable with the limitations.

BAILEE'S RIGHT TO COMPENSATION A bailee who by express or implied agreement undertakes to perform work on or render services in connection with the bailed goods is entitled to reasonable compensation for those services or that work. In most cases, the agreement between bailor and bailee fixes the amount of compensation and provides how it shall be paid. In the absence of a contrary agreement, the compensation is payable when the bailee completes the work or performs the services. If after such completion or performance but before the redelivery of the goods to the bailor the goods are lost or damaged through no fault of the bailee, the bailee is still entitled to compensation for his work and services.

Practical Advice

If you are a bailee, specify in your contract what your compensation will be.

FIGURE 47-2 **Duties in a Bailment**

Type of Bailment	Bailor's Duty	Bailee's Duty of Care
For Sole Benefit of Bailor	Slight care	To warn of defects of which she knew or should have known
For Sole Benefit of Bailee	Utmost care	To warn of known defects
For Mutual Benefit	Ordinary care	To warn of defects of which she knew or should have known

Most bailees who are entitled to compensation for work and services performed in connection with bailed goods acquire a possessory lien on the goods to secure the payment of such compensation. In most jurisdictions, the bailee has a statutory right to obtain a judicial foreclosure of his lien and a sale of the goods. Many statutes also provide that the bailee does not lose his lien on redelivery of the goods to the bailor, as was the case at common law. Instead, the lien will continue for a specified period after redelivery, if the bailee timely records with the proper authorities an instrument claiming such a lien.

BAILOR'S DUTIES In a bailment for the sole benefit of the bailee, the bailor warrants that she is unaware of any defects in the bailed property. In all other instances, the bailor has a duty to warn the bailee of all defects she knows of or should have discovered upon a reasonable inspection of the bailed property. A number of courts have extended strict liability in tort and the implied warranties under Article 2 of the UCC to leases and bailments. Article 2A imposes implied warranties on the lease of goods.

47-5c SPECIAL TYPES OF BAILMENTS

Although the general principles that apply to all bailees govern pledgees, warehousers, and safe deposit companies, certain special features about the transactions in which they respectively engage subject them to extraordinary duties of care and liability. Innkeepers and common carriers also may be said to be *extraordinary* bailees, whereas all other bailees are *ordinary* bailees. This distinction is based on the character and extent of the liability of these two classes of bailees for the loss of or injury to bailed goods. As we have seen, an **ordinary bailee** is liable only for the loss or injury that results from his failure to exercise ordinary or reasonable care. The liability of the **extraordinary bailee**, on the other hand, is, in general, *absolute*. Just as an insurer, in general, becomes automatically liable to the insured on the happening of the hazard insured against, regardless of the cause, the extraordinary bailee becomes liable to the bailor for any loss or injury to the goods, regardless of the cause and without regard to the question of his care or negligence. Thus, he insures the safety of the goods.

PLEDGES A **pledge** is a bailment for security in which the owner gives possession of her personal property to another (the secured party) to secure a debt or the performance of some obligation. The secured party does not have title to the property involved but merely a possessory security interest. Pledges of most types of personal property for security purposes are governed by Article 9 of the UCC, which we discussed in *Chapter 37*. In most respects, the secured party's duties and liabilities are the same as those of a bailee for compensation.

WAREHOUSING A **warehouser** is a bailee who, for compensation, receives goods to be stored in a warehouse. Under the common law, his duties and liabilities were identical to those of the ordinary bailee for compensation. Today, because a strong public interest affects their activities, warehousers are subject to extensive State and Federal regulation. Ware-housers also must be distinguished from ordinary bailees in that the receipts they issue for storage have acquired a special status in commerce. Regarded as documents of title, these receipts are governed by Article 7 of the UCC. (Documents of title are discussed later in this chapter.)

SAFE DEPOSIT BOXES A majority of States hold that a person who rents a safe deposit box from a bank enters into a bailment relationship. As this constitutes a bailment for the parties' mutual benefit, the bailee bank owes the customer the duty to act with ordinary due care and is liable only if negligent.

CARRIERS OF GOODS In the broadest sense, anyone who transports goods from one place to another, either gratuitously or for compensation, is a **carrier**. Carriers are classified primarily as common carriers and private carriers. A **common** carrier offers its services and facilities to the public on terms and under circumstances indicating that the offering is made to all persons. Stated somewhat differently, the criteria that define common carriers are as follows: (1) the carriage must be part of its business, (2) the carriage must be for remuneration, and (3) the carrier must represent to the general public that it is willing to serve the public in the transportation of property. Common carriers of goods include railroad, steamship, aircraft, public trucking, and pipeline companies. In contrast, a **private** or **contract carrier** is one who carries the goods of another on isolated occasions or who serves a limited number of customers under individual contracts without offering the same or similar contracts to the public at large.

The person who delivers goods to a carrier for shipment is known as the **consignor** or shipper. The person to whom the carrier is to deliver the goods is known as the **consignee**. The instrument containing the terms of the contract of transportation, which the carrier issues to the shipper, is called a **bill of lading** (discussed later in this chapter).

A common carrier is under a duty to serve the public to the limits of its capacity and, within those limits, to accept for carriage goods of the kind that it normally transports. A private carrier, by comparison, has no duty to accept goods for carriage, except where it agrees by contract to do so. Whether common or private, the carrier is under an absolute duty to deliver the goods to the person to whom the shipper has consigned them.

A private carrier, in the absence of special contract terms, is liable as a bailee for the goods it undertakes to carry. The liability of a common carrier, on the other hand, approaches that of an insurer of the safety of the goods, except when loss or damage is caused by an act of God, an act of a public enemy, the acts or fault of the shipper, the inherent nature of or a defect in the goods, or an act of public authority. The carrier, however, is permitted, through its contract with the shipper, to limit its liability, provided the carrier gives the shipper notice of this limitation and the opportunity to declare a higher value for the goods.

INNKEEPERS At common law, **innkeepers** (better known as hotel and motel owners or operators) are held to the same **strict** or **absolute liability** for their guests' belongings as are common carriers for the goods they carry. This rule of strict liability applies only to those who furnish lodging to the public for compensation as a regular business and extends only to the belongings of lodgers who are guests. In almost all jurisdictions, case law and statute have substantially modified the innkeeper's strict liability under common law.

47-6 Documents of Title

A **document of title**, which includes warehouse receipts and bills of lading, is a record evidencing a right to receive, control, hold, and dispose of the record *and* the goods it covers. Documents of title thus represent title to goods. To be a document of title, a document must be issued by or addressed to a bailee and must cover goods in the bailee's possession that are either identified or are fungible portions of an identified mass.

Briefly, a document of title symbolizes ownership of the goods it describes. Because of the document's legal characteristics, its ownership is equivalent to the ownership or control of the goods it represents, without the necessity of actual or physical possession of the goods. Likewise, it transfers the ownership or control of the goods without necessitating the physical transfer of the goods themselves. For these reasons, documents of title are a convenient means of handling the billions of dollars' worth of goods that are transported by carriers or are stored with warehousers. Documents of title also facilitate the transfer of title to goods and the creation of a security interest in goods. Article 7 of the UCC governs documents of title. In 2003, a revision of UCC Article 7 was promulgated to update the original Article 7 and provide a framework for the further development of electronic documents of title. All States have adopted Revised Article 7. This chapter covers Revised Article 7.

47-6a TYPES OF DOCUMENTS OF TITLE

To facilitate electronic documents of title, several definitions in Article 1 have been revised, including "bearer," "bill of lading," "delivery," "document of title," "holder," and "warehouse receipt." The term *electronic document of title* means "a document of title evidenced by a record consisting of information stored in an electronic medium." Revised Section 1-201(b)(16). The term *tangible document of title* means "a document of title evidenced by a record consisting of information that is inscribed in a tangible medium." Revised Section 1-201(b)(16). *Record* means "information that is inscribed on a tangible medium or that is stored in an electronic or other medium and is retrievable in perceivable form." Revised Article 7-102(10). The concept of an electronic document of title allows for commercial practice to determine whether records issued by bailees are "in the regular course of business or financing" and are "treated as adequately evidencing that the person in possession or control of the record is entitled to receive, control, hold, and dispose of the record and the goods the record covers." Preface to Revised Article 7.

WAREHOUSE RECEIPTS A warehouse receipt is a document of title issued by a person engaged in the business of storing goods for hire. A warehouser is liable for damages for loss or injury to the goods caused by his failure to exercise such care in regard to them as a reasonably careful person would exercise under the circumstances. The warehouser must deliver the goods to the person entitled to receive them under the terms of the warehouse receipt. Though a warehouser may limit his liability through a provision in the warehouse receipt fixing a specific maximum liability per article or item or unit of weight, this limitation does not apply when a warehouser converts goods to his own use.

Practical Advice

When dealing with warehousers, be alert as to whether they are attempting to limit their liability. If they are, carefully consider whether you are comfortable with the limitations.

To enforce the payment of her charges and necessary expenses in connection with keeping and handling the goods, a warehouser has a lien on the goods that enables her to sell them at public or private sale after notice and to apply the net proceeds of the sale to the amount of her charges. The Code, moreover, provides the warehouser a definite procedure for enforcing her lien against the goods stored and in her possession.

BILLS OF LADING A **bill of lading** is a document of title evidencing the receipt of goods issued by a person engaged in the business of directly or indirectly transporting or forwarding goods. It serves a threefold function: (1) as a receipt for the goods, (2) as evidence of the contract of carriage, and (3) as a document of title. A bill of lading is negotiable if, by its terms, the goods are deliverable to the bearer or to the order of a named person. Any other document is nonnegotiable.

Under the Code, bills of lading may be issued not only by common carriers but also by contract carriers, freight forwarders, or any person engaged in the business of transporting or forwarding goods.

The carrier must deliver the goods to the person entitled to receive them under the terms of the bill of lading. Common carriers are extraordinary bailees under the law and are subject to greater liability than are ordinary bailees, such as warehousers.

The Code allows a carrier to limit its liability by contract in all cases in which its rates depend on the value of the goods and the carrier allows the shipper an opportunity to declare a higher value. The limitation does not apply, however, when the carrier converts goods to its own use.

Practical Advice

When dealing with common carriers, be alert as to whether they are attempting to limit their liability. If they are, carefully consider whether you are comfortable with the limitations.

On goods in its possession that are covered by a bill of lading, the carrier has a lien for the charges and expenses necessary for its preservation of such goods. Against a purchaser for value of a negotiable bill of lading, this lien is limited to charges stated in the bill or in the applicable published tariff or, if no charges are so stated, to a reasonable charge.

The carrier may enforce its lien by public or private sale of the goods after notice to all persons known by the carrier to claim an interest in them. The sale must be on terms that are "commercially reasonable," and the carrier must conduct it in a "commercially reasonable manner."

A purchaser in good faith of goods sold to enforce the lien takes those goods free of any rights of persons against whom the lien was valid, even if the enforcement of the lien does not comply with Code requirements. This rule applies both to carrier's and to warehouser's liens. Good faith, as indicated in previous chapters, has been revised to mean "honesty in fact and the observance of reasonable commercial standards of fair dealing." Revised Section 7-102(6); Revised Section 1-201(b)(20).

47-6b NEGOTIABILITY OF DOCUMENTS OF TITLE

The concept of negotiability has long been established in law. It is important not only in connection with documents of title but also in connection with commercial paper and investment securities, topics treated in other chapters of this book.

Revised Article 7 provides that a document of title is negotiable if, by its terms, the goods are to be delivered to bearer or to the order of a named person. Revised Section 7-104(a).

Any other document is nonnegotiable. The negotiability of a document is determined at its time of issue. Revised Section 7-104, Comment 2. Revised Article 7 provides for the integration of electronic documents of title and, to the extent possible, applies the same rules for electronic and tangible documents of title.

A nonnegotiable document, such as a straight bill of lading or a warehouse receipt under which the goods are deliverable only to a person named in the bill, not to the order of any person or to bearer, may be transferred by assignment but may not be negotiated. Only a negotiable document or instrument may be negotiated.

An individual has "control" of an **electronic document of title** "if a system employed for evidencing the transfer of interests in the electronic document reliably establishes that person as the person to which the electronic document was issued or transferred." Revised Section 7-106(a). Control of an electronic document of title replaces the concept of possession and indorsement applicable to a tangible document of title. Thus, a person with a tangible document of title delivers the document by voluntarily transferring *possession* while a person with an electronic document of title delivers the document by voluntarily transferring *control*. Revised Section 7-106, Comment 2. The key to having a system of control under Revised Article 7 is the ability to show at any point in time the one person entitled to the goods under the electronic document. Revised Section 7-106, Comment 3. Revised Article 7 leaves to the marketplace the creation of systems that meet this standard.

47-6c DUE NEGOTIATION

The Code sets forth the manner in which a negotiable document of title may be negotiated and the requirements of due negotiation. Under Revised Article 7, an order form negotiable *tangible* document of title running to the order of a named person is negotiated by her indorsement and delivery. Revised Section 7-501(a). Delivery of a tangible document of title means voluntary transfer of possession. Revised Article 1-201(b)(15). After such indorsement in blank or to bearer, the document may be negotiated by delivery alone. A special indorsement, by which the document is indorsed over to a specified person, requires the indorsement of the special indorsee as well as delivery to accomplish a further negotiation.

A negotiable *electronic* document of title running to the order of a named person *or* to bearer is negotiated by delivery. Indorsement by the named person is not required to negotiate an electronic document of title. Revised Section 7-501(b). Delivery of an electronic document of title means voluntary transfer of control. Revised Article 1-201(b)(15).

Due negotiation, a term peculiar to Article 7, requires not only that the purchaser of the negotiable document take it in good faith, without notice of any adverse claim or defense, and pay value, but also that she take it in the regular course of business or financing, not in settlement or payment of a money obligation (in essence, a holder by due negotiation). Thus, a transfer for value of a negotiable document of title to a nonbanker or to a person not in business, such as a college professor or student, would not be a due negotiation.

Due negotiation creates new rights in the holder of the document. The transferee does not stand in the shoes of his transferor; in other words, the defects and defenses available against the transferor are not available against the new holder. Newly created by the negotiation, his rights are free of such defects and defenses. This enables bankers and businesspersons to extend credit on documents of title without concern about possible adverse claims or the rights of third parties.

The rights of a holder of a negotiable document of title to whom it has been duly negotiated include (1) title to the document; (2) title to the goods; (3) all rights accruing under the law of agency or estoppel, including rights to goods delivered to the bailee after the document was issued; and (4) the issuer's direct obligation to hold or deliver the goods according to the document's terms.

47-6d WARRANTIES

A person, other than a collecting bank or other intermediary, who either negotiates or delivers a document of title for value incurs certain warranty obligations, unless otherwise agreed. Such transferor warrants to her immediate purchaser (1) that the document is genuine, (2) that she had no knowledge of any fact that would impair its validity or worth, and (3) that

her negotiation or delivery is rightful and fully effective with respect to the title to the document and the goods it represents. Revised Article 7 makes it clear that these warranties only arise in the case of voluntary transfer of possession or control for value. Revised Section 7-507.

47-6e INEFFECTIVE DOCUMENTS OF TITLE

For a person to obtain title to goods through the negotiation of a document to him, the goods must have been delivered to the document's issuer by their owner or by either one to whom the owner has delivered the goods or one whom the owner has entrusted with actual or apparent authority to ship, store, or sell them. A warehouser or carrier, however, may deliver goods according to the terms of the document that it has issued or otherwise dispose of the goods as provided in the Code without incurring liability, even if the document did not represent title to the goods. The ware-houser or carrier need only have acted in good faith and complied with reasonable commercial standards in both the receipt and delivery or other disposition of the goods. Such a bailee has no liability even though the person from whom the bailee received the goods had no authority to obtain the issuance of the document or to dispose of the goods and the person to whom it delivered the goods had no authority to receive them.

Thus, a carrier or warehouser who receives goods from a thief or finder and later delivers them to a person to whom the thief or finder ordered them to be delivered is not liable to the true owner of the goods. Even a sale of the goods by the carrier or warehouser to enforce a lien for transportation or storage charges and expenses would not subject it to liability.

C H A P T E R   S U M M A R Y

INTRODUCTION TO PROPERTY AND PERSONAL PROPERTY

KINDS OF PROPERTY	**Definition** interest or group of interests that is legally protected **Tangible Property** physical objects **Intangible Property** property that does not exist in a physical form **Real Property** land and interests in land **Personal Property** all property that is not real property **Fixture** personal property so firmly attached to real property that an interest in it arises under real property law
TRANSFER OF TITLE TO PERSONAL PROPERTY	**Sale** transfer of property for consideration (price) **Gift** transfer of property without consideration • *Delivery* includes both manual transfer of the item and constructive delivery (delivery of something that symbolizes control over the item) • *Intent* • *Acceptance* • *Classification*

Will right to property acquired upon death of the owner

Accession right of a property owner to any increase in such property

Confusion intermixing of goods belonging to two or more owners such that they can identify their individual property only as part of a mass of like goods

- If due to mistake, accident, or agreement, loss shared proportionately
- If caused by an intentional or unauthorized act, wrongdoer bears loss

Possession a person may acquire title by taking possession of property

- *Abandoned Property* intentionally disposed of by the owner; the finder is entitled to the property
- *Lost Property* unintentionally left by the owner; the finder is generally entitled to the property
- *Mislaid Property* intentionally placed by the owner but unintentionally left; the owner of the premises is generally entitled to the property
- *Treasure Trove* coins or currency concealed by the owner for such a length of time that the owner is probably dead or undiscoverable; the finder is entitled to the property

PROPERTY INSURANCE

FIRE AND PROPERTY INSURANCE	**General Definition of Insurance** contractual arrangement that distributes risk of loss among a large number of members (the insureds) through an insurance company (the insurer) **Coverage** of fire and property insurance provides protection against loss due to fire or related perils **Types of Fire** • *Friendly Fire* fire contained in its intended location • *Hostile Fire* any fire outside its intended or usual location **Co-insurance** reduction in benefits for underinsuring the value of the property based on a percentage stated in the insurance policy and the amount underinsured **Multiple Insurers** if multiple insurers are involved, liability generally is distributed *pro rata* **Types of Policies** • *Valued Policy* covers full value of property as agreed upon by the parties at the time the policy is issued • *Open Policy* covers fair market value of property as calculated immediately prior to the loss
NATURE OF INSURANCE CONTRACTS	**General Contracts Law** basic principles of contract law apply **Insurable Interest** a financial interest or a factual expectancy in someone's property that justifies insuring the property; the interest must exist at the time the property loss occurs **Premiums** amount to be paid for an insurance policy **Defenses of the Insurer** • *Misrepresentation* false representation of a material fact made by the insured that is justifiably relied upon by the insurer; enables the insurer to rescind the contract within a specified time • *Breach of Warranty* the failure of a required condition; generally an insurer may avoid liability for a breach of warranty only if the breach is material • *Concealment* fraudulent failure of an applicant for insurance to disclose material facts that the insurer does not know; allows the insurer to rescind the contract • *Waiver* an insurer intentionally relinquishes the right to deny liability • *Estoppel* an insurer is prevented by its own conduct from asserting a defense **Termination** an insurance contract may be terminated by due performance or cancellation

BAILMENTS AND DOCUMENTS OF TITLE

BAILMENTS

Definition the temporary transfer of personal property by one party (the bailor) to another (the bailee)

Classification of Bailments
- *For the Bailor's Sole Benefit*
- *For the Bailee's Sole Benefit*
- *For Mutual Benefit* includes ordinary commercial bailments

Essential Elements
- *Delivery of Possession*
- *Personal Property*
- *Possession, but Not Ownership, for a Determinable Time*
- *Restoration of Possession to the Bailor*

Rights and Duties
- *Bailee's Duty to Exercise Due Care* the bailee must exercise reasonable care to protect the safety of the property and to return it to the proper person
- *Bailee's Absolute Liability* occurs when (1) the parties so agree; (2) the custom of the industry requires the bailee to insure the property against the risk in question, but he fails to do so; or (3) the bailee uses the bailed property in an unauthorized manner
- *Bailee's Right to Limit Liability* certain bailees are not permitted to limit their liability for breach of their duties, except as provided by statute
- *Bailee's Right to Compensation* entitled to reasonable compensation for work or services performed on the bailed goods
- *Bailor's Duties* in bailment for sole benefit of bailee, the bailor warrants that she is unaware of any defects; in all other bailments, the bailor has a duty to warn of all known defects and all defects she should discover upon a reasonable inspection

Special Types
- *Pledge* security interest by possession
- *Warehouser* storer of goods for compensation; warehouser must exercise reasonable care to protect the safety of the stored goods and to deliver them to the proper person
- *Carrier of Goods* transporter of goods; a common carrier is an extraordinary bailee, and a private carrier is an ordinary bailee
- *Innkeeper* hotel or motel operator; is an extraordinary bailee except as limited by statute or case law

DOCUMENTS OF TITLE

Definition an instrument evidencing ownership of the record and the goods it covers

Types
- *Warehouse Receipt* receipt issued by person storing goods
- *Bill of Lading* document issued to the shipper by the carrier (1) as a receipt for the goods, (2) as evidence of their carriage contract, and (3) as a document of title

Negotiability a document of title is negotiable if, by its terms, the goods are to be delivered to bearer or to the order of a named person

Due Negotiation delivery of a negotiable document in the regular course of business to a holder, who takes in good faith, for value, and without notice of any defense or claim

Warranties a person who negotiates or delivers a document of title for value, other than a collecting bank or other intermediary, incurs certain warranty obligations unless otherwise agreed

Ineffective Documents for a person to obtain title to goods by negotiation of a document, the goods must have been delivered to the issuer of the document by their owner or by one to whom the owner has entrusted actual or apparent authority

CASES

Fixtures
HERRON v. BARNARD
Missouri Court of Appeals, Western District, 2013
390 S.W.3d 901

CASE 47-1

Mitchell, J.

On March 1, 2007, Barnard, acting on behalf of Baltimore Avenue Investors, LLC (collectively "Barnard"), executed a written lease agreement for a 1,442-square-foot office space at 2000 Baltimore Avenue in Kansas City, Missouri, with Boka Powell, LLC, a Texas-based architectural design firm. Herron was employed by Boka Powell to run the Kansas City office.

The lease agreement was for a two-year term with a monthly rent payment of $1,562.17 and a right of first refusal regarding the lease of additional space within the building. The parties further agreed that Boka Powell, through Herron and at its own expense, would be permitted to remove existing partitions in order to reconfigure space for a kitchenette; relocate the plumbing, electrical, and waste lines for this purpose; add carpet; relocate the entry door; and paint the walls and ceiling. The lease further provided that Boka Powell was responsible for putting in a security system at its own expense. The space was then remodeled in accordance with the agreed-upon terms.

After the space was remodeled, Herron arranged for the installation of a sink, cabinetry (including a pull-out waste receptacle and storage bin), appliances, and shelving in the kitchenette area; he also arranged for the installation of a custom-made, tempered-glass door and matching transom for the entrance, as well as a variety of new light fixtures and bulbs, a picture-hanging mechanism, filing cabinets, and a security system. Of these items, Herron, himself, purchased the appliances, the sink, the bookshelves, the door and transom, the picture hanger, all of the lighting, the wire storage bin, and the wastebasket. Boka Powell purchased the filing cabinets, the storage cabinets, and the security system, but later transferred ownership of these items to Herron as part of a separation agreement. Herron later testified that the particular items he selected were for the purpose of creating an architectural showpiece for his customers to demonstrate what the architectural firm could do with a space.

* * *

Before the original two-year term expired, Boka Powell agreed to renew the lease. Barnard offered two options: the first was a two-year extension with an increased rent based upon an increase in the square footage of the space from renovations, and the second was a one-year extension at the same increased rental rate with the option for an additional extension of one year at an even higher rental rate. Although Herron was hoping

for the two-year extension, Boka Powell opted for the one-year extension with the one-year renewal option. When Herron conveyed Boka Powell's request to Barnard, Herron also told Barnard, "If at the end of the next year they decide to no longer participate or I have enough work to continue with my own company, I hope that we can still work out a future long term agreement." The term of the renewed lease was set to expire on April 30, 2010.

Sometime in November 2009, Boka Powell decided to cancel the lease agreement. Boka Powell paid, in a lump sum, the rent due through April 30, 2010, but terminated its lease as of January 30, 2010, advising Herron to vacate the premises no later than January 29th. In a separation agreement between Boka Powell and Herron, Boka Powell agreed to compensate Herron for outstanding expenses by giving him eight workstations, eight chairs, eight file cabinets, eight conference chairs, and two "L file" cabinets that were, at the time, located in the leased space, with those items to be removed at Herron's expense.

* * *

On February 24, 2010, Herron advised Barnard that he was unable to secure a co-tenant and could not afford the rent on his own. Herron indicated that, although the original lease expired on April 30, 2010, he could make arrangements to move his property before then, and he requested that Barnard identify what he considered a reasonable move-out date. In response, Barnard simply suggested that they meet up the next week but provided no move-out date. At that meeting, Herron returned his keys, but Barnard indicated that if Herron needed back in the space, all he needed to do was contact Barnard, and Barnard would let him in.

* * * While Herron (along with a small crew of workers) was in the process of removing the various items at issue in this appeal, Barnard showed up and advised Herron and his crew to stop what they were doing and leave because they were not authorized to be there, and Barnard considered them to be trespassing.

Thereafter, Herron filed a lawsuit for conversion and replevin (among other claims), alternatively seeking return of the property or damages. Barnard filed an answer and an amended answer, raising, as affirmative defenses, claims that he owned the property because: (1) the property constituted fixtures that transferred to Barnard pursuant to the terms of the lease agreement; and (2) Herron had abandoned the property by leaving it on the premises beyond the expiration of the lease. The trial court, after hearing testimony from both Herron and Barnard, and after viewing numerous exhibits consisting of photographs, blueprints, emails, and contracts, denied all of Herron's claims. Neither party requested findings of fact or conclusions of law, and, accordingly, the trial court provided none. Herron appealed the judgment.

"A fixture is an article of the nature of personal property [that] has been so annexed to the realty that it is regarded as part of the land and partakes of legal incidents of the freehold and belongs to the person owning the land." [Citation.] "The elements of a fixture are annexation, adaptability and intent." [Citation.] "Each of the elements … must be present to some degree, however slight." [Citation.] And "the general rule is that the burden of showing that the circumstances of the annexation are such as to make an article a fixture is on the party asserting it to be one." [Citation.]

* * *

The annexation element refers to the physical attachment of the property to the realty, and where structures are removable with minimal or no damage resulting, the mere fact of annexation does not support a finding that the item was a fixture. [Citation.] On the other hand, "[a]nnexation that may be slight and easily displaced does not prevent an article from becoming a fixture when the other elements are found." [Citation.]

The adaptation element means that "the characteristics of fitness or suitability for the building or premises in question are implied." [Citation.] In other words, if the premises were designed or built with the view of having the particular item made an integral part of the building, or if the alleged fixture was necessary for the particular use to which the premises are devoted, the element of adaptation is satisfied. [Citation.] But, to meet this element, one must prove that the property at issue is "peculiarly adapted to the real property," [citation], and "[a]n item usable at other locations is not peculiarly adapted for use on the land in question." [Citation.] Thus, although a space may be designed for the use of the property in question, unless there is something peculiar or unique about the property itself that requires only that particular item to be used in the space, the element of adaptation is not met. [Citation.]

The intent element is "of paramount importance, at least in the case of controversies between … landlord and tenant, where the controlling question is usually that of whether the intention in annexing the article to the realty was to make it a permanent accession to the land." [Citation.] * * *

"When an annexation is made by a tenant and is such that the chattel may be removed without material injury to the realty, there is a presumption that he did not intend to make a permanent annexation to the real estate but intended to reserve to himself the title to the chattel annexed. [Citation.] * * *

In the context of commercial tenancies, "[c]ase law appears to support the view that the extent of the furnishings necessary for the operation of a modern business negates an

intention … to make any gift to the landlord and that therefore all ordinary store fixtures, including showcases and shelving, business signs, and miscellaneous other appliances installed by (the tenant) may be considered to remain his personal property, 'unless substantial damage' would be the result of removal." [Citation.]

In examining the three elements, "[t]he latter two …, adaptation and intent, are more important in determining whether a chattel became a fixture than the method by which the chattel is affixed to a freehold." [Citation.]

* * *

We believe that there was substantial evidence to support adaptation, but only as to the custom door and transom. As for the remaining items, we do not believe that there was substantial evidence to support a finding that Barnard met his burden of demonstrating the element of adaptation.

The evidence demonstrated that the door and transom went from floor to ceiling, which was a height of approximately fourteen feet. The transom had to be specially built into the walls by setting it inside a custom-built wooden track and then enclosing and concealing the track within the dry-wall. Removing the transom would have caused significant damage to the property. It is apparent that the space housing the transom was designed with the view of having that particular transom become an integral part of the building itself. The transom was custom made for the space, and the size of the transom (approximately six feet tall) made it unique.

Although the door, itself, was only minimally attached to the space, it too was custom-built in combination with the transom. The two items were essentially a package set; thus, if the element of adaptation was met as to one of the items, it was satisfied for both. Thus, we believe that the evidence and reasonable inferences supported a finding by the trial court that the element of adaptation was met as to the door and transom.

As to the remaining items, the evidence did not demonstrate that there was anything peculiar or unique about them or that they were somehow made an integral part of the building. In fact, Barnard testified that the picture hanger did not constitute an improvement to the space and that neither the filing cabinets nor the refrigerator were integral parts of the building. And while it is true that the renovations to the space were made with the idea that the new space would be used as a kitchenette and storage, the facts that (1) the bookshelves, appliances, wood cabinetry, wastebasket, storage bin, sink, lighting, and alarm system could have easily been replaced by different bookshelves, appliances, cabinetry, wastebaskets, storage bins, sinks, lighting, and alarm systems, and (2) these particular items could have easily been used at a different location, establishes that these items were not "peculiarly adapted for use on the land in question." [Citation.] Consequently, in the present case, there was not substantial evidence to support a finding that the element of adaptation was met as to any of the items with the exception of the door and transom. And without evidence to support this element, the remaining items could not have constituted fixtures. [Citation.]

* * *

Here, we believe the evidence demonstrated that the majority of the items at issue constituted trade fixtures, * * * that Herron was permitted to remove at the conclusion of his tenancy pursuant to both the common law and the express term of the lease agreement.

* * *

* * * Consequently, we reverse the trial court's judgment as to all of the property except the door and transom, and we remand this matter to the trial court in order to determine Herron's remedy (whether it be return of the property, or if damages, what amount of damages to which Herron is entitled). We affirm the trial court's judgment with respect to the door and transom in light of the fact that substantial evidence supported a finding that these items constituted fixtures, thereby transferring ownership of them to Barnard.

CASE
47-2

Delivery of Gift
MIRVISH v. MOTT
Court of Appeals of New York, 2012
18 N.Y.3d 510, 965 N.E.2d 906

Read, J.

Jacques Lipchitz, the Russian-born cubist sculptor, died in 1973 at the age of 81. He was survived by his wife, Yulla H. Lipchitz, who inherited many valuable works of art from her husband, including "The Cry," a 1,100-pound bronze sculpture, cast three of seven, 1928-1929. After she was widowed, Yulla began a relationship with Biond Fury as early as 1980; the two of them lived together for 17 years prior to her death on July 20, 2003 at the age of 92.

From time to time, Yulla would make gifts to Fury, including art created by her late husband. She memorialized these gifts by giving Fury a picture of the artwork with a writing describing the piece and declaring that it was a gift. After Yulla's death, Fury produced a photograph of "The Cry" with the following notation on the back, in Yulla's handwriting: "I gave this sculpture 'The Cry' to my good friend Biond Fury in appreciation for all he did for me during my long illness. With love and my warm wishes for a Happy Future, Yulla Lipchitz October 2, 1997, New York." At the time, "The Cry" was apparently in storage in New York in the custody of the Marlborough Gallery, Inc. (Marlborough), the Manhattan art dealer.

About a year later, the French minister of culture and communication approached Pierre Levai, Marlborough's president, to ask about the possibility of placing "The Cry" on exhibit in Paris for a period of five years, "with a view to its ultimately being purchased." The minister proposed to include "The Cry" in a group of modern and contemporary works to be installed in the Tuileries Gardens near the Louvre Museum. On November 11, 1998, Levai wrote the minister that he had discussed the French government's request "with the Lipchitz family," who agreed to loan the sculpture for three years, unless Yulla died earlier. At the conclusion of the loan, Levai continued,

the family was "prepared to negotiate a sale of the work," but if "[a]t the conclusion of the loan, ... the sculpture [was] not purchased, it [was] to be returned to the Lipchitz family in New York at the borrower's cost."

Levai discussed the loan of "The Cry" to the French government only with Mott, never with Yulla. Mott, who at the time did not know about the handwritten gift instrument conveying "The Cry" to Fury, is the executor and a residuary beneficiary of one third of his mother's estate. He is an attorney, and he handled Yulla's financial affairs and held power of attorney from her for many years prior to her death. Mott also performed legal work for Marlborough, beginning as early as 1980.

According to Mott, he talked to his mother about the loan and, on her behalf, "consented that ['The Cry'] should be put on display in the [Tuileries Gardens] in Paris and it was and it had [Yulla's] name on the loan." The French government at some point also inquired if, once the exhibition was over, Yulla was willing to make a gift of "The Cry." Mott testified that Yulla told him "No, of course not, but if they want to buy it, they can buy it"—i.e., that "we would [give] ... a right of first refusal." "The Cry" was in Paris, subject to this agreement, when Yulla died. Her will did not mention "The Cry" or any other specific work of art. Fury claims not to have known that the sculpture was loaned to the French government in 1998.

* * *

[On March 9, 2004, Fury's attorney sent a letter and a copy of the deed of gift to Mott's attorney, demanding immediate delivery of "The Cry" to Fury. Mott claims to have sold "The Cry" and three other sculptures in a package deal in July 2004 to Marlborough International Fine Art Establishment (Marlborough International) for $1 million. But in a letter to the French minister dated January 10, 2005, six months *after* the purported sale of "The Cry" to Marlborough International, Mott informed the minister that Yulla had passed away in 2003; noted that "the agreement for the loan also provided that at its conclusion the Lipchitz family would be prepared to negotiate a sale of the Sculpture"; and inquired "[o]n behalf of the family… whether the Ministry [had] any interest in acquiring the Sculpture at this time before arrangements are made for its return."

On September 15, 2005, Fury sold his interest in "The Cry" to David Mirvish, an art collector and gallery owner in Toronto, for $220,000. On October 4, 2005, Mirvish's attorney notified Mott of the sale and demanded possession of the sculpture. In a letter dated October 14, 2005, the estate's attorney refused this demand, asserting "the Estate was the true owner of ['The Cry'], which was never subject of a valid *inter vivos* gift from [Yulla] to Biond Fury."

Both Mott, as executor of Yulla's estate, and Mirvish filed petitions with the Surrogate's Court seeking resolution of their conflicting claims of ownership of "The Cry." The Surrogate's Court ruled in favor of Mirvish, concluding that Yulla had made a valid *inter vivos* gift of "The Cry" to Fury because the wording of the deed of gift was "in the past tense, *i.e.*, 'I gave this sculpture "The Cry" to my good friend Biond Fury,'" which was not only "indicative of an antecedent transfer," but also "clearly identifie[d] the intended object and [was] consistent with [Yulla's] long pattern of making gifts of similar items to her companion." The Appellate Division reversed the Surrogate Court's decree.]

* * *

The principles of law that control the outcome of this appeal are a good deal less complicated than the history of the dispute, as is the application of those principles to the facts. In [citation] we held that

[f]irst, to make a valid inter vivos gift there must exist the intent on the part of the donor to make a present transfer; delivery of the gift, either actual or constructive to the donee; and acceptance by the donee. Second, the proponent of a gift has the burden of proving each of these elements by clear and convincing evidence [citations].

Relatedly, mere possession of a gift after the donor's death creates a presumption of delivery to the donee during the donor's lifetime. * * *

Here, Yulla's intent to make a present transfer of "The Cry" was clear on the face of the gift instrument, as the surrogate concluded. There is no suggestion Yulla was coerced; there is no question about her capacity. Nor is there any dispute that Fury accepted the gift. * * * Mott has not raised a triable issue of fact so as to overcome the presumption of delivery; Mirvish has established each of the elements of a valid inter vivos gift—intent, delivery and acceptance—by clear and convincing evidence. * * *

* * * Accordingly, the order of the Appellate Division should be reversed, with costs, and the order of Surrogate's Court reinstated.

CASE
47-3

Bailments: Classification/Essentials/Duties of Bailee
HADFIELD v. GILCHRIST
Court of Appeals of South Carolina, 2000
343 S.C. 88, 538 S.E.2d 268

Anderson, J.

Mark Hadfield filed this action against Sam Gilchrist, d/b/a Gilchrist's Service Center, and d/b/a Gilchrist Towing Company (Gilchrist) for damages sustained by Hadfield's vehicle while impounded on Gilchrist's lot. * * *

Facts/Procedural Background

Gilchrist owns a motor vehicle towing service and maintains a storage facility for the retention of the towed vehicles. Gilchrist operates under a license issued by the City of Charleston.

Hadfield, a medical student at MUSC, went to retrieve his 1988 Lincoln Continental from the parking spot where his wife parked the vehicle. The parking spot, located near MUSC, was on private property owned by Allen Saffer. Hadfield's wife parked the vehicle on Saffer's property without Saffer's permission. The vehicle was not in the parking spot when Hadfield arrived as Saffer had called Gilchrist to have the vehicle removed.

Gilchrist towed Hadfield's car to his storage facility. Gilchrist maintained a chain link fence around the storage area, and had an employee on the lot around the clock. The employee's duties included periodically leaving the office to check on the storage area, which was some distance away from the office.

Hadfield called to retrieve his vehicle, but was informed he would have to wait until the next morning and pay towing and storage fees. Upon Hadfield's arrival to pick up his car the following morning, he paid the fees. When he went to the storage area to collect his vehicle, Hadfield discovered the vehicle had been extensively vandalized. The vandals stole the radio/compact disc player, smashed windows, and pulled many electrical wires out of the dashboard. The vehicle depended heavily upon computers and never functioned properly after the incident. The vandals entered the storage area by cutting a hole in the fence. They vandalized between six and eight vehicles on the lot that night.

The magistrate, in summarizing Hadfield's testimony, concluded Hadfield's attempts to persuade Gilchrist to pay for the damages were futile. Hadfield secured estimates for the damage to the automobile * * * at $4,021.43. * * * After more than 60 days elapsed, Hadfield sold the vehicle for $1,000.00.

The magistrate found Gilchrist liable for the damages as a bailee, and entered judgment in favor of Hadfield for $4,035.00. Gilchrist appealed to the Circuit Court, which affirmed the decision of the magistrate.

* * *

Issues

(i) Did the Circuit Court err in applying the law of bailments?
(ii) Did the Circuit Court err in finding Gilchrist was responsible for damages?

Law/Analysis

Neither the magistrate nor the Circuit Court judge made a finding as to the type of bailment created in this case. The type of bailment created may determine the standard of care the bailee, Gilchrist, must meet. Therefore, we review the law of bailments.

Bailments

A bailment is created by the delivery of personal property by one person to another in trust for a specific purpose, pursuant to an express or implied contract to fulfill that trust. [Citations.] Bailments are generally classified as being for (1) the sole benefit of the bailor; (2) the sole benefit of the bailee; or (3) the mutual benefit of both. [Citation.] Bailments which benefit only one of the parties, the first and second classifications, are often described as gratuitous. [Citation.]

A. Gratuitous Bailment

"A gratuitous bailment is, by definition, one in which the transfer of possession or use of the bailed property is without compensation." [Citation.] For instance, a gratuitous bailment arises if the bailment is undertaken as a personal favor or is involuntary. [Citations.]

A "gratuitous bailee" acts without expectation of reward or compensation. [Citation.] To show the bailment was for the sole benefit of the bailor, the bailee must establish that it was not expecting compensation. * * *

Bailment for Mutual Benefit

By contrast, a bailment for the mutual benefit of the parties arises when one party takes the personal property of another into his or her care or custody in exchange for payment or other benefit. [Citations.]

Constructive Bailment

Although a bailment is ordinarily created by the agreement of the parties, the agreement of the parties may be implied or constructive, and the bailment may arise by operation of law. [Citation.] Such a constructive bailment arises when one person has lawfully acquired possession of another's personal property, other than by virtue of a bailment contract, and holds it under such circumstances that the law imposes on the recipient of the property the obligation to keep it safely and redeliver it to the owner. [Citations.] A constructive bailment may occur even in the absence of the voluntary delivery and acceptance of the property which is usually necessary to create a bailment relationship.

Gilchrist argues he towed the vehicle pursuant to the Charleston Municipal Ordinances, and the ordinances are for the sole benefit of the vehicle owners. Accordingly, he contends, the relationship created is a gratuitous bailment. We disagree. * * *

Clearly, the [applicable Charleston] ordinances provide for the payment to the city or its agent, the towing service, for the costs of towing and storage. Gilchrist charged Hadfield towing and storage fees.

* * * We conclude a constructive bailment, for the mutual benefit of Hadfield and Gilchrist, was created.

Bailment Action/Nature of Theory

Although contractual in nature, and involving the conveyance of personal property, an action for breach of the duty of care by a bailor sounds in tort. [Citations.] * * *

Bailee's Degree of Care/Burden of Proof

The degree of care required of a bailee for mutual benefit is defined as ordinary care, or due care, or the degree of care which would be exercised by a person of ordinary care in the protection of his own property. [Citations.]

In a bailment action alleging a breach of the duty of care, the bailor is entitled to be compensated for all losses that are the natural consequence and proximate result of the bailee's negligence. [Citation.] * * *

* * *

Hadfield testified before the magistrate regarding the "nice" condition of the vehicle prior to being towed, and the damage to his vehicle, and the other vehicles on the lot. In addition, he introduced photographs depicting the damage. Thus, Hadfield made out his *prima facie* case. * * * The burden then shifted to Gilchrist to show that he used ordinary care in protecting the vehicle while in his care.

Gilchrist impounded the cars in a storage lot surrounded by a chain link fence. There was an individual on the clock at all times. The person on duty spent time in the office and only visited the storage lot to check on it. The vandal cut a hole in the fence and broke into six to eight cars on the night in question. The fact the guard was not on duty at the impound lot and, considering the only other security for the vehicles was the chain link fence, the magistrate and Circuit Court judge could have concluded Gilchrist failed to exercise ordinary care. * * *

* * *

Accordingly, the order of the Circuit Court is AFFIRMED.

QUESTIONS

1. In January, Roger Burke loaned his favorite nephew, Jimmy White, his valuable Picasso painting. Knowing that Jimmy would celebrate his twenty-first birthday on May 15, Burke sent a letter to Jimmy on April 14 stating:

    Dear Jimmy,

    Tomorrow I leave on my annual trip to Europe, and I want to make you a fitting birthday gift, which I do by sending you my enclosed promissory note. Also I want you to keep the Picasso that I loaned you last January, and you may now consider it yours. Happy birthday!

    Affectionately,

    /s/ Uncle Roger

    The negotiable promissory note for $5,000 sent with the letter was signed by Roger Burke, payable to Jimmy White or bearer, and dated May 15. On May 21, Burke was killed in an automobile accident while motoring in France.

    First Bank was appointed administrator of Burke's estate. Jimmy presented the note to the administrator and demanded payment, which was refused. Jimmy brought an action against First Bank as administrator, seeking recovery on the note. The administrator in turn brought an action against Jimmy, seeking the return of the Picasso.

    a. What decision in the action on the note?

    b. What decision in the action to recover the painting?

2. Several years ago, Pierce purchased a tract of land on which stood an old, vacant house. Recently, Pierce employed Fried, a carpenter, to repair and remodel the house. While Fried was tearing out a partition to enlarge one of the rooms, he found a metal box hidden in the wall. After breaking open the box and discovering that it contained $2,000 in gold and silver coins and old-style bills, Fried took the box and its contents to Pierce and told her where he had found it. When Fried handed the box and the money over to Pierce, he said, "If you do not find the owner, I claim the money." Pierce placed the money in an envelope and deposited it in her safe deposit box, where it presently remains. No one has ever claimed the money, but Pierce refuses to give it to Fried. Will Fried be able to recover the money from Pierce? Why or why not?

3. Gable, the owner of a lumber company, was cutting trees over the boundary line between his property and property owned by Lane. Although he realized he had crossed onto Lane's property, Gable continued to cut trees of the same kind as those he had cut on his own land. While on Lane's property, he found a diamond ring on the ground, which he took home. All of the timber Gable cut that day was commingled. Explain what Lane's rights are, if any (a) in the timber and (b) in the ring.

4. Decide and explain your decision for each of the following problems:

    a. A chimney sweep found a jewel and took it to a goldsmith, whose apprentice removed the stone and refused to return it. The chimney sweep sues the goldsmith.

    b. One of several boys walking along a railroad track found an old stocking. All started playing with it until it burst in the hands of its discoverer, revealing several hundred dollars. The original discoverer claims all of the money; the other boys claim it should be divided equally.

    c. A traveling salesperson leaving a store notices a parcel of bank notes on the floor. He picks them up and gives them to the owner of the store to keep for the true owner. After three years, they have not been reclaimed and the salesperson sues the storekeeper.

    d. Frank is hired to clean the swimming pool at the country club. He finds a diamond ring on the bottom of the pool. The true owner cannot be found. The country club sues Frank for possession of the ring.

    e. A customer found a pocketbook lying on a barber's table. He gave it to the barber to hold for the true owner, who failed to appear. The customer sues the barber.

5. Jones had fifty crates of oranges equally divided between grades A, B, and C, grade A being the highest quality and C being the lowest. Smith had one thousand crates of oranges, about 90 percent of which were grade A, but some of which were grades B and C, the exact percentage of each being unknown. Smith willfully mixed Jones's crates with his own so that it was impossible to identify any particular crate. Jones seized the whole lot. Smith demanded nine hundred crates of grade A and fifty crates each of grades B and C. Jones refused to give them up unless Smith could identify particular crates. This Smith could not do. Smith brought an action against Jones to recover what he demanded or its value. Judgment for whom and why?

6. Barnes, the owner and operator of Blackacre, decided to cease farming operations and liquidate his holdings. Barnes sold fifty head of yearling Merino sheep to Billing and then sold Blackacre to Clifton. He executed and delivered to Billing a bill of sale for the sheep and was

paid for them. It was understood that Billing would send a truck for the sheep within a few days. At the same time, Barnes executed a warranty deed conveying Blackacre to Clifton. Clifton took possession of the farm and brought along one hundred head of his yearling Merino sheep and turned them into the pasture, not knowing the sheep Barnes sold Billing were still in the pasture. After the sheep were mixed, it was impossible to identify the fifty head belonging to Billing. Explain whether Billing will recover the fifty head of sheep from Clifton.

7. Susan permitted Kevin to take her very old grandfather clock on the basis of Kevin's representations that he was skilled at repairing such clocks and restoring them to their original condition and could do the job for $60. The clock had been badly damaged for years. Kevin immediately sold the clock to Fixit Shop for $30. Fixit Shop was in the business of repairing a large variety of items and also sold used articles. Three months later, Susan was in the Fixit Shop and clearly identified a grandfather clock Fixit Shop had for sale as the one she had given Kevin to repair. Fixit Shop had replaced more than half of the moving parts by having exact duplicates custom-made, the clock's exterior had been restored by a skilled cabinetmaker, and the clock's face had been replaced by a duplicate. All materials belonged to Fixit Shop, and its employees accomplished the work. Fixit Shop asserts it bought the clock in the normal course of business from Kevin, who represented that it belonged to him. The fair market value of the clock in its damaged condition was $30, and the value of repairs made is $220.

    Susan sued Fixit Shop for return of the clock. Fixit Shop defended that it then had title to the clock and, in the alternative, that Susan must pay the value of the repairs if she is entitled to regain possession. Who will prevail? Why?

8. Under an oral agreement, Hyer rented from Bateman a vacant lot for a filling station. Hyer placed on the lot a lightly constructed building bolted to a concrete slab and several storage tanks laid on the ground in a shallow excavation. Later, Hyer prepared a lease that contained a provision allowing him to remove the equipment at the termination of the lease. This lease was not executed, having been rejected by Bateman due to a renewal clause it contained. Several years later, another lease was prepared, which both Hyer and Bateman did sign. This lease did not mention removal of the equipment. At the termination of this lease, Hyer removed the equipment, and Bateman brought an action to recover possession of the equipment. What judgment? Explain.

9. Elvers sold a parcel of real estate, describing it by its legal description and making no mention of any improvements or fixtures on it. The land had upon it a residence, a barn, a rail fence, a stack of hay, some growing corn, and a windmill. The residence had a mirror built into the west wall of the living room and a heating system consisting of a furnace, steam pipes, and coils. In the house were chairs, beds, tables, and other furniture. On the house was a lightning rod. In the basement were screens for the windows. Which of these things passed by the deed and which did not?

10. John Swan rented a safe deposit box at the Tenth Citizens Bank of Emanon, State of X. On December 17, 2018, Swan went to the bank with stock certificates to place in the safe deposit box. After he was admitted to the vault and had placed the stock certificates in the box, Swan found lying on a chair in the privacy booth of the vault a $5,000 negotiable bearer bond issued by the State of Wisconsin with coupons attached, due June 30, 2025. Swan picked up the bond and, observing that it did not carry the name of the owner, left the vault and went to the office of the president of the bank. He told the president what had occurred and delivered the bond to the president only after obtaining his promise that should the owner not call for the bond or become known to the bank by June 30, 2019, the bank would redeliver the bond to Swan. On July 1, 2019, Swan learned that the owner of the bond had not called for it, nor was his identity known to the bank. Swan then asked that the bond be returned to him. The bank refused, stating that it would continue to hold the bond until the owner claimed it. Explain whether Swan will prevail in his action to recover possession of the bond.

11. Lile, an insurance broker who handled all insurance for Tempo Co., purchased a fire policy from Insurance Company insuring Tempo Co.'s factory against fire in the amount of $1.5 million. Before the policy was delivered to Tempo and while it was still in Lile's hands, Tempo advised Lile to cancel the policy. Prior to cancellation, however, Tempo suffered a loss. Tempo now makes a claim against Insurance Company on the policy. The premium had been billed to Lile but was unpaid at the time of loss. In an action by Tempo Co. against Insurance Company, what judgment? Explain.

12. On July 15, Adler purchased in Chicago a Buick sedan, intending to drive it that day to St. Louis, Missouri. He telephoned a friend, Maruchek, who was in the insurance business, and told him that he wanted liability insurance on the automobile, limited in amount to $50,000 for injuries to one person and to $100,000 for any one accident. Maruchek took the

order and told Adler over the telephone that he was covered and that his policy would be written by the Young Insurance Company. Later that same day and before Maruchek had informed the Young Insurance Company of Adler's application, Adler negligently operated the automobile and seriously injured Brown, who brings suit against Adler. Is Adler covered by liability insurance? Explain.

13. Graham owns a building having a fair market value of $120,000. She takes out a fire insurance policy from the Bentley Insurance Company for $72,000; the policy contains an 80 percent co-insurance clause. The building is damaged by fire to the extent of $48,000. How much insurance is Graham entitled to collect? Explain.

14. Phil was the owner of a herd of twenty highly bred dairy cows. He was a prosperous farmer, but his health was very poor. On the advice of his doctor, Phil decided to winter in Arizona. Before he left, he made an agreement with Freya under which Freya was to keep the cows on Freya's farm through the winter, be paid the sum of $800 by Phil, and return to Phil the twenty cows at the close of the winter. For reasons that Freya thought made good farming sense, Freya sold six of the cows and replaced them with six other cows. After winter was over, Phil returned from Arizona. Is Freya liable for conversion of the original six cows? Why or why not?

15. Hines stored her furniture, including a grand piano, in Arnett's warehouse. Needing more space, Arnett stored Hines's piano in Butler's warehouse next door. As a result of a fire, which occurred without any fault of Arnett or Butler, both warehouses and their contents were destroyed. Is Arnett liable to Hines for the value of her piano and furniture? Explain.

16. Curtis rented a safe deposit box from Reliable Safe Deposit Company, in which he deposited valuable securities and $4,000 in cash. Later, after opening the box and discovering $1,000 missing, Curtis brought an action against Reliable. At the trial, the company showed that its customary procedure was as follows: that there were two keys for each box furnished to each renter; that if a key was lost, the lock was changed; that new keys were provided for each lock each time a box was rented; that there were two clerks in charge of the vault; and that one of the clerks was always present to open the box. Reliable Safe Deposit Company also proved that two keys were given to Curtis at the time he rented his box, that his box could not be opened without the use of one of the keys in his possession, and that the company had issued no other keys to Curtis's box. Explain whether Reliable is obligated to pay Curtis for the missing $1,000.

17. A, B, and C each stored five thousand bushels of yellow corn in the same bin in X's warehouse. X wrongfully sold ten thousand bushels of this corn to Y. A contends that inasmuch as his five thousand bushels of corn were placed in the bin first, the remaining five thousand bushels belong to him. Explain what are the rights of the parties.

18. a. On April 1, Mary Rich, at the solicitation of Super Fur Company, delivered a $13,000 mink coat to the company at its place of business for storage in its vaults until November 1. On the same day, she paid the company its customary charge of $50 for such storage. After Mary left the store, the general manager of the company, on finding that its storage vaults were already filled to capacity, delivered Mary's coat to Swift Trucking Company for shipment to Fur Storage Company. En route, the truck in which Mary's coat was being transported was badly damaged by fire caused by the driver's negligence, and Mary's coat was totally destroyed. Is Super Fur Company liable to Mary for the value of her coat? Why or why not?

    b. Would your answer be the same if Mary's coat had been safely delivered to Fur Storage Company and had been stolen from the company's storage vaults without negligence on its part? Why or why not?

19. Rich, a club member, left his golf clubs with Bogan, the pro at the Happy Hours Country Club, to be refinished at Bogan's pro shop. The refinisher employed by Bogan suddenly left town, taking Rich's clubs with him. The refinisher had previously been above suspicion, although Bogan had never checked on the man's character references. A valuable sand wedge that Bogan had borrowed from another member, Smith, for his own use in an important tournament was also stolen by the refinisher, as well as several pairs of golf shoes that Bogan had checked for members without charge as an accommodation. The club members concerned each made claims against Bogan for their losses. Can (a) Rich, (b) Smith, and (c) the other members compel Bogan to make good their respective losses? Explain.

20. Donna drove an automobile into Terry's garage and requested him to make repairs for which the charge would be $125. Donna, however, never returned to get the automobile. Two months later, Carla saw the automobile in Terry's garage and claimed it as her own, asserting that it had been stolen from her. Terry told Carla that she could have the automobile if she paid for the repairs and storage. One week later, Molly appeared and proved that the automobile was hers, that it had

been stolen from her, and that neither Donna nor Carla had any rights in it. Discuss whether Terry is liable for conversion of the automobile.

21. On June 1, Cain delivered his 2013 automobile to Barr, the operator of a repair shop, for necessary repairs. Barr put the car in his lot on Main Street. The lot, which is fenced on all sides except along Main Street, holds one hundred cars and is unguarded at night, although the police make periodic checks. The lot is well lit. The cars do not have the keys in them when left out overnight. At some time during the night of June 4, the hood, starter, alternator, and gearshift were stolen from Cain's car. The car remained on the lot, and during the evening of June 5,

the transmission was stolen from the car. Discuss whether Barr exercised due care in taking care of the automobile.

22. Seton in Phoenix, according to a contract with Rider in New York, ships to Rider goods conforming to the contract and takes from the carrier a shipper's order bill of lading that Seton indorses in blank and forwards by mail to Clemson, his agent in New York, with instructions to deliver the bill of lading to Rider on receipt of payment of the price for the goods. Forest, a thief, steals the bill of lading from Clemson and transfers it for value to Pace, a *bona fide* purchaser. Before the goods arrive in New York, Rider is insolvent. What are the rights of the parties? Explain.

C A S E   P R O B L E M S

23. Scarola purchased an automobile for value and without knowledge that it was stolen. After he insured the car with Insurance Company of North America (INA), the car was stolen once again. When INA refused to reimburse Scarola for the loss, contending that he did not have an insurable interest in the car, Scarola brought an action. Did Scarola have an insurable interest in the automobile? Why or why not?

24. Sears had sold to and installed in the Seven Palms Motor Inn a number of furnishings, including drapes and bedspreads, in connection with the construction of a motel on land Seven Palms owned. Sears did not receive payment in full for the materials and labor and brought suit to recover $8,357.49, with interest, and to establish a mechanic's lien on the motel and land for the unpaid portion of the furnishings. Seven Palms asserted that neither the drapes nor bedspreads were fixtures and that, thus, Sears could not obtain a mechanic's lien on them. Explain whether the drapes and bedspreads are fixtures.

25. David E. Ross, his two brothers, and their families operated and owned the entire stock of five businesses. Ross had three children: Rod, David II, and Betsy. David II and Betsy were not involved in the operation of the companies, but Rod began working for one of the firms, Equitable Life and Casualty Insurance Company, in 2014. Between 2016 and 2020, the elder Ross informed a number of persons of his desire to reward Rod for his work with Equitable Life by giving him stock in addition to the stock he would inherit. He subsequently executed several stock transfers to Rod, representing shares in

various family businesses, which were reflected by appropriate entries on the corporate books. Certificates were issued in Rod's name and placed in an envelope identified with the name Rod Ross, but they were kept with the other family stock certificates in an office safe to which Rod did not have access. In all, one-fourth of the stock holdings of David E. Ross were transferred to Rod in this manner. This fact is consistent with the elder Ross's expressed intention that Rod should ultimately receive a total of one-half of the stock upon his father's death. David E. died in April 2020. His will divided the estate equally among the three children and made no reference to prior gifts of stock to Rod. David II and Betsy brought an action contesting the validity of the stock transfers. Are the *inter vivos* gifts of the stock valid? Explain.

26. Laval was a patient of Dr. Leopold, a practicing psychiatrist. Dr. Leopold shared an office with two associates practicing in the same field. No receptionist or other employee attended the office. Laval placed her coat in the clothes closet in the office reception room. Later, when she returned to retrieve the coat to leave, she found it missing. Is Dr. Leopold liable to Laval for the value of her coat? Explain.

27. Sewall left his car in a parking lot owned by Fitz-Inn Auto Parks, Inc. The lot was approximately one hundred by two hundred feet in size and had a chain link fence along the rear boundary to separate the lot from a facility of the Massachusetts Bay Transportation Authority. Although the normal entrance and exit were located at the front of the

lot, it was also possible to leave by way of small side streets on either side of the lot. Upon entering the lot, the driver would pay the attendant on duty a fee of $5 to park. The attendant's duties were limited to collecting money from patrons and directing them to parking spaces. Ordinarily, the attendant remained on duty until 11:00 A.M., after which time the lot was left unattended. Furthermore, a patron could remove his car from the lot at any time without interference by any employee of the parking lot.

On the morning of April 15, Sewall entered the lot, paid the $5 fee, parked his car in a space designated by the attendant, locked it, and took the keys with him. This was a routine he had followed for several years. When he returned to the unattended lot that evening, however, he found that his car was gone, apparently having been stolen by an unidentified third person. Is Fitz-Inn, the owner of the lot, liable for the value of the car? Why or why not?

28. Mieske delivered 32 fifty-foot reels of developed movie film to the Bartell Drug Company to be spliced together into four reels for viewing convenience. She placed the films, which contained irreplaceable pictures of her family's activities over a period of years, into the order in which they were to be spliced and then delivered them to the manager of Bartell. The manager placed a film-processing packet on the bag of films and gave Mieske a receipt that stated, "We assume no responsibility beyond retail cost of film unless otherwise agreed to in writing." Although the disclaimer was not discussed, Mieske's parting words to the store manager were, "Don't lose these. They are my life."

Bartell sent the film to its processing agent, GAF Corporation, which intended to send them to another processing lab for splicing. While at the GAF laboratory, however, the film was accidentally placed in the garbage dumpster and was never recovered. Upon learning of the loss of their film, the Mieskes brought action to recover damages from Bartell and GAF. The defendants argued that their liability was limited to the cost of the unexposed film. Are GAF or Bartell liable to the Mieskes? If so, for how much? Explain.

29. Plaintiff, Heath Benjamin (Benjamin), found more than $18,000 in currency inside the wing of an airplane. At the time of this discovery, State Central Bank (State) owned the plane and it was being serviced by Lindner Aviation, Inc. (Lindner). Benjamin at the time was employed by Lindner and was conducting a routine annual inspection of the plane.

As part of the inspection, Benjamin removed panels from the underside of the wings. Although these panels were to be removed annually as part of the routine inspection, a couple of the screws holding the panel on the left wing were so rusty that Benjamin had to use a drill to remove them. Benjamin testified that the panel probably had not been removed for several years. Inside the left wing Benjamin discovered two packets approximately four inches high and wrapped in aluminum foil. He removed the packets from the wing and took off the foil wrapping. Inside the foil was approximately $18,000 tied in string and wrapped in handkerchiefs.

The money was eventually turned over to the Keokuk police department.

No one came forward within twelve months claiming to be the true owner of the money. Explain who is entitled to receive the money.

30. Calvin Klein, Ltd., a New York clothing company, had used the services of Trylon Trucking Corporation for more than three years, involving hundreds of shipments, prior to the lost shipment at issue. After completing each carriage, Trylon would forward to Calvin Klein an invoice that contained a limitation of liability provision. The provision stated, "In consideration of the rate charged, the shipper agrees that the carrier shall not be liable for more than $50 on any shipment accepted for delivery to one consignee unless a greater value is declared, in writing, upon receipt at time of shipment and charge for such greater value paid, or agreed to be paid, by shipper."

On April 2, Trylon dispatched its driver Jamahl Jefferson to the John F. Kennedy International Airport to pick up 2,833 blouses sent from Hong Kong, China, to Calvin Klein. The driver disappeared, stealing both the truck and the blouses. Calvin Klein sued Trylon for the full value of the blouses. Does the limitation of liability provision extend to the shipment? Explain.

31. Francis B. Freeman, Jr., purchased a cattle scale for $11,000. The scale, which weighs approximately six thousand five hundred pounds, was sold as a portable model. The manufacturer sold additional items that permitted the scale to be moved. Freeman did not buy that equipment. Freeman placed the scale in a barn on a concrete pad poured for the scale, then poured concrete ramps that would allow cattle to enter and exit the scale. Freeman further welded an iron fence into place to help funnel the cattle through the scale area. Although the scale was designed to be portable, 70 percent of the scales sold were installed the same way Freeman installed his. The

scale has remained in place since its installation. The scale could be moved by cutting away a welded metal fence and lifting the scale with heavy machinery. The removal of the fence would take approximately one hour with use of a cutting torch, after which the scale could be moved within fifteen minutes. Mary Ann Barrs purchased the land—including the barn that housed the cattle scale—from Freeman for $3.5 million. Barrs claims that the cattle scale was a fixture that was part of the land and passed to her in the sale. Explain whether the cattle scale is a fixture.

T A K I N G   S I D E S

The plaintiffs are public utilities providing telecommunications services in New Hampshire. The plaintiffs commenced separate actions for abatement of real estate taxes against sixteen municipalities. The plaintiffs disputed the defendants' treatment of its communications equipment as real estate, thereby challenging their authority to tax its equipment. The communications equipment at issue involves two basic categories: (1) distribution plant, which includes telephone poles, wires, and underground conduits, and (2) central office equipment, consisting of frames, switches, and other power equipment.

The plaintiffs submitted affidavits setting forth the following facts. All of the plaintiffs' poles, wires, and underground conduits located in the municipalities are placed either on public rights of way or on private property owned by third parties. Approximately 90 percent of the poles are located on public rights of way pursuant to licenses issued by the state or the municipalities. The remaining 10 percent of the poles are placed on private property either by consent of the property owner or pursuant to an easement. The poles, wires, and underground conduits are installed in a manner that permits and facilitates their removal and relocation. Consequently, removal of that equipment is neither complicated nor timeconsuming and does not harm the underlying land or change its usefulness. The plaintiffs remove and relocate their poles, wires, and underground conduits at the request of the state or the applicable private landowner or municipality. In obtaining the licenses, consents, or easements for their poles, wires, and underground conduits, the plaintiffs insist on maintaining ownership of that equipment and refuse any requests to make the equipment a permanent part of the realty. The plaintiffs' central office equipment, most of which is located in buildings owned by the plaintiffs, is portable and is designed to permit removal and relocation. The plaintiffs' practice and policy is to move pieces of central office equipment among buildings in response to changes in technology or system use. Although certain frames are bolted to the buildings, their removal is achieved without affecting the usefulness of the buildings or the frames themselves. When the plaintiffs ultimately vacate a building used as a central office, they remove all of their equipment and merely transfer the building "as a shell." The vacated building, though devoid of central office equipment, retains utility for other commercial or professional uses. The defendants did not dispute the specific facts set forth by the plaintiffs.

a. What are the arguments that the property is not real property and therefore not subject to taxation by the municipalities?

b. What are the arguments that the property is real property and can be taxed by the municipalities?

c. Who is correct? Explain.

Interests in Real Property

Interests in real property may be classified as possessory or nonpossessory interests. Possessory interests in real property, called estates, are classified to indicate the quantity, nature, and extent of the rights they involve. The two major categories are freehold estates (those existing for an indefinite time or for the life of a person) and estates less than freehold (those that exist for a predetermined time), called leasehold estates. Both freehold estates and leasehold estates are regarded as possessory interests in property. Also, there are several nonpossessory interests in property, including easements and *profits à prendre*. In addition, a person may have a privilege or a license to go on the property for a certain purpose. The ownership of an interest in property may be held by one individual or concurrently by two or more persons, each of whom is entitled to an undivided interest in the entire property. This chapter considers these topics.

48-1 Freehold Estates

As stated previously, a freehold estate is a right of ownership of real property for an indefinite time or for the life of a person. Of all the estates in real property, the most valuable usually are those estates that combine the enjoyment of immediate possession with ownership at least for life. These estates are either some form of fee estates or estates for life. In addition, either type of estate may be created without immediate right to possession; such an estate is known as a future interest. Estates are classified according to their duration.

48-1a FEE ESTATES

Fee estates include the right to immediate possession for an indefinite time and the right to transfer the interest by deed or will. Fee estates include both fee simple and qualified fee estates.

FEE SIMPLE ESTATE When a person says that he has "bought" a house or a corporation informs its shareholders that it has "purchased" an industrial site, the property generally is held in fee simple. A **fee simple estate** means that the property is owned absolutely and can be sold or passed on by will or inheritance; this estate provides the greatest possible ownership interest. The absolute rights to transfer ownership and to transmit that ownership through inheritance are basic characteristics of a fee simple estate. The estate signifies full control over the property, which can be sold or disposed of as desired. Fee simple is the most extensive and comprehensive estate in land; all other estates are derived from it.

A fee simple is created by any words that indicate an intent to convey absolute ownership. "To B in fee simple" will accomplish this, as will "To B forever." The general presumption is that a conveyance is intended to convey full and absolute title in the absence of a clear intent to the contrary. The grantor must possess or have the right to transfer a fee simple interest to transfer such an interest.

QUALIFIED OR BASE FEE ESTATE A **qualified fee estate** is an estate in land that is less than a fee simple estate because it will terminate on the happening of a contingent event. A qualified fee estate is also known as a base fee, conditional fee, or fee simple defeasible. For example, Abe may provide in his will that his daughter is to have his house and lot in "fee simple forever so long as she does not use it to sell alcoholic beverages, in which case the house shall revert to Abe's estate." If his daughter dies without using the house to sell alcoholic beverages, the property is transferred to her heirs as though she owned it absolutely. If, however, Abe's daughter uses the house to sell alcoholic beverages, the daughter will lose her title to the land, and it will revert to Abe's heirs.

The holder of a qualified fee interest may transfer the property by deed or will, and the property will pass by intestate succession. All transferees, however, take the property subject to the initial condition imposed upon the interest.

48-1b LIFE ESTATES

A grant or a devise (grant by will) "to Alex for life" creates in Alex an estate that terminates on his death. Such a provision may stand alone, in which case the property will revert to the grantor and his heirs, or as is more likely, it will be followed by a subsequent grant to another party, such as "to Alex for life and then to Benjamin and his heirs." Alex is the life tenant, and Benjamin is generally described as the remainderman. Alex's life, however, need not be the measure of his life estate, as where an estate is granted "to Alex for the life of Dale." Upon Dale's death, Alex's interest terminates; if Alex dies before Dale, Alex's interest passes to his heirs or as he directs in his will for the remainder of Dale's life. Thus, a life estate is an ownership right in property for the life of a designated individual, while a remainder is the ownership estate that takes effect when a prior life estate terminates.

No particular words are necessary to create a life estate, so long as the words chosen clearly reflect the intent of the grantor. Life estates arise most frequently in connection with the creation of trusts, a subject considered in *Chapter 50.*

Generally, a life tenant may make reasonable use of the property as long as he does not commit "waste." Any act or omission that permanently injures the realty or unreasonably changes its characteristics or value constitutes **waste**. For example, failing to repair a building, cutting timber excessively without replanting, or neglecting to observe adequate conservation techniques may subject the life tenant to an action by the remainderman to recover damages for waste.

A conveyance by the life tenant passes only her interest. The life tenant and the remainderman may, however, join in a conveyance to pass the entire fee to the property, or the life tenant may terminate her interest by conveying it to the remainderman.

Practical Advice
The use of a life estate with a remainder is a useful way of providing income to one person with the ability to control the distribution of the corpus upon the termination of the life estate.

48-1c FUTURE INTERESTS

Not every interest in property carries the right to immediate possession, even though the right and title to the interest are absolute. Thus, where property is conveyed or devised by will "to Anderson during his life and then to Brown and her heirs," Brown has a definite presently existing *interest* in the property, but she is not entitled to immediate *possession*. This right and similar rights, generically referred to as **future interests**, are of two principal types: reversions and remainders.

REVERSIONS If Anderson conveys property "to Brown for life" and makes no disposition of the remainder of the estate, Anderson holds the **reversion**—the grantor's right to the property upon the death of the life tenant. Thus, Anderson would regain ownership to the property when Brown dies. Furthermore, because the grantor has only to allow his grantee's estate to expire before he may regain ownership, a reversion in Anderson also is created if he conveys property "to Caldwell for ten years." Reversions may be transferred by deed or will and pass by intestate succession.

A **possibility of reverter**, or a conditional reversionary interest, exists where property *may* return to the grantor or his successor in interest because an event upon which a fee simple estate was to terminate has occurred. This potential for reversion is present in the grant of a base or qualified fee, previously discussed in this chapter. Thus, Ellen has a possibility of reverter if she dedicates property to a public use "so long as it is used as a park" and indicates that if it is not so used, it will revert to her heirs. If in one hundred years the city ceases to use the property for a park, Ellen's heirs will be entitled to the property. A possibility of a reverter may pass by will or intestate succession. In some States, it may be transferred by deed.

REMAINDERS A remainder, as discussed, is an estate in property that, like a reversion, will take effect in possession, if at all, upon the termination of a prior estate created by the *same instrument.* Unlike a reversion, a remainder is held by a person other than the grantor or his successors. A grant from Gwen to "William for his life and then to Charles and his heirs" creates a remainder in Charles. Upon the termination of the life estate, Charles will be entitled to possession as remainderman, taking his title not from William, but from the original grantor, Gwen. Remainders are of two kinds: vested remainders and contingent remainders.

A **vested remainder** is one in which the only contingency to possession by the remainderman is the termination of all preceding estates created by the transferor. When Jalen has a remainder in fee, subject only to a life estate in Carol, the only obstacle to the right of immediate possession by Jalen or his heirs is Carol's life. Carol's death is sufficient and necessary to place Jalen in possession. The law considers this unconditional or vested remainder as a fixed, present interest to be enjoyed in the future. Such an interest in property is just as transferable as the life estate that precedes it, and it is characteristic of a vested remainder that the owner of the preceding estate can do nothing to defeat the remainder.

A **contingent remainder**, by comparison, is one in which the right to possession is dependent or conditional on the happening of some event in addition to the termination of the preceding estates. The contingent remainder may be conditioned on the existence of some person not yet born or on the happening of an event that may never occur. A provision in a will "to Sandy for life and then to her children, but if she has no children then to Douglas" creates contingent remainders both as to the children and as to Douglas. If Sandy marries and has a child, the remainder then vests in that child, and Douglas's expectancy is closed out. If Sandy dies without having had a child, then and only then will an estate vest in Douglas. It is, of course, possible for a contingent remainder to become vested while possession is still in the preceding life estate, as evidenced by the birth of a child to Sandy in the above example. In most States, a contingent remainder is transferable by deed. It also is inheritable, unless by limitation it terminates before the death of the remainderman.

♦ **SEE FIGURE 48-1:** *Freehold Estates*

48-2 Leasehold Estates

A **lease** is both a contract and a conveyance of an estate in land. It is a contract, express or implied, by which the owner of the land, the **landlord (lessor)**, grants to another, the tenant (lessee), an exclusive right to use and possession of the land for a definite or ascertainable time, or term. The possessory term thus granted is an estate in land called a **leasehold**, which is a nonfreehold estate. The landlord retains an interest in the property, called a *reversion*. A leasehold estate has two principal characteristics: it continues for a definite or ascertainable term and carries with it the tenant's obligation to pay rent to the landlord. Thus, if Linda, the owner of a house and lot, rents both to Ted for a year, Linda, of course, retains the title to the property, but she has sold to Ted the right to occupy it. During the term of the lease, Ted's right to occupy the property is superior to that of Linda, and as long as he occupies in accordance with the lease contract, he has, as a practical matter, exclusive possession against all the world as though he were the actual owner.

The law of leasehold estates has changed considerably over the past few decades. Traditionally, the common law viewed a leasehold estate less as a contract than as a conveyance of the use of land. In the twenty-first century, the landlord-tenant relationship is primarily viewed as a contract and therefore subject to the contract doctrines of unconscionability, implied warranties, and constructive conditions.

Moreover, numerous ordinances and statutes, such as the 1972 Uniform Residential Landlord and Tenant Act (Act), now protect tenants' rights, thereby further modifying the landlord-tenant relationship. The Act, promulgated by the Uniform Law Commission, has been enacted in whole or in part by at least twenty-six States and has influenced statutory developments in many other States. It provides a comprehensive system for regulating the relationship between landlords and tenants and governs most persons who reside in rental housing. The Act does not apply to commercial or industrial properties, the occupancy of hotels or motels, mobile home park tenants, and recreational vehicle long-term tenants. The Act contains detailed requirements regarding the landlord's obligations (restrictions on security deposits and methods for providing notices to tenants and prohibitions on certain provisions in rental agreements), the landlord's rights (collection of rent, eviction, entering the premises, and termination of the lease), the tenant's obligations (payment of rent and compliance with rules), and the tenant's rights (possession, termination of the lease, receipt of essential services, and avoidance of unlawful eviction). Finally, the Act provides remedies for noncompliance by either the landlord or the tenant. The Revised Residential Landlord and Tenant Act of 2015 includes new articles covering the disposition of tenant property, lease termination in case of domestic violence or sexual assault, and security deposits. As of July 2021, it had not been adopted by any State.

48-2a CREATION AND DURATION

Because they are created by contract, the usual requirements for contract formation apply to leaseholds. In most jurisdictions, leases for a term longer than a statutorily specified period, generally fixed at either one or three years, must be in writing. A few States require that all leases be in writing. Leasehold interests have historically been divided into four categories: (1) definite term, (2) periodic tenancy, (3) tenancy at will, and (4) tenancy at sufferance. These tenancies most significantly vary in their duration and their manner of termination.

DEFINITE TERM A lease for a definite term automatically expires at the end of the term. Such a lease is frequently termed a tenancy for years, even though its duration may be one year or less. It is created by express agreement, oral or written. No notice to terminate is required since the lease established its termination date.

PERIODIC TENANCY A **periodic tenancy** is a lease of indefinite duration that continues for successive periods unless one party terminates it by notice to the other. For example, a lease to Ted "from month to month" or "from year to year" creates a periodic tenancy. Periodic tenancies are generally express, oral, or written, but also arise by implication. If Laura leases to Ted without stating any term in the lease, this creates

FIGURE 48-1 Freehold Estates

Interest	Complementary Estate	Duration	Transfer by Deed	Transfer by Will or Intestacy
Fee Simple	None	Perpetual	Yes	Yes
Qualified Fee	Possibility of reverter	Until contingency occurs	Yes	Yes
Life Estate	Reversion or remainder	Life of indicated person	Yes	No, unless measuring life is not life tenant's
Reversion	Life estate	Perpetual	Yes	Yes
Possibility of Reverter	Qualified fee	Perpetual if contingency occurs	In some States	Yes
Vested Remainder	Life estate	Perpetual	Yes	Yes
Contingent Remainder	Life estate	Perpetual if contingency occurs	In most States	Yes, unless it is limited such that it terminates before the death of the remainderman

a tenancy at will. If, moreover, Ted pays rent to Laura at the beginning of each month (or some other regular time) and Laura accepts such payments, most courts would hold that the tenancy at will has been transformed into a tenancy from month to month.

Either party may terminate a periodic tenancy at the expiration of any one period, but only upon adequate notice to the other party. In the absence of an express agreement in the lease, the common law requires six months' notice in tenancies from year to year. In most jurisdictions, this period has been shortened by statute to periods ranging between thirty and ninety days. In periodic tenancies involving periods of less than one year, the notice required at common law is one full period in advance, but again, this requirement may be subject to statutory regulation.

TENANCY AT WILL A lease containing a provision that either party may terminate at any time creates a tenancy at will. A lease that does not specify duration likewise creates a tenancy at will. At common law, such tenancies were terminable without any prior notice, but many jurisdictions now have statutes requiring a period of notice before termination, usually ten to ninety days.

TENANCY AT SUFFERANCE A **tenancy at sufferance** arises when a tenant fails to vacate the premises at the expiration of the lease and thereby becomes a holdover tenant. The common law gives the landlord the right to elect either to dispossess such tenant or to hold her for another term. Until the landlord makes this election, a tenancy at sufferance exists.

Practical Advice

When entering into a lease, specify the duration of the lease and any optional periods of extension.

48-2b TRANSFER OF INTERESTS

Both the tenant's possessory interest in the leasehold and the landlord's reversionary interest in the property may be freely transferred in the absence of contractual or statutory prohibition. This general rule is subject to one major exception: the tenancy at will. Any attempt by either party to transfer her interest is usually considered an expression of the intent (will) to terminate the tenancy.

TRANSFERS BY LANDLORD After conveying the leasehold interest, a landlord is left with a reversionary interest in the property plus the right to rent and other benefits acquired under the lease. The landlord may transfer either or both of these interests. The party to whom the reversion is transferred takes the property subject to the tenant's leasehold interest, if the transferee has actual or constructive notice of the lease. For example, Linda leases Whiteacre to Tina for five years, and Tina records the lease with the register of deeds. Linda then sells Whiteacre to Arthur. Tina's lease is still valid and enforceable against Arthur, whose right to possession of Whiteacre begins only after the lease expires.

TRANSFERS BY TENANT   In the absence of a prohibitive lease or statutory provision, a tenant, except for a tenant at will, may dispose of his interest either by (1) assignment or by (2) sublease. As a result, most standard leases expressly require the consent of the landlord to an assignment or subletting of the premises. Under the majority view, a covenant against assignment of a lease does not prohibit the tenant from subleasing the premises. Conversely, a prohibition against subleasing is not considered a restriction upon the right to assign the lease.

If a tenant transfers *all* his interest in a leasehold, thereby forfeiting his reversionary rights, he has made an assignment. Many leases prohibit assignment without the landlord's written consent.

If the tenant assigns the lease without consent, the assignment is not void, but it may be avoided by the landlord. In other words, the prohibition of assignment in a lease is solely for the landlord's benefit; the assignor, therefore, cannot rely upon the prohibition in attempting to terminate an otherwise valid assignment on the ground that the landlord did not consent. If, however, the landlord accepts rent from the assignee, he will be held to have waived the restriction.

The tenant's agreement to pay rent and other contractual **covenants** (express promises) pass to and obligate the assignee of the lease as long as the assignee remains in possession of the leasehold estate. Although the assignee is thus bound to pay rent, the original tenant is not thereby relieved of his contractual obligation to do so. If the assignee fails to pay the stipulated rent, the original tenant will have to pay, though he will have a right to be reimbursed by the assignee. Thus, after an assignment of a tenant's interest, both the original tenant and the assignee are liable to the landlord for failure to pay rent.

A **sublease** differs from an assignment in that the tenant transfers *less* than all of her rights in the lease and thereby retains a reversion in the leasehold. For example, Mary is a tenant under a lease from Leon which is to terminate on December 31, 2021. If Mary leases the premises to Tony for a period shorter than that covered by her own lease (e.g., until November 30, 2021), Mary has subleased the premises because she has transferred less than her whole interest in the lease.

The legal effects of a sublease are entirely different from those of an assignment. In a sublease, the sublessee (Tony, in this example) has no obligation to Mary's landlord, Leon. Tony's obligations run solely to Mary, the original tenant, and Mary is not relieved of any of her obligations under the lease. Thus, Leon has no right of action against Mary's sublessee, Tony, under any covenants contained in the original lease between him and Mary because that lease has not been assigned to Tony. Mary, of course, remains liable to Leon for the rent and for all other covenants in the original lease.

Practical Advice

As the landlord, clearly specify in the lease whether it may be assigned or sublet and, if so, whether your written consent is required.

♦ **SEE FIGURE 48-2:** *Assignment Compared with Sublease*

FIGURE 48-2   Assignment Compared with Sublease

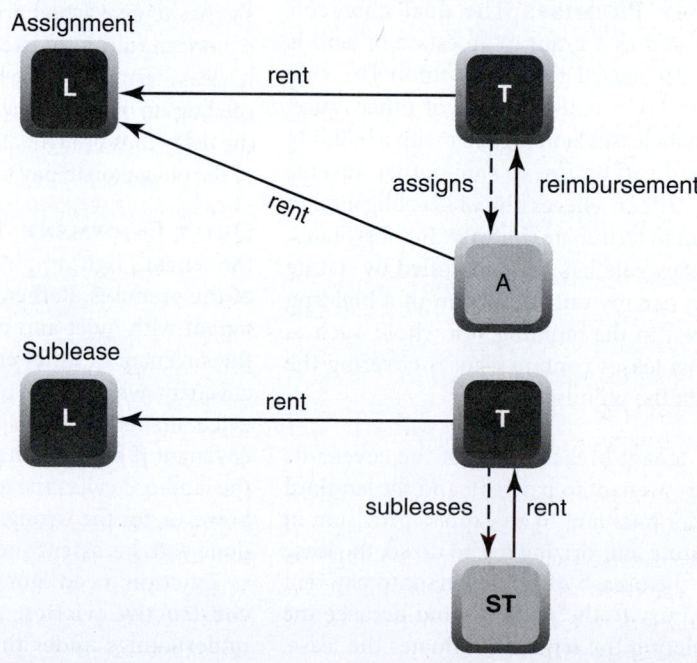

48-2c TENANT'S OBLIGATIONS

While the leasehold estate carries with it only an implied obligation on the part of the tenant to pay reasonable rent, the lease contract almost always contains an express promise or covenant by the tenant to pay rent in specified amounts at specified times. In the absence of a specific covenant providing the amount of rental and the times for payment, the rent will be a *reasonable* amount *payable only at the end of the term*.

Most leases provide that if the tenant breaches any of the covenants in the lease, the landlord may declare the lease at an end and regain possession of the premises. The tenant's express undertaking to pay rent thus becomes one of the covenants upon which this provision can operate. Where the lease makes no such provision, at common law, the tenant's failure to pay rent when due gives the landlord only the right to recover a judgment for the amount of such rent; it gives him no right to oust the tenant from the premises. In most jurisdictions, however, the common law rule has been changed by statute to entitle the landlord to dispossess the tenant for nonpayment of rent, even if the lease does not provide for such action.

Unless the lease contains express provisions to the contrary, a tenant is under no duty to make any repairs to the leased premises. He is not obliged to repair or restore substantial or extraordinary damage occurring without his fault, nor must he repair damage caused by ordinary wear and tear. The tenant is obliged, however, to use the premises in a manner that causes them no substantial injury. The law reimposes this duty; it need not be expressly stipulated in the lease. For example, a tenant who overloads an electrical connection, thereby damaging a wiring system, is liable to the landlord.

DESTRUCTION OF THE PREMISES The dual character of a lease as a contract and as a grant of an estate in land is particularly evident with regard to the common law rule governing the destruction of premises by fire or other cause. In cases in which the tenant leases land together with a building and the building is destroyed by fire or some other adverse cause, the common law neither relieves him of his obligation to pay rent nor permits him to terminate the lease. In most States, however, the common law rule has been modified by statute to exclude tenants who occupy only a portion of a building and who have no interest in the building as a whole, such as apartment tenants. Most leases contain clauses covering the accidental destruction of the premises.

EVICTION When the tenant breaches one of the covenants in her lease, such as the covenant to pay rent, and the landlord evicts or dispossesses her pursuant to an express provision in the lease or under a statute authorizing her to do so, the lease is terminated. Because the breach of the covenant to pay rent does not involve any injury to the premises and because the landlord's action in evicting the tenant terminates the lease, the evicted tenant is not liable to the landlord for any future installments of rent. Most long-term leases, however, contain a survival clause providing that the eviction of the tenant for nonpayment of rent will not relieve her of liability for damages equal to the difference between the rent reserved in the lease and the rent the landlord is able to obtain when reletting the premises. The landlord generally can terminate the tenancy if a tenant repeatedly disturbs other tenants and neighbors, such as by throwing loud parties or selling drugs, or otherwise violates the lease or the law. If the landlord wrongfully evicts the tenant, the tenant's obligations under the lease are terminated and, as will be discussed, the landlord is liable for breach of the tenant's right of quiet enjoyment.

ABANDONMENT If the tenant wrongfully abandons the premises before the term of the lease expires and the landlord reenters the premises or relets them to another, a majority of the courts hold that the tenant's obligation to pay rent after reentry terminates. The landlord, if he desires to hold the tenant to his obligation to pay rent, either must leave the premises vacant or must have in the lease another "survival clause" that covers this situation.

48-2d LANDLORD'S OBLIGATIONS

Under the Federal Fair Housing Act, a landlord cannot discriminate against a tenant with regard to race, color, sex, religion, national origin, disability, or familial status (except under the housing for older persons exception). Nevertheless, absent express provisions in the lease, the landlord, under the common law, has few obligations to her tenant. Under the majority (American) rule, at the beginning of the lease, she has only to give the tenant the right to possession. In a minority of States (the English rule), she has to give actual possession. Thus, in States following the American rule, if the previous tenant refuses to move out when his lease terminates, the landlord must bring dispossession proceedings to oust him; she is not responsible to the new tenant for the delay thus brought about, and the new tenant is not relieved of the obligation to pay rent from the starting date of the lease.

QUIET ENJOYMENT The landlord may not interfere with the tenant's right to physical possession, use, and enjoyment of the premises. Rather, the landlord is bound to provide the tenant with quiet and peaceful enjoyment, a duty known as the covenant of **quiet enjoyment**. The landlord breaches this covenant, which arises by implication, whenever he wrongfully evicts the tenant. He is also regarded as having breached this covenant if someone having better title to the property than the landlord evicts the tenant. The landlord is not responsible, however, for the wrongful acts of third parties unless they are done with his assent and under his direction.

Eviction need not be actual. Under the doctrine of **constructive eviction**, a failure by the landlord in any of her undertakings under the lease that causes a substantial and lasting injury to the tenant's beneficial enjoyment of the premises is regarded as being, in effect, an eviction of the tenant. Under such circumstances, the courts permit the tenant to abandon the premises and terminate the lease. The tenant must abandon possession within a reasonable time, however, to claim that a constructive eviction occurred.

♦ **See Case 48-1**

FITNESS FOR USE Historically, as the primary value of the lease to the tenant was the land, the landlord, under the common law, is under no obligation to provide or maintain the premises in a tenantable (livable) condition or to make them fit for any purpose, unless there is a specific provision in the lease. Most States, however, have abandoned this rule in residential leases by imposing an **implied warranty of habitability** that requires the leased premises to be fit for ordinary residential purposes, having adequate weatherproofing; heat, water, and electricity; as well as clean, sanitary, and structurally safe premises. These courts also have held that the covenant to pay rent is conditioned upon the landlord's performance of this implied warranty of habitability. Courts reaching these results have emphasized that the tenant's interest is in a place to live, not merely in land. The common law assumption that the value of the leasehold is the land may have been valid in an agricultural society and may continue to be valid with regard to certain farm leases, but it is not applicable in the case of a modern apartment rental.

A number of States have statutes requiring landlords to keep residential premises fit for occupation. Zoning ordinances, health and safety regulations, and building and housing codes may also impose certain duties upon the landlord.

If the landlord violates the warranty of habitability, the tenant may terminate the lease and avoid further liability for rent and in some States withhold rent and sue for damages.

♦ **See Case 48-2**

REPAIR Under the common law, in the absence of an express provision in the lease or a statutory duty to do so, the landlord has no obligation to repair or restore the premises. The landlord does, however, have a duty to maintain, repair, and keep in safe condition those portions of the premises that remain under her control. For example, an apartment house owner who controls the lobbies, stairways, elevators, and other common areas of the building is liable for their maintenance and repair and is responsible for injuries that occur as a result of her failure to do so. With respect to apartment buildings, the courts presume that any portion of the premises that is not expressly leased to the tenants remains under the landlord's control. Thus, the landlord, in such cases, is liable to make external repairs, including repairs to the roof.

While at common law in a number of States the landlord is under no duty to repair, restore, or keep the premises in a tenantable condition, she may and often does assume those duties in the lease. Her breach of any such undertakings does not, however, entitle the tenant to abandon the premises and refuse to pay rent. Unless an express provision in the lease gives the tenant this right, the common law allows him only an action for damages. As mentioned, a number of States now have statutes that require the landlord to keep residential premises fit for occupancy and accordingly have imposed upon the landlord a duty to repair those items.

LANDLORD'S LIABILITY FOR INJURY CAUSED BY THIRD PARTIES Some States hold landlords liable for injuries their tenants and others suffer as a result of the foreseeable criminal conduct of third parties. Although landlords cannot be insurers of their tenants' safety, courts have held landlords liable for failure "to take minimal precautions to protect members of the public from the reasonably foreseeable criminal acts of third persons." *Ianelli v. Powers*, 498 N.Y.S.2d 377 (N.Y. App. Div. 1986).

Practical Advice
In your written lease, attempt to provide for the landlord's duty to repair, the landlord's liability to third parties, and the landlord's obligation to maintain the premises in habitable condition.

48-3 Concurrent Ownership

Property may be owned by one individual or by two or more persons concurrently. Two or more persons who hold title concurrently are generally referred to as co-tenants. Each is entitled to an undivided interest in the entire property, and neither has a claim to any specific portion of it. Each may have equal undivided interests, or one may have a larger undivided share than the other. Regardless of the particular relationships between the co-tenants, this form of ownership is distinct from the separate ownership of specific parts of property by different persons. Thus, Anne, Barbara, and Carol each may own separate parts of Blackstone Manor, or each may own, as a co-tenant, an undivided one-third interest in all of Blackstone Manor. Their being co-tenants or the owners of specific portions depends on the manner and form in which they acquired their interests.

The two major types of concurrent ownership are tenancy in common and joint tenancy. Both provide an undivided interest in the whole, the right of both tenants to possession, and the right of either to sell his interest during life and thus terminate the original relationship. Other forms of co-ownership of both real and personal property are tenancy by the entireties and community property. In addition, real property may be owned concurrently in the form of condominiums and cooperatives.

48-3a TENANCY IN COMMON

Under a **tenancy in common**, the most frequently used form of concurrent ownership, each co-owner has both an undivided interest in the property with no right of survivorship and the right to possession and use, but none claim any specific portion of the property. Tenants in common need not have acquired their interests at the same time or by the same instrument, and their interests may differ as to duration and scope. Because there is no right of survivorship, the interests of tenants in common may be devised by will or pass by intestate succession. By statute in all States, a transfer of title to two or more persons is presumed to create a tenancy in common. Tenants in common may terminate their tenancy either by transferring all of their co-interests to one person or by partitioning the property among themselves. Partition is the act of physically dividing the property and thereby changing undivided interests into smaller parcels that each person owns individually. The size of an individual parcel is based upon the size of the owner's prior share of the undivided interest. If physical division of the property (e.g., a house) is not practicable, the property will be sold and the proceeds divided.

48-3b JOINT TENANCY

A **joint tenancy** is co-ownership whereby each tenant holds an undivided interest with a right of survivorship. The most significant feature of joint tenancy is the right of *survivorship*: upon the death of a joint tenant, title to the entire property passes by operation of law to the survivor or survivors. Neither the heirs of the deceased joint tenant nor his general creditors have a claim to his interest after his death, and a joint tenant cannot transfer his interest by executing a will. Nevertheless, a joint tenant may sever the tenancy by conveying or mortgaging his interest to a third party. Furthermore, the interest of either co-tenant is subject to levy and sale upon execution. To sever a joint tenancy is to forfeit the right of survivorship: following severance, the tenancy becomes a tenancy in common among the remaining joint tenants and the transferee. A joint tenancy may be terminated by partitioning the property among the tenants, making each the exclusive owner of a specific part of the entire property.

To sustain a joint tenancy, the common law requires the presence of what are known as the *four unities* of time, title, interest, and possession:

1. the unity of time means that the interests of all tenants must vest at the same time;
2. the unity of title means that all tenants must acquire title by the same instrument;
3. the unity of interest means that the tenants' interests must be identical in duration and scope; and
4. the unity of possession means that the tenants have identical rights of possession and enjoyment.

While the absence of any unity will prevent the creation of a joint tenancy, the presence of the fourth unity and any two of the others will result in the creation of a tenancy in common, because the only unity required of a tenancy in common is the unity of possession.

Practical Advice
If you jointly hold property with another, specify the type of joint ownership.

◆ *See Case 48-3*

48-3c TENANCY BY THE ENTIRETIES

Tenancy by the entireties, which is recognized in some States, is created only by a conveyance to a *husband and wife*. It is distinguished from joint tenancy by the inability of either spouse to convey separately his or her interest during life and thus destroy the right of survivorship. Likewise, the interest of either spouse cannot be attached by creditors. By the nature of the tenancy, divorce would terminate the relationship, and partition would then be available as a method of creating separate interests in the property.

◆ SEE FIGURE 48-3: *Rights of Concurrent Owners*

FIGURE 48-3 Rights of Concurrent Owners

	Undivided Interest	Right to Possession	Right to Sell	Right to Mortgage	Levy by Creditors	Right to Will	Right of Survivorship
Joint Tenancy	Yes	Yes	Yes	Yes	Yes	No	Yes
Tenancy in Common	Yes	Yes	Yes	Yes	Yes	Yes	No
Tenancy by Entireties	Yes	Yes	No	No	No	No	Yes

48-3d COMMUNITY PROPERTY

In Arizona, California, Idaho, Louisiana, Nevada, New Mexico, Puerto Rico, Texas, Washington, and Wisconsin, one-half of any property acquired by either a husband or a wife belongs to each spouse. Originating in the civil law of continental Europe, this system, known as **community property**, has been modified by U.S. common law and by statutes as well.

In most instances, the only property belonging separately to either spouse is that acquired prior to the marriage or acquired subsequent to it by gift or devise. Upon the death of either spouse, one-half of the community property belongs outright to the survivor, and the interest of the deceased spouse in the other half may go to the heirs of the decedent or as directed by will. Under certain conditions in a few jurisdictions, however, the surviving spouse may also claim an interest in the decedent's one-half share of the property.

48-3e CONDOMINIUMS

Condominiums embody a form of co-ownership now widely utilized in the United States. All States have enacted statutes authorizing this form of ownership. The 1980 Uniform Condominium Act (UCA), promulgated by the Uniform Law Commission, contains comprehensive provisions for creation, management, and termination of condominium associations, including point-of-sale consumer protection. At least fourteen States have adopted the UCA. The purchaser of a condominium acquires separate ownership to the unit and becomes a tenant in common with respect to its common facilities, such as the land upon which the project is built, recreational facilities, hallways, parking areas, and spaces between the units. A condominium association, funded by assessments levied on each unit, maintains the common elements. The transfer of a condominium conveys both the separate ownership of the unit and the share in the common elements.

48-3f COOPERATIVES

Cooperatives involve an indirect form of common ownership. A cooperative, usually a corporation, purchases or constructs the dwelling units and then leases the units to its shareholders as tenants, who acquire the right to use and occupy their units.

48-4 Nonpossessory Interests

Although a nonpossessory interest in land entitles the holder to use the land or to take something from it, the interest does not give him the right to possess the land. Nonpossessory interests include easements, *profits à prendre*, and licenses, all of which differ from a tenancy because the tenant has an exclusive *possessory* interest.

48-4a DEFINITION OF EASEMENTS

An easement is a limited right to use the land of another in a manner specified by the acts of the parties or by operation of law and possessing all the attributes of an estate in the land itself. The easement can involve all or a specific portion of the property. For example, a typical easement exists where Liz sells part of her land to Neal and expressly provides in the same or a separate document that Neal, as the adjoining landowner, shall have a right-of-way over a strip of Liz's remaining parcel of land. Neal's land is said to be the **dominant** parcel (land whose owner has rights in other land), and Liz's land, which is subject to the easement, is the servient parcel. Easements may, of course, involve a multitude of different uses, as, for example, a right to run a ditch across another's land; to lay pipe under the surface; to erect power lines; or, in the case of adjacent buildings, to use a stairway or a common or "party" wall.

Because the owner of the entire servient tract retains the title to the servient parcel, she may make any use of or allow others the use of the tract as long as this use does not interfere with the easement. Thus, crops may be grown over an easement for a pipeline, but livestock cannot be pastured on an easement for a driveway. Although the owner of the servient parcel is under a duty not to interfere with the use of the easement, the owner of the dominant parcel generally is responsible for maintaining the easement and keeping it in repair.

48-4b TYPES OF EASEMENTS

Easements fall into two classes: appurtenant easements and easements in gross. **Appurtenant** easements are by far the more common type; the rights and duties they create pertain to the land itself, not to the individuals who have created such easements. Therefore, the easement usually stays with the land when it is sold. For example, if Liz (from the previous example) sells her servient parcel to Kyle, who has actual notice of the easement for the benefit of Neal's land or constructive notice by means of the local recording act, Kyle takes the parcel subject to the easement. Likewise, if Neal conveys his dominant parcel to Daniel, the deed from Neal to Daniel need contain no specific reference to the easement to give to Daniel, as the dominant parcel's new owner, the right to use the right-of-way over the servient parcel. As Neal does not then own the dominant parcel, he has no further right to use the right-of-way. Neal could not, however, transfer the benefit of the easement to a party who did not acquire an interest in the dominant parcel of land. Most frequently, a deed conveying certain land "together with all appurtenances" is sufficient to transfer an easement. This characteristic of an appurtenant easement is described by the statement that both the burden and the benefit of an appurtenant easement pass with the land.

The second type of easement is an **easement in gross**, which is personal to the particular individual who receives the right.

It, in effect, amounts to little more than an irrevocable personal right to use.

◆ See Case 48-4

48-4c CREATION OF EASEMENTS

Easements may be created by (1) express grant or reservation, (2) implied grant or reservation, (3) necessity, (4) dedication, and (5) prescription.

EXPRESS GRANT OR RESERVATION The most common way to create an easement is to convey it by deed. In an easement by **express grant**, one party expressly transfers the easement to another party. For example, when Amy conveys part of her land to Robert, she may, in the same deed, expressly grant him an easement over her remaining property. Alternatively, Amy may grant an easement to Robert in a separate document. This document must comply with all the formalities of a deed. An easement is an interest in land subject to the statute of frauds.

In other instances, when an owner transfers land, she may wish to retain certain rights in it. In an easement by **reservation**, one party expressly reserves the right to retain an easement in property that is being transferred. In the example given, Amy may want to "reserve" over the land she grants to Robert an easement in favor of the land she retains. Amy may reserve this right by express words in the deed of conveyance to Robert.

APPLYING THE LAW

Interests in Real Property

FACTS In 1998, the Padgetts bought a two-acre lot in the mountains from the Morgans. Almost immediately, the Padgetts built a weatherized cabin on the property, which they used every summer for a few months and every winter for a few weeks. They also built a small barn on the eastern edge of the property, behind their garage. After a couple years, the Padgetts improved their access to the barn by extending the gravel drive that started at the street to beyond the garage, along the property's eastern border, and into the barn.

About the time the Padgetts built the barn, the property owners to their east—the Martingales—built a summer home on their one-acre parcel, with a three-car garage in the far westernmost corner of their property. While the Martingales had originally envisioned accessing their garage by way of a spur off the concrete circular drive in front of the house, they did not immediately build the garage access driveway because two huge trees needed to be removed to do so. In the interim, easy access to the Martingale garage was available via the Padgetts' driveway, and the Padgetts did not seem to mind Mrs. Martingale driving the length of their gravel drive and then cutting back onto her own property behind the large trees.

The Martingales and Padgetts were quite friendly. More often than not, when Mrs. Martingale used the Padgetts' gravel drive to get to her garage, Mrs. Padgett would be out gardening. Mrs. Martingale would stop and talk to Mrs. Padgett for a few minutes and then continue driving back to the garage. The subject of Mrs. Martingale's use of the gravel drive never came up in conversation.

The Martingales never removed the big trees and never built any formal access to their garage. Then in late 2020, the Padgetts converted their vacation home in the mountains to their primary residence. They demolished the barn and built a bigger one on the other side of their property. In the spring of 2021, Mrs. Padgett had the gravel leading to the spot where the barn had been removed, and she planted a vegetable garden in the area where the driveway had previously existed. When Mrs. Martingale arrived for her twenty-second consecutive summer in the mountains, she could no longer access her garage.

ISSUE Does Mrs. Martingale have an easement over the Padgetts' property?

RULE OF LAW Easements arise in several ways. First, and most commonly, easements are granted expressly by the landowner. Second, they can arise by implication if an owner of adjacent properties establishes a use that is apparent and permanent and then conveys one of the properties without mention of the easement. Easements can also spring from necessity; conveyance of a portion of a parcel with no access to roads may require the seller also to convey an easement across his remaining land to give the purchaser ingress and egress. Finally, the law of most States contemplates easements by prescription. To establish a prescriptive easement, the one claiming it must prove that she has regularly used the other's land openly and adversely over a specific time period established by the relevant State's adverse possession laws.

APPLICATION The Padgetts did not expressly grant the Martingales an easement over their land. Moreover, no easement by implication can be established because the Padgetts did not buy their land from the Martingales, nor did the gravel driveway or the Martingales' garage exist until a few years after each couple had purchased their parcels. Furthermore, necessity cannot be shown since the Martingale property has street frontage, and all that would be required to give the Martingales easy vehicular access to their garage is removal of two trees on their own property.

The only possibility of establishing a permanent legal right-of-way across the Padgetts' land, perhaps suggested by the decades over which Mrs. Martingale used the gravel drive, is easement by prescription. The first requirement, open and generally known use, presents no hurdle here. Mrs. Padgett was quite aware of Mrs. Martingale's use of the gravel drive because the two women spoke briefly almost every time Mrs. Martingale drove down the Padgetts' gravel path to her own garage. Second, the use must have been adverse to that of the owner. Adverse use of an easement does not require exclusion of the owner. However, it does require that the use be hostile to the wishes of the rightful

owner. Thus, if permission is given, the "adverse" element cannot be proven. Here, Mrs. Padgett apparently approved of Mrs. Martingale's use. Therefore, it cannot be said Mrs. Martingale's use was adverse. The third element of a prescriptive easement is use, consistent with the nature of the right-of-way, without interruption over the statutorily established prescription period. The prescriptive periods in most states are between five and twenty years. If Mrs. Martingale successfully used the Padgetts' gravel drive every time she drove into her garage over a twenty-one year interval, she has probably satisfied the time requirement in even the State with the longest prescriptive period.

CONCLUSION The Martingales' use of the Padgetts' gravel drive was not adverse. Therefore, the Martingales cannot establish an easement over the Padgetts' former gravel drive, despite Mrs. Martingale's openly using the right-of-way regularly for a period of twenty-one years.

IMPLIED GRANT OR RESERVATION EASEMENTS by implied grant or implied reservation arise whenever an owner of adjacent properties establishes an *apparent* and *permanent* use in the nature of an easement and then conveys one of the properties without mention of any easement. For example, suppose that Andrew owns two adjacent lots, Nos. 1 and 2. There is a house on each lot. Behind each house is a garage. Andrew has constructed a driveway along the boundary between the two lots, partly on lot 1 and partly on lot 2, which leads from the street in front of the houses to the two garages in the rear. Andrew conveys lot 2 to Michael without any mention of the driveway. Andrew is held to have *impliedly granted* an easement to Michael over the portion of the driveway that lies on Andrew's lot 1, and he is held to have *impliedly reserved* an easement over the portion of the driveway that lies on Michael's lot 2.

NECESSITY If Sharon conveys part of her land to Terry and the part conveyed to Terry is so situated that he would have no access to it except across Sharon's remaining land, the law implies a grant by Sharon to Terry of an easement by necessity across her remaining land. An easement by necessity usually will not arise if an alternative, albeit circuitous, approach to the land is available.

An easement by necessity may also arise by implied reservation. This would be the case in a situation in which Sharon conveys part of her land to Terry, and her remaining property would be wholly landlocked unless she were given a right-of-way across the land conveyed to Terry.

DEDICATION When an owner of land subdivides it into lots and records the plan or plat of the subdivision, she is held, both by common law and now more frequently by statute,

to have dedicated *to the public* all of the streets, alleys, parks, playgrounds, and beaches shown on the plat. In addition, when the subdivider sells the lots by reference to the plat, it is now generally recognized that the purchasers acquire easements by implication over the areas shown to be dedicated to the public.

PRESCRIPTION An easement may arise by prescription in most States if certain required conditions are met. To obtain an easement by prescription, a person must use a portion of land owned by another in a way (1) that is adverse to the rightful owner's use; (2) that is open and notorious; and (3) that continues, uninterrupted, for a specific period that varies from State to State. The claimant acquires no easement by prescription, however, if given the owner's permission to use the land.

Practical Advice
Be sure to have any easement you obtain put in writing and properly file it with the recorder of deeds.

48-4d PROFITS À PRENDRE
The French phrase *profit à prendre* describes the right to remove the natural resources such as petroleum, minerals, timber, and wild game from the land of another. An example would be the grant by Jack to Roger, an adjoining landowner, of the right to remove coal, fish, or timber from Jack's land or to graze his cattle on Jack's land. Like an easement, a *profit à prendre* may arise by prescription, but if it comes about through an act of the parties, it must be created with all the formalities accorded the grant of an estate in real property. Unless the right is clearly designated as exclusive, the owner of the land

is entitled to exercise it as well. Furthermore, even one who does not own adjacent land may hold the right to take profits. Thus, Norman may have a right to remove crushed gravel from John's acreage even though Norman lives in another part of the county.

48-4e LICENSES

Real interests in property such as easements or *profits à prendre* are considered interests in land. On the other hand, a license, which is created by a contract granting permission to make use of an owner's land, does not create an interest in the property. A license is usually exercised only at the will of the owner and subject to revocation by him at any time. For example, if Carter tells Karen she may cut across Carter's land to pick hickory nuts, Karen has nothing but a license subject to revocation at any time. It is possible that upon the basis of a license, Karen may expend funds to exercise the right, and the courts may prevent Carter from revoking the license simply because it would be unfair to penalize Karen under the circumstances. In such a case, Karen's interest is practically indistinguishable from an easement.

A common example of a license is a theater ticket or the use of a hotel room. No interest is acquired in the premises; there is simply a right of use for a given length of time, subject to good behavior. No formality is required to create a license; a shopkeeper licenses persons to enter his establishment merely by being open for business.

CHAPTER SUMMARY

FREEHOLD ESTATES

Fee Estates right to immediate possession of real property for an indefinite time
- *Fee Simple* absolute ownership of property
- *Qualified Fee* ownership subject to its being taken away upon the happening of an event

Life Estates ownership right in property for the life of a designated person, while the remainder is the ownership estate that takes effect when the prior estate terminates

Future Interests
- *Reversion* grantor's right to property upon termination of another estate
- *Remainders* are of two kinds: vested remainders (unconditional remainder that is a fixed, present interest to be enjoyed in the future) and contingent remainders (remainder interest conditional upon the happening of an event in addition to the termination of the preceding estate)

LEASEHOLD ESTATES

Lease both (1) a contract for use and possession of land and (2) a grant of an estate in land for a period of time
- *Landlord* owner of land who grants a leasehold interest to another while retaining a reversionary interest in the property
- *Tenant* possessor of the leasehold interest in the land Duration of Leases

Duration of Leases
- *Definite Term* lease that automatically expires at the end of the term
- *Periodic Tenancy* lease that continues for successive periods unless terminated by notice to the other party
- *Tenancy at Will* lease that is terminable at any time
- *Tenancy at Sufferance* possession of real property without a lease

Transfer of Tenant's Interest
- *Assignment* transfer of all of the tenant's interest in the leasehold
- *Sublease* transfer of less than all of the tenant's interest in the leasehold

Tenant's Obligations the tenant has an obligation to pay a specified rent at specified times or, if none is specified, to pay a reasonable amount at the end of the term
- *Destruction of the Premises* under the common law, if the premises are destroyed the tenant is not relieved of his obligation to pay rent and cannot terminate the lease
- *Eviction* if the tenant breaches one of the covenants of her lease, the landlord may terminate the lease and evict (remove) her from the premises
- *Abandonment* if tenant abandons property and the landlord reenters or relets it, tenant's obligation to pay rent terminates

Landlord's Obligations
- *Quiet Enjoyment* the right of the tenant to have physical possession of the premises free of landlord interference
- *Fitness for Use* most courts impose for residential leases an implied warranty of habitability that the leased premises are fit for ordinary residential purposes
- *Repair* unless there is a statute or a specific provision in the lease, the landlord has no duty to repair or restore the premises

---

CONCURRENT OWNERSHIP

Tenancy in Common co-ownership in which each tenant holds an undivided interest with no right of survivorship

Joint Tenancy co-ownership with the right of survivorship; requires the presence of the four unities (time, title, interest, and possession)

Tenancy by the Entireties co-ownership by spouses in which neither may convey his or her interest during life

Community Property spouses' rights in property acquired by the other during their marriage

Condominium separate ownership of an individual unit with tenancy in common with respect to common areas

Cooperative the corporate owner of the property leases units to its shareholders as tenants

---

NONPOSSESSORY INTERESTS

Easement limited right to use the land of another in a specified manner
- *Appurtenant* rights and duties created by the easement pertain to and run with the land of the owner of the easement (dominant parcel) and the land subject to the easement (servient parcel)
- *In Gross* rights and duties created by the easement are personal to the individual who received the right
- *Creation of Easements* easements may be created by (1) express grant or reservation, (2) implied grant or reservation, (3) necessity, (4) dedication, and (5) prescription (adverse use)

Profits à Prendre right to remove natural resources from the land of another

Licenses permission to use the land of another

C A S E S

CASE 48-1

Constructive Eviction
HOME RENTALS CORP. v. CURTIS
Appellate Court of Illinois, Fifth District, 1992
236 Ill.App.3d 994, 602 N.E.2d 859, 176 Ill. Dec 913

Harrison, J.

[In February 1989, Home Rentals agreed to rent a single-family residence to Chris Curtis, Ed Domaracki, Mike Fraser, and Carson Flugstad (tenants), all of whom were students at Southern Illinois University. The terms of the written lease stated that the lease was to commence on August 17, 1989, and to expire on August 13, 1990. The tenants were to receive the premises in "good order and repair," rent was to be $740 per month, and

a $500 deposit was required. The tenants initially paid $1,980 to cover the deposit and advance rent for the last two months of the lease.

Although the house was fine when the tenants signed the lease in February, when they arrived on August 15, it was not. The electricity had not yet been turned on. Roaches had overrun the rooms, and the kitchen was so filthy and so infested by bugs that food could not be stored there. The carpet smelled, and one could see outside through holes in the wall. The bathrooms were unsanitary, no toilets worked, one of the bathtubs did not drain, and an open sewage drain emptied bathroom wastewater onto the basement floor. The tenants notified Home Rentals on the 16th that the place was uninhabitable because of the filth and roaches. Home Rentals responded that the tenants should just clean the place up and that it would reimburse them. Accordingly, the tenants attempted to clean the house, but the roach problem continued even after professional extermination, and Home Rentals did nothing about the plumbing. The tenants were never able to stay in the house. On August 21, the tenants finally sought housing elsewhere. They advised Home Rentals that they would not be living in the house, returned the keys, and reported the condition of the house to the city of Carbondale's Code Enforcement Division. The city notified Home Rentals on August 25, 1989, that it had found numerous city code violations and warned the corporation that the house would be posted "occupancy prohibited" unless all violations were corrected within 72 hours. By August 28, 1989, eleven days after the tenants' lease was to have commenced, Home Rentals had finally remedied all the violations. The city withdrew its threat, but Home Rentals did not rent the house to anyone else. Instead, it sued the tenants for breach of the lease and claimed $6,900 for all twelve months under the lease, less the deposit. The tenants denied the allegations and raised as affirmative defenses breach of the implied warranty of habitability and constructive eviction. Based on the latter theory, they asserted a counterclaim seeking the return of the $500 deposit and the $1,480 they had paid in advance rent. The circuit court of Jackson County found for the tenants in the amount of $1,980, and Home Rentals appealed.]

A constructive eviction occurs where a landlord has done "something of a grave and permanent character with the intention of depriving the tenant of enjoyment of the premises." [Citation.] Because persons are presumed to intend the natural and probable consequences of their acts, constructive eviction does not require a finding that the landlord had the express intention to compel a tenant to leave the demised premises or to deprive him of their beneficial enjoyment. All that is necessary is that the landlord committed acts or omissions which rendered the leased premises useless to the tenant or deprived the tenant of the possession and enjoyment of the premises, in whole or part, making it necessary for the tenant to move. * * *

At oral argument, counsel for Home Rentals asserted that defendants did what they did simply because "the premises did not meet their expectations." The inference, of course, was that defendants were overly particular and that their expectations were unrealistic. It is scarcely unreasonable, however, for tenants paying $740 per month to expect flushing toilets, sewage-free basements, and kitchens that are not overrun with roaches. These are things that Home Rentals failed to provide. What Home Rentals did provide was a house that was clearly and unquestionably unfit for people to live in. As a result, defendants had no alternative but to vacate the premises.

Home Rentals correctly points out that a tenant may not abandon premises under the theory of constructive eviction without first affording the lessor a reasonable opportunity to correct the defects in the property [citation], but such an opportunity existed here. Home Rentals' president, Henry Fisher, admitted that he actually inspected the premises as early as August 13. * * *

Considering the magnitude of the problems, four days was opportunity enough for Home Rentals to act. Constructive eviction has been found in analogous circumstances where an even shorter period was involved. [Citation.] We note, moreover, that there is no indication that giving Home Rentals additional time would have made any difference. In the four days before defendants left, the only action the company took at all was to send someone out to spray for bugs, which did not work, and to dispatch a man with a plunger. In the end, it was only because of the intervention by the City of Carbondale that Home Rentals implemented the necessary remedial measures.

* * *

For the foregoing reasons, the judgment of the circuit court of Jackson County is affirmed.

Affirmed.

CASE 48-2

Fitness for Use
TUCKER v. HAYFORD
Washington Court of Appeals, Division 3, 2003
118 Wash. App. 246, 75 P.3d 980

Sweeney, J.

We * * * note that a claim for personal injuries by a tenant can be premised on three distinct legal theories: contract (a rental agreement), common law obligations imposed on a landlord, and the Washington Residential Landlord-Tenant Act of 1973 (Landlord-Tenant Act), [citation], * * *

Here, the tenants claim that they became sick part of their tenancy. The trial judge dismissed all of their causes of action—contract, Landlord-Tenant Act, and common law—concluding that the Landlord-Tenant Act limited all rights to those specifically enumerated in the act. We conclude that the tenants' showing on summary judgment is sufficient to support causes of action based on contract, the Landlord-Tenant Act, and the common law. We therefore reverse the summary dismissal of their claims.

Facts

Robert Hayford bought a lot and mobile home in Kennewick, Washington from Mike Kirby in 1994. A domestic well supplied water to the home. The well water was tested on December 8, 1993. On March 15, 1994, the Benton Franklin District Health Department wrote to Mr. Kirby that: (1) the nitrate level of the well water was 8.8 mg/L; (2) the well was free of bacterial contamination; (3) the sanitary seal was improperly installed and maintained; and (4) chemicals were stored within 100 feet of the well. And "to protect and improve" the water system, the health department recommended that: (1) the sanitary seal be properly installed; and (2) the chemicals be stored at least 100 feet from the well. The health department also recommended that the well be tested yearly. * * *

Mr. Hayford "thumbed through" the report but depended on his real estate agent to call any problems to his attention. And the agent apparently did not.

Mr. Hayford leased the home to Don Tucker and Shalee Miller (now Tucker) in October of 1998. Mr. and Ms. Tucker asked if the well water was drinkable. Mr. Hayford said it was as long as a "Brita" filter was used. He said that the nitrates were a bit high.

The Tuckers have four children, one was born after they moved out of the home. The Tuckers signed a written residential lease prepared by Mr. Hayford. They ultimately extended the tenancy through August 1, 2000. The Tucker family all became ill. The family's pediatric nurse practitioner suggested that they test their well water. The test, dated March 28, 2000, showed bacteria in the water. The Tuckers told Mr. Hayford. He had the well repaired and that solved the problem.

The Tuckers moved out of the home on May 15, 2000. They sued Mr. Hayford for damages for personal injury arising from contaminated water. [The trial court granted Hayford's motion for summary judgment.]

Discussion

The Tuckers sued for damages based on their contract (obligation to perform major maintenance and repair, and covenant of quiet enjoyment); violation of the Landlord-Tenant Act; and negligent misrepresentation as to the water quality. * * *
* * *

Contract Claims
Obligations Imposed by This Contract * * *
* * *

> The tenant may recover for personal injuries caused by the landlord's breach of a repair covenant only if the unrepaired defect created an unreasonable risk of

harm to the tenant. The *Restatement (Second) of Torts* §357 (1965) provides that the lessor of land is liable if (a) the lessor has contracted to keep the land in repair; (b) the disrepair creates an unreasonable risk that performance of the lessor's agreement would have prevented; and (c) the lessor fails to exercise reasonable care in performing the agreement.

[Citation.] The contract defines the extent of the duty when a landlord's duty arises out of a covenant.
* * *

Notice * * * under this provision of the *Restatement* becomes an issue when the particular condition under consideration is *inside* the residence where the landlord has no right to enter. But that is not the case here. The source of water here was an outside well, which the landlord had physical access to. Actual notice is not then required.

Here the lease includes (1) an express covenant of quiet enjoyment and (2) requires that the lessor maintain and repair the leased premises.

* * *

Quiet Enjoyment.
No Washington case directly addresses the impact of drinking water on one's quiet enjoyment of his home. Washington does, however, recognize the relationship of water and habitability. In [citation] the court held that without water, a property is uninhabitable. [Citation.] * * *

Other jurisdictions have also held that a property without potable water is uninhabitable.

It is well settled that unsafe drinking water renders a home uninhabitable. And that by definition interferes with the quiet enjoyment of the home. * * *

Major Maintenance and Repair.
A health inspector recommended that this well be tested at least annually for bacteria. The question then is whether a reasonable person knew or in the exercise of ordinary care should have known that this well should have been tested annually—as part of the major maintenance of this home. Again, the evidence, viewed in a light most favorable to the Tuckers, includes high nitrate levels together with a recommendation for yearly bacteria testing. That is a sufficient showing to support a breach of the major maintenance and repair covenant of this lease, if proved.

Duties at Common Law
Traditional Common Law Landlord Liability.
Common law landlord liability requires a showing: "(1) latent or hidden defects in the leasehold (2) that existed at the commencement of the leasehold (3) of which the landlord had actual knowledge (4) and of which the landlord failed to inform the tenant." [Citation.] The landlord need not discover obscure defects or dangers, nor does the law impose any duty

to repair defective conditions. [Citation.] A "landlord is liable only for failing to inform the tenant of known dangers which are not likely to be discovered by the tenant." [Citation.]

The Tuckers moved into this home in 1998. The well was last tested in 1993. It was not tested again until after the Tuckers tested it in 2000. But this was after the Tuckers got sick. It had not then been tested for the five years prior to the Tuckers' moving in despite a recommendation by the health department that it be tested annually. This well was not then maintained at the time the property was leased to the Tuckers. And the condition of the water was certainly hidden or latent as to the Tuckers. Mr. Hayford did not warn the Tuckers. Mr. Hayford was aware of the report that required the annual testing. * * *

* * *

Implied Warranty of Habitability.
A landlord is subject to liability for physical harm caused to the tenant and others upon the leased property with the consent of the tenant or his subtenant by a dangerous condition existing before or arising after the tenant has taken possession, if he has failed to exercise reasonable care to repair the condition and the existence of the condition is in violation of:

1. an *implied duty of habitability;* or
2. *a duty created by a statute* or administrative regulation.

Restatement (Second) of Property §17.6 (1977).
* * *

Residential Landlord-Tenant Act
* * *

The Uniform Residential Landlord and Tenant Act (Uniform Landlord-Tenant Act) was drafted by the National Conference of Commissions on Uniform State Laws in 1972. [Citation.] While Washington made "substantial changes" to the Uniform Landlord-Tenant Act when it adopted its own Landlord-Tenant Act, our state's version still reflects a "strong [Uniform Landlord-Tenant Act] influence." [Citation.] * * * The purpose of the Uniform Landlord-Tenant Act was twofold: "'simplify, clarify, modernize and revise'" landlord and tenant law, and to "*encourage landlords to maintain and improve the quality of housing.*" [Citation.]

Washington's Landlord-Tenant Act
The Landlord-Tenant Act requires the landlord to "keep the premises fit for human habitation" and to particularly maintain the premises in substantial compliance with health or safety codes for the benefit of the tenant. [Citation.] It requires the landlord to make repairs, except in the case of normal wear and tear, "necessary to put and keep the premises in as good condition as it by law or rental agreement should have been, at the commencement of the tenancy." [Citation.]

It lists the landlord's obligations. [Citation.] And it lists the tenant's remedies: (1) terminate the rental agreement; (2) "[b]ring an action in an appropriate court, or at arbitration if so agreed, for any remedy provided under this chapter *or otherwise provided by law;*" or (3) pursue the other remedies available under the Landlord-Tenant Act. [Citation.]

* * * [Many] jurisdictions allow a tenant's cause of action arising from statutory duties under its versions of the Uniform Landlord-Tenant Act. And Washington commentators appear to agree. We conclude that the Washington Residential Landlord-Tenant Act of 1973 provides a cause of action for the injury sustained here.

* * *

We reverse the trial court's summary judgment order.

CASE 48-3

Concurrent Ownership
WOOD v. PAVLIN
Court of Appeals of Missouri, Southern District, Division One, 2015
467 S.W. 3d 323

Scott, J.
In 1991, Mr. and Mrs. Wood effectively gift-deeded a 266-acre farm to their sons, Johnny and Russell, as joint tenants with right of survivorship. Five months before Russell died in 2011, he transferred his interest into his revocable trust without notice to Johnny.

Johnny sought judicial relief in 2013, alleging Russell's transfer was ineffective and that Johnny owned the whole farm as surviving joint tenant. Alternatively, if the transfer was effective, Johnny sought half the farm's value from Russell's successor trustee on an unjust enrichment theory.

The trial court dismissed for failure to state a claim. An amended petition likewise was dismissed with prejudice. This appeal follows.

* * *

"Joint tenancy is based on the theory that the tenants share one undivided estate, with the distinctive characteristic of the right of survivorship." [Citation.] Such tenancies may be severed by one co-tenant's conveyance, which "destroys the joint tenancy and thereby destroys the right of survivorship." [Citation.]

As Johnny acknowledges, Missouri has recognized this right to sever since before the Civil War. [Citation.] "As therefore a joint tenancy of this nature may be destroyed at the pleasure of either tenants [Citation.]"

A right to sever also is our national norm. "Any joint tenant may unilaterally sever his or her joint tenancy interest, and the consent of the other tenants to the severance or termination is not required. Therefore, a joint tenant has the absolute right to terminate a joint tenancy unilaterally." [Citation.] "It is not necessary that consent to the termination of a joint tenancy be obtained from the other joint tenants." [Citation.]

* * *

We affirm the judgment of dismissal.

CASE
48-4

Types of Easements
BORTON v. FOREST HILLS COUNTRY CLUB
Missouri Court of Appeals, Eastern District, Division Five, 1996
926 S.W. 232

Ahrens, J.

Plaintiffs, Gene and Deborah Borton, appeal from the trial court's grant of summary judgment in favor of defendant, Forest Hills Country Club on plaintiffs' claims for injunctive relief and money damages due to golf balls hit onto their property from defendant's golf course. Plaintiffs also appeal from the summary judgment in favor of defendant on its counterclaim asserting it had gained an easement allowing its members to hit errant golf balls onto plaintiffs' property. We reverse and remand.

The developer of defendant's golf course began to sell lots for residential use adjacent to the golf course in 1963. The developer filed and recorded a set of deed restrictions on all the residential lots adjacent to the golf course in November, 1963. Paragraph 11 of these deed restrictions recites:

> All owners and occupants of any lot in the Forest Hills Club Estates Subdivision shall extend to one person, in a group of members or guests playing a normal game of golf on the Forest Hills Golf and Country Club, or their caddy, the courtesy of allowing such person or caddy the privilege of retrieving any and all errant golf balls which may have landed or remained on any lot in the subdivision. However, care shall be exercised in the retrieving of such golf ball to prevent damage to any lawn, flowers, shrubbery, or other improvement on the lot.

Plaintiffs purchased a residence adjacent to the fairway on the eleventh hole on defendant's golf course in March, 1994. The general warranty deed to plaintiffs provided that the property was subject to the set of deed restrictions and covenants. Because of the proximity of the tee boxes on the eleventh hole to plaintiffs' home, thousands of errant golf balls have been hit onto plaintiffs' property since they purchased their residence.

* * *

Plaintiffs concede that paragraph 11 of the deed restriction gives defendant and its members some right with respect to retrieving errant golf balls. Plaintiffs argue, however, that the right created in paragraph 11 is simply a license. Defendant contends it has an easement over the Borton's property, either by express grant via paragraph 11 in the deed restriction or by prescription.

Both a license and easement give the grantee the right to go onto the grantor's property for a limited use. [Citations.] A license is a personal right and as such, may be revoked at the will of the licensor. [Citation.] An easement, by contrast, gives the grantee an interest in the property of the grantor and thus runs with the land and is binding upon successive landowners. [Citations.]

In the instant case, since the original developer of the property properly recorded and filed the deed restrictions, those restrictions created property interests that run with the land and are binding on successive landowners. [Citations.] Thus, plaintiffs do not have the power to revoke or modify the rights granted to defendant in paragraph 11 of the deed restrictions. Therefore, the deed restrictions in paragraph 11 are in the nature of an easement in favor of defendant and its members to retrieve errant golf balls hit onto plaintiffs' property during a normal game of golf.

* * *

Since the terms of paragraph 11 are binding upon the parties and run with the land, we hold that defendant was granted an express easement by paragraph 11 of the deed restrictions.

* * *

Plaintiffs may recover * * * if they can demonstrate that defendant's current use of the easement constitutes a greater burden to their land than what was contemplated or intended. [Citations.] The defendant did not address plaintiffs' [claims] in its cross motion for summary judgment, and did not submit summary judgment facts to demonstrate that there is no material issue of fact in dispute as to this issue. Thus, the trial court's dismissal of plaintiffs' [claim] was premature and must be reversed.

The trial court's judgment granting defendant an easement over plaintiffs' property is reversed with instructions to enter judgment that defendant was granted an express easement by paragraph 11 of the deed restrictions. The trial court's dismissal of plaintiffs' [claim] is reversed and remanded for further proceedings.

1. Kirkland conveyed a farm to Adland to have and to hold for and during his life and upon his death to Rubin. Some years thereafter, oil was discovered in the vicinity. Adland thereupon made an oil and gas lease, and the oil company set up its machinery to commence drilling operations. Rubin thereupon filed suit to enjoin the operations. Assuming an injunction to be the proper form of remedy, what decision? Explain.

2. Smith owned Blackacre in fee simple absolute. In section 3 of a properly executed will, Smith devised Blackacre as follows: "I devise my farm Blackacre to my son Darwin so long as it is used as a farm." Sections 5 and 6 of the will made gifts to persons other than Darwin. The last and residuary clause of Smith's will provided "All the residue of my real and personal property not disposed of heretofore in this will, I devise and bequeath to Stanford University." Explain what interests in Blackacre were created by Smith's will.

3. Panessi leased to Barnes for a term of ten years beginning May 1 certain premises that were improved with a three-story building, the first floor being occupied by stores and the upper stories by apartments. On May 1 of the following year, Barnes leased one of the apartments to Charles for one year. On July 5, a fire destroyed the second and third floors of the building. The first floor was not burned but was rendered untenantable. Neither the lease from Panessi to Barnes nor the lease from Barnes to Charles contained any provision in regard to the fire loss. Discuss the liability of Barnes and Charles to continue to pay rent.

4. Ames leased an apartment to Boor at $200 a month, payable the last day of each month. The term of the written lease was from January 1, 2020, through April 30, 2021. On March 15, 2020, Boor moved out, telling Ames that he disliked all the other tenants. Ames replied, "Well, you're no prize as a tenant; I probably can get more rent from someone more agreeable." Ames and Boor then had a minor physical altercation in which neither was injured. Boor sent the apartment keys to Ames by mail. Ames wrote Boor, "It will be my pleasure to hold you for every penny you owe me. I am renting the apartment on your behalf to Clay until April 30, 2021, at $175 a month." Boor had paid his rent through February 28, 2020. Clay entered the premises on April 1, 2020. How much rent, if any, may Ames recover from Boor? Explain.

5. Jay signed a two-year lease containing a clause that expressly prohibited subletting. After six months, Jay asked the landlord for permission to sublet the apartment for one year. The landlord refused. This angered Jay, and he immediately assigned his right under the lease to Kay. Kay was a distinguished gentleman, and Jay knew that everyone would consider him a desirable tenant. Explain whether Jay's assignment of his lease to Kay is valid.

6. In 2009, Roy Martin and his wife, Alice, their son, Hiram, and Hiram's wife, Myrna, acquired title to a 240-acre farm. The deed ran to Roy Martin and Alice Martin, the father and mother, as joint tenants with the right of survivorship, and to Hiram Martin and Myrna Martin, the son and his wife, as joint tenants with the right of survivorship. Alice Martin died in 2017, and in 2020, Roy Martin married Agnes Martin. By his will, Roy Martin bequeathed and devised his entire estate to Agnes Martin. When Roy Martin died in 2022, Hiram and Myrna Martin assumed complete control of the farm. State the interest in the farm, if any, of Agnes, Hiram, and Myrna Martin immediately upon the death of Roy Martin. Explain.

7. In her will, Teressa granted a life estate to Amos in certain real estate, with remainder to Brenda and Clive in joint tenancy. All the residue of Teressa's estate was left to Hillman College. While going to Teressa's funeral, the car in which Amos, Brenda, and Clive were driving was wrecked. Brenda was killed instantly, Clive died a few minutes later, and Amos died on his way to the hospital. Discuss who is entitled to the real estate in question and why.

8. Otis Olson, the owner of two adjoining city lots, A and B, built a house on each. He laid a drainpipe from lot B across lot A to the main sewer pipe under the alley beyond lot A. Olson then sold and conveyed lot A to Fred Ford. The deed, which made no mention of the drainpipe, was promptly recorded. Ford had no actual knowledge or notice of the drainpipe, although it would have been apparent to anyone inspecting the premises because it was only partially buried. Later, Olson sold and conveyed lot B to Luke Lane. This deed also made no reference to the drainpipe and was promptly recorded. A few weeks thereafter, Ford discovered the drainpipe across lot A and removed it. Did he have the right to do so? Explain.

9. At the time of his marriage to Ann, Robert owned several parcels of real estate in joint tenancy with his brother, Sam. During his marriage, Robert purchased a house and put the title in his name and his wife's name as joint tenants, not as tenants in common. Robert died; within a month of his death, Smith obtained a judgment against the estate of Robert. Discuss the relative rights of Sam, Smith, and Ann.

10. In 1993, Ogle was the owner of two adjoining lots numbered 6 and 7 fronting at the north on a city street. In that year, she laid out and built a concrete driveway along and two feet in front of what she erroneously believed to be the west boundary of lot 7. Ogle used the driveway for access to buildings situated at the southern end of both lots. Later in the same year, she conveyed lot 7 to Dale, and thereafter in the same year, she conveyed lot 6 to Pace. Neither deed made any reference to the driveway, and after the conveyance, Dale used it exclusively for access to lot 7. In 2021, a survey by Pace established that the driveway encroached six inches on lot 6, and he brought an appropriate action to establish his lawful ownership of the strip upon which the driveway approaches, to enjoin its use by Dale, and to require Dale to remove the overlap. Will Pace prevail? Why or why not?

11. Temco, Inc., conveyed to the Wynns certain property adjoining an apartment complex being developed by Sonnett Realty Company. Although nothing to this effect was contained in the deed, the sales contract gave the purchaser of the property use of the apartment's swimming pool. Temco's sales agent also emphasized that use of the pool would be a desirable feature in the event that the Wynns decided to sell the property.

   Seven years later, the Bunns contracted to buy the property from the Wynns through the latter's agent, Sonnett Realty. Although both the Wynns and Sonnett Realty's agent told the Bunns that the use of the apartment's pool went with the purchased property, neither the contract nor the deed subsequently conveyed to the Bunns so provided. When the Bunns requested pool access passes from Temco and Offutt, the company that owned the apartments, their request was refused. Discuss whether the Bunns have a right to use the apartment's pool.

12. On January 1, Mrs. Irene Kern leased an apartment from Colonial Court Apartments, Inc., for a one-year term. When the lease was entered into, Mrs. Kern asked for a quiet apartment, and Colonial assured her that the assigned apartment was in a quiet, well-insulated building. In fact, however, the apartment above Mrs. Kern's was occupied by a young couple, the Lindgrens. From the start of her occupancy, Mrs. Kern complained of their twice-weekly parties and other actions that so disturbed her sleep that she had to go elsewhere for rest. After Mrs. Kern had lodged several complaints, Colonial terminated the Lindgrens' lease

effective February 28. The termination of the lease was prolonged, however, and Mrs. Kern vacated her apartment, claiming that she was no longer able to endure the continued disturbances. Colonial then brought this action to recover rent owed by Mrs. Kern. Will Colonial prevail? Has Mrs. Kern been constructively evicted? Explain.

13. In 1978, a deed for land in Pitt County was executed and delivered by Joel and Louisa Tyson "unto M. H. Jackson and wife Maggie Jackson, for and during the term of their natural lives and after their death to the children of the said M. H. Jackson and Maggie Jackson that shall be born to their inter-marriage as shall survive them and their heirs and assigns in fee simple forever." Thelma Jackson Vester, a daughter of M. H. and Maggie Jackson, died in 2020, survived by three children. M. H. Jackson, who survived his wife, Maggie Jackson, died in 2021, survived by four sons. The children of Thelma Jackson Vester brought this action against M. P. Jackson, a son of and executor of the will of M. H. Jackson. The children of Vester contended that through their deceased mother, they were entitled to one-fifth interest in the land conveyed by the deed of 1978. The executor contended that the deed conveyed a contingent remainder and only those children who survived the parents took an interest in the land. Discuss the contentions of both of the parties.

14. Robert and Majorie Wake owned land that they used as both a cattle ranch and a farm. Each spring and autumn, the Wakes would drive their cattle from the ranch portion of the operation across an access road on the farmland to Butler Springs, which was also on the farmland.

   In December 1998, the Wakes sold the farm to Jesse and Maud Hess but retained for themselves a right-of-way over the farm access road and the right to use Butler Springs for watering their livestock. In 2005, the Hesses sold the farm to the Johnsons, granting them uninterrupted possession of the property "excepting only that permissive use of the premises" owned by the Wakes.

   The Wakes continued to use the access road and Butler Springs until 2006, when they sold their ranch and granted the new owners "their rights to the water of Butler Springs," but they said nothing about the access road. The ranch was subsequently sold several times, and all the owners used the access road and watering hole. In 2020, the Nelsons purchased the ranch. Shortly thereafter, the Johnsons notified the Nelsons that they had revoked the Nelsons' right to use the access road and Butler Springs. In 2021, the Johnsons closed the access road by locking the gates across the road. The Nelsons brought this action, claiming easements to both the access road and Butler Springs. Does an easement in favor of the Nelsons exist? Why or why not?

15. Clayton and Margie Gulledge owned a house at 532 Somerset Place, N.W. (the Somerset property) as tenants by the entirety. They had three children: Bernis Gulledge, Johnsie Walker, and Marion Watkins. When Margie Gulledge died in 1994, Clayton became the sole owner of the Somerset property. The following year, Clayton remarried, but the marriage was unsuccessful. To avoid a possible loss of the Somerset property, Bernis forwarded Clayton funds to satisfy the second wife's financial demands. In exchange, Clayton conveyed the property to Bernis and himself as joint tenants. In 2015, Clayton conveyed his interest in the Somerset property to his daughter, Marion Watkins. In 2015, Clayton died. Bernis died in 2021, and Johnsie Walker died in 2018. In these proceedings, Marion Watkins claims to be a tenant in common with the estate of Bernis Gulledge. The estate claims that when Clayton died, Watkins' interest was extinguished and Bernis became the sole owner of the Somerset property. Who is correct? Explain.

16. By separate leases, Javins and a few others rented an apartment at the Clifton Terrace apartment complex. When they defaulted on their rent payments, the landlord, First National Realty, brought an action to evict them. The tenants admitted to the default but defended on the ground that the landlord had failed to maintain the premises in compliance with the Housing Code of Washington, D.C. They alleged that approximately 1,500 violations of this code had arisen since the term of their lease began. Discuss the merits of this case.

17. On January 14, 2017, Eura Mae Redmon deeded land to her daughter, Melba Taylor, and two sons, W. C. Sewell and Billy Sewell, "jointly and severally, and unto their heirs, assigns and successors forever," with the grantor retaining a life estate. W. C. Sewell died on November 18, 2018, and Billy Sewell died on May 11, 2019. Mrs. Redmon died on February 17, 2021. Melba Taylor then sought a declaration that her mother had intended to convey the property to the grantees as joint tenants, thereby making her, by virtue of her brothers' deaths, sole owner of the property. Descendants of W. C. and Billy Sewell opposed the complaint on the ground that the deed created a tenancy in common among the grantees. Who is correct? Explain.

18. Fay and Loretta O'Connell were married and owned several bank accounts as joint tenants with rights of survivorship. While accompanied by Loretta's sister, Mary Ann, Fay went to the banks where Fay and Loretta had joint accounts and withdrew all the funds from those accounts. Fay deposited the funds into new accounts in his name alone and designated all but the money market account as payable on death to Mary Ann. Did Fay sever and destroy the joint tenancy? What rights, if any, does Loretta have to the withdrawn funds? Explain.

TAKING SIDES

On June 30, 2012, Martin Hendrickson and Solveig Hendrickson were married, and on January 3, 2013, a home previously owned by Martin was conveyed to them as joint tenants and not as tenants in common. Solveig Hendrickson paid no part of the consideration for the premises. On August 3, 2020, Martin Hendrickson duly executed a Declaration of Election to Sever Survivorship of Joint Tenancy by which he endeavored to preserve an interest in the premises for Ruth Halbert, his daughter by a previous marriage. On the same day, he executed his last will and testament, by the terms of which he directed that his wife, Solveig Hendrickson, receive the minimum amount to which she was entitled under the laws of the State of Minnesota. Martin Hendrickson died with a valid will on October 9, 2020.

a. What are the arguments that the joint ownership was severed by Martin Hendrickson's declaration, thus creating a tenancy in common?

b. What are the arguments that the joint tenancy was not severed by Martin Hendrickson's declaration and thus the property passed to Solveig Hendrickson by survivorship upon Martin Hendrickson's death?

c. Which argument should prevail? Explain.

CHAPTER 49

Transfer and Control of Real Property

CHAPTER OUTCOMES

After reading and studying this chapter, you should be able to:

- Explain (1) the essential elements of a contract of sale of an interest in real property, (2) the meaning and importance of marketable title, and (3) the concept of implied warranty of habitability.

- Describe the fundamental requirements of a warranty, special warranty, and quitclaim deed.

- Explain (1) the elements of a secured transaction, (2) the distinction between a mortgage and a deed,

and (3) the distinction between an assumption of a mortgage and buying subject to a mortgage.

- Explain with examples (1) adverse possession, (2) a variance, (3) a nonconforming use, and (4) eminent domain.

- Describe the nature and types of restrictive covenants.

The law has always been, and still is, extremely cautious about the transfer of title to real estate. Personal property may, for the most part, be passed from owner to owner easily and informally, but real property can be transferred only through compliance with a variety of formalities. Such protocol is apparent in the transfer of property at death, where strict formalities are relaxed only with respect to personal property; it is most evident in a transfer of land during the owner's lifetime.

Title to land may be transferred in three principal ways: (1) by deed; (2) by will or by the law of descent upon the death of the owner; and (3) by open, continuous, and adverse possession by a nonowner for a statutorily prescribed period of years. This chapter discusses the first and third methods of transfer—transfer by deed and adverse possession. The second method is covered in *Chapter 50*.

In addition to the legal restrictions placed on the transfer of real property, a number of other controls apply to the use of privately owned property. Government units impose some of these, including zoning and the taking of property by eminent domain. Private parties through restrictive covenants impose others. These three controls are considered in the second part of this chapter.

TRANSFER OF REAL PROPERTY

The most common way in which real property is transferred is by deed. Such transfers usually involve a contract for the sale of the land, the subsequent delivery of the deed, and payment of the agreed consideration. The transfer of real estate by deed,

however, does not require consideration to be valid; it may be made as a gift. In most cases, the real estate purchaser must borrow part of the purchase price, using the real property as security. A far less usual method of transferring title, called *adverse possession*, requires no contract, deed, or other formality.

49-1 Contract of Sale

As indicated in the chapter on contracts, general contract law governs the sale of real property. In general, the seller agrees to convey the land and the buyer agrees to pay for it. In addition, the Federal Fair Housing Act (Title VIII of the Civil Rights Act, as amended) prohibits discrimination in the real estate market on the basis of race, color, religion, sex, national origin, disability, or familial status. The Act exempts the sale or rental of a single-family house owned by a private individual who owns fewer than four houses, provided that the owner does not use a broker or discriminatory advertising. Nevertheless, these exemptions do not apply to discrimination based on race or color; in the sale or rental of property, the Act prohibits all discrimination based on these factors.

49-1a FORMATION

Because an oral agreement for the sale of an interest in land is not enforceable under the statute of frauds, the buyer and seller must reduce the agreement to writing and have it signed by the other party to be able to enforce the agreement against that party. The simplest agreement should contain (1) the names and addresses of the parties, (2) a description of the property to be conveyed, (3) the time for the conveyance (called the *closing*), (4) the type of deed to be given, and (5) the price and manner of payment. To avoid dispute and to protect the rights of both parties adequately, a properly drawn contract for the sale of land will cover many other points as well.

A majority of jurisdictions adhere to the common law rule that the risk of loss or destruction of the property, not caused through the fault of the seller, rests with the purchaser after the contract is formed. The contract of sale may, of course, provide that such risk shall remain with the seller until she conveys the deed to the purchaser, that the seller must obtain insurance for the benefit of the purchaser, or that the risk is allocated in some other manner on which the parties have agreed.

49-1b MARKETABLE TITLE

The law of conveyancing has firmly established that a contract for the sale of land carries with it an implied obligation on the part of the seller to transfer marketable title. Marketable title means that the title is free from (1) encumbrances (such as mortgages, easements, liens, leases, and restrictive covenants); (2) defects in the chain of title appearing in the land records (such as a prior recorded conveyance of the same property by the seller); and (3) events depriving the seller of title, such as adverse possession or eminent domain. The seller's obligation to convey marketable title is significant, for if a title search reveals any flaw not specifically excepted in the contract, the seller has materially breached the contract. The buyer's remedies for breach include specific performance with a price reduction, rescission and restitution, or damages for loss of bargain. There are two important exceptions to this rule. First, most courts hold that the seller's implied or express obligation to convey marketable title does not include the obligation to convey title free from existing zoning restrictions. Second, some courts also hold that the seller's implied or express obligation to convey marketable title does not require him to convey title free from open and visible public rights-of-way or easements, such as public roads and sewers.

Before title to the property passes, the buyer should ensure that she is receiving good title by having the title searched. A title search involves examining prior transfers of and encumbrances to the property. Such an examination does not guarantee rightful ownership, however; consequently, most buyers purchase **title insurance** as well. Issued in the amount of the purchase price of the property, title insurance indemnifies the owner against any loss due to defects in the title to the property or due to liens or encumbrances, except for those stated in the policy as existing at the time the policy is issued. Such policies also may be issued to protect the interests of mortgagees or tenants of property.

> *Practical Advice*
> *Before title to the property passes, the buyer should have the title searched to ensure that she is receiving good title.*

> *Practical Advice*
> *As a buyer, obtain title insurance on the property to be purchased to insure against loss from defective title.*

49-1c IMPLIED WARRANTY OF HABITABILITY

Because the obligation of marketable title involves only the title to the property conveyed, such an obligation does not apply to the quality of any improvements to the land. The traditional common law rule is *caveat emptor*—let the buyer beware. Under this rigid maxim, the buyer must inspect the property thoroughly before completing the sale, as any defect discovered only after the transaction is complete would not be the seller's responsibility. The seller is liable only for any misrepresentation or express warranty he may have made about the property.

> *Practical Advice*
> *As a buyer, carefully inspect any dwelling prior to purchasing it. Also seek to have the seller expressly warrant the dwelling's condition and habitability.*

A majority of States have relaxed the harshness of the common law in sales made by one who builds and then sells residential dwellings. In such a sale, the builder-seller impliedly warrants a newly constructed house to be free of latent defects, that is, those defects not apparent upon a reasonable inspection of the house at the time of sale. In some States, this implied warranty of habitability benefits only the original purchaser. In other States, the warranty has been extended to subsequent purchasers for a reasonable time.

In addition, many jurisdictions now require *all* sellers to disclose hidden defects that materially affect the property's value and that would remain undetected following a reasonable examination. See *Chapter 11* for a discussion of misrepresentation.

♦ *See Case 49-1*

49-2 Deeds

A **deed** is a formal document transferring any interest in land upon delivery and acceptance. The party who transfers property by a deed is called the **grantor**; the transferee of the property is the **grantee**.

49-2a Types of Deeds

The rights conveyed by a deed vary, depending on the type of deed used. Deeds are of three basic types: warranty, special warranty, and quitclaim.

WARRANTY By a warranty deed (also called a general warranty deed), the grantor promises the grantee that the grantor has a valid title to the property. In addition, under a warranty deed, the grantor, either expressly or impliedly, obliges herself to make the grantee whole for any damage the grantee might suffer should the grantor's title prove to be defective. Aside from rendering the grantor liable for any defects in her title, the general warranty deed is distinct in that it will convey after-acquired title. For example, on January 30, Andrea conveys Blackacre by warranty deed to Bob. On January 30, Andrea's title to Blackacre is defective, but by February 14, Andrea has acquired a good title. Without more, Bob has acquired Andrea's good title under the January 30 warranty deed.

> **Practical Advice**
> *As a buyer, have the seller grant a general warranty deed that specifically provides for the seller's liability if the title is defective.*

SPECIAL WARRANTY Whereas a warranty deed contains a general warranty of title, a special warranty deed warrants only that the title has not been impaired, encumbered, or rendered defective because of any act or omission of the grantor. The grantor merely warrants the title so far as his acts or omissions are concerned. He does not warrant the title to be free of defects caused by the acts or omissions of others.

QUITCLAIM By a quitclaim deed, the grantor, in effect, says no more than "I make no promise as to what interest I have in this land, but whatever it is I convey it to you." Quitclaim deeds most commonly are used as a means for persons apparently having an interest in land to release their interest.

> **Practical Advice**
> *As a buyer, have the seller grant a general warranty deed that specifically provides for the seller's liability if the title is defective.*

49-2b FORMAL REQUIREMENTS

As noted, any transfer of an interest in land that is of more than a limited duration falls within the statute of frauds and must therefore be in writing. The wording of nearly all deeds, whatever the type, follows substantially the same pattern, though the words used will vary, depending upon whether the instrument is a warranty deed, a special warranty deed, or a quitclaim deed. Moreover, statutes in most States suggest that certain words of conveyance be used to make the deed effective. A common phrase for a warranty deed is "convey and warrant," although in

a number of States, the phrase "grant, bargain, and sell" is used together with a covenant by the seller later in the deed that she will "warrant and defend the title." A quitclaim deed generally will provide that the grantor "conveys and quitclaims" or, more simply, "quitclaims all interest" in the property.

DESCRIPTION OF THE LAND The description must be sufficiently clear to permit identification of the property conveyed. A common test of clarity is to ask whether a subsequent purchaser or a surveyor employed by him could mark off the land using the description.

QUANTITY OF THE ESTATE After describing the property, the deed usually will describe the quantity of estate conveyed to the grantee. Thus, either "to have and to hold to himself and his heirs forever" or "to have and to hold in fee simple" would vest the grantee with absolute title to the land. A deed conveying title to "George for life and to Elliott upon George's death," by comparison, would grant a life estate to George and a remainder interest to Elliott.

COVENANTS OF TITLE Customarily, in making a deed, the grantor makes certain promises concerning her title to the land. Such promises or covenants, the most usual of which are title (*seisen*), **against encumbrances**, **quiet enjoyment**, and **warranty**, ensure that the grantee will have undisturbed possession of the land and will, in turn, be able to transfer it free of the adverse claims of third parties. For the grantor's breach of covenant, the grantee is, moreover, entitled to be indemnified. In many States, all or many of these covenants are implied from the words of conveyance themselves—for example, *warrants* or *grant, bargain, and sell*.

EXECUTION Deeds generally end with the signature of the grantor, a seal, and an acknowledgment before a notary public or other official authorized to attest to the authenticity of documents. The grantor's signature can be made by an agent having written authority from the grantor in a form required by law. Today the seal has lost most of its former significance, and in those few jurisdictions in which it is required, the seal is sufficient if the word *Seal* or the letters L.S. appear next to the signature.

49-2c DELIVERY OF DEEDS

A deed does not transfer title to land until it is delivered. Delivery consists of the grantor's *intent* that the deed shall take effect, as evidenced by his acts or statements. Indispensable to delivery is the grantor's parting with control of the deed with the intention that it immediately will become operative to convey the estate it describes. Physical transfer of the deed is usually the best evidence of this intent, but it is not necessary. For example, the act of the grantor in placing a deed in a safe deposit box may or may not constitute delivery, depending on such facts as whether the grantee did or did not have access to the box and whether the grantor acts as if the property is the grantee's. A deed conceivably may be "delivered" even when kept in the grantor's possession; just as conceivably, physical delivery of a deed to a grantee may fail to transfer title. Frequently, in a transfer known as an escrow, a grantor will turn a deed over to a third party, the escrow agent, to hold until the grantee performs certain conditions. Upon the performance of the condition, the escrow agent must turn the deed over to the grantee.

49-2d RECORDATION

In almost all States, recording a deed is not necessary to pass title from grantor to grantee. Unless the grantee has the deed recorded, however, a subsequent good faith purchaser for value of the property will acquire title superior to that of the grantee. Recordation consists of delivering a duly executed and acknowledged deed to the recorder's office in the county where the property is located. There, a copy of the instrument is inserted in the current deed book and indexed.

In some States, called **notice** States, unrecorded instruments are invalid against any subsequent purchaser without notice. In **notice-race** States, an unrecorded deed is invalid against any subsequent purchaser without notice of who records first. Finally, in a few States, known as race States, an unrecorded deed is invalid against any deed recorded before it.

At least thirty-five States have adopted the Uniform Real Property Electronic Recording Act. This Act permits the electronic filing of real property instruments as well as systems for searching for and retrieving these land records.

Practical Advice
Promptly record your deed with the recorder of deeds; if possible, do this before or simultaneously with the seller's receipt of the purchase price.

49-3 Secured Transactions

The purchase of real estate usually involves a relatively large outlay of money, and few people pay cash for a house or business real estate. Most people must borrow part of the purchase price or defer payment over time. In these cases, the real estate itself is used to secure the obligation, which is evidenced by a note and either a mortgage or a deed of trust. The debtor is referred to as the **mortgagor** and the creditor as the **mortgagee**.

A secured transaction includes two elements: (1) a debt or obligation to pay money and (2) the creditor's interest in specific property that secures performance of the obligation. A security interest in property cannot exist apart from the debt it secures; consequently, discharging the debt in any manner terminates the interest. Transactions involving the use of real estate as security for a debt are subject to real estate law, which consists of statutes and rules developed by the common law of mortgages and trust deeds. The Uniform Commercial Code (UCC) does not apply to real estate mortgages or deeds of trust.

49-3a FORM OF MORTGAGES

The instrument creating a mortgage is in the form of a conveyance from the mortgagor to the mortgagee and must meet all the requirements for such documents: it must be in writing, it must contain an adequate description of the property, and it must be executed and delivered. The usual mortgage, however, differs from an outright conveyance of property by providing, in a condition referred to as a "defeasance," that, upon the performance of the promise by the mortgagor, the conveyance is void and of no effect. Although the defeasance normally appears on the face of the mortgage, it may be in a separate document.

The concept of a **mortgage** as a lien upon real property for the payment of a debt applies with equal force to transactions having the same purpose but possessing a different name and form. A **deed of trust** is fundamentally identical to a mortgage, the most striking difference being that under a deed of trust, the property is conveyed not to the creditor as security, but to a third person who acts as trustee for the creditor's benefit. The deed of trust creates rights substantially similar to those created by a mortgage. In some States, it is customary to use a deed of trust in lieu of the ordinary form of mortgage.

As with all interests in realty, the mortgage or deed of trust should be promptly recorded to protect the mortgagee's rights against third persons who acquire an interest in the mortgaged property without knowledge of the mortgage.

49-3b RIGHTS AND DUTIES

The rights and duties of the parties to a mortgage may depend upon whether it is viewed as creating a lien or as transferring legal title to the mortgagee. Most States have adopted the **lien** theory. The mortgagor retains title and, even in the absence of any stipulation in the mortgage, is entitled to possession of the premises to the exclusion of the mortgagee, even if the mortgagor defaults. Only through foreclosure or sale or through the court appointment of a receiver can the right of possession be taken from the mortgagor. A minority of States have adopted the common law **title** theory, which gives the mortgagee the right of ownership and possession. In most cases, as a practical matter, the mortgagor retains possession simply because the mortgagee has little interest in possession unless the mortgagor defaults.

Even though the mortgagor is generally entitled to possession and to many of the advantages of unrestricted ownership, he has a responsibility to deal with the property in a manner that will not impair the security. In most instances, **waste** (impairment of the security) results from the mortgagor's failure to prevent the actual or threatened action of third parties against the land. Thus, the debtor's failure to pay taxes or to discharge a prior lien may seriously impair the security of the mortgagee. In such cases, the courts generally permit the mortgagee to pay the obligation and add it to his claim against the mortgagor.

The mortgagor has the right to relieve his mortgaged property from the lien of a mortgage by paying the debt that it secures. Characteristic of a mortgage, this right of **redemption** can be extinguished only by operation of law. The right to redeem carries with it the obligation to pay the debt, and payment in full, with interest, is prerequisite to redemption.

Complete payment of a mortgage loan **satisfies** the mortgage. All States have statutes requiring the mortgagee to act within a specified time to document in the public land record that the lien of the mortgage has been satisfied. However, the State legislation varies considerably with respect to the length of this grace period. In 2004, the Uniform Law Commission promulgated the Model Residential Mortgage Satisfaction Act to provide rules and procedures for clearing fully paid residential real estate mortgages from the real property records. At least four States have adopted it.

49-3c MORTGAGE REGULATION

In July 2010, President Obama signed into law the Dodd-Frank Wall Street Reform and Consumer Protection Act (Dodd-Frank), the most significant change to U.S. financial regulation since the New Deal during the 1930s. One of the many standalone statutes included in the Dodd-Frank is the Mortgage Reform and Anti-Predatory Lending Act of 2010, which modifies the Truth-in-Lending Act to make mortgage brokers and lenders more accountable for the loans they make. The Dodd-Frank requires that lenders ensure a borrower's reasonable ability to repay the loan; prohibits unfair and deceptive lending practices (especially with respect to subprime mortgages); expands protection for borrowers of high-cost loans; and requires lenders to disclose the maximum amount a consumer could pay on a variable rate mortgage, with a warning that payments will vary based on interest rate changes.

The Economic Growth, Regulatory Relief, and Consumer Protection Act of 2018 amended the Truth in Lending Act to exempt banks with assets below $250 billion from some requirements for residential mortgage loans.

♦ **SEE FIGURE 49-1:** *Fundamental Rights of Mortgagor and Mortgagee*

49-3d TRANSFER OF MORTGAGE INTERESTS

The original mortgagor and mortgagee can transfer their interests to assignees whose rights and obligations will depend primarily upon (1) the agreement of the parties to the assignment and (2) the legal rules protecting the interest of one who is party to the mortgage but not to the transfer.

BY MORTGAGOR If the mortgagor conveys the land, the purchaser is not personally liable for the mortgage debt unless she expressly assumes the mortgage. If she **assumes the mortgage**, she is personally obligated to pay the debt the mortgagor owes to the mortgagee, who can also hold the mortgagor on his promise to pay. A transfer of mortgaged property **subject to the mortgage** does not personally obligate the transferee to pay the mortgage debt. In such a case, the transferee's risk of loss is limited to the realty.

BY MORTGAGEE A mortgagee has the right to assign the mortgage to another person without the consent of the mortgagor. An assignee of a mortgage is well advised to protect her rights against persons who subsequently acquire an interest in the mortgaged property without knowledge of the assignment by obtaining the assignment in a writing duly executed by the mortgagee and recording it promptly with the proper public official. Failure to record an assignment may cause an assignee of a mortgage note to lose her security. For example, Dylan buys land from Owen, relying upon a release executed and recorded by the mortgagee, Kristi. Kristi, however, had previously assigned the mortgage to Ali, who failed to have her assignment recorded. In the absence of Dylan's actual knowledge of the assignment by Kristi, Ali has no claim against the property.

FIGURE 49-1 Fundamental Rights of Mortgagor and Mortgagee

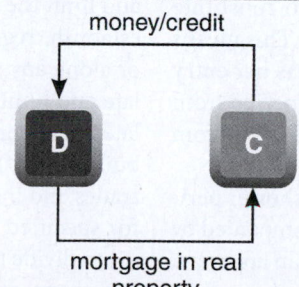

money/credit

Debtor/Mortgagor (D)

(1) To redeem property by payment of debt

(2) To possess general rights of ownership as limited by mortgage

Creditor/Mortgagee (C)

(1) To recover amount of debt

(2) To foreclose the mortgaged property upon default to satisfy debt

mortgage in real property

49-3e FORECLOSURE

The right to foreclose usually arises upon default by the mortgagor. Foreclosure is an action through which the mortgage holder takes the property from the mortgagor, ends the mortgagor's rights in the property, and sells the property to pay the mortgage debt. The mortgagor's failure to perform other promises in the mortgage also may give the mortgagee this right. Thus, a mortgage may provide that the mortgagor's failure to pay taxes constitutes a default that permits foreclosure. Mortgages also commonly provide that default in the payment of an installment makes the entire unpaid balance of the debt immediately due and payable, permitting foreclosure for the entire amount.

Whether foreclosure is by sale under judicial proceeding or by grant of power in the mortgage itself, the transaction is still a procedure to obtain satisfaction of a debt. If the proceeds are insufficient to satisfy the debt in full, the debtor-mortgagor remains liable for paying the balance. Generally, the mortgagee will obtain a *deficiency judgment* for any unsatisfied balance of the debt and may proceed to enforce the payment of this amount out of the mortgagor's other assets.

49-4 Adverse Possession

It is possible, although very rare, for title to land to be transferred **involuntarily**, without deed or other formality, by "adverse possession." In most States, a person who openly and continuously occupies the land of another for a statutorily prescribed time, typically five to twenty years, will gain title to the land. The possession must be actual, not merely constructive. Courts have held that living on land, farming it, building on it, or maintaining structures on it are sufficient to constitute possession. Possession, however, must be adverse. This means that any act of dominion by the true owner, such as her entry on the land or assertion of ownership, will stop the period from running. In such event, the period will commence anew from the point at which the owner interrupted it.

By statute, some jurisdictions have established shorter periods of adverse possession where possession is accompanied by some other claim, such as the payment of taxes or an apparent, even if invalid, claim of title.

PUBLIC AND PRIVATE CONTROLS

As discussed in *Chapter 7*, the law of nuisance imposes controls upon a landowner's use of her property. In exercising its police power for the benefit of the community, the State also can and does place controls upon the use of privately owned land. Moreover, the State does not compensate an owner for loss or damage he sustains by reason of such legitimate controls. The enforcement of zoning laws, which is a proper exercise of the police power, is not a taking of property but a regulation of its use. The taking of private property for a public use or purpose under the State's power of eminent domain is not, however, an exercise of the police power, and the owners of the property so taken are entitled to be paid its fair and reasonable value. In addition, private owners are entitled to control the use of privately owned property by means of restrictive covenants. This section addresses these various methods of State and private control of property.

49-5 Zoning

Zoning is the principal method of public control over land use. The validity of zoning is rooted in the police power of the State, the inherent power of government to provide for the public health, safety, morals, and welfare. Police power can be used only to regulate private property, never to "take" it. It is firmly established that regulation which has no reasonable relation to public health, safety, morals, or welfare is unconstitutional as a denial of due process of law.

49-5a ENABLING ACTS AND ZONING ORDINANCES

The power to zone is generally delegated to local authorities by statutes known as enabling statutes. A typical enabling statute grants municipalities the following powers: (1) to regulate and limit the height and bulk of buildings to be erected; (2) to establish, regulate, and limit the building or setback lines on or along any street, traffic way, drive, or parkway; (3) to regulate and limit the intensity of the use of lot areas and to regulate and determine the area of open spaces within and around buildings; (4) to classify, regulate, and restrict the location of trades and industries and the location of buildings designated for specified industrial, business, residential, and other uses; (5) to divide the entire municipality into districts of such number, shape, area, and class (or classes) as may be deemed best suited to carry out the purposes of the statute; and (6) to fix standards to which buildings or structures must conform.

Under these powers, the local authorities may enact zoning ordinances consisting of a map and correlating descriptive text. The map divides the municipality into districts, which are designated principally as industrial, commercial, or residential, with possible subclassifications. A well-drafted zoning ordinance will carefully define the uses permitted in each area.

Practical Advice

Prior to buying or developing real property, make sure that your plans conform with all zoning ordinances and private restrictive covenants.

49-5b VARIANCE

Enabling statutes empower zoning authorities to grant variances where the application of a zoning ordinance to specific property would cause its owner "particular hardship" unique or peculiar to the property. A **variance** permits a deviation from the zoning ordinance. Special circumstances applicable to particular property might include its unusual shape, topography, size, location, or surroundings. A variance is not available, however, if the hardship is caused by conditions general to the neighborhood or by the actions of the property owner. It must affirmatively appear that the property as presently zoned cannot yield a reasonable return upon the owner's investment.

49-5c NONCONFORMING USES

A zoning ordinance may not immediately terminate a lawful use that existed before it was enacted. Rather, such a nonconforming use must be permitted to continue—at least for a reasonable time. Most ordinances provide that nonconforming use may be eliminated (1) when the use is discontinued, (2) when a nonconforming structure is destroyed or substantially damaged, or (3) when a nonconforming structure has been permitted to exist for the period of its useful life as fixed by municipal authorities.

49-5d JUDICIAL REVIEW OF ZONING

Although the zoning process is traditionally viewed as legislative, it is subject to judicial review on a number of grounds, including claims that the zoning ordinance is invalid or amounts to a taking of property.

INVALIDITY OF ZONING ORDINANCE A zoning ordinance may be invalid as a whole because it bears no reasonable relation to public health, safety, morals, or welfare; because it involves the exercise of powers not granted to the municipality by the enabling act; or because it violates the State or U.S. Constitution.

ZONING AMOUNTS TO A TAKING Another form of attack is to show that zoning restrictions amount to confiscation or a "taking." It is not sufficient that the property owner will sustain a financial loss if the restrictions are not lifted. But when the owner can show that the restrictions make it impracticable for him to use the property for *any* beneficial purpose, he should prevail. Deprivation of all beneficial use is confiscation.

49-5e SUBDIVISION MASTER PLANS

A growing municipality has a special interest in regulating new housing developments so that they will harmonize with the rest of the community; so that streets within the development are integrated with existing streets or planned roads; and so that adequate provision is made for water, drainage, and sanitary facilities, as well as for traffic, recreation, light, and air. Accordingly, most States have legislation enabling local authorities to require municipal approval of every land subdivision plat. These enabling statutes provide penalties for failure to secure such approval where required by local ordinance. Some statutes provide that selling lots by reference to unrecorded plats is a criminal offense and provide further that such plats may not be recorded unless approved by the local planning board. Other statutes provide that building permits will not be issued unless the plat is approved and recorded.

49-6 Eminent Domain

The power to take private property for public use, known as the power of **eminent domain**, is recognized as one of the inherent powers of government both in the U.S. Constitution and in the constitutions of the States. At the same time, however, the power is carefully circumscribed and controlled. The Fifth Amendment to the U.S. Constitution provides, "[N]or shall private property be taken for public use, without just compensation." Similar or identical provisions are found in the constitutions of the States. There is, therefore, a direct constitutional prohibition against taking private property without just compensation and an implicit prohibition against taking private property for other than public use. Moreover, under both Federal and State constitutions, the individual from whom property is to be taken is entitled to due process of law.

49-6a PUBLIC USE

As noted, there is an implicit constitutional prohibition against taking private property for other than public use. Most States interpret public use to mean "public advantage." Thus, the power of eminent domain may be delegated to railroad and public utility companies. Because it enables such companies to offer continued and improved service to the public, the reasonable exercise of this power is upheld as being for a public advantage. As society grows more complex, other public purposes become legitimate grounds for exercising the power of eminent domain. One such use is in the area of urban renewal. Most States have legislation permitting the establishment of housing authorities with the power to condemn slum, blighted, and vacant areas and to finance, construct, and maintain housing projects. Some States recently have gone further by permitting private companies to exercise the power of eminent domain, provided the use is primarily for a public benefit, such as the alleviation of unemployment or economic decay within the community.

♦ *See Case 49-2*

In Kelo v. City of New London (*Case 49-2*), the U.S. Supreme Court held that governments have broad discretion in taking private property for a public purpose, which includes economic development. In response to *Kelo*, at least forty-five States have revised their eminent domain laws to limit or prohibit the use of eminent domain for economic development, although many provide an exception for condemnations to eliminate blight.

49-6b JUST COMPENSATION

When the power of eminent domain is exercised, just compensation must be made to the owners of the property taken. The measure of compensation is the fair market value of the property as of the time of taking. The compensation goes to holders of vested interests in the condemned property.

♦ SEE FIGURE 49-2: *Eminent Domain*

49-7 Private Restrictions Upon Land Use

Owners of real property may impose private restrictions, called **restrictive covenants** (or negative covenants), on the use of land. Historically, two types of private restrictions developed—real covenants and equitable servitudes. The two had different, although overlapping, requirements. Equitable servitudes now have nearly replaced real covenants. Accordingly, this section covers only equitable servitudes, which will be referred to by the more general term *restrictive covenant*.

49-7a COVENANTS RUNNING WITH THE LAND

If certain conditions are satisfied, a restrictive covenant will bind not only the original parties to it but also remote parties who subsequently acquire the property. A restrictive covenant that binds remote parties is said to "run with the land." To run with the land, the restrictive covenant must involve promises that are enforceable under the law of contracts. A majority of courts hold that the covenant must be in writing. The parties who agree to the restrictive covenant must intend that the covenant will bind their successors. Moreover, the covenant must "touch and concern" the land by affecting its use, utility, or value. Finally, a restrictive covenant will bind only those successors who have actual or constructive notice of the covenant.

FIGURE 49-2　Eminent Domain

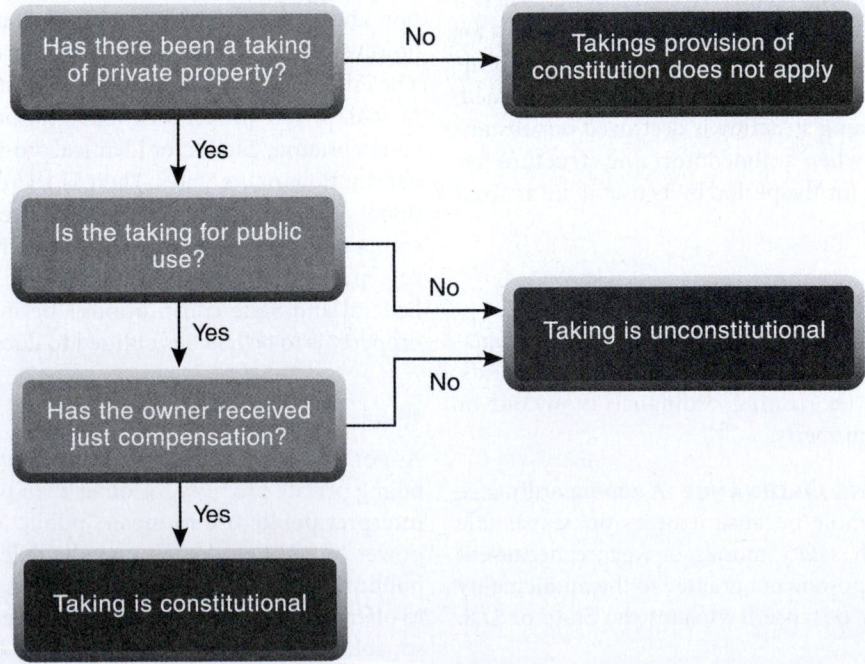

49-7b RESTRICTIVE COVENANTS IN SUBDIVISIONS

Restrictive covenants are widely used in subdivisions. The owners of lots are subject to restrictive covenants that, if actually brought to the attention of subsequent purchasers or recorded either by original deed or by means of a recorded plat or separate agreement, bind purchasers of lots in the subdivision as though the restrictions had been inserted in their own deeds. If the entire subdivision has been subjected to a general building plan designed to benefit all of the lots, any lot owner in the subdivision has the right to enforce the restriction against a purchaser whose title descends from a common grantor. If a restriction clearly is intended to benefit an entire tract, the covenant will be enforced against a subsequent purchaser of one of the lots in the tract if (1) the restriction apparently was intended to benefit the purchaser of any lot in the tract and (2) the restriction appears somewhere in the chain of title to which the lot is subject.

Subdivisions may involve many types of restrictive covenants. The more common ones limit the use of property to residential purposes, restrict the area of the lot on which a structure can be built, or provide for a special type of architecture. Frequently, a subdivider will specify a minimum size for each house in an attempt to maintain structural unity in a neighborhood.

49-7c TERMINATION OF RESTRICTIVE COVENANTS

A restrictive covenant may end by the terms of the original agreement. For example, the developer of a subdivision may provide that the restrictive covenant will terminate after thirty-five years unless a specified majority of the property owners reaffirm the covenant. In addition, a court will not enforce a restrictive covenant if changed circumstances make enforcement inequitable and oppressive. Evidence of changed conditions may be found either within the tract covered by the original covenant or within the area adjacent to or surrounding the tract.

Practical Advice

Prior to buying or developing real property make sure that your plans conform with all zoning ordinances and private restrictive covenants.

♦ *See Case 49-3*

49-7d VALIDITY OF RESTRICTIVE COVENANTS

Although restrictions upon land use have never been popular in the law, the courts will enforce a restriction that apparently will operate to the general benefit of the owners of all the land the restriction is intended to affect. The usual method of enforcing such agreements is by an injunction restraining violation.

The law for many years has held, however, that under the Fourteenth Amendment to the U.S. Constitution, a State or municipality cannot impose any racial restrictions by statute or ordinance. In 1947, the U.S. Supreme Court held that because State courts are an arm of State government, such courts cannot enforce private racial restrictive covenants. This effectively invalidated private racial restrictive covenants.

C H A P T E R   S U M M A R Y

TRANSFER OF REAL PROPERTY

CONTRACT OF SALE
Formation a contract to transfer any interest in land must be in writing to be enforceable
Marketable Title the seller must transfer marketable title, which is a title free from any defects or encumbrances
Quality of Improvements
* *Common Law Rule* under *caveat emptor* ("let the buyer beware"), the seller is not liable for any undiscovered defects
* *Implied Warranty of Habitability* in a number of States, the builder-seller of a dwelling impliedly warrants that a newly constructed house is free from latent defects

DEEDS
Definition a formal document transferring any type of interest in land
Types
* *Warranty Deed* the grantor (seller) promises the grantee (buyer) that she has valid title to the property without defect
* *Special Warranty Deed* the seller promises that he has not impaired the title

- *Quitclaim Deed* the seller transfers whatever interest she has in the property

Requirements the deed must (1) be written; (2) contain certain words of conveyance and a description of the property; (3) end with the signature of the grantor, a seal, and an acknowledgment before a notary public; and (4) be delivered

Delivery intent that the deed take effect, as evidenced by acts or statements of the grantor

Recordation required to protect the buyer's interest against third parties; consists of delivery of a duly executed and acknowledged deed to the appropriate recorder's office

SECURED TRANSACTIONS
- **Elements** a secured transaction involves (1) a debt or obligation to pay money, (2) an interest of the creditor in specific property that secures performance, and (3) the debtor's right to redeem the property (remove the security interest) by paying the debt

Mortgage interest in land created by a written document that provides security to the mortgagee (secured party) for payment of the mortgagor's debt

Deed of Trust an interest in real property that is conveyed to a third person as trustee for the benefit of the creditor

Transfer of Mortgage Interests
- *Assumes the Mortgage* the purchaser of mortgaged property becomes personally liable to pay the debt
- *Subject to the Mortgage* the purchaser is not personally liable to pay the debt, but the property remains subject to the mortgage

Foreclosure upon default, sale of the mortgaged property to satisfy the debt

ADVERSE POSSESSION
Definition acquisition of title to land by open, continuous, and adverse occupancy for a statutorily prescribed period

Possession must be actual and without intervening domination by true owner

PUBLIC AND PRIVATE CONTROLS

ZONING
Definition principal method of public control over private land use; involves regulation of land but may not constitute a taking of the property

Authority the power to zone is generally delegated to local authorities by statutes known as *enabling acts*

Variance a use differing from that provided in the zoning ordinance and granted to avoid undue hardship

Nonconforming Use a use not in accordance with, but existing prior to, a zoning ordinance; permitted to continue for at least a reasonable time

Judicial Review zoning ordinances may be reviewed to determine whether they are invalid or a confiscation of property

EMINENT DOMAIN
Definition the power of a government to take (buy) private land for public use

Public Use public advantage

Just Compensation the owner of the property taken by eminent domain must be paid the fair market value of the property

PRIVATE RESTRICTIONS UPON LAND USE
Definition private restrictions on property contained in a conveyance

Covenants Running with the Land covenants that bind not only the original parties but also subsequent owners of the property

Covenants in Subdivision bind purchasers of lots in the subdivision as if the restrictions had been inserted in their own deeds

CASES

CASE
49-1

Implied Warranty of Habitability
CONWAY v. CUTLER GROUP, INC.
Supreme Court of Pennsylvania, 2014
99 A. 3d 67

McCaffery, J.

In September 2003, The Cutler Group, Inc. ("Appellant") sold a new house in Bucks County to Davey and Holly Fields. After living in the house for three years, Mr. and Mrs. Fields sold the house to Michael and Deborah Conway ("Appellees"). In 2008, Appellees discovered water infiltration around some of the windows in the home, and, after consultation with an engineering and architectural firm, concluded that the infiltration was caused by several construction defects. On June 20, 2011, Appellees filed a one-count complaint against Appellant, alleging that its manner of construction breached the home builders' implied warranty of habitability recognized by this Court in *Elderkin v. Gaster*, [citation]. Appellant filed preliminary objections in the nature of a demurrer, arguing, *inter alia*, that, as a matter of law, the warranty recognized in *Elderkin* extends from the builder *only* to the first purchaser of a newly constructed home because there is no contractual relationship between the builder and second or subsequent purchasers of the home. Recognizing that courts have traditionally required a showing of privity of contract before permitting a party to proceed with a warranty claim, the trial court concluded that the question presented was "one of policy as to who will bear the burden for damages caused by latent defects … [in] relatively new residential dwellings." [Citation.] The trial court sustained Appellant's preliminary objections on the ground of lack of privity between the parties, and dismissed Appellees' complaint with prejudice. Appellees appealed to the Superior Court.

In a unanimous, published opinion, the Superior Court reversed. * * *

Appellant then petitioned for allowance of appeal in this Court, and we accepted the following issue for review:

Did the Superior Court wrongly decide an important question of first impression in Pennsylvania when it held that any subsequent purchaser of a used residence may recover contract damages for breach of the builder's implied warranty of habitability to new home purchasers?

In *Elderkin*, [citation] this Court adopted the implied warranty of habitability in the context of new home sales: "We thus hold that the builder-vendor impliedly warrants that the home he has built and is selling is constructed in a

reasonably workmanlike manner and that it is fit for the purpose intended—habitation." [Citation.] With the adoption of this warranty, the *Elderkin* Court rejected as anachronistic, in the context of residential real estate transactions, the traditional doctrine of *caveat emptor—the* rule that "in the absence of fraud or misrepresentation[,] a vendor is responsible for the quality of the property being sold … only to the extent … he expressly agrees to be responsible." [Citation.] The *Elderkin* Court explained that the doctrine of *caveat emptor* was rooted in the view that a vendor and a purchaser were on equal footing, with equal knowledge and bargaining power regarding the transaction at issue. However, residential real estate purchases in the modern era are transactions not just for land, but for a reasonably constructed and habitable home, for which the purchaser "justifiably relies on the skill of the developer," who not only "hold[s] himself out as having the necessary expertise with which to produce an adequate dwelling, but [also] has by far the better opportunity to examine the suitability of the home site and to determine what measures should be taken to provide a home fit for habitation." [Citation.] Accordingly, the *Elderkin* Court concluded that "[a]s between the builder-vendor and the vendee, the position of the former, even though he exercises reasonable care, dictates that he bear the risk that a home which he has built will be functional and habitable in accordance with contemporary community standards." [Citation.]

* * *

Here, the Superior Court extended that implied warranty to circumstances where the parties were not in privity of contract and the residence was not newly constructed, but rather had been occupied for several years. The Superior Court concluded that the public policy considerations that compel the implied warranty of habitability were not attenuated merely because the original buyer sold the residence to a subsequent buyer. [Citation.]

* * *

Although neither this Court nor the Superior Court has previously addressed the specific issue raised here, courts in many other jurisdictions have addressed it and have reached varying resolutions. * * * While noting that states had split on this issue, the Iowa court emphasized that the implied warranty did not arise from any language in the contract between the builder and the original purchaser, but rather was a judicial creation. Thus, the court reasoned, the implied warranty was not extinguished when the original purchaser sold the home to a subsequent purchaser, and contractual privity was not required for maintenance of an implied warranty action against the builder. * * *

* * *

A different result was reached by the Vermont Supreme Court, which recently declined to eliminate the requirement for contractual privity in a claim for breach of the implied warranty of habitability. [Citation.] The Vermont court reasoned that the existence of the implied warranty of habitability and the rationale underlying it are "founded on a sale." * * *

* * *

After careful review of the arguments of the parties, the comments of **amici**, and the reasoned decisions of our sister states on this issue, we conclude that the question of whether and/or under what circumstances to extend an implied warranty of habitability to subsequent purchasers of a newly constructed residence is a matter of public policy properly left to the General Assembly. * * *

It is well established that the courts' authority to declare public policy is limited.

* * *

The right of a court to declare what is or is not in accord with public policy does not extend to specific economic or social problems which are controversial in nature and capable of solution only as the result of a study of various factors and conditions. It is only when a given policy is so obviously for or against the public health, safety, morals or welfare that there is a virtual unanimity of opinion in regard to it, that a court may constitute itself the voice of the community in so declaring.

* * *

The order of the Superior Court is reversed.

CASE 49-2

Eminent Domain
KELO v. CITY OF NEW LONDON
Supreme Court of the United States, 2005
545 U.S. 469, 125 S.Ct. 2655, 162 L.Ed.2d 439

Stevens, J.
In 2000, the city of New London approved a development plan that, in the words of the Supreme Court of Connecticut, was "projected to create in excess of 1,000 jobs, to increase tax and other revenues, and to revitalize an economically distressed city, including its downtown and waterfront areas." [Citation.] [The plan proposed to replace a faded residential neighborhood—Fort Trumbull—with office space for research and development, a conference hotel, new residences, and a pedestrian "river-walk" along the Thames River. The project, to be built by private developers, is intended to build upon a $350 million research center built nearby by the Pfizer pharmaceutical company.

In assembling the land needed for this project, the city's development agent has purchased property from willing sellers and proposes to use the power of eminent domain to acquire the remainder of the property from unwilling owners of fifteen properties in exchange for just compensation. The unwilling owners claimed that the taking of their properties would violate the "public use" restriction in the Fifth Amendment of the United States Constitution. The trial court granted a permanent restraining order prohibiting the taking of some of the properties located in parcel. The Supreme Court of Connecticut held that all of the City's proposed takings were valid. The United States Supreme Court granted certiorari to determine whether a city's decision to take property for the purpose of economic development satisfies the "public use" requirement of the Fifth Amendment.]

* * *

Two polar propositions are perfectly clear. On the one hand, it has long been accepted that the sovereign may not take the property of A for the sole purpose of transferring it to another private party B, even though A is paid just compensation. On the other hand, it is equally clear that a State may transfer property from one private party to another if future "use by the public" is the purpose of the taking; the condemnation of land for a railroad with common-carrier duties is a familiar example. Neither of these propositions, however, determines the disposition of this case.

* * *

The disposition of this case therefore turns on the question whether the City's development plan serves a "public purpose." Without exception, our cases have defined that concept broadly, reflecting our longstanding policy of deference to legislative judgments in this field.

* * *

Those who govern the City were not confronted with the need to remove blight in the Fort Trumbull area, but their determination that the area was sufficiently distressed to justify a program of economic rejuvenation is entitled to our deference. The City has carefully formulated an economic development plan that it believes will provide appreciable benefits to the community, including—but by no means limited to—new jobs and increased tax revenue. As with other exercises in urban planning and development, the City is endeavoring to coordinate a variety of commercial, residential, and recreational uses of land, with the hope that they will form a whole greater than the sum of its parts. To effectuate this plan, the City has invoked a state statute that specifically authorizes the use of eminent domain to promote economic development. Given the comprehensive character of the plan, the thorough deliberation that preceded its adoption, and the limited scope of our review, it is appropriate for us, as it was in [citation], to resolve the challenges of the individual owners, not on a piecemeal basis, but rather in light of the entire plan. Because that plan unquestionably serves a public purpose, the takings challenged here satisfy the public use requirement of the Fifth Amendment.

To avoid this result, petitioners urge us to adopt a new bright-line rule that economic development does not qualify as a public use. Putting aside the unpersuasive suggestion that the City's plan will provide only purely economic benefits, neither precedent nor logic supports petitioners' proposal. Promoting economic development is a traditional and long accepted function of government. There is, moreover, no principled way of distinguishing economic development from the other public purposes that we have recognized. * * * Petitioners contend that using eminent domain for economic development impermissibly blurs the boundary between public and private takings. Again, our cases foreclose this objection. Quite simply, the government's pursuit of a public purpose will often benefit individual private parties. * * * Our rejection of that contention has particular relevance to the instant case: "The public end may be as well or better served through an agency of private enterprise than through a department of government—or so the Congress might conclude. We cannot say that public ownership is the sole method of promoting the public purposes of community redevelopment projects." [Citation.]

* * *

Alternatively, petitioners maintain that for takings of this kind we should require a "reasonable certainty" that the expected public benefits will actually accrue. Such a rule, however, would represent an even greater departure from our precedent. "When the legislature's purpose is legitimate and its means are not irrational, our cases make clear that empirical debates over the wisdom of takings—no less than debates over the wisdom of other kinds of socioeconomic legislation—are not to be carried out in the federal courts." [Citation.] * * * A constitutional rule that required postponement of the judicial approval of every condemnation until the likelihood of success of the plan had been assured would unquestionably impose a significant impediment to the successful consummation of many such plans.

Just as we decline to second-guess the City's considered judgments about the efficacy of its development plan, we also decline to second-guess the City's determinations as to what lands it needs to acquire in order to effectuate the project. "It is not for the courts to oversee the choice of the boundary line nor to sit in review on the size of a particular project area. Once the question of the public purpose has been decided, the amount and character of land to be taken for the project and the need for a particular tract to complete the integrated plan rests in the discretion of the legislative branch." [Citation.]

In affirming the City's authority to take petitioners' properties, we do not minimize the hardship that condemnations may entail, notwithstanding the payment of just compensation. We emphasize that nothing in our opinion precludes any State from placing further restrictions on its exercise of the takings power. Indeed, many States already impose "public use" requirements that are stricter than the federal baseline. * * *

The judgment of the Supreme Court of Connecticut is affirmed.

CASE 49-3	Termination of Restrictive Covenants **CAPPO v. SUDA** Appellate Court of Connecticut, 2011 126 Conn.App. 1, 10 A.3d 560	

Dupont, J.

[Plaintiffs, Thomas Cappo and certain other neighbors who reside on Ox Yoke Lane in Norwalk, Connecticut, seek to enforce a restrictive covenant against the defendants, Mark R. Suda, Jr., and Michelle L. Suda, from resubdividing the defendants' property and from constructing a second dwelling. The defendants admit that the properties belonging to the plaintiffs and the defendants are depicted on a "Map Showing Section Two of Cricklewood, Norwalk… as Map No. 3714" (Section Two) and admit that their deed contains a reference to restrictive covenants as set forth in volume 416 at page 118 of the Norwalk land records. This restriction, as provided in their warranty deed, states, "Said tract is subject to the following restrictions: 1. No more than one dwelling together with an attached garage shall be constructed thereon." The trial court granted summary judgment in favor of the plaintiffs, and the defendants appealed.]

In general, restrictive covenants fall into three classes: (1) mutual covenants in deeds exchanged by adjoining landowners; (2) uniform covenants contained in deeds executed by the owner of property who is dividing his property into building lots under a general development scheme; and (3) covenants exacted by a grantor from his grantee presumptively or actually for the benefit and protection of his adjoining land which he retains.... With respect to the second class of covenants, any grantee under such a general or uniform development scheme may enforce the restrictions against any other grantee. [Citation.]

It is undisputed that the restrictive covenants pertaining to the plaintiffs' and defendants' properties are in the second class of covenants.

* * *

The defendants claim that, although a restrictive covenant that prohibits resubdivision for the purpose of building an additional dwelling was contained in their deed, that restriction has been abandoned because resubdivisions have occurred in surrounding properties, which the defendants contend are part of the same subdivision as their property. The parties reside in a subdivision referred to as Section Two. All thirteen of the lots in Section Two have been developed, and none of the lots contain more than one dwelling. Two other parcels originating from the same grantor and developed into abutting subdivisions exist, namely, "Cricklewood" and "Bow End Road." Resubdivisions have occurred in Cricklewood. The court held that the three subdivisions, Section Two, Cricklewood and Bow End Road, were not a single general plan of development and, accordingly, rendered summary judgment in favor of the plaintiffs. We agree that the subdivisions are separate and not part of one plan of development and, therefore, agree with the court that the Section Two restrictions have not been extinguished or abandoned as a result of resubdivisions that occurred in Cricklewood.

* * *

When uniform covenants are contained in deeds executed by the owner of property who is dividing his property into building lots under a general development scheme, any grantee under such a general or uniform development scheme may enforce the restrictions against any other grantee. [Citation.] The owner's intent to develop the property under a common scheme is evidenced by the language in the deeds. [Citation.] * * *

"There are several factors that help to establish the existence of a common grantor's intent to develop the land according to a uniform plan. These factors include (1) the common grantor's selling or stating an intention to sell an entire tract of land, (2) the common grantor's exhibiting a map or plot of the entire tract at the time of the sale of one of the parcels, (3) the actual development of the tract in accordance with the restrictions, and (4) a substantial uniformity in the restrictions imposed in the deeds executed by the common grantor." [Citation.]

"The factors that help to negate the presence of a development scheme are: (1) the grantor retains unrestricted adjoining land; (2) there is no plot of the entire tract with notice on it of the restrictions; and (3) the common grantor did not impose similar restrictions on other lots." [Citation.]

Once a common scheme has been established, it is possible to find that the restrictive covenants are not enforceable because they have been abandoned.

[W]hen presented with a violation of a restrictive covenant, the court is obligated to enforce the covenant unless the defendant can show that enforcement would be inequitable.... [A] [c]hange in circumstances... may justify the withholding of equitable relief to enforce a covenant.... Such a change in circumstances is decided on a case by case basis, and the test is whether the circumstances show an abandonment of the original restriction making enforcement inequitable because of the altered condition of the property involved. [Citation.]

Any such change in conditions must be so substantial so as to frustrate completely the intent of the original covenant so that it would be inequitable to enforce it. [Citation.] Such a change in circumstances includes repeated violations of the restrictions without effective action to enforce them. [Citation.]

* * * The defendants admitted that the thirteen parcels in Section Two were developed under a common scheme using substantially uniform restrictions. Excepting the defendants' property, none of the owners of the parcels in Section Two have sought or received resubdivision approval, nor have repeated violations of the restrictions occurred in Section Two. Thus, the deed restrictions have not been abandoned. The plaintiffs met their burden to obtain summary judgment by demonstrating the absence of any genuine issue of material fact and showing, as a matter of law, that they were entitled to enjoin the defendants from resubdividing their lot and building a second dwelling in contravention of the restrictive covenant.

* * *

We agree with the trial court that the restrictions in the Section Two deeds have not been extinguished or abandoned as a result of resubdivisions that occurred in Cricklewood, and we agree that the two subdivisions were not developed under a common scheme. Thus, the defendants' claims fail.

QUESTIONS

1. Arthur was the father of Bridgette, Clay, and Dana and the owner of Redacre, Blackacre, and Greenacre.

   Arthur made and executed a warranty deed conveying Redacre to Bridgette. The deed provided that "this deed shall become effective only on the death of the grantor." Arthur retained possession of the deed and died, leaving the deed in his safe deposit box.

   Arthur made and executed a warranty deed conveying Blackacre to Clay. This deed also provided that "this deed shall become effective only on the death of the grantor." Arthur delivered the deed to Clay. After Arthur died, Clay recorded the deed.

   Arthur made and executed a warranty deed conveying Greenacre to Dana. Arthur delivered the deed to Lesley with specific instructions to deliver the deed to Dana on Arthur's death. Lesley duly delivered the deed to Dana when Arthur died.

   a. What is the interest of Bridgette in Redacre, if any?

   b. What is the interest of Clay in Blackacre, if any?

   c. What is the interest of Dana in Greenacre, if any?

2. Arkin, the owner of Redacre, executed a real estate mortgage to the Shawnee Bank and Trust Company for $100,000. After the mortgage was executed and recorded, Arkin constructed a dwelling on the premises and planted a corn crop. After Arkin defaulted in the payment of the mortgage debt, the bank proceeded to foreclose the mortgage. At the time of the foreclosure sale, the corn crop was mature and unharvested. Arkin contends that the mortgage should not apply to (a) the dwelling and (b) the corn crop. Explain whether Arkin is correct.

3. Robert and Stanley held legal title of record to adjacent tracts of land, each consisting of a number of five acres. Stanley fenced his five acres in 1996, placing his east fence fifteen feet onto Robert's property. Thereafter, he was in possession of this fifteen-foot strip of land and kept it fenced and cultivated continuously until he sold his tract of land to Nathan on March 1, 2001. Nathan took possession under deed from Stanley and continued possession and cultivation of the fifteen-foot strip that was on Robert's land until May 27, 2021, when Robert, having on several occasions strenuously objected to Nathan's possession, brought suit against Nathan for trespass. Explain whether Nathan has gained title by adverse possession.

4. Marcia executed a mortgage on Blackacre to secure her indebtedness to Ajax Savings and Loan Association in the amount of $125,000. Later, Marcia sold Blackacre to Morton. The deed contained the following provision: "This deed is subject to the mortgage executed by the Grantor herein to Ajax Savings and Loan Association."

   The sale price of Blackacre to Morton was $150,000. Morton paid $25,000 in cash, deducting the $125,000 mortgage debt from the purchase price. Upon default in the payment of the mortgage debt, Ajax brings an action against Marcia and Morton to recover a judgment for the amount of the mortgage debt and to foreclose the mortgage. Can Ajax recover from Marcia and Morton? Explain.

5. On January 1, 2021, Davis and Hershey owned Blackacre as tenants in common. On July 1, 2021, Davis made a written contract to sell Blackacre to Grigg for $250,000. Pursuant to this contract, Grigg paid Davis $250,000 on August 1, 2021, and Davis executed and delivered to Grigg a warranty deed to Blackacre. On February 1, 2022, Hershey quitclaimed his interest in Blackacre to Davis. Grigg brings an action against Davis for breach of warranty of title. Explain what judgment should be rendered.

6. Barker operated a retail bakery, Davidson a drugstore, Farrell a food store, Gibson a gift shop, and Harper a hardware store in adjoining locations along one side of a single suburban village block. As the population grew, the business section developed at the other end of the village, and the establishments of Barker, Davidson, Farrell, Gibson, and Harper were surrounded for at least a mile in each direction solely by residences. The village adopted a typical zoning ordinance, the provisions of which declared the area including the five stores to be a "residential district for single-family dwellings." Thereafter, Barker tore down the frame building that housed the bakery and began to construct a modern brick bakery. Davidson found her business increasing to such an extent that she began to build an addition that would extend the drug-store to the rear alley. Farrell's building was destroyed by fire, and he started to reconstruct it with the intention of restoring it to its former condition. Gibson changed the gift shop into a sporting goods store and after six months of operation decided to go back into the gift shop business. Harper sold his hardware store to Hempstead. The village building commissioner brings an action under the zoning ordinance to enjoin the construction work of Barker, Davidson, and Farrell and to enjoin the carrying on of any business by Gibson

and Hempstead. Assume the ordinance is valid. Explain the result.

7. Alda and Mattingly are residents of phase I of the Chimney Hills subdivision. The lots owned by Alda and Mattingly are subject to the following restrictive covenant: "Lots shall be for single-family residence purposes only." Alda intends to convert her carport into a beauty shop, and Mattingly brings suit against Alda to enjoin her from doing so. Alda argues that the covenant restricts only the type of building that can be constructed, not the incidental use to which residential structures are put. Will Alda be able to operate a beauty shop on the property? Why or why not?

C A S E   P R O B L E M S

8. The city of Boston sought to condemn land in fee simple for use in constructing an entrance to an underground terminal for a subway. The owners of the land contend that no more than surface and subsurface easements are necessary for the terminal entrance and seek to retain air rights above thirty-six feet. The city argues that any building utilizing this airspace would require structural supports that would interfere with the city's plan for the terminal. The city concedes that the properties around the condemned property could be assembled and structures could be designed to span over the condemned property, in which case the air rights would be quite valuable. Can the city condemn the property? Explain.

9. In May 2011, Fred Parramore executed four deeds, each conveying a life estate in his land to him and his wife and a remainder interest in one-fourth of his land to each of his four children: Alney, Eudell, Bernice, and Iris. Although Fred executed and acknowledged the four deeds as part of his plan to distribute his estate at his death, he did not deliver them to his children at this time. Instead, he placed the deeds with his will in a safe deposit box and instructed the children to pick up their deeds upon his death. Fred later conveyed Alney's deed to Alney, thereby vesting Alney's interest in that parcel, but Eudell's, Bernice's, and Iris's deeds were never handed over to them during Fred's lifetime. Fred, however, acted as if the land were beyond his control and on one occasion told a prospective buyer that the land had already been deeded away. When Fred died in November 2021, Alney brought this action, claiming that the deeds to Eudell, Bernice, and Iris were ineffective because they had never been handed over during Fred's lifetime. Accordingly, Alney argued, the remaining land should pass in equal shares to each of the four children under the residuary clause of Fred's will. Who will prevail? Why?

10. The Gerwitz family resides on a piece of land known as Lot #24 of the Belleville tract, which they acquired by deed in 2002. Shortly thereafter, the Gerwitzes began to use the adjacent vacant Lot #25. At various times, they planted grass seed, flowers, and shrubs on the land and used it for picnics and cook-outs. In 2021, Gelsomin acquired Lot #25 and constructed a foundation on it so that he could place a house there. The Gerwitzes then brought this action to stop him, claiming title to Lot #25 by adverse possession. Discuss whether the Gerwitzes have obtained title by adverse possession.

11. Leo owned a one-story, one-family dwelling in a single-family residential zoning district in Detroit. He attempted to sell the house with its adjoining lot for $138,500. Houses in the neighborhood generally sold for $120,000 to $125,000. Immediately to the west of Leo's property was a gasoline service station. In addition, Leo's property was located on a corner frequented with heavy traffic. Having received no offers from residential use buyers during the period of over a year that the property was listed and offered for sale, Leo applied to the board of zoning appeals for a variance to permit the use of the property as a dental and medical clinic and to use the side yard for off-street parking. The variance would be subject to certain conditions, including the preservation of the building's exterior as that of a one-family dwelling. Puritan-Greenfield Improvement Association, a nonprofit corporation, filed a complaint against Leo's variance request. Discuss whether the variance should be granted.

12. The Glendale Church purchased a twenty-one-acre parcel of land in a canyon along the banks of Mill Creek in Angeles National Forest. The church used the twelve flat acres next to the stream to operate a campground for disabled children. This area had a number of improved buildings located on it. In July, a forest fire destroyed all ground cover upstream from the church's campground, and a subsequent flood destroyed all the buildings. In response, the county of Los Angeles enacted an interim ordinance that temporarily prohibited the church from constructing new buildings. Is the church entitled to compensation for a temporary taking of its property? Why or why not?

13. Robert V. Gross owned certain land on which he proposed to construct an eighty-three-unit apartment

house. The land, however, was subject to a restriction imposed by a deed to a predecessor in title that provided that no part of the premises could be used for business purposes other than raising, growing, and selling live bait; selling fishing tackle; and selling sporting goods. Explain whether the restriction prohibits the construction and operation of an apartment house.

14. For seven years, Desford Potts had owned a six-acre tract of land within the corporate limits of the city of Franklin. The tract contained a livestock barn in which Potts stored lumber and other building materials. Bricks were also stored in stacks four or five feet high outside and behind the barn. Franklin passed a zoning ordinance by virtue of which Potts's lot was classified as residential property. Soon afterward, Potts moved some saw logs onto his back lot, and the city complained that Potts's use of his property for storage of building materials was a "nonconforming use." Potts then brought an action to enjoin interference by the city of Franklin. Explain whether Potts will prevail.

15. Sam and Eleanor Gaito purchased a home from Howard Frank Auman, Jr., in the spring of 2018. Auman had completed the construction of the house in November 2013. In the interim, three different parties had lived in the house for brief periods, but Auman had retained ownership. The last tenants, the Ashleys, experienced difficulties with the home's air-conditioning system. Repairs were attempted, but no effort was made to change the capacity of the air-conditioning unit. When the Gaitos moved into the house in June 2018, they too had problems with the air conditioning. The system created only a ten-degree difference between the outside and inside temperatures. The Gaitos complained to Auman on a number of occasions, but extensive repairs failed to correct the cooling problem. In May 2021, the Gaitos brought an action against Auman, alleging that the purchase price of the home included central air conditioning and that Auman had breached the implied warranty of habitability. At trial, an expert in the field of heating and air conditioning testified that a four-ton air-conditioning system, rather than the three-and-one-half-ton system

originally installed, was appropriate for the Gaitos' house. Explain who should prevail.

16. In 1972, South Carolina enacted a Coastal Zone Management Act requiring any person using land in a "critical area" to obtain a permit for any uses other than those to which the critical area was devoted when the Act went into effect on September 28, 1977. In 1986, Lucas paid $975,000 for two residential lots on the Isle of Palms in Charleston County, South Carolina, on which he intended to develop a residential subdivision known as "Beachwood East." Because no portion of those lots was included in a "critical area" at that time, Lucas was not required to obtain a permit. In 1988, however, South Carolina enacted the Beachfront Management Act, which established a "baseline" for the landward-most points of erosion and in effect barred the erection of any permanent habitable structures on his two parcels. Lucas filed suit in state court, claiming that the new statute violated his Fifth and Fourteenth Amendment rights by taking property without compensation. Explain.

17. Barba & Barba Construction, Inc., constructed a multilevel addition to a single-family house in Glenview, Illinois. Before the addition, the residence consisted of approximately 2,300 square feet. After the addition, the house consisted of approximately 3,200 square feet. More than eleven years later, John W. VonHoldt purchased the house. Shortly after taking occupancy, VonHoldt noticed a deflection of the wood flooring at the partition wall separating the master bedroom from an adjoining bathroom. This deflection created a depression in the floor plane. VonHoldt maintained that due to the thickness of the carpet, the depression was nearly concealed. An investigation revealed that the addition had not been constructed in accordance with the architectural plans approved by the Village of Glenview or with the Glenview Building Code. This variance resulted in excessive stress on the floor joists and inadequate support for a portion of the roof and ceiling, causing a greater-than-expected floor deflection. VonHoldt brought a lawsuit against Barba & Barba for breach of an implied warranty of habitability. Explain who should prevail.

Playtime Theaters and Sea-First Properties purchased two theaters in Renton, Washington, with the intention of exhibiting adult films. About the same time, they filed suit seeking injunctive relief and a declaratory judgment that the First and Fourteenth Amendments were violated by a city of Renton ordinance that prohibits adult motion picture theaters from locating within one thousand feet of any residential zone, single- or multiple-family dwelling, church, park, or school.

a. What are the arguments that the city has the right to enforce such an ordinance?

b. What are the arguments that the city does not have the right to enforce such an ordinance?

c. What result? Explain.

CHAPTER 50

Trusts and Decedents' Estates

CHAPTER OUTCOMES

After reading and studying this chapter, you should be able to:

- Explain the following types of trusts: (1) express, (2) testamentary, (3) *inter vivos*, (4) charitable, (5) spendthrift, (6) Totten, (7) implied, (8) constructive, and (9) resulting.

- Describe the powers and duties of a trustee.

- Explain the formal requirements for making a valid will and the various ways in which a will may be revoked.

- Define the following types of wills: (1) nuncupative, (2) holographic, and (3) soldiers' and sailors' wills.

- Describe intestate succession and the administration of decedents' estates.

In previous chapters, we saw that real and personal property may be transferred in a number of ways, including by sale and by gift. Another important way in which a person may convey property or allow others to use or benefit from it is through trusts and wills. Trusts may take effect during the transferor's lifetime, or when used in a will, they may become effective upon his death. Wills enable individuals to control the transfer of their property at their death. Upon a person's death, his or her property must pass to someone, and individuals are well advised to decide how their property should be distributed. Except for statutory or common law rights of spouses, the law permits individuals to make such distributions by sale, gift, trust, and will. If, however, an individual dies without a will—that is, intestate—State law prescribes who shall be entitled to the property that the individual owned at death. This chapter examines trusts and wills as well as the manner in which property descends when a person dies without leaving a will.

TRUSTS

A **trust** is a *fiduciary relationship* in which one or more persons hold *legal title* to property while its use, enjoyment, and benefit (*equitable title*) belong to another. A trust may be created for any purpose that is not against the law or public policy and may be established by agreement of the parties, by bequest in a will, or by a court decree. However created, the relationship is known as a trust. The party creating the trust is the creator or **settlor**, the party holding the legal title to the property is the **trustee** of the trust, and the person who receives the benefit of the trust is the **beneficiary**.

In 2000, the Uniform Law Commission promulgated the Uniform Trust Code (UTC), which has been adopted by at least thirty-five States and applies to express trusts and trusts created pursuant to a statute, judgment, or decree that requires the trust to be administered in the manner of an express trust. Excluded from the UTC's coverage are resulting and constructive trusts. Almost all of the rules in the UTC are default rules that apply if the terms of the trust fail to address or insufficiently cover a particular issue. UTC Section 105. Much of the UTC is a codification of the common law of trusts.

◆ **SEE FIGURE 50-1:** *Trusts*

50-1 Types of Trusts

All trusts may be divided into two major groups: express and implied. Implied trusts, which are imposed upon property by court order, are categorized as either "constructive" or "resulting" trusts.

50-1a EXPRESS TRUSTS

An **express trust** is a trust established by voluntary action and is represented by a written document, an oral statement, or conduct of the settlor. In a majority of jurisdictions, an express trust of real property must be in writing to meet the requirements of the statute of frauds. Trusts of personal property and implied trusts do not fall within the requirements of the statute of frauds.

No particular words are necessary to create a trust, provided that the intent of the settlor to establish a trust is unmistakable. Sometimes a settlor will offer a gift accompanied by words of request or recommendation implying or expressing the settlor's hope that the gift should or will be used for a particular purpose. Thus, instead of clearly creating a trust by leaving property "to X for the benefit and use of Y," a settlor may leave property to X "in full confidence and with hope that he will care for Y." Such a "**precatory expression**" (words of request) may be so definite as to impose a trust upon the property for the benefit of Y. Whether it creates a trust or is considered nothing more than a gratuitous wish depends on whether the court concludes from all the facts that the settlor genuinely intended a trust. Generally, courts hold that words such as request, hope, and rely place no legal obligation upon the recipient of a gift and therefore do not create a trust.

TESTAMENTARY TRUST Trusts employed in wills are known as **testamentary trusts** because they become effective after the settlor's death.

INTER *VIVOS* TRUST A trust established during the settlor's lifetime is referred to as an ***inter vivos***, or "between the living," trust.

> ### Practical Advice
>
> *As your estate grows, you should determine whether tax or other legal considerations make it beneficial to use a trust as a vehicle to distribute your assets.*

CHARITABLE TRUSTS A **charitable trust** may be created for the relief of poverty, the advancement of education or religion, the promotion of health, governmental or municipal purposes, or other purposes the achievement of which is beneficial to the community. UTC Section 405. Gifts for public museums, for park maintenance, and for the dissemination of a particular political doctrine or religious belief have been upheld as charitable.

SPENDTHRIFT TRUSTS A **spendthrift trust** restrains both voluntary and involuntary transfers of a beneficiary's interest. UTC Sections 103(16) and 502. A spendthrift trust prevents creditors of a beneficiary from attaching a trust distribution until it is actually made to that beneficiary. UTC Section 502. In a spendthrift trust, the trust estate is removed both from the beneficiary's control and disposition and from liability for her individual debts. Once the beneficiary actually receives income from the trust, however, creditors may seize the income or the beneficiary may use it as she pleases.

TOTTEN TRUSTS A **Totten trust** or **savings account trust** involves a bank account opened by the settlor of the trust. For example, Joanne deposits a sum of money into a savings account in the name of "Joanne, in trust for Justin." The settlor, Joanne, may make additional deposits in the account from time to time and may withdraw money from it whenever she pleases. Because the settlor may revoke the Totten trust by withdrawing the funds or by changing the form of the account, the courts have held such a trust to be tentative. Usually the transfer of ownership becomes complete only upon the depositor's death, when the beneficiary is entitled to the balance of the account.

50-1b IMPLIED TRUSTS

In some cases, the courts, in the absence of any express intent to create a trust, will impose a trust upon property because the acts of the parties appear to warrant such a construction. An

FIGURE 50-1 Trusts

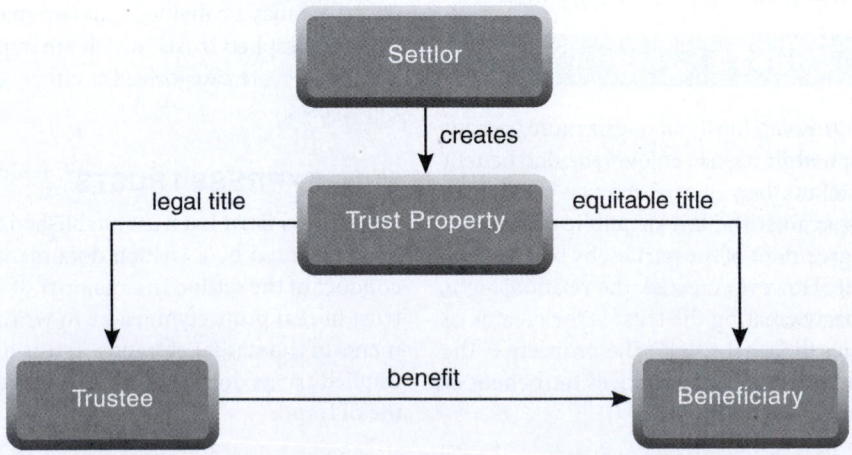

implied trust owes its existence to the law. As previously stated, implied trusts generally are divided into two classes: constructive trusts and resulting trusts.

CONSTRUCTIVE TRUSTS A court of equity creates a **constructive** trust to rectify misconduct, to prevent unjust enrichment, or to undo a morally wrong situation. Misconduct includes abuse of a confidential relationship, actual fraud, undue influence, and duress. Justice Cardozo referred to a constructive trust as "the formula through which the conscience of equity finds expression. When property has been acquired in such circumstances that the holder of the legal title may not in good conscience retain the beneficial interest, equity converts him into a trustee." *Beatty v. Guggenheim Exploration Co.*, 225 N.Y. 380, 122 N.E. 378 (1919). Rather than reflect the intent of the parties, a constructive trust represents a court's attempt to achieve an equitable and just result. The Restatement (Third) of Restitution and Unjust Enrichment provides that "[i]f a defendant is unjustly enriched by the acquisition of title to identifiable property at the expense of the claimant or in violation of the claimant's rights, the defendant may be declared a constructive trustee, for the benefit of the claimant, of the property in question and its traceable product."

Business and personal affairs provide many examples of constructive trusts. A director of a corporation who takes advantage of a "corporate opportunity" or who makes an undisclosed profit in a deal with the corporation will be treated as a trustee for the corporation with respect to the property or profits he acquires. Likewise, a trustee under an express trust who permits a lease held by the trust to expire and then acquires a new lease of the property in his individual capacity will be required to hold the new lease in trust for the beneficiary. If an agent who is given money by his principal to purchase property in the name of the principal instead uses the funds to acquire title in himself, courts will treat him as a trustee for the principal.

As previously indicated, the courts also invoke constructive trusts in situations involving those who use positions of friendship or marriage to their unjust advantage.

♦ *See Case 50-1*

RESULTING TRUSTS A **resulting trust** serves to effect the inferred or presumed intent of parties who have inadequately expressed their actual wishes. A resulting trust does not depend on contract or agreement and, as it is created by implication and by operation of law, it does not need to be evidenced in writing. The essence of a resulting trust is the presumption made by the law that the holder of legal title does not hold the property personally but as a trustee for another party. The most common example of a resulting trust is where Joel pays the purchase price for property and takes title in the name of Ann. The presumption here is that the parties intended Ann

to hold the property for Joel's benefit, and Ann will be treated as a trustee. The presumption, however, may be rebutted by evidence that Joel intended to make a gift to Ann. A second example of a resulting trust occurs when an express trust fails; then the trustee holds the property in trust for the settlor, to whom the property reverts.

50-2 Creation of Express Trusts

Each express trust has (1) a creator or settlor, (2) a "corpus" or trust property, (3) a trustee, and (4) a beneficiary. An express trust is created only if: (1) the settlor has capacity to create a trust, (2) the settlor indicates an intention to create the trust, (3) the trust has a definite beneficiary or is a charitable trust, (4) the trustee has duties to perform, and (5) the same person is not the sole trustee and sole beneficiary. UTC Section 402. No particular words are necessary to create a trust, provided that the settlor's intent to establish a trust is unmistakable. Consideration is not essential to an enforceable trust. A trust may be created only to the extent its purposes are lawful, not contrary to public policy, and possible to achieve. UTC Section 404.

50-2a SETTLOR

A **settlor** is a person, who creates, or contributes property to, a trust. UTC Section 103(15). Any person legally capable of making a contract may create a trust. But if the settlor's contract would be voidable or void because of infancy, incompetency, or some other reason, her declaration of trust is also voidable or void. In addition, a trust is void to the extent its creation was induced by fraud, duress, or undue influence. UTC Section 406.

50-2b TRUST CORPUS OR PROPERTY

One essential characteristic of a trust is a trust corpus or *res* consisting of definite and specific property. The *res* may be any type of property that exists and is assignable. A trust cannot be effective immediately for property not yet in existence or yet to be acquired.

50-2c TRUSTEE

Anyone legally capable of holding title to the trust property may be a trustee. Furthermore, the lack of a trustee will not destroy a trust. If the settlor neglects to appoint one, if the named trustee does not qualify, or if the named trustee declines to serve, the court will appoint an individual or institution to act as trustee. A trustee can, of course, decline to serve, and before the property will vest in her, it is necessary that she accept the trust. If the terms of a trust do not specify the trustee's compensation, a trustee is entitled to compensation that is reasonable under the circumstances. UTC Section 708.

DUTIES OF THE TRUSTEE A trustee has three primary duties:

1. to carry out the purposes of the trust,
2. to act with prudence and care in the administration of the trust, and
3. to exercise a high degree of loyalty toward the beneficiary.

Under ordinary circumstances, no special skills are required of a trustee, who is required simply to act with the same degree of care that a **prudent person** would exercise with respect to his personal affairs. UTC Section 804. The trustee has a duty to make the trust property productive and thus to invest it in income-producing assets.

The duty of loyalty arises from and illustrates the fiduciary character of the relationship between the trustee and the beneficiary. In all his dealings with the trust property, the beneficiary, and third parties, the trustee must act exclusively in the interest of the beneficiary. UTC Section 802. A failure to so act may arise from obvious self-dealing, or it may be entirely innocent; in either event, the trustee can be charged with lack of loyalty.

A trustee who fails to comply with the trust agreement or the statute is personally liable for any loss. UTC Section 1001.

◆ *See Case 50-2*

POWERS OF THE TRUSTEE The **powers** of a trustee are determined by (1) the authority granted him by the settlor in the instrument creating the trust and (2) the rules of law in the jurisdiction in which the trust is established. UTC Section 815. State laws affecting the powers of trustees have their greatest impact upon the investments a trustee may make with trust funds. Most States have adopted a prudent investor rule. UTC Section 804. Some States, however, still follow the historical test, which prescribes a list of types of securities qualified for trust investment. In some jurisdictions, this list is permissive; in others, it is mandatory. If the list is permissive, the trustee may invest in types of securities not listed but carries the burden of showing that he made a prudent choice. The trust instrument may give the trustee wide discretion as to investments; in such an event, the trustee need not adhere to the list deemed advisable under the statute.

Practical Advice

When creating a trust, carefully consider which powers you grant to your trustee in the trust instrument.

ALLOCATION OF PRINCIPAL AND INCOME Trusts often settle a life estate in the trust corpus on one beneficiary and a remainder interest on another beneficiary. For example, on his death, a man leaves his property to a trustee who is instructed to pay the income from the property to his widow during her life and to distribute the property to his children upon her death. In these instances, the trustee must distribute the principal to one party (the remainderman) and the income to another (the life tenant or income beneficiary). The trustee also must allocate receipts and charge expenses between the income beneficiary and the remainderman. If the trust agreement does not specify how the funds should be allocated, the trustee is provided statutory guidance, derived in at least forty-six States from the **Uniform Principal and Income Act**. The Act was amended and updated in 2008 to implement technical changes related to developments and interpretations relating to tax matters. At least thirty-six States have adopted the 2008 amendments.

The general rule in allocating benefits and burdens between income beneficiaries and remaindermen is that *ordinary* or current receipts and expenses are chargeable to the income beneficiary, whereas *extraordinary* receipts and expenses are allocated to the remainderman. Ordinary income is money paid for the use of trust property and any gain from the use of the trust property, while property received as a substitute for or a change in the form of the trust property is allocated to the trust principal.

◆ *See Figure 50-2: Allocation of Principal and Income*

50-2d BENEFICIARY

There are very few restrictions on who (or what) may be a beneficiary. Charitable uses are a common purpose of trusts, and if the settlor's object does not outrage public policy or morals, the courts will uphold almost any purpose that happens to strike a settlor's fancy.

A person named as a beneficiary of a trust may accept or reject the trust. In the absence of restrictive provisions in the trust instrument, such as a spendthrift clause, a beneficiary's interest may be reached by his creditors, or the beneficiary may sell or dispose of his interest. Upon his death, if the beneficiary held more than a life estate in the trust, the beneficiary's interest, unless disposed of by his will, passes to his heirs or personal representatives.

50-3 Termination of a Trust

Unless the terms of a trust expressly provide that the trust is irrevocable, the settlor may revoke or amend the trust. UTC Section 602.

A trust terminates to the extent the trust is revoked or expires pursuant to its terms, no purpose of the trust remains to be achieved, or the purposes of the trust have become unlawful, contrary to public policy, or impossible to achieve. UTC Section 410. The death of the trustee or beneficiary does not terminate the trust if neither of their lives delimits the duration of the trust.

FIGURE 50-2 Allocation of Principal and Income

	Receipts	Expenses
Ordinary—Income Beneficiary	Rents	Interest payments
	Royalties	Insurance
	Cash dividends (regular and extraordinary)	Ordinary taxes
	Interest	Ordinary repairs
		Depreciation
Extraordinary—Remainderman	Stock dividends	Extraordinary repairs
	Stock splits	Long-term improvements
	Proceeds from sale or exchange of corpus	Principal amortization
	Settlement of claims for injury to corpus	Costs incurred in the sale or purchase of corpus
		Business losses

If the purpose for which a trust has been established is fulfilled before the specified termination date, a court may decree the trust terminated. Most courts will not order the termination of a trust, even at the request of all the beneficiaries, if any of its purposes remain unfulfilled. The purposes the settlor set forth in the trust instrument, not the beneficiaries' wishes, will govern the court's actions. If the trustee acquires both the equitable and legal title to the trust res, the merger doctrine applies, and the trust terminates as the trustee and beneficiary must be different persons for a trust to exist.

DECEDENTS' ESTATES

When a person dies, the title to his property must pass to someone. If the decedent leaves a valid will, his property will pass as he directs, subject only to certain limitations imposed by the State. If, however, no valid will has been executed, the decedent is said to have died "intestate," and the State prescribes who shall be entitled to the property. If a decedent dies leaving a valid will that disposes of less than all of her net probate estate, intestacy laws govern the portion not effectively devised by the will. If a person dies without a will and leaves no heirs or next of kin, her property escheats (reverts) to the State. The procedure of managing the distribution of decedents' estates is referred to as probate, and the court that supervises the procedure is often designated the probate court.

Nonetheless, not all of the decedent's property will pass through probate. Certain property will pass through arrangements unaffected by probate. Asset-specific mechanisms for the non-probate transfer of property to a beneficiary at death—called "will substitutes"—are common. For instance, the decedent's life insurance policy or pension plan will pass to the beneficiary of the policy or plan, property the decedent jointly owned with a right of survivorship will pass to the survivor, and property subject to a trust will be governed by the trust instrument. Additional examples include securities registered in transfer on death (TOD) form and funds held in payable on

death (POD) bank accounts. In 2009, the Uniform Law Commission promulgated the **Uniform Real Property Transfer on Death Act**, which enables an owner to pass real property to a beneficiary at the owner's death without probate by executing and recording a TOD deed. At least seventeen States have adopted the Act, three States are considering adopting it, and a number of States have passed substantially similar laws.

50-4 Wills

A **will** is a written instrument, executed according to statutorily imposed formalities, whereby a person makes a disposition of his property that is to take effect after his death. A will is also called a **testament**; the maker of the will is called a testator; and gifts made in a will are called devises or bequests. A **bequest** or **legacy** is a gift by will of personal property; a devise is a gift by will of real property.

One major characteristic of a will sets it apart from other transactions such as deeds and contracts: a will is revocable at any time during life. There is no such thing as an irrevocable will. A document binding during life (such as a promise to make a will) may be a contract or a deed (conveying, for instance, a vested remainder after a life estate in the grantor), but it is not a will. Even a testator who by executing a joint or mutual will contractually promises not to revoke her will retains the power to revoke. Nonetheless, such a testator may be liable for breach of contract, and the courts may impose a constructive trust upon the beneficiaries of her estate. A will takes effect only on the death of the testator.

In 1969, the Uniform Law Commission and the American Bar Association approved the Uniform Probate Code (UPC), an attempt to encourage throughout the United States the adoption of a uniform, flexible, speedy, efficient, and, in most cases, less expensive system of settling a decedent's estate. At least nineteen States have adopted the UPC. The UPC, which has been updated a number of times, is based on the major premise that the probate court's appropriate role in the settlement of an estate is to offer assistance as requested or required, not to impose supervision or pointlessly detailed formality upon completely noncontentious settlements. The following discussion summarizes the general principles and procedures applicable to decedents' estates and notes the parallel principles and procedures under the UPC.

50-4a   MENTAL CAPACITY

The law of wills is based upon implementing the testator's intent and therefore requires that the testator have the mental capacity to form such an intent. Thus, a minor does not have the legal capacity to make a will. To make a valid will, the testator must have both the "power" and the "capacity" to do so. The requisite testamentary intent must always be present to create a valid will.

TESTAMENTARY CAPACITY For a will to be valid, testator must be capable of (1) knowing and understanding in a general way (a) the nature and extent of his or her property, (b) the natural objects of his or her bounty, and (c) the disposition that he or she is making of that property and (2) relating these elements to one another and forming an orderly desire regarding the disposition of the property. *Restatement (Third) of Property:* Wills and Other Donative Transfers.

Under the UPC, any person eighteen or more years of age who is of sound mind may make a will. Section 2-501.

CONDUCT INVALIDATING A WILL Any document that appears to be a will but reflects an intent other than the testator's is not a valid will. This is the basis for the rule that a transfer of property by will is invalid to the extent the transfer was a result of duress, undue influence, or fraud. A party contesting a will on one of these grounds has the burden of establishing duress, undue influence, or fraud. UPC Section 3-407.

A transfer of property by will is invalidated by **duress** if a person threatened to perform or did perform a wrongful act that coerced the testator into making a transfer that the testator would not otherwise have made. *Restatement (Third) of Property:* Wills and Other Donative Transfers, Section 8.3.

A transfer of property by will is invalidated by **undue influence** if a person exerted such influence over the testator that it overcame the testator's free will and caused the testator to make a transfer that the testator would not otherwise have made. "In the absence of direct evidence of undue influence, circumstantial evidence is sufficient to raise an inference of undue influence if the contestant proves that (1) the donor was susceptible to undue influence, (2) the alleged wrongdoer had

an opportunity to exert undue influence, (3) the alleged wrongdoer had a disposition to exert undue influence, and (4) there was a result appearing to be the effect of the undue influence." *Restatement (Third) of Property:* Wills and Other Donative Transfers, Section 8.3.

◆ *See Case 50-3*

A transfer of property by will is invalidated by **fraud** if a person knowingly or recklessly made a false representation to the testator about a material fact that was intended to and did lead the testator to make a transfer that the testator would not otherwise have made. *Restatement (Third) of Property:* Wills and Other Donative Transfers, Section 8.3. For example, Brian dies, leaving all his property to Mark upon Mark's representation that he is Brian's long-lost son. Mark in fact is not Brian's son. In such a case, the will may be set aside because the misrepresentation was made with the intent to deceive, and Brian justifiably relied upon it.

See Chapter 11 for a more complete discussion of duress, undue influence, and fraud.

◆ *See Case 50-1*

50-4b   FORMAL REQUIREMENTS OF A WILL

By statute in all jurisdictions, a will must comply with certain formalities to be valid. These formalities are intended both to ensure that the testator understood what she was doing and to help prevent fraud. As discussed later, some States permit specific types of wills that do not meet all of these requirements to be enforced with respect to testamentary dispositions of certain property.

WRITING A basic requirement of a valid will is that it be in writing. UPC, Section 2-502. The writing may be informal, as long as it substantially meets the basic statutory requirements. Pencil, ink, typewriting, and photocopy are equally valid media, and valid wills have been made on scratch paper and on an envelope.

It is also valid to incorporate into a will by reference another document that in itself is not a will for lack of proper execution. For a memorandum to be thus incorporated, the following four conditions must exist: (1) the memorandum must be in writing; (2) it must be in existence when the will is executed; (3) it must be adequately described in the will; and (4) in some States, it must be described in the will as being in existence. UPC, Section 2-510.

SIGNATURE A will must be signed by the testator or in the testator's name by some other individual in the testator's presence and at the testator's direction. UPC, Section 2-502. A fundamental requirement in almost all jurisdictions, the signature verifies that the will has been executed. The testator's initials, a single word, such as "father," or a mark at the end of a will in the testator's handwriting are adequate if intended as an execution.

Most statutes require the signature to be at the end of the will. Even in jurisdictions that do not so require, placing the signature at the end will preclude the charge that the portions of a will that follow the signature were written subsequent to its execution and are therefore invalid.

ATTESTATION Except for a few isolated types of wills (discussed later in this chapter) that are valid in a limited number of jurisdictions, a written will must be attested, or certified, by witnesses. The number and qualifications of witnesses and the manner of attestation are generally specified by statute. Usually two or three witnesses are required. Section 2-502 of the UPC requires that at least two persons, each of whom witnessed either the signing or the testator's acknowledgment of the will, act as witnesses to the will.

The most common restriction on the ability to act as a witness is that a witness must not have any interest under the will. This requirement takes at least two forms under statutes. One type of statute disqualifies a witness who is also a beneficiary under the will. The other type voids the bequest or devise to the interested witness, thus making him a disinterested and thereby qualified witness. Defining what constitutes an "interest" sufficient to disqualify a witness is not always easy. The spouse of a beneficiary under a will has been held to be "interested" and thus not qualified. Usually, though, the courts will not disqualify a person simply because he is named as executor in the will. The attorney who drafts the will generally is a qualified witness. Under the UPC, attestation by an interested witness does not invalidate a will or any provision thereof. Section 2-505(b).

> ### Practical Advice
> *Store your will in a safe place and make sure that others know where it is kept. In addition, place an inventory of your assets where you store your will.*

50-4c REVOCATION OF A WILL

A will is revocable by the testator, and under certain circumstances, a will may be revoked by operation of law. Most jurisdictions specify by statute the methods by which a will may be revoked. The five generally accepted methods for revoking a will are as follows:

DESTRUCTION OR ALTERATION Tearing, burning, or otherwise destroying a will is an effective way of revoking a will, unless such destruction is shown to be inadvertent or without intent. UPC, Section 2-507. In some States, partial revocation may be accomplished by erasing or obliterating a part of the will. In no case, however, will a substituted or additional bequest by interlineation be effective without reexecution and reattestation.

Courts occasionally face the difficult question of determining whether a will was revoked by destruction or simply mislaid.

♦ *See Case 50-4*

SUBSEQUENT WILL The execution of a second will does not in itself constitute a revocation of an earlier will. The first will is revoked to the extent that the second will is inconsistent with the first. UPC, Section 2-507. The most certain manner of revocation is the execution of a later will containing a declaration that all former wills are revoked. In some but not all jurisdictions, a testator may revoke a will by a written declaration to this effect in a subsequent document, such as a letter, even though the document does not meet the formal requirements of a will.

> ### Practical Advice
> *If you wish to revoke a previous will (1) make sure that your new will indicates that it revokes all prior wills, (2) destroy or cancel all prior wills, and (3) make sure that your witnesses and others know that you have intentionally revoked all prior wills.*

CODICILS A **codicil** is a written amendment or addition to an existing will executed with all the formal requirements of a will. The most frequent problem such an instrument raises involves the extent to which its terms, if not absolutely clear, revoke or alter provisions in the will. For the purpose of determining the testator's intent, the codicil and the will are regarded as a single instrument.

> ### Practical Advice
> *If you wish to alter your will, you will need to either execute a codicil or a new will. In either case you need to comply with all the requirements of a new will.*

OPERATION OF LAW A *marriage* generally revokes a will executed before the marriage. Almost all States treat *divorce* as revoking a testamentary bequest to a former spouse. Section 2-508. Moreover, at least twenty-seven States (including the nineteen States that have adopted the Uniform Probate Code) provide that divorce revokes not just testamentary bequests but also beneficiary designations to a former spouse in "will substitutes," such as revocable trusts, pension accounts, and life insurance policies. In 2018, a Minnesota statute with such a provision was challenged as violating the U.S. Constitution's Contracts Clause, which bars the States from enacting any laws "impairing the obligation of contracts." In an 8–1 decision, the U.S. Supreme Court upheld the statute's constitutionality. *Sveen v. Melin*, 584 U. S. ____.

The *birth* of a child after execution of a will may revoke a will at least as far as that child is concerned if it appears that the testator omitted to make a provision for the child. In some jurisdictions and under the UPC, the subsequent birth of a child will not revoke the will; rather, unless it appears from the will that the omission was intentional, the child is entitled to a share the same as the one he would receive were the testator to die without a will. Section 2-302.

50-4d EFFECTIVENESS OF TESTAMENTARY PROVISIONS

RENUNCIATION BY THE SURVIVING SPOUSE Statutes generally provide a surviving spouse the right to renounce a will and set forth the method by which the spouse may do so. Such statutory provisions enable the spouse to decide which method of taking—under the will or under intestate succession—would be most advantageous. Only those whom the statute designates may exercise the right to renounce a will, and the right conferred on the surviving spouse is personal. Upon renunciation of the will, the law of intestate succession determines the share of the estate taken by the surviving spouse.

ABATEMENT AND ADEMPTION OF A BEQUEST Abatement is the reduction or elimination of gifts by category upon the reduction in the value of the estate of the testator after the execution of his will. It can have serious implications. The first items to abate in a will are the **residue**, or those items remaining after provisions for specific and general gifts. **Specific gifts**, which must be satisfied first, involve particular or uniquely identifiable items; **general gifts** do not. For example, if John, a widower, after making specific gifts, leaves "all the rest, residue, and remainder of my estate to my daughter, Mary," Mary may receive a great deal less than her deceased father intended. Suppose at the time John executes his will he estimates his worth at $150,000. He leaves $20,000 to his church, $10,000 to the Salvation Army, and his car, worth $10,000, to his business partner, and he assumes that Mary will receive approximately $110,000. Having suffered substantial business and market reverses, John dies five years later without having changed his will. His executor reports that there is only $50,000 in the estate. Mary will receive only $10,000 because the specific devise of the car and the general devises of the $20,000 and $10,000 will abate only after the residue is depleted.

Ademption, or the removal or extinction of a gift by act of the testator, occurs when a testator neglects to change his will after changed circumstances have made the performance of a provision in the will impossible. For example, Hope buys a farm, Blackacre, wishing it to go upon her death to a favorite nephew who is studying agriculture at college. After so providing in her will, she sells Blackacre and uses the money to buy Greenacre. The general rule is that the nephew will not be entitled to Greenacre. Nonetheless, the courts sometimes have modified this doctrine to reflect the perceived intent of the decedent. Under the "modified intention theory," through which a court attempts to effectuate the decedent's presumed intent, no ademption occurs where the property in question is missing from the estate because of some involuntary act of the decedent or some event over which he had no control.

50-4e SPECIAL TYPES OF WILLS

There are a number of special types of wills, including nuncupative wills, holographic wills, soldiers' and sailors' wills, conditional wills, joint and reciprocal wills, and living wills.

NUNCUPATIVE WILLS A nuncupative will is an unwritten oral declaration made before witnesses. In the few jurisdictions that authorize them, such declarations usually can be made only when the testator is in his last illness. Under most statutes permitting nuncupative wills, only limited amounts of personal property, generally under $1,000, may be passed by such wills. Under the UPC, all wills must be in writing. Section 2-502.

HOLOGRAPHIC WILLS In approximately one-half of the jurisdictions, a signed will *entirely* in the handwriting of the testator is a valid testamentary document even if the will is not witnessed. Under the UPC, Section 2-503, the signature and *material* provisions must be in the testator's handwriting. Such an instrument, referred to as a **holographic will**, must comply strictly with the statutory requirements for such wills.

SOLDIERS' AND SAILORS' WILLS For soldiers on active duty and sailors at sea, most statutes relax the formal requirements for a will and permit a testamentary disposition to be valid regardless of the informality of the document. In most jurisdictions, however, such a will cannot pass title to real estate.

CONDITIONAL WILLS A contingent or conditional will is one that takes effect only upon the happening of a specified contingency, which is a condition precedent to the operation of the will.

JOINT AND MUTUAL OR RECIPROCAL WILLS A joint will consists of a single instrument that is made the will of two or more persons and is signed by them jointly. By comparison, in making mutual or reciprocal wills, two or more persons execute separate instruments with reciprocal terms in which each testator makes a testamentary disposition in favor of the other.

LIVING WILLS   Almost all States have adopted statutes that permit an individual to execute a **living will**. A living will is a form of advance health care directive by which individuals specify what actions should be taken for their health if they are no longer able to make decisions for themselves because of illness or incapacity. (A living will is not a *will* that acts as a disposition of property after death, but rather a *directive* about medical care to be provided before death.) Through a living will and other forms of advance directives, which must comply with applicable statutory requirements, an individual may reject the use of life-prolonging procedures that artificially delay the dying process and ask to be allowed to die naturally should she contract an incurable illness or suffer an incurable injury.

Practical Advice

You should prepare a living will that specifically states your wishes concerning extraordinary medical treatment to preserve your life.

50-5 Intestate Succession

Property not effectively disposed of before death or by will passes in accordance with the law of intestate succession. (**Intestate** means dying without a valid will.) The rules set forth in statutes for determining, in case of intestacy, to whom the decedent's property shall be distributed not only ensure an orderly transfer of title to property but also purport to effect what would probably be the wishes of the decedent. Nonetheless, the intestacy statute will govern the distribution of the estate even if such distribution is contrary to the clear intention of the decedent.

The rules specifying the **course of descent** vary widely from State to State, but as a general rule and except for the specific statutory or dower rights of the widow, the intestate property passes in equal shares to each child of the decedent living at the time of his death, with the share of any predeceased child to be divided equally among the children of such predeceased child. For example, if Arthur dies intestate leaving a widow and children, his widow generally will receive one-third of his real estate and personal property, and the remainder will pass to his children in the manner stated above. If his wife does not survive Arthur, his entire estate passes to their children. If Arthur dies leaving two surviving children, Belinda and Carl, and two grandchildren, Donna and David, the children of a predeceased child Darwin, the estate will go one-third to Belinda, one-third to Carl, and one-sixth each to Donna and David, the grandchildren, who divide equally their parent's one-third share. This result is described legally by the statement that *lineal descendants* of predeceased children take **per stirpes**, or by representation of their parent. If Arthur had executed a will, he

may have provided that all his lineal descendants, regardless of generation, would share equally. In that case, Arthur's estate would be divided into four equal parts, and his descendants would be said to take **per capita**.

If only the widow and relatives other than his children survive the decedent, a larger share is generally allotted the widow. She may receive all the decedent's personal property and one-half his real estate or, in some States, his entire estate.

At common law, property could not ascend lineally; parents of an intestate decedent did not share in his estate. Today, in many States, if a decedent has no lineal descendants or a surviving spouse, the statute provides that parents are the next to share.

Most statutes make some provision for brothers and sisters if no spouse, parents, or children survive the decedent. Brothers and sisters, together with nieces, nephews, aunts, and uncles, are termed collateral heirs. Beyond these limits, most statutes provide that if there are no survivors in the named classes, the property shall be distributed equally among the next of kin in equal degree.

The common law did not consider a stepchild as an heir or next of kin, that is, as one to whom property would descend by operation of law, and this rule prevails. Legally adopted children are, however, recognized as lawful heirs of their adoptive parents.

These generalities should be accepted as such; few fields of the law of property are so strictly a matter of statute, and the rights of heirs cannot reasonably be predicted without a knowledge of the exact terms of the applicable statute.

Under the UPC, if the decedent dies without a will, (1) if there is no descendant and no parent surviving or if all surviving children are children of the decedent and the spouse, the surviving spouse is entitled to the entire estate;(2) if there is a parent surviving but no descendants, the spouse is entitled to the first $200,000 plus three-quarters of the remaining estate;(3) if the decedent is survived by one or more descendants who are also descendants of the surviving spouse and also by descendants who are not descendants of the surviving spouse, the spouse is entitled to the first $150,000 plus one-half of the remaining estate; and(4) if the decedent is survived by descendants who are not also descendants of the surviving spouse, the spouse is entitled to the first $100,000 plus one-half of the remaining estate.

♦ **SEE FIGURE 50-3:** *Per Stirpes and Per Capita*

50-6 Administration of Estates

Because they are statutory, the rules and procedures controlling the management of a decedent's estate vary somewhat from State to State. In all jurisdictions, the estate is managed and finally disbursed under the supervision of a court. The procedure for managing the distribution of decedents' estates is

FIGURE 50-3 *Per Stirpes* and *Per Capita*

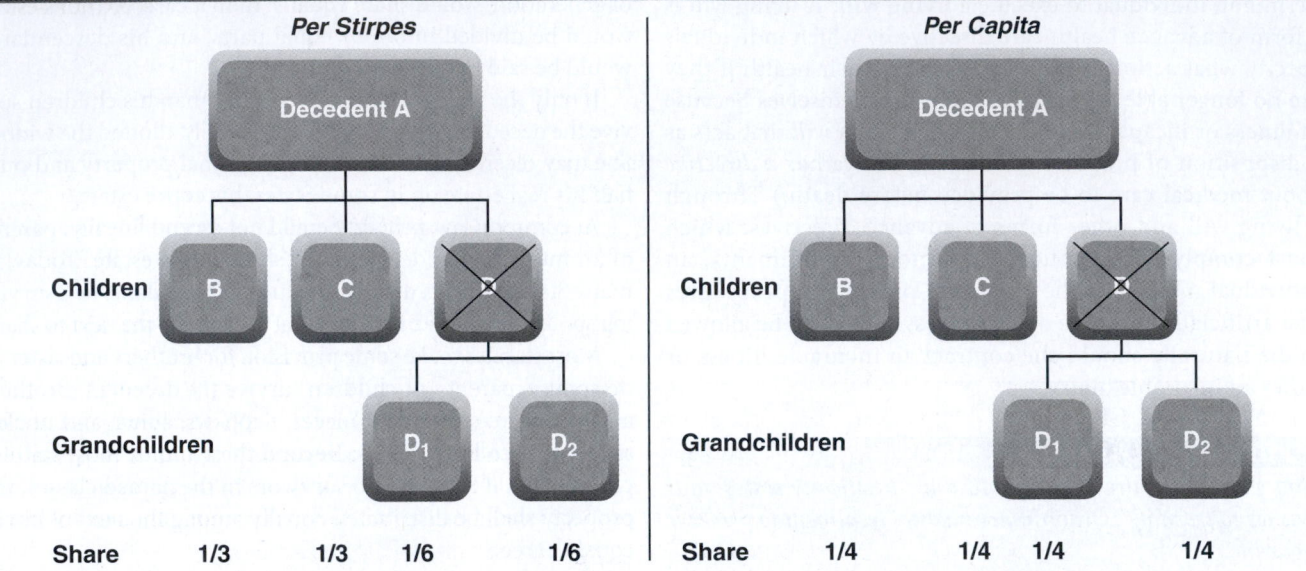

known as **probate**, and the court that supervises the procedure is often designated the probate court.

The first legal step after death is usually to determine whether or not the deceased left a will. If a will exists, the testator likely has named her executor in it. If there is no will or if a will exists but fails to name an executor, the court will, upon petition, appoint an administrator. The closest adult relative who is a resident of the State is entitled to such appointment.

Once approved or appointed by the court, the **executor** or **administrator** holds title to all the personal property of the deceased and is accountable to the creditors and the beneficiaries. The estate is his responsibility.

If there is a will, the witnesses must prove it before the court by testifying to the signing of the will by all signatories and by confirming the mental condition of the testator at the time she executed the will. If the witnesses are dead, proof of their handwriting is necessary. If satisfied that the will is proved, the court will enter a formal decree admitting the will to probate.

Soon after the admission of the will to probate, the decedent's personal representative—the executor or administrator—must file an inventory of the estate. The personal representative will then commence her duties of collecting the assets, paying the debts, and disbursing the remainder. The executor or administrator occupies a fiduciary position not unlike that of a trustee, and his responsibility for investing proceeds and otherwise managing the estate is equally demanding.

The administration of every estate involves probate expenses as well as fees to be paid to the executor or administrator and to the attorney who handles the estate. In addition, taxes are imposed at death by both the Federal and State governments. The Federal government imposes an **estate tax** on the transfer of property at death, while most State governments impose an **inheritance tax** on the privilege of an heir or beneficiary to receive the property. These taxes are separate from the basic income tax that the estate must pay on income received during estate administration.

C H A P T E R   S U M M A R Y

TRUSTS

TYPES OF TRUSTS   **Definition** a trust is a fiduciary relationship in which legal title to property (trust corpus) is held by one or more parties (the trustee) for the use, enjoyment, and benefit of another (the beneficiary)

Express Trust a trust established by voluntary action by the creator (settlor); usually in writing, although it may be oral

- *Testamentary Trust* a trust employed in a will; it becomes effective after the creator's death
- *Inter Vivos* **Trust** a trust established during the settlor's lifetime
- *Charitable Trust* a trust that has as its purpose the benefit of humankind
- *Spendthrift Trust* a trust designed to remove the trust estate from the beneficiary's control and from liability for his individual debts
- *Totten Trust* a tentative trust consisting of a joint bank account opened by the settlor (creator of the trust)

Implied Trust a trust created by operation of law

- *Constructive Trust* an implied trust imposed to rectify fraud or to prevent unjust enrichment
- *Resulting Trust* an implied trust imposed to fulfill the presumed intent of the settlor

CREATION AND TERMINATION OF TRUSTS

Settlor creator of a trust; anyone legally capable of making a contract may be a settlor

Trustee anyone legally capable of holding title to and dealing with property may be a trustee

- *Duties* the three primary duties of a trustee are to (1) carry out the purposes of the trust, (2) act prudently, and (3) act with utmost loyalty
- *Powers* generally established by the trust instrument and State law
- *Allocation of Principal and Income* see Figure 50-2

Beneficiary equitable owner of the trust property for whose use, enjoyment, and benefit the trust was created

Termination the general rule is that a unless the terms of a trust expressly provide that the trust is irrevocable, the settlor may revoke or amend the trust

DECEDENTS' ESTATES

WILLS

Definition a will (or testament) is a written instrument, executed with the formalities required by statute, whereby a person makes a disposition of his property to take effect after his death

Mental Capacity

- *Testamentary Capacity* for a will to be valid, the testator must be sufficiently competent to intend the document to be her will
- *Conduct Invalidating a Will* a will that is the product of duress, undue influence, or fraud is invalid and of no effect
- *Formal Requirements* a will must be (1) in writing, (2) signed, and (3) attested to by witnesses

Revocation a will is revocable by the testator and under certain circumstances may be revoked by operation of law

- *Destruction or Alteration* revokes a will
- *Subsequent Will* revokes prior wills to the extent they are inconsistent
- *Codicil* an addition to or revision of a will executed with all the formalities of a will
- *Marriage* generally revokes a will executed before the marriage
- *Divorce* generally revokes testamentary bequests and, in half the States, beneficiary designations to a former spouse
- *Birth of a Child* may revoke a will at least as far as that child is concerned
- *Renunciation by Surviving Spouse* surviving spouse may elect to take under laws of descent

Special Types of Wills generally binding only in specific situations and may have limitations upon their use

INTESTATE SUCCESSION	**Intestate** condition of person who dies without a valid will
	Course of Descent each State prescribes rules for the passage of property not governed by a valid will; as a general rule, the property passes in equal shares to each child after the widow's statutory or dower rights have been settled

ADMINISTRATION OF ESTATES	**Probate** the court's supervision of the management and distribution of the estate
	Executor or Administrator a person who is responsible for collecting the assets, paying the debts, and disbursing the remainder according to the will or intestate statute
	• *Executor* the person named in the will and appointed by the court to administer the will
	• *Administrator* a person appointed by the court to administer the estate when there is no will or when the person named in the will fails to qualify

C A S E S

CASE 50-1

Constructive Trusts
KEENEY v. KEENEY
Court of Appeals of Kentucky, 2007
223 S.W.3d 843

Acree, J.

This appeal from a judgment entered by the Pulaski Circuit Court began as Barbara Joanne Keeney's petition for dissolution of her marriage to Milton Keeney. Barbara [joined] * * * as additional defendants Milton's parents, Winfred (now deceased) and Ruth Keeney, and to establish her rights to 6.6629 acres near Nancy, Kentucky, titled in Winfred's and Ruth's names. The parties and trial court refer to this property as the "Nancy property" or, more frequently, the "Barlow property." * * *

Essential to Barbara's claims is the premise that Milton, aided by Winfred and Ruth, intentionally avoided direct ownership of real and/or personal property in his name. The obvious purpose was to avoid, and in fact, to defraud at least one particular creditor who was in a position to execute on any property she could have found belonging to Milton. As it happens, Milton was involved in a two-vehicle accident in the early 1970s when he was 18 years old. * * * Despite the passage of more than thirty years, the Smith judgment has never been satisfied.

On June 22, 1982, a decade or so after Milton's accident, Barbara and Milton were married. Before and during their marriage, Milton was self-employed. He had begun and continued establishing a business known as K-Bar Trailer Manufacturing Company. He built cattle, horse, and flatbed trailers. Additionally, Milton started a pig farm, but that venture eventually failed.

Barbara worked with her husband on many of his K-Bar ventures. * * *

Not long after their marriage, in February of 1983, and without Barbara's knowledge, Milton and his father attended a real estate auction where they were the successful bidders to purchase the Barlow property. Their winning bid was $61,700. * * *

* * *

Despite the fact that the funds to purchase the Barlow property came from Milton and Barbara's K-Bar checking account, the property was deeded to Winfred and Ruth. * * *

* * *

Barbara and Milton separated in January 1995. She filed for divorce on April 17, 1995. It was not until then that Milton represented to Barbara that his parents actually owned the Barlow property. * * *

* * *

The [trial] court concluded Barbara was unaware that the Barlow property was placed in the name of Winfred and Ruth. To the contrary, the court found that Barbara "was informed … that Milton had bought the Barlow property at Nancy" and that the property was paid for with funds from the K-Bar checking account controlled by Milton. The trial court ruled "as a matter of law that clear and convincing evidence [was] presented warranting the imposition of a constructive trust on the 'Nancy or Barlow Property.'" The court also ordered the property to be sold and the proceeds divided equally between Barbara and Milton. * * *

* * *

In summary, the Appellants * * * assert the trial court erred because "a constructive trust must result from an act of fraud, or, in the absence of fraud, must grow out of a fiduciary relationship." [Citation.] We reiterate what our predecessor court said in response to that argument.

* * *

The rule perhaps is best stated in [citation], wherein, after citing authorities, the Court said:

> These texts and authorities state the rule to be that a constructive trust is created by equity regardless of any actual or presumed intention of the parties to create a trust where the legal title to property is obtained through fraud, misrepresentation, concealment, undue influence or taking advantage of one's weakness or necessities, *or through similar means or circumstances rendering it unconscionable for the holder of the legal title to retain the property.*

[Citation] (emphasis added). When legal title to property has been acquired or held under such circumstances that the holder of that legal title may not in good conscience retain the beneficial interest, equity converts him into a trustee. [Citation.] Constructive trusts are created by the courts "in respect of property which has been acquired by fraud, or where, though acquired originally without fraud, it is against equity that it should be retained by him who holds it." [Citations.] "The fraud may occur in *any form of unconscionable conduct*; taking advantage of one's weaknesses or necessities, or in any way violating equity in good conscience." [Citations.] In fact, a court exercising its equitable power may impress a constructive trust upon one who obtains legal title, "not only by fraud or by violation of confidence or of fiduciary relationship, but *in any other unconscientious manner,* so that he cannot equitably retain the property which really belongs to another[.]" [Citation.]

It is true, * * * that Kentucky courts have required the party seeking the imposition of a trust to establish a "confidential relationship" with the party upon whom the trust is to be imposed. * * * Furthermore, "[t]he tendency of the courts is to construe the term 'confidence' or 'confidential relationship' liberally in favor of the confider and against the confidant, for the purpose of raising a constructive trust on a violation or betrayal thereof." [Citation.]

* * *

A careful review of this matter indicates there is no reason to believe that the circuit court was clearly erroneous in any of its findings of fact. The collaboration of Milton and his parents to avoid execution of the Smith judgment unquestionably falls in that category of behavior described variously in our case law as "unconscientious," "unconscionable," and "violating equity in good conscience." * * * Winfred's and Ruth's efforts to hide Milton's beneficial ownership of property from Mary Smith had an obvious and even greater dispossessory effect on Barbara than it had on its target.

Even if defrauding Barbara of her beneficial interest was not Winfred's and Ruth's original intention, it became so when she decided to divorce their son. Their retention of the property thus deprived Barbara of her beneficial ownership of the marital residence. [Citation.]

* * *

In this case, the trial court found that Winfred and Ruth placed the Barlow property in their names to conceal the identity of the beneficial owners; that Barbara and Milton were the beneficial owners of the subject property; that Barbara and Milton paid for the property; and that Winfred (or Winfred's estate) and Ruth would be unjustly enriched by retaining it. We cannot say that the circuit court's creation of a constructive trust, or its finding of any of the underlying facts necessary to support it, are clearly erroneous.

* * *

Affirmed.

CASE
50-2

Duties of the Trustee
IN THE MATTER OF THE ESTATE OF ROWE
Supreme Court, Appellate Division, Third Department, 2000
274 A.D.2d 87, 712 N.Y.S.2d 662; appeal denied, 96 N.Y.2d 707, 749 N.E.2d 206, 725 N.Y.S.2d 637 (2001)

Mercure, J. P.

Petitioner [Wilbur National Bank] was appointed trustee of a charitable lead trust created under the will of Frances E. Rowe, deceased (hereinafter decedent). The trust was funded solely by 30,000 shares of International Business Machines (hereinafter IBM) common stock, which was trading for approximately $113 per share at the time of decedent's death in April 1989 and approximately $117 per share when the trust was funded in September 1989. Under the terms of the trust instrument, petitioner was required to make annual distributions to qualified charities of 8% of the estate tax value of the trust assets, or $270,300; at the end of 15 years, the balance remaining in the trust, if any, was payable to respondents, who are decedent's nieces, or their issue.

In August 1994, respondents made a demand pursuant * * * that petitioner file an intermediate accounting, claiming that petitioner's failure to diversify the trust assets had resulted in a decline in yield and forced sales of trust principal, thereby threatening the depletion of the trust corpus by the end of the trust term. In December 1994, Surrogate's Court required petitioner to prepare an intermediate accounting for the period from September 8, 1989 to December 31, 1994 (hereinafter the accounting period). Petitioner filed its accounting and then commenced this proceeding for a judicial settlement thereof. Respondents objected to the accounting upon the grounds (among others) that petitioner's failure to diversify the trust was imprudent in that it violated petitioner's own policy requiring diversification, the policy of the Comptroller of Currency, and regulations of the Federal Reserve Bank.

The evidence adduced at the July 1996 trial of the proceeding to settle petitioner's intermediate account showed that petitioner's own written policy required diversification of the trust assets. At the time of the original funding of the trust in 1989, petitioner's Trust Policy Manual provided: "[I]t is the [Trust] Committee's recommendation that where practicable, the Investment staff follow a balanced and diversified approach in the management of those funds. Any trust accounts not conforming to this principle must be brought to the Committee's attention with supporting data as to the reason for these exceptions." The policy became even more specific in 1994, then providing: "[I]t is the Committee's recommendation that the Investment staff adhere to the principles of the 'Prudent Investor' rule by using modern portfolio theory and following a balanced and diversified approach in the management of those funds. Any trust accounts not conforming to these principles must be brought to the Committee's attention with supporting data as to the reason for these exceptions. Exceptions to diversification may be made when an agency customer or the trust instrument specifically permits, or where large capital gains would be incurred, or when the cost basis of the property has the potential to be written up in the near future." Further, the 1994 policy advised that existing holdings exceeding 10% of a portfolio should be trimmed down over a period of time, supported by several research houses and reviewed annually by petitioner's Trust Committee (hereinafter the Committee).

As for the actual investment activity engaged in by petitioner, the evidence showed that the Committee reviewed the trust in October 1989. Because the value of the stock had dropped from the time the trust was funded, the Committee felt that it would be imprudent to diversify immediately, but gave its approval to a plan of diversifying at a later time when the stock had reached a higher price. In the meantime, petitioner generated some income by selling various call options, and several small sales and in-kind distributions were made of IBM stock in order to fulfill the annual payout requirements.

The first move toward diversification came in February 1991, when petitioner sold 5,000 shares of IBM stock at $125 per share and an additional 2,959 shares at $136 per share. As of the close of the accounting period on December 31, 1994, petitioner still held 19,398 shares of IBM stock valued at $74 per share. Over the course of the accounting period, the market value of the trust assets had dropped from $3,521,250 to $1,853,937.

In August 1997, Surrogate's Court rendered its decision that, from the period September 8, 1989 to December 31, 1994, petitioner was negligent, that it had violated its own policy manual and that it should have diversified most of the trust's holdings in IBM in January 1990. Ultimately, Surrogate's Court ordered that petitioner's Letters of Trusteeship be revoked, appointed successor cotrustees, directed petitioner to turn over the trust property to them, ordered petitioner to refund its commissions to the trust and directed that petitioner pay damages of $496,259, together with $133,990 in interest, for a total of $630,249. Petitioner appeals.

Initially, we are unpersuaded by petitioner's various challenges to the finding by Surrogate's Court that petitioner acted imprudently in failing to diversify the trust's investments. During petitioner's administration of the trust, New York followed the "prudent person rule" of investment [citation], which provided: "A fiduciary holding funds for investment may invest the same in the kinds and classes of securities described in the succeeding subparagraphs, provided that investment is made only in such securities as would be acquired by prudent [persons] of discretion and intelligence in such matters who are seeking a reasonable income and the preservation of their capital." To determine whether the prudent person standard has been violated, the court should engage in "'a balanced and perceptive analysis of [the trustee's] consideration and action in the light of the history of each individual investment, viewed at the time of its action or its omission to act'" [citation]. All of the facts and circumstances of the case must be examined to determine whether a concentration of a particular stock in an estate's portfolio violates the prudent person standard [citation]. Further, each individual investment decision should be examined in relation to the entire portfolio as an entity [citation], and a trustee can be found to have been imprudent for losses resulting from negligent inattentiveness, inaction or indifference [citation].

At trial, the generalized testimony of Herbert Simmerly, who was petitioner's vice-president and trust officer and a supervisor of the trust, Benjamin Nesbitt, petitioner's senior vice-president and senior trust officer, and investment officers Lynda Peet and Erica Decker was directly contradicted by the testimony of respondent's expert, Loren Ross. Significantly, Ross expressed the strong opinion that petitioner had acted imprudently in failing to diversify the trust's assets immediately upon receipt of the IBM stock, in furtherance of its initial goal of creating a diversified portfolio of fixed income oriented assets and equity or growth assets. According to Ross, both the 15-year duration of the trust and the 8% annual payout requirement made the investment in IBM stock particularly inappropriate. First, IBM's dividends of less than $5 per share fell far short of satisfying the "extremely heavy burden" of having to pay out "an unvarying $270,300 a year" to charities, thereby requiring that capital be depleted to supplement the shortfall. Second, the extreme volatility and over-all downward trend of IBM stock during this period and the fact that IBM itself was undergoing an "extremely stressful time" made it unsuitable for fulfilling the trust's investment goals. Moreover, Ross stated that petitioner's tactic of waiting for the IBM stock to rise was based on "wishful hoping" and that any hesitancy on the part of petitioner to sell the IBM stock below acquisition costs was a "cosmetic kind of consideration." Finally, Ross testified that the use of call options increased the risk of the portfolio.

In addition to Ross's testimony describing petitioner's decision to delay diversification as unwise and unreasonably risky, the evidence reveals that petitioner failed to follow its own internal protocol during the administration of the trust up to the time of the intermediate accounting, that petitioner failed to conduct more than routine reviews of the IBM stock and that the target prices set for the trust's IBM stock were department-wide positions affecting many accounts, giving no particular consideration to the unique needs of this particular trust [citation]. Finally, we note that neither adverse tax consequences nor any provision of the trust instrument restricted petitioner's freedom to sell the IBM stock and diversify the trust's investments. In view of the foregoing, * * * we perceive no basis for disturbing the determination of Surrogate's Court that petitioner acted imprudently in retaining the IBM stock.

* * *

Ordered that the order is affirmed, with costs.

CASE 50-3

Conduct Invalidating a Will
PRINE v. BLANTON
Supreme Court of Georgia, 2012
290 Ga. 307, 720 S.E.2d 600

Hunstein, J.

[Debra Prine challenged the validity of her father's will on the grounds that he lacked testamentary capacity and was operating under undue influence. Testator Melvin H. Blanton's 1990 will and family trust divided the majority of his assets equally among his four surviving children and a granddaughter who was the child of his deceased daughter. In August 2008, Blanton met with his attorney and directed him to change his will and trust to exclude Debra Prine, his one surviving daughter. On September 17, 2008, while in the hospital, Blanton executed a new will and trust that left most of his property to his three sons through the Blanton Trust and excluded Debra Prine as a beneficiary. The following day, Blanton was placed in intensive care. He was discharged three weeks later to hospice care and died in February 2009. Blanton's sons and co-executors, Timmy M. Blanton and Greg Blanton, filed a petition to probate the will. Following a bench trial, the probate court found that Melvin Blanton was of sufficient sound and disposing mind and was not subjected to undue or illegal influence at the time he executed his will and trust amendment. Debra Prine appealed to the superior court, and the executors filed a motion for summary judgment, which the superior court granted.]

* * *

A testator possesses the mental capacity to make a will if he understands that he is executing a document that will dispose of his property after death, is capable of remembering the property that is subject to his disposition and the persons related to him by blood and affection, and "'has sufficient intellect to enable him to have a decided and rational desire as to the disposition of his property.'" [Citation.] "The controlling question … is whether the testator had sufficient testamentary capacity at the time of executing the will." [Citation.]

* * *

In this case, the propounders [supporters of the will] presented the affidavit of the attorney who drafted and witnessed the will stating that Blanton was of a sufficient sound and disposing mind and memory at the time he instructed the attorney on how to prepare the will and at the time he executed it. The other subscribing witness and the notary public who executed the self-proving affidavit attached to the will also verified that Blanton knew he was signing his last will and testament and he appeared to be of sound and disposing mind and memory at the time.

His treating physician testified in a deposition that during office visits in 2008 Blanton was "sharp as a tack," showing no symptoms of mental instability, confusion, dementia, hallucinations, or declining mental condition. Blanton was admitted to the hospital on September 15, 2008, after he complained of abdominal pain and fever. Two days later he executed the new will and trust amendment. His physician testified that Blanton was his usual self on the morning the will was executed, his condition was improving, and his medications would not have affected his mental ability. During his rounds on the following morning, the physician found that Blanton had declined sharply and referred him to a specialist for a neurology consultation and admitted him into the hospital's intensive care unit.

* * *

The caveator [opponent of the will] * * * relies on the affidavits of four lay witnesses. These witnesses either did not see Blanton until after he was admitted into intensive care or were vague about when they had seen him confused or hallucinating. The caveator testified that she did not see her father in the hospital until after work on the day he executed his will, he knew who she was at that time, and she had no knowledge of his mental condition earlier in the day. Evidence that the testator was aged, ill, and in pain when he executed his will or that his medical condition deteriorated while he was in the hospital does not show lack of testamentary capacity to make a will. * * * Construing the evidence in this case in the light most favorable to the caveator, she has not presented a genuine issue

of material fact that the testator lacked the requisite mental capacity when he signed his will.

To invalidate a will, undue influence must amount to deception or coercion that destroys the testator's free agency. [Citation.] The testator's choice of naming one relative instead of another as the favored beneficiary is an insufficient reason to deny probate of the will. [Citation.]

The caveator has not presented a genuine issue of material fact on the question of undue influence. Blanton's attorney and the subscribing witnesses attested that they believed he signed his will freely and voluntarily. His treating physician and other witnesses described the testator as strong-willed, stubborn, opinionated, and not susceptible to influence. There is no evidence that the propounders exerted any power or control over Blanton, coerced him into signing the will, or prevented the caveator and others from visiting him in the hospital or at his home. * * *

Judgment affirmed. * * *

C A S E
50-4

Revocation of a Will
WHATLEY v. ESTATE OF MCDOUGAL
Court of Appeals of Arkansas, 2013
430 S.W.3d 875

Gruber, J.

Bettye McDougal died at home on February 17, 2011, at age sixty-four. She had become unable to leave her recliner or bed in her final days, was under the care of hospice, received visits from a home health-care nurse, and was constantly cared for by close friends and relatives. The Circuit Court of Union County admitted to probate a copy of an April 6, 2007 will proffered on March 21, 2011, by her brother, Bobby Long, as her last will and testament. The will nominated Mr. Long as executor; left the bulk of the estate to him; excluded Ms. McDougal's only child and intestate beneficiary, Todd Whatley; and made specific bequests to friends including Albert Warren, who had lived with her for twelve years, as well as to a trust for her two grandchildren.

Mr. Whatley objected to probation of the copy of the will, stating that the original had not been located and that he believed his mother had intentionally destroyed it before her death. He asked the court to find that she died intestate and—because Mr. Long had a conflict of interest with the estate—to appoint a different executor. At trial—conducted on February 6 and June 11, 2012—Mr. Whatley stipulated that his mother properly executed a will on April 6, 2007, at the office of her lawyer. The parties did not dispute that Ms. McDougal left the lawyer's office with the original will and that it was not found after her death.

Much of the testimony at trial focused on decedent's strong-willed personality and business acumen; on knowing what she wanted; on her fifteen-year strained relationship with her son; and on the fact that she often publicized her intention to cut him out of her will. Her estrangement with him began after his wife, Regina Whatley, stole money from decedent's trucking business and his relationship with his wife continued despite decedent's wishes. From then on, neither Todd Whatley nor his and Regina's young son visited decedent again until the week before her death. She began spending all holidays with her brother and his wife, Janice Long, and never had a visit with her second grandchild, who was born after the estrangement began.

* * *

[The trial court concluded that the estate had satisfied the statutory requirements of Arkansas Code and had sufficiently rebutted the presumption of revocation by destruction. Therefore, the original will was found to have been in existence at the time of her death and to have been lost or misplaced.] Mr. Whatley appeals, contending that the circuit court clearly erred in admitting the copy of the will to probate.

* * *

Under [the Arkansas] statute, the proponent of a lost will must prove two things: first, the will's execution and its contents by strong, cogent, and convincing evidence; second, that the will was still in existence at the time of the testator's death (i.e., had not been revoked by the testator) or was fraudulently destroyed during the testator's lifetime. [Citation.] Proof of the second statutory element is necessary because the law presumes that an original will that cannot be found after a testator's death has been revoked. [Citation.] * * *

It will be presumed that a testator destroyed a will executed by the testator in his or her lifetime, with the intention of revoking same, if he or she retained custody thereof or had access thereto, and it could not be found after the testator's death. [Citations.] The burden is upon the proponent of the will to prove by a preponderance of the evidence that the decedent did not revoke it during his or her lifetime. [Citation.] Thus, it is not necessary for the trial court to determine what became of the will; it is enough that the court determine that the will was not revoked or cancelled by the decedent. [Citation.]

* * *

In the present case, the circuit court found that the second prong of the statute was established by indirect evidence that the original will was in existence at the time of decedent's death. Decedent's safe was secured by both a key and a combination lock, and it was accessible only by her or someone at her direction. Albert Warren knew how to access the safe and had done so before at her direction; Bobby Long knew the location of the key, but decedent kept the combination to the safe. Todd Whatley visited her only the one time after their estrangement,

was never alone with her, and was never alone in the house. Family and friends who were periodically alone with her in her last days were the beneficiaries under the will. Decedent had told them that all the papers for her estate were in the safe; other documents were found in there, but not the will. Decedent kept valuables in odd places, Albert Warren had the onset of dementia during her last year, and no one made a thorough and exhaustive search of the house.

* * *

In the present case, * * * the testimony and attending circumstances were sufficient to overcome the presumption of revocation. It was up to the circuit court to determine the credibility of the witnesses and the weight to be accorded their testimony. There was ample evidence that decedent was determined that her son inherit nothing upon her death; that she believed, and told many people, that her plans for distribution of her estate were taken care of; and that she, as well as relatives and friends attending her in her final days, believed the necessary papers were in her safe or her attorney's office. This evidence argues against revocation or destruction of the will that insured her plan would be carried out, and it supports a conclusion that the will was in existence at the time of her death. It was not necessary that the circuit court determine what happened to decedent's original will; it was enough that the court found that the will was not revoked or cancelled by her.

Affirmed.

QUESTIONS

1. State and explain whether or not a trust is created in each of the following situations:
   a. A declares herself trustee of "the bulk of my securities" in trust for B.
   b. A, the owner of Blackacre, purports to convey to B in trust for C "a small part" of Blackacre.
   c. A deposits $100,000 in a savings bank. He declares himself trustee of the deposit in trust to pay B $50,000 out of the deposit, reserving the power to withdraw from the deposit any amounts not in excess of $50,000.
2. Testator gives property to Tim in trust for Barney's benefit, providing that Barney cannot anticipate the income by assignment or pledge. Barney borrows money from Linda, assigning his future income under the trust for a stated period. Can Linda obtain any judicial relief to prevent Barney from collecting this income? Why or why not?
3. Collins was trustee for the beneficiary Indolent under the will of Indolent's father. Indolent, a middle-age doctor, gave little concern to the management of the trust

fund, contenting himself with receiving the income paid him by the trustee. Among the assets of the trust were one thousand shares of ABC Corporation and one thousand shares of XYZ Corporation. About two years before the termination of the trust, Collins, at a fair price and after full explanation to Indolent, purchased from the trust the ABC stock. At the same time but without saying anything to Indolent, he purchased the XYZ stock at a price in excess of its then market value. At the termination of the trust, both stocks had advanced in market value well beyond the prices paid by Collins, and Indolent demanded that Collins either account for this advance in the value of both stocks or replace the stocks. What are Indolent's rights? Explain.

4. Joe Brown gave to his wife, Mary Brown, $350,000 with which to buy real property. They orally agreed that title to the real property should be taken in the name of Mary Brown but that she should hold the property in trust for Joe Brown. There were two witnesses to the oral agreement, both of whom are still living. Mary purchased the property on September 2, and a deed to it with Mary Brown as the grantee was delivered.

Mary died ten years later without a will. The real property is now worth $800,000. Joe Brown is claiming the property as the beneficiary of a trust. Mary's children are claiming that the property belongs to Mary's estate and have pleaded the statute of limitations and the statute of frauds as defenses to the claim of Joe. There is no evidence to prove whether Mary would or would not have conveyed the property to Joe during her lifetime if she had been requested to do so. Explain what Joe's ownership rights are to this particular real property.

5. On March 10, John Carver executed his will, which was witnessed by William Hobson and Sam Witt. By his will, Carver devised his farm, Stonecrest, to his nephew, Roy White. The residue of his estate was given to his sister, Florence Carver. A codicil to his will executed April 15 of that year provided that $25,000 be given to Carver's niece, Mary Jordan, and $25,000 to Wanda White, Roy White's wife. The codicil was witnessed by Roy White and Harold Brown. John Carver died September 1 of that year, and the will and codicil were admitted to probate. Explain how Carver's estate should be distributed.

6. Edwin Fuller, a bachelor, prepared his will in his office. The will, which contained no residuary clause, provided that one-third of his estate would go to his nephew, Tom Fuller, one-third to the city of Emanon to be used for park improvements, and one-third to his brother, Kurt. He signed the will in his office and then went to the office of his nephew, Tom Fuller, who, at Edwin's request, signed the will as a witness. As no other persons were available in Tom's office, Edwin then went to the bank, where Frank Cash, the cashier, at Edwin's request, also signed as a witness. In each instance, Edwin stated that he had signed the document but did not state that it was his will. Edwin returned to his office and placed the will in his safe. Subsequently, Edwin died, survived by Kurt, his only heir-at-law. Explain how the estate should be distributed.

7. Arnold executed a one-page will, in which he devised his farm to Burton. Later, as the result of a quarrel with Burton, Arnold wrote the words, "I hereby cancel and revoke this will /s/ Arnold," in the margin of the will but did not destroy the will. Arnold then executed a deed to the farm, naming Connie as grantee, and placed the deed and will in his safe. Shortly afterwards, Arnold married Donna, with whom he had one child, Ernest. Thereafter, Arnold died, and the deed and will were found in his safe. Burton, Connie, and Ernest claim the farm, and Donna claims dower. Discuss the validity of each claim.

8. The validly executed will of John Dane contained the following provision: "I give and devise to my daughter, Mary, Redacre for and during her natural life and, at her death, the remainder to go to Wilmore College." The will also provided that the residue of his estate should go to Wilmore College. Thereafter, Dane sold Redacre and then added a validly executed codicil to his will, "Due to the fact that I have sold Redacre which I previously gave to my daughter, Mary, I now give and devise Blackacre to Mary in place and instead of Redacre."

   Another clause of the codicil provided: "I give to my son, Henry, my one-half interest in the oil business, which I own in common with William Steele." Subsequently, Dane acquired all of the interest in the oil business from his partner, Steele, and at the time of his death, Dane owned the entire oil business. The will and codicil have been admitted to probate.

   a. Explain what interest, if any, Mary acquires in Blackacre.

   b. Explain what interest, if any, Henry acquires in the oil business.

9. Leonard Wolfe was killed in an automobile accident while driving his Toyota Camry. The car was rendered a total loss, and Wolfe's insurance carrier paid his estate $18,550 for damage to the vehicle. Under the terms of Wolfe's will, any car owned at his death was to be given to his brother, David. Wolfe's daughter, Carol, however, brought an action, claiming that the gift of the car to David was adeemed by its total destruction and that she, as the residuary legatee under the will, was entitled to the insurance proceeds. Who is entitled to the insurance proceeds? Explain.

10. Grace Peterson, a never-married and childless woman, then age seventy-four, asked Chester Gustafson, a Minneapolis attorney, to draw a will for her. Gustafson, who had also probated Peterson's sister's estate, drew this first will and six subsequent wills and codicils free of charge because he claimed that she had no money to pay for his services. Over the five-year period during which Gustafson redrew Peterson's will, an increasing amount of property was devised to Gustafson's children, until, finally, the seventh will so devised Peterson's entire estate. Peterson, however, hardly knew the children except from several chance encounters ten years before. She died without ever having changed the seventh will, and Gustafson, who was named as executor, now seeks to have the will admitted to probate. Discuss whether the seventh will should be probated.

C A S E   P R O B L E M S

11. Rodney Sharp was a fifty-six-year-old dairy farmer whose education did not go beyond the eighth grade. Upon the death of his wife of thirty-two years, Sharp developed a very close relationship with Jean Kosmalski, a schoolteacher sixteen years his junior. Sharp eventually proposed to Kosmalski, but when she refused, he continued to make gifts to her in hopes of changing her mind. He also gave her access to his bank account, from which she withdrew substantial amounts of money; made a will naming her as sole beneficiary; and executed a deed naming her as a joint owner of his farm. Then, in September 2019, Sharp transferred his remaining joint interest in the farm to Kosmalski. In February 2021, Kosmalski ordered Sharp to move out of his home and to vacate the farm. She then took possession of both, leaving Sharp with assets of $300. Discuss whether a constructive trust should be imposed on the property transferred to Kosmalski.

12. By his last will and testament, Henry Nussbaum made a residual bequest and devise of his estate to his niece, Jane Blair, as trustee, in trust for the education of his grandchildren. If the trust could not be fulfilled, the residue was to revert to the plaintiff, Dorothy Witmer. After Nussbaum died in 2009, the plaintiff contended that the trustee had breached her fiduciary duty by failing to invest the trust corpus. A considerable portion of the trust funds were held in a checking account from 2012 to 2021. The trustee claimed that the will failed to specify when and what investments were to be made, and hence, such matters were left to her good-faith discretion. She also explained the large checking account balances by the fact that she thought she would need access to the funds to pay for college in the near future. Decision?

13. John Hobelsberger lived alone on his farm near Kranzburg, South Dakota. A grandniece, Phyllis Raml, and her husband, Ralph, lived on and operated a farm about two miles away. Hobelsberger and the Ramls had a friendly and cordial relationship. The Ramls visited him rather frequently and largely cared for him during his later years. Hobelsberger was hospitalized on October 23, and his condition was diagnosed as intermittent cerebral insufficiency. During his hospitalization, he requested that the Ramls send an attorney to see him about the preparation of a will. Thomas Green, an attorney, interviewed the testator on or about November 10 and prepared a will in compliance with his instructions.

Hobelsberger was transferred to a nursing home on November 19. On November 22, Green and a secretary went to the nursing home and witnessed his signing of the will. Hobelsberger was then eighty years old. He subscribed the will with a mark because he was having trouble with his hands. Hobelsberger died on July 19 of the following year, survived by twenty-seven nieces and nephews and seven grandnieces and grandnephews. The will, after providing for the payment of debts and funeral expenses, left Hobelsberger's entire estate to Phyllis Raml. Nine of the nieces and nephews contested the will, claiming lack of testamentary capacity, undue influence by the Ramls, and improper execution. Should the court admit the will to probate? Explain.

14. Mamie Henry, a widow, died leaving no children, but she was survived by several nieces and nephews. At first, no will was found, and Joe Barksdale, a nephew, was appointed administrator of Mrs. Henry's estate. Later, Rita Pendergrass produced a copy of a will allegedly made by Mrs. Henry. The will left all of Mrs. Henry's property to Mrs. Pendergrass and appointed her as executrix. When Mrs. Pendergrass sought to have the will admitted to probate, Joe Barksdale and Olen Barksdale filed a contest on the grounds that the purported will was never duly executed or, if executed, was destroyed by Mrs. Henry prior to her death. Should the will be probated? Explain.

15. George Washington Croom died testate. In his will, Croom left various bequests of real and personal property to his children and a grandchild. In Item Eight of his will, Croom stated "I leave nothing whatsoever to my daughter Kathryn Elizabeth Turner, and my son Ernest Edward Croom." At his death, Croom also left three optional share certificates in Carolina Savings & Loan Association issued to George W. Croom or Kimberly Joyce Croom, the deceased's minor daughter. Each of these certificates had attached to it an "Agreement Concerning Stock in Carolina Savings and Loan Association" which purported to create a joint account with a right of survivorship. Two of these agreements were signed by George Croom only, and the third agreement was not signed at all. None of these certificates were specifically devised by Croom's will, and the will contained no residuary clause. Who is entitled to share in these assets? Explain.

16. Willie Mae Arant executed her Last Will and Testament in her home with two witnesses present. The original will could not be found after Arant's death, so a copy of the will was filed and admitted in Probate Court. The will left the bulk of the estate to Melvin Bolton, Arant's

nephew, and Kent Sutcliffe, Arant's grandson. The evidence tended to show that the last verifiable location of the will was in Arant's attorney's office. Moreover, Arant told the witnesses to the will that she intended to have the will left with her attorney. Arant's only surviving daughter filed a suit challenging the probate of the will on the ground that because the original will could not be found, it had been destroyed with the intent to revoke. What factors should the court consider in deciding whether to probate the will? Explain.

T A K I N G   S I D E S

Upon George Welch's death, he was survived by his third wife, Dorothy Welch, and his daughter by his first marriage, Patricia Fisher. At the time George and Dorothy were married, George was in very poor health and he relied on Dorothy to care for him. George was suicidal and an alcoholic and suffered from severe depression. During the eight months George and Dorothy were married, George became isolated from his family and his health deteriorated. Prior to his death, George transferred the bulk of his assets to Dorothy. Dorothy assisted in the transfer of George's assets and often completed checks and other papers for George's signature. Although George and Dorothy had executed a prenuptial agreement, during the month preceding his death, George made a new will that named Dorothy as his sole beneficiary. Patricia had been the sole beneficiary of his prior will. Through the transfers of assets and the new will, Dorothy received $570,000.

a. What are the arguments that Patricia is entitled to the $570,000?

b. What are the arguments that Dorothy is entitled to the $570,000?

c. Who should prevail? Why?

Appendices

A THE CONSTITUTION OF THE UNITED STATES OF AMERICA

B DICTIONARY OF LEGAL TERMS

The Constitution of the United States of America

We the People of the United States, in Order to form a more perfect Union, establish Justice, insure domestic Tranquility, provide for the common defense, promote the general Welfare, and secure the Blessings of Liberty to ourselves and our Posterity, do ordain and establish this Constitution for the United States of America.

ARTICLE I

Section 1

All legislative Powers herein granted shall be vested in a Congress of the United States, which shall consist of a Senate and House of Representatives.

Section 2

The House of Representatives shall be composed of Members chosen every second Year by the People of the several States, and the Electors in each State shall have the Qualifications requisite for Electors of the most numerous Branch of the State Legislature.

No Person shall be a Representative who shall not have attained to the Age of twenty five Years, and been seven Years a Citizen of the United States, and who shall not, when elected, be an Inhabitant of that State in which he shall be chosen.

Representatives and direct Taxes shall be apportioned among the several States which may be included within this Union, according to their respective Numbers, which shall be determined by adding to the whole Number of free Persons, including those bound to Service for a Term of Years, and excluding Indians not taxed, three fifths of all other Persons. The actual Enumeration shall be made within three Years after the first Meeting of the Congress of the United States, and within every subsequent Term of ten Years, in such Manner as they shall by Law direct. The number of Representatives shall not exceed one for every thirty Thousand, but each State shall have at Least one Representative; and until such enumeration shall be made, the State of New Hampshire shall be entitled to chuse three, Massachusetts eight, Rhode Island and Providence Plantations one, Connecticut five, New-York six, New Jersey four, Pennsylvania eight, Delaware one, Maryland six, Virginia ten, North Carolina five, South Carolina five, and Georgia three.

When vacancies happen in the Representation from any State, the Executive Authority thereof shall issue Writs of Election to fill such vacancies.

The House of Representatives shall chuse their Speaker and other Officers; and shall have the sole Power of Impeachment.

Section 3

The Senate of the United States shall be composed of two Senators from each State, chosen by the Legislature thereof, for six Years; and each Senator shall have one Vote.

Immediately after they shall be assembled in Consequence of the first Election, they shall be divided as equally as may be into three Classes. The Seats of the Senators of the first Class shall be vacated at the Expiration of the second Year, of the second Class at the Expiration of the fourth Year, and of the third Class at the Expiration of the sixth Year, so that one third may be chosen every second Year; and if Vacancies happen by Resignation or otherwise, during the Recess of the Legislature of any State, the Executive thereof may make temporary Appointments until the next Meeting of the Legislature, which shall then fill such Vacancies.

No Person shall be a Senator who shall not have attained to the Age of thirty Years, and been nine Years a Citizen of the United States, and who shall not, when elected, be an Inhabitant of that State for which he shall be chosen.

The Vice President of the United States shall be President of the Senate, but shall have no Vote, unless they be equally divided.

The Senate shall chuse their other Officers, and also a President pro tempore, in the Absence of the Vice President, or when he shall exercise the Office of President of the United States.

The Senate shall have the sole power to try all Impeachments. When sitting for that Purpose, they shall be on Oath or Affirmation. When the President of the United States is tried, the Chief Justice shall preside: And no Person shall be convicted without the Concurrence of two thirds of the Members present.

Judgment in Cases of Impeachment shall not extend further than to removal from Office, and disqualification to hold and enjoy any Office of honor, Trust or Profit under the United States: but the Party convicted shall nevertheless be liable and subject to Indictment, Trial, Judgment and Punishment, according to Law.

Section 4

The Times, Places and Manner of holding Elections for Senators and Representatives, shall be prescribed in each State by the Legislature thereof: but the Congress may at any time by Law make or alter such Regulations, except as to the Places of chusing Senators.

The Congress shall assemble at least once in every Year, and such Meeting shall be on the first Monday in December, unless they shall by Law appoint a different Day.

Section 5

Each House shall be the Judge of the Elections, Returns and Qualifications of its own Members, and a Majority of each shall constitute a Quorum to do Business; but a smaller Number may adjourn from day to day, and may be authorized to compel the Attendance of absent Members, in such Manner, and under such Penalties as each House may provide.

Each House may determine the Rules of its Proceedings, punish its Members for disorderly Behaviour, and, with the Concurrence of two thirds, expel a Member. Each House shall keep a Journal of its Proceedings, and from time to time publish the same, excepting such Parts as may in their Judgment require Secrecy; and the Yeas and Nays of the Members of either House on any question shall, at the Desire of one fifth of those Present, be entered on the Journal.

Neither House, during the Session of Congress, shall, without the Consent of the other, adjourn for more than three days, nor to any other Place than that in which the two Houses shall be sitting.

Section 6

The Senators and Representatives shall receive a Compensation for their Services, to be ascertained by Law, and paid out of the Treasury of the United States. They shall in all Cases, except Treason, Felony and Breach of the Peace, be privileged from Arrest and Breach of the Peace, be privileged from Arrest during their Attendance at the Session of their respective Houses, and in going to and returning from the same; and for any Speech or Debate in either House, they shall not be questioned in any other Place.

No Senator or Representative shall, during the Time for which he was elected, be appointed to any civil Office under the Authority of the United States, which shall have been created, or the Emoluments whereof shall have been encreased during such time; and no Person holding any Office under the United States, shall be a Member of either House during his Continuance in Office.

Section 7

All Bills for raising Revenue shall originate in the House of Representatives; but the Senate may propose or concur with Amendments as on other Bills.

Every Bill which shall have passed the House of Representatives and the Senate, shall, before it become a Law, be presented to the President of the United States; If he approve he shall sign it, but if not he shall return it, with his Objections to that House in which it shall have originated, who shall enter the Objections at large on their Journal, and proceed to reconsider it. If after such Reconsideration two thirds of that House shall agree to pass the Bill, it shall be sent, together with the Objections, to the other House, by which it shall likewise be reconsidered, and if approved by two thirds of that House, it shall become a Law. But in all such Cases the Votes of both Houses shall be determined by Yeas and Nays, and the Names of the Persons voting for and against the Bill shall be entered on the Journal of each House respectively. If any Bill shall not be returned by the President within ten Days (Sundays excepted) after it shall have been presented to him, the Same shall be a Law, in like Manner as if he had signed it, unless the Congress by their Adjournment prevent its Return, in which Case it shall not be a Law.

Every Order, Resolution, or Vote to which the Concurrence of the Senate and House of Representatives may be necessary (except on a question of Adjournment) shall be presented to the President of the United States; and before the Same shall take Effect, shall be approved by him, or being disapproved by him, shall be repassed by two thirds of the Senate and House of Representatives, according to the Rules and Limitations prescribed in the Case of a Bill.

Section 8

The Congress shall have Power to lay and collect Taxes, Duties, Imposts and Excises, to pay the Debts and provide for the common Defense and general Welfare of the United States; but all Duties, Imposts and Excises shall be uniform throughout the United States;

To borrow Money on the credit of the United States;

To regulate Commerce with foreign Nations, and among the several States, and with the Indian Tribes;

To establish an uniform Rule of Naturalization, and uniform Laws on the subject of Bankruptcies throughout the United States;

To coin Money, regulate the Value thereof, and of foreign Coin, and fix the Standard of Weights and Measures;

To provide for the Punishment of counterfeiting the Securities and current Coin of the United States;

To establish Post Offices and post Roads;

To promote the Progress of Science and useful Arts, by securing for limited Times to Authors and Inventors the exclusive Right to their respective Writings and Discoveries;

To constitute Tribunals inferior to the supreme Court;

To define and punish Piracies and Felonies committed on the high Seas, and Offenses against the Law of Nations;

To declare War, grant Letters of Marque and Reprisal, and make Rules concerning Captures on Land and Water;

To raise and support Armies, but no Appropriation of Money to that Use shall be for a longer Term than two Years;

To provide and maintain a Navy;

To make Rules for the Government and Regulation of the land and naval Forces;

To provide for calling forth the Militia to execute the Laws of the Union, suppress Insurrections and repel Invasions;

To provide for organizing, arming, and disciplining, the Militia, and for governing such Part of them as may be employed in the Service of the United States, reserving to the States respectively, the Appointment of the Officers, and the Authority of training the Militia according to the discipline described by Congress;

To exercise exclusive Legislation in all Cases whatsoever, over such District (not exceeding ten Miles square) as may, by Cession of particular States, and the Acceptance of Congress, become the Seat of the Government of the United States, and to exercise like Authority over all Places purchased by the Consent of the Legislature of the State in which the Same shall be, for the Erection of Forts, Magazines, Arsenals, dock-Yards, and other needful Buildings;—And

To make all Laws which shall be necessary and proper for carrying into Execution the foregoing Powers, and all other Powers vested by this Constitution in the Government of the United States, or in any Department or Officer thereof.

Section 9

The Migration or Importation of such Persons as any of the States now existing shall think proper to admit, shall not be prohibited by the Congress prior to the Year one thousand eight hundred and eight, but a Tax of Duty may be imposed on such Importation, not exceeding ten dollars for each Person.

The Privilege of the Writ of Habeas Corpus shall not be suspended, unless when in Cases of Rebellion or Invasion the public Safety may require it.

No Bill of Attainder or ex post facto Law shall be passed.

No Capitation, or other direct, Tax shall be laid, unless in Proportion to the Census or Enumeration herein before directed to be taken.

No Tax or Duty shall be laid on Articles exported from any State.

No Preference shall be given by any Regulation of Commerce or Revenue to the Ports of one State over those of another; nor shall Vessels bound to, or from, one State, be obliged to enter, clear, or pay Duties in another.

No Money shall be drawn from the Treasury, but in Consequence of Appropriations made by Laws; and a regular Statement and Account of the Receipts and Expenditures of all public Money shall be published from time to time.

No Title of Nobility shall be granted by the United States: And no Person holding any Office of Profit or Trust under them, shall, without the Consent of the Congress, accept of any present, Emolument, Office, or Title, of any kind whatever, from any King, Prince, or foreign State.

Section 10

No State shall enter into any Treaty, Alliance, or Confederation; grant Letters of Marque and Reprisal; coin Money; emit Bills of Credit; make any Thing but gold and silver Coin a Tender in Payment of Debts; pass any Bill of Attainder, ex post facto Law, or Law impairing the Obligation of Contracts, or grant any Title of Nobility.

No State shall, without the Consent of the Congress, lay any Imposts or Duties on Imports or Exports, except what may be absolutely necessary for executing its inspection Laws: and the net Produce of all Duties and Imposts, laid by any State on Imports or Exports, shall be for the Use of the Treasury of the United States; and all such Laws shall be subject to the Revision and Controul of the Congress.

No State shall, without the Consent of Congress, lay any Duty of Tonnage, keep Troops, or Ships of War in time of Peace, enter into any Agreement or Compact with another State, or with a foreign Power, or engage in War, unless actually invaded, or in such imminent Danger as will not admit of delay.

ARTICLE II

Section 1

The executive Power shall be vested in a President of the United States of America. He shall hold his Office during the Term of four Years, and, together with the Vice President, chosen for the same Term, be elected, as follows:

Each State shall appoint, in such Manner as the Legislature thereof may direct, a Number of Electors, equal to the whole Number of Senators and Representatives to which the State may be entitled in the Congress: but no Senator or Representative, or Person holding an Office of Trust or Profit under the United States, shall be appointed an Elector.

The Electors shall meet in their respective States, and vote by Ballot for two Persons, of whom one at least shall not be an Inhabitant of the same State with themselves. And they shall make a list of all the Persons voted for, and of the Number of Votes for each; which List they shall sign and certify, and transmit sealed to the Seat of the Government of the United States, directed to the President of the Senate. The President of the Senate shall, in the presence of the Senate and House of Representatives, open all the Certificates, and the Votes shall be counted. The Person having the greatest Number of Votes shall be the President, if such Number be a Majority of the whole Number of Electors appointed; and if there be more than one who have such Majority, and have an equal Number of Votes, then the House of Representatives shall immediately chuse by Ballot one of them for President; and if no Person have a Majority, then from the five highest on the List the said House shall in like Manner chuse the President. But in chusing the President, the Votes shall be taken by States, the Representation from each State having one Vote; A quorum for this Purpose shall consist of a Member or Members from two thirds of the States, and a Majority of all the States shall be necessary to a Choice. In every Case, after the Choice of the President, the Person having the Greatest Number of Votes of the Electors shall be the Vice President. But if there should remain two or more who have equal Votes, the Senate shall chuse from them by Ballot the Vice President.

The Congress may determine the Time of Chusing the Electors, and the Day on which they shall give their Votes; which Day shall be the same throughout the United States.

No Person except a natural born Citizen, or a Citizen of the United States, at the time of the Adoption of this Constitution, shall be eligible to the Office of President; neither shall any Person be eligible to that Office who shall not have attained to the Age of thirty five Years, and been fourteen Years a Resident within the United States.

In Case of the Removal of the President from Office, or of his Death, Resignation, or Inability to discharge the Powers and Duties of the said Office, the Same shall devolve on the Vice President, and the Congress may by Law provide for the Case of Removal, Death, Resignation or Inability, both of the President and Vice President, declaring what Officer shall then act as President, and such Officer shall act accordingly, until the Disability be removed, or a President shall be elected.

The President shall, at stated Times, receive for his Services, a Compensation, which shall neither be encreased nor diminished during the Period for which he shall have been elected, and he shall not receive within that Period any other Emolument from the United States, or any of them.

Before he enter on the Execution of his Office, he shall take the following Oath or Affirmation:—"I do solemnly swear (or affirm) that I will faithfully execute the Office of President of the United States, and will to the best of my Ability, preserve, protect and defend the Constitution of the United States."

Section 2

The President shall be Commander in Chief of the Army and Navy of the United States, and of the Militia of the several States, when called into the actual Service of the United States; he may require the Opinion, in writing, of the principal Officer in each of the executive Departments, upon any Subject relating to the Duties of their respective Offices, and he shall have Power to grant Reprieves and Pardons for Offences against the United States, except in Cases of Impeachment.

He shall have Power, by and with the Advice and Consent of the Senate, to make Treaties, providing two thirds of the Senators present concur; and he shall nominate, and by and with the Advice and Consent of the Senate, shall appoint Ambassadors, other public Ministers and Consuls, Judges of the supreme Court, and all other Officers of the United States, whose Appointments are not herein otherwise provided for, and which shall be established by Law: but the Congress may by Law vest the Appointment of such inferior Officers, as they think proper, in the President alone, in the Courts of Law, or in the Heads of Departments.

The President shall have Power to fill up all Vacancies that may happen during the Recess of the Senate, by granting Commissions which shall expire at the End of their next Session.

Section 3

He shall from time to time give to the Congress Information of the State of the Union, and recommend to their Consideration such Measures as he shall judge necessary and expedient; he may, on extraordinary Occasions, convene both Houses, or either of them, and in Case of Disagreement between them, with Respect to the Time of Adjournment, he may adjourn them to such Time as he shall think proper, he shall receive Ambassadors and other public Ministers; he shall take Care that the Laws be faithfully executed, and shall Commission all the Offices of the United States.

Section 4

The President, Vice President and all civil Officers of the United States, shall be removed from Office on Impeachment for, and Conviction of, Treason, Bribery, or other high Crimes and Misdemeanors.

ARTICLE III

Section 1

The judicial Power of the United States, shall be vested in one supreme Court, and in such inferior Courts as the Congress may from time to time ordain and establish. The Judges, both of the supreme and inferior Courts, shall hold their Offices during good Behaviour, and shall, at Times, receive for their Services, a Compensation, which shall not be diminished during their Continuance in Office.

Section 2

The judicial Power shall extend to all Cases, in Law and Equity, arising under this Constitution, the Laws of the United States, and Treaties made, or which shall be made, under their Authority;—to all Cases affecting Ambassadors, other public Ministers and Consuls;—to all Cases of admiralty and maritime Jurisdiction;—to Controversies to which the United States shall be a Party;—to controversies between two or more States;—between a State and Citizens of another State;— between Citizens of different States;—between Citizens of the same State claiming Lands under Grants of different States; and between a State, or the Citizens thereof, and foreign States, Citizens or Subjects.

In all Cases affecting Ambassadors, other public Ministers and Consuls, and those in which a State shall be Party, the supreme Court shall have original Jurisdiction. In all the other Cases before mentioned, the supreme Court shall have appellate Jurisdiction, both as to Law and Fact, with such Exceptions, and under such Regulations as the Congress shall make.

The Trial of all Crimes, except in Cases of Impeachment, shall be by Jury; and such Trial shall be held in the State where the said Crimes shall have been committed; but when not committed within any State, the Trial shall be at such Place or Places as the Congress may by Law have directed.

Section 3

Treason against the United States, shall consist only in levying War against them, or in adhering to their Enemies, giving them Aid and Comfort. No Person shall be convicted of Treason unless on the Testimony of two Witnesses to the same overt Act, or on Confession in open Court.

The Congress shall have Power to declare the Punishment of Treason, but no Attainder of Treason shall work Corruption of Blood, or Forfeiture except during the Life of the Person attainted.

ARTICLE IV

Section 1

Full Faith and Credit shall be given in each State to the public Acts, Records, and judicial Proceedings of every other State. And the Congress may by general Laws prescribe the Manner in which such Arts, Records and Proceedings shall be proved, and the Effect thereof.

Section 2

The Citizens of each State shall be entitled to all Privileges and Immunities of Citizens in the several States.

A Person charged in any State with Treason, Felony, or other Crime, who shall flee from Justice, and be found in another State, shall on Demand of the executive Authority of the State from which he fled, be delivered up, to be removed to the State having Jurisdiction of the Crime.

No Person held to Service or Labour in one State, under the Laws thereof, escaping into another, shall, in Consequence of any Law or Regulation therein, be discharged from such Service or Labour, but shall be delivered up on Claim of the Party to whom such Service or Labour may be due.

Section 3

New States may be admitted by the Congress into this Union; but no new State shall be formed or erected within the Jurisdiction of any other State; nor any State be formed by the Junction of two or more States, or Parts of States, without the Consent of the Legislatures of the States concerned as well as the Congress.

The Congress shall have Power to dispose of and make all needful Rules and Regulations respecting the Territory or other Property belonging to the United States; and nothing in this Constitution shall be so construed as to Prejudice any Claims of the United States, or of any particular State.

Section 4

The United States shall guarantee to every State in this Union a Republican Form of Government, and shall protect each of them against Invasion; and on Application of the Legislature, or of the Executive (when the Legislature cannot be convened) against domestic Violence.

ARTICLE V

The Congress, whenever two thirds of both Houses shall deem it necessary, shall propose Amendments to this Constitution, or, on the Application of the Legislatures of two thirds of the several States, shall call a Convention for proposing Amendments, which, in either Case, shall be valid to all Intents and Purposes, as Part of this Constitution, when ratified by the Legislatures of three fourths of the several States, or by Conventions in three fourths thereof, as the one or the other Mode of Ratification may be proposed by the Congress; Provided that no Amendment which may be made prior to the Year One thousand eight hundred and eight shall in any Manner affect the first and fourth Clauses in the Ninth Section of the first Article; and that no State, without its Consent, shall be deprived of its equal Suffrage in the Senate.

ARTICLE VI

All Debts contracted and Engagements entered into, before the Adoption of this Constitution, shall be as valid against the United States under this Constitution, as under the Confederation.

This Constitution, and the Laws of the United States which shall be made in Pursuance thereof; and all Treaties made, or which shall be made, under the Authority of the United States, shall be the supreme Law of the Land; and the Judges in every State shall be bound thereby, any Thing in the Constitution or Laws of any State to the Contrary notwithstanding.

The Senators and Representatives before mentioned, and the Members of the several State Legislatures, and all executive and judicial Officers, both of the United States and of the Several States, shall be bound by Oath or Affirmation, to support this Constitution; but no religious Test shall ever be required as a Qualification to any Office or public Trust under the United States.

ARTICLE VII

The Ratification of the Conventions of nine States, shall be sufficient for the Establishment of this Constitution between the States so ratifying the Same.

Amendment I [1791]

Congress shall make no law respecting an establishment of religion, or prohibiting the free exercise thereof; or abridging the freedom of speech, or the press; or the right of the people peaceably to assemble, and to petition the Government for a redress of grievances.

Amendment II [1791]

A well regulated Militia, being necessary to the security for a free State, the right of the people to keep and bear Arms, shall not be infringed.

Amendment III [1791]

No Soldier shall, in time of peace be quartered in any house, without the consent of the Owner, nor in time of war, but in a manner to be prescribed by law.

Amendment IV [1791]

The right of the people to be secure in their persons, houses, papers, and effects, against unreasonable searches and seizures, shall not be violated, and no Warrants shall issue, but upon probable cause, supported by Oath or Affirmation, and particularly describing the place to be searched, and the persons or things to be seized.

Amendment V [1791]

No person shall be held to answer for a capital, or otherwise infamous crime, unless on a presentment or indictment of a Grand Jury, except in cases arising in the land or naval forces, or in the Militia, when in actual service in time of War or public danger; nor shall any person be subject for the same offense to be twice put in jeopardy of life or limb; nor shall be compelled in any criminal case to be a witness against himself, nor be deprived of life, liberty, or property, without due process of law; nor shall private property be taken for public use, without just compensation.

Amendment VI [1791]

In all criminal prosecutions, the accused shall enjoy the right to a speedy and public trial, by an impartial jury of the State and district wherein the crime shall have been committed, which district shall have been previously ascertained by law, and to be informed of the nature and cause of the accusation; to be confronted with the Witnesses against him; to have compulsory process for obtaining witnesses in his favor, and to have the Assistance of counsel for his defense.

Amendment VII [1791]

In suits at common law, where the value in controversy shall exceed twenty dollars, the right of trial by jury shall be preserved, and no fact tried by a jury, shall be otherwise re-examined in any Court of the United States, than according to the rules of the common law.

Amendment VIII [1791]

Excessive bail shall not be required, no excessive fines imposed, nor cruel and unusual punishments inflicted.

Amendment IX [1791]

The enumeration in the Constitution, of certain rights, shall not be construed to deny or disparage others retained by the people.

Amendment X [1791]

The powers not delegated to the United States by the Constitution, nor prohibited by it to the States, are reserved to the States respectively, or to the people.

Amendment XI [1798]

The judicial power of the United States shall not be construed to extend to any suit in law or equity, commenced or prosecuted against one of the United States by Citizens of another State, or by Citizens or Subjects of any Foreign State.

Amendment XII [1804]

The Electors shall meet in their respective states and vote by ballot for President and Vice-President, one of whom, at least, shall not be an inhabitant of the same state with themselves; they shall name in their ballots the person voted for as President, and in distinct ballots the person voted for as Vice-President, and they shall make distinct lists of all persons voted for as President, and of all persons voted for as Vice-President, and of the number of votes for each, which lists they shall sign and certify, and transmit sealed to the seat of the government of the United States, directed to the President of the Senate;—The President of the Senate shall, in the presence of the Senate and House of Representatives, open all the certificates and the votes shall then be counted;—The person having the greatest number of votes for President, shall be the President, if such a number be a majority of the whole number of Electors appointed; and if no person have such majority, then from the persons having the highest numbers not exceeding three on the list of those voted for as President, the House of Representatives shall choose immediately, by ballot, the President. But in choosing the President, the votes shall be taken by states, the representation from each state having one vote; a quorum for this purpose shall consist of a member or members from two-thirds of the states, and a majority of all the states shall be necessary to a choice. And if the House of Representatives shall not choose a President whenever the right of choice shall devolve upon them, before the fourth day of March next following, then the Vice-President shall act as President, as in the case of the death or other constitutional disability of the President. The person having the greatest number of votes as Vice-President, shall be the Vice-President, if such number be a majority of the whole number of Electors appointed, and if no person have a majority, then from the two highest numbers on the list, the Senate shall choose the Vice-President; a quorum for the purpose shall consist of two-thirds of the whole number of Senators, and a majority of the whole number shall be necessary to a choice. But no person constitutionally ineligible to the office of President shall be eligible to that of the Vice-President of the United States.

Amendment XIII [1865]

Section 1. Neither slavery nor involuntary servitude, except as a punishment for crime whereof the party shall have been duly convicted, shall exist within the United States, or any place subject to their jurisdiction.
Section 2. Congress shall have power to enforce this article by appropriate legislation.

Amendment XIV [1868]

Section 1. All persons born or naturalized in the United States, and subject to the jurisdiction thereof, are citizens of the United States and of the State wherein they reside. No State shall make or enforce any law which shall abridge the privileges or immunities of citizens of the United States; nor shall any State deprive any person of life, liberty, or property, without due process of law; nor deny to any person within its jurisdiction the equal protection of the laws.
Section 2. Representatives shall be appointed among the several States according to their respective numbers, counting the whole number of persons in each State, excluding Indians not taxed. But when the right to vote at any election for the choice of electors for President and Vice President of the United States, Representatives in Congress, the Executive and Judicial officers of a State, or the members of the Legislature thereof, is denied to any of the male inhabitants of such State, being twenty-one years of age, and citizens of the United States, or in any way abridged, except for participation in rebellion, or other crime, the basis of representation therein shall be reduced in the proportion which the number of such male citizens shall bear the whole number of male citizens twenty-one years of age in such State.
Section 3. No person shall be a Senator or Representative in Congress, or elector of President and Vice President, or hold any office, civil or military, under the United States, or under any State, who, having previously taken an oath, as a member of Congress, or as an officer of the United States, or as a member of any State legislature, or as an executive or judicial officer of any State, to support the Constitution of the United States, shall have engaged in insurrection or rebellion against the same, or given aid or comfort to the enemies thereof. But Congress may by a vote of two-thirds of each House, remove such disability.
Section 4. The validity of the public debt of the United States, authorized by law, including debts incurred for payment of pensions and bounties for services in suppressing insurrection or rebellion, shall not be questioned. But neither the United States nor any State shall assume or pay any debt or obligation incurred in aid of insurrection of rebellion against the United States, or any claim for the loss or emancipation of any slave; but all such debts, obligations and claims shall be held illegal and void.
Section 5. The Congress shall have power to enforce, by appropriate legislation, the provisions of this article.

Amendment XV [1870]

Section 1. The right of citizens of the United States to vote shall not be denied or abridged by the United States or by any State on account of race, color, or previous condition of servitude.

Section 2. The Congress shall have power to enforce this article by appropriate legislation.

Amendment XVI [1913]

The Congress shall have power to lay and collect taxes on incomes, from whatever source derived, without apportionment among the several States, and without regard to any census or enumeration.

Amendment XVII [1913]

The Senate of the United States shall be composed of two Senators from each State, elected by the people thereof, for six years; and each Senator shall have one vote. The electors in each State shall have the qualifications requisite for electors of the most numerous branch of the State legislatures.

When vacancies happen in the representation of any State in the Senate, the executive authority of each State shall issue writs of election to fill such vacancies; Provided, That the legislature of any State may empower the executive thereof to make temporary appointments until the people fill the vacancies by election as the legislature may direct.

This amendment shall not be construed as to affect the election or term of any Senator chosen before it becomes valid as part of the Constitution.

Amendment XVIII [1919]

Section 1. After one year from the ratification of this article the manufacture, sale, or transportation of intoxicating liquors within, the importation thereof into, or the exportation thereof from the United States and all territory subject to the jurisdiction thereof for beverage purposes is hereby prohibited.

Section 2. The Congress and the several States shall have concurrent power to enforce this article by appropriate legislation.

Section 3. This article shall be inoperative unless it shall have been ratified as an amendment to the Constitution by the legislatures of the several States, as provided in the Constitution, within seven years from the date of the submission hereof to the States by the Congress.

Amendment XIX [1920]

The right of citizens of the United States to vote shall not be denied or abridged by the United States or by any State on account of sex.

Congress shall have power to enforce this article by appropriate legislation.

Amendment XX [1933]

Section 1. The terms of the President and Vice President shall end at noon on the 20th day of January, and the terms of Senators and Representatives at noon on the 3d day of January, of the years in which such terms would have ended if this article had not been ratified; and the terms of their successors shall then begin.

Section 2. The Congress shall assemble at least once in every year, and such meeting shall begin at noon on the 3d day of January, unless they shall by law appoint a different day.

Section 3. If, at the time fixed for the beginning of the term of the President, the President elect shall have died, the Vice President elect shall become President. If a President shall not have been chosen before the time fixed for the beginning of his term, or if the President elect shall have failed to qualify, then the Vice President elect shall act as President until a President shall have qualified; and the Congress may by law provide for the case wherein neither a President elect nor a Vice President elect shall have qualified, declaring who shall then act as President, or the manner in which one who is to act shall be selected, and such person shall act accordingly until a President or Vice President shall have qualified.

Section 4. The Congress may by law provide for the case of the death of any of the persons from whom the House of Representatives may choose a President whenever the right of choice shall have devolved upon them, and for the case of the death of any of the persons from whom the Senate

may choose a Vice President whenever the right of choice shall have devolved upon them.

Section 5. Sections 1 and 2 shall take effect on the 15th day of October following the ratification of this article.

Section 6. This article shall be inoperative unless it shall have been ratified as an amendment to the Constitution by the legislatures of three-fourths of the several States within seven years from the date of its submission.

Amendment XXI [1933]

Section 1. The eighteenth article of amendment to the Constitution of the United States is hereby repealed.

Section 2. The transportation or importation into any State, Territory, or possession of the United States for delivery or use therein of intoxicating liquors, in violation of the laws thereof, is hereby prohibited.

Section 3. This article shall be inoperative unless it shall have been ratified as an amendment to the Constitution by conventions in the several States, as provided in the Constitution, within seven years from the date of the submission hereof to the States by the Congress.

Amendment XXII [1951]

Section 1. No person shall be elected to the office of the President more than twice, and no person who has held the office of President, or acted as President, for more than two years of a term to which some other person was elected President shall be elected to the office of the President more than once. But this Article shall not apply to any person holding the office of President when this Article was proposed by the Congress, and shall not prevent any person who may be holding the office of President, or acting as President, during the term within which this Article becomes operative from holding the office of President, or acting as President during the remainder of such term.

Section 2. This article shall be inoperative unless it shall have been ratified as an amendment to the Constitution by the legislatures of three-fourths of the several States within seven years from the date of its submission to the States by the Congress.

Amendment XXIII [1961]

Section 1. The District constituting the seat of Government of the United States shall appoint in such manner as the Congress may direct:

A number of electors of President and Vice President equal to the whole number of Senators and Representatives in Congress to which the District would be entitled if it were a State, but in no event more than the least populous State; they shall be in addition to those appointed by the States, but they shall be considered, for the purposes of the election of President and Vice President, to be electors appointed by a State; and they shall meet in the District and perform such duties as provided by the twelfth article of amendment.

Section 2. The Congress shall have power to enforce this article by appropriate legislation.

Amendment XXIV [1964]

Section 1. The right of citizens of the United States to vote in any primary or other election for President or Vice President, for electors for President or Vice President or for Senator or Representative in Congress, shall not be denied or abridged by the United States or any State by reason of failure to pay any poll tax or other tax.

Section 2. The Congress shall have power to enforce this article by appropriate legislation.

Amendment XXV [1967]

Section 1. In case of the removal of the President from office or of his death or resignation, the Vice President shall become President.

Section 2. Whenever there is a vacancy in the office of the Vice President, the President shall nominate a Vice President who shall take office upon confirmation by a majority vote of both Houses of Congress.

Section 3. Whenever the President transmits to the President pro tempore of the Senate and the Speaker of the House of Representatives his written declaration that he is unable to discharge the powers and duties of his office, and until he transmits to them a written declaration to the contrary, such powers and duties shall be discharged by the Vice President as Acting President.

Section 4. Whenever the Vice President and a majority of either the principal officers of the executive departments or of such other body as Congress may by law provide, transmit to the President pro tempore of the Senate and the Speaker of the House of Representatives their written declaration that the President is unable to discharge the powers and duties of his office, the Vice President shall immediately assume the powers and duties of the office as Acting President.

Thereafter, when the President transmits to the President pro tempore of the Senate and the Speaker of the House of Representatives his written declaration that no inability exists, he shall resume the powers and duties of his office unless the Vice President and a majority of either the principal officers of the executive department or of such other body as Congress may by law provide, transmit within four days to the President pro tempore of the Senate and the Speaker of the House of Representatives their

written declaration that the President is unable to discharge the powers and duties of his office. Thereupon Congress shall decide the issue, assembling within forty-eight hours for that purpose if not in session. If the Congress, within twenty-one days after receipt of the latter written declaration, or, if Congress is not in session, within twenty-one days after Congress is required to assemble, determines by two-thirds vote of both Houses that the President is unable to discharge the powers and duties of his office, the Vice President shall continue to discharge the same as Acting President; otherwise, the President shall resume the powers and duties of his office.

Amendment XXVI [1971]

Section 1. The right of citizens of the United States, who are eighteen years of age or older, to vote shall not be denied or abridged by the United States or by any State on account of age.

Section 2. The Congress shall have power to enforce this article by appropriate legislation.

Amendment XXVII [1992]

No law, varying the compensation for the services of the Senators and Representatives, shall take effect, until an election of Representatives shall have intervened.

Dictionary of Legal Terms

abatement Reduction or elimination of gifts by category upon the reduction in value of the estate.

absolute surety Surety liable to a creditor immediately upon the default of the principal debtor.

acceptance

Commercial paper Acceptance is the drawee's signed engagement to honor the draft as presented. It becomes operative when completed by delivery or notification. UCC §3-410.

Contracts Compliance by offeree with terms and conditions of offer.

Sale of goods UCC §2-606 provides three ways a buyer can accept goods: (1) by signifying to the seller that the goods are conforming or that he will accept them in spite of their nonconformity, (2) by failing to make an effective rejection, and (3) by doing an act inconsistent with the seller's ownership.

acceptor Drawee who has accepted an instrument.

accession An addition to one's property by increase of the original property or by production from such property. For example, A innocently converts the wheat of B into bread. UCC §9-315 changes the common law where a perfected security interest is involved.

accident and health insurance Provides protection from losses due to accident or sickness.

accommodation An arrangement made as a favor to another, usually involving a loan of money or commercial paper. While a party's intent may be to aid a maker of a note by lending his credit, if he seeks to accomplish thereby legitimate objects of his own and not simply to aid the maker, the act is not for accommodation.

accommodation indorser Signer not in the chain of title.

accommodation party A person who signs commercial paper in any capacity for the purpose of lending his name to another party to an instrument. UCC §3-415.

accord and satisfaction A method of discharging a claim whereby the parties agree to accept something in settlement, the "accord" being the agreement and the "satisfaction" its execution or performance. It is a new contract that is substituted for an old contract, which is thereby discharged, or for an obligation or cause of action and that must have all of the elements of a valid contract.

account Any account with a bank, including a checking, time, interest or savings account. UCC §4-194. Also, any right to payment, for goods or services, that is not evidenced by an instrument or chattel paper; for example, account receivable.

accounting Equitable proceeding for a complete settlement of all partnership affairs.

act of state doctrine Rule that a court should not question the validity of actions taken by a foreign government in its own country.

actual authority Power conferred upon agent by actual consent given by principal.

actual express authority Actual authority derived from written or spoken words of principal.

actual implied authority Actual authority inferred from words or conduct manifested to agent by principal.

actual notice Knowledge actually and expressly communicated.

actus reas Wrongful or overt act.

ademption The removal or extinction of a devise by act of the testator.

adequacy of consideration Not required where parties have freely agreed to the exchange.

adhesion contract Standard "form" contract, usually between a large retailer and a consumer, in which the weaker party has no realistic choice or opportunity to bargain.

adjudication The giving or pronouncing of a judgment in a case; also, the judgment given.

administrative agency Governmental entity (other than courts and legislatures) having authority to affect the rights of private parties.

administrative law Law dealing with the establishment, duties, and powers of agencies in the executive branch of government.

administrative process Entire set of activities engaged in by administrative agencies while carrying out their rulemaking, enforcement, and adjudicative functions.

administrator A person appointed by the court to manage the assets and liabilities of an intestate (a person dying without a will). A person named in the will of a testator (a person dying with a will) is called the executor. Female designations are administratrix and executrix.

adversary system System in which opposing parties initiate and present their cases.

adverse possession A method of acquiring title to real property by possession for a statutory period under certain conditions. The periods of time may differ, depending on whether the adverse possessor has color of title.

affidavit A written statement of facts, made voluntarily, confirmed by oath or affirmation of the party making it, and taken before an authorized officer.

affiliate Person who controls, is controlled by, or is under common control with the issuer.

affirm Uphold the lower court's judgment.

affirmative action Active recruitment of minority applicants.

affirmative defense A response that attacks the plaintiff's legal right to bring an action as opposed to attacking the truth of the claim. For example, accord and satisfaction; assumption of risk; contributory negligence; duress; estoppel.

affirmative disclosure Requirement that an advertiser include certain information in its advertisement so that the ad is not deceptive.

after-acquired property Property the debtor may acquire at some time after the security interest attaches.

agency Relation in which one person acts for or represents another by the latter's authority.

Actual agency Exists where the agent is really employed by the principal.

Agency by estoppel One created by operation of law and established by proof of such acts of the principal as reasonably lead to the conclusion of its existence.

Implied agency One created by acts of the parties and deduced from proof of other facts.

agent Person authorized to act on another's behalf.

allegation A statement of a party setting out what he expects to prove.

allonge Piece of paper firmly affixed to the instrument.

annuity contract Agreement to pay periodic sums to insured upon reaching a designated age.

annul To annul a judgment or judicial proceeding is to deprive it of all force and operation.

answer The answer is the formal written statement made by a defendant setting forth the ground of his defense.

antecedent debt Preexisting obligation.

anticipatory breach of contract (or **anticipatory repudiation**) The unjustified assertion by a party that he will not perform an obligation that he is contractually obligated to perform at a future time. See UCC §§610 & 611.

apparent authority Such principal power that a reasonable person would assume an agent has in light of the principal's conduct.

appeal Resort to a superior (appellate) court to review the decision of an inferior (trial) court or administrative agency.

appeal by right Mandatory review by a higher court.

appellant A party who takes an appeal from one court to another. He may be either the plaintiff or defendant in the original court proceeding.

appellee The party in a cause against whom an appeal is taken; that is, the party who has an interest adverse to setting aside or reversing the judgment. Sometimes also called the "respondent."

appropriation Unauthorized use of another person's name or likeness for one's own benefit.

appurtenances Things appurtenant pass as incident to the principal thing. Sometimes an easement consisting of a right of way over one piece of land will pass with another piece of land as being appurtenant to it.

APR Annual percentage rate.

arbitration The reference of a dispute to an impartial (third) person chosen by the parties, who agree in advance to abide by the arbitrator's award issued after a hearing at which both parties have an opportunity to be heard.

arraignment Accused is informed of the crime against him and enters a plea.

articles of incorporation (or **certificate of incorporation**) The instrument under which a corporation is formed. The contents are prescribed in the particular state's general incorporation statute.

articles of partnership A written agreement by which parties enter into a partnership, to be governed by the terms set forth therein.

as is Disclaimer of implied warranties.

assault Unlawful attempted battery; intentional infliction of apprehension of immediate bodily harm or offensive contact.

assignee Party to whom contract rights are assigned.

assignment A transfer of the rights to real or personal property, usually intangible property such as rights in a lease, mortgage, sale agreement, or partnership.

assignment of rights Voluntary transfer to a third party of the rights arising from a contract.

assignor Party making an assignment.

assumes Delegatee agrees to perform the contractual obligation of the delegator.

assumes the mortgage Purchaser of mortgaged property becomes personally liable to pay the debt.

assumption of risk Plaintiff's express or implied consent to encounter a known danger.

attachment The process of seizing property, by virtue of a writ, summons, or other judicial order, and bringing the same into the custody of the court for the purpose of securing satisfaction of the judgment ultimately to be entered in the action. While formerly the main objective was to coerce the defendant debtor to appear in court, today the writ of attachment is used primarily to seize the debtor's property in the event a judgment is rendered.

Distinguished from execution See **execution**.

Also, the process by which a security interest becomes enforceable. Attachment may occur upon the taking of possession or upon the signing of a security agreement by the person who is pledging the property as collateral.

authority Power of an agent to change the legal status of his principal.

authorized means Any reasonable means of communication.

automatic perfection Perfection upon attachment.

award The decision of an arbitrator.

bad checks Issuing a check with funds insufficient to cover it.

bailee The party to whom personal property is delivered under a contract of bailment.

Extraordinary bailee Absolutely liable for the safety of the bailed property without regard to the cause of loss.

Ordinary bailee Must exercise due care.

bailment A delivery of personal property in trust for the execution of a special object in relation to such goods, beneficial either to the bailor or bailee or both, and upon a contract to either redeliver the goods to the bailor or otherwise dispose of the same in conformity with the purpose of the trust.

bailor The party who delivers goods to another in the contract of bailment.

bankrupt The state or condition of one who is unable to pay his debts as they are, or become, due.

Bankruptcy Code The Act was substantially revised in 1978, effective October 1, 1979. Straight bankruptcy is in the nature of a liquidation proceeding and involves the collection and distribution to creditors of all the bankrupt's nonexempt property by the trustee in the manner provided by the Act. The debtor rehabilitation provisions of the Act (Chapters 11 and 13) differ from straight bankruptcy in that the debtor looks to rehabilitation and reorganization, rather than liquidation, and the creditors look to future earnings of the bankrupt, rather than to property held by the bankrupt, to satisfy their claims.

bargain Negotiated exchange.

bargained exchange Mutually agreed-upon exchange.

basis of the bargain Part of the buyer's assumption underlying the sale.

battery Unlawful touching of another; intentional infliction of harmful or offensive bodily contact.

bearer Person in possession of an instrument.

bearer paper Payable to holder of the instrument.

beneficiary One who benefits from act of another. See also **third-party beneficiary**.

Incidental A person who may derive benefit from performance on contract, though he is neither the promisee nor the one to whom performance is to be rendered. Since the incidental beneficiary is not a donee or creditor beneficiary (see **third-party beneficiary**), he has no right to enforce the contract.

Intended beneficiary Third party intended by the two contracted parties to receive a benefit from their contract.

Trust As it relates to trust beneficiaries, includes a person who has any present or future interest, vested or contingent, and also includes the owner of an interest by assignment or other transfer and, as it relates to a charitable trust, includes any person entitled to enforce the trust.

beyond a reasonable doubt Proof that is entirely convincing and satisfying to a moral certainty; criminal law standard.

bilateral contract Contract in which both parties exchange promises.

bill of lading Document evidencing receipt of goods for shipment issued by person engaged in business of transporting or forwarding goods; includes airbill. UCC §1-201(6).

> *Through bill of lading* A bill of lading which specifies at least one connecting carrier.

bill of sale A written agreement, formerly limited to one under seal, by which one person assigns or transfers his right to or interest in goods and personal chattels to another.

binder A written memorandum of the important terms of a contract of insurance which gives temporary protection to an insured pending investigation of risk by the insurance company or until a formal policy is issued.

blue law Prohibition of certain types of commercial activity on Sunday.

blue sky laws A popular name for state statutes providing for the regulation and supervision of securities offerings and sales, to protect citizen-investors from investing in fraudulent companies.

bona fide In good faith.

bond A certificate or evidence of a debt on which the issuing company or governmental body promises to pay the bondholders a specified amount of interest for a specified length of time and to repay the loan on the expiration date. In every case, a bond represents debt—its holder is a creditor of the corporation, not a part owner, as the shareholder is.

boycott Agreement among parties not to deal with a third party.

breach Wrongful failure to perform the terms of a contract.

> *Material breach* Nonperformance which significantly impairs the aggrieved party's rights under the contract.

bribery Offering property to a public official to influence the official's decision.

bulk transfer Transfer not in the ordinary course of the transferor's business of a major part of his inventory.

burglary Breaking and entering the home of another at night with intent to commit a felony.

business judgment rule Protects directors from liability for honest mistakes of judgment.

business trust A trust (managed by a trustee for the benefit of a beneficiary) established to conduct a business for a profit.

but for rule Person's negligent conduct is a cause of an event if the event would not have occurred in the absence of that conduct.

buyer in ordinary course of business Person who buys in ordinary course, in good faith, and without knowledge that the sale to him is in violation of anyone's ownership rights or of a security interest.

by-laws Regulations, ordinances, rules, or laws adopted by an association or corporation for its government.

callable bond Bond that is subject to redemption (reacquisition) by the corporation.

cancellation One party's putting an end to a contract because of a breach by other party.

capital Accumulated goods, possessions, and assets, used for the production of profits and wealth. Owners' equity in a business. Also used to refer to the total assets of a business or to capital assets.

capital surplus Surplus other than earned surplus.

carrier Transporter of goods.

casualty insurance Covers property loss due to causes other than fire or the elements.

cause of action The ground on which an action may be sustained.

caveat emptor "Let the buyer beware." This maxim is more applicable to judicial sales, auctions, and the like than to sales of consumer goods, where strict liability, warranty, and other laws protect.

certificate of deposit A written acknowledgment by a bank or banker of a deposit with promise to pay to depositor, to his order, or to some other person or to his order. UCC §3-104(2)(c).

certificate of title Official representation of ownership.

certification Acceptance of a check by a drawee bank.

certification of incorporation See **articles of incorporation**.

certification mark Distinctive symbol, word, or design used with goods or services to certify specific characteristics.

certiorari "To be informed of." A writ of common law origin issued by a superior to an inferior court requiring the latter to produce a certified record of a particular case tried therein. It is most commonly used to refer to the Supreme Court of the United States, which uses the writ of certiorari as a discretionary device to choose the cases it wishes to hear.

chancery Equity; equitable jurisdiction; a court of equity; the system of jurisprudence administered in courts of equity.

charging order Judicial lien against a partner's interest in the partnership.

charter An instrument emanating from the sovereign power, in the nature of a grant. A charter differs from a constitution in that the former is granted by the sovereign, while the latter is established by the people themselves.

> *Corporate law* An act of a legislature creating a corporation or creating and defining the franchise of a corporation. Also a corporation's constitution or organic law; that is to say, the articles of incorporation taken in connection with the law under which the corporation was organized.

chattel mortgage A pre-Uniform Commercial Code security device whereby the mortgagee took a security interest in personal property of the mortgagor. Such security device has generally been superseded by other types of security agreements under UCC Article 9 (Secured Transactions).

chattel paper Writings that evidence both a debt and a security interest.

check A draft drawn upon a bank and payable on demand, signed by the maker or drawer, containing an unconditional promise to pay a sum certain in money to the order of the payee. UCC §3-104(2)(b).

> *Cashier's check* A bank's own check drawn on itself and signed by the cashier or other authorized official. It is a direct obligation of the bank.

C. & F. Cost and freight; a shipping contract.

C.I.F. Cost, insurance, and freight; a shipping contract.

civil law Laws concerned with civil or private rights and remedies, as contrasted with criminal laws.

The system of jurisprudence administered in the Roman empire, particularly as set forth in the compilation of Justinian and his successors, as distinguished from the common law of England and the canon law. The civil law (Civil Code) is followed by Louisiana.

claim A right to payment.

clearinghouse An association of banks for the purpose of settling accounts on a daily basis.

close corporation See **corporation**.

closed-ended credit Credit extended to debtor for a specific period of time.

closed shop Employer can only hire union members.

C.O.D. Collect on delivery; generally a shipping contract.

code A compilation of all permanent laws in force consolidated and classified according to subject matter. Many states have published official codes of all laws in force, including the common law and statutes as judicially interpreted, which have been compiled by code commissions and enacted by the legislatures.

codicil A supplement or an addition to a will; it may explain, modify, add to, subtract from, qualify, alter, restrain, or revoke provisions in an existing will. It must be executed with the same formalities as a will.

cognovit judgment Written authority by debtor for entry of judgment against him in the event he defaults in payment. Such provision in a debt instrument on default confers judgment against the debtor.

collateral Secondarily liable; liable only if the party with primary liability does not perform.

collateral (security) Personal property subject to security interest.
　Banking Some form of security in addition to the personal obligation of the borrower.

collateral promise Undertaking to be secondarily liable, that is, liable if the principal debtor does not perform.

collecting bank Any bank, except the payor bank, handling the item for collection. UCC §4-105(d).

collective mark Distinctive symbol used to indicate membership in an organization.

collision insurance Protects the owner of an automobile against damage due to contact with other vehicles or objects.

commerce power Exclusive power granted by the U.S. Constitution to the federal government to regulate commerce with foreign countries and among the states.

commercial bailment Bailment in which parties derive a mutual benefit.

commercial impracticability Performance can only be accomplished with unforeseen and unjust hardship.

commercial law A phrase used to designate the whole body of substantive jurisprudence (*e.g.*, Uniform Commercial Code; Truth in Lending Act) applicable to the rights, intercourse, and relations of persons engaged in commerce, trade, or mercantile pursuits. See **Uniform Commercial Code**.

commercial paper Bills of exchange (*i.e.*, drafts), promissory notes, bank checks, and other negotiable instruments for the payment of money, which, by their form and on their face, purport to be such instruments. UCC Article 3 is the general law governing commercial paper.

commercial reasonableness Judgment of reasonable persons familiar with the business transaction.

commercial speech Expression related to the economic interests of the speaker and its audience.

common carrier Carrier open to the general public.

common law Body of law originating in England and derived from judicial decisions. As distinguished from statutory law created by the enactment of legislatures, the common law comprises the judgments and decrees of the courts recognizing, affirming, and enforcing usages and customs of immemorial antiquity.

community property Rights of a spouse in property acquired by the other during marriage.

comparable worth Equal pay for jobs of equal value to the employer.

comparative negligence Under comparative negligence statutes or doctrines, negligence is measured in terms of percentage, and any damages allowed shall be diminished in proportion to amount of negligence attributable to the person for whose injury, damage, or death recovery is sought.

complainant One who applies to the courts for legal redress by filing a complaint (*i.e.*, plaintiff).

complaint The pleading that sets forth a claim for relief. Such complaint (whether it be the original claim, counterclaim, cross-claim, or third-party claim) shall contain (1) a short, plain statement of the grounds upon which the court's jurisdiction depends, unless the court already has jurisdiction and the claim needs no new grounds of jurisdiction to support it, (2) a short, plain statement of the claim showing that the pleader is entitled to relief, and (3) a demand for judgment for the relief to which he deems himself entitled. Fed.R. Civil P. 8(a). The complaint, together with the summons, is required to be served on the defendant. Rule 4.

composition Agreement between debtor and two or more of her creditors that each will take a portion of his claim as full payment.

compulsory arbitration Arbitration required by statute for specific types of disputes.

computer crime Crime committed against or through the use of a computer or computer/services.

concealment Fraudulent failure to disclose a material fact.

conciliation Nonbinding process in which a third party acts as an intermediary between disputing parties.

concurrent jurisdiction Authority of more than one court to hear the same case.

condition An uncertain event that affects the duty of performance.
　Concurrent conditions The parties are to perform simultaneously.
　Express condition Performance is contingent on the happening or non-happening of a stated event.

condition precedent An event that must occur or not occur before performance is due; event or events (presentment, dishonor, notice of dishonor) that must occur to hold a secondary party liable to commercial paper.

condition subsequent An event that terminates a duty of performance.

conditional acceptance An acceptance of an offer contingent upon the acceptance of an additional or different term.

conditional contract Obligations are contingent upon a stated event.

conditional guarantor of collection Surety liable to creditor only after creditor exhausts his legal remedies against the principal debtor.

confession of judgment Written agreement by debtor authorizing creditor to obtain a court judgment in the event debtor defaults. See also **cognovit judgment**.

confiscation Governmental taking of foreign-owned property without payment.

conflict of laws That branch of jurisprudence, arising from the diversity of the laws of different nations, states, or jurisdictions, that reconciles the inconsistencies, or decides which law is to govern in a particular case.

confusion Results when goods belonging to two or more owners become so intermixed that the property of any of them no longer can be identified except as part of a mass of like goods.

consanguinity Kinship; blood relationship; the connection or relation of persons descended from the same stock or common ancestor.

consensual arbitration Arbitration voluntarily entered into by the parties.

consent Voluntary and knowing willingness that an act should be done.

conservator Appointed by court to manage affairs of incompetent or to liquidate business.

consideration The cause, motive, price, or impelling influence that induces a contracting party to enter into a contract. Some right, interest, profit, or benefit accruing to one party or some forbearance, detriment, loss, or responsibility given, suffered, or undertaken by the other.

consignee One to whom a consignment is made. Person named in bill of lading to whom or to whose order the bill promises delivery. UCC §7-102(b).

consignment Ordinarily implies an agency; denotes that property is committed to the consignee for care or sale.

consignor One who sends or makes a consignment; a shipper of goods. The person named in a bill of lading as the person from whom the goods have been received for shipment. UCC §7-102(c).

consolidation In *corporate law*, the combination of two or more corporations into a newly created corporation. Thus, A Corporation and B Corporation consolidate to form C Corporation.

constitution Fundamental law of a government establishing its powers and limitations.

constructive That which is established by the mind of the law in its act of *construing* facts, conduct, circumstances, or instruments. That which has not in its essential nature the character assigned to it, but acquires such character in consequence of the way in which it is regarded by a rule or policy of law; hence, inferred, implied, or made out by legal interpretation; the word "legal" being sometimes used here in lieu of "constructive."

constructive assent An assent or consent imputed to a party from a construction or interpretation of his conduct; as distinguished from one which he actually expresses.

constructive conditions Conditions in contracts that are neither expressed nor implied but rather are imposed by law to meet the ends of justice.

constructive delivery Term comprehending all those acts that, although not truly conferring a real possession of the vendee, have been held by construction of law to be equivalent to acts of real delivery.

constructive eviction Failure by the landlord in any obligation under the lease that causes a substantial and lasting injury to the tenant's enjoyment of the premises.

constructive notice Knowledge imputed by law.

constructive trust Arising by operation of law to prevent unjust enrichment. See also **trustee**.

consumer goods Goods bought or used for personal, family, or household purposes.

consumer product Tangible personal property normally used for family, household, or personal purposes.

contingent remainder Remainder interest, conditional upon the happening of an event in addition to the termination of the preceding estate.

contract An agreement between two or more persons which creates an obligation to do or not to do a particular thing. Its essentials are competent parties, subject matter, a legal consideration, mutuality of agreement, and mutuality of obligation.

> *Destination contract* Seller is required to tender delivery of the goods at a particular destination; seller bears the expense and risk of loss.
>
> *Executed contract* Fully performed by all of the parties.
>
> *Executory contract* Contract partially or entirely unperformed by one or more of the parties.
>
> *Express contract* Agreement of parties that is expressed in words either in writing or orally.
>
> *Formal contract* Agreement that is legally binding because of its particular form or mode or expression.
>
> *Implied-in-fact contract* Contract where agreement of the parties is inferred from their conduct.
>
> *Informal contract* All oral or written contracts other than formal contracts.
>
> *Installment contract* Goods are delivered in separate lots.
>
> *Integrated contract* Complete and total agreement.
>
> *Output contract* A contract in which one party agrees to sell his entire output and the other agrees to buy it; it is not illusory, though it may be indefinite.
>
> *Quasi contract* Obligation not based upon contract that is imposed to avoid injustice.
>
> *Requirements contract* A contract in which one party agrees to purchase his total requirements from the other party; hence, such a contract is binding, not illusory.
>
> *Substituted contract* An agreement between the parties to rescind their old contract and replace it with a new contract.
>
> *Unconscionable contract* One that no sensible person not under delusion, duress, or in distress would make, and such as no honest and fair person would accept. A contract the terms of which are excessively unreasonable, overreaching, and one-sided.
>
> *Unenforceable contract* Contract for the breach of which the law does not provide a remedy.
>
> *Unilateral and bilateral* A unilateral contract is one in which one party makes an express engagement or undertakes a performance, without

receiving in return any express engagement or promise of performance from the other. Bilateral (or reciprocal) contracts are those by which the parties expressly enter into mutual engagements.

contract clause Prohibition against the states' retroactively modifying public and private contracts.

contractual liability Obligation on a negotiable instrument, based upon signing the instrument.

contribution Payment from cosureties of their proportionate share.

contributory negligence An act or omission amounting to a want of ordinary care on the part of the complaining party, which, concurring with defendant's negligence, is proximate cause of injury.

The defense of contributory negligence is an absolute bar to any recovery in some states; because of this, it has been replaced by the doctrine of comparative negligence in many other states.

conversion Unauthorized and wrongful exercise of dominion and control over another's personal property, to exclusion of or inconsistent with rights of the owner.

convertible bond Bond that may be exchanged for other securities of the corporation.

copyright Exclusive right granted by the federal government to authors of original works including literary, musical, dramatic, pictorial, graphic, sculptural, and film works.

corporation A legal entity ordinarily consisting of an association of numerous individuals. Such entity is regarded as having a personality and existence distinct from that of its several members and is vested with the capacity of continuous succession, irrespective of changes in its membership, either in perpetuity or for a limited term of years.

> *Closely held or close corporation* Corporation that is owned by few shareholders and whose shares are not actively traded.
>
> *Corporation de facto* One existing under color of law and in pursuance of an effort made in good faith to organize a corporation under the statute. Such a corporation is not subject to collateral attack.
>
> *Corporation de jure* That which exists by reason of full compliance with requirements of an existing law permitting organization of such corporation.
>
> *Domestic corporation* Corporation created under the laws of a given state.
>
> *Foreign corporation* Corporation created under the laws of any other state, government, or country.
>
> *Publicly held corporation* Corporation whose shares are owned by a large number of people and are widely traded.
>
> *Subchapter S corporation* A small business corporation which, under certain conditions, may elect to have its undistributed taxable income taxed to its shareholders. I.R.C. §1371 et seq. Of major significance is the fact that Subchapter S status usually avoids the corporate income tax, and corporate losses can be claimed by the shareholders.
>
> *Subsidiary and parent* Subsidiary corporation is one in which another corporation (called parent corporation) owns at least a majority of the shares and over which it thus has control.

corrective advertising Disclosure in an advertisement that previous ads were deceptive.

costs A pecuniary allowance, made to the successful party (and recoverable from the losing party), for his expenses in prosecuting or defending an action or a distinct proceeding within an action. Generally, "costs" do not include attorneys' fees unless such fees are by a statute denominated costs or are by statute allowed to be recovered as costs in the case.

cosureties Two or more sureties bound for the same debt of a principal debtor.

co-tenants Persons who hold title concurrently.

counterclaim A claim presented by a defendant in opposition to or deduction from the claim of the plaintiff.

counteroffer A statement by the offeree which has the legal effect of rejecting the offer and of proposing a new offer to the offeror. However, the provisions of UCC §2-207(2) modify this principle by providing that the "additional terms are to be construed as proposals for addition to the contract."

course of dealing A sequence of previous acts and conduct between the parties to a particular transaction that is fairly to be regarded as establishing a common basis of understanding for interpreting their expressions and other conduct. UCC §1-205(1).

course of performance Conduct between the parties concerning performance of the particular contract.

court above—court below In appellate practice, the "court above" is the one to which a cause is removed for review, whether by appeal, writ of error, or certiorari, while the "court below" is the one from which the case is being removed.

covenant Used primarily with respect to promises in conveyances or other instruments dealing with real estate.

Covenants against encumbrances A stipulation against all rights to or interests in the land that may subsist in third persons to the diminution of the value of the estate granted.

Covenant appurtenant A covenant that is connected with land of the grantor, not in gross. A covenant running with the land and binding heirs, executors, and assigns of the immediate parties.

Covenant for further assurance An undertaking, in the form of a covenant, on the part of the vendor of real estate to do such further acts for the purpose of perfecting the purchaser's title as the latter may reasonably require.

Covenant for possession A covenant by which the grantee or lessee is granted possession.

Covenant for quiet enjoyment An assurance against the consequences of a defective title, and against any disturbances thereupon.

Covenants for title Covenants usually inserted in a conveyance of land, on the part of the grantor, and binding him for the completeness, security, and continuance of the title transferred to the grantee. They comprise covenants for seisin, for right to convey, against encumbrances, or quiet enjoyment, sometimes for further assurance, and almost always of warranty.

Covenant in gross Such as do not run with the land.

Covenant of right to convey An assurance by the covenantor that the grantor has sufficient capacity and title to convey the estate that he by his deed undertakes to convey.

Covenant of seisin An assurance to the purchaser that the grantor has the very estate in quantity and quality which he purports to convey.

Covenant of warranty An assurance by the grantor of an estate that the grantee shall enjoy the same without interruption by virtue of paramount title.

Covenant running with land A covenant which goes with the land, as being annexed to the estate, and which cannot be separated from the land or transferred without it. A covenant is said to run with the land when not only the original parties or their representatives, but each successive owner of the land, will be entitled to its benefit, or be liable (as the case may be) to its obligation. Such a covenant is said to be one which "touches and concerns" the land itself, so that its benefit or obligation passes with the ownership. Essentials are that the grantor and grantee must have intended that the covenant run with the land, the covenant must affect or concern the land with which it runs, and there must be privity of estate between the party claiming the benefit and the party who rests under the burden.

covenant not to compete Agreement to refrain from entering into a competing trade, profession, or business.

cover Buyer's purchase of goods in substitution for those not delivered by breaching seller.

credit beneficiary See **third-party beneficiary**.

creditor Any entity having a claim against the debtor.

crime An act or omission in violation of a public law and punishable by the government.

criminal duress Coercion by threat of serious bodily injury.

criminal intent Desired or virtually certain consequences of one's conduct.

criminal law The law that involves offenses against the entire community.

cure The right of a seller under the UCC to correct a nonconforming delivery of goods to buyer within the contract period. §2-508.

curtesy Husband's estate in the real property of his wife.

cy-pres As near (as possible). Rule for the construction of instruments in equity, by which the intention of the party is carried out *as near as may be*, when it would be impossible or illegal to give it literal effect.

damage Loss, injury, or deterioration caused by the negligence, design, or accident of one person, with respect to another's person or property. The word is to be distinguished from its plural, "damages," which means a compensation in money for a loss or damage.

damages Money sought as a remedy for breach of contract or for tortious acts.

Actual damages Real, substantial, and just damages, or the amount awarded to a complainant in compensation for his actual and real loss or injury, as opposed, on the one hand, to "nominal" damages and, on the other, to "exemplary" or "punitive" damages. Synonymous with "compensatory damages" and "general damages."

Benefit-of-the-bargain damages Difference between the value received and the value of the fraudulent party's performance as represented.

Compensatory damages Compensatory damages are such as will compensate the injured party for the injury sustained, and nothing more; such as will simply make good or replace the loss caused by the wrong or injury.

Consequential damages Such damage, loss, or injury as does not flow directly and immediately from the act of the party, but only from some of the consequences or results of such act. Consequential damages resulting from a seller's breach of contract include any loss resulting from general or particular requirements and needs of which the seller at the time of contracting had reason to know and which could not reasonably be prevented by cover or otherwise, and injury to person or property proximately resulting from any breach of warranty. UCC §2-715(2).

Exemplary or punitive damages Damages other than compensatory damages which may be awarded against a person to punish him for outrageous conduct.

Expectancy damages Calculable by subtracting the injured party's actual dollar position as a result of the breach from that party's projected dollar position had performance occurred.

Foreseeable damages Loss of which the party in breach had reason to know when the contract was made.

Incidental damages Under UCC §2-710, such damages include any commercially reasonable charges, expenses, or commissions incurred in stopping delivery, in the transportation, care, and custody of goods after the buyer's breach, in connection with the return or resale of the goods, or otherwise resulting from the breach. Also, such damages, resulting from a seller's breach of contract, include expenses reasonably incurred in inspection, receipt, transportation, and care and custody of goods rightfully rejected, any commercially reasonable charges, expenses, or commissions in connection with effecting cover, and any other reasonable expense incident to the delay or other breach. UCC §2-715(1).

Irreparable damages In the law pertaining to injunctions, damages for which no certain pecuniary standard exists for measurement.

Liquidated damages and penalties Damages for breach by either party may be liquidated in the agreement but only at an amount which is reasonable in the light of the anticipated or actual harm caused by the breach, the difficulties of proof of loss, and the inconvenience or non-feasibility of otherwise obtaining an adequate remedy. A term fixing unreasonably large liquidated damages is void as a penalty. UCC §2-718(1).

Mitigation of damages A plaintiff may not recover damages for the effects of an injury that she reasonably could have avoided or substantially ameliorated. This limitation on recovery is generally denominated as "mitigation of damages" or "avoidance of consequences."

Nominal damages A small sum awarded where a contract has been breached but the loss is negligible or unproven.

Out-of-pocket damages Difference between the value received and the value given.

Reliance damages Contract damages placing the injured party in as good a position as he would have been in had the contract not been made.

Treble damages Three times actual loss.

de facto "In fact, in deed, actually." This phrase is used to characterize an officer, a government, a past action, or a state of affairs which must be accepted for all practical purposes but which is illegal or illegitimate. See also **corporation**, *corporation de facto*.

de jure Descriptive of a condition in which there has been total compliance with all requirements of law. In this sense it is the contrary of *de facto*. See also **corporation**, *corporation de jure*.

de novo Anew; afresh; a second time.

debenture Unsecured bond.

debt security Any form of corporate security reflected as debt on the books of the corporation in contrast to equity securities such as stock; for example, bonds, notes, and debentures are debt securities.

debtor Person who owes payment or performance of an obligation.

deceit A fraudulent and cheating misrepresentation, artifice, or device used to deceive and trick one who is ignorant of the true facts, to the prejudice and damage of the party imposed upon. See also **fraud**; **misrepresentation**.

decree Decision of a court of equity.

deed A conveyance of realty; a writing, signed by a grantor, whereby title to realty is transferred from one party to another.

deed of trust Interest in real property that is conveyed to a third person as trustee for the creditor.

defamation Injury of a person's reputation by publication of false statements.

default judgment Judgment against a defendant who fails to respond to a complaint.

defendant The party against whom legal action is sought.

definite term Lease that automatically expires at end of the term.

delectus personae Partner's right to choose who may become a member of the partnership.

delegatee Third party to whom the delegator's duty is delegated.

delegation of duties Transferring to another all or part of one's duties arising under a contract.

delegator Party delegating his duty to a third party.

delivery The physical or constructive transfer of an instrument or of goods from one person to another. See also **constructive delivery**.

demand Request for payment made by the holder of the instrument.

demand paper Payable on request.

demurrer An allegation of a defendant that even if the facts as stated in the pleading to which objection is taken be true, their legal consequences are not such as to require the demurring party to answer them or to proceed further with the cause.

The Federal Rules of Civil Procedure do not provide for the use of a demurrer, but provide an equivalent to a general demurrer in the motion to dismiss for failure to state a claim on which relief may be granted. Fed.R. Civil P. 12(b).

deposition The testimony of a witness taken upon interrogatories, not in court, but intended to be used in court. See also **discovery**.

depository bank The first bank to which an item is transferred for collection even though it may also be the payor bank. UCC §4-105(a).

descent Succession to the ownership of an estate by inheritance or by any act of law, as distinguished from "purchase."

Descents are of two sorts, *lineal* and *collateral*. Lineal descent is descent in a direct or right line, as from father or grandfather to son or grandson. Collateral descent is descent in a collateral or oblique line, that is, up to the common ancestor and then down from him, as from brother to brother, or between cousins.

design defect Plans or specifications inadequate to ensure the product's safety.

devise A testamentary disposition of land or realty; a gift of real property by the last will and testament of the donor. When used as a noun, means a testamentary disposition of real or personal property; when used as a verb, means to dispose of real or personal property by will.

dictum Generally used as an abbreviated form of *obiter dictum*, "a remark by the way"; that is, an observation or remark made by a judge that does not embody the resolution or determination of the court and that is made without argument or full consideration of the point.

directed verdict In a case in which the party with the burden of proof has failed to present a prima facie case for jury consideration, the trial judge may order the entry of a verdict without allowing the jury to consider it because, as a matter of law, there can be only one such verdict. Fed.R. Civil P. 50(a).

disaffirmance Avoidance of a contract.

discharge Termination of certain allowed claims against a debtor.

disclaimer Negation of warranty.

discount A discount by a bank means a drawback or deduction made upon its advances or loans of money, upon negotiable paper or other evidences of debt payable at a future day, which are transferred to the bank.

discovery The pretrial devices that can be used by one party to obtain facts and information about the case from the other party in order to assist the party's preparation for trial. Under the Federal Rules of Civil Procedure, tools of discovery include depositions upon oral and written questions, written interrogatories, production of documents or things, permission to enter upon land or other property, physical and mental examinations, and requests for admission. Rules 26–37.

dishonor To refuse to accept or pay a draft or to pay a promissory note when duly presented. UCC §3-507(1); §4-210. See also **protest**.

disparagement Publication of false statements resulting in harm to another's monetary interests.

disputed debt Obligation whose existence or amount is contested.

dissenting shareholder One who opposes a fundamental change and has the right to receive the fair value of her shares.

dissolution The dissolution of a partnership is the change in the relation of the partners caused by any partner's ceasing to be associated with the carrying on, as distinguished from the winding up, of the business. See also **winding up**.

distribution Transfer of partnership property from the partnership to a partner; transfer of property from a corporation to any of its shareholders.

dividend The payment designated by the board of directors of a corporation to be distributed *pro rata* among a class or classes of the shares outstanding.

document Document of title.

document of title Instrument evidencing ownership of the document and the goods it covers.

domicile That place where a person has his true, fixed, and permanent home and principal establishment, and to which whenever he is absent he has the intention of returning.

dominant Land whose owner has rights in other land.

donee Recipient of a gift.

donee beneficiary See **third-party beneficiary**.

donor Maker of a gift.

dormant partner One who is both a silent and a secret partner.

dower A species of life-estate that a woman is, by law, entitled to claim on the death of her husband, in the lands and tenements of which he was seised in fee during the marriage, and which her issue, if any, might by possibility have inherited.

Dower has been abolished in the majority of the states and materially altered in most of the others.

draft A written order by the first party, called the drawer, instructing a second party, called the drawee (such as a bank), to pay a third party, called the payee. An order to pay a sum certain in money, signed by a drawer, payable on demand or at a definite time, and to order or bearer. UCC §3-104.

drawee A person to whom a bill of exchange or draft is directed, and who is requested to pay the amount of money therein mentioned. The drawee of a check is the bank on which it is drawn.

When a drawee accepts, he engages that he will pay the instrument according to its tenor at the time of his engagement or as completed. UCC §3-413(1).

drawer The person who draws a bill or draft. The drawer of a check is the person who signs it.

The drawer engages that upon dishonor of the draft and any necessary notice of dishonor or protest, he will pay the amount of the draft to the holder or to any indorser who takes it up. The drawer may disclaim this liability by drawing without recourse. UCC §3-413(2).

due negotiation Transfer of a negotiable document in the regular course of business to a holder, who takes in good faith, without notice of any defense or claim, and for value.

duress Unlawful constraint exercised upon a person, whereby he is forced to do some act against his will.

Physical duress Coercion involving physical force or the threat of physical force.

duty Legal obligation requiring a person to perform or refrain from performing an act.

earned surplus Undistributed net profits, income, gains, and losses.

earnest The payment of a part of the price of goods sold, or the delivery of part of such goods, for the purpose of binding the contract.

easement A right in the owner of one parcel of land, by reason of such ownership, to use the land of another for a special purpose not inconsistent with a general property right in the owner. This right is distinguishable from a "license," which merely confers a personal privilege to do some act on the land.

Affirmative easement One where the servient estate must permit something to be done thereon, as to pass over it, or to discharge water on it.

Appurtenant easement An incorporeal right that is attached to a superior right and inheres in land to which it is attached and is in the nature of a covenant running with the land.

Easement by necessity Such arises by operation of law when land conveyed is completely shut off from access to any road by land retained by the grantor or by land of the grantor and that of a stranger.

Easement by prescription A mode of acquiring title to property by immemorial or long-continued enjoyment; refers to personal usage restricted to claimant and his ancestors or grantors.

Easement in gross An easement in gross is not appurtenant to any estate in land or does not belong to any person by virtue of ownership of an estate in other land but is a mere personal interest in or a right to use the land of another; it is purely personal and usually ends with death of grantee.

Easement of access Right of ingress and egress to and from the premises of a lot owner to a street appurtenant to the land of the lot owner.

ejectment An action to determine whether the title to certain land is in the plaintiff or is in the defendant.

electronic funds transfer A transaction with a financial institution by means of computer, telephone, or other electronic instrument.

emancipation The act by which an infant is liberated from the control of a parent or guardian and made his own master.

embezzlement The taking, in violation of a trust, of the property of one's employer.

emergency Sudden, unexpected event calling for immediate action.

eminent domain Right of the people or government to take private property for public use upon giving fair consideration.

employment discrimination Hiring, firing, compensating, promoting, or training of employees based on race, color, sex, religion, or national origin.

employment relationship One in which employer has right to control the physical conduct of employee.

endowment contract Agreement to pay insured a lump sum upon reaching a specified age or in event of death.

entirety Used to designate that which the law considers as a single whole incapable of being divided into parts.

entrapment Induced by a government official into committing a crime.

entrusting Transfer of possession of goods to a merchant who deals in goods of that kind and who may in turn transfer valid title to a buyer in the ordinary course of business.

equal pay Equivalent pay for the same work.

equal protection Requirement that similarly situated persons be treated similarly by government action.

equipment Goods used primarily in business.

equitable Just, fair, and right. Existing in equity; available or sustainable only in equity, or only upon the rules and principles of equity.

equity Justice administered according to fairness, as contrasted with the strictly formulated rules of common law. It is based on a system of rules and principles that originated in England as an alternative to the harsh rules of common law and that were based on what was fair in a particular situation.

equity of redemption The right of the mortgagor of an estate to redeem the same after it has been forfeited, at law, by a breach of the condition of the mortgage, upon paying the amount of debt, interest, and costs.

equity securities Stock or similar security, in contrast to debt securities such as bonds, notes, and debentures.

error A mistake of law, or a false or irregular application of it, such as vitiates legal proceedings and warrants reversal of the judgment.

Harmless error In appellate practice, an error committed in the progress of the trial below which was not prejudicial to the rights of the party assigning it and for which, therefore, the appellate court will not reverse the judgment.

Reversible error In appellate practice, such an error as warrants the appellate court's reversal of the judgment before it.

escrow A system of document transfer in which a deed, bond, or funds is or are delivered to a third person to hold until all conditions in a contract are fulfilled; for example, delivery of deed to escrow agent under installment land sale contract until full payment for land is made.

estate The degree, quantity, nature, and extent of interest that a person has in real and personal property. An estate in lands, tenements, and hereditaments signifies such interest as the tenant has therein.

Also, the total property of whatever kind that is owned by a decedent prior to the distribution of that property in accordance with the terms of a will or, when there is no will, by the laws of inheritance in the state of domicile of the decedent.

Future estate An estate limited to commence in possession at a future day, either without the intervention of a precedent estate or on the determination by lapse of time, or otherwise, of a precedent estate created at the same time. Examples include reversions and remainders.

estoppel A bar or impediment raised by the law that precludes a person from alleging or from denying a certain fact or state of facts, in consequence of his or her previous allegation, denial, conduct, or admission, or in consequence of a final adjudication of the matter in a court of law. See also **waiver**.

eviction Dispossession by process of law; the act of depriving a person of the possession of lands that he has held, pursuant to the judgment of a court.

evidence Any species of proof or probative matter legally presented at the trial of an issue by the act of the parties and through the medium of witnesses, records, documents, concrete objects, and so on, for the purpose of inducing belief in the minds of the court or jury as to the parties' contention.

exception A formal objection to the action of the court, during the trial of a cause, in refusing a request or overruling an objection; implying that the party excepting does not acquiesce in the decision of the court but will seek to procure its reversal, and that he means to save the benefit of his request or objection in some future proceeding.

exclusionary rule Prohibition of illegally obtained evidence.

exclusive dealing Sole right to sell goods in a defined market.

exclusive jurisdiction Such jurisdiction that permits only one court (state or federal) to hear a case.

exculpatory clause Excusing oneself from fault or liability.

execution

Execution of contract includes performance of all acts necessary to render it complete as an instrument; implies that nothing more need be done to make the contract complete and effective.

Execution upon a money judgment is the legal process of enforcing the judgment, usually by seizing and selling property of the debtor.

executive order Legislation issued by the president or a governor.

executor A person appointed by a testator to carry out the directions and requests in his will and to dispose of the property according to his testamentary provisions after his decease. The female designation is executrix. A person appointed by the court in an intestacy situation is called the administrator(rix).

executory That which is yet to be executed or performed; that which remains to be carried into operation or effect; incomplete; depending upon a future performance or event. The opposite of executed.

executory contract See **contracts**.

executory promise Unperformed obligation.

exemplary damages See **damages**.

exoneration Relieved of liability.

express Manifested by direct and appropriate language, as distinguished from that which is inferred from conduct. The word is usually contrasted with "implied."

express warranty Explicitly made contractual promise regarding property or contract rights transferred; in a sale of goods, an affirmation of fact or a promise about the goods or a description, including a sample, of goods which becomes part of the basis of the bargain.

expropriation Governmental taking of foreign-owned property for a public purpose and with payment.

ex-ship Risk of loss passes to buyer when the goods leave the ship. See UCC §2-322. See also **F.A.S.**

extortion Making threats to obtain property.

fact An event that took place or a thing that exists.

false imprisonment Intentional interference with a person's freedom of movement by unlawful confinement.

false light Offensive publicity placing another in a false light.

false pretenses Intentional misrepresentation of fact in order to cheat another.

farm products Crops, livestock, or stock used or produced in farming.

F.A.S. Free alongside. Term used in sales price quotations indicating that the price includes all costs of transportation and delivery of the goods alongside the ship. See UCC §2-319(2).

federal preemption First right of the federal government to regulate matters within its powers to the possible exclusion of state regulation.

federal question Any case arising under the Constitution, statutes, or treaties of the United States.

fee simple

Absolute A fee simple absolute is an estate that is unlimited as to duration, disposition, and descendibility. It is the largest estate and most extensive interest that can be enjoyed in land.

Conditional Type of transfer in which grantor conveys fee simple on condition that something be done or not done.

Defeasible Type of fee grant that may be defeated on the happening of an event. An estate that may last forever, but that may end upon the happening of a specified event, is a "fee simple defeasible."

Determinable Created by conveyance that contains words effective to create a fee simple and, in addition, a provision for automatic expiration of the estate on occurrence of stated event.

fee tail An estate of inheritance, descending only to a certain class or classes of heirs; for example, an estate is conveyed or devised "to A. and the heirs of his body," or "to A. and the heirs male of his body," or "to A. and the heirs female of his body."

fellow servant rule Common law defense relieving employer from liability to an employee for injuries caused by negligence of fellow employee.

felony Serious crime.

fiduciary A person or institution who manages money or property for another and who must exercise in such management activity a standard of care imposed by law or contract; for example, executor of estate; receiver in bankruptcy; trustee.

fiduciary duty Duty of utmost loyalty and good faith, such as that owed by a fiduciary such as an agent to her principal.

field warehouse Secured party takes possession of the goods but the debtor has access to the goods.

final credit Payment of the instrument by the payor bank.

financing statement Under the Uniform Commercial Code, a financing statement is used under Article 9 to reflect a public record that there is a security interest or claim to the goods in question to secure a debt. The financing statement is filed by the security holder with the secretary of state or with a similar public body; thus filed, it becomes public record. See also **secured transaction**.

fire (property) insurance Provides protection against loss due to fire or other related perils.

firm offer Irrevocable offer to sell or buy goods by a merchant in a signed writing that gives assurance that it will not be rescinded for up to three months.

fitness for a particular purpose Goods are fit for a stated purpose, provided that the seller selects the product knowing the buyer's intended use and that the buyer is relying on the seller's judgment.

fixture An article in the nature of personal property that has been so annexed to realty that it is regarded as a part of the land. Examples include a furnace affixed to a house or other building, counters permanently affixed to the floor of a store, and a sprinkler system installed in a building. UCC §9-313(1)(a).

Trade fixtures Such chattels as merchants usually possess and annex to the premises occupied by them to enable them to store, handle, and display their goods, which generally are removable without material injury to the premises.

F.O.B. Free on board at some location (for example, F.O.B shipping point; F.O.B destination); the invoice price includes delivery at seller's expense to that location. Title to goods usually passes from seller to buyer at the F.O.B location. UCC §2-319(1).

foreclosure Procedure by which mortgaged property is sold on default of mortgagor in satisfaction of mortgage debt.

forgery Intentional falsification of a document with intent to defraud.

four unities Time, title, interest, and possession.

franchise A privilege granted or sold, such as to use a name or to sell products or services. The right given by a manufacturer or supplier to a retailer to use his products and name on terms and conditions mutually agreed upon.

fraud Elements include false representation; of a present or past fact; made by defendant; action in reliance thereon by plaintiff; and damage resulting to plaintiff from such misrepresentation.

fraud in the execution Misrepresentation that deceives the other party as to the nature of a document evidencing the contract.

fraud in the inducement Misrepresentation regarding the subject matter of a contract that induces the other party to enter into the contract.

fraudulent misrepresentation False statement made with knowledge of its falsity and intent to mislead.

freehold An estate for life or in fee. It must possess two qualities: (1) immobility, that is, the property must be either land or some interest issuing out of or annexed to land; and (2) indeterminate duration.

friendly fire Fire contained where it is intended to be.

frustration of purpose doctrine Excuses a promisor in certain situations when the objectives of contract have been utterly defeated by circumstances arising after formation of the agreement, and performance is excused under this rule even though there is no impediment to actual performance.

full warranty One under which warrantor will repair the product and, if unsuccessful, will replace it or refund its cost.

fungibles With respect to goods or securities, those of which any unit is, by nature or usage of trade, the equivalent of any other like unit. UCC §1-201(17); for example, a bushel of wheat or other grain.

future estate See **estate**.

garnishment A statutory proceeding whereby a person's property, money, or credits in the possession or control of another are applied to payment of the former's debt to a third person.

general intangible Catchall category for collateral not otherwise covered.

general partner Member of either a general or limited partnership with unlimited liability for its debts, full management powers, and a right to share in the profits.

gift A voluntary transfer of property to another made gratuitously and without consideration. Essential requisites of "gift" are capacity of donor, intention of donor to make gift, completed delivery to or for donee, and acceptance of gift by donee.

gift causa mortis A gift in view of death is one which is made in contemplation, fear, or peril of death and with the intent that it shall take effect only in case of the death of the giver.

good faith Honesty in fact in conduct or in a transaction.

good faith purchaser Buyer who acts honestly, gives value, and takes the goods without notice or knowledge of any defect in the title of his transferor.

goods A term of variable content and meaning. It may include every species of personal property, or it may be given a very restricted meaning. Sometimes the meaning of "goods" is extended to include all tangible items, as in the phrase "goods and services."

All things (including specially manufactured goods) that are movable at the time of identification to a contract for sale other than the money in which the price is to be paid, investment securities, and things in action. UCC §2-105(1).

grantee Transferee of property.

grantor A transferor of property. The creator of a trust is usually designated as the grantor of the trust.

gratuitous promise Promise made without consideration.

group insurance Covers a number of individuals.

guaranty A promise to answer for the payment of some debt, or the performance of some duty, in case of the failure of another person who, in the first instance, is liable for such payment or performance.

The terms *guaranty* and *suretyship* are sometimes used interchangeably; but they should not be confounded. The distinction between contract of suretyship and contract of guaranty is whether or not the undertaking is a joint undertaking with the principal or a separate and distinct contract; if it is the former, it is one of "suretyship," and if the latter, it is one of "guaranty." See also **surety**.

guardianship The relationship under which a person (the guardian) is appointed by a court to preserve and control the property of another (the ward).

heir A person who succeeds, by the rules of law, to an estate in lands, tenements, or hereditaments, upon the death of his ancestor, by descent and right of relationship.

holder Person who is in possession of a document of title or an instrument or an investment security drawn, issued, or indorsed to him or to his order, or to bearer, or in blank. UCC §1-201(20).

holder in due course A holder who takes an instrument for value, in good faith, and without notice that it is overdue or has been dishonored or of any defense against or claim to it on the part of any person.

holograph A will or deed written entirely by the testator or grantor with his own hand and not witnessed (attested). State laws vary with respect to the validity of the holographic will.

homicide Unlawful taking of another's life.

horizontal privity Who may bring a cause of action.

horizontal restraints Agreements among competitors.

hostile fire Any fire outside its intended or usual place.

identified goods Designated goods as a part of a particular contract.

illegal per se Conclusively presumed unreasonable and therefore illegal.

illusory promise Promise imposing no obligation on the promisor.

implied-in-fact condition Contingencies understood but not expressed by the parties.

implied-in-law condition Contingency that arises from operation of law.

implied warranty Obligation imposed by law upon the transferor of property or contract rights; implicit in the sale arising out of certain circumstances.

implied warranty of habitability Leased premises are fit for ordinary residential purposes.

impossibility Performance that cannot be done.

in personam "Against the person." Action seeking judgment against a person involving his personal rights and based on jurisdiction of his person, as distinguished from a judgment against property (*i.e.*, in rem).

in personam jurisdiction Jurisdiction based on claims against a person, in contrast to jurisdiction over his property.

in re In the affair; in the matter of; concerning; regarding. This is the usual method of entitling a judicial proceeding in which there are no adversary parties, but merely some res concerning which judicial action is to be taken, such as a bankrupt's estate, an estate in the probate court, or a proposed public highway.

in rem A technical term used to designate proceedings or actions instituted *against the thing*, in contradistinction to personal actions, which are said to be *in personam*.

> *Quasi in rem* A term applied to proceedings which are not strictly and purely *in rem*, but are brought against the defendant personally, though the real object is to deal with particular property or subject property to the discharge of claims asserted; for example, foreign attachment, or proceedings to foreclose a mortgage, remove a cloud from title, or effect a partition.

in rem jurisdiction Jurisdiction based on claims against property.

incidental beneficiary Third party whom the two parties to a contract have no intention of benefiting by their contract.

income bond Bond that conditions payment of interest on corporate earnings.

incontestability clause The prohibition of an insurer to avoid an insurance policy after a specified period of time.

indemnification Duty owed by principal to agent to pay agent for losses incurred while acting as directed by principal.

indemnify To reimburse one for a loss already incurred.

indenture A written agreement under which bonds and debentures are issued, setting forth maturity date, interest rate, and other terms.

independent contractor Person who contracts with another to do a particular job and who is not subject to the control of the other.

indicia Signs; indications. Circumstances which point to the existence of a given fact as probable, but not certain.

indictment Grand jury charge that the defendant should stand trial.

indispensable paper Chattel paper, instruments, and documents.

indorsee The person to whom a negotiable instrument, such as a promissory note or bill of lading is assigned by indorsement.

indorsement The act of a payee, drawee, accommodation indorser, or holder of a bill, note, check, or other negotiable instrument, in writing his name upon the back of the same, with or without further or qualifying words, whereby the property in the same is assigned and transferred to another. UCC §3-202 *et seq.*

> *Blank indorsement* No indorsee is specified.
>
> *Qualified indorsement* Without recourse, limiting one's liability on the instrument.
>
> *Restrictive indorsement* Limits the rights of the indorser in some manner.
>
> *Special indorsement* Designates an indorsee to be paid.

infliction of emotional distress Extreme and outrageous conduct intentionally or recklessly causing severe emotional distress.

information Formal accusation of a crime brought by a prosecutor.

infringement Unauthorized use.

injunction An equitable remedy forbidding the party defendant from doing some act which he is threatening or attempting to commit, or restraining him in the continuance thereof, such act being unjust and inequitable, injurious to the plaintiff, and not such as can be adequately redressed by an action at law.

innkeeper Hotel or motel operator.

inquisitorial system System in which the judiciary initiates, conducts, and decides cases.

insider Relative or general partner of debtor, partnership in which debtor is a partner, or corporation in which debtor is an officer, director, or controlling person.

insiders Directors, officers, employees, and agents of the issuer as well as those the issuer has entrusted with information solely for corporate purposes.

insolvency Under the UCC, a person is insolvent who either has ceased to pay his debts in the ordinary course of business or cannot pay his debts as they fall due or is insolvent within the meaning of the Federal Bankruptcy Law. UCC §1-201(23).

> *Insolvency (bankruptcy)* Total liabilities exceed total value of assets.
>
> *Insolvency (equity)* Inability to pay debts in ordinary course of business or as they become due.

inspection Examination of goods to determine whether they conform to a contract.

instrument Negotiable instruments, stocks, bonds, and other investment securities.

insurable interest Exists where insured derives pecuniary benefit or advantage by preservation and continued existence of property or would sustain pecuniary loss from its destruction.

insurance A contract whereby, for a stipulated consideration, one party undertakes to compensate the other for loss on a specified subject by specified perils. The party agreeing to make the compensation is usually called the "insurer" or "underwriter"; the other, the "insured" or "assured"; the written contract, a "policy"; the events insured against, "risks" or "perils"; and the subject, right, or interest to be protected, the "insurable interest." Insurance is a contract whereby one undertakes to indemnify another against loss, damage, or liability arising from an unknown or contingent event.

> *Co-insurance* A form of insurance in which a person insures property for less than its full or stated value and agrees to share the risk of loss.
>
> *Life insurance* Payment of a specific sum of money to a designated beneficiary upon the death of the insured.
>
> *Ordinary life* Life insurance with a savings component that runs for the life of the insured.
>
> *Term life* Life insurance issued for a limited number of years that does not have a savings component.

intangible property Protected interests that are not physical.

intangibles Accounts and general intangibles.

intent Desire to cause the consequences of an act or knowledge that the consequences are substantially certain to result from the act.

inter alia Among other things.

inter se or **inter sese** "Among or between themselves." Used to distinguish rights or duties between two or more parties from their rights or duties to others.

interest in land Any right, privilege, power, or immunity in real property.

interest in partnership Partner's share in the partnership's profits and surplus.

interference with contractual relations Intentionally causing one of the parties to a contract not to perform the contract.

intermediary bank Any bank, except the depositary or payor bank, to which an item is transferred in the course of collection. UCC §4-105(c).

intermediate test Requirement that legislation have a substantial relationship to an important governmental objective.

international law Deals with the conduct and relations of nation-states and international organizations.

interpretation Construction or meaning of a contract.

interpretative rules Statements issued by an administrative agency indicating its construction of its governing statute.

intestate A person is said to die intestate when he dies without making a will. The word is also often used to signify the person himself. *Compare* **testator**.

intrusion Unreasonable and highly offensive interference with the seclusion of another.

inventory Goods held for sale or lease or consumed in a business.

invitee A person is an "invitee" on land of another if (1) he enters by invitation, express or implied, (2) his entry is connected with the owner's business or with an activity the owner conducts or permits to be conducted on his land, and (3) there is mutual benefit or a benefit to the owner.

joint liability Liability where creditor must sue all of the partners as a group.

joint and several liability Liability where creditor may sue partners jointly as a group or separately as individuals.

joint stock company A general partnership with some corporate attributes.

joint tenancy See **tenancy.**

joint venture An association of two or more persons to carry on a single business transaction for profit.

judgment The official and authentic decision of a court of justice upon the respective rights and claims of the parties to an action or suit therein litigated and submitted to its determination.

judgment in personam A judgment against a particular person, as distinguished from a judgment against a thing or a right or *status.*

judgment in rem An adjudication pronounced upon the status of some particular thing or subject matter, by a tribunal having competent authority.

judgment n.o.v. Judgment *non obstante veredicto* in its broadest sense is a judgment rendered in favor of one party notwithstanding the finding of a verdict in favor of the other party.

judgment notwithstanding the verdict A final binding determination on the merits made by the judge after and contrary to the jury's verdict.

judgment on the pleadings Final binding determination on the merits made by the judge after the pleadings.

judicial lien Interest in property that is obtained by court action to secure payment of a debt.

judicial review Power of the courts to determine the constitutionality of legislative and executive acts.

jurisdiction The right and power of a court to adjudicate concerning the subject matter in a given case.

jurisdiction over the parties Power of a court to bind the parties to a suit.

jury A body of persons selected and summoned by law and sworn to try the facts of a case and to find according to the law and the evidence. In general, the province of the jury is to find the facts in a case, while the judge passes upon pure questions of law. As a matter of fact, however, the jury must often pass upon mixed questions of law and fact in determining the case, and in all such cases the instructions of the judge as to the law become very important.

justifiable reliance Reasonably influenced by a misrepresentation.

labor dispute Any controversy concerning terms or conditions of employment or union representation.

laches Based upon maxim that equity aids the vigilant and not those who slumber on their rights. It is defined as neglect to assert a right or claim which, taken together with a lapse of time and other circumstances causing prejudice to the adverse party, operates as a bar in a court of equity.

landlord The owner of an estate in land, or a rental property, who has leased it to another person, called the "tenant." Also called "lessor."

larceny Trespassory taking and carrying away of the goods of another with the intent to permanently deprive.

last clear chance Final opportunity to avoid an injury.

lease Any agreement that gives rise to relationship of landlord and tenant (real property) or lessor and lessee (real or personal property).

The person who conveys is termed the "lessor," and the person to whom conveyed, the "lessee"; and when the lessor conveys land or tenements to a lessee, he is said to lease, demise, or let them.

> *Sublease,* or *underlease* One executed by the lessee of an estate to a third person, conveying the same estate for a shorter term than that for which the lessee holds it.

leasehold An estate in realty held under a lease. The four principal types of leasehold estates are the estate for years, periodic tenancy, tenancy at will, and tenancy at sufferance.

leasehold estate Right to possess real property.

legacy A legacy is a gift or bequest by will of personal property, whereas a devise is a testamentary disposition of real estate.

> *Demonstrative legacy* A bequest of a certain sum of money, with a direction that it shall be paid out of a particular fund. It differs from a specific legacy in this respect: that, if the fund out of which it is payable fails for any cause, it is nevertheless entitled to come on the estate as a general legacy. And it differs from a general legacy in this: that it does not abate in that class, but in the class of specific legacies.
>
> *General legacy* A pecuniary legacy, payable out of the general assets of a testator.
>
> *Residuary legacy* A bequest of all the testator's personal estate not otherwise effectually disposed of by his will.
>
> *Specific legacy* One which operates on property particularly designated. A legacy or gift by will of a particular specified thing, as of a horse, a piece of furniture, a term of years, and the like.

legal aggregate A group of individuals not having a legal existence separate from its members.

legal benefit Obtaining something to which one had no legal right.

legal detriment Doing an act one is not legally obligated to do or not doing an act one has a legal right to do.

legal entity An organization having a legal existence separate from that of its members.

legal sufficiency Benefit to promisor or detriment to promisee.

legislative rules Substantive rules issued by an administrative agency under the authority delegated to it by the legislature.

letter of credit An engagement by a bank or other person made at the request of a customer that the issuer will honor drafts or other demands for payment upon compliance with the conditions specified in the credit.

letters of administration Formal document issued by probate court appointing one an administrator of an estate.

letters testamentary The formal instrument of authority and appointment given to an executor by the proper court, empowering him to enter upon the discharge of his office as executor. It corresponds to letters of administration granted to an administrator.

levy To assess; raise; execute; exact; tax; collect; gather; take up; seize. Thus, to levy (assess, exact, raise, or collect) a tax; to levy an execution, that is, to levy or collect a sum of money on an execution.

liability insurance Covers liability to others by reason of damage resulting from injuries to another's person or property.

liability without fault Crime to do a specific act or cause a certain result without regard to the care exercised.

libel Defamation communicated by writing, television, radio, or the like.

liberty Ability of individuals to engage in freedom of action and choice regarding their personal lives.

license License with respect to real property is a privilege to go on premises for a certain purpose, but does not operate to confer on or vest in the licensee any title, interest, or estate in such property.

licensee Person privileged to enter or remain on land by virtue of the consent of the lawful possessor.

lien A qualified right of property that a creditor has in or over specific property of his debtor, as security for the debt or charge or for performance of some act.

lien creditor A creditor who has acquired a lien on the property by attachment.

life estate An estate whose duration is limited to the life of the party holding it or of some other person. Upon the death of the life tenant, the property will go to the holder of the remainder interest or to the grantor by reversion.

limited liability Liability limited to amount invested in a business enterprise.

limited partner Member of a limited partnership with liability for its debts only to the extent of her capital contribution.

limited partnership See **partnership**.

limited partnership association A partnership that closely resembles a corporation.

liquidated Ascertained; determined; fixed; settled; made clear or manifest. Cleared away; paid; discharged.

liquidated damages See **damages**.

liquidated debt Obligation that is certain in amount.

liquidation The settling of financial affairs of a business or individual, usually by liquidating (turning to cash) all assets for distribution to creditors, heirs, and others. To be distinguished from dissolution.

loss of value Value of promised performance minus value of actual performance.

lost property Property with which the owner has involuntarily parted and that she does not know where to find or recover, not including property that she has intentionally concealed or deposited in a secret place for safekeeping. Distinguishable from mislaid property, which has been deliberately placed somewhere and forgotten.

main purpose rule Where object of promisor/surety is to provide an economic benefit for herself, the promise is considered outside of the statute of frauds.

maker One who makes or executes; as the maker of a promissory note. One who signs a check; in this context, synonymous with drawer. See **draft**.

mala in se Morally wrong.

mala prohibita Wrong by law.

mandamus "We command." A legal writ compelling the defendant to do an official duty.

manslaughter Unlawful taking of another's life without malice.
  Involuntary manslaughter Taking the life of another by criminal negligence or during the course of a misdemeanor.
  Voluntary manslaughter Intentional killing of another under extenuating circumstances.

manufacturing defect Not produced according to specifications.

mark Trade symbol.

market allocations Division of market by customers, geographic location, or products.

marketable title Free from any defects, encumbrances, or reasonable objections to one's ownership.

marshaling of assets Segregating the assets and liabilities of a partnership from the assets and liabilities of the individual partners.

master See **principal**.

material Matters to which a reasonable investor would attach importance in deciding whether to purchase a security.

material alteration Any change that changes the contract of any party to an instrument.

maturity The date at which an obligation, such as the principal of a bond or a note, becomes due.

maxim A general legal principle.

mechanic's lien A claim created by state statutes for the purpose of securing priority of payment of the price or value of work performed and materials furnished in erecting or repairing a building or other structure; as such, attaches to the land as well as buildings and improvements erected thereon.

mediation Nonbinding process in which a third party acts as an intermediary between the disputing parties and proposes solutions for them to consider.

mens rea Criminal intent.

mentally incompetent Unable to understand the nature and effect of one's acts.

mercantile law An expression substantially equivalent to commercial law. It designates the system of rules, customs, and usages generally recognized and adopted by merchants and traders that, either in its simplicity or as modified by common law or statutes, constitutes the law for the regulation of their transactions and the solution of their controversies. The Uniform Commercial Code is the general body of law governing commercial or mercantile transactions.

merchant A person who deals in goods of the kind involved in a transaction or who otherwise by his occupation holds himself out as having knowledge or skill peculiar to the practices or goods involved in the transaction or to whom such knowledge or skill may be attributed by his employment of an agent or broker or other intermediary who by his occupation holds himself out as having such knowledge or skill. UCC §2-104(1).

merchantability Merchant seller guarantees that the goods are fit for their ordinary purpose.

merger The fusion or absorption of one thing or right into another. In corporate law, the absorption of one company by another, the latter retaining its own name and identity and acquiring the assets, liabilities, franchises, and powers of the former, which ceases to exist as separate business entity. It differs from a consolidation, wherein all the corporations terminate their separate existences and become parties to a new one.
  Conglomerate merger An acquisition, which is not horizontal or vertical, by one company of another.
  Horizontal merger Merger between business competitors, such as manufacturers of the same type of products or distributors selling competing products in the same market area.
  Short-form merger Merger of a 90 percent subsidiary into its parent.
  Vertical merger Union with corporate customer or supplier.

midnight deadline Midnight of the next banking day after receiving an item.

mining partnership A specific type of partnership for the purpose of extracting raw minerals.

minor Under the age of legal majority (usually eighteen).

mirror image rule An acceptance cannot deviate from the terms of the offer.

misdemeanor Less serious crime.

mislaid property Property that an owner has put deliberately in a certain place that she is unable to remember, as distinguished from lost property, which the owner has left unwittingly in a location she has forgotten. See also **lost property**.

misrepresentation Any manifestation by words or other conduct by one person to another that, under the circumstances, amounts to an assertion not in accordance with the facts. A "misrepresentation" that justifies the rescission of a contract is a false statement of a substantive fact, or any conduct which leads to a belief of a substantive fact material to proper understanding of the matter in hand. See also **deceit; fraud**.
  Fraudulent misrepresentation False statement made with knowledge of its falsity and intent to mislead.
  Innocent misrepresentation Misrepresentation made without knowledge of its falsity but with due care.
  Negligent misrepresentation Misrepresentation made without due care in ascertaining its falsity.

M'Naughten Rule Right/wrong test for criminal insanity.

modify Change the lower court's judgment.

money Medium of exchange issued by a government body.

monopoly Ability to control price or exclude others from the marketplace.

mortgage A mortgage is an interest in land created by a written instrument providing security for the performance of a duty or the payment of a debt.

mortgagor Debtor who uses real estate to secure an obligation.

multinational enterprise Business that engages in transactions involving the movement of goods, information, money, people, or services across national borders.

multiple product order Order requiring an advertiser to cease and desist from deceptive statements on all products it sells.

murder Unlawful and premeditated taking of another's life.

mutual mistake Where the common but erroneous belief of both parties forms the basis of a contract.

necessaries Items needed to maintain a person's station in life.

negligence The omission to do something that a reasonable person, guided by those ordinary considerations that ordinarily regulate human affairs, would do, or the doing of something that a reasonable and prudent person would not do.

　Culpable negligence Greater than ordinary negligence but less than gross negligence.

negligence per se Conclusive on the issue of negligence (duty of care and breach).

negotiable Legally capable of being transferred by indorsement or delivery. Usually said of checks and notes and sometimes of stocks and bearer bonds.

negotiable instrument Signed document (such as a check or promissory note) containing an unconditional promise to pay a "sum certain" of money at a definite time to order or bearer.

negotiation Transferee becomes a holder.

net assets Total assets minus total debts.

no arrival, no sale A destination contract, but if goods do not arrive, seller is excused from liability unless such is due to the seller's fault.

no-fault insurance Compensates victims of automobile accidents regardless of fault.

nonconforming use Preexisting use not in accordance with a zoning ordinance.

nonprofit corporation One whose profits must be used exclusively for the charitable, educational, or scientific purpose for which it was formed.

nonsuit Action in form of a judgment taken against a plaintiff who has failed to appear to prosecute his action or failed to prove his case.

note See **promissory note**.

novation A novation substitutes a new party and discharges one of the original parties to a contract by agreement of all three parties. A new contract is created with the same terms as the original one; only the parties have changed.

nuisance Nuisance is that activity which arises from the unreasonable, unwarranted, or unlawful use by a person of his own property, working obstruction or injury to the right of another or to the public, and producing such material annoyance, inconvenience, and discomfort that law will presume resulting damage.

obiter dictum See **dictum**.

objective fault Gross deviation from reasonable conduct.

objective manifestation What a reasonable person under the circumstances would believe.

objective satisfaction Approval based upon whether a reasonable person would be satisfied.

objective standard What a reasonable person under the circumstances would reasonably believe or do.

obligee Party to whom a duty of performance is owed (by delegator and delegatee).

obligor Party owing a duty (to the assignor).

offer A manifestation of willingness to enter into a bargain, so made as to justify another person in understanding that his assent to that bargain is invited and will conclude it. Restatement, Second, Contracts, §24.

offeree Recipient of the offer.

offeror Person making the offer.

open-ended credit Credit arrangement under which debtor has rights to enter into a series of credit transactions.

opinion Belief in the existence of a fact or a judgment as to value.

option Contract providing that an offer will stay open for a specified period of time.

order A final disposition made by an agency.

order paper Payable to a named person or to anyone designated by that person.

order to pay Direction or command to pay.

original promise Promise to become primarily liable.

output contract See **contracts**.

palpable unilateral mistake Erroneous belief by one party that is recognized by the other.

parent corporation Corporation that controls another corporation.

parol evidence Literally oral evidence, but now includes prior to and contemporaneous, oral, and written evidence.

parol evidence rule Under this rule, when parties put their agreement in writing, all previous oral agreements merge in the writing and the contract as written cannot be modified or changed by parol evidence, in the absence of a plea of mistake or fraud in the preparation of the writing. But the rule does not forbid a resort to parol evidence not inconsistent with the matters stated in the writing. Also, as regards sales of goods, such written agreement may be explained or supplemented by course of dealing, usage of trade, or course of conduct, and by evidence of consistent additional terms, unless the court finds the writing to have been intended also as a complete and exclusive statement of the terms of the agreement. UCC §2-202.

part performance In order to establish part performance taking an oral contract for the sale of realty out of the statute of frauds, the acts relied upon as part performance must be of such a character that they reasonably can be naturally accounted for in no other way than that they were performed in pursuance of the contract, and they must be in conformity with its provisions. See UCC §2-201(3).

partial assignment Transfer of a portion of contractual rights to one or more assignees.

partition The dividing of lands held by joint tenants, copartners, or tenants in common into distinct portions, so that the parties may hold those lands in severalty.

partnership An association of two or more persons to carry on, as co-owners, a business for profit.

　Partnerships are treated as a conduit and are, therefore, not subject to taxation. The various items of partnership income (gains and losses, etc.) flow through to the individual partners and are reported on their personal income tax returns.

　Limited partnership Type of partnership comprised of one or more general partners who manage business and who are personally liable for partnership debts, and one or more limited partners who contribute capital and share in profits but who take no part in running business and incur no liability with respect to partnership obligations beyond contribution.

　Partnership at will One with no definite term or specific undertaking.

partnership capital Total money and property contributed by partners for permanent use by the partnership.

partnership property Sum of all of the partnership's assets.

past consideration An act done before the contract is made.

patent Exclusive right to an invention.

payee The person in whose favor a bill of exchange, promissory note, or check is made or drawn.

payer or **payor** One who pays or who is to make a payment, particularly the person who is to make payment of a check, bill, or note. Correlative to "payee."

payor bank A bank by which an item is payable as drawn or accepted. UCC §4-105(b). Correlative to "drawee bank."

per capita This term, derived from the civil law and much used in the law of descent and distribution, denotes that method of dividing an intestate estate by which an equal share is given to each of a number of persons, all of whom stand in equal degree to the decedent, without reference to their stocks or the right of representation. The opposite of *per stirpes*.

per stirpes This term, derived from the civil law and much used in the law of descent and distribution, denotes that method of dividing an intestate estate where a class or group of distributees takes the share to which its deceased would have been entitled, taking thus by its right of representing such ancestor and not as so many individuals. The opposite of *per capita*.

perfect tender rule Seller's tender of delivery must conform exactly to the contract.

perfection of security interest Acts required of a secured party in the way of giving at least constructive notice so as to make his security interest effective at least against lien creditors of the debtor. See UCC §§9-302 through 9-306. In most cases, the secured party may obtain perfection either by filing with the secretary of state or by taking possession of the collateral.

performance Fulfillment of one's contractual obligations. See also **part performance**; **specific performance**.

periodic tenancy Lease with a definite term that is to be continued.

personal defenses Contractual defenses that are good against holders but not holders in due course.

personal property Any property other than an interest in land.

petty crime Misdemeanor punishable by imprisonment of six months or less.

plaintiff The party who initiates a civil suit.

pleadings The formal allegations by the parties of their respective claims and defenses.

> *Rules or codes of civil procedure* Unlike the rigid technical system of common law pleading, pleadings under federal and state rules or codes of civil procedure have a far more limited function, with determination and narrowing of facts and issues being left to discovery devices and pretrial conferences. In addition, the rules and codes permit liberal amendment and supplementation of pleadings. Under rules of civil procedure, the pleadings consist of a complaint, an answer, a reply to a counterclaim, an answer to a cross-claim, a third-party complaint, and a third-party answer.

pledge A bailment of goods to a creditor as security for some debt or engagement.

> Much of the law of pledges has been replaced by the provisions for secured transactions in Article 9 of the UCC.

possibility of reverter The interest which remains in a grantor or testator after the conveyance or devise of a fee simple determinable and which permits the grantor to be revested automatically of his estate on breach of the condition.

possibility test Under the statute of frauds, asks whether performance could possibly be completed within one year.

power of appointment A power of authority conferred by one person by deed or will upon another (called the "donee") to appoint, that is, to select and nominate, the person or persons who is or are to receive and enjoy an estate or an income therefrom or from a fund, after the testator's death, or the donee's death, or after the termination of an existing right or interest.

power of attorney An instrument authorizing a person to act as the agent or attorney of the person granting it.

power of termination The interest left in the grantor or testator after the conveyance or devise of a fee simple on condition subsequent or conditional fee.

precatory Expressing a wish.

precedent An adjudged case or decision of a court, considered as furnishing an example or authority for an identical or similar case afterwards arising or a similar question of law. See also **stare decisis**.

preemptive right The privilege of a stockholder to maintain a proportionate share of ownership by purchasing a proportionate share of any new stock issues.

preference The act of an insolvent debtor who, in distributing his property or in assigning it for the benefit of his creditors, pays or secures to one or more creditors the full amount of their claims or a larger amount than they would be entitled to receive on a *pro rata* distribution. The treatment of such preferential payments in bankruptcy is governed by the Bankruptcy Act, §547.

preliminary hearing Determines whether there is probable cause.

premium The price for insurance protection for a specified period of exposure.

preponderance of the evidence Greater weight of the evidence; standard used in civil cases.

prescription Acquisition of a personal right to use a way, water, light, and air by reason of continuous usage. See also **easement**.

presenter's warranty Warranty given to any payor or acceptor of an instrument.

presentment The production of a negotiable instrument to the drawee for his acceptance, or to the drawer or acceptor for payment; or of a promissory note to the party liable, for payment of the same. UCC §3-504(1).

presumption A presumption is a rule of law, statutory or judicial, by which a finding of a basic fact gives rise to the existence of presumed fact, until presumption is rebutted. A presumption imposes on the party against whom it is directed the burden of going forward with evidence to rebut or meet the presumption, but does not shift to such party the burden of proof in the sense of the risk of nonpersuasion, which remains throughout the trial upon the party on whom it was originally cast.

price discrimination Price differential.

price fixing Any agreement for the purpose and effect of raising, depressing, fixing, pegging, or stabilizing prices.

prima facie (Latin) At first sight; on the first appearance; on the face of it; so far as can be judged from the first disclosure; presumably; a fact presumed to be true unless disproved by some evidence to the contrary.

primary liability Absolute obligation to pay a negotiable instrument.

principal

> *Law of agency* The term "principal" describes one who has permitted or directed another (*i.e.*, an agent or a servant) to act for his benefit and subject to his direction and control. Principal includes in its meaning the term "master" or employer, a species of principal who, in addition to other control, has a right to control the physical conduct of the species of agents known as servants or employees, as to whom special rules are applicable with reference to harm caused by their physical acts.
>
> *Disclosed principal* One whose existence and identity are known.
>
> *Partially disclosed principal* One whose existence is known but whose identity is not known.
>
> *Undisclosed principal* One whose existence and identity are not known.

principal debtor Person whose debt is being supported by a surety.

priority Precedence in order of right.

private carrier Carrier which limits its service and is not open to the general public.

private corporation One organized to conduct either a privately owned business enterprise for profit or a nonprofit corporation.

private law The law involving relationships among individuals and legal entities.

privilege Immunity from tort liability.

privity Contractual relationship.

privity of contract That connection or relationship that exists between two or more contracting parties. The absence of privity as a defense in actions for damages in contract and tort actions is generally no longer viable with the enactment of warranty statutes (*e.g.*, UCC §2-318), acceptance by states of the doctrine of strict liability, and court decisions that have extended the right to sue to third-party beneficiaries and even innocent bystanders.

probable cause Reasonable belief of the offense charged.

probate Court procedure by which a will is proved to be valid or invalid, though in current usage this term has been expanded to include generally all matters and proceedings pertaining to administration of estates, guardianships, etc.

procedural due process Requirement that governmental action depriving a person of life, liberty, or property be done through a fair procedure.

procedural law Rules for enforcing substantive law.

procedural rules Rules issued by an administrative agency establishing its organization, method of operation, and rules of conduct for practice before it.

procedural unconscionability Unfair or irregular bargaining.

proceeds Consideration for the sale, exchange, or other disposition of collateral.

process
> *Judicial process* In a wide sense, this term may include all the acts of a court from the beginning to the end of its proceedings in a given cause; more specifically, it means the writ, summons, mandate, or other process that is used to inform the defendant of the institution of proceedings against him and to compel his appearance, in either civil or criminal cases.
>
> *Legal process* This term is sometimes used as equivalent to "lawful process." Thus, it is said that legal process means process not merely fair on its face but valid in fact. But properly it means a summons, writ, warrant, mandate, or other process issuing from a court.

profit corporation One founded for the purpose of operating a business for profit.

profit a prendre Right to make some use of the soil of another, such as a right to mine metals; carries with it the right of entry and the right to remove.

promise to pay Undertaking to pay an existing obligation.

promisee Person to whom a promise is made.

promisor Person making a promise.

promissory estoppel Arises where there is a promise which promisor should reasonably expect to induce action or forbearance on part of promisee and which does induce such action or forbearance, and where injustice can be avoided only by enforcement of the promise.

promissory note An unconditional written promise to pay a specified sum of money on demand or at a specified date. Such a note is negotiable if signed by the maker and containing an unconditional promise to pay a sum certain in money either on demand or at a definite time and payable to order or bearer. UCC §3-104.

promoters In the law relating to corporations, those persons who first associate themselves for the purpose of organizing a company, issuing its prospectus, procuring subscriptions to the stock, securing a charter, and so on.

property Interest that is legally protected.
> *Abandoned property* Intentionally disposed of by the owner.
>
> *Lost property* Unintentionally left by the owner.
>
> *Mislaid property* Intentionally placed by the owner but unintentionally left.

prosecute To bring a criminal proceeding.

protest A formal declaration made by a person interested or concerned in some act about to be done, or already performed, whereby he expresses his dissent or disapproval or affirms the act against his will. The object of such a declaration usually is to preserve some right that would be lost to the protester if his assent could be implied, or to exonerate him from some responsibility that would attach to him unless he expressly negatived his assent.
> *Notice of protest* A notice given by the holder of a bill or note to the drawer or indorser that the bill has been protested for refusal of payment or acceptance. UCC §3-509.

provisional credit Tentative credit for the deposit of an instrument until final credit is given.

proximate cause Where the act or omission played a substantial part in bringing about or actually causing the injury or damage and where the injury or damage was either a direct result or a reasonably probable consequence of the act or omission.

proxy (Contracted from "procuracy.") Written authorization given by one person to another so that the second person can act for the first, such as that given by a shareholder to someone else to represent him and vote his shares at a shareholders' meeting.

public corporation One created to administer a unit of local civil government or one created by the United States to conduct public business.

public disclosure of private facts Offensive publicity given to private information about another person.

public law The law dealing with the relationship between government and individuals.

puffery Sales talk that is considered general bragging or overstatement.

punitive damages Damages awarded in excess of normal compensation to punish a defendant for a serious civil wrong.

purchase money security interest Security interest retained by a seller of goods in goods purchased with the loaned money.

qualified fee Ownership subject to its being taken away upon the happening of an event.

quantum meruit "As much as he deserves." Describes the extent of liability on a contract implied by law. Elements essential to recovery under quantum meruit are (1) valuable services rendered or materials furnished (2) for the person sought to be charged, (3) which services and materials such person accepted, used, and enjoyed, (4) under such circumstances as reasonably notified her that plaintiff, in performing such services, was expected to be paid by the person sought to be charged.

quasi As if; almost as it were; analogous to. Negatives the idea of identity but points out that the conceptions are sufficiently similar to be classed as equals of one another.

quasi contract Legal fiction invented by common law courts to permit recovery by contractual remedy in cases where, in fact, there is no contract, but where circumstances are such that justice warrants a recovery as though a promise had been made.

quasi in rem See *in rem*.

quasi in rem jurisdiction Jurisdiction over property not based on claims against it.

quiet enjoyment Right of a tenant not to have his physical possession of premises interfered with by the landlord.

quitclaim deed A deed of conveyance operating by way of release; that is, intended to pass any title, interest, or claim that the grantor may have in the premises but neither professing that such title is valid nor containing any warranty or covenants for title.

quorum When a committee, board of directors, meeting of shareholders, legislature, or other body of persons cannot act unless at least a certain number of them are present.

rape Unlawful, nonconsensual sexual intercourse.

ratification In a broad sense, the confirmation of a previous act done either by the party himself or by another; as, for example, confirmation of a voidable act.

In the law of principal and agent, the adoption and confirmation by one person, with knowledge of all material facts, of an act or contract performed or entered into in his behalf by another who at the time assumed without authority to act as his agent.

rational relationship test Requirement that legislation bear a rational relationship to a legitimate governmental interest.

real defenses Defenses that are valid against all holders, including holders in due course.

real property Land, and generally whatever is erected or growing upon or affixed to land. Also, rights issuing out of, annexed to, and exercisable within or about land. See also **fixture**.

reasonable man standard Duty of care required to avoid being negligent; one who is careful, diligent, and prudent.

receiver A fiduciary of the court, whose appointment is incident to other proceedings wherein certain ultimate relief is prayed. He is a trustee or ministerial officer representing the court, all parties in interest in the litigation, and the property or funds entrusted to him.

recognizance Formal acknowledgment of indebtedness made in court.

redemption (a) The realization of a right to have the title of property restored free and clear of a mortgage, performance of the mortgage obligation being essential for such purpose. (b) Repurchase by corporation of its own shares.

reformation Equitable remedy used to reframe written contracts to reflect accurately real agreement between contracting parties when, either through mutual mistake or unilateral mistake coupled with actual or equitable fraud by the other party, the writing does not embody the contract as actually made.

regulatory license Requirement to protect the public interest.

reimbursement Duty owed by principal to pay back authorized payments agent has made on principal's behalf. Duty owed by a principal debtor to repay surety who pays principal debtor's obligation.

rejection The refusal to accept an offer; manifestation of an unwillingness to accept the goods (sales).

release The relinquishment, concession, or giving up of a right, claim, or privilege, by the person in whom it exists or to whom it accrues, to the person against whom it might have been demanded or enforced.

remainder An estate limited to take effect and be enjoyed after another estate is determined.

remand To send back. The sending by the appellate court of a cause back to the same court out of which it came, for the purpose of having some further action taken on it there.

remedy The means by which the violation of a right is prevented, redressed, or compensated. Though a remedy may be by the act of the party injured, by operation of law, or by agreement between the injurer and the injured, we are chiefly concerned with one kind of remedy, the judicial remedy, which is by action or suit.

rent Consideration paid for use or occupation of property. In a broader sense, it is the compensation or fee paid, usually periodically, for the use of any property, including land, buildings, or equipment.

replevin An action whereby the owner or person entitled to repossession of goods or chattels may recover those goods or chattels from one who has wrongfully distrained or taken such goods or chattels or who wrongfully detains them.

reply Plaintiff's pleading in response to the defendant's answer.

repudiation Repudiation of a contract means refusal to perform duty or obligation owed to other party.

requirements contract See **contracts**.

res ipsa loquitur "The thing speaks for itself." Permits the jury to infer both negligent conduct and causation.

rescission An equitable action in which a party seeks to be relieved of his obligations under a contract on the grounds of mutual mistake, fraud, or impossibility.

residuary Pertaining to the residue; constituting the residue; giving or bequeathing the residue; receiving or entitled to the residue. See also **legacy, residuary legacy**.

respondeat superior "Let the master answer." This maxim means that a master or employer is liable in certain cases for the wrongful acts of his servant or employee, and a principal for those of his agent.

respondent In equity practice, the party who makes an answer to a bill or other proceeding. In appellate practice, the party who contends against an appeal; that is, the "appellee". The party who appeals is called the "appellant."

restitution An equitable remedy under which a person who has rendered services to another seeks to be reimbursed for the costs of his acts (but not his profits) even though there was never a contract between the parties.

restraint on alienation A provision in an instrument of conveyance which prohibits the grantee from selling or transferring the property which is the subject of the conveyance. Many such restraints are unenforceable as against public policy and the law's policy of free alienability of land.

restraint of trade Agreement that eliminates or tends to eliminate competition.

restrictive covenant Private restriction on property contained in a conveyance.

revenue license Measure to raise money.

reverse An appellate court uses the term "reversed" to indicate that it annuls or avoids the judgment, or vacates the decree, of the trial court.

reverse discrimination Employment decisions taking into account race or gender in order to remedy past discrimination.

reversion The term reversion has two meanings. First, it designates the estate left in the grantor during the continuance of a particular estate; second, it denotes the residue left in grantor or his heirs after termination of a particular estate. It differs from a remainder in that it arises by an act of law, whereas a remainder arises by an act of the parties. A reversion, moreover, is the remnant left in the grantor, while a remainder is the remnant of the whole estate disposed of after a preceding part of the same has been given away.

revocation The recall of some power, authority, or thing granted, or a destroying or making void of some deed that had existence until the act of revocation made it void.

revocation of acceptance Rescission of one's acceptance of goods based upon a nonconformity of the goods that substantially impairs their value.

right Legal capacity to require another person to perform or refrain from performing an act.

right of entry The right to take or resume possession of land by entering on it in a peaceable manner.

right of redemption The right (granted by statute only) to free property from the encumbrance of a foreclosure or other judicial sale, or to recover the title passing thereby, by paying what is due, with interest and other costs. Not to be confounded with the "equity of redemption," which exists independently of statute but must be exercised before sale. See also **equity of redemption**.

right to work law State statute that prohibits union shop contracts.

rights in collateral Personal property the debtor owns, possesses, or is in the process of acquiring.

risk of loss Allocation of loss between seller and buyer where the goods have been damaged, destroyed, or lost.

robbery Larceny from a person by force or threat of force.

rule Agency statement of general or particular applicability designed to implement, interpret, or process law or policy.

rule against perpetuities Principle that no interest in property is good unless it must vest, if at all, not later than twenty-one years, plus period of gestation, after some life or lives in being at time of creation of interest.

rule of reason Balancing the anticompetitive effects of a restraint against its procompetitive effects.

sale Transfer of title to goods from seller to buyer for a price.

sale on approval Transfer of possession without title to buyer for trial period.

sale or return Sale where buyer has option to return goods to seller.

sanction Means of enforcing legal judgments.

satisfaction The discharge of an obligation by paying a party what is due to him (as on a mortgage, lien, or contract) or what has been awarded to him by the judgment of a court or otherwise. Thus, a judgment is satisfied by the payment of the amount due to the party who has recovered such judgment, or by his levying the amount. See also **accord and satisfaction**.

scienter Knowingly.

seal Symbol that authenticates a document.

secondary liability Obligation to pay is subject to the conditions of presentment, dishonor, notice of dishonor, and sometimes protest.

secret partner Partner whose membership in the partnership is not disclosed.

Section 402A Strict liability in tort.

secured bond A bond having a lien on specific property.

secured claim Claim with a lien on property of the debtor.

secured party Creditor who possesses a security interest in collateral.

secured transaction A transaction founded on a security agreement. Such agreement creates or provides for a security interest. UCC §9-105(h).

securities Stocks, bonds, notes, convertible debentures, warrants, or other documents that represent a share in a company or a debt owed by a company.

   Certificated security Security represented by a certificate.

   Exempt security Security not subject to registration requirements of 1933 Act.

   Exempt transaction Issuance of securities not subject to the registration requirements of 1933 Act.

   Restricted securities Securities issued under an exempt transaction.

   Uncertificated security Security not represented by a certificate.

security agreement Agreement that grants a security interest.

security interest Right in personal property securing payment or performance of an obligation.

seisin Possession with an intent on the part of him who holds it to claim a freehold interest.

self-defense Force to protect oneself against attack.

separation of powers Allocation of powers among the legislative, executive, and judicial branches of government.

service mark Distinctive symbol, word, or design that is used to identify the services of a provider.

servient Land subject to an easement.

setoff A counterclaim demand that defendant holds against plaintiff, arising out of a transaction extrinsic to plaintiff's cause of action.

settlor Creator of a trust.

severance The destruction of any one of the unities of a joint tenancy. It is so called because the estate is no longer a joint tenancy, but is severed.

   Term may also refer to the cutting of crops or to the separation of anything from realty.

share A proportionate ownership interest in a corporation.

Shelley's case, rule in Where a person takes an estate of freehold, legally or equitably, under a deed, will, or other writing, and in the same instrument there is a limitation by way of remainder of any interest of the same legal or equitable quality to his heirs, or heirs of his body, as a class of persons to take in succession from generation to generation, the limitation to the heirs entitles the ancestor to the whole estate.

   The rule was adopted as a part of the common law of this country, though it has long since been abolished by most states.

shelter rule Transferee gets rights of transferor.

shipment contract Seller is authorized or required only to bear the expense of placing goods with the common carrier and bears the risk of loss only up to such point.

short-swing profits Profits made by insider through sale or other disposition of corporate stock within six months after purchase.

sight draft An instrument payable on presentment.

signature Any symbol executed with intent to validate a writing.

silent partner Partner who takes no part in the partnership business.

slander Oral defamation.

small claims courts Inferior civil courts with jurisdiction limited by dollar amount.

social security Measures by which the government provides economic assistance to disabled or retired employees and their dependents.

sole proprietorship A form of business in which one person owns all the assets of the business, in contrast to a partnership or a corporation.

sovereign immunity Foreign country's freedom from a host country's laws.

special warranty deed Seller promises that he has not impaired title.

specific performance The doctrine of specific performance is that where damages would compensate inadequately for the breach of an agreement, the contractor or vendor will be compelled to perform specifically what he has agreed to do; for example, ordered to execute a specific conveyance of land.

   With respect to the sale of goods, specific performance may be decreed where the goods are unique or in other proper circumstances. The decree for specific performance may include such terms and conditions as to payment of the price, damages, or other relief as the court may deem just. UCC §§2-711(2)(b), 2–716.

standardized business form A preprinted contract.

stare decisis Doctrine that once a court has laid down a principle of law as applicable to a certain state of facts, it will adhere to that principle and apply it to all future cases having substantially the same facts, regardless of whether the parties and property are the same or not.

state action Actions by governments, as opposed to actions taken by private individuals.

state-of-the-art Made in accordance with the level of technology at the time the product is made.

stated capital Consideration, other than that allocated to capital surplus, received for issued stock.

statute of frauds A celebrated English statute, passed in 1677, which has been adopted, in a more or less modified form, in nearly all of the United States. Its chief characteristic is the provision that no action shall be brought on certain contracts unless there be a note or memorandum thereof in writing, signed by the party to be charged or by his authorized agent.

statute of limitation A statute prescribing limitations to the right of action on certain described causes of action; that is, declaring that no suit shall be maintained on such causes of action unless brought within a specified period after the right accrued.

statutory lien Interest in property, arising solely by statute, to secure payment of a debt.

stock "Stock" is distinguished from "bonds" and, ordinarily, from "debentures" in that it gives a right of ownership in part of the assets of a corporation and a right to interest in any surplus after the payment of debt. "Stock" in a corporation is an equity, representing an ownership interest. It is to be distinguished from obligations such as notes or bonds, which are not equities and represent no ownership interest.

Capital stock See **capital**.

Common stock Securities that represent an ownership interest in a corporation. If the company has also issued preferred stock, both common and preferred have ownership rights. Claims of both common and preferred stockholders are junior to claims of bondholders or other creditors of the company. Common stockholders assume the greater risk, but generally exercise the greater control and may gain the greater reward in the form of dividends and capital appreciation.

Convertible stock Stock that may be changed or converted into common stock.

Cumulative preferred Stock having a provision that if one or more dividends are omitted, the omitted dividends must be paid before dividends may be paid on the company's common stock.

Preferred stock is a separate portion or class of the stock of a corporation that is accorded, by the charter or by-laws, a preference or priority in respect to dividends, over the remainder of the stock of the corporation, which in that case is called *common stock*.

Stock warrant A certificate entitling the owner to buy a specified amount of stock at a specified time(s) for a specified price. Differs from a stock option only in that options are granted to employees and warrants are sold to the public.

Treasury stock Shares reacquired by a corporation.

stock option Contractual right to purchase stock from a corporation.

stop payment Order for a drawee not to pay an instrument.

strict liability A concept applied by the courts in product liability cases in which a seller is liable for any and all defective or hazardous products that unduly threaten a consumer's personal safety. This concept applies to all members involved in the manufacture and sale of any facet of the product.

strict scrutiny test Requirement that legislation be necessary to promote a compelling governmental interest.

subagent Person appointed by agent to perform agent's duties.

subject matter jurisdiction Authority of a court to decide a particular kind of case.

subject to the mortgage Purchaser is not personally obligated to pay the debt, but the property remains subject to the mortgage.

subjective fault Desired or virtually certain consequences of one's conduct.

subjective satisfaction Approval based upon a party's honestly held opinion.

sublease Transfer of less than all of a tenant's interest in a leasehold.

subpoena A subpoena is a command to appear at a certain time and place to give testimony upon a certain matter. A *subpoena duces tecum* requires production of books, papers, and other things.

subrogation The substitution of one thing for another, or of one person into the place of another with respect to rights, claims, or securities.

Subrogation denotes the putting of a third person who has paid a debt in the place of the creditor to whom he has paid it, so that he may exercise against the debtor all the rights which the creditor, if unpaid, might have exercised.

subscribe Literally, to write underneath, as one's name. To sign at the end of a document. Also, to agree in writing to furnish money or its equivalent, or to agree to purchase some initial stock in a corporation.

subscriber Person who agrees to purchase initial stock in a corporation.

subsidiary corporation Corporation controlled by another corporation.

substantial performance Equitable doctrine protects against forfeiture for technical inadvertence, trivial variations, or omissions in performance.

substantive due process Requirement that governmental action be compatible with individual liberties.

substantive law The basic law of rights and duties (contract law, criminal law, tort law, law of wills, etc.), as opposed to procedural law (law of pleading, law of evidence, law of jurisdiction, etc.).

substantive unconscionability Oppressive or grossly unfair contractual terms.

sue To begin a lawsuit in a court.

suit A generic term of comprehensive signification that applies to any proceeding in a court of justice in which the plaintiff pursues, in such court, the remedy that the law affords him for the redress of an injury or the recovery of a right.

Derivative suit Suit brought by a shareholder on behalf of a corporation to enforce a right belonging to the corporation.

Direct suit Suit brought by a shareholder against a corporation based upon his ownership of shares.

summary judgment Rule of Civil Procedure 56 permits any party to a civil action to move for a summary judgment on a claim, counterclaim, or cross-claim when he believes that there is no genuine issue of material fact and that he is entitled to prevail as a matter of law.

summons Writ or process directed to the sheriff or other proper officer, requiring him to notify the person named that an action has been commenced against him in the court from which the process has issued and that he is required to appear, on a day named, and answer the complaint in such action.

superseding cause Intervening event that occurs after the defendant's negligent conduct and relieves him of liability.

supreme law A law that takes precedence over all conflicting laws.

surety One who undertakes to pay money or to do any other act in event that his principal debtor fails therein.

suretyship A guarantee of debts of another.

surplus Excess of net assets over stated capital.

tangible property Physical objects.

tariff Duty or tax imposed on goods moving into or out of a country.

tenancy Possession or occupancy of land or premises under lease.

Joint tenancy Joint tenants have one and the same interest, accruing by one and the same conveyance, commencing at one and the same time, and held by one and the same undivided possession. The primary incident of joint tenancy is survivorship, by which the entire tenancy on the decease of any joint tenant remains to the survivors, and at length to the last survivor.

Tenancy at sufferance Only naked possession that continues after tenant's right of possession has terminated.

Tenancy at will Possession of premises by permission of owner or landlord, but without a fixed term.

Tenancy by the entirety A tenancy that is created between a husband and wife and by which together they hold title to the whole with right of survivorship so that, upon death of either, the other takes the whole to the exclusion of the deceased's heirs. It is essentially a "joint tenancy," modified by the common law theory that husband and wife are one person.

Tenancy for a period A tenancy for years or for some fixed period.

Tenancy in common A form of ownership whereby each tenant (*i.e.,* owner) holds an undivided interest in property. Unlike the interest of a joint tenant or a tenant by the entirety, the interest of a tenant in common does not terminate upon his or her prior death (*i.e.,* there is no right of survivorship).

tenancy in partnership Type of joint ownership that determines partners' rights in specific partnership property.

tenant Possessor of a leasehold interest.

tender An offer of money; the act by which one produces and offers to a person holding a claim or demand against him the amount of money which he considers and admits to be due, in satisfaction of such claim or demand, without any stipulation or condition.

Also, there may be a tender of performance of a duty other than the payment of money.

tender of delivery Seller makes available to buyer goods conforming to the contract and so notifies the buyer.

tender offer General invitation to all shareholders to purchase their shares at a specified price.

testament Will.

testator One who makes or has made a testament or will; one who dies leaving a will.

third-party beneficiary One for whose benefit a promise is made in a contract but who is not a party to the contract.

Creditor beneficiary Where performance of a promise in a contract will benefit a person other than the promisee, that person is a creditor beneficiary if no purpose to make a gift appears from the terms of the promise, in view of the accompanying circumstances, and performance of the promise will satisfy an actual, supposed, or asserted duty of the promisee to the beneficiary.

Donee beneficiary The person who takes the benefit of the contract even though there is no privity between him and the contracting parties. A third-party beneficiary who is not a creditor beneficiary. See also **beneficiary**.

time paper Payable at definite time.

time-price doctrine Permits sellers to have different prices for cash sales and credit sales.

title The means whereby the owner of lands or of personalty has the just possession of his property.

title insurance Provides protection against defect in title to real property.

tort A private or civil wrong or injury, other than breach of contract, for which a court will provide a remedy in the form of an action for damages.

Three elements of every tort action are the existence of a legal duty from defendant to plaintiff, breach of that duty, and damage as proximate result.

tortfeasor One who commits a tort.

trade acceptance A draft drawn by a seller that is presented for signature (acceptance) to the buyer at the time goods are purchased and that then becomes the equivalent of a note receivable of the seller and the note payable of the buyer.

trade name Name used in trade or business to identify a particular business or manufacturer.

trade secrets Private business information.

trademark Distinctive insignia, word, or design of a good that is used to identify the manufacturer.

transferor's warranty Warranty given by any person who transfers an instrument and receives consideration.

treaty An agreement between or among independent nations.

treble damages Three times actual loss.

trespass At common law, trespass was a form of action brought to recover damages for any injury to one's person or property or relationship with another.

Trespass to chattels or personal property An unlawful and serious interference with the possessory rights of another to personal property.

Trespass to land At common law, every unauthorized and direct breach of the boundaries of another's land was an actionable trespass. The present prevailing position of the courts finds liability for trespass only in the case of intentional intrusion, or negligence, or some "abnormally dangerous activity" on the part of the defendant. *Compare* **nuisance**.

trespasser Person who enters or remains on the land of another without permission or privilege to do so.

trust Any arrangement whereby property is transferred with the intention that it be administered by a trustee for another's benefit.

A trust, as the term is used in the Restatement, when not qualified by the word "charitable," "resulting," or "constructive," is a fiduciary relationship with respect to property, subjecting the person by whom the title to the property is held to equitable duties to deal with the property for the benefit of another person, which arises through a manifestation of an intention to create such benefit. Restatement, Second, Trusts §2.

Charitable trust To benefit humankind.

Constructive trust Wherever the circumstances of a transaction are such that the person who takes the legal estate in property cannot also enjoy the beneficial interest without necessarily violating some established principle of equity, the court will immediately raise a *constructive trust* and fasten it upon the conscience of the legal owner, so as to convert him into a trustee for the parties who in equity are entitled to the beneficial enjoyment.

Inter vivos trust Established during the settlor's lifetime.

Resulting trust One that arises by implication of law, where the legal estate in property is disposed of, conveyed, or transferred, but the intent appears or is inferred from the terms of the disposition, or from the accompanying facts and circumstances, that the beneficial interest is not to go or be enjoyed with the legal title.

Spendthrift trust Removal of the trust estate from the beneficiary's control.

Testamentary trust Established by a will.

Totten trust A tentative trust that is a joint bank account opened by the settlor.

Voting trust A trust that holds the voting rights to stock in a corporation. It is a useful device when a majority of the shareholders in a corporation cannot agree on corporate policy.

trustee In a strict sense, a "trustee" is one who holds the legal title to property for the benefit of another, while, in a broad sense, the term is sometimes applied to anyone standing in a fiduciary or confidential relation to another, such as agent, attorney, bailee, etc.

trustee in bankruptcy Representative of the estate in bankruptcy who is responsible for collecting, liquidating, and distributing the debtor's assets.

tying arrangement Conditioning a sale of a desired product (tying product) on the buyer's purchasing a second product (tied product).

ultra vires Acts beyond the scope of the powers of a corporation, as defined by its charter or by the laws of its state of incorporation. By the doctrine of ultra vires, a contract made by a corporation beyond the scope of its corporate powers is unlawful.

unconscionable Unfair or unduly harsh.

unconscionable contract See **contracts**.

underwriter Any person, banker, or syndicate that guarantees to furnish a definite sum of money by a definite date to a business or government in return for an issue of bonds or stock. In insurance, the one assuming a risk in return for the payment of a premium.

undisputed debt Obligation whose existence and amount are not contested.

undue influence Term refers to conduct by which a person, through his power over the mind of a testator, makes the latter's desires conform to his own, thereby overmastering the volition of the testator.

unemployment compensation Compensation awarded to workers who have lost their jobs and cannot find other employment.

unenforceable Contract under which neither party can recover.

unfair employer practice Conduct in which an employer is prohibited from engaging.

unfair labor practice Conduct in which an employer or union is prohibited from engaging.

unfair union practice Conduct in which a union is prohibited from engaging.

Uniform Commercial Code One of the Uniform Laws, drafted by the National Conference of Commissioners on Uniform State Laws, governing commercial transactions (sales of goods, commercial paper, bank deposits and collections, letters of credit, bulk transfers, warehouse receipts, bills of lading, investment securities, and secured transactions).

unilateral mistake Erroneous belief on the part of only one of the parties to a contract.

union shop Employer can hire nonunion members, but such employees must then join the union.

universal life Ordinary life divided into two components, a renewable term insurance policy and an investment portfolio.

unliquidated debt Obligation that is uncertain or contested in amount.

unqualified indorsement (see **indorsement**) One that imposes liability upon the indorser.

unreasonably dangerous Danger beyond that which the ordinary consumer contemplates.

unrestrictive indorsement (see **indorsement**) One that does not attempt to restrict the rights of the indorsee.

usage of trade Any practice or method of dealing having such regularity of observance in a place, vocation, or trade as to justify an expectation that it will be observed with respect to the transaction in question.

usury Collectively, the laws of a jurisdiction regulating the charging of interest rates. A usurious loan is one whose interest rates are determined to be in excess of those permitted by the usury laws.

value The performance of legal consideration, the forgiveness of an antecedent debt, the giving of a negotiable instrument, or the giving of an irrevocable commitment to a third party. UCC §1-201(44).

variance A use differing from that provided in a zoning ordinance in order to avoid undue hardship.

vendee A purchaser or buyer; one to whom anything is sold. See also **vendor**.

vendor The person who transfers property by sale, particularly real estate; "seller" being more commonly used for one who sells personalty. See also vendee.

venue "Jurisdiction" of the court means the inherent power to decide a case, whereas "venue" designates the particular county or city in which a court with jurisdiction may hear and determine the case.

verdict The formal and unanimous decision or finding of a jury, impaneled and sworn for the trial of a cause, upon the matters or questions duly submitted to it upon the trial.

vertical privity Who is liable to the plaintiff.

vertical restraints Agreements among parties at different levels of the distribution chain.

vested Fixed; accrued; settled; absolute. To be "vested," a right must be more than a mere expectation based on an anticipation of the continuance of an existing law; it must have become a title, legal or equitable, to the present or future enforcement of a demand, or a legal exemption from the demand of another.

vested remainder Unconditional remainder that is a fixed present interest to be enjoyed in the future.

vicarious liability Indirect legal responsibility; for example, the liability of an employer for the acts of an employee or that of a principal for the torts and contracts of an agent.

void Null; ineffectual; nugatory; having no legal force or binding effect; unable, in law, to support the purpose for which it was intended.

This difference separates the words "void" and "voidable": *void* in the strict sense means that an instrument or transaction is nugatory and ineffectual, so that nothing can cure it; *voidable* exists when an imperfection or defect can be cured by the act or confirmation of the person who could take advantage of it.

Frequently, the word "void" is used and construed as having the more liberal meaning of "voidable."

voidable Capable of being made void. See also **void**.

voir dire Preliminary examination of potential jurors.

voluntary Resulting from free choice. The word, especially in statutes, often implies knowledge of essential facts.

voting trust Transfer of corporate shares' voting rights to a trustee.

wager (gambling) Agreement that one party will win or lose depending upon the outcome of an event in which the only interest is the gain or loss.

waiver Terms "estoppel" and "waiver" are not synonymous; "waiver" means the voluntary, intentional relinquishment of a known right, and "estoppel" rests upon principle that, where anyone has done an act or made a statement that would be a fraud on his part to controvert or impair, because the other party has acted upon it in belief that what was done or said was true, conscience and honest dealing require that he not be permitted to repudiate his act or gainsay his statement. See also **estoppel**.

ward An infant or insane person placed by authority of law under the care of a guardian.

warehouse receipt Receipt issued by a person storing goods.

warehouser Storer of goods for compensation.

warrant, v. In contracts, to engage or promise that a certain fact or state of facts, in relation to the subject matter, is, or shall be, as it is represented to be.

In conveyancing, to assure the title to property sold, by an express covenant to that effect in the deed of conveyance.

warranty A warranty is a statement or representation made by a seller of goods, contemporaneously with and as a part of a contract of sale, though collateral to express the object of the sale, having reference to the character, quality, or title of goods, and by which the seller promises or undertakes to ensure that certain facts are or shall be as he then represents them.

The general statutory law governing warranties on sales of goods is provided in UCC §2-312 *et seq.* The three main types of warranties are (1) express warranty; (2) implied warranty of fitness; (3) implied warranty of merchantability.

warranty deed Deed in which grantor warrants good clear title. The usual covenants of title are warranties of seisin, quiet enjoyment, right to convey, freedom from encumbrances, and defense of title as to all claims.

Special warranty deed Seller warrants that he has not impaired title.

warranty liability Applies to persons who transfer an instrument or receive payment or acceptance.

warranty of title Obligation to convey the right to ownership without any lien.

waste Any act or omission that does permanent injury to the realty or unreasonably changes its value.

white-collar crime Corporate crime.

will A written instrument executed with the formalities required by statutes, whereby a person makes a disposition of his property to take effect after his death.

winding up To settle the accounts and liquidate the assets of a partnership or corporation, for the purpose of making distribution and terminating the concern.

without reserve Auctioneer may not withdraw the goods from the auction.

workers' compensation Compensation awarded to an employee who is injured, when the injury arose out of and in the course of his employment.

writ of certiorari Discretionary review by a higher court. See also **certiorari**.

writ of execution Order served by sheriff upon debtor demanding payment of a court judgment against debtor.

zoning Public control over land use.

Source: Many of the definitions are abridged and adapted from *Black's Law Dictionary*, 5th edition, West Publishing Company, 1979.

Index

A

Abandoned property, 1077
Abatement, 1146
Abbreviated rule of reason standard, 897
Abnormally dangerous activities, 157
 strict liability, 1036
Abrams v. United States, 73
Absolute liability, 1085
Absolute privilege, 129
Abuse, occurrence, 487
Acceleration, 543
Acceptance, 585, 586
 addressing, 428
 authorization, reasonable manner, 198
 conditional acceptance, 196
 goods, 450
 manner, 429
 revocation, 450
 sale of goods, 295
 variant acceptances, 428–429
 wholesale funds transfers, 611
Acceptance (offer), 190
 communication, 197–198
 silence, usage, 197
Accepted goods breach, damages
  recovery, 519
Acceptors, 585
Accession, 808, 1077
Accommodation party, 569
Accord, 339
Accountability (social responsibility
  arguments), 21
Accountants
 accountant-client privilege, 1024
 audit requirements, 1026
 client information, 1023–1024
 criminal liability, 1026
 legal liability, 1021, 1025
 liability
  federal securities law, 1026
  third parties, 1022f
 Sarbanes-Oxley Act, 1026–1027
 Working papers, 1023
Account, duty, 376
Accounting, FIFO method, 561

Accounting Oversight Board, 110
Accredited investors, 990
 limited offers, 990
ACH. *See* Automated clearinghouse
ACH Network, 539
Acid rain, 1040
Act for Prevention of Frauds and Perjuries,
  An, 289
Action, private causes (problems), 1036
Act of state doctrine, 1058
Actual authority, 396, 685
Actual express authority, 396
 officers, 765
Actual implied authority, 396
 officers, 765
 partnership, 650
Actual notice, requirement, 399–400
Actus reas (nonmental criminal elements), 108
Act utilitarianism, 16
ADA. *See* Americans with Disabilities Act of
  1990
ADAAA. *See* Americans with Disabilities Act
  Amendments Act
Additional terms, 428
ADEA. *See* Age Discrimination in
  Employment Act of 1967
Adelphia, violations/scandal, 14, 20, 110,
  754, 984
Ademption, 1146
Adequacy (legal sufficiency), 234–235
Adhesion contract, 258
Adjudicated in competent (ward), 278
Adjudication (administrative agencies),
  93–94
Adjustable rate mortgages (ARMs), 928
Administrative agencies
 adjudication, 93–94
 enforcement, 92–93
 executive branch control, 95–96
 information, disclosure, 96
 judicial review, 94–95
 legislative control, 95
 limits, 94–96, 94f, 97
 operation, 91–94, 96–97
 procedural rules, 92
 rulemaking, 91–92

Administrative Dispute Resolution Act, 93
Administrative law, 9, 89
Administrative law judge (ALJ), 93, 906
Administrative Procedure Act (APA), 91–94
Administrative process, 91
Administrative rulemaking, 93f
Administrators, 293, 1148
Admission, request, 51
Ad substantiation, 921
Adversary system, 7
Adverse possession, 1126, 1130
Advertisements
 correction, 921
 offer, 192
*A.E. Robinson Co., Inc. v. County Forest
  Products, Inc.*, 415
Affiliated directors, 762
Affiliates, 993
Affirm, action, 53
Affirmance, 359
Affirm, appellate court action, 43
Affirmative action, 951
 plan, usage, 953
Affirmative defense, 51
Affirmative disclosure, 921
After-acquired property, 811
Age Discrimination in Employment Act of
  1967 (ADEA), 953
Age, misrepresentation (liability), 277
Agency
 agency by estoppel, 374
 circumstances, change, 382
 consensual relationship, 372
 creation, 374–375, 383
  capacity, 375
  formalities, 374–375
 gratuitous agency, 374
 interest, coupling, 382
 irrevocable powers, 382
 law, operation, 380–381
 legal relationships, 373–374
 nature, 372–374, 382
 parties, acts, 380
 purposes, scope, 373
 termination, 380–384
  impact, 399–400

Agent, 374, 603
  apparent authority, 404
  authorized acts, 402–403
  authorized contracts, 406
  contract liability, 406–407
  disclosed principal, contract liability,
      406–407
  duties, 379f
  liability
    assumption, 406
    tort, 407
    undisclosed principal, relationship,
        406–407
    unidentified principal, relationship, 406
  misrepresentation, 406
  nonexistent/incompetent principal,
      contract liability, 407
  principal
    duties, 284, 378–379
    relationship, 372, 381
  renunciation, 380
  respondeat superior, 403–404
  subagent, 398
  third persons, relationship, 406, 409
  unauthorized acts, 403
    impact, 403–404
  unauthorized contracts, 406–407
Agreements, validity, 176f
Air pollutant, definition, 1040
Alcoa Concrete & Masonry v. Stalker Bros.,
    260–262
Alcohol testing, employee privacy, 956
Aldana v. Colonial Palms Plaza, Inc., 324–325
*Alexander v. Fedex Ground Package System,
    Inc.*, 384–386
ALJ. *See* Administrative law judge
Allonge, 557–558
Alternative B, 490
Alternative C, 490
Alternative dispute resolution (ADR), 53–56,
    58
Alzado v. Blinder, Robinson & Co., Inc.,
    691–692
American Institute of Certified Public
    Accountants (AICPA), 1024
*American Manufacturing Mutual Insurance
    Company v. Tison Hog Market, Inc.*,
    833–834
*American Needle, Inc. v. National Football
    League*, 907–909
Americans with Disabilities Act Amendments
    Act (ADAAA), 953
Americans with Disabilities Act of 1990
    (ADA), 949, 953
Andean Common Market (ANCOM), 1056
Anderson v. McOskar Enterprises, Inc.,
    266–267
Animals
  keeping, 157–158
  nontrespassing animals, 157–158
  trespassing animals, 157

Annual meetings, 756
Annual percentage rate (APR), 928
Annual percentage yield (APY),
    607–608
Annuity contracts, securities, 988
Antecedent debt, 561, 652
Antibribery, FCPA provision, 1006
Anticipatory repudiation, 337–338, 453,
    463–464
Anti-counterfeiting Amendments Act
    (2004), 880
Antifraud provisions, 996, 1003–1005
Antitrusts, 895
  laws, 1061
Any Kind Checks Cashed, Inc. v. Talcott,
    575–577
APA. *See* Administrative Procedure Act
Apparent authority, 396, 399, 658
  agent, 404
  occurrence, 396–397
  officers, 765–766
  partnership, 650
Appeal, 52–53
Appeal by right, 43
Appellant, 10
Appellate courts, 45
Appraisal remedy, 790–791
Appropriation (privacy), 130
Appurtenant easements, 1109
Arbitrary and capricious test, 95
Arbitration, 54–56
  comparison, 55f
  compulsory arbitration, 55
  consensual arbitration, 55
  court-annexed arbitration, 56
  international arbitration, 56
  nonbinding arbitration, 56
  procedure, 55–56
  rules, 1060
  types, 55
ARMs. *See* Adjustable rate mortgages
Arraignment, 116
Arrangement of Nice Concerning the
    International Classification of Goods
    and Services, 875, 1063
Arthur Andersen, violations/scandal, 14, 20,
    110, 984
Article 2 (UCC), 424–427
Article 2A (UCC), 424–427
ASEAN. *See* Association of Southeast Asian
    Nations
Asian Pacific Economic Cooperation
    (APEC), 1056
*Aspen Skiing Co. v. Aspen Highlands Skiing
    Corp.*, 900
Assault (person), 128
Assault of Non-Solicited Pornography and
    Marketing Act, 111
Assent (invalidation), conduct
    (impact), 213
  application, 219

Assets
  distribution, 654–655, 658
    limited liability company (LLC), 686
    limited partnerships, 680
  marshaling, 655, 658
  net assets, 738
  test, 739
  purchase/lease, 787–788
Assignee, 315
  first assignee in point of time, 318
  rights, 317–318
    assignor, rights (obtaining), 317–318
    notice, 317
Assignments, 553
  assignment of rights, 315
  express prohibition, 317
  law, 316, 531
  negotiation, comparison, 537
  partial assignments, 316
  personal rights, 317
  prohibition, law (impact), 317
  requirements, 316
  revocability, 316
  rights, 321–322
    assignment, 315–319
    successive assignments, 318–319
Assignor, 315
  express warranties, 318
  implied warranties, 318
  rights, obtaining, 317–318
  stands in the shoes, 317
Associates, selection, 678
  right, 637
*Association for Molecular Pathology v. Myriad
    Genetics, Inc.*, 889–891
Association of Southeast Asian Nations
    (ASEAN), 1056
Attachment jurisdiction, 48, 49
AT&T Mobility LLC v. Concepcion, 55
Auctions, 429
Auction sales
  offer, 192
  with/without reserve, 429
Audit requirements, 1026
Austin v. Michigan Chamber of Commerce, 74
Authenticating record, 810
  requirement, absence, 810–811
Authenticity, term (usage), 562
Authority, 654. *See also* Officers
  actual authority, 396, 686
  actual express authority, 396
  actual implied authority, 396, 650
  agency termination, impact, 399–400
  apparent authority, 396–397, 399, 650, 658
  contractual liability, rules, 401
  delegation, 398–399
  express warranty, 405
  implied authority, 405–406
  ratification, 400–401
    impact, 401
    requirements, 400–401

revocation, 380
second restatement, 399–501
third restatement, 400
types, 396–398
Authorized means (offer), 198
Authorized signatures, 584
Automated clearinghouse (ACH), 602
Automated teller machines (ATMs), 609
Automatic perfection, 813–814
Automatic stays, Chapter 3 bankruptcy, 841
Award, 55

B

Bad checks, 115
Bagley v. Mt. Bachelor, Inc., 267–270
Bail bond, 822
Bailee
    absolute liability, 1083–1084
    bailments, 1081
    compensation right, 1083
    duty, 1082
    extraordinary bailee, 1084
    liability limitation right, 1083
    ordinary bailee, 1084
    professional bailees, 1083
    rights/duties, 1082–1083
Bailee, goods, 471–472
Bailments, 490, 1074, 1081–1083, 1087–1088
    commercial bailment, 1082
    constructive bailment, 1082
    determinable time, possession, 1082
    duties, 1083f
    elements, 1081–1082
    goods, carriers, 1084
    implied bailment, 1082
    innkeepers, 1084
    mutual benefits, 1081
    personal property, 1082
    pledges, 1084
    possession, delivery, 1082
    safe deposit boxes, 1084
    types, 1084
    warehousing, 1084
Bailor
    bailments, 1081
    possession, restoration, 1082
    rights/duties, 1082–1083
Bank fraud, 112
Bankruptcy, 340–341, 839–840, 1064
    Chapter 3 bankruptcy, case administration,
        840–841
    creditor rights, 856–857, 860
        post judgment remedies, 857
        prejudgment remedies, 856–857
    debtor relief, 856–858, 860
        assignments, 857–858
        compositions, 857
        equity receiverships, 858
    debt payment promise, 240
    federal bankruptcy law, 839–840, 858–860

insolvency meaning, 512
law, application, 850–851
ordinary bankruptcy, 840
proceedings, comparison, 856f
straight bankruptcy, 840
trustee in bankruptcy, 817–818
Bankruptcy Code, 840, 843–844
Banks
    collecting banks, 604–606
    collections, 605f, 614
    deposits, 603, 614
    intermediary banks, 604
    pay or banks, 604–605
Bargained-for exchange, 239–240, 243
    past consideration, 239
    third parties, 239–240
Base fee estate, 1101–1102
BAT. *See* Best available technology
Battery, 127–128
BCT. *See* Best conventional pollution control
        technology
Beam v. Stewart, 779–781
Bearer
    paper, 553f
        negotiation, 553f
    payment, 544
Beatty v. Guggenheim Exploration Co., 1141
Beckman v. Dunn, 129
Behrman, Jack, 19
*Belden Inc. v. American Electronic
        Components, Inc.*, 498–499
Beneficiary, 320, 612, 1142
    defenses, 322
    incidental beneficiary, 321, 322
    intended beneficiary, 320–322
        rights, 322
    third-party beneficiary contracts, 320–322
Beneficiary's bank, 612
Benefit-of-the-bargain rule, 353
Bequest, 1143
    abatement/ademption, 1146–1147
Berardi v. Meadow brook Mall Company,
        221–223
Berg v. Traylor, 280–282
Berle, Adolf, 20
Berne Convention for the Protection of
        Literary and Artistic Works, 1063
Best available technology (BAT), 1041
Best conventional pollution control
        Technology (BCT), 1041
Best practicable control technology (BPT),
        1041
Beyond a reasonable doubt, definition, 5
Bibi v. Elfrink, 262–263
Bigelow-Sanford, Inc. v. Gunny Corp., 525–526
Bilateral contracts, 176–177
    consideration, 236f
    legal sufficiency, 235–236
Billing errors (consumer credit transactions),
        929
Bill of Rights, 67, 115

Bills of lading, 1084–1086
Binder, 1079
Blank indorsements, 556
Blue Laws, 256
Blue-sky laws (blue sky laws), 730, 984
Board of directors, 753
    action, meeting (absence), 764
    capital structure, 762
    changes, 762
    classification, 757
    compensation, 763
    competition duty, absence, 768
    corporate opportunity, 768
    diligence, duty, 766–767
    dividends, 762
    duties, 765–770
    election, 763
    function, 761–763
        exercise, 770
    indemnification, 768
    inspection rights, 765
    liability limitation statutes, 768–769
    loans, 767–768
    loyalty, duty, 767–768
    management compensation, 762–763
    number, 763
    obedience, duty, 766
    officers, selection/removal, 762
    powers, delegation, 764–765
    quorum/voting, 764
    role, 761, 770
    tenure, 763
    vacancies/removal, 763
    votes, plurality, 757
Bona fide intent, demonstration, 876
Bona fide occupational qualification (BFOQ),
        950, 952
Bona fide seniority system, 952
Bonds
    callable, 732
    convertible, 731
    income bonds, 731
    mortgage bonds, 731
    participating bonds, 731
    secured bonds, 731
    unsecured bonds, 731
Books, inspection right, 760
*Border State Bank of Greenbush v. Bagley
        Livestock Exchange, Inc.*, 829–831
Borrowing, 71
Borton v. Forest Hills Country Club,
        1117–1118
Bouton v. Byers, 183–185
Boycotts (Sherman Act), 899–900
BPT. *See* Best practicable control technology
Breach, 174, 334
    absence, loss risk (passage), 473f
    breach of duty, plaintiff proof, 148
    discharge by breach, 336–338, 342
    duty of care, 148–153, 158–159
    impact, 357

Breach (*continued*)
  law, application, 338
  loss, risk, 470
  material breach, 336–337
  parties, agreement, 470
Brehm v. Eisner, 776–778
*Brentwood Academy v. Tennessee Secondary
    School Athletic Association*, 80–81
Bribery, 114
  commercial bribery, 114
Brown v. Board of Education of Topeka, 76,
    84–86
*Brown v. Entertainment Merchants
    Association*, 83–84
Bubble concept, 1039
Bulk transfer, 472
Burden (material increase), assignments
    (impact), 317
Burlington N. & S. F.R. Co. v. White,
    963–965
Burningham v. Westgate Resorts, Ltd.,
    227–228
Bush, George W., 110, 953
Business
  bad checks, 114
  bribery, 114
  burglary, 113
  business for profit, 630–631
  buyer in ordinary course of business, 469
  control, 626, 631–632
  crimes, 111–114, 118
  embezzlement, 112
  ethical responsibilities, 19–20
  ethical standards, 18–19
  ethics, 14
  external liability, 626
  extortion, 114
  false pretenses, 112
  forgery, 114
  judgment rule, 767–768
  larceny, 111–112
  management, 626, 631–632
  ordinary course, buyers (impact),
      816–817
  regular course, 787
  regulation, 19–20
  robbery, 112
  sale, 252
  selection factors, 625–626
  social responsibility, 14
  transacting, 1059–1066
  transferability, 626
  trusts, 627–628
Business association
  continuity, 626
  formation, ease, 625
  forms, 626–628
  general partnership, 626
  joint venture, 626–627
  selection, 624–625
  sole proprietorship, 626

  taxation, 625–626
  unincorporated business association, types,
      686–687
Business enterprise, reorganization, 851
  acceptance of, 853
  confirmation of, 853–854
  conversion or dismissal, 852–853
  effect, confirmation, 854
  plan of, 853
  proceedings, 852
Business Ethics (DeGeorge), 14
But-for test, 153
Buyers
  acceptance, 450
    revocation, 450–451
  accepted goods breach, damages
      recovery, 519
  breach, 470
  buyer in ordinary course of business, 469
  collateral, 817
  competing interests, 816–817
  consequential damages, recovery, 520
  consumer goods, 817
  contract, cancellation, 517
  cover, 517–518
  goods, security interest (enforcement), 519
  impact, 816–817
  incidental damages, recovery, 519–520
  insolvency, goods reclamation, 516
  inspection, 449
  nondelivery/repudiation, damages
      recovery, 518
  payment
    obligation, 451
    recovery, 517
  performance, 449–451, 454–455
  flowchart, 452f
  lawsuit, 519
  rejection, 449–450
  remedies, 516–520, 523
    example, 521f
  replevin, lawsuit, 518
  seller insolvency, identified goods
      recovery, 518
  warranty examination, 488–489
Bylaws, charter (comparison), 713f

C

CACM. *See* Central American Common
    Market
Callable bonds, 732
Cancellation, 1081
  definition, 515
CAN-SPAM Act, 111
Capacity (contracts), 175
Capital
  flow, 1059
  return, right, 636
  structure, 762
  surplus, 733, 737

Cappo v. Suda, 1133–1134
Care
  duty of care, breach, 148–153, 158–159
  duty, plaintiff proof, 148
Carelessness, 108
Caribbean Community (CARICOM), 1056
Carriers, 1084
  involvement, 470
Carson, Rachel, 1042
Carter v. Tokai Financial Services, Inc.,
    434–435
Caselaw, 7
Cash dividends, 737
  legal restrictions, 738–739
Cashier's check, 539
Catalano, Inc. v. Target Sales, Inc., 898
Catamount Slate Products, Inc. v. Sheldon,
    201–203
Causa mortis, 1077
Cause, challenges, 51
Caveat emptor, 919, 1122
CDA. *See* Communications Decency
    Act of 1996
Cease-and-desist order, 920
Central American Common Market
    (CACM), 1056
*Central Hudson Gas and Electric Corp. v.
    Public Service Commission*, 74
Certificated security, 809
Certificate of deposit (CD), 540
  example, 541f
  payment promissory, 540f
Certificate of title, 811
Certification, 585
  mark, 875
C.&F. contract, 445
CFCs. *See* Chlorofluorocarbons
CFPB. *See* Consumer Financial Protection
    Bureau
Challenges, cause, 51
Chapa v. Traciers & Associates, 832–833
Chapter 3 bankruptcy
  automatic stays, 841
  case administration, 840–842, 858
  commencement, 841
  creditors, meetings, 842
  dismissal, 841
  involuntary petitions, 841
  trustees, 841–842
  voluntary petitions, 841
Chapter 5 bankruptcy, 842–847, 858–859
  administration, expenses, 842–843
  claims
    priority, 842–843
    proof, 842
    subordination, 843
  creditors, 842–843
  debtors, 843–845
    discharge, 844–845
    duties, 843

estate, administration expenses, 842–843
  exemptions, 843–844
  property transfer, trustee recovery, 846
domestic support obligations, 842
estate, 842, 845–847
  transfers, fraud, 846–847
  trustee, lien creditor role, 845
  voidable preferences, 845–846
gap creditors, unsecured claims, 843
nondischargeable debts, 844–845
prebankruptcy transfers, exceptions, 846
secured claims, 842
unsecured claims, 842, 843
Chapter 7 bankruptcy
  conversion, 848
  debtor estate assets, trustee collection/
    distribution, 848, 849f
  discharge, 849–851
  dismissal, 848–849
  estate, distribution, 849
  liquidation, 848–852, 859
  means test, scenarios, 849
  proceedings, 848
Chapter 11 bankruptcy
  cash payments, 853
  confirmation, impact, 854
  corporation usage, 852
  creditor acceptance, 853–854
  feasibility, 853
  good faith, 853
  proceedings, 852–853
  reorganization, 851–853, 858
  reorganization plan, 852
    acceptance, 853
    confirmation, 853–854
  trustee, duties, 852
Chapter 13 bankruptcy
  confirmation, impact, 855–856
  conversion/dismissal, 854
  discharge, 855–856
  individual debts, adjustment, 854–856,
    859–860
  plan, 854–855
    confirmation, 855
    requirements, 854
  proceedings, 854
Charging order, 635
Charitable trusts, 1140
Charter, 713
  amendments, 785–786, 793
    combinations, 786–792
    director/shareholder approval,
      785–786
  bylaws, comparison, 713f
  opt-in, 733
  opt-out, 732–733
Check, 539, 586
  bad checks, 114
  cashier's check, 539
  example, 539f
  payment order, 538f

presentation, 586
  substitute check, 606–607
Check Clearing for the 21st Century Act
    (Check 21) (Check Truncation
    Act), 539
Chicago Board of Trade v.
    United States, 897
Children, reasonable person standard,
    148–149
CHIPS. See Clearing House Interbank
    Payment System
Chlorofluorocarbons (CFCs), 1046
C.I.F. contract, 445
Citizenship, diversity, 46
Citizens United v. Federal Election
    Commission, 73–74
Civil dispute resolution, 42, 49, 58–59
Civil law, 5
  criminal law, comparison, 5f
  systems, 7
Civil liability, 1007f
Civil monetary penalty, 1006
Civil procedure, 50–53
  appeal, 52–53
  enforcement, 53
  pleadings, 50–51
  pretrial procedure, 51
  trial, 51–52
Civil Rights Act of 1964, 949–952
  comparable worth, 952
  disability law, 953–954
  discrimination, proving, 950–951
  remedies, 951
  reverse discrimination, 951–952
  sexual harassment, 952
  Title VII, 1064
Civil Rights Act of 1991, 951, 955
Claims, 562, 842. See also Chapter 5
    bankruptcy
Class action, 50
Class suit, 760
Claw back, Dodd-Frank requirements, 762
Clayton Act, 895, 900–905
  exclusive dealing, 900–901
  mergers, 901–903
  tying contracts, 900–901
Clean Air Act, 1038–1040, 1047
  National Ambient Air Quality Standards
    (NAAQSs), 1038–1039
  nonattainment areas, 1039
  prevention of significant deterioration
    (PSD) areas, 1039
  state implementation plan (SIP), 1039
Clean Power Plan, 1038
Clean Water Act, 1040–1042, 1047
  amendments (1977), 1041
  new source performance standards,
    1041–1042
  nonpoint source pollution, 1041
  point sources, 1041
Clearing house, 603

Clearing House Interbank Payment System
    (CHIPS), 609–611
Client information, 1023–1024
Closed-end credit, 928
Closed shop, 948
Closely held corporations, 701–702,
    715–716, 753
  management structure, 755f
  supermajority, imposition, 756
Closing argument, 52
Coastal Leasing Corporation v. T-Bar S
    Corporation, 528–529
Codicils, 1145
  exclusion, 291
Co-insurance clauses, 1078–1079
Coleman, Inc. v. Nufarm Americas, Inc.,
    436–438
Collateral, 292, 807
  acceptance, 820
  authenticating record, 810
    requirement, absence, 810–811
  buyers, 817
  classification, 807–809, 827
  debtor rights, 810
  impact, 811
  junk collateral, 811
  kinds, 809
  rights, 810
  sale, 819–820
    proceeds, application, 820
  security agreement, 810
Collecting banks, 603–605
  agent, 603
  duty of care, 603
  duty to act, timeliness, 603–604
  final payment, 605
  indorsements, 604–605
  warranties, 605
Collection, 602
  guarantor, 821
  indorsements, 556
Collective bargaining agreements,
    rejection, 852
Collective mark, 875
College v. Woodward, 706
Commerce
  federal commerce power, 70
  state regulation, 70–71
  taxation, 70–71
Commerce Clause, U.S. Supreme Court
    interpretation, 70–71
Commerce & Industry Insurance Company v.
    Bayer Corporation, 438–440
Commercial bailment, 1082
Commercial bribery, 114
Commercial impracticability, 452
Commercially reasonable, term, 1087
Commercial practices, expansion, 426
Commercial speech, 74
Commercial unit, 446
Commissions, unsecured claims, 843

Common carrier, 1084
Common law, 7, 173, 1021–1024, 1027–1028
    actions, 1035, 1047
    approach (incorporation), 714
    composition, 857
    offer, 198
    restraint (trade), 256–257
    system, 7
    title theory, 1124
Common Market for Eastern and Southern
        Africa (COMESA), 1056
Common stock, 735
Communication (offer), 191–192
Communications Decency Act of 1996
        (CDA), 129–130
Community property, 1109
Community Reinvestment Act (CRA), 927
Comparable worth, 952
Comparative negligence, 158
    warranties, 492
Comparative responsibility, 492
Compensation, 5, 378
    bailee right, 1083
    board of directors, 763
    right, 636
    workers' compensation, 957
Compensatory damages, 353
    consequential damages, 353
    cost avoidance, 353
    incidental damages, 353
Competing interests
    buyers, 816–817
    lien creditors, 817
    priorities, 814–818, 819f, 828
    secured creditors, 814–816
    trustee in bankruptcy, competing interests,
        817–818
    unsecured creditors, 814
Competition
    meeting (Robinson-Patman Act),
        904–905
        defense, 905f
    unfair methods, 905
Complaint
    filing, 50
    responses, 50–51
Compliance
    methods, 296–297, 302
    program, elements, 109
Compositions (debtors/creditors), 857
Comprehensive Environmental Response,
        Compensation, and Liability Act
        (CERCLA), 1042–1043
Compulsory arbitration, 55
Compulsory licenses, 879
Compulsory share exchange, 788–789
Computer crime, 110–111
Computer, target, 110–111
Concealment, 216, 1081
Concerted action, 897–898
Concerted refusal to deal, 898

Conciliation, 56
    comparison, 55f
Concurrent conditions, 336
Concurrent federal jurisdiction, 46
Concurrent ownership, 1107–1109, 1113
    types, 1107–1108
Concurrent owners, rights, 1108f
Conditional acceptance, 196
Conditional privilege, 129
Conditional promises (legal sufficiency), 237
Conditional wills, 1146
Conditions, 334–336, 341–342
    concurrent conditions, 336
    constructive condition, 335
    defective condition, 157, 491
    express condition, 335
    implied-in-fact conditions, 335
    implied-in-law conditions, 335
    precedent, 335, 587–589
    presupposed condition, nonhappening,
        452–453
    subsequent, 335
Condominiums, 1109
Confidential information, 377
Confidential nonpublic review, 988
Confidential relationship, 214
Conflict-of-interest transactions,
        validation, 768
Conflict of laws rule, 46
Conflicts of interest, 377, 767
Confusion, impact, 1077
Conglomerate merger, 901
Conklin Farm v. Doris Leibowitz, 663–665
Connes v. Molalla Transport System, Inc.,
        413–415
Conscious parallelism, 898
Consensual arbitration, 55
Consent, 134
Consequential damages, recovery, 520
Consideration, 234, 243, 429–430
    absence, 240–242
    bilateral contracts, 236f
    contracts, 175
    flowchart, 242f
    irrevocable offers, 242
    past consideration, 239
    promissory estoppel, 241
    unilateral contracts, 236f
Consignee, 1084
Consignment, 471
Consignor, 1084
Consolidated corporation, 789
Consolidation, 789
Constitutional law, 6–7, 67
    federalism, 68
    federal supremacy, 68
    judicial review, 68
    powers, separation, 68–69
    preemption, 68
    principles, 68–69
    state action, 69

Constitutional privilege, 129
Constitution, definition/function, 6
Constructive bailment, 1082
Constructive condition, 335
Constructive delivery, 1076
Constructive eviction, 1106
Constructive notice, 399
Constructive trusts, 1139
Consumer credit contract, 566–567
Consumer credit transactions, 927–932, 934
    billing errors, 929
    consumer credit card fraud, 930–931
    contract terms, 930
    credit accounts, 928–929
    credit cards, bill of rights, 931–932
    disclosure requirements, 928–929f
    fair credit reportage, 931
    home equity loans, 929
    market access, 927–928
    Mortgage Disclosure Improvement Act
        (MDIA), 930
    Mortgage Reform and Anti-Predatory
        Lending Act, 930
    settlement charges, 929
Consumer financial product/service, 922
Consumer Financial Protection Bureau
        (CFPB), 55, 609, 922–923, 931
Consumer funds transfers, 609–610, 614
    consumer liability, 610
    disclosure, 609
    documentation, 609
    error resolution, 609–610
    financial institution, liability, 610
    periodic statements, 609
    preauthorized transfers, 609
Consumer goods, 808, 811
    buyers, 817
    obligation, debtor payment, 820
    PMSI, 813–814
    warranties, federal legislation, 489
Consumer Product Safety Act (CPSA), 921
Consumer Product Safety Commission
        (CPSC), 921–922
Consumer protection, 609, 919, 933
    affirmative disclosure, 921
    Consumer Financial Protection Bureau
        (CFPB), 922
    Consumer Product Safety Commission
        (CPSC), 921–922
    corrective advertising, 921
    federal consumer protection agencies,
        919–923
    Federal Trade Commission (FTC)
        impact, 920–921
        remedies, 921
        standards, 920–921
    local consumer protection agencies,
        919–920
    multiple product order, 921
    state consumer protection agencies,
        919–923

Consumer purchases, 923–926, 933
　disclaimers, limitations, 924
　federal warranty protection, 923–924
　labeling requirements, 924
　presale disclosure, 924
　rescission, consumer rights, 925, 926f
　state "Lemon Laws," 924–925
Consumers
　debts, prebankruptcy transfer
　　exception, 846
　leases, 423
Content, 536
Contingent remainder, 1103
Continuing general lien, 811
Contract carrier, 1084
Contracting party, satisfaction, 335
Contract liability, 275–277, 1021–1023
　agent, 405–407
　disclosed principal, 397fd
　example, 649f
　principal, 395–401, 407–408
　undisclosed principal, 399f
　unidentified principal, 398f
Contracts, 178f
　adhesion contract, 258
　admission, 432
　adoption, 401
　authorized contracts (agent), 405
　bilateral contracts, 176–177
　cancellation, 515, 517
　capacity, 175, 275
　carriers, involvement, 471
　classification, 175–180
　clause, 73
　consideration, 175
　　absence, 240–244
　consumer credit contract, 566–567
　contract within the statute, 291
　definition, 174, 179
　destination contract, 466, 471
　disaffirmance, 275–276
　discharge, 341f
　employment contracts, 256–257
　exceptions, 432
　exclusive dealing contracts,
　　236–237
　executed contracts, 177
　executory contracts, 177
　express contracts, 175–176
　form, 431–432, 434
　　statute of frauds, 431–432
　formal contracts, 178
　freedom, 427
　goods identification, 513
　governing, laws (usage), 174f
　implied contracts, 175–176
　informal contracts, 178
　instruments, material alteration, 824
　international contracts, 173–174,
　　1060–1062
　interpretation, 299–303

introduction, 172
law
　development, 172–174, 179
　UCC law of sales and leases,
　　comparison, 432f
modifications, 241, 296, 431
mutual assent, 174
object, legality, 175
option contracts, 194–195
oral contract, 290
parol evidence, 432
partnership, 648–651
preexisting contracts, modification,
　237, 238f
preexisting contractual obligation, 237–239
price
　cost of cover, difference, 517
　market price, difference, 518
privity, 489
quasi contracts (restitution), 178–179,
　178f, 180
ratification, 275–277
remedies, 352, 358f
requirements, 174–175, 179
rescission, 296
restitution, 276
rule, 298
　nonapplication, 298–299
shipment contract, 466, 471
statute of frauds, 291–296, 301–302
　writings/record, 431–432
substituted contracts, 238, 339
supplemental evidence, 299–301
terms (consumer credit transactions), 929
third parties
　impact, 315
　law, application, 320
third-party beneficiary contracts, 320–322
types, 173
unauthorized contracts (agent), 405–406
unconscionable contracts, 257–258
unenforceable contracts, 177
unilateral contracts, 176–177
valid contracts, 177
voidable contracts, 177, 272, 351
voidable promises, 240
void contracts, 177
writing, 290
written contract, unauthorized material
　alteration, 338
Contracts for the International Sales of Goods
　(CISG), 1061
Contractual covenants, 1105
Contractual defenses, 563
Contractual duties, 378
　compensation, 378
　indemnification/reimbursement, 378
Contractual liability, 583, 593–594
　principles, 593
　rules, 401
　types, 588f

Contractual promises, 175f
Contractual provisions, impact, 520–522
Contractual relations, interference, 132–133
Contribution (surety right), 823
Contributory infringer, 881
Contributory negligence, 155, 158, 957
　warranties, 492
Control, 993
Conventional level, 18
Convention on the Settlement of Investment
　Disputes between States and Nationals
　of Other States, 1060
Conversion, 112
Conversion (corporations), 789
Conversion, liability (usage), 588, 594
Convertible bonds, 731
Conway v. Cutler Group, Inc., 1131–1132
Cooke v. Fresh Express Foods Corporation,
　Inc., 798–800
Cooperation, right, 453
Cooperative Centrale Raiffeisen-
　Boerenleenbank B.A. v. Bailey,
　548–549
Cooperatives, 1109
Coopers & Lybrand v. Fox, 721–722
Copartners, 632
Copperwald Corp. v. Independence Tube
　Corp., 898
Copyright Act, 879
Copyright Alternative in Small-Claims
　Enforcement Act of 2019 (the CASE
　Act), 879
Copyrights, 877–880, 883
　infringement, 879–880
　intellectual property, protection, 1062
　ownership, 879
　registration, 878
　remedies, 879–880
　rights, 878–879
Corporate governance, 20–22, 753–755
Corporateness, recognition/disregard,
　714–715, 720
Corporate opportunity, 768
　advantage, 1141
Corporate political speech, 73–74
Corporate powers, 716, 719
　purposes, 716
　sources, 716, 719
Corporate shares, free transferability, 707
Corporate veil, piercing, 684, 715–716, 719
Corporations, 627
　attributes, 707–708, 718–719
　bylaws, 713
　characteristics, 625f
　as a citizen, status, 708
　classification, 708–710, 719
　closely held corporations, 709–710,
　　715–716
　consolidated corporation, 789
　consolidation, 789
　conversion, 789

Corporations (*continued*)
corporation by estoppel, 714
corporation *de facto*, 714
corporation *de jure*, 714
creature of the state, 707
criminal offense conviction, 109
de facto corporations, 714
defective corporation, 714
de jure corporations, 714
directors/officers, role, 760
dissolution, 791–793
doing business, 709
domestication, 789
domestic corporations, 709
financial structure, law (application), 740
foreign corporations, 709
formation, 710, 719–720
going private transactions, 789–790
incorporation, states election, 712
legal entity, 707
liability, 109–110
limited liability, 707
management
centralization, 708
structure, statutory model, 755f
merged corporation, 789
moral agents, 19–20
name, promoter preincorporation
contracts, 711f
nature, 707, 718–719
nonprofit corporations, 708
organization, 710–712, 718
parent corporation, 716
parent-subsidiary corporations, 716
perpetual existence, 707–708
as a person, status, 708
private corporations, 708
professional corporations, 710
profit corporations, 708
promoters, 710–711
contracts, 710–711
fiduciary duty, 711
public corporations, 708
publicly held corporations, 709–710
regulation, scope, 709
sanctions, 709
shares, free transferability, 707
subchapter S corporation, 710
subscribers, 712
subsidiary corporation, 716
surviving corporation, 788
ultra vires acts, effect, 717
Corrective advertising, 921
Cost avoidance, 353
Cost-benefit analysis, 16
Cost justification (Robinson-Patman Act), 904
Cost of cover, contract price (difference), 517
Cosureties, 821
Co-tenants, 1107
Council on Environmental Quality
(CEQ), 1037

Counterclaim, 51
Counterfeit mark, 877
Counteroffer, 196
County of Washington v. Gunther, 952
Course of dealing, 299, 426
Course of descent, 1147–1148
Course of performance, 299
Courts
adjudication, comparison, 55f
court-annexed arbitration, 56
courts of appeal, 42–43
district courts, 42
federal courts, 42–44
inferior trial courts, 44
orders, usage, 653–654
special courts, 43–44
stare decisis (dual court system), 47, 48f
state courts, 44–45
Supreme Court, 43
system, 42
trial courts, 44
U.S. circuit courts, 44f
Covenant not to compete, 256
Covenants, 1105
Covenants (land), 1128
restrictive covenants
termination, 1129
validity, 1129
subdivisions, restrictive covenants, 1129
Coverage wills, exclusion, 291
*Cox Enterprises, Inc. v. Pension Benefit
Guaranty Corporation*, 745–746
Credit accounts (consumer credit
transactions), 928–929
*Credit Alliance Corp. v. Arthur Andersen &
Co.*, 1022
Credit Card Accountability, Responsibility,
and Disclosure Act (Credit Card Bill
of Rights) (CARD), 931
Credit Card Fraud Act, 930
Credit cards, bill of rights, 931–932
Credit obligation, rescission, 926
Creditors, 292
acceptance, 853–854
bankruptcy rights, 856–857, 860
beneficiary, 321
benefit, debtor assignments, 857–858
Chapter 5 bankruptcy, 842–843
gap creditors, unsecured claims, 843
meetings (Chapter 3 bankruptcy), 842
principal debtor, relationship, 820–821
protection, 686, 793
remedies, 932–934
rights, 634–635, 658
secured creditors, competing interests,
814–816
surety, relationship, 821
unsecured creditors, competing
interests, 814
Credit rating agencies, 731
Credit transaction, 613f

Crimes, 107
bad checks, 114
bribery, 114
burglary, 113
business crimes, 111–114, 118
classification, 109
computer crime, 110–111
defenses, 114–115, 118
duress, 114
elements, 108
embezzlement, 112
entrapment, 115
extortion, 114
false pretenses, 112
forgery, 114
instrument, 110
liability, 717, 718
mental fault, degrees, 108f
mistake of fact, 114
nature, 107–110, 117
person/property, defense, 114
robbery, 112
vicarious liability, 109
white-collar crime, 110–111
Criminal defendant, constitutional
protection, 115f
Criminal law, 5, 107
application, 113
civil law, comparison, 5f
Criminal liability, 1023
principal, 404–405, 409
Criminal procedure, 115–118
Fifth Amendment, 117
Fourth Amendment, 116–117
Sixth Amendment, 117
Criminal prosecution, steps, 115–116
Criminal sanctions, 996–998
IRC imposition, 1023
Cross-examination, 51
Crowd funding exemption, 991–992
Cumulative stock, 736
Cumulative-to-the-extent-earned stock, 736
Cumulative voting, 758
Customers
death/incompetence, 607
duties, 607–608
pay or banks, relationship, 605–608
Cybercrime, 110

D

Dahan v. Weiss, 307–308
Damages
award, 874
certainty, 355–356
compensatory damages, 353
consequential damages, 353
foreseeability, 355
incidental damages, 353
limitations, 355–356, 494
liquidated damages, 354–355

liquidation/limitation, 520–521
mitigation, 356
monetary damages, 352–356
nominal damages, 353–354
punitive damages, 354
recovery, 513, 518
reliance damages, 354
treble damages, 895
Davis v. Watson Brothers Plumbing, Inc.,
    596–597
Deal, concerted refusal, 898
Death
    agency, 380
    offer, 196
Debt
    antecedent debt, 561, 652
    collection practices, 933
    liquidated debt, settlement, 238–239
    payment promise
        bankruptcy discharge, 240
        statute of limitations, impact, 240
    subsequent debts, 652
    unliquidated debt, settlement, 239
Debtor-creditor, change, 604
Debtors, 807
    bankruptcy relief, 856–858, 860
    Chapter 5 bankruptcy, 842–845
        discharge, 844–845
        duties, 843
    exemptions, 843–844
    debt, reorganization, 840
    estate
        administration expenses, 841–842
        assets, trustee collection/distribution,
            847, 848f
    location, change, 813
    principal debtor, 292, 820
    property transfer, trustee recovery, 845
    rights, 807f
Debt securities, 731, 742
    callable bonds, 732
    convertible bonds, 731
    income bones, 731
    issuance, authority, 731
    secured bonds, 731
    types, 731–732, 737f, 742
    unsecured bonds, 731
Decedents, estates, 1139, 1143, 1149
Deception
    intention, 217
    meaning, 920
    occurrence, 920
Deeds, 1122–1123, 1128–1129
    deed of trust, 1123
    delivery, 1123
    estate, quantity, 1122
    execution, 1122–1123
    formal requirements, 1122–1123
    land, description, 1122
    quit claim, 1122
    recordation, 1123

title, covenants, 1122
types, 1122
warranty, 1122
Deepwater Horizon, disaster, 1041–1042
De facto corporations, 714
Defamation, 74–75, 129–130
    defenses, 129–130
    elements, 129
Default, 818–820, 828
Default judgment, 50
Defeasance, 1124
Defective condition, 157, 490, 491
Defective corporation, 714
Defective goods, leases/bailments, 490
Defective incorporation, 714–715
Defects
    design defect, 491
    manufacturing defect, 491
Defendant, 10
    innocence, presumption, 116
    last clear chance, 166
Defend Trend Secrets Act (DTSA), 874
Defense, 562
    contractual defenses, 564
    personal defenses, 564–566
    real defenses, 564–565
Deficiency judgment, 1126
Definiteness, 192–193
    open terms, 193
Definite time, 542–543
DeGeoge, Richard T., 14
Deiter v. Coons, 475–477
De jure corporations, 612
Delectus personae, 751
Delegable duties, 319
Delegated duty, assumption, 319
Delegatee, 316, 319
Delegation of duties, 315, 319–320, 323
Delegator, 316, 319
Delivery, tender, 444
Demand note, 539
    dishonoring, 585
Demand paper, 542, 562
Demand, payable on demand, 542
Demurrer, 50
Denial, 51
Denney v. Reppert, 245–246
Department of Revenue of Kentucky v. Davis,
    81–83
Depositions, 51
Deposits
    bank deposits, 602
    indorsements, 556
Derivative actions, 679
    limited liability company (LLC), 682
Derivative law suits, 753
Descent, course, 1123–1124
Design defect, 492, 495–496
Design patent, 881
Destination contract, 466, 471

Detroit Lions, Inc. v. Argovitz, 388–389
*Diamond, Commissioner of Patents and
    Trademarks v. Chakrabarty*, 880
Different terms, 428
Digital Millennium Copyright Act (DMCA),
    878–879
Dignity, right (harm), 129–131
Diligence, duty, 376
    directors/officers, 766–767
DiLorenzo v. Valve and Primer Corporation,
    248–249
Direct deposits/withdrawals, 609
Directed verdict, 52
Direct examination, 51
Direct export sales, 1064
Direct infringer, 881
Direct liability (principal), 402–403
Directors, 741. *See also* Board of directors
    business judgment rule, 767–768
    charter amendment approval, 785–786
    reliance, 767
    role, 762, 771
Direct TV, Inc. v. Imburgia, 62–63
Disability Insurance (DI), 957
Disability law, 953–954
Disaffirmance, 275–276
Discharge, 334
    bankruptcy, 340–341
    contracts, 341f
    impossibility, 339–340
    law, application, 338
Discharge by agreement, 338–339, 342
    accord/satisfaction, 339
    mutual rescission, 338
    novation, 339
    substituted contract, 339
Discharge by breach, 336–338, 342
Discharge by operation of law, 339–343
Discharge by performance, 336, 342
    anticipatory repudiation, 337–338
    material breach, 336–337
    substantial performance, 337
    written contract, unauthorized material
        alteration, 338
Disclaimers, limitations, 925
Disclosed principal, 395
    agent, contract liability, 405–406
    contract liability, 397f
Disclosure requirements, 986
Discovery, 51
Discrimination, 1064
    defenses, 951
    disparate impact, 951
    disparate treatment, 949
    employment discrimination law, 948–954
    past discrimination, present effects,
        949–950
    price discrimination, prohibition, 903
    proving, 949–950
    reverse discrimination, 950–951
Disparagement (economic interests), 133

Dispatch, 198
Dissenters, rights
    purpose, 790
    transactions, 790–791
Dissociated partners, liability, 656–657
Dissociation, 652–653, 660–661
    continuation, 655–656
    dissolution, avoidance, 655–658, 661
    effects, 653
    general partnerships (RUPA), 656
    impact, absence, 655–656
    rightful dissociations, 652–653
    RUPA rules, 657f
    wrongful dissociations, 652
Dissolution, 653–655, 658, 660–661, 794
    authority, 654
    causes, 656–658
        dissociations, impact (absence), 655–656
    continuation, 658–659
    corporations, 790–792
    court orders, usage, 653–654
    dissociations, impact (absence), 655–656
    effects, 654, 658
    general partnerships, RUPA (usage), 652
    involuntary dissolution, 790–791
    judicial dissolution, 791
    law, operation (impact), 653
    liability, 654
    limited partnership, 681
    outcomes, 659
    partners, impact, 653
    RUPA rules, 657f
    term partnership, 653
    UPA definition, 658
    usage, avoidance, 655–658
    voluntary dissolution, 791
    winding up, 654–655
Distributions, 743
    declaration, 741, 743
    definitions, 738
    legal restrictions, 738–741
        concepts, 739f
    liquidation, legal restrictions, 739
    payment, 741, 743
    problems, liability, 741, 742f, 743
    Revised Act definition, 737
    sharing, rights, 636–637
    types, 737–738, 743
Distributive justice, 17
District courts, 42
Diversity of citizenship, 46
Dividends, 736–737, 743, 763
    cash dividends, 737
    compelling, shareholder right, 741
    declaration, effect, 741
    definitions, 738
    legal restrictions, 738–741, 743
    liquidating dividends, 738
    preferences, 736
    problems, liability, 741, 743
    property dividends, 737

    stock dividends, 737–738
    types, 737–738, 743
Dixon, Laukitis and Downing v. Busey Bank,
        615–616
DMCA. See Digital Millennium Copyright
        Act
Documents, 808–809
    production, 51
Documents of title. See Title documents
Dodd-Frank Act, 922
Dodd-Frank Wall Street Reform and
        Consumer Protection Act
        (Dodd-Frank Act), 20, 609, 731,
        755, 983, 1062
    amendments, 998–999
    CFPB establishment, 922
    enactment, 786
    provisions, 1001
    requirement, 989
    rules authorization, 758, 762, 764–765
Dodge v. Ford Motor Co., 747–749
Doing business (corporations), 709
DOMA. See Federal Defense of Marriage Act
Domestic animals, definition, 157–158
Domestication (corporations), 789
Domestic banks, securities, 988
Domestic corporations, 709
Domestic support obligations, prebankruptcy
        transfer exception, 846
Dominant parcel, 1109
Donahue v. Rodd Electrotype Co., Inc.,
        774–775
Donald R. Hessler v. Crystal Lake Chrysler-
        Plymouth, Inc., 459–460
Donee beneficiary, 321, 1076
Donor, 1076
Drafts, 538
    example, 539f
    orders, drawers, 585–586
    payment order, 538f
    sight draft, 538
    time draft, 538, 586
    unaccepted draft, 586–587
        drawees, 591–592
Drake Mfg. Co., Inc. v. Poly flow, Inc.,
        720–721
Drawee, 538, 539
    acceptance, 586
    bank, 606
Drawers, 538, 585–586
Drug testing, employee privacy, 956
Dual priority rule, 658
Due care, bailee duty, 1082
Due diligence
    defense, 996
    requirements, 1024
Due negotiation, 1086
Due performance, termination, 1081
Due process, 75
    procedural due process, 75
    substantive due process, 75

Due Process Clause, 71
    U.S. Supreme Court interpretation, 76
Dumping, violation, 1059
Durable power of attorney, 375
Duress, 114, 213–214, 220, 824
    exertion, 825
    impact, 1144
    improper threats, 213–214
    physical compulsion, 213
Duties of possessors of land, 151–153
    second restatement, 151–152
    third restatement, 152–153
Duty (duties)
    board of directors, 766–769
    breach, plaintiff proof, 148
    contractual duties, 378
    definition, 4
    delegable duties, 319
    delegated duty, assumption, 319
    delegation, 315, 319–320, 323
    fiduciary duty, 375–377
    limited partnership, 679
    material increase, assignments
        (impact), 317
    officers, 766–770
    parties, 319–320
    partners, fiduciary duty, 633–634
    preexisting contractual duty, 237
    public duty, 237
Duty not to compete, 376
Duty of care, 603
    breach, 148–153, 158–159
    duties of possessors of land, 151–153
    duty to act, 150–151
    partners, 634
    plaintiff proof, 148
    reasonable person standard, 148–149
Duty of diligence, 375
Duty of good conduct, 375
Duty of obedience, 374–375
Duty to account, 375
Duty to act, 150–151
    timeliness, 603–604
Duty to inform, 375

E

Earned surplus, 738
    test, 738–739
Easements
    appurtenant easements, 1109
    creation, 1109–1110
    dedication, 1110
    definition, 1108
    dominant parcel, 1108
    easement in gross, 1108
    easement in reservation, 1109
    express grant/reservation, 1109
    implied grant/reservation, 1110
    licenses, 1111
    necessity, 1111

prescription, 1111
servient parcel, 1108
types, 1108
Eastman Kodak Co. v. Image Technical Services, Inc., 911–913
ECOA. *See* Equal Credit Opportunity Act
Economic coercion, 213
Economic Community of West African States (ECOWAS), 1056
Economic interests
contractual relations, interference, 132–133
disparagement, 133
fraudulent misrepresentation, 133
harm, 132–133, 135
Economic loss, unintentional infliction (avoidance), 148
Economies of scale, usage, 706
EDGAR. *See* Electronic Data Gathering, Analysis, and Retrieval
Ed Nowogroski Insurance, Inc. v. Rucker, 884–886
EEOC v. Abercrombie & Fitch Stores, Inc., 951
Effective moment (offer), 198
Effluent limitations, 1041
Electioneering communication, 74
Electronic chattel paper, 810
Electronic Data Gathering, Analysis, and Retrieval (EDGAR), 983, 990, 997
Electronic document of title, 1086
control, 1087
negotiation, 1087
Electronic filing, facilitation, 811
Electronic fund transfer (EFT), 602, 609, 611, 615
automated teller machines (ATMs), 609
direct deposits/withdrawals, 609
nature/types, 615
online banking, 609
pay-by-phone systems, 609
personal computer (online) banking, 609
point-of-sale system, 609
wholesale, 609
Electronic Fund Transfer Act (EFTA), 602, 609
Electronic fund transfer system (EFTS), 609
Electronic records, 291–292
Electronic Signatures in Global and National Commerce (E-Sign), 292, 431, 707
Embezzlement, 112
Emergencies, standard, 149
Emerging growth companies (EGCs), 988
Eminent domain, 71–72, 1127–1128
flowchart, 1128f
public use, 1127–1128
Emotional distress, infliction, 129
Employee benefit plans, 843, 922
Employee privacy, 956–957
drug/alcohol testing, 956
lie detector tests, 956–957
Employee protection, 955–958
judicial limitations, 955
statutory limitations, 955

Employee termination at will, 955
Employment
comparable worth, 952
contracts, 256–257
discrimination, 1064
prohibition, 949
discrimination law, 949–955
executive order, 953
disparate impact, 950
disparate treatment, 950
federal employment discrimination laws, 954f
law, 947
past discrimination, present effects, 950
relationship, 373
remedies, 951
reverse discrimination, 951–952
Enabling statute, 90–91
Encumbrances, 1122, 1123
Enforcement, 53
administrative agencies, 92–93
rights (shareholders), 760–761
Engagement letter, 1021
Enron, violations/scandal, 14, 20, 110, 984
Entities
merged entity, 686
merger, 686
surviving entity, 686
Entity theory, 628–629
Entrapment, 115
Environment
federal regulation, 1036–1037, 1047–1048
international environment, 1055–1057
Environmental damage, common law actions, 1035, 1047
Environmental impact statements (EISs), 1037–1038
content, 1038
preparation, procedure, 1037
requirement
nature, 1038
scope, 1037–1038
Environmental law, 1035
abnormally dangerous activities, strict liability, 1036
action, private causes (problems), 1036–1037
Environmental Protection Agency (EPA), 1037
Environmental Protection Agency v. EME Homer City Generation, L.P., 1048–1049
EPA. *See* Environmental Protection Agency
Equal Credit Opportunity Act (ECOA), 927
Equal Employment Opportunity Commission (EEOC), 949, 952
charges, filing, 951f
Equal Pay Act, 949
Equal protection, 75–77
intermediate test, 77
rational relationship test, 76
strict scrutiny test, 76–77

Equipment, 808
Equitable title, 1139
Equity, 7–8
balance, 1040
insolvency meaning, 512
insolvency test, 738
receiverships, 857
remedies, 352, 356
injunctions, 357
specific performance, 356–357
securities, 732, 736
shares, 732
types, 737f
Ernst & Ernst v. Hochfelder, 1030–1032
Error resolution (consumer funds transfers), 610
Estate of Countryman v. Farmers Coop. Ass'n, 697–698
Estates
administration, 1147–1148, 1150
decedents, estates, 1143
quantity, 1123
Estate tax, imposition, 1148
Estoppel
corporation by, 714
partnership by, 650–651, 659
person, 564
Ethical behavior, theories, 18
Ethical fundamentalism, 15
Ethical relativism, 16
Ethical system, selection, 18
Ethical theories, 15–18
Ethics
business, ethics, 14
law, contrast, 15
program, elements, 109
situational ethics, 16
social ethics theories, 17–18
Error resolution, 610
European Union (EU), 1056
Eviction (tenants), 1106
Examination, 51
cross-examination, 51
direct examination, 51
Exclusionary rule, 116
Exclusive dealing (Clayton Act), 901
Exclusive dealing agreement, 237, 906
Exclusive dealing contracts, 236–237
Exclusive federal jurisdiction, 46
Exclusive state jurisdiction, 46
Exculpatory clauses, 257
Executed contracts, 177
Execution
fraud, 215
writ, 53
Executive branch control (administrative agencies), 95–96
Executive orders, 9, 953
Executor-administrator provision, 293
Executors, 293, 1148
Executory contracts, 177

Executory promise, 561
Exempt securities, 988, 1008
   short-term commercial paper, 988
Exoneration, surety right, 823
Expectation interest, 352
Expertise (social responsibility arguments), 21
Export controls, 1059
Express assumption, 155
Express condition, 335
Express contracts, 175–176
Express exclusions, 487–488
Express grant/reservation, 1110
Express insider trading liability, 1005, 1009
Express promises, 1105
Express trusts, 1139–1140
Express warranties, 485–486
   express warranty of authority, 405
Express warranties (assignor), 315
Ex-ship, 446
External liability, 626
Extortion, 114
Extraordinary bailee, 1084

F

FAA. *See* Federal Arbitration Act
Fact, 216–217
   affirmation, 487
   mistakes, 114
   notice, 380, 400
   questions, 95
   representation, prediction (contrast), 216
Factual cause, 153, 159
   plaintiff proof, 148
Failure-to-warn cases, 492
Fair and equitable, term, 852
Fair Credit and Charge Card Disclosure
   Act, 928
Fair Credit Billing act, 930
Fair Credit Reporting Act (FRCA), 931
Fair Debt Collection Practices Act
   (FDCPA), 933
Fair disclosure, 1004
Fair Labor Standards Act (FLSA), 958, 960
Fair use, 879
Fair value, 797, 798
False imprisonment, 129
False light, 132
False pretenses, 112
False registration statements, 995–996
False representation, 215–216
False statement, inclusion, 679, 680
Falsity, knowledge, 217
Family and Medical Leave Act, 958
Family Entertainment and Copyright Act
   (2005), 880
Faragher v. City of Boca Raton, 969–971
Farm products, 808
   buyers, 816–817
F.A.S. port of shipment, 445
Fault, types, 108

FCC v. Fox Television Stations, Inc., 101–103
FCPA. *See* Foreign Corrupt Practices Act
FDA. *See* Food and Drug Administration
FDCPA. *See* Fair Debt Collection
   Practices Act
Feasibility, 853
Federal Alternative Fines Act, 996, 1023,
   1038, 1043
Federal Arbitration Act (FAA), 55–56
Federal Bankruptcy Act, 43
Federal bankruptcy law, 839–840, 858–860
Federal commerce power, 70
Federal Communications Commission
   (FCC), 923
Federal Computer Fraud and Abuse Act, 111
Federal Consumer Credit Protection Act
   (FCCPA), 926, 927, 930, 932
Federal courts, 42–44, 57–58
Federal Defense of Marriage Act (DOMA),
   overturning, 75, 76
Federal employment discrimination laws, 954f
Federal environmental statutes, 1045f
Federal Fair Housing Act (Title VIII), 1121
Federal fiscal powers, 71–72
   borrowing, 71
   eminent domain, 71–72
   money, coining, 71
   spending power, 71
   taxation, 71
Federal Food, Drug, and Cosmetic Act, 1043
Federal Ins. Co. v. Winters, 326–327
Federal Insecticide, Fungicide, and
   Rodenticide Act (FIFRA), 1042–1043
Federalism, 68
Federal judicial system, 43f
Federal jurisdiction, 45–46, 47f
   concurrent federal jurisdiction, 46
   exclusive federal jurisdiction, 46
Federally regulated common carriers,
   securities, 988
Federal Organizational Corporate Sentencing
   Guidelines, 109
Federal question, 46
Federal Reporter, 9
Federal Securities and Exchange Act
   (1934), 709
Federal Securities Code, 9
Federal securities law, 1024–1028
Federal Supplement, 9
Federal supremacy, 68
Federal Trade Commission (FTC),
   904–905, 907
   rule, holder in due course rights, 566f
Federal Trade Commission (FTC) Act,
   904–905, 907
   remedies, 924
   standards, 924
Federal Trade Commission v. Ruberoid Co.,
   9, 90
Federal Trademark Dilution Act (1995), 877
Federal Trust Indenture Act (1939), 731

Federal Unemployment Tax Act, 957, 958
Federal warranty protection, 924–925
Federal Water Pollution Control Act, 1040
Fee estates, 1101–1102
   base fee estate, 1101–1102
   qualified fee estate, 1101–1102
Fee simple estates, 1101
Fellow servant rule, 957
Felony, 109
Ferrell v. Mikula, 138–139
Fictitious payee rule, 554–555
Fidelity bond, 821
Fiduciary, 216, 375
   duty, RUPA provision, 633
   relationship, 1139
Fiduciary duty, 376–378, 767
   confidential information, 377
   conflicts of interest, 377
   duty not to compete, 377
   duty to account for financial benefits,
      377–378
   financial benefits, accounting duty, 377–378
   misappropriation, 377
   partners, 633–634
   principal, remedies, 378
   promoters, 712
   self-dealing, 377
Fifth Amendment, 117
Filing time priority, 814
Final credit, 603
Finance leases, 423–424
Financial benefits, accounting duty, 377–378
Financial institution, liability, 611
Financial interest, 682
Financial structure, 730–741
Financing function, 536
Financing statement, filing, 811–813
   content, 812
   duration, 812–813
   place, 813
Fire
   coverage, types, 1078
   friendly fire, 1078
   hostile fire, 1078
Fire and property insurance, 1078–1079, 1088
   co-insurance clauses, 1078–1079
Firm name, 629
Firm offers, 194, 428
First Amendment, 73–75
   commercial speech, 74
   corporate political speech, 73–74
   defamation, 74–75
First assignee in point of time, 318
First-in, first-out (FIFO) accounting
   method, 561
First sale doctrine, 879
First Bank v. Brumitt, 327–328
First State Bank of Sinai v. Hyland, 285–286
Fisher v. University of Texas at Austin, 77
Fish producers, unsecured claims, 843
Fitness, implied warranty, 487, 488

Fixtures, 808, 1075–1076
  factors, relevance, 1075
Flagrant trespassers, 152
F.O.B. place of destination, 446
F.O.B. place of shipment, 445
Food and Drug Administration (FDA), 922–923
Food Quality Protection Act (FQPA), 1042
Foreclosure, 1126
Foreign agents, 1064
Foreign corporations, 709
Foreign Corrupt Practices Act, 997, 1002, 1063
  antibribery provision, 1006
Foreign governments, actions (jurisdiction), 1057–1059, 1065
Foreign investment property, taking, 1058
Foreign limited liability companies, 680–682
Foreign limited partnerships, 677
Foreign official, definition, 1006
Foreseeability, 153–154
Foreseeable plaintiffs, 1022–1023
Foreseen class of users test, 1022
Foreseen users test, 1022
Forged signature, negligence (impact), 584
Forgery, 114
Form, 430f, 536
  battle, 200, 428
Formal contracts, 178
Formal rulemaking, 92
Forward-looking statements, 995, 1002
Fourteenth Amendment, 708, 1074
Fourth Amendment, 116
Fox v. Mountain West Electric, Inc., 180–182
FQPA. *See* Food Quality Protection Act
Frank B. Hall & Co., Inc. v. Buck, 139–140
Frankfurter, Felix, 8
Fraud, 214–217, 220–221, 824
  antifraud provisions, 996
  bank fraud, 112
  exertion, 825
  fraud in the execution, 215
  impact, 1142
  mail fraud, 112
  nonfraudulent misrepresentation, 217–218
  statute of frauds, 290, 824
  tort, damages, 360
  wire fraud, 112
Fraud in the inducement, 215–217
  deception, intention, 217
  fact, 216–217
  false representation, 215–216
  falsity, knowledge, 217
  justifiable reliance, 217
  materiality, 217
Fraudulent misrepresentation (economic interests), 133
Fraudulent transfers, 847
Freedom of contract, 427
Freedom of Information Act (FOIA), 96

Freehold estates, 1101–1103, 1112
  types, 1104f
Freeman v. Quicken Loans, Inc., 937–938
Free-writing prospectus, 987
Friendly fire, 1078
Frustration of purpose doctrine, 340
F.T.C. Motion Picture Advertising Service Co., 905
FTC v. Wyndham Worldwide Corp., 935–937
Full faith and credit, 53
Full performance, 825–826
  noncompliance, effect, 297
Full warranty, 924
Funds transfers, 602
  consumers, 609–611
  parties, involvement, 613f
Fungible goods, 466, 1082
Furlong v. Alpha Chi Omega Sorority, 456–457
Future interests, 1102
  remainders, 1102–1103
  reversions, 1102
Future services, contracts, 734

G

Gaddy v. Douglass, 389–390
Galleon Group, violations, 14
Galler v. Galler, 709, 759
Gambling statutes, 255
Gap creditors, unsecured claims, 843
Garnishment, 53
  prejudgment garnishment, remedy, 856
GCC. *See* Gulf Cooperation Council
General contracts provisions, 296–297
General gifts, 1146
General intangibles, 809
Generally Accepted Auditing Standards (GAAS), 1021
General partners, 677–679
  limited partners, comparison, 680f
General partnerships, 626
  characteristics, 625f
  dissolution, 648, 660–661
    RUPA, usage, 652
  dissolution (UPA), 657–658, 660–661
  formation, 624, 628, 638
  internal relations, 624
  operation, 648
  selection, factors, 625–626
General verdict, 52
Generic name, 875–876
Genetic Information Discrimination Act (GINA), 954–955
Geographic market, 900
Georg v. Metro Fixtures Contractors, Inc., 573–575
Gift, 1076–1077
  acceptance, 1077
  classification, 1077
  delivery, 1076
  general gifts, 1146

  intent, 1077
  specific gifts, 1146
Global Crossing, scandal, 20, 110, 1003
Going private transactions, 789–790
  management buyout, 789, 790
Golden Rule, 17
Good conduct, duty, 376
Good faith, 193, 425, 766
  Chapter 11 bankruptcy, 852
  conflict of interests, absence, 767
  holder in due course, 561
  purchaser, 467
Good persons, 18
Goods, 295, 808
  acceptance, 432, 450
  accepted goods breach, damages recovery, 519
  bulk, sales, 472, 474
  carriers, 1084
  consumer goods, 808, 811
  damages, recovery, 513
  definition, 423
  delivery, 432
    cessation, 512
    stopping, 512–513
    withholding, 512
  description, 486
  entrusting, 469, 469f
  fungible goods, 466, 1082
  goods in possession of bailee, 471–472
  goods-oriented remedies, 512, 517
  identification, 513
  identified goods, casualty, 451
  movement, absence, 466
  noninventory goods, PMSI, 816
  partial destruction/deterioration, 451
  physical movement, 466
  reclamation, 516
  resale, 513
  sale, 295, 297
  sale or return, 471
  security interest, 932
    enforcement, 519
  title transfer, power, 466
  totally lost/damaged, 451
  value
    affirmation, 486
    differences, 519
  voidable title, 467–469
  void title, 467–469
Governing law, 424
Government
  contract clause, 73
  due process, 75
  First Amendment, 73–75
  foreign governments, actions (jurisdiction), 1057–1059
  fourth branch, 90
  limitations, 72–77, 73f, 78
  powers, 69–72, 72f, 78
  regulation, reduction (social responsibility arguments), 22

Government in the Sunshine Act, 96
Grain producers, unsecured claims, 843
Gramm-Leach-Bliely Financial
    Modernization Act (GLBA), 923
Grant, bargain, and sell (phrase usage), 1123
Gratuitous agency, 375, 376
Greene v. Boddie-Noell Enterprises, Inc.,
    504–505
Greenhouse gases, 1040
Griffin v. Jones, 695–697
Gross v. FBL Financial Services, Inc., 953
Guarantors, 821
Gulf Cooperation Council (GCC), 1056

H

Habitability, implied warranty, 1107, 1122
Hadfield v. Gilchrist, 1093–1094
Hadley v. Baxendale, 355
Halla Nursery, Inc. v. Baumann-Furrie & Co.,
    1022
Hamilton v. Lanning, 864–866
Handicapped person, definition, 953
Hardship
    discharge, 853
        granting, 855
    particular hardship, 1127
Harm, 154–155, 159
    economic interests, 132–133, 135
    person, 127–128, 135
    personal property, 132
    plaintiff proof, 148
    property, 131–132, 135
    right of dignity, 129–131, 135
Harris v. Looney, 722–723
Harris v. Viegelahn, 863–864
Hart-Scott-Rodino Act of 1976, 902
Hazardous air pollutants, 1040, 1047
Hazardous substances, 1042–1045
    Federal Insecticide, Fungicide, and
        Rodenticide Act (FIFRA), 1042–1043
    Resource Conservation and Recovery Act
        (RCRA), 1044
    Superfund, 1044
    Toxic Substances Control Act (TSCA),
        1042, 1043
Heinrich v. Titus-Will Sales, Inc., 478–479
Herfindahl-Hirschman Index (HHI), 902
Heritage Bank v. Bruha, 546–547
Herrod v. Barnard, 1090–1092
Hochster v. De La Tour, 344–345
Hoffmann-La Roche Ltd. v. Empagran S.A.,
    1061
Holder, 552, 560
    defenses, availability, 568f
    negotiation, 552–555
    notice, discharge, 564
Holder in due course, 537, 559, 570
    alterations, 567f
        effects, 566f
    antecedent debt, 561

authenticity, questioning, 562–563
claim/defense, notice, 562
defenses, availability, 568f
execution, fraud, 564
executory promise, 561
fraudulent alteration, 565
good faith, 561
infancy, 564
insolvency proceedings, discharge, 564
instrument
    notice, 562
    overdue, notice, 562
notice, absence, 561–562
payee, comparison, 563
personal defenses, 565–566
preferred position, 563–566, 570
real defenses, 563–565
requirements, 559–563, 570
rights
    FTC rule, 568f
    limitations, 566–570
rules, demonstration, 565
shelter rule, 563
status, 563, 570
transferee requirement, 559–560
unauthorized signature, 564–565
value, 560–561
void obligations, 564
Holdover securities, 763
Holographic wills, 1146
Home equity line of credit (HELOC), 929
Home Equity Loan Consumer Protection Act
    (HELCPA), 929
Home equity loans (consumer credit
    transactions), 928
Home Mortgage Disclosure Act (HMDA), 927
Home Rentals Corp. v. Curtis, 1113–1114
Horizontal agreements, 898
Horizontal merger, 901
Horizontal privity, 490
Horizontal restraints, 897
Hospital Corporation of America v. FTC,
    913–915
Hospitalization Insurance (Medicare), 957
Hostile fire, 1078
Household Credit Services, Inc. v. Pfennig,
    937–938
Hun v. Cary, 766
Husky International Electronics, Inc. v. Ritz,
    860–861
Hybrid rulemaking, 92

I

Ianelli v. Powers, 1107
Identification, 465–466
Identified goods
    casualty, 451
    recovery, 518
Illegal agreement, 254
Illegal bargains, 254

Illegality
    effect, 258–260
    exceptions, 259
    restitution, 259
    subsequent illegality, 340
    unenforceability, general rule, 259
Illegal per se, 897
Illinois v. Gates, 116
Illusory promises (legal sufficiency),
    236–237
Image replacement document (IRD),
    539, 607
Imminently hazardous products, recall, 921
Impairment of recourse, 824–825
Implied assumption, 155
Implied bailment, 1082
Implied contracts, 175–176
Implied grant/reservation, 1111
Implied-in-fact conditions, 335
Implied-in-law conditions, 335
Implied trusts, 1140–1141
Implied warranties, 486–487, 1122
    fitness, 487, 488
    implied warranty of authority, 405–406
    implied warranty of habitability, 1107
Implied warranties (assignor), 318
Import-Export Clause, 70–71
Impossibility, 339–340
    commercial impractability, 340
    objective impossibility, 339
    purpose, frustration, 340
    restitution, availability, 340
    subjective impossibility, 339
    subsequent illegality, 340
Impostor rule, 554
Improper means, 874
Improper threats, 213–214
Incidental beneficiary, 321, 322
Incidental damages, 353
    recovery, 514, 519
Income, allocation, 1142, 1143f
Income bonds, 731
Incoming partner, liability, 652, 660
Incompetency (offer), 196
Incompetent persons, 278, 279
    mental illness/defect, 278
    nonadjudicated incompetents,
        incapacity, 279f
    person underguardianship, 278
Incompetent principal, contract liability, 407
Incorporation
    articles, 713
    charter, bylaws (comparison), 713f
    common law approach, 714
    defects, 714–715, 719
    formalities, 712–713, 718–719
    incorporators, impact, 712
    name, selection, 712
    organizational meeting, 713
    state selection, 712
    statutory approach, 714–715

Incorrect indorsements, 558
Indemnification, 379
    mandatory indemnification, 768
    right, 403, 636
Indenture, 731
Independent contractor, 373, 403
    torts, 404
Indictment, 116
Indirect infringer, 882
Indispensable paper, 808–809
Individual debtor, discharge (absence), 854
Individual mandate, 70
Indorsements, 555–558, 569–570, 604
    blank indorsements, 556
    collecting banks, 604–605
    formal requirements, 557–558
    incorrect indorsements, 558
    misspelled indorsements, 558
    placement, 557–558, 558f
    qualified indorsements, 557
    restrictions, problems, 557
    restrictive indorsements, 556–557
    special indorsements, 556
    types, 557f
    unauthorized indorsement, 608
    unqualified indorsements, 557
Indorsers, 585–586
Inducement, fraud, 215–217
Infancy, 564
Inferior trial courts, 44
Informal contracts, 178
Informal rulemaking, 92
Information, 116
    disclosure, 96
    Freedom of Information Act (FOIA), 96
    Government in the Sunshine Act, 96
    Privacy Act of 1974, 96
Inform, duty, 376
Inheritance tax, imposition, 1148
Initial public offering (IPO), 987
Injunctions, 7, 357
    issuance, 874
Innkeepers, 1084
Innocent misrepresentation, 218
In personam jurisdiction (personal
        jurisdiction), 48
Inquisitorial system, 7
In Re Apa assessment fee litigation, 185–186
In Re L.B. Trucking, Inc., 499–500
In Re Magness, 324
In rem jurisdiction, 49
In Re The Score Board, Inc., 281–283
Inside information, trading (party ban), 1004f
Insider trading, 1002
    civil monetary penalties, 1005
    express insider trading liability, 1004
Insolvency, 846
    bankruptcy meaning, 512
    definition, 512
    equity meaning, 512
    goods reclamation, 516

proceedings, discharge, 564
    seller insolvency, identified goods
        recovery, 518
Insolvent, term, 738
Inspection, 449–450
Instruments, 110, 808
    acceleration, 543
    forging, 825
    negotiation, criteria, 540
Insurable interest, 466, 1080
Insurance
    clauses, 1079
    co-insurance clauses, 1078–1079
    concealment, 1081
    contracts, 1079–1081, 1088
        insurable interest, 1080
        offer/acceptance, 1079
        termination, 1081
    contractual undertaking, 1078
    estoppel, 1081
    fire and property insurance, 1078–1079
    insurer, defenses, 1080–1081
    misrepresentation, 1080
    other insurance clauses, 1079
    policies
        securities, 988
        types, 1079
    premiums, 1080
    private nuisance, 1035–1036
    property insurance, 1074
    waiver, 1081
Insurer, defenses, 1080–1081
Intangible property, 1075
Intangibles, 809
    accounts, 809
    general intangibles, 809
Intellectual property (IP)
    characteristics, 883f
    protection, 872, 1062
Intended beneficiary, 320–322
    rights, 322
Intent, 126–127
    flowchart, 127f
    offer, 191–192
Intentional torts, 125
    consent, 134
    defenses, 134–135
    list, 134f
    privilege, 134–135
Intention to deceive, 217
Interest
    competing interests, 814–818
    contract remedies protection, 352
    financial interest, 682, 683
    future interest, 1102
    insurable interest, 466
    management interest, 683
    nonpossessory interests, 1109–1112
    security interest, 466
    unity, 1108
Intermediary banks, 603, 612

Intermediate test, 72, 77
Internal Revenue Service (IRS) Restructuring
        and Reform Act, 1024
International Anti-Bribery and Fair
        Competition Act, 1063
International arbitration, 56
International business law, 1055
International Centre for the Settlement of
        Investment Disputes, creation, 1060
International Chamber of Commerce,
        arbitration rules, 1060
International contracts, 173–174, 1061
International Court of Justice (ICJ),
        1055–1056
International environment, 1055–1057, 1064
International Monetary Fund (IMF),
        1059, 1060
International treaties, 1056–1057
Interpretation, defining, 299–300
Interstate Land Sales Full Disclosure Act
        (ILSA), 925
Inter-Tel Technologies, Inc. v. Linn Station
        Properties, LLC, 723–725
Inter vivos gift, 1077
Inter vivos trust, 1140
Intestate, meaning, 1146
Intestate succession, 1147, 1150
In the Matter of 1545 Ocean Ave., LLC,
        698–700
In the Matter of the Estate of Rowe, 1151–1153
Intoxicated persons, 278
    incapacity, 279f
Intrastate issues, 993
Intuitionism, 18
Inventory, 808
    PMSI, 816
Investment contract, 985
Investment property, 809
Investor Protection and Securities Reform
        Act (2010), 755
Invisible hand, 20
Invitee, 152
Involuntary dissolution, 791–792
Involuntary petitions (Chapter 3
        bankruptcy), 841
Irrevocable offers, 428
    consideration, 242
    unilateral contracts, 194
Irrevocable powers, 382
Issuers
    advertising notice, 992
    aggregate amount, raising, 991
    categories, 986
    exempt securities, 988
    exempt transactions (Securities Act of
        1933), 994f, 1008
    ineligibility, 991
    information, filing, 991
    nonreporting issuers, 986, 993, 994
    proxy materials, 1000
    reporting issuers, 994

Items
    alteration, 608
    collection, 602–606, 614
    payment, 606

J
Jasper v. H. Nizam, Inc., 974–977
Jenkins v. Eckerd Corporation, 308–309
Jerman v. Carlisle, McNellie, Rini, Kramer & Ulrich LPA, 940–942
Johnson v. Transportation Agency, 952
Joint adventurers, 633
Joint and mutual wills, 1146
Joint and several liability, 648–649
Joint liability, 649
Joint tenancy, 1108
    sustenance, 1108
Joint venture, 626, 1063
Jones v. Star Credit Corp., 425
Judge-made law, 7
Judgment
    decision, affirming, 43
    default judgment, 50
    judgment on pleadings, 51
    remand, action, 43
    reverse/modify, action, 43
    summary judgment, 51
Judicial bonds, 822
Judicial dissolution, 791–792
Judicial law, 7–8
Judicial lien, 842, 847
Judicial review, 7, 68
    administrative agencies, 94–95
    fact, questions, 95
    law, questions, 95
    requirements, 94–95
Jumpstart Our Business Startups Act of 2012 (JOBS Act), 987, 989, 1003
    private right of action, addition, 991
    Regulation A, 991
    Section 4(a)(6), addition, 988, 991
Junk bond, 731
Junk collateral, 811
Jurisdiction, 45, 58
    attachment jurisdiction (quasi in rem jurisdiction), 48, 49
    concurrent federal jurisdiction, 46
    exclusive federal jurisdiction, 46
    exclusive state jurisdiction, 46
    federal jurisdiction, 45–46, 47f
    flowchart, 49f
    jurisdiction over the defendant, 48
    jurisdiction over the parties, 47–49
    in personam jurisdiction, 48
    in rem jurisdiction, 49
    state jurisdiction, 46–47, 47f
    subject matter jurisdiction, 45–47, 47f
    venue, contrast, 49
Jury instructions, 52
Just compensation, 1128

Justice
    distributive justice, 17
    law, relationship, 3–4
Justifiable reliance, 217
J.W. Hampton Co. v. United States, 71

K
Kalas v. Cook, 306–307
Kant, Immanuel, 17
Keeney v. Keeney, 1150–1151
Kelo v. City of New London, 1132–1133
Kelso v. Bayer Corporation, 503–504
Kimbrell's of Sanford, Inc. v. KPS, Inc., 831
King v. Burwell, 91
King v. Verifone Holding, Inc., 771–772
Kirtsaeng v. John Wiley & Sons, Inc., 887–888
Klein v. Pyrodyne Corporation, 165–167
Kohlberg, Lawrence, 18
    moral development, stages, 19f
Kyoto Protocol, 1046

L
Labor
    dispute, 947–948
    Fair Labor Standards Act (FLSA), 958
    flow, 1059
    law, 947–960
    unfair practices, 949f
Labor Management Relations Act (LMRA) (Taft-Hartley Act), 948
Labor-Management Reporting and Disclosure Act, 948–949
Lading, bills, 1084–1086
Land
    contract provision, 294
    covenants, 1128
    description, 1123
    use, private restrictions, 1128–1130
Landlords, 1103
    fitness for use, 1107
    obligations, 1106–1107
    quiet enjoyment, 1106–1107
    repair, 1107
    transfers, 1104
Land, possessors (duties), 151–153
    second restatement, 151–152
    third restatement, 152–153
Landreth Timber Co. v. Landreth, 985
Landrum-Griffin Act, 948–949
Lanham Act, 874–877
Lapse of time (offer), 193
Larceny, 111–112
Last clear chance, 155
Law
    administrative law, 9
    application, 10
    choice, 46
    civil law, 5
    classification, 4–5, 4f

common law, 7, 173
    offer, 198
constitutional law, 6–7
criminal law, 5
    application, 113
    definition, 2–3
environmental law, 1035
ethics, contrast, 15
functions, 3
governing law, 424
hierarchy, 6f
international business law, 1055
judicial law, 7–8
justice, relationship, 3–4
legislative law, 8–9
morals, relationship, 3, 4f
nature, 2–4
operation, 380–381
private law, 5
procedural law, 5
public law, 5
questions, 95
representations, 217
restatements, 8
sources, 5–9
substantive law, 5
Lawyers Edition, 9
Lead plaintiff, 50
Leahy-Smith America Invents Act, 881
Leasehold estates, 1103–1107, 1112–1113
    creation/duration, 1103–1104
    definite term, 1104
    interests, transfer, 1104–1105
    landlord obligations, 1106–1107
    landlord transfers, 1104
    periodic tenancy, 1104
    tenancy at will, 1104
    tenant obligations, 1106
Leaseholds, 1103
Leases, 422, 491
    consumer leases, 423
    contracts, formation, 427, 434
    definitions, 422–424, 429
    finance leases, 423–424
    law, 423f
    nature, 423, 429
    sublease, 1105
Leegin Creative Leather Products, Inc. v. PSKS, Inc., 898, 909–911
Lefkowitz v. Great Minneapolis Surplus Store, Inc., 9, 203–204
Legacy, 1143
Legal aggregate (partnership), 628–629
Legal analysis, 9–10
Legal benefit, 234
Legal detriment, 234
Legal entity, 707
Legal liability (accountants), 1021, 1025
Legal monopolies, 20
Legal procedure, misuse, 131
Legal sanctions, 3

Legal sufficiency, 234–239, 243
  adequacy, 234–235
  bilateral contracts, 235–236
  conditional promises, 237
  exclusive dealing contracts, 237
  illusory promise, 236–237
  liquidated debt, settlement, 238–239
  output contract, 236
  preexisting contracts, modification,
    237, 238f
  preexisting contractual obligation,
    237–239
  preexisting public obligation, 237
  requirements contracts, usage, 236
  substituted contracts, 238
  unilateral contracts, 235
  unliquidated debt, settlement, 239
Legislative control (administrative
    agencies), 95
Legislative law, 8–9
*Leibling, P.C. v. Mellon PSFS (NJ) National
    Association*, 616–617
"Lemon Laws," 910–925
Lessee, 1103
Lessor, 1103
Letters of credit, 1061
Leveraged buyout (LBO), 790
Liability
  absolute liability, 1084
  agent assumption, 406
  civil liability, 1005
  conditions precedent, 586–588
  contractual liability, 401, 583
    types, 588f
  corporation, liability, 109–110
  crimes, 717, 719
  criminal liability (principal), 404–405
  direct liability (principal), 402–403
  dishonor, 586–587
    notice, 587–588
    presentment/notice, 588
  dissolution, 654
  external liability, 626
  fault, absence, 108
  financial institutions, 611
  imposition, 492
  joint and several liability, 648–649
  joint liability, 649
  liability without fault, 108
  limitation, 686, 686f
    bailee right, 1083
  limited partnership, 679
  parties, 583
  primary liability, 583
  primary parties, 585
  products liability, 484
  scope, 159
    plaintiff proof, 148
    proximate cause, 153–154
  secondary liability, 583
  secondary parties disclaimer, 586

shares, 735
strict liability, 147, 157–158
termination, 588–589, 594
  cancellation/renunciation, 589
  payment, 589
  payment tender, 589
tort liability (principal), 402–404
torts, 717, 719
transfer, 591f
unlimited personal liability, 651
usage, 588
vicarious liability, 109
  principal, 403–404
warranty basis, 589
warranty liability, 583
Libel, 129
Libertarians, impact, 17
Liberty, 75
Licensee, 152
Licenses
  compulsory licenses, 879
  regulatory license, 255
  revenue license, 255
Licensing statutes, 254–255
Lie detector tests, 956–957
Lien creditors
  competing interests, 817
  priority, 817–818
Lien theory, adoption, 1124
Life estates, 1102
Limited liability, 679, 707
Limited liability company (LLC), 625–627,
    675, 680–686, 688–690
  assets, distribution, 685
  authority, 685
  causes, 684
  characteristics, 625f
  contribution, 681
  conversions, 686
  creditor protection, 685
  definition, 681
  derivative actions, 683
  dissociation, 684
  dissolution, 684–685
  distributions, 682
  duties, 683
  exceptions, 684
  filing, 681
  foreign limited liability companies, 682
  formation, 681–682
    authorization, 624
  information, 683
  interest, 985
    assignment, 683–684
  law, application, 683
  liabilities, 684
  management, 682
  manager-managed LLCs, 683
  member-managed LLCs, 683
  members, 681
    rights, 682–683

mergers, 686
name, 681
operating agreement, 681
profit and loss (P&L) sharing, 682
voting, 683
winding up, 684–685
withdrawal, 682
Limited liability limited partnership (LLLP),
    627, 687
Limited liability partnership (LLP), 627,
    686–687, 687f
  designation, 686
  formalities, 686
  liability limitation, 686–687, 686f
Limited offers, 989–990
  excess, limit, 989–990
  private placements, 989
Limited partners, general partners
    (comparison), 680f
Limited partnership, 626–627, 675–680,
    687–688
  assets distribution, 680
  associates, selection, 678
  certificate, filing, 676
  characteristics, 625f
  contributions, 676
  control, 677
  definition, 676
  derivative actions, 679
  dissolution, 680
  distribution, 678–679
  duties, 679
  foreign limited partnerships, 677
  formation, 676–677
    defect, 676–677
  general partner, 679
  information, 679
  interest, assignment, 678
  law, application, 683
  liabilities, 679–680
  loans, 679
  name, 676
  profit and loss (P&L) sharing, 678
  rights, 678–679
  voting rights, 678
  winding up, 680
  withdrawal, 678
Limited warranty, 924
Liquidated damages, 354–355
Liquidated debt, settlement, 238–239
Liquidating dividends, 738
Liquidation, 793, 847–851
  conversion, 848
  discharge, 849, 851
  dismissal, 848
  estate distribution, 848–849
  preferences, 736
  proceedings, 847
Living wills, 1147
Long-arm statutes, 48
Long-run profits (social responsibility
    arguments), 22

Loss, risk, 465, 469–472, 474
  breaches, 470
    absence, 470–471
    buyer breach, 470
    passage, 473f
    seller breach, 470
    trial sales, 470–471
Lost profit, 514
Lost property, 1077
Louisiana v. Hamed, 121–122
Love v. Hardee's Food Systems, Inc., 161–163
Loyalty, duty, 1141–1142
Loyalty, duty (directors/officers), 767–768
  interests, conflict, 767

M

Mackay v. Four Rivers Packing Co., 305–306
Madison Square Garden Corp., Ill. v. Carnera, 366–367
Madoff, Bernie, 14
Madrid Protocol, 876, 1063
Magnetic Ink Character Recognition (MICR), 605, 607
Magnuson-Moss Warranty Act, 489
  flowchart, 925f
  provisions, 923–924
Mail fraud, 112
Main purpose doctrine, 293
Major rule, 95
Makers, 539–540, 579
Mala in se, 109
Mala prohibita, 109
Management
  buyout, 790
  compensation, 762–763
  interest, 682
  partnership participation right, 637
  structure, 753
    examples, 755f
Manager-managed LLCs, 683
  member-managed LLCs, comparison, 684f
Mandatory indemnification, 768
Mandatory safety standards, 922
Manifest system, 1044
Manufacturing defect, 492, 494
Marbury v. Madison, 68
Marketable title, 1122
Market price
  contract price, difference, 518
  unpaid contract price, difference, 513
Market rent
  old rent due, present values (difference), 513
  present value, old rent due (difference), 518
Markets
  access (consumer credit transactions), 927–932
  allocation (Sherman Act), 898
  concentration, 902

Market share, 900
Mark Line Industries, Inc. v. Murillo Modular Group, Ltd., 594–596
Marks, 875, 876
  usage, 876
Maroun v. Wyreless Systems, Inc., 225–226
Marriage provision, 293–294
Marsh v. Alabama, 69
Martin v. Melland's Inc., 480
Mass layoff, definition, 958
Material breach, 336–337
Materiality, 217
Material matters, 995
Material misrepresentation, 217
Material misstatement, 1002
Material omission, 1002
Matrixx Initiatives, Inc. v. Siracusano, 1013–1015
Maxims, 8
Mayo Foundation for Medical Education and Research v. United States, 97–98
McCarran-Ferguson Act, 1078
McCormick on Evidence, 94
McCulloch v. Maryland, 68
McCutcheon v. Federal Election Commission, 74
McDonnell Douglas Corp. v. Green, 950
McDowell Welding & Pipefitting, Inc. v. United States Gypsum Co., 345–346
Means test, 848
Mediation, 56
  comparison, 55f
Mediation-arbitration (med-arb), 56
Member-managed LLCs, 684
  comparison, 684f
Memorandum, 296
Mens rea (mental fault), 108
Mental capacity, 1144
Mental disability, 149
Mental fault, degrees, 108f
Mental illness/defect, 278
Mercado Comun del Cono Sur (MERCO-SUR), 1056
Merchants
  definition, 194, 426, 472
  goods
    buyer, 450
    entrusting, 469, 469f
  rules, applicability, 426f
  sales, 426
  sellers, 491
    implied warranty, 486
  written confirmation, 297
  written merchant confirmation, 431
Merged corporation, 788–789
Merged entity, 685
Mergers, 788–789
  concentration, change, 902
  conglomerate merger, 901
  horizontal merger, 901
  merger clause, 298

short-form merger, 789
vertical merger, 901
Mergers (Clayton Act), 901–903
Merit system, 949
Merritt v. Craig, 362–363
Metropolitan Life Insurance Company v. RJR Nabisco, Inc., 743–745
Midnight (banking day), 605
Midnight deadline, 603–604
Midwest Hatchery v. Doorenbos Poultry, 526–528
Miller v. McDonald's Corporation, 386–388
Mims v. Arrow Financial Services, LLC, 59
Minimum price, indication, 733
Mini-trial, 56
Minors, 275–279
  age, misrepresentation (liability), 277
  contracts
    liability, 275–277
    tort, connection (liability), 277–278
  disaffirmance, 275–276
  incapacity, 279f
  necessaries, liability, 277
  sales, 468
Mirror image (offer), 198
Mirror image rule, 428
Mirvish v. Mott, 1092–1093
Misappropriation, 377
  DTSA definition, 874
Misdemeanor, 109
Mislaid property, 1077
Misleading proxy statements, 1005–1006
Misrepresentation, 218f
  innocent misrepresentation, 218
  material misrepresentation, 217
  negligent misrepresentation, 218
  nonfraudulent misrepresentation, 217–218, 221
  remedies, 359–360, 362
    contract law, 360
    restitution, 360
    tort law, 360
Misspelled indorsements, 558
Mistake, 218–221
  fault, effect, 220
  mistake of fact, 114
  mutual mistake, 218–219
  risk, assumption, 220
  terms, meaning, 220
  unilateral mistake, 219
Misuse, occurrence, 494
Mixed-motive case, 951
Mode Code of Evidence, 9
Model Business Corporation Act (MBCA), 706, 710, 733
  Amendments (1969), 753
Model Land Development Code, 9
Model Penal Code, 9, 109
Model Professional Corporation Supplement, 710
Modification, agreement, 824

Modified comparative responsibility, 493
Modify, judicial action, 43
Monetary damages, 352–356, 360
    certainty, 355–356
    compensatory damages, 353
    foreseeability, 355
    limitations, 355–356
    liquidated damages, 354–355
    mitigation, 356
    nominal damages, 353–354
    punitive damages, 354
    reliance damages, 354
Money
    coining, 71
    money-oriented remedies, 512, 517
    term, usage, 542
Monopolies, 899–900
    creation, 901
    power, 900, 901
    types, 20
Monopolization, 899–900
    attempts, 900–901
    conspiracies, 901
Montana Food, LLC v. Todosijevic, 693–694
Montreal Protocol on Substances that Deplete
        the Ozone Layer, 1046
Moore v. Kitsmiller, 164–165
Moral agents, 19
Moral development
    levels, 18
    stages (Kohlberg), 19f
Moral obligation, 240–241
Morals, law (relationship), 3, 4f
Morrison v. National Australia Bank Ltd.,
        1068–1069
Mortgage
    assumption, 821, 822f
    bonds, 731
    concept, 1124
    form, 1124
    interests, transfer, 1125
    regulation, 1125
Mortgage Disclosure Improvement Act
        (MDIA), 929–930
Mortgagee, 1124
    fundamental rights, 1125f
    mortgage interests transfer, 1125
Mortgage Reform and Anti-Predatory
        Lending Act, 930
Mortgagor, 1124
    fundamental rights, 1125f
    mortgage interests transfer, 1125
Most-favored nation provision, GATT, 1057
Motion for a new trial, granting, 52
Motion for judgment notwithstanding the
        verdict, granting, 52
Motor vehicles, usage, 1038–1039
*Mountain Peaks Financial Services, Inc. v.
        Roth-Steffen*, 325–326
Multilateral Investment Guarantee Agency
        (MIGA), 1059

Multinational enterprises (MNEs), forms,
        1064
Multiple product order, 921
Murphy v. BDO Seidman, LLP, 1028–1030
Mutual assent, 174, 190
    application, 195
    flowchart, 199f
    manifestation, 427–429, 433–434
Mutuality of obligation, 236
Mutual mistake, 218–219
Mutual rescission, 338

N

Named plaintiff, 50
National Ambient Air Quality Standards
        (NAAQSs), 1038–1039
National Association of Attorney General
        (NAAG), activity, 919–920
National Business Services, Inc. v. Wright, 257
National Conference of Commissioners on
        Uniform State Laws, 55
National Contingency Plan (NCP), 1044
National Cooperative Research Act, 898
National Environmental Policy Act (NEPA),
        1037–1038, 1046–1047
National environmental policy, NEPA
        declaration, 1037
*National Federation of Independent Business v.
        Sebelius*, 71
National Highway Traffic Safety
        Administration (NHTSA), 923
National Labor Relations Act (NLRA),
        947–948
National Labor Relations Board (NLRB), 948
Nationally Recognized Statistical Rating
        Organizations (NRSROs), 731
National Pollutant Discharge Elimination
        System (NPDES), 1041
National Reporter System, 9
National Securities Markets Improvement Act
        (1996), 997, 1003
Nationsbank of Virginia, N.A. v. Barnes, 547
Natural monopolies, 20
Necessaries, liability, 277
Necessary and Proper Clause, 68
Necessary, term, 277
Negligence, 108, 147, 148, 1022
    action, defenses, 156f
    comparative negligence, 158
    contributory negligence, 155, 158
    defenses, 155–157, 159
    flowchart, 150f
    impact, 565, 584
    negligence per se, 149
        flowchart, 150f
    pure comparative negligence, 155
    risk, assumption, 155–156
Negligent hiring, 403
Negligent misrepresentations, 218
    third parties, accountant liability, 1023f

Negotiability, 536–538, 545
    terms/omissions, impact, 544–545
    title documents, 1086
    words, 544
Negotiable instruments
    agreements, reference, 541–542
    ambiguity, 544
    certificates of deposit, 540
    checks, 539
    completion, absence, 544–545
    credit function, 536
    dating, 544
    definite time requirement, 543
    drafts, 538f
    financing function, 537
    fixed amount, requirement (purpose), 542
    formal requirements, 540–546
    law, development, 537
    money, term (usage), 542
    notes, 539–540
    order/bearer, payment, 544
    particular fund doctrine, 542
    payable on demand requirement, 542–543
    payment promise/order, 541
    requirement list, 540
    signature, 541
    transfer, law (application), 559
    types, 538–540, 545
    unconditional promise/order, 541–542
    undertaking/instruction, absence, 542
    usage, 537f
    writing, 540
Negotiated Rulemaking Act, 92
Negotiation, 56, 569
    assignment, comparison, 537–538
    bearer paper, 553
    due negotiation, 1086
    fictitious payee rule, 554–555
    holder, 552–555
    impostor rule, 554
    order paper, 553–555
    preliminary negotiations (offer), 192
    rescission, impact, 555
Net assets, 738
    test, 739
Neugebauer v. Neugebauer, 223–224
*New England Rock Services, Inc. v. Empire
        Paving, Inc.*, 246–248
New rent, 513
    present values, old rent due (difference),
        517–518
New source performance standards, 1041
New source standards, 1040
    hazardous air pollutants, 1040
    new vehicles, 1040
New York Stock Exchange, 790
New York Times Co. v. Sullivan, 74
Nichols v. Healthsouth Corporation, 773–774
No arrival, no sale terms, 446
No Electronic Theft Act (NET Act), 880
Nominal damages, 353–354

Nonacceptance, damages recovery, 513–514
Nonadjudicated incompetents, incapacity, 279f
Nonattainment areas, 1039
Nonbinding arbitration, 56
Noncompliance, effect, 297–298, 302
  full performance, 297
  parol evidence rule, 298
  promissory estoppel, 298
  restitution, 297
Nonconforming uses (zoning), 1127
Nonconstruction contractors, affirmative action plan, 953
Nonconsumer debts, prebankruptcy transfer exception, 846
Nonconsumer transaction, 563–564
Noncontractual promises, 175f
Noncumulative stock, 736
Nondelivery, damages recovery, 518
Nondischargeable debts, 844–845
Nondisclosure (silence), 215
Nonexistent principal, contract liability, 407
Nonfraudulent misrepresentation, 217–218, 221
  tort, damages, 360
Nonfungible securities, 995
Noninventory goods, PMSI, 816
Non-investment-grade bond (junk bond), 731
Nonissuers, exempt transactions, 993–995, 1008
Nonobviousness (patentability criteria), 881
Nonpoint source, 1040
Nonpoint source pollution (Clean Water Act), 1041
Nonpossessory interests, 1109–1113
Nonprofit corporations (not-for-profit corporation), 709
Nonreporting issuers, 986, 993, 994
Nonstatutory composition, 857
Nontariff barriers, governmental usage, 1059
No par value stock, 733
Norcia v. Samsung telecommunications America, LLC, 206–208
Norris-La Guardia Act, 947
North American Free Trade Agreement (NAFTA), 1056
Northern Corp. v. Chugach Electrical Association, 346–347
Northern Pacific Railway Co. v. United States, 897
Notes, 539
  demand note, 539, 586
  example, 539f
  makers, 585
  promissory note, payment promise, 539f
  time note, 539
Not-for-profit charitable organizations, securities, 987
Notice, 381, 1124
  actual notice, 399
  constructive notice, 399–400
  definition, 562
  filing, 811–812

notice of a fact, 380, 400
notice-race states, 1124
Novation, 339
Novelty (patentability criteria), 881
Nozick, Robert, 17
Nuisance, 1035–1036, 1046
  private nuisance, 1035–1036
  property, 131
  public nuisance, 1036
Nuncupative wills, 1146

O
OBB Personenverkehr AG v. Sachs, 1067–1068
Obedience, duty, 376
  directors/officers, 766
  partners, 634
Obergefell v. Hodges, 75, 76
Objective fault, 108
Objective impossibility, 339
Objective satisfaction, 335
Objective standard, 190
Object, legality, 175
Obligation
  advances, 811
  full performance, 825–826
  moral obligation, 240–241
  mutuality, 236
  obligation-oriented remedies, 512, 517
  preexisting contractual obligation, 237–239
  preexisting public obligation, 237
  prior unenforceable obligations, performing (promises), 240–241
  void obligations, 564
Obligee, 315, 316, 319
Obligor, 315, 807
  secondary obligor, 807, 820
Occupational Safety and Health Act, 955–956
Occupational Safety and Health Administration (OSHA), 955–956
Offer, acceptance, 196–197, 201
  communication, 197–198, 201
  effective moment, 198
  general rule, 197
  list, 199f
  prior rejection, 198
  requirements, 201
  silence, usage, 197
Offeree, 190, 235
Offeror, 190, 235
Offers, 190–191
  advertisements, 192
  auction sales, 192
  authorized means, 198
  common law, 198
  communication, 191
  counteroffer, 196
  death/incompetency, 196
  definiteness, 192–193, 427–428
  duration, 193–197, 200–201
  essentials, 191–193, 200

firm offers, 194, 428
intent, 191–192
irrevocable offers, 428
  consideration, 242
  unilateral contracts, 194
lapse of time, 193
limited offers, 989–991
mirror image, 198
offer of proof, 52
option contracts, 194–195
output, 193
preliminary negotiations, 192
promissory estoppel, 195
received, 194
rejection, 196
requirements contracts, 193
revocable offers, duration, 197f
revocation, 193–194
statutory irrevocability, 194
stipulated provisions, 198
subject matter, destruction, 196
subsequent illegality, 196
unauthorized means, 198
variant acceptances, 198–200
Office of Federal Contract Compliance Programs (OFCCP), 953
Officers, 765, 770
  actual express authority, 765
  actual implied authority, 765
  apparent authority, 765
  authority, 765
  business judgment rule, 766–767
  competition duty, absence, 768
  corporate opportunity, 768
  diligence, duty, 766–767
  duties, 765–770
  indemnification, 768
  liability limitation statutes, 768–769
  loans, 767–768
  loyalty, duty, 767–768
  obedience, duty, 766
  ratification, 765
  reliance, 766
  role, 761, 765
  selection/removal, 762, 765
Official bonds, 822
Old-Age and Survivors Insurance (OASI), 957
Old rent due
  new rent present values, difference, 517–518
  present values, difference, 513
Old rent, present values (difference), 513
Omnicare, Inc. v. Laborers District Council Construction Industry Pension Fund, 1011–1013
O'Neil v. Crane Co., 502–503
Open delivery, 427
Open-end credit account, 928
Opening statement, 51
Open policy, 1079
Open price, 427

Open quantity, output/requirement contracts, 427–428
Open terms, 428
    definiteness, 193
Operation of law, usage, 339–341
Opinion, statement, 216
Option contracts, 194–195, 428
Opt out legislation, 844
Oral argument, 53
Oral contract, 290
Order for relief, 841
Order paper
    negotiation, 553–555, 553f
    stolen order paper, 554f
Orders, 93
    charging order, 635
    payment, 544
    stop payment orders, 607
Order to pay, 538f
Ordinary bailee, 1084
Ordinary bankruptcy, 840
Ordinary course, payments, 846
Original promise, 292
Originator, 612
Originator's bank, 612
Orr v. Orr, 77
Other insurance clauses, 1079
Out-of-pocket rule, 360
Output
    contract, legal sufficiency, 236
    offer, 193
Outside directors, 761
Overseas Private Investment Corporation (OPIC), 1058
Ozone layer, international protection, 1046, 1047

P

Palsgraf v. Long Island Railroad Co., 163
Palumbo v. Nikirk, 167
Paper
    demand paper, 542, 562
    time paper, 543, 562
Paperless filing, facilitation, 812
Parent corporation, 716
Parent-subsidiary corporations, 716
Paris Climate Change Conference, 1046
Paris Convention for the Protection of Industrial Property, 875, 882, 1062
Parker v. Twentieth Century-Fox Corp., 61–62
Parlato v. Equitable Life Assurance Society of the United States, 411–412
Parmalat, violations, 14
Parol evidence, 298, 432
Parol evidence rule, 298, 302
    flowchart, 300f
    situations, nonapplication, 298–299
Partial assignments, 316
Participating bonds, 731
Participating preferred shares, 736

Particular fund doctrine, 542
Particular hardship, 1127
Parties, 612
    accommodation party, 583
    acts, 380
    agreement, 470
        absence, 467f
    cooperation, right, 453
    default, 357–358
    discharge by agreement, 338–339, 342
    duties, 319–320
    injury, breach (impact), 357
    involvement, 613f
    jurisdiction, 47–49
    liability, 583
        signature, 583–584
    mutual agreement, 380
    obligations, 451–455
    primary parties, liability, 585
    secondary parties, liability, 585–588
Partners
    care, duty, 634
    comparison, 680f
    copartners, 633
    dissociated partner, binding power, 656
    duties, 633–634, 639
    fiduciary duty, 633–634
    incoming partner, liability, 652, 660
    interest, partnership property (comparison), 636f
    notice, 652, 660
    obedience, duty, 376, 634
    relationships, 632–633, 639, 659–660
    rights, 634–639
    transferable interest, 635
Partnership
    actual implied authority, 650
    agreement, 629–630, 634
        components, 629
    apparent authority, 650
    assignability, 635
    associates, selection right, 637
    association, 630
    binding, authority, 649–650
    books, information/inspection (right), 637–638
    business for profit, 630–631
    capital, 631–632
        return, right, 636
    compensation, right, 637
    continuation, right, 658
    contracts, 648–651, 659
    co-ownership, 631
    creditors, rights, 635
    crimes, 659
        torts, relationship, 651
    definition, 628
    dissociated partners, binding power, 656
    dissociation, 652–653
        effects, 653

    dissolution, 652–655
        effects, 654
        occurrence, 653
    distributions, sharing (right), 636–637
    enforcement rights, 637–638
    entity theory, 628–629
    estoppel, usage, 650–651
    existence, tests, 630–631, 630f
    firm name, 630
    formation, 629–633, 638–639
    general partnership, 626
    indemnification, 651
        right, 636
    interest, assignment, 678
    legal aggregate, 628–629
    limited liability limited partnership (LLLP), 627
    limited partnership, 627
    liquidation, 680
    loyalty, partner duty, 633
    management, participation right, 637
    nature, 628–629, 638
    ownership, characteristics, 635
    partnership at will, 652–653
    partners with third parties, relationship, 648
    partner, transferable interest, 635–636
    profits, sharing (rights), 636
    property, 631–632
        partner interest, comparison, 636f
        rights, 634–635
    statute of frauds, 629–630
    torts, 659
    winding up, 654–655
Partners with third parties, partnership (relationship), 648
Part performance exception, application, 294
Par value stock, 733
Pass-through basis, 625
Patentability, 881
    criteria, 880
Patent Cooperation Treaty, 1062
Patent Law Treaty (PLT), 882, 1062–1063
Patents, 880–882, 884
    design patent, 882
    infringement, 882
    intellectual property, protection, 1062
    issuance, 882
    plant patent, 882
    remedies, 882
Patient Protection and Affordable Care Act (Obamacare), 70, 71
    U.S. Supreme Court examination, 91
Payable on demand requirement, 542–543
Payable to bearer, 544
Payable to order, 544
Pay-by-phone systems, 609
Payee, 538, 540
    fictitious payee rule, 554–555
    indorsement, 554

Payment, 586
  acceptance, 432
  improper payment, subrogation (bank
      right), 607
  noncash means, 536
  obligation, 451
  order, 538f, 612
      execution, errors, 613
      unauthorized payment orders, 613
  ordinary course, prebankruptcy transfer
      exception, 846
  promise, example, 540f
  recovery, 517
  tender, 589
Payor banks, 605–606
  customers
      death/incompetence, 607–608
      duties, 608
      relationship, 606, 614
  disclosure requirements, 607–608
  improper payment, subrogation (bank
      right), 607
  item, payment, 606
  stop payment orders, 607
  substitute check, 606–607
  wholesale electronic funds transfers, 609
Payroll Advance, Inc. v. Yates, 264–265
Peace, breach, 818
Peace River Seed Co-Op. v. Proseeds Mktg,
      524–525
Per capita, 1147, 1148f
Peremptory challenges, 51
Perez v. Mortgage Bankers Ass'n., 99–100
Perfected security interests, 817
  perfected security interests, contrast,
      814–816
  unperfected security interests, contrast, 814
Perfection, 811–814, 828
  automatic perfection, 813–814
  control, 814
  methods, 811, 815f, 828
  priority, 814
  temporary perfection, 814
Perfect tender rule, 337
Performance, 334, 444
  assurance, right, 453
  bonds, 822
  buyer, 449–451
  course, 299
  discharge, 336
  flowchart, 452f
  law, application, 338
  lawsuit, 519
  prevention, 337
  seller, 444–449
  specific performance, 356–357
  substantial performance, 337
  substituted performance, 453
  time, extension, 824
Periodic reporting requirements,
      998–1000

Periodic statements (consumer funds
      transfers), 610
Periodic tenancy, 1104
Perpetual existence, 707
Person
  assault, 128
  battery, 127–128
  defense, 114
  emotional distress, infliction, 128
  estoppel, 564
  false imprisonment, 128
  harm, 127–128, 135
  incompetent persons, 278
  intoxicated persons, 278
  person under guardianship, 278
Personal computer (online) banking, 609
Personal defenses, 564–566
Personal identification number (PIN), 609
Personal jurisdiction, 48
Personal property (chattel), 1075,
      1087–1088
  conversion, 132
  harm, 132
  sale, 356–357
  secured transactions, 806–807, 826–828
  tangible personal property, sale, 1076
  title transfer, 1076–1078, 1087–1088
      will/descent, usage, 1077
  trespass, 132
Personal rights, assignments, 317
Per Stirpes, 1148f
Philip Morris USA v. Williams, 136–137
Physical compulsion, 213
Physical disability, 149
Physical force, 213
Pittsley v. Houser, 435–436
Plaintiff, 5, 10
  conduct (warranties), 490, 493–494
  foreseeable plaintiffs, 1022
Plant patent, 882
Pleadings, 50–51
  appeal, 52–53
  discovery, 51
  enforcement, 53
  judgment, 51
Pledges, 810–811, 813, 1084
PLT. *See* Patent Law Treaty
PMSI. *See* Purchase money security interest
Point-of-sale (POS) systems, 609
Point source, 1040
Point sources (Clean Water Act), 1041
  effluent limitations, 1041
  National Pollutant Discharge Elimination
      System (NPDES), 1041
Possession, 813, 1082
  adverse possession, 1126, 1130
  unity, 1108
Possibility of reverter, 1102
Postconventional level, 18
Postincorporation subscription, 712
Postjudgment remedies, 857

Power
  commerce, state regulation, 70–71
  concentrations, 758–759
  control, 993
  federal commerce power, 70
  federal fiscal powers, 71–72
  government powers, 69–72
  separation, 68–69
      checks/balances, 69f
  spending power, 71
  statutory powers, 716–717
Power given as security, 383
Power of attorney, 374–375
  durable power of attorney, 375
Power of avoidance, loss, 359–360
  delay, 359
  third parties, rights, 359–360
Precatory expression, 1140
Preconventional level, 18
Prediction, fact representation (contrast), 216
Preemption, 68
Preemptive rights, 732–733
Preexisting contracts, modification, 237, 238f
Preexisting contractual duty, 237
Preexisting contractual obligation, 237–239
Preexisting public obligation, 237
Preferential transfers, avoidance, 818
Preferred position (holder in due course),
      563–566
Pregnancy Discrimination Act, 950
Preincorporation subscription, 712
Prejudgment garnishment, remedy, 857
Prejudgment remedies, 856–857
Preliminary hearing, 115
Premises, destruction, 1106
Premiums, 1080
Preponderance, 5
Presale disclosure, 924
Presentment, 586
  warranties on presentment, 591
Prestenbach v. Collins, 365–366
Presupposed condition, failure of, 452–453
Pretrial motions, 50
Pretrial procedure, 51
  summary judgment, 51
Prevention of significant deterioration (PSD)
      areas, 1039
Price discrimination, prohibition, 903
Price fixing, 898
Price recovery, 514
Prima facie case, 950
Prima facie evidence, 876
Primary-benefit test, 1022
Primary liability, 583
Primary-line injury (Robinson-Patman
      Act), 904
Primary parties, liability, 585, 593
Principal, 375
  allocation, 1142, 1143f
  contract liability, 395–401, 407–408
  criminal liability, 404–405, 409

direct liability, 402–403
disclosed principal, 395
    contract liability, 397
duties, 379f, 380
incapacity, 381
remedies, 378
respondeat superior, 403–404
third persons, relationship, 395, 407–409
tort liability, 401–404, 408
torts, 379–380
undisclosed principal, 396
    contract liability, 399f
unidentified principal, 395
    contract liability, 398f
vicarious liability, 403–404
Principal agent
authorized acts, 402–403
duties, 375–378, 383
relationship, 373, 381
unauthorized acts, 403
Principal debtor, 292, 820, 825f
creditor
    relationship, 820–821
    release, 826
defenses, 824, 825f, 825–826, 829
full payment/performance, tender, 826
incapacity, 824
personal defenses, 824–825
surety, relationship, 821
Prine v. Blanton, 1153–1154
Priorities (competing interests), 814–818, 819f
Priority, 842
Prior unenforceable obligations, performing
    (promises), 240–241
Privacy, 131f
appropriation, 130
defenses, 131
false light, 131
intrusion, 130
invasion, 130–131
legal procedure, misuse, 131
private facts, public disclosure, 130–131
Privacy Act of 1974, 96
Private carrier, 1084
Private corporations, 708
Private facts, public disclosure, 130–131
Private insurance, 1035–1036
Private law, 5
Private nuisance, 1035–1036
trespass, difference, 1036
Private placements, 989
Private Securities Litigation Reform Act
    (1995), 1002, 1026
Privilege, 134–135
defense, 129
types, 129
Privity
contracts, 489–490
horizontal privity, 490
vertical privity, 490, 493
Privity (warranties), 493

Probable cause, 116
Probate, 1147–1148
Procedural due process, 75–76
Procedural law, 5
Procedural rules (administrative
    agencies), 92
Procedural unconscionability, 258, 425
Production (documents), 51
Products
alteration, 494
damages, limitations, 494
design defect, 492, 495–496
failure to warn, 495
farm products, 808
    buyers, 816–817
liability, 484
    torts, third restatement, 494–495, 497
    types, 495f
manufacturing defect, 492, 494
misuse/abuse, 494
multiple product order, 921
product line exception, 787
unreasonably dangerous product, 492
Professional bailees, 1083
Professional corporations, 710
Profitability (social responsibility
    arguments), 21
Profit and loss (P&L) sharing, 678
limited liability company (LLC), 682
Profit-and-loss statements, 998
Profit corporations, 708–709
Profits
long-run profits, 22
lost profit, 514
recovery, 1002
share, 631
sharing, right, 636
short-swing profits, 1002–1003
Profits à prendre, 1101, 1111–1112
Promisee, 235, 292, 320
Promises, 235
affirmation, 485–486
collateral, 292
debt payment, 240
enforceability, statute (impact), 241–242
promises made under seal, 241
renunciations, 241
voidable promises, 240
Promisor, 235, 292, 320
Promissory estoppel, 178, 178f, 180, 241
noncompliance, effect, 298
offer, 195
Promissory note, 734
payment promise, 540f
Promoters, 711
contracts, 710–711
fiduciary duty, 712
preincorporation contracts, 711f
Proof, offer, 52
Proper purpose, 760
books/records, 760

Property, 1074, 1087–1088
abandoned property, 1077
accession, 1077
after-acquired property, 811
community property, 1109
confusion, impact, 1077
defense, 114
definition, 75
dividends, 737
fixtures, 1075–1076
harm, 131–132, 135
insurance, 1074, 1078, 1088
intangible property, 1075
investment property, 809
lost property, 1077
mislaid property, 1077
nuisance, 131
personal property, 132, 1075
possession, 1077–1078
real property, 131, 1075
return, bailee absolute liability, 1083
tangible property, 1075
title transfer, gift (usage), 1076
types, 1075–1076, 1076f
Prosecuted, definition, 5
Prospectus, 730, 985
free-writing prospectus, 987
Prosser, William, 150
Providence & Worcester Co. v. Baker, 756
Provision
executor-administrator provision, 293
general contracts provision, 296–297
land contract provision, 294
marriage provision, 293–294
one-year provision, 294
statute of frauds, 292–293
time computation, 294–295
Provisional crediting, 603
Proxies, 682, 758
form, 1000
misleading proxy statements, 1005–1006
solicitations, 1000
statements, 1000
usage, 754
Proximate cause (scope of liability),
    153–154
Prudent person, 1141
Public advantage, meaning, 1128
Public corporations, 708
Public disclosure, private facts, 130–131
Public duty, 237
Public figure, definition, 75
Public float requirement, 986
Public invitee, 152
Publicity, right, 130
Public law, 5
Publicly Available Consumer Product Safety
    Information Database, 922
Publicly held corporations, 709–710, 754
management structure, 755f
Public nuisance, 1036

Public policy
exculpatory clauses, 257
public officials, corruption, 258
tortious conduct, 258
trade, common law restraint, 256–257
unconscionable contracts, 257–258
violations, 256–258, 260
Puffery, 920
Punitive award, 136
Punitive damages, 354
Purchase money security interest (PMSI), 807
inventory, 816
noninventory goods, 815–816
Pure comparative negligence, 155
Pure comparative responsibility, 493
Purpose, frustration, 340

Q
Qualified directors, 767
Qualified fee estate, 1101–1102
Qualified indorsements, 557
Qualified privilege, 129
Quasi contracts (restitution), 178–179, 178f, 180
Quasi in rem jurisdiction (attachment jurisdiction), 49
Questions of fact, 95
Questions of law, 95
Quiet enjoyment, 1106–1107, 1123
Quitclaim, 1123
Quorum, 756, 764
Quo warranto, 714

R
Racketeer Influenced and Corrupt Organizations Act (RICO), 111, 1023
Radlax Gateway Hotel, LLC v. Amalgamated Bank, 861–862
Raffles v. Wichelhaus (Peerless Case), 220
Ratification, 400–401
impact, 401
occurrence, 276
requirements, 400–401
Ratify, term, 275
Rational relationship test, 72, 76
Rawls, John, 17
Raytheon Co. v. Hernandez, 950
Real defenses, 564–565
Real Estate Settlement Procedures Act (RESPA), 929
Real property (realty), 131, 173, 808, 1075
adverse possession, 1126
control, 1121
filings, 812
interests, 1101
law, application, 1110–1111
nuisance, 131

sale, 357
contract, 1121–1122
transfer, 1121, 1129–1130
trespass, 131
zoning, 1126–1127
Reasonable manner, 198
Reasonable person standard, 148–149
children, 148–149
emergencies, standard, 149
mental disability, 149
physical disability, 149
skill/knowledge, superiority, 149
statute, violation, 149
Receipt, 196
Receiving bank, 612
Reciprocal wills, 1146
Recklessness, 128
Record, 296
inspection right, 760
meaning, 1085
Recordation, 1124
Recourse, impairment, 824
Recovery, calculation, 1079
Redemption, right, 1125
Reed v. King, 226–227
Reformation, 7, 356
Regional trade communities, 1056
Registered limited liability partnership (RLLP), 686
Registration, Evaluation and Authorization of Chemicals (REACH), 1043
Regulation A, 991–992, 995
Regulation A+, 991–992
Tier 1, 992
Tier 2, 992
Regulation B, 927
Regulation Crowdfunding, provisions, 991
Regulation D, 989
Regulation FD, 1004
Regulations, 70
commerce, state regulation, 70
Regulation X, amendment, 929
Regulation Z, 928
amendment, 929
Regulatory license, 255
Rehabilitation Act, 953
Reimbursement, 379
surety right, 823
Rejection (buyer), 449–450
Rejection (offer), 196
Re Keytronics, 640–642
Reliance damages, 354
Reliance interest, 352
Remainders, 1102–1103
contingent remainder, 1103
vested remainder, 1102–1103
Remand, judicial action, 43, 53
Remedies, 352, 356–357, 358f
contract law, 360
contractual provisions, impact, 520–523
creditor remedies, 932–933

damages, liquidation/limitation, 520–521
election, 358–359
liberal administration, 427
limitations, 358–359, 362
modification/limitation, agreement (usage), 521
postjudgment remedies, 857
power of avoidance, loss, 359
prejudgment remedies, 857
restitution, 357–358, 360
sales remedies, 512
statute of frauds, 358
statute of limitations, 522
tort law, 360
ultra vires acts, 717
usage, 360, 512
Remittance transfer, 610
Remove, defendant action, 46
Rent
new rent due, 513
old rent, present values (difference), 513
Renunciations, 241
Reorganization. *See* Chapter 11 bankruptcy
Replevin, lawsuit, 518
Reply, 51
Reporting issuers, 994
Reports, misleading statements, 1002
Repose, statute, 494
Repossession, 818–819
Repudiation, damages recovery, 513–514, 518
Request for admissions, 51
Requirements contracts, 193
legal sufficiency, 236
open quantity, relationship, 427–428
Rescission, 925
consumer rights, 925,
contracts, 296
impact, 555
Reservation, 1110
Residue, 1145
Res ipsa loquitur, 153
Resource Conservation and Recovery Act (RCRA), 1042, 1044
Respondeat superior, 403–404
Restatement of Torts, 126, 494–495
Restitution, 361–362
availability, 340
contracts, 276
interest, 352
noncompliance, effect, 297–298
public policy, 259
quasi contracts, 178–179, 178f, 180
Restraint of trade, 256
Restrictive covenants
subdivision involvement, 1129
termination, 1129
validity, 1129
Restrictive indorsements, 556–557
Resulting trusts, 1139, 1141
Revenue license, 255

Reverse discrimination, 951–952
Reverse, judicial action, 43, 53
Reversions, 1102
Reverter, possibility, 1102
Revised Model Business Corporation Act
        (RMBCA), 706–707, 710,
        712–713
    pre-1999 changes, 792f
Revised Residential Landlord and Tenant
        Act, 1104
Revised Uniform Limited Partnership Act
        (ReRULPA), 675–676
Revised Uniform Limited Partnership Act
        (RULPA), 675–678
Revised Uniform Partnership Act (RUPA),
        628–630, 648, 686
    fiduciary duty, 633
    presumptions, 631, 632
Revised Uniform Unincorprated Nonprofit
        Association Act (RUUNAA), 631
Revocable offers, duration, 197f
Revocation
    acceptance, 450
    offer, 193–194
Ricci v. DeStefano, 967–969
Rightful dissociations, 652–653
Right of dignity
    defamation, 129–130
    harm, 129–131
    privacy, invasion, 130–131
Right of publicity, 130
Rights
    assignability, 316
    assignment, 315–319, 322–323
    definition, 4
    intended beneficiary, 322
    nonassignability, 316–317
    successive assignments, 318–319
    vesting, 322
Right-to-work law, 948
Risk
    material increase, assignments
        (impact), 317
    variation (surety), 824
    voluntary assumption, 490,
        493–494, 957
Risk, assumption, 494
    express assumption, 155
    implied assumption, 155–156
    mistakes, 220
    negligence, defenses, 155–156
    strict liability, defenses, 158
*RNR Investments Limited Partnership v.
        Peoples First Community Bank*,
        661–663
Road show, 987
Robbery, 112
Robertson v. Jacobs Cattle Co., 665–666
Robinson-Patman Act, 882, 903–904, 916
    competition, meeting, 904
    cost justification, 904

    primary-line injury, 904
    secondary-line injury, 904
    tertiary-line injury, 904
    violation, 903
Robinson v. Durham, 477
Roosevelt, Franklin Delano, 110
Rosewood Care Center, Inc. v. Caterpillar, Inc.,
        303–304
Rule 10b5-2, 1002, 1026
Rule 10B-5, requisites, 1002
Rule 144, 993
Rule 144A, 994–995
Rule 147, 993
Rule 504, 989
Rule 505, 989–990
Rule 506, SEC amendment, 989
Rulemaking
    administrative agencies, 91–92
    administrative rulemaking, 93f
    formal rulemaking, 92
    hybrid rulemaking, 92
    informal rulemaking, 92
Rule of law, 10
Rule of reason test, 897
Rule utilitarianism, 16
Run with the land, phrase, 1128

S

Sackett v. Environmental Protection Agency,
        100–101
Safe deposit boxes, 1084
Safe harbor, 995
    nonexclusive list, 709
    provision, 677, 1001
Salaries, unsecured claims, 843
Sale
    components, 173
    definition, 423
    sale on approval, 471
    sale or return, 471
Sale of goods, 295, 297
    acceptance, 295
    admission, 295
    delivery/payment, 295
    specially manufactured goods, 295
Sales, 422, 472
    contracts, 1121–1123, 1129
        formation, 427, 433–434, 1121–1122
        habitability, implied warranty, 1122
        validation/preservation, 427
    definitions, 423–424, 429
    law, 423f
    nature, 423, 433
    remedies, 512
        law, application, 515
    trial sales, 470–471
    unregistered sales, 995
Sales (merchants), 426
Salman v. United States, 1015–1016
Sample, usage, 486

Sanctions, 3. *See also* Legal sanctions
Sarbanes-Oxley Act (SOX), 20, 110, 762,
        1026–1027
    audit committee impact, 764
    clawback requirements, 763
    rules, adoption, 998
Satisfaction, 339
    objective satisfaction, 335
    subjective satisfaction, 335
Savings account trust, 1140
Savings and loan associations,
        securities, 987
Schmerber v. California, 117
Schoenberger v. Chicago Transit Authority,
        409–410
Schreiber v. Burlington Northern, Inc.,
        1016–1017
Schuette v. BAMN, 77
Scienter, 217, 1002
Scope of liability (proximate cause),
        153–154, 159
    foreseeability, 153–154
    superseding cause, 154
Seasoned issuer, 986
Secondary activity, 948
Secondary liability, 583
Secondary-line injury (Robinson-Patman
        Act), 904
Secondary meaning, 875
    prima facie evidence, 876
Secondary obligor, 807, 820
Secondary parties, liability, 585–588, 593
    acceptance, effect, 586
    conditions, 586–588
    conversion, liability, 588
    disclaimer, 586
    drawers, 585–586
    indorsers, 585–586
Second Prospective Report (EPA), 1038
Section 4(a)(5), 990
Section 12(A)(2), 996
Section 17(A), 996
Section 402A, 490–491
Secured bonds, 731
Secured claims (Chapter 5
        bankruptcy), 842
Secured creditors, competing interests,
        814–816
Secured party, 807
    debtor location, change, 813
    possession, 813
    rights, 807f
Secured transactions, 806–807,
        1124–1126, 1130
    essentials, 807, 826–827
    foreclosure, 1126
    mortgages
        form, 1124
        interests, transfer, 1125
        regulation, 1125
        rights/duties, 1124–1125

Securities
  Civil Liability Under the 1933 and 1934
      Acts, 1007
  civil sanctions, 996, 1006
  communications, 987
  criminal sanctions, 996–997
  definition, 985, 1006
  disclosure, 997–998
      requirements, 986
  emerging growth companies (EGCs), 987
  entitlement, 809
  exempt securities, 987–988, 1008
  false registration statements, 995–996
  federal securities law, 1024–1027
  holders, 992
  integrated disclosure, 986
  liability, 995–997, 1002–1008
  periodic reporting requirements, 998–1000
  registration, 985–987, 1006
      requirements, 998
  regulation, 1002, 1061
  shelf registrations, 987
Securities Act of 1933, 730, 984, 1008, 1024
  applicability, 997f
  disclosure, 999f
  issuers, exempt transactions, 994f
  registration/exemption, 988f
  registration/liability provisions, 997f
Securities and Exchange Commission (SEC)
  rules, 986
  statutes, 1002
Securities and Exchange Commission v. W.J.
      Howey Co., 985
Securities Enforcement Remedies and Penny
Securities Exchange Act of 1934, 758, 996,
      1008, 1024–1027
  civil liability, 1005
  disclosure, 1009
  liability, 1008
Securities Litigation Uniform Standards Act
      (1998), 984
Security agreement, 807, 810
Security interest, 466, 807
  enabling, prebankruptcy transfer
      exception, 846
  enforceability, requisites, 812f
  enforcement, 519
  holder in due course, 561
  perfected security interests
      perfected security interests, contrast,
          814–816
      unperfected security interests,
          contrast, 814
  perfecting, methods, 811, 815f
  perfection, control (usage), 816
  unperfected security interests,
      unperfected
      security interests (contrast), 816
SEC v. Edwards, 1010–1011
Self-dealing, 377
Self-defense, privilege, 134

Seller
  breach, 470
  contract
      cancellation, 515
      goods identification, 513
  damages recovery, 513–514
  failure to warn, 492
  goods, delivery
      cessation, 512
      stopping, 512–513
      withholding, 512
  goods resale, 513
  incidental damages, recovery, 514
  insolvency, identified goods
      recovery, 518
  liabilities, 787
  nonacceptance/repudiation, damages
      recovery, 513–514
  not a merchant status, 472
  opinion/recommendation, 486
  performance, 444–449, 454
  price recovery, 514
  remedies, 512, 518–519
      examples, 516f
Sender, 612
Seniority system, 949
Service mark, 876
Servient parcel, 1109
Settlement charges (consumer credit
      transactions), 929
Settlor, 1141
Sexual discrimination, Title VII
      prohibition, 949
Sexual harassment, 952
Shareholders
  books/records, inspection right, 760
  changes, approval, 757–758
  charter amendment approval, 785–786
  derivative lawsuits, 761
  direct lawsuits, 760–761
  directors
      election, 757
      removal, 757
  dissension, 790–791
      appraisal remedy, 790–791
      procedure, 790
      right, 761
  enforcement rights, 759–761, 769–770
  lawsuits, 760–761, 760f
  meetings, 756
  proposals, 1000–1001
  proxies, 758
  quorum, 756
  repayment obligation, 741
  rights, 741
  role, 756, 769–770
  special meetings, 756
  voting, 756
      agreements, 758–759
      power, concentrations, 758–759
      rights, 756–759, 769

Shares
  acquisition, 738
      legal restrictions, 739–740
  classes, 735–737, 742
  common stock, 735
  compulsory exchange, 788
  control, sale, 788
  dividend preferences, 736
  liability, 735
  liquidation preferences, 736
  participating preferred shares, 736
  preferred stock, 735–736
  purchase, 787–788
  redemption, 738
      legal restrictions, 739–740
  rights/limitation, 736
  tender offer, 788
  transactions, 768
  transfer, restrictions, 759
Shares, issuance, 732–735, 742
  amount, consideration, 733–734
  authority, 732
  example, 734f
  functions, exercise, 763–765
  preemptive rights, 732–733
Shares, payment, 734–735
  consideration
      types, 734
      valuation, 735
Shawnee Telecom Resources, Inc. v. Brown,
      796–798
Shaw v. United States, 118–119
Shelf registrations, 987
Shelter rule, 553, 563
Sherman Antitrust Act, 882–900, 905
  amendments, 1061
  boycotts, 899
  market allocation, 898
  monopolies, 899–900
  monopolization, 899–900
  price fixing, 898
  strengthening, 900
  trade, restraint, 896–899, 900f
      concerted action, 897–898
  tying arrangements, 899
  violation, 109
Sherrod v. Kidd, 204–205
Shipment contract, 466, 471
Short-form merger, 789
Short-swing profits, 1002–1003
Short-term commercial paper, 987
Sight draft, 538
Signature, 541, 564–565, 583–584
  authentic signatures, 590
  authorized signatures, 584, 590
  forged signature, negligence (impact), 584
  unauthorized signature, 564–565, 584
Signed writing, 194
Silence (nondisclosure), 215
Silent Spring (Carson), 1042
Silvestri v. Optus Software, Inc., 343–344

Situational ethics, 16
Sixth Amendment, 117
Slander, 129
Small Business Liability Relief and
       Brownfields Revitalization
       Act, 1045
Small claims courts, 44
Smith, Adam, 19
Social coercion, 213
Social contract (social responsibility
       arguments), 21–22
Social egalitarians, 17
Social ethics theories, 17–18
Social responsibility, arguments, 21–22
Social Security, 955
Social security, 957–958
Social Security Act of 1935, 957
Soldano v. O'Daniels, 160–161
Soldiers' and sailors' wills, 1146
Sole proprietorship, 626
Solicitation, 1000
*South Florida Water Management District
       v. Miccosukee Tribe of Indians*,
       1050–1052
Sovereign immunity, 1057–1058
Spam, 111
Special courts, 43–45
Special indorsements, 556
Specially manufactured goods, 295
Special meetings, 756
Special property interest, 466
Special verdict, 52
Special warranty, 1123
Specific gifts, 1145
Specific performance, 7, 356–357,
       518–519
Specified period, 193
Speech, corporate political speech, 73–74
Spending power, 71
Spendthrift trusts, 1140
Stakeholder model, 22, 22f
Stands in the shoes, 317
Stare decisis (dual court system), 7, 47, 48f
State action, 69
State courts, 44–45, 58
   appellate courts, 45
   inferior trial courts, 44
   law, choice, 46
   special courts, 45
   system, 45f
   trial courts, 44
State, creature, 707
State implementation plan (SIP), 1039
State jurisdiction, 46–47, 47f
   exclusive state jurisdiction, 46
State "Lemon Laws," 910–925
Statement of opinion, 216
*State of Qatar v. First American Bank of
       Virginia*, 572–573
State of South Dakota v. Morse, 119–121
State of the art, demonstration, 492

Stationary sources, 1038–1039
Status-based duty rules, 152
Statute of frauds, 290, 358, 824
   compliance, 296–297
   contracts, 291–296, 301–302
      modification/rescission, 296
   electronic records, 291–292
   executor-administrator provision, 293
   general contracts provisions, 296–297
   land contract provision, 294
   marriage provision, 293–294
   one-year provision, 294–295
   partnership, 629–630
   sale of goods, 295, 297
   suretyship provision, 292–293
   types, 295f
Statute of limitations, 341
   impact, 240
   remedies, 522
Statutes
   enabling statute, 90–91
   gambling statutes, 255
   impact, 241–242
   licensing statutes, 254–255
   statute of repose, 494
   Sunday statutes, 256
   usury statutes, 255–256
   violation, 149, 254–256, 259–260
Statutory Close Corporation Supplement,
       710, 713, 754, 791
Statutory irrevocability, 194
Statutory liens, 847
Statutory model, 755f
Statutory powers, 716–717
Steinberg v. Chicago Medical School,
       182–183
Stewart, Marta, 14
Stipulated provisions (offer), 198
Stock Reform Act, 1002
Stocks
   common stock, 735
   distributions, 736–737
   dividends, 736–737
   no par value stock, 733
   options, 736
   par value stock, 733
   preferred stock, 735–736
   right, 736
   splits, 737–738
   Treasury stock, 733–734
   warrants, 736
Stolen order paper, 554
Stone v. Mississippi, 73
Stop payment orders, 607
Stop Trading on Congressional Knowledge
       Act of 2012, 1004
Straight bankruptcy, 840
Strict liability, 147, 156–160, 1084
   abnormally dangerous activities, 157
   animals, keeping, 157–158
   comparative negligence, 158

   contributory negligence, 158
   defective condition, 491
   defenses, 158, 160
   requirements, 491–493
   rise, activities (impact), 157–159
   risk, assumption, 158
   tort usage, 484, 490–491, 497
Strict scrutiny test, 72, 76
Subagent, 398
Subdivision master plans, 1127
Subdivisions, restrictive covenants, 1129
Subjective fault, 108
Subjective impossibility, 339
Subjective satisfaction, 335
Subject matter
   destruction, 196, 339–340
   jurisdiction, 45–47, 47f
Sublease, assignment, 1105f
Subrogation
   bank right, 607
   surety right, 823
Subscribers, 712
Subsequent debts, 652
Subsequent illegality, 196
Subsequent will, 1145
Subsidiary corporation, 716
Subsidiary debts, criteria, 716
Substantial evidence, 95
Substantial performance, 337
Substantive due process, 75
Substantive law, 5
Substantive unconscionability, 258, 425
Substitute check, 606–607
Substituted contracts, 238, 339
Substituted performance, 453
Sue, term, 5
Summary jury trial, 56
Summons, issuance, 50
Sunday statutes, 256
Superfund, 1042, 1044
Superfund Amendments and Reauthorization
       Act (SARA), 1044
Superfund Recycling Act, 1044
Superior skill/knowledge, 149
Superseding cause, 154
Supplemental Security Income (SSI), 957
Supplementary proceeding, 857
Supremacy Clause, 68
Surety, 292
   contract, 824
   contribution, 823
   cosureties, 821
   creditor, relationship, 821
   defenses, 823, 824f, 825–826, 829
   duties, 822, 829
   exoneration, 823
   identification, 821
   obligation, claim setoff, 824, 825
   personal defenses, 824–826
   principal debtor, relationship, 821
   reimbursement, 823

Surety (*continued*)
  rights, 823, 829
  risk, variation, 824–825
  subrogation, 823
  types, 821
Suretyship, 806, 820, 828–829
  formation, 820, 822, 828–829
  nature, 820–822, 828–829
  parties, involvement, 820–821
  relationship, 821f
  types, 821–822
Suretyship provision, 292–293
  main purpose doctrine, 293
  original promise, 292
Surplus, 738
  capital surplus, 738
  earned surplus, 738
  test, 739
Surviving corporation, 788, 789
Surviving entity, 685
Surviving spouse, renunciation, 1145

T

Taft-Hartley Act, 948
Takings Clause, 71–72
Tangible document of title, 1085
Tangible personal property,
    sale, 1075
Tangible property, 1075
Target, 110
Tariff, 1059
  commerce, state regulation,
    70–71
  federal fiscal powers, 71
Taxation, 675
"Television Test," 18
Telex Corp. v. IBM, 900
Temporary perfection, 814
Tenancy
  joint tenancy, 1108
  tenancy at sufferance, 1104
  tenancy at will, 1104
  tenancy by the entireties, 1108
  tenancy in common, 1108
Tenants, 1102, 1103
  abandonment, 1106
  co-tenants, 1107
  eviction, 1106
  obligations, 1106
  premises, destruction, 1106
  tenant in partnership, 635
  transfers, 1105
Tender, 336, 444
Tender offers, 788, 1001–1002
  defensive tactics, 1001–1002
  disclosure requirements, 1001
  fraud, 1003
  required practices, 1001
  state regulation, 1000–1002
Term partnership, dissolution, 653

Terms
  additional terms, 429
  different terms, 429
  meaning, mistake (impact), 220
Tertiary-line injury, 904
Testamentary provisions, effectiveness,
    1145–1146
Testamentary trust, 1140
  exclusion, 291
*Texas Department of Housing and Community
    Affairs v. Inclusive Communities
    Project*, 951
Theft, Economic Espionage Act definition, 874
*The Hyatt Corporation v. Palm Beach National
    Bank*, 571
Third parties (third persons)
  accountant liability, 1023f
  agent
    relationship, 405
    rights, 407
  bargained-for exchange, 240
  contracts, 315
    law, application, 320
  dissociated partners, liability, 656–657
  injury, landlord liability, 1107
  partnership/partners, relationship, 659–660
  principal, relationship, 395
  priority, 814
  relationship, 395
  satisfaction, 335
Third-party beneficiary, 1021–1022
  contracts, 320–323
    intended beneficiary, 321–322
Thomas v. Lloyd, 642–643
Thor Properties v. Willspring Holdings LLC,
    205–206
Time draft, 538, 586
Time is of the essence, 337
Time, lapse
  agency, 380
  offer, 193
Time note, 540
Time paper, 543, 562
Time, unity, 1108
Title
  certificate, 811
  covenants, 1123
  electronic document of title, 1085
  equitable title, 1139
  identification, 465–466
  insurable interest, 466
  insurance, purchase, 1122
  marketable title, 1122
  passage, 466
    party agreement, absence, 467f
  personal property transfer, 1076–1078
  tangible document of title, 1085
  theory, 1124
  transfer, 465–469, 474
    power, 466–469
    seller right, 466

unity, 1108
  warranty, 485, 488
Title documents, 1074, 1081, 1085–1089
  bills of lading, 1085–1086
  due negotiation, 1086–1087
  ineffectiveness, 1087
  negotiability, 1086
  symbolization, 1085
  types, 1085–1086
  warehouse receipts, 1085
  warranties, 1087
Title IX, 957
Title VII, 1064
Title VIII, 1121
Tortious conduct, 258
Tortious interference, example, 1334
Tort liability, 651f
  principal, 401–404, 408
    example, 402f
Torts
  contracts, connection (liability), 277–278
  damages, 360
  disparagement, 133
  independent contractor, 404
  intentional torts, 125
    defenses, 134–135
  liability, 651, 717, 719, 1022
  partnership crimes, relationship, 651
  reform, 126
  restatement, 126, 494–495
  strict liability, 484, 490–491, 497
  third restatement, 494–495, 497
  warranties, 484
Totten trusts, 1140
Toxic Substances Control Act (TSCA), 1043
Trade
  acceptance, 538
  common law restraint, 256–257
  dress, 875
  flow, 1059
  horizontal restraints, 897
  restraint (Sherman Act), 895–899,
    896f, 900f
    standards, 896–897
  restraint of trade, 256
  unreasonable restraints, 896
  usage, 299, 426
  vertical restraints, 897
Trademark Cyberpiracy Prevention Act
    (1999), 876–877
Trademark Law Treaty, 875, 1063
Trademarks
  distinctiveness, 875
  intellectual property, protection, 1062
  registrations, 876
Trade names, 877, 883
Trade-Related Aspects of Intellectual
    Property Rights (TRIPS), 1062
Trade secrets, 872–874, 883
  civil remedies, 874
  criminal penalties, 873–874

Economic Espionage Act definition, 873
federal protection, 873–874
misappropriation, 873
remedies, 873
state protection, 873
theft, Economic Espionage Act definition, 874
UTSA definition, 873
Trade symbols, 874–877, 883
infringement, 876–877
registration, 875–876
remedies, 877
types, 875
Transfer, 552, 569–570, 846
bulk transfer, 472
meaning, 590
warranties on transfer, 589–590
Transferees
application, 654
requirements, 559–560
rights, 560f
Transferor, warranties, 589–590
Transfers by landlord, 1104
Transfers by tenant, 1105
Travelers Indemnity Co. v. Stedman, 597–599
Treasure trove, 1077
Treasury stock, 733–734
Treaties, 9
Treble damages, 882
Trespass
personal property, 132
private nuisance, difference, 1036
real property, 131
Trespasser, 151–152
Trespass to land, 1036
Trial, 51–52
conduct, 51–52
mini-trial, 56
new motion, 52
summary jury trial, 56
Trial sales, 470–471
Triffin v. Cigna Insurance, 577–578
Troubled Asset Relief Program (TARP), 927
Trump administration, CFPB, 922
Trustee in bankruptcy
competing interests, 817–818
preferential transfers, avoidance, 818
unperfected security interest, priority, 817–818
Trustees, 1141–1142
Chapter 3 bankruptcy, 841–842
duties, 1142
lien creditor role, 845
powers, 1142
principal/income, allocation, 1142, 1143f
Trusts, 1139, 1148
beneficiary, 1142
breach, 651
charitable trusts, 1140
constructive, 1141
corpus/property, 1141

creation, 1141–1142, 1148
decedent's property, 1143
deed of trust, 1123, 1124
express trusts, 1139–1140
flowchart, 1140f
implied trusts, 1140–1141
indorsements, 556–557
inter vivos trust, 1140
resulting trusts, 1141
settler, 1141
spendthrift trusts, 1140
termination, 1142–1143, 1148
testamentary trust, 1140
totten trusts, 1140
trustee, 1141–1142
types, 1139–1141, 1148
Truth-in-Lending Act (TILA), 927
Truth in Securities Act, 984–985
Tucker v. Hayford, 1114–1116
Tying arrangements (Sherman Act), 899, 901
Tying contracts (Clayton Act), 901
Tying product, 899

U

Ultramares Corporation v. Touche, 1022
Ultra vires acts, 717, 719, 761
effect, 717
remedies, 717
Ultra vires doctrine, 717
Unaccepted drafts, 586–587
drawees, 591–592
Unaffiliated directors, 761
Unauthorized indorsement, 608
Unauthorized means (offer), 198
Unauthorized payment order, 613
Unauthorized signature, 584, 608
holder in due course, 564–565
impact, 565
ratification, 584
Uncertificated security, 809
Unconditional promise/order, 541–542
Unconscionability, 425
procedural unconscionability, 258, 425
substantive unconscionability, 258, 425
Undisclosed principal, 396
agent, contract liability, 406–407
contract liability, 399f
Undue influence, 214, 220, 1144
Unemployment insurance, 955, 957–958
Unenforceability, general rule, 259
Unenforceable contracts, 177
Unfair conduct, 900
Unfair labor practices, 948
Unfairness
meaning, 920
social responsibility arguments, 21
Unidentified principal, 395
agent, contract liability, 406
contract liability, 398f
Uniform Arbitration Act (UAA), 55

Uniform Commercial Code (UCC), 8, 173, 198, 200
Article 2, principles, 424–427, 433
Article 4A
coverage, examples, 612
scope, 611–612
Article 2A, principles, 424–427, 433
consideration, 429–430
law of sales and leases, contract law (comparison), 432f
Uniform Consumer Credit Code (UCCC), 927
Uniform Durable Power of Attorney Act, 399
Uniform Electronic Transactions Act (UETA), 291, 292, 431, 707
Uniform Law Commission (ULC), 55, 675, 984, 1143
Uniform Limited Liability Company Act (ULLCA), 680–681
Uniform Limited Partnership Act (ULPA), 9, 675
Uniform Partnership Act (UPA), 9, 628, 634, 649
usage, 657–658
Uniform Power of Attorney Act (UPOAA), 376, 399
Uniform Principal and Income Act, 1142
Uniform Probate Code (UPC), 9, 1143
Uniform Real Property Electronic Recording Act, 1124
Uniform Residential Landlord and Tenant Act, enactment, 1103
Uniform Trade Secrets Act (UTSA), 872
Uniform Unincorprated Nonprofit Association Act (UUNAA), 631
Unilateral contracts, 176–177
consideration, 236f
irrevocable offers, 194
legal sufficiency, 235
Unilateral mistake, 219
Unincorporated business association, types, 686–687, 690
Union Planters Bank, National Association v. Rogers, 617–619
Union shop, 948
United Nations Commission on International Trade Law (UNCITRAL), 56, 292, 840, 1060, 1064
United Nations Committee on International Trade Law, 1060
United Nations Convention on Contracts for the International Sale of Goods (CISG), 174, 424, 1060
United Nations Convention on the Law of the Sea (UNCLOS), 1057
United Nations Framework Convention on Climate Change (UNFCCC),1046
United States Bankruptcy Abuse Prevention and Consumer Protection Act (2005), 840
United States, circuit courts, 44f
United States Court of Appeals, 43–44

United States Court of Federal Claims, 43
United States Court of International Trade, 43
United States Patent and Trademark Office
    (USPTO), 882
United States Supreme Court, 43
    Reports, 9
    Supreme Court Reporter, 9
United States Tax Court, 43
United States v. Socony-Vacuum, 898
United States v. Windsor, 75, 76
United Travel Service, Inc. v. Weber, 257
Universal Copyright Convention, 1063
Unlimited personal liability, 651
Unliquidated debt, settlement, 239
Unpaid contract price, market price
    (difference), 513
Unperfected security interests
    perfected security interests, contrast,
        814–816
    priorities, 817–818
    unperfected security interests, contrast, 816
Unqualified indorsements, 557
Unreasonably dangerous product, 492
Unregistered sales, 995
Unseasoned issuer, 986
Unsecured bonds, 731
Unsecured claims (Chapter 5 bankruptcy), 842
Unsecured creditors, competing interests, 814
Unwarranted by the facts test, 95
Usage of trade, 299, 426
Usury statutes, 255–256
Utilitarianism, 16
    act utilitarianism, 16
    rule utilitarianism, 16
Utility (patentability criteria), 881
Utility Air Regulatory Group v. EPA, 1040

V

Valid contracts, 177
Value, 560–561, 809–810
    electronic payments, 536
Valued policy, 1079
Vance v. Ball State University, 964–967
Vanegas v. American Energy Services,
    244–245
Variant acceptances, 428–429
Venue, jurisdiction (contrast), 49
Verdict, 52
    challenge, motions (impact), 52
    directed verdict, 52
    general verdict, 52
    special verdict, 52
Vertical merger, 901
Vertical privity, 490, 493
Vertical restraints, 897
Vertical territorial/customer restrictions, 898
Vest, 322
Vested remainder, 1102–1103
Vicarious liability, 109
    principal, 403–404

Vienna Trademark Agreement, 875, 1063
Vietnam Veterans Readjustment Act, 954
Voidable contracts, 177, 278, 358
Voidable dominant party, 214
Voidable mistake, 218
Voidable promises, 240
Voidable title (goods), 467–469
Void agreement, 213
Void contracts, 177
Void obligations, 564
Void title (goods), 467–469
    example, 468f
Voir dire, 51
Voluntary dissolution, 791
Voluntary petitions (Chapter 3
    bankruptcy), 841
Voluntary safety standards, 922
Voting, 764
    shareholder voting agreements, 758–759
    trusts, 758
Voting power
    concentrations, 758–759
        characteristics, 758f
    dissenting, shareholder rights, 761
Voting rights
    limited partnership, 677–678
    shareholders, 756–759

W

Waddell v. L.V.R.V. Inc., 457–458
Wages
    assignments/garnishment, 932
    unsecured claims, 842
Waiver, 1081
Wal-Mart Stores, Inc. v. Samara Brothers, Inc.,
    886–887
Wards Cove Packing Co. v. Antonio, 950
Warehouse receipts, 1085
Warehousing, 1084
WARN. *See* Worker Adjustment and
    Retraining Notification Act
Warnick v. Warnick, 667–669
Warranties, 484, 496, 1123
    actions, obstacles, 487–491, 496–497
    alteration, 494
    basis, 590
    breach, 1080–1081
        notice, 490
    buyer examination, 488
    collecting banks, 605
    comparative negligence, 493
    contract, privity, 489–490
    contributory negligence, 493
    disclaimers, 487–489, 493
    examination, refusal, 488–489
    express exclusions, 485
    express warranties, 485–486
    failure to warn, 495
    federal legislation, relationship, 489
    federal warranty protection, 924–925

implied warranties, 486–487
    fitness, 487
liability, 583
limitation, 489
limited warranty, 923
modification, 489
notice, 493
plaintiff conduct, 490, 493–494
privity, 493
recovery, obstacles, 493–494, 497
risk, voluntary assumption, 493–494
special warranty, 1123
title, 485, 488
transferor, 589–590
types, 485–487, 489f, 496
Warranties on presentment, 590–594
    payors, 593
    unaccepted drafts, drawees, 591–592
Warranties on transfer, 589–590, 594
    alteration, absence, 590
    authentic/authorized signatures, 590
    defenses, absence, 590
    enforcement, entitlement, 589–590
    insolvency, knowledge (absence), 590
Waste, 1102, 1124
Wealth *of Nations, The (Smith)*, 19
Wealth, transfer, 902
Well-known seasoned issuer, 987
Whatley v. Estate of McDougal, 1154–1155
Whistle blow, 392
    awards, Dodd-Frank Act, 1005
White v. Samsung Electronics America, Inc.,
    140–142
White-collar crime, 110–111, 118
    computer crime, 110–111
    Racketeer Influenced and Corrupt
        Organizations Act (RICO), 111
Wholesale electronic funds transfers, 609
Wholesale funds transfers, 611–613, 615
    acceptance, 612–613
    Article 4A, scope, 611–612
    parties, 612, 613t
    payment order, 612
        execution, errors, 613
    transactions, exclusion, 612
    unauthorized payment orders, 613
Wholly owned subsidiaries, 1064
Wild animals, definition, 157–158
Williams Act, 1001, 1002
Williamson v. Mazda Motor of America, Inc.,
    78–79
Wills, 1143–1147, 1149
    attestation, 1144
    bequest, abatement/ademption, 1146
    codicils, 1145
    conditional wills, 1146
    destruction/alteration, 1145
    formal requirements, 1144–1145
    holographic wills, 1146
    joint and mutual wills, 1146
    law, operation, 1145–1146

living wills, 1147
mental capacity, 1144
nuncupative wills, 1146
reciprocal wills, 1146
revocation, 1145
signature, 1144–1145
soldiers' and sailors' wills, 1146
subsequent will, 1145
surviving spouse, renunciation, 1146
testamentary provisions, effectiveness, 1146
types, 1146–1147
writing, 1144
Wilson v. Campoli, 455–456
Winding up, 658
    assets
        distribution, 654–655
        marshaling, 655, 658
    limited liability company (LLC), 685
    participation, 654
Wire fraud, 111, 112
Without reserve, term, 192
Womco, Inc. v. Navistar International Corporation, 501

Wood v. Pavlin, 1116–1117
Words of negotiability, 543
Worker Adjustment and Retraining Notification Act (WARN), 958
Workers' compensation, 957
Working papers, 1023
Works for hire, 879
World Intellectual Property Organization (WIPO)
    Copyright Treaty of 1996, 1063
    Performances and Phonograms Treaty (1996), 878
World Trade Organization (WTO), 1057
    Antidumping Code, 1059
World-wide Volkswagen Corp. v. Woodson, 60–61
WorldCom, violations/scandal, 984
Writ of certiorari, 43, 53
Writ of execution, 53
Written confirmation, 297
Written contract, unauthorized material alteration, 338
Written interrogatories, 51

Written merchant confirmation, 431
Written warranties, 924
Wrongful dissociations, 652
WTO. *See* World Trade Organization
Wyler v. Feuer, 692–693

Y
Young v. United Parcel Service, Inc., 971–974

Z
Zarda v. Altitude Express, Inc., 960–962
Zelnick v. Adams, 283–285
Zoning, 1126–1127, 1130
    acts, enabling, 1126
    judicial review, 1127
    nonconforming uses, 1127
    ordinances, enabling, 1126–1127
    subdivision master plans, 1127
    variance, 1127